ISBN 978-1-390-99285-4
PIBN 11190762

English
Français
Deutsche
Italiano
Español
Português

www.forgottenbooks.com

Mythology Photography **Fiction**
Fishing Christianity **Art** Cooking
Essays Buddhism Freemasonry
Medicine **Biology** Music **Ancient**
Egypt Evolution Carpentry Physics
Dance Geology **Mathematics** Fitness
Shakespeare **Folklore** Yoga Marketing
Confidence Immortality Biographies
Poetry **Psychology** Witchcraft
Electronics Chemistry History **Law**
Accounting **Philosophy** Anthropology
Alchemy Drama Quantum Mechanics
Atheism Sexual Health **Ancient History**
Entrepreneurship Languages Sport
Paleontology Needlework Islam
Metaphysics Investment Archaeology
Parenting Statistics Criminology
Motivational

epigram of Xeinagoras, a Greek mathematician, who measured the height of Olympus from these parts (ap. Plut. Aemil. Paul. 15). Games were also celebrated here in honour of Apollo. (Steph. B. s. v. Πύθιον.) Pythium commanded an important pass across Mount Olympus. This pass and that of Tempe are the only two leading from Macedonia into the north-east of Thessaly. Leake therefore places Pythium on the angle of the plain between *Kokkinopló* and *Livádhi*, though no remains of the ancient town have been discovered there. (Liv. xlii. 53; Plut., Steph. B., *ll. cc.*; Ptol. iii. 13. § 42; Leake, *Northern Greece*, vol. iii. p. 341, seq.)

PYTHO. [DELPHI.]

PYTHO'POLIS. [MYTHEPOLIS.]

PYXIRATES. [EUPHRATES.]

PYXITES (Πυξίτης), a small river in the east of Pontus, emptying itself into the Euxine 60 stadia on the north-east of Prytanis. (Plin. vi. 4; Arrian, *Peripl. P. E.* p. 6; Anonym. *Peripl. P. E.* p. 15.) It is possibly the same as the Cissa mentioned by Ptolemy (v. 6. § 6), and is commonly identified with the modern *Vitzeh*.   [L. S.]

PYXUS. [BUXENTUM.]

Q.

QUACERNI. [QUERQUERNI.]

QUADI (Κουάδοι), a great German tribe in the south-east of Bohemia, in Moravia and Hungary, between Mons Gabreta, the Hercynian and Sarmatian mountains, and the Danube. (Tac. *Germ.* 42, *Ann.* xii. 29, *Hist.* iii. 5, 21; Ptol. ii. 11. § 26; Plin. iv. 25.) They were surrounded on the north-west by the Marcomanni, with whom they were always closely connected, on the north by the Gothini and Osi, on the east by the Jazyges Metanastae, and on the south by the Pannonians. It is not known when they came to occupy that country, but it seems probable that they arrived there about the same time when the Marcomanni established themselves in Bohemia. At the time when the Marcomannian king Maroboduus and his successor Catualda, on being driven from their kingdom, implored the protection of the Romans, the latter in A. D. 19 assigned to them and their companions in exile the districts between the rivers Marus and Cusus, and appointed Vannius, a Quadian king of the territory (Tac. *Ann.* ii. 63; Plin. iv. 25). This new kingdom of the Quadi, after the expulsion of Vannius, was divided between his nephews Vangio and Sido, who, however, continued to keep up a good understanding with the Romans. (Tac. *Ann.* xii. 29, 30.) Tacitus (*Germ. l. c.*) says that down to his own time the Marcomanni and Quadi had been governed by kings of the house of Maroboduus, but that then foreigners ruled over them, though the power of these rulers was dependent on that of the Roman emperors. At a later time the Quadi took an active part in the war of the Marcomanni against the Romans, and once nearly annihilated the whole army of M. Aurelius, which was saved only by a sudden tempest. (Dion Cass. lxxi. 8). Notwithstanding the peace then concluded with them, they still continued to harass the Romans by renewed acts of hostility, and the emperor was obliged, for the protection of his own dominions, to erect several forts both in and around their kingdom, in consequence of which the people were nearly driven to abandon their country. (Dion Cass. lxxi. 11, 13, 20.) In

A. D. 180 the emperor Commodus renewed the peace with them (Dion Cass. lxxii. 2; Lamprid. *Com.* 3; Herodian, i. 6), but they still continued their inroads into the Roman empire (Eutrop. ix. 9; Vopisc. *Aurel.* 18; Amm. Marc. xvii. 12, xxix. 6). Towards the end of the fourth century the Quadi entirely disappear from history; they had probably migrated westward with the Suevi, for Quadi are mentioned among the Suevi in Spain. (Hieron. *Ep.* 9.) According to Ammianus Marcellinus (xvii. 12) the Quadi resembled in many respects the Sarmatians, for they used long spears and a coat of mail consisting of linen covered with thin plates of horn; they had in war generally three swift horses for every man, to enable him to change them, and were on the whole better as skirmishers than in an open battle in the field. Ptolemy (*l. c.*) mentions a considerable number of towns in their country, such as Eburodunum, Meliodunum, Caridorgis, Medoslanium, &c.; the Celtic names of which suggest that those districts previous to the arrival of the Quadi had been inhabited by Celts, who were either subdued by them or had become amalgamated with them. The name Quadi itself seems to be connected with the Celtic word *col*, cold, or *coad*, that is, a wood or forest, an etymology which receives support from the fact that Strabo (vii. p. 290), the first ancient author that notices them, mentions them under the name of Κόλδουοι. Tacitus evidently regards them as Germans, but Latham (*ad Tac. Germ.* p. 154) is inclined to treat them as Sarmatians. (Comp. Wilhelm, *Germanien*, p. 223, fol.)   [L. S.]

QUADIA'TES. In the inscription on the arch of Susa, published by Maffei, there is a list of the Alpine peoples who were under the dominion of Cottius. The first name is the Seguvii, and the last is the Quadiates. There is nothing that enables us to fix the position of the Quadiates.

Pliny (iii. 4) mentions a people in Gallia Narbonensis under the name of Quariates. After naming the Oxybii and Lingauni [LINGAUNI], he adds: "Super quos Suetri, Quariates, Adunicates." The valley of *Queiras* on the left bank of the *Durance*, below *Briançon*, and a little above *Embrun*, is supposed to represent the position of the Quariates. D'Anville conjectures that the Quiadiates of the inscription may be the same as the Quariates, for the B of the inscription, if it is not very clear, may have been taken for a D; or the complete name may have been Quadriates, the name of *Queiras* in old records being Quadriatium.   [G. L.]

QUADRA'TA (sc. Castra). 1. A Roman fort in Upper Pannonia, on the river Savus, between the towns of Noviodunum and Siscia. (*It. Ant.* pp. 260, 274; Geogr. Rav. iv. 19; *Tab. Peut.*) No remains appear to be extant, and the site accordingly is unknown.

2. A fort in Upper Pannonia, on the road between Arrabona and Carnuntum, not far from the banks of the Danube. (*It. Ant.* p. 247.) Muchar (*Noricum*, p. 264) identifies it with a place between *Ovar* and *Oroszvar*, now occupied by a large farm of Count Zitsi.   [L. S.]

QUADRA'TAE, a village or station in Gallia Cisalpina, on the road from Augusta Taurinorum to Ticinum. The Itineraries place it 22 or 23 miles from the former city and 16 or 19 from Rigomagus (*Itin. Ant.* pp. 340, 356; *Itin. Hier.* p. 557); but the latter station is itself of uncertain site. Quadratae must have been situated between *Chivasso* and *Crescentino*, near the confluence of the *Dora Baltea* with the *Po*; but the exact site has not been determined. Though the name is not mentioned by any of the geographers, it would seem to have been in the later ages of the Empire a place or station of importance, as we learn from the Notitia that a body of troops (Sarmatae Gentiles) was permanently stationed there. (*Notit. Dign.* vol. ii. p. 121.)   [E. H. B.]

QUADRIBU'RGIUM. Ammianus Marcellinus (xviii. 2) mentions Quadriburgium among the fortresses on the Rhine which Julian repaired : " Civitates occupatae sunt septem, Castra Herculis, Quadriburgium, Tricesimae, Novesium, Bonna, Antunnacum et Bingio." There is however some corruption in the passage (note of Lindenbrog). The places seem to be mentioned in order from north to south. D'Anville conjectures that Quadriburgium is the same place as Burginatium [BURGINA-TIUM], following Cluver and Alting. (Ukert, *Gallien*, p. 528.) Other geographers conjecture solely from the resemblance of name that it may be *Qualburg*, not far from *Clève*, which appears to have been a Roman place, for Roman coins and inscriptions have been found there.   [G. L.]

QUARIA'TES. [QUADIATES.]

QUARQUERNI, a people in Istria, of uncertain site. (Plin. iii. 19. s. 23.)

QUARQUERNI. [QUERQUERNI.]

QUARTENSIS LOCUS, a place mentioned in the Not. Imp. as under the command of the governor of Belgica Secunda : " Praefectus classis Sambricae in loco Quartensi sive Hornensi." The place seems to be *Quarte* on the *Sambre*, which keeps the ancient name. The word *Quarte* indicates a distance of iv. from some principal place, it being usual for chief towns to reckon distances along the roads which led from them to the limits of their territory. This principal place to which Quartensis belonged was Bagacum (*Bavai*), and the distance from *Quarte* to *Bavai* is four Gallic leagues. The great Roman road from Durocortorum (*Reims*) to *Bavai* passed by *Quarte*. "Quartensis" is the adjective of a form "Quartus" or "Quarta," and Quarta occurs in an old record of the year 1125, "Altare de Quarta supra Sambram," which is the church of *Quarte*.   [G. L.]

QUERQUERNI (Plin. iii. 3. s. 4; Quarquerni, *Inscr. ap. Gruter*, p. 245. 2; Quacerni, Κουακερνοί, Ptol. ii. 6. § 47), a people in the NW. of Hispania Tarraconensis, a subdivision of the Gallaeci Bracarii.

QUERQUETULA (*Eth.* Querquetulanus ; Κορκοτουλανός, Dionys.), an ancient city of Latium, mentioned only by Pliny among the populi Albenses, or extinct communities of Latium, and by Dionysius among the the Latin cities which constituted the league against Rome. (Plin. iii. 5. s. 9; Dionys. v. 61.) Neither passage affords the slightest clue to its position, and the name is not elsewhere mentioned; indeed, it seems certain that the place was not in existence at a later period. It is undoubtedly erroneous to connect (as Gell has done) the name of the Porta Querquetulana at Rome with this city (Becker, *Handbuch*, vol. i. p. 170); and we are absolutely in the dark as to its position. It has been placed by Gell and Nibby at a place called *Corcollo*, about 3 miles NE. of Gabii and the same distance from Hadrian's villa near *Tivoli*; but this is a mere conjecture. (Gell, *Top. of Rome*, p. 369; Nibby, *Dintorni*, vol. ii. p. 668.)   [E. H. B.]

QUINDA. [ANAZARBUS.]

QUINTA'NAE or AD QUINTA'NAS, a station on the Via Labicana or Latina, 15 miles from Rome, and at the foot of the hill occupied by the ancient city of Labicum, now *La Colonna*, from which it was about a mile distant. (*Itin. Ant.* p. 304; Gell, *Top. of Rome*, p. 5.) Under the Roman Empire it became the site of a village or suburb of Labicum, the inhabitants of which assumed the name of Lavicani Quintanenses. [LA-BICUM.]   [E. H. B.]

QUINTIA'NA CASTRA, a fort in the east of Vindelicia, not far from the banks of the Danube, between Batava Castra and Augustana Castra. Its garrison consisted of a troop of Rhaetian horsemen. (*It. Ant.* p. 249; *Notit. Imp.*, where it is called Quartana Castra ; comp. Eugipp. *Vit. S. Severini*, 15, 27.) Muchar (*Noricum*, p. 285) identifies its site with that of the modern village of *Künzen*.   [L. S.]

QUIZA (Κούϊζα, also Βούϊζα, Ptol. iv. 2. § 3), a place on the coast of Mauretania Caesariensis, called by Ptolemy a colonia, and in the Antonine Itinerary a municipium, but in Pliny designated as "Quiza Xenitana preregrinorum oppidum." It was situated between Portus Magnus and Arsenaria, at the distance of 40 stadia from either. It is the modern *Giza* near *Oran*. (Ptol. *l. c.* ; *It. Ant.* p. 13; Plin. v. 2; Mela, i. 6.)

R.*

RAAMAH. [RHEGMA.]

RAAMSES (Ῥαμεσσῆ, LXX., *Exod.* i. 11, xii. 37; *Numb.* xxxiii. 3, 5), was, according to D'Anville (*Mém. sur l'Egypte*, p. 72), identical with Heroopolis in the Delta; but according to other writers (Jablonsky, *Opusc.* ii. p. 136; Winer, *Bibl. Realwörterbuch*, vol. ii. p. 351) the same as Heliopolis in the same division of Aegypt. [W.B.D.]

RABBATH-AMMON. [PHILADELPHIA.]

RABBATH-MOAB, a town in the country of Moab, stated by Stephanus, who is followed by Reland, Raumer, Winer, and other moderns, to be identical with Ar of Moab, the classical Areopolis. This identification is almost certainly erroneous ; and indeed it is very doubtful whether a Rabbath did exist at all in the country of Moab All the notices of such a name in the Bible are identified with Rabbath-Ammon, except in Joshua (xiii. 25), where Aroer is said to be "before Rabbah," which may possibly be Rabbath-Ammon, and certainly cannot, in the absence of other ancient evidence, be admitted to prove the existence of a Rabbath in Moab. There is, however, some evidence that such a town may have existed in that country, in the modern site of *Rabba*, marked in Zimmerman's map about halfway between *Kerak* (Kir of Moab) and the *Mojeb* (Arnon), and by him identified with Areopolis, which last, however, was certainly identical with Ar of Moab, and lay further north, on the south bank of the Arnon, and in the extreme border of Moab (*Numb.* xxi. 15, xxii. 36). [AREOPOLIS.] Rabba is placed by Burckhardt 3 hours north of *Kerak* (*Syria*, p. 377), and is doubtless the site noticed in Abulfeda's *Tabula Syriae* as *Rabbath* and *Mab* (90). Irby and Mangles

* For those articles not found under RA-, RE-, RI-, &c., see RHA-, RHE-, RHI-, &c.

passed it two hours north of *Kerak.* "The ruins," they say, "are situated on an eminence, and present nothing of interest, except two old ruined Roman temples and some tombs. The whole circuit of the town does not seem to have exceeded a mile, which is a small extent for a city that was the capital of Moab, and which bore such a high-sounding Greek name." (*Journal,* June 5, p. 457.) They must not be held responsible for the double error involved in the last cited words, regarding the etymology of the name Areopolis, and its identity with Rabbath, which are almost universal.　　　　　　[G. W.]

RAGAE. [RHAGAE.]

RAGANDO or RAGINDO, a town in the south-east of Noricum, on the great road leading from Celeia to Poetovium, between the rivers Savus and Dravus. (*It. Ant.* p. 129; *It. Hieros.* p. 561; *Tab. Peut.*) Muchar (*Noricum,* p. 240) looks for its site near *Mount Studenitz;* but other geographers entertain different opinions, and nothing certain can be said.　　　　　　　　　　　　　　[L. S.]

RAGAU ('Ραγαΰ, Isidor. *Stathm. Parth.* § 13), a town mentioned by Isidorus in the district of Parthia called Apavarctene. It is probably the same place as the Ragaea of Ptolemy ('Ραγαία, vi. 5. § 4). It is not clear whether there exist at present any remains of this town. but it must have been situated to the E. of *Nishápur,* between that town and *Herát.*　　　　　　　　　　[V.]

RAGIRAVA. [RAPAVA.]

RAMAH ('Ραμά). 1. A city of the tribe of Benjamin, mentioned with Gibeon and Beeroth (*Josh.* xviii. 25), and elsewhere with Bethel, as in or near Mount Ephraim. (*Judges,* iv. 5.) From xix. 13 of Judges it would appear to have been not far north of Jerusalem, and lying near to Gibeah of Benjamin. Being a border city between the king-doms of Israel and Judah, it was fortified by Baasha king of Israel, "that he might not suffer any to go out or come in to Asa, king of Judah." (1 *Kings,* xv. 17, comp. xii. 27.) It is placed by Eusebius 6 miles north of Jerusalem, over against Bethel (*Onomast.* s. r.), and by S. Jerome 7 miles from Jerusalem near Gabaa, and was a small village in his day. (*Comment. in Hos.* cap. v., *in Sophon.* cap. i.) Josephus places it 40 stadia from Jeru-salem. (*Ant.* viii. 12. § 3.) Its site is still marked by the miserable village of *Er-Rám,* situated on a hill on the east of the *Nablús* road, 2 hours north of Jerusalem, and half an hour west of *Jeba',* the ancient Gibeah. Its situation is very com-manding, and it retains a few scattered relics of its ancient importance. (Robinson, *Bibl. Res.* vol. ii. pp. 315, 316.)

2. See also RAMATHA and RAMOTH.　　[G. W.]

RAMATH-LEHI, or simply LEHI (translated in LXX. 'Αναίρεσις σιαγόνος), where Samson slew the Philistines with the jaw-bone of an ass. (*Judges,* xv. 14—19.) The name *Ramleh* appears so like an abbreviation or contraction — perhaps a corruption — of this name, that it may well be identified as the scene of this slaughter. And here probably was the Ramah in the Thamnitic toparchy in which Eusebius and S. Jerome found the Ramathaim Sophim of Samuel, and the Arimathaea of the Evan-gelists, which they place near to Lydda in the plain. (*S. Matth.* xxvii. 57; *S. Mark,* xv. 42; *S. Luke,* xxiii. 50; *S. John,* xix. 38, 'Αριμαθαία; Eusebius, *Onomast. s. v. Armatha Sophim ;* S. Jerome, *Epi-taph. Paulae,* p. 673.) Dr. Robinson, indeed, con-troverts all these positions; but his arguments cannot

prevail against the admitted facts, "that a place called Ramathem or Ramatha did anciently exist in this region, somewhere not far distant from Lydda" (*Bibl. Res.* vol. iii. p. 40), and that no other place can be found answering to this description but *Ramleh,* which has been regarded from very early times as the place in question. The facts of *Ramleh* having been built by Suliman, son of the khalif Abd-el-Malik, after the destruction of Lydda in the early part of the 8th century, and that the Arabic name signifies " the sand," will not seriously mili-tate against the hypotheses with those who con-sider the great probability that the khalif would fix on an ancient, but perhaps neglected, site for his new town, and the common practice of the Arabs to modify the ancient names, to which they would attach no meaning, to similar sounds intelligible to them, and in this instance certainly not less appro-priate than the ancient name; although the situation of the town " on a broad low swell in the sandy though fertile plain," would satisfy the condition re-quired by its presumed ancient designation. (*Bibl. Res.* vol. iii. p. 25—43.) It may be questioned whether the *nomus* of Ramathem, mentioned with those of Apheirema and Lydda, as taken from Samaritis and added to Judaea (1 *Maccab.* xi. 34; Josephus, *Ant.* 2. § 3, 4. § 9), derived its name from this or from one of the other Ramahs, in Benjamin.　[G. W.]

RAMATHA ('Ραμαθά), the form in which Jo-sephus represents the name of Samuel's native city, Ramathaim Sophim (LXX. 'Αρμαθαίμ Σιφά) of Mount Ephraim (1 *Sam.* i. 1), perhaps identical with Ramah, where was his ordinary residence (vii. 17, viii. 4, xix. 18—24, xxv. 1), but distinct from the Ramah above named. Ancient tradition has fixed this city at *Neby Samwil,* i. e. " The Prophet Samuel," a village situated on a very high and commanding hill, two hours to the NNW. of Jeru-salem, where the place of his sepulture is shown. Eusebius and S. Jerome, however, found it in the western plain, near Lydda (*Onomast. s. v. Armatha Sophim ;* see RAMATH-LEHI). Dr. Robinson has stated his objections to the identification of Ra-mathaim Sophim with *Neby Samwil,* and has endea-voured to fix the former much further to the south, on the hill called *Sôba,* a little to the south of the *Jaffa* road, about 3 hours from Jerusalem; while Mr. Wolcott has carried it as far south as the vicinity of Hebron. (Robinson, *Bibl. Res.* vol. ii. pp. 139—144, 330—334, *Bibl. Sacra,* vol. i. pp. 44—52.) These objections are based on the hypothesis that the incidents attending Saul's unction to the king-dom, narrated in 1 *Sam.* ix. x., took place in Ramah of Samuel, of which, however, there is no evidence; and his difficulty would press almost with equal weight on *Sôba,* as the direct route from *Sôba* to Gibeah (*Jeba*) would certainly not have conducted Saul by Rachel's sepulchre. Neither can the district of Mount Ephraim be extended so far south. Indeed, this last seems to be the strongest objection to *Neby Samwil,* and suggests a site further north, perhaps *Ram-Ullah,* in the same parallel of latitude as the other Ramah and Bethel, which were certainly in Mount Ephraim. (*Judges,* iv. 5.) On the other hand, the name Ramah, signifying "a height," is so remarkably applicable to *Neby Samwil,* which is evidently the site of an ancient town, which could not, as Dr. Robinson suggests, have been Mizpah, that it would be difficult to find a position better suited to Ramathaim Sophim than that which tra-dition has assigned it. [MIZPAH.]　　　[G. W.]

y y 2

RAMATHAIM-ZOPHIM. [RAMATHA.]

RAMBA'CIA ('Ραμβακία, Arrian, *Anab.* vi. 21), a village of the Oritae, the first which was taken by Alexander the Great in his march westwards from the Indus. There can be no certainty as to its exact position, but the conjecture of Vincent seems well grounded that it is either the *Ram-nagar* or the *Ram-gur* of the *Ayin Akbarî.* (Vincent, *Voyage of Nearchus,* vol. i. p. 185.)   [V.]

RAME, a place in Gallia Narbonensis, which the Itins. fix on the road between Embrodunum (*Embrun*) and Brigantium (*Briançon*). D'Anville says that there is a place called *Rame* on this road near the *Durance,* on the same side as *Embrun* and *Briançon,* and at a point where a torrent named *Biesse* joins the *Durance.*   [G. L.]

RAMISTA or REMISTA, a place in Upper Pannonia, on the road running along the river Savus to Siscia (*It. Hieros.* p. 561; Geogr. Rav. iv. 19; *Tab. Peut.*) Its site has not yet been ascertained with certainty.   [L. S.]

RAMOTH, identical in signification with Râm and Ramah, equivalent in Hebrew to "an eminence," and hence a generic name for towns situated on remarkable heights, as so many in Palestine were. Besides those above named [RAMAH; RAMATHA] was a Ramah in the tribe of Asher, not far from Tyre; and another in Naphthali (*Josh.* xix. 29, 36) in the north and a Ramath in the tribe of Simeon, appropriately called "Ramath of the South" (ver. 8.), to which David sent a share of the spoils of Ziklag (1 *Sam.* xxx. 27), and yet a Ramoth in Issachar, assigned to the Levites of the family of Gershom. (1 *Chron.* vi. 74.) More important than the foregoing was—

RAMOTH-GILEAD ('Ραμώθ ἐν Γαλαάδ), a city of the tribe of Gad, assigned as a city of refuge, first by Moses and subsequently by Joshua. (*Deut.* iv. 43; *Josh.* xx. 8, 'Αρημώθ.) It was also a Levitical city of the family of Merari. (*Josh.* xxi. 38.) The Syrians took it from Ahab, who lost his life in seeking to recover it. (1 *Kings,* xxii.) Eusebius places it 15 miles west of Philadelphia (*Onomast. s. v.,* where S. Jerome erroneously reads east; Reland, p. 966), in the Peraea, near the river *Jabok.* Its site is uncertain, and has not been recovered in modern times.   [G. W.]

RANILUM, a town in the interior of Thrace. (*Tab. Peut.*)   [T. H. D.]

RAPHANAEA ('Ραφαναία), a maritime city of Syria, only once named by Josephus, who states that the Sabbatic river flowed between Arcaea and Raphanaea. (*B. J.* vii. 5. § 1.) [SABBATICUS.]   [G. W.]

RAPHIA ('Ραφία, 'Ράφεια), a maritime city in the extreme south of Palestine, between Gaza and Rhinocorura, a day's march from both, reckoned by Josephus, Polybius, and others, as the first city of Syria. (Joseph. *B. J.* iv. 11. § 5; Polyb. v. 80.) It was taken from the Egyptians by Alexander Jannaeus, and held by the Jews for some time. It was one of the ruined and depopulated cities restored by Gabinius. (*Ant.* xiii. 13. § 3, 15. § 4, xiv. 5. § 3.) It is mentioned also by Strabo (xvi. p. 759) and in the Itinerary of Antoninus, between the above-named towns. Coins of Raphia still exist, and it was represented by its bishop in the council of Ephesus, and in those of Constantinople, A. D. 536 and 553. (Reland, *s. v.* pp. 967, 968; Le Quien, *Oriens Christianus,* vol. iii. pp. 629, 630.) It was in the neighbourhood of this city that a great battle was fought

between Ptolemy Philopator and Antiochus the Great, in which the latter was routed with immense loss. (3 *Maccab.* i. 2; Polyb. v. 80, &c.; Hieron. *ad Dan.* cap. xi.) Its site is still marked by the name *Refah,* and two ancient granite columns *in situ,* with several prostrate fragments, the remains apparently of a temple of considerable magnitude. (Irby and Mangles' *Journal,* October 8.)   [G. W.]

RAPPIA'NA, a town on the river Margus in Moesia Superior, now *Alexinitsa.* (*Itin. Hieros.* p. 566.)   [T. H. D.]

RAPRAUA ('Ράπραυα, Marcian, *Peripl.* ii. § 32, ed. Müller), a small place on the coast of Gedrosia, between the river Arabis and the Portus Mulierum. It is probably the same as that called by Ptolemy Ragirava ('Ραγίραυα, vi. 21. § 2). It may be doubted whether it can now be recognised, unless indeed the name has been preserved in that of *Arabat,* a bay in the immediate neighbourhood. (See Müller, *ad Arrian. Indic.* § 26.)   [V.]

RARA'PIA (*Itin. Ant.* p. 426, where the reading varies between Scalacia, Serapia, Sarapia, and Rarapia), a town of Lusitania, on the road from Ossonoba to Ebora, and 95 miles N. of the former place; now *Ferreira.* (Comp. Florez. *Esp. Sagr.* xiv. p. 202.)   [T. H. D.]

RARASSA ('Ράρδωσα or 'Ηράρασα, Ptol. vii. 1. § 50), a place which Ptolemy calls the metropolis of the Caspeirnei in India intra Gangem. Its exact situation cannot be determined; but there can be no doubt that it was in Western India, not far from the *Vindya Ms.* Lassen places it a little S. of *Ajmir.*   [V.]

RA'SENA. [ETRURIA, pp. 855, 859.)

RATAE (*Itin. Ant.* pp. 477, 479: *Ράτε,* Ptol. ii. 3. § 20, where some read 'Ράγε), a town of the Coritani in the interior of Britannia Romana, and on the road from *London* to *Lincoln.* It is called Ratecorion in the Geogr. Rav. (v. 31). Camden (p. 537) identifies it with *Leicester.*   [T. H. D.]

RATA'NEUM (Plin. iii. 22. s. 26; 'Ράτινον, Dion Cass. lvi. 11), a town of Dalmatia, which was burnt by its inhabitants, when it was taken by Germanicus in the reign of Augustus. (Dion Cass. *l. c.*)

RATIA'RIA ('Ρατιαρία, Procop. *de Aed.* iv. 6, p. 290; 'Ρατιαρία Μυσῶν, Ptol. iii. 9. § 4, viii. 11. § 5; 'Ραζαρία, Hierocl. p. 655; 'Ραγηρία, Theophylact. i. 8; Ratiaris, Geogr. Rav. iv. 7), a considerable town in Moesia Superior on the Danube, and the head-quarters of a Roman legion; according to the Itinerary (p. 219), the Leg. XIV. Gemina, according to the Not. Imp. (c. 30), the Leg. XIII. Gemina. It was also the station of a fleet on the Danube (*ibid.*). Usually identified with *Arzar-Palanca.* [T. H. D.]

RATIA'TUM ('Ρατίατον), a town of the Pictones (Ptol. ii. 7. § 6). Ptolemy mentions it before Limonum, and places it north of Limonum, and further west. Some editions of Ptolemy place Ratiatum in the territory of the Lemovices, but this is a mistake. In the records of a council held at *Orléans* in A. D. 511, the bishop of the Pictavi signs himself "de civitate Ratiatica." The name was preserved in that of the Pagus Ratiatensis, from which comes the modern name of *Pays de Retz.* Gregory of Tours speaks of Ratiatum as "infra terminum Pictavorum qui adjacet civitati Namneticae." The district of *Retz* was taken from the diocese of *Poitiers* and attached to the diocese of *Nantes* in the time of Charles the Bald. Belley (*Mém. de l'Acad. des Inscript.* tom. xix. p. 729) fixes Ratiatum at the site of the two churches of *St. Pierre* and *St. Op-*

portus de Retz, which are near *Machecoul* and on the *Tenu*, a small river in the department of *La Vendée*. The *Tenu* enters the sea near *Bourgneuf*, opposite to the *Isle Noirmoutier* (D'Anville, *Notice, &c.*; Ukert, *Gallien*, p. 393). [G. L.]

RATOMAGUS. [ROTOMAGUS.]

RAUDA ('Pαῦδα, Ptol. ii. 6. § 50), a town of the Vaccaei in Hispania Tarraconensis, on the road from Asturica to Caesar Augusta (*Itin. Ant.* p. 440), now *Roa*, on the *Douro*. (Comp. Florez. *Esp. Sagr.* vii. p. 274.) [T. H. D.]

RAU'DII CAMPI. [CAMPI RAUDII.]

RAVENNA ('Pαούεννα, Strab.; 'Pάβεννα, Ptol. *et al.*: *Eth.* Ravennas -ātis: *Ravenna*), one of the most important cities of Gallia Cispadana, situated a short distance from the sea-coast, at the southern extremity of the extensive range of marshes and lagunes, which occupied the whole coast of Venetia from thence to Altinum. (Strab. v. p. 213; *Itin. Ant.* p. 126.) It was 33 miles N. of Ariminum. Though included within the limits of Cisalpine Gaul, according to the divisions established in the days of Strabo and Pliny, it does not appear to have ever been a Gaulish city. Strabo tells us that it was a Thessalian colony, which probably meant that it was a Pelasgic settlement, and was connected with the traditions that ascribed to the Pelasgi the foundation of the neighbouring city of Spina. [SPINA.] But they subsequently, according to the same writer, received a body of Umbrian colonists, in order to maintain themselves against the growing power of the Etruscans, and thus became an Umbrian city, to which people they continued to belong till they passed under the Roman government. (Strab. v. pp. 214, 217.) Pliny, on the other hand, calls it a *Sabine* city, — a strange statement, which we are wholly unable to explain. (Plin. iii. 15. s. 20.) It seems probable that it was really an Umbrian settlement, and retained its national character, though surrounded by the Lingonian Gauls, until it received a Roman colony. No mention of the name is found in history till a late period of the Roman Republic, but it appears to have been then already a place of some consequence. In B. C. 82, during the civil wars of Marius and Sulla, it was occupied by Metellus, the lieutenant of the latter, who made it the point of departure from whence he carried on his operations. (Appian, *B. C.* i. 89.) Again it was one of the places which was frequently visited by Caesar during his command in Gaul, for the purpose of raising levies, and communicating with his friends at Rome (Cic. *ad Att.* vii. 1, *ad Fam.* i. 9, viii. 1); and just before the outbreak of the Civil War it was there that he established his head-quarters; from whence he carried on negotiations with the senate, and from whence he ultimately set out on his march to Ariminum. (Id. *ib.* ii. 32; Caes. *B. C.* i. 5; Suet. *Caes.* 30; Appian, *B. C.* ii. 32.) Its name again figures repeatedly in the civil wars between Antony and Octavian, especially during the war of Perusia (Appian, *B. C.* iii. 42, 97, v. 33, 50, &c.); and it is evident that it was already become one of the most important towns in this part of Cisalpine Gaul.

It is uncertain at what period Ravenna received a Roman colony. Strabo speaks of it as having in his time, as well as Ariminum, received a body of Roman colonists (v. p. 217); but the date is not mentioned, and it certainly did not, like Ariminum, pass into the condition of a regular Colonia, numerous inscriptions being extant which give it the title

of a Municipium. It is probable that the settlement alluded to by Strabo took place under Augustus, and it is certain that it was to that emperor that Ravenna was indebted for the importance which it subsequently enjoyed during the whole period of the Roman Empire. The situation of the city was very peculiar. It was surrounded on all sides by marshes, or rather lagunes, analogous to those which now surround the city of *Venice*, and was built, like that city, actually in the water, so that its houses and edifices were wholly constructed on piles, and it was intersected in all directions by canals, which were crossed either by bridges or ferries. The lagunes had a direct communication with the sea, so that the canals were scoured every day by the flux and reflux of the tides, — a circumstance to which Strabo attributes, no doubt with justice, the healthiness of the city, which must otherwise have been uninhabitable from malaria. (Strab. v. p. 213; Jornand. *Get.* 29; Sidon. Apoll. *Epist.* i. 5; Procop. *B. G.* i. 1; Claudian, *de VI. Cons. Hon.* 495.) The old city had a small port at the mouth of the river Bedesis, mentioned by Pliny as flowing under its walls (Plin. iii. 15. s. 20); but Augustus, having determined to make it the permanent station of his fleet in the Adriatic, constructed a new and spacious port, which is said to have been capable of containing 250 ships of war (Jornand. *l. c.*), and was furnished with a celebrated Pharos or lighthouse to mark its entrance. (Plin. xxxvi. 12. s. 18.) This port was near 3 miles distant from the old city, with which it was connected by a long causeway: a considerable town rapidly grew up around it, which came to be known by the name of PORTUS CLASSIS or simply CLASSIS; while between the two, but nearer to the city, there arose another suburb, scarcely less extensive, which bore the name of Caesarea. (Jornand. *l. c.*; Sidon. Apoll. *l. c.*; Procop. *B. G.* ii. 29; Geogr. Rav. iv. 31.) In addition to these works Augustus constructed a canal, called from him the Fossa Augusta, by which a part of the waters of the Padus were carried in a deep artificial channel under the very walls of Ravenna and had their outlet at the port of Classis. (Plin. iii. 16. s. 20; Jornand. *l. c.*)

From this time Ravenna continued to be the permanent station of the Roman fleet which was destined to guard the Adriatic or Upper Sea, as Misenum was of that on the Lower (Tac. *Ann.* iv. 5, *Hist.* ii. 100, iii. 6, 40; Suet. *Aug.* 49; Veget. *de R. Mil.* v. 1; *Not. Dign.* ii. p. 118); and it rose rapidly into one of the most considerable cities of Italy. For the same reason it became an important military post, and was often selected by the emperors as their head-quarters, from which to watch or oppose the advance of their enemies into Italy. In A. D. 193 it was occupied by Severus in his march upon Rome against Didius Julian (Spartian, *Did. Jul.* 6; Dion Cass. lxxiii. 17); and in 238 it was there that Pupienus was engaged in assembling an army to oppose the advance of Maximin when he received the news of the death of that emperor before Aquileia. (Herodian, viii. 6, 7; Capit. *Maximin.* 24, 25, *Max. et Balb.* 11, 12.) Its strong and secluded position also caused it to be selected as a frequent place of confinement for prisoners of distinction, such as the son of the German chieftain Arminius, and Maroboduus, chief of the Suevi. (Tac. *Ann.* i. 58, ii. 63; Suet. *Tib.* 20.) The same circumstances at a later period led to its selection by the feeble and timid Honorius as the place of his residence: his example was followed by his successors; and from the year 404, when Honorius first established himself there, to the close of the Western Empire, Ravenna continued to be the permanent imperial residence and the place from whence all the laws and rescripts of the emperors were dated. (Jornand. *Get.* 29 ; Gibbon, c. 30.) Even before this period we are told that it was a very rich and populous city, as well as of great strength (Zosim. ii. 10): it was the capital of Picenum (as that name was then used) and the residence of the Consularis or governor of that province. (Orell. *Inscr.* 3649; Böcking, *ad Not. Dign.* ii. pp. 359, 443.) But the establishment of the imperial court there naturally added greatly to its prosperity and splendour, while its inaccessible situation preserved it from the calamities which at this period laid waste so many cities of Italy. Yet Ravenna as a place of residence must always have had great disadvantages. Sidonius Apollinaris, who visited it late in the fifth century, complains especially of the want of fresh water, as well as the muddiness of the canals, the swarms of gnats, and the croaking of frogs. (Sidon. Apoll. *Ep.* i. 5, 8.) Martial, at a much earlier period, also alludes to the scarcity of fresh water, which he jestingly asserts was so dear that a cistern was a more valuable property than a vineyard. (Martial, iii. 56, 57.)

After the fall of the Western Empire Ravenna continued to be the capital of the Gothic kings. Odoacer, who had taken refuge there after repeated defeats by Theodoric, held out for near three years, but was at length compelled to surrender. (Jornand. *Get.* 57; Cassiod. *Chron.* p. 649.) Theodoric himself established his residence there, and his example was followed by his successors, until, in 539, Vitiges was after a long siege compelled by famine to surrender the city to Belisarius. (Procop. *B. G.* ii. 28, 29.) It now became the residence of the governors who ruled a part of Italy in the name of the Byzantine emperors, with the title of exarchs, whence the whole of this province came to be known as the Exarchate of Ravenna. The Byzantine governors were in a state of frequent hostility with the Lombard kings, and were gradually stripped of a large portion of their dominions; but Ravenna itself defied their arms for more than two centuries. It was besieged by Liutprand about 750, and its important suburb of Classis totally destroyed (P. Diac. vi. 49); but it was not till the reign of his successor Astolphus that Ravenna itself fell into the hands of the Lombards. But the exact date, as well as the circumstances of its final conquest, are uncertain. (Gibbon, c. 49.)

The situation of Ravenna at the present day presents no resemblance to that described by ancient writers. Yet there is no doubt that the modern city occupies the same site with the ancient one, and that the change is wholly due to natural causes. The accumulation of alluvial deposits, brought down by the rivers and driven back by the waves and tides, has gradually filled up the lagunes that surrounded and canals that intersected the city; and the modern Ravenna stands in a flat and fertile plain, at a distance of 4 miles from the sea, from which it is separated by a broad sandy tract, covered in great part with a beautiful forest of stone pines. Though Ravenna is one of the most interesting places in Italy for its mediaeval and early Christian antiquities, it presents few remains of the Roman period, and those for the most part belong to the

declining years of the Empire. A triumphal arch, known by the name of Porta Aurea, was destroyed in 1585: it stood near the modern gate called *Porta Adriana*. Several of the ancient basilicas date from the Roman period; as does also the sepulchral chapel containing the tomb of Galla Placidia, the sister of Honorius, and mother of Valentinian III. A portion of the palace of Theodoric still remains in its original state, and the mausoleum of that monarch, just without the walls, is a monument of remarkable character, though stripped of its external ornaments. An ancient basilica, still called *S. Apollinare in Classe*, about 3 miles from the southern gate of the city, preserves the memory and marks the site of the ancient port and suburb of Classis ; while another basilica, which subsisted down to the year 1553, bore the name of *S. Lorenzo in Cesarea :* and thus indicated the site of that important suburb. It stood about a quarter of a mile from the south gate of the city, between the walls and the bridge now called *Ponte Nuovo*. This bridge crosses the united streams of the *Ronco* and *Montone*, two small rivers which previously held separate courses to the sea, but were united into one and confined within an artificial channel by Clement XII. in 1736. The *Ronco*, which is the southernmost of the two, is probably the same with the Bedesis of Pliny; indeed Cluverius says that it was in his time still called *Bedeso*. Hence the *Montone* must be identified with the Vrvus of the same author. The Anemo, which he places next in order, is clearly the same now called the *Amone* or *Lamone*, which flows under the walls of *Faenza*. (Plin. iii. 15. s. 20; Cluver. *Ital.* p. 300.)

The natural causes which have produced these changes in the situation and environs of Ravenna were undoubtedly in operation from an early period. Already in the fifth century the original port constructed by Augustus was completely filled up, and occupied by orchards. (Jornand. *Get.* 29.) But Ravenna at that period had still a much frequented port, where the fleets of Belisarius and Narses could ride at anchor. The port of Classis itself is now separated from the sea by a strip of sandy and marshy plain about 2 miles broad, the greater part of which is occupied by a forest of stone pines, which extends for many miles along the sea-coast both to the S. and N. of Ravenna. The existence of this remarkable strip of forest is attested as early as the fifth century, the name of Pineta being already found in Jornandes, who tells us that Theodoric encamped there when he besieged Odoacer in Ravenna. (Jornand. 57.) But it is probable that it has extended its boundaries and shifted its position as the land has gradually gained upon the sea.

The territory of Ravenna was always fertile, except the sandy strip adjoining the sea, and produced abundance of wine of good quality, but it was remarked that the vines quickly decayed. (Strab. v. p. 214; Plin. xiv. 2. s. 4.) Its gardens also are noticed by Pliny as growing the finest asparagus, while the adjoining sea was noted for the excellence of its turbot. (Plin. ix. 54. s. 79, xix. 4. s. 19.)　　　　　　　　　　　　　　　　[E. H. B.]

RAVIUS (Ῥάούιος, Ptol. ii. 2. § 4), a river on the W. coast of Hibernia, according to Camden (p. 1385) the *Trobis*. Others identify it with the *Guebara*.　　　　　　　　　　　　　　[T. H. D.]

RAURACI, or RAURICI (Ῥαυρικοί). The form Raurici appears in Ptolemy (ii. 9. § 18), in Pliny (iv.

17), and in some inscriptions. Ptolemy mentions two towns of the Rauraci, Rauricorum Augusta and Argentovaria [AUGUSTA RAURACORUM; ARGEN-TARIA]. Augusta is *Augst* near *Bâle*, in the Swiss Canton of *Bâle*, and Argentovaria may be *Artsenheim*. The position of these places helps us to form a measure of the extent of the territory of the Rauraci, which may have nearly coincided with the bishopric of *Bâle*.

The Rauraci joined the Helvetii in their emigration, B. C. 58. [HELVETII.]　　　　　　[G. L.]

RAURANUM, in Gallia, is placed by the Table and the Antonine Itin. on a direct road from Mediolanum Santonum (*Saintes*) to Limonum (*Poitiers*). It is Raurana in the Table, but the name Rauranum occurs in a letter of Paulinus to Ausonius (*Ep. IV. ad Auson.* v. 249), who places it "Pictonicis in arvis." The place is *Rom* or *Raum*, near *Chenay*, nearly due south of *Poitiers*. (D'Anville, *Notice, &c.*; Ukert, *Gallien*, p. 392.)　　[G. L.]

RAURARIS. [ARAURIS.]

REATE ('Ρέατε, Strab.; 'Ρέατος, Dionys.: *Eth.* 'Ρεατίνος, Reatinus: *Rieti*), an ancient city of the Sabines, and one of the most considerable that belonged to that people. It was situated on the Via Salaria, 48 miles from Rome (*Itin. Ant.* p. 306), and on the banks of the river Velinus. All writers agree in representing it as a very ancient city: according to one account, quoted by Dionysius from Zenodotus of Troezen, it was one of the original abodes of the Umbrians, from which they were expelled by the Pelasgi; but Cato represented it as one of the first places occupied by the Sabines when they descended from the neighbourhood of Amiternum, their original abode. (Dionys. ii. 49.) Whatever authority Cato may have had for this statement, there seems no reason to doubt that it was substantially true. The fertile valley in which Reate was situated lay in the natural route of migration for a people descending from the highlands of the central Apennines; and there is no doubt that both Reate and its neighbourhood were in historical times occupied by the Sabines. It was this migration of the Sabines that led to the expulsion of the Aborigines, who, according to Dionysius, previously occupied this part of Italy, and whose most ancient metropolis, Lista, was only 24 stadia from Reate. (Dionys. i. 14, ii. 49.) Silius Italicus appears to derive its name from Rhea, and calls it consecrated to the Mother of the Gods; but this is probably a mere poetical fancy. (Sil. Ital. viii. 415.) No mention of Reate occurs in history before the period when the Sabines had been subjected to the Roman rule, and admitted to the Roman Franchise (B. C. 290); but its name is more than once incidentally noticed during the Second Punic War. In B. C. 211 Hannibal passed under its walls during his retreat from Rome, or, according to Coelius, during his advance upon that city (Liv. xxvi. 11); and in B. C. 205 the Reatini are specially mentioned as coming forward, in common with the other Sabines, to furnish volunteers to the armament of Scipio. (Id. xxviii. 45.) We are wholly ignorant of the reasons why it was reduced to the subordinate condition of a Praefectura, under which title it is repeatedly mentioned by Cicero, but we learn from the great orator himself, under whose especial patronage the inhabitants were placed, that it was a flourishing and important town. (Cic. *in Cat.* iii. 2, *pro Scaur.* 2. § 27, *de Nat. Deor.* ii. 2.) Under the Empire it certainly obtained the ordinary municipal privileges, and had

its own magistrates (Zumpt, *de Col.* pp. 98, 188; Gruter, *Inscr.* p. 354. 3, &c.): under Vespasian it received a considerable number of veteran soldiers as colonists, but did not obtain the rank or title of a Colonia. (*Lib. Col.* p. 257; Orell. *Inscr.* 3685; Gruter, *Inscr.* p. 538. 2; &c.)

The territory of Reate included the whole of the lower valley of the Velinus, as far as the falls of that river; one of the most fertile, as well as beautiful, districts of Italy, whence it is called by Cicero the Reatine Tempe (*ad Att.* iv. 15.) But the peculiar natural character of this district was the means of involving the citizens in frequent disputes with their neighbours of Interamna. (Varr. *R. R.* iii. 2. § 3.) The valley of the Velinus below Reate, where the river emerges from the narrow mountain valley through which it has hitherto flowed, and receives at the same time the waters of the *Salto* and *Turano*, both of them considerable streams, expands into a broad plain, not less than 5 or 6 miles in breadth, and almost perfectly level; so that the waters of the Velinus itself, and those of the smaller streams that flow into it, have a tendency to stagnate and form marshes, while in other places they give rise to a series of small lakes, remarkable for their picturesque beauty. The largest of these, now known as the *Lago di Piè di Lugo*, seems to have been the one designated in ancient times as the LACUS VELINUS; while the fertile plains which extended from Reate to its banks were known as the ROSEI or more properly ROSEAE CAMPI, termed by Virgil the "Rosea rura Velini." (Virg. *Aen.* vii. 712; Cic. *ad Att.* iv. 15; Varro, *R. R.* i. 7. § 10, ii. 1. § 16, iii. 2. § 10; Plin. xvii. 4. s. 3.) But this broad and level valley is at an elevation of near 1000 feet above that of the Nar, into which it pours its waters by an abrupt descent, a few miles above Interamna (*Terni*); and the stream of the Velinus must always have constituted in this part a natural cascade. Those waters, however, are so strongly impregnated with carbonate of lime, that they are continually forming an extensive deposit of travertine, and thus tending to block up their own channel. The consequence was, that unless their course was artificially regulated, and their channel kept clear, the valley of the Velinus was inundated, while on the other hand, if these waters were carried off too rapidly into the Nar, the valley of that river and the territory of Interamna suffered the same fate. The first attempt to regulate the course of the Velinus artificially, of which we have any account, was made by M'. Curius Dentatus, after his conquest of the Sabines, when he carried off its waters by a deep cut through the brow of the hill overlooking the Nar, and thus gave rise to the celebrated cascade now known as the *Falls of Terni*. (Cic. *ad Att.* iv. 15; Serv. *ad Aen.* vii. 712.) From the expressions of Cicero it would appear that the Lacus Velinus, previous to this time, occupied a much larger extent, and that a considerable part of the valley was then first reclaimed for cultivation.

But the expedient thus resorted to did not fully accomplish its object. In the time of Cicero (B. C. 54) fresh disputes arose between the citizens of Reate and those of Interamna; and the former appealed to the great orator himself as their patron, who pleaded their cause before the arbiters appointed by the Roman senate. On this occasion he visited Reate in person, and inspected the lakes and the channels of the Velinus. (Cic. *pro Scaur.* 2. § 27, *ad Att.* iv. 15.) The result of the arbitration is unknown: but in the reign of Tiberius the Reatines had to contend against a more formidable danger, arising from the project which had been suggested of blocking up the outlet of the Lacus Velinus altogether; a measure which, as they justly complained, would undoubtedly have inundated the whole valley. (Tac. *Ann.* i. 79.) Similar disputes and difficulties again arose in the middle ages; and in A. D. 1400 a new channel was opened for the waters of the Velinus, which has continued in use ever since.

No other mention occurs of Reate under the Roman Empire; but inscriptions attest its continued municipal importance: its name is found in the Itineraries (*Itin. Ant.* p. 306), and it early became the see of a bishop, which it has continued ever since. Throughout the middle ages it was, as it still continues to be, the capital of the surrounding country. No ancient remains are now visible at *Rieti.*

The territory of Reate was famous in ancient times for its breed of mules and asses; the latter were particularly celebrated, and are said to have been sometimes sold for a price as high as 300,000 or even 400,000 sesterces (Varr. *R.R.* ii. 8. § 3; Plin. viii. 43. s. 68), though it is difficult not to suppose some error in these numbers. Hence, Q. Axius, a friend of Varro, who had a villa on the Lacus Velinus, and extensive possessions in the Reatine territory, is introduced by Varro in his dialogues *De Re Rustica,* as discoursing on the subject of breeding horses, mules, and asses. (Varr. *R. R.* ii. 1. § 8; Strab. v. p. 228.) It was at the villa of this Q. Axius that Cicero lodged when he visited Reate. (Cic. *ad Att.* iv. 15.) The SEPTEM AQUAE, mentioned by him in the same passage, and alluded to also by Dionysius (i. 14), were evidently some springs or sources, which supplied one of the small lakes in the valley of the Velinus.   [E. H. B.]

RECHIUS. [BOLBE.]

REDINTUINUM ('Ρεδιντούινον), a town in the northern part of the country occupied by the Marcomanni (*Bohemia*), is mentioned only by Ptolemy (ii. 11. § 29). Some geographers regard it as having occupied the site of the modern *Prague,* and others identify it with *Horsies;* but nothing certain can be said about the matter.   [L. S.]

RE'DONES ('Ρήδονες, 'Ρηΐδονες), in the Celtogalatia Lugdunensis of Ptolemy (ii. 8. § 12), are placed by him west of the Senones and along the Liger. Their capital is Condate (*Rennes*). But the Redones were not on the *Loire.* Pliny (iv. 18) enumerates the Rhedones among the peoples of Gallia Lugdunensis: "Diablindi, Rhedones, Turones." After the bloody fight on the *Sambre* (B. C. 57) Caesar sent P. Crassus with a single legion into the country of the Veneti, Redones, and other Celtic tribes between the *Seine* and the *Loire*, all of whom submitted. (*B. G.* ii. 34.) Caesar here enumerates the Redones among the maritime states whose territory extends to the ocean. In B. C. 52 the Redones with their neighbours sent a contingent to attack Caesar during the siege of Alesia. In this passage also (*B. G.* vii. 75), the Redones are enumerated among the states bordering on the ocean, which in the Celtic language were called the Armoric States. D'Anville supposes that their territory extended beyond the limits of the diocese of *Rennes* into the dioceses of *St. Malo* and *Dol.* Their chief town, *Rennes*, is the capital of the department of *Ille-et-Vilaine.*   [G. L.]

REGANUM, a northern tributary of the Danube,

the modern *Regen* in *Bavaria,* is noticed only once. (Geogr. Rav. iv. 25.)   [L. S.]

RE'GIA ('Ρηγία, Ptol. ii. 2. § 10). A place in the interior of Hibernia, no doubt so named by the Romans from its being a royal residence, the proper name of which was unknown to them. It was perhaps seated on the river *Culmore,* in the neighbourhood of *Omagh.*

2. ('Ετέρα 'Ρηγία, Ptol. *l. c.*), another place of the same description, conjectured to have been on the river *Dur.*

3. Regia Carissa. [CARISSA.]   [T. H. D.]

REGIA'NA (called by Ptol. ii. 4. § 13, 'Ρήγινα; comp. Geogr. Rav. iv. 44, and Regina, Plin. iii. 3), a town of Baetica, on the road from Hispalis to Emerita. (*Itin. Ant.* p. 415.) Usually identified with *Puebla de la Reyna,* where there are Roman remains.   [T. H. D.]

REGIA'NUM ('Ρηγιανον, Ptol. iii. 10. § 10), a place on the Danube in Moesia Inferior. It is probably the same place as the Augusta of the Itinerary (p. 220; comp. *Tab. Peut.*) and the Αὐγούστον of Procopius (*de Aed.* iv. 6); in which case it may be identified with *Cotoszlin* at the confluence of the *Ogristul* and *Danube.*   [T. H. D.]

REGILLUM ('Ρήγιλλον), a town of the Sabines mentioned by several ancient writers as the place of residence of Atta or Attius Clausus, who migrated to Rome about B. C. 505, with a large body of clients and followers, where he adopted the name of Appius Claudius and became the founder of the Claudian tribe and family. (Liv. ii. 16; Dionys. v. 40; Suet. *Tib.* 1; Serv. *ad Aen.* vii. 706.) About 60 years afterwards C. Claudius, the uncle of the decemvir Appius Claudius, withdrew into retirement to Regillum, as the native place of his forefathers ("antiquam in patriam," Liv. iii. 58; Dionys. xi. 15). The name is not noticed on any other occasion, nor is it found in any of the geographers, and we are wholly without a clue to its position.   [E. H. B.]

REGILLUS LACUS (ἡ 'Ρηγίλλη λίμνη, Dionys.: *Lago di Cornufelle*), a small lake in Latium, at the foot of the Tusculan hills, celebrated for the great battle between the Romans and the Latins under C. Mamilius, in B. C. 496. (Liv. ii. 19; Dionys. vi. 3; Cic. *de Nat. D.* ii. 2, iii. 5; Plin. xxxiii. 2. s. 11; Val. Max. i. 8. § 1; Vict. *Vir. Ill.* 16; Flor. i. 11.) Hardly any event in the early Roman history has been more disguised by poetical embellishment and fiction than the battle of Regillus, and it is impossible to decide what amount of historical character may be attached to it: but there is no reason to doubt the existence of the lake, which was assigned as the scene of the combat. It is expressly described by Livy as situated in the territory of Tusculum ("ad lacum Regillum in agro Tusculano," Liv. ii. 19); and this seems decisive against the identification of it with the small lake called *Il Laghetto di Sta Prassede,* about a mile to the N. of *La Colonna;* for this lake must have been in the territory of Labicum, if that city be correctly placed at *La Colonna* [LABICUM], and at all events could hardly have been in that of Tusculum. Moreover, the site of this lake being close to the Via Labicana would more probably have been indicated by some reference to that high-road than by the vague phrase "in agro Tusculano." A much more plausible suggestion is that of Gell, that it occupied the site of a volcanic crater, now drained of its waters, but which was certainly once occupied by a lake, at a place called *Cornufelle,* at the foot of the hill on which stands the modern town of *Frascati*. This crater, which resembles that of Gabii on a much smaller scale, being not more than half a mile in diameter, was drained by an artificial emissary as late as the 17th century: but its existence seems to have been unknown to Cluverius and other early writers, who adopted the lake or pool near *La Colonna* for the Lake Regillus, on the express ground that there was no other in that neighbourhood. (Cluver. *Ital.* p. 946; Nibby, *Dintorni*, vol. iii. pp. 8—10; Gell, *Top. of Rome*, pp. 186, 371.) Extensive remains of a Roman villa and baths may be traced on the ridge which bounds the crater, and an ancient road from Tusculum to Labicum or Gabii passed close by it, so that the site must certainly have been one well known in ancient times.   [E. H. B.]

REGINA. [ERGINUS ; REGIANA.]

REGINEA, in Gallia Lugdunensis, is placed in the Table on a road from Condate (*Rennes*). The first station is Fanum Martis, and the next is Reginea, 39 Gallic leagues from Condate. D'Anville fixes Reginea at *Erquies* on the coast, between *S. Brieuc* and *S. Malo*. [FANUM MARTIS.]   [G. L.]

REGINUM, a town in the northern part of Vindelicia, on the southern bank of the Danube, on the road leading to Vindobona. This town, the modern *Ratisbon*, or *Regensburg*, is not mentioned by the Roman historians, but it was nevertheless an important frontier fortress, and, as we learn from inscriptions, was successively the station of the 1st, 3rd, and 4th Italian legions, and of a detachment of cavalry, the Ala II. Valeria. The town appears to have also been of great commercial importance, and to have contained among its inhabitants many Roman families of distinction. (*It. Ant.* p. 250; *Tab. Peut.*, where it is called Castra Regina; comp. Rayser, *Der Oberdonaukreis Bayerns*, iii. p. 38, &c.)   [L. S.]

REGIO, a town of Thrace on the river Bathynias, and not far from Constantinople (*Itin. Hieros.* p. 570), with a roadstead, and handsome country houses. (Agath. v. p. 146; comp. Procop. *de Aed.* iv. 8; Theophan. p. 196.) Now *Koutschuk-Tzschekmetsche*.   [T. H. D.]

REGIS VILLA (Ῥηγισούιλλα, Strab.), a place on the coast of Etruria, which, according to Strabo, derived its name from its having been the residence of the Pelasgic king or chief Maleas, who ruled over the neighbouring Pelasgi in this part of Etruria. (Strab. v. p. 225.) None of the other geographers mentions the locality; but Strabo places it between Cosa and Graviscae; and it is therefore in all probability the same place which is called in the Maritime Itinerary REGAE, and is placed 3 miles S. of the river Armenta (*Fiora*) and 12 miles from Graviscae. (*Itin. Marit.* p. 499.) The site is now marked only by some projecting rocks called *Le Murelle*. (Dennis's *Etruria*, vol. i. p. 398; Westphal, *Ann. d. Inst.* 1830, p. 30.)   [E. H. B.]

REGISTUS or RESISTUS. [BISANTHE.]

RE'GIUM LE'PIDI or RE'GIUM LE'PIDUM (Ῥήγιον Λέπιδον, Strab.; Ῥήγιον Λεπίδιον, Ptol.: *Eth.* Rogiensis: *Reggio*), sometimes also called simply REGIUM, a town of Gallia Cispadana, situated on the Via Aemilia, between Mutina and Parma, at the distance of 17 miles from the former and 18 from the latter city. (*Itin. Ant.* pp. 99, 127; Strab. v. p. 216.) We have no account of its foundation or origin; but the name would raise a presumption that it was founded, or at least settled and enlarged, by Aemilius Lepidus when he constructed the Aemi-

lian Way ; and this is confirmed by a passage of Festus, from which it appears that it was originally called Forum Lepidi. (Fest. *s. v. Rhegium*, p. 270.) The origin of the appellation of Regium, which completely superseded the former name, is unknown. It did not become a colony like the neighbouring cities of Mutina and Parma, and evidently never rose to the same degree of opulence and prosperity as those cities, but became, nevertheless, a flourishing municipal town. It is repeatedly mentioned during the civil war with M. Antonius, both before and after the battle of Mutina (Cic. *ad Fam.* xi. 9, xii. 5); and at a somewhat earlier period it was there that M. Brutus, the father of the murderer of Caesar, was put to death by Pompey in B. C. 79. (Oros. v. 22; Plut. *Pomp.* 16.) Its name scarcely occurs in history during the Roman Empire ; but its municipal consideration is attested by inscriptions, and it is mentioned by all the geographers among the towns on the Via Aemilia, though ranked by Strabo with those of the second class. (Strab. v. p. 216; Plin. iii. 15. s. 20; Ptol. iii. 1. § 46; Orell. *Inscr.* 3983, 4133 ; Tac. *Hist.* ii. 50; Phlegon, *Macrob.* 1.) Ptolemy alone gives it the title of a Colonia, which is probably a mistake ; it was certainly not such in the time of Pliny, nor is it so designated in any extant inscription. Zumpt, however, supposes that it may have received a colony under Trajan or Hadrian. (Zumpt, *de Colon.* p. 403.) St. Ambrose notices Regium as well as Placentia and Mutina among the cities which had fallen into great decay before the close of the fourth century. (Ambros. *Ep.* 39.) It was not long before this that an attempt had been made by the emperor Gratian to repair the desolation of this part of Italy by settling a body of Gothic captives in the territory of Regium, Parma, and the neighbouring cities. (Ammian. xxxi. 9. § 4.) The continued existence of Regium at a late period is proved by the Itineraries and Tabula (*Itin. Ant.* pp. 283, 287; *Itin. Hier.* p. 616; *Tab. Peut.*), and it is mentioned long after the fall of the Western Empire by Paulus Diaconus among the "locupletes urbes" of Aemilia. (P. Diac. *Hist. Lang.* ii. 18.) In the middle ages it rose to a great degree of prosperity, and *Reggio* is still a considerable town with about 16000 inhabitants. Its episcopal see dates from the fifth century.

The tract called the CAMPI MACRI, celebrated for the excellence of its wool, was apparently included in the territory of Regium Lepidum.   [E. H. B.]

REGNI (Ῥῆγνοι, Ptol. ii. 3. § 28), a people on the S. coast of Britannia Romana, seated between the Cantii on the E. and the Belgae on the W., in the modern counties of *Surrey* and *Sussex*. Their chief town was Noviomagus. (Comp. Camden, p. 179.)   [T. H. D.]

REGNUM, a town of the Belgae in the S. of Britannia Romana, and seemingly a place of some importance, since there was a particular road to it. (*Itin. Ant.* p. 477.) Camden (p. 133) identifies it with *Ringwood* in *Hampshire*. Horsley, on the contrary (p. 441), conjectures it to have been *Chichester ;* but, though Roman antiquities have been found at *Chichester*, its situation does not suit the distances given in the Itinerary.   [T. H. D.]

REGU'LBIUM, a town of the Cantii on the E. coast of Britannia Romana, now *Reculver*. (*Not. Imp.*; comp. Camden, p. 236.)   [T. H. D.]

REHOB (Ῥοώβ, al. Ῥαδέ, al. Ἐρεώ), a town in the tribe of Asher, occupied by the Canaanites. (*Josh.* xix. 28; *Judg.* i. 31.) A second city of the same name is reckoned among the 22 cities of the same tribe (*Josh.* xix. 30); but neither of these can be identified with the Rhoob ('Ροώβ) noticed by Eusebius, 4 miles distant from Scythopolis.   [G. W.]

REHOBOTH (translated εὑρυχωρία in LXX.), one of the wells dug by Isaac in the country of Gerar, — after Esek (contention) and Sitnah (hatred), — for which the herdsmen did not strive: so he called it Rehoboth: "And he said, For now the Lord hath made room for us, and we shall be fruitful in the land." (*Gen.* xxvi. 18, 20—22.) There was a town in the vicinity of the well, the traces of which were recovered, with the well itself, by Mr. Rowlands, in 1843. " About a quarter of an hour beyond *Sebâta*, we came to the remains of what must have been a very well-built city, called now *Rohébeh.* This is undoubtedly the ancient Rehoboth, where Abraham, and afterwards Isaac, digged a well. This lies, as Rehoboth did, in the land of Gerar. Outside the walls of the city is an ancient well of living and good water called *Bir-Rohébeh.* This most probably is the site, if not the well itself, digged by Isaac." (Williams's *Holy City,* vol. i. Appendix, i. p. 465.)   [G. W.]

REII APOLLINA'RES (*Riez*), in Gallia Narbonensis. Among the Oppida Latina of Gallia Narbonensis, or those which had the Latinitas, Pliny (iii. c. 4) enumerates " Alebece Reiorum Apollinarium." The old reading, " Alebeceriorum Apollinarium," is a blunder made by joining two words together, which has been corrected from the better MSS., from the inscription COL. REIOR. APOLLINAR., and from the Table, which has Reis Apollinaris. The place may have taken its name from a temple of Apollo built after the town became Roman. The name Alebece may be corrupt, or it may be a variation of the form Albici or Albioeci. [ALBICI.] As Pliny calls the place an Oppidum Latinum, we might suppose that it was made a Colonia after his time, but the name Col. Jul. Aug. Apollinar. Reior., which appears in an inscription, shows it to have been a colony of Augustus.

Riez is in the arrondissement of *Digne* in the department of *Basses Alpes.* There are four columns standing near the town, which may be the remains of a temple. The bases and the capitals are marble: the shafts are a very hard granite, and about 18 feet high. There is also a small circular building consisting of eight columns resting on a basement, but it has been spoiled by modern hands. There now stands in it a rectangular altar of one block of white marble, which bears an inscription to the Mother of the Gods and the Great Goddess. At *Riez* there have been discovered an enormous quantity of fragments of granite columns; and it is said that there have been a circus and a theatre in the town. (*Guide du Voyageur,* Richard et Hocquart, p. 792.)   [G. L.]

REMESIA'NA ('Ρεμεσίανα, Hierocl. p. 654; called Romesiana in *Tab. Peut.* and in Geogr. Rav. iv. 7; 'Ρουμισίανα in Procopius, *de Aed.* iv. 1, p. 268, ed. Bonn), a town of Moesia Superior, between Naissus and Serdica. (*Itin. Ant.* p. 135.) Now *Mustapha Palanca.*   [T. H. D.]

REMETODIA (called Remetodion in Geogr. Rav. iv. 7), a place in Moesia Superior on the Danube. (*Tab. Peut.*)   [T. H. D.]

REMI ('Ρημοί), a people of Gallia Belgica (Ptol. ii. 9. § 12) along the Sequana (*Seine*). Their capital was Durocortorum (*Reims*). This is Ptolemy's description (ii. 9. § 12).

Caesar (*B. G.* ii. 3) says that the Remi were the nearest to the Celtae of all the Belgae, and he makes the Sequana and Matrona (*Marne*) the boundary between the Belgae and the Celtae. The Suessiones were the neighbours of the Remi. (*B. G.* ii. 12.) When Caesar had entered the country of the Remi from the south (B. C. 57), he came to the Axona (*Aisne*), which he says is on the borders of the Remi. Eight miles from the *Aisne* and north of it was Bibrax, a town of the Remi. The Remi then extended as far north as the *Aisne,* and beyond it. Their capital, Durocortorum, is between the *Aisne* and the *Marne.*

When the Belgae in the beginning of B. C. 57 were collecting their forces to attack Caesar, the Remi were traitors to their country. They submitted to the Roman proconsul and offered to supply him with corn, to give hostages, to receive him in their towns and to help him against the rest of the Belgae and the Germans with all their power. (*B. G.* ii. 3.) The Suessiones who were in political union with the Remi joined the Belgae. When the great meeting of the Gallic states was held at Bibracte in B. C. 52 to raise troops to attack Caesar at Alesia, the Remi did not come, and they continued faithful to Caesar. When Caesar entered Gallia in B. C. 58, the Aedui and the Sequani were the leading nations; but when the Sequani were humbled, the Remi took their place, and those nations that did not like to attach themselves to the political party of the Aedui, joined the Remi. Thus the Aedui were the first of the Gallic political communities and the Remi were the second. (Caes. *B. G.* vi. 12.) Even the Carnutes, a Celtic people, had attached themselves to the Remi. (*B. G.* vi. 4.) Caesar rewarded the fidelity of the Remi by placing the Suessiones in dependence on them (viii. 6).

Pliny (iv. 17) mentions the Remi as one of the Foederati Populi of Belgica. When Strabo wrote (p. 194) the Remi were a people in great favour with the Romans, and their city Durocortorum was the occasional residence of the Roman governors. [DUROCORTORUM.]

Lucan (*Pharsal.* l. 424) has a line on the Remi:—

" Optimus excusso Leucus Rhemusque lacerto."

But the military skill of the Remi is otherwise unknown. They were a cunning people, who looked after themselves and betrayed their neighbours.   [G. L.]

REPANDUNUM, a town of the Coritani in Britannia Romana, probably *Repton* in *Derbyshire.* (*Not. Imp.*: Camden, p. 586.)   [T. H. D.]

REPHAIM VALLIS (γῆ 'Ραφαίν, 'Εμεκ 'Ραφαίν, κοιλὰς τῶν Τιτάνων, LXX.; κ. Γιγάντων, Joseph.), a valley mentioned in the north border of the tribe of Judah, the south of Benjamin (*Josh.* xv. 8, xviii. 18), in the vicinity of Jerusalem. It is translated " the valley of the giants" in the authorised version, except in 2 *Sam.* v. 18, 22, where we find that the valley of Rephaim was a favourite camping ground for the Philistines, soon after David had got possession of the stronghold of Sion; and in *Isaiah,* xvii. 5, where it is represented as a fruitful corn-bearing tract of land, well answering to the wide valley, or rather plain, immediately south of the valley of Hinnom, traversed by the Bethlehem road, which is commonly identified by travellers as the " valley of the giants," although Eusebius places it in Benjamin (*Onomast. s. v.*).

It evidently derived its name from the Rephaim, a family of the Amalekites (*Gen.* xiv. 5) settled in Ashteroth Karnaim, supposed by Reland to be of the race of the Gephyraei, who came with Cadmus from Phoenicia to Greece. (Herod. v. 57; Reland, *Palaest.* p. 141, comp. pp. 79,355.) The Philistines who are said to have encamped there may have bequeathed their name to the valley.   [G. W.]

REPHIDIM ('Ραφιδείν), the eleventh encampment of the Israelites after leaving Egypt, the next before Sinai, " where was no water for the people to drink." (*Numb.* xxxiii. 14.) Moses was accordingly instructed to smite the rock in Horeb, which yielded a supply for the needs of the people, from whose murmurings the place was named Massah and Meribah. Here also it was that the Israelites first encountered the Amalekites, whom they discomfited ; and here Moses received his father-in-law Jethro. (*Exod.* xvii.) Its position, Dr. Robinson surmises, must have been at some point in *Wady-esh-Sheikh*, not far from the skirts of Horeb (which he takes to be the name of the mountain district), and about a day's march from the particular mountain of Sinai. Such a spot exists where *Wady-esh-Sheikh* issues from the high central granite cliffs ; which locality is more fully described by Burckhardt, and Dr. Wilson, who agrees in the identification, and names the range of rocky mountains *Wateiyah.* He says that " water from the rock in Horeb could easily flow to this place." (Robinson, *Bib. Res.* vol. i. pp. 178, 179 ; Burckhardt, *Travels in Syria, &c.* p. 488 ; Wilson, *Lands of the Bible,* vol. i. p. 254.) Dr. Lepsius controverts this position and proposes *El-Hessue,* only a mile distant from the convent-mountain of *Pharán,* as the Rephidim (= " the resting-place ") of the Exodus. This is at the foot of *Gebel Serbal,* which he regards as the mountain of the law, and finds the stream opened by Moses " in the clear-running and well-flavoured spring of *Wádi Firán,* which irrigates the fertile soil of *El-Hessue,* and causes it to exhibit all the riches of the gardens of *Farán* for the space of half a mile." (Lepsius, *A Tour from Thebes to the Peninsula of Sinai,* pp. 74—82.)   [G. W.]

RERIGO'NIUM ('Ρεριγόνιον, Ptol. ii. 3. § 7), a town of the Novantae in the province of Valentia in the SW. part of Britannia Barbara, which seems to have been seated at the S. extremity of the Sinus Rerigonius (*Loch Ryan*) near *Stanraer.* Camden identifies it with *Bargeny* (p. 1203).   [T. H. D.]

RERIGONIUS SINUS ('Ρεριγόνιος κόλπος, Ptol. ii. 3. § 1), a bay in the country of the Novantae, so named from the town of Rerigonium (*q. v.*). Now *Loch Ryan,* formed by the *Mull of Galloway.* (Horsley, p. 375.)   [T. H. D.]

RESAINA.   [RHESAENA.]

RESAPHA *al.* REZEPH ('Ρησάφα), a city of Syria, reckoned by Ptolemy to the district of Palmyrene (v. 15. § 24), the Risapa of the Peutinger Tables, 21 miles from Sure ; probably identical with the Rossafat of Abulfeda (*Tab. Syr.* p. 119), which he places near *Rakka,* not quite a day's journey from the Euphrates. It is supposed to be identical with the Rezeph of Scripture ('Ραφις, LXX.), taken by Sennacherib, king of Assyria, as he boasts in his insulting letter to Hezekiah. (2 *Kings,* xix. 12.) It has been identified with Sergiopolis, apparently without sufficient reason. (Mannert, *Geographie von Syrien,* p. 413.)   [G. W.]

REUDIGNI, a German tribe on the right bank of the river Albis, and north of the Longobardi,

which may have derived its name from its inhabiting a marshy district, or from *reed* or *ried.* (Tac. *Germ.* 40.) Various conjectures have been hazarded about their exact abodes and their name, which some have wished to change into Reudingi or Deuringi, so as to identify them with the later Thuringi; but all is uncertain.   [L. S.]

REVESSIO ('Ρύεσσιον), in Gallia, is the city of the Vellavi, or Velauni, as the name is written in Ptolemy (ii. 7. § 20). Revessio is the name of the place in the Table. In the Not. Provinc. it is written Civitas Vellavorum. Mabillon has shown that the place called Civitas Vetula in the middle ages is *S. Paulien* or *Paulham,* and the Civitas Vetula is supposed to be the ancient capital of the Vellavi. *S. Paulien* is in the department of *Haute Loire,* north of *Le Puy.*   [G. L.]

RHA ('Ρα ποταμός, Ptol. v. 9. §§ 12, 17, 19, 21, vi. 14. §§ 1, 4; Amm. Marc. xxii. 8. § 28 ; 'Ρῶς, Agathem. ii. 10: *Volga*) a river of Asiatic Sarmatia, which according to Ptolemy (*l. c.*), the earliest geographer who had any accurate knowledge of this longest of European streams, had its twin sources in the E. and W. extremities of the Hyperborean mountains, and discharged itself into the Hyrcanian sea. The affluents which Ptolemy (vi. 14. § 4) describes as falling into it from the Rhymnici Montes, and which must not be confounded with the river Rhymnus [RHYMMUS], are the great accession made to the waters of the Volga by the *Kama* in the government of *Kasan.* Ammianus Marcellinus (*l. c.*) says that its banks were covered with the plant which bore the same name as the river — the " rha " or " rheon " of Dioscorides (ῥᾶ, ῥῆον, iii. 11) and " rhacoma " of Pliny (xxvii. 105), or officinal rhubarb. (Comp. Pereira, *Mat. Med.* vol. ii. pt. 1. p. 1343.) The old reading Rha in the text of Pomponius Mela (iii. 5. § 4) has been shown by Tzschucke (*ad loc.*) to be a mistake of the earlier editors, for which he substitutes Casius, a river of Albania. The OARUS ("Oapos, Herod. iv. 123, 124), where, according to the story of the Scythian expedition, the erection of eight fortresses was supposed to mark the extreme point of the march of Dareius, has been identified by Klaproth, and Schafarik (*Slav. Alt.* vol. i. p. 499)—who mentions that in the language of some tribes the *Volga* is still called " Rhau"—with that river.   [E. B. J.]

RHAABE'NI ('Ρααβηνοί), a people of Arabia Deserta, next to the Agabeni, who were on the confines of Arabia Felix. (Ptol. v. 19. § 2.) Above them were the Masani ; the Orcheni lay between them and the NW. extremity of the *Persian Gulf.* Mr. Forster justly remarks that " the description of Ptolemy rather indicates the direction, than defines the positions, of these several tribes." (*Geog. of Arabia,* vol. ii. p. 238.)   [G. W.]

RHA'BDIUM ('Ράβδιον, Procop. *B. P.* ii. 19, *de Aedif.* ii. 4), a strongly fortified height, in an inaccessible part of Mesopotamia, two days' journey from Dara in the direction of Persia. The works were placed on the brow of very steep rocks which overlook the surrounding country. Justinian added additional works to it. It has not been identified with any modern place.   [V.]

RHACALA'NI.   [ROXOLANI.]

RHACATAE ('Ρακάται), a German tribe mentioned by Ptolemy (ii. 11. § 26) as occupying, together with the Teracatriae, the country on the south of the Quadi, on the frontiers of Pannonia;

but nothing further is known about either of them.   [L. S.]

BHACOTIS. [ALEXANDREIA, p. 95.]

RHAEBA ('Ραΐ6a, Ptol. ii. 2. § 10), a town in the interior of Hibernia, according to Camden (p. 1357) *Rheban* in *Queen's County*.   [T. H. D.]

RHAEDESTUS. [BISANTHE.]

RHAE'TEAE ('Ραιτέαι), a place in the Arcadian district of Cynuria, at the confluence of the Gortynius and Alpheius. (Paus. viii. 28. § 3.)

RHAETIA ('Ραιτία). The name of this country, as well as of its inhabitants, appears in ancient inscriptions invariably without the *h*, as Raetia and Raeti, while the MSS. of Latin authors commonly have the forms Rhaetia and Rhaeti,—a circumstance which goes far to show that the more correct spelling is without the *h*. Rhaetia was essentially an Alpine country, bordering in the north on Vindelicia, in the west on the territory inhabited by the Helvetii, in the south on the chain of the Alps from Mons Adula to Mons Ocra, which separated Rhaetia from Italy, and in the east on Noricum and Venetia ; hence it comprised the modern *Grisons*, the *Tyrol*, and some of the northern parts of *Lombardy*. This country and its inhabitants did not attract much attention in ancient times until the reign of Augustus, who determined to reduce the Alpine tribes which had until then maintained their independence in the mountains. After a struggle of many years Rhaetia and several adjoining districts were conquered by Drusus and Tiberius, B. C. 15. Rhaetia, within the boundaries above described, seems then to have been constituted as a distinct province (Suet. *Aug.* 21; Vell. Pat. ii. 39; Liv. *Epit.* 136; Aurel. Vict. *Epit.* 1). Vindelicia, in the north of Rhaetia, must at that time likewise have been a separate province ; but towards the end of the first century A. D. the two provinces appear united as one, under the name of Rhaetia, which accordingly, in this latter sense, extended in the north as far as the Danube and the Limes. At a still later period, in or shortly before the reign of Constantine, the two provinces were again divided, and ancient Rhaetia received the name Rhaetia Prima, its capital being called Curia Rhaetorum (*Chur*); while Vindelicia was called Rhaetia Secunda. The exact boundary line between the two is not accurately defined by the ancients, but it is highly probable that the Alpine chain extending from the *Lake of Constance* to the river *Inn* was the natural line of demarcation; it should, however, be observed that Ptolemy (ii. 12) includes under the name of Rhaetia all the country west of the river Licus as far as the sources of the Danubius and Rhenus, while he applies the name of Vindelicia to the territory between the Licus and Oenus.

Ancient Rhaetia or Rhaetia Proper was throughout an Alpine country, being traversed by the Alpes Rhaeticae and Mons Adula. It contained the sources of nearly all the Alpine rivers watering the north of Italy, such as the Addua, Sarius, Olbius, Cleusis, Mincius, and others ; but the chief rivers of Rhaetia itself were the Athesis with its tributary the Isargus (or Ilargus), and the Aenus or Oenus. The magnificent valleys formed by these rivers were fertile and well adapted to agricultural pursuits ; but the inhabitants depended mainly upon their flocks (Strab. vii. p. 316). The chief produce of the valleys was wine, which was not at all inferior to that grown in Italy ; so that Augustus was particularly partial to it (Strab. iv. p. 206; Plin. xiv. 3, 5, 8; Virg. *Georg.* ii. 96; Colum. iii. 2 ; Martial, xiv. 100; Suet. *Aug.* 77).

Besides this Rhaetia produced abundance of wax, honey, pitch, and cheese, in which considerable commerce was carried on.

The ancient inhabitants of Rhaetia have in modern times attracted more than ordinary attention from their supposed connection with the ancient Etruscans. They are first mentioned by Polybius (xxxiv. 10; comp. Strab. iv. p. 204, vii. pp. 292, 313). According to tradition the Rhaetians were Etruscans who had originally inhabited the plains of Lombardy, but were compelled by the invading Gauls to quit their country and take refuge in the Alps, whereby they were cut off from their kinsmen, who remained in Italy and finally established themselves in Etruria. (Justin, xx. 5; Plin. iii. 24; Steph. B. *s. v.* 'Ραιτοί.) This tradition derives some support from the fact recorded by Dionysius of Halicarnassus (i. 24) that the Etruscans in Etruria called themselves Rasena, which is believed to be only another form of the name Rhaeti. A decision of this question is the more difficult because at the time when the Romans conquered Rhaetia the bulk of its inhabitants were Celts, which in the course of a few centuries became entirely Romanised. But, assuming that the Rhaeti were a branch of the Etruscan nation, it is not very likely that on the invasion of Italy by the Gauls they should have gone back to the Alps across which they had come into Italy ; it seems much more probable to suppose that the Etruscans in the Alps were a remnant of the nation left behind there at the time when the Etruscans originally migrated into Italy. But, however this may be, the anxiety to obtain a key to the mysterious language of the Etruscans has led modern inquirers to search for it in the mountains and valleys of ancient Rhaetia; for they reasonably assumed that, although the great body of the population in the time of Augustus consisted of Celts, who soon after their subjugation adopted the language of the conquerors, there may still exist some traces of its original inhabitants in the names of places, and even in the language of ordinary life. In the districts where the nation has remained purest, as in the valley of *Engadino* and in the *Grödnerthal*, the language spoken at present is a corruption of Latin, the Romaunsh as it is called, intermixed with some Celtic and German elements, and a few words which are believed to be neither Celtic, nor German, nor Latin, and are therefore considered to be Etruscan. Several names of places also bear a strong resemblance to those of places in Etruria ; and, lastly, a few ancient monuments have been discovered which are in some respects like those of Etruria. The first who, after many broad and unfounded assertions had been made, undertook a thorough investigation of these points, was L. Steub, who published the results of his inquiries in a work *Uber die Urbewohner Raetiens und ihren Zusammenhang mit den Etruskern*, Munich, 1843, 8vo. A few years ago another scholar, Dr. W. Freund, during a residence in Rhaetia collected a vast number of facts, well calculated to throw light upon this obscure subject, but the results of his investigations have not yet been published.

As to the history of the ancient Rhaetians, it has already been intimated that they became known to the Romans in the second century B. C. They were a wild, cunning, and rapacious mountain people, who indulged their propensity to rob and plunder even at the time when they were subject to Rome, and when their rulers had made a great road through their country into Noricum (Dion Cass. liv. 22;

Hor. Carm. iv. 14. 15). Like all mountaineers, they cherished great love of freedom, and fought against the Romans with rage and despair, as we learn from Florus (iv. 12), who states that the Rhaetian women, who also took part in the war, after having spent their arrows, threw their own children in the faces of the Romans. Still, however, they were obliged to yield, and in B. C. 15 they were finally subdued, and their country was made a Roman province. During the later period of the Empire their territory was almost entirely depopulated; but it somewhat recovered at the time when the Ostrogoths, under Theodoric, took possession of the country, and placed its administration into the hands of a Dux (Euipp. *Vit. S. Severini*, 29; Cassiod. *Var.* iv. 4). After the death of Theodoric, the Boioarii spread over Rhaetia and Noricum, and the river Licus became the boundary between the Alemanni in Vindelicia, and the Boioarii in Rhaetia. (Egin. *Vit. Carol. M.* 11.) The more important among the various tribes mentioned in Rhaetia, such as the LEPONTII, VIBERI, CALUCONES, VENNONES, SARUNETES, ISARCI, BRIXENTES, GENAUNI, TRIDENTINI, and EUGANEI, are discussed in separate articles. Tridentum was the most important among the few towns of the country ; the others are known almost exclusively through the Itineraries, two roads having been made through Rhaetia by the Romans, the one leading from Augusta Vindelicorum to Comum, and the other from the same town to Verona; Paulus Diaconus, however, mentions a few towns of the interior which were not situated on these high-roads, such as the town of Maia, which was destroyed in the eighth century by the fall of a mountain, and the site of which is now occupied by the town of *Meran*.   [L. S.]

RHAGAE ('Ραγαί, Arrian, *Anab.* iii. 30; Strab. xi. pp. 514, 524; 'Ράγεια, Isidor. Char. § 7; ἡ 'Ράγα, Steph. *B. s. v.*; 'Ράγαια, Ptol. vi. 5. § 4; Rhages, *Tobit,* i. 14: *Eth.* 'Ραγηνός), a great town of Media Magna, the capital of the province of Rhagiana, which is first known to us in history as the place to which the Jewish exiles were sent. (*Tobit,* i. 14, iv. 20, ix. 2.) It was situated in the eastern part of the country towards Parthia, one day's journey from the Pylae Caspiae (Arrian, *Anab.* iii. 20) and 10 days' march from Ecbatana (*Hamadán*). The name of the place is stated by Strabo to have been derived from the frequent earthquakes to which it had been subject, but this is contrary to all probability (Strab. xi. p. 514); he adds, also, that, like many other places in the neighbourhood, it had been built (or rather rebuilt) by the Greeks (p. 524). In later times it appears to have been re-built by Seleucus Nicator, who called it Europus. (Strab. *l. c.*) Still later it appears to have been again rebuilt by one of the house of Arsaces, who named it in consequence Arsacia. (Strab. *l. c.*; Steph. B. *s. v.*) In modern times the ancient name has returned; and the ruins of *Rhey,* which have been visited and described by many travellers, no doubt represent the site of the ancient Rhagae. (Ker Porter, *Travels,* vol. i. p. 358.) Pliny mentions a town of Parthia, which he calls Apameia Rhagiane (vi. 14. § 17). Some geographers have contended that this is the same as Rhagae; but the inference is rather that it is not.   [V.]

RHAGIA'NA. [RHAGAE.]

RHAMAE, a town in the interior of Thrace. (*Itin. Hieros.* p. 568.)   [T. H. D.]

RHAMANI'TAE. 1. ('Ραμανῖται, Strab. xvi. p. 782), supposed by Mr. Forster to be identical with the Rhabanitae of Ptolemy ('Ραβανῖται, vi. 7. § 24), whom that geographer places under Mount Climax. He says "their common position, north of Mount Climax, concurs with the resemblance of the two names to argue the identity" (*Geog. of Arabia,* vol. i. p. 68, note); but it is by no means clear that the Rhamanitae lay near Mount Climax. All that Strabo says of them is, that Marsiaba, the limit of the expedition of Aelius Gallus, the siege of which he was forced to raise for want of water, lay in the country of the Rhamanitae ; but nothing in geography is more difficult to determine than the situation of that town. [MARSYABA.]

2. A people of the same name is mentioned by Pliny, as existing on the Persian Gulf, identical with the Anariti of Ptolemy and the EPIMARANITAE.   [G. W.]

RHAMIDAVA. [DACIA, p. 744, b.]

RHAMNUS. 1. ('Ραμνοῦς, -οῦντος: *Eth.* 'Ραμνούσιος, fem. 'Ραμνουσία, 'Ραμνουσίς), a demus of Attica, belonging to the tribe Aeantis (Steph. B., Harpocr., Suid., *s. v.*), which derived its name from a thick prickly shrub, which still grows upon the site. ('Ραμνοῦς, contr. of ῥαμνόεις from ῥάμνος.) The town stood upon the eastern coast of Attica, at the distance of 60 stadia from Marathon, and upon the road leading from the latter town to Oropus. (Paus. i. 33. § 2.) It is described by Scylax (p. 21) as a fortified place; and it appears from a decree in Demosthenes (*pro Cor.* p. 238, Reiske) to have been regarded as one of the chief fortresses in Attica. It was still in existence in the time of Pliny ("Rhamnus pagus, locus Marathon," iv. 7. s. 11). Rhamnus was the birthplace of the orator Antipho [*Dict. of Biogr. s. v.*]; but it was chiefly celebrated in antiquity on account of its worship of Nemesis, who was hence called by the Latin poets *Rhamnusia virgo* and *Rhamnusia dea*. (Catull. lxvi. 71; Claud. *B. Get.* 631; Ov. *Met.* iii. 406, *Trist.* v. 8. 9; Stat. *Silv.* iii. 5. § 5.) The temple of the goddess was at a short distance from the town. (Paus. *l. c.*; comp. Strab. ix. p. 399.) It contained a celebrated statue of Nemesis, which, according to Pausanias, was the work of Pheidias, and was made by him out of a block of Parian marble, which the Persians had brought with them for the construction of a trophy. The statue was of colossal size, 10 cubits in height (Hesych. *s. v.*; Zenob. *Prov.* v. 82), and on its basis were several figures in relief. Other writers say that the statue was the work of Agoracritus of Paros, a disciple of Pheidias. (Strab. ix. p. 396; Plin. xxxvi. 5. s. 4. § 17, Sillig.) It was however a common opinion that Pheidias was the real author of the statue, but that he gave up the honour of the work to his favourite disciple. (Suid. *s. v.*; Zenob. *l. c.*; Tzetz. *Chil.* vii. 960.) Rhamnus stood in a small plain, 3 miles in length, which, like that of Marathon, was shut out from the rest of Attica by surrounding mountains. The town itself was situated upon a rocky peninsula, surrounded by the sea for two-thirds of its circumference, and connected by a narrow ridge with the mountains, which closely approach it on the land side. It is now called *Ovrió-Kastro*. ('Οβριό-Καστρο, a corruption of 'Εβραιόν-Καστρον, *Jews'-Castle,* a name frequently applied in Greece to the ruins of Hellenic fortresses.) It was about half a mile in circuit, and its remains are considerable. The principal gate was situated upon the narrow ridge already mentioned, and is still preserved; and adjoining it is the southern wall, about 20 feet in height. At the head of a narrow glen, which leads to the principal gate, stand the ruins of the temple of Nemesis upon a large artificial platform, supported by a wall of pure white marble. But we find upon this platform, which formed the τέμενος or sacred enclosure, the remains of *two* temples, which are almost contiguous, and nearly though not quite parallel to each other. The larger building was a peripteral hexastyle, 71 feet long and 33 broad, with 12 columns on the side, and with a pronaus, cella, and posticum in the usual manner. The smaller temple was 31 feet long by 21 feet broad, and consisted only of a cella, with a portico containing two Doric columns *in antis.* Among the ruins of the larger temple are some fragments of a colossal statue, corresponding in size with that of the Rhamnusian Nemesis; but these fragments were made of Attic marble, and not of Parian stone as stated by Pausanias. It is, however, not improbable, as Leake has remarked, that the story of the block of stone brought by the Persians was a vulgar fable, or an invention of the priests of Nemesis by which Pausanias was deceived. Among the ruins of the smaller temple was found a fragment, wanting the head and shoulders, of a statue of the human size in the archaic style of the Aeginetan school. This statue is now in the British Museum. Judging from this statue, as well as from the diminutive size and ruder architecture of the smaller temple, the latter appears to have been the more ancient of the two. Hence it has been inferred that the smaller temple was anterior to the Persian War, and was destroyed by the Persians just before the battle of Marathon; and that the larger temple was erected in honour of the goddess, who had taken vengeance upon the insolence of the barbarians for outraging her worship. In front of the smaller temple are two chairs (θρόνοι) of white marble, upon one of which is the inscription Νεμέσει Σώστρατος ἀνέθηκεν, and upon the other Θέμιδι Σώστρατος ἀνέθηκεν, which has led some to suppose that the smaller temple was dedicated to Themis. But it is more probable that both temples were dedicated to Nemesis, and that the smaller temple was in ruins before the larger was erected. A difficulty, however, arises about the time of the destruction of the smaller temple, from the fact that the forms of the letters and the long vowels in the inscriptions upon the chairs clearly show that those inscriptions belong to an era long subsequent to the battle of Marathon. Wordsworth considers it ridiculous to suppose that these chairs were dedicated in this temple after its destruction, and hence conjectures that the temple was destroyed towards the close of the Peloponnesian War by the Persian allies of Sparta. (Leake, *Demi of Attica,* p. 105, seq., 2nd ed., *Northern Greece,* vol. ii. p. 434, seq.; Wordsworth, *Athens and Attica,* p. 34, seq.; *Unedited Antiquities of Attica,* c. vi. p. 41, seq.)

2. A harbour on the W. coast of Crete near the promontory Chersonesus. (Ptol. iii. 17. § 2.) Pliny, on the contrary, places it in the interior of the island (iv. 12. s. 20).

RHAPSII AETHIOPES. [RHAPTA.]

RHAPTA (τὰ Ῥαπτά, Ptol. i. 9. § 1, 14. § 4; *Peripl. Mar. Erythr.* p. 10), was, according to the author of the Periplus, the most distant station of the Arabian trade with Aegypt, Aethiopia, and the ports of the Red Sea. Its correct lat. is 15′ 5″. The name is derived from the peculiar boats in use there. These are termed by the natives dows

(δάϋ), and, like the modern boats of *Pata* on the *Mozambique* coast, were frequently of 100 or 150 tons burden. But whether vessels of this size or merely canoes, all the craft at this part of the E. coast of Africa were formed of the hollowed trunks of trees and joined together by cords made of the fibres of the cocoa instead of iron or wooden pins, and hence the Greeks gave them, and the harbour which they principally frequented, the name of " the sewed " (τὰ ῥαπτά). Ptolemy speaks (i. 17. § 7, iv. 7. § 28, vii. 3. § 6, i. 17. § 12, &c.) of a promontory RHAPTUM, a river RHAPTUS, and a tribe of Aethiopians named RHAPSII. All these may probably be referred to the immediate neighbourhood of the town Rhapta, since the emporium was doubtless the most striking object to the caravans trading there and to the Greek merchants accompanying the caravans. The *promontory* was one of the numerous bluffs or headlands that give to this portion of the E. coast of Africa the appearance of a saw, the shore-line being everywhere indented with sharp and short projections. The *river* was one of the many streams which are broad inland, but whose mouths, being barred with sand or coral reefs, are narrow and difficult to be discovered. This portion of the coast, indeed, from lat. 2° S. to the mouth of the *Govind,* the modern appellation of the Rhaptus of Ptolemy and the Periplus, is bordered by coral reefs and islands, — e. g. the *Dundas* and *Jubak* islands, — generally a league or even less from the mainland. Some of these islands are of considerable height; and through several of them are arched apertures large enough to admit the passage of a boat. As the shore itself also is formed of a coral conglomerate, containing shells, madrepore, and sand, it is evident that there has been a gradual rising of the land and corresponding subsidence of the sea. The reefs also which have been formed on the main shore have affected materially the course of the rivers, — barring the mouths of many, among them the Rhaptus, and compelling others, e. g. the *Webbé,* to run obliquely in a direction parallel to the coast. Another result of the reefs has been that many rivers having no or insufficient outlets into the sea, have become marshes or shallow lakes; and, consequently, streams that in Ptolemy's age were correctly described as running into the ocean, are now meres severed from it by sand and ridges of coral.

Rhapta seems, from the account in the Periplus, to have been, not so much the name of a single town, as a generic term for numerous villages inhabited by the builders of the " seamed boats." These were probably situated nearly opposite the modern island of *Pata;* and whether it implies one or many places, Rhapta certainly was on the coast of Azania. The Rhapsii Aethiopes are described in the Periplus as men of lofty stature; and in fact the natives of E. Africa, at the present day, are generally taller than the Arabs. Each village had its chief, but there was a principal shiekh or chief to whom all were subject. This division into petty communities under a general head also still subsists. In the first century B. C. the Rhapsii were held in subjection by the shiekh and people of Muza, whence came ships with Arab masters, and pilots who understood the language of the Rhapsii and were connected with them by intermarriage. The Arabs brought to Rhapta spear-heads, axes, knives, buttons, and beads; sometimes also wine and wheaten bread, not so much indeed for barter, as for presents to the

Rhapsian chiefs. From Rhapta they exported ivory (inferior to that of Adulis), tortoise-shell (the next best in quality to that of India), rhinoceros-horn, and nauplius (a shell probably used in dyeing). These commercial features are nearly repeated at the present day in this region. The African still builds and mans the ship; the Arab is the navigator and supercargo. The ivory is still of inferior quality, being for the most part found in the woods, damaged by rain, or collected from animals drowned by the overflow of the rivers at the equinoxes. The hawksbill turtle is still captured in the neighbourhood of the river *Govind*, and on the shore opposite the island of *Pata*. (See Vincent, *Voyage of Nearchus*, vol. ii. pp. 169—183; Cooley, *Claudius Ptolemy and the Nile*, pp. 68—72.) [W. B. D.]

RHAPTUM PROMONTORIUM. [RHAPTA.]

RHAPTUS FLUVIUS. [RHAPTA.]

RHASTIA ('Ραστία), a town in the country of the Trocmi in Galatia, in Asia Minor, which is noticed only by Ptolemy (v. 4. § 9). [L. S.]

RHATOSTATHYBIUS ('Ρατοσταθύβιος, Ptol. ii. 3. § 3), a river on the W. coast of Britannia Romana, according to Camden (p. 733) the *Taf*. [T. H. D.]

RHAUCUS ('Ραῦκος, Scyl. p. 19; Polyb. xxxi. 1. § 1, xxxiii. 15. § 1: *Eth.* 'Ραύκιος, fem. 'Ραυκία, Steph. B. *s. v.*). From the story told about the Cretan bees by Antenor in his "Cretica" (*ap. Aelian. N. A.* xvii. 35; comp. Diodor. v. 70), it seems that there were two cities of this name in Crete. The existence of two places so called in the island might give rise to some such legend as that which he mentions. Pashley (*Crete*, vol. i. p. 235) fixes the site of one Rhaucus at *Hághio Mýro*, between Cnossus and Gortyna, and from its proximity to Mt. Ida infers that it is the more ancient. [E. B. J.]

COIN OF RHAUCUS.

RHEBAS ('Ρήβας), a very small river on the coast of Bithynia, the length of which amounts only to a few miles; it flows into the Euxine, near the entrance of the Bosporus, north-east of Chalcedon, and still bears the name of *Riva*. (Scylax, p. 34; Dionys. Per. 794; Ptol. v. 1. § 5; Arrian, *Peripl. P. E.* p. 13; Marcian, p. 69; Plin. vi. 1; Steph. B. *s. v.*) This little river, which is otherwise of no importance, owes its celebrity to the story of the Argonauts. (Orph. *Arg.* 711; Apollon. Rhod. ii. 650, 789.) It also bore the names of Rhessaeus and Rhesus (Plin. *l c.*; Solin. 43), the last of which seems to have arisen from a confusion with the Rhesus mentioned by Homer. [L. S.]

RHE'DONES. [REDONES.]

RHE'GIUM ('Ρήγιον : *Eth.* 'Ρηγῖνος, Rheginus: *Reggio*), an important city of Magna Graecia, situated near the southern end of the Bruttian peninsula, on the E. side of the Sicilian straits, and almost directly opposite to Messana in Sicily. The distance between the two cities, in a direct line, is only about 6 geog. miles, and the distance from Rhegium to the nearest point of the island is somewhat less. There is no doubt that it was a Greek colony, and we have no account of any settlement previously existing on the site; but the spot is said to have been marked by the tomb of Jocastus, one of the sons of Aeolus. (Heraclid. *Polit.* 25.) The foundation of Rhegium is universally ascribed to the Chalcidians, who had, in a year of famine, consecrated a tenth part of their citizens to Apollo; and these, under the direction of the oracle at Delphi, proceeded to Rhegium, whither they were also invited by their Chalcidic brethren, who were already established at Zancle on the opposite side of the strait. (Strab. vi. p. 257; Heraclid. *l c.*; Diod. xiv. 40; Thuc. vi. 4; Scymn. Ch. 311.) With these Chalcidians were also united a body of Messenian exiles, who had been driven from their country at the beginning of the First Messenian War, and had established themselves for a time at Macistus. They were apparently not numerous, as Rhegium always continued to be considered a Chalcidic city; but they comprised many of the chief families in the new colony; so that, according to Strabo, the presiding magistrates of the city were always taken from among these Messenian citizens, down to the time of Anaxilas, who himself belonged to this dominant caste. (Strab. vi. p. 257; Paus. iv. 23. § 6; Thuc. vi. 4; Heraclid. *l. c.* 1.) The date of the foundation of Rhegium is uncertain; the statements just mentioned, which connect it with the First Messenian War would carry it back as far as the 8th century B.C.; but they leave the precise period uncertain. Pausanias considers it as founded after the end of the war, while Antiochus, who is cited by Strabo, seems to refer it to the beginning; but his expressions are not decisive, as we do not know how long the exiles may have remained at Macistus; and it is probable, on the whole, that we may consider it as taking place shortly after the close of the war, and therefore *before* 720 B.C. (Paus. *l. c.*; Antioch. *ap. Strab. l. c.*). In this case it was probably the most ancient of all the Greek colonies in this part of Italy. Various etymologies of the name of Rhegium are given by ancient authors; the one generally received, and adopted by Aeschylus (*ap. Strab. l. c.*), was that which derived it from the bursting asunder of the coasts of Sicily and Italy, which was generally ascribed to an earthquake. (Diod. iv. 85; Justin. iv. 1, &c.) Others absurdly connected it with the Latin *regium* (Strab. *l. c.*), while Heraclides gives a totally different story, which derived the name from that of an indigenous hero. (Heraclid. *Polit.* 25.)

There seems no doubt that Rhegium rose rapidly to be a flourishing and prosperous city; but we know almost nothing of its history previous to the time of Anaxilas. The constitution, as we learn from Heraclides, was aristocratic, the management of affairs resting wholly with a council or body of 1000 of the principal and wealthiest citizens. After the legislation of Charondas at Catana, his laws were adopted by the Rhegians as well as by the other Chalcidic cities of Sicily. (Heraclid. *l. c.*; Arist. *Pol.* ii. 12, v. 12.) The Rhegians are mentioned as affording shelter to the fugitive Phocaeans, who had been driven from Corsica, previous to the foundation of Velia. (Herod. i. 166, 167.) According to Strabo they extended their dominion over many of the adjoining towns, but these could only have been small places, as we do not hear of any colonies of importance founded by the Rhegians; and their territory extended only as far as the Halex on the E., where they adjoined the Locrian territory, while the Locrian colonies of Medma and Hipponium prevented their extension on the N. Indeed, from the position of Rhegium it seems to have always maintained closer relations with Sicily, and taken more part in the politics of that island than in those of the other Greek cities in Italy. Between the Rhegians and Locrians, however, there appears to have been a constant spirit of enmity, which might be readily expected between two rival cities, such near neighbours, and belonging to different races. (Thuc. iv. 1, 24.)

Rhegium appears to have participated largely in the political changes introduced by the Pythagoreans, and even became, for a short time after the death of Pythagoras, the head-quarters of his sect (Iambl. *Vit. Pyth.* 33, 130, 251); but the changes then introduced do not seem to have been permanent.

It was under the reign of Anaxilas that Rhegium first rose to a degree of power far greater than it had previously attained. We have no account of the circumstances attending the elevation of that despot to power, an event which took place, according to Diodorus, in B.C. 494 (Diod. xi. 48); but we know that he belonged to one of the ancient Messenian families, and to the oligarchy which had previously ruled the state. (Strab. vi. p. 257; Paus. iv. 23. § 6; Arist. *Pol.* v. 12; Thuc. vi. 4.) Hence, when he made himself master of Zancle on the opposite side of the straits, he gave to that city the name of Messana, by which it was ever afterwards known. [MESSANA.] Anaxilas continued for some years ruler of both these cities, and thus was undisputed master of the Sicilian straits: still further to, strengthen himself in this sovereignty, he fortified the rocky promontory of Scyllaeum, and established a naval station there to guard the straits against the Tyrrhenian pirates. (Strab. vi. p. 257.) He meditated also the destruction of the neighbouring city of Locri, the perpetual rival and enemy of Rhegium, but was prevented from carrying out his purpose by the intervention of Hieron of Syracuse, who espoused the cause of the Locrians, and whose enmity Anaxilas did not choose to provoke. (Schol. *ad Pind. Pyth.* ii. 34.) One of his daughters was, indeed, married to the Syracusan despot, whose friendship he seems to have sought assiduously to cultivate.

Anaxilas enjoyed the reputation of one of the mildest and most equitable of the Sicilian rulers (Justin. iv. 2), and it is probable that Rhegium enjoyed great prosperity under his government. At his death, in B.C. 476, it passed without opposition under the rule of his two sons; but the government was administered during their minority by their guardian Micythus, who reigned over both Rhegium and Messana for nine years with exemplary justice and moderation, and at the end of that time gave up the sovereignty into the hands of the two sons of Anaxilas. (Diod. xi. 48, 66; Herod. vii. 170; Justin. iv. 2; Macrob. *Sat.* i. 11.) These, however, did not hold it long: they were expelled in B.C. 461, the revolutions which at that time agitated the cities of Sicily having apparently extended to Rhegium also. (Diod. xi. 76.)

The government of Micythus was marked by one great disaster: in B.C. 473, the Rhegians, having sent an auxiliary force of 3000 men to assist the Tarentines against the Iapygians, shared in the great defeat which they sustained on that occasion [TARENTUM]; but the statement of Diodorus that

the barbarians not only pursued the fugitives to the gates of Rhegium, but actually made themselves masters of the city, may be safely rejected as incredible. (Diod. xi. 52; Herod. vii. 170; Grote's *Hist. of Greece,* vol. v. p. 319.) A story told by Justin, that the Rhegians being agitated by domestic dissensions, a body of mercenaries, who were called in by one of the parties, drove out their opponents, and then made themselves masters of the city by a general massacre of the remaining citizens (Justin. iv. 3), must be placed (if at all) shortly after the expulsion of the sons of Anaxilas; but the whole story has a very apocryphal air; it is not noticed by any other writer, and it is certain that the old Chalcidic citizens continued in possession of Rhegium down to a much later period.

We have very little information as to the history of Rhegium during the period which followed the expulsion of the despots; but it seems to have retained its liberty, in common with the neighbouring cities of Sicily, till it fell under the yoke of Dionysius. In B.C. 427, when the Athenians sent a fleet under Laches and Charoeades to support the Leontines against Syracuse, the Rhegians espoused the cause of the Chalcidic cities of Sicily, and not only allowed their city to be made the head-quarters of the Athenian fleet, but themselves furnished a considerable auxiliary force. They were in consequence engaged in continual hostilities with the Locrians. (Diod. xii. 54; Thuc. iii. 86, iv. 1, 24, 25.) But they pursued a different course on occasion of the great Athenian expedition to Sicily in B.C. 415, when they refused to take any part in the contest; and they appear to have persevered in this neutrality to the end. (Diod. xiii. 3; Thuc. vi. 44, vii. 1, 58.)

It was not long after this that the increasing power of Dionysius of Syracuse, who had destroyed in succession the chief Chalcidic cities of Sicily, became a subject of alarm to the Rhegians; and in B.C. 399 they fitted out a fleet of 50 triremes, and an army of 6000 foot and 600 horse, to make war upon the despot. But the Messenians, who at first made common cause with them, having quickly abandoned the alliance, they were compelled to desist from the enterprise, and made peace with Dionysius. (Diod. xiv. 40.) The latter, who was meditating a great war with Carthage, was desirous to secure the friendship of the Rhegians; but his proposals of a matrimonial alliance were rejected with scorn; he in consequence concluded such an alliance with the Locrians, and became from this time the implacable enemy of the Rhegians. (*Ib.* 44, 107.) It was from hostility to the latter that he a few years later (B.C. 394), after the destruction of Messana by the Carthaginians, restored and fortified that city, as a post to command the straits, and from which to carry on his enterprises in Southern Italy. The Rhegians in vain sought to forestal him; they made an unsuccessful attack upon Messana, and were foiled in their attempt to establish a colony of Naxians at Mylae, as a post of offence against the Messenians. (*Ib.* 87.) The next year Dionysius, in his turn, made a sudden attack on Rhegium itself, but did not succeed in surprising the city; and after ravaging its territory, was compelled to draw off his forces. (*Ib.* 90.) But in B.C. 390 he resumed the design on a larger scale, and laid regular siege to the city with a force of 20,000 foot, 1000 horse, and a fleet of 120 triremes. The Rhegians, however, opposed a vigorous resistance: the fleet of Dionysius suffered severely from a storm, and the approach of winter at length compelled him to abandon the siege. (*Ib.* 100.) The next year (B.C. 389) his great victory over the confederate forces of the Italiot Greeks at the river Helorus left him at liberty to prosecute his designs against Rhegium without opposition: the Rhegians in vain endeavoured to avert the danger by submitting to a tribute of 300 talents, and by surrendering all their ships, 70 in number. By these concessions they obtained only a precarious truce, which Dionysius found a pretext for breaking the very next year, and laid siege to the city with all his forces. The Rhegians, under the command of a general named Phyton, made a desperate resistance, and were enabled to prolong their defence for eleven months, but were at length compelled to surrender, after having suffered the utmost extremities of famine (B.C. 387). The surviving inhabitants were sold as slaves, their general Phyton put to an ignominious death, and the city itself totally destroyed. (Diod. xiv. 106—108, 111, 112; Strab. vi. p. 258; Pseud.-Arist. *Oecon.* ii. 21.)

There is no doubt that Rhegium never fully recovered this great calamity, but so important a site could not long remain unoccupied. The younger Dionysius partially restored the city, to which he gave the name of Phoebias, but the old name soon again prevailed. (Strab. *l.c.*) It was occupied with a garrison by the despot, but in B.C. 351 it was besieged and taken by the Syracusan commanders Leptines and Callippus, the garrison driven out, and the citizens restored to independence. (Diod. xvi. 45.) Hence they were, a few years later (B.C. 345), among the foremost to promise their assistance to Timoleon, who halted at Rhegium on his way to Sicily, and from thence, eluding the vigilance of the Carthaginians by a stratagem, crossed over to Tauromenium. (Diod. xvi. 66, 68; Plut. *Timol.* 9, 10.) From this time we hear no more of Rhegium, till the arrival of Pyrrhus in Italy (B.C. 280), when it again became the scene of a memorable catastrophe. The Rhegians on that occasion, viewing with apprehension the progress of the king of Epirus, and distrusting the Carthaginians, had recourse to the Roman alliance, and received into their city as a garrison, a body of Campanian troops, 4000 in number, under the command of an officer named Decius. But these troops had not been long in possession of the city when they were tempted to follow the example of their countrymen, the Mamertines, on the other side of the strait; and they took advantage of an alleged attempt at defection on the part of the Rhegians, to make a promiscuous massacre of the male citizens, while they reduced the women and children to slavery, and established themselves in the sole occupation of the town. (Pol. i. 7; Oros. iv. 3; Appian, *Samnit.* iii. 9; Diod. xxii. *Exc. H.* p. 494, *Exc. Vales,* p. 562; Dion Cass. *Fr.* 40. 7; Strab. v. p. 258.) The Romans were unable to punish them for this act of treachery so long as they were occupied with the war against Pyrrhus; and the Campanians for some years continued to reap the benefit of their crime. But as soon as Pyrrhus had finally withdrawn from Italy, the Romans turned their arms against their rebellious soldiers; and in B.C. 270, being actively supported by Hieron of Syracuse, the consul Genucius succeeded in reducing Rhegium by force, though not till after a long siege. Great part of the Campanians perished in the defence; the rest were executed by order of the Roman people. (Pol. i. 6, 7; Oros. iv. 3; Dionys. *Fr. Mai.* xix. 1, xx. 7.)

Rhegium was now restored to the survivors of its former inhabitants (Pol. i. 7; Liv. xxxi. 31; Appian, *l.c.*); but it must have suffered severely, and does not seem to have again recovered its former prosperity. Its name is hardly mentioned during the First Punic War, but in the second the citizens distinguished themselves by their fidelity to the Roman cause, and repeated attempts of Hannibal to make himself master of the city were uniformly repulsed. (Liv. xxiii. 30, xxiv. 1. xxvi. 12, xxix. 6.) From this time the name of Rhegium is rarely mentioned in history under the Roman Republic; but we learn from several incidental notices that it continued to enjoy its own laws and nominal liberty as a "foederata civitas," though bound, in common with other cities in the same condition, to furnish an auxiliary naval contingent as often as required. (Liv. xxxi. 31, xxxv. 16, xxxvi. 42.) It was not till after the Social War that the Rhegians, like the other Greek cities of Italy, passed into the condition of Roman citizens, and Rhegium itself became a Roman Municipium. (Cic. *Verr.* iv. 60, *Phil.* i. 3, *pro Arch.* 3.) Shortly before this (B.C. 91) the city had suffered severely from an earthquake, which had destroyed a large part of it (Strab. vi. p. 258; Jul. Obseq. 114); but it seems to have, in great measure, recovered from this calamity, and is mentioned by Appian towards the close of the Republic as one of the eighteen flourishing cities of Italy, which were promised by the Triumvirs to their veterans as a reward for their services. (Appian, *B. C.* iv. 3.) Rhegium, however, had the good fortune to escape on this occasion by the personal favour of Octavian (*Ib.* 86); and during the war which followed between him and Sextus Pompeius, B.C. 38—36, it became one of the most important posts, which was often made by Octavian the headquarters both of his fleet and army. (Strab. vi. p. 258; Appian, *B. C.* v. 81, 84; Dion Cass. xlviii. 18, 47.) To reward the Rhegians for their services on this occasion, Augustus increased the population, which was in a declining state, by the addition of a body of new colonists; but the old inhabitants were not expelled, nor did the city assume the title of a Colonia, though it adopted, in gratitude to Augustus, the name of Rhegium Julium. (Strab. *l.c.*; Ptol. iii. 1. § 9; Orell. *Inscr.* 3838.) In the time of Strabo it was a populous and flourishing place, and was one of the few cities which, like Neapolis and Tarentum, still preserved some remains of its Greek civilisation. (Strab. vi. pp. 253, 259.) Traces of this may be observed also in inscriptions, some of which, of the period of the Roman Empire, present a curious mixture of Greek and Latin, while others have the names of Roman magistrates, though the inscriptions themselves are in Greek. (Morisani, *Inscr. Reginae,* 4to. Neap. 1770, pp. 83, 126, &c.; Boeckh, *C. I.* 5760—5768.)

Its favourable situation and its importance, as commanding the passage of the Sicilian straits, preserved Rhegium from falling into the same state of decay as many other cities in the south of Italy. It continued to exist as a considerable city throughout the period of the Roman Empire (Plin. iii. 5. s. 10; Ptol. *l. c.*; *Itin. Ant.* pp. 112, 115, 490), and was the termination of the great highway which led through the southern peninsula of Italy, and formed the customary mode of communication with Sicily. In A.D. 410 Rhegium became the limit of the progress of Alaric, who after the capture of Rome advanced through Campania, Lucania, and Bruttium, laying waste those provinces on his march, and made himself master of Rhegium, from whence he tried to cross over into Sicily, but, being frustrated in this attempt, retraced his steps as far as Consentia, where he died. (*Hist. Miscell.* xiii. p. 535.) Somewhat later it is described by Cassiodorus as still a flourishing place (*Var.* xii. 14), and was still one of the chief cities of Bruttium in the days of Paulus Diaconus. (*Hist. Lang.* ii. 17.) During the Gothic wars after the fall of the Western Empire, Rhegium bears a considerable part, and was a strong fortress, but it was taken by Totila in A. D. 549, previous to his expedition to Sicily. (Procop. *B. G.* i. 8, iii. 18, 37, 38.) It subsequently fell again into the hands of the Greek emperors, and continued subject to them, with the exception of a short period when it was occupied by the Saracens, until it passed under the dominion of Robert Guiscard in A. D. 1060. The modern city of *Reggio* is still a considerable place, with a population of about 10,000 souls, and is the capital of the province of *Calabria Ultra*; but it has suffered severely in modern times from earthquakes, having been almost entirely destroyed in 1783, and again in great part overthrown in 1841. It has no remains of antiquity, except a few inscriptions, but numerous coins, urns, mosaics, and other ancient relics have been brought to light by excavations.

Rhegium was celebrated in antiquity as the birthplace of the lyric poet Ibycus, as well as that of Lycus the historian, the father of Lycophron. (Suid. *s. v.* Ἴβυκος; Id. *s. v.* Λύκος.) It gave birth also to the celebrated sculptor Pythagoras (Diog. Laërt. viii. 1. § 47; Paus. vi. 4. § 4); and to several of the minor Pythagorean philosophers, whose names are enumerated by Iamblichus (*Vit. Pyth.* 267), but none of these are of much note. Its territory was fertile, and noted for the excellence of its wines, which were especially esteemed for their salubrity. (Athen. i. p. 26.) Cassiodorus describes it as well adapted for vines and olives, but not suited to corn. (*Var.* xii. 14.) Another production in which it excelled was its breed of mules, so that Anaxilas the despot was repeatedly victor at the Olympic games with the chariot drawn by mules (ἀπήνη), and his son Leophron obtained the same distinction. One of these victories was celebrated by Simonides. (Heraclid. *Polit.* 25; Athen. i. p. 3; Pollux, *Onomast.* v. 75.)

Rhegium itself was, as already mentioned, the termination of the line of high-road which traversed the whole length of Southern Italy from Capua to the Sicilian strait, and was first constructed by the praetor Popilius in B. C. 134. (Orell. *Inscr.* 3308; Mommsen, *Inscr. R. N.* 6276; Ritschel, *Mon. Epigr.* pp. 11, 12.) But the most frequented place of passage for crossing the strait to Messana was, in ancient as well as in modern times, not at Rhegium itself, but at a spot about 5 miles further N., which was marked by a column, and thence known by the name of COLUMNA RHEGINA. (*Itin. Ant.* pp. 98, 106, 111; Plin. iii. 5. s. 10; ἡ Ῥηγίνων στυλίς, Strab. v. p. 257.) The distance of this from Rhegium is given both by Pliny and Strabo at 12½ miles or 100 stadia, and the latter places it only 6 stadia from the promontory of Caenys or *Punta del Pezzo*. It must therefore have been situated in the neighbourhood of the modern village of *Villa San Giovanni*, which is still the most usual place of passage. But the distance from Rhegium is overstated by both geographers, the *Punta del Pezzo* itself being less

than 10 miles from *Reggio*. On the other hand the inscription of *La Polla* (Forum Popilii) gives the distance from the place of passage, which it designates as "Ad Statuam," at only 6 miles. (Mommsen, *Inscr. R. N.* 6276.) Yet it is probable that the spot meant is really the same in both cases, as from the strong current in the straits the place of embarkation must always have been nearly the same.   [E. H. B.]

COIN OF RHEGIUM.

RHEGMA (Ῥῆγμα), the name of a lake or lagune formed by the river Cydnus in Cilicia, at its mouth, about 5 stadia below Tarsus; the inhabitants of this city used it as their port. (Strab. xiv. p. 672; *Stadiasm. Mar. Mag.* §§ 155, 156, where it is called Ῥηγμοί; *It. Hieros.* p. 579.) The two last authorities place the Rhegma 70 stadia from Tarsus, which may possibly refer to a particular point of it, as the Rhegma was very extensive.   [L. S.]

RHEGMA. [EPIMARANITAE.]

RHEI'MEA (Ῥειμέα, Böckh, *Inscr.* no. 4590), a town of Auranitis, as appears from an inscription found by Burckhardt (*Travels,* p. 69) at *Deir-el-Lebcn,* situated three-quarters of an hour from the modern village of *Rima-el-Luhf,* where there stands a building with a flat roof and three receptacles for the dead, with an inscription over the door. (Böckh, *Inscr.* 4587—4589 ; comp. Buckingham, *Arab Tribes,* p. 256.)   [E. B. J.]

RHEI'THRUM. [ITHACA, p. 98, a.]

RHEITI. [ATTICA, p. 328, a.]

RHENI. [RENI.]

RHENEIA. [DELOS, p. 760.]

RHENUS (Ῥῆνος), one of the largest rivers in Europe, is not so long as the Danube, but as a commercial channel it is the first of European rivers, and as a political boundary it has been in ancient and modern times the most important frontier in Europe. The Rhine rises in the mountains which belong to the group of the *St. Gothard* in Switzerland, about 46° 30′ N. lat. There are three branches. The *Vorder-Rhein* and the *Mittel-Rhein* meet at *Dissentis,* which is only a few miles from their respective sources. The united stream has an east by north course to *Reichenau,* where it is joined by the *Hinter-Rhein.* At *Chur* (Curia), which is below the junction of the *Hinter-Rhein,* the river becomes navigable and has a general northern course to the *Bodensee* or *Lake of Constanz,* the Lacus Brigantinus or Venetus. This lake consists of two parts, of which the western part or *Untersee,* is about 30 feet lower than the chief part, called the *Lake of Constanz.* The course of the Rhine from the *Untersee* is westward, and it is navigable as far as the falls of *Schaffhausen,* which are not mentioned by any of the ancient geographers. It is interrupted by a smaller fall at *Laufenburg,* and there is a rapid near *Rheinfelden,* 10 miles below *Laufenburg.* The course is still west to

Basle (Basilia), where the Rhine is about 800 feet above the sea, and here we may fix the termination of the Upper Rhine. The drainage of all that part of Switzerland which lies north of the *Lake of Geneva* and the Bernese Alps is carried to the Rhine by the *Aar*, which joins it on the left bank at *Coblens*, one of the Roman Confluentes.

From *Basle* the Rhine has a general north course to *Bonn*, where it enters the low country which forms a part of the great plain of Northern Europe. This may be called the Middle Rhine. In this part of its course the river receives few streams on the left bank. The chief river is the *Mosel* (Mosella), which joins it at *Coblens* (Confluentes). On the right bank it is joined by the *Neckar* (Nicer), the *Main* (Moenus), which joins it at *Mains* (Moguntiacum), and the *Lahn* (Laugana), which joins it at *Niederlahnstein*.

Below *Bonn* the river has still a general north course past *Cologne* (Colonia Agrippinensis) as far as *Wesel*, where it is joined on the right bank by the *Lippe* (Luppia), and higher up by the *Roer* or *Ruhr* (Rura). Between *Cologne* and *Wesel* it is joined on the west side by the *Erft*. From *Wesel* its course is NW. and then west to *Pannerden* in the kingdom of the Netherlands. At *Pannerden* it divides into two branches, of which the southern is called the *Waal* (Vahalis), and the northern retains the name of Rhine. The *Waal* has the greater volume of water. It runs westward, and is joined at *Gorcum* on the left bank by the *Maas* (Mosa). The *Maas* itself divides several times after its junction with the *Waal*. The main branch is joined on the right side by the *Leck*, a branch which comes from the Rhine Proper at *Wyck* by *Duurstede*, and flows past *Rotterdam* into the *North Sea*.

The Rhine, which is divided at *Pannerden*, runs north to *Arnheim* (Arenacum), above which town it communicates with the *Yssel* at *Doesburg* by a channel which is supposed to be the Fossa Drusiana, the canal of Drusus. [FLEVO LACUS.] The *Yssel* runs north from *Doesburg* to the *Zuider Zee*, which it enters on the east side below the town of *Kampen*. The Rhine runs westward from *Arnheim*, and at *Wyck* by *Duurstede*, as already said, sends off the branch called the *Leck*, which joins the *Maas*. The Rhine divides again at *Utrecht* (Trajectum): one branch called the *Vecht* runs northward into the *Zuider Zee*; the other, the Rhine, or Old Rhine, continues its course with diminished volume, and passing by *Leiden* enters the *North Sea* at *Katwyck*. The whole course of the Rhine is estimated at about 950 miles.

The delta of the Rhine lies between the *Yssel*, which flows into the *Zuider Zee*, and the *Maas*, if we look at it simply as determined by mere boundaries. But all this surface is not alluvial ground, for the eastern part of the province of *Utrecht* and that part of Guelderland which is between the Rhine, the *Zuider Zee*, and the *Yssel* contains small elevations which are not alluvial.

This description of the Rhine is necessary in order to understand what the ancient writers have said of it.

The first description of the Rhine that we possess from any good authority is Caesar's, though he had not seen much of it. He says (*B. G.* iv. 15) that it rises in the Alpine regions of the Lepontii, and passes in a long course along the boundaries of the Nantuates, Helvetii, Sequani, Mediomatrici, Triboci, and Treviri, in a rapid course. The name Nantuates is corrupt [NANTUATES]. If we make the limits of the Treviri extend nearly to the Netherlands or the commencement of the low country, Caesar has shown pretty clearly the place where the Rhine enters the great plain. On approaching the ocean, he says, it forms many islands, and enters the sea by several mouths (capita). He knew that the Rhine divided into two main branches near the sea; and he says that one of the branches named the Vahalis (*Waal*) joined the Mosa (*Maas*), and formed the Insula Batavorum [BATAVORUM INSULA]. He speaks of the rapidity of the river, and its breadth and depth in that part where he built his wooden bridge over it. (*B. G.* iv. 17.) He made the bridge between *Coblens* and *Andernack*, higher up than the place where the river enters the low country. He crossed the Rhine a second time by a bridge which he constructed a little higher up than the first bridge. (*B. G.* vi. 9.)

Those persons, and Caesar of course, who said that the Rhine had more than two outlets were criticised by Asinius Pollio (Strab. iv. p. 192); and Virgil (*Aen.* viii. 724, Rhenique bicornis) follows Pollio's authority. But if the Mosa divided as it does now, Caesar was right and Pollio was wrong.

Strabo, who had some other authorities for his description of the Rhine besides Caesar, and perhaps besides Caesar and Pollio, does not admit Pollio's statement of the Rhine having a course of 6000 stadia; and yet Pollio's estimate is much below the truth. Strabo says that the length of the river in a right line is not much above one-half of Pollio's estimate, and that if we add 1000 stadia for the windings, that will be enough. This assertion and his argument founded on the rapidity of the stream, show that he knew nothing of the great circuit that the Rhine makes between its source and *Basle*. He knew, however, that it flowed north, but unluckily he supposed the *Seine* also to flow north. He also made the great mistake of affirming that the county of *Kent* may be seen from the mouths of the Rhine. He says that the Rhine had several sources, and he places them in the Adulas, a part of the Alps. In the same mountain mass he places the source of the Aduas, or Addua (*Adda*), which flows south into the lake Larius (*Lago di Como*). [ADDUA.]

The most difficult question about the Rhine is the outlets. When Pliny and Tacitus wrote, Drusus the brother of Tiberius had been on the lower Rhine, and also Germanicus, the son of Drusus, and other Roman commanders. Pliny (iv. 14) speaks of the Rhenus and the Mosa as two distinct rivers. In another passage (iv. 15) he says that the Rhine has three outlets: the western, named Helium, flows into the Mosa; the most northerly, named Flevum, flows into the lakes (*Zuider Zee*); and the middle branch, which is of moderate size, retains the name Rhenus. He supposed that there were islands in the Rhine between the Helium and the Flevum; and the Batavorum Insula, in which were the Canninefates also, is one of them. He also places between these two branches the islands of the Frisii, Chauci, Frisiabones, Sturii, and Marsacii. The Flevum of Pliny corresponds to the Flevo of Mela [FLEVO LACUS], who mentions this branch and only another, which he calls the Rhenus, which corresponds to Pliny's Rhenus. Mela mentions no other outlets. He considered the third to be the Mosa, we may suppose, if he knew anything about it

Tacitus (*Ann.* ii. 6) observes that the Rhine

z z 2

divides into two branches at the head of the Batavorum Insula. The branch which flows along the
German bank keeps its name and its rapid course to
the Ocean. The branch which flows on the Gallic
bank is broader and less rapid: this is the Vahalis
(*Waal*), which flows into the Mosa. (*Hist.* v. 23.)
[BATAVORUM INSULA.] He knows only two outlets of the Rhine, and one of them is through the
Mosa. The Rhine, as he calls the eastern branch,
is the boundary between Gallia and Germania. East
of this eastern branch he places the Frisii (*Ann.*
iv. 72); and herein he agrees with Pliny, who
places them between the Middle Rhine and the
Flevum. Accordingly the Rhenus of Tacitus is
the Rhenus of Mela and Pliny.

This third branch of the Rhine seems to be that
which Tacitus calls the work of Drusus (*Ann.* ii.
6), and which Sentonius (*Claudius*, c. 1) mentions
without saying where it was: "Drusus trans Rhenum
fossas novi et immensi operis effecit, quae nunc adhuc
Drusinae vocantur." Germanicus in his expedition
against the northern Germans (Tac. *Ann.* ii. 6), ordered his fleet to assemble at the Batavorum Insula,
whence it sailed through the Fossa Drusiana, and
the lakes into the Ocean and to the river Amisia
(*Ems*). This course was probably taken to avoid
the navigation along the sea-coast of Holland. On
a former occasion Germanicus had taken the same
course (*Ann.* i. 60), and his father Drusus had
done the same.

Ptolemy (ii. 9. § 4), who wrote after Tacitus and
Pliny, is acquainted with three outlets of the Rhine.
He places first the outlet of the Mosa in 24° 40'
long., 53° 20' lat. He then comes to the Batavi
and to Lugdunum, which town he places in 26° 30'
long., 53° 20' lat. The western mouth of the Rhine
is in 26° 45' long., 53° 20' lat. The middle mouth
is in 27° long., 53° 30' lat.; and the eastern in 28°
long., 54° lat. His absolute numbers are incorrect,
and they may be relatively incorrect also. His
western outlet is a little east of Lugdunum, and
this should be the Old Rhine or Rhine Proper.
The middle mouth is further east, and the eastern
mouth further east still. The eastern mouth may
be the *Yssel*, but it is difficult to say what Ptolemy's
middle mouth is. Gosselin supposes that Ptolemy's
western mouth may have been about *Zandwoord*.
He further supposes that the Middle Mouth according to his measures was about the latitude of
Bakkum, about 4 leagues above *Zandwoord*, and
he adds that this mouth was not known to those
writers who preceded Ptolemy, and we may conjecture that it was little used, and was the first
of the outlets that ceased to be navigable. The
third mouth he supposes to correspond to the passage of the *Vlie*. But nothing can be more vague
and unsatisfactory than this explanation, founded
on Ptolemy's measurements and pure conjecture.
So much as this is plain. Ptolemy does not reckon
the Mosa as one of the outlets of the Rhine, as the
Roman writers do; and he makes three outlets besides the outlet of the Mosa.

This country of swamps, rivers, and forests through
which the Lower Rhine flowed has certainly undergone great changes since the Roman period, owing
to the floods of the Rhine and the inundations of
the sea, and it is very difficult, perhaps impossible,
to make the ancient descriptions agree with the
modern localities. Still it was a fixed opinion that
the Rhine divided into two great branches, as Caesar
says, and this was the division of the Rhine from

the *Waal* at *Pannerden*, or wherever it may have
been in former times. One of the great outlets was
that which we call the *Maas* that flows by Rotterdam; the other was the Rhine Proper that entered the
sea near *Leiden*, and it was the stream from *Pannerden* to *Leiden* that formed the boundary between
Gallia and Germania. (Servius, *ad Aeneid.* viii.
727.) Ptolemy places all his three outlets in Gallia, and it is the eastern mouth which he makes
the boundary between Roman Gallia and Great Germania (ii. 11. § 1). If his eastern mouth is the
Yssel, he makes this river from *Arnheim* to the
outlet of the *Yssel* the eastern limit of Roman
Gallia in his time. This may be so, but it was
not so that Pliny and Tacitus understood the boundary. Whatever changes may have taken place
in the Delta of the Rhine, D'Anville's conclusion
is just, when he says that we can explain the
ancient condition of the places sufficiently to make
it agree with the statements of the ancient authors.

The floods of the Rhine have been kept in their
limits by embankments of earth which begin at
Wesel, in the Prussian province of *Düsseldorf*, and
extend along the Rhine and its branches to the sea.
The Romans began these works. In the time of
Nero, Pompeius Paullinus, to keep his soldiers employed, finished an embankment ("agger") on the
Rhine which Drusus had begun sixty-three years
before. (Tac. *Ann.* xiii. 53.) It has sometimes been
supposed that this "agger" is the "moles" which
Civilis broke down in the war which he carried on
against the Romans on the Lower Rhine. (Tac. *Hist.*
v. 19.) The consequence of throwing down this
"moles" was to leave nearly dry the channel between
the Batavorum Insula and Germania, which channel
is the Proper Rhine. The effect of throwing down
the "moles" was the same as if the river had been
driven back ("velut abacto amne"). This could not
have been effected by destroying an embankment;
but if the "moles" of Drusus was a dike which projected into the river for the purpose of preventing
most of the water from going down the *Waal*, and
for maintaining the channel of the Rhine on the north
side of the Batavorum Insula, we can understand
why Civilis destroyed and why Drusus had constructed it. Drusus constructed it to keep the
channel full on the north side of the Batavorum
Insula, and to maintain this as a frontier against
the Germans; and so we have another proof that
the Rhine Proper or the Middle Rhine was the
boundary between Gallia and Germania in this part,
as every passage of Tacitus shows in which he
speaks of it. Civilis destroyed the "moles" to stop
the Romans in their pursuit of him; for they were
on the south side of the island, and had no boats
there to make a bridge with. Ukert understands it
so, and he is probably right.

Another great Roman work in the Delta of the
Rhine was the canal of Corbulo. The Roman conquerors left durable monuments of their dominion in
all the countries which they invaded, even in the
watery regions of the Rhine, where they had to fight
with floods, with the tempests of the ocean, and a warlike people whose home was in the marshes and
forests.

The Rhine was the great frontier of the Romans
against the German tribes. All the cities on the
west or Gallic side, from *Leiden* to *Basle*, were either
of their foundation or were strengthened and fortified
by them. In the time of Tiberius eight legions
guarded the frontier of the Rhine.

This article may be read with the articles BATA-
VORUM INSULA, FLEVO LACUS, FOSSA CORBULO-
NIS, MOSA, MOSELLA, and GALLIA TRANSALPINA.
(D'Anville, *Notice, &c.*, "Rhenus"; *Penny Cyclopaedia*, art. "Rhine"; and Ukert, *Gallien*,—who
has collected all the ancient and many modern authorities.)   [G. L.]

RHENUS (*Reno*), a river of Gallia Cispadana,
and one of the southern tributaries of the Padus.
(Plin. iii. 16. s. 20.) It flowed within about a mile
of the walls of Bononia (*Bologna*), on the W. side
of the city, and is celebrated in history on account
of the interview between Antony, Octavian, and Lepidus, which is generally believed to have taken place
in a small island formed by its waters. [BONONIA.]
It has its sources in the Apennines nearly 50 miles
above *Bologna*, and is a considerable stream, though
called by Silius Italicus "parvus," to distinguish it
from its far greater namesake, the *Rhine*. (Sil. Ital.
viii. 599.) In the time of Pliny it is probable that
it discharged its waters into the principal channel of
the Padus, but at the present day they are turned
aside into an artificial channel before reaching that
river, and are thus carried into the arm now known
as the *Po di Primaro*. Hence the mouth of that
branch of the Po is now called the *Foce del Reno*.
Pliny tells us that the reeds which grew on the banks
of the Rhenus were superior to all others for making
arrows. (Plin. xvi. 36. s. 65.)   [E. H. B.]

RHESAENA ('Ρέσαινα, Ptol. v. 18. § 13; 'Ρέσινα,
Steph. B. *s. v.*; Amm. Marc. xxxii. 5; Ressaina,
Tab. Peut.; Rasin, *Notit. Imp.*: Eth. 'Ρεσιναΐτης,
Steph. B. *s. v.*), a town of considerable importance
at the northern extremity of Mesopotamia; it was situated near the sources of the Chaboras (*Khabúr*), on
the great road which led from Carrhae to Nicepho-
rium, about 88 miles from Nisibis and 40 from
Dara. (Procop. *B. P.* ii. 19, *de Aedif.* ii. 2.) It
was near this town that Gordian the Younger fell in
a battle with the Persians. (Amm. Marc. *l. c.*) A
coin exists of the emperor Decius, bearing the legend
CEΠ. ΚΟΛ. ΡΗCΑΙΝΗCΙΩΝ., which may in all
probability be referred to this town. In the Notit.
Imp. the place is subject to the government of the
Dux Osrhoenae (*Notit. Dign.* ed. Böcking, i. p. 400),
and a bishop of Resaina is mentioned among those
who subscribed their names at the Council of Nicaea.
Under Theodosius, the town appears to have been
partially rebuilt, and to have received the title of
THEODOSIOPOLIS. (Hierocl. p. 793.) There can
be no doubt that it is at present represented by
Ras-al-Ain, a considerable entrepôt of commerce
in the province of *Diarbekr*. It was nearly destroyed by the troops of *Timúr*, in A.D. 1393.
(D'Herbelot, *Dict. Orient.* i. p. 140, iii. p. 112;
Niebuhr, ii. p. 390.)   [V.]

COIN OF RHESAENA.

RHETICO, a mountain of Germany, mentioned
only by Pomp. Mela (iii. 3), along with Mount
Taunus. As no particulars are stated it is impos-

sible to identify it, and German writers are so divided
in their opinions that some take Rhetico to be the
name of the *Siebengebirge*, near *Bonn*, while others
identify it with a mountain in the *Tirol*. [L. S.]

RHIDAGUS (Curt. vi. 4. § 7), a river of Hyrcania, which flows from the mountains NW. to the
Caspian. Alexander crossed it on his march in
pursuit of Dareius. It appears to be the same as
the Choatres of Ammianus (xxiii. 24), and may
perhaps be represented by the present *Adjius*. [V.]

RHINOCORU'RA or RHINOCOLU'RA ('Ρινο-
κόρουρα, Polyb. Ptol. Joseph.; 'Ρινοκόλουρα, Strab.:
Eth. 'Ρινοκουραΐος, 'Ρινοκουρουρίτης), a maritime
city on the confines of Egypt and Palestine, and consequently reckoned sometimes to one country, sometimes to the other. Strabo, going south, reckons
Gaza, Raphia, Rhinocolura (xvi. p. 759); Polybius,
going north, reckons it to Egypt, calling Raphia the
first city of Coelesyria (v. 80). Ptolemy also
reckons it to Egypt, and places it in the district of
Cassiotis (iv. 5. § 12), between Ostracine and Anthedon. The Itinerarium Antonini (p. 151) places
it xxii. M.P. south of Rafia, and the same distance
north of Ostracena. The following curious account
of its origin and name is given by Diodorus Siculus.
Actisanes, king of Aethiopia, having conquered
Egypt, with a view to the suppression of crime in his
newly-acquired dominion, collected together all the
suspected thieves in the country, and, after judicial
conviction, cut off their noses and sent them to
colonise a city which he had built for them on the
extremity of the desert, called, from their mishap,
Rhinocolura (quasi ῥῖνος κόλουροι=curti, al. ῥ. κεί-
ρασθαι), situated on the confines of Egypt and Syria,
near the shore; and from its situation destitute of
nearly all the necessaries of life. The soil around it
was salt, and the small supply of well water within
the walls was bitter. Necessity, the mother of
invention, led the inhabitants to adopt the following
novel expedient for their sustenance. They collected a quantity of reeds, and, splitting them very
fine, they wove them into nets, which they stretched
for many stadia along the sea-shore, and so snared
large quantities of quails as they came in vast
flights from the sea (i. 60). Strabo copies this account of its origin (*l. c.*); Seneca ascribes the act
to a Persian king, and assigns the city to Syria
(*de Ira*, iii. 20). Strabo (xvi. p. 781) mentions it
as having been the great emporium of Indian and
Arabian merchandise, which was discharged at
Leuce Come, on the eastern coast of the Red Sea,
whence it was conveyed, via Petra, to Rhinocolura,
and thence dispersed to all quarters. In his day,
however, the tide of commerce flowed chiefly down
the Nile to Alexandria. The name occurs in Josephus, but unconnected with any important event.
It is known to the ancient ecclesiastical writers as
the division between the possessions of the sons of
Noah. S. Jerome states that the "River of Egypt"
flowed between this city and Pelusium (Reland,
Palaest. pp. 285, 286, 969—972); and in one passage the LXX. translate "the River of Egypt"
by Rhinocorura." (*Isaiah*, xxvii. 12.) It is remarkable that this penal colony, founded for mutilated convicts, should have become fruitful in saints;
and its worthy and exemplary bishop Melas, in the
time of the Arian persecution, who was succeeded by
his brother Solon, became the founder of a succession
of religious men, which, according to the testimony
of Sozomen, continued to his time. (*Hist. Eccles.*
vii. 31.) Rhinocorura is now *El-Arish*, as the

River of Egypt is *Wady-el-Arish*. The village is situated on an eminence about half a mile from the sea, and is for the most part enclosed within a wall of considerable thickness. There are some Roman ruins, such as marble columns, &c., and a very fine well of good water. (Irby and Mangles, *Travels*, p. 174, October 7.)   [G. W.]

RHIPE. [ENISPE.]

RHIPAEI MONTES (τὰ 'Ριπαῖα ὄρη), a name applied by Grecian fancy to a mountain chain whose peaks rose to the N. of the known world. It is probably connected with the word *ῥιπαί*, or the chill rushing blasts of Βορέας, the mountain wind or "tramontana" of the Greek Archipelago, which was conceived to issue from the caverns of this mountain range. Hence arose the notion of the happiness of those living beyond these mountains — the only place exempt from the northern blasts. In fact they appear in this form of *'Ριπαί*, in Alcman (*Fragm.* p. 80, ed. Welcker), a lyric poet of the 7th century B. C., who is the first to mention them. The contemporary writers Damastes of Sigeum (*ap.* *Steph. B. s. v.* 'Υπερβόρεοι) and Hellanicus of Lesbos (*ap. Clem. Alex. Strom.* i. p. 305) agree in their statements in placing beyond the fabled tribes of the N. the Rhipaean mountains from which the north wind blows, and on the other side of these, on the sea-coast, the Hyperboreans. The legends connected with this imagined range of mountains lingered for a long period in Grecian literature, as may be seen from the statements of Hecataeus of Abdera (*ap. Aelian. H. A.* xi. 1) and Aristotle (*Met.* i. 13; comp. Soph. *Oed. Col.* 1248; Schol. *ad loc.*; Strab. vii. pp. 295, 299.) Herodotus knows nothing of the Rhipaean mountains or the Alps, though the positive geography of the N. begins with him. It would be an idle inquiry to identify the Rhipaean range with any actual chain. As the knowledge of the Greeks advanced, the geographical "mythus" was moved further and further to the N. till it reached the 48th degree of latitude N. of the Maeotic lake and the Caspian, between the *Don*, the *Volga*, and the *Jaik*, where Europe and Asia melt as it were into each other in wide plains or steppes. These "mountains of the winds" followed in the train of the meteorological "mythus" of the Hyperboreans which wandered with Heracles far to the W. Geographical discovery embodied the picture which the imagination had formed. Poseidonius (*ap. Athen.* vi. p. 223, d.) seems to have considered this range to be the Alps. The Roman poets, borrowing from the Greeks, made the Rhipaean chain the extreme limit to the N. (Virg. *Georg.* i. 240; Propert. i. 6. 3; Sil. It. xi. 459;) and Lucan (iii. 273) places the sources of the Tanais in this chain. (Comp. Mela, i. 19. § 18; Plin. iv. 24; Amm. Marc. xxii. 8. § 38; Procop. *B. G.* iv. 6; Sid. Apoll. ii. 343; Jornand. *Get.* 16; Oros. i. 2.) In the earlier writers the form is Ripaei, but with Pliny and those who followed him the *p* becomes aspirated. In the geography of Ptolemy (iii. 5. §§ 15, 19) and Marcian (*Peripl.* § 39, ed. Didot) the Rhipaean chain appears to be that gently rising ground which divides the rivers which flow into the Baltic from those which run to the Euxine.   [E. B. J.]

RHISPIA ('Ρισπία), a place in Upper Pannonia, of uncertain site (Ptol. ii. 15. § 4; Orelli, *Inscript.* n. 4991), though it is commonly identified with *Csur*. (Schönwisner, *Antiquitates Sabariae*, p. 41.)   [L. S.]

RHITHYMNA ('Ρίθυμνα), a town of Crete, which

is mentioned by Ptolemy (iii. 17. § 7) and Pliny (iv. 20) as the first town on the N. coast to the E. of Amphimalla, and is spoken of as a Cretan city by Steph. B., in whose text its name is written Rhithymnia ('Ριθυμνία: *Eth.* 'Ριθυμνιάτης, 'Ριθύμνιος). It is also alluded to by Lycophron (76). The modern *Rhithymnos* or *Retimo* retains the name of the ancient city upon the site of which it stands. Eckhel (*Numi Vet. Anecdoti*, p. 155; comp. Rasche, vol. iv. pt. i. p. 1024) first assigned to Rhithymna its ancient coins; maritime emblems are found on them. (Pashley, *Creta*, vol. i. p. 101.)   [E. B. J.]

COIN OF RHITHYMNA.

RHIUM ('Ρίον). 1. A promontory in Achaia. [Vol. I. p. 13, a.]

2. A town in Messenia, in the Thuriate gulf, and also the name of one of the five divisions into which Cresphontes is said to have divided Messenia. (Strab. viii. pp. 360, 361.) Strabo describes Rhium as over against Taenarum (ἀπεναντίον Ταινάρου), which is not a very accurate expression, as hardly any place on the western coast, except the vicinity of Cape Acritas, is in sight from Taenarum. (Leake, *Morea*, vol. i. p. 459.)

RHIUSIAVA. [RIUSIAVA.]

RHIZANA ('Ρίζανα, Ptol. vi. 21. § 2; 'Ρίζανα, Marcian, *Peripl.* i. § 33, ed. Müller), a town on the coast of Gedrosia, in the immediate neighbourhood of the most western mouth of the Indus. The differences between Ptolemy and Marcian with regard to distances do not seem here reconcileable.   [V.]

RHIZE'NIA ('Ριζηνία, Steph. B. *s. v.*), a town of Crete of which nothing is known; there is an "eparkhía" now called *Rhisó-kastron*, but it is a mere guess to identify it with this.   [E. B. J.]

RHIZIUS ('Ρίζιος), a small coast river of Pontus, between the Iris and Acampsis, still bearing the name of *Riseh*. (Arrian, *Peripl. P. E.* p. 7; Anonym. *Peripl. P. E.* p. 12.)   [L. S.]

RHIZON ('Ρίζων, Polyb. ii. 11; Strab. vii. p. 316; Liv. xlv. 26; Steph. B. *s. v.*; 'Ρίζανα, Ptol. ii. 17. § 12; Rhizinium, Plin. iii. 26; Rucimum, Geogr. Rav. v. 14; ad Zizio [ad Rhisio?], *Peut. Tab.*), a town of Dalmatia, situated upon a gulf which bore the name of RHIZONICUS SINUS ('Ριζονικὸς κόλπος, Strab. vii. pp. 314, 316; Ptol. ii. 17. § 5). Teuta, the Illyrian queen, took refuge in this her last stronghold, and obtained peace upon the conqueror's terms. Scylax (p. 9) has a river Rhizus ('Ριζοῦς, comp. Polyb. *l. c.*; Philo, *ap. Steph. B. s. v.* Βουθόη), but this can be no other than the *Bocche di Cattaro*, celebrated for its grand scenery, which gives this gulf with its six mouths the appearance of an inland lake, and hence the mistake of Scylax and Polybius, who says that Rhizon was at a distance from the sea. In *Risano*, standing on rising ground at the extremity of a beautiful bay that runs to the N. from *Perasto*, are remains of the Roman colony. A Mosaic pavement and coins have been found there. Near *Risano* is a cavern from which a torrent runs in winter, and falls into the bay, but it is not known whether this be the Dalmatian cavern mentioned by Pliny (ii. 44). It is here that Cadmus is said to have retired among the Encheleee. (Scylax, *l. c.*) Whether the Phoenicians had reached the E. shore of the Adriatic does not appear, but it could only be from traces of Phoenician settlements that this term was assigned to his wanderings. (Wilkinson, *Dalmatia*, vol. i. p. 381; Neigebaur, *Die Süd-Slaven*, p. 30.)   [E. B. J.]

RHIZONICUS SINUS. [RHIZON.]

RHIZO'PHAGI AETHIOPES ('Ριζοφάγοι, Diodor. iii. 23; Strab. xvii. p. 770, seq.; Ptol. iv. 8. § 29), one of the numerous tribes of Aethiopia, whom the Greeks named after the diet peculiar to them. The root-eating Aethiopians dwelt above Meroë, on either bank of the Astaboras (*Tacazzé*), and derived their principal sustenance from a kind of cake or *polenta*, made from the reeds and bulrushes that covered that alluvial region. The roots were first scrupulously cleansed, then powdered between stones, and the pulp thus obtained was dried in the sun. The Rhizophagi are described as a mild and harmless race, living in amity with their neighbours, and, probably because they had nothing to lose, unmolested by them. Their only foes were lions, who sometimes committed the greatest havoc among this unarmed race; and their best friends, according to Diodorus (comp. Agatharch. *ap. Hudson, Geog. Graec. Min.* p. 37), were a species of gnat, or more probably gadfly, which at the summer solstice (ὑπὸ τὴν ἀνατολὴν τοῦ κυνὸς) assailed the lions in such numbers, that they fled from the marshes, and permitted the Rhizophagi to recruit their losses. The site of this obscure tribe probably corresponds with that of the *Shikos* (Bruce, *Travels*, vol. iii. pp. 69—72), who now occupy the southern part of the territory of *Taka* or *Atbara*, on the upper *Tacazzé*. [W. B. D.]

RHIZUS ('Ριζοῦς), a port-town of Pontus, at the mouth of the river Rhizius, about 120 stadia to the east of the river Calus, and 30 stadia west of the mouth of the Ascurus. In the time of Procopius (*Bell. Goth.* iv. 2) the place had risen to considerable importance, so that Justinian surrounded it with strong fortifications. The Table mentions on its site a place under the name of Reila, which is probably only a corruption of the right name, which still exists in the form of *Rizeh*, though the place is also called *Irrisk*. (Comp. Procop. *de Aed.* iii. 4; Ptol. v. 6. § 6.)   [L. S.]

RHIZUS ('Ριζοῦς: *Eth.* Ριζούντιος), a town of Magnesia in Thessaly, whose inhabitants were transported to Demetrias upon the foundation of the latter city. (Strab. ix. pp. 436, 443; Steph. B. *s. v.*; Plin. iv. 9. s. 16.) We learn from Scylax (p. 24) that Rhizus was outside the Pagasaean gulf upon the exterior shore; but its exact position is uncertain. Leake places it at the ruins eastward of *Nakhóri* (*Northern Greece*, vol. iv. p. 383).

RHOCCA ('Ρόκκα), a town of Crete, where there was a temple to Artemis Rhoccaea (Aelian, *N. A.* xii. 22). Pococke (vol. ii. p. 247) found remains at the village which still bears the name of *Rhokka*, to the S. of the ancient Methymna; and there can be little doubt but that this is the site of Rhocca, which, as is shown by Aelian (*N. A.* xiv. 20), was near Methymna (Höck, *Kreta*, vol. i. p. 391; Pashley, *Crete*, vol. ii. p. 41.)   [E. B. J.]

RHODA or RHODUS ('Ρόδη, Steph. B. *s. v.*; Rhoda, Mela, ii. 6; Liv. xxxiv. 8; 'Ρόδος, Strab. xiv. p. 654; Eustath. *ad Dion. Per.* 504; called by Ptol. ii. 6. § 20, 'Ροδίπολις, where we should probably read 'Ρόδη πόλις), a Greek emporium on the coast of the Indigetae in Hispania Tarraconensis,

founded according to Strabo (*l. c.*) by the Rhodians, and subsequently taken possession of by the Massiliots. It is the modern *Rosas ;* but tradition says that the old town lay towards the headland at *San Pedro de Roda*. (Ford, *Handbook of Spain*, p. 249; comp. Meurs. *Rhod.* i. 28; Marca, *Hisp.* ii. 18; Martin, *Hist. des Gaules*, p. 218; Florez, *Med.* iii. p. 114; Mionnet, i. p. 148.)   [T. H. D.]

RHO'DANUS ('Ροδανός: *Rhône*). The Rhone rises in Switzerland, in a glacier west of the pass of *St. Gothard* and south of the *Gallenstock*, a mountain above 12,000 feet high. It has a general course, first SW., then W. by S. as far as *Martigny*, the Octodurus of Caesar (*B. G.* iii. 1). The course from *Martigny* to the *Lake of Geneva* forms nearly a right angle with the course of the river above *Martigny*. The length of the valley through which the Rhone flows to the *Lake of Geneva* is above 90 miles. This long valley called Wallis, or the *Vallais*, is bounded by the highest Alpine ranges: on the north by the Bernese Alps, which contain the largest continuous mass of snow and ice in the Swiss mountains, and on the south by the Lepontian and Pennine Alps. The *Lake of Geneva*, the Lacus Lemannus of the Romans [LEMANUS], which receives the Rhone at its eastern extremity, is more than 1200 feet above the surface of the Mediterranean.

The *Lake of Geneva* lies in the form of a crescent between Switzerland and Savoy. The convex part of the crescent which forms the north side is above 50 miles in length; the concave or southern side is less than 50 miles in length. The widest part, which is about the middle, is 8 or 9 miles. The greatest depth, which is near some high cliffs on the south coast, is stated variously by different authorities, some making it as much as 1000 feet. The Rhone enters the lake at the east end a muddy stream, and the water flows out clear at the western extremity past Geneva, an ancient city of the Allobroges. [GENEVA.]

Below Geneva the Rhone runs in a rapid course and in a SW. direction past *Fort l'Ecluse*. *Fort l'Ecluse* is at the point described by Caesar (*B. G.* i. 9) where the Jura overhangs the course of the Rhone. [HELVETII.] The river then runs south past *Seyssel*, and making a bend turns north again, and flowing in an irregular western course to *Lyon* (Lugdunum) is joined there by the Saône, the ancient Arar [ARAR; LUGDUNUM]. The length of the course of the Rhone from the *Lake of Geneva* to *Lyon* is about 130 miles. The *Saône*, as Caesar says, is a slow river, but the current is seen very plainly under the bridges in *Lyon*. The Rhone is a rapid stream, and violent when it is swelled by the rains and the waters from the Alpine regions.

From *Lyon* the Rhone flows in a general southern course. The direct distance is about 150 miles from *Lyon* to *Arles* (Arelate) where the river divides into two large branches which include the isle of *Camargue*. The whole course of the Rhone from the ice-fields of Switzerland to the low shores of the Mediterranean is above 500 miles.

The valley of the Rhone below *Lyon* is narrow on the west bank as far as the junction of the *Ardèche*, and it is bounded by high, bare, and rocky heights. Some of the hill slopes are planted with vines. All the rivers which flow into the Rhone from the highlands on the west are small: they are the *Ardèche*, *Cèze*, *Gardon* (Vardo), and some smaller streams. The left bank of the Rhone from

Lyon downwards is generally flat, but there are several parts where the rocks rise right above the water, and in these places the railway from *Lyon* to *Marseille* is cut in the rocks close to the river. At *St. Andeol*, a small town on the west bank above the *Ardèche*, the plain country begins on the west side of the Rhone. On the east side the hills are seen in the distance. From one of the middle-age towers built on the amphitheatre of *Arles*, there is a view of the great plain which lies all round that city to the north, west, and east, and stretches southward to the coast of the Mediterranean. The two large affluents of the Rhone on the east side are the *Isère* (Isara) and the *Durance* (Druentia).

The Rhone was earlier known to the Greeks and Romans than any other of the large rivers of Western Europe. The oldest notices of this river must have come from the Phocaeans and the Greeks of Massilia. What Avienus has collected from some source (*Or. Marit.* 623—690) is unintelligible. Pliny (iii. 4) very absurdly derives the name Rhodanus from a town which he names *Rhoda*; but the name Rhodanus is older than any city, and, like the names of other European rivers, it is one of the oldest memorials that we have of the languages of the West. Polybius (iii. 47) supposed that the Rhone rose further east than it does, but he knew that it flowed down a long valley (*αὐλῶν*) to the west, though he does not mention the *Lake of Geneva*. Ptolemy (ii. 10), the latest of the classical geographers, had no exact notion of the sources of the Rhone, though the Romans long before his time must have known where to look for them. He makes the sources of the Arar come from the Alps, by which the Jura is meant, and in this statement and what he says of the course of the Arar and Dubis he may have followed Strabo (iv. p. 186), as it has been supposed. The blunders about the sources of this river are singular. Mela (iii. 3) mentions the Danubius and Rhodanus among the rivers of Germany; and in another passage he says that it rises not far from the sources of the Ister and the Rhenus (ii. 5).

There is much difference in the statements about the number of the mouths of the Rhone. Timaeus, quoted by Strabo (p. 183), says that there were five outlets, for which Polybius reproves Timaeus, and says there were only two. Polybius (iii. 41) names the eastern branch the Massaliotic. Artemidorus, as cited by Strabo, made five mouths. Strabo does not state how many he supposed that there were. He says that above the mouths of the Rhone, not far from the sea, is a lake called Stomalimne, which some make one of the outlets of the Rhone, and those particularly do who enumerate seven outlets of the river. But he shows that this was a mistaken opinion. Caesar built ships at Arelate when he was going to besiege Massilia, and he brought them down the river to that city, and by the eastern branch, as we may assume.

The Rhone was navigated by the people on its banks at the time when Hannibal with his army came to cross it, and much earlier. Polybius is the earliest extant writer who has given us any precise information about this river. Hannibal (B.C. 218) crossed it at a point above the division of the stream, and of course higher than *Arles*, for we assume that the bifurcation was not higher than that city in his time, if it ever was. (Polyb. iii. 43.) He probably crossed the river at *Beaucaire* and below the junction of the *Gardon*. He then marched northwards on the east side of the river to the In-

sula. [INSULA ALLOBROGUM.] Much has been written on this passage of Polybius and on Livy (xxi.), who also describes the same passage. (*The March of Hannibal from the Rhone to the Alps*, by H. L. Long, Esq., 1831; Ukert, *Gallien*, p. 561, &c.; and the modern writers quoted by each.)

Pliny (iii. 4) enumerates three mouths of the Rhone. He calls the two smaller "Libyca" (if the reading is right): one of these is the Hispaniense os, which we may assume to be the nearest to Spain; the other is Metapinum, and the third and largest is the Massaliot. Some modern maps represent three mouths of the river. Ptolemy (ii. 10) mentions only a western and an eastern mouth, and he makes a mistake in placing the Fossae Marianae [FOSSAE MARIANAE] west of the western mouth. The channels of the Rhone below *Arles* may have been changed in some parts, even in historical periods, and the bed of the river above *Arles* has not always been where it is now. But there is no evidence for any great changes in the river's course since the time when Polybius wrote, though it is certain that the alluvium brought down the river must have enlarged the Delta of the Rhone.

The canal of Marius, which was on the east side of the eastern outlet of the Rhone, is described under FOSSA MARIANA; and the stony plain is described under LAPIDEI CAMPI.   [G. L.]

RHODANU'SIA. Pliny (iii. 4) mentions Rhoda in Gallia Narbonensis as a colony of the Rhodii He places it on the coast east of Agathe (*Agde*), and says that it gave the name to the Rhodanus. [RHODANUS.] Hieronymus, in his Prologue to the Second Epistle to the Galatians, copies Pliny. This may be the place which Stephanus (*s. v.* ῾Ροδανουσία) names Rhodanusia, and calls "a city in Massalia;" by which the Massaliotic territory must be meant. The passage in Strabo (iv. p. 180) τὴν δὲ ῾Ρόην ᾿Αγαθὴν τοῖς, in which he intends to speak of one of the Massiliotic settlements, is corrupt. Casaubon (*Comment. in Strab.* p. 83) sometimes thought that we ought to read τὴν δὲ ῾Ρόην καὶ ᾿Αγαθὴν τοῖς. Groskurd (*Strab.* Transl. i. p. 310) thinks that Pliny has called this place Rhoda because he confounded it with Rhode or Rhodus in Iberia, which he does not mention. He observes that Scymnus (v. 208), Stephanus, and Sidonius Apollinaris (i 5) rightly name it Rhodanusia; and he has no doubt that Strabo wrote it so. But it is by no means certain that Strabo did write it so. Groskurd's argument is this: there never was a town Rhoda in Gallia, and Strabo mentions the Iberian Rhode or Rhodus. Since then Strabo is acquainted with both places, he has not made a mistake like Pliny; rather must we with Vossius (*Note on Mela*, ii. 6) alter the corrupt ῾Ρόην into ῾Ροδανουσίαν; and Koray is mistaken in rejecting ῾Ρόην altogether as not genuine. We know nothing of this Gallic Rhode or Rhodanusia. The place is gone and has left no trace.   [G. L.]

RHODE. [RHODANUSIA.]
RHODE FLUVIUS. [SAGARIS.]

RHO'DIA (῾Ροδία: Eth. ῾Ροδιεύς), a town of Lycia, situated in the mountains on the north of Corydallus. (Steph. B. *s. v.*; Ptol. v. 3. § 6; Phot. *Cod.* 176.) At the time when Col. Leake wrote his work on Asia Minor (p. 186) the site of this town was not yet ascertained, and Sir C. Fellows did not examine the district; but the inscriptions which have since been found fix its site at the place now called *Eski Hissar*. (Spratt and Forbes, *Tra-*

vois in Lycia, i. pp. 166, 181.) The town had a temple of Asclepius, and its citizens are not called, as Stephanus Byz. asserts, 'Ροδιεῖς, but 'Ροδιαπολῖται or 'Ροδιοπολῖται, whence it appears that Pliny (v. 28) correctly calls the town Rhodiopolis. A plan of the numerous remains of this town is given by Spratt, according to whom it was not surrounded by walls: the theatre stands nearly in the centre, and is small, having a diameter of only 136 feet; but many of the seats remain, and the basement of the proscenium is perfect. In the front of it is a terrace, with seats along the parapet. Remains of churches show that the place was inhabited in Christian times. There are also traces of an aqueduct. The town being situated on a lofty eminence, commands an extensive southern prospect.　　　　　　　　　　　　[L. S.]

RHODIO'RUM REGIO. [PERAEA.]

RHO'DIUS ('Ρόδιος), a river of Troas, having its sources in Mount Ida, a little above the town of Astyra; it flows in a north-western direction, and after passing by Astyra and Cremaste, discharges itself into the Hellespont between Dardanus and Abydus. (Hom. *Il.* xii. 20, xx. 215; Hesiod, *Theog.* 341; Strab. xii. p. 554, xiii. pp. 595, 603; Plin. v. 33.) Strabo (xiii. p. 595) states that some regarded the Rhodius as a tributary of the Aesepus; but they must have been mistaken, as the river is mentioned on the coins of Dardanus. (Sestini, *Geog. Numis.* p. 39.) Pliny (l. c.) states that this ancient river no longer existed; and some modern writers identify it with the Pydius mentioned by Thucydides (viii. 106; comp. Hesych. and Phavorin. s. v. Πύδιον). Richter (*Wallfahrten*, p. 457) describes its present condition as that of a brook flowing into the *Dardanelles* by many mouths and marshes. [L. S.]

RHO'DOPE ('Ροδόπη, Herod. vi. 49; Thuc. ii. 96; Polyb. xxxiv. 19; Strab. iv. p. 208, vii. pp. 313, 329, 331; Mela, ii. 2. § 2; Plin. iii. 29, iv. 5. s. 17; Amm. Marc. xxi. 10. § 3; Malchus, *ap. Exc. de Leg. Rom.* p. 90), a mountain chain forming the W. continuation of Haemus, and the frontier between Thrace and Macedonia, of which little more is known than the name. On its desolate heights, the lurking places of the fierce Satrae, was the great sanctuary and oracle of the Thracian Dionysus. As the Strymon took its sources in Rhodope (Strab. viii. p. 331) the high ridges round *Dúpnitza* and *Ghiustendíl* must be assigned to Rhodope, which may roughly be said to belong to the central of the three continuous chains, which under the name of the *Despoto Dagh* branches out to the S. of the *Balkan* (Haemus) at about 23° E. long.　　　　　　　　[E. B. J.]

RHODU'NTIA ('Ροδουντία: Eth. 'Ροδούντιος), a fortress on Mt. Callidromus, defending one of the passes to Thermopylae. (Strab. ix. p. 428; Liv. xxxvi. 16, 19; Steph. B. s. v.; Leake, *Northern Greece*, vol. ii. pp. 10, 62, 64.)

RHODUS ('Ρόδος: Eth. 'Ρόδιος: *Rhodes*), one of the chief islands of the Aegean, or more properly of that part of the Aegean which is called the Carpathian sea, about 9 or 10 miles from the coast of Caria. In the earliest times it is said to have borne the names of Ophiussa (Steph. B. s. v. 'Ρόδος), Stadia, Telchinis (Strab. xvi. p. 653), Asteria, Aethraea, Trinacria, Corymbia, Poïeessa, Atabyria, Macaria, and Oloëssa. (Plin. v. 36.) It extends from south to north, and is 920 stadia in circumference (Strab. xiv. p. 605), or, according to Pliny, 125 Roman miles, though others reduced it to 103. The island is traversed from north to south by a chain of mountains, the highest point of which was called Atabyris or Atabyrion, and the towns were all situated on the coast. Mount Atabyris is 4560 feet above the level of the sea, and on the top of it stood a temple of Zeus Atabyrius. Rhodes was believed to have at one time risen out of the sea, and the Telchines, its most ancient inhabitants, are said to have immigrated from Crete. (Pind. *Olymp.* vii. 23, &c.; Plin. ii. 87; Aristid. *Orat.* xliii. p. 653, ed. Dind.; Strab. l. c.; Diod. v. 55.) The Telchines, about whom many fabulous stories are related, are said to have been nine in number, and their sister Halia or Amphitrite became by Poseidon the mother of six sons and one daughter, Rhodos, from which in the end the island received the name it still bears. Others, however, with better reason, derive the name Rhodus from ῥόδον, a rose, for the rose appears as a symbol on coins of the island, so that Rhodus would be "the island of Roses." (Eckhel, vol. ii. p. 602; Sestini, *Num. Vet.* p. 382.) These most ancient and fabulous Telchines are said to have perished or been driven from the island during an inundation, and Helios then created a new race of inhabitants, who were called after him Heliadae; they were seven in number, and became ancestors of seven tribes, which partly peopled Rhodus itself and partly emigrated to Lesbos, Cos, Caria, and Egypt. The Heliadae are said to have greatly distinguished themselves by the progress they made in the sciences of astronomy and navigation. (Pind. l. c. 160, &c.; Diod. v. 56; Conon, *Narrat.* 47; Strab. xiv. p. 654.) After this various immigrations from foreign countries are mentioned: Egyptians under Danaus, Phoenicians under Cadmus, Thessalians and Carians, are each said to have furnished their contingent to the population of Rhodes. Whatever we may think of these alleged immigrations, they can have but little affected the national character of the Rhodians, which in fact did not become fixed until a branch of the Doric race took possession of the island, after which event the Doric character of its inhabitants became thoroughly established. Some Dorians or Heracleidae appear to have been settled there as early as the Trojan War, for the Heracleid Tlepolemus is described as having sailed to Troy with nine ships. (*Il.* ii. 653; Diod. iv. 58, v. 59; Apollod. ii. 8. § 2.) After the Trojan War Aethaemenes, a Heracleid from Argos, led other settlers to Rhodus. (Strab. xiv. p 653; Diod. xv. 59; Apollod. iii. 2. § 1; comp. Thuc. vii. 57; Aristid. *Orat.* xliv. p. 839.) After this time the Rhodians quietly developed the resources of their island, and rose to great prosperity and affluence.

The three most ancient towns of the island were LINDUS, IALYSUS, and CAMIRUS, which were believed to have been founded by three grandsons of the Heliad Ochimus bearing the same names, or, according to others, by the Heracleid Tlepolemus. (Diod. iv. 58, v. 57.) These three towns, together with Cos, Cnidus, and Halicarnassus, formed what was called the Doric hexapolis, which had its common sanctuary on the Triopian headland on the coast of Caria, Apollo being the tutelary deity of the confederation. (Herod. i. 144.) The rapid progress made by the Rhodian towns at a comparatively early period is sufficiently attested by their colonies in the distant countries of the west. Thus they founded settlements in the Balearic islands, Rhode on the coast of Spain, Parthenope, Salapia, Siris, and Sybaris in Italy, and Gela in

Sicily; while the countries nearer home were not neglected, for Soli in Cilicia, and Gagae and Corydalla in Lycia, were likewise Rhodian colonies. But notwithstanding this early application to navigation and commerce, for which Rhodes is so admirably situated between the three ancient continents, the Rhodians were not ranked with the great maritime powers of Greece. Herodotus speaks of them only as forming a part of the Doric confederacy, nor does Thucydides mention their island more frequently. The Rhodians, in fact, did not attain to any political eminence among the states of Greece until about B. C. 408, when the three ancient towns conjointly built the city of Rhodes at the northern extremity of the island, and raised it to the rank of a capital. During the first period of the Peloponnesian War the towns of Rhodes paid tribute to Athens, and were reluctantly compelled to serve against Syracuse and Gela in Sicily (Thuc. vii. 57); but in B. C. 412 they joined the Peloponnesians. The popular party being favourable to Athens, soon afterwards attempted a reaction, but it was crushed (Diod. xiii. 38, 45). In B. C. 396, however, when Conon appeared with his fleet in the waters of Rhodes, the Rhodians again embraced the cause of Athens (Diod. xiv. 79; Paus. vi. 7. § 6); but the democracy which was now established was ill managed, and did not last long; and as early as B. C. 390, the exiled aristocrats, with the assistance of Sparta, recovered their former ascendancy. (Aristot. Polit. v. 4. 2; Xenoph. Hellen. iv. 8. § 20, &c.; Diod. xiv. 97.) The fear of Sparta's growing power once more threw Rhodes into the hands of the Athenians, but soon after the battle of Leuctra a change again took place; at least the Thebans, in B. C. 364, were zealously engaged in sowing discord for the purpose of drawing Rhodes, Chios, and Byzantium over to their own side. During the Social War, from B. C. 357 to 355, the Rhodians were arrayed against Athens, being instigated by the dynast of Caria and his successor Artemisia. But as they became alarmed by the growing power of the Carian dynasty, they solicited the protection of Athens through the eloquence of Demosthenes. (Demos. de Libert. Rhodior.) The form of government throughout this period was oligarchical, which accounts for the insolent conduct of Hegesilochus, as described in Athenaeus (x. p. 444). Rhodes furnished Darius, the last king of Persia, with one of his bravest and ablest generals in the person of Memnon, who, if he had had the sole direction of affairs, might have checked the victorious career of Alexander, and saved the Persian empire. But as it was, Rhodes, like the rest of Greece, lost its independence, and received a Macedonian garrison (Curt. iv. 5). The expulsion of this garrison after the death of Alexander was the beginning of a glorious epoch in the history of Rhodes; for during the wars against the successors of Alexander, and especially during the memorable siege of the city of Rhodes by Demetrius Poliorcetes, the Rhodians gained the highest esteem and regard from all the surrounding princes and nations. During the period which then followed, down to the overthrow of the Macedonian monarchy, Rhodus, which kept up friendly relations with Rome, acted a very prominent part, and extended its dominion over a portion of the opposite coasts of Caria and Lycia—a territory which is hence often called the Περαία τῶν 'Ροδίων [PERAEA]— and over several of the neighbouring islands, such as Casus, Carpathus, Telos, and Chalce. After the

defeat of Perseus the Romans deprived the Rhodians of a great amount of territory and power, under the pretext that they had supported Macedonia; but the anger of Rome was propitiated, and in the war against Mithridates the Rhodians defended themselves manfully against the Pontian king. During the civil war between Caesar and Pompey they sided with the former, and their adherence to him led them, after his death, to resist Cassius; but the republican, after defeating them in a naval engagement, entered the city of Rhodes by force, and having put to death the leaders of the hostile party, carried off all the public property, even the offerings and ornaments of the temples (Appian, Bell. Civ. iv. 72; Plut. Brut. 30; Dion Cass. xlvii. 32). This calamity in B. C. 42 broke the power of the Rhodians, but it still remained one of the great seats of learning. Tiberius, before his accession to the imperial throne, resided at Rhodes for several years. The emperor Claudius deprived it of all political independence (Dion Cass. lx. 24); but although he afterwards restored its liberty, it was at all times a very precarious possession, being taken away and given back as circumstances or the caprices of the emperors suggested (Tac. Ann. xii. 58; comp. Suet. Vesp. 8; Eutrop. vii. 13). In the arrangements of Constantine, Rhodus, like other islands, belonged to the Provincia Insularum, of which it was the metropolis (Hierocles, p. 685, &c.). During the middle ages it continued to enjoy a considerable degree of prosperity, and was the last place in Western Asia that yielded to the Mohammedans.

The great prosperity which the Rhodians enjoyed during the best period of their history was owing in the first place to their extensive navigation and commerce, and in the second to their political institutions. In respect to the former they were particularly favoured by the situation of their island, and during the Macedonian and Roman periods no Greek state could rival them in the extent and organisation of their commerce; their sailors were regarded as the best, and their laws relating to navigation were thought models worthy of being adopted by the Romans. The form of government of the Rhodians was indeed founded upon a popular basis, but their democracy was tempered by an admixture of oligarchy. Such at least we find it during the Macedonian period, at a time when the ancient Doric institutions had given way to a form of government more suited to the actual circumstances. (Strab. xii. p. 575, xiv. p. 652; Cic. de Re Publ. i. 31; Dion Chrys. Orat. xxxi.; Aristid. Orat. xliv. p. 831.) The sovereign power belonged to the assembly of the people, which had the final decision of everything; but nothing was brought before it which had not previously been discussed by the senate or βουλή. (Polyb. xvi. 35, xxiii. 3, xxvii. 6, xxviii. 15, xxix. 5; Cic. de Re Publ. iii. 35.) The executive was in the hands of two magistrates called πρυτάνεις, each of whom governed for six months in the year as eponymus. Next to these, the admirals (ναύαρχοι) possessed the most extensive power. Other officers are mentioned in inscriptions, but their character and functions are often very uncertain. The Rhodian constitution had its safest foundation in the character and habits of the people, who, although the vicinity of Asia had a considerable influence and created a love of splendour and luxury, yet preserved many of their ancient Doric peculiarities, such as earnestness, perseverance, valour, and patriotism, combined with an active zeal for literature, philosophy, and art. The intellectual activity maintained itself in Rhodes long after it had died away in most other parts of Greece.

The island of Rhodes, which appears even in the earliest traditions as extremely wealthy (Hom. *Il.* ii. 670; Pind. *Olymp.* vii. 49; Philostr. *Imag.* ii. 27), is in many parts indeed rough and rocky, especially the coast near the city of Rhodes, and the district about Lindus, but on the whole it was extremely fertile: its wine, dried raisins and figs, were much esteemed, and its saffron, oil, marble, achate, sponges, and fish, are often spoken of. The most important productions of Rhodian industry were ships, arms, and military engines. Besides the places already mentioned, the ancients notice Ixia and Mnasyrium, two forts in the south, and a place called Achaia.

By far the most important place was the city of Rhodus at the north-eastern extremity of the island. It was built in B. C. 408 upon a regular plan formed by the architect Hippodamus, the same who built the walls of Peiraeeus. (Strab. xiv. p. 654; Diod. xix. 45, xx. 83; Harpocrat. *s. v.*; Ἱπποδάμεια.) It was constructed in the form of an amphitheatre rising from the coast, and was protected by strong walls and towers, while nature provided it with two excellent harbours. The acropolis rose at the south-western extremity, and on the slope of it was the theatre. According to Strabo, Rhodus surpassed all other cities for the beauty and convenience of its ports, streets, walls, and public edifices, all of which were adorned with a profusion of works of art both in painting and sculpture. The principal statues were in the temple of Dionysus and the gymnasium; but the most extraordinary statue, which is described as one of the seven wonders of the ancient world, was the brazen statue of Helios, commonly called the Colossus of Rhodes. It was the work of Chares of Lindus, who employed upon its execution twelve years. It cost 300 talents, and was 70 cubits in height: its gigantic size may be inferred from the fact that few men were able to encompass one of its thumbs with their arms. (Plin. xxxiv. 18; Strab. *l. c.*) The Colossus stood at the entrance of one of the ports, but the statement that it stood astride over the entrance, and that the largest ships could sail between its legs, is in all probability a mere fable. It was overthrown by an earthquake, 56 years after its erection, that is, in B. C. 224, or according to others a few years later. Ptolemy promised the Rhodians, among other things, 3000 talents for its restoration (Polyb. v. 89), but it is said not to have been attempted in consequence of an oracle (Strab. *l. c.*). Later authorities, however, speak of it as standing erect: the emperor Commodus is said to have ordered his own bust to be put upon it; and Cedrenus relates that a king of the Saracens sold the fragments to a merchant who employed upwards of 900 camels to carry them away. Notwithstanding the great splendour of the city, the number of its inhabitants does not appear to have been very great, for during the siege of Demetrius Poliorcetes no more than 6000 citizens capable of bearing arms are mentioned. (Diod. xx. 84.) But Rhodus has nevertheless produced many men of eminence in philosophy and literature, such as Panaetius, Stratocles, Andronicus, Eudemus, Hieronymus, Peisander, Simmias, and Aristides; while Poseidonius, Dionysius Thrax, and Apollonius, surnamed the Rhodian, resided in the island for a

considerable time. The present town of Rhodes contains very few remains of the ancient Greek city. (Comp. P. D. Paulsen, *Descriptio Rhodi Maced. Asiata*, Göttingen, 1818; H. Rost, *Rhodus, ein Hist. Arch. Fragment*, Altona, 1823; Th. Menge, *Vorgeschichte von Rhodus*, Cöln, 1827; Rottier, *Descript. des Monuments de Rhodes*, Bruxelles, 1828; Ross, *Reisen auf den Griech. Inseln*, iii. pp. 70—113, which contains a good account of the middle-age history and the present condition of the island and city with maps and plans; Sestini, *Mon. Vet.* p. 91.) [L. S.]

COIN OF RHODUS.

RHODUSSA, an island off the southern coast of Caria, near the entrance of the port of Panormus. (Plin. v. 35; *Stadiasm. Mar. Mag.* p. 248, where the name is written Ῥοποῦσα.) It is marked in modern charts by the name of *Limosa* or *Karagash*. [L. S.]

RHODUSSAE, a group of small islands in the Propontis, south of Pityussa, is mentioned only by Pliny (v. 44). [L. S.]

RHOE (Ῥόη), a place on the coast of Bithynia, 20 stadia to the east of Calpe, on a steep promontory, contained a road fit only for small vessels. (Arrian, *Peripl. P. E.* p. 13; Anonym. *Peripl. P. E.* p. 3.) [L. S.]

RHOETACES. [ALBANIA, p. 89, b.]

RHOETEUM (τὸ Ῥοίτειον or Ῥοίτιον ἄκρον), a promontory, or rather a rocky headland, running out in several points in Mysia or Troas, at the entrance of the Hellespont, north of Ilion; it contained a small town of the same name situated on an eminence. The place is very often mentioned by the ancients. (Herod. vii. 43; Scylax, p. 35; Strab. xiii. p. 595; Steph. B. *s. v.*; Pomp. Mela, i. 18; Plin. v. 33; Thucyd. iv. 52, viii. 101; Apollon. Rhod. i. 929; Tryphiod. 216; Virg. *Aen.* vi. 595; Liv. xxxvii. 37.) The promontory is now called *Intepeh*, and the site of the ancient town is believed to be occupied by *Paleo Castro*, near the village of *It-ghelmes*. (Richter, *Wallfahrten*, p. 475; Leake, *Asia Minor*, p. 275.) [L. S.]

RHOGANA (Ῥόγανα, Ptol. vi. 8. § 7; Marcian, *Peripl.* i. § 28, ed. Müller), a small place on the coast of Carmania, between the promontories of Carpella and Alambater. It is perhaps the same place as the Gogana of Arrian. [GOGANA.] [V.]

RHOGANDA'NI (Ῥογανδανοί, Ptol. vii. 4. § 9), a tribe of ancient *Ceylon*, at the southern end of the island. Ptolemy mentions that in this part of the island were the best pastures for the elephants, which is the case, too, at the present time. [V.]

RHOGE (Ῥόγη), an island off the coast of Lycia, not far from the entrance of the Phoenicus Portus. (Plin. v. 35; Steph. B. *s. v.*; *Stadiasm. Mar. Mag.* §§ 217, 218, where it is called Rhope, Ῥόπη.) [L. S.]

RHO'GONIS (Ῥόγονις, Arrian, *Ind.* c. 39), a river of ancient Persis, which flows into the Persian

Gulf in lat. 29° 20', long. 48° 25' E. It was little better than a torrent, and is now doubtless marked by the present *Bender-rik.* Ptolemy (vi. 4. § 2) and Ammianus (xxiii. 6) call it Rhogomanis ('Ρο-γομάνις), and Marcianus (*Peripl.* i. § 24, ed Müller) Rhogomanius ('Ρογομάνιος). (Vincent, vol. i. p. 401; Thevenot, v. p. 535.)   [V.]

RHOSCOPUS ('Ροσκόπους), a place on the coast of Pamphylia, near the mouth of the Cestrus, is mentioned only in the Stadiasmus (§§ 199, 200).   [L. S.]

RHOSOLOGIACUM or RHOSOLOGIA ('Ροσο-λογία), a small place in the country of the Tectosages in Galatia, on the road from Ancyra to Caesareia Mazaca, not far from the river Halys. · (*It. Ant.* pp. 143, 206 ; Ptol. v. 4. § 8, where some read 'Οροσολογία or 'Οροσολαγιακόν; *It. Hieros.* p. 575, where it is called Rosolodiacum.)   [L. S.]

RHOSUS. [ISSUS.]

RHOXOLA'NI.   [ROXOLANI.]

RHUANA ('Ρούδνα al. 'Ράδανα βασίλειον), an inland town of Arabia, placed by Ptolemy (vi. 7. § 33) in long. 87°, lat. 22°. Apparently not far distant from the SW. bay of the *Persian Gulf,* and on the river *Lar.*   [G. W.]

RHUBON, RHUDON ('Ρούβωνος ἐκβ., Ptol. iii. 5. § 2 ; 'Ρουδῶνος ἐκβ., Marcian. Heracl. *Peripl.* § 39, ed. Müller), a river of European Sarmatia which took its source in Alaunus Montes and discharged itself into the Venedicus Sinus. Schafarik (*Slav. Alt.* vol. i. p. 497) has identified it with the *Düna,* which, taking a direction generally W., falls into the *Gulf of Riga* below *Fort Dünamunde,* after a course of 655 miles. This same ethnologist connects the mythic Eridanus, and the trees that wept amber, with the Rhudon of Marcian (Rhubon appears to be a corrupted form), which Sabinus, a commentator upon Virgil, A. D. 1544, calls Rhodanus. The amber could be brought by land, or by water from the coasts where it was collected to the *Düna,* and thence by boats conveyed to the Borysthenes and the coasts of the Euxine. The name "Eri-danus," closely connected with Rhodanus, is composed of the words "Rha" and "Don," roots which, in several of the Indo-European languages, signify "water," "river," as for instance in "Rha," the old name for the *Volga,* and Danubius, Tanais, Danapris, Danastris, and the like.   [E. B. J.]

RHUBRICATUS ('Ρούβρικατος, Ptol. iv. 3. § 5), a river of Numidia, the same as the UBUS of the Peut. Tab., which flowed 5 M. P. to the E. of Hippo Regius, now called the *Seibouse* (Barth, *Wanderungen,* p. 70).   [E. B. J.]

RHU'DIAE or RU'DIAE ('Ρουδία, Ptol.; 'Ρωδίαι, Strab.: *Eth.* Rudinus: *Rugge),* an ancient city of the Salentines, in the interior of the Roman province of Calabria, and in the immediate vicinity of Lupiae (*Lecce).* (Strab. vi. p. 281; Ptol. iii. 1. § 76.) Strabo calls it a *Greek* city (πόλις Ἑλληνίς); but we have no other indication of this fact, and all the other notices we find of it would lead us to infer that it was a native Salentine or Messapian town. Under the Romans it appears to have enjoyed municipal rank (an inscription has "Municipes Rudini," Orell. 3858); but in other respects it was a place of little importance, and derived its sole celebrity from the circumstance of its being the birthplace of the poet Ennius. (Strab. *l. c.* Mel. ii. 4. § 7; Sil. Ital. xii. 393; Cic. *de Or.* iii. 42.) That author is repeatedly termed a *Calabrian* (Hor. *Carm.* iv. 8; Ovid. *A. A.*

iii. 409; Sil. Ital. *l. c.*; Acron, *ad Hor. l. c.*), and these passages confirm the accuracy of Ptolemy, who assigns Rhudiae to the Salentines, and therefore to the Calabrians according to the Roman use of the name. Pliny and Mela, on the contrary, enumerate Rudiae among the towns of the Pediculi together with Barium and Egnatia, and the latter author expressly excludes it from Calabria (Plin. iii. 11. s. 16; Mel. *l. c.*). But it seems impossible to reconcile this statement with that of Strabo, who places it near Lupiae, in the interior of the peninsula, or with the actual situation of Rudiae, which is clearly ascertained at a place still called *Rugge,* though now uninhabited, about a mile from *Lecce,* where the inscription above cited was discovered, as well as several others in the Messapian dialect, and many vases and other objects of antiquity. The identity of this place with the municipal town of Rudiae can therefore admit of no doubt ; nor is there any reason to question the fact that this was also the birthplace of Ennius : but considerable confusion has arisen from the mention in the Tabula of a place called "Rudae," which it places 12 miles W. of Rubi, on the road to Canusium. As this place would have been within the limits of the Pediculi or Peucetii, it has been supposed by some writers to be the same with the Rudiae of Pliny and Mela, and therefore the birthplace of Ennius ; but the claims of *Rugge* to this distinction appear unquestionable. (Galateo, *de Sit. Iapyg.* p. 77; Romanelli, vol. ii. pp. 93—102; Mommsen, *Unter Ital. Dialekte,* p. 58.)

The Rudae or Rudiae of the Tabula, which is otherwise quite unknown, must have been situated somewhere in the neighbourhood of the modern *Andria.*   [E. H. B.]

RHUS.   [MEGARA, p. 313, b.]

RHU'SIUM ('Ρούσιον, Anna Comn. vii. pp. 210, 215), a town in Thrace on the road from Siracellae to Aenos. Now *Ruskoi.*   [T. H. D.]

RHUTUPIAE   [RUTUPIAE.]

RHY'MMICI MONTES ('Ρυμμικὰ ὄρη, Ptol. vi. 14. §§ 4, 10, 11), a mountain chain of Asiatic Sarmatia, of which no nearer indication can be given than that it belongs to the great meridian chain, or rather assemblage of nearly parallel mountain chains, of the *Ural.*

The river RHYMMUS ('Ρυμμὸς ποταμός, Ptol. vi. 14. §§ 2, 4), which has been a sore puzzle to geographers, took its source in these mountains and discharged itself into the Caspian between the Rha (*Volga)* and the Daix (*Ural).* In the present day there is, W. of the *embouchure* of the *Ural* to the great delta of the *Volga,* only one small stream which reaches the Caspian, under the name of the *Naryn Chara* (Goebel, *Reise in die Steppen,* vol. ii. p. 342). This river is probably the Rhymmus of Ptolemy. (Humboldt, *Asie Centrale,* vol. ii. p. 187.)   [E. B. J.]

RHY'NDACUS ('Ρυνδακός), an important river in the province of Hellespontus, which has its sources at the foot of Mount Olympus in Phrygia Epictetus, near the town of Azani. (Scylax, p. 35 ; Plin. v. 40 ; Pomp. Mela, i. 19 ; Strab. xii. p. 576.) According to Pliny, it was at one time called Lycus, and had its origin in the lake of Miletopolis ; but this notion is incorrect. The river flows at first in a north-western direction, forming the boundary between Mysia and Bithynia, through the lake of Apollonia, and in the neighbourhood of Miletopolis receives the river Megistus, and discharges itself into the Propontis opposite the island of Besbicus.

The Scholiast on Apollonius Rhodius (i. 1165) states that in later times the Rhyndacus, after receiving the waters of the Megistus, was itself called Megistus; but Eustathius (ad Hom. Il. xiii. 771) assures us that in his time it still bore the name of Rhyndacus. According to Valerius Flaccus (iii. 35) its yellow waters were discernible in the sea at a great distance from its mouth. In B. C. 73 Lucullus gained a victory over Mithridates on the banks of this river. (Plut. Luc. 11; comp. Polyb. v. 17; Ptol. v. 1. §§ 4, 8; Steph. B. s. v.) The Rhyndacus is now called Lupad, and after its union with the Megistus (Susugherli) it bears the name of Mohalidsh or Micalitza. (See Hamilton's Researches, i. p. 83, &c.) [L. S.]

RHYPES ('Ρύπες, 'Ρύπαι, Steph. B. s. v.: Eth. 'Ρύψ, 'Ρῦπος), a city of Achaia, 30 stadia W. of Aegium, was originally one of the twelve Achaean cities. It had ceased to be a member of the League in the time of Polybius, who mentions Leontium in its place. Rhypes, however, continued to exist down to the time of Augustus; but this emperor transferred its inhabitants to Patrae, and its territory ('Ρυπίς, or ἡ 'Ρυπική) was divided between Aegium and Pharae. Its ruins were seen by Pausanias at a short distance from the main road from Aegium to Patrae. We learn from Strabo that this town was mentioned by Aeschylus as κεραυνίας 'Ρύπας, or " Rhypes stricken by the thunderbolt." It was the birthplace of Myscellus, the founder of Croton. (Herod. i. 145; Paus. vii. 6. § 1, vii. 18. § 7, vii. 23. § 4; Strab. viii. pp. 386, 387.) In the territory of Rhypes there was a demus called LEUCTRUM (Λεῦκτρον, Strab. p. 387), and also a seaport named ERINEUM ('Ερινεόν, or 'Ερινεὸς Λιμήν), which is mentioned by Thucydides, and which is described by Pausanias as 60 stadia from Aegium. (Thuc. vii. 34; Paus. vii. 22. § 10; Plin. iv. 6.) The geographers of the French Commission place Rhypes at some ruins on the right bank of the river Tholo, where it issues into the plain; and the distance of the position on the Tholo from Vostitza (Aegium) is that which Pausanias assigns as the interval between Aegium and Rhypes. But Leake, thinking it highly improbable that two of the chief cities of Achaia should have been only 30 stadia from each other, suspects the accuracy of Pausanias or his text, as to the distance between Rhypes and Aegium. He accordingly places Rhypes further W. on the banks of the river of Salmeniko, and supposes Erineum to have been its port and to have been situated immediately above it at the harbour of Lambiri. The position of Lambiri answers very well to that of Erineum; but the reason given by Leake does not appear sufficient for rejecting the express statement of Pausanias as to the distance between Aegium and Rhypes. (Leake, Peloponnesiaca, p. 408, seq.; comp. Curtius, Peloponnesos, vol. i. p. 458, seq.)

RHY'TIUM ('Ρύτιον, Steph. B.; Plin. iv. 20: Eth. 'Ρυτιεύς), a town of Crete which Homer (Il. ii. 648) couples with Phaestus as " well-peopled cities." The city belonged to the Gortynians (Strab. x. p. 479; Nonnus, Dionys. xiii. 233.) The corrupt reading 'Ρυθίμνη in Steph. B. (s. v. Στῆλαι) should be emended into 'Ρύτιον. (Höck, Kreta, vol. i. p. 414.) The city must have existed somewhere on or close to the route which leads from Kasteliand to Haghtus Dhéka; but Pashley (Crete, vol. i. p. 293) could find no vestiges of antiquity in the neighbourhood. [E. B. J.]

RIBLAH ('Ρεβλαθά), a city " in the land of Hamath," where Jehoahaz or Shallum was cast into chains by Pharaoh Necho, and where Nebuchadnezzar subsequently gave judgment on Zedekiah. (2 Kings, xxiii. 33, xxv. 6.) We find Nebuchadnezzar there again, after an interval of ten years, when the last remnant was carried captive and slain there. (Jerem. lii. 27.) [G. W.]

RICCIACUM, in North Gallia. The Table has a road from Divodurum (Metz) to Augusta Trevirorum (Trier). From Divodurum to Caranusca is xlii., from Caranusca to Ricciacum x., and from Ricciacum to Augusta x. D'Anville guessed Ricciacum to be Remich on the Mosel; but it is only a guess. There is evidently an error in the Table in the distance between Divodurum and Ricciacum, which is a great deal too much. The geographers have handled this matter in various ways. [CARANUSCA.] (See also Ukert, Gallien, p. 512, and the note.) [G. L.]

RICINA. 1. (Eth. Ricinensis: Ru. near Macerata), a municipal town of Picenum, situated on a hill above the right bank of the river Potentia (Potenza), about 15 miles from the sea. Pliny is the only geographer that mentions it (iii. 13. s. 18); but the " ager Ricinensis" is noticed also in the Liber Coloniarum (p. 226), and we learn from an inscription that it received a colony under the emperor Severus, and assumed in consequence the title of " Colonia Helvia Ricina" (Orell. Inscr. 915; Cluver. Ital. p. 739.) Its ruins are still visible, and include the remains of a theatre and other buildings. They are situated about 3 miles from Macerata, and 6 from Recanati, which has preserved the traces of the ancient name. though it does not occupy the ancient site. (Holsten. Not. ad Cluver. p. 137.) The Tabula correctly places it at a distance of 12 miles from Septempeda (S. Severino.) (Tab. Peut.)

2. A small town on the coast of Liguria, mentioned only in the Tabula, which places it on the coast to the E. of Genoa. It is commonly identified with Recco, a town about 12 miles from Genoa, but the Tabula gives the distance as only 7, so that the identification is very doubtful. (Tab. Peut.; Geogr. Rav. iv. 32.) [E. H. B.]

RICINA ('Ρικίνα, Ptol. ii. 2. § 11), one of the Ebudae insulae or Hebrides. [T. H. D.]

RIDUNA, one of the islands off that part of the Gallic coast which was occupied by the Armoric states. As the Marit. Itin. mentions Caesarea (Jersey), Sarnia (Guernsey), and Riduna, it is concluded that Riduna is Aurigny or Alderney off Cap de la Hague. [G. L.]

RIGODULUM, a place on the Mosella (Mosel), " protected either by mountains or the river." (Tacitus, Hist. iv. 71.) In the war with Civilis this place was occupied by Valentinus with a large force of Treviri. Civilis, who was at Mains, marched to Rigodulum in three days (tertiis castris) and stormed the place. On the following day he reached Colonia Trevirorum (Trier). It is supposed that Rigodulum may be Reol on the Mosel. Lipsius assumes Rigodulum to be Rigol near Confluentes (Coblenz), but that is impossible. Ammianus Marcellinus (xvi. 6) places Rigodulum near Confluentes, but his authority is small; and there may be some corruption in the text. [G. L.]

RIGODU'NUM ('Ριγόδουνον, Ptol. ii. 3. § 16), a town of the Brigantes in the N. of Britannia Romana. Camden (p. 974) conjectures it might have been *Ribble-chester* or *Rixton*; others identify it with *Richmond.*   [T. H. D.]

RIGOMAGUS, a village of Cisalpine Gaul, forming a station on the road from Ticinum (*Pavia*) to Augusta Taurinorum (*Turin*.) It is placed by the Itineraries 36 M. P. from Laumellum (*Lomello*), and 36 M. P. from Augusta or Taurini: these distances coincide with the site of *Trino Vecchio*, a village a little to the S. of the modern town of *Trino*, on the left bank of the *Po* (*Itin. Ant.* p. 339; Cluver. *Ital.* p. 234; Walckenaer, *Géogr. des Gaules,* vol. iii. p. 23).   [E. H. B.]

RIGOMAGUS (*Remagen*), on the Rhine. The Table places it between Bonna (*Bonn*) and Antunnacum (*Andernach*), viii. from Bonna and ix. from Antunnacum. The Antonine Itin., which omits Rigomagus, makes the distance xvii. from Bonna to Antunnacum. *Remagen* is on the Rhine and on the north side of the *Ahr* near its junction with the Rhine. Ukert (*Gallien,* p. 518, note) speaks of a milestone found at *Remagen* with the inscription " a Col. Agripp. M. P. XXX."   [G. L.]

RIMMON (Έρεμμών), a city of the tribe of Simeon (*Josh.* xix. 7), mentioned by Zechariah as the extremity of the land of Judah (xiv. 10). Placed by Eusebius S. of Daroma, 16 miles from Eleutheropolis. (*Onomast. s. vv.* Έρεμθών, Ρεμμά.) He places another town of the same name 15 miles north of Jerusalem. (*Ib. s. v.* Ρεμμούς.) [G. W.]

RIOBE, in North Gallia, a name which appears in the Table on a road which passes from Augustomagus (*Senlis*) through Calagum (*Chailli*). Riobe comes after Calagum, but the distance is not given. A road, which appears to be in the direction of a Roman road, runs from *Chailli* to *Orbi*, a few miles north of the *Seine*; and D'Anville thinks that the name *Orbi* and the distance from Riobe to Condate (*Montereau-sur-Yonne*) enable us to fix Riobe at *Orbi.* [CONDATE, No. 2; CALAGUM.] [G. L.]

RIPA (Plin. iii. 1. s. 3, according to the Codex Reg., though the common reading is Ripepora), a place in Hispania Baetica, which according to Rezzonico (*Disquisit. Plin.* ii. p. 11) occupied the site of the modern *Castro del Rio.* (Comp. Ukert, vol. ii. part i. p. 380.)   [T. H. D.]

RIRA, a river on the E. coast of Thrace. (Plin. iv. 11. s. 18.) Reichards conjectures it to be the *Kamczik.*   [T. H. D.]

RISARDIR (Polyb. *ap. Plin.* v. 1), a harbour on the W. coast of Mauretania, which may be identified with the ACRA of the Ship-journal of Hanno (Άκρα, *Peripl.* § 5, ed. Müller). It now bears the name of *Agader*, signifying in the Berber language (Paradis, *Dictionnaire Berbère,* p. 110) "a fortress,' and is described as being the best roadstead along t e coast of *Marocco. Agader* or *Santa Cruz*, which was called Guertguessem in the time of Leo Africanus, was walled round and strengthened by batteries in 1503 by Emanuel, king of Portugal; but was taken from the Portuguese by the Moors in 1536. (Jackson, *Marocco,* p. 113; *Journ. of Geogr. Soc.* vol. vi. p. 292.)   [E. B. J.]

RITHYMNA. [RHITHYMNA.]

RITTIUM (Ρίττιον), a place in the south-east of Lower Pannonia, situated close to the Danube, and on the road leading to Taurunum. (*It. Ant.* p. 242; Ptol. ii. 16. § 5; *Tab. Peut.*) It contained a garrison of Dalmatian cavalry. (*Not. Imp.*, where the name is mis-spelt Rictium.) According to Muchar (*Noricum,* i. p. 265), its site is now occupied by the town of *Titel.*   [L. S.]

RITUMAGUS, in Gallia, a Mansio which is placed in the Anton. Itin. and in the Table on a road on the north side of the *Seine* from Rotomagus (*Rouen*) to Lutetia (*Paris*) ; and between Rotomagus and Petromantalum. The distance of Ritumagus from Rotomagus is viii. in the Table and ix. in the Itin., which distance fixes Ritumagus near *Radepont,* at the passage of the *Andelle,* a small stream which flows into the *Seine.*   [G. L.]

RIUSIAVA (Ριουσίαυα), a town in the Agri Decumates, in Germany (Ptol. ii. 11. § 30), is commonly believed to have been situated in the *Riesgau,* or *Ries,* which may possibly derive its name from it.   [L. S.]

ROBOGDII (Ροβόγδιοι, Ptol. ii. 2. § 3), a people in the northernmost part of Hibernia, whose name, according to Camden (p. 1411), is still perpetuated in that of a small episcopal town called *Robogh* in Ulster.   [T. H. D.]

ROBOGDIUM PROM. (Ροβόγδιον άκρον, Ptol. ii. 2. § 2), a promontory on the N. coast of Hibernia in the territory of the Robogdii, conjectured by Camden (p. 1411) to be *Fair Head.*   [T. H. D.]

ROBORARIA, a station on the Via Latina, 16 miles from Rome, the site of which is probably marked by the *Osteria della Molara,* at the back of the hill of Tusculum (*Itin. Ant.* p. 305; Westphal, *Röm. Kampagne,* pp. 76, 97.) [VIA LATINA.]   [E.H.B.]

ROBORETUM (GALLAECIA, Vol. I. p. 934, a.]

ROBRICA, in Gallia, is placed by the Table on the north side of the *Loire*, on a road from Juliomagus (*Angers*) to Caesarodunum (*Tours*). The distance of Robrica from Juliomagus is xvii. and xxviiii. from Caesarodunum. D'Anville fixed Robrica at the distance of 16 Gallic leagues from *Angers* at the bridges of *Longué*, over the *Latan*, which flows into the *Loire.* He conjectures that Robrica contains the Celtic element *Briga,* a bridge or river ford, which is probable. Though D'Anville cannot make the two actual distances severally correspond to those of the Table, he finds that the whole distance between *Angers* and *Tours* agrees with the whole distance in the Table between Juliomagus and Caesarodunum. Walckenaer has shown in a Mémoire cited by Ukert (*Gallien,* p. 481), that the ancient road deviated in many places from the modern road.   [G. L.]

ROBUR. Ammianus Marcellinus (xxx. 3) mentions a fortress named Robur, which Valentinian I., A.D. 374, built near Basilia (*Basle*) on the Rhine in Switzerland. Schoepflin guessed that Robur was on the site of the cathedral of *Basle,* but the words of Ammianus do not give much support to this conjecture : "Prope Basiliam, quod appellant accolae Robur." Others have made other guesses. [G. L.]

RODIUM, in North Gallia, is placed in the Table on a road between Samarobriva (*Amiens*) and Augusta Suessionum (*Soissons*). It is xx. from Samarobriva to Rodium, a distance which followed along the ancient road brings us to *Roie,* which represents Rodium ; but D'Anville says that to make the ancient and modern distances agree we must go further, and as far as the belfry named *Roic-église.*   [G. L.]

RODUMNA (Ροδούμνα), in Gallia, is one of the towns of the Segusiani. (Ptol. ii. 8. § 14.) Rodumna appears in the Table on a road which leads to Lugdunum (*Lyon*) through Forum Segusianorum. Rodumna is *Roanne* on the west bank of the *Loire*, which gave name to the former district of *Roannais.*   [G. L.]

ROMA ('Ρώμη, Strab. Ptol. et alii : *Eth.* Romanus), the chief town of Italy, and long the mistress of the ancient world.

CONTENTS.

	Page
Situation	- 7.9
Climate	- 721

PART I.—HISTORY OF THE CITY.

I. Traditions respecting the foundation of Rome	722
II. The city of Romulus	- 724
Pomoerium	- 724
Gates of the Palatine city	- 727
III. Progress of the city till the building of the walls of Servius Tullius	- 729
Legend of Tarpeia—Porta Janualis, and Temple of Janus	- 729
Regions of Servius	- 733
Septimontium	- 734
IV. Progress of the city till the time of Augustus	735
Regions of Augustus	- 737
His municipal regulations	- 739
Augustan Rome	- 740
V. History of the city till the building of the walls of Aurelian	- 741
Fire under Nero	- 741
Changes under subsequent Emperors	- 741
VI. Decline and Fall of the city	- 742
Rome in the time of Constantius II.	- 742
The Barbarians at Rome	- 743
Rome under the Popes	- 745
VII. Population of Rome	- 746

PART II.—TOPOGRAPHY.

I. Walls and gates of Servius Tullius	- 748
Survey under Vespasian, and circumference of the city	- 756
False and doubtful gates	- 757
Transtiberine wall	- 757
II. Walls and gates of Aurelian and Honorius	- 758
III. The Capitol	- 761
IV. The Forum and its environs	- 772
The Sacra Via	- 773
Vicus Jugarius and Vicus Tuscus	- 775
The Comitium	- 775
The Forum under the Kings	- 778
during the Republic	- 783
under the Empire	- 789
V. The imperial Fora	- 797
VI. The Palatine, Velia, and Nova Via	- 802
VII. The Aventine	- 810
VIII. The Velabrum, Forum Boarium, and Circus Maximus	- 812
IX. The Caelian hill	- 817
X. The district S. of the Caelian	- 819
XI. The Esquiline and its neighbourhood	- 822
XII. The Viminal, Quirinal, and Pincian hills	- 828
XIII. The Campus Martius, Circus Flaminius, and Via Lata	- 832
XIV. The Transtiberine district	- 840
XV. Circi, Theatres, and Amphitheatres	- 843
XVI. Baths	- 847
XVII. Bridges	- 848
XVIII. Aqueducts	- 850
Sources and Literature of Roman Topography	- 851

SITUATION.

Rome was seated on the Tiber, and principally on its left bank, at a distance of about 15 miles from its mouth. The observatory of the *Collegio Romano*, which is situated in the ancient Campus Martius, lies in 41° 53′ 52″ N. lat., and 12° 28′ 40″ long. E. of Greenwich.

Rome lies in the vast plain now called the *Campagna*, which extends in a south-easterly direction about 90 miles from *Cape Linaro*, a little S. of *Civitá Vecchia*, to the Circaean promontory; whilst its breadth is determined by the mountains on the NE. and by the Mediterranean on the SW., in which direction it does not exceed about 27 miles in its greatest extent. Looking from any of the heights of Rome towards the E., the horizon is bounded from the N. almost to the S. by a nearly continuous chain of mountains, at a distance varying from about 10 to 20 miles. This side offers a prospect of great natural beauty, which, to the lover of antiquity, is still further enhanced by the many objects of classical interest which it presents. In the extreme north, at a distance of about 20 miles, lies the round and isolated mass of Soracte. Then follows the picturesque chain of the Sabine Apennines, in which the peaked and lofty summit of Lucretilis, now *Monte Gennaro*, forms a striking feature. A few miles farther S., at the spot where the Anio precipitates its waters through the chain, lies Tibur, embosomed in its grey and sombre groves of olives. More southward still, and seated on the last declivities of the Sabine mountains, is the "frigidum Praeneste," celebrated for its Sortes and its temple of Fortune (Cic. *Div.* ii. 41), and, like the neighbouring Tibur, one of the favourite resorts of Horace. (*Od.* iii. 4.) A plain of 4 or 5 miles in breadth now intervenes, after which the horizon is again intercepted by the noble form of Mons Albanus (*Monte Cavo*), which closes the line of mountains towards the S. This mass is clearly of volcanic origin, and totally unconnected with the Apennines. The mountain awakens many historical recollections. Its summit was crowned by the temple of Jupiter Latiaris, the common sanctuary and meeting place of the Latin cities, conspicuous from the surrounding plain, and even visible to the mariner. Beneath lay Alba Longa with its lake; at its southern foot Lanuvium, and on its northern declivity Tusculum, consecrated by the genius and philosophy of Cicero. To the S. and SW. of Mons Albanus there is nothing to obstruct the view over the undulating plain till it sinks into the sea; but on the W. and NW. the prospect is bounded to a very narrow compass by the superior elevation of Mons Janiculus and Mons Vaticanus.

The plain marked out by these natural boundaries is intersected by two considerable rivers, the Tiber and the Anio. The former, at first called Albula, and afterwards Tiberis or Tibris (Liv. i. 3 ; Plin. iii. 5. s. 9; Virg. *Aen.* viii. 330, &c.), entering the plain between Soracte and the Sabine chain before described, bends its yellow course to the S. At a distance of about 3 miles from Rome, it receives the Anio flowing from the eastward, and then with increased volume passes through the city and discharges itself into the sea at Ostia. The course of the Tiber marked the limits of Etruria : the angular territory between it and the Anio is attributed to the Sabines; whilst on the southern side the line of the Anio and of the Tiber formed the boundary of Latium.

The *Campagna* of Rome consists of undulating ridges, from which scanty harvests are gathered; but the chief use to which it is applied is the pasturing of vast herds of cattle. These, with the picturesque herdsmen, mounted on small and half wild horses and armed with long poles or lances, are almost the only objects that break the monotony of a scene where scarce a tree is visible, and where even the solitary houses are scattered at wide intervals. Yet anciently the Campagna must have presented a very different aspect. Even within sight of Rome it was thickly studded with cities at first as flourishing as herself; and in those times, when "every rood of ground maintained its man," it must have presented an appearance of rich cultivation.

Such is the nature of the country in the immediate neighbourhood of Rome. The celebrated group of seven hills—the site on which the eternal city itself was destined to rise—stands on the left bank of the Tiber. To the N. of them is another hill, the Mons Pincius or Collis Hortorum, which was excluded from the ancient city, but part of it was enclosed in the walls of Aurelian. The Tiber, at its entrance into Rome, very nearly approaches the foot of this hill, and then describes three bold curves or reaches; first to the SW., then to the SE., and again to the SW. The distance from the spot where the Tiber enters the city to the SW. point of the Aventine is, in a direct line, about 2 miles. At the extremity of the second, or most eastern reach, it divides itself for a short space into two channels and forms an island, called the Insula Tiberina. At this spot, at about 300 paces from its eastern bank, lies the smallest but most renowned of the seven hills, the Mons Capitolinus. It is of a saddle-back shape, depressed in the centre, and rising into two eminences at its S. and N. extremities. On its N. or rather NE.

side, it must in ancient times have almost touched the Collis Quirinalis, the most northerly of the seven, from which a large portion was cut away by Trajan, in order to construct his forum. The Quirinalis is somewhat in the shape of a hook, running first to the SW., and then curving its extreme point to the S. Properly speaking, it is not a distinct hill, but merely a tongue, projecting from the same common ridge which also throws out the adjoining Viminal and the two still more southern projections of the Esquiline. It will be seen from the annexed plan, without the help of which this description cannot be understood, that the Quirinal, and the southernmost and most projecting tongue of the Esquiline, almost meet at their extremities, and enclose a considerable hollow—which, however, is nearly filled up by the Viminal, and by the northern and smaller tongue of the Esquiline. These two tongues of the Esquiline were originally regarded as distinct hills, under the names of Cispius, the northern projection, and Op-

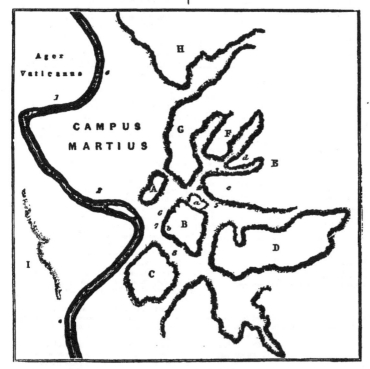

PLAN OF THE ROMAN HILLS.

A. Mons Capitolinus.
B. Mons Palatinus.
C. Mons Aventinus.
D. Mons Caelius.
E. Mons Esquilinus.
F. Collis Viminalis.
G. Collis Quirinalis.
H. Collis Hortorum (or Mons Pincius).
I. Mons Janiculus.
a. Velia.
b. Germalus.

c. Oppius.
d. Cispius.
e e. Tiberis Fl.
1. Prata Quinctia.
2. Prata Flaminia.
3. Subura.
4. Carinae.
5. Caeroliensis.
6. Velabrum.
7. Forum Boarium.
8. Vallis Murcia.

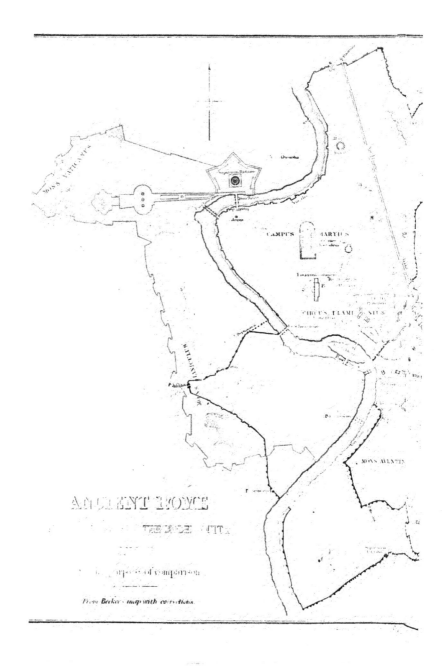

ANCIENT ROME
THE WHOLE CITY

purpose of comparison

From Becker's map with corrections.

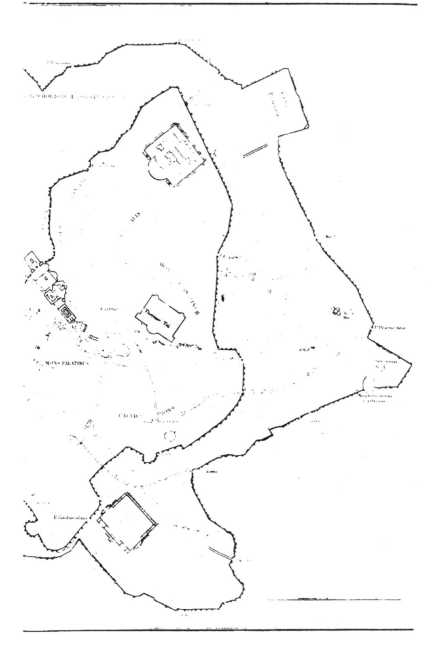

pius the southern one; but they were afterwards considered as one hill, in order not to exceed the prescriptive number of seven. S. of the Esquiline lies Mons Caelius, the largest of the seven; and to the W. of it Mons Aventinus, the next largest, the NW. side of which closely borders on the Tiber. In the centre of this garland of hills lies the lozenge-shaped Mons Palatinus, facing on the NW. towards the Capitoline, on the NE. towards the Esquiline, on the SE. towards the Caelian, and on the SW. towards the Aventine.

It may be observed that, of the seven hills above described, the Quirinal and Viminal are styled *colles*, whilst the others, though without any apparent reason for the distinction, are called *montes*. It cannot depend upon their height, since those called *colles* are as lofty as those dignified with the more imposing name of *montes*; whence it seems probable that the difference originated in the ancient traditions respecting the Septimontium. A less important eminence, called Velia, which was not reckoned as a distinct hill, projected from the NE. side of the Palatine towards the Esquiline, and separated the two valleys which in after times became the sites of the Forum Romanum and of the Colosseum. The Germalus was another but still smaller offshoot, or spur, of the Palatine, on its western side.

On the opposite bank of the Tiber, Mons Vaticanus and Mons Janiculus rise, as before remarked, to a considerably greater height than the hills just described. The former of these lies opposite to the Pincian, but at a considerable distance from the river, thus leaving a level space, part of which was called the Ager Vaticanus, whilst the portion nearest the river obtained the name of Prata Quinctia. To the S. of Mons Vaticanus, and close to the river, at the extreme western point of its first reach, the Mons Janiculus begins to rise, and runs almost straight to the S. till it sinks into the plain opposite to Mons Aventinus. The open space between this hill and the southernmost curve of the Tiber formed the Regio Transtiberina. The sinuous course of the river from the Pincian to the Capitoline left a still more extensive plain between its left bank and the hills of Rome, the northern and more extensive portion of which formed the Campus Martius, whilst its southern part, towards the Capitoline, was called the Prata Flaminia.

From the preceding description it will be perceived that the Capitoline, Aventine, Caelian, and Palatine were completely isolated hills, separated from one another by narrow valleys. Those valleys which lay nearest the Tiber seem, in their original state, to have formed a marsh, or even a lake. Such was the Vallis Murcia, between the Palatine and Aventine, in later times the seat of the Circus Maximus; as well as the low ground between the Palatine and river, afterwards known as the Velabrum and Forum Boarium; and perhaps even part of the Forum Romanum itself. Thus, in the combat between the Romans and Sabines, on the spot afterwards occupied by the forum, the affrighted horse of Mettius Curtius, the Sabine leader, is described as carrying him into a marsh. (Liv. i. 12.) Nay, there are grounds for believing that the Tiber, in the neighbourhood of Rome, formed at a very remote period an arm of the sea, as pure marine sand is often found there. (Niebuhr, *Lect. on Ethnogr.* vol. ii. p. 39.)

In order to assist the reader in forming a clear idea of the nature of the Roman hills, we shall here

insert a few measurements. They are taken from a paper by Sir George Schukburg in the "Philosophical Transactions," An. 1777 (vol. lxvii. pt. 2. p. 594), and have been esteemed the most accurate. (Becker, *Handbuch,* vol. i. p. 83, note.) Other measurements by Calandrelli are also annexed. The latter are according to the Paris foot, which equals 12·785 inches English.

Height above the Mediterranean:—

	Feet.
Janiculum, near the *Villa Spada*	260
Aventine, near *Priory of Malta*	117
Palatine, floor of imperial palace	133
Caelian, near the Claudian aqueduct	125
Esquiline, floor of *S. Maria Maggiore*	154
Capitoline, W. end of the Tarpeian rock	118
Viminal and Quirinal at their junction, in the Carthusian church, baths of Diocletian	141
Pincian, garden of the *Villa Medici*	165
Tiber, above the Mediterranean	33
Convent of St. Clare in the *Via de' Specchi*	27
Forum, near the arch of Severus	34

Measurements from Calandrelli, in his and Conti's *Opuscoli astronomici e fisici* (ap. Sachse, *Gesch. der Stadt Rom.* vol. i. p. 697):—

	Paris feet
Janiculum, floor of the church of *S. Pietro in Montorio* (not the highest point of the hill)	185
Aventine, floor of *S. Alessio*	146
Palatine, floor of *S. Bonaventura*	160
Caelian, floor of *S. Giovanni Laterano*	158
Esquiline, floor of *S. Maria Maggiore*	177
Capitol, floor of *S. Maria d' Araceli*	151
Viminal, floor of *S. Lorenzo*	160
Quirinal, *Palazzo Quirinale*	148
Pincian, floor of *S. Trinità de' Monti*	150
Vatican, floor of *S. Pietro*	93

In ancient times, however, the hills must have appeared considerably higher than they do at present, as the valleys are now raised in many places from 15 to 20 feet above their former level, and in some parts much more. (Lumisden, *Ant. of Rome,* p. 137.) This remark is more particularly applicable to the forum, which is covered with rubbish to a great depth; a circumstance which detracts much from the apparent height of the Capitoline: whose sides, too, must formerly have been much more abrupt and precipitous than they now are. The much superior height of the Janiculum to that of any of the hills on the W. bank of the Tiber, will have been remarked. Hence it enjoyed a noble prospect over the whole extent of the city and the *Campagna* beyond, to the mountains which bound the eastern horizon. The view has been celebrated by Martial (iv. 64), and may be still enjoyed either from the terrace in front of *S. Pietro in Montorio,* or from the spot where the *Fontana Paolina* now pours its abundant waters:—

" Hinc septem dominos videre montes
  Et totam licet aestimare Romam,
  Albanos quoque Tusculosque colles
  Et quodcunque jacet sub urbe frigus."

CLIMATE.

The climate of Rome appears to have been much colder in ancient times than it is at present. Dionysius (xii. 8) records a winter in which the snow lay more than 7 feet deep at Rome, when houses were destroyed and men and cattle perished. Another severe winter, if it be not the same, is mentioned by Livy (v. 13) as occurring B.C. 398, when the Tiber was frozen over and the roads rendered impassable. (Cf. xl. 45, &c.) A very severe winter is also alluded to by St. Augustin (de Civ. Dei, iii. 17). That such instances were rare, however, appears from the minuteness with which they are recorded. Yet there are many passages in the classics which prove that a moderate degree of winter cold was not at all unusual, or rather that it was of ordinary occurrence. Thus Pliny (xvii. 2) speaks of long snows as being beneficial to the corn; and allusions to winter will be found in Cicero (ad Qu. Fr. ii. 12), Horace (Od. i. 9, iii. 10), Martial (iv. 18), and in numerous other passages of ancient writers. At the present time the occurrence of even such a degree of cold as may be inferred from these passages is extremely rare. One or two modern instances of severe winters are indeed recorded; but, generally speaking, snow seldom falls, and never lies long upon the ground. This change of climate is accounted for by Dr. Arnold as follows: " Allowing that the peninsular form of Italy must at all times have had its effect in softening the climate, still the woods and marshes of Cisalpine Gaul, and the perpetual snows of the Alps, far more extensive than at present, owing to the uncultivated and uncleared state of Switzerland and Germany, could not but have been felt even in the neighbourhood of Rome. Besides, even in the Apennines, and in Etruria and in Latium, the forests occupied a far greater space than in modern times ; this would increase the quantity of rain, and consequently the volume of water in the rivers; the floods would be greater and more numerous, and before man's dominion had completely subdued the whole country, there would be a large accumulation of water in the low grounds, which would still further increase the coldness of the atmosphere." (Hist. of Rome, vol. i. p. 449.)

But if the Roman climate is ameliorated with regard to the rigour of its winters, there is no reason to believe that the same is the case with respect to that unhealthy state of the atmosphere called malaria. In ancient times, Rome itself appears to have been tolerably free from this pestilence, which was confined to certain tracts of the surrounding country. This may have been partly owing to its denser population; for it is observed that in the more thickly inhabited districts of Rome there is even at present but little malaria. Strabo, speaking of Latium, observes that only a few spots near the coast were marshy and unwholesome (v. p. 231), and a little further on gives positive testimony to the healthiness of the immediate neighbourhood of Rome (ἐφεξῆς δ᾽ ἐστὶ πεδία, τὰ μὲν πρὸς τὴν Ῥώμην συνάπτοντα καὶ τὰ προάστεια αὐτῆς, τὰ δὲ πρὸς τὴν θάλατταν· τὰ μὲν οὖν πρὸς τὴν θάλατταν ἧττόν ἐστιν ὑγιεινά, τὰ δὲ ἄλλα εὐάγωγά τε καὶ παραπλησίως ἐξησκημένα, ib. p. 239). To the same purpose is the testimony of Livy, who represents Camillus describing the hills of Rome as "saluberrimos colles;" and of Cicero (de Rep. ii. 6): " locumque delegit et fontibus abundantem et in regione pestilenti salubrem: colles enim sunt, qui cum perflantur ipsi, tum afferunt umbram vallibus." It is surprising how Becker (Handbuch, p. 82) can interpret Cicero's meaning in this passage to be that the lower parts of Rome were unhealthy, when it is

obvious that he meant just the reverse, — that the shade of the hills secured their healthiness. Little can be inferred with regard to any permanent malaria from the altars which we are told were erected to the goddesses Orbona and Febris on the Esquiline and in other places. (Cic. N. D. ii. 25; Plin. ii. 5; Valer. Max. ii. 5. § 6.) Even the most healthy spots are not always exempt from fevers, much less a populous city during the heats of autumn. The climate of Rome is at present reckoned unhealthy from June till October; but Horace dreaded only the autumnal heats. (Od. ii. 14. 15; Sat. ii. 6. 19.) The season is more accurately defined in his Epistle to Maecenas, where he places it at the ripening of the fig : —

> " dum ficus prima calorque
> Designatorem decorat lictoribus atris."
>
> (Ep. i. 7. 5.)

In the same epistle (v. 10) he seems to expect as a usual occurrence that the Alban fields would be covered with snow in the winter.

PART I. HISTORY OF THE CITY.

I. TRADITIONS RESPECTING THE FOUNDATION OF ROME.

The history of the foundation of Rome is lost in the darkness of remote antiquity. When the greatness of the city, and its progress in arts and letters, awakened curiosity respecting its origin, authentic records on the subject, if indeed they had ever existed, were no longer to be found. Hence a license of conjecture which has produced at the least no fewer than twenty-five distinct legends respecting the foundation of Rome. To record all these, many of which are merely variations of the same story, would be beside the purpose of the present article. The student who desires a complete account of them will find them very clearly stated in Sir G. Cornewall Lewis's Inquiry into the Credibility of the early Roman History (vol. i. p. 394, seq.), and also, though not so fully, in Niebuhr's History of Rome (Eng. Transl. vol. i. p. 214, seq.), chiefly derived from the following ancient sources: Dionys. Halic. i. c. 72 —74; Plut. Rom. 1, 2; Servius, ad Virg. Aen. i. 273; and Festus, s. v. Roma. The importance of the subject, however, and the frequent allusions to it in the classical writers, will not permit us to pass it over in perfect silence; and we shall therefore mention, as compendiously as possible, some of the principal traditions.

All the theories on the subject may be reduced to three general heads, as follows :—I. That Rome was founded in the age preceding the Trojan War. II. That it was founded by Aeneas, or other persons, a little after the fall of Troy. III. That Romulus, grandson of Numitor, king of Alba Longa, was its founder, several centuries after the Trojan War.

Many who held the first of these opinions ascribed the building of Rome to the Pelasgi, and thought that its name was derived from the force (ῥώμη) of their arms. (Plut. Rom. 1.) Others regarded it as having been founded by an indigenous Italian tribe, and called Valentia, a name of the same import, which, after the arrival of Evander and other Greeks, was translated into Rome. (Niebuhr, Hist. vol. i. p. 214.) A more prevalent tradition than either of the preceding was, that the city was first founded by the Arcadian Evander, about sixty years before the Trojan War. The fact that Evander settled on the Palatine hill seems also to have been sometimes accepted by those who referred the real foundation of Rome to 'a much later period. The tradition respecting this settlement is interesting to the topographer, as the names of certain places at Rome were said to be derived from circumstances connected with it. The Palatium, or Palatine hill, itself was thought to have been named after the Arcadian town of Pallantium, the *n* and one *l* having been dropped in the course of time; though others derived the appellation in different ways, and especially from Pallas, the grandson of Evander by his daughter Dyna and Hercules (Paus. viii. 43; Dionys. i. 32.) So, too, the Porta Carmentalis of the Servian city derived its name from a neighbouring altar of Carmentis, or Carmenta, the mother of Evander. (Dionys. *l c.*; Virg. *Aen.* viii. 338.) Nothing indeed can be a more striking proof of the antiquity of this tradition, as well as of the deep root which it must have taken among the Roman people, than the circumstance that to a late period divine honours continued to be paid to Carmenta, as well as to Evander himself. Another indication of a similar tendency was the belief which prevailed among the Romans, and was entertained even by such writers as Livy and Tacitus, that letters and the arts of civilisation were first introduced among them by Evander. (Liv. i. 7; Tac. *Ann.* xi. 14; Plut. *Q. R.* 56.)

The greater part of those who held the second opinion regarded Aeneas, or one of his immediate descendants, as the founder of Rome. This theory was particularly current among Greek writers. Sometimes the Trojans alone were regarded as the founders; sometimes they are represented as uniting in the task with the Aborigines. Occasionally, however, Greeks are substituted for Trojans, and the origin of Rome is ascribed to a son of Ulysses and Circe; nay, in one case Aeneas is represented as coming into Italy in company with Ulysses. But though this view was more particularly Grecian, it was adopted by some Latin writers of high repute. Sallust (*Cat.* 6) ascribes a Trojan origin to Rome; and Propertius (iv. 1), without expressly naming Aeneas as the founder, evidently refers its origin to him:—

"Hoc quodcunque vides, hospes, qua maxima Roma
    est,
Ante Phrygem Aenean collis et herba fuit;"

though in the same passage he also refers to the occupation of the Palatine hill by Evander. One very prevalent form of this tradition, which appears to have been known to Aristotle (Dionys. i. 72), represents either a matron or a female slave, named Romé, as burning the ships after the Trojans had landed. They were thus compelled to remain; and when the settlement became a flourishing city, they named it after the woman who had been the cause of its foundation.

The third form of tradition, which ascribed the origin of Rome to Romulus, was by far the most universally received among the Romans. It must be regarded as ultimately forming the national tradition; and there is every probability that it was of native growth, as many of its incidents serve to explain Roman rites and institutions, such as the worship of Vesta, the Lupercalia, Larentalia, Lemuria, Arval Brothers, &c. (Lewis, vol. i. p. 409.) The legend was of high antiquity among the Romans, although inferior in this respect to some of the Greek

accounts. It was recorded in its present form by Fabius Pictor, one of the earliest Roman annalists, and was adopted by other ancient antiquarians and historians (Dionys. i. 79). Nay, from the testimony of Livy we may infer that it prevailed at a much earlier date, since he tells us (x. 23) that an image of the she-wolf suckling the two royal infants was erected near the Ficus Ruminalis by the curule aediles, B. C. 296.* The story is too well known to be re-

THE CAPITOLINE WOLF.

peated here. We shall merely remark that although according to this tradition Aeneas still remains the mythical ancestor of the Romans, yet that the building of two cities and the lapse of many generations intervene between his arrival in Italy and the foundation of Rome by his descendant Romulus. Aeneas himself founds Lavinium, and his son Ascanius Alba Longa, after a lapse of thirty years. We are little concerned about the sovereigns who are supposed to have reigned in the latter city down to the time of Numitor, the grandfather of Romulus, ex-

---

* It has been conjectured that this was probably the same statue mentioned by Cicero (*de Div.* i. 12, *Cat.* iii. 8), and described as having been struck by lightning; but this can hardly be the case, as the image described by Cicero stood in the Capitol. A bronze statue answering Cicero's description is still preserved in the Capitoline Museum at Rome, which is regarded by Niebuhr as a genuine relic (*Hist.* vol. i. p. 210), and has been immortalised in the verse of Byron. A modern critic finds in it a production too clumsy for the state of Roman art at the time assigned by Livy, and thinks that the holes in the hind-leg of the wolf were not produced by lightning, but arise from a defect in the casting. (Braun, *Ruins and Museums of Rome*, p. 81.) Fabius Pictor, however, who mentions this statue in the passage cited from his work by Dionysius (*l c.*), expressly remarks the primitive nature of its workmanship,— χάλκεα ποιήματα παλαιᾶς ἐργασίας,—though considerably less than a century must have elapsed between his time and the date of its erection. It was rude, therefore, even when compared with the state of Roman art towards the end of the third century B. C., though it had been erected only at the beginning of that century. Mommsen is inclined to believe that the Capitoline wolf is the genuine one erected by the Ogulnii and described by Livy, from the circumstance of its having been found near the arch of Severus. (*De Comitio Rom.*, in the *Annali dell' Instituto*, 1844, vol. xvi. p. 300.) Whoever has seen the group will perhaps at all events agree with Winckelmann that the twins are evidently of a different period from the wolf.

cept in so far as they may serve to ascertain the era of Rome. The account which has the most pretensions to accuracy is that given by Dionysius (i. 65, 70, 71) and by Diodorus (*Fr.* lib. viii. vol. iv. p. 21, Bipont). The sum of the reigns here given, allowing five years for that of Aeneas, who died in the seventh year after the taking of Troy, is 432 years — that is, down to the second year of Numitor, when Rome was founded by Romulus, in the first year of the 7th Olympiad. Now this agrees very closely with Varro's era for the foundation of Rome, viz., 753 B. C. For Troy having been taken, according to the era of Eratosthenes, in 1184 B. C., the difference between 1184 and 753 leaves 431 years for the duration of the Alban kingdom.

Varro's date for the foundation of Rome is that generally adopted. Other authorities place it rather later: Cato, in 751 B. C.; Polybius, in 750; Fabius Pictor, in 747.

This is not the place to enter into the question whether these dates of the Alban kings were the invention of a later age, in order to satisfy the requirements of chronology. It will suffice to remark that the next most prevalent opinion among those Romans who adopted the main points of this tradition assigned only three centuries to the Alban kings before the foundation of Rome. This was the opinion of Virgil (*Aen.* i. 272),—

"Hic jam tercentum totos regnabitur annos,"

— of Justin, of Trogus Pompeius (xliii. 1), and of Livy (i. 29), who assigns a period of 400 years for the existence of Alba, and places its destruction a century after the foundation of Rome. At all events the preponderance of testimony tends very strongly to show that Rome was not founded till several centuries after the Trojan War. Timaeus seems to have been the first Greek writer who adopted the account of the foundation of Rome by Romulus. (Niebuhr, *Hist.* vol. i. p. 218.)

II. The City of Romulus.

The Roman historians almost unanimously relate that Rome originally consisted of the city founded by Romulus on the Palatine. (*Liv.* i. 7; *Vell.* i. 8; *Tac. Ann.* xii. 24; Dionys. i. 88; Gell. xiii. 14; *Ov. Tr.* iii. 1. 29, &c.) The ancient settlement of Evander on the same hill, as well as a city on the Capitoline called Saturnia (Varr. *L. L.* v. § 42, Müll.; Festus, p. 322, Müll.), and another on Mons Janiculus called Aenea or Antipolis (Dionys. i. 73; Plin. iii. 9), must be supposed to have disappeared at the time of its foundation, if indeed they had ever existed. It seems probable enough, as Dionysius says, that villages were previously scattered about on the seven hills ; but the existence of a place called Vatica or Vaticum, on the right bank of the Tiber, and of a Quirium on the Quirinal, rests solely on the conjecture of Niebuhr (*Hist.* vol. i. p. 223, seq., 289, seq., Eng. Trans.)

Pomoerium.—Tacitus has given in the following passage the fullest and most authentic account of the circuit of the Romulean city: "Sed initium condendi, et quod pomoerium Romulus posuerit, noscere haud absurdum reor. Igitur a foro Boario, ubi aereum tauri simulacrum adspicimus, quia id genus animalium aratro subditur, sulcus designandi oppidi coeptus, ut magnam Herculis aram amplecteretur. Inde certis spatiis interjecti lapides, per ima montis Palatini ad aram Consi, mox ad Curias Veteres, tum ad sacellum Larum; forumque Romanum et Capitolium non a Romulo sed a Tito Tatio additum urbi credidere." (*Ann.* xii. 24.)

According to this description, the point where the furrow of the pomoerium commenced was marked by the statue of a bull, whence the name of the Forum Boarium was by some writers afterwards derived. The Forum Boarium lay under the westernmost angle of the Palatine ; and the furrow probably began a little beyond the spot where the Arcus Argentarius now stands, close to the church of *S. Giorgio in Velabro*, embracing the altar of Hercules, or Ara Maxima, which stood in the same forum :—

"Constituitque sibi, quae Maxima dicitur, aram,
Hic ubi pars urbis de bove nomen habet."

(Ov. *Fast.* i. 581.)

Hence it proceeded along the north side of the Vallis Murcia (Circus Maximus), as far as the Ara Consi. According to Becker (*Handbuch*, p. 98, *de Muris, &c.* p. 11), this altar must be sought towards the lower end of the Circus, near the southernmost angle of the Palatine ; but he gives no authority for this opinion, which is a mere assumption, or rather a *petitio principii* from the passage of Tacitus before quoted, whence he thinks that it must necessarily be referred to the spot indicated. (*Handb.* p. 468, and p. 665, note 1438.) But there is nothing at all in the words of Tacitus to warrant this inference ; and there seems to be no good reason why we should dispute the authority of Tertullian, from whom we learn that the Ara Consi stood near the first *meta* of the circus, and therefore somewhere *near the middle* of the SW. side of the Palatine ("et nunc ara Conso illi in Circo defossa est ad primas metas," *de Spect.* 5). Hence, after turning, of course, the southernmost point of the Palatine, where the Septizonium of Severus afterwards stood, the pomoerium proceeded through the valley between the Palatine and Caelius (*Via de S. Gregorio*) to the Curiae Veteres. The situation of this last place has been the subject of much dispute. Niebuhr (*Hist.* vol. i. p. 288), though with some hesitation (*ib.* note 735), and Bunsen (*Beschreibung*, vol. i. p. 138), place the Curiae Veteres near the baths of Titus on the Esquiline, and they are followed by Müller (*Etrusker*, vol. ii. p. 143). This view appears, however, to be founded on no authority, except that of the modern writers Blondus Flavius and Lucius Faunus, who state that the part of the Esquiline called Carinae, and even the baths of Titus themselves, were designated in ancient notarial documents as "Curia Vetus." But, first, it is highly improbable that Tacitus, in his description, should have taken so long a stride as from the Ara Consi, in the middle of the SW. side of the Palatine, to the Esquiline, without mentioning any intervening place. Again: if the line of the pomoerium had proceeded so far to the N., it must have embraced the Velia as well as the Palatine, as Bunsen assumes (*l. c.*); and this must have destroyed that squareness of form which, as we shall see further on, procured for the city of Romulus the appellation of "Roma Quadrata." That the furrow was drawn at right angles following the natural line of the hill we are assured by more than one authority (περιγράφει τετράγωνον σχῆμα τῷ λόφῳ, Dionys. i. 88; antiquissimum pomoerium, quod a Romulo institutum est, Palatini montis radicibus terminabatur, Gell. xiii. 14). But, further, it may be shown from satisfactory testimony that the Curiae Veteres were not seated on the Esquiline, but between the Palatine and Caelian. Thus the *Notitia*, in describing the 10th Regio, or Palatium, marks the boundaries as follows, taking the reverse direction of that followed by Tacitus: "Continet casam Romuli, aedem Matris Deum et Apollinis Rhamnusii, Pentapylum, domum Augustinianam et Tiberianam, Auguratorium, aream Palatinam, aedem Jovis Victoris, domum Dionia, Curiam Veterem, Fortunam Respicientem, Septizonium Divi Severi, Victoriam Germanicianam, Lupercal." The Curiae Veteres are here mentioned in the singular number; but there is some authority for this deviation. Thus Ovid (*Fast.* iii. 139) says:—

"Janna tunc regis posita viret arbore Phoebi;
Ante tuas fit idem, Curia prisca, fores,"

where the Curia Prisca is identified with the Curiae Veteres by the following passage in Macrobius:— "Eodem quoque ingrediente mense tam in *Regia Curiisque* atque flaminum domibus, laureae veteres novis laureis mutabantur." (*Sat.* i. 12.) Now, in order to determine the precise situation of the Curia Vetus of the *Notitia,* it must be borne in mind that the "Domus Augustiniana," or palace of Augustus, occupied a considerable portion of the NE. side of the Palatine, commencing at the N. corner, as will be shown in treating the topography of the later city, and ending probably opposite to the arch of Titus, where the entrance was situated. Proceeding eastward, along the same side of the hill, we find enumerated the Auguratorium and Area Palatina. Then follows the temple of Jupiter Victor, which we must not confound, as Becker does (*Handb.* p. 100, cf. p. 422, note 847; see Preller, *Regionen,* p. 186), with that of Jupiter Stator, since the latter, according to the *Notitia,* lay rather more northwards in the 4th Regio, and probably on or near the Summa Sacra Via. That of Jupiter Victor, then, must have lain to the E. of the palace, and, as there is but a short space left on this side of the hill, it is probable that the Domus Dionis must be placed at least at its extreme NE. angle, if not on the side facing the Caelian. The Curia Vetus, of course, lay more to the S., and perhaps towards the middle of the E. side of the Palatine. Its site near the temple (or statue) of Fortuna Respiciens is confirmed by the *Basis Capitolina,* which mentions in the 10th Regio a "Vicus Curiarum" near to another of Fortuna Respiciens. (Gruter, *Inscr.* ccl.) The fourth point mentioned by Tacitus — the Aedes Larum — lay on the Summa Sacra Via, and therefore at about the middle of the NE. side of the Palatine hill. ("Aedem Larum in Summa Sacra Via," *Mon. Ancyr.*; "Ancus Martius (habitavit) in Summa Sacra Via, ubi aedes Larum est," Solin. i. 24.) At this point the historian finishes his description of the pomoerium of Romulus, and proceeds to say that the forum and Capitol were believed to have been added to the city not by that monarch but by Titus Tatius. Hence he is charged with leaving about a third of the pomoerium undefined; and, in order to remedy this defect, Becker (*de Muris, &c.* p. 14, *Handb.* p. 102), not without the sanction of other critics and editors, proposes to alter the punctuation of the passage, and to read "tum ad sacellum Larum forumque Romanum; et Capitolium non a Romulo," &c. But in truth little is gained by this proceeding — only the short space from the arch of Titus to the N. point of the Palatine, whilst the remaining part of the line from thence to the Forum Boarium still remains undescribed. But what is worse, even this little is gained at the expense of truth; since, strictly speak-

ing, a line drawn from the Aedes Larum to the forum would include the temple of Vesta (*S. Maria Liberatrice*), which, as we learn from Dionysius (ii. 65), lay *outside* the walls of Romulus. Moreover, according to the emended punctuation, it might be doubtful whether Tacitus meant that the forum was included in the Romulean city, or not; and it was apparently to obviate this objection that Becker proposed to insert *hoc* before *et* (hoc et Capitolium). But these are liberties which sober criticism can hardly allow with the text of such a writer. Tacitus was not speaking like a common topographer or regionary, who is obliged to identify with painful accuracy every step as he proceeds. It is more consistent with his sententious style that, having carried the line thus far, he left his readers to complete it from the rough indication — which at the same time conveyed an important historical fact — that the forum and Capitol, which skirted at some distance the northern angle of the hill, were added by Tatius, and lay therefore outside the walls of Romulus. His readers could not err. It was well known that the original Rome was square; and, having indicated the *middle point* in each of the sides, he might have been charged with dulness had he written, "tum ad sacellum Larum, inde ad forum

PLAN OF THE ROMULEAN CITY.

A. Mons Palatinus.	g g. Nova Via.
B. B. Mons Capitolinus.	h. Clivus Victoriae.
C. Collis Quirinalis.	1. Porta Janualis.
D. Mons Aventinus.	2. Porta Carmentalis.
E. Forum Romanum.	3. Sacellum Larum.
a a. Velia.	4. Porta Mugionis.
b. Inter duos Lucos.	5. Porta Romanula.
c. Germalus.	6. Lupercal.
d d. Clivus Capitolinus.	7. Ara Consi.
e e e. Sacra Via.	8. Porta Ferentina?
f. Summa Sacra Via.	9. Curiae Veteres.

Boarium." Bunsen, however, has assumed from the omission that the line of wall never proceeded beyond the Sacellum Larum, and that, indeed, it was not needed; the remaining space being sufficiently defended by a marsh or lake which surrounded it. (*Beschr.* vol. i. p. 138.) But, as the Sacellum Larum lay on high ground, on the top of the Velian ridge, this could not have been a reason for not carrying the wall farther; and even if there was a marsh lower down, we cannot but suppose, as Becker observes (*de Mur.* p. 14), that the pomoerium must have been carried on to its termination. Indeed the Porta Romanula, one of the gates of the Romulean city, lay, as we shall presently see, on the NW. side, a little to the N. of the spot whence Tacitus commences his description; and if there was a gate there, *à fortiori* there was a wall.

The line described by Tacitus is that of the furrow, not of the actual wall; but, in the case at least of a newly founded city, the wall must have very closely followed this line. The space between them — the wall being inside — was the pomoerium, literally, "behind the wall" (post moerum = murum); and this space could not be ploughed or cultivated. The line of the furrow, or boundary of the pomoerium, was marked by stones or *cippi*. The name pomoerium was also extended to another open space within the walls which was kept free from buildings. The matter is very clearly explained by Livy in the following passage:—"Pomoerium, verbi vim solum intuentes, postmoerium interpretantur esse. Est autem magis circa murum locus, quem in condendis urbibus olim Etrusci, qua murum ducturi essent, certis circa terminis inaugurato consecrabant: ut neque interiore parte aedificia moenibus continuarentur, quae nunc vulgo etiam conjungunt; et extrinsecus puri aliquid ab humano cultu pateret soli. Hoc spatium, quod neque habitari neque arari fas erat, non magis quod post murum esset, quam quod murus post id, pomoerium Romani appellarunt: et in urbis incremento semper, quantum moenia processura erant, tantum termini hi consecrati proferebantur" (i. 44). Every city founded, like Rome, after the Etruscan manner, had a pomoerium. The rites observed in drawing the boundary line, called "primigenius sulcus" (Paul. Diac. p. 236, Müll.), were as follows: the founder, dressed in Gabinian fashion (cinctu Gabino), yoked to a plough, on an auspicious day, a bull and a cow, the former on the off side, the latter on the near side, and, proceeding always to the left, drew the furrow marking the boundary of the pomoerium. There was a mystical meaning in the ceremony. The bull on the outside denoted that the males were to be dreadful to external enemies, whilst the cow inside typified the women who were to replenish the city with inhabitants. (Joann. Lydus, *de Mens.* iv. 50.) The furrow represented the ditch; the clods thrown up, the wall; and persons followed the plough to throw inwards those clods which had fallen outwards. At the places left for the gates, the plough was lifted up and carried over the profane space. (Varr. *L. L.* v. § 143, Müll.; Plut. *Q. R.* 27, *Rom.* 11.) The whole process has been summed up in the following vigorous words of Cato:—"Qui urbem novam condet, tauro et vacca aret; ubi araverit, murum faciat; ubi portam vult esse, aratrum sustollat et portet, et portam vocet." (ap. Isidor. xv. 2, 3.)

The religious use of the pomoerium was to define the boundary of the auspicia urbana, or city auspices. (Varr. *l. c.*) So Gellius, from the books of

the Roman augurs: "Pomoerium est locus intra agrum effatum per totius urbis circuitum pone muros regionibus certis determinatus, qui facit finem urbani auspicii" (xiii. 14). From this passage it appears that the pomoerium itself stood within another district called the "ager effatus." This was also merely a religious, or augural, division of territory, and was of five kinds, viz. the ager Romanus, Gabinus, peregrinus, hosticus, and incertus, or the Roman, Gabinian, foreign, hostile, and doubtful territories. (Varr. v. § 33, Müll.) These agri or territories were called "effati," because the augurs declared (effati sunt) after this manner the bounds of the celestial auguries taken beyond the pomoerium. (Id. vi. § 53, Müll.) Hence in this sense the Ager Romanus is merely a religious or augural division, and must not be confounded with the Ager Romanus in a political sense, or the territory actually belonging to the Roman people. It was the territory declared by the augurs as that in which alone auguries might be taken respecting foreign and military affairs; and hence the reason why we find so many accounts of generals returning to Rome to take the auguries afresh. (Liv. viii. 30, x. 3, xxiii. 19, &c.)

It is impossible to determine exactly how much space was left for the pomoerium between the furrow and the wall. In the case of the Romulean city, however, it was probably not very extensive, as the nature of the ground, especially on the side of Mons Caelius, would not allow of any great divergence from the base of the hill. Besides, the boundaries already laid down on the N. side, as the Sacellum Larum and Aedes Vestae, show that the line ran very close under the Palatine. This question depends upon another, which there is no evidence to determine satisfactorily, namely, whether the wall crowned the summit of the hill or ran along its base. The former arrangement seems the more probable, both because it was the most natural and usual mode of fortification, and because we should otherwise in some parts hardly find room enough for the pomoerium. Besides, one at least of the gates of the Romulean city, as we shall see further on, was approached by steps, and must therefore have stood upon a height. There seems to be no good authority for Niebuhr's assumption (*Hist.* vol. i. p. 287, seq.) that the original city of Romulus was defended merely by the sides of the hill being escarped, and that the line of the pomoerium was a later enlargement to enclose a suburb which had sprung up round about its foot. It is surprising how Niebuhr, who had seen the ground, could imagine that there was room for such a suburb with a pomoerium. Besides, we are expressly told by Tacitus (*l. c.*) that the line of the pomoerium which he describes was *the beginning* of building the city (initium condendi). Indeed Niebuhr seems to have had some extraordinary ideas respecting the nature of the ground about the Palatine, when he describes the space between that hill and the Caelius, now occupied by the road called *Via di S. Gregorio*, as "a wide and convenient plain!" (*Hist.* i. 390, cf. p. 391.) An obscure tradition is mentioned indeed by Greek writers, according to which there was a Roma Quadrata distinct from and older than the city of Romulus (πρὸ δὲ τῆς μεγάλης ταύτης Ῥώμης, ἣν ἔκτισε Ῥωμύλος περὶ τὴν Φαυστύλου οἰκίαν ἐν ὄρει Παλατίῳ, τετράγωνος ἐκτίσθη Ῥώμη παρὰ Ῥώμου ἢ Ῥώμους παλαιοτέρου τούτων, Dion Cass. *Fr. Vales.* 3, 5, p. 10, St.; cf. Tzetzes, *ad Lycophr.* v. 1232). But, as Becker observes (*Handb.*

p. 106), we should infer from these words that the Rome alluded to was not on the Palatine, but on some other hill Plutarch, indeed, also alludes to the same tradition (*Rom.* 9), and describes Romulus as building this Roma Quadrata and afterwards enlarging it. We also find some obscure hints to the same purpose in Latin authors. Thus Solinus: "Nam ut affirmat Varro, auctor diligentissimus, Romam condidit Romulus, Marte genitus et Rhea Silvia, vel ut nonnulli, Marte et Ilia, dictaque est primum Roma quadrata, quod ad aequilibrium foret posita. Ea incipit a silva, quae est in area Apollinis, et ad supercilium scalarum Caci habet terminum, ubi tugurium fuit Faustuli" (i. 2). Now we must not take the whole of this account to be Varro's, as Becker does. (*De Muris, &c.* p. 18, seq., *Handb.* p. 106.) All that belongs to Varro seems to be taken from a passage still extant respecting the parentage of Romulus (*L. L.* v. § 144, Müll.), and the words after "vel ut nonnulli," &c. belong to Solinus himself. Varro, therefore, is not, as Becker asserts, a witness to Rome having been called *quadrata*. The following passage in Festus, however, manifestly alludes to another sense of Roma Quadrata, namely, as a certain hallowed place which every city built with Etruscan rites possessed, and in which were deposited such things as were considered of good omen in founding a city, and which are described by Ovid (*Fasti,* iv. 821; cf. Plut. *Rom.* 11): "Quadrata Roma in Palatio ante templum Apollinis dicitur, ubi reposita sunt quae solent boni ominis gratia in urbe condenda adhiberi, quia saxo munitus est initio in speciem quadratam. Ejus loci Ennius meminit, cum ait: 'et quis est erat Romae regnare quadratas'" (p. 258, Müll.). The place here described was, in fact, the *mundus* of the Romulean city. The words of Solinus, though we are ignorant of the exact position of the places which he mentions, seem to denote too large an area ·to be reconciled with the description of Festus. In confirmation of the latter, however, Becker (*Handb.* p. 107) adduces a fragment of the Capitoline plan (Bellori, *Tab.* xvi.), with the imperfect inscription RRA APO (area Apollinis), and, on the space beside it, a plan of a square elevation with steps at two of its sides. This, he observes, exactly answers to the description of Festus, being a "locus saxo munitus in speciem quadratam;" and the area Apollinis was naturally before his temple. That *the whole* of the Romulean city, however, was also called *quadrata,* is evident, not only from a passage of Dionysius before cited, where he speaks of the temple of Vesta being outside of the Rome called Quadrata (ὅτι τῆς τετραγώνου καλουμένης Ῥώμης, ἣν ἐκεῖνος ἐτείχισεν, ἐκτός ἐστιν, ii. 65), but also from the mutilated fragment of Ennius, quoted by Festus in the passage just cited. It is without sense as it stands, and Müller's emendation appears certain:—

"Et qui se sperat Romae regnare quadratae,"

where the meaning is inapplicable to a mere *mundus,* and must be referred to the entire city.

Gates of the Palatine city.— It was required that in a town built, like Rome, with Etruscan rites, there should be at least three gates and three temples, namely, to Jupiter, Juno, and Minerva (Serv. *ad Aen.* i. 422); and we learn from Pliny (iii. 9) that the city of Romulus had, in fact, three if not four gates. In the time of Varro, three gates existed at Rome besides those of the Servian walls, and two of these can be referred with certainty to the Palatine city. "Praeterea intra muros video portas dici. In palatio Mucionis, a mugitu, quod ea pecus in bucita circum antiquom oppidum exigebant. Alteram Romanulam ab Roma dictam, quae habet gradus in Nova Via ad Volupiae sacellum. Tertia est Janualis dicta ab Jano; et ideo ibi positum Jani signum ; et jus institutum a Pompilio, ut scribit in Annalibus Piso, ut sit aperta semper, nisi quom bellum sit nusquam." (*L. L.* v. §§ 164, 165, Müll.) The gate here called Mucio by Varro is the same as that called Mugio by other writers, by an ordinary interchange of *c* and *g*, as in Caius for Gaius, Cermalus for Germalus, &c. Thus Varro himself, as cited by Nonius (xii. 51. p. 531, M.) is made to call it Mugio. In Paulus Diaconus (p. 144, Müll.) we find the adjective form Mugionia, erroneously formed, however, from Mugius, the name of a man; and lastly, the form Mugonia in Solinus (i. 24).

The most important passage for determining the situation of this gate is Livy's description (i. 12) of the battle between the Sabines and Romans. The former occupy the Capitoline hill, the latter are arrayed in the valley beneath. The Romans mount to the attack, but are repulsed and driven back towards the "old gate" ("ad veterem portam") of the Palatium. Romulus, who is stationed on the high ground near it (the summit of the Velia), vows to erect on this spot a temple to Jupiter, under the name of "Stator," if he arrest the flight of the Romans. At this time the Sabines had driven back the Romans to the extremity of what was afterwards the forum, and their leader Metius Curtius had even penetrated nearly to the gate of the Palatium. The Romans, however, rally; the Sabines are repulsed, and the combat is renewed in the valley between the two hills. Dionysius confirms the site of the gate by describing it as leading to the Palatium from the Summa Sacra Via; which street, as will be seen when we come to describe the topography of the later city, crossed the ridge of the Velia at this spot (Ῥώμυλος μὲν Ὀρθωσίῳ Διΐ (ἱερὸν ἱδρύσατο) παρὰ ταῖς καλουμέναις Μυκώνισι πύλαις, αἱ φέρουσιν εἰς τὸ Παλάτιον ἐκ τῆς ἱερᾶς ὁδοῦ, ii. 50). The spot is further identified by a graphic passage in Ovid, where the citizen who serves as *Cicerone* to his book conducts it from the fora of the Caesars along the Sacra Via, and, having crossed the eastern extremity of the Forum Romanum, arrives at the temple of Vesta; then proceeding onwards up the Sacra Via, first points out the former residence of Numa, and then, *turning to the right,* indicates the gate of the palace:—

" Paruit et ducens, ' Haec sunt fora Caesaris, inquit;
    Haec est a sacris quae via nomen habet.
Hic locus est Vestae, qui Pallada servat et ignem;
    Hic fuit antiqui regia parva Numae.'
Inde petens dextram, ' Porta est, ait, ista Palati:
    Hic Stator; hoc primum condita Roma loco
    est.' "   (*Trist.* iii. 1. 27.)

The site of the temple of Jupiter Stator here given is confirmed by other writers. Thus it is described by Livy (i. 41) as near the palace of Tarquinius Priscus, from the windows of which, overhanging the Nova Via, Tanaquil addressed the people. Now, as will be shown in its proper place, the Nova Via ran for some distance parallel with the Sacra Via, and between it and the Palatine, and, at its highest point near this gate, was called "Summa," like the Sacra Via. Thus Solinus (i. 24): "Tarquinius Priscus ad Mugoniam Portam supra · Summam

Novam Viam (habitavit)." The site of the temple of Jupiter Stator near the Summa Sacra Via is sufficiently certain without adopting the proof adduced by Becker from the equestrian statue of Cloelia, the history of which he completely misunderstands. The passage from Pliny (xxxiv. 13) which he quotes (note 156) relates to another and apparently a rival statue of Valeria, the daughter of Publicola, who disputed with Cloelia the honour of having swum the Tiber, and escaped from the custody of Porsena. Indeed, the two rival legends seem to have created some confusion among the ancients themselves ; and it was a disputed point in the time of Plutarch whether the existing statue was that of Cloelia or Valeria. (*Popl.* 19.) Becker confounds these two statues, and asserts (note 155) that Pliny, as well as Dionysius, speaks of the statue of Cloelia as no longer existing in his time. But Pliny, on the contrary, in the very chapter quoted, mentions it as still in being : " Cloeliae etiam statua *est* equestris." It was the statue of Valeria that had disappeared, if indeed it had ever existed except in the account of Aunius Fetialis. Pliny, therefore, must share the castigation bestowed by Becker on Plutarch and Servius for their careless topography : whose assertion as to the existence of the statue in their time he will not believe, though the latter says he had seen it with his own eyes (*ad Aen.* viii. 646). The only ground which Becker has for so peremptorily contradicting these three respectable authorities is a passage in Dionysius (v. 35); who, however, only says that when he was at Rome the statue no longer stood in its place (ταύτην ἡμεῖς μὲν οὐκ ἔτι κειμένην εὕρομεν), and that on inquiry he was told that it had been destroyed (ἠφανίσθη) in a fire that had raged among the surrounding houses. But Dionysius may have been misinformed; or perhaps ἠφανίσθη is to be taken in its literal sense, and the statue was only removed for a while out of sight. We may assume, therefore, that it had been restored to its original position in the period which elapsed between Dionysius and Pliny, and that it continued to adorn the Summa Sacra Via for some centuries after the time of the former writer.

The preceding passages abundantly establish the site of the Porta Mugionis at that spot of the Palatine which faces the Summa Sacra Via, or present arch of Titus; nor does it seem necessary, by way of further proof, to resort to the far-fetched argument adduced by Becker from the nature of the ground (*Handb.* p. 113), namely, that this is the only spot on the NE. face of the hill which offers a natural ascent, by the road (*Via Polveriera*) leading up to the Convent of S. Bonaventura. That road, indeed, has all the appearance of being an artificial rather than a natural ascent, and may have been made centuries after the time of Romulus. Unfortunately, too, for Becker's round assertion on this subject (*Handb.* p. 109), that we must *ab initio* embrace as an incontrovertible principle that gates are to be sought only where the hill offers natural ascents, we find that the only other known gate, the Porta Romanula, was, on his own showing, accessible only by means of steps. For the situation of this gate Varro is again our principal authority. We have seen in the passage before quoted from that author that it opened into the Nova Via, near the Sacellum Volupiae, by means of steps. Varro again alludes to it in the following passage : " Hoc sacrificium (to Acca Larentia) fit in Velabro, qua in Novam Viam

exitur, ut aiunt quidam, ad sepulcrum Accae, ut quod ibi prope faciunt Diis Manibus Servilibus sacerdotes; qui uterque locus extra urbem antiquam fuit non longe a Porta Romanula, de qua in priore libro dixi." (*L. L.* vi. § 24, Müll.) The site of the Sacellum Volupiae cannot be determined; but the Velabrum is one of the most certain spots in Roman topography, and is still indicated by the church which bears its name, *S. Giorgio in Velabro.* We learn from both these passages of Varro—for Scaliger's emendation of Nova Via for Novalia in the former is incontestable—the exact site of the Porta Romanula ; for as the sacrifice alluded to was performed in the Velabrum near the spot where the Nova Via entered it, and as the P. Romanula was not far from this place, it follows that it must have been at the lower end of the street or in the *infima Nova Via.* Varro's account is confirmed by Festus (p. 262, Müll.), who, however, calls the gate *Romana* instead of *Romanula*: " Sed porta Romana instituta est a Romulo infimo clivo Victoriae, qui locus gradibus in quadram formatus est : appellata autem Romana a Sabinis praecipue, quod ea proximus aditus erat Romam." Here the same steps are alluded to that are mentioned by Varro. The Clivus Victoriae was that part of the NW. declivity of the Palatine which overhung the Nova Via. It was so named either from a temple of Victory seated on the top of the hill (" in aedem Victoriae, quae est in Palatio, pertulere deam," Liv. xxix. 14), or more probably — as this temple was not dedicated by L. Postumius till B. c. 295—from an ancient grove, sacred to Victory, on this side of the Palatine, near the Lupercal (Dionys. i. 32), the tradition of which, though the grove itself had long disappeared, probably led to the temple being founded there.

The Romulean city must undoubtedly have had at least a third gate, both from the testimony of Pliny and because it cannot be supposed that its remaining two sides were without an exit; but there is no authority to decide where it lay. Becker thinks that it was seated at the southernmost point of the hill; but this, though probable enough, is nothing more than a conjecture. The Porta Janualis, the third gate mentioned by Varro, was most probably as old as the time of Romulus, though it certainly never belonged to the Palatine city. Its situation and true nature will be discussed presently. We find, however, a gate called Ferentina mentioned by Plutarch (*Rom.* 20), who relates that Romulus, after the murder of Tatius, which was followed by visible signs of the divine anger, purified Rome and Laurentum by rites which still continued to be observed at that gate. We also find an account in Festus (p. 213) of a Porta Piacularis, which was so called " propter aliqua piacula quae ibidem fiebant ;" and some have assumed (v. Müller, *ad Fest. l c.*) that these two gates were identical. It is well known that the Roman gates had sometimes two names; and this seems especially probable in the case of those which had some religious ceremony connected with them. Becker (*Handb.* p. 177) rejects, however, with something like indignation the idea that such a gate could have belonged to the Romulean city, and would therefore either place it in the Lucus Ferentinae, or alter the text of Plutarch, his usual expedient. Altogether, however, it does not seem quite so improbable that it may have been the third and missing gate of Romulus, since its name indicates its site near the S. extremity of the Palatine, just where we are in want of one.

III. Progress of the City till the Time
of Servius Tullius.

We can only pretend to give a probable account
of the progress of the city under the first five kings.
The statements on the subject in ancient authors are
divergent, though the contradiction is often rather
apparent than real. In the course of his reign Romulus added to his original city on the Palatine, the
Capitoline hill, then called Saturnius, the Caelian,
then called Querquetulanus, and the Aventine. But
we must distinguish the nature of these additions.
Dionysius (ii. 37) represents the Capitoline and
Aventine as enclosed by Romulus with a strong fortification consisting of a ditch and palisades, chiefly as
a protection for herdsmen and their flocks, and not
as surrounded with a wall, like the Palatine. Yet
it is evident from the account of the attack by the
Sabines on the Capitoline (Liv. i. 11) that it must
have been regularly fortified, and have had a gate.
Romulus had already marked it out as the *arx* or citadel of his future city; and when he had defeated the
Caeninenses and slain their king, he carried thither
and dedicated the first spolia opima at an oak-tree
held sacred by the shepherds, but which now became
the site of the temple of Jupiter Feretrius (Ib. c. 10).
When Livy tells us that this was the first temple
consecrated at Rome, he probably means with the
exception of those which were usually erected at the
foundation of every city. That the Capitoline was
a much more important hill in the time of Romulus
than the Aventine and Caelian is also shown by the
fact of his opening upon it the asylum for slaves and
fugitives, in order to increase the population of his
city. This asylum was situated somewhere in the
hollow between the two eminences of the Capitoline,
and the site retained till a late period the name of
" Inter duos lucos" (Ib. c. 10; Dionys. ii. 15; Strab.
v. 230; Plut. *Rom.* 9; Ov. *Fast.* iii. 431, &c.).

The Capitoline hill, or Mons Saturnius, appears
then to have been a real addition to the Romulean
city; but the Aventine seems to have remained
down to the time of Ancus Martius a mere rudely
fortified enclosure for the protection of the shepherds.
Various etymologies, all perhaps equally unsatisfactory, have been invented for the name of Aventinus. One legend derived it from an Alban king
so called, who was buried on the hill (Liv. i. 3;
Varr. *L. L.* v. § 43, Müll.; Paul. Diac. p. 19, Müll.),
another from a descendant of Hercules, mentioned
by Virgil (*Aen.* vii. 656). Servius in his commentary on this passage makes Aventinus a king of the
Aborigines, but adds from Varro that the Aventine
was assigned by Romulus to the Sabines, who named
it after the Avens, one of their rivers. This account
is not found in the remains which we possess of
Varro, who, however (*l. c.*), adds a few more etymologies to that already given. One of these, taken
from Naevius, derives the name of the hill from the
birds (aves) that resorted thither from the Tiber, to
which Virgil also seems to allude (*Aen.* viii. 233).
Varro himself thinks that it was so called "ab
adventu," because, being formerly separated from the
other hills by a marsh or lake, it was necessary to
go to it in boats: whilst others derived the name
"ab adventu hominum," because, having upon it
a temple of Diana common to all the Latin people,
it was a place of great resort. But these various
etymologies only prove that nothing certain was
known.

The preponderance of authority tends to show that
the Caelian hill was also colonised in the time of
Romulus. Caelius Vibennus, or Caeles Vibenna, an
Etruscan general who came to the assistance of Romulus against Tatius and the Sabines, had this hill
assigned to him and settled upon it with his army;
whence it derived its name of " Caelius," it having
been previously called Querquetulanus from its woods
of oak. (Varr. *L. L.* v. § 46, Müll.; Dionys. ii. 36;
Paul. Diac. p. 44, Müll.) The traditions respecting
the incorporation of this hill are, however, very various. Some authors relate that it was added by
Tullus Hostilius (Liv. i. 30; Eutrop. i. 4; Aur.
Vict. *Vir. Ill.* 4), others by Ancus Martius (Cic.
Rep. ii. 18; Strab. v. p. 234); whilst some, again,
place the arrival of Caeles as low down as the reign
of Tarquinius Priscus. (Tac. *Ann.* iv. 65; Festus,
p. 355, Müll.) The last account probably arose
from some confusion between the arrival of the Tuscans under Romulus, and a subsequent one under
the Tuscan king Tarquinius. But the sacred books
relating to the Argive chapels established by Numa
mention the hill under the name of Caelius (Varr.
ib. § 47), and it therefore seems probable that the
arrival of Vibenna must be placed under Romulus.
This Tuscan settlement appears, however, not to have
been permanent. After the death of their leader a
portion of his followers incurred the suspicion of the
Romans, and were removed from the hill to a less
defensible position on the plain, apparently between
the Palatine and Capitoline, where they founded the
Vicus Tuscus; whilst the remainder were transferred
to the adjoining hill called Caeliolus (Varr. *ib.* §
46). Whence also Propertius:—

" Et tu, Roma, meis tribuisti praemia Tuscis
Unde hodie vicus nomina Tuscus habet;
Tempore quo sociis venit Lycomedius armis,
Atque Sabina feri contudit arma Tati."—
(iv. 2. 49.)

Here the Tuscan general is named Lycomedius,
which seems to be derived from Lucumo, the name
given to him by Dionysius (ii. 42, 43), and which
was probably only an appellative for an Etruscan
prince. The hill having been vacated by this removal of the Tuscans, was again colonised under a
subsequent king, which in some degree reconciles the
conflicting accounts: but all we shall say further
about it at present is, that in the reign of Tiberius
an attempt was made to change its name again, and
to call it Mons Augustus, either because Tiberius
had laid out a great deal of money there in repairing
the damage occasioned by a fire, or from a decree of
the senate, which appointed that name to be used
because a statue of Tiberius had been saved from the
flames. (Tac. *Ann.* iv. 64; Suet. *Tib.* 48.) But
this name never came into common use.

*Legend of Tarpeia.—Porta Janualis and Temple
of Janus.*—The story of Tarpeia involves two or three
points of topographical interest. It shows that the
Capitoline hill was regularly fortified, and had a gate.
The deed of Tarpeia, whether treacherous or patriotic, for there are two versions of her history, occasioned a change in the name of the hill. It had
previously been called Mons Saturnius, from Saturn,
to whom it was sacred (Fest. p. 322); and there
was a tradition that some Eleans, who had obtained
their dismissal from the army of Hercules on his
return from his western expedition, had been attracted
to settle upon it by the resemblance of its name to
that of Κρόνιος, a mountain of their own country.
(Dionys. i. 34.) After the foundation of the Capitol

Its appellation, as we shall have occasion to relate further on, was again altered to that which it ever afterwards continued to bear; yet one part of the southern portion of the hill still retained the name of Rupes Tarpeia, from the vestal having been buried on it. (Varr. *L.L.* v. § 41, Müll.) Dionysius (ii. 40) adopted the account of Piso, who attributed the death of Tarpeia to a patriotic attempt to deceive the Sabines, in preference to that of Fabius, which brands her with disloyalty. The latter, however, seems to have obtained most currency among the Romans; and Propertius even derives the name of the hill from her father, Tarpeius, who commanded the Roman garrison,—"A duce Tarpeio mons est cognomen adeptus" (v. 4. 93),—whilst he brands the tomb of the vestal with infamy. ("Tarpeiae turpe sepulcrum," v. 4. 1). The obscure legend of the Porta Pandana, which existed somewhere on the Capitol in the time of Varro (*L.L.* v. § 42), is also connected with the story of Tarpeia; and Tatius is said to have stipulated, in the treaty which he made with Romulus, that this gate should always be left open. (Fest. p. 363, and Paul. Diac. p. 220, Müll.) According to an incredible account in Solinus (i. 13), it was a gate of the old Saturnian city, and was originally called Porta Saturnia; nor is the version of Polyaenus more satisfactory (*Stratag.* viii. 35), who refers the story of the Porta Pandana to the treaty with the Gauls, by which the Romans engaged always to leave one gate open, but, in order to evade the consequences, built it in an inaccessible place.

After peace had been concluded between Romulus and Tatius, they possessed two distinct but united cities,—the former reigning on the Palatine, the latter on the Capitoline, and dwelling on the spot where the temple of Juno Moneta afterwards stood (Plut. *Rom.* 2; Sol. i. 21.) When Tacitus says, in the passage before cited, that Tatius added the Capitoline to the city, we are perhaps therefore to understand that he built upon it and made it habitable, whilst previously it had been only a sort of military outpost. The valley between the two hills formed a kind of neutral ground, and served as a common market-place. The gate called Janualis, mentioned by Varro in the passage cited from him when treating of the Romulean gates, seems undoubtedly to have belonged to the Sabine town. Niebuhr, who is followed by Bunsen (*Beschr.* vol. i. p. 145), is of opinion (*Hist.* i. 292) that it was built by the two cities as a barrier of their common liberties; that it was open in time of war in order that succour might pass from one to the other, and shut during peace, either to prevent the quarrels which might arise from unrestricted intercourse, or as a token that the cities, though united, were distinct. Becker, on the other hand, denies that it ever was a gate at all, maintaining that it only got that name *catachrestically*, from the temple which it subsequently formed being called "Porta Belli" (pp. 118, 119, and note 167). But there seems to be ample evidence that it was originally a gate. Varro, in the passage cited, evidently considered it as such; and it is also mentioned by Macrobius as a real gate, though the situation which he assigns to it will hardly be allowed even by those who give the greatest extention to the walls of the Romulean city ("Cum bello Sabino—Romani portam, quae sub radicibus collis Viminalis erat, quae postea ex eventu *Janualis* vocata est, claudere festinarent," *Sat.* i. 9). We may learn from Ovid, not only its real situation, but also that it was the very gate which Tarpeia betrayed to the Sabines. The passage fixes its site so accurately, and consequently also that of the temple of Janus,— an important point in Roman topography,— that it is necessary to quote it at length :—

"Presserat ora deus.   Tunc sic ego nostra resolvo,
    Voce mea voces eliciente dei:
Quum tot sint Jani cur stas sacratus in uno,
    Hic ubi templa foris juncta duobus habes?
Ille manu mulcens propexam ad pectora barbam
    Protinus Oebalii retulit arma Tati,
Utque levis custos, armillis capta Sabinis,
    Ad summae Tatium duxerit arcis iter.
Inde, velut nunc est, per quem descenditis, inquit,
    Arduus in valles et fora clivus erat.
Et jam contigerat portam, Saturnia cujus
    Dempserat oppositas insidiosa seras.
Cum tanto veritus committere numine pugnam.
    Ipse meae movi callidus artis opus,
Oraque, qua pollens ope sum, fontana reclusi
    Sumque repentinas ejaculatus aquas.
Ante tamen calidis subjeci sulphura venis,
    Clauderet ut Tatio fervidus humor iter.
Cujus ut utilitas pulsis percepta Sabinis,
    Quae fuerat, tuto reddita forma loco est.
Ara mihi posita est, parvo conjuncta sacello.
    Haec adolet flammis cum strue farra suis."
                              (*Fast.* i. 255. seq.)

We see from these lines, that the gate attacked by the Sabines lay at the bottom of a path leading down from the Capitoline, which path still existed in the time of Ovid, and was situated between the forum of Caesar and the Forum Romanum. The gate was consequently at the bottom of the NE. slope of the Capitoline hill, a little to the N. of the present arch of Septimius Severus. We also learn that a small temple or sacellum was dedicated to Janus at this spot. Whether the ancient gate was incorporated in this temple, or whether it was pulled down, or whether the temple was erected by the side of the gate, cannot be determined; but at all events its former existence was commemorated by the title of Porta Janualis. It is no objection to Ovid's account, as far as the topographical question is concerned, that it differs from the one usually received, which represents the Sabines as successful through the treachery of Tarpeia, and not as repulsed through the intervention of Janus. He seems to have combined two different legends; but all that we are here concerned for is his accurate description of the site of the temple, and consequently of the gate.

Its site is further confirmed by Procopius (*B. G.* i. 25. p. 122, Dind.), who mentions it as situated a little beyond the statues of the three Fates, as will appear in the second part of this article. The temple was dedicated by the peace-loving Numa, who made the opening and shutting of it the sign of war and peace. (Liv. i. 19.) Niebuhr, therefore, besides assigning an inadmissible and even absurd meaning to this custom, has forestalled its date, when he mentions it as coming into use at the union of the two independent cities.

After writing what precedes, the compiler of this article met with an essay by Dr. Th. Mommsen, published in the *Annali dell' Instituto* for the year 1844 (vol. xvi.), and entitled *De Comitio Romano*, in which that writer (p. 306, seq.) considers that he has irrefragably established that the temple of

Janus was not situated in the place here assigned to it, but in the Forum Olitorium outside the Porta Carmentalis. As the opinion of so distinguished a scholar as Mommsen is entitled to great attention, we shall here briefly review his arguments. They may be stated as follows. That the temple of Janus was in the Forum Olitorium may be shown from Tacitus: "Et Jano templum, quod apud Forum Olitorium C. Duilius struxerat (dedicavit Tiberius)," (*Ann.* ii. 49); and also from Festus: "Religioni est quibusdam porta Carmentali egredi et in aede Jani, quae est extra eam, senatum haberi, quod ea egressi sex et trecenti Fabii apud Cremeram omnes interfecti sunt, cum in aede Jani S. C. factum esset, ut proficiscerentur" (p. 285, Müll.). But this temple was undoubtedly the same as the famous one founded by Numa, and Duilius could only have *restored*, not *built* it ; since it can be shown that there was only one Temple of Janus at Rome before the time of Domitian. Thus Ovid (as may be seen in the passage before quoted) asks Janus, —

" Cum tot sint Jani cur stas sacratus, *in uno*,
  Hic ubi juncta foris templa duobus habes ? "

The same thing appears from the following passage of Martial (x. 28. 2), which shows that, before Domitian erected the Janus Quadrifrons in the Forum Transitorium, the god had only one little temple : —

" Pervius exiguos habitabas ante Penates
  Plurima qua medium Roma terebat iter."

The same situation of this only temple is also testified by Servius (*ad Aen.* vii. 607): " Sacrarium (Jani) Numa Pompilius fecerat — Quod Numa instituerat, translatum est ad Forum Transitorium." And again " Sacrarium hoc Numa Pompilius fecerat circa imum Argiletum juxta theatrum Marcelli." Thus the situation of the sole temple of Janus is proved by the preponderance of the best authority, and does not rest on mere conjecture.

In these remarks of Mommsen's we miss that accuracy of interpretation which is so necessary in treating questions of this description. The word "struxerat," used by Tacitus, denotes the erection of a new building, and cannot be applied to the mere restoration of an ancient one. Nor, had there been no other temple of Janus, would it have been necessary to designate the precise situation of this by the words "apud Forum Olitorium." Again, the words of Ovid refer, not to one temple, but to one Janus, which, however, as we have seen, was converted into a sort of small temple. "When there are so many Jani, why is your image consecrated only in one ?" This, then, was not a temple in the larger sense of the word ; that is, a building of such a size as to be fit for assemblies of the senate, but merely the little sacellum described by Ovid. Let us hear Mommsen's own description of it, drawn from this passage, and from that of Martial just quoted: " Fuit enim Jani aedes (quod luculentissime apparet ex Ovidii verbis supra laudatis) non nisi Janus aliquis, sive bifrons sive quadrifrons, Dei statua ornatus, Ea, quam Numa fecit, fornix erat pervius ad portam Carmentalem applicatus, quo transibant omnes qui a Campo Martio Foroque Olitorio venientes Boarium Romanumve petebant " (p. 307). But — overlooking the point how the building of Numa could have been attached to a gate erected in the time of Servius — how is it possible to conceive that, as Mommsen infers from the words of Festus, the senate could have been assembled in a little place of this description,

the common thoroughfare of the Romans? Besides, we have the express testimony of Livy, that the Senatus Consultum, sanctioning the departure of the Fabii, was made in the usual place for the meetings of the senate,—the Curia Hostilia. "Consul e Curia egressus, comitante Fabiorum agmine, qui in vestibulo curiae, senatus consultum exspectantes, steterant, domum rediit" (ii. 48). Livy is certainly a better witness on such a point than Festus; whose account, therefore, is overthrown, not only by its inherent improbability, but also by the weight of superior authority. All that we can infer from his words is, that the temple of Janus, outside the Porta Carmentalis, was sufficiently large to hold an assembly of the senate ; but this circumstance itself is sufficient proof that it could not have been the original little temple, or sacellum, of Numa. There are other objections to the account of Festus. It was not ominous, as he says, to go out at the Carmental gate. but to go out through the right arch of the gate (" infelici via dextro Jano portae Carmentalis profecti, ad Cremeram flumen perveniunt," Ib. c. 49). If the whole gate had been accursed, how could a sacred procession like that of the virgins from the temple of Apollo to that of Juno Regina, described by Livy (xxvii. 37), have passed through it ? Nor can it be told whether the relative *ea* refers to the Porta Carmentalis, as sense, or to aedes Jani, as grammar, requires. Further, it would be contrary to the usual custom, as Becker correctly remarks (*Handbuch*, p. 139, note), for the senate to assemble outside of the gates to deliberate on a domestic matter of this nature. Then, with reference to Ovid's description, he could not have mentioned the sacellum of Janus as adjoining two fora, had it stood where Mommsen places it, where it would have been separated from the Forum Romanum by the whole length of the Vicus Jugarius. Besides, it is plain from the passage of the Fasti before quoted that the original temple stood at the foot of a clivus, or descent from the Capitoline. Yet Mommsen puts it at the very top of the hill over the Carmental gate (" in ipso monte," p. 310, vide his plan at the end of the volume), where the hill is most abrupt, and where there could not possibly have been any clivus, and the Porta Janualis at the bottom. We should remark, too, that the reading, "arduus in valles et fora clivus erat," is not a mere conjecture of Becker, as Mommsen seems to think (p. 310), but the common reading; and that to substitute " *per fora* " instead would make evident nonsense. Nor in that case do we see how the temple could have been " apud Forum Olitorium," as Tacitus says, even if *apud* only means *near*, not *at :* and still less how it could have adjoined the theatre of Marcellus (" juxta theatrum Marcelli "), as indicated by Servius. What has been said will also be sufficient to refute the last named commentator in stating this to be the *original* temple. He has evidently confounded the two.

We can therefore only agree in part with the somewhat severe censure which Mommsen has pronounced on Becker on this occasion. "At quod somniavit de aede Jani sine simulacro (p. 259), quod Festum, quod Servium gravissimi erroris incusavit (p. 139, n. 254. seq.), id vix condono homini philologo " (p. 307). It appears, we trust, pretty plainly, that Festus and Servius must have been in error; but we cannot admit a temple without an image. The explanation we have already given, that Ovid is alluding to a Janus, not to a proper temple, may obviate the difficulty. But we see no reason why Janus, a very ancient Latin divinity, and to whom the Mons Janiculus appears to have been sacred before the building of Rome, should not have been honoured with a regular temple besides the little affair which was the index of peace and war. As the question, however, is connected with the situation of the Argiletum and Forum Caesaris, we shall have occasion to revert to it, and have mentioned it here only because the legend of Tarpeia, and consequent building of the temple, are closely connected with the history of the city.

Romulus, after his mysterious disappearance, was deified under the name of Quirinus, and his successor, Numa, erected a temple to the new God on the Quirinal. (Dionys. ii. 63; Ov. *Fast.* ii. 509). This hill, which was previously named Agonus (Fest. p. 254; Dionys. ii. 37), appears in the time of Numa to have been divided into four distinct eminences, each named after some deity, namely, Quirinalis, Salutaris, Mucialis, and Latiaris (Varr. *L. L.* v. § 51, Müll.); but from what deity the name of Mucialis was derived remains inexplicable. The name of Quirinalis, which, however, some derive from the Quirites, who had come with Tatius from Cures, and settled on the hill (Varr. and Fest. *ll. cc.*), ultimately swallowed up the other three. The temple of Quirinus probably stood near the present church of *S. Andrea del Noviziato.* This question, however, as well as that concerning the sites of the other three temples, will recur when treating of the topography of the city. Numa, who was himself a Sabine, also founded a capitol (Hieron. i. p. 298), subsequently called, by way of distinction, "vetus Capitolium," on the Quirinal, which hill had been chiefly colonised by his countrymen. Of course the name of "Capitolium" could not have been applied to it till after the foundation of the Roman Capitol, and originally it was the *arx* of the city, containing the three usual temples of Jupiter, Juno, and Minerva. (Varr. *L.L.* v. § 158, Müll.) This ancient temple of Jupiter is alluded to by Martial (v. 22. 4), and probably stood on the southern part of the Quirinal on the present height of *Magnanapoli.*

Tullus Hostilius is said to have added the Caelian hill to the city after the destruction of Alba Longa, when the population of Rome was doubled by the inhabitants of Alba being transferred thither; and in order to render the Caelian still more thickly inhabited Tullus chose it for his own residence. (Liv. i. 30; Eutrop. i. 4; Victor, *Vir. Ill.* 4.) The two accounts of the incorporation of this hill by Romulus and Tullus contain, as we have before remarked, nothing contradictory; otherwise Dionysius Halicarnassensis would hardly have committed himself by adopting them both (ii. 36, 50, iii. 1). The first Tuscan settlement had been transferred to another place. But when Cicero (*de Rep.* ii. 18) and Strabo (v. p. 234) state that the Caelian was added to the city by Ancus Martius, this is a real divergence for which we cannot account; as the hill could hardly have been incorporated by Tullus and again by Ancus.

Ancus is also said, by the two authorities just quoted, to have added the Aventine; and there is no improbability in this, for Romulus never made it a proper part of his city, and we learn from Plutarch (*Num.* 15) that it was uninhabited in the time of Numa. We must remember that the earlier enclosures were made rather to assert a future claim to the ground when the number of citizens was in-

creased, than that they were absolutely wanted at the time of making them ("Crescebat interim urbs, munitionibus alia atque alia appetendo loca; quum in spem magis futurae multitudinis, quam ad id quod tum hominum erat, munirent," Liv. i. 8). The account of Ancus having added the Aventine is confirmed by Dionysius (iii. 43) and by Livy (i. 33), who state that it was assigned to the citizens of the conquered Politorium. Yet the history of the Aventine is more mysterious than that of any other of the Roman hills. At the end of the third century of the city we find it, as an *ager publicus*, taken possession of by the patricians, and then, after a hard contest, parcelled out among the plebeians by a Lex Icilia (Dionys. x. 31, 32; cf. Liv. iii. 31, 32), by whom it was afterwards principally inhabited. It remained excluded from the pomoerium down to the time of Claudius, though the most learned Romans were ignorant of the reason. After some further victories over the Latins, Ancus brought many thousands more of them to Rome; yet we can hardly understand Livy's account (*l. c.*) that he located them in the Vallis Murcia; not only because that spot seems too limited to hold so large a number, but also because the Circus Maximus seems already to have been designed, and even perhaps begun, at that spot. (Dionys. iii. 68.) At all events they could not have remained there for any length of time, since Livy himself mentions that the circus was laid out by Tarquinius Priscus (i. 35). The fortifying of the Janiculum on the right bank of the Tiber, the building of the Sublician bridge to connect it with Rome, and the foundation of the port of Ostia at the mouth of the river, are also ascribed to Ancus Martius, as well as the fortification called the Fossa Quiritium. (Liv. i. 33; Dionys. 44, 45; Victor, *Vir. Ill.* 5; Flor. i. 4.)

The circuit of Rome, then, at the time of the accession of Tarquinius Priscus, appears to have embraced the Quirinal, Capitoline, Palatine, Aventine, and Caelian hills, and the Janiculum beyond the Tiber. The Viminal and Esquiline are not mentioned as having been included, but there can be no doubt that they were partially inhabited. Whether the first named hills were surrounded with a common wall it is impossible to say; but the fortifications, whatever their extent, seem to have been of a very rude and primitive description (τείχη—αβροσχίδια καὶ φαῦλα ταῖς ἐργασίαις ὄντα, Dionys. iii. 67). Tarquinius does not appear to have made any additions to the city, but he planned, and perhaps partly executed, what was of much more utility, a regular and connected wall to enclose the whole city. (Liv. i. 36, 38; Dionys. iii. 67.) Nay, according to Victor (*Vir. Ill.* 6), he actually completed this wall, and Servius only added the *agger* (*Ib.* c. 7.) The reign of Tarquin was indeed a remarkable epoch in the architectural progress of the city. We must remember that he was of Tuscan birth, and even of Greek descent; and therefore it is natural to suppose that his knowledge of architecture and of the other arts of civilised life was far superior to that of the Romans and Latins; and hence the improvements which he introduced at Rome. It is satisfactory to discover and point out undesigned coincidences of this description, which greatly add to the credibility of the narratives of ancient writers, since there is too much disposition at the present day to regard them as the inventors or propagators of mere baseless fables. Tarquin also constructed those wonderful sewers for draining the Velabrum and forum which exist even to the present day ; he improved the Circus Maximus, planned the temple of the Capitoline Jupiter, and erected the first porticoes and tabernae around the forum (Liv. i. 35, 38 ; Dionys. iii. 67—69 ; Tac. *Hist.* iii. 72) ; in short, he must be regarded as the founder of the subsequent architectural splendour of Rome.

The additional space included by Servius Tullius in the line of wall which he completed is variously stated in different authors. Dionysius (iv. 13) and Strabo (v. p. 234) relate that he added the Viminal and Esquiline hills: Livy states that the hills which he added were the Quirinal and Viminal, and that he enlarged or improved the Esquiline ("auget Esquilias," i. 44); while Victor (*Vir. Ill.* 7) mentions that he added all three. It is possible that Livy means all that back or eastern portion of the Quirinal and Esquiline which run together into one common ridge, and which was fortified by the agger of Servius Tullius; and in this way we may account for his expression of "auget Esquilias," which alludes to this extension of the hill, and the consequent amalgamation of its previously separate tongues, the Oppius and Cispius. Hence there is but little real contradiction in these apparently divergent statements. Though the elder Tarquin may dispute with Servius the honour of having built the walls of Rome, yet the construction of the agger is unanimously ascribed to Servius, with the single exception of Pliny (iii. 9), who attributes it to Tarquin the Proud. The custom, however, has prevailed of ascribing not only this, but the walls also, to Servius. A description of these walls and of their gates, and an inquiry into the circumference of the Servian city, will be found in the second part of this article; but there are two other points, in some degree connected with one another, which require investigation here, namely, the Regiones of Servius and the Septimontium.

Regions of Servius. — Servius divided the city into four *political* districts or regions, which, however, were not commensurate with its extent. Their number seems to have been connected with that of the city tribes; but there are many particulars concerning them which cannot be explained. Our knowledge of them is chiefly derived from Varro (*L. L.* § 45, seq., Müll.), from whom we learn that they were : I. The *Suburana*, the limits of which cannot be precisely determined, but which embraced the Caelian hill, the valley of the Colosseum, and part of the Sacra Via, that western portion of the southern tongue of the Esquiline (Mons Oppius) known as the Carinae, the Ceroliensis,—which seems to have been the valley or part of the valley between the Esquiline and Caelian,—and the Subura, or valley north of the Oppius. II. The *Esquilina* or *Esquiliae*, which comprehended the smaller or N. tongue of the Esquiline (Mons Cispius) and its eastern back or ridge, as far as the rampart or agger of Servius, and perhaps also the eastern back of the Oppius. III. The *Collina*, so called from its embracing the Quirinal and Viminal hills, which, as we have before said, were called *colles*, in contradistinction to the other hills called *montes*. The intervening valleys were, of course, included. IV. The *Palatina* or *Palatium*, embraced that hill with its two spurs or offshoots, Velia and Germalus.

When we compare these regions with the map of Rome we are immediately struck with some remarkable omissions. Thus, the Capitoline hill, with the valley to the E. (forum), and valley to the S. (Velabrum and Forum Boarium), together with the

Aventine, are entirely excluded. Various conjectures have been proposed to account for these omissions. Some have imagined that the Capitol was excluded because the division of Servius regarded only the plebeian tribes, and that the Capitol was inhabited solely by patricians. Becker (*Handb.* p. 386) rightly rejects this hypothesis; but another, which he prefers to it, seems hardly better founded, namely, that the hill, as being the citadel, was occupied with public buildings to the exclusion of all private ones, or, at all events, as being common to all, could not be incorporated with any one region. But this would have been a better reason for the exclusion of the Quirinal, which was at that time the proper capitol of the city ; nor does it seem to be a fact that private buildings were excluded from the Capitol. Various reasons have also been assigned for the exclusion of the Aventine ; the principal of which are, the unfavourable auguries which had appeared upon it to Remus, and the circumstance of its containing a temple of Diana, which was common to all the Latin nation, and therefore prevented the hill from being made a portion of the city.

But if we attentively read the account given by Varro of the Servian Regions (*L. L.* v. §§ 41—54, Müll.), we shall perceive that the division was entirely guided by the distribution of the Argive chapels, instituted probably by Numa ; though Varro does not explain why they should have had this influence. Thus, after giving an account of the Capitoline and Aventine, he proceeds to say (§ 45): "Reliqua urbis loca olim discreta, quom Argeorum sacraria in septem et xx. partis urbis sunt disposita. Argeos dictos putant a principibus qui cum Hercule Argivo venere Romam et in Saturnia subsederunt. E quis prima est scripta Regio Suburana, secunda Exquilina, tertia Collina, quarta Palatina." He then proceeds to enumerate the sacraria or chapels in each regio, mentioning six in each, or twenty-four in all, though he had called them twenty-seven in the passage just quoted.

The obvious meaning of this passage is, that "the other parts of the city were formerly separated (i. e. from the Capitoline and Aventine) at the time when the Argive chapels were distributed into twenty-seven parts of the city." It would hardly, perhaps, be necessary to state this, had not some eminent scholars put a different interpretation on the passage. Thus Bunsen (*Beschreibung der Stadt Rom*, vol. i. p. 147), whose general view of the matter seems to be approved of by Becker (*Handb.* p. 127, note 183), takes Varro's meaning to be, that the remaining parts of the city did not originally form each a separate district, like the Capitol and Aventine, but were divided into smaller parts, with different names. This view has been already condemned by Müller (*ad loc.*), and indeed its improbability is striking ; but it requires a somewhat minute examination of the passage to show that it is altogether untenable. Livy also mentions these chapels as follows : "Multa alia sacrificia locaque sacris faciendis, quae Argeos pontifices vocant, dedicavit (Numa)." (i. 21.) Now Bunsen is of opinion that the statements of Livy and Varro are inconsistent, and that whilst the former under the name of *Argei* means *places*, the latter alludes to *men*. In conformity with this view he proceeds to construe the passage in Varro as follows : "The name of *Argives* is derived from the *chiefs* who came with the *Argive Hercules* to Rome and settled in Saturnia. *Of these parts of the city* we find first described (viz. in the Sacris Argeorum)

the Suburan Region, as second, &c." ("Den Namen
Argeer leitet man ab von den Anführern die mit
dem Argiver Hercules nach Rom kamen, und sich in
Saturnia niederliessen. Von diesen Stadttheilen
findet sich zuerst verzeichnet (nämlich in den Sacris
Argeorum) die Suburanische Region, als zweite,
&c." (*Beschr.* i. 690, cf. p. 148.) But to say
that the name of Argives was derived from other
Argives can hardly be what the author intended.
Besides, the sense is disjointed ; for the relative *quis*
(wrongly translated " of these parts of the city ")
cannot be made to refer to an antecedent that is
separated from it by a long sentence. As the text
stands, *quis* must necessarily refer to *Argeos* in the
sentence immediately preceding. It might be thought
that this sentence has been interpolated, since Varro
called an Argive *Argus*, not *Argivus*. " Itaque dicimus 'hic Argus' cum hominem dicimus ; cum oppidum,
Graecanice ' hoc Argos,' cum Latine, ' Argei.' (*L. L.*
ix. § 89, Müll.) We see from this passage that the more
ancient Latin name for the town of Argos was *Argei*
(*masc. plur.*), and hence it might be inferred to be
Livy's meaning that the chapels were called *Argos*
or *Argoses*, not *Argives*. But *Argei*, in still more
ancient Latin than that of Varro, was also the name
for *Argives* as we find from a verse which he quotes
from Ennius (vii. § 44) : —

" Libaque, fictores, Argeos et tutulatos ;"

whence we are disposed to think that the name of
Argives, however anomalous the usage may appear,
was really applied to these chapels, just as a modern
Italian calls a church *S. Pietro* or *S. Paolo*, and
that the meaning of Varro in the second sentence of
the passage quoted, is : " It is thought that these
Argei (i. e. the *sacraria* so called) were named
after the chiefs who came to Rome with the Argive
Hercules ;" in which manner Varro would coincide
with Livy in making these Argei *places*. How else,
too, shall we explain Ovid (*Fast.* iii. 791) : —

" Itur ad Argeos, *qui* sint sua pagina dicet ?"

And in like manner Masurius Sabinus, quoted by
Gellius (*N. A.* x. 15): "Atque etiam cum (Fla-
minica) it ad Argeos." A passage in Paulus Diaconus throws a gleam of light upon the matter ;
though, with more grammatical nicety than knowledge of antiquity, he has adopted, apparently from
the Greek, a neuter form unknown to any other
writer : " Argea loca appellantur Romae, quod in
his sepulti essent quidam Argivorum illustres viri,"
(p. 19, Müll.) Hence it appears that these chapels
were the (reputed) burial places of these Argive
heroes, and their *masculine* appellation thus gains
still further probability. " E quis," &c. would mean,
therefore, that the different Servian Regions were
marked off and named according to these chapels.

We have already remarked that though Varro
mentions 27 of these chapels, he enumerates only
24. Hence Becker (*Handb.* p. 386), as well as
Bunsen, are of opinion that the three odd ones
were upon the Capitol. The only reason assigned
for this conjecture is that the hill had three
natural divisions — two heights with a depression
between them. But if we have rightly explained
Varro's meaning, it is impossible that the Capitol
should have had any of these chapels. Bunsen,
however, goes still further, and, connecting the
chapels with the Argive men of straw which were
annually precipitated into the Tiber, thinks that
their number might have been 30, allotting the

remaining three to the ancient Capitol on the Quirinal, although Varro had already accounted for his
usual number of six in that district. (*Beschr.* i.
149.) However, it is not at all improbable that the
tradition of the Argive mannikins was connected
with that of the chapels, since it may be inferred
from the context of the passage in Varro, explaining
the line of Ennius before quoted, that they were instituted by Numa. Thus the preceding line (§ 43),
" mensas constituit idemque ancilia," refers to Numa's institutions, who is again alluded to in § 45,
" eundem Pompilium ait fecisse flamines." In § 44
Varro describes the custom regarding the men of
straw as follows : " Argei ab Argis ; Argei fiunt e
scirpeis, simulacra hominum xxiiii. ; ea quotannis de
ponte sublicio a sacerdotibus publice deici solent in
Tiberim." The origin of the custom is variously explained ; but the most probable account is that it
was intended to commemorate the abolition by the
Argives of human sacrifices once offered to Saturn,
for which these men of straw were substituted. None
of the MSS. of Varro, however, gives the number of
27 or 30 ; though the latter was introduced into the
text by Aldus from the account of Dionysius (i. 38).
Hence it would perhaps be more in accordance with
the principles of sound criticism to reduce the number of chapels given by Varro (v. § 45) from 27
to 24, instead of increasing them to 30 ; as they
would then not only correspond with the number of
these Argive mannikins, but also with that of the
chapels which Varro separately enumerates.

Septimontium.—The *Septimontium* seems also to be
in some degree connected with these Argive chapels
and the Servian divisions of the city. The word Septimontium had two meanings ; it signified both the complex of seven hills on which Rome stood, and a festival
(Septimontiale sacrum, Suet. *Dom.* 4) celebrated in
commemoration of the traditions connected with them.
Now it is remarkable that Antistius Labeo, quoted
by Festus (p. 348, Müll.) in his account of the places
where this festival was celebrated, omits all mention
of the Capitoline and Aventine, just as they seem to
have been left out of Numa's town and the regions of
Servius subsequently formed according to it: " Septimontium, ut ait Antistius Labeo, hisce montibus
feriae: Palatio, cui sacrificium quod fit, Palatuar
dicitur. Veliae, cui item sacrificium Fagutali, Suburae, Cermalo, Oppio Caelio monti, Cispio monti."
There were Argive chapels at all these places, and
hence a strong presumption that the festival of the
Septimontium was founded by Numa, the author of
most of the ancient Roman solemnities. That Labeo
considered the places he enumerates to be hills is
evident, not only as a direct inference from the term
Septimontium itself, but also from his express words,
" hisce montibus feriae,"—"there are holidays on the
hills here recited." Moreover, we know as a certainty
that five of the places mentioned *were* hills, namely,
the Palatium, Velia, Oppius, Cispius, and Caelius,—
a strong presumption that the others also were
heights. Yet Niebuhr (*Hist.* i. 389), Bunsen,
(*Beschr.* i. 685), and Becker (*Handb.* p. 124),
assume that one or two of them were no hills at all.
The places about which there can be any doubt are
Fagutal and Germalus. Respecting Subura there can
be no doubt at all ; it was certainly a valley. Now
the Fagutal was a ridge of the Esquiline containing
the Lucus Fagutalis. It was the residence of
Tarquinius Superbus: " Esquiliis (habitavit) supra
clivum Pullium, ad Fagutalem lucum" (Solin. i.
25). But if the grove was above the clivus it must

have been on a height. Servius had occupied a residence not far from it, over the Clivus Urbius (*Ib.*; Liv. i. 48), and it was probably situated at or near the spot now occupied by the church of *S. Martina.* There is not the slightest ground for Niebuhr's assumption (*Hist.* i. 390) that the Fagutal was what he calls "the plain" between the Caelian and Palatine. The Cermalus or Germalus — for originally *c* and *g* were the same letter — was, like the Velia, only a distinct portion of the Palatine hill. ("Huic (Palatio) Cermalum et Velias conjunxerunt," Varr. v. § 64, Müll.) Preller (*Regionen,* p. 180) considers the Germalus to be that side of the Palatine which overhangs the Velabrum between the modern churches of *S. Giorgio in Velabro* and *S. Anastasia;* and it is not improbable, as Becker conjectures (p. 418), that the hill formerly projected further to the W. than it now does, and descended in shelves or ledges. It does not appear on what grounds Niebuhr (*l. c.*) assumed the Germalus to be a "spot *at the foot* of the Palatine." It contained the Lupercal, which, being a cave or grotto, must have been excavated in a hill or cliff, as indeed Dionysius states in his description of it : ἦν δὲ τὸ ἀρχαῖον, ὡς λέγεται σπήλαιον ὑπὸ τῷ λόφῳ μέγα (i. 32).

All the places, then, enumerated by Labeo appear to have been heights, with the exception of the Subura. But on counting the names, we find that he mentions eight places instead of seven, or one more than is required to make a Septimontium. Hence Niebuhr (*Ib.* p. 389) omitted the Subura,— not, however, because it was situated in the plain,— and was followed by Bunsen (*Beschr.* i. 141), who afterwards altered his mind, and struck out the Caelius (*Ib.* p. 685); and this last opinion is also followed by Becker (*Handb.* p. 124) and Müller (*ad Fest.* p. 341). The chief reason assigned for this view is that a principal part of the first regio (Suburana) was called Caelimontium,— a name afterwards preserved as that of one of the regions of Augustus; and on comparing this name with that of Septimontium it is inferred that, like the latter, it must have indicated a distinct and independent city union, and could not therefore have been included in any ante-Servian union. But if there had been any distinct and independent township of this kind, we must surely have heard of it in some of the ancient authors. We do not know when the term *Caelimontium* first came into use; but it is not improbable that it arose from another small hill, the Caelius Minor or Caeliolum, having been annexed to the larger one. Martial mentions them both in the following lines:—

"Dum per limina te potentiorum
   Sudatrix toga ventilat, vagumque
   Major Caelius et minor fatigat."—(xii. 18.)

We learn from Varro that the junction of these two hills had taken place in or before his time : "Caeliolus cum Caelio *nunc* conjunctum" (*L. L.* v. § 46, Müll.), though popular use, as we see from the lines of Martial, sometimes still continued to regard them as distinct ; nor can we tell for what purpose they had been united. Little can be inferred from the order in which the hills are mentioned in the text of Festus, as local sequence is entirely disregarded ; or from the circumstance that Cispius is called "mons" and Oppius not, unless we leave out "Caelio;" or from the omission of Caelius in *some* of the MSS. of Paulus Diaconus. On the whole it seems most probable that *Suburae* may be the redundant word ; unless indeed we might suppose that there were two Fagutals or groves of Jupiter, and that Suburae was inserted here to define the place of the one which overhung it.

Becker regards the Septimontium not as a proper city festival, but as commemorating traditions connected with the site of Rome long previous to the building of the city. In confirmation of this he refers (*Handb.* p. 125) to a passage in Varro (*L. L.* v. § 41, Müll.) and to another in Festus (p. 321), where it is said that a people of Reate, called Sacrani, drove the Ligurians and Sicilians out of Septimontium; and a third passage is adduced from Servius (*ad Aen.* xi. 317) to prove that the Sicilians once occupied the site of Rome; that they were expelled thence by the Ligurians, and the Ligurians in their turn by the Sacrani. Now, without entering into the historical questions connected with these obscure traditions, it may be allowed in general to be probable enough that such traditions were afloat ; and when, as we have ventured to assume, Numa instituted the festival, he made them the basis of it; just as he instituted the Argive chapels and the twenty-four mannikins to commemorate the tradition of the Argive chiefs and their abolishment of human sacrifices. But the festival, nevertheless, was a proper city festival. Becker urges (*Handb.* p. 124) that the Septimontium described by Labeo could not have been in commemoration of a city union immediately preceding that of Servius, because it included the Oppius and Cispius, which were first added to the city by Servius. A great deal depends upon what we understand by the words "added to the city" (" zur Stadt gezogen"). To say that they were not included in the wall and agger afterwards completed by Servius would be a mere puerility; but they must have been inhabited and formed part of the city before his time, since there were Argive chapels upon them (Varr. v. § 50); and these chapels, as we have seen, formed the basis of the city union formed by him. The festival must certainly have been *post-Romulean,* since some of the names of places where it was celebrated were not known before the time of Romulus. Caelius occupied the Caelian hill in his reign; the name of Germalus is said to be derived from the twins (germani) Romulus and Remus, who were landed there (Varr. v. § 54); whilst Oppius and Cispius are said by Festus (p. 348, Müll.), on the authority of Varro, not to have been so named till the reign of Tullus Hostilius. But as they are mentioned by those names in the sacred books of the Argives (Varr. v. § 50) it is probable that they were so called at least as early as the time of Numa.

Such, then, was the ancient Septimontium. The walls of Servius included a different group of seven hills which came to be regarded by the later Romans as the real Septimontium. They are those already described at the beginning of this article, namely, the Quirinal, Viminal, Esquiline, Caelian, Aventine, Capitoline, and Palatine.

IV. PROGRESS OF THE CITY TILL THE TIME OF AUGUSTUS.

Having thus brought down the history of the city to the foundation of the Servian walls, we shall proceed to sketch its progress to the time of Augustus, and then till the walls of Aurelian. The former walls marked the rise and consolidation of a city, which, though soon to become formidable to its neighbours, was not yet secure from their attacks. The latter, enclosing an area more than twice as large as that defended by the Servian walls, betokened the capital of a large state, which, after becoming the mistress of the world, was beginning to totter under the weight of its own greatness, and found itself compelled to resort to the same means of defence which had protected its infancy — no longer, however, to ward off the attacks of its immediate neighbours, but those of the remotest tribes of Asia and Europe. Thus the history of the city, during this period of eight centuries, reflects in some degree the history of the Roman people, and exhibits the varying fortunes of the greatest of all human empires. Unfortunately, however, the materials even for a slight sketch of so vast a subject and so long a period are scanty and inadequate ; nor, even were they more abundant, would our present limits allow more than an attempt to draw such an outline as may serve to illustrate the topography of the city.

Tarquin the Proud, the last of the Roman kings, seems to have effected little for the city, except by completing or improving the works of his predecessors. Of these the most important was the temple of the Capitoline Jove, the description of which will be found in the second part of this article. The expulsion of the Tarquins (B. C. 510) restored to the Roman people the use of the Campus Martius. This ground, which from the earliest times had probably been sacred to Mars (Dionys. v. 13), had been appropriated by the Tarquins, and at the time of their expulsion was covered with the crops which they had sown. The unholy nature of this property prevented its distribution among the people, like that of the other royal goods. The corn was ordered to be cut down and thrown into the Tiber ; and according to the legend its quantity was so great that it caused the island afterwards known as the Insula Tiberina, or that of Aesculapius. (Liv. ii. 5; Dionys. l. c. Plut. Publ. 8.)

The defeat of the Etruscans under Aruns, who had espoused the royal cause, was, according to the usual principle of the Romans of incorporating the vanquished nations, the means of adding a fresh supply of citizens, as there will be occasion to relate in another place.

We have little or nothing to record respecting the history of the city from this period till its capture by the Gauls B. C. 390. After the fatal battle at the Allia, the Romans returned dispirited. The city, together with the older inhabitants, was abandoned to its fate; many families escaped to Veii and other neighbouring towns ; whilst the men of an age to bear arms occupied the Capitol, which they prepared to defend. The flight of the Vestal virgins, who succeeded in escaping to Caere, is connected with a topographical legend. Being unable to carry away all their sacred utensils, they buried some of them in casks (doliolis), in a chapel near the house of the Flamen Quirinalis ; whence the place, which seems to have been near the Cloaca Maxima. in the Forum Boarium, obtained the name of Doliola, and was held so sacred that it was forbidden to spit upon it. (Liv. v. 40; Val. Max. i. 1. § 10.) Varro, however (LL. v. § 157, Müll.), did not recognise this story, but attributed the name either to some bones having been deposited there, or to the burial at an earlier period of some sacred objects belonging to Numa Pompilius.

The Gauls entered the city unopposed. and through

the open Porta Collina. (Liv. v. 41.) The time during which they held it is variously given at from six to eight months. (Polyb. ii. 22; Flor. i. 13; Plut. Cam. 30; Serv. Aen. viii. 652.) Their attempt on the Capitol is alluded to elsewhere. They set fire to and otherwise devastated the city; but perhaps we are not to take literally the words of Livy and other writers, to the effect that they completely destroyed it (v. 42, 43; Flor. i. 13; Plut. Cam. 21). It is at least apparent, from Livy's own narrative (c. 55), that the Curia Hostilia was spared ; and it seems probable that the Gauls would have preserved some of the houses for their own sakes. We may, however, conclude that the destruction was very great and terrible, as otherwise the Romans would not have discussed the project of emigrating to Veii. The firmness and judicious advice of Camillus persuaded them to remain. But the pressing necessity of the case, which required the new buildings to be raised with the greatest haste, was fatal to the beauty and regularity of the city. People began to build in a promiscuous manner, and the materials, afforded at the public expense, were granted only on condition that the houses should be ready within a year. No general plan was laid down ; each man built as it suited him; the ancient lines of streets were disregarded, and houses were erected even over the cloacae. Hence down to the time of Augustus, and perhaps later, the city, according to the forcible expression of Livy (v. 55), resembled in arrangement rather one where the ground had been seized upon than where it had been distributed. It may be inferred from a statement of Cornelius Nepos, as quoted by Pliny, that the greater part of the city was roofed with shingles. (" Scandula contectam fuisse Romam, ad Pyrrhi usque bellum, annis DCCCLXX., Cornelius Nepos auctor est," xvi. 15.) Livy indeed mentions the public distribution of tiles, but these perhaps may have been applied to other purposes besides roofing, such as for making the floors, &c.; and the frequent and destructive fires which occurred at Rome lead to the belief that wood was much more extensively used in building than is customary in modern times. Within a year the new city was in readiness ; and it must have been on a larger scale than before the Gallic invasion, since it had acquired a great accession of inhabitants from the conquered towns of Veii, Capena, and Falisci. Those Romans who, to avoid the trouble of building, had occupied the deserted houses of Veii were recalled by a decree by which those who did not return within a fixed time were declared guilty of a capital offence. (Liv. vi. 4.) The walls of Rome seem to have been left uninjured by the Gauls, notwithstanding Plutarch's assertion to the contrary. (Cam. 32.) We nowhere read of their being repaired on this occasion, though accounts of subsequent restorations are frequent, as in the year B. C. 351 (Liv. vii. 20), and again in 217, after the defeat at Trasimene. (Id. xxii. 8.) Nothing can convey a higher notion of Roman energy than the fact that in the very year in which the city was thus rising from its ashes, the Capitol was supported by a substructure of square and solid masonry, of such massiveness as to excite wonder even in the Augustan age. (Liv. l. c.; Plin. xxxvi. 24. s. 2.)

The censorship of Appius Claudius Caecus, B. C. 312, forms a marked epoch in the progress of the city. By his care Rome obtained its first aqueduct, and its first regularly constructed high-road, the Aqua and Via Appia. (Liv. ix. 29.). But the war with Pyrrhus which soon ensued, and afterwards the still larger and more destructive ones waged with the Carthaginians, prevented the progress which might have been anticipated from these beginnings. The construction of a second aqueduct, the Anio Vetus, in the censorship of Man. Curius Dentatus and L. Papirius Cursor, B. C. 272, testifies, however, that the population of the city must have continued to increase. In the year B. C. 220 we find the censor C. Flaminius constructing the Flaminian Way, as well as the circus which bore his name. (Liv. *Epit.* xx.; Paul Diac. p. 89.) But it was the conquests of the Romans in Lower Italy, in Sicily, and Greece, which first gave them a taste for architectural magnificence. The first basilica was erected at Rome in the year B. C. 184, and was soon followed by others, as there will be occasion to relate when we come to speak of the forum. But it was not till ten years later that the city was first paved by the care of the censors Q. Fulvius Flaccus and A. Postumius Albinus. They also paved the public highways, constructed numerous bridges, and made many other important improvements, both in the city and its neighbourhood. (Liv. xli. 27.) Yet, notwithstanding these additions to the public convenience and splendour, the private houses of the Romans continued, with few exceptions, to be poor and inconvenient down to the time of Sulla. The house of Cn. Octavius, on the Palatine, seems to have exhibited one of the earliest examples of elegant domestic architecture. (Cic. *de Off.* i. 39.) This was pulled down by Scaurus in order to enlarge his own house. The latter seems subsequently to have come into the possession of Clodius (Ascon. *ad Cic. Mil. Arg.*), and its magnificence may be inferred from the circumstance that he gave 14,800,000 sesterces for it, or about 130,000*l.* (Plin. xxxvi. 24. s. 2.) Indeed, as we approach the imperial times, the dwellings of the leading Romans assume a scale of extraordinary grandeur, as we see by Pliny's description of that of Crassus the orator, who was censor in B. C. 92. It was also on the Palatine, and was remarkable for six magnificent lotus-trees, which Pliny had seen in his youth, and which continued to flourish till they were destroyed in the fire of Nero. It was also distinguished by four columns of Hymettian marble, the first of that material erected in Rome. Yet even this was surpassed by the house of Q. Catulus, the colleague of Marius in the Cimbrian war, which was also on the Palatine; and still more so by that of C. Aquilius on the Viminal, a Roman knight, distinguished for his knowledge of civil law. (Plin. xvii. 1.) M. Livius Drusus, tribune of the people in B. C. 93, also possessed an elegant residence, close to that of Catulus. After his death it came into the possession of the wealthy M. Crassus, of whom it was bought by Cicero for about 30,000*l.* (*ad Fam.* v. 6). It seems to have stood on the N. side of the Palatine, on the declivity of the hill, not far from the Nova Via, so that it commanded a view of the forum and Capitol. It was burnt down in the Clodian riots, and a temple of Freedom erected on the spot; but after the return of Cicero was restored to him, rebuilt at the public expense. (Cic. *ad Att.* ii. 24, *Fam.* v. 6.; Vell. Pat. ii. 45; Dion Cass. xxxviii. 17, xxxix. 11, 20; App. *B. C.* ii. 15, &c.) The house of Lepidus, consul in B. C. 77, was also remarkable for its magnificence, having not only columns, but even its thresholds, of solid Numidian marble. (Plin. xxxvi. 8.) The luxury of private residences at Rome seems to have attained

its acme in those of Sallust and Lucullus. The distinguishing feature of the former, which lay on the Quirinal, was its gardens (Horti Sallustiani), which probably occupied the valley between the Quirinal and Pincian, as well as part of the latter hill. (Becker, *Handb.* p. 583.) The house of Lucullus, the conqueror of Mithridates and Tigranes, was situated on the Pincian, and was also surrounded with gardens of such remarkable beauty, that the desire of possessing them, which they awakened in the breast of Messalina, caused the death of their subsequent owner, P. Valerius Asiaticus. (Tac. *Ann.* xi. 1; Dion Cass. lx. 31.) From this period they formed one of the most splendid possessions of the imperial family. (Plut. *Lucull.* 39.)

The ambitious designs entertained by the great leaders of the expiring Republic led them to court public favour by the foundation of public buildings rather than to lay out their immense wealth in adorning their own residences. The house inhabited by Pompey in the Carinae was an hereditary one; and though, after his triumph over Mithridates and the pirates, he rebuilt it on a more splendid scale and adorned it with the beaks of ships, yet it seems even then to have been far from one of the most splendid in Roma. (Plut. *Pomp.* 40, seq.) On the other hand, he consulted the taste and convenience of the Romans by building a theatre, a curia, and several temples. In like manner Caesar, at the height of his power, was content to reside in the ancient Regia; though this indeed was a sort of official residence which his office of Pontifex Maximus compelled him to adopt. (Suet. *Caes.* 46.) But he formed, and partly executed, many magnificent designs for the embellishment of the city, which his short tenure of power prevented him from accomplishing. Among these were a theatre of unexampled magnitude, to be hollowed out of the Tarpeian rock; a temple of Mars, greater than any then existing; the foundation of two large public libraries; the construction of a new forum; besides many other important works, both at Rome and in the provinces. (Suet. *Caes.* 26, 44; App. *B. C.* ii. 102, &c.)

The firm and lengthened hold of power enjoyed by Augustus, and the immense resources at his disposal, enabled him not only to carry out several of his uncle's plans, but also some new ones of his own; so that his reign must be regarded as one of the most important epochs in the history of the city. The foundation of new temples and other public buildings did not prevent him from repairing and embellishing the ancient ones; and all his designs were executed with so much magnificence that he could boast in his old age of having found Rome of brick and left it of marble. (Suet. *Aug.* 28.) In these undertakings he was assisted by the taste and munificence of his son-in-law Agrippa, who first founded public and gratuitous baths at Rome (Dion Cass. liv. 29); but as we shall have occasion to give an account of these works, as well as of those executed by Pompey and Caesar, in the topographical portion of this article, it will not be necessary to enumerate them here; and we shall proceed to describe the important municipal reforms introduced by Augustus, especially his new division of the city into Vici and Regions.

Regions of Augustus.—Although Rome had long outgrown its limits under Servius Tullius, yet the municipal divisions of that monarch subsisted till the time of Augustus, who made them his model, so far as the altered circumstances of the city would

permit. Servius had formed the different Vici into
religious corporations somewhat analogous with our
parishes, with an appointed worship of the Lares,
and proper feasts or Compitalia. During the Republic these corporations became a kind of political
clubs, and were often made the engines of designing
demagogues. (Preller, *Regionen*, p. 81.) Augustus, in his new distribution, also adopted the
scheme of embodying the Vici as religious corporations, and for this purpose erected chapels in the
crossways, and set up images of the gods *vicatim*, as
the Apollo Sandaliarius and the Jupiter Tragoedus.
(Suet. *Aug.* 57.) Many bases of these statues have
been discovered. By the term *Vicus* we are to
understand a certain collection of houses insulated
by streets running round all its sides ; whence the
term came also to be applied to the streets themselves
("altero vici appellantur, cum id genus aedificiorum
definitur, quae continentia sunt in oppidis, quaeve
itineribus regionibusque distributa inter se distant,
nominibusque dissimilibus discriminis causa sunt
dispartita," Fest. p. 371, et ibi Müll). *Compitum*,
which means properly a cross-road, was also,
especially in ancient times, only another name for
Vicus ; and thus we find Pliny describing Rome
as divided into Compita Larum instead of Vici (iii.
9). The Vici and Compita, regarded as streets,
were narrrower than the Viae and Plateae. (Suet.
Aug. 45; Amm. Marc. xxviii. 4. § 29.) They were
named after temples and other objects. The Vici
were composed of two classes of houses called respectively *insulae* and *domus*. The former were so called
because, by a law of the XII. Tables, it was ordained
that they should be separated from one another by an
interval of 2½ feet, called *ambitus*, and by later authors
circuitus (Varr. *L. L.* v. § 22, Müll.; Paul. Diac. p.
16, 111 Müll.) This law, which seems to have been
designed for purposes of health and for security against
fire, was disregarded during the Republic, but again
enforced by Nero when he rebuilt the city (Tac. *Ann.*
xv. 43); and there is an ordinance on the subject by
Antoninus and Verus (*Dig.* viii. 2. 14). By *insulae*,
therefore, we are to understand single houses divided
by a small space from the neighbouring ones, not
a complex of houses divided by streets. The latter
division formed a *Vicus*. Yet some insulae were so
large and disposed in such a manner that they almost
resembled Vici (vide Fest. p. 371, et ibi Müll).
The insulae were inhabited by the middling and lower
classes, and were generally let out in floors ("coenacula meritoria," *Dig.* xix. 2. 30). It appears from
the same authority that they were farmed by persons
who underlet them; but sometimes the proprietors
kept stewards to collect their rents. Insulae were
named after their owners, who were called "domini
insularum" (Suet. *Caes.* 41, *Tib.* 48). Thus we
hear of the insula Eucarpiana, Critonia, Arriana,
&c. (vide Gruter, 611. 13 ; Murat. 948. 9.) Rent
was high (Juv. iii. 166), and investments in houses
consequently profitable, though hazardous, since the
principle of insurance was altogether unknown.
(Gell. xv. 1, 2.) Crassus was a great speculator in
houses, and was said to possess nearly half Rome.
(Plut. c. 2.) The *domus*, on the contrary, were the
habitations or palaces of the rich and great, and
consequently much fewer in number than the insulae,
the proportion in each Region being as 1 to 25 or 30.
The domus were also commonly insulated, but not by
any special law, like the insulae. They were also
composed of floors or stages, but were occupied by a
single family (Petron. 77); though parts of them,

especially the postica, were sometimes let out (Plaut.
Trin. i. 2. 157; Suet. *Nero*, 44. *Vitell.* 7).

The number of insulae and domus in each Vicus
would of course vary. Augustus appointed that each
should be under the government of magistrates elected
from its plebeian inhabitants ("magistri e plebe
cujusque viciniae lecti,"—where *vicinia* has its original meaning of the householders composing a Vicus,
Suet. *Aug.* 30). Hence Livy calls them "infimum genus magistratuum" (xxxiv. 7). They were
called Magistri, Magistri Vicorum, Curatores Vicorum, and Magistri Larum, and their number varied
from two to four in each Vicus. In the *Basis
Capitolina* each Vicus has 4 Magistri ; but the
Notitia and *Curiosum* mention 48 Vico-magis-
tri in each Region, without reference to the number of Vici. On certain days, probably the Compitalia (Ascon. *in Cic. Pis.* p. 7), these magistrates
were allowed to assume the *toga praetexta*, and to be
attended by two lictors; and the public slaves of each
Region were at their command, who were commonly at
the disposal of the aediles in case of fire. (Dion Cass.
lv. 8 ; Liv. *l. c.*) The principal duties of their
office were to attend to the worship of the Lares, re-
censions of the people, &c. For Augustus restored
the Ludi Compitalicii and the regular worship of the
Lares in spring and summer (Suet. *Aug.* 31), and
caused his own Genius to be added to the two Lares
which stood in the aedicula or chapel of each compitum. (Ov. *Fast.* v. 145.) The Vicomagistri
likewise superintended the worship of the popular
deities Stata Mater and Vulcanus Quietus, to whom,
as protectors against fire, chapels were erected, first
in the forum, and afterwards in the different streets.
(Fest. p. 317, Müll.; cf. Preller, *Regionen*, p. 84.)

A certain number of Vici, varying according to
the *Notitia* and *Curiosum* from 7 to 78 constituted a
Regio ; and Augustus divided Rome into 14 of these
Regions. The 4 Servian Regions were followed in
the first 6 of Augustus. In determining the boundaries of the Regions Augustus seems to have caused
them to be measured by feet, as we see them enumerated in the *Notitia* and *Curiosum*. The limits appear
to have been marked by certain public buildings, not
by *cippi*. We may safely assume that Augustus included the suburbs in his city, but not within a pomoerium, since the Porticus Octaviae is mentioned, as being
outside of the pomoerium, although it lay far within
the 9th Region. (Dion Cass. liv. 8.) The Regions
appear at first to have been distinguished only by
numbers; and officially they were perhaps never
distinguished otherwise. Some of the names of
Regions found in the *Notitia* and *Curiosum* are post-
Augustan, as those of Isis and Serapis and Forum
Pacis. The period when names were first applied to
them cannot be determined. They are designated
only by numbers in Tacitus and Frontinus, and even
in the *Basis Capitolina* which belongs to the time of
Hadrian. We find, indeed, in Suetonius "Regio
Palatii" (*Aug.* 5, *Ill. Gramm.* 2); but so also he
says "Regio Martii Campi," which never was a
Region (*Caes.* 39, *Nero*, 12); and in these instances *Regio* seems to be used in its general
sense.

The boundaries of the Regions cannot be traced
with complete accuracy; but, as it is not our intention to follow those divisions when treating of the
topography of the city, we shall here insert such a
general description of them as may enable the reader
to form some notion of their situation and relative
size. *Regio I.*, or *Porta Capena*, embraced the

suburb lying outside of that gate, to the E. of the baths of Antoninus. It contained 10 Vici, and among its principal objects were, the temple of Mars, the arch of Drusus, and the sepulchre of the Scipios. *Regio II.*, or *Caelimontana*, lay to the N. of this, and comprehended the whole extent of the Caelian hill. It had 7 Vici, and among its monuments may be mentioned the Arcus Dolabellae and the aqueduct of Nero. *Regio III.*, called *Isis and Serapis*, lay to the N. of the Caelimontana, and embraced the valley of the Colosseum, and that southern portion of the Esquiline anciently known as Mons Oppius. It comprehended 12 Vici, and its principal objects were the baths of Titus and the Flavian amphitheatre or Colosseum. *Regio IV.*, called *Templum Pacis* and *Sacra Via*, was situated to the W. of that of Isis and Serapis, and comprehended the Velian ridge and the greater part of the valley between the Palatine, Esquiline, Viminal, and Quirinal, to the exclusion, however, of that western portion which lay immediately under the Capitoline. Yet it embraced the buildings on the N. side of the forum, including the temple of Faustina, the Basilica Paulli, and the Area Vulcani. Its eastern boundary ran close to the Colosseum, since it included the Colossus and the Meta Sudans, both which objects stood very near that building. Its principal monuments, besides those already mentioned, were the temple of Venus and Rome, and the basilica of Constantine. It embraced the Subura, the greater portion of the Sacra Via, and the Forum Transitorium, and contained 8 Vici. *Regio V.*, or *Esquilina*, included the northern portion of the Esquiline (Mons Cispius) and the Viminal, besides a vast tract of suburbs lying to the E. of the Servian walls and agger. Thus it extended so far as to embrace the Amphitheatrum Castrense, which adjoins the modern church of *S. Croce in Gerusalemme*, and the so-called temple of Minerva Medica, near the *Porta Maggiore*. It had 15 Vici, and among its remaining principal objects were the gardens of Maecenas, the arch of Gallienus, and the Nymphaeum of Alexander Severus. *Regio VI.*, called *Alta Semita*, embraced the Quirinal, and extended to the E. so as to include the Praetorian camp. It had 17 Vici, and its chief objects were the baths of Diocletian, the house and gardens of Sallust, and the ancient Capitol. *Regio VII.*, or *Via Lata*, was bounded on the E. by the Quirinal, on the N. by the Pincian, on the S. by the Servian wall between the Quirinal and Capitoline, and on the W. by the road called Via Lata till it joined the Via Flaminia—a point which cannot be accurately ascertained. The Via Lata was the southern portion of the modern *Corso*, and probably extended to the N. nearly as far as the Antonine column. The Region comprehended 15 Vici. Being without the Servian walls, part of this district was anciently a burying place, and the tomb of Bibulus is still extant. *Regio VIII.*, or *Forum Romanum Magnum*, was one of the most important and populous in Rome. The ancient forum obtained the name of " Magnum " after the building of that of Caesar. (Dion Cass. xliii. 22.) This Region, which formed the central point of all the rest, embraced not only the ancient forum, except the buildings on its N. side, but also the imperial fora, the Capitoline hill, and the valley between it and the Palatine as far as the Velabrum. It contained 34 Vici, among which were the densely populated ones Jugarius and Tuscus. The monuments in this district are so numerous and well

known that it is unnecessary to specify them. *Regio IX*, called *Circus Flaminius*, comprehended the district lying between the Via Lata on the E., the Tiber on the W., the Capitoline hill and Servian wall on the S.; whilst on the N. it seems to have extended as far as the present *Piazza Navona* and *Piazza Colonna*. It contained 35 Vici, and among its objects of interest may be named the circus from which it derived its name, the three theatres of Balbus, Pompey, and Marcellus, the Pantheon, and many other celebrated monuments. The Campus Martius, or northern part of the area between the hills and the Tiber, was not comprehended in any of the 14 Regions. *Regio X.*, or *Palatium*, consisted of the Palatine hill and its declivities. It had 20 Vici. Its boundaries are so well marked that we need not mention its numerous and well-known monuments till we come to describe its topography. *Regio XI.*, or *Circus Maximus*, derived its name from the circus, which occupied the greater part of it. It comprehended the valley between the Palatine and Aventine, and also apparently the northern declivities of the latter hill, as far as the Porta Trigemina. On the N., where it met the Region of the Forum Romanum, it seems to have included the Velabrum. It contained 19 Vici according to the *Notitia*, 21 according to the *Curiosum*. *Regio XII.*, called *Piscina Publica*, was bounded on the W. by the Aventine, on the N. by the Caelian, on the E. by *Regio I*, or Porta Capena, and on the S. it probably extended to the line of the Aurelian walls. It had 17 Vici, and its most remarkable monument was the baths of Caracalla. *Regio XIII.*, or *Aventinus*, included that hill and the adjoining banks of the Tiber. It had 17 Vici according to the *Notitia*, 18 according to the *Curiosum*. *Regio XIV.*, *Transtiberina*, or *Transtiberim*, comprehended all the suburb on the W., or right bank of the Tiber, including the Vatican, the Janiculum, with the district between them and the river, and the Insula Tiberina. This, therefore, was by far the largest of all the Regions, and contained 78 Vici.

Municipal Regulations of Augustus.—All these Regions were under the control of magistrates chosen annually by lot. (Suet. *Aug.* 30.) The government of the Regions was not corporative, like that of the Vici, but administrative ; and one or more Regions seem to have been intrusted to a single magistrate chosen among the aediles, tribunes, or praetors. (Preller, *Regionen*, p. 77.) The supreme administration, however, was vested in the Praefectus Urbi. At a later period other officers were interposed between the praefect and these governors. Thus the *Basis Capitolina* mentions a Curator and Denunciator in each Region. Subsequently, however, the latter office seems to have been abolished, and the *Notitia* and *Curiorum* mention two curators in each Region. There were also subordinate officers, such as *praecones* or criers, and a number of imperial slaves, or libertini, were appointed to transact any necessary business concerning the Regions. (Preller, p. 79.)

One of the chief objects of Augustus in establishing these Regions seems to have been connected with a reform of the city police. For this purpose he established 7 Cohortes Vigilum, whose stations were so disposed that each cohort might be available for two Regions. Each was under the command of a tribune, and the whole was superintended by a Praefectus Vigilum. (Suet. *Aug.* 30;

Dion Cass. lv. 26; Paulus, *de Offic. Praef. Vigil.,
Dig.* i. 15.) As these stations were necessarily
near the borders of Regions, we find them frequently
mentioned in the *Notitia* and *Curiosum.* They
seem to have been a sort of barracks. But besides
the 7 principal stations, the *Breviarium* mentions
14 *excubitoria*, or outposts, which seem to have been
placed in the middle of each region. The *corps* of
which they were composed were probably supplied
from the main stations. The duties of the vigiles
were those of a night-police, namely, to guard against
fires, burglaries, highway robberies, &c. The first
of these duties had anciently been performed by
certain triumviri, called from their functions Noc-
turni, who were assisted by public slaves stationed
at the gates and round the walls. The same office
was, however, sometimes assumed by the aediles
and tribunes of the people. (Paulus, *l. c.*) The
vigiles were provided with all the arms and tools
necessary for their duties; and from a passage in
Petronius (c. 79) seem to have possessed the power
of breaking into houses when they suspected any
danger. The numbers of the vigiles amounted at
last to 7000 men, or 1000 in each cohort. Augustus
also established the Cohortes Praetoriae, or imperial
guard, of which 9 cohorts were disposed in the
neighbourhood of Rome, and 3 only, the Cohortes
Urbanae, were permitted within the city. (Tac. *Ann.*
iv. 5; Suet. *Aug.* 49.) These cohorts of Augustus
were under the command of the Praefectus Urbi.
(Tac. *Hist.* iii. 64.) It was his successor, Tiberius,
who, by the advice of Sejanus, first established a
regular Praetorian camp at Rome, a little to the
eastward of the agger of Servius, and placed the
bands under the command of a Praefectus Praetorio.
(Tac. *Ann.* iv. 2; Suet. *Tib.* 37.)

Augustus also paid considerable attention to the
method of building, and revived the regulations laid
down by P. Rutilius Rufus with regard to this subject in the time of the Gracchi (Suet. *Aug.* 89); but
all we know of these regulations is, that Augustus
forbade houses to be built higher than 70 feet, if
situated in a street. (Strab. v. p. 235.) The
height was subsequently regulated by Nero and
Trajan, the last of whom fixed it at 60 feet. (Aur.
Vict. *Epit.* c. 13.) Yet houses still continued to
be inconveniently high, as we see from the complaints
of Juvenal, in the time, probably, of Domitian, and
dangerous alike in case of fire or falling, especially
to a poor poet who lived immediately under the
tiles: —

" Nos urbem colimus tenui tibicine fultam
Magna parte sui; nam sic labentibus obstat
Villicus, et veteris rimae quum texit hiatum
Securos pendente jubet dormire ruina.
Vivendum est illic ubi nulla incendia, nulli
Nocte metus. Jam poscit aquam, jam frivola
transfert
Ucalegon: tabulata tibi jam tertia fumant:
Tu nescis; nam si gradibus trepidatur ab imis
Ultimus ardebit, quem tegula sola tuetur
A pluvia, molles ubi reddunt ova columbae."
(iii. 193.)

Augustan Rome. — Strabo, who visited Rome in
the reign of Augustus, and must have remained
there during part of that of Tiberius, has left us
the following lively picture of its appearance at
that period: " The city, having thus attained such
a size, is able to maintain its greatness by the
abundance of provisions and the plentiful supply
of wood and stone for building, which the constant fires and continual falling and pulling down
of houses render necessary; for even pulling down
and rebuilding in order to gratify the taste is but
a sort of voluntary ruin. Moreover the abundant
mines and forests, and the rivers which serve to
convey materials, afford wonderful means for these
purposes. Such is the Anio, flowing down from Alba
(Fucensis), a Latin city lying towards the territory
of the Marsians, and so through the plain till it falls
into the Tiber: also the Nar and the Tenea, which
likewise join the Tiber after flowing through Umbria; and the Clanis, which waters Etruria and the
territory of Clusium. Augustus Caesar took great
care to obviate such damages to the city. To guard
against fires he appointed a special corps composed
of freedmen; and to prevent the falling down of
houses he ordained that no new ones should be built,
if they adjoined the public streets, of a greater
height than 70 feet. Nevertheless the renovation of
the city would have been impossible but for the
before-mentioned mines and forests, and the facility
of transport.

" Such, then, were the advantages of the city from
the nature of the country; but to these the Romans
added those which spring from industry and art.
Although the Greeks are supposed to excel in
building cities, not only by the attention they pay to
the beauty of their architecture and the strength of
their situation, but also to the selection of a fertile
country and convenient harbours, yet the Romans have
surpassed them by attending to what they neglected,
such as the making of high-roads and aqueducts,
and the constructing of sewers capable of conveying
the whole drainage of the city into the Tiber. The
high-roads have been constructed through the country
in such a manner, by levelling hills and filling-up
hollows, that the waggons are enabled to carry
freight sufficient for a vessel; whilst the sewers,
vaulted with hewn blocks of masonry, are sometimes
large enough to admit the passage of a hay-cart.
Such is the volume of water conveyed by the
aqueducts that whole rivers may be said to flow
through the city, which are carried off by the
sewers. Thus almost every house is provided with
water-pipes, and possesses a never-failing fountain.
Marcus Agrippa paid particular attention to this
department, besides adorning the city with many
beautiful monuments. It may be said that the ancient Romans neglected the beauty of their city,
being intent upon greater and more important objects; but later generations, and particularly the
Romans of our own day, have attended to this point
as well, and filled the city with many beautiful
monuments. Pompey, Julius Caesar, and Augustus,
as well as the children, friends, wife and sister of
the last, have bestowed an almost excessive care and
expense in providing these objects. The Campus
Martius has been their special care, the natural
beauties of which have been enhanced by their designs. This plain is of surprising extent, affording
unlimited room not only for the chariot races and
other equestrian games, but also for the multitudes
who exercise themselves with the ball or hoop, or in
wrestling. The neighbouring buildings, the perpetual verdure of the grass, the hills which crown
the opposite banks of the river and produce a kind
of scenic effect, all combine to form a spectacle from
which it is difficult to tear oneself. Adjoining this
plain is another, and many porticoes and sacred
groves, three theatres, an amphitheatre, and temples

so rich and so close to one another that they might appear to exhibit the rest of the city as a mere supplement. Hence this place is considered the most honourable and sacred of all, and has been appropriated to the monuments of the most distinguished men and women. The most remarkable of these is that called the Mausoleum, a vast mound near the river raised upon a lofty base of white stone, and covered to its summit with evergreen trees. On the top is a bronze statue of Augustus: whilst under the mound are the tombs of himself, his relatives, and friends, and at the back of it a large grove, affording delightful promenades. In the middle of the Campus is an enclosed space where the body of Augustus was burnt, also constructed of white stone, surrounded with an iron rail, and planted in the interior with poplar trees. Then if we proceed to the ancient forum, and survey the numerous basilicae, porticoes, and temples which surround it, and view the Capitol and its works, as well as those on the Palatine and in the portico of Livia, we might easily be led to forget all other cities. Such is Rome" (v. pp. 235, 236).

In spite, however, of this glowing picture, or rather perhaps from the emphasis which it lays on the description of the Campus Martius, whilst the remainder of the city is struck off with a few light touches, it may be suspected that in the time of Augustus the ancient part of Rome, with the exception of the immediate vicinity of the forum and Capitol, did not present a spectacle of any great magnificence. The narrowness and irregularity of the streets, the consequence of the hasty manner in which the city was rebuilt after its destruction by the Gauls, still continued to disfigure it in the time of Augustus, as is shown by a passage in Livy (v. 55), already cited (cf. Tacitus, *Ann.* xv. 38: " Obnoxia urbe artis itineribus, hucque et illuc flexis, atque enormibus vicis, qualis *vetus* Roma fuit"—that is, before the fire). This defect was not remedied till the great fire in the reign of Nero, which forms the next remarkable epoch in the history of the city.

V. THE CITY TILL THE TIME OF AURELIAN.

Fire under Nero.—There had been a destructive fire in the reign of Tiberius, which burnt down all the buildings on the Caelian hill (Tac. *Ann.* iv. 64); but this was a mere trifle compared with the extensive conflagration under Nero. The latter, the most destructive calamity of the kind that had ever happened at Rome, is unequivocally said by Suetonius (*Nero*, 38) to have been caused by the wilful act of the emperor, from disgust at the narrow and winding streets. Nero is represented by that historian as contemplating the flames with delight from the tower of Maecenas on the Esquiline, and as converting the awful reality into a sort of dramatic spectacle, by singing as the fire raged, in proper scenic attire, the Sack of Troy ; nor does the more judicious Tacitus altogether reject the imputation (*Ann.* xv. 38, seq.) The fire commenced at the lower part of the Circus Maximus, where it adjoins the Caelian and Palatine, in some shops containing combustible materials. Thence it spread through the whole length of the circus to the Forum Boarium, and northwards over the whole Palatine till it was arrested at the foot of the Esquiline. It lasted six days and seven nights, and its extent may be judged from the fact that out of the fourteen Regions three were completely destroyed, and seven very nearly so, whilst only three escaped altogether untouched.

The three Regions utterly destroyed must have been the xith, x th, and ivth, or those called Circus Maximus, Palatium, and Templum Pacis. The forum must have suffered considerably, but the Capitol seems to have escaped, as the Capitoline temple, after its first destruction in the time of Sulla, remained entire till burnt by the Vitellians. The narrow and crooked streets, and the irregular Vici of which ancient Rome was composed, rendered it impossible to arrest the conflagration. Nero was at Antium when it broke out, and did not return to Rome till the flames were threatening his own palace, which he had not the power to save. This was the *Domus Transitoria*, the domain of which he had extended from the Palatine to the gardens of Maecenas on the Esquiline. What chiefly directed suspicion against Nero, as having wilfully caused the fire, was the circumstance of its breaking out afresh in the Aemilian property of his minion Tigellinus.

Much irreparable loss was occasioned by this fire, such as the destruction of several time-honoured fanes, of many master-pieces of Greek art, besides a vast amount of private property. Among the venerable temples which perished on this occasion, were that of Luna, erected by Servius Tullius, the altar and fane of Hercules in the Forum Boarium, the temple of Jupiter Stator, founded by Romulus, those of Vesta and of the Penates Populi Romani, and the Regia of Numa. Yet, on the other hand, the fire made room for great improvements. Nero caused the town to be rebuilt on a regular plan, with broad streets, open spaces, and less lofty houses. All the buildings were isolated, and a certain portion of each was constructed with Alban or Gabinian stone, so as to be proof against fire; to guard against which a plentiful supply of water was laid on. As a means of escape and assistance in the same calamity, as well as for the sake of ornament, Nero also caused porticoes to be built at his own expense along the fronts of the insulae. He supplied the proprietors with money for building, and specified a certain time by which the houses were to be completed (Tac. *Ann.* xv. 38—43; Suet. *Nero*, 38). Thus Rome sprung a second time from her ashes, in a style of far greater splendour than before. The new palace, or *domus aurea*, of the emperor himself kept pace with the increased magnificence of the city. Its bounds comprehended large parks and gardens, filled with wild animals, where solitude might be found in the very heart of the city; a vast lake, surrounded with large buildings, filled the valley in which the Flavian amphitheatre was afterwards erected ; the palace was of such extent as to have triple porticoes of a thousand feet ; in the vestibule stood a colossal figure of Nero himself, 120 feet in height ; the ceilings were panelled, the chambers gilt, and inlaid with gems and mother-of-pearl; and the baths flowed both with fresh and sea water. When this magnificent abode was completed, Nero vouchsafed to honour it with his qualified approbation, and was heard to observe, " that he was at last beginning to lodge like a man." (Suet. *Nero*, 31; Mart. *de Spect.* 2.)

Changes under subsequent Emperors. — The two predecessors of Nero, Caligula and Claudius, did not effect much for the city ; and the short and turbulent reigns of his three successors, Galba, Otho, and Vitellius, were characterised rather by destruction than improvement. Caligula indeed perfected some of the designs of Tiberius (Suet. *Cal.*

3 B 3

21); and the reign of Claudius was distinguished by the completion of two aqueducts and the construction of several beautiful fountains (Id. *Claud.* 20). The factious struggles between Otho and Vitellius were marked by the ominous burning of the Capitol. At length the happier era of the public-spirited Vespasian was distinguished alike by his regard for the civil liberties of the Romans, and for their material comforts, by the attention which he paid to the improvement of the city, and by his restoring to the public use and enjoyment the vast space appropriated by Nero for his own selfish gratification. The bounds of the imperial palace were again restricted to the limits of the Palatine, and on the site of Nero's lake rose a vast amphitheatre destined for the amusement of so many thousands of the Roman people, whose ruins we still gaze at with wonder and admiration. Vespasian was likewise the founder of the temple of Peace, near the Forum, and of a temple to Claudius on the Caelian hill. Titus pursued the popular designs of his father, and devoted a large portion of the former imperial gardens on the Esquiline to the foundation of public baths. (Suet. *Tit.* 7; Mart. iii. 20. 15.) Under this emperor another destructive fire raged for three days and nights at Rome, and again laid a great part of the city in ashes. (Suet. *Tit.* 8.) The chief works of Domitian were the rebuilding of the temple of Jupiter Capitolinus, which had again been burnt, on the mere external gilding of which he is said to have expended 12,000 talents, or nearly three millions sterling; and the foundation of a new forum, which, however, was not finished till the time of Nerva, whose name it bore. (Id. *Dom.* 5.) Trajan constructed the last of the imperial fora, with which was connected the Basilica Ulpia. (Dion Cass. lxix. 4.) Rome probably attained its highest pitch of architectural splendour under the reign of his successor Hadrian. That emperor had a passion for building, and frequently furnished his own designs, which, however, were not always in the best taste. His most remarkable works were the Mausoleum on the right bank of the Tiber, now the *Castello di S. Angelo*, the Temple of Venus and Rome near the Colosseum, and the enormous villa whose ruins may still be seen at the foot of the ascent which leads to *Tivoli*. (Spart. *Hadr.* 19; Procop. *B. G.* i. 22.)

It would be tedious and unprofitable to recount the works of succeeding emperors down to the time of Aurelian; and it may suffice to mention that those who most contributed to renovate or adorn the city were Septimius Severus, Caracalla, and Alexander Severus. During this period Rome betrayed unequivocal symptoms of her approaching decline and fall. Large bodies of the barbarians had already penetrated into Italy, and, in the reign of the accomplished but feeble Gallienus, a horde of the Alemanni had menaced and insulted Rome itself. After a lapse of eight centuries its citizens again trembled for the safety of their families and homes; and the active and enterprising Aurelian, whilst waging successful wars in Egypt and the East, found himself compelled to secure his capital by fortifying it with a wall.

This great undertaking, commenced A. D. 271, was completed in the reign of Probus, the successor of Aurelian. (Vopisc. *Aur.* 21, 39; Aur. Vict. *Caes.* 35; Eutrop. ix. 15; Zosim. i. 49). The accounts of the circumference of this wall are discrepant and improbable. Vopiscus (*Aurel.* c. 39) mentions the absurd and extravagant measure of nearly 50 miles; which,

however, has been adopted by Lipsius and Isaac Vossius, as well as by Nibby (*Mura, &c.* p. 120, seq.). The walls of Aurelian were repaired by Honorius, and with the exception of that part beyond the Tiber, and some modern additions by the Popes, are substantially the same as those which now exist, as appears from the inscriptions on the gates. Without the additions referred to, their circumference would be between 11 and 12 miles, thus reducing the city to about the same dimensions as those given by Pliny in the time of Vespasian; nor is there any reason to believe that, in the sinking state of the Empire, the city would have received any increase of inhabitants. Another measurement by Ammon, the geometrician, just before the siege of the city by Alaric, gave a circumference of 21 miles (Phot. *Bibl.* 80, p. 63, ed. Bekk.); but this number, though adopted by Gibbon, and nearer to the truth, cannot be accepted any more than that of Vopiscus. (Gibbon, *Decl. and Fall*, vol. ii. p. 17, ed. Smith, and notes.) Piale suggested that Vopiscus meant *pedes* instead of *passus*, and other emendations of both the passages have been proposed; but without discussing the merit of these, it is sufficient to know that the texts are undoubtedly either corrupt or erroneous. This may be briefly but decisively shown from the following considerations, which will, for the most part, apply to both the statements:— 1st, the incredible extent of the work; 2nd, the absence of any traces of such walls; 3rd, or of any buildings within their supposed limits, such as would naturally belong to a city; 4th, the fact that the extant inscriptions ascribe to Honorius the *restoration* of an old line of walls and towers, not the *construction* of a new one. (Bunbury, in *Class. Mus.* iii. p. 368.)

VI. DECLINE AND FALL OF THE CITY.

The history of the city from the time of Aurelian presents little more than a prospect of its rapid decline. The walls of that emperor were ominous of its sinking fortunes; but the reign of Diocletian forms the first marked aera of its decay. The triumph of that emperor and of his colleague Maximian, A. D. 303, was the last ever celebrated at Rome, but was distinguished by the trophies of an important Persian victory. (Eutrop. ix. 27.) The Roman emperors had long ceased to be of Roman extraction; Diocletian, the descendant of slaves, was born in Dalmatia; Maximian, the son of a peasant, was his fellow countryman; and thus neither was wedded by any ties of birth or patriotism to the ancient glories of the eternal city. These were the first emperors who deserted the capital to fix their residence in the provinces. Maximian established his court at Milan, whilst Diocletian resided at Nicomedia, on the embellishment of which he lavished all the treasures of the East, in endeavouring to render it a rival worthy of Rome. His only visit to the ancient capital seems to have been on the occasion of his triumph; it was not prolonged beyond two months, and was closed with unexpected precipitation and abruptness. (Lact. *Mort. Pers.* c. 17.) Yet his reign is distinguished as having conferred upon the city one of the latest, but most magnificent of its monuments, — the baths on the Quirinal which bear his name, by far the largest at Rome, whose enormous ruins may still be traced, and afford room enough for various churches, convents, and gardens. (Vopisc. *Prob.* 2; Orell. *Inscr.* 1056.) Subsequently, indeed, Maxentius, the partner and rival of Constantine, resided at Rome during the six years of his reign, and affected to prize the elegance of the ancient metropolis; whilst his lust and tyranny, supported by squandering its treasures, created more disgust among the Romans than the absence of their former sovereigns. Maxentius, however, adorned the city which he polluted by his vices, and some of his works are among the last monuments worthy to be recorded. He restored the temple of Venus and Rome, which had been damaged by a fire, and erected that magnificent basilica, afterwards dedicated in the name of Constantine, whose three enormous arches may still be viewed with admiration. (Aur. Vict. *Caes.* c. 40. § 26.) The final transfer of the seat of empire to Byzantium by Constantine gave the last fatal blow to the civic greatness of Rome. Yet even that emperor presented the city — we can hardly say adorned it — with a few monuments. One of them, the arch which records his triumph over Maxentius, still subsists, and strikingly illustrates the depth of degradation to which architectural taste had already sunk. Its beauties are derived from the barbarous pillage of former monuments. The superb sculptures which illustrated the acts and victories of Trajan, were ruthlessly and absurdly constrained to typify those of Constantine; whilst the original sculptures that were added, by being placed in juxtaposition with those beautiful works, only serve to show more forcibly the hopeless decline of the plastic arts, which seem to have fallen with paganism.

Rome in the Time of Constantius II. — From this period the care of the Romans was directed rather towards the preservation than the adornment of their city. When visited by the Second Constantius, A. D. 357, an honour which it had not received for two and thirty years, Rome could still display her ancient glories. The lively description of this visit by Ammianus Marcellinus, though written in a somewhat inflated style, forms a sort of pendant to Strabo's picture of Rome in the age of Augustus, and is striking and valuable, both as exhibiting the condition of the eternal city at that period, and as illustrating the fact that the men of that age regarded its monuments as a kind of Titanic relics, which it would be hopeless any longer to think of imitating. "Having entered Rome," says the historian, "the seat of empire and of every virtue, Constantius was overwhelmed with astonishment when he viewed the forum, that most conspicuous monument of ancient power. On whatever side he cast his eyes, he was struck with the thronging wonders. He addressed the senate in the Curia, the people from the tribunal; and was delighted with the applause which accompanied his progress to the palace. At the Circensian games which he gave, he was pleased with the familiar talk of the people, who, without betraying pride, asserted their hereditary liberty. He himself observed a proper mean, and did not, as in other cities, arbitrarily terminate the contests, but, as is customary at Rome, permitted them to end as chance directed. When he viewed the different parts of the city, situated on the sides of the seven hills and in the valleys between them, he expected that whatever he first saw must be superior to everything else: such as the temple of the Tarpeian Jove, whose excellence is like divine to human; the baths which occupy whole districts; the enormous mass of the amphitheatre, built of solid Tiburtine stone, the height of which almost baffles

the eye; the Pantheon, which may be called a circular Region, vaulted with lofty beauty; the high, but accessible mounds, bearing the statues of preceding princes; the temple of Rome, the forum of Peace; the theatre of Pompey, the odeum, the stadium, and other similar ornaments of the eternal city. But when he came to the forum of Trajan, which we take to be a structure unparalleled in the whole world, he was confounded with astonishment as he surveyed those gigantic proportions, which can neither be described nor again imitated by man. Wherefore, laying aside all hope of attempting anything of the kind, he merely expressed the power and the wish to imitate the horse of Trajan, on which that prince is seated, and which stands in the middle of the Atrium. Hereupon prince Hormisda, who stood near him, exclaimed with national gesticulation: 'First of all, emperor, order such a stable to be made for it, if you can, that the horse you propose making may lodge as magnificently as the one we behold.' The same prince being asked his opinion of Rome said that the only thing which displeased him was to perceive that men died there as well as in other places. So great was the emperor's surprise at all these sights that he complained that rumour, which commonly magnifies everything, had here shown itself weak and malignant, and had given but a feeble description of the wonders of Rome. Then, after much deliberation, he resolved that the only way in which he could add to the ornaments of the city would be by erecting an obelisk in the Circus Maximus" (xvi. 10).

The same historian from whom the preceding topographical picture has been transcribed has also left some lively and interesting notices of the manners of the Romans at this period. These have been paraphrased in the eloquent language of Gibbon, to whose work the reader is referred for many interesting particulars concerning the state of Rome at this time (vol. iv. pp. 70—89, ed. Smith). We may here observe with surprise that whilst Alaric, like another Hannibal, was threatening her gates, her nobles were revelling in immoderate wealth, and squandering the revenues of provinces on objects of pomp and luxury, though, as we have seen, the arts had fallen to so low an ebb that there was no longer any hope of rivalling the works of their ancestors. The poorer citizens, few of whom could any longer boast a pure Roman descent, resembled the inmates of a poorhouse, except that their pleasures were provided for as well as their wants. A liberal distribution of corn and bacon, and sometimes even of wine, relieved their necessities, whilst health and recreation were promoted by gratuitous admittance to the baths and public spectacles. Yet Rome was now struggling for her existence. We have already mentioned the restoration of the walls by Honorius. It was under the same emperor that the first example occurs of that desecration by which the Romans stripped and destroyed their own monuments. If we may credit Zosimus (v. 38), Stilicho was the first to lay violent hands on the temple of the Capitoline Jove, by stripping off the plates of gold which lined its doors, when the following inscription was found beneath them: "Misero regi servantur." In after times this example was but too frequently followed; and it may be said with truth that the Romans themselves were the principal destroyers of their own city.

The Barbarians at Rome. — After two sieges, or rather blockades, in 408 and 409, by the Goths under Alaric, Rome was captured and sacked on a third occasion in 410 (A. U. C. 1163)—the first time since the Gallic invasion that the city had actually been in the hands of an enemy. But though it was plundered by the Goths, it does not appear to have sustained much damage at their hands. They evacuated it on the sixth day, and all the mischief they seem to have done was the setting fire to some houses near the Salarian gate, by which they had entered, which unfortunately spread to and destroyed the neighbouring palace of Sallust (Procop. *B. V.* i. 2.) Nearly half a century later, in the reign of Maximus, Rome was again taken, and sacked by the Vandals, under Genseric, A. D. 455. This time the pillage lasted a fortnight; yet the principal damage inflicted on the monuments of the city was the carrying off by Genseric of the curious tiles of gilt bronze which covered the temple of the Capitoline Jupiter (*Ib.* 5). That edifice, with the exception, perhaps, of the spoliation by Stilicho, appears to have remained in much the same state as after its last rebuilding by Domitian; and though paganism had been abolished in the interval, the venerable fane seems to have been respected by the Roman Christians. Yet, as may be perceived from an edict of the emperor Majorian, A. D. 457, the inhabitants of Rome had already commenced the disgraceful practice of destroying the monuments of their ancestors. The zeal of the Christians led them to deface some of the temples; others, which had not been converted into Christian churches, were suffered to go to ruin, or were converted into quarries, from which building materials were extracted. Petitions for that purpose were readily granted by the magistrates; till Majorian checked the practice by a severe edict, which reserved to the emperor and senate the cognisance of those cases in which the destruction of an ancient building might be allowed, imposed a fine of 50 lbs. of gold (2000*l.* sterling) on any magistrate who granted a license for such dilapidations, and condemned all subordinate officers engaged in such transactions to be whipped, and to have their hands amputated (*Nov. Major.* tit. vi. p. 35: "Antiquarum aedium dissipatur speciosa constructio; et ut earum aliquid reparetur magna diruuntur," &c.)

In the year 472, in the reign of Olybrius, Rome was for the third time taken and sacked by Ricimer; but this calamity, like the two former ones, does not appear to have been productive of much damage to the public monuments. These relics of her former glory were the especial care of Theodoric, the Ostrogoth, when he became king of Italy, who, when he visited the capital in the year 500, had surveyed them with admiration. "The Gothic kings, so injuriously accused of the ruin of antiquity, were anxious to preserve the monuments of the nation whom they had subdued. The royal edicts were framed to prevent the abuses, the neglect, or the depredations of the citizens themselves; and a professed architect, the annual sum of 200 lbs. of gold, 25,000 tiles, and the receipt of customs' from the Lucrine port, were assigned for the ordinary repairs of the walls and public edifices. A similar care was extended to the statues of metal or marble, of men or animals. The spirit of the horses, which have given a modern name to the Quirinal, was applauded by the barbarians; the brazen elephants of the Via Sacra were diligently restored; the famous heifer of Myron deceived the cattle as they were driven through the forum of Peace; and an officer was created to protect those works of art, which Theodoric considered as

the noblest ornament of his kingdom." (Gibbon, *Decline and Fall*, vol. v. p. 21, ed. Smith ; cf. *Excerpt. de Odoac. Theod.* 67.) The letters of Cassiodorus, the secretary of Theodoric, show that Rome had received little or no injury from its three captures. The Circus Maximus was uninjured, and the Ludi Circenses were still exhibited there (*Variar.* iii. 51); the thermae and aqueducts were intact (*Ib.* vii. 6); the Claudian aqueduct was still in play, and discharged itself on the top of the Aventine as if it were a valley (*Ib.*). That the aqueducts were perfect also appears from Procopius (*B. G.* i. 19), who says that in the subsequent siege under Vitiges, the Goths broke them down, to deprive the inhabitants of their supply of water. The theatres had suffered only from the effects of time, and were repaired by Theodoric (Cassiod. *ib.* iv. 51.)

In the year 536 the Gothic garrison, with the exception of their commander Leuderis, who preferred captivity to flight, evacuated Rome on the approach of Belisarius, the lieutenant of Justinian. Belisarius entered by the Asinarian gate, and, after an alienation of sixty years, Rome was restored to the imperial dominion. But in a few months the city was beleaguered by the numerous host of Vitiges, the newly elected king of the Goths; and its defence demanded all the valour and ability of Belisarius. For this purpose he repaired the walls, which had again fallen into decay. Regular bastions were constructed; a chain was drawn across the Tiber ; the arches of the aqueducts were fortified; and the mole of Hadrian was converted into a citadel. That part of the wall between the Flaminian and Pincian gates, called *muro torto*, was alone neglected (Procop. *B. G.* i. 14, sqq.), which is said to have been regarded both by Goths and Romans as under the peculiar protection of St. Peter. As we have before said, the Goths invested the city in six divisions, from the Porta Flaminia to the Porta Praenestina ; whilst a seventh encampment was formed near the Vatican, for the purpose of commanding the Tiber and the Milvian bridge. In the general assault which followed, a feint was made at the Salarian gate, but the principal attacks were directed against the mole of Hadrian and the Porta Praenestina. It was on this occasion that at the former point the finest statues, the works of Praxiteles and Lysippus, were converted into warlike missiles, and hurled down upon the besiegers. When the ditch of St. Angelo was cleansed in the pontificate of Urban VIII., the Sleeping Faun of the Barberini Palace was discovered, but in a sadly mutilated state. (Winckelmann, *Hist. de l'Art,*vol. ii. p. 52, seq.) But the assault was not successful, and after a fruitless siege, which lasted a year, the Goths were forced to retire.

After the recall of Belisarius the Goths recovered strength and courage, and, under Totila, once more threatened the walls of Rome. In 544 Belisarius was again despatched into Italy, to retrieve the faults of the generals who had succeeded him; but on this occasion he was deserted by his usual fortune, and, after a fruitless attempt to relieve the city, was compelled to retreat to Ostia. (Procop. *B. G.* iii. 19.) In December, 546, the Goths were admitted into the city by the treachery of some Isaurian sentinels posted at the Asinarian gate. Rome was again subjected to pillage, and appears to have suffered more than on any former occasion. A third part of the walls was destroyed in different places, and a great many houses were burnt.

(Procop. *ib.* c. 22; Marcell. *Chron.* p. 54.) Totila threatened to destroy the finest works of antiquity, and even issued a decree that Rome should be turned into a pasture. Yet he was not deficient in magnanimity and clemency, and was diverted from these designs by the remonstrances of Belisarius, who warned him not to sully his fame by such wanton barbarity. Upon Totila's marching into Lucania, Belisarius, at the head of 1000 horse, cut his way through the Goths who had been left to guard the city. He repaired with rude and heterogeneous materials the walls which had been demolished; whilst the gates, which could not be so suddenly restored, were guarded by his bravest soldiers. Totila returned to Rome by forced marches, but was thrice repulsed in three general assaults. Belisarius, however, being commanded by Justinian to proceed into Lucania, left a garrison of 3000 of his best troops at Rome under the command of Diogenes. The city was again betrayed by some Isaurians in 549, who opened the gate of St. Paul to Totila and his Goths. Totila, who seems now to have considered himself as in confirmed possession of Italy, no longer exhibited any desire to destroy the edifices of Rome, which he regarded as the capital of his kingdom, and he even exhibited the equestrian games in the Circus. (Procop. *B. G.* iv. 22.) But in 552 he was defeated and slain by the eunuch Narses in the battle of Tagina. Narses then marched to Rome, and once more sent its keys to Justinian, during whose reign the city had been no fewer than five times taken and recovered. (*Ib.* 26—35; Theoph. *Chron.* vol. i. p. 354, ed. Bonn.)

Rome under the Popes.—Towards the close of the sixth century Rome had touched the lowest point of degradation. The Roman citizens lived in continual fear of the attacks of the Lombards; the inhabitants of the surrounding country, who no longer dared to devote themselves to the pursuits of agriculture, took refuge within the walls; and the *Campagna* of Rome became a desert, exhaling infectious vapours. The indigence and the celibacy of a great part of the inhabitants produced a rapid decrease of population, though their scanty numbers did not protect them from famine. The edifices of Rome fell into decay; and it is commonly believed that Pope Gregory the Great, who filled the papal chair from 590 to 604, purposely defaced the temples and mutilated the statues,—a charge, however, which rests on doubtful evidence, and which has been strenuously repelled by Gregory's biographer Platina (ap. Bayle, *Grégoire Ier.*). Bargaeus, in his epistle on the subject (in Graevius, *Thesaur. Ant.* vol. iv.), says that the Circus Maximus, the baths and theatres, were certainly overthrown designedly, and that this is particularly evident in the baths of Caracalla and Diocletian (p. 1885). He attributes this, *as a merit*, to Gregory and one or two subsequent popes, and assigns as a reason that the baths were nothing but schools of licentiousness (p. 1889, seq.). It seems more probable, however, that the destruction of the baths arose from the failure of the aqueducts — a circumstance which would have rendered them useless — and from the expense of keeping them up. Bargaeus himself attributes the ruin of the aqueducts to the latter cause (p. 1891); but they must also have suffered very severely in the Gothic wars. Hence perhaps the huge foundations of the thermae, having become altogether useless, began to be used as stone quarries, a circumstance which would account for

the appearance of wilful damage. That ruin had made great progress at Rome before the time of Gregory, is manifest from some passages in his own works in which he deplores it. Thus in one of his homilies he says: "Qualis remanserit Roma, conspicimus. Immensis doloribus multipliciter attrita, desolatione civium, impressione hostium, *frequentia ruinarum.*" And again: "Quid autem ista de hominibus dicimus, cum ruinis crebrescentibus ipsa quoque destrui aedificia videmus?" (*Hom.* 18 *in Ezech.* ap. Donatum, *de Urbe Roma*, i. 28, sub fin.) He would hardly have written thus had he himself been the cause of these ruins. The charge probably acquired strength from Gregory's avowed antipathy to classical literature.

Whilst the dominion of Italy was divided between the Lombards and the exarchs of Ravenna, Rome was the head of a duchy of almost the same size as her ancient territory, extending from Viterbo to Terracina, and from Narni to the mouth of the Tiber. The fratricide Constans II. is said to have entertained the idea of restoring the seat of empire to Rome (A. D. 662). (*Hist. Misc.* ap. Muratori, *Scrip. R. I.* iii. pt. i. p. 137.) But the Lombard power was too strong; and, after a visit of a few days to the ancient capital, he abandoned it for ever, after pillaging the churches and carrying off the bronze roof of the Pantheon. (Schlosser. *Gesch. d. bilder-stürmenden Kaiser*, p. 80.) In the eighth century the Romans revived the style of the Republic, but the Popes had become their chief magistrates. During this period Rome was constantly harassed and suffered many sieges by the Lombards under Luitprand, Astolphus, and other kings. In 846 the various measure of its calamities was filled up by an attack of the Saracens — as if the former mistress of the world was destined to be the butt of wandering barbarians from all quarters of the globe. The disciples of Mahomet pillaged the church of St. Peter, as well as that of St. Paul outside the Porta Ostiensis, but did not succeed in entering the city itself. They were repulsed by the vigilance and energy of pope Leo IV., who repaired the ancient walls, restored fifteen towers which had been overthrown, and enclosed the quarter of the Vatican; on which in 852 he bestowed his blessing and the title of *Città Leonina*, or Leonine city (now the *Borgo di S. Pietro*). (Anastasius, *V. Leon. IV.*) In the period between 1081 and 1084 Rome was thrice fruitlessly besieged by the emperor Henry IV., who, however, by means of corruption at last succeeded in gaining possession of it; but the ruins of the Septizonium, defended by the nephew of Pope Gregory VII., resisted all the attacks of Henry's forces. Gregory shut himself up in the castle of S. Angelo, and invoked the assistance of his vassal, Robert Guiscard. Henry fled at the approach of the warlike Norman; but Rome suffered more at the hands of its friends than it had ever before done from the assaults of its enemies. A tumult was excited by the imperial adherents, and the Saracens in Robert's army, who despised both parties, seized the opportunity for violence and plunder. The city was fired; a great part of the buildings on the Campus Martius, as well as the spacious district from the Lateran to the Colosseum, was consumed, and the latter portion has never since been restored. (Malaterra, iii. c. 37; Donatus, iv. 8.)

But Rome has suffered more injury from her own citizens than from the hands of foreigners; and its ruin must be chiefly imputed to the civil dissensions of the Romans, and to the use which they made of the ancient monuments to serve their own selfish and mercenary purposes. The factions of the Guelphs and Ghibelines, of the Colonna and Ursini, which began in the tenth century and lasted several hundred years, must have been very destructive to the city. In these sanguinary quarrels the ancient edifices were converted into castles; and the multitude of the latter may be estimated from the fact that the senator Brancaleone during his government (1252—1258) caused 140 towers, or fortresses, the strongholds of the nobility, to be demolished in Rome and its neighbourhood; yet subsequently, under Martin V., we still hear of forty-four existing in one quarter of the city alone. (Matthew Paris, *Hist. Maj.* p. 741, seq.) Some of these were erected on the most celebrated buildings, as the triumphal monuments of Caesar, Titus, and the Antonines. (Montfaucon, *Diar. Ital.* p. 186; Anonymus, *ib.* p. 285.) But still more destructive were the ravages committed on the ancient buildings during times of peace. The beautiful sculptures and architectural members, which could no longer be imitated, were seized upon and appropriated to the adornment of new structures. We have seen that this barbarous kind of spoliation was exercised as early as the reign of Constantine, who applied the sculptures of some monument of Trajan's to adorn his own triumphal arch. In after ages Charlemagne carried off the columns of Rome to decorate his palace at Aix-la-Chapelle (Sigebert, *Chron.* in Bouquet, *Historiens de France,* v. p. 378); and several centuries later Petrarch laments that his friend and patron, Robert, king of Sicily, was following the same pernicious example. ("Itaque nunc, heu dolor! heu scelus indignum! de vestris marmoreis columnis, de liminibus templorum (ad quae nuper ex orbe toto concursus devotissimus fiebat), de imaginibus sepulcrorum sub quibus patrum vestrorum venerabilis cinis erat, ut reliquas sileam, desidiosa Napolis adornatur," Petrar. *Opp.* p. 536, seq.) It would be endless to recount the depredations committed by the popes and nobles in order to build their churches and palaces. The abbé Barthélemi (*Mém. de l'Acad. des Inscr.* xxviii. p. 585) mentions that he had seen at Rome a manuscript letter relating to a treaty between the chiefs of the factions which desolated Rome in the 14th century, in which, among other articles, it is agreed that the Colosseum shall be *common* to all parties, who shall be at liberty to take stones from it. (De Sade; *Vie de Pétrarque,* i. 328, note.) Sixtus V. employed the stones of the Septizonium in building St. Peter's. (Greg. Leti, *Vita di Sisto V.* iii. p. 50.) The nephews of Paul III. were the principal destroyers of the Colosseum, in order to build the Farnese palace (Muratori, *Ann. d' Italia,* xiv. p. 371); and a similar reproach was proverbially applied to those of Urban VIII. ("Quod non fecerunt Barbari, fecere Barberini," Gibbon, viii. p. 284, note.) But even a worse species of desecration than this was the destruction of the most beautiful marble columns, by converting them into lime. Poggio complains (A. D. 1430) that the temple of Concord, which was almost perfect when he first came to Rome, had almost disappeared in this manner. ("Capitolio contigua forum versus superest porticus aedis Concordiae, quam cum primum ad urbem accessi, vidi fere integram, opere marmoreo admodum specioso; Romani postmodum, ad calcem, aedem totam et porticûs partem, disjectis columnis, sunt demoliti," *de Var. Fort.* p. 12.) And the same practice

is reprobated in the verses of Aeneas Sylvius, afterwards Pope Pius II.:—

"Sed tuos hic populus, muris defossa vetustis,
Calcis in obsequium marmora dura coquit.
Impia tercentum si sic gens egerit annos
Nullum hic indicium nobilitatis erit."
(In Mabillon, *Mus. Ital.* i. 97.)

The melancholy progress of the desolation of Rome might be roughly traced from some imperfect memorials. The account of the writer called the Anonymus Einsiedlensis, who visited Rome early in the 9th century, which has been published by Mabillon (*Anal.* iv. p. 502), and by Hänel (*Archiv. f. Philol. u. Pädag.* i. p. 115), exhibits a much more copious list of monuments than that of another anonymous writer, who compiled a book *De Mirabilibus Romae,* in the 12th or 13th century. (Montfaucon, *Diar. Ital.* p. 283, seq.; Nibby, *Effem. Lett. di Roma,* 1820, Fasc. i.—iv.) Several passages in the works of Petrarch exhibit the neglected and desolate state of Rome in the 14th century,—the consequence of the removal of the holy see to Avignon. Thus, in a letter to Urban V., he says: "Jacent domus, labant maenia, templa ruunt, sacra pereunt, calcantur leges." And a little after: "Lateranum humi jacet et Ecclesiarum mater omnium tecto carens ventis patet ac pluviis," &c. (Cf. lib. ix. ep. 1.) Yet the remains of ancient Roman splendour were still considerable enough to excite the wonder and admiration of Manuel Chrysoloras at the commencement of the 15th century, as may be seen in his epistle to the emperor John Palaeologus. (subjoined to Codinus, *de Antiq. C. P.* p. 107, seq.) Much destruction must have been perpetrated from this period to the time, and even during the life, of Poggio. But the progress of desolation seems to have been arrested subsequently to that writer, whose catalogue of the ruins does not exhibit a great many more remains than may yet be seen. Care is now taken to arrest as far as possible even the inevitable influence of time; and the antiquarian has at present nothing to regret except that more active means are not applied to the disinterment of the ancient city. The funds devoted to the re-erection of a magnificent basilica far without the walls, and on so unwholesome a site that the very monks are forced to desert it during the heats of summer, might, in the eye at least of transmontane taste, have been more worthily devoted to such an object.

VII. POPULATION OF ROME.

Before we close this part of the subject it will be expected that we should say something respecting the probable amount of the population of Rome. The inquiry is unfortunately involved in much obscurity, and the vagueness of the *data* upon which any calculation can be founded is such that it is impossible to arrive at any wholly satisfactory conclusion. The latitude hence allowed may be judged from the fact that the estimates of some of the best modern scholars are about four times as great as those of others; and whilst Dureau de la Malle, in his *Economie politique des Romains* (i. p. 340, seq.), sets down the population at 562,000 souls, Höck, in his *Römische Geschichte* (vol. i. pt. ii. p. 383, seq.), estimates it at 2,265,000; nay Lipsius, in his work *De Magnitudine Romana* (iii. 3), even carried it up to the astounding number of 8,000,000. But this is an absurd exaggeration; whilst, on the other hand, the estimate of Dureau de la Malle is undoubtedly much too low.

The only secure *data* which we possess on the subject are the records of the number of citizens who received the *congiaria* or imperial largesses, for it is only during the imperial times that we can profess to make any calculation. We learn from the *Monumentum Ancyranum* that Augustus, in his 12th consulate, distributed a pecuniary gift to 320,000 of the *plebs urbana*. (" Consul XII. trecentis et viginti millibus plebei urbanae sexagenos denarios viritim dedi," tab. iii.) The recipients of this bounty were all males, and probably formed the whole free male population of Rome, with the exception of the senators, knights, and aliens. Women and boys of a tender age did not participate in these distributions. It had been customary for the latter to be admitted to participation after the age of ten; but Augustus appears to have extended his liberality to still younger children. (" Ne minores quidem pueros praeteriit, quamvis nonnisi ab undecimo aetatis anno accipere consuessent," Suet. *Aug.* 41.) The distributions of corn seem to have been regulated on stricter principles, as these were regular, not extraordinary like the largesses. From these the children were probably excluded, and there was, perhaps, a stricter inquiry made into the titles of the recipients. Thus we learn from the *Mon. Ancyranum* that those who received corn in the 13th consulate of Augustus amounted to rather more than 200,000. (Cf. Dion Cass. lv. 10.) From the same document it appears that three largesses made by Augustus, of 400 sesterces per man, were never distributed to fewer than 250,000 persons. (" Quae mea congiaria pervenerunt ad hominum millia nunquam minus quinquaginta et ducenta," *Ib.*, where Höck, *Röm. Gesch.* i. pt. ii. p. 388, by erroneously reading *sestertium* instead of *hominum*, has increased the number of recipients to 625,000.) From a passage in Spartian's life of Septimius Severus (c. 23) it would seem that the number entitled to receive the distributions of corn had increased. That author says that Severus left at his death wheat enough to last for seven years, if distributed according to the regular canon or measure of 75,000 *modii* daily. Now, if we calculate this distribution according to the system of Augustus, of five modii per man monthly, and reckon thirty days to the month, then this would leave the number of recipients at 450,000 (75,000 × 30 = 2,250,000 ÷ 5 = 450,000). According to these statements we can hardly place the average of the male plebeian population of Rome during the first centuries of the Empire at less than 350,000; and at least twice as much again must be added for the females and boys, thus giving a total of 1,050,000. There are no very accurate *data* for arriving at the numbers of the senators and knights. Bunsen (*Beschr.* i. p. 184), without stating the grounds of his calculation, sets them down, including their families, at 10,000. But this is evidently much too low an estimate. We learn from Dionysius Halicarnassensis (vi. 13) that in the annual procession of the knights to the temple of Castor they sometimes mustered to the number of 5000. But this must have been very far from their whole number. A great many must have been absent from sickness, old age, and other causes; and a far greater number must have been in the provinces and in foreign countries, serving with the armies, or employed as *publicani*, and in other public capacities. Yet their families would probably, for the most part,

reside at Rome. We see from the complaints of Horace how the equestrian dignity was prostituted in the imperial times to *liberti* and aliens, provided they were rich enough for it. (*Epod.* iv. in Menam; cf. Juv. i. 28.) We should, perhaps, therefore be below the mark in fixing the number of knights and senators at 15,000. If we allow a wife and one child only to each, this would give the number of individuals composing the senatorial and equestrian families at 45,000, which is a small proportion to 1,050,000 freemen of the lower class. It may be objected that marriage was very much out of fashion with the higher classes at Rome during the time of Augustus; but the omission was supplied in another manner, and the number of kept women and illegitimate children, who would count as population just as well as the legitimate ones, must have been considerable. In this calculation it is important not to underrate the numbers of the higher classes, since they are very important factors in estimating the slave population, of which they were the chief maintainers. The preceding sums, then, would give a total of 1,095,000 free inhabitants of Rome, of all classes. To these are to be added the aliens residing at Rome, the soldiers, and the slaves. The first of these classes must have been very numerous. There must have been a great many provincial persons settled at Rome, for purposes of business or pleasure, who did not possess the franchise, a great many Greeks, as tutors, physicians, artists, &c., besides vast numbers of other foreigners from all parts of the world. The Jews alone must have formed a considerable population. So large, indeed, was the number of aliens at Rome, that in times of scarcity we sometimes read of their being banished. Thus Augustus on one occasion expelled all foreigners except tutors and physicians. (Suet. *Aug.* 42.) According to Seneca, the greater part of the inhabitants were aliens. " Nullum non hominum genus concurrit in urbem et virtutibus et vitiis magna praemia ponentem. Unde domo quisque sit, quaere; videbis majorem partem esse, quae relictis sedibus suis venerit in maximam quidem et pulcherrimam urbem, non tamen suam." (*Cons. ad Helv.* c. 6.) In this there is no doubt some exaggeration; yet we find the same complaints reiterated by Juvenal:—

" Jam pridem Syrus in Tiberim defluxit Orontes."

" Hic alta Sicyone, ast hic Amydone relicta,
　Hic Andro, ille Samo, hic Trallibus aut Alabandis,
　Esquilias dictumque petunt a Vimine collem,
　Viscera magnarum domuum, dominique futuri '　　　　　　(iii. 62, seq.).

It would perhaps, then, be but a modest estimate to reckon the aliens and foreigners resident at Rome, together with their wives and families, at 100,000. The soldiers and the *vigiles*, or police, we can hardly estimate at less than 25,000; and as many of these men must have been married, we may reckon them, with their families, at 50,000. Hence 100,000 aliens and 50,000 military, &c., added to the foregoing sum of 1,095,000, makes 1,245,000 for the total miscellaneous free population of Rome.

There are great difficulties in the way of estimating the slave population, from the total absence of any accurate data. We can only infer generally that it must have been exceedingly numerous—a fact that is evident from many passages of the ancient authors

The number of slaves kept as domestic servants must have been exceedingly large. Horace mentions (*Sat.* i. 3. 12) that the singer Tigellius had sometimes as many as 200 slaves; but when he was taken with a sudden fit of economy, he reduced them to the very modest number of 10. No doubt, however, he was a first-rate vocalist, and, like his brethren in modern times, a man of fortune. Tillius the praetor, who was a stingy churl, when he went to Tibur, had 5 slaves at his heels to carry his cooking utensils and wine. (*Ib.* i. 6. 107.) Horace himself, who of course was not so rich a man as Tigellius, when he sat down to his frugal supper of cakes and vegetables, was waited upon by 3 slaves ; and we may presume that these did not compose his entire household. (*Ib.* v. 115.) In the reign of Nero, 400 slaves were maintained in the palace of Pedanius Secundus, who were all put to death, women and children included, because one of them had murdered his master. (Tac. *Ann.* xiv. 42, seq.) The slaves no longer consisted of those born and bred on the estates of their masters, but were imported in multitudes from all the various nations under the wide-spread dominion of the Romans. ("Postquam vero nationes in familiis habemus, quibus diversi ritus, externa sacra, aut nulla sunt, colluviem istam non nisi metu coercueris." (*Ib.* c. 44.) The case of Pedanius, however, was no doubt an extraordinary one. It cannot be imagined that the plebs urbana, who received the public rations, were capable of maintaining slaves; nor probably are many to be assigned to the aliens. But if we place the patrician and equestrian families at 15,000, and allow the moderate average number of 30 slaves to each family, this would give a total number of 450,000. Some also must be allowed to the richer part of the *plebs*—to persons who, like Horace, were not patrician nor equestrian, yet could afford to keep a few slaves ; as well as to the aliens resident at Rome, so that we can hardly compute the number of domestic slaves at less than 500,000. To these must be added the public slaves at the disposal of the various municipal officers, also those employed in handicraft trades and manufactures, as journeymen carpenters, builders, masons, bakers, and the like. It would not perhaps be too much to estimate these at 300,000, thus making the total slave population of Rome 800,000. This sum, added to that of the free inhabitants, would give a total of 2,045,000.

The *Notitia* and *Curiosum* state the number of *insulae* at Rome at 46,602, and the number of *domus* at 1790, besides *balnea*, *lupanaria*, military and police stations, &c. If we had any means of ascertaining the average number of inhabitants in each *insula*, it would afford a valuable method of checking the preceding computation. But here again we are unfortunately reduced to uncertainty and conjecture. We may, however, pretty surely infer that each *insula* contained a large number of inmates. In the time of Augustus the yearly rent of the *coenacula* of an *insula* ordinarily produced 40,000 sesterces, or between 300*l.* and 400*l.* sterling. (*Dig.* 19. tit. 2. s. 30, ap. Gibbon, ch. 31, note 70.) Petronius (c. 95, 97), and Juvenal (*Sat.* iii. passim) describe the crowded state of these lodgings. If we take them at an average of four stories, each accommodating 12 or 13 persons, this would give say 50 persons in each insula; and even then the inmates, men, women and boys, would be paying an average yearly rent of about 7*l.* per head. The inmates of each *domus* can hardly be set down at less, since the

family, with tutors and other hangers on, may perhaps be fairly estimated at 10, and the slaves in each *domus* at 40. We learn from Valerius Maximus (iv. 4. § 8), that sixteen men of the celebrated Gens Aelia lived in one small house with their families; but this seems to have been an exceptional case even in the early times, and cannot be adopted as a guide under the Empire, Now, taking the *insulae* actually inhabited at 40,000 — since some must have been to let, or under repair — and the inhabited *domus* at 1500 = 41,500, and the number of inmates in each at 50, we should have a total population of 2,075,000, a sum not greatly at variance with the amount obtained by the previous method. But the reader will have seen on what data the calculation proceeds, and must draw his own conclusions accordingly. (Cf. Bunsen, *Beschreibung der Stadt Rom*, i. p. 183, seq.; Dureau de la Malle, *Economie politique des Romains* i. p. 340. seq.; Mommsen, *Die Römischen Tribus*, p. 187, seq.; Höck, *Römische Geschichte*, i. pt. ii. p. 383, seq.; Zumpt, *Ueber den Stand der Bevölkerung im Alterthum*, Berlin, 1841; Gibbon, *Decline and Fall*, vol. iv. p. 87, seq., with the note of Smith.)

PART II. TOPOGRAPHY.

Having thus given an account of the rise and progress, the decline and fall of the Roman city, we shall now proceed to describe its topography. In treating this part of the subject we shall follow those divisions which are marked out either by their political importance or by their natural features rather than be guided by the arbitrary bounds laid down in the Regions of Augustus. The latter, however convenient for the municipal purposes which they were intended to serve, would be but ill calculated to group the various objects in that order in which they are most calculated to arrest the attention of the modern reader, and to fix them in his memory. We shall therefore, after describing the walls of Servius Tullius and those of Aurelian, proceed to the Capitol, one of the most striking objects of ancient Rome, and then to the Forum and its environs, the remaining hills and their valleys, with the various objects of interest which they present.

I. WALLS AND GATES OF SERVIUS TULLIUS.

At the commencement of the Roman Empire the walls of Servius Tullius could no longer be traced. Instead of dreading the assaults of the surrounding petty nations of Italy, Rome had now extended her frontiers to the Euphrates and the Atlantic; her ancient bulwarks were become entirely useless, and the increase of her population had occasioned the building of houses close to and even over their remains; so that in the time of Dionysius of Halicarnassus, who came to Rome in the reign of Augustus, it was difficult to discover their course (iv. 13). To attempt now to trace their exact outline would therefore be a hopeless task. The remains of the *agger* of Servius are still, however, partly visible, and the situation of a few of the ancient gates is known with certainty, whilst that of others may be fixed with at least some approach to accuracy from notices of them contained in ancient authors. It is from these materials that we must endeavour to reconstruct the line of the Servian walls, by first determining the probable sites of the gates, and by then drawing the wall between them, according to indications offered by the nature of the ground.

We learn from Cicero that Servius, like Romulus, was guided in the construction of his wall by the outline of the hills: " Cujus (urbis) is est tractatus ductusque muri quum Romuli tum etiam reliquorum regum sapientia definitus ex omni parte arduis praeruptisque montibus, ut unus aditus, qui esset inter Esquilinum Quirinalemque montem, maximo aggere objecto fossa cingeretur vastissima ; atque ut ita munita arx circumjectu arduo et quasi circumciso saxo niteretur, ut etiam in illa tempestate horribili Gallici adventus incolumis atque intacta permanserit." (De Rep. ii. 6.) Becker (de Muris, p. 64, Handb. p. 129) asserts that Cicero here plainly says that Servius erected walls only where there were no hills, or across the valleys, and concludes that the greater part of the defences of the city consisted of the natural ones offered by the hills alone. Becker, however, appears to have formed no very clear ideas upon the subject; for notwithstanding what is here said, we find him a few pages further on, conducting the line of wall not only along the height of the Quirinal, but even over the summit of the Capitoline hill itself ! (Handb. pp. 131, 136, de Muris, pp. 65, 70.) Neither his first, or theoretical, nor his second, or practical, view, is correct. The former is in direct contradiction to his authority; for Cicero says that the other kings did like Romulus; and he, as we have seen, and as Becker himself has shown, walled in his city all round. Cicero says, as plainly as he can speak, that there was a wall, and that it was defined along its whole extent (" definitus ex omni parte ") by the line of the hills. If it did not run along their summit, we cannot explain Pliny's assertion (iii. 9) that the agger equalled the height of the walls (" Namque eum (aggerem) muris aequavit qua maxime patebat (urbs) aditu plano : caetero munita erat praecelsis muris, aut abruptis montibus," &c.), since it would be a no great extolling of its height to say that it was raised to the level of a wall in the valley. Cicero, however, notices two exceptions to the continuous line, and the fact of his pointing these out proves the continuity of the wall in the remainder of the circuit. The first exception is the agger just mentioned, upon the top of which, however, according to Dionysius (ix. 68), there seems also to have been a sort of wall, though probably not of so great a height as the rest, at least he uses the comparative when speaking of it : τεῖχος ἀνεγείρας ὑψηλότερον (iv. 54). The second exception was the Arx, or Capitoline hill, which, being on its western side much more abrupt and precipitous than the other hills, was considered as sufficiently defended by nature, with a little assistance from art in escarping its sides. That there was no wall at this spot is also proved, as Niebuhr remarks (Hist. vol. i. p. 396) by the account of the Gauls scaling the height. (Liv. v. 47; comp. Bunbury, Class. Mus. vol. iii. p. 347.) The Capitoline, therefore, must have been the spot to which Dionysius alluded, when he said that Rome was partly defended by its hills, and partly by the Tiber (ix. 68); as well as Pliny in the passage just cited, where we must not infer from the plural (montibus) that he meant more than one hill. This is merely, as in Dionysius also, a general mode of expression; and we have before observed that Pliny's own account shows that the wall crowned the hills. Lastly, had there been no wall upon them, it is difficult to

see how there could have been gates; yet we find Becker himself placing gates at spots where, according to his theoretical view, there could have been no wall. Niebuhr (l. c.), who, like Becker, does not confine the escarpment to the Capitol, but thinks that the greater part of the city was fortified solely by the steepness of its hills, places towers, walls, and gates just at the different ascents; but this view, improbable in itself, and unsupported by any authority, cannot be maintained against the express testimony of Cicero. There seems, however, to have been an interior fortification on the E. side of the Capitoline, protecting the ascent by the clivus, as we shall see in the sequel. It was probably intended to secure the citadel, in case an enemy succeeded in forcing the external walls. We have seen before that the hill was fortified by Romulus; but whether these ancient fortifications, as well as those on the Palatine, were retained by Servius, it is impossible to say.

We may assume then that the wall of Servius, or his predecessor,—which seems to have been built of stone (" muro lapideo," Liv. i. 15),—surrounded the whole city, with the exception of the Capitoline hill and a small part defended by the Tiber,—thus justifying the noble lines of Virgil (Georg. ii. 533.) :—

" rerum facta est pulcerrima Roma
Septemque una sibi muro circumdedit arces."

Our next task will be to determine the outline of this wall by means of the site of the different gates ; though, of course, where the outline of the hills is well defined this alone will be a guide. The situation of two of the gates may be considered certain,— that of the PORTA COLLINA, at the N. extremity of the agger, and that of the Esquiline at its southern end. Taking, therefore, the former as a starting-point, and proceeding continually to the left, we shall make the circuit of the whole city, till we again arrive at the Porta Collina.

This, the most northerly of all the gates, lay near the point where the Via Salaria branches off from the Via Nomentana. From this spot the first gate to the W. was probably the Porta Salutaris, so named, apparently, from its being on that division of the Quirinal which in the time of Numa and in the sacred books of the Argives was called Collis Salutaris, from an ancient sacellum of Salus which stood upon it (Varr. L. L. v. § 51). When Paulus Diaconus tells us (p. 327, Müll.) that it was named after the temple of Salus, he seems to be alluding to the later and more famous temple dedicated by C. Junius Bubulcus in B. C. 303, which we shall have occasion to describe in the sequel : but it is probable that it obtained its name, as we have said, at a much earlier period. As the new temple probably stood at or near the site of the ancient one, and as the Notitia in describing the 6th Regio, or Alta Semita, takes this temple for a starting point, and, proceeding always in a circuit to the left, arrives at last at the baths of Diocletian, it may be assumed that this gate was the first important object westward of the baths. It seems to have spanned a Clivus Salutis, which Canina (Roma Antica, p. 187) places, with much probability in the Via delle Quattro Fontane, where it ascends from the Piazza Barberina. (Cf. Preller, Regionen, p. 134.)

The next gate to the left seems to have been the PORTA SANQUALIS, so named from the temple of Sancus. (Paul. Diac. p. 345, Müll.) This was the same divinity as Deus Fidius (Fest. p. 241, Müll.), whose sacellum is mentioned by Livy (viii. 20) as situated near the temple of Quirinus. It is also recorded in the fragments of the Argive books as seated on the Collis Mucialis (Varr. *L.L.* v. § 62, Müll.), which hill comes next in order after the Collis Salutaris. We have already mentioned the temple of Quirinus as having been situated near the present church of *S. Andrea* and it may therefore be assumed that the Porta Sanqualis spanned the ascent to it at or near the modern *Via della Dataria.*

Between the Porta Sanqualis and the Capitoline hill there were probably two gates ; at all events there must undoubtedly have been one in the very narrow ravine which in early times separated the Capitoline from the Quirinal, and which afforded the only outlet from the neighbourhood of the forum. This was, perhaps, the PORTA RATUMENA, which we learn from Pliny (viii. 65: "unde postea nomen *est* ") and Plutarch (*Popl.* 13: παρὰ τὴν πύλην, ἣν νῦν Ῥατουμέναν καλοῦσιν) was still existing in their time. Becker, indeed, disputes the inference of its existence from Pliny's words, and disbelieves the assertion of Plutarch. But there is nothing at all incredible in the fact, and therefore no reason why we should disbelieve it. We know, from the example of London and other cities, that a gate, and especially the name of a gate marking its former site, may remain for ages after the wall in which it stood has been removed. Even the local tradition of its name would have sufficed to mark its site ; but it seems highly probable, from the nature of the ground where it stood, that the gate itself had been preserved. The road through so narrow a gorge could never have been disturbed for building or other purposes ; and it is probable that the gate remained standing till the ravine was enlarged by cutting away the Quirinal in order to make room for Trajan's forum. We learn from the passages just cited, as well as from Festus (p. 274), that the gate derived its name from a charioteer, who, returning victorious from the Circensian games at Veii, was thrown out of his chariot and killed at this spot, whilst the affrighted horses, thus freed from all control, dashed up the Capitoline hill, and, as the legend runs, did not finish their mad career till they had thrice made the circuit of the temple of Jupiter Capitolinus. (Plin. viii. 65.) So remarkable an omen would have been quite a sufficient ground in those days for changing the name of the gate. But it matters little what faith we may be disposed to place in the legend ; for

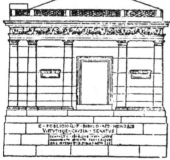

TOMB OF CAIUS BIBULUS.

even if it was an invention, it must have been framed with that regard to local circumstances which would have lent it probability, and no other gate can be pointed out which would have so well suited the tenor of the story. Its existence at this spot is further confirmed by the tomb of Bibulus, one of the few remaining monuments of the Republic, which stands in the *Macel dei Corvi,* and by the discovery of the remains of another sepulchral monument a little farther on, in the *Via della Pedacchia.* It is well known that, with a few rare exceptions, no interments were allowed within the walls of Rome ; the tomb of Bibulus must therefore have been a little without the gate, and its front corresponds to the direction of a road that would have led from the forum into the Campus Martius (Canina, *Roma Antica,* p. 218). Bunsen, however, is of opinion (*Beschr.* vol. iii. p. 35) that it lay within the walls, and infers from the inscription, which states that the ground was presented as a burial-place to Bibulus and his descendants by the Senate and people " honoris virtutisque caussa," that he was one of those rare exceptions mentioned by Cicero (*Leg.* ii. 23) of persons who obtained the privilege of being buried within the city. A more unfortunate conjecture was hardly ever hazarded. Becker has justly pointed out that the words of the inscription merely mean that the ground was presented to Bibulus, without at all implying that it was within the walls ; and an attentive consideration of the passage in Cicero will show that it could not possibly have been so. Ever since the passing of the law of the XII. Tables against interment within the walls, Cicero could find only one example in which it had been set aside, namely, in honour of C. Fabricius. Now if Bibulus had lived in the period between the composition of the *De Legibus* and the final abolishment of the Republic, we could not have failed to hear of an individual who had achieved so extraordinary a mark of distinction ; and if, on the other hand, he lived before that work was written, — of which there can scarcely be a doubt, — then Cicero would certainly have mentioned him.

Besides the gates already enumerated between the spot from which we started and the Capitoline hill, there seems also to have been another for which we can find no more convenient site than the SW. side of the Quirinal, between the Porta Ratumena and Porta Sanqualis, unless indeed we adopt the not improbable conjecture of Preller (Schneidewin's *Philologus,* p. 84), that the Ratumena was one of the gates of the fortification on the Clivus Capitolinus, and that the PORTA FONTINALIS was the gate in the gorge between the Quirinal and the Capitoline. This latter gate is mentioned by Paulus Diaconus (p. 85, Müll.), in connection with a festival called Fontinalia. It is also mentioned by Varro (*LL.* vi. § 22, Müll.) and other writers ; and we learn from Livy (xxxv. 10) that a portico was constructed from it to the altar of Mars, forming a thoroughfare into the Campus Martius. The same historian again mentions the Ara Martis as being in the Campus (xl. 45), but there is nothing to indicate its precise situation. Numa instituted a festival to Mars, as a pledge of union between the Romans and Sabines (Fest. p. 372, Müll.), and it was probably on this occasion that the altar was erected. It is impossible to place any gate and portico leading from it in the short strip of wall on the S. side of the Capitoline, and therefore its site was perhaps that already indicated. The altar must have stood at no great distance from the gate, and could hardly have been so far to the W. as the

Piazza di Venezia, as Urlichs assumes (*Beschr.* vol. v. p. 17), since in that case the portico must have crossed the road leading out of the Porta Ratumena.

A little beyond the last named gate the wall must have joined the Capitoline hill, along which, as we have said, there was no other fortification but the precipitous nature of the ground, rendered here and there still more abrupt by escarpment. At the SW. extremity of the hill the wall must have been resumed, and must undoubtedly have run in a direct line across the short space between the Capitoline hill and the Tiber. Between this spot and the Aventine the wall was discontinued; and this is the part alluded to by Dionysius (*l. c.*) as sufficiently defended by the river. The piece of wall just mentioned must have shut out the Forum Olitorium and Circus Flaminius, since Asconius (*ad Cic. Tog. Cand.* p. 90, Orell.) mentions a temple of Apollo, which was situated between those places, as being outside the PORTA CARMENTALIS. This gate lay just at the foot of the Capitol, and is one of the most certain entrances to the Servian city. It was named after a fane or altar of Carmenta, the mother of Evander, which stood near it. This altar is mentioned by Dionysius (i. 32), and appears to have existed long after his time, since it was seen by A. Gellius (xviii. 7) and by Servius (*ad Virg. Aen.* viii. 337.) The street called Vicus Jugarius ran from the Porta Carmentalis round the base of the Capitoline to the Forum, as we learn from Livy's description (xxvii. 37) of the procession of the virgins to the temple of Juno Regina on the Aventine, when two white heifers were led from the temple of Apollo before mentioned through the Porta Carmentalis and Vicus Jugarius to the forum. The exact site of the gate was probably a little to the NW. of the church of *S. Omobono.*

The principal gates of Rome had commonly more than one thoroughfare. These archways, or passages, were called Fornices and Jani. Cicero's etymology of the latter word shows the meaning attached to it, though the etymology itself is absurd ("Ab eundo nomen est ductum: ex quo transitiones perviae Jani, foresque in liminibus profanarum aedium *januae* nominantur," *Nat. Deor.* ii. 27). We have already said that the right *Janus* of the Porta Carmentalis, on going out of the town, was regarded as ill-omened, and branded with the name of *Porta Scelerata*, from its having been that through which the Fabii passed on their fatal expedition to the Cremera. (Liv. ii. 49.) So Ovid (*Fast* i. 201):—

* Carmentis portae dextro via proxima Jano est:
  Ire per hanc noli, quisquis es, omen habet."

Festus (p. 285, Müll.), Servius (*Aen.* viii. 337,) and Orosius (ii. 5) have completely misunderstood these passages in applying the epithet *scelerata* to the whole gate, as we have before remarked.

In the short piece of wall between the Capitoline hill and the Tiber there must have been at least another gate besides the Carmentalis, namely the PORTA FLUMENTANA. It is mentioned by Cicero (*ad Att.* vii. 3), and its situation near the river may be inferred not only from its name, but also from passages in Livy, which mention it in connection with inundations (xxxv. 9, 21). Plutarch also (*Otho,* 4) records a great inundation which had caused much damage in the corn-market, at that time held in the Porticus Minucia Frumentaria, near the Forum Olitorium (*Not. Reg.* ix.); but the words of Paulus Diaconus are incomprehensible, who says that a part

of the Tiber once actually flowed through this gate ("Flumentana Porta Romae appellata, quod Tiberis partem ea fluxisse affirmant," p. 89, Müll.) The site is further confirmed by a passage in Varro alluding to the populousness of the suburb just outside the gate: "Nam quod extra urbem est aedificium, nihilo magis ideo est villa, quum eorum aedificia qui habitant extra portam Flumentanam, aut in Aemilianis " (*R. R.* iii. 2). This neighbourhood had early become very thickly inhabited, as is evident from the many porticoes, theatres, temples and other buildings, which are mentioned there (see Preller, *Regionen,* p. 156, seq.) But Livy's narrative of the trial of Manlius (vi. 20) is one of the most striking proofs of the situation of the P. Flumentana, though it is a stumbling-block to those who hold that the temple of Jupiter was on the SW. summit of the Capitoline hill. A spot near the place where the Circus Flaminius afterwards stood was at that time used for the assemblies of the Comitia Centuriata, by which Manlius was tried. From this place both the Capitol and the Arx were visible; and Manlius had produced a great effect upon his judges by calling upon them to pronounce their verdict in the sight of those very gods whose temple he had preserved: "Ut Capitolium atque arcem intuentes, ut ad deos immortales versi, de se judicarent." In order to deprive him of this appeal the tribunes adjourned the assembly to a spot just outside the Porta Flumentana, called "lucus Poetelinus," whence the Capitol could not be seen (" unde conspectus in Capitolium non esset "). A glance at any map of Rome will show that this was the only spot in the Campus Martius where the temple, from its being hidden by the SW. summit, which we assume to have been the Arx, was concealed from view. The tribunes would doubtless have been glad to conceal the Arx also, had it been in their power; but an appeal to the Arx alone would have lacked the effect of the *religio* which swayed so much with the superstitious Romans. They were no longer in the presence of those rescued deities in whose sight Manlius had invoked their judgment. There is no occasion therefore to try, with Becker, to alter Livy's text, by reading Frumentaria for Flumentana, or seek to place the scene of the trial at another spot. since the Comitia Centuriata were usually assembled in the Campus.

The ancient topographers, as well as the modern Italians (Nibby, *Mura, &c.* p. 132 ; Canina, *Indicazione Topografica,* pp. 34, 632, ed. 1850), place another gate, the PORTA TRIUMPHALIS. between the Carmentalis and the Flumentana. That there was such a gate is certain, since it is frequently mentioned in classical authors, but unfortunately in such a manner that no decided inference can be drawn respecting its situation. Hence various theories have been advanced on the subject, which have led to warm controversies. The German school of topographers, though not united among themselves, have agreed in departing from the Italian view, chiefly because it appears to them absurd to imagine that there could have been three gates in so short a piece of wall. If, however, as it will be shown to be probable, the Porta Triumphalis was opened only on occasions of state, there really seems to be very little force in this objection. Bunsen and his followers allow that it formed a real entrance into the city, but strangely enough make it lead into the Circus Maximus; whilst Becker, on the other hand, holds that it was no gate at all properly so called, but a mere triumphal arch situated in the Campus Martius. The theory of Bunsen necessarily rests on the assumption of a different line of wall from that laid down in the preceding account; and as another line is also adopted by Niebuhr (*Hist.* i. p. 397, *Ethnogr.* ii. p. 49), it will be necessary to examine this point before proceeding to the question of the gate. Niebuhr and Bunsen are, however, far from coinciding. The line drawn by the former proceeds along the banks of the river; that drawn by the latter runs from the Porta Carmentalis to the N. angle of the Circus Maximus, and, adopting the NW. front of the circus, or what was called the *Oppidum*, as part of the line, proceeds onwards to the Aventine, thus shutting the greater part of the Forum Boarium out of the city. Both these theories, however, agree in so far as they assume an *enceinte continue*, or continued line of wall; and therefore, if this notion can be shown to be false, both fall to the ground. Now it can be proved on the very best evidence that there was no wall in this part of the city, which was defended solely by the Tiber. We have already adduced a passage from Dionysius in confirmation of this statement; and the same author in another passage repeats the same thing in so plain a manner that there can be no reasonable doubt of the fact : ἐδέησεν ἡ πόλις ἁλῶναι κατὰ κράτος ἀτείχιστος οὖσα ἐκ τῶν παρὰ τὸν ποταμὸν μερῶν (v. 23). But Dionysius does not stand alone. We have Livy also as a voucher for the same fact, who, in narrating the enterprise of Porsena against Rome, observes that the citizens regarded some parts of their city as secured by the wall, and other parts by the Tiber: "Alia muris, alia Tiberi objecto videbantur tuta." (ii. 10). The same fact appears, though not in so direct a manner, from the same author's account of the procession of the virgins from the temple of Apollo, outside the Carmental gate, to that of Juno Regina on the Aventine, to which we have before briefly alluded. The route is described as follows : "A porta (Carmentali) Jugario vico in forum venere. Inde vico Tusco Velabroque per Boarium forum in clivum Publicium atque aedem Junonis Reginae perrectum" (xxvii. 37). Now the small space allotted by Bunsen to the Forum Boarium must have been *inside* of the wall, since the temples of Fortune and Mater Matuta, which stood upon it (Liv. xxxiii. 27), were within the Porta Carmentalis (Id. xxv. 7). The procession, then, after passing through that forum, must have gone out of the city at another gate,—Bunsen's Flumentana,—and have entered it again by the Trigemina, before it could reach the Clivus Publicius,— facts which are not mentioned by Livy in his very precise description of the route.

Having thus shown on the best evidence that no wall existed at this point, it would be a mere waste of time to refute arguments intended to show that it possibly might have existed,—such as whether a wall with a gate would keep out an inundation, whether the Fabii went over the Sublician bridge, and others of the like sort, which would have puzzled an ancient haruspex. We will therefore proceed to examine Becker's hypothesis, that the Porta Triumphalis was, in fact, no gate at all, but merely an arch in the Campus Martius, a theory which is also adopted, though with some little variation, by Preller (*Regionen*, p. 162, and Anhang, p. 239).

Becker places this arch at the spot where the Campus Martius joins the Regio called Circus Flaminius, and takes it to be the same that was rebuilt by Domitian (of course he must mean *rebuilt*, though it is not very clearly expressed. *De Muris*, p. 92, *Handb.* p. 153). His conjecture is founded on the following lines in a poem of Martial's (viii. 65) in which he describes the erection of this arch and of some other buildings near it :—

" Haec est digna tuis, Germanice, porta triumphis,
   Hos aditus urbem Martis habere decet."

Becker, however, is totally unable to prove that this arch and the temple of Fortuna Redux near it were even in the Campus Martius at all. Thus he says (*Handb.* p. 642): " It is not indeed expressly said that the Ara of Fortuna Redux was in the Campus Martius; but it *becomes probable* from the circumstance that Domitian built here. and, as we have *conjectured* at p. 153, close to the Porta Triumphalis, a temple to the same goddess." The argument then proceeds as follows: " We *know* from Martial that Domitian built a temple to Fortuna Redux where her altar formerly stood, and also a triumphal arch near it. We do *not know* that this altar was in the Campus Martius; but it is *probable* that it was, because Domitian built this temple close to it, and also close to the arch, which, as *I conjectured*, was the Porta Triumphalis !"

There is, however. another passage of Martial, either overlooked or ignored by Becker, which tends very strongly to show that this arch of Domitian's really was in the Campus Martius, but at quite a different spot from that so conveniently fixed upon by him. It is the following (x. 6): —

" Felices quibus urna dedit spectare coruscum
   Solibus Arctois aideribusque ducem.
Quando erit ille dies quo Campus et arbor et
   omnis
Lucebit Latia culta fenestra nuru ?
Quando moras dulces, longusque a Caesare
   pulvis,
Totaque Flaminia Roma videnda via ?"

There can be no doubt that these lines refer to the same triumphal entry of Domitian's as those quoted by Becker; and they pretty plainly show, as Canina, without any view to the present question, justly observes (*Indicazione, &c.* p. 437), that the arch and other monuments stood on the Via Flaminia, and therefore at a very considerable distance from the spot assigned to them by Becker.

This arch having broken down, Preller comes to the rescue, and places the Porta Triumphalis near the Villa Publica and temple of Bellona, close to the Via Lata. For this site he adduces several plausible arguments : near the temple of Bellona was the piece of ager hostilis, where the Fetiales went through the formalities of declaring war; as well as the Columna Bellica, whence a lance was thrown when the army was going to take the field ; also a Senaculum " citra aedem Bellonae," in which audience was given to foreign ambassadors whom the senate did not choose to admit into the city. The Villa Publica also served for the reception of the latter, and probably also of Roman generals before their triumph, and of all who, being cum imperio, could not cross the pomoerium, and therefore in the ordinary course took up their abode there. After this ceased to exist, the Diribitorium was used in its stead, in which Claudius passed some nights, and in which probably Vespasian and Titus slept before their triumph. This spot therefore had the significance of a kind of out-post of the city.

As this theory is evidently framed with a view to the triumph of Vespasian and Titus, and as the account of that triumph is also one of the main arguments adduced by Becker for his Porta Triumphalis, it will be necessary to examine it. The narrative of Josephus runs as follows (*Bell. Jud.* vii. 5. § 4, p. 1305, Huds.); " The emperor and his son Titus spent the night preceding their triumph in a public building in the Campus Martius, near the temple of Isis, where the army was assembled and marshalled. At break of day the emperors came forth and proceeded to the Porticus Octaviae (near the theatre of Marcellus), where, according to ancient custom, the senate were assembled to meet them. Vespasian, after offering the usual prayer, and delivering a short address, dismissed the troops to their breakfast, whilst he himself *returned* to the gate named after the triumphal processions that used to pass through it. Here the emperor break-fasted, and, having put on the triumphal dress, and sacrificed to the gods whose shrines were at the gate, caused the pageant to proceed through the circi." Becker concludes from this narrative that the Porta Triumphalis must have been outside the town, in the Campus Martius, and near the public building where the emperor had slept. A further proof is, he contends, that the procession went through the *circi*, which must mean the Circus Flaminius and Circus Maximus; and that this was so may be shown from Plutarch (*Aem. Paull.* 32), who says that Paullus went through the Circi, and in another passage expressly relates (*Lucull.* 37) that Lucullus adorned the Circus Flaminius with the arms, &c. which he had taken, which it would be absurd to suppose he would have done unless the procession passed through that circus. Then comes the supposition we have already noticed, that the procession of Vespasian passed through the arch re-erected by his younger son Domitian some years after his father's death. After passing through the Circus Flaminius, Becker thinks that the pro-cession went through the P. Carmentalis, and by the Vicus Jugarius to the forum, along the latter *sub Veteribus*, and finally through the Vicus Tuscus, the Velabrum, and Forum Boarium, into the Circus Maximus. Having conducted the emperors thus far, Becker takes leave of them, and we remain com-pletely in the dark as to the manner in which they got out of the circus and found their way back again to the forum and Capitol, the usual destina-tion of triumphant generals.

Admitting that Becker has here given a true inter-pretation of the text of Josephus as it stands, we shall proceed to examine the conclusions that have been drawn from it, beginning with those of Preller. That writer has very properly assumed (*Regionen*, p. 240) that if the triumphal arch did not actually cross the pomoerium it led at all events into a terri-tory subject to the jurisdiction of the city, into which it was unlawful for a general cum imperio to pass without the permission of the senate. Had not this been so the whole business would have been a mere vain and idle ceremony. The account of Vespasian's tri-umph seems indeed a little repugnant to this view, since he met the senate in the Porticus Octaviae, which on this supposition was considerably beyond the boundary; and which he had therefore crossed before he had obtained authority to do so. Still more re-pugnant is Dion's account of the triumph of Tiberius,

who, we are told, assembled the senate at the same place precisely on the ground that it was outside of the pomoerium, and that consequently he did .not violate their privileges by assembling them there (ἔς τε τὸ 'Οκταούειον τὴν βουλὴν ἤθροισε διὰ τὸ ἔξω τοῦ πωμηρίου αὐτὸ εἶναι, lv. 8). But as these instances occurred in the imperial times, when it may be said with Becker (*Handb.* p. 151, note) that the ceremony no longer had any meaning, we will go back for an example to the early ages of the Republic. First, however, we must demand the acknowledgment that the triumphal gate passed by Vespasian was the same, or at least stood on the same spot, as that which had been in use from time immemorial. We cannot allow it to be shifted about like a castle on a chessboard, to suit the convenience of commentators; and we make this demand on the authority of Josephus himself in the very passage under discussion, who tells us that it took its name from the circumstance that the triumphal processions had *always* passed through it (ἀπὸ τοῦ πέμπεσθαι δι' αὐτῆς ἀεὶ τοὺς θριάμβους τῆς προσηγορίας ἀπ' αὐτῶν τετυχυῖαν). Now Livy, in his account of the triumph of the consuls Valerius and Horatius, relates that they assembled the senate in the Campus Martius to solicit that honour; but when the senators complained that they were overawed by the presence of the military, the consuls called the senate away into the Prata Flaminia, to the spot occupied in the time of the historian by the temple of Apollo. (" Consules 'ex composito eodem biduo ad urbem accessere, sena-tumque in Martium Campum *evocavere*. Ubi quum de rebus a se gestis agerent, questi primores Patrum, senatum inter milites dedita opera terroris causa haberi. Itaque inde Consules, ne criminationi esset locum, in prata Flaminia, ubi nunc aedes Apollinis (jam tum Apollinare appellabant) *avocavere* se-natum," iii. 63.) This temple was situated close to the Porticus Octaviae (Becker, *Handb.* p. 605), and therefore considerably nearer the city than the spot indicated either by Becker or Preller. The consuls therefore must have already passed beyond the Porta Triumphalis before they began to solicit the senate for leave to do so!

Becker, however, has been more careful, and has not extended the jurisdiction of the city beyond the walls of Servius, at this part of the Campus, before the time of the emperor Claudius. But what re-sults from his view? That the whole affair of the Porta Triumphalis was mere farce, — that it led nowhere, — that the triumphant general, when he had passed through it by permission of the senate, was as much outside the city boundary as he was before. But that it afforded a real entrance into the town clearly appears from the passage in Cicero's oration against Piso (c. 23): "Cum ego Caelimon-tana porta introisse dixissem, sponsione me, ni Esquilina introisset, homo promtissimus lacessivit. Quasi vero id aut ego scire debuerim, aut vestrum quispiam audierit, aut ad rem pertineat qua tu porta introieris, modo ne triumphali; quae porta Macedonicis semper proconsulibus ante te patuit." The Porta Triumphalis being here put on a level with the Caelimontana and Esquilina, the natural conclu-sion is that, like them, it afforded an actual, though not customary, entrance within the walls. We further learn from the preceding passage that this same Porta Triumphalis had been open to every proconsul of Macedonia before Piso, including of course L. Aemi-lius Paullus, who triumphed over Perseus B. C. 167

(Liv. xlv. 39), thus establishing the identity of the gate to at least that period.

But to return to Becker's explanation of the passage of Josephus. Admitting Plutarch's account of the triumphs of Paullus and Lucullus, namely, that they passed through the Circus Flaminius, yet what does this prove? how is it connected with the Porta Triumphalis? Those generals may have marshalled their processions in the Campus and passed through the Circus Flaminius in their way to the Porta Triumphalis. The procession would have been equally visible in the Circus as in the streets of Rome, just as the Lord Mayor's show may, or might, be seen at Westminster as well as in the city. It is possible indeed that in the case of Vespasian there was no procession till he arrived at the gate; but it does not necessarily follow that the same line was always precisely observed. In truth we may perceive a difference between the expressions of Josephus and those of Plutarch. The former says that Vespasian went διὰ τῶν Sedτρων; whilst Plutarch says, of Paullus, that the people assembled ἐν τοῖς ἱππικοῖς Sedτροις, ἃ Κίρκους καλοῦσιν; of Lucullus, that he adorned τὸν Φλαμίνειον ἱππό-δρομον. Here the circi are precisely designated as hippodromes; but Josephus uses the general term Sedτρων, which may include theatres of all kinds. Now we will suggest a more probable route than that given by Becker, according to which the pageant must have crossed the forum twice. After coming out at the further end of the circus, Vespasian turned down to the left, between the Palatine and Caelian, the modern Via di S. Gregorio. This would bring him out opposite his own magnificent amphitheatre, the Colosseum, then in course of construction. Even if it had not risen much above its foundations, still its ample area by means of scaffoldings, would have accommodated a vast number of spectators; and as to Vespasian personally, it would have imparted no small relish to his triumph to pass through so magnificent a work of his own creation. Hence his road lay plain and direct over the Summa Sacra Via to the forum and Capitol.

Now, taking all these things into consideration, we will venture to suggest a very slight change in the text of Josephus, a change not so great as some of those often proposed by Becker upon much smaller occasions, and which will release us from a great deal of perplexity. The alteration is that of an N into a Π, a very slight one in the uncial character; and, by reading ἀπεχώρει for ἀνεχώρει, we would make Vespasian depart from the Porticus Octaviae towards the gate which had always been used for triumphs, instead of retracing his steps towards one of which nobody can give any account. But whatever may be thought of the individual case of Vespasian, still we hold it to be incontestable that the ancient Porta Triumphalis, against which the sole objection seems to be that it was near two other gates, is to be sought in that part of the Servian wall between the P. Carmentalis and the P. Flumentana. The objection just alluded to would indeed have some force, if we could assume, with Becker (Handb. p. 154), that the Porta Triumphalis, just like an ordinary one, lay always open for common traffic. But it is surprising how anybody could come to that conclusion after reading the passages which Becker has himself cited from Suetonius, Tacitus, and Dion Cassius, or that in Cicero's oration against Piso before quoted. The first of these authors relates that after the death of Augustus

the senate voted, or proposed to vote, that, as an extraordinary mark of honour, his funeral should pass through the triumphal gate, preceded by the statue of Victory which stood in the curia: "Ut censuerint quidam funus triumphali porta ducendum, praecedente Victoria, quae est in Curia" (Aug. 100; cf. Tac. Ann. i. 8); and Dion says (lvi. 42) that this was actually done, and the body burned in the Campus Martius. Now if the Porta Triumphalis had been an ordinary gate and common thoroughfare, what honour would there have been in passing through it? or how should the spectator have discovered that any distinction had been conferred? Wherefore Preller (Regionen, p. 240) has rightly come to the conclusion that it was usually kept shut.

Between the Capitoline and the Aventine, along the banks of the river, the wall, as we have shown, was discontinued, but it was recommenced at the spot where the latter hill approaches the Tiber. This may be shown from the well-ascertained position of the PORTA TRIGEMINA, which, as we learn from a passage in Frontinus, lay just under the Clivus Publicius, at the northernmost point of the hill ("incipit distribui Appia (aqua) imo Publicio Clivo ad Portam Trigeminam," Aq. 3); and the Clivus Publicius, as we know from a passage in Livy respecting the procession of the virgins before alluded to, formed the ascent to the Aventine from the Forum Boarium ("inde vico Tusco Velabroque per Boarium forum in clivum Publicium atque aedem Junonis Reginae perrectum," xxvii. 37). There are some difficulties connected with the question of this gate, from its being mentioned in conjunction with the Pons Sublicius; but there will be occasion to discuss the situation of that bridge in a separate section; and we shall only remark here that the narratives alluded to seem to show that it was at no great distance from the gate. It is probable that the latter derived its name from its having three Jani or archways.

A little beyond the Porta Trigemina most topographers have placed a PORTA NAVALIS, which is mentioned only once, namely, by P. Diaconus in the following passage: "Navalis Porta a vicinia Navalium dicta" (p. 179, Müll.), where we are told that it derived its name from the vicinity of the government dockyards. It has been assumed that these docks lay to the S. of the Aventine, in the plain where Monte Testaccio stands; but Becker has the merit of having shown, as will appear in its proper place, that they were in the Campus Martius. There was, however, a kind of emporium or merchant dock, between the Aventine and Tiber, and, as this must have occasioned considerable traffic, it is probable that there was a gate leading to it somewhere on the W. side of the hill, perhaps near the Priorato, where there seems to have been an ascent, but whether it was called Porta Navalis it is impossible to say. The writer of this article is informed by a gentleman well acquainted with the subject, that traces of the Servian wall have very recently been discovered at the NW. side of the Aventine, below S. Sabina and S. Alessio.

The line of wall from this point to the Caelian hill cannot be determined with any certainty. Round the Aventine itself it doubtless followed the configuration of the hill; but its course from the S. point of the Aventine has been variously laid down. Hence the question arises whether it included the nameless height on which the churches of S. Sabina and *S. Saba* now stand. It seems probable that it must, at all events, have included a considerable portion of it, since, had it proceeded along the valley, it would have been commanded by the hill; and indeed the most natural supposition is that it enclosed the whole, since the more extended line it would thus have described affords room for the several gates which we find mentioned between the Porta Trigemina and the Porta Capena near the foot of the Caelian.

Among these we must, perhaps, assume a PORTA MINUCIA or MINUTIA, which is twice mentioned by Paulus (pp. 122, 147), and whose name, he says, was derived from an ara or sacellum of Minucius, whom the Romans held to be a god. We hear nowhere else of such a Roman deity; but we learn from Pliny (xviii. 4) that a certain tribune of the people, named Minutius Augurinus, had a statue erected to him, by public subscription, beyond the Porta Trigemina, for having reduced the price of corn. This occurred at an early period, since the same story is narrated by Livy (iv. 13—16) n. c. 436, with the additional information that it was Minutius who procured the condemnation of the great corn monopoliser, Maelius, and that the statue alluded to was a gilt bull. It is possible therefore that the gate may have been named after him; and that from the extraordinary honours paid to him, he may have come in process of time to be vulgarly mistaken for a deity. If there is any truth in this view, the gate may be placed somewhere on the S. side of the Aventine.

In the mutilated fragment which we possess of Varro's description of the Roman gates (*L.L.* v. § 163, Müll.) he closes it by mentioning three, which it is impossible to place anywhere except in the line of wall between the Aventine and Caelian. He had been speaking of a place inhabited by Ennius, who lived on the Aventine (Hieron. *Chron.* 134, vol. i. p. 369, Ronc.), and then mentions consecutively a PORTA NAEVIA, PORTA RAUDUSCULA, and PORTA LAVERNALIS. He must therefore be enumerating the gates in the order from W. to E., since it would be impossible to find room for three more gates, besides those already mentioned, on the Aventine. The P. Naevia, therefore, probably lay in the valley between that hill and the adjoining height to the E. It could not have been situated on the Aventine itself, since the *Basis Capitolina*, mentions in the 12th Regio, or Piscina Publica, a vicus Porta Naevia, as well as another of Porta Raudusculana. But the exact position of the latter gate, as well as of the Porta Lavernalis, it is impossible to determine further than that they lay in the line of wall between the Aventine and Caelian.

After so much uncertainty it is refreshing to arrive at last at a gate whose site may be accurately fixed. The PORTA CAPENA lay at the foot of the Caelian hill, at a short distance W. of the spot where the Via Latina diverged from the Via Appia. The latter road issued from the P. Capena, and the discovery of the first milestone upon it, in a vineyard a short distance outside of the modern *Porta di S. Sebastiano*, has enabled the topographer accurately to determine its site to be at a spot now marked by a post with the letters P. C., 300 yards beyond the *Via S. Gregorio*, and 1480 within the modern gate. That it was seated in the valley, appears from the fact that the Rivus Herculaneus, probably a branch of the Aqua Marcia, passed over it; which we are expressly told, lay too low to

supply the Caelian hill. (Front. *Aq.* 18.) Hence Juvenal (iii. 11):—

" Substitit ad veteres arcus madidamque Capenam,"

where we learn from the Scholia that the gate, which in later times must have lain a good way within the town, was called " Arcus Stillans." So Martial (iii. 47):—

" Capena grandi porta qua pluit gutta."

A little way beyond this gate, on the Via Appia, between its point of separation from the Via Latina and the *P. S. Sebastiano*, there still exists one of the most interesting of the Roman monuments — the tomb of the Scipios, the site of which is marked by a solitary cypress.

From the Porta Capena the wall must have ascended the Caelian hill, and skirted its southern side; but the exact line which it described in its progress towards the agger can only be conjectured. Becker (*Handb.* p. 167), following Piale and Bunsen, draws the line near the *Ospedale di S. Giovanni*, thus excluding that part of the hill on which the Lateran is situated, although, as Canina observes (*Indicazione*, p. 36), this is the highest part of the hill. There was perhaps a gate at the bottom of the present *Piazza di Navicella*, but we do not know its name; and the next gate respecting which there is any certainty is the PORTA CAELIMONTANA. Bunsen (*Beschr.* i. p. 638) and Becker, in conformity with their line of wall, place it by the hospital of *S. Giovanni*, now approached by the *Via S. S. Quattro Coronati*, the ancient street called Caput Africae. The PORTA QUERQUETULANA, if it was really a distinct gate and not another name for the Caelimontana, must have stood a little to the N. of the latter, near the church of *S. S. Pietro e Marcellino*, in the valley which separates the Caelian from the Esquiline. This gate, which was also called Querquetularia, is several times mentioned, but without any more exact definition. (Plin. xvi. 15; Festus, p. 261.) The Caelian hill itself, as we have before remarked, was anciently called Querquetulanus. From this point the wall must have run northwards in a tolerably direct line till it joined the southern extremity of the agger, where the PORTA ESQUILINA was situated, between which and the Querquetulana there does not appear to have been any other gate. The Esquilina, like the others on the agger, is among the most certain of the Roman gates. We learn from Strabo (v. p. 237) that the Via Labicana proceeded from it; whilst at a little distance the Praenestina branched off from the Labicana. It must therefore have lain near the church of *S. Vito* and the still existing arch of Gallienus; but its exact site is connected with the question respecting the gates in the Aurelian wall which corresponded with it, and cannot therefore at present be determined. The site of the PORTA COLLINA, the point from which we started, is determined by the fact mentioned by Strabo (*Ib.* p. 228) that both the Via Salaria and Via Nomentana started from it; and it must consequently have stood near the northern corner of the baths of Diocletian at the commencement of the present *Via del Macao*. We learn from Paulus Diaconus (p. 10) that this gate was also called Agonensis and Quirinalis. Agonos, as we have said, was the ancient name of the Quirinal hill.

The Porta Collina, then, and the Porta Esquilina were seated at the northern and southern extremities of the agger. But besides these, Strabo (*Ib.* p. 234) mentions another lying between them, the PORTA VIMINALIS; which is also recorded by Festus (p. 376) and by Frontinus (*Aq.* 19). It must have lain behind the SE. angle of the baths of Diocletian, where an ancient road leads to the rampart, which, if prolonged, would run to the PORTA CLAUSA of the walls of Aurelian, just under the southern side of the Castra Praetoria. It is clear from the words of Strabo, in the passage just cited (ὑπὸ μεσῷ δὲ τῷ χώματι τρίτη ἐστὶ πύλη ὁμώνυμος τῷ Οὐϊμιναλίῳ λόφῳ), that there were only three gates in the agger, though some topographers have contrived to find room for two or three more in this short space, the whole length of the agger being but 6 or 7 stadia (Strab. *l. c.*; Dionys. ix. 68), or about ¾ of a mile. Its breadth was 50 feet, and below it lay a ditch 100 feet broad and 30 feet deep. Remains of this immense work are still visible near the baths of Diocletian and in the grounds of the *Villa Negroni*, especially at the spot where the statue of Roma now stands.

Survey under Vespasian and Circumference of the City.—In the preceding account of the gates in the Servian wall we have enumerated twenty, including the Porta Triumphalis. Some topographers have adopted a still greater number. When we consider that there were only nine or ten main roads leading out of ancient Rome, and that seven of these issued from the three gates Capena, Esquilina, and Collina alone, it follows that five or six gates would have sufficed for the main entrances, and that the remainder must have been unimportant ones, destined only to afford the means of convenient communication with the surrounding country. Of those enumerated only the Collina, Viminalis, Esquilina, Caelimontana, Capena, Trigemina, Carmentalis, and Ratumena seem to have been of any great importance. Nevertheless it appears from a passage in Pliny (iii. 9) that in his time there must have been a great number of smaller ones, the origin and use of which we shall endeavour to account for presently. As the passage, though unfortunately somewhat obscure, is of considerable importance in Roman topography, we shall here quote it at length : " Urbem tres portas habentem Romulus reliquit, aut (ut plurimas tradentibus credamus) quatuor. Moenia ejus collegere ambitu Imperatoribus Censoribusque Vespasianis anno conditae DCCCXXVII. pass. XIIIM.CC. Complexa montes septem, ipsa dividitur in regiones quattuordecim, compita Larium CCLXV. Ejusdem spatium, mensura currente a milliario in capite Romani fori statuto, ad singulas portas, quae sunt hodie numero triginta septem, ita ut duodecim semel numerentur, praetereanturque ex veteribus septem, quae esse desierunt, efficit passuum per directum XXXM.DCCLXV. Ad extrema vero tectorum cum castris Praetoriis ab eodem milliario per vicos omnium viarum mensura colligit paulo amplius septuaginta millia passuum." Now there seems to be no reason for doubting the correctness of this account. Pliny could have had no reason for exaggeration, against which, in the account of the Romulean gates, he carefully guards himself. Again, he seems to have taken the substance of it from the official report of a regular survey made in his own time and in the reign of Vespasian. The only room for suspicion therefore seems to be that his text may have been corrupted, and that instead of thirty-seven as the number of the gates we should insert some smaller one. But an examination of his figures does

not tend to show that they are incorrect. The survey seems to have been made with a view to the three following objects : 1. To ascertain the actual circumference of the city, including all the suburbs which had spread beyond the walls of Servius. It is well known that *moenia* signifies the buildings of a city as well as the walls (" muro moenia amplexus est," Flor. i. 4, &c.), and therefore this phrase, which has sometimes caused embarrassment, need not detain us. Now the result of this first measurement gave 13,200 *passus*, or 13¼ Roman miles—a number to which there is nothing to object, as it very well agrees with the circumference of the subsequent Aurelian walls. 2. The second object seems to have been to ascertain the actual measure of the line of street within the old Servian walls. The utility of this proceeding we do not immediately recognise. It may have been adopted out of mere curiosity; or more probably it may have been connected with questions respecting certain privileges, or certain taxes, which varied according as a house was situated within or without the walls. Now the sum of the measurements of all these streets, when put together as if they had formed a straight line (" per directum"), amounted to 30,765 *passus*, or 30 Roman miles and about ¾. Such we take to be the meaning of " per directum;" though some critics hold it to mean that the distance from the milliarium to these gates was measured in a straight line, as the crow flies, without taking into the calculation the windings of the streets. But in that case it would surely have been put earlier in the sentence —" mensura currente per directum ad singulas portas." This, however, would have been of little consequence except for the distinction drawn by Becker (*Handb.* p. 185, note 279), who thinks that the measurement proceeds on two different principles, namely *per directum*, or as the crow flies, from the milliarium to the Servian gates, and, on the contrary, by all the windings of the streets from the same spot to the furthest buildings outside the walls. Such a method, as he observes, would afford no true ground of comparison, and therefore we can hardly think that it was adopted, or that such was Pliny's meaning. Becker was led to this conclusion because he thought that " per vicos omnium viarum " stands contrasted with " per directum;" but this contrast does not seem necessarily to follow. By *viae* here Pliny seems to mean all the roads leading out of the thirty-seven gates; and by " ad extrema tectorum per vicos omnium viarum " is signified merely that the measure was further extended to the end of the streets which lined the commencements of these roads. Such appears to us to be the meaning of this certainly somewhat obscure passage. Pliny's account may be checked, roughly indeed, but still with a sufficient approach to accuracy to guarantee the correctness of his text. If a circumference of 13¼ miles yielded 70 miles of street, and if there were 30 miles of street within the Servian walls, then the circumference of the latter would be to the former as 3 to 7, and would measure rather more than 5¾ miles. Now this agrees pretty well with the accounts which we have of the size of the Servian city. Becker, following the account of Thucydides (ii. 13), but without allowing for that part of the walls of Athens described as unguarded, with the whole circuit of which walls Dionysius (iv. 13, and ix. 68) compares those of ancient Rome, sets the latter down at 43 stadia, or 5⅜ miles. On Nolli's great plan of Rome they are given at a measurement equal to 10,230 English yards (Burgess, *Topography and Antiquities of Rome*, vol. i. p. 458), which agrees as nearly as possible with the number above given of 5¾ miles. Nibby, who made a laborious but perhaps not very accurate attempt to ascertain the point by walking round the presumed line of the ancient walls, arrived at a considerably larger result, or nearly 8 miles. (*Mura, &c.* p. 90.)

False and doubtful Gates. — But our present business is with the gates of the Servian town; and it would really appear that in the time of Vespasian there were no fewer than thirty-seven outlets from the ancient walls. The seven old gates to which Pliny alludes as having ceased to exist, may possibly have included those of the old Romulean city and also some in the Servian walls, which had been closed. In order to account for the large number recorded by Pliny, we must figure to ourselves what would be the natural progress of a city surrounded with a strong wall like that of Servius, whose population was beginning to outgrow the accommodation afforded within it. At first perhaps houses would be built at the sides of the roads issuing from the main gates; but, as at Rome these sites were often appropriated for sepulchres, the accommodation thus afforded would be limited. In process of time, the use of the wall becoming every day more obsolete, fresh gates would be pierced, corresponding with the line of streets inside, which would be continued by a line of road outside, on which houses would be erected. Gradually the walls themselves began to disappear; but the openings that had been pierced were still recorded, as marking, for fiscal or other purposes, the boundary of the city wards. Hence, though Augustus had divided the city and suburbs into fourteen new Regions, we find the ancient boundary marked by these gates still recorded and measured in the time of Vespasian; and indeed it seems to have been kept up for a long while afterwards, since 'we find the same number of thirty-seven gates recorded both in the *Notitia* and *Curiosum*.

Hence we would not tamper with the text of Pliny, as Nibby has done with very unfortunate success (*Mura, &c.* p. 213, seq.) — a remedy that should never be resorted to except in cases of the last necessity. Pliny's statement may be regarded as wholly without influence with respect to the *original* Servian gates, the number of which we should rather be inclined to reduce than to increase. We find, indeed, more names mentioned than those enumerated, but some of them were ancient or obsolete names; and, again, we must remember that " porta " does not always signify a city gate. Of the former kind was the PORTA AGONENSIS, which, as we learn from Paulus Diaconus (p. 10), was another appellation for the Porta Collina. The same author (p. 255) also mentions a PORTA QUIRINALIS as a substantive gate; though possibly, like Agonensis, it was only a duplicate name for one of the gates on the Quirinal. The term " porta " was applied to any arched thoroughfare, and sometimes perhaps to the arch of an aqueduct when it spanned a street in the line of wall; in which case it was built in a superior manner, and had usually an inscription. Among internal thoroughfares called " portae " were the STERCORARIA on the Clivus Capitolinus, the LIBITINENSIS in the amphitheatre, the FENESTELLA, mentioned by Ovid (*Fast.* vi. 569) as that by which Fortuna visited Numa, &c. The last of these formed

the entrance to Numa's regia, as we learn from Plutarch (*de Fort. Rom.* 10). Among the arches of aqueducts to which the name of gate was applied, may perhaps be ranked that alluded to by Martial (iv. 18): —

" Qua vicina pluit Vipsanis porta columnis," &c.

Respecting the gates called FERENTINA and PIACULARIS we have before offered a conjecture. [See p. 728.] The PORTA MICTIA rests solely on a false reading of Plautus. (*Cas.* ii. 6. 2. *Pseud.* i. 3. 97.) On the other hand, a PORTA CATULARIA seems to have really existed, which is mentioned by Paulus Diaconus (p. 45; cf. Festus, p. 285) in connection with certain sacrifices of red-coloured dogs. This must be the sacrifice alluded to by Ovid (*Fast.* iv. 905), in which the entrails of a dog were offered by the flamen in the Lucus Robiginis. It is also mentioned in the *Fasti Praenestini*, vii. Kal. Mai, which date agrees with Ovid's: " Feriae Robigo Via Claudia, ad miliarium v., ne robigo frumentis noceat." But this is at variance first, with Ovid, who was returning to Rome by the Via Nomentana, not the Via Claudia, and, secondly, with itself, since the Via Claudia did not branch off from the Via Flaminia till the 10th milestone, and, consequently, no sacrifice could be performed on it at a distance of 5 miles from Rome. However this discrepancy is to be reconciled, it can hardly be supposed that one of the Roman gates derived its name from a trifling rustic sacrifice; unless, indeed, it was a duplicate one, used chiefly with reference to sacerdotal customs, as seems to have been sometimes the case, and in the present instance to denote the gate leading to the spot where the annual rite was performed. Paulus Diaconus also mentions (p. 37) a PORTA COLLATINA, which he affirms to have been so called after the city of Collatia, near Rome. But when we reflect that both the Via Tiburtina and the Via Praenestina issued from the Porta Esquilina, and that a road to Collatia must have run between them, the impossibility of a substantive Porta Collatina is at once apparent. The DUODECIM PORTAE are placed by Bunsen (*Beschr.* i. p. 633) in the wall of the Circus Maximus; but as it appears from Pliny (*l. c.*) that they stood on the ancient line of wall, and as we have shown that this did not make part of the wall of the circus, this could not have been their situation. We do not see the force of Piale's celebrated discovery that the Duodecim Portae must have been a *place* at Rome, because Julius Obsequens says that a mule brought forth there; which it might very well have done at one of the gates. Becker's opinion (*Handb.* p. 180) that it was an arch, or arches, of the Aqua Appia seems as unfounded as that of Bunsen (vide Preller, *Regionen*, p. 193). It is mentioned by the *Notitia* in the 11th Regio, and therefore probably stood somewhere near the Aventine; but its exact site cannot be determined. It seems probable, as Preller remarks, that it may have derived its name from being a complex of twelve arched thoroughfares like the 'Εννεάπυλον of the Pelasgicon at Athens.

Transtiberine Wall. — Ancus Marcius, as we have related, fortified the JANICULUM, or hill on the right bank of the Tiber commanding the city. Some have concluded from Livy (i. 33: " Janiculum quoque adjectum, non inopia locorum, sed ne quando ea arx hostium esset. Id non muro solum, sed etiam ob commoditatem itineris ponte Sublicio tum primum in Tiberi facto conjungi urbi placuit "), that a wall was built from the fortress on the top of the hill down to the river, but the construction of *conjungi* in this passage may be a zeugma. It seems strange that Ancus should have built a wall on the *right* bank of the Tiber when there was yet none on the *left* bank; and it is remarkable that Dionysius (iii. 45), in describing the fortification of the Janiculum, makes no mention of a wall, nor do we hear of any gates on this side except that of the fortress itself. The existence of a wall, moreover, seems hardly consistent with the accounts which we have already given from the same author of the defenceless state of the city on that side. Niebuhr (*Hist.* i. p. 396) rejected the notion of a wall, as utterly erroneous, but unfortunately neglected to give the proofs by which he had arrived at this conclusion. The passage from Appian (Κλαύδιον δ' Άππιον χιλίαρχον τειχοφυλακοῦντα τῆς Ῥώμης τὸν λόφον τὸν καλούμενον Ἰανουκλον εὖ ποτε παθόντα ὑφ' ἑαυτοῦ τῆς εὐεργεσίας ἀναμνήσας ὁ Μάριος, ἐς τὴν πόλιν ἐσῆλθεν, ὑπανοιχθείσης αὐτῷ πύλης, *B. C.* i. 68) which Becker (p. 182, note) seems to regard as decisive proves little or nothing for the earlier periods of the city; and, even had there been a wall, the passing it would not have afforded an entrance into the city, properly so called.

II. Walls and Gates of Aurelian and Honorius.

In the repairs of the wall by Honorius all the gates of Aurelian vanished; hence it is impossible to say with confidence that any part of Aurelian's wall remains; and we must consider it as represented by that of Honorius. Procopius (*B. G.* iii. 24) asserts that Totila destroyed all the gates; but this is disproved by the inscriptions still existing over the *Porta S. Lorenzo*, as well as over the closed arch of the *Porta Maggiore;* and till the time of Pope Urban VIII. the same inscription might be read over the Ostiensis (*P. S. Paolo*) and the ancient Portuensis. It can hardly be imagined that these inscriptions should have been preserved over restored gates. The only notice respecting any of the gates of Aurelian on which we can confidently rely is the account given by Ammianus Marcellinus (xvii. 4. § 14) of the carrying of the Egyptian obelisk, which Constantius II. erected in the Circus Maximus, through the Porta Ostiensis. It may be assumed, however, that their situation was not altered in the new works of Honorius. By far the greater part of these gates exist at the present day, though some of them are now walled up, and in most cases the ancient name has been changed for a modern one. Hence the problem is not so much to discover the sites of the ancient gates as the ancient names of those still existing; and these do not admit of much doubt, with the exception of the gates on the eastern side of the city.

Procopius, the principal authority respecting the gates in the Aurelian (or Honorian) wall, enumerates 14 principal ones, or πύλαι, and mentions some smaller ones by the name of πυλίδες (*B. G.* i. 19). The distinction, however, between these two appellations is not very clear. To judge from their present appearance, it was not determined by the size of the gates; and we find the Pinciana indifferently called πυλίς and πύλη. (Urlichs, *Class. Mus.* vol. iii. p. 196.) The conjecture of Nibby (*Mura, &c.* p. 317) may perhaps be correct, that the πύλαι were probably those which led to the great highways. The unknown writer called the Anonymus Einsiedlensis, who flourished about the beginning of

the ninth century, also mentions 14 gates, and includes the Pinciana among them; but his account is not clear.

Unlike Servius, Aurelian did not consider the Tiber a sufficient protection; and his walls were extended along its banks from places opposite to the spots where the walls which he built from the Janiculum began on the further shore. The wall which skirted the Campus Martius is considered to have commenced not far from the *Palazzo Farnese*, from remains of walls on the right bank, supposed to have belonged to those of the Janiculum; but all traces of walls on the left bank have vanished beneath the buildings of the new town. It would appear that the walls on the right and left banks were connected by means of a bridge on the site of the present *Ponte Sisto* — which thus contributed to form part of the defences; since the arches being secured by means of chains drawn before them, or by other contrivances, would prevent an enemy from passing through them in boats into the interior of the city: and it is in this manner that Procopius describes Belisarius as warding off the attacks of the Goths (*B. G.* i. 19).

From this point, along the whole extent of the Campus Martius, and as far as the Porta Flaminia, the walls appear, with the exception of some small posterns mentioned by the Anonymous of Einsiedlen to have had only one gate, which is repeatedly mentioned by Procopius under the name of Porta Aurelia (*B. G.* i. c. 19, 22, 28); though he seems to have been acquainted with its later name of Porta Sti Petri, by which it is called by the Anonymous (*Ib.* iii. 36). It stood on the left bank, opposite to the entrance of the Pons Aelius (*Ponte di S. Angelo*), leading to the mausoleum of Hadrian. The name of Aurelia is found only in Procopius, and is somewhat puzzling, since there was another gate of the same name in the Janiculum, spanning the Via Aurelia, which, however, is called by Procopius (*Ib.* i. 18) by its modern name of Pancratiana; whilst on the other hand the Anonymous appears strangely enough to know it only by its ancient appellation of Aurelia. The gate by the bridge, of which no trace now remains, may possibly have derived its name from a Nova Via Aurelia (Gruter, *Inscr.* ccccli. 6), which passed through it; but there is a sort of mystery hanging over it which it is not easy to clear up. (Becker, *Handb.* p. 196, and note.)

The next gate, proceeding northwards, was the Porta Flaminia, which stood a little to the east of the present *Porta del Popolo*, erected by Pope Pius IV. in 1561. The ancient gate probably stood on the declivity of the Pincian (ἐν χώρῳ κρημνώδει, Procop. *B. G.* i. 23), as the Goths did not attack it from its being difficult of access. Yet Anastasius (*Vit. Gregor II.*) describes it as exposed to inundations of the Tiber; whence Nibby (*Mura, &c.* p. 304) conjectures that its site was altered between the time of Procopius and Anastasius, that is, between the sixth and ninth centuries. Nay, in a great inundation which happened towards the end of the eighth century, in the pontificate of Adrian I., the gate was carried away by the flood, which bore it as far as the arch of M. Aurelius, then called *Tres Fucciccllae*, and situated in the Via Flaminia, where the street called *della Vite* now runs into the *Corso*. (*Ib.*) The gate appears to have retained its ancient name of Flaminia as late as the 15th century, as appears from a life of Martin V. in Muratori (*Script. Rer. Ital.* t. iii. pt. ii. col.

864). When it obtained its present name cannot be determined; its ancient one was undoubtedly derived from the Via Flaminia, which it spanned. In the time of Procopius, and indeed long before, the wall to the east had bent outwards from the effects of the pressure of the Pincian hill, whence it was called *murus fractus* or *inclinatus*, just as it is now called *muro torto*. (Procop. *B. G.* i. 23.)

The next gate, proceeding always to the right, was the PORTA PINCIANA, before mentioned, which was already walled up in the time of the Anonymous of Einsiedlen. It of course derived its name from the hill on which it stood. Belisarius had a house near this gate (Anastas. *Silverio*, pp. 104, 106); and either from this circumstance, or from the exploits performed before it by Belisarius, it is supposed to have been also called *Belisaria*, a name which actually occurs in one or two passages of Procopius (*B. G.* i. 18, 22; cf. Nibby, *Mura, &c.* p. 248). But the Salaria seems to have a better claim to this second appellation as the gate which Belisarius himself defended; though it is more probable that there was no such name at all, and that Βελισαρία in the passages cited is only a corruption of Σαλαρία. (Becker, *de Muris*, p. 115; Urlichs in *Class. Mus.* vol. iii. p. 196.)

Respecting the two gates lying between the Porta Pinciana and the Praetorian camp there can be no doubt, as they stood over, and derived their names from, the Via Salaria and Via Nomentana. In earlier times both these roads issued from the Porta Collina of the Servian wall; but their divergence of course rendered two gates necessary in a wall drawn with a longer radius. The PORTA SALARIA still subsists with the same name, although it has undergone a restoration. Pius IV. destroyed the PORTA NOMENTANA, and built in its stead the present *Porta Pia*. The inscription on the latter testifies the destruction of the ancient gate, the place of which is marked with a tablet bearing the date of 1564. A little to the SE. of this gate are the walls of the Castra Praetoria, projecting considerably beyond the rest of the line, as Aurelian included the camp in his fortification. The PORTA DECUMANA, though walled up, is still visible, as well as the PRINCIPALES on the sides.

The gates on the eastern tract of the Aurelian walls have occasioned considerable perplexity. On this side of the city four roads are mentioned, the Tiburtina, Collatina, Praenestina, and Labicana, and two gates, the PORTA TIBURTINA and PRAENESTINA. But besides these gates, which are commonly thought to correspond with the modern ones of *S. Lorenzo* and *Porta Maggiore*, there is a gate close to the Praetorian camp, about the size of the Pinciana, and resembling the Honorian gates in its architecture, which has been walled up from time immemorial, and is hence called PORTA CLAURA, or *Porta Chiusa*. The difficulty lies in determining which were the ancient Tiburtina and Praenestina. The whole question has been so lucidly stated by Mr. Bunbury that we cannot do better than borrow his words: "It has been generally assumed that the two gates known in modern times as the *Porta S. Lorenzo* and the *Porta Maggiore* are the same as were originally called respectively the Porta Tiburtina and Praenestina, and that the roads bearing the same appellations led from them directly to the important towns from which they derived their name. It is admitted on all hands that they appear under these

names in the *Anonymus*; and a comparison of two passages of Procopius (*B. G.* i. 19, *Ib.* p. 96) would appear to lead us to the same result. In the former of these Procopius speaks of the part of the city attacked by the Goths as comprising *five gates* (πύλαι), and extending from the Flaminian to the Praenestine. That he did not reckon the Pinciana as one of these seems probable, from the care with which, in the second passage referred to, he distinguishes it as a πυλίς, or minor gate. Supposing the closed gate near the Praetorian camp to have been omitted for the same reason, we have just the five required, viz., Flaminia, Salaria, Nomentana, Tiburtina (*Porta S. Lorenzo*), and Praenestina (*Maggiore*). On this supposition both these ancient ways (the Tiburtina and Praenestina) must have issued originally from the Esquiline gate of the Servian walls. Now we know positively from Strabo that the Via Praenestina did so, as did also a third road, the Via Labicana, which led to the town of that name, and afterwards rejoined the Via Latina at the station called Ad Pictas (v. p. 237). Strabo, on the other hand, does not mention from what gate the road to Tibur issued in his time. Niebuhr has therefore followed Fabretti and Piale in assuming that the latter originally proceeded from the Porta Viminalis, which, as we have seen, stood in the middle of the agger of Servius, and that it passed through the walls of Aurelian by means of a gate now blocked up, but still extant, just at the angle where those walls join on to the Castra Praetoria. . . . . . .

Assuming this to have been the original Tiburtina, Niebuhr (followed by MM. Bunsen and Urlichs) considers the *Porta S. Lorenzo* to have been the Praenestina, and the *Porta Maggiore* to have been the Labicana; but that when the gate adjoining the Praetorian camp was blocked up, the road to *Tivoli* was transferred to the *Porta S. Lorenzo*, and that to Praeneste to the gate next in order, which thus acquired the name of Praenestina instead of its former one of Labicana (*Beschreibung*, i. p. 657, seq). To this suggestion there appear to be two principal objections brought forward by M. Becker, neither of which M. Urlichs has answered: the first, that, supposing the Via Tiburtina to have been so transferred, which taken alone might be probable enough, there is no apparent reason why the Via Praenestina should have been also shifted, instead of the two thenceforth issuing together from the same gate, and diverging immediately afterwards; and secondly, that there is no authority for the existence of such a *gate* called the Labicana at all. The passage of Strabo, already cited, concerning the *Via* Labicana, certainly seems to imply that that road in his time separated from the Praenestina immediately after leaving the Esquiline gate; but there is no improbability in the suggestion of M. Becker, that its course was altered at the time of the construction of the new walls, whether under Aurelian or Honorius, in order to avoid an unnecessary increase of the number of gates. Many such changes in the direction of the principal roads may have taken place at that time, of which we have no account, and on which it is impossible to speculate. Westphal, in his *Römische Campagne* (p. 78), has adopted nearly the same view of the case: but he considers the Via Labicana to have originally had a gate assigned to it, which was afterwards walled up, and the road carried out of the same gate with the Via Praenestina. The only real difficulty in the ordinary view of the subject, supported by M. Becker, appears to be that, if the Via Tiburtina always issued from the Porta S. Lorenzo, we have no road to assign to the now closed gate adjoining the Praetorian camp, nor yet to the Porta Viminalis of the Servian walls, a circumstance certainly remarkable, as it seems unlikely that such an opening should have been made in the agger without absolute necessity. On the other hand, the absence of all mention of that gate prior to the time of Strabo would lead one to suspect that it was not one of the principal outlets of the city; and a passage from Ovid, quoted by M. Becker, certainly affords some presumption that the road from Tibur, in ancient times, actually entered the city by the Porta Esquilina (*Fast.* v. 684). This is, in fact, the most important, perhaps the only important, point of the question; for if the change in the names had already taken place as early as the time of Procopius, which Niebuhr himself seems disposed to acknowledge, it is hardly worth while to inquire whether the gates had borne the same appellations during the short interval from Honorius to Justinian" (*Class. Mus.* vol. iii. p. 369, seq.).

The Porta Tiburtina (*S. Lorenzo*) is built near an arch of the Aquae Marcia, Tepula, and Julia, which here flow over one another in three different canals. The arch of the gate corresponds with that of the aqueduct, but the latter is encumbered with rubbish, and therefore appears very low, whilst the gate is built on the rubbish itself. As the inscription on it appeared on several of the other gates, we shall here insert it : *S.P.Q.R. Impp. DD. NN. invictissimis principibus Arcadio et Honorio victoribus et triumphatoribus semper Augg. ob instauratos urbis aeternae muros portas ac turres egestis immensis ruderibus ex suggestione V.C. et inlustris comitis et magistri utriusque militiae Fl. Stilichonis ad perpetuitatem nominis eorum simulacra constituit curante Fl. Macrobio Longiniano V.C. Praef. Urbi D. N. M. Q. eorum.* In like manner the magnificent double arch of the Aqua Claudia and Anio Novus, which flow over it, was converted into the Porta Praenestina (*Maggiore*). The right arch, from the city side, is walled up, and concealed on the outside by the Honorian wall. Just beyond the gate is the curious tomb of Eurysaces, the baker, sculptured with the instru-

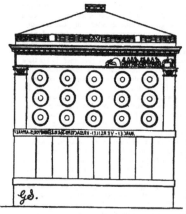

TOMB OF EURYSACES.

ments of his trade, which was brought to light in 1838, by the pulling down of a tower which had been built over it in the middle ages. Over the closed Honorian arch was the same inscription as over the Porta Tiburtina. On the aqueduct are three inscriptions, which name Claudius as its builder, and Vespasian and Titus as its restorers. The gate had several names in the middle ages.

Hence the wall follows for some distance the line of the Aqua Claudia, till it reaches its easternmost point; when, turning to the S. and W., and embracing the curve of what is commonly called the Amphitheatrum Castrense, it reaches the ancient PORTA ASINARIA, now replaced by the *Porta di S. Giovanni,* built a little to the E. of it in 1574, by Pope Gregory XIII. It derived its name from spanning the Via Asinaria (Festus, p. 282, Müll.), and is frequently mentioned by Procopius. (*B. G.* i. 14, iii. 20, &c.) In the middle ages it was called Lateranensis from the neighbouring palace of the Lateran.

After this gate we find another mentioned, which has entirely vanished. The earliest notice of it appears in an epistle of Gregory the Great (ix. 69), by whom it is called PORTA METRONIS; whilst by Martinus Polonus it is styled Porta Metroni or Metronii, and by the Anonymous, Metrovia. (Nibby, *Mura, &c.* p. 365.) It was probably at or near the point where the *Marrana* (Aqua Crabra) now flows into the town. (Nibby, *l. c.*; Piale, *Porte Merid.* p. 11.)

The two next gates were the PORTA LATINA and PORTA APPIA, standing over the roads of those names, which, as we have before said, diverged from one another at a little distance outside the Porta Capena, for which, therefore, these gates were substitutes. The Porta Latina is now walled up, and the road to Tusculum (*Frascati*) leads out of the Porta S. Giovanni The Porta Appia, which still retained its name during the middle ages, but is now called *Porta di S. Sebastiano,* from the church situated outside of it, is one of the most considerable of the gates, from the height of its towers, though the arch is not of fine proportions. Nibby considers it to be posterior to the Gothic War, and of Byzantine architecture, from the Greek inscriptions and the Greek cross on the key-stone of the arch. (*Mura, &c.* p. 370.) A little within it stands the so-called arch of Drusus.

A little farther in the line of wall to the W. stands an arched gate of brick, ornamented with half columns, and having a heavy architrave. The Via Ardeatina (Fest. p. 282, Müll.) proceeded through it, which issued from the Porta Raudusculana of the Servian walls. (Nibby, p. 201, seq.) We do not find this gate named in any author, and it was probably walled up at a very early period. The last gate on this side is the PORTA OSTIENSIS, now called *Porta di S. Paolo,* from the celebrated basilica about a mile outside of it, now in course of reconstruction in the most splendid manner. The ancient name is mentioned by Ammianus Marcellinus (xvii. 4), but that of S. Pauli appears as early as the sixth century. (Procop. *B. G.* iii. 36.) It had two arches, of which the second, though walled up, is still visible from the side of the town, though hidden from without by a tower built before it. Close to it is the pyramid, or tomb, of Cestius, one of the few monuments of the Republic. It is built into the wall. From this point the walls ran to the river, inclosing *Monte Testaccio,* and then northwards along its banks, till they reached the point opposite to the walls of the Janiculum. Of this last portion only a few fragments are now visible.

On the other side of the Tiber only a few traces of the ancient wall remain, which extended lower down the stream than the modern one. Not far from the river lay the PORTA PORTUENSIS, which Urban VIII. destroyed in order to build the present *Porta Portese.* This gate, like the Ostiensis and Praenestina, had two arches, and the same inscription as that over the Tiburtina. From this point the wall proceeded to the height of the Janiculum, where stood the PORTA AURELIA, so named after the Via Aurelia (vetus) which issued from it. We have already mentioned that its modern name (*Porta di S. Pancrazio*) was in use as early as the time of Procopius; yet the ancient one is found in the Anonymous of Einsiedlen, and even in the *Liber de Mirabilibus.* The walls then again descended in a NE. direction to the river, to the point opposite to that whence we commenced this description, or between the *Farnese Palace* and *Ponte Sisto.* It is singular that we do not find any gate mentioned in this portion of wall, and we can hardly conceive that there should have been no exit towards the Vatican. Yet neither Procopius (*B. G.* i. 19, 23) nor the writers of the middle ages recognise any. We find, indeed, a Transtiberine gate mentioned by Spartianus (*Sever.* 19) as built by Septimius Severus, and named after him (Septimiana); but it is plain that this could not have been, originally at least, a city gate, as there were no walls at this part in the time of Severus. Becker conjectures (*de Muris,* p. 129, *Handb.* p. 214) that it was an archway belonging to some building erected by Severus, and that it was subsequently built into the wall by Aurelius or Honorius; of the probability of which conjecture, seeing that it is never once mentioned by any author, the reader must judge.

III. THE CAPITOL.

In attempting to describe this prominent feature in the topography of Rome, we are arrested on the threshold by a dispute respecting it which has long prevailed and still continues to prevail, and upon which, before proceeding any further, it will be necessary to declare our opinion. We have before described the Capitoline hill as presenting three natural divisions, namely, two summits, one at its NE. and the other at its SW. extremity, with a depression between them, thus forming what is commonly called a saddle-back hill. Now the point in dispute is, which of these summits was the Capitol, and which the Arx? The unfortunate ambiguity with which these terms are used by the ancient writers, will, it is to be feared, prevent the possibility of ever arriving at any complete and satisfactory solution of the question. Hence the conflicting opinions which have prevailed upon the subject, and which have given rise to two different schools of topographers, generally characterised at present as the German and the Italian school. There is, indeed, a third class of writers, who hold that both the Capitol and Arx occupied the same, or SW. summit; but this evidently absurd theory has now so few adherents that it will not be necessary to examine it. The most conspicuous scholars of the German school are Niebuhr, and his followers Bunsen, Becker, Preller, and others; and these hold that the temple of Jupiter Capitolinus was seated on the SW. summit of the hill. The Italian view, which is directly

contrary to this, was first brought into vogue by Nardini in the last century, and has since been held by most Italian scholars and topographers. It is not, however, so exclusively Italian but that it has been adopted by some distinguished German scholars, among whom may be named Göttling, and Braun, the present accomplished Secretary of the Archaeological Institute at Rome.

Every attempt to determine this question must now rest almost exclusively on the interpretation of passages in ancient authors relating to the Capitoline hill, and the inferences to be drawn from them; and the decision must depend on the preponderance of probability on a comparison of these inferences. Hence the great importance of attending to a strict interpretation of the expressions used by the classical writers will be at once apparent; and we shall therefore preface the following inquiry by laying down a few general rules to guide our researches.

Preller, who, in an able paper published in Schneidewin's *Philologus,* vol. i., has taken a very moderate and candid view of the question, consoles himself and those who with him hold the German side, by remarking that no passage can be produced from an ancient and trustworthy writer in which Capitolium is used as the name of *the whole hill.* But if the question turns on this point — and to a great extent it certainly does — such passages may be readily produced. To begin with Varro, who was both an ancient and a trustworthy writer. In a passage where he is expressly describing *the hills* of Rome, and which will therefore admit neither of misapprehension nor dispute, Varro says: "Septimontium nominatum *ab tot montibus,* quos postea urbs muris comprehendit. E *quis Capitolium* dictum, quod hic, quom fundamenta foderentur aedis Jovis, caput humanum dicitur inventum. Hic *mons* ante Tarpeius dictus," &c. (*L.L.* v. § 41, Müll.) Here Capitolium can signify nothing but the Capitoline hill, just as Palatium in § 53 signifies the Palatine. In like manner Tacitus, in his description of the Romulean pomoerium before cited: " Forumque Romanum et Capitolium non a Romulo sed a Tito Tatio additum urbi credidere" (*Ann.* xii. 24), where it would be absurd to restrict the meaning of *Capitolium* to the Capitol properly so called, for Tatius dwelt on the Arx. So Livy in his narrative of the exploit of Horatius Cocles: " Si transitum a tergo reliquissent, jam plus hostium in Palatio Capitolioque, quam in Janiculo, fore" (ii. 10), where its union with Palatium shows that the hill is meant; and the same historian, in describing Romulus consecrating the spolia opima to Jupiter Feretrius a couple of centuries before the Capitoline temple was founded, says, " in Capitolium escendit " (i. 10). The Greek writers use τὸ Καπιτώλιον in the same manner: 'Ρώμυλος μὲν τὸ Παλάτιον κατέχων — Τάτιος δὲ τὸ Καπιτώλιον. (Dionys. ii. 50.) Hence we deduce as a first general rule that the term *Capitolium* is sometimes used of the whole hill.

Secondly, it may be shown that the whole hill, when characterised generally as the Roman citadel, was also called *Arx:* " Atque ut ita munita arx circumjectu arduo et quasi circumciso saxo niteretur, ut etiam in illa tempestate horribili Gallici adventus incolumis atque intacta permanserit." (Cic. *Rep.* ii. 6.) " Sp. Tarpeius Romanae praeerat arci." (Liv. i. 11.) But there is no need to multiply examples on this head, which is plain enough.

But, thirdly, we must observe that though the terms Capitolium and Arx are thus used generally

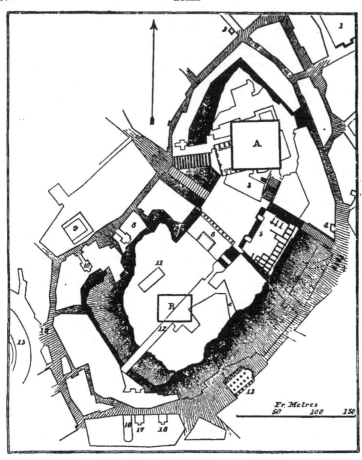

PLAN OF THE CAPITOLINE HILL.

A. Temple of Jupiter Capitolinus.
B. Temple of Juno Moneta.
1. Forum Trajani.
2. Sepulcrum Bibuli.
3. Capitoline Museum.
4. S. Pietro in Carcere.
5. Palazzo Senatorio.
6. Palazzo de' Conservatori.
7. Arcus Severi.
8. S. Nicola de' Funari.
9. Tor de' Specchi.
10. S. Andrea in Vincis.
11. Palazzo Cafarelli.

12. Monte Caprino.
13. S. Maria della Consolazione.
14. Piazza Montanara.
15. Theatrum Marcelli.
16. S. Omobuono.
17. S. Maria in Portica.
18. S. Salvatore in Statera.
a a. Via di Macel de' Corvi.
b b. Salita di Marforio.
c c. Via della Pedacchia.
d d. Via della Bufola.
e e. Via di Monte Tarpeo.

to signify the whole hill, they are nevertheless frequently employed in a stricter sense to denote respectively one of its summits, or rather, the temple of Jupiter Capitolinus and the opposite summit; and in this manner they are often found mentioned as two separate localities opposed to one another: "De arce capta Capitolioque occupato — nuntii veniunt." (Liv. iii. 18.) "Est autem etiam aedes Vejovis Romae inter arcem et Capitolium." (Gell. N. A. v.

12.) On this point also it would be easy to multiply examples, if it were necessary.

The preceding passages, which have been purposely selected from prose writers, suffice to show how loosely the terms Arx and Capitolium were employed; and if we were to investigate the language of the poets, we should find the question still further embarrassed by the introduction of the ancient names of the hill, such as Mons Tarpeius, Rupes Tarpeia,

&c., which are often used without any precise signification.

With these preliminary remarks we shall proceed to examine the question as to which summit was occupied by the Capitoline temple. And as several arguments have been adduced by Becker (*Handb.* pp. 387—395) in favour of the SW. summit, which he deems to be of such force and cogency as "completely to decide" the question, it will be necessary to examine them *seriatim*, before we proceed to state our own opinion. They are chiefly drawn from narratives of attempts to surprise or storm the Capitol, and the first on the list is the well-known story of Herdonius, as related by Dionysius of Halicarnassus (x. 14): "Herdonius," says Becker, "lands by night at the spot where the Capitol lies, and where the hill is not the distance of a stadium from the river, and therefore manifestly opposite to its western point. He forces a passage through the Carmental gate, which lay on this side, ascends the height, and seizes the fortress (φρούριον). Hence he presses forwards still farther to the neighbouring citadel, of which he also gains possession. This narrative alone suffices to decide the question, since the Capitol is expressly mentioned as being next to the river, and the Carmental gate near it: and since the band of Herdonius, after taking possession of the western height, proceeds to the adjoining citadel" (p. 388).

In this interpretation of the narrative some things are omitted which are necessary to the proper understanding of it, and others are inserted which are by no means to be found there. Dionysius does not say that Herdonius landed at the spot *where the Capitol lies*, and where the hill is only a stade from the river, but that he landed at that part of Rome where the *Capitoline hill* is, at the distance of not quite a stade from the river. Secondly, Becker assumes that φρούριον is the Capitol, or, as he calls it, by begging the whole question, "the *western* height." But his greatest misrepresentation arises from omitting to state that Dionysius, as his text stands, describes the Carmental gate as left open in pursuance of some divine or oracular command (κατά τι θέσφατον); whereas Becker's words ("er dringt durch das Carmentalische Thor") would lead the reader to believe that the passage was *forced* by Herdonius. Now it has been shown that the Porta Carmentalis was one of the city gates; and it is impossible to believe that the Romans were so besotted, or rather in such a state of idiotcy, that, after building a huge stone wall round their city at great expense and trouble, they should leave one of their gates open, and that too without a guard upon it; thus rendering all their elaborate defences useless and abortive. We have said *without a guard*, because it appears from the narrative that the first obstacle encountered by Herdonius was the φρούριον, which according to Becker was the Capitol; so that he must have passed through the Vicus Jugarius, over the forum, and ascended the Clivus Capitolinus without interruption. It is evident, however, that Dionysius could not have intended the Carmental gate, since he makes it an entrance not to the city but to the Capitol (ἱεραὶ πύλαι τοῦ Καπιτωλίου); and that he regarded it as seated upon an eminence, is plain from the expression that Herdonius made his men *ascend* through it (ἀναβιβάσας τὴν δύναμιν). The text of Dionysius is manifestly corrupt or interpolated; which further appears from the fact that when he was describing the real Carmental gate

(i. 32), he used the adjective form Καρμεντίς (παρὰ ταῖς Καρμεντίσι πύλαις), whilst in the present instance he is made to use the form Καρμέντινος. Herdonius must have landed *below* the line of wall running from the Capitoline to the river, where, as the wall was not continued along its banks, he would have met with no obstruction. And this was evidently the reason why he brought down his men in boats; for if the Carmental gate had been always left open it would have been better for him to have marched overland, and thus to have avoided the protracted and hazardous operation of landing his men. It is clear, as Preller has pointed out (Schneidewin's *Philologus* i. p. 85, note), that Dionysius, or rather perhaps his transcribers or editors, has here confounded the Porta Carmentalis with the Porta Pandana, which, as we have before seen, was seated on the Capitoline hill, and always left open, for there could hardly have been two gates of this description. The Porta Pandana, as we have already said, was still in existence in the time of Varro (*L. L.* v. § 42, Müll.), and was in fact the entrance to the ancient fort or castellum — the φρούριον of Dionysius — which guarded the approach to the Capitoline hill, of course on its E. side, or towards the forum, where alone it was accessible. Thus Solinus: "Iidem (Herculis comites) et montem Capitolinum Saturnium nominarunt, Castelli quoque, quod excitaverunt, portam Saturniam appellaverunt, quae postmodum Pandana vocitata est" (i. 13). We also learn from Festus, who mentions the same castrum, or fort, that it was situated in the lower part of the Clivus Capitolinus. "Saturni quoque dicebantur, qui castrum in imo clivo Capitolino incolebant" (p. 322, Müll.). This, then, was the φρούριον first captured by Herdonius, and not, as Becker supposes, the Capitol: and hence, as that writer says, he pressed on to the *western* height, which, however, was not the Capitol but the Arx. When Dionysius says of the latter that it adjoined, or was connected with, the Capitolium, this was intended for his Greek readers, who would otherwise have supposed, from the fashion of their own cities, that the Arx or Acropolis formed quite a separate hill.

The story of Herdonius, then, instead of being "alone decisive," and which Becker (*Warnung*, pp. 43, 44) called upon Braun and Preller to explain, before they ventured to say a word more on the subject, proves absolutely nothing at all; and we pass on to the next, that of Pontius Cominius and the Gauls. "The messenger climbs the rock at the spot nearest the river, by the Porta Carmentalis, where the Gauls, who had observed his footsteps, afterwards make the same attempt. It is from this spot that Manlius casts them down" (p. 389). This is a fair representation of the matter; but the question remains, when the messenger had clomb the rock was he in the Capitol or in the Arx? The passages quoted as decisive in favour of the former are the following: "Inde (Cominius) qua proximum fuit a ripa, per praeruptum eoque neglectum hostium custodiae saxum in Capitolium evadit." (Liv. v. 46.) "Galli, seu vestigio notato humano, seu sua sponte animadverso ad Carmentis saxorum adscensu aequo — in summum evasere" (*Ib.* 47). Now, it is plain, that in the former of these passages Livy means the Capitoline hill; and not the Capitol strictly so called; since, in regard to a small space, like the Capitol Proper, it would be a useless and absurd distinction, if it lay, and was known to lie, next the river, to say that Cominius mounted it "where it was nearest to the river. "Cominius in Capitolium evadit" is here equivalent to "Romulus in Capitolium escendit," in a passage before cited. (Liv. i. 10.) Hence, to mark the spot more precisely, the historian inserts "ad Carmentis" in the following chapter. There is nothing in the other authorities cited in Becker's note (no. 750) which yields a conclusion either one way or the other. We might, with far superior justice, quote the following passage of Cicero, which we have adduced on another occasion, to prove that the attempt of the Gauls was on the *Arx* or citadel: "Atque ut ita munita Arx circumjectu arduo et quasi circumciso saxo niteretur, ut etiam in illa tempestate horribili Gallici adventus incolumis atque intacta permanserit" (*De Rep.* ii. 6). But, though we hold that the attempt was really on the Arx, we are nevertheless of opinion that Cicero here uses the word only in its general sense, and thus as applicable to the whole hill, just as Livy uses *Capitolium* in the preceding passage. Hence, Mr. Bunbury (*Class. Mus.* vol. iv. p. 430) and M. Preller (*l. c.*) have justly regarded this narrative as affording no evidence at all, although they are adherents of the German theory. We may further observe, that the house of Manlius was on the Arx; and though this circumstance, taken by itself, presents nothing decisive, yet, in the case of so sudden a surprise, it adds probability to the view that the Arx was on the southern summit.

We now proceed to the next illustration, which is drawn from the account given by Tacitus of the attack of the Vitellians on the Capitol. Becker's interpretation of this passage is so full of errors, that we must follow him sentence by sentence, giving, first of all, the original description of Tacitus. It runs as follows: "Cito agmine forum et imminentia foro templa praetervecti erigunt aciem per adversum collem usque ad primas Capitolinae arcis fores. Erant antiquitus porticus in latere clivi, dextrae subeuntibus: in quarum tectum egressi saxis tegulisque Vitellianos obruebant. Neque illis manus nisi gladiis armatae; et arcessere tormenta aut missilia tela longum videbatur. Faces in prominentem porticum jecere et sequebantur ignem; ambustasque Capitolii fores penetrassent, ni Sabinus revulsas undique statuas, decora majorum in ipso aditu vice muri objecisset. Tum diversos Capitolii aditus invadunt, juxta lucum asyli, et qua Tarpeia rupes centum gradibus aditur. Improvisa utraque vis : propior atque acrior per asylum ingruebat. Nec sisti poterant scandentes per conjuncta aedificia, quae, ut in multa pace, in altum edita solum Capitolii aequabant. Hic ambigitur, ignem tectis oppugnatores injecerint, an obsessi, quae crebrior fama est, quo nitentes ac progressos depellerent. Inde lapsus ignis in porticus appositas aedibus : mox sustinentes fastigium aquilae vetere ligno traxerunt flammam alueruntque. Sic Capitolium clausis foribus indefensum et indireptum conflagravit." (*Hist.* iii. 71.)

"The attack," says Becker, "is directed solely against the Capitol; that is, the height containing the temple, which latter is burnt on the occasion" (p. 390). This is so far from being the case, that the words of Tacitus would rather show that the attack was directed against the Arx. The temple is represented as having been shut up, and neither attacked nor defended : "clausis foribus, indefensum et indireptum conflagravit." Such a state of things is inconceivable, if, as Becker says, the attack was directed solely against the Capitol. That part of the hill was evidently deserted, and

left to its fate; the besieged had concentrated themselves upon the Arx, which thus' became the point of attack. By that unfortunate ambiguity in the use of the word Capitolium, which we have before pointed out, we find Tacitus representing the gates of the Capitolium as having been burnt ("ambustasque Capitolii fores ") which, if Capitolium meant the same thing in the last sentence, would be a direct contradiction, as the gates are there represented as shut. But in the first passage he means the gates of the fortification which enclosed the whole summit of the hill; and in the second passage he means the gates of the temple. The meaning of Tacitus is also evident in another manner; for if the Vitellians were attacking the temple itself, and burning its gates, they must have already gained a footing on the height, and would consequently have had no occasion to seek access by other routes — by the steps of the Rupes Tarpeia, and by the Lucus Asyli. Becker proceeds : "Tacitus calls this (*i. e.* the height with the temple), indifferently Capitolina Arx and Capitolium." This is quite a mistake. The Arx Capitolina may possibly mean the *whole summit* of the hill; but if it is to be restricted to one of the two eminences, it means the Arx proper rather than the Capitol. "The attacking party, it appears, first made a lodgment on the Clivus Capitolinus. Here the portico *on the right* points distinctly to the SW. height. Had the portico been to the right of a person ascending in the contrary direction, it would have been separated from the besieged by the street, who could not therefore have defended themselves from its roof." If we thought that this argument had any value we might adopt it as our own : for we also believe that the attack was directed against the SW. height, but with this difference, that the Arx was on this height, and not the Capitol. But, in fact, there was only one *principal* ascent or clivus,—that leading towards the western height; and the only thing worth remarking in Becker's observations is that he should have thought there might be *another* Clivus Capitolinus leading in the opposite direction. We may remark, by the way, that the portico here mentioned was probably that erected by the great-grandson of Cn. Scipio. (Vell. Pat. ii. 3.) "As the attack is here fruitless, the Vitellians abandon it, and make another attempt at two different approaches ("diversos aditus"); at the Lucus Asyli, that is, on the side where at present the broad steps lead from the *Palazzo de' Conservatori* to *Monte Caprino*, and again where the Centum Gradus led to the Rupes Tarpeia. Whether these Centum Gradus are to be placed by the church of *Sta Maria della Consolazione*, or more westward, it is not necessary to determine here, since that they led to the *Caffarelli* height is undisputed. On the side of the asylum (*Palazzo de' Conservatori*) the danger was more pressing. Where the steps now lead to *Monte Caprino*, and on the whole side of the hill, were houses which reached to its summit. These were set on fire, and the flames then caught the adjoining portico, and lastly the temple."

Our chief objection to this account is, its impossibility. If the Lucus Asyli corresponded to the steps of the present *Palazzo de' Conservatori*, which is seated in the depression between the two summits, or present *Piazza del Campidoglio*, then the besiegers must have forced the passage of the Clivus Capitolinus, whereas Tacitus expressly says that they were repulsed. Being repulsed they must have retreated *downwards*, and renewed the attempt at lower points; at the foot of the Hundred Steps, for instance, on one side, and at the bottom of the Lucus Asyli on another; on both which sides they again attempted to mount. The *Palazzo de' Conservatori*, though not the highest point of the hill, is *above* the *clivus*. Becker, as we have shown, has adopted the strangely erroneous opinion that the "Capitolinae arcis fores" belonged to the Capitol itself (note 752), and that consequently the Vitellians were storming it from the *Piazza del Campidoglio* (note 754). But the portico from which they were driven back was on the clivus, and consequently they could not have reached the top of the hill, or *piazza*. The argument that the temple must have been on the SW. height, because the Vitellians attempted to storm it by mounting the Centum Gradus (Becker, *Warnung*, p. 43), may be retorted by those who hold that the attack was directed against the Arx. The precise spot of the Lucus Asyli cannot be indicated; but from Livy's description of it, it was evidently somewhere on the *descent* of the hill ("locum qui nunc septus *descendentibus* inter duos lucos est, asylum aperit," i. 8). It is probable, as Preller supposes (*Philol.* p. 99), that the "aditus juxta lucum Asyli" was on the NE. side of the hill near the present arch of Severus. The Clivus Asyli is a fiction; there was only one clivus on the Capitoline.

We have only one more remark to make on this narrative. It is plain that the fire broke out near the Lucus Asyli, and then spreading-from house to house, caught at last the *front* of the temple. This follows from Tacitus' account of the portico and the eagles which supported the *fastigium* or pediment, first catching fire. The back-front of the Capitoline temple was plain, apparently a mere wall; since Dionysius (iv. 61) does not say a single word about it, though he particularly describes the front as having a triple row of columns and the sides double rows. But as we know that the temple faced the south, such an accident could not have happened except it stood on the NE. height, or that of *Araceli*.

We might, therefore, by substituting *Caffarelli* for *Araceli*, retort the triumphant remark with which Becker closes his explanation of this passage: "To him, therefore, who would seek the temple of Jupiter on the height of *Caffarelli*, the description of Tacitus is in every respect inexplicable."

Becker's next argument in favour of the W. summit involves an equivocation. It is, "that the temple was built *on that summit* of the hill which bore the name of Mons Tarpeius." Now it is notorious—and as we have already established it, we need not repeat it here—that before the building of the Capitol the *whole hill* was called Mons Tarpeius. The passages cited by Becker in note 755 (Liv. i. 55; Dionys. iii. 69) mean nothing more than this; indeed, the latter expressly states it (ὃς [λόφος] τότε μὲν ἐκαλεῖτο Ταρπήϊος, νῦν δὲ Καπιτωλῖνος). Capitolium gradually became the name for the whole hill; but who can believe that the name of Tarpeia continued to be retained at that very portion of it where the Capitoline temple was built? The process was evidently as follows: the northern height, on which the temple was built, was at first alone called Capitolium. Gradually its superior importance gave name to the whole hill; yet a particular portion, the most remote from the temple, retained the primitive name of Rupes Tarpeia. And thus Festus in a mutilated fragment,—

not however so mutilated but that the sense is plain —"Noluerunt funestum locum [cum altera parte] Capitoli conjungi" (p. 343), where Müller remarks, "non multum ab Ursini supplemento discedere licebit."

Becker then proceeds to argue that the temple of Juno Moneta was built on the site of the house of M. Manlius Capitolinus, which was on the Arx (Liv. v. 47; Plut. *Cam.* 36; Dion Cass. *Fr.* 31, &c.); and we learn from Ovid (*Fast.* i. 637) that there were steps leading from the temple of Concord, to that of Juno Moneta. Now as the former temple was situated under the height of *Araceli*, near the arch of Severus, this determines the question of the site of Juno Moneta and the Arx. Ovid's words are as follows:—

> "Candida, te niveo posuit lux proxima templo
> Qua fert sublimes alta Moneta gradus;
> Nunc bene prospicies Latiam, Concordia, turbam," &c.

This is very obscure; but we do not see how it can be inferred from this passage that there were steps from one temple to the other. We should rather take it to mean that the temple of Concord was placed close to that of Moneta, which latter was approached by a flight of lofty steps. Nor do we think it very difficult to point out what these steps were. The temple of Juno was on the Arx; that is, according to our view, on the SW. summit; and the lofty steps were no other than the Centum Gradus for ascending the Rupes Tarpeia, as described by Tacitus in the passage we have just been discussing. Had there been another flight of steps leading up to the top of the Capitoline hill, the Vitellians would certainly have preferred them to clambering over the tops of houses. But it will be objected that according to this view the temple of Concord is placed upon the Arx, for which there is no authority, instead of on the forum or clivus, for which there is authority. Now this is exactly the point at which we wish to arrive. There were several temples of Concord, but only two of any renown, namely, that dedicated by Furius Camillus, B. C. 367, and rededicated by Tiberius after his German triumph, which is the one of which Dion speaks; and another dedicated by the consul Opimius after the sedition and death of Gracchus. Appian says that the latter temple was *in* the forum: ἡ δὲ βουλὴ καὶ νεὼν Ὁμονοίας αὐτὸν ἐν ἀγορᾷ προσέταξεν ἐγεῖραι (*B.C.* i. 26). But in ordinary language the clivus formed part of the forum; and it would be impossible to point out any place in the forum, strictly so called, which it could have occupied. It is undoubtedly the same temple alluded to by Varro in the following passage: "Senaculum supra Graecostasim ubi aedis Concordiae et basilica Opimia" (*L.L.* v. p. 156, Müll.); from which we may infer that Opimius built at the same time a basilica, which adjoined the temple. Becker (*Handb.* p. 309) denied the existence of this basilica; but by the time he published his *Warnung* he had grown wiser, and quoted in the Appendix (p. 58) the following passage from Cicero (*p. Sest.* 67): "L. Opimius cujus monumentum celeberrimum in foro, sepulcrum desertissimum in littore Dyrrhachino est relictum;" maintaining, however, that this passage related to Opimius' temple of Concord. But Urlichs (*Röm. Top.* p. 26), after pointing out that the epithet *celeberrimum*, "very much frequented," suited better with a basilica than with a temple, produced

two ancient inscriptions from Marini's *Atti de' Fratelli Aroali* (p. 212); in which a basilica Opimia is
recorded; and Becker, in his *Antwort* (p. 33), con-
fessing that he had overlooked these inscriptions,
retracted his doubts, and acknowledged the existence
of a basilica. According to Varro, then, the Aedis
Concordiae and basilica of Opimius were close to
the senaculum; and the situation of the senaculum
is pointed out by Festus between the Capitol and
forum: "Unum (Senaculum) ubi nunc est aedis
Concordiae, inter Capitolium et Forum" (p. 347,
Müll). This description corresponds exactly with the
site where the present remains of a temple of Concord are unanimously agreed to exist: remains, however, which are supposed to be those of the temple
founded by Camillus, and not of that founded by
Opimius. According to this supposition there must
have been two temples of Concord on the forum.
But if these remains belong to that of Camillus,
who shall point out those of the temple erected by
Opimius? Where was its site? What its history?
When was it demolished, and its place either left
vacant or occupied by another building? Appian,
as we have seen, expressly says that the temple built
by Opimius was in the forum; where is the evidence
that the temple of Camillus was also in the forum?
There is positively none. Plutarch, the only direct
evidence as to its site, says no such thing, but only
that it looked down upon the forum: ἐψηφίσαντο
τῆς μὲν Ὁμονίας ἱερὸν, ὥσπερ ηὔξατο ὁ Κάμιλλος,
εἰς τὴν ἀγορὰν καὶ εἰς τὴν ἐκκλησίαν ἄποπτον ἐπὶ
τοῖς γεγενημένοις ἱδρύσασθαι (*Camill.* 42). Now
ἄφορᾶν means *to view from a distance*, and especially *from a height*. It is equivalent to the Latin
prospicere, the very term used by Ovid in describing
the same temple:—

"Nunc bene prospicies Latiam, Concordia, turbam."

These expressions, then, like Ovid's allusion to the
"sublimes gradus" of Moneta, point to the Arx as
the site of the temple. It is remarkable that Lucan
(*Phars.* i. 195) employs the same word when describing the temple of Jupiter Tonans, erected by
Augustus, also situated upon the Arx, or Rupes
Tarpeia:—

"—— O magnae qui moenia prospicis urbis
Tarpeia de rupe Tonans."

This temple indeed, has also been placed on the
clivus, on the authority of the pseudo-Victor, and
against the express evidence of the best authorities.
Thus an inscription in Gruter (lxxii. No. 5), consisting of some lines addressed to Fortuna, likewise
places the Jupiter Tonans on the Tarpeian rock:—

"Tu quae Tarpeio coleris vicina Tonanti
Votorum vindex semper Fortuna meorum," &c.

Suetonius (*Aug.* c. 29 and 91), Pliny (xxxvi. 6)
and the *Mon. Ancyranum,* place it "in Capitolio," meaning the Capitoline hill. It has been
absurdly inferred that it was on the clivus, because Dion says that those who were going up to
the great temple of Jupiter met with it first,—ὅτι
πρῶτοι οἱ ἀνιόντες ἐς τὸ Καπιτώλιον ἐνετύγχανον
(liv. 4), which they no doubt would do, since the
clivus led first to the western height.

On these grounds, then, we are inclined to believe
that the temple of Concord erected by Camillus stood
on the Arx, and could not, therefore, have had any
steps leading to the temple of Juno Moneta. The
latter was likewise founded by Camillus, as we
learn from Livy and Ovid:—

"Arce quoque in summa Junoni templa Monetae
Ex voto memorant facta, Camille, tuo;
Ante domus Manli fuerant" (*Fast.* vi. 183);

and thus these two great works of the dictator
stood, as was natural, close together, just as the
temple of Concord and the basilica subsequently
erected by Opimius also adjoined one another on or
near the clivus. It is no objection to this view
that there was another small temple of Concord on
the Arx, which had been vowed by the praetor
Manlius in Gaul during a sedition of the soldiers.
The vow had been almost overlooked, but after a
lapse of two years it was recollected, and the temple
erected in discharge of it. (Liv. xxii. 33.) It seems,
therefore, to have been a small affair, and might
very well have coexisted on the Arx with another
and more splendid temple.

But to return to Becker's arguments. The next
proof adduced is Caligula's bridge. "Caligula,"
he says, as Bunsen has remarked, "caused a bridge
to be thrown from the Palatine hill over the temple
of Augustus (and probably the Basilica Julia) to
the Capitoline temple, which is altogether inconceivable if the latter was on the height of
Araceli, as in that case the bridge must have been
conducted over the forum" (p. 393). But here
Becker goes further than his author, who merely
says that Caligula threw a bridge from the Palatine
hill to the Capitoline: "Super templum Divi Augusti ponte transmisso, Palatium Capitoliumque
conjunxit." (Suet. *Cal.* 22.) Becker correctly
renders Palatium by the "Palatine hill," but
when he comes to the other hill he converts it
into a temple. Suetonius offers a parallel case
of the use of these words in a passage to which
we had occasion to allude just now, respecting the
temple of Jupiter Tonans : "Templum Apollinis in
Palatio (extruxit), aedem Tonantis Jovis in Capitolio" (*Aug.* 29); where, if Becker's view was
right, we might by analogy translate,—"he erected
a temple of Apollo in the palace."

The next proof is that a large piece of rock fell
down from the Capitol ("ex Capitolio") into the Vicus
Jugarius (Liv. xxxv. 21); and as the Vicus Jugarius
ran under the S. summit, this shows that the Capitoline temple was upon it. But pieces of rock fall
down from hills, not from buildings, and, therefore,
Capitolium here only means the hill. In like
manner when Livy says (xxxviii. 28), "substruc-
tionem super Aequimelium in Capitolio (censores
locaverunt)," it is plain that he must mean the
hill; and consequently this passage is another proof
of this use of the word. The Aequimelium was in or
by the Vicus Jugarius, and could not, therefore, have
been on the Capitol properly so called, even if the latter
had been on the SW. height. Becker wrongly translates this passage,—" a substruction *of the Capitol*
over the Aequimelium" (p. 393.) Then comes the
passage respecting the statue of Jupiter being turned
towards the east, that it might behold the forum
and curia; which Becker maintains to be impossible
of a statue erected on the height of *Araceli.* Those
who have seen the ground will not be inclined to
coincide in this opinion. The statue stood on a
column (Dion Cass. xxxvii. 9 ; Cic. *Div.* i. 12 ; cf.
Id. *Cat.* iii. 8), and most probably *in front of* the
temple—it could hardly have been placed *behind*
it ; and, therefore, if the temple was on the S.
height, the statue must have been at the extremity
of it ; a site which certainly would not afford a
very good view of the forum. Next the direction

of the Clivus Capitolinus is adduced, which ran to the Western height, and must have led directly to the temple, whence it derived its name. But this is a complete begging of the question, and the clivus more probably derived its name from the hill. If the direction of the clivus, however, proves anything at all—and we are not disposed to lay much stress upon it—it rather proves the reverse of Becker's case. The clivus was a continuation of the Sacra Via, by which, as we shall have occasion to show when treating of that road, the augurs descended from the Arx after taking the auguries, and by which they carried up their new year's offerings to king Tatius, who lived upon the Arx: and hence in sacerdotal language the clivus itself was called Sacra Via. (Varro, L.L. v. § 47, Müll.; Festus, p. 290, id.). Lastly, " the confined height of *Araceli* would not have afforded sufficient room for the spacious temple of Jupiter, the Area Capitolina, where meetings of the people were held, and at the same time be able to display so many other temples and monuments." There is some degree of truth in this observation, so far at least as the Area Capitolina is concerned. But when we come to describe the temple of Jupiter Capitolinus, an acquaintance with which is necessary to the complete understanding of the present question, though Becker has chosen to omit it, " as lying out of the plan of his book" (p 396), we shall endeavour to show how this objection may be obviated. Meanwhile, having now discussed all Becker's arguments in favour of the SW. summit as the site of the Capitoline temple, it will be more convenient shortly to review the whole question, and to adduce some reasons which have led us to a directly contrary conclusion. In doing this we do not presume to think, with Becker, that we have "completely decided" the question. It is one, indeed, that will not admit of complete demonstration ; but we venture to hope that the balance of probability may be shown to predominate very considerably in favour of the NE. height.

The greater part of Becker's arguments, as we trust that we have shown, prove nothing at all, while the remainder, or those which prove something, may be turned against him. We must claim as our own the proof drawn from the storm of the Capitol by the Vitellians, as described by Tacitus, as well as that derived from Mons Tarpeius being the name of the SW. height, and that from the westerly direction of the Clivus Capitolinus. Another argument in favour of the NE. height may be drawn from Livy's account of the trial of Manlius Capitolinus, to which we have already adverted when treating of the Porta Flumentana [supra, p. 751], and need not here repeat. To these we shall add a few more drawn from probability.

Tatius dwelt on the Arx, where the temple of Juno Moneta afterwards stood. (Plut. *Rom.* 20; Solinus, i. 21.) "This," says Becker (p. 388), "is the height of *Araceli*, and always retained its name of Arx after the Capitol was built, since certain sacred customs were attached to the place and appellation." He is here alluding to the Arx being the auguraculum of which Festus says : " Auguraculum appellabant antiqui quam nos arcem dicimus, quod ibi augures publice auspicarentur " (p. 18, where Müller observes : " non tam *arcem* quam *in arce* fuisse arbitror auguraculum "). The templum, then, marked out from the Arx, from which the city auspices were taken, was defined by a peculiar and

appropriate form of words, which is given by Varro, (L.L. vii. § 8, Müll.) It was bounded on the left hand and on the right by a distant tree ; the tract between was the *templum* or *tescum* (country region) in which the omens were observed. The augur who inaugurated Numa led him to the Arx, seated him on a stone, with his face turned towards the South, and sat down on his left hand, capite velato, and with his lituus. Then, looking forwards over the city and country — " prospectu in urbem agrumque capto"— he marked out the temple from east to west, and determined in his mind the sign (signum) to be observed as far as ever his eyes could reach : " quo longissime conspectum oculi ferebant." (Liv. i. 18; cf. Cic. *de Off.* iii. 16.) The great extent of the prospect required may be inferred from an anecdote related by Valerius Maximus (viii. 2. § 1), where the augurs are represented as ordering Claudius Centumalus to lower his lofty dwelling on the Caelian, because it interfered with their view from the Arx,—a passage, by the way, which shows that the auguries were taken from the Arx till at all events a late period of the Republic. Now, supposing with Becker, that the Arx was on the NE. summit, what sort of prospect would the augurs have had? It is evident that a large portion of their view would have been intercepted by the huge temple of Jupiter Capitolinus. The SW. summit is the only portion of the hill which, in the words of Livy, would afford a noble prospect, " in urbem agrumque." It was doubtless this point to which the augur conducted Numa, and which remained ever afterwards the place appointed for taking the auguries. Preller is of opinion that Augustus removed them to a place called the Auguratorium on the Palatine. (*Philologus*, i. p. 92.) But the situation laid down for that building scarcely answers to our ideas of a place adapted for taking the auguries, and it seems more probable that it was merely a place of assembly for the college of augurs.

Another argument that has been adduced in favour of the SW. summit being the Arx, is drawn from its proximity to the river, and from its rocky and precipitous nature, which made it proper for a citadel. But on this we are not inclined to lay any great stress.

Other arguments in favour of the Italian view may be drawn from the nature of the temple itself ; but in order to understand them it will first be necessary to give a description of the building. The most complete account of the TEMPLUM JOVIS CAPITOLINI is that given by Dionysius (iv. 61), from which we learn that it stood upon a high basis or platform, 8 plethra, or 800 Greek feet square, which is nearly the same in English measure. This would give about 200 feet for each side of the temple, for the length exceeded the breadth only by about 15 feet. These are the dimensions of the original construction ; and when it was burnt down a generation before the time of Dionysius,— that is, as we learn from Tacitus (*Hist.* iii. 72), in the consulship of L. Scipio and Norbanus (B. C. 83),—it was rebuilt upon the same foundation. The materials employed in the second construction were, however, of a much richer description than those of the first. The front of the temple, *which faced the south*, had a portico consisting of three rows of columns, whilst on the flanks it had only two rows : and as the back front is not said to have had any portico, we may conclude that there was nothing on this side but a plain wall. The interior contained three cells

parallel to one another with common walls, the centre
one being that of Jove, on each side those of Juno
and Minerva. In Livy, however (vi. 4), Juno is
represented as being in the same cella with Jupiter.
But though the temple had three cells, it had but
one *fastigium*, or pediment, and a single roof.

Now the first thing that strikes us on reading this
description is, that the front being so ornamented,
and the back so very plain, the temple must have
stood in a situation where the former was very conspicuous, whilst the latter was but little seen. Such
a situation is afforded only by the NE. summit of
the Capitoline. On this site the front of the temple,
being turned to the south, would not only be visible
from the forum, but would also present its best
aspect to those who had ascended the Capitoline hill;
whilst on the other hand, had it stood on the SW.
summit, the front would not have been visible from
the forum, and what is still worse, the temple would
have presented only its nude and unadorned back
to those who approached it by the usual and most
important ascent, the Clivus Capitolinus. Such a
state of things, in violation of all the rules which
commonly regulate the disposition of public buildings,
is scarcely to be imagined.

We will now revert to Becker's objection respecting
the AREA CAPITOLINA. It must be admitted that
the dimensions of the temple would have allowed but
little room for this area on the height of *Araceli*,
especially as this must have contained other small
temples and monuments, such as that of Jupiter
Feretrius, &c. Yet the Area Capitolina, we know, was
often the scene not only of public meetings but even
of combats. There are very striking indications that
this area was not confined to the height on which
the temple stood, but that it occupied part at least of
the extensive surface of lower ground lying between
the two summits. One indication of this is the great
height of the steps leading up to the vestibule of the
temple, as shown by the story related by Livy of
Annius, the ambassador of the Latins; who being
rebuked by Manlius and the fathers for his insolence,
rushed frantically from the vestibule, and falling
down the steps, was either killed or rendered insen-
sible (viii. 6). That there was a difference in the
level of the Capitol may be seen from the account
given by Paterculus of Scipio Nasica's address to
the people in the sedition of the Gracchi. Standing
apparently on the same lofty steps,—" ex *superiore
parte Capitolii* summis gradibus insistens" (ii. 3),—
Nasica incited by his eloquence the senators and
knights to attack Gracchus, who was standing in
the area below, with a large crowd of his adherents,
and who was killed in attempting to escape down
the Clivus Capitolinus. The area must have been

of considerable size to hold the catervae of Gracchus;
and the same fact is shown by several other passages
in the classics (Liv. xxv. 3, xlv. 36, &c.). Now
all these circumstances suit much better with a
temple on the NE. summit than with one on the
opposite height. An area in front of the latter, besides being out of the way for public meetings, would
not have afforded sufficient space for them; nor
would it have presented the lofty steps before described, nor the ready means of escape down the
clivus. These, then, are the reasons why we deem
the NE. summit the more probable site of the
Capitoline temple.

We have already mentioned that this famous
temple was at least planned by the elder Tarquin;
and according to some authors the foundation was
completely laid by him (Dionys. iv. 59), and the
building continued under Servius (Tac. *Hist.* iii. 72).
However this may be, it is certain that it was not
finished till the time of Tarquinius Superbus, who
tasked the people to work at it (Liv. i. 56): but
the tyrant was expelled before it could be dedicated,
which honour was reserved for M. Horatius Pulvillus,
one of the first two consuls of the Republic (Polyb.
iii. 22; Liv. ii. 8; Plut. *Popl.* 14). When the
foundations were first laid it was necessary to exau-
gurate the temples of other deities which stood upon
the site destined for it; on which occasion Terminus
and Juventas, who had altars there, alone refused
to move, and it became necessary to enclose their
shrines within the temple; a happy omen for the
future greatness of the city! (Liv. v. 54; Dionys. iii.
69.) It is a well-known legend that its name of
Capitolium was derived from the finding of a human
head in digging the foundation (Varr. *L. L.* v.
§ 41, Müll.; Plin. xxviii. 4, &c.) The image
of the god, originally of clay, was made by Turanius
of Fregellae, and represented him in a sitting
posture. The face was painted with vermilion, and
the statue was probably clothed in a tunica palmata
and toga picta, as the costume was borrowed by
triumphant generals. On the acroterium of the
pediment stood a quadriga of earthenware, whose
portentous swelling in the furnace was also regarded as an omen of Rome's future greatness (Plin.
xxviii. 4; Plut. *Popl.* 13). The brothers C. & Q.
Ogulnius subsequently placed a bronze quadriga with
a statue of Jupiter on the roof; but this probably did
not supersede that of clay, to which so much ominous
importance was attached. The same aediles also
presented a bronze threshold, and consecrated some
silver plate in Jupiter's cella (Liv. x. 23; cf. Plaut.
Trin. i. 2. 46.) By degrees the temple grew exceedingly rich. Camillus dedicated three golden
paterae out of the spoils taken from the Etruscans
(Liv. vi. 4), and the dictator Cincinnatus placed in
the temple a statue of Jupiter Imperator, which he
had carried off from Praeneste (Id. vi. 29). At
length the pediment and columns became so encumbered with shields, ensigns, and other offerings that
the censors M. Fulvius Nobilior and M. Aemilius
Lepidus were compelled to rid the temple of these
superfluous ornaments (Id. xl. 51).

As we have before related, the original building lasted till the year B. C. 83, when it was burnt
down in the civil wars of Sulla, according to Tacitus
by design (" privata fraude," *Hist.* iii. 72). Its
restoration was undertaken by Sulla, and subsequently confided to Q. Lutatius Catulus, not without
the opposition of Caesar, who wished to obliterate the
name of Catulus from the temple, and to substitute

his own. (Plut. *Popl.* 15; Suet. *Caes.* 15; Dion Cass. xxxvii. 44 ; Cic. *Verr.* iv. 31, &c.) On this occasion Sulla followed the Roman fashion of despoiling Greece of her works of art, and adorned the temple with columns taken from that of the Olympian Zeus at Athens. (Plin. xxxvi. 5.) After its destruction by the Vitellians, Vespasian restored it as soon as possible, but still on the original plan, the haruspices allowing no alteration except a slight increase of its height. (Tac. *Hist.* iv. 53; Suet.

Vesp. 8; Dion Cass. lxvi. 10, &c.) The new building, however, stood but for a very short period. It was again destroyed soon after Vespasian's death in a great fire which particularly desolated the 9th Region, and was rebuilt by Domitian with a splendour hitherto unequalled. (Suet. *Dom.* 15; Dion Cass. lxvi. 24.) Nothing further is accurately known of its history ; but Domitian's structure seems to have lasted till a very late period of the Empire.

TEMPLE OF JUPITER CAPITOLINUS RESTORED.

The Area Capitolina, as we have already seen, was frequently used for meetings or *contiones*; but besides these, regular comitia were frequently holden upon it. (Liv. xxv. 3, xxxiv. 53, xliii. 16, xlv. 36 ; Plut. *Paul. Aem.* 30 ; App. *B. C.* i. 15, &c.) Here stood the CURIA CALABRA, in which on the Calends the pontifices declared whether the Nones would fall on the fifth or the seventh day of the month. (Varr. *L. L.* vi. § 27, Müll.; Macrob. *Sat.* i. 15.) Here also was a CASA ROMULI, of which there were two, the other being in the 10th Region on the Palatine; though Becker (*Handb.* p. 401 and note) denies the existence of the former in face of the express testimony of Macrobius (*l. c.*) Seneca (*Controv.* 9) ; Vitruvius (ii. 1) ; Martial (viii. 80) ; Conon (*Narrat.* 48), &c. (v. Preller in Schneidewin's *Philologus*, i. p. 83). It seems to have been a little hut or cottage, thatched with straw, commemorative of the lowly and pastoral life of the founder of Rome. The area had also rostra, which are mentioned by Cicero (*ad Brut.* 3).

Besides these, there were several temples and sacella on the NE. summit. Among them was the small temple of JUPITER FERETRIUS, one of the most ancient in Rome, in which spolia opima were dedicated first by Romulus, then by Cossus, and lastly by Marcellus (Liv. i. 10; Plut. *Marcell.* 8; Dionys. ii. 34, &c.) The last writer, in whose time only the foundations remained, gives its dimensions at 10 feet by 5. It appears, however, to have been subsequently restored by Augustus. (Liv. iv. 20; *Mon. Ancyr.*) The temple of FIDES, which stood close to the great temple, was also very ancient, having been built by Numa, and afterwards restored by M. Aemilius Scaurus. (Liv. i. 21 ; Cic. *N. D.* ii. 23, *Off.* iii. 29, &c.) It was roomy enough for assemblies of the senate. (Val. Max. iii. 2. § 17; App. *B. C.* i. 16.) The two small temples of MENS and of VENUS ERYCINA stood close together, separated only by a

trench. They had both been vowed after the battle at the Trasimene lake and were consecrated two years afterwards by Q. Fabius Maximus and T. Otacillius Crassus. (Liv. xxii. 10, xxiii. 51; Cic. *N. D.* ii. 23.) A temple of VENUS CAPITOLINA and VENUS VICTRIX are also mentioned, but it is not clear whether they were separate edifices. (Suet. *Cal.* 7, *Galb.* 18; *Fast. Amit. VIII. Id. Oct.*) We also hear of two temples of JUPITER (Liv. xxxv. 41), and a temple of OPS (xxxix. 22.) It by no means follows, however, that all these temples were on the Capitol, properly so called, and some of them might have been on the other summit, Capitolium being used generally as the name of the hill. This seems to have been the case with the temple of FORTUNE, respecting which we have already cited an ancient inscription when discussing the site of the temples of Concord and Jupiter Tonans. It is perhaps the temple of Fortuna Primigenia mentioned by Plutarch (*Fort. Rom.* 10) as having been built by Servius on the Capitoline, and alluded to apparently by Clemens. (*Protrept.* iv. 51. p. 15. Sylb.) The temple of HONOS AND VIRTUS, built by C. Marius, certainly could not have been on the northern eminence, since we learn from Festus (p. 34, Müll.) that he was compelled to build it low lest it should interfere with the prospect of the augurs, and he should thus be ordered to demolish it. Indeed Propertius (iv. 11. 45) mentions it as being on the Tarpeian rock, or southern summit:—

" Foedaque Tarpeio conopia tendere saxo
    Jura dare et statuas inter et arma Mari."

Whence we discover another indication that the auguraculum could not possibly have been on the NE. height; for in that case, with the huge temple of Jupiter before it, there would have been little cause to quarrel with this bagatelle erected by Marius. It must have stood on a lower point of the hill than the auguraculum, and probably near its declivity. The building of it by Marius is testified by Vitruvius (iii. 2, 5), and from an inscription (Orelli, 543) it appears to have been erected out of the spoils of the Cimbric and Teutonic war. We learn from Cicero that this was the temple in which the first senatus consultum was made decreeing his recall. (Sest. 54, Planc. 32, de Div. i. 28.)

We have already had occasion to allude to the temple erected by Augustus to JUPITER TONANS. Like that of Fortune it must have stood on the SW. height and near the top of the ascent by the Clivus, as appears from the following story. Augustus dreamt that the Capitoline Jove appeared to him and complained that the new temple seduced away his worshippers; to which having answered that the Jupiter Tonans had been merely placed there as his janitor or porter, he caused some bells to be hung on the pediment of the latter temple in token of its janitorial character. (Suet. Aug. 91.) That the same emperor also erected a temple to MARS ULTOR on the Capitoline, besides that in his forum, seems very doubtful, and is testified only by Dion Cassius (lv. 10). Domitian, to commemorate his preservation during the contest with the Vitellians, dedicated a sacellum to JUPITER CONSERVATOR, or the Preserver, in the Velabrum, on the site of the house of the aedituus, or sacristan, in which he had taken refuge; and afterwards, when he had obtained the purple, a large temple to JUPITER CUSTOS on the Capitoline, in which he was represented in the bosom of the god. (Tac. H. iii. 74; Suet. Dom. 5.) We also hear of a temple of BENEFICENCE (Εὐεργεσία) erected by M. Aurelius. (Dion, lxxi. 34.)

But one of the most important temples on the SW. summit or Arx was that of JUNO MONETA, erected, as we have said, in pursuance of a vow made by Camillus on the spot where the house of M. Manlius Capitolinus had stood. (Liv. vii. 28.) The name of Moneta, however, seems to have been conferred upon the goddess some time after the dedication of the temple, since it was occasioned by a voice heard from it after an earthquake, advising (monens) that expiation should be made with a pregnant sow. (Cic. de Div. i. 45.) The temple was erected in B. C. 345. The Roman mint was subsequently established in it. (Liv. vi. 20; cf. Suidas, Μονῆτα.) It was rebuilt B. C. 173. (Liv. xlii. 7.) Near it, as we have before endeavoured to establish, must be placed the temple of Concord erected by Camillus and restored by Tiberius; as well as the other smaller temple to the same deity, of no great renown, dedicated during the Second Punic War, B. C. 217. (Liv. xxii. 33.)

Such were the principal temples which occupied the summit of the Capitoline hill. But there were also other smaller temples, besides a multitude of statues, sacella, monuments, and offerings. Among these was the temple of VEJOVIS, which stood in the place called "inter duos lucos" between the Capitol and the Tarpeian height. An ara JOVIS PISTORIS and aedes VENERIS CALVAE must also be reckoned among them. (Ovid. F. vi. 387; Lactant. i. 20.) Among the statues may be mentioned those of the ROMAN KINGS in the temple of Fides (App. B. C. i. 16; Dion, xliii. 45), and on the hill the two colossal statues of APOLLO and JUPITER. The former of these, which was 30 cubits high, was brought by M. Lucullus from Apollonia in Pontus. The Jupiter was made by Sp. Carvilius out of the armour and helmets of the conquered Samnites, and was of such a size that

it could be seen from the temple of Jupiter Latiaris on the Alban Mount. (Plin. xxxiv. 18.) It would be useless to run through the whole list of objects that might be made out. It will suffice to say that the area Capitolina was so crowded with the statues of illustrious men that Augustus was compelled to remove many of them into the Campus Martius. (Suet. Cal. 34.)

We know only of one profane building on the summit of the Capitoline hill—the TABULARIUM, or record office. We cannot tell the exact site of the original one; but it could not have stood far from the Capitoline temple, since it appears to have been burnt down together with the latter during the civil wars of Sulla. Polybius (iii. 26) mentions the earlier one, and its burning, alluded to by Cicero (N. D. iii. 30, pro Rabir. Perd. 3), seems to have been effected by a private hand, like that of the Capitol itself. (Tac. Hist. iii. 72.) When rebuilt by Q. Lutatius Catulus it occupied a large part of the eastern side of the depression between the two summits of the Capitoline, behind the temple of Concord, and much of it still exists under the Palazzo Senatorio. In the time of Poggio it was converted into a salt warehouse, but the inscription recording that it was built by Catulus, at his own expense (de suo) was still legible, though nearly eaten away by the saline moisture. (De Variet. Fort. lib. i. p. 8.) This inscription, which was extant in the time of Nardini, is also given by him (Rom. Ant. ii. p. 300) and by Gruter (clxx. 6; cf. Orell. 31), with slight variations, and shows that the edifice, as rebuilt by Catulus, must have lasted till the latest period of the Empire. It is often called aerarium in Latin authors. (Liv. iii. 69 &c.)

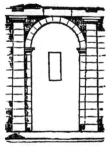

ARCH OF TABULARIUM.

We shall now proceed to consider some of the most remarkable spots on the hill and its declivities. And first of the ASYLUM. Becker (Handb. p. 387) assumes that it occupied the whole depression between the two summits, and that this space, which by modern topographers has been called by the unclassical name of Intermontium, was called "inter duos lucos." But here his authorities do not bear him out. Whether the whole of this space formed the original asylum of Romulus, it is impossible to say; but it is quite certain that this was not the asylum of later times. It would appear from the description of Dionysius (ii. 15) that in its original state (ἦν τότε, κ. τ. λ.) the grove may have extended from one summit to the other; but it does not appear that it occupied the whole space. It was convenient for Becker to assume this, on account of his interpretation of the passage in Tacitus respecting the assault of the Vitellians, where he makes them storm the SW. height from the grove of the asylum, which he places where the steps now lead up to the *Palazzo de' Conservatori*. But, first, it is impossible to suppose that in the time of Vitellius the whole of this large area was a grove. Such an account is inconsistent with the buildings which we know to have been erected on it, as the Tabularium, and also with the probable assumption which we have ventured to propose, that a considerable part of it was occupied by the Area Capitolina. But, secondly, the account of Tacitus, as we have already pointed out, is quite incompatible with Becker's view. The Vitelliana, being repulsed near the summit of the Clivus, retreat *downwards*, and attempt two other ascents, one of which was by the Lucus Asyli. And this agrees with what we gather from Livy's description of the place: "Locum, qui nunc septus *descendentibus* inter duos lucos est, asylum aperit" (i. 8.) Whence we learn that the place called "inter duos lucos" contained the ancient asylum, the enclosure of which asylum was seen by those who *descended* the "inter duos lucos." Thirdly, the asylum must have been near the approach to it; and this, on Becker's own showing (*Handb.* p. 415), was under the NE. summit, namely, between the carcer and temple of Concord and behind the arch of Severus. This ascent has been erroneously called Clivus Asyli, as there was only one clivus on the Capitoline hill. But it is quite impossible that an ascent on this side of the hill could have led to a Lucus Asyli where the *Palazzo de' Conservatori* now stands. It was near the asylum, as we have seen, that the fire broke out which destroyed the temple of Jupiter Capitolinus; and the latter, consequently, must have been on the NE. summit. With respect to the asylum, we need only

farther remark, that it contained a small temple, but to what deity it was dedicated nobody could tell (ναὸν ἐπὶ τούτῳ κατασκευασάμενος· ὅτῳ δὲ ἄρα θεῶν ἢ δαιμόνων οὐκ ἔχω σαφὲς εἰπεῖν, Dionys. ii. 15); and he was therefore merely called the divinity of the asylum (θεὸς ἀσύλαιος, Plut. *Rom.* 9).

Another disputed point is the precise situation of the RUPES TARPEIA, or that part of the summit whence criminals were hurled. The prevalent opinion among the older topographers was that it was either at that part of the hill which overhangs the *Piazza Montanara*, that is, at the extreme SW. point, or farther to the W., in a court in the *Via di Tor de' Specchi*, where a precipitous cliff, sufficiently high to cause death by a fall from it, bears at present the name of *Rupe Tarpea.* That this was the true Tarpeian rock is still the prevalent opinion, and has been adopted by Becker. But Dureau de la Malle (*Mémoire sur la Roche Tarpéienne*, in the *Mém. de l'Acad.*, 1819) has pointed out two passages in Dionysius which are totally incompatible with this site. In describing the execution of Cassius, that historian says that he was led to the precipice *which overhangs the forum*, and cast down from it *in the view of all the people* (τοῦτο τὸ τέλος τῆς δίκης λαβούσης, ἀγαγόντες οἱ ταμίαι τὸν ἄνδρα ἐπὶ τὸν ὑπερκείμενον τῆς ἀγορᾶς κρημνὸν, ἀπάντων ὁρώντων, ἔρριψαν κατὰ τῆς πέτρας, viii. 78, cf. vii. 35, seq.). Now this could not have taken place on the side of the *Tor de' Specchi*, which cannot be seen from the forum; and it is therefore assumed that the true Rupes Tarpeia must have been on the E. side, above *S. Maria della Consolazione.* The arguments adduced by Becker to controvert this assumption are not very convincing. He objects that the hill is much less precipitous here than on the other side. But this

SUPPOSED TARPEIAN ROCK.

proves nothing with regard to its earlier state. Livy, as we have seen, records the fall of a vast mass of rock into the Vicus Jugarius. Such landslips must have been frequent in later times, and it is precisely where the rock was most precipitous that they would occur. Thus, Flavius Blondus (*Inst. Rom.* ii. 58) mentions the fall in his own time of a piece as large as a house. Another objection advanced by Becker is that the criminal would have fallen into the Vicus Jugarius. This, however, is absurd; he would only

have fallen at the back of the houses. Nothing can be inferred from modern names, as that of a church now non-extant, designated as *sub Tarpeio*, as we have already shown that the whole S. summit was Mons Tarpeius. Becker's attempt to explain away the words ἀπάντων ὁρώντων is utterly futile. On the whole, it seems most probable that the rock was on the SE. side, not only from the express testimony of Dionysius, which it is difficult or impossible to set aside, but also from the inherent probability that among a people like the Romans a public execution would take place at a public and conspicuous spot. The CENTUM GRADUS, or Hundred Steps, were probably near it; but their exact situa-

tion it is impossible to point out. The other objects on the Clivus and slopes of the hill will be described in the next section.

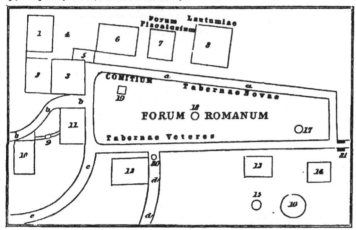

PLAN OF THE FORUM DURING THE REPUBLIC.

1. Basilica Opimia.
2. Aedes Concordiae.
3. Senaculum.
4. Vulcanal.
5. Graecostasis.
6. Curia.
7. Basilica Porcia.
8. Basilica Aemilia.
9. Porta Stercoraria.
10. Schola Xantha.
11. Templum Saturni.
12. Basilica Sempronia.
13. Aedes Castoris.
14. Regia.
15. Fons Juturnae.
16. Aedes Vestae.
17. Puteal Libonis.
18. Lacus Curtius.
19. Rostra.
20. Signum Vertumni.
21. Fornix Fabianus.
a a. Sacra Via.
b b b. Clivus Capitolinus.
c c. Vicus Jugarius.
d d. Vicus Tuscus.

IV. THE FORUM AND ITS ENVIRONS.

The forum, the great centre of Roman life and business, is so intimately connected with the Capitol that we are naturally led to treat of it next. Its original site was a deep hollow, extending from the eastern foot of the Capitoline hill to the spot where the Velia begins to ascend, by the remains of the temple of Antoninus and Faustina. At the time of the battle between the Romans and Sabines this ground was in its rude and natural state, partly swampy and partly overgrown with wood. (Dionys. ii. 50.) It could, however, have been neither a thick wood nor an absolute swamp, or the battle could not have taken place. After the alliance between the Sabines and Romans this spot formed a sort of neutral ground or common meeting-place, and was improved by cutting down the wood and filling up the swampy parts with earth. We must not, indeed, look for anything like a regular forum before the reign of Tarquinius Priscus; yet some of the principal lines which marked its subsequent extent had been traced before that period. On the E. and W. these are marked by the nature of the ground; on the former by the ascent of the Velia, on the latter by the Capitoline hill. Its northern boundary was traced by the road called Sacra Via. It is only of late years, however, that these boundaries have been recognised. Among the earlier topographers views equally erroneous and discordant

prevailed upon the subject; some of them extending the forum lengthways from the Capitoline hill to the summit of the Velia, where the arch of Titus now stands; whilst others, taking the space between the Capitoline and temple of Faustina to have been its breadth, drew its length in a southerly direction, so as to encroach upon the Velabrum. The latter theory was adopted by Nardini, and prevailed till very recently. Piale (Del Foro Romano, Roma, 1818, 1832) has the merit of having restored the correct general view of the forum, though his work is not always accurate in details. The proper limits of the forum were established by excavations made between the Capitol and Colosseum in 1827, and following years, when M. Fea saw opposite to the temple of Antoninus and Faustina, a piece of the pavement of the Sacra Via, similar to that which runs under the arch of Severus. (Bunsen, Le For. Rom. expliqué, p. 7.) A similar piece had been previously discovered during excavations made in the year 1742, before the church of S. Adriano, at the eastern corner of the Via Bonella, which Ficoroni (Vestigie di Roma antica, p. 75) rightly considered to belong to the Sacra Via. A line prolonged through these two pieces towards the arch of Severus will therefore give the direction of the street, and the boundary of the forum on that side. The southern side was no less satisfactorily determined by the excavations made in 1835, when the Basilica Julia was discovered; and in front of its steps another paved street, enclosing the area of the forum, which was distinguishable by its being paved with slabs of the ordinary silex. This street continued eastwards, past the ruin of the three columns or temple of Castor, as was shown by a similar piece of street pavement having been discovered in front of them. From this spot it must have proceeded eastwards, past the church of *Sta. Maria Liberatrice*, till it met that portion of the Sacra Via which ran in a southerly direction opposite the temple of Faustina (*S. Loerenso in Miranda*), and formed the eastern boundary of the forum. Hence. according to the opinion now generally received, the forum presented an oblong or rather trapezoidal figure, 671 English feet in length, by 202 at its greatest breadth under the Capitol, and 117 at its eastern extremity. (Bunsen, *Les Forum de Rome*, p. 15.)

THE FORUM IN ITS PRESENT STATE.

Sacra Via. — The SACRA VIA was thus intimately connected with the forum; and as it was both one of the most ancient and one of the most important streets of Rome. it will demand a particular description. Its origin is lost in obscurity. According to some accounts it must have been already in existence when the battle before alluded to was fought, since it is said to have derived its name of the "Sacred Way" from the treaty concluded upon it between Romulus and Tatius. (Dionys. ii. 46; Festus, p. 290, Müll.) This, however, seems highly improbable; not only because the road could hardly have existed at so early a period, when the site of the forum itself was in so rude a state, but also because a public highway is not altogether the place in which we should expect a treaty of peace to be concluded. The name of the comitium has also been derived, perhaps with no greater probability, from the same event. It is more likely that the road took its origin at a rather later period, when the Sabine and Roman cities had become consolidated. Its name of Sacra Via seems to have been derived from the sacred purposes for which it was used. Thus we learn from Varro (*L. L.* § 47, Müll.) that it began at the sacellum of the goddess Strenia, in the Carinae; that it proceeded thence as far as the arx, or citadel on the Capitoline hill; and that certain sacred offerings, namely, the white sheep or lamb (ovis idulis), which was sacrificed every ides to Jove (Ovid, *F.* i. 56; Macrob. *S.* i. 15; Paul. Diac. p. 104, Müll.), were borne along it monthly to the arx. It was also the road by which the augurs descended from the arx when, after taking the auguries, they proceeded to inaugurate anything in the city below. It likewise appears that Titus Tatius instituted the custom that on every new year's day the augurs should bring him presents of verbenae from the grove of Strenia, or Strenua, to his dwelling on the arx ("ab exortu poene urbis Martiae Streniarum usus adolevit, auctoritate regis Tatii, qui verbenas felicis arboris ex luco Strenuae anni novi auspicia primus accepit," Symm. *Epist.* x. 35). This custom seems to have been retained in later times in that known as the augurium salutis. (Cic. *Leg.* ii. 8; Tac. *Ann.* xii. 23; Lucian, *Pseudol.* 8.) Hence perhaps the appellation of 'sacra;" though the

3 D 3

whole extent of road was called Sacra Via only in sacerdotal language, between which and the common usage we have already had occasion to note a diversity when giving an account of the Servian gates. In common parlance only that portion of the road was called Sacra Via which formed the ascent of the Velia, from the forum to its summit ("Hujus Sacrae Viae pars haec sola vulgo nota quae est a foro eunti primore clivo," Varr, *l. c.*). Hence by the poets it is sometimes called "Sacer Clivus:" "Inde sacro veneranda petes Palatia clivo." (Mart. i. 70. 5); and—

> "—— quandoque trahet feroces
> Per sacrum clivum, imerita decorus
> Fronde, Sicambros."
>   (Hor. *Od.* iv. 2. 34.)

compared with—

> "Intactus aut Britannus ut *descenderet*
> Sacra catenatus via."   (Id. *Epod.* vii. 7.)

(Comp. Ambrosch, *Studien und Andeut.* p. 78, seq.) The origin of the vulgar opinion is explained by Festus in the following passage: "Itaque ne eatenus quidem, ut vulgus opinatur, sacra appellanda est, a regia ad domum regis sacrificuli; sed etiam a regis domo ad sacellum Streniae, et rursus a regia usque in arcem" (p. 290, Müll.). Whence it appears that only the part which lay between the Regia, or house of the pontifex maximus, and that of the rex sacrificulus, was commonly regarded, and probably for that very reason, as "sacra." This passage, however, though it shows plainly enough that there must have been a space between these two residences, has caused some embarrassment on account of a passage in Dion Cassius (liv. 27), in which he says that Augustus presented the house of the rex sacrificulus (τοῦ βασιλέως τῶν ἱερῶν) to the Vestals because it adjoined their residence (ὁμότοιχος ἦν); and as we know from Pliny (*Ep.* vii. 19) that the vestals dwelt close to the temple, it seems impossible, if Dion is right, that there should have been a street lying between the two places mentioned. But the matter is plain enough; though Becker (*de Muris*, pp. 30—35, *Handb.* pp. 226—237) wastes several pages in most far-fetched reasonings in order to arrive at a conclusion which already lies before us in a reading of the text of Dion for which there is actually MS. authority. Augustus was chosen pontifex maximus (ἀρχιερεύς), not rex sacrificulus, as Dion himself says in this passage. But the two offices were perfectly distinct ("Regem sacrificulum creant. Id sacerdotium pontifici subjecere," Liv. ii. 2). Augustus would hardly make a present of a house which did not belong to him; and therefore in Dion we must read, with some MSS., τοῦ βασιλέως τῶν ἱερέων, for ἱερῶν: Dion thus, in order perhaps to convey a lively notion of the office to his Greek readers, designating the Roman pontifex maximus as "king of the priests," instead of using the ordinary Greek term ἀρχιερεύς. The matter therefore lies thus. Varro says that in ordinary life, only the clivus, or ascent from the forum to the Summa Sacra Via, obtained the name of Sacra Via. Festus repeats the same thing in a different manner; designating the space so called as lying between the Regia, or house of the pontifex maximus, and that of the rex sacrificulus. Whence it follows that the latter must have been on the Summa Sacra Via. It can scarcely be doubted that before the time of Augustus

the Regia was the residence of the pontifex maximus. The building appears to have existed till a late period of the Empire. It is mentioned by the younger Pliny (*Ep.* iv. 11) and by Plutarch (*Q. R.* 97, *Rom.* 18) as extant in their time, and also probably by Herodian (i. 14) in his description of the burning of the temple of Peace under Commodus. After the expulsion of the kings, the rex sacrificulus, who succeeded to their sacerdotal prerogatives, was probably presented with one of the royal residences, of which there were several in the neighbourhood of the Summa Sacra Via; that being the spot where Ancus Marcius, Tarquinius Priscus, and Tarquinius Superbus had dwelt. (Liv. i. 41; Solin. i. 23, 24 ; Plin. xxxiv. 13.) We cannot tell the exact direction in which the Sacra Via traversed the valley of the Colosseum and ascended to the arch of Titus, nor by what name this part of the road was commonly called in the language of the people ; but it probably kept along the base of the Velia. At its highest point, or Summa Sacra Via, and perhaps on the site afterwards occupied by the temple of Venus and Rome, there seems to have been anciently a market for the sale of fruit, and also probably of nick-nacks and toys. "Summa Sacra Via, ubi poma veneunt." (Varr. *R. R.* i. 2.) Hence Ovid (*A. A.* ii. 265.) :—

> "Rure suburbano poteris tibi dicere missa
> Illa, vel in Sacra sint licet emta Via."

Whilst the nick-nacks are thus mentioned by Propertius (iii. 17. 11.) : —

> "Et modo pavonis caudae flabella superbae
> Et manibus dura frigus habere pila,
> Et cupit iratum talos me poscere eburnos
> Quaeque nitent Sacra vilia dona Via."

The direction of the Sacra Via is indicated by Horace's description of his stroll: "Ibam forte Via Sacra," &c. (*S.* i. 9.) He is going down it towards the forum, having probably come from the villa of Maecenas, on the Esquiline, when he is interrupted by the eternal bore whom he has pilloried. The direction of his walk is indicated by his unavailing excuse that he is going to visit a sick friend over the Tiber (v. 17) and by the arrival at the temple of Vesta (v. 35); the Sacra Via having been thus quitted and the forum left on the right. The two extremities of the street, as commonly known, are indicated in the following passage of Cicero: "Hoc tamen miror, cur tu huic potissimum irascere, qui *longissime* a te *abfuit*. Equidem, si quando ut fit, jactor in turba, non *illum* accuso, *qui est in Summa Sacra Via*, cum *ego* ad *Fabium Fornicem impellor*, sed eum qui in me ipsum incurrit atque incidit" (*p. Planc.* 7). The Fornix Fabius, as it will be seen hereafter, stood at the eastern extremity of the forum ; and Cicero has made the most of his illustration by taking the whole length of the street. Beyond this point, where it traversed the N. side of the forum, we are at a loss to tell what its vulgar appellation may have been; and if we venture to suggest that it may have been called "Janus," this is merely a conjecture from Horace (*Epist.* i. 1. 54), where "haec Janus summus ab imo" seems to suit better with a street—just as we should say, "all Lombard street"—than with two Jani, as is commonly interpreted, or than with a building containing several floors let out in counting houses. (Cf. *Sat.* ii. 3. 18.) This view is supported by the Scholia on the first of these passages, where it is said :

" Janus autem hic *platea* dicitur, ubi mercatores et fœneratores sortis causa convenire solebant." In fact it was the Roman Change. The ascent from the forum to the summit of the Capitoline hill, where the Sacra Via terminated, was, we know, called Clivus Capitolinus.

It only remains to notice Becker's *dictum* (*de Muris*, p. 23) that the name of this street should always be written Sacra Via, and not in reversed order Via Sacra. To the exceptions which he noted there himself, he adds some more in the *Handbuch* (p. 219, note), and another from Seneca (*Controv.* xxvii. p. 299, Bip.) in his *Addenda;* and Urlichs (*Röm. Topogr.* p. 8) increases the list. On the whole, it would seem that though Sacra Via is the more usual expression, the other cannot be regarded as unclassical.

Vicus Jugarius — Of the name of the street which ran along the south side of the forum we are utterly ignorant; but from it issued two streets, which were among the most busy, and best known, in Rome. These were the Vicus Jugarius and Vicus Tuscus. We have before had occasion to mention that the former ran close under the Capitoline hill, from the forum to the Porta Carmentalis. It was thought to derive its name from an altar which stood in it to Juno Juga, the presiding deity of wedlock. (Paul. Diac. p. 104, Müll.) It does not appear to have contained any other sacred places in ancient times; but Augustus dedicated in it altars to Ceres and Ops Augusta. (*Fast. Amit. IV. Id. Aug.*) At the top of the street, where it entered the forum, was the fountain called Lacus Servilius, which obtained a sad notoriety during the proscriptions of Sulla, as it was here that the heads of the murdered senators were exposed. (Cic. *Rosc. Am.* 32; Senec. *Prov.* 3.) M. Agrippa adorned it with the effigy of a hydra (Festus, p. 290, Müll.). Between the Vicus Jugarius and Capitoline hill, and close to the foot of the latter, lay the Aequimaelium (Liv. xxxviii. 28), said to have derived its name from occupying the site of the house of the demagogue, Sp. Maelius, which had been razed (Varr. *L.L.* v. 157, Müll.; Liv. iv. 16). It served as a market-place, especially for the sale of lambs, which were in great request for sacrifices, and probably corresponded with the modern *Via del Monte Tarpeo.* (Cic. *Div.* ii. 17.)

Vicus Tuscus.—In the imperial times the Vicus Jugarius was bounded at its eastern extremity by the Basilica Julia; and on the further side of this building, again, lay the Vicus Tuscus. According to some authorities this street was founded in B. C. 507, being assigned to such of the Etruscans in the vanquished host of Aruns as had fled to Rome, and felt a desire to settle there (Liv. ii. 15; Dionys. v. 36); but we have before related, on the authority of Varro and Tacitus, that it was founded in the reign of Romulus. These conflicting statements may, perhaps, be reconciled, by considering the later settlement as a kind of second or subsidiary one. However this may be, it is with the topographical facts that we are here more particularly concerned, about which Dionysius communicates some interesting particulars. He describes the ground assigned to the Tuscans as a sort of hollow or gorge situated between the Palatine and Capitoline hills; and in length nearly 4 stadia, or half a Roman mile, from the forum to the Circus Maximus (v. 36). We must presume that this measurement included all the windings of the street; and even then it would

seem rather exaggerated, as the whole NW. side of the Palatine hill does not exceed about 2 stadia. We must conclude that it was continued through the Velabrum to the circus. Its length as Canina observes (*For. Rom.* pt. i. p. 67) is a proof that the forum must have extended from NW. to SE., and not from NE. to SW.; as in the latter case, the space for the street, already too short, would have been considerably curtailed. This street, probably from the habits of its primitive colonists, became the abode of fishmongers, fruiterers, bird-fanciers, silk-mercers, and perfumers, and enjoyed but an indifferent reputation (" Tusci turba impia vici," Hor. *S.* ii. 3. 29.) It was here, however, that the best silks in Rome were to be procured (" Nec nisi prima velit de Tusco serica vico," Mart. xi. 27. 11). In fact, it seems to have been the great shopping street of Rome; and the Roman gentlemen, whose ladies, perhaps, sometimes induced them to spend more than what was agreeable there, vented their ill humour by abusing the tradesmen. According to the scholiast on the passage of Horace just cited, the street was also called Vicus Turarius. This appellation was doubtless derived from the frankincense and perfumes sold in it, whence the allusion in Horace (*Ep.* i. 1. 267):—

" Ne capsa porrectus aperta
Deferar in vicum vendentem tus et odores,
Et piper, et quicquid chartis amicitur ineptis."

Being the road from the forum to the circus and Aventine, it was much used for festal processions. Thus it was the route of the Pompa Circensis, which proceeded from the Capitol over the forum, and by the Vicus Tuscus and Velabrum to the circus. (Dionys. vii. 72.) We have seen that the procession of the virgins passed through it from the temple of Apollo outside the Porta Carmentalis to that of Juno Regina on the Aventine. Yet notwithstanding these important and sacred uses, it is one of the charges brought by Cicero against Verres that he had caused it to be paved so villanously that he himself would not have ventured to ride over it. (*Verr.* i. 59.) We see from this passage that a statue of Vertumnus, the national Etruscan deity, stood at the end of the street next the forum. Becker (*Handb.* p. 308) places him at the other extremity near the Velabrum. But all the evidence runs the other way; and the lines of Propertius (iv. 2. 5), who puts the following words into the god's mouth, are alone sufficient to decide the matter (*Class. Mus.* vol. iv. p. 444):—

" Nec me turs juvant, nec templo laetor eburno
Romanum satis est posse videre forum."

Comitium.—Having thus described the streets which either encircled the forum or afforded outlets from it, we will now proceed to treat of the forum itself, and the objects situated upon and around it, and endeavour to present the reader with a picture of it as it existed under the Kings, during the Republic, and under the Empire. But here, as in the case of the Capitol, we are arrested in the outset by a difficult investigation. We know that a part of the forum, called the comitium, was distinguished from the rest by being appropriated to more honourable uses; but what part of the forum it was has been the subject of much dispute. Some, like Canina, have considered it to be a space running parallel with the forum along its whole southern extent; whilst others, like Bunsen and Becker, have thought that it formed a section of the area at its eastern extremity, in size about one-third of the whole forum. An argument advanced by Becker himself (*Handb.* p. 278) seems decisive against both these views, namely, that we never hear any building on the S. side of the forum spoken of as being on the comitium. Yet in spite of this just remark, he ends by adopting the theory of Bunsen, according to which the comitium began at or near the ruin of the three columns and extended to the eastern extremity of the forum: and thus both the temple of Vesta and the Regia must have stood very close to it. The two chief reasons which seem to have led him to this conclusion are, the situation of the rostra, and that of the Tribunal Praetoris. Respecting the former, we shall have occasion to speak further on. The argument drawn from the latter, which is by far the more important one, we shall examine at once. It proceeds as follows (*Handb.* p. 280): "The original Tribunal Praetoris was on the comitium (Liv. vi. 15, xxix. 16; Gell. xx. 1, 11, 47 (from the XII. Tables); Varro, *L. L.* v. 32. p. 154; Plaut. *Poen.* iii. 6. 11; Macrob. *Sat.* ii. 12), which, however, is also mentioned as being merely on the forum. (Liv. xxvii. 50, xl. 2, 44.) But close to the tribunal was the Puteal Libonis or Scribonianum, and this is expressly mentioned as being near the Fornix Fabius, the Atrium Vestae, the rostra, and lastly the aedes Divi Julii (Porphyr. *ad Hor. Ep.* i. 19. 8; Schol. Cruq. *Ib.* Id. *ad. Sat.* ii. 6. 35; Fest. p. 333; Schol. *ad Pers. Sat.* iv. 49); consequently the comitium also must have been close to all these objects."

We presume that Becker's meaning in this passage is, that the *first* or *original* tribunal was on the comitium, and that it was afterwards moved into the forum. It could hardly have been both on the comitium and forum, though Becker seems to hint at such a possibility, by saying that it is "also mentioned as being merely on the forum;" and indeed there seems to be no physical impossibility in the way, since it is evident that the tribunal at first was merely a movable chair ("dictator — stipatus ea multitudine, sella in comitio posita, viatorem ad M. Manlium misit: qui — agmine ingenti ad tribunal venit," Liv. vi. 15). But if that was his meaning, the passages he cites in proof of it do not bear him out. In the first Livy merely says that a certain letter was carried *through* the forum to the tribunal of the praetor, the latter of course being on the comitium ("eae literae per forum ad tribunal praetoris latae," xxvii. 50). The other two passages cited contain nothing at all relative to the subject, nor can there be any doubt that in the early times of the Republic the comitium was the usual place on which the praetor took his seat. But that the tribunal was moved from the comitium to the forum is shown by the scholiasts on Horace whom Becker quotes. Thus Porphyrio says: "Puteal autem Libonis sedes praetoris fuit prope Arcum Fabianum, dictumque quod a Libone illic primum tribunal et subsellia locata sint." *Primum* here is not an adjective to be joined with *tribunal* — i. e. "that the first or original tribunal was placed there by Libo;" but an adverb — "that the tribunal was first placed there by Libo." The former version would be nonsense, because Libo's tribunal could not possibly have been the first. Besides the meaning is unambiguously shown by the Schol. Cruq.: "puteal Libonis; tribunal: Quod autem ait *Libonis*, hinc sumsit, quod *is primus* tribunal *in foro statuerit.*" If the authority

of these scholiasts is suspicious as to the fact of this removal, though there are no apparent grounds for suspicion, yet Becker at all events is not in a condition to invalidate their testimony. He has quoted them to prove the situation of the puteal; and if they are good for that, they are also good to prove the removal of the tribunal. Yet with great inconsistency, he tacitly assumes that the tribunal had always stood in its original place, that is, on the comitium, and by the puteal, contrary to the express evidence that the latter was on the forum. ("Puteal locus erat *in foro*," Sch. Cruq. *ad Sat.* ii. 6. 35.) Libo flourished about a century and a half before Christ. [See *Dict. of Biogr.* Vol. II. p. 779.] Now all the examples cited by Becker in which the tribunal is alluded to as being on the comitium, are previous to this date. The first two in note 457 might be passed over, as they relate not to the praetor but to the dictator and consuls; nevertheless, they are both anterior to the time of Libo, the first belonging to the year B. C. 382 and the second to 204. The passage from Gellius "ad praetorem in comitium," being a quotation from the XII. Tables, is of course long prior to the same period. The passage in Varro (v. § 155, Müll.), which derives the name of comitium from the practice of coming together there (coire) for the decision of suits, of course refers to the very origin of the place. A passage from Plautus can prove nothing, since he died nearly half a century before the change effected by Libo. The passage alluded to in Macrobius (ii. 12) must be in the quotation from the speech of C. Titius in favour of the Lex Fannia: "Inde ad comitium vadunt, ne litem suam faciant; veniunt in comitium tristes, &c." But the Lex Fannia was passed in B. C. 164 (Macrob. ii. 13); or even if we put it four years later, in B. C. 160, still before the probable date of Libo's alteration; who appears to have been tribune in B. C. 149. Thus the argument does not merely break down, but absolutely recoils against its inventor; for if, as the Scholia Cruquiana inform us, Libo moved the tribunal from the comitium to the forum, and placed it near the puteal, then it is evident that this part of the area could not have been the comitium.

The comitium, then, being neither on the south nor the east sides of the forum, we must try our fortune on the north and west, where it is to be hoped we shall be more successful. The only method which promises a satisfactory result is, to seek it with other objects with which we know it to have been connected. Now one of these is the Vulcanal. We learn from Festus that the comitium stood *beneath* the Vulcanal: "in Volcanali, quod est supra Comitium" (p. 290, Müll.). In like manner Dionysius describes the Vulcanal as standing a little above the forum, using, of course, the latter word in a general sense for the whole area, including the comitium: καὶ τὰς συνόδους ἐνταῦθα ἐποιοῦντο, ἐν 'Ηφαίστου χρηματίζοντες ἱερῷ, μικρὸν ἐπανεστηκότι τῆς ἀγορᾶς (ii. 50). Where ἱερόν is not to be taken of a proper temple (ναός), but signifies merely an area consecrated to the god, and having probably an altar. It was a rule that a temple of Vulcan should be outside the town (Vitruv. i. 7): and thus in later times we find one in the Campus Martius ("tactam de caelo aedem in campo Vulcani," Liv. xxiv. 10). That the Vulcanal was merely an open space is manifest from its appellation of *area*, and from the accounts we read of rain falling upon it (Liv. xxxix. 46, xl. 19), of buildings being erected upon it (Id. ix. 46), &c. But that it had an altar appears from the circumstance that sacrifices of live fish taken in the Tiber were here made to Vulcan, in propitiation for human souls. (Festus in *Piscatorii Ludi*, p. 238, Müll.) Another fact which shows it to have been an open space, and at the same time tends to direct us to its site, is the lotus-tree which grew upon it, the roots of which are said to have penetrated as far as the forum of Caesar, which, as we shall show in its proper section, lay a little N. of the Forum Romanum. " Verum altera lotus in Vulcanali, quod Romulus constituit ex victoria de decumis, aequaeva urbi intelligitur, ut auctor est Masurius. Radices ejus in forum usque Caesaris per stationes municipiorum penetrant." (Plin. xvi. 86.) From which passage — whatever may be thought of the tale of the tree — we deduce these facts : that the Vulcanal existed in the time of Pliny; that it had occupied the same spot from time immemorial; that it could not have been at any very great distance from the forum of Caesar, otherwise the roots of the tree could not possibly have reached thither. Let those consider this last circumstance who hold with Canina that the comitium was on the south side of the forum; or even with Bunsen and Becker that it was on the east. The Vulcanal must originally have occupied a considerable space, since it is represented as having served for a place of consultation between Romulus and Tatius, with their respective senates. (Dionys. ii. 50; Plut. *Rom.* 20.) Its extent, however, seems to have been reduced in process of time, since the Graecostasis was taken out of its area; a fact which appears from Livy mentioning the Aedes Concordiae, built by Flavius, as being " in area Vulcani " (ix. 46); whilst Pliny says that it was on the Graecostasis (" aediculam aeream (Concordiae) fecit in Graecostasi, quae *tunc* supra comitium erat," xxxiii. 6): whence the situation of the Vulcanal may be further deduced ; since we know that the Graecostasis adjoined the curia, and the latter, as will be shown presently, lay on the N. side of the forum. Hence the Vulcanal also must have been close to the curia and forum; whence it ran back in a N. direction towards the spot subsequently occupied by the Forum Caesaris. This site is further confirmed by the *Notitia*, which places the Area Vulcani, as well as the Templum Faustinae and Basilica Paulli in the 4th Regio. Preller indeed says (*Regionen*, p. 128), that the area cannot possibly be mentioned in its right place here, because it stood immediately over the forum in the neighbourhood of the temple of Faustina, where the old Curia Hostilia stood; but his only reason for this assertion is Becker's dictum respecting the Vulcanal at p. 286, of which we have already seen the value. The comitium, then, would occupy that part of the forum which lay immediately under the Vulcanal, or the W. part of its N. side; a situation which is confirmed by other evidence. Dionysius says that, as the judgment-seat of Romulus, it was in the most conspicuous part of the forum (*ἐν τῷ φανερωτάτῳ τῆς ἀγορᾶς*, ii. 29), a description which corresponds admirably with the site proposed. Livy (i. 36) says that the statue of Attius Navius was on the steps of the comitium on *the left* of the curia, whence it may be inferred that the comitium extended on both sides of the curia. Pliny (xxxiv. 11) speaking of the same statue, says that it stood *before* the curia, and that its basis was burnt in the same fire which consumed that building when the body of Clodius was burnt there.

Hence, we are led to suppose that the comitium occupied a considerable part of the N. side of the forum; but its exact limits, from the want of satisfactory evidence, we are unable to define. It must have been a slightly elevated place, since we hear of its having steps; and its form was probably curvilinear, as Pliny (xxxiv. 12) speaks of the statues of Pythagoras and Alcibiades being at *its horns* (" in cornibus Comitii"); unless this merely alludes to the angle it may have formed at the corner of the forum. It has been sometimes erroneously regarded as having a roof; a mistake which seems to have arisen from a misinterpretation of a passage in Livy, in which that author says that in B. c. 208 the comitium was covered for the first time since Hannibal had been in Italy (" Eo anno primum, ex quo Hannibal in Italiam venisset, comitium tectum esse, memoriae proditum est," xxvii. 36). Hence, it was thought, that from this time the comitium was covered with a permanent roof. But Piale (*del Foro Rom.* p. 15, seq.) pointed out that in this manner there would be no sense in the words " for the first time since Hannibal was in Italy," which indicate a repeated covering. The whole context shows that the historian is alluding to a revived celebration of the Roman games, in the usual fashion; and that the covering is nothing more than the *vela* or canvas, which on such occasions was spread over the comitium, to shade the spectators who occupied it from the sun. That the comitium was an open place is evident from many circumstances. Thus, the prodigious rain, which so frequently falls in the narrative of Livy, is described as wetting it (Liv. xxxiv. 45; Jul. Obseq. c. 103), and troops are represented as marching over it. It was here, also, that the famous Ruminalis Arbor grew (Tac. *Ann.* xiii. 58), which seems to have been transplanted thither from the Palatine by some juggle of Attius Navius, the celebrated augur (Plin. xv. 20; ap. Bunsen, *Les Forum de Rom.* p. 43, seq.), though we can by no means accede to Bunsen's emendation of that passage.

The principal destination of the comitium was for holding the comitia curiata, and for hearing lawsuits (" Comitium ab eo quod coibant eo, comitiis curiatis, et litium causa," Var. *L. L.* v. § 155, Müll.), and it must, therefore, have been capable of containing a considerable number of persons. The comitia centuriata, on the other hand, were held in the Campus Martius ; and the tributa on the forum proper. The curiata were, however, sometimes held on the Capitol before the Curia Calabra. The comitium was also originally the proper place for *contiones,* or addresses delivered to the assembled people. All these customs caused it to be regarded as more honourable and important than the forum, which at first was nothing more than a mere market-place. Hence, we frequently find it spoken of as a more distinguished place than the forum ; and seats upon it for viewing the games were assigned to persons of rank. Its distinction from the forum, as a place of honour for the magistrates, is clearly marked in the following passage of Livy, describing the alarm and confusion at Rome after the defeat at Trasimene : " Romae ad primum nuntium cladis ejus cum ingenti terrore ac tumultu concursus *in forum* populi est factus. Matronae vagae per vias, quae repens clades adlata, quaeve fortuna exercitus esset, obvios percontantur. Et quum frequentis contionis modo *turba in comitium et curiam versa magistratus vocaret*," &c. (xxii. 7). When not occupied by the magistrates it appears to have been open to the people. Thus, the senate being assembled in the curia to hear the ambassadors of those made prisoners at the battle of Cannae, the people are represented as filling the comitium: "Ubi is finem fecit, extemplo ab ea turba, quae in comitio erat, clamor flebilis est sublatus, manusque ad curiam tendentes, &c." (Id. xxii. 60.) Being the place for the contiones it of course had a suggestum, or rostra, from which speeches were delivered; but we shall have occasion to describe this and other objects on and around the comitium and forum when we arrive at them in their chronological order.

It was not till after the preceding account of the comitium had been committed to paper that the writer of it met with the essay on the comitium by Mommsen in the *Annali dell' Instituto* (vol. xvi.), to which reference has before been made. The writer was glad to perceive that his general view of the situation of the comitium had been anticipated, although he is unable to concur with Mommsen respecting some of the details; such as the situation of the Curia Hostilia, of the temple of Janus, of the Forum Caesaris, and some other objects. In refuting Becker's views, Mommsen has used much the same arguments, though not in such detail, as those just adduced; but he has likewise thought it worth while to refute an argument from a passage in Herodian incidentally adduced by Becker in a note (p. 332). As some persons, however, may be disposed to attribute more weight to that argument than we do ourselves, we shall here quote Mommsen's refutation: "Minus etiam probat alterum, quod à Beckero, p. 332, n. 612, affertur, argumentum desumtum ex narratione Herodiani, i. 9, Severam in somnio vidisse Pertinacem equo vectum διὰ μέσης τῆς ἐν Ῥώμῃ ἱερᾶς ὁδοῦ; qui cum venisset κατὰ τὴν ἀρχὴν τῆς ἀγορᾶς, ἔνθα ἐπὶ δημοκρατίας πρότερον δῆμος συνιὼν ἐκκλησίαζεν, equum eo excusso subiisse Severo eumque vexisse ἐπὶ τῆς ἀγορᾶς μέσης. Non intelligo cur verba ἔνθα — ἐκκλησίαζεν referantur ad τὴν ἀρχὴν neque ad τῆς ἀγορᾶς, quod multo est simplicius. Nam ut optime quasi in foro insistere videtur qui rerum Romanarum potiturus est, ita de comitio eo tempore inepte haec dicerentur; accedit quod, si ad τὴν ἀρχὴν τῆς ἀγορᾶς omen pertineret, Severus ibi constiturus fuisset, neque in foro medio.—Nullis igitur idoneis argumentis topographi Germani comitium eam partem fori esse statuerunt quae Veliis subjacet" (p. 289).

So much for the negative side of the question: on the positive side Mommsen adduces (p. 299) an argument which had not occurred to the writer of the present article in proof of the position above indicated for the comitium. It is drawn from the Sacrum Cluacinae. That shrine, Mommsen argues, stood by the Tabernae Novae, that is, near the arch of Severus, as Becker has correctly shown (*Handb.* p. 321) from Livy iii. 48; but he has done wrong in rejecting the result that may be drawn from the comparison of the two legends; first, that the comitium was so called because Romulus and Tatius met upon it after the battle (p. 273); second, that the Romans and Sabines cleansed themselves, after laying aside their arms, at the spot where the statue of Venus Cluacina afterwards stood (Plin. xv. 18. s. 36); whence it follows that the statue was on the comitium. A fresh confirmation, Mommsen continues, may be added to this discovery

of the truth. For that the Tabernae were on the comitium, and not on the forum, as Becker supposes, is pretty clearly shown by Dionysius (τὴν τε ἀγορὰν ἐν ᾗ δικάζουσι καὶ ἐκκλησιάζουσι, καὶ τὰς ἄλλας ἐπιτελοῦσι πολιτικὰς πράξεις, ἐκείνως ἐκόσμησεν, ἐργαστηρίοις τε καὶ τοῖς ἄλλοις κόσμοις περιλαβών, iii. 67).

We are not, however, disposed to lay any great stress on this argument. We think, as we have already said, that Varro's etymology of the comitium, from the political and legal business transacted there rendering it a place of great resort, is a much more probable one; since, as the forum itself did not exist at the time when Romulus and Tatius met after the battle, it is at least very unlikely that any spot should afterwards have been marked out upon it commemorative of that event. It is, nevertheless, highly probable that the statue of Cluacina stood on the comitium, but without any reference to these traditions. We do not, however, think that the tabernae occupied the comitium. By ἀγορά Dionysius means the whole forum, as may be inferred from περιλαβών.

The Forum under the Kings.—In the time of Romulus, then, we must picture the forum to ourselves as a bare, open space, having upon it only the altar of Saturn at about the middle of its western side, and the Vulcanal on its NW. side. Under Numa Pompilius it received a few improvements. Besides the little temple of Janus, which

TEMPLE OF JANUS. (From a Coin.)

did not stand far from the forum, but of which we have already had occasion to speak, when treating of the Porta Janualis in the first part of this article, Numa built near it his Regia, or palace, as well as the celebrated temple of Vesta. Both these objects stood very near together at the SE. extremity of the forum. The AEDES VESTAE was a round building (Festus, p. 262; Plut. *Num.* 11), but no temple in the Roman sense of the word; since it had been purposely left uninaugurated, because, being the resort of the vestal virgins, it was not deemed right that the senate should be at liberty to meet in it (Serv. *Aen.* vii. 153). Its site may be inferred from

TEMPLE OF VESTA (From a Coin.)

several passages in ancient authors. Thus we learn from Dionysius (ii. 66) that it was in the forum, and that the temple of the Dioscuri, whose site we shall point out further on, was subsequently built close to it (Id. vi. 13; Mart. i. 70. 2). It is also said to have been near the lake, or fountain, of Juturna. (Val. Max. i. 8. 1; Ov. F. i. 707.) All these circumstances indicate its site to have been near the present church of *St. Maria Liberatrice;* where, indeed the graves of twelve vestal virgins, with inscriptions, were discovered in the 16th century. (Aldroandus, *Memorie,* n. 3; Lucio Fauno, *Antich. di Roma,* p. 206.) In all its subsequent restorations the original round form was retained, as symbolical of the earth, which Vesta represented (Ov. F. vi. 265). The temple itself did not immediately abut upon the forum, but lay somewhat back towards the Palatine; whilst the REGIA, which lay in front, and a little to the E. of it, marked the boundary of the forum on that side. The latter, also called Atrium Vestae, and Atrium Regium, though but a small building, was originally inhabited by Numa. (Ov. ib. 265; Plut. *Num.* 14, &c.). That it lay close to the forum is shown by the account of Caesar's body being burnt before it (App. *B. C.* ii. 148); and, indeed, Servius says expressly that it lay "in radicibus Palatii finibusque Romani fori" (*ad Aen.* viii. 363). At the back of both the buildings must have been a sacred grove which ran towards the Palatine. It was from this grove that a voice was heard before the capture of the city by the Gauls, bidding the Romans repair their walls and gates. The admonition was neglected; but this impiety was subsequently expiated by building at the spot an altar or sacellum to Aius Loquens. (Cic. *Div.* i. 45.)

Tullus Hostilius, after the capture of Alba Longa, adorned the forum with a curia or senate-house, which was called after him the CURIA HOSTILIA, and continued almost down to the imperial times to be the most usual place for holding assemblies of the senate. (Varr. *L. L.* v. § 155, Müll.; Liv. i. 30.) From the same spoils he also improved the comitium: "Fecitque idem et sepsit de manubiis comitium et curiam" (Cic. *Rep.* ii. 17); whence we can hardly infer that he surrounded the comitium with a fence or wall, but more probably that he marked it off more distinctly from the forum by raising it higher, so as to be approached by steps. The Curia Hostilia, which from its pre-eminence is generally called simply curia, must have adjoined the eastern side of the Vulcanal. Niebuhr (*Beschr.* vol. iii. p. 60) was the first who indicated that it must have stood on the N. side of the forum, by pointing out the following passage in Pliny, in which the method of observing noon from it is described:— "Duodecim tabulis ortus tantum et occasus nominantur; post aliquot annos adjectus est meridies, accenso consulum id pronuntiante, cum a curia inter rostra et graecostasim prospexisset solem." (vii. 60.) Hence, since the sun at noon could be observed from it, it must have faced the south. If its front, however, was parallel with the northern line of the forum, as it appears to have been, it must have looked a little to the W. of S.; since that line does not run due E., but a few degrees to the S. of E. Hence the necessity, in order to observe the true meridian, of looking between the Graecostasis and rostra. Now the Graecostasis— at a period of course long after Tullus Hostilius, and when mid-day began to be observed in this

manner—was a lofty substruction on the *right* or W. side of the curia; and the rostra were also an elevated object situated directly *in its front.* This appears from the passage in Varro just alluded to: —"*Ante hanc* (curiam) rostra: quojus loci id vocabulum, quod ex hostibus capta fixa sunt rostra. *Sub dextra hujus* (curiae) a comitio locus substructus, ubi nationum subsisterent legati, qui ad senatum essent missi. Is graecostasis appellatus, a parte ut multa. Senaculum supra Graecostasim, ubi aedis Concordiae et Basilica Opimia." (*L. L.* v. § 155, 156.) When Varro says that the Graecostasis was *sub dextra curiae,* he is of course looking towards the south, so that the Graecostasis was on his right. This appears from his going on to say that the senaculum lay above the Graecostasis, and towards the temple of Concord; which, as we have had occasion to mention, was seated on the side of the Capitoline hill. It further appears from this passage that the Graecostasis was a substruction, or elevated area (locus substructus) at the side of, or adjoining the comitium (comp. Plin. xxxiii. 6); and must have projected in front of the curia. The relative situation of these objects, as here described, is further proved by Pliny's account of observing midday, with which alone it is consistent. For, as all these objects faced a little to the W. of S., it is only on the assumption that the Graecostasis lay to the W. of the curia, that the meridian sun could be observed with accuracy from any part of the latter between the Graecostasis and rostra.

A singular theory is advanced by Mommsen respecting the situation of the Curia Hostilia, which we cannot altogether pass over in silence. He is of opinion (*l. c.* p. 289, seq.) that it lay on the Capitoline hill, just above the temple of Concord, which he thinks was built up in front of it; and this he takes to be the reason why the curia was rebuilt on the forum by Sulla. His only authority for this view is the following passage in Livy: "(Censores) et clivum Capitolinum silice sternendum curaverunt et porticum ab aede Saturni in Capitolium ad Senaculum ac super id Curiam" (xli. 27). From these words, which are not very intelligible, Mommsen infers (p. 292) that a portico reached from the temple of Saturn to the senaculum, and thence to the curia above it, which stood on the Capitol on the spot afterwards occupied by the Tabularium (p. 292). But so many evident absurdities follow from this view, that Mommsen, had he given the subject adequate consideration, could hardly, we think, have adopted it. Had the curia stood behind the temple of Concord, the ground plan of which is still partly visible near the arch of Severus, it is quite impossible that, according to the account of Pliny, mid-day could have been observed from it between the rostra and Graecostasis, since it would have faced nearly to the east. Mommsen, indeed (p. 296), asserts the contrary, and makes the Carcer Mamertinus and arch of Titus lie almost due N. and S., as is also shown in his plan at the end of the volume. But the writer can affirm from his own observation that this is not the fact. To a person standing under the Capitol at the head of the forum, and opposite to the column of Phocas, the temple of Faustina bears due E. by the compass, and the arch of Titus a few degrees to the S. of E. To a person standing by the arch of Severus, about the assumed site of the curia, the arch of Titus would of course bear a little more S. still. Something must be allowed for variation of the compass, but these are trifles. The correct bearings are given in Canina's large plan and in Becker's map, and are wholly at variance with those laid down by Mommsen. Again, it is not to be imagined that Opimius would have built up his temple of Concord immediately in front of the ancient curia, thus screening it entirely from the view of the forum and comitium; a state in which it must have remained for nearly half a century, according to the hypothesis of Mommsen. Another decisive refutation of Mommsen's view is that the Basilica Porcia, as we shall see further on, was situated on the forum close by the curia, whilst according to Mommsen the two buildings were separated by a considerable interval. We hold it, therefore, to be quite impossible that the curia could have stood where Mommsen places it; but at the same time we confess our inability to give a satisfactory explanation of the passage in Livy. A word, or several words, seem to have dropped out, as is the case frequently in the very same sentence, where the gaps are marked in the editions with asterisks. Such a corrupt sentence, therefore, does not suffice as authority for so important a change, in the teeth of all evidence to the contrary.

We shall only further observe that the preceding passages of Varro and Pliny thus appear, when rightly interpreted, mutually to support and explain one another, and show the Graecostasis to have stood to the W. of the curia, first from its proximity to the senaculum and temple of Concord, and secondly, from the mid-day line falling between it and the rostra. That the curia was considerably raised appears from the circumstance that Tarquin the Proud nearly caused the death of Servius Tullius by hurling him down the steps in front of it, which led to the comitium. (Dionys. iv. 38; Liv. i. 48.) It was an inaugurated temple in order that the senate might hold their meetings in it, but not a sacred one. (Liv. i. 30; Varr. l. c.) In the reign of Tullus the forum was adorned with the trophy called PILA HORATIANA, consisting of the spoils won from the Curiatii; but where it stood cannot be determined. (Dionys. iii. 22; Liv. i. 26.)

The SENACULUM referred to in the preceding account appears to have been a raised and open area, adjoining the Graecostasis and curia, on which the senators were accustomed to assemble before they entered the curia to deliberate. Thus Varro: "Senaculum vocatum ubi senatus aut ubi seniores consisterent: dictum ut Gerusia apud Graecos" (v. § 156, Müll.). Valerius Maximus gives a still more explicit account: "Senatus assiduam stationem eo loci peragebat qui hodieque Senaculum appellatur: nec exspectabat ut edicto contraheretur, sed inde citatus protinus in Curiam veniebat" (ii. 2. § 6). Festus mentions that there were three Senacula in all; namely, besides the one alluded to, another near the Porta Capena, and a third by the temple of Bellona, in the Campus Martius. But as his account is in some respects contradictory of the two preceding authorities, we shall here insert it: "Senacula tria fuisse Romae, in quibus senatus haberi solitus sit, memoriae prodidit Nicostratus in libro qui inscribitur de senatu habendo: unum, ubi nunc est aedis Concordiae inter Capitolium et Forum; in quo solebant magistratus D. T. cum Senioribus deliberare; alterum ad portam Capenam; tertium, citra aedem Bellonae, in quo exterarum nationum legatis, quos in urbem admittere nolebant, senatus dabatur" (p. 347, Müll.).

Here the senaculum is represented, not as a place in which the senate assembled previously to deliberation, but as one in which it actually deliberated. It is impossible, however, that this could have been so. For in that case what would have been the use of the curia? in which the senate is constantly represented as assembling, except in cases where they held their sittings in some other temple. Besides we have no accounts of the senaculum being an inaugurated place, without which it would have been unlawful for the senate to deliberate in it. Nicostratus therefore, who, from his name, seems to have been a Greek, probably confounded the senacula with the curia, and other temples in which the senate assembled; and at all events his account cannot be set against the more probable one of Varro and Valerius Maximus. There is, however, one part in the account of Festus, which seems to set the matter in a different point of view. The words, "in quo solebant magistratus D.T. cum senioribus deliberare," seem to point to the senaculum not as a place where the senators deliberated among themselves, but where they conferred with the magistrates; such magistrates we may suppose as were not entitled to enter the curia. Such were the tribunes of the people, who, during the deliberations of the senate, took their seats before the closed doors of the curia; yet as they had to examine and sign the decrees of the Fathers before they became laws, we may easily imagine that it was sometimes necessary for the tribunes and senators to confer together, and these conferences may have taken place at the senaculum ("Tribunis plebis intrare curiam non licebat: ante valvas autem positis subselliis, decreta patrum attentissima cura examinabant; ut, si qua ex eis improbassent, rata esse non sinerent. Itaque veteribus senatus consultis T. litera subscribi solebat: eaque nota significabatur, ita tribunos quoque censuisse," Val. Max. ii. 2. § 7.) In this manner the senacula would have answered two purposes; as places in which the senators met previously to assembling in the curia, and as a sort of neutral ground for conferences with the plebeian magistrates.

With regard to the precise situation of the senaculum belonging to the Curia Hostilia, we can hardly assume, with Mommsen, that it occupied the spot on which the temple of Concord was afterwards actually built; nor do the words of Varro and Festus,— "Senaculum ubi aedis Concordiae"—seem to require so very rigorous an interpretation. It is sufficient if it adjoined the temple; though it is not improbable that the latter may have encroached upon some part of its area. After the temple was erected there still appears to have been a large open space in front of it, part of the ancient senaculum, but which now seems to have obtained the name of "Area Concordiae." Its identity with the senaculum appears from its adjoining the Vulcanal, like the latter: "In area Vulcani et Concordiae sanguinem pluit." (Liv. xl. 19.) "In area Vulcani per biduum, in area Concordiae totidem diebus sanguinem pluit." (Jul. Obseq. 59.) The temple of Concord became a very usual place for assemblies of the senate, as appears from many passages in ancient authors. (Cic. Phil. ii. 7; Lampr. Alex. 6, &c.) From the area a flight of steps led up to the vestibule of the temple: "(Equites Romani) qui frequentissimi in gradibus Concordiae steterunt." (Cic. Phil. viii. 8.) According to Macrobius the temple of Saturn also had a senaculum

("Habet aram et ante senaculum," i. 8). This must have been near the senaculum of the Curia Hostilia, but could hardly have been the same. If Macrobius is right, then Festus is wrong in limiting the senacula to three; and it does not seem improbable that the areae near temples, where the senate was accustomed to meet, may have been called senacula.

To Ancus Marcius we can only ascribe the CAR-CER MAMERTINUS, or prison described by Livy as overhanging the forum ("media urbe, imminens foro," i. 33). It is still to be seen near the arch of Severus, under the church of S. Giuseppe dei Falegnami.

We have before remarked that a new architectural era began at Rome with the reign of Tarquinius Priscus; and if he had not been interrupted by wars, he would doubtless have carried out many of those grand schemes which he was destined only to project. He may almost be called the founder of the forum, since it was he who first surrounded it with private houses and shops. According to Varro (ap. Macrob. § i. 8), he also founded the TEMPLE OF SATURN on the forum at the spot where the altar stood; though, according to another account, it was begun by Tullus Hostilius. At all events, it does not seem to have been dedicated before the expulsion of the kings (Macrob. l. c.), and according to Livy (ii. 21), in the consulship of Sempronius and Minucius, B. C. 497. According to Becker (Handb. p. 312) the ruin of the three columns under the Capitol are remains of it, and this, he asserts, is a most decided certainty, which can be denied only by persons who prefer their own opinion to historical sources, or wilfully shut their eyes. It appears to us, however, judging from these very historical sources, that there is a great deal more authority for the Italian view than for Becker's; according to which the temple of Saturn is the ruin of the eight columns, at the foot of the clivus. All the writers who speak of it mention it as being at the lower part of the hill, and beneath the clivus, while the three columns are a good way up, and above the clivus. Thus Servius (Aen. ii. 115, viii. 319) says that the temple of Saturn was "ante clivum Capitolini;" and in the Origo gentis Romanae (c. 3) it is said to be "sub clivo Capitolino." In like manner Varro (L. L. v. § 42, Müll.) places it "in faucibus (montis Saturni);" and Dionysius, παρὰ τῇ ῥίζῃ τοῦ λόφου, κατὰ τὴν ἄνοδον τὴν

ἀπὸ τῆς ἀγορᾶς φέρουσαν εἰς τὸ Καπιτώλιον (i. 34). Festus (p. 322, Müll.) describes the ara as having been "in imo clivo Capitolino." Moreover, the miliarium aureum, which stood at the top of the forum (Plin. iii. 9) was under the temple of Saturn: "ad miliarium aureum, sub aedem Saturni" (Tac.H. i. 27); "sub aedem Saturni, ad miliarium aureum" (Suet. Otho. c. 6.) Further, the Monumentum Ancyranum mentions the Basilica Julia as "inter aedem Castoris et aedem Saturni." Now what has Becker got to oppose to this overwhelming mass of the very best evidence? His objections are, first, that Servius (Aen. ii. 116) mentions the temple of Saturn as being "juxta Concordiae templum;" and though the eight columns are near the temple of Concord, yet they cannot, without awkwardness, be called juxta! Secondly, the Notitia, proceeding from the Carcer Mamertinus, names the temples in the following order: Templum Concordiae et Saturni et Vespasiani et Titi. Now, as the three columns are next to the temple of Concord, it follows that they belong to the temple of Saturn. The whole force of the proof here adduced rests on the assumption that the Notitia mentions these buildings precisely in the order in which they actually occurred. But it is notorious that the authority of the Notitia in this respect cannot be at all depended on, and that objects are named in it in the most preposterous manner. We need no other witness to this fact than Becker himself, who says of this work, "Propterea cavendum est diligenter, ne, quoties plura simul templa nominantur, eodem ea ordine juncta fuisse arbitremur." (De Muris, &c., p. 12, nota.) But thirdly, Becker proceeds: "This argument obtains greater certainty from the inscriptions collected by the Anonymous of Einsiedlen. Fortunately, the entire inscriptions of all the three temples are preserved, which may be still partly read on the ruins. They run as follows: 'Senatus populusque Romanus incendio consumptum restituit Divo Vespasiano Augusto‖. s. p. q. r. impp. Caess. Severus et Antoninus pii felic Aug. restituerunt.‖ s.p.q.r. aedem Concordiae vetustate collapsam in meliorem faciem opere et cultu splendidiore restituerunt." Now as the whole of the first inscription, with the exception of the last three words, "Divo Vespasiano Augusto," are still to be read over the eight columns, and the letters ESTITVER, a fragment of "restituerunt" in the second inscrip-

TABULARIUM AND TEMPLES OF VESPASIAN, SATURN AND CONCORD.

tion, over the three columns, Becker regards the order of the *Notitia* as fully confirmed, and the three temples to be respectively those of Concord, Vespasian and Titus, and Saturn.

With regard to these inscriptions all are agreed that the third, as here divided, belongs to the temple of Concord; but with regard to the proper division of the first two, there is great difference of opinion. Bunsen and Becker divide them as above, but Canina (*Foro Rom.* p. 179) contends that the first finishes at the word " restituit," and that the words from " Divo Vespasiano" down to " restituerunt " form the second inscription, belonging to the temple of Vespasian and Titus. In the original codex containing the inscriptions, which is in the library of Einsiedlen, they are written consecutively, without any mark where one begins and another ends; so that the divisions in subsequent copies are merely arbitrary and without any authority. Now it may be observed that the first inscription, as divided by Canina, may still be read on the architrave of the eight columns, which it exactly fills, leaving no space for any more words. Becker attempts to evade this difficulty by the following assertion: " There is no room," he says (*Handb.* p. 357), " for the dedication ' Divo Vespasiano,' on the front of the temple; and although it is unusual for one half of an inscription to be placed on the back, yet on this occasion the situation of the temple excuses it ! " We are of opinion, then, that the whole of the words after " restituit " down to the beginning of the inscription on the temple of Concord, belong to the temple of Vespasian, or that of which three columns still remain.   Another proof that the words " Divo Vespasiano Augusto " could never have existed over the temple with the eight columns is that Poggio (*de Variet. Fort.* p. 12), in whose time the building was almost entire, took it to be the temple of Concord, which he could not have done had the dedication to Vespasian belonged to it. (Bunbury, in *Class. Mus.* iv. p. 27, note.) Thus two out of Becker's three arguments break down, and all that he has to adduce against the mass of evidence, from the best classical authorities, on the other side, is a stiff and pedantic interpretation of the preposition *juxta* in such a writer as Servius ! Thus it is Becker himself who is amenable to his own charge of shutting his eyes against historical evidence. His attempt to separate the altar from the temple (*Handb.* p. 313), at least in locality, is equally unfortunate.

TEMPLE OF SATURN.

The remains of the temple of Saturn, or the portico with the eight columns at the head of the forum, are in a rude and barbarous style of art, some of the columns being larger in diameter than others.   Hence Canina infers that the restoration was a very late one, and probably subsequent to the removal of the seat of empire to Constantinople.   From the most ancient times the temple of Saturn served as an *aerarium*, or state treasury, where the public money, the military ensigns, and important documents were preserved (Liv. iii. 69; Plut. *Q. R.* 42; Macrob. i. 8; Solin. i. 12, &c.).   On account of its Grecian origin sacrifices were performed at the altar of Saturn after the Greek rite, that is, *capite aperto*, instead of *capite velato* as among the Romans (Macrob. *l. c.*).

Adjoining the temple of Saturn was a small cella or AEDES OF OPS, which served as a bank for the public money.   The *Fasti Amiternini* and *Capranicorum* mention it as being " ad Forum," and " in Vico Jugario," which determines its position here (*Calend. Amit. Dec.; Cal. Capran. Aug.*).   It is several times alluded to by Cicero: " Pecunia utinam ad Opis maneret" (*Phil.* i. 7, cf. ii. 14).   Before the temple stood a statue of Silvanus and a sacred fig-tree, which it was necessary to remove in B. C. 493, as its roots began to upset the statue (Plin. xv. 20).   Behind the temple, in a small lane or Angiportus, and about midway up the ascent of the clivus, was the PORTA STERCORARIA, leading to a place where the ordure from the temple of Vesta was deposited on the 15th of June every year. (Varr. *L. L.* vi. § 32, Müll.; Festus, p. 344.) This custom seems to have been connected with the epithet of Stercutus applied to Saturn by the Romans, as the inventor of applying manure to the fields (Macrob. *Sat.* i. 7.)   Close to the Ara Saturni there was a SACELLUM DITIS, in which wax masks were suspended during the Saturnalia. (*Ib.* 11.)

But the most important alteration made by Tarquinius Priscus with regard to the forum was the causing of porticoes and shops to be erected around it (Liv. i. 35; Dionys. iii. 67).   This gave the forum a fixed and unalterable shape.   We may wonder at the smallness of its area when we reflect that this was the great centre of politics and business for the mistress of the world.   But we must recollect that its bounds were thus fixed when she herself was not yet secure against the attempts of surrounding nations. As her power and population gradually increased various means were adopted for procuring more accommodation — first, by the erection of spacious basilicae, and at last, in the imperial times, by the construction of several new fora.   But at first, the structures that arose upon the forum were rather of a useful than ornamental kind; and the *tabernae* of Tarquin consisted of butchers' shops, schools, and other places of a like description, as we learn from the story of Virginia. These TABERNAE were distinguished by the names of *Veteres* and *Novae*, whence it seems probable that only the former were erected in the time of Tarquin.   The two sides of the forum, lengthways, derived their names from them, one being called *sub Veteribus*, the other *sub Novis*. A passage in Cicero, where he compares these tabernae with the old and new Academy, enables us to determine their respective sites: " Ut ii, qui sub Novis solem non ferunt, item ille cum aestu aret, veterum, ut Maenianorum, sic Academicorum umbram secutus est " (*Acad.* iv. 22).   Hence it appears that the *Novae*, being exposed to the sun, must have been on the northern side of the forum, and the *Veteres* of course on the south side. This relative situation is also established by the accounts which we have of basilicae being built either on or near their sites, as will appear in the sequel. Their arrangement cannot be satisfactorily ascertained, but of course they could not have stood before the curia and comitium. In process of time the forum began to put on a better appearance by the conversion of the butchers' shops into those of silversmiths ("Hoc intervallo primum forensis dignitas crevit, atque ex tabernis lanieniis argentariae factae," Varro *in Non.* p. 532, M.). No clue, however, is given to the exact date of this change. The earliest period at which we read of the *argentariae* is in Livy's description of the triumph of Papirius Cursor, B. C. 308 (ix. 40). When the comitia were declared it seems to have been customary for the argentarii to close their shops. (Varr. *L. L.* vi. § 91, Müll.) The tabernae were provided with *Maeniana* or balconies, which extended beyond the columns supporting the porticoes, and thus formed convenient places for beholding the games on the forum (Festus, p. 134, Müll.; Isid. *Orig.* xv. 3, 11.) These Maeniana appear to have been painted with subjects. Thus Cicero: "Demonstravi digito pictum Gallum in Mariano scuto Cimbrico sub Novis" (*de Or.* ii. 66). Pliny mentions another picture, or rather caricature, of a Gaul *sub Veteribus*, and also a figure of an old shepherd with a stick. The latter appears to have been considered by the Romans as a valuable work, as some of them asked a German ambassador what he valued it at? But the barbarian, who had no taste for art, said he would not have it as a gift, even if the man was real and alive (xxxv. 8). According to Varro, quoted by the same author (*Ib.* 37), the Maeniana sub Veteribus were painted by Serapion.

Another service which Tarquin indirectly rendered to the forum was by the construction of his cloacae, which had the effect of thoroughly draining it. It was now that the LACUS CURTIUS, which had formerly existed in the middle of the forum, disappeared ("Curtium in locum palustrem, qui tum fuit in foro, antequam cloacae sunt factae, secessisse," Piso *ap.* Varr. *L. L.* v. § 149, seq. Müll.) This, though not so romantic a story as the self-immolation of Curtius, is doubtless the true representation; but all the three legends connected with the subject will be found in Varro (*l. c.*) It was perhaps in commemoration of the drainage that the shrine or sacellum of VENUS CLUACINA was erected on the N. side of the forum, near the Tabernae Novae, as appears from the story of Virginius snatching the butcher's knife from a

SHRINE OF CLUACINA. (From a Coin.)

shop close to it. (Liv. iii. 48 ; cf. Plin. xv. 36.) The site of the Lacus Curtius after its disappearance was commemorated in another manner. Having been struck with lightning, it seems to have been converted into a dry *puteal*, which, however, still continued to bear the name of Lacus Curtius (cf. Varr. v § 150):

"Curtius ille lacus, siccas qui sustinet aras,
Nunc solida est tellus, sed lacus ante fuit."
(Ov. *Fast.* vi. 397.)

Every year the people used to throw pieces of money into it, a sort of augurium salutis, or new year's gift for Augustus. (Suet. *Aug.* 57.) Close to it grew a fig-tree, a vine, and an olive, which had been fortuitously planted, and were sedulously cultivated by the people; and near them was an altar, dedicated to Vulcan, which was removed at the time of the gladiatorial games given at Caesar's funeral. (Plin. xv. 20; cf. Gruter, *Inscr.* lxi. 1, 2.)

Servius Tullius probably carried on and completed the works begun by his predecessor around the forum, just as he finished the wall; but he does not appear to have undertaken anything original excepting the adding of a lower dungeon, called after him TULLIANUM, to the Mamertine prison. ("In hoc (carcere) pars quae sub terra Tullianum, ideo quod additum a Tullio rege," Varr. *L. L.* v. § 151.) This remains to the present day, and still realises to the spectator the terrible description of Sallust (*Cat.* 55).

The Roman *Ciceroni* point out to the traveller the SCALAE GEMONIAE inside the Mamertine prison, where there are evident remains of an ancient staircase. But it appears from descriptions in ancient authors that they were situated in a path leading down from the Capitol towards the prison, and that they were visible from the forum. (Dion Cass. lviii. 5; Valer. Max. vi. 9. § 13; Tac. *Hist.* iii. 74.) Traces of this path were discovered in the 16th century (Luc. Fauno, *Ant. di Roma*, p. 32), and also not many years ago in excavating the ground by the arch of Severus.

It does not appear that any additions or improvements were made in the forum during the reign of Tarquinius Superbus.

The Forum during the Republic. — One of the earliest buildings erected near the forum in the republican times was the temple of CASTOR AND POLLUX. After the battle at lake Regillus, the Dioscuri, who had assisted the Romans in the fight, were seen refreshing themselves and their horses, all covered with dust and sweat, at the little fountain of Juturna, near the temple of Vesta. (Dionys. vi. 13 ; Val. Max. i. 8. § 1 ; Cic. *N. D.* ii. 2, &c.) A temple had been vowed to those deities during the Latin War by Postumius the dictator; and the spot where this apparition had been observed was chosen for its site. It was dedicated by the son of Postumius B. C. 484. (Liv. ii. 42.) It was not a temple of the largest size; but its conspicuous situation on the forum made it one of the best known in Rome. From the same circumstance the flight of steps leading up to it served as a kind of suggestum or rostra from which to address the people in the forum; a purpose to which it seems to have been sometimes applied by Caesar. (Dion Cass. xxxviii. 6 ; cf. Cic. *p. Sest.* 15 ; Appian, *B. C.* iii. 41.) The temple served for assemblies of the senate, and for judicial business. Its importance is thus described by Cicero: "In aede Castoris, celeberrimo clarissimoque monumento, quod templum in oculis quotidianoque conspectu populi Romani est positum ; quo saepenumero senatus convocatur ; quo maximarum rerum frequentissimae quotidie advocationes fiunt" (*in Verr.* i. 49). Though dedicated to the twin gods, the temple was commonly called only *Aedes Castoris*, as in the preceding passage ; whence Bibulus, the colleague of Caesar in the aedileship, took occasion to compare himself to Pollux, who, though he shared the temple in common with his brother, was never once named. (Suet. *Caes.* 10.) It was restored by

Metellus Dalmaticus (Cic. *Scaur.* 46, et ibi Ascon), and afterwards rebuilt by Tiberius, and dedicated in his and Drusus's name, A. D. 6. (Suet. *Tib.* 20; Dion Cass. lv. 27.) Caligula connected it with his palace by breaking through the back wall, and took a foolish pleasure in exhibiting himself to be adored between the statues of the twin deities. (Suet. *Cal.* 22; Dion Cass. lix. 28.) It was restored to its former state by Claudius (Id. lx. 6). We learn from Dionysius that the Roman knights, to the number sometimes of 5000, in commemoration of the legend respecting the foundation of the temple, made an annual procession to it from the temple of Mars, outside of the Porta Capena. On this occasion, dressed in their state attire and crowned with olive, they traversed the city and proceeded over the

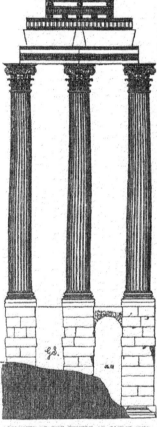

COLUMNS OF THE TEMPLE OF CASTOR AND POLLUX.

forum to the temple (vi. 13). Its neighbourhood was somewhat contaminated by the offices of certain persons who trafficked in slaves of bad character, who might be found there in shoals. ("Num moleste feram si mihi non reddiderit nomen aliquis ex his, qui ad Castoris negotiantur, nequam mancipia ementes vendentesque, quorum tabernae pessimorum servorum turba refertae sunt," Senec. *de Sapient.* 13; cf. Plaut. *Curc.* iv. 1. 20.) The three elegant columns near the forum, under the Palatine, are most probably remains of this temple. We have seen in the preceding account that it stood close to the forum, as well as to the temple of Vesta, a position which precisely agrees with that of the three columns. None of the other various appropriations of this ruin will bear examination. Poggio (*de Var. Fort.* p. 22) absurdly considered these columns to be remains of Caligula's bridge. By the earlier Italian topographers they were regarded as belonging to the temple of Jupiter Stator; but it has been seen that this must have stood a good deal higher up on the Velia. Nardini thought they were remains of the comitium, and was followed by Nibby (*Foro Rom.* p. 60) and Burgess (*Antiq. of Rome,* i. p. 365). We have shown that the comitium was not at this side of the forum. Canina takes them to have belonged to the Curia Julia (*Foro Rom.* parte i. p. 132), which, however, as will appear in its proper place, could not have stood here. Bunsen (*Les Forum de Rome,* p. 58) identifies them with a temple of Minerva, which, as he himself observes (p. 59), is a "*dénomination entièrement nouvelle,*" and indeed, though new, not true. It arises from his confounding the Chalcidicum mentioned in the *Monumentum Ancyranum* with the Atrium Minervae mentioned by the *Notitia* in the 8th Region. But we have already observed that the curia and Chalcidium, which adjoined it, would be quite misplaced here. The *Curiosum,* indeed, under the same Region, mentions besides the Atrium Minervae a Templum Castorum et Minervae, but this does not appear in the *Notitia.* Bunsen was more correct in his previous adoption of the opinion of Fea, that the columns belonged to the temple of Castor. (*Bullettino dell' Inst.* 1835; cf. Bunbury in *Class. Mus.* iv. p. 19.)

The capture of the city by the Gauls, B. C. 390, which, as we have before said, inflicted so much injury that the Romans entertained serious thoughts of migrating to Veii, must of course have occasioned considerable damage in the vicinity of the forum. The Curia Hostilia, however, must have escaped, since Livy represents the senate as debating in it respecting this very matter (v. 5). Such shops and private houses as had been destroyed were probably restored in the fashion in which they had previously existed. It was now that the little temple to AIUS LOQUENS, or LOCUTIUS, to which we have before alluded, was erected on the Nova Via, not far from the temple of Vesta (*Ib.* 50). From this period the forum must have remained without any important alterations down to the time of M. Porcius Cato, when basilicas first began to be erected. During this interval all that was done was to adorn it with statues and other ornaments, but no building was erected upon it; for the small ex voto temple to Concord, which appears to have been made of bronze, erected on the Vulcanal by the aedile C. Flavius, B. C. 303 (Id. ix. 46), can hardly come under that denomination. It was probably also during this period that the GRAECOSTASIS, or elevated area, which served as a waiting-place for foreign ambassadors before they were admitted to an audience of the senate, was constructed on the Vulcanal close to the curia, as before described. The adornment of the suggestum or oratorical platform on the comitium with the beaks of the ships taken from the Antiates, forms, from the connection of this celebrated object with the history of republican Rome, and the change of name which it underwent on the occasion, a sort of epoch in the history of the forum. This occurred B. C. 337. (Plin. xxxiv. 11.) The Rostra at this time stood, as we have said, on the comitium before the curia—a position which they continued to occupy even after the time that new ones were erected by Julius Caesar. (Dion Cass. xliii. 49 ; Ascon. ad Cic. Milon. 5.) The rostra were a templum, or place consecrated by auguries (" Rostrisque earum (navium) suggestum in foro extructum, adornari placuit : Rostraque id templum appellatum," Liv. viii. 14 ; comp. Cic. in Vatin. 10.) They are distinguished by Dion Cassius (lvi. 34) from those erected by Caesar, by the epithet of βῆμα δημηγορικόν, and by Suetonius by that of vetera. (Suet. Aug. 100.) It may be inferred from a passage in a letter of Fronto's to the emperor Antoninus, that the rostra were not raised to any very great height above the level of the comitium and forum (" Nec tantulo superiore, quanto rostra foro et comitio excelsiora ; sed altiores antemnae sunt prora vel potius carina," lib. i. ep. 2). When speaking from the rostra it was usual in the more ancient times for the orator to turn towards the comitium and curia,—a custom first neglected by C. Licinius Crassus in the consulship of Q. Maximus Scipio and L. Mancinus, who turned towards the forum and addressed himself to the people (Cic. Am. 25) ; though, according to Plutarch (Gracch. 5), this innovation was introduced by C. Gracchus.

ROSTRA. (From a Coin.)

The erecting of columns in honour of military achievements came very early into use at Rome, and seems to have preceded the triumphal arch. The first monument of this sort appears to have been the column on the forum called the COLUMNA MAENIA, commemorative of the victory gained by C. Maenius over the Latins, B. C. 338. (Liv. viii. 13.) Livy, indeed, in the passage cited says that the monument was an equestrian statue ; whilst Pliny on the other hand (xxxiv. 11) states that it was a column, which is also mentioned by Cicero. (Sest. 58.) Niebuhr would reconcile both accounts, by assuming that the statue was on a column. (Hist. vol. iii. p. 145.) Pliny in another place (vii. 60) says that the column afforded the means of determining the last hour of the day ("A columna Maenia ad carcerem inclinato sidere supremam pronuntiabat (accensus)") ; but it is very difficult to see how a column standing on the forum could

have thrown a shadow towards the carcer in the evening.

Another celebrated monument of the same kind was the Duilian column, also called COLUMNA ROSTRATA, from its having the beaks of ships sculptured upon it. It was erected in honour of C. Duilius, who gained a great naval victory over the Carthaginians, B. C. 260. According to Servius (Georg. iii. v. 29) there were two of these columns, one on or near the rostra, the other in front of the circus. Pliny, indeed (xxxiv. 11), and Quintilian (Inst. i. 7) speak of it as " in foro ;" but forum is a generic name, including the comitium as a part, and therefore, as used by these authors, does not invalidate the more precise designation of Servius. The basis of this column was found at no great distance from the arch of Severus (Ciacconio, Columnae Rostratae Inscrip. Explicatio, p. 3, ap. Canina, Foro Rom. p. 301, note), a fact which confirms the position which we have assigned to the comitium and curia. The inscription in a fragmentary state is still preserved in the Palazzo de' Conservatori.

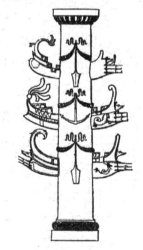

COLUMNA DUILIA.

On the forum in front of the rostra stood the statue of MARSYAS with uplifted hand, the emblem of civic liberty. (Serv. ad Aen. iv. 58 ; cf. Macrob. Sat. iii. 12.) Here was the great resort of the causidici, and also of the Roman courtesans. Hence Martial (ii. 64. 8) :—

" Ipse potest fieri Marsya causidicus."

Horace (Sat. i. 6. 120) has converted the pointed finger of the Satyr into a sign of scorn and derision against an obnoxious individual :—

" —— obeundus Marsya, qui se
Vultum ferre negat Noviorum posse minoris."

It was here that Julia, the daughter of Augustus, held her infamous orgies, in company with the vilest of the Roman prostitutes. (Senec. *Ben.* vi. 32 ; Plin. xxi. 6.) The account given by Servius of this statue has been the subject of much discussion, into which the limits of this article will not permit us to enter. The whole question has been exhausted by Creuzer. (*Stud.* ii. p. 282, seq.; cf. Savigny, *Gesch. des Röm. Rechts*, i. 52.)

Near the rostra were also the statues of the THREE SIBYLS (Plin. xxxiv. 11), which are apparently the same as the three Μοῖραι or Fates, mentioned by Procopius. (*B. Goth.* i. 25.) These also were at the head of the forum, towards the temple of Janus, a position which points to the same result as the Duilian column with respect to the situation of the comitium.

Livy's description of a great fire which broke out about the forum B. C. 211 affords some topographical particulars: " Interrupit hos sermones nocte, quae pridie Quinquatrus fuit, pluribus simul locis circa forum incendium ortum. Eodem tempore septem Tabernae, quae postea quinque, et argentariae, quae nunc Novae appellantur, arsere. Comprehensa postea privata aedificia, neque enim tum basilicae erant: comprehensae Lautumiae, forumque piscatorium, et atrium regium. Aedis Vestae vix defensa est" (xxvi. 27). As the fire, wilfully occasioned, broke out in several places, and as the Curia Hostilia does not seem to have been endangered, we may perhaps conclude that the Septem Tabernae here mentioned were on the S. side of the forum. The argentariae afterwards called Novae were undoubtedly on the N. side, and, for the reason just given, they perhaps lay to the E. of the curia, as the fire seems to have spread to the eastward. It was on the N. side that the greatest damage was done, as the fire here spread to the Lautumiae and Forum Piscatorium. The Septem Tabernae appear to have been the property of the state, as they were rebuilt by the censors at the public expense, together with the fish-market and Atrium Regium (" Locaverunt inde reficienda quae circa forum incendio consumpta erant, *septem* tabernas, macellum, atrium regium," Id xxvii. 11). This passage would seem to show that the reading *quinque* (tabernae) in that previously cited is corrupt. Muretus has observed that one codex has "quae postea *vet.*," which in others was contracted into v., and thus taken for a numeral. (Becker, *Handb.* p. 297, notes). Hence we may infer that the Veteres Tabernae on the S. side of the forum were seven in number, and from the word *postea* applied to them, whilst *nunc* is used of the Novae, it might perhaps be inferred that the distinctive appellation of *Veteres* did not come into use till after this accident.

It also appears from this passage, that there were no basilicae at Rome at this period. It was not long afterwards, however, namely B. C. 184, that the first of these buildings was founded by M. Porcius Cato in his censorship, and called after him BASILICA PORCIA. In order to procure the requisite ground, Cato purchased the houses of Maenius and Titius in the Lautumiae, and four tabernae. (Liv. xxxix 44.) Hence we may infer that the Lautumiae lay close at the back of the forum; which also appears from the circumstance that Maenius, when he sold his house, reserved for himself one of its columns, with a balcony on the top, in order that he and his posterity might be able to view from it the gladiatorial shows on the forum. (Ps. Ascon. *ad Cic. Div. in Caecil.* 16; cf. Schol. *ad Hor. Sat.* i. 3. 21.) This column must not be confounded with

the monument called the Columna Maenia, which stood on the forum. The Basilica Porcia must have stood close to the curia, since it was destroyed by the same fire which consumed the latter, when the body of Clodius was burnt in it (Ascon. *ad Cic. pro Mil. Arg.* p. 34, Orell.); but it must have been on the eastern side, as objects already described filled the space between the curia and the Capitoline hill. The FORUM PISCATORIUM stood close behind it, since Plautus describes the unsavoury odours from that market as driving away the frequenters of the basilica into the forum:—

" Tum piscatores, qui praebent populo pisces foetidos
 Qui advehuntur quadrupedanti crucianti canterio
 Quorum odos subbasilicanos omnes abigit in forum."
  (*Capt.* iv. 2. 33.)

In the time of Cicero, the tribunes of the people held their assemblies in the Basilica Porcia. (Plut. *Cato Min.* 5.) After its destruction by fire at the funeral of Clodius it does not appear to have been rebuilt; at all events we do not find any further mention of it.

The state of the forum at this period is described in a remarkable passage of Plautus ; in which, as becomes a dramatist, he indicates the different localities by the characters of the men who frequented them (*Curc.* iv. 1):—

" Qui perjurum convenire volt hominem mitto in
  comitium ;
Qui mendacem et gloriosum, apud Cloacinae sacrum
Ditis damnosos maritos sub basilica quaerito ;
Ibidem erunt scorta exoleta, quique stipulari solent :
Symbolarum collatores apud Forum Piscarium ;
In foro infimo boni homines atque dites ambulant ,
In medio propter canalem, ibi ostentatores meri ;
Confidentes garrulique et malevoli supra lacum,
Qui alteri de nihilo audacter dicunt contumeliam
Et qui ipsi sat habent, quod in se possit vere dicier.
Sub Veteribus ibi sunt, qui dant quique accipiunt
  foenere ;
Pone aedem Castoris ibi sunt, subito quibus credas
  male,
In Tusco Vico ibi sunt homines, qui ipsi sese ven-
  ditant.
In Velabro vel pistorem, vel lanium, vel aruspicem,
Vel qui ipsi vortant, vel qui aliis ut vorsentur prae-
  beant.
[Ditis damnosus maritos apud Leucadiam Oppiam]."

This is such a picture as Greene might have drawn of Paul's, or Ben Jonson of Moor Fields. The good men walking quietly by themselves in the obscurest part of the forum, whilst the flash gentlemen without a denarius in their purses, are strutting conspicuously in the middle; the *gourmands* gathering round the fishmarket and clubbing for a dinner ; the gentlemen near the Lacus Curtius, a regular set of scandal-mongers, so ready to speak ill of others, and so wholly unconscious that they live in glass-houses themselves ; the perjured witness prowling about the comitium, like the man in Westminster Hall in former days with a straw in his shoe; the tradesman in the Vicus Tuscus, whose spirit of trading is so in-bred that he would sell his very self ; all these sketches from life present a picture of manners in " the good old times " of the Roman Republic, when Cato himself was censor, which shows that human nature is very much the same thing in all ages and countries. In a topographical point of view there is little here but what confirms what has been already said respecting the forum and its environs; except that the usurers *sub Veteribus* show that the bankers' shops were not confined to the N. side of the forum. What the *canalis* was in the middle of the forum is not clear, but it was perhaps a drain. The passage is, in some places, probably corrupt, as appears from the two obscure lines respecting the *maritæ Ditis*, the second of which is inexplicable, though they probably contain some allusion to the Sacellum Ditis which we have mentioned as adjoining the temple of Saturn. Mommsen, however (*l. c.* p. 297), would read "dites damnosos marito," &c., taking these "dites" to be the rich usurers who resorted to the basilica and lent young men money for the purpose of corrupting city wives. But what has tended to throw doubts upon the whole passage is the mention of the basilica, since, according to the testimony of Cicero (*Brut.* 15), Plautus died in the very year of Cato's censorship. Yet the basilica is also alluded to in another passage of Plautus before quoted; so that we can hardly imagine but that it must have existed in his lifetime. If we could place the basilica in Cato's aedileship instead of his censorship, every difficulty would vanish; but for such a view we can produce no authority.

Mommsen (*Ib.* p. 301) has made an ingenious, and not improbable attempt to show, that Plautus, as becomes a good poet, has mentioned all these objects on the forum in the order in which they actually existed; whence he draws a confirmation of the view respecting the situation of the comitium. That part of the forum is mentioned first as being the most excellent. Then follows on the *left* the Sacrum Cluacinae, the Basilica Porcia, and Forum Piscatorium, and the Forum Infimum. Returning by the middle he names the canalis, and proceeds down the forum again on the *right*, or southern side. In the "malevoli supra lacum" the Lacus Servilius is alluded to at the top of the Vicus Jugarius. Then we have the Veteres Tabernae, the temple of Castor, the Vicus Tuscus, and Velabrum.

The Basilica Porcia was soon followed by others. The next in the order of time was the BASILICA FULVIA, founded in the censorship of M. Aemilius Lepidus, and M. Fulvius Nobilior, B.C. 179. This was also "post Argentarias Novas" (Liv. xl. 51), and must therefore have been very close to the Basilica Porcia. From the two censors it was sometimes called Basilica Aemilia et Fulvia. (Varr. *L.L.* vi. § 4, Müll.) All the subsequent embellishments and restorations appear, however, to have proceeded from the Gens Aemilia. M. Aemilius Lepidus, consul with Q. Lutatius in B.C. 78, adorned it with bronze shields bearing the effigies of his ancestors. (Plin. xxxv. 4.) It appears to have been entirely rebuilt by L. Aemilius Paullus, when aedile, B.C. 53. This seems to have been the restoration alluded to by Cicero (*ad Att.* iv. 16), from which passage — if the punctuation and text are correct, for it is almost a locus desperatus — it also appears that Paullus was at the same time constructing another new and magnificent basilica. Hence a difficulty arises respecting the situation of the latter, which we are unable to solve, since only one BASILICA PAULLI is mentioned by ancient authors; and Plutarch (*Caes.* 29) says expressly that Paullus expended the large sum of money which he had received from Caesar as a bribe in building on the forum, in place of the Basilica Fulvia, a new one which bore his own name. (Cf. Appian, *B. C.* ii. 26.) It is certain at least that we must not assume with Becker (*Handb.* p. 303) that the latter was but a poor affair in comparison with the new one because it was built with the ancient columns. It is plain that in the words "nihil gratius illo monumento, nihil gloriosius," Cicero is alluding to the restoration of the ancient basilica, since he goes on to mention it as one which used to be extolled by Atticus, which would not have been possible of a new building; and the employment of the ancient columns only added to its beauty. The building thus restored, however, was not destined to stand long. It seems to have been rebuilt less then twenty years afterwards by Paullus Aemilius Lepidus (Dion Cass. xlix. 42); and in about another twenty years this second restoration was destroyed by a fire. It was again rebuilt in the name of the same Paullus, but at the expense of Augustus and other friends (Id. liv. 24), and received further embellishments in the reign of Tiberius, A. D. 22. (Tac. *Ann.* iii. 72.) It was in this last phase that Pliny saw it when he admired its magnificence and its columns of Phrygian marble (xxxvi. 24).

BASILICA AEMILIA. (From a Coin.)

The third building of this kind was the BASILICA SEMPRONIA, erected by T. Sempronius Gracchus in his censorship, B.C. 169. For this purpose he purchased the house of Scipio Africanus, together with some adjoining butchers' shops, behind the Tabernae Veteres, and near the statue of Vertumnus, which, as we have said, stood near the forum at the end of the Vicus Tuscus. (Liv. xliv. 16.) This, therefore, was the first basilica erected on the S. side of the forum. We hear no further mention of it, and therefore it seems probable that it altogether disappeared, and that its site between the Vicus Tuscus and Vicus Jugarius was subsequently occupied in the imperial times by the Basilica Julia.

The LAUTUMIAE, of which we have had occasion to speak when treating of the Basilica Porcia, was not merely the name of a district near the forum, but also of a prison which appears to have been constructed during the Republican period. The Lautumiae are first mentioned after the Second Punic War, and it seems very probable, as Varro says (*L. L.* v. § 151, Müll.), that the name was derived from the prison at Syracuse; though we can hardly accept his second suggestion, that the etymology is to be traced at Rome, as well as in the Sicilian city, to the circumstance that stone quarries formerly existed at the spot. The older topographers, down to the time of Bunsen, assumed that Lautumiae was only another appellation for the Carcer Mamertinus, a misconception perhaps occasioned by the abruptness with which Varro (*l. c.*) passes from his account of the Tullianum to that of the Lautumiae. We read of the latter as a place for the custody of hostages and prisoners of war in Livy (xxxii. 26, xxxvii. 3); a purpose to which neither the size nor the dungeon-like con-

struction of the carcer would have adapted it.
That the Lautumiae was of considerable size may
also be inferred from the circumstance that when
the consul Q. Metellus Celer was imprisoned there
by the tribune L. Flavius, Metellus attempted to
assemble the senate in it. (Dion Cass. xxxvii. 50.)
Its distinctness from the Carcer Mamertinus is also
shown by Seneca (*Controv.* 27, p. 303, Bipont).

An important alteration in the arrangement of
the forum, to which we have before alluded, was
the removal of the TRIBUNAL PRAETORIS from
the comitium to the eastern end of the forum
by the tribune L. Scribonius Libo, apparently in
B. C. 149. It now stood near the Puteal, a place
so called from its being open at the top like a well,
and consecrated in ancient times either from the
whetstone of the augur Navius having been buried
there, or from its having been struck by lightning.
It was repaired and re-dedicated by Libo; whence it
was afterwards called PUTEAL LIBONIS, and PU-
TEAL SCRIBONIANUM. After this period, its vicinity
to the judgment-seat rendered it a noted object at
Rome, and we find it frequently alluded to in the
classics. (Hor. *Ep.* i. 19. 8, *Sat.* ii. 6. 35 ; Cic. *p.*

PUTEAL LIBONIS OR SCRIBONIANUM.

Sest. 8, &c.) The tribunal of the praetor urbanus
seems, however, to have remained on the comitium.
Besides these we also find a TRIBUNAL AURELIUM
mentioned on the forum, which seems to have stood
near the temple of Castor (Cic. *p. Sest.* 15, *in
Pis.* 5, *p. Cluent.* 34), and which, it is conjectured,
was erected by the consul M. Aurelius Cotta B. C.
74. These tribunals were probably constructed of
wood, and in such a manner that they might be
removed on occasion, as for instance, when the whole
area of the forum was required for gladiatorial shows
or other purposes of the like kind; at least it appears
that the tribunals were used for the purpose of
making the fire in the curia when the body of Clodius was burnt in it. (Ascon. *ad Cic. Mil. Arg.*
p. 34.)

In the year B. C. 121 the TEMPLE OF CONCORD was
built by the consul L. Opimius on the Clivus Capitolinus just above the senaculum (Varr. *L. L.* v.
§ 156, Müll.); but, as we have already had occasion
to discuss the history of this temple when treating
of the Capitol and of the senaculum, we need not
revert to it here. At the same time, or a little
afterwards, he also erected the BASILICA OPIMIA,
which is mentioned by Varro in close connection
with the temple of Concord, and must therefore
have stood on its northern side, since on no other
would there have been space for it. Of this basilica
we hear but very little, and it seems not improbable

that its name may have been afterwards changed to
that of " Basilica Argentaria," perhaps on account
of the silversmiths' and bankers' shops having been
removed thither from the *tabernae* on the forum.
That a Basilica Argentaria, about the origin of which
nobody can give any account, existed just at this
spot is certain, since it is mentioned by the *Notitia*,
in the 8th Regio, when proceeding from the forum
of Trajan, as follows: " Cohortem sextam Vigilum,
Basilicam Argentariam, Templum Concordiae, Um-
bilicum Romae," &c. The present *Salita di Marforio*, which runs close to this spot, was called in
the middle ages " Clivus Argentarius;" and a whole
plot of buildings in this quarter, terminating, according to the *Mirabilia* (Montf. *Diar. Ital.* p. 293),
with the temple of Vespasian, which, as we shall
see in the sequel, stood next to the temple of
Concord, bore the name of " Insula Argentaria "
(Becker, *Handb.* p. 413, seq.).

In the same year the forum was adorned with the
triumphal arch called FORNIX FABIUS or FABIANUS,
erected by Q. Fabius Allobrogicus in commemoration of his triumph over the Allobroges. This was
one of the earliest, though not precisely the first, of
this species of monuments at Rome, it having been
preceded by the three arches erected by L. Stertinius
after his Spanish victories, of which two were
situated in the Forum Boarium and one in the
Circus Maximus. (Liv. xxxiii. 27.) We may
here remark that fornix is the classical name for
such arches ; and that the term arcus, which, however, is used by Seneca of this very arch (*Const.
Sap.* 1), did not come into general use till a late
period. The situation of this arch is indicated by
several passages in Roman authors. We have
already cited one from Cicero (*p. Planc.* 7), and in
another he says that Memmius, when coming down
to the forum (that is, of course, down the Sacra Via),
was accustomed to bow his head when passing
through it (" Ita sibi ipsum magnum videri Mem-
mium, ut in forum descendens caput ad fornicem
Fabii demitteret," *de Orat.* ii. 66). Its site is still
more clearly marked by the Pseudo-Asconius (*ad
Cic. Verr.* i. 7) as being close to the Regia, and by
Porphyrio (*ad Hor. Epist.* i. 19. 8) as near the
Puteal Libonis.

The few other works about the forum during the
remainder of the Republican period were merely
restorations or alterations. Sulla when dictator
seems to have made some changes in the curia
(Plin. xxxiv. 12), and in B. C. 51, after its destruction in the Clodian riots, it was rebuilt by his son
Faustus. (Dion Cass. xl. 50.) Caesar, however,
caused it to be pulled down in B. C. 45, under pretence of having vowed a temple to Felicitas, but in
reality to efface the name of Sulla. (Id. xliv. 5.)
The reconstruction of the Basilica Fulvia, or rather
the superseding of it by the Basilica Paulli, has
been already mentioned.

It now only remains to notice two other objects
connected with the Republican Forum, the origin of
which cannot be assigned to any definite period.
These were the SCHOLA XANTHA and the JANI.
The former, which lay back considerably behind the
temple of Saturn and near the top of the Clivus Capitolinus, consisted of a row of arched chambers, of which
three are still visible. They appear from inscriptions to have been the offices of the scribes, copyists,
and *praecones* of the aediles, and seem to be alluded to
by Cicero. (*Philipp.* ii. 7, *p. Sest.* 12.) Another row
was discovered in 1835 at the side of the temple of

Vespasian and against the wall of the Tabularium, with a handsome though now ruined portico before them, from which there was an entrance into each separate chamber. From the fragments of the architrave an inscription could still be deciphered that it was dedicated to the twelve Dei Consentes. (Canina, *Foro Rom.* p. 207, *Bullet. d. Inst.* 1835.) This discovery tallies remarkably with the following passage in Varro: "Et quoniam (ut aiunt) Dei facientes adjuvant, prius invocabo eos; nec ut Homerus et Ennius, Musas, sed XII. deos consentis; neque tamen eos urbanos, *quorum imagines ad forum auratae stant*, sex mares et feminae totidem, sed illos XII. deos, qui maxime agricolarum duces sunt" (*R. R.* i. 1). We may, however, infer that the inscription was posterior to the time of Varro, probably after some restoration of the building; since in his *De Lingua Latina* (viii. § 71) he asks: "Item quaerunt, si sit analogia, cur appellant omnes aedes Deum Consentum et non Deorum Consentium?" whereas in the inscription in question we find it written "Consentium." We may further remark that the former of these passages would sanction the including of the whole Clivus Capitolinus under the appellation of "forum."

With respect to the Jani on the forum, it seems rather problematical whether there were three of them. There appear to have been two Jani before the Basilica Paulli, to which the money-lenders chiefly resorted. (Schol. *ad Hor. Ep.* i. 1. 54.) But when Horace (*Sat.* ii 3. 18) says —

    " —— postquam omnis res mea Janum
    Ad medium fracta est,"

he probably means, as we said before, the middle of the street, and not a Janus which lay between two others, as Becker thinks must necessarily follow from the use of the word *medius.* (*Handb.* p. 327, note.)

The Forum under the Empire. — The important alterations made by Julius Caesar in the disposition of the forum were the foundation of its subsequent appearance under the Empire. These changes were not mere caprices, but adaptations suited to the altered state of political society and to Caesar's own political views. But the dagger of the assassin terminated his life before they could be carried out, and most of them were left to be completed by his successor Augustus. One of the most important of these designs of Caesar's was the building of a new curia or senate-house, which was to bear his name. Such a building would be the badge of the senate's servitude and the symbol of his own despotic power. The former senate-house had been erected by one of the kings; the new one would be the gift of the first of the emperors. We have mentioned the destruction of the old curia by fire in the time of Sulla, and the rebuilding of it by his son Faustus; which structure Caesar caused to be pulled down under a pretence, never executed, of erecting on its site a temple of Felicitas.

The curia founded by Pompey near his theatre in the Campus Martius—the building in which Caesar was assassinated — seems to have been that commonly in use; and Ovid (*Met.* xv. 801), in describing that event, calls it simply Curia:—

    " —— neque enim locus ullus in urbe
    Ad facinus diramque placet, nisi Curia, caedem."

We may suppose that when Caesar attained to supreme power he was not well pleased to see the

meetings of the senate held in a building dedicated by his great rival.

A new curia was voted a little before Caesar's death, but he did not live to found it; and the *Monumentum Ancyranum* shows that it was both begun and completed by Octavianus.

Respecting the site of the CURIA JULIA the most discordant opinions have prevailed. Yet if we accept the information of two writers who could not have been mistaken on such a subject, its position is not difficult to find. We learn from Pliny that it was erected on the comitium: "Idem (Augustus) in Curia quoque quam in Comitio consecrabat, duas tabulas impressit parieti" (xxxv. 10); and this site is confirmed by Dion Cassius: τὸ βουλευτήριον τὸ Ἰούλιον, ἀπ' αὐτοῦ κληθὲν παρὰ τῷ Κομιτίῳ ἀνοιμασμένῳ ἀκοδόμουν, ὅσπερ ἐψήφιστο (xlvii. 19). It is impossible to find any other spot for it on the comitium than that where the old curia stood. Besides the author last quoted expressly informs us that in consequence of some prodigies that occurred in the year before Caesar's murder it had been resolved to rebuild the Curia Hostilia (καὶ διὰ τοῦτο τό τε βουλευτήριον τὸ Ὁστίλιον ἀνοικοδομηθῆναι ἐψήφισθη, *Ib.* xlv. 17.) At the time when this decree was made Caesar was himself pontifex maximus; it would have been a flagrant breach of religion to neglect a solemn vow of this description; and we cannot therefore accept Becker's assertion that this vow was never accomplished. (*Handb.* p. 331, note 608.) We cannot doubt that the curia erected by Augustus was in pursuance of this decree, for Caesar did not live even to begin it ("Curiam et continens ei Chalcidicum — feci," *Mon. Ancyr*); but though the senate-house was rebuilt, it was no longer named Hostilia, but, after its new founder, Julia. Now what has Becker got to oppose to all this weight of testimony? Solely a passage in Gellius,— which, however, he misapprehends,— in which it is said, on the authority of Varro, that the new curia had to be inaugurated, which would not have been the case had it stood on the ancient spot ("Tum adscripsit (Varro) de locis in quibus senatus consultum fieri jure posset, docuitque confirmavitque, nisi in loco per augures constituto, quod templum appellaretur, senatusconsultum factum esset, justum id non fuisse. Propterea et in Curia Hostilia et in Pompeia, *et post in Julia*, cum profana ea loca fuissent, templa esse per augures constituta," xiv. 7. § 7.) But Becker has here taken only a half view of these augural rites. As a temple could not be built without being first inaugurated, so neither could it be pulled down without being first exaugurated. This is evident from the accounts of the exauguration of the fanes in order to make room for the temple of the Capitoline Jupiter. ("Et, ut libera a caeteris religionibus area esset tota Jovis templique ejus, quod inaedificaretur, exaugurare fana sacellaque statuit, quae aliquot ibi a Tatio rege, consecrata inaugurataque postea fuerant," Liv. i. 55, cf. v. 54; Dion. Halic. iii. 69.) When Caesar, therefore, pulled down the curia of Faustus he first had it exaugurated, by which the site again became a *locus profanus*, and would of course require a fresh inauguration when a new temple was erected upon it. The curia in use in the time of Propertius (iv. 1. 11) must have been the Curia Julia; and the following lines seem to show that it had risen on the site of the ancient one:—

    "Curia praetexto quae nunc nitet alta Senatu
    Pellitos habuit, rustica corda, Patres."

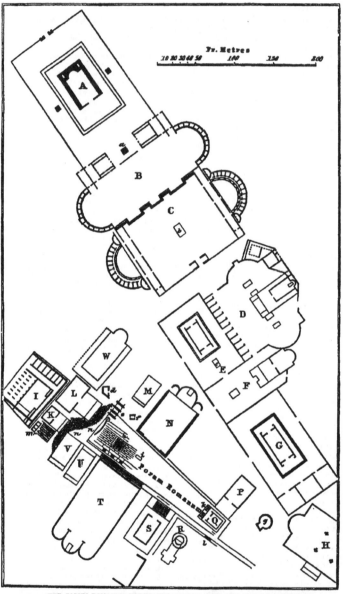

THE FORUM ROMANUM UNDER THE EMPIRE, AND THE IMPERIAL FORA.

A. Templum Divi Trajani	K. Templum Vespasiani et Titi.	R. Aedes Vestae.
B. Basilica Ulpia.		S. Aedes Castoris.
C. Forum Trajani.	L. Templum Concordiae.	T. Basilica Julia.
D. Forum Augusti.	M. Curia or Senatus.	U. Graecostasis.
E. Forum Julium.	N. Basilica Aemilia seu Paulli.	V. Templum Saturni.
F. Forum Transitorium.		a. Columna Trajani.
G. Templum Pacis.	P. Templum Antonini et Faustinae.	b. Equus Trajani.
H. Basilica Constantini.		c. Equus Caesaris.
I. Tabularium.	Q. Aedes Divi Julii	d. Carcer Mamertinus.

e. Arcus Severi.
f. Templum Jani.
g. Aedes Penatium.
h. Columna Phocae.
i. Equus Domitiani.
k. Rostra Julia.
l. Fornix Fabii.
m. Schola Xantha.
n n. Clivus Capitolinus.

A further confirmation that the new curia stood on the ancient spot is found in the fact that down to the latest period of the Empire that spot continued to be the site of the senate-house. The last time that mention is made of the Curia Julia is in the reign of Caligula (" Consensit (senatus) ut consules non in Curia, quia Julia vocabatur, sed in Capitolium convocarent," Suet. Cal. 60); and as we know that the curia was rebuilt by Domitian, the Julia must have been burnt down either in the fire of Nero, or more probably in that which occurred under Titus. It is not likely, as Becker supposes (Handb. p. 347), that Vespasian and Titus would have suffered an old and important building like the curia to lie in ashes whilst they were erecting their new amphitheatre and baths. The new structure of Domitian, called Senatus in the later Latin (" Senatum dici et pro loco et pro hominibus," Gell. xviii. 7, 5), is mentioned by several authorities (Hieronym. an. 92. i. p. 443, ed. Ronc.; Cassiod. Chron. ii. p. 197; Catal. Imp. Vienn. p. 243.) The place of this senatus is ascertained from its being close to the little temple of Janus Geminus, the index belli pacisque (ἔχει δὲ τὸν νεὼν (ὁ Ἰανὸς) ἐν τῇ ἀγορᾷ πρὸ τοῦ βουλευτηρίου, Procop. B. G. i. 25); and hence from its proximity to Numa's sacellum it was sometimes called " Curia Pompiliana" (Vopisc. Aurel. 41, Tacit. 3.) The same situation is confirmed by other writers. Thus Dion Cassius mentions that Didius Julianus, when he first entered the curia as emperor, sacrificed to the Janus which stood before the doors (lxxiii. 13). In the same manner we find it mentioned in the Notitia in the viiith Region. That it occupied the site of the ancient church of S. Martina, subsequently dedicated to and now known as S. Luca, close to the arch of Severus, appears from an inscription (Gruter, clxx. 5) which formerly existed in the Ambo, or hemicycle, of S. Martina, showing that this hemicycle, which was afterwards built into the church, originally formed the Secretarium Senatus (Urlichs, Röm. Top. p. 37, seq.; Preller, Regionen, p. 142.) The Janus temple seems to have been known in the middle ages under the appellation of templum fatale, by which it is mentioned in the Mirabilia Urbis. (" Juxta eum templum fatale in S. Martina, juxta quod est templum refugii, i. e., S. Adrianus," Ib.) In the same neighbourhood was a place called in the later ages " Ad Palmam," which also connects the senatus with this spot, as being both near to that place and to the Arcus Severi. Thus Ammianus: " Deinde ingressus urbem Theodoricus, venit ad Senatum, et ad Palmam populo alloquutus," &c. (Excerpt. de Odo. 66.) And in the Acta SS., Mai. vii. p. 12: " Ligaverunt ei manus a tergo et decollaverunt extra Capitolium et extrahentes jactaverunt eum juxta arcum triumphi ad Palmam." (cf. Anastas. V. Sist. c. 45.) The appellation " ad Palmam " was derived from a statue of Claudius II. clothed in the tunica palmata, which stood here: " Illi totius orbis judicio in Rostris posita est columna cum palmata statua superfixa." (Treb. Pollio, Claud. c. 2.)

We cannot doubt, therefore, that the curia or senatus built by Domitian was near the arch of Severus; which is indeed admitted by Becker himself (Handb. p. 355). But, from his having taken a wrong view of the situation of the comitium, he is compelled to maintain that this was altogether a new site for it; and hence his curia undergoes no fewer than three changes of situation, receiving a new one almost every time that it was rebuilt,

namely, first, on the N. side of his comitium, secondly on the S. side, and thirdly near the Arcus Severi, for which last site the evidence is too overwhelming to be rejected. We trust that our view is more consistent, in which the senate-house, as was most probable, appears to have always retained its original position. And this result we take to be no slight confirmation of the correctness of the site which we have assigned to the comitium. In their multitudinous variations, Bunsen and Becker are sore puzzled to find a place for their second curia—the Julia—on their comitium, to which the passages before cited from Pliny and Dion inevitably fix them. Bunsen's strange notions have been sufficiently refuted by Becker (Handb. p. 333), and we need not therefore examine them here. But though Becker has succeeded in overthrowing the hypothesis of his predecessor, he has not been able to establish one of his own in its place. In fact he gives it up. Thus he says (p. 335) that, in the absence of all adequate authority, he will not venture to fix the site of the curia ; yet he thinks it probable that it may have stood where the three columns are ; or if that will not answer, then it must be placed on the (his) Vulcanal. But his complaint of the want of authorities is unfounded. If he had correctly interpreted them, and placed the comitium in its right situation, and if he had given due credit to an author like Dion Cassius when he says (l. c.) that it was determined to rebuild the Curia Hostilia, he had not needed to go about seeking for impossible places on which to put his Curia Julia.

There are three other objects near the forum into which, from their close connection with the Basilica Julia, we must inquire at the same time. These are the CHALCIDICUM, the IMPERIAL GRAECOSTASIS, and a TEMPLE OF MINERVA. We have already seen that the first of these buildings is recorded in the Monumentum Ancyranum as erected by Augustus adjoining the curia ; and the same edifice is also mentioned by Dion Cassius among the works of Augustus: τό τε Ἀθήναιον καὶ τὸ Χαλκιδικὸν ὠνομασμένον, καὶ τὸ βουλευτήριον, τὸ Ἰουλίειον, τὸ ἐπὶ τοῦ πατρὸς αὐτοῦ τιμῇ γενόμενον, καθιέρωσεν (li. 22). But regarding what manner of thing the Chalcidicum was, there is a great diversity of opinion. It is one of those names which have never been sufficiently explained ; but it was perhaps a sort of portico, or covered walk (deambulatorium), annexed to the curia. Bunsen, as we have mentioned when treating of the temple of Castor in the preceding section, considers the Athenaeum and Chalcidicum to have been identical; and as the Notitia mentions an Atrium Minervae in the 8th Region, and as a Minerva Chalcidica is recorded among the buildings of Domitian, he assumes that these were the same, and that the unlucky ruin of the three columns, which has been so transmuted by the topographers, belonged to it. In all which we can only wonder at the uncritical spirit that could have suggested such an idea; for in the first place the Monumentum Ancyranum very distinctly separates the aedes Minervae, built by Augustus, from the Chalcidicum, by mentioning it at a distance of five lines apart; secondly, the aedes Minervae is represented to be on the Aventine, where we find one mentioned in the Notitia (cf. Ov. Fast. vi. 728; Festus, v. Quinquatrus, p. 257, Müll.), and consequently a long way from the curia and its adjoining Chalcidicum ; thirdly, they are also mentioned separately by Dion Cassius. in the passage before cited, whose text is not to be capriciously meddled with by reading, τό τε 'Αθήναιον τὸ καὶ Χαλκιδικὸν ὠνομασμένον, in order to prop a theory which cannot support itself. We need not, therefore, enter further into this view. That of Becker (*Handb.* p. 335) seems probable enough, that the Chalcidicum usurped the place of the senaculum of the curia, though we should be more inclined to say that of the Graecostasis, as the position of the latter seems at all events to have been shifted about this period. We learn from Pliny (xxxiii. 6) that in his time it no longer stood " supra Comitium." Yet such a place seems to have existed to the latest period, and is mentioned in the *Notitia* (Regio viii.) under the altered name of Graecostadium, close to the Basilica Julia, though the MSS. vary with regard to the position. It had probably, therefore, been removed before the time of Pliny to the south side of the forum, and perhaps at the time when the new curia and Chalcidicum were built. If this was so, it would tend to prove that the comitium did not extend across the whole breadth of the forum. The Atrium Minervae of the *Notitia* must have been of a later period.

Another change in the disposition of the forum, with reference to the politics of the times, which was actually carried out by Caesar in his lifetime, was the removal of the ancient rostra. The comitium, which may be called the aristocratic part of the forum, had become in a great measure deserted. The popular business was now transacted at the lower end of the forum; and Caesar, who courted the mob, encouraged this arrangement. The steps of the temple of Castor had been converted into a sort of extempore rostra, whence the demagogues harangued the people, and Caesar himself had sometimes held forth from them. (Dion Cass. xxxviii. 6; cf. Cic. *p. Sest.* 15; App. *B. C.* iii. 41.) Dion Cassius expressly mentions that the ROSTRA were changed by Caesar (xliii. 49). The change is also mentioned by Asconius: " Erant enim tunc rostra non eo loco quo nunc sunt, sed ad Comitium prope juncta Curiae" (*ad Cic. Mil.* 5), where, by this absolute and unqualified mention of the curia, he must of course have meant the curia *existing* in his time, which was the Julia; and this shows that it stood on the ancient site of the Hostilia. Another proof that the rostra were moved in Caesar's lifetime may be derived from Livy (*Epit.* cxvi.): " Caesaris corpus a plebe ante Rostra crematum est." For, as Appian (*B. C.* ii. 148) indicates the place in another manner, and says that the burning of the body took place before the Regia, it is plain that the rostra mentioned in the *Epitome* just cited must have been very near the Regia. But we have seen that the ancient rostra were on the comitium, at the other end of the forum. There are other passages from which we may arrive at the exact situation of the new rostra. Thus Suetonius, in his account of the funeral of Augustus, says that a panegyric was pronounced upon him by Drusus from the rostra under the Tabernae Veteres (" pro Rostris sub Veteribus," *Aug.* 100; cf. Dion Cass. lvi. 34). It should be stated, however, that the common reading of this passage is " pro Rostris veteribus," that is, from the old rostra on the comitium; and we shall see further on that the old rostra appear to have existed after the erection of the new. It is not, however, probable that they would be used on this occasion, even if they were ever used at all; and we see from Dion Cassius's account of the

funeral of Octavia, the sister of Augustus, that Drusus also on that occasion pronounced a panegyric from the new rostra, or those commonly used, as we must conclude from Dion's mentioning them without any distinctive epithet (ἐπὶ τοῦ βήματος). Canina (*Foro Rom.* p. 129) adopted the common reading, with the omission of *sub*, because he imagined that " sub Veteribus " must mean " under some old building," instead of its being a designation for the S. side of the forum. And Cicero, when pronouncing one of his invectives against Antony from the rostra, bids his audience look *to the left* at the gilt equestrian statue of Antony, which, as appears from what Cicero says a little further on, stood before the temple of Castor. (*Phil.* vi. 5.) From a comparison of all these passages we may state with precision that the new rostra were established by Caesar on the SE. side of the forum, between the temple of Castor and the Regia, a spot which, as we have said, had previously become the regular place for the contiones. But, as this spot was on Becker's comitium,— his lower end of the forum being our upper end,— he could not of course admit that this was the place on which the new rostra were erected, and he is therefore obliged to place them a great deal higher up towards the Capitol, and to the W. of the temple of Castor. As, however, in questions of this sort, one error always begets another, he is thus puzzled to account for the circumstance how Cicero, speaking from these rostra, could allude to the statue of Antony as being on his left (*Handb.* p. 337); and, in order to avoid this contradiction, asserts that Dion Cassius was mistaken, in saying that the rostra were removed in Caesar's lifetime. It must be the old rostra, those on the (his) comitium, before which Caesar's body was burnt, and then everything goes right. Unfortunately, however, the testimony of Dion is confirmed by the expressive silence of the *Monumentum Ancyranum*. That record, in which Augustus so ostentatiously recites his buildings, his repairs, and his alterations, says not a word about the rostra. We have seen a little while ago that Becker contradicts Dion respecting the Curia Julia, and now he contradicts both that author and the *Monumentum Ancyranum*, and solely because he has adopted a wrong site for his comitium. How shall we characterise a topographical system which at every turn comes into collision with the best authorities? On the other hand, if there is any truth in the system we have adopted, all the merit we can claim for it is derived from paying due respect to these authorities, and implicitly following what they say, without presuming to set our own opinion above their teaching. Before we quit this subject it may be as well to say that, though these new rostra of Caesar's became the ordinary *suggestum*, or platform, for the orators, yet the old ones do not appear to have been demolished. We have before seen, from a passage in Trebellius Pollio, that the old rostra *ad Palmam*, or near the arch of Severus, existed in the time of Claudius II.; and the *Notitia* and *Curiosum* expressly mention three rostra on the forum.

In a bas-relief on the arch of Constantine Canina has correctly recognised a representation of this part of the forum, with the buildings on the Clivus Capitolinus. Constantine is seen addressing the people from a raised platform or *suggestum*, provided with a balustrade, which is undoubtedly intended for the ancient rostra. Canina is further of opinion that an elevated terrace, presenting the segment of a circle, which was excavated at this part of the forum some years ago, is the actual rostra (*Indicazione*, p. 270, ed. 1850, and his Dissertation " *Sui Rostri del Foro Romano*" in the *Atti dell' Accademia Rom. di Archeologia*, viii. p. 107, seq. ; cf. Becker, *Handbuch*, p. 359). It seems also to have been here that Augustus received the homage of Tiberius, when the latter was celebrating his German triumph: " Ac priusquam in Capitolium flecteret, descendit e curru, seque praesidenti patri ad genua submisit." (Suet. *Tib.* 20.) The scene is represented on the large Vienna Cameo. (Eckhel, *Pierres gravées*, 1 ; Mongez, *Iconogr. Rom.* 19, vol. ii. p. 62.) If these inferences are just the ancient rostra would appear to have been used occasionally after the erection of the new ones.

The STATUES OF SULLA AND POMPEY, of which the former appears to have been a gilt equestrian one, were re-erected near the new rostra, as they had formerly stood by the old ones. After the battle of Pharsalus they were both removed, but Caesar replaced them. Besides these there were two STATUES OF CAESAR, and an equestrian STATUE OF OCTAVIAN. (Dion Cass. xlii. 18, xliii. 49, xliv. 4 ; Suet. *Caes.* 75 ; App. *B. C.* i. 97.)

Caesar also began the large basilica on the S. side of the forum, called after him the BASILICA JULIA; but, like most of his other works, he left it to be finished by Augustus (" Forum Julium et Basilicam quae fuit inter aedem Castoris et aedem Saturni, coepta profligataque opera à patre meo perfeci," *Mon. Ancyr.*). Its situation is here so accurately fixed

```
. . . . . . . A . .
. . . . . . . . ASILICA .
. . . . . . . . . . ER
REPARATAE . . .
. . . . . SET ADIECIT
. . . . . . . . .
```

thus leaving no doubt that they were the same. (*Bullettino dell' Inst. Marzo*, 1835) Panvinius, whose work was written in 1558, as appears from the dedicatory epistle, says that the inscription was found " paulo ante in foro Romano prope columnam," that is, the column of Phocas. The basis on which it stood must therefore have been again covered with rubbish, till the inscription was re-discovered in its more imperfect form after a lapse of nearly three centuries. Anulinus and Fronto were consuls A. D. 199, and consequently in the reign of Septimius Severus, when the basilica appears to have been repaired.

Altogether, therefore, the site of the basilica may be considered as better ascertained than those of most of the imperfect monuments. It must have been bounded on the E. and W., like the basilica Sempronia, by the Vicus Tuscus and the Vicus Jugarius. It appears from the *Monumentum Ancyranum* that the original building, begun by Caesar, and completed by Augustus, was burnt down during the reign of the latter, and again rebuilt by him on a larger scale, with the design that it should be dedicated in the names of his grandsons Caius and Lucius (" Et eandem basilicam consumptam incendio ampliato ejus solo sub titulo nominis filiorum

that it cannot possibly be mistaken, namely, between the temple of Saturn, which, as we have seen, stood at the head of the forum, and the temple of Castor, which lay near that of Vesta; and the *Notitia* indicates the same position; so that it must have been situated between the Vicus Jugarius and Vicus Tuscus. It has been seen before that this was the site of the ancient Basilica Sempronia, a building of which we hear no more during the imperial times : whence it seems probable that it was either pulled down by Caesar in order to erect his new basilica upon the site, or that it had previously gone to ruin. And this is confirmed by the fact that, in the excavations made in 1780, it was ascertained that the basilica was erected upon another ancient foundation, which Canina erroneously supposes to have been that of the comitium. (Fredenheim, *Exposé d'une Découverte faite dans le Forum Romain*, Strasbourg, 1796; Fea, *Varietà di Notizie e della Basilica Giulia ed alcuni Siti del Foro Romano*, ap. Canina, *Foro Romano*, p. 118.) In some excavations made in 1835 near the column of Phocas, another proof of the site of the basilica was discovered. It was the following fragment of an inscription, which taken by itself seems too mangled and imperfect to prove anything:

. . . A . . . ASILICA . . . ER REPARATAE . . . SET ADIECIT. It was recollected, however, that this must be the fragment of an inscription discovered in the 16th century at this spot, which is recorded by Gruter (clxxi. 7) and by Panvinius in his *Descriptio Urbis Romae* (Graevius, iii. p. 300). The two inscriptions, when put in juxta-position, appear as follows :—

```
        GABINIUS VETTIUS
   PROBIANUS . V. C. PRAEF. VRB
   STATUAM QVAE BASILICAE
     IVLIAE A SE NOVITER
   REPARATAE . ORNAMENTO
        ESSET ADIECIT
   DEDIC . XV. KAL . FEBRVARI
      . . . . . PVBLICORVM
   CORNELIO ANNVLINO II
   ET. AVFID . FRONTONE    COS.
```

[meorum] inchoavi et, si vivus non perfecissem, perfici ab heredibus [meis jussi]." But, from a supplement of the same inscription recently discovered, it appears that Augustus lived to complete the work (" Opera fecit nova—forum Augustum, Basilicam Juliam," etc. ; Franz, in Gerhard's *Archäolog. Zeit.* No. ii. 1843). Nevertheless it seems to have anciently borne the names of his grandsons: " Quaedam etiam opera sub nomine alieno, nepotum scilicet et uxoris sororisque fecit: ut porticum basilicamque Lucii et Caii, &c." (Suet. *Aug.* 29). The addition which Augustus mentions having made to the building (" ampliato ejus solo ") may probably have been the portico here mentioned. In A. D. 282 it was again destroyed by fire, and was rebuilt by Diocletian (*Catal. Imp. Vienn.* p. 247, Ronc.)

The Basilica Julia was chiefly used for the sittings of law-courts, and especially for the causae centumvirales (Plin. *Epist.* v. 21, ii. 14.) Its immense size may be inferred from another passage in Pliny (vi.33), from which we learn that 180 judices, divided into 4 concilia, or courts, with 4 separate tribunals, and numerous benches of advocates, besides a large concourse of spectators, both men and women, were accustomed to assemble here. The 4 tribunals are also mentioned by Quintilian (*In. Or.* xii. 5, 6).

The funeral of Caesar was also that of the Republic. After his death and apotheosis, first an ALTAR and then an ÆDES DIVI JULIA were erected to him, on the spot where his body had been burnt (Βωμόν τινα ἐν τῷ τῆς πυρᾶς χωρίῳ ἱδρυσάμενοι, Dion Cass. xliv. 51; καὶ ἡρῷον οἵ ἔν τε τῇ ἀγορᾷ καὶ ἐν τῷ τόπῳ ἐν ᾧ ἐκέκαυτο προκατεβάλλοντο, Id. xlvii. 18: "Aedem Divi Juli—feci," Mon. Ancyr.) We also find mention of a column of Numidian marble nearly 20 feet high, erected to him on the forum by the people, with this inscription: "Parenti Patriae," (Suet. Caes. 88.) This, however, seems to have been the same monument sometimes called ara; for Suetonius goes on to say that the people continued for a long while to offer sacrifice and make vows at it ("Apud eandem longo tempore sacrificare, vota suscipere, controversias quasdam interposito per Caesarem jurejurando distrahere perseveravit"). This ara or columna was afterwards overthrown by Dolabella (Cic. Phil. i. 2, ad Att. xiv. 15). We have before seen that Caesar's body was burnt on the forum, before the Regia and the new rostra which he had erected, and we must therefore conclude that this was the spot where the altar was set up by the people, and subsequently the temple by Augustus. But this has been the subject of a warm controversy. Bunsen placed the temple on the Velian ridge, so that its front adjoined the Sacra Via where it crosses the eastern boundary of the forum, whilst Becker (Handb. p. 336) placed it on the forum itself, so that its back adjoined the same road. The authorities are certainly in favour of the latter view; and the difficulties raised by Urlichs (Röm. Top. p. 21, seq.), who came to the rescue of Bunsen's theory, arise from the mistake shared alike by all the disputants, that this end of the forum was the comitium. Urlichs might have seen that this was not so from a passage he himself quotes (p. 22) from the Fasti Amiternini, XV. Kal. Sept., showing that the temple stood on the forum ("Divo Julio ad Forum"). He seeks, however, to get rid of that passage by an unfortunate appeal to the Schol. Cruq. ad Hor. S. i. 6. 35, in order to show that after the time of Caesar there was no longer any distinction made between the forum and comitium, since the puteal is there named as being on the forum, instead of on the comitium as Urlichs thinks it should be. But this is only trying to support one error by another, since we have already shown that the puteal really was on the forum and not on the comitium. We need not therefore meddle with this controversy, which concerns only those who have taken a wrong view of the comitium.

We will, however, remark that the passage adduced by Becker in his Antwort, p. 41, from the Scholiast on Persius (iv. 49), where the puteal is mentioned as "in porticu Julia ad Fabianum arcum," confirms the sites of these places: from which passage we also learn that the temple had a portico. Vitruvius says (iii. 3) that the temple, which must have been a small one, was of the order called peripteros pycnostylos, that is, having columns all round it, at a distance of one diameter and a half of a column from one another. It must have been raised on a lofty base or substruction, with its front towards the Capitol, as we see from the following lines of Ovid (Met. xv. 841):—

> "—— ut semper Capitolia nostra forumque
> Divus ab excelsa prospectet Julius aede."

The same circumstance, as well as its close proximity to the temple of Castor, are indicated in the following verses of the same poet (Ex Pont. ii 285):—

> "Fratribus assimilis, quos proxima templa tenentes
> Divus ab excelsa Julius aede videt."

This substruction, or κρηπίς, as it is called by Dion, served, as we have seen, for a third rostra and, after the battle of Actium, was adorned by Augustus with the beaks of the captured Egyptian ships, from which time it was called ROSTRA JULIA. (Dion Cass. li. 19.)

Such were the alterations made by Julius Caesar in the forum, and by Augustus in honour of his adoptive father. The latter also made a few other additions. He erected at the head of the forum, under the temple of Saturn, the MILIARIUM AUREUM, which we have before had occasion to mention. (Dion Cass. liv. 8; Suet. Otho, 6; Tac. H. i. 27.) It was in shape like a common milestone, but seems to have been of bronze gilt. Its use is not very

THE MILIARIUM.

clear, as the milestones along the various roads denoted the distances from the gates. But when we recollect that Augustus included a great extent of new streets in his Regions, it seems not improbable that it was intended as a measure of distances within the city; and indeed we find that it was made the starting point in the survey of the city under Vespasian. (Plin. iii. 9.) Hence it might be regarded, as Plutarch says (Galb. 24), the common centre at which all the roads of Italy terminated. The UMBILICUS ROMAE which Becker confounds with it (p. 344) appears to have been a different thing, as the Notitia mentions both of them separately under Regio viii. The piece of column excavated near the arch of Severus must have belonged to this umbilicus, or to some other monument, not to the miliarium, which appears from the Notitia and Curiosum to have retained till a late period its original position near the temple of Saturn at the head of the forum.

We also read of a FORNIX AUGUSTI or triumphal arch erected on the forum in honour of Augustus, but its position is nowhere accurately defined; though from some Scholia on Virgil (Aen. viii. v. 606) edited by Mai, it is supposed to have been near the temple of Julius (Canina, Foro Rom. p. 139 note.)

The ARCUS TIBERII, another triumphal arch, dedicated to Tiberius, was erected at the foot of the Clivus Capitolinus near the temple of Saturn, in commemoration of the recovery of the Roman standards lost with the army of Varus. (Tac. *Ann.* ii. 41.) Tiberius also restored the temple of Castor in the name of himself and of his brother Drusus, as well as the temple of Concord, as we have before had occasion to remark.

Under the following emperors down to the time of Domitian we do not read of many alterations on the forum. The fire of Nero seems to have chiefly destroyed its lower part, where the temple of Vesta and the Regia lay; the upper portion and the Capitol appear to have escaped. The Curia Julia was probably burnt down in the fire which occurred in the reign of Titus; at all events it was certainly rebuilt by Domitian. The celebrated STATUE OF VICTORY, consecrated in the curia by Augustus, appears, however, to have escaped, since Dion Cassius expressly says that it existed in his time, and we find it mentioned even later. (Suet. *Aug.* 100; Dion Cass. li. 22; Herodian, v. 5.) It was this statue, or more correctly perhaps the altar which stood before it, that occasioned so warm a contention between the Christian and heathen parties in the time of Theodosius and Valentinian II., the former being led by Ambrosius, the latter by Symmachus, the praefectus urbi. (Symmach. *Epist.* x. 61; cf. Ambros. *Epist. ad calcem Symm.* ed. Par. i. p. 740, ii. pp. 473, 482; Gibbon, *Decline and Fall,* vol. iii. p. 409, seq., ed. Smith.) Ambrose is said to have obtained its removal; though this, perhaps, relates only to the altar, since the statue is mentioned by Claudian as still existing in the time of Honorius. (*De VI. Cons. Hon.* v. 597):—

"Adfuit ipsa suis ales Victoria templis
Romanae tutela togae: quae divite penna
Patricii reverenda fovet sacraria coetus."

Domitian had a peculiar predilection for two deities, Janus and Minerva. He erected so many archways all over the city that an ancient pasquinade, in the form of a Greek pun, was found inscribed upon one of them: "Janos arcusque cum quadrigis et insignibus triumphorum per Regiones urbis tantos ac tot extruxit ut cuidam Graece inscriptum sit, ἀρκεῖ." (Suet. *Dom.* 13; cf. Dion Cass. lvii. 1.) Among other temples of Minerva he is said by some authorities to have erected one on the forum between those of Vesta and Castor. (Becker, *Handb.* p. 356.) But there seems to have been hardly room for one at this spot; and, as we have before remarked, the *Notitia* does not mention it. Domitian also built, in honour of his father and brother, the TEMPLE OF VESPASIAN AND TITUS, next to the temple of Concord. The three columns on the Clivus Capitolinus most probably belong to it. The opinion that the eight Ionic columns are remains of this temple has been already discussed.

Such was the state of the forum when the colossal equestrian STATUE OF DOMITIAN was erected on it near the Lacus Curtius. Statius (*Silvae* i. 1) has written a small poem on this statue, and his description of it affords many interesting topographical particulars, which fully confirm what has been already said respecting the arrangement of the forum:—

"Quae superimposito moles geminata colosso
Stat Latium complexa forum? coelone peractum

Fluxit opus? Siculis an conformata caminis
Effigies, lassum Steropem Brontemque reliquit?

Par operi sedes. Hinc obvia limina pandit,
Qui fessus bellis, adscitae munere prolis,
Primus iter nostris ostendit in aethera divis.

At laterum passus hinc Julia tecta tuentur
Illinc belligeri sublimis regia Paulli.
Terga pater blandoque videt Concordia vultu.
Ipse autem puro celsum caput aere septus
Templa superfulges, et prospectare videris
An nova contemptis surgant palatia flammis
Pulcrius; an tacita vigilet face Troïcus ignis
Atque exploratas jam laudet Vesta ministras," &c.

The statue, therefore, must have faced the east, with the head slightly inclined to the right, so as to behold the temple of Vesta and the Palatine. Directly in front of it rose the temple of Divus Julius; on the right was the Basilica Julia, on the left the Basilica Aemilia; whilst behind, in close juxtaposition, were the temples of Concord and of Vespasian and Titus. The site of the statue near the Lacus Curtius is indicated in the poem (v. 75, seq.).

The next important monument erected on the forum after the time of Domitian appears to have been the TEMPLE OF ANTONINUS AND FAUSTINA, considerable remains of which still exist before and in the walls of the modern church of *S. Lorenzo in Miranda.* It stood at the eastern extremity of the N. side of the forum. These remains, which are now sunk deep in the earth, consist of the *pronaos* or vestibule. composed of eight columns of cipollino marble supporting an architrave, also part of the cella, built of square blocks of piperino. The architrave is ornamented with arabesque candelabra and griffins. On the front the inscription is still legible:—

DIVO . ANTONINO . ET
DIVAE . FAVSTINAE . EX . S . C .

TEMPLE OF ANTONINUS AND FAUSTINA.

But as a temple was decreed both to Antoninus Pius and his wife, the elder Faustina (Capitol. *Anton. P.* c. 6, 13), and to the younger Faustina, their daughter (*Ib.* c. 26), and as divine honours were also rendered after his death to M. Aurelius Antoninus, the husband of the latter, it becomes doubtful to which pair the temple is to be referred (Nibby, *Foro Rom.* p. 183). It seems, however, most probable that it was dedicated to Antoninus Pius and the elder Faustina. It is stated by Pirro Ligorio (ap. Canina, *Foro Rom.* p. 192) that in the excavations made here in 1547, the basis of a statue was discovered with an inscription purporting that it was erected by the guild of bakers to Antoninus Pius. In the time of Palladio the temple was a great deal more perfect than it is at present, and had an atrium in front, in the middle of which stood the bronze equestrian statue of M. Aurelius, which now adorns the Capitol. (*Architettura*, lib. iv. c. 9.) The inscription in Gruter (cclix. 6) probably belonged to the pedestal of this statue. It was found in the Sacra Via in 1562. Some difficulty, however, arises with regard to this account, since from various other sources we learn that the statue stood for a long while before the church of St. John Lateran. From Palladio's account of the *cortile*, or court, it would appear that the building lay some distance back from the Sacra Via.

In the reign of Commodus a destructive fire, which lasted several days, occasioned much damage in the neighbourhood of the forum, and destroyed among other things the temple of Vesta. (Herodian, i. 14.) According to Dion Cassius the same fire extended to the Palatine and consumed almost all the records of the empire (lxxii. 24). It was on the same occasion that the shop of Galen, which stood on the Sacra Via, was burnt down, and also the Palatine Library, as he himself assures us. (*De Compos. Medicam.* i. c. 1.)

This damage seems to have been repaired by Septimius Severus, the munificent restorer of the Roman buildings, who with a rare generosity commonly refrained from inscribing his own name upon them, and left their honours to the rightful founders ("Romae omnes aedes publicas, quae vitio temporum labebantur, instauravit; nusquam prope suo nomine inscripto, servatis tamen ubique titulis conditorum," Spart. *Sever.* c. ult.). Of the original monuments erected by that emperor the principal one was the Arcus Severi or triumphal arch, which still exists in good preservation at the top of the Roman forum. The inscription informs us that it was dedicated to Severus, as well as to his two sons, Caracalla and Geta, in his third consulate and the 11th year of his reign, consequently in A. D. 203. Between the temple of Concord and the arch, the church of *SS. Sergio e Bacco* was built in the middle ages, with its tower

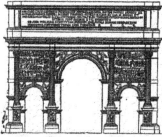

ARCH OF SEPTIMIUS SEVERUS.

resting upon the arch. It appears from a medal of Caracalla that a chariot with six horses and persons within it stood on the summit of the arch, and other persons on horseback at the sides, supposed to be the emperor's sons. It was erected partly in front of the temple of Concord, so as in some degree to conceal the view of that building, and thus to dis-

turb the whole arrangement of the edifices at this part of the forum. Originally it does not seem to have spanned any road, as the latest excavations show that it stood somewhat elevated above the level of the forum, and that the two side arches were approached by means of steps. (Canina, *Foro Rom.* p. 202.) The paved road that may be now seen under it must have been made at a later period. It would be quite a mistake to suppose that the Sacra Via passed under it. This road (here the *Clivus Capitolinus*) began to ascend the hill in front of the temple of Saturn and under the arch of Tiberius.

There seem to have been several other arches in the neighbourhood of the curia or senatus, and further on in the street which led into the Campus Martius; but whether these belonged to the numerous ones before alluded to as erected by Domitian, or were the works of a later age, cannot be determined, nor are they of such importance as to justify any extended research in this place. The haphazard names bestowed on them in the middle ages, as *Arcus manus carneae*, and perhaps also *panis aurei*, afford no clue by which to determine their meaning with any certainty.

Aurelian erected a golden statue of the GENIUS OF THE ROMAN PEOPLE on the rostra; and that these were the ancient rostra may be inferred from this statue being mentioned as close to the *senatus*, or curia, in the *Notitia*. ("Aurelianus—Genium Populi Romani in Rostra posuit," *Catal. Imp. Vienn.* t. ii. p. 246, ed. Ronc.; "continet,—Genium Populi Romani aureum et Equum Constantini, Senatum, Atrium Minervae," &c. *Not. Reg.* viii.) The same inference may be deduced from a passage in Dion Cassius (xlvii. 2), which describes some vultures settling on the temple of Concordia, as also on the sacellum of the Genius of the People; but as this passage relates to Augustus and Antony, it likewise proves that the sacellum must have been there long previously to the time of Aurelian, though when it was erected cannot be determined. The *Equus Constantini*, recorded in the preceding passage of the *Notitia*, is also mentioned by the Anonymus Einsiedlensis near the arch of Severus, under the title of *Cavallus Constantini.*

We shall here mention three other statues which stood in this neighbourhood, since they serve to confirm the topography of it as already described. Pliny mentions three STATUES OF THE SIBYL as standing near the rostra. ("Equidem et Sibyllae juxta Rostra esse non miror, tres sint licet," xxxiv. 11.) That he meant the ancient rostra is evident from his going on to say that he considered these statues to be among the earliest erected in Rome. At a late period of the Empire these seem to have obtained the name of the Fates (Μοῖραι or Parcae). They are mentioned by Procopius, in a passage before alluded to, as in the vicinity of the curia and temple of Janus (ἔχει δὲ τὸν νεὼν ἐν τῇ ἀγορᾷ πρὸ τοῦ βουλευτηρίου ὀλίγον ὑπερβάντι. τὰ τρία φᾶτα· οὕτω γὰρ Ῥωμαῖοι τὰς Μοίρας νενομίκασι καλεῖν, B. G. i. 25.) A whole street or district in this quarter seems to have been named after them, since both the modern church of S. Adriano, at the eastern corner of the Via Bonella, and that of SS. Cosmo e Damiano, which stands a little beyond the temple of Faustina, and consequently out of the proper boundaries of the forum, are said to have been founded in it. ("Fecit ecclesiam beato Adriano martyri in tribus Fatis," Anastas. V. Honor. i. p.

121, Blanch; " In ecclesia vero beatorum Cosmae et Damiani in tribus Fatis," &c. Id. *V. Hadr. ib.* p. 254.) Hence perhaps the name of *templum fatale* applied to the temple of Janus.

The last object which we shall have to describe on the forum is the COLUMN OF PHOCAS. Whilst the glorious monuments of Julius and Augustus, the founders of the empire, have vanished, this pillar, erected in the year 608 by Smaragdus, exarch of Ravenna, to one of the meanest and most hateful of their successors, still rears its head to testify the low abyss to which Rome had fallen. It appears from the inscription, which will be found in Canina (*Foro Rom.* p. 213) and Bunsen (*Beschr.* vol. iii. p. 271), that a gilt statue of Phocas stood upon the summit. The name of Phocas has been erased from this column, probably by Heraclius; but the date sufficiently shows that it must have been dedicated to him. Previously to the discovery of this inscription, which happened in 1813, it was thought that the column belonged to some building; and indeed it was probably taken from one, as the workmanship is much superior to what could have been executed in the time of Phocas. Byron alludes to it as the "nameless column with a buried base." In the excavations made in 1816, at the expense of the duchess of Devonshire, the pedestal was discovered to be placed on a raised basis with steps of very inferior workmanship. (Murray's *Handbook of Rome,* p. 62.) It may be remarked that this column proves the forum to have been in its ancient state, and unencumbered with rubbish, at the commencement of the 7th century. Between this pillar and the steps of the Basilica Julia are three large bases intended for statues.

V. THE IMPERIAL FORA.

Forum Julium.—As Rome increased in size, its small forum was no longer capable of accommodating the multitudes that resorted to it on mercantile or legal business; and we have seen that attempts were early made to afford increased accommodation by erecting various basilicae around it. Under the Empire, when Rome had attained to enormous greatness, even these did not suffice, and several new fora were constructed by various emperors; as the Forum Caesaris or Julium, the Forum Augusti, the Forum Nervae or Transitorium, and lastly the Forum Trajani. The political business, however, was still confined to the ancient forum, and the principal use of the new fora was as courts of justice. Probably another design of them was that they should be splendid monuments of their founders. In most cases they did not so much assume the aspect of a forum as that of a temple within an enclosed space, or τέμενος,—the forum of Trajan being the only one that possessed a basilica. From this characteristic of them, even the magnificent temple of Peace, erected by Vespasian without any design of its being appropriated to the purposes of a forum, obtained in after times the names of Forum Vespasiani and Forum Pacis.

The first foundation of this kind was that of Caesar, enclosing a TEMPLE OF VENUS GENITRIX, which he had vowed before the breaking out of the Civil War. After the battle of Pharsalus the whole plan of it was arranged. It was dedicated after his triumph in B. C. 45, before it was finished, and indeed so hastily that it was necessary to substitute a plaster model for the statue of Venus, which afterwards occupied the cella of the temple. (Plin. xxxv.

45.) Caesar did not live to see it completed, and it was finished by Augustus, as we learn from the *Monumentum Ancyranum.* We are told by Appian (*B. C.* ii. 102) that the temple was surrounded with an open space, or τέμενος, and that it was not destined for traffic but for the transaction of legal business. As it stood in the very heart of the city Caesar was compelled to lay out immense sums in purchasing the area for it, which alone is said to have cost him " super H. S. millies," or about 900,000*l.* sterling. (Suet. *Caes.* 26; Plin. xxxvi. 24.) Yet it was smaller than the ancient forum, which now, in contradistinction to that of Caesar, obtained the name of Forum Magnum. (Dion Cass. xliii. 22.)

No vestige of the Forum Julium has survived to modern times, and very various opinions have been entertained with regard to its exact site; although most topographers have agreed in placing it behind the N. side of the Forum Romanum, but on sites varying along its whole extent. Nardini was the first who pointed to its correct situation behind the church of *Sta Martina,* but it was reserved for Canina to adduce the proof.

We must here revert to a letter of Cicero's (*ad Att.* iv. 16), which we had occasion to quote when speaking of the restoration of the Basilica Aemilia under the forum of the Republic. It has an important passage with regard to the situation of the Forum Julium, but unfortunately so obscurely worded as to have proved quite a *crux* to the interpreters. It appears to have been written in B. C. 54, and runs as follows : " Paullus in medio foro basilicam jam paene texuit iisdem antiquis columnis; illam autem quam locavit facit magnificentissimam. Quid quaeris ? nihil gratius illo monumento, nihil gloriosius. Itaque Caesaris amici (me dico et Oppium, dirumparis licet) in monumentum illud, quod tu tollere laudibus solebas, ut forum laxaremus et usque ad atrium Libertatis explicaremus, contempsimus sexcenties H. S. Cum privatis non poterat transigi minore pecunia. Efficiemus rem gloriosissimam : nam in Campo Martio septa tributis comitiis marmorea sumus et tecta facturi eaque cingemus excelsa porticu," &c. Of these words Becker has given two different interpretations. He first imagined (*Handb.* p. 302, seq.) that Cicero was speaking only of two buildings : the Basilica Aemilia, which Paullus was restoring, and a new basilica, which the same person was building with Caesar's money, and which was afterwards named the Basilica Julia. But before he had finished his work he altered his mind, and at p. 460 pronounces his opinion that Cicero was speaking of no fewer than four different edifices : 1st, the Basilica Paulli (" Paullus—Columnis"); 2nd, the Basilica Julia (" illam—gloriosius"); 3rd, the Forum Julium (" Itaque—pecunia"); 4th, the Septa Julia (" Efficiemus," &c.). With all these views, except the second, we are inclined to agree; but we do not think it probable that Paullus would be constructing two basilicae at the same time; nor do we perceive how a new one only then in progress could have been a monument that Atticus had been accustomed to praise. The chief beauty of the basilica of Paullus was derived from its columns (" Nonne inter magnifica dicamus basilicam Paulli columnis e Phrygibus mirabilem," Plin. xxxvi. 24. s. 1); and though it had undergone two or three subsequent restorations before the time of Pliny, we are nevertheless inclined to think that the columns praised by him were the very same which Atticus had so often admired. However this may be, we see through the obscurity of Cicero's letter the rough sketch of a magnificent design of Caesar's, which had not yet been perfectly matured. The whole space from the back of the Basilica Aemilia as far as the Septa Julia in the Campus Martius was to be thrown open; and perhaps even the excavation of the extremity of the Quirinal, ultimately executed by Trajan, may have been comprised in the plan. Cicero is evidently half ashamed of this vast outlay in favour of Caesar, and seeks to excuse it with Atticus by leading him to infer that it will place his favourite monument in a better point of view. When Cicero wrote the plan was evidently in a crude and incipient state. The first pretence put forth was probably a mere extension of the Forum Romanum; but when Caesar a few years later attained to supreme power the new foundation became the Forum Julium. In his position some caution was requisite in these affairs. Thus the curia of Faustus was pulled down under pretence of erecting on its site a temple of Felicitas—a compliment to the boasted good fortune of Sulla, and his name of Felix. But instead of it rose the Curia Julia. The discrepancy in the sums mentioned by Cicero and Suetonius probably arose from the circumstance that as the work proceeded it was found necessary to buy more houses. If this buying up of private houses was not for the Forum Julium, for what purpose could it possibly have been? The Curia Julia stood on the site of the Curia Hostilia, the Basilica Julia on that of the Sempronia, and we know of no other buildings designed by Caesar about the forum.

With regard to the situation of the ATRIUM LIBERTATIS, to which Cicero says the forum was to be extended, we are inclined to look for it, with Becker, on that projection of the Quirinal which was subsequently cut away in order to make room for the forum of Trajan. The words of Livy, "Censores extemplo in atrium Libertatis escenderunt" (xliii. 16), seem to point to a height. A fragment of the Capitoline plan, bearing the inscription LIBERTATIS, seems to be rightly referred by Canina to the Basilica Ulpia. (Foro Rom. p. 185; cf. Becker, Antwort, &c. p. 29.) Now. if our conjecture respecting the site of the Atrium Libertatis is correct, it would have been occupied by the forum of Trajan and its appurtenances; and it therefore appears probable that the Atrium was comprehended in the Basilica Ulpia. Nor is this a mere unfounded guess, since it appears from some lines of Sidonius Apollinaris (Epig. 2), that in his time the Basilica Ulpia was the place where slaves received their manumission. And that the old Atrium Libertatis was devoted to manumission and other business respecting slaves appears from several passages of ancient authors. Thus Livy: "Postremo eo descensum est, ut ex quatuor urbanis tribubus unam palam in Atrio Libertatis sortirentur, in quam omnes, qui servitutem servissent, conjicerent" (xlv. 15). And Cicero: "Sed quaestiones urgent Milonem, quae sunt habitae nunc in Atrio Libertatis: Quibusnam de servis?" &c. (Mil. 22). Lastly, it may be mentioned that the following fragment of an inscription was found near the church of S. Martina, and therefore near this spot: —

SENATVS . POPVLVSQVE [ROMANVS]
LIBERTATI.

(Canina, Foro Rom. p. 391).

The preceding letter of Cicero's points to the

Forum Julium as closely adjoining the Basilica Aemilia, and there are other circumstances that may be adduced in proof of the same site. Ovid (Fast. i. 258) alludes to the temple of Janus as lying between two fora, and these must have been the Forum Romanum and the Forum Caesaris. Pliny's story (xvi. 86) of the lotus-tree on the Vulcanal, the roots of which penetrated to the forum of Caesar, whatever may be its absolute truth, must at all events have possessed sufficient probability to be not actually incredible; and there is no situation for Caesar's forum which tallies with that story better than that here assigned to it with relation to the site of the Vulcanal, as established in the preceding pages. Our Vulcanal need not have been distant more than about 30 yards from the Forum Julium; that of Becker lies at about five times that distance from it, and would render Pliny's account utterly improbable.

Palladio mentions that in his time considerable remains of a temple were discovered behind the place where the statue of Marforio then stood, near the church of S. Martina, which, from the cornice being adorned with sculptures of dolphins and tridents, he took to be one dedicated to Neptune. But as we have no accounts of a temple of Neptune in this neighbourhood, and as these emblems would also suit the sea-born goddess, it seems probable that the remains belonged to the temple of Venus Genitrix. This is still more strikingly confirmed by Palladio's account of its style of architecture, which was pycnostyle, as we know that of Venus to have been. (Archit. lib. iv. 31; comp. Vitruv. iii. 23.)

We can hardly doubt, therefore, that the forum of Caesar lay on this spot, as is indicated by so many various circumstances. The only objection that has been urged against it is the following passage of Servius, which places the ARGILETUM, a district which undoubtedly adjoined the Forum Julium, in quite a different part of the town: "Sunt geminae belli portae—Sacrarium hoc Numa Pompilius fecerat circa imum Argiletum juxta theatrum Marcelli, quod fuit in duobus brevissimis templis. Duobus autem propter Janum bifrontem. Postea captis Faliscis, civitate Tusciae, inventum est simulacrum Jani cum frontibus quatuor. Unde quod Numa instituerat translatum est ad forum Transitorium et quatuor portarum unum templum est institutam" (ad Virg. Aen. vii. 607). That the Argiletum adjoined the forum of Caesar is evident from the following epigram of Martial's (i. 117. 8):—

" Quod quaeris propius petas licebit
  Argi nempe soles subire letum:
  Contra Caesaris est forum taberna
  Scriptis postibus hinc et inde totis
  Omnes ut cito perlegas poetas.
  Illinc me pete, ne roges Atrectum;
  Hoc nomen dominus gerit tabernae."

Hence, if Servius is right, the forum of Caesar could not have been where we have placed it, but on the S. side of the Capitoline hill; and this opinion has found some defenders (Mommsen, Annali dell' Instit. vol. xvi. p. 311, seq.) We trust, however, that the situation of the small temple of Janus, the index belli pacisque, has been clearly established by what we have said in the former part of this article. Servius is evidently confounding this little temple with the larger one near the theatre of Marcellus; and indeed the whole passage is a heap of trash. For how can we connect such remote events as the taking of Falisci, or rather Falerii, and the erection of a Janus Quadrifrons on the Forum Transitorium, which did not exist till many centuries afterwards? Livy also indicates the Janus-temple of Numa as being in the Argiletum (" Janum ad infimum Argiletum indicem pacis bellique fecit," i. 19); whence we must conclude that it was a district lying on the N. side of the forum. We do not think, however, with Becker (*Handb.* p. 261), that any proof can be drawn from the words of Virgil (*Aen.* viii. 345, seq.), where, with a poetical license, the various places are evidently mentioned without regard to their order. But how far the district called Argiletum may have been encroached upon by the imperial fora it is impossible to say.

The forum of Caesar must have been very splendid. Before the temple of Venus stood a statue of the celebrated horse which would suffer nobody but Caesar to mount him, and whose fore-feet are said to have resembled those of a human being (Suet. *Caes.* 61; Plin. viii. 64). The temple was adorned with pictures by the best Greek artists, and enriched with many precious offerings (Plin. vii. 38, ix. 57, xxxvii. 5, &c.). It was one of the three fora devoted to legal business, the other two being the Forum Romanum and Augusti: —

" Causas, inquis, agam Cicerone disertius ipso
　Atque erit in triplici par mihi nemo foro."
　　　　　　　　　　　　　(Mart. iii. 38. 2.)

Whether it was ever used for assemblies of the senate seems doubtful; at all events the passage cited by Becker (*Handb.* p. 369) from Tacitus (*Ann.* xvi. 27) proves nothing, as the word *curia* there seems to point to the Curia Julia. Of the subsequent history of the Forum Caesaris but little is known. It appears to have escaped the fire of Nero; but it is mentioned among the buildings restored by Diocletian after the fire under Carinus (" Opera publica arserunt Senatum, Forum, Caesaris patrimonium, Basilicam Juliam et Graecostadium. *Catal. Imp. Vienn.* where, according to Preller, *Reg.* p. 143, we must read " Forum Caesaris, Atrium Minervae.") It is mentioned in the *Ordo Romanus*, in the year 1143, but may then have been a ruin.

Forum Augusti.—This forum was constructed for the express purpose of affording more accommodation for judicial business, which had now increased to such an extent that the Forum Romanum and Forum Julium did not suffice for it. It included in its area a TEMPLE OF MARS ULTOR, vowed by Augustus in the civil war which he had undertaken to avenge his father's death:—

" Mars ades, et satia scelerato sanguine ferrum,
　Stetque favor causa pro meliore tuus.
Templa feres, et, me victore, vocaberis Ultor.
　Voverat, et fuso laetus ab hoste redit."
　　　　　　　　　　　　　(Ov. *Fast.* v. 575, seq.)

This temple was appointed to be the place where the senate should consult about wars and triumphs, where provinces cum imperio should be conferred, and where victorious generals should deposit the insignia of their triumphs (Suet. *Aug.* 29). The forum was constructed on a smaller scale than Augustus had intended, because he could not obtain the consent of some neighbouring householders to part with their property (*Ib.* 56). It was opened for business before the temple was finished, which was dedicated B. C. 1 (*Ib.* 29; Vell Pat. ii. 100). The forum extended on each side of the temple in a semicircular

shape (Palladio, *Archit.* iv.), with porticoes, in which Augustus erected the statues of the most eminent Roman generals. On each side of the temple were subsequently erected triumphal arches in honour of Germanicus and Drusus, with their statues (Tac. *Ann.* ii. 64). The temple is said to have been very splendid (Plin. xxxvi. 54), and was adorned, as well as the forum, with many works of art (*Ib.* vii. 53, xxxiv. 18, xxxv. 10; Ov. *Fast.* v. 555, &c.). The Salii were accustomed to banquet here; and an anecdote is recorded of the emperor Claudius, that once when he was sitting in judgment in this forum, he was so attracted by the savoury odour of the dinner preparing for these priests, that he quitted the tribunal and joined their party. (Suet. *Claud.* 33.) This anecdote has partly served to identify the site of the temple, an inscription having been discovered on one of the remaining walls in which the Salii and their *Mansiones* are mentioned (Canina, *Foro Rom.* p. 150).

The remains of three of the columns, with their entablature, of the temple of Mars Ultor are still to be seen near the place called the *Arco de' Pantani.* It must therefore have adjoined the back of the Forum Caesaris. These three columns, which are tall and handsome, are of the Corinthian order. All we know respecting the history of the Forum Augusti is that it was restored by Hadrian (Spart. *Hadr.* 19). The church of *S. Basilio* was probably built on the site of the temple (*Ordo Rom.* 1143; Mabill. *Mus. Ital.* ii. p. 143).

TEMPLE OF MARS ULTOR.

Forum Transitorium or Forum Nervae.—This forum was begun by Domitian, but completed and dedicated by Nerva (Suet. *Dom.* 5; Aur. Vict. *Caes.* 12). We have said that Domitian had a particular predilection for Minerva, and he founded a large AEDES MINERVAE in this forum (" Dedicato prius foro, quod appellatur Pervium, quo aedes Minervae eminentior consurgit et magnificentior," A. Vict. *Ib.*). From this circumstance it was also called Forum Palladium (" Limina post Pacis Palladiumque forum," Mart. i. 2. 8); besides which it also had the name of Pervium or Transitorium, apparently because it was traversed by a street which connected the N. and S. sides of the city, which was not the case with the other fora (Niebuhr, in the *Beschreibung Roms,* iii. p. 282). Thus Lampridius (*Alex. Sev.* 28): " In foro Divi Nervae, quod Transitorium dicitur;" and Aurelius Victor in the passage just cited. From the line of Martial's before quoted, it appears to have adjoined the temple of Peace, erected by Vespasian, which we shall have occasion to describe in another section. There appears to have stood upon it a temple, or rather perhaps fourfold archway of Janus Quadrifrons, probably somewhat resembling that which still exists near *S. Georgio in Velabro,* connecting the roads which led to the four different forums, namely, the Forum Romanum, Forum Caesaris, Forum Nervae, and Forum Pacis, as Vespasian's temple of Peace was sometimes called. The passage before quoted from Servius (*ad Aen.* vii. 607), however absurd in other respects, may at least be received as evidence of the existence of such a Janus here, especially as it is confirmed by other writers. Thus Joannes Lydus: καὶ τοιοῦτον αὐτοῦ ἄγαλμα (τετράμορφον) ἐν τῷ φόρῳ τοῦ Νερβᾶ ἔτι καὶ νῦν λέγεται σεσωσμένον (*de Mens.* iv. 1). So also Martial:—

" Nunc tua Caesareis cinguntur limina donis
  Et fora tot numeros, Jane, quot ora geris "
                    (x. 28. 5).

In the middle ages this Janus-temple appears to have borne the name of *Noah's Ark.*

In the time of Pope Paul V. considerable remains existed of the *pronaos*, or vestibule of this temple of Minerva, consisting of several columns with their entablature, with the following inscription: IMP. NERVA. CAESAR. AVG. PONT. MAX. TRIB. POT. II. IMP. II. PROCOS. (Canina, *Foro Rom.* p. 171.) Paul took these columns to adorn his fountain, the *Acqua Paolo*, on the Janiculum. In the *Via Alessandrina* there are still remains of the wall of peperino which formed the enclosure of the forum, together with two large Corinthian columns half buried in the earth, now called the *Colonnacce.* Their entablature is covered with mutilated reliefs, and over them is an Attic, with a figure of Minerva, also in relief. The situation of the forum of Nerva, and the remains of it existing in his time, are described by Palladio (*Architettura*, lib. iv.), also by Du Pérac (tom. vi.), who observes, that it was then the most complete ruin of a forum in Rome. The *Colonnacce* are represented by Gamucci, *Antichità di Roma*, p. 55; Desgodetz, p. 159, seq.; Overbeke, pl. 39. There is a good description of the fora of Augustus and Nerva by Niebuhr in the *Beschreibung Roms*, vol. iii. p. 275.

Forum Trajani.—Thus between the Capitoline and Palatine hills, the Velian ridge and the ascent of the Quirinal, the valley was almost filled with a splendid series of public places, which we might imagine could hardly be surpassed. Yet it was reserved for Trajan to complete another forum, still more magnificent than any of the preceding ones, for the construction of which the Quirinal itself was forced to yield up part of its mass. Previously to the time of Trajan that hill was connected with the Capitoline by a sort of isthmus, or slender neck; the narrow and uneven defile between them was covered with private houses, and traversed only by a single road of communication between the forum and Campus Martius. But on the western side of this defile lay one of the handsomest quarters of Rome, containing the Septa Julia, the Flaminian circus, the theatres of Balbus, Pompey, and Marcellus, together with those temples and porticoes which so much excited the admiration of Strabo, and which he has described in a passage quoted in the former part of this article. The design of the forum of Trajan was, therefore, to connect this quarter of the town with the imperial fora in a manner not unworthy of the magnificent structures on either side of it. This gigantic work, a portion of which still remains, though the greater part has disappeared under the united influences of time and barbarism, is supposed to have been projected, and even begun, by Domitian. (Aur. Vict. *Caes.* 13; Hieron. i. p. 443, Ronc.; Cassiod. *Chron.* ii. p. 197.) It was, however, executed by Trajan, with the assistance of the celebrated architect Apollodorus of Damascus. (Dion Cass. lxix. 4.) But no

ancient author has left us a satisfactory description of it, and we are obliged to make out the plan, as best we may, from what we can trace of the remains; a task somewhat aided by the excavations made by the French when they had possession of Rome at the commencement of the present century. (See Tournon, *Etudes Statist. Rome*, tom. ii. p. 253, pl. 28, 29; Fea, *Notizie degli scavi nell' Anfiteatro Flavio e nel Foro Traiano*, Rom. 1813; Bunsen, *Les Forum de Rome*, ii^{de} partie, p. 24, seq.) This immense work consisted of the following parts :—

1. The forum, properly so called, a large open area immediately adjoining the NW. sides of the fora of Caesar and Augustus, and filling the whole space between the Capitoline and Quirinal, — much of the latter hill, indeed, and some of the former, having been cut away in order to make room for it. This part, which was called the area or atrium fori (Gell. xiii. 24; Amm. Marc. xvi. 10), contained, in the middle, an equestrian statue of Trajan, and was adorned with many other statues. The SW. and NE. sides of this square, where the ground had been cut away from the hills, was occupied with semicircular buildings. There are still large remains of that under the Quirinal, which are vulgarly called the baths of Paullus Aemilius. The lower part of this edifice, which has only been laid open within the last few years, consists of quadrangular niches, which probably served as little shops; above them was a vaulted portico, with rooms and staircases leading to the upper floors. Piranesi and other topographers conjectured that there was another similar building on the side of the Capitol, at the place called the *Chiavi d' Oro*; but Canina was the first to demonstrate its existence in his *Indicazione Topografica.* Along the front of each of the crescents thus formed there seems to have been a portico, which gave the forum its proper rectangular form. The forum was thus divided into three parts, through both the exterior ones of which there was a road for carriages, as appears from traces of pavement; whilst the square, or middle division was paved with flag-stones. In the middle of the SE. side there seems to have been a triumphal arch. vestiges of which were discovered in the time of Flaminio Vacca (*Memorie*, no. 40), forming the principal entrance on the side of the imperial fora.

FORUM TRAJANI.

2. Next to the forum on the NW. side lay the BASILICA ULPIA, which extended across it lengthways, and thus served to form one of its sides. The basilica was called Ulpia from Trajan's family name. The plan of the middle part is now laid entirely open. It seems to have been divided internally by four rows of columns, thus forming five aisles, with circular *absides* or *chalcidica* at each end. During the ex-

cavations the bases of these columns were discovered partly in their original situation. But it is doubtful whether the fragments of columns of gray granite now seen there belonged to the interior of the basilica ; it is more probable that it had columns of *giallo antico* and *paonezzato*, remains of which have been found (Nibby, *For. Trajano*, p. 353). The floor was paved with slabs of the same marbles. It is supposed from the authority of two passages in Pausanias to have had a bronze roof (v. 12, x. 5). On the side which faced the forum were three magnificent entrances, a large one in the middle and two smaller on each side, decorated with columns, as may be seen on medals.

BASILICA ULPIA.

On the NW. side of the basilica stood, and still stands, the COLUMN OF TRAJAN, the finest monument of the kind in the world. This column was intended to answer two purposes : to serve as a sepulchre for Trajan, and to indicate by its height the depth of soil excavated in order to make room for the forum and its buildings. The latter object is expressed by the inscription, which runs as follows :—

SENATVS . POPVLVSQVE . ROMANVS .
IMP. CAESARI . DIVI . NERVAE . F. NERVAE
TRAIANO . AVG. GERM. DACICO . PONTIF.
MAXIMO . TRIB. POT. XVII. IMP. VI. COS. VI. P. P.
AD . DECLARANDVM . QVANTAE . ALTITVDINIS
MONS . ET . LOCVS . TANT[IS . OPERI]BVS . SIT
[EGESTVS.

(Cf. Aur. Vict. *Epit.* 13; Dion Cass. lxviii. 16). The height of the column, including the pedestal, is 127½ English feet. The diameter at the base is between 12 and 13 feet, and rather more than a foot less at the top. The shaft consists of 19 cylindrical pieces of white marble, in which steps are cut for ascending the interior. On the top was a statue of Trajan, now replaced by that of St. Peter, erected by Pope Sixtus V. When the tomb beneath was opened by the same pontiff, in 1585, it was discovered to be empty. Round the column runs a spiral band of admirable reliefs, representing the wars of Trajan against Decebalus, and containing no fewer than 2500 human figures. The height of the reliefs at the bottom is 2 feet, increasing to nearly double that size at the top ; thus doing away with the natural effect of distance, and presenting the figures to the spectator of the same size throughout. The best descriptions of this magnificent column will be found in Fabretti, *De Columna Trajani*, Rome, 1690, with plates by Pietro Santi Bartoli ; Piranesi, *Trofeo, o sia magnifica Colonna Coclide, &c.*, with large folio drawings ; De Rossi, *Colonna Trajana designata*.

The column stood in an open space of no great extent, being 66 feet long and 56 broad. This

space was bounded on its two sides by porticoes with double columns. In the NW. side of the ba-

COLUMN OF TRAJAN.

silica,* on either side of the column, were two libraries, the BIBLIOTHECA GRAECA AND LATINA, as indicated by Sidonius :—

" Cum meis poni statuam perennem
  Nerva Trajanus titulis videret
  Inter auctores utriusque fixam
              Bibliothecae."—(ix. *Epigr.* 16.)

* It is remarkable, however, that the library is called by A. Gellius, " Bibliotheca *templi* Trajani " (xi. 17).

3. There are evident traces that Trajan's forum extended still farther to the NW., though it is doubtful whether this extension was owing to Trajan himself or to Hadrian. Excavations in this direction have brought to light enormous granite pillars belonging probably to the temple which Hadrian dedicated to Trajan (Spart. *Hadr.* 19), and which

TEMPLE OF TRAJAN.

TEMPLE OF TRAJAN.

is mentioned in the *Notitia* in conjunction with the column. This is further confirmed by some inscriptions bearing the name of Hadrian which have been discovered in this quarter. (Bunsen, *Les Forum Romains*, ii⁴ᵉ partie, p. 35.) Thus the space occupied by these noble structures extended from the fora of Caesar and Augustus almost to the Via Lata, or to the modern *Piazza degli Apostoli.*

How long the forum of Trajan existed is uncertain. The Anonymous of Einsiedlen mentions it in the way from Porta Nomentana to the Forum Romanum. In the *Mirabilia* it seems to be spoken of as a thing that has disappeared.

VI. THE PALATINE AND VELIA.

After the Capitol and forum, the Palatine hill is undoubtedly the most interesting spot at Rome, both from its having been the cradle of the eternal city, and also the seat of its matured power—the residence of the emperors when those emperors ruled the world, or, in the words of Tacitus, "ipsa imperii arx" (*H.* iii. 70),—a circumstance from which it has given name to the residences of subsequent princes. (Dion Cass. liii. 16.) In treating of the topography of this region, and indeed of that of the remainder of the city, we shall not endeavour to observe a chronological order, as was desirable in treating of the forum, in order that the reader might gain a clear idea of its appearance in the various periods of Roman history; but shall follow the most convenient method without regard to the dates of the

different objects mentioned. We have already described the situation and height of the hill. The latter, however, cannot be very accurately given, as the soil is covered to a great depth with rubbish, the sole remains of those magnificent edifices which once stood upon it. On the side of the Circus Maximus, indeed, in the *Vigna del Collegio Inglese,* these ruins assume something of a more definite form; but the gigantic arches and terraces at that part, though they may still excite our wonder, are not sufficiently perfect to enable us to trace any plan of the buildings which they once formed. However, they must all have been subsequent to the time of Nero; since the ravages of the fire under that emperor were particularly destructive on the Palatine hill. Hence the chief topographical interest attaches to the declivities of the hill, which present more facilities for ascertaining spots connected with and sanctified by the early traditions of the city,—of which several have already been discussed, as the Porta Romanula and Clivus Victoriae, the Porta Mugionis, the Curiae Veteres, &c.

We have already seen that the declivity towards the Capitoline hill was called GERMALUS or CERMALUS; but though in ancient times this was regarded as a separate hill, the reason is not clear, since it by no means presents any distinct features, like the Velia. Here was the LUPERCAL, according to tradition a grotto sacred to Pan ever since the time of the Arcadians (Dionys. i. 32, 79), and near it the FICUS RUMINALIS, or sacred fig-tree, under which Romulus and Remus were discovered suckled by the wolf. It is difficult to determine the exact spot of the Lupercal. Evander points it out to Aeneas as lying " gelida sub rupe " (Virg. *Aen.* viii. 343), and Dionysius (*l. c.*) describes it as on *the road* (κατὰ τὴν ὁδὸν) leading to the Circus Maximus; and his authority is preferable to that of Servius, who describes it as " in Circo " (*ad Aen.* viii. 90). Its most probable site therefore is at the western angle of the hill, towards the circus. Its situation is in some degree connected with that of the CASA ROMULI. The description of the 10th Regio, or Palatine, in the *Notitia* begins at the Casa Romuli, and proceeding round the base of the hill to the N. and E. ends, in coming from the circus, with the Lupercal; whence it is plain that the Casa Romuli must have stood a little to the N. of it. Plutarch notices the Casa Romuli, which was also called Tugurium Faustuli, in the following manner: Ῥωμύλος δὲ (ᾤκει) παρὰ τοὺς λεγομένους Βαθμοὺς Καλῆς Ἀκτῆς · οὗτοι δέ εἰσι περὶ τὴν εἰς τὸν ἱππόδρομον τὸν μέγαν ἐκ Παλαντίου κατάβασιν (*Rom.* 20). Here the expression Καλὴ Ἀκτή is puzzling, as an equivalent name does not occur in any Latin author. Properly ἀκτή signifies *the sea-shore,* and cannot therefore be applied to the banks of the Tiber: nor, in prose at least, to an inland bank. Hence Preller is inclined to think that it is merely Plutarch's awkward translation of the Roman name for a place called *Pulcra Rupes,* which obtained this appellation after the Lupercal had been restored by Augustus and adorned with architectural elevations. (*Regionen,* p. 181.) But Plutarch was surely master of his own language; and though he may not have been a very profound Latin scholar, yet as he lived some time in Rome and occupied himself with studying the history and manners of the people, we may perhaps give him credit for knowing the difference between *rupes* and *littus.* It seems more probable therefore that the Roman name of the place alluded to was PULCRUM LITTUS than *Pulcra Rupes* (though unfortunately we do not find it mentioned in any Latin author), and that, like the Casa Romuli and Lupercal, it was a traditionary name, as old as the story of Romulus and Remus itself. According to that story, we must recollect that the Tiber had overflowed its banks and formed a lake here, and that the cradle was washed ashore at the foot of the Palatine; whence the name *littus*, which is frequently used of the shores of a lake, might without impropriety be applied to this spot. The βαθμοί or steps mentioned by Plutarch in the preceding passage were of course a more recent work, but their date cannot be fixed. Propertius (v. l. 9) seems to allude to them in the following passage as existing even in the time of Romulus and Remus:—

" Qua gradibus domus ista Remi se sustulit olim
    Unus erat fratrum maxima regna focus."

But though we can hardly imagine their existence at that time, yet the passage at all events suffices to prove the existence of the steps in the time of Augustus. Becker, however, will by no means allow this. (*Handb.* p. 420 and note.) Plutarch goes on to say that in the neighbourhood of the Casa Romuli stood the cherry-tree said to have sprung from the lance hurled by Romulus from the Aventine to the Palatine; and that the tree withered and died from the roots having been injured when Caius Caesar (Caligula) caused the steps to be made there. (Γαίου δὲ Καίσαρος, ὥς φασι, τὰς ἀναβάσεις ἐπισκευάζοντος καὶ τῶν τεχνιτῶν περιορρυττόντων τὰ πλησίον, ἔλαθον αἱ ρίζαι κακωθεῖσαι παντάπασι, καὶ τὸ φυτὸν ἐμαράνθη.) Hence Becker draws the conclusion that this was the origin of the steps, and that they did not exist before the time of Caligula. But this is by no means a necessary consequence from Plutarch's words, since ἐπισκευάζω often signifies *to repair* or *make better*. We find the same steps mentioned by Solinus under the name of Scalae Caci: " Ad supercilium scalarum Caci habet terminum (Roma Quadrata), ubi tugurium fuit Faustuli. Ibi Romulus mansitavit," &c. (i. 18). It cannot be doubted that these are the same steps mentioned by Propertius and Plutarch. Gerhard proposed to *emend* this passage by reading Caii for Caci; an emendation of which Becker of course approved, as it suits his view that the steps did not exist before the time of Caligula. But unfortunately he was not aware of a passage in Diodorus Siculus which also mentions these steps in a manner confirmatory of the account of Solinus and Propertius: τοῦ δὲ Κακίου ἐν τῷ Παλατίῳ καταβασίς ἐστιν ἔχουσα λιθίνην κλίμακα τὴν ὀνομαζομένην ἀπ' ἐκεινοῦ Κακίαν (iv. 21). And as Diodorus wrote in the age of Augustus, the existence of the steps before the time of Caligula is thus proved.

An AEDES ROMULI is also mentioned on the Germalus in the sacred books of the Argives quoted by Varro (*L. L.* v. § 54, Müll.); but it is not found in any other author, and hence it may appear doubtful whether it is not the same as the Casa Romuli. The round church of *S. Teodoro* on the W. side of the Palatine has frequently been identified with this Aedes Romuli, and it is very probable that it was built over the remains of some ancient temple; but it is too far from the circus to have been the Casa Romuli, which lay more towards *S. Anastasia.* Besides the Casa seems to have been nothing more than a little thatched hut; of which, as we have

seen, there appears to have been a duplicate on the Capitol.

In the dearth of any more accurate information we cannot fix the situation of these venerable relics of Roman antiquity more precisely than may be gathered from the preceding general indications. M. Valerius Messala and C. Cassius Longinus, who were censors in B. C. 154, projected, and even began, a theatre at this spot, which was to extend from the Lupercal on the Germalus towards the Palatine. But this scheme was opposed by the rigid morality of Scipio Nasica, and all the works were put up to auction and sold. (Vell. Pat. i. 15; Val. Max. ii. 4. § 2; Appian, *B. C.* i. 28.) The Lupercal is mentioned in the *Monumentum Ancyranum*, as reconstructed by Augustus; whence Canina infers that the ancient one must have been destroyed when this theatre was commenced. (*Indicazione Topogr.* p. 460, 1850.) The Casa Romuli is represented by Fabius Pictor, as translated by Dionysius of Halicarnassus (i. 79), to have been carefully preserved in his time, the damage occasioned by age or tempests being made good according to the ancient pattern. Whether the building mentioned in the *Notitia* was still the same it is impossible to say.

We have already noticed, when treating of the city of Romulus, the SANCTUARY OF VICTORIA—most probably a sacred grove—and the CLIVUS VICTORIAE on the NW. slope of the Palatine. At or near this spot an AEDES MATRIS DEUM was erected B. C. 191, to contain the image of the Mater Idaea, which Scipio Nasica had brought from Asia thirteen years before. (Liv. xxxvi. 35; Cic. *Har. R.* 12.) It must have been to the N. of the Casa Romuli, since it is mentioned after it in the *Notitia*, when proceeding in that direction, yet at some distance from the N. point of the hill, between which and the temple the Domus Tiberiana must have intervened. It is recorded as having been twice burnt down; once in B. C. 110, when it was rebuilt by Metellus (Jul. Obs. 99), and again in A. D. 2, in the same fire which destroyed the palace of Augustus, by whom it was restored. (Val. Max. i. 8. § 11; Dion Cass. lv. 12; *Mon. Ancyr.*). It must also have been destroyed in the conflagration under Nero, and again rebuilt. Becker (*Handb.* p. 421) observes that its front must have faced the E., as the statue of the Magna Mater Idaea is described by Dion Cassius as looking that way (xlvi. 43). But this relates only to the statue; and we fancy that there is some reason to believe, from a passage in Martial, that the temple was a round one, and could not therefore be properly said to face any way. In this passage two temples are mentioned (i. 70. 9):—

" Flecte vias hac qua madidi sunt tecta Lyaei
    Et Cybeles picto stat Corybante tholus."

Becker observes (p. 422) that the age and situation of the temples here mentioned cannot be determined, as they occur nowhere else; and this seems to be true of the temple of Bacchus; but there appears to be no reason why the THOLUS CYBELES—which Becker writes *Torus*, without any apparent meaning—may not have been the Aedes Matris Deum before referred to. The description of the road to the house of Proculus given in this epigram suits the situation of this temple; and the house itself is mentioned as " nec propior quam Phoebus amat." Now, the temple of Apollo, built by Augustus, lay close to that of the Idaean Mother, as we shall see presently; and,

3 F 2

indeed, they are mentioned in one breath in the *Notitia*. ("Aedem Matris Deum et Apollinis Rhamnusii.") That this Tholus Cybeles may have been the temple which once occupied the site of the present circular church of *S. Teodoro* before referred to, we can only offer a conjecture; its situation, at least, admirably corresponds with that of the temple of the Idaean Mother.

We find a temple of this deity, as well as one of JUVENTAS mentioned in the *Monumentum Ancyranum* (tab. iv. l. 8) as erected by Augustus on the Palatine. The first of these may, however, have been only a restoration of the ancient temple. We can hardly conclude from the word *feci* that it was an entirely new and separate structure; since we find the same word used in that record with relation to other edifices which were among the most ancient in Rome, and of which it is not likely that there should have been duplicates: such as the temple of Jupiter Feretrius on the Capitol, that of Quirinus, that of Juno Regina on the Aventine, and others. In these cases it seems probable that the edifices were in such a ruinous state from long neglect that Augustus found it necessary to rebuild them from their foundations; which would justify the use of the word *feci* instead of *refeci*, but hardly the regarding of them as entirely new temples. The great care used by Augustus in restoring the ancient temples is alluded to by Horace (*Od.* iii. 6). The temple of Juventas may possibly have been new; at all events it could hardly have been the one dedicated by C. Licinius Lucullus about the same time as that of the Mater Magna Idaea, since the former was in the Circus Maximus. (Liv. xxxvi. 36; cf. Cic. *Brut.* 18, *ad Att.* i. 18.)

What the PENTAPYLUM may have been which is mentioned in the *Notitia* between the temple of Apollo and the palace of Augustus, it is difficult to say, except that it was probably a building with five gates. Preller (*Regionen*, p. 183) cites a passage from an anonymous describer of the Antiquities of Constantinople in Banduri (*Imp. Orient.* i. p. 21), in which a building in that city called *Tetrapylum*, which was used for depositing and bewailing the corpse of the emperor, or of that of any member of his family, is mentioned; and as this building is said to have been imitated from one at Rome, Preller thinks it highly probable that the Pentapylum in question may have afforded the model, and been used for a similar purpose.

Of the temples of JUPITER VICTOR and JUPITER STATOR — the former near the Nova Via and Porta Mugionis, the latter farther off towards the Sacra Via — we have already spoken when describing the Romulean city: besides which there seems to have been a temple of JUPITER PROPUGNATOR, probably of the time of the Antonines, known only from an inscription. (Gruter. ccc. 2; Orell. 42; Canina, *Indicazione*, p. 469.) We have also had occasion to mention the CURIAE VETERES and the sacellum of FORTUNA RESPICIENS. Other ancient buildings and shrines on the Palatine, the sites of which cannot be exactly determined, were the CURIA SALIORUM (Palatinorum), where the ancilia and the lituus Romuli were preserved, probably not far from the temple of Vesta (Dionys. ii. 70; Cic. *Div.* i. 17; Gruter, *Inscr.* clxiii. 5; Orell. 2244); a fanum, or ARA FEBRIS (Cic. *Leg.* ii. 11; Val. Max. ii. 5. § 6; Plin. ii. 5), an ancient sacellum of the DEA VIRIPLACA, the appeasing deity of connubial quarrels (Val. Max. ii. 1. § 6); and an

᾿Αφροδίσιον, or TEMPLE OF VENUS (Dion Cass. lxxiv. 3).

When the Romans began to improve their domestic architecture, and to build finer houses than those which had contented their more simple ancestors, the Palatine, from its excellent and convenient situation, early became a fashionable quarter. We have already alluded slightly to some of the more noted residences on this hill. The house of VITRUVIUS VACCUS is one of the most ancient which we find mentioned in this quarter. It was pulled down in B. C. 330 in consequence of the treasonous practices of its owner; after which the site remained unbuilt upon, and obtained the name of VACCI PRATA (Liv. viii. 19; Ps. Cic. *p. Dom.* 38); but how long it remained in this state it is impossible to say. The PORTICUS CATULI rose on the Palatine from a similar cause. Its site had previously been occupied by the house of M. Fulvius Flaccus, who perished in the sedition of C. Gracchus: the house was then razed, and the ground on which it stood called FLACCIANA AREA, till this portico was erected on it by Q. Lutatius Catulus, after his Cimbric victory. (Val. Max. vi. 3. § 1; Ps. Cic. *p. Dom.* 43.) Near it stood the HOUSE OF CICERO which he bought of Crassus, — probably not the celebrated orator, — the fate of which we have already related. It seems to have been on the NE. side of the Palatine, as Cicero is described by Plutarch as traversing the Sacra Via in order to arrive at the forum (*Cic.* 22): and Vettius calls Cicero "vicinum consulis," that is, of Caesar, who then dwelt in the Regia (*ad Att.* ii. 24). CATILINE's HOUSE was also on the Palatine, and was annexed by Augustus to his residence. (Suet. *Ill. Grumm.* 17.) Here also was a HOUSE OF ANTONIUS, which Augustus presented to Agrippa and Messala (Dion Cass. liii. 27); and also the HOUSE OF SCAURUS, famed for its magnificence. (Cic. *Scaur.* 27; Plin. xxxvi. 3.)

With the reign of Augustus a new era commenced for the Palatine. It was now marked out for the imperial residence; and in process of time, the buildings erected by successive emperors monopolised the hill, and excluded all private possessions. Augustus was born in this Region, at a place called AD CAPITA BUBULA, the situation of which we are unable to determine (Suet. *Aug.* 5). In early manhood he occupied the house of the orator C. Licinius Calvus "juxta forum super scalas anularias" (*Ib.* 72); but neither can the site of this be more definitely fixed. Hence he removed to the Palatine, where he at first occupied the HOUSE OF HORTENSIUS, a dwelling conspicuous neither for size nor splendour. (*Ib.*) After his victory over Sextus Pompeius, he appears to have purchased several houses adjoining his own, and to have vowed the TEMPLE OF APOLLO, which he afterwards built (Vell. Pat. ii. 81; Dion Cass. lxix. 15.) This temple, the second dedicated to that deity at Rome — the earlier one being in the Circus Flaminius — does not, however, appear to have been begun till after the battle of Actium, or at all events the plan of it was extended after that event. It is well known that after that victory Augustus dedicated a temple to the Leucadian Apollo near Actium, and in like manner the new structure on the Palatine was referred to the same deity; whence the phrases "Actius Apollo" (Virg. *Aen.* viii. 704; Prop. iv. 6. 67), and "Phoebus Navalis " (—"ubi Navali stant sacra Palatia Phoebo," Prop. iv. 1. 3). It was dedicated in B. C. 27. It was surrounded with a portico containing the BIBLIOTHECAE GRAECA

ET LATINA (Suet. *Aug.* 29; Dion Cass. Hil. 1; *Mon. Ancyr.*) These far-famed libraries were quite distinct institutions, as appears from monumental inscriptions to slaves and freedmen attached to them, who are mentioned as " a Bibliotheca Latina Apollinis," or, " a Bibliotheca Graeca Palatina" (Panvinius in Graevius, *Thes.* iii. col. 305; Orell. *Inscr.* 40, 41). In them were the busts or *clipeatae imagines* of distinguished authors. (Tac. *Ann.* ii. 83.) Propertius, in a short poem (iii. 29), has given so vivid a description of the whole building, that we cannot do better than insert it:—

" Quaeris cur veniam tibi tardior? Aurea Phoebo
    Porticus a magno Caesare aperta fuit.
Tota erat in speciem Poenis digesta columnis
    Inter quas Danai femina turba senis.
Hic equidem Phoebo visus mihi pulchrior ipso
    Marmoreus tacita carmen hiare lyra.
Atque aram circum steterant armenta Myronis
    Quatuor artificis, vivida signa, boves.
Tum medium claro surgebat marmore templum
    Et patria Phoebo carius Ortygia.
In quo Solis erat supra fastigia currus
    Et valvae Libyci nobile dentis opus.
Altera dejectos Parnassi vertice Gallos
    Altera moerebat funera Tantalidos.
Deinde inter matrem deus atque inter sororem
    Pythius in longa carmina veste sonat."

Hence we learn that the columns of the portico were of African marble, and between them stood statues of the fifty daughters of Danaus (cf. Ovid. *Amor.* ii. 2. 4.) According to Acron, fifty equestrian statues of the sons of Danaus also stood in the open space. (Schol. *ad Pers.* ii. 56.) The temple itself was of solid white marble from Luna (*Carrara*). (Serv. Virg. *Aen.* viii. 720.) The statue alluded to by Propertius as " Phoebo pulchrior ipso " was that of Augustus himself, which represented him in the dress and attitude of Apollo. (Schol. Cruq. *ad Hor. Ep.* i. 3, 17: Serv. *ad Virg. Ec.* iv. 10.) In the library was also a colossal bronze statue of Apollo, 50 feet in height (Plin. xxxiv. 18), as well as many precious works of art. (Ib. xxxiv. 8, xxxvii. 5, &c.) The Sibylline books were preserved in the temple (Suet. *Aug.* 31; Amm. Marc. xxiii. 3) before which was the spacious place called the AREA APOLLINIS.

From all these notices we may gather some idea of the splendour of this celebrated temple; but its exact site, as well as that of the PALACE OF AUGUSTUS, is nowhere clearly intimated. From several passages, however, which have been cited when discussing the situation of the Porta Mugionis, we may infer pretty accurately that the latter must have stood at the NE. side of the Palatine, between the arch of Titus and the temple of Vesta. (*S. Maria Liberatrice.*) It appears from a passage in Ovid (" Inde tenore pari," &c., *Trist.* iii. 1. 59), that the temple must have lain some way beyond the palace, and there seems to be no reason why we may not place it near *S. Teodoro*, though it stood perhaps on the summit of the hill. This seems to be the spot indicated in the *Notitia.* The temple is there called " aedis Apollinis *Rhamnusii*"—an epithet not easily explained, notwithstanding the attempt of Preller (*Regionen,* p. 182); although there can be no doubt that the temple built by Augustus is meant.

In the same document a DOMUS TIBERIANA, or palace of Tiberius, is mentioned as distinct from that of Augustus; a house, indeed, which he probably inherited, as he was born on the Palatine. (Suet. *Tib.* 5.) In his youth, when he lived in a quiet, retired manner, he first inhabited the house of Pompey in the Carinae, and afterwards that of Maecenas on the Esquiline (*Ib.* 15); but when he became emperor, it is most probable that he resided on the Palatine, till he secluded himself in the island of Capreae. The Domus Tiberiana must have stood near the NW. corner of the Palatine, since it is described as affording an exit into the Velabrum (" per Tiberianam domum in Velabrum," Tac. *Hist.* i. 27). Suetonius, speaking of the same departure of Otho, says that he hastened out at the back of the palace (" proripuit se a postica parte Palatii," *Otho,* 6); from which passages it would appear that the two palaces were connected together, that of Augustus being the more conspicuous towards the forum, whilst that of Tiberius formed the back front. It was from the latter that Vitellius surveyed the storming of the Capitol. (Suet. *Vit.* 15.) At a later period of the Empire we find a BIBLIOTHECA mentioned in the palace of Tiberius, which had probably superseded the Palatine Library, as the latter is no longer mentioned. (A. Gell. xiii. 19; Vopisc. *Prob.* 2.) All these buildings must, of course, have been destroyed in the fire of Nero; but we must assume that, after they were rebuilt, the Domus Augusti et Tiberii still continued to be distinguished, as they are mentioned as separate buildings in the *Notitia;* and indeed Josephus expressly says that the different parts of the complex of buildings forming the imperial palace were named after their respective founders. (*Ant. Jud.* xix. 1. § 15).

On or near the Palatine we must also place the TEMPLUM AUGUSTI — one of the only two public works which Tiberius undertook at Rome, the other being the *scena* of the theatre of Pompey Even these he did not live to finish, but left them to be completed and dedicated by Caligula. (Tac. *Ann.* vi. 45; Suet. *Tib.* 47, *Cal.* 21.) The circumstance of Caligula using this temple as a sort of pier for his bridge to the Capitoline makes it doubtful whether it could have stood on the Palatine hill. (Suet. *Ib.* 22.) Yet Pliny (xii. 42) alludes to it as " in Palatii templo;" and if it was not exactly on the summit of the hill, it could not have been very far from it. Becker conjectures that the BRIDGE OF CALIGULA passed over the Basilica Julia; but the only proof is, that Caligula was accustomed to fling money to the people from the roof of the basilica, which he might have ascended without a bridge. (Suet. *Cal.* 37, Jos. *Ant. Jud.* xix. 1. § 11.) The bridge, perhaps, did not stand very long. Caligula seems to have made extensive alterations in the imperial palace, though we cannot trace them accurately. (" Bis vidimus urbem totam cingi domibus principum Caii et Neronis," Plin. xxxvi. 24. s. 5.) We have already mentioned that he connected the temple of Castor with it. Yet in his time there must have been still some private dwellings on the NE. side of the Palatine, as Pliny mentions that the lotus-trees belonging to the house of Crassus at that spot lasted till the fire of Nero. (Ib. xvii. 1.) The enormous buildings of the last-named emperor probably engrossed the whole of the Palatine; at all events we hear no more of private houses there after the commencement of his reign. We have already adverted to Nero's two palaces. The first of these, or DOMUS TRANSITORIA, with its gardens, though not finished in the same style of splendour

3 Y 3

as its successor, the *domus aurea*, seems to have occupied as large an extent of ground, and to have reached from the Palatine to the gardens of Maecenas and the agger of Servius on the Esquiline. (Suet. *Nero*, 31; Tac. *Ann.* xv. 39.) The AUREA DOMUS was a specimen of insane extravagance. Its atrium or vestibule was placed on the Velia, on the spot where the temple of Venus and Rome afterwards stood, and in it rose the colossal STATUE OF NERO, 120 feet high, the base of which is still visible at the NW. side of the Colosseum. We may gain an idea of the vastness of this residence by comparing the prose description of Suetonius with the poetical one of Martial, when we shall see that the latter has not abused the privilege of his calling. (Suet. *Nero*, 31; Mart. *de Spect.* 2). It was never perfectly finished, and Vespasian, as we have said, restored the ground to the public. We know but little of the arrangement of the buildings on the Palatine itself under Nero, except that the different parts appear to have retained their former names. Domitian added much to the palace, now again confined to this hill, and fitted it up in a style of extraordinary magnificence; but, though we frequently hear of single parts, such as baths, *diaetae*, a portico called *Sicilia*, a dining-room dignified with the appellation of *Coenatio Jovis*, &c., yet we are nowhere presented with a clear idea of it as a whole (cf. Plut. *Popl.* 15; Plin. xxxv. 5. s. 38; Capit. *Pert.* 11; Mart. viii. 36; Stat. *Silv.* iii. 4. 47, iv. 2. 18, &c.) The anxiety and terror of the tyrant are strikingly depicted in the anecdote told by Suetonius (*Dom.* 14), that he caused the walls of the portico in which he was accustomed to walk to be covered with the stone, or crystallised gypsum, called *phengites*, in order that he might be able to see what was going on behind his back. It is uncertain where the ADONAEA, or gardens of Adonis, lay, in which Domitian received Apollonius of Tyana, and which are marked on a fragment of the Capitoline plan (Bellori, tab. xi.) Of the history of the palace little more is known. Several accounts mention the domus aurea as having been burnt down in the reign of Trajan (Oros. vii. 12; Hieron. an. 105, p. 447, Ronc.), and the palace which succeeded it appears to have been also destroyed by fire in the reign of Commodus (Dion Cass. lxxii. 24; Herodian, i. 14.)

At the southern extremity of the Palatine, Septimius Severus built the SEPTIZONIUM, considerable remains of which existed till near the end of the

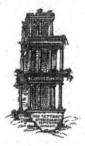

THE SEPTIZONIUM.

16th century, when Pope Sixtus V. caused the pillars to be carried off to the Vatican. Representations of the ruins will be found in Du Pérac (tav. 13) and Gamucci (*Antichità di Roma*, p. 83, *Speculum Rom. Magnificentiae*, t. 45). The name of the building, which, however, is very variously written in the MSS. of different authors, is by some supposed to have been derived from its form, by others from the circumstance of seven roads meeting at this spot. It seems not improbable that a similar place existed before the time of Severus, since Suetonius mentions that Titus was born near the Septizonium (c. 2); though topographers, but without any adequate grounds, have assigned this to the 3rd Region. It has been inferred from the name that the building had seven rows of columns, one above another, but this notion seems to be without foundation, as the ruins never exhibited traces of more than three rows. The tomb of Severus must not be confounded with it, which, as we learn from Spartianus, was on the Via Appia, and built so as to resemble the Septizonium. The same author informs us (*Sev.* 24) that the design of Severus was to make the Septizonium an atrium of the palace, so that it should be the first object to strike the eyes of those coming from Africa, his native country. But the true nature and destination of the building remain enigmatical.

We know of no other alterations in the palace except some slight ones under the emperors Elagabalus and Alexander Severus. The former consecrated there the TEMPLE OF HELIOGABALUS (Lampr. *Heliog.* 3; Herodian, v. 5) and opened a public bath, also destined apparently as a place of licentiousness (Lampr. *Ib.* 8). Of the buildings of Alexander Severus we hear only of a *diaeta*, erected in honour of his mother Julia Mammaea, and commonly called " ad Mammam " (Id. *Al. Sev.* 26). These diaetae were small isolated buildings, commonly in parks, and somewhat resembled a modern Roman *casino* or pavilion (Plin. *Ep.* ii. 17, v. 6). It is also related of both these emperors that they caused the streets of the Palatine to be paved with porphyry and *verde antico* (Lampr. *Hel.* 24, *Al. Sev.* 25). The Palatium was probably inhabited by Maxentius during his short reign, after which we hear no more of it. That emperor is said to have founded baths there. (*Catal. Imp. Vienn.* t. ii. p. 248, Ronc.)

The VICTORIA GERMANICIANA, the only object recorded in the *Notitia* between the Septizonium and the Lupercal, and which must therefore have stood on the side next the circus, was probably one of those numerous monuments erected either in honour of Germanicus, of which Tacitus speaks (*Ann.* ii. 83), or else to Caracalla, who likewise bore the name of Germanicus (Preller, *Regionen*, p. 187).

We have already treated generally of the Velia and Sacra Via, and of some of the principal objects connected with them, as well as of the Nova Via under the Palatine. The NOVA VIA was not a very important road, and we have little more to add respecting it. It seems to have begun at the Porta Mugionis, where, like the Sacra Via, at the same spot, it was called *Summa* Nova Via (Solin. i. 1). From this place it ran almost parallel with the Sacra Via, and between it and the hill, as far as its northern point, where it turned to the S., and still continued to run along the base of the Palatine, as far at least as the Porta Romanula (near *S. Giorgio in Velabro*). Some, indeed, carry it on as far as the Circus Maximus (Canina, *Indic. Top.* p. 331); a view which does not seem to be supported by any authority. The lower part of it, both on the side of the forum and of the Velabrum, was called Infima Nova Via. (Varro, v. § 43, Müll.) Ovid describes it as touching the forum (" Qua Nova Romano nunc Via juncta foro est," *Fast.* vi. 389); whence we must conclude that not only the open space itself, but also the ground around it on which the temples and basilicae stood, was included under the appellation of forum. A road appears, however, to have led from the Nova Via to the forum between the temples of Vesta and Castor, as is shown by remains of pavement discovered there; and this may have been the *junction* alluded to by Ovid, which from his words would seem to have been comparatively recent. The LUCUS VESTAE must have lain behind the Nova Via, towards the Palatine, and indeed on the very slope of the hill, as appears from the following passages: " Exaudita vox est a luco Vestae, qui a Palatii radice in Novam Viam devexus est " (Cic. *Div.* i. 45); " M. Caedicius de plebe nuntiavit tribunis, se in Nova Via, ubi nunc sacellum est supra aedem Vestae vocem noctis silentio audisse clariorem humana " (Liv. v. 32). The sacellum here alluded to was that of Aius Loquens. (Cic. *l c.* and ii. 32.) It is described by Varro (*ap. Gell.* xvi. 17) as " in infima Nova Via "; whence we must conclude that it was in the part near the forum that Caedicius heard the voice. Though called *Nova*, the road must have been of high antiquity, since Livy mentions that Tarquinius lived in it (i. 47); and perhaps it received its name from its newness in comparison with the Sacra Via.

Before we proceed to describe the monuments on the VELIA, we must observe that some writers, and especially the Italian school of topographers (Canina, *Foro Rom.* p. 60, seq., *Indic. Top.* p. 462), do not allow that the Velia consisted of that height which lies between the Palatine, the Esquiline, and the eastern side of the forum, but confine the application to the northern angle of the Palatine, which, it is contended, like the Germalus, was in ancient times considered as distinct from the remainder of the hill. Indeed it appears that Niebuhr first applied the name of Velia to the ridge in question (*Hist.* i. p. 390, Eng. trans.), in which view he was of course followed by Bunsen (*Beschr.* iii. p. 81). One of the chief arguments adduced against it is the account given of the house of Valerius Publicola. Valerius is said to have begun building a house on the same spot where Tullus Hostilius had previously dwelt (Cic. *Rep.* ii. 31); and the residence of Tullus Hostilius again is recorded to have been on the Velia, on the spot *afterwards* occupied by the Aedis Deum Penatium (Varro, *ap. Non.* xii. 51, p. 363, Gerl.; " Tullus Hostilius in Velia, ubi postea Deum Penatium aedes facta est," Solin. i. 22). Now Bunsen (*Ib.* p. 85), and after him Becker (*de Muris*, p. 43, *Handb.* p. 249), hold that the Aedes Deum Penatium here alluded to was that mentioned by Dionysius Halicarnassensis (i. 68) as standing in the short cut which led from the forum to the Carinae, in the district called 'Τπελαίαις. The MSS. vary in the spelling of this name; but we think with Becker that the Velia, or rather " Sub Velia," is meant, as Cujacius has translated the word: and Casaubon (*ad Mon. Anyr.*) reads Οὐέλιαι. But, whatever opinion may be entertained on that point, the other part of the description of Dionysius, namely, that the temple stood in the short cut between the forum and the

Carinae, sufficiently indicates the locality; and we are of opinion, with Becker, that Bunsen arrived at a very probable conclusion in identifying this temple with the present circular vestibule of the church of *SS. Cosma e Damiano*. Yet, if we assume with those writers that this was the only temple of the Penates on the Velia, and consequently the spot on which the house of Publicola stood, then we must confess that we see considerable force in the objection of Canina, that such a situation does not correspond with the descriptions given by Cicero, Livy, and other writers. All those descriptions convey the idea that Publicola's house stood on a somewhat considerable, though not very great, elevation. Thus Dionysius characterises the spot as λόφον ὑπερκείμενον τῆς ἀγορᾶς ὑψηλὸν ἐπιεικῶς καὶ περίτομον ἀκλεξάμενος (v. 19). And Cicero says of the house: " Quod in excelsiore loco coepisset aedificare " (*Rep.* ii. 31). A still more decisive passage is that of Livy: " Aedificabat in *summa Velia* " (ii. 7). For how can that spot be called the *top* of the Velia, which was evidently *at the bottom*, and, according to Becker's own showing, in a district called *sub* Velia? His attempts to evade these difficulties are feeble and unsatisfactory (*de Muris*, p. 45). Yet they are not incapable of solution, without abandoning Niebuhr's theory respecting the Velia, which we hold to be the true one. There were in fact two temples of the Penates on the Velia, namely, that identified by Bunsen with *SS. Cosma e Damiano*, and another " in Summa Velia," as Livy says; which latter occupied the site of the residence of Tullus Hostilius, and of the subsequent one of Valerius Publicola. Thus Solinus: " Tullus Hostilius in Velia (habitavit), ubi *postea* Deum Penatium aedes facta est " (i. 22). We cannot determine the length of this *postea*; but it was most probably after the time of Publicola, and perhaps a great deal later. But the other temple was certainly older, as it is mentioned in the sacred books of the Argives (*ap.* Varro, *L.L.* v. § 54: " In Velia apud aedem Deum Penatium"); and thus it is plain that there must have been two temples. The one in the Summa Velia is the Sacellum Larum mentioned by Tacitus, in describing the pomoerium of Romulus (*Ann.* xii. 24): and this is another proof that there were two temples; for it is impossible to imagine that the pomoerium could have extended so far to the N. as the church of *SS. Cosma e Damiano*. The situation of this sacellum would answer all the requirements of the passages before cited. For there is still a very considerable rise from the forum to the arch of Titus, near to which the sacellum must have stood, which rise was of course much more marked when the forum was in its original state, or some 20 feet below its present level. Indeed the northern angle of the Palatine, which Canina supposes to have been the Velia, does not present any great difference of height: and thus the objections which he justly urges against the aedes near the temple of Faustina do not apply to one on the site that we have indicated. Besides it appears to us an insuperable objection to Canina's view that he admits the spot near the temple of Faustina to have been called Sub Velia, though it is separated by a considerable space and by the intervening height, from the N. angle of the Palatine. The account of Asconius (*ad Cic. Pis.* 22) of a house of P. Valerius " sub Velia, ubi nunc aedis Victoriae est," is too confused and imperfect to draw any satisfactory conclusion from it. By all other authorities the

Aedis Victoriae is said to be not at the *foot of the Velia*, but on the *summit of the Palatine*.

But there is another argument brought forwards by Canina against the height in question being the Velia. He observes that the area on which the temple of Venus and Rome stands is divided from the Palatine by the Sacra Via, and hence could not have belonged to the Velia ; since the Sacra Via, and all the places on the opposite (northern) side of it, were comprehended in the 1st Regio of Servius, or the Suburana, whilst the Palatine, including the Velia, were contained in the 4th Regio (*Indicas. Topogr.* p. 462, cf. *Foro Rom.* p. 61). Now if this were so, it would certainly be a fatal objection to Niebuhr's view; but we do not think that any such thing can be inferred from Varro's words. In describing the 1st Region, in which a place called Ceroliensis was included, he says, " Ceroliensis a Carinarum junctu dictus Carinae, postea Cerolia, quod hinc oritur caput Sacrae Viae ab Streniae sacello," &c. (*L. L.* v. § 47.) The passage is obscure, but we do not see how it can be inferred from it that the Sacra Via formed the boundary between the 1st and 4th Servian Regions. Varro seems rather to be explaining the origin of the name Cerolia, which he connects with the Sacra Via, but in a manner which we cannot understand. The Sacra Via traversed the highest part of the ridge, and thus on Canina's own showing must have included some part of it in the 4th Region, making a division where no natural one is apparent, which is not at all probable. Besides, if this height was not called Velia, what other name can be found for it ? And it is not at all likely that an eminence of this sort, which is sufficiently marked, and lies in the very heart of the city, should have been without a name.

Assuming the Velia, therefore, to have been that rising ground which lies between the valley of the forum on the one hand, and that of the Colosseum on the other, we shall proceed to describe its monuments. The AEDES PENATIUM, before referred to as standing on the declivity of the ridge, or Sub Velia, and described by Dionysius (i. 68), seems to have been one of the most venerable antiquity. In it were preserved the images of the household gods said to have been brought from Troy, having upon them the inscription ΔΕΝΑΣ, which has given rise to so much controversy ; namely, whether it is a scribe's error for ΠΕΝΑΣ, that is ΠΕΝΑΣΙ = Penatibus, or whether it should have been ΔΙΣ ΜΑΓΝΙΣ (Diis Magnis), &c. &c. (See Ambrosch, *Stud. u. Andeut.* p. 231, seq.; Clausen, *Aeneas u. die Penaten*, ii. p. 624, n. 1116; Hertzberg, *de Diis Rom. Patriis*, lib. ii. c. 18.) We shall here follow our usual rule, and give Dionysius credit for understanding what he was writing about, as there does not appear to be any grave objection to doing so ; and as he immediately adds, after citing the above epigraph, that it referred to the Penates (ΔΕΝΑΣ *ἐπιγραφὴν ἔχουσαι, δηλοῦσαν τοὺς Πενάτας*), we shall assume that this was really the temple of the Trojan household gods. The Italian writers regard it as the temple of Remus.

We do not find any large buildings mentioned upon the Velia till the time of Nero, who, as we have seen, occupied it with the vestibule of his palace. A considerable part of it had perhaps been a market previously. Close to its NW. foot, immediately behind the Aedes Penatium just indicated, Vespasian, after his triumph over Jerusalem, built his celebrated TEMPLE OF PEACE, to which we have already had occasion to allude, when describing the imperial fora.

(*Joseph. B. J.* vii. 5. § 7; Suet. *Vesp.* 9; Dion Cass. lxvi. 15.) It stood in an enclosed space, much like the temple of Venus Genitrix in Caesar's forum, or that of Mars Ultor in the forum of Augustus; and hence though not designed like them as a place for legal business, it was nevertheless sometimes called Forum Pacis. The temple was built with the greatest splendour, and adorned with precious works of art from Nero's palace, as well as with the costly spoils brought from the temple of Jerusalem, which made it one of the richest and most magnificent sanctuaries that the world ever beheld. (Joseph. *l. c.*; Plin. xxxiv. 8. s. 84, xxxvi. 24; Herodian, i. 14.) Hence its attraction and notoriety gave a new name to the 4th Region, in which it stood, which was previously called " Sacra Via," but now obtained the name of " Templum Pacis." The exact site of this temple was long a subject of dispute, the older topographers maintaining that the remains of the three vast arches a little to the E. of the spot just described, and now universally allowed to belong to the basilica of Constantine, were remnants of it. Piranesi raised some doubts on the point, but Nibby was the first who assigned to these two monuments their true position (*Foro Rom.* p. 189, seq.); and his views have been further developed and confirmed by Canina. (*Indicas. Topogr.* p. 131, seq.) As Becker has also adopted the same conclusion, it will not be necessary to state the grounds which led to it, as they would occupy considerable space ; and we shall therefore refer those readers who desire more information on the subject to the works just mentioned. Annexed to the temple was a library, in which the learned were accustomed to meet for the purposes of study and literary intercourse. (A. Gell. v. 21, xvi. 8.) The temple was burnt down a little before the death of Commodus. (Dion Cass. lii. 24; Herodian, i. 14; Galen, *de Comp. Med.* i. 1.) It does not appear to have been restored, but the ruins still remained undisturbed, and the spot is several times mentioned in later writers under the name of Forum Pacis, or Forum Vespasiani (Amm. Marc. xvi. 10 ; Procop. *B. G.* iv. 21 ; Symm. *Ep.* x. 78; *Catal. Imp. Viene.* p. 243.)

The three arches just alluded to as standing near the temple of Peace, and apparently at the commencement of a road branching off from the Sacra Via, belonged, as is almost universally admitted, to the BASILICA CONSTANTINI, erected by Maxentius, and dedicated after his death in the name of Constantine. Their architecture has all the characteristics of a basilica, and could not possibly have been adapted to a temple. (Canina, *Indicas.* p. 124.) The first notice which we find of this building is in Aurelius Victor (*Caesar*, 40, 26), who mentions it as having been erected by Maxentius; and this account is confirmed by an accident which happened in 1828, when on the falling in of a part of an arch a coin bearing the name of Maxentius was discovered in the masonry. (*Beschr.* iii. 298.) In the *Cat. Imp. Viene.* p. 243, it is mentioned as occupying the site of the *horrea piperataria*, or spice warehouses of Domitian (" horrea piperataria ubi modo est Basilica Constantiniana et Forum Vespasiani "). These spice warehouses must have been the same that are related by Dion Cassius (lxxii. 24) to have first caught the flames when the temple of Peace was burnt, A. D. 192, and are described as τὰς ἀποθήκας τῶν τε 'Αραβίων καὶ τῶν Αἰγυπτίων φορτίων ; whence, as the fire spread towards the Palatine, it may be presumed that they stood on the site of the basilica.

Between the basilica of Constantine and the Colosseum, and consequently on the eastern side of the Velian height, Hadrian built the splendid TEMPLE OF ROMA AND VENUS, commonly called at a later period Templum Urbis, considerable remains of which still exist behind the convent of *S. Francesca Romana.* In the middle ages it was called Templum Concordiae et Pietatis (*Mirabilia Rom.* in *Effemerid. Letter.* i. p. 385); the older topographers gave it various names, and Nardini was the first to designate it correctly. The remains exhibit the plan of a double temple, or one having two cellas, the semicircular tribunes of which are joined together back to back, so that one cella faced the Capitol and the other the Colosseum; whence the description of Prudentius (*Contra Symm.* i. 214):—

"Atque Urbis Venerisque pari se culmine tollunt
Templa, simul geminis adolentur tura deabus."

The cella facing the Colosseum is still visible, but the other is enclosed in the cloisters of *S. Francesca.* In them were colossal statues of the goddesses in a sitting posture. Hadrian is related to have planned this temple himself, and to have been so offended with the free-spoken criticisms of the great architect Apollodorus upon it that he caused him to be put to death. (Dion Cass. lxix. 4.) Apollodorus is related to have particularly criticised the extravagant size of the two goddesses, who he said were too large to quit their seats and walk out of the temple, had they been so minded. The temple was of the style technically called *pseudo-dipteros decastylos,* that is, having only one row of ten columns, but at the same distance from the cella as if there had been

two rows. With its porticoes it occupied the whole space between the Sacra Via and the street which ran past the front of the Basilica Constantini. For a more detailed description of it see Nibby, *Foro Romano,* p. 209, seq., and Canina, *Edifizj di Roma,* classe ii. A ground plan, and elevations and sections of it as restored, will be found in Burgess, *Antiquities and Topography of Rome,* i. pp. 268, 280. Servius (*ad Aen.* ii. 227) speaks of snakes on the statue of Roma similar to those on that of Minerva. From some coins of Antoninus Pius the temple appears to have been restored by that emperor. Silver statues were erected in it to M. Aurelius and Faustina, as well as an altar on which it was customary for brides to offer sacrifice after their marriage. (Dion Cass. lxxi. 31.) It was partly burnt down in the reign of Maxentius, but restored by that emperor.

The ARCH OF TITUS, to which from its conspicuous position we have so frequently had occasion to allude, stood close to the SW. angle of this temple, spanning the Sacra Via at the very summit of the Velian ridge. Its beautiful reliefs, which are unfortunately in a bad state of preservation, represent the Jewish triumphs of Titus. The arch could not have been completed and dedicated till after the death of that emperor, since he is called Divus in the inscription on the side of the Colosseum, whilst a relief in the middle of the vault represents his apotheosis. It has undergone a good deal of restoration of a very indifferent kind, especially on the side which faces the forum. During the middle ages it was called Septem Lucernae and Arcus Septem Lucernarum, as we see from the Anonymus.

ARCH OF TITUS RESTORED.

We shall here mention two other monuments which, though strictly speaking they do not belong to the Palatine, yet stand in such close proximity to it that they may be conveniently treated of in this place. These are the ARCH OF CONSTANTINE and the Meta Sudans. The former, which stands at the NE. corner of the Palatine, and spans the road now called *Via di S. Gregorio,* between that hill and the Caelian, was erected, as the inscription testifies, in honour of Constantine's victory over Maxentius. It is adorned with superb reliefs relating to the history of Trajan, taken apparently from some arch or other monument of that emperor's. They contrast strangely with the tasteless

and ill-executed sculptures belonging to the time of Constantine himself, which are inserted at the lower part of the arch. This monument is in a much better state of preservation than the arch of Titus, a circumstance which may perhaps be ascribed to the respect entertained for the memory of the first Christian emperor. For detailed descriptions and drawings of this arch see Niebuhr (*Beschr.* iii. p. 314, seq.), Canina (*Edifizj Antichi,* classe xii.), Overbeke (*Restes de l' An. Rome,* ii. t. 8, 9), Piranesi (*Ant. Rom.* i.).

The META SUDANS, so called from its resemblance to the metae of the circus, was a fountain erected by Domitian, remains of which are still to be seen between the arch of Constantine and the Colosseum. (Hieron. p. 443, Ronc.; Cassiod. *Chron.* ii. p. 198.) It stands in the middle of a large circular basin, which was discovered in the last excavations at that spot, as well as traces of the conduit which con-

veyed the water. A meta sudans is mentioned in Seneca (*Ep.* 56), whence we might infer that the one now existing superseded an earlier one (v. *Beschr.* iii. 312, seq.; Canina, *Indicaz.* p. 119).

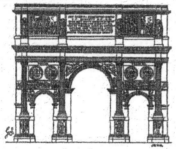

ARCH OF CONSTANTINE.

VII. THE AVENTINE.

We have already adverted to the anomalous character of this hill, and how it was regarded with suspicion in the early times of Rome, as ill-omened. Yet there were several famous spots upon it, having traditions connected with them as old or older than those relating to the Palatine, as well as several renowned and antique temples. One of the oldest of these legendary monuments was the ALTAR OF EVANDER, which stood at the foot of the hill, near the Porta Trigemina. (Dionys. i. 32.) Not far from it, near the Salinae, was the CAVE OF CACUS, a name which a part of the hill near the river still retains. (Solinus, i. 8; cf. Virg. *Aen.* viii. 190, seq.; Ovid, *Fast.* i. 551, seq.) Here also was the altar said to have been dedicated by Hercules, after he had found the cattle, to JUPITER INVENTOR. (Dionys. i. 39.) A spot on the summit of the hill, called REMORIA, or Remuria, preserved the memory of the auspices taken by Remus. (Paul. Diac. p. 276; Dionys. i. 85, seq.) Niebuhr, however, assumes another hill beyond the basilica of *St. Paolo*, and consequently far outside the walls of Aurelian, to have been the place called Remoria, destined by Remus for the building of his city. (*Hist. i.* p. 293, seq. and note 618.) Other spots connected with very ancient traditions, though subsequent to the foundation of the city, were the Armilustrium and the Lauretum. The ARMILUSTRUM, or Armilustrium, at first indicated only a festival, in which the soldiers, armed with *ancilia*, performed certain military sports and sacrifices; but the name was subsequently applied to the place where it was celebrated. (Varr. *L.L.* v. § 153, vi. § 22, Müll.; Liv. xxvii. 37; Plut. *Rom.* 23.) Plutarch (*l. c.*) says that king Tatius was buried here; but the LAURETUM, so named from its grove of laurels, is also designated as his place of sepulture. (Varr. *L.L.* v. § 152; Plin. xv. § 40; Dionys. iii. 43; Festus, p. 360.) There was a distinction between the Lauretum Majus and Minus (*Cal. Capran. Id. Aug.*); and the *Basis Capitolina* mentions a Vicus Loreti Majoris and another Loreti Minoris. The same document also records a Vicus Armilustri. Numa dedicated an altar to JUPITER ELICIUS on the Aventine. (Varr. *L. L.* vi.

§ 54; Liv. i. 20; cf. Ov. *F.* iii. 295, seq.); and the Calendars indicate a sacrifice to be performed there to Consus (*Fast. Capran. XII. Kal. Sep; Fast. Amitern. Pr. Id. Dec.*); but this is probably the same deity whose altar we have mentioned in the Circus Maximus.

The TEMPLE OF DIANA, built by Servius Tullius as the common sanctuary of the cities belonging to the Latin League, with money contributed by them, conferred more importance on the Aventine (Varr. *L.L.* v. § 43; Liv. i. 45; Dionys. iv. 26). This union has been compared with, and is said to have been suggested by, that of the Ionians for building the Artemisium, or temple of Diana, at Ephesus. It has been justly observed that Rome's supremacy was tacitly acknowledged by the building of the temple on one of the Roman hills (Liv. *l. c.*; Val. Max. vii. 3. § 1). Dionysius informs us that he saw in this temple the original *stele* or pillar containing the Foedus Latinum, as well as that on which the Lex Icilia was engraved. It appears, from Martial (vi. 64. 12), to have been situated on that side of the Aventine which faced the Circus Maximus, and hence it may have stood, as marked in Bufalini's plan, at or near the church of *S. Prisca* (cf. Canina, *Indicazione*, p. 532). We may further observe that Martial calls the Aventine "Collis Dianae," from this temple (vii. 73, xii. 18. 3). We learn from Suetonius that it was rebuilt by L. Cornificius, in the reign of Augustus (*Aug.* 29). That emperor does not appear to have done anything to it himself, as it is not mentioned in the *Monumentum Ancyranum*.

Another famous temple on the Aventine was that of JUNO REGINA, built by Camillus after the conquest of Veii, from which city the wooden statue of the goddess was carried off, and consecrated here; but the temple was not dedicated by Camillus till four years after his victory (Liv. v. 22, seq.; Val. Max. i. 8. § 3). Hence, probably, the reason why "cupresses simulacra," or images of cypress, were subsequently dedicated to this deity (Liv. xxvii. 37; Jul. Obs. 108); although a bronze statue appears to have been previously erected to her. (Liv. xxi. 62.) We have already seen from the description of the procession of the virgins in Livy (xxvii. 37) that the temple was approached by the CLIVUS PUBLICIUS, which ascent lay at the northern extremity of the Aventine, near the Porta Trigemina; but its situation cannot be accurately inferred from this circumstance. The Clivus Publicius, made, or rather perhaps widened and paved, by the aediles L. and M. Publicii Malleoli, was the main road leading up the hill. (Festus, p. 238; Varr. *L. L.* v. § 158; Front. *Aq.* 5.) Canina places the temple near the church of *S. Sabina*, where there are traces of some ancient building (*Indicazione*, p. 536). This is one of the temples mentioned as having been rebuilt by Augustus (*Mon. Ancyr.* tab. iv.)

From the document last quoted it would appear that there was a TEMPLE OF JUPITER on the Aventine; and its existence is also testified by the *Fasti Amiternini* (*Id. Aug.* FER. IOVI. DIANAE. VORTVMNO. IN . AVENTINO.); but we do not find it mentioned in any author. The passage just quoted likewise points probably to a sacellum or ARA OF VORTUMNUS, which the *Fasti Capranici* mention as being in the Loretum Majus. The TEMPLE OF MINERVA, also mentioned in the *Mon. Ancyranum* as having been repaired by Augustus, is better known, and seems to have been in existence at all events as early as the Second Punic War, since on account of some verses which Livius Andronicus had written to be sung in celebration of the better success of the war, this temple was appointed as a place in which *scribes*, as it appears poets were then called, and actors should meet to offer gifts in honour of Livius. (Festus, p. 333.) From an imperfect inscription (Gruter, xxxix. 5) it would appear that the temple was near the Armilustrium, and indeed it is named in conjunction with it in the *Notitia*.

There was a part of the Aventine called "SAXUM," or "SAXUM SACRUM" (Cic. *Dom.* 53), on which Remus was related to have stood when he took the auguries, which must therefore be considered as identical with, or rather perhaps as the highest and most conspicuous part of, the place called Remuria, and consequently on the very summit of the hill. Hence Ovid (*Fast.* v. 148, seq.):—

"——interea Diva canenda Bona est.
Est moles nativa, loco res nomina fecit,
Appellant Saxum; pars bona montis ea est.

On this spot was erected a TEMPLE OF THE BONA DEA, as Ovid proceeds to say " leniter acclivi jugo." From the expression *jugum*, we may conclude that it lay about the middle of the hill; but Hadrian removed it (" Aedem Bonae Deae transtulit," Spart. *Hadr.* 19), and placed it under the hill; whence it subsequently obtained the name of Templum Bonae Deae Subsaxoneae, and now stood in the 12th Region, or Piscina Publica, where it is mentioned in the *Notitia*, probably under the SE. side of the Aventine. For a legend of Hercules, connected with the rites of the Bona Dea, see Propertius (v. 9) and Macrobius (*Sat.* i. 12).

Besides these we find a TEMPLE OF LUNA and one of Libertas mentioned on the Aventine. The former of these is not to be confounded with the temple of Diana, as Bunsen has done (*Beschr.* iii. p. 412), since we find it mentioned as a substantive temple in several authors. (Liv. xl. 2; Aur. Vict. *Vir. Ill.* 65; *Fast. Praen. Prid. Kal. Apr.* " Lunae in Ave . . . ;" whilst in the *Capran.*, *Amitern.* and *Antiat.* we find, under *Id. Aug.*, " Dianae in Aventino.") It probably stood on the side next the circus. The TEMPLE OF LIBERTAS was founded by

T. Sempronius Gracchus, the father of the conqueror of Beneventum; the latter caused a picture representing his victory to be placed in the temple. (Liv. xxiv. 16.) Some difficulty has been occasioned by the manner in which the restoration of this temple by Augustus is mentioned in the *Monumentum Ancyranum*, namely, " Aedes Minervae et Junonis Reginae et Jovis Libertatis in Aventino (feci)" (tab. iv. l. 6). In the Greek translation of this record, discovered in the temple at Ancyra, and communicated by Hamilton (*Researches in Asia Min.* ii. n. 102), the words " Jovis Libertatis " are rendered Διὸς Ἐλευθερίου, whence Franz assumed that the Latin text was corrupt, and that we ought to read " Jovis Liberatoris." (Gerhard's *Archäolog. Zeitung,* no. ii. p. 25.) But there is no mention of any such temple at Rome, though Jupiter was certainly worshipped there under the title of Liberator (see the section on the Circus Maximus); whilst the existence of a temple of Libertas on the Aventine is attested not only by the passage just cited from Livy, but also by Paulus Diaconus. (" Libertatis templum in Aventino fuerat constructum," p. 121.) Hence it seems most probable that the Greek translation is erroneous, and that the reading " Jovis Libertatis " is really correct, the copula being omitted, as is sometimes the case; for example, in the instance " Honoris Virtutis," for Honoris et Virtutis, &c. And thus, in like manner, we find a temple of Jupiter Libertas indicated in inscriptions belonging to municipal towns of Italy (v. Orell. *Inscr.* no. 1249, 1282; cf. Becker, *Handb. Nachträge,* p. 721; Zumpt, *in Mon. Ancyr. Commentar.* p. 69). Another question concerning this Templum Libertatis, namely, whether there was an Atrium Libertatis connected with it, has occasioned much discussion. The Atrium Libertatis mentioned by Cicero (*ad Att.* iv. 16), the situation of which we have examined in a preceding section, could not possibly have been on the Aventine; yet the existence of a second one adjoining the temple of Libertas on that hill has been sometimes assumed, chiefly from Martial (xii. 3). The question turns on the point whether the words " Domus alta Remi," in that epigram, necessarily mean the Aventine; for our own part we think they do not. The question, however, is somewhat long; and they who would examine it more minutely may refer to Becker (*Handb.* p. 458, seq.; Urlichs, *Röm. Topogr.* p. 31, seq.; Becker, *Antwort,* p. 25, seq.; Canina, *Indicazione,* p. 536, seq.; Urlichs, *Antwort,* p. 5, seq.)

As the *Basis Capitolina* names among the Vici of the 13th Region, a VICUS FIDII and a VICUS FORTUNAE DUBIAE, we may perhaps assume that there were temples to those deities on or near the Aventine; but nothing further is known respecting them. The *Notitia* mentions on the Aventine, " THERMAE SURIANAE ET DECIANAE." The former of these baths seem to have been built by Trajan, and dedicated in the name of his friend Licinius Sura, to whom he was partly indebted for the empire. (" Hic ob honorem Surae, cujus studio imperium arripuerat, lavacra condidit," Aur. Vict. *Epit.* 13; cf. Dion Cass. lxviii. 15; Spart. *Adri.* 2, seq.) The dwelling of Sura was on that side of the Aventine which faced the Circus Maximus, and probably, as we have said, near the temple of Diana:—

"Quique videt propius Magni certamina Circi
Laudat Aventinae vicinus Sura Dianae."
　　　　　　　　　　　　　　(Mart. vi. 64. 12.)

Whence we may perhaps conclude that the baths also were near the same spot (v. Preller, *Regionen*, p. 300; Canina, *Indicas.* p. 533, seq.), where they seem to be indicated by the Capitoline plan (Bellori, tav. 4) and by traces of ruins. The baths of Decius are mentioned by Eutropius (ix. 4). Near the same spot appears to have been the HOUSE OF TRAJAN before he became emperor, designated in the *Notitia* as *Privata Trajani*, in which neighbourhood an inscription relating to a Domus Ulpiorum was found. (Gruter, xlv. 10.) Hence we may conclude that under the Empire the Aventine had become a more fashionable residence than during the Republic, when it seems to have been principally inhabited by plebeian families. The residence of Ennius, who, as we have said, possessed a house here, was, however, sufficient to ennoble it.

The narrow strip of ground between the hill and the Tiber also belonged to the district of the Aventine. In ancient times it was called "EXTRA PORTAM TRIGEMINAM," and was one of the busiest parts of the city, in consequence of its containing the emporium, or harbour of discharge for all laden ships coming up the river. Here also was the principal corn-market, and the *Basis Capitolina* mentions a Vicus Frumentarius in this neighbourhood. The period of its development was between the Second and Third Punic Wars, when the aediles M. Aemilius Lepidus and L. Aemilius Paullus first founded a regular EMPORIUM, and at the same time the PORTICUS AEMILIA. (Liv. xxxv. 10.) Their successors, M. Tuccius and P. Junius Brutus, founded a second portico *inter lignarios*, which epithet seems to refer to the timber yards at this spot. (Id. xxxv. 41.) Subsequently, in the censorship of M. Aemilius Lepidus and M. Fulvius Nobilior, the building of a harbour and of a bridge over the Tiber was commenced, as well as the foundation of a market and of other porticoes. (Liv. xl. 51.) The next censors, Q. Fulvius Flaccus and A. Postumius Albinus, paved the emporium with slabs of stone, constructed stairs leading down to the river, restored the Porticus Aemilia, and built another portico on the summit of the Aventine. (Liv. xli. 27.) The neighbourhood still bears the name of *La Marmorata;* and as numerous blocks of unwrought marble have at different times been discovered near the *Vigna Cesarini*, sometimes bearing numbers and the names of the exporters, it seems to have been the principal place for landing foreign marbles, and perhaps also for the workshops of the sculptors. (Vacca, *Mem.* 95—98; Fea, *Miscell.* i. p. 93; Bunsen, *Beschr.* iii. p. 432.) Just in this neighbourhood stood a temple of JUPITER DOLICHENUS or Dolicenus, indicated' in the *Notitia* under the name of *Dolocenum.* It is connected with the worship of the sun-god, brought from Heliopolis in Syria, concerning which there are numerous inscriptions, treated of by Marini (*Atti, &c.* pp. 538—548). In these the god is called Jup. O. M. Dolichenus, and sometimes a Juno Assyria Regina Dolichena is also mentioned. The worship resembled that brought to Rome by Elagabalus, but was previous to it, as some of the inscriptions relate to the time of Commodus. The temple seems to have been· in the neighbourhood of *S. Alessio*, as several inscriptions relating to the god were found here. (Preller, *Regionen*, p. 202.)

The broad level to the S. of the hill in which the *Monte Testaccio* stands, probably contained the large and important magazines mentioned in the *Notitia*, such as the HORREA GALBIANA ET ANICIANA, which

seem to have been a kind of warehouses for storing imported goods. They are sometimes mentioned in inscriptions. (Gruter, lxxv. 1; Orell. 45.) The *Monte Testaccio* itself is an artificial hill of potsherds, 153 ft. high according to Conti, and about one-third of a mile in circumference. Its origin is enveloped in mystery. According to the vulgar legend it was composed of the fragments of vessels in which the subject nations brought their tribute. A more plausible opinion was that this was the quarter of the potteries, and that the hill rose from the pieces spoiled in the process of manufacture; but this notion was refuted by the discovery of a tomb, during the excavation of some caves in the interior to serve as wine-cellars. (*Beschr.* iii. p. 434.) The whole district round the hill is strewed to a depth of 15 or 20 feet with the same sort of rubbish; the Porta Ostiensis, built by Honorius, stands on this factitious soil, which is thus proved to have existed at the beginning of the fifth century; but its origin will never, perhaps, be explained.

The last object we need mention here is the FORUM PISTORIUM, or Bakers' Market, so named apparently not because they made or sold their goods here, but because this was the place in which they bought their corn. We may remark that it was just opposite this point, under the Janiculum, that the corn-mills lay. (Preller, *Regionen*, p. 205.)

VIII. THE VELABRUM, FORUM BOARIUM, AND CIRCUS MAXIMUS.

Between the Palatine, the Aventine, and the Tiber, the level ground was occupied by two districts called the Velabrum and the Forum Boarium, whilst the valley between the two hills themselves was the site of the Circus Maximus. It will be the object of the present section to describe these districts and the monuments which they contained. They were comprehended in the 11th Region of Augustus, called "Circus Maximus," of which the Velabrum formed the boundary on the N., where it joined the 8th Region, or "Forum Romanum."

All accounts conspire in representing the VELABRUM as a marsh, or lake, at the time when Rome was founded, whence we may conclude that it could not have been built upon till the ground had been thoroughly drained by the construction of the Cloaca Maxima. Thus Tibullus (ii. 5. 33) :—

"At qua Velabri regio patet, ire solebat
    Exiguus pulsa per vada linter aqua."

(Cf. Varr. *L. L.* v. 43, seq. Müll.; Prop. v. 9. 5; Ov. *Fast.* vi. 399, &c.) Its situation between the Vicus Tuscus and Forum Boarium is ascertained from the descriptions of the route taken by triumphal and festal processions. · (Liv. xxvii. 37; Ov. *l. c.*; Plut. *Rom.* v. &c.) Its breadth, that is, its extension between the Vicus Tuscus and the Forum Boarium, cannot be accurately determined, but seems not to have been very great. Its termination on the S. was by the Arcus Argentarius, close to the modern church of *S. Giorgio in Velabro*, which marked the entrance into the Forum Boarium. This site of the Velabrum is also proved by testimonies which connect it with the Nova Via, the Porta Romanula, and the sepulchre of Acca Larentia. (Varr. *L. L.* vi. § 24, Müll.; cf. Cic. *ad Brut.* 15; Macrob. *S.* i. 10.) It is uncertain whether the SACELLUM VOLUPIAE, which also lay on the Nova Via, should be assigned to the Velabrum or to the Palatine. (Varr. *Ib.* v. § 164; Macrob. *Ib.*)

There was also a Velabrum Minus, which it is natural to suppose was not far distant from the Velabrum Majus. Varro says that there was in the Velabrum Minus a lake or pond formed from a hot spring called LAUTOLAE, near the temple of Janus Geminus (*Ib.* § 156); and Paulus Diaconus (p. 118) describes the Latulae as being "locus extra urbem." Hence it would seem that the Janus Geminus alluded to by Varro, must have been the temple near the Porta Carmentalis; but both the spring and the lake had vanished in the time of Varro, and were no longer anything but matters of antiquity.

The ARCUS ARGENTARIUS already mentioned as standing near the church of *S. Giorgio in Velabro* appears, from the inscription, to have been erected by the Negotiantes and Argentarii of the Forum Boarium in honour of Septimius Severus and his family. (Gruter, cclxv. 2; Orell. 913.) Properly speaking, it is no arch, the lintel being horizontal instead of vaulted. It is covered with ill-executed sculptures. Close to it stands the large square building called JANUS QUADRIFRONS, vaulted in the interior, and having a large archway in each front. The building had an upper story, which is said to have been used for mercantile purposes. The architecture belongs to a declining period of art, and the arch seems to have been constructed with fragments of other buildings, as shown by the inverted bas-reliefs on some of the pieces. (*Beschr.* iii. p. 339.) The *Notitia* closes the description of Regio xi. by mentioning an "Arcus Constantini," which cannot, of course, refer to the triumphal arch on the other side of the Palatine. The conjecture of Bunsen, therefore (*Beschr.* Anh. iii. p. 663), does not seem improbable, that this Janus was meant; and from its style of architecture it might very well belong to the time of Constantine.

The FORUM BOARIUM, one of the largest and most celebrated places in Rome, appears to have extended from the Velabrum as far as the ascent to the Aventine, and to have included in breadth the whole space between the Palatine and Circus Maximus on the E. and the Tiber on the W. Thus it must not be conceived as a regular forum or market surrounded with walls or porticoes, but as a large irregular space determined either by natural boundaries or by those of other districts. Its connection with the river on the one side and the circus on the other is attested by the following lines of Ovid (*Fast.* vi. 477):—

> "Pontibus et Magno juncta est celeberrima Circo
> Area quae posito de bove nomen habet."

Its name has been variously derived. The referring of it to the cattle of Hercules is a mere poetical legend (Prop. v. 9. 17, seq.); and the derivation of it from the statue of a bronze bull captured at Aegina and erected in this place, though apparently more plausible, is equally destitute of foundation, since the name is incontestably much older than the Macedonian War. (Plin. xxxiv. 5; Ov. *l. c.*; Tac. *Ann.* xii. 24.) It seems, therefore, most probable, as Varro says (*L.L.* v. § 146; cf. Paul. Diac. p. 30), that it derived its name from the use to which it was put, namely, from being the ancient cattle-market; and it would appear from the inscription on the Arcus Argentarius before alluded to that this traffic still subsisted in the third century. The Forum Boarium was rich in temples and monuments of the ancient times. Amongst the most famous were those of Hercules, Fortuna, and

Mater Matuta; but unfortunately the positions of them are not very precisely indicated. There seems to have been more than one TEMPLE OF HERCULES in this district, since the notices which we meet with on the subject cannot possibly be all referred to the same temple. The most ancient and important one must have been that connected with the MAGNA ARA HERCULIS, which tradition represented as having been founded by Evander. ("Et magna ara fanumque, quas praesenti Herculi Arcas Evander sacraverat," Tac. *Ann.* xv. 41; cf. *Ib.* xii. 24; Solin. i. 10.) This appears to have been the Hercules styled *triumphalis*, whose statue, during the celebration of triumphs, was clothed in the costume of a triumphant general; since a passage in Pliny connects it with that consecrated by Evander. ("Hercules ab Evandro sacratus ut produnt, in Foro Boario, qui triumphalis vocatur atque per triumphos vestitur habitu triumphali," xxxiv. 16.) It was probably this temple of Hercules into which it was said that neither dogs nor flies could find admittance (Ib. x. 41; Solin. i. 10), and which was adorned with a painting by Pacuvius the poet (Plin. xxxv. 7). A ROUND TEMPLE OF HERCULES, also in the Forum Boarium, seems to have been distinct from this, since Livy (x. 23) applies apparently the epithet "rotunda" to it, in order to distinguish it from the other. ("Insignem supplicationem fecit certamen in sacello Pudicitiae Patriciae, quae in Foro Boario est ad aedem rotundam Herculis, inter matronas ortum.") Canina (*Indicazione*, p. 338) assumes from this passage that the temple to which it refers must have been in existence at the time of the contest alluded to, namely, B. C. 297; but this, though a probable inference, is by no means an absolutely necessary one, since Livy may be merely indicating the locality as it existed in his own time. The former of these temples, or that of Hercules Triumphalis, seems to be the one mentioned by Macrobius (*Sat.* iii. 6) under the name of Hercules Victor; and it appears from the same passage that there was another with the same appellation, though probably of less importance, at the Porta Trigemina. Besides these we hear of a "Hercules Invictus" by the Circus Maximus (*Fast. Amitern; Prid. Id. Aug.*), and of another at the same place "in aede Pompeii Magni" (Plin. xxxiv. 8. a. 57), which seems to refer to some Aedes Herculis built or restored by Pompey, though we hear nothing more of any such temple. Hence there would appear to have been three or four temples of Hercules in the Forum Boarium. The conjecture of Becker seems not improbable, that the remains of a round temple now existing at the church of *S. Maria del Sole*, commonly supposed to have belonged to a

TEMPLE OF HERCULES.

temple of Vesta, may have been that of Hercules, and the little temple near it, now the church of S. Maria Egiziaca, that of Pudicitia Patricia. (Handb. p. 478, seq.)

This question is, however, in some degree connected with another respecting the sites of the TEMPLES OF FORTUNA and MATER MATUTA. Canina identifies the remains of the round temple at the church of S. Maria del Sole with the temple of Mater Matuta; whilst the little neighbouring temple, now the church of S. Maria Egiziaca, he holds to have been that of FORTUNA VIRILIS. His chief reason for maintaining the latter opinion is the following passage of Dionysius, which points, he thinks, to a temple of Fortuna Virilis, built by Servius Tullius close to the banks of the Tiber, a position which would answer to that of S. Maria Egiziaca: καὶ ναοὺς δύο κατασκευασάμενος Τύχης, τὸν μὲν ἐν ἀγορᾷ τῇ καλουμένη Βοαρίᾳ, τὸν δ' ἕτερον ἐπὶ ταῖς ᾐόσι τοῦ Τιβέριος, ἣν Ἀνδρείαν προσηγόρευσαν, ὡς καὶ νῦν ὑπὸ τῶν Ῥωμαίων καλεῖται. (Ant. Rom. iv. 27.) It should be premised that Canina does not hold the two temples in question to have been in the Forum Boarium, but only just at its borders. ("Corrispondevano da vicino al Foro Boario," Indicas. p. 338.) The temple of Fortuna Virilis here mentioned by Dionysius was, he contends, a distinct thing from the temple of Fors Fortuna, which he allows lay outside of the city on the other bank of the Tiber (p. 506). Indeed the distinction between them is shown from the circumstance that their festivals were celebrated in different months: that of Fortuna Virilis being in April, that of Fors Fortuna in June. (Comp. Ov. Fast. iv. 145, seq., with the Fasti Praenestini in April: "Frequenter mulieres supplicant . . . Fortunae Virili humiliores." Also comp. Ov. Fast. vi. 773, seq., with the Fasti Amiternini, VIII. Kal. Jul.: "Forti Fortunae Transtiber. ad Milliar. Prim. et Sext.")

Now these passages very clearly show the distinction between Fortuna Virilis and Fors Fortuna; and it may be shown just as clearly that Dionysius confounded them, as Plutarch has also done. (De Fort. Rom. 5.) Servius Tullius, as Dionysius says, built a temple of Fortuna in the Forum Boarium; but this Fortuna was not distinguished by any particular epithet. Dionysius gives her none in the passage cited; nor does any appear in passages of other authors in which her temple is mentioned. Thus Livy: "De manubiis duos fornices in foro Boario ante Fortunae aedem et Matris Matutae, unam in Maximo Circo fecit" (xxxiii. 27). So also in the passages in which he describes the fire in that district (xxiv. 47, xxv. 7). One of the two temples of Fortuna built by Servius Tullius was then that on the Forum Boarium, as shown in the preceding passages from Livy and from Dionysius: that the other was a temple of Fors Fortuna and not of Fortuna Virilis appears from Varro: "Dies Fortis Fortunae appellatus ab Servio Tullio Rege, quod is fanum Fortis Fortunae secundum Tiberim extra Urbem Romam dedicavit Junio mense" (L.L. vi. § 17, Müll.) Hence it is plain that both Dionysius and Plutarch have made a mistake which foreigners were likely enough to fall into. Temples being generally named in the genitive case, they have taken fortis to be an adjective equivalent to ἀνδρεῖος or virilis (v. Bunsen, Beschr. iii. Nachtr. p. 665; Becker, Handb. p. 478, note 998), and thus confounded two different temples. But as this temple of Fors Fortuna was "extra Urbem," it could not have been the same as that with which Canina indentifies it, which, as Livy expressly says, was "intra portam Carmentalem" (xxv. 7). The site of the temple of Fortuna Virilis cannot be determined, and Bunsen (l. c.) denies that there was any such temple: but it seems probable from the passage of Ovid referred to above that there was one, or at all events an altar; and Plutarch (Quaest. Rom. 74) mentions a Τύχης Ἄρρενος ἱερόν. On the other hand, there seem to have been no fewer than three temples of Fors Fortuna on the right bank of the Tiber. First, that built by Servius Tullius, described by Varro as "extra Urbem secundum Tiberim." Second, another built close to that of Servius by the consul Sp. Carvilius Maximus (B. C. 293): "De reliquo aere aedem Fortis Fortunae de manubiis faciendam locavit, prope aedem ejus Deae ab rege Ser. Tullio dedicatam." (Liv. x. 46.) Third, another dedicated under Tiberius (A. D. 16) near the Tiber in the gardens of Caesar, and hence, of course, on the right bank of the river: "Aedis Fortis Fortunae, Tiberim juxta, in hortis quos Caesar dictator populo Romano legaverat." (Tac. Ann. ii. 41.) That the Horti Caesaris were on the right bank of the Tiber we know from Horace (S. i. 9. 18) and Plutarch. (Brut. 20.) The temple built by Servius must also have been on the right bank, as it seems to be referred to in the following passage of Donatus: "Fors Fortuna est cujus diem festum colunt qui sine arte aliqua vivunt: hujus aedes trans Tiberim est" (ad Terent. Phorm. v. 6. 1). The same thing may be inferred from the Fasti Amiternini: "Forti Fortunae Transtiber. ad Milliar. Prim. et Sextam" (VIII. Kal. Jul.). The temple in the gardens of Caesar seems here to be alluded to as at the distance of one mile from the city, whilst that of Servius, and the neighbouring one erected by Carvilius appear to have been at a distance of six miles. But this need not excite our suspicion. There are other instances of temples lying at a considerable distance from Rome, as that of Fortuna Muliebris at the fourth milestone on the Via Latina. (Fest. p. 542; cf. Val. Max. i. 8. § 4, v. 2. § 1; Liv. ii. 40, &c.) It would appear, too, to have been some way down the river, as it was customary to repair thither in boats, and to employ the time of the voyage in drinking (Fast. vi. 777):—

" Pars pede, pars etiam celeri decurrite cymba
　Nec pudeat potos inde redire domum.
Ferte coronatae juvenum convivia lintres
　Multaque per medias vina bibantur aquas."

We have entered at more length into this subject than its importance may perhaps seem to demand, because the elegant remains of the temple now forming the Armenian church of S. Maria Egiziaca cannot fail to attract the notice of every admirer of classical antiquity that visits Rome. We trust we have shown that it could not possibly have been the temple of Fortuna Virilis, as assumed by Canina and others. The assumption that the neighbouring round temple was that of Mater Matuta may perhaps be considered as disposed of at the same time. The only grounds for that assumption seem to be its vicinity to the supposed temple of Fortuna Virilis. Livy's description (xxxiii. 27) of the two triumphal arches erected in the Forum Boarium before the two temples appearing to indicate that they lay close together.

With regard to the probability of this little church

having been the temple of PUDICITIA PATRICIA, it might be objected that there was in fact no such temple, and that we are to assume only a statue with an altar (Sachse, *Gesch. d. S. Rom.* i. p. 365). Yet, as Becker remarks (*Handb.* p. 480, note 100), Livy himself (x. 23) not only calls it a *sacellum*, a name often applied to small temples, but even in the same chapter designates it as a *templum* ("Quum se Virginia, et patriciam et pudicam in Patriciae Pudicitiae templum ingressam vero gloriaretur "); and Propertius (ii. 6. 25) also uses the same appellation with regard to it. On the other hand some have fixed on *S. Maria in Cosmedin* as the site of this temple, but with little appearance of

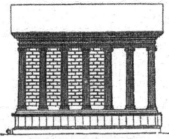

TEMPLE OF PUDICITIA PATRICIA.

probability. Becker seeks in the church just named the temple of Fortuna built by Servius Tullius in the Forum Boarium. The church appears to have been erected on the remains of a considerable temple, of which eight columns are still perceptible, built into the walls. This opinion may be as probable as any other on the subject; but as on the one hand, from our utter ignorance of the site of the temple, we are unable to refute it, so on the other we must confess that Becker's long and laboured argument on the subject is far from being convincing (*Handb.* p. 481, seq.). The site of the TEMPLE OF MATER MATUTA is equally uncertain. All that we know about it is that it was founded by Servius Tullius, and restored by Camillus after the conquest of Veii (Liv. v. 17), and that it lay somewhere on the Forum Boarium (Ovid, *Fast.* vi. 471). If we were inclined to conjecture, we should place both it and the temple of Fortuna near the northern boundary of that forum; as Livy's description of the ravages occasioned by the fire in that quarter seems to indicate that they lay at no great distance within the Porta Carmentalis (xxiv. 47, xxv. 7). The later history of both these temples is unknown.

In the Forum Boarium, near the mouth of the Cloaca Maxima, was also the place called DOLIOLA, mentioned in the former part of this article as regarded with religious awe on account of some sacred relics having been buried there, either during the attack of the Gauls, or at a still more ancient period. (Liv. v. 40; Varr. *L.L.* v. § 157, Müll.) When

CLOACA MAXIMA.

the Tiber is low, the mouth of the CLOACA MAXIMA may be seen from the newly erected iron bridge connecting the *Ponte Rotto* with the left bank. The place called AD BUSTA GALLICA where it is said that the bodies of the Gauls were burnt who died during or after the siege of the Capitol, has also been assumed to have been in this neighbourhood because it is mentioned by Varro (*Ib.*) between the Aequimelium and the Doliola (cf. Liv. v. 48, xxii. 14). But such an assumption is altogether arbitrary, as Varro follows no topographical order in naming places. Lastly, we shall mention two objects named in the *Notitia*, which seem to have stood on the Forum Boarium. These are the APOLLO COELISPEX, and the HERCULES OLIVARIUS, apparently two of those statues which Augustus dedicated in the different Vici. Becker (*Handb.* p. 493) places them in the Velabrum, and thinks that the epithet of Olivarius was derived from the oil-market, which was established in the Velabrum (Plaut. *Capt.* iii. 1. 29), but it seems more probable that it denoted the crown of olive worn by Hercules as Victor (Preller, *Regionen*, p. 194). The Forum Boarium was especially devoted to the worship of Hercules, whence it seems probable that his statue stood there; besides both that and the Apollo are mentioned in the *Notitia* in coming from the Porta Trigemina, before the Velabrum.

Before we quit the Forum Boarium we must advert to a barbarous custom of which it appears to have been the scene even to a late period of Roman history. Livy relates that after the battle of Cannae a Gallic man and woman and a Greek man and woman were, in accordance with the commands of the Sibylline books, buried alive in a stone sepulchre constructed in the middle of the Forum Boarium, and that this was not the first time that this barbarous and un-Roman custom had been practised (xxii. 57). Dion Cassius adverts to the same instance in the time of Fabius Maximus Verrucosus (*Fr. Vales.* 12), and Pliny mentions another which had occurred even in his own time (" Boario vero in foro Graecum Graecamque defossos, aut aliarum gentium, cum quibus tum res esset, etiam nostra aetas vidit," xxviii. 3; cf. Plut. *Q. R.* 83). It may also be remarked that the first exhibition of gladiatorial combats at Rome took place on the Forum Boarium, at the funeral of the father of Marcus and Decimus Brutus, B. C. 264. (Val. Max. ii. 4. § 7.)

The valley between the Palatine and Aventine, occupied by the Circus Maximus was, as we have had occasion to mention in the former part of this article, in earlier times called VALLIS MURCIA, from an altar of the Dea Murcia, or Venus, which stood there. He who mounts the enormous mass of ruins which marks the site of the imperial palace on the S. side of the Palatine hill may still trace the extent and configuration of the circus, the area of which is occupied by kitchen gardens, whilst a gas manufactory stands on the site of the carceres. The description of the circus itself will be reserved for a separate section devoted to objects of the same description, and we shall here only treat of the different monuments contained in it as a Region or district. The whole length of the circus was 3½ stadia, or nearly half a mile, the circular end being near the Septizonium, and the carceres or starting place nearly under the church of S. Anastasia, where the circus adjoined the Forum Boarium. Its proximity to the latter is shown by the circumstance that the Maxima Ara Herculis before alluded to is sometimes mentioned as being at the entrance of the Circus Maximus, and sometimes as on the Forum Boarium ("Ingens ara Herculis pos januas Circi Maximi," Serv. ad Aen. viii. 271; cf. Dionys. i. 40; Ovid, Fast. i. 581; Liv. i. 7, &c.) The large TEMPLE OF HERCULES must undoubtedly have been close to this altar, but on the Forum Boarium.

The Vallis Murcia contained several old and famous temples and altars, some of which were included in the circus itself. Such was the case with the altar or SACELLUM OF MURCIA herself ("Intumus Circus ad Murcim vocatur — ibi sacellum etiam nunc Murteae Veneris," Varr. L. L. v. § 154, Müll.); but its exact site cannot be determined. Consus had also a subterranean altar in the circus, which was opened during the games and closed at other times. It is described by Tertullian as being "ad primas metas," and therefore probably at a distance of about one-third of the whole length of the circus from the carceres, and near the middle of the S. side of the Palatine hill. (Tert. de Spect. 5; Varr. L. L. vi. § 20, Müll.; Tac. Ann. xii. 24; Plut. Rom. 14.) But the chief temple on the circus was the TEMPLE OF THE SUN, to which deity it was principally consecrated ("Circus Soli principaliter consecratur: cujus aedes medio spatio et effigies de fastigio aedis emicat," Tert. Spect. 8). Tacitus mentions the same ancient temple as being "apud Circum" (Ann. xv. 74); and from a comparison of these passages we may conclude that it stood in the middle of one of its sides, and probably under the Aventine. The Notitia and Curiosum mention it ambiguously in conjunction with a TEMPLE OF LUNA, so that it might possibly be inferred that both deities had a common temple ("Templum Solis et Lunae," Reg. xi.). It seems, however, more probable that there were two distinct temples, as we frequently find them mentioned separately in authors, but never in conjunction. It is perhaps the same temple of Luna which we have already mentioned on the Aventine, in which case it might have been situated on the declivity of that hill facing the circus, and behind the temple of Sol. Luna, like Sol, was a Circensian deity, both performing their appointed circuits in quadrigae. (Joh. Lydus, de Mens. i. 12; Tert. Spect.

9; Cass. Var. iii. 51.) The situation of the TEMPLE OF MERCURY, mentioned next to the two preceding ones in the Curiosum, may be determined with more accuracy, if we may believe an account recorded by Nardini (Rom. Ant. lib. vii. c. 3) on the authority of a certain Francesco Passeri, respecting the discovery of the remains of a small temple of that deity in a vineyard between the Circus Maximus and the Aventine. The remains were those of a little tetrastyle temple, which was identified as that of Mercury from an altar having the caduceus and petasus sculptured on it. The temple is represented on a medal of M. Aurelius, who appears to have restored it. The site agrees with that described by Ovid (Fast. v. 669):—

"Templa tibi posuere patres spectantia Circum
Idibus: ex illo est haec tibi festa dies."

A comparison of this passage with Livy, "aedes Mercurii dedicata est Idibus Maiis" (ii. 21), shows that the same ancient sanctuary is alluded to, the dedication of which caused a dispute between the consuls, B. C. 495 (Ib. c. 27). We next find mentioned in the Notitia an AEDES MATRIS DEUM, and another of JOVIS ARBORATORIS, for which we should probably read "Liberatoris.". The Magna Mater was one of the Circensian divinities. Her image was exhibited on the spina (Tert. Spect. 8), and it would appear that she had also a temple in the vicinity. Of a temple of Jupiter Liberator we know nothing further, though Jove was certainly worshipped at Rome under that name (Tac. Ann. xv. 64, xvi. 35), and games celebrated in his honour in the month of October. (Calend. Vindob. ap. Preller, Reg. p. 192.)

Next to these an AEDES DITIS PATRIS is named in the Notitia, but does not appear in the Curiosum. Some writers would identify Dispater with SUMMANUS. quasi Summus Manium (v. Gruter, MXV. 7; Mart. Capell. ii. 161); but there was a great difference of opinion respecting this old Sabine god, and even the Romans themselves could not tell precisely who he was. Thus Ovid (Fast. vi. 725):—

"Reddita, quisquis is est, Summano templa feruntur
Tunc cum Romanis, Pyrrhe, timendus eras."

The temple to him here alluded to was, however, certainly near the Circus Maximus, since Pliny mentions some annual sacrifices of dogs as made "inter aedem Juventatis et Summani" (xix. 4); and that the TEMPLE OF JUVENTAS was at the Circus Maximus we learn from Livy: "Juventatis aedem in Circo Maximo C. Licinius Lucullus triumvir dedicavit" (xxxvii. 36; cf. Calend. Amert. XII. Kal. Jul.: "Summano ad Circ. Max."). The temple of Summanus, therefore, must have been dedicated during the war with Pyrrhus, and that of Juventas in B. C. 192.

Close to the W. extremity of the circus, and towering as it were over the carceres, from its being built apparently on the slope of the Aventine (ὑπὲρ αὐτὰς ἱδρυμένος τὰς ἀφέσεις, Dionys. vi. 94), stood a famous TEMPLE OF CERES, dedicated also to LIBER AND LIBERA. Thus Tacitus, relating the dedication of the temple by Tiberius, it having been restored by Augustus, says: "Libero, Liberaeque et Cereri, juxta Circum Maximum, quam A. Postumius dictator voverat (dedicavit)" (Ann. ii. 49). It is mentioned by other writers as "ad Circum Maximum"; whence Canina's identification of it with the church of S. Maria in Cosmedin seems improbable (Indicaz.

p. 498), since that building is at some little distance from the circus, and certainly does not stand on higher ground. The temple of Ceres contained some precious works of art (Plin. xxxv. 10. s. 36. § 99), especially a picture of Dionysus by Aristides, which Strabo mentions that he saw (viii. p. 381), but which was afterwards destroyed in a fire which consumed the temple.

We also find a TEMPLE OF VENUS mentioned at the circus, founded by Q. Fabius Gurges, B. C. 295, very appropriately out of the money raised by fines levied on certain matrons for incontinence. (Liv. x. 31.) It seems to have been at some distance from the Forum Boarium, since the censors M. Livius and C. Claudius contracted for the paving of the road between the two places. (Id. xxix. 37.) Yet we have no means of defining its site more accurately, nor can we even tell whether it may not have been connected with the altar of Venus Murcia before mentioned. But the TEMPLE OF FLORA, founded by the aediles L. and M. Publicius, the same who constructed the clivus or ascent to the Aventine which bore their name, must have lain close to that ascent, and consequently also to the temple of Ceres just described; since Tacitus, after relating the re-dedication of the latter under Tiberius, adds: " eodemque in loco aedem Florae (dedicavit), ab Lucio et Marco Publiciis aedilibus constitutam." (Ann. ii. 49.) The Publicii applied part of the same money — raised by fines — with which they had constructed the clivus, in instituting floral games in honour of the divinity which they had here consecrated, as we learn from the account which Ovid puts into the mouth of the goddess herself (Fast. v. 283).

These are all the temples that we find mentioned in this quarter; but before we leave it there are one or two points which deserve to be noticed. The CAVE OF CACUS was reputed to have been near the Clivus Publicius. Solinus mentions it as being at the Salinae, near the Porta Trigemina (i. 8); a situation which agrees with the description in Virgil of the meeting of Aeneas and Evander at the Ara Maxima of Hercules, from which spot Evander points out the cave on the Aventine (Aen. viii. 190, seq.):—

" Jam primum saxis suspensam hanc adspice
    rupem," &c.

Of the DUODECIM PORTAE mentioned in the Notitia in this Region we have already spoken [Part II. p. 757].

IX. THE CAELIAN HILL.

The Caelius presents but few remains of ancient buildings, and as the notices of it in the classics are likewise scanty its topography is consequently involved in considerable obscurity. According to Livy (i. 30) Tullus Hostilius fixed his residence upon it; but other accounts represent him as residing on the Velia. (Cic. Rep. ii. 31.) We find a SACELLUM DIANAE mentioned on the Caeliolus — an undefined part of the eastern ridge (de Har. Resp. 15); another of the DEA CARNA " in Caelio monte" (Macrob. S. i. 12); and a little TEMPLE OF MINERVA CAPTA situated on the declivity of the hill:—

" Caelius ex alto qua Mons descendit in aequum,
    Hic ubi non plana est, sed prope plana via est,
    Parva licet videas Captae delubra Minervae."
        (Ov. Fast. iii. 837, seq.)

Hence it was probably the same ancient sanctuary, called " Minervium " in the sacred books of the Argives, which lay on the northern declivity of the Caelian towards the Tabernola (" Circa Minervium qua e Caelio monte iter in Tabernola est," Varr. L. L. v. § 47), and probably near the modern street Via della Navicella.

The most considerable building known on the Caelian in later times was the TEMPLE OF DIVUS CLAUDIUS, begun by Agrippina, destroyed by Nero, and restored by Vespasian. (Suet. Vesp. 9; Aur. Vict. Caes. 9.) The determination of its site depends on the question how far Nero conducted the Aqua Claudia along the Caelius, since we learn from Frontinus that the arches of that aqueduct terminated at the temple in question. (Front. Aq. 20, 76.) These Arcus Neroniani (also called Caelimontani, Gruter, Inscr. clxxxvii. 3) extend along the ridge of the narrow hill, supposed to be the Caeliolus, from the Porta Maggiore to the Santa Scala opposite the Lateran, where they are interrupted by the piazza and buildings belonging to that basilica. They recommence, however, on the other side in the Via di S. Stefano Rotondo, and proceed with a small gap as far as that church. There are further traces of them on the W. side of the arch of Dolabella; and the opinion of Canina seems probable enough, that they terminated near the garden of the convent of SS. Giovanni e Paolo, and that the remains of a huge substruction at this spot belonged to the temple of Claudius. (Indicaz. p. 73, seq.) Canina is further of opinion that the Aqua Claudia was distributed a little beyond this spot, and that one of the uses to which it was applied by Nero was to replenish his lake, which occupied the site of the Flavian amphitheatre. Others, however, are of opinion that the aqueduct did not proceed beyond the church of S. Stefano Rotondo, and therefore that the temple of Claudius stood near that spot, or that the church may even have been built on its foundations. But there are no sufficient grounds for arriving at any satisfactory conclusion on these points, and altogether the view of Canina is perhaps the more probable one.

The ARCH OF DOLABELLA, just alluded to, appears from the inscription on it to have been erected in the consulship of Dolabella and Silanus, A. D. 10. Its destination has been the subject of various conjectures. Some have imagined it to be a restoration of the Porta Caelimontana; but this can hardly be the case, since, if the Servian walls had run in this direction, half of the Caelian hill would have been shut out of the city. On the other hand, its appearance excludes the notion of a triumphal arch; and it could not originally have formed part of an aqueduct, since it was erected previously to the construction of the Aqua Claudia. It seems most probable therefore that it was designed as an entrance to some public place; but there are appearances that Nero subsequently conducted his aqueduct over it. (Canina, Indicaz. p. 77.) The road which led up to it from the Via di S. Gregorio seems in ancient times to have been called CLIVUS SCAURI. It is mentioned under that name in the Epistles of S. Gregory (vii. 13), and the Anonymus Einsiedlensis calls it Clivus Tauri, which is probably a scribe's error.

Next to the temple of Claudius, the Notitia mentions a MACELLUM MAGNUM, probably the market recorded by Dion Cassius as founded by Nero (τὴν ἀγορὰν τῶν ὄψων, τὸ μάκελλον ὀνομασμένον, καθίφωσε, lxi. 18). Nardini, who is followed by Canina (*Indicazione*, p. 83), is of opinion that the church of *S. Stefano Rotondo* was part of the macellum, perhaps a slaughter-house with a dome, and surrounded with porticoes.

MACELLUM.

The CASTRA PEREGRINA recorded in the *Notitia* are not mentioned by any author except Ammianus Marcellinus, who relates that Chnodomar, when conquered by Julian, was conducted to and died in this camp on the Caelian (xvi. 12, extr.) The name, however, occurs in inscriptions, and sometimes in connection with a temple of Jupiter Redux, as in that found in the church of *S. Maria in Domnica* (Gruter, xxii. 3; Orell. 1256). These inscriptions also mention a Princeps Peregrinorum, the nature of whose office we are unacquainted with; but it seems probable that he was the commander of the foreign troops stationed in this camp. Near the same church were found several little marble ships, apparently votive offerings, and one which stood a long while before it gave to the church and to the surrounding place the name of *della Navicella*.

An ISIUM, or temple of Isis, is mentioned by Treb. Pollio (*XXX. Tyran.* 25) on the Caelian, but it occurs nowhere else. It was probably one of the many temples erected to this goddess by Caracalla (Lampr. *Carac.* 9.) The spring called the AQUA MERCURII recorded by Ovid near the Porta Capena (*Fasti,* v. 673) was rediscovered by M. Fea in 1828, in the vigna of the *Padri Camaldolesi di S. Gregorio.* On the Caelian was also the CAMPUS MARTIALIS in which the Equiria were held in March, in case the Campus Martius was overflowed (Ovid, *Fast.* v. 673; Paul. Diac. p. 161). Its situation rests chiefly on conjecture; but it was probably near the Lateran; where the neighbouring church of *S. Gregorio,* now *S. Maria Imperatrice,* was called in the middle ages " in Campo Martio " (Canina, *Indicazione,* p. 84.)

In the Imperial times the Caelian was the residence of many distinguished Romans; and it is here that Martial places the " limina potentiorum " (xii. 8). We have already had occasion to allude to the HOUSE OF CLAUDIUS CENTUMALUS on this hill, which was of such an extraordinary height that the augurs commanded him to lower it; but this was during the Republic. Under the Empire we may mention the HOUSE OF MAMURRA, a Roman knight of Formiae, and praefectus fabrum of Caesar in his Gallic wars, the splendour of which is described by Pliny (xxxvi. 7), and lampooned by Catullus (xlii. 4). Here also was the HOUSE OF ANNIUS VERUS, the grandfather of Marcus Aurelius, in which that emperor was educated, situated near the house of the Laterani (Jul. Capit. *M. Ant.* 1.) It appears to have been surrounded with gardens; and according to the Italian writer Vacca (*Memor.* 18) the noble eques-

trian statue of Marcus Aurelius which now adorns the Capitol was discovered in a vineyard near the *Scala Santa.* On the same hill were the AEDES VICTILIANAE where Commodus sought refuge from the uneasy thoughts which tormented him in the palace, but where he could not escape the snares of the assassin (Lampr. *Comm.* 16; Jul. Capitol. *Pert.* 5). But the most remarkable of all these residences was the PALACE OF THE LATERANI, characterised by Juvenal (x. 18) as the " egregiae Lateranorum aedes," the residence of the consul Plautius Lateranus, whose participation in Piso's conspiracy against Nero cost him his life (Tac. *Ann.* xv. 49, 60). After this event the palace of the Laterani seems to have been confiscated, and to have become imperial property, since we find Septimius Severus presenting it to his friend Lateranus, probably a descendant of the family to which it had once belonged (Aur. Vict. *Epit.* 20). Subsequently, however, it appears to have been in the possession of the emperor Constantine, who erected upon its site the celebrated basilica which still bears the name of the Lateran, and presented it to the bishop of Rome (Niceph. vii. 49). The identity of the spot is proved by several inscriptions found there, as well as by the discovery of chambers and baths in making the façade of the modern basilica. (Venuti, *Roma Ant.* P. i. c. 8; Canina, *Indic.* p. 85). The DOMUS PHILIPPI mentioned in the *Notitia* was probably the private house of the emperor of that name. Lastly, we may mention that on the Caelian was the HOUSE OF SYMMACHUS, the strenuous defender of paganism in the reign of Valentinian (Symm. *Epist.* iii. 12, 88, vii. 18, 19).

There are a few other objects on the Caelian mentioned in the *Notitia,* some of which, however, hardly admit of explanation. Such is the ATRIUM or ANTRUM CYCLOPIS, respecting which we cannot say whether it was a cavern, or an area surrounded with porticoes. Whatever it was it seems to have stood on the S. side of the hill, since the vicus Ab Cyclopis in the 1st Region, or Porta Capena, was probably named after it (Preller, *Reg.* p. 119.) The CAPUT AFRICAE of the *Notitia,* which likewise appears in several inscriptions (Orell. 2685, 2934, 2935), is thought to have been a street in the neighbourhood of the Colosseum, since the Anonymus Einsiedlensis mentions it between the Meta Sudans and the church of SS. Quattro Coronati; whence it is held to have corresponded with the modern street which bears the name of that church (Nibby, *Mura di Roma,* p. 173, note 140; Urlichs, *Röm. Topogr.* p. 101). Becker observes (*Handb.* p. 508), that the name does not appear in any earlier writer, and connects it with some building founded by Septimius Severus, in order to strike his countrymen, the Africans, who arrived at Rome by the Via Appia; though, as Urlichs observes, they must have gone rather out of their way " to be imposed upon." Varro mentions a Vicus Africus on the Esquiline, so named because the African hostages in the Punic War were said to have been detained there (" Exquilis vicus Africus, quod ibi obsides ex Africa bello Punico dicuntur custoditi," *L. L.* v. § 159). Hence it is very probable, as Canina remarks (*Indicas.* p. 91), that the head, or beginning, of this street stood at the spot indicated by the Anonymus, namely, near the Colosseum, whence it ran up in the direction of the Esquiline, although Becker (*Handb.* p. 560) denies that the Caput Africae had any connection with the Vicus Africus. The ARBOR SANCTA is inexplicable

The LUDUS MATUTINUS ET GALLICUS (or Dacicus), the SPOLIARIUM, SANIARIUM, and ARMAMENTARIUM, were evidently gladiatorial schools with their appurtenances, situated apparently on the northern side of the Caelian, not far from the amphitheatre. Officers attached to these institutions are frequently mentioned in inscriptions. The Spoliarium and Armamentarium speak for themselves. The Saniarium is a word that does not occur elsewhere, and is thought by Preller to denote a hospital (a sanie) where the wounded gladiators were received. For a further account of these institutions see Preller, *Regionen*, pp. 120—122. Lastly, the MICA AUREA appears from an epigram of Martial's to have been a banqueting room of Domitian's (ii. 59): —

" Mica vocor; quid sim cernis; coenatio parva.
   Ex me Caesareum prospicis, ecce, tholum."

It is also mentioned, along with the Meta Sudans, as built by Domitian in the *Chronica Regia Coloniensis*, in Eccard's *Corpus Historicum* (vol. i. p. 745.)

X. THE DISTRICT TO THE S. OF THE CAELIAN.

To the S. of the Caelian lies a somewhat hilly district, bounded on the W. by the Aventine, and comprehending the 1st and 12th Regions of Augustus, or those called Porta Capena and Piscina Publica. The latter of these is decidedly the least important district of Rome, but the former presents several objects of considerable interest. Of the Porta Capena we have already treated. In its immediate vicinity stood the double TEMPLE OF HONOS AND VIRTUS, vowed by Marcellus in his Gallic wars, but not erected till after his conquest of Syracuse. It was the first intention of Marcellus that both the deities should be under the same roof; and, indeed, the temple seems to have been a mere restitution of an ancient one dedicated to Honos by Q. Fabius Verrucosus many years before. (Cic. *N. D.* ii. 23.) But when Marcellus was about to dedicate it, and to introduce the statue of another deity within the sanctuary, the pontifices interposed, and forbade him to do so, on the ground that the *procuratio*, or expiation of any prodigy occurring in a temple so constructed, would be difficult to perform. (Liv. xxvii. 25.) Hence, Marcellus was constrained to add another temple of Virtus, and to erect two images of the deities " separatis aedibus;" but though the work was pressed on in haste, he did not live to dedicate them. (Liv. *l. c.*; Val. Max. i. 1. § 8.) Nevertheless, we frequently find the temple mentioned in the singular number, as if it had formed only one building (" ad aedem Honoris atque Virtutis," Cic. *Verr.* iv. 54; cf. Ascon. *ad Cic. in Pis.* 19; also the *Notitia* and *Curiosum*.) Hence, perhaps, the most natural conclusion is that it consisted of two *cellae* under the same roof, like the temple of Venus and Rome, a form which agrees with the description of Symmachus: " Majores nostri—aedes Honori ac Virtuti gemella facie junctim locarunt." (*Epist.* i. 21.) The temple was adorned with the spoils of Grecian art brought by Marcellus from Syracuse; an instance noted and condemned by Livy as the first of that kind of spoliation, which he observes was subsequently inflicted upon the Roman temples themselves, and especially upon this very temple of Marcellus; for, in Livy's time, few of those ornaments remained, which had previously rendered it an object of attraction to all strangers who visited Rome (xxv. 40, cf. xxxiv. 4).

They probably disappeared during the Civil Wars, in which the Roman temples seem to have suffered both from neglect and spoliation; for in the time of Cicero the Syracusan spoils still existed in the temple (*in Verr.* iv. 54). It appears to have been burnt in the fire of Nero, since it is mentioned as having been restored by Vespasian. (Plin. xxxv. 37.)

According to Aurelius Victor (*Vir. Ill.* 32) the annual procession of the Roman knights to the temple of Castor started from this temple of Honos and Virtus, whereas Dionysius (xi. 13) names the temple of Mars as the starting-place. Becker (*Handb.* p. 311) regards the discrepancy between these accounts as tending to prove the correctness of his assumption that the temples must have lain close together. That one of the accounts is erroneous is a more probable conclusion, and it is a certain one that it is fallacious to draw any topographical deductions from such very shadowy premises. The true site of the TEMPLE OF MARS has been ascertained as satisfactorily as that of any of the monuments which do not actually speak for themselves ; such, we mean, as the Colosseum, Trajan's column, the Pantheon, and others of the like description. There can be no doubt that the temple of Mars, instead of being close to the Porta Capena, or at *S. Sisto*, as Becker places it (*Handb.* p. 513), lay on the Via Appia, at the distance of about 1½ miles from that gate. The proofs are overwhelming. In the first place an inscription, still preserved in the Vatican, recording the levelling of the Clivus Martis, was found in the *Vigna Nari*, outside of the Porta Appia (the modern *S. Sebastiano*). Secondly, another inscription, in the *Palazzo Barberini*, recorded by Fabretti (*Inscr.* p. 724, no. 443), Marini (*Fratr. Arv.* p. 8), and others, testifies that Salvia Marcellina gave a piece of ground to the Collegium of Aesculapius and Hygia for a small temple, close to the temple of Mars, between the first and second milestone on the Via Appia, on the left-hand side in going from the city. Thirdly, both the *Notitia* and *Curiosum* place the Aedes Martis at the extremity of the first Regio, close to the Flumen Almonis. The Almo flows outside the Porta Appia, near the *Vigna Nari* :—

" Est locus ante urbem, qua primum nascitur ingens
   Appia, quaque Italo gemitus Almone Cybebe
   Ponit, et Idaeos jam non reminiscitur amnes."
                                    (Stat. *Silv.* v. 1. 222.)

A brook now flows between the *Porta S. Sebastiano* and the church of *Domine quo vadis*, which, with great probability, has been identified with the Almo. (Cluver, *Ital. Ant.* p. 718; Westphal, *Röm. Campagna*, p. 17.) Fourthly, the same locality is indicated by several documents of the middle ages. Thus, in the *Acts of the Martyrs* : " Tunc B. Stephanus ductus a militibus foras muros Appiae portae ad T. Martis " (*Act of S. Stephanus and S. Julius*). " Diacones duxerunt in clivum Martis ante templum et ibidem decollatus est " (*Act of S. Sixtus*). And the *Mirabilia* (in Montfaucon, *Diar. Ital.* p. 283) : " Haec sunt loca quae inveniuntur in passionibus sanctorum foris portam Appiam, ubi beatus Syxtus decollatus fuit, et ubi Dominus apparuit Petro, *Domine quo vadis?* Ibi templum Martis, intus portam, arcus Syllae." Now, the passages in the classics which relate to the subject do not run counter to these indications, but, on the contrary tend to confirm them. Appian (*B. C.* iii. 41) mentions a temple of Mars 15 stadia distant from the city, which would answer pretty nearly to the distance of between 1 and 2 miles given in the inscription quoted. Ovid says (*Fast.* vi. 191):—

" Lux eadem Marti festa est; quem prospicit extra
    Appositum tectae Porta Capena viae."

The word *prospicit* denotes a long view; and as the temple of Mars stood on a hill, as is evident from the Clivus Martis, it might easily be visible at the distance of a mile or two. The words of Statius (" qua primum nascitur," &c.) must be corrupt, being both tautological and contrary to fact. The paving of the road from the Porta Capena to the temple would not have been worth twice recording by Livy, had it lain only at a distance of some 300 yards (x. 23, xxxviii. 28). The only way in which Becker can escape from the legitimate conclusion is by assuming two temples of Mars in this quarter; in which few, we suspect, will be inclined to follow him, and which may be regarded as equivalent to a confession of defeat. (Becker, *Handb.* p. 511, seq.; *Antw.* p. 63, seq.; Urlichs, *Röm. Topogr.* p. 105, seq.; Preller, *Regionen*, p. 116, seq.; Canina, *Indicazione*, p. 56, seq.)

Close to the Porta Capena and the temple of Honos et Virtus lay the VALLEY OF EGERIA with the LUCUS and AEDES CAMENARUM, the traditionary spot where Numa sought inspiration and wisdom from the nymph Egeria. (Liv. i. 21; Plut. *Num.* 13.) In the time of Juvenal, whose description of the spot is a locus classicus for its topography, the grove and temple had been profaned and let out to the Jews:—

" Substitit ad veteres arcus madidamque Capenam
    Hic ubi nocturnae Numa constituebat amicae.
    Nunc sacri fontis nemus et delubra locantur
    Judaeis, quorum cophinus foenumque supellex.
    Omnis enim populo mercedem pendere jussa est
    Arbor, et ejectis mendicat silva Camenis.
    In vallem Egeriae descendimus et speluncas
    Dissimiles veris. Quanto praestantius esset
    Numen aquae, viridi si margine clauderet undas
    Herba, nec ingenuum violarent marmora tophum."   (*Sat.* iii. 10, seq.)

It is surprising how Becker could doubt that there was an Aedes Camenarum here, since it is not only alluded to in the preceding passage, but also expressly mentioned by Pliny (xxxiv. 10.) The modern *Ciceroni* point out to the traveller as the valley of Egeria a pretty retired spot some distance outside of the *Porta S. Sebastiano*, in the valley called *La Caffarella*, near which are the remains of a little temple, called by some the temple of Honos et Virtus, by others a temple of Bacchus, with a grove said to be sacred to the latter deity. But though at present our imagination would more gladly fix on this spot as the scene of the conferences between Numa and his nymph, and though respectable authorities are not wanting in favour of this view (Venuti, *Descr. di Rom.* ii. p. 18; Guattani, *Rom. Descr.* ii. p. 45), yet the preceding passages, to which may be added Symmachus (" Sed enim propter eas (aedes Honoris et Virtutis) Camenarum religio sacro fonti advertitur," *Epist.* i. 21) and the *Notitia*, which places the templo of the Camenae

close to that of Honour and Valour, are too decisive to allow us to do so; and we must therefore assume the valley of Egeria to have been that near the church of *S. Sisto*, opposite to the baths of Caracalla. The little fountain pointed out as that of Egeria in the valley *Caffarella*, is perhaps the remains of a nymphaeum. Here was probably a sanctuary of the Almo, which waters the valley.

Near the temple of Mars, since it is mentioned in the *Notitia* in conjunction with it, lay the TEMPLE OF TEMPESTAS, built by L. Cornelius Scipio, the victor of Aleria, in commemoration of the escape of the Roman fleet from shipwreck off the island of Corsica, as appears from the inscription on his tomb. The temple and the occasion of its foundation are alluded to by Ovid (*Fasti*, vi. 193) in the following lines:—

" Te quoque, Tempestas, meritam delubra fatemur,
    Cum paene est Corsis obruta classis aquis."

But of the TEMPLE OF MINERVA, also mentioned at the same time with that of Mars, we know nothing more. Near the last was preserved the LAPIS MANALIS, a large cylindrical stone so called from *manare*, " to flow," because during seasons of drought it was carried in procession into the city, for the sake of procuring rain. (Paul. Diac. p. 128; Varr. *ap. Non.* xv. p. 375, Gerl.)

Close to the Porta Capena, and probably outside of it, lay one of the three SENACULA mentioned by Festus; but the only time at which we find meetings of the senate recorded there is during the year following the battle of Cannae, when they appear to have been regularly held at this place. (Liv. xxiii. 32.) During the same period the tribunal of the praetor was erected at the PISCINA PUBLICA. This last object, which seems to have been a swimming-place for the people in the Republican times (Festus, p. 213), gave name to the 12th Regio, which adjoined the 1st, or that of Porta Capena, on the W. (Amm. Marc. xvii. 4; cf. Cic. *ad Quint. Fr.* iii. 7.) The pond had, however, vanished in the time of Festus, and its exact situation cannot be determined. There are several other objects in this district in the like predicament, such as the LACUS PROMETHEI, the BALNEUM TORQUATI, and others mentioned in the *Notitia.* The Thermae Commodianae and Severianae will be considered under the section which treats of the thermae. The MUTATORIUM CAESARIS, perhaps a kind of imperial villa (Preller, *Reg.* p. 115), appears to have been situated near the modern church of *S. Balbina.* (Montfaucon, *ap. Urlichs Röm. Topogr.* p. 112.) The three TRIUMPHAL ARCHES OF TRAJAN, VERUS, AND DRUSUS, mentioned by the *Notitia* in the 1st Regio, probably spanned the Via Appia in the space between the temple of Mars and the Porta Capena. The arch still existing just within the *Porta S. Sebastiano* is generally thought to be that of Drusus, the father of the emperor Claudius. (" Praeterea Senatus, inter alia complura, marmoreum arcum cum tropaeis via Appia decrevit (Druso)," Suet. *Claud.* 1.)

For many miles the tombs of distinguished Romans skirt both sides of the Via Appia; and these remains are perhaps better calculated than any other object to impress the stranger with an adequate idea of Rome's former greatness. For the most part, however, they lie beyond the bounds of the present subject, and we shall therefore content ourselves

ARCH OF DRUSUS.

with mentioning a few which were contained within the actual boundaries of the city. They appear to have commenced immediately outside the Porta Capena ("An tu egressus porta Capena, cum Calatini, Scipionum, Serviliorum, Metellorum sepulcra vides, miseros putas illos?" Cic. Tusc. i. 7); and hence many of them were included in the larger circuit of the walls of Aurelian. The tomb of Horatia, slain by the hand of her victorious brother, seems to have been situated just outside the gate. (Liv. i. 26.) Fortunately the most interesting of those mentioned by Cicero—the TOMB OF THE SCIPIOS —is still in existence. It was discovered in 1780 in the Vigna Sassi, on the left-hand side of the Via Appia, a little beyond the spot where the Via Latina branches off from it, and about 400 paces within the Porta S. Sebastiano. Its entrance is marked by a single tall cypress tree. In Livy's time the tomb was still adorned with three statues, said to be those of Publius and Lucius Scipio, and of the poet Ennius, who was interred in the sepulchre of his patrona. (Hieron. Chron. p. 379, Ronc.) It was here that the sarcophagus of L. Scipio Barbatus, consul in B. C. 298, now preserved in the Vatican, was discovered, together with several monumental stones with inscriptions relating to other members of the family, or to their connections and freedmen. The originals were carried off to the Vatican and copies inserted in their stead. The most remarkable of these inscriptions are that of Scipio Barbatus; of his son Lucius Cornelius Scipio, the conqueror of Corsica, consul in B. C. 259; of Publius Scipio, son of Africanus Major, whose feeble state of health is alluded to by Cicero (Cato Maj. 11), and whose touching epitaph shows that he died young; of L. Cornelius Scipio, grandson of the conqueror of Spain, gathered to his fathers at the early age of 20; and of another of the same name, the son of Asiaticus, who died aged 33, whose title to honour is summed up in the laconic words, "Pater regem Antiochum subegit." A complete account of this tomb will be found in Visconti (Mon. degli Scipioni, Rom. 1785)

and in the Beschreibung Roms (vol. iii. p. 612, seq.), where the various epitaphs are given.

Also on the left-hand side of the Via Appia in going from the Porta Capena was the MAUSOLEUM OF SEPTIMIUS SEVERUS, which he caused to be erected for himself in his lifetime, in imitation of his Septizonium, but probably on a reduced scale. (Spart. Geta, 7.) In the same neighbourhood are some of those COLUMBARIA, or subterranean chambers, which formed the common resting-places for the ashes of persons of a lower condition. One of these, not far from the tomb of the Scipios, is said to contain the remains of the courtiers and domestics of the Caesars, from Julius to Nero. Among others there is an inscription to M. Valerius Creticus, with a bust. The walls, as well as a large pier in the middle, are hollowed throughout with vaulted recesses like large pigeon-holes,—whence the name,—in which are contained the ashes of the dead. The MAUSOLEUM OF CAECILIA METELLA, which stands on the Via Appia, about 2 miles outside the Porta S. Sebastiano, though it does not properly belong to our subject, demands, from the magnificence of its construction, as well as from Byron's well-known lines (Childe Harold, canto iv.), a passing word of notice here.

The remaining part of the district, or that forming the 12th Regio, and lying to the W. of the Via Appia, does not present many monuments of interest. The most striking one, the Thermae Antoninianae, or baths of Caracalla, will be spoken of under its proper head. We have already treated of the Bona Dea Subsaxanea and of the Isium. Close to the baths just mentioned Caracalla built the street called NOVA VIA, reckoned one of the handsomest in Rome. (Spart. Carac. 2; Aur. Vict. Caes. 21.) Respecting the FORTUNA MAMMOSA, we know nothing more than that the Basis Capitolina mentions a street of the same name in this neighbourhood. In the later period of the Empire this district appears to have contained several splendid palaces, as the SEPTEM DOMUS PARTHORUM, the

TOMB OF METELLA CAECILIA.

Domus Cilonis, and Domus Cornificies. The Domus Parthorum and Cilonis seem to have been some of those palaces erected by Septimius Severus, and presented to his friends. (Aur. Vict. *Epit.* 20.) Cilon is probably the same person mentioned by Dion (lxxvii. 4), Spartian (*Carac.* 3), and in the *Digest* (i. 12. 1, and 15. 4.) The Parthi seem to have been Parthian nobles, whom Severus brought with him to Rome, and of whose luxurious habits Tertullian has drawn a characteristic picture. (*De Hab. Mul.* 7.) The Privata Adriani and the Domus Cornifi-cies (Cornificiae) mentioned in the *Notitia*, lay doubtless close together. The former must have been the private residence of Hadrian, where M. Antoninus dwelt after his adoption by that emperor. (Jul. Capit. *M. Anton.* 5.) M. Antoninus had a younger sister named Anna Cornificia, to whom the house bearing her name doubtless belonged. (*Ib.* c. 1; Preller, *Regionen,* p. 198.)

XI. The Esquiline and its Neighbourhood.

The Esquiline (*Esquiliae,* or in a more ancient form *Exquiliae*) was originally covered with a thick wood, of which, in the time of Varro, the only re-mains were a few sacred groves of inconsiderable extent, the rest of the hill having been cleared and covered with buildings. (Varr. *L. L.* v. § 49, Müll.) Yet the derivation of the name of the hill from *aesculetum* seems to have been unknown to an-tiquity, and is a mere conjecture of Müller's (*ad loc.*); the ancient etymology being derived either from *excubiae regis,* because Servius Tullius had fixed his abode there, or from *excolere,* because the hill was first cleared and settled by that king. (Varr. *l. c.*; Ov. *Fast.* iii. 245.)

We have already described the Esquiline as throwing out two tongues or projections, called respectively, in the more ancient times of Rome, Oppius and Cispius. Their relative situation is in-dicated in the following passage of Festus: " Op-pius autem appellatus est, ut ait Varro rerum humanarum L. viii., ab Opita Oppio Tusculano, qui cum praesidio Tusculanorum missus ad Romam tuendam, dum Tullus Hostilius Veios oppugnaret, consederat in Carinis et ibi castra habuerat. Simi-

liter Cispium a Laevio Cispio Anagnino, qui ejus-dem rei causa eam partem Æsquiliarum, quae jacet ad vicum Patricium versus, in qua regione est aedis Mefitis, tuitus est " (p. 348, Müll.). Hence we learn that the Cispius was that projection which adjoined the Vicus Patricius, and must conse-quently have been the northern one, since the Vicus Patricius is known to have corresponded with the modern streets called *Via Urbana* and *Via di S. Pu-denziana,* which traverse the valley lying between the Viminal and the Esquiline. The following passage of Paulus Diaconus shows that the Vicus Patricius must have lain in a valley: " Patricius vicus Romae dictus eo, quod ibi patricii habitaverunt, jubente Servio Tullio, ut, si quid molirentur adversus ipsum, ex locis superioribus opprimerentur " (p. 221, Müll.); and its identity with the modern streets just mentioned appears from Anastasius (*Vita Pii I.*) : " Hic ex rogatu beatae Praxedis dedicavit ecclesiam thermas Novati in vico Patricii in honorem sororis suae sanctae Potentianae " (p. 14). This church of *S. Pudenziana* still exists in the street of the same name. It is also mentioned by the Anonymous of Einsiedlen, in whose time most of the streets still bore their ancient names, as being " in vico Pa-tricii." That the Cispius was the smaller and more northern tongue likewise appears from the sacred books of the Argives (ap. Varr. *L. L.* v. § 50), which, in proceeding northwards from the Caelian, first name the Oppius, which had four sacraria or chapels, and then the Cispius, which, being the smaller hill, had only two, namely, the Lucus Poe-telius and the Aedes Junonis Lucinae.

From the passage of Festus just quoted, it ap-pears that part of Mons Oppius bore the name of Carinae; and this appellation continued to exist when the names Oppius and Cispius had fallen out of use and been superseded by the general name of *Esquiliae.* Yet it is one of the contested points of Roman topography whether the Carinae formed part of the hill. The Italians still cling to the an-cient opinion that under that name was compre-hended the low ground from the Forum Transi-torium to the Colosseum. Becker (*Handb.* p. 522 seq.) partly adopted this view, but at the same time extended the district so as to embrace the western extremity of the Oppius; whilst Urlichs, on the contrary, confined the Carinae entirely to that hill. (*Beschr.* vol. iii. part ii. p. 119, seq.) That the Italian view is, at all events, partly erroneous, can hardly admit of a question. Besides the preceding passage of Festus, which clearly identifies the Carinae as part of the Oppius, there are other places in ancient writers which show that a portion at least of the district so called lay on a height. Thus Dionysius, speaking of the Tigillum Sororium, says that it was situated in the lane which *led down from the Carinae* to the Vicus Cyprius (ἔστι δ' ἐν τῷ στενωπῷ τῷ φέροντι ἀπὸ Καρίνης κάτω τοῖς ἐπὶ τὸν Κύπριον ἐρχομένοις στενωπόν, iii. 22). Again Varro (*L. L.* v. § 48), in describing the Subura or valley at the foot of the Oppius, says that it lay " sub muro terreo Carinarum;" obviously indicating that the latter place was on a height. Becker, indeed, maintains that walls of earth or aggeres were used in fortification only where the ground was level. But a wall on a height was certainly the usual mode of fortification in ancient Italy; and, as Mr. Bunbury justly remarks (*Class. Mus.* vol. v. p. 222), the peculiar appellation of " murus terreus " clearly distinguishes this wall from a common *agger.* Nor, as the Subura lay behind the gorge between the Esquiline and Quirinal, is it easy to see how any murus terreus in the district of the Carinae could have been so situated as to overhang the Subura, except upon the hill. The following words of Varro (*l. c.*) are even perhaps still more conclusive. He identifies the Subura with the Pagus Succusanus, — the ancient name of Subura being Succusa, by an interchange of *b* and *c*, — and holds it was thus named " quod succurrit Carinis:" where, whatever we may think of his etymology, it is plain that he regarded the Carinae as a height. It may be added that the western part of the Oppius, where the church of S. Pietro *in Vincoli* now stands, bore the name of *le Carre* as late as the 16th century. (And. Fulvius, *de Urb. Ant.* p. 304; cf. Niebuhr, *Hist.* i. p. 390, seq.)

It cannot therefore be doubted that the Carinae occupied the extremity of the Oppius; but how far that district extended eastwards cannot be said. It is a more difficult question to determine whether part of the valley lying at the western foot of the hill also bore the name of Carinae. Its solution is connected with another question respecting the site of the TEMPLE OF TELLUS. We know that this temple—which was a considerable one, since assemblies of the senate were sometimes held in it — lay in the Carinae, and that it was built on the site of the house of Sp. Cassius, which was confiscated and pulled down when that demagogue was convicted of a design to make himself sovereign of Rome. (Liv. ii. 41; Val. Max. vi. 3. § 1; Plin. xxxiv. 14.) That event took place B. C. 485; but the temple does not seem to have been built till B. C. 269. Its site is further determined by notices respecting the house of Pompey, which subsequently came into the possession of M. Antony, the situation of which is known to have been in the Carinae, and at the same time close to the temple of Tellus: " Docuit (Lenaeus) in Carinis, ad Telluris aedem, in qua regione Pompeiorum domus fuerat." (Suet. *Ill. Gramm.* 15, cf. Id. *Tib.* 15; Vell. Pat. ii. 77; Aur. Vict. *Vir. Ill.* 84; Dion Cass. xlviii. 38.) And Servius says expressly, though in some respects unintelligibly, " Carinae sunt aedificia facta in Carinarum modum,

quae erant circa templum Telluris " (*ad Aen.* viii. 361).

There is nothing in the preceding passages to exclude the possibility of the Templum Telluris having been on the summit of the hill; since it is not necessary to assume with Urlichs that it stood on its very edge (*Röm. Topogr.* p. 117); in which case, as there was an area attached to the temple, its back front must have been turned towards the road leading up to it from the valley, and the area have lain before it on the summit of the hill—a disposition which does not appear very probable. Yet there are some other circumstances tending to the inference that the temple was situated in the valley. Dionysius mentions it as being, not in the Carinae, but on the road leading to the Carinae (κατὰ τὴν ἐπὶ Καρίνας φέρουσαν ὁδόν, viii. 79.) A curious view, taken by Urlichs (*l. c.*) of the construction of ἐπί in this passage is one of the reasons which led him to place the temple on the hill. He thinks that it must necessarily mean " up to : " but it might just as well be said that it means " down to," in a passage quoted a little while ago from the same author respecting the situation of the Carinae and the Vicus Cyprius. In both cases it simply means " to." It will be perceived that Dionysius is here at variance with the authorities before quoted respecting the site of the temple. If the appellation of Carinae extended over some part of the adjacent valley it is possible that Dionysius, as a foreigner, might have been unaware of that fact, and have attached the name only to the more striking part of the district which lay on the hill. And there is a passage in Varro, a very obscure one indeed, from which it might be inferred that part of the Ceroliensis, which seems to have been the name of the valley between the Caelian, the Esquiline, and the Velian ridge, had likewise borne the name of Carinae (" Ceroliensis a Carinarum junctu dictus Carinae, postea Cerolia, quod hinc oritur caput Sacrae Viae," *L.L.* v. § 47). These passages would seem to indicate that the temple of Tellus lay in the valley between S. *Maria de' Monti* and the *Tor de' Conti*, where indeed we find traces of the name : since the churches of S. *Salvatore* and of S. *Pantaleone*, the latter of which still exists near the *Via del Colosseo*, bore in the middle ages the epithet of " in Tellure." Passages are also adduced from the *Acts of the Martyrs* to show that the temple of Tellus stood opposite to that of Pallas in the Forum Transitorium. (" Clementianus praecepit ei caput amputari ante templum in Tellure, corpusque ejus projici ante Palladis aedem in locum supradictum," *Act. S. Gordian.*) Hence it seems not improbable that the district of the Carinae, in which the temple undoubtedly stood, may have extended over a considerable part of the valley; but the passages relating to the subject are far from being decisive ; and the question is one of that kind in which much may be said on both sides.

Two striking legends of early Roman history are connected with the Esquiline and its vicinity ; that of the murder of Servius Tullius by his inhuman daughter, and that of the Tigillum Sororium, or typical yoke, by passing under which Horatius expiated the murder of his sister. We have before related that Servius Tullius resided on the Esquiline, and that he was the first to clear that hill and make it habitable. It was on his return to his residence on it, after his ejection from the curia by his son-in-law, Tarquinius Superbus, that he was murdered by the hirelings of that usurper. Livy's account of the transaction is clear and graphic, and the best guide to the topography of the neighbourhood. The aged monarch had reached the top of the VICUS CYPRIUS ("ad summum Cyprium vicum") when he was overtaken and slain. His daughter followed in her carriage, and, having arrived at the same spot where stood a temple of Diana a little before the time when Livy wrote, she was just *turning to the right* in order to ascend the CLIVUS URBIUS, which led to the summit of the Esquiline, when the affrighted driver reined his horses, and pointed out to Tullia the bleeding corpse of her murdered father; but the fiend-like Tullia bade him drive on, and arrived at home bespattered with the blood of her parent. From this unnatural deed the street which was the scene of it obtained the name of VICUS SCELERATUS (i. 48). The question that has been sometimes raised whether Tullia was returning to her father's or to her husband's house, does not seem to be of much importance. Solinus, indeed (i. 25), represents Servius Tullius as residing "supra clivum Urbium," and Tarquinius Superbus, also on the Esquiline, but, "Supra clivum Pullium ad Fagutalem lucum." The house of the latter therefore must have been upon the Oppius, on which the Lucus Fagutalis was situated, and most probably upon the southern side of it; but he may not have resided here till after he became king. On the other hand, as Tullia is represented as turning to the right in order to ascend the Clivus Urbius to the royal residence, it is plain that the Vicus Cyprius must have lain on the *north side* of one of the tongues of the Esquiline; and as we are further informed by Dionysius, in a passage before quoted (iii. 22), that there was a lane which led down from the Carinae, or western extremity of the Oppius, to the Vicus Cyprius, the conclusion is forced upon us that the palace of Servius Tullius must have been situated upon the eastern part of the northern side of the Oppius, and that consequently the Vicus Cyprius must have corresponded with the modern *Via di S. Lucia in Selci*. The Summus Cyprius Vicus was evidently towards the head of the valley, the lower part of the street running under the Carinae; and hence the Clivus Urbius and the residence of Servius may be placed somewhere near the church of *S. Martino.* Before the usurpation of Tarquin, he and his wife may have resided near his father-in-law, or even under the same roof; or, what is still more probable, Tullia, as Ovid represents her ("patrios initura Penates," *Fast.* vi. 602), was proceeding to take possession of her father's palace, since his deposition had been effected in the senate before his murder. Urlichs (*Röm. Topogr.* p. 119) admits that the Vicus Cyprius answered to the *Via di S. Lucia,* yet holds that Servius resided on the Cispius; a view utterly irreconcilable with the fact that the Clivus Urbius and palace lay on the right of that street. The passages before adduced prove the direction of the Vicus Cyprius as clearly as any locality in Rome can be proved which depends for its determination solely on notices in the classics. Yet Becker shuts his eyes to this satisfactory evidence, and maintains that the Vicus Cyprius corresponded with the modern *Via del Colosseo* (*Antwort*, p. 78); although in that case also it would have been impossible for Tullia to have ascended the Esquiline by turning to the right. The only ground he assigns for this incomprehensible view is an arbitrary estimate of the distances between the objects mentioned in *Regio IV.* of the *Notitia*, founded also on the assumption that

these objects are enumerated strictly in the order in which they actually followed one another. But we have already shown from Becker himself that this is by no means always the case, and it is evidently not so in the present instance; since, after mentioning the Tigillium Sororium, which lay in or near the Subura, the order of the catalogue leaves that spot and proceeds onwards to the Colosseum, and then again at the end of the list reverts to the Subura. The chief objection to placing the Vicus Cyprius under this side of the Oppius is, as Mr. Bunbury observes (*Class. Mus.* vol. v. p. 227), that it would thus seem to interfere with the Subura. But this objection is not urged either by Becker or Urlichs; and indeed the Subura, like the Velabrum, seems to have been a district rather than a street, so that we may conceive the Vicus Cyprius to have run through it.

The position of the TIGILLUM SORORIUM is determined by what has been already said; namely, in a narrow street leading down from the Carinae to the Vicus Cyprius. It seems to have been a wooden beam erected across the street. As it is mentioned in the *Notitia*, this monument, connected with one of Rome's early legends, must have existed down to the 5th century; and indeed Livy (i. 26) informs us that it was constantly repaired at the public expense. We learn from Dionysius (iii. 22) and Festus (p. 297, Müll.) that on each side of it stood an altar; one to JUNO SORORIA, the other to JANUS CURIATIUS.

Having had occasion to mention the SUBURA, it may be as well to describe that celebrated locality before proceeding further with the topography of the Esquiline. We have already seen from Varro that it was one of the most ancient districts in Rome; and its importance may be inferred from its having given name to the 1st Servian Region. We have also alluded to a passage in the same author (*L.L.* v. § 48, Müll.) which shows it to have been originally a distinct village, called Succusa or Pagus Succusanus, lying under the Carinae. Varro adds, that the name still continued to be written with a C instead of a B; a statement which is confirmed by the fact that in inscriptions the Tribus Suburana is always denoted by the abridged form TRIB. SVC. (Cf. Festus, *s. v. Subura*, p. 309, Müll.; Quintil. *Inst. Or.* i. 7. § 29; Mommsen, *Die Röm. Tribus,* p. 79, seq.) A *piazza* or place under the church of *S. Pietro in Vincoli* still bears the name of *Subura;* and the church of *S. Agata* over the *Via de' Serpenti,* which skirts the eastern foot of the Quirinal hill, bore in the middle ages the name of "in Suburra" or "super Suburra." Hence it seems probable that the Subura occupied the whole of the valley formed by the extremities of the Quirinal, Viminal, and Esquiline, and must consequently have been, not a street but, a region of some extent; as indeed we find it called by Gregory the Great in the 6th century ("in regione urbis illa quae Subura dicitur," *Dial.* iii. c. 30). But that it extended westward as far as the Forum Transitorium, a supposition which seems to rest solely on the order of the the names in the 4th Region of the *Notitia,* we can hardly conceive. We have shown that the district between the back of the imperial fora and the western extremity of the Esquiline may perhaps have formed part of the Carinae; but it can hardly have been called both Carinae and Subura. The latter seems to have properly begun at the point where the Quirinalis approaches the extremity of the Oppius; and this seems to have been the spot called by Martial the *primae fauces* of the Subura (ii. 17):—

" Tonstrix Suburae faucibus sedet primis,
　Cruenta pendent qua flagella tortorum
　Argique letum multus obsidet sutor."

Juvenal (v. 106) represents the Cloaca Maxima as penetrating to the middle of the Subura, and this fact was established by excavations made in the year 1743. (Ficoroni, *Vestigia di Roma*, ap. Bunbury, *Class. Mus.* vol. v. p. 219.)

From its situation between the imperial fora and the eastern hills, the Subura must have been one of the most frequented thoroughfares in Rome; and hence we are not surprised to find many allusions to its dirt and noise. It was the peculiar aversion of Juvenal,— a man, indeed, of many aversions (" Ego vel Prochytam praepono Suburae," *Sat.* iii. 5); a trait in his friend's character which had not escaped the notice of Martial (xii. 18):—

" Dum tu forsitan inquietus erras
　Clamosa, Juvenalis, in Subura."

The epithet *clamosa* here probably refers to the cries of itinerant chapmen: for we learn from other passages in Martial that the Subura was the chief place in which he used to market (vii. 31, x. 94, &c.; cf. Juv. xi. 136, seq.) It appears also to have been the abode of prostitutes (vi. 66; comp. Hor. *Epod.* v. 58). It was therefore what is commonly called a low neighbourhood; though some distinguished families seem to have resided in it, even Caesar himself in his early life (Suet. *Caes.* 46), and in the time of Martial, L. Arruntius Stella (xii. 3. 9). The Suburanenses, or inhabitants of the Subura, kept up to a late period some of the ancient customs which probably belonged to them when they formed a distinct village; especially an annual contest with the Sacravienses, or inhabitants of the Sacra Via, for the head of the horse sacrificed to Mars in the Campus Martius every October. If the Suburanenses gained the victory they fixed the head on a tower in the Subura called TURRIS MAMILIA, whilst the Sacravienses, if successful, fixed it on the Regia. (Festus, *s. v. October Equus*, p. 178, Müll.; Paul. Diac. p. 131.)

Throughout the time of the Republic the Esquiline appears to have been by no means a favourite or fashionable place of residence. Part of it was occupied by the CAMPUS ESQUILINUS, a place used as a burying-ground, principally for the very lowest class of persons, such as paupers and slaves; whose bodies seem to have been frequently cast out and left to rot here without any covering of earth. But under the Empire, and especially the later period of it, many palaces were erected on the Esquiline. Maecenas was the first to improve it, by converting this field of death, and probably also part of the surrounding neighbourhood, — the pauper burial-ground itself appears to have been only 1000 feet long by 300 deep,— into an agreeable park or garden. Horace (*S.* i. 8. 14) mentions the laying out of these celebrated HORTI MAECENATIS:—

" Nunc licet Esquiliis habitare salubribus atque
　Aggere in aprico spatiari, qua modo tristes
　Albis informem spectabant ossibus agrum."

It appears from these lines that the Campus Esquilinus adjoined the *agger* of Servius Tullius, which, by the making of these gardens, was converted into a cheerful promenade, from which people were no longer driven by the disgusting spectacle of mouldering bones. The Campus Esquilinus being a cemetery, must of course have been on the outside of the *agger*, since it was not lawful to bury within the pomoerium; and Varro (*L.L.* v. § 25) mentions it as " ultra Exquilias," by which he must mean the Servian Region so called, which was bounded by the *agger*. Its situation is also determined by a passage in Strabo (v. p. 237), where the Via Labicana, which issued from the Esquiline gate at the southern extremity of the *agger*, is said to leave the campus on the left. It appears to have also been the place of execution for slaves and ignoble criminals (Suet. *Claud.* 25; Tac. *Ann.* ii. 32, xv. 60; Plaut. *Mil.* ii. 4. 6, ed. Ritschl.). There does not seem to be any authority for Becker's assumption that the whole of the Esquiline outside of the Servian walls was called Campus Esquilinus (*Handb.* p. 554), nor that after the laying out of the gardens of Maecenas the ancient place of execution was transferred to the Sessorium, near *S. Croce in Gerusalemme.* Part of the campus was the field given, as the scholiast on Horace says, by some person as a burying-place. The Sessorium mentioned in the *Excerpta Valesiana de Odoacre* (69) was a palace; and though Theodoric ordered a traitor to be beheaded there it can hardly have been the ordinary place of execution for common malefactors. Besides the Sessorium mentioned by the scholiasts on Horace (*Epod.* v. 100, *Sat.* i. 8. 11) was close to the Esquiline gate, a full mile from *S. Croce*, and seems, therefore, to have been another name for the Campus Esquilinus, if the scholiasts are right in calling it Sessorium. The executions recorded in the passages before quoted from Suetonius and Tacitus took place long after the gardens of Maecenas were made; yet when Tacitus uses the words " extra Portam Esquilinam," there can be no doubt that he means *just without* the gate. It would be a wrong conception of the Horti Maecenatis to imagine that they resembled a private garden, or even a gentleman's park. They were a common place of recreation for the Roman populace. Thus Juvenal describes the *agger* as the usual resort of fortune-tellers. (*S.* vi. 588.) We see from the description of Horace that not even all the tombs had been removed. Canidia comes there to perform her incantations and evoke the *manes* of the dead; at sight of which infernal rites the moon hides herself behind the sepulchres (v. 35):—

"—— lunamque rubentem,
Ne foret his testis, post magna latere sepulcra."

Such a place, therefore, might still have been used for executions; though, doubtless, bodies were no longer exposed there, as they had formerly been. These " magna sepulcra " would also indicate that some even of the better classes were buried here; and the same thing appears from Cicero. (*Phil.* ix. 7.)

The Horti Maecenatis probably extended within the *agger* towards the baths of Titus, and it was in this part that the HOUSE OF MAECENAS seems to have been situated. Close to these baths, on the NE. side, others, built by Trajan, existed in ancient times, although all traces of them have now vanished. They have sometimes been confounded with those of Titus; but there can be no doubt that they were distinct and separate foundations. Thus the *Notitia* mentions in the 3rd Region the " Thermae Titianae et Trajanae ;" and their distinction is also shown by the inscription of Ursus Togatus: THERMIS TRAIANI THERMIS AGRIPPAE ET TITI, &c. (Gruter, dcxxxvii. 1). The site of the baths of Trajan, close to the church of *S. Martino*, may be determined from another inscription found near that church, in the pontificate of Paul III., which records some improvements made in them; as well as from a notice by Anastasius, in his Life of Symmachus (p. 88, Blanch.), stating that the church alluded to was erected "juxta Thermas Trajanas." It is a very common opinion that the house of Maecenas occupied part of the site of the baths of Titus, and this opinion is as probable as any other. It was a very lofty building. Horace describes it as a "molem propinquam nubibus arduis" (*Od.* iii. 20. 10), and from its situation and height must no doubt have commanded a view of Tibur and its neighbourhood; though we do not draw that conclusion from the immediately preceding lines, where we think the far better reading is, "*Ut* semper udum Tibur," &c., the *semper* belonging to "udum," and not to "contemplere" (cf. Tate's *Horace, Prel. Diss.* p. 24). We have before related how Nero beheld the fire of Rome from the house of Maecenas. Suetonius, in his account of that scene, calls the house "turris Maecenatiana" (*Nero*, 38), by which, perhaps, we are not to understand a tower, properly so called, but a lofty superstructure of several stories over the lower part of the house (Becker, *Charikles*, i. p. 195). Maecenas bequeathed his house and gardens to Augustus; and Tiberius lived there after his return from Rhodes, and before he succeeded to the empire (Suet. *Tib.* 15). The subsequent history of the house is unknown; but, as we have said, it may probably have been included in the baths of Titus.

Close to the gardens of Maecenas lay the HORTI LAMIANI (Philo Jud. vol. ii. p. 597, Mang.), belonging perhaps, to the Aelius Lamia celebrated by Horace (*Od.* i. 26, &c.). We learn from Valerius Maximus (iv. 4. 8) that the ancient family of the Aelii dwelt where the monument of Marius afterwards stood; whence it seems probable that the Horti Lamiani may have lain to the E. of those of Maecenas, towards the church of *S. Bibiana*. It was here that the body of Caligula was first hastily buried, which was afterwards burnt and reinterred by his sisters (Suet. *Cal.* 59).

There appear to have been several more gardens between the Porta Esquilina and the modern *Porta Maggiore;* as the HORTI PALLANTIANI, founded apparently by Pallas, the powerful freedman of Claudius (Tac. *Ann.* xi. 29; Suet. *Claud.* 28; Plin. *Ep.* viii. 6); and which, from several passages of Frontinus (*Aq.* 19, seq.), appear to have been situated between *P. Maggiore*, the Marian monument, and the church of *S. Bibiana*. Frontinus also mentions (*Aq.* 68) certain HORTI EPAPHRODITIANI, perhaps belonging to Epaphroditus, the *libertus* of Nero, who assisted in putting that emperor to death (Suet. *Ner*.49, Dom. 14; Tac. *Ann.* xv. 55); as well as some HORTI TORQUATIANI (c. 5), apparently in the same neighbourhood. The CAMPUS VIMINALIS SUB AGGERE of the *Notitia* was probably an exercise ground for the Praetorian troops on the outside of the agger near the Porta Viminalis. Hence the eastern ridge of the Viminal and Esquiline beyond the Servian walls must have been very open and airy.

The Esquiline derives more interest from its having been the residence of several distinguished poets and authors than the most splendid palaces could have conferred upon it. Virgil dwelt upon the Esquiline,

close to the gardens of his patron Maecenas. Whether Horace also had a house there cannot be said; but he was certainly a frequent guest with Maecenas; he loved to saunter on "the sunny agger," and he was at last buried close to the tomb of his munificent benefactor at the extremity of the hill. (Suet. *V. Hor.* 20.) Propertius himself informs us that his abode was on the Esquiline (iii. (iv.). 23. 23); where also dwelt the younger Pliny, apparently in the house formerly belonging to the poet Pedo Albinovanus (Plin. *Ep.* iii. 21; Mart. x. 19). Its precise situation will be examined a little further on, when treating of the Lacus Orphei.

The Esquiline and its neighbourhood did not contain many temples of note. That of Tellus, already mentioned, was the most important one; the rest seem for the most part to have been more remarkable for antiquity than for size or beauty. We have already adverted to the ancient *sacraria* mentioned here by Varro (*L. L.* v. 49, seq.); as the LUCUS AND SACELLUM OF JUPITER FAGUTALIS, on the southern side of the Oppius; the LUCUS ESQUILINUS, probably near the Esquiline gate; a LUCUS POETELIUS; a LUCUS MEFITIS, with an aedes, lying near the Vicus Patricius (Festus, *s. v. Septimontio,* p. 351, Müll.); and a LUCUS OF JUNO LUCINA, where, according to Pliny (xvi. 85), a temple was built to that goddess, B. C. 374; although it would appear from Dionysius (iv. 15) that there must have been one there previously in the time of Servius Tullius. An inscription relating to this temple was found in 1770, in digging the foundations of the monastery *delle Paollotte*, in the road which separated the Oppius and Cispius. We learn from Ovid (*Fast.* ii. 435) that the grove lay beneath the Esquiline; but as it appears from Varro that the temple stood on the Cispius, whilst the stone with the inscription in question was found on the side of the Oppius: it is probable that it may have rolled down from the monastery of the *Filippine* on the opposite height (Nibby, *Roma nel Anno* 1838, p. 670; Urlichs, *Röm. Top.* p. 120; Canina, *Indic.* p. 151). The SACELLUM STRENIAE, where the Sacra Via began, probably lay on the S. side of the Carinae, near the Colosseum. It seems not improbable that the LUCUS VENERIS LIBITINAE may also have been situated on the Esquiline, on account of the neighbourhood of the Campus Esquilinus; but there are no authorities by which its site can be satisfactorily determined. It was the great magazine for funereal paraphernalia (cf. Dionys. iv. 15; Festus, *s. v. Rustica Vinalia*, p. 265; Plut. *Q. R.* 23). On the Esquiline were also ALTARS OF MALA FORTUNA and of FEBRIS, the latter close to the Marian monument (Cic. *N. D.* iii. 25; Plin. ii. 5; Val. Max. ii. 5. § 6). We may likewise mention a TEMPLE OF FORTUNA RESPICIENS (Plut. *Fort. R.* 10), of FORTUNA SEIA in the Vicus Sandaliarius (*Inscr. ap. Graev. Thes.* iii. p. 288; Plin. xxxvi. 46), and one of DIANA in the Vicus Patricius, from which men were excluded (Plut. *Q. R.* 3). The HERCULES VICTOR or HERCULES SULLANUS of the *Notitia* was perhaps only a statue. We shall close this list by mentioning a TEMPLE OF SPES VETUS, near the Horti Pallantiani, several times alluded to by Frontinus; of ISIS PATRICIA, probably in the Vicus Patricius; and of MINERVA MEDICA, commonly identified with the ruins of a large circular building in a vineyard near the *Porta Maggiore*. This building bore, in the middle ages, the name of *Le Galuzze*, whence Canina is of opinion that it was the place where the emperor Gallienus was accustomed to divert himself with his court. (Treb. Pollio, *Gall. Duo*, c. 17.) The temple of Minerva Medica mentioned in the *Notitia* may probably have stood in the neighbourhood; but the building in question seems too large to be identified with it.

Among the profane monuments of this district we have had occasion to mention once or twice an object called the TROPHIES OF MARIUS. Valerius Maximus relates that Marius erected two *tropaea* (vi. 9. § 14); and that these must have been on the Esquiline appears from a passage of the same author (ii. 5. § 6), quoted a little while ago respecting the site of the altar of Febris. A building which stands at the junction of the *Via di S. Bibiana* and *Via di P. Maggiore* a little way outside the ancient Porta Esquilina bore during the middle ages the name of Templum Marii, or Cimbrum. and was adorned with those sculptured trophies which were removed in the pontificate of Sixtus V. to the balustrade of the *Piazza del Campidoglio*, where they still remain. (*Ordo Rom.* an. 1143, ap. Mabill. *Mus. Ital.* ii. p. 141; Poggio, *de Var. Fort.* p. 8, ed. Par. 1723.) There can be no doubt, however, that the building so called was no temple, but the *castellum* of an aqueduct, and is in all probability the object mentioned in the *Notitia* as the NYMPHEUM DIVI ALEXANDRI. It must have been one of the principal castella of the Aqua Julia, and from the trophies which stood in the neighbourhood having been applied to its adornment it was mistaken in a later age for a temple erected by Marius. (Canina, *Indicaz.* p. 156, seq. ; Preller, *Regionen*, p. 131.)

Between this Nymphaeum and the Porta Esquilina stands the ARCUS GALLIENI, which must have spanned the ancient Via Praenestina. It is a simple arch of travertine, and we learn from the inscription upon it, which is still legible, that it was erected by a certain M. Aurelius Victor in honour of the emperor Gallienus and his consort Salonina. Originally there were smaller arches on each side of it (*Spec. Rom. Magn.* tab. 24), but at present only the middle one remains.

Close to this arch and between it and the basilica of *S. Maria Maggiore*, lay the FORUM ESQUILINUM and MACELLUM LIVIANUM. This position of the macellum is certain. The basilica just named was built "juxta Macellum Liviae." (Anastas. *V. Liberii* and *V. Sist. III.*) That it was close to the arch of Gallienus appears from the *Ordo Romanus*. ("Intrans sub arcum (Gallieni) ubi dicitur Macellum Lunanum (Livianum) progreditur ante templum Marii quod dicitur Cimbrum," *Ann.* 1143, p. 141.) And the church of *S. Vito* close to the arch was designated as " in Macello." (An. Fulvius, *Ant. R.* ii. c. 6.) But it is a more difficult question to determine whether the Forum Esquilinum and Macellum Livianum were distinct objects or one and the same. We know that the Forum Esquilinum was in existence in B. C. 88, since it is mentioned by Appian (*B. C.* i. 58) as the scene of the struggle between Marius and Sulla. Hence Nibby (*Roma nell' Anno* 1838, tom. ii. p. 25), assuming that the macellum and forum were identical, regarded it as founded by M. Livius Salinator, who was censor with Claudius Nero, B. C. 204. But this view is unsupported by any authority, nor is it probable that the forum had two appellations; whence it seems most likely that the macellum was quite a distinct but adjoining market

founded by Augustus, and named after his consort Livia. (Preller, *Regionen*, p. 131.)

There was also a PORTICUS LIVIAE somewhere on the Esquiline, named in the *Notitia* in the 3rd Region after the baths of Titus. It was a quadrangular porticus (περίστερον), built by Augustus, B. C. 14, on the site of the house of Vedius Pollio, which he had inherited. (Dion Cass. liv. 23.) As the same author (lv. 8) calls it a τεμένισμα, we may conclude that it contained the TEMPLE OF CONCORD mentioned by Ovid. (*Fast.* vi. 633.) It is alluded to by Strabo (v. p. 236), and by both the Plinys. (xiv. 3; *Ep.* i. 5; cf. Becker, *Handb.* p. 542, *Antw.* p. 78.) We also read of a PORTICUS JULIA, built in honour of Caius and Lucius Caesar (Dion Cass. lvi. 27, as emended by Merkel *ad Ov. Fast.* p. cxli.), but its situation cannot be determined.

Near the church of *S. Croce in Gerusalemme*, towards the side of the *Porta Maggiore*, lie the ruins of a large building already alluded to, which in the middle ages bore the name of SESSORIUM. We have remarked that in the *Excerpta Valesiana* at the end of Ammianus Marcellinus it is called a palace (" in palatio, quod appellatur Sessorium," *de Odoac.* 69). It is identified by a passage in Anastasius stating that the church of *S. Croce* was erected there. (*Vit. Silvest* p. 45, Blanch.) Also near the same church, but on the other side of it, and built into the wall of Aurelian, are the remains of a considerable amphitheatre which are usually identified as the AMPHITHEATRUM CASTRENSE of the *Notitia*. Becker, however (*Handb.* p. 552, seq.), denies this identity, his chief objection being the great space which the 5th Regio must have occupied if this building is included in it, and holds that the true Amphitheatrum Castrense must have been near the Castra Praetoria. There are, however, no traces of the remains of an amphitheatre in that direction, and Becker acknowledges (*Handb.* p. 558) that he is unable to give any name to that by *S. Croce*. But there could not have been many structures of this description in Rome, and on the whole it seems most reasonable to conclude with Preller (*Regionen*, p. 132) that the one in question was the Castrense; especially as we know from Procopius (*B. G.* i. 22, seq.) that there was a vivarium, or place for keeping wild beasts used in the sports of the amphitheatre, close to the Porta Praenestina.

In the valley under this amphitheatre were the GARDENS AND CIRCUS OF ELAGABALUS (Lampr. *Heliog.* 14, 23), where the obelisk was found which now stands on the promenade on the Pincian (Ligorio, *Sui Cerchi*, p. 3 ; Canina, *Indic.* p. 178). Just outside the *Porta Maggiore* is the curious MONUMENT OF EURYSACES the baker, which has been spoken of above, p. 760.

The remaining monuments in the district under consideration are few and unimportant. The APOLLO SANDALIARIUS mentioned in the *Notitia* in the 4th Region was one of those statues which Augustus erected in the different Vici. (Suet. *Aug.* 57.) We have said that the temple of Fortuna Seia stood in the Vicus Sandaliarius; and as this temple was included in the domain of the golden house of Nero (Plin. xxxvi. 46) we may conclude that it was in or near the Carinae. (Becker, *Handb.* p. 561.) The COLOSSEUM will be described in a separate section. The 3rd Region, in which it was situated, must doubtless have contained a splendid TEMPLE OF

Isis and Serapis, from which the Region derived its name, but the history of the temple is unknown. The same remark applies to the Moneta mentioned in this Region, which seems to have been the imperial mint. (Preller, *Reg.* p. 124.) It is mentioned in inscriptions of the time of Trajan. (Marini, *Atti, &c.* p. 488.) The Summum Choragium is inexplicable. The Lacus Pastorum or Pastoris was a fountain near the Colosseum, as appears from the *Acta Sanctorum* (*in Eusebio*). The Domus Brutti Praesentis probably lay on the Esquiline. Marcus Aurelius affianced Commodus with the daughter of a Bruttus Praesens. (Capitol. *M. Anton. Ph.* c. 27.) A Porticus Claudia stood at the extremity of Nero's golden house, not far from the colossus of that emperor:—

"Claudia diffusas ubi porticus explicat umbras
     Ultima pars aulae deficientis erat."
                          (Mart. *de Spec.* 2.)

It is mentioned by the Anonymus Einsiedlensis and in the *Mirabilia* under the name of "Palatium Claudii," between the Colosseum and *S. Pietro in Vincoli.* The Ludus Magnus was a gladiatorial school apparently near the *Via di S. Giovanni.* (Canina, *Indic.* p. 108.) The Schola Quaestorum et Caplatorum or Capulatorum seems to have been an office for the scribes or clerks of the quaestors, as the Schola Xantha on the Capitoline was for those of the curule aediles. The Capulatores were those officers who had charge of the *capides* or *capulae*, that is, the bowls with handles used in sacrifices (Varr. *L.L.* v. § 121); but where this schola may have been cannot be said. The Castra Misenatium were the city station for what we may call the marines, or soldiers attached to the fleet and naval station at Misenum, established by Augustus. (Tac. *Ann.* iv. 5; Suet. *Aug.* 49.) This camp appears to have been situated near the church of *S. Vito* and *Via Merulana*, where also there was an *aedicula* of Neptune. (Canina, *Indicax*, p. 110.) The Balneum Daphnidis, perhaps alluded to by Martial (iii. 5. 6), was probably near the Subura and Carinae. Lastly the Lacus Orphei, or fountain of Orpheus, seems to have lain near the church of *S. Lucia*, which bore the epithet *in Orfeo*, or, as the Anonymous calls it, *in Orthea.* It is described in the lines of Martial, in which he desires Thalia to carry his book to Pliny (x. 19. 4, seq.):—

"I, perfer, brevis est labor peractae
     Altum vincere tramitem Suburae.
     Illic Orphea protenus videbis
     Udi vertice lubricum theatri,
     Mirantesque feras avemque regis
     Raptum quae Phryga pertulit Tonanti.
     Illic parva tui domus Pedonis
     Caelata est aquilae minore penna."

From this description it would appear that the fountain was in a circular basin—for such seems to be the meaning of "udum theatrum," because a statue of Orpheus playing on the lyre stood high in the midst of the basin, wet and shining with spray, and surrounded by the fascinated beasts as an audience. (Becker, *Handb.* p. 559, note.) The situation of the fountain near the church mentioned is very clearly indicated in these lines. As Martial lived on the southern extremity of the Quirinal the way from his house to that spot would of course lie through the Subura. At the top of the street leading through it, which, as we have seen, must have been the Vicus Cyprius, a short but steep ascent brought the pedestrian to the top of the Esquiline, where the first object that met his eyes was the fountain in question. The locality is identified by another poem of Martial's addressed to Paulus, who also lived on the Esquiline (v. 22. 4):—

"Alta Subursani vincenda est semita clivi
     Et nunquam sicco sordida saxa gradu;"

where we must not take Clivus Suburanus to be the name of a road, like Clivus Capitolinus, Publicius, &c., but merely a synonymous appellative with what Martial calls "altus trames" in the other poem. It may be further observed that this situation of the fountain agrees with the order of the *Notitia*, where it is named immediately before the Macellum Livianum. Close to it lay the small house formerly inhabited by Pedo Albinovanus, and in Martial's time the residence of his friend the younger Pliny.

XII   The Colles, or the Viminal, Quirinal, and Pincian Hills.

We have already remarked that the three northernmost hills of Rome were called *Colles*, in contradistinction to the others, which were called *Montes.* Only two of the former, the Viminal and Quirinal, were enclosed within the walls of Servius Tullius, and considered as properly belonging to the city; but part of the Pincian was included within the walls of Aurelian.

The Collis Viminalis, the smallest of the three hills, is separated from the Esquiline by the valley through which ran the Vicus Patricius, and by a hollow running towards the rampart of Servius. On the other side, towards the Quirinal, is another valley, which divides it from that hill, at present traversed by the streets called *Via de' Serpenti* and *Via di S. Vitale.* The most northern part of the valley, through which the latter street runs, was the ancient Vallis Quirini (Juv. ii. 133). The hill derived its name from the osiers with which it was anciently covered ("dictum a vimine collem," Id. iii. 71); and upon it was an Altar of Jupiter Viminalis, answering to the Jupiter Fagutalis of the Esquiline. (Varr. *L. L.* v. § 51; Fest. p. 373.) The Viminal was never a district of much importance, and seems to have been chiefly inhabited by the lower classes. The only remarkable building which we find recorded on it is the splendid Palace of C. Aquilius (Plin. xvii. 2). The existence of some baths of Agrippina upon it rests only on traditions of the middle ages. The baths of Diocletian, which lay on the ridge which united the Viminal and Quirinal, will be described in the section on the thermae. The Sacellum of Naenia lay without the Porta Viminalis. (Paul. Diac. p. 163.)

After the Palatine and Capitoline hills, the Quirinal was the most ancient quarter of the city. As the seat of the Sabine part of the population of Rome, it acquired importance in the period of its early history, which however it did not retain when the two nations had become thoroughly amalgamated. The Quirinal is separated from the Pincian on the N. by a deep valley; its western side is skirted by the Campus Martius; the manner in which it is parted from the Viminal by the Vallis Quirini has been already described. The street which ran through this last valley was called VICUS LONGUS, as we learn from the Anonymous of Einsiedlen, who mentions the church of S. Vitalis as situated " in vico longo." We find its name recorded in Livy (x. 23), and Valerius Maximus (ii. 5. § 6). Of the different ancient divisions of the Collis Quirinalis and of the origin of its name, we have already spoken in the former part of this article.

The Quirinal abounded in ancient fanes and temples. One of the earliest foundations of this sort was the TEMPLE OF QUIRINUS, erected by Numa to Romulus after his apotheosis. The first practical notice that we find of it is, however, in B. C. 435, when Livy (iv. 21) records a meeting of the senate in it; a fact which shows that it must have been a considerable building. A new one was dedicated, probably on the same spot, by L. Papirius Cursor, B. C. 292. (Liv. x. 46; Plin. vii. 60.) This structure appears to have been burnt in B. C. 48, and we do not hear of its re-erection till B. C. 15, when Augustus rebuilt it, as recorded in the *Monumentum Ancyranum*, and by Dion Cassius (liv. 19). Yet in the interval between these dates we find it alluded to as still existing (*Id.* xliii. 45; Cic. *ad Att.* xiii. 28), whence we may conclude that it had been only partially destroyed. Dion (liv. 19) describes the new structure of Augustus as having 76 columns, equalling the years which he had lived. Hence, it appears to have been the same building as that adduced by Vitruvius (iii. 2, 7) as an example of the *dipteros octastylos;* for that kind of temple had a double row of columns all round; namely, two rows of 8 each at the front and back; and, without counting the outside ones of these over again, two rows of 11 each at the sides (32 + 44 = 76). This noble portico appears to have been the same alluded to by Martial as the resort of the idlers of the vicinity (ix. 1. 9). Topographers are universally agreed that it was situated on the height over *S. Vitale* in the neighbourhood of *S. Andrea del Noviziato.* (Becker, *Handb.* p. 573; Urlichs, *Beschr.* iii. 2, 366; Canina, *Indic.* p. 185.) There appears to have been also a SACELLUM QUIRINALIS near the Porta Collina.

All the more interesting traditions respecting the Quirinal belong to the reign of Numa. One of the residences of that Sabine monarch was situated on this hill (Plut. *Num.* 14; Solin. i. 21), where he also founded a citadel, or capitol; and where his successor Tullus Hostilius, in pursuance of a vow made in the Sabine War, repeated, as it were in duplicate, Numa's peculiar institution of the Salian worship (Liv. i. 27; Dionys. ii. 70). All these things show very clearly the distinction between the Roman and Sabine cities during the reigns of the first monarchs. On the Quirinal, the Salian priests with their ancilia were attached to the worship of Quirinus, as, in the Romulean city, they were to that of Mars (" Quid de ancilibus vestris, Mars Gradive, tuque Quirine pater (loquar)?" Liv. v. 52); and the priests were called, by way of distinction, Salii Agonenses, or Collini, from the name of the hill (" In libris Saliorum quorum cognomen Agonensium," Varr. *L. L.* vi. § 14; cf. Dionys. *l. c.*, where, however, he erroneously speaks of a λόφος Κολλῖνος.)

Next to the temple of Quirinus, proceeding in a westerly direction, as may be inferred from the order in which the objects are mentioned in the *Curiosum* (the *Notitia* somewhat differs), stood a STATUE OF MAMURIUS; and then, after an interval occupied in

later times by the baths of Constantine, — the site of the present *Palazzo Rospigliosi.* — followed the VETUS CAPITOLIUM, or citadel of Numa. Whether Mamurius was another name for Mamers, the Sabine god of war, of which, according to Varro (*L. L.* v. § 73), the Roman name of Mars was only a corruption, or whether it was the name of the reputed maker of the ancilia (Paul. Diac. p. 131, Müll.), matters but little; the statue is equally connected with the ancient Salian rites, and therefore one of the most venerable objects in the city. We find a CLIVUS MAMURI mentioned in the middle ages in the neighbourhood of *S. Vitale* (Anastas. *V. Innoc. I.* p. 64, Blanch.), which no doubt took its name from this statue; whence we may infer that it stood near the temple of Quirinus; since the church of *S. Vitale* and that of *S. Andrea*, where the temple stood, are close together.

We have remarked in the former part of this article that the ancient Capitol of Numa probably stood on the height of *Magnanapoli.* It contained, like the Palatine before it and the Capitoline subsequently, a temple to the three divinities, Jupiter, Juno, and Minerva, as we learn from Varro: " Clivos proximus a Flora susus versus Capitolium vetus, quod ibi sacellum Jovis, Junonis, Minervae; et id antiquius quam aedis, quae in Capitolio facta" (*L. L.* v. § 158). Its site may be determined by that of another ancient sanctuary, the TEMPLE OF FLORA. In the order of the *Curiosum* and *Notitia* that temple stands between the Capitolium Vetus and the temple (or temples) of Salus and Serapis. The temple of Salus must undoubtedly have been situated near the Porta Salutaris, which, as we have before remarked, took its name from that sanctuary; and we must consequently seek for the temple of Flora on the W. side of the Quirinal, or that which faced towards the Campus Martius. That it stood on this side is confirmed by what Martial says respecting the situation of his house, which, as we learn from one of his epigrams, lay near the temple of Flora (v. 22. 2):—

" Sed Tiburtinae sum proximus accola pilae
    Qua videt antiquum rustica Flora Jovem."

(Cf. vi. 27.) From which we also learn that the temple of Flora could not have been very far from that of Jupiter in Numa's Capitol; as indeed likewise appears from the passage of Varro before quoted, with the addition that it must have lain on a lower part of the hill. But as Martial's house is thus shown to have been near the temple of Flora, so also that it was on the W. side of the hill appears from another epigram (i. 108. 2):—

" At mea Vipsanas spectant coenacula lauros
    Factus in hac ego sum jam regione senex."

It can hardly be doubted that this passage contains an allusion to some laurel trees growing near the Porticus Vipsania, erected, as will appear in a subsequent section, near the Via Lata by Agrippa, whose family name was Vipsanius. This portico is plainly alluded to in another passage of Martial (iv. 18), under the name of Vipsaniae Columnae. There is nothing surprising in Martial's indicating a locality by certain trees. In ancient Rome trees were noted objects, and claimed a considerable share of public attention, as we have already seen with regard to several that grew in or about the forum. Two laurel trees grew before the imperial palace (Tert. *Apol.* 35); and in front of the temple of Quirinus just described were two sacred myrtles, which were characterised by distinctive appellations as *patricia* and *plebeia*. But, to have faced the Porticus Vipsania, Martial's house must not only have been situated on the western side of the Quirinal, but also towards its southern extremity; which likewise appears from what has been said in the preceding section respecting the *route* from it to that of his friend Pliny being through the Subura and Vicus Cyprius; for this would have been a roundabout way had Martial dwelt towards the northern part of the hill.

All these circumstances tend to show that Numa's Capitol must have stood on the spot before indicated, and the temple of Flora a little to the N. of it. The part of the hill which it occupied was probably that called LATIARIS in the Argive fragments. The part styled COLLIS SALUTARIS must have been that near the gate of the same name, derived from the ancient SACELLUM OF SALUS, which stood near it; in place of which a regular TEMPLE OF SALUS was dedicated by C. Junius Bubulcus, B. C. 203 (Liv. ix. 43, x. 1), and adorned with paintings by Fabius Pictor. These were still to be seen in the time of Pliny, when the temple was destroyed by fire in the reign of Claudius (xxxv. 7; cf. Val. Max. viii. 14. § 6).

Cicero's friend Atticus lived close to the temple of Salus (" —tuae vicinae Salutis," *ad Att.* iv. 1), and at the same time near that of Quirinus: " Certe non longe a tuis aedibus inambulans post excessum suum Romulus Proculo Julio dixerit, se deum esse et Quirinum vocari, templumque sibi dedicari in eo loco jusserit." (*De Leg.* i. 1.) The vicinity of the temples is likewise indicated in another passage relating to a statue of Caesar, which had been erected in that of Quirinus: " De Caesare *vicino* scripseram ad te, quia cognoram ex tuis literis: eum σύνναον Quirino malo quam Saluti" (*ad Att.* xii. 45). Hence the sites of the two temples in question are still further established. For as that of Salus lay on the N. side of the hill, near the Porta Salutaris, and that of Quirinus some 200 yards to the S. of it, at the church of *S. Andrea*, so we may assume that the house of Atticus lay between the two, and he would thus be a close neighbour to both.

Another ancient sacrarium on the Quirinal was that of SEMO SANCUS or DIUS FIDIUS. We have shown, when treating of the Servian gates, that the Porta Sanqualis took its name from this sacellum; and Livy (viii. 20) describes it as facing the temple of Quirinus. Hence it must have stood on or near the site of the *Palazzo Quirinale*, between the temple of Salus and that of Flora. It had a perforated roof, for the deity loved the open air, whence his title of Dius; and some thought that no oath by this god should be sworn under a roof. (Varr. *L. L.* v. § 66.) Sancus was an old Sabine deity, and his temple at Rome appears to have been founded by Tatius. (Ov. *Fast.* vi. 213; Prop. v. 9. 74; Tertull. *ad Nat.* ii. 9.) Its antiquity is attested by the circumstance that the distaff and sandals of Tanaquil, the wife of Tarquinius Priscus, are recorded to have been preserved in it, and are said to have been in existence down to the time of Augustus. (Plin. viii. 74; Plut. *Q. R.* 30.) It appears to have been rebuilt by Tarquinius Superbus, but its dedication was reserved for Sp. Postumius. (Dionys. ix. 60.) The part of the hill where it stood must have been the COLLIS MUCIALIS of the Argive fragments. (Varr. v. § 52.)

There were several TEMPLES OF FORTUNA on the Quirinal, but they do not seem to have been of much importance; and the notices respecting them are very obscure. Vitruvius (iii. 2) mentions three which stood close together at the Porta Collina, belonging perhaps to those alluded to by Ovid under the name of FORTUNA PUBLICA (*Fast.* iv. 375, v. 729), and by Livy, who mentions a temple of FORTUNA PRIMIGENIA on this hill (xxxiv. 53). There was also an ALTAR OF FORTUNA in the Vicus Longus. (Plut. *Fort. Rom.* 10.)

In the street just named stood also a SACELLUM PUDICITIAE PLEBEIAE, founded by Virginia, the daughter of Aulus, after the quarrel between the matrons in that of Pudicitia Patricia alluded to in a former section (Liv. x. 23). Outside of the Porta Collina was a temple of VENUS ERYCINA, near which the Ludi Apollinares were held when the circus had been overflowed by the Tiber. (Liv. xxx. 38; Appian, *B. C.* i. 93.) Of the TEMPLE OF SERAPIS, mentioned in the *Notitia* along with that of Salus, nothing further is known, except that from the fragment of an inscription found near the church of *S. Agata alla Subura*, where possibly the temple may have stood, it may be inferred that it was dedicated by Caracalla. (Gruter, lxxxv. 6; Preller, *Reg.* p. 124.)

These are all the ascertained temples that lay on the Quirinal; for it is a disputed point whether we are to place on this hill the splendid TEMPLE OF SOL, erected by Aurelian. (Aur. Vict. *Caes.* 25; Eutrop. ix. 15 (9); Vopisc. *Aurel.*) Altogether, however, the most probable conclusion is that it stood there, and Becker's objections admit of an easy answer (*Handb.* p. 587, seq.). By those who assume it to have been on the Quirinal it is commonly identified with the remains of a very large building, on the declivity of the hill, in the *Colonna* gardens, on which spot a large Mithraic stone was discovered with the inscription "Soli Invicto." (Vignoli, *de Columna Antoniniana*, p. 174.) This position may be very well reconciled with all the ancient accounts respecting the temple. Becker objects that it is mentioned in the *Notitia* in the 7th Region (Via Lata). But this Region adjoined the western side of the Quirinal, and the temple of the Sun may have been recorded in it, just as many buildings on the declivity of the Aventine are enumerated in the 11th Region, or Circus Maximus. In the *Catalogus Imperatorum Vienn.* (ii. p. 246, Ronc.) it is said of Aurelian, "Templum Solis et Castra in Campo Agrippae dedicavit;" and it will appear in the next section that the Campus Agrippae must have been situated under this part of the Quirinal. Becker assumes from the description given by Vopiscus of his ride with Tiberianus, the conversation during which was the occasion of his writing the life of Aurelian, that the temple in question could not have been so near the Palatine as the spot indicated (" Ibi quum animus a causis atque a negotiis publicis solutus ac liber vacaret, sermonem multum a Palatio usque ad hortos Valerianos instituit, et in ipso praecipue de vita principum. Quumque ad templum Solis venissemus ab Aureliano principe consecratum quod ipse nonnihilum ex ejus origine sanguinem duceret, quaesivit," &c., Vopisc. *Aurel.* 1). We do not know where the Horti Valeriani lay; they might possibly, as assumed by Preller, have been identical with those of Lucullus on the Pincian, subsequently in the possession of Valerius Asiaticus (Tac. *Ann.* xi. 1), though these continued to bear in general the name of Lucullus. But Becker interprets the passage wrongly when he thinks that the temple of Sol lay beyond these gardens: on the contrary, the passing that temple gave rise to the conversation, which lasted till Vopiscus and his friend arrived at the Horti Valeriani, wherever these may have been; and if they were on the Pincian, the temple of Sol, in the locality indicated, would have been on the road to them from the Palatium. Lastly, we may observe that the Quirinal had, in very early times, been dedicated to the worship of Sol, who was a Sabine deity (Varro, *L. L.* v. § 74); and there was a PULVINAR SOLIS in the neighbourhood of the temple of Quirinus. (Quint. *Inst. Or.* i. 7; *Fast. Capran. Id. Aug.*; cf. Urlichs, *Beschr.* iii. 2. p. 386; Canina, *Indic.* p. 210, seq.; Preller, *Regionen*, p. 137.)

Such were the sanctuaries of the Quirinal. The ancient topographers, who are followed by the modern Italians, have assigned two circi to this quarter: the CIRCUS FLORAE near the temple of the same name, and the CIRCUS SALLUSTII in the gardens of Sallust, between the Quirinal and Pincian. The former has certainly been invented by misconstruing an inscription relating to the games of Flora in the Circus Maximus. (Becker, *Handb.* p. 673.) It is more doubtful whether a Circus Sallustii may not have existed. We have seen from a passage of Livy that the Ludi Apollinares were performed outside the Porta Collina when the overflowing of the Tiber prevented their performance in the usual place; and, according to Canina (*Indicas.* p. 199), traces of a circus are still visible in that locality. But none is mentioned in the catalogues of the Regions, nor does it occur in any ancient author. The HORTI SALLUSTIANI, however, undoubtedly lay in the valley between the Quirinal and Pincian, but their exact extent cannot be determined. They were formed by Sallust the historian with the money which he had extorted in Numidia. (Dion Cass. xliii. 9.) The house of Sallust lay near to the (subsequent) Porta Salaria, as we learn from Procopius, who relates that it was burnt in the storm of the city by Alaric, and that its half-consumed remains still existed in his time. (*B. V.* i. 2.) The Anonymous of Einsiedlen mentions some THERMAE SALLUSTIANAE near the church of *S. Susanna;* and the older topographers record that the neighbourhood continued to be called *Salustricum* or *Salustium* even in their days. (Andr. Fulvius, *de Urb. Ant.* p. 140; Luc. Fauno, *Ant. di R.* iv. 10. p. 120.) Becker (*Handb.* p. 585) raises a difficulty about the situation of these gardens from a passage in Tacitus (*Hist.* iii. 82), which, however, presents none if rightly understood. The Flavian troops which had penetrated to the gardens of Sallust *on their left* were those which marched on the Flaminian, not the Salarian, way, just as Nero is described as finding his way back to these gardens from the same road. (Tac. *Ann.* xiii. 49.)

The Horti Sallustiani subsequently became imperial property, though in what manner is unknown. The first notice which we find of them as such occurs under Nero in the passage just cited from Tacitus. Several emperors are described as residing in them, as Vespasian, Nerva, and Aurelian. (Dion Cass. lxvi. 10; Vopisc. *Aur.* 49; Hieron. p. 445, Ronc.)

Also close to the Porta Collina, but inside and to the right of it, lay the CAMPUS SCELERATUS, im-

mediately under the *agger*. The spot obtained its name from being the place where Vestal Virgins convicted of unchastity were buried alive; for even in this frightful punishment they retained their privilege of being interred within the walls. Dionysius attributes the introduction of this mode of execution to Tarquinius Priscus; and, according to Livy, the first example of its application was in the case of Minucia, B. C. 348. Dionysius, however, calls the first vestal who suffered Pinaria. (Dionys. ii. 67, iii. 67; Liv. viii. 15; Plut. *Num.* 10.)

The emperors appear to have shared with the vestals the privilege of intramural interment, although they did not always avail themselves of it. Indeed, according to Hieronymus (vol. i. p. 449, Ronc.), Trajan was the only emperor buried within the walls; but this statement is certainly erroneous, since Domitian erected a magnificent mausoleum for the Flavian family somewhere between the gardens of Sallust and the spot subsequently occupied by the baths of Diocletian. It is the object mentioned under the name of "Gens Flavia" in the *Notitia*, and is alluded to in several epigrams of Martial, in one of which he designates it as being near his own dwelling (v. 64. 5):—

      " Tam vicina jubent nos vivere Mausolea,
         Quum doceant ipsos posse perire deos."

(Cf. ix. 2 and 35; Stat. *Silv.* iv. 3. 18.) It was commonly called TEMPLUM GENTIS FLAVIAE, as appears from Suetonius (*Dom.* 17); but the same passage shows it to have been a sepulchre also, since the ashes of Julia, the daughter of Titus, as well as those of Domitian himself, were deposited in it. (Cf. Becker, *de Muris,* &c. p. 69.) It was erected on the site of the house in which Domitian was born, designated as being AD MALUM PUNICUM (Suet. *Dom.* 1); which name occurs again in the *Notitia*, and could not, therefore, have been applied to the whole Region, as Preller supposes (*Regionen*, p. 69), but must have denoted some particular spot, perhaps a vicus, called after a pomegranate tree that grew there. We have already adverted to the importance attached to trees growing within the city.

The only other object that remains to be noticed on the Quirinal is the PRAETORIAN CAMP, since the baths of Diocletian will be described under the proper head. We have related in the former part of this article that the Castra Praetoria were established in the reign of Tiberius outside the Porta Collina, to the eastward of the agger. They were arranged after the usual model of a Roman camp, and were enclosed within a brick wall, of which there are still some remains. (Canina, *Indicas.* p. 194.) They were included within the wall of Aurelian, which preserved their outline. We need only add that the 6th Region of Augustus, of which the Esquiline formed the principal part, was called ALTA SEMITA, from a road which ran along the whole back of the hill, answering to the modern *Strada di Porta Pia*.

The PINCIAN HILL presents but few objects of importance. Its earlier name was COLLIS HORTORUM, or HORTULORUM, derived from the gardens which covered it; and it was not till a late period of the empire that it obtained the name of Mons Pincius, from a magnificent palace of the Pincian family which stood upon it. (Urlichs, *Beschr.* vol. iii. part. ii. p. 572, *Röm. Top.* p. 136.) This DOMUS PINCIANA is rendered interesting from its having been the residence of Belisarius during his defence of Rome. It is the same building mentioned by Procopius under the name of παλάτιον. (Procop. *B. G.* ii. 8. 9 ; Anastasius, *V. Silver.* pp. 104, 106, Blanch.) The part of the hill included within the later city was bounded by the wall of Aurelian, by the valley which separates the Pincian from the Quirinal, and by the Campus Martius on the west.

The most famous place on the Pincian was the GARDENS OF LUCULLUS. Their situation is determined by a passage in Frontinus, from which we learn that the arches of the Aqua Virgo began under them. (*Aq.* 2.) This must have been in the street called *Capo le Case*, since the arches are still in existence from that spot to the *Fontana di Trevi.* (Canina, *Indic.* p. 395.) The early history of these gardens is obscure. They were probably formed by a Lucullus, and subsequently came into the possession of Valerius Asiaticus, by whom they were so much improved that Messalina's desire of possessing them caused the death of Valerius. (Tac. *Ann.* xi. 1, 32, 37.) They appear to have been also called after him " Horti Asiatici " (Becker, *Handb.* p. 591), and it is possible, as we have said before, that they may sometimes have borne the name of " Horti Valeriani." They were the scene of Messalina's infamous marriage with Silius (Juv. *S.* x. 334) and of her death by the order of Claudius. (Tac. *Ann.* xi. 37.) The gardens remained in the possession of the imperial family, and were reckoned the finest they had. (Plut. *Lucull.* 39.) The family of the Domitii, to which Nero belonged, had previously possessed property, or at all events a sepulchre, on the Pincian; and it was here that the ashes of that emperor were deposited. (Suet. *Ner.* 50.) Popular tradition places it on that part of the hill which overhangs the church of *S. Maria del Popolo* near the gate of the same name.

XIII. THE CAMPUS MARTIUS, CIRCUS FLAMINIUS, AND VIA LATA.

The whole plain which lies between the Pincian, Quirinal, and Capitoline hills on the E. and the Tiber on the W.,—on which the principal part of modern Rome stands,—may be designated generally by the name of CAMPUS MARTIUS, though strictly speaking it was divided into three separate districts. It is narrow at the northern part between the Pincian and the river, but afterwards expands to a considerable breadth by the winding of the Tiber. It is terminated by the approach of the latter to the Capitoline hill, between which and the stream a part of the Servian wall forming its southern boundary anciently ran. It was cut through its whole length by a straight road, very nearly corresponding with the modern *Corso*, running from the Porta Flaminia to the foot of the Capitol. The southern part of the district lying between this road and the hills formed, under the name of Via Lata, the 7th of the Augustan Regions; but how far it extended to the N. cannot be determined. From its northern boundary, wherever it may have been, to the Porta Flaminia and beyond that gate, the road before described was called Via Flaminia. The southern portion of the Campus Martius lying between the same road and the Tiber, as far N. as the modern *Piazza Navona* and *Piazza Colonna*, constituted the 9th Region of Augustus, under the name of CIRCUS FLAMINIUS.

In the earlier times all this district between the

hills and the river was private property, and was applied to agricultural purposes. We have already related in the former part of this article, how, after the expulsion of the Tarquins, the Campus Martius was assigned, or rather perhaps restored, to the public use. But the southern portion of the plain appears still to have belonged to private owners. The most considerable of these possessions was the PRATA FLAMINIA, or CAMPUS FLAMINIUS, which, however, must soon have become public property, since we find that assemblies of the people were held here under the decemvirs. (Liv. iii. 54.) Among these private estates must have been the AGER CATI, in which was a fountain whence the stream called Petronia flowed into the Tiber, and seems to have formed the southern boundary of the proper Campus Martius (" Petronia amnis est in Tiberim perfluens, quam magistratus auspicato transeunt cum in Campo quid agere volunt," Fest. p. 250; cf. Paul. Diac. p. 45); also the CAMPUS TIBERINUS, the property of the vestal Taracia, or Suffetia, which she presented to the people. (Plin. xxxiv. 11.)

We shall begin the description of this district from its southern side; that is, from the Servian wall between the Capitoline hill and the Tiber. Immediately before the Porta Carmentalis lay the FORUM OLITORIUM. It was, as its name implies, the vegetable market. (Varr. *L.L.* v. § 146.) The ELEPHAS HERBARIUS, or bronze statue of an elephant, which stood near the boundary of the 8th Region (v. *Notitia*) has by some topographers been connected with this forum, merely, it would seem, from the epithet *herbarius*; but the wall must have made here a decided separation between the 8th and 9th Regions. There were several temples in the Forum Olitorium, as those of Spes, of Juno Sospita, of Pietas, and of Janus. The TEMPLE OF SPES was founded by M. Atilius Calatinus in the First Punic War. (Tac. *Ann.* ii. 49; Cic. *N. D.* ii. 23; Liv. xxi. 62.) It was destroyed in the great fire which devastated this neighbourhood during the Second Punic War (Liv. xxiv. 47), and though soon rebuilt, was again burnt down in B. C. 30; after which the restored temple was dedicated by Germanicus. (Tac. *l. c.*) The TEMPLE OF JUNO was consecrated by C. Cornelius Cethegus in B. C. 195. There is a confusion in Livy between the names of SOSPITA and MATUTA applied to this deity (xxxii. 30, xxxiv. 53); and it is difficult to decide which epithet may be the correct one. The TEMPLE OF PIETAS is connected with the well-known legend of the Roman daughter who nourished her father (or mother) when in prison with the milk of her breast, and is said to have resided on the spot where the temple was erected. (Festus, p. 209; Val. Max. ii. 5. § 1.) It was dedicated in B. C. 180 by the son of M. Acilius Glabrio, in pursuance of a vow made by his father, on the day when he engaged king Antiochus at Thermopylae. (Liv. xl. 34.) It was pulled down in order to make room for the theatre of Marcellus. (Plin. vii. 36.) There appears, however, to have been another temple of Pietas in the Circus Flaminius itself. (Jul. Obs. 114.) Close by was the TEMPLE OF JANUS, to which we have already adverted in the former part of this article. The greater portion of the Forum Olitorium must have been engrossed by the THEATRE OF MARCELLUS, of which we shall speak in another section; and it may therefore be doubted whether it continued to serve the purposes of a market when the theatre was erected.   On the Forum Olitorium also stood the COLUMNA LACTARIA, so called because children were provided with milk at that spot.   (Paul. Diac. p. 118.)   The supposition that there was likewise a FORUM PISCARIUM in this neighbourhood rests only on a doubtful reading in Varro. (*L. L.* v. § 146.)

The Campus Flaminius began at an early period to be occupied with temples and other public buildings.   One of the most ancient and renowned of the former was the TEMPLE OF APOLLO.   The site appears to have been sacred to that deity from very early times, and was called APOLLINARE, probably from some altar which stood there. (Liv. iii. 63.) The temple was dedicated in B. C. 430, in consequence of a vow made with the view of averting a pestilence. (Liv. iv. 25, 29.)   It remained down to the time of Augustus the only temple of Apollo at Rome, and must have been of considerable size, since the senate frequently assembled in it.   It lay between the Forum Olitorium and Circus Flaminius, or, according to Pliny's designation, which amounts to the same thing, close to the Porticus Octaviae. (Ascon. *ad Cic. in Tog. Cand.* p. 90, Orell.; Plin. xxxvi. 5. s. 34.)

Another celebrated and important temple was the AEDES BELLONAE, since it was the chief place for assemblies of the senate when it was necessary for them to meet outside of the *pomoerium ;* as, for instance, when generals *cum imperio* were soliciting them for a triumph, for the reception of foreign ambassadors whom it was not advisable to admit into the city, and other similar occasions.   Close to it was one of the three SENACULA mentioned by Festus (p. 347).   The temple of Bellona is said to have been built in pursuance of a vow made by Appius Claudius Caecus, in the battle against the Etruscans, B. C. 297 (Liv. x. 19); but according to Pliny (xxxv. 3) it was built by Appius Claudius Regillensis two centuries earlier, who placed the images of his forefathers in it, B. C. 494; in which case the vow of Appius Claudius Caecus must have been accomplished by restoring the former temple.   In front of the temple lay a small area, on which stood the COLUMNA BELLICA, so called because it was the spot whence the Fetialis threw a lance in the ceremony of declaring war. When the war with Pyrrhus broke out this custom could not be observed in the usual manner by throwing the lance into the enemy's country; wherefore, a captured soldier of Pyrrhus's was made to buy a piece of ground near the temple, which symbolised the territory of the enemy; and into this the lance was flung on all subsequent occasions of declaring war against a people whose country lay beyond the sea. (Serv. *ad Aen.* ix. 53.)   This custom was observed as late as the time of Marcus Aurelius. (Dion Cass. lxxi. 33.)   There are two points in dispute about this temple; first, whether the area containing the Columna Bellica stood before or behind it; and secondly, whether the temple itself stood at the eastern or western end of the Circus Flaminius; which latter question also concerns the site of the temple of HERCULES CUSTOS, as will be seen from the following lines of Ovid (*Fast.* vi. 206) :—

" Prospicit a templo summum brevis area Circum:
   Est ibi non parvae parva columna notae.
 Hinc solet hasta manu, belli praenuntia, mitti,
   In regem et gentes quam placet arma capi.
 Altera pars Circi custode sub Hercule tuta est
   Quod deus Euboico carmine munus habet."

In the first line Becker (*Handb.* p. 607) reads " a tergo," with Merkel, instead of " a templo," which is the reading of Heinsius, and of most editions, and thus places the *area* behind the temple.   But this was not the usual situation for an area, and there is express authority that the column stood *before* the temple. (Paul. Diac. p. 33; Serv. *l. c.,* where Becker admits that we should read " ante aedem " for " ante pedem.")   The other point respecting the site of the temple depends on whether " summus circus " means the part where the *carceres* were, or the circular end.   Becker adopts the former meaning, and consequently places the temple of Bellona at the eastern end of the circus, and that of Hercules Custos at the western end.   Urlichs reverses this order, and quotes in support of his view Salmasius, *ad Solin.* p. 639, A.: " Pars circi, ubi metae ultimae *superior* dicitur; *inferior* ad carceres." (*Antic.* p. 31.)   This is a point that is not altogether established; but Becker's view seems in this case the more probable one, as will appear a little further on, when we come to treat of the Villa Publica.

The CIRCUS FLAMINIUS itself, which will be described in another section, lay under the Capitol, on which side its *carceres* were, and extended in a westerly direction towards the river.   Between it and the theatre of Marcellus lay the PORTICUS OCTAVIAE,— which must be carefully distinguished from the Porticus Octavia, built by Cn. Octavius,— enclosing TEMPLES of JUPITER STATOR and JUNO. This portico occupied the site of a former one built by Q. Caecilius Metellus, after his Macedonian triumph, and called after him PORTICUS METELLI. It seems most probable that the two temples before alluded to were in existence before the time when Metellus erected his portico; but the notices on this subject in ancient authors are obscure and contradictory. (Becker, *Handb.* p. 608, seq.)   There can be no doubt, however, that the Porticus Octaviae superseded that of Metellus. (Plin. xxxiv. 14; cf. Plut. *C. Gracch.* 4.)   It was erected by Augustus, and dedicated in the name of his sister; but at what date is uncertain. (Suet. *Aug.* 29; Ov. *A. A.* iii. 391.)   It contained a library, which was destroyed in the great fire in the reign of Titus, with all its literary treasures. (Dion Cass. xlix. 43, lxvi. 24; Suet. *Ill. Gramm.* 21.)   This library was probably in the part called the " Schola in porticibus Octaviae," and, like the Palatine library, was sometimes used for assemblies of the senate. (Plin. xxxv. 10. s. 114, xxxvi. 5, s. 22. s. 28; Dion Cass. lv. 8.)   Hence, it was even called Octavia Curia, and sometimes Octaviae Opera.   The church of *S. Angelo in Pescaria* now stands opposite to its principal entrance towards the river.

Close to the Porticus Octaviae, on its western side, lay the PORTICUS PHILIPPI, enclosing a temple of HERCULES MUSARUM.   This temple was built by M. Fulvius Nobilior, the conqueror of the Aetolians (Cic. *p. Arch.* 11), and rebuilt by L. Marcius Philippus, the step-father of Augustus, who also surrounded it with the portico.   (Suet. *Aug.* 29.) The name of the temple does not signify, as Becker supposes (*Handb.* p. 613), that it was dedicated to Hercules *and* the Muses, but to Hercules as leader of the Muses (Μουσαγέτης), the genitive, *Musarum,* depending on Hercules, as appears from coins of the Gens Pomponia, where he is represented in that character, with the legend HERCULES MUSARUM, as well as from an inscription in Gruter (mlxx,

5) HERCVLI . MVSARVM . PYTHVS (Urlichs, *Röm. Topogr.* p. 140, and *Antw.* p. 32). Indeed Eumenius expressly says that Fulvius Nobilior when in Greece had heard "Herculem Musagetem esse comitem ducemque Musarum" (*pro Inst. Schol. Aug.* p. 195, Arntz.); and we learn from Ovid that the statue of Hercules represented him with a lyre (*Fast.* vi. 810) : —

"Annuit Alcides, increpuitque lyram."

The vicinity of the temple and portico is indicated in Martial (v. 49. 8).

It is supposed that the THEATRUM BALBI lay close to the western side of this portico, and, a little farther on, opposite the round end of the circus, but rather to the north of it, the THEATRUM POMPEII; of which latter there are still some remains at the *Palazzo Pio.* Pompey's theatre must have lain close to the boundary between the Campus Martius and Circus Flaminius since Pliny mentions that a colossal statue of Jupiter, erected by the emperor Claudius in the Campus, was called Pompeianus from its vicinity to the theatre ("Talis in Campo Martio Jupiter a Divo Claudio Caesare dicatus, qui vocatur Pompeianus a vicinitate theatri," xxxiv. 18). The same thing might also be inferred from Cicero (" Quid enim loci natura afferre potest, ut in porticu Pompeii potius quam in Campo ambulemus," *de Fato,* 4.) Hence it would appear that the boundary of the two districts, after proceeding along the northern side of the Circus Flaminius, took a north-westerly direction towards the river. The PORTICUS POMPEII adjoined the *scena* of his theatre, and afforded a shelter to the spectators in the event of bad weather. (Vitruv. v. 9.) But what conferred the greatest interest on this group of buildings was the CURIA POMPEII, a large hall or hexedra in the portico itself, sometimes used for the representation of plays as well as for assemblies of the senate. It was here that Caesar was assassinated, at the base of Pompey's statue; an event which caused it to be regarded as a *locus sceleratus,* and to be walled up in consequence. (Cic. *Div.* ii. 9; Dion Cass. xliv. 16, 52; Suet. *Caes.* 80, 88; Plut. *Brut.* 14, *Caes.* 66, &c.) The statue of Pompey, however, was first taken out by order of Augustus, and placed under a marble arch or Janus, opposite the portico. (Suet. *Aug.* 31.) It is a question whether the portico styled HECATOSTYLON, from its having a hundred columns, was only another name for the portico of Pompey, or quite a distinct building. It is sometimes mentioned in a manner which would seem to intimate that it was identical with the Porticus Pompeii. Thus both are said to have had groves of plane-trees (Prop. ii. 32. 11), and to have been consumed in one and the same fire. (Hieron. *Chron.* p. 475, Ronc.) The following lines of Martial, however, appear to show that they were separate, but adjoining buildings (ii. 14. 6) : —

"Inde petit centum pendentia tecta columnis;
Illinc Pompeii dona nemusque duplex "

From these lines, and from two fragments of the Capitoline Plan, Canina has correctly inferred that there were two distinct porticoes, and that the Hecatostylon adjoined the N. side of that of Pompey. (*Indic.* p. 373.) Pompey also built a private dwelling-house near his theatre, in addition to the house which he possessed in the Carinae. The former of these seems to have been situated in some gardens.

(Plut. *Pomp.* 40, 44.) We find other HORTI POMPEII mentioned with the epithet of *superiores,* probably from their lying on the Pincian hill. (Ascon. *ad Cic. Mil. Arg.* p. 37, and c. 25. p. 50, Orell.)

Near the theatre of Pompey was also the PORTICUS OCTAVIA, which, as we have said, must be carefully distinguished from the Porticus Octaviae. It was a double portico originally erected by Cn. Octavius after his triumph over Perseus. It was likewise called CORINTHIA, from its columns being adorned with bronze capitals. (Plin. xxxiv. 7: Vell. Pat. ii. 1; Fest. p. 178.) Augustus rebuilt it, but dedicated it again in the name of its founder. Also near the theatre was the TRIUMPHAL ARCH OF TIBERIUS, erected by Claudius. (Suet. *Claud.* 11.)

Other temples in the district of the Circus Flaminius, besides those already enumerated, were a TEMPLE OF DIANA, and another of JUNO REGINA, — different from that of Juno in the Porticus Octaviae,— both dedicated by M. Aemilius Lepidus, B. C. 179. (Liv. xl. 52.) An AEDES FORTUNAE EQUESTRIS vowed by Q. Fulvius Flaccus in a battle against the Celtiberians, B. C. 176. (Liv. xl. 40, 44, xlii. 3, 10.) It stood near the theatre of Pompey in the time of Vitruvius (iii. 3. § 2, Schn.), but seems to have disappeared before that of Tacitus. (*Ann.* iii. 71.) A TEMPLE OF MARS, founded by D. Junius Brutus Callaicus (Plin. xxxvi. 5. s. 26); one of NEPTUNE, cited as "delubrum Cn. Domitii" (*Ib.*; Gruter, *Inscr.* cccxviii. 5); one of CASTOR AND POLLUX (Vitruv. iv. 8. 4); and probably also one of VULCAN. (*Fast. Capran. X. Kal. Sep.*) Some of these last, however, were perhaps, mere *sacella* in the circus itself.

A few profane objects will close the list of public buildings in this quarter. The STABULA IV. FACTIONUM of the *Notitia* must have been the stables in which the horses of the four factions or colours of the circus, albata, prasina, russata, and veneta, were kept. Domitian added two more colours, the aurata and purpurea, and another reading of the *Curiosum* mentions six stables, whilst the *Notitia* — certainly erroneously — names eight; but it seems most probable that there were only four. (Preller, *Regionen,* p. 167.) Some of the emperors paid great attention to these stables. Tacitus represents Vitellius as building some (*Hist.* ii. 94); and Caligula was constantly dining and spending his time in the stables of the Green Faction. (Suet. *Cal.* 55.) The four in question were probably situated under the Capitol, near the carceres of the Circus Flaminius. Between the Porticus Philippi and the theatre of Balbus lay two PORTICUS MINUCIAE, styled respectively VETUS and FRUMENTARIA, both built by Minucius who was consul in B. C. 111. (Vell. Pat. ii. 8.) The *Frumentaria* appears to have been the place in which the *tesserae* were distributed to those entitled to share the public gifts of corn. (Appul. *de Mund.* extr. p. 74. 14, Elm.; cf. Cic. *Phil.* ii. 34; Lampr. *Comm.* 16.) The CRYPTA BALBI mentioned in the *Notitia* was probably a peculiar species of portico, and most likely attached to the theatre of Balbus. A *crypta* differed from a portico by having one of its sides walled, and by being covered with a roof, in which were windows. (Urlichs, *Beschr.* vol. iii. pt. ii. p. 62.)

Such were the public buildings in the district called Circus Flaminius; immediately to the N. of which lay the CAMPUS MARTIUS, sometimes called merely Campus. The purposes to which this plain was applied were twofold; it served for gymnastic and warlike exercises, and also for large political assemblies of the people, as the *comitia* and *contiones*. At first it must have been a completely open field with only a few scattered sacred places upon it; and it was not till the 6th century of the city that regular temples began to be built there. By degrees it became covered with buildings, except in that part devoted to the public games and exercises, and especially the *equiria*, or horse-races, instituted by Romulus in honour of Mars. (Varr. *L. L.* vi. § 13; Paul. Diac. p. 81.) The spot where these took place is indicated by Ovid (*Fast.* iii. 519):—

" Altera gramineo spectabis Equiria campo
  Quem Tiberis curvis in latus urget aquis.
  Qui tamen ejecta si forte tenebitur unda
  Caelius accipiet pulverulentus equos."

The part of the Campus the side of which may be said to be " pressed upon " by the stream of the Tiber, is that lying between *Piazza Navona* and the bridge of *S. Angelo*, where the ground forms an angle opposed to the descending waters. Here also was the bathing-place of the Roman youth. (Hor. *Od.* iii. 7. 25 ; Comp. Cic. *pro Coel.* 15.)

Some writers have assumed that this spot was regarded as forming a distinct division called CAMPUS MINOR, whilst the remainder of the plain was called CAMPUS MAJOR. (Preller, *Regionen*, p. 160 ; Urlichs, *Röm. Marsfeld*, p. 19 ; Canina, *Indic*, pp. 384, 412.) But this distinction does not appear to rest on adequate authority. It is derived from a passage in Catullus : " Te campo quaesivimus minore " (liii. (lv.). 3); and from another in Strabo, quoted in the former part of this article, where, in describing the Campus Martius, he speaks of another field, or plain, near it (πλησίον δ' ἐστὶ τοῦ πεδίου τούτου καὶ ἄλλο πεδίον, καὶ στοαὶ κύκλῳ παμπληθεῖς, κ. τ. λ.). But, as Becker observes (*Handb.* p. 599), Strabo has already described the Campus Martius as the usual place for gymnastic exercises, and therefore his ἄλλο πεδίον cannot be the part of it just described. It seems most probable that he meant the Campus Flaminius, which still retained its ancient name, though for the most part covered with the porticoes and other buildings which he describes ; just as we have a Moorfields and Goodman's Fields in the heart of London. The Campus Minor of Catullus may have been the Campus Martialis on the Caelian ; or, as Preller observes, the punctuation may be :—

" Te campo quaesivimus, minore
  Te in circo."

The ancient *loci religiosi* on the Campus Martius were the following :—The PALUS CAPREAE, or CAPRAE, where Romulus is said to have disappeared during the holding of an assembly of the people: its situation is unknown ; but it does not seem improbable, as Preller suggests (*Regionen*, p. 137), that its site may have been marked by the AEDICULA CAPRARIA, mentioned in the *Notitia* in the 7th Region, and that it may consequently have lain somewhere under the Quirinal. (Liv. i. 16; Ov. *Fast.* ii. 489, &c.) A place called TARENTUM, or TERENTUM, which appears to have been volcanic (campus ignifer), with a subterranean ARA DITIS PATRIS ET PROSERPINAE, where the ludi saeculares were performed. The legend of Valesius and his children, and an account of the institution of the games, will be found in the *Dictionary of Antiqui-*

ties, p. 716. We are here only concerned for the situation of the place, which is very variously assigned by different writers. Urlichs placed it in the Forum Boarium, which, however, must be wrong, as it was undoubtedly in the Campus Martius (Val. Max. ii. 4. § 5; Festus, p. 329), though at one extremity of it. (Zos. ii. 4.) Hence Becker placed it near the mausoleum of Augustus, being led to this conclusion by the Sibylline oracle recorded by Zosimus (*l.c.*) :—

'Ρέζειν ἐν πεδίῳ παρὰ Θύμβριδος ἄπλετον ὕδωρ
  "Οππῃ στεινότατον.

Becker refers the word στεινότατον in this passage to πεδίον, and hence selects the northern part of the Campus for the site of Tarentum, as being the narrowest. But it may equally well refer to ὕδωρ; and the narrowest part of the Tiber in its course through the Campus Martius — taking that appellation in its more extended sense—is where it is divided by the Insula Tiberina. Other passages adduced are undecisive, as those of Ovid (*Fast.* i. 501) and Seneca (*de Morte Claudii*, 13); and therefore though Preller (*Regionen*, Anhang, p. 241) pronounces against Becker's site, we must leave the question undetermined.

The ARA MARTIS, near which, when the *comitia* were ended the newly-elected censors took their seats in curule chairs, was probably the earliest holy place dedicated to the god on the Campus which bore his name. We have already observed, when treating of the Porta Fontinalis, that it must have been near that gate, and that it was perhaps erected by Numa. There was also an AEDES MARTIS on the Campus, probably at the spot where the *equiria* were celebrated. (Dion Cass. lvi. 24; Ov. *Fast.* ii. 855.) It seems to have been a distinct temple from that already mentioned in the Circus Flaminius. The site of the TEMPLE OF THE LARES PERMARINI, dedicated by the censor M. Aemilius Lepidus, B. C. 179, in pursuance of a vow made by L. Aemilius Regillus after his naval victory over the fleet of Antiochus, cannot be determined (Liv. xl. 52; Macrob. *Sat.* i. 10); but it may probably have stood, as Preller conjectures, near the Navalia. The AEDES JUTURNAE, built by Q. Lutatius Catulus towards the end of the Republic, stood near the arches of the Aqua Virgo, and consequently near the Septa. (Serv. *ad Aen.* xii. 139; Ov. *Fast.* i. 463; Cic. *pro Cluent.* 36.)

Such was the Campus Martius down to the imperial times ; when the great works undertaken there by Julius Caesar and Augustus gave it quite a new appearance. But, before we proceed to describe these, we must say a few words respecting the NAVALIA, or government dockyards. The older topographers placed them under the Aventine, from confounding them with the Emporium or commercial docks. Piale first pointed out the incorrectness of this view; but erred himself in placing the Navalia on the opposite bank of the Tiber, from his ignorance of certain passages which determine them to have been in the Campus Martius. These passages, which were first adduced by Becker (*de Muris, &c.* p. 96, *Handb.* p. 159), are the following : " Spes unica imperii populi Romani, L. Quinctius, trans Tiberim contra eum ipsum locum, ubi nunc Navalia sunt, quatuor jugerum colebat agrum, quae prata Quinctia vocantur." (Liv. iii. 26.) This passage shows the Navalia to have been on the left bank of the Tiber, opposite some fields called prata Quinctia; and the following one from Pliny fixes the situation of these fields in the district called Vaticanus: "Aranti quatuor sua jugera in Vaticano, quae prata Quinctia appellantur, Cincinnato viator attulit dictataram" (xviii. 4). That the Navalia were in the Campus Martius may also be inferred from Livy (xlv. 42): "Naves regiae captae de Macedonibus inusitatae ante magnitudinis in Campo Martio subductae sunt"; and from Plutarch's account of the return of the younger Cato from Cyprus, in which he relates that although the magistrates and senate, as well as a great part of the Roman population, were ranged along both banks of the Tiber in order to greet him, yet he did not stop the course of his vessels till he arrived at the Navalia (*Cot. Min.* 39); a circumstance which shows that this arsenal must have lain towards the upper part of the stream's course through the city. Hence, though we cannot define the boundary between the Janiculum and the Vatican, nor consequently the exact situation of the Prata Quinctia, yet the site fixed upon by Becker for the Navalia, namely, between the *Piazza Navona* and *Porto di Ripetta*, seems sufficiently probable. Preller is disposed to place them rather lower down the stream, but without any adequate reason (*Regionen,* Anh. p. 242).

It was Caesar who began the great changes in the Campus Martius to which we have before alluded. He had at one time meditated the gigantic plan of diverting the course of the Tiber from the Milvian bridge to the Vatican hill, by which the Ager Vaticanus would have been converted into a new Campus Martius, and the ancient one appropriated to building; but this project was never carried into execution. (Cic. *ad Att.* xiii. 33.) The only building which he really began in the Campus was the SEPTA JULIA. It has been said, when treating of the Porta Flumentana, that a spot near the Circus Flaminius was appropriated to the holding of the Comitia Centuriata. In early times it was enclosed with a rude kind of fence or boundary, probably of hurdles: whence, from its resemblance to a sheep-fold, it obtained the name of OVILE, and subsequently of Septa. (Liv. xxvi. 22; Juv. vi. 528; Serv. *ad Virg. Ec.* i. 34.) For this simple and primitive fence Caesar substituted a marble building (Septa marmorea), which was to be surrounded with a portico a mile square, and to be connected with the Villa Publica. (Cic. *ad Att.* iv. 16.) It was probably not much advanced at the time of Caesar's assassination; since we find that it was continued by the triumvir Lepidus, and finally dedicated by Agrippa (Dion Cass. liii. 23); but whether it was completed on the magnificent plan described by Cicero cannot be said. Its situation may be determined by a passage in Frontinus, in which he says that the arches of the Aqua Virgo ended in the Campus Martius in front of the Septa. (*Aq.* 22.) These arches, which, as we have seen before, began under the gardens of Lucullus on the Pincian, were conducted to the baths of Agrippa. Donati mentions that remains of them were discovered in his time in front of the church of *S. Ignazio* (near the *Collegio Romano*). (*De Urb. R.* iii. 18.) This coincides with remains of the portico of the Septa existing under the *Palazzo Doria* and church of *S. Maria in Via Lata* in the *Corso* (Canina, *Indic.* 400); and we may therefore conclude that the Septa Julia stood at this spot. The portico must have enclosed a large open space where the assemblies were held, and in which gladiatorial shows, and on

one occasion even a naumachia, were exhibited. (Suet. *Aug.* 43, *Cal.* 18, *Ner.* 12; Dion Cass. lv. 8, lix. 10.) There was of course a suggestum or rostra, for haranguing the people. (Dion Cass. lvi. 1.) The Septa were destroyed in the great fire under Titus (Dion Cass. lvi. 24), but must have been restored, since, in the time of Domitian, when they had lost their political importance, they appear to have been used as a market, in which the most valuable objects were exposed for sale. (Mart. ix. 60.) They appear to have undergone a subsequent restoration under Hadrian. (Spart. *Hadr.* 19.)

The VILLA PUBLICA adjoined the Septa Julia, and must have been on its S. side, since it is described by Varro (*R. R.* iii. 2) as being " in Campo Martio extremo," and must consequently have lain between the Septa and the Circus Flaminius, near the *Palazzo di Venezia.* The original one was an ancient and simple building, and is mentioned by Livy (iv. 22) as early as the year B. C. 436. It was used by the consuls for the levying of troops, and by the censors for taking the census (Varr. *l. c.*); also for the reception of foreign ambassadors whom it was not thought advisable to admit into the city, and of Roman generals before they obtained permission to enter the gates in triumph (Liv. xxx. 21, xxxiii. 24, &c.). It was the scene of the massacre of the four Marian legions by Sulla (Val. Max. ix. 2. § 1; Liv. *Epit.* lxxxviii.; Strab. v. 249). A passage in Lucan respecting this horrible transaction confirms the position of the Villa Publica close to the Septa (ii. 196): —

" Tunc flos Hesperiae, Latii jam sola juventus
Concidit et miserae maculavit Ovilia Romae"

And another passage in Plutarch shows that it must have adjoined the Circus Flaminius on the other side (Οὐ μὴν ἀλλὰ καὶ τούτους καὶ τῶν ἄλλων τοὺς περιγενομένους εἰς ἑξακισχιλίους ἀθροίσας παρὰ τὸν ἱππόδρομον, ἐκάλει τὴν σύγκλητον εἰς τὸ τῆς Ἐνυοῦς ἱερόν, Sull. 30.) Seneca (*de Clem.* i. 12) likewise mentions the assembling of the senate in the neighbouring temple of Bellona, where the cries of the massacred soldiers were heard; and this circumstance would rather lead us to suppose that the temple in question was situated at the eastern end, or towards the *carceres,* of the Circus Flaminius, since the Septa and Villa Publica must have lain towards that end of it nearest to the Capitol. The simple building described by Varro must have been that rebuilt in the censorship of S. Aelius Paetus and C. Cornelius Cethegus, B. C. 194. Caesar could hardly have done anything to it, since a coin of C. Fonteius Capito, consul in B. C. 33, testifies that the latter either restored or rebuilt it.

The name of M. Vipsanius Agrippa, the son-in-law of Augustus, is connected with the principal changes and the most important buildings in the Campus Martius. The latter consisted of the Pantheon, the thermae, a portico, and the large structure called the Diribitorium. The Campus Agrippae and its buildings will be described when we come to treat of that part of the district under consideration called Via Lata.

The PANTHEON of Agrippa, which is still in so good a state of preservation that it serves for public worship, is one of the finest monuments of ancient Rome. An inscription on the frieze of the portico testifies that it was erected by Agrippa in his third consulate; whilst another below records repairs by the emperors Septimius Severus and Caracalla. From a very corrupt passage in Pliny (xxxvi. 24. s. 1), topographers have related that the temple was dedicated to Jupiter Ultor; but this is altogether inconsistent with other accounts of its destination; and it appears from an emendation of Jan, derived from the Codex Bambergensis, that we should read *Diribitorii* for *Jovi Ultori* (Becker, *Handb.* p. 635). Dion Cassius states that it received the name of Pantheon because it contained the images of many gods (liii. 27), which, however, seem to have been those of the deities mythically connected with the Julian race, and among them that of Caesar himself. The temple is circular, and its magnificent portico with triple row of columns, though perhaps not quite in harmony with the main building, cannot fail to excite the admiration of the beholder. It owes its

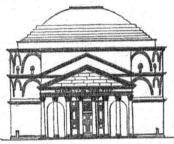

PANTHEON OF AGRIPPA.

excellent state of preservation partly to the solidity of its construction, partly to its having been consecrated as a Christian church as early as the reign of Phocas, under the title of *S. Maria ad Martyres*, or *della Rotonda*. To the lover of the fine arts it is doubly interesting from containing the tomb of Raphael. Some architects have thought that it was not originally intended for a temple, but as part of the baths; a notion, however, that is refuted by passages in ancient writers, where it is styled *templum* (Plin. xxxvi. 5. s. 38; Macrob. *Sat.* ii. 13). The Pantheon stood in the centre of the Campus Martius, taking that name in its widest sense. The THERMAE, of which only a few unimportant remains exist, adjoined it on the S., and must have extended to near the Hecatostylon. The DIRIBITORIUM was a large building destined, according to Becker (*Handb.* p. 638), to the examination of the voting tablets used in the comitia, in order to determine the result of elections, and therefore have been situated near the Septa. It seems to have been left unfinished at Agrippa's death, and was dedicated by Augustus, B. C. 7. Its vast unsupported roof was one of the wonders of Rome, and, when destroyed in the fire of Titus, could not be replaced. (Dion Cass. lv. 8; Plin. xvi. 40.) In hot weather Caligula sometimes converted it into a theatre (Dion Cass. lix. 7). The portico which Agrippa erected in the Campus Martius appears to have been called PORTICUS ARGONAUTARUM, from its being adorned with a picture of the Argonauts, and was erected in commemoration of Agrippa's naval victories (Dion Cass. liii. 27; Mart. iii. 20. 11). Becker (*Handb.* p. 637) contends that this was the same building called Basilica Neptuni by Spartian (*Hadr.* 19), and Ποσειδώνιον by Dion Cassius (lxvi. 24). But a basilica is not equivalent to a portico, nor can we imagine that Dion would have used the term Ποσειδώνιον of a στοά; whence it seems more probable, as assumed by Canina (*Indic.* p. 406) and other topographers, that Agrippa also erected a TEMPLE OF NEPTUNE, which was connected with, or probably surrounded by the portico. Nardini and Canina— the latter from recent researches—are of opinion that the eleven columns now existing in the front of the *Dogana di Terra* in the *Piazza di Pietra*, near the Antonine column, belonged to this temple. Of a PORTICUS MELEAGRI mentioned in the *Notitia* in connection with that of the Argonautarum, we know nothing further.

Augustus also erected a few monuments on the Campus Martius. Among them was the SOLARIUM AUGUSTI, an obelisk which now stands on *Monte Citorio*, which served as a gigantic gnomon, and, on an immense marble flooring that surrounded it, exhibited not only the hours, but also the increase and decrease of the days (Plin. xxxvi. 15). In the northern part of the Campus, between the Via Flaminia and the Tiber, he caused to be constructed during his life-time that superb MAUSOLEUM, a description of which by Strabo has already been cited in the former part of this article. This district had for some time previously served as a burying place for the most distinguished persons. Among others buried near this spot were Sulla, Caesar together with his aunt and daughter, and the two consuls Hirtius and Pansa, who fell at Mutina. Several members of the family of Augustus had been entombed in the mausoleum before the ashes of Augustus himself were deposited within it; as Marcellus, Agrippa, Octavia, and Drusus (Dion Cass. liii. 30; Virg. *Aen.* vi. 873, seq.; Ov. *Cons. ad Liv.* 67). By the time of Hadrian it was completely filled; which caused him to build a new one on the opposite side of the river (Dion Cass. lxix. 23). There are still considerable remains of the monument of Augustus. The area on which the sepulchre of the Caesars stood is now converted into a sort of amphitheatre for spectacles of the lowest description: sic transit gloria mundi. It is doubtful whether a third building of Augustus called PORTICUS AD NATIONES, or XIV. NATIONES, stood in the Campus Martius or in the Circus Flaminius. It appears to have been near the theatre of Pompey, and contained statues representing different nations (Plin. xxxvi. 5. s. 4; Serv. *ad Aen.* viii. 721.)

Near the Mausoleum appears to have been a portico called VIA TECTA, the origin of which is unknown. Its situation near the place assigned is determined by the following passage in Seneca's *Apocolocyntosis:* " Injicit illi (Claudio) manum Talthybius deorum nuntius et trahit capite obvoluto, ne quis eum possit agnoscere, per Campum Martium ; et inter Tiberim et Viam Tectam descendit ad inferos " (p. 389, Bip.). If this descent to the infernal regions was at the subterranean altar of Pluto and Proserpine before mentioned, it would go far to fix the situation of the Tarentum in the northern part of the Campus ; but this, though probable, is not certain. The Via Tecta is mentioned once or twice by Martial (iii. 5, viii. 75).

Among the other monuments relating to Augustus in the Campus Martius, was an ARA PACIS, dedicated to Augustus on his return from Germany, B. C. 13. (Dion Cass. liv. 25; Ov. *Fast.* iii. 882 ; *Fast. Praen. III. Kal. Feb.*) The ARA FORTUNAE REDUCIS was another similar altar (Dion Cass. liv. 19); but there is nothing to prove that it was on the Campus Martius.

In the reign of Augustus, Statilius Taurus erected an AMPHITHEATRE on the Campus,—the first built of stone at Rome ; but its situation cannot be determined. (Dion Cass. li. 23; Suet. *Aug.* 29.)

A long interval ensued after the reign of Augustus before any new public buildings were erected on the Campus Martius. Caligula began, indeed, a large amphitheatre near the Septa ; but Cladius caused it to be pulled down. Nero erected, close to the baths of Agrippa, the THERMAE NERONIANAE, which seem to have been subsequently enlarged by Alexander Severus, and to have obtained the name of THERMAE ALEXANDRINAE. The damage occasioned in this district by the fire of Nero cannot be stated, since all that we certainly know is that the amphitheatre of Statilius Taurus was destroyed in it (Dion Cass. lxii. 18). The fire under Titus was considerably more destructive in this quarter (Id. lxvi. 24); but the damage appears to have been made good by Domitian. Among the buildings restored by him on this occasion we find the TEMPLES OF ISIS AND SERAPIS mentioned ; but we have no accounts respecting their foundation. Their site may, however, be fixed between the Septa Julia and the baths of Agrippa, near the modern church of S. *Maria sopra Minerva.* Thus Juvenal (vi. 527):—

" A Meroe portabit aquas, ut spargat in aedem
    Isidis, antiquo quae proxima surgit Ovili."

(Cf. Joseph. *B. Jud.* vii. 5. § 4.) It was near the spot indicated that the celebrated group of the Nile was discovered which now adorns the Vatican (Braun, *Museums of Rome*, p. 160), together with several other Egyptian objects (Flaminio Vacca, *Mem.* nos. 26, 27; Bartoli, *Mem.* no. 112, &c.). Alexander Severus devoted much attention to these temples (Lampr. *A. Sev.* 26), and they must have existed till a late period, since they are enumerated in the *Notitia.*

Domitian also restored a temple of Minerva which stood near the same spot, the MINERVA CHALCIDICA of Cassiodorus (*Chron. sub Domit.*) and of the *Notitia.* (Montf. *Diar. Ital.* p. 292). It must have been the temple originally founded by Pompey in commemoration of his eastern victories, the inscription on which is recorded by Pliny (vii. 27). It was from this temple that the church of *S. Maria* just mentioned derived its epithet of *sopra Minerva ;* and it seems to have been near this spot that the celebrated statue of the Giustiniani Pallas, now in the *Braccio Nuovo* of the Vatican,

was discovered ; though according to other, but less probable, accounts, it was found in the circular temple near the *Porta Maggiore* (Braun, *Museums, &c.* p. 154). Some topographers assume that the temple built by Pompey was a different one from the above, with the barbarous title of Minerva Campensis, but in the same neighbourhood ; which does not seem probable (Canina, *Indicas.* p. 405).

Domitian also founded in the Campus Martius an ODEUM and a STADIUM (Suet. *Dom.* 5), which will be described in the proper sections. The situation of the former cannot be determined. The Stadium, in all probability, occupied the site of the *Piazza Navona,* the form of which shows that it must have been a circus. The name of *Navona* is a corruption of *in Agone,* and important remains of this Stadium

ANTONINE COLUMN.   (COLUMN OF M. AURELIUS.)

were in existence in the time of the Anonymous of Einsiedlen (Preller, *Regionen*, p. 171). The assumption that this place was occupied by a stadium built by Alexander Severus — in which case that of Domitian must be sought in some other part of the Campus — rests only on traditions of the middle ages (Canina, *Indic.* p. 392).

Trajan is said to have built a theatre in the Campus Martius, which, however, was destroyed by Hadrian. (Spart. *Hadr.* 8.) The same emperor probably erected what is called in the *Notitia* the BASILICA MARCIANES (Marcianae), which was probably a temple in honour of his sister, Marciana. The Antonines appear to have adorned this quarter with many buildings. The BASILICA MATIDIES (Matidiae) was perhaps erected by Antoninus Pius, and consecrated to Matidia, the wife of Hadrian; as well as the HADRIANUM, or temple to Hadrian himself, also mentioned in the *Notitia*. (Preller, p. 175.) The TEMPLUM ANTONINI and COLUMNA COCHLIS were the temple and pillar erected in honour of M. Aurelius Antoninus. (Capitol. *M. Ant.* 18; Aur. Vict. *Epit.* 16.) All these buildings stood near together in the vicinity of the *Piazza Colonna*, on which the column (Columna Antoniniana) still exists. For a long while this column was thought to be that of Antoninus Pius, and was even declared to be such in the inscription placed on the pedestal during the pontificate of Sixtus V. But the sculptures on the column were subsequently perceived to relate to the history of Antonine the philosopher; and this view was confirmed not only by the few remaining words of the original inscription, but also by another inscription found in the neighbouring *Piazza di Monte Citorio*, regarding a permission granted to a certain Adrastus, a freedman of Septimius Severus and Caracalla, to erect a small house in the neighbourhood of the column, as curator of it. This inscription, which is now preserved in the corridor of the Vatican, twice mentions the column as being that " Divi Marci." (Canina, *Indic.* p. 417, seq.) The column is an imitation of that of Trajan, but not in so pure a style of art. Both derive their name of *cochlis* from the spiral staircase (cochlea, κοχλίας) in the interior of them. (Isid. *Orig.* xv. 2, 38.) The COLUMNA ANTONINI PII was a large pillar of red granite, erected to

PEDESTAL OF COLUMN OF ANTONINUS PIUS.

him, as appears from the inscription, by M. Aurelius and L. Verus. It was discovered in the pontificate of Clement XI., in the garden of the *Padri della Missione*, on the E. side of the *Palazzo di Monte Citorio*. It broke in the attempt to erect it in the *Piazza di Monte Citorio*, where the obelisk now stands; but the pedestal with the inscription is

still preserved in the garden of the Vatican. (Canina *Indic.* p. 419.) The sculptures on the pedestal represent the Apotheosis of Antoninus Pius and Faustina.

The THERMAE COMMODIANAE and ALEXANDRINAE will be treated of in the section on the baths. After the time of Alexander Severus we find but few new buildings mentioned in this district. Gordian III. is said to have entertained the design of building an enormous portico under the Pincian hill, but it does not appear that it was ever executed. (Capitol. *Gord. III.* c. 32.) Respecting the Porticus Flaminia, see the article PONS MILVIUS. Some porticoes near the Pons Aelius, which appear to have borne the name of *Maximae*, were terminated by the TRIUMPHAL ARCH OF GRATIAN, VALENTINIAN, AND THEODOSIUS; the inscription on which will be found in the Anonymous of Einsiedlen, and in Gruter (clxxii. 1). Claudius, who was prefect of the city under Valentinian I., erected a portico near the baths of Agrippa, which he called PORTICUS BONI EVENTUS, after a neighbouring temple with the same name (Amm. Marc. xxix. 6. § 19); but with regard to this temple we have no information.

We shall now proceed to that part of the district under consideration comprised in the 7th Region of Augustus, and subsequently called VIA LATA, from the road which bounded its western side, and which formed the southern extremity of the Via Flaminia. The most important topographical question connected with this district is the situation of the CAMPUS AGRIPPAE, and the buildings connected with it. We have already shown from the situation of Martial's house, as well as from the probable site of the temple of Sol, that the Campus Agrippae must have lain under the western side of the Quirinal, and not under the Pincian, where Becker places it. It is probable, too, that it lay on a line with the Pantheon and thermae of Agrippa, although divided from them by the Via Lata; and hence Canina correctly describes it as facing the *Septa* (*Indic.* p. 215), whilst Urlichs and Preller, in like manner, place it between the *Piazza degli Apostoli* and the *Fontana Trevi*. (*Beschr.* vol. iii. pt. iii. p. 112; *Regionen*, p. 138.) The Campus Agrippae contained gardens, porticoes, and places for gymnastic exercises, and was, in short, a kind of Campus Martius in miniature. It was also a favourite lounge and promenade. (A. Gell. xiv. 5.) It appears from a passage in Dion Cassius, that the Campus was not finished before Agrippa's death, and that it was opened to the public by Augustus (lv. 8.) It contained a PORTICUS POLAE, so named after Agrippa's sister Pola or Polla; which is probably the same as that alluded to by Martial, in some passages before quoted, under the name of VIPSANIA. The latter name seems to be corrupted in the *Notitia* into *Porticus Gypsiani*. Becker (*Handb.* p. 596) would identify the Porticus Polae with the PORTICUS EUROPAE, but they seem to be different structures. (Urlichs, *Röm. Topogr.* p. 139.) The latter, which derived its name from a picture of the rape of Europa, is frequently mentioned by Martial (ii. 14, iii. 20, xi. 1). Its situation cannot be determined; but most topographers place it in the Campus Martius, among the other buildings of Agrippa. (Canina, *Indicaz.* p. 409; Urlichs, *Röm. Marsfeld*, p. 116.) It appears from the *Notitia* that the Campus Agrippae contained CASTRA, which, from the *Catalogus Imperat. Views.* (t. ii. p. 246, Ronc.), appear to have been dedicated by Aurelian; but the Porticus Vipsania served as a sort of barracks as early as the time of Galba. (Tac. *H.* i. 31; Plut. *Galb.* 25.)

Several objects mentioned in this district are doubtful as to site, and even as to meaning, and are not important enough to demand investigation. It contained TRIUMPHAL ARCHES OF CLAUDIUS AND M. AURELIUS. The latter subsisted in a tolerably perfect state near the *Piazza Fiano* in the *Corso*, till the year 1662, when pope Alexander VII. caused it to be pulled down. Its reliefs still adorn the staircase of the *Palazzo de' Conservatori.* (Canina, *Indicaz.* p. 220.)

ARCH OF AURELIUS.

We shall conclude this section with noticing a very humble but very useful object, the FORUM SUARIUM. Bacon was an article of great consumption at Rome. It was distributed, as well as bread, among the people, and its annual consumption in the time of Valentinian III. was estimated at 3,628,000 pounds. (Gibbon, *Decline and Fall,* vol. iv. p. 85, ed. Smith.) The custom of distributing it had been introduced by Aurelian. (Vopisc. *Aurel.* 25.) A country in which hogs'-flesh is the cheapest meat betrays a low state of farming. The swine still abounds in Italy; but in ancient times the Roman market was principally supplied from the forests of Lucania. The market was important enough to have its special tribune, and the " pigmen of the eternal city" ("Porcinarii Urbis aeternae") were considered such a useful body that peculiar privileges were granted to them. (*Cod.* xi. tit. 16; *Not. Dignit. Part. Occ.* p. 16; Gruter, *Inscr.* cclxxx. 4.) The market is alluded to in a sort of proverbial manner by Philostratus (ἄτιμά τε καὶ κοινὰ φύσιν᾽ ἐν, ὅσπερ ἐν οὐῶν ἀγορᾷ, *Heroic.* p. 283. 19, ed. Kayser.). It is supposed to have stood near the present church of *S. Croce dei Lucchesi*, which was substituted for that of *S. Nicolò in Porcilibus.* (Canina, *Indic.* p. 209; Preller, *Regionen,* p. 139.)

XIV. THE TRANSTIBERINE DISTRICT.

Although the district beyond the Tiber formed one of the 14 Regions of Augustus, and although part of it may perhaps have been enclosed with a wall as early as the time of Ancus Marcius, and was certainly included in that of Aurelian, yet, while it was considered a part of Rome, it never belonged to the Urbs, properly so called. The distinction be-

tween *Roma* and *Urbs* was at least as old as the time of Augustus, and was thus laid down by Alfenus Varus: "Ut Alfenus ait, Urbs est Roma, qua muro cingeretur; Roma est etiam, qua continentia aedificia essent." (*Digest.* l. tit. 16. l. 87.) This circumstance rather tends to strengthen Niebuhr's opinion that Ancus Marcius only built a citadel on the Janiculum, without any walls extending to the river. [See above, Part II. Sect. I. sub fin.] The district in question is naturally divided into three parts, the Mons Janiculus (or Janiculum), the Mons Vaticanus, — each with their respective plains towards the river, — and the Insula Tiberina. We shall begin with the last.

We have already mentioned the legend respecting the formation of the INSULA TIBERINA through the corn belonging to the Tarquins being thrown into the river. In the year B. C. 291 the island became sacred to Aesculapius. In consequence of a pestilence an embassy was despatched to Epidaurus to bring back to Rome the image of that deity ; but instead of the statue came a snake, into which it was perfectly known that the god himself had entered. As the vessel was passing the Tiberine island the snake swam ashore and hid itself there; in consequence of which a TEMPLE OF AESCULAPIUS was built upon it, and the island ever afterwards bore the name of the god. (*Liv. Epit.* xi.; *Ov. Met.* xv. 739; Val. Max. i. 8. § 2; Dionys. v. 13; Suet. *Claud.* 25.) Sick persons resorted to this temple for a cure; but it does not appear that there was any hospital near it, as was the case at Epidaurus. There is no classical authority for the fact that the sides of the island were afterwards walled round in the shape of a ship, with the prow against the current, typifying the vessel which brought the deity; but it is said that vestiges of this substruction are still visible. (Canina, *Indic.* p. 574.) The island also contained a TEMPLE OF JUPITER and a TEMPLE OF FAUNUS, both dedicated in B. C. 193. (Liv. xxxiii. 42, xxxiv. 53.) The temple of Jupiter appears to have adjoined that of Aesculapius. (*Ov. Fast.* i. 293.) It has been concluded, from the following verses of Ovid, that the temple of Faunus must have stood on the upper part of the island (*Fast.* ii. 193):—

" Idibus agrestis fumant altaria Fauni
    Hic, ubi discretas insula rumpit aquas ; "

but this, though a probable, is not a necessary inference. SEMO SANCUS, or Deus Fidius, seems also to have had a sacellum here, as well as TIBERINUS, as the river-god is called in the *Indigitamenta,* or religious books. (*Fast. Amit. VI. Id. Dec.*) By a curious error the early Christian writers confounded the former deity with Simon Magus, and thought that he was worshipped on the island. (Just. Mart. *Apol.* 2; Euseb. *H. Eccl.* ii. 12.) After the building of the two bridges which connected the island on either side with the shore, it seems to have obtained the name of " INTER DUOS PONTES" (Plut. *Publ.* 8); and this part of the river was long famous for the delicious pike caught in it; which owed their flavour apparently to the *rich* feeding afforded by the proximity of the banks. (Plut. *Popl.* 8; Macrob. *Sat.* ii. 12.) In the *Acta Martyrum* the island is repeatedly styled *Insula Lycaonia ;* it is at present called *Isola di S. Bartolommeo,* from the church and convent of that name.

The JANICULUM begins at that point opposite the Campus Martius where the Tiber reaches farthest to the W., whence it stretches in a southerly direction to a point opposite the Aventine. The masculine form of the name (Janiculus), though employed as a substantive by some modern writers, seems to rest on no classical authority, and can only be allowed as an adjective form with *mons* or *collis*. (Becker, *Handb.* p. 653.) The name *Janiculum* is usually derived from Janus, who is said to have had an *arx* or citadel here. (Ov. *Fast.* i. 245; Macrob. *Sat.* i. 7.) As the ridge runs in a tolerably straight line nearly due S. from the point where it commences, the curve described by the Tiber towards the E. leaves a considerable plain between the river and the hill, which attains its greatest breadth at the point opposite to the Forum Boarium. This was the original REGIO TRANSTIBERINA. It appears to have been covered with buildings long before the time of Augustus, and was principally inhabited by the lower classes, especially fishermen, tanners, and the like, though it contained some celebrated gardens. Hence the *Ludi Piscatorii* were held in this quarter. (Ov. *Fast.* vi. 237; Fest. pp. 210, 238.) It was the ancient *Ghetto*, or Jews' quarter, which now lies opposite to it. (Philo, *de Virt.* ii. p. 568, Mangey.)

The Regio Transtiberina contained but few temples or other public buildings. Of the temple of FORS FORTUNA we have already spoken when discussing the question respecting that of Pudicitia Patricia [supra, p. 814]. Of other *loci religiosi* in this quarter little more is known than the name. Such was the LUCUS FURINAE, mentioned in the narratives of the death of C. Gracchus. (Aur. Vict. *Vir. Ill.* 65; Plut. *C. Gracch.* 17.) Cicero connected this grove with the Eumenides, or Furies (*Nat. Deor.* iii. 18); but there is no account of those Attic deities having been naturalised at Rome, and we should rather infer from Varro that the grove was consecrated to some ancient indigenous goddess. (*L. L.* vi. § 19, Müll.) It was a universal tradition that Numa was buried in the Janiculum (Dionys. ii. 76; Plut. *Num.* 22; Val. Max. i. 1. § 12). Cicero, in a corrupt passage, places his tomb "haud procul a FONTI ARA" (or Fontis Aris) (*de Leg.* ii. 22); but of such a deity or altar we have no further account. We also find a LUCUS CORNISCARUM DIVARUM mentioned by Paulus Diaconus (p. 64, Müll.) as "trans Tiberim;" but though the names of these goddesses are also found in an inscription (Gruter, lxxxviii. 14), what they were cannot be told. Lastly, as the *Basis Capitolina* records a VICUS LARUM RURALIUM in this district, we may conclude that they had a *sacellum* here.

Among the profane places *trans Tiberim* were the MUCIA PRATA and the field called CODETA. The former—the land given to Mucius Scaevola by the Senate as a reward of his valour (Liv. ii. 13) —may, however, have lain beyond the district now under consideration, and probably farther down the Tiber. The Codeta, or Ager Codetanus, was so named from a plant that grew there resembling a horse's tail (coda) (Paul. Diac. pp. 38 and 58, Müll.), — no doubt the *Equisetis*, or *Equisetum palustre* of Linnaeus. (" Invisa et equisetis est, a similitudine equinae setae," Plin. xviii. 67. s. 4.) There seems to have been a Codeta Major and a Minor, since Suetonius relates that Caesar exhibited a naval combat in the latter, where he had formed a lake (" in minore Codeta defosso lacu," *Caes.* 39) Dion Cassius, on the other hand, represents this

naumachia as taking place in the Campus Martius (xliii. 23). Becker (*Handb.* p. 656, note) would reconcile these divergent accounts by assuming that the Codeta Minor lay in the Campus Martius, and the Codeta Major opposite to it, on the other side of the Tiber. (Cf. Preller, *Regionen*, p. 218.) But there seem to be some grave objections to this assumption. It is not probable that two places bearing the same name should have been on different sides of the river, nor that there should have been a marshy district, as the Codeta evidently was, in the Campus Martius, in the time of Caesar. Besides, had the latter contained a place called Codeta Minor, — which must have been of considerable size to afford room for the exhibition of a naval combat,— we should surely have heard of it from some other source. Becker adduces, in proof of his view, another passage from Suetonius (*Ib.* c. 44), from which it appears that Caesar contemplated building a magnificent temple of Mars, on the site of the lake, after causing it to be filled up; a project, however, which does not seem to have been carried into execution. Becker assumes that this temple must of course have been in the Campus Martius; though on what grounds does not appear, as we have already seen that there was a temple of Mars a long way outside the Porta Capena, besides a subsequent one in the forum of Augustus. We are, therefore, of opinion, that the word 'Αρείῳ, in Dion Cassius, must be a mistake either of his own, or of his copyists, and that the Campus Codetanus of the *Notitia* must have lain below the city, on the right bank of the Tiber. (Cf. Canina, *Indic.* p. 566, seq.) The *Notitia* mentions a CAMPUS BRUTTIANUS in connection with the Campus Codetanus, but what it was cannot be said. Some have conjectured that it was called after the Bruttii, who were employed at Rome as public servants. (Paul. Diac. p. 31.)

Near the same spot must have been the HORTI CAESARIS, which Caesar bequeathed to the Roman people. (Suet. *Caes.* 83; Tac. *Ann.* ii. 41; Cic. *Phil.* ii. 42.) According to Horace, they must have lain at some distance:—

" Trans Tiberim longe cubat is, prope Caesaris
    hortos."   (*Sat.* i. 9. 18.)

And it may be inferred from the situation of the TEMPLE OF FORS FORTUNA, which we have already discussed [supra, p. 814], that they must have been at about a mile's distance from the Porta Portuensis. (*Fast. Amit. VIII. Kal. Jul.*) It seems probable that they were connected with the NEMUS CAESARUM, where Augustus exhibited a *naumachia*, and where a grove or garden was afterwards laid out. (" Navalis proelii spectaculum populo dedi trans Tiberim, in quo loco nunc nemus est Caesarum" *Mon. Ancyr.*) This would rather tend to confirm the view that the codeta was in this neighbourhood. In Tacitus (*Ann.* xii. 56: " Ut quondam Augustus structo cis Tiberim stagno ") we are therefore probably to read *uls* for *cis*, which ancient form seems to have been retained in designating the Transtiberine district (" Dicebatur cis Tiberim et uls Tiberim," Aul. Gell. xii. 13; cf. Varr. *L.L.* v. § 83, Müll.; Pompon. *Dig.* i. tit. 2. l. 2. § 31.) The Nemus Caesarum seems to have been so called from Caius and Lucius Caesar. (Dion Cass. lxvi. 25.) We are not to suppose that it occupied the site of the lake excavated for the *naumachia*, but was planted round it as we learn from Tacitus (—" apud nemus quod navali stagno circumposuit Augustus," *Ann.* xiv. 15). There are several passages which show that the lake existed long after the time of Augustus. Thus Statius (*Silv.* iv. 4. 5):—

" Continuo dextras flavi pete Tybridis oras,
  Lydia qua penitus stagnum navale coercet
  Ripa, suburbanisque vadum praetexitur hortis."

This passage likewise confirms the situation of the lake on the right, or Etruscan, bank (Lydia ripa) with the Nemus round it (cf. Suet. *Tib.* 72). It was used by Titus to exhibit a *naumachia* (Suet. *Tit.* 7; Dion Cass. *l. c.*); and remains of it were visible even in the time of Alexander Severus (Id. lv. 10). Although the passage in the *Monumentum Ancyranum* in which Augustus mentions this lake or basin is rather mutilated, we may make out that it was 1800 feet long by 1200 broad.

The *Notitia* mentions five NAUMACHIAE in the 14th Region, but the number is probably corrupt, and we should read two. (Preller, *Regionen*, p. 206.) We know at all events that Domitian also made a basin for ship-fights in the Transtiberine district. (Suet. *Dom.* 4.) The stone of which it was constructed was subsequently employed to repair the Circus Maximus (*Ib.* 5). That it was in a new situation appears from Dion Cassius (ἐν καινῷ τινι χωρίῳ, lxvii. 8). It probably lay under the Vatican, since St. Peter's was designated in the middle ages as "apud Naumachiam." (Flav. Blond. *Instaur. R.* i. 24; Anastas. *V. Leo. III.* p. 306, Blanch.; Manif. *Diar. Ital.* p. 291.) The *naumachia* ascribed to the emperor Philip (Aur. Vict. *Caes.* 28) was perhaps only a restoration of this, or of that of Augustus.

Among other objects in the district of the Janiculum, we need only mention the HORTI GETAE and the CASTRA LECTICARIORUM. The former were probably founded by Septimius Severus, and inherited by his son Geta. We know at all events that

Severus founded some baths in this district (Spart. *Sept. Sev.* 19; cf. Becker, *de Muris*, p. 127) and the arch called PORTA SEPTIMIANA; and it likewise appears that he purchased some large gardens before his departure into Germany. (Spart. *Ib.* c. 4.) The *Lecticarii* were either sedan-chairmen, or men employed to carry biers, and their *castra* means nothing more than a station for them, just as we hear of the Castra Tabellariorum, Victimariorum, &c. (Preller, *Regionen*, p. 218.)

The MONS or COLLIS VATICANUS rises a little to the NW. of the Mons Janiculus, from which it is separated only by a narrow valley, now *Valle d' Inferno* The origin of the name of this district, at present the most famous in Rome, cannot be determined. The most common derivation of it is from a story that the Romans gained possession of it from the Etruscans through an oracular response ("Vatum responso expulsis Etruscis," Paul. Diac. p. 379.) We have already remarked that there is no ground for Niebuhr's assumption respecting the existence here of an Etruscan city called *Vatica* or *Vaticum* [see p. 724]. This district belonged still less than the Janiculum to the city, and was not even included in the walls of Aurelian. It was noted for its unhealthy air (Tac. *H.* ii. 93), its unfruitful soil (Cic. *de Leg. Agr.* ii. 35), and its execrable wine. ("Vaticana bibis, bibis venenum," Mart. vi. 92. 93; cf. x. 45.) In the Republican times the story so beautifully told by Livy (iii. 26) of the great dictator L. Quinctius Cincinnatus who was saluted dictator here whilst cultivating his farm of four acres, the PRATA QUINCTIA, lends the only interest to the scene, whether it may belong to the romance of history or not. There were no buildings in this quarter before the time of the emperors, and almost the only one of any note in all antiquity was a sepulchre—the MAUSOLEUM or MOLES HADRIANI, now the *Castello di S. Angelo*. (Dion Cass. lxix. 23;

MOLE OF HADRIAN RESTORED.

Spart. *Hadr.* 19.) Among the ancient notices of it the most important is that of Procopius. (*B. G.* i. 22. p. 106. ed. Bonn.) A complete history of it is given by Bunsen (*Beschr.* vol. ii. p. 404, seq.), and descriptions will be found in all the guide-books. Hadrian's mausoleum was the tomb of the following

emperors and their families, certainly till the time of Commodus, and perhaps till that of Caracalla (v. Becker *Handb.* note 1430). It was built in the HORTI DOMITIAE (Capitol. *Ant. P.* 5), if we are to understand the word *collocavit* in that passage of an actual entombment, and not of a lying-in-state.

These gardens of the Domitian family are frequently mentioned in inscriptions; and those who are curious respecting their history will find a long account of them in Preller's *Regionen* (p. 207, seq.). They appear to have existed under the same name in the time of Aurelian. (Vopisc. *Aurel.* 49.) In the same district were also the HORTI AGRIPPINAE. These came into the possession of her son, Caligula, who built a circus in them, afterwards called the Circus Neronis. It will be treated of in another section; and we shall only mention here that this was the place in which the Christians, having previously been wrapped in the *tunica molesta* or *picata*, were burnt, to serve as torches for the midnight games. (Tac. *Ann.* xv. 44.) Both the gardens mentioned came into the possession of Nero, and may therefore have also been called HORTI NERONIS. (Tac. *Ib.* and c. 39.)

The neighbourhood seems to have been a chosen spot for the sepulchres of the great. One of them, a pyramid larger than the still existing monument of Cestius, existed till the end of the 15th century, and was absurdly regarded sometimes as the *sepulcrum Romuli*, sometimes as the *sepulcrum Scipionis Africani*. It appears from notices belonging to the middle ages that on or near the spot where St. Peter's now stands, there was anciently a TEMPLUM APOLLINIS, or more probably of Sol. (Anastasius, *Vit. Silvestri*, p. 42; Montf. *Diar.* i. p. 155.)

Having thus gone over the various districts of the city, and noted the principal objects of interest which they contained, we shall now proceed to give an account of certain objects which, from their importance, their general similarity, and the smallness of their number, may be most conveniently ranged together and treated of in distinct sections. Such are, — (1) the structures destined for public games and spectacles, as the Circi, Theatres, and Amphitheatres; (2) the Thermae or Baths; (3) the Bridges; and, (4) the Aqueducts.

The general characteristics of these objects have been so fully described in the *Dictionary of Antiquities* that it will be unnecessary to repeat the descriptions here, and we shall therefore confine ourselves to what may be called their topographical history; that is, an account of their origin and progress, their situation, size, and other similar particulars.

XV. THE CIRCI, THEATRES, AND AMPHITHEATRES.

Horse and chariot races were the earliest kind of spectacle known at Rome. The principal circus in which these sports were exhibited, and which by way of pre-eminence over the others came ultimately to be distinguished by the title of CIRCUS MAXIMUS, was founded, as we have already related, by the elder Tarquin, in the valley between the Palatine and Aventine. That king, however, probably did little more than level and mark out the ground; for certain spaces around it were assigned to the patricians and knights, and to the 30 curiae, on which, at the time of the games, they erected their own seats or scaffolds, called *spectacula* and *fori*. (Liv. i. 35; cf. Dionys. iii. 68.) According to Livy, the same custom continued to prevail under Tarquinius Superbus (*Ib.* c. 56); though Dionysius represents that monarch as surrounding the circus with por-

ticoes (iv. 44). It was not till the year B. C. 228 that *carceres* for the chariots were built. (Liv. viii. 20.) We cannot tell what the original number of *carceres* may have been, but it was probably adapted to that of the chariots which started in the race. According to Tertullian (*de Spect.* 9) there were originally only two Circensian factions, or colours, the *albata* and *russata*—that is, winter and summer; but these distinctions of colours and factions do not seem to have been known till the time of the Empire. Joannes Lydus (*de Mens.* iv. 25, Beck.) states the original number of the factions to have been three, the *russata*, *albata* and *prasina*; and this seems to agree with the following passage in Cicero—if, indeed, it is to be interpreted strictly, and is anything more than a fortuitous coincidence: "Neque enim in quadrigis eum secundum numeraverim, aut tertium, qui vix e carceribus exierit, cum palmam jam primus acceperit." (*Brut.* 47.) However this may be, we know that in the early part of the Empire there were four colours, though by whom the fourth, or *veneta*, was added, cannot be said. Domitian added two more the *aurata* and *purpurata* (Suet. *Dom.* 7), but these do not seem to have come into customary use. The usual *missus*, or start, consisted of four chariots, as we learn from Virgil with the note of Servius:—

"Centum quadrijugos agitabo ad flumina currus"
　　　　　　　　　　　　　　　　(*Georg.* iii. 18);

where the commentator remarks from Varro:—"Id est, unius diei exhibebo circenses ludos, quia, ut Varro dicit in libris de gente populi Romani, olim xxv. missus fiebant." It appears probable that the *carceres* were twice the number of the chariots which started, in order to afford egress to those which had finished the course, whilst fresh charioteers were waiting in those which were closed to begin a new course (v. Becker, *de Muris*, p. 87). Thus in the Lyons mosaic eight *carceres* are represented; but in the Circus Maximus, after the increase of the factions to six, there were probably twelve *carceres*; and such also appears to have been the number in the circus on the Via Appia. (Cf. Cassiod. *Var.* iii. 51.) The Circus Maximus seems to have remained in a very rude and imperfect state till the time of Julius Caesar. He increased it by adding to both its extremities; and its size when thus enlarged appears to have been 3 stadia in length and 1 in breadth. Caesar also surrounded it with a canal, called EURIPUS, in order to protect the spectators from the fury of the elephants; but this was filled up by Nero and converted into seats for the equites, whose increased numbers probably required more accommodation. (Suet. *Caes.* 39; Plin. viii. 7, xxxvi. 24. a. 1.) The description of the circus by Dionysius (iii. 68) is the clearest and longest we possess, but the measurements which he gives differ from those of Pliny, as he makes it 3½ stadia long and 4 *plethra*, or ⅔ds of a stade, broad. But perhaps these authorities may be reconciled by assuming that one took the inner and the other the outer circumference. The reader will find a lengthened examination of these different measures in Canina's *Indicazione Topografica*, p. 491, seq. In Caesar's circus it was only the lower rows of seats that were built of stone; the upper rows were of wood, which accounts for the repeated fires that happened there. The first of these occurred in B. C. 31, a little before the battle of Actium, and destroyed a considerable part of the building. (Dion Cass. l. 10.) Augustus rebuilt the *Pulvinar*, or place on which the images of the gods were laid, and erected the first obelisk between the *metae*. (*Mon. Ancyr.*; Suet. *Aug.* 45; Plin. xxxvi. 14. s. 5.) The side towards the Aventine was again burnt in the reign of Tiberius. (Tac. *Ann.* vi. 45.) Claudius much improved the appearance of the circus by substituting marble *carceres* for those of tufo, and *metae* of gilt bronze for the previous ones of wood. He also appropriated certain seats to the senators. (Suet. *Claud.* 21.) We have seen that the fire of Nero broke out in the circus, whence it is natural to conclude that it must have been completely destroyed. Yet it must have been soon restored, since Nero caused his ridiculous triumphal procession to pass through it, and hung his triumphal wreaths round the obelisk of Augustus. (Dion Cass. lxiii. 21.) The effects of another fire under Domitian were repaired with the stone from his *naumachia*, and it was now, perhaps, that 12 *carceres* were first erected. (Suet. *Dom.* 5, 7.) We read of another restoration on a still more magnificent scale by Trajan. (Dion Cass. lviii. 7.) During the celebration of the Ludi Apollinares in the reign of Antoninus Pius, some of the rows of seats fell in and killed a large number of persons. (Capitol. *Anton. P.* 9; *Catal. Imp. Vienn.* ii. p. 244.) We know but little more of the history of the Circus Maximus. Constantine the Great appears to have made some improvements (Aur. Vict. *Caes.* 40. § 27), and we hear of the games being celebrated there as late as the 6th century. (Cassiod. *Var.* iii. 51.) The circus was used for other games besides the chariot races, as the *Ludus Trojae*, *Certamen Gymnicum*, *Venatio*, *Ludi Apollinares*, &c. The number of persons it was capable of accommodating was variously stated. Pliny (xxxvi. 24. s. 1) states it at 260,000. One codex of the *Notitia* mentions 485,000, another 385,000 ; the latter number is probably the more correct. (Preller, *Regionen*, p. 191.) The circus seems to have been enlarged after the time of Pliny, in the reign of Trajan.

The CIRCUS FLAMINIUS· was founded in B.C. 220 by the censor of that name. (Liv. *Epit.* xx.; Cass. *Chron.* p. 178.) We have but few notices respecting this circus, which lay under the Capitoline, with its *carceres* towards the hill, and its circular end towards the river. The *Ludi Plebeii*, and those called *Taurii*, were celebrated here (Val. Max. i. 7. § 4; Varr. *L.L.* v. § 154), and Augustus afforded in it the spectacle of a crocodile chase. (Dion Cass. lv. 10.) It also served for meetings of the people, which had previously been held in the *Prata Flaminia*. (Liv. xxvii. 21; Cic. *ad Att.* i. 14.) We find no mention of the Circus Flaminius after the first century of our era; and in the early part of the 9th century it had been so completely forgotten that the Anonymous of Einsiedlen mistook the *Piazza Navona* for it. Yet remains of it are said to have existed till the 16th century, at the church of *S. Caterina de' Funari* and the *Palazzo Mattei*. (And. Fulvio, *Ant. Urb.* lib. iv. p. 264; Lucio Fauno, *Ant. di Roma*, iv. 23. p. 138.)

What is sometimes called by modern topographers the CIRCUS AGONALIS, occupied, as we have said, the site of the *Piazza Navona*. But the *Agonalia* were certainly not celebrated with Circensian games, and there are good reasons for doubting whether this was a circus at all. Its form, however, shows that it was a place of the same kind,

and hence Becker's conjecture seems not improbable (*Handb.* p. 670), that it was the STADIUM founded by Domitian. The Grecian foot-races had been introduced at Rome long before the time of Domitian. Both Caesar and Augustus had built temporary *stadia* in the Campus Martius (Suet. *Caes.* 39; Dion Cass. liii. 1), and Domitian seems to have constructed a more permanent one. (Suet. *Dom.* 5; Cassiod. *Chron.* t. ii. p. 197.) We are not indeed told that it was in the Campus Martius, but this is the most probable place for it; and the *Notitia* after mentioning the three theatres and the *Odeum* in the 9th Region names the Stadium. It is also mentioned in conjunction with the Odeum by Ammianus Marcellinus (xvi. 10. § 14). It is discriminated from the circi by Lampridius: "Omnes de circo, de theatro, de stadio — meretrices collegit." (*Heliog.* 26.) In the middle ages it seems to have been called "Circus Alexandrinus," an appellation doubtless derived from the neighbouring thermae of Alexander Severus. By the Anonymus Einsiedlensis it was confounded, as we have said, with the Circus Flaminius.

Putting this on one side, therefore, the third circus, properly so called, founded at Rome, would be that which Caligula built in the gardens of his mother Agrippina in the Vatican. (Plin. xvi. 40, xxxvi. 11; Suet. *Claud.* 21.) From him the place subsequently obtained the name of CAIANUM (Dion Cass. lix. 14), by which we find it mentioned in the *Notitia*. (*Reg.* xiv.) This circus was also used by Nero, whence it commonly obtained the name of CIRCUS NERONIS. (Plin. *l. c.*; Suet. *Ner.* 22; Tac. *Ann.* xiv. 14.) In the middle ages it was called *Palatium Neronis*. Some writers assume another circus in this neighbourhood, which Canina (*Indic.* p. 590) calls CIRCUS HADRIANI, just at the back of the mausoleum of that emperor; but this seems hardly probable. (Cf. Urlichs, in *Class. Mus.* vol. iii. p. 202.) The chief passage on which this assumption is founded is Procopius, *de Bell. Goth.* ii. 1 (Preller, *Regionen*, p. 212).

A fourth circus was that of MAXENTIUS about two miles on the Via Appia, near the tomb of Caecilia Metella. It used to be commonly attributed to Caracalla; but an inscription dug up in 1825 mentions Romulus, the son of Maxentius (Orell. *Inscr.* 1069); and this agrees with the *Catalogus Imperatorum Viennensis*, which ascribes the building of a circus to Maxentius (ii. p. 248, Ronc.). This building is in a tolerable state of preservation; the spina is entire, and great part of the external walls remains; so that the spectator can here gain a clear idea of the arrangements of an ancient circus. A complete description of it has been published by the Rev. Richard Burgess (London, Murray, 1828.)

The fifth and last of the circuses at Rome, which can be assumed with certainty, is the CIRCUS HELIOGABALI, which lay near the Amphitheatrum Castrense, outside the walls of Aurelian. (Urlichs, *Röm. Topogr.* p. 126, seq.; Becker, *Antwort*, p. 81.) We have already said that the existence of a CIRCUS FLORAE in the 6th Region, is a mere invention; and that of a CIRCUS SALLUSTII, in the same district, rests on no satisfactory authority.

Although theatrical entertainments were introduced at Rome at an early period, the city possessed no permanent theatre before the THEATRUM POMPEII, built in the second consulship of Pompey, B.C. 55. (Vell. Pat. ii. 48; Plut. *Pomp.* 52.) Previously to this period, plays were performed in wooden theatres, erected for the occasion. Some of these temporary buildings were constructed with extravagant magnificence, especially that of M. Aemilius Scaurus in B. C. 59, a description of which is given by Pliny (xxxvi. 24. s. 7). An attempt, to which we have before alluded, was indeed made by the censor Cassius, B. C. 154, to erect a stone theatre near the Lupercal, which was defeated by the rigid morality of Scipio Nasica (Vell. Pat. i. 15; Val. Max. ii. 4. § 2; Liv. *Epit.* xlviii.; Oros. iv. 21). A good deal of this old Roman feeling remained in the time of Pompey; and in order to overcome, or rather to evade it, he dedicated a temple to VENUS VICTRIX on the summit of his theatre, to which the rows of seats appeared to form an ascent (Tac. *Ann.* xiv. 20; Tert. *de Spect.* 10; Plin. viii. 7). Gellius places the dedication of the theatre in the third consulship of Pompey, which is at variance with the other authorities (*N. A.* x. 1). We have spoken of its situation in a preceding section, and shall refer the reader who desires any further information on this head to Canina (*Indicaz.* p. 368, seq.), who has bestowed much labour in investigating the remains of this building. There is great discrepancy in the accounts of the number of spectators which this theatre was capable of accommodating. According to Pliny, in whose MSS. there are no variations, it held 40,000 persons (xxxvi. 24. s. 7); and the account of Tacitus of the visit of the German ambassadors seems to indicate a large number (" Intravere Pompeii theatrum, quo magnitudinem populi viserent," *Ann.* xiii. 54). Yet one of the codices of the *Notitia* assigns to it only 22,888 seats, and the *Curiosum* still fewer, or 17,580. It was called *theatrum lapideum*, or *marmoreum*, from the material of which it was built; which, however, did not suffice to protect it from the ravages of fire. The *scena* was destroyed in the reign of Tiberius, and rededicated by Claudius (Tac. *Ann.* iii. 72; Dion Cass. lx. 6). The theatre was burnt in the fire under Titus, and again in the reign of Philip; but it must have been restored on both occasions, as it is mentioned by Ammianus Marcellinus among the objects most worthy of notice in his account of the visit of Constantius II. (xvi. 10). We learn from the *Catalogus Imperatorum*, that it had been repaired by Diocletian and Maximian; and it was also the object of the care of Theodoric (Cassiod. *Var.* iv. 51).

The THEATRE OF BALBUS, dedicated in B.C. 12 (Suet. *Aug.* 29; Dion Cass. liv. 25), was a building of much less importance, and but few accounts have been preserved of it; yet it must have lasted till a late period, as it is recorded in the *Notitia*. According to the *Curiosum* it accommodated 11,600 persons; whilst the MSS. of the *Notitia* mention 11,510 and 8088.

The THEATRUM MARCELLI was begun by Caesar (Dion Cass. xliii. 49), and dedicated by Augustus, B. C. 12, to the memory of his nephew, Marcellus. (*Mon. Ancyr.*; Suet. *Aug.* 29; Dion Cass. liv. 26.) We have already mentioned its situation in the Forum Olitorium; and very considerable remains of it are still to be seen in the *Piazza Montanara*. Its arches are now occupied by dirty workshops. It does not seem to have enjoyed so much celebrity as Pompey's theatre. According to the *Curiosum* it was capable of accommodating 20,000 spectators. The *scena* was restored by Vespasian (Suet. *Vesp.* 19); and Lampridius mentions that Alexander

Severus contemplated a renovation of the theatre (*Alex.* 44.)

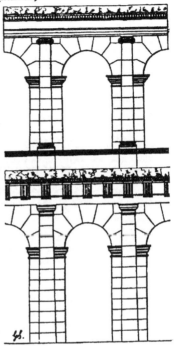

THEATRE OF MARCELLUS.

These were the three Roman theatres, properly so called (Ov. *Tr.* iii. 12. 24.):—

" Proque tribus resonant terna theatra foris."

Some of the MSS. of the *Notitia* mention four theatres, including, of course, the ODEUM, which was a roofed theatre, intended for musical performances. According to the most trustworthy accounts, it was built by Domitian, to be used in the musical contests of the Capitoline games which he instituted (Suet. *Dom.* 4; Cassiod. *Chron.* p. 197, Ronc.); and when Dion Cassius (lxix. 4) ascribes it to Trajan, we may perhaps assume that it was finished or perfected by him. Nero appears to have first introduced musical contests (Tac. *Ann.* xiv. 20), but the theatre in which they were held was probably a temporary one. The Odeum was capable of holding 10,000 or 12,000 persons. It is mentioned by Ammianus Marcellinus (xvi. 10).

The AMPHITHEATRE OF STATILIUS TAURUS was the first permanent building of that kind erected at Rome. After the chariot races, the gladiatorial combats were the most favourite spectacle of the Romans; yet it was long before any peculiar building was appropriated to them. We have already related that the first gladiators were exhibited in the Forum Boarium in B. c. 264; and subsequently these combats took place either in the circus or in the Forum Romanum: yet neither of these places was well adapted for such an exhibition. The former was inconvenient, from its great length, and the *metae* and *spinae* were in the way; whilst the latter, besides its moral unsuitableness for such a spectacle, became by degrees so crowded with monuments as to leave but little space for the evolutions of the combatants. The first temporary amphitheatre was the wonderful one built of wood by Caesar's partisan, C. Scribonius Curio. It consisted of two separate theatres, which, after dramatic entertainments had been given in them, were turned round, with their audiences, by means of hinges or pivots, and formed an amphitheatre (Plin. xxxvi. 24. s. 8). Caesar himself afterwards erected a wooden amphi-

theatre (Dion Cass. xliii. 22); but that of Statilius Taurus was the first built of stone, and continued to be the only one down to the time of Vespasian. We have mentioned that it was in the Campus Martius. It was dedicated in the fourth consulship of Augustus, B. C. 30. (Dion Cass. li. 23; Suet. *Aug.* 29.) The amphitheatre erected by Nero in the Campus Martius was a temporary one of wood. (Suet. *Nero*, 12.) The amphitheatre of Taurus, which does not appear to have been very magnificent (Dion Cass. lix. 10), was probably destroyed in the fire of Nero; at all events we hear no more of it after that event. The AMPHITHEATRUM FLAVIUM,

COLOSSEUM.

erected by Vespasian, appears to have been originally designed by Augustus. (Suet. *Vesp.* 9.) It stood on the site previously occupied by the lake of Nero, between the Velia and the Esquiline. (Mart. *Spect.* 2. 5), and was capable of containing 87,000 persons. (*Notitia, Reg.* iii.) A complete description of this magnificent building will be found in the *Dictionary of Antiquities*, and need not be re-

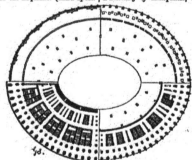

GROUND PLAN OF THE COLOSSEUM.

peated here. It was not completely erected, till the reign of Domitian; though Titus dedicated it in the year 80. (Suet. *Tit.* 7; Aur. Vict. *Caes.* 9. 7.) In the reign of Macrinus it was so much damaged by a fire, occasioned by lightning, that it was necessary to exhibit the *gladiatores* and *venationes* for several years in the Stadium. (Dion Cass. lxxviii. 25.) The restoration was undertaken by

Elagabalus, and completed by Alexander Severus. (Lampr. *Hel.* 17, *Alex.* 24.) It suffered a similar calamity under Decius (Hieron. *Chron.* p. 475); but the damage was again made good, and *venationes*, or combats with wild beasts, were exhibited in it as late as the 6th century. In the middle ages it was converted into a fortress; and at a later period a great part of it was destroyed by the

Romans themselves, in order to build the *Cancelleria* and the *Palazzo Farnese* with the materials. Enough, however, is still left to render it one of the

most striking and important monuments of imperial Rome. Its name of *Colosseum*, first mentioned by Bede (ap. Ducange, *Gloss.* ii. p. 407, ed. Bas.)

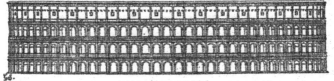

ELEVATION OF COLOSSEUM.

under the form *Colyseus*, was either derived from the vast size of the building, or, more probably, from the colossus of Nero, which stood close to it. (See Nibby, *Dell' Anfiteatro Flavio*, in the Appendix to Nardini, i. p. 238, which contains the best history of the building down to modern times.) Of the AMPHITHEATRUM CASTRENSE, near S. *Croce*, we have already spoken [p. 827].

XVI. THE THERMAE, OR BATHS.

We, of course, propose to speak here only of those large public institutions which were open either *gratis* or for a mere trifle to all, and of which the first were the THERMAE AGRIPPAE, near his Pantheon. The thermae must not be regarded as mere *balneae*, or places for bathing. They likewise contained *gymnasia*, or places for gymnastic exercises; *hexedrae*, or rooms for the disputations of philosophers; as well as apartments for the delivery of lectures, &c. The *thermae* of Agrippa do not seem to have been so splendid as some of the subsequent ones; yet, though they suffered in the fire under Titus, they were preserved till a late period, and are mentioned more than once by Martial (iii. 20. 15, 36. 6). The THERMAE NERONIANAE were erected by Nero very near to those of Agrippa (Tac. *Ann.* xiv. 47; Suet. *Nero*, 12). After their restoration by Alexander Severus, who appears, however, to have also enlarged them (Lamprid. *Alex.* 25), they obtained the name of THERMAE ALEXANDRINAE (Cassiod. *Chron.* vol. ii. p. 194, Ronc.). They must have lain between the *Piazza Navona* and the Pantheon, as they are thrice mentioned by the Anonymous of Einsiedlen between the latter building and the Circus Flaminius, which was the name he applied to the *Piazza Navona*. Hence the probability that the place just named was the Stadium of Nero. The Thermae Neronianae are frequently mentioned in a way that indicates considerable splendour (Mart. ii. 38. 8, vii. 34. 5; Stat. *Silv.* i. 5. 62); but their name was obliterated by that of the Thermae Alexandrinae, by which they appear in the *Notitia*.

The third baths erected at Rome were the THERMAE TITI, or the Esquiline, near the Flavian amphitheatre. (Mart. *Spect.* 2). There are still considerable remains of these baths; but the plan of them is difficult to make out, from their having been erected on the site of a large previous building. Canina's account of them is the best (vide *Memorie Romane di Antichità*, vol. ii. p. 119, *Indicas.* p. 101). The site on which they stand was perhaps previously occupied by the golden house of Nero. Near them stand the THERMAE TRAJANI, which Canina has correctly distinguished from those of Titus (Preller, *Regionen*, p. 126; Becker, *Handb.* p. 687). They are named in the *Notitia* as distinct,

and also in the Chroniclers, who however, singularly enough, place the building of both in the reign of Domitian. (Cassiod. *Chron.* vol. ii. p. 197, Ronc.; Hieron. vol. i. p. 443.) The baths of Titus had been run up very expeditiously (" *velocia munera*," Mart. *Spect.* 2; " thermis juxta *celeriter* extructis," Suet. *Tit.* 7), and might consequently soon stand in need of restorations; and it seems not improbable, as Becker suggests (*Handb.* p. 687), that Trajan, whilst he repaired these, also built his own at the side of them, before he had yet arrived at the imperial dignity. Cassiodorus (*l. c.*) expressly mentions the year 90. Those actually built by Trajan must have been the smaller ones lying to the NE. of those of Titus, since Anastasius mentions the church of *S. Martino de' Monti* as being built "juxta thermas Trajanas" (*Vit. Symmachi*, p. 88, Blanch.). His object in building them may have been to separate the baths of the sexes; for the men and women had hitherto bathed promiscuously: and thus the *Catal. Imp. Vienn.* notes, under Trajan: "Hoc Imperat. mulieres in Termis Trajanis laverunt."

The emperor Commodus, or rather his freedman Cleander in his name, is related to have built some baths (Lampr. *Comm.* 17; Herod. i. 12); and we find the THERMAE COMMODIANAE set down in the 1st Region in the *Notitia*; whilst, by the Anonymous of Einsiedlen, on the contrary, they are three or four times mentioned as close to the Rotunda. Their history is altogether obscure and impenetrable. The THERMAE SEVERIANAE are also recorded in the *Notitia* in the 1st Region in connection with the Commodianae. They are mentioned by Lampridius (*Sever.* 19); but no traces of them remain.

The THERMAE ANTONINIANAE or CARACALLAE present the most perfect remains of any of the Roman baths, and from their vastness cannot fail to strike the spectator with astonishment. The large hall was regarded in antiquity as inimitable. (Spart. *Carac.* 9, *Sever.* 21.) They were dedicated by Caracalla; but Elagabalus commenced the outer porticoes, which were finished by Alexander Severus. (Lampr. *Hel.* 17, *Alex.* 25.) They are situated under the church of S. *Balbina*, on the right of the Via Appia.

But the largest of all the baths at Rome were the THERMAE DIOCLETIANAE. Unfortunately they are in such a ruined state that their plan cannot be traced so perfectly as that of the baths of Caracalla, though enough remains to indicate their vast extent. They are situated on the inside of the *agger* of Servius, between the ancient Porta Collina and Porta Viminalis. Vopiscus mentions them in connection with the Bibliotheca Ulpia, which they contained (*Prob.* 2). These were followed by the

THERMAE CONSTANTINIANAE, the last erected at Rome. They are mentioned by Aurelius Victor as an "opus caeteris haud multo dispar" (*Caes.* 40. 27). In the time of Du Pérac, there were still some vestiges of them on the Quirinal, on the site of the present *Palazzo Rospigliosi*; but they have now entirely disappeared. At one time the colossal figures on *Monte Cavallo* stood near these baths, till Sixtus V. caused them to be placed before the Quirinal palace. Tradition connects them with the *Equi Tiridatis Regis Armeniorum*, mentioned in the *Notitia* in the 7th Region; in which case they would belong to the time of Nero. On the other hand they claim to be the works of Phidias and Praxiteles; but there is no means of deciding this matter.

Besides the baths here enumerated, the *Notitia* and *Curiosum* mention, in the 13th Region, but under mutilated forms, certain THERMAE SURANAE ET DECIANAE, to which we have already alluded in the 5th Section. They do not, however, seem to have been of much importance, and their history is unknown.

XVII. THE BRIDGES.

Rome possessed eight or nine bridges; but the accounts of them are so very imperfect that there are not above two or three the history of which can be satisfactorily ascertained. The PONS SUBLICIUS, the oldest and one of the most frequently mentioned of all the Roman bridges, is precisely that whose site is most doubtful. It was built of wood, as its name imports, by Ancus Marcius, in order to connect the Janiculum, which he had fortified, with the city. (Liv. i. 33; Dionys. iii. 45.) It was considered of such religious importance that it was under the special care of the pontifices (Varr. *L. L.* v. § 83), and was repaired from time to time, even down to the reign of Antoninus Pius. (Capitol. *Ant. P.* 8.) Nay that it must have existed in the time of Constantine is evident, not only from its being mentioned in the *Notitia*, but also from the fact of a bridge at Constantinople being named after it, no doubt to perpetuate in that city the remembrance of its sacred character. (*Descr. Const. Reg.* xiv.) Yet the greatest difference of opinion prevails with regard to its situation; and as this question also involves another respecting the site of the PONS AEMILIUS, we shall examine them both together.

We shall first consider the circumstances under which the Sublician bridge was built; and then inquire into the passages in ancient authors regarding it. Whether Ancus Marcius likewise built walls on the *right* bank of the Tiber when he built the bridge is, as we have before observed, very problematical. seeing that in his time there were none on the *left* bank, and therefore there could have been no impediment to his choosing whatever site he pleased for his bridge, due regard being paid to the nature of the ground. But, as before the time of Tarquinius Priscus, the district about the Forum Boarium and circus was little better than a swamp, it does not seem probable that such a spot should have been selected as the approach to a bridge. The ground beyond the subsequent Porta Trigemina lies higher and drier, and would consequently have afforded a more eligible site. Then comes the question whether, when Servius Tullius built his walls he included the Sublician bridge within them, or contrived that it should be left outside of the gate. As the intention of walls is to defend a city, it is evident that the latter course would be the safer one; for had the bridge afforded a passage to a spot within the walls, an enemy, after forcing it, would have found himself in the heart of the city. And if we examine the passages in ancient authors relating to the subject we shall find that they greatly preponderate in favour of this arrangement. Polybius expressly says that the bridge was πρὸ τῆς πόλεως, *before* or *outside of* the city (vi. 55). Becker, indeed (p. 697), would rob πρό of its usual meaning here, and contends that the expression cited is by no means equivalent to πρὸ τῶν πυλῶν or ἔξω τῆς πόλεως; but he does not support this assertion with any examples, nor would it be possible to support it. The narratives of the flight of Caius Gracchus likewise prove that the bridge must have been outside of the town. Thus Valerius Maximus: "Pomponius, quo is (Gracchus) facilius evaderet, concitatum sequentium agmen in Porta Trigemina aliquamdiu acerrima pugna inhibuit — Laetorius autem in ponte Sublicio constitit, et eum, donec Gracchus transiret, ardore spiritus sui sepsit" (iv. 7. § 2). In like manner the account of Aurelius Victor (*Vir. Ill.* c. 65) plainly shows that Gracchus must have passed the gate before he arrived at the bridge. There is nothing in Livy's narrative of the defence of the bridge by Horatius Cocles to determine the question either one way or

PONS SUBLICIUS, RESTORED BY CANINA.

the other. An inference might perhaps be drawn from a passage in Seneca, compared with another in Plautus, in favour of the bridge being outside of the Porta Trigemina: "In Sublicium Pontem me transfer et inter egentes me abige: non ideo tamen me despiciam, quod in illorum numero consideo, qui manum ad stipem porrigunt." (Sen. *de V. Beat.* 25.) As the Pons Sublicius is here shown to have been the haunt of beggars, so Plautus intimates that their

station was beyond the P. Trigemina (*Capt.* i. 1. 22): —

"Ire extra Portam Trigeminam ad saccum licet."

When the Tiber is low the piles of a bridge are still visible that existed just outside of the Porta Trigemina, near the *Porto di Ripa Grande* (Canina, *Indica.* p. 557); and the Italian topographers, as well as Bunsen, have assumed them to be the remains of the Sublician bridge; whilst Becker, in his *De Muris*, held them to belong to the Pons Aemilius. That writer in the treatise alluded to (p. 78, seq.) made three assertions respecting the Aemilian bridge: (1) That it was not the same as the Sublician; (2) that it stood where the Sublician is commonly placed, i. e. just below the Porta Trigemina; (3) that it was distinct from the Pons Lapideus, or Lepidi. But in his *Handbuch*, published only in the following year, he rejected all these assertions except the first.

According to the most probable view of this intricate and much disputed question at which we can arrive, the matter appears to us to have stood as follows: the Pons Sublicius was outside of the Porta Trigemina, at the place where remains of a bridge still exist. The reasons for arriving at this conclusion have been stated at the beginning of this discussion. Another bridge, of stone, also called Sublicius, was erected close to it to serve the purposes of traffic; but the wooden one was still preserved as a venerable and sacred relic, and as indispensable in certain ancient religious ceremonies, such as the precipitating from it the two dozen men of straw. But the stone bridge had also another name, that of *Lapideus*, by way of distinction from the wooden bridge.

Becker is of opinion that the notion of Aethicus, or Julius Orator, that *Pons Lapideus* was only a vulgar error for *Pons Lepidi*, is a " false eruditionis conjectura," and we think so too. We do not believe that the bridge ever bore the name of Lepidus. We may see from the account given of the wooden bridge by Dionysius, that, though preserved in his time, it was useless for all practical purposes (iii. 45).

We may be sure that the pontifices would not have taken upon themselves the repairs of a bridge subject to the wear and tear of daily traffic. Ovid (*Fast.* v. 622) adverts to its existence, and to the sacred purposes to which it was applied : —

" Tunc quoque priscorum virgo simulacra virorum
  Mittere roboreo scirpea *ponte* solet."

The coexistence of the two bridges, the genuine wooden Sublician, and its stone substitute, is shown in the following passage of Plutarch : οὐ γάρ θεμιτὸν, ἀλλ' ἐπάρατον ἡγεῖσθαι Ῥωμαίους τὴν κατάλυσιν τῆς ξυλίνης γεφύρας ... Ἡ δὲ λιθίνη πολλοῖς ὕστερον ἐξειργάσθη χρόνοις ὑπ' Αἰμιλίου ταμιεύοντος. (*Num.* 9.) Still more decisive is the testimony of Servius : " Cum per Sublicium pontem, hoc est ligneum, qui modo lapideus dicitur, transire conaretur (Porsena)" (*ad Aen.* viii. 646). There must certainly have been a strong and practicable bridge at an early period at this place, for the heavy traffic occasioned by the neighbourhood of the Emporium; but when it was first erected cannot be said. The words of Plutarch, ὑπ' Αἰμιλίου ταμιεύοντος, are obscure, and perhaps corrupt; but at all events we must not confound this notice with that in Livy respecting the building of the Pons Aemilius ; the piles of which were laid in the censorship of M. Aemilius Lepidus and M. Fulvius Nobilior, B.C. 179, and the arches completed some years afterwards, when P. Scipio Africanus and L. Mummius were censors (xl. 51). There is no proof that the *Ponte Rotto* is the Pons Aemilius; but Becker, in his *second* view, and Canina assume that it was; and this view is as probable as any other.

There were several bridges at Rome before the Pons Aemilius was built, since Livy (xxxv. 21) mentions that *two* were carried away by the stream in B.C. 193; and these could hardly have been all, or he would undoubtedly have said so. The Insula Tiberina was, in very early times, connected with each shore by two bridges, and hence obtained the name of INTER DUOS PONTES. (Plut. *Popl.* 8; Macrob. *Sat.* ii. 12.) That nearest the city (now *Ponte Quattro Capi*) was the PONS FABRICIUS, so named from its founder, or probably its restorer,

L. Fabricius, as appears from the inscription on it, and from Dion Cassius (xxxvii. 45). It was the favourite resort of suicides:—

" —— jussit sapientem pascere barbam
Atque a Fabricio non tristem ponte reverti."
      (Hor. *S.* ii. 3. 36.)

The bridge on the farther side of the island (now *Ponte S. Bartolommeo*) is commonly called PONS CESTIUS, and appears to have borne that name in the middle ages. In the inscription, however, which is still extant upon it, it is called PONS GRATIANUS, and its restoration by Valentinian, Valens, and Gratian is commemorated (Canina, *Indic.* p. 576; cf. Amm. Marc. xxvii. 3; Symm. *Epist.* v. 76, x. 45).

Besides these bridges we find four others recorded in the summary of the *Notitia*, namely, the Aelius, Aurelius, Probi, and Milvius. The last of these lay two miles N. of Rome, at the point where the Flaminian Way crossed the Tiber, and has been already described in this dictionary. [PONS MILVIUS.] The PONS AELIUS (now *Ponte S. Angelo*) was built by Hadrian when he founded his mausoleum, to which it directly leads. (Spart. *Hadr.* 19.) In the time of the Anonymous of Einsiedlen, who has preserved the inscription, it was called Pons S. Petri. But before the time of Hadrian there was a bridge which connected the district of the Vatican with the city near the gardens of Caligula and Nero, remains of which still exist near *S. Spirito.* This is probably the bridge which is called in the *Mirabilia* " PONS NERONIANUS," and by the ancient topographers " PONS VATICANUS." The PONS TRIUMPHALIS has also been sometimes identified with this bridge; but Piranesi, who is followed by Bunsen, places the Pons Triumphalis above the Aelian bridge; and it is said that there are still remains of one of the piles near *Tor di Nona.* But in the time of Procopius these had disappeared, and the Pons Aelius formed the only communication between the city and the Vatican district.

The PONS AURELIUS was most probably the present *Ponte Sisto*, leading to the Janiculum and the Porta Aurelia. It appears to have been called PONS ANTONINUS in the middle ages. What the PONS PROBI may have been it is impossible to say. Becker assigns the name to the bridge by the Porta Trigemina, but merely because, having denied that to be the Sublicius, he has nowhere else to place it. Canina, on the contrary (*Indic.* p. 609), places it where we have placed the Pons Aurelius.

XVIII. AQUEDUCTS.

In the time of Frontinus there were at Rome nine principal aqueducts, viz., the Appia. Anio Vetus, Marcia, Tepula, Julia, Virgo, Alsietina, Claudia, Anio Novus; and two subsidiary ones, the Augusta and Rivus Herculaneus. (*Aq.* 4.) Between the time of Frontinus and that of Procopius their number had considerably increased, since the latter historian relates that the Goths destroyed 14 aqueducts that were without the walls. (*B. G.* i. 19.) The *Notitia* enumerates 19, viz. the Trajana, Annia, Attica, Marcia, Claudia, Herculea, Cerulea, Julia, Augustea, Appia, Alseatina, Ciminia, Aurelia, Damnata, Virgo, Tepula, Severiana, Antoniniana, Alexandrina. To enter into a complete history of all these would almost require a separate treatise; and we shall therefore confine ourselves to a statement of the more important particulars concerning them, referring those readers who are desirous of more information on the subject to the *Dictionary of Antiquities,* art. AQUAEDUCTUS.

The AQUA APPIA was, as we have already related, the first aqueduct conferred on Rome by the care of the censor Appius Claudius Caecus, after whom it was named. It commenced on the Via Praenestina, between the 7th and 8th milestone, and extended to the Salinae, near the Porta Trigemina. The whole of it was underground, with

the exception of sixty *passus* conducted on arches from the Porta Capena. Its water began to be distributed at the imus Clivus Publicius, near the Porta Trigemina. (Front. *Aq.* 5.)

The ANIO VETUS was commenced by the censor M'. Curius Dentatus in B.C. 273, and completed by M. Fulvius Flaccus. (*Ib.* 6; Aur. Vict. *Vir. Ill.* 33.) It began above Tibur, and was 43 miles long; but only 221 *passus*, or less than a quarter of a mile, was above ground. It entered the city a little N. of *Porta Maggiore.*

The AQUA MARCIA, one of the noblest of the Roman aqueducts, was built by Q. Marcius Rex, in pursuance of a commission of the senate, B. C. 144. It began near the Via Valeria at a distance of 36 miles from Rome ; but its whole length was nearly 62 miles, of which 6935 *passus* were on arches. Respecting its source, see the article FUCINUS LACUS [Vol. I. p. 918]. It was lofty enough to supply the Mons Capitolinus. Augustus added another source to it, lying at the distance of nearly a mile, and this duct was called after him, AQUA AUGUSTA, but was not reckoned as a separate aqueduct. (Frontin. *Aq.* 12 ; Plin. xxxi. 24 ; Strab. v. p. 240.)

The AQUA TEPULA was built by the censors Cn. Servilius Caepio and L. Cassius Longinus, B. C. 127. Its source was 2 miles to the right of the 10th milestone on the Via Latina.

The preceding aqueduct was united by Agrippa with the AQUA JULIA, which began 2 miles farther down ; and they flowed together as far as the Piscina on the Via Latina. From this point they were conducted in separate channels in conjunction with the Aqua Marcia, so that the Aqua Julia was in the uppermost canal, the Marcia in the lowest, and the Tepula in the middle. (Front. *Aq.* 8, 9, 19.) Remains of these three aqueducts are still to be seen at the *Porta S. Lorenzo* and *Porta Maggiore.*

The AQUA VIRGO was also conducted to Rome by Agrippa in order to supply his baths. According to Frontinus (*Aq.* 10) its name was derived from its source having been pointed out by a young maiden, but other explanations are given. (Plin. xxxi. 25; Cassiod. *Var.* vii. 6.) It commenced in a marshy district at the 8th milestone on the Via Collatina, and was conducted by a very circuitous route, and mostly underground, to the Pincian hill; whence, as we have before mentioned, it was continued to the Campus Martius on arches which began under the gardens of Lucullus. It is the only aqueduct on the left bank of the Tiber which is still in some degree serviceable, and supplies the *Fontana Trevi.*

The AQUA ALSIETINA belonged to the Transtiberine Region. It was constructed by Augustus, and had its source in the Lacus Alsietinus (now *Lago di Martignano*), lying 6½ miles to the right of the 14th milestone on the Via Claudia. Its water was bad, and only fit for watering gardens and such like purposes. (Front. 11.)

The AQUA CLAUDIA was begun by Caligula, and dedicated by Claudius, A. D. 50. This and the Anio Novus were the most gigantic of all the Roman aqueducts. The Claudia was derived from two abundant sources, called Caerulus and Curtius, near the 38th milestone of the Via Sublacensis, and in its course was augmented by another spring, the Albudinus. Its water was particularly pure, and the best after that of the Marcia.

The ANIO NOVUS began 4 miles lower down the Via Sublacensis than the preceding, and was the longest and most lofty of all the aqueducts, being 58,700 passus, or nearly 59 miles, long, and its arches were occasionally 109 feet high. (Front. 15.) This also was completed by the emperor Claudius, as appears from the inscription still extant upon its remains over the *Porta Maggiore*; where both enter the city on the same arch, the Anio Novus flowing over the Claudia. Hence it was conducted over the Caelian hill on the ARCUS NERONIANI or CAELIMONTANI, which terminated, as we have already said, near the temple of Claudius.

As Procopius mentions fourteen aqueducts, five new ones must have been added between the time of Frontinus and of that historian; but respecting only two have we any certain information. The first of these is probably the AQUA TRAJANA, which we find recorded upon coins of Trajan, and which is also mentioned in the *Acta Martyr. S. Anton.* The water was taken from the neighbourhood of the Lacus Sabatinus (*Lago di Bracciano*), and, being conducted to the height of the Janiculum, served to turn the mills under that hill. (Procop. *B. G.* i. 19.) This duct still serves to convey the *Acqua Paola*, which, however, has been spoilt by water taken from the lake. It was also called CIMINIA.

The AQUA ALEXANDRINA was constructed by the emperor Alexander Severus for the use of his baths. (Lamprid. *Alex.* 25.) Originally it was the same as that now called *Acqua Felice*, but conducted at a lower level.

The AQUA SEVERIANA is supposed to have been made by the emperor Septimius Severus for the use of his baths in the 1st Region; but there is no evidence to establish its execution.

The AQUA ANTONINIANA was probably executed by Caracalla for the service of his great baths in the 12th Region; but this also is unsupported by any satisfactory proofs. (Canina, *Indic.* p. 620.) The names and history of a few other aqueducts which we sometimes find mentioned are too obscure to require notice here.

It does not belong to this subject to notice the Roman VIAE, an account of which will be found under that head.

SOURCES AND LITERATURE OF ROMAN TOPOGRAPHY.

With the exception of existing monuments, the chief and most authentic sources for the topography of Rome are the passages of ancient authors in which different localities are alluded to or described. Inscriptions also are a valuable source of information. By far the most important of these is the MONUMENTUM ANCYRANUM, or copy of the record left by Augustus of his actions; an account of which is given elsewhere. [Vol. I. p. 134.] To what is there said we need only add that the best and most useful edition of this document is that published at Berlin with the emendations of Franz, and a commentary by A. W. Zumpt (1845, 4to. pp. 120). Another valuable inscription, though not nearly so important as the one just mentioned, is that called the BASIS CAPITOLINA (Gruter, ccl.), containing the names of the Vici of 5 Regions (the 1st, 10th, 12th, 13th, and 14th), whose curatores and vicomagistri erected a monument to Hadrian. It will be found at the end of Becker's *Handbuch*, vol. i. We may also mention among sources of this description the fragments of Calendars which have been found in various places, and which are frequently useful by marking the sites of temples where certain sacrifices were performed. For the most part the original marbles of these fragments have disappeared, and the inscriptions on them are consequently only extant in MS. copies. One of the most ancient monuments of this kind is the FASTI MAFFEORUM or CALENDARIUM MAFFEANUM, so called from its having been preserved in the *Palazzo Maffei*. With a few *lacunae*, it contains all the twelve months; but what little information that is to be found in it, besides the principal festivals, relates chiefly to Augustus. The next in importance is the FASTI PRAENESTINI, discovered at Praeneste (*Palestrina*) in 1774. Verrius Flaccus, the celebrated grammarian, arranged and annotated it, caused it to be cut in marble, and erected it in the forum at Praeneste. (Suet. *Ill. Gramm.* c. 17.) Only four or five months are extant, and those in an imperfect state. The CALENDARIUM AMITERNINUM was discovered at Amiternum in 1703, and contains the months from May to December, but not entire. The calendar called FASTI CAPRANICORUM, so named from its having formerly been preserved in the *Palazzo Capranica*, contains August and September complete. Other calendars of the same sort are the ANTIATINUM, VENUSINUM, &c. Another lapidary document, but unfortunately in so imperfect a state that it often serves rather to puzzle than to instruct, is the CAPITOLINE PLAN. This is a large plan of Rome cut upon marble tablets, and apparently of the age of Septimius Severus, though with subsequent additions. It was discovered by the architect Giovanni Antonio Dosi, in the pontificate of Pius IV., under the church of SS. *Cosmo e Damiano*; where, broken into many pieces, it was used as a covering of the walls. It came into the possession of Cardinal Farnese, but was put away in a lumber room and forgotten for more than a century. Being rediscovered, it was published in 1673, in 20 plates, by Giovanni Pietro Bellori, librarian to Queen Christina; and subsequently at the end of the 4th volume of the *Thesaurus* of Graevius. The original fragments were carried to Naples with the other property of the Farnese family, and were subsequently given by the king of Naples to Pope Benedict XIV. In 1742 Benedict presented them to the Capitoline Museum at Rome, where they now appear on the wall of the staircase; but several of the pieces had been lost, for which copies, after the designs of Bellori and marked with a star, were substituted. On these fragments the plans of some ancient buildings may be made out, but it is very seldom that their topographical connection can be traced.

Amongst the literary records relating to Roman topography, the first place must be assigned to the NOTITIA. The full title of this work is: *Notitia Dignitatum utriusque Imperii, or in Partibus Orientis et Occidentis*; and it is a statistical view of the Roman empire, of which the description of Rome forms only a small portion or appendix. It cannot be later than the reign of Constantine, since no Christian church is mentioned in it, and indeed no building later than that emperor; nor, on the other hand, can it be earlier, since numerous buildings of the 3rd century, and even some of Constantine's, are named in it. The design of it seems to have been, to name the principal buildings or other objects which marked the boundaries of the different Regions; but we are not to assume that these objects are always named in the order in which they occurred, which is far from being the case. This catalogue has come down to us in various shapes. One of the simplest and most genuine seems to be that entitled *Curiosum Urbis Romae Regionum XIIII. cum Breviariis suis*, the MS. of which is in the Vatican. Some of the other MSS. of the *Notitia* seem to have been interpolated. The spelling and grammar betray a late and barbarous age; but it is impossible that the work can have been composed at the time when the MS. was written.

Besides these there are two catalogues of the so-called REGIONARII, PUBLIUS VICTOR, and SEXTUS RUFUS, which till a very recent period were regarded as genuine, and formed the chief basis of the works of the Italian topographers. It is now, however, universally allowed that they are compilations of a very late date, and that even the names of the writers of them are forgeries. It would be too long to enter in this place into the reasons which have led to this conclusion; and those readers who are desirous of more information will find a full and clear statement of the matter in a paper of Mr. Bunbury's in the *Classical Museum* (vol. iii. p. 373, seq.).

The only other authorities on Roman topography that can be called original are a few notices by travellers and others in the middle ages. One of the principal of these is a collection of inscriptions, and of routes to the chief churches in Rome, discovered by Mabillon in the monastery of Einsiedlen, whence the author is commonly cited as the ANONYMUS EINSIEDLENSIS. The work appears to belong to the age of Charlemagne, and is at all events older than the Leonine city, or the middle of the 9th century. It was published in the 4th vol. of Mabillon's *Analecta*; but since more correctly, according to the arrangement of Gustav Haenel, in the *Archiv für Philologie und Pädagogik*, vol. v. p. 115, seq. In the Routes the principal objects on the right and left are mentioned, though often lying at a considerable distance.

The treatise called the MIRABILIA ROMAE, prefixed to the *Chronicon Romualdi Salernitani* in a MS. preserved in the Vatican, and belonging apparently to the 12th century, seems to have been the first attempt at a regular description of ancient Rome. It was compiled from statistical notices, narratives in the *Acta Martyrum*, and popular legends. It appears, with variations, in the *Liber Censuum* of Cencius, and in many subsequent manuscripts, and was printed as early as the 16th century. It will be found in Montfaucon, *Diarium Ital.* p. 283, seq., and in Nibby's *Effemeridi Letterarie*, Rome, 1820, with notes. A work ascribed to MARTINUS POLONUS, belonging probably to the latter part of the 13th century, seems to have been chiefly founded on the *Mirabilia*. Accounts of some of the gates of Rome will be found in WILLIAM OF MALMESBURY's work *De Gestis Regum Anglorum* (book iv.).

The Florentine POGGIO, who flourished in the 15th century, paid great attention to Roman antiquities. His description of Rome, as it existed in his time, is a mere sketch, but elegant, scholar-like, and touching. It is contained in the first book of his work entitled *De Varietate Fortunae Urbis Romae*, and will be found in Sallengre, *Nov. Thesaur. Ant. Rom.* vol. i. p. 501. A separate edition of his work was also published in Paris, 1723. His predecessor, PETRARCH, has given a few particulars respecting the state of the city in his time; but he treats the subject in an uncritical manner.

The traveller KYRIACUS, called from his native town Anconitanus, who accompanied the emperor Sigismund, passed a few days in Rome during the time that Poggio was also there, which he spent in collecting inscriptions, and noting down some remarks. His work, entitled *Kyriaci Anconitani Itinerarium*, was published at Florence in 1742.

Such are the chief original sources of Roman topography. The literature of the subject is abundantly copious, but our space will permit us to do little more than present the reader with a list of the principal works. The first regular treatise on the antiquities of Rome was that of Biondo Flavio (Blondus Flavius) (1388—1463), who was at once a man of business and a man of letters. His work entitled *Roma Instaurata*, a gigantic step in Roman topography, was published by Froben at Basle, 1513, fol. An Italian translation by Lucio Fauno, but imperfect, appeared at Venice in 1548. Towards the end of the 15th century, Julius Pomponius Laetus founded the Roman Academy. Laetus was an enthusiastic collector of inscriptions, but his fondness for them was such that he sometimes invented what he failed in discovering, and he is accused of having forged the inscription to the statue of Claudian found in the forum of Trajan. (Tiraboschi, *Storia della Lett.* vol. ii. lib. iv.) His book, *De Romanae Urbis vetustate*, is uncritical, and of small value. Janus Parrhasius had a little previously published the pseudo-Victor. To the same period belong the *De Urbe Roma Collectanea* of the bishop Fabricius Varranus, a compilation chiefly borrowed from Biondo, and published, like the work of Laetus, in the collection of Mazocchi, Rome, 1515, 4to. Bernardo Ruccellai, a friend of Lorenzo de' Medici, commenced a description of Rome, by way of commentary on the so-called Victor. It was never completed, and the MS., which is of considerable value, was first printed among the Florentine "Scriptores," in an Appendix to Muratori's collection (vol. ii. p. 755).

The next work that we need mention is the *Antiquitates Urbis Romae* of Andreas Fulvius, Rome, 1527, fol. Bresc. 1545, 8vo. This production is a great step in advance. Fulvius procured from Raphael a sketch of the 14 Regions, according to the restoration of them by himself, but it does not seem to have been preserved. In 1534 the Milanese knight Bartholomaeus Marlianus published his *Urbis Romae Topographia*, a work in many points still unsurpassed. An augmented and much improved edition was published in 1544; but that of 1588 is a mere reprint of the first. It will also be found in the *Thesaurus* of Graevius, vol. iii. Marliano was the first to illustrate his work with plans and drawings, though they are not of a very superior kind. Lucio Fauno's *Delle Antichità della Città di Roma* appeared at Venice in 1548. It contains a few facts which had been overlooked by his predecessors. The celebrated hermit Onuphrius Panvinius of Verona, published at Venice in 1558 his *Commentarium Reipublicae Romanae Libri III.* The first book, entitled *Antiquae Urbis Imago*, which is the topographical part, is written with much learning and acuteness. It was intended merely as a preface to a complete description of Rome according to the Regions of Augustus, but the early death of Panvinius prevented the execution of this plan. His work is contained in the collection of Graevius, vol. iii. It was Panvinius who first published Sextus Rufus, and he also greatly augmented Publius

Victor. George Fabricius, of Chemnits, author of *Antiquitatum Libri II.*, Basle, 1550, accused Panvinius of stealing from him; but if such was the case, he greatly improved what he purloined. Jean Jacques Boissard, of Besançon, published at Frankfort in 1597 a *Topographia Romanae Urbis*, which is not of much value; but the sketches in his collection of inscriptions have preserved the aspect of many things that have now disappeared. The next work of any note is the *Roma Vetus et Recens* of the Jesuit Alex. Donatus of Siena, in which particular attention was paid to the illustration of Roman topography by passages in ancient authors. It was published at Rome, 1638, 4to, and also in the *Thesaurus* of Graevius, vol. iii. But this production was soon obscured by the more celebrated work of Faminiano Nardini, the *Roma Antica*, which marks an epoch in Roman Topography, and long enjoyed a paramount authority. So late as the year 1818, Hobhouse characterised Nardini as "to this day the most serviceable conductor." (*Hist. Illustrations of Childe Harold*, p. 54.) Yet, in many respects, he was an incompetent guide. He knew no Greek; he took the works of the pseudo-Regionaries for the foundation of his book; and it is even affirmed that, though he lived in Rome, he had never visited many of the buildings which he describes. (Bunsen, *Vorrede zur Beschreibung*, p. xxxix.) His work was published at Rome, 1668, 4to; but the best edition of it is the 4th, edited by Nibby, Rome. 1818, 4 vols. 8vo. There is a Latin translation of it in Graevius, vol. iv. In 1680, Raphael Fabretti, of Urbino, secretary to Cardinal Ottoboni, published a valuable work, *De Aquaeductibus*, which will also be found in the same volume of Graevius.

Towards the end of the 17th century two learned French Benedictines, Mabillon and Montfaucon, rendered much service to Roman topography. Mabillon first published the Anonymus Einsiedlensis in his *Analecta* (vol. iv. p. 50, seq.) Montfaucon, who spent two years and a half in Rome (1698—1700). inserted in his *Diarium Italicum* a description of the city divided into twenty days. The 20th chapter contains a copy of the *Mirabilia*. In 1687 Olaus Borrichius published a topographical sketch of Rome, according to the Regions. It is in the 4th volume of Graevius. The work of the Marquis Ridolfino Venuti, entitled *Accurata e succinta Descrizione Topografica delle Antichità di Roma* (Roma, 1763, 2 vols. 4to.), is a book of more pretensions. Venuti took most of his work from Nardini and Piranesi, and the new matter that he added is generally erroneous. The 4th edition by Stefano Piale, Rome, 1824, is the best. Francesco Ficoroni's *Vestigia e Rarità di Roma Antica* (Roma, 1744, 4to.) is not a very satisfactory performance. The most useful portions of it have been inserted in the *Miscellanea* of Fea (part i. pp. 118—178). The work of our countryman Andrew Lumisden, *Remarks on the Antiquities of Rome and its Environs* (London, 1797, 4to.) was, in its day, a book of some authority. Many valuable observations on Roman topography are scattered in the works of the learned Gaetano Marini, and especially in his *Atti de' Fratelli Arvali*; but he treated the subject only incidentally. The same remark applies to Visconti. The *Roma descritta ed illustrata* (Roma, 1806, 2 vol. 4to.), of the Abbate Guattani is the parent of most of the modern guide books. Antonio Nibby has published several useful works on Roman topography, which, if sometimes deficient in accurate

scholarship, display nevertheless considerable acuteness and knowledge of the subject. His principal works are, *Del Foro Romano, della Via Sacra, &c.*, Roma, 1819, 8vo.; *Le Mura di Roma, disegnate da Sir W. Gell, illustr. da A. Nibby*, Roma, 1820; and his *Roma Antica*, published in 1838. Sir Wm. Gell's *Topography of Rome and its Vicinity* (2nd Edit., revised and enlarged by Bunbury, London, 1846) contains some useful information. The *Miscellanea filologica, critica ed antiquaria* (Rome, 1790), and the *Nuova Descrizione di Roma* (Rome, 1820, 3 vols. 8vo.), by Carlo Fea, are useful works. Hobhouse's *Historical Illustrations of Childe Harold, with Dissertations on the Ruins of Rome* (London, 2nd ed. 1818, 8vo.) are chiefly valuable for their account of the gradual destruction of the city. The works of two other Englishmen are now out of date viz. Edward Burton's *Description of the Antiquities of Rome* (Oxf. 1821 ; London, 1828, 2 vols. 8vo.); and the Rev. Richard Burgess's *Topography and Antiquities of Rome* (London, 1831, 2 vols. 8vo.). Forsyth's *Italy* is of little service for Rome. Sachse's *Geschichte und Beschreibung der alten Stadt Rom* (Hanover, 1824—1828, 2 vols. 8vo.), though still in some respects a useful production, must now be regarded as superseded by more recent works.

We are now arrived at the *Beschreibung der Stadt Rom*, with which may be said to commence the modern epoch of Roman topography. This work was projected in 1817 by some German *literati* then residing at Rome, among whom were the present Chevalier Bunsen, and Ernst Platner, Eduard Gerhard and Wilhelm Röstell. They were joined by the celebrated historian B. G. Niebuhr, who undertook the superintendence of the ancient part; for the scheme of the book embraced a complete description of the modern city, with all its treasures of art, besides an account of ancient Rome. It is, however, of course only with the latter that we are here concerned, which was undertaken by Niebuhr. Bunsen, and subsequently L. Urlichs. Niebuhr's connection with the work was not of long duration, and only a few of the descriptions are from his hand, which form the most valuable portion of the book. The views of the German scholars threatened a complete revolution in Roman topography. They seemed to have come to Rome with the express design of overturning the paper city, as their ancestors many centuries before had subverted the stone one. In extent and accuracy of erudition they were far superior to their Italian antagonists; but this advantage is often more than counterbalanced by that want of sober and critical good sense which so frequently mars the productions of German scholars. They have succeeded in throwing doubt upon a great deal, but have established very little in its place. To Piale, and not to the Germans, belongs the merit of having reestablished the true situation of the forum, which may be considered as the most important step in the modern topography of Rome. The German views respecting the Capitol, the comitium, and several other important points, have found many followers; but to the writer of the present article they appear for the most part not to be proved; and he has endeavoured in the preceding pages to give his reasons for that opinion.

It cannot be denied, however, that the appearance of the *Beschreibung* did good service to the cause of Roman topography, by awakening a sharper and more extended spirit of inquiry. The first volume appeared at Stuttgard in 1829, the last in 1842. As a literary production — we are speaking of course of the ancient parts — it is of little service to the scholar. The descriptions are verbose, and the ancient ones being intermingled with the modern have to be sought through a voluminous work. A still graver defect is the almost entire absence, especially in the earlier volumes, of all citation of authorities.

At this period in the history of Roman topography W. A. Becker, paid a short visit to Rome. Becker took up the subject of his researches as a point of national honour; and in his first tract, *De Romae Veteris Muris atque Portis* (Leipzig, 1842), devoted two pages of the preface to an attack upon Canina, whom he suspected of the grave offence of a want of due reverence for German scholarship. But with an inborn pugnacity his weapons were also turned against his own countrymen. Amid a little faint praise, the labours of Bunsen and Urlichs were censured as incomplete and unsatisfactory. In the following year (1843) Becker published the first volume of his *Handbuch der Römischen Alterthümer*, containing a view of the topography of Rome. A review of his work by L. Preller, which appeared in the *Neue Jenaische Allgemeine Literatur-Zeitung*, though written with candour and moderation, seems to have stung Becker into fury. He answered it in a pamphlet entitled *Die Römische Topographie in Rom, eine Warnung* (Leipzig, 1844), in which he accused Preller of having taken up the cudgels in favour of Canina, though that gentleman is a moderate adherent of the German school of topographers. Nothing can exceed the arrogant tone of this pamphlet, the very title of which is offensive. It was answered by Urlichs in his *Römische Topographie in Leipzig* (Stuttgart, 1845), in which, though Becker well deserved castigation, the author adopted too much of the virulent and personal tone of his adversary. The controversy was brought to a close by a reply and rejoinder, both written with equal bitterness; but the dispute has served to throw light on some questions of Roman topography. In a purely literary point of view, Becker's *Handbuch* must be allowed to be a very useful production. His views are arranged and stated with great clearness, and the constant citation of authorities at the bottom of the page is very convenient to the student. The writer of this article feels himself bound to acknowledge that it would not have been possible for him to have prepared it without the assistance of Becker's work. Nevertheless he is of opinion that many of Becker's views on the most important points of Roman topography are entirely erroneous, and that they have gained acceptation only from the extraordinary confidence with which they are asserted and the display of learning by which they are supported. Amongst other German topographers we need only mention here L. Preller, who has done good service by some able papers and by his useful work on the Regions of Augustus (*Die Regionen der Stadt Rom*, Jena, 1846, 8vo.). We may add that the English reader will find a succinct and able sketch of the views of the German school, and particularly of Becker, in a series of very valuable papers by Mr. Bunbury, published in the *Classical Museum* (vols. iii. iv. and v.).

We shall close this list with the names of two modern Italian topographers. Between the years 1820 and 1835, Stefano Piale published some very useful dissertations on various points of Roman to-pography, among which the following may be particularly mentioned: *Delle Porte settentrionali del Recinto di Servio; Delle Porte orientali, delle meridionali, e di quelle del Monte Aventino della stessa cinta; Della grandezza di Roma al tempo di Plinio; Del Foro Romano; Delle Mura Aureliane; e degli antichi Arsenali detti Navalia, &c.* But at the head of the modern Italian school must be placed the Commendatore, Luigi Canina. Canina has a real enthusiasm for his subject, which, from his profession, he regards from an architectural rather than a philological point of view; and this, combined with the advantages of a residence at Rome, goes far to compensate the absence of the profounder, but often unwieldy, erudition of the Germans. The later editions of his works have been freed from some of the errors which disfigured the early ones, and contain much useful information, not unmixed sometimes with erroneous views; a defect, however, which in a greater or less degree must be the lot of all who approach the very extensive and very debatable subject of Roman topography. Canina's principal works are the *Indicazione topografica di Roma antica*, 4th ed. Rome, 1850, 8vo.; *Del Foro Romano e sue Adjacenze*, 2nd ed. 1845; and especially his magnificent work in four large folio volumes entitled *Gli Edifizi di Roma antica*, with views, plans, and restorations.

It now only remains to notice some of the principal maps and other illustrations of Rome. The Florentine San Gallo, who flourished in the 15th century, drew several of the most remarkable monuments. The sketches and plans of Antonio Labacco, executed at the beginning of the 16th century, are valuable but scarce. We have already mentioned that Raphael designed, or thought of designing, a plan of the restored city. This plan, if ever executed, is no longer in existence; but a description of it will be found in a letter addressed by Castiglione to Pope Leo X. (Published in the works of Castiglione, Padua, 1733. There is a translation of it in the *Beschreibung*, vol. i. p. 266. seq.) Serlio of Bologna, architect to Francis I., gave many plans and sketches of ancient Roman buildings in the 3rd book of his work on architecture (Venice, 1544, fol.), to which, however, he added *restorations*. Leonardo Buffalini's great plan of Rome, as it was in 1551, was most important for Roman topography. It was drawn on wood in 24 plates; but unfortunately all that now remains of it is an imperfect copy in the Barberini palace. Pirro Ligorio and Bernardo Gamucci published several views in Rome about the middle of the 16th century. In 1570 appeared the great work of Palladio, *Libri IV. dell' Architettura, &c.* (Venice, fol.), in the 4th book of which are several plans of ancient temples; but the collection is not so rich as that of Serlio. Scamozzi's *Discorsi sopra le Antichità di Roma* (Venice, 1852, fol.) contains some good views, but the letter-press is insignificant. In 1574 Fulvius Ursinus assisted the Parisian architect Du Pérac in drawing up a plan of the restored city, which was published in several sheets by Giacomo Lauro. It is erroneous, incomplete, and of little service. Of much more value are the views of ancient monuments published by Du Pérac in 1573, and republished by Losai in 1773. In the time of Du Pérac several monuments were in existence which have now disappeared, as the forum of Nerva, the Septizonium, and the trophies of Marius. The sketches of Pietro Santi Bartoli, first published in 1741, are clever but full of mannerism.

Antoine Desgodetz, sent to Rome by Colbert, published at Paris in 1682 his work in folio, entitled *Les Édifices antiques de Rome mesurés et dessinés*. The measurements are very correct, and the work indispensable to those who would thoroughly study Roman architecture. Nolli's great plan of Rome, the first that can be called an accurate one, appeared in 1748. In 1784 Piranesi published his splendid work the *Antichità Romane* (Rome, 4 vols. fol.), containing the principal ruins. It was continued by his son, Francesco Piranesi. The work of Mich. d'Overbeke, *Les restes de l'ancienne Rome* (à la Haye, 1673, 2 vols. large fol.), is also of great value. In 1822 appeared the *Antichità Romane* of Luigi Rossini (Rome, 1822, large fol.). To the plans and restorations of Canina in his *Edifizi* we have already alluded. His large map of Rome represents of course his peculiar views, but will be found useful and valuable. Further information on the literature of Roman topography will be found in an excellent preface to the *Beschreibung* by the Chevalier Bunsen.						[T. H. D.]

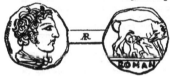

COIN OF ROME.

ROMATI'NUS. [CONCORDIA.]

ROME'CHIUM, a place on the E. coast of the Bruttian peninsula, mentioned only by Ovid, in his description of the voyage of the Epidaurian serpent to Rome (Ovid. *Met.* xv. 705). The geography of the passage is by no means very precise; but according to local topographers the name of *Romechi* is still retained by a place on the sea-coast near *Roccella*, about 12 miles N. of the ruins of Locri (Romanelli, vol. i. p. 156; Quattromani, *Not. ad Barrii Calabr.* iii. 13.)						[E. H. B.]

RO'MULA, a place in Upper Pannonia, on the road leading from Aemona along the river Savus to Sirmium. (*It. Ant.* p. 274; *Tab. Peut.*) It is perhaps the modern *Carlstadt*, the capital of *Croatia*.						[L. S.]

RO'MULA. [DACIA, p. 744. b.]

ROMU'LEA ('Ρωμυλία, Steph. B.: *Bisaccia*), a city of Samnium, mentioned by Livy (x. 17), as being taken by the Roman consul P. Decius, or according to others by Fabius, in the Third Samnite War, B. C. 297. It is described as being a large and opulent place; but seems to have afterwards fallen into decay, as the name is not noticed by any other writer, except Stephanus of Byzantium, and is not found in any of the geographers. But the Itineraries mention a station Sub Romula, which they place on the Appian Way, 21 miles beyond Aeculanum, and 22 miles from the Pons Aufidi (*Itin. Ant.* p. 120). Both these stations being known, we may fix Romulea, which evidently occupied a hill above the road, on the site of the modern town of *Bisaccia*, where various ancient remains have been discovered. (Romanelli, vol. ii. p. 348; Cluver. *Ital.* p. 1204; Pratilli, *Via Appia*, iv. 5).				[E. H. B.]

ROSCIA'NUM (*Rossano*), a town of Bruttium, situated on a hill about 2 miles from the sea-coast, on the gulf of Tarentum, and 12 miles from the mouth of the Crathis. The name is not found in the geographers, or mentioned by any earlier writer; but it is found in the Itinerary of Antoninus, which places it 12 miles from Thurii, and is noticed by Procopius during the Gothic wars as a strong fortress, and one of the most important strongholds in this part of Italy. (*Itin. Ant.* p. 114; Procop. *B. G.* iii. 30.) It was taken by Totila in A. D. 548, but continued throughout the middle ages to be a place of importance, and is still one of the most considerable towns in this part of *Calabria*.		[E.H.B.]

ROSTRUM NEMAVIAE, a place in the central part of Vindelicia, on the river Virdo. (*It. Ant.* pp. 237, 258.)						[L. S.]

ROTOMAGUS ('Ρατόμαγος), in Gallia Lugdunensis, is mentioned by Ptolemy (ii. 8. § 8) as the capital of the Veneliocasi, as the name is written in some editions. [VELLOCASSES.] In the Table the name is written Rattomagus, with the mark which indicates a capital town; and in the Antonine Itin. it occurs in the corrupted form Latomagus on the road which runs from a place called Carocotinum. Ammianus (xv. 11) speaks of it in the plural number Rotomagi. There are said to be coins with the legend Ratumacos.

Rotomagus is *Rouen* on the north side of the Seine, and the capital of the department of *Seine Inférieure*. The old Gallic name was shortened to Rotomum or Rodomum, and then to *Rouen*, as Rodumna has been shortened to *Roanne*. The situation of *Rouen* probably made it a town of some importance under the Roman Empire, but very few Roman remains have been found in *Rouen*. Some Roman tombs have been mentioned.		[G. L.]

ROXOLA'NI ('Ρωξολανοί), a people belonging to the Sarmatian stock, who first appear in history about a century before Christ, when they were found occupying the steppes between the *Dnieper* and the *Don*. (Strab. ii. p. 214, vii. pp. 294, 306, 307, 309; Plin. iv. 12; Ptol. iii. 5. §§ 19, 24, 25.) Afterwards some of them made their footing in Dacia and behind the Carpathians. Strabo (vii. p. 306) has told the story of the defeat of the Roxolani and their leader Tasius by Diophantus, the general of Mithridates, and takes the opportunity of describing some of their manners which resembled those of the Sarmatian stock to which they belonged. Tacitus (*Hist.* i. 79) mentions another defeat of this people, when making an inroad into Moesia during Otho's short lease of power. From the inscription (Orelli, *Inscr.* 750) which records the honours paid to Plautius Silvanus, it appears that they were also defeated by him. Hadrian, who kept his frontier quiet by subsidising the needy tribes, when they complained about the payment came to terms with their king (Spartian, *Hadr.* 6) — probably the Rasparasanus of the inscription (Orelli, *Inscr.* 833). When the general rising broke out among the Sarmatian, German and Scythian tribes from the Rhine to the Tanais in the reign of M. Aurelius, the Roxolani were included in the number. (Jul. Capit. *M. Anton.* 22.) With the inroads of the Goths the name of the Roxolani almost disappears. They probably were partly exterminated, and partly united with the kindred tribes of the Alani, and shared the general fate when the Huns poured down from the interior of Asia, crossed the *Don*, and oppressed the Alani, and, later, with the help of these, the Ostro-Goths.

It has been assumed that the name of the RHACALANI ('Ρακαλανοί, Ptol. iii. 5. § 24) is not different from that of the Roxolani, who, according to

3 I 4

Schafarik (*Slav. Alt.* vol. i. p. 342), received their appellation from the Sarmatian " Raxa,"— perhaps the *Volga* or some other river in their settlements.   [E. B. J.]

RUADITAE. [MARMARICA, p. 278, a.]

RUBI (*Eth.* 'Ρυβαστεινός, Rubastinus: *Ruvo*), a city of Apulia, situated on the branch of the Appian Way between Canusia and Butuntum, and about 10 miles distant from the sea-coast. It is mentioned by Horace, as one of the places where Maecenas and his companions slept on the journey from Rome to Brundusium. (Hor. *Sat.* i. 5. 94.) The distance from Canusium is given as 23 miles in the Antonine Itinerary, and 30 in the Jerusalem Itinerary, which is the more correct, the direct distance on the map being above 28 miles. (*Itin. Ant.* p. 116; *Itin. Hier.* p. 610.) Neither Strabo nor Ptolemy notices the existence of Rubi, but the inhabitants are mentioned under the name of Rubustini by Pliny, among the municipal towns of Apulia, and the " Rubustinus Ager" is enumerated in the Liber Coloniarum among the " Civitates Apuliae." (Plin. iii. 11. s. 16; *Lib. Colon.* p. 262.) An inscription also attests the municipal rank of Rubi in the reign of the younger Gordian. (Mommsen, *Inscr. R. N.* 624.) The singular ethnic form given by Pliny is confirmed by the evidence of coins which have the name P V BA Ξ-ΤΕΙΝΩΝ at full. These coins show also that Rubi must have received a considerable amount of Greek influence and cultivation ; and this is still more strongly confirmed by the discoveries which have been recently made by excavations there of numerous works of Greek art in bronze and terra cotta, as well as of vast numbers of painted vases, of great variety and beauty. These, however, like all the others found in Apulia and Lucania, are of inferior execution, and show a declining state of art as compared with those of Nola or Volci. All these objects have been discovered in tombs, and in some instances the walls of the tombs themselves have been found covered with paintings. (Romanelli, vol. ii. p. 172; *Bullett. dell' Inst. Arch.* 1829, p. 173, 1834, pp. 36, 164, 228, &c.) The modern town of *Ruvo* is still a considerable place, with an episcopal see. [E. H. B.]

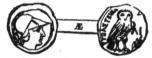

COIN OF RUBI.

RUBICON ('Ρουβίκων), a small river on the E. coast of Italy, flowing into the Adriatic sea, a few miles N. of Ariminum. It was a trifling stream, one of the least considerable of the numerous rivers that in this part of Italy have their rise in the Apennines, and discharge their waters into the Adriatic; but it derived some importance from its having formed the boundary between Umbria, or the part of the Gaulish territory included in that province, and Cisalpine Gaul, properly so called. Hence, when the limits of Italy were considered to extend only to the frontiers of Cisalpine Gaul, the Rubicon became on this side the northern boundary of Italy. (Strab. v. p. 217; Plin. iii. 15. s. 20; Lucan. i. 215.) This was the state of things at the outbreak of the Civil War between Caesar and Pompey: Cisalpine Gaul was included in the government of the former, and the Rubicon was therefore the limit of his province; it was this which rendered the passage of

this trifling stream so momentous an event, for it was, in fact, the declaration of war. Caesar himself makes no mention of its passage, and it is difficult to believe that he would have set out on his march from Ravenna without being fully prepared to advance to Ariminum; but the well-known story of his halt on its banks, his hesitation and ultimate decision, is related in detail by Suetonius and Plutarch, as well as by Lucan, and has given a proverbial celebrity to the name of the Rubicon. (Suet. *Caes.* 31; Plut. *Caes.* 32; Appian, *B. C.* ii. 35; Lucan, i. 185, 213—227.) The river is alluded to by Cicero a few years later as the frontier of Gaul; and M. Antonius was ordered by a decree of the senate to withdraw his army across the Rubicon, as a proof that he abandoned his designs on the Gaulish province. (Cic. *Phil.* vi. 3.) Strabo still reckons the Rubicon the limit between Gallia Cisalpina and Umbria; but this seems to have been altered in the division of Italy by Augustus; and though Pliny alludes to the Rubicon as " quondam finis Italiae," he includes Ariminum and its territory as far as the river Crustumius, in the 8th Region or Gallia Cispadana. (Plin. *l. c.*; Ptol. iii. 1. § 23.) Its name, however, was not forgotten; it is still found in the Tabula, which places it 12 miles from Ariminum (*Tab. Peut.*), and is mentioned by Sidonius Apollinaris. (*Ep.* i. 5.) But in the middle ages all trace of it seems to have been lost ; even the Geographer of Ravenna does not notice it, notwithstanding its proximity to his native city.

In modern times the identification of this celebrated stream has been the subject of much controversy, and cannot yet be considered as fully determined. But the question lies within very narrow compass. We know with certainty that the Rubicon was intermediate between Ariminum and Ravenna, and between the rivers Sapis (*Savio*), which flowed some miles S. of the latter, and the Ariminus or *Marecchia*, which was immediately to the N. of the former city. Between these two rivers only two streams now enter the Adriatic, within a very short distance of each other. The southernmost of these is called the *Luso* or *Lusa*, a considerable stream, which crosses the high-road from *Rimini* to *Ravenna* about 10 miles from the former city. A short distance further N. the same road crosses a stream now called *Fiumicino*, which is formed by the united waters of three small streams or torrents, the most considerable of which is the *Pisatello* (the uppermost of the three); the other two are the *Rigosa* or *Rigone*, called also, according to some writers, the *Rugone*, and the *Plusa*, called also the *Fiumicino*. These names are those attested by the best old maps as well as modern ones, especially by the Atlas of Magini, published in 1620, and are in accordance with the statements of the earliest writers on Italian topography, Flavio Biondo and Leandro Alberti. Cluverius, however, calls the northernmost stream the *Rugone*, and the one next to it the *Pisatello*. This point is, however, of little importance, if it be certain that the two streams always united their waters as they do at the present day before reaching the sea. The question really lies between the *Luso* and the *Fiumicino*, the latter being the outlet both of the *Rugone* and the *Pisatello*. A papal bull, issued in 1756, pronounced in favour of the *Luso*, which has, in consequence, been since commonly termed the Rubicon, and is still called by the peasants on its banks *Il Rubicone*. But it is evident that such an authority has no real weight. The name of *Rugone*, applied to one of the three branches of the *Fiumicino*, would be of more value, if it were certain that this name had not been distorted by antiquarians to suit their own purposes. But it appears that old maps and books write the name *Rigosa*. Two arguments, however, may be considered as almost decisive in favour of the *Fiumicino* as compared with the *Luso*: 1st. The distance given in the Tabula of 12 miles from Ariminum, coincides exactly with the distance of the *Fiumicino* from that city, as stated by Cluverius, who examined the question on the spot; and 2ndly, the redness of the gravel in the bed of the stream, from which it was supposed to have derived its name, and which is distinctly alluded to by Sidonius Apollinaris, as well as by Lucan (Sidon. *Ep.* i. 5; Lucan, i. 214), was remarked by Cluverius as a character of the *Fiumicino*, which was wholly wanting in the *Luso*. The circumstance which has been relied on by some authors, that the latter river is a more considerable and rapid stream than the other, and would therefore constitute a better frontier, is certainly of no value, for Lucan distinctly speaks of the Rubicon as a trifling stream, with little water in it except when swollen by the winter rains.

The arguments in favour of the *Fiumicino* or *Pisatello* (if we retain the name of the principal of its three confluents) thus appear decidedly to preponderate; but the question still requires a careful examination on the spot, for the statements of Cluverius, though derived from personal observation, do not agree well with the modern maps, and it is not improbable that the petty streams in question may have undergone considerable changes since his time: still more probable is it that such changes may have taken place since the time of Caesar. (Cluver. *Ital.* pp. 296 — 299; Blondi Flavii *Italia Illustrata*, p. 343; Alberti, *Descrizione d' Italia*, p. 246; Magini, *Carta di Romagna*; Mannert, *Geographie von Italien*, vol. i. p. 234; Murray's *Handbook for Central Italy* p. 104. The older dissertations on the subject will be found in Graevius and Burmann's *Thesaurus*, vol. vii. part 2.)　[E. H. B.]

RUBRAE and AD RUBRAS, a town in Hispania Baetica, now *Cabezas Rubias*. (*It. Ant.* p. 431.)　　　　　　　　　　　　[T. H. D.]

RUBRESUS LACUS. [ATAX.]

RUBRICATA ('Ρουβρίκατα, Ptol. ii. 6. § 74), an inland city of the Laeëtani in the NE. part of Hispania Tarraconensis, on the river Rubricatus, according to Reichard, *Olesa*.　　[T. H. D.]

RUBRICATUS or -UM ('Ρουβρίκατος, Ptol. ii. 6. § 18), a river of Hispania Tarraconensis flowing into the Mare Internum a little W. of Barcino, the modern *Llobregat*. (Mela, ii. 6. § 5; Plin. iii. 3. s. 4.)　　　　　　　　　　　　[T. H. D.]

RUBRICATUS, in Numidia. [RHUBRICATUS.]

RUBRUM MARE, or ERYTHRAEUM MARE (ἡ ἐρυθρὰ θάλασσα, Herod. i. 180, 202, ii. 8, 158, 159, iv. 39; Polyb. v. 54. § 12, ix. 43. § 2; Strab. i. pp. 32, 33, 50, 56, xvi. pp. 765, 779, xvii. pp. 804, 815; Pomp. Mela, iii. 8. § 1; Plin. vi. 2. s. 7). The sea called Erythra in Herodotus has a wide extension, including the *Indian Ocean*, and its two gulfs the *Red Sea* and the *Persian Gulf* [PERSICUS SINUS], which latter he does not seem to have considered as a gulf, but as part of a continuous sea-line; when the *Red Sea* specifically is meant it bears the name of Arabicus Sinus [ARABICUS SINUS]. The thick, wall-like masses of coral which form the shores or fringing reefs of the cleft by which the

waters of the *Indian Ocean* advance through the straits of *Bab-el-Mandeb*, with their red and purple hues, were no doubt the original source of the name. Thus also in Hebrew (*Exod.* x. 19, xiii. 18; *Ps.* cvi. 7, 9, 22) it was called "yam sûph," or the "weedy sea," from the coralline forests lying below the surface of the water. Ramses Miamoum (Sesostris) was the first (from 1388 to 1322, B. C.) — so said the priests — who with long ships subjected to his dominion the dwellers on the coast of the Erythraean, until at length sailing onwards, he arrived at a sea so shallow as to be no longer navigable. Diodorus (i. 55, 56; comp. Herod. ii. 102) asserts that this conqueror advanced in India beyond the Ganges, while Strabo (xvi. p. 760) speaks of a memorial pillar of Sesostris near the strait of Deire or *Bab-el-Mandeb*. It appears that the *Persian Gulf* had been opened out to Phoenician navigation as three places were found there which bore similar if not identical names with those of Phoenicia, Tylus or Tyrus, Aradus, and Dora (Strab. xvi. pp. 766, 784, comp. i. p. 42), in which were temples resembling those of Phoenicia (comp. Kenrick, *Phoenicia*, p. 48). The expeditions of Hiram and Solomon, conjoint undertakings of the Tyrians and Israelites, sailed from Ezion Geber through the Straits of *Bab-el-Mandeb* to Ophir, one locality of which may be fixed in the basin of the Erythraean or *Indian Ocean* [OPHIR]. The Lagid kings of Aegypt availed themselves with great success of the channel by which nature brought the traffic and intercourse of the *Indian Ocean*, within a few miles of the coast of the Interior Sea. Their vessels visited the whole western peninsula of India from the gulf of Barygaza, *Guzerat*, and *Cumbay*, along the coasts of *Malabar* to the Brahminical sanctuaries of *Cape Comorin*, and to the great island of Taprobane or *Ceylon*. Nearchus and the companions of Alexander were not ignorant of the existence of the periodical winds or monsoons which favour the navigation between the E. coast of Africa, and the N. and W. coasts of India. From the further knowledge acquired by navigators of this remarkable local direction of the wind, they were afterwards emboldened to sail from Ocelis in the straits of *Bab-el-Mandeb* and hold a direct course along the open sea to Muziris, the great mart on the *Malabar* coast (S. of *Mangalor*), to which internal traffic brought articles of commerce from the E. coast of the Indian peninsula, and even gold from the remote Chryse. The Roman empire in its greatest extent on its E. limit reached only to the meridian of the *Persian Gulf*, but Strabo (i. p. 14, ii. p. 118, xvi. p. 781, xvii. pp. 798, 815) saw in Aegypt with surprise the number of ships which sailed from Myos Hormos to India. From the Zend and Sanscrit words which have been preserved in the geographical nomenclature of Ptolemy, his tabular geography remains an historic monument of the commercial relations between the West and the most distant regions of Southern and Central Asia. At the same time Ptolemy (iv. 9, vii. 3. § 5) did not give up the fable of the "unknown southern land" connecting Prasum Prom. with Cattigara and Thinae (Sinarum Metropolis), and therefore joined E. Africa with the land of Tsin or *China*. This isthmus-hypothesis, derived from views which may be traced back to Hipparchus and Marinus of Tyre, in which, however, Strabo did not concur, made the *Indian Ocean* a Mediterranean sea. About half a century later than Ptolemy a minute, and as it appears a very faithful, account of the coast was given in the Periplus of the Erythraean Sea (a work erroneously attributed to Arrian, and probably not anterior to Septimius Severus and his son Caracalla) (comp. Cooley, *Claudius Ptolemy and the Nile*, p. 56). During the long wars with Persia, the Aegyptian and Syrian population, cut off from their ordinary communication with Persia and India, were supplied by the channel which the shores of the *Persian Gulf* and the Red Sea afforded; and in the reign of Justinian this commerce was very important. After the disturbances caused by the wars of Heraclius and Chosroes, the Arabs or Saracens placed upon the confines of Syria, Aegypt, and Persia, had the greatest portion of the rich trade with Aethiopia, S. Africa, and India thrown into their hands. From the middle of the ninth century the Arab population of the *Hedjas* maintained commercial relations with the northern countries of *Europe* and with *Madagascar*, with *E. Africa*, *India*, and *China*, diffusing their language, their coins, and the Indian system of numbers. But from the time that the Kaliph Al-Mansur closed the canal connecting the Red Sea with the Nile, the important line of communication between the commerce of Aegypt and India and the E. coast of S. Africa has never been restored. For all that concerns the data furnished by the ancient writers to the geography of the Erythraean sea the Atlas appended by Müller to his *Geographi Graeci Minores* (Paris, 1855) should be consulted. He has brought together the positions of Agatharchides, Artemidorus, Pliny, Ptolemy, and the Pseudo-Arrian, and compared them with the recent surveys made by Moresby, Carless, and others.   [E. B. J.]

RUCCO'NIUM. [DACIA, p. 744, b.]

RUESSIUM. [REVESSIO.]

RUFINIA'NA (*Ρουφινιανα*). Ptolemy (ii.9.§17) names Noeomagus [NOVIOMAGUS, No. 2.] and Rufiniana as the two towns of the Nemetes, a people on the Rhine in Gallia Belgica. If we place Rufiniana with D'Anville and others at *Ruffach* in *Upper Alsace* and in the present department of *Haut Rhin*, we must admit that Ptolemy has made a great mistake, for *Ruffach* is within the territory of the Rauraci. But D'Anville observes that it is not more extraordinary to find Rufiniana misplaced in Ptolemy than to find him place Argentoratum in the territory of the Vangiones.   [G. L.]

RUFRAE, a town of the Samnites on the borders of Campania, mentioned by Virgil (*Aen.* vii. 739) in a manner that would lead us to suppose it situated in Campania, or at least in the neighbourhood of that country; while Silius Italicus distinctly includes it among the cities of the Samnites (viii. 568), and Livy also mentions Rufrium (in all probability the same place) among the towns taken from the Samnites' at the commencement of the Second Samnite War, B. c. 326. (Liv. viii. 25.) None of these passages afford any clue to its position, which cannot be determined; though it must certainly be sought for in the region above indicated. The sites suggested by Romanelli (vol. ii. p. 463) and other local topographers are mere conjectures. [E. H. B.]

RUFRIUM. [RUFRAE.]

RUGII, RUGI (*Ρούγοι* or *Ρόγοι*), an important people in the north of Germany, occupying a considerable part of the coast of the Baltic. (Tac. *Germ.* 43.) Their country extended from the river Viadus in the west to the Vistula in the east, and was surrounded in the west by the Sideni, in the

south by the Helvecones, and in the east by the Sciri, who were probably a Sarmatian tribe. Strabo does not mention them, and Ptolemy (ii. 11. § 14) speaks of a tribe *Ρουτίκλειοι*, who are probably the same as the Rugii. After their first appearance in Tacitus, a long time passes away during which they are not noticed, until they suddenly reappear during the wars of Attila, when they play a conspicuous part. (Sidon. Apoll. *Paneg. ad Avit.* 319; Paul. Diac. *de Gest. Rom.* p. 534, ed. Erasm.) After the death of Attila, they appear on the north side of the Danube in Austria and Upper Hungary, and the country there inhabited by them was now called Rugia, and formed a separate kingdom. (Procop. *Bell. Goth.* ii. 14, iii. 2; Paul. Diac. *Longob.* i. 19.) But while in this latter country no trace of their name is now left, their name is still preserved in their original home on the Baltic, in the island of *Rügen*, and in the town of *Rügenwalde*, and perhaps also in *Rega* and *Regenwalde*. (Comp. Latham on *Tac. l. c.*, and Prolegom. p. xix., who strangely believes that the Rugii of Tacitus dwelt on the *Gulf of Riga*.)   [L. S.]

RUGIUM (*Ρούγιον*), a town in the north of Germany on the coast of the Baltic (Ptol. ii. 11. § 27), the site of which seems to correspond exactly with that of the modern *Regenwalde*, on the river *Rega*, though others seek it elsewhere. (Wilhelm, *Germanien*, p. 273.)   [L. S.]

RUNICATAE (*Ρουνικᾶται*), an Alpine tribe in the north-east of Vindelicia between the Oenus and Danubius. (Ptol. ii. 13. § 1.) In the inscription of the Alpine trophy quoted by Pliny (iii. 24) they are called Rucinates.   [L. S.]

RURA (*Ruhr*), a river of Western Germany, which flows into the Rhine from the east near the town of *Duisburg*. (Geogr. Rav. iv. 24.) [L. S.]

RURADA (Ruradensis Resp?), a place in Hispania Baetica, the name of which appears only upon coins, the present *Rus* near *Baeza*. (Florez, *Esp. Sagr.* vii. p. 98.)   [T. H. D.]

RUSADIR (Plin. v. 1; *Ρυσσάδειρον*, Ptol. iv. 1. § 7; Russader, *Itin. Ant.*), a colonia of Mauretania, situated near *Metagonites Prom.*, which appears sometimes to have been called from the town Rusadir (Ptol. iv. 1. § 12). It is represented by the "barádero" of *Melilla*, or Spanish penal fortress, on the bight formed between *C. Tres Forcas* and the *Mláia*.   [E. B. J.]

RUSAZUS. [MAURETANIA, p. 298, b.]

RUSCINO (*Ρουσκινών, Ρουσκινών*), a city of the Volcae Tectosages in Gallia Narbonensis. (Ptol. ii. 10. § 9.) When Hannibal entered Gallia by the Pyrenees, he came to Illiberis (*Elne*), and thence marched past Ruscino (Liv. xxi. 24). Ruscino stood on a river of the same name (Ptol. Strab.): "There was a lake near Ruscino, and a swampy place a little above the sea full of salt and containing mullets (*κεστρεῖς*), which are dug out; for if a man digs down two or three feet, and drives a trident into the muddy water, he may spear the fish, which is of considerable size: and it feeds on the mud like the eels." (Strab. iv. p. 182.) Polybius (xxxiv. 10, ed. Bekker) has the same about the river and the fish, which, however, he says, feed on the plant agrostis. (Athen. viii. p. 332.) The low tract which was divided by the Ruscino is the Cyneticum Littus of Avienus (*Or. Mar.* v. 565):—

"post Pyrenaeum jugum,

Jacent arenae littoris Cynetici,

Easque late sulcat amnis Roschinus."

Mela (ii. 5) names the place a Colonia, and so the title appears on coins, COL. RUS. LEG. VI. Pliny calls it "Oppidum Latinorum." It seems to have been a Colonia Latina.

The name is incorrectly written Ruscione in the Antonine Itin. and in the Table. It is placed between Combusta [COMBUSTA] and Illiberis, and it is represented by *Castel-Roussillon* or the *Tour de Roussillon* on the *Tet*, the ancient Ruscino, a short distance from *Perpignan*, the capital of the French department of the *Pyrénées Orientales*. *Perpignan* lies on the high-road from France into Spain, and there is no other great road in this part of the Pyrenees.

Ruscino is named Rosciliona in middle age documents, and from this name the modern name *Roussillon* is derived. *Roussillon* was a province of the ante-revolutionary history of France, and it corresponds to the modern department of *Pyrénées Orientales*.

The river Ruscino or Ruscinus is the Telis of Mela (ii. 5), the *Tet*; and we may probably conclude that the true reading in Mela is Tetis. The *Tet* rises in the Pyrenees, and flows past *Perpignan* into the Mediterranean, after a course of about 70 miles. Sometimes it brings down a great quantity of water from the mountains.　　　　[G. L.]

RUSELLAE ('Ρουσέλλαι: Eth. Rusellanus: *Roselle*), an ancient and important city of Etruria, situated about 14 miles from the sea, and 3 from the right bank of the river *Ombrone* (Umbro). In common with several of the ancient Etruscan cities, we have very little information concerning its early history, though there is no doubt of its great antiquity and of its having been at a very early period a powerful and important city. There is every probability that it was one of the twelve which formed the Etruscan League (Müller, *Etrusker*, vol. i. p. 346). The first mention of it in history is during the reign of Tarquinius Priscus, when it united with Clusium, Arretium, Volaterrae, and Vetulonia, in declaring war against the Roman king, apart from the rest of the confederacy,—a sufficient proof that it was at that time an independent and sovereign state. (Dionys. iii. 51.) From this time we hear no more of it until the Romans had carried their arms beyond the Ciminian forest, when, in B. C. 301, the dictator M. Valerius Maximus carried his arms, apparently for the first time, into the territory of the Rusellae, and defeated the combined forces of the Etruscans who were opposed to him. (Liv. x. 4, 5.) A few years later, in B. C. 294, the consul L. Postumius Megellus not only laid waste the territory of Rusellae, but took the city itself by storm, taking more than 2000 of the inhabitants captives (Id. x. 37). No other mention of it occurs during the period of Etruscan independence; but during the Second Punic War the Rusellani are mentioned among the "populi Etruriae" who came forward with voluntary supplies to equip the fleet of Scipio (B. c. 205), and furnished him with timber and corn (Id. xxviii. 45). It is evident that at this time Rusellae was still one of the principal cities of Etruria. We find no subsequent notice of it under the Roman Republic, but it was one of the places selected by Augustus to receive a colony (Plin. iii. 5. s. 8; Zumpt, *de Colon.* p. 347); notwithstanding which it seems to have fallen into decay; and though the name is noticed by Ptolemy (iii. 1. § 48) we meet with no later notice of it in ancient times. It did not, however, altogether cease to exist till a much later period, as it retained its episcopal see down to the twelfth century, when it was transferred to the neighbouring town of *Grosseto*. (Repetti, *Diz. Top.* vol. ii. pp. 526, 822.)

The site of Rusellae is now wholly desolate and overgrown with thickets, which render it very difficult of access. But the plan may be distinctly traced, and the line of the ancient walls may be followed in detached fragments throughout their entire circuit. It stood on the flat top of a hill of considerable elevation, about 6 miles from the modern city of *Grosseto*, overlooking the broad valley of the *Ombrone* and the level plain of the *Maremma*, which extends from thence to the sea. The walls follow the outline of the hill, and enclose a space of about 2 miles in circuit. They are constructed of very rude and massive stones, in some places with an approach to horizontal structure, similar to that at *Volterra* and Populonia; but in other parts they lose all traces of regularity, and present (according to Mr. Dennis) a strong resemblance to the rudest and most irregular style of Cyclopian construction, as exemplified in the walls of Tiryns in Argolis. (Dennis's *Etruria*, vol. ii. pp. 248, 249.) The sites of six gates may be traced; but there are no indications of the manner in which the gateway itself was formed. Within the walls are some fragments of rectangular masonry and some vaults of Roman construction. It is remarkable that no traces of the necropolis — so often the most interesting remnant of an Etruscan city— have yet been discovered at Rusellae. But the site is so wild and so little visited, that no excavations have been carried on there. (Dennis, *l. c.* p. 254.)

About 2 miles from the ruins, and 4 from *Grosseto*, are some hot-springs, now called *I Bagni di Roselle*. On a hill immediately above them are the mediaeval ruins of a town or castle called *Moscona*, which have been often mistaken for those of Rusellae. (Dennis, *l. c.*)　　　　[E. H. B.]

RUSGU'NIA (*Itin. Ant.*; 'Ρουσόνιον, Ptol. iv. 2. § 6), a town of Mauretania, and a colonia, which lay 15 M. P. to the E. of Icosium. Its ruins have been found near *Cape Matafu* or *Temendfus* (Barth, *Wanderungen*, p. 55). For an account of these, see *Ausland*, 1837, No. 144.　　　　[E. B. J.]

RUSICADE (Plin. v. 2; Mela, i. 7. § 1; 'Ρουσίκαδα, Ptol. iv. 3. § 3; Rusiccade, *Itin. Ant.*, *Peut. Tab.*), the harbour of Cirta in Numidia, and a Roman colonia, at the mouth of the small river THAPSUS (Vib. Seq. *de Flum.* p. 19: *U. Safsa*), and probably therefore identical with the THAPSA (Θάψα), a harbour-town, of Scylax (p. 50). Its site is near *Stora*; and the modern town of *Philippeville*, the *Rás-Skikda* of the Arabs, is made in part of the materials of the old Rusicade (Barth, *Wanderungen*, p. 66).　　　　[E. B. J.]

RUSIDA'VA. [DACIA, p. 744, b.]

RUSPE (*Peut. Tab.*; 'Ρούσπαι al. 'Ρούσπε, Ptol. iv. 3. § 10), a town of Numidia between Acholla and Usilla, near the CAPUT VADORUM (Corippus, *Johann.* i. 366: *C. K'abúdiah*), and the see of Fulgentius, well-known in the Pelagian controversy; he was expelled from it by the Vandal Thrasimund. Barth (*Wanderungen*, p. 177) found remains at *Schebba*.　　　　[E. B. J.]

RUSPI'NUM ('Ρουσπῖνον, Strab. xvii. p. 831; Ruspina, Auct. *B. Afr.* 6; Plin. v. 3; *Peut. Tab.*), a town of Africa Proper, where Caesar defeated Scipio, and which he afterwards made his position while waiting for reinforcements. It is probably the same place as the THERMAE of the Coast-describer (*Stadiasm.* § 114, ed. Müller), near the ruins of Leptis Parva. [E. B. J.]

RUSTICIA'NA ('Ρουστίκανα, Ptol. ii. 5. § 7), a city of the Vettones in Lusitania, on the right bank of the Tagus. Variously identified with *Corchuela* and *Galisteo.* (*It. Ant.* p. 433.) [T. H. D.]

RUSUCU'RRIUM, RUSSUCU'RRIUM (Plin. v. 1; *It. Ant.*; 'Ρουσσοκκόραι, Ptol. iv. 2. § 8), a town of Mauretania, which Claudius made a municipium (Plin. *l. c.*), but which was afterwards a colonia (*Itin. Ant.*). Barth (*Wanderungen*, p. 60) has identified it with the landing-place *Dellys* in *Algeria*, where there is good anchorage. [E. B. J.]

RUTE'NI ('Ρουτῆνοι), and 'Ρουτανοί in Ptolemy (ii. 7. § 21), who places them in Gallia Aquitania. Pliny (iv. 19) says that the Ruteni border on the Narbonensis Provincia ; and Strabo (iv. p. 191) places them and the Gabaleis or Gabali next to the Narbonensis. Their country was the old province of *Rouergue*, which extended from the *Cévennes*, its eastern boundary, about 90 miles in a western direction. The chief town was *Rhodes*. The modern department of *Aveyron* comprehends a large part of the *Rouergue.* There were silver mines in the country of the Ruteni and their neighbours the Gabali [GABALI], and the flax of this country was good.

The Arverni and Ruteni were defeated by Q. Fabius Maximus, B. C. 121, but their country was not reduced to the form of a Roman province (Caes. *B. G.* i. 45). In Caesar's time part of the Ruteni were included in the Provincia under the name of Ruteni Provinciales (*B. G.* vii. 5, 7). Vercingetorix in B. C. 52 sent Lucterius of the Cadurci into the country of the Ruteni to bring them over to the Gallic confederation, which he did. Caesar, in order to protect the Provincia on this side, placed troops in the country of the Ruteni Provinciales, and among the Volcae Arecomici and Tolosates. Pliny, who enumerates the Ruteni among the people of Aquitania, also mentions Ruteni in the Narbonensis (iii. 4), but he means the town Segodunum [SEGODUNUM]. The Ruteni Provinciales of course were nearer to the Tectosages than the other Ruteni, and we may perhaps place them in that part of the departments of *Aveyron* and *Tarn* which is south of the Tarnis (*Tarn*). It may be conjectured that part of the Ruteni were added to the Provincia, either after the defeat of the Ruteni by Maximus, or after the conquest of Tolosa by Caepio (B.C. 106.) [G.L.]

RUTICLEI. [RUGII.]

RUTUBA (*Roja*), a river of Liguria, which rises in the Maritime Alps, near the *Col de Tende*, and flows into the sea at *Vintimiglia* (Albium Intemelium). Its name is found in Pliny (iii. 5. s. 7), who places it apparently to the W. of Albium Intemelium, whereas it really flows on the E. side of that town; Lucan also notices it among the streams which flow from the Apennines (ii. 422), and gives it the epithet of "cavus," from its flowing through a deep bed or ravine. From the mention of the Tiber just after, some writers have supposed that he must mean another river of the name; but there is no reason to expect such strict geographical order from a poet, and the mention of the Macra a few lines lower down sufficiently shows that none such was intended. Vibius Sequester (p. 17) who makes the Rutuba fall into the Tiber, has obviously misunderstood the passage of Lucan. [E. H. B.]

RUTUBIS (Polyb. *ap. Plin.* v. 1; 'Ρουσίβίς, Ptol.

iv. 5. § 1), a port of Mauretania, which must be identified with the low rocky point of *Mazagan.* The town situated upon this was the last possessed by the Portuguese in *Morocco*, and was abandoned by them in 1769. (Jackson, *Morocco*, p. 104; *Journ. of Geogr. Soc.* vol. vi. p. 306.) [E. B. J.]

RU'TULI ('Ρούτουλοι), a people of ancient Italy, who, according to a tradition generally received in later times, were settled at a very early period in a part of Latium, adjoining the sea-coast, their capital city being Ardea. The prominent part that they and their king Turnus bear in the legendary history of Aeneas and the Trojan settlement, especially in the form in which this has been worked up by Virgil, has given great celebrity to their name, but they appear to have been, in fact, even according to these very traditions, a small and unimportant people. Their king Turnus himself is represented as dependent on Latinus ; and it is certain that in the historical period Ardea was one of the cities of the Latin League (Dionys. v. 61), while the name of the Rutuli had become merged in that of the Latin people. Not long before this indeed Livy represents the Rutuli as a still existing people, and the arms of Tarquinius Superbus as directed against them when he proceeded to attack Ardea, just before his expulsion. (Liv. i. 56, 57.) According to this narrative Ardea was not taken, but we learn from much better authority (the treaty between Rome and Carthage preserved by Polybius, iii. 22) that it had fallen under the power of the Romans before the close of the monarchy, and it is possible that the extinction of the Rutuli as an independent people may date from this period. The only other mention of the Rutuli which can be called historical is that their name is found in the list given by Cato (*ap. Priscian.* iv. 4. p. 629) of the cities that took part in the foundation of the celebrated temple of Diana at Aricia, a list in all probability founded upon some ancient record ; and it is remarkable that they here figure as distinct from the Ardeates. There were some obscure traditions in antiquity that represented Ardea as founded by a colony from Argos [ARDEA], and these are regarded by Niebuhr as tending to prove that the Rutuli were a Pelasgic race. (Nieb. vol. i. p. 44, vol. ii. p. 21.) Schwegler, on the other hand considers them as connected with the Etruscans, and probably a relic of the period when that people had extended their dominion throughout Latium and Campania. This theory finds some support in the name of Turnus, which may probably be connected with Tyrrhenus, as well as in the union which the legend represents as subsisting between Turnus and the Etruscan king Mezentius. (Schwegler, *Röm. Gesch.* vol. i. pp. 330, 331.) But the whole subject is so mixed up with fable and poetical invention, that it is impossible to feel confidence in any such conjectures. [E. H. B.]

RUTU'NIUM (*It. Ant.* p. 469), apparently a town of the Cornavii in the W. part of Britannia Romana. Camden (p. 651) identifies it with *Rowton* in *Shropshire*, Horsley (p. 418) with *Wem.* [T. H. D.]

RUTU'PIAE ('Ρουτούπιαι, Ptol. ii. 3. § 27; in the *Tab. Peut.* and *Not. Imp.* Rutupae; in the *Itin. Ant.* Ritupae, also Portus Rutupensis and Portus Ritupius: *Adj.* Rutupinus, Luc. *Phars.* vi. 67 ; Juv. iv. 141), a town of the Cantii on the E. coast of Britannia Prima, now *Richborough* in *Kent.* Rutupiae and Portus Rutupensis were probably distinct, the former being the city, the latter its harbour at some little distance. The harbour was probably

Stonar, not *Sandwich*; which latter town seems to have sprung up under the Saxons, after Rutupiae had begun to fall into decay, and was indeed probably built with materials taken from it. According to Camden (p. 244) the etymology of the name of Rutupiae is analogous to that of *Sandwich*, being derived from the British *Rhydtufeth*, signifying "sandy bottoms"; a derivation which seems much more probable than that from the Ruteni, a people who occupied the district in France now called *La Roergue*. The territory around the town was styled Rutupinus Ager (Auson. *Parent.* xviii. 8) and the coast Rutupinus Littus (Luc. *l. c.*). The latter was celebrated for its oysters, as the coast near *Margate* and *Reculver* is to the present day. Large beds of oyster-shells have been found in the neighbourhood, at a depth of from 4 to 6 feet under ground. The port is undoubtedly that mentioned by Tacitus (*Agric.* 38), under the erroneous name of Trutulensis Portus, as occupied by the fleet of Agricola. It was a safe harbour, and the usual and most convenient one for the passage between France and England. (Amm. Marc. xx. 1, xxvii. 8. § 6.) The principal Roman remains at *Richborough* are those of a castrum and of an amphitheatre. The walls of the former present an extensive ruin, and on the N. side are in some places from 20 to 30 feet in height. Fragments of sculptured marbles found within their circuit show that the fortification must have contained some handsome buildings. The foundation walls of the amphitheatre were excavated in 1849, and are the first remains of a walled building of that description discovered in England. There is a good description of *Richborough*, as it existed in the time of Henry VIII., in Leland's *Itinerary* (vol. vii. p. 128, ed. Hearne). Leland mentions that many Roman coins were found there, which still continues to be the case. Other Roman antiquities of various descriptions have been discovered, as pottery, fibulae, ornaments, knives, tools, &c. Rutupiae was under the jurisdiction of the Comes litoris Saxonici, and was the station of the Legio IIda Augusta. (*Notitia*, c. 52.) A complete account of its remains will be found in Roach Smith's *Antiquities of Richborough*, London, 1850.   [T. H. D.]

RYSSADIUM ('Ρυσσάδιον ὄρος, Ptol. iv. 6. § 8), "a mountain of Interior Libya, from which flows the Stacheir (*Gambia*), making near it the lake Clonia; the middle of the mountain (or lake?) 17° E. long., 11° N. lat." (Ptol. *l. c.*) This mountain terminated in the headland also called Ryssadium ('Ρυσσάδιον ἄκρον), the position of which is fixed by Ptolemy (iv. 6. § 6) at 8° 30′ E. long., and 11° 30′ N. lat. We assume, with Rennell and Leake, that Arsinarium is *C. Verde*, a conjecture which can be made with more confidence because it is found that Ptolemy's difference of longitude between Arsinarium and Carthage is very nearly correct,—according to that assumption this promontory must be looked for to the N. of the mouth of the *Gambia*. The mountain and lake must be assigned to that elevated region in which the *Senegal* and the *Gambia* take their rise, forming an appendage to the central highlands of Africa from which it projects northwards, like a vast promontory, into the *Great Sahara*.   [E. B. J.]

S.

SABA, SABAEI (Σάβη or Σαβαί: *Eth.* Σαβαῖος, fem. Σαβαία), were respectively the principal city and nation in *Yemen*, or Arabia Felix. [ARABIA.] Ancient geographers differ considerably as to the extent of territory occupied by the Sabaeans, Eratosthenes assigning to it a much larger area than Ptolemy. The difference may perhaps be reconciled by examining their respective accounts.

Our knowledge of the Sabaeans is derived from three sources: the Hebrew Scriptures, the Greek historians and geographers, and the Roman poets and encyclopedists, Pliny, Solinus, &c. The Arabian geographers, also, throw some light upon this ancient and far-extending race.

1. In the Hebrew genealogies (*Genesis*, x. 6, xxv. 3) the Sabaeans are described as the descendants of Cush, the son of Ham. This descent was probably not so much from a single stem, as from several branches of Hamite origin; and as the tribes of the Sabaeans were numerous, some of them may have proceeded immediately from Cush, and others from later progenitors of the same stock. Thus one tribe descended from Seba, the son of Cush, another from Jokshan, Abraham's son by Keturah; a third from Sheba, the son of Raamah—the 'Ρεγμά of the LXX. (Compare *Psalm* lxxii. 10; *Isaiah*, xlv. 14; *Ezekiel*, xxvii. 22, 23, xxxviii. 13.) The most material point in this pedigree is the fact of the pure Semitic blood of the Sabaeans. The Hebrew prophets agree in celebrating the stature and noble bearing, the enterprise and wealth of this nation, therein concurring with the expression of Agatharchides, who describes the Sabaeans as having τὰ σώματα ἀξιολογώτερα. Their occupations appear to have been various, as would be the case with a nation so widely extended ("Sabaei ... ad utrumque maria porrecti," Plin. vi. 28. s. 32): for there is no doubt that in the south they were actively engaged in commerce, while in the north, on the borders of Idumea, they retained the predatory habits of nomades. (*Job*, ii. 15.) The "Queen of the South," i. e. of *Yemen* or Sabaea, who was attracted to Palestine by the fame of Solomon, was probably an Arabian sovereign. It may be observed that *Yemen* and Saba have nearly the same import, each signifying the right hand; for a person turning his face to the rising sun has the south on his right, and thus Saba or *Yemen*, which was long regarded as the southern limit of the habitable zone, is the left-hand, or southern land. (Comp. Herod. iii. 107—113; Forster's *Geogr. of Arabia*, vol i. pp. 24—38.) A river Sabis, in Carmania (Mela, iii. 8. § 4), and a chain of mountains Sabo, at the entrance of the *Persian Gulf* (Arrian, *Periplus. M. Erythr.*, ὄρη μέγιστα λεγόμενα Σάβα; comp. Ptol. vi. 7. § 23), apparently indicate an extension of the Sabaeans beyond Arabia Proper. That they reached to the eastern shore of the Red Sea is rendered probable by the circumstance that a city named Sabu or Sabe stood there, about 36 miles S. of Podnu, in lat. 14° N. (Ptol. vi. 7. § 38, v. 22. § 14.)

2. The first Greek writer who mentions the Sabaeans by name is Eratosthenes. His account, however, represents a more recent condition of this nation than is described by Artemidorus, or by Agatharchides, who is Strabo's principal authority in his narrative of the Sabaeans. On the other hand, Diodorus Siculus professes to have compiled his

accounts of them from the historical books of the Aegyptian kings, which he consulted in the Alexandreian Library. (Diod. iii. 38, 46.) There can be little question that Herodotus, although he does not name the Sabaeans, describes them in various passages, when speaking of the Arabians, the southernmost people of the earth. (Herod. ii. 86, iii. 107 —113.) The commerce of *Yemen* with Phoenicia and Aegypt under the Pharaohs would render the name of the Sabaeans familiar in all the havens of the Red Sea and the eastern Mediterranean. The Aegyptians imported spices largely, since they employed them in embalming the dead; and the Phoenicians required them for the Syrian markets, since perfumes have in all ages been both favourite luxuries and among the most popular medicines of the East. At the time when Ptolemy wrote (in the second century A.D.) their trade with Syria and Aegypt, as the carriers of the silks and spices so much in request at Rome, brought the Sabaeans within ken of the scientific geographer and of the learned generally.

3. Accordingly, we meet in the Roman poets with numerous, although vague, allusions to the wealth and luxury of the Sabaeans. "Molles," "divites," "beati," are the epithets constantly applied to them. (See Catull. xi. 5; Propert. ii. 10. 16, *ib.* 29. 17, iii. 13. 8; Virgil, *Georg.* i. 57, ii. 150, *Aeneid.* i. 416; Horace, *Carm.* i. 29. 2, ii. 12. 24; Id. *Epist.* i. 6. 6, *ib.* 7. 36; Statius, *Silv.* iv. 8. 1; Senec. *Hercules, Oet.* v. 376.) The expedition of Aelius Gallus, indeed (B. C. 24), may have tended to bring Southern Arabia more immediately under the notice of the Romans. But their knowledge was at best very limited, and rested less on facts than on rumours of Sabaean opulence and luxury. Pliny and the geographers are rather better informed, but even they had very erroneous conceptions of the physical or commercial character of this nation. Not until the passage to India by the Cape had been discovered was Sabaea or *Yemen* really explored by Europeans.

Assuming, then, that the Sabaeans were a widely-spread race, extending from the *Persian Gulf* to the Red Sea, and running up to the borders of the desert in the Arabian peninsula, we proceed to examine the grounds of their reputation for excessive opulence and luxury. A portion of their wealth was undoubtedly native; they supplied Aegypt and Syria from the remotest periods with frankincense and aromatics; and since the soil of *Yemen* is highly productive, they took in exchange, not the corn or wine of their neighbours, but the precious metals. But aromatics were by no means the capital source of their wealth. The Sabaeans possessed for many centuries the keys of Indian commerce, and were the intermediate factors between Aegypt and Syria, as these countries were in turn the Indian agents for Europe. During the Pharaonic eras of Aegypt, no attempt was made to disturb the monopoly of the Sabaeans in this traffic. Ptolemy Philadelphus (B. C. 274) was the first Aegyptian sovereign who discerned the value of the Red Sea and its harbours to his kingdom. He established his Indian emporium at Myos-Hormus or Arsinoe, and under his successors Berenice, which was connected with Coptos on the Nile by a canal, shared the profits of this remunerative trade. But even then the Sabaeans lost a small portion only of their former exclusive advantages. They were no longer the carriers of Indian exports to Aegypt, but they were still the importers of them from India itself. The Aegyptian fleets proceeded no further than the haven of Sabbatha or Mariaba; while the Sabaeans, long prior even to the voyage of Nearchus (B. C. 330), ventured across the ocean with the monsoon to *Ceylon* and the *Malabar* coast. Their vessels were of larger build than the ordinary merchant-ships of the Greeks, and their mariners were more skilful and intrepid than the Greeks, who, it is recorded, shrunk back with terror from the Indian Ocean. The track of the Sabaean navigators lay along the coast of Gedrosia, since Nearchus found along its shores many Arabic names of places, and at *Possem* engaged a pilot acquainted with those seas. In proportion as luxury increased in the Syro-Macedonian cities (and their extravagance in the article of perfumes alone is recorded by Athenaeus, xii.), and subsequently in Rome, the Indian trade became more valuable to the Sabaeans. It was computed in the third century of the Empire, that, for every pound of silk brought to Italy, a pound of silver or even gold was sent to Arabia; and the computation might fairly be extended to the aromatics employed so lavishly by the Romans at their banquets and funerals. (Comp. Petronius, c. 64, with Plutarch, *Sulla*, c. 38.) There were two avenues of this traffic, one overland by Petra and the Elanitic gulf, the other up the Red Sea to Arsinoe, the Ptolemaic canal, and Alexandreia. We may therefore fairly ascribe the extraordinary wealth of the Sabaeans to their long monopoly of the Indian trade. Their country, however, was itself highly productive, and doubtless, from the general character of the Arabian peninsula, its southern extremity was densely populated. The Sabaeans are described by the Hebrew, the Greek, and the Arabian writers as a numerous people, of lofty stature, implying abundance of the means of life; and the recurrence of the name of Saba throughout the entire region between the Red Sea and Carmania shows that they were populous and powerful enough to send out colonies. The general barrenness of the northern and central districts of Arabia drove the population down to the south. The highlands that border on the *Indian Ocean* are distinguished by the plenty of wood and water; the air is temperate, the animals are numerous (the horses of *Yemen* are strong and serviceable), and the fruits delicious. With such abundance at home the Sabaeans were enabled to devote themselves to trade with undivided energy and success.

Nothing more strikingly displays the ignorance of the ancient geographers as regards Sabaea than their descriptions of the opulence of the country. Their narratives are equally pompous and extravagant. According to Agatharchides and Diodorus, the odour of the spice-woods was so potent that the inhabitants were liable to apoplexies, and counteracted the noxious perfumes by the ill odours of burnt goats'-hair and asphaltite. The decorations of their houses, their furniture, and even their domestic utensils were of gold and silver: they drank from vases blazing with gems; they used cinnamon chips for firewood; and no king could compete in luxury with the merchant-princes of the Sabaeans. We have only to remember the real or imputed sumptuousness of a few of the Dutch and English East India Companies' merchants in the 18th century, while the trade of the East was in a few hands, in order to appreciate the worth of these descriptions by Agatharchides and Diodorus.

The delusions of the ancients were first dis-pelled by the traveller Niebuhr. (*Description de l'Arabie*, p. 125.) He asserts, and he has not been contradicted, that *Yemen* neither produces now, nor ever could have produced, gold; but that, in the district of *Saade*, it has iron-mines,—a fact unnoticed by earlier describers,—which were worked when he visited the country. He states, moreover, that the native frankincense is of a very ordinary quality, Sabaea yielding only the species called Liban, while the better sorts of that gum are imported from *Sumatra*, *Siam*, and *Java*. The distance from which the superior kinds of myrrh, frankincense, nard, and cassia were fetched, probably gave rise to the strange tales related about the danger of gathering them from the trees, with which the Sabaeans regaled the Aegyptian and Greek merchants, and through them the Greek geographers also. One cause of danger alone is likely to have been truly reported: the spice-woods were the abode of venomous reptiles; one of which, apparently a purple cobra, was aggressive, and, springing on intruders, inflicted an incurable wound. The ancients, however, said and believed that cinnamon was brought to *Yemen* by large birds, which build their nests of its chips, and that the *ledonum* was combed from the beards of he-goats. The Sabaeans were governed by a king. (Dion Cass. liii. 29.) One inexorable condition of the royal office was, that he should never quit his palace: found beyond its precincts, it was allowable to stone him to death. The rule which governed the succession to the throne was singular. A certain number of noble families possessed equal claims to the crown: and the first child (females were eligible) born after an accession was presumptive heir to the reigning monarch. This seclusion of the king, and the strange mode of electing him, seem to indicate a sacerdotal influence, similar to that which regulates the choice of the Grand Lama and the homage paid to him by the Thibetians.

The precise boundaries of Sabaea it is impossible to ascertain. The area we have presumed is comprised within the *Arabian Sea* W., the *Persian Gulf* E., the *Indian Ocean* S., and an irregular line skirting the Desert, and running up in a narrow point to Idumea N.

For the principal divisions of the Sabaeans see the articles on Arabia; Adramitae; Minaei.

The decline of the Sabaeans seems to have proceeded from two causes: (1) the more direct intercourse of the Aegypto-Greeks with India, and (2) the rivalry of the powerful tribe of the Homeritae, who subjugated them. In the account of their eastern traffic, and of the characteristics of their land, we have traced the features of the race. Compared with the Arabs of the Desert, the Sabaeans were a highly civilised nation, under a regular government, and, as a mercantile community, jealous of the rights of property. The author of the Periplus remarks upon similar security among the Adramitae; the interests of the merchant had curbed and softened the natural ferocity of the Arab. This also, according to Niebuhr (*Descript. de l'Arabie*, p. 315), is still observable in *Yemen*, in comparison with the inland provinces of *Hejaz*, and *Nejed*.   [W. B. D.]

SABA. Three cities of this name are distinguished by ancient geographers: the name indeed was a common appellation of towns, and signified head of the province, or of its lesser divisions. (Comp. Plin. vi. 28. s. 32.)

1. (Σαβαί, Steph. B. *s. v.* Σαβάς, Agatharch. *ap. Phot.* p. 63), was the chief city of the Sabaeans. It

is described by Diodorus (iii. 46) as situated upon a lofty wooded hill, and within two days' journey of the frankincense country. The position of Saba is, however, quite uncertain: Mannert (*Geogr. der Griech. u. Röm.* vol. vi. pt. i. p. 66) places it at the modern *Saade*: other geographers identify it with *Mareb* [Mariaba]; and again Sabbatha, both from its site in the interior and its commercial importance, seems to have a good title to be considered as Saba (Σαβή of Agatharchides) or Sheba, the capital of the Sabaeans.

2. (Σαβή, Ptol. vi. 7. §§ 38, 42; Plin. vi. 23. s. 34), was also seated in the interior of the Sabaean territory, 26 miles NE. of *Aden*. Niebuhr (*Descript. de l'Arabie*, vol. ii. p. 60) identifies it with the modern *Saaba*.

3. (Σάβαι, Strab. xvii. p. 771; Σαβάτ, Ptol. iv. 7. § 8), on the western shore of the Red Sea, was the capital city of the Sabaeans, and its harbour was the Sabaiticum Os (Σαβαϊτικον στόμα, Strab. xvii. p. 770). The position of Sabae, like that of so many Aethiopian races and cities, is very uncertain. Some writers place it at the entrance of the Arabian gulf (Heeren, *Histor. Researches*, vol. i. p. 333); others carry it up as high as the bay of Adule, lat. 15° N. Bruce (*Travels*, vol. iii. p. 144) identifies the modern *Azab* with the Sabae, and places it between the tropics and the Abyssinian highlands. Combes and Tamisier (*Voyages*, vol. i. p. 89) consider the island *Massowa* to have a better claim: while Lord Valentia (*Travels*, vol. ii. p. 47) finds Sabae at *Port Mornington*. But although neither ancient geographers nor modern travellers are agreed concerning the site of the Aethiopian Sabae, they accord in placing it on the sea-coast of the kingdom or island of Meroe, and between the Sinus Avalites and the bay of Adule, i. e. between the 12th and 15th degrees of N. latitude. On the opposite shore were seated the Sabaeans of Arabia, and as there was much intercourse between the populations of the opposite sides of the Red Sea, the Aethiopian Sabaeans may have been a colony from Arabia. Both races are described as lofty in stature and opulent (*Psalm* lxxii.; 1 *Kings*, x. 1; *Isaiah*, xlv. 14), and this description will apply equally to the Sabaeans who dwelt in the spice country of Arabia, and to those who enjoyed almost a monopoly of the Libyan spice-trade, and were not far removed from the gold-mines and the emerald and topaz-quarries of the Aegyptian and Aethiopian mountains. The remarkable personal beauty of the Sabaeans is confirmed by the monuments of Upper Nubia, and was probably reported to the Greek geographers by the slave-dealers, to whom height and noble features would be a recommendation. The Sabaeans, at least in earlier periods, may be regarded as one of the principal tribes of the Aethiopian kingdom of Meroe. [Meroe.] Josephus (*Antiq.* ii. 5) affirms that the Queen of Sheba or Saba came from this region, and that it bore the name of Saba before it was known by that of Meroe. There seems also some affinity between the word Saba and the name or title of the kings of the Aethiopians, Saba-co.   [W. B. D.]

SABADI'BAE (Σαβαδείβαι νῆσοι, Ptol. vii. 2. § 28), three islands, mentioned by Ptolemy, in the neighbourhood of the Aurea Chersonesus in India extra Gangem. From the great resemblance of the name, it is not unlikely that he has confounded it with that of the island of Iabadius (or Sabadius), now *Java*, which he mentions in his next section. [Iabadius.]   [V.]

SABAGE'NA (Σαβάγηνα, Σαβάγεινα, or Σαβάγυνα), a town in Lesser Armenia, is mentioned only by Ptolemy (v. 7. § 10) as belonging to the prefecture of Laviniane.   [L. S.]

SABALINGII (Σαβαλίγγιοι), a German tribe, placed by Ptolemy (ii. 11. § 11) above the Saxones in the Cimbrian peninsula, the modern *Schleswig*. In the absence of all further information about them, it has been inferred, from the mere resemblance of name, that they dwelt in and about the place called *Sabyholm* in the island of *Laland*.   [L. S.]

SABA'RIA (Σαουαρία), an important town in the north of Upper Pannonia, was situated in a plain between the river Arrabo and the Deserta Boiorum, on the road from Carnuntum to Poetovium. The town, which seems to have been an ancient settlement of the Boii, derived its importance partly from the fertility of the plain in which it was situated, and partly from the fact that it formed a kind of central point at which several roads met. The emperor Claudius raised it to the rank of a Roman colony, whence it received the surname of Claudia. (Plin. iii. 27; Ptol. ii. 15. § 4.) In this town Septimius Severus was proclaimed Augustus (Aurel. Vict. *Epit.* 19), and the emperor Valentinian resided there some time. (Amm. Marc. xxx. 5.) Owing to this and other circumstances, the town rose to a high degree of prosperity during the latter period of the Roman Empire; and its ancient greatness is still attested by its numerous remains of temples and aqueducts. Many statues, inscriptions, and coins also have been found at *Stein am Anger*, which is the modern name, or, as the Hungarians call it, *Szombathely*. (*It. Ant.* pp. 233, 261, 262, 434; Orelli, *Inscript.* n. 200 and 1789; Schönwisner, *Antiquitates Sabariae,* p. 45; Muchar, *Noricum,* i. p. 167.) [L. S.]

SABARICUS SINUS. [INDICUS OCEANUS.]

SABATA or SABDATA (Plin. vi. 27. s. 31), a town of Assyria, probably the same place as the Σαβαθά of Zosimus (iii. 23), which that writer describes as 30 stadia from the ancient Seleuceia. It is also mentioned by Abulfeda (p. 253) under the name of Sabath.

SABA'TIA VADA. [VADA SABATIA.]

SABATI'NUS LACUS (Σαβάτα λίμνη, Strab.: *Lago di Bracciano*), one of the most considerable of the lakes of Etruria, which, as Strabo observes, was the most southerly of them, and consequently the nearest to Rome and to the sea. (Strab. v. p. 226.) It is, like most of the other lakes in the same region, formed in the crater of an extinct volcano, and has consequently a very regular basin-like form, with a circuit of about 20 miles, and is surrounded on all sides by a ridge of hills of no great elevation. It is probable that it derived its name from a town of the name of SABATE, which stood on its shores, but the name is not found in the geographers, and the only positive evidence of its existence is its mention in the Tabula as a station on the Via Claudia. (*Tab. Peut.*) The lake itself is called Sabata by Strabo, and Sabate by Festus, from whom we learn that it gave name to the Sabatine tribe of the Roman citizens, one of those which was formed out of the new citizens added to the state in B. C. 387. (Liv. vi. 4, 5; Fest. *s. v. Sabatina,* pp. 342, 343.) Silius Italicus speaks of the "Sabatia stagna" in the plural (viii. 492), probably including under the name the much smaller lake in the same neighbourhood called the Lacus Alsietinus or *Lago di Martignano*. The same tradition was reported of this lake as of the Ciminian, and of many others, that there was a city

swallowed up by it, the remains of which could still occasionally be seen at the bottom of its clear waters. (Sotion, *de Mir. Font.* 41, where we should certainly read Ἰδάατος for Ἰδκατος.) It abounded in fish and wild-fowl, and was even stocked artificially with fish of various kinds by the luxurious Romans of late times. (Columell. viii. 16.)

The Tabula places Sabate at the distance of 36 miles from Rome, but this number is much beyond the truth. The true distance is probably 27 miles, which would coincide with a site near the W. extremity of the lake about a mile beyond the modern town of *Bracciano*, where there are some ruins of Roman date, probably belonging to a villa. (*Tab. Peut.*; Holsten. *Not. ad Cluver.* p. 44; Westphal, *Röm. Kampagne,* pp. 156, 158.) The town of *Bracciano*, which now gives name to the lake, dates only from the middle ages and probably does not occupy an ancient site.   [E. H. B.]

SABATUS. 1. (*Sabbato*), a river of Samnium, in the country of the Hirpini, and one of the tributaries of the Calor (*Calore*), with which it unites under the walls of Beneventum. [CALOR.] The name of the river is not found in any ancient author, but Livy mentions the Sabatini among the Campanians who were punished for their defection to Hannibal in the Second Punic War. (Liv. xxvi. 33, 34.) These may mean generally the people of the valley of Sabatus, or there may have been, as supposed by Cluver, a town of the same name on the banks of the river. (Cluver. *Ital.* p. 1199.)

2. (*Savuto*), a river of Bruttium, on the W. coast of the peninsula, flowing into the sea between Amantea and Capo Suvero. Its name is known only from the Itineraries, from which we learn that it was crossed by the high-road to Rhegium 18 miles S. of Consentia (*Cosenza*), a distance which, combined with the name, clearly identifies it with the modern *Savuto*. (*Itin. Ant.* pp. 105, 110.) It is generally identified by geographers with the Ocinarus of Lycophron, on the banks of which the Greek city of Terina was situated; but this assumption rests on no sufficient grounds. [TERINA.]   [E. H. B.]

SA'BBATA or SABBA'TIA. [VADA SABATIA.]

SA'BBATHA (Σάββαθα, Ptol. vi. 7. § 38; Sabotha, Plin. vi. 28. s. 32), was the capital of the Adramitae, a Sabaean tribe inhabiting the S. coast of Arabia Felix (lat. 14° N.). [ADRAMITAE.] Its inhabitants are called Sabbathae by Festus Avienus (*Descr. Orb. Terr.* v. 1136). Sabbatha was seated far inland, on the coast of a navigable river (Prion?) — an unusual circumstance in that region, where the streams are brief in their course and seldom navigable. (*Peripl. Mar. Erythr.* p. 15.) If it really contained sixty temples within its walls, Sabbatha must have ranked second to none of the cities of Arabia. Its monopoly of the Indian trade doubtless rendered it a wealthy and important place. At no other haven on the coast were the spices, gums, and silks of India permitted to be landed: if exposed to sale elsewhere, they were confiscated, and their vendors punished with death. They were conveyed up the river to Sabbatha in boats made of leather, strained over wooden frames. One gate alone — probably for the convenience of detecting fraud — of Sabbatha was assigned to this branch of commerce; and after the bales had been examined, the goods were not handed over to their owners until a tithe had been deducted for a deity named Sabis (= dominus), and also a portion for the king.

Geographers attempt to identify Sabbatha with Mariaba (*Mareb*), but the proofs of their identity are unsatisfactory ; and it may even be questioned whether Sabbatha be not an elongated form of Saba, a common appellation for cities in Arabia Felix. The Καβάταυον of Strabo (xvi. p. 768) is supposed by his translator Groskurd (vol. iii. p. 287) to be an error for Σαβάταυον, and the latter to be a form of Sabbatha. [See MARIABA, Vol. II. p. 274.]   [W. B. D.]

SABI'NI (Σαβῖνοι), a people of Central Italy, who inhabited the rugged mountain country on the W. of the central chain of the Apennines, from the sources of the Nar and Velinus to the neighbourhood of Reate, and from thence southwards as far as the Tiber and the Anio. They were bounded on the N. and W. by the Umbrians and Etruscans, on the NE. by Picenum, from which they were separated by the main ridge of the Apennines; on the E. by the Vestini, the Marsi and Aequiculi, and on the S. by Latium. Their country thus formed a narrow strip, extending about 85 miles in length from the lofty group of the Apennines above Nursia, in which the Nar takes its rise (now called the *Monti della Sibilla*), to the junction of the Tiber and Anio, within a few miles of Rome. The southern limit of the Sabines had, however, undergone many changes; in Pliny's time it was fixed as above stated, the Anio being generally received as the boundary between them and Latium; hence Pliny reckons Fidenae and Nomentum Sabine cities, though there is good ground for assigning them both in earlier times to the Latins, and Ptolemy again includes them both in Latium. Strabo, on the other hand, describes the Sabine territory as extending *as far as* Nomentum, by which he probably means to include the latter city; while Eretum, which was only about 3 miles N. of Nomentum, seems to have been universally considered as a Sabine city. (Strab. v. p. 228; Plin. iii. 5. s. 9, 12. s. 17; Ptol. iii. 1. § 62.) In like manner Pliny includes the important city of Tibur among the Sabines, though it was certainly commonly reckoned a Latin city, and never appears in the early history of Rome in connection with the Sabines. The fact appears to be, that the frontier between the Sabines and Latins was in early times constantly fluctuating, as the Sabines on the one hand were pressing down from the N., and on the other were driven back in their turn by the arms of the Romans and Latins. But on the division of Italy into regions by Augustus, the Anio was established as the boundary of the First Region, and for this reason was considered by Pliny as the limit also between the Latins and Sabines. (Plin. *l. c.*) It is remarkable that no name for the *country* is found in ancient writers, standing in the same relation to that of the people which Samnium does to Samnites, Latium to Latini, &c.: it is called only " the land of the Sabines " (Sabinorum ager, or Sabinus ager, Liv. i. 36, ii. 16, &c.; Tac. *Hist.* iii. 78), and Roman writers would say " in Sabinis versari, in Sabinos proficisci," &c. The Greeks indeed used ἡ Σαβίνη for the name of the country (Strab. v. pp. 219, 228, &c.; Steph. Byz. *s. v.*), which is called to the present day by the Roman peasantry *La Sabina*, but we do not find any corresponding form in Latin authors.

All ancient authors agree in representing the Sabines as one of the most ancient races of Italy, and as constituting one of the elements of the Roman people, at the same time that they were the progenitors of the far more numerous races which had

spread themselves to the E. and S., under the names of Picentes, Peligni, and Samnites, the last of whom had in their turn become the parents of the Frentani, the Lucanians, Apulians and Bruttians. The minor tribes of the Marsi, Marrucini and Vestini, were also in all probability of Sabine origin, though we have no distinct testimony to this effect [MARSI]. These various races are often comprehended by modern writers under the general name of Sabellian, which is convenient as an ethnic designation; but there is no ancient authority for this use of the word, which was first introduced by Niebuhr (vol. i. p. 91). Pliny indeed in one passage says that the Samnites were also called Sabelli (Plin. iii. 12. s. 17), and this is confirmed by Strabo (v. p. 250). Sabellus is found also in Livy and other Latin writers, as an *adjective* form for Samnite, though never for the name of the nation (Liv. viii. 1, x. 19); but it is frequently also used, especially by the poets, simply as an equivalent for the adjective Sabine. (Virg. *G.* ii. 167, *Aen.* vii. 665; Hor. *Carm.* iii. 6. 37; Juv. iii. 169.)

But notwithstanding the important position of the Sabines in regard to the early history and ethnography of Italy, we have very little information as to their own origin or affinities. Strabo calls them a very ancient race and autochthons (v. p. 228), which may be understood as meaning that there was no account of their immigration or origin which he considered worthy of credit. He distinctly rejects as a fiction the notion that they or their Samnite descendants were of Laconian origin (*Ib.* p. 250); an idea which was very probably suggested only by fancied resemblances in their manners and institutions to those of Sparta (Dionys. ii. 49). But this notion, though not countenanced by any historian of authority, was taken up by the Roman poets, who frequently allude to the Lacedaemonian descent of the Sabines (Ovid. *Fast.* i. 260, iii. 230; Sil. Ital. ii. 8, viii. 412, &c.), and adopted also by some prose writers (Plut. *Rom.* 16; Hygin. *ap. Serv. ad Aen.* viii. 638). A much more important statement is that preserved to us by Dionysius on the authority of Zenodotus of Troezen, which represents the Sabines as an offshoot of the Umbrian race (Dionys. ii. 49). The authority of Zenodotus is indeed in itself not worth much, and his statement as reported to us is somewhat confused; but many analogies would lead us to the same conclusion, that the Sabines and Umbrians were closely cognate races, and branches of the same original stock. We learn from the Eugubine tables that Sancus, the tutelary divinity of the Sabine nation, was an object of especial worship with the Umbrians also; the same documents prove that various other points of the Sabine religion, which are spoken of as peculiar to that nation, were in fact common to the Umbrians also (Klenze, *Philol. Abhandl.* p. 80). Unfortunately the Sabine language, which would have thrown much light upon the subject, is totally lost; not a single inscription has been preserved to us; but even the few words recorded by ancient writers, though many of them, as would naturally be the case in such a selection, words *peculiar* to the Sabines, yet are abundantly sufficient to show that there could be no essential difference between the language of the Sabines and their neighbours, the Umbrians on the one side, and the Oscans on the other (Klenze, *l. c.*; Donaldson, *Varronianus*, p. 8). The general similarity between their dialect and that of the Oscan was probably the cause that they adopted with facility in the more southern regions of Italy, which they had conquered,

the language of their Oscan subjects; indeed all the
extant inscriptions in that language may be considered as Sabello-Oscan, and have probably received
some influence from the language of the conquerors,
though we have no means of estimating its amount.
The original Sabines appear to have early lost the
use of their own language, and adopted the general
use of Latin; which, considering the rugged and
secluded character of their country, and their primitive habits of life, could hardly have been the
case, had the two languages been radically distinct.
On the whole, therefore, we may fairly conclude
that the Sabines were only a branch of the same
great family with the Oscans, Latins, and Umbrians,
but apparently most closely related to the last of
the three. Their name is generally derived from
that of Sabus, who is represented as a son of Sancus,
the chief tutelary divinity of the nation. (Cato, ap.
Dionys. ii. 49; Sil. Ital. viii. 422; Serv. ad Aen. viii.
638.) But another etymology given by ancient
writers derives it from their religious habits and
devotion to the worship of the gods. (Varr. ap. Fest.
p. 343; Plin. iii. 12. s. 17.) This last derivation
in fact comes to much the same thing with the
preceding one, for the name of Sabus (obviously a
mythological personage) is itself connected with the
Greek σέβω, and with the word "sevum" found in
the Eugubine tables in the sense of venerable or
holy, just as Sancus is with the Latin "sanctus,"
"sancire," &c. (Donaldson, l. c.)

The original abode of the Sabines was, according
to Cato, in the upper valley of the Aternus, about
Amiternum, at the foot of the loftiest group of the
Apennines. We cannot indeed understand literally,
at least as applying to the whole nation, his assertion (as quoted by Dionysius) that they proceeded
from a village called Testrina, near Amiternum
(Cato, ap. Dionys. i. 14, ii. 49); though this may
have been true of the particular band or clan which
invaded and occupied Reate. But there is no reason
to doubt the general fact that the Sabines, at the
earliest period when their name appears in history,
occupied the lofty mountain group in question with
its adjacent valleys, which, from the peculiar configuration of this part of the Apennines, would afford
natural and convenient outlets to their migrations
in all directions. [APENNINUS.] The sending forth
of these migrations, or national colonies, as they
may be called, was connected with an ancient
custom which, though not unknown to the other
nations of Italy, seems to have been more peculiarly
characteristic of the Sabines — the Ver Sacrum or
"sacred spring." This consisted of dedicating, by a
solemn vow, usually in time of pressure from war or
famine, all the produce of the coming year, to some
deity: Mamers or Mars seems to have been the one
commonly selected. The cattle born in that year
were accordingly sacrificed to the divinity chosen,
while the children were allowed to grow up to man's
estate, and were then sent forth in a body to find
for themselves new places of abode beyond the limits
of their native country. (Strab. v. p. 250; Fest.
s. vv. Mamertini, p. 158, Sacrani, p. 321, Ver
Sacrum, p. 379; Sisenna, ap. Non. p. 522; Varr.
R. R. iii. 16. § 29; Liv. xxii. 9, 10.) Such colonies
were related by tradition to have given origin to
the nations of the Picentes, the Samnites, and the
Hirpini, and in accordance with the notion of their
consecration to Mars they were reported to have
been guided by a woodpecker, or a wolf, the animals
peculiarly connected with that deity. (Strab. v.

pp. 240, 250; Fest. pp. 106, 212.) We have no
statements of the period at which these successive
emigrations towards the E. and S. took place: all
that is known of the early history of the nations
to which they gave rise will be found in the respective articles, and we shall here content ourselves
with tracing that of the Sabines themselves, or the
people to whom that appellation continued to be
confined by the Romans.

These, when they first emerged from their upland
valleys into the neighbourhood of Reate, found that
city, as well as the surrounding territory, in the possession of a people whom Dionysius calls Aborigines,
and who, finding themselves unable to withstand the
pressure of the Sabines, withdrew, after the capture
of their capital city of Lista, towards the lower
valley of the Tiber, where they settled themselves in
Latium, and finally became one of the constituent
elements of the Latin people. (Cato, ap. Dionys.
i. 14, ii. 48, 49.) [ABORIGINES; LATIUM.] Meanwhile the Sabines, after they had firmly established
themselves in the possession of Reate and its neighbourhood, gradually pressed on towards the S. and
W., and occupied the whole of the hilly and rugged
country which extends from Reate to the plain of
the Tiber, and from the neighbourhood of Ocriculum
to that of Tibur (Tivoli.) (Dionys. ii. 49.) The
conquest and colonisation of this extensive tract
was probably the work of a long time, but at the
first dawn of history we find the Sabines already
established on the left bank of the Tiber down to
within a few miles of its confluence with the Anio;
and at a period little subsequent to the foundation
of Rome, they pushed on their advanced posts still
further, and established themselves on the Quirinal
hill, at the very gates of the rising city. The history of the Sabines under Titus Tatius, of the wars
of that king with Romulus, and of the settlement
of the Sabines at Rome upon equal terms with the
Latin inhabitants, so that the two became gradually
blended into one people, has been so mixed up with
fables and distorted by poetical and mythological
legends, that we may well despair of recovering the
truth, or extricating the real history from the maze
of various and discordant traditions; but it does not
the less represent a real series of events. It is an
unquestionable historical fact that a large part of
the population of the city was of Sabine origin, and
the settlement of that people on the Quirinal is
attested by numerous local traditions, which there is
certainly no reason to doubt. (Schwegler, Röm.
Gesch. vol. i. pp. 243, 478, &c.)

We cannot attempt here to discuss the various
theories that have been suggested with a view to
explain the real nature of the Sabine invasion, and
the origin of the legends connected with them. One
of the most plausible of these is that which supposes Rome to have been really conquered by the
Sabines, and that it was only by a subsequent
struggle that the Latin settlers on the Palatine
attained an equality of rights. (Ihne, Researches
into the History of the Roman Constitution, p. 44,
&c.; Schwegler, vol. i. pp. 491—493.) It cannot
be denied that this view has much to recommend
it, and explains many obscure points in the early
history, but it can be scarcely regarded as based on
such an amount of evidence as would entitle it to be
received as a historical fact.

The Sabine influence struck deep into the character of the Roman people; but its effect was especially prominent in its bearing on their sacred rites, and on their sacerdotal as well as religious institutions. This is in entire accordance with the character given of the Sabines by Varro and Pliny; and it is no wonder therefore that the traditions of the Romans generally ascribed to Numa, the Sabine king, the whole, or by far the greater part, of the religious institutions of their country, in the same manner as they did the military and political ones to his predecessor Romulus. Numa, indeed, became to a great extent the representative, or rather the impersonation of the Sabine element of the Roman people; at the same time that he was so generally regarded as the founder of all religious rites and institutions, that it became customary to ascribe to him even those which were certainly not of Sabine origin, but belonged to the Latins or were derived from Alba. (Ambrosch, *Studien*, pp. 141 —148; Schwegler, *R. G.* vol. i. pp. 543, 554.)

Throughout these earliest traditions concerning the relations of the Sabines with Rome, Cures is the city that appears to take the most prominent part. Tatius himself was king of Cures (Dionys. ii. 36); and it was thither also that the patricians sent, after the interregnum, to seek out the wise and pacific Numa. (Liv. i. 18; Dionys. ii. 58.) A still more striking proof of the connection of the Roman Sabines with Cures was found in the name of Quirites, which came to be eventually applied to the whole Roman people, and which was commonly considered as immediately derived from that of Cures. (Liv. i. 13; Varr. *L. L.* vi. 68; Dionys. ii. 46; Strab. v. p. 228.) But this etymology is, to say the least, extremely doubtful; it is far more probable that the name of Quirites was derived from " quiris," a spear, and meant merely " spearmen " or " warriors," just as Quirinus was the " spear-god," or god of war, closely connected, though not identical with, Mamers or Mars. It is certain also that this superiority of Cures, if it ever really existed, ceased at a very early period. No subsequent allusion to it is found in Roman history, and the city itself was in historical times a very inconsiderable place. [CURES.]

The close union thus established between the Romans and the Sabines who had settled themselves on the Quirinal did not secure the rising city from hostilities with the rest of the nation. Already in the reign of Tullus Hostilius, the successor of Numa, we find that monarch engaged in hostilities with the Sabines, whose territory he invaded. The decisive battle is said to have taken place at a forest called Silva Malitiosa, the site of which is unknown. (Liv. i. 30; Dionys. iii. 32, 33.) During the reign of Ancus Marcius, who is represented as himself of Sabine descent (he was a grandson of Numa), no hostilities with the Sabines occur ; but his successor Tarquinius Priscus was engaged in a war with that people which appears to have been of a formidable description. The Sabines, according to Livy, began hostilities by crossing the Anio ; and after their final defeat we are told that they were deprived of Collatia and the adjoining territory. (Liv. i. 36—38 ; Dionys. iii. 55—66.) Cicero also speaks of Tarquin as repulsing the Sabines from the very walls of the city. (Cic. *de Rep.* ii. 20.) There seems therefore no doubt that they had at this time extended their power to the right bank of the Anio, and made themselves masters of a considerable part of the territory which had previously belonged to the Latins. From this time no further mention of them occurs in the history of Rome till after the expulsion of the kings ; but in B. C. 504, after the repulse of Porsena,

a Sabine war again broke out, and from this time that people appears almost as frequently among the enemies of Rome, as the Veientes or the Volscians. But the renewal of hostilities was marked by one incident, which exercised a permanent effect on Roman history. The whole of one clan of the Sabines, headed by a leader named Atta Clausus, dissenting from the policy of their countrymen, migrated in a body to Rome, where they were welcomed as citizens, and gave rise to the powerful family and tribe of the Claudii. (Liv. ii. ; Dionys. v. 40 ; Virg. *Aen.* vii. 708; Tac. *Ann.* xi. 24; Appian, *Rom.* i. Fr. 11.) It is unnecessary to recapitulate in detail the accounts of the petty wars with the Sabines in the early ages of the Republic, which present few features of historical interest. They are of much the same general character as those with the Veientes and the Volscians, but for some reason or other seem to have been a much less favourite subject for popular legend and national vanity, and therefore afford few of those striking incidents and romantic episodes with which the others have been adorned. Livy indeed disposes of them for the most part in a very summary manner; but they are related in considerable detail by Dionysius. One thing, however, is evident, that neither the power nor the spirit of the Sabines had been broken ; as they are represented in B. C. 469, as carrying their ravages up to the very gates of Rome; and even in B. C. 449, when the decisive victory of M. Horatius was followed by the capture of the Sabine camp, we are told that it was found full of booty, obtained by the plunder of the Roman territories. (Liv. ii. 16, 18, &c., iii. 26, 30, 38, 61— 63 ; Dionys. v. 37—47, vi. 31, &c.) On this, as on several other occasions, Eretum appears as the frontier town of the Sabines, where they established their head-quarters, and from whence they made incursions into the Roman territory.

There is nothing in the accounts transmitted to us of this victory of M. Horatius over the Sabines to distinguish it from numerous other instances of similar successes, but it seems to have been really of importance ; at least it was followed by the remarkable result that the wars with the Sabines, which for more than fifty years had been of such perpetual recurrence, ceased altogether from this time, and for more than a century and a half the name of the Sabines is scarcely mentioned in history. The circumstance is the more remarkable, because during a great part of this interval the Romans were engaged in a fierce contest with the Samnites, the descendants of the Sabines, but who do not appear to have maintained any kind of political relation with their progenitors. Of the terms of the peace which subsisted between the Sabines and Romans during this period we have no account. Niebuhr's conjecture that they enjoyed the rights of isopolity with the Romans (vol. ii. p. 447) is certainly without foundation; and they appear to have maintained a position of simple neutrality. We are equally at a loss to understand what should have induced them at length suddenly to depart from this policy, but in the year B. C. 290 we find the Sabines once more in arms against Rome. They were, however, easily vanquished. The consul M'. Curius Dentatus, who had already put an end to the Third Samnite War, next turned his arms against the Sabines, and reduced them to submission in the course of a single campaign. (Liv. *Epit.* xi.; Vict. *Vir. Ill.* 33 ; Oros. iii. 22; Flor. i. 15.) They were severely punished for their defection; great numbers of prisoners were sold as slaves; the remaining citizens were admitted to the Roman franchise, but without the right of suffrage, and their principal towns were reduced to the subordinate condition of Praefecturae. (Vell. Pat. i. 14; Festus, s. v. Praefecturae; Serv. ad Aen. vii. 709, whose statement can only refer to this period, though erroneously transferred by him to a much earlier one.) The right of suffrage was, however, granted to them about 20 years later (B. C. 268); and from this time the Sabines enjoyed the full rights of Roman citizens, and were included in the Sergian tribe. (Vell. Pat. l. c.; Cic. pro Balb. 13, in Vatin. 15.) This circumstance at once separated them from the cause of the other nations of Italy, including their own kinsmen the Samnites, Picentes, and Peligni, during the great contest of the Social War. On that occasion the Sabines, as well as the Latins and Campanians, were arrayed on behalf of Rome.

The last occasion on which the name of the Sabines as a people is found in history is during the Second Punic War, when they came forward in a body to furnish volunteers to the army of Scipio. (Liv. xxviii. 45.) After their incorporation with the Roman state, we scarcely meet with any separate notice of them, though they continued to be regarded as among the bravest and hardiest of the subjects of Rome. Hence Cicero calls them "florem Italiae ac robur rei publicae." (Pro Ligar. 11.)

Under the Empire their name did not even continue to be used as a territorial designation. Their territory was included in the Fourth Region by Augustus. (Plin. iii. 12. s. 17.) It was subsequently reckoned a part of the province of Valeria, and is included with the rest of that province under the appellation of Picenum in the Liber Coloniarum. (Lib. Col. pp. 253. 257, &c.; P. Diac. Hist. Lang. ii. 20; Mommsen, ad Lib. Col. p. 212.) But though the name of the Sabines thus disappeared from official usage, it still continued in current popular use. Indeed it was not likely that a people so attached to ancient usages, and so primitive in their habits, would readily lose or abandon their old appellation. Hence it is almost the only instance in which the ancient name of a district or region of Italy has been transmitted without alteration to the present day: the province of La Sabina still forms one of the twelve into which the States of the Church are divided, and is comprised within very nearly the same limits as it was in the days of Strabo. (Rampoldi, Diz. Corog. d'Italia, s. v.)

The country of the Sabines was, as already mentioned, for the most part of a rugged and mountainous character; even at the present day it is calculated that above two-thirds of it are incapable of any kind of cultivation. But the valleys are fertile, and even luxuriant; and the sides of the hills, and lower slopes of the mountains, are well adapted for the growth both of vines and olives. The northernmost tract of their territory, including the upper valleys of the Nar and Velinus, especially the neighbourhood of Nursia, was indeed a cold and bleak highland country, shut in on all sides by some of the highest ranges of the Apennines; and the whole broad tract which extends from the group of the Monte Velino, SE. of Reate, to the front of the mountain ranges that border the Campagna of Rome, is little more than a mass of broken and rugged mountains, of inferior elevation to the more

central ranges of the Apennines, but still far from inconsiderable. The Monte Gennaro (the Mons Lucretilis of Horace), which rises directly from the plain of the Campagna, attains to an elevation of 4285 English feet above the sea. But the isolated mountain called Monte Terminillo near Leonessa, NE. of Rieti, which forms a conspicuous object in the view from Rome, rises to a height of above 7000 feet, while the Monte Velino, SE. of Rieti, on the confines of the Sabines and the Vestini, is not less than 8180 feet in height. The whole of the ridge, also, which separates the Sabines from Picenum is one of the most elevated of the Apennines. The Monti della Sibilla, in which the Nar takes its rise, attain the height of 7200 feet, while the Monte Vettore and Pizzo di Sevo, which form the continuation of the same chain towards the Gran Sasso, rise to a still greater elevation. There can be no doubt that these lofty and rugged groups of mountains are those designated by the ancients as the Mons Fiscellus, Tetrica ("Tetricae horrentes rupes," Virg. Aen. vii. 713), and Severus; but we are unable to identify with any certainty the particular mountains to which these names were applied. The more westerly part of the Sabine territory slopes gradually from the lofty ranges of these central Apennines towards the valley of the Tiber, and though always hilly is still a fertile and productive country, similar to the part of Umbria, which it adjoins. The lower valley of the Velinus about Reate was also celebrated for its fertility, and even at the present day is deservedly reckoned one of the most beautiful districts in Italy.

The physical character of the land of the Sabines evidently exercised a strong influence upon the character and manners of the people. Highlanders and mountaineers are generally brave, hardy, and frugal; and the Sabines seem to have possessed all these qualities in so high a degree that they became, as it were, the types of them among the Romans. Cicero calls them "severissimi homines Sabini," and Livy speaks of the "disciplina tetrica ac tristis veterum Sabinorum." (Cic. in Vatin. 15, pro Ligar. 11; Liv. i. 18.) Cato also described the severe and frugal mode of life of the early Romans as inherited from the Sabines (ap. Serv. ad Aen. viii. 638). Their frugal manners and moral purity continued indeed, even under the Roman government, to be an object of admiration, and are often introduced by the poets of the Empire as a contrast to the luxury and dissoluteness of the capital. (Hor. Carm. iii. 6. 38 — 44, Epod. 2. 41, Epist. ii. 1. 25; Propert. iii. 24. 47; Juv. iii. 169.) With these qualities were combined, as is not unfrequently found among secluded mountaineers, an earnest piety and strong religious feeling, together with a strenuous attachment to the religious usages and forms of worship which had been transmitted to them by their ancestors. The religion of the Sabines does not appear to have differed essentially from that of the other neighbouring nations of Italy; but they had several peculiar divinities, or at least divinities unknown to the Latins or Etruscans, though some of them seem to have been common to the Umbrians also. At the head of these stood Sancus, called also Semo Sancus, who was the tutelary divinity of the nation, and the reputed father of their mythical progenitor, or eponymous hero Sabus. He was considered as the peculiar guardian of oaths, and was thence generally identified by the Romans with Dius Fidius; while others, for less obvious reasons, identified him with

Hercules. (Ovid. *Fast.* vi. 215 ; Sil. Ital. viii. 420; Lactant. i. 15 ; Augustin, *Civ. Dei*, xviii. 19; Ambrosch. *Studien.* p. 170, &c.) Among the other deities whose worship is expressly said to have been introduced at Rome by the Sabines, we find Sol, Feronia, Minerva and Mars, or Mamers, as he was called by the Sabines and their descendants. (Varr. *L. L.* v. 74.) Minerva was, however, certainly an Etruscan divinity also; and in like manner Vejovis, Ops, Diana, and several other deities, which are said to be of Sabine extraction, were clearly common to the Latins also, and probably formed part of the mythology of all the Italian nations. (Varro, *l. c.*; Augustin, *C. D.* iv. 23 ; Schwegler, *Röm.* Gesch. i. p. 250 ; Ambrosch. *l. c.* pp. 141—176.) On the other hand Quirinus was certainly a Sabine deity, notwithstanding his subsequent identification with the deified Romulus. His temple, as well as that of Sancus, stood on the Quirinal hill, to which indeed it probably gave name. (Varr. *L. L.* v. 51 ; Ambrosch, pp. 149, 169.)

Connected with the religious rites of the Sabines may be mentioned their superstitious attachment to magical incantations, which they continued to practise down to a late period, as well as their descendants the Marsi and other Sabellian tribes. (Hor. *Epod.* 17. 28, *Sat.* i. 9. 29.) They were noted also for their skill, or pretended skill, in divination by dreams. (Fest. p. 335.) The rites of augury, and especially of auspices, or omens from the flight of birds, were also considered to be essentially of Sabine origin, though certainly common in more or less degree to the other nations of Central Italy. Attus Navius, the celebrated augur in the reign of Tarquin the Elder, who was regarded by many as the founder of the whole science of augury (Cic. *de Div.* ii. 38), was a Sabine, and the institution of the "auspicia majora" was also referred to Numa. (Cic. *de Rep.* ii. 14.)

The Sabine language, as already observed, is known to us only from a few words preserved by ancient writers, Varro, Festus, &c. Some of these, as "multa," "albus," "imperator," &c., are well known to us as Latin words, though said to have originally passed into that language from the Sabines. Others, such as "hirpus" or "irpus" for a wolf, "curis" or "quiris" (a spear), "nar" (sulphur), "teba" (a hill), &c., were altogether strange to the Latin, though still in use among the Sabines. A more general peculiarity of the Sabine dialect, and which in itself proves it to have been a cognate language with the Latin, is that it inserted the digamma or F at the commencement of many words instead of the rough aspirate ; thus they said "fircus," "fedus," "fostis," "fostia," &c., for the Latin "hircus," "hedus," "hostis," "hostia," &c. (Varro, *L. L.* v. 97; Fest. pp. 84, 102 ; Klenze, *Philolog. Abhandl.* pp. 70—76; Mommsen, *U. I. Dialekte*, pp. 335—359.) The two last authors have well brought together the little that we really know of the Sabine language. It is not quite clear from the expressions of Varro how far the Sabine language could be considered as still existing in his time; but it seems probable that it could no longer be regarded as a living language, though the peculiar expressions and forms referred to were still in use as provincialisms. (Klenze, *l. c.*)

The Sabines, we are told, dwelt principally in villages, and even their towns in the earliest times were unwalled. (Strab. v. p. 228 ; Dionys. ii. 49.) This is one of the points in which they were thought to resemble the Lacedaemonians (Plut. *Rom.* 16); though it probably arose merely from their simplicity of manners, and their retaining unchanged the habits of primitive mountaineers. In accordance with this statement we find very few towns mentioned in their territory ; and even of these REATE appears to have been the only one that was ever a place of much importance. INTEROCREA, about 14 miles higher up the valley of the Velinus (the name of which is still preserved in *Antrodoco*), seems never to have been a municipal town ; and it is probable that the whole upper valley of the Velinus was, municipally speaking, included in the territory of Reate, as we know was the case with the lower valley also, down to the falls of the river, which formed the limit of the territory of the Sabines on this side; Interamna, as well as Narnia and Ocriculum, being included in Umbria. FALACRINUM, the birthplace of Vespasian, situated near the sources of the Velinus, was certainly a mere village; as was also FORULI (*Civita Tommasa*), situated in the cross valley which led from Interocrea to Amiternum and formed the line of communication between the valley of the Velinus and that of the Aternus. AMITERNUM itself, though situated in the valley of the Aternus, so that it would seem to have more naturally belonged to the Vestini, was certainly a Sabine city (Plin. iii. 12. s. 17; Strab. v. p. 228), and was probably, next to Reate, the most considerable that they possessed. NURSIA, in the upper valley of the Nar, was the chief town of the surrounding district, but was never a place of much importance. The lower country of the Sabines, between Reate and Rome, seems to have contained several small towns, which were of municipal rank, though said by Strabo to be little more than villages. Among these were FORUM NOVUM, the site of which may be fixed at *Vescovio*, on the banks of the *Imele*, and FORUM DECII, the situation of which is wholly unknown. Both these were, as the names show, Roman towns, and not ancient Sabine cities ; the former appears to have replaced the Sabine CASPERIA, which was probably situated at *Aspra*, in the same neighbourhood. On the other hand CURES, the supposed metropolis of the Sabines that had settled at Rome, still retained its municipal rank, though not a place of much importance. The same was the case with ERETUM, which was, as already observed, the last of the strictly Sabine towns in proceeding towards Rome ; though Pliny includes Nomentum and Fidenae also among the Sabines. Besides these there were two towns of the name of Trebula, both of which must probably be placed in the southern part of the land of the Sabines. Of these TREBULA MUTUSCA (the Mutuscae of Virgil, *Aen.* vii. 711) is represented by *Monte Leone*, about 15 miles S. of *Rieti*, and on the right of the Salarian Way; while TREBULA SUFFENAS may perhaps be placed at *S. Antimo* near *Stroncone*, in the hills W. of *Rieti*. Lastly, VARIA, in the valley of the Anio, 4 miles above Tibur, still called *Vicovaro*, would appear to have been certainly a Sabine town; the whole valley of the Digentia *(Licenza)*, with its villages of Mandela, Digentia, and Fanum Vacunae (the well-known neighbourhood of Horace's Sabine farm), being included among its dependencies. [DIGENTIA.]

The territory of the Sabines was traversed throughout its whole extent by the Salarian Way, which was from an early period one of the great highroads of Italy. This proceeded from Rome

3 K 3

direct to Reate, and thence ascended the valley of
the Velinus by Interocrea and Falacrinum, from
whence it crossed the ridge of the Apennines into
the valley of the Truentus in Picenum, and thus
descended to Asculum and the Adriatic. The
stations between Rome and Reate were Eretum,
which may be fixed at *Grotta Marozza*, and Vicus
Novus, the site of which is marked by the *Osteria
Nuova*, or *Osteria dei Massacci*, 32 miles from
Rome. (Westphal, *Röm. Kamp.* p. 128.)   [VIA
SALARIA.]

Notwithstanding its mountainous character the
Sabine territory was far from being poor. Its productions consisted chiefly of oil and wine, which,
though not of first-rate quality, were abundant, and
supplied a great part of the quantity used by the
lower classes at Rome. (Hor. *Carm.* i. 9. 7, 20. 1;
Juv. iii. 85.) The Sabine hills produced also in
abundance the plant which was thence known as
Sabina herba (still called *Savin*), which was used
by the natives for incense, before the more costly
frankincense was introduced from the East. (Plin.
xvi. 20. s. 33, xxiv. 11. s. 61; Virg. *Cul.* 402; Ovid,
Fast. i. 342.) The neighbourhood of Reate was
also famous for its breed of mules and horses; and
the mountains afforded excellent pasturage for
sheep. The wilder and more inaccessible summits
of the Apennines were said still to be frequented by
wild goats, an animal long since extinct throughout
the continent of Italy. (Varr. *R. R.* ii. 1. § 5,
3. § 3.)   [E. H. B.]

SABIS (Σάβις), a small river of Carmania, which
is mentioned by Mela in connection with two other
small streams, the Andanis and Coros (iii. 8).
It is also noticed by Pliny, who places it in the
neighbourhood of Harmuza (*Ormúz*, vi. 23. s. 27).
Ptolemy speaks of a town in Carmania of the same
name with this river (vi. 8. § 14).   [V.]

SABIS (*Sambre*), a river of Belgica, which joins
the Mosa (*Maas*) at *Charleroi*. Caesar (B. C. 57)
marched against the Nervii and their confederates
from the south, and he found the enemy posted on
the north side of the Sabis (*B. G.* ii. 16). In this
battle the Belgae were defeated with great slaughter.
[NERVII.]   [G. L.]

SABLONES, in Gallia Belgica, is placed by the
Antonine Itin. on a road from Colonia Trajana
(*Kelln*) to Juliacum (*Juliers*) and Colonia Agrippinensis (*Cologne*). Sablones is supposed to be a
place named *Int-Sandt* near *Strälen*, a town on
the river *Niers*, a branch of the *Maas*. But see
MEDIOLANUM in Gallia, No. 3.   [G. L.]

SABOCI (Σαβῶκοι al. Σαβόκοι, Ptol. iii. 5.
§ 20), a people of European Sarmatia, who from the
termination "boki," "bank," so often occurring in
Russian and Polish local names, must be looked for
in the basin of the river *Sun*, one of the largest
affluents of the *Vistula*, and which drains a greater
part of *Galizia*. (Schafarik, *Slav. Alt.* vol. i.
p. 206.)   [E. B. J.]

SABORA, a place in Hispania Baetica, in the
mountains above *Malaga*, near *Cannete*; known
only from inscriptions. (Carter, *Travels*, p. 252;
Ukert, vol. ii. pt. i. p. 360.)   [T. H. D.]

SABRACAE, a people who dwelt, according to
Curtius, in the southern part of the *Punjáb*, in the
neighbourhood of the Insula Pattalene (ix. 8. § 4).
They are mentioned in connection with the Praesti
as forming part of the realm of Musicanus. (Arrian, *Anab.* vi. 15; Diod. xvii. 102.)   [V.]

SABRATA (Σαβράτα, Ptol. iv. 3. § 41, Plin. v. 4.

s. 5; Solin. 37; *Itin. Anton.*; *Peut. Tab.*; Σαβαραθά,
Procop. *de Aed.* vi. 4; Σαβράθα, *Stadiasm.* §§ 99,
100), a Phoenician town (Sil. Ital. iii. 256) on the
coast of N. Africa between the Syrtes. The name,
which is Phoenician and occurs on coins (Movers,
Die Phönis. vol. ii. p. 491), received the Graecised
form ABROTONUM; for although Pliny (*l. c.*) distinguishes the two towns they are undoubtedly the
same places. It became afterwards a Roman colonia, and was the birthplace of Flavia Domitilla,
the first wife of Vespasian, and mother of Titus and
Domitian. (Sueton. *Vespas.* 3). Justinian fortified
it (Procop. *l. c.*), and it remained during the middle
ages one of the most frequented markets upon this
coast, to which the natives of central Africa brought
their grain (comp. Ibn Abd-el-Hakem, *Journal
Asiatique*, 1844, vol. ii. p. 358). Barth (*Wanderungen*, p. 277) has given an account of the extensive
ruins of Sabrata, which he found to the W. of
Tripoli, at *Tripoli Vecchio*, or *Sodra-esch-Schurkía*,
lat. 32° 49′, long. 12° 26′. (Smyth, *Mediterranean*,
p. 456.)   [E. B. J.]

SABRINA (called by Ptolemy Σαβρίνα, ii. 3.
§ 3; probably also the Sarva of the Geog. Rav. v. 31),
a river on the W. coast of Britannia Romana, which
falls into the sea near Venta Silurum, now the
Severn. Its mouth formed an estuary of the same
name. (Comp. Tac. *Ann.* xii. 31.)   [T. H. D.]

SABUS, a fortified place in Armenia Minor, at
the foot of Antitaurus. (*It. Ant.* p. 209; *Not.
Imp.* c. 27.) In the Peuting. Table it is called
Saba.   [L. S.]

SACAE. [SCYTHIA.]

SACALA (τὰ Σάκαλα), a desert spot on the sea-
shore of Gedrosia which was visited by the fleet of
Nearchus (Arrian, *Ind.* c. 22). It is not satisfactorily identified with any modern place. (Vincent,
Voyage of Nearchus, i. p. 202.)   [V.]

SACANI. [SARMATIA.]

SACAPENE. [SACASENE.]

SACARAULI (Σακαραῦλοι, Strab. xi. p. 511.), a
nomad people of Central Asia, belonging to the
oldest stock of the *Turks* of the *Altai*. In Ptolemy
(vi. 14. § 4) this people appear under the name of
Sagaraucae (Σαγαραῦκαι) (comp. Ritter, *Erdkunde*,
vol. vii. p. 696).   [E. B. J.]

SACASSE'NE (Σακασσηνή, Strab. ii. p. 73, xi.
pp. 509, 511, 529: *Eth.* Sacassaani, Plin. vi. 11), a
province of Armenia, on the borders of Gogarene,
which it separated from the valley of the Araxes,
and which extended to the river Cyrus. St. Martin
(*Mém. sur l'Arménie*, vol. i. pp. 143, 209, 210)
identifies it with the Armenian province of *Siounik'h*,
which was governed up to the 12th century by a
race of princes who traced their descent to Haig, first
king of Armenia, and who in the 9th century had
political relations with the Byzantine court. (Const.
Porph. *de Caeren. Aul. Byz.* vol. i. p. 397.) The
SACAPENE of Ptolemy (v. 13. § 9) appears to be
the same as this province.   [E. B. J.]

SACASTE'NE (Σακαστηνή), a district of the
interior of Drangiana, which was occupied by the
Sacae or Scythians, who appear to have descended
through the *Punjáb*, and to have settled there.
(Isidor. *Mans. Parth.* c. 18.) According to Isidorus, it bore also the name of Paraetacene. It has
been supposed that the modern name of this country,
Segestan or *Seistan*, is derived from Sacastene (Wahl,
Vorder u. Mittel-Asien, i. p. 569; comp. Ritter,
viii. p. 120). Four towns, Baida, Min, Palacenti,
and Sigal, are mentioned in it : of these, Min may

bɔ compared with Min-nagara, a town on the Indus belonging to the same people. (Arrian, *Peripl. Mar. Eryth.* § 38.) [MINNAGARA.] [V.]

SACCASE'NA, a place in Cappadocia, probably in the neighbourhood of the modern *Urgub* or *Urkup.* (*It. Ant.* p. 296.) [L. S.]

SACCO'PODES (Σακκοπόδες), according to Strabo, a name given to the people of Adiabene in Assyria (xvi. p. 745). There has been a great dispute among learned men as to this name, which does not appear to be a genuine one. Bochart has suggested Saucropodes (Σαυκρόπoδes). On the whole, however, it would seem that the emendation of Tzschukke is the best, who reads Σαυλόπoδes. (Groskurd, *ad Strab.* vol. iii. p. 225.) [V.]

SACER MONS (τὸ 'Ιερὸν ὄρος) was the name given to a hill about 3 miles from Rome, across the Anio and on the right of the Via Nomentana. It is mentioned only on occasion of the two secessions of the plebeians from Rome : the first of which, in B. C. 494, was terminated by the dexterity of Menenius Agrippa, and gave occasion to the election of the first tribunes of the people. (Liv. ii. 32; Dionys. vi. 45; Appian, *B. C.* i. 1.) In memory of this treaty and the "Lex Sacrata" which was passed there to confirm it, an altar was erected on the spot, which thenceforth always bore the name of "the Sacred Mount." (Dionys. vi. 90; Appian, *l. c.*) The second occasion was during the Decemvirate; when the plebeians, who had at first seceded only to the Aventine, on finding that this produced no effect, withdrew to the Sacred Mount (Liv. iii. 52). Cicero, on the contrary, represents the secession on this occasion as taking place first to the Sacred Mount, and then to the Aventine (Cic. *de R. P.* ii. 37). Hardly any spot in the neighbourhood of Rome, not marked by any existing ruins, is so clearly identified by the descriptions of ancient writers as the Sacer Mons. Both Livy and Cicero concur in placing it 3 miles from Rome, across the Anio ; and the former expressly tells us that the plebeians, on the second occasion, proceeded thither by the Via Nomentana, which was then called Ficulensis (Liv. ii. 32, iii. 52; Cic. *Brut.* 14, *pro Cornel.*, ap. Ascon. p. 76). Now the third mile along the Via Nomentana brings us to a point just across the Anio; and on the right of the road at this point is a hill overlooking the river, in some degree isolated from the *plateau* beyond, with which it is, however, closely connected, while its front towards the valley of the Anio is steep and almost precipitous.

On its E. side flows a small stream, descending from the *Casale dei Pazzi* (apparently the one known in ancient times as the Rivus Ulmanus); so that the position is one of considerable strength, especially on the side towards Rome. The site is now uninhabited, and designated by no peculiar appellation. (Nibby, *Dintorni di Roma*, vol. iii. pp. 54, 55.) [E. H. B.]

SACHALI'TAE (Σαχαλῖται), a people upon the S. coast of Arabia Felix (Ptol. vi. 7. §§ 11, 24, 25), and upon the bay called after them SACHALITES SINUS (Σαχαλίτης κόλπος). Respecting the position of this bay there was a difference of opinion among the ancient geographers, Marinus placing it towards the west, and Ptolemy towards the east, of the promontory Syagrus (*Ras Fartak*). (Ptol. i. 17. § 2, comp. vi. 7. §§ 11, 46.) Marcianus (p. 23) agrees with Ptolemy; and says that the bay extended from this promontory to the mouth of the Persian gulf (comp. Steph. B. *s. v.* Σαχαλίτης κόλπος). Arrian

(*Peripl. Mar. Erythr.* p. 17. § 29) on the other hand agrees with Marcian, and places the bay between Cane and the promontory Syagrus. (See C. Müller, *ad Arrian, l. c.*)

SACILI or SACILI MARTIALIUM (Plin. iii. 1. s. 3; called by Ptolemy Σακιλίs, ii. 4. § 11), a town of the Turduli in Hispania Baetica, at a place near *Perabad*, now called *Alcorrucen.* (Morales, *Antig.* p. 96 : Florez, *Esp. Sagr.* p. 147.) [T. H. D.]

SA'CORA (Σάκορα), a town in the interior of Paphlagonia, is mentioned only by Ptolemy (v. 4. § 5). [L. S.]

SACORSA (Σάκορσα), a town in the interior of Paphlagonia, is mentioned only by Ptolemy (v. 4. § 6). [L. S.]

SACRA'NI, was the name given by a tradition, probably of very ancient date, to a conquering people or tribe which invaded Latium at a period long before the historical age. Festus represents them as proceeding from Reate, and expelling the Siculi from the Septimontium, where Rome afterwards stood. He tells us that their name was derived from their being the offspring of a "ver sacrum." (Fest. *s. v.* *Sacrani*, p. 321.) It hence appears probable that the Sacrani of Festus were either the same with the people called Aborigines by Dionysius (i. 16) [ABORIGINES], or were at least one clan or tribe of that people. But it is very doubtful whether the name was ever really used as a national appellation. Virgil indeed alludes to the Sacrani as among the inhabitants of Latium in the days of Aeneas (*Sacranae acies, Aen.* vii. 796), but apparently as a small and obscure tribe. Servius in his commentary on the passage gives different explanations of the name, all varying from one another, and from that given by Festus, which is the most distinct statement we have upon the subject. In another passage (*ad Aen.* xi. 317) Servius distinguishes the Sacrani from the Aborigines, but little value can be attached to his statements on such subjects. [E. H. B.]

SACRARIA. [CLITUMNUS.]

SACRIPORTUS (ὁ 'Ιερὸς λιμήν, Appian, *B. C.* i. 87), a place in Latium, between Signia and Praeneste, celebrated as the scene of the decisive battle between Sulla and the younger Marius, in which the latter was totally defeated, and compelled to take refuge within the walls of Praeneste, B. C. 82. (Liv. *Epit.* lxxxvii.; Appian, *B. C.* i. 87; Vell. Pat. ii. 26, 28; Flor. iii. 21. § 23; Vict. *Vir. Ill.* 68, 75; Lucan, ii. 134.) The scene of the battle is universally described as "apud Sacriportum," but with no more precise distinction of the locality. The name of Sacriportus does not occur upon any other occasion, and we do not know what was the meaning of the name, whether it were a village or small town, or merely a spot so designated. But its locality may be approximately fixed by the accounts of the battle; this is described by Appian as taking place *near* Praeneste, and by Plutarch (*Sull.* 28) as *near* Signia. We learn moreover from Appian that Sulla having besieged and taken Setia, the younger Marius, who had in vain endeavoured to relieve it, retreated step by step before him until he arrived in the neighbourhood of Praeneste, when he halted at Sacriportus, and gave battle to his pursuer. It is therefore evident that it must have been situated in the plain below Praeneste, between that city and Signia, and probably not far from the opening between the Alban hills and the Volscian mountains, through which must have lain the line of retreat of Marius;

but it is impossible to fix the site with more precision. [E. H. B.]

SACRUM PR. 1. (τὸ ἱερὸν ἀκρωτήριον, Strab. iii. p. 137), the SW. extremity of Lusitania ; according to Strabo (*l. c.*), the most W. point, not only of Europe but of the known world; the present *Cape St. Vincent.* Strabo adds that the surrounding district was called in Latin "Cuneus." Strabo also says that the geographer Artemidorus, who had been there, compared the promontory with the bow of a ship, and said that there were three small islands there ; which, however, are not mentioned by any other writer, nor do they now exist. (Cf. Mela, ii. 1 ; Plin. iv. 22. s. 35, &c.)

2. (τὸ ἱερὸν ἄκρον, Ptol. ii. 2. § 6) the SE. point of Hibernia, now *Carnsore Point.* [T. H. D.]

SACRUM PROM. (τὸ ἱερὸν ἄκρον, Ptol. iii. 5. § 8), the western point of the ACHILLEOS DROMOS. [E. B. J.]

SACRUM PROM., a promontory of Lycia upon the borders of Pamphylia, opposite the Chelidoniae Insulae, whence the promontory is called by Livy Chelidonium Prom. [For details, see Vol. I. p. 606, b.]

SADACORA (Σαδάκορα), a town of Cappadocia, situated on the great road from Coropassus and Garsabora to Mazaca. (Strab. xiv. p. 663.) [L.S.]

SADAME (*Itin. Ant.* p. 230; in Geog. Rav. 4, 6, written Sadanua), a town in the NE. part of Thrace, on the road from Hadrianopolis to Develtus, its distance from the latter, according to the Itinerary, being 18,000 paces. This would give as its site the present town of *Kanareh,* situated near the source of a small river which runs through a narrow valley and falls into the Black Sea at *Cape Zaitan,* according to Reichard it was in the neighbourhood of *Omar-Fakhi,* which is perhaps the *Sarbasan* of Voudoucourt. [J. R.]

SADOS (Σάδος), a small river of the Aurea Chersonesus, which fell into the *Bay of Bengal* (Ptol. vii. 2. § 3). It has been supposed by Forbiger to be the same as the present *Sundoway.* Ptolemy mentions also in the same locality a town called Sada, which was, in all probability, on or near the river. [V.]

SAELI'NI. [ASTURES, Vol. I. p. 249.]

SAEPI'NUM or SEPI'NUM (the name is variously written both in MSS. and even inscriptions, but Saepinum is probably the most correct form: Σαίπινον, Ptol.: *Eth.* Saepinas: *Altilia* near *Sepino*), a city of Samnium, in the country of the Pentri, on the E. slope of the great group of the *Monte Matese,* and near the sources of the *Tamaro* (Tamarus). It seems to have been in early times one of the chief towns of the Samnites, or rather one of the five which they possessed worthy of the name. From its position in the heart of their country it was not till the Third Samnite War that it was attacked by the Roman arms; but in B.C. 293 it was besieged by the consul L. Papirius Cursor, and though vigorously defended by a garrison amounting almost to an army, was at length carried by assault. (Liv. x. 44, 45.) From this time the name of Saepinum disappears from history, but it is found again at a later period among the municipal towns of Samnium under the Roman Empire. Its name is not indeed mentioned by Strabo, among the few surviving cities of Samnium in his day: but it received a colony under Nero (*Lib. Colon.* p. 237), and appears for a time to have recovered some degree of importance. Its name is found both in Ptolemy and Pliny among

the municipal towns of Samnium; and it is certain from inscriptions that it did not bear the title of a Colonia. (Plin. iii. 12. s. 17; Ptol. iii. 1. § 67; Orell. *Inscr.* 140; Mommsen, *Inscr. R. N.* 4918, 4929, 4934, &c.) Its name is mentioned also in the Tabula, which places it 30 M. P. from Beneventum, the intermediate station being a place called Sirpium, the site of which is unknown. (*Tab. Peut.*)

Saepinum became an episcopal see before the fall of the Roman Empire; it had, however, fallen into great decay in the time of the Lombards, but was repeopled by Romoaldus, duke of Beneventum (P. Diac. v. 30), and survived till the 9th century, when it was taken and plundered by the Saracens; after which it seems to have been abandoned by the inhabitants, who withdrew to the site occupied by the modern town of *Sepino,* about 2 miles from the site of the ancient one. The ruins of the latter, which are now called *Altilia,* are evidently of Roman date, and, from their regularity and style of construction, render it probable that the town was entirely rebuilt at the time of the establishment of the Roman colony, very probably not on the same site with the ancient Samnite city. The existing walls, which remain in almost complete preservation throughout their whole circuit, and which, as we learn from an inscription over one of the gates, were certainly erected by Nero (Mommsen, *I. R. N.* 4922), enclose a perfect square, with the angles slightly rounded off, and four gates, placed at the four cardinal points, flanked by massive square towers. The masonry is of reticulated work, the arches only of the gates being of massive stone. Within the enclosure are the remains of a theatre, besides the substructions and vestiges of several other buildings, and numerous fragments of an architectural character, as well as inscriptions. Of these last the most interesting is one which is still extant at the gate leading to Bovianum, and has reference to the flocks which then, as now, passed annually backwards and forwards from the thirsty plains of Apulia to the upland pastures of Samnium, especially of the *Matese;* and which appear to have even then followed the same line of route: the *trattura* or sheep-track still in use passing directly through the ruins of *Altilia.* (Craven's *Abruzzi,* vol. ii. pp. 130—135; Romanelli, vol. ii. pp. 444—448; Mommsen, *I. R. N.* 4916.) [E. H. B.]

SAEPONE, an inland town of Hispania Baetica, near *Cortes* in the *Sierra de Ronda.* (Plin. iii. 1. s. 3.) [T. H. D.]

SAETABICULA (Σαιταβίκουλα, Ptol. ii. 6. s. 62), a town of the Contestani in Hispania Tarraconensis, probably the present *Alcira* in *Valentia.* (Laborde. *Itin.* i. p. 266.) [T. H. D.]

SAETABIS, SETABIS, or SAETABI (Σαίταβις, Strab. iii. p. 160), a town of the Contestani in Hispania Tarraconensis. It was a Roman municipium in the jurisdiction of Carthago (Murat. *Inscr.* ii. p. 1183. 6), and had the surname of Augustanorum. (Plin. iii. 3. s. 4.) It lay upon an eminence (Sil. Ital. iii. 372) to the S. of the Sucro, and was famed for its flax and linen manufacture. (Plin. xix. 2. s. 1; Catull. xii. 14, &c.) Now *Jativa.* (Cf. Laborde, *Itin.* i. p. 266 ; Marca, *Hisp.* ii. 6. p. 118.) [T. H. D.]

SAE'TABIS (Σαιταβίς, Ptol. ii. 6. § 14), a river S. of the Sucro in the territory of the Contestani, on the E. coast of Hispania Tarraconensis. Most probably the *Alcoy.* (Ukert, ii. pt. i. p. 294.) [T.H.D.]

SAETIANI. [SCYTHIA.]

SAETTAE. [SETAE.]

SAGALASSUS (Σαγαλασσός: Eth. Σαγαλασσεύς or Σαγαλασσηνός), an important town and fortress near the north-western frontier of Pisidia, or, as Strabo (xii. p. 569) less correctly states, of Isauria, while Ptolemy (v. 3. § 6) erroneously mentions it among the towns of Lycia. (Comp. Steph. B. *s. v.*) Alexander the Great took the town by assault, having previously defeated its brave Pisidian inhabitants, who met the aggressor drawn up on a hill outside their town. (Arrian, *Anab.* i. 28.) Livy (xxxviii. 15), in his account of the expedition of Cn. Manlius, describes Sagalassus as situated in a fertile plain, abounding in every species of produce; he likewise characterises its inhabitants as the bravest of the Pisidians, and the town itself as most strongly fortified. Manlius did not take it, but by ravaging its territory compelled the Sagalassians to come to terms, to pay a contribution of 50 talents, 20,000 medimni of wheat, and the same quantity of barley. Strabo states that it was one of the chief towns of Pisidia, and that after passing under the dominion of Amyntas, tetrarch of Lycaonia and Galatia, it became part of the Roman province. He adds that it was only one day's march from Apamea, whereas we learn from Arrian that Alexander was five days on the road between the two towns; but the detention of the latter was not occasioned by the length of the road but by other circumstances, so that Strabo's account is not opposed to that of Arrian. (Comp. Polyb. xxii. 19; Plin. v. 24.) The town is mentioned also by Hierocles (p. 693), in the Ecclesiastical Notices, and the Acts of Councils, from which it appears to have been an episcopal see.

The traveller Lucas (*Trois Voyages*, i. p. 181, and *Second Voyage*, i. c. 34) was the first that reported the existence of extensive ruins at a place called *Aglasoun*, and the resemblance of the name led him to identify these ruins with the site of the ancient Sagalassus. This conjecture has since been fully confirmed by Arundell (*A Visit to the Seven Churches*, p. 132, foll.), who describes these ruins as situated on the long terrace of a lofty mountain, rising above the village of *Aglasoun*, and consisting chiefly of massy walls, heaps of sculptured stones, and innumerable sepulchral vaults in the almost perpendicular side of the mountain. A little lower down the terrace are considerable remains of a large building, and a large paved oblong area, full of fluted columns, pedestals, &c., about 240 feet long; a portico nearly 300 feet long and 27 wide; and beyond this some magnificent remains either of a temple or a gymnasium. Above these rises a steep hill with a few remains on the top, which was probably the acropolis. There is also a large theatre in a fine state of preservation. Inscriptions with the words Σαγαλασσέων πόλις leave no doubt as to these noble ruins belonging to the ancient town of Sagalassus. (Comp. Hamilton, *Researches*, vol. i. p. 486, foll.; Fellows, *Asia Minor*, p. 164, foll.)   [L. S.]

SAGANUS (Σαγανός, Marcian, *Peripl.* p. 21., ed. Hudson), a small river on the coast of Carmania, about 200 stadia from Harmuza. It is mentioned also by Ptolemy (vi. 8. § 4), and Pliny (vi. 25). It is probably the same stream which is called by Ammianus Marcellinus, Saganis (xxiii. 6). Vincent thinks that it may be represented by a small river which flows into the *Persian Gulf*, near *Gomeroon*. (*Voy. of Nearchus*, vol. i. p. 370.)   [V.]

SAGA'POLA (Σαγάπολα al. Σαγάπολα ὄρος,

Ptol. iv. 6. §§ 8, 14, 16, 17), a mountain of Interior Libya, from which flows the Subus, the position of which is fixed by Ptolemy (*l. c.*) 13° E. long., 22° N. lat. It may be assumed that the divergent which Ptolemy describes as ascending to this mountain from the Nigeir is one of the tributaries which flow into the *Djoübá* or *Quorra*, from the highlands to the N. of that river (comp. *Journ. Geog. Soc.* vol. ii. p. 13.)   [E. B. J.]

SAGARAUCAE. [SACARAULI.]

SAGARIS, a river of European Sarmatia (Ov. *ex Pont.* iv. 1047), which has been assumed, from the name, to have discharged itself into the SINUS SAGARIUS. (Plin. iv. 26.)   [E. B. J.]

SAGA'RTII. [PERSIS.]

SAGIDA (Σάγιδα or Σάγηδα, Ptol. vii. 1. § 71), a metropolis of Central India, which is perhaps the same as the present *Sohajpur*, near the sources of the river *Soane*.   [V.]

SAGRAS (ἡ Σάγρας, Strab. vi. p. 261), a river of Bruttium, on the E. coast of the peninsula, to the S. of Caulonia, between that city and Locri. It is celebrated in history for the great battle fought on its banks, in which an army of 130,000 Crotoniats is said to have been totally defeated by 10,000 Locrians: an event regarded as so extraordinary that it passed into a kind of proverb for something that appeared incredible, though true. (ἀληθέστερα τῶν ἐπὶ Σάγρᾳ, Suid. *s. v.*; Strab. vi. p. 261; Cic. *de N. D.* iii. 5; Justin. xx. 3; Plin. iii. 10. s. 15.) The victory was ascribed by the Locrians to the direct intervention of the Dioscuri, to whom they in consequence erected altars on the banks of the river, which were apparently still extant in the time of Strabo. It was added that the news of the victory was miraculously conveyed to the Greeks assembled at Olympia the same day that the battle was fought. (Strab. *l. c.*; Cic. *de N. D.* ii. 2.) But notwithstanding the celebrity thus attached to it, the date and occasion of the battle are very uncertain: and the circumstances connected with it by Strabo and Justin would lead to opposite conclusions. [CROTONA.] The date assigned by Heyne is B. C. 560, while Strabo certainly seems to imply that it took place *after* the fall of Sybaris in B. C. 510. (Grote's *Greece*, vol. iv. p. 552, note.) But whatever uncertainty prevailed concerning the battle, it seems certain that the Sagras itself was a well known stream in the days of Strabo and Pliny; both of whom concur in placing it to the N. of Locri and S. of Caulonia, and as the latter city was a colony and perhaps a dependency of Crotona, it is probable that the battle would be fought between it and Locri. Unfortunately the site of Caulonia cannot be determined [CAULONIA], and we are therefore quite at a loss which of the small streams flowing into the sea between Locri and the *Punta di Stilo* should be identified with the celebrated Sagras. The *Alaro* has been generally fixed upon by local writers, but has really no better claim than any other. (Romanelli, vol. i. p. 161; Swinburne's *Travels*, vol. i. p. 340.).   [E. H. B.]

SAGRUS (Σάγρος: *Sangro*), one of the most considerable of the rivers of Samnium, which has its sources in the lofty group of the Apennines S. of the *Lago di Fucino*, and has a course of above 70 miles from thence to the Adriatic. It flows at first in a SE. direction, passes under the walls of Aufidena as well as of the modern *Castel di Sangro*, and in this part of its course flows through a broad and level, but upland valley, bounded on both sides by lofty mountains. After passing Aufidena it turns abruptly to the NE., and pursues this course till it reaches the sea. In the lower part of its course it enters the territory of the Frentani, which it traverses in its whole breadth, flowing into the sea between Histonium and Ortona. Strabo indeed represents it as forming the boundary between the Frentani and the Peligni, but this is certainly a mistake, as the Peligni did not in fact descend to the sea-coast at all, and Ortona, one of the chief towns of the Frentani, was situated to the N. of the Sagrus. (Strab. v. p. 242; Ptol. iii. 1. § 19; where the name is erroneously written Ἴσαρος.) The upper valley of the ·Sagrus, with its adjoining mountains, was the territory of the Samnite tribe of the Caraceni. (Ptol. iii. 1. § 66.)   [E. H. B.]

SAGU'NTIA. 1. (Σαγουντία, Ptol. ii. 4. § 13), a town in the SW. part of Hispania Baetica. (Liv. xxxiv. 12; Plin. iii. 1. s. 3.) Now Xigonza or Gigonza, NW. from Medina Sidonia, where there are many ruins. (Morales, Antig. p. 87; Florez, Esp. Sagr. x. p. 47.)

2. A town of the Arevaci, in Hispania Tarraconensis, SW. from Bilbilis. It was in the jurisdiction of Clunia, on the road from Emerita to Caesaraugusta, and was the scene of a battle between Sertorius and Metellus. (Plut. Sert. 21; App. B. C. i. 110.) The name is written Segontia in the Itin. Ant. pp. 436 and 438, and in the Geog. Rav. iv. 43; but must not be confounded with that of a town of the Celtiberi. Now Siguenza on the Henares. (Florez, Esp. Sagr. viii. p. 18; Morales, Antig. p. 87.)   [T. H. D.]

SAGUNTUM (Σάγουντον, Ptol. ii. 6. § 63), also called SAGUNTUS (Mela, ii. 6; Σάγουντος, Steph. B. s. v.), a town of the Edetani or Sedetani in Hispania Tarraconensis, seated on an eminence on the banks of the river Pallantias, between Sucro and Tarraco, and not far from the sea. Strabo (iii. p. 159) erroneously places it near the mouth of the Iberus, though it lies near 100 miles to the SW. of it. The same author states that it was founded by Greeks from Zacynthus; and we find that Stephanus calls it Ζάκανθα and Ζάκυνθος. Livy adds that the founders were mixed with Rutuli from Ardea (Liv. xxi. 7); whence we sometimes find the city called Ausonia Saguntus. (Sil. Ital. i. 332.) Another tradition ascribed its foundation to Hercules. (Ib. 263, 505.) Saguntum lay in a very fertile district (Polyb. xvii. 2), and attained to great wealth by means of its commerce. It was the immediate cause of the Second Punic War, from its being besieged by Hannibal when it was in the alliance of the Romans. The siege is memorable in history. The town was taken, after a desperate resistance, in B. c 218, and all the adult males put to the sword; but how long the siege lasted is uncertain. (Liv. xxi. 14, 15; Cf. Sil. Ital. i. 271, seq.) Eight years afterwards Saguntum was recovered by the Romans. The Carthaginians had partly destroyed it, and had used it as a place for the custody of their hostages. (Polyb. iii. 98; Liv. xxiv. 42.) The city was restored by the Romans and made a Roman colony. (Liv. xxviii. 39; Plin. iii. 3. s. 4.) Saguntum was famous for its manufacture of earthenware cups (calices Saguntini) (Plin. xxxv. 12. s. 46; Mart. iv. 46, xiv. 108), and the figs grown in the neighbourhood were considered very fine. (Plin. xv. 18. s. 19.) Its site is now occupied by the town of Murviedro, which derives its name from the ancient

fortifications (muri veteres). But little now remains of the ruins, the materials having been unsparingly used by the inhabitants for the purpose of building. "The great temple of Diana stood where the convent of La Trinidad now does. Here are let in some six Roman inscriptions relating to the families of Sergia and others. At the back is a water-course, with portions of the walls of the Circus Maximus. In the suburb San Salvador, a mosaic pavement of Bacchus was discovered in 1745, which soon afterwards was let go to ruin, like that of Italica. The famous theatre is placed on the slope above the town, to which the orchestra is turned; it was much destroyed by Suchet, who used the stones to strengthen the castle, whose long lines of wall and tower rise grandly above; the general form of the theatre is, however, easily to be made out. . . . . The local arrangements are such as are common to Roman theatres, and resemble those of Merida. They have been measured and described by Dean Marti; Pons, iv. 232, in the Esp. Sagr. viii. 151." (Ford's Handbook for Spain, p. 206.) For the coins of Saguntum see Florez, Med. ii. p. 560; Mionnet, i. p. 49, Suppt. i. p. 98. The accompanying coin of Saguntum contains on the obverse the head of Tiberius, and on the reverse the prow of a ship.   [T. H. D.]

COIN OF SAGUNTUM.

SAGUTE SINUS (Polyb. ap. Plin. v. 1), a gulf on the W. coast of Mauretania, S. of the river Lixus, which must be identified with the EMPORICUS SINUS. The Phoenician word "Sacharut" signifies "Emporia," and by an elision not uncommon among the Africans assumed the form under which it appears in Polybius. (Movers, Die Phönis. ii. p. 541.)   [E. B. J.]

SAGY'LIUM (Σαγύλιον), a castle situated on a steep rock in the interior of Pontus, which was one of the strongholds of the Pontian kings. (Strab. xii. pp. 560, 561.)   [L. S.]

SAIS (Σάϊς, Herod. ii. 28, 59, 152, 169; Strab. xvii. p. 802; Steph. B. s. v.; Mela, i. 9. § 9; Plin. v. 10. s. 11: Eth. Σαΐτης, fem. Σαΐτις), the capital of the Saitic Nome in the Delta, and occasionally of Lower Aegypt also, stood, in lat. 31° 4' N., on the right bank of the Canopic arm of the Nile. The site of the ancient city is determined not only by the appellation of the modern town of Sa-el-Hadjar, which occupies a portion of its area, but also by mounds of ruin corresponding in extent to the importance of Sais at least under the later Pharaohs. The city was artificially raised high above the level of the Delta to be out of the reach of the inundations of the Nile, and served as a landmark to all who ascended the arms of the river from the Mediterranean to Memphis. Its ruins have been very imperfectly explored, yet traces have been found of the lake on wh ch the mysteries of Isis were performed, as well as of the temple of Neith (Athenè) and the necropolis of the Saite kings. The wall of unburnt brick which surrounded the principal buildings of the city was 70 feet thick, and probably therefore at least 100 feet high. It enclosed an area 2325 feet in length by 1960 in breadth. Beyond this enclosure were also two large cemeteries, one for the citizens generally, and the other reserved for the nobles and priests of the higher orders. In one respect the Saites differed from the other Aegyptians in their practice of interment. They buried their kings within the precincts of their temples. The tomb of Amasis attracted the attention of Herodotus (ii. 169), and Psammitichus, the conqueror and successor of that monarch, was also buried within the walls of the temple of Neith.

Sais was one of the sacred cities of Aegypt: its principal deities were Neith, who gave oracles there, and Isis. The mysteries of the latter were celebrated annually with unusual pomp on the evening of the Feast of Lamps. Herodotus terms this festival (ii. 59) the third of the great feasts in the Aegyptian calendar. It was held by night; and every one intending to be present at the sacrifices was required to light a number of lamps in the open air around his house. The lamps were small saucers filled with salt and oil, on which a wick floated, and which continued to burn all night. At what season of the year the feast of burning lamps was celebrated Herodotus knew, but deemed it wrong to tell (ii. 62); it was, however, probably at either the vernal or autumnal equinox, since it apparently had reference to one of the capital revolutions in the solar course. An inscription in the temple of Neith declared her to be the Mother of the Sun. (Plutarch, *Is. et Osir.* p. 354, ed. Wyttenbach; Proclus, *in Timaeum*, p. 30.) It ran thus: " I am the things that have been, and that are, and that will be; no one has uncovered my skirts ; the fruit which I brought forth became the Sun." It is probable, accordingly, that the kindling of the lamps referred to Neith as the author of light. On the same night apparently were performed what the Aegyptians designated the "Mysteries of Isis." Sais was one of the supposed places of the interment of Osiris, for that is evidently the deity whom Herodotus will not name (ii. 171) when he says that there is a burial-place of *him* at Sais in the temple of Athene. The mysteries were symbolical representations of the sufferings of Osiris, especially his dismemberment by Typhon. They were exhibited on the lake behind the temple of Neith. Portions of the lake may be still discerned near the hamlet of *Sa-el-Hadjar.*

Sais was alternately a provincial city of the first order and the capital of Lower Aegypt. These changes in its rank were probably the result of political revolutions in the Delta. The nome and city are said by Manetho to have derived their appellation from Saites, a king of the xviith dynasty. The xxivth dynasty was that of Bocchoris of Sais. The xxvith dynasty contained nine Saite kings; and of the xxviiith Amyrtaeus the Saite is the only monarch: with him expired the Saite dynasty, B. C. 408.

Bocchoris the Wise, the son of Tnephactus (Diodor. i. 45. § 2, 79. § 1), the Technatis of Plutarch (*Is. et Osir.* p. 354; comp. Athen. x. p. 418; Aelian, *H. A.* xi. 11), and the Aegyptian *Pehor*, was remarkable as a judge and legislator, and introduced, according to Diodorus, some important amendments into the commercial laws of Sais. He was put to death by burning after revolting from Sabaco the Aethiopian. During the Aethiopian dynasty Sais

seems to have retained its independence. The period of its greatest prosperity was between B. C. 697—524, under its nine native kings. The strength of Aegypt generally had been transferred from its southern to its northern provinces. Of the Saite monarchs of Aegypt Psammitichus and Amasis were the most powerful. Psammitichus maintained himself on the throne by his Greek mercenaries. He established at Sais the class of interpreters, caused his own sons to be educated in Greek learning, and encouraged the resort of Greeks to his capital. The intercourse between Sais and Athens especially was promoted by their worshipping the same deity — Neith-Athene; and hence there sprung up, although in a much later age, the opinion that Cecrops the Saite led a colony to Athens. The establishment of the Greeks at Cyrene was indirectly fatal to the Saitic dynasty. Uaphris, Apries, or Hophra, was defeated by the Cyrenians, B. C. 569; and his discontented troops raised their commander Amasis of Siouph to the throne. He adorned Sais with many stately buildings, and enlarged or decorated the temple of Neith; for he erected in front of it propylaea, which for their height and magnitude, and the quality of the stones employed, surpassed all similar structures in Aegypt. The stones were transported from the quarries of *El-Mokattam* near Memphis, and thence were brought also the colossal figures and androsphinxes that adorned the Dromos. To Sais Amasis transported from Elephantine a monolithal shrine of granite, which Herodotus especially admired (ii. 175). Though the ordinary passage from Elephantine to Sais was performed in twenty days, three years were employed in conveying this colossal mass. It was, however, never erected, and when Herodotus visited Aegypt was still lying on the ground in front of the temple. It measured, according to the historian, 30 feet in height, 12 feet in depth from front to back, and in breadth 21 feet. After the death of Amasis, Sais sank into comparative obscurity, and does not seem to have enjoyed the favour of the Persian, Macedonian, or Roman masters of Aegypt.

Sais indeed was more conspicuous as a seat of commerce and learning, and of Greek culture generally, than as the seat of government. Nechepsus, one of its kings, has left a name for his learning (Auson. *Epigram.* 409), and his writings on astronomy are cited by Pliny (ii. 23. s. 21). Pythagoras of Samos visited Sais in the reign of Amasis (comp. Plin. xxxvi. 9. s. 14); and Solon the Athenian conversed with Sonchis, a Saite priest, about the same time (Plut. *Solon*, 26; Herod. ii. 177; Clinton, *Fast. Hellen.* vol. ii. p. 9). At Sais, if we may credit Plato (*Timaeus*, iii. p. 25), Solon heard the legend of Atlantis, and of the ancient glories of Athens some thousand years prior to Phoroneus and Niobe and Deucalion's flood. The priests of Sais appear indeed to have been anxious to ingratiate themselves with the Athenians by discovering resemblances between Attic and Aegyptian institutions. Thus Diodorus (i. 28), copying from earlier narratives, says that the citizens of Sais, like those of Athens were divided into eupatrids, or priest-nobles; geomori, land-owners liable to military service ; and craftsmen or retail traders. He adds that in each city the upper town was called *Astu.* The Greek population of Sais was governed, according to Manetho, by their own laws and magistrates, and had a separate quarter of the city assigned to them. So strong indeed was the Hellenic element in Sais that it was doubted whether the Saites colonised Attica, or the Athenians Sais; and Diodorus says inconsistently, in one passage, that Sais sent a colony to Athens (i. 28. § 3), and in another (v. 57. § 45) that it was itself founded by Athenians. The principal value of these statements consists in their establishing the Graeco-Aegyptian character of the Saite people.

The ruins of Sais consist of vast heaps of brick, mingled with fragments of granite and Syenite marble. Of its numerous structures the position of one only can be surmised. The lake of *Sa-el-Hadjar*, which is still traceable, was at the back of the temple of Neith: but it remains for future travellers to determine the sites of the other sacred or civil structures of Sais. (Champollion, *l'Egypte*, vol. ii. p. 219; Id. *Lettres*, 50—53; Wilkinson, *Mod. Egypt and Thebes*.) [W. B. D.]

SALA (Σάλας). 1. A river in Germany, between which and the *Rhine*, according to Strabo (vii. p. 291), Drusus Germanicus lost his life. That the river was on the east of the Rhine is implied also in the account which Livy (*Epit.* 140) and Dion Cassius give of the occurrence; and it has therefore been conjectured with some probability that the Sala is the same river as the modern *Snale*, a tributary of the *Elbe*, commonly called the *Thuringian Saale;* though others regard the Sala as identical with the *Yssel.*

2. A river of Germany, alluded to by Tacitus (*Ann.* xiii. 57), who, without mentioning its name, calls it " flumen gignendo sale fecundum." It formed the boundary between the country of the Chatti and Hermunduri and near its banks were great salt-works, about which these two tribes were perpetually involved in war. From this circumstance it is clear that the river alluded to by Tacitus is none other but the *Saale* in Franconia, a tributary of the Moenus or *Main;* and that the salt-springs are, in all probability, those of the modern town of *Küssingen.*

3. A town in Upper Pannonia, on the road from Sabaria to Poetovium (Ptol. ii. 15. § 4; *It. Ant.* p. 262, where it is called Salle; Geogr. Rav. iv. 19, where it is called Salla). Some identify the place with the town of *Szala Egerszek*, and others with *Lüvir* on the river *Szala.* (Comp. Muchar, *Noricum*, i. p. 261.)

4. A town in the south-western part of Phrygia, on the frontiers of Caria and Pisidia, on the north-west of Cibyra. (Ptol. v. 2. § 26.)

5. A town in the north-western part of Armenia Minor, on the eastern slope of Mount Moschus. (Ptol. v. 13. § 10.) [L. S.]

SALA (Σάλα, Ptol. ii. 4. § 12), a town of the Turdetani in Hispania Baetica between Ptucci and Nabrissa. [T. H. D.]

SALA (Σάλα, Ptol. iv. 1. § 2; Plin. v. 1), a town of Mauretania, on the W. coast of Africa, situated near a river of the same name, " noticed by the Romans as the extreme object of their power and almost of their geography." (Gibbon, c. i.) In the Antonine Itinerary the name occurs as Salaconia, which has been supposed to be a corruption of Sala Colonia; but from the Vienna MS. it appears that the word " conia" has been inserted by a later hand. (*Itin. Anton.* ed. Parthey, p. 3.) The modern *Slá* or *Saliée*, near the mouth of the river *Bu-Regráb*, retains the name, though the site of the ancient town must be sought at *Rabat*, on the S. side of the river, where there are Roman remains. (Barth, *Wanderungen*, pp. 32, 37, 50.) [E. B. J.]

SALACIA. 1. (Σαλακεία, Ptol. ii. 5. § 3), a municipal town of Lusitania, in the territory of the Turdetani, to the NW. of Pax Julia and to the SW. of Ebora. It appears from inscriptions to have had the surname of Urbs Imperatoria. (Gruter, p. 13. 16; Mionnet, i. p. 4; Sestini, p. 16.) Salacia was celebrated for its manufacture of fine woollen cloths. (Plin. viii. 48. s. 73; Strab. iii. p. 144, with the note of Groskurd.) Now *Alaçer do Sal.* (Florez, *Esp. Sagr.* xiii. p. 115, xiv. p. 241; comp. Mela, iii. 1; *It. Ant.* pp. 417, 418, and 422.)

2. A town of the Callaici Bracarii in the NW. of Hispania Tarraconensis. (*Itin. Ant.* p. 422.) Identified either with *Salamonde* or *Pombeiro.* [T. H. D.]

SALAMBOREIA (Σαλαμβόρεια), a town of Cappadocia, in the district Garsauritis. (Ptol. v. 6. § 14; *Tab. Peut.*, where it is called Salaberina.) [L. S.]

SALAMI'NIA. [SALAMIS.]

SALAMI'NIAS, a town in Coele-Syria in the district Chalybonitis (*It. Anton.* p. 197; *Not. Imp.*), which Reland (*Palaest.* i. p. 217) identifies with Salamias (Σαλάμιας) in the *Not. Leonis Imp.*, and with *Salemjat* in Abulfeda (*Tab. Syr.* p. 105). It is said still to bear the name *Selmen.* (Richter, *Wallfahrten*, p. 238.)

SA'LAMIS (Σαλαμίς, Aesch. *Pers.* 880; Scyl. p. 41; Ptol. v. 14. § 3, viii. 20. § 5; *Stadiasm.* §§ 288, 289; Pomp. Mela, ii. 7. § 5; Plin. v. 35; Horat. *Carm.* i. 729; Σαλαμίν, Eustath *ad Il.* ii. 558; Σαλαμίας, Malala, *Chron.* xii. p. 313, ed. Bonn: *Eth.* Σαλαμίνιος, Böckh, *Inscr.* nos. 2625, 2638, 2639), a city on the E. coast of Cyprus, 18 M. P. from Tremithus, and 24 M. P. from Chytri. (*Peut. Tab.*) Legend assigned its foundation to the Aeacid Teucer, whose fortunes formed the subject of a tragedy by Sophocles, called Τεῦκρος, and of one with a similar title by Pacuvius. (Cic. *de Orat.* i. 58, ii. 46.) The people of Salamis showed the tomb of the archer Teucer (Aristot. *Anthologia*, i. 8, 112), and the reigning princes at the time of the Ionic revolt were Greeks of the Teucrid "Gens," although one of them bore the Phoenician name of Siromus (Hiram). (Herod. v. 104.) In the 6th century B. C. Salamis was already an important town, and in alliance with the Battiad princes of Cyrene, though the king Evelthon refused to assist in reinstating Arcesilaus III. upon the throne. (Herod. iv. 162.) The descendant of this Evelthon—the despot Gorgus—was unwilling to join in the Ionic revolt, but his brother Onesilus shut him out of the gates, and taking the command of the united forces of Salamis and the other cities, flew to arms. The battle which crushed the independence of Cyprus was fought under the walls of Salamis, which was compelled to submit to its former lord, Gorgus. (Herod. v. 103, 104, 108, 110.) Afterwards it was besieged by Anaxicrates, the successor of Cimon, but when the convention was made with the Persians the Athenians did not press the siege. (Diod. xii. 13.) After the peace of Antalcidas the Persians had to struggle for ten years with all their forces against the indefatigable and gentle Evagoras. Isocrates composed a panegyric of this prince addressed to his son Nicocles, which, with every allowance for its partiality, gives an interesting picture of the struggle which the Hellenic Evagoras waged against the Phoenician and Oriental influence under which Salamis and Cyprus had languished. (Comp. Grote, *Hist. of Greece*, vol. x. c. lxxvi.)

Evagoras with his son Pnytagoras was assassinated by a eunuch, slave of Nicocreon (Aristot. *Pol.* v. 8. § 10; Diodor. xv. 47; Theopomp. *Fr.* iii. ed. Didot), and was succeeded by another son of the name of Nicocles. The Graeco-Aegyptian fleet under Menelaus and his brother Ptolemy Soter was utterly defeated off the harbour of Salamis in a sea-fight, the greatest in all antiquity, by Demetrius Poliorcetes, B. C. 306. (Diodor. xx. 45—53.) The famous courtezan Lamia formed a part of the booty of Demetrius, over whom she soon obtained unbounded influence. Finally, Salamis came into the hands of Ptolemy. (Plut. *Demetr.* 35; Polyaen. *Strateg.* 5.) Under the Roman Empire the Jews were numerous in Salamis (*Acts*, xiii. 6), where they had more than one synagogue. The farming of the copper mines of the island to Herod (Joseph. *Antiq.* xv. 14. § 5) may have swelled the numbers who were attracted by the advantages of its harbour and trade, especially its manufactures of embroidered stuffs. (Athen. ii. p. 48.) In the memorable revolt of the Jews in the reign of Trajan this populous city became a desert. (Milman, *Hist. of the Jews*, vol. iii. pp. 111, 112.) Its demolition was completed by an earthquake; but it was rebuilt by a Christian emperor, from whom it was named CONSTANTIA. It was then the metropolitan see of the island. Epiphanius, the chronicler of the heretical sects, was bishop of Constantia in A. D. 367. In the reign of Heraclius the new town was destroyed by the Saracens.

The ground lies low in the neighbourhood of Salamis, and the town was situated on a bight of the coast to the N. of the river Pediaeus. This low land is the largest plain—SALAMINIA—in Cyprus, stretching inward between the two mountain ranges to the very heart of the country where the modern Turkish capital—*Nicosia*—is situated. In the *Life and Epistles of St. Paul*, by Coneybeare and Howson (vol. i. p. 169), will be found a plan of the harbour and ruins of Salamis, from the survey made by Captain Graves. For coins of Salamis, see Eckhel, vol. iii. p. 87.   [E. B. J.]

SA'LAMIS (Σαλαμίς, -ῖνος: *Eth.* and *Adj.* Σαλαμίνιος, Salaminius: *Adj.* Σαλαμινιακός, Salaminiacus: *Kulúri*), an island lying between the western coast of Attica and the eastern coast of Megaris, and forming the southern boundary of the bay of Eleusis. It is separated from the coasts both of Attica and of Megaris by only a narrow channel. Its form is that of an irregular semicircle towards the west, with many small indentations along the coast. Its greatest length, from N. to S., is about 10 miles, and its width, in its broadest part, from E. to W., is a little more. Its length is correctly given by Strabo (ix. p. 393) as from 70 to 80 stadia. In ancient times it is said to have been called Pityussa (Πιτυοῦσσα), from the pines which grew there, and also SCIRAS (Σκιράς) and CYCHREIA (Κυχρεία), from the names of two heroes Scirus and Cychreus. The former was a native hero, and the latter a seer, who came from Dodona to Athens, and perished along with Erechtheus in fighting against Eumolpus. (Strab. ix. p. 393; Paus. i. 36. § 1; Philochor. *ap. Plut. Thes.* 17.) The latter name was perpetuated in the island, for Aeschylus (*Pers.* 570) speaks of the ἀκτὴ Κυχρεία, and Stephanus B. mentions a Κυχρεῖος πάγος. The island is said to have obtained the name of Salamis from the mother of Cychreus, who was also a daughter of Asopus.

(Paus. i. 35. § 2.) It was colonised at an early period by the Aeacidae of Aegina. Telamon, the son of Aeacus, fled thither after the murder of his half-brother Phocus, and became sovereign of the island. (Paus. i. 35. § 1.) His son Ajax accompanied the Greeks with 12 Salaminian ships to the Trojan War. (Hom. *Il.* ii. 557.) Salamis continued to be an independent state till about the beginning of the 40th Olympiad (B. C. 620), when a dispute arose for its possession between the Athenians and Megarians. After a long struggle, it first fell into the hands of the Megarians, but was subsequently taken possession of by the Athenians through a stratagem of Solon. (Plut. *Sol.* 8, 9; Paus. i. 40. § 5.) Both parties appealed to the arbitration of Sparta. The Athenians supported their claims by a line in the Iliad, which represents Ajax ranging his ships with those of the Athenians (*Il.* ii. 558), but this verse was suspected to have been an interpolation of Solon or Peisistratus; and the Megarians cited another version of the line. The Athenians, moreover, asserted that the island had been made over to them by Philaeus and Eurysaces, sons of the Telamonian Ajax, when they took up their own residence in Attica. These arguments were considered sufficient, and Salamis was adjudged to the Athenians. (Plut. *Sol.* 10; Strab. ix. p. 394.) It now became an Attic demus, and continued incorporated with Attica till the times of Macedonian supremacy. In B. C. 318, the inhabitants voluntarily received a Macedonian garrison, after having only a short time before successfully resisted Cassander. (Diod. xviii. 69; Polyaen. *Strat.* iv. 11. § 2; Paus. i. 35. § 2.) It continued in the hands of the Macedonians till B. C. 232, when the Athenians, by the assistance of Aratus, purchased it from the Macedonians together with Munychia and Sunium. Thereupon the Salaminians were expelled from the island, and their lands divided among Athenian cleruchi. (Plut. *Arat.* 34; Paus. ii. 8. § 6; Böckh, *Inscr.* vol. i. p. 148, seq.) From that time Salamis probably continued to be a dependency of Athens, like Aegina and Oropus; since the grammarians never call it a δῆμος, which it had been originally, but generally a πόλις.

The old city of Salamis, the residence of the Telamonian Ajax, stood upon the southern side of the island towards Aegina (Strab. ix. p. 393), and is identified by Leake with the remains of some Hellenic walls upon the south-western coast near a small port, where is the only rivulet in the island, perhaps answering to the BOCARUS or BOCALIAS of Strabo (ix. p. 394; Leake, *Demi*, p. 169). The Bocarus is also mentioned by Lycophron (451). In another passage, Strabo (ix. p. 424) indeed speaks of a river Cephissus in Salamis; but as it occurs only in an enumeration of various rivers of this name, and immediately follows the Athenian Cephissus without any mention being made of the Eleusinian Cephissus, we ought probably to read with Leake ἐν Ἐλευσῖνι instead of ἐν Σαλαμῖνι.

When Salamis became an Athenian demus, a new city was built at the head of a bay upon the eastern side of the island, and opposite the Attic coast. In the time of Pausanias this city also had fallen into decay. There remained, however, a ruined agora and a temple of Ajax, containing a statue of the hero in ebony; also a temple of Artemis, the trophy erected in honour of the victory gained over the Persians, and a temple of Cychreus. (Paus. i. 35. § 3, 36. § 1.) Pausanias has not mentioned the statue of Solon, which was erected in the agora, with one hand covered by his mantle. (Dem. *de Fals. Leg.* p. 420; Aeschin. *in Tim.* p. 52.) There are still some remains of the city close to the village of *Ambelákia.* A portion of the walls may still be traced; and many ancient fragments are found in the walls and churches both of *Ambelákia* and of the neighbouring village of *Kulúri,* from the latter of which the modern name of the island is derived. The narrow rocky promontory now called *Cape of St. Barbara,* which forms the SE. entrance to the bay of *Ambelákia,* was the SILENIAE (Σιληνίαι) of Aeschylus, afterwards called TRO-PAEA (Τροπαία), on account of the trophy erected there in memory of the victory. (Aesch. *Pers.* 300, with Schol.) At the extremity of this promontory lay the small island of PSYTTALEIA (Ψυττάλεια), now called *Lípsokutáli,* about a mile long, and from 200 to 300 yards wide. It was here that a picked body of Persian troops was cut to pieces by Aristeides during the battle of Salamis. (Herod. viii. 95; Aesch. *Pers.* 447, seq.; Plut. *Arist.* 9; Paus. i. 36. § 2, iv. 36. § 3; Strab. ix. p. 393; Plin. iv. 12. s. 20; Steph. B. *s. v.*)

In Salamis there was a promontory SCIRADIUM (Σκιράδιον), containing a temple of the god of war, erected by Solon, because he there defeated the Megarians. (Plut. *Sol.* 9.) Leake identifies this site with the temple of Athena Sciras, to which Adei-

mantus, the Corinthian, is said to have fled at the commencement of the battle of Salamis (Herod. viii. 94); and, as the Corinthians could not have retreated through the eastern opening of the strait, which was the centre of the scene of action, Leake supposes Sciradium to have been the south-west promontory of Salamis, upon which now stands a monastery of the Virgin. This monastery now occupies the site of a Hellenic building, of which remains are still to be seen.

BUDORUM (Βούδορον or Βούδωρον) was the name of the western promontory of Salamis, and distant only three miles from Nisaea, the port of Megara. On this peninsula there was a fortress of the same name. In the attempt which the Peloponnesians made in B. C. 429 to surprise Peiraeeus, they first sailed from Nisaea to the promontory of Budorum, and surprised the fortress; but after overrunning the island, they retreated without venturing to attack Peiraeeus. (Thuc. ii. 93, 94, iii. 51; Diod. xii. 49; Strab. xi. p. 446; Steph. B. *s. v.* Βούδωρον.)

Salamis is chiefly memorable on account of the great battle fought off its coast, in which the Persian fleet of Xerxes was defeated by the Greeks, B. C. 480. The details of this battle are given in every history of Greece, and need not be repeated here. The battle took place in the strait between the eastern part of the island and the coast of Attica, and the position of the contending forces is

MAP OF SALAMIS.

A. A. A. Persian fleet.
B. B. B. Grecian fleet.
C. C. C. The Persian army.
    D. Throne of Xerxes.
    E. New Salamis.
    F. Old Salamis.
    G. The Island Psyttaleia.
    H. Peiraeeus.
    I. Phalerum.
    1. Athenian ships.
    2. Lacedaemonian and other Peloponne-
        sian ships.

3. Aeginetan and Euboean ships.
4. Phoenician ships.
5. Cyprian ships.
6. Cilician and Pamphylian ships.
7. Ionian ships.
8. Persian ships.
9. Egyptian ships.
a. Prom. Sileniae or Tropaea. (*Cape of St. Barbara.*)
b. Prom. Sciradium.
c. Prom. Budorus.

shown in the annexed plan. The Grecian fleet was drawn up in the small bay in front of the town of Salamis, and the Persian fleet opposite to them off the coast of Attica. The battle was witnessed by Xerxes from the Attic coast, who had erected for himself a lofty throne on one of the projecting declivities of Mt. Aegaleos. Colonel Leake has discussed at length all the particulars of the battle, but Mr. Blakesley has controverted many of his views, following the authority of Aeschylus in preference to that of Herodotus. In opposition to Col. Leake and all preceding authorities, Mr. Blakesley supposes, that though the hostile fleets occupied in the afternoon before the battle the position delineated in the plan annexed, yet that on the morning of the battle the Greeks were drawn up across the southern entrance of the strait, between the *Cape of St. Barbara* and the Attic coast, and that the Persians were in the more open sea to the south. Into the discussion of this question our limits prevent us from entering; and we must refer our readers for particulars to the essays of those writers quoted at the close of this article. There is, however, one difficulty which must not be passed over in silence. Herodotus says (viii. 76) that on the night before the battle, the Persian ships stationed about Ceos and Cynosura moved up, and beset the whole strait as far as Munychia. The only known places of those names are the island of Ceos, distant more than 40 geographical miles from Salamis, and the promontory of Cynosura, immediately N. of the bay of Marathon, and distant more than 60 geographical miles from Salamis. Both of those places, and more especially Cynosura, seem to be too distant to render the movement practicable in the time required. Accordingly many modern scholars apply the names Ceos and Cynosura to two promontories, the southernmost and south-easternmost of the island of Salamis, and they are so called in Kiepert's maps. But there is no authority whatever for giving those names to two promontories in the island; and it is evident from the narrative, as Mr. Grote has observed, that the names of Ceos and Cynosura must belong to some points in Attica, not in Salamis. Mr. Grote does not attempt to indicate the position of these places; but Mr. Blakesley maintains that Ceos and Cynosura are respectively the well-known island and cape, and that the real difficulty is occasioned, not by their distance, but by the erroneous notion conceived by Herodotus of the operations of the Persian fleet. (Leake, *Demi of Attica*, p. 166, seq., and Appendix II. *On the Battle of Salamis ;* Blakesley, *Excursus on Herodotus,* viii. 76, vol. ii. p. 400, seq.; Grote, *Hist. of Greece,* vol. v. p. 171, seq.)

COIN OF SALAMIS.

SALANIA'NA, a town of the Callaici Bracarii in Gallaecia (*Itin. Ant.* p. 427.) Variously identified with *Cela Nova, Moymenta,* and *Portela de Abade.* [T. H. D.]

SALA'PIA (Σαλαπία: *Eth.* Σαλαπῖνος; Salapinus: *Salpi*), one of the most considerable cities of Apulia, situated on the coast of the Adriatic, but separated from the open sea by an intervening lagune, or salt-water lake, which was known in ancient times as the SALAPINA PALUS (Lucan, v. 377; Vib. Seq. p. 26), and is still called the *Lago di Salpi.* This lagune has now only an artificial outlet to the sea through the bank of sand which separates them ; but it is probable that in ancient times its communications were more free, as Salapia was certainly a considerable sea-port and in Strabo's time served as the port both of Arpi and Canusium (Strab. vi. p. 284). At an earlier period it was an independent city, and apparently a place of considerable importance. Tradition ascribed its foundation, as well as that of the neighbouring cities of Canusium and Arpi, to Diomedes (Vitruv. i. 4. § 12); or, according to others, to a Rhodian colony under Elpias (Id. *ib.*; Strab. xiv. p. 654).* There is no trace of its having received a Greek colony in historical times, though, in common with many other cities of the Daunian Apulians, it seems to have imbibed a large amount of Hellenic influence. This was probably derived from the Tarentines, and did not date from a very early period.

The name of Salapia is not mentioned in history till the Second Punic War, in which it bears a considerable part. It was evidently one of the cities of Apulia which revolted to Hannibal after the battle of Cannae (Liv. xxii. 61); and a few years after we find it still in his possession. It was apparently a place of strength, on which account he collected there great magazines of corn, and established his winter quarters there in B. C. 214. (Id. xxiv. 20.) It remained in his hands after the fall of Arpi in the following year (Id. xxiv. 47); but in B. C. 210 it was betrayed into the power of Marcellus by Blasius, one of its citizens, who had been for some time the leader of the Roman party in the place, and the Numidian garrison was put to the sword. (Id. xxvi. 88; Appian, *Annib.* 45—47.) Its loss seems to have been a great blow to the power of Hannibal in this part of Italy ; and after the death of Marcellus, B. C. 208, he made an attempt to recover possession of it by stratagem ; but the fraud was discovered, and the Carthaginian troops were repulsed with loss. (Liv. xxvii. 1, 28; Appian, *Annib.* 51.) No subsequent mention of it is found till the Social War, in the second year of which, when the tide of fortune was beginning to turn in favour of Rome, it was taken by the Roman praetor C. Cosconius, and burnt to the ground (Appian, *B. C.* i. 51). After this time it appears to have fallen into a state of decay, and suffered severely from malaria in consequence of the exhalations of the neighbouring lagune. Vitruvius tells us, that at length the inhabitants applied to M. Hostilius, who caused them to remove to a more healthy situation, about 4 miles from the former site, and nearer the sea, while be at the same time opened fresh communications between the lagune and the sea (Vitruv. i. 4. § 12). We have no clue to the time at which this change took place, but it could hardly have been till after the town had fallen into a declining condition. Cicero, indeed, alludes to Salapia as in his day notorious for its pestilential climate (*de Leg. Agr.* ii. 27); but this may be understood as relating to its territory rather than the actual town. Vitruvius is the only author who notices the change of site ; but if his account can be depended

* Lycophron, on the other hand, seems to assign it a Trojan origin ; though the passage, as usual, is somewhat obscure. (Lycophr. *Alex.* 1129.)

upon, the Salapia mentioned by Pliny and Ptolemy as well as Strabo, must have been the new town, and not the original city of the name. (Strab. vi. p. 284; Plin. iii. 12. s. 17; Ptol. iii. 1. § 16.) The Liber Coloniarum also speaks of it as a colony adjoining the sea-coast, which doubtless refers to the new town of the name. This does not, however, seem to have ever risen into a place of much importance, and the name subsequently disappears altogether.

Extensive ruins of Salapia are still visible on the southern shore of the *Lago di Salpi*, in a tract of country now almost wholly desolate. They evidently belong to a city of considerable size and importance, and must therefore be those of the ancient Apulian city. This is further confirmed by the circumstance that the coins of Salapia, which of course belong to the period of its independence, are frequently found on the spot. (Swinburne's *Travels*, vol. i. p. 81.) The site of the Roman town founded by M. Hostilius is said to be indicated by some remains on the sea-shore, near the *Torre di Salpi*. (Romanelli, vol. ii. p. 201.)

The lagune still called the *Lago di Salpi* is about 12 miles in length by about 2 in breadth. At its eastern extremity, where it communicates with the sea by an artificial cut, are extensive salt-works, which are considered to be the representatives of those noticed in the Itineraries under the name of Salinae. It is by no means certain (though not improbable) that these ancient salt-works occupied the same site as the modern ones ; and the distances given in the Itineraries along this line of coast, being in any case corrupt and confused, afford no clue to their identification. (*Itin. Ant.* p. 314; *Tab. Peut.*) It is probable that the name of Salapia itself is connected with *sal*, the lagune having always been well adapted for the collection of salt.

The coins of Salapia, as well as those of Arpi and Canusium, have Greek legends, and indicate the strong influence of Greek art and civilisation, though apparently at a late period, none of them being of an archaic style. The magistrates' names which occur on them (ΔΑΖΟΣ, ΠΤΑΛΟΣ, &c.) are, on the contrary, clearly of native origin. (Mommsen, *U. I. D.* pp. 82, 83.)   [E. H. B.]

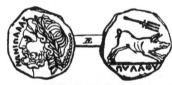

COIN OF SALAPIA.

SALA'RIA. 1. (Σαλάρια, Ptol. ii. 6. § 61), a town of the Bastitani, in the SE. part of Hispania Tarraconensis. According to Pliny it was a Roman colony. (Colonia Salariensis, iii. 3. s. 4.) Ukert (ii. pt. i. p. 407) identifies it with *Sabiote*, between *Ubeda* and *Baeza*.

2. A town of the Oretani, in the same neighbourhood. (Ptol. ii. 6. § 59.)   [T. H. D.]

SALAS. [SALA.]

SALASSI (Σαλασσοί), one of the most powerful of the Alpine tribes in the N. of Italy, who occupied the great valley of the Durias or *Dora Baltea*, now called the *Val d'Aosta*, from the plains of the Po to the foot of the Graian and Pennine Alps. Their country is correctly described by Strabo as a deep

and narrow valley, shut in on both sides by very lofty mountains. (Strab. iv. p. 205.) This valley, which extends above 60 miles in length from its entrance at *Ivrea* to its head among the very highest ranges of the Alps, must always have been one of the natural inlets into the heart of those mountains: hence the two passes at its head, now called the *Great and Little St. Bernard*, seem to have been frequented from a very early period. If we may trust to Livy, it was by the former of these passes, or the Pennine Alps, that the Boii and Lingones crossed when they first migrated into the plains of the N. of Italy. (Liv. v. 35.) It was the same pass by which Hannibal was commonly supposed in the days of Livy to have crossed those mountains, while Coelius Antipater represented him as passing the *Little St. Bernard*, an opinion commonly adopted by modern writers, though still subject to grave difficulties. One of the most serious of these arises from the character of the Salassi themselves, who are uniformly described as among the fiercest and most warlike of the Alpine tribes, and of inveterate predatory habits, so that it is difficult to believe they would have allowed an army like that of Hannibal to traverse their country without opposition, and apparently without molestation. (See Arnold's *Rome*, vol. iii. p. 481.)

The Salassi are commonly reckoned a Gaulish people, yet there are reasons which render it more probable that they were in fact, like their neighbours the Taurini, a Ligurian race. The Ligurians indeed seem, at a very early period, to have spread themselves along the whole of the western chain of the Alps, and the Gaulish tribes which occupied the plains of the Padus passed through their country. But the ethnical relations of all these Alpine races are very obscure. No mention of the Salassi is found in history till B. C. 143, when they were attacked without provocation by the consul Appius Claudius, who was, however, punished for his aggression, being defeated with the loss of 5000 men. But he soon repaired this disaster, and having in his turn slain 5000 of the mountaineers, claimed the honour of a triumph. (Dion Cass. *Fr.* 79; Liv. *Epit.* liii.; Oros. v. 4.) From this time they appear to have frequently been engaged in hostilities with Rome, and though nominally tributary to the republic, they were continually breaking out into revolt, and ravaging the plains of their neighbourhood, or plundering the Roman convoys, and harassing their troops as they marched through their country. As early as B. C. 100 a Roman colony was established at Eporedia (*Ivrea*), at the mouth of the valley (Vell. Pat. i. 15), with the view of keeping them in check, but it suffered severely from their incursions. Even at a much later period the Salassi plundered the baggage of the dictator Caesar when marching through their country, and compelled Decimus Brutus, on his way into Gaul after the battle of Mutina, to purchase a passage with a large sum of money. (Strab. iv. p. 205.) In B. C. 35 they appear to have broken out afresh into revolt, and for some time were able to defy the efforts of Antistius Vetus; but the next year they were reduced to submission by Valerius Messala. (Dion Cass. xlix. 34, 38; Appian, *Illyr.* 17.) Still, however, their subjection was imperfect, till in B. C. 25 Terentius Varro was sent against them, who having compelled the whole nation to lay down their arms, sold them without distinction as slaves. The number of captives thus sold is said to have amounted to

36,000 persons, of whom 8000 were men of military age. The tribe of the Salassi being thus extirpated, a Roman colony was settled at Praetoria Augusta (*Aosta*), and a highroad made through the valley. (Dion Cass. liii. 25; Strab. iv. p. 205; Liv. *Epit.* cxxxv.) The name of the Salassi, however, still remained, and is recognised as a geographical distinction both by Pliny and Ptolemy, but no subsequent trace of them is found as an independent tribe. (Plin. iii. 17. s. 21; Ptol. iii. 1. § 34.)

One of the main causes of the disputes between the Salassi and Romans had arisen from the goldwashings which were found in the valley, and which are said to have been extremely productive. These were worked by the Salassi themselves before the Roman invasion; but the Romans seem to have early taken possession of them, and they were farmed out with the other revenues of the state to the Publicani. But these were, as might be expected, involved in constant quarrels with the neighbouring barbarians, who sometimes cut off their supplies of water, at other times attacked them with more open violence. (Strab. iv. p. 205; Dion Cass. *Fr.* 79.)

The line of road through the country of the Salassi, and the passes which led from Augusta Praetoria over the Pennine and Graian Alps, are described in the article ALPES [Vol. I. p. 110].   [E. H. B.]

SALA'SSII. [MAURETANIA, Vol. II. p. 298, b.]

SALATARAE (Σαλατάραι, Ptol. vi. 11. § 6), a tribe of the Bactrians who lived along the banks of the Oxus. Forbiger suspects that they are the same as the Saraparae, noticed by Pliny (vi. 16. s. 18).   [V.]

SALATHUS (Σάλαθος, Ptol. iv. 6. § 5), a river on the W. coast of Africa, with a town of the same name. This river, which took its rise in Mt. Mandrus, is represented by one of the *Wadys*, which flows into the sea in the district occupied by the ancient Autololes, on the coast to the N. of *Cape Mirik.*   [E. B. J.]

SALAURIS, a town on the coast of Hispania Tarraconensis, mentioned in the *Ora Marit.* of Avienus (v. 518).   [T. H. D.]

SALDA, a town in the south of Lower Pannonia, on the southern bank of the Savus, and on the great highroad from Siscia to Sirmium. (*Tab. Peut.*; Geogr. Rav. iv. 19, where it is called Saldum.) It is very probably the same as the town of Sallis (Σαλλίς) mentioned by Ptolemy (ii. 16. § 8). The site is commonly believed to be occupied by the modern *Szlatina.*   [L. S.]

SALDAE (Σάλδαι, Strab. xvii. p. 831; Ptol. iv. 2. § 9, viii. 13. § 9; Plin. v. 1; *Itin. Anton.; Peut. Tab.*), a town on the coast of Mauretania Caesariensis, with a spacious harbour, which was in earlier times the E. boundary between the dominions of Juba and those of the Romans. (Strab. *l. c.*) Under Augustus it became a Roman "colonia." (Plin. *l. c.*) In later times it was the W. limit of Mauretania Sitifensis, against Mauretania Caesariensis in its more contracted sense. It is identified with *Bujeiyah*, the flourishing city of the *Kaliphat*, taken by Pedro Navarro, the general of Ferdinand the Catholic, after two famous battles, A. D. 1510 (comp. Prescott's *Ferdinand and Isabella*, vol. ii. p. 457), or the *C. Bongie* of the French province. (Barth, *Wanderungen*, p. 62.)   [E. B. J.]

SALDAPA, a town of Moesia (Theophyl. Simocat. i. 8), which was ravaged by the Avars in their wars with the emperor Maurice (Le Beau, *Bas Empire*, vol. x. pp. 248, 369). Schafarik (*Slav. Alt.* vol. ii. p. 158) has fixed the site at the ruins of *Dikelrick* upon the *Danube*.   [E. B. J.]

SALDUBA. 1. A small river in the territory of the Turduli in Hispania Baetica, probably the same called Σαδούκα, (with *var. lect.*) by Ptolemy (ii. 4. § 7). Now *Rio Verde.*

2. A town at the mouth of the preceding river (Σάλδουκα, Ptol. ii. 4. § 11), of no great importance (Mela, ii. 6; Plin. iii. 1. s. 3), near the present *Marbella.*

3. [CAESARAUGUSTA.]   [T. H. D.]

SALE, a town on the S. coast of Thrace, near the W. mouth of the Hebrus, and nearly equidistant from Zone and Doriscus. It is mentioned by Herodotus (vii. 59) as a Samothracian colony. [J. R.]

SALEM. [JERUSALEM.]

SALENI, a people of Hispania Tarraconensis, probably in Cantabria, mentioned by Mela (iii. 1). They are perhaps the same as the Σαλίνοί of Ptolemy (ii. 6. § 34).   [T. H. D.]

SALENTI'NI or SALLENTI'NI (both forms seem to rest on good authority), (Σαλεντῖνοι), a people of Southern Italy, who inhabited a part of the peninsula which forms the SE. extremity, or as it is very often called the *heel*, of Italy. Their territory was thus included in the region known to the Greeks by the name of Iapygia, as well as in the district called by the Romans Calabria. Strabo remarks that the peninsula in question, which he considers as bounded by a line drawn across from Tarentum to Brundusium, was variously called Messapia, Iapygia, Calabria, and Salentina; but that some writers established a distinction between the names. (Strab. vi. p. 282.) There seems no doubt that the names were frequently applied irregularly and vaguely, but that there were in fact two distinct tribes or races inhabiting the peninsula, the Salentines and the Calabrians (Strab. vi. p. 277), of whom the latter were commonly known to the Greeks as the Messapians [CALABRIA]. Both were, however, in all probability kindred races belonging to the great family of the Pelasgian stock. Tradition represented the Salentines as of Cretan origin, and, according to the habitual form of such legends, ascribed them to a Cretan colony under Idomeneus after the Trojan War. (Strab. vi. p. 282; Virg. *Aen.* iii. 400; Fest. *s. v. Salentini*, p. 329; Varr. *ap. Prob. ad Virg. Ecl.* vi. 31.) They appear to have inhabited the southern part of the peninsula, extending from its southern extremity (the *Capo di Leuca*), which was thence frequently called the Salentine promontory ("Salentinum Promontorium," Mel. ii. 4. § 8; Ptol. iii. 1. § 13), to the neighbourhood of Tarentum. But we have no means of distinguishing accurately the limits of the two tribes, or the particular towns which belonged to each.

The name of the Salentines does not seem to have been familiarly known to the Greeks, at least in early times: as we do not hear of their name in any of the wars with the Tarentines, though from their position they must have been one of the tribes that early came into collision with the rising colony. They were probably known under the general appellation of Iapygians, or confounded with their neighbours the Messapians. On the contrary, as soon as their name appears in Roman history, it is in a wider and more general sense than that to which it is limited by the geographers. Livy speaks of the Salentini as acceding to the Samnite alliance in B. C. 306, when the consul L. Volumnius was sent into their country, who defeated them in several battles, and took some of their towns. (Liv. ix. 42.) It is almost impossible to believe that the Romans had as early as this pushed their arms into the Iapygian peninsula, and it is probable that the Salentines are here confounded with the Peucetians, with whom, according to some accounts, they were closely connected. (Plin. iii. 11. s. 16.) But the name is used with still greater laxity shortly after, when Livy speaks of Thuriae as "urbem in Sallentinis" (x. 2), if at least, as there seems little doubt, the place there meant is the well-known city of Thurii in Lucania [THURII].

The name of the Sallentines does not again occur in history till the Fourth Samnite War, when they joined the confederacy formed by the Samnites and Tarentines against Rome; and shared in their defeat by the consul L. Aemilius Barbula in B. C. 281, as we find that general celebrating a triumph over the Tarentines, Samnites, and Sallentines. (*Fast. Capit.* ann. 473.) For some time after this the appearance of Pyrrhus in Italy drew off the attention of the Romans from more ignoble adversaries, but when that monarch had finally withdrawn from Italy, and Tarentum itself had fallen into the hands of the Romans, they were left at leisure to turn their arms against the few tribes that still maintained their independence. In B. C. 267 war was declared against the Salentines, and both consuls were employed in their subjugation. It was not likely that they could offer much resistance, yet their final conquest was not completed till the following year, when both consuls again celebrated triumphs "de Messapiis Sallentinisque." (*Fast. Capit.*; Zonar. viii. 7; Liv. *Epit.* xv; Florus, i. 20; Eutrop. ii. 17.) All the Roman writers on this occasion mention the Salentines alone; the Triumphal Fasti, however, record the name of the Messapians in conjunction with them, and it is certain that both nations were included both in the war and the conquest, for Brundusium, which is called by Florus "caput regionis," and the occupation of which was evidently the main object of the war (Zonar. *l. c.*), seems to have been at that period certainly a Messapian city. The Salentines are again mentioned as revolting to Hannibal during the Second Punic War (B.C. 213), but seem to have been again reduced to subjection without difficulty. (Liv. xxv. 1, xxvii. 36, 41.) From this time their name disappears from history, and is not even found among the nations of Italy that took up arms in the Social War. But the "Sallentinus ager" continued to be a recognised term, and the people are spoken of both by Pliny and Strabo as distinct from their neighbours the Calabri. (Strab. vi. p. 277; Plin. iii. 11. s. 16; Ptol. iii. 1. § 13; Mel. ii. 4; Cic. *pro Rosc. Am.* 46.) The "regio Salentina" is even mentioned as a distinct portion of Calabria as late as the time of the Lombards. (P. Diac. *Hist. Lang.* ii. 21.)

The physical character and topography of the country of the Salentines are given in the article CALABRIA. The following towns are assigned by Pliny to the Salentines, as distinguished from the Calabrians, strictly so called: ALETIUM, BASTA, NERETUM, UXENTUM, and VERETUM. All these are situated in the extreme southern end of the Iapygian peninsula. The list given by Ptolemy nearly agrees with that of Pliny; but he adds Rhudiae, which was considerably further N., and is reckoned on good authority a Calabrian city [RHUDIAE]. The place he calls Banota is probably the Basta of Pliny. To these inland towns may probably be added the seaports of CALLIPOLIS, CASTRUM MINERVAE, and perhaps HYDRUNTUM also, though

the last seems to have early received a Greek colony. But it is probable that at an earlier period the territory of the Salentines was considerably more extensive. Stephanus of Byzantium speaks of a *city* of the name of Sallentia, from which was derived the name of the Sallentines, but no mention of this is found in any other writer, and it is probably a mere mistake.   [E. H. B.]

SALERNUM (Σάλερνον: *Eth.* Salernitanus: *Salerno*), a city of Campania, but situated in the territory of the Picentini, on the N. shore of the gulf of Posidonia, which now derives from it the name of the *Gulf of Salerno*. We have no account of its origin or early history; it has been supposed that it was like the neighbouring Marcina a Tyrrhenian or Pelasgic settlement [MARCINA]; but there is no authority for this, and its name is never mentioned in history previous to the settlement of a Roman colony there. But when this was first decreed (in B. C. 197, it was not actually founded till B. C. 194), Livy speaks of the place as Castrum Salerni, whence we may infer that there was at least a fortress previously existing there (Liv. xxxii. 29, xxxiv. 45; Vell. Pat. i. 14; Strab. v. p. 251.) The Roman colony was established, as we are expressly told by Strabo, for the purpose of holding the Picentines in check, that people having actively espoused the cause of Hannibal during the Second Punic War (Strab. *l. c.*) Their town of Picentia being destroyed, Salernum became the chief town of the district; but it does not appear to have risen to any great importance. In the Social War it was taken by the Samnite general C. Papius (Appian, *B. C.* i. 42): but this is the only occasion on which its name is mentioned in history. Horace alludes to it as having a mild climate, on which account it had apparently been recommended to him for his health (Hor. *Ep.* i. 15. 1.) It continued to be a municipal town of some consideration under the Roman Empire, and as we learn from inscriptions retained the title of a Colonia (Plin. iii. 5. s. 9; Ptol. iii. 1. § 7; *Itin. Ant.*; *Tab. Peut.*; Mommsen, *Inscr. R. N.* pp. 9 —12.) But it was not till after the Lombard conquest that it became one of the most flourishing cities in this part of Italy; so that it is associated by Paulus Diaconus with Caprea and Neapolis among the "opulentissimae urbes" of Campania (P. Diac. *Hist. Lang.* ii. 17). It retained this consideration down to a late period of the middle ages, and was especially renowned for its school of medicine, which, under the name of Schola Salernitana, was long the most celebrated in Europe. But it seems certain that this was derived from the Arabs in the 10th or 11th century, and was not transmitted from more ancient times. Salerno is still the see of an archbishop, with a population of about 12,000 inhabitants, though greatly fallen from its mediaeval grandeur.

The ancient city, as we learn from Strabo (v. p. 251), stood on a hill at some distance from the sea, and this is confirmed by local writers, who state that many ancient remains have been found on the hill which rises at the back of the modern city, but no ruins are now extant. (Romanelli, vol. iii. p. 612.) From the foot of this hill a level and marshy plain extends without interruption to the mouth of the Silarus, the whole of which seems to have been included in the municipal territory of Salernum, as Lucan speaks of the Silarus as skirting the cultivated lands of that city (Lucan, ii. 425.) The distance from Salernum itself to the mouth of the

Silarus is not less than 18 miles, though erroneously given in the Tabula at only 9. (*Tab.Peut.*) [E. H. B.]

SALE'TIO, in Gallia. This name occurs in the Not. Imp., in the Antonine Itin. and in the Table. Ammianus (xvi. 2) names it Saliso: "Argentoratum, Brocomagum, Tabernas, Salisonem, &c." The Itin. places Saletio between Argentoratum (*Strassburg*) and Tabernae; and the Table places it between Tabernae and Brocomagus (*Brumath*), which is north of *Strassburg*. The numbers are not correct in the Itin.; but there is no doubt that the place is *Sets* near the Rhine. A diploma of Otho the Great names it "Salise in Elisazium," in *Elsax* or *Alsace*. (D'Anville, *Notice, &c.*)　　[G. L.]

SALGANEUS (Σαλγανεύς; Liv. uses the Gr. acc. Salganea: *Eth.* Σαλγάνιος), a town upon the eastern coast of Boeotia, and between Chalcis and Anthedon, is said to have derived its name from a Boeotian, who served as pilot to the Persian fleet of Xerxes, and was put to death upon suspicion of treachery, because no outlet appeared to the channel of the Euripus; but the Persian commander, having found out his mistake, erected a monument on the spot, where the town was afterwards built. (Strab. ix. p. 403; Dicaearch. *Stat. Graec.* p. 19; Steph. B. *s. v.*). Salganeus was considered an important place from its commanding the northern entrance to the Euripus. (Diod. xix. 77; Liv. xxxv. 37, 46, 51.) The remains of the town stand directly under the highest summit of Mount Messapium, in the angle where the plain terminates, and upon the side of a small port. The citadel occupied a height rising from the shore, 90 yards in length, and about 50 broad, and having a flat summit sloping from the SE. towards the sea. There are remains of walls on the crest of the summit, and on the SE. side of the height. (Leake, *Northern Greece*, vol. ii. p. 267.)

SALI (Σάλοι, Ptol. iii. 5. § 22), a people of European Sarmatia, whom Schafarik (*Slav. Alt.* vol. i. p. 302) places on the river *Salis* in the Baltic province of *Livonia*.　　　　　[E. B. J.]

SA'LIA, a river in the territory of the Astures, on the N. coast of Hispania Tarraconensis. (Mela, iii. 1.) Now the *Sella*.　　　[T. H. D.]

SA'LIA, a branch of the Mosella (*Mosel*), mentioned by Venant. Fortun. (iii. 12. 5), which must be the *Seille* (Forbiger, vol. iii. p. 126). The *Seille* joins the *Mosel* at *Metz*.　　　　[G. L.]

SALICA (Σάλικα, Ptol. ii. 6. § 59), a town of the Oretani in Hispania Tarraconensis. [T. H. D.]

SALICE. [TAPROBANE.]

SALICES (AD), a place in Moesia which the Antonine Itinerary places not far from the mouths of the Danube at 43 M. P. from Halmyris, and 62 M. P. from Tomi. The low and marshy meadows which surrounded it were the scene of the sanguinary battle between the great Fridigern and the legions of Valens. (Amm. Marc. xxxi. 7. § 5; Gibbon, c. xxvi.; Le Beau, *Bas Empire*, iv. p. 112; Greenwood, *Hist. of the Germans*, p. 328.) [E. B. J.]

SALIENTIS (Salientibus, *Itin. Ant.* p. 428), a place in Gallaecia, on the road from Bracara to Asturica; variously identified with *Caldelas* and *Orense*.　　　　　　[T. H. D.]

SALINAE, in Gallia, the chief town of the Suetri or Suctrii (Ptol. iii. 1. § 42), a people in the Provincia E. of the Rhone. An inscription in Spon, "Deco. civitatis Salin.," is said to belong to this place; and another inscription has been found at *Lucerano* near the sources of the *Paglione*: "C. Julio Valenti

J. F. Fabr vi. viro civitat. Saliniens. ... Alpium maritimarum patrono optimo." Some place Salinae at *Castellan* in the diocese of *Senes* in the Maritime Alps, where there are salt springs, and where Spon's inscription is said to have been found. D'Anville places it at *Seillans* in the diocese of *Fréjus*, near Faventia (*Fayence*); and he observes that all the old towns of this country preserve their names. (D'Anville, *Notice, &c.*; Ukert, *Gallien*, p. 438.) [G. L.]

SALI'NAE (Σαλῖναι, Ptol. ii. 3. § 21), a town of the Catyeuchlani or Capelani, towards the E. coast of Britannia Romana. Camden (p. 339) identifies it with *Salndy* or *Sandye*, near *Potton* in *Bedfordshire*; others have sought it in the S. part of *Lincolnshire*.　　　　[T. H. D.]

SALI'NAE (Σαλῖναι, Ptol. iii. 8. § 7; *Peut. Tab.*; Geog. Rav. iv. 7), a town of Dacia identified with *Thorda*, on the *Aranyos* in *Transylvania*, where there are Roman remains. (Comp. Paget, *Hungary and Transylvania*, vol. ii. p. 259.)　[E. B. J.]

SALINSAE. [MAURETANIA, Vol. II. p. 299, a.]

SALI'NUM (Σαλῖνον), a place on the right bank of the Danube, a little below Aquincum, on the road from this town to Mursa in Lower Pannonia. (Ptol. ii. 16. § 4; *It. Ant.* p. 245, where it is called Vetus Salina.) On the Peut. Table we find in that spot the corrupt name Vetusalium. Its site must have been in the neighbourhood of the modern *Hanszabek*.　　　　　　　[L. S.]

SALIOCANUS. [STALIOCANUS.]

SALIOCLITA, in Gallia, is placed by the Antonine Itin. on the road from Genabum (*Orléans*) to Lutetia (*Paris*). It is *Saclas*, a little south of *Etampes*, on the *Juine*, a branch of the *Seine*. The Itin. makes the distance the same from Genabum, and Lutetia, which we must take to be *La Cité de Paris*; but there is an error in the Itin., as D'Anville shows, in the distance from Salioclita to Lutetia, and he proposes to correct it. [G. L.]

SALISSO, in north Gallia, is placed by the Antonine Itin. on a road from Augusta Trevirorum (*Trier*) to Bingium (*Bingen*). The places reckoned from Augusta are Baudobrica xviii., Salisso xxii, Bingium xxiii. This Baudobrica is not the place described under the article BAUDOBRICA (*Boppart*). These 63 Gallic leagues exceed the real distance from *Trier* to *Bingen* considerably. The site of Salisso is uncertain.　　　[G. L.]

SALLAECUS (Σάλλαικος, Ptol. ii. 5. § 8), a town in the S. of Lusitania.　　　[T. H. D.]

SALLENTI'NI. [SALENTINI.]

SALLUNTUM. [DALMATIA.]

SALMA'NTICA (Σαλμάντικα, Ptol. ii. 5. § 9; in the *Itin. Ant.* called Salmatice; in Polyaenus *Strat.* viii. 48, Σαλματίς), an important town of the Vettones in Lusitania, on the S. bank of the Durius, on the road from Emerita to Caesaraugusta. It is incontestibly identical with the Ἑλμαντική of Polybius (iii. 14), and the Hermandica or Helmantica of Livy (xxi. 5; cf. Nonius, *Hisp.* c. 38). It is the celebrated modern town of *Salamanca*, where the piers of a bridge of twenty-seven arches over the *Tormes*, built by Trajan, are still in existence. (Cf. Miñano, *Diccion.* vii. p. 402; Florez, *Esp. Sagr.* xiv. p. 267.)　　　　[T. H. D.]

SALMO'NA, a branch of the Mosella (*Mosel*).

"Nec fastiditos Salmonae usurpo fluores."

(Ausonius, *Mosell.* 366.)

The Salmona is the *Salme*, which flows into the *Mosel*, near the village of *Neumagen*.　　[G. L.]

SALMO'NE (Σαλμώνη, Steph. B. *s. v.*; Strab.; Σαλμωνία, Diod. iv. 68: *Eth.* Σαλμωνεύς, Σαλμωνείτης, Steph. B.; the form Σαλμωνείτης presupposes a form Σαλμώνεια, which probably ought to be read in Diodorus instead of Σαλμωνία), an ancient town of Pisatis in Elis, said to have been founded by Salmoneus, stood near Heracleia at the sources of the Enipeus or Barnichius, a branch of the Alpheius. Its site is uncertain. (Strab. viii. p. 356; Diod. *l. c.*; Apollod. i. 9. § 7; Steph. B. *l. c.*)

SALMONE. [SAMONIUM PROMONTORIUM.]

SALMYCA (Σάλμυκα, Steph. B. *l. c.*) a city of Spain near the Pillars of Hercules; perhaps in the Campus Spartiarius near Carthago Nova, if the reading of Brodaeus in Oppian (*Cyneg.* iv. 222) is correct. (Comp. Ukert, ii. pt. i. p. 402.)   [T. H. D.]

SALMYDESSUS ('Αλμυδισσός ἤτοι Σαλμυδησσός, Ptol iii. 11. § 4; Halmydessos, Plin. iv. 11. s. 18; Mela, ii. 2. § 5), a coast-town or district of Thrace, on the Euxine, about 60 miles NW. from the entrance of the Bosporus, probably somewhere in the neighbourhood of the modern *Midjeh*. The eastern offshoots of the Haemus here come very close to the shore, which they divide from the valley of the Hebrus. The people of Salmydessus were thus cut off from communication with the less barbarous portions of Thrace, and became notorious for their savage and inhuman character, which harmonised well with that of their country, the coast of which was extremely dangerous.

Aeschylus (*Prom.* 726*) describes Salmydessus as "the rugged jaw of the sea, hostile to sailors, step-mother of ships;" and Xenophon (*Anab.* vii. 5. § 12, seq.) informs us, that in his time its people carried on the business of wreckers in a very systematic manner, the coast being marked out into portions by means of posts erected along it, and those to whom each portion was assigned, having the exclusive *right* to plunder all vessels and persons cast upon it. This plan, he says, was adopted to prevent the bloodshed which had frequently been occasioned among themselves by their previous practice of indiscriminate plunder. Strabo (vii. p. 319) describes this portion of the coast of the Euxine as "desert, rocky, destitute of harbours, and completely exposed to the north winds;" while Xenophon (*l. c.*) characterises the sea adjoining it as "full of shoals."

The earlier writers appear to speak of Salmydessus as a district only, but in later authors, as Apollodorus, Pliny. and Mela, it is mentioned as a town.

Little is known respecting the history of this place. Herodotus (iv. 93) states that its inhabitants, with some neighbouring Thracian tribes, submitted without resistance to Darius when he was marching through their country towards the Danube. When the remnant of the Greeks who had followed Cyrus the Younger entered the service of Seuthes, one of the expeditions in which they were employed under Xenophon was to reduce the people of Salmydessus to obedience; a task which they seem to have accomplished without much difficulty. (*Anab. l. c.*)   [J. R.]

SALQ, a tributary of the Iberus in Celtiberia, which flowed past the town of Bilbilis (whence

---

* In this passage the poet, strangely enough, places Salmydessus in Asia Minor near the Thermodon.

Justin, xliv. 3, calls the river itself Bilbilis), and entered the Iberus at Allabon. (Mart. i. 49, x. 20, 103, iv. 55.) Now the *Xalon.*   [T. H. D.]

SALODU'RUM, in Gallia, is placed in the Antonine Itin. x. from Petinesca [PETINESCA]. and the distance from Salodurum to Augusta Rauracorum (*Augst* near *Basle*) is xxii.

Salodurum is *Solothurn*, as the Germans call it, or *Soleure*, and though the distance between *Basle* and *Solothurn* is somewhat less than that in the Itins., this may be owing to the passage over the hills which separate the cantons of *Basle* and *Solothurn*.

It is said that there are Roman remains at *Soleure*, and an inscription of the year B. C. 219, "Vico Salod.", has been found there. Salodurum is one of the towns of the Helvetii with a Celtic termination (*dur*). Cluver conjectured that Ptolemy's Ganodurum [GANODURUM] might be Salodurum. (D'Anville, *Notice &c.*; Ukert, *Gallien.*)   [G. L.]

SALOE (Σαλόη, Paus. vii. 24. § 7), or **SALE** (Plin. v. 31), a small lake of Lydia at the foot of Mount Sipylus, on the site of Tantalis or Sipylas, the ancient capital of Maeonia, which had probably perished during an earthquake. (Strab. i. p. 58, xii. p. 579.)

The lake was surrounded by a marsh; and the Phyrites, which flowed into it as a brook, issued at the other side as a river of some importance. [L. S.]

SALOMACUM, or **SALAMOCUM**, is placed by the Antonine Itin. on a road from Aquae Tarbellicae (*Dax*) to Burdigala (*Bordeaux*). Salomacum is the next place on the road to Burdigala and xviii. distant. The distance and the name *Sales* show that *Sales* is Salomacum.   [G.L.]

SALO'NA, **SALO'NAE** (Σαλῶνα, Σαλῶναι; this latter is the more usual form, as found in Inscriptions, Orelli, *Inscr.* nos. 502, 3833, 4995; and on coins, Rasche. vol. iv. pt. i. p. 1557: *Eth.* Σαλωνίτης, Σαλωνεύς), a town and harbour of Dalmatia, which still bears its ancient name, situated on the SE. corner of the gulf into which the Adriatic breaks (*Can. di Castelli*) on the N. of the river IADER (*il Giad. o*). Lucan's description (viii. 104) —

" Qua maris Adriaci longas ferit unda Salonas
Et tepidum in molles Zephyros excurrit Iader" —

agrees with its oblong form, still traceable in the ruins, and with the course of the river. Though the public buildings and houses of ancient Salonae have been destroyed, enough remains of the wall to show the size, as well as position, of the city; and the arch of the bridge proves that the course of the river is unchanged.

The city consisted of two parts, the eastern and the western; the latter stands on rather higher ground, sloping towards the N., along which the wall on that side is built. Little is known of Salonae before the time of Julius Caesar; after the fall of Dalminium it became the chief town of Dalmatia, and the head-quarters of L. Caecilius Metellus, B. C. 117. (Appian, *Illyr.* 11.) It was besieged a second time, and opened its gates to Cn. Cosconius, B. C. 78. (Eutrop. vi. 4; Oros. v. 23.) When the Pompeian fleet swept the Ionian gulf from Corcyra to Salonae, M. Octavius, who commanded a squadron for Pompeius, was compelled to retreat with loss from before this stronghold of

Caesar's. (Caes. *B. C.* iii. 9.) The profligate Gabinius, after being cooped up for months in the fortress, died here. (Auct. *B. Alex.* 43 ; Dion Cass. xlii. 12.) In B. C. 39 Asinius Pollio defeated the Partheni, who had espoused the cause of Brutus and Cassius, and took Salonae, in commemoration of which his son Asinius Gallus bore the "agnomen" Saloninus. (Comp. Virg. *Bucol.* viii. 7 ; Hor. *Carm.* ii. 1. 14—16.) From the time it received a colony it was looked upon as the great bulwark of the Roman power on that side the Adriatic, and was distinguished for its loyalty, as was shown in the siege it maintained against Bato the native leader, A. D. 6. All the great Roman roads in Dalmatia met at this point, and when the country was divided into three "conventus," or assize towns, as many as 382 "decuriae" were convened to it. (Plin. iii. 26.) Under the earlier emperors the town was embellished with many public buildings, the number of which was greatly increased by Diocletian, who, according to Porphyrogenitus (*de Adm. Imp.* 29), completely rebuilt the city. No great change took place for nearly two centuries after the death of that emperor ; but if we are to believe Porphyrogenitus (*l. c.*) the "long Salonae" attained to half the size of Constantinople. In A. D. 481 Salonae was taken by Odoacer, king of the Heruli, but was recovered from the Goths by the Gepid prince Mundus, the general of Justinian. Totila occupied it for a time. Little is known of these sieges, except that it was partially destroyed. (Procop. *B. G.* i. 5, 7, 11, &c.) It soon recovered from these diasters; and it was from Salonae that Belisarius in 544, and Narses in 552, set out to reconquer Italy from Totila and the Goths. (Comp. Gibbon, c. xliii.) The Avars invaded Dalmatia in 639, and, advancing upon Salonae, pillaged and burnt the town, which from that time has been deserted and in ruins. (Const. Porph. *l. c.*) The town possessed a dockyard, which, from Strabo's (vii. p. 315) account, seems to have been the only one deserving that name on the Dalmatian coast. The present state of the place offers many illustrations of past events ; the following works touch very fully upon the remains of the fortifications and other ruins : Wilkinson, *Dalmatia*, vol. i. pp. 151—164; Neigebaur, *Die Sud-Slaven*, pp. 151—164 ; Lanza, *Antiche lapide Salonitane inedite*, Zara, 1850 ; F. Carrara, *Topografia e Scavi di Salona*, Trieste, 1850.

The fame of Salonae mainly rests upon its neighbourhood having been chosen by Diocletian as the place of his retirement. That emperor, after his resignation, spent the last nine years of his life in the seclusion of the palace which has given its name to *Spalato*. *Spalato*, often erroneously called *Spalatro*, in Illyric *Split*, is a corrupted form of Salonae Palatium or S. Palatium. The building of the palace, within the precincts of which the greater part of the modern town is constructed, occupied twelve years. The stone, which was very little inferior to marble itself, was brought from the quarries of Tragurium. After the death of Diocletian, but little is known of the palace or its occupants. Part of it was kept by the magistrats of Salonae, as a state palace; and part was occupied by the "Gynaecium," or cloth manufactory, in which women only were employed,—whence the name. It was tenanted by the phantom emperors of the West, Glycerius and Julius Nepos, the latter of whom was murdered here. When Salonae was captured by the Avars, the houseless citizens fled to the massive structure of the palace for shelter : the settlement swelled by the arrival of their countrymen became a Roman city under the name of ASPALATHUM, and paid an annual tribute of 200 pieces of gold to the Eastern emperors. (Const. Porph. *l. c.*)

The palace is nearly a square, terminated at the four corners by a quadrangular tower. According to the latest and most accurate admeasurements, the superficial content, including the towers, occupies a space of a little more than eight acres. (Wilkinson, *Dalmatia*, vol. i. pp. 114—143 ; Neigebaur. *Die Sud-Slaven*, pp. 134—151.) The entire building was composed of two principal sections, of which the one to the S. contained two temples — one dedicated to Jupiter the other to Aesculapius — and the private rooms of the emperor. Two streets intersected each other at right angles, nearly in the centre of it; the principal one led from the Porta Aurea, the main entrance on the N. front, to a spacious court before the vestibule; the other ran in a direct line from the W. to the E. gate, and crossed the main street just below the court. What remains is not enough to explain the distribution of the various parts of the interior. By a comparison of what existed in his time with the precepts of Vitruvius, Adams (*Antiquities of Diocletian's Palace*, 1764) has composed his ingenious restoration of the palace. (Comp. Gibbon, c. xiii.) All the gates, except the Porta Argentea, were defended by two octagonal towers; the principal or "golden gate" still remains nearly perfect. The temple of Jupiter is now the "Duomo," and that of Aesculapius is a baptistery dedicated to St. John. Diocletian's palace marks an aera; — columnar was so combined with arched architecture, that the arches were at first made to rest upon the entablature, and afterwards were even forced immediately to spring from the abacus, in violation of the law of statics, which requires undiminished and angular pillars under the arch; at length the entablature itself took the form of an arch. (Müller, *Ancient Art*, § 193.) But although this architecture offends against the rules of good taste, yet these remains may serve to show how directly the Saracens and Christian architects borrowed from Roman models many of the characteristics which have been looked upon as the creation of their own imagination. (Comp. Hope, *Architecture*, vol. i. c. viii.; Freeman, *Hist. of Architecture*, p. 152.) A plan of the palace of Diocletian, taken from Adams, will be found in Fergusson's *Handbook of Architecture*, vol. i. p. 356, accompanied by an account of the general arrangements of the building. [E.B.J.]

SALPESA, a Roman municipium in Hispania Baetica, SE. of Hispalis, at the ruined *Facialcazar*, between *Utrera* and *Coronil.* (Florez, *Esp. Sagr.* ix. p. 17; Mionnet, *Suppl.* i. p. 44.) [T. H. D.]

SALPI'NUM (*Eth.* Salpinas), an ancient city of Etruria, mentioned only by Livy (v. 31, 32), who speaks of the Salpinates as assisting the Volsinians in their war against Rome in B. C. 389. It is clear from the manner in which they are here spoken of that they were an independent people, with a considerable territory and a fortified city ; and the manner in which they are associated with the powerful Volsinians would lead to the inference that they also must have been a people of considerable power. Yet no subsequent mention of their name is found, and all trace of their existence disappears. Niebuhr conjectures that Salpinum occupied the site of the modern *Orvieto*, the name of which is evidently a corruption of Urbs Vetus, the form used by Paulus Diaconus in the seventh century (P. Diac. iv. 33): there is, therefore, little doubt that the site was one of a more ancient Etruscan city ; and its proximity to Volsinii renders it probable enough that it may have been Salpinum. But no reliance can be placed upon any such conclusion. (Niebuhr, vol. ii. p. 493.)   [E. H. B.]

SALSAS or SALSA, a river of Carmania, noticed by Pliny (vi. 25). Reichard imagines that this is the same stream as that called by Marcian, Cathraps (p. 21, ed. Hudson), and by Ptolemy, Araps or Cathraps (vi. 8. § 4); and he identifies it with the modern *Shir ;* but this seems very doubtful. [V.]

SALSULAE, in Gallia. Mela (ii. 5) describes the Salsulae Fons as not sending forth fresh water, but water salter than the sea. He places the Fons south of the lake Rubresus, and near the shore which he calls Leucate [LEUCATE]. Salsulae is in the Antonine Itin. on the road from Narbo to the Pyrenees. Salsulae is *Salses* or *Salçes*, where there is a salt-spring. Near the Fons, says Mela, is a plain very green with fine and slender reeds, under which is water. This is the place, he says, where fish are got by striking down with a prong or something of the sort; and this is the origin of the fables told by the Greeks and some Romans about fishes being dug out of the ground. He alludes to Polybius (xxxiv. 10). [RUSCINO.]   [G. L.]

SALSUM FLUMEN, a tributary of the Baetis in Hispania Baetica, between Attegua and Attubis. (Hirtius, *B. A.* c. 7, 8.) Variously identified with the *Guadajoz* and *Salado.*   [T. H. D.]

SALSUS. [STACHIR.]

SALTIATES (Σαλτιῆται, Strab. iii. p. 144), according to Strabo a people of Spain celebrated for their woollen manufacture. But we must probably read in this passage Σαλακιῆται.   [T. H. D.]

SALTICI, a town of the Celtiberi in Hispania Tarraconensis. (*Itin. Ant.* p. 447.) Variously identified with *Jorquera* and *S. Maria del Campo.* [T. H. D.]

SALTIGA (Σάλτιγα, Ptol. ii. 6. § 61), a town of the Bastitani in Hispania Tarraconensis. [T. H. D.]

SALTOPYRGUS. [TEGLICIUM.]

SALURNIS (*Salurn*), a town in Rhaetia, on the river Athesis, in the north of Tridentum, is mentioned only by Paulus Diaconus. (*Hist. Langob.* iii. 9.)   [L. S.]

SALUTARIS PHRYGIA. [PHRYGIA, p. 625.]

SALVA (Σαλούα), a town in the north-eastern extremity of Lower Pannonia, on the right bank of the Danube. (Ptol. ii. 16. § 4; *Itin. Ant.* pp. 266, 267.) According to the Notitia Imperii, where it is called Solva, it contained a garrison of a body of horsemen. The site of this place cannot be ascertained with certainty.   [L. S.]

SA'LYES (Σάλυες), SA'LYI, SALLU'VII, or SA'LLYES (Steph. Byz. *s. v.*), a Ligurian people in Gallia. There are other varieties in the writing of the word. The early Greeks gave the name of Ligyes to these Salyes; and their territory, which was in the possession of the Massaliots, when Strabo wrote, was originally called Ligystice. (Strab. iv. p. 203.) The geographer means to say that the old Greeks were not acquainted with the name of Salyes, but only with the name of the nation to which they belonged. Livy (v. 34) speaks of the Phocaeans who founded Massilia being attacked by the Salyes, for in his time the name Salyes was familiar to the Romans.

Strabo speaks of the Salyes in his description of the Alps. He makes their country extend from Antipolis to Massilia, and even a little further. They occupied the hilly country which lies inland and some parts of the coast, where they were mingled with the Greeks (iv. p. 203). They extended west as far as the Rhone. The Salyes had also the country north of Massilia as far as the Druentia (*Durance*), a distance of 500 stadia; but on crossing the Druentia at Cabellio or Caballio (*Cavaillon*) a man would be in the country of the Cavares (Strab. iv. p. 185), who extended from the Druentia to the Isara (*Isère*). [CAVARES.] Strabo adds that the Salyes occupy both plains and the mountains above the plains. In this passage (Οἱ μὲν οὖν Σάλυες ἐν αὐτοῖς) Groskurd (*Transl. Strab.* vol. i. p. 318) has altered Σάλυες into Καουαροι, and so he has spoiled the meaning. Ukert has defended the true reading, though he has not correctly explained *ἐν αὐτοῖς.* The Salyes occupied the wide plains east of Tarascon and *Arles*, one of the best parts of the country between the *Durance* and the Mediterranean; and so Strabo could correctly say that the Volcae Tectosages who reach to the Rhone had the Salyes extending along their border and opposite to them on the other side of the river, and the Cavares opposite to them (north of the *Durance*).

The Salyes are sometimes distinguished from the Ligures, as when Strabo (iv. p. 178) speaks of the coast which the Massaliots possess and the Salyes as far as the Ligyes to the parts towards Italy and the river Varus, the boundary of the Narbonitis (Provincia Narbonensis) and Italy. Livy also (xxi. 26) speaks of P. Cornelius Scipio sailing along the coast of Etruria and of the Ligures, and then the coast of the Salyes till he came to Massilia. This shows that the Ligurians of Gallia, or the country west of the *Var*, became known to the Romans by the name of Salyes. Strabo's remark that these Salyes, whom the early Greeks named Ligures, were called Celtoligyes by the later Greeks, may explain how Livy or his Epitomiser has called the Salyes both Ligurians ("Transalpinos Ligures," *Epit.* 47) and Galli (*Epit.* 60). They were a mixed race of Galli and Ligures.

The Salyes were a warlike people. They had both infantry and cavalry, distributed into ten tribes or divisions. They were the first of the Transalpine nations which the Romans subdued. (Florus, iii. 2.) The Romans fought for a long time with the Ligurians east of the *Var*, and with the Salyes west of it, for these people being in possession of the sea-coast closed against the Romans the way into Spain. They plundered both by sea and land, and were so formidable that the road through their land was hardly safe for a large army. After eighty years of fighting the Romans with difficulty succeeded in getting a road of 12 stadia in width allowed for the free passage of those who went on the public service.

Livy (xxxi. 10) tells us that in the Second Punic War the Insubres, Cenomani, and Boii stirred up the Salyes and other Ligurians to join them; and all together under Hamilcar attacked Placentia. There is no ground, as Ukert remarks, to alter the reading "Salyis," for we see no reason why the Salyes as well as other Ligurians or mixed Ligurians should not aid the enemies of Rome. Both the Ligurians and the Cisalpine Galli dreaded the arms and the encroachment of the Romans. The alliance with

Massilia first brought the Romans into the country of the Salyes; and in B. C. 154 the Oxybii and Deceates, or Deciates, who were threatening Massilia, were defeated by the consul Q. Opimius. The Salyes or Salluvii are not named on this occasion by the historians, and the Deceates and Oxybii, who were certainly Ligurians, may have been two smaller tribes included under the general name of Salyes or Salluvii. [DECIATES; OXYBII.] The consul M. Fulvius Flaccus in B. C. 125 defeated the Salyes, and in B. C. 123 the consul C. Sextius Calvinus completed the subjugation of this people, and founded Aquae Sextiae (*Aix*) in their territory.

Ptolemy (ii. 10. § 15) enumerates Tarascon, Glanum, Arelatum (Arelate) Colonia, Aquae Sextiae Colonia, and Ernaginum as the towns of the Salyes. Tarascon, Glanum (*St. Remi*), Arelate, and Ernaginum [ERNAGINUM] all lie west of Aquae Sextiae (*Aix*) and of *Marseille*; and we may conclude that the country of the Salyes is the western half of the tract between the *Var* and the Rhone, and between the *Durance* and the Mediterranean.

The tribes east of the Salyes, the Albici, Suetri, Neruai, Oxybii, and Deciates, and there may be some others [COMMONI], were perhaps sometimes included under the name of the more powerful nation of the Salyes; but Strabo's statement does not appear to be strictly correct, when he makes the Salyes extend along the coast to Antipolis. The coast immediately west of the *Var* belonged to the Deceates and Oxybii. Pliny says " Ligurium celeberrimi ultra Alpes, Salluvii, Deciates, Oxybii " (iii. 5); the three tribes of Transalpine Ligures whose names occur in the history of the Roman conquest of this country. In Pliny's list of the Coloniae in the interior of Narbonensis east of the Rhone there is " Aquae Sextiae Salluviorum," and we may conclude that the head-quarters of the Salyes or Salluvii were in the plain country above *Aix*, and thence to *Arles*. Owing to their proximity to the Greeks of Massilia they would be the first of the Ligures or the mixed Galli and Ligurians who felt the effect of Greek civilisation, and there can be no doubt that their race was crossed by Greek blood. Possessing the town of Arelate, at the head of the delta of the Rhone, they would have in their hands the navigation of the lower part of the river. The history of this brave and unfortunate people is swallowed up in the blood-stained annals of Rome; and the race was probably nearly extirpated by the consul Calvinus selling them after his conquest. [G. L]

· SAMAICA (Σαμαϊκή, Ptol. iii. 11. § 9), is described by Ptolemy as a στρατηγία of Thrace, on the borders of Macedonia and the Aegean. [J. R.]

SAMACHONI'TIS LACUS (Σαμαχωνῖτις λίμνη al. Σεμεχωνῖτις), the name given by Josephus to the small lake of the Upper Jordan, called in Scripture the "waters of Merom," where Joshua routed the army of Jabin, king of Hazor, which city, according to Josephus, was situated above the lake. (Comp. *Josh.* xi. 5, 7, and *Judg.* iv. with Josephus, *Ant.* v. 5. § 1.) He elsewhere describes the lake as 60 stadia long by 30 broad, extending its marshes to a place called Daphne, which Reland is probably right in altering to Dane, i. e. Dan, as Josephus immediately identifies it with the temple of the Golden Calf. (Joseph. *B. J.* iv. 1. § 1; Reland, *Palaest.* p. 263.) The name, which is not elsewhere found, has been variously derived, but the most probable etymology would connect it in sense with the Hebrew name Merom = *aquae superiores*, deriving the word from the Arabic " samaca," *altus fuit.* (Reland, *l. c.* p. 262.) It is singular that no other notices occur of this lake in sacred or in other writings. Its modern name is *Bahr-el-Huleh.* Pococke writes: " Josephus says the lake was 7 miles long, but it is not above 2 miles broad, except at the north end, where it may be about 4. The waters are muddy and esteemed unwholesome, having something of the nature of the water of a morass." (*Observations on Palaestine,* vol. ii. p. 73.) Dr. Robinson " estimated its length at about 2 hours, or from 4 to 5 geographical miles; its breadth at the northern end is probably not less than 4 miles." It had the appearance almost of a triangle, the northern part being far the broadest; " or rather the map gives to it in some degree the shape of a pear." (*Bibl. Res.* vol. iii. pp. 339, 340, *Biblioth. Sacr.* vol. i. p. 12; Stanley, *Sinai and Palestine,* p. 383, n. 1.) [G. W.]

SAMAMYCIL. [SYRTICA.]

SA'MARA. [FEUDIS; SAMAROBRIVA.]

SAMA'RIA (Σαμαρεῖτις, LXX., Joseph.; χώρα Σαμαρέων, Σαμαρίς, Σαμάρεια, Ptol.). The district has been already described in general, under PALAESTINA [p. 518], where also the notice of Josephus has been cited [p. 532]. It remains to add a few words concerning its extent, its special characteristics, and its place in classical geography. It lay, according to Josephus, "between Judaea and Galilee (comp. *St. John,* iv. 4), extending from a village called Ginaea in the great plain (Esdraelon) to the toparchy of Acrabatta." Ginaea there can be no difficulty in identifying with the modern *Jenin,* at the southern extremity of the plain, on the road from *Nablûs* to *Nazareth.* The toparchy of Acrabatta, mentioned also by Pliny, it is difficult to define: but it certainly lay between *Nablûs* and Jericho, and therefore probably east of the toparchy of Gophna and in the same parallel of latitude. (Eusebius, *Onomast. s. v.* 'Ακραββεὶν; Reland, *Palaest.* p. 192.) The northern boundary of Samaria is well defined by a continuous line of hills, which, commencing with Mount Carmel on the W., runs first in a SW direction and then almost due E. to the valley of the Jordan, bounding the great plain of Esdraelon on the S. Its southern boundary is not so distinctly marked, but was probably conterminous with the northern limits of the tribe of Benjamin. It comprehended the tribe of Ephraim, and the half of Manasseh on this side Jordan, and, if it be extended as far E. as Jordan, included also some part of Issachar, that skirted these two tribes on the E. Pliny (v. 13) reckons to Samaria the towns Neapolis, formerly called Mamortha, Sebaste, and Gamala, which last is certainly erroneous. [GAMALA.] Ptolemy names Neapolis and Thena (Θῆνα, v. 16. § 5), which last is evidently identical with Thanath (Θανὰθ) of the tribe of Joseph, mentioned by Eusebius (*Onomast. s. v.*), and still existing in a village named *Thena,* 10 miles E. of Neapolis, on the descent to the Jordan. St. Jerome notes that the most precious oil was produced in Samaria (*in Hoseam,* cap. xii.), and its fertility is attested by Josephus. [G. W.]

SAMARIA, SEBASTE (Σαμάρεια, Σεβάστη), the Hebrew SHOMRON, the capital city of the kingdom of Israel, and the royal residence from the time of Omri (cir. B. C. 925). of whom it is said that " he bought the hill Samaria of Shemer for two talents of silver, and built on the hill, and called the name of the city which he built after the name of Shemer, owner of the hill, Samaria " (Heb. *Shemeron*). (1 *Kings,* xvi. 24.) Mr. Stanley thinks that Omri built it merely as a palatial residence (*Sinai and Palestine*, p. 240); but Dr. Robinson perhaps more justly concludes that it was chosen as the site of the capital, and remarks that "it would be difficult to find in all Palestine a situation of equal strength, fertility, and beauty combined." (*Bibl. Res.* iii. p. 146.) Its great strength is attested by the fact that it endured a siege from all the power of the Syrian army under Hazael, in the days of Jehoram (cir. B. C. 892), little more than 30 years after its first foundation, and was not taken notwithstanding the frightful effects of the famine within the walls (2 *Kings*, vii. 24—viii. 20); and when subsequently besieged by the Assyrians (cir. B. C. 721) it was only reduced after a siege of three years (xviii. 9, 10). After the captivity it was taken by John Hyrcanus, after a year's siege, when he is said to have sapped the foundations of it with water and destroyed all traces of a city. It was subsequently occupied by the Jews until Pompey restored it to its own inhabitants. It was further restored by Gabinius. (Joseph. *Ant.* xiii. 10. § 3, 15. § 4, xiv. 4. § 4, 5. § 3, xiii. 10. § 3, 15. § 4.) It was granted to Herod the Great by Augustus on the death of Antony and Cleopatra, and by him converted into a Roman city under the name of Sebaste =Augusta, in honour of his imperial patron. (*Ant.* xv. 3. §§ 3, 7, 8. § 5, *B. J.* i. 20. § 3.) The town was surrounded with a wall 20 stadia in length: in the middle of the town was a temple built in honour of Caesar, itself of large dimensions, and standing in a *temenos* of 1½ stadium square. It was colonised with 6000 veterans and others, to whom was assigned an extremely fertile district around the city. (*B. J.* i. 21. § 2.) Dr. Robinson imagines that it was in this city that Philip first preached the Gospel, and that the church was founded by the apostles St. Peter and St. John (*Acts*, viii. 5, &c.); but considering the absence of the article in the original, supplied in the English translation, and comparing the passage with the identical expression in St. John (iv. 5), it is more probable that the same town is intended, viz. Sychar, or Neapolis, the chief seat of the Samaritan worship. Nor does the expression in Acts (viii. 14), that "Samaria had received the word of God," militate against this view; for here also the country may be very well understood, and it is well remarked by Dr. Robinson that "it is sometimes difficult to distinguish whether, under the name Samaria, the city or the region is meant." (*Bibl. Res.* iii. p. 146.) It is most probable, however, that the sacred writers would have used the classical name then in vogue had they had occasion to mention the city. Septimius Severus gave a colony there in the beginning of the third century (Ulpian, quoted by Robinson, *l. c.* p 148, n. 1), and it was probably at that time an episcopal see; for its bishop, Marius or Marinus, was present at the Council of Nicaea and subscribed its acts. (Le Quien, *Oriens Christianus*, vol. iii. col. 549—552.) The tradition which assigns Sebaste as the place of St. John Baptist's imprisonment and martyrdom is first found in St. Jerome (*Comment in Osee*, i. 5), who also places there the tombs of Obadiah and Elisha (*Comment. in Abdiam*, i. 1, *Epitaph. Paulae*, c. 6), and militates against Josephus, whose statement, however, is inadmissible. [MACHAERUS.] The modern village which represents in its name and site the magnificent city of Herod the Great is situated on an isolated hill 6 miles N. of *Nablus*, reckoned by Josephus a day's journey from Jerusalem. (*Ant.* xv. 11.)

The village occupies only the eastern extremity of the hill, and stands at the height of about 926 feet above the sea. Its only conspicuous building is the ruined church of St. John, overhanging the brow of the eastern declivity: at the further extremity of the hill, are the remains of an ancient gateway, and near it stand 60 columns *in situ*, the commencement apparently of a colonnade which extended the whole length of the hill, for at some distance eastward 20 more still stand, and others, whole or in fragments, lie prostrate over the whole hill, while the *débris* of the buildings have raised the surrounding valleys, remarkably fulfilling the prophecy of Micah (i. 6): "I will make Samaria as an heap of the field, as plantings of a vineyard; and I will pour down the stones thereof into the valley, and I will discover the foundations thereof." At about half its height the hill is girt about with a distinct belt of level ground, while similar terraces, not so well defined, may be traced above and below, which it is thought may have once served as the streets of the city. (Ritter, *Erdkunde Palästina*, iii. pp. 661—666.) Coins of the city are quoted by Vaillant, Noris, Eckhel, and others, chiefly of the earlier emperors.   [G. W.]

SAMARIANE, a town of Hyrcania, mentioned by Strabo (xi. p. 508). It is no doubt the same as that called Samaranne by Ptolemy (vi. 9. § 2), and by Ammianus Marcellinus, Saramanna (xxiii. 6). It cannot be identified with any modern place. [V.]

SAMAROBRI'VA, in Gallia, the ford or passage of the Samara, was a town of the Ambiani on the Samara (*Somme*). Caesar held a meeting of the states of Gallia at Samarobriva in the autumn of B. C. 54, before putting his troops in winter-quarters. Caesar himself stayed at Samarobriva, as his narrative shows (*B. G.* v. 24, 46, 47, 53), and as appears from those letters of Cicero addressed to his friend Trebatius, who was about Caesar at that time (*ad Fam.* vii. 11, 12, 16). Ptolemy mentions Samarobriva as the chief town of the Ambiani (ii. 9. § 8). The town afterwards took the name of "Ambiani urbs inter alias eminens" (Amm. Marc. xv. 11), or "Civitas Ambianorum" in the Notitia Prov. Gallia. The name of Samarobriva appears in the Antonine Itin. and in the Table; but in the Itin. has Amiani also. There seems no reason for fixing Samarobriva at any other site than *Amiens*, though some geographers would do so.   [G. L.]

SAMBANA (Σάμβανα), a small place mentioned by Diodorus Siculus (xvii. 27). There can be little doubt that it is the same as the Sabata of Pliny (vi. 27. § 31). It was situated about two days' journey N. of Sittake and E. of Artemita.   [V.]

SAMBASTAE (Σαμβασταί), one of the many small tribes in the district of Pattalene mentioned by Arrian (vi. 15) as noticed by Alexander and his troops near the mouths of the Indus. It has been conjectured that the present ruins of *Sevistan* or *Schwan* indicate the site of the chief fortress of this people; and Burnes appears to believe that this is the same place noticed by Curtius (ix. 8) as a stronghold of the Brachmani (Burnes, *Travels in Bokhara*, iii. p. 57).   [V.]

SAMBRACITA'NUS SINUS, in Gallia, is placed in the Maritime Itin. between Forum Julii and Heraclea. It is the gulf of *Grimaud*.   [G. L.]

SA'MBROCA (Σάμβροκα, Ptol. ii. 6. § 20), a river of Hispania Tarraconensis, which entered the sea between the Pyrenees and the Iberus. Ukert (ii. pt. i. p. 292) takes it to be the same river called Alba by Pliny (iii. 3. s. 4); the modern *Ter*.   [T. H. D.]

SAMBULOS. [BAGISTANUS MONS.]

SAMBUS (Σάμβος), a small river which forms one of the tributaries of the *Jumna*. It is mentioned by Arrian in his list of Indian rivers (*Ind.* c. 4.). [V.]

SAME or **SAMOS** (Σάμη, Σάμος: *Eth.* Σαμαῖος: *Samo*), the most ancient city in Cephallenia, which is also the name of this island in the poems of Homer. [CEPHALLENIA.] The city stood upon the eastern coast, and upon the channel separating Cephallenia and Ithaca. (Strab. x. p. 455.) Along with the other Cephallenian towns it joined the Athenian alliance in B.C. 431. (Thuc. ii. 30.) When M. Fulvius passed over into Cephallenia in B.C. 189, Samos at first submitted to the Romans along with the other towns of the island; but it shortly afterwards revolted, and was not taken till after a siege of four months, when all the inhabitants were sold as slaves. (Liv. xxxviii. 28, 29.) It appears from Livy's narrative that Same had two citadels, of which the smaller was called Cyatis; the larger he designates simply as the major arx. In the time of Strabo there existed only a few vestiges of the ancient city. (Strab. *l. c.*; comp. Plin. iv. 12. s. 19.)

Same has given its name to the modern town of *Samo*, and to the bay upon which it stands. Its position and the remains of the ancient city are described by Leake. It stood at the northern extremity of a wide valley, which borders the bay, and which is overlooked to the southward by the lofty summit of Mount Aenus (*'Elato*). It was built upon the north-western face of a bicipitous height, which rises from the shore at the northern end of the modern town. "The ruins and vestiges of the ancient walls show that the city occupied the two summits, an intermediate hollow, and their slope as far as the sea." On the northern of the two summits are the ruins of an acropolis, which seems to have been the major arx mentioned by Livy. On the southern height there is a monastery, on one side of which are some remains of a Hellenic wall, and which seems to be the site of the Cyatis, or smaller citadel. There are considerable remains of the town walls. The whole circuit of the city was barely two miles. (Leake, *Northern Greece.* vol. iii. p. 55.)

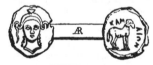

COIN OF SAME.

SA'MIA. [SAMICUM.]

SA'MICUM (Σαμικόν: *Eth.* Σαμικεύς), a town of Triphylia in Elis, situated near the coast about half-way between the mouths of the Alpheius and the Neda, and a little north of the Anigrus. It stood upon a projecting spur of a lofty mountain, which here approaches so near the coast as to leave only a narrow pass. From its situation commanding this pass, it is probable that a city existed here from the earliest times; and it was therefore identified with the Arene of Homer (*Il.* ii. 591, xi. 723), which the poet places near the mouth of the Minyeius, a river supposed to be the same as the Anigrus [ARENE.] According to Strabo the city was originally called SAMOS (Σάμος), from its being situated upon a hill, because this word formerly signified "heights." Samicum was at first the name of the fortress, and the same name was also given to the surrounding plain. (Strab. viii. pp. 346, 347; Paus. v. 5. § 3.) Pausanias speaks (v. 6. § 1) of a city SAMIA (Σαμία), which he apparently distinguishes from Samicum; but Samicum is the only place mentioned in history. [See some remarks under MACISTUS.] Samicum was occupied by the Aetolian Polysperchon against the Arcadians, and was taken by Philip, B.C. 219. (Paus. v. 6. § 1; Polyb. iv. 77, 80.) The ruins of Samicum are found at *Khaiáffa* (written Χαϊάφφα), which is only the name of the guarded pass. The ruined walls are 6 feet thick, and about 1½ mile in circumference. They are of the second order of Hellenic masonry, and are evidently of great antiquity. The towers towards the sea belong to a later age.

Near Samicum upon the coast was a celebrated temple of the Samian Poseidon, surrounded by a grove of wild olives. It was the centre of the religious worship of the six Triphylian cities, all of whom contributed to its support. It was under the superintendence of Macistus, the most powerful of the Triphylian cities. (Strab. viii. pp. 344, 346, 347.) In a corrupt passage of Strabo (p. 344) this temple is said to be 100 stadia equidistant from Lepreum and the Annius (τοῦ 'Αννίου); for the latter name we ought to read Alpheius and not Anigrus, as some editors have done.

In the neighbourhood of Samicum there were celebrated medicinal springs, which were said to cure cutaneous diseases. Of the two lagoons which now stretch along the coast, the larger, which extends as far as the mouth of the Alpheius, begins at the northern foot of the hill upon which Samicum stands; the southern extends along the precipitous sides of the hill, which were called in antiquity the Achaean rocks. (Strab. viii. p. 347.) The river Anigrus flows into the latter of these lagoons, and from thence flows out into the sea. The lagoon is deep, being fed with subterraneous sources; in summer it is said to be very fetid, and the air extremely unwholesome. Strabo relates that the waters of the lake were fetid, and its fish not eatable, which he attributes to the Centaurs washing their wounds in the Anigrus. Pausanias mentions the same circumstances; and both writers describe the efficacy of the water in curing cutaneous diseases. There were two caves, one sacred to the Nymphs Anigrides ('Ανιγρίδες, Paus.; 'Ανιγριάδες, Strab.), and the other to the Atlantides; the former was the more important, and is alone mentioned by Pausanias. It was in the cave of the Anigrides that the persons who were going to use the waters first offered up their prayers to the Nymphs. (Strab. viii. p. 346, seq.; Paus. v. 5. §§ 7—11.) These two caves are still visible in the rocks; but they are now accessible only by a boat, as they are immediately above the surface of the lake. General Gordon, who visited these caverns in 1835, found in one of them water distilling from the rock, and bringing with it a pure yellow sulphur. (Leake, *Morea*, vol. i. p. 54, seq., *Peloponnesiaca*, p. 108; Boblaye, *Recherches*, &c., p. 133, seq.; Curtius, *Peloponnesos*, vol. ii. p. 78, seq.)

SAMINTHUS (Σάμινθος), a town in the Argeia, on the western edge of the Argive plain, which was taken by Agis, when he marched from Phlius into the territory of Argos in B.C. 418. (Thuc. v. 58.) Its position is uncertain. Leake, who supposes Agis to have marched over Mt. Lyrceium and the adjoining hills, places it at *Kutzopódhi* (*Morea*, vol. ii. p. 415), and Ross at the village of *Phiklia*, on the southern side of Mt. Tricaranon, across which is the shortest pass from the Phliasia into the Argive plain. (*Peloponnes*, p. 27.)

SAMMO'NIUM. [SAMONIUM.]

SA'MNIUM (ἡ Σαυνῖτις, Pol., Strab.; *Eth.* SAM-NIS, pl. SAMNITES, Σαυνῖται, Pol., Strab., &c.; Σαυ-νῖται, Ptol.), one of the principal regions or districts of Central Italy. The name was sometimes used in a more extensive, sometimes in a more restricted, sense, the Samnites being a numerous and powerful people, who consisted of several distinct tribes, while they had founded other tribes in their immediate neighbourhood, who were sometimes included under the same appellation, though they did not properly form a part of the nation. But Samnium proper, according to the more usual sense of the name (exclusive of the Frentani, but including the Hirpini), was a wholly inland district, bounded on the N. by the Marsi, Peligni, and Frentani, on the E. by Apulia, on the S. by Lucania, and on the SW. and W. by Campania and Latium.

I. GENERAL DESCRIPTION.

The territory thus limited was almost wholly mountainous, being filled up with the great mountain masses and ramifications of the Apennines, which in this part of their course have lost even more than elsewhere the character of a regular chain or range, and consist of an irregular and broken mass, the configuration of which it is not very easy to understand. But as the whole topography of Samnium depends upon the formation and arrangement of these mountain groups, it will be necessary to examine them somewhat in detail.

1. In the northern part of the district, adjoining the Marsi and Peligni, was a broken and irregular mass of mountains, containing the sources of the Sagrus (*Sangro*), and extending on both sides of the valley of that river, as far as the frontiers of the Frentani. This was the land of the CARACENI, the most northerly of the Samnite tribes, whose chief city was Aufidena, in the valley of the Sagrus, about 5 miles above *Castel di Sangro*, now the chief town of the surrounding district.

2. The valley of the Sagrus was separated by a mountain pass of considerable elevation from the valley of the Vulturnus, a river which is commonly considered as belonging to Campania; but its sources, as well as the upper part of its course, and the valleys of all its earliest tributaries, were comprised in Samnium. Aesernia, situated on one of these tributaries, was the principal town in this part of the country; while Venafrum, about 15 miles lower down the valley, was already reckoned to belong to Campania. This portion of Samnium was one of the richest and most fertile, and least mountainous of the whole country. From its proximity to Latium and Campania, the valley of the Vulturnus was one of the quarters which was most accessible to the Roman arms, and served as one of the highroads into the enemy's country.

3. From Aesernia a pass, which was probably used from very early times, and was traversed by a road in the days of the Roman Empire, led to Bovianum in the valley of the Tifernus. This city was situated in the very heart of the Samnite country, surrounded on all sides by lofty mountains. Of these the most important is that on the SW., the *Monte Matese*, at the present day one of the most celebrated of the Apennines,

but for which no ancient name has been preserved. The name of Mons Tifernus may indeed have been applied to the whole group; but it is more probable that it was confined, as that of *Monte Biferno* is at the present day, to one of the offshoots or minor summits of the *Matese*, in which the actual sources of the Tifernus were situated. The name of *Matese* is given to an extensive group or mass of mountains filling up the whole space between *Bojano* (Bovianum) and the valley of the Vulturnus, so that it sends down its ramifications and underfalls quite to the valley of that river, whence they sweep round by the valley of the Calor, and thence by *Morcone* and *Sepino* to the sources of the Tamarus. Its highest summit, the *Monte Miletto*, SW. of *Bojano*, rises to a height of 6744 feet. This rugged group of mountains, clothed with extensive forests, and retaining the snow on its summits for a large part of the year, must always have been inaccessible to civilisation, and offered a complete barrier to the arms of an invader. There could never have been any road or frequented pass between that which followed the valley of the Vulturnus and that which skirts the eastern base of the *Matese*, from the valley of the *Calore* to that of the *Tamaro*. This last is the line followed by the modern road from *Naples* to *Campobasso*.

4. N. of *Bojano* the mountains are less elevated, and have apparently no conspicuous (or at least no celebrated) summits; but the whole tract, from *Bojano* to the frontier of the Frentani, is filled up with a mass of rugged mountains, extending from *Agnone* and the valley of the *Sangro* to the neighbourhood of *Campobasso*. This mountainous tract is traversed by the deep and narrow valleys of the *Trigno* (Trinius) and *Biferno* (Tifernus), which carry off the waters of the central chain, but without affording any convenient means of communication. The mountain tracts extending on all sides of Bovianum constituted the country of the PENTRI, the most powerful of all the Samnite tribes.

5. S. of the *Matese*, and separated from it by the valley of the Calor (*Calore*), is the group of the MONS TABURNUS, still called *Monte Taburno*, somewhat resembling the *Matese* in character, but of inferior elevation as well as extent. It formed, together with the adjoining valleys, the land of the CAUDINI, apparently one of the smallest of the Samnite tribes, and the celebrated pass of the Caudine Forks was situated at its foot. Closely connected with Mount Taburnus, and in a manner dependent on it, though separated from it by the narrow valley of the *Isclero*, is a long ridge which extends from *Arpaja* to near Capua. It is of very inferior elevation, but rises boldly and steeply from the plain of Campania, of which it seems to form the natural boundary. The extremity of this ridge nearest to Capua is the MONS TIFATA, so celebrated in the campaigns of Hannibal, from which he so long looked down upon the plains of Campania.

6. At the eastern foot of Mons Taburnus was situated Beneventum, the chief town of the HIRPINI, and which, from its peculiar position, was in a manner the key of the whole district inhabited by that people. It stood in a plain or broad valley formed by the Calor with its tributaries the Sabatus and Tamarus, so that considerable valleys opened up from it in all directions into the mountains. The Calor itself is not only the most considerable of the tributaries of the Vulturnus, but at the point of its junction with that river, about 20 miles below

Beneventum, is little if at all inferior to it in magnitude and volume of waters. The Calor itself rises in the lofty group of mountains between *S. Angelo dei Lombardi* and *Eboli*. This group, which is sometimes designated as *Monte Irpino*, and is the most elevated in this part of the Apennines, sends down its waters to the N. in the Calor and its tributary the Sabatus; while on the E. it gives rise to the Aufidus, which flows into the Adriatic sea, after traversing more than two-thirds of the breadth of Italy; and on the S. the Silarus flows by a much shorter course into the *Gulf of Salerno*. From this point, which forms a kind of knot in the main chain of the Apennines, the mountains sweep round in a semicircle to the NE. and N. till they reach the head waters of the Tamarus, and adjoin the mountains already described in the neighbourhood of *Bojano* and *Campobasso*. In this part of its course the main chain sends down the streams of the *Ufita* and the *Miscano* on the W. to swell the waters of the *Calore*, while on the E. it gives rise to the Cerbalus or *Cervaro*, a stream flowing into the Adriatic.

7. From the *Monte Irpino* towards the E. the whole of the upper valley of the Aufidus was included in Samnium, though the lower part of its course lay through Apulia. The exact limit cannot be fixed,—the confines of the Hirpini towards Apulia on the one side, and Lucania on the other, being, like the boundaries of Samnium in general, almost wholly arbitrary, and not marked by any natural limit. It may be considered, indeed, that in general the mountain country belonged to Samnium, and the lower falls or hills to Apulia; but it is evident that such a distinction is itself often arbitrary and uncertain. In like manner, the rugged mountain chain which extends along the right bank of the Aufidus appears to have been included in Samnium; but the line of demarcation between this and Lucania cannot be determined with accuracy. On the other hand, the detached volcanic mass of Mons Vultur, with the adjacent city of Venusia, was certainly not considered to belong to Samnium.

II. HISTORY.

All ancient writers agree in representing the Samnites as a people of Sabine origin, and not the earliest occupants of the country they inhabited when they first appear in history, but as having migrated thither at a comparatively late period. (Varr. *L. L.* vii. 29; Appian, *Samnit., Fr.* 4, 5; Strab. v. p. 250; Fest. *s. v. Samnites*, p. 326; A. Gell. xi. 1.) This account of their origin is strongly confirmed by the evidence of their name; the Greek form of which, Σαυνῖται, evidently contains the same root as that of Sabini (*Sav*-nitae or *Saf*-nitae, and *Sab*-ini or *Saf*-ini); and there is reason to believe that they themselves used a name still more closely identical. For the Oscan form "Safinim," found on some of the denarii struck by the Italian allies during the Social War, cannot refer to the Sabines usually so called, as that people was long before incorporated with the Romans, and is, in all probability, the Oscan name of the Samnites. (Mommsen, *Unter Ital. Dialekte*, p. 293; Friedländer, *Oskische Münzen*, p. 78.) The adjective form Sabellus was also used indifferently by the Romans as applied to the Sabines and the Samnites. [SABINI.]

The Samnite emigration was, according to Strabo (v. p. 250), one of those sent forth in pursuance of a vow, or what was called a "ver sacrum." It was, as usual, under the special protection of Mars, and was supposed to have been guided by a bull. (Strab. *l. c.*) It is probable from this statement that the emigrants could not have been numerous, and that they established themselves in Samnium rather as conquerors than settlers. The previously existing population was apparently Oscan. Strabo tells us that they established themselves in the land of the Oscans (*l. c.*); and this explains the circumstance that throughout the Samnite territory the language spoken was Oscan. (Liv. x. 20.) But the Oscans themselves were undoubtedly a cognate tribe with the Sabines [ITALIA]; and whatever may have been the circumstances of the conquest (concerning which we have no information), it seems certain that at an early period both branches of the population had completely coalesced into one people under the name of the Samnites.

The period at which the first emigration of the Samnites took place is wholly unknown; but it is probable that they had not been long in possession of their mountainous and inland abodes before they began to feel the necessity of extending their dominion over the more fertile regions that surrounded them. Their first movements for this purpose were probably those by which they occupied the hilly but fertile tract of the Frentani on the shores of the Adriatic, and the land of the Hirpini on the S. Both these nations are generally admitted to be of Samnite origin. The Frentani, indeed, were sometimes reckoned to belong to the Samnite nation, though they appear to have had no political union with them [FRENTANI]: the Hirpini, on the contrary, were generally regarded as one of the component parts of the Samnite nation; but they appear to have been originally a separate colony, and the story told by Strabo and others of their deriving their name from the wolf that had been their leader, evidently points to their having been the result of a separate and subsequent migration. (Strab. v. p. 250; Serv. *ad Aen.* xi. 785.) The period of this is, however, as uncertain as that of the first settlement of the other Samnites: it is not till they began to spread themselves still further both towards the S. and W., and press upon their neighbours in Lucania and Campania, that the light of history begins to dawn upon their movements. Even then their chronology is not clearly fixed; but the conquest and occupation of Campania may be placed from about B.C. 440 to B.C. 420, and was certainly completed by the last of these dates. [CAMPANIA.] That of Lucania must probably be placed somewhat later; but whatever were the causes which were at this time urging the movements of the Sabellian tribes towards the S., they seem to have continued steadily in operation; and within less than half a century (B.C. 410—360) the Samnites spread themselves through the whole of Lucania, and almost to the southern extremity of Italy. [LUCANIA.] The subsequent fortunes of these conquering races, and their contests with the cities of Magna Graecia, do not belong to our present subject, for the Lucanians seem to have early broken off all political connection with their parent nation, the Samnites, just as the latter had done with their Sabine ancestors. This laxity in their political ties, and want of a common bond of union, seems to have been in great measure characteristic of the Sabellian races, and was one of the causes which undoubtedly paved the way for their final subjection under the Roman yoke. But the Samnites seem to have retained possession, down to a much later period, of the tract of country from the Silarus to the Sarnus, which was subsequently occupied by the Picentini. (Scylax, p. 3. § 11; Niebuhr, vol. i. p. 94.) They certainly were still in possession of this district in the Second Samnite War; and it is probable that it was not till the close of their long struggles with Rome that it was wrested from them, when the Romans transplanted thither a colony of Picentines, and thus finally cut off the Samnites from the sea. On the side of Apulia the progress of the Samnites was less definite; and it does not appear that they established themselves in the permanent possession of any part of that country, though they were certainly pressing hard upon its frontier cities; and it was probably the sense of this and the fear of the Samnite arms that induced the Apulians early to court the alliance of Rome. [APULIA.]

The Samnite nation, when it first appears in Roman history, seems to have consisted of four different tribes or cantons. Of these the PENTRI and the HIRPINI were much the most powerful; so much so indeed that it is difficult to understand how such petty tribes as the CARACENI and CAUDINI could rank on terms of equality with them. The FRENTANI are frequently considered as forming a fifth canton; but though that people were certainly of Samnite race, and must have been regarded by Scylax as forming an integral part of the Samnite nation, as he describes the Samnites as occupying a considerable part of the coast of the Adriatic (Peripl. p. 5. § 15), they seem to have already ceased to form a part of their political body at the time when they first came into contact with Rome. [FRENTANI.] We have no account of the nature and character of the political constitution that bound together these different tribes. It seems to have been a mere federal league, the bonds of which were drawn closer together in time of war, when a supreme general or commander-in-chief was chosen to preside over the forces of the whole confederacy, with the title of Embratur, the Sabellian form corresponding to the Latin Imperator. (Liv. ix. 1; Niebuhr, vol. i. p. 107.) But we find no mention, even on occasions of the greatest emergency, of any regular council or deliberative assembly to direct the policy of the nation; and the story told by Livy of the manner in which Herennius Pontius was consulted in regard to the fate of the Roman army at the Caudine Forks seems to negative the supposition that any such body could have existed. (Liv. ix. 3; see also viii. 39.)

The first mention of the Samnites in Roman history, is in B. C. 354, when we are told that they concluded a treaty of alliance with the republic, the progress of whose arms was already beginning to attract their attention (Liv. vii. 19; Diod. xvi. 45). It is probable that the Samnites, who were already masters of Aesernia and the upper valley of the Vulturnus, were at this time pushing forward their arms down the course of that valley, and across the mountain country from thence to the Liris, then occupied by the Volscians, Auruncans, and other tribes, of Ausonian or Oscan origin. It was not long before these onward movements brought them into collision with the Romans, notwithstanding their recent alliance. Among the minor tribes in this part of Italy were the Sidicini, who, though situated on the very borders of Campania, had hitherto preserved their independence, and were not included in the Campanian people [SIDICINI]. This petty people having been assailed by the Samnites, upon

what cause or pretext we know not, and finding themselves unable to cope with such powerful neighbours, invoked the assistance of the Campanians. The latter, notwithstanding their connection with the Samnites, readily espoused the cause of the Sidicini, but it was only to bring the danger upon their own heads; for the Samnites now turned their arms against the Campanians, and after occupying with a strong force the ridge of Mount Tifata, which immediately overlooks Capua, they descended into the plain, defeated the Campanians in a pitched battle at the very gates of Capua, and shut them up within the walls of the city (Liv. vii. 29). In this extremity the Campanians in their turn applied for assistance to Rome, and the senate, after some hesitation on account of their recent alliance with the Samnites, granted it (Ib. 30, 31). Thus began the First Samnite War (B. C. 343), the commencement of that long struggle which was eventually to decide whether the supremacy of Italy was to rest with the Romans or the Samnites.

This first contest was, however, of short duration. In the first campaign the two consuls M. Valerius Corvus and A. Cornelius Cossus gained two decisive victories; the one at the foot of Mount Gaurus, the other near Saticula. The first of these, as Niebuhr observes (vol. iii. p. 119), was of especial importance; it was the first trial of arms between the two rival nations, and might be taken as a sort of omen of the ultimate issue of the contest. A third battle near Suessula, where the remains of the army that had been defeated at Mount Gaurus, after having been reinforced, again attacked Valerius, terminated in an equally decisive victory of the Romans; and both consuls triumphed over the Samnites (Liv. vii. 32—38; Fast. Capit.). The next year the military operations of the Romans were checked by a mutiny of their own army, of which the commons at Rome took advantage; and the city was divided by dissensions. These causes, as well as the increasing disaffection of the Latins, naturally disposed the Romans to peace, and a treaty was concluded with the Samnites in the following year, B. C. 341. The account which represents that people as humiliated and suing for peace, is sufficiently refuted by the fact that the Romans abandoned the Sidicini to their fate, and left the Samnites free to carry out their aggressive designs against that unfortunate people (Liv. viii. 1, 2).

The peace which terminated the First Samnite War renewed the alliance previously existing between the Romans and the Samnites. In consequence of this the latter took part in the great war with the Latins and Campanians, which almost immediately followed, not as the enemies, but as the allies, of Rome; and the Roman armies were thus enabled to reach Campania by the circuitous route through the country of the Marsi and Peligni, and down the valley of the Vulturnus (Liv. viii. 6). During the fifteen years that followed, down to the renewal of the contest between Rome and Samnium, the course of events was almost uniformly favourable to the former power. The successful termination of tho war with the Latins and Campanians, and the consolidation of the Roman power in both those countries had added greatly to the strength of the republic; and the latter had followed up this advantage by the reduction of several of the smaller independent tribes in the same neighbourhood — the Ausones, Sidicini, and the Privernates, who appear on this occasion as independent of, and separate from, the other Volscians [PRIVERNUM]. But the power of the Volscians seems to have been by this time very much broken up; and it was apparently during this interval that the Samnites on their side carried on successful hostilities against that people, and wrested from them or destroyed the cities of Sora and Fregellae in the valley of the Liris, while they threatened Fabrateria with the same fate (Liv. viii. 19, 23, x. 1). This movement, however, gave umbrage to the Romans, while the Samnites on their side could not view with indifference the reduction of the Sidicini, and it was evident that a fresh rupture between the two nations could not be long delayed (Id. viii. 17, 19). The attention of the Samnites was, however, drawn off for a time by the danger that threatened them from another quarter, and they joined with their kinsmen the Lucanians to oppose the arms of Alexander, king of Epirus, who was advancing from Paestum into the heart of the country. Both Samnites and Lucanians were defeated by him in a pitched battle; but he subsequently turned his arms towards the south, and his death in B. C. 326 relieved the Samnites from all apprehension in that quarter. (Liv. viii. 17, 24.)

The same year (B. C. 326) witnessed the outbreak of the Second Samnite War. The immediate occasion of this was the assistance furnished by the Samnites to the Greek cities of Palaepolis and Neapolis, against which the Romans had declared war, when the Samnites and Nolans (who were at this time in alliance with Samnium) threw into their cities a strong body of auxiliaries as a garrison. They did not, however, avert the fall of Palaepolis; while Neapolis escaped a similar fate, only by espousing the alliance of Rome, to which it ever after steadily adhered (Liv. viii. 22—26). The Romans had about the same time secured a more important alliance in another quarter; the Lucanians and Apulians, with whom, as Livy remarks, the republic had previously had no relations, either friendly or hostile, now concluded an alliance with Rome (Ib. 25). The Lucanians indeed were soon persuaded by the Tarentines to abandon it again (Ib. 27), but the Apulians continued steadfast; and though it is evident that the whole nation was not united, and that many of the chief towns took part with the Samnites, while others continued to side with Rome, yet such a diversion must have been of the greatest consequence. Hence throughout the war we find the contest divided into two portions, the Romans on the one side being engaged with the Samnites on the frontiers of Campania, and in the valley of the Vulturnus, from whence they gradually pushed on into the heart of Samnium; and on the other carrying on the war in Apulia, in support of their allies in that country, against the hostile cities supported by the Samnites. It is evident that the Frentani must have at this time already separated themselves from the Samnite alliance, otherwise it would have been impossible for the Romans to march their armies, as we find them repeatedly doing, along the coast of the Adriatic into Apulia. (Liv. ix. 2, 13.)

The first operations of the war were unimportant; the Romans conquered some small towns in the valley of the Vulturnus (Liv. viii. 25); and we are told that Q. Fabius and L. Papirius gained repeated victories over the Samnites, so that they even sued for peace, but obtained only a truce for a year, and, without observing even this, resumed the contest with increased forces. (Ib. 30, 36, 37.) It is evident therefore that no real impression had been made

upon their power. Nor did the victory of A. Cornelius Arvina in the following year (B. C. 322), though it again induced them to sue for peace without success, produce any permanent effect; for the very next year (B. C. 321) the Samnites under the command of C. Pontius were not only able to take the field with a large army, but inflicted on the Romans one of the severest blows they had ever sustained in the celebrated pass of the Caudine Forks. [CAUDIUM.] There can be little doubt that the circumstances and character of that disaster are greatly disguised in the accounts transmitted to us; but, whatever may have been its true nature, it is certain that it caused no material interruption of the Roman arms, and that, after repudiating the treaty or capitulation concluded by the consuls, the Romans renewed the contest with undiminished vigour. It is impossible here to follow in detail the operations of the succeeding campaigns, which were continued for seventeen years with many fluctuations of fortune. The disaster at Caudium shook the faith of many of the Roman allies, and was followed by the defection even of their own colonies of Satricum, Fregellae, and Sora. Some years later (B. C. 315) the capture of Saticula by the Romans and of Plistia by the Samnites shows that both armies were still engaged on the very frontiers of Samnium; while the advance of the Samnites to the pass of Lautulae, and the victory which they there a second time obtained over the Romans (Liv. ix. 22, 23; Diod. xix. 72), once more gave a shock to the power of the latter, and for a moment endangered their supremacy in Campania. But they speedily recovered the advantage, and the victory gained by them at a place called Cinna (of uncertain site) decided the submission of the revolted Campanians. (Liv. ix. 27; Diod. xix. 76.) Their arms had meanwhile been successful in Apulia, and had ultimately effected the reduction of the whole province, so that in B. C. 316 the consul Q. Aemilius Barbula was able to carry the war into Lucania, where he took the town of Nerulum. (Liv. ix. 20.) The decisive victory of the consuls of B. C. 314 had also for the first time opened the way into the heart of Samnium, and they laid siege to Bovianum, the capital of the Pentri. The next year was marked by the fall of Nola, followed by that of Atina and Calatia (Cajazzo): and it seemed probable that the war was at length drawing to a close in favour of the Romans, when the outbreak of a fresh war with the Etruscans in B. C. 311 divided the attention of that people, and, by occupying a large part of their forces in another quarter, operated a powerful diversion in favour of the Samnites. To these additional enemies were added the Umbrians as well as the Marsi and Peligni; yet the Romans not only made head against all these nations, but at the same time carried their victorious arms into the heart of Samnium. Bovianum, the capital city of the Pentri, was twice taken and plundered, once in 311 by C. Junius, and again in 305 by T. Minucius. At the same time Sora and Arpinum were finally added to the Roman dominion. These successive defeats at length compelled the Samnites to sue for peace, which was granted them in B. C. 304; but on what terms is very uncertain. It seems impossible to believe that the Romans, as asserted by Livy, should have restored them their ancient treaty of alliance, and it is probable that they in some form consented to acknowledge the supremacy of Rome. (Liv. ix. 45; Dionys. Exc. p. 2331; Niebuhr, vol. iii. p. 259.)

But the peace thus concluded was of short duration. Little more than five years elapsed between
the close of the Second Samnite War and the commencement of the Third. It might well have been
thought that, after a struggle of more than twenty
years' duration, the resources of the Samnites, if not
their spirit, would have been exhausted; but they
seem to have been actively engaged, even before the
actual outbreak of hostilities, in organising a fresh
coalition against Rome. A new and formidable
auxiliary had appeared in a large body of Gauls,
which had recently crossed the Alps, and, uniting
with their countrymen the Senones, threatened the
Romans from the N. Rome was at this time engaged in war with the Etruscans and Umbrians,
and the Etruscans hastened to secure the services of
the Gauls. Meanwhile the Samnites, deeming the
attention of the Romans sufficiently engaged elsewhere, attacked their neighbours the Lucanians,
probably with the view of restoring the power in
that country of the party favourable to the Samnite
alliance. The opposite party, however, called in
the Romans to their assistance, who declared war
against the Samnites, and thus began the Third
Samnite War, B. C. 298. (Liv. x. 11.) The
contest had now assumed larger dimensions; the
Samnites concluded a league with the Etruscans,
Umbrians, and Gauls, and for several successive campaigns the operations in Samnium were subordinate
to those in the valley of the Tiber. But the territory of Samnium itself was at the same time ravaged
by the Roman generals in so systematic a manner,
that it is clear they had obtained a decided superiority in the field; and though the Samnites on one
occasion retaliated by laying waste the Campanian
and Falernian plains, they were soon again driven
back to their mountain fastnesses. (Liv. x. 15, 17,
20.) At length, in B. C. 295, the great battle of
Sentinum, in which the united forces of the Gauls and
Samnites were totally defeated by the Roman consul
Q. Fabius, decided the fortune of the war. Gellius
Egnatius, the Samnite general, who had been the
main organiser of the confederacy, was slain, and the
league itself virtually broken up. (Liv. x. 27—30.)
Nevertheless the Samnites continued to carry on the
war with unabated energy; and in B. C. 293 they
raised a fresh army of 40,000 men, levied with
solemn sacred rites, and arrayed in a peculiar garb.
These circumstances sufficiently prove the importance which they attached to this campaign, yet its
result was not more successful than those which
had preceded it, and the Samnite armies were again
defeated by the consuls L. Papirius Cursor and Sp.
Carvilius in two successive battles near Aquilonia
and Cominium. (Liv. x. 38—45.) The operations of the subsequent campaigns are imperfectly
known to us, from the loss of the books of Livy in
which they were related: but the next year (B. C.
292) C. Pontius, the victor of the Caudine Forks,
reappears, after a long interval, at the head of the
Samnite armies; he defeated Q. Fabius, but was in
his turn defeated in a far more decisive engagement,
in which it is said that 20,000 Samnites were slain,
and 4000 taken prisoners, including C. Pontius
himself, who was led in triumph by Fabius, and then
put to death. (Oros. iii. 22; Liv. Epit. xi.) It is
probable that this battle gave the final blow to the
Samnite power, yet their resistance was still prolonged for two years more; and it was not till B. C.
290 that they consented to lay down their arms
and sue for peace. Even in that year the consul

M'. Curius Dentatus could still earn the honour of
a triumph, and the fame of having put an end to
the Samnite wars after they had lasted for more
than fifty years. (Liv. Epit. xi.; Eutrop. ii. 9.)

The conclusion of the Third Samnite War is regarded by some of the Roman historians as the close
of the struggle between Rome and Samnium, and
not without reason, for though the name of the
Fourth Samnite War is given by modern writers to
the war that broke out afresh in B. C. 282, the
Samnites on that occasion certainly figure rather as
auxiliaries than as principals. They, however, joined
the league which was formed at the instigation of
the Tarentines against Rome; and bore a part in
all the subsequent operations of the war. They
seem indeed to have at first looked with jealousy or
suspicion upon the proceedings of Pyrrhus; and it
was not till after the battle of Heraclea that they
sent their contingent to his support. (Plut. Pyrrh.
17.) But in the great battle at Asculum the following year (B. C. 278) the Samnites bore an important part, and seem to have sustained their
ancient reputation for valour. (Dionys. xx. Fr.
Didot.) The departure of Pyrrhus for Sicily
shortly after, and his final defeat by M'. Curius at
Beneventum after his return (B. C. 274), left the
Samnites and their allies to bear the whole brunt
of the war, and they were wholly unable to contend with the power of Rome. We know nothing
in detail of these last campaigns: we learn only
that in B. C. 272, just before the fall of Tarentum,
the Samnites, as well as their allies the Lucanians
and Bruttians, made their final and absolute submission; and the consul Sp. Carvilius celebrated the
last of the long series of triumphs over the Samnites.
(Zonar. viii. 6; Liv. Epit. xiv.; Fast. Capit.) A fresh
revolt indeed broke out in the N. of Samnium three
years afterwards, among the petty tribe of the Caraceni, but was speedily suppressed, before it had attained any more formidable character. (Zonar.
viii. 7; Dionys. xx. 9, Fr. Mai.)

We have no account of the terms on which the
Samnites were received to submission by the Romans,
or of their condition as subjects of the republic. But
there can be no doubt that the policy of the dominant people was to break up as much as possible
their national organisation and all bonds of union
between them. At the same time two colonies were
established as fortresses to keep them in check: one
at Beneventum, in the country of the Hirpini (B. C.
268), and the other at Aesernia, in the valley of the
Vulturnus (B. C. 264). All these precautions, however, did not suffice to secure the fidelity of the
Samnites during the Second Punic War. After
the battle of Cannae (B. C. 216), the Hirpini were
among the first to declare themselves in favour of
Hannibal, and their example is said to have been
followed by all the Samnites, except the Pentriani.
(Liv. xxii. 61.) It is singular that this tribe, long
the most powerful and warlike of all, should have
thus held aloof; but the statement of Livy is confirmed by the subsequent course of the war, during
which the Pentrians never seem to have taken any
part, while the land of the Hirpini, and the southern
portions of Samnium bordering on Lucania, were
frequently the scene of hostilities. But the Roman
colonies Aesernia and Beneventum never fell into
the hands of the Carthaginians; and the latter was
through a great part of the war held by one of the
Roman generals, as a post of the utmost military
importance. In B. C. 214 and again in B. C. 212,

the land of the Hirpini was still in the hands of the Carthaginians, and became the scene of the operations of Hannibal's lieutenant Hanno against Sempronius Gracchus. It was not till B.C. 209 that, Hannibal having been finally compelled to relinquish his hold upon Central Italy, the Hirpini (and apparently the other revolted Samnites also) renewed their submission to Rome. (Liv. xxvii. 15.)

From this time we hear no more of the Samnites in history till the great outbreak of the Italian nations, commonly known as the Social War, B.C. 90, in which they once more took a prominent part. They were not indeed among the first to take up arms, but quickly followed the example of the Picentes and Marsi; and so important an element did they constitute of the confederation, that of the two consuls chosen as the leaders of the allies, one was a Samnite, Caius Papius Mutilus. (Diod. xxxvii. 2. p. 539.) Besides Papius, several of the most distinguished of the Italian generals, Marius Egnatius, Pontius Telesinus, and Trebatius, were also of Samnite origin; and after the fall of Corfinium, the seat of government and head-quarters of the allies was transferred to the Samnite town of Bovianum, and from thence subsequently to Aesernia. The Samnites indeed suffered severely in the second campaign of the war, being attacked by Sulla, who defeated Papius Mutilus, took Aeculanum and Bovianum by assault, and reduced the Hirpini to submission. The other Samnites, however, still held out, and an army which had thrown itself into Nola was able to prolong its resistance against all the efforts of Sulla. Hence at the end of the second year of the war (B.C. 89), when all the other nations of Italy had successively submitted and been admitted to the Roman franchise, the Samnites and Lucanians were still unsubdued, and maintained a kind of guerilla warfare in their mountains, while the strong fortress of Nola enabled them still to maintain their footing in Campania. (Vell. Pat. ii. 17; Liv. Epit. lxxx; Diod. xxxvii. 2. p. 540; Appian, B.C. i. 53.) In this state of things the civil war which broke out between Sulla and Marius altered the nature of the contest. The Samnites warmly espoused the Marian cause, from a natural feeling of enmity towards Sulla, from whose arms they had recently suffered so severely; and so important was the share they took in the struggle that ensued after the return of Sulla to Italy (B.C. 83), that they in some measure imparted to what was otherwise a mere civil war, the character of a national contest. A large number of them served in the army of the younger Marius, which was defeated by Sulla at Sacriportus (Appian, B.C. i. 87); and shortly afterwards an army, composed principally of Samnites and Lucanians, under the command of C. Pontius Telesinus, made a desperate attempt to relieve Praeneste by marching suddenly upon Rome. They were met by the army of Sulla at the very gates of the city, and the battle at the Colline gate (Nov. 1, B.C. 82), though it terminated in the complete victory of Sulla, was long remembered as one of the greatest dangers to which Rome had ever been exposed. (Vell. Pat. ii. 27; Appian, B.C. i. 93; Plut. Sull. 28; Lucan, ii. 135—138.) Pontius Telesinus fell in the field, and Sulla displayed his implacable hatred towards the Samnites by putting to the sword, without mercy, 8000 prisoners who had been taken in the battle. (Appian, l.c.; Strab. v. 249; Plut. Sull. 30.) He had already put to death all the Samnites whom he had taken prisoners at the

battle of Sacriportus, alleging that they were the eternal enemies of the Roman name; and he now followed up this declaration by a systematic devastation of their country, carried on with the express purpose of extirpating the whole nation. (Strab. l.c.) It can hardly be believed that he fully carried out this sanguinary resolution, but we learn from Strabo that more than a century afterwards the province was still in a state of the utmost desolation,—many of what had once been flourishing cities being reduced to the condition of mere villages, while others had altogether ceased to exist. (Strab. l.c.)

Nor is it probable that the province ever really recovered from this state of depression. The rhetorical expressions of Florus point to its being in his day still in a state of almost complete desolation. (Flor. i. 16. § 8.) Some attempts seem indeed to have been made under the Roman Empire to recruit its population with fresh colonists, especially by Nero, who founded colonies at Saepinum, Telesia, and Aesernia (Lib. Colon. pp. 259, 260, &c.); but none of these attained to any great prosperity, and the whole region seems to have been very thinly populated and given up chiefly to pasturage. Beneventum alone retained its importance, and continued to be a flourishing city throughout the period of the Roman Empire. In the division of Italy under Augustus the land of the Hirpini was separated from the rest of Samnium, and was placed in the Second Region with Apulia and Calabria, while the rest of the Samnites were included in the Fourth Region, together with the Sabines, Frentani, Peligni, &c. (Plin. iii. 11. s. 16, 12. s. 17.) At a later period this district was broken up, and Samnium with the land of the Frentani constituted a separate province. This is the arrangement which we find in the Notitia, and it was probably introduced at an earlier period, as the Liber Coloniarum in one part gives under a separate head the "Civitates Regionis Samnii," including under that name the towns of the Peligni, as well as the Frentani. (Notit. Dign. ii. pp. 9, 10; Lib. Colon. p. 259.) In another part of the same document, which is undoubtedly derived from different sources, the Samnite towns are classed under the head of Campania; but this union, if it ever really subsisted, could have been but of very brief duration. The "Provincia Samnii" is repeatedly mentioned in inscriptions of the 4th century, and was governed by an officer styled "Praeses." (Mommsen, Die Lib. Col. p. 206.) The same appellation continued in use after the fall of the Roman Empire, and the name of Samnium as a separate province is found both in Cassiodorus and Paulus Diaconus. (Cassiod. Var. xi. 36; P. Diac. Hist. Lang. ii. 20.) The only towns in it that retained any consideration in the time of the last writer were Aufidena, Aesernia, and Beneventum. The last of these cities became under the Lombards the capital of an independent and powerful duchy, which long survived the fall of the Lombard kingdom in the N. of Italy. But in the revolutions of the middle ages all trace of the name and ancient limits of Samnium was lost. At the present day the name of Sannio is indeed given to a province of the kingdom of Naples; but this is merely an official designation, recently restored, to the district, which had previously been called the Contado di Molise. This and the adjoining province of the Principato Ultra comprise the greater part of the ancient Samnium; but the modern boundaries have no reference to the ancient divisions, and a considerable portion of the Samnite territory is included in the *Terra di Lavoro*, while a corner in the NW. is assigned to the *Abruzzi*.

Of the national character of the Samnites we learn little more than that they were extremely brave and warlike, and had inherited to a great degree the frugal and simple habits of their ancestors the Sabines. We find also indications that they retained the strong religious or superstitious feelings of the Sabines, of which a striking instance is given by Livy in the rites and ceremonies with which they consecrated the troops that they levied in B. C. 293. (Liv. x. 38.) But they had almost ceased to exist as a nation in the days of the Latin poets and writers that are preserved to us; and hence we cannot wonder that their name is seldom alluded to. They are said to have dwelt for the most part, like the Sabines, in open villages; but it is evident, from the accounts of their earliest wars with the Romans, that they possessed towns, and some of them, at least, strongly fortified. This is confirmed by the remains of walls of a very ancient style of construction, which are still preserved at Aesernia and Bovianum, and still more remarkably at Aufidena. (Abeken, *Mittel Italien*, pp. 142, 148.) But from the very nature of their country the Samnites must always have been, to a great extent, a rude and pastoral people, and had probably received only a faint tinge of civilisation, through their intercourse with the Campanians and Apulians.

III. TOPOGRAPHY.

The rivers of the Samnite territory have been already noticed in connection with the mountain chains and groups in which they take their rise. From the purely inland character of the region, none of these rivers, with the exception of the Calor and its tributaries, belong wholly to Samnium, but traverse the territories of other nations before they reach the sea. Thus the Sagrus and Trinius, after quitting the mountains of Samnium, flow through the land of the Frentani to the Adriatic; the Tifernus separates the territory of that people from Apulia, while the Frento and the Aufidus traverse the plains of Apulia. On the other side of the central chain the Vulturnus, with its affluent the Calor, and the tributaries of the latter, the Sabatus and Tamarus, carry down the whole of the waters of the Apennines of Samnium, which flow to the Tyrrhenian sea.

The topography of Samnium is the most obscure and confused of any part of Italy. The reason of this is obvious. From the continued wars which had devastated the country; and the state of desolation to which it was reduced in the time of the geographers, only a few towns had survived, at least in such a state as to be deemed worthy of notice by them; and many of the names mentioned by Livy and other authors during the early wars of the Romans with the Samnites never reappear at a later period. It is indeed probable that some of these were scarcely towns in the stricter sense of the term, but merely fortified villages or strongholds, in which the inhabitants collected their cattle and property in time of war. Those which are mentioned by the geographers as still existing under the Roman Empire, or the site of which is clearly indicated, may be briefly enumerated. AUFIDENA, in the upper valley of the Sagrus, is the only town that can be assigned with any certainty to the Caraceni. In the upper valley of the Vulturnus was AESERNIA, the terri-

tory of which bordered on that of Venafrum in Campania. At the northern foot of the *Monte Matese* was BOVIANUM; and in the mountain tract between it and the Frentani was TREVENTUM or TEREVENTUM (*Trivento*). SE. of Bovianum lay SAEPINUM, the ruins of which are still visible near *Sepino*; and at the southern foot of the *Monte Matese*, in the valley of the Calor, was TELESIA. ALLIFAE lay to the NW. of this, in the valley of the Vulturnus, and at the foot of the *Matese* in that direction. In the country of the Hirpini were BENEVENTUM, the capital of the whole district; AECULANUM, near *Mirabella*, about 15 miles to the SW.; EQUUS TUTICUS, near the frontiers of Apulia; AQUILONIA, at *Lacedogna*, on the same frontier; ABELLINUM, near the frontiers of Campania; and COMPSA, near the sources of the Aufidus, bordering on Lucania, so that it is assigned by Ptolemy to that country. On the borders of Campania, between Beneventum and the plains, were Caudium, apparently once the capital of the Caudine tribe; and SATICULA, the precise site of which has not been determined, but which must have been situated in the neighbourhood of Mount Tifata. The Samnite CALATIA, on the other hand, was situated N. of the Vulturnus, at *Cajazzo*; and COMPULTERIA, also a Samnite city, was in the same neighbourhood. The group of hills on the right bank of the Vulturnus, extending from that river towards the Via Latina, must therefore have been included in Samnium; but Teanum and Cales, situated on that highroad, were certainly both of them Campanian towns. It is probable, however, that in early times the limits between Campania and Samnium were subject to many fluctuations; and Strabo seems to regard them as imperfectly fixed even in his day. (Strab. v. p. 249.)

Of the minor towns of Samnium, or those which are mentioned only in history, may be noticed: DURONIA (Liv. x. 39), identified, but on very slight grounds, with *Civita Vecchia*, N. of *Bojano*; MURGANTIA (Liv. x. 17), supposed to be *Baselice*, on the frontiers of Apulia, near the sources of the Frento (*Fortore*); ROMULEA, on the frontiers of Apulia, between Aeculanum and Aquilonia; TRIVICUM, in the same neighbourhood, still called *Trevico*; PLISTIA, near *Sta Agata dei Goti*, on the frontiers of Campania; CALLIFAE and RUFRIUM, both of them mentioned by Livy (viii. 25) in connection with Allifae, and probably situated in the neighbourhood of that city; COMINIUM (Liv. x. 39, 44), of very uncertain site; AQUILONIA (Liv. l. c.), also of uncertain site, but which must be distinguished from the city of the same name in the country of the Hirpini; Maronea, noticed by Livy in the Second Punic War, when it was recovered by Marcellus, in B. C. 210 (Liv. xxvii. 1); MELAE, Fulfulae, and Orbitanium, all of which are noticed on only one occasion (Liv. xxiv. 20), and the sites of which are wholly undetermined.* To these must be added Cluvia, Cimetra, Volana, Palumbinum, and Herculaneum, all of them mentioned as towns taken from the Samnites (Liv. ix. 31, x. 15, 45), but of which nothing more is known; Imbrinium (Liv. viii. 30), where Fabius gained a victory over the Samnites in B. C. 325; Cinna, which is repre-

---

* It has been thought unnecessary to repeat in these and other similar cases the modern sites assigned by Italian or German topographers, where these rest on no other foundation than mere conjecture.

sented by Diodorus as the scene of the decisive victory in B. C. 314 (Diod. xix. 76); and several places of which the names are found only in Virgil and Silius Italicus,—MUCRAE, RUFRAE, BATULUM, and CELENNA (Virg. Aen. vii. 739; Sil. Ital. viii. 564), which seem to have been situated on the borders of Campania, so that it is doubtful to which country they are to be assigned. The minor towns of the Hirpini have been already discussed in that article; Pauna, or Panna, a name found in Strabo (v. p. 250) as that of a place still existing in his time, is probably corrupt, but we are wholly at a loss what to substitute. On the other hand, inscriptions attest the existence under the Roman Empire of a town called Juvavium, or Juvanum, of municipal rank, which is not mentioned by any of the geographers, but is probably the one meant by the Liber Coloniarum, which notices the "Iobanus ager" among the "civitates Samnii." (Lib. Col. p. 260.) It was probably situated in the neighbourhood of Sta Maria di Palazzo, a few miles N. of the Sagrus, and on the very frontiers of the Marrucini. (Mommsen, Inscr. R. N. p. 271.) The existence of a town named Tifernum is very doubtful [TIFERNUS]; and that of a city of the name of Samnium, though adopted by many local writers (Romanelli, vol. ii. p. 490), certainly rests on no adequate authority.

Samnium was traversed in ancient times by several lines of highway. One of these, following nearly the same line with the modern road from Naples to Aquila, proceeded up the valley of the Vulturnus from Venafrum to Aesernia, thence crossed the mountain ridge to Aufidena in the valley of the Sagrus, and from thence again over another mountain pass to Sulmo in the land of the Peligni. Another branch led from Aesernia to Bovianum, and from thence to Equus Tuticus, where it joined the Via Appia or Trajana. A third followed the valley of the Vulturnus from Aesernia to Allifae, and thence by Telesia to Beneventum. There seems also to have been a cross line from the latter place by Saepinum to Bovianum. (Itin. Ant. p. 102; Tab. Peut.) But these different lines are very confusedly laid down in the Tabula, and the distances given are often either corrupt or erroneous. The course of the Via Appia, and its branch called the Via Trajana, through the land of the Hirpini, has been already noticed in that article. [See also VIA APPIA.]   [E. H. B.]

SAMO'NIUM, SAMMO'NIUM, SALMO'NIUM, SALMO'NE PROM. (Σαμώνιον, Σαλμώνιον, Strab. ii. p. 106, x. pp. 474, 475, 478, 489; Σαλμώνη, Acts, xxvii. 7; comp. Ptol. iii. 15. § 5; Pomp. Mela, ii. 7. § 12; Plin. iv. 20. s. 21; Stadiasm. § 318: Eth. Σαλμώνιος, Σαλμώνις, Apoll. Rhod. iv. 1693; Dionys. Per. 110; Inscrip. ap. Böckh, Corpus, vol. ii. p. 409), the E. promontory of Crete, to which the seamen of the Alexandrian vessel which conveyed Paul to Rome, thinking they could pursue their voyage under the lee of the island, ran down. (Acts, l. c.) Much difference of opinion has been entertained relative to the identification of this celebrated foreland, the position of which would seem to be incontrovertibly ascertained by the existence of the modern name C. Salomon. (Comp. Höck, Kreta, vol. i. p. 427.) But though the name is certainly in favour of this site, the statements of the ancients as to its position, and of the seven islets or rocks which surround it, determine conclusively that it must be C. S. Sidero. It is true that by the recent Admiralty survey it is not

quite so far to the E. as C. Salomon (the difference is, however, only a few seconds of longitude); but by its extreme extension from the mainland it would be considered as the principal promontory at this end of the island, and known as the "E. foreland." (Comp. Museum of Class. Antiquities, vol. ii. p. 302.)   [E. B. J.]

SAMOS or SAMUS (Σάμος: Eth. and Adj. Σάμιος, Samius, Σαμαῖος, Σαμιακὸς in Steph.: Σαμιώτης in the language of the modern Greeks, who call the island Samo, Σάμω: the Turks call it Susam Adassi), a large island in that part of the Aegaean which is called the Icarian sea, and the most important of the Sporades next after Rhodes. The word denotes a height, especially by the sea-shore. (See Const. Porphyrog. de Them. 16. p. 41, ed. Bonn.) Hence SAMOTHRACIA, or the Thracian Samos, which is said by Pausanias (vii. 4. § 3) to have been colonised and named by certain fugitives from the Icarian Samos,—and SAME, one of the names of Cephalonia, which is inversely connected with it by one of Strabo's conjectures (x. p. 457). How applicable the idea of elevation is to the island before us may be seen in the narratives and views given by Dr. Clarke (Travels, vol. ii. p. 192, vol. iii. p. 366), who uses the strongest language in describing the conspicuous height of Samos above the surrounding islands.

The following earlier names of Samos are mentioned by Pliny (v. 37) and other writers, — Parthenia, Anthemus, Melamphylus, Drynsa and Cyparissia. Some of these have evidently arisen from the physical characteristics of the island. Samos was, and is, well-wooded. It is intersected from E. to W. by a chain of mountains, which is in fact a continuation of the range of Mycale, being separated from it only by the narrow channel, hardly a mile in breadth, which the Turks call the Little Boghaz. Here was fought the decisive victory against the Persians, B. C. 479. The Great Boghaz, which is nearly 10 miles in breadth, separates the other extremity of Samos from the comparatively low island of ICARIA. The length of Samos, from E. to W., is about 25 miles. Its breadth is very variable. Strabo reckons the circuit at 600 stadia, Pliny at 87 miles, though he says that Isidorus makes it 100. These differences may be readily accounted for by omitting or including Port Vathy, which is a wild-looking bay, though a very serviceable harbour, on the north. Here the modern capital is situated: but in ancient times the bay of Vathy seems to have been comparatively deserted—perhaps, as Tournefort suggests, because it was peculiarly exposed to pirates, who infested the straits and bays of an island which lay in the route of commerce between the Bosporus and Egypt. What Tournefort tells us of his travels through Samos gives us the idea of a very rugged, though picturesque and productive, island. (Possibly the Palinurus and Panormus of Samos, mentioned by Livy, xxxvii. 11, may have been in the bay of Vathy.) The highest point, Mount Kerkis, the ancient Cerceteus (Strab. x. p. 488), which is nearly always covered with snow, and reaches the height of 4725 English feet, is towards the west. A ridge, which branches off in a south-easterly direction from the main range, and ends in the promontory of Poseidium, opposite Mycale, was called Ampelus, which name seems also to have been given to the whole mountain-system (Strab. xiv. p. 637). The westernmost extremity of the island, opposite Icaria was anciently called Cantharium. Here the cliffs are very bare and lofty. A landslip, which has taken place in this part of the island, has probably given rise to the name by which it is now called (ἡ καττωβατή).

The position of Samos was nearly opposite the boundary-line of Caria and Ionia; and its early traditions connect it, first with Carians and Leleges, and then with Ionians. The first Ionian colony is said to have consisted of settlers from Epidaurus, who were expelled from thence by the Argives. However this may be, we find Samos at an early period in the position of a powerful member of the Ionic confederacy. At this time it was highly distinguished in maritime enterprise and the science of navigation. Thucydides tells us (i. 13) that the Samians were among the first to make advances in naval construction, and that for this purpose they availed themselves of the services of Ameinocles the Corinthian shipbuilder. The story of Pliny (vii. 57), that either they or Pericles the Athenian first constructed transports for the conveyance of horses, though less entitled to literal acceptance, is well worthy of mention ; and Samos will always be famous for the voyage of her citizen Colaeus, who, "not without divine direction" (Herod. iv. 152), first penetrated through the Pillars of Hercules into the Ocean, and thus not only opened out new fields of commercial enterprise, but enlarged the geographical ideas of the Greeks by making them for the first time familiar with the phenomenon of the tides.

Under the despot Polycrates, Samos was in fact the greatest Greek maritime power. This famous man, about ten years after the taking of Sardis by Cyrus, held Samos in a position of proud independence, when Lesbos and Chios had submitted to the Persians. He had 1000 bowmen in his pay; he possessed 100 ships of war, and made considerable conquests both among the islands and the mainland. He fought successfully against the Milesians and Lesbians, and made a treaty with Amasis, king of Egypt. Whether we are to take the story in the poetical form in which it is presented to us by Herodotus, or to attribute the change to the more probable motive of self-interest, this treaty was broken off for an alliance with Cambyses. In connection with this monarch's expedition to the Nile, some Samian malcontents were so treacherously treated by Polycrates, that they sought and obtained assistance from Greece. A joint force of Lacedaemonians and Corinthians besieged Polycrates in Samos for forty days: but in this struggle also he was successful. At last his own cupidity, acted on by the fraud of Oroetes, a neighbouring satrap, brought him to a wretched death on the mainland. The time which succeeded was full of crime and calamity for Samos. In the end, Syloson, the brother of Polycrates (whose association with Cambyses is the subject of another romantic story in Herodotus), landed with a Persian army on Samos, and became a tributary despot; but not till his native island had been so depopulated as to give rise to the proverb ἕκητι Συλοσῶντος εὐρυχωρίη. For details see the lives of POLYCRATES and SYLOSON in the Dict. of Biography. It was at this period that Pythagoras, who was a native of Samos, left the island to travel in foreign countries, being partly urged to leave his home (according to Plutarch, Placit. i. 3) through discontent under the government of Polycrates, who, however, was a patron of literature, and had Anacreon many years at his court. For the chronology of this period see Clinton, Fast. Hell. vol. ii. note B. pp. 230—232.

Samos was now Persian. It was from Samos that

Datis sailed to Marathon, taking Naxos on his way. But the dominion of the Persians did not last long. When their fleet was gathered at Samos again, after the battle of Salamis, to the number of 400 sail, it was in a great measure the urgency of Samian envoys which induced the commanders of the Greek fleet at Delos to go across to the eastern side of the Aegaean. Then followed that battle in the strait, which completed the liberation of the Greeks.

In the maritime confederacy which was organised soon afterwards under Athenian rule, Samos seems to have been the most powerful of the three islands which were exempted from paying tribute. It was at the instance of her citizens that the common treasure was removed from Delos to Athens. But this friendship with Athens was turned into bitter enmity in consequence of a conflict with Miletus about the territory of Priene. Samos openly revolted; and a large force was despatched from Athens against it under the command of ten generals, two of whom were Sophocles and Pericles. The latter pronounced in the Cerameicus the funeral oration over those who had fallen in the war which, after a resistance of nine months, reduced Samos to complete subjection.

From 439 to 412 Samos remained without fortifications and without a fleet. But about this latter date it became the hinge upon which all the concluding events of the Peloponnesian War really turned. The first movements towards the establishment of an oligarchy at Athens began at Samos through the intrigues of Alcibiades ; and yet this island was practically the home of the Athenian democracy during the struggle which ensued. It was at Samos that Alcibiades rejoined his fellow-citizens ; and from Samos that he finally sailed for the Peiraeus in 407. Even till after the battle of Arginusae Samos was, more than any other place, the headquarters and base of operations for the Athenian fleet.

Our notices of the island now become more fragmentary. After the death of Alexander the Great it was for a time subject to the kings of Egypt. (Polyb. v. 35.) Subsequently, it took the part of Antiochus the Great in his war with Rome. It also acted with Mithridates against Rome; but was finally united with the province of Asia B. C. 84. After the battle of Actium, Augustus passed the winter there. Under the Roman emperors it was on the whole a place of no great importance, though it had the honour of being a free state. (Plin. v. 37.) This privilege was taken away under Vespasian. (Suet. Vesp. 8.) In the division of the Empire contained in the Synecdemus we find it placed with Rhodes, Cos, Chios, &c., in the Province of the Islands. In the later division into themes, it seems to be again raised to a distinguished position. It gave its name to a separate theme, which included a large portion of the mainland, and was divided into the two turms of Ephesus and Adramyttium, the governor having his residence (πραιτώριον) at Smyrna; and this arrangement is spoken of in such a way (Const. Porphyrog. de Them. l. c.) as distinctly to connect it with the ancient renown of Samos.

It would be difficult to follow the fortunes of Samos through the middle ages. (See Finlay's History of the Byzantine and Greek Empires, vol. ii. p. 112.) There are some points of considerable interest in its modern history. In 1550, after being sacked by the Ottomans, it was given by Selim to the Capitan Pacha Ochiali, who introduced colonists from various other places; whence the names of some of the modern villages in the island, *Metelinous*, *Albaniticori*, and *Vourlotes* (*Vourla* giving the name to some islands at the entrance of the bay of Smyrna). Samos was much injured by the ravages of Morosini. In Tournefort's time the largest part of the island was the property of ecclesiastics; and the number of convents and nunneries was considerable. He reckoned the population to be 12,000; now it is estimated at 50,000, nearly the whole being Christian. Samos performed a distinguished part in the War of Independence. The Turks often attempted to effect a landing: the defences constructed by the Samiotes are still visible on the shore; and the Greek fleet watched no point more carefully than this important island. On the 17th of August, 1824, a curious repetition of the battle of Mycale took place. Formidable preparations for a descent on the island were made by Tahir-Pacha, who had 20,000 land-troops encamped on the promontory of Mycale. Canaris set fire to a frigate near Cape Trogillium, and in the confusion which followed the troops fled, and Tahir-Pacha sailed away. At this time the Logothete Lycurgus was τύραννος of the island " in the true classical sense of the word," as is observed by Ross, who describes the castle built by Lycurgus on the ruins of a mediaeval fort, adding that he was then (1841) residing with the rank of Colonel at Athens, and that he was well remembered and much regretted in Samos. This island was assigned to Turkey by the treaty which fixed the limits of modern Greece; but it continued to make struggles for its independence. Since 1835 it has formed a separate Beylick under a Phanariot Greek named Stephen Vogorides, who resides in Constantinople with the title of " Prince of Samos," and sends a governor as his deputy. Besides other rights, the island has a separate flag exhibiting the white Greek cross on a blue ground, with a narrow red stripe to denote dependence on the Porte. It does not appear, however, that this government of Greeks by a Greek for the Sultan is conducive to contentment.

The present inhabitants of this fruitful island are said to be more esteemed for their industry than their honesty. They export silk, wool, wine, oil, and fruits. If the word *Sammet* is derived from this place, it is probable that silk has been an object of its industry for a considerable time. Pliny (xiii. 34) mentions pomegranates among its fruits. At the present day the beans of the carob-tree are exported to Russia, where a cheap spirit for the common people is made from them. We might suppose from the name of Mount Ampelus, that the wine of the island was celebrated in the ancient world; but such a conclusion would be in direct contradiction to the words of Strabo, who notices it as a remarkable fact, that though the wine of the surrounding islands and of the neighbouring parts of the mainland was excellent, that of Samos was inferior. Its grapes, however, under the name of ὁμομηλίδες or ἁμαμηλίδες, are commended by Athenaeus (xiv. p. 653; see Poll. *Onomast.* vi. 11), and now they are one of the most valued parts of its produce. Ross saw these grapes (σταφίδα) drying in large quantities in the sun; and other authorities speak highly of the Malmsey or sweet muscato wine exported in large quantities from Samos. Its marble is abundant; but it has a greater tendency to split into small fragments than that of Pentelicus or Paros. A stone found in the island is

said by Pliny (xxxvi. 40) to have been used for polishing gold. He also mentions in several places (*l. c.*, also xxviii. 53, 77, xxxi. 46, xxxv. 19, 53) the various medicinal properties of its earth. The Samian earthenware was in high repute at Rome (" Samia etiamnum in esculentis laudantur," Plin. xxxv. 46), and the name has been traditionally given by modern writers to the " red lustrous pottery " made by the Romans themselves for domestic use. (See Marryatt's *Pottery and Porcelain*, London 1850, pp. 286, 290.) For the natural Flora and Fauna of the island we must be content to refer to Tournefort, who says, among other facts, that tigers sometimes swim across to it from Mycale, which Chandler describes as a mountain infested with wild beasts. The woody flanks of *Mount Kerkis* still supply materials for shipbuilding. It is said in Athenaeus (*l. c.*) that the roses and fruits of Samos came to perfection twice a year; and Strabo informs us that its general fruitfulness was such as to give rise to the proverb φέρει καὶ ὀρνίθων γάλα.

The archaeological interest of Samos is almost entirely concentrated in that plain on the S., which contained the sanctuary of Hera at one extremity and the ancient city on the other. This plain is terminated at the SW. by a promontory, which from its white cliffs is called ἄκρον κᾶδο by the Greeks, but which received from the Genoese the name of Cape *Colonna*, in consequence of the single column of the Heraeum which remains standing in its immediate neighbourhood. Virgil tells us (*Aen.* i. 16), that Samos was at least second in the affections of Juno; and her temple and worship contributed much to the fame and affluence of Samos for many centuries. Herodotus says that the temple was the largest he had seen. It was of the Ionic order; in form it was decastyle dipteral, in dimensions 346 feet by 189. (See Leake, *Asia Minor*, p. 348.) It was never entirely finished. At least, the fluting of the columns was left, like the foliage on parts of our cathedrals, incomplete. The original architect was Rhoecus, a Samian. The temple was burnt by the Persians. After its restoration it was plundered by pirates in the Mithridatic War, then by Verres, and then by M. Antony. He took to Rome three statues attributed to Myron: of these Augustus restored the Athene and Heracles, and retained the Zeus to decorate the Capitol. The image of the goddess was made of wood, and was supposed to be the work of Smilis, a contemporary of Daedalus. In Strabo's time the temple, with its chapels, was a complete picture gallery, and the hypaethral portion was full of statues. (See Orig. c. *Cels.* 4.) In the time of Tacitus, this sanctuary had the rights of asylum. (*Ann.* iv. 14.) When Pausanias was there, the people pointed out to him the shrub of Agnus Castus, under the shade of which, on the banks of the river Imbrasus, it was believed that Hera was born. (Paus. *l. c.*) Hence the river itself was called Parthenias, and the goddess Imbrasia. (Comp. Apoll. Rhod. i. 187, Ἰμβρασίης ἔδος Ἥρης.) The anchorage in front of the sanctuary was called ὅρμος Ἡραῖτης. (Athen. xv. p. 672.) The temple was about 200 paces from the shore, according to Ross, who found its whole basement covered with a mass of small fragments of marble, among which are portions of the red tiles with which the temple was roofed. He discovered hardly anything of interest, except an inscription with the word ναοποῖαι.

The appearance of the watercourses of the Imbrasus shows that they are often swollen by rains,

3 м 2

and thus harmonises with the natural derivation of the word. In the plain which extends along the base of the mountains eastwards towards the city, Ross says that there are traces of ancient channels made for the purpose of irrigation. He regards the marshy places near the temple to be the Κάλαμοι and the Ἕλος mentioned by Athenaeus (xiii. p. 572) in connection with the expedition of Pericles. (The former place is likewise referred to by Herodotus, ix. 96.) Across this plain, which is about two miles in length, there is no doubt that a Sacred Way extended from the sanctuary to the city, like that which connected Athens with Eleusis. Somewhere on this line (κατὰ τὴν ὁδὸν τὴν εἰς τὸ Ἡραῖον, Paus. vii. 5. § 6) was the tomb of Rhadine and Leontichus, where lovers used to make their vows; and traces of funeral monuments are still seen at the extremity of the line, close to the city-wall.

The modern town of Chora, close to the pass leading through the mountains to Vathy, is near the place of the ancient city, which was situated partly in the plain and partly on the slope of the hill. The western wall runs in a straight line from the mountain towards the sea, with the exception of a bend inwards near the tombs just mentioned. Here is a brackish stream (ἡ γλυφάδα), which is the Chesius, the second of the three streams mentioned by Pliny. (See Etym. Magn. s. v. Ἀστυπαλαία.) The southern wall does not touch the sea in all its length, and is strengthened by being raised on vaulted substructions. Here and elsewhere the ruins of Samos touch the question of the use of the arch among the Greeks. On the east side of the city the walls are very considerable, being 10 or 12 feet thick, and about 18 feet high. The masonry is partly quadrangular and partly polygonal; there are round towers at intervals on the outside of the wall, and in one place are traces of a gate. In the eastern part of the city was the steep citadel of Astypalaea, which was fortified by Polycrates (Polyaen. Strat. i. 23. § 2), and here probably was what Suetonius calls the palace of Polycrates. (Suet. Calig. 21.) In the higher part of the town the theatre is distinctly visible; the marble seats are removed; underneath is a large cistern. The general area is covered with small fragments, many of the best having furnished materials for the modern castle of Lycurgus near the shore on the SE.; and little more remains of a city which Herodotus says was, under Polycrates, the greatest of cities, Hellenic or Barbarian, and which, in the time of comparative decay, is still called by Horace Concinna Samos.

Herodotus makes especial mention of the harbour and of an immense tunnel which formed an aqueduct for the city. The former of these works (τὸ τίγάνι, as it is now called, from being shaped like a frying-pan) is below Astypalaea; and, though it is now accessible only to small craft, its famous moles remain, one extending eastwards from the castle of Lycurgus, the other extending to meet it from the extremity of the east city-wall southwards. Here Ross saw subterranean passages hewn in the rock, one of which may possibly be the κρυπτὴ διῶρυξ ἐκ τῆς ἀκροπόλεος φέρουσα ἐπὶ Σάλασσαν (Herod. iii. 146), constructed by Maeandrius after the death of Polycrates. The tunnel has not been clearly identified; but, from what M. Musurus told Prof. Ross, it is probable that it is where Tournefort placed it, and that it penetrated the hill from Metelinous to Chora, and that thence the water was taken into the city by a covered channel, traces of which re-

main. It is clear that it cannot be in the quarry pointed out to Ross; both because the cleavage of the rock is in the wrong direction, and because water from such a height would fall like a cascade on the city.

The authorities, to which reference has been made in this article, are, Tournefort (Voyage du Levant, 1717, pp. 404—436), who has given a very copious account of the island; and Ross (Reisen auf den Griechischen Inseln des Aegäischer Meeres, vol. ii. 1843, pp. 139—155), who has examined the sites and remains of the ancient city and Heraeum more carefully than any one else. (See also Clarke, Travels, vol. ii. pp. 192—194, vol. iii. pp. 364—367.) Maps of the island will be found in Tournefort and Choiseul-Gouffier; but the best delineation of it is given in three of the English Admiralty charts. There is a small sketch of the neighbourhood of the city in Kiepert's Hellas (1841), and a larger one in Ross. In Kiepert's general map the rivers Imbrasus and Chesius are wrongly placed, and also (probably) the ridge of Ampelus. It is very questionable whether the point called Poseidion can be where it is (doubtfully) placed in Ross's plan: the position of the little island Narthecis in the strait seems to show that this promontory ought to be further to the east. (See Strab. xiv. p. 637.) A little volume was published in London, and dedicated to James Duke of York, in 1678, entitled "A Description of the present State of Samos, Nicaria, Patmos, and Mount Athos, by Joseph Georgirenes (Γεωργιρήνης), Archbishop of Samos, now living in London, translated by one that knew the author in Constantinople." From this book it appears that Dapper has taken much directly, and Tournefort indirectly. Panofka has written a book on Samos (Res Samiorum, Berlin, 1822): and more recently (1856) Guérin has published a work on this island and Patmos.   [J. S. H.]

COIN OF SAMOS.

SAMOS, in Triphylia. [SAMICUM.]
SAMOS or SAME, in Cephallenia. [SAME.]
SAMOSATA (Σαμόσατα), a strongly fortified city of Syria, placed by Ptolemy (v. 15. § 11) and Strabo in the district of Commagene. It contained the royal residence, and was a province in the time of Strabo, surrounded by a small but very rich country, and situated at the bridge of the Euphrates. (Strab. xvi. 2. § 3, p. 749.) Its distance from the borders of Cappadocia in the vicinity of Tomisa across Mount Taurus was 450 stadia. (Ib. xiv. 2. § 29, p. 664.) It was besieged and taken by Mark Antony during his campaign in Syria. (Joseph. Ant. xiv. 15. § 8.) Its strategic importance is intimated by Caesennius' Paetus, prefect of Syria under Vespasian, who, having represented that Antiochus, king of Commagene, was meditating an alliance with the Parthians to enable him to throw off the Roman yoke, warned his imperial master "that Samosata, the largest city of Commagene, was situated on the Euphrates, and would therefore secure the Parthians an easy passage

of the river and a safe asylum on the western side." The legate was therefore instructed to seize and hold possession of Samosata. (*B. J.* vii. 7. § 1.) This town gave birth to Lucian, and became infamous in the third century in connection with the heretical bishop "Paul of Samosata," who first broached the heresy of the simple humanity of our Lord; and was condemned in a council assembled at Antioch (A. D. 272, Euseb. *H. E.* vii. 27, 28). The modern name of the town is *Sempeat* or *Somisat*, about 40 miles S. of the cataracts of the Euphrates, where it passes Mount Taurus, but Pococke could hear of no ruins there. (*Observations on Syria*, vol. ii. pt. 1, p. 156.)   [G. W.]

SAMOTHRA'CE, SAMOTHRA'CA, or SAMO-THRA'CIA (Σαμοθράκη : Eth. Σαμόθραξ; Σαμο-θρηΐκη in Herodotus, who uses the adjective Σαμο-θρηΐκιος, and calls the inhabitants Σαμοθρήϊκες. In Pliny (iv. 23) we find the form Samothrace; in the *Itin. Ant.* (p. 522, Wess.), Samothraca; in Livy (xlii. 25, 50, xliv. 45, 46), both Samothraca and Samothracia. Properly it is "the Thracian Samos." Thus Homer calls it sometimes Σάμος Θρηϊκίη, sometimes simply Σάμος. Hence the line in Virgil (*Aen.* vii. 208):

"Threiciamque Samum quae nunc Samothracia fertur."

By the modern Greeks it is called *Samothraki*, and often also *Samandraki* (ἐς τὸ μανδράκι), which is merely a corruption of the other, formed in ignorance, after the analogy of *Stamboul* and *Stalimni*,—μαν-δράκι denoting "a sheepfold"). An island in the north of the Aegaean, opposite the mouth of the He-brus, and lying N. of Imbrus, and NE. of Lemnos. Its distance from the coast of Thrace is estimated at 38 miles by Pliny (*l. c.*), who says its circuit is 32 miles. It is of an oval shape, and, according to the English survey, 8 miles in length and 6 in breadth. It was traditionally said to have been diminished in size, in consequence of an outburst of waters from the Hellespont; and perhaps some great physical changes took place in this part of the Aegaean at no very remote period. (See Admiral Smyth's *Medi-terranean*, pp. 74, 119.) However this may be, Sa-mothrace is remarkable for its extreme elevation. No land in the north of the Archipelago is so conspicu-ous, except Mt. Athos; and no island in the whole Archipelago is so high, except *Candia*. The eleva-tion of the highest point, called Saoce by Pliny (*l. c.*), is marked 5240 feet in the Admiralty Chart (No. 1654). The geographical position of this point (the modern name of which is *Mt. Fingares*) is 40° 26' 57" N. lat., and 25° 36' 23" E. long. Though there are several anchorages on the coast of Samothrace, there is an entire absence of good harbours. a circum-stance in harmony with the expression of Pliny, who calls it "importuosissima omnium." Scylax, however

(p. 280, ed. Gail), mentions a port, which possibly was identical with the harbour Demetrium spoken of by Livy. The ancient city (of the same name as the island) was on the north, in the place marked *Palaeopolis* on the chart.

The common name of the Thracian and the Ionian Samos was the occasion of speculation to Strabo and Pausanias. The latter (vii. 4. § 3) says that the Thracian island was colonised by emigrants from the other. The former (x. pp. 457, 472) mentions a theory that it might be named from the Saii, a people of Thrace. Scymnus Chius (692) says, that aid came from Samos to Samothrace in a time of famine, and that this brought settlers from the Ionian to the Thracian Island. The truth seems to be, that σάμος denotes any elevated land near the sea, and that the name was therefore given to the island before us, as well as to others. [CEPHALLENIA; SAMOS.] The earlier names of Sa-mothrace were Dardania, Electris, Melite, and Leu-cosia. Diodorus Siculus (v. 47) speaks of its in-habitants as Autochthons, and dwells on peculiarities of their language as connected with their religious worship. The chief interest of this island is con-nected with the CABEIRI. For these mysterious divinities we must refer to the *Dict. of Biography and Mythology*. Pelasgians are said by Herodotus (ii. 51) to have first inhabited the island, and to have introduced the mysteries.

The lofty height of Samothrace appears in Homer in a very picturesque connection with the scenery of Troy. He describes Poseidon as gazing from this throne on the incidents of the war: and travellers in the Troad have noticed the view of Samothrace towering over Imbros as a proof of the truthfulness of the Iliad. Bearing in mind this geographical affinity (if we may so call it) of the mountain-tops of Saoce and Ida, we shall hardly be surprised to find Scymnus Chius (678) calling Samothrace a Trojan island (νῆσος Τρωϊκή). The tradition was that Dardanus dwelt there before he went to Troy, and that he introduced the Cabeiric mysteries from thence into Asia.

A few detached points may be mentioned which connect this island with Greek and Roman history. Its inhabitants joined Xerxes in his expedition against Greece; they are spoken of as skilful in the use of the javelin; and a Samothracian ship is said to have sunk an Athenian ship, and to have been sunk in turn by an Aeginetan one, at the battle of Salamis. (Herod. viii. 90.) At that time the Samothracians possessed forts erected on the mainland. (Ib. vii. 108.) Philip of Macedon and his wife Olympias were both initiated in the mysteries. It would seem that such initiation was regarded as a preservation from danger. (Aristoph. *Pax*, 277, and Schol.) Samothrace appears also to have had the rights of asylum; for Perseus took refuge there, after he was defeated by the Romans in the battle of Pydna. (Liv. xlv. 6.) Germanicus sailed to the island with the view of being initiated: but he was prevented by an omen. (Tac. *Ann.* ii. 54.) St. Paul passed the night at anchor here on his first voyage from Asia to Europe. (*Acts*, xvi. 11.) In Pliny's time Samothrace was a free state (*l. c.*). In the Synecdemus we find it, with Thasos, in the province of Illyricum. (Wess. p. 640.) In the later division described by Constant. Porphyrog. (*De Them.* p. 47, ed. Bonn) it is in the Thracian subdivision of the First Eu-ropean or Thracian Theme.

Samothrace appears to have no modern history

and no present importance. Pliny (xxxvii. 67) makes mention of a gem which was found there; and in the Middle Ages its honey and goats are said to have been celebrated. No traveller seems to have explored and described this island. [J.S.H.]

SAMULOCENAE, according to the Peut. Tab., or more correctly according to inscriptions found on the spot, SUMLOCENNE, was apparently a Roman colony of some importance in the Agri Decumates of Germany. The Table erroneously places the town in Vindelicia, whence some antiquarians have regarded Samulocenae and Sumlocenne as two different places. But there can be no doubt that they are only two forms of the same name belonging to one town, the site of which is occupied by the modern *Sülchen*, near *Rottenburg* on the *Neckar*, where many Roman remains, such as coins, inscriptions, and arms, have been found. (Comp. Jaumann, *Colonia Sumlocenne, &c.*, Stuttgart, 1840, 8vo.; Leichtlen, *Schwaben unter den Römern*, p. 107, foll.) [L.S.]

SAMUS. [SAMOS.]

SAMUS, a river of Hispania Baetica. (Geog. Rav. iv. 45.) Ancient Spanish coins indicate a town of the same name. (Flores, *Med.* iii. p. 142.) [T.H.D.]

SAMYDACE (Σαμυδάκη), a town on the coast of Carmania, noticed by Marcian (c. 28. ed. Didot) and Ptolemy (vi. 8. § 7). It appears to have been placed near the mouth of the river Samydacus. (See also Steph. B. *s. v.*) It is possible, as suggested by Forbiger, that the river is the same as the present *Sadji.* [V.]

SANAUS (Σαναός), a town of Phrygia, in the neighbourhood of Laodiceia. (Strab. xii. p. 576; Hierocl. p. 666.) In the acts of the Council of Chalcedon (p. 674), it is called Σαναῶν πόλις, and is probably mentioned by Ptolemy (v. 2. § 26) under the name of Sanis. [L.S.]

SANCTIO, a place in the Agri Decumates, in the south-west of Germany, was situated on the banks of the Rhine, but is mentioned only by Ammianus Marcellinus (xxi. 3), and in such a manner that it is not easy to identify its site; it is possible, however, that the modern *Seckingen* may correspond with it. [L.S.]

SANDA, a river on the N. coast of Hispania Tarraconensis (Plin. iv. 20. s. 34.) Probably the *Miera.* [T.H.D.]

SANDA'LIUM (Σανδάλιον), a mountain fortress of Pisidia, mentioned only by Strabo (xii. p. 169) and Stephanus B. (*s. v.*). [L.S.]

SANDANES (Σανδάνες, *Peripl. Mar. Erythr.* c. 52). There has been some question whether this is the name of a man or of a place. As the text stands in the Periplus, it would seem to be that of a ruler of the coast-region in the neighbourhood of *Bombay*. On the other hand, Ptolemy speaks of the same territory under the title of 'Αριακή Σαδινῶν; whence Benfey (Ersch and Grüber, *Encycl.* art. *Indien*) argues, with strong probability, that the reading in the Periplus is incorrect, and that Ptolemy is right in making the name that of a people rather than of a chief. [V.]

SANDARACA (Σανδαράκη), a coast-town of Bithynia, at a distance of 90 stadia to the east of the river Oxines. (Arrian, *Peripl. P. E.* p. 14 ; Anonym. *Peripl. P. E.* p. 4.) [L.S.]

SANDOBANES. [ALBANIA, Vol. I. p. 89, b.]

SANDRIZETES, according to some editions of Pliny (iii. 28), the name of a tribe in Pannonia on

the river Dravus; but a more correct reading gives the name Andizetes, which is no doubt the same as the Andizetii ('Ανδιζήτιοι) mentioned by Strabo (vii. p. 314) among the tribes of Pannonia. [L.S.]

SANE. 1. (Σάνη: *Eth.* Σάνιος, Σηναῖος, Σαναῖος, Herod. vii. 22 ; Thuc. iv. 109 ; Steph. B. *s. v.*), a colony of Andros, situated upon the low, undulating ground, forming the isthmus which connects the peninsula of Acte with Chalcidice, through which the canal of Xerxes passed. Masses of stone and mortar, with here and there a large and squared block, and foundations of Hellenic walls, which are found upon this *Próvlaka* or neck of land, mark the site of ancient Sane, which was within Acte and turned towards the sea of Euboea. (Leake, *Northern Greece,* vol. iii. p. 143.)

2. It appears from Herodotus (vii. 123; comp. Thuc. v. 18) and the Epitomiser of Strabo (vii. p. 330, *Fr.* 27), that there was another town of this name in Pallene. According to the position assigned to it in the list of Herodotus, the site must be sought for between C. *Posidhi* and the W. side of the isthmus of *Porto.* Mela (ii. 3. § 1) is opposed to this position of Sane, as he places it near Canastraeum Prom. (*C. Paliúri*). [E.B.J.]

SANGALA (τὰ Σάγγαλα), a place mentioned by Arrian to the NW. of the Malli (or *Multán*), apparently near the junction of the Hydraotes and Acesines (v. 22). There can be little doubt that it is the same place as that noticed by Ptolemy under the name Σάγαλα ἡ καὶ Εὐθυμηδία (vi. 1. § 46). The position, however, of the latter is assigned with this difference, that it is placed below the junction of the Hydaspes and Acesines, whereas the former would seem to have been to the E. of the Hydraotes. Burnes has identified Sagala with the present *Lahore*, which is probable enough (*Travels,* vol. iii. p. 82). It may be remarked, that the Εὐθυμηδία of Ptolemy ought in all probability to be Εὐθυδημία, the name being derived from the well-known Bactrian king, Euthydemus. [V.]

SANGA'RIUS (Σαγγάριος : *Sakarya* or *Sakari; Turkish Ayala*), one of the principal rivers of Asia Minor, is mentioned in the Iliad (iii. 187, xvi. 719) and in Hesiod (*Theog.* 344). Its name appears in different forms as Sagraphos (Schol. *ad Apollon. Rhod.* ii. 724), Sangaris (Constant. Porphyr. i. 5), or Sagaris (Ov. *ex Pont.* iv. 10. 17; Plin. vi. 1; Solin 43). This river had its sources on Mount Adoreus, near the town of Sangia in Phrygia, not far from the Galatian frontier (Strab. xii. p. 543), and flowed in a very tortuous course, first in an eastern, then in a northern, then in a north-western, and lastly again in a northern direction through Bithynia into the Euxine. In one part of its course it formed the boundary between Phrygia and Bithynia; and in early times Bithynia was bounded on the east by the Sangarius. [BITHYNIA.]

The Bithynian part of the river was navigable, and was celebrated from the abundance of fish found in it. Its principal tributaries were the Alander, Bathys, Thymbres, and Gallus. (Comp. Scylax, p. 34 ; Apollon. Rhod. ii. 724 ; Scymnus. 234, foll.; Strab. xii. pp. 563, 567; Dionys. Perieg. 811; Ptol. v. 1. § 6; Steph. B. *s. v.*; Liv. xxxviii. 18; Plin. v. 43; Amm. Marc. xxii. 9.) [L.S.]

SA'NGIA (Σαγγία), a small place in the east of Phrygia, near Mount Adoreus and the sources of the Sangarius. (Strab. xii. p. 543.) [L.S.]

SANIA'NA (Σανίανα, Const. Porph. *Them.* i. p. 28, *de Adm. Imp.* c. 50, p. 225, Bonn.), a place in the interior of Thrace, probably the modern *Esenga* or *Zingane*.　　　　　　　　[J. R.]

SANIGAE (Σανίγαι, Arrian, *Peripl. Pont. Eux.* p. 12; Σάννιγαι, Steph. B. *s. v.*; Σαγίδαι, Procop. *B. G.* iv. 3), a tribe of Mt. Caucasus, who were found in the neighbourhood of DIOSCURIAS or the Roman SEBASTOPOLIS.　　　　　　　[E. B. J.]

SANISERA, a city in the island Balearis Minor (Plin. iii. 5. s. 11), the modern *Alajor*. (Cf. Wernsd. *Ant. Bal.* p. 57; Salmas. *ad Solin.* c. 34, p. 401.)　　　　　　　　　　[T. H. D.]

SANITIUM (Σανίτιον), is placed in the Alpes Maritimae by Ptolemy (iii. 1. § 43), and named as one of the towns of the Vesdiantii or Vediantii. Cemenelium is the other town which he names [CEMENELIUM]. If Sanitium is *Senez*, which is west of the *Var*, part of this people were east of the *Var* and part of them were west of it.　　[G. L.]

SANNI. [MACRONES.]

SANTICUM (Σαντικόν, Ptol. ii. 14. § 3), a town of Noricum, on the south-west of Virunum, on the road from this place to Aquileia (*It. Ant.* p. 276). The exact site of the place is utterly uncertain, but conjecture has fixed upon four or five different places that might be identified with Santicum with equal probability.　　　　　　　　　[L. S.]

SA'NTONES or SA'NTONI (Σάντονες, Σάντονοι, Σάντωνες), a people of South-western Gallia, in the Celtogalatia Aquitania of Ptolemy (ii. 7. § 7), who names their capital Mediolanium. [MEDIOLANUM.] They were in the Celtica of Caesar, being north of the Garumna (*Garonne*). The Roman poets make the quantity of the word suit their verse, as Lucan does when he says (i. 422), "gaudetque amoto Santonus hoste;" and Juvenal and Martial when they use the word Santonicus.

Caesar, who first mentions the Santones (*B. G.* i. 10), says that when the Helvetii were preparing to leave their country with their families and moveables, their intention was to make their way to the territory of the Santones, "who are not far distant from the borders of the Tolosates." He gives us no means for conjecturing why the Helvetii proposed to cross the whole width of Gallia and settle themselves in a country on the coast of the Atlantic which was full of people. The position of the Santones is defined by Ptolemy, who places them between the Pictones and the Bituriges Vivisci, one of whose towns was Burdigala (*Bordeaux*). Strabo (iv. pp. 190, 208) fixes the position of the Santones still clearer when he says that the Garumna flows into the sea between the Bituriges Iosci (Vivisci) and the Santones, both of which are Celtic nations. In another passage he places the Pictones and Santones on the shores of the Atlantic, and the Pictones north of the Santones; which completes the description of their position.

Caesar never made any campaign against the Santones, or, if he did, he has said nothing about it. He got ships from the Pictones and Santones for his naval war with the Veneti (*B. G.* iii. 11), from which we learn that the Santones and Pictones were a maritime people. When Vercingetorix (B. C. 52) was stirring up the Gallic nations against Caesar, he secured the assistance of the Pictones and "all the rest of the states that border on the ocean," an expression which includes the Santones, though they are not mentioned. But the Santones sent 12,000 men to the siege of Alesia. (*B. G.* vii. 75.) In Pliny's enumeration of the Gallic people (iv. 33) the Santones are named Liberi.

The Santones gave name to that division of France before the revolution which was named *Saintonge*, the chief part of which is included in the French department of *Charente Inférieure*. The coast of the territory of the Santones is low and marshy; the interior is generally level and fertile. D'Anville supposed that the territory of the Santones comprehended the diocese of *Saintes*, and the small province of *Aunis* on the north-west.

The wormwood of this country is spoken of by various writers, Pliny (xxvii. 38), and Martial (*Ep.* ix. 95):—

"Santonica medicata dedit mihi pocula virga."

Martial (xiv. 128) and Juvenal (viii. 145) mention a "cucullus" with the name "Santonicus." It appears that some thick coarse woollen cloths were imported from Gallia into Italy.

Havercamp in his edition of Orosius (vi. 7) gives a coin with the name "Arivos," and on the other side the legend "Santonos" in Roman capitals with the figure of a horse in action. He gives also another coin with the same legend; and a third with the abbreviated name "Sant" and the name of "Q. Doci" on it.　　　　　　　[G. L.]

SA'NTONUM PORTUS (Σαντόνων λιμήν). Ptolemy in his description of the coast of Celtogalatia Aquitania (ii. 7. § 1) proceeds from south to north. Next to the outlets of the *Garonne* he places Santonum Portus, and next to it Santonum Promontorium (Σαντόνων ἄκρον). The outlet of the river Canentelus is placed north of the promontorium. The Carantonus of Ausonius is certainly the *Charente* [CARANTONUS]; and Ptolemy's Canentelus is a different river, or, if it is the same river, he has placed it wrong.

It is impossible to determine what is the Santonum Portus of Ptolemy. If it is *Rochelle*, as some geographers maintain, and if Ptolemy's Canentelus is the *Charente*, he has placed their positions in wrong order. It seems very unlikely that Ptolemy should mention a river between the *Garonne* and *Loire*, and not mention the *Charente*. The only other large river between the *Garonne* and the *Loire* is the *Sèvre Niortaise*, which is north of *La Rochelle*, and if Ptolemy's Canentelus is the *Sèvre*, the Santonum Portus might be *La Rochelle*. D'Anville supposes Santonum Portus to be the embouchure of the *Seudre*, which opens into the sea opposite the southern extremity of the *Isle d'Oléron*; but he does not undertake to fix the position of the Santonum Promontorium. The latitudes of Ptolemy cannot be trusted, and his geography of Gallia is full of errors. [G. L.]

SA'NTONUM PROMONTO'RIUM. [SANTONUM PORTUS.]

SAOCE. [SAMOTHRACE.]

SAO'CORAS (Σαόκορας, Ptol. v. 18. § 3), a river of Mesopotamia, mentioned by Ptolemy, which appears to have had its source in the M. Masius near Nisibis, and to have flowed to the SW. into the Euphrates. There has been much dispute, as to what river Ptolemy intended by this name, as at present there is no stream existing which corresponds with his description. Forbiger has conjectured with some reason that it is the same as the Mascas of Xenophon (*Anab.* i. 5. § 4), which flowed about 35 parasangs to the E. of the Chaboras (*Khabúr*), and surrounded the town of Corsote: Ptolemy would seem to have confounded it with the Mygdonius. [MYGDONIUS.]　　　　　　　　[V.]

SAPAEI (Σαπαῖοι or Σάπαιοι), a Thracian people, occupying the southern portion of the Pan-

3 M 4

gaeus, in the neighbourhood of Abdera. (Strab. xii. p. 549.) In this passage, however, Strabo calls them Sapae (Σάπαι), and assumes their identity with the Sinti, which in another place (x. p. 457) he treats as a mere matter of conjecture. The Via Egnatia ran through their country, and especially through a narrow and difficult defile called by Appian (B. C. iv. 87, 106) the pass of the Sapaei, and stated by him to be 18 miles from Philippi; so that it must have been nearly midway between Neapolis and Abdera. The Sapaei are mentioned, and merely mentioned, by Herodotus (vii. 110) and by Pliny (iv. 11. s. 18). Their town is called Sapaica (Σαπαϊκή) by Steph. B. (s. v.).   [J. R.]

SAPAICA. [SAPAEI.]

SAPARNUS (Σάπαρνος), a small tributary of the Indus, in the upper Panjáb, noticed by Arrian (Indic. c. 4). It is probably the present Abbasin.   [V.]

SAPAUDIA. This name occurs in Ammianus Marcellinus (xv. 11), in his description of Gallia. He says of the Rhone that after flowing through the Lake of Geneva " per Sapaudiam fertur et Sequanos." In the Notit. Imp. we read: " in Gallia Ripense praefectus militum Barcariorum Ebruduni Sapaudiae," where Ebrudunum appears to be Yverdun, which is at one end of the Lake of Neufchâtel. In another passage of the Notit. there occurs : " tribunus cohortis primae Sapaudiae Flaviae Calarone," or " Calarone," which is Grenoble [CULARO]. Thus Sapaudia extended northward into the country of the Helvetii and southward into the territory of the Allobroges. The name Sapaudia is preserved in Saboia, or Savoy, but in a much more limited signification ; and in the country now called Savoy there is said to be a canton which bears the particular name of Savoy. (D' Anville, Notice, &c.)   [G. L.]

SAPHAR. [SAPPHAR.]

SAPHE. [BEZABDA.]

SAPHRI (Σάφρι), a small village of Parthyene mentioned by Isidorus (Stath. Parth. c. 12). It may be the same place as that called by Ptolemy Σόρβα (vi. 9. § 6), which he places in Hyrcania, close to the Astabeni. Forbiger identifies it with the modern Shoffri.   [V.]

SAPIRI'NE (Plin. vi. 29. s. 33.; Σαππειρήνη ἢ Σασπειρήνη νῆσος, Ptol. iv. 5. § 77; Σαπφειρηνή, Steph. B. s. v.), an island in the Arabian gulf, NE. of Myos Hormos and S. of the promontory Pharan, from which sapphires were obtained according to Stephanus. Now Sheduan.

SAPIS (Σάπις, Strab.: Savio), a small river of Cisalpine Gaul, not far from the frontiers of Umbria. It rises in the Umbrian Apennines, a few miles above Sarsina, flows under the walls of that town, and afterwards, pursuing a course nearly due N., crosses the Aemilian Way close to the town of Caesena (Cesena), and falls into the Adriatic about 10 miles S. of Ravenna. (Strab. v. p. 217; Plin. iii. 15. s. 20; Lucan. ii. 406; Sil. Ital. viii. 448; Tab. Peut.) It is called in the Tabula Sabis; and the name is written Isapis in several editions of Lucan and Strabo; but there seems little doubt that Sapis is the true form of the name. It is still called the Savio. There can be little doubt that the SAPINIA TRIBUS, mentioned by Livy (xxxi. 2, xxxiii. 37), as one of the tribes or divisions of the Umbrian nation, immediately adjoining the Gaulish tribe of the Boii, derived its name from the Sapis, and must have dwelt on the banks of that river. [E. H. B.]

SAPPHAR METROPOLIS (Σαπφάρα μητρό-

πολις), placed by Ptolemy in long. 88°, lat. 14° 30'; doubtless the capital of the Sappharitae (Σαπφαρῖται), whom the same geographer places near the Homeritae (vi. 6. § 25), which Bochart identifies with the " Sephar " called by Moses " a mount of the East," and which was the limit of the children of Joktan. (Gen. x. 30.) This Forster further identifies with the Mount Climax of Ptolemy, which Niebuhr judged to be the Sumdra or Nakil Sumara of modern Arabia, the highlands of Yemen, on the E. of which that same traveller found some ruins, half a day's journey SW. of Jerim, named Saphar, which he says is without doubt Aphar, or Dhafar. (Forster, Geogr. of Arabia, vol. i. pp. 94, 105, 127 notes, 175, vol. ii. pp. 154, 172.) Aphar was the metropolis of the Sabaeans according to the author of the Periplus ascribed to Arrian, and distant 12 days' journey eastward from Musa on the Arabian gulf; Mr. Forster remarks " that the direction and the distance correspond with the site of Dhafar " (vol. ii. p. 166, note *). It is to be regretted that this important and well marked site has not yet been visited and explored.   [G. W.]

SAPPHARI'TAE. [SAPPHAR.]

SAPPIRE'NE. [SAPIRINE.]

SAPRA PALUS. [BUCES.]

SARACE'NI (Σαρακηνοί). This celebrated name, which became so renowned and dreaded in Europe, is given to a tribe of Arabia Felix by the classical geographers, who do not, however, very clearly define their position in the peninsula, and indeed the country of Saracene in Ptolemy seems scarcely reconcileable with the situation assigned to the Saraceni by the same geographer. Thus he, consistently with Pliny, who joins them to the Nabataei (vi. 28. s. 32), places the Saraceni south of the Scenitae, who were situated in the neighbourhood of the northern mountains of the Arabian peninsula (vi. 7. § 21); but the region Saracene he places to the west of the black mountains (μελανὰ ὄρη)— by which name he is supposed to designate the range of Sinai, as he couples it with the gulf of Pharan — and on the confines of Egypt (v. 17. § 3). St. Jerome also calls this district the " mons et desertum Saracenorum, quod vocatur Pharan " (Onomast. s. v. Χωρήβ, Choreb), in agreement with which Eusebius also places Pharan near the Saraceni who inhabit the desert (s. v. Φαράν). According to these writers their country corresponds with what is in Scripture called Midian (Exod. ii.15, iii. 1; see MIDIAN), which, however, they place incorrectly on the east of the Red Sea; and the people are identified with the Ishmaelites by St. Jerome (Onomast. l. c.), elsewhere with Kedar (Comment. in Ies. xlii. and in Loc. Heb. ad voc.), with the Midianites by St. Augustine (in Numer.), with the Scenitae by Ammianus Marcellinus, who, however, uses the name in a wider acceptation, and extends them from Assyria to the cataracts of the Nile (xiv. 4). Their situation is most clearly described by the author of the Periplus. " They who are called Saraceni inhabit the parts about the neck of Arabia Felix next to Petraea, and Arabia Deserta. They have many names, and occupy a large tract of desert land, bordering on Arabia Petraea and Deserta, on Palaestina and Persis, and consequently on the before-named Arabia Felix." (Marcian. apud Geog. Min. vol. i. p. 16, Hudson.) The fact seems to be that this name, like that of Scenitae (with whom, as we have seen, the Saraceni are sometimes identified), was used either in a laxer or more restricted sense for various wandering tribes. As their nomadic and migratory habits were described by the latter, so their predatory propensities, according to the most probable interpretation of the name, was by the former, for the Arabic verb Saraka, according to lexicographers, signifies "to plunder." (Bochart, Geog. Sac. lib. iv. cap. 2, pp. 213, 214.) The derivation of the name from Sarah has been rejected by nearly all critics as historically erroneous; and the fact that the name was in use many centuries before Mohammed, at once negatives the theory that it was adopted by him or his followers, in order to remove the stigma of their servile origin from Hagar the bondwoman. (Reland, Palaestina, p. 87.) This author maintains that "Saraceni nil nisi orientales populos notat:" deriving the word from the Arabic sharaka == ortus fuit; and as unhappily the Greek alphabet cannot discriminate between sin and shin, and the name does not occur in the native authors, there is nothing to determine the etymology. Mr. Forster, in defiance of Bochart's severe sentence, "Qui ad Saram referunt, nugas agunt" (Geog. Sac. i. 2, p. 213), argues for the matronymic derivation from Sarah, and shows that the country of Edom, or the mountains and territory bordering on the Saracena of classic authors, are called "the country, mountains, &c. of Sarah" by the Jews; and he maintains that, as this tract derived its name of Edom and Idumaea from the patriarch Esau, so did it that of Sarah from Sarah the wife of Abraham, the acknowledged mother of the race. (Geog. of Arabia, vol. ii. pp. 17—19.) His attempt to identify the Saraceni with the Amalekites is not so successful; for however difficult it may be to account for the appearance of the latter in the Rephidim (Exod. xvii. 1, 8; REPHIDIM), which was the country of Saracens, yet their proper seat is fixed beyond doubt in the south of the promised land, in the hill-country immediately north of the wilderness of Paran, near to Kadesh (Numb. xiii. 29); and it is impossible to understand "the valley" in xiv. 25, and "the hill" in xiv. 45, of Horeb, as Mr. Forster does, since the whole context implies a position far to the north of the district of Horeb, marked by the following stations: Taberah, 3 days' journey from "the Mount of the Lord" (x. 33, xi. 3); Kibroth-hattaavah, Hazeroth, the wilderness of Paran (xi. 34, 35, xii. 16, compare xxxiii. 16—18). It must indeed be admitted that the name of the Amalekites is occasionally used, in a much wider acceptation than its proper one, of all the Edomite tribes, throughout Northern Arabia, as e. g. in 1 Sam. xv. 7; and similarly the name Saraceni is extended in Marcian's Periplus, already cited: but it seems more natural to interpret the words οἱ καλούμενοι Σαρακηνοί, πλείονας ἔχοντες προσηγορίας of the general name of several specific tribes, marking common habits or common position rather than common origin, according to the analogy of the Scenitae in old times and of Bedawín == "deserti incolae," in modern times; particularly as it does not appear that the name was ever adopted by the Arabs themselves, who would not have been slow to appropriate an honourable appellation, which would identify them with the great patriarch. That their predatory character had become early established is manifest from the desperate expedient resorted to by the emperor Decius in order to repress their encroachments. He is said to have brought lions and lionesses from Africa and turned them loose on the borders of Arabia and Palestine, as far as the Circisium Castrum,

that they might breed and propagate against the Saracens. (Chron. Alex. in A. M. 5760, Olymp. 257, Ind. xiv. == A. D. 251.) This strong fortress, called by Procopius Circesium (Κιρκήσιον φρούριον), the most remote of the Roman garrisons, which was fortified by Diocletian (Amm. Marc. xxiii. 5), was situated on the angle formed by the confluence of the Aborrhas (Khabour) and the Euphrates (it is still called Karkisia), so that it is clear that, in the time of Procopius, the name of Saraceni was given to the Arab tribes from Egypt to the Euphrates. Consistently with this view, he calls Zenobia's husband Odonathes, "king of the Saracens in those parts" (Bell. Pers. ii. 5, p. 288); and Belisarius's Arab contingent, under their king Aretas (Ἀρέθας) he likewise calls Saracens (ii. 16, p. 308). That Roman general describes them (c. 19, p. 312) as incapable of building fortifications, but adepts at plunder, which character again justifies the etymology above preferred; while it is clear from these and other passages that the use of the name had become established merely as a general name, and precisely equivalent to Arab (see Bell. Pers. i. 19, p. 261), and was accordingly adopted and applied indifferently to all the followers of Mohammed by the writers of the middle ages.   [G. W.]

SARALA. [SARDINIA.]

SARA'LIUM or SARALUS (Σάραλος), a town of the Trocmi in Galatia, on the east of the river Halys. (Tab. Peut.; Ptol. v. 9. § 4.)   [L. S.]

SARAME'NE (Σαραμήνη), a district of Pontus, on the bay of Amisus. (Strab. xii. p. 547; comp. PONTUS.)   [L. S.]

SARANGA (τὰ Σάραγγα), a small place on the coast of Gedrosia between the Indus and the Arabis. It was visited by Nearchus in his coast voyage to Persia (Arrian, Ind. c. 22). It has been conjectured by Müller (Geogr. Graec. Min. l. c., ed. Paris) that it is the same as the 'Ρίζανα of Ptolemy (vi. 21. § 2).   [V.]

SARANGAE. [DRANGIANA.]

SARANGES (Σαράγγης), a small tributary of the Hydraotes (Irávati), mentioned by Arrian (Ind. c. 4) in his list of Indian rivers. It is doubtless the Sanscrit Saranga, though it has not been determined to what stream this Indian name applies.   [V.]

SARAPANA (Σαραπανά, Strab. xi. p. 500; Σαραπανίς, Procop. B. G. iv. 14), a strong position in Iberia, upon the river Phasis, identified with Scharapani in Imiretia, on the modern road which leads from Mingrelia into Georgia over Suram. (Comp. Journ. Geog. Soc. vol. iii. p. 34.)   [E. B. J.]

SARAPARAE (Σαραπάραι, Strab. xi. p. 531; Plin. vi. 16. s. 18), a Thracian people, dwelling beyond Armenia near the Guranii and Medi, according to Strabo, who describes them as a savage, lawless, and mountainous people, who scalped and cut off heads (περισκυθιστὰς καὶ ἀποκεφαλιστάς). The latter is said by Strabo to be the meaning of their name, which is confirmed by the fact that in the Persian sar means "head" and para "division." (Anquetil, Sur les anc. Langues de la Perse, in Mém. de l'Acad. &c. vol. xxxi. p. 419, quoted in Kramer's Strab. vol. ii. p. 500; comp. Groskurd's Strab. vol. ii. p. 439.)

SARAPIONIS PORTUS. [NICONIS DROMUS.]

SARAPIS INS. (Σαράπιδος νῆσος), an island off the South Coast of Arabia, mentioned by the author of the Periplus ascribed to Arrian (Geog. Graec. Min. vol. i. p. 19, Hudson) as situated 2000 stadia east of the seven islands of Zenobia, which are identified with the islands of *Kurian Murian*. The island of Sarapis is therefore correctly placed by D'Anville at *Mazeira*. It is described in the Periplus as about 120 stadia distant from the coast, and about 200 stadia wide. It had three villages, and was inhabited by the sacred caste of the Ichthyophagi. They spoke Arabic, and wore girdles of cocoa leaves. The island produced a variety and abundance of tortoises, and was a favourite station for the merchant vessels of Cane.   [G. W.]

SARA'VUS, a river of Gallia, a branch of the Mosella (*Mosel*). The Itins. place the Pons Saravi on the Saravus, on a road from Divodurum (*Metz*) to Argentoratum (*Strassburg*). [PONS SARAVI.]

The Saravus is mentioned in the poem of Ausonius on the Mosella (v. 367):—

" Naviger undisona dudum me mole Saravus
 Tota veste vocat, longum qui distulit amnem,
 Fessa sub Augustis ut volveret ostia muris."

The Saravus is the *Sarre*, which joins the *Mosel* on the right bank a few miles above Augusta Trevirorum (*Trier*). In an inscription the river is named Sarra.   [G. L.]

SARBACUM (Σάρβακον, Ptol. iii. 5. § 29), a town of Sarmatia, upon an affluent of the Tanais, probably a Graecised form of the Slavonic *Srbec*. (Schafarik, *Slav. Alt.* vol. i. pp. 512, 514.) [E. B. J.]

SARDABALE. [SIGA.]

SARDEMISUS, a southern branch of Mount Taurus on the frontiers of Pisidia and Pamphylia, extending as far as Phaselis; it is also connected with Mount Climax on the frontiers between Milyas and Pisidia Proper. (Pomp. Mela, i. 14; Plin. v. 26.)   [L. S.]

SARDE'NE (Σαρδόνη), a mountain of Mysia, on the northern bank of the Hermus, in the neighbourhood of Cyme; at its foot was the town of Neonteichos. (Hom. *Ep.* i. 3; *Vit. Hom.* 9.) [L. S.]

SARDES (Σάρδεις or Σάρδις: *Eth.* Σαρδιανός), the ancient capital of the kingdom of Lydia, was situated at the northern foot of Mount Tmolus, in a fertile plain between this mountain and the river Hermus, from which it was about 20 stadia distant. (Arrian, *Anab.* i. 17.) The small river Pactolus, a tributary of the Hermus, flowed through the agora of Sardes. (Herod. v. 101.) This city was of more recent origin, as Strabo (xiii. p. 625) remarks, than the Trojan times, but was nevertheless very ancient, and had a very strong acropolis on a precipitous height. The town is first mentioned by Aeschylus (*Pers.* 45); and Herodotus (i. 84) relates that it was fortified by a king Meles, who, according to the Chronicle of Eusebius, preceded Candaules. The city itself was, at least at first, built in a rude manner, and the houses were covered with dry reeds, in consequence of which it was repeatedly destroyed by fire; but the acropolis, which some of the ancient geographers identified with the Homeric Hyde (Strab. xiii. p. 626; comp. Plin. v. 30; Eustath. *ad Dion. Per.* 830), was built upon an almost inaccessible rock, and surrounded with a triple wall. In the reign of Ardys, Sardes was taken by the Cimmerians, but they were unable to gain possession of the citadel. The city attained its greatest prosperity in the reign of the last Lydian king, Croesus. After the overthrow of the Lydian monarchy, Sardes became the residence of the Persian satraps of Western Asia. (Herod. v 25; Paus. iii. 9. § 3.) On the revolt of the Ionians, excited by Aristagoras

and Histiaeus, the Ionians, assisted by an Athenian force, took Sardes, except the citadel, which was defended by Artaphernes and a numerous garrison. The city then was accidentally set on fire, and burnt to the ground, as the buildings were constructed of easily combustible materials. After this event the Ionians and Athenians withdrew, but Sardes was rebuilt; and the indignation of the king of Persia, excited by this attack on one of his principal cities, determined him to wage war against Athens. Xerxes spent at Sardes the winter preceding his expedition against Greece, and it was there that Cyrus the younger assembled his forces when about to march against his brother Artaxerxes. (Xenoph. *Anab.* i. 2. § 5.) When Alexander the Great arrived in Asia, and had gained the battle of the Granicus, Sardes surrendered to him without resistance, for which he rewarded its inhabitants by restoring to them their freedom and their ancient laws and institutions. (Arrian, i. 17.) After the death of Alexander, Sardes came into the possession of Antigonus, and after his defeat at Ipsus into that of the Seleucidae of Syria. But on the murder of Seleucus Ceraunus, Achaeus set himself up as king of that portion of Asia Minor, and made Sardes his residence. (Polyb. iv. 48, v. 57.) Antiochus the Great besieged the usurper in his capital for a whole year, until at length Lagoras, a Cretan, scaled the ramparts at a point where they were not guarded. On this occasion, again, a great part of the city was destroyed. (Polyb. vii. 15, &c. viii. 23.) When Antiochus was defeated by the Romans in the battle of Magnesia, Sardes passed into the hands of the Romans. In the reign of Tiberius the city was reduced to a heap of ruins by an earthquake; but the emperor ordered its restoration. (Tac. *Ann.* ii. 47; Strab. xiii. p. 627.) In the book of Revelation

COIN OF SARDES.

(iii. 1, &c.), Sardes is named as one of the Seven Churches, whence it is clear that at that time its inhabitants had adopted Christianity. From Pliny (v. 30) we learn that Sardes was the capital of a conventus: during the first centuries of the Christian era we hear of more than one council held there; and it continued to be a wealthy city down to the end of the Byzantine empire. (Eunap. p. 154; Hierocl. p. 669.) The Turks took possession of it in the 11th century, and two centuries later it was almost entirely destroyed by Tamerlane. (Anna Comn. p. 323 ; M. Ducas, p. 39.) Sardes is now little more than a village, still bearing the name of Sart, which is situated in the midst of the ruins of the ancient city. These ruins, though extending over a large space, are not of any great consequence; they consist of the remains of a stadium, a theatre, and the triple walls of the acropolis, with lofty towers.

The fertile plain of Sardes bore the name of Sardiene or Σαρδιανὸν πεδίον, and near the city was the celebrated tomb of Alyattes. Sardes was believed to be the native place of the Spartan poet Alcman, and it is well known that the two rhetoricians Diodorus and the historian Eunapius were natives of Sardes. (Chandler, *Travels in Asia Minor*, p. 316, foll. ; Leake, *Asia Minor*, p. 342, foll. ; Richter, *Wallfahrten*, p. 511, foll. ; Prokesch, *Denkwürdigk.* vol. iii. p. 31, foll.]   [L. S.]

SARDI'NIA (ἡ Σαρδώ: Eth. Σαρδῷος, Sardus: *Sardinia*), one of the largest and most important islands in the Mediterranean sea, situated to the S. of Corsica (from which it was separated only by a narrow strait, now called the *Strait of Bonifazio*) and NW. of Sicily. Its most southern extremity, *Cape Spartivento*, was distant only 120 geog. miles from *Cape Serrat* in Africa.

I. GENERAL DESCRIPTION.

It was a disputed point in ancient times whether Sicily or Sardinia was the largest. Herodotus calls Sardinia "the largest of islands" (νῆσον δπασέων μεγίστην, i. 170, νῆσον τὴν μεγίστην, v. 106), but in passages where it is not certain that the expression is to be construed quite strictly. Scylax, however, distinctly calls Sardinia the largest of all the islands in the Mediterranean, assigning to Sicily only the second rank (Scyl. p. 56. § 113); and Timaeus seems to have adopted the same view (ap. *Strab.* xiv. p. 654). But the general opinion was the other way: the comic poet Alexius already enumerated the seven great islands, as they were called, placing Sicily first and Sardinia second (Alex. *ap. Const. Porphyr. de Prov.* ii. § 10): and this view is followed by Scymnus Chius, as well as by the later geographers. (Scymn. Ch. p. 223; Strab. ii. p. 123; Plin. iii. 7. s. 13, 8. s. 14; Diod. v. 17). Diodorus, however, justly remarks, that it is very nearly equal to Sicily in magnitude (Diod. v. 16): and this opinion, which was adopted by Cluverius (*Sicil. Ant.* p. 478), continued to prevail down to a very recent period. But modern researches have proved that Sardinia is actually the larger of the two, though the difference is but trifling. (Smyth's *Sardinia*, p. 66.) Its general form is that of an oblong parallelogram. above 140 geog. miles in its greatest length, by about 60 in its average breadth, which, however, attains to as much as 77 in one part. The measurements given by Pliny, of 188 miles (148⅔ geog. miles) in length along the E. coast, and 175 on the W., are therefore very fair approximations (Plin.

iii. 7. s. 13), while those of Strabo, who calls the island 220 miles in length by 98 in breadth, are considerably overstated. (Strab. v. p. 224.)

Sardinia is a much more fertile and less mountainous island than Corsica. It is, however, traversed throughout its whole length from N. to S. by a chain of mountains which commence at the headland called *Capo Lungo Sardo*, and extend along the eastern side of the island, as far as *Capo Carbonara*, which forms the SE. extremity of the island. This range, which is composed of granitic and other primary rocks, is undoubtedly a continuation, in a geological sense, of the mountains of Corsica, and produces a rugged and difficult country forming much the wildest and most uncivilised part of Sardinia. The mountain summits, however, are far from attaining the same elevation as those of Corsica, the highest point, called *Monte Genargentu*, rising only to 5276 feet, while the *Monte di Sta Vittoria*, in the same neighbourhood, rises to 4040 feet, and the peak of *Limbarra* (the most northerly group of the chain) to 3686 feet: but the general elevation of the range rarely exceeds 3000 feet. (Smyth, p. 67.) West of this mountain district, which may be considered on a rough estimate as comprising about one half of the whole island, are situated three detached groups of mountains; the most considerable of which is that in the SW., which extends from *Capo Spartivento* to *Capo della Frasca* on the *Gulf of Oristano*, and the highest summits of which attain to an elevation of nearly 4000 feet. In the extreme NW. of the island is another isolated range of less extent, called the *Monti della Nurra*, extending from the *Capo della Caccia* to the *Capo del Falcone*. Both these groups are, like the mountains in the E. of the island, composed of primary rocks; but N. of the river *Tirso*, and extending from thence to the N. coast of the island beyond *Sassari*, is an extensive volcanic tract, occupied in considerable part by a range of extinct volcanoes, one of which, the *Monte Urticu*, rises to an elevation of 3430 feet. There is no trace of any volcanic action having taken place within the historical period, but extensive tracts are still covered with broad streams and fields of lava. Notwithstanding this abundance of mountains, Sardinia possesses several plains of considerable extent. The largest of these is that called the *Campidano*, which extends from the *Gulf of Cagliari* to that of *Oristano*, thus separating entirely the range of mountains in the SW. from those in the E. of the island; it is a tract of great fertility. A similar plain, though of less extent, stretches across from the neighbourhood of *Alghero* to that of *Porto Torres*, thus isolating the chain of the *Monti della Nurra ;* while several smaller ones are found in other parts of the island. The general character of Sardinia is therefore well summed up by Strabo, when he says, " the greater part of it is a rugged and wild country, but a large part contains much fertile land, rich in all kinds of produce, but most especially in corn." (Strab. v. p. 224.)

The great disadvantage of Sardinia, in ancient as well as modern times, was the insalubrity of its climate. This is repeatedly alluded to by ancient writers, and appears to have obtained among the Romans an almost proverbial notoriety. Mela calls it " soli quam coeli melioris, atque ut foecunda, ita pene pestilens." Strabo gives much the same account, and Martial alludes to it as the most deadly climate he can mention. (Strab. v. p. 225; Mel. ii. 7. § 19; Paus. x. 17. § 11; Martial, iv. 60. 6;

Cic. *ad Q. Fr.* ii. 3; Tac. *Hist.* ii. 85; Sil. Ital. xii. 371.) There can be no doubt that this was mainly owing to the extensive marshes and lagunes on the coast, formed at the mouths of the rivers; and as these naturally adjoined the more level tracts and plains, it was precisely the most fertile parts of the island that suffered the most severely from malaria. (Strab. *l. c.*) The more elevated and mountainous tracts in the interior were doubtless then, as now, free from this scourge; but they were inhabited only by wild tribes, and rarely visited by the more civilised inhabitants of the plains and cities. Hence the character of unhealthiness was naturally applied to the whole island.

II. HISTORY.

The statements of ancient writers concerning the origin of the population of Sardinia are extremely various and conflicting, and agree only in representing it as of a very mixed kind, and proceeding from many different sources. According to Pausanias, who has given these traditions in the greatest detail, its first inhabitants were Libyans, who crossed over under the command of Sardus, the son of a native hero or divinity, who was identified by the Greeks with Hercules. (Paus. x. 17. § 2.) This Sardus was supposed to have given name to the island, which was previously called, or at least known to the Greeks, by that of Ichnusa ('Ἰχνοῦσα), from the resemblance of its general form to the print of a man's foot. (Paus. *l. c.* § 1; Sil. Ital. xii. 358—360; Pseud. Arist. *Mirab.* 104.) Timaeus, according to Pliny, called it Sandaliotis from the same circumstance (Plin. iii. 12. s. 17); but it is clear that neither of these names was ever in general use. The fact that the earliest population came from Africa is intrinsically probable enough, though little value can be attached to such traditions. Pausanias indeed expressly tells us (*l. c.* § 7) that the population of the mountain districts (the people whom he calls Ilienses) resembled the Libyans both in their physical characters and their habits of life. The next settlers, according to Pausanias, were a Greek colony under Aristaeus, to whom some writers ascribe the foundation of Caralis; and these were followed by a body of Iberians under a leader named Norax, who founded the city called Nora in the SW. part of the island. Next to these came a body of Greeks from Thespiae and Attica, under the command of Iolaus, who founded a colony at Olbia in the NE. corner of the island. After this came a body of Trojans, a part of those who had escaped from the destruction of their city, and established themselves in the southern part of the island. It was not till long afterwards that they were expelled from thence by a fresh body of Libyans, who drove them up into the more rugged and inaccessible parts of the island, where they retained down to a late period the name of Ilienses ('Ἰλιεῖς, Paus. x. 17. §§ 2—7; Sil. Ital. xii. 360—368). The existence of a mountain tribe of this name is a well-attested fact, as they are mentioned by Livy as well as by the geographers; and it is probable that the casual resemblance of name gave occasion to the fable of their Trojan origin. [ILIENSES.] The Iolai or Iolaenses, on the other hand, had lost their name in the time of Strabo, and were called, according to him, Diaghesbians (Διαγησβεῖς, v. p. 225), a name which is, however, not found in any other ancient author. Another tribe, whose name is found in historical times, is that of the Balari, who, according to Pau-

sanias, derived their origin from a body of mercenaries in the service of Carthage, that had fled for refuge to the mountains. (Paus. *l. c.* § 9.) To these must be added the Corsi, whose origin is sufficiently indicated by their name. They dwelt in the mountains in the N. of the island (the *Montagne di Limbarra*), and had evidently crossed over from the adjacent island of Corsica, as they are described by Pausanias as having done. (Paus. *l. c.*)

It is idle to attempt to criticise such traditions as these; they are related with many variations by other writers, some of whom term the Iolaenses, others the Ilienses, the most ancient inhabitants of the island (Diod. iv. 29, v. 15; Mel. ii. 7. § 19; Strab. v. p. 225; Sil. Ital. *l. c.*); and it is clear that the different mountain tribes were often confounded with one another. Strabo alone has a statement that the earliest inhabitants of Sardinia (before the arrival of Iolaus) were Tyrrhenians (v. p. 225), by which he must probably mean Pelasgians, rather than Etruscans. We have no account of any Greek colonies in Sardinia during the historical period; though the island was certainly well known to them, and seems to have been looked upon as affording a tempting field for colonisation. Thus we are told by Herodotus that when Phocaea and Teos were taken by Harpagus (B. c. 545) the project was suggested that all the remaining Ionians should proceed in a body to Sardinia, and establish themselves in that island. (Herod. i. 170.) Again in B. c. 499, Histiaeus of Miletus promised Darius to subdue the whole island for him; and it appears that the project of emigrating there was seriously entertained. (Id. v. 106, 124.) Pausanias indeed represents the Messenians as thinking of emigrating there at a much earlier period, just after the close of the Second Messenian War, B. c. 668 (Paus. iv. 23. § 5); but none of these projects were realised, and it seems certain that there were no Greek settlements in the island at the time when it fell into the hands of the Carthaginians.

The Carthaginian conquest is indeed the first fact in the history of Sardinia that can be considered as resting on any sure historical foundation; and even of this the date cannot be fixed with certainty. It is probable indeed that at a much earlier period the Phoenicians had not only visited the coasts of Sardinia for commercial purposes, but had established trading stations or factories there. Diodorus indeed expressly tells us that they planted colonies in Sardinia, as well as in Sicily, Spain, and Africa (Diod. v. 35); and there seems some reason to ascribe to them the first foundation of the important cities of Caralis, Nora, and Sulci. (Movers, *die Phönizier*, vol. iii. pp. 558, 573.) But in this case, as in many others, it is impossible to separate distinctly what was done by the Phoenicians themselves and what by their descendants the Carthaginians. It is, however, certain that it was reserved for the latter to form extensive and permanent settlements in the island, of which they reduced the greater part under their authority. According to Justin, the first Carthaginian expedition took place under a leader named Malchus, who was, however, defeated in a great battle by the native barbarians. (Justin, xviii. 7.) The next invasion was conducted by Hasdrubal, the son of Mago, and the elder brother (if we may trust to the accuracy of Justin) of Hamilcar, who was killed at Himera, B. c. 480. Hasdrubal himself, after many successes, was slain in battle; but the Carthaginians seem to have from this time maintained their footing in the island. (Id. xix. 1.) The chronology of Justin does not claim much confidence; but it seems probable that in this instance it is not far from correct, and that we may place the Carthaginian conquest about 500—480 B.C. It can hardly have taken place much earlier, as the Ionian Greeks still looked upon the island as open to colonisation in the reign of Darius Hystaspis.

Of the details and circumstances of the Carthaginian conquest we have no account; but we are told in general terms that they made themselves masters of the whole island, with the exception of the rugged mountain districts which were held by the Ilienses and Corsi. (Paus. x. 17. § 9; Pol. I. 10.) They founded many towns, and from their superior civilisation struck such deep root into the country, that even in the time of Cicero the manners, character, and institutions of the Sardinians were still essentially Punic. It even appears that a considerable part of the population was of Punic origin, though this was doubtless confined to the towns and the more settled districts in their immediate neighbourhood. (Cic. pro Scaur. §§ 15, 42, 45.) But notwithstanding these clear evidences of the extent of the Carthaginian influence, we have scarcely any account of the long period of above two centuries and a half, during which they continued masters of all the more important portions of the island. An isolated notice occurs in B.C. 379 of a great revolt in Sardinia, the inhabitants of which took advantage of a pestilence that had afflicted the Carthaginians, and made a vigorous effort to shake off their yoke, but without success. (Diod. xv. 24.) We learn also that already at this period Sardinia was able to export large quantities of corn, with which it supplied the fleets and armies of Carthage. (Diod. xiv. 63, 77.) The story current among the Greeks, of the Carthaginians having systematically discouraged agriculture in the island (Pseud. Arist. de Mirab. 104), is therefore, in all probability, without foundation. During the First Punic War (B.C. 259) L. Cornelius Scipio, after the conquest of Aleria in Corsica, directed his course to Sardinia, where he defeated the Carthaginian fleet near Olbia, but did not venture to attack that city. (Zonar. viii. 11.) Having, however, received reinforcements from Rome, he landed in the island, totally defeated the Carthaginian general Hanno, and took the city of Olbia, as well as several minor towns. The next year C. Sulpicius followed up this advantage, and ravaged the greater part of the island, apparently with little opposition. (Zonar. viii. 11, 12; Pol. i. 24; Oros. iv. 7, 8; Flor. ii. 2. § 16; Val. Max. v. 1. § 2.)

No real footing was, however, gained by the Romans in Sardinia during the First Punic War; and the peace which put a close to that contest left the island subject to Carthage as before. But a few years afterwards the Carthaginian mercenaries in Sardinia followed the example of their brethren in Africa, and raised the standard of revolt; they were indeed overpowered by the natives, and driven out of the island, but their cause was espoused by the Romans, who undertook to restore them, and threatened the Carthaginians with war if they attempted the restoration of their own dominion in Sardinia. The latter were exhausted with the long and fierce contest with their mercenary troops in Africa, and were in no condition to resist. They consequently submitted to the demands of the Romans, and agreed by treaty to abandon all claims to Sardinia, B.C.

238. (Pol. i. 79, 88; Appian, Pun. 5; Liv. xxi. 1.) But the Carthaginians could cede no more than they possessed, and the whole island was at this time in the hands of the natives. Its subjugation was not effected by the Romans till after several campaigns; and though in B.C. 235 T. Manlius Torquatus triumphed over the Sardinians, and is said to have reduced the whole island to subjection (Eutrop. iii. 3; Oros. iv. 12; Vell. Pat. ii. 38; Fast. Capit.), it is clear that this statement must be understood with considerable limitation, as the consuls of the two succeeding years, Sp. Carvilius and Pomponius Matho, were still able to earn the distinction of a triumph "de Sardis." (Fast. Capit.) The conquest of the island was now considered complete; and it was reduced to the condition of a province, to which a praetor was annually sent. Corsica was soon after annexed to his jurisdiction. But it is certain that the wilder mountain tribes of the interior, though they may have tendered a nominal submission, were not really subdued, and continued long after to molest the settled parts of the island by their depredations, as well as to find employment for the arms of the praetor by occasional outbreaks of a more serious description.

During the Second Punic War, Sardinia was naturally watched with considerable jealousy, lest the Carthaginians should attempt to regain possession of what they had so long held. But the war which broke out there in B.C. 215, under a native chief named Hampsicora, is attributed by the Roman writers themselves in great measure to the severity of taxation and the exactions of their governors. T. Manlius Torquatus, the same who as consul had already triumphed over the Sardinians, was appointed to quell this insurrection. He defeated the Sardinians under Hiostus, the son of Hampsicora, in the neighbourhood of Cornus: but the arrival of a Carthaginian force under Hasdrubal gave fresh spirit to the insurgents, and the combined armies advanced to the very gates of Caralis. Here, however, they were met by Torquatus in a pitched battle and totally defeated. Hasdrubal was taken prisoner, Hiostus slain in the battle, and Hampsicora in despair put an end to his own life. The remains of the defeated army took refuge in the fortress of Cornus; but this was soon reduced by Manlius, and the other towns of Sardinia one after the other made their submission. (Liv. xxiii. 32, 40, 41.)

From this time we hear no more of any general wars in Sardinia; and the large supplies of corn which the island began to furnish to Rome and to the armies in Italy (Liv. xxv. 22, xxx. 24) sufficiently prove that a considerable part of it at least was in the peaceable possession of the Roman authorities. The mountain tribes were, however, still unsubdued; and in B.C. 181 the Ilienses and Balari broke out into a fresh insurrection, which assumed so formidable a character that the consul Tib. Sempronius Gracchus was expressly sent to Sardinia to carry on the war. He defeated the insurgents with heavy loss, and followed up his victory with such vigour that he put to the sword or took prisoners not less than 80,000 persons. (Liv. xl. 19, 34, xli. 6, 12, 17, 28.) The number of captives brought to Rome on this occasion was so great that it is said to have given rise to the proverb of "Sardi venales" for anything that was cheap and worthless. (Vict. Vir. Ill. 65.) Another serious outbreak occurred in Sardinia as late as B.C. 114, to repress which M. Caecilius Metellus was sent as proconsul to the island, and after two years of continuous warfare he earned the distinction of a triumph, a sufficient proof of the formidable character of the insurrection. (Eutrop. iv. 25; Ruf. Fest. 4.) This is the last time we hear of any war of importance in Sardinia; but even in the time of Strabo the mountaineers were in the habit of plundering the inhabitants of the more fertile districts, and the Roman praetors in vain endeavoured to check their depredations. (Strab. v. p. 225.)

The administration of the province was entrusted throughout the period of the Republic to a praetor or propraetor. Its general system was the same as that of the other provinces; but Sardinia was in some respects one of the least favoured of all. In the time of Cicero it did not contain a single free or allied city (*civitas foederata*) (Cic. *pro Scaur.* § 44): the whole province was regarded as conquered land, and hence the inhabitants in all cases paid the tenth part of their corn in kind, as well as a *stipendium* or annual contribution in money. (Cic. *pro Balb.* 18; Liv. xxiii. 41.) From the great fertility of the island in corn, the former contribution became one of the most important resources of the Roman state, and before the close of the Republic we find Sardinia, Sicily, and Africa alluded to as the " tria frumentaria subsidia reipublicae." (Cic. *pro Leg. Manil.* 12; Varr. *R. R.* ii. Pr. § 3; Valerius Maximus also terms them " benignissimae urbis nostrae nutrices," vii. 6. § 1.) For this reason, as soon as Pompeius was appointed to the command against the pirates, one of his first cares was to protect the coasts of these three provinces. (Cic. *l. c.*) Among the eminent persons who at different times filled the office of praetor or propraetor in Sardinia, may be mentioned the elder Cato in B. C. 198 (Liv. xxxii. 8, 27); Q. Antonius Balbus, who was appointed by Marius to the government of the island, but was defeated and killed by L. Philippus, the legate of Sulla, B. C. 82 (Liv. *Epit.* lxxxvi.); M. Atius Balbus, the grandfather of Augustus, who was praetor in B. C. 62, and struck a coin with the head of Sardus Pater, which is remarkable as the only one belonging to, or connected with, the island [*Biogr. Dict.* Vol. I. p. 455]; and M. Aemilius Scaurus, who was praetor in B. C. 53, and was accused by the Sardinians of oppression and peculation in his government, but was defended by Cicero in an oration of which some fragments are still extant, which throw an important light on the condition and administration of the island. (Cic. *pro Scaur.* ed. Orell.; Ascon. *in Scaur.*)

In B. C. 46 the island was visited by Caesar on his return from Africa, and the Sulcitani severely punished for the support they had given to Nasidius, the admiral of Pompey. (Hirt. *B. Afr.* 98.) The citizens of Caralis, on the contrary, had shown their zeal in the cause of Caesar by expelling M. Cotta, who had been left by Pompey in charge of the island. (Caes. *B. C.* i. 30.) Sardinia was afterwards occupied by Menodorus, the lieutenant of Sextus Pompeius, and was one of the provinces which was assigned to the latter by the treaty of Misenum, B. C. 39; but it was subsequently betrayed by Menodorus himself into the hands of Octavian. (Dion Cass. xlviii. 30, 36, 45; Appian, *B. C.* v. 56. 66, 72, 80.) It was probably for some services rendered on one or other of these occasions that the citizens of Caralis were rewarded by obtaining the rights of Roman citizens, a privilege apparently conferred on them by Augustus. (" Caralitani civium Roma-

norum," Plin. iii. 7. s. 13.) This was in the days of Pliny the only privileged town in the island: but a Roman colony had been planted in the extreme N. at a place called Turris Libysonis. (Plin. *l. c.*) Two other colonies were established in the island at a later period (probably under Hadrian), one at Usellis, on the W. coast, the other at Cornus. (Ptol. iii. 3. § 2; Zumpt, *de Col.* p. 410.)

Under the Roman Empire we hear but little of Sardinia, which continued to be noted chiefly for its abundant supply of corn, and for the extreme unhealthiness of its climate. In addition to the last disadvantage, it suffered severely, as already mentioned, from the perpetual incursions of the wild mountain tribes, whose depredations the Roman governors were unable to repress. (Strab. v. p. 225.) With the view of checking these marauders, it was determined in the reign of Tiberius to establish in the island a body of 4000 Jews and Egyptians, who, it was observed, would be little loss if they should perish from the climate. (Tac. *Ann.* ii. 85.) We have no account of the success of this experiment, but it would seem that all the inhabitants of the island were gradually brought under the Roman government, as at the present day even the wildest mountaineers of the interior speak a dialect of purely Latin origin. (De la Marmora, *Voy. en Sard.* vol. i. pp. 198, 202.) It is clear also from the number of roads given in the Itineraries, as well as from the remains of them still existing, and the ruins of aqueducts and other ancient buildings still extant, that the island must have enjoyed a considerable degree of prosperity under the Roman Empire, and that exertions were repeatedly made for its improvement. At the same time it was frequently chosen as a place of exile for political offenders, and nobles who had given umbrage to the emperors. (Tac. *Ann.* xiv. 62, xvi. 9, 17; Dion Cass. lvi. 27; Martial, viii. 32.) Its great importance to Rome down to the latest period of the Empire, as one of the principal sources from which the capital was supplied with corn, is attested by many writers, so that when at length it was occupied by the Vandals, it seemed, says a contemporary writer, as if the life-blood of the city had been cut off. (Prudent. *adv. Symmach.* ii. 942; Salvian. *de Provid.* vi.)

During the greater part of the Roman Empire Sardinia continued to be united with Corsica into one province: this was one of those assigned to the senate in the division under Augustus (Dion Cass. liii. 12); it was therefore under the government of a magistrate styled proconsul; but occasionally a special governor was sent thither by the emperor for the repression of the plundering natives. (Id. lv. 28; Orell. *Inscr.* 74, 2377.) After the time of Constantine, Sardinia and Corsica formed two separate provinces, and had each its own governor, who bore the title of Praeses, and was dependent on the Vicarius Urbis Romae. (*Not. Dign.* ii. p. 64; Böcking, *ad loc.*; Ruf. Fest. 4.) It was not till A. D. 456 that Sardinia was wrested from the Roman Empire by Genseric, king of the Vandals; and though recovered for a time by Marcellianus, it soon fell again into the hands of the barbarians, to whom it continued subject till the fall of the Vandal monarchy in Africa, when Cyrillus recovered possession of the island for Justinian, A. D. 534. (Procop. *B. V.* i. 6, 10, 11, ii. 5.) It was again conquered by the Gothic king Totila in A. D. 551 (Id. *B.G.* iv. 24), but was recovered by Narses after the death of that monarch, and seems from this period to have remained a dependency of the Byzantine Empire down to a late period. But in the 8th century, after having suffered severely from the incursions of the Saracens, it passed for the most part into the hands of that people, though the popes continued to assert a nominal sovereignty over the island.

III. TOPOGRAPHY.

The principal physical features of Sardinia have been already described. Of the numerous ranges, or rather groups, of mountains in the island, the only ancient name that has been preserved to us is that of the INSANI MONTES (Liv. xxx. 39; Claudian, *B. G.* 513; τὰ Μαινόμενα ὄρη, Ptol.), and even of these it is not easy to determine the position with any degree of accuracy: the name was apparently applied to the mountains in the N. and NE. of the island, which seem to have been regarded (though erroneously) as more elevated than those farther S., so that the unhealthiness of the southern part of the island was popularly attributed to the shutting out of the bracing north winds by this range of lofty mountains. (Claudian, *l. c.* 513—515.) From its extent and configuration, Sardinia could not possess any very considerable rivers. The largest were, the THYRSUS (Θύρσος, Ptol.: *Tirso*), which rises in the mountains in the NE. of the island, and flows into the *Gulf of Oristano* on the W. coast; the SACER FLUVIUS ('Ιερὸς ποταμός, Ptol.), which falls into the same gulf near Neapolis, now called the *R. di Pabillonis;* the TEMUS or TERMUS (Τέρμος, Ptol.), still called the *Temo,* and falling into the sea near *Bosa,* to the N. of the Thyrsus; the CAEDRIUS (Καἴδριος, Ptol.), on the E. coast of the island, now the *Fiume di Orosei;* and the Saeprus (Σαιπρός, Ptol.), now the *Flumendosa,* in the SE. quarter of the island. No ancient name has been preserved for the *Rio Samassi,* which flows into the *Gulf of Cagliari,* near the city of that name, though it is a more considerable stream than several of those named.

Ptolemy has preserved to us (iii. 3) the names of several of the more important promontories and headlands of the coast of Sardinia; and from its nature and configuration, most of these can be identified with little difficulty. The most northern point of the island, opposite to Corsica, was the promontory of Errebantium ('Ἐρρεβάντιον ἄκρον, Ptol.), now called the *Punta del Falcone,* or *Longo Sardo.* The NW. point, forming the western boundary of an extensive bay, now called the *Golfo dell' Asinara,* is the Gorditanum Prom. (Γορδίτανον ἄκρον) of Ptolemy: immediately opposite to it lies the *Isola dell' Asinara,* the HERCULIS INSULA ('Ηρακλέους νῆσος) of Ptolemy and Pliny, and one of the most considerable of the smaller islands which surround Sardinia. This headland forms the N. extremity of the ridge of mountains called *Monti della Nurra:* the S. end of the same range forms a bold headland, now called *Capo della Caccia,* immediately adjoining which is a deep land-locked bay, the Nymphaeus Portus of Ptolemy (Νύμφαιος λιμήν), now called *Porto Conte.* The Hermaeum Prom. ('Ἑρμαίον ἄκρον) of the same author is evidently the *Capo di Marragiu,* about 12 miles N. of the river *Temo:* the Coracodes Portus (Κορακώδης λιμήν), which he places between that river and Tharros, is probably the small bay that is found S. of *Capo Mannu.* The Prom. Crassum (Παχεῖα ἄκρα) must be *Capo Altano,* from whence the coast trends to the SE. as far as the *Capo di Teulada,* the extreme S. point of the whole island, which must be the one called Cher-

sonesus by Ptolemy; but his positions for this part of the coast are very inaccurate. Opposite to this SW. corner of the island lay two small islands, one of them, called by Ptolemy the Island of Hawks ('Ιεράκων νῆσος), is the *Isola di S. Pietro;* the other, now known as the *Isola di S. Antioco,* is called by him Plumbaria Insula (Μολιβώδης νῆσος), while it is named by Pliny Enosis. It was joined to the mainland by a narrow strip of sand, and was the site of the celebrated town of Sulci, from whence the adjoining bay (now known as the *Golfo di Palmas*) derived the name of Sulcitanus Portus. Two other small ports mentioned by Ptolemy between *Cape Teulada* and the site of Nora (at *Capo di Pula*), Bitiae Portus and Herculis Portus, must be the small coves at *Isola Rossa di Teulada* and *Porto Malfattano.* The next headland, named Cunicularium Prom. (Κουνικουλάριον ἄκρον, but the reading is doubtful), is the *Punta della Savorra;* and the promontory of Caralis must be the headland immediately adjoining the city of that name, now called the *Capo di S. Elia.* Pliny, however, gives the name of Caralitanum Prom. to the SE. headland of Sardinia, for which (singularly enough) Ptolemy furnishes us with no name. The small island lying off it, called both by him and Pliny Ficaria, is a mere rock, now known as the *Isola dei Cavoli.* Proceeding along the E. coast of the island, we find the Sulpicius Portus (Σουλπίκιος λιμήν), which cannot be identified with certainty, and the Portus Olbianus ('Ολβιανὸς λιμήν), which is certainly the *Gulf of Terranova;* while towards the NE. extremity of the island are two headlands called Columbarium and Arcti Promontorium. The latter is still called *Capo dell' Orso,* from its fancied resemblance to the figure of a bear; the former cannot be clearly identified, though it is most probably the *Capo di Ferro.* Opposite this corner of Sardinia lie several small islands, of which the *Isola della Maddalena* is the most considerable, and next to it the *Isola di Caprera.* These are probably the Phintonis and Ilva of Ptolemy, while Pliny terms them Phintonis and Fossa. The Cuniculariae Insulae of Pliny are the small islets N. of these, now called the *Isole dei Budelli.*

The towns of Sardinia were not numerous, and but few of them attained to any importance, at least down to a late period. Hence they are very summarily dismissed by Strabo, who notices only Caralis and Sulci by name, while Pliny tells us the island contained eighteen "oppida," that is, towns of municipal rank, but enumerates only six, besides the colony of Turris Libysonis (Strab. v. p. 22; Plin. iii. 7. s. 13). The only towns which appear to have ever really been places of importance are: CARALIS, the capital of the whole island, in ancient as in modern times; SULCI, in the extreme SW. of the island, on the *Isola di S. Antioco;* NORA, on the coast between Caralis and Sulci at the *Capo di Pula;* NEAPOLIS, on the W. coast, at the mouth of the Sacer Fluvius; THARROS, on a promontory at the N. extremity of the *Gulf of Oristano;* CORNUS, on the W. coast, about 16 miles further N.; BOSA (Βῶσα, Ptol. iii. 3. § 7; *Itin. Ant.* p. 83), also on the W. coast, at the mouth of the river Temus, still called *Bosa;* TURRIS LIBYSONIS (*Porto Torres*), on the N. coast of the island; TIBULA, at *Longo Sardo,* near the extreme N. point or Cape Errebantium; and OLBIA, on the *Gulf of Terranova,* in the NE. corner of the island. In the interior were: FORUM TRAJANI (*Fordungianus*), situated on the river Thyrsus about 18 miles from its mouth; USELLIS, about 15 miles to the S. of the preceding; VALENTIA, to the SE. of Usellis: and GURULIS VETUS and NOVA, both of which were situated between the rivers Thyrsus and Temus.

Of the minor towns mentioned by Ptolemy or the Itineraries, the following may be noticed: 1. On the W. coast, were Tilium (Ptol.), which must have been near the Capo Negretto: Osaca or Hosaca (Id.) at Flumentorgiu, a few miles W. of Neapolis; and Othoca (Itin. Ant.) apparently the modern Oristano, near the mouth of the river Thyrsus. 2. On the S. coast, Pupulum (Ptol.) may probably be placed at Massacara, a few miles N. of Sulci; Bitia (Ptol.) at S. Isidoro di Teulada; and Tegula (Itin. Ant.) at the Capo di Teulada, the extreme S. point of the island. 3. On the E. coast, Feronia (Ptol.) must have been at or near Posada, 25 miles S. of Olbia, and is apparently the same place called in the Itineraries Portus Lugudonis. The other small places mentioned in the same Itinerary were probably mere stations or villages. 4. On the N. coast, besides the two considerable towns of Tibula and Turris Libysonis, Ptolemy places two towns, which he calls Juliola (probably the same with the Viniola of the Itinerary, still called Torre Vignola) and Plubium, which may probably be fixed at Castel Sardo. The small towns of the interior are for the most part very uncertain, the positions given by Ptolemy, as well as the distances in the Itineraries, varying so much as to afford us in reality but little assistance; and of the names given by Ptolemy, Erycinum, Heraeum, Macopsisa, Saralapis or Sarala, and Lesa, not one is mentioned in the Itineraries. The Aquae Lesitanae (Ptol.) are probably the Acqui di Benetutti in the upper valley of the Thyrsus: the Aquae Hypsitanae are those of Fordungiasus, and the Aquae Neapolitanae the Bagni di Sardara. There remain considerable ruins of a Roman town at a place called Castro on the road from Terranova (Olbia) to Oristano. These are supposed to mark the site of a place called in the Itineraries Lugudonec, probably a corruption of Lugudo or Lugudonis. In the SW. portion of the island, also, between Neapolis and Sulci, are considerable Roman remains at a place called Antas, probably the Metalla of the Itineraries. (Itin. Ant. p. 84.).

The Itineraries give several lines of road through the island of Sardinia. (Itin. Ant. pp. 78—85.) One of these proceeded from Tibula, at the N. extremity of the island, which was the usual place of landing from Corsica, along the whole length of the E. coast to Caralis. It did not accurately follow the line of coast, though it seldom departed far from it, but struck somewhat inland from Tibula to Olbia, and from thence with some exceptions followed the line of coast. A more circuitous, but probably more frequented, route was that which led from Tibula to Turris Libysonis, and thence along the W. coast of the island by Bosa, Cornus, and Tharros to Othoca (Oristano), from which one branch led direct across the island through the plain of the Campidano to Caralis, while another followed nearly the line of the coast by Neapolis to Sulci, and from thence round the southern extremity of the island by Tegula and Nora to Caralis. Besides these, two other cross lines of road through the interior are given: the one from Olbia to Caralis direct, through the mountain country of the interior, and the other crossing the same wild tract from Olbia direct to Othoca. Very few of the stations on these lines of road can be identified, and the

names themselves are otherwise wholly unknown. The reader will find them fully discussed and examined by De la Marmora (Voy. en Sardaigne, vol. ii. pp. 418—457), who has thrown much light on this obscure subject; but the results must ever remain in many cases uncertain.

We learn from the geographers that even under the Roman Empire several of the wild tribes in the interior of the island retained their distinctive appellations; but these are very variously given, and were probably subject to much fluctuation. Thus Strabo gives the names of four mountain tribes, whom he calls Parati, Sossinati, Balari and Aconites (Strab. v. p. 225), all of which, with the exception of the Balari, are otherwise entirely unknown. Pliny mentions only three, the Ilienses, Balari, and Corsi, which he calls "celeberrimi in ea populorum" (Plin. iii. 12. s. 17), and which are in fact all three well known names. The existence of the Ilienses under the Empire is also distinctly attested by Pausanias (x. 17. § 7): yet neither their name nor that of the Balari is noticed by Ptolemy, though he gives those of no less than eighteen tribes as existing in his time. These are, beginning at the N. point of the island and proceeding from N. to S.: "the Tibulatii and Corsi, the Coracenses; then the Carenses and Cunusitanae; next to these the Salcitani and Luquidonenses; then the Aesaronenses; after them the Cornenses (called also Aechilenses); then the Ruacenses; next to whom follow the Celaitani and Corpicenses; after them the Scapitani and Siculenses; next to these the Neapolitani and Valentini, and furthest to the S. the Sulcitani and Noritani." (Ptol. iii. 3. § 6). Of these the Corsi are otherwise well known [see above, pp. 908,909]; the four last names, as well as the Tibulates and Cornenses, are evidently derived from the names of towns, and are probably the inhabitants of districts municipally dependent upon them, rather than tribes in the proper sense of the term. The other names are wholly unknown. After the fall of the Western Empire we find for the first time the name of Barbaricini (Βαρβαρικίνοι, Procop. B. V. ii. 13) applied to the mountaineers of the interior. This appellation, which appears to be merely a corruption of "Barbari vicini," was retained throughout the middle ages, and is still preserved in the name of Barbargia, given to the wild mountain tract which extends from the neighbourhood of Cagliari towards the sources of the Tirso. These mountaineers were not converted to Christianity till the close of the sixth century, and even at the present day retain many curious traces of paganism in their customs and superstitious usages. (De la Marmora, vol. i. p. 30.)

IV. NATURAL PRODUCTIONS, ETC.

The chief produce of Sardinia in ancient times was, as already mentioned, its corn, which it produced in large quantities for exportation even before the period of the Roman conquest. Its mountain tracts were also well adapted for pasturage, and the native tribes subsisted mainly on the produce of their flocks and herds (Diod. v. 15), while they clothed themselves with the skins, whence they were sometimes called "pelliti Sardi." The island also possessed mines both of silver and iron, of which the first are said to have been considerable. (Solin. 4. § 4.) They were undoubtedly worked by the Romans, as we learn from existing traces, and from the name of Metalla given to a place in the SW. of the island, between Neapolis and Sulci. (Itin.

Ant. p. 84; De la Marmora, vol. ii. p. 453.) It had also extensive fisheries, especially of tunny; and of the murex, or shell-fish which produced the purple dye (Suid. *s. v.*). But its most peculiar natural productions were the wild sheep, or moufflon, called by the Greeks μουσμόν (*Ovis Ammon* Linn.), which is still found in large herds in the more unfrequented parts of the island (Strab. v. p. 225; Paus. x. 17. § 12; Aelian, *H. A.* xvi. 34), and a herb, called *Herba Sardoa,* the bitterness of which was said to produce a kind of convulsive grin on the countenances of those that tasted it, which was generally considered as the origin of the phrase, a Sardonic smile (risus Sardonicus; Σαρδόνιος γέλωs, Paus. x. 17. § 13; Suid. *s. v.* Σαρδάνιος; Serv. *ad Virg. Ecl.* vii. 41; Solin. 4. § 4.) But the etymology and origin of this phrase are exceedingly dubious, and the peculiar herb alluded to by the ancients cannot be now identified. The bitterness of the Sardinian honey (Hor. *A. P.* 375), which was supposed to result from the same herb, is, however, a fact still observable at the present day. (Smyth's *Sardinia,* p. 104.) Pausanias mentions that the island was free from wolves, as well as from vipers and other venomous serpents, an advantage that it still enjoys (Paus. x. 17. § 12; Solin. 4. § 3; De la Marmora, vol. i. pp. 173, 177); but it contained a venomous spider, apparently a kind of tarantula, called Solifuga, which was peculiar to the island. (Solin. *l. c.*)

The native population of Sardinia seem to have enjoyed a very evil reputation among the Romans. The harsh expressions of Cicero (*pro Scaur.* 9. §§ 15, 42, &c.) must, indeed, be received with considerable allowance, as it was his object in those passages to depreciate the value of their testimony; but the proverbial expression of "Sardi venales" was generally understood as applying to the worthlessness of the individuals, as well as to the cheapness and abundance of slaves from that country. ("Habes Sardos venales, alium alio nequiorem," Cic. *ad Fam.* vii. 24.) The praetors, even in the days of Augustus, seem to have been continually making inroads into the mountain territories for the purpose of carrying off slaves (Strab. v. p. 255); but as these mountaineers according to Strabo and Diodorus, lived in caves and holes in the ground, and were unacquainted with agriculture (Strab. *l. c.*; Diod. iv. 30), it is no wonder that they did not make useful slaves.

Of the antiquities found in Sardinia, by far the most remarkable are the singular structures called by the inhabitants Nuraghe or Nuraggis, which are almost entirely peculiar to the island. They are a kind of towers, in the form of a truncated cone, strongly built of massive stones, arranged in layers, but not of such massive blocks, or fitted with such skill and care, as those of the Cyclopean structures of Greece or Italy. The interior is occupied with one or more vaulted chambers, the upper cone (where there are two, one over the other, as is frequently the case) being approached by a winding stair or ramp, constructed in the thickness of the walls. In some cases there is a more extensive basement, or solid substruction, containing several lateral chambers, all constructed in the same manner, with rudely pointed vaultings, showing no knowledge of the principle of the arch. The number of these singular structures scattered over the island is prodigious; above 1200 have been noticed and recorded, and in many cases as many as twenty or thirty are found in the same neighbourhood: they are naturally found in very different degrees of preservation, and many varieties of arrangement and construction are observed among them; but their purpose and destination are still unknown. Nor can we determine to what people they are to be ascribed. They are certainly more ancient than either the Roman or Carthaginian dominion in the island, and are evidently the structures alluded to by the author of the treatise *de Mirabilibus,* which he describes as θόλοι, or vaulted chambers, the construction of which he ascribes to Iolaus. (Pseud. Arist. *de Mirab.* 104.) Diodorus also speaks of great works constructed by Daedalus for Iolaus, which must evidently refer to the same class of monuments. (Diod. iv. 30.) Both traditions are valuable at least as evidence of their reputed high antiquity; but whether they are to be ascribed to the Phoenicians or to the native inhabitants of the island, is a point on which it is very difficult to form an opinion. They are fully described by De la Marmora in his *Voyage en Sardaigne,* vol. ii. (from which work the annexed figure is taken), and more briefly by Capt. Smyth (*Sardinia,* pp. 4—7) and Valéry (*Voy. en Sardaigne*).

The work of De la Marmora, above cited, contains a most complete and accurate account of all the antiquities of Sardinia, as well as the natural history, physical geography, and present state of the island. Its authority has been generally followed throughout the preceding article, in the determination of ancient names and localities. The works of Captain Smyth (*Present State of Sardinia,* 8vo. London, 1828), Valéry (*Voyage en Corse et en Sardaigne,* 2 vols. 8vo. Paris, 1838), and Tyndale (*Island of Sardinia,* 3 vols. 8vo. London, 1849), though of much interest, are of inferior value.　　　　[E. H. B.]

NURAGHE IN SARDINIA.

SARDONES. [SORDONES.]

SARDO'NYX (Σαρδόνυξ), a mountain or chain of mountains in *Hindostan*, noticed by Ptolemy (vii. 1. §§ 20 and 65). It would seem to have been part of the range now known by the name of the *Vindhya Mountains*. Lassen, in his map, has identified them with the *Pâgapippali Mountains* on the right bank of the Narmada (*Nerbudda*), and Forbiger has supposed them to be the *Sâtpura Mountains*, a continuation of the same chain.   [V.]

SARDO'UM or **SARDO'NIUM MARE** (τὸ Σαρδῷον πέλαγος, Strab., Pol., but τὸ Σαρδόνιον πέλαγος, Herod. i. 166), was the name given by the ancients to the part of the Mediterranean sea adjoining the island of Sardinia on the W. and S. Like all similar appellations it was used with considerable vagueness and laxity; there being no natural limit to separate it from the other parts of the Mediterranean. Eratosthenes seems to have applied the name to the whole of the sea westward of Sardinia to the coast of Spain (*ap. Plin.* iii. 5. s. 10), so as to include the whole of what was termed by other authors the MARE HISPANUM or BALEARICUM; but this extension does not seem to have been generally adopted. It was, on the other hand, clearly distinguished from the Tyrrhenian sea, which lay to the E. of the two great islands of Sardinia and Corsica, between them and Italy, and from the Libyan sea (Mare Libycum), from which it was separated by the kind of strait formed by the Lilybaean promontory of Sicily, and the opposite point (*Cape Bon*) on the coast of Africa. (Pol. i. 42; Strab. ii. pp. 105, 122; Agathem. ii. 14; Dionys. Per. 82.) Ptolemy, however, gives the name of the Libyan sea to that immediately to the S. of Sardinia, restricting that of Sardoum Mare to the W., which is certainly opposed to the usage of the other geographers. (Ptol. iii. 3. § 1.) Strabo speaks of the Sardinian sea as the deepest part of the Mediterranean; its greatest depth was said by Posidonius to be not less than 1000 fathoms. (Strab. ii. pp. 50, 54.) It is in fact quite unfathomable, and the above estimate is obviously a mere guess.   [E. H. B.]

SAREPTA (Σάρεφθα), the "Zarephath, a city of Sidon" of the Old Testament (1 *Kings*, xvii. 9, 10; comp. *St. Luke*, iv. 26), apparently at the most extreme north (*Obad.* 20), celebrated in the history of Elijah the prophet. It is said by Josephus to be not far from Tyre and Sidon, lying between the two. (*Ant.* viii. 13. § 2.) Pliny places it between Tyre and Ornithon, on the road to Sidon (v. 19. § 17). In the Itinerarium Hierosolymitanum the name does not occur, but it is described by a periphrasis and placed viii. M. P. from Sidon (p. 583). The Arabian geographer Sherif Ibn Idris, quoted by Reland, places *Zaraphand* 20 miles from Tyre, 10 from Sidon. (*Palaestina*, p. 985.) It was formerly celebrated for its wine, and is supposed to be intended by Pliny under the name of Tyrian, which he commends with that of Tripolis and Berytus (xiv. 7). Several of the later Latin poets have also sung the praises of the "dulcia Bacchi munera, quae Sarepta ferax, quae Gaza crearet," the quantity of the first syllable being common (ap. Reland, p. 986). The place is noticed by modern travellers. Dr. Robinson found "a large village bearing the name of *Sûrapend*," five hours north of Tyre, three south of Sidon, near the sea-shore, where is a saint's tomb called *El-Khûdr* (= *St. George*), which he imagined to mark the site of a

Christian chapel mentioned by travellers in the middle ages. (*Bibl. Res.* vol. iii. pp. 412, 413.)   [G. W.]

SARGANTHA. [SERGUNTIA.]

SARGARAUSE'NE (Σαργαραυσηνή), a district of Cappadocia, on the east of Commagene and near the frontiers of Pontus, containing, according to Ptolemy (v. 6. § 13), the towns of Phiara, Sadagena, Gauraena, Sabalassus, Ariarathira, and Maroga. (Strab. xii. pp. 534, 537; Plin. vi. 3.) [L.S.]

SARGE'TIA (Σαργετία, Dion Cass. lxviii. 14; Σαργεττία, Tzetz. *Chil.* ii. 61; Σαργέντιος, Tzetz. *Chil.* vi. 53), a river of Dacia, upon which stood the royal palace of Decebalus. This river must be identified with the *Strel* or *Strey*, a tributary of the *Marosch*, since we know that Sarmizegethusa was the residence of Decebalus. [SARMIZEGETHUSA.] (Ukert, vol. iii. pt. ii. p. 603.)

SARIPHI MONTES (τὰ Σάριφα ὄρη), a chain of mountains, extending, according to Ptolemy, between Margiana and Ariana, and the watershed of several small streams. They are probably those now called the *Hazâras*. Mannert (v. 2. p. 65), has supposed them the same as the Σαπφείροι (see Dion. Perieg. v. 1099), but this is contrary to all probability.   [V.]

SARMA'LIUS (*It. Ant.* p. 203) or **SARMA'LIA** (Σαρμαλία, Ptol. v. 4. § 8), a town in Galatia, on the road from Ancyra to Tavia or Tavium, is supposed by some to be the modern *Karadjelek*. [L.S.]

SARMA'TIA (Σαρματία: Eth. Σαρμάται), the name of a country in Europe and Asia. For the earlier and Greek forms of the word see SAUROMATAE.

That *S-rm* is the same root as *S-rb*, so that *Sarmatae* and *Serbi, Servi, Sorabi, Srb,* &c., may be, not only the name for the same populations, but also the same name, has been surmised, and that upon not unreasonable grounds. The name seems to have first reached the Greeks through the Scythians of the lower *Dnieper* and *Don*, who applied it to a non-Scythic population. Whether this non-Scythic population used it themselves, and whether it was limited to them by the Scythians, is uncertain. It was a name, too, which the Getae used; also one used by some of the Pannonian populations. It was, probably, the one which the Sarmatians themselves used partially, their neighbours generally, just like Galli, Graeci, and many others.

More important than the origin of the name are the questions concerning (1) the area, (2) the population to which it applied. Our chief authority on this point is Ptolemy; Strabo's notices are incidental and fragmentary.

The area given by Strabo to the Galatae and Germani, extends as far as the Borysthenes, or even the *Don*, the Tyrigetae being the most western of the non-German countries of the southeast, and the Bastarnae being doubtful,—though, perhaps, German (vii. p. 289). Of a few particular nations, such as the Jazyges, Hamaxobii, and Roxolani, a brief notice is given, without, however, any special statement as to their Sarmatian or non-Sarmatian affinities. In Asia, the country of the Sauromatae is called the plains of the Sarmatae, as opposed to the mountains of Caucasus. The inordinate size given to Germany by Strabo well nigh obliterates, not only Sarmatia, but Scythia in Europe as well.

Pliny's notices are as incidental as Strabo's, and nearly as brief,—the development of Germany eastwards being also inordinate. He carries it as far as the country of the Bastarnae.

The Germany of Tacitus is bounded on the east by the Sarmatae and Daci. The Sarmatae here are the population of a comparatively small area between the *Danube* and *Theiss*, and on the boundaries of *Hungary*, *Moldavia*, and *Gallicia*. But they are something more. They are the type of a large class widely spread both eastward and northward; a class of equal value with that of the Germani. This, obviously, subtracts something from the vast extent of the Germania of *Strabo* (which nearly meant Northern Europe); but not enough. The position of the Bastarnae, Peucini, Venedi, and Finni, is still an open question. [SCYTHIA.]

This prepares us for something more systematic, and it is in Ptolemy that we find it. The SARMATIAE of Ptolemy fall into (1) the EUROPEAN, and (2) the ASIATIC.

I. SARMATIA EUROPAEA.

The western boundary is the *Vistula*; the northern the *Baltic*, as far as the *Venedic* gulf and a tract of unknown country; the southern, the country of the Jazyges Metanastae and Dacia; the eastern, the isthmus of the *Crimea*, and the *Don*. This gives us parts of *Poland* and *Gallicia*, *Lithuania*, *Esthonia*, and *Western Russia*. It includes the Finni (probably a part only), and the Alauni, who are Scythians *eo nomine* (Ἀλαῦνοι Σκίθαι). It includes the Bastarnae, the Peucini, and more especially the Venedi. It also includes the simple Jazyges, as opposed to the Jazyges Metanastae, who form a small section by themselves. All these, with the exception of the Finni, are especially stated to be the *great* nations of Sarmatia (to which add the Roxolani and Hamaxobii), as opposed to the smaller ones.

Of the *greater* nations of Sarmatia Europaea, the Peucini and Bastarnae of Ptolemy are placed further north than the Peucini and Bastarnae of his predecessors. By later writers they are rarely mentioned. [VENEDI.] Neither are the Jazyges, who are the Jazyges Sarmatae of Strabo. These, along with the Roxolani, lay along the whole side (δλην τὴν πλευρὰν) of the Maeotis, say in *Kherson*, *Tauris* and *Ekaterinoslav*. [ROXOLANI.] Hamaxobii is merely a descriptive term. It probably was applied to some Scythian population. Pliny writes Hamaxobii aut Aorsi, a fact of which further notice is taken below. The Alauni, notwithstanding an Ἀλαῦνον ὄρος, and other complications, can scarcely be other than the Alani of Caucasus; the ἀλκήεντες Ἀλαυνοι of the Periegesis (l. 302) are undoubted Scythians. Nestor, indeed, has a population otherwise unknown, called *Uliczi*, the *csi* being non-radical, which is placed on the *Dniester*. It does not, however, remove the difficulty.

The Peucini were best known as the occupants of one of the islands at the mouth of the Danube. They may also, however, have extended far into *Bessarabia*. So manifold are the changes that a word with Sarmatian or Scythian inflexion can undergo, that it is not improbable that Peuc-ini may be the modern words *Budjack* and *Bess*, in *Bess*-arabia. The following are the *actual* forms which the name of the Patz-inacks, exactly in the country of the *Peuc*-ini, undergoes in the mediaeval and Byzantine writers. Πατζ(υνᾶκται, *Pecenatici*, *Pizenaci*, *Pincenates*, *Postinagi*, *Peczenjezi* (in Slavonic), *Petinei*, *Pecinei* (the nearest approach to

Peucini.) Then, in the direction of *Budziak* and *Bessi*, *Beknakije*, *Petschnakije*, *Pezina*-völlr (in Norse), *Bisseni* and *Bessi*, (Zeuss, *Die Deutschen*, &c. *s. vv.* Pecinaci and *Cumani*). The Patzinaks were Scythians, who cannot be shown to be of recent origin in Europe. They may, then, have been the actual descendants of the Peucini; though this is not necessary, for they may have been a foreign people who, on reaching the country of the *Peuc*-ini, took the name; in such a case being *Peuc*-ini in the way that an Englishman is a Briton, i. e. not at all. The difference between the Peucini and Bastarnae was nominal. Perhaps the latter were Moldavian rather than Bessarabian. The Atmoni and Siaones of Strabo were Bastarnae.

The geography of the minor nations is more obscure, the arrangement of Ptolemy being somewhat artificial. He traces them in two parallel columns, from north to south, beginning, in both cases with the country of the Venedi, and taking the eastern bank of the Vistula first. The first name on this list is that of the Gythones, south of the Venedi. It is not to be understood by this that the Venedi lay between the Gythones and the Baltic, so as to make the latter an inland people, but simply that the Venedi of the parts about *Memel* lay north of the Gythones of the parts about *Elbing*. Neither can this people be separated from the Guttones and Aestyii, i. e. the populations of the amber country, or *East Prussia*.

The Finni succeed (Γύθωνες εἶτα Φίννοι). It is not likely that these Finns (if Finns of Finland) can have laid due south of *East Prussia*; though not impossible. They were, probably, on the east.

The Bulanes (Sulones?), with the Phrugundiones to the south, and the Avareni at the head of the Vistula, bring us to the Dacian frontier. The details here are all conjectural. Zeuss has identified the Bulanes with the Borani of Zosimus, who, along with the Goths, the Carpi, and the Urugundi, attacked the empire under Gallus. In Nestor a population called *Sul*-iczi occupies a locality between the *Dnieper* and *Dniester*: but this is too far east. In *Livonia*, Henry the Lett gives prominence to the nation of the *Selones*, a likelier identification.

For Bulanes (supposing this to be the truer reading) the word *Polyane* gives us the most plausible signification. Nestor uses it frequently. It is *Pole*, primarily meaning *occupants of plains*. Wherever, then, there were plains they might be *Polyane*; and Nestor actually mentions two divisions of them; the *Lekhs*, or *Poles* of the *Vistula*, and the *Polyane* of the *Dnieper*.

The Phrugundiones of Ptolemy have always been a *crux geographica*. Name for name, they are so like Burgundiones as to have suggested the idea of a migration from *Poland* to *Burgundy*. Then there are the Urugundi and Burgundi of the Byzantine writers (see Zeuss, *s. vv.* Borani, *Urugundi*), with whom the Ptolemaean population is, probably, identical. The writer who is unwilling to assume migrations unnecessarily will ask whether the several Burgundys may not be explained on the principle suggested by the word *Polyane*, i. e. whether the word may not be the name of more than one locality of the same physical conditions. Probably, this is the case. In the German, and also in the Slavonic languages, the word *Fairguni*, *Fergund*, *Vergunt*, *Virgunda*, *Virgunndia*, and *Viraunnia*, mean *hill-range*, *forest*, *elevated tract*.

Of these there might be any amount,—their occurrence in different and distant parts by no means implying migrations.

The Avareni may be placed in *Gallicia*.

South of them come the Ombrones, and the Anarto-phracti. Are these the Arnartes of Caesar? The Anartes of Caesar were on the eastern confines of the Hercynian forest (*Bell. Gall.* vi. 24, 25), conterminous with the Daci, a fact which, taken along with the physical conditions of the country, gives us *Western Gallicia*, or *Austrian Silesia*, for the Anarto-phracti. Then come the Burgiones, then the Arsiaetae (compare with *Aorsi*), then the Saboki, then the Piengitae, and then the Bessi, along the *Carpathian Mountains*. *Gallicia*, with parts of *Volhynia*, and *Podolia* give us ample room for these obscure, and otherwise unnamed, populations.

The populations of the second column lie to the east of those just enumerated, beginning again with the Venedi (ὑπὸ τοὺς Ὀυενέδας πᾶλιν). *Vilna*, *Grodno*, with parts of *Minsk*, *Volhynia*, *Podolia*, and *Kiev* give us an area over which we have six names to distribute. Its southern boundary are the Peucinian mountains (*Bukhovinia ?*).

(1.) The Galindae.—These are carried too far east, i. e. if we are right in identifying them with the Galinditae of the *Galandia* and *Golens* of the middle ages, who are East Prussians on the *Spirding Lake*.

(2.) The Sudeni.—These, again, seem to be the *Sudo*-vitae (the termination is non-radical in several Prussian names) conterminous with the Galinditae, but to the north-east of them. Their district is called *Sudovia*.

(3.) The Stavani.—Concerning these, we have the startling statement, that they extend as far as the Alauni (μέχρι τῶν ᾽Αλαύνων). Is not ῎Αλαυνοι an erroneous name developed out of some form of Γαλίν-δαι ? The extension of either the Stavani to Caucasus, or of the Alani to *Prussia*, is out of the question.

(4.) The Igylliones.—Zeuss has allowed himself (*s. v. Jazwingi*) to hold that the true form of this word is ᾽Ιτυγγιόνες, and to identify this with a name that appears in so many forms as to make almost any conjecture excusable, — *Jazwingi*, *Jacwingi*, *Jaczwingi*, *Jecwesin*, *Getuinzitae*, *Getwezitae*, *Jentwisiones*, *Jentwosi*, *Jacintiones*, *Jatwjazi*, *Jatwjezi*, or *Getwesia*, and *Gotwezia*, all actual forms. The area of the population, which was one of the most powerful branches of the Lithuanian stock in the 13th century, was part of *Grodno*, *Minsk*, and *Volhynia*, a locality that certainly suits the Igylliones.

(5.) The Costoboci in *Podolia*.

(6.) The Transmontani. — This is a name from the Latin of the Dacians,—perhaps, however, a translation of the common Slavonic *Za-volovsknje*, i. e. *over-the-watershed*. It was applied, perhaps, to the population on the northern frontier of Dacia in general.

The third list, beginning also with the Venedi, follows the line of the Baltic from *Vilna* and *Courland* towards *Finland*, and then strikes inland, eastwards and southwards. Immediately on the Venedic gulf lie the

(1.) Veltae (Ὀυέλται). Word for word, this is the *Vylte* and *Wilzi* of the middle ages ; a form which appears as early as Alfred. It was German, i. e. applied by the Franks to certain Slavonic population. It was also native, its plural being *Weletabi*. Few

nations stand out more prominently than these *Wilts* of the Carlovingian period. They lie, however, to the *west* of *Prussia*, and indeed of *Pomerania*, from which the *Oder* divided them. In short, they were in *Mecklenburg*, rather than in *Livonia* or *Esthonia*, like the Veltae of Tacitus. Word for word, however, the names are the same. The synonym for these western *Wiltae* or *Welatabi* was *Liut-ici* (*Lutizi*). This we know from special evidence. A probable synonym for the Veltae of Tacitus was also some form of *Lit-*. This we infer from their locality being part of the present *Lith*-nania and *Lett*-land. Add to this that one writer at least (Adam of Bremen) places Wilzi in the country of Ptolemy's Veltae. The exact explanation of this double appearance of a pair of names is unknown. It is safe, however, to place the Veltae in *Lett*-land, i. e. in the southern parts of *Livonia*, and probably in parts of *Lithuania Proper* and *Courland*. Constantine Porphyrogeneta mentions them as Veltini. North of the Veltae —

(2.) The Osii (Ossii), probably in the isle of *Oesel*. It should be added, however, the root *ves-*, *wes-*, appears frequently in the geography of *Prussia*. *Osilii*, as a name for the occupants of *Oesel*, appears early in mediaeval history.

(3.) The Carbones, north of the Osii. This is a name of many explanations. It may be the Finn word for *forest* = *Carbo*. It may be the root *Cur-* (or *K-r*), which appears in a great number of Finn words,— *Coralli* (*Karelian*), *Cur-* (in *Cur-land*), *Kur-* (in *Kur-sk*), &c. The forms *Curones* and *Curonia* (*Courland*) approach it, but the locality is *south* instead of north. It more probably = *Kar-elia*. It almost certainly shows that we have passed from the country of the Slavonians and Lithuanians to that of the Esthonians, Ingrians, and Finlanders. Then, to the east, —

(4.) The Kar-eotae. — Here the *Kar-* is the common Finn root as before. Any part of the government of *Novogorod* or *Olonets* might have supplied the name, the present Finns of both belonging to the *Karelian* division of the name (the *-el-* being non-radical). Then —

(5, 6, 7, 8, 9, 10, 11, &c.) The Salii, south of whom the Agathyrsi, then the Aorsi and Pagyritae, south of whom the Savari, and Borusci as far as the Rhipaean mountains. Then the Akibi and Naski, south of whom the Vibiones and Idrae, and south of the Vibionea, as far as the Alauni, the Sturni. Between the Alauni and Hamaxobii the Karyones and Sargatii. At the bend of the Tanais the Ophlones and Tanaitae.

There are few points in this list which are fixed. The bend of the Tanais (= *Don*) would place the Ophlones in *Ekaterinoslav*. The Borusci, if they reached the Rhipaean mountains, and if these were the *Uralian* rather than the *Valdai* range, must have extended far beyond both European and Asiatic Sarmatia. The Savari bear a name very like one in Nestor — the *Sjevera*, on the *Desna*, *Sem*, and *Sula*,— a word that may merely mean *northern*. It is a name that reappears in Caucasus — Sabeiri.

The Aorsi may be the *Ersad* (the *d* is inflexional), a branch of the Mordvins, occupant at the present time of a tract on the *Oka*. The *Pa-gyritae* may have been the tribes *on* (*po* = *on*) the Gerrhus, such compounds being common in Slavonic, e. g *Po*-labi (*on* the Elbe), *Po*-morania (*on* the sea), &c. The whole geography, however, is indefinite and uncertain.

For *Agathyrsi*, see HUNNI. The *Sargatii* are mentioned in Ptolemy.

South of the Tanaitae came the Osuli (? *Sul*-icsi of Nestor), reaching as far as the Roxolani, i. e. occupying parts of *Cherson* and *Ekaterinoslav*.

Between the Roxolani and Hamaxobii the Rhakalani and Exobugitae. The statement of Pliny that the Hamaxobii were Aorsi, combined with similarity of name between Aorsi and *Ersad*, will not help us here. The *Ersad* are in the governments of *Penza* and *Tamlov ;* the direction of the Hamaxobii is more westward. Rhakalani seems but another form of Roxolani. In *Exo-bug*-itae the middle syllable may give us the root *Bug*, the modern name of the Hypanis. It has been surmised that this is the case with Sa-*bok*-ae, and Costo-*boc*-i. The locality would suit.

Between the Peucini and Basternae (this difference between two nations otherwise identified creates a complication) lie the Carpiani, above whom the Gevini and Budini.

The Carpi must have been near or on the *Carpathian Mountains*. They appear as a substantive nation in the later history of Rome, in alliance with the Sarmatae, &c. of the Dacian frontier. We have a *Victoria Carpica Arpi;* Carpiani and Καρποδάκαι (which Zeuss renders Carpathian Dacians) are several forms of this name [CARPI]. They, along with the Costoboci, Armadoci, and Astingi, appear as the most important frontagers of Northern Dacia.

Between the Basternae and Roxolani the Chuni, and under their own mountains (ὑπὸ τὰ ἴδια ὄρη) the Amadoci and Navari, and along the lake (marsh) of Byke the Torekkadae, and along the Achillaean Course ('Αχιλλέως δρόμον) the Tauroscythae, and south of the Basternae in the direction of Dacia the Tagri, and south of them the Tyrangetae.

For *Tauroscythae* and *Tyrangetae*, see *s. vv.* and SCYTHIA.

Tagri looks like a modified form of *Zagora* (*tramontane*), a common Slavonic geographical name, applicable to many localities.

The Amadoci occupied ἴδια ὄρη, or the Mons Amadocus of Ptolemy. There was also a λίμνη 'Αμαδόκη. This juxta-position of a mountain and lake (pool, or swamp, or fen) should fix their locality more closely than it does. Their history connects them with the Costoboci. (Zeuss, *s. vv.* Costo*boci, Amadoci*.) The physical conditions, however, come out less clearly than our present topographical knowledge of *Podolia, Minsk*, &c. explains. For the Navari see NEURI.

The name Chuni is important. [See HUNNI.]

In Torek-kad-ae and Exo-bug-itae we have two elements of an apparent compound that frequently occurs in Scytho-Sarmatian geography—*Tyn-get-ae*, &c., *Costo-bok-i. Sa-boc-i.* The geography is quite compatible in the presence of these elements.

RIVERS.—From the Vistula eastwards, the Chronus, the Rhubon, the Turuntus, the Chersinos,—the order of the modern names being the *Pregel, Memel, Duna, Aa*, and *Neva*. For the drainage of the *Black Sea*, see SCYTHIA.

MOUNTAINS.—Peuce, the Montes Amadoci, the Mons Budinus, the Mons Alaunus, the Mons Carpathus, the Venedic mountains, the Rhipaean mountains. None of these are definitely identified. It is difficult to say how Ptolemy named the most important range of so flat a tract as Russia, viz., the *Valdai Mountains*. On the other hand, the names of his text imply more mountains than really exist. All his mountains were, probably, spurs of the Carpathians, just as in Sarmatia Asiatica they were of Caucasus.

TOWNS.—See SCYTHIA.

II. SARMATIA ASIATICA.

The boundaries are—the Tanais, from its sources to its mouth, European Sarmatia from the sources of the Tanais northwards, the Maeotis and Cimmerian Bosporus, the Euxine as far as the river Corax, the range of Caucasus, the Caspian as far as the river Soana, the Volga as far as its bend (Scythia being on the east of that river), — and on the north an Unknown Land. Without knowing the point at which this terra incognita begins, it is impossible to give the northern limits of Sarmatia Asiatica. It is included, however, in the governments of *Caucasus, Circassia, Astrakhan, Don Kosaks, Saratov, Simbirsk, Kazan, Viatka, Kostroma, Vladimir* (?), *Nizhni Novogorod, Riazan* (?), *Tambov*, and *Penza ;* all the governments, in short, on the water system of the *Volga;* a view which makes the watershed between the rivers that empty themselves into the White Sea and the rivers that fall into the Caspian and Euxine a convenient provisional boundary.

For the obscure geography of Asiatic Sarmatia, the bend of the Tanais is our best starting point. To the north of it dwelt the Perierbidi, a great nation; to the south the Iaxamatae, the former in *Don Kosaks, Voronezh*, and *Tambov, Saratov*, the latter in *Astrakhan*. North of the Perierbidi come the Asaei, the Suardeni, the Zacatae, the Hippophagi Sarmatae, the Modocae, the Royal Sarmatians, the Hyperborean Sarmatians, the Unknown Land. In *Kazan* and *Simbirsk* we may place the Chaenides, and on the east of the *Volga* the Phtheirophagi and Materi. The Νησιῶτις χώρα must be at the mouth of the *Volga*. If so, the order in which the names have been given is from north to south, and the Phtheirophagi are in *Eastern Kazan*, the Materi in *Saratov*.

The remaining populations are all (or nearly all) in the governments of *Caucasus* and *Circassia*, in the northern spurs of the Caucasian range. They are the Siraceni, the Psessii, the Thymeotae, the Turambae, the Asturicani, the Arichi, the Zicchi, the Conapoeni, the Meteibi, the Agoritae, the Melanchlaeni, the Sapothraeni, the Scymnitae, the Amazones, the Sunani, the Sacani, the Orinaei, the Vali, the Servi, the Tusci, the Diduri, the Vodae, the Olondae, the Isondae, the Gerrhi. The Achaei, Kerketi, Heniochi, Suanocolchi, and Sanaraei are truly Caucasian, and belong to the geography of the mountain range rather than the Sarmatian plains and steppes — for such they are in physical geography, and such was the view of Strabo, so far as he noticed Sarmatia at all.

It is difficult to determine the source of Ptolemy's information, difficult to say in what language we are to seek for the meaning of his names. The real populations, as they actually existed, were not very different from those of the Herodotean Scythia; yet the Herodotean names are wanting. These were, probably, Scythian, — the northern populations to which they applied being Ugrian. Are the names native? For the parts due north of Caucasus they may be so; indeed it is possible that the greater number of them may be due to a Caucasian source. At the present time, when we are fairly supplied with

3 N 3

data both as to the names by which the populations of the parts in question designate themselves, as well as those by which they are designated by their neighbours, there are no satisfactory identifications at all. There are some that we may arrive at by a certain amount of assumption; but it is doubtful whether this is legitimate. In the names, for instance, beginning with *sa-* (*Sa-*boci, &c.) we may see the Slavonic for *trans*; in those with *po-* the Slavonic *ad*,—both of which are common in the geographical terminology of the Russians, &c. But these are uncertain, as are the generality of the other coincidences.

In Siberia, for instance, a Samoyed tribe is named *Motor-si* : name for name, this may be Materi ; whether, however, it denote the same population is another question.

Are the Sarmatiae of Ptolemy natural divisions ? Subject to an hypothesis, which will be just stated in the present article, but which will be exhibited in full in SCYTHIA, the Sarmatiae of Ptolemy are objectionable, both for what it contains and what it omits. The whole of Asiatic Sarmatia is, more or less, arbitrary. It seems to be a development of the area of the Herodotean Sauromatae. In the north it comprised Finn or Ugrian, in the south Circassian and Georgian, populations. The Alauni were Scythian, as were several other tribes. It is therefore no ethnological term. Neither are its boundaries natural, if we look at the physical conditions of the country. It was defined upon varying and different principles,—sometimes with a view to physical, sometimes to ethnological, sometimes to political geography. It contains *more* than a natural Sarmatia.

On the other hand, the Vistula was no ethnological line of demarcation. The western half of Poland was Sarmatian, in respect to its climate, surface, and the manners of its inhabitants. The Lygii, however, having been made part of Germania, remained so in the eyes of Ptolemy. That the populations on each side of the *Lower Vistula*, i. e. of *West* and *East Prussia*, were the same, is certain ; it is certain, at least, that they were so at the beginning of the historical period, and all inference leads us to hold that they were so before. The Vistula, however, like the Rhine, was a good natural boundary.

The Jazyges Metanastae were most probably Sarmatian also. Pliny calls them Jazyges Sarmatae (iv. 25); the name Metanastae being generally interpreted *removed*. It is, however, quite as likely to be some native adjunct misunderstood, and adapted to the Greek language.

The other Jazyges (i. e. of the Maeotis) suggested the doctrine of a migration. Yet, if the current interpretation be right, there might be any amount of Jazyges in any part of Sarmatia. It is the Slavonic for language, and, by extension, for the people who speak a language:—" a po Oije rjeje, gde wteczet' w Welgu, *jazyk* swoj Muroma, i Czeremisi swoj *jazyk*; e Mordwa swoj *jazyk*;"—translated, "On the Oka river, where it falls into the Volga, a particular people, the Muroma, and the Tsheremis, a peculiar people, and the Mordwins, a peculiar people." (Zeuss, *s. v. Ostfinnen*). Hence it has at least a Slavonic gloss. On the other hand, it has a meaning in the Magyar language, where *Jassag* = *bowman*, a fact which has induced many scholars to believe that there were Magyars in Hungary before the great Magyar invasion, indeed before the Hun. Be this as it may, the district of the Jazyges Me-

tanastae is called the *Jassag* district at the present moment.

More than one of the Dacian populations were Sarmatian,—the difference between Dacia, the name of the Roman Province, and Sarmatia, the country of an independent and hostile population, being merely political. Indeed, if we look to the distribution of the Sarmatae, their south-eastern limit must have the parts about Tormi. [See SAUROMATAE.] Here, however, they were intrusive.

ETHNOLOGY.—The doctrine upon this point is merely stated in the present notice. It is developed in the article on SCYTHIA. It is to the effect that, in its proper application, *Sarmatian* meant one, many, or all of the north-eastern members of the Slavonic family, probably, with some members of the Lithuanic, included.

HISTORY.—The early Sarmatian history is Scythian as well [SCYTHIA], and it is not until Pannonia becomes a Roman province that the Sarmatian tribes become prominent in history, and, even then, the distribution of the several wars and alliances between the several nations who came under the general denomination is obscure. In doing this there is much that in a notice like the present may be eliminated. The relations of the Greeks and earlier Romans with Sarmatia were with Scythia and the Getae as well, the relations of the latter being with the provincials of Pannonia, with the Marcomanni, and Quadi, &c. Both are neighbours to a tribe of Jazyges.

The great Mithridatic Empire, or, at any rate, the Mithridatic Confederacy, contained Sarmatians *eo nomine*, descendants of the Herodotean Sauromatae. Members of this division it must have been whom the Marcus, the brother of Lucius Lucullus, chastised and drove beyond the Danube, in his march through Moesia. Those, too, it was with whom the Cis-Danubian nations in general were oftenest in contact,—Jazyges, Roxolani, Costoboci, &c., who though (almost certainly) Sarmatian in their ethnological affinities, are not, *eo nomine*, Sarmatian, but, on the contrary, populations with more or less of an independent history of their own. Thirdly, the Sarmatians, who, in conjunction with Getae, Daci, Moesians, Thracians, &c., may have been found in the districts south of the Danube, must be looked upon as intrusive and foreign to the soil on which they are found.

On the other hand, it must be remembered that the Sarmatae *eo nomine* fall into two divisions, divided from each other by the whole extent of the Roman province of Dacia, the area of those of the east being the parts between the Danube and the *Don*, the area of those of the west being the parts between the Danube and *Theiss*. The relations of the former are with the Scythians, Roxolani, the kings of Pontus, &c., over whom, some years later, M. Crassus triumphed. His actions, however, as well as those of M. Lucullus, so far as they were against the Sarmatae, were only accidental details in the campaigns by which Moesia was reduced. The whole of the Trans-Danubian frontier of Moesia, east of Viminiacum, was formed by Dacia.

The point at which the Romans and Sarmatians would more especially come in contact was the country about Sirmium, where the three provinces of Pannonia, Illyricum, and Moesia joined, and where the pre-eminently Sarmatian districts of the nations between the Danube and *Theiss* lay northwards — pre-eminently Sarmatian as opposed to the Dacians, on one side, and the Quadi, &c., of the Regnum Vannianum, on the other. In the general Pannonian and Dalmatian outbreak of A. D. 6, the Sarmatians of these parts took a share (Vell. Pat. ii. 110), as they, doubtlessly, did in the immediately previous war of the Marcomanni, under Maroboduus; the Marcomanni, Quadi, Jazyges, and western Daci, and Sarmatae being generally united, and, to all appearances, the members of a definite confederacy.

The Regnum Vannianum gives us the continuation of the history of these populations (A. D. 19—50). It is broken up; Vannius (? the Ban) himself displaced, and Vangio and Sido, strongly in the interest of Rome, made kings of the parts between the Marus and Cusus (Moravia) instead. To the Vannian confederacy (a Ban-at) the Sarmatae and Jazyges supply the cavalry, the occupants of the Banat itself the infantry (Tac. Annal. xii. 29).

For A. D. 35, we find an interesting notice in Tacitus, which gives definitude to the Sarmatia Asiatica of Ptolemy. It is to the effect that, in a war with Parthia, Pharasmanes entered into an alliance with the Albanians of the coast of the Caspian and the Sarmatae Sceptuchi (? Βασίλειοι). (Tac. Ann. vi. 33.)

A. D. 69. Two pregnant sentences tell us the state of the Sarmatian frontier at the accession of Galba: "Coortae in nos Sarmatarum ac Suevorum gentes; nobilitatus cladibus mutuis Dacus" (Hist. i. 2). The Suevi (who here mean the Quadi and Marcomanni) and Sarmatae (foot and horse) are united. Dacia is paving the way to its final subjection. The Jazyges seem to fall off from the alliance; inasmuch as they offer their services to Rome, which are refused. The colleague of Sido is now Italicus, equally faithful to Rome. (Hist. iii. 5.) In the following year it is Sarmatae and Daci who act together, threatening the fortresses of Moesia and Pannonia (iv. 54).

An invasion of Moesia by the Roxolani took place A. D. 69. This is a detail in the history of the Eastern branch.

The conquest of Dacia now draws near. When this has taken place, the character of the Sarmatian area becomes peculiar. It consists of an independent strip of land between the Roman Province and Quado-Marcomannic kingdom (Banat); its political relations fluctuating. When Tacitus wrote the Germania, the Gothini paid tribute to both the Quadi and Sarmatae; a fact which gives us a political difference between the two, and also a line of separation. The text of Tacitus is ambiguous: "Partem tributorum Sarmatae, partem Quadi, ut alienigenis imponunt" (Germ. 43). Were the Sarmatae and Quadi, or the Quadi alone, of a different family from that of the Gothini? This is doubtful. The difference itself, however, is important.

There were Sarmatians amongst the subjects as well as the allies of Decebalus; their share in the Dacian War (A. D. 106) being details of that event. They were left, however, in possession of a large portion of their country, i. e. the parts between the Vallum Romanum and the frontier of the Suevi, Quadi, or occupants of Regnum Vannianum; the relations of this to the Roman and non-Roman areas in its neighbourhood being analogous to that of the Decumates Agri, between the Rhine and Upper Danube.

In the Marcomannic War (under M. Antoninus) the Sarmatae are as prominent as any members of the confederacy: indeed it is probable that some of the Marcomanni may have been Sarmatae, under another name. This is not only compatible with the undoubtedly German origin of the name Marcomanni (Marchmen), but is a probable interpretation of it. German as was the term, it might be, and very likely was, applied to a non-German population. There were two Marches: one held by Germans for Rome and against the Sarmatians, the other held by the Sarmatians for themselves. The former would be a March, the other an Ukraine. In the eyes of the Germans, however, the men of the latter would just as much be Marchmen as themselves. What the Germans in the Roman service called a neighbouring population the Romans would call it also. We shall soon hear of certain Borderers, Marchmen, or men of the Ukraine, under the name of Limigantes (a semi-barbarous form from Limes); but they will not be, on the strength of their Latin names, Latins. The Solitudines Sarmatarum of the Roman maps was more or less of a Sarmatian March. The Jazyges and Quadi are (as usual) important members of the confederacy.

A. D. 270. Aurelian resigns the province of Dacia to the Barbarians; a fact which withdraws the scene of many a Sarmatian inroad from the field of observations,—the attacks of the Barbarians upon each other being unrecorded. Both before and after this event, however, Sarmatian inroads along the whole line of the Danube, were frequent. Sarmatians, too, as well as Daci (Getae) were comprehended under the general name of Goth in the reigns of Decius, Claudius, &c. Add to this that the name of Vandal is now becoming conspicuous, and that under the name of Vandal history we have a great deal that is Sarmatian.

The most important effect of the cession of Dacia was to do away with the great block of Roman, Romanising, or Romanised territory which lay between the Sarmatians of Pannonia and the Sarmatians of Scythia. It brought the latter within the range of the former, both being, then, the frontagers of Moesia. Add to this the fact of a great change in the nomenclature being effected. The German portion of the Marcomanni (Thervings and Grutungs) has occupied parts of Dacia. The members of this section of the German name would only know the Sarmatae as Vandals. Again, the Hun power is developing itself; so that great material, as well as nominal, changes are in the process of development. Finally, when the point from which the Sarmatae come to be viewed has become Greek and Constantinopolitan, rather than Latin and Roman, the names Slaveni and Servi will take prominence. However, there is a great slaughter of the Sarmatians by Carus, on his way eastwards. Then there is the war, under Constantine, of the Sarmatae of the Border,—the Sarmatae Limigantes, — a Servile War. [See LIMIGANTES.] The authors who tell us of this are the writers of the Historia Augusta and Ammianus; after whose time the name is either rarely mentioned, or, if mentioned, mentioned on the authority of older writers. The history is specific to certain divisions of the Sarmatian population. This was, in its several divisions, hostile to Rome, and independent; still, there were Sarmatian conquests, and colonies effected by the transplantation of Sarmatae. One lay so far east as Gaul.

"Arvaque Sauromatum nuper metata coloni"
(Auson. Mosella)

applies to one of these. There were more of them. The general rule, however, is, that some particular division of the name takes historical prominence, and that the general name of *Sarmatia*, as well as the particular *Sarmatae* of the parts between Dacia and Pannonia, and those between Scythia and Persia, disappears. [See VANDALI; THAIFA-LAE.]   [R. G. L.]

SARMA'TICA I'NSULA, an island at that mouth of the Danube called Kalonstoma (τὸ καλὸν στόμα). (Plin. iv. 24. s. 24.)   [T. H. D.]

SARMA'TICAE PORTAE (αἱ Σαρματικαὶ πύλαι, Ptol. v. 9. §§ 11, 15), a narrow pass of the Caucasus, whence it is also called Caucasiae Portae. (Plin. vi. 11. s. 12, 15. s. 15.) From its vicinity to the Caspian sea, it was also called by some of the ancients Portae Caspiae (Suet. *Nero*, 19), Claustra Caspiarum (Tac. *H.* i. 6), and Via Caspia (Id. *Ann.* vi. 33); but Pliny (*l. c.*) notes this as an error; and the proper Portae Caspiae were in the Taurus (Forbiger, *Geogr.* vol. ii. p. 47, note 92). The Sarmaticae Portae formed the only road between Sarmatia and Iberia. Ptolemy (*l. c.*) distinguishes from this pass another in the same mountain, which he calls αἱ Ἀλβάνιαι Πύλαι (Portae Albaniae), and places the latter in the same latitude as the former, namely the 47th degree, but makes its longitude 3 degrees more to the E. The Albaniae Portae are those on the Alazon, leading over the mountain from *Derbend* to *Berdan*. At both spots there are still traces of long walls 120 feet in height; and on this circumstance seems to have been founded a legend, prevalent in that neighbourhood, of the *Black Sea* and the Caspian having been at one time connected by such a wall. (Forbiger, *Ibid.* p. 55, note 13, b.; comp. Ritter, *Erdkunde*, ii. p. 837.) [T. H. D.]

SARMA'TICI MONTES (Σαρματικὰ ὄρη), a range of mountains on the eastern frontier of Germany, mentioned only by Ptolemy (ii. 11. § 6, viii. 10. § 2), according to whom it appears to have extended north of the Danube as far as the sources of the Vistula, and therefore consisted of the mountains in *Moravia* and a part of the *Carpathians*.   [L. S.]

SARMA'TICUM MARE (ὁ Σαρματικὸς ὠκεανός, Ptol. vii. 5. §§ 2, 6), a sea in the N. of Europe, washing the coast of Sarmatia, and which must thus have been the *Baltic* (Tac. *Germ.* 45). But sometimes the *Black Sea* is designated by the poets under this name, as by Ovid (*ex Pont.* iv. 10. 38) and by Valerius Flaccus (Sarmaticus Pontus, viii. 207.)   [T. H. D.]

SARMATINA, a town of Ariana, mentioned by Ammianus (xxiii. 6). It is probably the same as the Sarmagana of Ptolemy (vi. 17. § 4), as both he and Ammianus place it next to Bitaxa, in the same province.   [V.]

SARMIZEGETHU'SA (Σαρμιζεγέθουσα, Ptol. iii. 8. § 9: Ζερμιζεγέθουσα, Dion Cass. lviii. 9), one of the most considerable towns of Dacia, and the residence of the Dacian kings (βασίλειον, Ptol. *l. c.*) It is called Sarmategis in the *Tabula Peut.*, and Sarmazege by the Geogr. Rav. (iv. 7). It is incontestably the same place as that called τὰ βασίλεια Δακῶν by Dion Cassius (lxvii. 10; lxviii. 8), who places it on the river Sargetia (*Ib. c.* 14); a situation which is also testified by ruins and inscriptions. At a later period a Roman colony was founded here by Trajan, after he had expelled and killed Decebalus king of the Dacians; as is testified by its name of Colonia Ulpia Trajana Augusta and may be inferred

from Ulpian (*Dig.* 50. tit. 15. l. 1.), from whom we also learn that it possessed the Jus Italicum. It was the head-quarters of the Legio xiii. Gemina (Dion Cass. lv. 23), and at first probably there was only a Roman encampment here (Id. lviii. 9; Aur. Vict. *Caes.* xiii. 4). Hadrian conferred an aqueduct upon it, as appears from an inscription (Gruter, p. 177. 3; Orelli, No. 812), and that emperor seems to have retained the colony, on account of its numerous Roman inhabitants, when he resolved to abandon the rest of Dacia to the barbarians. From an inscription to Trajan and his sister Marciana, there would appear to have been baths here (Orell. 791). Sarmizegethusa occupied the site of the present *Varhély* (called also *Gradischte*), on the river *Strel* or *Strey*, about 5 Roman miles from the Porta Ferrea, or Vulcan Pass. (Comp. *Inscr.* Gruter, p. 272; Orelli, Nos. 831, 3234, 3433, 3441, 3527, 3686, 4552; Zamosc. *Ann.* pp. 40, 74; Marsili, *Danub.* tab. 24, 55, &c.; Ukert, iii. 2. p. 616, seq.; Zumpt, in *Rhein. Mus.* 1843, p. 253—259.) [T. H. D.]

SARNEIUS (Σάρνειος), a small stream of Hyrcania mentioned by Strabo (x. p. 511), which, after rising in M. Coronus, flowed in a westerly direction into the Caspian. Professor Wilson considers that it must be either the *Atrek* or the *Gurgan*.   [V.]

SA'RNIA or SARMIA, is named in the Msritume Itin. among the islands of the Ocean between Gallia and Britannia. Supposed to be *Guernsey*. [G. L.]

SARNUS (ὁ Σαρνός: *Sarno*), a river of Campania, flowing into the *Bay of Naples*. It has its sources in the Apennines, above Nuceria (*Nocera*), near which city it emerges into the plain, and, after traversing this, falls into the sea a short distance S. of Pompeii. Its present mouth is about 2 miles distant from that city, but we know that in ancient times it flowed under the walls of Pompeii, and entered the sea close to its gates. [POMPEII.] The change in its course is doubtless owing to the great catastrophe of A. D. 79, which buried Pompeii and Herculaneum. Virgil speaks of the Sarnus as flowing through a plain (*quae rigat aequora Sarnus, Aen.* vii. 738); and both Silius Italicus and Statius allude to it as a placid and sluggish stream. (Sil. Ital. viii. 538; Stat. *Silv.* i. 2. 265; Lucan, ii. 422.) According to Strabo it was navigable, and served both for the export and import of the produce of the interior to and from Pompeii. (Strab. v. p. 247; Plin. iii. 5. s. 9; Ptol. iii. 1. § 7: Suet. *Clar. Rhet.* 4.) Vibius Sequester tells us (p. 18) that it derived its name as well as its sources from a mountain called Sarus. or Sarnus, evidently the same which rises above the modern town of *Sarno*, and is still called *Monte Saro* or *Sarno*. One of the principal sources of the *Sarno* does, in fact, rise at the foot of this mountain, which is joined shortly after by several confluents, the most considerable of these being the one which flows, as above described, from the valley beyond Nuceria.

According to a tradition alluded to by Virgil (*l. c.*), the banks of the Sarnus and the plain through which it flowed, were inhabited in ancient times by a people called SARRASTES, whose name is evidently connected with that of the river. They are represented as a Pelasgian tribe, who settled in this part of Italy, where they founded Nuceria, as well as several other cities. (Conon, *ap. Serv. ad Aen. l. c.*; Sil. Ital. viii. 537.) But their name seems to have quite disappeared in the historical period; and we find Nuceria occupied by the Alfaterni, who were an Oscan or Sabellian race. [NUCERIA.]

No trace is found in ancient authors of a town of the name of Sarnus; but it is mentioned by the Geographer of Ravenna (iv. 32), and seems, therefore, to have grown up soon after the fall of the Roman Empire.　　　　　　　　　　　[E. H. B.]

SARON. [SHARON.]

SARON. [SARONICUS SINUS.]

SARO'NICUS SINUS (Σαρωνικὸς κόλπος, Aeschyl. Agam. 317; Strab. viii. pp. 335, 369, 374, 380; Σαρωνικὸς πόρος, Strab. viii. p. 335; Σαρωνικὸν πέλαγος, Strab. viii. pp. 335, 369; Σαρωνὶς θάλασσα, Dionys. Per. 422; also called Σαλαμινιακὸς κόλπος, Strab. viii. p. 335: *Gulf of Egina*), a gulf of the Aegaean sea, extending from the promontories of Sunium in Attica and Scyllaeum in Troezenia up to the isthmus of Corinth. The length of the gulf, according to Scylax (p. 20, Hudson), is 740 stadia. It washes the coasts of Attica, Megaris, Corinth, Epidaurus and Troezen, and contains the islands of Aegina and Salamis. It was said to have derived its name from Saron, a king of Troezen, who was drowned while hunting in a lagoon upon the Troezenian coast called Phoebaea and afterwards Saronia. (Paus. ii. 30. § 7; *Etym. M.* p. 708. 52; Leake, *Morea*, vol. ii. p. 448.) A Troezenian river Saron is also mentioned (Eustath. *ad Dionys. Per.* 422), and likewise a town of the same name. (Steph. B. *s. v.*) Some derived the name of the gulf from σαρωνίς, " an oak." (Plin. iv. 5. s. 18.)

SARPE'DON (Σαρπηδών or Σαρπηδονία ἄκρα), a promontory on the coast of Cilicia, 80 stadia to the west of the mouth of the Calycadnus, and 120 from Seleuceia. In the peace between the Romans and Antiochus the Great this promontory and Cape Calycadnus were made the frontier between the kingdom of Syria and the free countries of Asia Minor. (Strab. xiv. p. 670; Ptol. v. 8. § 3; Appian, *Syr.* 39; Pomp. Mela, i. 13; Liv. xxxviii. 38; Plin. v. 22; *Stadiasm. Mar. Magni*, § 163.) It now bears the name of *Lissan-el-Kahpe*. (Leake, *Asia Minor*, p. 203.)　　　　　　　　　[L. S.]

SARPEDO'NIUM PROM. (Σαρπηδονίη ἄκρη, Herod. vii. 58), the NW. extremity of the gulf of Melas, and due north of the eastern end of the island of Imbros, now *Cape Paxi*.　　　　　　　[J. R.]

SARRASTES. [SARNUS.]

SARRUM, in Gallia, is placed by the Table between Condate (*Cognac*) [CONDATE, No. 5] and Vesunna (*Perigueux*). It is supposed to be *Charmans*, but the real distances do not agree with the numbers in the table.　　　　　　　　[G. L.]

SARS, a river on the W. coast of Hispania Tarraconensis, between the Prom. Nerium and the Minius. (Mela, iii. 1.) Incontestably the modern *Sar*, which does not reach the sea, but falls into the ancient Ulla at Turris Augusti (*Torres de Este*). (Comp. Florez, *Esp. Sagr.* xv. p. 41.) [T. H. D.]

SA'RSINA (Σάρσινα, Strab.: *Eth.* Sarsinas: *Sarsina*), a city of Umbria, situated in the Apennines, on the left bank of the river Sapis (*Sario*), about 16 miles above Caesena. It seems to have been in very early times a powerful and important city, as it gave name to the tribe of the Sarsinates (Σαρσινάτοι, Pol.), who were one of the most considerable of the Umbrian tribes. Indeed some authors speak of them as if they were not included in the Umbrian nation at all, but formed a separate tribe with an independent national character. Thus Polybius, in enumerating the forces of the Italian nations, speaks of the Umbrians *and* Sarsinates, and Plautus,

in one passage, makes a similar distinction. (Pol. ii. 24; Plaut. *Mostell.* iii. 2. 83.) The Fasti Capitolini, also, in recording the conquest of the Sarsinates, speak of the two consuls as triumphing " de Sarsinatibus," without any mention of the Umbrians; but the Epitome of Livy, in relating the same event, classes them generally among the Umbrians. (Liv. *Epit.* xv.; *Fast. Capit.*) The probable conclusion is that they were a tribe of the Umbrian race; but with a separate political organisation. We have no particulars of the war which ended in their subjection, which did not take place till B. C. 266, so that they were one of the last of the Italian states that submitted to the Roman yoke. From this time Sarsina was certainly included in Umbria in the Roman sense of the term, and became an ordinary municipal town, apparently not of much importance. (Strab. v. p. 227; Plin. iii. 14. s. 19.) It derived its chief celebrity from its being the birthplace of the celebrated comic poet Plautus, who was born there about B. C. 254, very shortly after the Roman conquest. (Hieron. *Chron.* ad Ol. 145; Fest. *s. v. Plotus*, p. 238.) Its territory contained extensive mountain pastures, — whence it is called by Silius Italicus " dives lactis " (Sil. Ital. viii. 461),—as well as forests, which abounded in dormice, so much prized by the Romans. (Martial, iii. 58. 35.) Various inscriptions attest the municipal rank of Sarsina under the Roman Empire (Orell. *Inscr.* 4404; Gruter, *Inscr.* p. 522. 8, p. 1095. 2); but its name is not again found in history. In the middle ages it sunk into complete decay, but was revived in the 13th century, and is now a small town of 3000 inhabitants, which retains the ancient site as well as name.　　　　　　　　　　　　　[E. H. B.]

SARTA (Σάρτη, Herod. vii. 122; Steph. B. *s. v.*), a maritime town on the Singitic gulf between Singus and Ampelus Prom; now *Kartáli*. (Leake, *North. Greece*, vol. iii. p. 154.)　　　　[E. B. J.]

SARUE'NA (Σαρούηνα), a town of Cappadocia, in the district Chamane or Chamanene, on the northeastern slope of Mount Argaeus, celebrated for its hot springs (Ptol. v. 6. § 12; *Tab. Peut.*, where it is called Arauenia, whence Aquae Arauenae; *It. Ant.* p. 202, where its name is Sacoena). It is by some believed to be the modern *Baslyan*. (L. S.]

SARUNE'TES, the name of an Alpine people (Plin. iii. 20. s. 24) in the valley near the sources of the Rhine. There seems no reason to doubt the correctness of the name, and it may be preserved in *Sargans*, which is north of *Chur*, and between *Chur* and the *Lake of Constans*. In a passage of Caesar (*B. G.* iv. 10) he mentions the Nantuates as a people in the upper part of the Rhine, above the Helvetii. The name Nantuates [NANTUATES] is corrupt; and it is possible that the name Sarunetes should be in its place.　　　　　　　　　　　　　　[G. L.]

SARUS (Σάρος), one of the principal rivers in the south-east of Asia Minor, having its sources in Mount Taurus in Cataonia. It first flows in a southeastern direction through Cappadocia by the town of Comana; it then passes through Cilicia in a southwestern direction, and, after flowing by the town of Adana, empties itself into the Cilician sea, on the south of Tarsus, after dividing itself into several branches. (Liv. xxxiii. 41.) According to Xenophon (*Anab.* i. 4. § 1) its breadth at its mouth was 3 plethra or 300 feet; and Procopius (*de Aedif.* v. 4) says it was a navigable river. (Comp. Strab. xii. p. 535; Ptol. v. 8. § 4; Appian, *Syr.* 4; Plin. vi. 3; Eustath. *ad Dion. Per.* 867, who erroneously calls it

Sinarus.) The modern name of the Sarus is *Sihun* or *Seihan.*   [L. S.]

SARXA, a station on the road from Philippi to Heracleia (*Peut. Tab.*), to the N. of the Lake Cercinites, between Strymon and Scotussa. Now *Zikhna.* (Leake, *North. Greece,* vol. iii. p. 227.) [E. B. J.]

SASI'MA (Σάσιμα), a town of Cappadocia, 24 Roman miles to the south of Nazianzus; the place contained the first church to which Gregory of Nazianzus was appointed, and he describes it as a most miserable town. (*It. Ant.* p. 144; *It. Hieros.* p. 577; Hierocl. p. 700, with Wesseling's note.) Some look for its site near the modern *Babloma.*   [L. S.]

SASO (Σασώ, Ptol. iii. 13. § 47; Σασών, Strab. vi. p. 281), a small, rocky island, lying off the coast of Grecian Illyria, N. of the Acroceraunian promontory, and possessing a landing-place which served as a station for pirates. (Comp. Polyb. v. 110; Mela, ii. 7; Plin. iii. 26. s. 30; *Itin. Ant.* p. 489.) It is still called *Saseno, Sassono,* or *Sassa.* [T. H. D.]

SASPI'RES, or SASPI'RI (Σάσπειρες, Σάσπειροι, Herod. i. 104, iv. 37, 40, vii. 79: Apoll. Rhod. ii. 397, 1242; Steph. B. *s. v.:* cf. Amm. Marc. xxii. 8. § 21), a Scythian people, dwelling to the S. of Colchis and N. of Media. According to Herodotus and Stephanus (*ll. cc.*) they were an inland people, but Apollonius places them on the seacoast. They belonged to the 18th satrapy of the Persian kingdom (Herod. iii. 94), and were armed in the same manner as the Colchians, that is, with wooden helmets, small shields of untanned hide, short lances, and swords (Ib. vii. 79). The Parisian scholiast on Apollonius derives their name from the abundance of supplies found in their country. The Saspeires appear to have inhabited that district of *Georgia* lying on the upper course of the river Cyrus, in which *Tiflis* lies, which is still called *Tschin Kartuel ;* and as the district contains several other places, the names of which begin with the syllable *Tschin,* Ritter conjectures that the Saspeires were identical with the eastern Iberians, respecting whom the Greeks invented so many fables. (Rennell, *Geogr. of Herod.* p. 503; Ritter, *Erdkunde,* ii. p. 922; Bähr, *ad Herod.* i. 104.) [T. H. D.]

SA'SSULA, a town of Latium, situated in the neighbourhood of Tibur, of which city it was a dependency. It is mentioned only by Livy (vii. 19) among the towns taken from the Tiburtines in B. C. 354, and was probably always a small place. The site has been identified by Gell and Nibby with the ruins of an ancient town, at the foot of the hill of *Siciliano,* between 7 and 8 miles from *Tivoli* (Tibur). The ruins in question, consisting of a line of walls of polygonal construction, surrounding a hill of small extent, unquestionably indicate the site of an ancient town; but as we know that the Tiburtine territory contained several other towns besides Empulum and Sassula, the only two whose names are known to us, the identification of the latter is wholly arbitrary. (Gell, *Top. of Rome,* p. 394: Nibby, *Dintorni,* vol. iii. p. 63.) [E.H.B.]

SATACHTHA (Σατάχθα, or Σατάχθαι, Ptol. iv. 7. § 17), a place in Aethiopia, on the left bank of the Nile, probably near the present *Korti,* or else somewhat more to the S., near the half-destroyed village of *Ambucote.*   [T. H. D.]

SA'TALA (Σάταλα), an important town of Armenia Minor, as may be inferred from the numerous routes which branched off from thence to Pontus and Cappadocia. Its distance from Caesareia was 325 miles, and 124 or 135 from Trapezus. The

town was situated in a valley surrounded by mountains, a little to the north of the Euphrates, and was of importance, being the key to the mountain passes leading into Pontus; whence we find that in later times the Legio XV. Apollinaris was stationed there. In the time of Justinian its walls had fallen into decay, but that emperor restored them. (Ptol. i. 15. § 9, v. 7. § 3, viii. 17. § 41; Dion Cass. lxviii. 18; Procop. *de Aed.* iv. 3; *It. Ant.* pp. 181, 183, 206, 207, 216, 217; *Notit. Imp.; Tab. Peut.*) The site of this town has not yet been discovered with certainty, though ruins found in various parts of the country have been identified with it by conjecture. (Tournefort, *Voyages,* Letter 21, c. 2. p. 17; Rennell, *Asia Minor,* ii. p. 219 ; Cramer, *Asia Minor,* ii. p. 152, foll.)   [L. S.]

SATARCHAE, a Scythian people on the E. coast of the Tauric Chersonesus, who dwelt in caves and holes in the ground, and in order to avoid the rigour of winter, even clothed their faces, leaving only two small holes for their eyes. (Mela, ii. 1.) They were unacquainted with the use of gold and silver, and carried on their traffic by means of barter. They are mentioned by Pliny under the name of Scythi Satarchi (iv. 26). According to Ptolemy (iii. 6. § 6) there was a town in the Tauric peninsula called Satarche (Σατάρχη), which the scholiast (*ad loc.*) says was subsequently called Matarcha (Μάταρχα); but the account of the Satarchae living in caverns seems inconsistent with the idea of their having a town. Yet Valerius Flaccus also mentions a town —or perhaps a district—called Satarche, which, from his expression, " ditant sua mulctra Satarchen," we may conclude to have been rich in herds of cattle. (*Argon.* vi. 145.) The same poet describes the Satarchae as a yellow-haired race. (*Ib.*) [T.H.D.]

SATI'CULA (Σατίκολα, Diod.: *Eth.* Σατικολανός, Steph. B.; Saticulanus, Liv.; but Saticulus, Virg.), a town of Samnium, nearly on the frontiers of Campania. It is first mentioned at the outbreak of the First Samnite War (B. C. 343), when the consul Cornelius established his camp there, apparently to watch the movements of the Samnites in that quarter, and from thence subsequently advancing into their territory, was drawn into a defile, where he narrowly escaped the loss of his whole army, but was saved by the courage and ability of Decius. (Liv. vii. 32, 34.) Again, in B. C. 315, during the Second Samnite War, it was besieged by the Roman dictator L. Aemilius, and was considered of sufficient importance to engage a Roman army for nearly a year, when it was taken by Q. Fabius. The Samnites made a vigorous attempt to relieve it, but without effect, and it fell into the hands of the Romans. (Id. ix. 21, 22; Diod. xix. 72.) From this time it continued in their power; and before the close of the war it was one of the places which they determined to occupy with a colony, which was established there in B. C. 313. (Vell. Pat. i. 14; Fest. *s. v. Saticula,* p. 340, M.) Livy does not notice the establishment of a colony there on this occasion, but he afterwards mentions it as one of the "coloniae Latinae," which distinguished themselves in the Second Punic War by their zeal and fidelity. (Liv. xxvii. 10.) It is remarkable, however, that a few years before the name of Saticula is found among the towns that had revolted to Hannibal, and were recovered by Fabius in B. C. 215. (Liv. xxiii. 39.) But it appears that all the MSS. have " Austicula " (Alschefski, *ad loc.*); and though this name is otherwise quite unknown, it is certainly not safe to alter it, when, by so doing, we involve ourselves in a great historical difficulty; for the revolt of one of the Latin colonies is in itself most improbable, and was certainly not an event to be passed over with such slight notice. The territory of Saticulum ("ager Saticulanus") is again noticed during the same war in conjunction with that of Trebula (Liv. xxiii. 14); but from the end of the Second Punic War all trace of it disappears. The name is not found in any of the geographers, and its site is extremely uncertain. But the passages in Livy (ix. 21, 22) seem to point to its being situated not far from Plistia, which may very probably be placed at *Prestia* near *Sta Agata dei Goti*; while the description of the march of Marcellus in B. C. 216, shows clearly that it must have been situated S. of the Vulturnus, and probably in the valley at the back of Mount Tifata, between that ridge and the underfalls of Mount Taburnus. It may be added that such a position would be a very natural one for the Roman consul to occupy at the first outbreak of the Samnite wars, from its proximity to Capua.　　　　　　　　[E. H. B.]

SATION. [DASSARETAE, Vol. I. p. 756, a.]

SATNIOEIS (Σατνιόεις: *Tuzla* or *Tusla*), a small river in the southern part of Troas, having its sources in Mount Ida, and flowing in a western direction between Hamaxitus and Larissa, discharges itself into the Aegean. It owes its celebrity entirely to the Homeric poems. (*Il.* vi. 34, xiv. 445, xxi. 87; Strab. xiii. pp. 605, 606, who states that at a later time it was called Σαφνίοεις.)　　　　　[L. S.]

SATRAE (Σάτραι, Herod. vii. 110—112), a Thracian people who occupied a portion of the range of the Pangaeus, between the Nestus and the Strymon. Herodotus states that they were the only Thracian tribe who had always preserved their freedom; a fact for which he accounts by the nature of their country, —a mountainous region, covered with forests and snow—and by their great bravery. They alone of the Thracians did not follow in the train of Xerxes, when marching towards Greece. The Satrae were in possession of an oracle of Dionysus, situated among the loftiest mountain peaks, and the interpreters of which were taken from among the Bessi,— a circumstance which has suggested the conjecture that the Satrae were merely a clan of the Bessi,— a notion which is rendered more probable by the fact that Herodotus is the only ancient writer who mentions them; whereas the Bessi are repeatedly spoken of. We may infer from Pliny's expression, "Bessorum multa nomina" (iv. 11. s. 18), that the Bessi were divided into many distinct clans. Herodotus says that to the Satrae belonged the principal part of the gold and silver mines which then existed in the Pangaeus.　　　　　　　　[J. R.]

SATRICUM (*Eth.* Σατρικανός, Satricanus: *Casale di Conca*), an ancient city of Latium, situated on the frontier of the Volscian territory, between the Alban hills and the sea. This position rendered it a place of importance during the wars between the Romans and Volscians, and it is frequently mentioned in history at that period. It appears to have been originally a Latin city, as Diodorus mentions its name among the reputed colonies of Alba, and Dionysius also includes it in the list of the thirty cities of the Latin League. (Diod. vii. Fr. 3; Dionys. v. 61.) But when it first appears in history it is as a Volscian town, apparently a dependency of Antium. It had, however, been wrested from that people by the Romans at the same time with Corioli, Pollusca, &c; and hence it is one of

the towns the recovery of which by the Volscians is ascribed to Coriolanus. (Liv. ii. 39.) It seems to have continued in their power from this time till after the Gaulish invasion, as in B. C. 386 it was made the head-quarters of the Volscians and their allies on the outbreak of a war with Rome, and, after their defeat by Camillus, was assaulted and taken by that general. (Id. vi. 7, 8.) It would appear that it must on this occasion have for the first time received a Roman colony, as a few years later (B. C. 381) it is styled a "colonia populi Romani." In that year it was attacked by the Volscians in concert with the Praenestines, and, after an obstinate defence, was carried by assault, and the garrison put to the sword. (Id. vi. 22.) It is subsequently mentioned on two occasions as affording shelter to the Volscian armies after their defeat by the Romans (Id. vi. 22, 32); after the last of these (B. C. 377) it was burnt by the Latins, who considered themselves betrayed by their Volscian allies. (*Ib.* 33.) It was not till B. C. 348 that the city was rebuilt by the Antiates, who established a colony there; but two years later it was again taken by the Romans under M. Valerius Corvus. The garrison, to the number of 4000 men, were made prisoners, and the town burnt and destroyed, with the exception of a temple of Mater Matuta. (Id. vii. 27; *Fast. Capit.*) A few years later it was the scene of a victory of the Romans, under C. Plautius, over the Antiates (id. viii. 1), and seems to have been soon after restored, and received a fresh colony, as it was certainly again inhabited at the commencement of the Second Samnite War. In B. C. 320, after the disaster of the Caudine Forks, the Satricans revolted from Rome and declared in favour of the Samnites; but they were soon punished for their defection, their city being taken by the consul Papirius, and the Samnite garrison put to the sword. (Liv. ix. 12, 16; Oros, iii. 15.) From this time it seems to have continued subject to Rome: but its name disappears from history, and it probably sunk rapidly into decay. It is incidentally mentioned during the Second Punic War (B. C. 206) on occasion of a prodigy which occurred in the temple of Mater Matuta, already noticed (Liv. xxviii. 11); but it seems certain that it ceased to exist before the close of the Republic. Cicero indeed alludes incidentally to the name in a manner that shows that the site at least was well known in his time (*ad Q. Fr.* iii. 1. § 4); but Pliny reckons it among the celebrated towns of Latium, of which, in his days, no vestige remained (Plin. iii. 5. s. 9); and none of the other geographers allude to its name. The site, like that of most of the Latin cities which disappeared at an early period, is a matter of much doubt; but several passages in Livy tend to prove that it must have been situated between Antium and Velitrae, and its site has been fixed with much probability by Nibby at the farm or *casale*, now called *Conca*, about half way between *Anzo* and *Velletri*. The site is an isolated hill of tufo, of somewhat quadrangular form, and about 2500 feet in circuit, with precipitous sides, and presents portions of the ancient walls, constructed in much the same style as those of Ardea, of irregular square blocks of tufo. The sites of two gates, one on the E. the other to the W., may also be distinctly traced. There is therefore no doubt that the site in question is that of an ancient city, and the position would well accord with the supposition that it is that of Satricum. (Nibby, *Dintorni di Roma*, vol. iii. p. 64, a.)　　　　　　[E. H. B.]

SA'TTALA. [SETAE.]

SA'TURAE PALUS. [POMPTINAE PALUDES.]

SA'TURIUM. [TARENTUM.]

SATURNI PROMONTORIUM, a headland in Hispania Tarraconensis, not far from Carthago Nova. (Plin. iii. 3. s. 4.) It must be the same promontory called Σκομβραρία ἄκρα by Ptolemy (ii. 6. § 14). Now *Cabo de Palos*. [T. H. D.]

SATU'RNIA (Σατουρνία: *Saturnia*), an ancient city of Etruria, situated in the valley of the Albinia (*Albegna*), about 24 miles from its mouth. There is no doubt that it was an ancient Etruscan city; and as Pliny tells us that it was previously called Aurinia (iii. 5. s. 8), it is probable that this was its Etruscan name, and that it first received that of Saturnia at the time of the Roman colony. But no mention of it is found in history during the period of Etruscan independence; and there is certainly no ground for the supposition of Müller that it was one of the twelve cities of the Etruscan League. (Müller, *Etrusker*, vol. i. p. 350.) Dionysius indeed mentions it as one of the cities founded by the Pelasgians, and subsequently taken from them by the Tyrrhenians and Etruscans (Dionys. i. 20); but though this is strong evidence for the antiquity of the city, there is no proof that it was ever a place of importance under the Etruscans; and it even seems probable that before the close of their rule, Saturnia had sunk into the condition of a subordinate town, and a mere dependency of Caletra. At least it is remarkable that Livy, in speaking of the establishment of the Roman colony there, says that it was settled "in agro Caletrano." (Liv. xxxix. 55.) The foundation of this colony, which was established in B.C. 183, is the only historical fact recorded to us concerning Saturnia; it was a "colonia civium," and therefore would naturally retain its colonial rank even at a late period. Pliny, however, calls it only an ordinary municipal town, but Ptolemy gives it the rank of a colony, and it is mentioned as such in an inscription of Imperial times. (Plin. iii. 5. s. 8; Ptol. iii. 1. § 49; Gruter. *Inscr.* p. 1093. 8.) It is probable therefore that it received a fresh colony under the Roman Empire, though we have no account of the circumstance. But it seems not to have been a place of any importance, and the existing remains which belong to this period are of little interest.

The modern town of *Saturnia*, which retains the ancient site as well as name, is but a very poor place; but its mediaeval walls are based on those of the ancient city, and the circuit of the latter may be distinctly traced. It occupied the summit of a conical hill, surrounded by steep cliffs, about 2 miles in circuit. Considerable portions of the walls remain in several places: these are constructed of polygonal masonry, resembling that of Cosa, but built of travertino; they are supposed by Micali to belong to the Roman colony, though other writers would assign them to the Pelasgians, the earliest inhabitants of Saturnia. (Micali, *Ant. Pop. Ital.* vol. i. pp. 152, 210; Dennis, *Etruria*, vol. ii. pp. 308—310.) Numerous tombs are also found in the neighbourhood of the town, but which more resemble the cromlechs of northern Europe than the more regular sepulchres of other Etruscan cities. (Dennis, *l. c.* pp. 314—316.) [E. H. B.]

SATYRI MONUMENTUM (τὸ Σατύρου μνῆμα, Strab. xi. p. 494), a monument consisting of a vast mound of earth, erected in a very conspicuous situation on a promontory on the E. side of the Cim-

merian Bosporus, 90 stadia S. of Achilleum. It was in honour of a king of Bosporus, whom Dubois de Montpéreux identifies with Satyrus I., who reigned B.C. 407—393. (*Voyage autour du Caucase*, v. p. 48.) The same authority (*Ib.* p. 36) identifies the mound with the hill *Koukouoba*. [T. H. D.]

SATYRO'RUM I'NSULAE (Σατύρων νῆσοι, Ptol. vii. 2. § 30), a group of three Indian islands, lying E. of the Chersonesus Aurea, in the same degree of latitude as its southern point. They were said to be inhabited by a race of men having tails like Satyrs; that is, probably, by apes resembling men. Perhaps the *Anamba* islands. [T. H. D.]

SATYRO'RUM PROMONTO'RIUM (Σατύρων ἄκρον, Ptol. vii. 3. § 2), a promontory on the coast of Sinae (*China*), forming the southern extremity of the bay Theriodes, and placed by Ptolemy directly under the equator. It is probably the present *Cape St. James*. (Forbiger, *Geogr.* ii. p. 477, note 51.) [T. H. D.]

SAVA. [MAPHARITIS.]

SAVARI (Σάβαροι, Ptol. iii. 5. § 22), a people in the N. of European Sarmatia, between the rivers Turuntus and Chesinus. Schafarik (*Slav. Alterth.* i. p. 212) identifies them with the *Sjewer*, a powerful Slavonian race which dwelt on the rivers *Desna, Sem,* and *Sula*, and possessed the towns *Tschernigow* and *Ljubotsch*, both of which are mentioned by Constantine Porphyrogenitus (*de Adm. Imp.* c. 9). The name of the *Sjewer* does not occur in history after the year 1024, though their land and castles are frequently mentioned subsequently in Russian annals. (*Ibid.* ii. p. 129.) [T. H. D.]

SAVARIA. [SABARIA.]

SAUCONNA. [ARAR.]

SAVIA (Σαουία, Ptol. ii. 6. § 56), a town of the Pelendones in Hispania Tarraconensis, the site of which is undetermined. [T. H. D.]

SAVINCA'TES, a name which occurs in the inscription on the arch of Susa, and is placed next to the Adanates, whom D'Anville supposes to be the same as the Edenates [EDENATES]. His reasons for placing the Savincates below *Embrun* and on the *Durance*, are not satisfactory. He finds a name *Savines* there, and that is all the proof except the assumption of the correctness of the position which he has assigned to the Adanates, and the further assumption that the two people were neighbours. [G. L.]

SAULOE PARTHAYNISA (Σαυλόη Παρθαύνισα), this curiously mixed name which has passed into treatises of geography from the editions of Isidorus in the Geographi Graeci Minores of Hudson and Müller, appears to have rested on a bad reading of the Greek text. The amended text of the passage in question is Παρθυνηνὴ σχοῖνοι κέ, ἣν αὐλών (Isidor. *Stath. Parth.* c. 12), which is probably correct (see *Geog. Graec.* ed. Müller, Paris, 1855.) [V.]

SAUNARIA (Σαυναρία), a town of unknown site in Pontus Polemoniacus, is mentioned only by Ptolemy (v. 6. § 10). [L. S.]

SAUNIUM, a little river on the N. coast of Hispania Tarraconensis, in the territory of the Concani and Saleni; now *Saja*. (Mela, iii. 1.) [T. H. D.]

SAVO. [VADA SABBATA.]

SAVO (*Savone*), a small river of Campania, which appears to have formed the boundary between that country and Latium, in the most extended sense of the term. It is a small and sluggish stream ("piger Savo," Stat. *Silv.* iv. 3. 66), flowing into the sea between Sinuessa and the mouth of the Vulturnus (Plin. iii. 5. s. 9), and was crossed by the Appian Way, a few miles from its mouth, by a bridge called the Pons Campanus, from its forming the frontier of that country.　　　　[E. H. B.]

SAURO'MATAE (Σαυρομάται), probably the form which the root *Sarmat*- took in the languages from which the information of the Greeks of the parts about Olbiopolis was derived. It is the only form found in Herodotus, who knows nothing of the later name Sarmatae. When this latter term, however, came into use, Sauromatae, especially with the Roman writers, became archaic and poetical, or exotic. This is the case in the line —

" Ultra *Sauromatas*, fugere hinc libet," &c.
(Juv. *Sat.* ii. 1),

and elsewhere.

The Greeks of the *Black Sea* would take the name from either the Scythians or the Getae; and it is probably to the language of the latter, that the form belonged. Hence, it is a form of Samar-tae, taken from one of the eastern dialects of Dacia by the Greeks (possibly having passed through a Scythian medium as well) as opposed to Sarmatae, which is from the western parts of the Dacian area, and adopted by the Romans. Its first and most convenient application is to the Asiatic branch of the Sarmatians. These may be called Sarmatians as well, as they are by Ptolemy. On the contrary, it is rare, even in a Greek author, to apply Sauromatae to the Sarmatians of the Panno-nian frontier. The evidence as to the identity of the words is superabundant. Besides the internal probability, there is the statement of Pliny—" Sar-matae, Graecis Sauromatae" (iv. 25).

With the writers of the Augustan age the use of the two forms fluctuates. It is exceptional, how-ever, for a Greek to write Sarmatae, or a Roman Sauromatae. Exceptional, however, as it is, the change is frequent. Diodorus writes Sauromatae (ii. 44), speaking of the Asiatic branch; Strabo writes Sauromatae under the same circumstances; also when following Greek authorities. For the western tribes he writes Sarmatae.

Ovid uses the term that best suits his metre, giving *Sarmatae* the preference, *caeteris paribus*.

" *Sarmaticae* major Geticaeque frequentia gentes."
(*Trist.* v. 7. 13.)

" Jam didici Getice *Sarmaticeque* loqui."
(*Ibid.* v. 12. 58.)

" Stridula *Sauromates* paustra bubulcus agit."
(*Ibid.* iii. 12. 30.)

The Sauromatae of Herodotus were the occupants of a Adξιs, a word evidently used in a technical sense, and perhaps the term by which his informants trans-lated the Scythian or Sarmatian equivalents to our word *March*; or it may = *street.* The *Bashkir* country, at the present moment, is divided into four *streets, roads,* or *ways,* according to the countries to which they lead. The number of these Adξιs were two; the first being that of the Sauromatae, bounded on the south and west by the Tanais and Maeotis, and extending northwards fifteen days' journey. The country was treeless. The second Adξιs, that of the Budini, followed. This was a wooded country. There is no necessity for con-necting the Budini with Sarmatae, on the strength of their both being occupants of a Adξιs. All that comes out of the text of Herodotus is, that the

Scythians near Olbiopolis knew of a Adξιs of the Sauromatae and a Adξιs of the Budini. The former seems to have been the north-eastern part of the *Don Kozak* country, with a portion of *Saratov* (iv. 21).

When Darius invaded Scythia, the Sauromatae, Ge-loni, and Budini acted together, and in opposition to the Agathyrsi, Neuri, Androphagi, Melanchlaeni, and Tauri; the former agreeing to help the Scythians, the latter to leave them to their fate. This suggests the probability that, politically, the Adξιes were con-federate districts (Herod. iv. 119).

The language of the Sauromatae was *Scythian with solecisms,* a statement which leads to the strange story of the Amazons (iv. 110—116), with whom the Sauromatae were most especially con-nected (iv. 117). The women amongst them re-mained unmarried until they had slain an enemy.

The account of Hippocrates is substantially that of Herodotus, except that he especially calls the Sauromatae European and Scythian; though, at the same time, different from other nations. He makes the number, too, of enemies that the virgins must slay before they can marry, three.

For further details, see SARMATIA.　　[R. G. L.]

SAVUS (Σάος or Σάονος: *Save*), a great and navigable tributary of the Danube; it has its sources in the Carnian Alps (Plin. iii. 28; Jornand. *de Reb. Get.* 56), and, flowing in an eastern direction almost parallel with the more northern Dravus, reaches the Danube at Singidunum. A portion of its upper course forms the boundary between No-ricum and Pannonia, but the whole of the lower part of the river belongs to the southern part of Pannonia, and some of the most important towns of that country, as Siscia, Servitium, and Sirmium, were situated on its banks. (Strab. iv. p. 207, vii. p. 314; Appian, iii. 22; Ptol. ii. 16. § 1, iii. 9. § 1; Justin, xxxii. 3, 8, 16; Claud. *de Laud. Stilich.* ii. 192.)　　　　　　[L. S.]

SAXA RUBRA (*Prima Porta*), a village and station on the Flaminian Way, 9 miles from Rome. It evidently derived its name from the redness of the tufo rocks, which is still conspicuous in the neighbourhood of *Prima Porta.* The name is written " Ad Rubras " in the Tabula, while Martial calls the place simply " Rubrae;" and this form is found also in the Jerusalem Itinerary. (Martial, iv. 64. 15; *Itin. Hier.* p. 612.) But the proper form of it seems to have been Saxa Rubra, which is used both by Livy and Cicero. The former mentions it during the wars of the Romans with the Veientes, in connection with the operations on the Cremera (Liv. ii. 49); and Cicero notices it as a place in the immediate vicinity of Rome, where M. Antonius halted before entering the city. (Cic. *Phil.* ii. 31.) It was there also that Antonius, the general of Vespasian, arrived on his march upon Rome, when he learnt the successes of the Vitellians and the death of Sabinus. (Tac. *Hist.* iii. 79.) At a much later period also (B. C. 32) it was the point to which Maxentius advanced to meet Constantine previous to the battle at the Milvian bridge. (Vict. *Caes.* 40. § 23.) We learn from Martial (*l. c.*), that a village had grown up on the spot, as would naturally be the case with a station so immediately in the neighbour-hood of the city.

On a hill on the right of the Via Flaminia, a little beyond *Prima Porta,* are considerable ruins, which are believed to be those of the villa of Livia, known by the name of " Ad Gallinas," which was situated 9 miles from Rome, on the Via Flaminia. (Plin. xv. 30. s. 40; Suet. *Galb.* 1.)   [E. H. B.]

SAXETANUM, a place in Hispania Baetica (*Itin. Ant.* p. 405), called Sex (Σέξ) by Ptolemy (ii. 4. § 7), Hexi by Mela (ii. 6), and by Pliny (iii. 3) Sexti Firmum Julium. It is the 'Εξιταυῶν πόλις of Strabo (iii. p. 156). On the name see Casaubon (*ad Strab.* i. p. 50), and Tzschuck (*ad Melam*, vol. ii. pt. 2. p. 447). It was renowned for its salt-fish. (Strab. iii. p. 156; Athen. iii. p. 121; Plin. xxxii. 11. s. 53; Mart. vii. 78, &c.) Now most probably *Motril.* (Cf. Florez, *Esp. Sagr.* xii. p. 101.)   [T. H. D.]

SA'XONES (Σάξονες: *Saxons*), a German tribe, which, though it acted a very prominent part about the beginning and during the early part of the middle ages, yet is not even mentioned in ancient history previous to A. D. 287. In that year, we are told by Eutropius (vii. 13; comp. Oros. vii. 25), the Saxons and Franks infested the coasts of Armorica and Belgica, the protection of which was intrusted to Carausius. The fact that Pliny and Tacitus do not mention them in the country in which we afterwards find them, does not prove that they did not exist there in the time of those writers. For the inhabitants of the Cimbrian Chersonesus, where subsequently we find the Saxons, are mentioned by those writers only under the general appellation of the Cimbri, without noticing any special tribes under separate names. Ptolemy (ii. 11. § 11; comp. Steph. B. s. v.) is the first authority describing the habitations of the Saxons, and according to him they occupied the narrow neck of the Cimbrian Chersonesus, between the river Albis (*Elbe*) and Chalusus (*Trave*), that is, the country now called *Holstein*. Their neighbours on the south of the Albis were the Chauci, in the east the Suardones, and in the north the Singulones, Angli, and other smaller tribes of the peninsula. But besides this portion of the continent, the Saxons also occupied three islands, called "Saxon islands," off the coast of *Holstein* (Σαξόνων νῆσοι, Ptol. ii. 11. § 31), one of which was no doubt the modern *Helgoland*; the two others must either be supposed to have been swallowed up by the sea, or be identified with the islands of *Dycksand* and *Vielschovel*, which are nearer the coast than *Helgoland*.

The name Saxones is commonly derived from *Sahs* or *Sachs*, a battle-knife, but others connect it with *seax* (earth) or *seat*, according to which Saxons would describe the people as living in fixed seats or habitations, as opposed to the free or wandering Franks. The former, however, is the more probable origin of the name; for the living in fixed habitations was certainly not a characteristic mark of the ancient Saxons.

They appear to have gradually spread along the north-western coast of Germany, and to have gained possession of a large extent of country, which the Ravenna Geographer (iv. 17, 18, 23) calls by the name of Saxonia, but which was certainly not inhabited by Saxons exclusively In A. D. 371 the Saxons, in one of their usual ravaging excursions on the coasts of Gaul, were surrounded and cut to pieces by the Roman army under Valentinian (Oros. vii. 32; Amm. Marc. xxviii. 2, 5; comp. xxvi. 4, xxvii. 8; Zosim. iii. 1, 6); and about the middle of the fifth century a band of Saxons led by Hengist and Horsa crossed over into Britain, which had been completely given up by the Romans, and now fell into the hands of the roving Saxons, who in con-

nection with other German tribes permanently established themselves in Britain, and there developed the great features of their national character. (Beda, *Hist. Eccles.* i. 12). As the Romans never invaded the original country of the Saxons, we know of no towns or places in it, with the exception perhaps of the town of Treva (Τρήουα) mentioned by Ptolemy (ii. 11. § 27). Besides those already mentioned, there are but few passages in ancient writers in which the Saxons are mentioned, such as Marcian, p. 53; Claud. *de Laud. Stil.* ii. 255; Sidon. Apoll. vii. 90, 369. Among modern writers the reader may consult Kufahl, *De Saxonum Origine*, Berlin, 1830, 8vo., and the best works on the early history of England and Germany.   [L. S.]

SA'XONUM I'NSULAE.   [SAXONES.]

SCAIDA'VA, a town in Moesia Inferior, between Novae and Trimammium. *Itin. Ant.* p. 222.) It is called Scedeba (Σκεδεβά) by Procopius (*de Aed.* iv. 11). Variously identified with *Ratonou* and *Rustchuck*.   [T. H. D.]

SCA'LABIS, a town of Lusitania, on the road from Olisipo to Emerita and Bracara. (*Itin. Ant.* pp. 420, 421.) Pliny (iv. 21. s. 35) calls it a Roman colony, with the surname Praesidium Julium, and the seat of one of the three "conventus juridici" of Lusitania. It is undoubtedly the same place which Ptolemy (ii. 5. § 7) erroneously calls Σκαλαβίσκος, which is probably a corruption of Σκαλαβίς κολ. (κολωνία) The modern *Santarem.* (Cf. Wesseling, *ad Itin. l. c.*; Isidor. *de Vir. Ill.* c. 44; Florez, *Esp. Sagr.* xiii. p. 69.)   [T. H. D.]

SCALDIS (*Schelde, Escaut*) a river in North Gallia. Caesar (*B. G.* vi. 33), the first writer who mentions the Scaldis, says, when he was pursuing Ambiorix, that he determined to go "as far as the Scaldis which flows into the Mosa (*Maas*) and the extremity of the Arduenna" (*Ardennes*). All the MSS. quoted by Schneider (*B. G.* vi. 33) have the reading "Scaldem," "Schaldem," "Scaldin," and other trifling varieties, except one MS. which has "Sambim;" so that, as Schneider concludes, we cannot doubt that Caesar wrote "Scaldis" in this passage. Pliny (iv. 17) describes the Scaldis as the boundary between the Gallic and Germanic nations, and says nothing of its union with the Mosa: "A Scalde ad Sequanam Belgica;" and "a Scaldi incolunt extera Toxandri pluribus nominibus." Some geographers suppose that the Tabuda of Ptolemy is the *Schelde.* [TABUDA.]

The passage of Caesar is most easily explained by supposing that he knew nothing of the lower course of the Schelde, and only reported what he heard. It is possible that the East Schelde was once the chief outlet of the Schelde, and it may have had some communication with the channels about the islands between the *East Schelde* and the lower course of the Mosa, which communication no longer exists. There is at least no reason for taking, in place of "Scaldim" or "Scaldem," the reading "Sabin" (Σαβιν), from the Greek version of the Commentaries.

The *Schelde* rises in France, in the department of *Aisne.* Below *Antwerp* it enters the sea by two aestuaries, the *Hond* or *West Schelde* and the *East Schelde.*   [G. L.]

SCAMANDER (Σκάμανδρος: *Mendere Su*, or the river of *Bunarbaschi*), a famous little stream in the plain of Troy, which according to Homer (*Il.* xx. 74) was called Xanthus by the gods and Scamander by men; though it probably owed the name Xanthus to the yellow or brownish colour of its water (comp. *Il.* vi. 4, xxi. 8). Notwithstanding this distinct declaration of the poet that the two names belonged to the same river, Pliny (v. 33) mentions the Xanthus and Scamander as two distinct rivers, and describes the former as flowing into the Portus Achaeorum, after having joined the Simoeis. In regard to the colour of the water, it was believed to have even the power of dyeing the wool of sheep which drank of it. (Aristot. *Hist. Anim.* iii. 12; Aelian, *Hist. Anim.* viii. 21; Plin. ii. 106; Vitruv. viii. 3,14.) Homer (*Il.* xxii.147, &c.) states that the river had two sources close to the city of Ilion, one sending forth hot water and the other cold, and that near these springs the Trojan women used to wash their clothes. Strabo (xiii. p. 602) remarks that in his time no hot spring existed in those districts; he further asserts that the river had only one source; that this was far away from Troy in Mount Ida; and lastly that the notion of its rising near Troy arose from the circumstance of its flowing for some time under ground and reappearing in the neighbourhood of Ilion. Homer describes the Scamander as a large and deep river (*Il.* xx. 73, xxi. 15, xxii. 148), and states that the Simoeis flowed into the Scamander, which after the junction still retained the name of Scamander (*Il.* v. 774, xxi. 124; comp. Plin. ii. 106; Herod. v. 65; Strab. xiii. p. 595.) Although Homer describes the river as large and deep, Herodotus (vii.42) states that its waters were not sufficient to afford drink to the army of Xerxes. The Scamander after being joined by the Simoeis has still a course of about 20 stadia eastward, before it reaches the sea, on the east of Cape Sigeum, the modern *Kum Kale.* Ptolemy (v. 2. § 3), and apparently Pomp. Mela (i. 18), assign to each river its own mouth, the Simoeis discharging itself into the sea at a point north of the mouth of the Scamander. To account for these discrepancies, it must be assumed that even at that time the physical changes in the aspect of the country arising from the muddy deposits of the Scamander had produced these effects, or else that Ptolemy mistook a canal for the Scamander. Even in the time of Strabo the Scamander reached the sea only at those seasons when it was swollen by rains, and at other times it was lost in marshes and sand. It was from this circumstance, that, even before its junction with the Simoeis, a canal was dug, which flowed in a western direction into the sea, south of Sigeum, so that the two rivers joined each other only at times when their waters were high. Pliny, who calls the Scamander a navigable river, is in all probability thinking of the same canal, which is still navigable for small barges. The point at which the two rivers reach the sea is now greatly changed, for owing to the deposits at the mouth, the coast has made great advances into the sea, and the Portus Achaeorum, probably a considerable bay, has altogether disappeared. (Comp. Leake, *Asia Minor,* p. 289, foll., and the various works and treatises on the site and plain of ancient Troy.)　　　　　　　　　　　　　　　[L. S.]

SCAMA'NDRIA, a small town of Mysia, no doubt situated on the river Scamander in the plain of Troy (Plin. v. 33; Hierocl. p. 662, where it is called Scamandros). Leake (*Asia Minor,* p. 276) conjectures that it stood on a hill rising below *Bunarbaschi.* An inscription referring to this town is preserved in the museum at Paris (Choiseul-Gouffier, *Voyage Pittoresque,* tom. ii. p. 288.)　[L. S.]

SCAMBO'NIDAE. [ATHENAE, p. 302, a.]

SCAMPAE. [ILLYRICUM, Vol. II. p. 36, b.]
SCANDARIUM. [Cos.]
SCANDEIA. [CYTHERA.]

SCA'NDIA (Σκανδία) or SCANDINA'VIA. Until about the reign of Augustus the countries north of the Cimbrian Chersonesus were unknown to the ancients, unless we assume with some modern writers that the island of Thule, of which Pytheas of Massilia spoke, was the western part of what is now sometimes called Scandinavia, that is *Sweden* and *Norway.* The first ancient writer who alludes to these parts of Europe, Pomp. Mela, in the reign of Claudius, states (iii. 3) that north of the Albis there was an immense bay, full of large and small islands, between which the sea flowed in narrow channels. No name of any of these islands is mentioned, and Mela only states that they were inhabited by the Hermiones, the northernmost of the German tribes. In another passage (iii. 6) the same geographer speaks of an island in the Sinus Codanus, which, according to the common reading, is called Codanonia, or Candanovia, for which some have emended Scandinavia. This island is described by him as surpassing all others in that sea both in size and fertility. But to say the least it is very doubtful as to whether he alludes to the island afterwards called Scandia or Scandinavia, especially as Mela describes his island as inhabited by the Teutones. The first writer who mentions Scandia and Scandinavia is Pliny, who, in one passage (iv. 27), likewise speaks of the Sinus Codanus and its numerous islands, and adds that the largest of them was called Scandinavia; its size, he continues, is unknown, but it is inhabited by 500 *pagi* of Helleviones, who regard their island as a distinct part of the world (*alter terrarum orbis*). In another passage (iii. 30) he mentions several islands to the east of Britannia, to one of which he gives the name of Scandia. From the manner in which he speaks in this latter passage we might be inclined to infer that he regarded Scandinavia and Scandia as two different islands; but this appearance may arise from the fact that in each of the passages referred to he followed different authorities, who called the same island by the two names Scandia and Scandinavia. Ptolemy (ii. 11. §§ 33, 34, 35) speaks of a group of four islands on the east of the Cimbrian Chersonesus, which he calls the Scandiae Insulae (Σκανδίαι νῆσοι), and of which the largest and most eastern one is called Scandia, extending as far as the mouth of the Vistula. In all these accounts there is the fundamental mistake of regarding Scandinavia as an island, for in reality it is connected on the northeast with the rest of Europe. Pliny speaks of an immense mountain, Sevo, in Scandinavia, which may possibly be *Mount Kjölen,* which divides Sweden from Norway, and a southern branch of which still bears the name of *Seve-Ryggen.* The different tribes mentioned by Ptolemy as inhabiting Scandia are the Chaedini (Χαιδεινοί), Phavonae (Φαυόναι), Phiraesi (Φιραῖσοι), Gutae (Γοῦται), Dauciones (Δαυκίωνες), and Levoni (Λευῶνοι). At a later time, Jornandes (*de Reb. Get.* p. 81, &c.) enumerates no less than twenty-eight different tribes in Scandinavia. Tacitus does not indeed mention Scandia, but the Sitones and Suiones (whence the modern name *Swedes*) must unquestionably be conceived as the most northern among the German tribes and as inhabiting Scandia (*Germ.* 44, 45). It is well known that according to Jornandes the Goths, and according to Paulus Diaconus (v. 2) the

Longobardi, originally came from Scandinavia. It deserves to be noticed that the southern part of the supposed island of Scandia, the modern *Sweden*, still bears the name *Scania*, *Scone*, or *Schonen*. Pliny (viii. 16) mentions a peculiar animal called achlis, and resembling the alcis, which was found only in Scandinavia. For further discussions about the various tribes of Scandinavia, which all the ancients treat as a part of Germania Magna, see Wilhelm, *Germanien*, p. 343, &c.; Zeuss, *Die Deutschen, &c.* pp. 77, 156, &c. [L. S.]

SCA'NDILA, a small island in the northern part of the Aegaean sea, between Peparethus and Scyros, now *Skandole*. (Plin. iv. 12. s. 23; Mela, ii. 7. § 8:)

SCANDINAVIA. [SCANDIA.]

SCAPTE HYLE (Σκαπτὴ ὕλη, Plut. *Cim.* 4, *de Exilio*, p. 605; Marcellin. *Vit. Thucyd.* § 19), or the " foss wood," situated on the confines of Macedonia and Thrace, in the auriferous district of Mt. Pangaeum, to which Thucydides was exiled, and where he composed his great legacy for all ages — the history of the war in which he had served as general. [E. B. J.]

SCA'PTIA (*Eth.* Σκαπτήριος, Scaptiensis: *Passerano*), an ancient city of Latium, which appears to have ceased to exist at a very early period. Its name is found in Dionysius among the thirty cities of the Latin League (Dionys. v. 61); and it therefore seems probable that it was at that time a considerable, or at all events an independent, town. No mention of it is subsequently found in history, but after the great Latin War it was included in one of the new Roman tribes created on that occasion (B. C. 332), to which it gave the name of Scaptian. (Fest. *s. v.* *Scaptia*, p. 343; Liv. viii. 17.) No subsequent mention is found of the town, and it is only noticed by Pliny among the " clara oppida " of Latium, which in his time had utterly disappeared (Plin. iii. 5. s. 9). Silius Italicus also alludes to the " Scaptia pubes," but in a passage from which no inference can be derived (viii. 395). The Scaptienses noticed by Suetonius (*Aug.* 40) and elsewhere were the members of the Scaptian tribe. There is no real clue to its position; that derived from the passage of Festus, from which it has been commonly inferred that it was in the neighbourhood of Pedum, being of no value. The words " quam Pedani incolebant," found in all the ordinary editions of that author, are in fact merely a supplement of Ursinus, founded on an inference from Livy (viii. 14, 17), which is by no means conclusive. (See Müller's note.) But supposing that we are justified in placing Scaptia in this neighbourhood, the site suggested by Nibby, on the hill now occupied by a farm or *casale* called *Passerano*, is at least probable enough; the position is a strong one, on the point of one of those narrow ridges with precipitous sides between two ravines, which abound in this part of the Campagna. It is about 3 miles NW. of *Gallicano*, the presumed site of Pedum; and the existence of an ancient town on the spot is attested by the fragments of ancient walls, the large, roughly-hewn masses of which are found worked up into more recent buildings. Its situation closely resembles that of *Gallicano* itself, as well as that of *Zagarolo*, about 3 miles further S. (where there are also indications of ancient habitation); and the identification of any of the three can be little more than conjectural. (Nibby, *Dintorni*, vol. iii. pp. 70, 71.) [E. H. B.]

SCARABA'NTIA (Σκαραβαντία, Ptol. ii. 15. § 5), a town on the western bank of Lake Pelso in Upper Pannonia, on the road leading from Carnuntum to Sabaria. (Plin. iii. 27; *It. Ant.* pp. 233, 261, 262, 266; *Tab. Peut.*) According to coins and inscriptions found at the place, it was a municipium with the surname of Flavia Augusta. Hence it appears that the reading in Pliny, " Scarabantia Julia," is not correct, and that we must read either Scarabantia Flavia, or Scarabantia et Julia. Its site is now occupied by the town of *Oedenburg*, in Hungarian *Soprony* or *Sopron*. (Comp. Muchar, *Norikum*, i. p. 168; Schönwisner, *Antiquitates Sabariae*, p. 31; Orelli, *Inscript.* n. 4992.) [L. S.]

SCA'RBIA, a town in Rhaetia, between Partenum and Veldidena, on the road leading from Augusta Vindelicorum into Italy, occupied the site of the modern *Scharnitz*. (*Tabula Peutingeriana*.) [L. S.]

SCARDO'NA (Σκαρδῶνα, Ptol. ii. 17. § 3; Procop. *B. G.* i. 7, 16, iv. 23; Plin. iii. 26; Geogr. Rav. v. 14; Σκάρδων, Strab. vii. p. 315; Sardona, *Peut. Tab.*), a town in the territory of the Liburnii on the Titius, 12 M. P. from where that river meets the sea. From the circumstance of its having been one of the three " conventus " of Dalmatia, it must have been a place of importance, and was used from early times as a depôt for the goods which were transported by the Titius to the inland Dalmatians. (Strab. *l.c.*) The modern *Scardóna* in Illyric *Scardin* or *Scradin*, retains the name of the old city, though it does not occupy the site, which was probably further to the W. (Wilkinson, *Dalmatia*, vol. i. p. 191.) Ptolemy (ii. 17. § 13) has an island of the same name off the Liburnian coast,—perhaps the rocky and curiously-shaped island of *Pago*. [E. B. J.]

SCARDUS, SCODRUS, SCORDUS MONS (τὸ Σκάρδον ὄρος, Polyb. xxviii. 8; Ptol. ii. 16. § 1), the desolate heights which are mentioned incidentally by Livy (xliii. 20, xliv. 31) as lying in the way from Stymbara to Scodra, and as giving rise to the Oriuna. They seem to have comprehended the great summits on either side of the Drilo, where its course is from E. to W. (Leake, *Northern Greece* vol. iii. p. 477.) In Kiepert's map (*Europaischen Turkei*) Scardus (*Schar-Dagh*) extends from the *Ljubatrin* to *Shalesh*; over this there is a " col" from *Kalkandele* to *Prisdren* not less than 5000 feet above the level of the sea. According to the nomenclature of Grisebach, Scardus reaches from the *Ljubatrin* at its NE. extremity to the SW. and S. as far as the *Klissoura of Devol*; S. of that point Pindus commences in a continuation of the same axis. [E. B. J.]

SCARNIUNGA, a river of Pannonia, mentioned only by Jornandes (*de Reb. Get.* 52), which it is impossible to identify from the vague manner in which it is spoken of. [L. S.]

SCARPHE (Σκάρφη), in Boeotia. [ETEONUS.]

SCARPHE or SCARPHEIA (Σκάρφη, Hom.; Σκάρφεια, Strab., Paus., Steph. B.: *Eth.* Σκαρφεύς, Σκαρφαιεύς), a town of the Locri Epicnemidii, mentioned by Homer. (*Il.* ii. 532.) According to Strabo it was 10 stadia from the sea, 30 stadia from Thronium, and a little less from some other place of which the name is lost, probably Nicaea. (Strab. ix. p. 426.) It appears from Pausanias that it lay on the direct road from Elateia to Thermopylae by Thronium (viii. 15. § 3), and likewise from Livy, who states that Quintius Flamininus marched from Elateia by Thronium and

Scarpheia to Heracleia (xxxiii. 3). Hence the town may be placed between the modern villages of 'Andera and Molo. (Leake, Northern Greece, vol. ii. p. 178.) Scarpheia is said by Strabo to have been destroyed by an inundation of the sea caused by an earthquake (i. p. 60), but it must have been afterwards rebuilt, as it is mentioned by subsequent writers down to a late period. (Plin. iv. 7. s. 12; Ptol. iii. 15. § 11; Hierocl. p. 643; Geog. Rav. iv. 10; Const. Porphyr. de Them. ii. 5. p. 51, Bonn.) Scarpheia is also mentioned by Lycophr. 1147; Appian, Syr. 19; Paus. ii. 29. § 3, x. 1. § 2.

SCARPO'NA or SCARPONNA, in Gallia, is placed in the Antonine Itin. and in the Table on a road between Tullum (Toul) and Divodurum (Mets). The two authorities agree in placing it at the distance of x. from Tullum; but the Itin. makes the distance from Scarpona to Divodurum xii., and the Table makes it xiiii. The larger number comes nearer to the truth, for the place is Charpagne, on the Mosel. An inscription has been found at Charpagne, which is as follows : " IIIIvir viarum curand. Sabell. V. S. P. M. Scarp. Civit. Leuc." Scarpona was in the territory of the Leuci. [LEUCI.] Jovinus, Equitum Magister, defeated the Alemanni near Scarponna in A. D. 366. in the reign of Valentinian and Valens. (Amm. Marc. xxvii. 2; D'Anville, Notice, &c.; Ukert, Gallien, p. 506.)　　[G. L.]

SCENAE (Σκηναί), a town of Mesopotamia on a canal from the Euphrates, and on the borders of Babylonia, 18 schoeni from Seleucia, and 25 days' journey from the passage of the Euphrates at Zeugma. (Strab. xvi. p. 748.) It belonged to the peaceful and nomadic tribe of the Scenitae, and therefore, though called by Strabo ἀξιόλογος πόλις, was probably only a city of tents, as, indeed, its name implies.

2. SCENAE MANDRAE, a place in Middle Egypt, on the right bank of the Nile, between Aphroditopolis and Babylon, a little SE. of Memphis. (Itin. Ant. p. 169.) It had a Roman garrison, and in later times became the see of a Christian bishop. (Not. Imp.; comp. Wesseling, ad Itin. l. c.)

3. SCENAE VETERANORUM, a place in Lower Egypt, on an arm of the Nile, and on the road from Heliopolis to Vicus Judaeorum. (Itin. Ant. pp. 163, 169.) It lay SW. of Bubastus.　　[T. H. D.]

SCENITAE (Σκηνῖται), a general name for various Arab tribes in Pliny, often distinguished by some other appellation. Thus, towards the lower part of the Euphrates, beyond the " Attali latrones, Arabum gens," he places the Scenitae (vi. 26), whom he mentions again more fully (c. 28), " Nomadas inde infestatoresque Chaldaeorum Scenitas, ut diximus cludunt, et ipsi vagi, sed a tabernaculis cognominati, quae ciliciis metantur, ubi libuit. Deinde Nabataei," &c. Then again below the confluence of the Euphrates and Tigris he places the Nomades Scenitae on the right bank of the river, the Chaldaei on the left. He speaks also of the Scenitae Sabaei. Strabo also uses the name in the same latitude of application of many various tribes of Arabia, Syria, and Mesopotamia (see Index, s. v.); but Ptolemy assigns them a definite seat near the mountains which stretch along the north of the peninsula, north of the Thaditae (al. Oaditae) and Saraceni (vi. 7. § 21); and in this vicinity, towards the Red Sea, it is that Ammianus Marcellinus places the Scenite Arabs, whom posterity called Saracens (xxiii. 6.) [SARACENI.] The remark of Bochart is therefore borne out by authorities: " Ubi Sce-

nitas Eratosthenes, ibi Saracenos ponunt Procopius et Marcianus. Saraceni nimirum a Scenitis hoc solum differunt, quod Scenitarum nomen est vetustius." (Geogr. Sacr. iv. 2. p. 213.)　　[G.W.]

SCEPSIS (Σκῆψις : Eth. Σκήψιος), a town in the SE. of Mysia, on the river Aesepus, 150 stadia to the SE. of Alexandria Troas, and not far from Dicte, one of the highest points of Mount Ida. It was apparently a place of the highest antiquity; for it was believed to have been founded immediately after the time of the Trojan War, and Demetrius, a native of the place, considered it to have been the capital of the dominions of Aeneas. (Strab. xiii. p. 607). The same author stated that the inhabitants were transferred by Scamandrius, the son of Hector, and Ascanius, the son of Aeneas, to another site, lower down the Aesepus, about 60 stadia from the old place, and that there a new town of the same name was founded. The old town after this was distinguished from the new one by the name of Palaescepsis. For two generations the princes of the house of Aeneas maintained themselves in the new town ; but the form of government then became an oligarchy. During this period, colonists from Miletus joined the Scepsians, and instituted a democratic form of government. The descendants of the royal family, however, still continued to enjoy the regal title and some other distinctions. (Strab. l. c. comp. xiii. p 603; xiv. p. 635; Plin. v. 2; Steph. B. s. v.) In the time of Xenophon (Hell. iii. 1. § 15), Scepsis belonged to Mania, a Dardanian princess ; and after her death it was seized by Meidias, who had married her daughter; but Dercyllidas, who had obtained admission into the town under some pretext, expelled Meidias, and restored the sovereign power to the citizens. After this we hear no more of Scepsis until the time of the Macedonian supremacy, when Antigonus transferred its inhabitants to Alexandria Troas, on account of their constant quarrels with the town of Cebrene in their neighbourhood. Lysimachus afterwards allowed them to return to their ancient home, which at a later time became subject to the kings of Pergamum. (Strab. xiii. p. 597.) This new city became an important seat of learning and philosophy, and is celebrated in the history of the works of Aristotle. Strabo (xiii. p. 608) relates that Neleus of Scepsis, a pupil of Aristotle and friend of Theophrastus, inherited the library of the latter, which also contained that of Aristotle. After Neleus' death the library came into the hands of persons who, not knowing its value, and being unwilling to give them up to the library which the Pergamean kings were collecting, concealed these literary treasures in a pit, where they were exposed to injury from damp and worms. At length, however, they were rescued from this place and sold to Apellicon of Teos. The books, in a very mutilated condition, were conveyed to Athens, and thence they were carried by Sulla to Rome. It is singular that Scylax (p. 36) enumerates Scepsis among the Aeolian coast-towns ; for it is evident from Strabo (comp. Demosth. c. Aristocr. p. 671) that it stood at a considerable distance from the sea. The town of Palaescepsis seems to have been abandoned entirely, for in Pliny's time (v. 33) not a vestige of it existed, while Scepsis is mentioned by Hierocles (p. 664) and the ecclesiastical notices of bishoprics. In the neighbourhood of Scepsis there existed very productive silver mines. It was the birthplace of Demetrius and Metrodorus. The former, who bestowed much labour on the topography of Troas, spoke of

3 o

a district, Corybissa, near Scepsis, of which otherwise nothing is known. Extensive ruins of Scepsis are believed to exist on an eminence near the village of *Eskiupshi.* These ruins are about 3 miles in circumference, and 8 gates can be traced in its walls. (Forbiger, *Handbuch der Alt. Geogr.* vol. ii. p. 147.)   [L. S.]

SCHE'DIA (Σχεδία, Strab. xvii. pp. 800, 803), a large town-like village of Lower Egypt, situated on the great canal which connected Alexandria with the Canopic arm of the Nile, near Andropolis. At Schedia was the general custom-house for goods, ascending or descending the river, and also the station for the splendid vessels in which the prefects visited the upper country; whence it is singular that it is not mentioned by any later writer than Strabo. Mannert (x. pt. i. p. 601) seeks it on the lake of *Aboukir;* whilst Reichardt, from the similarity of the name, takes it to have been the modern *Dejedie.*   [T. H. D.]

SCHE'RIA. [CORCYRA.]

SCHINUSSA, a small island in the Aegaean sea, one of the Sporades, S. of Naxos. (Plin. iv. 12. s. 68.)

SCHISTE (ἡ σχιστὴ ὁδός), the name of the road leading from Delphi into Central Greece, was more particularly applied to the spot where the road divided into two, and which was called τρεῖς κέλευθοι, reckoning the road to Delphi as one of the three. Of the other two roads. the NE. led to Daulis; the SE. parted into two, one leading to Trachis and Lebadeia, the other to Ambrysus and Stiris. At the spot where the three roads met was the tomb of Laius and his servant, who were here slain by Oedipus. It must have stood at the entrance of the *Zimenó Dervéni,* or opening between the mountains Cirphis and Parnassus, which leads to Delphi. The road from this point becomes very steep and rugged towards Delphi, as Pausanias has described it. (Aeschyl. *Oed. Tyr.* 733; Eurip. *Phoen.* 38; Paus. ix. 2. § 4, x. 5. § 3; Leake, *Northern Greece,* vol. ii. p. 105.)

SCHOENUS (Σχοινοῦς), the name of several towns, from the reeds or rushes growing in their neighbourhood. 1. (usually Σχοῖνος), a town in Boeotia, mentioned by Homer (*Il.* ii. 497), and placed by Stabo upon a river of the same name in the territory of Thebes, upon the road to Anthedon, and at the distance of 50 stadia from Thebes. (Strab. ix. p. 408; Eustath. *ad loc.*; Steph. B. *s. v.*; Nicander, *Theriac.* 887; Plin. iv. 7. s. 12.) This river is probably the stream flowing into the lake of Hylica from the valley of *Moriki,* and which near its mouth is covered with rushes. Nicander is clearly wrong, who makes (*l. c.*) the Schoenus flow into the lake Copais. (Ulrichs, *Reisen,* p. 258; Leake, *Northern Greece,* vol. ii. p. 320.) Schoenus was the birthplace of the celebrated Atalanta, the daughter of Schoenus (Paus. viii. 35. § 10); and hence Statius gives to Schoenus the epithet of " Atalantaeus." (Stat. *Theb.* vii. 267.)

2. A town in the centre of Arcadia near Methydrium, which was said to have derived its name from the Boeotian Schoenus. (Paus. viii. 35. § 10; Steph. B. *s. v.*; Leake, *Peloponnesiaca,* p. 240.)

3. A harbour in the Corinthia. [CORINTHUS, p. 683, a.]

4. A river near Maroneia in Thrace, mentioned only by Mela (ii. 2. § 8).

SCHOENUS, a bay on the west coast of Caria, on the south-east of the Cnidian Chersonesus, and opposite the island of Syme. (Pomp. Mela, i. 16;

Plin. v. 29.) It should be observed, however, that this description of the bay of Schoenus is only conjectural, and based upon the order in which Pliny mentions the places in that locality.   [L. S.]

SCIA (Σκία; *Eth.* Σκιεύς), a small town in Euboea (Steph. B. *s. v.* Σκιάς), probably in the territory of Eretria, since Pausanias (iv. 2. § 3) mentions Scium as a district belonging to Eretria.

SCIAS. [MEGALOPOLIS, p. 309, b.]

SCIATHIS. [PHENEUS, p. 595, a.]

SCI'ATHUS (Σκίαθος: *Eth.* Σκιάθιος: *Skiatho*), a small island in the Aegaean sea, N. of Euboea, and a little E. of the Magnesian coast of Thessaly, is described by Pliny as 15 miles in circumference (iv. 12. s. 23). It is said to have been originally colonised by Pelasgians from Thrace, who were succeeded by Chalcidians from Euboea. (Scymn. Ch. 584.) It possessed two towns, one of which was also called Sciathus, but the name of the other is unknown. (Scylax, p. 23, Hudson; Strab. ix. p. 436; Ptol. iii. 13. § 47.) It is frequently mentioned in the history of the invasion of Greece by Xerxes, since the Persian and Grecian fleets were stationed near its coasts. (Herod. vii. 176, 179, 182, 183, viii. 7.) It afterwards became one of the subject allies of Athens, but was so insignificant that it had to pay only the small tribute of 200 drachmae yearly. (Franz, *Elem. Epigr.* 52.) The town of Sciathus was destroyed by the last Philip of Macedonia, B. C. 200, to prevent its falling into the hands of Attalus and the Romans. (Liv. xxxi. 28, 45.) In the Mithridatic War it was one of the haunts of pirates. (Appian, *Mithr.* 29.) It was subsequently given by Antony to the Athenians. (Appian, *B. C.* v. 7.) Sciathus was celebrated for its wine (Athen. i. p. 30, f.), and for a species of fish found off its coasts and called κεστρεύς. (Athen. i. p. 4, c.; Pollux, vi. 63.) The modern town lies in the SE. part of the island, and possesses an excellent harbour. The inhabitants have only been settled here since 1829, previous to which time their town stood in the NE. part of the island upon a rock projecting into the sea, and accessible only upon one side, as more secure against the pirates. Ross says that the new town stands upon the site of the ancient city, but the latter was not the homonymous capital of the island, which occupied the site of the old town in the NE. part of the island, as appears from an inscription found there by Leake. The ancient city in the SE. of the island, upon which the modern town now stands, is probably the second city mentioned by Scylax, but without a name. (Ross, *Wanderungen in Griechenland,* vol. ii. p. 50; Leake, *Northern Greece,* vol. iii. p. 111.)

SCIDRUS (Σκίδρος: *Eth.* Σκιδρανός, Steph. B.: *Sapri*), a Greek city on the coast of Lucania, on the Tyrrhenian sea, between Pyxus (Buxentum) and Latis. It is mentioned only by Herodotus (vi. 21), from whom we learn that it was, as well as Latis, a colony of Sybaris, and was one of the places to which the surviving inhabitants of that city retired, after its destruction by the Crotoniats. It does not appear from his expressions whether these towns were then first founded by the fugitives, or had been previously settled as regular colonies; but the latter supposition is much the more probable. It is singular that no subsequent trace is found of Scidrus; its name is never again mentioned in history, nor alluded to by the geographers, with the exception of Stephanus of Byzantium

(s. v.), who calls it merely a "city of Italy." We have therefore no clue to its position; for even its situation on the Tyrrhenian sea is a mere inference from the manner in which it is mentioned by Herodotus in conjunction with Latis. But there exist at *Sapri*, on the *Gulf of Policastro*, extensive remains of an ancient city, which are generally considered, and apparently not without reason, as indicating the site of Scidrus. They are said to consist of the remains of a theatre and other public buildings of the ancient walls, and constructions around the port. (Antonini, *Lucania*, part ii. c. 11; Romanelli, vol. i. p. 377.) This last is a remarkable landlocked basin, though of small extent; and it is singular that, even if the town had ceased to exist, no allusion should be found to the existence of this secure port, on a coast almost wholly destitute of natural harbours. But the high mountains which shut it in and debar it from all communication with the interior probably prevented it from ever attaining to any importance. *Sapri* is at the present day a mere fishing village, about 6 miles E. of *Policastro*.   [E. H. B.]

SCILLUS (Σκιλλοῦς: *Eth.* Σκιλλούντιος), a town of Triphylia, a district of Elis, situated 20 stadia south of Olympia. In B.C. 572 the Scilluntians assisted Pyrrhus, king of Pisa, in making war upon the Eleians; but they were completely conquered by the latter, and both Pisa and Scillus were razed to the ground. (Paus. v. 6. § 4, vi. 22. § 4.) Scillus remained desolate till about B.C. 392, when the Lacedaemonians, who had a few years previously compelled the Eleians to renounce their supremacy over their dependent cities, colonised Scillus and gave it to Xenophon, then an exile from Athens. Xenophon resided here more than twenty years, but was expelled from it by the Eleians soon after the battle of Leuctra, B.C. 371. He has left us a description of the place, which he says was situated 20 stadia from the Sacred Grove of Zeus, on the road to Olympia from Sparta. It stood upon the river Selinus, which was also the name of the river flowing by the temple of Artemis at Ephesus, and like the latter it abounded in fish and shell-fish. Here Xenophon, from a tenth of the spoils acquired in the Asiatic campaign, dedicated a temple to Artemis, in imitation of the celebrated temple at Ephesus, and instituted a festival to the goddess. Scillus stood amidst woods and meadows, and afforded abundant pasture for cattle; while the neighbouring mountains supplied wild hogs, roebucks, and stags. (Xen. *Anab.* v. 3. §§ 7—13.) When Pausanias visited Scillus five centuries afterwards the temple of Artemis still remained, and a statue of Xenophon, made of Pentelic marble. (Paus. v. 6. § 5, seq.; comp. Strab. viii. pp. 344, 387; Plut. *de Exsil.* p. 603.) There are no remains to identify Scillus, but there can be no doubt that it stood in the woody vale, in which is a small village called *Rasa*, and through which flows a river falling into the Alpheius nearly opposite the Cladens. (Leake, *Morea*, vol. ii. p. 213, seq., *Peloponnesiaca*, p. 9; Boblaye, *Recherches*, &c. p. 133; Curtius, *Peloponnesos*, vol. ii. p. 91.)

SCINCOMAGUS (Σκιγγόμαγος). This place is first mentioned by Strabo (iv. p. 179), who says, when he is speaking of one of the passes of the Alps, that from Ebrodunum (*Embrun*) on the Gallic side through Brigantium (*Briançon*) and Scincomagus and the pass of the Alps to Ocelum, the limit of the land of Cottius is 99 miles; and at Scincomagus Italy begins: and the distance from Scincomagus to Ocelum is 27 miles. (See Groskurd's note on the passage, *Transl. Strab.* i. p. 309.) Pliny also (ii. 108) makes Italy extend to the Alps at Scincomagus, and then he gives the breadth of Gallia from Scincomagus to the Pyrenees and Illiberis. (See the notes and emendations in Harduin's edition.) It appears then that Scincomagus was at the foot of the Alps on the Italian side; and if the position of Ocelum were certain, we might probably determine that of Scincomagus, which must be on the line of the passage over the Alps by the *Mont Genèvre*. It was a great mistake of Bouche and Harduin to suppose that Scincomagus was the same as Segusio or *Susa*. D'Anville guesses that Scincomagus may be a place which he calls "*Chamlat de Siguin*, at the entrance of the *Col de Cestrières*, which leads from the valley of *Sézane* (Cesano) into that of *Pra-gelas*." As usual, he relies on the resemblance of the ancient and modern names, which is often useful evidence; for "magus" in Scincomagus is merely a common Gallic name for town. D'Anville also supposes that this position of Scincomagus is confirmed by the site of Ocelum, as he has fixed it. [OCELUM.] But all this is vague.   [G. L.]

SCIO'NE (Σκιώνη, Herod. vii. 123, viii. 128; Thuc. iv. 120—123, 133, v. 32; Strab. vii. p. 330; Pomp. Mela, ii. 2. § 11; Plin. iv. 17: *Eth.* Σκιωναῖος, Herod.; Σκιωνεύς, Steph. B. *s. v.*), the chief town on the isthmus of Pallene in Macedonia. Although it called itself Achaean, like many other colonial towns, in default of any acknowledged mother-city, it traced its origin to warriors returning from Troy. Under concert with Brasidas the Scionaeans proclaimed their revolt from Athens, two days after the truce was sworn, March, B.C. 421. Brasidas, by a speech which appealed to Grecian feeling, wound up the citizens to the highest pitch of enthusiasm. The Athenians, furious at the refusal of the Lacedaemonians to give up this prize, which they had gained after the truce, passed a resolution, under the instigation of Cleon to kill all the grown-up male inhabitants of the place, and strictly besieged the town, which Brasidas was unable to relieve, though he had previously conveyed away the women and children to a place of safety. After a long blockade Scione surrendered to the Athenians, who put all the men of military age to death, and sold the women and children to slavery. The site of this ill-fated city must be sought for between the capes *Paliuri* and *Posidhi*. (Leake, *Northern Greece*, vol. iii. p. 157.)   [E. B. J.]

SCIRA'DIUM. [SALAMIS.]

SCIRI or SCIRRI, a population variously placed by various authors. The first who mentions them is Pliny (iv. 13. s. 27), who fixes them in Eningia, i. e. in the parts to the NE. of the extreme frontier of what he and his contemporaries call Germania, i. e. *East Prussia*, *Courland*, *Livonia*, *Esthonia*, and part of *Finnland*, "quidam haec habitari ad Vistulam usque fluvium a Sarmatia, Venedis, Sciris, Hirris, tradunt." No other author either mentions the Hirri or places the Sciri thus far northward.

The most interesting notice of them is in the so-called Olbian inscription (Böckh, *Inscr.* no. 2058), wherein they are mentioned as dangerous neighbours to the town of Olbia along with the Galatae, the Thisamatae, the Scythae, and the Saudaratae (Zeuss, *Die Deutschen*, &c., *s. v. Galatae*); and, doubtless, the neighbouring town of Olbia was their true locality.

The evidence of Jornandes makes them Alans ("Sciri et Satagarii et ceteri Alanorum," *Reb. Get.* 49), evidence which is important, since Peria, the notary of the Alan king Candax, was the writer's grandfather. They are made by Sidonius (*Carm.* vii. 322) part of Attila's army, by Jornandes subjects of Odoacer, by Procopius members of the Goth and Alan alliance. They were, almost certainly, a Scythian tribe of *Kherson*, who during the period of the Greek settlements harassed Olbia, and, during the Byzantine period, joined with the other barbarians of the Lower Danube against Rome. Of these, the chief confederates were the Heruli and Turcilingi; with whom they found their way as far west as *Bavaria*. The present country of *Styria* (*Styermark*)=the *March* of the Stiri or Sciri, the change from *Sc* to *St* being justified by the Bavarian Count *Von Schiern* in one part of a document of the 10th century being made a *Comes de Stira* in another. Add to this the existence of a *Nemus Scirorum* in *Bavaria*. (See Zeuss, *s. v. Sciri*).

The Sciri of the later writers were probably a portion of the Scythians of the parts between the Danube and *Don*, under a newer and more specific name. The transplantation into *Styria* along with an inroad of Uldis, king of the Huns, seems to have broken up the name and nation. Sozomenes saw the remnants of them labouring as slaves in the mines of Mount Olympus in Bithynia (ix. 5). [R. G. L.]

SCIRITIS (ἡ Σκιρῖτις: *Eth.* Σκιρίτης, fem. Σκιρῖτις), a rugged and barren mountainous district, in the north of Laconia, between the upper Eurotas on the west and the Oenus on the east, and extending north of the highest ridge of the mountains, which were the natural boundary between Laconia and Arcadia. The name probably expressed the wild and rugged nature of the country, for the word signified hard and rugged (σκίρον, σκεῖρον, σκληρόν, Hesych.). It was bounded by the Maenalians on the north, and by the Parrhasians on the west, and was originally part of Arcadia, but was conquered at an early period, and its inhabitants reduced to the condition of Lacedaemonian Perioeci. (Steph. B. *s. v.* Σκῖρος; Thuc. v. 33.) According to Xenophon they were subjected to Sparta even before the time of Lycurgus. (*De Rep. Lac.* c. 12.) They were distinguished above all the other Perioeci for their bravery; and their contingent, called the Σκιρίτης λόχος, 600 in number, usually occupied the extreme left of the Lacedaemonian wing. (Thuc. v. 67, 68.) They were frequently placed in the post of danger, and sometimes remained with the king as a body of reserve. (Xen. *Cyr.* iv. 2. § 1, *Hell.* v. 2. § 24, v. 4. § 52; Diod. xv. 32.) On the first invasion of Laconia by the Thebans the Sciritae, together with the Perioeci of Caryae and Sellasia, revolted from Sparta, in consequence of which their country was subsequently ravaged by the Lacedaemonians. (Xen. *Hell.* vii. 24. § 1.) The only towns in the Sciritis appear to have been SCIRUS and OEUM, called Ium by Xenophon. The latter is the only place in the district mentioned in historical times [OEUM]. Scirus may perhaps have been the same as Scirtonium (Σκιρτώνιον), in the district of Aegytis. (Paus. viii. 27. § 4; Steph. B. *s. v.*)

The road from Sparta to Tegea, which is the same as the present road from Sparta to *Tripolitzá*, led through the Sciritis. (Leake, *Morea*, vol. iii. p. 28; Boblaye, *Recherches, &c.* p. 75; Ross, *Reisen im Peloponnes*, p. 178; Curtius, *Peloponnesos*, vol. ii. p. 263.)

SCIRO'NIA SAXA. [MEGARA, p. 316, b.]

SCIRRI. [SCIRI.]

SCIRTIA'NA, a station on the Egnatian road, between Brucida (*Presba*) and Castra or Parembole. The name is no doubt connected with that of the SCIRTONES (Σκίρτονες), whom Ptolemy (iii. 17. § 8) couples with the Dassaretian Pirustae as Illyrian tribes near Macedonia.   [E. B. J.]

SCIRTONES. [SCIRTIANA.]

SCIRTO'NIUM. [SCIRITIS.]

SCIRTUS (Σκίρτος, Procop. *de Aed.* ii. 7), a river of Mesopotamia, a western tributary of the Chaboras (*Chabur*). It flowed from 25 sources, and ran past Edessa. (*Chron. Edess.* in Asseman, *Bibl. Or.* i. p. 388.) Its name, which signifies the skipping or jumping (from σκιρτάω), is said to have been derived from its rapid course and its frequent overflowings; and its present name of *Daisan* means the same thing.   [T. H. D.]

SCIRUM. [ATTICA, p. 326, a.]

SCISSUM. [CISSA.]

SCI'TTIUM. [SOTIATES.]

SCODRA (ἡ Σκόδρα, Ptol. ii. 16. (17.) § 12; Σκόδραι, Hierocl. p. 656: *Eth.* Scodrenses, Liv. xlv. 26), one of the more important towns of Roman Illyricum (*Montenegro*), the capital of the Labeates, seated at the southern extremity of the lake Labeatis, between two rivers, the Clausula on the E., and the Barbanna on the W. (Liv. xliv. 31), and at a distance of 17 miles from the sea-coast (Plin. iii. 22. s. 26). It was a very strong place, and Gentius, king of the Illyrians, attempted to defend it against the Romans, B. C. 168, but was defeated in a battle under the walls. Pliny erroneously places it on the Drilo (*l. c.*). At a later period it became the chief city of the province Praevalitana. It is the present *Scutari*, which is also the name of the lake Labeatis. (Wilkinson, *Dalmatia and Montenegro*, vol. i. p. 476.)   [T. H. D.]

SCOLLIS (Σκόλλις), a mountain between Elis and Achaia, now called *Sandameriótiko*, 3333 feet high, from which the river Larissus rises, that forms the boundary between Achaia and Elis. Strabo describes it as adjacent to Mount Lampeia, which was connected with the range of Erymanthus. (Strab. viii. p. 341.) Strabo also identifies it with the "Olenian Rock" of Homer. (*Il.* ii. 617; Strab. viii. p. 387; Leake, *Morea*, vol. ii. pp. 184, 230; *Peloponnesiaca*, p. 203.)

SCOLOTI. [SCYTHIA.]

SCOLUS (Σκῶλος, Thuc. v. 18; Strab. ix. p. 408), a town of Chalcidice near Olynthus, mentioned together with Spartolus, in the treaty between Athens and Sparta in the tenth year of the Peloponnesian War.   [E. B. J.]

SCOLUS (Σκῶλος: *Eth.* Σκώλιος, Σκωλιεύς), a town of Boeotia, mentioned by Homer (*Il.* ii. 497), and described by Strabo as a village of the Parasopia below Cithaeron (ix. p. 408). Pausanias, in his description of the route from Plataea to Thebes, says, that if the traveller were, instead of crossing the Asopus, to follow that river for about 40 stadia, he would arrive at the ruins of Scolus, where there was an unfinished temple of Demeter and Core (ix. 4. § 4). Mardonius in his march from Tanagra to Plataea passed through Scolus. (Herod. ix. 15.) When the Lacedaemonians were preparing to invade Boeotia, B. C. 377, the Thebans threw up an intrenchment in front of Scolus, which probably extended from Mt. Cithaeron to the Asopus. (Xen. *Hell.* v. 4. § 49, *Agesil.* 2.) Strabo says that

Scolus was so disagreeable and rugged (τραχύs) that it gave rise to the proverb, "never let us go to Scolus, nor follow any one there" (ix. p. 408). Leake places Scolus just below the projection of Cithaeron, on a little rocky table-height, overlooking the river, where stands a *metôkhi* dependent on a convent in the Eleutheris, called St. Meletius. (*Northern Greece*, vol. ii. p. 330.)

SCOMBRA'RIA (Σκομβραρία, Strab. iii. p. 159), an island on the S. coast of Spain, in front of the bay which formed the harbour of Carthago Nova, and 24 stadia, or 3 miles, distant from the coast. It derived its name from the scombei, tunny-fish, or mackarel, which were found here in great quantities, and from which the Romans prepared their garum. (Plin. xxxi. 8. s. 43.) It was also called Herculis Insula. Now *Islote*.　　　[T. H. D.]

SCOMBRA'SIA. [SATURNI PROM.]

SCOMBRUS, SCO'MIUS (Σκόμβροs, al. Σκόμιοs, Thuc. ii. 96; Aristot. *Meteor.* i. 13; Scopius, Plin. iv. 17: *Eth.* Σκόμβροι, Hesych.), an outlying mountain of the chain of Haemus, or that cluster of great summits between *Ghiustendil* and *Sofia*, which sends tributaries to all the great rivers of the N. of European Turkey. As the most central point, and nearly equidistant from the Euxine, the Aegean, the Adriatic, and the Danube, it is probably the Haemus of the traveller's tale in Livy (xl. 21), to which Philip, son of Demetrius, king of Macedonia, made a fruitless excursion with the expectation of beholding from thence at once the Adriatic and the Euxine (*Black Sea*), the Danube and the Alps. (Leake. *Northern Greece*, vol. iii. p. 474.) [E. B. J.]

SCOMIUS. [SCOMBRUS.]

SCOPAS (Σκόπαs), an eastern tributary of the Sangarius in Galatia, which according to Procopius (*de Aed.* v. 4) joined the Sangarius, 10 miles east of the town of Juliopolis. Pliny (v. 43) calls it Scopius, and according to Procopius this river frequently overflowed the country, which is perhaps alluded to in the Jerusalem Itinerary (p. 574), where a station called Hycronpotamum (i. e. ὑγρὸν ποταμόν) is mentioned about 13 miles to the east of Juliopolis. The modern name of the river is *Aladan*. (Comp. Leake, *Asia Minor*, p. 79; Eckhel, *Doctr. Num.* iii. p. 101.)　　　　[L. S.]

SCO'PELUS. [HALONNESUS.]

SCOPI. [SCUPI.]

SCO'PIA (Σκοπία ἄκρα), a headland on the west coast of Caria, to the west of Myndus, and opposite the island of Cos. (Ptol. v. 2. § 10.) Strabo (xiv. p. 658) mentions two headlands in the same vicinity, Astypalaea and Zephyrium, one of which may possibly be the same as Scopia. 　　[L. S.]

SCORDISCI (Σκορδίσκοι), a powerful Celtic tribe, in the southern part of Lower Pannonia, between the rivers Savus, Dravus, and Danubius. They and the Boii were overpowered by the Dacians. (Strab. vii. pp. 293, 313.) Some call them an Illyrian tribe, living on the borders of Illyricum, they were much mixed up with them. They were in the end greatly reduced by their struggles with the Dacians and the Triballi, so that when they came in contact with the Romans they were easily subdued. (Appian, *Illyr.* 3; Liv. xli. 23; Justin, xxxii. 3; Plin. iii. 28; Ptol. ii. 16. § 3.) In Pannonia they seem to have gradually become assimilated to the Pannonians, whence in later times they disappear from history as a distinct nation or tribe.　　　　　[L. S.]

SCORDISCUS. [SCYDISES.]

SCORDUS MONS. [SCARDUS.]

SCOTANE. [CLEITOR, p. 633, a.]

SCOTI. The Scoti were the ancient inhabitants of Hibernia, as appears from notices in some of the Latin writers. (Claudian, *de IV. Cons. Honor.* 33, *de Laud. Stil.* ii. 251; Oros. i. 2.) For several centuries Ireland was considered as the land of the Scoti, and the name of Scotia was equivalent to that of Hibernia. (Isid. *Orig.* xiv. 6; Beda, i. 1, ii. 4; Geogr. Rav. i. 3, v. 32; Alfred the Great, *ap. Oros.* p. 30, &c.) We have no accounts respecting the subdivisions of the Scoti; but perhaps they are to be sought in the names of the Irish counties, as *Munster, Leinster, Ulster, Connaught.* Ammianus mentions the Scoti, in conjunction with the Attacotti, as committing formidable devastations (xxvii. 8. § 4). According to St. Jerome (*adv. Jovin.* v. 2. 201, ed. Mart.) they had their wives in common; a custom which Dion Cassius represents as also prevailing among the kindred race in Caledonia (lxxvi. 12). At a later period the names of Scotia and Scoti vanish entirely from Ireland, and become the appellations of the neighbouring Caledonia and its inhabitants. This was effected through a migration of the Scoti into Caledonia, who settled to the N. of the *Clyde;* but at what time this happened, cannot be ascertained. Beda (i. 1) states that it took place under a leader called Reuda. The new settlement waged war with the surrounding Picts, and even against the Anglo-Saxons, but at first with little success. (Id. i. 24, iv. 36.) Ultimately, however, in the year 839, under king Keneth, they succeeded in subduing the Picts (Fordun, *Scot. Hist.* ap. Gale, i. 659, seq.); and the whole country N. of *Solway Frith* subsequently obtained the name of *Scotland.* (Comp. Zeuss, *Die Deutschen u. die Nachbarstämme*, p. 568; Gibbon, vol. iii. p. 268, and *notes*, ed. Smith.) [T. H. D.]

SCOTITAS. [LACONIA, p. 113, b.]

SCOTUSSA (*Peut. Tab.*; Scotusa, Plin. iv. 17. s. 18: *Eth.* Scotussaei, Plin. iv. 17. s. 18), a station on the road from Heracleia Sintica to Philippi, which passed round the N. of the lake Cercinites, answering to the place where the Strymon was crossed just above the lake. (Leake, *Northern Greece*, vol. iii. p. 227.)　　　　　[E. B. J.]

SCOTUSSA (Σκοτοῦσσα or Σκοτοῦσα : *Eth.* Σκοτουσσαῖος), an ancient town of Pelasgiotis in Thessaly, lying between Pherae and Pharsalus, near the frontiers of Phthiotis. Scotussa is not mentioned in Homer, but according to some accounts the oracle of Dodona in Epeirus originally came from this place. (Strab. vii. p. 329.) In B. C. 394 the Scotussaei joined the other Thessalians in opposing the march of Agesilaus through their country. (Xen. *Hell.* iv. 3. § 3.) In B. C. 367 Scotussa was treacherously seized by Alexander, tyrant of the neighbouring town of Pherae. (Diod. xv. 75.) In the territory of Scotussa were the hills called Cynoscephalae, which are memorable as the scene of two battles, one fought in B. C. 364, between the Thebans and Alexander of Pherae, in which Pelopidas was slain, and the other, of still greater celebrity, fought in B. C. 197, in which the last Philip of Macedonia was defeated by the Roman consul Flamininus. (Plut. *Pelop.* 32; Strab. ix. p. 441; Polyb. xviii. 3, seq.; Liv. xxxiii. 6, seq.) In B. C. 191 Scotussa surrendered to Antiochus, but was recovered shortly afterwards, along with Pharsalus and Pherae, by the consul Acilius. (Liv. xxxvi. 9, 14.) The ruins of Scotussa are found at

Suppl. The city was about two or three miles in circumference; but of the walls only a few courses of masonry have been preserved. The acropolis stood at the south-western end of the site, below which, on the east and north, the ground is covered with foundations of buildings, heaps of stones, and fragments of tiles and pottery. (Leake, *Northern Greece*, vol. iv. p. 454, seq.)

SCULTENNA (Σκούλταννα, Strab.: *Panaro*), a river of Gallia Cispadana, and one of the principal of the southern tributaries of the Padus. (Plin. iii. 16. s. 20 ; P. Diac. *Hist. Lang.* iv. 47.) It crosses the Aemilian Way about 5 miles E. of Mutina (*Modena*), and falls into the Po a little below *Bondeno*, being the last of the tributaries of that river which now flow into its main stream. In the lower part of its course it now bears the name of *Panaro*, but in the upper part, before it leaves the valleys of the Apennines, it is still known as the *Scoltenna*. It has its sources in one of the loftiest and most rugged groups of the Apennines, at the foot of the *Monte Cimone*, and from thence flows for many miles through a deep and winding valley, which appears to have been the abode of the Ligurian tribe of the Friniates. The district still bears on old maps the title of *Frignano*. (Magini, *Carte d' Italia*, tav. 16.) In B. C. 177 the banks of the Scultenna were the scene of a decisive conflict between the Ligurians and the Roman consul G. Claudius, in which the former were defeated with great slaughter (Liv. xli. 12, 18); but the site of the battle is not more exactly indicated. Strabo speaks of the plains on the banks of the Scultenna, probably in the lower part of its course, as producing wool of the finest quality. (Strab. v. p. 218.)   [E. H. B.]

SCUPI (Σκούποι, Ptol. iii. 9. § 6, viii. 11. § 5; Hierocl.; Niceph. Bryenn. iv. 18; Geog. Rav. iv. 15; τὰ Σκόπια, Anna Comn. ix. p. 253; Σκούπιον, Procop. *de Aed.* iv. 4; Orelli, *Inscr.* 1790: *Uschküb*), a town which, from its important position at the *débouché* from the Illyrian into the plains of Paeonia and the Upper Axius, was in all ages the frontier town of Illyricum towards Macedonia. There is no evidence of its ever having been possessed by the kings of Macedonia or Paeonia. Under the Romans it was ascribed to Dardania, as well in the time of Ptolemy as in the fifth century, when it was the capital of the new diocese of Dardania (Marquardt, in Becker's *Röm. Alt.* iii. pt. i. p. 110). The Roman road from Stobi to Naissus passed by Scupi, which was thus brought into connection with the great SE. route from Viminacium on the Danube to Byzantium. It was probably seldom under the complete authority of Constantinople, though after the memorable victory in which, under its walls, Basil, the "Slayer of the Bulgarians", in the beginning of the eleventh century, avenged the defeat he had suffered from Samuel, king of Bulgaria, twenty-one years before, in the passes of Mt. Haemus, this city surrendered to the Byzantine army (Cedren. p. 694). In the reign of Michael Palaeologus it was wrested from the emperor by the Servians, and became the residence of the Kral (Cantacuzenus, p. 778.) Finally, under Sultan Bayezid, Scupi, or the "Bride of Rúmili," received a colony of Ottoman Turks (Chalcondyles, p. 31). (Leake, *Northern Greece*, vol. iii. p. 478.)   [E. B. J.]

SCURGUM (Σκούργον), a town in the north of Germany, in the territory of the Helvecones, between the Viadus and the Vistula, the exact site of which is unknown. (Ptol. ii. 11. § 27; comp. Wilhelm, *Germanien*, p. 253.)   [L. S.]

SCYDISES (Σκυδίσης), a chain of rugged mountains in the east of Pontus, which was connected in the north with the Moschici Montes on the east, and with Mons Paryadres on the north-west, while in the south-west it was connected with Antitaurus. (Strab. xi. p. 497, xii. p. 548; Ptol. v. 6. § 8, where it is called Σκορδίσκος.) Modern travellers identify it with the *Tshambü Bel* (*Wiener Jahrbücher*, vol. cv. p. 21.)   [L. S.]

SCYDRA (Σκύδρα: Eth. Σκυδραῖος), a town of Emathia in Macedonia, which Ptolemy places between Tyrissa and Mieza. (Steph. B. *s. v.*; Ptol. iii. 13. § 39; Plin. iv. 10. s. 17.) It is perhaps the same as the station Scurio in the Jerusalem Itinerary (p. 606), where it is placed between Edessa and Pella, at the distance of 15 miles from either. (Cramer, *Ancient Greece*, vol. i. p. 228.)

SCYLACE (Σκυλάκη), an ancient Pelasgian town of Mysia, on the coast of the Propontis, east of Cyzicus. (Steph. B. *s. v.*) In this place and the neighbouring Placia, the Pelasgians, according to Herodotus (i. 57), had preserved their ancient language down to his time. Scylax (p. 35) mentions only Placia, but Mela (i. 19) and Pliny (v. 40) speak of both as still existing. These towns never to have been of any importance, and to have decayed at an early period.   [L. S.]

SCYLA'CIUM or SCYLLETIUM (Σκυλλήτιον, Steph. B., Strab.; Σκυλάκιον, Ptol.: Eth. Σκυλλήτινος: *Squillace*), a town on the E. coast of Bruttium, situated on the shores of an extensive bay, to which it gave the name of SCYLLETICUS SINUS. (Strab. vi. p. 261.) It is this bay, still known as the *Gulf of Squillace*, which indents the coast of Bruttium on the E. as deeply as that of Hipponium or Terina (the *Gulf of St. Eufemia*) does on the W., so that they leave but a comparatively narrow isthmus between them. (Strab. *l. c.* ; Plin. iii. 10. s. 15.) [BRUTTIUM.] According to a tradition generally received in ancient times, Scylletium was founded by an Athenian colony, a part of the followers who had accompanied Menestheus to the Trojan War. (Strab. *l. c.* ; Plin. *l. c.* ; Serv. *ad Aen.* iii. 553.) Another tradition was, however, extant, which ascribed its foundation to Ulysses. (Cassiod. *Var.* xii. 15; Serv. *l. c.*) But no historical value can be attached to such statements, and there is no trace in historical times of Scylletium having been a Greek colony, still less an Athenian one. Its name is not mentioned either by Scylax or Scymnus Chius in enumerating the Greek cities in this part of Italy, nor is there any allusion to its Athenian origin in Thucydides at the time of the Athenian expedition to Sicily. We learn from Diodorus (xiii. 3) that it certainly did not display any friendly feeling towards the Athenians. It appears, indeed, during the historical period of the Greek colonies to have been a place of inferior consideration, and a mere dependency of Crotona, to which city it continued subject till it was wrested from its power by the elder Dionysius, who assigned it with its territory to the Locrians. (Strab. vi. p. 261.) It is evident that it was still a small and unimportant place at the time of the Second Punic War, as no mention is found of its name during the operations of Hannibal in Bruttium, though he appears to have for some time had his head quarters in its immediate neighbourhood, and the place called Castra Hannibalis must have been very near to Scylacium. [CASTRA HAN-

MIRALIS.] In B. C. 124 the Romans, at the instigation of C. Gracchus, sent a colony to Scylacium, which appears to have assumed the name of Minervium or Colonia Minervia. (Vell. Pat. i. 15; Mommsen, in *Berichte der Sächsischen Gesellschaft der Wissenschaften*, 1849, pp. 49—51.) The name is written by Velleius "Scolatium;" and the form "Scolacium" is found also in an inscription of the reign of Antoninus Pius, from which it appears that the place must have received a fresh colony under Nerva. (Orell *Inscr.* 136; Mommsen, *l. c.*). Scylacium appears to have become a considerable town after it received the Roman colony, and continued such throughout the Roman Empire. (Mel. ii. 4. § 8; Plin. iii. 10. s. 15; Ptol. iii. 1. § 11.) Towards the close of this period it was distinguished as the birthplace of Cassiodorus, who has left us a detailed but rhetorical description of the beauty of its situation, and fertility of its territory. (Cassiod. *Var.* xii. 15.)

The modern city of *Squillace* is a poor place, with only about 4000 inhabitants, though retaining its episcopal see. It stands upon a hill about 3 miles from the sea, a position according with the description given by Cassiodorus of the ancient city, but it is probable that this occupied a site nearer the sea, where considerable ruins are said still to exist, though they have not been described by any modern traveller.

The SCYLLETICUS SINUS (Σκυλλητικὸς κόλπος), or *Gulf of Squillace*, was always regarded as dangerous to mariners; hence Virgil calls it "navifragum Scylaceum." (*Aen.* iii. 553.) There is no natural port throughout its whole extent, and it still bears an evil reputation for shipwrecks. The name is found in Aristotle as well as Antiochus of Syracuse, but would seem to have been unknown to Thucydides; at least it is difficult to explain otherwise the peculiar manner in which he speaks of the *Terinaean* gulf, while relating the voyage of Gylippus along the E. coast of Bruttium. (Thuc. vi. 104; Arist. *Pol.* vii. 10; Antioch. *ap.* Strab. vi. p. 254.)   [E. H. B.]

SCYLAX (Σκύλαξ), the chief tributary of the Iris in Pontus; it had its sources in the east of Galatia, and flowing in a north-western direction, emptied itself into the Iris near Eupatoria or Magnopolis. (Strab. xii. p. 547.) Its modern name is *Tchoterlek Irmak.* (Hamilton, *Researches*, vol. i. pp. 365, 374.)   [L. S.]

SCYLLAE (*Tab. Peut.*; Geogr. Rav. iv. 6, v. 12), a town of Thrace, on the Euxine, where the long wall, erected by the emperor Anastasius Dicorus for the defence of Constantinople, terminated. This wall commenced at Selymbria, on the Propontis, and was carried across the narrow part of Thrace, at the distance of about 40 miles from Constantinople, its length being 2 days' journey (Procop. *de Aed.* iv. 9; Gibbon, *Decline and Fall*, c. 40.)   [J. R.]

SCYLLAEUM (τὸ Σκύλλαιον; *Scilla*), a promontory, and town or fortress, on the W. coast of Bruttium, about 15 miles N. of Rhegium, and almost exactly at the entrance of the Sicilian strait. The promontory is well described by Strabo (vi. p. 257) as a projecting rocky headland, jutting out boldly into the sea, and united to the mainland by a narrow neck or isthmus, so as to form two small but well sheltered bays, one on each side. There can be no doubt that this rocky promontory was the one which became the subject of so many fables, and which was represented by Homer and other poets as

the abode of the monster Scylla. (Hom. *Od.* xii. 73, &c., 235, &c.; *Biogr. Dict.* art. SCYLLA.) But the dangers of the rock of Scylla were far more fabulous than those of its neighbour Charybdis, and it is difficult to understand how, even in the infancy of navigation, it could have offered any obstacle more formidable than a hundred other headlands whose names are unknown to fame. (Senec. *Ep.* 79; Smyth's *Sicily*, p. 107.) At a later period Anaxilas, the despot of Rhegium, being struck with the natural strength of the position, fortified the rock, and established a naval station there, for the purpose of checking the incursions of the Tyrrhenian pirates. (Strab. vi. p. 257.) In consequence of this a small town grew up on the spot; and hence Pliny speaks of an "oppidum Scyllaeum;" but it was probably always a small place, and other writers speak only of the promontory. (Plin. iii. 5. s. 10; Mel. ii. 4. § 8; Ptol. iii. 1. § 9.; Steph. Byz. *s. v.*) At the present day the rock is still occupied by a fort, which is a post of considerable strength, while a small town stretches down the slopes towards the two bays. The distance from the castle to the opposite point of the Sicilian coast, marked by the *Torre del Faro*, is stated by Capt. Smyth at 6047 yards, or rather less than 3½ Eng. miles, but the strait afterwards contracts considerably, so that its width between the *Punta del Pezzo* (Caenys Prom.) and the nearest point of Sicily does not exceed 3971 yards. (Smyth's *Sicily*, p. 108.)   [E. H. B.]

SCYLLAEUM (Σκύλλαιον), a promontory of Troezenia, and the most easterly point of the Peloponnesus, is said to have derived its name from Scylla, the daughter of Nisus, who, after betraying Megara and Nisaea to Minos, was thrown by the latter into the sea, and was washed ashore on this promontory. Scyllaeum formed, along with the opposite promontory of Sunium in Attica, the entrance to the Saronic gulf. It is now called *Kavo-Skyli;* but as Pausanias, in the paraplus from Scyllaeum to Hermione, names Scyllaeum first, and then Bucephala, with three adjacent islands, it is necessary, as Leake has observed, to divide the extremity now known as *Kavo-Skyli* into two parts; the bold round promontory to the N. being the true Scyllaeum, and the acute cape a mile to the S. of it Bucephala, since the three islands are adjacent to the latter. (Paus. ii. 34. §§ 7, 8; Scylax, p. 20, Hudson; Strab. viii. p. 373; Thuc. v. 53; Plin. iv. 5. s. 9; Mela, ii. 3; Leake, *Morea*, vol. ii. p. 462, *Peloponnesiuca*, p. 282; Boblaye, *Recherches*, p. 59; Curtius, *Peloponnesos*, vol. ii. p. 452.)

SCYLLE'TICUS SINUS. [SCYLLACIUM.]

SCYRAS. [LACONIA, p. 114, b.]

SCYROS or SCYRUS (Σκῦρος: *Eth.* Σκύριος: *Skyro*), an island in the Aegaean sea, and one of the northern Sporades, was so called from its ruggedness. It lay east of Euboea, and contained a town of the same name (Strab. ix. p. 436; Scylax, p. 23; Ptol. iii. 13. § 47), and a river called Cephissus. (Strab. ix. p. 424.) Scyros is frequently mentioned in the stories of the mythical period. Here Thetis concealed her son Achilles in woman's attire among the daughters of Lycomedes, in order to save him from the fate which awaited him under the walls of Troy. (Apollod. iii. 13. § 8; Paus. i. 22. § 6; Strab. ix. p. 436.) It was here also that Pyrrhus, the son of Deidamia by Achilles, was brought up, and was fetched from thence by Ulysses to the Trojan War. (Hom. *Il.* xix. 326, *Od.* xi. 507; Soph. *Phil.* 239, seq.) According to another tradi

3 O 4

tion Scyros was conquered by Achilles (Hom. *Il.*
i. 668; Paus. i. 22. § 6); and this conquest was
connected in the Attic legends with the death of
Theseus. After Theseus had been driven out of
Athens he retired to Scyros, where he was first
hospitably received by Lycomedes, but was afterwards treacherously hurled into the sea from one
of the rocks in the island. It was to revenge his
death that Peleus sent Achilles to conquer the
island. (Plut. *Thes.* 35; Paus. i. 22. § 6; Philostr.
Heroic. 19) Scyros is said to have been originally
inhabited by Pelasgians, Carians, and Dolopians;
and we know from Thucydides that the island was
still inhabited by Dolopians, when it was conquered
by Cimon after the Persian wars. (Nicolaus Damasc.
ap. Steph. B. *s. v.*; Scymn. Ch. 580, seq.; Thuc. i.
98; Diod. xi. 60.) In B. C. 476 an oracle had
directed the Athenians to bring home the bones of
Theseus; but it was not till B. C. 469 that the
island was conquered, and the bones conveyed to
Athens, where they were preserved in the Theseium.
Cimon expelled the Dolopians from the island, and
peopled it with Athenian settlers. (Thuc. Diod. *ll.cc.*;
Plut. *Thes.* 36, *Cim.* 8; on the date of the conquest
of Scyros, which Clinton erroneously places in B. C.
476, see Grote, *History of Greece*, vol. v. p. 409.)
From this time Scyros was subject to Athens, and
was regarded even at a later period, along with
Lemnos and Imbros, as a possession to which the
Athenians had special claims. Thus the peace of
Antalcidas, which declared the independence of all
the Grecian states, nevertheless allowed the Athenians
to retain possession of Scyros, Lemnos, and Imbros
(Xen. *Hell.* iv. 8. § 15, v. 1. § 31); and though the
Macedonians subsequently obtained possession of
these islands, the Romans compelled Philip, in the
peace concluded in B. C. 196, to restore them to the
Athenians. (Liv. xxxiii. 30.) The soil of Scyros
was unproductive (Dem. *c. Callip.* p. 1238; Eustath.
ad Hom. Il. ii. p. 782; Suidas, *s. v.* ἀρχὴ Σκυρία); but
it was celebrated for its breed of goats, and for its
quarries of variegated marble. (Strab. ix. p. 437;
Athen. i. p. 28, xii. p. 540; Zenob. ii. 18; Plin.
xxxvi. 16. s. 26.)

Scyros is divided into two parts by a narrow
isthmus, of which the southern half consists of high
rugged mountains. The northern half is not so
mountainous. The modern town of *St. George*, on
the eastern side of the island, stands upon the site
of the ancient town. It covers the northern and
western sides of a high rocky peak, which to the
eastward falls steeply to the sea; and hence Homer
correctly describes the ancient city as the lofty
Scyros (Σκῦρον αἰπεῖαν, *Il.* i. 664). The Hellenic
walls are still traceable in many parts. The city was
barely 2 miles in circumference. On the isthmus
south of Scyros a deep bay still retains the name of
Achilli (Ἀχίλλι), which is doubtless the site of the
Achilleion, or sanctuary of Achilles, mentioned by
Eustathius (*ad Il.* ix. 662). Athena was the
divinity chiefly worshipped at Scyros. Her temple
stood upon the shore close to the town. (Stat.
Achill. i. 285, ii. 21.) Tournefort says that he
saw some remains of columns and cornices of white
marble, close by a forsaken chapel, on the left hand
going into the fort of *St. George*; these are probably
remains of the temple of Athena. (Tournefort,
Voyage, vol. i. p. 334, trans.; Leake, *Northern
Greece*, vol. iii. p. 106. seq.; Fiedler, *Reise*, vol. ii.
p. 66; Ross, *Wanderungen in Griechenland*, vol. ii.
p. 32, seq.)

SCYRUS (Σκῦρος), a tributary of the Alpheius,
in southern Arcadia. [MEGALOPOLIS, p. 309, b.]

SCYTHIA (ἡ Σκυθία, ἡ Σκυθική: *Eth.* Σκύθης,
Scytha), the country of the Scythae, a vast area in
the eastern half of Northern Europe, and in Western
and Central Asia. Its limits varied with the differences of date, place, and opportunities of information
on the part of its geographers. Indeed, to a great
extent, the history of Scythia is the history of a

Name.—It is obvious that the term came from the
Greeks to the Romans; in this respect unlike Sarmatia, Dacia, and others, which, in form at least, are
Roman rather than Greek. But whence did the
Greeks get it? for it is by no means either significant
in their tongue, or a Greek word at all. They took
it from one or more of the populations interjacent
between themselves and the Scythae; these being
Thracians, Sarmatians, and Getae. Probably all
three used it; at any rate, it seems to have been
used by the neighbours of the Greeks of Olbiopolis,
and by the Thracians on the frontiers of the Greeks
of Macedonia. This is in favour of its having been
a term common to *all* the forms of speech between
Macedonia and the Borysthenes. *Scyth-*, then, is a
Sarmatian, Thracian, and Getic term in respect to its
introduction into the Greek language. Was it so
in its *origin?* The presumption as well as the evidence is in favour of its having been so. There is
the express evidence of Herodotus (iv. 6) that the
population which the Greeks called Scythae called
themselves Scoloti. There is the fact that the Persian equivalent to Scythae was Sakae. Thirdly,
there is the fact that in the most genuine-looking of
the Scythic myths there is no such eponymus as
Scytha or Scythes, which would scarcely have been
the case had the name been native. *Scyth-*, then,
was a word like *German* or *Allemand*, as applied to
the *Deutsche*, a word strange to the language of the
population designated by it, but not strange to the
language of the neighbouring countries. To whom
was it applied? To the tribes who called themselves
Scoloti.

What was the extent of the term? Did it apply
not only to the Scoloti, but to the whole of the
class to which the Scoloti belonged? It is safe
to say that, at *first*, at least, there were many
congeners of the Scoloti whom no one called
Scythae. The number, however, increased as the
term became general. Did the name denote any
populations of a different family from the Scoloti?
Rarely, at first; afterwards, frequently. If the
populations designated by their neighbours as Scythae called themselves by some other name, what was
that name? Scoloti applied only to a part of them.
Had the word *Scyth-* a meaning in any language? if
so, what was it, and in what tongues? Both these
points will be noticed in the sequel, the questions involved in them being at present premature, though
by no means unimportant.

The knowledge of the Scythian family dates from
the beginning of Greek literature.

SCYTHIANS OF HESIOD, ETC.—Populations belonging to the Scythian family are noticed by Homer under
the names of Abii, Glactophagi, and Hippemolgi,
the habit of milking their mares being as definite a
characteristic of a Scythian as anything in the way
of manners and customs can be. Hesiod gives us
Scythae under that name, noting them also as Hippemolgi. The Scythians of Homer and Hesiod are
poetical rather than historical nations. They are
associated with the Mysi of Bulgaria (not of Asia),

a point upon which Strabo enlarges (vii. 3. §§ 7, 8). They are Hamaxobii (ἐν ἀκήναις οἰκί ἔχοντες), and ἀγαῦοι. Aeschylus mentions them as εὔνομοι. The apparent simplicity of their milk-drinking habits got them the credit of being men of mild and innocent appetites with Ephorus (Strab. vii. p. 302), who contrasts them with the cannibal Sarmatae. There was also an apparent confusion arising out of the likeness of Νόμαδες to Νόμοι (from νόμος = law). The Prometheus of Aeschylus is bound to one of the rocks of Caucasus, on the distant border of the earth, and the inaccessible desert of the Scythians.

Such are the Scythae of Aeschylus and Hesiod. The writers of the interval, who knew them as the invaders of Asia, and as historical agents, must have had a very different notion of them. Fragmentary allusions to the evils inflicted during their inroads are to be found in Callinus, Archilochus, &c. The notice of them, however, belongs to the criticism of the historical portion of the account of

TRANS-DANUBIAN SCYTHIANS OF HERODOTUS: SCOLOTI: SCYTHIANS OF HIPPOCRATES.—Much of the Herodotean history is simple legend. The strange story of an intermarriage of the females who, whilst their husbands were in Asia, were left behind with the slaves, and of the rebellion therein originating having been put down by the exhibition, on the part of the returning masters, of the whips with which the backs of the rebels had been previously but too familiar, belongs to the Herodotean Scythians (iv. 1—6). So do the myths concerning the origin of the nation, four in number, which may be designated as follows:—

1. *The Account of the Scythians themselves.*—This is to the effect that Targitaus, the son of Zeus by a daughter of the river Borysthenes, was the father of Leipoxais, Arpoxais, and Colaxais. In their reign, there fell from heaven a yoke, an axe (σάγαρις), a plough-share, and a cup, all of gold. The two elder failed in taking them up; for they burnt when they approached them. But the younger did not fail; and ruled accordingly. From Leipoxais descended the Auchaetae (γένος); from Arpoxais the Catiari and Traspies; from Colaxais the Paralatai. The general name for all is "Scoloti, whom the Greeks call Scythae." This was exactly 1000 years before the invasion of Darius. The gold was sacred; the country large. It extended so far north that the continual fall of feathers (snow) prevented things from being seen. The number of the kingdoms was three, the greatest of which had charge of the gold. Of this legend, the elements seem partly Scythian, and partly due to the country in which the Scythians settled. The descent from the Borysthenes belongs to this latter class. The story of the sons of Targitaus is found, in its main features, amongst the present Tartars. In *Targitaus* more than one commentator has found the root *Turk.* The threefold division reminds us to the Great, Middle, and Little Hordes of the *Kirghis;* and it must be observed that the words *greatest* and *middle* (μεγίστη and μέση) are found in the Herodotean account. They may be more technical and definite than is generally imagined. In the account there is no Eponymus, no *Scytha,* or even *Scolotus.* There is also the statement that the Scythians are the *youngest* of all nations. This they might be, as immigrants.

2. *The Account of the Pontic Greeks.*—This is to the effect that Agathyrsus, Gelonus, and Scythes (the *youngest*) were the sons of Hercules and Echidna, the place where they met being the Hylæa. The son that could draw the bow was to rule. This was Scythes, owing to manoeuvres of his mother. He stayed in the land: the others went out. The cup appears here as an emblem of authority.

3. *The Second Greek Account.*—This is historical rather than mythological. The Massagetae press the Scythians upon the Cimmerii, the latter flying before them into Asia. This connects the history of the parts about the Bosporus with Media. The inference from the distribution of the signs of Cimmerian occupancy confirms this account. There were the burial-places of the Cimmerii on the Tyras; there was the Cimmerian Bosporus, and between them, with Cimmerian walls, Scythia (ἡ Σκυθική). This is strong evidence in favour of Scythian extension and Cimmerian preoccupancy.

4. *The Account of Aristeas of Proconnesus.*—This is a speculation rather than either a legend or a piece of history. Aristeas (Mure, *History of Greek Literature,* vol. ii. 469, seq.) visited the country of the Issedones. North of these lay the Arimaspi ; north of the Arimaspi the Monophthalmi; north of the Monophthalmi the Gold-guarding Griffins (Γρύπες χρυσοφαλάκοι); and north of these, the Hyperborei. The Hyperborei made no movements; but the Griffins drove the Monophthalmi, the Monophthalmi the Arimaspi, the Arimaspi the Issedones, the Issedones the Scythians, the Scythians the Cimmerians, the Cimmerians having to leave their land; but they, as we learn elsewhere, attack the Medes. (Herod. iv. 5—16). No one had ever been further north than Aristeas, an unsafe authority. The information of Herodotus himself is chiefly that of the Greeks of the Borysthenes. He mentions, however, conversations with the steward of one of the Scythian kings.

The Emporium of the Borystheneitae was central to the Scythia of the sea-coast. In the direction of the Hypanis, i. e. west and north-west, the order of the population was as follows: the Callipidae and Alazones (Ἕλληνες Σκυθαί), sowers and consumers of corn; to the north of whom lay the Scythae Aroteres, not only sowers of corn, but sellers of it; to the north of these the Neuri; to the north of the Neuri either a desert or a terra incognita (iv. 17, 18.) The physical geography helps us here. The nearer we approach the most fertile province of *Modern Russia, Podolia,* wherein we place the Scythae Aroteres, the more the Scythian character becomes agricultural. The Hellenes Scythae (Callipidae and Alazones) belong more to *Kherson.* That the Hellenes Scythae were either a mixed race, or Scythicised Greeks, is unlikely. The doctrine of the present writer is as follows: seeing that they appear in two localities (viz. the Governments of *Kherson* and *Caucasus*); seeing that in each of these the populations of the later and more historical periods are Alani (Ptolemy's form for those of *Kherson* is Alauni); seeing that even the Alani of Caucasus are by one writer at least called ἀλάνωντες Ἀλαῦνοι; seeing that the root Αλαν might have two plurals, one in -οι and one in -ες, he ends in seeing in the Hellenic Scythians simply certain Scythians of the Alan name. Neither does he doubt about Geloni being the same word,—forms like Chuni and Hunni, Arpi and Carpi being found for these parts. At any rate, the locality for the Callipidae and Alazones suits that of Ptolemy's Alauni, whilst that of the Scythian Greeks and Geloni of Caucasus suits that of the Alans of the fourth and fifth centuries.

The Scythian affinities of the Neuri are implied rather than categorically stated; indeed, in another part there is the special statement that the Tyras rises out of a great lake which separates the Scythian and Neurid countries (τὴν Σκυθικὴν καὶ τὴν Νευρίδα γῆν). This, however, must not be made to prove too much ; since the Scythians that were conterminous with the Neuri were known by no special name, but simply by the descriptive term Scythae Aroteres. [Exampaeus; Neuri.] In Siberian geography *Narym = marsh.* Hence *Neuri* may be a Scythian gloss. There may also have been more Neuri than one, e. g. on the *Narym* of the head-waters of the *Dnieper*, i. e. of *Pinsk.* A fact in favour of the Neuri being Scythian is the following. The occupants of *Volhynia,* when its history commences, which is as late as the 13th century, are of the same stock with the Scythians, i. e. Comanian Turks. Not only is there no evidence of their intro-duction being recent, but the name Omani (Lygii Omani) appears about the same parts in Ptolemy.

East of the Borysthenes the Agricultural Scythae occupy the country as far as the Panticapes, 3 days distant. Northwards they extend 11 days up the Borysthenes, where they are succeeded by a desert; the desert by the Androphagi, a nation peculiar and by no means Scythian (c. 19). Above the Androphagi is a desert.

The bend of the *Dnieper* complicates the geo-graphy here. It is safe, however, to make *Eka-terinoslav* the chief Georgic area, and to add to it parts of *Kiev, Kherson,* and *Poltava,* the agricul-tural conditions increasing as we move northwards. The two deserts (ἐρῆμοι) command notice. The first is, probably, a March or political frontier, such as the old Suevi used to have between themselves and neighbours; at least, there is nothing in the conditions of the soil to make it a natural one. It is described as ἐρῆμος ἐπὶ πολλόν. The other is ἐρῆμος ἀληθέως, — a distinction, apparently, of some value. To be natural, however, it must be inter-preted *forest* rather than *steppe. Kursk* and *Tsher-nigov* give us the area of the Androphagi; *Kursk* having a slight amount of separate evidence in fa-vour of its having been " by no means Scythian " (c. 18).

The Hylaea, or wooded district of the *Lower Dnieper,* seems to have been common ground to the Scythae Georgi and Scythae Nomades; or, perhaps it was uninhabited. The latter extend 14 days east-ward. i. e. over Taurida, part of *Ekaterinoslav,* and *Don Kosaks,* to the Gerrhus.

The Palaces (τὰ καλεύμενα βασιλήῒα) succeed; their occupants being the Royal Scythians, the best and most numerous of the name, who look upon the others as their slaves. They extend, southwards, into the *Crimea* (τὴν Ταυρικήν), and, eastwards, as far as the ditch dug by the offspring of the blind slaves (the statement that the Scythians blinded their slaves on account of the milk being one of the elements of the strange Servile legend previously noticed), and the Maeotic Emporium called Kremni. Some touch the Tanais.

North of the Royal Scythians lie the Melanchlaeni (a probable translation of *Karakalpak = black bonnet*), a different nation and not Scythian (c. 20), with marshes, and either a desert or a terra incog-nita above them. This distinction is, almost cer-tainly, real. At the present moment a population, to all appearances aboriginal, and neither Slavonic nor Scythian (but Ugrian or Finn), occupies parts of *Penza* and *Tambov* having, originally, extended both further west and further south. To the north the forest districts attain their *maximum* development. [Melanchlaeni.] The Royal Scythians may have occupied parts of *Voronezh.*

East of the Tanais it was no longer Scythia, but the *Adiges* of the Sauromatae. [See Sauromatae; Budini; Geloni; Thyssagetae; Iurcae.] The want of definite boundaries makes it difficult to say where the Iurcae end. Beyond them to the *east* lay other Scythians, who, having revolted from the Royal, settled there. Up to their districts the soil was level and deep, beyond it rough and stony, with mountains beyond. These are occupied by a nation of Bald-heads, flat-nosed and bearded, Scy-thians in dress, peculiar in language, collectors of a substance called ἄσχυ from a tree called *ποντικόν* (c.23). Their flocks and herds are few; their manners so simple that no one injures them, &c. [Argippaei; Issedones; Hyperborei; Arimaspi.] In the parts about the mountains of the Argippaei trade was carried on by means of *seven interpreters.* Let this be the caravan trade of *Orenburg,* near its ter-minus on the *Volga,* and we shall find that seven is about the number of languages that could at the present moment be brought together at a fair in the centre of *Orenburg.* For the modern Rus-sian take the language of the Sauromatae; for the Scythian that of the modern Tartars. To these we can add four Ugrian forms of speech,— the Tshu-wash, the Mordwin, the Tsheremiss, and the Votiak, with the two forms of speech akin to the Ostiak and Permian to choose the fifth from. The Tshuwash of *Kasan* and the Bashkirs of *Orenburg* have mixed characters at the present time,—Turk and Ugrian.

Rivers.—The chief river of the Herodotean Scy-thia was the Ister [Danubius], with its five mouths; and then the Tyras (*Dniester*), the Hypanis (*Bog*), the Borysthenes (*Dnieper*), the Panticapes [see s. v.], the Hypacyris [see Carcina], the Gerrhus [see s. v.], and the Tanais (*Don*); the feeders of the Ister (i. e. the rivers of the present Danubian Principalities) being the Porata (Scythic, in Greek Puretus), the Tiarantos, the Araros, the Naparis, and the Ordessus (cc. 47, 48). To these add, from the country of the Agathyrsi, the Maris (c. 49), or modern *Maros* of *Transylvania.* The difference between the ancient and modern names of rivers is nowhere greater than here,—the *Maros* being the only name now in use which represents the original one; unless we choose to hold that, word for word, *Aluta = Araros. Word for word,* indeed, Naparis *is Dnieper;* but then the rivers are different. This creates a grave difficulty in the determination of the language to which the names of the Scythian rivers should be referred. Yet the question is important, inasmuch as, in the names, as they come down to us, we have so many glosses of some language or other. Upon the whole, however, the circumstances under which they reached Herodotus suggest the notion that they are Scythian: e. g. the express statement that Porata is a Scythian form. Again ; Hypanis is, word for word, *Kuban,*— a word of which the appearance in both Asia and Europe is best explained by supposing it to be Scythian. On the other hand, they are as little significant in the language which, amongst those at present existing, best explains the *undoubted* Scythian glosses, as they are in the Slavonic, Latin, or Greek.

The physical geography of Herodotean Scythia was a steppe, with occasional districts (chiefly along the courses of the rivers and at their head-waters) of a more practicable character.

MOUNTAINS.—These were the eastern continuation of the Carpathians, and the hills of the *Crimea* or *Tauris*. These were but imperfectly known to Herodotus.

LAKES. [See EXAMPAEUS and BUCE.]

TOWNS, exclusively Greek colonies. [See OLBI-OPOLIS; PANTICAPAEUM.]

Beyond the Sauromatae (*s. v.*) lay "other Scythians, who, having revolted from the Royal, reached this country," i. e. some part of *Orenburg* (c. 22).

Thirdly, there were the SACAE, whom we may call the Scythians of the Persian frontier. Their occupancy was the parts conterminous with Bactria, and it was under Darius, the son of Hystaspes, that they, along with the Bactrians, joined in the invasion of Greece. Their dress was other than Bactrian, consisting of a pointed turban, a bonnet, leggings, native bows, daggers, and the axe called *σάγαρις* —a word which is probably technical. There were Scythae Amyrgii, truly, however, Scythae, inasmuch as the Persians called all the Scythians by the name SACAE. Under the reign of Cyrus they were independent. Under Darius, they, along with the Caspii, formed the 15th satrapy (iii. 93). This connects them with their frontagers on the west, rather than the east.

There is no difficulty, however, in fixing them. From *Asterabad* to *Balk* they extended along the northern frontier of Persia, in the area, and probably as the ancestors, of the present Turcomans and Uzbeks. The name Amyrgii will be noticed in the sequel.

The Sacae, if not separated from the "other Scythians" by the greater part of *Independent Tartary*, were, at any rate, a population that presented itself to the informants of Herodotus under a different aspect. The Sacae were what the Persians found on their northern frontier. The eastern Scythae were the Scythians beyond the Sauromatae, as they appeared to the occupants of the parts about the Tanais.

It is not difficult to see the effect of these three points of view upon future geographers. With Scythians in *Transylvania*, Scythians in *Orenburg*, with Scythians (even though called Sacae) in *Khorasan* and *Turcomania*, and with a terra incognita between, the name cannot but fail to take upon itself an inordinate amount of generality. The three isolated areas will be connected; and the historical or ethnological unity will give way to a geographical. At present, however, there is a true unity over the whole of Scythia in the way both of

PHYSIOGNOMY AND MANNERS.—The physical conformation of the Scythians is not only mentioned incidentally by Herodotus, but in a more special manner by Hippocrates: "The Scythian *γένος* is widely different from the rest of mankind, and is like to nothing but itself, even as is the Aegyptian. Their bodies are thick and fleshy, and their limbs loose, without tone, and their bellies the smoothest (?), softest (?), moistest (?) (*κοίλιαι ὑγρόταται*) of all bellies as to their lower parts (*πασέων κοιλέων αἱ κάτω*); for it is not possible for the belly to be dried in such a country, both from the soil and climate, but on account of the fat and the smoothness of their flesh, they are all like each other, the men like the men, the women like the women." (Hippocr. *de Aere*, &c. pp. 291, 292.)

Coming as this notice does from a physician, it has commanded considerable attention; it has, however, no pretensions to be called a description, though this has often been done. In the hands of later writers its leading features become exaggerated, until at length the description of a Scythian becomes an absolute caricature. We may see this by reference to Ammianus Marcellinus and Jornandes, in their accounts of the Huns. The real fact inferred from the text of Hippocrates is, that the Scythians had a peculiar physiognomy, a physiognomy which the modern ethnologist finds in the population of Northern and Central Asia, as opposed to those of Persia, Caucasus, Western and Southern Europe.

Their general *habits* were essentially nomadic, pastoral, and migratory; the commonest epithets or descriptive appellations being Ἀμαξόβιοι, Φερόοικοι, Ἱπποτόξοται, and the like.

Concerning their RELIGION, we have something more than a mere cursory notice (iv. 59). (i.) Tabiti (Ταβίτι): This was the Scythian name for the nearest equivalent to the Greek *Hestia* (*Vesta*), the divinity whom they most especially worshipped. (ii.) Papaeus : "Most properly, in my mind, is Zeus thus called." So writes Herodotus, thinking of the ideas engendered by such exclamations as Παπᾶς. (iii.) Apia: This is the name for earth: as (iv.) Oeto-syrus (Οἰτόσυρος) is for Apollo, and (v.) Artimpasa for Aphrodite, and (vi.) Thamimasaada for Poseidon, the God of the Royal Scythians most especially. To Oestosyrus we have the following remarkable inscription (*Gud. Inscrip. Antiq.* p. 56. 2; see Zeuss, *s. v. Skythen*): ΘΕΛ. ΞΕΛΟΙΤΟΞΚΤΡΑ (? ΞΕΛ-ηνη) ΚΑΙ APOLLΩΝΩ. OITOΞΚΤΡΩ. ΜΙΘΡΑ. Μ. ΟΤΛΠΙΟΞ. ΠΛΟΚΑΜΟΞ. ΝΕΩΚΟΡΟΞ. ΑΝΕΘ (ηκε). Here the connection is with the Persian god Mithras.

The Scoloti sacrificed to all their gods, but to Mars the most especially; for, besides the deities which have been mentioned under their several Scythian names, Mars and Heracles were objects of particular adoration. The Scythian Venus, too, was the Ἀφροδίτη οὐρανίη. To Ares, however, they sacrificed most especially and most generally; for there was a place of worship to him in every *νόμος* (mark the use of this word, which is applied to the divisions of the Persian empire as well), where horses, sheep, and captives were sacrificed, and where the emblem of the god was an iron sword,—even as it was with the Alani of Ammianus and the Huns of Priscus.

Human beings were sacrificed, but no swine. Neither were swine eaten, nor were they tolerated in the country. This is noticed, because in many of the nations of Northern Asia, e. g. the Wotiaks and others, the hog, even now, is held in abomination, and that by Pagan tribes untinctured with Mahometanism.

Notwithstanding the praises of the earlier poets, the wars of the "just and illustrious" Scythians were of a piece with the worship of their war-god. They scalped their enemies, and they used their skulls as drinking cups (cc. 64—65). Once a year the monarch of each nome filled a vast vat with wine and apportioned it to the warriors who had killed most enemies during the year. Those whose hands were unstained got none, and were disgraced; those who had killed many took a double allowance (c. 66).

Their soothsayers, amongst other superstitions, practised rhabdomancy, amongst whom the *Enarees*

(ἀνδρόγονοι) are the most famous. They got
their art from Aphrodite, as they got their ailment.
During the Scythian invasion of Asia, a portion of
the conquerors plundered the temple of the Aphrodite Urania in Ascalon, for which sacrilege they and
their children were afflicted with θήλεια νοῦσος, the
names of the sufferers being 'Ενάρεες (i. 105, 106).
The nature of this θήλεια νοῦσος has yet to be
satisfactorily explained.

The sacerdotal and regal relations are curious.
When the king ails he calls his priests, who tell him
that his ailment comes from some one having fore-
sworn himself in the greatest oath a Scythian can
take. This is " by the hearth of the king." Take
it falsely, and the king will sicken. Upon sickening,
however, he sends for the offender, whom the priests
have indicated. The charge is denied. Other priests
are sent for. If their vaticinations confirm the
earlier ones, death and confiscation are the fate of
the perjurer. Otherwise, a third set is called.
If these agree in the condemnation of the first, a
load of faggots, drawn by bullocks, is brought in,
the lying priests have their hands bound behind
them, the faggots are set a-light to, the beasts are
goaded into a gallop, the flames catch the wind, the
men are burnt to death, and the bullocks scorched,
singed, or burnt to death also. The sons of the of-
fending perjurer are killed, his daughters left
unhurt.

Their oaths were made over a mixture of wine
and blood. The swearers to them punctured themselves, let their blood fall into a vat of wine, drank
the mixture, and dipped in it their daggers, arrows,
javelin, and σάγαρις.

The ferocity exhibited in their burials was of the
same kind. The tombs of the kings were on the
Gerrhus. Thither they were brought to be buried,
wherever they might die. They were entombed
with sacrifices both of beasts and men, Hippo-
thusia, Anthropothysia, and Suttee — all these characterised the funeral rites of the Scythians θικαιότα-
τοι ἀνθρώπων.

LANGUAGE.—The specimens of this fall into two
divisions, the Proper and the Common Names. The
former are the names of geographical localities and
individuals. In one way or the other, they are numerous; at least they appear so at first. But we
rarely are sure that the fact itself coincides with
the first presumptions. The names of the rivers
have been noticed. Of those of the gods, none have
been definitely traced to any known language in respect to their meaning. Neither have they been
traced to any known mythology as Proper Names.
Next come the names of certain kings and other
historical individuals, none of which have given any
very satisfactory place for the old Scythian.

With the Common Names (and under the class of
Common Names we may place such Proper Names
as are capable of being translated) the results improve, though only slightly. Of these terms the
chief are the following:—

(i.) 'Εξαμπαῖος = Sacred Ways="Ιραι "Οδοι, the
name of a well-head. [See s. v.] (ii.) Οἰόρπατα=
ἀνδροκτόνοι = Men-killers, a name applied by the
Scythians to the Amazons. Here οἰόρ = man,
πατά = kill (iv. 110). (iii.) Temerinda = Mater
Maris, applied to the Euxine. This is not from
Herodotus, but from Pliny (vi. 7). (iv.) Arimaspi
=Μονόφθαλμοι, = one-eyed = ἄριμα = one, σπου=
eye. (Herod. iv. 27.) These will be considered
under the head of Ethnology.

HISTORY.—The Herodotean view of the Scythians
is incomplete without a notice of the historical portion
of his account; not that the two parts are, by any
means, on the same level in the way of trustworthy
information. The geography and descriptions are
from contemporary sources. The history is more or
less traditional. Taking it, however, as we find it,
it falls into two divisions:—1, The Invasion of Asia
by the Scythians; and 2, The Invasion of Scythia
by Darius.

1. *Invasion of Asia by the Scythians.*—In the
reigns of Cyaxares king of Media and of Sadyattes
king of Lydia, the Scythians invade Asia, bodily and
directly. They had previously invaded the country
of the Cimmerians, whom they had driven from their
own districts on the Maeotis, and who were thus
thrown southwards. The Scythians pressed the Cimmerians, the Massagetae the Scythians. Chains of
cause and effect of this kind are much loved by
historians. It is only, however, in the obscure portions of history that they can pass unchallenged.
The Cimmerians take Sardis during the last years
of the reign of Ardys (B. C. 629.) They are expelled by Alyattes, his son. (Herod. i. 15, 16.)
It seems that the Cimmerians were followed up by
their ejectors; inasmuch as five years afterwards
(B. C. 624) the Scythians themselves are in Media;
Cyaxares, who was engaged upon the siege of Nineveh (Ninus), being called back to oppose them. He
is defeated; and the Scythians occupy Asia for 28
years, Cyaxares surviving their departure. From
Media they direct their course towards Egypt; from
the invasion of which they are diverted by Psammitichus. Their attack upon the temple of the
Venus Urania, in Ascalon, during their passage
through Palestine, along with its mysterious sequelae,
has been already noticed. The king who led them
was named Madyes. (Herod. i. 103, seqq.) They
were ejected B.C. 596.

There was a band of Scythians, however, in Media,
in the reign of Croesus, B. C. 585, the account of
which is as follows. Cyaxares, still reigning, receives a company (εἴλη) of Scythians, as sup-
pliants, who escape (ὑπεξῆλθε) from Lydia into
Media. He treats them well, and sends his son to
them to learn the use of the bow, along with the
Scythian language, until he finds that their habits
of hunting and robbing are intolerable. This, along
with a particular act of atrocity, determines Cyaxares to eject them. They fly back to Alyattes,
who refuses to give them up. But Alyattes dies,
and the quarrel is entailed upon his son, Croesus.
The battle that it led to was fought May 28, B. C.
585, when the eclipse predicted by Thales interrupted it.

The Scythian invasion might easily be known
in its general features to both the Greeks of Asia
and the Jews; and, accordingly, we find sufficient
allusions to an invasion of northern barbarians, both
in the Scriptures and in the fragments of the early
Greek poets, to justify us in treating it as a real
fact, however destitute of confirmation some of the
Herodotean details may have been. (See Mure's
Critical History, &c. vol. iii. p. 133, seq.) Though
further removed from his time than

2. *Invasion of Scythia by Darius.*—It is, probably,
a more accurate piece of history. Darius invades
Scythia for the sake of inflicting a chastisement
for the previous invasion of Asia. This had been
followed, not by any settlement of the Scythians
elsewhere, but by a return home. The strange

story of the Servile War of Whips belongs to this period.

When the approach of Darius becomes threatening, the Geloni, Budini, and Sauromatae join with the Scythians in resisting it; the Agathyrsi, Neuri, Androphagi, Melanchlaeni, and Tauri reserving themselves for the defence of their own territory if attacked (iv. 119). To the three constituents of the confederacy there are three kings, Scopasis, Ianthyrsus, and Taxacis, each with an allotted district to defend. This was done by destroying the grass and tillage, driving off the flocks and herds, and *corrupting* (we can scarcely translate συγχού by *poisoning*) the wells. The points whereon attack was anticipated were the frontiers of the *Danube* and the *Don*. These they laid waste, having sent their own wives and children northwards. The first brunt of the war fell upon the Budini, whose Wooden City was burnt. Darius then moved southward and westward, pressing the other two divisions upon the countries of the Melanchlaeni, Neuri, and Agathyrsi. The latter warn the Medes against encroaching on the frontier. Idanthyrsus answers enigmatically to a defiance of Darius. Scopasis tampers with the Ionians who have the custody of the bridge over the Danube. The Medes suffer from dearth, and determine to retreat across the Danube. The Scythians reach the passage before them, and require the Ionians to give it up. And now appears, for the first time, the great name of Miltiades, who is one of the commanders of the guard of the bridge. He advises that the Scythians should be conciliated, Darius weakened. A half-measure is adopted, by which the Scythians are taught to distrust the Ionians, and the Medes escape into Thrace —so ending the Scythian invasion of Darius. (Herod. iv. 120—142.)

Criticism of the Herodotean Accounts.—The notices of Herodotus upon the Scythae, though full, are excursive rather than systematic. Part of their history appears as Lydian, part as Scythian Proper. There is much legend in his accounts ; but the chief obscurities are in the geography. Even here the details are irregular. One notice arises out of the name Scythae, another out of the geography of their rivers, a third out of the sketch of Tauris. [See TAURIS and TAUROSCYTHAE.] In this we hear that Scythia is bounded first by the Agathyrsi, next by the Neuri, then by the Androphagi, and lastly by the Melanchlaeni. The area is four-cornered ; the longest sides being the prolongations along the coast and towards the interior. From the Ister to the Borysthenes is 10 days; 10 days more to the Maeotis ; from the coast to the Melanchlaeni, 20 days ;—200 stadia to each day's journey. If this measurement be exact, it would bring *Tula, Tambov, Riazan,* &c., within the Scythian area,—which is going too far. The days' journeys inland were probably shorter than those along the coast.

The Agathyrsi were in *Transylvania,* on the *Maros.* The evidence, or want of evidence, as far as the text of Herodotus goes, is the same as it is with the Neuri. Their frontagers were known as Scythae Aroteres, i. e., the generic name was with them specific. Hence any Scythians whatever with a specific name must have been contrasted with them; and this seems to have been the case with the Agathyrsi. [HUNNI, p. 1097.] Assuming, however, the Agatnyrsi to have been Scythian, and to have lain on the *Maros,* we carry the Herodotean Scythae as far west as the *Theiss ;* nor can we ex-

clude them from any part of *Wallachia* and *Moldavia.* Yet these are only known to Herodotus as the country of the SIGYNNES. The frontier, then, between the Scythae and Getae is difficult to draw. Herodotus has no Getae, *eo nomine,* north of the Danube : yet such there must have been. Upon the whole, we may look upon the Danubian Principalities as a tract scarcely known to Herodotus, and make it Scythian, or Getic, or mixed, according to the evidence of other writers, as applicable at the time under consideration. It was probably Getic in the East, Sarmatian in the West, and Scythian in respect to certain districts occupied by intrusive populations.

Thucydides mentions the Getae and Scythians but once (ii. 96), and that together. The great alliance that Sitalces, king of Thrace, effects against Perdiccas of Macedon includes the Getae beyond Mount Haemus, and, in the direction of the Euxine sea, the Getae who were conterminous (ὅμοροι) with the Scythians, and whose armour was Scythian (ὁμόσκενοι). They were each archers and horsemen (ἱπποτοξόται); whereas the Dii and the mountaineers of Rhodope wore daggers. According to Ovid (*Trist.* v. 7. 19), the occupants of the level country do so too :—

"Dextera non segnis fixo dare vulnera cultro,
Quem vinctum lateri barbara omnis habet."

THE SCYTHIANS OF THE MACEDONIAN PERIOD. —Passing over the notices of Xenophon, which apply to Thrace Proper rather than to the parts north of Mount Haemus, and which tell us nothing concerning the countries beyond the Danube, -- passing, also, over the notices of a war in which Philip king of Macedon was engaged against Atheas, and in which he crossed Mount Haemus into the country of the Triballi, where he received a wound, —we come to the passage of the Danube by Alexander. In the face of an enemy, and without a bridge, did the future conqueror of Persia cross the river, defeat the Getae on its northern bank, destroy a town, and return. (Arrian, *Anab.* i. 2—7.) This was an invasion of Scythia in a geographical sense only ; still it was a passage of the Danube. The Getae of Alexander may have been descendants of the Sigynnes of Herodotus. They were not, *eo nomine,* Scythians.

When Alexander was on the Danube the famous embassy of the Galatae reached him. They had heard of his fame, and came to visit him. They were men of enormous stature, and feared only that the heavens should fall. This disappointed Alexander, who expected that they would fear *him.* Much has been written concerning the embassy as if it came from Gaul. Yet this is by no means necessary. Wherever there is a *Halicz* or *Galacz* in modern geography, there may have been a *Galat*-ian locality in ancient; just as, wherever there is a *Kerman* or *Carman*-ia, there may have been a German one, and that without any connection with the Galli or Germani of the West. The roots *G-l-t* and *K-ron-n,* are simply significant geographical terms in the Sarmatian and Turk tongues — tongues to which the Getic and Scythian may most probably be referred.

Such is the present writer's opinion respecting the origin of the statements that carry certain Galatae as far as the Lower Danube, and make the Basternae, and even the occupants of the Tanais, Germans — not to mention the Caramanians of Asia Minor and Carmanians of Persia. In the present instance, however, the statement of Strabo is very specific. It is to the effect that the ambassadors to Alexander were Κέλτοι περὶ τὸν 'Αδρίαν (vii. p. 301), and that Ptolemy was the authority. Nevertheless, Ptolemy may have written Γαλάται, and such Galatae may have been the Galatae of the Olbian Inscription. [See *infra* and SCIRI.]

The next Macedonian who crossed the Danube was Lysimachus, who crossed it only to re-cross it in his retreat, and who owed his life to the generosity of a Getic prince Dromichaetes. This was about B. C. 312.

Our next authorities (fragmentary and insufficient) for the descendants of the Herodotean Scythians are the occupants of the Greek towns of the Euxine. Even those to the south of the Danube, Callatis, Apollonia, &c., had some Scythians in the neighbourhood, sometimes as enemies, sometimes as protectors,—sometimes as protectors against other barbarians, sometimes as protectors of Greeks against Greeks, as was the case during the Scythian and Thracian wars of Lysimachus. The chief frontagers, however, were Getae. Between Olbia, to the north of the Danube (=Olbiopolis of Herodotus), and the native tribes of its neighbourhood, the relations are illustrated by the inscription already noticed. (Böckh, *Inscr. Graec.* no. 2058.) It records a vote of public gratitude to Protogenes, and indicates the troubles in which he helped his fellow-citizens. The chief of those arose from the pressure of the barbarians around, by name Saudaratae, Thisametae, Sciri [see SCIRI], Galatae, and Scythae. The date of this inscription is uncertain; but we may see the import of the observations on the word Galatae when we find the assumption that they were Gauls of Gallia used as an instrument of criticism:—" The date of the above inscription is not specified; the terror inspired by the Gauls, even to other barbarians, seems to suit the second century B. C. better than it suits a later period." (Grote, *Hist. of Greece*, vol. xii. p. 644, note.) What, however, if the Galatae of *Wallachia* were as little Galli as the Cermanians of Persia are Germans, or as *Galacs* is the same as *Calais*? The present writer wholly disconnects them, and ignores the whole system of hypothetical migrations by which the identity is supported.

A second Olbia in respect to its Helleno-Scythic relations, was Bosporus, or Panticapaeum, a Greek settlement which lasted from B. C. 480 till the reign of Mithridates. [PANTICAPAEUM.]

From Bosporus there was a great trade with Athens in corn, hides, and *Scythian* slaves,—Scythes, as the name of a slave, occurring as early as the time of Theognis, and earlier in the Athenian drama than those of Davus and Geta (Dacian and Getic) which belong to the New Comedy,—Scythes and Scythaena being found in the Old.

The political relations were those of independent municipalities; sometimes sovereign, sometimes protected. The archons of Bosporus paid tribute to the Scythian princes of their neighbourhood, when they were powerful and united; took it, when the Scythians were weak and disunited. Under this latter category came the details of the division of the Maeotae, viz., Sindi, Toraeti, Dandarii, Thetes, &c. Of these, Parysades I. (a Scythic rather than a Greek name) was *king*, being only *archon* of his native town. In the civil wars, too, of Bosporus, the Scythians took a part; nor were there wanting examples of Scythian manners even in the case of the

Panticapaean potentates. Eumelus lost his life by being thrown out of a four-wheeled wagon-and-four with a tent on it.

SCYTHIANS OF THE MITHRIDATIC PERIOD, ETC. — The Scythians pressed on Parysades IV., who called in Mithridates, who was conquered by Rome. The name now becomes of rare occurrence, subordinate to that of the Sarmatae, Daci, Thracians, &c. In fact, instead of being the nearest neighbours to Greece, the Scythae were now the most distant enemies of Rome.

In the confederacy of the Dacian Boerebistes, in the reign of Augustus, there were Scythian elements. So there were in the wars against the Thracian Rhescuporis and the Roxolani. So there were in the war conducted by J. Plautius in the reign of Vespasian, as shown by the following inscription: REGIBUS BASTERNARUM ET RHOXOLANORUM FILIOS DACORUM . . . EREPTOS REMISIT . . . SCYTHARUM QUOQUE REGE A CHERSONESI QUÆ EST ULTRA BORYSTHENEM OBSIDIONE SUMMOTO. (Grut. p. 453; Böckh, vol. ii. pt. 1. p. 82; Zeuss, *s. v. Skythen.*)

Though the history of the Scythians, *eo nomine*, be fragmentary, the history of more than one Scythian population under a change of name is both prominent and important. In the article HUNNI reasons are given for believing that the descendants of the Herodotean Agathyrsi, of Scythian blood, were no unimportant element in the Dacian nationality.

After the foundation of Constantinople the Scythian nations appear with specific histories and names, Hun, Avar, &c.

The continuity of the history of the name of the Herodotean Scythians within the Herodotean area is of great importance; as is the explanation of names like Galatae and Germani; as also is the consideration of the sources whence the nomenclature and information of the different authorities is derived. It is important, because, when we find one name disappearing from history, and another appearing, there is (according to, at least, the current criticism) a presumption in favour of a change of population. Sometimes this presumption is heightened into what is called a proof ; yet the presumption itself is unreal. For one real change of name referrible to an actual change of population there are ten where the change has been merely one in respect to the sources whence the information was derived, and the channels through which it came. This is what occurs when the same country of *Deutschland* is called *Germany* by an Englishman, *Allemagne* in France, *Lamagna* in Italy. This we know to be nominal. We ought at least to ask whether it may not be so in ancient history — and that not once or twice, but *always* — before we assume hypothetical movements and migrations.

Now in the case of Scythia we can see our way to great nominal and but slight real changes. We see the sources of information changed from Greek to Latin, and the channels from Getic and Macedonian to Dacian.

If so, the occupants of *Hungary*, the Principalities, and South-western *Russia* under the Caesars may be the descendants of the occupants of the same districts in the time of Herodotus. That there are *some* differences is not only likely but admitted,—differences in the way of admixture of blood, modification of nationality, changes of frontier, differences of the kind that time always effects, even in a stationary condition of nations. It is only denied that any wholesale change can be proved, or even reasonably supposed. Who can be shown to have eliminated any definite Scythian population from any definite Scythian occupancy? With the Greeks and Romans the negative evidence is nearly conclusive to the fact that no such elimination ever took place. That the Barbarians might have displaced each other is admitted; but there is no trustworthy evidence to their having done so in any single instance. All opinions in favour of such changes rest upon either the loose statements of insufficiently-informed writers, or the supposed necessity of accounting for the appearance and change of certain names by means of certain appearance and changes of population.

The bearings of this will appear in the notice of the Ethnology of Scythia. They appear also under HUNNL.

Of the SACAE, *eo nomine*, the history is obscure. In one sense, indeed, it is a nonentity. There is no classical historian of the Sacae. How far the ethnologist can *infer* them is a question which will be treated in the sequel.

Of the history of the populations akin to the Sacae, the details are important; but then it is a history of the Massagetae, Parthi, &c., a history full of critical preliminaries and points of inference rather than testimony.

The Scythia of all the authors between Herodotus and Ptolemy means merely the country of the Scythae, the Scythae being such northern nations as, without being, *eo nomine*, Sarmatian, were Hamaxobii and Hippemolgi; their habits of milking their mares and travelling in tented wagons being their most genuine characteristic. These it was which determined the views of even Strabo, whose extension of Germania and Galatia (already noticed) left him no room for a Scythia or even a Sarmatia; Sarmatia, which is to Ptolemy as Germania was to Strabo: for the Sarmatia of Ptolemy leaves no room in Europe for a Scythia; indeed, it cuts deeply into Asiatic Scythia, the only

SCYTHIA OF PTOLEMY.—The Scythia of Ptolemy is exclusively Asiatic, falling into, 1. The Scythia within the Imaus. 2. The Scythia beyond the Imaus.

This is a geographical division, not an ethnological one. Scythae Alauni are especially recognised as a population of European Sarmatia.

As Ptolemy's Sarmatia seems to have been formed out of an extension of the area of the Herodotean Sauromatae, his Scythia seems to have grown out of the eastern Scythae of the Herodotean Scythia, i. e. the Scythae of *Orenburg*. It did not grow out of the country of the Sacae, inasmuch as they are mentioned separately; even as the Jazyges of the *Theiss* were separated from the Sarmatians. The continuator, however, of the Herodotean account must make the Sacae Scythians. They may be disposed of first.

THE SACAE OF PTOLEMY were bounded by the Sogdians on the west, the Scythians on the north, and the Seres on the east. They were nomads, without towns, and, resident in woods and caves. The mountain-range of the Comedi (ἡ Κωμηδῶν ὀρεινή) was in their country; so was the Stone Tower (Λίθινος Πύργος). The populations were: 1, 2. The Caratae and Comari along the Jaxartes. 3. The Comedae, on the Comedian mountain. 4. The Massagetae along the range of the Ascatancas ('Ασκατάγκας). 5. In the interjacent country, the

Grynaei Scythae; and, 6, the Toornae; south of whom, along the Imaus, 7, the Byltae. (Ptol. vi. 13.)

SCYTHIA INTRA IMAUM.—Bounded on the S. and E. by Sogdiana, Margiana, and the Sacae; on the W. by the Caspian and Sarmatia Asiatica; on the N. by a terra incognita; and on the E. by the northern prolongation of the Imaus. (Ptol. vi. 14.)

Rivers.— The Rhymmus, the Daix, the Jaxartes, the Iastus, and the Polytimetus.

Mountains.— The eastern part of the Montes Hyperborei, the Montes Alani (observe the reappearance of this name), the Montes Rhymmici, the Mons Norossus, the MM. Aspisii, Tapyri, Syebi, Anarei,— all W. of the Imaus.

Populations.—The Alani Scythae (on the confines of the terra incognita), the Suabeni, the Alanorsi, S. of whom the Saetiani, and Massaei, and Syebi; and (along the Imaus) the Tectosaces and (on the eastern head-waters of the Rha) the Rhobosci, S. of whom the Asmani; and then the Paniardi, S. of whom, along the river, the district called Canodipsas, S. of which the Coraxi; then the Orgasi, after whom, as far as the sea (i. e. the Caspian, in this chapter called Hyrcanian), the Erymmi, with the Asiotae on the E. of them, succeeded by the Aorsi; after whom the Jaxartae, a great nation along the river of the same name; then S. of the Saetiani, the Mologeni and Samnitae, as far as the MM. Rhymmici. Then, S. of the Massaei and MM. Alani, the Zaratae and Sasones; and further W. and as far as the MM. Rhymmici, the Tybiacae, succeeded by the Tabieni, S. of the Zaratae, and the Iastae and Machaetegi along the Mons Norossus; S. of whom the Norosbes and Norossi, and the Cachagae Scythae along the Jaxartae. On the W. of the MM. Aspisii, the Aspisii Scythae; on the E. the Galactophagi Scythae; E. of the MM. Tapuri and the Suebi, the Tapurei; and above the MM. Anarei and the Mons Ascatancas, the Scythae Anarei, and the Ascatancae and Ariacae along the Jaxartes, S. of whom the Namastae; then the Sagaraucae, and, along the Oxus, the Rhibii, with their town Davaba.

SCYTHIA EXTRA IMAUM was bounded by Scythia intra Imaum, the Sacae, the Terra Incognita, and the Seres. It contained the western part of MM. Auxacii, Casii and Emodi, with the source of the river Oechardus. (Ptol. vi. 15.)

Its *Populations* were the Abii Scythae, the Hippophagi Scythae, the Chatae Scythae, the Charaunaei Scythae; the designation Scythae being applied to each.

Districts.—The Auxacitis, the Casia (ἡ Καρία χώρα), the Achasa (ἡ Ἀχάσα χώρα).

Towns.—Auxacia, Issedon, Scythica, Chaurana, Soeta.

The remarks that applied to the Sarmatia Asiatica of Ptolemy apply here. Few names can be safely identified. Neither is it safe to say through what languages the information came. Some words suggest a Persian, some a Turk source, some are Mongol. Then the geography is obscure. That the range of *Pamer* was unduly prolonged northwards is evident [IMAUS]; this being an error of the geographer. The courses, however, of the Oxus and Jaxartes may themselves have changed.

The prolongation of the *Pamer* range being carried in a northern and north-eastern direction, so as to include not only the drainages of the Oxus and Jaxartes, but that of the *Balkash Lake* as well, gives us the line of the Imaus; the terra incognita to the

N. being supposed to begin with the watershed of the *Irtish, Obi,* and other rivers falling into the Arctic Ocean. Within the limits thus described we may place the *Nor-osbi* and *Nor-oasi,* on the eastern edge, i. e. in the parts where at the present moment the lakes distinguished by the name *Nor* occur. It should be added, however, that the syllable *is* generally final, as in *Koko-nor,* &c. Still it is a prominent element in compound names, and indicates Mongol occupancy. The Byltae may be placed in *Bulti-stan,* i. e. the country of the *Bulti — Little Tibet,* the gloss being Persian.

In Ascatancas (the Greek spelling is the more convenient Ασκα-τάγκ-ας), we have the Turkish *-tagh = mountain* just as it actually occurs in numberless compounds.

Karmit is a name of common application, chiefly to members of the Mongol family.

Mass-agetae is a term full of difficulty. Can it have arisen out of the common name *Mus-tag?*

In *Scythia extra Imaum,* the Casia and Achassa (χώραι) may be made one and identified with the Cesii of Pliny. The most reasonable explanations of these names is to be found in the suggestion of Major Cunningham's valuable work on *Ladak* (p. 4), where the Achassa Regio = *Ladakh,* and the Chatae, and Chauronse Scythae = *Chang-thang* and *Khor* respectively.

Roughly speaking, we may say that the country of the Sacae was formed by an irregular tract of land on the head-waters of the Oxus and the watershed between it and the Jaxartes, a tract which included a portion of the drainage of the Indus. It is only a portion of this that could give the recognised conditions of Scythian life, viz. steppes and pasturages. These might be founded on the great table land of *Pamer,* but not in the mountain districts. Those, however, were necessary for "residences in woods and caves"; at the same time, the population that occupied them might be pastoral rather than agricultural. Still they would not be of the Scythian type. Nor is it likely that the Sacae of Ptolemy were so. They were not, indeed, the Sacae of Herodotus, except in part, i. e. on the desert of the Persian frontier. They were rather the mountaineers of *Kaferistan, Wakhan, Shugnan, Roshan, Astor, Huns-Nagor,* and *Little Tibet,* partly Persian, partly Bhot (or Tibetan), in respect to their ethnology.

The Scythians beyond the Imaus.—These must be divided between *Ladakh, Tibet, Chinese Tartary,* and *Mongolia* in respect to their geography. Physically they come within the conditions of a Scythian occupancy; except where they are true mountaineers. Ethnologically they may be distributed between the Mongol, Bhot, and Turk families — the Turks being those of Chinese Tartary.

The Turcoman districts of the Oxus, *Khiva,* the *Kirghis* country, *Ferghana, Tashkend,* with the parts about the *Balkash,* give us the Scythia within the Imaus. It coincides chiefly with *Independent Tartary,* with the addition of a small portion of *Mongolia* and southern *Siberia.* Its conditions are generally Scythian. In the upper part, however, of the Jaxartes, the districts are agricultural at present; nine-tenths of this area is Turk, part of the population being Nomades, part industrial and agricultural.

THE SCYTHIA OF THE BYZANTINE AUTHORS.— This means not only Hunns, Avars, Alans, and Sarmatians, but even Germans, Goths, and Vandals.

It is used, however, but rarely. It really existed only in books of geography. Every division of the Scythian name was known under its specific designation.

ETHNOLOGY.—If any name of antiquity be an ethnological, rather than a geographical, term, that name is Scythia. Ptolemy alone applies it to an area, irrespective of the races of its occupants. With every earlier writer it means a number of populations connected by certain ethnological characteristics. These were physical and moral—physical, as when Hippocrates describes the Scythian physiognomy; moral, as when their nomadic habits, as Hamaxobii and Hippemolgi, are put forward as distinctive. Of language as a test less notice is taken; though (by Herodotus at least) it is by no means overlooked. The division between Scythian and non-Scythian is always kept in view by him. Of the non-Scythic populations, the Sauromatae were one; hence the ethnology of Scythia involves that of Sarmatia, both being here treated together.

In respect to them, there is no little discrepancy of opinion amongst modern investigators. The first question respecting them, however, has been answered unanimously.

Are they represented by any of the existing divisions of mankind, or are they extinct? It is not likely that such vast families as each is admitted to have been has died out. Assuming, then, the present existence of the congeners of both the Sarmatae and the Scythae, in what family or class are they to be found? The Scythae were of the Turk, the Sarmatae of the Slavono-Lithuanic stock.

The evidence of this, along with an exposition of the chief differences of opinion, will now be given, Scythia being dealt with first. Premising that *Turk* means all the populations whose language is akin to that of the Ottomans of Constantinople, and that it comprises the Turcomans, the Independent Tartars, the Uzbeks, the Turks of Chinese Tartary, and even the Yakuts of the Lena, along with several other tribes of less importance, we may examine the *à priori* probabilities of the Scythae having been, in this extended sense, Turks.

The *situs* of the nations of South-western Russia, &c., at the beginning of the proper historical period, is a presumption in favour of their being so. Of these the best to begin with are the Cumanians (12th century) of *Volhynia.* That they were Turk we know from special statements, and from samples of their language compared with that of the *Kirghis* of *Independent Tartary.* There is no proof of their being new comers, however much the doctrine of their recent emigration may have been gratuitously assumed. The Uzes were what the Cumanians were; and before the Uzes, the Patzinaks (10th century) of *Bessarabia* and the Danubian Principalities were what the Uzes were. Earlier than the Patzinaks, the Chazars ruled in *Kherson* and Taurida (7th and 8th centuries) like the Patzinaks, in the same category with definitely known Cumanians and Uzes. These four populations are all described by writers who knew the true Turks accurately, and, knowing them, may be relied on. This knowledge, however, dates only from the reign of Justinian [TURCAE]. From the reign, then, of Justinian to the 10th century (the date of the break-up of the Cumanians), the Herodotean Scythia was Turk — Turk without evidence of the occupation being recent.

The Avars precede the Chazars, the Huns the

Avars, the Alani the Huns. [HUNNI; AVARES]. The migrations that make the latter, at least, recent occupants being entirely hypothetical. The evidence of the Huns being in the same category as the Avars, and the Avars being Turk, is conclusive. The same applies to the Alani — a population which brings us to the period of the later classics.

The conditions of a population which should, at one and the same time, front Persia and send an offset round the Caspian into Southern Russia, &c., are best satisfied by the present exclusively Turk area of *Independent Tartary*.

Passing from the presumptuous to the special evidence, we find that the few facts of which we are in possession all point in the same direction.

Physical Appearance. — This is that of the *Kirghis* and *Uzbeks* exactly, though not that of the Ottomans of *Rumelia*, who are of mixed blood. Allowing for the change effected by Mahomet, the same remark applies to their

Manners, which are those of the *Kirghis* and *Turcomans.*

Language.—The Scythian glosses have not been satisfactorily explained, i. e. Temerinda, Arimaspi, and Exampaeus have yet to receive a derivation that any one but the inventor of it will admit. The *oior-*, however, in *Oior-pata* is exactly the *er*, *aer*, =*man*, &c., a term found through all the Turk dialects. It should be added, however, that it is Latin and Keltic as well (*vir*, *fear*, *gwr*). Still it is Turk, and that unequivocally.

The evidence, then, of the Scythae being Turk consists in a series of small particulars agreeing with the *à priori* probabilities rather than in any definite point of evidence. Add to this the fact that no other class gives us the same result with an equally small amount of hypothesis in the way of migration and change. This will be seen in a review of the opposite doctrines, all of which imply an unnecessary amount of unproven changes.

The Mongol Hypothesis.—This is Niebuhr's, developed in his *Researches into the History of the Scythians, &c.*; and also Neumann's, in his *Hellenen im Skythenlande.* It accounts for the manners and physiognomy, as well as the present doctrine; but not for anything else. It violates the rule against the unnecessary multiplication of causes, by bringing from a distant area, like Mongolia, what lies nearer, i. e. in Tartary. With Niebuhr the doctrine of fresh migrations to account for the Turks of the Byzantine period, and of the extirpation of the older Scythians, takes its *maximum* development, the least allowance being made for changes of name. " This " (the time of Lysimachus) "is the last mention of the Scythian nation in the region of the Ister; and, at this time, there could only be a remnant of it in Budzack " (p. 63).

The Finn Hypothesis.—This is got at by making the Scythians what the Huns were, and the Huns what the Magyars were—the Magyars being Finn. It arises out of a wrong notion of the name, *Hungary*, and fails to account for the *difference* between the Scythians and the nations to their north.

The Circassian Hypothesis.—This assumes an extension of the more limited area of the northern occupants of Caucasus in the direction of *Russia* and *Hungary.* Such an extension is, in itself, probable. It fails, however, to explain any one fact in the descriptions of Scythia, though valid for some of the older populations.

The Indo-European Hypothesis. — This doctrine takes many forms, and rests on many bases. The

-*get-* in words like Massa-*get-ae*, &c., is supposed to == *Goth* == *German*. Then there are certain names which are Scythian and Persian, the Persian being Indo-European. In the extreme form of this hypothesis the *Sacae* == *Saxons*, and the *Yuche* of the Chinese authors == *Goths*.

If the Scythians were intruders from Independent Tartary, whom did they displace ? Not the Sarmatians, who were themselves intruders. The earlier occupants were in *part* congeners of the Northern Caucasians. They were chiefly, however, Ugrians or Finns; congeners of the Mordvins, Tsheremess, and Tshuwashes of *Penza, Saratov, Kazan*, &c.: Dacia, Thrace, and Sarmatia being the original occupancies of the Sarmatae.

If so, the ethnographical history of the Herodotean Scythia runs thus : — there was an original occupancy of Ugrians; there was an intrusion from the NE. by the Scythians of Independent Tartary, and there was intrusion from the SW. by the Sarmatians of Dacia. The duration of the Scythian or Turk occupancy was from the times anterior to Herodotus to the extinction of the Cumanians in the 14th century. Of internal changes there was plenty; but of any second migration from Asia (with the exception of that of the Avars) there is no evidence. Such is the history of the Scythae.

The Sacae were, perhaps, less exclusively Turk, though Turk in the main. Some of them were, probably, Mongols. The Sacae Amyrgii may have been Ugrians; the researches of Norris upon the second of the arrow-headed alphabets having led him to the opinion that there was at least one invasion of Persia analogous to the Magyar invasion of Hungary, i. e. effected by members of the Ugrian stock, probably from *Orenburg* or *Kazan.* With them the root *m-rd* == *man.* History gives us no time when the Turks of the Persian frontier, the Sacae, were not pressing southwards. Sacastene (== *Segestan*) was one of their occupancies; Carmania probably another. The Parthians were of the Scythian stock; and it is difficult to believe that, word for word, Persia is not the same as Parthia. The history, however, of the Turk stock is one thing; the history of the Scythian name another. It is submitted, however, that the two should be connected. This being done, the doctrine of the recent diffusion of the Turks is a doctrine that applies to the name only. There were Turk invasions of Hungary, Turk invasions of Persia, Turk invasions of China, Assyria, Asia Minor, and even north-eastern Africa, from the earliest period of history. And there were Sarmatian invasions in the opposite direction, invasions which have ended in making Scythia Slavonic, and which (in the mind of the present writer) began by making parts of Asia Median. Lest this be taken for an exaggeration of the Turk influence in the world's history, let it be remembered that it is only a question of *date*, and that the present view only claims for the Turk conquests the place in the antehistorical that they are *known* to have had in the historical period. With the exception of the Mongol invasions of the 13th century and the Magyar occupancy of Hungary, every conquest in Southern Asia and Europe, from the North, has been effected by members of the stock under notice. [See SARMATIA; VENEDI; FENNI; SITONES; TURCAE.]   [R. G. L.]

SCYTHI'NI (Σκυθινοί, Xen. *Anab.* iv. 7. § 18; Σκουθινοι, Diod. xiv. 29; Σκυθηνοί, Steph. B. *s. v.*), an Asiatic people dwelling on the borders of Armenia, between the rivers Harpasus on the E. and

Asparus on the W., and bounded by the mountains of the Chalybes on the S. The Ten Thousand Greeks, in their retreat under Xenophon, were compelled to march four days through their territory. Rennell (*Geogr. of Herod.* p. 243) seeks them in the province of *Kars* (comp. Ritter, *Erdkunde*, vol. i. p. 764). [T. H. D.]

SCYTHO'POLIS. [BETHSAN.]

SCYTHOTAURI. [TAUROSCYTHAE.]

SEBAGE'NA (Σεβάγηνα, or, as others read, 'Εβάγηνα), a town in Cappadocia, of uncertain site. (Ptol. v. 6. § 15.) [L. S.]

SEBASTE (Σεβαστή). 1. A town in a small island off the coast of Cilicia, built by Archelaus king of Cappadocia, to whom the Romans had given Cilicia Aspera. (Strab. xiv. p. 671.) It seems to have received its name Sebaste in honour of Augustus ; for, until his time, both the island and the town were called Eleusa, Elaeusa, or Elaeussa (Joseph. *Ant.* xvi. 4. § 6, *Bell.* i. 23. § 4 ; comp. Ptol. v. 8. § 4 ; Hierocl. p. 704 ; *Stadiasm. Mar. Magn.* § 172, where it is called 'Ελεοῦς ; Steph. B. *s. vv.* Σεβαστή and 'Ελαιοῦσσα), a name which Pliny (v. 22) still applies to the town, though he erroneously places it in the interior of Caria. Stephanus, in one of the passages above referred to, calls Sebaste or Elaeussa an island, and in the other a peninsula, which may be accounted for by the fact that the narrow channel between the island and the mainland was at an early period filled up with sand, as it is at the present, — for the place no longer exists as an island. Sebaste was situated between Corycus and the mouth of the river Lamus, from which it was only a few miles distant. Some interesting remains of the town of Sebaste still exist on the peninsula near *Ayash*, consisting of a temple of the composite order, which appears to have been overthrown by an earthquake, a theatre, and three aqueducts, one of which conveyed water into the town from a considerable distance. (Comp. Beaufort, *Karamania*, p. 250, foll.; Leake, *Asia Minor.* p. 213.)

2. A town in Phrygia Pacatiana, between Alydda and Eumenia, is noticed only by Hierocles, (p. 667) and in the Acts of the Council of Constantinople (iii. p. 674); but its site has been identified with that of the modern *Segikler*, where inscriptions and coins of the town have been found. The ancient name of the place is still preserved in that of the neighbouring stream, *Sebasli Su.* (Comp. Hamilton's *Researches*, i. p. 121, &c.; Arundell, *Discoveries*, i. p. 136, who erroneously takes the remains at *Segikler* for those of the ancient Eucarpia.)

3. [CABIRA, Vol. I. p. 462.] [L. S.]

SEBASTE. [SAMARIA.]

SEBASTEIA (Σεβάστεια), a town in the south of Pontus, on the north bank of the Upper Halys. As it was near the frontier, Pliny (vi. 3) regards it as not belonging to Pontus, but to Colopene in Cappadocia. (Ptol. v. 6. § 10; Hierocl. p. 702; *It. Ant.* pp. 204, 205.) The town existed as a small place before the dominion of the Romans in those parts, but its ancient name is unknown. Pompey increased the town, and gave it the name of Megalopolis (Strab. xii. p. 560). The name Sebastia must have been given to it before the time of Pliny, he being the first to use it. During the imperial period it appears to have risen to considerable importance, so that in the later division of the Empire it was made the capital of Armenia Minor. The identity of Sebastia with the modern *Siwas* is established partly by the resemblance of the names, and partly by the agreement

of the site of *Siwas* with the description of Gregory of Nyssa, who states that the town was situated in the valley of the Halys. A small stream, moreover, flowed through the town, and fell into a neighbouring lake, which communicated with the Halys (*Orat. I. in XL. Mart.* p. 501, *Orat. II.* p. 510; comp. Basil. M. *Epist.* viii.). In the time of the Byzantine empire Sebasteia is mentioned as a large and flourishing town of Cappadocia (Nicet. *Ann.* p. 76; Ducas, p. 31); while Stephanus B. (*s. v.*) and some ecclesiastical writers refer it to Armenia. (Sozom. *Hist. Eccl.* iv. 24; Theodoret. *Hist. Eccl.* ii.. 24.) In the Itinerary its name appears in the form of Sevastia, and in Abulfeda it is actually written Siwas. The emperor Justinian restored its decayed walls. (Procop. *de Aed.* iii. 4.) The town of *Siwas* is still large and populous, and in its vicinity some, though not very important, remains of antiquity are seen. (Fontanier, *Voyages en Orient.* i. p.179, foll.) [L. S.]

SEBASTO'POLIS (Σεβαστόπολις.) 1. A town in Pontus Cappadocicus (Ptol. v. 6. § 7), which, according to the Antonine Itinerary (p. 205), was situated on a route leading from Tavium to Sebastia, and was connected by a road with Caesareia (p. 214). Pliny (vi. 3) places it in the district of Colopene, and agrees with other authorities in describing it as a small town. (Hierocl. p. 703; *Novell.* 31; Gregor. Nyssen. *in Macrin.* p. 202.) The site of this place is still uncertain, some identifying the town with Cabira, which is impossible, unless we assume Sebastopolis to be the same town as Sebaste, and others believing that it occupied the site of the modern *Turchal* or *Turkhal.*

2. A town in Pontus, of unknown site (Ptol. v. 6. § 9), though, from the place it occupies in the list of Ptolemy, it must have been situated in the south of Themiscyra.

3. About Sebastopolis on the east coast of the Euxine see DIOSCURIAS, and about that in Mysia, see MYRINA. [L. S.]

SEBASTOPOLIS (Hierocl. p. 638), a place in the interior of Thrace, near Philippopolis. [J. R.]

SEBATUM, a town situated either in the southwestern part of Noricum, or in the east of Rhaetia, on the road from Aemona to Veldidena (*It. Ant.* p. 280), seems to be the modern *Sachrs.* (Comp. Muchar, *Norikum*, i. p. 250.) [L. S.]

SEBENDU'NUM (Σεβένδουνον, Ptol. ii. 6. § 71), a town of the Castellani in Hispania Tarraconensis. There is a coin of it in Sestini (p.164). [T.H.D.]

SEBENNYTUS (Σεβέννυτος, Ptol. iv. 5. § 50; Steph. B. *s. v.*; ἡ Σεβεννυτικὴ πόλις, Strab. xvii. p. 802: *Eth.* Σεβεννύτης), the chief town of the Sebennytic nome in the Egyptian Delta, situated on the Sebennytic arm of the Nile, nearly due E. of Sais, in lat. 31° N.. The modern hamlet of *Semenhoud*, where some ruins have been discovered, occupies a portion of its site. Sebennytus was anciently a place of some importance, and standing on a peninsula, between a lake (λίμνη Σεβεννυτικὴ: *Burlos*) and the Nile, was favourably seated for trade and intercourse with Lower Aegypt and Memphis. The neglect of the canals, however, and the elevation of the alluvial soil have nearly obliterated its site. (Champollion, *l'Egypte*, vol. ii. p. 191, seq.) [W. B. D.]

SEBE'THUS (*Fiume della Maddalena*), a small river of Campania, flowing into the *Bay of Naples*, immediately to the E. of the city of Neapolis. It is alluded to by several ancient writers in connection with that city (Stat. *Silv.* i. 2. 263; Colum. x. 134;

Vib. Sequest. p. 18), and is generally considered to be the same with the stream which now falls into the sea a little to the E. of Naples, and is commonly called the Fiume della Maddalena. This rivulet, which rises in a fountain or basin called La Bolla, about 5 miles from Naples, is now a very trifling stream, but may have been more considerable in ancient times. The expressions of poets, however, are not to be taken literally, and none of the geographers deem the Sebethus worthy of mention. Virgil, however, alludes to a nymph Sebethis, and an inscription attests the local worship of the river-god, who had a chapel (aedicula) erected to him at Neapolis. (Gruter, *Inscr.* p. 94. 9.)　　　[E. H. B.]

SEBI'NUS LACUS (*Lago d' Iseo*), a large lake in the N. of Italy, at the foot of the Alps, formed by the waters of the river Ollius (*Oglio*), which after flowing through the land of the Camuni (the *Val Camonica*), are arrested at their exit from the mountains and form the extensive lake in question. It is not less than 18 miles in length by 2 or 3 in breadth, so that it is inferior in magnitude only to the three great lakes of Northern Italy; but its name is mentioned only by Pliny (ii. 103. s. 106, iii. 19. s. 23), and seems to have been little known in antiquity, as indeed is the case with the *Lago d' Iseo* at the present day. It is probable that it derived its name from a town called Sebum, on the site of the modern *Iseo*, at its SE. extremity, but no mention of this name is found in ancient writers. (Cluver, *Ital.* p. 412.)　　　[E. H. B.]

SEBRIDAE (Σεβρίδαι, Ptol. iv. 7. § 33), or SOBORIDAE (Σοβορίδαι, Ptol. iv. 7. § 29), an Aethiopian race, situated between the Astaboras (*Tacazze*) and the Red Sea. They probably correspond with the modern *Samhar*, or the people of the "maritime tract." There is some likelihood that the Sembritae, Sebridae, and Soboridae are but various names, or corrupted forms of the name of one tribe of Aethiopians dwelling between the upper arms of the Nile and the Red Sea. [W. B. D.]

SEBURRI (Σεβουρροί and Σεουρροί, Ptol. ii. 6. § 27), a people in the NW. of Hispania Tarraconensis, on both banks of the Minius, probably a subdivision of the Callaici Bracarii.　　　[T. H. D.]

SECELA or SECELLA. [ZIKLAG.]

SECERRAE, called by the Geogr. Rav. (iv. 42) and in a Cod. Paris. of the *Itin. Ant.* (p. 398) SETERRAE, a town of the Lacëtani in Hispania Tarraconensis, on the road from the Summum Pyrenaeum and Juncaria to Tarraco. Variously identified with *S. Pere de Sercada, Arbucias,* and *San Seloni* (properly *Santa Colonia Sejerra*). The last identification seems the most probable.　　　[T. H. D.]

SE'CIA (*Secchia*), a river of Gallia Cispadana, one of the southern tributaries of the Padus, which crosses the Via Aemilia a few miles W. of *Modena*. It is evidently the same stream which is called by Pliny the Gabellus; but the name of Secia, corresponding to its modern appellation of *Secchia*, is found in the Jerusalem Itinerary, which marks a station called Pons Secies, at a distance of 5 miles from Mutina. (*Itin. Hier.* p. 606.) The same bridge is called in an inscription which records its restoration by Valerian, in A. D. 259, Pons Seculae. (Murat. *Inscr.* p. 460. 5; Orell. *Inscr.* 1002.) The *Secchia* is a considerable stream, having the character, like most of its neighbours, of a mountain torrent.　　　[E. H. B.]

SECOANUS (Σηκοανός, Steph. s. v.), a river of the Massaliots, according to one reading, but accord-

ing to another reading, a city of the Massaliots, " from which comes the ethnic name Sequani, as Artemidorus says in his first book." Nothing can be made of this fragment further than this; the name Sequanus belonged both to the basin of the *Rhone* and of the *Seine*.　　　[G. L.]

SECOR or SICOR (Σηκώρ ἢ Σικόρ λιμήν), a port which Ptolemy (ii. 7. § 2) places on the west coast of Gallia, between the Pictonium or Pictonium Promontorium and the mouth of the Ligeris (*Loire*). The name also occurs in Marcianus. The latitudes of Ptolemy cannot be trusted, and we have no other means of fixing the place except by a guess. Accordingly D'Anville supposes that Secor may be the port of the *Sables d'Olonne;* and other conjectures have been made.　　　[G. L.]

SECURISCA (Σεκούρισκα, Procop. *de Aed.* iv. 7. p. 292, ed. Bonn.), a town in Moesia Inferior, lying S. of the Danube, between Oescus and Novae. (*Itin. Ant.* p. 221; comp. Geogr. Rav. iv. 7; Theophyl. vii. 2.) Variously identified with *Sohegurli, Sistov,* and *Tcherezelan.*　　　[T. H. D.]

SEDELAUCUS. [SIDOLOCUS.]

SEDETA'NI. [EDETANI.]

SEDIBONIA'TES, are placed by Pliny in Aquitania (iv. c. 19). He says, " Aquitani, unde nomen provinciae, Sediboniates. Mox in oppidum contributi Convenae, Begerri." The Begarri are the Bigerriones of Caesar. [BIGERRIONES.] We have no means of judging of the position of the Sediboniates except from what Pliny says, who seems to place them near the Bigerriones and Convenae. [CONVENAE.]　　　[G. L.]

SEDU'NI, a people in the valley of the Upper Rhone, whom Caesar (*B. G.* iii. 1, 7) mentions: " Nantuates Sedunos Veragrosque." They are also mentioned in the trophy of the Alps (Plin. iii. 20) in the same order. They are east of the Veragri, and in the *Valais*. Their chief town had the same name as the people. The French call it *Sion*, and the Germans name it *Sitten*, which is the ancient name, for it was called Sedunum in the middle ages. An inscription has been found at *Sion:* " Civitas Sedunorum Patrono." *Sitten* is on the right bank of the Rhone, and crossed by a stream called *Sionne*. The town-hall is said to contain several Roman inscriptions. [NANTUATES; OCTODURUS.]　　　[G. L.]

SEDU'SII, a German tribe mentioned by Caesar (*B. G.* i. 51) as serving under Ariovistus; but as no particulars are stated about them, and as they are not spoken of by any subsequent writer, it is impossible to say to what part of Germany they belonged. Some regard them as the same as the Edusones mentioned by Tacitus (*Germ.* 40), and others identify them with the Phundusi whom Ptolemy (ii. 11. § 12) places in the Cimbrian Chersonesus ; but both conjectures are mere fancies, based on nothing but a faint resemblance of names. [L. S.]

SEGALLAUNI (Σεγαλλαυνοί, Ptol. ii. 10. § 11). Ptolemy places them west of the Allobroges, and he names as their town Valentia Colonia (*Valence*), near the Rhone. Pliny (iii. 4) names them Segovellauni, and places them between the Vocontii and the Allobroges; but he makes Valentia a town of the Cavares. [CAVARES.]　　　[G. L.]

SEGASAMUNCLUM (Σεγισαμόγκουλον, Ptol. ii. 6. § 53), a town of the Autrigones in Hispania Tarraconensis. (*Itin. Ant.* p. 394.) Variously identified with *S. Maria de Ribaredonda, Cameno,* and *Balluercanes.*　　　[T. H. D.]

3 P 2

SE'GEDA AUGURI'NA, an important town of Hispania Baetica, between the Baetis and the coast. (Plin. iii. 1. s. 3.) Commonly supposed to be *S. Iago della Higuera* near *Jaen*.   [T. H. D.]

SEGELOCUM (*Itin. Ant.* p. 475, called also AGELOCUM, *Ib.* p. 478), a town in Britannia Romana, on the road from Lindum to Eboracum, according to Camden (p. 582) *Littleborough* in *Nottinghamshire.*   [T. H. D.]

SEGE'SAMA (Σεγεσάμα, Strab. iii. p. 162), or SEGESAMO and SEGISAMO (*Itin. Ant.* pp. 394, 449, 454; Orell. *Inscr.* no. 4719), and SEGISAMONENSES of the inhabitants (Plin. iii. 3. s. 4), a town of the Murbogi or Turmodigi in Hispania Tarraconensis, on the road from Tarraco to Asturica, now called *Sasamo*, to the W of *Briviesca.* (Florez, *Esp. Sagr.* vi. p. 419, xv. p. 59.)   [T. H. D.]

SEGESSERA, in Gallia, is placed in the Table between Corobilium (*Corbeil*) and Andomatunum (*Langres*), and the distance of Segessera from each place is marked xxi. The site of Segessera is not certain. Some fix it at a place named *Suzannecourt*. [COROBILIUM.]   [G. L.]

SEGESTA (Σέγεστα: Eth. Σεγεστανός, Segestanus: Ru. near *Calatafimi*), a city of Sicily in the NW. part of the island, about 6 miles distant from the sea, and 34 W. of Panormus. Its name is always written by the Attic and other contemporary Greek writers EGESTA ("Εγεστα: Eth. 'Εγεσταῖος, Thuc. &c.), and it has hence been frequently asserted that it was first changed to Segesta by the Romans, for the purpose of avoiding the ill omen of the name of Egesta in Latin. (Fest. s.v. *Segesta*, p. 340.) This story is, however, disproved by its coins, which prove that considerably before the time of Thucydides it was called by the inhabitants themselves Segesta, though this form seems to have been softened by the Greeks into Egesta. The origin and foundation of Segesta is extremely obscure. The tradition current among the Greeks and adopted by Thucydides (Thuc. vi. 2; Dionys. i. 52; Strab. xiii. p. 608), ascribed its foundation to a band of Trojan settlers, fugitives from the destruction of their city; and this tradition was readily welcomed by the Romans, who in consequence claimed a kindred origin with the Segestans. Thucydides seems to have considered the Elymi, a barbarian tribe in the neighbourhood of Eryx and Segesta, as descended from the Trojans in question; but another account represents the Elymi as a distinct people, already existing in this part of Sicily when the Trojans arrived there and founded the two cities. [ELYMI.] A different story seems also to have been current, according to which Segesta owed its origin to a band of Phocians, who had been among the followers of Philoctetes; and, as usual, later writers sought to reconcile the two accounts. (Strab. vi. p. 272; Thuc. l. c.) Another version of the Trojan story, which would seem to have been that adopted by the inhabitants themselves, ascribed the foundation of the city to Egestus or Aegestus (the Acestes of Virgil), who was said to be the offspring of a Trojan damsel named Segesta by the river god Crimisus. (Serv. *ad Aen.* i. 550, v. 30.) We are told also that the names of Simois and Scamander were given by the Trojan colonists to two small streams which flowed beneath the town (Strab. xiii. p. 608); and the latter name is mentioned by Diodorus as one still in use at a much later period. (Diod. xx. 71.) It is certain that we cannot receive the statement of the Trojan origin of Segesta as historical; but what-

ever be the origin of the tradition, there seems. no doubt on the one hand that the city was occupied by a people distinct from the Sicanians, the native race of this part of Sicily, and on the other that it was not a Greek colony. Thucydides, in enumerating the allies of the Athenians at the time of the Peloponnesian War, distinctly calls the Segestans barbarians; and the history of the Greek colonies in Sicily was evidently recorded with sufficient care and accuracy·for us to rely upon his authority when he pronounces any people to be non-Hellenic. (Thuc. vii. 57.) At the same time they appear to have been, from a very early period, in close connection with the Greek cities of Sicily, and entering into relations both of hostility and alliance with the Hellenic states, wholly different from the other barbarians in the island. The early influence of Greek civilisation is shown also by their coins, which are inscribed with Greek characters, and bear the unquestionable impress of Greek art.

The first historical notice of the Segestans transmitted to us represents them as already engaged (as early as B. C. 580) in hostilities with the Selinuntines, which would appear to prove that both cities had already extended their territories so far as to come into contact with each other. By the timely assistance of a body of Cnidian and Rhodian emigrants under Pentathlus, the Segestans at this time obtained the advantage over their adversaries. (Diod. v. 9.) A more obscure statement of Diodorus relates that again in B. C. 454, the Segestans were engaged in hostilities with the *Lilybaeans* for the possession of the territory on the river Mazarus. (Id. xi. 86.) The name of the Lilybaeans is here certainly erroneous, as no town of that name existed till long afterwards [LILYBAEUM]; but we know not what people is really meant, though the presumption is that it is the Selinuntines, with whom the Segestans seem to have been engaged in almost perpetual disputes. It was doubtless with a view to strengthen themselves against these neighbours that the Segestans took advantage of the first Athenian expedition to Sicily under Laches (B. C. 426), and concluded a treaty of alliance with Athens. (Thuc. vi. 6.) This, however, seems to have led to no result, and shortly after, hostilities having again broken out, the Selinuntines called in the aid of the Syracusans, with whose assistance they obtained great advantages, and were able to press Segesta closely both by land and sea. In this extremity the Segestans, having in vain applied for assistance to Agrigentum, and even to Carthage, again had recourse to the Athenians, who were, without much difficulty, persuaded to espouse their cause, and send a fleet to Sicily, B. C. 416. (Thuc. vi. 6; Diod. xii. 82.) It is said that this result was in part attained by fraud, the Segestans having deceived the Athenian envoys by a fallacious display of wealth, and led them to conceive a greatly exaggerated notion of their resources. They, however, actually furnished 60 talents in ready money, and 30 more after the arrival of the Athenian armament. (Thuc. vi. 8, 46; Diod. xii. 83, xiii. 6.)

But though the relief of Segesta was thus the original object of the great Athenian expedition to Sicily, that city bears little part in the subsequent operations of the war. Nicias, indeed, on arriving in the island, proposed to proceed at once to Selinus, and compel that people to submission by the display of their formidable armament. But this advice was overruled: the Athenians turned their arms against Syracuse, and the contest between Segesta and Selinus was almost forgotten in the more important struggle between those two great powers. In the summer of B. C. 415 an Athenian fleet, proceeding along the coast, took the small town of Hyccara, on the coast, near Segesta, and made it over to the Segestans. (Thuc. vi. 62; Diod. xiii. 6.) The latter people are again mentioned on more than one occasion as sending auxiliary troops to assist their Athenian allies (Thuc. vii. 57; Diod. xiii. 7); but no other notice occurs of them. The final defeat of the Athenians left the Segestans again exposed to the attacks of their neighbours the Selinuntines; and feeling themselves unable to cope with them, they again had recourse to the Carthaginians, who determined to espouse their cause, and sent them, in the first instance, an auxiliary force of 5000 Africans and 800 Campanian mercenaries, which sufficed to ensure them the victory over their rivals, B. C. 410. (Diod. xiii. 43, 44.) But this was followed the next year by a vast armament under Hannibal, who landed at Lilybaeum, and, proceeding direct to Selinus, took and destroyed the city. (Ib. 54—58.) This was followed by the destruction of Himera; and the Carthaginian power now became firmly established in the western portion of Sicily. Segesta, surrounded on all sides by this formidable neighbour, naturally fell gradually into the position of a dependent ally of Carthage. It was one of the few cities that remained faithful to this alliance even in B. C. 397, when the great expedition of Dionysius to the W. of Sicily and the siege of Motya seemed altogether to shake the power of Carthage. Dionysius in consequence laid siege to Segesta, and pressed it with the utmost vigour, especially after the fall of Motya; but the city was able to defy his efforts, until the landing of Himilco with a formidable Carthaginian force changed the aspect of affairs, and compelled Dionysius to raise the siege. (Id. xiv. 48, 53—55.) From this time we hear little more of Segesta till the time of Agathocles, under whom it suffered a great calamity. The despot having landed in the W. of Sicily on his return from Africa (B. c. 307), and being received into the city as a friend and ally, suddenly turned upon the inhabitants on a pretence of disaffection, and put the whole of the citizens (said to amount to 10,000 in number) to the sword, plundered their wealth, and sold the women and children into slavery. He then changed the name of the city to Dicaeopolis, and assigned it as a residence to the fugitives and deserters that had gathered around him. (Diod. xx. 71.)

It is probable that Segesta never altogether recovered this blow; but it soon resumed its original name, and again appears in history as an independent city. Thus it is mentioned in B. c. 276, as one of the cities which joined Pyrrhus during his expedition into the W. of Sicily. (Diod. xxii. 10. Exc. H. p. 498.) It, however, soon after fell again under the power of the Carthaginians; and it was probably on this occasion that the city was taken and plundered by them, as alluded to by Cicero (Verr. iv. 33); a circumstance of which we have no other account. It continued subject to, or at least dependent on that people, till the First Punic War. In the first year of that war (B. c. 264) it was attacked by the consul Appius Claudius, but without success (Diod. xxiii. 3. p. 501); but shortly after the inhabitants put the Carthaginian garrison to the sword, and declared for the alliance of Rome. (Ib. 5. p. 502; Zonar. viii. 9.) They were in con-

sequence besieged by a Carthaginian force, and were at one time reduced to great straits, but were relieved by the arrival of Duilius, after his naval victory, B. C. 260. (Pol. i. 24.) Segesta seems to have been one of the first of the Sicilian cities to set the example of defection from Carthage; on which account, as well as of their pretended Trojan descent, the inhabitants were treated with great distinction by the Romans. They were exempted from all public burdens, and even as late as the time of Cicero continued to be "sine foedere immunes ac liberi." (Cic. Verr. iii. 6, iv. 33.) After the destruction of Carthage, Scipio Africanus restored to the Segestans a statue of Diana which had been carried off by the Carthaginians, probably when they obtained possession of the city after the departure of Pyrrhus. (Cic. Verr. iv. 33.) During the Servile War also, in B. c. 102, the territory of Segesta is again mentioned as one of those where the insurrection broke out with the greatest fury. (Diod. xxxvi. 5, Exc. Phot. p. 534.) But with the exception of these incidental notices we hear little of it under the Roman government. It seems to have been still a considerable town in the time of Cicero, and had a port or emporium of its own on the bay about 6 miles distant (τὸ τῶν Αἰγεστέων ἐμπόριον, Strab. vi. pp. 266, 272; Σεγεστανῶν ἐμπόριον, Ptol. iii. 4. § 4). This emporium seems to have grown up in the days of Strabo to be a more important place than Segesta itself: but the continued existence of the ancient city is attested both by Pliny and Ptolemy; and we learn from the former that the inhabitants, though they no longer retained their position of nominal independence, enjoyed the privileges of the Latin citizenship. (Strab. l. c.; Plin. iii. 8. s. 14; Ptol. iii. 4. § 15.) It seems, however, to have been a decaying place, and no trace of it is subsequently found in history. The site is said to have been finally abandoned, in consequence of the ravages of the Saracens, in A. D. 900 (Amico, ad Fazell. Sic. vii. 4. not. 9), and is now wholly desolate ; but the town of Castell 'a Mare, about 6 miles distant, occupies nearly, if not precisely, the same site as the ancient emporium or port of Segesta.

The site of the ancient city is still marked by the ruins of a temple and theatre, the former of which is one of the most perfect and striking ruins in Sicily. It stands on a hill, about 3 miles NW. of Calatafimi, in a very barren and open situation. It is of the Doric order, with six columns in front and fourteen on each side (all, except one, quite perfect, and that only damaged), forming a parallelogram of 162 feet by 66. From the columns not being fluted, they have rather a heavy aspect; but if due allowance be made for this circumstance, the architecture is on the whole a light order of Doric; and it is probable, therefore, that the temple is not of very early date. From the absence of fluting, as well as other details of the architecture, there can be no doubt that it never was finished,—the work probably being interrupted by some political catastrophe. This temple appears to have stood, as was often the case, outside the walls of the city, at a short distance to the W. of it. The latter occupied the summit of a hill of small extent, at the foot of which flows, in a deep valley or ravine, the torrent now called the Fiume Gaggera, a confluent of the Fiume di S. Bartolomeo, which flows about 5 miles E. of Segesta. The latter is probably the ancient Crimisus [CRIMISUS], celebrated for the great victory of Timoleon over the Carthaginians, while the Gaggera must probably be the stream called by Diodorus (xx. 71) the Scamander

3 P 3

Two other streams are mentioned by Aelian (*V. H.* ii. 33) in connection with Segesta, the Telmessus and the Porpax; but we are wholly at a loss to determine them. Some vestiges of the ancient walls may still be traced; but almost the only ruins which remain within the circuit of the ancient city are those of the theatre. These have been lately cleared out, and exhibit the *praecinctio* and sixteen rows of seats, great part in good preservation. The general form and arrangement are purely Greek; and the building rests at the back on the steep rocky slope of the hill, out of which a considerable part of it has been excavated. It is turned towards the N. and commands a fine view of the broad bay of *Castell 'a Mare*. (For a more detailed account of the antiquities of Segesta, see Swinburne's *Travels*, vol. ii. pp. 231—235; Smyth's *Sicily*, pp. 67, 68; and especially *Serra di Falco, Antichità della Sicilia*, vol. i. pt. ii.) Ancient writers mention the existence in the territory of Segesta of thermal springs or waters, which seem to have enjoyed considerable reputation (τὰ θερμὰ θάτρα Αἰγεσταῖα, Strab. vi. p. 275; θερμὰ λουτρὰ τὰ Ἐγεσταῖα, Diod. iv. 23). These are apparently the sulphureous springs at a spot called *Calametti*, about a mile to the N. of the site of the ancient city. (Fasell. *Sic.* vii. 4.) They are mentioned in the Itinerary as "Aquae Segestanae sive Pincianae" (*Itin. Ant.* p. 91); but the origin of the latter name is wholly unknown.

The coins of Segesta have the figure of a dog on the reverse, which evidently alludes to the fable of the river-god Crimisus, the mythical parent of Aegestus, having assumed that form. (Serv. *ad Aen.* i. 550, v. 30; Eckhel, vol. i. 234.) The older coins (as already observed) uniformly write the name ΣΕΙΕΣΤΑ, as on the one annexed: those of later date, which are of copper only, bear the legend ΕΓΕΣΤΑΙΩΝ (Eckhel, *l. c.* p. 236). [E. H. B.]

COIN OF SEGESTA.

SEGESTA (*Sestri*), a town on the coast of Liguria, mentioned by Pliny, in describing the coast of that country from Genua to the Macra. (Plin. iii. 5. s. 7.) He calls it Segesta Tigulliorum; so that it seems to have belonged to a tribe of the name of the Tigullii, and a town named Tigullia is mentioned by him just before. Segesta is commonly identified with *Sestri* (called *Sestri di Levante* to distinguish it from another place of the name), a considerable town about 30 miles from *Genoa*, while Tigullia is probably represented by *Tregoso*, a village about 2 miles further inland, where there are considerable Roman remains. Some of the MSS. of Pliny, indeed, have "Tigullia intus, et Segesta Tigulliorum," which would seem to point clearly to this position of the two places. (Sillig, *ad loc.*) It is probable, also, that the Tegulata of the Itineraries (*Itin. Ant.* p. 293) is identical with the Tigullia of Pliny. [E. H. B.]

SEGESTA, or SEGESTICA. [SISCIA.]
SEGIDA (Σέγιδα, Strabo, iii. p. 162). 1. A

town of the Arevaci in Hispania Tarraconensis. According to Appian, who calls it Σεγήδη (vi. 44), it belonged to the tribe of the Belli, and was 40 stadia in circumference. Stephanus B. (*s. v.*) calls it Σεγίδη, and makes it a town of the Celtiberians, of whom indeed the Arevaci and Belli were only subordinate tribes. Segida was the occasion of the first Celtiberian War (Appian, *l. c.*), and was probably the same place called Segestica by Livy (xxxiv. 17).

2. A town of Hispania Baetica, with the surname Restituta Julia. (Plin. iii. 1. s. 3.) [T. H. D.]

SEGISA (Σέγισα, Ptol. ii. 6. § 61), a town of the Bastitani in Hispania Tarraconensis, perhaps the modern *Sehegin*. [T. H. D.]

SEGI'SAMA and SEGISAMA JU'LIA (Σεγίσαμα Ἰουλία, Ptol. ii. 6. § 50), a town of Hispania Tarraconensis. We find the inhabitants mentioned by Pliny as Segisamajulienses (iii. 3. s. 4). Ptolemy ascribes the town to the Vaccaei, but Pliny to the Turmodigi, whence we may probably conclude that it lay on the borders of both those tribes. The latter author expressly distinguishes it from Segisamo. [T. H. D.]

SEGISAMO. [SEGESAMA.]
SEGISAMUNCLUM. [SEGASAMUNCLUM.]

SEGNI, a German tribe in Belgium, mentioned by Caesar (*B. G.* vi. 32) with the Condrusi, and placed between the Eburones and the Treviri. In *B. G.* ii. 4 Caesar speaks of the Condrusi, Eburones, Caeraesi, and Paemani, "qui uno nomine Germani appellantur;" but he does not name the Segni in that passage. There is still a place named *Sinei* or *Signei* near *Condros*, on the borders of *Namur*; and this may indicate the position of the Segni. [G. L.]

SEGOBO'DIUM, in Gallia, placed in the Table on a road from Andomatunum (*Langres*) to Vesontio (*Besançon*). The Itin. gives the same road, but omits Segobodium. D'Anville supposes Segobodium to be *Seveux*, which is on the *Saône*, and in the direction between *Besançon* and *Langres*. [G. L.]

SEGOBRI'GA (Σεγόβριγα, Ptol. ii. 6. § 58). 1. The capital of the Celtiberi in Hispania Tarraconensis. (Plin. iii. 3. s. 4.) It lay SW. of Caesaraugusta, and in the jurisdiction of Carthago Nova. (Plin. *l. c.*) The surrounding district was celebrated for its talc or selenite. (Id. xxxvi. 22. s. 45.) It must have been in the neighbourhood of *Priego*, where, near *Pennaescrite*, considerable ruins are still to be found. (Florez, *Esp. Sagr.* vii. p. 61.) For coins see Sestini, i. p. 193. (Cf. Strab. iii. p. 162; Front. *Strat.* iii. 10. 6.)

2. A town of the Edetani in Hispania Tarraconensis, known only from inscriptions and coins, the modern *Segorbe*. (Florez, *Esp. Sagr.* v. p. 21, viii. p. 97, and *Med.* pp. 573, 650; Mionnet, i. p. 50, and Supp. i. p. 102.) [T. H. D.]

COIN OF SEGOBRIGA.

SEGOBRI'GIL. [MASSILIA, p. 290.]

SEGODU'NUM (Σεγόδουνον). Ptolemy (ii. 7. § 21) calls Segodunum the chief town of the Ruteni [RUTENI], a Gallic people west of the Rhone, in the Aquitania of Ptolemy. In some editions of Ptolemy the reading is Segodunum or Etodunum. In the Table the name is Segodum, which is probably a corrupt form; and it has the mark of a chief town. It was afterwards called Civitas Rutenorum, whence the modern name *Rodez*, on the *Aveyron*, in the department of *Aveyron*, of which it is the chief town. [G. L.]

SEGODU'NUM (Σεγόδουνον), a town of southern Germany, probably in the country of the Hermunduri, is, according to some, the modern *Würzburg*. (Ptol. ii. 11. § 29; comp. Wilhelm, *Germanien*, p. 209.) [L. S.]

SEGO'NTIA. 1. A town of the Celtiberi in Hispania Tarraconensis, 16 miles from Caesaraugusta. (*Itin. Ant.* pp. 437, 439.) Most probably identical with the Seguntia of Livy (xxxiv. 19). The modern *Rueda*, according to Lapie.

2. (Σεγοντία Παράμικα, Ptol. ii. 6. § 66), a town of the Barduli in Hispania Tarraconensis. [T. H. D.]

SEGONTIACI, a people in the S. part of Britannia, in *Hampshire*. (Camden, pp. 84, 146; Caes. *B. G.* v. 21; Orelli, *Inscr.* 2013.) [T. H. D.]

SEGO'NTIUM, a city in the NW. part of Britannia Secunda, whence there was a road to Deva. (*Itin. Ant.* p. 482.) It is the modern *Caernarvon*, the little river by which is still called *Sejont*. (Camden, p. 798.) It is called Seguntio by the Geogr. Rav. (v. 31). [T. H. D.]

SEGORA, in Gallia, appears in the Table on a road from Portus Namnetum (*Nantes*) to Limunum, or Limonum (*Poitiers*). D'Anville supposes that Segora is *Bressuire*, which is on the road from *Nantes* to *Poitiers*. [G. L.]

SEGOSA, in Gallia, is placed by the Antonine Itin. on a road from Aquae Tarbellicae (*Dax*) to Burdigala (*Bordeaux*). The first station from Aquae Tarbellicae is Mosconnum, or Mostomium, the site of which is unknown. The next is Segosa, which D'Anville fixes at a place named *Escousse* or *Escoursé*. But he observes that the distance, 28 Gallic leagues, between Aquae and Segosa is less than the distance in the Itin. [G. L.]

SEGOVELLAUNI. [SEGALLAUNI.]

SEGO'VIA (Σεγούβια, Ptol. ii. 6. § 56). 1. A town of the Arevaci in Hispania Tarraconensis, on the road from Emerita to Caesaraugusta. (*Itin. Ant.* p. 435; Plin. iii. 3. s. 4; Flor. iii. 22.) It still exists under the ancient name. For coins see Florez (*Med.* ii. p. 577), Mionnet (i. p. 51, and Suppl. i. p. 104), and Sestini (p. 196).

2. A town of Hispania Baetica, on the river Silicense. (Hirt. *B. A.* 57.) In the neighbourhood of Secili or the modern *Perabad*. [T. H. D.]

SEGUSIA'NI (Σεγοσιανοί or Σεγουσιανοί), a Gallic people. When Caesar (B. C. 58) was leading against the Helvetii the troops which he had raised in North Italy, he crossed the Alps and reached the territory of the Allobroges. From the territory of the Allobroges he crossed the Rhone into the country of the Segusiani: "Hi sunt extra Provinciam trans Rhodanum primi." (*B. G.* i. 10.) He therefore places them in the angle between the *Rhone* and the *Saône*, for he was following the Helvetii, who had not yet crossed the *Saône*. In another place (vii. 64) he speaks of the Aedui and Segusiani as bordering on the Provincia, and the Segusiani were dependents of the Aedui (vii. 75). Strabo (iv. p. 186) places the

Segusiani between the Rhodanus and the Dubis (*Doubs*), on which D'Anville remarks that he ought to have placed them between the Rhone and the *Loire*. But part of the Segusiani at least were west of the Rhone in Caesar's time, as he plainly tells us, and therefore some of them were between the Rhone and the *Doubs*, though this is a very inaccurate way of fixing their position, for the *Doubs* ran through the territory of the Sequani. Lugdunum was in the country of the Segusiani. [LUGDUNUM.] Pliny gives to the Segusiani the name of Liberi (iv. 18).

In Cicero's oration *Pro P. Quintio* (c. 25), a Gallic people named Sebaguinos, Sebaginnos, with several other variations, is mentioned. The reading "Sebusianos" is a correction of Lambinus. Baiter (Orelli's Cicero, 2nd ed.) has written "Seguslavos" in this passage of Cicero on his own authority; but there is no name Segusiavi in Gallia. It is probable that the true reading is "Segusianos." Ptolemy (ii. 8. § 14) names Rodumna (*Roanne*) and Forum Segusianorum as the towns of the Segusiani, which shows that the Segusiani in his time extended to the *Loire* [RODUMNA]; and the greater part of their territory was probably west of the *Rhone* and *Saône*. Mionnet, quoted by Ukert (*Gallien*, p. 320), has a medal which he supposes to belong to the Segusiani. [G. L.]

SEGU'SIO (Σεγούσιον : Eth. Σεγουσιανός, Segusinus : *Susa*), a city of Gallia Transpadana, situated at the foot of the Cottian Alps, in the valley of the Duria (*Dora Riparia*), at the distance of 35 miles from Augusta Taurinorum (*Turin*). It was the capital of the Gaulish king or chieftain Cottius, from whom the Alpes Cottiae derived their name, and who became, in the reign of Augustus, a tributary or dependent ally of the Roman Empire. Hence, when the other Alpine tribes were reduced to subjection by Augustus, Cottius retained the government of his territories, with the title of Praefectus, and was able to transmit them to his son, M. Julius Cottius, upon whom the emperor Claudius even conferred the title of king. It was not till after the death of the younger Cottius, in the reign of Nero, that this district was incorporated into the Roman Empire, and Segusio became a Roman municipal town. (Strab. iv. pp. 179, 204; Plin. iii. 20. s. 24; Amm. Marc. xv. 10.)

It was probably from an early period the chief town in this part of the Alps and the capital of the surrounding district. It is situated just at the junction of the route leading from the *Mont Genèvre* down the valley of the *Dora* with that which crosses the *Mont Cenis*; both these passages were among the natural passes of the Alps, and were doubtless in use from a very early period, though the latter seems to have been unaccountably neglected by the Romans. The road also that was in most frequent use in the latter ages of the Republic and the early days of the Empire to arrive at the pass of the Cottian Alps or *Mont Genèvre*, was not that by Segusio up the valley of the Dura, but one which ascended the valley of *Fenestrelles* to Ocelum (*Uxeau*), and from thence crossed the *Col de Sestrières* to Scingomagus (at or near *Cesanne*), at the foot of the actual pass of the *Genèvre*. This was the route taken by Caesar in B. C. 58, and appears to have still been the one most usual in the days of Strabo (Caes. *B. G.* i. 10; Strab. iv. p. 179); but at a later period the road by Segusio seems to have come into general use, and is that given in the Itineraries. (*Itin. Ant.* pp. 341,

357.) Of Segusio as a municipal town we hear little ; but it is mentioned as such both by Pliny and Ptolemy, and its continued existence is proved by inscriptions as well as the Itineraries ; and we learn that it continued to be a considerable town, and a military post of importance, as commanding the passes of the Alps, until long after the fall of the Western Empire. (Plin. iii. 17. s. 21; Ptol. iii. 1. § 40; Gruter, *Inscr.* p. 111. 1 ; Orell. *Inscr.* 1690, 3803 ; Amm. Marc. xv. 10; *Itin. Hier.* p. 556 ; P. Disc. *Hist. Lang.* iii. 8; Greg. Tur. iv. 39.)

Ammianus tells us that the tomb of Cottius was still visible at Segusio in his time, and was the object of much honour and veneration among the inhabitants (Amm. *l. c.*). A triumphal arch erected by him in honour of Augustus is still extant at *Susa ;* it enumerates the names of the " Civitates " which were subject to his rule, and which were fourteen in number, though Pliny speaks of the " Cottianae civitates xii." (Plin. iii. 20. s. 24; Orell. *Inscr.* 626.) All these are, however, mere obscure mountain tribes, and the names of most of them entirely unknown. His dominions extended, according to Strabo, across the mountains as far as Ebrodunum in the land of the Caturiges (Strab. iv. p. 179); and this is confirmed by the inscription which enumerates the Catariges and Medulli among the tribes subject to his authority. These are probably the two omitted by Pliny. Ocelum, in the valley of the *Clusone,* was comprised in the territory of Cottius, while its limit towards the Taurini was marked by the station Ad Fines, placed by the Itineraries on the road to Augusta Taurinorum. But the distances given in the Itineraries are incorrect, and at variance with one another. Ad Fines may probably be placed at or near *Avigliana,* 15 miles from *Turin,* and 20 from *Susa.* The mountain tribes called by Pliny the " Cottianae civitates," when united with the Roman government, at first received only the Latin franchise (Plin. *l. c.*); but as Segusio became a Roman municipium, it must have received the full franchise.   [E. H. B.]

SEGUSTERO, a name which occurs in the Antonine Itin. and in the Table, is a town of Gallia Narbonensis, and the name is preserved in *Sisteron,* the chief town of an arrondissement in the department of *Basses Alpes,* on the right bank of the *Durance.* Roman remains have been found at *Sisteron.* The name in the Notit. Prov. Galliae is Civitas Segesteriorum. It was afterwards called Segesterium, and Sistericum, whence the modern name comes. (D'Anville, *Notice,* &c.)   [G. L.]

SEIR, M. (Σηείρ, LXX. Σάειρα, Σήειρον, Joseph). " The land of Seir " is equivalent to " the country of Edom." (*Gen.* xxxii. 3.) Mount Seir was the dwelling of Esau and his posterity (xxxvi. 8, 9 ; *Deut.* ii. 4, 5), in the possession of which they were not to be disturbed. (*Josh.* xxiv. 4.) Its general situation is defined in *Deuteronomy* (i. 2) between Horeb and Kadesh Barnea. The district must have been extensive, for in their retrograde movement from Kadesh, which was in Seir (i. 44), the Israelites compassed Mount Seir many days (ii. 1, 3). The original inhabitants of Mount Seir were the Horims; " but the children of Esau succeeded them, when they had destroyed them from before them, and dwelt in their stead " (ii. 12, 22 ; comp. *Gen.* xiv. 6). It obviously derived its name from " Seir the Horite " (xxxvi. 20, 21), and not, as Josephus erroneously supposes, from the Hebrew שָׂעִיר = hirsutus. (*Ant.* i. 20. § 3.) The range bordering *Wady Araba* is marked *M. Shehr* in some modern maps,

but without sufficient authority for the name. Dr. Wilson confines the name to the eastern side of the *Araba,* from a little north of Petra to the *Gulf of Akabah,* which range he names *Jebel-esh-Sherah* (*Lands of the Bible,* vol. i. pp. 289, 290, 337, 340); but since Kadesh was in Seir, it is obvious that this name must have extended much more widely, and on both sides the *Araba.* Mr. Rowlands heard the name *Es-Serr* given to an elevated plain to the east of Kadesh, which must, he thinks, be the Seir alluded to in *Deut.* i. 44, where the Israelites were chased before the Amalekites. (Williams's *Holy City,* vol. i. appendix, p. 465.)   [G. W.]

SEIRAĒ. [PROPHIS.]

SELACHUSA, an island lying off the Argolic promontory of Speiraeum, mentioned only by Pliny (iv. 12. s. 57).

SELAH. [PETRA.]

SELAMBINA (Σηλάμβινα, Ptol. ii. 4. § 7), a town on the coast of Hispania Baetica between Sex and Abdera. (Plin. iii. 1. s. 3.) Florez (*Esp. Sagr.* xii. pp. 3, 6) identifies it with *Calabreña,* but, according to Ukert (ii. p. i. p. 351), it is to be sought in the neighbourhood of *Sorbitan.*   [T. H. D.]

SELAS. [MESSENIA, p. 342, b.]

SELASIA. [SELLASIA.]

SELEMNUS. [ACHAIA, p. 13, b. No. 10.]

SELENTIS or SELENITIS (Σελεντὶς or Σελενιτίς) a district in the south-west part of Cilicia, extending along the coast, but also some distance in the interior; it derived its name from the town of Selinus. (Ptol. v. 8. §§ 2, 5.)   [L. S.]

SELENU'SIAE (Σελενούσιαι) or SELENNUTES two lakes formed by the sea, north of the mouth of the Caystrus, and not far from the temple of the Ephesian Artemis. These two lakes, which communicated with each other, were extremely rich in fish, and formed part of the revenue of the temple of Artemis, though they were on several occasions wrested from it. (Strab. xiv. p. 642 ; Plin. v. 31.) The name of the lakes, derived from Selene, the moon-goddess, or Artemis, probably arose from their connection with the great goddess of Ephesus. (Comp. Chandler's *Travels in Asia Minor,* vol. i. p. 162.)   [L. S.]

SELEUCEIA or SELEUCIA, two towns in Syria. 1. AD BELUM (Σελεύκεια πρὸς Βήλῳ), sometimes called SELEUCOBELUS, situated in the district of Cassiotis, placed by Ptolemy in long. 69° 30', lat. 34° 45'. The Belus was a tributary of the Orontes, running into it from the W., and since, as Pococke remarks, Seleucia was exactly in the same latitude as Paltos, it must have been due E. of it. Now *Boldo,* the ancient Paltos, lies two hours S. of *Jebilee,* ancient Gabala, on the coast. Seleucia ad Belum must be looked for 1° 10' to the E., according to Ptolemy's reckoning, who places Paltos in long. 63° 20', lat. 34° 45'. Modern conjecture has identified it with *Shogh* and *Divertigi,* which is placed 30 miles E. of Antioch. (Ptol. v. 15. § 16 ; Pococke, *Syria.* vol. ii. p. 199.) Pliny mentions it with another not elsewhere recognised, in the interior of Syria: " Seleucias praeter jam dictam (i. e. Pieria), duas, quae ad Euphratem, et quae ad Belum vocantur " (v. 23. § 19).

2. PIERIA (Σελεύκεια Πιερία : Eth. Σελευκεύς), a maritime city of Syria, placed by Ptolemy in long. 68° 36', lat. 35° 26', between Rhossus and the mouths of the Orontes. Its ancient name, according to Strabo, was " Rivers of Water " ("Ὕδατος ποταμοί), a strong city, called Free by Pompey (Strab. xvi. 2. § 8). Its position is fully described by Polybius.

It was situated on the sea between Cilicia and Phoenice, over against a large mountain called Coryphaeum, the base of which was washed on its W. side by the sea, towards the E. it dominated the districts of Antioch and Seleucis. Seleucia lay on the S. of this mountain, separated from it by a deep and rugged valley. The city extended to the sea through broken ground, but was surrounded for the most part by precipitous and abrupt rocks. On the side towards the sea lay the factory (τὰ ἐμπορεῖα) and suburb, on the level ground, strongly fortified. The whole hollow (κῆτος) of the city was likewise strongly fortified with fine walls, and temples, and buildings. It had one approach on the sea side, by an artificial road in steps (κλιμακωτὴν), distributed into frequent and continuous slopes (cuttings?—ἐγκλίμασι) and curves (tunnels?—σκαιώμασι). The embouchure of the Orontes was not far distant—40 stadia, according to Strabo (xvi. p. 750). It was built by Seleucus Nicator (died B. C. 280), and was of great importance, in a military view, during the wars between the Seleucidae and the Ptolemies. It was taken by Ptolemy Euergetes on his expedition into Syria, and held by an Egyptian garrison until the time of Antiochus the Great, who, at the instigation of Apollophanes, a Seleucian, resolved to recover it from Ptolemy Philopator (cir. B. C. 220), in order to remove the disgrace of an Egyptian garrison in the heart of Syria, and to obviate the danger which it threatened to his operations in Coele-Syria, being, as it was, a principal city, and well nigh, so to speak, the proper home of the Syrian power. Having sent the fleet against it, under the admiral Diognetus, he himself marched with his army from Apameia, and encamped near the Hippodrome, 5 stadia from the city. Having in vain attempted to win it by bribery, he divided his forces into three parts, of which one under Zeuxis made the assault near the gate of Antioch, a second under Hermogenes near the temple of the Dioscuri, the third under Ardys and Diognetus by the arsenal and suburb, which was first carried, whereupon the garrison capitulated (Polyb. v. 58—60). It was afterwards a place of arms in the further prosecution of the war against Ptolemy (66). The Mount Coryphaeum of Polybius is the Pieria of Ptolemy and Strabo, from which the town derived its distinguishing appellation. Strabo mentions, from Posidonius, that a kind of asphaltic soil was quarried in this place, which, when spread over the roots of the vine, acted as a preservative against blight (vii. p. 316.) He calls it the first city of the Syrians, from Cilicia, and states its distance from Soli, in a straight course, a little less than 1000 stadia (xiv. p. 676). It was one of the four cities of the Tetrapolis, which was a synonym for the district of Seleucis, the others being Antioch, Apameia, and Laodiceia, which were called sister cities, being all founded by Seleucus Nicator, and called by the names respectively of himself, his father, his wife, and his mother-in-law; that bearing his father's name being the largest, that bearing his own, the strongest. (Strab. xvi. p. 749.) The auguries attending its foundation are mentioned by John Malalas (Chronographia, lib. viii. p. 254). It became the port of Antioch, and there it was that St. Paul and Barnabas embarked for Cyprus, on their first mission to Asia Minor (Acts, xiii. 4), the Orontes never having been navigable even as far as Antioch for any but vessels of light draught. Pliny calls it "Seleucia libera Pieria," and describes it as situated on a promontory (v. 21) clxxv. M. P. distant from Zeugma on the Euphrates (12). He de-

signates the Coryphaeum of Polybius, the Pieria of Strabo, Mount Casius, a name also extended by Strabo to the mountains about Seleucia, where he speaks of the Antiocheans celebrating a feast to Triptolemus as a demigod, in Mount Cassius around Seleucia (xvi. p. 750). The ruins of the site have been fully explored and described in modern times, first by Pococke (Observations on Syria, chap. xxii. p. 182, &c.), who identified many points noticed by Polybius, and subsequently by Col. Chesney (Journal of the R. Geog. Society, vol. viii. p. 228, &c.). The mountain range noticed by Polybius is now called Jebel Musa; and the hill on which the city stood appears to be the "low mountain, called Bin-Killisch," or the 1000 churches. Part of the site of the town was occupied, according to Pococke, by the village of Kepse, situated about a mile from the sea. The masonry of the once magnificent port of Seleucia is still in so good a state that it merely requires trifling repairs in some places, and to be cleaned out; a project contemplated, but not executed, by one Ali Pasha, when governor of Aleppo. The plan of the port, with its walls and basins, its piers, floodgates, and defences, can be distinctly traced. The walls of the suburb, with its agora, the double line of defence of the inner city, comprehending in their circumference about 4 miles, which is filled with ruins of houses ; its castellated citadel on the summit of the hill, the gate of Antioch on the SE. of the site, with its pilasters and towers, near which is a double row of marble columns; large remains of two temples, one of which was of the Corinthian order; the amphitheatre, near which Antiochus encamped, before his assault upon the city, with twenty-four tiers of benches still to be traced; the numerous rocky excavations of the necropolis, with the sarcophagi, always of good workmanship, now broken and scattered about in all directions, all attest the ancient importance of the city, and the fidelity of the historian who has described it. Most remarkable of all in this view is the important engineering work, to which Polybius alludes as the only communication between the city and sea, fully described by Col. Chesney, as the most striking of the interesting remains of Seleucia. It is a very extensive excavation, cut through the solid rock from the NE. extremity of the town almost to the sea, part of which is a deep hollow way, and the remainder regular tunnels, between 20 and 30 feet wide, and as many high, executed with great skill and considerable labour. From its eastern to its western extremity is a total length of 1088 yards, the greater part of which is traversed by an aqueduct carried along the face of the rock, considerably above the level of the road. Its termination is rough and very imperfect, about 30 feet above the level of the sea ; and while the bottom of the rest of the excavation is tolerably regular, in this portion it is impeded by large masses of rock lying across it at intervals: which would imply either that it was never completed, or that it was finished in this part with masonry, which may have been carried off for building purposes. It is, perhaps, in this part that the stairs mentioned by Polybius may have been situated, in order to form a communication with the sea. There can be no doubt whatever that this excavation is the passage mentioned by him as the sole communication between the city and the sea ; and it is strange that any question should have arisen concerning its design. A rough plan of the site is given by Pococke (p. 183); but a much more carefully executed plan, with drawings and sections of the tunnels, &c., has lately been published by Captain Allen, who surveyed the site of the harbour, but not of the town, in 1850. (*The Dead Sea, &c.*, Map at end of vol. i., and vol. ii. pp. 208—230.) [G. W.]

reign of Augustus, and the sophist Alexander, who taught at Antioch, and was private secretary to the emperor M. Aurelius (Philostr. *Vit. Soph.* ii. 5.) According to some authorities, lastly, the emperor Trajan died at Seleuceia (Eutrop. viii. 2, 16; Oros. *l. c.*), though others state that he died at Selinus.

COIN OF SELEUCEIA IN SYRIA.   COIN OF SELEUCEIA IN CILICIA.

SELEUCEIA or SELEUCIA (Σελεύκεια). 1. A town near the northern frontier of Pisidia, surnamed Sidera (ἡ Σιδηρᾶ, Ptol. v. 5. § 4; Hierocl. p. 673), probably on account of iron-works in its vicinity. There are some coins of this place with the image of the Asiatic divinity Men, who was worshipped at Antioch, and bearing the inscription Κλαυδιοσσελευκέων, which might lead to the idea that the place was restored by the emperor Claudius. (Sestini, *Mon. Vet.* p. 96.) Its site is now occupied by the town of *Ejerdir*.

2. A town in Pamphylia between Side and the mouth of the river Eurymedon, at a distance of 80 stadia from Side, and at some distance from the sea. (*Stadiasm. Mar. Mag.* § 216.)

3. An important town of Cilicia, in a fertile plain on the western bank of the Calycadnus, a few miles above its mouth, was founded by Seleucus I., surnamed Nicator. A town or towns, however, had previously existed on the spot under the names of Olbia and Hyria, and Seleucus seems to have only extended and united them in one town under the name Seleucia. The inhabitants of the neighbouring Holmi were at the same time transferred to the new town, which was well built, and in a style very different from that of other Cilician and Pamphylian cities. (Steph. B. *s. v.*; Strab. xiv. p. 670.) In situation, climate, and the richness of its productions, it rivalled the neighbouring Tarsus, and it was much frequented on account of the annual celebration of the Olympia, and on account of the oracle of Apollo. (Zosim. i. 57; Basil. *Vita S. Theclae,* i. p. 275, *Orat.* xxvii. p. 148.) Pliny (v. 27) states that it was surnamed Tracheotis; and some ecclesiastical historians, speaking of a council held there, call the town simply Trachea (Sozom. iv. 16; Socrat. ii. 39; comp. Ptol. v. 8. § 5; Amm. Marc. xiv. 25; Oros. vii. 12.) The town still exists under the name of *Selefkieh*, and its ancient remains are scattered over a large extent of ground on the west side of the Calycadnus. The chief remains are those of a theatre, in the front of which there are considerable ruins, with porticoes and other large buildings: farther on are the ruins of a temple, which had been converted into a Christian church, and several large Corinthian columns. Ancient Seleuceia, which appears to have remained a free city ever since the time of Augustus, remained in the same condition even after a great portion of Cilicia was given to Archelaus of Cappadocia, whence both imperial and autonomous coins of the place are found. Seleuceia was the birthplace of several men of eminence, such as the peripatetics Athenaeus and Xenarchus, who flourished in the

4. Seleucia in Caria [TRALLES.]   [L. S.]

SELEUCEIA or SELEUCIA (Σελεύκεια, Polyb. v. 48; Strab. xi. p. 521; Ptol. v. 18. § 8), a large city near the right bank of the Tigris, which, to distinguish it from several other towns of the same name, is generally known in history by the title of Σελεύκεια ἐπὶ τῷ Τίγρητι. (Strab. xvi. p. 738; Appian, *Syr.* 57.) It was built by Seleucus Nicator (Strab. *l. c.*; Plin. vi. 26. s. 30; Tacit. *Ann.* vi. 42; Joseph. *Ant. Jud.* xviii. 9. § 8; Amm. Marc. xxiii. 20), and appears to have been placed near the junction with the Tigris, of the great dyke which was carried across Mesopotamia from the Euphrates to the Tigris, and which bore the name of *Nahar Malcha* (the royal river). (Plin. *l. c.*, and Isid. Char. p. 5.) Ptolemy states that the artificial river divided it into two parts (v. 18. § 8). On the other hand, Theophylact states that both rivers, the Tigris and Euphrates, surrounded it like a rampart —by the latter, in all probability, meaning the *Nahar Malcha* (v. 6). It was situated about 40 miles NE. of Babylon (according to Strabo, 300 stadia, and to the Tab. Peutinger., 44 M.P.). In form, its original structure is said to have resembled an eagle with its wings outspread. (Plin. *l. c.*) It was mainly constructed of materials brought from Babylon, and was one principal cause of the ruin of the elder city, as Ctesiphon was (some centuries later) of Seleuceia itself. (Strab. xvi. p. 738.) It was placed in a district of great fertility, and is said, in its best days, to have had a population of 600,000 persons. (Plin. *l. c.*) Strabo adds, that it was even larger than Antiocheia Syriae,—at his time probably the greatest commercial entrepôt in the East, with the exception of Alexandreia (xvi. p. 750). Even so late as the period of its destruction its population is still stated to have amounted to half a million. (Eutrop. v. 8; comp. Oros. viii. 5.) To its commercial importance it doubtless owed the free character of its local government, which appears to have been administered by means of a senate of 300 citizens. Polybius states that, on the overthrow of Molon, the Median rebels Antiochus and Hermeias descended on Seleuceia, which had been previously taken by Molon, and, after punishing the people by torture and the infliction of a heavy fine, exiled the local magistracy, who were called Adeiganae. (Ἀδειγᾶναι, Polyb. v. 54.) Their love of freedom and of independent government was, however, of longer duration. (Plin. *l. c.*; Tacit. *Ann.* vi. 42.)

Seleuceia owed its ruin to the wars of the Romans with the Parthians and other eastern nations. It is first noticed in that between Crassus and Orodes (Dion Cass. xl. 20); but it would seem that Crassus did not himself reach Seleuceia. On the advance of Trajan from Asia Minor, Seleuceia was taken by Erucius Clarus and Julius Alexander, and partially burnt to the ground (Dion Cass. lxviii. 30); and a few years later it was still more completely destroyed by Cassius, the general of Lucius Verus, during the war with Vologeses. (Dion Cass. lxxi. 2; Eutrop. v. 8; Capitol. Verus, c. 8.) When Severus, during the Parthian War, descended the Euphrates, he appears to have found Seleuceia and Babylon equally abandoned and desolate. (Dion Cass. lxxv. 9.) Still later, in his expedition to the East, Julian found the whole country round Seleuceia one vast marsh full of wild game, which his soldiers hunted. (Amm. Marc. xxiv. 5.) It would seem from the indistinct notices of some authors, that Seleuceia once bore the name of Coche. [Coche.]   [V.]

SELEUCIS (Σελευκίς), a district of Syria, mentioned by Ptolemy, as containing the cities of Gephyra, Gindarus, and Imma (v. 15. § 15). Strabo calls it the best of all the districts: it was also called Tetrapolis, on account of its four most important cities, for it had many. These four were, Antioch, Seleuceia in Pieria, Apameia, and Laodiceia (xvi. p. 749). It also comprehended, according to Strabo, four satrapies; and it is clear that he uses the name in a much wider sense than Ptolemy, who places the four cities of the tetrapolis of Strabo's Seleucis in so many separate districts; Antioch in Cassiotis, Apameia in Apamene, Laodiceia in Laodicene, while he only implies, but does not state, that Seleuceia lies in Seleucis.   [G. W.]

SELGE (Σέλγη: Eth. Σελγεύς), an important city in Pisidia, on the southern slope of Mount Taurus, at the part where the river Eurymedon forces its way through the mountains towards the south. The town was believed to be a Greek colony, for Strabo (xii. p. 520) states that it was founded by Lacedaemonians, but adds the somewhat unintelligible remark that previously it had been founded by Calchas (Comp. Polyb. v. 76; Steph. B. s. v.; Dion. Per. 858). The acropolis of Selge bore the name of Cesbedium (Κεσβέδιον; Polyb. l. c.) The district in which the town was situated was extremely fertile, producing abundance of oil and wine, but the town itself was difficult of access, being surrounded by precipices and beds of torrents flowing towards the Eurymedon and Cestrus, and requiring bridges to make them passable. In consequence of its excellent laws and political constitution, Selge rose to the rank of the most powerful and populous city of Pisidia, and at one time was able to send an army of 20,000 men into the field. Owing to these circumstances, and the valour of its inhabitants, for which they were regarded as worthy kinsmen of the Lacedaemonians, the Selgians were never subject to any foreign power, but remained in the enjoyment of their own freedom and independence. When Alexander the Great passed through Pisidia, the Selgians sent an embassy to him and gained his favour and friendship. (Arrian, Anab. i. 28.) At that time they were at war with the Telmissians. At the period when Achaeus had made himself master of Western Asia, the Selgians were at war with Pednelissus, which was besieged by them; and Achaeus, on the invitation of Pednelissus, sent a large force against Selge. After a long and vigorous siege, the Selgians, being betrayed and despairing of resisting Achaeus any longer, sent deputies to sue for peace, which was granted to them on the following terms: they agreed to pay immediately 400 talents, to restore the prisoners of Pednelissus, and after a time to pay 300 talents in addition. (Polyb. v. 72—77.) We now have for a long time no particulars about the history of Selge: in the fifth century of our era Zosimus (v. 15) calls it indeed a little town, but it was still strong enough to repel a body of Goths. It is strange that Pliny does not notice Selge, for we know from its coins that it was still a flourishing town in the time of Hadrian; and it is also mentioned in Ptolemy (v. 5. § 8) and Hierocles (p. 681). Independently of wine and oil, the country about Selge was rich in timber, and a variety of trees, among which the storax was much valued from its yielding a strong perfume. Selge was also celebrated for an ointment prepared from the iris root. (Strab. l. c.; Plin. xii. 55, xxi. 19; comp. Liv. xxxv. 13.) Sir C. Fellows (Asia Minor, p. 171, foll.) thinks that he has discovered the ruins of Selge about 10 miles to the north-east of the village of Boojak. They are seen on a lofty promontory "now presenting magnificent wrecks of grandeur." "I rode," says Sir Charles, "at least 3 miles through a part of the city, which was one pile of temples, theatres, and buildings, vying with each other in splendour..... The material of these ruins had suffered much from the exposure to the elements, being grey with a lichen which has eaten into the marble, and entirely destroyed the surface and inscriptions; but the scale, the simple grandeur, and the uniform beauty of style bespeak its date to be the early Greek. The sculptured cornices frequently contain groups of figures fighting, wearing helmets and body-armour, with shields and long spears; from the ill-proportioned figures and general appearance, they must rank in date with the Aegina marbles. The ruins are so thickly strewn, that little cultivation is practicable; but in the areas of theatres, cellas of temples, and any space where a plough can be used, the wheat is springing up. The general style of the temples is Corinthian, but not so florid as in less ancient towns. The tombs are scattered for a mile from the town, and are of many kinds, some cut in chambers in face of the rock, others sarcophagi of the heaviest form: they have had inscriptions, and the ornaments are almost all martial; several seats remain among the tombs. I can scarcely guess the number of temples or columned buildings in the town, but I certainly traced fifty or sixty.... Although apparently unnecessary for defence, the town has had strong walls, partly built with large stones in the Cyclopean mode.... I never conceived so high an idea of the works of the ancients as from my visit to this place, standing as it does in a situation, as it were, above the world." It is to be regretted that it was impossible by means of inscriptions or coins to identify this place with the ancient Selge more satisfactorily. (Comp. Von Hammer, in the Wiener Jahrbücher, vol. cvi. p. 92.)   [L. S.]

COIN OF SELGE.

SELGOVAE (Σελγοούαι, Ptol. ii. 3. § 8), a people on the SW. coast of Britannia Barbara, in the E. part of *Galloway* and in *Dumfries-shire*. Camden (p. 1194) derives the name of *Solway* from them.   [T. H. D.]

SELI'NUS (Σελινοῦς) 1. A village in the north of Laconia, described by Pausanias as 20 stadia from Geronthrae; but as Pausanias seems not to have visited this part of Laconia, the distances may not be correct. Leake, therefore, places Selinus at the village of *Kosmas*, which lies further north of Geronthrae than 20 stadia, but where there are remains of ancient tombs. (Paus. iii. 22. § 8; Leake, *Peloponnesiaca*, p. 363; Boblaye, *Recherches, &c.* p. 97; Curtius, *Peloponnesos*, vol. ii. p. 304.)

2. A river in the Triphylian Elis, near Scillus. [SCILLUS.]

3. A river in Achaia. [ACHAIA, p. 13, b. No. 6.]

SELI'NUS (Σελινοῦς: Eth. Σελινούντιος, Selinuntius: Ru. at *Torre dei Pulci*), one of the most important of the Greek colonies in Sicily, situated on the SW. coast of that island, at the mouth of the small river of the same name, and 4 miles W. of that of the Hypsas (*Belici*). It was founded, as we learn from Thucydides, by a colony from the Sicilian city of Megara, or Megara Hyblaea, under the conduct of a leader named Pammilus, about 100 years after the settlement of that city, with the addition of a fresh body of colonists from the parent city of Megara in Greece. (Thuc. vi. 4, vii. 57; Scymn. Ch. 292; Strab. vi. p. 272.) The date of its foundation cannot be precisely fixed, as Thucydides indicates it only by reference to that of the Sicilian Megara, which is itself not accurately known, but it may be placed about B. C. 628. Diodorus indeed would place it 22 years earlier, or B. C. 650, and Hieronymus still further back, B. C. 654; but the date given by Thucydides, which is probably entitled to the most confidence, is incompatible with this earlier epoch. (Thuc. vi. 4; Diod. xiii. 59; Hieron. *Chron.* ad ann. 1362; Clinton, *Fast. Hell.* vol. i. p. 208.) The name is supposed to have been derived from the quantities of wild parsley (σέλινον) which grew on the spot; and for the same reason a leaf of this parsley was adopted as the symbol of their coins.

Selinus was the most westerly of the Greek colonies in Sicily, and for this reason was early brought into contact and collision with the Carthaginians and the barbarians in the W. and NW. of the island. The former people, however, do not at first seem to have offered any obstacle to their progress; but as early as B. C. 580 we find the Selinuntines engaged in hostilities with the people of Segesta (a non-Hellenic city), whose territory bordered on their own. (Diod. v. 9). The arrival of a body of emigrants from Rhodes and Cnidus who subsequently founded Lipara, and who lent their assistance to the Segestans, for a time secured the victory to that people; but disputes and hostilities seem to have been of frequent occurrence between the two cities, and it is probable that in B. C. 454, when Diodorus speaks of the Segestans as being at war with the *Lilybaeans* (xi. 86), that the Selinuntines are the people really meant. [LILYBAEUM.] The river Mazarus, which at that time appears to have formed the boundary between the two states, was only about 15 miles W. of Selinus; and it is certain that at a somewhat later period the territory of Selinus extended to its banks, and that that city had a fort

and emporium at its mouth. (Diod. xiii. 54.) On the other side its territory certainly extended as far as the Halycus or *Salso*, at the mouth of which it had founded the colony of Minoa, or Heracleia, as it was afterwards termed. (Herod. v. 46.) It is evident, therefore, that Selinus had early attained to great power and prosperity; but we have very little information as to its history, We learn, however, that, like most of the Sicilian cities, it had passed from an oligarchy to a despotism, and about B. C. 510 was subject to a despot named Peithagoras, from whom the citizens were freed by the assistance of the Spartan Euryleon, one of the companions of Dorieus: and thereupon Euryleon himself, for a short time, seized on the vacant sovereignty, but was speedily overthrown and put to death by the Selinuntines. (Herod. v. 46.) We are ignorant of the causes which led the Selinuntines to abandon the cause of the other Greeks, and take part with the Carthaginians during the great expedition of Hamilcar, B. C. 480; but we learn that they had even promised to send a contingent to the Carthaginian army, which, however did not arrive till after its defeat. (Diod. xi. 21, xiii. 55.) The Selinuntines are next mentioned in B. C. 466, as co-operating with the other free cities of Sicily in assisting the Syracusans to expel Thrasybulus (Id. xi. 68); and there is every reason to suppose that they fully shared in the prosperity of the half century that followed, a period of tranquillity and opulence for most of the Greek cities in Sicily. Thucydides speaks of Selinus just before the Athenian expedition as a powerful and wealthy city, possessing great resources for war both by land and sea, and having large stores of wealth accumulated in its temples. (Thuc. vi. 20.) Diodorus also represents it at the time of the Carthaginian invasion, as having enjoyed a long period of tranquillity, and possessing a numerous population. (Diod. xiii. 55.)

In B. C. 416, a renewal of the old disputes between Selinus and Segesta became the occasion of the great Athenian expedition to Sicily. The Selinuntines were the first to call in the powerful aid of Syracuse, and thus for a time obtained the complete advantage over their enemies, whom they were able to blockade both by sea and land; but in this extremity the Segestans had recourse to the assistance of Athens. (Thuc. vi. 6; Diod. xii. 82.) Though the Athenians do not appear to have taken any measures for the immediate relief of Segesta, it is probable that the Selinuntines and Syracusans withdrew their forces at once, as we hear no more of their operations against Segesta. Nor does Selinus bear any important part in the war of which it was the immediate occasion. Nicias indeed proposed, when the expedition first arrived in Sicily (B. C. 415), that they should proceed at once to Selinus and compel that city to submit on moderate terms (Thuc. vi. 47); but this advice being overruled, the efforts of the armament were directed against Syracuse, and the Selinuntines in consequence bore but a secondary part in the subsequent operations. They are, however, mentioned on several occasions as furnishing auxiliaries to the Syracusans; and it was at Selinus that the large Peloponnesian force sent to the support of Gylippus landed in the spring of 413, having been driven over to the coast of Africa by a tempest. (Thuc. vii. 50, 58; Diod. xiii. 12.)

The defeat of the Athenian armament left the Segestans apparently at the mercy of their rivals; they in vain attempted to disarm the hostility of the

Selinuntines by ceding without further contest the frontier district which had been the original subject of dispute. But the Selinuntines were not satisfied with this concession, and continued to press them with fresh aggressions, for protection against which they sought assistance from Carthage. This was, after some hesitation, accorded them, and a small force sent over at once, with the assistance of which the Segestans were able to defeat the Selinuntines in a battle. (Diod. xiii. 43, 44.) But not content with this, the Carthaginians in the following spring (B. C. 409) sent over a vast army amounting, according to the lowest estimate, to 100,000 men, with which Hannibal (the grandson of Hamilcar that was killed at Himera) landed at Lilybaeum, and from thence marched direct to Selinus. The Selinuntines were wholly unprepared to resist such a force; so little indeed had they expected it that the fortifications of their city were in many places out of repair, and the auxiliary force which had been promised by Syracuse as well as by Agrigentum and Gela, was not yet ready, and did not arrive in time. The Selinuntines, indeed, defended themselves with the courage of despair, and even after the walls were carried, continued the contest from house to house; but the overwhelming numbers of the enemy rendered all resistance hopeless; and after a siege of only ten days the city was taken, and the greater part of the defenders put to the sword. Of the citizens of Selinus we are told that 16,000 were slain, 5000 made prisoners, and 2600 under the command of Empedion escaped to Agrigentum. (Diod. xiii. 54—59.) Shortly after Hannibal destroyed the walls of the city, but gave permission to the surviving inhabitants to return and occupy it, as tributaries of Carthage, an arrangement which was confirmed by the treaty subsequently concluded between Dionysius and the Carthaginians, in B. C. 405. (Id. xiii. 59, 114.) In the interval a considerable number of the survivors and fugitives had been brought together by Hermocrates, and established within its walls. (Ib. 63.)

There can be no doubt that a considerable part of the citizens of Selinus availed themselves of this permission, and that the city continued to subsist under the Carthaginian dominion; but a fatal blow had been given to its prosperity, which it undoubtedly never recovered. The Selinuntines are again mentioned in B. C. 397 as declaring in favour of Dionysius during his war with Carthage (Diod. xiv. 47); but both the city and territory were again given up to the Carthaginians by the peace of 383 (Id. xv. 17); and though Dionysius recovered possession of it by arms shortly before his death (Id. xv. 73), it is probable that it soon again lapsed under the dominion of Carthage. The Halycus, which was established as the eastern boundary of the Carthaginian dominion in Sicily by the treaty of 383, seems to have generally continued to be so recognised, notwithstanding temporary interruptions; and was again fixed as their limit by the treaty with Agathocles in B. C. 314. (Id. xix. 71.) This last treaty expressly stipulated that Selinus, as well as Heracleia and Himera, should continue subject to Carthage, as before. In B. C. 276, however, during the expedition of Pyrrhus to Sicily, the Selinuntines voluntarily submitted to that monarch, after the capture of Heracleia. (Id. xxii. 10. Exc. H. p. 498.) During the First Punic War we again find Selinus subject to Carthage, and

its territory was repeatedly the theatre of military operations between the contending powers. (Id. xxiii. 1, 21; Pol. i. 39.) But before the close of the war (about B. C. 250), when the Carthaginians were beginning to contract their operations, and confine themselves to the defence of as few points as possible, they removed all the inhabitants of Selinus to Lilybaeum and destroyed the city. (Diod. xxiv. 1. Exc. H. p. 506.)

It seems certain that it was never rebuilt. Pliny indeed, mentions its name ("Selinus oppidum," iii. 8. s. 14), as if it was still existing as a town in his time, but Strabo distinctly classes it with the cities which were wholly extinct; and Ptolemy, though he mentions the river Selinus, has no notice of a town of the name. (Strab. vi. p. 272; Ptol. iii. 4. § 5.) The THERMAE SELINUNTIAE, which derived their name from the ancient city, and seem to have been much frequented in the time of the Romans, were situated at a considerable distance from Selinus, being undoubtedly the same as those now existing at Sciacca: they are sulphureous springs, still much valued for their medical properties, and dedicated, like most thermal waters in Sicily, to St. Calogero. At a later period they were called the Aquae Labodes or Larodes, under which name they appear in the Itineraries. (Itin. Ant. p. 89; Tab. Peut.) They are there placed 40 miles W. of Agrigentum, and 46 from Lilybaeum; distances which agree well with the position of Sciacca. This is distant about 20 miles to the E. of the ruins of Selinus.

The site of the ancient city is now wholly desolate, with the exception of a solitary guardhouse, and the ground is for the most part thickly overgrown with shrubs and low brushwood; but the remains of the walls can be distinctly traced throughout a great part of their circuit. They occupied the summit of a low hill, directly abutting on the sea, and bounded on the W. by the marshy valley through which flows the river Madiuni, the ancient Selinus; on the E. by a smaller valley or depression, also traversed by a small marshy stream, which separates it from a hill of similar character, where the remains of the principal temples are still visible. The space enclosed by the existing walls is of small extent, so that it is probable the city in the days of its greatness must have covered a considerable area without them; and it has been supposed by some writers that the present line of walls is that erected by Hermocrates when he restored the city after its destruction by the Carthaginians. (Diod. xiii. 63.) No trace is, however, found of a more extensive circuit, though the remains of two lines of wall, evidently connected with the port, are found in the small valley E. of the city. Within the area surrounded by the walls are the remains of three temples, all of the Doric order, and of an ancient style; none of them are standing, but the foundations of them all remain, together with numerous portions of columns and other architectural fragments, sufficient to enable us to restore the plan and design of all three without difficulty. The largest of them (marked C. on the plan) is 230 feet long by 85 feet broad, and has 6 columns in front and 18 in length, a very unusual proportion. All these are hexastyle and peripteral. Besides these three temples there is a small temple or Aedicula (marked B.), of a different plan, but also of the Doric order. No other remains of buildings, beyond mere fragments and foundations, can be traced within the walls; but the outlines of two large edifices, built of squared stones and in a massive style, are distinctly traceable outside the walls, near the NE. and NW. angles of the city, though we have no clue to their nature or purpose.

But much the most remarkable of the ruins at

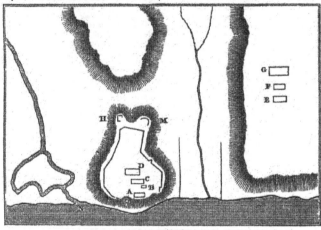

PLAN OF SELINUS.

A C D. Temples within the city.
B. Small temple or aedicula in the city.
E F G. Great temples without the city.

H M. Remains of edifices outside the walls.
N. River Selinus, now the *Madiuni.*

Selinus are those of three temples on the hill to the E., which do not appear to have been included in the city, but, as was often the case, were built on this neighbouring eminence, so as to front the city itself. All these temples are considerably larger than any of the three above described; and the most northerly of them is one of the largest of which we have any remains. It had 8 columns in front and 17 in the sides, and was of the kind called pseudo-dipteral. Its length was 359 feet, and its breadth 162, so that it was actually longer than the great temple of Jupiter Olympius at Agrigentum, though not equal to it in breadth. From the columns being only partially fluted, as well as from other signs, it is clear that it never was completed; but all the more important parts of the structure were finished, and it must have certainly been one of the most imposing fabrics in antiquity. Only three of the columns are now standing, and these imperfect; but the whole area is filled up with a heap of fallen masses, portions of columns, capitals, &c., and other huge architectural fragments, all of the most massive character, and forming, as observed by Swinburne, "one of the most gigantic and sublime ruins imaginable." The two other temples are also prostrate, but the ruins have fallen with such regularity that the portions of almost every column lie on the ground as they have fallen; and it is not only easy to restore the plan and design of the two edifices, but it appears as if they could be rebuilt with little difficulty. These temples, though greatly inferior to their gigantic neighbour, were still larger than that at Segesta, and even exceed the great temple of Neptune at Paestum; so that the three, when standing, must have presented a spectacle unrivalled in antiquity. All these buildings may be safely referred to a period anterior to the Carthaginian conquest (B. C. 409), though the three temples last described appear to have been all of them of later date than those within the walls of the city. This is proved, among other circumstances, by the sculptured metopes, several of which have been discovered and extricated from among the fallen fragments. Of these sculptures, those which belonged to the temples within the walls, present a very peculiar and archaic style of art, and are universally recognised as among the earliest extant specimens of Greek sculpture. (They are figured by Müller, *Denkmäler,* pl. 4, 5, as well as in many other works, and casts of them are in the British Museum.) Those, on the contrary, which have been found among the ruins of the temple marked E. on the opposite hill, are of a later and more advanced style, though still retaining considerable remains of the stiffness of the earliest art. Besides the interest attached to these Selinuntine metopes from their important bearing on the history of Greek sculpture, the remains of these temples are of value as affording the most unequivocal testimony to the use of painting, both for the architectural decoration of the temples, and as applied to the sculptures with which they were adorned. A very full and detailed account of the ruins at Selinus is given in the Duke of Serra di Falco's *Antichità Siciliane,* vol. ii., from which the preceding plan is derived. A more general description of them will be found in Swinburne's *Travels,* vol. ii. pp. 242—245; Smyth's *Sicily,* pp. 219—221; and other works on Sicily in general.

The coins of Selinus are numerous and various. The earliest, as already mentioned, bear merely the figure of a parsley-leaf on the obverse. Those of somewhat later date (including the one figured below) represent a figure sacrificing on an altar, which is consecrated to Aesculapius, as indicated by the cock which stands below it. The subject of this type evidently refers to a story related by Diogenes Laertius (viii. 2. § 11) that the Selinuntines were afflicted with a pestilence from the marshy character of the lands adjoining the neighbouring river, but that this was cured by works of drainage, suggested by Empedocles. The figure standing on the coin is the river-god Selinus, which was thus made conducive to the salubrity of the city.   [E. H. B.]

COIN OF SELINUS

SELI′NUS (Σελινοῦς: Eth. Σελινοὑντιος or Σελινοὑσιος: Selenti), a port-town on the west coast of Cilicia, at the mouth of a small river of the same name, which is now called Selenti. (Scylax, p. 40; Liv. xxxiii. 20; Strab. xiv. p. 682; Ptol. v. 8. § 2, viii. 17. § 42; Plin. v. 22.) This town is memorable in history as the place where, in A. D. 117, the emperor Trajan is said to have died (Dion Cass. lxviii. 33). After this event the place for a time bore the name of Trajanopolis; but its bishops afterwards are called bishops of Selinus. (Hierocl. p. 709.) Basil of Seleucia (Vita S. Theclae, ii. 17) describes the place as reduced to a state of insignificance in his time, though it had once been a great commercial town. (Comp. Stadiasm. Mar. Mag. §§ 203, 204; Lucan, viii. 260; Chron. Paschale, p. 253.) Selinus was situated on a precipitous rock, surrounded on almost every side by the sea, by which position it was rendered almost impregnable. The whole of the rock, however, was not included in the ancient line of fortifications; inside the walls there still are many traces of houses, but on the outside, and between the foot of the hill and the river, the remains of some large buildings are yet standing, which appear to be a mausoleum, an agora, a theatre, an aqueduct, and some tombs (Beaufort, Karamania, p. 186, foll.)

Respecting the small river Selinus, flowing by Pergamum, see PERGAMUM, p. 575.   [L. S.]

SELLA′SIA (Σελλασία, Xen. Polyb. Diod.; Σελασία, Steph. B., Hesych. s. v.; the latter is perhaps the correct form, and may come from σέλας; the name is connected by Hesychius with Artemis Selasia: Eth. Σελλασιεύς, Σελασιεύς), a town of Laconia, situated in the valley of the Oenus, on the road leading from Tegea and Argos, and one of the bulwarks of Sparta against an invading army. Its distance from Sparta is nowhere mentioned; but from the description which Polybius gives of the celebrated battle fought in its neighbourhood between Antigonus and Cleomenes, it is probable that the plain of Krevatá was the site of the battle. We learn from Polybius that this battle took place in a narrow opening of the vale of the Oenus, between two hills named Evas and Olympus, and that the river Gorgylus flowed across the plain into the Evenus. South of the Khan of

Krevatá is a small plain, the only one in the valley of the Oenus, about ten minutes in width and a quarter of an hour in length, at the end of which the rocks again approach so close as barely to leave room for the passage of the river. The mountain, which bounds this plain on the east, is Olympus, a continuation of the mountain of Vresthéna: it rises very steep on the left bank of the Oenus. The mountain on the western side is Evas, now Túrlaes, which, though not so steep, is still inaccessible to cavalry. Towards the north the plain is shut in by a mountain, over which the road leads to Tegea, and towards the south by a still higher mountain. The Oenus, which flows near the eastern edge of the plain, can be crossed at any point without difficulty. It receives on its right side a small brook, the Gorgylus, which descends from a ravine on the northern side of Mt. Evas. On the summit of the hill, more than 2800 feet above the sea, which shuts in the plain on the south, and over which the road leads to Sparta, are the ruins of Sellasia, described below.

The battle of Sellasia, of which Polybius gives a detailed account, requires a few words of explanation. In B. C. 221, Cleomenes, the Spartan king, expecting that Antigonus, the Macedonian king, and the Achaeans, would invade Laconia, fortified the other passes which led into the country, and took up his own position with the main body of his forces in the plain of Sellasia, since the roads to Sparta from Argos and Tegea united at this point. His army amounted to 20,000 men, and consisted of Lacedaemonians, Perioeci, allies, and mercenaries. His left wing, containing the Perioeci and allies, was stationed on Mt. Evas under the command of his brother Eucleidas; his right wing, consisting of the Lacedaemonians and mercenaries, encamped upon Mt. Olympus under his own command; while his cavalry and a part of the mercenaries occupied the small plain between the hills. The whole line was protected by a ditch and a palisade. Antigonus marched into Laconia from Argos with an army of 30,000 men, but found Cleomenes so strongly intrenched in this position, that he did not venture to attack him, but encamped behind the small stream Gorgylus. At length, after several days' hesitation, both sides determined to join battle. Antigonus placed 5000 Macedonian peltasts, with the greater part of his auxiliary troops, on his right wing to oppose Eucleidas; his cavalry with 1000 Achaeans and the same number of Megalopolitans in the small plain; while he himself with the Macedonian phalanx and 3000 mercenaries occupied the left wing, in order to attack Cleomenes and the Lacedaemonians on Mt. Olympus. The battle began on the side of Mt. Evas. Eucleidas committed the error of awaiting the attack of the enemy upon the brow of the hill, instead of availing himself of his superior position to charge down upon them; but while they were climbing the hill they were attacked upon the rear by some light troops of Cleomenes, who were stationed in the centre with the Lacedaemonian cavalry. At this critical moment, Philopoemen, who was in the centre with the Megalopolitan horse, diverted the attack of the light infantry by charging without orders the Lacedaemonian centre. The right wing of the Macedonians then renewed their attack, defeated the left wing of the Lacedaemonians, and drove them over the steep precipices on the opposite side of Mt. Evas. Cleomenes, perceiving that the only hope of retrieving the day was by the defeat

of the Macedonians opposed to him, led his men out
of the intrenchments and charged the Macedonian
phalanx. The Lacedaemonians fought with great
bravery; but after many vain attempts to break
through the impenetrable mass of the phalanx, they
were entirely defeated, and of 6000 men only 200
are said to have escaped from the field of battle.
Cleomenes, perceiving all was lost, escaped with a
few horsemen to Sparta, and from thence proceeded
to Gythium, where he embarked for Aegypt. Antigonus, thus master of the passes, marched directly
to Sellasia, which he plundered and destroyed, and
then to Sparta, which submitted to him after a
slight resistance. (Polyb. ii. 65—70; Plut. *Cleom.*
27, 28. *Philop.* 6; Paus. ii. 9. § 2, iii. 10. § 7, iv.
29. § 9, vii. 7. § 4, viii. 49. § 5.)

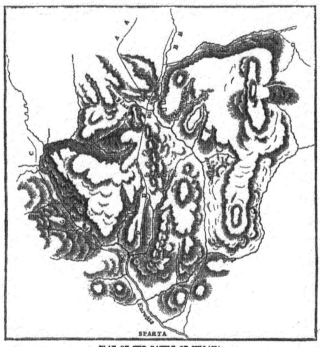

PLAN OF THE BATTLE OF SELLASIA.

a a a. Troops of Cleomenes.	B B. Road to Argos.
b b b. Troops of Antigonus.	C C. Road to Megalopolis.
A A. Road to Tegea.	D D. Road to Sparta.

In the preceding account of the battle we have
followed the excellent description of Ross. (*Reisen
im Peloponnes,* p. 181.) The French Commission
had previously supposed the plain of *Krevatá* to be
the site of the battle of Sellasia (Boblaye, *Recherches, &c.* p. 73); and the same opinion has been
adopted by Curtius. (*Peloponnesos,* vol. ii. p, 260.)
Leake, however, places Sellasia to the SE., near the
monastery of the Forty Saints ("Αγιοι Σαράντα),
and supposes the battle to have been fought in the
pass to the eastward of the monastery. The ruins
near the *Khan of Krevatá* he maintains to be those
of Caryae. (Leake, *Morea,* vol. ii. p. 529, *Peloponnesiaca,* p. 341, seq.) But Ross informs us that
in the narrow pass NE. of the monastery of the
Forty Saints there is barely room for a loaded mule
to pass; and we know moreover that Sellasia was
situated on the high road from Sparta to Tegea and
Argos, which must have led through the plain of
Krevatá. (κατὰ τὴν λεωφόρον, Paus. iii. 10. § 7;
Plut. *Cleom.* 23; Xen. *Hell.* vi. 5. § 27; Diod. xv.
64; Liv. xxxiv. 28.)

On leaving the plain of *Krevatá,* the road southwards ascends the mountain, and at the distance of
a quarter of an hour leaves a small ruin on the left,
called by the peasants *Palaeogúla* (ἡ Παλαιογούλα).
The remains of the walls are Hellenic, but they are
of very small extent, and the place was probably
either a dependency of Sellasia or one to which the
inhabitants of the latter fled for refuge at one of the
periods when their city was destroyed.

The ruins of Sellasia lie 1½ miles beyond *Palaeogúla* upon the summit of the mountain. The city
was about 1½ miles in circumference, as appears

from the foundations of the walls. The latter were from 10 to 11 feet thick, and consist of irregular but very small stones. The northern and smaller half of the city was separated by a wall from the southern half, which was on lower ground.

From its position Sellasia was always exposed to the attacks of an invading army. On the first invasion of Laconia by the Thebans in B. c. 369, Sellasia was plundered and burnt (Xen. *Hell.* vi. 5. § 27); and because the inhabitants at that time, together with several others of the Perioeci, went over to the enemy, the town was again taken and destroyed four years later by the Lacedaemonians themselves, assisted by some auxiliaries sent by the younger Dionysius. (Xen. *Hell.* vii. 4. § 12.) It suffered the same fate a third time after the defeat of Cleomenes, as has been already related. It appears to have been never rebuilt, and was in ruins in the time of Pausanias (iii. 10. § 7).

SELLE'IS (Σελλήεις). 1. A river in Elis, mentioned by Homer, upon which Ephyra stood. [EPHYRA, No. 2.]

2. A river in Sicyonia, upon which Strabo also places a town Ephyra. [EPHYRA, No. 3.]

SELLE'TAE (Plin. iv. 11. s. 18, init.), a people of Thrace, whose country was called SELLETICA (Σελλητική, Ptol. iii. 11. § 8). It was north of the Haemus, between that range of mountains and the Panysus. [J. R.]

SELLE'TICA. [SELLETAE.]

SELLI or HELLI, an ancient tribe in Epeirus, in whose country, called Hellopia, the oracle of Dodona was situated. [DODONA, p. 782, a.]

SE'LLIUM (Σέλιον, Ptol. ii. 5. § 7), a place in Lusitania, lying N. of Scalabis (*Itin. Ant.* p. 421). Identified with *Ceice* or *Seijo.* [T. H. D.]

SELLUS, according to Avienus (*Ora Marit.* 507) a high mountain in Hispania Tarraconensis, on which the city of Lebedontia once stood. Ukert (ii. pt. i. p. 484) identifies it with *C. Salou.* [T. H. D.]

SELY'MBRIA (Σηλυβρίη, Herod. vi. 33; Σηλυ6ρία, Xen. *Anab.* vii. 2. § 15, &c.; Strab. vii. p. 319; Ptol. iii. 11. § 6; Σηλυμβρία, Dem. *de Rhod. lib.* p. 198, Reiske), a Thracian town on the Propontis, 22 miles east from Perinthus, and 44 miles west from Constantinople (*Itin. Hier.* p. 570, where it is called Salamembria), near the southern end of the wall, built by Anastasius Dicorus for the protection of his capital. (Procop. *de Aed.* iv. 9; see SCYL-LAE).

According to Strabo (*l. c.*), its name signifies " the town of Selys;" from which it has been inferred that Selys was the name of its founder, or of the leader of the colony from Megara, which founded it at an earlier period than the establishment of Byzantium, another colony of the same Grecian state. (Scymn. 714.) In honour of Eudoxia, the wife of the emperor Arcadius, its name was changed to Eudoxiupolis (Hierocl. p. 632), which it bore for a considerable time; but its modern name, *Silivri,* shows that it subsequently resumed its original designation.

Respecting the history of Selymbria, only detached and fragmentary notices occur in the Greek writers. In Latin authors, it is merely named (Mela, ii. 2. § 6; Plin. iv. 11. s. 18, xxix. 1. s. 1; in the latter passage it is said to have been the birthplace of Prodicus, a disciple of Hippocrates). It was here that Xenophon met Medosades, the envoy of Seuthes (*Anab.* vii. 2, § 28), whose forces afterwards encamped in its neighbourhood (*Ib.* 5. § 15). When

Alcibiades was commanding for the Athenians in the Propontis (B. c. 410), the people of Selymbria refused to admit his army into the town, but gave him money, probably in order to induce him to abstain from forcing an entrance. (Xen. *Hell.* i. 1. § 21.) Some time after this, however, he gained possession of the place through the treachery of some of the townspeople, and, having levied a contribution upon its inhabitants, left a garrison in it. (*Ib.* 3. § 10; Plut. *Alcib.* 30.) Selymbria is mentioned by Demosthenes (*l. c.*) in B. c. 351, as in alliance with the Athenians; and it was no doubt at that time a member of the Byzantine confederacy. According to a letter of Philip, quoted in the oration *de Corona* (p. 251, R.), it was blockaded by him about B. c. 343; but Professor Newman considers that this mention of Selymbria is one of the numerous proofs that the documents inserted in that speech are not authentic. (*Class. Mus.* vol. i. pp. 153, 154.) [J. R.]

SEMACHIDAE. [ATTICA, p. 330, b.]

SEMA'NA SILVA (Σημανὰ or Σημανοὺς ὕλη), one of the mountain forests of ancient Germany, on the south of Mons Melibocus (Ptol. ii. 1. § 7), is perhaps only a part of the *Hars* mountain or of the *Thüringer Wald.* (Zeuss, *Die Deutschen,* p. 8; Wilhelm, *Germanien,* p. 38, &c.) [L. S.]

SEMANTHINI (Σημανθινοί, Ptol. vii. 3. § 4), a people dwelling in the land of the Sinae E. of the Semanthine mountains, which derived their name from them. [T. H. D.]

SEMANTHINI MONTES (τὸ Σημανθινὸν ὄρος, Ptol. vii. 2. § 8), a mountain chain in the country of the Sinae (*China*), which, according to Ptolemy, extended from the sources of the Aspithra in a NW. direction as far as those of the Serus. It is probably the chain which separates the Chinese province of *Yunnan* from the districts of *Mien* and *Laotschua.* [T. H. D.]

SEMBRITAE (Σεμβρίται, Strab. xvi. pp. 770 —786; SEMBERRITAE, Plin. vi. 30. s. 35), a people inhabiting the district of Tenesis in Aethiopia, although they seem to have been of Aegyptian origin. The first mention of the Sembritae occurs in Eratosthenes (ap. Strab. xvii. p. 786), who says that they occupied an island above Meroë; that their name implies " immigrants;" that they descended from the Aegyptian war-caste, who, in the reign of Psammitichus (B. c. 658), abandoned their native land; and that they were governed by a queen, although they were also dependent on the sovereigns of Meroë. Artemidorus, also quoted by Strabo (xvi. p. 770), says, on the contrary, that they were the ruling order in Meroë: these accounts, however, may be reconciled by the supposition that Eratosthenes and Artemidorus described them at different periods. If the Sembritae were the Aegyptian refugees, they were also the Automoloi ('Ασμάχ) noticed by Herodotus (ii. 30). Pliny (*l. c.*) speaks of four islands of the Sembritae, each containing one or more towns. These were therefore not islands in the Nile, or in any of its principal tributaries, the Astapus, or Astaboras, but tracts between rivers, mesopotamian districts like Meroë itself, which in the language of Nubia are still denominated " islands." The capital of the Sembritae was, according to Pliny, Sembobis. It stood on the left bank of the river, 20 days' journey above Meroë. Pliny names also, among other of their principal towns, Sai in Arabia, — i. e. on the right bank of the Nile, for he assumes that river as the boundary between Lybia and Arabia, — Esar or

Sape (*Sobah*), on the left bank, 17 days' journey above Meroë, and Daron again on the Arabian side.

Without being able to define the position of this tribe, or to state their relations to the Aethiopians of Meroë, we shall perhaps not err in placing them on the Blue Nile [ASTAPUS], and in the neighbourhood of Axume. The geographers (Heeren, &c.) who describe the Sembritae as dwelling near the White Nile, have forgotten both their vicinity to Arabia—i. e. the eastern portion of Meroë—and the character of the regions which the Astapus and Astaboras respectively water. The White Nile flows through lagoons and morasses unsuited for towns and permanent settlements; while the Blue Nile has always had on its banks a numerous population, dwelling in large villages and towns. Along the Blue Nile ran the principal highways of the trade of Aegypt with Southern Aethiopia, while the White Nile led off to the uncivilised and scattered tribes of the Libyans. The Sembritae, if seated on the latter river, would probably have eluded observation altogether; whereas on the former they would be as well known to the caravans and their guides as any other of the Aethiopian races. Moreover, the mesopotamian districts suited to towns lie to the east of Aethiopia Proper, and would afford a secure retreat to the refugees from Aegypt in search of a new habitation. (See Cooley's *Claudius Ptolemy and the Nile*, pp. 7—27.) The present *Senaar* corresponds nearly with the territory of the Sembritae. [W.B.D.]

SEMIRA'MIDIS MONS (Σεμειραμίδος ὄρος), a remarkable circular mountain on the N. side of the Persian gulf, and the eastern limit of Caramania. It is noticed both by Arrian (*Peripl. M. E.* p. 20, ed. Huds.) and by Marcian (*Peripl. M. Ext.* c. 27, ed. Müller, 1855), who states that it was opposite to Mt. Pasabo, in Arabia, and that these two mountains, with their promontories, form the straits at the entrance of the gulf of Persia. Ptolemy speaks of it, and states that it was also called Strongylus, probably from its form (vi. 8. § 11). Its modern name appears to be *Elbourz*. (Vincent, *Voyage of Nearchus*, i. p. 319—321.)   [V.]

SEMNONES (Σέμνωνες or Σέμνονες), or perhaps more correctly Sennones, are described as the most ancient and illustrious among the Suevi in the north of Germany. They dwelt between the Albis and Viadus, being surrounded on the west by the Cherusci, on the south by the Silingi, on the east by the Manimi and Burgundiones, and on the north-west by the Longobardi. (Tac. *Germ.* 39; Ptol. ii. 11. §§ 15, 17; Vell. Pat. ii. 106.) Their country accordingly extended from the hills of *Lusatia* in the south, as far as *Potsdam* in the north, and in it they formed 100 communities (*pagi*), which gave them such strength that they regarded themselves as the head of the Suevi. Their country contained an ancient forest (Semnonum Silva), hallowed by awful superstition and sacrificial rites; at stated seasons deputies from all the kindred tribes met in it, and commenced their proceedings with a human sacrifice. No one, moreover, was allowed to enter this forest except he was bound in chains, a mark of humiliation in the presence of the god; and if any one stumbled he was not permitted to rise, but had to crawl along. As to the history of the Semnones, we learn from Tacitus (*Ann.* ii. 45) and Strabo (vii. p. 290) that in the time of Augustus they were united with the Marcomanni under Maroboduus. In the Monumentum Ancyranum the Semnones, are mentioned

among the German tribes which sought the friendship of the emperor and the Romans. They appear to have been governed by kings, one of whom bore the name of Masyus, and reigned in the time of Domitian. (Dion Cass. lxvii. 5, comp. lxxi. 20.) After the reign of M. Aurelius they are no longer mentioned in history, from which circumstance some have unnecessarily inferred that the Semnones were not a distinct tribe, but only a general name for several kindred tribes. As to the Silva Semnonum, it is generally supposed to have existed near *Finsterwalde* or *Sonnenwalde*, between the rivers *Elster* and *Spree*, where three large places have been discovered, which were evidently intended as a sort of altars. (Kruse, *Deutsche Alterth.* vol. ii. part 2, p. 132; Zeuss, *Die Deutschen*, p. 130.) [L.S.]

SENA (Σήνη, Pol.: Σήνα, Strab.: *Eth.* Senensis), called also for distinction's sake SENA GALLICA (Σεναγάλλικα, Ptol.: *Sinigaglia*), a city of Umbria, but situated in the district known as the Gallicus Ager, on the coast of the Adriatic, at the mouth of a small river of the same name. The district in which it was situated had previously belonged to the Galli Senones, and there can be no doubt that both the river and town derived their name from that of this people. (Sil. Ital. viii. 453; Pol. ii. 19.) It is therefore probable that there was a Gaulish town of the name before the Roman conquest, but we have no account of it until the establishment of a Roman colony there, which seems to have taken place immediately after the final subjection of the Senones in B. c. 289. (Pol. ii. 19; Liv. *Epit.* xi.) The colony must have been a "colonia civium," as its name is not mentioned by Livy among the Latin colonies in the Second Punic War. It was at Sena that the two consuls Livius and Nero united their forces before the battle of the Metaurus, B. c. 207 (Liv. xxvii. 46; Appian, *Annib.* 52; Vict. *Vir. Ill.* 48), on which account that battle is described by some authors as being fought "ad Senam," and even Cicero alludes to it as the "Senense praelium." (Cic. *Brut.* 18; Eutrop. iii. 18; Oros. iv. 18.) Its name is not again mentioned in history till the Civil Wars between Marius and Sulla, when it was taken and plundered by Pompeius, the lieutenant of Sulla, B. c. 82. (Appian, *B. C.* i. 88.) It seems to have always continued to be a flourishing and considerable town, and under the Triumvirate received a fresh accession of colonists. (*Lib. Col.* pp. 226, 258.) Its name is mentioned by all the geographers, as well as in the Itineraries. It was situated on the line of road which led along the coast from Ancona to Fanum Fortunae, where it joined the Flaminian Way, properly so called. (Strab. v. p. 227; Plin. iii. 14. s. 19; Ptol. iii. 1. § 22; *Itin. Ant.* pp. 100, 316; *Tab. Peut.*) The name was early corrupted from Sena Gallica into the contracted form Senogallia, which is already found in Pliny, and appears also in the Itineraries. The Geographer of Ravenna has Senegallia, thus approaching still more closely to the modern form of *Sinigaglia.* The city is mentioned as still in existence during the Gothic Wars, after the fall of the Western Empire, and again under the Lombards (Procop. *B. G.* iv. 23; P. Diac. *Hist. Lang.* ii. 22); it was for some time also one of the cities of the Pentapolis under the exarchs of Ravenna, but fell into decay in the middle ages, and is alluded to by Dante in the 14th century as verging rapidly to extinction. (Dante, *Par.* xvi. 75.) It, however, revived again, and is now a flourishing town, with a considerable trade, but has no ancient remains.

The river Sena, alluded to by Silius Italicus and Lucan, must be the small stream now called the *Nevola* or *Nigola*, which falls into the sea at *Sinigaglia*. (Sil. Ital. viii. 453; Lucan, ii. 407.)　　[E. H. B.]

SENA (Σαῖνα, Ptol.: *Eth.* Senensis: *Siena*), a city of Etruria, sometimes called SENA JULIA, to distinguish it from the city of the same name on the Adriatic. It was situated nearly in the heart of Etruria, about 28 miles E. of Volaterrae and 40 S. of Florentia. There is no reason whatever to suppose that there was an Etruscan city on the site, and no allusion to its existence occurs before the establishment of the Roman colony. Even the date of this is not accurately known; but it is probable from the epithet of Julia that it was founded either by Caesar himself or by the Triumvirate in his honour. It is singular that its name is not found in the Liber Coloniarum; but its colonial rank is attested by Pliny, who calls it " colonia Senensis," as well as by Tacitus. (Plin. iii. 5. s. 8; Tac. *Hist.* iv. 45.) It is subsequently mentioned by Ptolemy, as well as in the Tabula, which places it on a line of road from Florentia to Clusium. (Ptol. iii. 1. § 49; *Tab. Peut.*) But it seems never to have been a place of much importance in ancient times, and it was not till the middle ages that it rose to be one of the first cities of Tuscany. It has no remains of antiquity. (Dennis's *Etruria*, vol. ii. p. 135.)　　[E. H. B.]

SENA INSULA, in Gallia. On this island, which was opposite to the coast of the Osismii, was an oracle of a Gallic goddess. Nine virgins named Gallicenae (Barrigenae, ed. I. Vossius) had the care of the oracle. They could raise storms by their verses, change themselves into beasts, heal diseases, and foretell the future, but they were only propitious to seamen who came to consult them. (Mela, iii. 6.) This is the island of *Sein*, incorrectly called on the maps *Isle des Saints*, which is at the entrance of the bay of *Douarnenez*, and separated from a point of land on the coast of Britany (*Pointe Raz*) by a narrow channel. D'Anville supposes that this may be the island which Strabo places opposite the mouth of the *Loire*. This island was inhabited only by women who were possessed by Dionysus. They allowed no man to enter their island; but so far from keeping their virginity, they used to visit the men on the mainland. These two stories are very different. Strabo names his island that of the Namnites, as Groskurd (*Strab. Transl.* i. p. 198) has it; but the name is Samnites in the common texts of Strabo. This seems to be the same island that Dionysius speaks of (*Perieg.* 571) as being visited by the women of the Amnitae for the purpose of performing the rites of Bacchus. D'Anville further thinks that Pliny (iv. 16) may be speaking of Sena when he mentions after the islands which are near to Britain, Siambis, or Amnis, as some MSS. have it, and Axantos, which is evidently Uxantis or *Ouessant.* Sina, as the Maritime Itin. names it, is mentioned there with Uxantis.　　[G. L.]

SENIA (Σενία, Ptol. ii. 16. (17.) § 2), a Roman colony on the coast of Liburnia (" Colonia Senensis," Tac. *H.* iv. 45), and on the road from Aquileia to Siscia. (*Itin. Ant.* p. 273.) It had a harbour. (Comp. Plin. iii. 21. s. 25; Geogr. Rav. iv. 31; *Tab. Peut.*) Variously identified with *Zeng* or *Senga.*　　[T. H. D.]

SENOMAGUS, in Gallia Narbonensis, is mentioned in the Table, and placed north of Avenio (*Avignon*), on a road along the east side of the

Rhone. Some geographers guess that it may be near the *Pont St. Esprit.*　　[G. L.]

SE'NONES (Σένονες, Σέννονες, Steph. B. *s. v.*). Polybius (ii. 17) names the Italian Senones, Σήνωνες. The Roman poets make the penultima short:—

" Ut Braccatorum pueri Senonumque minores."
(Juv. viii. 234.)

An absurd explanation of the name is quoted by Festus (*s. v. Senones*) and by Servius (*ad Aen.* viii. 656).

The Senones were one of the great Celtic nations who bordered on the Belgae. (Caes. *B. G.* ii. 2.) They were north-west of the Aedui and bordered on them. Their capital was Agedincum (*Sens*), on the right bank of the *Yonne*, which is a branch of the *Seine.* (Ptol. ii. 8. § 12.) The Senones are in the Lugdunensis of Ptolemy and Pliny. Besides Agedincum there were in the country of the Senones, Autissiodurum (*Auxerre*) and Melodunum (*Melun*) on the *Seine* not far from Paris, which shows that their territory extended from the neighbourhood of *Paris* along the *Seine* and along the *Yonne* to the borders of the small nation of the Mandubii [MANDUBII], whose town was Alesia, and to the borders of the Lingones. The railroad from *Paris* to *Dijon*, which passes near *Melun, Fontainebleau, Sens, Joigny, St. Florentin, Tonnerre* on the *Armançon*, a branch of the *Yonne*, runs through the country of the Senones. Between *St. Florentin* and *Flogny*, which is about half-way between *St. Florentin* and *Tonnerre*, extends a vast plain, level as the sea, fertile, and in summer covered with wheat. A large part of the territory of the Senones is a fertile country. In seems to have comprehended the dioceses of *Sens* and *Auxerre.* Besides Melodunum and Agedincum, Caesar mentions Vellaunodunum as a town of the Senones (vii. 11), on the side towards the Carnutes.

The Senones were at first well disposed to Caesar (*B. G.* ii. 2), probably through fear of their neighbours, the Belgae and the German people north of the *Marne.* Caesar had given them Cavarinus for a king, but the Senones expelled him (v. 54); and when the Roman proconsul ordered the senate of the Senones to come to him, they refused. In the spring of B. C. 53 Caesar summoned the states of Gallia to a meeting, but the Senones, Carnutes, and Treviri would not come (vi. 3), upon which he transferred the meeting of the states to Lutetia Parisiorum. He says that the Parisii bordered on the Senones, and " within the memory of their fathers they had united their state with that of the Senones; " but he does not explain the nature of this union. He marched from Lutetia (*Paris*) into the country of the Senones, which presents no difficulties for an army. The Senones yielded in spite of Acco, who was the leader in the revolt; and Caesar took with him Cavarinus and the cavalry of the Senones, in which force it is probable that they were strong, as their country is well adapted for grazing and corn. At the close of the year Caesar whipped Acco to death, and quartered six of his legions at *Sens* for the winter (vi. 44). In B. C. 52 the Senones sent 12,000 men with the rest of the Gallic forces to attack Caesar before Alesia (vii. 75). The Senones seem to have given Caesar no more trouble; but in B. C. 51 Drappes, a Senon, at the head of a number of desperate men, was threatening the Provincia. Drappes was caught and starved himself to death. (*B. G.* viii. 30, 44.) [G.L.]

SENONES (Σήνωνες), a nation of Gaulish origin, which was settled in Italy, on the coast of the Adriatic, extending from the river Aesis (*Esino*), a few miles N. of Ancona, to the Utis (*Montone*). (Liv. v. 35.) The history of their migration from Transalpine Gaul, their settlement in Italy, and their wars with the Romans, which ended in the extermination of the whole nation, are fully related under the article GALLIA CISALPINA (pp. 936— 938). After the conquest of the Senones, and their expulsion from their lands on the Adriatic, two colonies were founded in their territory, the one at Sena, the other at Ariminum; and at a later period the remainder of their lands was portioned out among the Roman citizens by an agrarian law of the tribune C. Flaminius. This district, which still retained the name of the "Gallicus ager," was afterwards considered as a part of Umbria, and included for all administrative purposes under that appellation. Its topography will therefore be most conveniently given in the article UMBRIA. [E. H. B.]

SE'NTICE (Σεντική, Ptol. ii. 6. § 50), a town of the Vaccaei in Hispania Tarraconensis, variously identified with *Los Santos, Zamora, Calzadilla de Mandiges*, and *Zarzosa*. [T. H. D.]

SE'NTIDES (Σέντιδες, Ptol. iv. 5. § 21), a people in the S. of Marmarica. [T. H. D.]

SE'NTII (Σέντιοι), a people of Gallia Narbonensis (Ptol. ii. 10. § 19), whose town Ptolemy names Dinia, which is *Digne*. [DINIA.] [G. L.]

SENTI'NUM (Σεντινον: Eth. Σεντινάτης, Sentinas -atis: *Sentino*), a city of Umbria, on the E. slope of the Apennines, but near the central ridge of those mountains, and not far from the sources of the Aesis (*Esino*). It is celebrated in history as the scene of a great battle fought in the Third Samnite War, B. C. 295, when the allied forces of the Samnites and Gauls were defeated by the Roman consul Q. Fabius. Gellius Egnatius, the Samnite general, was slain in the battle; while the Roman consul P. Decius followed the example of his father, and devoted himself for the safety of the Roman army. (Liv. x. 27 —30; Pol. ii. 19.) The scene of this decisive victory, one of the most memorable in the Roman annals, is placed by Livy "in Sentinati agro;" but we have no more precise clue to its position, nor do the details of the battle give us any assistance. Sentinum itself seems to have been a strong town, as in the Perusian War it was besieged by Octavian himself without success; though it was afterwards taken by surprise by his lieutenant, Salvidienus Rufus, by whom it was plundered and burnt to the ground. (Dion Cass. xlviii. 13.) It was subsequently revived, by receiving a body of colonists, under the Triumvirate (*Lib. Col.* p. 258), but did not obtain the title of a Colonia, and continued under the Roman Empire to be a town of municipal rank. (Plin. iii. 14. s. 19; Strab. v. p. 227; Ptol. iii. 1. § 53; Orell. *Inscr.* 3861, 4949.) Its site is marked by the village still called *Sentino*, on the river of the same name (a small stream falling into the *Esino*), a few miles below the modern town of *Sasso Ferrato*. [E. H. B.]

SENUS (Σίνος or Σαῖνος, Ptol. vii. 3. § 2), a river in the land of the Sinae (*China*) which ran into the Sinus Magnus between the *South-horn Cape* (Νότιον κέρας), S. of Ambastus, and Rabana. Probably the modern *Saigon* or *Saung*. (Comp. Forbiger, *Geogr.* ii. p. 478.) [T. H. D.]

SENUS (Σῆνος, Ptol. ii. 2. § 4), a river on the W. coast of Hibernia, in the territory of the Auteri. Camden identifies it with the *Shannon*. [T. H. D.]

SEPELACI, a town of the Edetani in Hispania Tarraconensis (*Itin.Ant.* p. 400), identified with *Burriana, Onda*, or *Castellon de la Plana*. [T. H. D.]

SE'PIA. [PHENEUS, p. 595, a.]

SE'PIAS (Σηπιάς), a promontory of Magnesia, opposite the island of Sciathos, and forming the SE. extremity of Thessaly. It is now called *C. St. George*. It is celebrated in mythology as the spot where Peleus laid in wait for Thetis, and from whence he carried off the goddess (Eurip. *Androm.* 1266), and in history as the scene of the great shipwreck of the fleet of Xerxes. (Herod. vii. 113, 188; Strab. ix. p. 443; Apoll. Rhod. i. 580; Ptol. iii. 13. § 16; Plin. iv. 9. s. 16; Mela, ii. 3; Leake, *Northern Greece*, vol. iv. p. 382.)

SEPONTIA PARAMICA (Σεπόντια Παράμικα, Ptol. ii. 6. § 50), a town of the Vaccaei in Hispania Tarraconensis lying to the W. of Lacobriga (or the modern *Lobera*). [T. H. D.]

SEPPHORIS (Σεπφώρις, al. Σέφφορις: Eth. Σεπφωρίτης), a town of Upper Galilee, not mentioned under this name in Scripture, but frequently by Josephus. It was garrisoned by Antigonus, in his war with Herod the Great, until the latter took it, early in his Galilean campaign (*Ant.* xiv. 15. § 4.) It seems to have been a place of arms, and to have been occasionally the royal residence, for in the troubles which arose in the country during the presidency of Varus, the robber-chief Judas, son of Ezekias, seized the palace of Sepphoris, and carried off the arms and treasure which it contained (xvii. 12. § 5). It was subsequently taken and burned by Varus (§ 9). Herod the tetrarch (Antipas) afterwards rebuilt and fortified it, and made it the glory of all Galilee, and gave it independence (xviii. 2. § 1); although, according to the statement of Justus the son of Pistus, he still maintained the superiority of his newly founded city Tiberias; and it was not until Nero had assigned Tiberias to Agrippa the Younger that Sepphoris established its supremacy, and became the royal residence and depository of the archives. It is termed the strongest city of Galilee, and was early taken by Gallus, the general of Cestius. (*B. J.* ii. 18. § 11.) It maintained its allegiance to the Romans after the general revolt of Galilee (*Ib.* iii. 2. § 4, 4. § 1), but did not break with the Jewish leaders. (*Vita*, 8, 9.) Its early importance as a Jewish town, attested by the fact that it was one of the five cities in which district sanhedrims were instituted by Gabinius (*B. J.* i. 8. § 5), was further confirmed by the destruction of Jerusalem, after which catastrophe it became for some years the seat of the Great Sanhedrim, until it was transferred to Tiberias. (Robinson, *Bibl. Res.* vol. iii. p. 202.) It was subsequently called Diocaesareia, which is its more common appellation in the ecclesiastical annals; while Epiphanius and S. Jerome recognise both names. A revolt of the Jewish inhabitants, in the reign of Constantius (A. D. 339), led to the destruction of the city by Constantius Gallus Caesar. (Socrates, *H. E.* ii. 33; Sozomen, *H. E.* iv. 7.) This town, once the most considerable city of Galilee, was situated according to S. Jerome 10 miles west of Mount Tabor. (*Onomast. s. v.* Θαβώρ; Procopius Gazaeus, *Comment. in Lib. Judicum*.) It was much celebrated in the history of the Crusaders, for its fountain — a favourite camping place of the Christians. It is still represented by a poor village bearing the name *Sephurieh*, distant about 5 miles to the north of Nazareth, retaining no vestiges of its former greatness, but conspicuous with a ruined tower and church, both of the middle ages; the latter professing to mark the site of the birthplace of the Virgin Mary, assigned by a late tradition to this locality. It became the see of a suffragan bishop, under the metropolitan of Scythopolis (Le Quien, *Oriens Christianus*, vol. iii. pp. 713, 714), and there are coins still extant of the reigns of Domitian, Trajan, &c. (Reland, *Palaestina*, pp. 199 —1003; Eckhel, *Doct. Vet. Num.* vol. iii. pp. 425, 426.)   [G. W.]

SEPTEM AQUAE. [REATE.]

SEPTEM ARAE, a place in Lusitania (*Itin. Ant.* pp. 419, 420). Variously identified with *Codesera* and *Arronches*.   [T. H. D.]

SEPTEM FRATRES ('Επτάδελφοι ὄρος, Ptol. iv. 1. § 5), a group of mountains in the northernmost part of Mauritania Tingitana, connected by a tongue of land with the promontory of Abyla (now *Ximiera* near *Ceuta*), and thus on the narrowest part of the Fretum Gaditanum (Plin. v. 1. s. 1; Solin. c. 28; Strab. xvii. p. 827.) One of these mountains, now called the *Ape Mountains* (Graberg Von Hemsö, *Empire of Morocco*, Germ. Tr. p. 24), bore, according to Strabo (*l.c.*) the name of the Elephant ('Ελέφας), probably from the number of elephants which were to be found there. (Plin. *l.c.*; Mart. Cap. vi. p. 216.) The Geogr. Rav. (iii. 11) also mentions in this neighbourhood a town called Septem Fratres, which is perhaps the same place mentioned in the Itin. Ant. (p. 9) as a station between Tingis and Abyle. Procopius also (*B. Vand.* i. 1; comp. ii. 5, and *de Aed.* vi. 7) mentions here a castle or fortress called Σέπτον; and Isidore (*Orig.* xv. 1) a castle and town called Septa, perhaps the modern *Ceuta*. (Comp. Mela, i. 5. § 5, et ibi Tzschucke.)   [T. H. D.]

SEPTEM MARIA ('Επτὰ πελάγη), was the name commonly given to the extensive lagunes at the mouth of the Padus, and the adjoining rivers, and which extend along a considerable part of the shores of the Adriatic from the mouths of the Padus to Altinum. Pliny indeed seems to use the term in a more restricted sense, as he speaks of "Atrianorum paludes, quae Septem Maria appellantur" (iii. 16. s. 20); but the Itinerary distinctly applies the name to the whole extent of the lagunes from Ravenna to Altinum (*Itin. Ant.* p. 126); and Herodian, who notices them particularly (viii. 7), clearly uses the term in the same sense.   [E. H. B.]

SEPTEM PAGI ('Επτὰ Πάγοι), was the name given to a district close to Rome, but on the right bank of the Tiber, which according to tradition had originally formed part of the territory of the Veientes, but was ceded by them to the Romans as early as the reign of Romulus. (Dionys. ii. 55; Plut. *Rom.* 25.) According to the authorities followed by Dionysius it was again surrendered to the Etruscans by the treaty concluded with Porsena, but was shortly after restored by that monarch to the Romans. (Dionys. v. 31, 36.) Livy mentions the same circumstances, but without giving the name of the district. (Liv. ii. 13, 15.) It is evident, however, that this was a well-known appellation, but we are unable to fix its boundaries more definitely.   [E. H. B.]

SEPTE'MPEDA (Σεπτέμπεδα, Strab., Ptol.: *Eth.* Septempedanus: *San Severino*), a town of Picenum, in the upper valley of the Potentia, 9 miles above Treia. It is mentioned by all the geographers, and the "ager Septempedanus" is noticed in the Liber Coloniarum. (Plin. iii. 13. s. 18; Strab. v. p. 241; Ptol. iii. 1. § 52; *Lib. Col.* p. 258.) Pliny assigns it the rank of a municipal town, and this is confirmed by inscriptions, one of which is of the age of Aurelian.

(Orell. *Inscr.* 1026; Gruter, *Inscr.* p. 308. 3.) It is placed by the Itinerary of Antoninus on that branch of the Flaminian Way which, quitting the main high road at Nuceria, crossed the Apennines to Prolaqueum and thence descended the valley of the Potentia by Septempeda and Treia to Auximum and Ancona. (*Itin. Ant.* p. 312.) It early became an episcopal see, and derives its modern name of *San Severino* from one of its bishops who flourished in the middle ages. It still retains its rank as an episcopal city, and is the capital of the surrounding city, though it has not more than 3000 inhabitants. (Rampoldi, *Dizion. Corogr.* vol. iii. p. 837.)   [E. H. B.]

SEPTIMANCA, a town of the Vaccaei in Hispania Tarraconensis (*Itin. Ant.* p. 435). Now *Simancas*.   [T. H. D.]

SEPULCHRUM EURIPIDIS (Amm. Marc. xxvii. 4. § 8; comp. Gell. xv. 20; Plut. *Lycurg.* 36; Vitruv. viii. 3; Plin. xxxi. 19; *Itin. Hierosol.*), the remarkable monument erected to Euripides in Macedonia, at the narrow gorge of Aulon or Arethusa (*Besikia* or *Rumili Bóghazi*), where the mountains close upon the road. The ancients (Vitruvius, *l. c.*; Plin. *l. c.*) placed it at the confluence of two streams, of which the water of one was poisonous, the other so sweet and health-giving that travellers were wont to halt and take their meals by its currents. In the Jerusalem Itinerary, a document as late as the 13th century, it occurs as a station between Pennana and Apollonia. (Comp. Clarke's *Travels*, vol. viii. pp. 9—13.)   [E. B. J.]

SE'QUANA (Σηκουάνας, Σηκοάνας, Ptol. ii. 8. § 2), the *Seine*, one of the large rivers of Gallia. The *Seine* rises in the highlands south of *Langres*, but in the department of *Côte d'Or*, and flows in a northwest direction past *Châtillon-sur-Seine*, *Troyes*, *Melun*, *Paris*, *Mantes*, *Elboeuf*, *Rouen*, and *Le Havre*. It enters the Atlantic below *Le Havre*. The course of the *Seine* is about 470 miles, and the area of its basin is about 26,000 English square miles, which is only one half of the area of the basin of the *Loire*. The chief branches of the *Seine* which join it on the right bank are the *Aube*, the *Marne*, and the *Oise*; on the left bank, the *Yonne*, the *Loing*, and the *Eure*. None of the hills which bound the basin of the *Seine*, or are contained within it, have a great elevation, and a large part of the country included within this basin is level.

Caesar (*B. G.* i. 1) makes the Sequana and the Matrona (*Marne*) the boundary between the Celtae and the Belgae. Strabo (iv. p. 192) says that the Sequana rises in the Alps, a statement which we must not altogether impute to an erroneous notion of the position of the river's source, though his knowledge of Gallia was in many respects inaccurate, but to the fact that he extended the name of Alps far beyond the proper limits of those mountains. But his inaccuracy is proved by his saying that the Sequana flows parallel to the Rhine, and through the country of the Sequani. He is more correct in fixing its outlet in the country of the Caleti and the Lexovii. The *Seine* was navigated in the time of Strabo and much earlier. [GALLIA TRANSALPINA, Vol. I.]

The Mátrona, as Ausonius names it (*Mosella*, v. 462),—

"Matrona non Gallos Belgasque intersita fines," —

joins the *Seine* a few miles above *Paris;* it is the largest of the affluents of the *Seine*.

Ammianus Marcellinus (xv. 11) says that the

united streams of the Sequana and Matrona entered the sea near Castra Constantia (*Coutances*), which is a great mistake. In the cosmography of Aethicus the Sequana is named Geon or Geobonna.   [G. L.]

SE′QUANI (Σηκουανοί), a Celtic nation in the upper valley of the Arar or *Saône*. Lucan (i. 425) follows the quantity of the Greek form: —

" Optima gens flexis in gyrum Sequana fraenis."

Caesar fixes the position of the Sequani. Their territory extended to the Rhine. (*B. G.* i. 1.) The Jura separated them on the east from the Helvetii; and the narrow pass between the Jura and the Rhone at *Fort l'Ecluse* was in the possession of the Sequani (*B. G.* i. 6, 8). The southern boundary of their territory from *Fort l'Ecluse* was the *Rhone*; but they did not possess all the country in the angle between the *Rhone* and the *Saône*, for part of it was held by the Allobroges (*B. G.* i. 12), and part by the Segusiani (*B. G.* i. 10) and by the Ambarri, who were dependent on the Aedui (*B. G.* i. 11). When Caesar describes the march of the Helvetii from *Fort l'Ecluse* to the *Saône*, he says that the Helvetii first passed through the territory of the Sequani, and then entered the territory of the Aedui, which they plundered. But they had not yet reached the *Saône*, as Caesar's narrative shows, and it is clear from this passage (*B. G.* i. 11) and those already cited, that a large tract of country between the *Rhone* and *Saône* did not belong to the Sequani, for the line of march of the Helvetii from *Fort l'Ecluse* to the *Saône* would probably bring them to the *Saône* at a point not much lower down than *Mâcon*. The western boundary of the Sequani was the Arar, also called the Sauconna, a name which appears to be the same as the name of the Sequani. Their neighbours on the west side of the *Saône* were the Aedui, with whom the Sequani had disputes about the river tolls (Strab. iv. p.192). On the north their neighbours were the Leuci and Lingones. Strabo (iv. p. 186) describes the Arar and Dubis (*Doubs*) as flowing through the country of the Sequani. D'Anville has an argument to show that the part of the dioceses of *Châlon-sur-Saône* and *Mâcon* which is east of the *Saône* belonged to the old territory of the Sequani, which may be true; but the towns Matisco (*Mâcon*) and Cabillonum (*Châlon*) were on the west side of the *Saône* and in the territory of the Aedui (*B. G.* vii. 90).

In another passage besides that already referred to, Caesar shows that the Sequani extended to the Rhine, for in describing the course of this river from south to north, he says that it passes by the territory of the Helvetii, Sequani, Mediomatrici and Tribocci. (*B. G.* iv. 10.)

The Sequani belonged to the division of Belgica under the Empire (Plin. iv. 17; Ptol. ii. 9. § 21). The territory of the Sequani contained much good land, some of the best in Gallia. Their chief town was Vesontio (*Besançon*) on the *Doubs*, and they had other towns also. They fed hogs, and their hams and bacon were exported to Rome as Strabo (iv. p.192) says; and Varro (*de R.R.* ii. 4) may mean to say the same, when he speaks of Gallic bacon.

The Sequani had kings, sometimes at least; for Gallic kings were not perpetual. (*B. G.* i. 3.) Before Caesar went into Gallia, the Arverni and Aedui had been the two most powerful peoples. The Sequani were in league with the Arverni, who occupied the centre of all Gallia, but hostile to their neighbours the Aedui. To maintain themselves against the

Aedui, the Arverni and Sequani hired Germans to come over the Rhine. The Germans came in great numbers, and in Caesar's time it was computed that there were 120,000 of them in Gallia. This is the first historical notice of a permanent settlement of Germans in these parts. The Sequani with the assistance of their allies defeated and humbled the Aedui, but they gained nothing by this victory. Ariovistus, the king of these German mercenaries, took from the Sequani a third part of their lands, and was threatening to take a second third, when Caesar drove the Germans into the Rhine, after defeating them near that river. If the Germans were all destroyed or driven away from the territory of the Sequani by Caesar, they came again, for the country on the west bank of the Rhine, which belonged to the Sequani, the *Upper Alsace*, has been German for many centuries.

In B. C. 52, the Sequani were among the nations who sent their contingent to attack Caesar before Alesia.   [G. L.]

SERA (Σῆρα, Ptol. i. 11. § 1, 17, § 5, vi. 13. § 1, 16. § 8, viii. 24. § 8), the capital of the country of Serica, and one of the chief commercial towns of the Seres. It was the remotest point of Eastern Asia with which the ancients had any commerce, or of which they possessed any knowledge. It was situated on the mountain Ottorocorras at the eastern source of the Bautisus. . Mannert (iv. p. 501) identifies it either with *Singan* in the province of *Schensi*, or with *Honan* on the *Hoang-ho*; but according to Heeren (*Ideen*, i. 2. p. 668) it is *Pekin* itself.   [T. H. D.]

SERACA (Σεράκα, Ptol. v. 9. § 28), a town in the S. of Asiatic Sarmatia.   [T. H. D.]

SERANUSA, perhaps more correctly Seramusa, a town of the interior of Pontus Polemoniacus, on the south-east of Comana Pontica. (*Tab. Peut.*; Ptol. v. 6. § 9, where it is written Σέμνουτα or Σέρμουντα.)   [L. S.]

SERAPIUM (*It. Anton.* p. 170; Serapiu, *Tab. Peut.*), a large village seated near the junction of the canal of the Ptolemies with the Bitter Lakes, east of the Delta. Serapium was 18 miles distant from Heroopolis and 50 from Clysma, at the top of the Sinus Heroopolites. Its temple of Serapis, and its position on the canal that connected the Nile with the Red Sea, rendered it a place of considerable traffic. It was probably founded, or at least enlarged, by the Ptolemies after Philadelphus (B. C. 274) had extended the canal to the Bitter Lakes.   [W. B. D.]

SERBES (Σέρβητος ἐκβολαί, Ptol. iv. 2. § 7), a small river on the N. coast of Mauritania, which fell into the sea to the W. of Rusuccurum; either the present *Massafran*, or, more probably, the *Isser*.   [T. H. D.]

SERBI or SIRBI (Σέρβοι or Σίρβοι, Ptol. v. 9. § 21), a people in Asiatic Sarmatia, according to Ptolemy (*l. c.*) between the Ceraunian mountains and the river Rha, above the Diduri and below the Vali. Pliny, however (vi. 7. s. 7), places them on the E. shore of the Maeotis, between the Vali and the Arrechi. (Comp. Schaffarik, *Slav. Alterth.* i. p. 165.)   [T. H. D.]

SERBO′NIS LACUS. [SIRBONIS LACUS.]

SE′RDICA or SA′RDICA (Σαρδική, Ptol. iii. 11. § 12) (the first of these forms is the more usual with the Romans, the latter with the Greeks), a considerable town of Upper Moesia, which in earlier times was regarded as belonging to Thrace (Ptol. *l.c.*), but which in the third century was attributed to Dacia Inferior, and made its capital. (Theodoret. *Hist. Eccl.* ii. 4.) It lay in a fruitful plain, at the spot where the sources of the Oescus united, and on the high-road from Naissus to Philippopolis, between Meldia and Burburaca. (*Itin. Ant.* p. 135; *Itin. Hierosol.* p. 567.) From the time of Aurelian it bore on its coins the surname of Ulpia; probably because, when Dacia was relinquished, the name of that Dacian town was transferred to it, and its inhabitants, perhaps, located there. The emperor Maximian was born in its neighbourhood. (Eutrop. ix. 14, 22.) It was destroyed by Attila (Priscus, *de Legat.* p. 49), but shortly afterwards restored. In the middle ages it occurs under the name of Triaditza (Τριάδιτζα, Niceph. *Chron. Ann. Is. Angeli*, iii. p. 214; Aposp. Geogr. in Hudson, iv. p. 43), which was perhaps its original Thracian appellation, and which is still retained in the dialect of the inhabitants. (See Wesseling, *ad Itin. Ant. l. c.*) Its extensive ruins lie to the S. of Sophia. (Comp. Procop. *de Aed.* iv. 1. p. 267, 4. p. 282; Hierocl. p. 654; Amm. Marc. xxxi. 16; Gruter, *Inscr.* p. 540. 2; Orelli, nos. 3548, 5013.) The Geogr. Rav. (iv. 7) incorrectly writes the name Sertica, since it was derived from the Thracian tribe of the Serdi. It is called by Athanasius (*Apol. contra Arianos*, p. 154) Σαρδῶν πόλις.   [T. H. D.]

SERE'NA, a town in Lower Pannonia, on the south bank of the Danube, on the road from Poetovium to Mursa. (*It. Hieros.* p. 562; Geog. Rav. iv. 19, where it is called Serenis; *Tab. Peut.*, where its name is Serona.) It is thought to have occupied the site of the modern *Moszlavina*   [L. S.]

SERES. [SERICA.]

SERE'TIUM (Σερέτιον, Dion Cass. lvi. 12), a fortified town of Dalmatia, which with Rhaetinus was captured by Germanicus in the campaign of A. D. 7.   [E. B. J.]

SERGU'NTIA (Σεργουντία, Strab. iii. p. 162), a small town of the Arevaci on the Durius, in Hispania Tarraconensis. Ukert (ii. pt. i. p. 455) takes it to have been the Σάργανθα of Stephanus B. (*s. v.*)   [T. H. D.]

SE'RIA (Σέρια, Ptol. ii. 4. § 12), a town of the Turdetani in Hispania Baetica, with the surname of Fama Julia. (Plin. iii. 1. s. 3.) It lay E. of the mouth of the Anas, and N. of the Baetis. [T.H.D.]

SERIA'NE, a city of Syria mentioned in the Itinerary of Antoninus as xviii. M. P. distant from Androna, which was xxvii. M.P. from Calcis, cxxxviii. M.P. from Dolicha, now *Doluc.* (*Itin. Ant.* pp. 194, 195.) Mannert thinks that it corresponds in situation with the Chalybon (Χαλυβών) of Ptolemy (v. 15. § 17), which gave its name to a district of Syria Chalybonitis. It is certainly identical with the modern *Siria*, 2 long days SE. of *Aleppo*, in the desert, the ruins of which were discovered and described by Pietro della Valle. (Mannert, *Geographie*, part vi. vol. i. p. 411.)   [G. W.]

SE'RICA (ἡ Σηρική, Ptol. vi. 16. §§ 1, 3 4, 6, vii. 2. § 1, 3. § 1, 5. § 1, viii. 24. §§ 1, 5, 27. § 2. &c.), a tract of country in the E. part of Asia, inhabited by the people called Seres. According to the description of Ptolemy, it was bounded on the W. by Scythia extra Imaum, on the NE. by an unknown land, on the E. by the Sinae, and on the S. by India. Pliny on the contrary (vi. 13. s. 15) seems to extend it on the E. as far as the coast of Asia, as he mentions an Oceanus Sericus, and in another place (*Ib.* 17. s. 20) speaks of a promontory and bay. Modern opinions vary respecting its site; but

the best geographers, as Rennell, D'Anville, and Heeren, concur in placing it at the NW. angle of the present empire of *China*. (See Yates, *Textrinum Antiq.* p. 232, note). The name of Serica, as a country, was not known before the first century of our era, though there are earlier accounts of the people called Seres. It seems highly improbable, however, that they were known to Hecataeus, and the passage on which that assumption is founded occurs only in one MS. of Photius. They are first mentioned by Ctesias (p. 371, n. 22, ed. Bähr); but according to Mela (iii. 7) they were in his time known to all the world by means of their commerce. On the nothern borders of their territories were the more eastern skirts of the mountains Annibi and Auxacii (the *Altai*), which stretched as far as here from Scythia. In the interior of the country were the Montes Asmiraei, the western part of the *Da-Uri* chain; and towards the southern borders the Casii Montes (now *Khara*, in the desert of *Gobi*), together with a southern branch called Thagurus, which trended towards the river Bautisus (*Hoang-ho*.) On the farther side of that river lay the Ottorocorras, the most eastern branch of the Emodi mountains, called by Ptolemy (vi. 16. § 5) τὰ Σηρικὰ ὄρη. Among the rivers of the country, the same author (*Ib.* § 3) names, in its northern part, the Oechardes (probably the *Selenga*), and, in the S., the Bautes or Bautisus (*Hoang-ho*), which flowed towards the land of the Sinae. Pliny, however (*l. c.*), mentions several other rivers, which seem to have been coast ones, as the Psitaras, Cambari, Lanos, and Atianos, as well as the promontory of Chryse and the bay of Cyrnaba. Serica enjoyed a serene and excellent climate, and possessed an abundance of cattle, trees, and fruits of all kinds (Amm. Marc. xxxiii. 6. § 64; Plin. *l. c.*). Its chief product, however, was silk, with which the inhabitants carried on a very profitable and most extensive commerce (Strab. xv p. 693; Arist. *Hist. Nat.* v. 19; Virg. *Georg.* ii. 121; Plin. and Amm. *ll. cc.* &c.). Pliny records (xi. 22. s. 26), that a Greek woman of Cos, named Pamphila, first invented the expedient of splitting these substantial silken stuffs, and of manufacturing those very fine and veil-like dresses which became so celebrated under the name of Coae vestes. Both Serica and its inhabitants are thought to have derived their name from their staple product, since, as we learn from Hesychius (*s. v.* Σῆρες), the insect, from the web of which the brilliant stuff called holosericon was prepared, was named Ser (Σῆρ). (Comp. Bähr, *Sur les Noms de la Chine* in the *Mém. rel. à l'Asie*, iii. p. 264; and *Tableaux Hist. de l'Asie*, pp. 57 and 68.) It has been doubted, however, from the apparent improbability that any people should call themselves Seres, or silkworms, whether the name of Seres was ever really borne by any nation; and it has been conjectured that it was merely a mercantile appellation by which the natives of the silk district were known. (Latham, in *Class. Mus.* vol. iii. p. 43, seq.) Lassen (*Ind. Alt.* i. p. 321) has produced from the *Mahabharata*, ii. 50, as the real names of the Seres, those of Caka, Tukhara, and Kanka, who are represented as bringing just the same goods to market as are ascribed by Pliny (xxxiv. 14. s. 41) to the Seres, namely, wool, skins, and silk. Yet, though it may be allowed to be improbable that a people should have called themselves " Silkworms," yet it seems hardly less so that such an appellation should have been given them by foreigners, and that they should have been known by it and no other for a period of several centuries. On the other hand, may it not be possible that the product was called after the people, instead of the people after the product? We are not without examples of an analogous procedure; as, for instance, the name of the phasis, or pheasant, from the river Phasis; of our own word *currants*, anciently and properly *Corinths*, from the place whence that small species of grape was originally brought, &c. However this may be, we may refer the reader who is desirous of a further account of the origin and manufacture of silk, to an excellent dissertation in the *Textrinum Antiquarum* of Mr. Yates (part i. p. 160, seq.), where he will find all the passages in ancient authors that bear upon the subject carefully collected and discussed.

Besides its staple article, Serica also produced a vast quantity of precious stones of every kind (*Expos. tot. Mundi*, ap. Hudson, iii. p. 1, seq.), as well as iron, which was esteemed of a better quality even than the Parthian (Plin. *l. c.*) and akins (*Per. M. Erythr.* p. 22; Amm. *l. c.*)

According to Pausanias (vi. 22. § 2) the Seres were a mixture of Scythians and Indians. They are mentioned by Strabo (xv. p. 701), but only in a cursory manner. It appears from Mela (iii. 7) and from Pliny (vi. 17. s. 24), compared with Eustathius (*ad Dionys. Per.* v. 753, seq.), and Ammianus Marcellinus (*l. c.*), that they were a just and gentle people, loving tranquillity and comfort. Although addicted to commerce, they were completely isolated from the rest of the world, and carefully avoided all intercourse with strangers. From these habits, they were obliged to carry on their commercial transactions in a very singular manner. They inscribed the prices of their goods upon the bales in which they were packed, and then deposited them in a solitary building called the Stone Tower; perhaps the same place mentioned by Ptolemy (vi. 15. § 3) under the name of Hormeterion, situated in a valley on the upper course of the Jaxartes, and in the Scythian district of Casia. The Scythian merchants then approached, and having deposited what they deemed a just price for the goods, retired. After their departure, the Seres examined the sum deposited, and if they thought it sufficient took it away, leaving the goods; but if not enough was found, they removed the latter instead of the money. In the description of this mode of traffic we still recognise the characteristics of the modern Chinese. The Parthians also traded with the Seres, and it was probably through the former that the Romans at a later period procured most of their silk stuffs; though the Parthians passed them off as Assyrian goods, which seems to have been believed by the Romans (Plin. xi. 22. s. 25). After the overthrow of the Parthian empire by the Persians, the silk trade naturally fell into the hands of the latter. (Vopisc. *Aurel.* c. 45; Procop. *B. Pers.* i. 20, &c.) With regard to their persons, the Seres are described as being of unusual size, with blue eyes, red hair, and a rough voice (Plin. vi. 22. s. 24), almost totally unacquainted with diseases and bodily infirmities (*Expos. tot. Mundi, l. c.*), and consequently reaching a very great age (Ctes. *l. c.*; Strab. xv. p. 701; Lucian, *Macrob.* 5). They were armed with bows and arrows (Hor. *Od.* i. 29. 9; Charic. vi. 3). Ptolemy (*ll. cc.*) enumerates several distinct tribes of them, as the Annibi, in the extreme N., on the mountains named after them; the Zizyges, between them and the Auxacian mountains; the Damnae, to the S. of these; and still further S.

down to the river Oechardes, the Pialae; the Oechardae, who dwelt about the river of the same name; and the Garenaei and Nabannae, to the E. of the Annibi. To the S. of these again was the district of Asmiraea, near the mountains of the same name, and still further in the same direction the Issedones; to the E. of whom were the Throani. To the S. of the Issedones were the Asparacae, and S. of the Throani the Ethaguri. Lastly, on the extreme southern borders were seated the Batae and the Ottorocorrae,—the latter, who must doubtless be the same people called by Pliny Attacori, on the like-named mountain. To the southern district must also be ascribed the Sesatae mentioned in Arrian's *Peripl. M. Erythr.* (p. 37), small men with broad foreheads and flat noses, and, from the description of them, evidently a Mongol race. They migrated yearly with their wives and children to the borders of the Sinae, in order to celebrate their festivals there; and when they had returned to the interior of their country, the reeds which they left behind them, and which had served them for straw, were carefully gathered up by the Sinae, in order to prepare from it the Malabathron, a species of ointment which they sold in India. (Comp. Ritter, *Erdkunde*, ii. p. 179, v. p. 443, 2nd ed.; Bohlen, *das Alte Indien*, ii. p. 173; Heeren's, *Ideen*, i. 2. p. 494). According to Ammianus (*l. c.*) the towns of Serica were few in number, but large and wealthy. Ptolemy, in the places cited at the head of this article, names fifteen of them, of which the most important seem to have been, Sera, the capital of the nation; Issedon; Throana, on the E. declivity of the Asmiraei mountains, and on the easternmost source of the Oechardes; Asmiraea, on the same stream, but somewhat to the NW. of the preceding town; Aspacara, on the left bank of the Bautisus, not far from its most western source; and Ottorocorra.   [T. H. D.]

SERIMUM (Σήριμον, Ptol. iii. 5. § 28), a town on the Borysthenes, in the interior of European Sarmatia.   [T. H. D.]

SERI'PHOS or SERI'PHUS (Σέριφος: *Eth.* Σερίφιος: *Serpho*), an island in the Aegaean sea, and one of the Cyclades, lying between Cythnos and Siphnos. According to Pliny (iv. 12. s. 22) it is 12 miles in circumference. It possessed a town of the same name, with a harbour. (Scylax, p. 22; Ptol. iii. 15. § 31.) It is celebrated in mythology as the place where Danaë and Perseus were driven to shore in the chest in which they had been exposed by Acrisius, where Perseus was brought up, and where he afterwards turned the inhabitants into stone with the Gorgon's head. (Apollod. ii. 4. § 3; Pind. *Pyth.* x. 72, xii. 18; Strab. x. p. 487; Ov. *Met.* v. 242.) Seriphos was colonised by Ionians from Athens, and it was one of the few islands which refused submission to Xerxes. (Herod. viii. 46, 48.) By subsequent writers Seriphos is almost always mentioned with contempt on account of its poverty and insignificance (Aristoph. *Acharn.* 542; Plat. *Rep.* i. p. 329; Plut. *de Exsil.* 7. p. 602; Cic. *de Nat. Deor.* i. 31, *de Senect.* 3); and it was for this reason employed by the Roman emperors as a place of banishment for state criminals. (Tac. *Ann.* ii. 85, iv. 21; Juv. vi. 564, x. 170; Senec. *ad Consol.* 6.) It is curious that the ancient writers make no mention of the iron and copper mines of Seriphos, which were, however, worked in antiquity, as is evident from existing traces, and which, one might have supposed, would have bestowed some prosperity upon the island.

But though the ancient writers are silent about the mines, they are careful to relate that the frogs of Seriphos differ from the rest of their fraternity by being dumb. (Plin. viii. 58. s. 83; Arist. *Mir. Ausc.* 70; Aelian, *Hist. An.* iii. 37; Suidas, *s. v.* Βάτραχος ἐκ Σερίφου.) The modern town stands upon the site of the ancient city, on the eastern side of the island, and contains upwards of 2000 inhabitants. It is built upon a steep rock, about 800 feet above the sea. There are only a few remains of the ancient city. (Ross, *Reisen auf den Griech. Inseln,* vol. i. p. 134, seq.; Fiedler, *Reise, &c.* vol. ii. p. 106, seq.)

COIN OF SERIPHOS.

SERMO, a town of the Celtiberi in Hispania Tarraconensis. (*Itin. Ant.* p. 447.) Variously identified with *Muel* and *Mezalocha.*   [T. H. D.]

SERMYLE (Σερμύλη, Herod. vii. 122; Thuc. v. 18; Σερμυλία, Scyl. p. 26; Hecataeus, *ap. Steph. B. s. v.;* Böckh, *Inscr. Graec.* vol. i. p. 304; *Eth.* Σερμύλιοι), a town of Chalcidice, between Galepsus and Mecyberna, which gave its name to the Toronaic gulf, which was also called SERMYLICUS SINUS (κόλπος Σερμυλικός, Scyl. *l. c.*). The modern *Ormylia,* between *Molyvó* and *Derna,* is identified from its name, which differs little from the ancient form, with the site of Sermyle. (Leake, *Northern Greece,* vol. iii. p. 155.)   [E. B. J.]

SERMY'LICUS SINUS. [SERMYLE.]

SEROTA, a town on the frontier between Upper and Lower Pannonia, on the right bank of the river Dravus. (*It. Ant.* p. 130; *It. Hieros.* p. 562; Geog. Rav. iv. 19, where it is called Sirore, while the Table calls it Sirota.) It is possible that this town may have belonged to the tribe of the Serretes mentioned by Pliny (iii. 28) as inhabiting a part of Pannonia. The town of Serota is commonly identified with the modern *Veröcze* or *Verovits.* [L. S.]

SERPA, a place in Hispania Baetica, on the Anas, and in the territory of the Turdetani. (*Itin. Ant.* p. 426.) It still bears its ancient name. See Resendi *Ant. Lusit.* p. 194.   [T. H. D.]

SERRAEPOLIS (Σερραίπολις κώμη, Ptol. v. 6. § 4), a village on the coast of Cilicia, lying between *Mallus* and Aegae (*Ayaz*).

SERRAPILLI, a tribe mentioned by Pliny (iii. 28), as dwelling on the river Dravus in Pannonia. The resemblance of name has induced some geographers to assume that they dwelt about the modern town of *Pilisch;* but this is a mere conjecture.   [L. S.]

SERRETES. [SEROTA.]

SERRHAE. [SIRIS.]

SERRHEUM or SERRHIUM (Σέρριον, Dem. p. 85, R.; Σέρρειον, Herod. vii. 59; Steph. B. *s. v.*), a promontory and town on the southern coast of Thrace, now *Cape Makri.* It lay to the west of Maroneia, and opposite to the island of Samothrace. It is repeatedly mentioned by Demosthenes (pp. 85, 114, 133, R.), as having been taken by Philip, contrary to his engagements with the Athenians; and Livy (xxxi. 16) states that it was one of the Thracian towns captured by Philip V. in the

year B. C. 200. (Plin. iv. 11. s. 18; Mela, ii. 2.) According to Stephanus Byz. (*l. c.*) a town on the island of Samothrace bore the same name.   [J. R.]

SERRI, a people of the Asiatic Sarmatia, on the Euxine. (Plin. vi. 5. s. 5.) Mela (l. 19) places them between the Melanchlaeni and Siraces. [T. H. D.]

SERRIUM. [SERRHEUM.]

SERVIODU'RUM, a town in the north-east of Vindelicia on the Danube, on the road from Reginum to Boiodurum, near Augustana Castra. (*Tab. Peut.; Not. Imp.*) It must have occupied the site of the modern *Straubing,* or some place in the neighbourhood, such as *Azelburg,* where ancient remains still exist.   [L. S.]

SERVI'TIUM, a town in the southern part of Upper Pannonia, on the river Dravus, on the road from Siscia to Sirmium. (*It. Ant.* p. 268; Geog. Rav. iv. 19, where it is called Serbetium; *Tab. Peut.*) Its site has been identified with several modern places; but the most probable conjecture is that it occupied the place of the modern *Sieverovcsi,* the point at which the roads leading from Sirmium and Siscia to Salona met.   [L. S.]

SESABIUS (Σησαμός), a small river on the coast of Paphlagonia, flowing into the Euxine near the town of Amastris, whence in later times the river itself was called Amastris. (Anonym. *Peripl. P. E.* p. 5; Marcian. p. 71; AMASTRIS.)   [L. S.]

SESARETHUS. [TAULANTII.]

SESATAE. [SERICA.]

SESECRI'ENAE (Σησεκρίεναι νῆσοι, Arrian, *Peripl. M. Erythr.* p. 30), a group of islands opposite to the S. coast of India intra Gangem, and probably in the Sinus Colchicus — where Ptolemy (vii. 1. § 10) places a town with the somewhat similar name of Σωσίκουραι. It must have been in the neighbourhood of Taprobane, since the Periplus mentions the Αἰγιδίων νῆσος as close to the Sesecrienae, whilst Ptolemy (vii. 4. § 11) places the same island amongst a number of others lying before Taprobane, many of which must undoubtedly have belonged to the Sesecrienae.   [T. H. D.]

SESSITES (*Sesia*), a river of Gallia Transpadana, and one of the most important of the northern tributaries of the Padus. It flows beneath the walls of Vercellae (*Vercelli*), and joins the Padus about 16 miles below that city. Its name is noticed only by Pliny (iii. 16. s. 20) and the Geographer of Ravenna (iv. 36), who writes the name Sisidus. [E. H. B.]

SESTIA'NAE ARAE (called by Ptolemy Σηστίου Βωμοὶ ἄκρον, ii. 5. § 3). the W. promontory of the N. coast of Gallaecia in Hispania Tarraconensis. It had three altars dedicated to Augustus, whence its name. (Plin. iv. 20. s. 34; Mela, iii. 1.) It is the present *Cabo Villano* (Florez, *Esp. Sagr.* xx. p. 44; Sestini, *Med. Isp.* p. 103.)   [T. H. D.]

SESTIA'RIA PROM. (Σηστιαρία ἄκρα, Ptol. iv. 1. § 7), a headland on the N. coast of Mauritania Tingitana, between capes Russadir and Abyla. It is probably the same that is called Cannarum Promontorium in the *Itin. Ant.* (p. 11), lying at a distance of 50 miles from Russadir, or the present *Cabo Quilates.*   [T. H. D.]

SESTI'NUM (*Eth.* Sestinas: *Sestino*), a town in the interior of Umbria, mentioned only by Pliny, who enumerates the Sestinates among the towns of that region (Plin. iii. 14. s. 19; Gruter, *Inscr.* p. 108. 7), but which still retains its ancient name. It is situated among the Apennines, at the source of the river *Foglia* (Pisaurus).   [E. H. B.]

SESTUS (Σηστός: Eth. Σήστιος), the principal town of the Thracian Chersonesus, and opposite to Abydus, its distance from which is variously stated by ancient writers, probably because their measurements were made in different ways; some speaking of the mere breadth of the Hellespont where it is narrowest; others of the distance from one city to the other; which, again, might be reckoned either as an imaginary straight line, or as the space traversed by a vessel in crossing from either side to the other, and this, owing to the current, depended to some extent upon which shore was the starting point. Strabo (xiii. p. 591) states that the strait is 7 stadia across near Abydus; but that from the harbour of Abydus to that of Sestus, the distance is 30 stadia.* (On this point the following references may be consulted: Herod. vii. 34; Xen. Hell. iv. 8. 5; Polyb. xvi. 29; Scyl. p. 28; Plin. iv. 11. s. 18. Ukert (iii. 2. § 137, note 41) has collected the various statements made by the moderns respecting this subject.)

Owing to its position, Sestus was for a long period the usual point of departure for those crossing over from Europe to Asia; but subsequently the Romans selected Callipolis as the harbour for that purpose, and thus, no doubt, hastened the decay of Sestus, which, though never a very large town, was in earlier times a place of great importance. According to Theopompus (ap. Strab. l. c.), it was a well-fortified town, and connected with its port by a wall 200 feet in length (σκέλει διπλέθρῳ). Dercyllidas, also, in a speech attributed to him by Xenophon (Hell. iv. 8. § 5), describes it as extremely strong.

Sestus derives its chief celebrity from two circumstances,—the one poetical the other historical. The former is its connection with the romantic story of Hero and Leander, too well known to render it necessary to do more than merely refer to it in this place (Ov. Her. xviii. 127; Stat. Silv. i. 3. 27, &c.); the latter is the formation (B. C. 480) of the bridge of boats across the Hellespont, for the passage of the army of Xerxes into Europe; the western end of which bridge was a little to the south of Sestus (Herod. vii. 33). After the battle of Mycale, the Athenians seized the opportunity of recovering the Chersonesus, and with that object laid siege to Sestus, into which a great many Persians had hastily retired on their approach, and which was very insufficiently prepared for defence. Notwithstanding this, the garrison held out bravely during many months; and it was not till the spring of B. C. 478 that it was so much reduced by famine as to have become mutinous. The governor, Artayctes, and other Persians, then fled from the town in the night; and on this being discovered, the inhabitants opened their gates to the Athenians. (Herod. ix. 115, seq.; Thuc. i. 89.) It remained in their possession till after the battle of Aegospotami, and used to be called by them the corn-chest of the Piraeeus, from its giving them the command of the trade of the Euxine. (Arist. Rhet. iii. 10. § 7.) At the close

of the Peloponnesian War (B. C. 404), Sestus, with most of the other possessions of Athens in the same quarter, fell into the hands of the Lacedaemonians and their Persian allies. During the war which soon afterwards broke out between Sparta and Persia, Sestus adhered to the former, and refused to obey the command of Pharnabazus to expel the Lacedaemonian garrison; in consequence of which it was blockaded by Conon (B. C. 394), but without much result, as it appears. (Xen. Hell. iv. 8. § 6.) Some time after this, probably in consequence of the peace of Antalcidas (B. C. 387), Sestus regained its independence, though only for a time, and perhaps in name merely; for on the next occasion when it is mentioned, it is as belonging to the Persian satrap, Ariobarzanes, from whom Cotys, a Thracian king, was endeavouring to take it by arms (B. C. 362 ?). He was, however, compelled to raise the siege, probably by the united forces of Timotheus and Agesilaus (Xen. Ages. ii. 26; Nep. Timoth. 1); the latter authority states that Ariobarzanes, in return for the services of Timotheus in this war, gave Sestus and another town to the Athenians *, from whom it is said to have soon afterwards revolted, when it submitted to Cotys. But his successor, Cersobleptes, surrendered the whole Chersonesus, including Sestus, to the Athenians (B. C. 357), who, on the continued refusal of Sestus to yield to them, sent Chares, in B. C. 353, to reduce it to obedience. After a short resistance it was taken by assault, and all the male inhabitants capable of bearing arms were, by Chares' orders, barbarously massacred. (Diod. xvi. 34.)

After this time we have little information respecting Sestus. It appears to have fallen under the power of the Macedonians, and the army of Alexander the Great assembled there (B. C. 334), to be conveyed from its harbour in a Grecian fleet, from Europe to the shores of Asia. By the terms of the peace concluded (B. C. 197) between the Romans and Philip, the latter was required to withdraw his garrisons from many places both in Europe and in Asia; and on the demand of the Rhodians, actuated no doubt by a desire for free trade with the Euxine, Sestus was included in the number. (Liv. xxxii. 33.) During the war with Antiochus, the Romans were about to lay siege to the town (B. C. 190); but it at once surrendered. (Liv. xxxvii. 9.) Strabo mentions Sestus as a place of some commercial importance in his time; but history is silent respecting its subsequent destinies. According to D'Anville its site is occupied by a ruined place called Zemenic; but more recent authorities name it Jalowa (Mannert, vii. p. 193). (Herod. iv. 143; Thuc. viii. 62; Polyb. iv. 44; Diod. xi. 37; Arrian, Anab. i. 11. §§ 5, 6; Ptol. iii. 12. § 4, viii. 11. § 10; Steph. B. s. v.; Scymn. 708; Lucan, ii. 674.)　　　　　　　　　　　　　　　　　　　　[J. R.]

SESUVII [Essui].

SETABIS. [Saetabis.]

SETAE, SETTAE, or SAETTAE (Σέται, Σέτται, or Σαίτται), a town in Lydia, near the sources of the river Hermus, which is not mentioned by any of the earlier writers. (Hierocl. p. 669; Ptol. v. 2. § 21; Concil. Constant. iii. p. 502; Concil. Nicaen.

---

* There is much obscurity in this part of Grecian history, and the statement of Nepos has been considered inconsistent with several passages in Greek authorities, who are undoubtedly of incomparably greater weight than the unknown compiler of the biographical notices which pass under the name of Nepos. (See Dict. Biogr. Vol. III. p. 1146, a.)

ii. p. 591; comp. Sestini, *Geog. Num.* p. 55.) It is commonly supposed to have occupied the site of the modern *Sidas Kaleh*.   [L. S.]

SETA'NTII (Σετάντιοι, Ptol. ii. 3. § 2), a tribe probably belonging to the Brigantes on the W. coast of Britannia Romana, and possessing a harbour (Σεταντίων λιμήν, Ptol. *l. c.*), commonly thought to have been at the mouth of the river *Ribble.* Reichard, however, places it on the S. coast of the *Solway Frith*, while Camden (p. 793) would read, with one of the MSS. of Ptolemy, " Segontiorum Portus," and seeks it near *Caernarvon.* [T. H. D.]

SETANTIORUM PORTUS. [SETANTII.]

SETEIA (Σετηΐα or Σεγηΐα είσχυσις, Ptol. ii. 3. § 2), an estuary on the W. coast of Britannia Romana, opposite the isle of Mona, into which the *Dee* discharges itself.   [T. H. D.]

SETELSIS (Σετελσίς or Σελευσίς, Ptol. ii. 6. § 72), a town of the Jaccetani in Hispania Tarraconensis, now *Solsona.* See a coin in Sestini, p. 189.   [T. H. D.]

SETHERIES, a river of Asiatic Sarmatia, on the E. coast of the Pontus Euxinus, and in the territory of the Sindi. (Plin. vi. 5. s. 5.)   [T. H. D.]

SE'TIA (Σητία: Eth. Setinus: *Sezze*), an ancient city of Latium, situated on the S. slope of the Volscian mountains, between Norba and Privernum, looking over the Pontine Marshes. It is probable that it was originally a Latin city, as its name is found in the list given by Dionysius of the thirty cities of the Latin League. (Dionys. v. 61.) But it must have fallen into the hands of the Volscians, at the time their power was at its height. No mention of it is, however, found during the wars of the Romans with that people until after the Gaulish invasion, when a Roman colony was established there in B. C. 392, and recruited with an additional body of colonists a few years afterwards. (Vell. Pat. i. 14; Liv. vi. 30.) At this time Setia must have been the most advanced point of the Roman dominion in this direction, and immediately adjoined the territory of the Privernates, who were still an independent and powerful people. [PRIVERNUM.] This exposed the new colonists to the incursions of that people, who, in B. C. 342, laid waste their territory, as well as that of Norba. (Liv. vii. 42, viii. 1.) The Privernates were, however, severely punished for this aggression, and from this time the Setini seem to have enjoyed tranquillity. But it is remarkable that a few years later L. Annius of Setia appears as one of the leaders of the Latins in their great war against Rome, B. C. 340. (Liv. viii. 3.) Setia was a Colonia Latina, and was one of those which, during the pressure of the Second Punic War (B. C. 209). declared its inability to furnish any further supplies either of men or money. (Liv. xxvii. 9.) It was, at a later period of the war, severely punished for this by the imposition of much heavier contributions. (Id. xxix. 15.) From its strong and somewhat secluded position, Setia was selected as the place where the Carthaginian hostages, given at the close of the war, were detained in custody, and in B. C. 198 became in consequence the scene of a very dangerous conspiracy among the slaves of that and the adjoining districts, which was suppressed by the energy of the praetor L. Cornelius Merula. (Id. xxxii. 26.) From this time we hear no more of Setia till the Civil Wars of Marius and Sulla, when it was taken by the latter after a regular siege, B. C. 82. (Appian, *B. C.* i. 87.) It appears therefore to have been at this

period a strong fortress, an advantage which it owed to its position on a hill as well as to its fortifications, the remains of which are still visible. Under the Empire Setia seems to have continued to be a flourishing municipal town, but was chiefly celebrated for its wine, which in the days of Martial and Juvenal seems to have been esteemed one of the choicest and most valuable kinds: according to Pliny it was Augustus who first brought it into vogue.   (Plin. xiv. 6. s. 8; Martial, x. 36. 6, xiii. 112; Juv. x. 27; Strab. v. pp. 234, 237; Sil. Ital. viii. 379.) We learn from the Liber Coloniarum that Setia received a colony under the Triumvirate; and it is probable that it subsequently bore the title of a Colonia, though it is not mentioned as such by Pliny. (Plin. iii. 5. s. 9; *Lib. Colon.* p. 237; Orell. *Inscr.* 2246; Zumpt, *de Colon.* p. 338.)

The position of Setia on a lofty hill, looking down upon the Pontine Marshes and the Appian Way, is alluded to by several writers (Strab. v. p. 237; Martial, x. 74. 11, xiii. 112), among others in a fragment of Lucilius (*ap. A. Gell.* xvi. 9), in whose time it is probable that the highroad, of the extreme hilliness of which he complains, passed by Setia itself. It was, however, about 5 miles distant from the Appian Way, on the left hand. There can be no doubt that the modern town of *Sezze* occupies the same site with the ancient one, as extensive remains of its walls are still visible. They are constructed of large polygonal or rudely squared blocks of limestone, in the same style as those of Norba and Cora. The substructions of several edifices (probably temples) of a similar style of construction, also remain, as well as so e inconsiderable ruins of an amphitheatre. (Westphal, *Röm. Kamp.* p. 53; Dodwell's *Pelasgic Remains,* pp. 115—120.)   [E. H. B.]

SE'TIA (Σέτια, Ptol. ii. 4. § 9). 1. A town of the Turduli in Hispania Baetica, between the Baetis and Mount Ilipula.

2. A town of the Vascones in Hispania Tarraconensis. (Ptol. ii. 6. § 67.)   [T. H. D.]

SE'TIDA (Σέτιδα, Ptol. ii. 4. § 12), a town of the Turdetani in the W. of Hispania Baetica. [T. H. D.]

SETIDA'VA (Σετίδαυα), a town in the northeast of ancient Germany, on the north of the sources of the Vistula, so that it belonged either to the Omani or to the Burgundiones. (Ptol. ii. 11. § 28.) Its exact site is not known, though it is commonly assumed to have occupied the place of the modern *Zydowo* on the south of *Gnesen.* (Wilhelm, *Germanien,* p. 253.)   [L. S.]

SETISACUM (Σετίσακον, Ptol. ii. 6. § 52), a town of the Murbogi in the N. of Hispania Tarraconensis.   [T. H. D.]

SETIUS MONS or PROM. [BLASCON; FECYI JUGUM.]

SETOTRIALLACTA (Σετοτριαλλάκτα, Ptol. ii. 6. § 56), a town of the Arevaci in Hispania Tarraconensis.   [T. H. D.]

SETO'VIA (Σετουΐα, Appian, *Illyr.* 27), a town of Dalmatia, situated in a well-wooded valley, which was besieged by Octavius in the campaign of B. C. 34. It has been identified with *Sign*, situated in the rich valley of the *Cettina*, and bounded by mountains to the right and left.   [E. B. J.]

SETUACO'TUM (Σετουάκωτον, or Σετουάκατον), a town in the south of Germany between the upper part of the Danube and the Silva Gabreta, perhaps belonging to the territory of the Narisci (Ptol. ii. 11 § 30); but its site is quite unknown.   [L. S.]

SETUIA (Σετουία), a town of the Quadi, in the south-east of Germany, apparently near the sources of the river Aucha, a tributary of the Danube, in the Carpathian mountains. (Ptol. ii. 11. § 29.) Its identification is only matter of conjecture. [L.S.]

SEVACES (Σεούακες), a tribe in the western part of Noricum, is mentioned only by Ptolemy (ii. 14. § 2.)   [L. S.]

SEVE'RI MURUS. [VALLUM.]

SEVE'RUS MONS, a mountain of Central Italy mentioned only by Virgil (Aen. vii. 713), who places it among the Sabines, and associates it with the Mons Tetrica. It therefore evidently belonged to the lofty central ranges of the Apennines, in that part of Italy, but cannot be identified with more accuracy. [APENNINUS.]   [E. H. B.]

SEUMARA or SEUSAMORA (Σεύμαρα and Σεύσμορα, Strab. xi. p. 501), a town in the Caucasian Iberia.   [T. H. D.]

SEVO, a lofty mountain in the extreme north of ancient Germany, in the island of Scandia, in the territory of the Ingaevones. It was believed to equal in extent and magnitude the Ripaei Montes. (Plin. iv. 27; Solin. 20.) There can be no doubt that this mountain is the same as Mount Kjölen which at present separates Sweden from Norway, and the southern branch of which still bears the name of Seve-Ryggen. [SCANDIA.]   [L. S.]

SEURRI. [SEBURRI.

SEX. [SAXETANUM.

SEXANTAPRISTA (Εξαντάπριστα, Procop. de Aed. iv. 11. p. 307), a town of Moesia Inferior, on the Danube, on the great high-road between Tri-mammium and Tigra. (Itin. Ant. p. 222.) According to the Notit. Imp. (where it is called Sexagintaprista), the 5th cohort of the 1st Legio Ital., together with a squadron of cavalry, lay in garrison here. Some identify it with Rustschuk, whilst others place it further to the E., near Lipnik. [T.H.D.]

SEXTANTIO, in Gallia Narbonensis. The true name of this place is preserved in an inscription found at Nemausus (Nîmes), and published by Ménard. The name is written Sextatio in the An-tonine Itin.; and Sostantio in the Jerusalem Itin. The remains of Sextantio are supposed to be those which are about 3 miles north of Montpellier, on the banks of the Ledus (Lez).   [G. L.]

SHAALABBIN (Σαλαμίν, LXX.), a city of the tribe of Dan (Josh. xix. 42) joined with Ajalon ('Iaaλών), and mentioned in the LXX. (not in the Hebrew) as one of the cities in which the Amorites continued to dwell, after the occupation of Canaan by the Israelites (xix. 48). This last fact identifies it with the Shaalbim (LXX. Θαλαβίν) of the book of Judges (i. 35), which is also joined with Aijalon, and of which the same fact is related. It is there placed in Mount Heres. Eusebius mentions a village named Salaba (Σαλαβά), in the borders of Sebaste (Onomast. s. v.), which could not be in Dan: but S. Jerome (Comment. in Ezech. xlviii.) mentions three towns in the tribe of Dan, Ailon, Selebi and Emaus. It is joined with Makaz and Beth-shemesh in 1 Kings iv. 9, which also indicates a situation in or near the plain of Sharon. In Mr. Smith's list of places in the district of Ramleh, is a village named Selbit, containing all the radicals of the Scripture name, and probably identical with Selebi of Josephus, as the modern Yalo is with Ajalon and 'Amwas with Emmaus. Its place is not definitely fixed. (Robinson, Bibl. Res. vol. iii. 2nd appendix, p. 120.)   [G. W.]

SHALISHA (LXX. Alex. Σείλισσα, Vat. Σαλχά), a district of Palestine, in or near Mount Ephraim (1 Sam. ix. 4), in which was probably situated Baal Shalisha. [BAAL SHALISHA.]   [G. W.]

SHARON (Σαρών: Eth. Σαρωνίτης). 1. Part of the great western plain of Palestine, distinguished for its fertility, mentioned by the prophet Isaiah with "the glory of Lebanon, and the excellency of Carmel and Sharon." (Isaiah, xxxv. 2.) "The rose of Sharon" is used proverbially in the Canticles (ii. 1.) It is remarkable that the name does not occur in either of these passages in the LXX., but in the latter is translated by ἄνθος τοῦ πεδίου, by which appellative Symmachus translates it in the former passage, while Theodotion and Aquila retain the proper name. Its richness as a pasture land is intimated in 1 Chronicles (xxvii. 29), where we read that "Shitrai the Sharonite" was overseer of David's "herds that fed in Sharon." It doubtless derived its name from a village mentioned only in the New Testament (Acts, ix. 35) in connection with Lydda, in a manner that intimates its vicinity to that town. Its site has not been recovered in modern times, but it occurred to the writer, on the spot, that it may possibly be represented by the village of Butus (= Peter), on the north of the road between Lydda and Bethoron, and may have changed its name in honour of the Apostle, and in commemoration of the miracle wrought by him. S. Jerome in his commentaries limits the name to the district about Joppa, Lydda, and Iamnia (ad Ies. xxxiii. lxv.) Eusebius calls the district Saronas (Σαρωνάς), and extends it from Joppa to Caesarea (of Palestine); while other writers reckon to it the whole of the coast north of Caesarea, as far as Carmel. (Ono-mast. sub voce.) The width of the plain about Jaffa is little less than 18 miles, and the luxuriance of its soil is still attested by the numerous wild flowers with which it is carpeted in the spring,—roses, lilies, tulips, narcissus, anemones, carnations, and a thousand others, no less than by the abundant vegetation and increase where the land is cultivated as garden or corn land. (Ritter, Palästina, &c. vol. iii. part i. pp. 25, 586—588.) Reland has shown that the classical name for this fruitful district was δρυμός, which Strabo joins with Carmel, as then in the power of the pirates who had Joppa for their port (xvi. 2. § 28, p. 759). Reland suggests an ingenious account of this synonym, which appears also in Josephus (who does not use the Scripture name) in connection with Carmel, in a manner that clearly points to the district described by Strabo under the same name. In one passage the name is used in the plural (Δρυμοὶ δὲ τὸ χωρίον καλεῖται, Ant. xiv. 13. § 3); in the parallel passage it is singular (ἐπὶ τὸ καλούμενον Δρυμόν, Bell. Jud. i. 13. § 2). Now δρυμός, according to ancient etymologists, signified any kind of wood, and, as Ritter remarks, the traces of the forests of Sharon are still to be discovered in the vicinity of Carmel; but according to Pliny the Sinus Saronicus derived its name from an oak grove, "its Graecia antiqua appellante quercum." (H. N. iv. 5. s. 9.) The very probable conjecture of Reland therefore is that Δρυμός is simply a translation of Saron or Sarona, for according to the Etymologicum Magnum Σαρωνίδες αἱ κοῖλαι δρύες (ad voc. Σαρούμενος).

2. Eusebius and St. Jerome recognise another Sharon, to which they apply the prophecy of Isaiah (xxxiii. 9), "Sharon is like a wilderness" (ἔλη ἐγένετο ὁ Σάρων, LXX.), which they refer to the

country between Tabor and the sea of Tiberias (*Onomast. s. v.*) But as the name is here introduced in connection with Lebanon and Carmel,—Bashan being also introduced,—and as no other notice of a Galilaean Sharon is to be met with, it seems more reasonable to refer the notice in Isaiah to the plain of Sharon on the west coast.

3. There was certainly another Sharon beyond Jordan, apparently near the region of Gilead, for the children of Abihail, of the tribe of Gad, are said to have "dwelt in Gilead in Bashan, and in her towns, and in all the suburbs of Sharon" (1 *Chron.* v. 16); and it is possible that "the herds that fed in Sharon," under charge of David's chief herdsman, Shitrai the Sharonite, may have pastured in this trans-Jordanic district, not in the plain of the Mediterranean. Reland indeed maintains that the mention of the suburbs of Sharon in connection with the Gadites, is no proof of the existence of a trans-Jordanic Sharon, for that, as the tribe of Gad was specially addicted to pastoral pursuits, they may have pastured their flocks in the suburbs of the towns of other and distant tribes. But this hypothesis seems much more forced than the very natural theory of a second Sharon in the tribe of Gad properly so called. (*Palaestina*, pp. 370, 371, 988.)   [G. W.]

SHAVEH (LXX. Vat. ἡ κοιλὰς τοῦ Σαβύ, Alex. ἡ Σαυή). "The valley of Shaveh, which is the king's dale," where Melchizedek met Abraham returning from the slaughter of the kings. (*Gen.* xiv. 17.) The learned are not agreed concerning the city of Melchizedek. They who regard his Salem as identical with Jerusalem, naturally identify "the king's dale," equivalent to "the valley of Shaveh," with "the king's dale" where Absalom erected his monument (2 *Sam.* xviii. 18), and place it in the vicinity of "the king's gardens," in the valley of the Kedron, where tradition points out "Absalom's hand" or place. [JERUSALEM, Vol. II. p. 17, a. and p. 23, b.]   [G. W.]

SHAVEH KIRJATHAIM (translated by the LXX. Σαυὴ ἡ πόλις), the original seat of that very ancient people the Emims, where they were smitten by Chedorlaomer, king of Elam. (*Gen.* xiv. 5.) It no doubt passed with the other possessions of the Emims to the Moabites (*Deut.* ii. 9—11), and is probably identical with the Kiriathaim (LXX. Καριαθαίμ) of Jeremiah (xlviii. 23) and Ezekiel (xxv. 9).   [G. W.]

SHEBA.   [SABAEA.]

SHECHEM.   [NEAPOLIS II.]

SHILOH.   [SILO.]

SHITTIM (LXX. Σαττείν al. Σαττίν), the last station of the Israelites before crossing the Jordan, described to be by Jordan in the plains of Moab. Abel-shittim was at one extremity of their vast encampment, as Beth-Jesimoth was at the other. (*Numb.* xxv. 1, xxxiii. 49.) It was from thence that Joshua sent the spies to reconnoitre Jericho (*Josh.* ii. 1), and from thence that they marched to their miraculous passage of the Jordan (iii. 1). In Micah (vi. 5) it is mentioned in connection with Gilgal, being the last encampment on the east of Jordan, as Gilgal was the first on the west. Here the LXX. render ἀπὸ τῶν σχοίνων ἕως τοῦ Γαλγάλ.   [G. W.]

SHUNEM (LXX. Σωμάν: Eth. Σωμανίτης, Σωμαντῖς), a village of Palestine celebrated as the birthplace of Abishag (1 *Kings*, i. 3), and for the miracle of Elisha. (2 *Kings*, iv.) It was situated in Issachar (*Josh.* xix. 18; LXX. Σουνάμ), near Gilboa, to the north; for when Saul and the Is-

raelites were encamped in Gilboa, the Philistines pitched in Shunem, so that he had to pass through their lines to come to Endor. (1 *Sam.* xxviii. 4.) Eusebius mentions a village named Sanim, in the borders of Sebaste, in the district of Acrabattene, which cannot be identical with this. But the Subem (Σουβήμ) of the same author, which he places v. M. P. south of Mount Tabor, corresponds very well with the site of the modern village of Sôlam, which still marks the site of ancient Shunem. It is a miserable village, situated above the plain of Esdraelon, on the road between Jenîn and Nazareth, about 1½ hour north of Zer'în, ancient Jezreel, on the steep slope of the western spur of Little Hermon (*Ed-Dûhy*).   [G. W.]

SHUR (Σούρ, LXX.), a place repeatedly mentioned to describe the western extremity of the borders of the posterity of Ishmael (*Gen.* xxv. 18), of the Amalekites only (1 *Sam.* xv. 7), of the Geshurites, Gezrites, and Amalekites (xxvii. 8), in all which passages it is placed "over against," "before," and on the way to Egypt. Hagar's well, afterwards called Beer-lahai-roi, between Kadesh and Bered, was "in the way to Shur." (*Gen.* xvi. 7, 14.) The name is still found in the south of Palestine. "Moilahhi (= Beer-lahai-roi) lies on the great road from Beersheba to Shur, or Jebel-es-Sur, which is its present name,—a grand chain of mountains running north and south, a little east of the longitude of Suez, lying, as Shur did, before Egypt. (*Gen.* xvi. 7.) It lies at the south-west extremity of the plain of Paran, as Kadesh does at its utmost north-east extremity. (Rowlands, in Williams's *Holy City*, vol. i. appendix No. 1. pp. 465, 466.)   [G. W.]

SHUSHAN.   [SUSA.]

SIAGUL (Σιαγούλ, Ptol. iv. 3. § 9, (the most easterly town of Zeugitana, only 3 miles from the coast, and to which Putput served as a harbour. Shaw (*Travels*, ch. 2) identifies it with some ruins at the village of *Kassir-Asseite*, from two inscriptions which he found there, with the words Civ. Siagitana; but which he must have read incorrectly, since the town would have been called Siagulitana. According to Maffei (*Mus. Veron.* p. 457. 2) there is also an inscription with the words Civ. Siagitana near *Turus* in Africa; which Orelli (i. p. 334) refers either to Sigus in Numidia or to Sigu in Mauritania Caesariensis.   [T. H. D.]

SIANTICUM.   [SANTICUM.]

SIARUM, a town of Hispania Baetica, SE. of Hispalis. Now *Saracatin*, in the territory of *Utrera*. (Plin. iii. 1. s. 3; Gruter, *Inscr.* p. 803; Florez, *Med.* ii. p. 571, iii. p. 117, *Esp. Sagr.* ix. p. 112, &c.)   [T. H. D.]

SIATA, an island on the Gallic coast, which is mentioned in the Maritime Itin. after Vindilis, or *Belle Isle*. D'Anville conjectures Siata to be the *Isle de Houat*, which is off the coast of the department of *Morbihan*, and between *Belle Isle* and the mainland.   [G. L.]

SIATUTANDA (Σιατούτανδα), is mentioned by Ptolemy (ii. 11. § 27) as a town of Germany; but had probably no existence at all, the geographer imagining that in the words of Tacitus (*Ann.* iv. 73), "ad sua tutanda digressis rebellibus" the name of some town was contained. Notwithstanding this evident origin of the name, some modern geographers still persist in assuming a town Siatutanda.   [L.S.]

SI'BAE (Σίβαι, Arrian, *Ind.* c.*5; Diod. xvii. 96; Strab. xv. p. 688), a nation of the *Panjáb.* below the junction of the Hydaspes and Acesines, encountered by Alexander in his attempt to invade India. They are described as a rude, warlike people, armed only with clubs for defensive weapons. The Greeks noticed this use of the club, and that the people were in the habit of branding the representation of a club on the backs of their cattle, and that they were clothed in the skins of wild animals. From these facts they inferred that they must be descendants of Hercules. There can be doubt that they are the same race as are called Sobii in Curtius (ix. 4. § 2). A tribe of similar character, called *Siapul* or *Siapuch*, still exists in that country, who use the club, and wear the skins of goats for clothing. (Ritter, vii. p. 279, v. p. 467; Bohlen, *Alte-Indien*, i. p. 208.) It is possible that they have derived their name from the god *Siva.* [V.]

SIBA'RIA, a town of the Vettones in Hispania Tarraconensis, N. of Salmantica, and on the road from Emerita to Caesaraugusta. (*Itin. Ant.* p. 434.) Variously identified with *Santiz, Fuente de Saburra, Peñausende,* and *Zamocina.* [T. H. D.]

SIBDA (Σίβδα: *Eth.* Σιβδανός, Σιβδίτης), a place in Caria, and one of the six towns which were given by Alexander the Great to Ada, a daughter of king Hecatomnus of Halicarnassus, and thus became subject to Halicarnassus. (Steph. B. *s. v.*; Plin. v. 29.) Its exact site cannot be ascertained. [L. S.]

SIBERE'NA (Σιβερήνη: *Sta Severina*), a town of Bruttium situated in the mountains about 15 miles NW. of Crotona. The name is mentioned only by Stephanus of Byzantium (*s. v.*), who calls it an Oenotrian city, but it is probable that it is the same place which is now called *Santa Severina,* an appellation that is already noticed by Constantine Porphyrogenitus in the tenth century. It was at that time apparently a place of importance, but is now much decayed. (Const. Porph. *de Adm. Imp.* ii. 10; Holsten. *Obs. in Steph. Byz. s. v.*) [E. H. B.]

SI'BERIS (Σίβερις), a river of Galatia, a tributary of the Sangarius; it flowed in a southwestern direction, and joined the main river near the little town of Syceon, not far from Juliopolis. (Procop. *de Aed.* v. 4.) Procopius also mentions that this river frequently overflowed its banks, a fact which is perhaps alluded to in the name of a station called Hycron Potamon, about 13 miles east of Juliopolis (*It. Hieros.* p. 574); though it is possible also that the name may be misspelt for Hieron Potamon, which is only another name for the Hieras of Pliny (v. 43), and unquestionably identical with the Siberis which now bears the name of *Kirmir.* [L. S.]

SIBUZA'TES, an Aquitanian people, who submitted to P. Crassus, Caesar's legatus in B. C. 56. (*B. G.* iii. 27.) There are many varieties in the manuscript readings of this name. It is merely by conjecture founded on resemblance of name, that they have been placed about *Saubusse* or *Sobuse,* on the *Adour,* between Aquae Tarbellicae (*Dax*) and *Bayonne.* [G. L.]

SIBYLLA'TES, one of the Aquitanian tribes mentioned by Pliny (iv. 19). D'Anville conjectures that the name is preserved in that of the Vallis Subola, mentioned by Fredegarius. He argues that they cannot be the same people as the Sibuzates who submitted to P. Crassus, because Caesar speaks of a few of the remotest Aquitanian tribes which did not submit to the Roman general, trusting to the approaching winter season (*B. G.* iii. 27); from which remark we may infer that these remotest tribes were in the valleys of the Pyrenees. "The people of the

valley of *Soule* might derive this advantage from their situation, which is shut in between *Low Navarre* and the high part of *Béarn.*" (D'Anville.) [G. L.]

SIBYRTUS. [SYBRITA.]

SICAMBRI, SYCAMBRI, SYGAMBRI, SUGAMBRI, or SUCAMBRI (Σύγαμβροι, Σούγαμβροι, or Σούκαμβροι), a powerful German tribe, occupying in the time of Caesar the eastern bank of the Rhine, and extending from the *Sieg* to the *Lippe.* It is generally assumed that this tribe derived its name from the little river *Sieg,* which falls into the Rhine a little below *Bonn,* and during the middle ages was called Sega, Segaha, but is not mentioned by any ancient writer; this assumption, however, is at least only a probable conjecture, though it must be admitted that in the time of Caesar they inhabited the country north and south of the *Sieg,* and to the north of the Ubii. (Caes. *B. G.* iv. 16, foll., vi. 35; Strab. vii. pp. 290, 291; Dion Cass. xxxix. 48, xl. 32, liv. 20, 32, 33, 36.) When the Usipetes and Tencteri were defeated by Caesar, the remnants of these tribes took refuge in the country of the Sicambri, who took them under their protection. Caesar then demanded their surrender; and this being refused, he built his famous bridge across the Rhine to strike terror into the Germans. The Sicambri, however, did not wait for his arrival, but, on the advice of the Usipetes and Tencteri, quitted their own country and withdrew into forests and uninhabited districts, whither Caesar neither would nor could follow them. A few years later, B. C. 51, during the war against the Eburones, we find Sicambri fighting against the army of Caesar on the left bank of the Rhine, and nearly defeating the Romans; Caesar's arrival, who had been in another part of Gaul, alone saved his legions. The Sicambri were then obliged to return across the Rhine. In B. C. 16 the Sicambri, with the Usipetes and Tencteri, again invaded Gallia Belgica, and M. Lollius, who had provoked the barbarians, sustained a serious defeat. A similar attack which was made a few years later, was repelled by Drusus, who pursued the Germans into their own country. After the withdrawal of the Romans, the Sicambri formed a confederation among their countrymen against the common enemy, and as the Chatti who had received the country of the Ubii on the right bank of the Rhine, refused to join them, the Sicambri made war upon them; and as they left their own territory unprotected, Drusus penetrated through it into the interior of Germany. After the death of Drusus, Tiberius undertook the completion of his plans against Germany. None of the tribes offered a more vigorous resistance than the Sicambri; but in the end they were obliged to submit, and 40,000 Sicambri and Suevi were transplanted into Gaul, where as subjects of Rome they received settlements between the lower course of the *Meuse* and the Rhine. In that country they subsequently formed an important part of the nation or confederacy of the Franks. Those Sigambri who were not transplanted into Gaul seem to have withdrawn into the hills of Mons Retico, and for a long time they are not mentioned in history; they reappear in the time of Ptolemy (ii. 11. § 8), when they are spoken of as neighbours of the Bructeri Minores. The Sicambri are described as bold, brave, and cruel, and we hear nothing of towns in their country; they seem in fact to have lived in villages and isolated farms. (Caes. *B. G.* iv. 19; comp. Tac. *Ann.* ii. 26, iv. 47, xii. 39; Suet. *Aug.* 21, *Tib.* 9; Eutrop. vii. 9; Oros. vi. 21; Horat. *Carm.* iv. 2. 36. 14.

51; Or. *Amor.* i. 14. 49; Venant. Fort. *de Charib. Regs*, vi. 4; Gregor. Turon. ii. 31; Procop. *Bell. Goth.* i. 12; Lydus, *de Magistr* i. 50, iii. 36; Zeuss, *Die Deutschen*, p. 83, foll.; Wilhelm, *Germanien*, p. 142, foll.)   [L. S.]

SICANL [Siculi.]

SICCA VENERIA (Σίκκα or Σίκα Ούενερία, Ptol. iv. 3. § 30, viii. 2. § 9), a considerable town of Numidia on the river Bagradas, and on the road from Carthago to Hippo Regius, and from Musti to Cirta. (*Itin. Ant.* pp. 41, 45.) It was built on a hill, and, according to Pliny (v. 3. s. 2), was a Roman colony. We learn from Valerius Maximus (ii. 6. § 15) that it derived its surname from a temple of Venus which existed there, in which, agreeably to a Phoenician custom, the maidens of the town, including even those of good family, publicly prostituted themselves, in order to collect a marriage portion; a circumstance which shows that the town was originally a Phoenician settlement, devoted to the worship of Astarte. (Comp. Sall. *Jug.* 56; Polyb. i. 66, 67.) Shaw (*Travels*, p. 87) takes it to be the modern *Keff*, where a statue of Venus has been found, and an inscription, with the words Ordo Siccensium. (Comp. Donati, *Suppl. Thes. Murat.* ii. pp. 266. 6; Orelli, *Inscr.* no. 3733.)   [T. H. D.]

SICELLA. [Ziklag.]

SICHEM. [Neapolis II.]

SICI'LIA (Σικελία: *Eth.* Σικελιώτης, Siciliensis: *Sicily*), one of the largest and most important islands in the Mediterranean. It was indeed generally reckoned the largest of all; though some ancient writers considered Sardinia as exceeding it in size, a view which, according to the researches of modern geographers, turns out to be correct. [Sardinia.]

I. General Description.

The general form of Sicily is that of a triangle, having its shortest side or base turned to the E., and separated at its NE. angle from the adjoining coast of Italy only by a narrow strait, called in ancient times the Fretum Siculum or Sicilian Strait, but now more commonly known as the *Straits of Messina*. It was generally believed in antiquity that Sicily had once been joined to the continent of Italy, and severed from it by some natural convulsion. (Strab. vi. p. 258; Plin. iii. 8. s. 14; Virg. *Aen.* iii. 414.) But though this is probably true in a geological sense, it is certain that the separation must have taken place at a very early period, not only long before the historical age, but before the first dawn of tradition. On the other side, the W. extremity of Sicily stretches out far towards the coast of Africa, so that the westernmost point of the island, the headland of Lilybaeum, is separated only by an interval of 80 geogr. miles from the Hermaean Promontory, or *Cape Bon* in Africa.

The general triangular form of Sicily was early recognised, and is described by all the ancient geographers. The three promontories that may be considered as forming the angles of the triangle, viz. Cape Pelorus to the NE., Cape Pachynus to the SE., and Lilybaeum on the W., were also generally known and received (Pol. i. 42; Strab. vi. pp. 265, 266; Plin. iii. 8. s. 14; Ptol. iii. 4; Mel. ii. 714). Its dimensions are variously given: Strabo, on the authority of Posidonius, estimates the side from Pelorus to Lilybaeum, which he reckons the longest, at 1700 stadia (or 170 geogr. miles); and that from Pachynus to Pelorus, the shortest of the three, at 1130 stadia. Pliny on the contrary reckons 186

Roman miles (149 geogr.) from Pelorus to Pachynus, 200 M.P. (160 geogr. miles) from Pachynus to Lilybaeum, and 170 M.P. (136 geogr.) from Lilybaeum to Pelorus: thus making the northern side the shortest instead of the longest. But Strabo's views of the proportion of the three sides are entirely correct; and his distances but little exceed the truth, if some allowance be made for the windings of the coast. Later geographers, from the time of Ptolemy onwards, erroneously conceived the position of Sicily as tending a great deal more to the SW. than it really does, at the same time that they gave it a much more regular triangular form; and this error was perpetuated by modern geographers down to the time of D'Anville, and was indeed not altogether removed till the publication of the valuable coast survey of the island by Captain Smyth. (See the map published by Magini in 1620, and that of D'Anville in his *Analyse Géographique de l'Italie*, Paris 1744.)

A considerable part of Sicily is of a mountainous character. A range of mountains, which are geologically of the same character as those in the southern portion of Bruttium (the group of *Aspromonte*), and may be considered almost as a continuation of the same chain, interrupted only by the intervening strait, rises near Cape Pelorus. and extends at first in a SW. direction to the neighbourhood of *Taormina* (Tauromenium) from whence it turns nearly due W. and continues to hold this course, running parallel with the N. coast of the island till it rises into the elevated group of the *Monte Madonia*, a little to the S. of *Cefalù* (Cephaloedium.) From thence it breaks up into more irregular masses of limestone mountains, which form the central nucleus of the W. portion of the island, while their arms extending down to the sea encircle the *Bay of Palermo*, as well as the more extensive *Gulf of Castellamare*, with bold and almost isolated headlands. The detached mass of Mount Eryx (*Monte di S. Giuliano*) rises near *Trapani* almost at the W. extremity of the island, but with this exception the W. and SW. coast round to *Sciacca*, 20 miles beyond the site of Selinus, is comparatively low and shelving, and presents no bold features. Another range or mass of mountains branches off from that of the *Monte Madonia* near *Polizzi*, and trends in a SE. direction through the heart of the island, forming the huge hills, rather than mountains, on one of which Enna was built, and which extend from thence to the neighbourhood of *Piazza* and *Aidone*. The whole of the SE. corner of the island is occupied by a mass of limestone hills, never rising to the dignity nor assuming the forms of mountains, but forming a kind of table-land, with a general but very gradual slope towards the S. and SE.; broken up, however, when viewed in detail, into very irregular masses, being traversed by deep valleys and ravines, and presenting steep escarpments of limestone rock, so as to constitute a rugged and difficult country.

None of the mountains above described attain to any great elevation. The loftiest group, that of the *Monte Madonia*, does not exceed 3765 feet, while the average height of the range which extends from thence to Cape Pelorus, is little, if at all, above 3000 feet high. *Monte S. Giuliano*, the ancient Eryx, erroneously considered in ancient times as the highest mountain in Sicily after Aetna [Eryx], is in reality only 2184 feet in height (Smyth's *Sicily*, p. 242). The ancient appellations given to these mountains seem to have been somewhat vague and fluctuating; but we may assign the name of NEPTUNIUS MONS to the chain which rises at Cape Pelorus, and extends from thence to the neighbourhood of Tauromenium; while that of MONS NEBRODES seems to have been applied in a more general sense to the whole northerly range extending from near Tauromenium to the neighbourhood of Panormus; and the HERAEI MONTES of Diodorus can be no others than a part of the same range. (See the respective articles.) But incomparably the most important of the mountains of Sicily, and the most striking physical feature of the whole island, is the great volcanic mountain of AETNA, which rises on the E. coast of the island, and attains an elevation of 10,874 feet, while its base is not less than 90 miles in circumference. It is wholly detached from the mountains and hills which surround it, being bounded on the N. by the river Acesines or Alcantara, and the valley through which it flows, and on the W. and S. by the Symaethus, while on the E. its streams of lava descend completely into the sea, and constitute the line of coast for a distance of near 30 miles. The rivers already mentioned constitute (with trifling exceptions) the limits of the volcanic district of Aetna, but volcanic formations of older date, including beds of lava, scorias, &c., are scattered over a considerable extent of the SE. portion of the island, extending from the neighbourhood of Palagonia to that of Palazzolo, and even to Syracuse. These indeed belong to a much more ancient epoch of volcanic action, and can never have been in operation since the existence of man upon the island. The extensive action of volcanic fires upon Sicily was, however, observed by the ancients, and is noticed by several writers. The apparent connection between Aetna and the volcanoes of the Aeolian Islands is mentioned by Strabo, and the same author justly appeals to the craters of the Palici, and to the numerous thermal springs throughout the island, as proofs that the subterranean agencies were widely diffused beneath its surface (Strab. vi. pp. 274, 275).

Few countries in Europe surpass Sicily in general productiveness and fertility. Its advantages in this respect are extolled by many ancient writers. Strabo tells us (vi. p. 273) that it was not inferior to Italy in any kind of produce, and even surpassed it in many. It was generally believed to be the native country of wheat (Diod. v. 2), and it is certain that it was not surpassed by any country either in the abundance or quality of this production. It was equally celebrated for the excellence of its honey and its saffron, both of which were extensively exported to Rome; as well as for its sheep and cattle, and excellent breeds of horses, among which those of Agrigentum seem to have been the most celebrated (Strab. l. c.; Sil. Ital. xiv. 23; Virg. Aen. iii. 704). There were indeed no extensive plains, like those of Campania or Cisalpine Gaul; the largest being that now called the Piano di Catania, extending along the banks of the Symaethus, and known in ancient times as the LEONTINUS or LAESTRYGONIUS CAMPUS. But the whole island was intersected by numerous streams, and beautiful valleys; and though a considerable part of its surface (as already observed) was occupied either by mountains or rocky hills, the slopes and underfalls of these abounded in scenery of the most charming description, and were adapted for the growth of vines, olives, and fruits of every description.

The climate of Sicily may be considered as intermediate between those of Southern Italy and Africa. The northern part of the island, indeed, closely resembles the portion of Italy with which it is more immediately in contact; but the southern and southwestern parts present strong indications of their more southerly latitude, and have a parched and arid appearance (at least to the eyes of northern travellers), except in winter and spring. The abundance also of the dwarf palm (Chamaerops humilis Linn.), a plant unknown to other parts of Europe, tends to give a peculiar aspect to these districts of Sicily. The climate of the island in general was certainly not considered unhealthy in ancient times; and though at the present day many districts of it suffer severely from malaria, there is good reason to believe that this would be greatly diminished by an increased population and more extensive cultivation. It is remarkable, indeed, in Sicily, as in the south of Italy, that frequently the very sites which are now considered the most unhealthy were in ancient times occupied by flourishing and populous cities. In many cases the malaria is undoubtedly owing to local causes, which might be readily obviated by draining marshes or affording a free outlet to stagnant waters.

II. HISTORY.

The accounts of the early population of Sicily are more rational and consistent than is generally the case with such traditions. Its name was obviously derived from that of the people who continued in historical times to be its chief inhabitants, the SICULI or SICELS (Σικελοί); and the tradition universally received represented these as crossing over from the mainland, where they had formerly dwelt, in the extreme southern portion of Italy. The traditions and notices of this people in other parts of Italy, and of their previous wanderings and migrations, are, indeed, extremely obscure, and will be discussed elsewhere [SICULI]; but the fact that they were at one time settled in the Bruttian peninsula, and from thence passed over into Sicily, may be safely received as historical. There is every probability also that they were not a people distinct in their origin from the races whom we subsequently find in that part of Italy, but were closely connected with the Oenotrians and their kindred tribes. Indeed, the names of Σικελός and Ἰταλός are considered by many philologers as of common origin. There seems, therefore, little doubt that the Sicels, or Siculi, may be regarded as one of the branches of the great Pelasgic race, which we find in the earliest times occupying the southern portion of Italy: and this kindred origin will account for the facility with which we find the Sicels subsequently adopting the language and civilisation of the Greek colonists in the island, at the same time that there remain abundant traces of their common descent with the people of Italy.

But the Sicels, who occupied in the historical period the greater part of the interior of the island, were not, according to the Greek writers, its earliest inhabitants. Thucydides indeed assigns their immigration to a period only three centuries before the settlement of the first Greek colonies (Thuc. vi. 2); and Diodorus, without assigning any date, agrees in representing them as the latest comers among the native population of the island (Diod. v. 6). The first notices of Sicily allude to the existence of races of gigantic men, of savage manners, under the

names of Laestrygones and Cyclopes ; but these
fabulous tales, preserved only by the early poets in a
manner that renders it impossible to separate truth
from falsehood, are justly discarded by Thucydides
as unworthy of serious consideration (Thuc. vi. 2).
It may suffice to remark, that Homer (of course, the
earliest authority on the subject) says nothing directly to prove that he conceived either the Cyclopes or Laestrygones as dwelling in Sicily; and
this is in both cases a mere inference of later writers,
or of some tradition now unknown to us. Homer
indeed, in one passage, mentions (but not in connection with either of these savage races), " the island
of Thrinakia " (Odyss. xii. 127), and this was generally identified with Sicily, though there is certainly
nothing in the Odyssey that would naturally lead to
such a conclusion. But it was a tradition generally
received that Sicily had previously been called TRI-
NACRIA, from its triangular form and the three
promontories that formed its extremities (Thuc. vi.
2 ; Diod. v. 2 ; Strab. vi. p. 265), and this name
was connected with the Homeric Thrinakia. It is
obvious that such a name could only have been
given by Greek navigators, and argues a considerable amount of acquaintance with the configuration
of its shores. It could not, therefore, have been (as
supposed even by Thucydides) the original or native
name of the island, nor could it have been in use
even among the Greeks at a very early period. But
we cannot discard the general testimony of ancient
writers, that this was the earliest appellation by
which Sicily was known to the Greeks.

Another people whom Thucydides, apparently
with good reason, regards as more ancient than the
Sicels, were the SICANI, whom we find in historical
times occupying the western and north-western parts
of the island, whither, according to their own tradition, they had been driven by the invading Sicels,
when these crossed the straits, though another tradition ascribed their removal to the terror and devastation caused by the eruptions of Aetna (Thuc. vi. 2;
Diod. v. 6). The Sicanians claimed the honour of
being autochthons, or the original inhabitants of the
island, and this view was followed by Timaeus ; but
Thucydides, as well as Philistus, adopted another
tradition, according to which they were of Iberian
extraction (Thuc. l. c.; Diod. l. c.). What the
arguments were which he regards as conclusive, we
are unfortunately wholly ignorant; but the view is
in itself probable enough, and notwithstanding the
close resemblance of name, it is certain that throughout the historical period the Sicani and Siculi are
uniformly treated as distinct races. Hence it is
improbable that they were merely tribes of a kindred
origin, as we should otherwise have been led to infer
from the fact that the two names are evidently only
two forms of the same appellation.

A third race which is found in Sicily within the
historical period, and which is regarded by ancient
writers as distinct from the two preceding ones,
is that of ELYMI, who inhabited the extreme north-
western corner of the island, about Eryx and Segesta. Tradition ascribed to them a Trojan origin
(Thuc. vi. 2; Dionys. i. 52), and though this story
is probably worth no more than the numerous similar tales of Trojan settlements on the coast of Italy,
there must probably have been some foundation for
regarding them as a distinct people from their neighbours, the Sicani. Both Thucydides and Scylax
specially mention them as such (Thuc. l. c.; Scyl.
p. 4. § 13): but at a later period, they seem to

have gradually disappeared or been merged into the
surrounding tribes, and their name is not again
found in history.

Such were the indigenous races by which Sicily
was peopled when its coasts were first visited, and
colonies established there, by the Phoenicians and the
Greeks. Of the colonies of the former people we
have little information, but we are told in general by
Thucydides that they occupied numerous points
around the coasts of the island, establishing themselves in preference, as was their wont, on projecting
headlands or small islands adjoining the shore.
(Thuc. vi. 2). But these settlements were apparently, for the most part, mere trading stations, and
as the Greeks came to establish themselves permanently and in still increasing numbers in Sicily, the
Phoenicians gradually withdrew to the NW. corner
of the island, where they retained three permanent
settlements, Motya, Panormus, and Soloeis or Soluntum. Here they were supported by the alliance of
the neighbouring Elymi, and had also the advantage
of the proximity of Carthage, upon which they all
became eventually dependent. (Thuc. l. c.)

The settlement of the Greek colonies in Sicily
began about the middle of the eighth century B. C.,
and was continued for above a century and a half.
Their dates and origin are known to us with much
more certainty than those which took place during
the corresponding period in the south of Italy. The
earliest were established on the E. coast of the island,
where the Chalcidic colony of NAXOS was founded
in B. C. 735, and that of SYRACUSE the following
year (B. C. 734), by a body of Corinthian settlers
under Archias. Thus the division between the Chalcidic and Doric colonies in Sicily, which bears so
prominent a part in their political history, became
marked from the very outset. The Chalcidians were
the first to extend their settlements, having founded
within a few years of the parent colony (about B. C.
730) the two cities of LEONTINI and CATANA, both
of them destined to bear an important part in the
affairs of Sicily. About the same time, or shortly
after (probably about B. C. 728), a fresh body of
colonists from Megara founded the city of the same
name, called, for distinction's sake, MEGARA HYB-
LAEA, on the E. coast, between Syracuse and Catana.
The first colony on the S. coast of the island was
that of GELA, founded in B. C. 690, by a body of
emigrants from Rhodes and Crete; it was, therefore,
a Doric colony. On the other hand, the Chalcidians
founded, at what precise period we know not, the
colony of ZANCLE (afterwards called MESSANA), in
a position of the utmost importance, as commanding
the Sicilian Straits. The rapid rise and prosperity
of these first settlements are shown by their having
become in their turn the parents of other cities,
which soon vied with them, and, in some cases, surpassed them in importance. Thus we find Syracuse
extending its power by establishing in succession the
colonies of ACRAE in B. C. 664, CASMENAE in B. C.
644, and CAMARINA in B. C. 599. Of these, the
last alone rose to be a flourishing city and the rival
of the neighbouring Gela. The latter city in its
turn founded the colony of AGRIGENTUM, in B. C.
580, which, though one of the latest of the Greek
colonies in the island, was destined to become one of
the most powerful and flourishing of them all. Still
further to the W., the colony of SELINUS, planted as
early as B. C. 628, by a body of settlers from the
Hyblaean Megara, reinforced with emigrants from
the parent city in Greece, rose to a state of power

and prosperity far surpassing that of either of its mother cities. Selinus was the most westerly of the Greek colonies, and immediately bordered on the territory of the Elymi and the Phoenician or Carthaginian settlements. On the N. coast of the island, the only independent Greek colony was HIMERA, founded about B. C. 648 by the Zanclaeans; MYLAE, another colony of the same people, having apparently continued, from its proximity, to be a mere dependency of Zancle. To the above list of Greek colonies must be added CALLIPOLIS and Euboea, both of them colonies of Naxos, but which never seem to have attained to consideration, and disappear from history at an early period.*

Our accounts of the early history of these numerous Greek colonies in Sicily are unfortunately very scanty and fragmentary. We learn indeed in general terms that they rose to considerable power and importance, and enjoyed a high degree of wealth and prosperity, owing as well to the fertility and natural advantages of the island, as to their foreign commerce. It is evident also that at an early period they extended their dominion over a considerable part of the adjoining country, so that each city had its district or territory, often of considerable extent, and comprising a subject population of native origin. At the same time the Sicels of the interior, in the central and northern parts of the island, and the Sicanians and Elymi in the W., maintained their independence, though they seem to have given but little trouble to their Greek neighbours. During the sixth century B. C. the two most powerful cities in the island appear to have been Agrigentum and Gela, Syracuse not having yet attained to that predominance which it subsequently enjoyed. Agrigentum, though one of the latest of the Greek colonies in Sicily, seems to have risen rapidly to prosperity, and under the able, though tyrannical government of the despot Phalaris (B. C. 570—554) became apparently for a time the most powerful city in the island. But we know very little about his real history, and with the exception of a few scattered and isolated notices we have hardly any account of the affairs of the Greek cities before B. C. 500. At or before that period we find that a political change had taken place in most of these communities, and that their governments, which had originally been oligarchical, had passed into the hands of despots or tyrants, who ruled with uncontrolled power. Such were Panaetius at Leontini, Cleander at Gela, Terillus at Himera, and Scythes at Zancle (Arist. Pol. v. 12; Herod. vi. 23, vii. 154). Of these Cleander seems to have been the most able, and laid the foundation of a power which enabled his brother and successor Hippocrates to extend his dominion over a great part of the island. Callipolis, Leontini, Naxos, Zancle, and Camarina successively fell under the arms of Hippocrates, and Syracuse itself only escaped subjection by the intervention of the Corinthians (Herod. vii. 154). But what Hippocrates had failed to effect was accomplished by Gelon, who succeeded him as despot of Gela, and by interposing in the civil dissensions of the Syracusans ultimately succeeded in making

himself master of that city also, B. C. 485. From this time Gelon neglected his former government of Gela, and directed all his efforts to the aggrandizement of his new acquisition. He destroyed Camarina, and removed all the inhabitants to Syracuse, together with a large part of those of Gela itself, and all the principal citizens of Megara Hyblaea and Euboea (Herod. vii. 156).

Syracuse was thus raised to the rank of the first city in Sicily, which it retained for many centuries afterwards. A few years before (B. C. 488), Theron had established himself in the possession of the sovereign power at Agrigentum, and subsequently extended his dominion over Himera also, from whence he expelled Terillus, B. C. 481. About the same time also Anaxilaus, despot of Rhegium, on the other side of the straits, had established a footing in Sicily, where he became master of Zancle, to which he gave the name of Messana, by which it was ever afterwards known [MESSANA]. All three rulers appear to have been men of ability and enlightened and liberal views, and the cities under their immediate government apparently made great progress in power and prosperity. Gelon especially undoubtedly possessed at this period an amount of power of which no other Greek state could boast, as was sufficiently shown by the embassy sent to him from Sparta and Athens to invoke his assistance against the threatened invasion of Xerxes (Herod. vii. 145, 157). But his attention was called off to a danger more immediately at hand. Terillus, the expelled despot of Himera, had called in the assistance of the Carthaginians, and that people sent a vast fleet and army under a general named Hamilcar, who laid siege to Himera, B. C. 480. Theron, however, was able to maintain possession of that city until the arrival of Gelon with an army of 50,000 foot and 5000 horse to his relief, with which, though vastly inferior to the Carthaginian forces, he attacked and totally defeated the army of Hamilcar. This great victory, which was contemporaneous with the battle of Salamis, raised Gelon to the highest pitch of reputation, and became not less celebrated among the Sicilian Greeks than those of Salamis and Plataea among their continental brethren. The vast number of prisoners taken at Himera and distributed as slaves among the cities of Sicily added greatly to their wealth and resources, and the opportunity was taken by many of them to erect great public works, which continued to adorn them down to a late period (Diod. xi. 25).

Gelon did not long survive his great victory at Himera: but he transmitted his power unimpaired to his brother Hieron. The latter, indeed, though greatly inferior to Gelon in character, was in some respects even superior to him in power: and the great naval victory by which he relieved the Cumaeans in Italy from the attacks of the Carthaginians and Tyrrhenians (B. C. 474) earned him a well-merited reputation throughout the Grecian world. At the same time the rule of Hieron was extremely oppressive to the Chalcidic cities of Sicily, the power of which he broke by expelling all the citizens of Naxos and Catana, whom he compelled to remove to Leontini, while he repeopled Catana with a large body of new inhabitants, at the same time that he changed its name to Aetna. Theron had continued to reign at Agrigentum until his death in B. C. 472, but his son Thrasydaeus, who succeeded him, quickly incurred the enmity of the citizens, who were enabled by the assistance of Hieron to expel him,

---

* The above summary of the progress of Greek colonisation in Sicily is taken almost wholly from Thucydides (vi. 3—5). See, however, Scymnus Chius (270—299) and Strabo (vi. pp. 267—272). The dates are fully discussed by Clinton (Fasti Hellenici, vol. i.).

and were thus restored to at least nominal freedom. A similar revolution occurred a few years later at Syracuse, where, on the death of Hieron (B. C. 467), the power passed into the hands of Thrasybulus, whose violent and tyrannical proceedings quickly excited an insurrection among the Syracusans. This became the signal for a general revolt of all the cities of Sicily, who united their forces with those of the Syracusans, and succeeded in expelling Thrasybulus from his strongholds of Ortygia and Achradina (Diod. xi. 67, 68), and thus driving him from Sicily.

The fall of the Gelonian dynasty at Syracuse (B. C. 466) became for a time the occasion of violent internal dissensions in most of the Sicilian cities, which in many cases broke out into actual warfare. But after a few years these were terminated by a general congress and compromise, B. C. 461 ; the exiles were allowed to return to their respective cities: Camarina, which had been destroyed by Gelon, was repeopled and became once more a flourishing city; while Catana was restored to its original Chalcidic citizens, and resumed its ancient name (Diod. xi. 76). The tranquillity thus reestablished was of unusual permanence and duration; and the half century that followed was a period of the greatest prosperity for all the Greek cities in the island, and was doubtless that when they attained (with the exception of Syracuse) their highest degree of opulence and power. This is distinctly stated by Diodorus (l. c.) and is remarkably confirmed by the still existing monuments,—all the greatest architectural works being referable to this period. Of the form of government established in the Sicilian cities at this time we have little information, but it seems certain that a democratic constitution was in almost all instances substituted for the original oligarchies.

But prosperous as this period (B. C. 461—409) undoubtedly was, it was by no means one of unbroken tranquillity. It was disturbed in the first instance by the ambitious schemes of Ducetius, a Siculian chief, who endeavoured to organise all the Sicels of the interior into one confederacy, which should be able to make head against the Greek cities. He at the same time founded a new city, to which he gave the name of Palice, near the sacred fountain of the Palici. But these attempts of Ducetius, remarkable as the only instance in the whole history of the island in which we find the Sicels attempting to establish a political power of their own, were frustrated by his defeat and banishment by the Syracusans in B. C. 451; and though he once more returned to Sicily and endeavoured to establish himself on the N. coast of the island, his projects were interrupted by his death, B. C. 445. (Diod. xi. 88, 90—92, xii. 8, 29.) He found no successor; and the Sicels of the interior ceased to be formidable to the Greek cities. Many of their towns were actually reduced to subjection by the Syracusans, while others retained their independent position; but the operation of Hellenic influences was gradually diffusing itself throughout the whole island.

The next important event in the history of Sicily is the great Athenian expedition in B. C. 415. Already, at an earlier period, soon after the outbreak of the Peloponnesian War, the Athenians had interfered in the affairs of Sicily, and, in B. C. 427, had sent a squadron under Laches and Charoeades to support the Ionic or Chalcidic cities in the island,

which were threatened by their more powerful Doric neighbours. But the operations of these commanders, as well as of Eurymedon and Sophocles, who followed them in B. C. 425 with a large force, were of an unimportant character, and in B. C. 424 a general pacification of the Greek cities in Sicily was brought about by a congress held at Gela (Thuc. iv. 58, 65). But the peace thus concluded did not remain long unbroken. The Syracusans took advantage of the intestine dissensions at Leontini to expel the democratic party from that city: while the Selinuntines were engaged in war with their non-Hellenic neighbours the Segestans, whom they pressed so hard that the latter were forced to apply for assistance to Athens. The Leontine exiles also sued for aid in the same quarter, and the Athenians, who were at this time at the height of their power, sent out an expedition on the largest scale, nominally for the protection of their allies in Sicily, but in reality, as Thucydides observes, in hopes of making themselves masters of the whole island (Thuc. vi. 6). It is impossible here to relate in detail the proceedings of that celebrated expedition, which will be more fully noticed in the article SYRACUSAE, and are admirably related in Grote's History of Greece, vol. viii. ch. 58—60. Its failure may be attributed in great measure to the delays and inactivity of Nicias, who lingered at Catana, instead of proceeding at once to besiege Syracuse itself, and thus gave the Syracusans time to strengthen and enlarge their fortifications, at the same time that they revived the courage of their allies. The siege of Syracuse was not actually commenced till the spring of 414 B. C., and it was continued till the month of September, 413 B. C., with the most unremitting exertions on both sides. The Syracusans were supported by the chief Dorian cities in the island, with the exception of Agrigentum, which stood aloof from the contest, as well as by a portion of the Sicel tribes : but the greater part of those barbarians, as well as the Chalcidic cities of Naxos and Catana and the Segestans, furnished assistance to the Athenians (Thuc. vii. 57, 58).

The total defeat of the Athenian armament (by far the most formidable that had been seen in Sicily since that of the Carthaginians under Hamilcar), seemed to give an irresistible predominance to the Dorian cities in the island, and to Syracuse especially. But it was not long before they again found themselves threatened by a still more powerful invader. The Selinuntines immediately took advantage of the failure of the Athenians to renew their attacks upon their neighbours of Segesta, and the latter, feeling their inability to cope with them, now applied for protection to Carthage. It is remarkable that we hear nothing of Carthaginian intervention in the affairs of Sicily from the time of the battle of Himera until this occasion, and they seem to have abandoned all ambitious projects connected with the island, though they still maintained a footing there by means of their subject or dependent towns of Panormus, Motya, and Soluntum. But they now determined to avail themselves of the opportunity offered them, and sent an armament to Sicily, which seemed like that of the Athenians, calculated not so much for the relief of Segesta as for the conquest of the whole island. Hannibal, the grandson of Hamilcar who had been slain at Himera, landed at Lilybaeum, in B. C. 409, with an army estimated at 100,000 men, and marching straight upon Selinus, laid siege at once to the city. Selinus was at this

3 R 2

time, next to Agrigentum and Syracuse, probably the most flourishing city in Sicily, but it was wholly unprepared for defence, and was taken after a siege of only a few days, the inhabitants put to the sword or made prisoners, and the walls and public buildings razed to the ground (Diod. xiii. 54—58). From thence Hannibal turned his arms against Himera, which was able to protract its resistance somewhat longer, but eventually fell also into his power, when in order to avenge himself for his grandfather's defeat, he put the whole male population to the sword, and so utterly destroyed the city that it was never again inhabited (Id. xiii. 59—62).

After these exploits Hannibal returned to Carthage with his fleet and army. But his successes had now awakened the ambition of the Carthaginian people, who determined upon a second invasion of Sicily, and in B. c. 406 sent thither an army still larger than the preceding, under the command of Hannibal. Agrigentum, at this time at the very highest point of its power and opulence, was on this occasion the first object of the Carthaginian arms, and though the citizens had made every preparation for defence, and in fact were enabled to prolong their resistance for a period of eight months they were at length compelled by famine to surrender. The greater part of the inhabitants evacuated the city, which shared the fate of Selinus and Himera (Diod. xiii. 81, 91).

Three of the principal Greek cities in Sicily had thus already fallen, and in the spring of B. c. 405, Himilco, who had succeeded Hannibal in the command, advanced to the attack of Gela. Meanwhile the power of Syracuse, upon which the other cities had in a great degree relied for their protection, had been in great measure paralysed by internal dissensions: and Dionysius now availed himself of these to raise himself to the possession of despotic power. But his first operations were not more successful than those of the generals he replaced, and after an ineffectual attempt to relieve Gela, he abandoned both that city and Camarina to their fate, the inhabitants of both emigrating to Leontini. Dionysius was able to fortify himself in the supreme power at Syracuse, and hastened to conclude peace with Himilco upon terms which left the Carthaginians undisputed masters of nearly half of Sicily. In addition to their former possessions, Selinus, Himera, and Agrigentum were to be subject to Carthage, while the inhabitants of Gela and Camarina were to be allowed to return to their native cities on condition of becoming tributary to Carthage (Diod. xiii. 114.)

From this time Dionysius reigned with undisputed authority at Syracuse for a period of 38 years (B. c. 405—367), and was able at his death to transmit his power unimpaired to his son. But though he raised Syracuse to a state of great power and prosperity, and extended his dominion over a large part of Sicily, as well as of the adjoining part of Italy, his reign was marked by great and sudden changes of fortune. Though he had dexterously availed himself of the Carthaginian invasion to establish his power at Syracuse, he had no sooner consolidated his own authority than he began to turn his thoughts to the expulsion of the Carthaginians from the island. His arms were, however, directed in the first instance against the Chalcidic cities of Sicily, Naxos, Catana, and Leontini, all of which successively fell into his power, while he extended his dominions over a great part of the Sicel

communities of the interior. It was not till he had effected these conquests, as well as made vast preparations for war, by enlarging and strengthening the fortifications of Syracuse and building an enormous fleet, that he proceeded to declare war against Carthage, B. c. 397. His first successes were rapid and sudden: almost all the cities that had recently been added to the Carthaginian dominion declared in his favour, and he carried his victorious arms to the extreme W. point of Sicily, where Motya, one of the chief strongholds of the Carthaginian power, fell into his hands after a long siege. But the next year (B. c. 396) the state of affairs changed. Himilco, who landed in Sicily with a large army, not only recovered Motya and other towns that had been taken by Dionysius, but advanced along the N. coast of the island to Messana, which he took by assault and utterly destroyed. Dionysius was even compelled to shut himself up within the walls of Syracuse, where he was closely besieged by Himilco, but a sudden pestilence that broke out in the Carthaginian camp reduced them in their turn to such straits that Himilco was glad to conclude a secret capitulation and retire to Africa (Diod. xiv. 47 —76). Hostilities with Carthage were renewed in B. c. 393, but with no very decisive result, and the peace concluded in the following year (B. c. 392) seems to have left matters in much the same state as before. In B. c. 383 war again broke out between Dionysius and the Carthaginians, but after two great battles, with alternate success on both sides, a fresh treaty was concluded by which the river Halycus was established as the boundary between the two powers. The limit thus fixed, though often infringed, continued to be recognised by several successive treaties. and may be considered as forming from henceforth the permanent line of demarcation between the Carthaginian and the Greek power in Sicily (Diod. xv. 17).

(For a more detailed account of the reign of Dionysius and his wars with the Carthaginians, see the article DIONYSIUS in the *Biogr. Dict.* Vol. I. p. 1033. The same events are fully narrated by Mr. Grote, vol. x. ch. 81, 82, and vol. xi. ch. 83.)

Several important towns in Sicily derived their origin from the reign of the elder Dionysius and the revolutions which then took place in the island. Among these were TAUROMENIUM, which arose in the place and not far from the site of the ancient Naxos, which had been finally destroyed by Dionysius : TYNDARIS, founded by the Syracusan despot on the N. coast of the island, with a body of colonists principally of Messenian origin ; ALAESA, in the same part of Sicily, founded by the Sicel chief Archonides; and LILYBAEUM, which grew up adjoining the port and promontory of that name, a few miles S. of Motya, the place of which it took as one of the principal Carthaginian ports and strongholds in the island.

The power of Syracuse over the whole of the eastern half of Sicily appeared to be effectually consolidated by the elder Dionysius, but it was soon broken up by the feeble and incompetent government of his son. Only ten years after the death of the father (B.c. 357), Dion landed in Sicily at the head of only a few hundred mercenary troops, and raised the standard of revolt; all the dependent subjects of Syracuse soon flocked around it, and Dion was welcomed into the city itself by the acclamations of the citizens. Dionysius himself was absent at the time, but the island-citadel of Ortygia was held by his garrison, and still secured him a footing in Sicily. It was not till after a long blockade that his son Apollocrates was compelled to surrender it into the hands of Dion, who thus became master of Syracuse, B. C. 356. But the success of Dion was far from restoring liberty to Sicily, or even to the Syracusans: the despotic proceedings of Dion excited universal discontent, and he was at length assassinated by Callippus, one of his own officers, B. C. 353. The period that followed was one of great confusion, but with which we are very imperfectly acquainted. Successive revolutions occurred at Syracuse, during which the younger Dionysius found means to effect his return, and became once more master of Ortygia. But the rest of the city was still held by a leader named Hicetas, who called in the assistance of the Carthaginians. Ortygia was now besieged both by sea and land by a Carthaginan fleet and army. It was in this state of things that a party at Syracuse, equally opposed to Hicetas and Dionysius, had recourse to the parent city of Corinth, and a small force of 1200 soldiers was sent to their assistance under Timoleon, B. C. 344. His successes were rapid and brilliant; and within less than two months from his landing in Sicily, he found himself unexpectedly in the possession of Ortygia, which was voluntarily surrendered to him by Dionysius. Hicetas and the Carthaginians were, however, still masters of the rest of the city; but mistrust and disunion enfeebled their defence: the Carthaginian general Magon suddenly withdrew his forces, and Timoleon easily wrested the city from the hands of Hicetas, B. C. 343.

Syracuse was now restored to liberty and a democratic form of government; and the same change was quickly extended to the other Greek cities of Sicily. These had thrown off the yoke of Syracuse during the disturbed period through which they had recently passed, but had, with few exceptions, fallen into the hands of local despots, who had established themselves in the possession of absolute power. Such were, Hicetas himself at Leontini, Mamercus at Catana, and Hippon at Messana, while minor despots, also of Greek origin, had obtained in like manner the chief power in the Sicilian cities of Apollonia, Centuripa and Agyrium. Timoleon now turned his arms in succession against all these petty rulers, and overthrew them one after another, restoring the city in each case to the possession of independent and free self-government. Meanwhile the Greeks had been threatened with a more general danger from a fresh Carthaginian invasion; but the total defeat of their generals Hasdrubal and Hamilcar at the river Crimisus (B. C. 340), one of the most brilliant and decisive victories ever gained by the Greeks over the Carthaginians, put an end to all fears from that quarter: and the peace that followed once more established the Halycus as the boundary between the two nations (Diod. xv. 17).

The restoration of the Sicilian Greeks to liberty by Timoleon, was followed by a period of great prosperity. Many of the cities had suffered severely, either from the exactions of their despotic rulers, or from the troubles and revolutions that had taken place, but these were now recruited with fresh colonists from Corinth, and other cities of Greece, who poured into the island in vast numbers; the exiles were everywhere restored, and a fresh impulse seemed to be given to the development of Hellenic influences in the island. Unfortunately this period of reviving prosperity was of short duration. Only

twenty three years after the battle of the Crimisus, a despotism was again established at Syracuse by Agathocles (B. C. 317), an adventurer who raised himself to power by very much the same means as the elder Dionysius, whom he resembled in energy and ability, while he even surpassed him in sanguinary and unsparing severity. The reign of Agathocles (B. C. 317—289) was undoubtedly a period that exercised the most disastrous influence over Sicily; it was occupied in great part with internal dissensions and civil wars, as well as by long continued struggles between the Greeks and Carthaginians. Like Dionysius, Agathocles had, in the first instance, made use of Carthaginian support, to establish himself in the possession of despotic power, but as he gradually extended his aggressions, and reduced one Greek city after another under his authority, he in his turn came into fresh collision with Carthage. In B. C. 310, he was defeated at the river Himera, near the hill of Ecnomus, by the Carthaginian general Hamilcar, in so decisive a battle that it seemed to extinguish all his hopes: his allies and dependent cities quickly threw off his yoke, and Syracuse itself was once more blockaded by a Carthaginian fleet. In this extremity Agathocles adopted the daring resolution of transporting his army to Africa, and carrying on the war at the very gates of Carthage. During his absence (which was protracted for nearly four years, B. C. 310—307) Hamilcar had brought a large part of Sicily under the dominion of Carthage, but was foiled in all his attempts upon Syracuse, and at length was himself taken prisoner in a night attack, and put to death. The Agrigentines, whose name had been scarcely mentioned for a long period, but whose city appears to have been revived under Timoleon, and now again appears as one of the most considerable in Sicily, made a fruitless attempt to raise the banner of freedom and independence, while the Syracusan exile Deinocrates, at the head of a large army of exiles and mercenaries, maintained a sort of independent position, aloof from all parties. But Agathocles, on his return from Africa, concluded peace with Carthage, and entered into a compromise with Deinocrates, while he established his own power at Syracuse by a fearful massacre of all that were opposed to him. For the last twelve years of his reign (B. C. 301—289), his dominion seems to have been firmly established over Syracuse and a great part of Sicily, so that he was at liberty to follow out his ambitious schemes in the south of Italy and elsewhere.

After the death of Agathocles (B. C. 289), Sicily seems to have fallen into a state of great confusion; Syracuse apparently still retained its predominant position among the Greek cities, under a despot named Hicetas: but Agrigentum, which had also fallen into the hands of a despot named Phintias, was raised to a position that almost enabled it to dispute the supremacy. Phintias extended his dominion over several other cities, and having made himself master of Gela, utterly destroyed it, in order to found and people a new city at the mouth of the river Himera, to which he gave the name of Phintias. This was the last Greek city founded in Sicily. Meanwhile the Carthaginians were becoming more and more preponderant in the island, and the Greeks were at length led to invoke the assistance of Pyrrhus, king of Epirus, who was at this time carrying on war in Italy against the Romans. He readily listened to their overtures, and landed in the island in the autumn of B. C. 278. Phintias was at this time dead, and Hicetas had not long before been expelled from Syracuse. Pyrrhus therefore had no Greek adversaries to contend with, and was able to turn all his efforts against the Carthaginians. His successes were at first rapid and decisive: he wrested one town after another from the dominion of Carthage, took Panormus, which had long been the metropolis of their Sicilian possessions, and had never before fallen into the hands of a Greek invader, and carried by assault the strong fortresses of Ercte and Eryx: but he was foiled in an attack on Lilybaeum; jealousies and dissensions now arose between him and his Sicilian allies, and after little more than two years he was fain to return to Italy (B. C. 276), abandoning all his projects upon Sicily (Diod. *Exc. Hoesch.* xxii. 10, pp. 497—499).

The departure of Pyrrhus left the Sicilian Greeks without a leader, but Hieron, who was chosen general by the Syracusans, proved himself worthy of the occasion. Meanwhile a new and formidable enemy had arisen in the Mamertines, a band of Campanian mercenaries, who had possessed themselves by treachery of the important city of Messana, and from thence carried their arms over a considerable part of Sicily, and conquered or plundered many of its principal towns. Hieron waged war with them for a considerable period, and at length obtained so decisive a victory over them, in the immediate neighbourhood of Messana, that the city itself must have fallen, had it not been saved by the intervention of the Carthaginian general Hannibal. Hieron was now raised to the supreme power at Syracuse, and even assumed the title of king, B. C. 270. A few years after this we find him joining his arms with the Carthaginians, to effect the expulsion of the Mamertines, an object which they would doubtless have accomplished had not that people appealed to the protection of Rome. The Romans, who had recently completed the conquest of Italy, gladly seized the pretext for interfering in the affairs of Sicily, and espoused the cause of the Mamertines. Thus began the First Punic War, B. C. 264.

It is impossible here to relate in detail the events of that long-protracted struggle, during which Sicily became for twenty-three years the field of battle between the Romans and Carthaginians. Hieron, who had found himself at the beginning engaged in active hostilities with Rome, after sustaining several defeats, and losing many of his subject towns, wisely withdrew from the contest, and concluded in B. C. 263 a separate peace with Rome, by which he retained possession in full sovereignty of Syracuse and its territory, including the dependent towns of Acrae, Helorus, Netum, Megara, and Leontini, together with Tauromenium (Diod. xxiii. *Exc. H.* p. 502). From this time to the day of his death Hieron remained the faithful ally of the Romans, and retained the sovereign power at Syracuse undisturbed. In the rest of Sicily all trace of independent action on the part of the several Greek cities disappears: Agrigentum was indeed the only one of these cities in the island which appears to have retained any considerable importance: it was not taken by the Roman consuls till after a long and obstinate siege, B. C. 262, and was severely punished for its protracted resistance, the inhabitants being sold as slaves. Agrigentum indeed at a later period fell again into the hands of the Carthaginians, B. C. 255, but on the other hand the Romans made themselves mas-

ters of Panormus, for a long time the capital of the Carthaginian dominion in the island, which was thenceforth occupied by a strong Roman garrison, and never again fell into the hands of its former masters. For several years before the conclusion of the war, the possessions of the Carthaginians in Sicily were confined to the mountain of Eryx, occupied by Hamilcar Barca, and to the two strongly fortified seaports of Lilybaeum and Drepanum, the former of which defied all the attacks of the Romans, as it had previously done those of Pyrrhus. The siege, or rather blockade, of Lilybaeum was continued for nearly ten years, until the destruction of the Carthaginian fleet off the islands of the Aegates, B. C. 241, compelled that people to purchase peace by the surrender of all their remaining possessions in Sicily.

The whole island was now reduced into the condition of a Roman province, with the exception of the territory still governed by Hieron as an allied, but independent sovereign. The province thus constituted was the first that had ever borne that name (Cic. *Verr.* ii. 1): it was placed under the government of a praetor, who was sent annually from Rome (Appian, *Sic.* 2). On the first outbreak of the Second Punic War (B. C. 218), the consul Sempronius was at first sent to Sicily as his province, to guard against any threatened invasion from Africa; but he was soon recalled to oppose Hannibal in Italy, and for some years Sicily bore but an unimportant part in the war. A great change, however, occurred in the fourth year of the war (B. C. 215), in consequence of the defection of Hieronymus, the grandson and successor of Hieron at Syracuse, who abandoned the alliance of Rome to which Hieron had continued constant throughout his long reign, and espoused the Carthaginian cause. Hieronymus indeed was soon after assassinated, but the Carthaginian party at Syracuse, headed by Hippocrates and Epicydes, still maintained the ascendency, and Marcellus, who had been sent in haste to Sicily to put down the threatened revolt, was compelled to form the siege of Syracuse, B. C. 214. But so vigorous was the resistance offered to him that he soon found himself obliged to convert the siege into a blockade, nor was it till the autumn of B. C. 212 that the city finally fell into his hands. Meanwhile the war had extended itself to all parts of Sicily: many cities of the Roman province had followed the example of Syracuse, and joined the alliance of Carthage, while that power spared no exertions for their support. Even after the fall of Syracuse, the war was still continued: the Carthaginian general Mutines, who had made himself master of Agrigentum, carried on a desultory warfare from thence, and extended his ravages over the whole island. It was not till Mutines had been induced to desert the Carthaginian cause, and betray Agrigentum into the hands of the Romans, that the consul Laevinus was able to reduce the revolted cities to submission, and thus accomplished the final conquest of Sicily, B. C. 210 (Liv. xxvi. 40; xxvii. 5).

From this time the whole of Sicily became united as a Roman province, and its administration was in most respects similar to that of the other provinces. But its lot was anything but a fortunate one. Its great natural fertility, and especially its productiveness in corn, caused it, indeed, to be a possession of the utmost importance to Rome; but these very circumstances seem to have made it a favourite field for speculators, who bought up large tracts of land, which they cultivated solely by means of slaves, so that the free population of the island became materially diminished. The more mountainous portions of the island were given up to shepherds and herdsmen, all likewise slaves, and accustomed to habits of rapine and plunder, in which they were encouraged by their masters. At the same time the number of wealthy proprietors, and the extensive export trade of some of the towns, maintained a delusive appearance of prosperity. It was not till the outbreak of the Servile War in B. C. 135 that the full extent of these evils became apparent, but the frightful state of things then revealed sufficiently shows that the causes which had produced it must have been long at work. That great outbreak, which commenced with a local insurrection of the slaves of a great proprietor at Enna, named Damophilus, and was headed by a Syrian slave of the name of Eunus, quickly spread throughout the whole island, so that the slaves are said to have mustered 200,000 armed men. With this formidable force they defeated in succession the armies of several Roman praetors, so that in B. C. 134, it was thought necessary to send against them the consul Fulvius Flaccus, and it was not till the year B. C. 132 that their strongholds of Tauromenium and Enna were taken by the consul P. Rupilius. (Diod. xxxiv. Exc. Phot., Exc. Vales.) The insurrection was now finally quelled, but the state of Sicily had undergone a severe shock, and the settlement of its affairs was confided to P. Rupilius, together with ten commissioners, who laid down a code of laws and rules for its internal government which continued to be observed in the days of Cicero (Cic. Verr. ii. 16).

But the outbreak of the second Servile War, under Salvius and Athenion, less than thirty years after the termination of the former one (B. C. 103), and the fact that the slaves were again able to maintain the contest against three successive consuls till they were finally vanquished by M. Aquilius, in B. C. 100, sufficiently proves that the evils in the state of society had been but imperfectly remedied by Rupilius; nor can we believe that the condition of the island was in reality altogether so flourishing as it is represented by Cicero during the interval which elapsed between this Servile War and the praetorship of Verres, B. C. 73. But that great natural resources of Sicily and its important position as the granary of Rome undoubtedly enabled it to recover with rapidity from all its disasters. The elder Cato had called it the store-room (cella penaria) of the Roman state, and Cicero observes that in the great Social War (B. C. 90—88) it supplied the Roman armies not only with food, but with clothing and arms also (Cic. Verr. ii. 2). But the praetorship of Verres (B. C. 73—70) inflicted a calamity upon Sicily scarcely inferior to the Servile wars that had so recently devastated it. The rhetorical expressions of Cicero must not indeed be always understood literally; but with every allowance for exaggeration, there can be no doubt that the evils resulting from such a government as that of Verres were enormous; and Sicily was just in such a state as to suffer from them most severely.

The orations of Cicero against Verres convey to us much curious and valuable information as to the condition of Sicily under the Roman republic as well as to the administration and system of government of the Roman provinces generally. Sicily at that time formed but one province, under the government

of a praetor or pro-praetor, but it had always two quaestors, one of whom resided at Syracuse, the other at Lilybaeum. This anomaly (for such it appears to have been) probably arose from the different parts of the island having been reduced into the form of a province at different periods. The island contained in all above sixty towns which enjoyed municipal rights: of these, three only, Messana, Tauromenium, and Netum, were allied cities (civitates foederatae), and thus enjoyed a position of nominal independence; five were exempt from all fiscal burdens and from the ordinary jurisdiction of the Roman magistrates (civitates immunes et liberae): the rest were in the ordinary position of provincial towns, but retained their own magistrates and municipal rights, as well as the possession of their respective territories, subject to the payment of a tenth of their produce to the Roman state. These tenths, which were paid in kind, were habitually farmed out, according to principles and regulations laid down in the first instance by Hieron, king of Syracuse, and which therefore continued to be known as the Lex Hieronica. For judicial purposes, the island appears to have been divided into districts or conventus, but the number of them is not stated; those of Syracuse, Agrigentum, Lilybaeum, and Panormus are the only ones mentioned.

Sicily took little part in the Civil War between Caesar and Pompey. It was at first held by M. Cato on behalf of the latter, but abandoned by him when Pompey himself had quitted Italy, and was then occupied by Curio, as pro-praetor, with four legions (Caes. B. C. i. 30, 31). Caesar himself visited it previous to his African war, and it was from Lilybaeum that he crossed over with his army into Africa (Hirt. B. Afr. 1.) After the death of Caesar, it fell into the hands of Sextus Pompeius, whose powerful fleet enabled him to defy all the efforts of Octavian to recover it, and was at length secured to him by the peace of Misenum, B. C. 39, together with Sardinia and Corsica. But Octavian soon renewed his attempts to dispossess him, and though he sustained repeated defeats at sea, and lost a great part of his fleet by a storm, the energy and ability of Agrippa enabled him to triumph over all obstacles; and the final defeat of his fleet at Naulochus compelled Pompeius to abandon Sicily, and take refuge in the east (Appian, B. C. v. 77—122; Dion Cass. xlix. 1—17). There seems no doubt that the island suffered severely from this contest, and from the rapacity or exactions of Sextus Pompeius: Strabo distinctly ascribes its decayed condition in his time principally to this cause (Strab. vi. pp. 270, 272). Augustus made some attempts to relieve it by sending colonies to a few cities, among which were Tauromenium, Catana, Syracuse, Thermae, and Tyndaris (Strab. vi. p. 272; Plin. iii. 8. s. 14); but the effect thus produced was comparatively small, and Strabo describes the whole island as in his time, with few exceptions, in a state of decay, many of its ancient cities having altogether disappeared, while others were in a declining condition, and the interior was for the most part given up to pasturage, and inhabited only by herdsmen (Strab. l. c.)

Augustus appears to have greatly remodelled the internal administration of Sicily: so that the condition of most of the towns had undergone a change between the time of Cicero and that of Pliny. Caesar had indeed proposed to give Latin rights to all the Sicilians, and M. Antonius even brought

3 R 4

forward a law to admit them without distinction to the Roman franchise (Cic. *ad Att.* xiv. 2), but neither of these measures was accomplished; and we learn from Pliny that Messana was in his day the only city in the island of which the inhabitants possessed the Roman citizenship: three others, Centuripa, Netum, and Segesta enjoyed the Jus Latii, while all the others (except the colonies already mentioned) were in the ordinary condition of "civitates stipendiariae" (Plin. iii. 8. s. 14). We hear very little of Sicily under the Empire; but it is probable that it never really recovered from the state of decay into which it had fallen in Strabo's time. Almost the only mention of it in history is that of an outbreak of slaves and banditti in the reign of Gallienus which seems to have resembled on a smaller scale the Servile wars that had formerly devastated it (Treb. Poll. *Gallien,* 4). The increasing importance of the supply of corn from Africa and Egypt renders it probable that that from Sicily had fallen off, and the small number of remains of the imperial period still existing in the island, though so many are preserved from a much earlier date, seems to prove that it could not then have been very flourishing. At a late period of the Empire, also, we find very few names of towns in the Itineraries, the lines of road being carried through stations or "mansiones" otherwise wholly unknown, a sufficient proof that the neighbouring towns had fallen into decay. (*Itin. Ant.* pp. 86—98.) In the division of the provinces under Augustus, Sicily was assigned to the senate, and was governed by a proconsul; at a later period it was considered as a part of Italy, and was governed by a magistrate named a Consularis, subject to the authority of the Vicarius Urbis Romae. (*Notit. Dign.* ii. p. 64; and Böcking, *ad loc.*)

Its insular position must have for a considerable time preserved Sicily from the ravages of the barbarians who devastated Italy towards the close of the Western Empire. Alaric indeed attempted to cross over the straits, but was foiled by a tempest. (*Hist. Miscell.* xiii. p. 535.) But Genseric, being master of a powerful fleet, made himself master of the whole island, which was held by the Vandals for a time, but subsequently passed into the hands of the Goths, and continued attached to the Gothic kingdom of Italy till it was conquered by Belisarius in A. D. 535. It was then united to the Eastern Empire, and continued to be governed as a dependency by the Byzantine emperors till the ninth century, when it fell into the hands of the Saracens or Arabs. That people first landed at Mazara, in the W. of the island in A. D. 827, and made themselves masters of Agrigentum; but their progress was vigorously opposed. They took Messana in 831, and Panormus in 835, but it was not till 878 that Syracuse, the last fortress in the island, fell into their hands. The island continued in the possession of the Saracens till the middle of the eleventh century, when it was partially recovered by the Byzantine emperors with the assistance of the Normans. But in 1061 the Norman Roger Guiscard invaded Sicily on his own account, and, after a long struggle, wholly reduced the island under his dominion. It has since remained attached, with brief exceptions, to the crown of Naples, the monarch of which bears the title of King of the Two Sicilies.

The extant remains of antiquity in Sicily fully confirm the inference which we should draw from the statements of ancient historians, as to the prosperity and opulence of the island under the Greeks, and its comparatively decayed condition under the Romans. The ruins of the latter period are few, and for the most part unimportant, the exceptions being confined to the three or four cities which we know to have received Roman colonies: while the temples, theatres, and other edifices from the Greek period are numerous and of the most striking character. No city of Greece, with the exception of Athens, can produce structures that vie with those of which the remains are still visible at Agrigentum, Selinus and Segesta. At the same time the existing relics of antiquity, especially coins and inscriptions, strongly confirm the fact that almost the whole population of the island had been gradually Hellenised. It is evident that the strong line of demarcation which existed in the days of Thucydides between the Greek cities and those of non-Hellenic or barbarian origin had been to a great degree effaced before the island passed under the dominion of Rome. The names of Sicilian citizens mentioned by Cicero in his Verrine orations are as purely Greek where they belong to cities of Siculian origin, such as Centuripa and Agyrium, or even to Carthaginian cities like Panormus and Lilybaeum, as are those of Syracuse or Agrigentum. In like manner we find coins with Greek legends struck by numerous cities which undoubtedly never received a Greek colony, such as Alaesa, Menaenum, and many others. It is probable indeed that during the Roman Republic the language of the whole island (at least the written and cultivated language) was Greek, which must, however, have gradually given way to Latin under the Empire, as the Sicilian dialect of the present day is one of purely Latin origin, and differs but slightly from that of the south of Italy. Of the language of the ancient Sicels we have no trace at all, and it is highly probable that it was never used as a written language.

III. TOPOGRAPHY.

The general description of the physical features of Sicily has been already given. But it will be necessary here to describe its coasts in somewhat more detail. The E. coast extending from Cape Pelorus to Pachynus, consists of three portions of a very different character. From Pelorus to Taurominium, a distance of about 40 miles, it is closely bordered by the chain of mountains called the Mons Neptunius, the slopes of which descend steeply to the sea, forming a very uniform line of coast, furrowed by numerous small torrents. Two of the small headlands between these valleys appear to have borne the names of Drepanum (Plin.) and Argennum (Ptol.), but their identification is quite uncertain. S. of Taurominium, from the mouth of the Acesines to that of the Symaethus, the whole coast is formed by beds of lava and other volcanic matters, which have flowed down from Aetna. Off this coast, about midway between Acium and Catana are some rocky islets of volcanic origin, called by Pliny the Cyclopum Scopuli: the name of Portus Ulyssis is given by the same author to a port in this neighbourhood, but it is impossible to say which of the many small sheltered coves on this line of coast he means to designate. S. of the Symaethus the coast is much varied, being indented by several deep bays and inlets, separated by projecting rocky headlands. The principal of these is the bay of Megara (Sinus Megarensis) so called from the Greek city of that name; it was bounded on the N. by the Xiphonian promontory, now *Capo di Sta Croce* (Ἱερωνίας ἀκρωτήριον, Strab. vi. p. 267), within which was the XIPHONIAN PORT (Λιμὴν Ξιφόνειος, Scyl. p. 4), evidently the harbour of *Augusta*, one of the finest natural harbours in the island. Between this and Syracuse is the remarkable peninsular promontory of THAPSUS (*Magnisi*), while immediately S. of Syracuse occurs the remarkable landlocked bay called the Great Harbour of that city, and the rocky headland of PLEMMYRIUM which bounds it on the S. From this point to Cape Pachynus no ancient names have been preserved to us of the headlands or harbours. From Cape Pachynus to the site of Gela the coast is low but rocky. Along this line must be placed the port of Ulysses (Portus Odysseae) mentioned by Cicero, and the promontory of Ulysses of Ptolemy, both apparently in the immediate neighbourhood of Cape Pachynus [PACHYNUS.] The Bucra promontory (Βούκρα ἄκρα) of Ptolemy, which he places further W., is wholly unknown, as is also the port of Caucana of the same author (Καυκάνα Λιμήν, Ptol. iii. 4. § 7). The remainder of the S. coast of Sicily from Gela to Lilybaeum presents on the whole a very uniform character; it has few or no natural ports, and no remarkable headlands. It is bounded for the most part by hills of clay or soft limestone, generally sloping gradually to the sea, but sometimes forming cliffs of no great elevation. The celebrated promontory of LILYBAEUM is a low rocky point, and its famous port, though secure, is of small extent. N. of Lilybaeum was the promontory of AEGITHALLUS, with the adjacent low islands, on one of which the city MOTYA was built; while the more considerable islands of the AEGATES lay a few miles further to the W., and the promontory of DREPANUM adjoining the city of the same name formed the NW. point of Sicily. It is remarkable that no ancient name is preserved to us for the deep gulf of *Castellamare* which occurs on the coast between *Trapani* and *Palermo*, though it is one of the most remarkable features of the N. coast of Sicily; nor are the two striking headlands that bound the *Bay of Palermo* itself known to us by their ancient names. The bold and insulated hill of *Monte Sta Rosalia* is, however, the ancient ERCTE. The northern coast of Sicily is bold and varied, formed by offshoots and ridges of the northern chain of mountains descending abruptly to the sea; hence it was always a rugged and difficult line of communication. But none of the rocky headlands that interrupt it are mentioned to us by their ancient names, till we come to that of Mylae adjoining the town of the same name (*Milazzo*), and the PHALACRIAN PROMONTORY (Ptol. iii. 4. § 2), apparently the *Capo di Rasocolmo* within a few miles of Cape Pelorus.

From the triangular form of Sicily and the configuration of the mountain chains which traverse it, it is evident that it could not have any rivers of importance. Most of them indeed are little more than mere mountain torrents, swelling with great rapidity after violent storms or during the winter rains, but nearly, if not wholly, dry during the summer months. The most important rivers of the island are: 1. The SYMAETHUS (*Simeto* or *Giarretta*), which rises in the northern chain of mountains (the Mons Nebrodes), and flows to the S. and SE. round the foot of Aetna, falling into the sea about 6 miles S. of Catania. It receives several tributaries, of which the *Dittaino* is certainly the ancient CHRYSAS, that flowed near the city of Assorus, while the ADRANUS of Stephanus can

be no other than the northern or main branch of the Symaethus itself. The Cyamosorus (Κυαμόσωρος) of Polybius, which appears to have been in the neighbourhood of Centuripa, must probably be the branch now called *Fiume Salso*, which joins the *Simeto* just below *Centorbi*. 2. The ACESINES or ASINES (*F. Cantara*), which rises very near the Symaethus, but flows along the northern foot of Aetna, and falls into the sea just below Tauromenium. 3. The HIMERA (*F. Salso*), the most considerable of two rivers which bore the same name, rising in the *Monte Madonia* (Mons Nebrodes) only about 15 miles from the N. coast, and flowing due S.; so that it traverses nearly the whole breadth of Sicily. and falls into the sea at *Alicata* (Phintias). 4. The HALYCUS (*Platani*), so long the boundary between the Carthaginian and Greek territories in the island, is also a considerable stream; it rises not far from the Himera, but flows to the SW., and enters the sea between Agrigentum and Selinus, close to the site of Heraclea Minoa. 5. The HYPSAS (*Belici*), falling into the sea on the S. coast, a few miles E. of Selinus; and 6, the ANAPUS (*Anapo*), which flows under the walls of Syracuse and falls into the great harbour of that city. It is unlike most of the rivers of Sicily, being a full clear stream, supplied from subterranean sources. The same character belongs still more strongly to its tributary the CYANE, which has a considerable volume of water, though its whole course does not exceed two miles in length.

The minor rivers of Sicily which are mentioned either in history or by the geographers are numerous, but in many cases are very difficult to identify. Beginning at Cape Pachynus and proceeding along the coast westward, we find: 1, the Motychanus (Μοτύχανος, Ptol. iii. 4. § 7), evidently so called from its flowing near Motyca, and therefore probably the stream now called *Fiume di Scicli*; 2, the Hirminius of Pliny, probably the *Fiume di Ragusa*, very near the preceding; 3, the HIPPARIS; and 4, the OANUS, two small streams which flowed under the walls of Camarina, now called the *F. di Camarana* and *Frascolari*; 5, the GELA or GELAS, which gave name to the city of Gela, and must therefore be the *Fiume di Terranova*; 6, the ACRAGAS, a small stream flowing under the walls of Agrigentum, to which it gave name, and receiving a tributary called the HYPSAS (*Drago*), which must not be confounded with the more important river of the same name already mentioned; 7, the CAMICUS, probably the *Fiume delle Canne*, about 10 miles W. of Girgenti; 8, the SELINUS, flowing by the city of that name, now the *Madiuni*; 9, the MAZARA or MAZARUS, flowing by the town of the same name, and still called *Fiume di Mazzara*. Besides these Ptolemy mentions the Isburus and Sosias or Sossius, two names otherwise wholly unknown, and which cannot be placed with any approach to certainty. Equally uncertain is the more noted river ACHATES, which is placed by Pliny in the same part of Sicily with the Mazara and Hypsas; but there is great confusion in his enumeration as well as that of Ptolemy. It is generally identified with the *Dirillo*, but this is situated in quite a different part of Sicily. The Acithius of Ptolemy, which he places between Lilybaeum and Selinus, may be the *Fiume di Marsala*.

Along the N. coast, proceeding from Lilybaeum to Cape Pelorus, we meet with a number of small streams, having for the most part a short torrent-like course, from the mountains to the sea. Their identification is for the most part very obscure and uncertain. Thus we find three rivers mentioned in connection with Segesta, and all of them probably flowing through its territory, the Porpax, Telmessus, and CRIMESSUS or CRIMISUS. The last of these is probably the *Fiume di S. Bartolomeo*, about 5 miles E. of Segesta: the other two, which are mentioned only by Aelian (*V. H.* ii. 33), cannot be identified, though one of them is probably the *Fiume Gaggera*, which flows beneath Segesta itself, and falls into the *F. di S. Bartolomeo* near its mouth. But, to complicate the question still more, we are told that the names of Scamander and Simois were given by the Trojan colonists to two rivers near Segesta; and the former name at least seems to have been really in use. (Strab. xiii. p. 608; Diod. xx. 71.) Proceeding eastward we find: 1, the Orethus (Vib. Sequest. p. 15), still called the *Oreto*, a small stream flowing under the walls of Panormus ; 2, the Eleutherus (Ἐλεύθερος, Ptol. iii. 4. § 3), placed by Ptolemy between Panormus and Soluntum, and which must therefore be the *Fiume di Bagaria*; 3, the northern HIMERA, commonly identified with the *Fiume di S. Leonardo*, near *Termini*, but more probably the *Fiume Grande*, about 8 miles further E. [HIMERA]; 4, the Monalus (Μόναλος, Ptol.), between Cephaloedium and Alaesa, now the *Pollina*; 5, the Halesus or Alaesus, flowing beneath the city of Alaesa, now the *Pettineo*; 6, the Chydas (Χύδας, Ptol.), between Alaesa and Aluntium ; 7, the Timethus (Τίμηθος, Id.), between Agathyrna and Tyndaris ; 8, the Helicon (Ἑλικών, Id.), between Tyndaris and Mylae ; 9, the Phacelinus (Vib. Sequest.), which was near Mylae, or between that city and Messana (the nearer determination of these four last is wholly uncertain); 10, the Melas of Ovid (*Fast.* iv. 476) is generally placed in the same neighbourhood, though without any obvious reason.

Along the E. coast the names may be more clearly identified. 1. The ONOBALAS of Appian (*B. C.* v. 109) is probably identical with the Acesines already noticed; 2, the ACIS, a very small stream, is the *Fiume di Jaci* ; 3, the AMENANUS, flowing through the city of Catana, is the *Giudicello;* 4, the TERIAS is the *Fiume di S. Leonardo*, which flows from the Lake of *Lentini*; 5, the PANTAGIAS is the *Porcari*; 6, the ALABUS is the *Cantaro*, a small stream flowing into the bay of *Augusta*. The Anapus and its confluent the Cyane have been already mentioned. S. of Syracuse occur three small rivers, memorable in the retreat of the Athenians: these are, 1, the CACYPARIS (*Cassibili*); 2, the ERINEUS (*Fiume di Avola*); and 3, the ASINARUS (*Falconara*). A few miles S. of this was the HELORUS, now called the *Abisso*, flowing by the city of the same name. No other stream occurs between this and Cape Pachynum.

Sicily contains no lakes that deserve the name; but there are a few pools or marshy lagoons, of which the names have been preserved to us. Of the latter description were the LYSIMELIA PALUS near Syracuse, and the CAMARINA PALUS adjoining the city of the same name. The LACUS PALICORUM, on the contrary, was a deep pool or basin of volcanic origin: while the small lake called by the poets Pergus or Pergusa is still extant in the neighbourhood of Enna. The *Lago di Lentini*, though much the most considerable accumulation of waters in Sicily, is not mentioned by any ancient author.

The towns and cities of Sicily were very numerous.

The Greek colonies and their offshoots or dependencies have been already mentioned in relating the history of their settlement; but the names of all the towns so far as they can be ascertained will be here enumerated in geographical order, without reference to their origin, omitting only the places mentioned in the Itineraries, which were probably mere villages or stations. 1. Beginning from Cape Pelorus and proceeding along the E. coast towards Cape Pachynus, were: MESSANA, TAUROMENIUM, NAXOS, ACIUM, CATANA and SYRACUSE. TROTILUM, destroyed at an early period, as well as MEGARA HYBLAEA, were situated between Catana and Syracuse. The Chalcidic colonies of CALLIPOLIS and EUBOEA, both of which disappeared at an early period, must have been situated on or near the E. coast of the island, and to the N. of Syracuse, but we have no further clue to their situation. S. of Syracuse, between it and Cape Pachynus, was HELORUS, at the mouth of the river of the same name. 2. W. of Cape Pachynus, proceeding along the S. coast, were CAMARINA, GELA, PHINTIAS, AGRIGENTUM, HERACLEA MINOA, THERMAE SELINUNTIAE, SELINUS, MAZARA, and LILYBAEUM. Besides these the more obscure towns of CAMICUS, CAENA, and INYCUM, the two former dependencies of Agrigentum, the latter of Selinus, must be placed on or near the S. coast of the island. 3. N. of Lilybaeum was MOTYA, which ceased to exist at a comparatively early period, and DREPANUM (*Trapani*) at the NW. angle of the island. Between this and Panormus, were ERYX at the foot of the mountain of the same name, and a short distance from the coast, the Emporium of Segesta, HYCCARA, and CETARIA. Proceeding eastward from PANORMUS, along the N. coast of the island, were SOLUNTUM, THERMAE, HIMERA, CEPHALOEDIUM, ALAESA, CALACTA, AGATHYRNA, ALUNTIUM, TYNDARIS, and MYLAE.

The towns in the interior are more difficult to enumerate: with regard to some of them indeed we are at a loss to determine, even in what region of the island they were situated. For the purpose of enumeration it will be convenient to divide the island into three portions; the first comprising the western half of Sicily as far as the river Himera, and a line drawn from its sources to the N. coast: the other two, the NE. and SE. portions, being separated by the course of the river *Dittaino* and that of the Symaethus to the sea. 1. In the western district were SEGESTA and HALICYAE, the most westerly of the inland cities; ENTELLA, on the river Hypsas, about midway between the two seas; IAETA and MACELLA, both of which may probably be placed in the mountainous district between Entella and Panormus; TRIOCALA, near *Calatabellotta*, in the mountains inland from the Thermae Selinuntiae; SCHERA, of very uncertain site, but probably situated in the same part of Sicily; HERBESSUS, in the neighbourhood of Agrigentum; PETRA, near the sources of the W. branch of the Himera in the *Madonia* mountains; and ENGYUM (*Gangi*), at the head of the *Fiume Grande*, the E. branch of the same river. PAROPUS must apparently be placed on the northern declivity of the same mountains, but further to the W.

A little to the E. of the Himera and as nearly as possible in the centre of the island, was situated the fortress of ENNA (*Castro Giovanni*), so that the boundary line between the NE. and NW. regions may be conveniently drawn from thence. 2. In the NE. region were : ASSORUS and AGYRIUM.

NE. of Enna, but W. of the valley of the Symaethus; CENTURIPA (*Centorbi*), nearly due E. of
Enna; ADRANUM (*Adernò*), on the E. bank of the
Symaethus, at the foot of Mount Aetna; HYBLA
MAJOR (which must not be confounded with the
city of the same name near Syracuse), and AETNA,
previously called INESSA, both situated on the
southern slope of the same mountain. N. of Agyrium, on the southern slopes of the Mons Nebrodes
were situated HERBITA, CAPITIUM, and probably
also GALARIA: while on the northern declivities of
the same mountains, fronting the sea, but at some
distance inland, were placed APOLLONIA (probably
Pollina), AMESTRATUS (*Mistretta*), ABACAENUM,
a few miles inland from Tyndaris, and NOAE, probably *Nuara*. Three other towns, IMACHARA,
ICHANA, and TISSA, may probably be assigned to
this same region of Sicily, though their exact position cannot be determined. 3. In the SE. portion
of Sicily, S. of the Symaethus and its tributary
the Chrysas or *Dittaino*, were situated ERGETIUM,
MORGANTIA, LEONTINI, and HYBLA: as well as
MENAENUM and HERBESSUS: but of all these
names Leontini (*Lentini*) and Menaenum (*Mineo*)
are the only ones that can be identified with anything like certainty. In the hills W. of Syracuse
were ACRAE (*Palazzolo*), BIDIS (*S. Gio. di Bidino*),
and CACYRUM (*Cassaro*); and W. of these again, in
the direction towards Gela, must be placed the He-
raean HYBLA, as well as ECHETLA, in the neighbourhood of *Gran Michele*. SW. of Syracuse, in the
interior, were NETUM or NEETUM (*Noto Vecchio*),
and MOTYCA (*Modica*), both of which are well
known. The Syracusan colony of CASMENAE must
probably have been situated in the same district
but its site has never been identified.

After going through this long list of Sicilian
towns, there remain the following, noticed either by
Cicero or Pliny, as municipal towns, to the position
of which we have no means of even approximating.
The ACHERINI (Cic.), TYRACINI (Cic.; Tyracienses,
Plin.), Acestaei (Plin.), Etini (Id.), Herbulenses
(Id.), Semellitani (Id.), Talarenses (Id.). Many of
the above names are probably corrupt and merely
false readings, but we are at a loss what to substitute. On the other hand, the existence of a town
called MUTISTRATUM or Mytistratum is attested by
both Cicero and Pliny, and there seems no sufficient
reason for rejecting it as identical with Amestratus,
as has been done by many modern geographers,
though its site is wholly uncertain. Equally unknown are the following names given by Ptolemy
among the inland towns of the island: Aleta
(Ἀλήτα), Hydra or Lydia (Ὕδρα or Λυδία), Patyorus (Πατίωρος), Coturga or Cortuga (Κότυργα or
Κόρτυγα), Legum or Letum (Λῆγον or Λῆτον),
Ancrina (Ἄγκρινα), Ina or Ena (Ἴνα or Ἥνα), and
Elœthium (Ἐλκέθιον). It would be a waste of time
to discuss these names, most of which are probably
in their present form corrupt, and are all of them
otherwise wholly unknown. On the other hand the
existence of NACONA, mentioned by Stephanus of
Byzantium, but not noticed by any other writer, is
confirmed by coins.

The topography of Sicily is still very imperfectly
known. The ruins of its more celebrated cities are
indeed well known, and have been often described;
especially in the valuable work of the Duke of
Serra di Falco (*Antichità della Sicilia*, 5 vols. fol.
Palermo, 1834—1839), as well as in the well-known
travels of Swinburne, Sir R. Hoare, &c. (Swinburne's

Travels in the Two Sicilies, 2 vols. 4to. Lond. 1783;
Sir R. Hoare's *Classical Tour through Italy and
Sicily*, 2 vols. 8vo. Lond. 1819; St. Non, *Voyage
Pittoresque de Naples et de la Sicile*, 5 vols. fol.
Paris, 1781; Biscari, Principe di, *Viaggio per le
Antichità della Sicilia*, 8vo. Palermo, 1817, &c.):
but the island has never been thoroughly explored
by an antiquarian traveller, like those to whom we
are indebted for our knowledge of Greece and Asia
Minor. The valuable work of Cluverius (*Sicilia
Antiqua*, fol. Lugd. Bat. 1619) must here, as well
as for Italy, be made the foundation of all subsequent
researches. But much valuable information is found
in the more ancient work of Fazello, a Sicilian monk
of the sixteenth century, as well as of his commentator Amico, and in the Topographical Dictionary of
the latter author. (Thomae Fazelli *de Rebus Siculis
Decades Duo*, first edit. in fol. Panormi, 1558,
republished with copious notes by Amico, 3 vols. fol.
Catanae, 1749—1753; Amico, *Lexicon Topogra-
phicum Siculum*, 3 vols. 4to. Catanae, 1759). Much,
however, still remains to be done. Many localities
indicated by Fazello in the sixteenth century as
presenting ancient remains have never (so far as we
are aware) been visited by any modern traveller: no
good map of the island exists, which can be trusted
for topographical details, and there can be little
doubt that a minute and careful examination of the
whole country, such as has been made of the neighbouring island of Sardinia by the Chev. De la Marmora, would well reward the labours of the explorer.
Even the ruins described by Sir R. Hoare as existing
in the neighbourhood of *Sta Croce*, or those situated
near *Vindicari*, a few miles N. of Cape Pachynus
and commonly ascribed to Imachara, have never
been examined in detail, nor has any clue been obtained to their identification.

The Itineraries give several lines of route through
the island, but many of the stations mentioned are
wholly uncertain, and were probably never more
than obscure villages or mere solitary posthouses.
The first line of route (*Itin. Ant.* pp. 86—89) proceeds from Messana along the E. coast by Tauromenium and Acium to Catana, and from thence strikes
inland across the centre of the island to Agrigentum;
the course of this inland route is wholly uncertain
and the names of the three stations upon it, Capi-
toniana, Gelasium Philosophiana and Petiliana, are
entirely unknown. From Agrigentum it followed
the line of coast to Lilybaeum; the stations given
are Cena [CAENA], Allava, Ad Aquas (i. e. the
Aquae Labodes or Thermae Selinuntiae), Ad fluvium
Lanarium, and Mazara; all except the 3rd and 5th
of very uncertain site. A second route (*Itin. Ant.*
pp. 89, 90) proceeds in the inverse direction from
Lilybaeum to Agrigentum, and thence by a more
southerly line, through Calvisiana, Hybla, and
Acrae (*Palazzolo*) to Syracuse, and from thence as
before along the E. coast to Messana. A third line
follows the N. coast of the island from Lilybaeum
by Panormus to Messana. The stations on this line
are better known and can for the most part be determined: they are, Drepana, Aquae Segestanae
(near Segesta), Parthenium (*Partinico*), Hyccara
(*Muro di Carini*), Panormus, Soluntum, Thermae,
Cephaloedium, Halesus (Alaesa), Calacte, Agatinnum,
(Agathyrnum), Tyndaris, and Messana. A fourth
route (*Itin. Ant.* p. 93) crossed the interior of the
island from Thermae, where it branched off from the
preceding, passing through Enna, Agyrium, Centuripa and Aetna to Catana. A fifth gives us a line

of strictly maritime route around the southern extremity of the island from Agrigentum to Syracuse;
but with the exception of Pintia, which is probably
Phintias (*Alicata*), none of the stations can be
identified. Lastly, a line of road was in use which
crossed the island from Agrigentum direct to Panormus (*Itin. Ant.* p. 96), but none of its stations
are known, and we are therefore unable to determine
even its general course. The other routes given in
the Itinerary of Antoninus are only unimportant
variations of the preceding ones. The Tabula gives
only the one general line around the island (crossing,
however, from Calvisiana on the S. coast direct to
Syracuse), and the cross line already mentioned from
Thermae to Catana. All discussion of distances
along the above routes must be rejected as useless,
until the routes themselves can be more accurately
determined, which is extremely difficult in so hilly
and broken a country as the greater part of the
interior of Sicily. The similarity of names, which
in Italy is so often a sure guide where all other indications are wanting, is of far less assistance in
Sicily, where the long period of Arabic dominion has
thrown the nomenclature of the island into great
confusion   [E. H. B.]

COIN OF SICILIA.

SICILIBBA or SICILIBBA (in the Geogr. Rav.
Siciliba, iii. 5), a place in Africa Propria (*Itin. Ant.*
pp. 25, 45), variously identified with *Basilbah* and
Haouch Alouina.   [T. H. D.]

SI'CINOS (Σίκινος: *Eth.* Σικινίτης: *Sikino*), a
small island in the Aegaean sea, one of the Sporades,
lying between Pholegandros and Ios, and containing
a town of the same name. (Scylax, p. 19; Strab.
x. p. 484; Ptol. iii. 15. § 31.) It is said to have
been originally called Oenoë from its cultivation of
the vine, but to have been named Sicinos after a son
of Thoas and Oenoë. (Steph. B. *s. v.*; Apoll. Rhod.
i. 623; Schol. *ad loc.*; Plin. iv. 12. s. 23; Etym.
M. p. 712. 49.) Wine is still the chief production
of the island. It was probably colonised by Ionians.
Like most of the other Grecian islands, it submitted
to Xerxes (Herod. viii. 4), but it afterwards formed
part of the Athenian maritime empire. There are
some remains of the ancient city situated upon a lofty
and rugged mountain, on whose summit stands the
church of *S. Marina*. There is also still extant an
ancient temple of the Pythian Apollo, now converted
into the church *Episkopi* (ἡ 'Επισκοπή). It stands
in a depression between the main range of mountains, and the summit lying more to the left, upon
which the ruins of the ancient city stand. We
learn from an inscription found there by Ross that
it was the temple of the Pythian Apollo. (Ross,
Reisen auf den Griech. Inseln, vol. ii. p. 149, seq.;
Fiedler, *Reise*, vol. ii. p. 151, seq.)

SICOR. [SEGOR.]

SI'CORIS (Σίκορις, Dion Cass. xli. 20), a tributary river of the Iberus in Hispania Tarraconensis.
It rose in the Pyrenees in the territory of the Cer-

retani, and separated the countries of the Ilergetes
and Lacetani. It flowed past Ilerda, and according
to Vibius Sequester (p. 224, ed. Bipont) bore the
name of that town. A little afterwards it received
the Cinga, and then flowed into the Iberus near
Octogesa. (Caes. *B. C.* i. 40, 48; Plin. iii. 3. s. 4;
Lucan. iv. 13, seq.) Ausonius describes it as flowing impetuously ("torrentem," *Epist.* xxv. 59).
Now the *Segre*.   [T. H. D.]

SI'CULI (Σικελοί), is the name given by ancient
writers to an ancient race or people that formed one
of the elements in the primitive population of Italy,
as well as Sicily. But the accounts given of them
are very confused and uncertain. We find the
Siculi mentioned: 1, as among the early inhabitants
of Latium; 2, in the extreme S. of Italy; 3, in
Sicily; 4, on the shores of the Adriatic. It will be
convenient to examine these notices separately.

1. The Siculi are represented by Dionysius as
the earliest inhabitants of the country subsequently
called Latium (i. 9), as well as of the southern part
of Etruria; they were an indigenous race, i. e. one
of whose wanderings and origin he had no account.
They held the whole country till they were expelled
from it by the people whom he calls Aborigines,
descending from the mountains of Central Italy
[ABORIGINES], who made war upon them, in conjunction with the Pelasgians; and after a long protracted struggle, wrested from them one town after
another (Id. i. 9, 16). Among the cities that are
expressly mentioned by him as having once been
occupied by the Siculi, are Tibur, where a part of
the city was still called in the days of Dionysius
Σικελιόν, Ficulea, Antemnae, and Tellenae, as well
as Falerii and Fescennium, in the country afterwards called Etruria (Id. i. 16, 20, 21). The
Siculi being thus finally expelled from their possessions in this part of Italy, were reported to have
migrated in a body to the southern extremity of the
peninsula, from whence they crossed over the straits,
and established themselves in the island of Sicily,
to which they gave the name it has ever since
borne. [SICILIA.] (Id. i. 22.) Dionysius is the
only author who has left us a detailed account of
the conquest and expulsion of the Siculi, but they
are mentioned by Pliny among the races that had
successively occupied Latium (Plin. iii. 5. s. 9);
and this seems to have been an established and
received tradition.

2. We find the Siculi frequently mentioned in the
southernmost portion of the Italian peninsula, where
they appear in close connection with the Oenotrians,
Morgetes, and Itali, all of them kindred tribes, which
there are good reasons for assigning to the Pelasgic
race. [OENOTRIA.] It is probable, as suggested by
Strabo, that the Siculi, more than once, mentioned
by Homer (*Odyss.* xx. 383, xxiv. 211, &c.), were
the inhabitants of the coast of Italy opposite to
Ithaca: and the traditions of the Epizephyrian Locrians, reported by Polybius, spoke of the Siculi as the
people in whose territory they settled, and with whom
they first found themselves engaged in war. (Polyb.
xii. 5, 6.) Numerous traditions also, reported by
Dionysius (i. 22, 73) from Antiochus, Hellanicus, and others, concur in bringing the Siculi and
their eponymous leader Siculus (Σικελός) into close
connection with Italus and the Itali: and this is
confirmed by the linguistic relation which may fairly
be admitted to exist between Σικελός and 'Ιταλός
(Niebuhr, vol. i. p. 47) though this is not close
enough to be in itself conclusive. So far as

our scanty knowledge goes, therefore, we must conclude that the two shores of the Sicilian strait were at one period peopled by the same tribe, who were known to the Greeks by the name of Sicels or Siculi; and that this tribe was probably a branch of the Oenotrian or Pelasgic race. The legends which connected these Siculi with those who were expelled from Latium seem to have been a late invention, as we may infer from the circumstance that Sicelus, who is represented by Antiochus as taking refuge with Morges, king of Italia, was called a fugitive *from Rome.* (Dionys. i. 73.)

3. The Siculi or Siceli were the people who occupied the greater part of the island of Sicily when the Greek colonies were first established there, and continued throughout the period of the Greek domination to occupy the greater part of the interior, especially the more rugged and mountainous tracts of the island. [SICILIA.] The more westerly portions were, however, occupied by a people called Sicani, whom the Greek writers uniformly distinguish from the Siculi, notwithstanding the resemblance of the two names. These indeed would seem to have been in their origin identical, and we find Roman writers using them as such; so that Virgil more than once employs the name of Sicani, where he can only mean the ancient Latin people called by Dionysius Siculi. (Virg. *Aen.* viii. 795, xi. 317.)

4. The traces of the Siculi on the western shores of the Adriatic are more uncertain. Pliny indeed tells us distinctly that Numana and Ancona were founded by the Siculi (Plin. iii. 13. s. 18); but it is by no means improbable that this is a mere confusion, as we know that the latter city at least was really founded by *Sicilian Greeks,* as late as the time of Dionysius of Syracuse [ANCONA]. When, however, he tells us that a considerable part of this coast of Italy was held by the Siculians and Liburnians, before it was conquered by the Umbrians (*Ib.* 14. s. 19), it seems probable that he must have some other authority for this statement; Pliny is, however, the only author who mentions the Siculi in this part of Italy.

From these statements it is very difficult to arrive at any definite conclusion with regard to the ethnographic affinities of the Siculi. On the one hand, the notices of them in Southern Italy, as already observed, seem to bring them into close connection with the Itali and other Oenotrian tribes, and would lead us to assign them to a Pelasgic stock: but on the other it must be admitted that Dionysius distinctly separates them from the Pelasgi in Latium, and represents them as expelled from that country by the Pelasgi, in conjunction with the so-called Aborigines. Hence the opinions of modern scholars have been divided: Niebuhr distinctly receives the Siculi as a Pelasgic race, and as forming the Pelasgic or Greek element of the Latin people; the same view is adopted by O. Müller (*Etrusker,* pp. 10—16, &c.) and by Abeken (*Mittel Italien,* p. 5); while Grotefend (*Alt Italien,* vol. iv. pp. 4—6), followed by Forbiger and others, regards the Siculi as a Gaulish or Celtic race, who had gradually wandered southwards through the peninsula of Italy, till they finally crossed over and established themselves in the island of Sicily. This last hypothesis is, however, purely conjectural. We have at least some foundation for supposing the Siculi as well as the Oenotrians to be of Pelasgic origin : if this be rejected, we are wholly in the dark as to their origin or affinities. [E. H. B.]

SI'CULUM MARE (τὸ Σικελικὸν πέλαγος, Pol. Strab. &c.), was the name given in ancient times to that portion of the Mediterranean sea which bathed the eastern shores of Sicily. But like all similar appellations, the name was used in a somewhat vague and fluctuating manner, so that it is difficult to fix its precise geographical limits. Thus Strabo describes it as extending along the eastern shore of Sicily, from the Straits to Cape Pachynus, with the southern shore of Italy as far as Locri, and again to the eastward as far as Crete and the Peloponnese; and as filling the Corinthian Gulf, and extending northwards to the Iapygian promontory and the mouth of the Ionian gulf. (Strab. ii. p. 123.) It is clear, therefore, that he included under the name the whole of the sea between the Peloponnese and Sicily, which is more commonly known as the Ionian sea [IONIUM MARE], but was termed by later writers the Adriatic [ADRIATICUM MARE]. Polybius, who in one passage employs the name of Ionian sea in this more extensive sense, elsewhere uses that of the Sicilian sea in the same general manner as Strabo, since he speaks of the island of Cephallenia as extending out towards the Sicilian sea (v. 3); and even describes the Ambracian gulf as an inlet or arm of the Sicilian sea (iv. 63, v. 5). Eratosthenes also, it would appear from Pliny, applied the name of Siculum Mare to the whole extent from Sicily to Crete. (Plin. iii. 5. s. 10.) The usage of Pliny himself is obscure; but Mela distinguishes the Sicilian sea from the Ionian, applying the former name to the western part of the broad sea, nearest to Sicily, and the latter to its more easterly portion, nearest to Greece. (Mel. ii. 4. § 1.) But this distinction does not seem to have been generally adopted or continued long in use. Indeed the name of the Sicilian sea seems to have fallen much into disuse. Ptolemy speaks of Sicily itself as bounded on the N. by the Tyrrhenian sea, on the S. by the African, and on the E. by the Adriatic; thus omitting the Sicilian sea altogether (Ptol. iii. 4. § 1); and this seems to have continued under the Roman Empire to be the received nomenclature.

Strabo tells us that the Sicilian sea was the same which had previously been called the Ausonian (Strab. ii. p. 133, v. p. 233); but it is probable that that name was never applied in the more extended sense in which he uses the Sicilian sea, but was confined to the portion more immediately adjoining the southern coasts of Italy, from Sicily to the Iapygian promontory. It is in this sense that it is employed by Pliny, as well as by Polybius, whom he cites as his authority. (Plin. *l. c.*) [E. H. R.]

SICUM (Σικοῦν, Ptol. ii. 16. § 4; Plin. iii. 22; Siclis, *Peut. Tab.*), a town of Dalmatia, to the E. of Tragurium, on the road to Salona, where Claudius is said to have quartered the veterans. (Plin. *l. c.*) From its position it cannot be *Sebenico,* with which it has been identified, but may be represented by the vestiges of a Roman station to the NW. of *Castel Vettúri,* on the *Riviere dei Castelli,* where a column with a dedicatory inscription to M. Julius Philippus has been lately found, as well as much pottery and Roman tiles. (Wilkinson, *Dalmatia,* vol. i. p. 176.) [E. B. J.]

SI'CYON (ὁ and ἡ Σικυών, also Σεκυών, Bekker, *Anecd.* p. 555: Eth. Σικυώνιος: the territory Σικυωνία: *Vasilikâ.*)

I. *Situation.*—Sicyon was an important city of Peloponnesus, situated upon a table-height of no great elevation, at the distance of about 2 miles from the

Corinthian gulf. Strabo (viii. p. 382) correctly describes it as occupying a strong hill distant 20 stadia from the sea, though he adds that others made the distance 12 stadia, which may, however, have reference to the lower town built at the foot of the table-height. Upon this height the modern village of *Vasilikâ* now stands. It is defended on every side by a natural wall of precipices, which can be ascended only by one or two narrow passages from the plain. A river flows upon either side of the hill, the one on the eastern side being the Asopus, and that on the western side the Helisson. When Sicyon was at the height of its power, the city consisted of three parts, the Acropolis on the hill of *Vasilikâ*, the lower town at its foot, and a port-town upon the coast. The port-town was well fortified. (Σικυ-ωνίων λιμήν, Xen. *Hell.* vii. 3. § 2; Polyb. v. 27; Paus. ii. 12. § 2; Strab. *l. c.*)

II. *History.* — Sicyon was one of the most ancient cities of Greece, and is said to have existed under the name of AEGIALEIA (Αἰγιάλεια, Paus. ii. 5. § 6) or AEGIALI (Αἰγιαλοί, Strab. viii. p. 382) long before the arrival of Pelops in Greece. It was also called MECONE (Μηκόνη), which was apparently its sacerdotal name, and under which it is celebrated as the "dwelling-place of the blessed," and as the spot where Prometheus instituted the Hellenic sacrifices and deceived Zeus. (Steph. B. *s. v.* Σικυών; Strab. viii. p. 382; Callim. *Fragm.* 195, p. 513, ed. Ernesti; Hesiod. *Theog.* 535.) Its name TELCHINIA (Τελχινία) has reference to its being one of the earliest seats of the workers in metal. (Steph. B. *s. v.* Σικυών). Its name Aegialeia was derived from a mythical autochthon Aegialeus, and points to the time when it was the chief city upon the southern coast of the Corinthian gulf, the whole of which was also called Aegialeia. Its later name of Sicyon was said to have been derived from an Athenian of this name, who became king of the city, and who is represented as a son of either Marathon or Metion. (Paus. ii. 6. § 5.) This legend points to the fact that the early inhabitants of Sicyon were Ionians. Aegialeus is said, in some traditions, to have been the son of Inachus, the first king of Argos, and the brother of Phoroneus. A long series of the successors of Aegialeus is given, among whom one of the most celebrated was the Argive Adrastus, who, being expelled from his own dominions, fled to Polybus, then king of Sicyon, and afterwards succeeded him on the throne. (Euseb. *Chron.* p. 11, seq.; August. *Civ. Dei,* xviii. 2; Paus. ii. 6. §§ 6, 7.) Homer indeed calls Adrastus first king of Sicyon (Hom. *Il.* ii. 572); and we know that in historical times this hero was worshipped in the city. (Herod. v. 67.) Sicyon was subsequently conquered by Agamemnon, who, however, left Hippolytus on the throne; but Sicyon became a tributary city to Mycenae. (Paus. ii. 6. §§ 6, 7: Hom. *Il.* ii. 572, xxiii. 299.) Hippolytus was the grandson of Phaestus, who was a son of Hercules ; and in consequence of this connection, the inhabitants were not expelled or reduced to subjection upon the conquest of the city by the Dorians under Phalces, the son of Temenus; for while the Dorian conquerors, as in all other Doric states, were divided into three tribes under the names of Hylleis, Pamphyli, and Dymanatae, the original Sicyonians were formed into a fourth tribe, under the name of Aegialeis, which possessed the same political rights as the other three. (Paus. ii. 6. § 7; Strab. viii. p. 389; Herod. v. 68.) Sicyon was now a Dorian

state; and from this time its real history begins. It was at first dependent upon Argos (Paus. *l. c.*), which was for some time the most powerful state in the Peloponnesus, Sparta being second to it. In the First Messenian War the Sicyonians fought on the side of the Messenians along with the Argives and Arcadians. (Paus. iv. 11. § 1.) In the Second Messenian War, about B. C. 676, Sicyon became subject to the tyranny of the Orthagoridae, who governed the city for more than 100 years, and whose rule is praised by Aristotle (*Pol.* v. 9. § 21) for its mildness. The family of the Orthagoridae belonged to the non-Dorian tribe, and the continuance of their power is to be accounted for by the fact of their being supported by the original population against the Dorian conquerors. Orthagoras, the founder of the dynasty, is said to have been originally a cook. (Aristot. *l. c.*; Hellad. *ap.* Phot. cod. 279, p. 530 ; Liban. vol. iii. p. 251, ed. Reiske.) In other accounts Andreas is mentioned as the first of the Sicyonian tyrants (Herod. vi. 126; Diod. *Fragm. Vat.* 14); and it is probable that he is the same person as Orthagoras, as the two names do not occur in the same author. He was succeeded by his son Myron, who gained a chariot victory at Olympia in B. C. 648; Myron by Aristonymus; and Aristonymus by Cleisthenes. (Herod. vi. 126; Paus. ii. 8. § 1, vi. 19. § 1.) The latter was celebrated for his wealth and magnificence, and was also distinguished by his bitter hatred against Argos, and his systematic endeavour to depress and dishonour the Dorian tribes. He changed the ancient and venerable names of the three Dorian tribes into the insulting names of Hyatae, Oneatae, and Choereatae, from the three Greek words signifying the sow, the ass, and the pig; while he declared the superiority of his own tribe by giving it the designation of Archelai, or lords of the people. Cleisthenes appears to have continued despot till his death, which may be placed about B. C. 560. The dynasty perished with him. He left no son; but his daughter Agariste, whom so many suitors wooed, was married to the Athenian Megacles, of the great family of the Alcmaeonidae, and became the mother of Cleisthenes, the founder of the Athenian democracy after the expulsion of the Peisistratidae. The names given to the tribes by Cleisthenes continued in use for sixty years after the death of the tyrant, when by mutual agreement the ancient names were restored. (Herod. vi. 126—131; Grote, *Hist. of Greece,* vol. iii. p. 43, seq.; *Dict. of Biogr.* art. CLEISTHENES.)

A Dorian reaction appears now to have taken place, for during a long time afterwards the Sicyonians were the steady allies of the Spartans. In the invasion of Greece by Xerxes (B. C. 480), the Sicyonians sent a squadron of 15 ships to Salamis (Herod. viii. 43), and a body of 3000 hoplites to Plataea. (Herod. ix. 28.) In the interval between the Persian and Peloponnesian wars the territory was twice invaded and laid waste by the Athenians, first under Tolmides in B. C. 456 (Thuc. i. 108; Paus. i. 27. § 5), and a second time under Pericles, B. C. 454 (Thuc. i. 111; Diod. xi. 88). A few years later (B. C. 445) the Sicyonians supported the Megarians in their revolt from Athens. (Thuc. i. 114.) In the Peloponnesian War they sided with Sparta, and sent a contingent of ships to the Peloponnesian fleet. (Thuc. ii. 9, 80, 83.) In B. C. 424 the Sicyonians assisted Brasidas in his operations against the Athenians in the Megarid

(Thuc. iv. 70), and in the same year they repulsed a descent of the Athenians under Demosthenes upon their territory. (Thuc. iv. 101.) In B.C. 419 they united with the Corinthians in preventing Alcibiades from erecting a fortress upon the Achaean promontory of Rhium. (Thuc. v. 52.) About this time a democratical revolution appears to have taken place, since we find the Lacedaemonians establishing an oligarchical government in Sicyon in B.C. 417. (Thuc. v. 82.) In the wars of Lacedaemon against Corinth, B. C. 394, and against Thebes, B. C. 371, the Sicyonians espoused the side of the Lacedaemonians. (Xen. Hell. iv. 2.§ 14, iv. 4. § 7, seq. vi. 4. § 18.) But in B. C. 368 Sicyon was compelled by Epaminondas to join the Spartan alliance, and to admit a Theban harmost and garrison into the citadel. Euphron, a leading citizen of Sicyon, taking advantage of these circumstances, and supported by the Arcadians and Argives, succeeded in establishing a democracy, and shortly afterwards made himself tyrant of the city. But being expelled by the Arcadians and Thebans, he retired to the harbour, which he surrendered to Sparta. By the assistance of the Athenians he returned to Sicyon; but finding himself unable to dislodge the Theban garrison from the Acropolis, he repaired to Thebes, in hopes of obtaining, by corruption and intrigue, the banishment of his opponents and the restoration of his own power. Here, however, he was murdered by some of his enemies. (Xen. Hell. vii. 1—3; Diod. xv. 69, 70; Dict. of Biogr. art. EUPHRON.) Sicyon seems, however, to have been favorable to tyrants; for, after a short time, we again find the city in their power. The facility with which ambitious citizens obtained the supreme power was probably owing to the antagonism between the Dorian and old Ionian inhabitants. Demosthenes mentions two Sicyonian tyrants, Aristratus and Epichares, in the pay of Philip (de Cor. pp. 242, 324). In the Lamian war, after the death of Alexander the Great, B.C. 323, the Sicyonians joined the other Greeks against the Macedonians. (Diod. xviii. 11.) The city subsequently fell into the hands of Alexander, the son of Polysperchon; and after his murder in B. C. 314, his wife Cratesipolis continued to hold the town for Cassander till B.C. 308, when she was induced to betray it to Ptolemy. (Diod. xix. 67, xx. 37.) In B. C. 303, Sicyon passed out of the hands of Ptolemy, being surprised by Demetrius Poliorcetes in the night. It appears that at this time Sicyon consisted of three distinct parts, as already mentioned, the Acropolis, on the hill of Vasiliká, the lower city at its foot, and the port-town. It is probable that formerly the Acropolis and the lower city were united with the port-town, by walls extending to the sea; but the three quarters were now separated from one another, and there was even a vacant space between the lower town and the citadel. Seeing the difficulty of defending so extensive a space with the diminished resources and population of the city, and anxious to secure a strongly fortified place, Demetrius compelled the inhabitants to remove to the site of the ancient Acropolis, which Diodorus describes as " a site very preferable to that of the former city, the inclosed space being an extensive plain, surrounded on every side by precipices, and so difficult of access that it would not be possible to attack the walls with machines." This new city was called Demetrias. (Diod. xx. 102; Plut. Demetr. 25; Paus. ii. 7. § 1; Strab. viii. p. 382.) The name Demetrias

soon disappeared; but the city continued to remain upon its lofty site, which was better adapted than most mountain heights in Greece for a permanent population, since it contained a good supply of water and cultivable land. Pausanias (l. c.) represents the lower town as the original city of Aegialeus; but Col. Leake justly remarks, it is more natural to conclude that the first establishment was made upon the hill Vasiliká, which, by its strength and its secure distance from the sea, possesses attributes similar to those of the other chief cities of Greece. Indeed, Pausanias himself confirms the antiquity of the occupation of the hill of Vasiliká, by describing all the most ancient monuments of the Sicyonians as standing upon it. (Leake, Morea, vol. iii. p. 367.)

After Demetrius quitted Sicyon, it again became subject to a succession of tyrants, who quickly displaced one another. Cleon was succeeded in the tyranny by Euthydemus and Timocleides; but they were expelled by the people, who placed Cleinias, the father of Aratus, at the head of the government. Cleinias was soon afterwards murdered by Abantidas who seized the tyranny, B. C. 264. Abantidas was murdered in his turn, and was succeeded by his father Paseas; but he again was murdered by Nicocles, who had held the sovereign power only four months, when the young Aratus surprised the citadel of Sicyon, and delivered his native city from the tyrant, B. C. 251. (Paus. ii. 8. §§ 1—3; Plut, Arat. 2.) Through the influence of Aratus, Sicyon now joined the Achaean League, and was one of the most important cities of the confederacy. (Paus. ii. 8. § 3; Plut. Arat. 9; Polyb. ii. 43.) In consequence of its being a member of the league, its territory was devastated, both by Cleomenes, B. C. 233 (Plut. Arat. 41, Cleom. 19; Polyb. ii. 52), and by the Aetolians, B. C. 221. (Polyb. iv. 13.) In the Roman wars in Greece, Sicyon was favoured by Attalus, who bestowed handsome presents upon it. (Polyb. xvii. 16; Liv. xxxii. 40.) The conquest of Corinth by the Romans, B. C. 146, was to the advantage of Sicyon, for it obtained the greater part of the neighbouring territory and the administration of the Isthmian games. (Paus. ii. 2. § 2.) But even before Corinth was rebuilt, Sicyon again declined, and appears in an impoverished state towards the end of the Republic. (Cic. ad Att. i. 19, 20, ii. 1.) After the restoration of Corinth, it still further declined, and its ruin was completed by an earthquake, which destroyed a great part of the city, so that Pausanias found it almost depopulated (ii. 7. § 1). The city, however, still continued to exist in the sixth century of the Christian era; for Hierocles (p. 646, Wess.) mentions New Sicyon (Νέα Σικυών) among the chief cities of Achaia. The maritime town was probably Old Sicyon. Under the Byzantine empire Sicyon was called Hellas, and the inhabitants Helladici, probably in contradistinction to the surrounding Slavonic inhabitants. (Σικυών, ἡ νῦν Ἑλλάς, Suidas; τῶν Σικυωνίων τῶν νυνὶ λεγομένων Ἑλλαδικῶν, Malala, iv. p. 68, Bonn.) The name Vasiliká (τὰ Βασιλικά) has reference to the ruins of the temples and other public buildings.

III. Art, &c.—Sicyon is more renowned in the artistic than in the political history of Greece. For a long time it was one of the chief seats of Grecian art, and was celebrated alike for its painters and sculptors. According to one tradition painting was invented at Sicyon, where Telephanes was the first to practise the monogram, or drawing in outline

(Plin. xxxv. 3. s. 15); and the city long remained the home of painting ("diu illa fuit patria picturae," Plin. xxxv. 11. s. 40). Sicyon gave its name to one of the great schools of painting, which was founded by Eupompus, and which produced Pamphilus and Apelles. (Plin. xxxv. 10. s. 36.) Sicyon was likewise the earliest school of statuary in Greece, which was introduced into the city by Dipoenus and Scyllis from Crete about B. C. 560 (Plin. xxxvi. 4); but its earliest native statuary of celebrity was Canachus. Lysippus was also a native of Sicyon. (*Dict. of Biogr. s. vv.*) The city was thus rich in works of art; but its most valuable paintings, which the Sicyonians had been obliged to give in pledge on account of their debts, were removed to Rome in the aedileship of M. Scaurus, to adorn his theatre. (Plin. xxxv. 11. s. 40.)

Sicyon was likewise celebrated for the taste and skill displayed in the various articles of dress made by its inhabitants, among which we find mention of a particular kind of shoe, which was much prized in all parts of Greece. (Athen. iv. p. 155; Pollux, vii. 93; Hesych. *s. v. Σικυωνία*; Auctor, *ad Herenn.* iv. 3, *de Orat.* i. 54; Lucret. iv. 1121; Fest. *s. v. Sicyonia.*)

IV. *Topography of the City.*—Few cities in Greece were more finely situated than Sicyon. The hill on which it stood commands a most splendid view. Towards the west is seen the plain so celebrated for its fertility; towards the east the prospect is bounded by the lofty hill of the Acrocorinthus; while in front lies the sea, with the noble mountains of Parnassus, Helicon, and Cithaeron rising from the opposite coast, the whole forming a charming prospect, which cannot have been without influence in cultivating the love for the fine arts, for which the city was distinguished. The hill of Sicyon is a tabular summit of a triangular shape, and is divided into an upper and a lower level by a low ridge of rocks stretching right across it, and forming an abrupt separation between the two levels. The upper level, which occupies the southern point of the triangle, and is about a third of the whole, was the Acropolis in the time of Pausanias (ἡ νῦν Ἀκρόπολις, ii. 7. § 5).

MAP OF THE SITE OF SICYON (from Leake).
A. *Vasiliká.*   *b b b.* Remains of ancient walls.

Pausanias came to Sicyon from Corinth. After crossing the Asopus, he noticed the Olympieum on the right, and a little farther on the left of the road

the tomb of Eupolis of Athens, the comic poet. After passing some other sepulchral monuments, he entered the city by the Corinthian gate, where was a fountain dropping down from the overhanging rocks, which was therefore called Stazusa (Στάζουσα), or the dropping fountain. This fountain has now disappeared in consequence of the falling in of the rocks. Upon entering the city Pausanias first crossed the ledge of rocks dividing the upper from the lower level, and passed into the Acropolis. Here he noticed temples of Tyche and the Dioscuri, of which there are still some traces. Below the Acropolis was the theatre, the remains of which are found, in conformity with the description of Pausanias, in the ledge of rocks separating the two levels On the stage of the theatre stood the statue of a man with a shield, said to have been that of Aratus. Near the theatre was the temple of Dionysus, from which a road led past the ruined temple of Artemis Limnaea to the Agora. At the entrance of the Agora was the temple of Peitho or Persuasion: and in the Agora the temple of Apollo, which appears to have been the chief sanctuary in Sicyon. The festival of Apollo at Sicyon is celebrated in the ninth Nemean ode of Pindar; and Aratus, when he delivered his native city from its tyrant, gave as the watchword Ἀπόλλων ὑπερδέξιος. (Plut. *Arat.* 7.) In the time of Polybius (xvii. 16) a brazen colossal statue of king Attalus I., 10 cubits high, stood in the Agora near the temple of Apollo; but this statue is not mentioned by Pausanias, and had therefore probably disappeared. (Paus. ii. 7. §§ 2—9.) Near the temple of Peitho was a sanctuary consecrated to the Roman emperors, and formerly the house of the tyrant Cleon. Before it stood the heroum of Aratus (Paus. ii. 8. § 8), and near it an altar of the Isthmian Poseidon, and statues of Zeus Meilichius and of Artemis Patroa, the former resembling a pyramid, the latter a column. In the Agora were also the council-house (βουλευτήριον), and a stoa built by Cleisthenes out of the spoils of Cirrha; likewise a brazen statue of Zeus, the work of Lysippus, a gilded statue of Artemis, a ruined temple of Apollo Lyceius, and statues of the daughters of Proetus, of Hercules, and of Hermes Agoraeus. (Paus. ii. 9. §§ 6, 7.) The Poecile Stoa or painted stoa, was probably in the Agora, but is not mentioned by Pausanias. It was adorned with numerous paintings, which formed the subject of a work of Polemon. (Athen. xiii. p. 577.)

Pausanias then proceeded to the Gymnasium, which he describes as not far from the Agora. The Gymnasium contained a marble statue of Hercules by Scopas; and in another part a temple of Hercules in a sacred inclosure, named Paedize. From thence a road led to two large inclosures, sacred to Aesclepius and Aphrodite, both of which were adorned with several statues and buildings. From the Aphrodisium Pausanias went past the temple of Artemis Pheraea to the gymnasium of Cleinias, which was used for the training of the Ephebi, and which contained statues of Artemis and Hercules. (Paus. ii. 10.) It is evident that this gymnasium was different from the one already described, as Pausanias continues his course towards the sea-side. From thence he turns towards the gate of the city called the Sacred, near which there formerly stood a celebrated temple of Athena, built by Epopeus, one of the mythical kings of Sicyon, but which had been burnt by lightning, and of which nothing then remained but the altar: this temple may perhaps have been the one sacred to Athena Colocasia, mentioned by Athenaeus (iii. p. 72). There were two adjoining temples, one sacred to Artemis and Apollo, built by Epopeus, and the other sacred to Hera, erected by Adrastus, who was himself worshipped by the people of Sicyon (Herod. v. 68; Pind. *Nem.* ix. 20). There can be little doubt that these ancient temples stood in the original Acropolis of Sicyon; and indeed Pausanias elsewhere (ii. 5. § 6) expressly states that the ancient Acropolis occupied the site of the temple of Athena. We may place these temples near the northern edge of the hill upon the site of the modern village of *Vasilikà;* and accordingly the

remarkable opening in the rocks near the village may be regarded as the position of the Sacred Gate, leading into the ancient Acropolis. (Leake, *Morea,* vol. iii. p. 372.)

In descending from the Heraeum, on the road to the plain, was a temple of Demeter; and close to the Heraeum were the ruins of the temple of Apollo Carneius and Hera Prodromia, of which the latter was founded by Phalces, the son of Temenus. (Paus. ii. 11. §§ 1, 2.)

The walls of Sicyon followed the edge of the whole hill, and may still be traced in many parts. The direction of the ancient streets may also still be

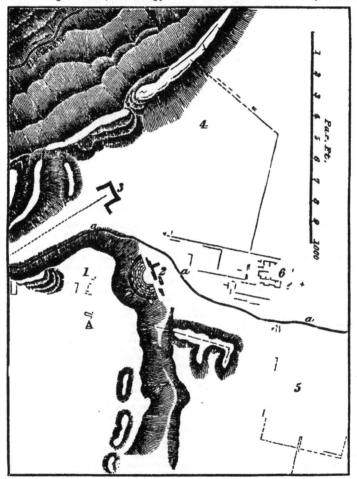

PLAN OF THE RUINS OF SICYON (from the French Commission).

A. Acropolis from the time of Demetrius.
1. Temple of Tyche and the Dioscuri.
2. Theatre.
3. Stadium.
4. Probable site of the Gymnasium.

5. Probable site of the Agora.
6. Roman Building.
a a Road from the lake of Stymphalus to *Vasilikà* and Corinth.

followed by the existing foundations of the houses: they run with mathematical precision from NE. to SW., and from NW. to SE., thus following the rule of Vitruvius. Few of the ruins rise above the ground; but there is a Roman building better preserved, and containing several chambers, which lies near the ridge separating the two levels of the hill. Leake supposes that this building was probably the praetorium of the Roman governor during the period between the destruction of Corinth by Mummius and its restoration by Julius Caesar, when Sicyon was the capital of the surrounding country; but more recent observers are inclined to think that the ruins are those of baths. West of this building are the theatre and the stadium; and the modern road which leads from *Vasilikó* to Stymphalus runs between this Roman building and the theatre and then through a portion of the stadium. The theatre was cut out of the rock, separating the two levels of the hill, as already described; its total diameter was about 400 feet, and that of the orchestra 100. Each wing was supported by a mass of masonry, penetrated by an arched passage. To the NW. of the theatre are the remains of the stadium, of which the total length, including the seats at the circular end, is about 680 feet. Col. Leake remarks that " the stadium resembles that of Messene, in having had seats which were not continued through the whole length of the sides. About 80 feet of the rectilinear extremity had no seats; and this part, instead of being excavated out of the hill like the rest, is formed of factitious ground, supported at the end by a wall of polygonal masonry, which still exists." There are also, in various parts of the hill, remains of several subterraneous aqueducts, which supplied the town with water. The opening of one of them is seen on the SE. side of the theatre; and there is another opening now walled up W. of the modern village. The tyrant Nicocles escaped through these subterraneous passages when Sicyon was taken by Aratus. (Plut. *Arat.* 9.)

V. *Topography of the Sicyonia.* — The territory of Sicyon was very small, and, in fact, was little more than the valley of the Asopus. In the upper part of its course the valley of the Asopus is confined between mountains, but near the sea it opens out into a wide plain, which was called ASOPIA. ('Ασωπία, Strab. viii. p. 382, ix. p. 408; Paus. ii. 1. § 1.) This plain was celebrated for its fertility (μέγα φρονεῖν ἐπὶ τῷ τὸ Σικυώνιον πεδίον γεωργεῖν, Lucian, *Icarom.* c. 18), and was especially adapted for the cultivation of the olive. (" Sicyonia bacca," Virg. *Georg.* ii. 519; Ov. *Ep. ex Pont.* iv. 15. 10; Stat. *Theb.* iv. 50.) The neighbouring sea supplied an abundance of excellent fish. (Athen. i. p. 27.) It was separated from the Corinthia on the E. by the river Nemea, and from the territory of Pellene on the W. by the Sythas; and on the S. it was bounded by the territories of Phlius and Cleonae. At one time the territory of Sicyon must have extended even beyond the Sythas, since GONUSSA or DONUSSA, which lay W. of this river, is described by Pausanias as belonging to the Sicyonians. [PELLENE, p. 571, a.] Between the Helisson and the Sythas was probably the river Selleeis, with the neighbouring village of Ephyra, mentioned by Strabo (viii. p. 338). [EPHYRA, No. 3.] Sixty stadia S. of Sicyon, and near the frontiers of Phliasia, was Titane or Titana, the most important of the dependencies of Sicyon. [TITANE.] Forty stadia beyond Titane was Phlius; but this road, which

was too narrow for carriages, was not the direct road from Sicyon to Phlius. The direct road was to the right of the Asopus; and the circuitous road through Titane to the left of that river. Between these two roads, at the distance of 20 stadia from Sicyon, was a sacred grove, containing a temple of the Eumenides. (Paus. ii. 11. § 3, seq.) East of Sicyon was Epieicia, on the river Nemea. [EPIEICIA.] In the same direction was the fortress DERAE. (Δέραι, Xen. *Hell.* vii. 1. § 22.) There was also a fortress Phoebia, taken by Epaminondas in his march through the valley of the Asopus: it is probably the same place as Buphia. [BUPHIA.] Strabo (ix. p. 412) mentions a demus Plataeae in the Sicyonia. (Hagen, *Sicyonia*, Regimont. 1831; Gompf, *Sicyoniacorum Spec.* Berol. 1832, Torg. 1834; Bobrik, *De Sicyoniae Topographia*, Regimont. 1839; Leake, *Morea*, vol. iii. p. 351, seq.; Boblaye, *Recherches, &c.* p. 30, seq.; Ross, *Reisen im Peloponnes*, p. 39, seq.; Curtius, *Peloponnesos*, vol. ii. p. 482, seq.; Boulé, *Etudes sur le Péloponnèse*, p. 343, seq.)

COIN OF SICYON.

SIDAE (Σίδαι), a place in Boeotia, celebrated for its pomegranates. Hence the Boeotians called this fruit σίδη, though the more usual name was ῥοιά. As the Athenians are said to have contended with the Boeotians for the possession of the place, it must have been upon the borders of Attica, but its exact site is unknown. (Athen. xiv. pp. 650, 651.)

SIDE (Σίδη: *Eth.* Σιδήτης), a town with a good harbour on the coast of Pamphylia, 50 stadia to the west of the river Melas, and 350 east of Attaleia. (*Stad. Mar. Mag.* § 214, foll.) The town was founded by Cumae in Aeolis. (Scylax, *Peripl.* p. 40; Strab. xiv. p. 567, comp. p. 664; Steph. B. *s. v.*; Pomp. Mela, i. 15.) Arrian (*Anab.* i. 26), who admits the Cumaean origin of the place, relates a tradition current at Side itself, according to which the Sidetae were the most ancient colonists sent out from Cumae, but soon after their establishment in their new home forgot the Greek language, and formed a peculiar idiom for themselves, which was not understood even by the neighbouring barbarians. When Alexander appeared before Side, it surrendered and received a Macedonian garrison. In the time of Antiochus the Great, a naval engagement took place off Side between the fleet of Antiochus, commanded by Hannibal, and that of the Rhodians, in which the former was defeated. (Liv. xxxv. 13, 18, xxxvii. 23, 24.) Polybius (v. 73) states that there existed great enmity between the people of Side and Aspendus. At the time when the pirates had reached their highest power in the Mediterranean, they made Side their principal port, and used it as a market to dispose of their prisoners and booty by auction. (Strab. xiv. p. 664.) Side continued to be a town of considerable importance under the Roman emperors, and in the ultimate division of the province it became the metropolis of Pamphylia Prima. (Hierocl.

p. 682; *Concil. Const.* ii. p. 240.) The chief divinity of this city was Athena, who is therefore seen represented on its coins, holding a pomegranate (σίδη) in her hand. (Sestini, *Num. Vet.* p. 392, foll.; comp. Xenoph. *Anab.* i. 2. § 12: Cicero, *ad Fam.* iii. 6; Athen. viii. p. 350; Paus. viii. 28. § 2; Ptol. v. 5. § 2, viii. 17. § 31.) The exact site of ancient Side, which is now called *Esky Adalia*, as well as its remains, have been described by modern travellers. Beaufort (*Karamania*, p. 146, foll), who gives an excellent plan of the present condition of the place, states that the city stood on a low peninsula, and was surrounded by walls; the part facing the land was of excellent workmanship, and much of it is still perfect. There were four gates, one from the country and three from the sea. The agora, 180 feet in diameter, was surrounded by a double row of columns. One side of the square is at present occupied by the ruins of a temple and portico. The theatre appears like a lofty acropolis rising from the centre of the town, and is by far the largest and best preserved of any seen in Asia Minor. The harbour consisted of two small moles, connected with the quay and principal sea gate. At the extremity of the peninsula were two artificial harbours for larger vessels. Both are now almost filled with sand and stones, which have been borne in by the swell. The earliest coins of Side are extremely ancient; the inscriptions are in very barbarous characters, resembling the Phoenician, and the imperial coins exhibit the proud titles of λαμπροτάτη and ἔνδοξος. (Eckhel, vol. iii. pp. 44, 161; Spanheim, *De Usu et Praest. Num.* p. 879; Fellows, *Asia Minor*, p. 201; Leake, *Asia Minor*, p. 195, foll.)

Respecting Side, the ancient name of Polemonium, see POLEMONIUM.　　　　　　　　[L. S.]

SIDE (Σίδη), a town on the eastern coast of Laconia, a little N. of the promontory Malea. It was said to have existed before the Dorian conquest, and to have derived its name from a daughter of Danaus. The inhabitants were removed by the Dorian conquerors to the neighbouring town of Boeae. It probably occupied the site of the monastery of *St. George*, where there is a port. (Scylax, p. 17; Paus. iii. 22. § 11; Boblaye, *Recherches, &c.* p. 99; Curtius, *Peloponnesos*, vol. ii. p. 297.)

SIDE'NE (Σιδήνη). 1. A town of Mysia, on the river Granicus, which was destroyed by Croesus, and was never rebuilt, in consequence of a curse pronounced on the site by the destroyer. (Strab. xiii. pp. 587, 601.)

2. A town in Lycia, mentioned only by Stephanus B. (*s. v.*) on the authority of the *Lydiaca* of Xanthus.

3. A district on the coast of Pontus, about the mouth of the river Sidenus, which derived its name from the town of Side, afterwards called Polemonium. The greater part of the district was formed by the deposits of the river (Strab. i. p. 52, ii. p. 126, xii. pp. 547, 548, 556; Plin. vi. 4.)　　　　[L. S.]

SIDE'NI (Σιδηνοί), a people of Arabia Felix, placed by Ptolemy between the Thamyditae on the north, and the Darrae on the south, on the Elanitic gulf (vi. 7. § 4). Mr. Forster identifies them with the *Djeheyne* tribe of Burckhardt, in the north of the *Hedjaz*, extending along the coast from *Jebel Hassane* (certainly identical with the Hippos Mons — both meaning Horse-mountain — of Ptolemy), to *Yembo*. "All the circumstances, of name, locality, and neighbourhood," he says, "concur to prove their identity." (*Arabia*, vol. i. p. 126.)　　　[G. W.]

SIDE'NI (Σιδεινοί, Σειδινοί, Σιδηνοί), a German tribe on the coast of the Baltic, between the mouth of the river Suebus and that of the Viadua. (Ptol. ii. 11. § 14.) It is possible that Sibini (Σίβινοι) is only a corrupt form of the name of this same tribe. (Zeuss, *Die Deutschen*, p. 154.)　　　[L. S.]

SIDE'NUS, a small river of Pontus, having its sources in Mount Paryadres, and flowing through the district of Sidene into the Euxine; at its mouth was the town of Side or Polemonium (Plin. vi. 4), from which the river is now called *Pouleman Chai.* (Comp. Hamilton, *Researches*, i. p. 270.) [L. S.]

SIDERIS, a river of Hyrcania, mentioned by Pliny (vi. 16. s. 18), which flowed into the Caspian sea. It cannot be now determined to which river he refers, but he states from it the Caspian sea was called the Hyrcanian.　　　　　　　　[V.]

SIDE'RUS (Σιδηροῦς), according to Scylax (p. 39) a promontory and a port-town on the coast of Lycia. The same place seems to be meant in Stephanus B. (*s. v.* Σιδαροῦς), when he calls Sidarus a town and harbour. Col. Leake (*Asia Minor*, p. 189) has shown that the town of Siderus is in all probability no other than Olympus, on the south of Phaselis.　　　　　　　　　　　　[L. S.]

SIDICI'NI (Σιδικῖνοι), a people of Central Italy bordering on the Samnites and Campanians. In the time of the geographers they had disappeared as a people, or become absorbed into the general appellation of Campanians (Strab. v. p. 237), but at an earlier period they appear as a wholly independent people. Their chief city was Teanum, on the E. slope of the volcanic mountain group of *Rocca Monfina*: but they had at one time extended their power considerably further to the N. and up the valley of the Liris, as the territory of Fregellae is said to have been subject to them, before they were dispossessed of it by the Volscians (Liv. viii. 22). It is clear however that this extension of their limits was of short duration, or at all events had ceased before they first appear in history. Strabo tells us expressly that they were an Oscan tribe (*l. c.*), and this is confirmed by the coins of Teanum still extant, which have Oscan inscriptions. They were therefore closely allied to the neighbouring tribes of the Campanians on the S. and the Aurunci and Ausones on the W. Hence Virgil associates the inhabitants of the Sidicinian plains (" Sidicina aequora," *Aen.* vii. 727) with the Auruncans and the inhabitants of Cales. The last city is assigned by Silius Italicus to the Sidicini, but this is opposed to all other authorities (Sil. Ital. viii. 511). The name of the Sidicini is first mentioned in history in B. C. 343, when they were attacked by the Samnites, who had been long pressing upon their neighbours the Volscians. Unable to contend with these formidable assailants, the Sidicini had recourse to the Campanians, who sent an army to their assistance, but were easily defeated (Liv. vii. 29, 30), and being in their turn threatened by the whole power of the Samnites, invoked the assistance of Rome. During the war which followed (the First Samnite War), we lose sight altogether of the Sidicini, but by the treaty which put an end to it (in B. C. 341) it was particularly stipulated that the Samnites should be at liberty to pursue their ambitious designs against that people (Id. viii. 1, 2). Thus abandoned by the Romans to their fate the Sidicini had recourse to the Latins (who were now openly shaking off their connection with Rome) and the Campanians: and the Samnites were a second time drawn off from their special attack on this petty people to oppose a more powerful coalition (*Ib.* 2, 4, 5). It is clear that the Sidicini took part as allies of the Latins and Campanians in the war that followed: but we have no account of the terms they obtained in the general settlement of the peace in B. C. 338. It is certain, however, that they retained their independence, as immediately afterwards we find them engaging in a war on their own account with their neighbours the Auruncans. The Romans espoused the defence of the latter people, but before they were able to take the field, the Auruncans were compelled to abandon their ancient city, which was destroyed by the Sidicini, and withdrew to Suessa. (Liv. viii. 15.) The Ausonians of Cales had on this occasion been induced to make common cause with the Sidicini, but their combined forces were easily defeated by the Roman consuls. Cales soon after fell into the hands of the Romans; but though the territory of the Sidicini was overrun by the consuls of B. C. 332, who established their winter-quarters there to watch the movements of the Samnites, their city of Teanum still held out (*Ib.* 16, 17). Nor do we know at what time it fell into the power of the Romans, or on what terms the Sidicini were ultimately received to submission. But it is probable that this took place before B. C. 297, when we are told that the consul Decius Mus advanced to attack the Samnites "per Sidicinum agrum" in a manner that certainly implies the district to have been at that time friendly, if not subject, to Rome (Liv. x. 14).

After this the name of the Sidicini never appears in history as that of a people, but their territory (the "Sidicinus ager") is mentioned during the Second Punic War, when it was traversed and ravaged by Hannibal on his march from Capua to Rome (Liv. xxvi. 9). The Sidicini seem to have gradually come to be regarded as a mere portion of the Campanian people, in common with the Ausonians of Cales and the Auruncans of Suessa, and the name still occurs occasionally as a municipal designation equivalent to the Teanenses (Liv. xxvi. 15; Cic. *Phil.* ii. 41). Strabo speaks of them in his time as an extinct tribe of Oscan race: and under the Roman Empire the only trace of them preserved was in the epithet of Sidicinum, which still continued to be applied to the city of Teanum. (Strab. v. p. 237; Plin. iii. 5. s. 9; Ptol. iii. 1. § 68; Sil. Ital. v. 551, xii. 524.)   [TEANUM.]   [E. H. B.]

SIDODO'NE (Σιδωδώνη or Σισιδών, Arrian, *Ind.* c. 37), a small place on the coast of Carmania, noticed by Arrian in Nearchus's voyage. Kempthorne thinks that it is represented by a small fishing village called *Mogou;* but Müller suggests, what seems more probable, that it is the present *Duan.* (*Geogr. Graec. Minor.* p. 359, ed. Müller, Paris, 1855.)   [V.]

SIDOLOCUS or SIDOLEUCUS, in Gallia, is mentioned by Ammianus Marcellinus when he is speaking of Julian's march from Augustodunum to Autissiodurum. Sidolocum is supposed to be *Saulieu* [CHORA.]   [G. L.]

SIDON (Σιδών: *Eth.* Σιδώνιος,), a very ancient and important maritime city of Phoenicia, which, according to Josephus, derived its origin and name from Sidon, the firstborn son of Canaan (*Gen.* x. 15; Joseph. *Ant.* i. 6. § 2), and is mentioned by Moses as the northern extremity of the Canaanitish settlements, as Gaza was the southernmost (*Gen.* x. 19); and in the blessing of Jacob it is said of Zebulun "his border shall be unto Sidon" (xlix.

13). At the time of the Eisodus of the children of Israel, it was already distinguished by the appellation of "the Great" (*Josh.* xi. 8; compare in LXX. ver. 2), and was in the extreme north border which was drawn from Mount Hermon (called Mount Hor in *Num.* xxxiv. 7) on the east to Great Sidon, where it is mentioned in the border of the tribe of Asher, as also is "the strong city of Tyre." (*Josh.* xix. 28, 29.) It was one of several cities from which the Israelites did not dispossess the old inhabitants. (*Judg.* i. 31.)

As the origin of this ancient city, its history, and manufactures, have been noticed under PHOE-NICIA, it only remains in this place to speak of its geographical position and relations so far as they either serve to illustrate, or are illustrated by, its history.

It is stated by Josephus to have been a day's journey from the site of Dan, afterwards Paneas (*Ant.* v. 3. § 1). Strabo places it 400 stadia S. of Berytus, 200 N. of Tyre, and describes it as situated on a fair haven of the continent. He does not attempt to settle the questions between the rival cities, but remarks that while Sidon is most celebrated by the poets (of whom Homer does not so much as name Tyre), the colonists in Africa and Spain, even beyond the Pillars of Hercules, showed more honour to Tyre (xvi. 2. §§ 22, 24). Herodotus's account of the origin of the race has been given under PHOENICIA [p. 607, b.], and is shown to be in accordance with that of other writers. Justin follows it, but gives a different etymology of the name: "Condita urbe, quam a piscium uberitate Sidona appellaverunt, nam piscem Phoenices Sidon vocant;" but this is an error corrected by Michaelis and Gesenius (*Lex. s. v.* צידון), who derive it from צוד, "to hunt or snare" game, birds, fish, &c., indifferently, so that the town must have derived its name from the occupation of the inhabitants as fishers, and not from the abundance of fish; and Ritter refers to the parallel case of Beth-saida on the sea of Tiberias. (*Erdkunde, Syrien.* vol. iv. p. 43.) Pliny, who mentions it as "artifex vitri Thebarum-que Boeotiarum parens," places "Sarepta and Ornithon oppida" between it and Tyre (v. 19). It is reckoned XXX. M. P. from Berytus, XXIV. from Tyre, in the Itinerary of Antoninus (p. 149). But the Itinerarium Hierosolymitanum reckons it xxviii. from Berytus, placing Heldua and Parphirion between (p. 584). Scylax mentions the closed harbour of Sidon (λιμὴν κλειτός, p. 42, ed. Hudson), which is more fully described by a later writer, Achilles Tatius (circ. A. D. 500), who represents Sidon as situated on the Assyrian sea, itself the metropolis of the Phoenicians, whose citizens were the ancestors of the Thebans. A double harbour shelters the sea in a wide gulf; for where the bay is covered on the right hand side, a second mouth has been formed, through which the water again enters, opening into what may be regarded as a harbour of the harbour. In this inner basin, the vessels could lie securely during the winter, while the outer one served for the summer. (Cited by Reland, *Palaes.* p. 1012). This inner port Reland conjectures, with great probability, is the closed port of Scylax, and to be identified with the second harbour described by Strabo at Tyre, where he says there was one closed and another open harbour, called the Egyptian. The best account of the site is given by Pococke. "It was situated," he says, "on a rising ground, defended by the sea on the north and west. The present city is mostly on the north side of the hill. The old city seems to have extended farther east, as may be judged from the foundations of a thick wall, that extends from the sea to the east; on the south it was probably bounded by a rivulet, the large bed of which might serve for a natural fosse; as another might which is on the north side, if the city extended so far, as some seem to think it did, and that it stretched to the east as far as the high hill, which is about three quarters of a mile from the present town. . . . On the north side of the town, there are great ruins of a fine fort, the walls of which were built with very large stones, 12 feet in length, which is the thickness of the wall; and some are 11 feet broad, and 5 deep. The harbour is now choked up. . . . This harbour seems to be the minor port mentioned by Strabo (xvi. p. 756) for the winter; the outer one probably being to the north in the open sea between Sidon and Tyre (?), where the shipping rides in safety during the summer season." (*Observations on Palestine*, p. 86.) The sepulchral grots are cut in the rock at the foot of the hills ; and some of them are adorned with pilasters, and handsomely painted.

The territory of the Sidonians, originally circumscribed towards the north by the proximity of the hostile Gibbites, extended southwards to the tribe of Zebulon, and Mount Carmel; but was afterwards limited in this direction also by the growing power of their rivals the Tyrians. (Ritter, *l. c.* p. 43, &c.)

COIN OF SIDON.

SIDO'NES (Σίδωνες), a tribe in the extreme east of Germany, about the sources of the Vistula (Ptol. ii. 11. § 21), and no doubt the same which appears in Strabo (vii. p. 306) under the name of Σίδωνες, as a branch of the Bastarnae.   [L. S.]

SIDO'NIA. [PEDONIA.]

SIDUS (Σιδοῦς, Σιδοῦντιὰς κώμη, Hesych.: *Eth.* Σιδούντιος), a village in the Corinthia, on the Saronic gulf, between Crommyon and Schoenus. It was taken by the Lacedaemonians along with Crommyon in the Corinthian War, but was recovered by Iphicrates. (Xen. *Hell.* iv. 4. § 13, iv. 5. § 19.) It probably stood in the plain of *Susâki.* (Scylax; Steph. B. *s. v.*; Plin. iv. 7. s. 11; Boblaye, *Recherches, &c.* p. 35; Leake, *Peloponnesiaca,* p. 397; Curtius, *Peloponnesos,* vol. ii. p. 555.)

SIDUSSA (Σίδουσσα), a small town of Ionia, belonging to the territory of Erythrae. (Thucyd. viii. 24; Steph. B. *s. v.*) Pliny (v. 38) erroneously describes it as an island off the coast of Erythrae. It is probable that the place also bore the name of Sidus (Σιδοῦς), as Stephanus B. (*s. v.*) mentions a town of this name in the territory of Erythrae.   [L. S.]

SIDYMA (Σίδυμα: *Eth.* Σιδυμεύς), a town of Lycia, on the southern slope of Mount Cragus, to the north-west of the mouth of the Xanthus. (Plin. v. 28; Steph. B. *s. v.*; Ptol. v. 3. § 5; Hierocles, p.

684; Cedrenus, p. 344.) The ruins of this city, on a lofty height of Mount Cragus, have first been discovered and described by Sir C. Fellows. (*Lycia,* p. 151, foll.) They are at the village of *Tortoorcar Hisâ,* and consist chiefly of splendidly built tombs, abounding in Greek inscriptions. The town itself appears to have been very small, and the theatre, agora, and temples, are of diminutive size, but of great beauty.   [L. S.]

SIELEDIVA. [TAPROBANE.]

SIGA (Σίγα, Ptol. iv. 2. § 2), a commercial town of Mauritania Caesariensis, seated near the mouth of a river of the same name in a large bay. The mouth of the river formed the port of the city, at a distance of 3 miles from it (Sigensis Portus, *Itin. Ant.* p. 13), opposite to the island of Acra, on the highroad, and near Cirta, the residence of Syphax. (Strab. xvii. p. 829; Plin. v. 2. s. 1.) In Strabo's time it was in ruins, but must have been subsequently restored, since it is mentioned in the Itinerary (p. 12) as a Roman municipium. (Comp. Ptol. *l. c.*; Mela, i. 5; Scylax, 51, 52.) According to Shaw (*Travels,* p. 12), who, however, did not visit the place, its ruins are still to be seen by the present *Tacumbrit;* others identify it with the *Areschkul* of the Arabs, at the mouth of the *Tafna,* near *Rasgun.*   [T. H. D.]

SIGA (Σίγα, Ptol. iv. 2. § 2), a river of Mauritania Caesariensis, falling into a bay of the sea opposite to the island of Acra (now *Caracoles*). Scylax (p. 51) calls it Σίγον. Probably the present *Tafna.*   [T. H. D.]

SIGE'UM (Σίγειον or ἡ Σιγειὰς ἄκρα), a promontory in Troas, forming the north-western extremity of Asia Minor, at the entrance of the Hellespont, and opposite the town of Elaeus, in the Thracian Chersonesus. Near it the naval camp of the Greeks was said to have been formed during the Trojan War. (Herod. v. 65, 94; Thucyd. viii. 101; Strab. xiii. pp. 595, 603; Pomp. Mela, i. 18; Plin. v. 33; Ptol. v. 2. § 3; Serv. *ad Aen.* ii. 312.) This promontory is now called *Yenisheri.*

Near the promontory was situated the town of Sigeum, which is said to have been an Aeolian colony, founded under the guidance of Archaeanax of Mytilene, who used the stones of ancient Troy in building this new place. But some years later the Athenians sent troops under Phrynon and expelled the Mytileneans ; and this act of violence led to a war between the two cities, which lasted for a long time, and was conducted with varying success. Pittacus, the wise Mytilenean, is said to have slain Phrynon in single combat. The poet Alcaeus also was engaged in one of the actions. The dispute was at length referred to Periander, of Corinth, who decided in favour of the Athenians. (Strab. xiii. p. 599; Herod. v. 95; Steph. B. *s. v.*; Diog. Laërt. i. 74.) Henceforth we find the Pisistratidae in possession of Sigeum, and Hippias, after being expelled from Athens, is known to have retired there with his family. (Herod. v. 65). The town of Sigeum was destroyed by the inhabitants of Ilium soon after the overthrow of the Persian empire, so that in Strabo's time it no longer existed. (Strab. xiii. p. 600; Plin. v. 33.) A hill near Sigeum, forming a part of the promontory, was believed in antiquity to contain the remains of Achilles, which was looked upon with such veneration that gradually a small town seems to have risen around it, under the name of Achilleum [ACHILLEUM]. This tomb, which was visited by Alexander the Great, Julius

Caesar, and Germanicus, is still visible in the form of a mound or tumulus.   [L. S.]

SIGMAN (Σίγμαν), a river in Gallia. Ptolemy (ii. 7. § 2) places the mouth of the Sigman between the Aturis (Adour) and the Garonne; and between the Sigman and the Garonne he places Curianum Promontorium. [CURIANUM.] Marcianus (Peripl.), who has the name Signatius, gives two distances between the mouth of the Adour and that of the Sigman, one of which is 500 and the other 450 stadia. We cannot trust either the latitudes of Ptolemy or the distances of Marcian along this coast. There is no river between the Adour and the Garonne that we can suppose to have been marked down by the ancient coasting ships to the exclusion of the Leyre, which flows into the Bassin d'Arcachon. But Gosselin supposes the Sigman to be the Mimian, which is about half-way between the Adour and the Bassin d'Arcachon.   [G. L.]

SI'GNIA (Σίγνια: Eth. Signinus: Segni), an ancient city of Latium, situated on a lofty hill at the NW. angle of the Volscian mountains, looking down upon the valley of the Sacco. It is represented by ancient authors as a Roman colony founded by Tarquinius Superbus, at the same time with Circeii. (Liv. i. 55; Dionys. iv. 63.) No trace of it is found before this; its name does not figure among the cities of the Latin League or those of which the foundation was ascribed to Alba; and the story told by Dionysius (l. c.), that it originated at first in a fortuitous settlement of some Roman troops encamped in the neighbourhood, which was afterwards enlarged and strengthened by Tarquin, certainly points to the fact of its being a new town, and not, like so many of the Roman colonies, a new settlement in a previously existing city. It passed, after the expulsion of Tarquin, into the hands of the Roman Republic, as it was attacked in B. C. 497 by Sextus Tarquinius, who in vain endeavoured to make himself master of it (Dionys. v. 58). A few years later, it received a fresh colony, to recruit its exhausted population (Liv. ii. 21). From this time it appears to have continued a dependency of Rome, and never, so far as we learn, fell into the power of the Volscians, though that people held all the neighbouring mountain country. Signia must indeed, from its strong and commanding position, overlooking all the valley of the Trerus and the broad plain between it and Praeneste, have been a point of the utmost importance for the Romans and Latins, especially as securing their communications with their allies the Hernicans. In B. C. 340 the Signians shared in the general defection of the Latins (Liv. viii. 3); but we have no account of the part they took in the war that followed, or of the terms on which they were received to submission. We know only that Signia became again (as it had probably been before) a Colonia Latina, and is mentioned as such during the Second Punic War. On that occasion it was one of those which continued faithful to Rome at the most trying period of the war (Liv. xxvii. 10), and must therefore have been still in a flourishing condition. On account of its strong and secluded position we find it selected as one of the places where the Carthaginian hostages were deposited for safety (Id. xxxii. 2): but this is the last mention of it that occurs in history, except that the battle of Sacriportus is described by Plutarch as taking place near Signia (Plut. Sull. 28). That decisive action was fought in the plain between Signia and Praeneste [SACRIPORTUS]. It, however, certainly continued during

the later ages of the Republic and under the Empire to be a considerable municipal town. It received a fresh body of colonists under the Triumvirate, but it is doubtful whether it retained the rank of a Colonia. Pliny does not reckon it as such, and though it is termed "Colonia Signina" in some inscriptions, these are of doubtful authenticity. (Strab. v. p. 237; Plin. iii. 5. s. 9; Sil. Ital. viii. 378; Lib. Colon. p. 237; Zumpt, de Col. p. 338; Gruter, Inscr. p. 490. 5, &c.)

Signia was chiefly noted under the Roman Empire for its wine, which, though harsh and astringent, was valued for its medical qualities, and seems to have been extensively used at Rome (Strab. v. p. 237; Plin. xiv. 6. s. 8; Athen. i. p. 27; Sil. Ital. l. c.; Martial, xiii. 116; Cels. de Med. iv. 5). Its territory produced also pears of a celebrated quality (Juv. xi. 73; Plin. xv. 15. s. 16; Colum. v. 10. § 18; Macrob. Sat. ii. 15), as well as excellent vegetables, which were sent in large quantities to Rome (Colum. x. 131). These last were grown on a hill near the city, called by Columella Mons Lepinus, apparently one of the underfalls of the Volscian mountains; but there is no authority for applying the name (as modern writers have frequently done) to the whole of that mass of mountains [LEPINUS MONS]. Signia also gave name to a particular kind of cement known as "opus Signinum," and extensively employed both for pavements and reservoirs of water (Plin. xxxv. 12. s. 46; Colum. i. 6. § 12, viii. 15. § 3; Vitruv. viii. 7. § 14).

The modern town of Segni (a poor place, with about 3500 inhabitants) occupies a part only of the site of the ancient city. The latter embraced within the circuit of its walls the whole summit of the hill, which stands boldly out from the Volscian mountains, with which it is connected only by a narrow neck or isthmus. The line of the ancient walls may be traced throughout its whole extent; they are constructed of large masses of stone (the hard limestone of which the hill itself consists, but of polygonal or rudely squared form, and afford certainly one of the most remarkable specimens of the style of construction commonly known as Cyclopean or Pelasgic, of which striking instances are found also in other cities in this part of Latium. The city had in all five gates, two of which still retain their primitive construction; and one of these, known as the Porta Saracinesca, presents a remarkable instance of the rudest and most massive Cyclopean construction. The architrave is formed of single masses of stone not less than 12 feet in length, laid across from one impost to the other. This gate has been repeatedly figured[*]; another, less celebrated but scarcely less remarkable, is found on the SE. side of the town, and is constructed in a style precisely similar. The age of these walls and gates has been a subject of much controversy; on the one hand the rude and massive style of their construction, and the absence of all traces of the arch in the gateways, would seem to assign them to a remote and indefinite antiquity; on the other hand, the historical notices that we possess concerning Signia all tend to prove that it was not one of the most ancient cities of Latium, and that there could not have existed a city of such magnitude previous to the settlement of the Roman colony under Tarquin. (For the discussion of this question as well as for

---

[*] The annexed figure is taken from that given by Abeken (Mittel Italien, pl. 2).

the description of the remains themselves, see the *Annali dell' Instituto Archeologico* for 1829, pp. 78—87, 357—360; *Classical Museum*, vol. ii. pp. 167—170; Abeken, *Mittel Italien*, p. 140, &c.) The only other remains within the circuit of the walls are a temple (now converted into the church of *S. Pietro*) of Roman date, and built of regularly squared blocks of tufo; and nearly adjoining it a circular reservoir for water, of considerable size and lined with the "opus Signinum." (*Annali, l. c.* p. 82.) Several inscriptions of imperial date are also preserved in the modern town.   [E. H. B.]

GATE OF SIGNIA.

SIGRIA'NE (ἡ Σιγριανή, Strab. xi. p. 525), a district of Media Atropatene, near the Caspian Gates. Ptolemy calls it Σιγριανική (vii. 2. § 6).   [V.]

SI'GRIUM (Σίγριον), the westernmost promontory of the island of Lesbos, which now bears the name of *Sigri* (Strab. xiii. pp. 616, 618.) Stephanus B. (*s. v.*) calls Sigrium a harbour of Lesbos. [L. S.]

SIGULO'NES (Σιγούλωνες), a German tribe mentioned by Ptolemy (ii. 11. § 11) as inhabiting the Cimbrian Chersonesus, to the north of the Saxones, but is otherwise unknown.   [L. S.]

SIGYNNES (Σιγύννες, Herod. v. 9; Σίγυνοι, Apoll. Rhod. iv. 320; Orph. *Arg.* 759; Σίγυννοι, Strab. xi. p. 520). The only name of any Trans-Danubian population, other than Scythian, known to Herodotus was that of the Sigynnes, whom he seems to have described as the Thracians described them to either himself or his informants. The Thracian notion of one of these Sigynnes was that he wore a Median dress, and considered himself a descendant of the Medes; though how this could be was more than Herodotus could say. "Anything, however, is possible in a long space of time." The horses of the Sigynnes were undersized — ponies, indeed, rather than horses. They were flatnosed and long-haired; their coat being five fingers deep. They were too weak to carry a man on their back; but not too weak for harness. In chariots they were light and quick; and in the drawing of chariots the Sigynnes took great delight.

We must look on Sigynnes as a general and collective name for a large assemblage of populations; inasmuch as their country is said to extend as far westwards as the Heneti on the Adriatic. Say that it reached what was afterwards the frontier of Pan-

nonia. On the north it must really have been bounded by some of the Scythian districts. In the language of the Ligyans above Massilia, the word *Sigynna* means a *merchant*, or *retail-dealer*, or *carrier*. In Cyprus they call *spears* by the name *Sigynna*. The resemblance of this word to the name *Zigeun=Gipsy* has often been noticed. Word for word, it may be the same. It may also have been applied to the gipsies with the meaning it has in Ligyan. It does not, however, follow that the Sigynnes were gipsies.   [R. G. L.]

SIHOR (Σιώρ). 1. The torrent more commonly known as "the River of Egypt," the southern boundary of the Promised Land, identified by the LXX. with Rhinocorura, the modern *Wady-el-Arish.* [RHINOCORURA.] (*Joshua*, xiii. 3; 1 *Chron.* xiii. 5; *Jeremiah*, ii. 18.) In the first cited passage, the LXX. read ἀπὸ τῆς ἀοικήτου τῆς κατὰ πρόσωπον Αἰγύπτου; in the second, ἀπὸ ὁρίων Αἰγύπτου, and only in the last is a proper name retained, and there it is changed to Γηών. St. Jerome (*Onomast. s. v.*), following Eusebius, describes it as before Egypt, and speaks of a village of the name between Aelia and Eleutheropolis, which it is difficult to imagine that they could have identified with the Sihor above named. St. Jerome says that he has said more on the subject "in libris Hebraicorum quaestionum," but the passage is not to be found there. In his "Epitaphium Paulae" he writes, "veniam ad Aegypti flumen Sior, qui interpretatur turbidus" (p. 677); but he here probably means the Nile, which is sometimes supposed to be called Sihor, as in the passage of Jeremiah above referred to. The village named by Eusebius and St. Jerome doubtless marked the site of the city of the tribe of Judah, situated in the mountains, and written Zior in the authorised version, but צִיאֹר in the original (*Joshua*, xv. 54), and in the LXX. Σίωρ, (al. Σωραίθ).

2. SIHOR or SHIHOR LIBNATH (LXX. Σιὼν καὶ Λαβανάθ), perhaps to be taken as two names, as by the LXX., Eusebius, and St. Jerome, who name "Sior in tribu Aser," without the addition of Libnath. It is mentioned only in the border of Asher. (*Joshua*, xix. 26.) The various conjectures concerning the place or places are stated by Bonfrerius (*Comment. in loc.*), but none are satisfactory, and the site or sites have still to be recovered.   [G. W.]

SILA (ἡ Σίλα; *Sila*) was the name given in ancient times to a part of the Apennines in the S. of Bruttium, which were clothed with dense forests, and furnished abundance of pitch, as well as timber for ship-building. Strabo tells us it was 700 stadia (70 geog. miles) in length, and places its commencement in the neighbourhood of Locri. (Strab. vi. p. 261.) It is evident, therefore, that he, as well as Pliny (iii. 5. s. 10), who notices it in connection with Rhegium and Leucopetra, assigned the name to the southernmost group of the Apennines (the range of *Aspromonte*), S. of the isthmus which separates the Terinaean and Scylletic gulfs. At the present day the name of *Sila* is given only to the detached and outlying mountain group N. of that isthmus, and E. of *Cosenza* (Consentia.) It is probable that the name, which evidently means only "the forest," and is connected with the Latin *silva*, and the Greek ὕλη, was originally applied in a more general sense to all the forest-covered mountains of this part of *Calabria*, though now restricted to the group in question.   [E. H. B.]

3 s 4

SILACE'NAE, a place in Lower Pannonia, on the south of Lake Peiso. (*It. Ant.* p. 233, where it appears in the ablat. form Silacenis). Its exact site is unknown.   [L. S.]

SILANA, a town in the NW. of Thessaly, near the frontiers of Athamania, mentioned along with Gomphi and Tricca by Livy. Leake conjectures that it occupied the site of *Polidna*, near which are several squared blocks of ancient workmanship. (Liv. xxxvi. 13; Leake, *Northern Greece*, vol. iv. p. 529.)

SI'LARUS (Σίλαρος, Ptol.; Σιλαρίς, Strab.: *Sele*), a considerable river of Southern Italy, flowing into the gulf of Posidonia, and forming the boundary between Campania and Lucania. It rises in the mountains near *Teora*, on the confines of the Hirpini, and not far from the sources of the Aufidus; thence flows for some distance in a southerly direction till it receives the waters of the Tanager (*Tanagro*), a considerable stream, which joins it from the SE.; it then turns to the SW. and pursues that direction to the sea, which it enters about 5 miles to the N. of the city of Paestum. About 5 miles from its mouth it receives another important tributary in the Calor (*Calore*), which joins it from the S. Between the Calor and Tanager, on the S. bank of the Silarus rises the mountain group of Mount Alburnus, mentioned by Virgil in connection with that river. The "luci Silari" of the same author are evidently the same with the extensive woods which still clothe the valley of the *Sele* from its confluence with the *Tanagro* to within a few miles of the sea. (Virg. *Georg.* iii. 146.) The Silarus was in the days of Strabo and Pliny the recognised boundary between Campania (including under that name the land of the Picentini) and Lucania; but this applies only to its course near its mouth, as Eburi (*Eboli*), though situated to the N. of it, is included by Pliny among the towns of Lucania. (Strab. v. p. 251, vi. p. 252; Plin. iii. 5. s. 9, 10, 11. s. 15; Ptol. iii. 1. § 8; Mel. ii. 4. § 9; *Tab. Peut.*.; Dionys. Per. 361.) A peculiarity of its waters, mentioned by several ancient writers, is that they had the power of petrifying sticks, leaves, and other substances immersed in them. (Strab. v. p. 251; Plin. ii. 103. s. 106; Sil. Ital. viii. 582.)

The name is written by Lucan and Columella Siler, and the same form is found in Vibius Sequester, indicating an approach to the modern name of *Sele*. (Lucan, ii. 426; Colum. x. 136; Vib. Seq. p. 18.)   [E. H. B.]

SILAS (Σιλᾶς, Arrian, *Ind.* c. 6; Strab. xv. p. 703; Diod. ii. 37), a river of the Upper *Panjáb*, the story of which, as told by ancient writers, is clearly fabulous. According to Arrian and others, the water of this river was so light that nothing could swim in it. Lassen, who has examined this story with his usual acuteness, has shown from the *Mahabhárata* that there was a stream in the northern part of India called the *Sila*, the water of which was endowed with a highly petrifying power, from which circumstance the river obtained its signification, *Sila* meaning in Sanscrit a stone. (*Zeitschr. f. Kunde des Morgenlands*, ii. p. 63.) It may be remarked that the name occurs differently written. Thus Diodorus writes Σίλλαν ποταμόν; Antigonus Σίλαν κρήνην. (*Mirab.* c. 161.) Pliny evidently refers to the same story, but calls the river Side in his quotation from Ctesias (xxxi. s. 18).   [V.]

SI'LBIUM (Σίλβιον: *Eth.* Silbianus), a small

town of Phrygia, on the east of Apamea and Celaenae, and beyond the source of the Maeander (Ptol. v. 2. § 25; Plin. v. 29). In the Byzantine writers it is sometimes mentioned under corrupt forms of its name, such as Silbia (Hierocl p. 667), Sublas (Cinnamus, vi. 15), or Sublium and Syblaea (*Oriens Christ.* p. 809). This place, which was the see of a bishop, belonged to the conventus of Apamea. Modern travellers seek its site in the neighbourhood of *Sandukli.* (Kiepert, in *Franz's Fünf Inschriften*, p. 37.)   [L. S.]

SILI or SIMI (Σίλοι or Σιμοί, Strab. xvi. p. 772), a tribe of Aethiopians, who used the horns of the oryx, a species of gazelle, as weapons. Some have considered them to be the same as the Αἰθίοπες Σιμοί of Agatharchides, p. 42. (Comp. Diodor. iii. 8.)   [T. H. D.]

SILICENSE FLUMEN, a river in Hispania Baetica, in the neighbourhood of Corduba, probably the *Guadajoz*, or one of its tributaries. (Hirt. *B. A.* 57.)   [T. H. D.]

SILINDIUM (Σιλίνδιον), a small town of Troas at the foot of Mount Ida, is mentioned only by Stephanus B. (*s. v.*) on the authority of Demetrius of Scepsis.   [L. S.]

SILINGAE (Σιλίγγαι), a tribe of Germany, on the south of the Semnones, between the western slopes of Mons Asciburgius and the river Albis. (Ptol. ii. 11. § 18.) It is generally supposed that this name is the one from which the modern *Silesia* or *Schlesien* is formed. (Latham, *Tacit. Germ.* p. 138; Palacky, *Gesch. von Böhmen*, vol. i. p. 68.)   [L. S.]

SILIS (*Sele*), a small river of Venetia, in the N. of Italy, which rises in the mountains above *Treviso* (Tarvisium), and flows into the lagunes at Altinum (*Altino*). It is still called the *Sele.* (Plin. iii. 18. s. 22.)   [E. H. B.]

SILLA (Σίλλα, Isid. Charax, § 2, ed. Müller, 1855), a river of Apolloniatis, a district of Assyria, which, according to Isidorus, flows through the centre of the town of Artemita. [ARTEMITA.] There can be little doubt that this is the river now called the *Diyaleh.* It is also, in all probability, the same as that called by Steph. B. (*s. v.* Ἀνθέμεια) the Delas. Forbiger imagines that the Diabus of Ammianus (xxiii. 6), the Durus of Zosimus (iii. 25), and the Gorgos of Ptolemy (iv. 1. § 7), refer to the same river. It is, however, more likely that the first of these streams is the same as that elsewhere called the Zabatus.   [V.]

SILO or SHILOH (Σηλώμ: *Eth.* Σηλωνίτης), a town of Palestine, in the tribe of Ephraim, in the mountain region according to Josephus (*Ant.* v. 1), where the ark and the tabernacle were first established by Joshua on the settlement of the land by the tribes of Israel. There also were assembled the national convocations for the division of the land and the transaction of other public business affecting the whole Union. (*Joshua*, xviii. 1, 10, xix. 51, xxi. 2, xxii. 9.) There Samuel ministered before the Lord in the days of Eli the high-priest (1 *Sam.* i.—iii.). There was the seat of the Divine worship until the disastrous battle of Aphek, from which period the decline of Shiloh must be dated (ch. iv.) until its desolation became proverbial in Israel. (*Psalm* lxxviii. 60; *Jeremiah*, vii. 12, xxvi. 6, 9.) Its situation is very particularly described in the book of Judges (xxi. 19), as "on the north side of Bethel, on the east side of the highway that goeth up from Bethel to Shechem, and on the south of Lebonah."

St. Jerome places it xii. M. P. from Neapolis (=Shechem = *Nablús*), in the toparchy of Acrabattena. (*Onomast. s. v.*) Its ruins were shown, and the remains of the altar among them, in his day. (*Comment. in Sophon.* i. 14, *Epitaph. Paulae.*) From these notes the site is easily identified with the modern *Silún*, on the east of the *Nablús* road, about four hours south of that town, situated over against a village named *El-Lebban* (Lebonah), which lends its name also to a Khan on the road-side. *Silún* is merely a heap of ruins lying on a hill of moderate elevation at the south-eastern extremity of a valley through which passes the great north road from Judaea to Galilee. "Among the ruins of modern houses are traces of buildings of greater antiquity, and at some distance, towards the east, is a well of good water, and in the valleys many tombs excavated in the rock." (Robinson, *Bibl. Res.* vol. iii. pp. 86—89.) Among the tombs of Shiloh, if Reland's conjecture is correct, is to be sought the very slender authority on which the pagans rested their assertion that their demigod Silenus was buried in the country of the Hebrews; and the fact of the effigy of this deity being found on the coins of Flavia Neapolis, certainly lends countenance to his ingenious hypothesis that the fable originated in the imaginary correspondence between this name and the town of Ephraim, (*Palaestina*, p. 1017.) But the error which he has copied from Benjamin of Tudela, of placing the tomb of Samuel in Shiloh, is obviously attributable to a lapse of memory on the part of that writer, as no one has ever identified Shiloh with the modern *Nebi Samwîl.* The error is corrected by Asher. (*Itinerary of R. Benjamin of Tudela,* ed. A. Asher, vol. i. p. 78, vol. ii. p. 95.) [G. W.]

SILOAM. [JERUSALEM, p. 28, b.]

SI'LPIA, a town in Hispania Baetica, N. of the Baetis, and apparently in the *Sierra Morena.* (Liv. xxviii. 12.) Probably *Linares.* [T. H. D.]

SI'LSILIS (*Not. Imp.*), a fort situated on the right bank of the Nile, between Ombos and Apollinopolis Magna in Upper Aegypt. The original name of this place is nearly preserved in the modern *Silili.* The fort of Silsilis stood at the foot of the mountain now called *Gebel Selsilek,* or " hill of the chain," and was one of the points which commanded the passage of the river. For at this spot the Arabian and Libyan hills approach each other so nearly that the Nile, contracted to about half its ordinary width, seems to flow between two perpendicular walls of sandstone. Silsilis was one of the principal seats for the worship of the Nile itself, and Rameses II. consecrated a temple to it, where it was worshipped under the emblem of a crocodile and the appellation of Hapimoou. The stone quarries of Silsilis were also celebrated for their durable and beautiful stone, of which the great temples and monuments of the Thebaid were for the most part built. (Wilkinson, *Mod. Egypt and Thebes,* vol. ii. p. 283.) [W. B. D.]

SILVANECTES. This name occurs in the Notitia of the Provinces of Gallia, where the chief town is called Civitas Silvanectium. In the Notit. Imp. the Silvanectes are placed in Belgica Secunda, but the name there denotes a town, according to the usage then established of giving to the capital towns the names of their people. It appears almost certain that the Subanecti of Ptolemy (ii. 9. § 11) is the same name as Silvanectae or Silvanectes. Ptolemy places the Subanecti east of the *Seine,* and makes Ratomagus their capital. But this Ratomagus is conjectured to be the same as the Augustomagus of the Itin. and of the Table, which is *Senlis* [AUGUSTOMAGUS].

Pliny (iv. c. 17) mentions the Ulmanetes in Gallia Belgica: " Suessiones liberi, Ulmanetes liberi, Tungri." It is possible that this too may be a corrupted form of Silvanectes, for the modern name *Senlis* confirms the form Silvanectes, and the name Ulmanetes is otherwise unknown. [G. L.]

SI'LVIA, a place in Illyria, on the road from Sirmium to Salona. (*Itin. Ant.* p. 269.) It is probably the same town as the Salvia of Ptolemy [SALVIA]. It is identified with *Kewpris* by Lapie. [T. H. D.]

SI'LVIUM (Σιλούϊον: *Eth.* Silvinus: *Garagnone*), a town of Apulia in the interior of the country. It is noticed by Strabo (vi. p. 283) as the frontier town of the Peucetii, and its name is noticed by Pliny among the municipal towns of Apulia (Plin. iii. 11. s. 16). But at a much earlier period it is mentioned by Diodorus as an Apulian town, which was wrested from the Samnites by the Romans in B. C. 306 (Diod. xx. 80). Our only clue to its position is derived from the Itineraries, which place it 20 miles from Venusia, on the branch of the Appian Way which led direct to Tarentum. This distance coincides with the site of a town (now destroyed) called *Garagnone,* situated about midway between *Spinazzolo* and *Poggio Orsino,* and nearly due E. of *Venosa* (Pratilli, *Via Appia,* iv. 6. p. 478; Romanelli, vol. ii p. 188). [E. H. B.]

SILURA, an island of Britain, separated only by a narrow strait from the coast of the Dumnonii, who inhabited the most SW. point of Britannia. (Solin. c. 22.) It is probably the same island which Sulpicius Severus (ii. 51) calls Sylina, and seems to mean the *Scilly Islands.* [T. H. D.]

SI'LURES (Σίλυρες, Ptol. ii. 3. § 24), a powerful and warlike people in the W. part of Britannia Romana, whose territory was bounded on the S. by the estuary of the Sabrina. The important towns of Isca and Venta belonged to them. Tacitus (*Agr.* 11) calls them descendants of the Iberi of Spain, and states that they had emigrated from Ireland into Britain; but there seems to be no foundation for this opinion. (Cf. Zeuss, *Die Deutschen,* p. 202.) Although subjugated by the Romans, they caused them continual alarm; and they were the only people of Britain who, at a later period, maintained their independence against the Saxons. (Beda, *Hist. Ecc.* i. 12, seq.; cf. Tac. *Ann.* xii. 2, 31; Plin. iv. 16. s. 30). [T. H. D.]

SIME'NA (Σίμηνα: *Eth.* Σιμηνεύς), a town on the coast of Lycia, 60 stadia from Aperlae (Plin. v. 27; Steph. B. s. v.; *Stadiasm. Mar. Mag.* §§ 239, 240, where it is called Somena, Σόμηνα; comp. Leake *Asia Minor,* p. 188; Spratt and Forbes, *Travels in Lycia,* vol. i. p. 137, vol. ii. pp. 86, 274.) [L. S.]

SI'MENI. [ICENI.]

SIMEON. [PALAESTINA, p. 529, b.]

SIMITTU (Σίμισθον, Ptol. iv. 3. § 29), called by Pliny (v. 4. § 4) Simittuense Oppidum, a Roman colony in the interior of Numidia, on the road from Cirta to Carthago, 7 miles to the W. of Bulla Regia. (*Itin. Ant.* p. 43.) There were some mineral waters 5 miles E. of the town (*Ib.*). It lay on the site of the present *Ain Semit,* on the *Qued-el-Bull,* 2 leagues to the W. of *Bull.* [T. H. D.]

SIMOIS (Σιμόεις), a small river of Troas, having its source in Mount Ida, or more accurately in Mount

Cotylus, which passed by Ilion, joined the Scamander below that city. This river is frequently spoken of in the Iliad, and described as a rapid mountain torrent. (*Il.* iv. 475, v. 774, xii. 22, xxi. 308; comp. Aeschyl. *Agam.* 692; Strab. xiii. p. 597; Ptol. v. 2. § 3; Steph. B. *s. v.*; Pomp. Mela, i, 18; Plin. v. 33; and SCAMANDER.) Its present name is *Dumbrek Chai*, and at present its course is so altered that it is no longer a tributary of the Scamander, but flows directly into the Hellespont.   [L. S.]

SIMUNDU.   [TAPROBANE.]

SIMYLLA (Σιμύλλα, Ptol. vii. 1. § 6), a commercial entrepôt on the western coast of *Hindostan*, in the district called 'Αριακὰ Σαδινῶν. It is noticed in the Periplus by the name of Σήμυλλα, and was probably at or near *Bassein*, a little N. of *Bombay*.   [V.]

SI'MYRA (Σιμύρα), a maritime city of Phoenicia mentioned by Pliny in connection with Marathus and Antaradus, N. of Tripolis, Orthosia, and the river Eleutherus (v. 20). It is placed by Ptolemy between the mouth of the Eleutherus and Orthosia, and, if the figures can be trusted, 10' west of the former, 14' north; in the same latitude with Orthosia (i. e. 34° 40'), but 40' east of it, which would seem either to imply an ignorance of the coast, or to intimate that Simyra lay at some distance from the shore, and that the Eleutherus ran southward to the sea. Strabo says that it was occupied by the Aradians, together with the neighbouring Marathus (xvi. p. 753), apparently placing it north of the Eleutherus. In addition to what has been said under MARATHUS, and in confirmation of the identification there attempted, the following may be cited from Shaw, and will serve to illustrate the situation of Simyra: "The ancient Marathus may be fixed at some ruins near the Serpent Fountain, which make, with *Rou-wadde* and Tortosa, almost an equilateral triangle. About 5 miles from the river *Akker*, and 24 to the SSE. of Tortosa, there are other considerable ruins known by the name of *Sumrah*, with several rich plantations of mulberry and other fruit trees growing in and round about them. These, from the very name and situation, can be no other than the remains of the ancient Simyra ... the seat formerly of the Zemarites. Pliny v. 20) makes Simyra a city of Coelesyria, and acquaints us that Mount Libanus ended there to the northward; but as *Sumrah* lies in the *Jeune* (i. e. the great plain), 2 leagues distant from that mountain, this circumstance will better fall in with Arca, where Mount Libanus is remarkably broken off and discontinued." (*Travels*, pp. 268, 269.) The ruins of Arca are 5 miles E. of *Sumrah*, and 2 leagues WSW. of *Arca* is the *Nahr-el-Berd*, the Cold River, which Shaw and others identify with the Eleutherus. It is manifest how irreconcilable all this is with Ptolemy and other ancient geographers. [ELEUTHERUS; ORTHOSIA; MARATHUS.] [G.W.]

SINA.   [SENA.]

SINAE (οἱ Σῖναι, Ptol. vii. 3, &c.), the ancient nation of the Chinese, whose land is first described by Ptolemy (*l. c.*) and Marcianus (p. 29, seq.), but in an unsatisfactory manner. Indeed, the whole knowledge of it possessed by the Greeks and Romans vested on the reports of individual merchants who had succeeded in gaining admittance among a people who then, as in modern times, isolated themselves as much as possible from the rest of the world. For the assumption which Deguignes sought to establish, that a political alliance was formed between

Rome and China, and that the emperor M. Aurelius Antoninus sent a formal embassy thither in the year 166, rests solely on the name of Yan-Tun, which that writer discovered in some ancient Chinese annals, and must therefore be regarded with great suspicion. (See Bohlen, *das Alte Indien*, i. p. 71.) According to the description of Ptolemy, the country of the Sinae extended very far to the S., and was connected with the E. coast of Africa by an unknown land, so that the Indian Ocean formed a large mediterranean sea. He does not venture to define its eastern boundary, but finishes his account of the known earth with the 180th degree of longitude, without, however, denying that there were tracts of unknown land still farther to the E. But Cosmas Indicopleustes (ap. Montfaucon, *N. Coll. Patrum*, ii. p. 337), who calls the country of the Sinae Τ(ίνιτζα, was the first who laid down its correct boundary by the ocean on the E. On the N. it was bounded by Serica, and on the S. and W. by India extra Gangem, from which it was divided by the river Aspithra (probably the *Bangpa-Kung*) and the Semanthine mountains. Thus it embraced the southern half of *China*, and the eastern part of Further India, as *Tongquin, Cochin-China, Camboja*, &c. Ptolemy mentions several large bays and promontories on the coast. At the extreme NE. of the Indian Ocean, where the land of the Sinae abutted on Further India, was the great gulf (of *Siam*), which on the coast of the Sinae was formed by the South Cape (τὸ Νότιον ἄκρον) (probably Cape *Caniboja*), and on the side of India by another large promontory (perhaps *Cape Romania*). To the S. of South Cape, and between it and the Cape of the Satyrs (Σατύρων ἄκρον), Ptolemy and Marcianus (p. 30) place another large bay called Theriodes (Θηριώδης κόλπος); and to the S. of the Cape of Satyrs, again, and between it and the mouth of the river Cottiaris, the Bay of the Sinae (Σινῶν κόλπος). These very vague and incorrect accounts do not permit us to decide with any confidence respecting the places indicated by Ptolemy; but it has been conjectured that the Cape of the Satyrs may have been *Cape St. James*, the Theriodes Sinus the bay between it and the mouth of the river *Camboja* or *Maykiang*, and the Bay of the Sinae the gulf of *Tongquin*. Among the mountains of the country Ptolemy names only the Montes Semanthini (Σημανθινὸν ὄρος), which formed its NW. boundary. Among the rivers indicated are the Aspithra ("Ασπιθρα), rising in the mountains just mentioned, to which we have already alluded; the Ambastus ("Αμβαστος), probably the *Camboja*, which fell into the Great Bay between the towns of Bramma and Rhabana; the Senos or Sainos (Σένος or Σαῖνος) more to the S.; and further still in the same direction the Cottiaris (Κοττίαρις), which emptied itself into the bay of the Sinae to the N. of the town of Cattigara. The last may perhaps be the *Si Kiang*, which discharges itself at *Canton*. Respecting the nation of the Sinae themselves, we have no information, though Ptolemy mentions several subdivisions of them; as in the N. the Semanthini, on the like named mountains; S. of them the Acadorae, with a town called Acadra, and again to the S. the Aspithrae, on the Aspithra, and having a city of the same name as the river. SE. of the latter, on the Great Bay, and dwelling on the river Ambastus, were the Ambastae. Lastly, in a still more southern district between the bay of Theriodes and that of the Sinae, were the Aethiopes

Ichthyophagi and the Sinæ Ichthyophagi. Among the 8 cities mentioned by Ptolemy, namely, Bramma, Rhabana, Cattigara, Acadra, Aspithra, Cocconagra, Sarata, and Thinæ or Sinæ, the last was undoubtedly the most important, and was regarded by him and others as the capital of the nation. It has been conjectured to be *Thsin*, in the province of *Chensi*, or even *Nankin* itself. It may be remarked that the Sinæ were anciently called Thinæ (Θῖναι); though it is said that this form of their name only arose from the Arabic pronunciation of Sinæ. (See Sickler, ii. p. 518; Gesenius, *Heb. Lex.* p. 788.) The next town in point of importance was Cattigara, which both Ptolemy and Marcianus regard as the chief place of trade. [CATTIGARA.]   [T.H.D.]

SINAI (Σινᾶ ὄρος), the celebrated mountain of Arabia Petraea. It, however, lent its name to the whole peninsula in which it was situated, which must therefore first be described. It is formed by the bifurcation of the Red Sea at its northern extremity, and is bounded by the Heroopoliticus Sinus (or *Sea of Suez*) on the west, and the Aelaniticus Sinus (the *Gulf of Akaba*) on the east, ending in the Posidium Promontorium (*Ras Mohammed*). At the northern extremity of the *Sea of Suez* stood Arsinoe (*Suez*), and Aelana (*Akaba*), at the extremity of the gulf that bears its name. The caravan road of the great *Haj*, which joins these two towns, traverses a high table-land of desert, now called *El-Tîh*="the Wilderness of the Wandering," part of ancient Idumaea. To the south of this road, the plateau of chalk formation is continued to *Jebel Tîh*, the μέλανα ὄρη of Ptolemy, extending from the eastern to the western gulf, in a line slightly curved to the south, and bounded in that direction by a belt of sandstone, consisting of arid plains, almost without water or signs of vegetation. To this succeeds the district of primitive granite formation, which extends quite to the southern cape, and runs into the *Gulf of Akaba* on the east, but is separated by a narrow strip of alluvial soil called *El-Káa* from the *Sea of Suez*. The northern part of the *Tîh* is called in Scripture " the wilderness of Paran" (*Numb.* xii. 16, xiii. 3, xxxii. 8, &c.), in which the Israelites abode or wandered during great part of the forty years; although Eusebius and St. Jerome, as will be presently seen, identify this last with the wilderness of *Sin*. This wilderness of *Sin* is commonly supposed to be connected, in name and situation, with Mount Sinai; but as the Israelites entered on the wilderness of Sin on leaving their encampment by the Red Sea, the next station to Elim (*Exod.* xvi. 1; *Numb.* xxxiii. 10, 11), and traversed it between Elim and Rephidim, where they had apparently left it (*Exod.* xvii. 1),—for Dophkah and Alush are inserted between the two in *Numbers* xxxiii. 12—14,— and yet had not arrived at Sinai (ver. 15; *Exod.* xvi. 1), it may be questioned whether the identification rests on solid ground. Eusebius and St. Jerome, who distinguish between the deserts of Sin and Sinai, yet appear to extend the former too far eastward. " The desert of Sin," they say, " extends between the Red Sea and the desert of Sina; for they came from the desert of Sin to Rephidim, and thence to the desert of Sinai, near Mount Sina, where Moses received the dispensation of the Law; but this desert is the same as that of Kaddes according to the Hebrew, but not according to the LXX." The confusion indicated by this last remark may be explained by the observations, 1st, that Zin, which is a synonym " for the wilderness of

Kadesh " (*Numb.* xx. 1, xxxiii. 36), is identical in Greek with the Sin (i. e. Σίν); the Σ representing both the צ (tsadi) of זין and the ס (samech) of סין; and, 2dly, that instead of making Zin identical with Kadesh, as it is in the Hebrew, the LXX. read so as to make " the desert of Paran," which they identify with " the desert of Kadesh," an intermediate station between Sin and Mount Hor (*Numb.* xxxiii. 36, in LXX.)

The wilderness of Sin, then, must be fixed to the northwest part of the granite district of the peninsula between *Serbal* and the Red Sea, while Zin is north of Ezion Geber, between it and Mount Hor,— the southern extremity in fact of *Wady Músa*, or the *Arabah*, north of *Akaba*.

With respect to Sinai, it is difficult to decide between the rival claims of the two mountains, which, in modern as in ancient times, have been regarded as the Mountain of the Law. The one is *Serbal* above-mentioned, situated towards the NW. extremity of the granite district, towering with its five sharp-pointed granite peaks above the fruitful and agreeable *oasis* of *Wady Pharan*, still marked by extensive ruins of the churches, convents, and buildings of the old episcopal town of Paran; the other between 30 and 40 miles south-east of *Serbal*, in the heart of the granite district, where native traditions, of whatever value, have affixed to the mountains and valleys names connected with the inspired narrative of the giving of the Law; and where the scenery is entirely in unison with the events recorded. Emerging from the steep and narrow valley *Nakba Hawa*, whose precipitous sides rise to the perpendicular height of 1000 feet, into the wide plain called *Wady Músa*, at the northern base of the traditionary Horeb, Russegger describes the scene as grand in the extreme. " Bare granite mountains, whose summits reach to a height of more than 7000 Paris feet above the level of the sea; wonderful, I might say fabulous, forms encompass a plain more than a mile in length, in the background of which lies the convent of St. Catharine, at the foot of *Jebel Músa*, between the holy Horeb on the west, and Ebestimmi on the east." In this valley, then, formed at the base of Horeb by what may be called a junction of the *Wady-er-Rahâh* and *Wady-esh-Sheikh*, but which, according to Russegger's express testimony, bears in this place the native name of *Wady Músa*, must the children of Israel have encamped before *Jebel Músa*, whose rugged northern termination, projected boldly into the plain, bears the distinctive name of *Ras Sasâfah*. *Jebel Músa* rises to the height of 5956 Paris feet above the sea, but is far from being the highest of the group. Towering high above it, on the south, is seen the summit of Horeb, having an elevation of 7097 Paris feet, and south of that again *Jebel Katherina*, more than 1000 feet higher still (viz. 8168 Paris feet), all outtopped by *Jebel-om-Shomer*, the highest of this remarkable group, which attains an altitude of 8300 Paris feet. Over against *Jebel Músa* on the north, and confining the valley in that direction, is the spur of a mountain which retains in its name, *Jebel Sena*, a memorial of the ancient Scripture appellation of the Mountain of the Law. To attempt anything like a full discussion of the questions at issue between the advocates of the conflicting traditions or hypotheses, would be as inconsistent with the character of such an article as this, as with the limits which must be assigned to it: a very few remarks must suffice. There seems, then, to be no question that the site of Horeb was traditionally known to the Israelites for many centuries after the Exodus (1 Kings, xix. 8); and if so, it is improbable that it was subsequently lost, since its proximity to Elath and Ezion Geber, which were long in their possession, would serve to ensure the perpetuity of the tradition. It is worthy of remark that Josephus nowhere uses the name Horeb, but in the passage parallel to that above cited from the 1st book of Kings, as uniformly throughout his history, substitutes τὸ Σιναῖον ὄρος,— so far confirming the identity of locality indicated by the two names, learnedly maintained by Dr. Lepsius, who holds Horeb to be an Amalekite appellative equivalent in signification with Sin, both signifying "earth made dry by draining off the water," which earth he finds in the large mounds of alluvial deposit in the bed of *Wady Faran*, at the northern base of *Serbal*, his Sinai. Buxtorf, however, cites rabbinical authorities for another etymology of Sinai, derived from the nature of the rock in the vicinity. (See *Shaw's Travels*, 4to. p. 443. and note 7.) Josephus does not in any way identify the site; but Eusebius and St. Jerome have been erroneously understood to describe Serbal under the name Sina, when they say that Pharan was south of Arabia, next to the desert of the Saracens, through which the children of Israel journeyed when they decamped from Sina (*Onomast. s. v. Pharan.*); for they obviously confound the city of Paran with the wilderness mentioned in Numbers (xii. 16, xiii. 3); and the description is so vague as to prove only their ignorance, if not of the true site of the city Pharan (which they place 3 days east of Aila), at least of the utter want of all connection between this and the desert of Zin, which is Paran; and in this, as in other passages, on which much reliance has been placed in this discussion, it is clear that they are not writing from any local knowledge, but simply drawing deductions from the Scripture narrative (see e. g. *Onomast. s. v. Raphadim*), which we are perhaps equally competent to do. The earliest Christian writer, then, who can be quoted as a witness to the true site of the "Mountain of the Law" is Cosmas Indicopleustes (circ. A. D. 530), who undoubtedly describes Mount Choreb, in the Sinaic (desert ?), as near to Pharan, about 6 miles distant; and this Pharan must be the Pharan of the ecclesiastical annals, whose ruins at the foot of Mount Serbal have been noticed above. This then is direct historical testimony in favour of a hypothesis first started by Burckhardt in modern times, advocated by Dr. Lepsius, and adopted by Mr. Forster and others. But then it appears to be the only clear historical evidence, and must therefore be compared with that in favour of the existing tradition, which, as it is accepted in its main features by Drs. Robinson and Wilson, Ritter, Mr. Stanley, and other eminent scholars, is obviously not unworthy of regard. That the present convent of St. Catharine was originally founded by the emperor Justinian (about A. D. 556), is as certain as any fact in history; and it is equally difficult to imagine that, at so short an interval after the journey of Cosmas, the remembrance of the true Sinai could have been lost, and that the emperor or the monks would have acquiesced in what they knew to be a fictitious site; for the mountain had long been regarded with veneration by the monks, who, however, had erected no monastery before this time, but dwelt in the mountains and valleys about the bush in which God appeared to Moses (Eutychii *Annales*, tom. ii. p. 163) comp. Procopius, *De Aedificiis Justiniani*, v. 8); so that when their monasteries are mentioned in earlier times, it is clear that the monastic cells only are to be understood. On the whole, then, the testimony of Cosmas can hardly avail against a tradition which was not originated, but only perpetuated, by the erection of Justinian's monastery. To this historical argument in favour of the existing traditions a topographical one may be added. If Rephidim is correctly placed by Dr. Lepsius and others at *Wady Faran*, at the foot of Serbal, it seems to follow incontestably that *Serbal* cannot be Sinai; for what occasion could there be for the people to decamp from Rephidim, and journey to Sinai, if Rephidim were at the very base of the mount ? (*Exod.* xix. 1, 2). Dr. Lepsius feels the difficulty, and attempts to remove it by insinuating that the sacred narrative is not to be implicitly trusted. That Horeb is mentioned in connection with Rephidim is certainly a palpable difficulty (*Exod.* xviii. 1—6), but in a choice of difficulties it is safer to adopt that which does least violence to the sacred text.

By far the strongest argument in favour of the identity of Serbal with Sinai is to be found in the celebrated inscriptions with which the rocks on that mountain and in the surrounding valleys are covered. Not that anything can be certainly determined from these mysterious records, while the art of deciphering them is still in its infancy. The various theories respecting them cannot here be discussed; the works containing them are referred to at the end of the article: but it may be well to put on record the whole of the earliest testimony concerning them, and to offer for their elucidation an observation suggested by an early writer which has been strangely overlooked in this discussion. It is an interesting theory of Cosmas Indicopleustes, that the Israelites, having been instructed in written characters in the Decalogue given in Horeb, were practised in writing, as in a quiet school, in the desert for forty years: "from whence it comes to pass," he proceeds, "that you may see in the desert of Mount Sinai, and in all the stations of the Hebrews, all the rocks in those parts, which have rolled down from the mountains, engraven with Hebrew inscriptions, as I myself, who journeyed in those parts, testify; which certain Jews also having read, interpreted to us, saying that they were written thus. 'The pilgrimage (ἄπεσις) of such an one, of such a tribe, in such a year, and such a month,'—as is frequently written in our hostelries. For they, having newly acquired the art, practised it by multiplying writing, so that all those places are full of Hebrew inscriptions, preserved even unto this time, on account of the unbelievers, as I think; and any one who wishes can visit those places and see them, or they can inquire and learn concerning it that I have spoken the truth." (Cosmas Indicopleustes, *de Mundo*, lib. v. apud Montfaucon, *Collectio Nova Patrum*, tom. ii. p. 205.) On this it may suffice to remark, that while it is certain that the characters are neither the original nor later Hebrew,— i. e. neither Phoenician nor Chaldaic,—still the Jews in Cosmas's company could decipher them. We know that they are for the most part similar to the ancient Arabian (the Hamyaritic or Hadramûtic) character, with which the whole region in the south of the Arabian peninsula teems. If, then, Mr. Forster's ingenious and very probable conjecture of the identity of the rock-hewn inscription of *Hism Ghorab* with that copied by Abderakhman from the southern coast of Arabia, preserved and translated by Schultens, be correct, it will follow that the old Adite character was decipherable even two centuries later than the date assigned to Cosmas, who could scarcely have failed to discover the Christian origin of these inscriptions, if they had been really Christian. Indeed it may well be questioned whether any Christians could have been sufficiently conversant with this ancient character to use it as freely as it is used on the rocks of the peninsula. Certainly if the hypothesis of this place having been resorted to as a place of pilgrimage by the pagan tribes of Arabia, and so having acquired a sanctity in the very earliest times, could be established, the fact might furnish a clue to the future investigation of this deeply interesting subject, and, as Ritter has suggested, might serve to remove some difficulties in the Sacred Narrative. Now the journal of Antoninus Placentinus does in fact supply so precisely what was wanting, that it is singular that his statement has attracted so little notice in connection with the Sinaitic inscriptions; which, however, he does not expressly mention or even allude to. But what we do learn from him is not unimportant, viz., that before the time of Islâm, in " the ages of ignorance," as the Mohammedans call them, the peninsula of Mount Sinai was a principal seat of the idolatrous superstition of the Arabians; and that a feast was held there in honour of their miraculous idol, which was resorted to by Ishmaelites, as he calls them, from all parts; the memorial of which feast seems still to be preserved by the Bedawin. (Burckhardt, Syria, pp. 566, 567.) Now when it is remembered that the eastern commerce of Greece and Rome, conducted by the Arabs of Yemen and Hadramant, must have brought their merchants and sailors to the vicinity of this ancient sanctuary at Arsinoe or at Elana, the pilgrimage becomes almost a matter of course; and the practice which we know prevailed in their own country of graving their memorials with an iron pen in the rock for ever, was naturally adopted by them, and imitated by the Christian pilgrims in after times. Undue stress has been laid on the frequency of the inscriptions about Serbal, contrasted with their rarity about Jebel Músa; but it should be remembered that they are executed almost entirely in the soft sandstone which meets the granite on and around Serbal, but which is scarcely found in the interior, where the hard, primitive rock did not encourage the scribbling propensities of the travellers, as the softer tablets in the more western part, where the blocks of trap-stone (which are also largely interspersed with the granite, and which present a black surface without, but are lemon-coloured within) were studiously selected for the inscriptions, which, in consequence, come out with the effect of a rubricated book or illuminated manuscript, the black surface throwing out in relief the lemon-coloured inscriptions.

This account of the peninsula must not be concluded without a brief notice of the very remarkable temple of Sarbut-el-Chádem, and the stelae which are found in such numbers, not only in the temple, but in other western parts of the peninsula, where large masses of copper, mixed with a quantity of iron ore, were and still are found in certain strata of the sandstone rocks along the skirts of the primeval chain, and which gave to the whole district the name still found in the hieroglyphics, Maphat, " the copper land," which was under the particular pro-

tection of the goddess Hathor, Mistress of Maphat. The temple, dedicated to her, stands on a lofty sandstone ledge, and is entirely filled with lofty stelae, many of them like obelisks with inscriptions on both sides; so crowded with them in fact, that its walls seem only made to circumscribe the stelae, although there are several erected outside it, and on the adjacent hills. The monuments belong, apparently, to various dynasties, but Dr. Lepsius has only specially mentioned three, all of the twelfth. The massive crust of iron ore covering the hillocks, 250 yards long and 100 wide, to the depth of 6 or 8 feet, and blocks of scoriae, prove that the smelting furnaces of the Egyptian kings were situated on these airy heights; but the caverns in which the ore was found contain the oldest effigies of kings in existence, not excepting the whole of Egypt and the pyramids of Gizeh.

The chief authorities for this article, besides those referred to in the text, are Niebuhr (Voyage en Arabie, vol. i. pp. 181—204); Seetzen (Reisen, vol. iii. pp. 55—121). For the physical history and description of the peninsula, Russegger is by far the fullest and most trustworthy authority (Reisen, vol. iii. pp. 22—58). Dr. Robinson has investigated the history and geography of the peninsula, with his usual diligence (Travels, vol. i. §§ 3, 4. pp. 87—241); and Dr. Wilson has added some important observations in the way of additional information or correction of his predecessor (Lands of the Bible, vol. i. chapters vi.—viii. pp. 160—275). Lepsius's Tour from Thebes to the Peninsula of Sinai (Letters, pp. 310—321, 556—562), which has been translated by C. H. Cottrell (London, 1846), argues for Serbal as the true Mountain of the Law; and his theory has been maintained with great learning and industry by Mr. John Hogg (Remarks on Mount Serbal, &c. in Transactions of the Royal Society of Literature, 1849). The graphic description of the country from Mr. A. P. Stanley's pen is the latest contribution to the general history of the peninsula (Sinai and Palestine, 1856). The decipherment of the inscriptions has been attempted by the learned Orientalists of Germany, Gesenius, Roediger, Beer, and others (Ch. Bunsen, Christianity and Mankind, vol. iii. pp. 231—234); and Mr. Forster has published a vindication of his views against the strictures of Mr. Stanley on his original work (The Voice of Israel from the Rocks of Sinai, 1851; The Israelitish Authorship of the Sinaitic Inscriptions, 1856).   [G. W.]

SINCHI, a sub-division of the Sarmatian tribe of the Tauri. (Amm. Mar. xxii. 8. § 33.) [T. H. D.]

SINDA (Σίνδα : Eth. Sindensis), a town which seems to have been situated on the western frontier of Pisidia, in the neighbourhood of Cibyra and the river Caularis (Liv. xxxviii. 15; Strabo, xii. p. 570, xiii. p. 630). Stephanus B. (s. v. Συνδία), who speaks of Sindia as a town of Lycia, is probably alluding to the same place. (Comp. Hierocl. p. 680; Polyb. Excerpt. de Leg. 30.) Some writers have confounded Sinda with Isionda, which is the more surprising, as Livy mentions the two as different towns in the same chapter. (Leake, Asia Minor, p. 152.)   [L. S.]

SINDA SARMATICA (Σίνδα κώμη, Ptol. v. 9. § 8), a town or village in Asiatic Sarmatia, in the territory of the Sindi, with an adjoining harbour (Σινδικὸς λιμήν, Ptol. Ib.), 180 stadia E. of the mouth of the Bosporus Cimmerius at Corocondama, and, according to Arrian (Per. P. Eux. p. 19), 500 stadia from Panticapaeum, and 300 from the Holy Harbour. But, according to Pliny, who calls it Civitas Sindica (vi. 5. s. 5), it was 67 miles from the latter. It lay apparently on the lake of Corocondametis. According to Scylax (p. 31) Sinda was a Greek colony; though Mela, who calls it Sindos (i. 19), regards it, with less probability, as a sea-port founded by the Sindi themselves. (Comp. Strab. xii. p. 496; Scymn. Fr. v. 154.)

2. A town of the Sindi, on the W. coast of the Sinus Magnus, or on the E. coast of the Aurea Chersonesus in India extra Gangem, between the mouths of the Dorias and Daonas. (Ptol. vii. 2. § 7; Steph. B. p. 602.)   [T. H. D.]

SINDI (Σινδοί, Herod. iv. 28), a people in Asiatic Sarmatia, on the E. coast of the Pontus Euxinus and at the foot of the Caucasus, in the district called Sindice. (Herod. l. c.; Hipponax. p. 71, ed. Welck.; Hellanic. p. 78; Dionys. Per. 681; Steph. B. p. 602 ; Amm. Marc. xxii. 8. § 41, &c.) Besides the sea-port of Sinda, other towns belonging to the same people were, Hermonassa, Gorgippia, and Aborace. (Strab. xi. p. 495.) They had a monarchical form of government (Polyaen, viii. 55), and Gorgippia was the residence of their kings. (Strab. l. c.) Nicolaus Damascenus (p. 160, ed. Orell.) mentions a peculiar custom which they had of throwing upon the grave of a deceased person as many fish as the number of enemies whom he had overcome. Their name is variously written, and Mela calls them Sindones (iii. 19), Lucian (Tox. 55), Σινδιανοί. Eichwald (Alt Geogr. d. Kasp. M. p. 356) holds them to have been a Hindoo colony. (Comp. Bayer, Acta Petrop. ix. p. 370; St. Croix, Mem. de l'Ac. des Inscr. xlvi. p. 403; Larcher, ad Herod. vii. p. 506; Ukert, vol. iii. pt. 2. p. 494, &c.)   [T. H. D.]

SI'NDICE (Σινδική, Strab. xi. pp. 492, 495, &c.), the tract of country inhabited by the Sindi, which, according to Scylax (p. 31), lay between that belonging to the Maeotae, on the Palus Maeotis, and that of the Cercetae (the modern Cherkas), and which must therefore be sought at or near the peninsula of Taman. According to Strabo (xi. p. 492) it reached to the Achaei, and extended in a southerly direction from the Hypanis. [T. H. D.]

SINDOCANDA (Σινδοκάνδα, Ptol. vii. 4. § 3), a city in the middle of the W. coast of Taprobane, belonging to the people called Sandocandae. Hence it has been conjectured, either that the name of the town should be changed into Sandocanda, or that the people should be called Sindocandae. [T. H. D.]

SINDOMANA (Σινδόμανα, Strab. xv. p. 701), a town on the lower course of the Indus, and in the neighbourhood of the island of Pattalene. (Comp. Arrian, Anab. vi. 15; Diod. xvii. 102; Curtius, ix. 8, 13, 17.)   [T.H.D.]

SINDUS (Σίνδος, Herod. vii. 123; Steph. B. s. v.), a maritime town of Mygdonia in Macedonia, between Therme (Thessalonica) and Chalastra. [E. B. J.]

SINGA (Σίγγα, Ptol. v. 15. § 10), a city of the Syrian province of Commagene, to the N. of Doliche, and situated on the river Singas (Ib. § 9), (now the Seneja), which had its source in Mount Pieria and flowed to the NW. till it fell into the Euphrates to the S. of Samosata.   [T. H. D.]

SINGAMES (Σιγγάμης, Arrian, Per. P. Eux. p. 10), a navigable river of Colchis, which entered the Pontus Euxinus 210 stadia N. of the Cobus, and 120 stadia SE. from the Tarsuras. (Plin. vi. 4. s. 4.) Now the Osingiri.   [T. H. D.]

SI'NGARA (τὰ Σίγγαρα, Dion Cass. xviii. 22), a strongly fortified post at the northern extremity of Mesopotamia, which for awhile, as appears from many coins still extant, was occupied by the Romans as an advanced colony against the Persians. Its position has not been clearly defined by ancient writers, Stephanus B. calling it a city of Arabia, near Edessa, and Ptolemy placing it on the Tigris (v. 18. § 9). There can, however, be no doubt that it and the mountain near it, called by Ptolemy ὁ Σίγγαρας ὄρος (v. 18. § 2), are represented at the present day by the district of the Singár. It appears to have been taken by Trajan (Dion Cass. lxviii. 22); and as the legend on some of the coins reads ΑΤΡ. ΣΕΠ. ΚΟΛ. ΣΙΝΓΑΡΑ. and bears the head of Gordian on the obverse, it appears to have formed a Roman colony under the emperors Severus and Gordian. It was the scene of a celebrated nocturnal conflict between Constantius and Sapor, the king of Persia, the result of which was so unsatisfactory that both sides claimed the victory. (Amm. Marc. xviii. 5; Eutrop. x. 10; Sext. Ruf. c. 27.) Still later, under the reign of Julian, it is recorded that it underwent a celebrated siege, and at length was carried by the Persians by storm, though gallantly defended by the townspeople and two legions. (Amm. Marc. xx. 6.) The country around it is stated by Ammianus and Theophylactus to have been extremely arid, which rendered it equally difficult to take or to relieve from a distance.   [V.]

SINGIDA'VA (Σιγγίδαυα, Ptol. iii. 8. § 8), a town in the interior of Dacia, between the rivers Tysia and Aluta, now Dora on the Marosch. [T.H.D.]

SINGIDU'NUM (Σιγγί(ν)δουνον, or Σιγινδουνον, Ptol. iii. 9. § 3), a town in Moesia Superior, at the spot where the Savus falls into the Danubius, and on the main road along the banks of the latter river, opposite to the town of Taurunum (Semlin) in Pannonia. (Itin. Ant. p. 132; Itin. Hierosol. p. 563.) By Procopius (de Aed. iv. 6. p. 287) it is called Σιγγηδών. It was a fortress, and the head-quarters of the Legio IV. Flavia Felix (Not. Imp.), the modern Belgrade.   [T. H. D.]

SI'NGILI or SINGILIS, a town of Hispania Baetica. (Plin. iii. 1. s. 3.) It lay near Castillon or Valsequilla, and D'Anville (l. p. 39) identifies it with Puente de don Gonzalo. Concerning its ruins and inscriptions, see Florez, Esp. Sagr. ix. p. 42, xii. 20; Morales, p. 21.   [T. H. D.]

SINGITICUS SINUS. [SINGUS.]

SI'NGONE (Σιγγόνη), a town of the Quadi in the south-east of Germany, mentioned by Ptolemy (ii. 11. § 30), but otherwise unknown. [L. S.]

SI'NGULIS, a tributary river of the Baetis, navigable as far up as Astigi. (Plin. iii. 1. s. 3.) Now the Xenil.   [T. H. D.]

SINGUS (Σίγγος, Herod. vii. 122; Thuc. v. 18; Böckh, Corp. Inscr. vol. i. p. 304; Ptol. iii. 13. § 11; Steph. B. s. v.; Plin. iv. 17: Εth. Σιγγαῖοι), a town of Sithonia in Macedonia, upon the gulf to which it gave its name, SINGITICUS SINUS (Σιγγιτικὸς κόλπος, Ptol. l. c.: Gulf of A'ghion Oros), identified with Sykia, probably a corrupted form of the old name. (Leake, Northern Greece, vol. iii. p. 153.)   [E. B. J.]

SINIAR, a district of Babylonia, which is mentioned in Genesis under the title of the "land of Shinar." It is noticed under the name of Σενναὰρ τῆς Βαβυλωνίας by Histiaeus and Eusebius, quoted by Josephus (Ant. Jud. i. 5) and Eusebius (Praepar. Evang. ix. 15; comp. Gen. xi. 2; Isaiah, xi. 11;

Zech. v. 11). It would seem to comprehend especially the great plain land of Babylonia, as distinguished from Assyria and Elymais (*Gen.* xiv. 1), and probably extended to the junction of the Tigris and Euphrates, if not as far as the Persian gulf. Some have, without reason, confounded it with Singara, the modern *Singár.*   [V.]

SINIS (Σίνις), a Roman colony in the district of Melitene in Armenia Minor. (Ptol. v. 7. § 5.) The place is not mentioned by any other writer, but it is possible that it may be the same place as the one which Procopius (*de Aed.* iii. 4) simply calls Κολωνία.   [L. S.]

SINNA. 1. (Σίννα, Ptol. v. 18. §§ 11, 12), the name of two towns in Mesopotamia, one on the S. declivity of Mount Masius, the other more to the SE., on the Tigris.

2. (Σιννᾶ, Strab. xvi. p. 755), a mountain fortress in Lebanon.   [T. H. D.]

SINO'NI·A (*Zannone*), was the name given in ancient times to the smallest of the three islands known as the *Isole di Ponza.* It is situated about 5 miles to the NE. of Pontia (*Ponza*), the principal island of the group (Plin. iii. 6. s. 12; Mel. ii. 7. § 18).   [E. H. B.]

SINO'PE (Σινώπη : *Eth.* Σινωπεύς), the most important of all the Greek colonies on the coast of the Euxine, was situated on a peninsula on the coast of Paphlagonia, at a distance of 700 stadia to the east of Cape Carambis (Strab. xii. p. 546 ; Marcian, p. 73 ; Eustath. *ad Dion. Per.* 775.) It was a very ancient place, its origin being referred to the Argonauts and to Sinope, the daughter of Asopus. (Apollon. Rhod. ii. 947 ; Val. Flacc. v. 108.) But the Sinopians themselves referred the foundation of their city to Autolycus, a companion of Heracles, and one of the Argonauts, to whom they paid heroic honours (Strab. *l. c.*). But this ancient town was small and powerless, until it received colonists from Miletus. The Milesians were in their turn dispossessed by the Cimmerians, to whom Herodotus (iv. 12) seems to assign the foundation of the city ; but when the Cimmerians were driven from Asia Minor, the Ephesians (in B. C. 632) recovered possession of their colony. (Scymn. 204, foll.: Anonym. *Peripl. P. E.* p. 8.) The leader of the first Milesian colony is called Ambron, and the leaders of the second Cous and Critines ; though this latter statement seems to be a mistake, as Eustathius and Stephanus B. (*s. v.*) call the founder Critius, a native of Cos. After this time Sinope soon rose to great power and prosperity. About the commencement of the Peloponnesian War the Sinopians, who were then governed by a tyrant, Timesileon, received assistance from the Athenians ; and after the expulsion of the tyrant, 600 Athenian colonists were sent to Sinope (Plut. *Pericl.* 20). At the time of the retreat of the Ten Thousand under Xenophon, Sinope was a wealthy and flourishing city, whose dominion extended to the river Halys, and which exercised great influence over the tribes of Paphlagonia and Cappadocia, independently of its colonies of Cerasus, Cotyora, and Trapezus. It was mainly owing to the assistance of the Sinopians, that the returning Greeks were enabled to procure ships to convey them to Heracleia (Xenoph. *Anab.* v. 5. § 3 ; Arrian, *Peripl. P. E.* p. 17 ; Diod. Sic. xiv. 30, 32 ; Amm. Marc. xxii. 8). Strabo also acknowledges that the fleet of the Sinopians held a distinguished position among the naval powers of the Greeks ; it was mistress of the Euxine as far as the entrance

of the Bosporus, and divided with Byzantium the lucrative tunny fisheries in that sea. In the time of Ptolemy Soter, Sinope was governed by a prince, Scydrothemis, to whom the Egyptian king sent an embassy. (Tac. *Hist.* iv. 82, foll.) Its great wealth, and above all its excellent situation, excited the cupidity of the kings of Pontus. It was first assailed in B. C. 220, by Mithridates IV., the great-grandfather of Mithridates the Great. Polybius (iv. 56), who is our principal authority for this event, describes the situation of Sinope in the following manner : It is built on a peninsula, which advances out into the sea. The isthmus which connects the peninsula with the mainland is not more than 2 stadia in breadth, and is entirely barred by the city, which comes up close to it, but the remainder of the peninsula stretches out towards the sea. It is quite flat and of easy access from the town ; but on the side of the sea it is precipitous all around, and dangerous for vessels, and presents very few spots fit for effecting a landing. This description is confirmed by Strabo (xii. p. 545), for he says that the city was built on the neck of the peninsula ; but he adds, that the latter was girt all around with rocks hollowed out in the form of basins. At high water these basins were filled, and rendered the shore inaccessible, especially as the rocks were everywhere so pointed that it was impossible to walk on them with bare feet. The Sinopians defended themselves bravely against Mithridates, and the timely aid of the Rhodians in the end enabled them to compel the aggressor to raise the siege. Pharnaces, the successor of Mithridates IV., was more successful. He attacked the city unexpectedly, and finding its inhabitants unprepared, easily overpowered it, B. C. 183. From this time Sinope became the chief town, and the residence of the kings of Pontus. (Strab. *l. c.*; Polyb. xxiv. 10.) Mithridates, surnamed Euergetes the successor of Pharnaces, was assassinated at Sinope in B. C. 120 (Strab. x. p. 477). His son, Mithridates the Great, was born and educated at Sinope, and did much to embellish and strengthen his birthplace : he formed a harbour on each side of the isthmus, built naval arsenals, and constructed admirable reservoirs for the tunny fisheries. After his disaster at Cyzicus, the king intrusted the command of the garrison of Sinope to Bacchides, who acted as a cruel tyrant ; and Sinope, pressed both from within and from without, was at last taken by Lucullus, after a brave resistance. (Strab. *l. c.*; Plut. *Lucull.* 18; Appian, *Bell. Mithr.* 83; Memnon, in Phot. *Cod.* p. 238, ed. Bekker.) Lucullus treated the Sinopians themselves mildly, having put the Pontian garrison to the sword ; and he left them in possession of all their works of art, which embellished the city, with the exception of the statue of Autolycus, a work of Sthenis, and the sphere of Billarus. (Strab. Plut. *ll. cc.*; Cic. *pro Leg. Man.* 8.) Lucullus restored the city to its ancient freedom and independence. But when Pharnaces, the son of Mithridates, had been routed at Zela, Caesar took Sinope under his protection, and established Roman colonies there, as we must infer from coins bearing the inscription Col. Jul. Caes. Felix Sinope. In the time of Strabo Sinope was still a large, splendid, and well fortified city ; for he describes it as surrounded by strong walls, and adorned with fine porticoes, squares, gymnasia, and other public edifices. Its commerce indeed declined, yet the tunny fisheries formed an inexhaustible source of revenue, which maintained the city in a tolerable state of prosperity. It possessed extensive suburbs, and numerous villas in its vicinity (Strab. *l. c.*; Plin. vi. 2). From Pliny's letter's (x. 91), it appears that the Sinopians suffered some inconvenience from the want of a good supply of water, which Pliny endeavoured to remedy by a grant from the emperor Trajan to build an aqueduct conveying water from a distance of 16 miles. In the time of Arrian and Marcian, Sinope still continued to be a flourishing town. In the middle ages it belonged to the empire of Trebizond, and fell into the hands of the Turks in A. D. 1470, in the reign of Mohammed II. Sinope is also remarkable as the birthplace of several men of eminence, such as Diogenes the Cynic, Baton, the historian of Persia, and Diphilus, the comic poet.

Near Sinope was a small island, called Scopelus, around which large vessels were obliged to sail, before they could enter the harbour; but small craft might pass between it and the land, by which means a circuit of 40 stadia was avoided (Marcian, p. 72, &c.) The celebrated Sinopian cinnabar (Σινωπικὴ μίλτος, Σινωπὶς or Σινωπικὴ γῆ) was not a product of the district of Sinope, but was designated by this name only because it formed one of the chief articles of trade at Sinope. (Groskurd *on Strabo*, vol. ii. p. 457, foll.) The imperial coins of Sinope that are known, extend from Augustus to Gallienus. (Sestini, *Num. Vet.* p. 63; Rasche, *Lex. Num.* iv. 2. p. 1105, foll.)

Sinope, now called *Sinab*, is still a town of some importance, but it contains only few remains of its former magnificence. The wall across the isthmus has been built up with fragments of ancient archi tecture, such as columns, architraves, &c., and the same is found in several other parts of the modern town; but no distinct ruins of its temples, porticoes, or even of the great aqueduct, are to be seen. (Hamilton, *Researches*, vol. i. p. 306, &c.)   [L. S.]

SINO'RIA (Σινορία, Strab. xii. p. 555), a town on the frontier of Armenia Major, a circumstance which gave rise to a pun of the historian Theophanes who wrote the name Σινόρια. The place is no doubt the same as the one called Sinorega by Appian (*Mithrid.* 101), by Ammianus Marcellinus (xvii. 7) Synhorium, by Ptolemy (v. 7. § 2) Sinibra or Sinera, and in the Antonine Itinerary (p. 208) Sinervas. The pun upon the name made by Theophanes seems to show that the form Sinoria, which Strabo gives, is the correct one. The town was a fortress built by Mithridates on the frontier between Greater and Lesser Armenia; but assuming that all the different names mentioned above are only varieties or corrup tions of one, it is not easy to fix the exact site of the town, for Ptolemy and the Antonine Itinerary place it to the south-west of Satala, on the road from this town to Melitene, and on the Euphrates, while the Table, calling it Sinara, places it 79 miles to the north-east of Satala, on the frontiers of Pontus; but there can be no doubt that the Sinara of the Table is altogether a different place from Sinoria, and the site of the latter place must be sought on the banks of the Euphrates between Satala and Melitene, whence some identify it with *Murad Chai* and others with *Seni Beli.*   [L. S.]

SINOTIUM. [SYNODIUM.]

SINSII (Σίνσιοι, Ptol. iii. 8. § 5), a people in the S. of Dacia.   [T. H. D.]

SINTI (Thuc. ii. 98; Steph. B. *s. v.*; Liv. xli. 51), a Thracian tribe who occupied the district lying between the ridge called Cercine and the right or W. bank of the Strymon, in the upper part of the course of that river, which was called from thence SINTICE (Σιντικὴ, Ptol. iii. 13. § 30). When Macedonia was divided into four provinces at the Roman conquest, Sintice was associated with Bisaltia in the First Macedonia, of which Amphipolis was the capital (Liv. xlv. 29). It contained the three towns HERACLEIA, PAROECOPOLIS, TRISTOLUS. [E.B.J.]

SINTIES. [LEMNOS.]

SINUESSA (Σινούεσσα or Σινύεσσα: Eth. Σινουεσσηνός, Sinuessanus: *Mondragone*), a city of Latium, in the more extended sense of the name, situated on the Tyrrhenian sea, about 6 miles N. of the mouth of the Vulturnus. It was on the line of the Via Appia, and was the last place where that great highroad touched on the sea-coast. (Strab. v. p. 233.) It is certain that Sinuessa was not an ancient city; indeed there is no trace of the existence of an Italian town on the spot before the foundation of the Roman colony. Some authors, indeed, mention an obscure tradition that there had previously been a Greek city on the spot which was called Sinope; but little value can be attached to this statement. (Liv. x. 21; Plin. iii. 5. s. 9.) It is certain that if it ever existed, it had wholly disappeared, and the site was included in the territory of the Ausonian city of Vescia, when the Romans determined to establish simultaneously the two colonies of Minturnae and Sinuessa on the Tyrrhenian sea. (Liv. x. 21.) The name of Sinuessa was derived, according to Strabo, from its situation on the spacious gulf (Sinus), now called the *Gulf of Gaeta.* (Strab. v. p. 234.) The object of establishing these colonies was chiefly for the purpose of securing the neighbouring fertile tract of country from the ravages of the Samnites, who had already repeatedly overrun the district. But for this very reason the plebeians at Rome hesitated to give their names, and there was some difficulty found in carrying out the colony, which was, however, settled in the following year, B. C. 296. (Liv. x. 21; Vell. Pat. i. 14.) Sinuessa seems to have rapidly risen into a place of importance; but its territory was severely ravaged by Hannibal in B. C. 217, whose cavalry carried their devastations up to the very gates of the town. (Liv. xxii. 13, 14.) It subsequently endeavoured, in common with Minturnae and other "coloniae maritimae," to establish its exemption from furnishing military levies; but this was overruled, while there was an enemy with an army in Italy. (Id. xxvii. 38.) At a later period (B. C. 191) they again attempted, but with equal ill success, to procure a similar exemption from the naval service. (Id. xxxvi. 3.) Its position on the Appian Way doubtless contributed greatly to the prosperity of Sinuessa; for the same reason it is frequently incidentally mentioned by Cicero, and we learn that Caesar halted there for a night on his way from Brundusium to Rome, in B. C. 49. (Cic. *ad Att.* ix. 15, 16, xiv. 8, *ad Fam.* xii. 20.) It is noticed also by Horace on his journey to Brundusium, as the place where he met with his friends Varius and Virgil. (*Sat.* i. 5. 40.) The fertility of its territory, and especially of the neighbouring ridge of the Mons Massicus, so celebrated for its wines, must also have tended to promote the prosperity of Sinuessa, but we hear little of it under the Roman Empire. It received a body of military colonists, apparently under the Triumvirate (*Lib. Col.* p. 237), but did not retain the rank of a Colonia, and is termed by Pliny as well as the Liber Coloniarum only an "oppidum," or ordinary municipal town. (Plin. iii. 5. s. 9; *Lib. Col. l. c.*) It was the furthest town in Latium, as that term was understood in the days of Strabo and Pliny, or "Latium adjectum," as the latter author terms it; and its territory extended to the river Savo, which formed the limit between Latium and Campania. (Strab. v. pp. 219, 231, 233; Plin. iii. 5. s. 9; Mel. ii. 4. § 9.) At an earlier period indeed Polybius reckoned it a town of Campania, and Ptolemy follows the same classification, as he makes the Liris the southern limit of Latium (Pol. iii. 91; Ptol. iii. 1. § 6); but the division adopted by Strabo and Pliny is probably the most correct. The Itineraries all notice Sinuessa as a still existing town on the Appian Way, and place it 9 miles from Minturnae, which is, however, considerably below the truth. (*Itin. Ant.* p. 108; *Itin. Hier.* p. 611; *Tab. Peut.*) The period of its destruction is unknown.

The ruins of Sinuessa are still visible on the sea-coast just below the hill of *Mondragone*, which forms the last underfall or extremity of the long ridge of *Monte Massico*. The most important are those of an aqueduct, and of an edifice which appears to have been a triumphal arch ; but the whole plain is covered with fragments of ancient buildings. (Cluver. *Ital.* p. 1080; Romanelli, vol. iii. p. 486.)

At a short distance from Sinuessa were the baths or thermal springs called AQUAE SINUESSANAE, which appear to have enjoyed a great reputation among the Romans. Pliny tells us they were esteemed a remedy for barrenness in women and for insanity in men. They are already mentioned by Livy as early as the Second Punic War; and though their fame was eclipsed at a later period by those of Baiae and other fashionable watering-places, they still continued in use under the Empire, and were resorted to among others by the emperor Claudius. (Liv. xxii. 13; Tac. *Ann.* xii. 66; Plin. xxxi. 2. s. 4.) It was there, also, that the infamous Tigellinus was compelled to put an end to his own life. (Tac. *Hist.* i. 72; Plut. *Oth.* 2.) The mild and warm climate of Sinuessa is extolled by some writers as contributing to the effect of the waters (Tac. *Ann.* xii. 66); hence it is called "Sinuessa tepens" by Silius Italicus, and "mollis Sinuessa" by Martial. (Sil. Ital. viii. 528; Mart. vi. 42.) The site of the waters is still called *I Bagni*, and the remains of Roman buildings still exist there.　　[E. H. B.]

SINUS AD GRADUS or AD GRADUS. [FOSSA MARIANA.]

SION, M. (Σιών), originally the name of a particular fortress or hill of Jerusalem, but often in the poetical and prophetic books extended to the whole city, especially to the temple, for a reason which will presently be obvious. Sion proper has been always assumed by later writers to be the SW. hill of Jerusalem, and this has been taken for granted in the article on Jerusalem [JERUSALEM, p. 18]. The counter hypothesis of a later writer, however, maintained with great learning, demands some notice under this head. Mr. Thrupp (*Antient Jerusalem*, 1855) admits the original identity of Sion and the city of David, but believes both to have been distinct from the upper city of Josephus, which latter he identifies with the modern *Sion*, in agreement with other writers. The transference of the name and position of Sion he dates as far back as the return from the Babylonish

captivity, believing that the Jews had lost the tradition of its identity with the city of David; so that, while they correctly placed the latter, they erroneously fixed the former where it is still found, viz., at the SW. of the Temple Mount, which mount was in fact the proper "Sion," identical with "the city of David;" for it is admitted that the modern Sion is identical not only with that recognised by the Christian (he might have added the Jewish) inhabitants of Jerusalem, and by all Christian (and Jewish) pilgrims and travellers from the days of Constantine, but with the Sion of the later Jewish days, and with that of the Maccabees. The elaborate argument by which it is attempted to remove this error of more than 2000 years' standing from the topography of Jerusalem, cannot here be stated, much less discussed; but two considerations may be briefly mentioned, which will serve to vindicate for the SW. hill of the city the designation which it has enjoyed, as is granted, since the time of the Babylonish captivity. One is grounded on the language of Holy Scripture, the other on Josephus. Of the identity of the original Sion with the city of David, there can be no doubt. Mr. Thrupp (pp. 12, 13) has adduced in proof of it three conclusive passages from Holy Scripture (2 *Sam.* v. 7; 1 *Kings*, viii. 1; 1 *Chron.* xi. 5). It is singular that he did not see that the second of these passages is utterly irreconcilable with the identity of the city of David with the Temple Mount; and that his own attempt to reconcile it with his theory, is wholly inadequate. According to that theory Mount Sion, or the city of David, extended from the NW. angle of the present Haram, to the south of the same enclosure; and the tombs of David, which were certainly in the city of David, he thinks might yet be discovered beneath the south-western part of the Haram (p. 161). That the temple lay on this same mount, between these two points, is not disputed by any one. Now, not to insist upon the difficulty of supposing that the threshing-floor of Araunah the Jebusite, where the temple was undoubtedly founded (2 *Chron.* iii. 1), lay in the very heart of the city of David, from which David had expelled the Jebusites, it is demonstrable, from the contents of the second passage above referred to, that the temple was in no sense in the city of David; for, after the completion of the temple, it is said in that and the parallel passage (2 *Chron.* v. 2, 5, 7) that Solomon and the assembled Israelites brought up the ark of the covenant of the Lord out of the city of David, which is Sion, into the temple which he had prepared for it on what Scripture calls Mount Moriah (2 *Chron.* iii. 1). Again, in 2 Samuel, v. 6—9, we have the account of David's wresting " the stronghold of Sion, the same is the city of David," out of the hands of the Jebusites; after which " David dwelt in the fort, and called it the city of David." Josephus, in recording the same events, states that David " laid siege to Jerusalem, and took the lower city by assault, while the citadel still held out." (*Ant.* vii. 3. § 2.) This citadel is clearly identified with the upper city, both in this passage and in his more detailed description of the city, where he says " that the hill upon which the upper city was built was by far the highest, and on account of its strength was called by King David the fortress" (φρούριον). (*Bell. Jud.* v. 4. § 1.) We are thus led to a conclusion directly opposite to that arrived at by Mr. Thrupp, who says that " the accounts in the books of Samuel and Chronicles represent David as taking the stronghold of Sion first and the Jebusite city afterwards; Josephus represents him as taking the lower city first, and afterwards the citadel. There can be no doubt, therefore, that in Josephus's view, Sion was the lower city, and the Jebusite city the citadel;" for a comparison of the 7th with the 9th verse in 2 *Sam.* v., and of the 5th with the 7th verse in 1 *Chron.* xi. can leave no doubt that the intermediate verses in both passages relate to the particulars of occupation of Sion, which particulars are narrated by Josephus of the occupation of the upper city, here called by him by the identical name used by the sacred writer, of the "castle in which David dwelt; therefore they called it the city of David;" and this φρούριον of Josephus is admitted by Mr. Thrupp to be the upper city (p. 56, note 2). That the name Sion was subsequently used in a much wider acceptation, and applied particularly to the sanctuary, is certain; and the fact is easily explained. The tent or tabernacle erected by David for the reception of the ark was certainly on Mount Sion, and in the city of David (2 *Sam.* vi. 12; 1 *Chron.* xv. 1, 29), and therefore in all the language of his own divine compositions, and of the other Psalmists of the conclusion of his and the commencement of Solomon's reign, Sion was properly identified with the sanctuary. What could be more natural than that, when the ark was transferred to the newly-consecrated temple on the contiguous hill, which was actually united to its former resting-place by an artificial embankment, the signification of the name should be extended so as to comprehend the Temple Mount, and continue the propriety and applicability of the received phraseology of David's and Asaph's Psalms to the new and permanent abode of the most sacred emblem of the Hebrew worship? But to attempt to found a topographical argument on the figurative and frequently elliptical expressions of Psalms or prophecies is surely to build on a foundation of sand. It was no doubt in order not to perplex the topography of Jerusalem by the use of ecclesiastical and devotional terminology that Josephus has wholly abstained from the use of the name Sion. [G. W.]

SIPH or ZIPH (LXX. Alex. Ζίφ, Vat. 'Οζίβ: *Eth.* Ζιφαῖος), a city of the tribe of Judah, mentioned in connection with Maon, Carmel, and Juttah (*Josh.* xv. 55). The wilderness of Ziph was a favourite hiding-place of David when concealing himself from the malice of Saul. (1 *Sam.* xxiii. 14, 26, xxvi. 1; *Psalm* liv. title.) This wilderness of Ziph was contiguous to the wilderness of Maon (1 *Sam.* xxiii. 25); and this Maon is connected with Carmel in the history of Nabal and Abigail (xxv. 2). The three names are still found a few miles south of Hebron, as *Kirmel, Main, Ziph.* The ruins lie on a low ridge between two small wadys, which commence here and run towards the Dead Sea. "There is here little to be seen except broken walls and foundations, most of them of unhewn stone, but indicating solidity, and covering a considerable tract of ground. Numerous cisterns also remain." (Robinson, *Bibl. Res.* vol. ii. p. 191). Ziph is placed by St. Jerome 8 miles E. of Hebron (S. would be more correct), and the desert of Ziph is frequently mentioned in the annals of the recluses of Palestine, while the site of the town was identified by travellers at least three centuries ago. (Fürer, *Itinerarium,* p. 68.) [G.W.]

SIPHAE or TIPHA (Σίφαι, Thuc. iv. 76; Scylax, p. 15; Steph. B. *s. v.*; Ptol. iii. 15. § 5; Plin. iv. 3. s. 4; Τίφα, Paus. ix. 32. § 4: *Eth.* Τιφαῖος, Τιφαιεύς), a town of Boeotia, upon the Corinthian gulf, which was said to have derived its name from Tiphys, the pilot of the Argonauts. In the time of Pausanias the inhabitants of Siphae pointed out the spot where the ship Argo anchored on its return from its celebrated voyage. The same writer mentions a temple of Hercules at Siphae, in whose honour an annual festival was celebrated. (Paus. *l.c.*) Thucydides (*l. c.*), Apollonius Rhodius (i. 105), and Stephanus B. (*s. v.* Σίφαι) describe Siphae as a dependency of Thespiae; and it is accordingly placed by Müller and Kiepert at *Alikés.* But Leake draws attention to the fact that Pausanias describes it as lying W. of Thisbe; and he therefore places it at port *Sarándi,* near the monastery dedicated to St. Taxiarches, where are the remains of a small Hellenic city. On this supposition the whole of the territory of Thisbe would lie between Thespiae and Siphae, which Leake accounts for by the superiority of Thespiae over all the places in this angle of Boeotia, whence the whole country lying upon this part of the Corinthian gulf may have often, in common acceptation, been called the Thespice. (Leake, *Northern Greece.* vol. ii. p. 515.)

SIPHNOS or SIPHNUS (Σίφνος: *Eth.* Σίφνιος: *Siphno* Gr., *Siphanto* Ital.), an island in the Aegaean sea, one of the Cyclades, lying SE. of Seriphos, and NE. of Melos. Pliny (iv. 12. s. 22. § 66) describes it as 28 miles in circuit, but it is considerably larger. The same writer says that the island was originally called Merope and Acis; its ancient name of Merope is also mentioned by Stephanus B. (*s. v.*). Siphnos was colonised by Ionians from Athens (Herod. viii. 48), whence it was said to have derived its name from Siphnos, the son of Sunius. (Steph. B. *s. v.*) In consequence of their gold and silver mines, of which remains are still seen, the Siphnians attained great prosperity, and were regarded, in the time of Polycrates (B. C. 520), as the wealthiest of all the islanders. Their treasury at Delphi, in which they deposited the tenth of the produce of their mines (Paus. x. 11. § 2), was equal in wealth to the treasuries of the most opulent states; and their public buildings were decorated with Parian marble. Their riches, however, exposed them to pillage; and a party of Samian exiles, in the time of Polycrates, invaded the island, and levied a contribution of 100 talents. (Herod. iii. 57, 58.) The Siphnians were among the few islanders in the Aegaean who refused tribute to Xerxes, and they fought with a single ship on the side of the Greeks at Salamis. (Herod. viii. 46, 48.) Under the Athenian supremacy the Siphnians paid an annual tribute of 3600 drachmae. (Franz, *Elem. Epigr. Gr.* n. 52.) Their mines were afterwards less productive; and Pausanias (*l. c.*) relates that in consequence of the Siphnians neglecting to send the tenth of their treasure to Delphi, the gods destroyed their mines by an inundation of the sea. In the time of Strabo the Siphnians had become so poor that Σίφνιον ἀστράγαλον became a proverbial expression. (Strab. x. p. 448; comp. Eustath. *ad Dionys. Per.* 525; Hesych. *s. v.* Σίφνιος ἀρραβών.) The moral character of the Siphnians stood low; and hence to act like a Siphnian (Σιφνιάζειν) was used as a term of reproach. (Steph. B.; Suid.; Hesych.) The Siphnians were celebrated in antiquity, as they are in the present day, for their skill in pottery. Pliny (xxxvi. 22. § 159, Sillig) mentions a particular kind of stone, of which drinking cups were made. This, according to Fiedler, was a species of talc, and is probably intended by

Stephanus B. when he speaks of Σίφνιον νσττά-
μιον.

Siphnos possessed a city of the same name (Ptol.
iii. 15. § 31), and also two other towns, Apollonia
and Minoa, mentioned only by Stephanus B. The
ancient city occupied the same site as the modern
town, called *Kastron* or *Seraglio*, which lies upon
the eastern side of the island. There are some remains of the ancient walls; and fragments of marble
are found, with which, as we have already seen, the
public buildings in antiquity were decorated. A
range of mountains, about 3000 feet in height, runs
across Siphnos from SE. to NW.; and on the high
ground between this mountain and the eastern side
of the island, about 1000 feet above the sea, lie five
neat villages, of which *Stavri* is the principal. These
villages contain from 4000 to 5000 inhabitants;
and the town of *Kastron* about another 1000. The
climate is healthy, and many of the inhabitants
live to a great age. The island is well cultivated,
but does not produce sufficient food for its population, and accordingly many Siphnians are obliged
to emigrate, and are found in considerable numbers in
Athens, Smyrna, and Constantinople. (Tournefort,
Voyage, &c. vol. i. p. 134, seq. transl.; Fiedler,
Reise, vol. ii. p. 125, seq.; Ross, *Reise auf den
Griech. Inseln,* vol. i. p. 138, seq.)

COIN OF SIPHNOS.

SIPIA, in Gallia, is placed by the Table on a
route from Condate (*Rennes*) to Juliomagus (*Angers*).
The distance from Condate to Sipia is xvi. and this
distance brings us to a little river *Seche* at a place
called *Vi-seche,* the *Vi* being probably a corruption
of Vadum. The same distance xvi. measured from
Vi-seche brings us to Combaristum (*Combré*) on the
road to *Angers.* But see the article COMBARISTUM.
The *Seche* is a branch of the *Vilaine* (D'Anville,
Notice, &c.).　　　　　　　　　　　　　[G. L.]

SIPONTUM, or SIPUNTUM, but in Greek always SIPUS (Σιποῦς -οῦντος: Eth. Σιπούντιος, Si-
pontinus: *Sta Maria di Siponto*), a city of Apulia,
situated on the coast of the Adriatic, immediately S.
of the great promontory of Garganus, and in the
bight of the deep bay formed by that promontory
with the prolongation of the coast of Apulia. (Strab.
vi. p. 284.) This bay is now called the *Gulf of
Manfredonia,* from the city of that name which is
situated within a few miles of the site of Sipontum.
The *Cerbalus,* or *Cervaro,* and the *Candelaro* fall
into this bay a short distance S. of Sipontum, and
form at their mouth an extensive lagune or salt-
water pool (στομαλίμνη, Strab. *l. c.*), now called the
Pantano Salso. Like most places in this part of
Apulia the foundation of Sipontum was ascribed to
Diomed (Strab. *l. c.*): but with the exception of this
vague and obscure tradition, which probably means
no more than that the city was one of those belonging
to the Daunian tribe of Apulians, we have no account of its being a Greek colony. The name is
closely analogous in form to others in this part of

Italy (Hydruntum, Butuntum, &c.): and its Greek
derivation from σηπία, a cuttle-fish (Strab. *l. c.*), is
in all probability fictitious. The Greek form Sipus,
is adopted also by the Roman poets. (Sil. Ital. viii.
633; Lucan. v. 377.) The only mention of Sipontum
in history before the Roman conquest is that of its
capture by Alexander, king of Epirus, about B. C.
330. (Liv. viii. 24.) Of the manner in which it
passed under the yoke of Rome we have no account;
but in B. C. 194 a colony of Roman citizens was
settled there, at the same time that those of Salernum
and Buxentum were established on the other sea.
(Liv. xxxiv. 45.) The lands assigned to the colonists are said to have previously belonged to the
Arpani, which renders it probable that Sipontum
itself had been merely a dependency of that city.
The new colony, however, does not seem to have
prospered. A few years later (B. C. 184) we are
told that it was deserted, probably on account of
malaria; but a fresh body of colonists was sent
there (Liv. xxxix. 22), and it seems from this time
to have become a tolerably flourishing town, and was
frequented as a seaport, though never rising to any
great consideration. Its principal trade was in
corn. (Strab. vi. p. 284; Mel. ii. 4. § 7; Plin. iii.
11. s. 16; Ptol. iii. 1. § 16; Pol. x. 1.) It is, however, mentioned apparently as a place of some importance, during the Civil Wars, being occupied
by M. Antonius in B. C. 40. (Appian, *B. C.* v.
56; Dion Cass. xlviii. 27.) We learn from inscriptions that it retained its municipal government and magistrates, as well as the title of a
colony, under the Roman Empire (Mommsen, *Inscr.
R. N.* 927—929); and at a later period Paulus
Diaconus mentions it as still one of the "urbes
satis opulentae" of Apulia. (P. Diac. *Hist. Lang.* ii.
21.) Lucan notices its situation immediately at the
foot of Mount Garganus ("subdita Sipus montibus,"
Lucan, v. 377). It was, however, actually situated
in the plain and immediately adjoining the marshes
at the mouth of the *Candelaro,* which must always
have rendered the site unhealthy; and in the middle
ages it fell into decay from this cause, till in 1250
Manfred king of Naples removed all the remaining
population to a site about a mile and a half further
N., where he built a new city, to which he gave the
name of *Manfredonia.* No ruins of the ancient city
are now extant, but the site is still marked by an
ancient church, which bears the name of *Sta Maria
di Siponto,* and is still termed the cathedral, the
archbishop of *Manfredonia* bearing officially the
title of Archbishop of Sipontum. (Craven's *Southern
Tour,* p. 67; Romanelli, vol. ii. p. 209.) The name
of Sipontum is found in the Itineraries (*Itin. Ant.*
p. 314; *Tab. Peut.*), which give a line of road proceeding along the coast from thence to Barium,
passing by the Salinae at the mouth of the Palus
Salapina, and therefore following the narrow strip of
beach which separated that lagune from the sea.
There is still a good horse-road along this beach; but
the distances given in the Itineraries are certainly
corrupt.　　　　　　　　　　　　　　　[E. H. B.]

SI'PYLUS (Σίπυλος), a mountain of Lydia between the river Hermus and the town of Smyrna; it
is a branch of Mount Tmolus, running in a north-
western direction along the Hermus. It is a rugged,
much torn mountain, which seems to owe its present
form to violent convulsions of the earth. The
mountain is mentioned even in the Iliad, and was
rich in metal. (Hom. *Il.* xxiv. 615; Strab. i. p. 58,
xii. p. 579, xiv. p. 680.) On the eastern slope of the

mountain, there once existed, according to tradition, an ancient city, called Tantalis, afterwards Sipylus, the capital of the Maeonians, which was believed to have been swallowed up by an earthquake, and plunged into a crater, afterwards filled by a lake, which bore the name of Sale or Saloë (Strab. i. p. 58, xii. p. 579; Steph. B. *s. v.*; Plin. v. 31; Paus. vii. 24. § 7). Pliny relates that the spot once occupied by Sipylus was successively occupied by other towns, which he calls Archaeopolis, Colpe and Lebade. Pausanias (v. 13. § 4) calls the lake the marsh of Tantalus, and adds that his tomb was conspicuous near it, and that the throne of Pelops was shown on the summit of the mountain above the temple of (Cybele) Plastene. The tops of the houses of Sipylus were believed to have been seen under the water for some time after (Paus. vii. 24. § 7); and some modern travellers, mistaking the ruins of old Smyrna for those of Sipylus, imagine that they have discovered both the remains of Sipylus and the tomb of Tantalus. Chandler (*Travels in Asia Minor*, p. 331) thought that a small lake of limpid water at the north-eastern foot of Mount Sipylus, not far from a sepulchre cut in the rock, might be the lake Sale; but Hamilton (*Researches*, i. p. 49, foll.) has shown that the lake must be sought for in the marshy district of Manissa.

In speaking of Mount Sipylus, we cannot pass over the story of Niobe, alluded to by the poets, who is said to have been metamorphosed into stone on that mountain in her grief at the loss of her children. (Hom. *Il.* xxiv. 614; Soph. *Antig.* 822; Ov. *Met.* vi. 310; Apollod. iii. 5; Paus. viii. 2. § 3.) Pausanias (i. 21. § 5) relates that he himself went to Mount Sipylus and saw the figure of Niobe formed out of the natural rock; when viewed close he saw only the rock and precipices, but nothing resembling a woman either weeping or in any other posture; but standing at a distance you fancied you saw a woman in tears and in an attitude of grief. This phantom of Niobe, says Chandler (p. 331), whose observation has been confirmed by subsequent travellers, may be defined as an effect of a certain portion of light and shade on a part of Sipylus, perceivable at a particular point of view. Mount Sipylus now bears the name of *Saboundji Dagh* or *Sipuli Dagh*.   [L. S.]

SIRACELLAE (*Itin. Ant.* p. 332; *Ib.* p. 333, Siracelle; *It. Hier.* p. 602, Sirogellae; *Tab. Peut.* Syrascellae; and in Geog. Rav. iv. 6, and v. 12, Syrascele), a place in Thrace, on the road from Trajanopolis to Callipolis, and on the main road to Constantinople. Its distance from Trajanopolis is variously given in the Itin. Ant., and the readings of the MSS. differ,— one stating the distance to be as much as 59,000 paces, another as little as 50,000. According to Mannert (vii. p. 205), its site is near the modern *Chachan* or *Rusqueur* (?) of P. Lucas (*Trois Voy.* p. 47); but Richard places it near *Zerna*, and Lapie near *Malgara* or *Migalgara;* the uncertainty of the Itinerary above mentioned being probably the cause of this discrepancy.   [J. R.]

SIRACE'NE. [SIROC.]

SIRACE'NI (Σιρακηνοί, Ptol. v. 9. §§ 17, 19), a great and mighty people of Asiatic Sarmatia on the east shore of the Maeotis, beyond the Rha and on the Achardeus, in the district called by Strabo (xi. 504) Siracene. They appear under various names. Thus Strabo (xi. p. 506) and Mela (i. 19) call them Siraces; Tacitus (*Ann.* xii. 15, seq.) Siraci (in Strabo, xi. p. 492, Σιρακοί); and in an inscription (Böckh, ii. p. 1009) we find the form Σιράχοι.

They were governed by their own kings, and the Romans were engaged in a war with them, A. D. 50. (Tac. *l. c.*; Strab. *ib.* p. 504.)   [T. H. D.]

SIRAE or SEIRAE. [PROPHIS.]

SIRAE, in Macedonia. [SIRIS.]

SIRANGAE (Σιράγγαι or Σηράγγαι, Ptol. iv. 6. § 17), a tribe in the interior of Libya.   [T. H. D.]

SIRBES. [XANTHUS.]

SIRBL [SERBI.]

SIRBITUM, a city of Aethiopia, above which the mountains cease, and at a distance of 14 days' sail from Meroë. (Plin. vi. 30. s. 35.) From these particulars Mannert (x. pt. i. p. 171) is induced to regard it as the modern *Senaar*.   [T. H. D.]

SIRBO'NIS LACUS (ἡ Σιρβωνίς or Σιρβωνίδος λίμνη, Herod. ii. 6; Diodur. i. 30; Ptol. iv. 5. §§ 12, 20; Strab. i. pp. 50, 65, xvii. 760—763; Σίρβων, Steph. B. *s. v.*; Plin. v. 12. s. 14: *Sebaket-Bardoil*), was a vast tract of morass, the centre of which formed the Sirbonian lake, lying between the eastern angle of the Delta, the *Isthmus of Suez*, Mount Casius, and the Mediterranean sea. With the latter it was at one time connected by a natural channel (τὸ ἔκρεγμα), running through bars of quicksand and shingle (τὰ βάραθρα), which separated the sea from the morass. The limits of the Serbonian bog have, however, been much contracted in later ages by the elevation of the sea-borde and the drifting of the sands, and the lake is now of inconsiderable extent. The Sirbonian region is celebrated in history for having been the scene of at least the partial destruction of the Persian army in B. C. 350, when Darius Ochus was leading it, after the storming of Sidon, to Aegypt, in order to restore the authority of Persia in that kingdom. Diodorus (i. 30) has probably exaggerated the serious disaster into a total annibilation of the invading host, and Milton (*P. L.* ii. 293) has adopted the statement of Diodorus, when he speaks of

"———— that Serbonian bog
Betwixt Damiata and Mount Casius old
Where armies whole have sunk."

The same Persian army, however, afterwards took Pelusium, Bubastis, and other cities of the Delta. The base of the Deltaic triangle of Aegypt was reckoned by Herodotus (ii. 6) from the bay of Plinthine to the lake of Serbonis.   [W. B. D.]

SIRENU'SAE I'NSULAE. [MINERVAE PROMONTORIUM].

SIRICAE, a place in Cappadocia on the road from Comana to Melitene, and 24 miles NW. of the first. (*Itin. Ant.* pp. 210, 211.) According to Lapie, near the *Benbodagh*.   [T. H. D.]

SIRIO, in Gallia, is placed by the Itins. on a road from Burdigala (*Bordeaux*) to Aginnum (*Agen*). The distance is probably corrupt in the Table, which places Sirio x. from *Bordeaux;* for the true distance is xv. or xvi. Gallic leagues. D'Anville fixes Sirio (the *Pont de Siron*) near the point where the small river *Siron* or *Ciron* joins the *Garonne* on the left bank.   [G. L.]

SIRIS (Σίρις: *Eth.* Σιρίτης, but also Σιρῖνος; Sirites), an ancient city of Magna Graecia, situated at the mouth of the river of the same name flowing into the Tarentine gulf, and now called the *Sinno.* There is no doubt that Siris was a Greek colony, and that at one time it attained to a great amount of wealth and prosperity; but its history is extremely obscure and uncertain. Its first origin was generally ascribed to a Trojan colony; and, as a proof of this, an ancient statue of Minerva was shown there which claimed to be the true Trojan Palladium (Strab. vi. p. 264; Lycophr. *Alex.* 978—985). Whatever may have been the origin of this legend, there seems no doubt that Siris was originally a city of the Chones, the native Oenotrian inhabitants of this part of Italy (Strab. *l. c.*). A legend found in the Etymologicon (*s. v.* Σίρις), according to which the city derived its name from a daughter of Morges, king of the Siculi, evidently points in the same direction, as the Morgetes also were an Oenotrian tribe. From these first settlers it was wrested, as we are told, by a body of Ionian colonists from Colophon, who had fled from their native city to avoid the dominion of the Lydians. (Strab. *l. c.*; Athenae. xii. p. 523.) The period of this emigration is very uncertain; but it appears probable that it must have taken place not long after the capture of the city by Gyges, king of Lydia, about 700—690 B. C. Archilochus, writing about 660 B. C., alludes to the fertility and beauty of the district on the banks of the Siris; and though the fragment preserved to us by Athenaeus does not expressly notice the existence of the *city* of that name, yet it would appear from the expressions of Athenaeus that the poet certainly did mention it; and the fact of this colony having been so lately established there was doubtless the cause of his allusion to it (Archil. *ap. Athen.* xii. p. 523). On the other hand, it seems clear from the account of the settlement at Metapontum (Strab. vi. p. 265), that the territory of Siris was at that time still unoccupied by any Greek colony. We may therefore probably place the date of the Ionian settlement at Siris between 690 and 660 B. C. We are told that the Ionic colonists gave to the city the name of Polieum (Πολίειον, Strab. vi. p. 264; Steph. B. *s. v.* Σίρις); but the appellation of Siris; which it derived from the river, and which seems to have been often given to the whole district (ἡ Σίρις, used as equivalent to ἡ Σιρῖτις), evidently prevailed, and is the only one met with in common use. Of the history of Siris we know literally nothing, except the general fact of its prosperity, and that its citizens indulged in habits of luxury and effeminacy that rivalled those of their neighbours the Sybarites. (Athen. xii. p. 523.) It may be received as an additional proof of their opulence, that Damasua, a citizen of Siris, is noticed by Herodotus among the suitors for the daughter of Cleisthenes of Sicyon, about 580—560 B. C., on which occasion Siris and Sybaris among the cities of Italy alone furnished claimants. (Herod. vi. 127.) This was probably about the period that Siris was at the height of its prosperity. But an Ionian city, existing as it did in the midst of the powerful Achaean colonies, must naturally have been an object of jealousy to its neighbours; and hence we are told that the Metapontines, Sybarites, and Crotoniats formed a league against Siris; and the war that ensued ended in the capture of the city, which appears to have been followed by the expulsion of the inhabitants (Justin. xx. 2). The date of the destruction of Siris cannot be fixed with any approach to certainty: it was probably *after* 550 B. C., and certainly preceded the fall of its rival Sybaris in B. C. 510. Its ruin appears to have been complete, for we meet with no subsequent mention of the city, and the territory is spoken of as open to colonisation at the time of the Persian War, B. C. 480. (Herod. viii. 62.)

Upon that occasion we learn incidentally that the Athenians considered themselves as having a claim of old standing to the vacant district of the Sirites,

and even at one time thought of removing thither with their wives and families. (Herod. *l. c.*) The origin of this claim is unknown; but it seems pretty clear that it was taken up by the Athenian colonists who established themselves at Thurii in B. C. 443, and became the occasion of hostilities between them and the Tarentines. These were at length terminated by a compromise, and it was agreed to found in common a fresh colony in the disputed territory. This appears to have been at first established on the site of the ancient city, but was soon after transferred to a spot 3 miles distant, where the new colony received the name of Heracleia, and soon rose to be a flourishing city. (Strab. vi. p. 264; Diod. xii. 36.) [HERACLEIA.] According to Strabo, Siris still continued to exist as the port or naval station of Heracleia; but no other mention of it is found, and it is not clear whether Strabo himself meant to speak of it as still subsisting in his day. No remains of it are extant, and the exact site does not appear to have been determined. But it may be placed on the left bank of the river Siris (now called the *Sinno*), at or near its mouth; a position which well accords with the distance of 24 stadia (3 miles) from Heracleia, the remains of which are visible at *Policoro*, near the river *Agri*, the ancient Aciris. [HERACLEIA.]

The river Siris is mentioned by Lycophron (*Alex.* 982), as well as by Archilochus in a passage already cited (*ap. Athen.* xii. p. 523); but the former author calls it Σίνις, and its modern name of *Sinno* would seem to be derived from an ancient period; for we find mention in the Tabula of a station 4 miles from Heracleia, the name of which is written Semnum, probably a corruption for Ad Simnum or Sinnum. The Siris and Aciris are mentioned in conjunction by Pliny as well as by Strabo, and are two of the most considerable streams in Lucania. (Plin. iii. 11. s. 15; Strab. vi. p. 264.) The name of the former river is noticed also in connection with the first great battle between Pyrrhus and the Romans, B. C. 280, which was fought upon its banks (Plut. *Pyrrh.* 16). It has been absurdly confounded by Florus and Orosius with the Liris in Campania. (Flor. i. 18. § 7; Oros. iv. 1.)

The fertile district of the Siritis (ἡ Σιρῖτις or Σειρῖτις) is a portion of the level tract or strip of plain which borders the gulf of Tarentum from the neighbourhood of *Rocca Imperiale* to the mouth of the *Bradano*. This plain stretches inland from the mouth of the *Sinno* to the foot of the hill on which stands the modern city of *Tursi*, about 8 miles from the sea. It is a tract of extraordinary natural fertility, but is now greatly neglected, and, in common with all this coast, desolated by malaria. [E. H. B.]

SIRIS, SIRAE, SERRHAE (Σίρις, Herod. viii. 115; Sirae, Liv. xlv. 4; Σέρβαι, Hierocl.: *Eth.* Σιρωπαίονεις, Herod. v. 15; Steph. B.: *Serrés*), a town of Macedonia, standing in the widest part of the great Strymonic plain on the last slopes of the range of mountains which bound it to the NE. Xerxes left a part of his sick here, when retreating to the Hellespont (Herod. *l. c.*): and P. Aemilius Paulus, after his victory at Pydna, received at this town, which is ascribed to Odomantice, a deputation from Perseus, who had retired to Samothrace. (Liv. *l. c.*) Little is known of Serrhae, which was the usual form of the name in the 5th century (though from two inscriptions found at *Serrés* it appears that Sirrha, or Sirrhae, was the more ancient orthography, and that which obtained at least until the division of the empire), until the great spread of the Servian kingdom. Stephen Dushan in the 14th century seized on this large and flourishing city, and assumed the imperial crown here, where he established a court on the Roman or Byzantine model, with the title of Emperor of Romania, Sclavonia, and Albania. (Niceph. Greg. p. 467.) After his death a partition of his dominions took place. but the Greeks have never since been able to recover their former preponderance in the provinces of the Strymonic valley. Sultan Murad took this town from the Servians, and when Sigismund, king of Hungary, was about to invade the Ottoman dominions, Bayezid (Bajazet Ilderim) summoned the Christian princes who were his vassals to his camp at Serrhae, previous to his victory at Nicopolis, A. D. 1396. (J. von Hammer, Gesch. des Osman. Reiches, vol. i. pp. 193, 246, 600.)

Besides the Macedonian inscriptions of the Roman empire found by Leake (Inscr. 126) and Cousinéry, the only other vestige of the ancient town is a piece of Hellenic wall faced with large quadrangular blocks, but composed within of small stones and mortar forming a mass of extreme solidity. Servian remains are more common. (Leake, Northern Greece, vol. iii. pp. 200—210.)   [E. B. J.]

SI'RMIO (Sermione), a narrow neck or tongue of land, projecting out into the Lake Benacus (Lago di Garda), from its southern shore. Though a conspicuous and picturesque object in all views of the lake from its southern shores, it is unnoticed by any of the geographers, and its name would probably have been unknown to us, but for the circumstance that Catullus, who was a native of the neighbouring Verona, had a villa on its shores, and has sung the praises of Sirmio in one of the most charming odes in the Latin language (Catull. xxxi.). The name of Sirmio is, however, found in the Itineraries, which place a "Sermione mansio" on the road from Brixia to Verona, and just midway between the two cities, 22 M. P. from each (Itin Ant. p. 127). This must, however, have been situated at the entrance of the peninsula, probably where a road turned off to it, as it is clear that the highroad could never have turned aside to the promontory itself.

Extensive substructions and other remains of an ancient villa are still visible at the extremity of the promontory, where it juts out into the lake: but these undoubtedly belong to an abode on a much more magnificent scale than the villa of Catullus, and probably belong to some villa of the imperial times, which had replaced the humbler dwelling of the poet.   [E. H. B.]

SI'RMIUM (Σίρμιον), an important city in the south-eastern part of Lower Pannonia, was an ancient Celtic place of the Taurisci, on the left bank of the Savus, a little below the point where this river is joined by the Bacuntius (Plin. iii. 28.) Zosimus (ii. 18) is mistaken when he asserts that Sirmium was surrounded on two sides by a tributary of the Ister. The town was situated in a most favourable position, where several roads met (It. Ant. pp. 124, 131; It. Hieros. p. 563), and during the wars against the Dacians and other Danubian tribes, it became the chief depôt of all military stores, and gradually rose to the rank of the chief city in Pannonia. (Herodian, vii. 2.) Whether it was ever made a Roman colony is not quite certain, though an inscription is said to exist containing the words Dec. Colon. Sirmiens. It contained a large manufactory of arms, a spacious forum, an imperial palace, and other public build-

ings, and was the residence of the admiral of the first Flavian fleet on the Danube. (Amm. Marc. xvii. 13, xix. 11; Notit. Imp.) The emperor Probus was born at Sirmium. (Vopisc. Prob. 3, 21; comp. Strab. ii. p. 134; Ptol. ii. 16. § 8, viii. 7. § 6; Steph. B. s. v.; Eutrop. ix. 17; Aethicus, p. 715, ed. Gronov.; Geog. Rav. iv. 19.) The city is mentioned for the last time by Procopius (B. Goth. iii. 33, 34), as being in the hands of the Avari, but when and how it perished are questions which history does not answer. Extensive ruins of it are still found about the modern town of Mitrovitz. (See Orelli, Inscript. n. 3617; Marsili, Danubius, p. 246, foll.)   [L. S.]

SIRNIDES, a group of small islands off the promontory Sammonium in Crete. (Plin. iv. 12. s. 20.)

SIROC (Σιρόκ), a town of Parthyene, noticed by Isidorus. (Stath. Parth. c. 12, ed. Müller.) It is not clear whether there is any corresponding modern town; but Rennell thinks it is represented by the present Serakhs. (Geog. Herod. p. 297.) Ptolemy places a district which he calls Siracene among the Astabeni, a people who occupied part of Hyrcania (vi. 9. § 5). It is not impossible that Siroc and Siracene may be thus connected.   [V.]

SISAPON (Σισαπών, Strab. iii. p. 142), a considerable town in Hispania Baetica. (Cic. Phil. ii. 19; Plin. iii. 1. s. 3.) It lay N. of Corduba, between the Baetis and the Anas, and was celebrated for its silver mines and veins of cinnabar (Strab. l. c.: Vitruv. vii. 9; Plin. xxxiii. 7. s. 40; Dioscor. v. 109.) The town of Almaden in the Sierra Morena, with which Sisapon is identified, still possesses a rich mine of quicksilver. "The mine is apparently inexhaustible, becoming richer in proportion as the shafts deepen. The vein of cinnabar, about 25 feet thick, traverses rocks of quarts and slate; and runs towards Almadenejos. Virgin quicksilver occurs also in pyrites and hornstein." "Between 20,000 and 25,000 quintals of mercury are now procured annually." (Ford, Handbook of Spain, p. 70; comp. Laborde, Itin. ii. p. 133; Dillon's Travels, ii. pp. 72, 77.) The name of this town is variously written It appears on coins as "Sisipo" (Sestini, p. 87), whilst others have the correct name. (Florez, Med. iii. p. 119; Mionnet, i. p. 25, and Supp. i. p. 114.) The form "Sisalone" (Itin. Ant. p. 444) is probably corrupt. It appears to be the same town called Σισαπόνη by Ptolemy (ii. 6. § 59), who, however, places it in the territory of the Oretani, in Hispania Tarraconensis, on which indeed it borders.   [T. H. D.]

SISAR. [USAR.]

SISARA (Σισάρα, Ptol. iv. 3. § 17), a lake in Africa Propria, in the neighbourhood of Hippo Diarrhytus. Now Benizert or Bizerta. [T. H. D.]

SISARACA (Σισάρακα, Ptol. ii. 6. § 52), a town of the Murbogi or Turmodigi in Hispania Tarraconensis. For coins, see Sestini, p. 197. [T.H.D.]

SISAURANUM (τὸ Σισαυράνων, Procop. Pers. ii. 19, de Aedif. ii. 4), a fortress of Mesopotamia, above Dara, noticed by Procopius. It is not elsewhere mentioned.   [V.]

SI'SCIA, SEGESTA, or SEGE'STICA (Σισκία, Σεγέστα, Σεγεστική), a great town in the south of Upper Pannonia, on the southern bank of the Savus, on an island formed by that river and two others, the Colapis and Odra, a canal dug by Tiberius completing the island. (Dion Cass. xlix. 37.) It was situated on the great road from Aemona to Sirmium.

(*It. Ant.* pp. 259, 260, 265, 266, 272, 274; Plin. iii. 28.) According to Pliny the name *Segestica* belonged only to the town, and the town was called Siscia; while Strabo (vii. p. 314) says that Siscia was a fort in the neighbourhood of Segestica; but if this was so, it must be supposed that subsequently the fort and town became united as one place. (Comp. Strab. iv. p. 202, v. p. 214, vii. p. 218; Appian, *Illyr.* 16, 23, &c.) Siscia was from the first a strongly fortified town; and after its capture by Tiberius, in the reign of Augustus (Appian, Dion Cass., *ll. cc.*; Vell. Pat. ii. 113), it became one of the most important places of Pannonia; for being situated on two navigable rivers, it not only carried on considerable commerce (Strab. v. pp. 207. 214), but became the central point from which Augustus and Tiberius carried on their undertakings against the Pannonians and Illyrians. Tiberius did much to enlarge and embellish the town, which as early as that time seems to have been made a colonia, for Pliny mentions it as such: in the time of Septimius Severus it received fresh colonists, whence in inscriptions it is called Col. Septimia Siscia. The town contained an imperial mint, and the treasury for what was at a later time called the province Savia; at the same time it was the station of the small fleet kept on the Savus. Siscia maintained its importance until Sirmium began to rise, for in proportion as Sirmium rose, Siscia sank and declined. (Comp. Zosim. ii. 48; Orelli, *Inscript.* n. 504, 505, 2703, 3075, 3346, 4993.) The modern town of *Sissek*, occupying the place of the ancient Siscia, contains many interesting remains of antiquity. (Marsili, *Danubius*, p. 47; Schönwisner, *Antiq. Sabariae*, p. 52, foll.; Muchar, *Noricum*, i. p. 159.) [L. S.]

SITACE (Σιτάκη), a large town, first noticed by Xenophon (*Anab.* ii. 4. § 13), situated about 8 parasangs from the Median Wall, and 15 from the Tigris and the mouth of the Physcus. The exact situation cannot be now determined, but several travellers have noticed, in this neighbourhood, extensive ancient remains, which may perhaps belong to this city. (Mannert, v. pt. ii. p. 281; Niebuhr, ii. p. 305; Ives, *Travels*, &c. p. 133.) [V.]

SITACUS (Σιτακός, Arrian, *Ind.* c. 38), a river of Persis, to which Nearchus came in his celebrated coasting voyage. It is in all probability the same as that called by Pliny Sitiogagus (vi. 23. s. 26); although his statement that, from its mouth, an ascent could be made to Pasargada in 7 days, is manifestly erroneous. There is no reason to doubt that it is at present represented by a stream called *Sita-Rhegian*. (Vincent, *Voy. of Nearchus*, i. p. 385; D'Anville, *Mém. de l'Acad.* xxx. p. 158; Ritter, *Erdkunde*, vii. p. 763.) [V.]

SITHO'NIA (Σιθωνίη, Herod. vii. 123; Steph. B.; Virg. *Bucol.* x. 66; Hor. *Carm.* i. 18. 9: Longos), the central of the three prongs which run out into the Aegean from the great peninsula of Chalcidice, forming a prolongation to the peak called *Solomón* or *Kholomón*. The Sithonian peninsula, which, though not so hilly as that of Acte, is not so inviting as Pallene, was the first, it appears, to be occupied by the Chalcidic colonists. A list of its towns is given in CHALCIDICE. [E. B. J.]

SITIA, a place in Hispania Baetica. (Plin. iii. 1. s. 3.) [T. H. D.]

SITIFI (Σίτιφι, Ptol. iv. 2. § 34), a town in the interior of Mauretania Caesariensis, situated in an extensive plain not far from the borders of Numidia, and on the road from Carthage to Cirta. (*Itin. Ant.* pp. 24, 29, 31, &c.; comp. Amm. Marc. xxviii. 6.) At first, under the Numidian kings, it was but an unimportant place; but under the Roman dominion it became the frontier town of the new province of Numidia, was greatly enlarged and elevated to be a colony; so that on the subsequent division of Mauretania Caesar. into two smaller provinces it became the capital of Mauretania Sitifensis. Under the dominion of the Vandals, it was the capital of the district Zabé. (Ζάβη, Procop. *B. Vand.* ii. 20.) It is still called *Setif*, and lies upon an eminence in a delightful neighbourhood. Some ruins of the ancient town are still to be seen. (Shaw's *Travels*, p. 49.) [T. H. D.]

SITILLIA, in Gallia, is placed by the Table on a road from Aquae Bormonis (*Bourbon l'Archambault*) to Pocrinium, supposed to be *Perrigni*. Sitilla is xvi. from Aquae Bormonis and xiiii. from Pocrinium. Sitillia is probably a place named *Tiel*. (D'Anville *Notice*, &c.) [G. L.]

SITIOGAGUS. [SITACUS.]

SITOMAGUS, a town of the Iceni or Simeni, in the E. part of Britannia Romana. (*Itin. Ant.* p. 480.) Camden (p. 456) identifies it with *Thetford* in Norfolk, whilst others seek it at *Stowmarket*, *Southwold*, and *Saxmundham*. In the *Tab. Peut.* it is erroneously written "Sinomachus." [T, H, D,]

SITONES, a population conterminous with the Suiones, from whom they differ only in being governed by a female: "in tantum non modo a libertate sed etiam a servitute degenerant. Hic Sueviae finis." (Tac. *Germ.* 45.) The Sitonian locality is some part of *Finland*; probably the northern half of the coast of the *Gulf of Bothnia*.

The statement that they were under a female rule is explained as follows. The name by which the East Bothnian Finlanders designate themselves is *Kainu*-laiset (in the singular *Kainu*-lainen). The Swedes call them *Qvaens* (*Kwains*). The mediaeval name for their country is *Cajan*-ia. Now *qvinna* in the Norse language = *woman*, being our words *queen* and *quean*; and in the same Norse tongue the land of the *Qvaens* would be *Cvena-land*; as it actually is, being *Cwaen-land* (*Queen-land*) in Anglo-Saxon. Hence the statement of Tacitus arises out of information concerning a certain *Cwaen*-land, erroneously considered to be a *terra feminarum*, instead of a *terra Quaenorum*. The reader who thinks this fanciful should be informed that in Adam of Bremen, writing in the 12th century, when the same country comes under notice, the same confusion appears, and that in a stronger form. The Sitonian country is actually *terra feminarum*. More than this, the *feminae* become *Amazons*: " circa haec litora Baltici maris ferunt esse *Amazonas*, quod nunc terra *feminarum* dicitur, quas aquae gustu aliqui dicunt concipere..... Hae simul viventes, spernunt consortia virorum, quos etiam, si advenerint, a se viriliter repellunt," c. 228. (Zeuss, *Die Deutschen*, &c., s. v. *Kwenen*.)

It is worth noticing that King Alfred's locality of the *Cwenas* is, in respect to their relations to the *Svias*, exactly that of Tacitus,—*Cwena*-land succeeding *Svea*-land.

The Sitones seem to have been the ancient representatives of the Finns of Finland,—the Fenni of the ancients being the Laps. This is not only what the words Sitones and Qvaen suggest, but the inference from the word Fenni also. To the Finlander, Fin is a strange name. The Swede calls him *Qvaen*;

3 T 4

he calls himself *Suoma-lainen* or *Hamelainen*. On the other hand, it is the Lap of *Finmark* that is called a Fin, and it is the Norwegian who calls him *uo*. [FENNI.]   [R. G. L.]

SITTACE (Σιττάκη, Ptol. vi. 1. § 5), a town of ancient Assyria, at the southern end of this province, on the road between Artemita and Susa. (Strab. xvi. p. 744.) It is called Sitta (Σίττα) by Diodorus (xvii. 110). It was the capital of the district of Sittacene, which appears to have been called in later times Apolloniatis (Strab. xi. p. 524), and which adjoined the province of Susis (xv. p. 732). Pliny, who gives the district of Sittacene a more northerly direction, states that it bore also the names of Arbelitis and Palaestine (vi. 27. a. 31). It is probably the same country which Curtius calls Satrapene (v. 2).   [V.]

SITTACE'NE. [SITTACE.]

SITTOCATIS (Σιττόκατις, Arrian, *Ind.* c. 4), a navigable river, which, according to Arrian, flowed into the *Ganges*. It has been conjectured by Mannert that it is the same as the present *Sind*, a tributary of the *Jumna*, near *Rampur* (v. pt. i. p. 69).   [V.]

SIUPH (Σιούφ, Herod. ii. 172), a town of the Saïtic nome in the Delta of Egypt. It does not appear to be mentioned by any other writer besides Herodotus.   [T. H. D.]

SIVA (Σίουα), a town in the prefecture of Cilicia in Cappadocia, on the road from Mazaca to Tavium, at a distance of 22 miles from Mazaca. (Ptol. v. 6. § 15; *Tab. Peut.*)   [L. S.]

SMARAGDUS MONS (Σμάραγδος ὄρος, Ptol. iv. 5. § 15), was a portion of the chain of hills which runs along the western coast of the Red Sea from the Heroopolite gulf to the straits of *Bab-el-Mandeb*. Between lat. 24° and 25° in this range is the Mount Smaragdus, the modern *Djebel Zabareh*, which derived its name from the emeralds found there, and early attracted by its wealth the Aegyptians into that barren region. The principal mine was at *Djebel-Zabareh*; but at *Bender-el-Sogheir* to N., and at *Sekket* to S., each a portion of Mount Smaragdus, there are traces of ancient mining operations. Small emeralds of an inferior quality are still found in this district. (Mannert, *Geograph.* vol. x. p. 21.) Strabo (xvii. p. 815) and Pliny (xxxvii. 15. s. 16) mention the wealth obtained from these mines. At *Sekket* there is a temple of the Ptolemaic era; but the mines were known and wrought at least as early as the reign of Amunoph III., in the 18th dynasty of the native kings of Aegypt.   [W. B. D.]

SMENUS. [LACONIA, p. 114, b.]

SMILA. [CROSSAEA.]

SMYRNA (Σμύρνα: Eth. Σμυρναῖος, Smyrnaeus: *Smyrna* or *Izmir*), one of the most celebrated and most flourishing cities in Asia Minor, was situated on the east of the mouth of the Hermus, and on the bay which received from the city the name of the Smyrnaeus Sinus. It is said to have been a very ancient town founded by an Amazon of the name of Smyrna, who had previously conquered Ephesus. In consequence of this Smyrna was regarded as a colony of Ephesus. The Ephesian colonists are said afterwards to have been expelled by Aeolians, who then occupied the place, until, aided by the Colophonians, the Ephesian colonists were enabled to re-establish themselves at Smyrna. (Strab. xiv. p. 633; Steph. B. *s. v.*; Plin. v. 31.) Herodotus, on the other hand (i. 150), states that Smyrna originally belonged to the Aeolians, who admitted into their city some Colophonian exiles; and that these Colophonians afterwards, during a festival which was celebrated outside the town, made themselves masters of the place. From that time Smyrna ceased to be an Aeolian city, and was received into the Ionian confederacy (Comp. Paus. vii. 5. § 1.) So far then as we are guided by authentic history, Smyrna belonged to the Aeolian confederacy until the year B. C. 688, when by an act of treachery on the part of the Colophonians it fell into the hands of the Ionians, and became the 13th city in the Ionian League. (Herod. *l. c.*; Paus. *l. c.*) The city was attacked by the Lydian king Gyges, but successfully resisted the aggressor (Herod. i. 14; Paus. ix. 29. § 2.) Alyattes, however, about B. C. 627, was more successful; he took and destroyed the city, and henceforth, for a period of 400 years, it was deserted and in ruins (Herod. i. 16; Strab. xiv. p. 646), though some inhabitants lingered in the place, living κωμηδόν, as is stated by Strabo, and as we must infer from the fact that Scylax (p. 37) speaks of Smyrna as still existing. Alexander the Great is said to have formed the design of rebuilding the city (Paus. vii. 5. § 1); but he did not live to carry this plan into effect; it was, however, undertaken by Antigonus, and finally completed by Lysimachus. The new city was not built on the site of the ancient one, but at a distance of 20 stadia to the south of it, on the southern coast of the bay, and partly on the side of a hill which Pliny calls Mastusia, but principally in the plain at the foot of it extending to the sea. After its extension and embellishment by Lysimachus, new Smyrna became one of the most magnificent cities, and certainly the finest in all Asia Minor. The streets were handsome, well paved, and drawn at right angles, and the city contained several squares, porticoes, a public library, and numerous temples and other public buildings; but one great drawback was that it had no drains. (Strab. *l. c.*; *Marm. Oxon.* n. 5.) It also possessed an excellent harbour which could be closed, and continued to be one of the wealthiest and most flourishing commercial cities of Asia; it afterwards became the seat of a conventus juridicus which embraced the greater part of Aeolis as far as Magnesia, at the foot of Mount Sipylus. (Cic. *p. Flacc.* 30; Plin. v. 31.) During the war between the Romans and Mithridates, Smyrna remained faithful to the former, for which it was rewarded with various grants and privileges. (Liv. xxxv. 42, xxxvii. 16, 54, xxxviii. 39.) But it afterwards suffered much, when Trebonius, one of Caesar's murderers, was besieged there by Dolabella, who in the end took the city, and put Trebonius to death. (Strab. *l. c.*; Cic. *Phil.* xi. 2; Liv. *Epit.* 119; Dion Cass. xlvii. 29.) In the reign of Tiberius, Smyrna had conferred upon it the equivocal honour of being allowed, in preference to several other Asiatic cities, to erect a temple to the emperor (Tac. *Ann.* iii. 63, iv. 56). During the years A. D. 178 and 180 Smyrna suffered much from earthquakes, but the emperor M. Aurelius did much to alleviate its sufferings (Dion Cass. lxxi. 32.) It is well known that Smyrna was one of the places claiming to be the birthplace of Homer, and the Smyrnaeans themselves were so strongly convinced of their right to claim this honour, that they erected a temple to the great bard, or a 'Ομήρειον, a splendid edifice containing a statue of Homer (Strab. *l. c.*; Cic. *p. Arch.* 8): they even showed a cave in the neighhourhood of their city, on the little river Meles, where the poet was said to have composed his works. Smyrna was at all times not only a great commercial place, but its schools of rhetoric and philosophy also were in great repute. The Christian Church also flourished through the zeal and care of its first bishop Polycarp, who is said to have been put to death in the stadium of Smyrna in A. D. 166 (Iren. iii. p. 176). Under the Byzantine emperors the city experienced great vicissitudes: having been occupied by Tzachas, a Turkish chief, about the close of the 11th century, it was nearly destroyed by a Greek fleet, commanded by John Ducas. It was restored, however, by the emperor Comnenus, but again subjected to severe sufferings during the siege of Tamerlane. Not long after it fell into the hands of the Turks, who have retained possession of it ever since. It is now the great mart of the Levant trade. Of Old Smyrna only a few remains now exist on the north-eastern side of the bay of Smyrna; the walls of the acropolis are in the ancient Cyclopean style. The ancient remains of New Smyrna are more numerous, especially of its walls which are of a solid and massive construction; of the stadium between the western gate and the sea, which, however, is stripped of its marble seats and decorations; and of the theatre on the side of a hill fronting the bay. These and other remains of ancient buildings have been destroyed by the Turks in order to obtain the materials for other buildings; but numerous remains of ancient art have been dug out of the ground at Smyrna. (Chandler's *Travels in Asia*, pp. 76, 87; Prokesch, *Denkwürdigkeiten*, i. p. 515, foll.; Hamilton, *Researches*, i. p. 46, foll.; Sir C. Fellows, *Asia Minor*, p. 10, foll.)   [L. S.]

COIN OF SMYRNA.

SMYRNAEUS SINUS (Σμυρναῖον κόλπος), also called the bay of Hermus (Ἑρμεῖος κόλπος), from the river Hermus, which flows into it, or the bay of Meles (Μελήτου κ.), from the little river Meles, is the bay at the head of which Smyrna is situated. From its entrance to the head it is 350 stadia in length, but is divided into a larger and a smaller basin, which have been formed by the deposits of the Hermus, which have at the same time much narrowed the whole bay. A person sailing into it had on his right the promontory of Celaenae, and on his left the headland of Phocaea; the central part of the bay contained numerous small islands. (Strab. xiv. p. 645; Pomp. Mela, i. 17; *Vit. Hom.* 2; Steph. B. *s. v.* Σμύρνα.)   [L. S.]

SOANAS (Σοάνας, Ptol. vii. 4. § 3), a small river of Taprobane (*Ceylon*), which flowed into the sea on the western side of the island. Lassen (in his map) calls it the *Kilau*. On its banks lived a people of the same name, the Soani. (Ptol. vii. 4. § 9.)   [V.]

SOANDA or SOANDUM (Σόανδα or Σόανδον), a castle of Cappadocia, between Therma and Sacoena. (Strab. xiv. p. 663; *It. Ant.* p. 202.) The

same place seems to be alluded to by Frontinus (iii. 2. § 9), who calls it Suenda. Hamilton (*Researches*, ii. p. 286, foll.) identifies it with *Saoghanli Dere*, a place situated on a rock, about 8 miles on the south-west of *Karahissar*, but other geographers place it in a different locality.   [L. S.]

SOAS. [SONUS.]

SOATRA (Σόατρα), or probably more correctly Savatra (Σάυατρα), as the name appears on coins, was an open town in Lycaonia, in the neighbourhood of Apameia Cibotus, on the road from thence to Laodiceia. The place was badly provided with water (Strab. xiv. p. 668; Ptol. v. 4. § 12; Hierocl. p. 672; *Tab. Peut.*), whence travellers are inclined to identify its site with the place now called *Su Vermess*, that is, "there is no water here."   [L. S.]

SOATRAE, a town in Lower Moesia (*Itin. Ant.* p. 229), variously identified with *Pravadi* and *Kiopikeni.* In the Tab. Peut. and by the Geogr. Rav. (iv. 6) it is called Scatrae.   [T. H. D.]

SOBU'RA (Σοβούρας ἐμπόριον), a place on the eastern coast of *Hindostan*, mentioned in the Periplus (p. 34). It is probably the same as the modern *Sabras*, between *Pondicherry* and *Madras*. (See Lassen's map.)   [V.]

SOCANAA or SOCANDA (Σωκανδα or Σωκάνδα), a small river of Hyrcania, noticed by Ptolemy (vi. 9. § 2). It is probably the present *Gurgan*. Ammianus Marcellinus speaks of a place called Socunda, on the shores of the Hyrcanian or Caspian sea (xxiii. 6).   [V.]

SO'CRATIS I'NSULA (Σωκράτους νῆσος), an island of the Sinus Arabicus (*Red Sea*), placed by Ptolemy (vi. 7. § 44), who alone mentions it, in long. 70°, lat. 16° 40', and therefore off the N. coast of his Elisari, the Sabaei of other geographers, 30' east of his Accipitrum Insula ('Ιεράκων) and 2° 20' south of them. They are probably identical with the *Farsan* islands, of the E. I. Company's Chart, described by commanders Moresby and Elwon, in their Sailing Directions for the Red Sea, as "the largest all along this coast, situated upon the extensive banks west of *Gheesan*. They are two in number, but may be considered as forming one island, being connected by a sandy spit of shoal-water, across which camels frequently pass from one to the other." The westernmost is *Farsan Kebeer* (= the greater), 31 miles in length, extending from lat. 16° 35' long. 42° 13' to lat. 16° 54' long. 41° 47'. *Farsan Seggeer* (= the smaller) is, on its NE. side, 18 miles in length, and extends to lat. 17° 1½': their whole breath is only 12 miles. The land is of considerable height, interspersed with some plains and valleys: the hilly parts are coral rock (pp. 38, 39; C. Müller, *Tabulas in Geog. Graec. Min.* tab. viii). In other comparative atlases, adopted by Arrowsmith, the modern name is given as *Kotumbul Is.*, considerably to the N. of the *Farsan*, described by the same writers as lying only 2 miles from the main, a small island about ½ a mile in length and therefore not likely to have been noticed by Ptolemy, who obviously mentions only the more important. (*Sailing Directions*, p. 50.) Mannert identifies the Socratis Insula with Niebuhr's *Firan*, where the traveller says the inhabitants of *Loheia* have a pearl fishery. This name does not occur in the "Sailing Directions," but is probably the same as *Farsan*. (Mannert, *Geographie von Arabien*, p. 49; Niebuhr, *Description de l'Arabie*, p. 201.)   [G. W.]

SOCUNDA. [SOCANAA.]

SODOM (τὰ Σόδομα, Strab. xv. p. 764; Steph. B.

s. v.; Sodoma, -orum, Tertul. *Apolog.* 40; Sodoma, -ae, Sever. Sulp. i. 6 ; Sedul. *Carm.* i. 105; Sodomum, Solin. 45. § 8; Sodomi, Tertull. *Carm. de Sodom.* 4), the infamous city of Canaan situated near the Dead Sea in an exceedingly rich and fruitful country, called in its early history " the plain of Jordan" and described as " well watered everywhere, before the Lord destroyed Sodom and Gomorrah, even as the garden of the Lord, like the land of Egypt, as thou comest to Zoar." (*Gen.* xiii. 10—12.) It is also reckoned one of " the cities of the plain" (xiii. 12. xix. 29), and was probably the capital of the Pentapolis, which consisted of Sodom, Gomorrah, Admah, Zeboiim, and Bela, afterwards Zoar (*Deut.* xxix. 23; *Gen.* xiv. 8, xix. 22), all of which towns, however, had their several petty kings, who were confederate together against Chedorlaomer king of Elam and his three allies, Amraphel king of Shinar, Arioch king of Ellasar, and Tidal king of nations. After Chedorlaomer had succeeded in reducing these sovereigns to subjection, they served him twelve years; in the thirteenth year they revolted, and in the fourteenth year were again vanquished by their northern enemies, when the conquerors were in their turn defeated by Abraham, whose nephew Lot had been carried captive with all his property. The sacred historian has preserved the names of four of the petty kings who at this time ruled the cities of the plain, viz. Bera of Sodom, Birsha of Gomorrah, Shinab of Admah, and Shemeber of Zeboiim; and the scene of the engagement was " the vale of Siddim, which is the salt sea" (*Gen.* xiv.), an expression which seems clearly to imply that the battle-field, at least, was subsequently submerged; the admission of which fact, however, would not involve the consequence that no lake had previously existed in the plain; although this too may be probably inferred from the earlier passage already cited, which seems to describe a wide plain watered by the river Jordan, as the plain of Egypt is irrigated by the Nile: and as this vale of Siddim was full of slime-pits (beds of bitumen), its subsidence naturally formed the Asphalt Lake. The catastrophe of the cities, as described in the sacred narrative, does not certainly convey the idea that they were submerged, for fire and not water was the instrument of their destruction (*Gen.* xix.; *S. Jude* 7); so that the cities need not necessarily have been situated in the middle of the valley, but on the sloping sides of the hills which confined the plain, from which they would still be appropriately denominated "cities of the plain." (Reland, *Palaestina*, p. 255.) This is remarked in order to remove what has been regarded as a fundamental objection to the hypotheses of a late traveller, who claims to have recovered the sites of all the cities of the Pentapolis, which, as he maintains, are still marked by very considerable ruins of former habitations. Whatever value may be attached to the identification of the other four, there is little doubt that the site of Sodom is correctly fixed near the south-western extremity of the lake, where the modern native name *Usdom* or *Esdom*, containing all the radicals of the ancient name, is attached to a plain and a hill (otherwise called *Khashm* or *Jebel-el-Milhh*, i. e. the salt hill), which consequently has long been regarded as marking the site of that accursed city. This singular ridge has been several times explored and described by modern travellers, whose testimony is collected and confirmed by Dr. Robinson (*Bibl. Res.* vol. ii. p. 481—483); but it was reserved for the diligence or imagination of M. de

Saulcy to discover the extensive *débris* of this ancient city, covering the small plain and mounds on the north and north-east of the salt-ridge, and extending along the bed of *Wady Zuweirah* (*Voyage autour de la Mer Morte*, vol. ii. pp. 71—74). On the other side of the question M. Van de Velde is the latest authority. (*Syria and Palestine* in 1851 and 1852, pp. 114, 115, note). Lieut. Lynch, of the American exploring expedition, has given a striking view of this salt mountain, illustrative of his description of the vicinity of Usdom. (*Expedition to the Dead Sea*, pp. 306—308.) [G.W.]

SODRAE (Σόδραι), a tribe met with by Alexander the Great in the lower *Panjáb*, near Pattalene, according to Diodorus (xvii. 102). The name is probably of Indian origin, and may represent the caste of the *Sudras.*   [V.]

SOGDI (Σόγδοι), one of the smaller tribes noticed by Arrian (*Anab.* vi. 15) as encountered by Alexander in the lower *Panjáb.* By their name, they would appear to represent an immigration from the north.   [V.]

SOGDIA'NA (ἡ Σογδιανή, Strab. ii. p. 73, xi. p. 516; Ptol. vi. 12, &c.), a widely extending district of Central Asia, the boundaries of which are not consistently laid down by ancient authors. Generally, it may be stated that Sogdiana lay between the Oxus and the Jaxartes, as its N. and S. limits, the former separating it from Bactriana and Ariana, the latter from the nomad populations of Scythia. (Strab. xi. pp. 511, 514; Ptol. vi. 12. § 1.) To the W. the province was extended in the direction of the Caspian sea, but, in early times at least, not to it; to the E. were the Sacae and the Seres. The district comprehended the greater part of the present *Turkestan*, with the kingdom of *Bokhara*, which bears to this day the name of *Sogd.* The character of the country was very diversified; some part of it being very mountainous, and some part, as the valley of *Bokhara*, very fertile and productive. The larger extent would seem to have been, as at present, a great waste. (Arrian, *Anab.* iv. 16; Curt. vii. 10. § 1.) At the time when Alexander visited the country, there appear to have been extensive forests, filled with all manner of game, and surrounded, at least in some parts, with walls, as preserves. Alexander is said to have hunted down 4000 wild beasts. (Curt. viii. 1. § 19.)

The principal mountain chains are those called the Montes Oxii to the N. (at present the *Pamer Mountains*,) the Comedarum Montes (probably the range of the *Ak-tagh* or *White Mountains*) to the S., and the Montes Sogdii (the modern name of which is not certain, there being a doubt whether they comprehend the *Behr-tagh* as well as the *Kara-tagh*). The two great rivers of the country were those which formed its boundaries; the Oxus (*Gihon* or *Amu-Darja*) and the Jaxartes (*Sihon* or *Syr-Darja*). There are, also, besides these main streams, several smaller ones, feeders of the great rivers, as the Demus, Bascatis, and the Polytimetus, the latter, doubtless, the stream which flows beside the town of *Sogd.* The generic name of the inhabitants of Sogdiana is Sogdii or Sogdiani (Arrian, iv. 16, 18; Plin. vi. 16 ; Curt. iii. 2. § 9, &c.), a race who, as is stated by Strabo (xi. p. 517), appear, in character at least, to have borne a great resemblance to their neighbours of Bactriana. Besides these, Ptolemy and other writers have given a list of other names,— those, probably, of local tribes, who occupied different parts of the province. Many of these show by the form of their name that if not directly of Indian descent, they are clearly connected with that country. Thus we have the Pasicae, near the Montes Oxii; the Thacori (*Takurs*) on the Jaxartes; the Oxydrancae, Drybactae, and Gandari (*Gandháras*), under the mountains; the Mardyeni (*Maáras*), Chorasmii (*Khwaresmians*), near the Oxus; and the Cirrodes (*Kirátas*) near the same river. (Wilson, *Ariana*, p. 164.)

The historians of Alexander's march leave us to suppose that Sogdiana abounded with large towns; but many of these, as Professor Wilson has remarked (*l. c.*), were probably little more than forts erected along the lines of the great rivers to defend the country from the incursions of the barbarous tribes to its N. and E. Yet these writers must have had good opportunity of estimating the force of these places, as Alexander appears to have been the best part of three years in this and the adjoining province of Bactriana. The principal towns of which the names have been handed down to us, were Cyreschata or Cyropolis, on the Jaxartes (Steph. B. *s. v.*; Curt. vi. 6); Gaza (*Ghas* or *Ghazna*, Ibn Haukfl, p. 270); Alexandreia Ultima (Arrian, iii. 30; Curt. *l. c.*; Amm. Marc. xxiii. 6), doubtless in the neighbourhood of, if not on the site of the present *Khojend*; Alexandreia Oxiana (Ptol. vi. 12. § 5; Steph. B. *s. v.*); Nautaca (Arrian, iii. 28, iv. 18), in the neighbourhood of *Karshi* or *Naksheb*; Branchidae (Strab. xi. p. 518), a place traditionally said to have been colonised by a Greek population; and Marginia (Curt. vii. 10. § 15), probably the present *Marghinan*. (Droysen, *Rhein. Mus.* 2 Jahr. p. 86; Mannert, iv. p. 452; Burnes, *Travels*, i. p. 350; *Memoirs of Báber*, p. 12; De Sacy, *Notices et Extraits*, iv. p. 354; Thirlwall, *Hist. of Greece*, vi. p. 284.)   [V.]

SOGDII MONTES. [SOGDIANA.]

SOGIU'NTII, an Alpine people mentioned by Pliny (iii. 20. s. 24). Nothing but resemblance of name gives us any indication of the position of many small mountain tribes, but the names remain frequently very little changed. The position of the Sogiuntii is conjectured to be shown by the name *Sause* or *Souches*, NE. of Briançon in the department of *Hautes Alpes*. But this is merely a guess; and even the orthography of the name Sogiuntii is not certain.   [G. L.]

SOLE, a small town in the interior of Hyrcania, mentioned by Ammianus (xxiii. 6).   [V.]

SOLEN (Σωλήν, Ptol. vii. 1. §§ 10, 34), a small river of S. India, which has its sources in M. Bettigo, and flows thence into the Sinus Colchicus or *Gulf of Manaar*. It is not certain which of two rivers, the *Vaiparu* or the *Tamraparni*, represent it at present: Lassen inclines to the latter.   [V.]

SOLENTA. [OLYNTA INSULA.]

SOLENTUM. [SOLUS.]

SOLETUM (*Soleto*), a town of Calabria, situated in the interior of the Iapygian peninsula, about 12 miles S. of Lupiae (*Lecce*). It is mentioned only by Pliny, in whose time it was deserted ("Soletum desertum," Plin. iii. 11. s. 16), but it must have been again inhabited, as it still exists under the ancient name. That the modern town occupies the ancient site is proved by the remains of the ancient walls which were still visible in the days of Galateo, and indicated a town of considerable magnitude (Galateo, *de Sit. Iapyg.* p. 81; Romanelli, vol. ii. p. 26.)[E. H. B.]

SOLI (Σόλοι: *Eth.* Σολεύς or Σόλιος), an im-

portant town on the coast of Cilicia, between the mouths of the rivers Lamus and Pyramus, from each of which its distance was about 500 stadia. (Strab. xiv. p. 675; *Stadiasm. Mar. Mag.* § 170, &c.) The town was founded by Argives joined by Lindians from Rhodes. (Strab. xiv. p. 671; Pomp. Mela, i. 13; Liv. xxxvii. 56.) It is first mentioned in history by Xenophon (*Anab.* i. 2. § 24) as a maritime town of Cilicia; it rose to such opulence that Alexander the Great could fine its citizens for their attachment to Persia with 200 talents. (Arrian, *Anab.* ii. 5. § 5; Curt. iii. 17.) During the Mithridatic War the town of Soli was taken and destroyed by Tigranes, king of Armenia, who probably transplanted most of its inhabitants to Tigranocerta. (Dion Cass. xxxvi. 20; Plut. *Pomp.* 28; Strab. xi. p. 532.) But the place was revived by Pompey, who peopled it with some of those pirates who had fallen into his hands, and changed its name into Pompeiupolis. (Πομπηιούπολις, Plut. *l. c.*; Strab. xiv. p. 671; Appian, *Mithr.* 105; Ptol. v. 8. § 4; Plin. v. 22; Steph. B. *s. v.*; Tac. *Ann.* ii. 58; Hierocl. p. 704.) Soli was the birthplace of Chrysippus the philosopher, and of two distinguished poets, Philemon and Aratus, the latter of whom was believed to be buried on a hill near the town. The Greek inhabitants of Soli are reported to have spoken a very corrupt Greek in consequence of their intercourse with the natives of Cilicia, and hence to have given rise to the term solecism (σολοικισμός), which has found its way into all the languages of Europe; other traditions, however, connect the origin of this term with the town of Soli, in Cyprus. (Diog. Laert. i. 2. § 4; Eustath. *ad Dion. Per.* 875; Suid. *s. v.* Σόλοι.) The locality and the remains of this ancient city have been described by Beaufort (*Karamania*, p. 261, foll.). "The first object that presented itself to us on landing," says he, "was a beautiful harbour or basin, with parallel sides and circular ends; it is entirely artificial, being formed with surrounding walls or moles, which are 50 feet in thickness and 7 in height. Opposite to the entrance of the harbour a portico rises from the surrounding quay, and opens to a double row of 200 columns, which, crossing the town, communicates with the principal gate towards the country. Of the 200 columns no more than 42 are now standing; the remainder lie on the spot where they fell, intermixed with a vast assemblage of other ruined buildings which were connected with the colonnade. The theatre is almost entirely destroyed. The city walls, strengthened by numerous towers, entirely surrounded the town. Detached ruins, tombs, and sarcophagi were found scattered to some distance from the walls, on the outside of the town, and it is evident that the whole country was once occupied by a numerous and industrious people." The natives now call the place *Mezetlu*. (Comp. Leake, *Asia Minor*, p. 213, foll.) The little river which passed through Soli was called Liparis, from the oily nature

COIN OF SOLI.

of its waters. (Vitruv. viii. 3; Antig. Caryst. 150; Plin. *l. c.*) Pliny (xxxi. 2) mentions bituminous springs in the vicinity, which are reported by Beaufort to exist at *Bikhordy*, about six hours' walk to the north-east of *Mezetlu*.   [L. S.]

SOLI or SOLOE (Σόλοι, Ptol. v. 14. § 4), an important seaport town in the W. part of the N. coast of Cyprus, situated on a small river. (Strab. xiv. p. 683.) According to Plutarch (*Sol.* 26) it was founded by a native prince at the suggestion of Solon and named in honour of that legislator. The sojourn of Solon in Cyprus is mentioned by Herodotus (v. 113). Other accounts, however, make it an Athenian settlement, founded under the auspices of Phalerus and Acamas (Strab. *l. c.*), or of Demophon, the son of Theseus (Plut. *l. c*). We learn from Strabo (*l. c.*) that it had a temple of Aphrodite and one of Isis; and from Galen (*de Simp. Med.* ix. 3, 8) that there were mines in its neighbourhood. The inhabitants were called Solii (Σόλιοι), to distinguish them from the citizens of Soli in Cilicia, who were called Σολεῖς (Diog. Laert. *V. Solon*, 4). According to Pococke (ii. p. 323), the valley which surrounded the city is still called *Solea;* and the ruins of the town itself may be traced in the village of *Aligora.* (Comp. Aesch. *Pers.* 889; Scyl. p. 41; *Stadiasm. M. Magni,* § 295, seq.; Const. Porphyr. *de Them.* i. p. 39, Lips.; Hierocl. p. 707, &c.).   [T. H. D.]

SOLIA. [ARAE HESPERI.]

SOLICI'NIUM, a town in the Agri Decumates, in South-western Germany, on Mount Pirus, where Valentinian in A. D. 369 gained a victory over the Alemanni. (Amm. Marc. xxvii. 10, xxviii. 2, xxx. 7.) A variety of conjectures have been made to identify the site of the town, but there are no positive criteria to arrive at any satisfactory conclusion.   [L. S.]

SOLIMARIACA, in Gallia, is placed in the Antonine Itin. on the road from Andomatunum (*Langres*) to Tullum Leucorum (*Toul*), and nearly half-way between Mosa (*Meuse*) and Tullum. There is a place named *Soulosse*, which in name and in position agrees with Solimariaca. "The trace of the Roman road is still marked in several places by its elevation, both on this side of *Soulosse* and beyond it on the road to *Toul*." (D'Anville, *Notice, &c.*) [G. L.]

SOLIMNIA, a small island of the Aegaean sea, off the coast of Thessaly, near Scopelos. (Plin. iv. 12. s. 23.)

SOLIS INSULA (Plin. vi. 22. s. 24), an island mentioned by Pliny between the mainland of *India* and *Ceylon*, in the strait. There can be no doubt that it is the present *Ramiseram Cor*, famous for a temple of Rama. It bore also the name of Κῶρυ [CORY.]   [V.]

SOLIS FONS. [OASIS, p. 458.]

SOLIS PORTUS (Ἡλίου λιμήν, Ptol. vii. 4. § 6), a harbour near the SE. corner of Taprobane (*Ceylon*). It has been conjectured by Forbiger that it is the present *Vendelusbai*,—a name we do not discover on the best maps. Its position, south of the Malea mountains (*Adam's Peak*), is certain.   [V.]

SOLIS PROMONTO'RIUM (Ἱερὰ Ἡλίου ἄκρα), " Sacra solis extrema," a promontory of the east coast of Arabia at the south of the Persian gulf, between the mouth of the river Lar and Rhegma, in the country of the Nariti. (Ptol. vi. 7. § 14.) [LAR; RHEGMA.]   [G. W.]

SO'LLIUM (Σόλλιον: Eth. Σολλιεύς), a town on the coast of Acarnania, on the Ionian sea.

Its exact site is uncertain, but it was probably in the neighbourhood of Palaerus, which lay between Leucas and Alyzia. [PALAERUS.] Leake, however, places it S. of Alyzia, at *Stravolimióna* (i. e. *Port Stravo*). Sollium was a Corinthian colony, and as such was taken by the Athenians in the first year of the Peloponnesian War (B. C. 431), who gave both the place and its territory to Palaerus. It is again mentioned in B. C. 426, as the place at which Demosthenes landed when he resolved to invade Aetolia. (Thuc. ii. 30, iii. 95, comp. v. 30; Steph. B. *s. v.*; Leake, *Northern Greece*, vol. iv. p. 18, seq.)

SOLMISSUS (Σολμισσός), a hill near Ephesus, rising above the grove of Leto, where the Curetes, by the loud noise of their arms, prevented Hera from hearing the cries of Leto when she gave birth to her twins. (Strab. xiv. p. 640.)   [L. S.]

SOLOMATIS (Σολόματις, Arrian, *Ind.* c. 4), a river named by Arrian as one of the feeders of the Ganges. There has been much difference of opinion as to what modern stream this name represents. Mannert thinks that it is one of the affluents of the *Jumna* (v. pt. i. p. 69); while Benfey, on the other hand, considers it not unlikely that under the name of Solomatis lurks the Indian *Saraswáti* or *Sarsooti*, which, owing to its being lost in the sands, is fabled by the Indians to flow under the earth to the spot where the *Ganges* and *Jumna* join, near *Allahabad*. (Benfey, art. *Indien*, in *Ersch und Gruber*, p. 4.)   [V.]

SOLO'NA (*Eth.* Solonas: *Città del Sole*), a town of Gallia Cispadana, mentioned only by Pliny among the municipal towns of the 8th region (Plin. iii. 15. s. 20), but the name of the Solonates is found also in an inscription, which confirms its municipal rank (Gruter, *Inscr.* p. 1095. 2). Unfortunately this inscription, which was found at Ariminum, affords no clue to the site of Solona: it is placed conjecturally by Cluver at a place called *Città del Sole* about 5 miles SW. of *Forli*: but this site would seem too close to the important town of Forum Livii. (Cluver. *Ital.* p. 291.)   [E. H. B.]

SOLO'NIUM (Σολόνιον), in Gallia Narbonensis, where C. Pomptinus defeated the Allobroges, B. C. 61. (Dion Cass. xxxvii. c. 48; Liv. *Epit.* 103, where it is said, " C. Pontinius Praetor Allobroges qui rebellaverant ad Salonem (Solonem ?) domuit.") It has been conjectured that Solonium is *Sallonax*, in the department of *Ain*, near the small river *Brivas;* but this is merely a guess. The narrative of Dion is useless, as usual, for determining anything with precision. Other guesses have been made about the position of Solonium ; one of which is too absurd to mention.   [G. L.]

SOLO'NIUS AGER (Σολόνιον, Plut.), was the name given to a district or tract in the plain of Latium, which appears to have bordered on the territories of Ostia, Ardea, and Lanuvium. But there is some difficulty in determining its precise situation or limits. Cicero in a passage in which he speaks of a prodigy that happened to the infant Roscius, places it " in Solonio, *qui est campus agri Lanuvini*" (*de Div.* i. 36); but there are some reasons to suspect the last words to be an interpolation. On the other hand, Livy speaks of the Antiates as making incursions "in agrum Ostiensem, Ardeatem, Solonium" (viii. 12). Plutarch mentions that Marius retired to a villa that he possessed there, when he was expelled from Rome in B. C. 88; and from thence repaired to Ostia. (Plut. *Mar.* 35.) But the most distinct indication of its locality is afforded by a passage of Festus (s. v. *Pomonal*, p. 250). where he tells us "Pomonal est in agro Solonio, via Ostiensi, ad duodecimum lapidem, diverticulo a miliario octavo." It is thence evident that the "ager Solonius" extended westward as far as the Via Ostiensis, and probably the whole tract bordering on the territories of Ostia, Laurentum, and Ardea, was known by this name. It may well therefore have extended to the neighbourhood of Lanuvium also. Cicero tells us that it abounded in snakes. (*De Div.* ii. 31.) It appears from one of his letters that he had a villa there, as well as Marius, to which he talks of retiring in order to avoid contention at Rome (*ad Att.* ii. 3).

The origin of the name is unknown; it may probably have been derived from some extinct town of the name; but no trace of such is found. Dionysius, indeed, speaks of an *Etruscan* city of Solonium, from whence the Lucumo came to the assistance of Romulus (Dionys. ii. 37.); but the name is in all probability corrupt, and, at all events, cannot afford any explanation of the *Latin* district of the name.　　　　　　　　　　　[E. H. B.]

SOLO'RIUS MONS, an offshoot of Mons Argentarius, running to the SW., on the borders of Hispania Tarraconensis and Baetica, and connecting Mount Ortospeda with Mount Ilipula. (Plin. iii. 1. s. 2.) It is probably the same mountain mentioned by Strabo (iii. p. 156) as rich in gold and other mines, and the present *Sierra Nevada.*　　　[T. H. D.]

SO'LUS or SOLUNTUM (Σολόεις, Thuc.; Σολοῦς, Diod.: *Eth.* Σολουντῖνος, Diod., but coins have Σολοντῖνος; Soluntinus: *Solanto*), a city of Sicily, situated on the N. coast of the island, about 12 miles E. of Panormus, and immediately to the E. of the bold promontory called *Capo Zaffarana.* It was a Phoenician colony, and from its proximity to Panormus was one of the few which that people retained when they gave way before the advance of the Greek colonies in Sicily, and withdrew to the NW. corner of the island. (Thuc. vi. 2.) It afterwards passed together with Panormus and Motya into the hands of the Carthaginians, or at least became a dependency of that people. It continued steadfast to the Carthaginian alliance even in B. C. 397, when the formidable armament of Dionysius shook the fidelity of most of their allies (Diod. xiv. 48); its territory was in consequence ravaged by Dionysius, but without effect. At a later period of the war (B. C. 396) it was betrayed into the hands of that despot (*Ib.* 78), but probably soon fell again into the power of the Carthaginians. It was certainly one of the cities that usually formed part of their dominions in the island; and in B. C. 307 it was given up by them to the soldiers and mercenaries of Agathocles, who had made peace with the Carthaginians when abandoned by their leader in Africa. (Diod. xx. 69.) During the First Punic War we find it still subject to Carthage, and it was not till after the fall of Panormus that Soluntum also opened its gates to the Romans. (Id. xxiii. p. 505.) It continued to subsist under the Roman dominion as a municipal town, but apparently one of no great consideration, as its name is only slightly and occasionally mentioned by Cicero. (*Verr.* ii. 42, iii. 43.) But it is still noticed both by Pliny and Ptolemy (Plin. iii. 8. s. 14; Ptol. iii. 4. § 3, where the name is corruptly written Ὀλουλίς), as well as at a later period by the Itineraries, which place it 12 miles from Panormus and 12 from Thermae (*Termini*).

(*Itin. Ant.* p. 91; *Tab. Peut.*) It is probable that its complete destruction dates from the time of the Saracens.

At the present day the site of the ancient city is wholly desolate and uninhabited. It stood on a lofty hill, now called the *Monte Catalfano*, at the foot of which is a small cove or port, with a fort, still called the *Castello di Solanto*, and a station for the tunny fishery. The traces of two ancient roads, paved with large blocks of stone, which led up to the city, may still be followed, and the whole summit of the hill is covered with fragments of ancient walls and foundations of buildings. Among these may be traced the remains of two temples, of which some capitals, portions of friezes, &c. have been discovered; but it is impossible to trace the plan and design of these or any other edifices. They are probably all of them of the period of the Roman dominion. Several cisterns for water also remain, as well as sepulchres; and some fragments of sculpture of considerable merit have been discovered on the site. (Fazell. *de Reb. Sic.* viii. p. 352; Amico, *Lex. Top.* vol. ii. pp. 192—195; Hoare's *Class. Tour*, vol. ii. p. 234; Serra di Falco, *Ant. della Sicilia*, vol. v. pp. 60—67.)　　　　　　　　　　　[E. H. B.]

COIN OF SOLUS.

SOLYGEIA, SOLYGEIUS. [CORINTHUS, pp. 684, b, 685, a.]

SOLYMA (τὰ Σόλυμα), a high mountain near Phaselis in Lycia. (Strab. xiv. p. 666.) As the mountain is not mentioned by any other writer, it is probably only another name for the Chimaera Mons, the Olympus, or the mountains of the Solymi, mentioned by Homer. (*Od.* v. 283.) In the Stadiasmus it is simply called the ὄρος μέγα: it extends about 70 miles northward from Phaselis, and its highest point, now called *Taghtalu*, rises immediately above the ruins of Phaselis, which exactly corresponds with the statement of Strabo. (Leake, *Asia Minor*, p. 189.)　　　　　　　　　[L. S.]

SOLYMI. [LYCIA.]

SOMENA. [SIMENA.]

SONAUTES, according to Pliny (vi. 1), a river in Pontus; while, according to Apollonius Rhodius (ii. 747), the Acheron in Bithynia was anciently called Soonautes (Σοωναύτης).　　　[L. S.]

SONEIUM, a place in Moesia Superior, on the borders of Thrace, at the pass of Mount Scomius, called Succi. (*Itin. Hieros.* p. 567.) Identified with *Bagna.*　　　　　　　　　　[T. H. D.]

SONISTA, a town in Upper Pannonia, on the road from Poetovium to Siscia. (Geog. Rav. iv. 19; *Tab. Peut.*; *It. Hieros.* p. 561, where it is written Sunista.) Its exact site is unknown.　　[L. S.]

SO'NTIA (*Eth.* Sontinus: *Sanza*), a town of Lucania, known only from Pliny. who enumerates the Sontini among the municipal towns of that province (Plin. iii. 11. s. 15). It is probable that it is the same place now called *Sanza*, situated in the mountains about 12 miles N. of the *Gulf of Policastro.*　　　　　　　　　　　　[E. H. B.]

SO'NTIUS (*Isonzo*), one of the most considerable of the rivers of Venetia, which has its sources in the Alps, at the foot of the lofty *Mt. Terglou*, and has from thence a course of above 75 miles to the sea, which it enters at the inmost bight of the Adriatic, between Aquileia and the Timavus. It receives at the present day the waters of the *Natisone* and *Torre*, the ancient NATISO and TURRIS, both of which in ancient times pursued independent courses to the sea under the walls of Aquileia, and from the E. those of the *Wippach* or *Vipao*, called by the ancients the FLUVIUS FRIGIDUS. Though so important a stream, the name of the Sontius is not mentioned by any of the geographers; but it is found in the Tabula, which places a station called Ponte Sonti (Ad Pontem Sonti) 14 miles from Aquileia on the highroad to Aemona (*Laybach*). This bridge, which lay on the main entrance into Italy on this side, was a military point of considerable importance. It checked for a time the march of the emperor Maximin when advancing upon Aquileia, in A. D. 238 (Herodian, viii. 4; Capit. *Maximin.* 22); and at a later period it was here that Odoacer took up his position to oppose the advance of Theodosius, by whom he was, however, defeated in a decisive battle, A. D. 489 (Cassiod. *Chron.* p. 472; Id. *Var.* i. 18; Jornand. *Get.* 57). The Sontius is correctly described by Herodian, though he does not mention its name, as a large and formidable stream, especially in spring and summer, when it is fed by the melting of the Alpine snows.   [E. H. B.]

SONUS (Σῶνος, Arrian, *Ind.* c. 4; Plin. vi. 18. s. 22), a principal affluent of the *Ganges*, which flows in a NE. direction to it from the *Vindhya Mountains*. Its modern name is *Soane*. There is no doubt that it has been contracted from the Sanscrit *Suvarna*, golden. The Soas (Σῶας) of Ptolemy (vii. 1. § 30) is certainly the same river.   [V.]

'SOPHE'NE (Σωφηνή, Strab. et alii; Σωφαρηνή, Dion Cass. xxxvi. 36; Procop. *de Aedif.* iii. 2, B. *Pers.* i. 21: *Eth.* Σωφηνός), a district of Armenia, lying between Antitaurus and Mount Masius, separated by the Euphrates from Melitene in Armenia Minor, and by Antitaurus from Mesopotamia. Its capital was Carcathiocerta. (Strab. xi. pp. 521, 522, 527.) It formed at one time, with the neighbouring districts, a separate west Armenian kingdom, governed by the Sophenian Artanes, but was annexed to the east Armenian kingdom by Tigranes. Sophene was taken away from Tigranes by Pompey. (Strab. xi. p. 532; Dion Cass. xxxvi. 26; Plut. *Lucull.* 24, *Pomp.* 33.) Nero gave Sophene as a separate kingdom to Sohaemus. (Tac. *Ann.* xiii. 7.)

SOPIA'NAE, a town in the central part of Lower Pannonia, on the road from Mursa to Sabaria (*It. Ant.* pp. 231, 232, 264, 267), was according to Ammianus Marcellinus (xxviii. 1) the birthplace of the emperor Maximinus. Its site is occupied by the modern *Fünfkirchen.*   [L. S.]

SORA (Σῶρα: *Eth.* Soranus: *Sora*), a city of Latium, situated in the valley of the Liris, on the right bank of that river, about 6 miles to the N. of Arpinum. Though included in Latium in the more extended sense of that term, as it was understood under the Roman Empire, Sora was originally a Volscian city (Liv. x. 1), and apparently the most northerly possessed by that people. It was wrested from them by the Romans in B. C. 345, being surprised by a sudden attack by the consuls Fabius Dorso and Ser. Sulpicius. (Liv. vii. 28.) It was subsequently occupied by the Romans with a colony:

the establishment of this is not mentioned by Livy, but in B. C. 315 he tells us the inhabitants had revolted and joined the Samnites, putting to death the Roman colonists. (Id. ix. 23; Diod. xix. 72.) The city was in consequence besieged by the dictator C. Fabius, and, notwithstanding the great defeat of the Romans at Lautulae, the siege was continued into the following year, when the city was at length taken by the consuls C. Sulpicius and M. Poetelius; the citadel, which was in a very strong and inaccessible position, being betrayed into their hands by a deserter. The leaders of the defection were sent to Rome and doomed to execution; the other inhabitants were spared. (Liv. ix. 23, 24.) Sora was now occupied by a Roman garrison; but notwithstanding this it again fell into the hands of the Samnites in B. C. 306, and it was not recovered by the Romans till the following year. (Id. ix. 43, 44; Diod. xx. 80, 90.) After the close of the Second Samnite War it was one of the points which the Romans determined to secure with a colony, and a body of 4000 colonists was sent thither in B. C. 303. (Id. x. 1.) From this time Sora became one of the ordinary " coloniae Latinae " and is mentioned in the Second Punic War among the refractory colonies, which in B. C. 209 refused any further contributions. (Liv. xxvii. 9, xxix. 15. The text of Livy gives *Cora* in the first passage, and *Sora* in the second, but the same place is necessarily meant in both passages, and it is probable that Sora is the true reading.) From this time we hear little more of Sora, which lapsed into the condition of an ordinary municipal town. (Cic. pro *Planc.* 9). Its rank of a Colonia Latina was merged in that of a municipium by the *Lex Julia*; but it received a fresh colony under Augustus, consisting, as we learn from an inscription, of a body of veterans from the 4th legion. (*Lib. Colon.* p. 237; Plin. iii. 5. s. 9; Orell. *Inscr.* 3681.) Juvenal speaks of it as a quiet country town, where houses were cheap (Juv. iii. 223); and it is mentioned by all the geographers among the towns of this part of Italy. (Strab. v. p. 238; Ptol. iii. 1. § 63; Sil. Ital. viii. 394; Orell. *Inscr.* 3972.) Nothing more is heard of it under the Roman Empire, but it survived the fall of the Western Empire, and continued throughout the middle ages to be a place of consideration. Sora is still an episcopal see, and much the most important place in this part of Italy, with about 10,000 inhabitants. The modern town undoubtedly occupies the same site with the ancient one, in the plain or broad valley of the Liris, resting upon a bold and steep hill, crowned by the ruins of a mediaeval castle. The ancient citadel, described by Livy, stood on a hill at the back of this, called the *Rocca di S. Angelo*, where some remains of the ancient walls, constructed of massive polygonal blocks, are still visible. No remains of Roman times are preserved, except a few inscriptions, and some foundations, supposed to be those of a temple. (Romanelli, vol. iii. pp. 362—366; Hoare's *Classical Tour*, vol. i. pp. 299—302.)   [E. H. B.]

SORA (Σόρα or Σῶρα), a town of Paphlagonia, noticed only by the latest writers of antiquity, and of unknown site. (Constant. Porph. *Them.* i. 7; *Novellae*, xxix. 1; Hierocl. p. 695; *Conc. Nicaen.* ii. p. 52; *Conc. Chalced.* p. 664, where it is called Sura.)   [L. S.]

SORA (Σῶρα, Ptol. vii. 1. § 68), a town in the southern part of India, between M. Bettigo and Adeisathron. It was the capital of a nomad race called Sorae (Ptol. l. c.), and the royal residence of a king named Arcates. The people are evidently the same as the Surae of Pliny (vi. 20. s. 23). Lassen places them in the mountains above *Madras* (see map). [V.]

SORACTE (*Monte S. Oreste*), a mountain of Etruria, situated between Falerii and the Tiber, about 26 miles N. of Rome, from which it forms a conspicuous object. It is detached from the chain of the Apennines, from which it is separated by the intervening valley of the Tiber; yet in a geological sense it belongs to the Apennine range, of which it is an outlying offset, being composed of the hard Apennine limestone, which at once distinguishes it from the Mons Ciminus and the other volcanic hills by which it is surrounded. Though of no great elevation, being only 2420 feet in height, it rises in a bold and abrupt mass above the surrounding plain (or rather table-land), which renders it a striking and picturesque object, and a conspicuous feature in all views of the *Campagna*. Hence the selection of its name by Horace in a well-known ode (*Carm.* i. 9) is peculiarly appropriate. It was consecrated to Apollo, who had a temple on its summit, probably on the same spot now occupied by the monastery of *S. Silvestro*, and was worshipped there with peculiar religious rites. His priests were supposed to possess the power of passing unharmed through fire, and treading on the hot cinders with their bare feet. (Virg. *Aen.* vii. 696, xi. 785—790; Sil. Ital. v. 175—181, vii. 662; Plin. vii. 2.) Its rugged and craggy peaks were in the days of Cato still the resort of wild goats. (Varr. *R. R.* ii. 3. § 3.)

Soracte stands about 6 miles from *Civita Castellana*, the site of the ancient Falerii, and 2 from the Tiber. It derives its modern appellation from the village of *Sant' Oreste*, which stands at its S. extremity on a steep and rocky hill, forming a kind of step or ledge at the foot of the more elevated peaks of Soracte itself. This site, which bears evident signs of ancient habitation, is supposed to be that of the ancient FERONIA or LUCUS FERONIAE. (Dennis's *Etruria*, vol. i. p. 179.) [E. H. B.]

SORBIODU′NUM, or SORVIODU′NUM, a town of Britannia Romana, in the territory of the Belgae. (*Itin. Ant.* pp. 483, 486.) It is identified with *Old Sarum*, where coins of several Roman emperors have been found, and where the traces of the ancient Roman walls show it to have been about half a mile in circumference. (Camden, p. 113.) [T.H.D.]

SORDICE, a lake in Gallia. A river Sordus ran out of the *E'tang* Sordice, in the country of the Sordones or Sordi. [SORDONES.]

"Stagnum hic palusque, quippe diffuse patet,
Et incolae istam Sordicen cognominant."

(Avienus, *Or. Mar.*, as I. Vossius reads it.)
The Sordice is supposed by some geographers to be the E'tang de Leucate; but others take it to be an étang further south, called E'tang de St. Nazaire, and the E'tang de Leucate to be that near Salsulae, which is described by Strabo, Mela, and others. [SALSULAE; RUSCINO.] [G. L.]

SORDONES, or SARDONES, as the name has sometimes been written, a people in Gallia. Mela (ii. 5) writes: after the Salsulae fons "is the ora Sordonum, and the small streams Telis and Tichis; the Colonia Ruscino, and the vicus Illiberis." Pliny (iii. 4) begins his description of Gallia Narbonensis from the foot of the Pyrenees. He says "On the coast is the regio Sordonum or Sardonum, and in the interior the Consuarani; the rivers Techum, Vernodubrum; towns, Illiberis and Ruscino." These Sordones are the Sordi of Avienus (*Or. Marit.* 562):—

"Sordus inde denique
Populus agebat inter avios locos
Ac pertinentes usque ad interius mare,
Qua pinifertae stant Pyrenae vertices,
Inter ferarum lustra ducebat greges,
Et arva late et gurgitem ponti premit:"

as I. Vossius reads the passage in his edition of Mela. The Sordi then occupied the coast of the Mediterranean from the Pyrenees northward, and the neighbouring part of the interior at the north foot of the Pyrenees. Ptolemy, as D'Anville observes, does not mention the Sordones, and he has made the territory of the Volcae Tectosages comprehend Illiberis and Ruscino. The Sordones probably occupied the whole of the territory called *Roussillon*, and they would be in possession of that pass of the Pyrenees called *Col de Pertus*, which is defended by the fort of *Bellegarde*. They bordered on the Consorani. [CONSORANI.] [G. L.]

SORICA′RIA, a place in Hispania Baetica, mentioned by Hirtius (*B. Hisp.* c. 24), and the same called also "Soritia" by that author (c. 27). Ukert (ii. pt. i. p. 361) seeks it in the neighbourhood of the Flumen Salsum (the *Salado*), S. of the Baetis, and between *Osuña* and *Antequera*. [T. H. D.]

SORINGI (Σώριγγοι, *Peripl. M. E.* p. 34), a people of the southern part of *Hindostan*, who apparently dwelt along the banks of the Chaberus (*Káveri*). Lassen places them below the Sorae, on the slopes of the hills above *Madras*. [V.]

SORITIA. [SORICARIA.]

SORNUM, (Σόρνον, Ptol. iii. 8. § 10), a city of Dacia; now *Gieritza*. [T. H. D.]

SORO′RES (AD), a station in Lusitania, N. of Emerita. (*Itin. Ant.* p. 433.) Variously identified with *Montanches* and *Aliseda*. [T. H. D.]

SOSTOMAGUS, in Gallia, is placed by the Jerusalem Itin. between Tolosa (*Toulouse*) and Carcaso (*Carcassone*), 38 miles from *Toulouse* and 24 from *Carcassone*. The road is nearly direct, and if the distances are correct, we might perhaps find some name like Sosto in the proper place. Some geographers have found Sostomagus near *Castelnaudari*. [G. L.]

SOTERA, a place in Ariana, mentioned by Ammianus (xxiii. 6). It is probably the same as that called by Ptolemy Σώτειρα (vi. 17. § 7). [V.]

SOTIA′TES or SONTIA′TES, a people of Aquitania. Schneider (*Caesar, B. G.* iii. 20) who writes "in Sontiatium fines" has a long note on the various forms of this word. Nicolaus Damascenus (quoted by Athenaeus, vi. p. 249) writes the name Sotiani, but as Caesar was his authority for what he says, he may have altered the form of the word. In Dion Cassius (xxxix. c. 46) the reading is 'Ασιάτας (ed. Reimarus); but there are other variations in the MSS. In Pliny (iv. 19) we find among the nations of Aquitania "Ausci, Elusates, Sottiates, Osquidates Campestres." Orosius (vi. 8, ed. Haverkamp) has Sontiates, but one MS. has Sotiates and others have Sociates.

In B. C. 56 Caesar sent P. Crassus into Aquitania. Crassus came from the north, and after summoning the men of fighting age who were on the muster rolls of *Toulouse, Carcassone,* and *Narbonne,* he entered the territory of the Sotiates, the first of the Aquitanian peoples whom he attacked. The Sotiates were the neighbours of the Elusates a name represented by the town of *Eause*. A line drawn from *Auch* (Ausci) on the *Gers* to *Bazas* in the department of *La Gironde*, passes near *Sos*, a town which is on the *Getise*, and in the *Gabaret*. In the middle ages it was called *Sotium*. Ancient remains have been found at *Sos*. Here we have an instance of the preservation of ancient names in this part of France, and there are many other instances.

D'Anville in determining the position of the Sotiates argues correctly that Crassus having passed through the Santones, a people who had submitted to Caesar (*B. G.* iii. 12) and would offer no resistance, entered Aquitania by the north, and the Sotiates who were only seven or eight leagues south of the *Garonne* would be the first tribe on whom he fell. He says that he has evidence of a Roman road very direct from *Sos* to *Eause* ; and he is convinced that this is part of the road described in the Jerusalem Itin. between Vasatae and Elusa. On this road the name Scittium occurs in the Itin., and as the distance between Scittium and Elusa corresponds very nearly to the distance between *Sos* and *Eause*, he conjectures that this word Scittium is written wrong, and that it should be Sotium.

The Sotiates, who were strong in cavalry, attacked the Romans on their march, and a battle took place in which they were defeated. Crassus then assaulted their town, which made a stout resistance. He brought up his vineae and towers to the walls, but the Sotiates drove mines under them, for as they had copper mines in their country they were very skilful in burrowing in the ground. At last they sent to Crassus to propose terms of surrender (*B. G.* iii. 21). While the people were giving up their arms on one side of the town, Adcantuannus, who was a king or chief, attempted to sally out on another side with his 600 "soldurii." The Romans met him there, and after a hard fight Adcantuannus was driven back into the town; but he still obtained the same easy terms as the rest.

These Soldurii were a body of men who attached themselves to a chief with whom they enjoyed all the good things without working, so long as the chief lived; but if any violence took off their leader it was their duty to share the same fate or to die by their own hand. This was an Iberian and also a Gallic fashion. The thing is easily understood. A usurper or any desperate fellow seized on power with the help of others like himself ; lived well, and fed his friends ; and when his tyranny came to an end, he and all his crew must kill themselves, if they wished to escape the punishment which they deserved. (Plut. *Sertor.* c. 14; Caesar, *B. G.* vii. 40 ; and the passage in Athenaeus.)

The MSS. of Caesar vary in the name of Adcantuannus. Schneider writes it Adiatunus, and in Athenaeus it is 'Αδιάτομον. Schneider mentions a medal of Pellerin, with REX ΔALETVΩNVΣ and a lion's head on one side, and on the other SO-TIOGA. Walckenaer (*Géogr. &c.* i. 284) may be speaking of the same medal, when he describes one which is said to have been found at *Toulouse*, with a head of Adictanus on one side and the word Sotiagae on the other. He thinks it " very suspected;" and it may be.   [G. L.]

SOZO'POLIS (Σωζόπολιs), a town noticed only by late writers as a place in Pisidia, on the north of Termessus, in a plain surrounded on all sides by

mountains. (Hierocl. p. 672; Evagr. *Hist. Eccles.* iii. 33.) It is possibly the same place which Stephanus B. notices under the name of Sozusa. Nicetas (*Ann.* p. 9) mentions that it was taken by the Turks, but recovered from them by John Comnenus. (Comp. *Ann.* p. 169; Cinnamus, p. 13.) The traveller Paul Lucas (*Sec. Voy.* vol. i. c. 33) observed some ancient remains at a place now called *Souzou*, south of *Aglasoun*, which probably belong to Sozopolis.   [L. S.]

SOZO'POLIS, a later name of Apollonia in Thrace. [Vol. I. p. 160.]   [J. R.]

SPALATHRA (Plin. iv. 9. s. 16; Σπάλαυθρα, Scylax, p. 25; Σπαλάθρη, Steph. B. *s. v.*; Σπάλαθρον, Hellanic. *ap. Steph. B. s. v.* : *Eth.* Σπαλαθραῖος), a town of Magnesia, in Thessaly, upon the Pagasaean gulf. It is conjectured that this town is meant by Lycophron (899), who describes Prothous, the leader of the Magnetes in the Iliad, as ὁ ἐκ Παλαύθρων (Σπαλαύθρων). (See Müller, *ad Scyl.* l. c.)

SPALATUM. [SALONA.]

SPANETA, a town in Lower Pannonia, of unknown site. (*It. Ant.* p. 268; *It. Hieros.* p. 563; Geog. Rav. iv. 19, who writes Spaneatis.   [L. S.]

SPARATA, a place in Moesia Superior, probably on the river *Isker*. (*Itin. Hieros.* p. 567.) By the Geogr. Rav. it is called Sparthon (iv. 7).   [T. H. D.]

SPARTA (Σπάρτη, Dor. Σπάρτα : *Eth.* Σπαρτιάτης, Spartiates, Spartanus), the capital of Laconia, and the chief city of Peloponnesus. It was also called LACEDAEMON (Λακεδαίμων: *Eth.* Λακεδαιμόνιος, Lacedaemonius), which was the original name of the country. [See Vol. II. p. 103, a.] Sparta stood at the upper end of the middle vale of the Eurotas, and upon the right bank of the river. The position of this valley, shut in by the mountain ranges of Taÿgetus and Parnon, its inaccessibility to invaders, and its extraordinary beauty and great fertility, have been described in a previous article [LACONIA]. The city was built upon a range of low hills and upon an adjoining plain stretching SE. to the river. These hills are offshoots of Mt. Taÿgetus, and rise almost immediately above the river. Ten stadia S. of the point where the Oenus flows into the Eurotas, the latter river is divided into two arms by a small island overgrown with the oleander, where the foundations of an ancient bridge are visible. This is the most important point in the topography of the site of Sparta. Opposite to this bridge the range of hills rises upon which the ancient city stood; while a hollow way (Map, *ff.*) leads through them into the plain to *Magula*, a village situated about half-way between *Mistrá* and the island of the Eurotas. Upon emerging from this hollow into the plain, there rises on the left hand a hill, the south-western side of which is occupied by the theatre (Map, A.). The centre of the building was excavated out of the hill ; but the two wings of the cavea were entirely artificial, being built of enormous masses of quadrangular stones. A great part of this masonry still remains ; but the seats have almost entirely disappeared, because they have for many ages been used as a quarry by the inhabitants of *Mistrá*. The extremities of the two wings are about 430 feet from one another, and the diameter or length of the orchestra is about 170 feet ; so that this theatre was probably the largest in Greece, with the exception of those of Athens and Megalopolis. There are traces of a wall around this hill, which also embraces a considerable part of the adjoining plain to the east. Within the space enclosed by this wall there are two terraces, upon one of which, amidst the ruins of a church, the French Commission discovered traces of an ancient temple. In this space there are also some ancient doors, formed of three stones, two upright with the architrave, buried in the ground; but no conjecture can be formed of the building to which they belonged without excavations.

The hill we have been describing is the largest of all the Spartan heights, and is distinguished by the wall which surrounds it, and by containing traces of foundations of some ancient buildings. From it two smaller hills project towards the Eurotas, parallel to one another, and which may be regarded as portions of the larger hill. Upon the more southerly of the two there are considerable remains of a circular brick building, which Leake calls a circus, but Curtius an amphitheatre or odeum (Map, 3). Its walls are 16 feet thick, and its diameter only about 100 feet; but as it belongs to the Roman period, it was probably sufficient for the diminished population of the city at that time. Its entrance was on the side towards the river. West of this building is a valley in the form of a horse-shoe, enclosed by walls of earth, and apparently a stadium, to which its length nearly corresponds.

To the north of the hollow way leading from the bridge of the Eurotas to *Magúla* there is a small insulated hill, with a flat summit, but higher and more precipitous than the larger hill to the south of this way. It contains but few traces of ancient buildings (Map, B.). At its southern edge there are the remains of an aqueduct of later times.

The two hills above mentioned, north and south of this hollow way, formed the northern half of Sparta. The other portion of the city occupied the plain between the southern hill and the rivulet falling into the Eurotas, sometimes called the *River of Magúla*, because it flows past that village, but more usually *Trypiótiko*, from *Trypí*, a village in the mountains (Map, cc). Two canals, beginning, at *Magúla*, run across this plain: upon the southern one (Map, bb), just above its junction with the *Trypiótiko*, stands the small village of *Psychikó* (Map, 6). Between this canal and the *Trypiótiko* are some heights upon which the town of New Sparta is now built (Map, D.). Here are several ancient ruins, among which are some remains of walls at the southern extremity, which look like city-walls. The plain between the heights of New Sparta and the hill of the theatre is covered with corn-fields and gardens, among which are seen fragments of wrought stones, and other ancient remains, cropping out of the ground. The only remains which make any appearance above the ground are those of a quadrangular building, called by the present inhabitants the tomb of Leonidas. It is 22 feet broad and 44 feet long, and is built of ponderous square blocks of stone. It was probably an heroum, but cannot have been the tomb of Leonidas, which we know, from Pausanias (iii. 14. § 1), was near the theatre, whereas this building is close to the new town.

This plain is separated from the Eurotas by a range of hills which extend from the Roman amphitheatre or circus to the village of *Psychikó*. Between the hills and the river is a level tract, which is not much more than 50 yards wide below the Roman amphitheatre, but above and below the latter it swells into a plain of a quarter of a mile in breadth. Beyond the river *Trypiótiko* there are a few traces of the foundations of ancient buildings near the little

village of *Kalagoniá* (Map, 7). Leake mentions an ancient bridge over the *Trypiótiko*, about a quarter of a mile NE. of the village of *Kalagoniá*. This bridge, which was still in use when Leake visited the district, is described by him as having a rise of about one-third of the span, and constructed of large single blocks of stone, reaching from side to side. The same traveller noticed a part of the ancient causeway remaining at either end of the bridge, of the same solid construction. But as this bridge is not noticed by the French Commission, it probably no longer exists, having been destroyed for its materials. (Leake, *Morea*, vol. i. p. 157, *Peloponnesiaca*, p. 115.)

Such is the site of Sparta, and such is all that now remains of this famous city. There cannot be any doubt, however, that many interesting discoveries might be made by excavations; and that at any rate the foundations of several ancient buildings might be found, especially since the city was never destroyed in ancient times. Its present appearance corresponds wonderfully to the anticipation of Thucydides, who remarks (i. 10) that " if the city of the Lacedaemonians were deserted, and nothing remained but its temples and the foundations of its buildings, men of a distant age would find a difficulty in believing in the existence of its former power, or that it possessed two of the five divisions of Peloponnesus, or that it commanded the whole country, as well as many allies beyond the peninsula,—so inferior was the appearance of the city to its fame, being neither adorned with splendid temples and edifices, nor built in contiguity, but in separate quarters, in the ancient method. Whereas, if Athens were reduced to a similar state, it would be supposed, from the appearance of the city, that the power had been twice as great as the reality." Compared with the Acropolis of Athens, which rises proudly from the plain, still crowned with the columns of its glorious temples, the low hills on the Eurotas, and the shapeless heap of ruins, appear perfectly insignificant, and present nothing to remind the spectator of the city that once ruled the Peloponnesus and the greater part of Greece. The site of Sparta differs from that of almost all Grecian cities. Protected by the lofty ramparts of mountains, with which nature had surrounded their fertile valley, the Spartans were not obliged, like the other Greeks, to live within the walls of a city pent up in narrow streets, but continued to dwell in the midst of their plantations and gardens, in their original village trim. It was this rural freedom and comfort which formed the chief charm and beauty of Sparta.

It must not, however, be supposed that Sparta was destitute of handsome public buildings. Notwithstanding the simplicity of the Spartan habits, their city became, after the Messenian wars, one of the chief seats of poetry and art. The private houses of the Spartans always continued rude and unadorned, in accordance with a law of Lycurgus, that the doors of every house were to be fashioned only with the saw, and the ceiling with the axe (Plut. *Lyc.* 13); but this regulation was not intended to discourage architecture, but to prevent it from ministering to private luxury, and to restrain it to its proper objects, the buildings for the gods and the state. The palace of the kings remained so simple, that its doors in the time of Agesilaus were said to be those of the original building erected by Aristodemus, the founder of the Spartan monarchy (Xen. *Ages.* 8. § 7); but the temples of the gods were built with great magnificence, and the spoils of the Persian wars were employed in the erection of a beautiful stoa in the Agora, with figures of Persians in white marble upon the columns, among which Pausanias admired the statues of Mardonius and Artemisia (iii. 11. § 3). After the Persian wars Athens became more and more the centre of Greek art; but Sparta continued to possess, even in the time of Pausanias, a larger number of monuments than most other Grecian cities.

Sparta continued unfortified during the whole period of autonomous Grecian history; and it was first surrounded with walls in the Macedonian period. We learn from Polybius (ix. 21) that its walls were 48 stadia in circumference, and that it was much larger than Megalopolis, which was 50 stadia in circuit. Its superiority to Megalopolis in size must have been owing to its form, which was circular. (Polyb. v. 22.) Leake remarks that, "as the side towards the Eurotas measured about two miles with the windings of the outline, the computation of Polybius sufficiently agrees with actual appearances, though the form of the city seems rather to have been semicircular than circular." (Morea, vol. i. p. 180.) Its limits to the eastward, at the time of the invasion of Philip (B. C. 218), are defined by Polybius, who says (v. 22) that there was a distance of a stadium and a half between the foot of the cliffs of Mt. Menelaium and the nearest part of the city. Livy also describes the Eurotas as flowing close to the walls (xxxiv. 28, xxxv. 29). When Demetrius Poliorcetes made an attempt upon Sparta in B. C. 296, some temporary fortifications were thrown up; and the same was done when Pyrrhus attacked the city in B. C. 272. (Paus. i. 13. § 6, vii. 8. § 5.) But Sparta was first regularly fortified by a wall and ditch by the tyrant Nabis in B. C. 195 (Liv. xxxiv. 27; Paus. vii. 8. § 5); though even this wall did not surround the whole city, but only the level parts, which were more exposed to an enemy's attack. (Liv. xxxiv. 38.) Livy, in his account of the attack of Sparta by Philopoemen in B. C. 192, alludes to two of the gates, one leading to Pharae, and the other to Mount Barbosthenes. (Liv. xxxv. 30.) After the capture of the city by Philopoemen, the walls were destroyed by the Achaean League (Paus. vii. 8. § 5); but they were shortly afterwards restored by order of the Romans, when the latter took the Spartans under their protection in opposition to the Achaeans. (Paus. vii. 9. § 5.) Its walls and gates were still standing when Pausanias visited Sparta in the second century of the Christian era, but not a trace of them now remains. When Alaric took Sparta in A. D. 396, it was no longer fortified, nor protected by arms or men (Zosim. v. 6); but it continued to be inhabited in the thirteenth century, as we learn from the "Chronicle of the Morea." It was then always called Lacedaemon, and was confined to the heights around the theatre. The walls which surrounded it at that time may still be traced, and have been mentioned above. It is to the medieval Lacedaemon that the ruins of the churches belong, of which no less than six are noticed by the French Commission. After the conquest of Peloponnesus by the Franks in the thirteenth century, William de Villehardouin built a strong fortress upon the hill of Misithrá, usually pronounced Mistrá, a little more than two miles west of Sparta, at the foot of Mt. Taygetus. The inhabitants of the medieval Lacedaemon soon abandoned their town and took refuge within the fortress

of Mistrá, which long continued to be the chief place in the valley of the Eurotas. The site of Sparta was occupied only by the small villages of Magúla and Psychikó, till the present Greek government resolved to remove the capital of the district to its ancient seat. The position of New Sparta upon the southern part of the ancient site has been already described.

It has been observed that Sparta resembled Rome in its site, comprehending a number of contiguous hills of little height or boldness of character. (Mure, Tour in Greece, vol. ii. p. 236.) It also resembled Rome in being formed out of several earlier settlements, which existed before the Dorian conquest, and gradually coalesced with the later city. which was founded in their midst. These earlier places, which are the hamlets or κῶμαι mentioned by Thucydides (i. 10), were four in number, Pitane, Limnae or Limnaeum, Mesoa, and Cynosura, which were united by a common sacrifice to Artemis. (Paus. iii. 16. § 9.) They are frequently called φυλαί, or tribes, by the grammarians (Müller, Dorians, iii. 3. § 7), and were regarded as divisions of the Spartans; but it is clear from ancient writers that they are names of places.* We are best informed about Pitane, which is called a πόλις by Euripides (Troad. 1112), and which is also mentioned as a place by Pindar (πρὸς Πιτάναν δὲ παρ' Εὐρώτα πόρον, Ol. vi. 46). Herodotus, who had been there, calls it a δῆμος (iii. 55). He also mentions a λόχος Πιτανάτης (ix. 53); and though Thucydides (i. 20) denies its existence, Caracalla, in imitation of antiquity, composed a λόχος Πιτανάτης of Spartans. (Herodian. iv. 8.) It appears from the passage of Pindar quoted above, that Pitane was at the ford of the Eurotas, and consequently in the northern part of the city. It was the favourite and fashionable place of residence at Sparta, like Collytus at Athens and Craneion at Corinth. (Plut. de Exsil. 6. p. 601.) We are also told that Pitane was near the temple and stronghold of Issorium, of which we shall speak presently. (Polyaen. ii. 1. § 14; Plut. Ages. 32.) Limnae was situated upon the Eurotas, having derived its name from the marshy ground which once existed there (Strab. viii. p. 363); and as the Dromus occupied a great part of the lower level towards the southern extremity, it is probable that Limnae occupied the northern. (Leake, Morea, vol. i. p. 177.) It is probable that Mesoa was in the SE. part of the city [see below, p. 1028, b.], and Cynosura in the SW.

In the midst of these separate quarters stood the Acropolis and the Agora, where the Dorian invaders first planted themselves. Pausanias remarks that the Lacedaemonians had no acropolis, towering above other parts of the city, like the Cadmeia at Thebes and Larissa at Argos, but that they gave this name to the loftiest eminence of the group (iii. 17. § 2). This is rather a doubtful description, as the great hill, upon which the theatre stands, and the hill at the northern extremity of the site, present nearly the same elevation to the eye. Leake places the Acropolis upon the northern hill, which, he observes, was

---

* Some modern writers mention a fifth tribe, the Aegeidae, because Herodotus (iv. 149) speaks of the Aegeidae as a great tribe (φυλή) in Sparta; but the word φυλή seems to be here used in the more general sense of family, and there is no evidence that the word Aegeidae was the name of a place, like the other four mentioned above.

better adapted for a citadel than any other, as being separated from the rest, and at one angle of the site; but Curtius supposes it to have stood upon the hill of the theatre, as being the only one with a sufficiently large surface on the summit to contain the numerous buildings which stood upon the Acropolis. The latter opinion appears the more probable; and the larger hill, cleared from its surrounding rubbish, surrounded with a wall, and crowned with buildings, would have presented a much more striking appearance than it does at present.

The chief building on the Acropolis was the temple of Athena Chalcioecus, the tutelary goddess of the city. It was said to have been begun by Tyndareus, but was long afterwards completed by Gitiadas, who was celebrated as an architect, statuary, and poet. He caused the whole building to be covered with plates of bronze or brass, whence the temple was called the Brazen House, and the goddess received the surname of Chalcioecus. On the bronze plates there were represented in relief the labours of Hercules, the exploits of the Dioscuri, Hephaestus releasing his mother from her chains, the Nymphs arming Perseus for his expedition against Medusa, the birth of Athena, and Amphitrite and Poseidon. Gitiadas also made a brazen statue of the goddess. (Paus. iii. 17. §§ 2, 3.) The Brazen House stood in a sacred enclosure of considerable extent, surrounded by a stoa or colonnade, and containing several sanctuaries. There was a separate temple of Athena Ergane. Near the southern stoa was a temple of Zeus Cosmetas, and before it the tomb of Tyndareus; the western stoa contained two eagles, bearing two victories, dedicated by Lysander in commemoration of his victories over the Athenians. To the left of the Brazen House was a temple of the Muses; behind it a temple of Ares Areia, with very ancient wooden statues; and to its right a very ancient statue of Zeus Hypatus, by Learchus of Rhegium, parts of which were fastened together with nails. Here also was the σκήνωμα, a booth or tent, which Curtius conjectures to have been the οἴκημα οὐ μέγα, ὃ ἦν τοῦ ἱεροῦ (Thuc. i. 134), where Pausanias took refuge as a suppliant. Near the altar of the Brazen House stood two statues of Pausanias, and also statues of Aphrodite Ambologēra (delaying old age), and of the brothers Sleep and Death. The statues of Pausanias were set up by order of the Delphian Apollo to expiate his being starved to death within the sacred precincts. (Paus. iii. 17. § 2—18. § 1.)

The Agora was a spacious place, surrounded, like other Greek market-places, with colonnades, from which the streets issued to the different quarters of the city. Here were the public buildings of the magistrates,—the council-house of the Gerusia and senate, and the offices of the Ephori, Nomophylaces, and Bidiaei. The most splendid building was the Persian stoa, which had been frequently repaired and enlarged, and was still perfect when Pausanias visited the city. The Agora contained statues of Julius Caesar and Augustus: in the latter was a brazen statue of the prophet Agias. There was a place called Chorus, marked off from the rest of the Agora, because the Spartan youths here danced in honour of Apollo at the festival of the Gymnopaedia. This place was adorned with statues of the Pythian deities, Apollo, Artemis, and Leto; and near it were temples of Earth, of Zeus Agoraeus, of Athena Agoraea, of Apollo, of Poseidon Asphaleius, and of Hera. In the Agora was a colossal statue

representing the people of Sparta, and a temple of the Moerae or Fates, near which was the tomb of Orestes, whose bones had been brought from Tegea to Sparta in accordance with the well-known tale in Herodotus. Near the tomb of Orestes was the statue of king Polydorus, whose effigy was used as the seal of the state. Here, also, was a Hermes Agoraeus bearing Dionysus as a child, and the old Ephoreia, where the Ephors originally administered justice, in which were the tombs of Epimenides the Cretan and of Aphareus the Aeolian king. (Paus. iii. 11. §§ 2—11.)

The Agora was near the Acropolis. Lycurgus, it is said, when attacked by his opponents, fled for refuge from the Agora to the Acropolis; but was overtaken by a fiery youth, who struck out one of his eyes. At the spot where he was wounded, Lycurgus founded a temple of Optiletis * or Ophthalmitis, which must have stood immediately above the Agora. Plutarch says that it lay within the temenos of the Brazen House; and Pausanias mentions it, in descending from the Acropolis, on the way to the so-called Alpium, beyond which was a temple of Ammon, and probably also a temple of Artemis Cnagia. (Plut. Lyc. 11; Apophth. Lac. p. 227, b.; Paus. iii. 18. § 2.) The Agora may be placed in the great hollow east of the Acropolis (Map, 2). Its position is most clearly marked by Pausanias, who, going westwards from the Agora, arrived immediately at the theatre, after passing only the tomb of Brasidas (iii. 14. § 1). The site of the theatre, which he describes as a magnificent building of white marble, has been already described.

The principal street, leading out of the Agora, was named Aphetais (Ἀφεταΐς), the Corso of Sparta (Map, dd). It ran towards the southern wall, through the most level part of the city, and was bordered by a succession of remarkable monuments. First came the house of king Polydorus, named Booneta (Βοώνητα), because the state purchased it from his widow for some oxen. Next came the office of the Bidiaei, who originally had the inspection of the race-course; and opposite was the temple of Athena Celeutheia, with a statue of the goddess dedicated by Ulysses, who erected three statues of Celeutheia in different places. Lower down the Aphetais occurred the heroa of Iops, Amphiaraus, and Lelex,—the sanctuary of Poseidon Taenarius,—a statue of Athena, dedicated by the Tarentini,—the place called Hellenium, so called because the Greeks are said to have held counsel there either before the Persian or the Trojan wars,—the tomb of Talthybius,—an altar of Apollo Acreitas,—a place sacred to the earth named Gaseptum,—a statue of Apollo Maleates,—and close to the city walls the temple of Dictynna, and the royal sepulchres of the Eurypontidae. Pausanias then returns to the Hellenium, probably to the other side of the Aphetais, where he mentions a sanctuary of Arsinoe, the sister of the wives of Castor and Pollux; then a temple of Artemis near the so-called Phruria (Φρούρια), which were perhaps the temporary fortifications thrown up before the completion of the city walls; next the tombs of the Iamidae, the Eleian prophets,— sanctuaries of Maro and Alpheius, who fell at Thermopylae,—the temple of Zeus Tropaeus, built by the Dorians after conquering the Achaean inhabitants of Laconia, and especially the Amyclaei,—the temple

* So called, because ὀπτίλοι was the Lacedaemonian form for ὀφθαλμοί, Plut. Lyc. 11.

of the mother of the gods,—and the heros of Hippolytus and Aulon. The Aphetais upon quitting the
city joined the great Hyacinthian road which led to
the Amyclaeum. (Paus. iii. 12. §§ 1—9.)

The next most important street leading from the
Agora ran in a south-easterly direction. It is
usually called Scias, though Pausanias gives this
name only to a building at the beginning of the
street, erected by Theodorus of Samos, and which
was used even in the time of Pausanias as a place
for the assemblies of the people. Near the Scias
was a round structure, said to have been built by
Epimenides, containing statues of the Olympian
Zeus and Aphrodite; next came the tombs of Cy-
nortas, Castor, Idas, and Lynceus, and a temple of
Core Soteira. The other buildings along this street
or in this direction, if there was no street, were the
temple of Apollo Carneius, who was worshipped
here before the Dorian invasion,—a statue of Apollo
Aphetaeus,—a quadrangular place surrounded with
colonnades, where small-wares (ρῶπος) were anciently sold,—an altar sacred to Zeus, Athena, and
the Dioscuri. all surnamed Ambulii. Opposite was
the place called Colona and the temple of Dionysus
Colonatas. Near the Colona was the temple of
Zeus Euanemus. On a neighbouring hill was the
temple of the Argive Hera, and the temple of Hera
Hypercheiria, containing an ancient wooden statue of
Aphrodite Hera. To the right of this hill was a
statue of Hetoemocles ,who had gained the victory in
the Olympic games. (Paus. iii. 12. § 10—iii. 13.)
Although Pausanias does not say that the Colona
was a hill, yet there can be no doubt of the fact, as
κολώνα is the Doric for κολώνη, a hill. This height
and the one upon which the temple of Hera stood
are evidently the heights NW. of the village of Psychikó between the Eurotas and the plain to the S.
of the theatre (Map, C.).

After describing the streets leading from the
Agora to the S. and SE. Pausanias next mentions a
third street, running westward from the Agora. It
led past the theatre to the royal sepulchres of the
Agiadae. In front of the theatre were the tombs of
Pausanias and Leonidas (iii. 14. § 1).

From the theatre Pausanias probably went by the
hollow way to the Eurotas, for he says that near the
Sepulchres of the Agiadae was the Lesche of the
Crotani, and that the Crotani were a portion of the
Pitanatae. It would appear from a passage in
Athenaeus (i. p. 31) that Pitane was in the neighbourhood of the Oenus; and its proximity to the
Eurotas has been already shown. [See above, p.
1026, a.] It is not improbable, as Curtius observes,
that Pitane lay partly within and partly without
the city, like the Cerameicus at Athens. After
proceeding to the tomb of Taenarus, and the sanctuaries of Poseidon Hippocurus and the Aeginetan
Artemis, Pausanias returns to the Lesche, near
which was the temple of Artemis Issoria, also called
Limnaea. Issorium, which is known as a stronghold
in the neighbourhood of Pitane (Polyaen. ii. 1. § 14;
Plut. Ages. 32), is supposed by Curtius to be the hill
to the north of the Acropolis (Map, C.). Leake, as we
have already seen, regards this hill as the Acropolis
itself, and identifies the Issorium with the height
above the ruined amphitheatre or circus. Pausanias next mentions the temples of Thetis, of
Demeter Chthonia, of Sarapis, and of the Olympian
Zeus. He then reached the Dromus, which was
used in his day as a place for running. It extended
along the stream southwards, and contained gym-

nasia, one of which was dedicated by a certain
Eurycles. The Roman amphitheatre and the sta-
dium, of which the remains have been already
described, were included in the Dromus. In the
Dromus was a statue of Hercules, near which, but
outside the Dromus, was the house of Menelaus.
The Dromus must have formed part of Pitane, as
Menelaus is called a Pitanatan. (Hesych. s. v.)
Proceeding from the Dromus occurred the temples
of the Dioscuri, of the Graces, of Eileithyia, of
Apollo Carneius, and of Artemis Hegemone; on the
right of the Dromus was a statue of Asclepius
Agnitas; at the beginning of the Dromus there
were statues of the Dioscuri Aphetarii; and a little
further the heroum of Alcon and the temple of
Poseidon Domatites. (Paus. iii. 14. §§ 2—7.)

South of the Dromus was a broader level, which
was called Platanistas, from the plane-trees with
which it was thickly planted. It is described as a
round island, formed by streams of running water,
and was entered by two bridges, on each of which
there was a statue of Hercules at one end and of
Lycurgus at the other. Two divisions of the Spartan
Ephebi were accustomed to cross these bridges and
fight with one another in the Platanistom; and,
though they had no arms, they frequently inflicted
severe wounds upon one another. (Paus. iii. 15. § 8,
seq.; Lucian, Anachars. 38; Cic. Tusc. Quaest. v.
27.) The running streams surrounding the Plataniston were the canals of the Trypiótiko, which were fed
by several springs in the neighbourhood, and flowed
into the Eurotas. Outside the city was the district
called Phoebaeum, where each division of the Ephebi
sacrificed the night before the contest. The Phoebaeum occupied the narrow corner south of the Plataniston formed by the Trypiótiko and the Eurotas.
Pausanias describes it as near Therapne, which was
situated upon the Menelaium, or group of hills
upon the other side of the Eurotas, mentioned below.
The proximity of the Phoebaeum to Therapne is
mentioned in another passage of Pausanias (iii. 19.
§ 20), and by Herodotus (vi. 61). The heroum of
Cynisca, the first female who conquered in the chariot-
race in the Olympic games, stood close to the Plataniston, which was bordered upon one side by a colonnade. Behind this colonnade there were several
heroic monuments, among which were those of Alci-
mus, Enaraephorus, of Dorceus, with the fountain
Dorceia, and of Sebrus. Near the latter was the
sepulchre of the poet Alcman; this was followed by
the sanctuary of Helena and that of Hercules, with
the monument of Oeonus, whose death he here avenged
by slaying the sons of Hippocoon. The temple of
Hercules was close to the city walls. (Paus. iii.
14. § 8—15. § 5.) Since the poet Alcman, whose
tomb was in this district, is described as a citizen of
Mesoa [Dict. of Biogr., art. ALCMAN], it is probable
that this was the position of Mesoa, the name of
which might indicate a tract lying between two rivers..
(Comp. Μεσηνή—ὑπὸ δύο ποταμῶν—μεσαζομένη,
Steph. B. s. v. Μεσσήνη.)

After reaching the SE. extremity of the city,
Pausanias returns to the Dromus. Here he mentions
two ways : the one to the right leading to a temple
of Athena Axiopoenus, and the other to the left to
another temple of Athena, founded by Theras, near
which was a temple of Hipposthenes, and an ancient
wooden statue of Enyalius in fetters. He then describes, but without giving any indication of its position, the painted Lesche, with its surrounding
heroa of Cadmus, Oeolycus, Aegeus, and Amphilo-

chus, and the temple of Hera Aegophagus. He afterwards returns to the theatre, and mentions the different monuments in its neighbourhood; among which were a temple of Poseidon Genethlius, heroa of Cleodaeus and Oebalus, a temple of Asclepius, near the Booneta, the most celebrated of all the temples of this god in Sparta, with the heroum of Teleclus on its left; on a height not far distant, an ancient temple of Aphrodite armed, upon an upper story of which was a second temple of Aphrodite Morpho; in its neighbourhood was a temple of Hilaeira and Phoebe, containing their statues, and an egg suspended from the roof, said to have been that of Leda. Pausanias next mentions a house, named Chiton, in which was woven the robe for the Amyclaean Apollo; and on the way towards the city gates the heroa of Cheilon and Athenaeus. Near the Chiton was the house of Phormion, who hospitably entertained the Dioscuri when they entered the city as strangers (Paus. iii. 15. § 6—16. § 4.) From these indications we may suppose that the Amyclaean road issued from this gate, and it may therefore be placed in the southern part of the city. In that case the double temple of Aphrodite probably stood upon one of the heights of New Sparta.

Pausanias next mentions a temple of Lycurgus; behind it the tomb of his son Eucosmus, and an altar of Lathria and Alexandra: opposite the temple were monuments of Theopompus and Eurybiades, and the heroum of Astrabacus. In the place called Limnaeum stood the temples of Artemis Orthia and Leto. This temple of Artemis Orthia was, as we have already remarked, the common place of meeting for the four villages of Pitane, Mesoa, Cynosura, and Limnae. (Paus. iii. 16. § 6, seq.) Limnae was partly in the city and partly in the suburbs. Its position to the N. of the Dromus has been mentioned above ; and, if an emendation in a passage of Strabo be correct, it also included a district on the left bank of the Eurotas, in the direction of Mt. Thornax (τὸ Λιμναῖον κατὰ τὸν [Θόρνα]κα, Meineke's emendation instead of [Θρᾷ]κα, Strab. viii. p. 364).

The most ancient topographical information respecting Sparta is contained in the answer of the Delphic oracle to Lycurgus. The oracle is reported to have directed the lawgiver to erect temples to Zeus and Athena, and to fix the seat of the senate and kings between the Babyca and Cnacion. (Plut. Lyc. 6.) These names were obsolete in the time of Plutarch. He says that the Cnacion was the Oenus, now the Kelefina; and he also appears to have considered the Babyca a river, though the text is not clear ; in that case the Babyca must be the Trypiótiko, which forms the southern boundary of the city. It appears, however, from the same passage of Plutarch, that Aristotle regarded the Babyca as a bridge, and only the Cnacion as a river; whence he would seem to have given the name of Cnacion to the Trypiótiko, and that of Babyca to the bridge over the Eurotas.

The left, or eastern bank of the Eurotas, was not occupied by any part of Sparta. When Epaminondas invaded Laconia in B. C. 370 he marched down the left bank of the Eurotas till he reached the foot of the bridge which led through the hollow way into the city. But he did not attempt to force the passage across the bridge; and he saw on the other side a body of armed men drawn up in the temple of Athena Alea. He therefore continued his march along the left bank of the river till he arrived opposite to Amyclae, where he crossed the river. (Xen. Hell.

vi. 5. § 27.) The account of Xenophon illustrates a passage of Pausanias. The latter writer, in describing (iii. 19. § 7) the road to Therapne, mentions a statue of Athena Alea as standing between the city and a temple of Zeus Plusius, above the right bank of the Eurotas, at the point where the river was crossed; and as only one bridge across the Eurotas is mentioned by ancient writers, there can be no doubt that the road to Therapne crossed the bridge which Xenophon speaks of, and the remains of which are still extant. Therapne stood upon the Menelaium or Mount Menelaius, which rose abruptly from the left hand of the river opposite the south-eastern extremity of Sparta. (Μενελάιον, Polyb. v. 22; Μενελάειον, Steph. B. s. v.; Menelaius Mons, Liv. xxxiv. 28.) The Menelaium has been compared to the Janiculum of Rome, and rises about 760 feet above the Eurotas. It derived its name from a temple of Menelaus, containing the tombs of Menelaus and Helen, whither solemn processions of men and women were accustomed to repair, the men imploring Menelaus to grant them bravery and success in war, the women invoking Helen to bestow beauty upon them and their children. (Paus. iii. 19. § 9; Herod. vi. 61; Isocr. Encom. Hel. 17; Hesych. s. v. Ἑλένια, Θεράπναι· τίδια.) The foundations of this temple were discovered in 1834 by Ross, who found amongst the ruins several small figures in clay, representing men in military costume and women in long robes, probably dedicatory offerings made by the poorer classes to Menelaus and Helen. (Ross, Wanderungen in Griechenland, vol. ii. p. 13, seq.) The temple of Menelaus is expressly said to have been situated in Therapne (Θεράπνη, Θεράπναι; Therapne, Plin. iv. 5. s. 8), which was one of the most ancient and venerable places in the middle valley of the Eurotas. It was said to have derived its name from a daughter of Lelex (Paus. iii. 19. § 9), and was the Achaean citadel of the district. It is described by the poets as the lofty well-towered Therapne, surrounded by thick woods (Pind. Isthm. i. 31; Coluth. 225), where slept the Dioscuri, the guardians of Sparta. (Pind. Nem. x. 55.) Here was the fountain of Messeïs, the water of which the captive women had to carry (Paus. iii. 20. § 1; Hom. Il. vi. 457); and it was probably upon this height that the temple of Menelaus stood, which excited the astonishment of Telemachus in the Odyssey. Hence Therapne is said to have been in Sparta, or is mentioned as synonymous with Sparta. (Θεράπναι, πόλις Λακωνική, ἥν τινες Σπάρτην φασίν, Steph. B. s. v.; ἐν Σπάρτῃ, Schol. ad Apoll. Rhod. ii. 162, Pind. Isthm. i. 31.) It is probable that further excavations upon this spot would bring to light some tombs of the heroic ages. The Phoebaeum, which has been already described as the open space on the right bank of the Eurotas [see p. 1028, b.], contained a temple of the Dioscuri. Not far from this place was the temple of Poseidon, surnamed Gaeaochus. (Paus. iii. 20. § 2.)

After the power of Sparta was destroyed by the battle of Leuctra, its territory was exposed to invasion and the city to attack. The first time that an enemy appeared before Sparta was when Epaminondas invaded Laconia in B. C. 390, as already related. After crossing the river opposite Amyclae, he marched against the city. His cavalry advanced as far as the temple of Poseidon Gaeaochus, which we have seen from Pausanias was in the Phoebaeum. We also learn from Xenophon that the Hippodrome was in the neighbourhood of the temple of Poseidon, and consequently must not be confounded with the Dromus. The Thebans did not advance further, for they were driven back by a body of picked hoplites, whom Agesilaus had placed in ambush in the sanctuary of the Tyndaridae (Dioscuri), which we likewise know from Pausanias was in the Phoebaeum. (Xen. *Hell.* vi. 5. §§ 31, 32.) In B. C. 362 Epaminondas made a daring attempt to surprise Sparta, and actually penetrated into the market-place; but the Spartans having received intelligence of his approach, the city had been put into a state of defence, and Epaminondas again withdrew without venturing upon an assault. (Xen. *Hell.* vii. 5. §§ 11—14; Polyb. ix. 8; Diod. xv. 83.) In B. C. 218 Philip unexpectedly entered Laconia, descended the vale of the Eurotas by the left bank of the river, passing by Sparta, and then laid waste the whole country as far as Taenarus and Malea. Lycurgus, the Spartan king, resolved to intercept him on his return: he occupied the heights of the Menelaium with a body of 2000 men, ordered the remaining forces of Sparta to be ready to take up their position between the city and the western bank of the river, and at the same time, by means of a dam, laid the low ground in that part under water.

Philip, however, contrary to the expectation of Lycurgus, stormed the Menelaium, and brought his whole army safely through the pass, and encamped two stadia above the city. (Polyb. v. 17—24.) In B. C. 195 Quinctius Flamininus attacked Sparta, because Nabis, the tyrant of the city, refused obedience to the terms which the Roman general imposed. With an army of 50,000 men Flamininus assaulted the city on its three undefended sides of Phoebaeum, Dictynnaeum, and Heptagoniae. He forced his way into the city, and after overcoming the resistance which he met with in the narrow ways at the entrance of the city, marched along the broad road (probably the Aphetais) leading to the citadel and the surrounding heights. Thereupon Nabis set fire to the buildings nearest to the city walls, which compelled the Romans to retreat. But the main object of Flamininus had been answered, for three days afterwards Nabis sent his son-in-law to implore peace. (Liv. xxxiv. 38, 39.) The position of the Phoebaeum has been already explained. The Dictynnaeum was so called from the temple of Artemis Dictynna, which Pausanias describes as situated at the end of the Aphetais, close to the walls of the city (iii. 12. § 8). Leake thinks that the name of the village of *Kalagoniá* may be a

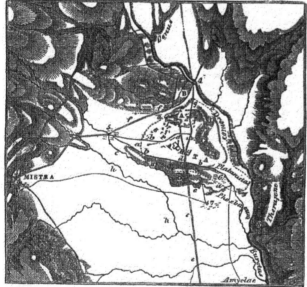

A. Acropolis.
B. M. Issorium.
C. Hill Colona.
D. New Sparta.
1. Theatre.
2. Agora.
3. Amphitheatre or Odeum.
4. Bridge across the Eurotas
5. Village of *Magúla.*
6. Village of *Psychikó.*
7. Village of *Kalagoniá.*

8. Temple of Menelaus.
a a a. Circuit of Walls.
b b. Canals.
c c. The Tiasa. River of *Trypiótiko* or *Magúla.*
d d. Street Aphetais.
e e. The Hyacinthian Road.
f f. Hollow Way leading from the Bridge of the Eurotas to *Magúla* and *Mistrá.*
g g. Modern Road.
h h. The *Pandeleimona.*

corruption of Heptagoniae; but it is more probable that the Heptagoniae lay further west in the direction of *Mistrá*, as it was evidently the object of Flamininus to attack the city in different quarters.

The small stream which encloses Sparta on the south, now called the *Trypiótiko* or river of *Magúla*, is probably the ancient Tiasa (Τίασα), upon which stood the sanctuary of Phaëna and Cleta, and across which was the road to Amyclae. (Paus. iii. 18. § 6.) Leake, however, gives the name of Tiasa to the *Pandeleímona*, the next torrent southwards falling into the Eurotas.

With respect to the gates of Sparta, the most important was the one opposite the bridge of the Eurotas: it was probably called the gate to Therapne. Livy mentions two others, one leading to the Messenian town of Pharae, and the other to Mount Barbosthenes (xxxv. 30). The former must have been upon the western side of the city, near the village of *Magúla*. Of the southern gates the most important was the one leading to Amyclae.

In this article it has not been attempted to give any account of the political history of Sparta, which forms a prominent part of Grecian history, and cannot be narrated in this work at sufficient length to be of any value to the student. A few remarks upon the subject are given under LACONIA.

The modern authority chiefly followed in drawing up the preceding account of the topography of Sparta is Curtius, *Peloponnesos*, vol. ii. p. 219, seq. Valuable information has also been derived from Leake, *Morea*, vol. i. p. 150, seq., *Peloponnesiaca*, p. 129, seq. See also Mure, *Tour in Greece*, vol. ii. p. 220, seq.; Ross, *Wanderungen in Griechenland*, vol. ii. p. 11, seq.; *Expédition scientifique de Morée*, vol. ii. p. 61, seq.; Boblaye, *Recherches, &c.*, p. 78, seq.; Beulé, *Etudes sur le Péloponèse*, p. 49, seq.

SPARTA'RIUS CAMPUS (Σπαρτάριον πεδίον, Strab. iii. p. 160), a district near Carthago Nova in Hispania Tarraconensis, 100 miles long and 30 broad, which produced the peculiar kind of grass called *spartum*, used for making ropes, mats, &c. (Plin. xix. 2. s. 8.) It is the *stipa tenacissima* of Linnaeus; and the Spaniards, by whom it is called *esparto*, still manufacture it for the same purposes as those described by Pliny. It is a thin wiry rush, which is cut and dried like hay, and then soaked in water and plaited. It is very strong and lasting, and the manufacture still employs a large number of women and children. It was no doubt the material of which the Iberian whips mentioned by Horace (*Epod.* iv. 3) were composed. (See Ford, *Handb. of Spain*, p. 168.) From this district Carthago Nova itself obtained the surname of "Spartaria." [T. H. D.]

SPARTO'LUS (Σπάρτωλος, Thuc. ii. 79, v. 18; Steph. B.), a town of the Chalcidic peninsula, at no great distance from Olynthus (Isaeus, *de Dicaeogen. Haered.* p. 55), under the walls of which the Athenian forces were routed, B. C. 249. It belonged to the Bottiaeans, and was perhaps their capital, and was of sufficient importance to be mentioned in the treaty between Sparta and Athens in the tenth year of the Peloponnesian War. [E.B.J.]

SPAUTA (Σπαῦτα), a lake in Media Atropatene, which is intensely salt, so as to cause the itch on the bodies of persons who have unwittingly bathed in it, with injury also to their clothes (Strab. xi. p. 523). Its present name is the *Sea of Urumiah*. Its earliest Armenian name is said to have been *Kaputan*, or *Kaputan Chow*, whence the Greek form would seem

to have been modified. (L. Ingigi, *Archaeol. Armen.* i. p. 160; St. Martin, *Mémoires*, i. p. 59.) It is probably the same as the Μαρτιανὴ λίμνη of Ptolemy (vi. 2. § 17). Many travellers have visited it in modern times. (Tavernier, i. ch. 4; Morier, *Sec. Voy.* ii. p. 179.)   [V.]

SPELAEUM, a place in Macedonia which Livy says was near Pella (xlv. 33).

SPELUNCA (*Sperlonga*), a place on the coast of Latium (in the more extended sense of that name), situated between Tarracina and Caieta. The emperor Tiberius had a villa there, which derived its name from a natural cave or grotto, in which the emperor used to dine, and where he on one occasion very nearly lost his life, by the falling in of the roof of the cavern (Tac. *Ann.* iv. 59; Suet. *Tib.* 39). The villa is not again mentioned, but it would appear that a village had grown up around it, as Pliny mentions it in describing the coast ("locus, Speluncas," Plin. iii. 5. s. 9), and its memory is still preserved by a village named *Sperlonga*, on a rocky point about 8 miles W. of *Gaëta*. Some Roman remains are still visible there, and the cave belonging to the Imperial villa may be identified by some remains of architectural decoration still attached to it (Craven's *Abruzzi*, vol. i. p. 73). [E. H. B.]

SPEOS ARTE'MIDOS, the present grottoes of *Beni-hassan*, was situated N. of Antinoe, in Middle Aegypt, on the eastern bank of the Nile, in lat. 27° 40′ N. The name is variously written: Peos in the Itinerary of Antoninus (p. 167, Wesseling); Pois in the Notitia Imperii; but Speos is probably the true form, implying an excavation (σπέος) in the rocks. Speos Artemidos was rediscovered by the French and Tuscan expedition into Aegypt early in the present century. It was constructed by some of the Pharaohs of the 18th dynasty in a desert-valley running into the chain of Arabian hills. The structure as a whole consists of a temple, and of between thirty and forty catacombs. The temple is dedicated to Pasht, Bubastis, the Artemis of the Greeks. (Herod. ii. 58.) The catacombs appear to have served as the general necropolis of the Hermopolite nome. For although Hermopolis and its district lay on the western bank of the Nile, yet as the eastern hills at this spot approach very closely to the stream, while the western hills recede from it, it was more convenient to ferry the dead over the river than to transport them across the sands. Some of these catacombs were appropriated to the mummies of animals, cats especially, which were worshipped by the Hermopolitans. In the general cemetery two of these catacombs merit particular attention : (1) the tomb of Neoopth, a military chief in the reign of Sesortasen I. and of his wife Rotei; (2) that of Amenheme, of nearly the same age, and of very similar construction. The tomb of Neoopth, or, as it is more usually denominated, of Rotei, has in front an architrave excavated from the rock, and supported by two columns, each 23 feet high, with sixteen fluted facelets. The columns have neither base nor capital; but between the architrave and the head of the column a square abacus is inserted. A denteled cornice runs over the architrave. The effect of the structure, although it is hardly detached from the rock, is light and graceful. The chamber or crypt is 30 feet square, and its roof is divided into three vaults by two architraves, each of which was originally supported by a single column, now vanished. The walls are painted in compartments of the most brilliant colours, and the

3 U 4

drawing is generally in the best style of Aegyptian art. They represent various events in the life of Neoopth. From the tomb of Rotei, indeed, might be compiled a very copious record of the domestic life of the Aegyptians. On its walls are depicted, among many others, the following subjects: the return of warriors with their captives; wrestlers; hunting wild beasts and deer; the Nile boats, including the *Bari* or high-prowed barge, and fisheries; granaries and flax-dressing; spinning and weaving; games with the lance, the ball, and the discus; and the rites of sepulture. The tomb of Amenheme is covered also with representations of men in various postures of wrestling; and the other grottoes are not less interesting for their portraitures of civil and domestic life. (Wilkinson, *Modern Egypt and Thebes*; Rosellini, *Mon. Civ.* vol. i.; Kenrick, *Anc. Egypt*, vol. i. p. 47, foll.)   [W.B.D.]

SPERCHEIUS (Σπερχειός: *Elládha*), a river in the S. of Thessaly, rising in Mount Tymphrestus (Strab. ix. p. 433), and flowing into the Maliac gulf. The Dryopes and Aenianes dwelt in the upper part of its course till it entered the plain of Malis, through which it flowed to the sea. In ancient times it joined the sea at Anticyra; and the rivers Dyras, Melas, and Asopus fell separately into the sea to the S. of the Spercheius. (Herod. vii. 198.) But the Spercheius has changed its course, and now falls into the sea much further south, about a mile from Thermopylae. The Dyras and Melas now unite their streams, and fall into the Spercheius, as does also the Asopus. [THERMOPYLAE.] Spercheius is celebrated in mythology as a river-god [*Dict. of Biogr. s. v.*], and is mentioned in connection with Achilles. (Hom. *Il.* xvii. 142.) Its name also frequently occurs in the other poets. (Aesch. *Pers.* 486; Sophocl. *Phil.* 722; Virg. *Georg.* ii. 488; Lucan, vi. 366.) (Leake, *Northern Greece*, vol. ii. pp. 8, 11, 15.)

SPERCHIAE, a place in Thessaly, which, according to the description of Livy (xxxii. 13), would seem to have been situated at no great distance from the sources of the Spercheius. Ptolemy (iii. 13. § 17) mentions a place Spercheia between Echinus and Thebes in Phthiotis; and Pliny (iv. 7. s. 13) places Sperchios in Doris. It is probable that these three names indicate the same place, but that its real position was unknown.

SPHACTE'RIA. [PYLUS.]
SPHAE'RIA. [CALAUREIA.]
SPHA'GIAE. [PYLUS.]
SPHENDALE. [ATTICA, p. 330, a.]
SPHENTZANIUM, a place in Dalmatia, SE. of the road from Scodra to Naissus. (Ann. Comn. 9. p. 252). Probably the modern *Pecciana*. [T. H. D.]
SPHETTUS. [ATTICA, p. 332, b.]
SPHI'NGIUM. [BOEOTIA, p. 412, a.]

SPINA (Σπίνα, Strab.; Σπίνα, Steph. B.: *Eth.* Σπινάτης and Σπινίτης), an ancient city of Italy, situated near the southernmost mouth of the Padus, within the limits of Gallia Cisalpina. It was, according to Dionysius, a Pelasgic settlement, and one of the most flourishing cities founded by that people in Italy, enjoying for a considerable time the dominion of the Adriatic, and deriving great wealth from its commercial relations, so that the citizens had a treasury at Delphi, which they adorned with costly offerings. They were subsequently expelled from their city by an overwhelming force of barbarians, and compelled to abandon Italy. (Dionys. i. 18, 28.) Strabo gives a similar account of the naval

greatness of Spina, as well as of its treasury at Delphi; but he calls it a Greek (Hellenic) city; and Scylax, who notices only Greek, or reputed Greek, cities, mentions Spina apparently as such. Its Greek origin is confirmed also by Justin, whose authority, however, is not worth much. (Strab. v. p. 214, ix. p. 421; Scyl. p. 6. § 19; Justin, xx. 1; Plin. iii. 16. s. 20.) But these authorities, as well as the fact that it had a treasury at Delphi, which is undoubtedly historical, seem to exclude the supposition that it was an Etruscan city, like the neighbouring Adria; and whatever be the foundation of the story of the old Pelasgic settlement, there seems no reason to doubt that it was really a Greek colony, though we have no account of the period of its establishment. Scylax alludes to it as still existing in his time: hence it is clear that the barbarians who are said by Dionysius to have driven out the inhabitants, can be no other than the neighbouring Gauls; and that the period of its destruction was not very long before the conquest of Cisalpine Gaul by the Romans. It does not appear to have ever been rebuilt or become a Roman town. Strabo speaks of it as in his time a mere village; and Pliny repeatedly alludes to it as a place no longer in existence. (Plin. iii. 16. s. 20, 17. s. 21; Strab. v. p. 214.) No subsequent trace of it is found, and its site has never been ascertained. We know, however, that it must have been situated on or near the southernmost arm of the Padus, which derived from it the name of SPINETICUM OSTIUM, and which probably corresponded with the modern *Po di Primaro*. [PADUS.] But the site of Spina must now be sought far from the sea: Strabo tells us that even in his time it was 90 stadia (11 miles) from the coast; though it was said to have been originally situated on the sea. It is probably now 4 or 5 miles further inland; but the changes which have taken place in the channels of the rivers, as well as the vast accumulations of alluvial soil, render it almost hopeless to look for its site.

Pliny tells us that the Spinetic branch of the Padus was the one which was otherwise called Eridanus; but it is probable that this was merely one of the attempts to connect the mythical Eridanus with the actual Padus, by applying its name to one particular branch of the existing river. It is, however, probable that the Spinetic channel was, in very early times, one of the principal mouths of the river, and much more considerable than it afterwards became. [PADUS.]   [E. H. B.]

SPINAE, a place in Britannia Romana, E. of Aquae Solis (*Bath*). (*Itin. Ant.* pp. 465, 486.) Now the village of *Spene* near *Newbury* in *Berkshire*, which has its name of *new* in regard to Spinae, the ancient borough. (Camden, p. 166.) [T. H. D.]

SPIRAEUM (Plin. iv. 5. s. 9) or SPEIRAEUM (Ptol. iii. 16. § 12), a promontory on the eastern coast of Peloponnesus upon the confines of the territories of Corinth and Epidaurus. For details, see Vol. I. p. 685, a.

SPOLE'TIUM (Σπωλήτιον: *Eth.* Spoletinus: *Spoleto*), a city of Umbria, situated between Interamna (*Terni*) and Trebia (*Trevi*), about 9 miles S. of the sources of the Clitumnus. Its name is not mentioned in history as an Umbrian town, nor have we any account of its existence previous to the establishment of the Roman colony, which was settled there in B. C. 240, just after the close of the First Punic War (Liv. *Epit.* xx.; Vell. Pat. i. 14). It was a Colonia Latina, and its name is repeatedly mentioned during the Second Punic War.

In B. C. 217, just after the battle at the Lake Trasimenus, Hannibal advanced to the gates of Spoletium, and made an assault upon the city, but was repulsed with so much vigour by the colonists, that he drew off his forces and crossed the Apennines into Picenum. (Liv. xxii. 9.) A few years later (B. C. 209) Spoletium was one of the colonies which distinguished themselves by their fidelity and zeal in the service of Rome, at the most trying moment of the war. (Id. xxvii. 10.) For some time after this we hear but little of Spoletium, though it seems to have been a flourishing municipal town. In B. C. 167 it was selected by the senate as the place of confinement of Gentius, king of Illyria, and his sons; but the citizens declined to take charge of them, and they were transferred to Iguvium (Liv. xlv. 43). But in the civil war between Marius and Sulla it suffered severely. A battle was fought beneath its walls in B. C. 82, between Pompeius and Crassus, the generals of Sulla, and Carrinas, the lieutenant of Carbo, in which the latter was defeated, and compelled to take refuge in the city. (Appian, B. C. i. 89.) After the victory of Sulla, Spoletium was one of the places severely punished, all its territory being confiscated, apparently for the settlement of a military colony. (Flor. iii. 21; Zumpt, de Colon. p. 254.) Florus calls Spoletium at this time one of the "municipia Italiae splendidissima;" but this is probably a rhetorical exaggeration. Cicero, however, terms it, in reference to a somewhat earlier period, "colonia Latina in primis firma et illustris." (Cic. pro Balb. 21.) It became a municipium (in common with the other Latin colonies) by virtue of the Lex Julia; and does not appear to have subsequently obtained the title of a colony, though it received a fresh accession of settlers. (Lib. Col. p. 225; Zumpt, l. c.) It is again mentioned during the Perusian War (B. C. 41), as affording a retreat to Munatius Plancus when he was defeated by Octavian (Appian, B. C. v. 33); and seems to have continued under the Empire to be a flourishing municipal town, though rarely mentioned in history. (Strab. v. p. 227; Plin. iii. 14. s. 19; Ptol. iii. 1. § 54; Orell. Inscr. 1100, 1103, 3966.) It was at or near Spoletium that the emperor Aemilianus was encamped, when the death of his rivals Gallus and Volusianus gave him temporary possession of the empire; and it was there also that he was himself put to death by his soldiers, after a reign of only three months. (Vict. Epit. 31.) Spoletium is again mentioned during the Gothic Wars, after the fall of the Western Empire, when it was taken by the Gothic king Totila (Procop. B. G. iii. 12), who partially destroyed its fortifications; but these were restored by Narses (Ib. iv. 33). It was at this time regarded as a strong fortress, and was a place of importance on that account. Under the Lombards it became the capital of a duchy (about A. D. 570), the dukes of which soon rendered themselves altogether independent of the Lombard kings, and established their authority over a considerable part of Central Italy. The duchy of Spoleto did not cease to exist till the 12th century.

Spoletium was not situated on the Via Flaminia, properly so called. That line of highroad proceeded from Narnia to Mevania (Bevagna) by a more direct course through Carsulae, thus leaving on the right hand the two important towns of Interamna and Spoletium. (Strab. v. p. 227.) We learn from Tacitus that this continued to be the line of the Flaminian Way as late as the time of Vespasian (Tac. Hist. iii. 60); but at a later period the road through Interamna and Spoletium came into general use, and is the one given in the Itineraries. (Itin. Ant. p. 125; Itin. Hier. p. 613.) This must have followed very nearly the same line with the modern road from Rome to Perugia, which crosses a steep mountain pass, called Monte Somma, between Spoleto and Terni; and this was probably the reason that this line was avoided in the first instance by the Via Flaminia. But there must always have been a branch road to Spoletium. and from thence, as we learn from Suetonius (Vesp. 1), another branch led to Nursia in the upper valley of the Nar.

Spoleto is still a tolerably flourishing place, with the rank of a city. It has several Roman remains, among which the most interesting is an arch commonly called the Porta d'Annibale, as being supposed to be the gate of the city from whence that general was repulsed. There is, however, no foundation for this: and it is doubtful whether the arch was a gateway at all. Some remains of an ancient theatre are still visible, and portions of two or three ancient temples are built into the walls of modern churches. A noble aqueduct, by which the city is still supplied with water, though often ascribed to the Romans, is not really earlier than the time of the Lombard dukes. Some remains of the palace inhabited by the latter, but first built by Theodoric, are also visible in the citadel which crowns the hill above the town.　　　　　　　　　　　[E. H. B.]

SPO'RADES (Σποράδες), or the "Scattered," a group of islands in the Aegaean, Cretan, and Carpathian seas, so called because they were scattered throughout these seas, in opposition to the Cyclades, which lay round Delos in a circle. But the distinction between these groups was not accurately observed, and we find several islands sometimes ascribed to the Cyclades, and sometimes to the Sporades. The islands usually included among the Cyclades are given under that article. [Vol. I. p. 723.] Scylax makes two groups of Cyclades; but his southern group, which he places off the coast of Laconia and near Crete, are the Sporades of other writers: in this southern group Scylax specifies. Melos, Cimolos, Oliaros, Sicinos, Thera, Anaphe, Astypalaea (p. 18, ed. Hudson). Strabo first mentions among the Sporades the islands lying off Crete,— Thera, Anaphe, Therasia, Ios, Sicinos, Lagusa, Pholegandros (x. pp. 484, 485). Then, after describing the Cyclades, he resumes his enumeration of the Sporades,—Amorgos, Lebinthos, Leria, Patmos, the Corassiae, Icaria. Astypalaea, Telos, Chalcia, Nisyros, Casos, the Calydnae (x. pp. 487— 489). Pliny (iv. 12. s. 23) gives a still longer list. An account of each island is given under its own name.

STABA'TIO, in Gallia, a name which occurs in the Table on a road from Vienna (Vienne) past Cularo (Grenoble) to the Alpis Cottia (Mont Genèvre). Stabatio is placed between Durotincum and Alpis Cottia. D'Anville fixed Stabatio at Monestier or Monetier near Briançon.　　　　　　　　　　[G. L.]

STA'BIAE (Στάβιαι: Eth. Stabianus; Ru. near Castell'a Mare), a city of Campania, situated at the foot of the Mons Lactarius, about 4 miles S. of Pompeii, and a mile from the sea. The first mention of it in history occurs during the Social War (B. C. 90), when it was taken by the Samnite general C. Papius (Appian, B. C. i. 42). But it was retaken by Sulla the following year (B. C. 89), and entirely destroyed

(Plin. iii. 5. s. 9). Nor was it ever restored, so as to resume the rank of a town; Pliny tells us that it was in his time a mere village, and the name is not mentioned by any of the other geographers. It is, however, incidentally noticed both by Ovid and Columella (Ovid. *Met.* xv. 711; Colum. *R. R.* x. 133), and seems to have been, in common with the whole coast of the *Bay of Naples*, a favourite locality for villas. Among others Pomponianus, the friend of the elder Pliny, had a villa there, where the great naturalist sought refuge during the celebrated eruption of Vesuvius in A. D. 79, and where he perished, suffocated by the cinders and sulphureous fumes (Plin. *Ep.* vi. 16). It is certain that Stabiae was on this occasion buried under the ashes and cinders of the volcano, though less completely than Pompeii and Herculaneum; but the site was again inhabited, and the name was retained throughout the period of the Roman Empire, though it appears to have never again risen into a place of any consideration. It was chiefly resorted to by invalids and others, on account of its neighbourhood to the Mons Lactarius, for the purpose of adopting a milk diet (Galen, *de Meth. Med.* v. 12; Cassiod. *Var.* xi. 10; Symmach. *Ep.* vi. 17). Its name is found also in the Tabula, and was preserved in that of *Castell 'a Mare di Stabia*, borne by the modern town. The Stabiae of the Lower Empire seems to have been situated *on* the coast, in the bight of the *Bay of Naples;* and probably did not occupy the same site with the older town, which seems to have been situated about a mile inland at the foot of the hill of *Gragnano.* The exact spot was forgotten till the remains were accidentally brought to light about 1750; and since that time excavations have been frequently made on the site, but the results are far less interesting than those of Pompeii and Herculaneum. They confirm the account of Pliny, by showing that there was no town on the spot, but merely a row of straggling villas, and these for the most part of an inferior class. They seem to have suffered severely from the earthquake of A. D. 63, which did so much damage to Pompeii also. (Swinburne's *Travels,* vol. i. p. 82.) [E. H. B.]

STA'BULA, in Gallia, is placed by the Antonine Itin. vi. from Cambes (*Gros Kembs*) and xviii. from Argentovaria (*Artzenheim*). These distances bring us to a place between *Otmarsheim* and *Bautzheim,* where Rhenanus, quoted by D'Anville, says that traces of an old place are found.

The word Stabula meant a station or resting place for travellers, a kind of inn, as we see from a passage of Ulpian (*Dig.* 47. tit. 5. s. 1): "qui naves, cauponas, stabula exercent;" and the men who kept these places were "Stabularii." [G. L.]

STA'BULUM, AD, in Gallia, is placed by the Antonine Itin. between Salsulae (*Salses*) and Summus Pyrenaeus, or the pass of the Pyrenees at *Bellegarde.* It is supposed to be *Le Boulu,* which looks like a part of the old name, on the left bank of the *Tech.* The distances in the Itin. both from Salsulae to Ad Stabulum, and from Ad Stabulum to Summus Pyrenaeus, are a great deal too much. The name, however, and the place *Le Boulu* on the *Tech* seem to fix the position of this Stabulum. [CENTURIONES, AD; STABULA.] [G. L.]

STA'BULUM DIOME'DIS (*Itin. Ant.* p. 331; *It. Hier.* p. 603), a place on the coast of Thrace, on the Via Egnatia, 18,000 paces, according to Itin. Ant., 12,000, according to It. Hier., from Porsula, or Maximianopolis; probably the same as Pliny (iv.

11. s. 18) calls Tirida: "Oppidum fuit Tirida, Dio medis equorum stabulis dirum." This Diomedes was king of the Bistones in Thrace, and was in the habit of throwing strangers to be devoured by his savage horses, till at length he himself was punished in the same way by Hercules. (Mela, ii. 2. § 8.) Lapie places it near the modern *Iassikeni.* [J. R.]

STA'BULUM NOVUM, a town probably of the Cosetani, in Hispania Tarraconensis. (*Itin. Ant.* p. 390.) Variously identified with *Villanueva de Sitges, Villanueva,* and *Solivela,* or *Sagarre.* [T. H. D.]

STACHIR (Στάχειρ, Ptol. iv. 6. §§ 7 and 8), a river on the W. coast of Libya Interior, which rose in Mount Ryssadium. Not far from its source it formed a lake named Clonia, and after flowing in a westerly direction, discharged itself into the Sinus Hesperius, to the SE. of the promontory of Ryssadium. It is probably the same river which Pliny (v. 1. s. 1) calls Salsus, and may be the modern *St. John* or *St. Antonio* river, also called *Rio de Guaon.* [T. H. D.]

STAGEIRA, STAGEIRUS (Στάγειρος, Herod. vii. 115; Thuc. iv. 88, v. 18; Strab. vii. p. 331, Fr. 33, 35; Στάγειρα, al. Στάγειρα, Ptol. iii. 13. § 10; Plin. iv. 17, xvi. 57), a town of Chalcidice in Macedonia, and a colony of Andros. The army of Xerxes, after passing through the plain of Syleus, passed through Stageirus to arrive at Acanthus. In the eighth year of the Peloponnesian War it surrendered to Brasidas, and two years afterwards was included in the treaty between Sparta and Athens. It was the birthplace of Aristotle. Alexander, from regard to his great teacher, restored this town, which with other Grecian colonies in that quarter had fallen into decay, when W. Thrace had become part of the Macedonian kingdom. (Plut. *Alex.* 7; Diog. Laert. v. § 4; Theophr. *H. P.* 102; Aelian, *V. H.* iii. 17.) But the improvement was not permanent, and no memorial of the birthplace of Aristotle remains, unless the coins inscribed 'Ορθαγορέων are of this place, as Eckhel (vol. ii. p. 73) supposed, on the authority of a fragment in the Geographi Minores (vol. iv. p. 42, ed. Hudson). Leake (*Northern Greece,* vol. iii. p. 168) has fixed the site at *Stavrós,* which he considers to be a contraction of the old name: it is almost presumption to differ with so great an authority in comparative geography; but it may be observed that the name *Stavrós* or "Cross" is common enough in Greece, and Mr. Bowen (*Mount Athos, &c.* p. 120, London, 1852) has shown, from a comparison with the passage in Herodotus (*l. c.*), that the traditional belief of the Macedonian peasants in identifying *Isboros* or *Nizoro,* as it is called by them, with Stageirus, rests upon satisfactory grounds. The position of this village, on the S. face of a wooded mountain which commands a view of Mt. Athos and the Aegean, is very much that of an Hellenic city, and there are vast substructions of Hellenic masonry all around. The Epitomiser of Strabo (vii. p. 331), who lived not long before the eleventh century, has a port and island called CAPRUS (Κάπρος) near Stageirus, which is probably the island of *Leftheridha* near *C. Marmári;* Leake (*l. c.*) prefers, in accordance with his views that *Stavrós* represents Stageirus, the port and island of *Lybtzádha.* [E. B. J.]

STAGNA VOLCARUM, on the coast of Gallia Narbonensis. Mela (ii. 5) speaks of the Stagna Volcarum, which he places W. of the Rhone. They are the long line of *étangs* between *Aigues-Morte* and *Agde*, separated from the land by a long, narrow, flat, which widens near *Cette*, where the Mons Setius is. These lagunes are the *E'tangs de Tau, de Frontignan, de Maguelone*, and others. Avienus (*Or. Marit.* 58) mentions the Taurus or *E'tang de Tau:*

"Taurum paludem namque gentiles vocant."

[FECTI JUGUM; LEDUS].　　　　　[G. L.]

STALIOCA'NUS PORTUS (Σ(τ)αλιοκανὸς Λιμήν). Ptolemy (ii. 8. § 2) places this port between Gobaeum Promontorium [GOBAEUM] and the mouth of the Tetus, on the coast of Gallia Lugdunensis. D'Anville (*Notice, &c.*) found in a manuscript plan of the *Anse du Conquet* the name of *Port Sliocan*, N. of *Cap Mahé*, at the bottom of the road of *Loo-Christ*. Lobineau in his *History of Bretagne* says that the name means White Tower, and that there were traces of a port there, constructed of brick and cement. Gosselin places the Staliocanus on the N. coast of *Bretagne*, at the outlet of the river on which *Morlaix* stands. It is impossible to determine which of the numerous bays on this irregular coast is Ptolemy's Staliocanus.　　[G. L.]

STANACUM, a place in Noricum, on the road leading along the Danube from Augusta Vindelicorum to Carnuntum and Vindobona. (*It. Ant.* p. 249; *Tab. Peut.*) Its exact site is uncertain. (Comp. Muchar, *Norikum*, i. p. 285.)　　[L. S.]

STATIELLI (Στατίελλοι), a tribe of Ligurians, who inhabited the northern slopes of the Apennines, on both sides of the valley of the *Bormida*. Their locality is clearly fixed by that of the town of Aquae Statiellae, now *Acqui*, which grew up under the Roman Empire from a mere watering place into a large and populous town, and the chief place of the surrounding district. The Statielli are mentioned by Livy in B. C. 173, as an independent tribe, who were attacked by the Roman consul, M. Popillius: after defeating them in the field, he attacked and took their city, which Livy calls Carystus, and, not content with disarming them, sold the captives as slaves. This proceeding was severely arraigned at Rome by the tribunes, especially on the ground that the Statielli had previously been uniformly faithful to the Roman alliance; but they did not succeed in enforcing reparation (Liv. xlii. 7, 8, 9, 21). Livy writes the name Statiellates, while Decimus Brutus, who crossed their territory on his march from Mutina, B. C. 44, and addresses one of his letters to Cicero from thence, dates it "finibus Statiellensium" (Cic. *ad Fam.* xi. 11). Pliny, who enumerates them among the tribes of Ligurians existing in his time, calls them Statielli, and their chief town Aquae Statiellorum (Plin. iii. 5. s. 7). The site of Carystus, mentioned only by Livy, in the passage above cited, is wholly unknown.　　[E. H. B.]

STATO'NIA (Στατωνία: Eth. Statoniensis), a town of Southern Etruria, which is mentioned by Strabo among the smaller towns (πολίχναι) in that part of Italy. (Strab. v. p. 226.) Pliny also mentions the Statones among the municipalities of Etruria (iii. 5. s. 8), but neither author affords any nearer clue to its situation. We learn, however, that it was celebrated for its wine, which was one of the most noted of those grown in Etruria (Plin. xiv. 6. s. 8), and that there were valuable stone-quarries in its territory. (Vitruv. ii. 7. § 3.) From the terms in which Vitruvius speaks of these, it seems probable that the district of Statonia, which he calls "praefectura Statoniensis," adjoined that of Tarquinii ; and both Pliny and Seneca allude to the

existence of a lake "in agro Statoniensi," in which there were floating islands. (Plin. ii. 95. s. 96; Senec. *N. Q.* iii. 25.) This can hardly be any other than the small *Lago di Mezzano*, a few miles W. of the more extensive *Lago di Bolsena*: we must therefore probably look for Statonia between this and Tarquinii. But within this space several sites have been indicated as possessing traces of ancient habitation; among others, *Farnese* and *Castro*, the last of which is regarded by Cluver as the site of Statonia, and has as plausible a claim as any other. But there is nothing really to decide the point. (Cluver, *Ital.* p. 517; Dennis's *Etruria*, vol. i. pp. 463 – 468.)　　　　[E. H. B.]

STATUAS (AD), the name of two places in Pannonia, one of which was situated on the Danube, a little to the west of Bregetio (*It. Ant.* p. 246; *Notit. Imp.*), and the other further southeast, in the neighbourhood of Alisca and Alta Ripa (*It. Ant.* p. 244), which Muchar (*Norikum*, i. p. 264) identifies with *Szekszard*.　　[L. S.]

STATUAS (AD), a town in the territory of the Contestani in Hispania Tarraconensis. (*Itin. Ant.* p. 400.) Variously identified with *Adsaneta* and *Xativa* or *S. Felipe*.　　[T. H. D.]

STAVANI (Σταυανοί, Ptol. iii. 5. § 25), a people in European Sarmatia, at the N. foot of Mons Bodinus. Ukert (iii. 2. § 435) conjectures that we should read Στλαυανοι, that is, Slavi, and seeks them on the *Duná* and the *Ilmensee*.　　[T. H. D.]

STECTO'RIUM (Στεκτόριον: Eth. Στεκτορηνός), a town of Phrygia, between Peltae and Synnada. (Ptol. v. 2. § 25; Paus x. 27. § 1.) Kiepert (in Franz's *Fünf Inschriften*, p. 36) identifies it with the modern *Afijum Karahissar*. (Comp. Sestini, *Num. Vet.* p. 126.)　　[L. S.]

STEI'RIA. [ATTICA, p. 332, a.]

STELAE (Στήλαι, Steph. B. s. v.), a Cretan city which is described by the Byzantine geographer as being near two towns, which are called, in the published editions of his work, Paraesus and Rhithymna. In Mr. Pashley's map the site is fixed at the Mohammedan village of *Philippo* on the route from *Kasteliana* (Inatus) to *Haghias Dhéka* (Gortyna).　　[E. B. J.]

STELLA'TIS CAMPUS was the name given to a part of the rich plain of Campania, the limits of which cannot be clearly determined, but which appears to have adjoined the "Falernus ager," and to have been situated likewise to the N. of the Vulturnus. Livy mentions it more than once during the wars of the Romans with the Samnites (ix. 44, x. 31), and again during the Second Punic War, when Hannibal found himself there by an error of his guides (Liv. xxii. 13). From his expressions it would appear to have adjoined the "Calenus ager," and apparently was the part of the plain lying between Cales and the Vulturnus. It was a part of the public lands of the Roman people, which the tribune Rullus proposed by his agrarian law to parcel out among the poorer citizens (Cic. *de Leg. Agr.* i. 7. ii. 31): this was for the time successfully opposed by Cicero, but the measure was carried into effect a few years later by the agrarian law of Caesar, passed in his consulship, B. C. 59 (Suet. *Caes.* 20). The statement of Suetonius that the district thus named was previously regarded by the Romans as consecrated, is clearly negatived by the language of Cicero in the passages just referred to. The name of Stellatinus Ager seems to have been given to a district in quite another part of Italy, forming a part of the territory of Capena in southern Etruria. It was from this district that the Stellatine tribe derived its name (Fest. *s. v. Stellatina*).   [E. H. B.]

STENA, a station in Macedonia, on the road from Tauriana (*Doïrán*) to Stobi (*Peut. Tab.*), which is evidently the pass now called *Demir kapi*, or " Iron Gate," where the river Axius is closely bordered by perpendicular rocks, which in one place have been excavated for the road (Leake, *Northern Greece*, vol. iii. p. 442.)   [E. B. J.]

STE'NTORIS LACUS (Στεντορὶς λίμνη, Herod. vii. 58; Acropol. p. 64), a lake on the south-east coast of Thrace, formed by the Hebrus, and opening into the Aegean near the town of Aenos. Pliny (iv. 11. s. 18) incorrectly places on it a STENTORIS PORTUS; and Mannert conjectures that perhaps the right reading in Herodotus (*l. c.*) is λιμένα, not λίμνην.   [J. R.]

STENUS, a river of Thrace, mentioned by Mela only (ii. 2. § 8) as near Maronea, on the south coast. The name is probably corrupt, as it occurs in the MSS. in a great variety of forms,—Stenos, Stonos, Schoenus, Scenus, Sithenos, &c. (See Tzschucke, *ad loc.*).   [J.R.]

STENYCLA'RUS (Στενύκλαρος, Στενύκληρος: *Eth.* Στενυκλήριος), a town in the north of Messenia, and the capital of the Dorian conquerors, built by Cresphontes. Andania had been the ancient capital of the country. (Paus. iv. 3. § 7; Strab. viii. p. 361.) The town afterwards ceased to exist, but its name was given to the northern of the two Messenian plains. (Paus. iv. 33. § 4, iv. 15. § 8; Herod. ix. 64.) [MESSENIA, p. 341.]

STEPHANAPHANA, more correctly, perhaps, Stephani Fanum, a place in Illyris Graeca, on the Via Egnatia (*Itin. Hieros.* p. 608). It was the castle of St. Stephen (τοῦ ἁγίου Στεφάνου), repaired by Justinian. (Procop. *de Aed.* iv. 4.) Lapie places it on the river *Boscovitza*.   [T. H. D.]

STEPHANE (Στεφάνη), a small port town on the coast of Paphlagonia, according to Arrian (*Peripl. P. E.* p. 15) 180 stadia east of Cimolis, but according to Marcian (p. 72) only 150. The place was mentioned as early as the time of Hecataeus as a town of the Mariandyni (Steph. B. *s. v.* Στεφανίς), under the name of Stephanis. (Comp. Scylax, p. 34; Ptol. v. 4. § 2.) The modern village of *Stephanio* or *Estifan* probably occupies the site of the ancient Stephane.   [L. S.]

STEREO'NTIUM (Στερεόντιον), a town in North-western Germany, probably in the country of the Bructeri or Marsi, the exact site of which cannot be ascertained. (Ptol. ii. 11. § 27.)   [L. S.]

STIPHANE (Στιφάνη), a lake in the north-western part of Pontus, in the district called Phazemonitis. The lake was extensive and abounded in fish, and its shores afforded excellent pasture (Strab. xii. p. 560.) Its modern name is *Boghas Kieui Ghieul.* (Hamilton, *Researches*, i. p. 336. foll.)   [L. S.]

STI'RIA. [ATTICA, p. 332, a.]

STIRIS (Στίρις: *Eth.* Στιρίτης), a town of Phocis situated 120 stadia from Chaeroneia, the road between the two places running across the mountains. The inhabitants of Stiris claimed descent from an Athenian colony of the Attic demus of Steiria, led by Peteus, when he was driven out of Attica by Aegeus. Pausanias describes the city as situated upon a rocky summit, with only a few wells, which did not supply water fit for drinking, which the inhabitants obtained from a fountain, four stadia below the city,

to which fountain there was a descent excavated among the rocks. The city contained in the time of Pausanias a temple of Artemis Stiritis, made of crude brick, containing two statues, one of Pentelic marble, the other of ancient workmanship, covered with bandages. (Paus. x. 35. §§ 8—10.) Stiris was one of the Phocian cities destroyed by Philip at the close of the Sacred War (Paus. x. 3. § 2); but it was afterwards rebuilt and was inhabited at the time of the visit of Pausanias. The ruins of Stiris, now called *Paleá khora*, are situated upon a tabular height defended by precipitous rocks, about a quarter of an hour's ride from the monastery of St. Luke. The summit is surrounded with a wall of loose construction, and the surface of the rock within the inclosure is excavated in many places for habitations. The fountain of water described by Pausanias is probably the copious source within the walls of the monastery issuing from the side of the hill. This fountain is mentioned in an inscription fixed in the outer wall of the church. (Leake, *Northern Greece*, vol. ii. p. 528, seq.)

STLUPI or STLUPPI (Στλοῦπι, Στλοῦπποι, Ptol. ii. 16. (17.) § 9), a place in Liburnia. The inhabitants are called Stlupini by Pliny (iii. 21. s. 25). Perhaps the present *Sluni.*   [T. H. D.]

STOBI (Στόβοι, Strab. vii. p. 329, *Fr.* 4, viii. p. 389; Ptol. iii. 13. § 4; Liv. xxxiii. 19, xxxix. 59, xl. 21, xlv. 29; Plin. iv. 17), a town in the NW. of Paeonia in Macedonia, which appears to have been a place of some importance under the Macedonian kings, although probably it had been greatly reduced by the incursions of the Dardani, when Philip had an intention of founding a new city near it in memory of a victory over these troublesome neighbours, and which he proposed to call Perseis, in honour of his son. At the Roman conquest, Stobi was made the place of deposit of salt, for the supply of the Dardani, the monopoly of which was given to the Third Macedonia. In the time of Pliny (*l. c.*) Stobi was a municipal town, but probably as late as the time of Heliogabalus it was made a " colonia." When about A. D. 400 Macedonia was under a " consular," Stobi became the chief town of Macedonia II or Salutaris (Marquardt, in *Becker's Röm. Alter.* vol. iii. pt. i. p. 118). According to the Tabular Itinerary it stood 47 M. P. from Heraclea of Lyncus, which was in the Via Egnatia, and 55 M. P. from Tauriana, and was therefore probably in the direct road from Heraclea to Serdica. The position must have been therefore on the Erigon, 10 or 12 miles above the junction of that river with the Axius, a situation which agrees with that of Livy, who describes it as belonging to Deuriopus of Paeonia, which was watered by the Erigon. Stobi was a point from which four roads issued. (*Peut. Tab.*) One proceeded NW. to Scupi, and from thence to Naissus on the great SE. route from Viminacium on the Danube to Byzantium; the second NE. to Serdica, 100 M. P. SE. of Naissus on the same route; the third SE. to Thessalonica; and the fourth SW. to Heraclea, the last forming a communication with that central point on the Via Egnatia leading through Stobi from all the places on the three former routes. In A. D. 479 Stobi was captured by Theodoric the Ostrogoth (Malch. Philadelph. *Exc. de Leg. Rom.* pp. 78—86, *ap. Müller, Fragm. Hist. Graec.* vol. iv. p. 125); and in the Bulgarian campaign of A. D. 1014, it was occupied by Basil II. and the Byzantine army (Στόπειον, Cedren. p. 709). The geography of the basin of the Erigon in which Stobi was situated is so imperfectly known that there is a difficulty in identifying its site: in Kiepert's map (*Europäische Turkei*) the ruins of Stobi are marked to the W. of *Demírkapí*, or the pass of the " Iron Gate." (Leake, *Northern Greece*, vol. iii. pp. 306, 440.) [E. B. J.]

STOBORRUM PROM. (Στόβορρον ἄκρον, Ptol. iv. 3. § 5), a headland of Numidia, between the promontory of Hippus and the town of Aphrodisium, at the E. point of the Sinus Olchacites. Now *Cap Ferro* or *Ras Hadid*. [T. H. D.]

STOE'CHADES (αἱ Στοιχάδες νῆσοι) or STI'-CHADES, on the S. coast of Gallia. Strabo (iv. p. 184) speaks of the Stoechades islands lying off the coast of Narbonensis, five in number, three larger and two smaller. They were occupied by the Massaliots. Steph. B. (*s. v.* Στοιχάδες) says, " islands near Massalia; and they are also named Ligystides." Ptolemy (ii. 10. § 21) also mentions five islands Stoechades, which he places in the meridian of the Citharistes Promontorium [CITHARISTES].

Pliny (iii. 5) mentions only three Stoechades, which he says were so named from being in a line (στοῖχος), and he gives to them the Greek names respectively Prote, Mese or Pomponiana, and Hypaea. These must be the islands now named *Isles d'Hières*, of which the most westerly is *Porqueroles*, the central is *Portcroz*, and the most easterly is *l'Isle du Levant* or *du Titan*, opposite to the town of *Hières*, in the department of *Var*. These islands are mere barren rocks. Besides the three larger islands, which have been enumerated, there are two others at least, mere rocks, *l'Esquillade* and *Bagneau*, which make up the number of five. Coral was got in the sea about the Stoechades (Plin. xxxii. 3), and is still got on this part of the French coast.

Agathemerus (*Geog. Min.* ii. p. 13, ed. Hudson) places the Stoechades along the coast which was occupied by the settlements of the Massaliots; but he fixes the two small Stoechades near Massilia. These are the two dismal rocks named *Ratoneau* and *Pomègue* which are seen as soon as you get out of the port of *Marseille*, with some still smaller rocks near them [MASSILIA, p. 292], one of which contains the small fort named *Château d'If*.

The Stoechades still belonged to the Massaliots in Tacitus' time (*Hist.* iii. 43). The Romans who were exiled from Rome sometimes went to Massilia, as L. Scipio Asiaticus did; if he did not go to the Stoechades as the Scholiast says (Cic. *pro Sest.* c. 3); but the Roman must have found the Stoechades a dull place to live in. When Lucan (iii. 516) says " Stoechados arva," he uses a poetic license; and Ammianus (xv. 11) as usual in his geography blunders when he places the Stoechades about Nicaea and Antipolis (*Nizza, Antibes*). [G. L.]

STOENI. [EUGANEI.]

STOMA, AD, a place in Moesia on the Southernmost arm of the Danube. (*Tab. Peut.*; Geogr. Rav. iv. 5.) Mannert (vii. p. 123) places it by the modern *Zof*. [T. H. D.]

STOMALIMNE. [FOSSA MARIANA.]

STRADELA, a town of Palestine mentioned only in the Itinerarium Hierosolymitanum as x. M.P. from Maximianopolis, and xii. M.P. from Sciopolis (i. e. Scythopolis), and identified by the writer with the place where Ahab abode and Elias prophesied, and —by a strange confusion—where David slew Goliath (p. 586, ed. Wesseling). The name is undoubtedly a corruption of Esdraela, the classical form of the Scriptural Jezreel. [ESDRAELA.] [G. W.]

STRA'GONA (Στραγόνα), a town in the south-

eastern part of Germany, either in the country of the Silingae or in that of the Diduni, on the northern slope of Mons Asciburgius. (Ptol. ii. 11. § 28.) If the resemblance of names be a safe guide, we might identify it with *Strigau*, though this hardly agrees with the degrees in which it is placed by Ptolemy; whence others suppose it to have been situated at *Strehlen*, between *Schweidnitz* and *Brieg*. [L. S.]

STRAPELLUM. [APULIA, p. 167.]

STRA'TIA. [ENISPE.]

STRATONI'CE (Στρατονίκη, Ptol. iii. 13. § 11), a town of Chalcidice in Macedonia, which Ptolemy places on the Singitic gulf. Leake (*Northern Greece*, vol. iii. p. 160) considers that there is here the same mistake as in the case of Acanthus [ACANTHUS], and refers it to the Hellenic remains on the coast of the Strymonic gulf in the confined valley of *Stratóni*. [E.B.J.]

STRATONICEIA (Στρατονίκεια or Στρατονίκη, Ptol. v. 2. § 20: *Eth.* Στρατονικεύς), one of the most important towns in the interior of Caria, was situated on the south-east of Mylasa, and on the south of the river Marsyas. It appears to have been founded by Antiochus Soter, who named it after his wife Stratonice. (Strab. xiv. p. 660; Steph. B. *s. v.*) The subsequent Syro-Macedonian kings adorned the town with splendid and costly buildings. At a later time it was ceded to the Rhodians. (Liv. xxxiii. 18, 30.) Mithridates of Pontus resided for some time at Stratoniceia, and married the daughter of one of its principal citizens. (Appian, *Mithr.* 20.) Some time after this it was besieged by Labienus, and the brave resistance it offered to him entitled it to the gratitude of Augustus and the Senate (Tac. *Ann.* iii. 62; Dion Cass. xlviii. 26). The emperor Hadrian is said to have taken this town under his special protection, and to have changed its name into Hadrianopolis (Steph. B. *l. c.*), a name, however, which does not appear to have ever come into use. Pliny (v. 29) enumerates it among free cities in Asia. Near the town was the temple of Zeus Chrysaoreus, at which the confederate towns of Caria held their meetings ; at these meetings the several states had votes in proportion to the number of towns they possessed. The Stratoniceans, though not of Carian origin, were admitted into the confederacy, because they possessed certain small towns or villages, which formed part of it. Menippus, surnamed Catochas, according to Cicero (*Brut.* 91) one of the most distinguished orators of his time, was a native of Stratoniceia. Stephanus B. (*s v.* Ἰδριάς) mentions a town of Idrias in Caria, which had previously been called Chrysaoris; and as Herodotus (v. 118) makes the river Marsyas, on whose banks stood the white pillars at which the Carians held their national meetings, flow from a district called Idrias, it is very probable that Antiochus Soter built the new city of Stratoniceia upon the site of Idrias. (Leake, *Asia Minor*, p. 235.) *Eskihissar*, which now occupies the place of Stratoniceia, is only a small village, the whole neighbourhood of which is strewed with marble fragments, while some shafts of columns are standing single. In the side of a hill is a theatre, with the seats remaining, and ruins of the proscenium, among which are pedestals of statues, some of which contain inscriptions. Outside the village there are broken arches, with pieces of massive wall and marble coffins. (Chandler, *Travels in Asia Minor*, p. 240; Leake, *Asia Minor*, p. 229; Fellows, *Asia Minor*,

p. 254, foll., *Lycia*, p. 80, foll.; Sestini, *Num. Vet.*
p. 90.)   [L. S.]

STRATO'NIS INSULA, an island in the Arabian gulf between the harbour Elaea and the harbour Saba. (Strab. xvi. p. 770; Plin. vi. 29. s. 34.)

STRATONIS TURRIS. [CAESAREIA, No. 4, p. 470.]

STRATUS (Στράτος: *Eth.* Στράτιος: its territory ἡ Στρατική: *Surovigli*), the chief town of Acarnania, was situated in the interior of the country, in a fertile plain on the right bank of the Achelous. It commanded the principal approaches to the plain from the northward, and was thus a place of great military importance. Strabo (x. p. 450) places it 200 stadia from the mouth of the Achelous by the course of the river. At the distance of 80 stadia S. of the town the river Anapus flowed into the Achelous; and 5 Roman miles to its N., the Achelous received another tributary stream, named Petitaurus. (Thuc. ii. 82; Liv. xliii. 22.) Stratus joined the Athenian alliance, with most of the other Acarnanian towns, at the commencement of the Peloponnesian War. In B.C. 429 it was attacked by the Ambraciots, with a number of barbarian auxiliaries, aided by some Peloponnesian troops, under the command of Cnemus; but they were defeated under the walls of Stratus, and obliged to retire. Thucydides describes Stratus at that time as the chief town of Acarnania, which it is also called by Xenophon in his account of the expedition of Agesilaus into this country. (Thuc. ii. 80, seq., iii. 106; Xen. *Hell.* iv. 6.) When the Aetolians extended their dominions, Stratus fell into the hands of this people, whence it is called by Livy a town of Aetolia. It is frequently mentioned during the Macedonian and Roman wars. Neither Philip V. nor his successor Perseus was able to wrest the town from the Aetolians; and it remained in the power of the latter till their defeat by the Romans, who restored it to Acarnania, together with the other towns, which the Aetolians had taken from the Acarnanians. (Polyb. iv. 63, v. 6, 7, 13, 14, 96; Liv. xxxvi. 11, xliii. 21, 22.) Livy (xliii. 21) gives an erroneous description of the position of Stratus when he says that it is situated above the Ambracian gulf, near the river Inachus.

There are considerable remains of Stratus at the modern village of *Surovigli*. The entire circuit of the city was about 2½ miles. The eastern wall followed the bank of the river. Leake discovered the remains of a theatre situated in a hollow: its interior diameter below is 105 feet, and there seem to have been about 30 rows of seats. (Leake, *Northern Greece*, vol. i. p. 137, seq.)

STRAVIA'NAE or STRAVIA'NA, a town in Lower Pannonia, on the road from Siscia to Mursa, of which the exact site has not been ascertained. (*It. Ant.* p. 265, where it appears in the ablat. form Stavianis.)   [L. S.]

STRENUS (Στρῆνος: *Eth.* Στρήνιος), a town of Crete, which Stephanus of Byzantium (*s. v.*) mentions on the authority of Herodian (others read Herodotus), but no further notice is found of it either in Herodotus or any other author. [E. B. J.]

STREVINTA (Στρεουίντα), a place in the southeast of Germany, near Mons Asciburgius, of uncertain site. (Ptol. ii. 11. § 29.)   [L. S.]

STRO'BILUS (Στρόβιλος), a peak of mount Caucasus, to which, according to the legend, Prometheus had been fastened by Hephaestus. (Arrian, *Peripl. P. E.* p. 12.)   [L. S.]

STRO'NGYLE. [AEOLIAE INSULAE.]

STRO'NGYLUS. [SEMIRAMIDIS MONS.]

STRO'PHADES (Στροφάδες: *Eth.* Στροφαδεύς: *Strofadia* and *Strivali*), formerly called Plotae (Πλωταί), two small islands in the Ionian sea, about 35 miles S. of Zacynthus, and 400 stadia distant from Cyparissia in Messenia, to which city they belonged. The sons of Boreas pursued the Harpies to these islands, which were called the "Turning" islands, because the Boreadae here returned from the pursuit. (Strab. viii. p. 359; Ptol. iii. 16. § 23; Steph. B. *s. v.*; Plin. iv. 12. s. 19; Mela, ii. 7; Apoll. Rhod. ii. 296; Apollod. i. 9. § 21; Virg. *Aen.* iii. 210; *It. Ant.* p. 523.)

STRUCHATES (Στρούχατες), one of the six tribes into which Herodotus divides the ancient inhabitants of Media. (Herod. i. 101.)   [V.]

STRUTHUS. [HERMIONE.]

STRYME (Στρύμη), a town on the S. coast of Thrace, a little to the W. of Mesembria, between which and Stryme flowed the small river Lissus, which the army of Xerxes is said to have drunk dry. (Herod. vii. 108.) Stryme was a colony of Thasos; but disputes seem to have arisen respecting it between the Thasii and the people of the neighbouring city of Maroneia. (Philip. *ap. Demos.* p. 163, R.)   [J. R.]

STRYMON (Στρυμών, Ptol. iii. 13. § 18), the largest river of Macedonia, after the Axius, and, before the time of Philip, the ancient boundary of that country towards the E. It rises in Mount Scomius near Pantalia (the present *Gustendil*) (Thuc. ii. 96), and, taking first an E. and then a SE. course, flows through the whole of Macedonia. It then enters the lake of Prasias, or Cercinitis, and shortly after its exit from it, near the town of Amphipolis, falls into the Strymonic gulf. Pliny, with less correctness, places its sources in the Haemus (iv. 10. s. 12). The importance of the Strymon is rather magnified in the ancient accounts of it, from the circumstance of Amphipolis being seated near its mouth; and it is navigable only a few miles from that town. Apollodorus (ii. 5. 10) has a legend that Hercules rendered the upper course of the river shallow by casting stones into it, it having been previously navigable much farther. Its banks were much frequented by cranes (Juv. xiii. 167; Virg. *Aen.* x. 269; Mart. ix. 308). The Strymon is frequently alluded to in the classics. (Comp. Hesiod. *Theog.* 339; Aesch. *Suppl.* 258, *Agam.* 192; Herod. vii. 75; Thuc. i. 200; Strab. vii. p. 323; Mela. ii. 2; Liv. xliv. 44. &c.) Its present name is *Struma*, but the Turks call it *Karasu*. (Comp. Leake, *North. Gr.* iii. pp. 225, 465, &c.)   [T. H. D.]

STRYMO'NICUS SINUS (Στρυμονικὸς κόλπος, Strab. vii. p. 330), a bay lying between Macedonia and Thrace, on the E. side of the peninsula of Chalcidice (Ptol. iii. 13. § 9). It derived its name from the river Strymon, which fell into it. Now the gulf of *Rendina*.   [T. H. D.]

STRYMO'NII (Στρυμόνιοι), the name by which, according to tradition, the Bithynians in Asia originally were called, because they had immigrated into Asia from the country about the Strymon in Europe. (Herod. vii. 75; Steph. B. *s. v.* Στρυμών.) Pliny (v. 40) further states that Bithynia was called by some Strymonia.   [L. S.]

STUBERA. [STYMBARA.]

STU'CCIA (Στουκκία, Ptol. ii. 3. § 3), a small river on the W. coast of Britain, identified by Camden (p. 772) with the *Ystwyth* in *Cardiganshire*.   [T. H. D.]

STURA (*Stura*), a river of Northern Italy, one of the confluents of the Padus (Plin. iii. 16. s. 20), which joins that river a few miles below *Turin* (Augusta Taurinorum), within a few miles of the Duria Minor or *Dora Riparia*. It still retains its ancient name and is a considerable stream, rising in the glaciers of the Alps, between the *Roche Melon* and *Mont Iseran*. [E. H. B.]

STURA (Στουρά), a small place in Pattalene, near the mouths of the Indus, mentioned by Arrian (*Ind.* c. 4). [V.]

STURIUM INSULA. [PHILA].

STU'RNIUM (Στούρνοι: *Eth.* Sturninus: *Sternaccio*), a town of Calabria, mentioned both by Pliny and Ptolemy among the municipal towns of that region. (Plin. iii. 11. s. 16; Ptol. iii. 1. § 77.) Its name is not otherwise known, but it is supposed to be represented by the modern village of *Sternaccio*, about 10 miles S. of *Lecce* (Lupiae) and a short distance NE. of *Soleto* (Soletum). (Cluver. *Ital.* p. 1231; Romanelli, vol. ii. p. 114.) There exist coins with the inscription ΣΤΤ, and types resembling those of the Tarentines, which are ascribed to Sturnium. [E. H. B.]

STYLLA'NGIUM (Στυλλάγγιον, Polyb. iv. 77, 80; Στυλλάγιον, Steph. B. s. v.: *Eth.* Στυλλάγιος, Στυλλαγιεύς), a town of Triphylia in Elis of uncertain site, which surrendered to Philip in the Social War.

STY'MBARA (Στύμβαρα, Strab. vii. p. 327; Στυβέρρα, Polyb. xxviii. 8. § 8; Stubera, Liv. xxxi. 39, xliii. 20, 22), a town on the frontier of regal Macedonia, which is by some assigned to Deuriopus, and by others to Pelagonia, which in the campaign of B. C. 400 was the third encampment of the consul Sulpicius; it must be looked for in the basin of the Erigon. (Leake, *Northern Greece*, vol. iii. p. 306.) [E. B. J.]

STYMPHA'LIS, a district annexed by the Romans, along with Atintania and Elimiotis, to Macedonia upon the conquest of this kingdom, A.D. 168. (Liv. xlv. 30.) From the mention of this district along with Atintania and Elimiotis, which were portions of Epeirus upon the borders of Thessaly, it would appear that Stymphalis is only another form of the more common name Tymphalis or Tymphaea; though, it is true, as Cramer has observed, that Diodorus has mentioned Stymphalia (Diod. xx. 28), and Callimachus speaks of the Stymphalian oxen in that territory (*Hymn. in Dian.* 179). Ptolemy (iii. 13. § 43) likewise mentions a town Gyrtona in Stymphalia, but in this passage other MSS. read Tymphalia. (Cramer, *Ancient Greece*, vol. i. p. 198.)

STYMPHA'LUS (Στύμφαλος, Στύμφηλος, Paus. et alii; τὸ Στύμφηλον, Schol. *ad Pind. Ol.* vi. 129; Stymphalum, Plin. iv. 6. s. 10; Stymphala, Lucret. v. 31: *Eth.* Στυμφάλιος, Στυμφήλιος), the name of a town, district, mountain, and river in the NE. of Arcadia. The territory of Stymphalus is a plain, about six miles in length, bounded by Achaia on the N., Sicyonia and Phliasia on the E., the territory of Mantineia on the S., and that of Orchomenus and Pheneus on the W. This plain is shut in on all sides by mountains. On the N. rises the gigantic mass of Cyllene, from which a projecting spur, called Mt. Stymphalus, descends into the plain. (Στύμφαλος ὄρος, Ptol. iii. 16. § 14; Hesych. s. v.; nivalis Stymphalus, Stat. *Silv.* iv. 6. 100.) The mountain at the southern end of the plain, opposite Cyllene, was called Apelaurum (τὸ 'Απέλαυρον,

Polyb. iv. 69) [*], and at its foot is the katavóthra or subterraneous outlet of the lake of Stymphalus (ἡ Στυμφαλὶς λίμνη, Strab. viii. p. 371; ἡ Στυμφηλίη λίμνη, Herod. vi. 76). This lake is formed partly by the rain-water descending from Cyllene and Apelaurum, and partly by three streams which flow into it from different parts of the plain. From the west descends a small stream, which rises in Mount Geronteium in the neighbourhood of *Kastania*; and from the east comes another stream, which rises near *Dusa*. But the most important of the three streams is the one which rises on the northern side of the plain, from a copious kefalóvrysi. In summer it flows about two miles through the plain into the katavóthra of Apelaurum; but in winter it becomes almost immediately a part of the waters of the lake, though its course may be traced through the shallower water to the katavóthra. This stream was called Stymphalus by the ancients; it was regarded by them as the principal source of the lake, and was universally believed to make its reappearance, after a subterranean course of 200 stadia, as the river Erasinus in Argolis. (Herod. vi. 76; Paus. ii. 3. § 5, ii. 24. § 6, viii. 22. § 3; Strab. viii. p. 371; ARGOS, Vol. I. p. 201, a.) The Stymphalii worshipped the Erasinus and Metope (Μετώπη, Aelian, *V. H.* ii. 33), whence it has been concluded that Metope is only another name of the river Stymphalus. Metope is also mentioned by Callimachus (*Hymn. in Jov.* 26), with the epithet pebbly (πολύστρειος), which, as Leake observes, seems not very appropriate to a stream issuing in a body from the earth, and flowing through a marsh. (*Peloponnesiaca*, p. 384.) The water, which formed the source of the Stymphalus, was conducted to Corinth by the emperor Hadrian, by means of an aqueduct, of which considerable remains may still be traced. The statement of Pausanias, that in summer there is no lake, is not correct, though it is confined at that time to a small circuit round the katavóthra. As there is no outlet for the waters of the lake except the katavóthra, a stoppage of this subterraneous channel by stones, sand, or any other substance occasions an inundation. In the time of Pausanias there occurred such an inundation, which was ascribed to the anger of Artemis. The water was said to have covered the plain to the extent of 400 stadia; but this number is evidently corrupt, and we ought probably to read τεσσαράκοντα instead of τετρακοσίους. (Paus. viii. 22. § 8.) Strabo relates that Iphicrates, when besieging Stymphalus without success, attempted to obstruct the katavóthra, but was diverted from his purpose by a sign from heaven (viii. p. 389). Strabo also states that originally there was no subterraneous outlet for the waters of the lake, so that the city of the Stymphalii, which was in his time 50 stadia from the lake, was originally situated upon its margin. But this is clearly an error, even if his statement refers to old Stymphalus, for the breadth of the whole lake is less than 20 stadia.

The city derived its name from Stymphalus, a son of Elatus and grandson of Arcas; but the ancient city, in which Temenus, the son of Pelasgus, dwelt, had entirely disappeared in the time of Pausanias,

---

[*] There was also a small town, Apelaurus, which is mentioned by Livy as the place where the Achaeans under Nicostratus gained a victory over the Macedonians under Androsthenes, B. C. 197. (Liv. xxxiii. 14.)

and all that he could learn respecting it was, that Hera was formerly worshipped there in three different sanctuaries, as virgin, wife, and widow The modern city lay upon the southern edge of the lake, about a mile and a half from the katavóthra, and upon a rocky promontory connected with the mountains behind. Stymphalus is mentioned by Homer (*Il.* ii. 608), and also by Pindar (*Ol.* vi. 169), who calls it the mother of Arcadia. Its name does not often occur in history, and it owes its chief importance to its being situated upon one of the most frequented routes leading to the westward from Argolis and Corinth. It was taken by Apollonides, a general of Cassander (Diod. xix. 63), and subsequently belonged to the Achaean League (Polyb. ii. 55, iv. 68, &c.). In the time of Pausanias it was included in Argolis (viii. 22. § 1). The only building of the city, mentioned by Pausanias, was a temple of Artemis Stymphalia, under the roof of which were figures of the birds Stymphalides; while behind the temple stood statues of white marble, representing young women with the legs and thighs of birds. These birds, so celebrated in mythology, the destruction of which was one of the labours of Heracles (*Dict. of Biogr.* Vol. II. p. 396), are said by Pausanias to be as large as cranes. but resembling in form the ibis, only that they have stronger beaks, and not crooked like those of the ibis (viii. 22. § 5). On some of the coins of Stymphalus, they are represented exactly in accordance with the description of Pausanias.

The territory of Stymphalus is now called the vale of *Zaraka*, from a village of this name, about a mile from the eastern extremity of the lake. The remains of the city upon the projecting cape already mentioned are more important than the cursory notice of Pausanias would lead one to expect. They cover the promontory, and extend as far as the fountain, which was included in the city. On the steepest part, which appears from below like a separate hill, are the ruins of the polygonal walls of a small quadrangular citadel. The circuit of the city walls, with their round towers, may be traced. To the east, beneath the acropolis, are the foundations of a temple in antis; but the most important ruins are those on the southern side of the hill, where are numerous remains of buildings cut out of the rock. About ten minutes N. of Stymphalus, are the ruins of the medieval town of *Krónia* (Leake, *Morea*, vol. iii. p. 108, seq.; *Peloponnesiaca,* p. 384; Boblaye, *Recherches, &c.,* p. 384; Ross, *Reisen im Peloponnes,* p. 54; Curtius, *Peloponnesos,* vol. i. p. 201, seq.).

STYRA (τὰ Στύρα: *Eth.* Στυρεύς: *Stura*), a town of Euboea, on the W. coast, N. of Carystus, and nearly opposite the promontory of Cynosura in Attica. The town stood near the shore in the inner part of the bay, in the middle of which is the island Aegileia, now called *Sturanisi*. Styra is mentioned by Homer along with Carystus (*Il.* ii. 539). Its inhabitants were originally Dryopians, though they denied this origin (Herod. viii. 46; Paus. iv. 34. § 11), and claimed to be descended from the demus of Steiria in Attica. (Strab. x. p. 446.) In the First Persian War (B. C. 490) the Persians landed at Aegileia, which belonged to Styra, the prisoners whom they had taken at Eretria. (Herod. vi. 107.) In the Second Persian War (B. C. 480, 479) the Styrians fought at Artemisium, Salamis, and Plataeae. They sent two ships to the naval engagements, and at Plataeae they and the Eretrians amounted together

to 600 men. (Herod. viii. 1, 46, ix. 28; Paus. v. 23. § 2.) They afterwards became the subjects of Athens, and paid a yearly tribute of 1200 drachmae. (Thuc. vii. 57; Franz, *Elem. Epigr. Gr.* n. 49.) The Athenian fleet was stationed here B. C. 356. (Dem. c. *Mid.* p. 568.) Strabo relates (x. p. 446) that the town was destroyed in the Maliac war by the Athenian Phaedrus, and its territory given to the Eretrians; but as the *Maliac* war is not mentioned elsewhere, we ought probably to substitute *Lamiac* for it. (Leake, *Northern Greece,* vol. ii. pp. 422, 432.)

STYX (Στύξ), a waterfall descending from a lofty rock in the Aroanian mountains, above Nonacris, a town in the NE. of Arcadia, in the district of Pheneus. The water descends perpendicularly in two slender cascades, which, after winding among a labyrinth of rocks, unite to form a torrent that falls into the Crathis. It is by far the highest waterfall in Greece; the scenery is one of wild desolation; and it is almost impossible to climb over the rocks to the foot of the cascade. The wildness of the scenery, the inaccessibility of the spot, and the singularity of the waterfall made at an early period a deep impression upon the Greeks, and invested the Styx with superstitious reverence. It is correctly described by both Homer and Hesiod. The former poet speaks of the "down-flowing water of the Styx" (τὸ κατειβόμενον Στυγὸς ὕδωρ, *Il.* xv. 37), and of the "lofty torrents of the Styx" (Στυγὸς ὕδατος αἰπὰ ῥέεθρα, *Il.* viii. 369). Hesiod describes it as "a cold stream, which descends from a precipitous lofty rock" (ὕδωρ ψυχρὸν ὅ τ᾽ ἐκ πετρῆς καταλείβεται ἠλιβάτοιο ὑψηλῆς, *Theog.* 785), and as "the perennial most ancient water of the Styx, which flows through a very rugged place" (Στυγὸς ἄφθιτον ὕδωρ ὠγύγιον, τὸ δ᾽ ἵησι καταστυφέλου διὰ χώρου, *Theog.* 805). The account of Herodotus, who does not appear to have visited the Styx, is not so accurate. He says that the Styx is a fountain in the town Nonacris; that only a little water is apparent; and that it dropt from the rock into a cavity surrounded by a wall (vi. 74). In the same passage Herodotus relates that Cleomenes endeavoured to persuade the chief men of Arcadia to swear by the waters of the Styx to support him in his enterprise. Among the later descriptions of this celebrated stream that of Pausanias (viii. 17. § 6) is the most full and exact. "Not far from the ruins of Nonacris," he says, "is a lofty precipice higher than I ever remember to have seen, over which descends water, which the Greeks call the Styx." He adds that when Homer represents Hera swearing by the Styx, it is just as if the poet had the water of the stream dropping before his eyes. The Styx was transferred by the Greek and Roman poets to the invisible world [see *Dict. of Gr. and Rom. Biogr. and Myth.* art. STYX]; but the waterfall of Nonacris continued to be regarded with superstitious terrors; its water was supposed to be poisonous; and it was believed that it destroyed all kinds of vessels, in which it was put, with the exception of those made of the hoof of a horse or an ass. There was a report that Alexander the Great had been poisoned by the water of the Styx. (Arrian, *Anab.* vii. 27; Plut. *Alex.* 77, de *Prim. Frig.* 20. p. 954; Paus. viii. 18. § 4; Strab. viii. p. 389; Aelian, *H. An.* x. 40; Antig. *Hist. Mirab.* 158 or 174; Stob. *Ecl. Phys.* i. 52. § 48; Plin. ii. 103. s. 106, xxx. 16. s. 53, xxxi. 2. s. 19; Vitruv. viii. 3; Senec. *Q. N.* iii. 25.) The belief in the deleterious nature of the water continues down to the present day, and the inhabitants of the surrounding villages relate that no vessel will hold the water. It is now called τὰ Μαυρανέρια, or the Black Waters, and sometimes τὰ Δρακο-νέρια, or the Terrible Waters. (Leake, *Morea*, vol. iii. p. 160, seq.; Fiedler, *Reise durch Griechenland*, vol. i. p. 400, who gives a drawing of the Styx: Curtius, *Peloponnesos*, vol. i. p. 195.)

SUA'GELA (Σουάγελα), a town of Caria, in which was shown the tomb of Car, the ancestor of all the Carians ; the place was in fact believed to have received its name from this circumstance, for in Carian σοῦα signified a tomb, and γέλας a king. (Steph. B. *s. v.*) Strabo, who calls the place Syangela (xiii. p. 611), states that this town and Myndus were preserved at the time when Mausolus united six other towns to form Halicarnassus. [L.S.]

SUANA (Σούανα, Ptol.: *Eth.* Suanensis: *Sovana*), a town of Southern Etruria, situated in the valley of the *Fiora* (*Arminia*), about 24 miles from the sea, and 20 W. of Volsinii (*Bolsena*). No mention of it is found in history as an Etruscan city, but both Pliny and Ptolemy notice it as a municipal town of Etruria under the Roman Empire. (Plin. iii. 5. s. 8; Ptol. iii. 1. § 49.) Its site is clearly marked by the modern town of *Sovana* or *Soana*, which was a considerable place in the middle ages, and still retains the title of a city, and the see of a bishop, though now a very poor and decayed place. It has only some slight remains of Roman antiquity, but the ravines around the town abound with tombs hewn in the rock, and adorned with architectural façades and ornaments, strongly resembling in character those at *Castel d' Asso* and *Bieda.* These relics, which are pronounced to be among the most interesting of the kind in Etruria, were first discovered by Mr. Ainsley in 1843, and are described by him in the *Annali dell' Instituto di Corrispondenza Archeologica* for 1843 (pp. 223—226); also by Mr. Dennis (*Etruria*, vol. i. pp. 480—500). [E. H. B.]

SUARDONES, a tribe of the Suevi in Northern Germany, on the right bank of the Albis, south of the Saxones, and north of the Langobardi. (Tac. *Germ.* 40.) Zeuss (*Die Deutschen*, p. 154), deriving their name from *suard* or *sword* (a sword), regards it as identical with that of the Pharodini, mentioned by Ptolemy (ii. 1L § 13) as living in nearly the same part of Germany. [L. S.]

SUARNI, a rude people of Asiatic Sarmatia, in the neighbourhood of the Portae Caucasiae and the Rha. They possessed gold mines (Plin. vi. 11. s. 12.) They are probably the same people whom Ptolemy calls Surani (Σουρανοί, v. 9. § 20) and places between the Hippic and Ceraunian mountains. [T. H. D.]

SUASA (Σούασα: *Eth.* Suasanus: Rn. near *Castel Leone*), a town of Umbria mentioned both by Ptolemy and Pliny, of whom the latter reckons it among the municipal towns of that country. Ptolemy places it, together with Ostra, in the district of the Senones, and it was therefore situated on the northern declivity of the Apennines. Its site is clearly identified at a spot between *S. Lorenzo* and *Castel Leone* in the valley of the *Cesano*, about 18 miles from the sea. Considerable ruins were still extant on the spot in the time of Cluver, including the remains of the walls, gates, a theatre, &c.; and inscriptions found there left no doubt of their identification. (Cluver, *Ital.* p. 620.) [E. H. B.]

SUASTE'NE (Σουαστηνη, Ptol. vii. 1. § 42), a district in the NW. of India, beyond the *Panjáb*, and above the junction of the *Kabúl* river and the

Indus. It derives its name from the small river Suastus (the *Swastú* or *Swoad*), which is one of the tributaries of the *Kabúl* river. [GOSYA.] [V.]

SUASTUS. [SUASTENE.]

SUBANECTI. [SILVANECTES.]

SUBATII. [TUBANTES.]

SUBDINNUM. [CENOMANI.]

SUBERTUM, another reading of SUDERTUM.

SUBI, a river on the E. coast of Hispania Tarraconensis, which entered the sea near the town of Subur. (Plin. iii. 3. s. 4.) Probably the modern *Francoli.* [T. H. D.]

SUBLA'QUEUM (*Subiaco*), a place in the valley of the Anio about 24 miles above Tibur (*Tivoli*). It derived its name from its situation below the lake or lakes formed by the waters of the Anio in this part of its course, and called the SIMBRUINA STAGNA or SIMBRIVII LACUS. These lakes have now entirely disappeared: they were evidently in great part artificial, formed as reservoirs for the Aqua Marcia and Aqua Claudia, both of which were derived from the Anio in this part of its course. There is no mention of Sublaqueum before the time of Nero, who had a villa there called by Frontinus "Villa Neronis Sublacensis;" and Tacitus mentions the name as if it was one not familiar to every one. (Tac. xiv. 22; Frontin. *de Aquaed.* 93.) It seems certain therefore that there was no town of the name, and it would appear from Tacitus (*l. c.*) that the place was included for municipal purposes within the territory of Tibur. Pliny also notices the name of Sublaqueum in the 4th Region of Augustus, but not among the municipal towns: as well as the lakes ("lacus tres amoenitate nobiles") from which it was derived. (Plin. iii. 12. s. 17.) It appears from mediaeval records that these lakes continued to exist down to the middle ages, and the last of them did not disappear till the year 1305. (Nibby, *Dintorni*, vol. iii. p. 125.) *Subiaco* obtained a great celebrity in the middle ages as the place of retirement of St. Benedict, and the cradle of the celebrated monastic order to which he gave his name. It seems probable that the site was in his time quite deserted, and that the modern town owes its origin to the monastery founded by him, and a castle which was soon after established in its neighbourhood. (Nibby, *l. c.* p. 123.) [E. H. B.]

SUBLA'VIO (*It. Ant.* p. 280) or SUBLA'BIO (*Tab. Peut.*), a place in Rhaetia, on the site of the modern convent of *Seben*, near the town of *Clausen.* Some suppose the correct name to be Subsavione, which occurs in a middle age document of the reign of the emperor Conrad II. [L. S.]

SUBUR (Σούβουρ, Ptol. ii. 6. § 17), a town of the Laeëtani in Hispania Tarraconensis lying E. of Tarraco. (Mela, ii. 6.) Ptolemy (*l. c.*) ascribes it to the Cosetani, and Pliny (iii. 3. s. 4) to the Ilergetes. It is mentioned in an inscription. (Gruter, p. 414.) Variously identified with *Sitges* and *Villanueva.* [T. H. D.]

SUBUR (Σούβουρ, Ptol. iv. 1. § 13). 1. A town in the interior of Mauretania Tingitana, near the river of the same name.

2. (Ptol. iv. 1. § 2), a river of Mauretania Tingitana. Pliny (v. 1. s. 1) calls it a fine navigable river. It fell into the Atlantic near Colonia Banasa, 50 miles S. of Lixus. It is still called *Subu* or *Cubu*, and rises among the forests of *Mount Salelo* in the province of *Sciaus* (Graberg of Hemsö, *Das Kaiserreich Marokko*, tr. by Reumont, p. 12). [T H. D.]

SUBUS (Σούβος, Ptol. iv. 6. § 8), a river on the

W. coast of Libya Interior, which had its source in
Mount Sagapola, and discharged itself to the S. of
the point of Atlas Major; now the *Sus.* [T. H. D.]

SUBZUPARA, a place in Thracia, on the road
from Philippopolis to Hadrianopolis (*Itin. Ant.* pp.
137, 231). It is called Castozobra or Castra Iarba
in the *Itin. Hieros.* (p. 568), and Καστράζαρβα by
Procopius (*de Aed.* iv. 11. p. 305, ed. Bonn), and
still retains the name of *Castro Zarvi,* or simply
Zarvi. It has, however, also been identified with
Hirmenly and *Coiunlou.* In the *Tab. Peut.* it is
called Castra Rubra.   [T. H. D.]

SU'CCABAR (Ζουχδβαρρι, Ptol. iv. 2. § 25, 3. §
20, xiii. 13. § 11), a town in the interior of Mauretania Caesariensis, lying to the SE. of the mouth
of the Chinalaph, and a Roman colony with the
name of Colonia Augusta (Plin. v. 2. s. 1). It
appears in Ammianus Marcellinus under the name
of Oppidum Sugabarritanum (xxix. 5). Mannert
(x. 2. p. 451) would identify it with the present
Masuna, where Leo Africanus (Lohrsbach, p. 382)
found considerable remains of an ancient city, with
inscriptions, &c.   [T. H. D.]

SUCCI or SUCCORUM ANGUSTIAE, the
principal pass of Mount Haemus in Thrace, between
Philippopolis and Serdica, with a town of the same
name. (Amm. Marc. xxi. 10. § 2, xxii. 2. § 2,
xxvi. 10. § 4.) It is called Σοῦκις by Sozomenus
(ii. 22), and Σουσδκεες by Nicephorus (ix 13).
Now the pass of *Snilu Derbend* or *Demir Kapi*
(Comp. V. Hammer, *Gesch. des Osman. Reichs,* i. p.
175.)   [T. H. D.]

SUCCO'SA (Σουκκῶσα, Ptol. ii. 6. § 68), a town
of the Ilergetes in Hispania Tarraconensis [T.H.D.]

SUCCOTH (LXX. Σοκχωθ, Vat., Σωχώ, Alex.),
a city of the tribe of Gad in the valley, formerly
part of the kingdom of Sihon king of Heshbon
(*Josh.* xiii. 27). It is connected with Zarthan in
1 *Kings,* vii. 46, where Hiram is said to have cast
his brasen vessels, &c. for Solomon's temple " in
the plain of Jordan, in the clay ground between
Succoth and Zarthan," elsewhere called Zaretan,
mentioned in the account of the miraculous passage
of the Israelites (*Josh.* iii. 16). The city doubtless derived its name from the incident in the life of
Jacob mentioned in Genesis (xxxiii. 17) where the
name is translated by the LXX. as in the parallel
passage in Josephus (*Ant.* i.21.§ 1), Σκηναί (booths).
It was therefore south of the Jabbok, and the last
station of Jacob before he crossed the Jordan towards Shechem. S. Jerome, in his commentary on
the passage, says, " Sochoth: est usque hodie civitas trans Jordanem hoc vocabulo in parte Scytho-
poleos," from which some writers have inferred that
Scythopolis may have derived its name from this
place in its vicinity (Robinson, *Bibl. Res.* vol. iii.
p. 175. n. 5), and this hypothesis is supported by
the respectable names of Reland, Gesenius, and
Rosenmüller. A place called *Succôt* is still pointed
out by the Arabs south of *Beisan* (=Bethshan=
Scythopolis), on the east side of Jordan, near the
mouth of *Wady Mûs.*   [G. W.]

SUCCUBO, a town in Hispania Baetica, in the
jurisdiction of Corduba. (Plin. iii. 1. s. 3.) Capitolinus mentions it under the name of Municipium
Succubitanum. (*Anton. Phil.* 1; cf. Florez, *Esp.
Sagr.* xii. p. 302.)   [T. H. D.]

SUCHE (τὸ Σούχου φρούριον, Strab. xvi. p.
770), the SUCHIM of the Hebrews (2 *Chron.* xii.
3), and the modern *Suachim,* was a harbour on the
western coast of the Red Sea, just above the bay of

Adule, lat. 16° N. It was occupied by the Aegyptians and Greeks successively as a fort and trading
station; but the native population of Suche were the
Sabae Aethiopians.   [W. B. D.]

SUCIDAVA (Σουκίδαυα, Ptol. iii. 10. § 11), a
town in Moesia Inferior, between Durostorum and
Axiopolis. (*Itin. Ant.* p. 224; *Tab. Peut.; Not.
Imp.*) Procopius calls it Σικιδάβα (*de Aed.* iv. 7.
p. 298, ed. Bonn) and Σικίβιδα (*Ib.* p. 291). Variously identified with *Osenik,* or *Assenik,* and *Sato-
nou.*   [T. H. D.]

SUCRO (Σούκρων, Ptol. ii. 6. § 14), a river of
Hispania Tarraconensis, which rose in the country
of the Celtiberi in a S. offshoot of Mount Idubeda,
and after a considerable bend to the SE. discharged
itself in the Sucronensis Sinus, to the S. of Valentia.
(Strab. iii. pp. 158, 159, 163, 167; Mela, ii. 6; Plin.
iii. 3. ss. 4, 5, 11.) Now the *Xucar.* [T. H. D.]

SUCRON (Σούκρων, Strab. iii. p. 158), a town of
the Edetani in Hispania Tarraconensis, on the river
of the same name, midway between Carthago Nova
and the river Iberus. (*Itin. Ant.* p. 400; cf. Cic.
Balb. 2; Liv. xxviii. 24, xxix. 19; App. *B. C.* i.
110; Plut. *Sert.* 19, &c.) It was already destroyed
in the time of Pliny (iii. 3. s. 4). Variously placed
at *Alcira, Sueca,* and *Cullera.* (Cf. Florez, *Esp.
Sagr.* v. p. 35; Marca, *Hisp.* ii. 5.)   [T. H. D.]

SUCRONENSIS SINUS, a bay on the E. coast
of Hispania Tarraconensis, now the *Gulf of Valencia.*
(Mela, ii. 6 and 7.)   [T. H. D.]

SUDE'NI (Σουδηνοί), a tribe in the east of
Germany, about the Gabreta Silva, and in close
proximity to the Marcomanni. (Ptol. ii. 11. § 15;
comp. SIDENI.)   [L. S.]

SUDERTUM (Σούδερτον: Eth. Sudertanus), a
town in the southern part of Etruria, apparently
situated between Volsinii and the sea-coast, but we
have no clue to its precise situation. The name
itself is uncertain. The MSS. of Pliny, who enumerates it among the municipal towns of Etruria,
vary between Sudertani and Subertani; and the
same variation is found in Livy (xxvi. 23), who
mentions a prodigy as occurring "in foro Sudertano."
Ptolemy on the other hand writes the name Σού-
δερνον, for which we should probably read Σούδερτον. (Ptol. iii. 1. § 50.) Cluver would identify
it, without any apparent reason, with the Maternum
of the Itineraries, and place it at *Farnese. Sorano,*
a few miles NE. of Sovana (Suana), would seem to
have a more plausible claim, but both identifications
are merely conjectural. (Cluver, *Ital.* p. 517;
Dennis's *Etruria,* vol. i. p. 478.)   [E. H. B.]

SUDE'TI MONTES (Σούδητα ὄρη), a range of
mountains in the SE. of Germany, on the N. of the
Gabreta Silva, thus forming the western part of the
range still called the *Sudeten,* in the NW. of *Bohemia.* (Ptol. ii. 11. §§ 7, 23.)   [L. S.]

SUE'BUS (Σούηβος), a river on the north coast
of Germany, between the Albis and Viadus, which
flows into the Baltic at a distance of 850 stadia to
the west of the mouth of the Viadus (Marcian. p. 53),
and which, according to Ptolemy (ii. 11. § 1),
divided at its mouth into several branches. Notwithstanding these explicit statements, it is extremely difficult to identify the river, whence some
regard it as the *Peene,* others as the *Warne,* and
others again as the Viadus or *Oder* itself, or rather
the central branch of it, which is called the *Swine*
or *Schweene.*   [L. S.]

SUEL (Σούελ, Ptol. ii. 4. § 7), a town of Hispania Baetica, on the road from Malaca to Gades.

(*Itin. Ant.* p. 405.) According to inscriptions it was a Roman municipium in which libertini had been settled. (Reines. pp. 13, 131; Spon, *Miscell.* v. p. 189; Orelli, *Inscr.* no. 3914; Mela, ii. 6; Plin. iii. 1. s. 3.) It is the modern *Fuengirola.* (*Inscr.* in Aldrete, *Orig. Ling. Cast.* i. 2.)   [T. H. D.]

SUELTERI, a people of Gallia Narbonensis, enumerated by Pliny (iii. 4), between the Camatullici and the Verrucini. The name Selteri is placed in the Table above Forum Julia (*Fréjus*). Nothing can be ascertained about the position of this people [CAMATULLICI].   [G. L.]

SUESIA PALUS, a large lake of Germany mentioned only by Pomponius Mela (iii. 3) along with two others, the Estia and Melsagium, but it is impossible to say what lake he is alluding to.   [L. S.]

SUESSA, sometimes called for distinction's sake SUESSA AURUNCA (Σούεσσα: Eth. Suessanus: *Sessa*), a city of Latium, in the widest sense of that term, but previously a city of the Aurunci, situated on the SW. slope of the volcanic mountain of *Rocca Monfina*, about 5 miles S. of the Liris, and 8 from the sea. Though it became at one time the chief city of the Aurunci, it was not a very ancient city, but was founded as late as B. C. 337, in consequence of the Aurunci having abandoned their ancient city (called from their own name Aurunca), which was situated a good deal higher up, and about 5 miles N. of Suessa. [AURUNCA.] Aurunca was now destroyed by the Sidicini, and Suessa became thenceforth the capital of the Aurunci (Liv. viii. 15). That people had, after their defeat by T. Manlius in B. C. 340, placed themselves under the protection of Rome, and we do not know by what means they afterwards forfeited it; perhaps, like the neighbouring Ausonians of Vescia and Minturnae, their fidelity had been shaken by the defeat of the Romans at Lautulae: but it is clear that they had in some manner incurred the displeasure of the Romans, and given the latter the right to treat their territory as conquered land, for in B. C. 313 a Roman colony was established at Suessa. (Liv. ix. 28; Vell. Pat. i. 14.) It was a colony with Latin rights, and is mentioned among those which in the Second Punic War professed their inability to furnish their required quota to the Roman armies. It was punished a few years later by the imposition of double contributions. (Liv. xxvii. 9, xxix. 15.) It is again mentioned in the Civil Wars of Marius and Sulla, when it espoused the party of the latter, but was surprised and occupied by Sertorius. (Appian, *B. C.* i. 85, 108). In the time of Cicero it had passed into the condition of a municipium by virtue of the Lex Julia, and is spoken of by that orator as a prosperous and flourishing town: it was the scene of a massacre by Antonius of a number of military captives. (Cic. *Phil.* iii. 4, iv. 2, xiii. 8.) It received a fresh colony under Augustus, and assumed in consequence the titles of "Colonia Julia Felix Classica," by which we find it designated in an inscription. (*Lib. Col.* p. 237; Plin. iii. 5. s. 9; Gruter, *Inscr.* p. 1093. 8; Orell. *Inscr.* 4047.) Numerous other inscriptions attest its continuance as a flourishing and important town under the Roman Empire (Orell. *Inscr.* 130, 836, 1013, 2284, 3042; Mommsen, *Inscr. R. N.* pp. 210—212); and this is confirmed by existing remains: but no mention of it is found in history. Nor is its name found in the Itineraries; but we learn from existing traces that there was an ancient road which branched off from the Via Appia at Minturnae and proceeded

by Suessa to Teanum, from which it was continued to Beneventum. (Hoare's *Class. Tour.* vol. i. p. 145. This is evidently the same line given in the *Itin. Ant.* p. 121, though the name of Suessa is not there mentioned.)

Suessa Aurunca was the birthplace of the celebrated satirical poet Lucilius, whence he is called by Juvenal "Auruncae alumnus." (Auson. *Epist.* 15. 9; Juv. i. 20.)

The modern city of *Sessa* undoubtedly occupies the ancient site: and considerable ruins are still visible, including, besides numerous inscriptions and other fragments, the remains of a temple incorporated into the church of the *Vescovado*, a remarkable cryptoporticus, and several extensive subterranean vaults under the church of *S. Benedetto*, constructed of reticulated masonry. Some remains of an amphitheatre are also visible, and an ancient bridge of 21 arches, constructed for the support of the road which leads into the town at the modern *Porta del Borgo.* It is still called *Ponte di Ronaco*, supposed to be a corruption of *Ponte Aurunco* (Hoare, *l. c.* pp. 145—147; Giustiniani, *Diz. Topogr.* vol. ix. p. 28, &c.).

The fertile plain which extends from the foot of the hills of *Sessa* to the Liris and the sea, now known as the *Demanio di Sessa*, is the ancient "Ager Vescinus," so called from the Ausonian city of Vescia, which seems to have ceased to exist at an early period [VESCIA]. The district in question was probably afterwards divided between the Roman colonies of Suessa and Sinuessa.   [E. H. B.]

COIN OF SUESSA AURUNCA.

SUESSA POME'TIA (Σούεσσα Πωμεντίдη, Dionys.: Eth. Πωμεντῖνος), an ancient city of Latium, which had ceased to exist in historical times, and the position of which is entirely unknown, except that it bordered on the "Pomptinus ager" or Pomptinae Paludes, to which it was supposed to have given name. Virgil reckons it among the colonies of Alba, and must therefore have considered it as a Latin city (*Aen.* vi. 776): it is found also in the list of the same colonies given by Diodorus (vii. Fr. 3); but it seems certain that it had at a very early period become a Volscian city. It was taken from that people by Tarquinius Superbus, the first of the Roman kings who is mentioned as having made war on the Volscians (Liv. i. 53; Strab. v. p. 231; Vict. *Vir. Ill.* 8): Strabo indeed calls it the metropolis of the Volscians, for which we have no other authority; and it is probable that this is a mere inference from the statements as to its great wealth and power. These represent it as a place of such opulence, that it was with the booty derived from thence that Tarquinius was able to commence and carry on the construction of the Capitoline temple at Rome. (Liv. *l. c.*; Dionys. iv. 50; Cic. *de Rep.* ii. 24; Plin. vii. 16. s. 15). This was indeed related by some writers of Apiolae, another city taken by Tarquin (Val. Antias, *ap. Plin.* iii. 5. s. 9), but the current tradition seems to have been that connected with Pometia (Tac. *Hist.* iii. 72). The name of Suessa Pometia is only once mentioned before this time, as the place where the sons of Ancus Marcius retired into exile on the accession of Servius. (Liv. i. 41). It is clear also that it survived its capture by Tarquin, and even appears again in the wars of the Republic with the Volscians, as a place of great power and importance. Livy indeed calls it a " Colonia Latina," but we have no account of its having become such. It, however, revolted (according to his account) in B. C. 503, and was not taken till the following year, by Sp. Cassius, when the city was destroyed and the inhabitants sold as slaves. (Liv. ii. 16, 17). It nevertheless appears again a few years afterwards (B. C. 495) in the hands of the Volscians, but was again taken and pillaged by the consul P. Servilius (*Ib.* 25; Dionys. vi. 29). This time the blow seems to have been decisive; for the name of Suessa Pometia is never again mentioned in history, and all trace of it disappears. Pliny notices it among the cities which were in his time utterly extinct (Plin. iii. 5. s. 9), and no record seems to have been preserved even of its site. We are, however, distinctly told that the Pomptinus ager and the Pomptine tribe derived their appellation from this city (Fest. *s. v. Pomptina,* p. 233), and there can therefore be no doubt that it stood in that district or on the verge of it; but beyond this all attempts to determine its locality must be purely conjectural.   [E. H. B.]

SUESSETA'NI, a people of Hispania Tarraconensis, mentioned only by Livy (xxv. 34, xxviii. 24, xxxiv. 20, xxxix. 42) and especially in connection with the Sedetani (or Edetani). Marca (*Hisp.* ii. 9. 4) takes them for a branch of the Cossetani; and Ukert (ii. pt. i. p. 318) seeks them near the Celtiberi, Lacetani, and Ilergetes. [T.H.D.]

SUESSIONES, or SUE'SSONES (*Ouéssones,* Ptol. ii. 9. § 11), a people of Gallia Belgica. The Remi told Caesar (*B. G.* ii. 3) in B. C. 57 that the Suessiones were their brothers and kinsmen, had the same political constitution and the same laws, formed one political body with them, and had the same head or chief: their territory bordered on the territory of the Remi, and was extensive and fertile: within the memory of man the Suessones had a king, Divitiacus, the most powerful prince in Gallia, who even had the dominion of Britannia; at this time (B. C. 57) they had a king named Galba, a very just and wise man, to whom the Belgae who were combining against Caesar unanimously gave the direction of the war. The Suessiones had twelve towns, and promised a contingent of 50,000 men for the war with Caesar.

Caesar (*B. G.* ii. 12) took Noviodunum, a town of the Suessiones, and the people submitted [NOVIODUNUM; AUGUSTA SUESSIONUM]. The Suessiones had the rich country between the *Oise* and the *Marne,* and the town of *Soissons* on the *Aisne* preserves their name unchanged. The Suessiones are mentioned (*B. G.* vii. 75) among the peoples who sent their contingent to attack Caesar at Alesia, B. C. 52; but their force was only 5000 men. Caesar paid the Suessiones for their pains by subjecting them to their brothers the Remi (*B. G.* viii. 6: "qui Remis erant attributi"); in which passage the word " attributi" denotes a political dependence, and in Gallia that signified payment of money. The Remi took care of themselves [REMI].

Pliny names the Suessiones Liberi (iv. 17), which, if it means anything, may mean that they were re-

leased in his time from their dependence on the Remi. In Pliny's text the name " Suecconi" stands between the name Veromandui and Suessiones; but nobody has yet found out what it means.

The orthography of this name is not quite certain; and the present name *Soissons* is as near the truth as any other form. In Strabo (iv. p. 195) it is Σουεσσίωνες, and Lucan (L. 423) has—

" Et Biturix, longisque leves Suessones in armis:"

Suessones is a correction; but there is no doubt about it (ed. Oudendorp).   [G. L.]

SUE'SSULA (Σουέσσουλα: *Eth.* Suessulanus: *Sessola*), a city of Campania, situated in the interior of that country, near the frontiers of Samnium, between Capua and Nola, and about 4 miles NE. of Acerras. It is repeatedly mentioned during the wars of the Romans with the Samnites, as well as in their campaigns against Hannibal. Thus in the First Samnite War (B. C. 343) it was the scene of a decisive victory by Valerius Corvus over the Samnites, who had gathered together the remains of their army which had been previously defeated at Mount Gaurus (Liv. vii. 37). In the great Campanian War shortly after, the Suessulani followed the fortunes of the citizens of Capua, and shared the same fate, so that at the close of the contest they must have obtained the Roman civitas, but without the right of suffrage (Id. viii. 14). In the Second Punic War the city bears a considerable part, though apparently more from its position than its own importance. The line of hills which rises from the level plain of Campania immediately above Suessula, and forms a kind of prolongation of the ridge of Mount Tifata, was a station almost as convenient as that mountain itself, and in B. C. 216, it was occupied by Marcellus with the view of protecting Nola, and watching the operations of Hannibal against that city (Liv. xxiii. 14, 17). From this time the Romans seem to have kept up a permanent camp there for some years, which was known as the Castra Claudiana, from the name of Marcellus who had first established it, and which is continually alluded to during the operations of the subsequent campaigns (Liv. xxiii. 31, xxiv. 46, 47, xxv. 7, 22, xxvi. 9). But from this period the name of Suessula disappears from history. It continued to be a municipal town of Campania, though apparently one of a secondary class; and inscriptions attest its municipal rank under the Empire. It had received a body of veterans as colonists under Sulla, but did not attain the colonial rank (Strab. v. p. 249; Plin. iii. 5. s. 9; Orell. *Inscr.* 129, 130, 2333; *Lib. Col.* p. 237). The Tabula places it on a line of road from Capua to Nola, at the distance of 9 miles from each of those cities (*Tab. Peut.*). It was an episcopal see in the first ages of Christianity, and its destruction is ascribed to the Saracens in the 9th century. Its ruins are still visible in a spot now occupied by a marshy forest about 4 miles S. of *Maddaloni,* and an adjacent castle is still called *Torre di Sessola.* Inscriptions, as well as capitals of columns and other architectural fragments, have been found there (Pratilli *Via Appia,* iii. 3. p. 347; Romanelli, vol. iii. p. 590).   [E. H. B.]

SUETRI (Σουητρίοι, Ptol. iii. 1. § 42, written Σουετρίοι in some editions), a Ligurian people, placed by Pliny (iii. 4) above the Oxybii, who were on the coast between *Fréjus* and *Antibes.* The Suetri are the last people named in the Trophy of the Alps. If the position of their town Salinae [SALINAE] is properly fixed, the Suetri were in the northern part of the diocese of *Frijus*.   [G. L.]

SUEVI (Σοῆβοι or Σουῆβοι), is the designation for a very large portion of the population of ancient Germany, and comprised a great number of separate tribes with distinctive names of their own, such as the Semnones. German authors generally connect the name Suevi with *Swiban*, i. e. to sway, move unsteadily, and take it as a designation of the unsteady and migratory habits of the people, to distinguish them from the Ingaevones, who dwelt in villages or fixed habitations (Zeuss, *Die Deutschen*, p. 55, foll.); others, however, and apparently with good reason, regard the name as of Celtic or even Slavonian origin; for the Romans no doubt employed the name, not because indigenous in Germany, but because they heard it from the Celts in Gaul. We must, however, from the first distinguish between the Suevi of Caesar (*B. G.* i. 37, 51, 54, iii. 7, iv. 1, &c.) and those of Tacitus (*Germ.* 38, &c.): the Suevi in Caesar occupied the eastern banks of the Rhine, in and about the country now called *Baden*, while Tacitus describes them as occupying the country to the north and east of the Suevi of Caesar, so that the two writers assign to them quite a different area of country. Strabo (vii. p. 290) again states that in his time the Suevi extended from the Rhenus to the Albis, and that some of them, such as the Hermunduri and Longobardi, had advanced even to the north of the Albis. Whether the nations called Suevi by Caesar and Tacitus are the same, and if so, what causes induced them in later times to migrate to the north and east, are questions to which history furnishes no answers. It is possible, however, that those whom Caesar encountered were only a branch of the great body, perhaps Chatti and Longobardi. That these latter were pure Germans cannot be doubted; but the Suevi of Tacitus, extending from the Baltic to the Danube, and occupying the greater part of Germany, no doubt contained many Celtic and still more Slavonic elements. It has in fact been conjectured, with great probability, that the name Suevi was applied to those tribes which were not pure Germans, but more or less mixed with Slavonians; for thus we can understand how it happened that in their habits and mode of life they differed so widely from the other Germans, as we see from Tacitus; and it would also account for the fact that in later times we find Slavonians peaceably established in countries previously occupied by Suevi. (Comp. Plin. iv. 28; Ptol. ii. 11. § 15; Oros. i. 2.) It deserves to be noticed that Tacitus (*Germ.* 2, 45) calls all the country inhabited by Suevian tribes by the name Suevia. The name Suevi appears to have been known to the Romans as early as B. C. 123 (Sisenna, *ap. Non. s. v. lancea*), and they were at all times regarded as a powerful and warlike people. Their country was covered by mighty forests, but towns (oppida) also are spoken of. (Caes. *B. G.* iv. 19.) As Germany became better known to the Romans, the generic name Suevi fell more and more into disuse, and the separate tribes were called by their own names, although Ptolemy still applies the name of Suevi to the Semnones, Longobardi, and Angli.

In the second half of the third century we again find the name Suevi limited to the country to which it had been applied by Caesar. (Amm. Marc. xvi. 10; Jornand. *Get.* 55; *Tab. Peut.*) These Suevi, from whom the modern *Suabia* and the *Suabians* derive their names, seem to have been a body of adventurers from various German tribes, who assumed the ancient and illustrious name, which was as applicable to them as it was to the Suevi of old. These later Suevi appear in alliance with the Alemannians and Burgundians, and in possession of the German side of Gaul, and Switzerland, and even in Italy and Spain, where they joined the Visigoths. Ricimer, who acts so prominent a part in the history of the Roman empire, was a Suevian. (Comp. Zeuss, *l. c.*; Wilhelm, *Germanien*, p. 101, &c.; Grimm, *Deutsche Gram.* i. pp. 8, 60. ii. p. 25, *Gesch. der Deutschen Spr.* i. p. 494; Latham, on *Tacit. Germ. Epileg.* p. lxxi.)   [L. S.]

SUEVICUM MARE, is the name given by Tacitus (*Germ.* 45) to the *Baltic Sea*, which Ptolemy calls the Σαρματικὸς Ὠκεανός (vii. 5. § 2, viii. 10. § 2.)   [L. S.]

SUFES a place in Byzacena (*Itin. Ant.* pp. 47, 48, 49, 51, 55). Now *Sbiba* or *Sbihah*. [T. H. D.]

SUFETULA a town of Byzacene, 25 miles S. of Sufes. In its origin it seems to have been a later and smaller place than the latter, whence its name as a diminutive—little Sufes. In process of time, however, it became a very considerable town, as it appears to have been the centre whence all the roads leading into the interior radiated. Some vast and magnificent ruins, consisting of the remains of three temples, a triumphal arch, &c., at the present *Sfaitla*, which is seated on a lofty plateau on the right bank of the *Wed Dschmila*, 80 kilomètres SW. of *Kairwan*, attest its ancient importance. (See Shaw's *Travels*, p. 107; Pelissier, in *Revue Archeol.* July 1847.) [T. H. D.]

SUIA (Συία, Steph. B. *s. v.*: Eth. Συιάτης, Συιεύς; Σύβα, Stadiasm, §§ 331, 332), the harbour of Elyrus in Crete, 50 stadia to the W. of Poecilassus, situated on a plain. It probably existed as late as the time of Hierocles, though now entirely uninhabited. Mr. Pashley (*Travels*, vol. ii. p. 100) found remains of the city walls as well as other public buildings, but not more ancient than the time of the Roman Empire. Several tombs exist resembling those of *Hághio Kýrko*; an aqueduct is also remaining.   [E. B. J.]

SUILLUM [HELVILLUM.]

SUINDINUM. [CENOMANI.]

SUIONES, are mentioned only by Tacitus (*Germ.* 44) as the most northern of the German tribes, dwelling on an island in the ocean. He was no doubt thinking of Scandia or Scandinavia; and Suiones unquestionably contains the root of the modern name *Sweden* and *Swedes*.   [L. S.]

SUISSA, a town in Armenia Minor (*It. Ant.* pp. 207, 216), where, according to the Notitia Imperii (p. 27), the Ala I. Ulpia Dacorum was stationed; but its site is now unknown. [L. S.]

SUISSATIUM (in Ptol. Σουεσσάσιον, ii. 6. § 65), a town of the Caristi in Hispania Tarraconensis. The Geogr. Rav. (iv. 45) calls it Seustatium. It is the modern *Vittoria*. [T. H. D.]

SULCI (Σολκοί, Steph. B., Ptol.; Σοῦλχοι, Strab.; Σύλκοι, Paus.: Eth. Sulcitanus: *S. Antioco*), one of the most considerable cities of Sardinia, situated in the SW. corner of the island, on a small island, now called *Isola di S. Antioco*, which is, however, joined to the mainland by a narrow isthmus or neck of sand. S. of this isthmus, between the island and the mainland, is an extensive bay, now called the *Golfo di Palmas*, which was known in ancient times as the Sulcitanus Portus (Ptol.). The foundation of Sulci is expressly attributed to the Cartha-

3 x 3

ginians (Paus. x. 17. § 9; Claudian. *B. Gild.* 518), and it seems to have become under that people one of the most considerable cities of Sardinia, and one of the chief seats of their power in the island. Its name was first mentioned in history during the First Punic War, when the Carthaginian general, Hannibal, having been defeated in a sea-fight by C. Sulpicius, took refuge at Sulci, but was slain in a tumult by his own soldiers (Zonar. viii. 12). No other mention of the name occurs in history till the Civil War between Pompey and Caesar, when the citizens of Sulci received in their port the fleet of Nasidius, the admiral of Pompey, and furnished him with supplies; for which service they were severely punished by Caesar, on his return from Africa, B. C. 46, who imposed on the city a contribution of 100,000 sesterces, besides heavily increasing its annual tribute of corn (Hirt. *B. Afr.* 98). Notwithstanding this infliction, Sulci seems to have continued under the Roman Empire to be one of the most flourishing towns in the island. Strabo and Mela both mention it as if it were the second city in Sardinia; and its municipal rank is attested by inscriptions, as well as by Pliny. (Strab. v. p. 225; Mel. ii. 7. § 19; Plin. iii. 7. s. 13; Ptol. iii. 3. § 3; *Inscr.* ap De la Marmora, vol. ii. pp. 479, 482.) The Itineraries give a line of road proceeding from Tibula direct to Sulci, a sufficient proof of the importance of the latter place. (*Itin. Ant.* pp. 83, 84.) It was also one of the four chief episcopal sees into which Sardinia was divided, and seems to have continued to be inhabited through a great part of the middle ages, but ceased to exist before the 13th century. The remains of the ancient city are distinctly seen a little to the N. of the modern village of *S. Antioco*, on the island or peninsula of the same name: and the works of art which have been found there bear testimony to its flourishing condition under the Romans. (De la Marmora, vol. ii. p. 357; Smyth's *Sardinia*, p. 317.) The name of *Sulcis* is given at the present day to the whole district of the mainland, immediately opposite to *S. Antioco*, which is one of the most fertile and best cultivated tracts in the whole of Sardinia. The Sulcitani of Ptolemy (iii. 3. § 6) are evidently the inhabitants of this district.

The Itineraries mention a town or village of the name of Sulci on the E. coast of Sardinia, which must not be confounded with the more celebrated city of the name. (*Itin. Ant.* p. 80.) It was probably situated at *Girasol*, near *Tortoli.* (De la Marmora, p. 443.)   [E. H. B.]

SULGAS, river. [GALLIA, p. 954; VINDALIUM.]

SU'LIA, SULE'NA (Σουλία, Σουλήνα, *Stadiasm.* §§ 324, 325), a promontory of Crete, 65 stadia from Matala, where there was a harbour and good water, identified by Mr. Pashley (*Travels*, vol. i. p. 304) with *Hághio Galéne*, the chief port of *Amári*, on the S. coast of the island.   [E. B. J.]

SULIS, in Gallia, is placed in the Table on a route from Dartoritum, which is Dariorigum [DARIORIGUM] the capital of the Veneti, to Gesocribate the western extremity of *Bretagne.* The distance from Dariorigum to Sulis is xx. By following the direction of the route we come to the junction of a small river named *Seuel* with the river of *Blavet.* The name and distance, as D'Anville supposes, indicate the position of Sulis.   [G. L.]

SULLONIACAE, a town in Britannia Romana (*Itin. Ant.* p. 471), now *Brockley Hill* in *Hertfordshire.* (Camden, p. 359.)   [T. H. D.]

SULMO (*Sermoneta*), an ancient city of Latium,

mentioned only by Pliny (iii. 5. s. 9) among those which were extinct in his time, and incidentally noticed by Virgil. (*Aen.* x. 517.) It is in all probability the same place with the modern *Sermoneta*, which stands on a hill between Norba and Setia, looking over the Pontine Marshes.   [E. H. B.]

SULMO (Σουλμῶν: Eth. Sulmonensis: *Sulmona*), a city of the Peligni, situated in the valley of the *Gizio*, in a spacious basin formed by the junction of that river with several minor streams. There is no doubt that it was one of the principal cities of the Peligni, as an independent tribe, but no notice of it is found in history before the Roman conquest. A tradition alluded to by Ovid and Silius Italicus, which ascribed its foundation to Solymus, a Phrygian and one of the companions of Aeneas, is evidently a mere etymological fiction (Ovid, *Fast.* iv. 79; Sil. Ital. ix. 70—76.) The first mention of Sulmo occurs in the Second Punic War, when its territory was ravaged by Hannibal in B. C. 211, but without attacking the city itself. (Liv. xxvi. 11.) Its name is not noticed during the Social War, in which the Peligni took so prominent a part; but according to Florus, it suffered severely in the subsequent civil war between Sulla and Marius, having been destroyed by the former as a punishment for its attachment to his rival. (Flor. iii. 21.) The expressions of that rhetorical writer are not, however, to be construed literally, and it is more probable that Sulmo was confiscated and its lands assigned by Sulla to a body of his soldiers. (Zumpt, *de Colon.* p. 261.) At all events it is certain that Sulmo was a well-peopled and considerable town in B. C. 49, when it was occupied by Domitius with a garrison of seven cohorts; but the citizens, who were favourably affected to Caesar, opened their gates to his lieutenant M. Antonius as soon as he appeared before the place. (Caes. *B. C.* i. 18; Cic. *ad Att.* viii. 4, 12 a.) Nothing more is known historically of Sulmo, which, however, appears to have always continued to be a considerable provincial town. Ovid speaks of it as one of the three municipal towns whose districts composed the territory of the Peligni ("Peligni pars tertia ruris," *Amor.* ii. 16. 1): and this is confirmed both by Pliny and the Liber Coloniarum; yet it does not seem to have ever been a large place, and Ovid himself designates it as a small provincial town. (*Amor.* iii. 15.) From the Liber Coloniarum we learn also that it had received a colony, probably in the time of Augustus (Plin. iii. 12. s. 17; *Lib. Colon.* pp. 229, 260); though Pliny does not give it the title of a Colonia. Inscriptions, as well as the geographers and Itineraries, attest its continued existence as a municipal town throughout the Roman Empire. (Strab. v. p. 241; Ptol. iii. 1. § 64; *Tab. Peut.*; Orell. *Inscr.* 3856 ; Mommsen, *Inscr. R. N.* pp. 287—289.) The modern city of *Sulmona* undoubtedly occupies the ancient site: it is a tolerably flourishing place and an episcopal see, having succeeded to that dignity after the fall of *Valva*, which had arisen on the ruins of Corfinium. (Romanelli, vol. iii. pp. 154—156.)

The chief celebrity of Sulmo is derived from its having been the birthplace of Ovid, who repeatedly alludes to it as such, and celebrates its salubrity, and the numerous streams of clear and perennial water in which its neighbourhood abounded. But, like the whole district of the Peligni, it was extremely cold in winter, whence Ovid himself, and Silius Italicus in imitation of him, calls it "gelidus

Sulmo" (Ovid, *Fast.* iv. 81, *Trist.* iv. 10. 3, *Amor.* ii. 16; Sil. Ital. viii. 511.) Its territory was fertile, both in corn and wine, and one district of it, the Pagus Fabianus, is particularly mentioned by Pliny (xvii. 26. s. 43) for the care bestowed on the irrigation of the vineyards.

The remains of the ancient city are of little interest as ruins, but indicate the existence of a considerable town ; among them are the vestiges of an amphitheatre, a theatre, and thermae, all of them without the gates of the modern city. About 2 miles from thence, at the foot of the *Monte Morrone*, are some ruins of reticulated masonry, probably those of a Roman villa, which has been called, without the slightest reason or authority, that of Ovid. (Romanelli, vol. iii. pp. 159, 161; Craven's *Abruzzi*, vol. ii. p. 32.)

Sulmo was distant seven miles from Corfinium, as we learn both from the Tabula and from Caesar. (Caes. *B. C.* i. 18; *Tab. Peut.*) Ovid tells us that it was 90 miles from Rome (*Trist.* iv. 10. 4), a statement evidently meant to be precise. The actual distance by the highroad would be 94 miles ; viz. 70 to Cerfennia, 17 from thence to Corfinium, and 7 from Corfinium to Sulmo. (D'Anville, *Anal. Géogr. de l'Italie*, pp. 175, 179.) There was, however, probably a branch road to Sulmo, after passing the Mons Imeus, avoiding the *détour* by Corfinium. [E. H. B.]

SUMATIA (Σουματία, Paus. viii. 3. § 4; Steph. B. *s. v.*; Σουμητία, Paus. viii. 36. § 7; Σουμάτειον, Paus. viii. 27. § 3; Σουμήτεια, Steph. B. *s. v.*), a town of Arcadia in the district Maenalia, on the southern slope of Mt. Maenalus. It was probably on the summit of the hill now called *Sylimna*, where there are some remains of polygonal walls. (Leake, *Morea*, vol. ii. p. 51; Ross, *Peloponnes*, p. 120.)

SUMMONTORIUM, a place in Vindelicia (*It. Ant.* p. 277), where, according to the Notitia Imperii, the commander of the 3rd legion was stationed. Its exact site is uncertain. [L. S.]

SUMMUS PYRENAEUS. One of the passes of this name mentioned in the Antonine Itin. and the Table was on the road from Narbo (*Narbonne*) to Juncaria (*Junquera*) in Spain. The road passed from Narbo through Ad Centuriones and Ad Stabulum ; but the distances in the Itins. are not correct; nor is the distance in the Itin. correct from Summus Pyrenaeus to Juncaria. The pass, however, is well marked; and it is the *Col de Pertus*, which is commanded by the fort of *Bellegarde*. This is the road by which Hannibal entered Gallia, and the Roman armies marched from Gallia into Spain. A second pass named Summus Pyrenaeus in the Antonine Itin. was on the road from Beneharnum [BENEHARNUM] in Aquitania to Caesaraugusta (*Saragosa*) in Spain. The road went through Iluro (*Oleron*) and Aspa Luca [ASPA LUCA] and Forum Ligneum [FORUM LIGNEUM], which is 5 from Summus Pyrenaeus. This road follows the *Gave d'Aspe* from *Oleron;* and on reaching the head of the valley there are two roads, one to the right and the other to the left. That to the right called *Port de Bernère* must be the old road, because it leads into the valley of *Aragues* and to *Beilo* in Spain, which is the Ebellinum of the Itin. on the road from Summus Pyrenaeus to *Saragosa*.

There is a third pass the most western of all also named Summus Pyrenaeus on the road from Aquae Tarbellicae (*Dax*) in Aquitania to Pompelon (*Pamplona*) in Spain. The Summus Pyrenaeus is the *Sommet de Castel-Pinon*, from which we descend into the valley of *Roncesvalles* on the road to *Pamplona* [IMUS PYRENAEUS]. (D'Anville, *Notice, &c.*) [G. L.]

SUNA [ABORIGINES.]

SU'NICI Tacitus (*Hist.* iv. 66) mentions the Sunici in the history of the war with Civilis. Civilis having made an alliance with the Agrippinenses (*Cöln*) resolved to try to gain over the nearest people to *Cöln*, and he first secured the Sunici. Claudius Labeo opposed him with a force hastily raised among the Betasii, Tungri and Nervii, and he was confident in his position by having possession of the bridge over the Mosa. [PONS MOSAE]. No certain conclusion as to the position of the Sunici can be derived from this; but perhaps they were between *Cöln* and the *Maas*. Pliny (iv. 17) mentions the Sunici between the Tungri and the Frisiabones. [G. L.]

SU'NIUM (Σούνιον: Eth. Σουνιεύs), the name of a promontory and demus on the southern coast of Attica. The promontory, which forms the most southerly point in the country, rises almost perpendicularly from the sea to a great height, and was crowned with a temple of Athena, the tutelary goddess of Attica. (Paus. i. 1. § 1; Σούνιον Ιρόν, Hom. *Od.* iii. 278 ; Soph. *Ajax*, 1235; Eurip. *Cycl.* 292; Vitruv. iv. 7). Sunium was fortified in the nineteenth year of the Peloponnesian War (B.C. 413) for the purpose of protecting the passage of the corn-ships to Athens (Thuc. viii. 4), and was regarded from that time as one of the principal fortresses of Attica (Comp. Dem. *pro Cor.* p. 238; Liv. xxxi. 25; Scylax, p. 21.) Its proximity to the silver mines of Laurium probably contributed to its prosperity, which passed into a proverb (Anaxand. *ap. Athen.* vi. p. 263, c.) ; but even in the time of Cicero it had sunk into decay (*ad Att.* xiii. 10). The circuit of the walls may still be traced, except where the precipitous nature of the rocks afforded a natural defence. The walls which are fortified with square towers, are of the most regular Hellenic masonry, and enclose a space of a little more than half a mile in circumference. The southern part of Attica, extending northwards from the promontory of Sunium as far as Thoricus on the east, and Anaphlystus on the west, is called by Herodotus the Suniac angle (τὸν γουνὸν τὸν Σουνιακόν, iv. 99). Though Sunium was especially sacred to Athena, we learn from Aristophanes (*Equit.* 557, *Aves*, 869) that Poseidon was also worshipped there.

The promontory of Sunium is now called *Cape Kolónnes*, from the ruins of the temple of Athena which still crown its summit. Leake observes that "the temple was a Doric hexastyle; but none of the columns of the fronts remain. The original number of those in the flanks is uncertain; but there are still standing nine columns of the southern, and three of the northern side, with their architraves, together with the two columns and one of the antae of the pronaus, also bearing their architraves. The columns of the peristyle were 3 feet 4 inches in diameter at the base, and 2 feet 7 inches under the capital, with an intercolumniation below of 4 feet 11 inches. The height, including the capital, was 19 feet 3 inches. The exposed situation of the building has caused a great corrosion in the surface of the marble, which was probably brought from the neighbouring mountains; for it is less homogeneous, and of a coarser grain, than the marble of Pentele. The walls of the fortress were faced with the same kind of stone. The entabla-

3 X 4

ture of the peristyle of the temple was adorned
with sculpture, some remains of which have been
found among the ruins. North of the temple, and
nearly in a line with its eastern front, are foundations of the Propylaeum or entrance into the sacred
peribolus: it was about 50 feet long and 30 broad,
and presented at either end a front of two Doric
columns between antae, supporting a pediment. The
columns were 17 feet high, including the capital,
2 feet 10 inches in diameter at the base, with an
opening between them of 8 feet 8 inches." (The
Demi of Attica, p. 63, 2nd ed.) Leake remarks
that there are no traces of any third building visible,
and that we must therefore conclude that here, as
in the temple of Athena Polias at Athens, Poseidon
was honoured only with an altar. Wordsworth,
however, remarks that a little to the NE. of the
peninsula on which the temple stands is a conical
hill, where are extensive vestiges of an ancient
building, which may perhaps be the remains of the
temple of Poseidon. (Athens and Attica, p. 207.)

SUNNESIA, a small island on the S. coast of
Spain (Geogr. Rav. v. 27.)   [T. H. D.]

SUNONENSIS LACUS, a lake in Bithynia,
between the Ascania Lacus and the river Sangarius.
(Amm. Marc. xxvi. 8.) It is probably the same
lake which is mentioned by Evagrius (Hist. Eccl.
ii. 14) under the name of Bodrη λίμνη in the neighbourhood of Nicomedeia, and which is at present
known under the name of Shabanja. It seems, also,
to be the same lake from which the younger Pliny
(x. 50) proposed to cut a canal to the sea. [L. S.]

SUPERAEQUUM or SUPEREQUUM (Eth.
Superaequanus: Castel Vecchio Subequo), a town of
the Peligni, one of the three which possessed municipal rights, and among which the territory of that
people was divided. [PELIGNI.] Hence it is mentioned both by Pliny and in the Liber Coloniarum,
where it is termed "Colonia Superaequana." It
received a colony of veterans, probably under Augustus, to which a fresh body of colonists was added
in the reign of M. Aurelius. (Plin. iii. 12. s. 17;
Lib. Colon. p. 229; Zumpt, de Colon. p. 361.) The
name is not mentioned by any other author, but
several inscriptions attest its municipal importance.
Its site, which was erroneously transferred by Cluverius to Palena, was clearly fixed by Holstenius
at a place still called Castel Vecchio Subequo (in
older documents Subrequo or Subrego), where the
inscriptions alluded to are still extant. It is situated
on a hill on the right bank of the Aternus, and about
4 miles on the left of the Via Valeria. Its territory probably comprised the hilly district between that
road and the Aternus. (Cluver, Ital. p. 758; Holsten.
Not. in Cluver. p. 145; Romanelli, vol. iii. pp. 134—
137; Mommsen, Inscr. R. N. p. 289.) [E. H. B.]

SUPERATII. [ASTURES.]

SUPERUM MARE. [ADRIATICUM MARE.]

SU'PPARA (Σούππαρα, Peripl. M. E. c. 52, ed.
Müll.), a place on the western coast of Hindostan,
at no great distance from Barygaza or Beroach.
Ptolemy calls it Σουπάρα (vii. 1. § 6). In Lassen's
map it is placed on the left bank of the Tápati or
Managúna, not far to the N. of Surat. This place
is also mentioned by Edrisi (i. p. 171), and by Cosmas Indicopleustes under the form of 'Οββαθὰ (p.
337, ed. Montfauc.). It has been suspected, with
much reason, by Benfey, that this is the "Ophir" of
the Bible,— the name in Sanscrit and Hebrew respectively offering some remarkable analogies. (Benfey, art. Indien, in Ersch und Gruber, p. 28.) [V.]

SURA (τὰ Σοῦρα: Eth. Σουρηνός), a city of Syria,
situated on the Euphrates, in the district of Palmyrene, long. 72° 40', lat. 35° 40' of Ptolemy, who
places it between Alalis and Alamata (v. 15. § 25);
apparently the Sure of the Peutinger Table, according to which it was 105 M.P. distant from Palmyra.
It is called in the Notitiae Imperii (§ 24) Flavia
Turina Sura (ap. Mannert, p. 408). It is probably identical with the Ura of Pliny, where, according to him, the Euphrates turns to the east from the
deserts of Palmyra (v. 24. s. 87). He, however,
mentions Sura (26. s. 89) as the nearest town to
Philiscum, a town of the Parthians on the Euphrates.
It was 126 stadia distant from Heliopolis, which was
situated in what was called "Barbaricus campus."
It was a Roman garrison of some importance in the
Persian campaigns of Belisarius; and a full account
is given of the circumstances under which it was
taken and burned by Chosroes I. (A. D. 532), who,
having marched three long days' journey from Circesium to Zenobia, along the course of the Euphrates,
thence proceeded an equal distance up the river to
Sura. Incidental mention of the bishop proves that
it was then an episcopal see. (Procop. Bell. Pers. i.
18, ii. 5.) Its walls were so weak that it did not
hold out more than half an hour; but it was afterwards more substantially fortified, by order of the
emperor Justinian. (Id. de Aedificiis Justiniani,
ii. 9.) "About 36 miles below Balis (the Alalis of
Ptolemy), following the course of the river, are the
ruins of Sura; and about 6 miles lower is the ford
of El-Hammám," which Col. Chesney identifies with
the Zeugma of Thapsacus, where, according to local
tradition, the army of Alexander crossed the Euphrates (Expedition for Survey, &c. vol. i. p. 416).
In the Chart (iii.) it is called Sooreah, and marked
as "brick ruins," and it is probable that the extensive brick ruins a little below this site, between it
and Phunsa (Thapsacus), may be the remains of
Alamata, mentioned in connection with Sura by
Ptolemy. Ainsworth is certainly wrong in identifying
the modern Suriyeh with the ancient Thapsacus
(p. 72).   [G. W.]

SURA, a branch of the Mosella in Gallia. Ausonius (Mosella, v. 354):— ·

  "Namque et Pronaeae Nemesaeque adjuta meatu
    Sura tuas properat non degener ire sub undas."

The Sura (Sour or Sure), comes from Luxembourg,
and after receiving the Pronaea (Prum) and Nemesa
(Nims), joins the Our, which falls into the Moselle on
the left bank above Augusta Trevirorum. [G. L.]

SURAE. [SORAE.]

SURASE'NAE (Σουρασῆναι, Arrian, Ind. c. 8),
an Indian nation, noticed by Arrian, who appear
to have dwelt along the banks of the Jumna. They
were famous for the worship of the Indian Hercules,
and had two principal cities, Methora (Madura)
and Cleisobora. The name is, pure Sanscrit, Sura-
sénakas.   [V.]

SURDAONES, a people of Hispania Tarraconensis,
seated near Ilerda, and probably belonging to the
Ilergetes. (Plin. iii. 3. s. 4.)   [T. H. D.]

SU'RIUM (Σούριον, Ptol. v. 10. § 6), a place in
Colchis, at the mouth of the Surius. (Plin. vi. 4. s.
4.) There is still at this spot a plain called Suram.
(Ritter, Erdkunde, ii. p. 809.)   [T. H. D.]

SU'RIUS a small tributary river of the Phasis in
Colchis. (Plin. vi. 4. s. 4.) According to the same
authority, its water had a petrifying power (ii. 103.
s. 106.)   [T. H. D.]

SURRENTINUM PROM. [MINERVAE PROM.]
SURRENTUM (Συρρεντόν, Strab.; Σούρεντον, Ptol.: *Eth.* Surrentinus : *Sorrento*), a city on the coast of Campania, on the southern side of the beautiful gulf called the Crater or *Bay of Naples*, about 7 miles from the headland called Minervae Promontorium, which forms the southern boundary of that bay. We have very little information as to its early history: its name is never mentioned till after the Roman conquest of Campania. Tradition indeed ascribed the foundation of Surrentum to the Greeks, but whether it was a colony from Cumae, or an earlier Greek settlement, we have no account: and there does not appear any evidence that it had, like many places in this part of Italy, a distinctly Greek character in historical times. Strabo calls it a Campanian city (Strab. v. p. 247), but this may very probably refer to its not being one of those occupied by the Picentines. According to the Liber Coloniarum a great part of its territory, and perhaps the town itself, was considered in a certain sense as consecrated to Minerva, on account of its proximity to her celebrated temple on the adjoining promontory, and was for that reason occupied by Greek settlers (*Lib. Col.* p. 236). It nevertheless received a partial colony under Augustus (*Ib.*), but without attaining the rank or character of a Colonia. Numerous inscriptions record its existence as a municipal town under the Roman Empire, and it is noticed by all the geographers: but its name is rarely mentioned in history (Strab. *l. c.*; Plin. iii. 5. s. 9; Mel. ii. 4. § 9; Ptol. iii. 1. § 7; Orell. *Inscr.* 3742; Mommsen, *Inscr. R. N.* 2111—2125). It was, however, resorted to by wealthy Romans on account of its beautiful scenery and delightful climate; among others Pollius Felix, the friend of Statius, had a villa there, which the poet has celebrated at considerable length in one of his minor poems (*Silv.* ii. 2). We are told also that Agrippa Postumus, when he first incurred the displeasure of Augustus, was ordered to retire to Surrentum, before he was consigned to more complete banishment in the island of Planasia (Suet. *Aug.* 65).

But the chief celebrity of Surrentum was derived from its wine, which enjoyed a high reputation at Rome, and is repeatedly alluded to by the poets of the Empire. It was considered very wholesome, and was in consequence recommended by physicians to convalescents and invalids. Tiberius indeed is said to have declared that it owed its reputation entirely to the physicians, and was in reality no better than vinegar. It did not attain its maturity till it had been kept 25 years (Plin. xiv. 6. s. 8; Athenae. i. p. 126; Ovid. *Met.* xv. 710; Martial, xiii. 110; Stat. *Silv.* iii. 5. 102; Strab. v. p. 243; Colum. *R. R.* iii. 2. § 10). We learn from Martial also (xiii. 110, xiv. 102) that Surrentum was noted for its pottery. The hills which produced the celebrated wine were those which encircle the plain in which the city was situated ("Surrentini colles," Ovid. *Met. l. c.*), and separate it from the gulf of Posidonia on the other side These hills form a part of the ridge which descends from the lofty mountain group of the *Monte S. Angelo* between *Castellamare* and *Amalfi*, and is continued as far as the headland opposite *Capri* This point, now called the *Punta della Campanella*, the ancient Promontorium Minervae, was known also by the name of Surrentinum Promontorium, from its close connection with the town of Surrentum (Tac. *Ann.* iv. 67; Stat. *Silv.* v. 3. 165). The celebrated sanctuary of the Sirens,

from which Surrentum itself was supposed to have derived its name, seems to have been situated (though the expressions of Strabo are not very clear) between this headland and the town (Strab. v. p. 247). But the islands of the Sirens (Sirenusae Insulae) were certainly the rocks now called *Li Galli*, on the opposite side of the promontory. The villa of Pollius, which is described by Statius as looking down upon the deep *Gulf of Puteoli*, stood upon the headland now called *Capo di Sorrento*, on the W. of the town, separating the *Bay of Sorrento* from that of *Massa:* extensive ruins of it are still visible, and attest the accuracy of the poet's description. (Stat. *Silv.* ii. 2; Swinburne's *Travels*, vol. i. pp. 88—90.)

The other ruins still visible at *Sorrento* and in its neighbourhood are of no great interest: they present numerous fragments of buildings of imperial times, to some of which the names of a temple of Hercules, temple of Neptune, &c. have been applied by local antiquarians, with no other foundation than the fact that we learn from Statius the existence of temples to those divinities at Surrentum. The most considerable relic of antiquity is a Piscina of large dimensions, which is in such good preservation that it still serves to supply the inhabitants with water. The modern town of *Sorrento* is a flourishing and populous place with a population of above 6000 souls: it is much resorted to by strangers on account of its mild and delicious climate, for which it is already extolled by Silius Italicus ("Zephyro Surrentum molle salubri," Sil. Ital. v. 466.) [E. H. B.]

SUSA (τὰ Σοῦσα, Aeschyl. *Pers.* 535, 730; Herod. i. 188; Xen. *Cyr.* viii. 6. § 8, &c.; in O. T. SHUSHAN, *Esther*, i. 2; *Nehemiah*, i. 1; *Daniel*, viii. 2), the chief city of the province of Susiana, on the eastern bank of the Choaspes (*Kerkhah*). There was considerable doubt among the ancient writers as to the exact position of this celebrated city. Thus Arrian (vii. 7), Pliny (vi. 27. s. 31), and Daniel (viii. 2) place it on the Eulaeus (Ulai in Daniel); while from other authors (Strab. xv. p. 728) it may be gathered that it was situated on the Choaspes. (For the probable cause of this confusion, see CHOASPES.) We may add, however, that, according to Curtius, Alexander on his way from Babylon had to cross the Choaspes before he could reach Susa (v. 2), and that the same inference may be drawn from the account of Aristagoras of the relative position of the places in Persia in his address to Cleomenes. (Herod. v. 52.) It appears to have been an early tradition of the country that Susa was founded by Dareius the son of Hystaspes (Plin. *l. c.*); and it is described by Aeschylus as μέγ' ἄστυ Σουσίδος (*Pers.* 119). By others it is termed Μεμνόνειον ἄστυ (Herod. v. 54), and its origin is attributed to Memnon, the son of Tithonus. (Strab. *l. c.*; Steph. B. *s. v.*) The name is said to have been derived from a native Persian word *Susan* (meaning *lily*), from the great abundance of those plants in that neighbourhood. (Steph. B. *s. v.*; Athen. xii. p. 513, ed. Cassaub.) Athenaeus also confirms the account of the excellence of the climate of Susa (*l. c.*). It may be remarked that the word Σούσινον was well known as applied to an unguent extracted from lilies. (Dioscor. iii. c. *de lilio*: Athen. xv. p. 609; Etymol. M. *s. v.* Σούσινον). The city was said to have been 120 stadia in circumference (Strab. *l. c.*), and to have been surrounded by a wall, built like that of Babylon of burnt brick. (Strab. *l. c.*; Paus. iv. 31.

§ 5.) Diodorus (xix. 16, xvii. 65) and Cassiodorus (vii. 15) speak of the strength and splendour of its citadel; and the latter writer affirms that there was a splendid palace there, built for Cyrus by Memnon. Besides this structure, Pliny speaks of a celebrated temple of Diana (*l. c.*; see also Mart. Capella, vi. *de India*, p. 225, ed. Grotius), in all probability that of the Syrian goddess Anaitis: while St. Jerome adds, that Daniel erected a town there (Hieronym. *in Dan.*), a story which Josephus narrates, with less probability, of Ecbatana. (*Ant.* x. 11.) Susa was one of the capitals at which the kings of Persia were wont to spend a portion of the year. Thus Cyrus, according to Xenophon, lived there during the three months of the spring. (*Cyrop.* viii. 6. § 22.) Strabo offers the most probable reason for this custom, where he states that Susiana was peculiarly well suited for the royal residence from its central position with respect to the rest of the empire, and from the quiet and orderly character of its government (*l. c.*) From these and other reasons, Susa appears to have been the chief treasury of the Persian empire (Herod. v. 49); and how vast were the treasures laid up there by successive kings, may be gathered from the narrative in Arrian, of the sums paid by Alexander to his soldiers, and of the presents made by him to his leading generals, on the occasion of his marriage at Susa with Barsine and Parysatis (Curt. vii. 4, 5): even long after Alexander's death, Antigonus found a great amount of plunder still at Susa. (Diod. xix 48.)

With regard to the modern site to be identified as that of the ruins of Susa, there has been considerable difference of opinion in modern times. This has, however, chiefly arisen from the scarcity of travellers who have examined the localities with any sufficient accuracy. The first who did so, Mr. Kinneir, at once decided that the modern *Sús*, situated at the junction of *Kerkhah* and river of *Díz*, must represent the Shushan of Daniel, the Susa of profane authors. (*Travels*, p. 99; comp. Malcolm, *Hist. Persia*, i. p. 256.) Rennell had indeed suspected as much long before (*Geogr. Herodot.* i. p. 302); but Vincent and others had advanced the rival claim of *Shuster*. (*Anc. Commerce*, i. p. 439.) The question has been now completely set at rest, by the careful excavations which have been made during the last few years, first by Colonel (now Sir W. F.) Williams, and secondly by Mr. Loftus. The results of their researches are given by Mr. Loftus in a paper read to the Royal Society of Literature in November, 1855. (*Transactions*, vol. v. new series.) Mr. Loftus found three great mounds, measuring together more than 3½ miles in circumference, and above 100 feet in height; and, on excavating, laid bare the remains of a gigantic colonnade, having a frontage of 343 feet, and a depth of 244, consisting of a central square of 36 columns, flanked to the N., E., and W. by a similar number—the whole arrangement being nearly the same as that of the Great Hall of Xerxes at Persepolis. A great number of other curious discoveries were made, the most important being numerous inscriptions in the cuneiform character. Enough of these has been already deciphered to show, that some of the works on the mound belong to the most remote antiquity. Among other important but later records is an inscription,— the only memorial yet discovered of Artaxerxes Mnemon, the conqueror of the Greeks at Cunaxa,— which describes the completion of a palace, commenced by Dareius the son of Hystaspes and

dedicated to the goddesses Tanaitis and Mithra. A Greek inscription was also met with, carved on the base of a column, and stating that Arreneides was the governor of Susiana. The natives exhibit a monument in the neighbourhood, which they call and believe to be the tomb of Daniel. There is no question, however, that it is a modern structure of the Mohammedan times.   [V.]

SUSIA'NA (ἡ Σουσιανή, Ptol. vi. 3. § 1; Polyb. v. 46; Strab. xv. 729, &c.; ἡ Σουσίς, Strab. xv. 731; ἡ Σουσιάς, Strab. ii. p. 134), an extensive province in the southern part of Asia, consisting in great measure of plain country, but traversed by some ranges of mountains. Its boundaries are variously given by different writers according as it was imagined to include more or less of the adjacent district of Persia. Generally, its limits may be stated to have been, to the N., Media with the mountains Charbanus and Cambalidus, part of the chain of the Parachoathras; to the E. the outlying spurs of the Parachoathras and the river Oroatis; to the S. the Persian gulf from the mouth of the Oroatis to that of the Tigris; and to the W. the plains of Mesopotamia and Babylonia. (Cf. Ptol. *l. c.* with Strab. *l. c.*, who, however, treats Susiana as part of Persia). As a province it appears to have been very fertile, especially in grain, but exposed along the coasts to intense heat. (Strab. xv. p. 731.) The vine, the Macedonians are said to have introduced. (Strab. *l. c.*) Its principal mountains are those on the N., called by Pliny Charbanus and Cambalidus (vi. 27. s. 31), while a portion of the Montes Uxii probably belonged to this province, as in them is a pass called Πύλαι Σουσίδες. (Polyaen. iv. 3. 27.)

Susiana was intersected by numerous rivers which flowed either to the Tigris or Persian gulf, from the high mountain watershed whereby it was surrounded. Of these the principal were the Eulaeus (*Karún*), the Choaspes (*Kerkhah*), the Coprates (river of *Diz*), the Hedyphon or Hedypnus (*Jerráhi*), and the Oroatis (*Táb*). The inhabitants of the district appear to have borne indifferently the names of Susii or Susiani, and, as inhabitants of the plain country, to have been devoted to agricultural employments; in the mountains, however, were tribes of robbers, who, from time to time, were strong enough to levy black mail even on their kings when traversing their passes. (Strab. xv. p. 728.) Another name, whereby the people were known, at least in early times, was Cissii (Aesch. *Pers.* 16), and the land itself Cissia (Strab. xv. p. 728; Herod. v. 49). This name is clearly connected with that of one of the chief tribes of the people, the Cossaei, who are repeatedly mentioned in ancient authors. (Strab. xi. p. 522; Arr. *Ind.* 40; Polyb. v. 54, &c.) There were many different tribes settled in different parts of Susiana; but it is hardly possible now to determine to what different races they may have belonged. Among these, the most prominent were the Uxii, a robber tribe on the mountain borders of Media; the Messabatae, who occupied a valley district, probably now that known as *Máh-Sabadan;* the Cossaei, in the direction along the Median mountains; and the Elymaei, inhabitants of Elymais, the remnant, in all probability, of the earliest dwellers in this province— ELAM being the name whereby this whole district is known in the sacred records. (*Isaiah*, xxi. 2; *Jerem.* xlix. 25.) Besides these, several smaller districts are noticed in different authors, as Cabandene, Corbiana, Gabiene, and Characene. Though Ptolemy has preserved the names of several small towns, there seems to have been no city of importance in Susiana, excepting Susa itself. [V.]

SUSUDATA (Σουσουδάτα), a place in the southeast of Germany, probably in the country inhabited by the Silingae, at the foot of the Vandalici Montes. (Ptol. ii. 11. § 28.) Its exact site cannot be ascertained.	[L. S.]

SUTHUL, a town and fortress in the interior of Numidia, where Jugurtha had a treasury. (Sall. *Jug.* 37.)	[T. H. D.]

SUTRIUM (Σούτριον: *Eth.* Sutriensis: *Sutri*), a city of Etruria, situated in the southern part of that country, 32 miles from Rome, on the line of the Via Cassia. There is no doubt that it was an ancient Etruscan site, but apparently a small town, and in all probability a mere dependency of one of its more powerful neighbours. It was not till after the fall of Veii that the Romans carried their arms as far as Sutrium, which they first attacked in B. C. 391, with what success is uncertain (Diod. xiv. 98); but it must have fallen into their hands either in that or the following year, as we find it in a state of dependency on Rome immediately after the Gaulish invasion. (Liv. vi. 3.) The very year after that event (B. C. 389) the neighbouring Etruscans laid siege to Sutrium with a large force; the city fell into their hands, but was recovered (as the tradition related) by the dictator Camillus on the same day. (Liv. vi. 3; Diod. xiv. 117.) Very nearly the same story is told again in B. C. 385, when the city was half taken by the Etruscans, but recovered by Camillus and Valerius. (Liv. vi. 9.) It was doubtless with a view to guard against the repetition of these surprises that two years afterwards Sutrium received a Roman colony, B. C. 383 (Vell. Pat. i. 14), and henceforth became, in conjunction with the neighbouring Nepete, one of the principal frontier fortresses of the Roman territory on this side; hence Livy terms it "claustra Etruriae." (Liv. ix. 32.) We do not find any subsequent mention of it in history till B. C. 311, when the Etruscans again laid siege to the city with their united forces, but were defeated in a great battle under its walls by Aemilius Barbula. (Liv. l. c.) The next year (B. C. 310) they were able to renew the siege at the opening of the campaign, but were once more defeated by the consul Q. Fabius Maximus, and took refuge in the Ciminian forest, which lay only a few miles distant. (*Ib.* 33, 35.) But this barrier was now for the first time passed by the Roman arms, and henceforth the wars with the Etruscans were transferred to a more northerly region. From this time, therefore, we hear but little of Sutrium, which was, however, still for a time the outpost of the Roman power on the side of Etruria. (Liv. x. 14.) Its name is next mentioned after a long interval during the Second Punic War, as one of the Coloniae Latinae, which, in B. C. 209, declared their inability to bear any longer the burdens of the war. It was in consequence punished at a later period by the imposition of still heavier contributions. (Liv. xxvii. 9, xxix. 15.) Its territory was one of those in which permission was given to the exiled citizens of Capua to settle. (Id. xxvi. 34.)

Sutrium continued under the Roman government to be a small and unimportant country town: it is only once again mentioned in history, at the outbreak of the Perusian War (B. C. 41), when it was occupied by Agrippa, in order to cut off the communications of Lucius Antonius with Rome. (Appian,

B. C. v. 31.) But its position on the Cassian Way preserved it from falling into decay, like so many of the Etruscan cities, under the Roman Empire: it is noticed by all the geographers, and its continued existence down to the close of the Western Empire is proved by inscriptions as well as the Itineraries. We learn that it received a fresh colony under Augustus, in consequence of which it bears in inscriptions the titles "Colonia Julia Sutrina." (Strab. v. p. 226; Plin. iii. 5. s. 8; Ptol. iii. 1. § 50; *Itin. Ant.* p. 286; *Tab. Peut.*; *Lib. Col.* p. 217; Gruter, *Inscr.* p. 302. 1; Zumpt, *de Col.* p. 351.)

The modern town of *Sutri* is but a poor place with only about 2000 inhabitants, but retains its episcopal see, which it has preserved throughout the middle ages. It occupies the site of the ancient city, as is shown by many fragments of columns and other architectural ornaments built into the modern houses, as well as by some portions of the ancient walls, which resemble in their style of construction those of Nepe and Falerii. The situation is, like that of most of the towns in this part of Etruria, on a nearly isolated hill bounded by precipitous cliffs or banks of tufo rock, of no great elevation, and surrounded by small glens or ravines on all sides. In the cliffs which bound these are excavated numerous tombs, of no great interest. But the most remarkable relic of antiquity at *Sutri* is its amphitheatre, which is excavated in the tufo rock, and is in this respect unique of its kind. It is, however, of small size, and, though irregular in construction, its architectural details are all of a late character: hence it is probable that it is really of Roman and Imperial times, though great importance has been sometimes attached to it as a specimen of an original Etruscan amphitheatre. Its anomalies and irregularities of structure are probably owing only to the fact that it was worked out of a previously existing stone-quarry. (Dennis's *Etruria*, vol. i. pp. 94—97; Nibby, *Dintorni*, vol. iii. pp. 142, 143.)	[E. H. B.]

SUZAEI (Σουζαῖοι), a tribe of ancient Persis, noticed by Ptolemy (vi. 4. § 3). Lassen considers from this name that they were connected with the people of Susa, and that they were of the same race as the Uxii, one of the mountain races of Susiana. (Ersch. u. Grüber's *Encycl.* iii. sect. vol. xvii. p. 438.)	[V.]

STYAGROS PROMONTORIUM (Σύαγρος ἄκρα), a promontory of the S. coast of Arabia, at the eastern extremity of the Adramitae, the westernmost of the gulf of the Sachalitae, placed by Ptolemy in long. 90°, lat. 14° (vi. 7. § 11). He comments on an error of his predecessor, Marinus, who, he says, places the gulf Sachalites on the W. of Cape Syagros, while all who had navigated those seas distinctly asserted that the country Sachalitis and its synonymous bay were to the E. of Syagros (i. 17. §§ 2, 3). Marcianus (p. 23, *ap. Hudson Geogr. Min.* tom. i.) agrees with Ptolemy. The author of the Periplus ascribed to Arrian seems, however, to confirm the testimony of Marinus, by placing the Sinus Sachalites next to Cane Emporium, between that and Syagros Promontorium, and naming the bay to the E. of Syagros, Omana, which he reckons as 600 stadia in width; but as he mentions still further to the E., Moscha Portus, as a magazine for the spicery of Sachalitis, which he there more fully describes, it is possible that he may have included all the country as far E. as Moscha under this name. It is at least clear that the Omana Sinus could be no part of the present district of *Oman*. The maps give no bay to the W. of Syagros, where the Tretus Portus was situated. The Periplus says that the cape extended eastward, places a castle with a harbour and magazine at Syagros, and describes, in connection with it, the Dioscoridis Insula (*Socotora*), which Pliny places at a distance of 2240 stadia.

There is no difficulty in identifying this promontory Syagros with the modern *Ras Fartask*, which derives its designation from *the snout* of the animal commemorated in its Greek name, which was probably a loose translation of its native appellation. The Periplus describes Syagros as the largest promontory in the world,—an hyperbolical expression, no doubt, but better suited to this cape than to any other on the coast, since the isolated mountain that forms *Ras Fartask* reaches an elevation of 2500 feet, and is visible at a distance of 60 miles; while those of *Ras Saugra* (al. *Saukira*), further to the E., sometimes identified with Syagros on account of the similarity of name, do not exceed 600 feet. The subject, it must be admitted, is not free from difficulty, mainly owing to the fact that Ptolemy places Moscha Portus,—which is usually supposed to be the same as the Moscha Portus of the Periplus, and is identified with *Dzafar* or *Saphar*,—W. of Syagros ; in which case *Ras Noos* (al. *Nous*), or *Ras Saugra* (al. *Saukira*), must be his Syagros, and the Sachalites Sinus still further E. But since the distance between Socatra and the coast at *Ras Fartask*, about 2000 stadia, approximates much more nearly to Pliny's figures, 240 M.P. (= 2240 stadia), than that between the same island and either of the other capes,—for *Ras Noos* is 3600 stadia distant, and *Ras Saugra* considerably more,—the most probable solution of the difficulty is found in the hypothesis adopted above, of two ports called Moscha on the same coast. [MOSCHA.] (See Müller's *Notes to Didot's ed. of the Geogr. Graec. Min.* vol. i. pp. 279, 280.) The question has been examined by Dean Vincent, who was the first to fix correctly this important point in Arabian geography, and his main conclusions are acquiesced in by Mr. Forster, who has corroborated them by fresh evidence from the researches of modern travellers ; and it is an interesting fact, that while the Greek geographers appear to have translated the native name of the cape, which it retains to this day, the natives would appear to have adopted a modification of that Greek translation as the name of the town situated, then as now, under the cape, which still bears the name of *Sugger*. (Vincent, *Periplus*, vol. ii. pp. 331—351 ; Forster, *Arabia*, vol. ii. pp. 166—177.) [G. W.]

SY'BARIS (Σύβαρις: Eth. Συβαρίτης, Sybarita), a celebrated city of Magna Graecia, situated on the W. shore of the Tarentine gulf, but a short distance from the sea, between the rivers Crathis and Sybaris. (Strab. vi. p. 263; Diod. xii. 9.) The last of these, from which it derived its name, was the stream now called the *Coscile*, which at the present day falls into the *Crati* about 3 miles from its mouth, but in ancient times undoubtedly pursued an independent course to the sea. Sybaris was apparently the earliest of all the Greek colonies in this part of Italy, being founded, according to the statement of Scymnus Chius, as early as B. C. 720. (Scymn. Ch. 360; Clinton, *F. H.* vol. i. p. 174.) It was an Achaean colony, and its Oekist was a citizen of Helice in Achaia: but with the Achaean emigrants were mingled a number of Troezenian citizens. The Achaeans, however, eventually ob-

tained the preponderance, and drove out the Troezenians. (Strab. *l. c.* ; Arist. *Pol.* v. 3.) The Sybarites indeed appear to have sought for an origin in heroic times; and Solinus has a story that the first founder of the city was a son of Ajax Oïleus (Solin. 2. § 10); but this is evidently mere fiction, and the city was, historically speaking, undoubtedly an Achaean colony. It rose rapidly to great prosperity, owing in the first instance to the fertility of the plain in which it was situated. Its citizens also, contrary to the policy of many of the Greek states, freely admitted settlers of other nations to the rights of citizenship, and the vast population of the city is expressly ascribed in great measure to this cause. (Diod. xii. 9.) The statements transmitted to us of the power and opulence of the city, as well as of the luxurious habits of its inhabitants, have indeed a very fabulous aspect, and are without doubt grossly exaggerated, but there is no reason to reject the main fact that Sybaris had in the sixth century B. C. attained a degree of wealth and power unprecedented among Greek cities, and which excited the admiration of the rest of the Hellenic world. We are told that the Sybarites ruled over 25 subject cities, and could bring into the field 300,000 of their own citizens (Strab. *l. c.*), a statement obviously incredible. The subject cities were probably for the most part Oenotrian towns in the interior, but we know that Sybaris had extended its dominion across the peninsula to the Tyrrhenian sea, where it had founded the colonies of Posidonia, Laüs, and Scidrus. The city itself was said to be not less than 50 stadia in circumference, and the horsemen or knights who figured at the religious processions are said to have amounted to 5000 in number (Athen. xii. p. 519), which would prove that these wealthy citizens were more than four times as numerous as at Athens. Smindyrides, a citizen of Sybaris, who was one of the suitors for the daughters of Cleisthenes of Sicyon, is said by Herodotus to have surpassed all other men in refined luxury. (Herod. vi. 127.) It was asserted that on this occasion he carried with him a train of 1000 slaves, including cooks, fishermen, &c. (Athen. vi. p. 273; Diod. viii. Fr. 19.) It is unnecessary to repeat here the tales that are told by various writers, especially by Athenaeus, concerning the absurd refinements of luxury ascribed to the Sybarites, and which have rendered their very name proverbial. (Athenae. xii. pp. 518—521; Diod. viii. Fr. 18—20 ; Suid. *s. v.* Συβαρτικαῖς.) They were particularly noted for the splendour of their attire, which was formed of the finest Milesian wool, and this gave rise to extensive commercial relations with Miletus, which produced a close friendship between the two cities. (Timaeus, *ap. Athen.* xii. p. 519; Herod. vi. 21.) As an instance of their magnificence we are told that Alcimenes of Sybaris had dedicated as a votive offering in the temple of the Lacinian Juno a splendid figured robe, which long afterwards fell into the power of Dionysius of Syracuse, and was sold by him for 120 talents, or more than 24,000*l.* sterling. (Pseud Arist. *Mirab.* 96; Athen. xii. p. 541.)

Notwithstanding these details concerning the wealth and luxury of Sybaris, we are almost wholly without information as to the history of the city until shortly before its fall. Herodotus incidentally refers to the time of Smindyrides (about 580—560, B. C.) as the period when Sybaris was at the height of its power. At a later period it seems to have been agitated by political dissensions, with the circumstances of which we are very imperfectly acquainted. It appears that the government had previously been in the hands of an oligarchy, to which such persons as Smindyrides and Alcimenes naturally belonged; but the democratic party, headed by a demagogue named Telys, succeeded in overthrowing their power, and drove a considerable number of the leading citizens into exile. Telys hereupon seems to have raised himself to the position of despot or tyrant of the city. The exiled citizens took refuge at Crotona; but not content with their victory, Telys and his partisans called upon the Crotoniats to surrender the fugitives. This they refused to do, and the Sybarites hereupon declared war on them, and marched upon Crotona with an army said to have amounted to 300,000 men. They were met at the river Traeis by the Crotoniats, whose army did not amount to more than a third of their numbers; notwithstanding which they obtained a complete victory, and put the greater part of the Sybarites to the sword, continuing the pursuit to the very gates of the city, of which they easily made themselves masters, and which they determined to destroy so entirely that it should never again be inhabited. For this purpose they turned the course of the river Crathis, so that it inundated the site of the city and buried the ruins under the deposits that it brought down. (Diod. xii. 9, 10; Strab. vi. p. 263; Herod. v. 44; Athenae. xii. p. 521; Scymn. Ch. 337—360.) This catastrophe occurred in B. C. 510, and seems to have been viewed by many of the Greeks as a divine vengeance upon the Sybarites for their pride and arrogance, caused by their excessive prosperity, more especially for the contempt they had shown for the great festival of the Olympic Games, which they are said to have attempted to supplant by attracting the principal artists, athletes, &c., to their own public games. (Scymn. Ch. 350—360; Athen. l. c.)

It is certain that Sybaris was never restored. The surviving inhabitants took refuge at Latis and Scidrus, on the shores of the Tyrrhenian sea. An attempt was indeed made, 58 years after the destruction of the city, to establish them anew on the ancient site, but they were quickly driven out by the Crotoniats, and the fugitives afterwards combined with the Athenian colonists in the foundation of Thurii. [Thurii.] At the present day the site is utterly desolate, and even the exact position of the ancient city cannot be determined. The whole plain watered by the rivers Coscile and Crati (the ancient Sybaris and Crathis), so renowned in ancient times for its fertility, is now a desolate swampy tract, pestilential from malaria, and frequented only by vast herds of buffaloes, the usual accompaniment in Southern Italy of all such pestiferous regions. The circumstance mentioned by Strabo that the river Crathis had been turned from its course to inundate the city, is confirmed by the accidental mention in Herodotus of the dry channel of the Crathis" (παρὰ τὸν ξηρὸν Κράθιν, Herod. v. 44): and this would sufficiently account for the disappearance of all traces of the city. Swinburne indeed tells us that some " degraded fragments of aqueducts and tombs " were still visible on the peninsula formed by the two rivers, and were pointed out as the ruins of Sybaris, but these, as he justly observes, being built of brick, are probably of Roman times, and have no connection with the ancient city. Keppel Craven, on the other hand, speaks of " a wall sometimes visible in the bed of the Crathis when the

waters are very low" as being the only remaining relic of the ancient Sybaris. (Swinburne's Travels, vol. i. pp. 290—292; Craven's Southern Tour, pp. 217, 218.) The ruins marked on Zannoni's large map as l'Antica Sibari are probably those of Thurii [Thurii.] But it is certain that the locality has never yet been thoroughly examined, and it is probable that some light may even yet be thrown upon the site of this celebrated city: especially if the marshy plain in which it is situated should ever be reclaimed and cultivated. There is no doubt that if this were done, it would again be a tract of surpassing fertility: it is cited as such by Varro, who tells us that " in Sybaritano" wheat was said to produce a hundred-fold. (Varr. R. R. i. 44.) Even at the present day the drier spots produce very rich crops of corn. (Swinburne, l. c.)

The river Sybaris was said to be so named by the Greek colonists from a fountain of that name at Bura in Achaia (Strab. viii. p. 386): it had the property, according to some authors, of making horses shy that drank of its waters. (Pseud. Arist. Mirab. 169; Strab. vi. p. 263.) It is a considerable stream, and has its sources in the Apennines near Murano, flows beneath Castrovillari, and receives several minor tributary streams before it joins the Crathis.　　　　　　　　　　　[E. H. B.]

COIN OF SYBARIS.

SY'BOTA. [Corcyra, p. 670.]

SYBRITA (Σύβριτα, Scyl. p. 18; Σούβριτα, Ptol. iii. 17. § 10; Σούβριτος, Hierocles; Σίβυρτος, Polyb. ap. Steph. B. s. v.: Eth. Σιβύρτιος, Böckh, Corp. Inscr. vol. ii. p. 637), a town of Crete, 8 M. P. from Eleutherna (Peut. Tab.), and famous for its numerous and beautiful silver coins, which, though some of them belong to a very early period, are the finest specimens of the Cretan mint; the types are always connected with the worship of Dionysus or Hermes. (Eckhel, vol. ii. p. 320.)　　[E. B. J.]

SYCAMINA (Συκαμίνων πόλις), a city of Palestine, placed by Strabo between Acre ("Ακη) and Caesareia Palaestinae (Στράτωνος πύργος), the name of which alone remained in his time. There were, he says, many such; of which he specifies this and Bucolon (Βουκόλων) and Crocodeilon (Κροκοδείλων). (Strab. xvi. p. 758.) It was here that Ptolemy Lathyrus, son of Cleopatra, landed the army of 30,000 men whom he had brought from Cyprus to besiege Ptolemais, which would imply that it was not far distant from Acre (Josephus, lib. xiii. 13. § 3). The Itinerary of Antoninus makes it xxiv. M. P. from Ptolemais, xx. M. P. from Caesareia; the Jerusalem Itinerary xv. M.P. from Ptolemais, xvi. from Caesareia. (Wesseling, pp. 149, 584.) The last-named authority places it at Mount Carmel, thereby justifying its identification with the modern Kaipha or Haifa, followed by Reichard, Mannert, and Kiepert, rather than with Atlit, suggested by Lapie. Indeed the testimony of Eusebius would seem to be conclusive on this point, as he speaks of a village of this name (Συκαμίνων πόλις) on the coast between Ptolemais and Caesareia, near Mount Carmel, called also Hepha ('Ηφὰ) in his day. (*Onomast. s. v.* 'Ιαφέθ.) Dr. Wilson, however, thinks that the modern *Haifa* "more probably occupies the site of the 'Mutatio Calamon,' given in the Jerusalem Itinerary as 12 Roman miles from Ptolemais, while the 'Mansio Sicamenos' of the same work was 3 miles farther on. Ruins have been discovered along the shore, about 2 Roman miles to the the W. of *Haifa ; . . .* these ruins may have been those of Sycaminos." (*Lands of the Bible*, vol. ii. p. 241.) *Haifa* is a small walled town to the S. of the *Bay of Acre*, at the northern base of the promontory of Mount Carmel, distant about 10 miles from Ptolemais (*Acre*); a distance far too small to satisfy the statement of the Itinerary of Antoninus, or even that of the Jerusalem Itinerary. But, notwithstanding this, its identity with Sycamina seems to be sufficiently established by the testimony of Eusebius, joined to the historical fact recorded by Josephus, which better suits this than any other place on the coast, being in fact the very place where Ibrahim Pasha, when engaged in a similar enterprise against *Acre*, landed some of his troops and concentrated his army, in 1831, preparatory to forming the siege of the town. (Alderson, *Notes on Acre*, pp. 23, 24.)   [G. W.]

SYCE (Σύκη), a town of Cilicia, which according to the Ravenna Geographer, who calls it Sycas (i. 17), was situated between Arsinoë and Celenderis. (Athen. iii. 5; Steph. s. v. Συκαί.) Leake (*Asia Minor*, p. 202) looks for its site near the moder *Kizliman.*   [L. S.]

SYCEON, a town of Galatia, situated at the point where the river Siberis flowed into the Sangarius. (Procop. *de Aed.* v. 4 ; *Vit. Theod. Syceotae*, 2 ; Wessel. *ad Hierocl.* p. 697.) [L. S.]

SYCU'RIUM, a town of Thessaly in the district Pelasgiotis, at the foot of Mt. Ossa, which Leake identifies with *Marmariani.* (Liv. xlii. 54; Leake, *Northern Greece*, vol. iii. p. 374.)

SYEBI MONTES (τὰ Σύηβα ὄρη, Ptol. vi. 14. § 8), a mountain chain in Scythia, running from the Tapuri mountains in a NE. direction towards Imaus.   [T. H. D.]

SYEDRA (Σύεδρα: *Eth.* Συεδρεύς), a coast-town in the west of Cilicia, between Coracesium and Selinus (Strab. xiv. p. 669, where the common but erroneous reading is Arsinoë ; Steph. B. s. v.; Ptol. v. 8. § 1; Hierocl. p. 683; Lucan, viii. 259; Flor. iv. 2.) It should, however, be observed that Stephanus B. calls it a town of Isauria, and that Hierocles assigns it to Pamphylia. Beaufort (*Karamania*, p. 178) observed some ruins on a steep hill in that district, which he thinks may mark the site of Syedra; and Mr. Hamilton, in his map of Asia Minor, also marks the ruins of Sydre on the same spot, a little to the south-east of *Alaya*, the ancient Coracesium.   [L. S.]

SYE'NE (Συήνη, Herod. ii. 30; Strab. ii. p. 133, xvii. p. 797, seq.; Steph. B. s. v.; Ptol. vii. 5. § 15, viii. 15. § 15; Plin. ii. 73. s. 75, v. 10. s. 11, vi. 29. s. 34; *It. Ant.* p. 164), the modern *Assouan*, was the frontier town of Aegypt to the S. Syene stood upon a peninsula on the right bank of the Nile, immediately below the Great Falls, which extend to it from Philae. It is supposed to have derived its name from Suan, an Aegyptian goddess, the Ilithya of the Greeks, and of which the import is "the opener;" and at Syene Upper Aegypt was

in all ages, conceived to open or begin. The quarries of Syene were celebrated for their stone, and especially for the marble called *Syenite.* They furnished the colossal statues, obelisks, and monolithal shrines which are found throughout Aegypt; and the traces of the quarrymen who wrought in these 3000 years ago are still visible in the native rock. They lie on either bank of the Nile, and a road, 4 miles in length, was cut beside them from Syene to Philae. Syene was equally important as a military station and as a place of traffic. Under every dynasty it was a garrison town; and here were levied toll and custom on all boats passing southward and northward. The latitude of Syene— 24° 5' 23" — was an object of great interest to the ancient geographers. They believed that it was seated immediately under the tropic, and that on the day of the summer solstice a vertical staff cast no shadow, and the sun's disc was reflected in a well at noonday. This statement is indeed incorrect; the ancients were not acquainted with the true tropic: yet at the summer-solstice the length of the shadow, or ₁₄th of the staff, could scarcely be discerned, and the northern limb of the sun's disc would be nearly vertical. The Nile is nearly 3000 yards wide above Syene. From this frontier town to the northern extremity of Aegypt it flows for more than 750 miles without bar or cataract. The voyage from Syene to Alexandreia usually occupied between 21 and 28 days in favourable weather. [W. B. D.]

SYGAMBRI. [SICAMBRI.]

SYLINA INSULA. [SILURA.]

SYLLIUM (Σύλλιον), a fortified town of Pamphylia, situated on a lofty height between Aspendus and Side, and between the rivers Eurymedon and Cestrus, at a distance of 40 stadia from the coast. (Strab. xiv. p. 667; Arrian, *Anab.* i. 25; Scylax, p. 40; Ptol. v. 5. § 1; Hierocl. p. 679; Polyb. xxii. 17; Steph. B. mentions it under the name Σύλειον, while in other passages it is called Σόλαιον, Σύλλον, and Σίλουον.) Sir C. Fellows (*Asia Minor*, p. 200) thinks that the remains of a Greek town which he found in a wood on the side of a rocky hill near *Bolcascooe* belong to the ancient Syllium; but from his description they do not appear to exist on a lofty height.   [L. S.]

SYMAETHUS (Σύμαιθος: *Simeto*), one of the most considerable rivers of Sicily, which rises in the chain of Mons Nebrodes, in the great forest now called the *Bosco di Caronia*, and flows from thence in a southerly direction, skirting the base of Aetna, till it turns to the E. and flows into the sea about 8 miles S. of *Catania*. In the lower part of its course it formed the boundary between the territory of Leontini and that of Catana. (Thuc. vi. 65.) It receives in its course many tributaries, of which the most considerable are, the *Fiume Salso*, flowing from the neighbourhood of *Nicosia* and *Traina*, probably the Cyamosorus of Polybius (i. 9), which he describes as flowing near Centuripa (*Centorbi*), and the *Dittaino*, which rises in the hills near *Asaro*, the ancient Assorus. This is undoubtedly the stream called in ancient times CHRYSAS. Stephanus of Byzantium apparently gives the name of Adranus to the upper part or main branch of the Symaethus itself, which flows under the walls of ADRANUM (*Adernò*). This part of the river is still called the *Simeto ;* but in the lower part of its course, where it approaches the sea, it is now known as the *Giarretta.* Such differences of name are common in modern, as well as in ancient times. The Symae-

Road to Catania

L O G N I N A

B A Y

Bay of Dascon

GREAT

P L E M M Y R I U M

1. Temple of Minerva.
2. Theatre.
3. Amphitheatre.
4. Latomie or Quarries.
5. Fountain of Arethusa.
6. Site of Apollo Temenitis.
7. Entrance to the Catacombs.
8. Ancient bridge over the Anapus.

PLAN
of
SYRACUS

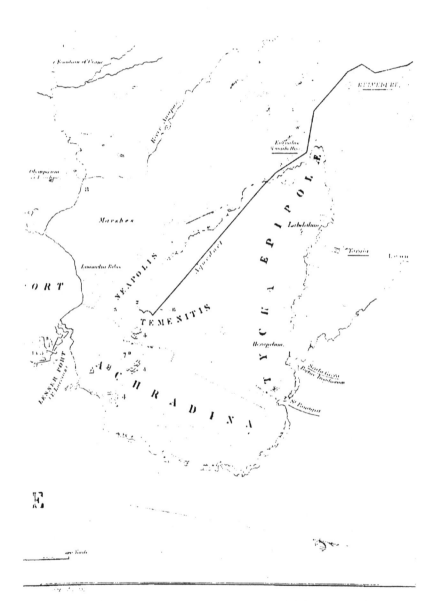

thus is much the most considerable river on the E. coast of Sicily, and is in consequence noticed by all the geographers (Scyl. p. 4. § 13; Strab. vi. p. 272; Plin. iii. 8. s. 14; Ptol. iii. 4. § 9). It is also repeatedly alluded to by the Roman poets (Virg. *Aen.* ix. 584; Ovid, *Fast.* iv. 472; Sil. Ital. xiv. 232.)   [E. H. B.]

SY'MBOLON PORTUS (Συμβόλων λιμήν, Ptol. iii. 6. § 2; Συμβόλου λιμήν, Arrian, *Per. Pont. Eux.* p. 20), a harbour with a narrow entrance on the S. coast of the Chersonesus Taurica, between the town of Chersonesus and the port of Cienus. In ancient times it was the chief station for the pirates of the Tauric peninsula. (Strab. vii. p. 309; Plin. iv. 12. s. 26; Anon. *Per. Pont. Eux.* p. 6.) Now the port of *Balaklava.* (Comp. Clarke's *Travels,* ii. p. 398; Pallas, ii. p. 128.)   [T. H. D.]

SY'MBOLUM (Σύμβυλον, Dion Cass. xlvii. 35), a place in the Thracian district of Edonis, in the neighbourhood of Philippi. (Comp. Leake, *North. Gr.* iii. p. 217.)   [T. H. D.]

SYMBRA (Σύμβρα), a small town in Babylonia mentioned by Zosimus (iii. 27). It is probably the same as that called by Ammianus, Hucumbra (xxiv. 8).   [V.]

SYME (Σύμη: *Symi*), an island off the coast of Caria, to the west of Cape Cynossema, between the Cnidian peninsula and Rhodes, at the entrance of the Sinus Schoenus. (Herod. i. 174; Thuc. viii. 41; Strab. xiv. p. 656; Scylax, p. 38; Athen. vi. p. 262.) The island is described as 37 Roman miles in circumference, and as possessing eight harbours (Plin. v. 31, 133) and a town of the same name as the island. The island itself is very high but barren. According to Stephanus B. (*s. v.*; comp. Athen. vii. p. 296) Syme was formerly called Metapontis and Aegle, and obtained its later name from Syme, a daughter of Ialysus, who, together with Chthonius, a son of Poseidon, is said to have first peopled the island. In the story of the Trojan war, Syme enjoys a kind of celebrity, for the hero Nireus is said to have gone with three ships to assist Agamemnon. (Hom. *Il.* ii. 671; Dictys. Cret. iv. 17; Dares Phryg. 21.) The first historical population of the island consisted of Dorians; but subsequently it fell into the hands of the Carians, and when they, in consequence of frequent droughts, abandoned it, it was for a long time uninhabited, until it was finally and permanently occupied by Argives and Lacedaemonians, mixed with Cnidians and Rhodians. (Diod. Sic. v. 33; Raoul-Rochette, *Hist. des Colon. Grecques,* i. p. 337, iii. p. 72.) There are still a few but unimportant remains of the acropolis of Syme, which, however, are constantly diminished, the stones being used to erect modern buildings. (Comp. Ross, *Reisen auf den Griech. Inseln.* vol. iii. p. 121, foll.)   [L. S.]

SYMPLE'GADES. [BOSPORUS, p. 424.]

SYNCA (Σύνκα), a small village of Babylonia noticed by Zosimus (iii. c. 28).   [V.]

SYNNADA (Σύνναδα: *Eth.* Συναδεύς), a town of Phrygia Salutaris, at the extremity of a plain about 60 stadia in length, and covered with olive plantations. It is first noticed during the march of the consul Manlius against the Gallograeci (Liv. xxxviii. 15, xlv. 34); and Cicero (*ad Att.* v. 20; comp. *ad Fam.* iii. 8. xv. 4) mentions that he passed through Synnada on his way from Ephesus to Cilicia. In Strabo's time (xii. p. 577) it was still a small town, but when Pliny wrote (v. 29) it was an important place, being the conventus juridicus for the

whole of the surrounding country. It was very celebrated among the Romans for a beautiful kind of marble furnished by the neighbouring quarries, and which was commonly called Synnadic marble, though it came properly from a place in the neighbourhood, Docimia, whence it was more correctly called Docimites lapis. This marble was of a light colour, interspersed with purple spots and veins. (Strab. *l. c.*; Plin. xxxv. 1; Stat. *Silv.* i. 5. 36; Comp. Steph. B. *s. v.*; Ptol. v. 2. § 24; Martial, ix. 76; Symmach. ii. 246.) There still are appearances of extensive quarries between *Kosru-Khan* and *Bulvudun,* which Col. Leake (*Asia Minor,* p. 36) is inclined to identify with those of Synnada or Docimia. Remains of the town of Synnada still exist under the name *Eski-kara-hissar* about 3 miles to the north-west of these quarries, where they were discovered by Texier. Earlier travellers imagined they had found them at *Surmina* or *Surmeneh,* or in the plain of *Sandakleh.* (Comp. Hamilton, *Researches,* i. p. 466, ii. 177; *Journal of the R. Geogr. Society,* vii. p. 58, viii. p. 144; Eckhel, *Doctr. Num.* iii. p. 172; Sestini, *Num. Vet.* p. 127.)   [L. S.]

SYNNAUS (Σύνναος), a town in Phrygia Pacatiana, not far from the sources of the Macestus, probably on the site of the modern *Simavsul.* (Ptol. v. 2. § 20; Socrat. *Hist. Eccl.* vii. 3, Niceph. *Hist. Eccles.* xiv. 11; Concil. Chalced. p. 674; Hamilton, *Researches,* ii. p. 124; Franz, *Fünf Inschriften,* p. 33.)   [L. S.]

SYNO'DIUM (Συνόδιον, Appian, *Illyr.* 27; Σινότιον, Strab. vii. p. 315), a town of Dalmatia, situated in a deep gorge between two hills, where Gabinius was defeated, and to which the Dalmatians retreated in the campaign of B. C. 34. Octavius, suspecting their intentions, sent skirmishers over the high ground while he advanced through the valley and burnt Synodium.   [E. B. J.]

SYRACU'SAE (Συρακούσαι: *Eth.* Συρακόσιος, Steph. B.; but Thucydides, Diodorus, &c. use the form Συρακόσιος, which, as we learn from coins and inscriptions, was the native form; Syracusanus: *Siracusa, Syracuse*), the most powerful and important of all the Greek cities in Sicily, situated on the E. coast of the island, about midway between Catana and Cape Pachynus. Its situation exercised so important an influence upon its history and progress, that it will be desirable to describe this somewhat more fully before proceeding to the history of the city, reserving, at the same time, the topographical details for subsequent discussion.

I. SITUATION.

Syracuse was situated on a table-land or tabular hill, forming the prolongation of a ridge which branches off from the more elevated table-land of the interior, and projects quite down to the sea, between the bay known as the Great Harbour of Syracuse, and the more extensive bay which stretches on the N. as far as the peninsula of THAPSUS or *Magnisi.* The broad end of the kind of promontory thus formed, which abuts upon the sea for a distance of about 2½ miles, may be considered as the base of a triangular plateau which extends for above 4 miles into the interior, having its apex formed by the point now called *Mongibellisi,* which was occupied by the ancient fort of EURYALUS. This communicates, as already stated, by a narrow ridge with the table-land of the interior, but is still a marked point of separation, and was the highest point of the ancient city, from whence the table-land slopes very gradually to the sea. Though of small elevation, this plateau is bounded on all sides by precipitous banks or cliffs, varying in height, but only accessible at a few points. It may be considered as naturally divided into two portions by a slight valley or depression running across it from N. to S., about a mile from the sea: of these the upper or triangular portion was known as EPIPOLAE, the eastern portion adjoining the sea bore the name of ACHRADINA, which thus forms in some degree a distinct and separate plateau, though belonging, in fact, to the same mass with Epipolae.

The SE. angle of the plateau is separated from the Great Harbour by a small tract of low and level ground, opposite to which lies the island of ORTYGIA, a low islet about a mile in length, extending across the mouth of the Great Harbour, and originally divided by only a narrow strait from the mainland, whilst its southern extremity was separated from the nearest point of the headland of Plemmyrium by an interval of about 1200 yards, forming the entrance into the Great Harbour. This last was a spacious bay, of above 5 miles in circumference; thus greatly exceeding the dimensions of what the ancients usually understood by a port, but forming a very nearly land-locked basin of a somewhat oval form, which afforded a secure shelter to shipping in all weather; and is even at the present day one of the finest harbours in Sicily. But between the island of Ortygia and the mainland to the N. of it, was a deep bight or inlet, forming what was called the Lesser Port or PORTUS LACCEIUS, which, though very inferior to the other, was still equal to the ordinary requirements of ancient commerce.

S. of the Great Harbour again rose the peninsular promontory of PLEMMYRIUM, forming a table-land bounded, like that on the N. of the bay, by precipitous escarpments and cliffs, though of no great elevation. This table-land was prolonged by another plateau at a somewhat lower level, bounding the southern side of the Great Harbour, and extending from thence towards the interior. On its NE. angle and opposite to the heights of Epipolae, stood the temple of Jupiter Olympius, or the OLYMPIEUM, overlooking the low marshy tract which intervenes between the two table-lands, and through which the river Anapus finds its way to the sea. The beautiful stream of the CYANE rises in a source about 1½ mile to the N. of the Olympieum, and joins its waters with those of the Anapus almost immediately below the temple. From the foot of the hill crowned by the latter extends a broad tract of very low marshy ground, extending along the inner side of the Great Harbour quite to the walls of the city itself. A portion of this marsh, which seems to have formed in ancient times a shallow pool or lagoon, was known by the name of LYSIMELEIA (Λυσιμέλεια, Thuc. vii. 53; Theocr. Id. xvi. 84), though its more ancient appellation would seem to have been SYRACO (Συρακώ), from whence the city itself was supposed to derive its name. (Steph. B. s. v. Συρακοῦσαι; Scymn. Ch. 281.) It is, however, uncertain whether the names of Syraco and Lysimeleia may not originally have belonged to different portions of these marshes. This marshy tract, which is above a mile in breadth, extends towards the interior for a considerable distance, till it is met by the precipitous escarpments of the great table-land of the interior. The proximity of these marshes must always have been prejudicial to the healthiness of the situation; and the legend, that when Archias and Myscellus were about to found Syracuse and Crotona, the latter chose health while the former preferred wealth (Steph. B. l. c.), points to the acknowledged insalubrity of the site even in its most flourishing days. But in every other respect the situation was admirable; and the prosperity of Syracuse was doubtless owing in a great degree to natural as well as political causes. It was, moreover, celebrated for the mildness and serenity of its climate, it being generally asserted that there was no day on which the sun was not visible at Syracuse (Cic. Verr. v. 10), an advantage which it is said still to retain at the present day.

II. HISTORY.

Syracuse was, with the single exception of Naxos, the most ancient of the Greek colonies in Sicily. It was a Corinthian colony, sent out from that city under a leader named Archias, son of Euagetes, who belonged to the powerful family of the Bacchiadae, but had been compelled to expatriate himself. According to some accounts the colony was strengthened by an admixture of Dorian or Locrian colonists with the original Corinthian settlers; but it is certain that the Syracusans regarded themselves in all ages as of pure Corinthian origin (Theocr. Id. xv. 91), and maintained relations of the closest amity with their parent city. The colony was founded in B. C. 734, and the first settlers established themselves in the island of Ortygia, to which it is probable that the city was confined for a considerable period. (Thuc. vi. 2; Strab. vi. p. 269; Scymn. Ch. 279—282; Marm. Par.; concerning the date, see Clinton, F. H. vol. i. p. 164.) The name of Ortygia is evidently Greek, and derived from the well-known epithet of Diana, to whom the island was regarded as consecrated (Diod. v. 3); but the city seems to have assumed from the very beginning the name of Syracusae, which was derived, as already mentioned, from the name of the adjoining marsh or lake, Syraco, doubtless an indigenous name, as it has no signification in Greek. It appears indeed that the form Syraco was used by Epicharmus for the name of the city itself, but this was evidently a mere poetic license. (Strab. viii. p. 364.)

As in the case of most of the Greek colonies in Sicily, we have very little information concerning the early history and progress of Syracuse; but we may infer that it rose steadily, if not rapidly, to prosperity, from the circumstance that it continued to extend its power by the foundation of fresh colonies: that of Acrae within 70 years after its own establishment (B. C. 664); Casmenae 20 years later (B. C. 644), and Camarina 45 years afterwards, or B. C. 599. None of these colonies, however, rose to any considerable power: it was obviously the policy of Syracuse to keep them in the position of mere dependencies; and Camarina, having given umbrage to the parent city, was destroyed only 46 years after its foundation. (Thuc. vi. 5; Scymn. Ch. 294—296.) Syracuse was not, however, free from internal dissensions and revolutions. An obscure notice preserved to us by Thucydides indicates the occurrence of these as early as B. C. 648, which led to the expulsion of a party or clan called the Myletidae, who withdrew into exile and joined in the foundation of Himera. (Thuc. vi. 5.) Another indication of such disputes is found in Aristotle (Pol. v. 4), but we are unable to assign any definite place in chronology to the occurrence there alluded to. At a later period we find the government in the hands of an exclusive oligarchy called the Geomori or Gamori, who, from their name, would appear to have been the descendants of the original colonists, around whom there naturally grew up a democracy or *plebs*, composed of the citizens derived from other sources. At length, about B. C. 486, a revolution took place; and the democracy succeeded in expelling the Geomori, who thereupon withdrew to Casmenae. (Herod. vii. 155; Dionys. vi. 62.) But this revolution quickly led to another; Gelon, the powerful despot of Gela, having espoused the cause of the exiles. Gela was at this time at least equal, if not superior, to Syracuse in power. Hippocrates, its late despot, had extended his power over many of the other cities in the east of Sicily, and defeated the Syracusans themselves in a great battle at the river Helorus. He would probably indeed have made himself master of Syracuse upon this occasion had it not been for the interposition of the Corinthians and Corcyraeans, who brought about a peace upon equitable terms. (Herod. vii. 154.) But the expulsion of the Geomori opened a fresh opportunity to Gelon, who, putting himself at the head of the exiles, easily effected their restoration, while the people of Syracuse readily admitted Gelon himself as their ruler with despotic authority. (*Ib.* 155.)

This revolution (which occurred in B. C. 485) seemed at first likely to render Syracuse subordinate to Gela, but it ultimately produced a directly contrary effect. Gelon seems to have been fully alive to the superior advantages of Syracuse, and from the moment he had established his power in that city, made it the chief object of his solicitude, and directed all his efforts to the strengthening and adorning his new capital. Among other measures, he removed thither the whole body of the citizens of Camarina (which had been repeopled by Hippocrates), and subsequently more than half of those of Gela itself, admitting them all to the full rights of Syracusan citizens. Afterwards, as he directed his arms successively against the Sicilian Megara and Euboea, he removed the wealthy and noble citizens of both those cities also to Syracuse. (*Ib.* 156.) That city now rose rapidly to a far greater amount of power and prosperity than it had previously enjoyed, and became, under the fostering care of Gelon, unquestionably the first of the Greek cities in Sicily. It was probably at this period that it first extended itself beyond the limits of the island, and occupied the table-land or heights of Achradina, which were adapted to receive a far more numerous population, and had already become thickly peopled before the time of Thucydides. (Thuc. vi. 3.) This portion of the city now came to be known as the Outer City (ἡ ἔξω πόλις), while the island of Ortygia was called the Inner City, though still frequently designated as "the Island." Strictly speaking, however, it had ceased to merit that term, being now joined to the mainland by an artificial dike or causeway. (Thuc. *l. c.*)

From the time of Gelon the history of Syracuse becomes inseparably blended with that of Sicily in general; its position in the island being so important that, as Strabo justly remarks, whatever vicissitudes of fortune befel the city were shared in by the whole island. (Strab. vi. p. 270.) Hence it would be useless to recapitulate the events of which a brief summary has been already given in

the article SICILIA, and which are more fully detailed by all the general historians of Greece. The following summary will, therefore, be confined to those historical events which more immediately affected the city itself, as distinguished from the political vicissitudes of the state.

There can be no doubt that Syracuse continued to flourish extremely throughout the reign of Gelon (B. C. 485—478), as well as that of his successor Hieron (B. C. 478—467), who, notwithstanding the more despotic character of his government, was in many respects a liberal and enlightened ruler. His patronage of letters and the arts especially rendered Syracuse one of the chief resorts of men of letters, and his court afforded shelter and protection to Aeschylus, Pindar, and Bacchylides. Nor was Syracuse itself deficient in literary distinction. Epicharmus, though not a native of the city, spent all the latter years of his life there, and Sophron, the celebrated writer of mimes, was a native of Syracuse, and exhibited all his principal works there. The care bestowed upon the arts is sufficiently attested by the still extant coins of the city, as well as by the accounts transmitted to us of other monuments; and there is every probability that the distinction of Syracuse in this respect commenced from the reign of Hieron. The tranquil reign of that monarch was followed by a brief period of revolution and disturbance; his brother Thrasybulus having, after a short but tyrannical and violent reign, been expelled by the Syracusans, who established a popular government, B. C. 466. This was for a time agitated by fresh tumults, arising out of disputes between the new citizens who had been introduced by Gelon and the older citizens, who claimed the exclusive possession of political power; but after some time these disputes were terminated by a compromise, and the new citizens withdrew to Messana. (Diod. xi. 67, 68, 72, 73, 76.)

The civil dissensions connected with the expulsion of Thrasybulus, which on more than one occasion broke out into actual hostilities, show how great was the extent which the city had already attained. Thrasybulus himself, and afterwards the discontented citizens, are mentioned as occupying the Island and Achradina, both of which were strongly fortified, and had their own separate walls (Diod. xi. 68, 73); while the popular party held *the rest of the city*. It is evident therefore that there were already considerable spaces occupied by buildings outside the walls of these two quarters, which are distinctly mentioned on one occasion as "the suburbs" (τὰ προαστεῖα, *Ib.* 68). Of these, one quarter called Tycha, which lay to the W. of Achradina, adjoining the N. slope of the table-land, is now first mentioned by name (*Ibid.*); but there can be no doubt that the plain between the heights of Achradina and the marshes was already occupied with buildings, and formed part of the city, though it apparently was not as yet comprised within the fortifications.

The final establishment of the democracy at Syracuse was followed by a period of about sixty years of free government, during which we are expressly told that the city, in common with the other Greek colonies in Sicily, developed its resources with great rapidity, and probably attained to its maximum of wealth and power. (Diod. xi. 68, 72.) Before the close of this period it had to encounter the severest danger it had yet experienced, and gave abundant proof of its great resources by coming off victorious in a contest with Athens, then at the very height of its power The circumstances of the great siege of Syracuse by the Athenians must here be related in some detail, on account of their important bearing on all questions connected with the topography of the city, and the interest they confer on its localities. At the same time it will obviously be impossible to do more than give a very brief sketch of that memorable contest, for the details of which the reader must refer to the narrative of Thucydides, with the copious illustrations of Arnold, Grote, and Col. Leake.

It was not till the spring of B. C. 414 that the siege of Syracuse was regularly commenced. But in the autumn of 415, the Athenians had already made a demonstration against the city, and sailing into the Great Harbour, effected a landing without opposition near the Olympieum, where they established their camp on the shore, and erected a temporary fort at a place called Dascon (Thuc. vi. 66; Diod. xii. 6), apparently on the inner bight of the harbour, between the mouth of the Anapus and the bay now called the *Bay of Maddalena*. But though successful in the battle that ensued, Nicias did not attempt to follow up his advantage, and withdrew to winter at Catana. The next spring the Athenians landed to the N. of Syracuse, at a place called Leon, about 6 or 7 stadia from the heights of Epipolae, while they established their naval station at the adjoining peninsula of Thapsus (*Magnisi*). The land troops advanced at once to occupy Epipolae, the military importance of which was felt by both parties, and succeeded in establishing themselves there, before the Syracusans could dislodge them. They then proceeded to build a fort at a place called Labdalum, which is described by Thucydides as situated " on the top of the cliffs of Epipolae, looking towards Megara " (Thuc. vi. 97), and having occupied this with a garrison, so as to secure their communications with their fleet, they advanced to a place called Syce (ἡ Σύκη), where they established themselves, and began to construct with great rapidity a line of circumvallation across the plateau of Epipolae.* The construction of such a line was the customary mode of proceeding in Greek sieges, and it was with the special object of guarding against it that the Syracusans had in the preceding winter extended their fortifications by running a new line of wall so as to enclose the temple of Apollo Temenites (Thuc. vi. 75), which probably extended from thence down to the Great Harbour. Nevertheless the Athenian line of circumvallation was carried on so rapidly as to excite in them the greatest alarm. Its northern extremity was made to rest on the sea at a point called Trogilus (probably near the *Scala Greca*), and it was from thence carried across the table-land

* The account here given of the Athenian operations assumes that " the circle " repeatedly spoken of by Thucydides (vi. 98, 99, &c.), is the circuit of the lines of circumvallation. This is the construction adopted by Göller, and all earlier editors of Thucydides, as well as by Col. Leake ; and appears to the writer of this article by far the most natural and intelligible interpretation. Mr. Grote, on the contrary, as well as Dr. Arnold in his later edition adopts the suggestion of M. Firmin Didot that " the circle " (ὁ κύκλος) was a particular intrenchment or fortified camp of a circular form. It is difficult to understand the military object of such a work, as well as to reconcile it with the subsequent details of the siege operations.

of the Epipolae, to the point nearest to the Great Harbour. Alarmed at the rapid progress of this wall, the Syracusans endeavoured to interrupt it by constructing a counter or cross wall (ὑποτείχισμα or ἐγκάρσιον τεῖχος), directed apparently from the wall recently erected around the temple of Apollo Temenites towards the southern cliff of Epipolae. (Thuc. vi. 99.) This wall was, however, carried by the Athenians by a sudden attack and destroyed, whereupon the Syracusans attempted a second counterwork, carried through the marshes and low ground, so as to prevent the Athenians from connecting their works on Epipolae with the Great Harbour. But this work was, like the preceding one, taken and destroyed; and the Athenians, whose fleet had meanwhile entered the Great Harbour, and established itself there, were able to construct a strong double line of wall, extending from the cliffs of Epipolae quite down to the harbour. (*Ib.* 100— 103.) On the table-land above, on the contrary, their works were still incomplete, and especially that part of the line of circumvallation near Trogilus was still in an unfinished state when Gylippus landed in Sicily, so that that commander was able to force his passage through the lines at this point, and effect an entry into Syracuse. (Id. vii. 2.) It is remarkable that the hill of Euryalus, though in fact the key of the position on the Epipolae, seems to have been neglected by Nicias, and was still undefended by any fortifications.

Gylippus immediately directed his efforts to prevent the completion of the Athenian lines across the table-land, and obtained in the first instance an important advantage by surprising the Athenian fort at Labdalum. He next began to erect another cross wall, running out from the walls of the city across the plateau, so as to cross and intersect the Athenian lines; and notwithstanding repeated efforts on the part of the Athenians, succeeded in carrying this on so far as completely to cut off their line of circumvallation, and render it impossible for them to complete it. (Id. vii. 4—6.) Both parties seem to have looked on the completion of this line as the decisive point of the siege ; Nicias finding himself unable to capture the outwork of the Syracusans, almost despaired of success, and wrote to Athens for strong reinforcements. Meanwhile he sought to strengthen his position on the Great Harbour by occupying and fortifying the headland of Plemmyrium, which completely commanded its entrance. (*Ib.* 4.) The Syracusans, however, still occupied the Olympieum (or Polichne, as it was sometimes called) with a strong body of troops, and having, under the guidance of Gylippus, attacked the Athenians both by sea and land, though foiled in the former attempt, they took the forts which had been recently erected on the Plemmyrium. (*Ib.* 4, 22— 24.) This was a most important advantage, as it rendered it henceforth very difficult for the Athenians to supply their fleet and camp with provisions; and it is evident that it was so regarded by both parties (*Ib.* 25, 31) : the Syracusans also subsequently gained a decisive success in a sea-fight within the Great Harbour, and were preparing to push their advantage further, when the arrival of Demosthenes and Eurymedon from Athens with a powerful fleet restored for a time the superiority of the Athenians. Demosthenes immediately directed all his efforts to the capture of the Syracusan counterwork on Epipolae; but meanwhile Gylippus had not neglected to strengthen his position there, by constructing three redoubts or forts, each of them occupied with a strong garrison, at intervals along the sloping plateau of Epipolae, while a fort had been also erected at the important post of Euryalus, at the extreme angle of the heights. (Thuc. vii. 43.) So strong indeed was their position that Demosthenes despaired of carrying it by day, and resolved upon a night attack, in which he succeeded in carrying the fort at Euryalus, but was foiled in his attempt upon the other outworks, and repulsed with heavy loss. (Ib. 43—45.)

The failure of this attack was considered by Demosthenes himself as decisive, and he advised the immediate abandonment of the siege. But the contrary advice of Nicias prevailed; and even when increasing sickness in the Athenian camp had induced him also to consent to a retreat, his superstitious fears, excited by an eclipse of the moon, again caused them to postpone their departure. The consequences were fatal. The Syracusans now became rather the besiegers than the besieged, attacked the Athenian fleet in the Great Harbour, and cut off and destroyed the whole of their right wing under Eurymedon, in the bay of Dascon. Elated with this success, they sought nothing less than the capture of the whole armament, and began to block up the mouth of the Great Harbour, from Ortygia across to Plemmyrium, by mooring vessels across it. The Athenians were now compelled to abandon all their outposts and lines on the heights, and draw together their troops as close to the naval camp as possible; while they made a final effort to break through the barrier at the entrance of the harbour. But this attempt proved unsuccessful, and led to a complete defeat of the Athenian fleet. There was now no course but to retreat. The army under Nicias and Demosthenes broke up from its camp, and at first directed their course along the valley of the Anapus, till they came to a narrow pass, commanded by a precipitous ridge called the Acraean Rock ('Ακραῖον λέπας, Thuc. vii. 78), which had been occupied in force by the Syracusans. Failing in forcing this defile, the Athenians changed their line of retreat, and followed the road to Helorus, but after forcing in succession, though not without heavy loss, the passage of the two rivers Cacyparis and Erineus, and reaching the banks of the Asinarus, the last survivors of the Athenian army were compelled to lay down their arms. The whole number of prisoners was said to amount to 7000. A trophy was erected by the Syracusans on the bank of the Asinarus, and a festival called the Asinaria instituted to commemorate their victory. (Thuc. vii. 78—87; Diod. xiii. 18, 19.)

The failure of the Athenian expedition against Syracuse seemed likely to secure to that city the unquestionable superiority among the Greek colonies in Sicily. But a new and formidable power now appeared—the Carthaginians, who were invited by the Segestans to support them against the Selinuntines, but who, not content with the destruction of Selinus and Himera (B. C. 410), and with that of Agrigentum (B. C. 406), pushed forward their conquests with a view of making themselves masters of the whole island. Dionysius, then a young man, took advantage of the alarm and excitement caused by this danger to raise himself to despotic power at Syracuse (B. C. 405), and he soon after concluded a peace with the Carthaginians, whose career of victory had been checked by a pestilence. The history of the reign of Dionysius at

Syracuse, which continued for a period of 38 years (B. C. 405—387), cannot be here related: it is briefly given in the Biogr. Dict., art. DIONYSIUS, and very fully in Grote's History of Greece, vols. x. and xi.; but its influence and effects upon the city itself must be here noticed. From a very early period he turned his attention to the strengthening and fortification of the city, and constructed great works, partly with a view to the defence of the city against external invasion, partly for the security of his own power. One of his first operations was to convert the island of Ortygia into a strong fortress, by surrounding it with a lofty wall, fortified with numerous towers, especially on the side where it adjoined the land, where he raised a strongly fortified front, called the Pentapyla; while, for still further security, he constructed an interior fort or citadel within the island, which became the acropolis of Syracuse, and at the same time the residence of Dionysius and his successors in the despotism. Adjoining this he constructed within the lesser port, or Portus Lacceius, docks for his ships of war on a large scale, so as to be capable of receiving 60 triremes: while they were enclosed with a wall, and accessible only by a narrow entrance. But not content with this, he a few years afterwards added docks for 160 more ships, within the Great Port, in the recess or bight of it which approaches most nearly to the Portus Lacceius, and opened a channel of communication between the two. At the same time he adorned the part of the city immediately outside the island with porticoes and public buildings for the convenience of the citizens. (Diod. xiv. 7.) But his greatest work of all was the line of walls with which he fortified the heights of Epipolae. The events of the Athenian siege had sufficiently proved the vital importance of these to the safety of the city; and hence before Dionysius engaged in his great war with Carthage he determined to secure their possession by a line of permanent fortifications. The walls erected for this purpose along the northern edge of the cliffs of Epipolae (extending from near Sta Panagia to the hill of Euryalus, or Mongibellisi) were 30 stadia in length, and are said to have been erected by the labour of the whole body of the citizens in the short space of 20 days. (Diod. xiv. 18.) It is remarkable that we hear nothing of the construction of a similar wall along the southern edge of the plateau of Epipolae; though the table-land is at least as accessible on this side as on the other; and a considerable suburb called Neapolis had already grown up on this side (Diod. xiv. 9), outside of the wall of Achradina, and extending over a considerable part of the slope, which descends from the Temenitis towards the marshy plain of the Anapus. But whatever may have been the cause, it seems certain that Syracuse continued till a later period to be but imperfectly fortified on this side.

The importance of the additional defences erected by Dionysius was sufficiently shown in the course of the war with Carthage which began in B. C. 397. In that war Dionysius at first carried his arms successfully to the western extremity of Sicily, but fortune soon turned against him, and he was compelled in his turn to shut himself up within the walls of Syracuse, and trust to the strength of his fortifications. The Carthaginian general Himilco entered the Great Port with his fleet, and established his head-quarters at the Olympieum, while he not only ravaged the country outside the walls, but made himself master of one of the suburbs, in which were situated the temples of Ceres and Proserpine, both of which he gave up to plunder. But the anger of the goddesses, brought on by this act of sacrilege, was believed to be the source of all the calamities that soon befel him. A pestilence broke out in the Carthaginian camp, from which they sustained very heavy losses, and Dionysius took advantage of their enfeebled state to make a general attack on their camp both by sea and land. The position occupied by the Carthaginians was very much the same as that which had been held by the Athenians: they occupied the headland of Plemmyrium, on which they had erected a fort, while they had also fortified the Olympieum, or Polichna, and constructed a third fort close to the edge of the Great Harbour for the protection of their fleet, which lay within the inner bay or harbour of Dascon. But Dionysius, by a sudden attack from the land side, carried both the last forts, and at the same time succeeded in burning a great part of the Carthaginian fleet, so that Himilco was compelled to abandon the enterprise, and by a secret capitulation secured a safe retreat for himself and the native Carthaginians in his army, abandoning his allies and mercenaries to their fate. (Diod. xiv. 62, 63, 70—75.)

The defeat of the Carthaginian armament left Dionysius undisputed master of Syracuse, while that city held as unquestioned a pre-eminence over the other cities of Sicily; and it is probable that the city itself continued to increase in extent and population. The impregnable citadel in the island of Ortygia constructed by the elder Dionysius continued to be the bulwark of his power, as well as that of his son and successor. Even when the citizens, in B. C. 357, opened their gates to Dion, who made a triumphal entry into Achradina, and made himself master with little difficulty of the fort on the summit of Epipolae, the island still held out, and Dion was compelled to resort to a blockade, having erected a line or wall of contravallation across from the lesser port to the greater, so as effectually to cut off the garrison from all communication with the interior. (Plut. Dion. 29; Diod. xvi. 12.) It was not till after the blockade had been continued for above a year that Apollocrates was compelled by scarcity of provisions to surrender this stronghold, and Dion thus became complete master of Syracuse, B. C. 356. But that event did not, as had been expected, restore liberty to Syracuse, and the island citadel still remained the stronghold of the despots who successively ruled over the city. When at length Timoleon landed in Sicily (B. C. 344) Ortygia was once more in the possession of Dionysius, while the rest of the city was in the hands of Hicetas, who was supported by a Carthaginian fleet and army, with which he closely blockaded the island fortress. But the arrival of Timoleon quickly changed the face of affairs: Ortygia was voluntarily surrendered to him by Dionysius; and Neon, whom he left there as commander of the garrison, by a sudden sally made himself master of Achradina also. Soon after Timoleon carried the heights of Epipolae by assault, and thus found himself master of the whole of Syracuse. One of the first measures he took after his success was to demolish the fortress erected by Dionysius within the Island, as well as the palace of the despot himself, and the splendid monument that had been erected to him by his son and successor. On the site were erected the new courts of justice. (Plut. Timol. 22.)

Syracuse had suffered severely from the long period of civil dissensions and almost constant hostilities which had preceded its liberation by Timoleon; and one of the first cares of its deliverer was to recruit its exhausted population, not only by recalling from all quarters the fugitive or exiled citizens, but by summoning from Corinth and other parts of Greece a large body of new colonists. Such was the success of his invitation that we are assured the total number of immigrants (including of course the restored exiles) amounted to not less than 60,000. (Plut. Timol. 22, 23.) The democratic form of government was restored, and the code of laws which had been introduced by Diocles after the Athenian expedition, but had speedily fallen into neglect under the long despotism of the two Dionysii, was now revived and restored to its full vigour. (Diod. xiii. 35, xvi. 70.) At the same time a new annual magistracy was established, with the title of Amphipolus of the Olympian Jove, who was thenceforth destined, like the Archon at Athens, to give name to the year. The office was apparently a merely honorary one, but the years continued to be designated by the names of the Amphipoli down to the time of Augustus. (Diod. xvi. 70; Cic. Verr. ii. 51, iv. 61.)

There can be no doubt that the period following the restoration of liberty by Timoleon was one of great prosperity for Syracuse, as well as for Sicily in general. Unfortunately it did not last long. Less than 30 years after the capture of Syracuse by Timoleon, the city fell under the despotism of Agathocles (B. C. 317), which continued without interruption till B. C. 289. We hear very little of the fortunes of the city itself under his government, but it appears that, like his predecessor Dionysius, Agathocles devoted his attention to the construction of great works and public buildings, so that the city continued to increase in magnificence. We are told, among other things, that he fortified the entrance of the lesser port, or Portus Lacceius, with towers, the remains of one of which are still visible. During the absence of Agathocles in Africa, Syracuse was indeed exposed to the assaults of the Carthaginian general Hamilcar, who encamped, as Himilco had formerly done, at Polichne, and from thence made desultory attacks upon the city, but without any important result; and having at length made a night attack upon the fort of Euryalus, he was defeated, and himself taken prisoner. (Diod. xx. 29.) After the death of Agathocles, Syracuse for a short time recovered its liberty, but soon fell again under the virtual despotism of Hicetas, and subsequently passed into the hands of successive military adventurers, till in B. C. 275, the government became vested in Hieron, the son of Hierocles, who, at first with the title of general autocrator, and afterwards with that of king, continued to reign over the city till B. C. 216. His wisdom and moderation proved a striking contrast to the despotism of several of the former rulers of Syracuse, and while his subjects flourished under his liberal and enlightened rule, external tranquillity was secured by the steadiness with which he adhered to the alliance of Rome, after having once measured his strength against that formidable power. By the treaty concluded between him and the Romans in B. C. 263, he was recognised as king of Syracuse, with the dependent towns of Acrae, Helorus, Netum, Megara, and Leontini, to which was annexed Tauromenium also, as an outlying dependency. (Diod. xxiii. Exc. H. p. 502.) Notwithstanding the small extent of his territory,

Hieron was undoubtedly a powerful prince, and Syracuse seems to have risen, during this long period of peace and tranquillity, to a high state of wealth and prosperity. Its commercial relations with foreign countries, especially with Egypt, were assiduously cultivated and extended, while the natural resources of its fertile territory were developed to the utmost by the wise and judicious regulations of Hieron, which, under the name of the Lex Hieronica, were subsequently introduced into all parts of Sicily, and continued to be observed by the Romans, in their administration of that province. At the same time the monarch adorned the city with many public works and buildings, including temples, gymnasia, &c., while he displayed his wealth and magnificence by splendid offerings, both at Rome and the most noted sanctuaries of Greece. On the whole it may probably be assumed that the reign of Hieron II. was the period when Syracuse attained its highest degree of splendour and magnificence, as well as of wealth and population.

But this state of things was abruptly changed after the death of Hieron. His grandson, Hieronymus, who succeeded him, deserted the alliance of Rome for that of Carthage, and though the young king was shortly after assassinated, the Carthaginian party continued to maintain its ascendency at Syracuse under two leaders named Hippocrates and Epicydes, who were appointed generals with supreme power. They shut the gates against Marcellus, who was in command of the Roman armies in Sicily, and having refused all terms of accommodation, compelled that general to form the siege of Syracuse, B. C. 214. (Liv. xxiv. 21—33.) The enterprise proved far more arduous than the Roman General seems to have anticipated. He established his camp, as the Carthaginians had repeatedly done, on the height of the Olympieum; but his principal attacks were directed against the northern walls, in the neighbourhood of Hexapylum (the outlet of the city towards Leontini and Megara), as well as against the defences of Achradina from the sea. His powerful fleet gave Marcellus the complete command of the sea, and he availed himself of this to bring up his ships with powerful battering engines under the very walls which bordered the rocks of Achradina; but all his efforts were baffled by the superior skill and science of Archimedes; his engines and ships were destroyed or sunk, and after repeated attempts, both by sea and land, he found himself compelled to abandon all active assaults and convert the siege into a blockade. (Liv. xxiv. 33, 34.)

During the winter he left the camp and army at the Olympieum, under the command of T. Quinctius Crispinus, while he himself took up his winter-quarters and established a fortified camp at Leon, on the N. side of the city. But he was unable to maintain a strict blockade by sea, and the Carthaginians succeeded in frequently throwing in supplies, so that the blockade was prolonged for more than two years; and Marcellus began to entertain little prospect of success, when in the spring of B. C. 212 an accident threw in his way the opportunity of scaling the walls by night, at a place called by Livy the Portus Trogiliorum (evidently the little cove called Scala Greca); and having thus surprised the walls he made himself master of the gate at Hexapylum, as well as of a great part of the slope of Epipolae. But the strong fort of Euryalus, at the angle of Epipolae, defied his efforts, and the walls of Achradina, which still retained its separate fortifications, enabled the

Syracusans to hold possession of that important part of the city, as well as of the island and fortress of Ortygia. The two quarters of Tycha and Neapolis were, however, surrendered to him, and given up to plunder, the citizens having stipulated only for their lives; and shortly after Philodemus, who commanded the garrison of Euryalus, having no hopes of relief, surrendered that important post also into the hands of Marcellus. (Liv. xxv. 23—25.) The Roman general was now in possession of the whole heights of Epipolae, and being secured from attacks in the rear by the possession of Euryalus, he divided his forces into three camps, and endeavoured wholly to blockade Achradina. At the same time Crispinus still held the old camp on the hill of the Olympieum. (Ib. 26.) In this state of things a vigorous effort was made by the Carthaginians to raise the siege: they advanced with a large army under Himilco and Hippocrates, and attacked the camp of Crispinus; while Bomilcar, with a fleet of 150 ships, occupied the Great Harbour, and took possession of the shore between the city and the mouth of the Anapus, at the same time that Epicydes made a vigorous sally from Achradina against the lines of Marcellus. But they were repulsed at all points, and though they continued for some time to maintain their army in the immediate neighbourhood of the city, it was soon attacked by a pestilence, arising from the marshy nature of the low grounds in which they were encamped, to which both Hippocrates and Himilco fell victims, with a great part of their troops. Bomilcar, also, who had quitted the port with the view of obtaining reinforcements from Carthage, never returned, and Epicydes, who had gone out to meet him, abandoned the city to its fate, and withdrew to Agrigentum. The defence of Syracuse was now entrusted to the leaders of the mercenary troops, and one of these, a Spaniard named Mericus, betrayed his post to Marcellus. A body of Roman troops was landed in the night at the extremity of the island, near the fountain of Arethusa, and quickly made themselves masters of the whole of Ortygia; while Marcellus, having at the same time made a general assault on Achradina, succeeded in carrying a portion of that quarter also. The remaining part of the city was now voluntarily surrendered by the inhabitants; and Marcellus, after taking precautions to secure the royal treasures, and the houses of those citizens who had been favourable to the Romans, gave up the whole city to be pillaged by his soldiers. Archimedes, who had contributed so much to the defence of the city, was accidentally slain in the confusion. The plunder was said to be enormous; and the magnificent statues, pictures, and other works of art which were carried by Marcellus to Rome, to adorn his own triumph, are said to have given the first impulse to that love of Greek art which afterwards became so prevalent among the Romans. (Liv. xxv. 26—31, 40; Plut. Marc. 14 —19; Diod. xxvi. Fr. 18—20.)

From this time Syracuse sank into the ordinary condition of a Roman provincial town; but it continued to be the unquestionable capital of Sicily, and was the customary residence of the Roman praetors who were sent to govern the island, as well as of one of the two quaestors who were charged with its financial administration. Even in the days of Cicero it is spoken of by that orator as "the greatest of Greek cities, and the most beautiful of all cities." (Cic. Verr. iv. 52.) Its public buildings had apparently suffered little, if at all, from its capture by

Marcellus, and were evidently still extant in the days of the orator, who enumerates most of them by name. All the four quarters of the city, the Island, Achradina, Tycha, and Neapolis, were still well inhabited; though as a measure of precaution no persons of native Syracusan extraction were permitted to dwell in the Island. (*Ib.* v. 32.) But the prosperity of Syracuse seems to have sustained a severe shock in the time of Sextus Pompeius, who, according to Strabo, inflicted upon it injuries, from which it appears never to have recovered. Such was its decayed condition that Augustus endeavoured to recruit it by sending thither a Roman colony (B. C. 21). But the new settlers were confined to the Island and to the part of the city immediately adjoining it, forming a portion only of Achradina and Neapolis. (Strab. vi. p. 270; Dion Cass. liv. 7; Plin. iii. 8. s. 14.) It is in this part of the town that the amphitheatre and other edifices of Roman construction are still found.

But though greatly fallen from its former splendour, Syracuse continued throughout the Roman Empire to be one of the most considerable cities of Sicily, and still finds a place in the 4th century in the Ordo Nobilium Urbium of Ausonius. The natural strength of the Island as a fortress rendered it always a post of the utmost importance. After the fall of the Western Empire, it fell with the rest of Sicily under the dominion of the Goths, but was recovered by Belisarius in A. D. 535, and annexed to the dominions of the Byzantine emperors, in whose hands it continued till the 9th century, when it was finally wrested from them by the Arabs or Saracens. Syracuse was, with the single exception of Tauromenium, the last place in Sicily that fell into the hands of those invaders: it was still a very strong fortress, and it was not till 878, more than fifty years after the Saracens first landed in the island, that it was compelled to surrender, after a siege of nine months' duration. The inhabitants were put to the sword, the fortifications destroyed, and the city given up to the flames. Nor did it ever recover from this calamity, though the Island seems to have always continued to be inhabited. Its fortifications were strengthened by Charles V., and assumed very much their present appearance. The modern city, which is still confined to the narrow limits of the Island, contains about 14,000 inhabitants. But the whole of the expanse on the opposite side of the strait, as well as the broad table-land of Achradina and Epipolae, are now wholly bare and desolate, being in great part uncultivated as well as uninhabited.

III. TOPOGRAPHY.

The topographical description of Syracuse as it existed in the days of its greatness cannot better be introduced than in the words of Cicero, who has described it in unusual detail. " You have often heard (says he) that Syracuse was the largest of all Greek cities, and the most beautiful of all cities. And it is so indeed. For it is both strong by its natural situation and striking to behold, from whatever side it is approached, whether by land or sea. It has two ports, as it were, enclosed within the buildings of the city itself, so as to combine with it from every point of view, which have different and separate entrances, but are united and conjoined together at the opposite extremity. The junction of these separates from the mainland the part of the town which is called the Island, but this is reunited to the continent by a bridge across the nar-

row strait which divides them. So great is the city that it may be said to consist of four cities, all of them of very large size; one of which is that which I have already mentioned, the Island, which is surrounded by the two ports, while it projects towards the mouth and entrance of each of them. In it is the palace of king Hieron, which is now the customary residence of our praetors. It contains, also, several sacred edifices, but two in particular, which far surpass the others, one a temple of Diana, the other of Minerva, which before the arrival of Verres was most highly adorned. At the extremity of this island is a fountain of fresh water, which bears the name of Arethusa, of incredible magnitude, and full of fish: this would be wholly overflowed and covered by the waves were it not separated from the sea by a strongly-built barrier of stone. The second city at Syracuse is that which is called Achradina, which contains a forum of very large size, beautiful porticoes, a most highly ornamented Prytaneum, a spacious Curia, and a magnificent temple of Jupiter Olympius; not to speak of the other parts of the city, which are occupied by private buildings, being divided by one broad street through its whole length, and many cross streets. The third city is that which is called Tycha, because it contained a very ancient temple of Fortune; in this is a very spacious gymnasium, as well as many sacred edifices, and it is the quarter of the town which is the most thickly inhabited. The fourth city is that which, because it was the last built, is named Neapolis: at the top of which is a theatre of vast size; besides this it contains two splendid temples, one of Ceres, the other of Libera, and a statue of Apollo, which is known by the name of Temenites, of great beauty and very large size, which Verres would not have hesitated to carry off if he had been able to remove it." (Cic. *Verr.* iv. 52, 53.)

Cicero here distinctly describes the four quarters of Syracuse, which were commonly compared to four separate cities; and it appears that Diodorus gave the same account. (Diod. xxvi. 19, ed. Didot.) In later times, also, we find it alluded to as "the quadruple city " ("quadruplices Syracusae," Auson. *Cl. Urb.* 11). Others, however, enumerated five quarters, as Strabo tells us that it was formerly composed of five cities (πεντάπολις ἦν τὸ παλαιόν, Strab. v. p. 270), probably because the heights of Epipolae towards the castle of Euryalus were at one time inhabited, and were reckoned as a fifth town. But we have no distinct statement to this effect. The several quarters of the city must now be considered separately.

1. ORTYGIA ('Ορτυγία, Pind., Diod., Strab., &c.), more commonly known simply as "the Island" (ἡ νῆσος, Thuc., &c., and in the Doric dialect Νᾶσος: hence Livy calls it Nasus, while Cicero uses the Latin Insula), was the original seat of the colony, and continued throughout the flourishing period of the city to be as it were the citadel or Acropolis of Syracuse, though, unlike most citadels, it lay lower than the rest of the city, its strength as a fortress being derived from its insular position. It is about a mile in length, by less than half a mile in breadth, and of small elevation, though composed wholly of rock, and rising perceptibly in the centre. There is no doubt that it was originally an island, naturally separated from the mainland, though in the time of Thucydides it was united with it (Thuc. vi. 3): probably, however, this was merely effected by an artificial mole or causeway,

for the purpose of facilitating the communication with "the outer city," as that on the mainland was then called. At a later period it was again severed from the land, probably by the elder Dionysius, when he constructed his great docks in the two ports. It was, however, undoubtedly always connected with the mainland by a bridge, or series of bridges, as it is at the present day. The citadel or castle, constructed by Dionysius, stood within the island, but immediately fronting the mainland, and closely adjoining the docks or *navalia* in the Lesser Port. Its front towards the mainland, which appears to have been strongly fortified, was known as the Pentapyla (τὰ πεντάπυλα, Plut. *Dion.* 29); and this seems to have looked directly upon the Agora or Forum, which we know to have been situated on the mainland. It is therefore clear that the citadel must have occupied nearly the same position with the modern fortifications which form the defence of Syracuse on the land side. These were constructed in the reign of Charles V., when the isthmus by which Ortygia had been reunited to the mainland was cut through, as well as a Roman aqueduct designed to supply this quarter of the city with water, constructed, as it appeared from an inscription, by the emperor Claudius. (Fazell. *Sic.* iv. i. p. 169.)

Ortygia was considered from an early time as consecrated to Artemis or Diana (Diod. v. 3), whence Pindar terms it "the couch of Artemis," and "the sister of Delos" (δέμνιον Ἀρτέμιδος, Δάλου κασιγνήτα, *Nem.* i. 3). Hence, as we learn from Cicero (*l. c.*), one of the principal edifices in the island was a temple of Diana. Some remains of this are supposed to be still extant in the NE. corner of the modern city, where two columns, with a portion of their architrave, of the Doric order, are built into the walls of a private house. From the style and character of these it is evident that the edifice was one of very remote antiquity. Much more considerable remains are extant of the other temple, noticed by the orator in the same passage—that of Minerva. This was one of the most magnificent in Sicily. Its doors, composed of gold and ivory, and conspicuous for their beautiful workmanship, were celebrated throughout the Grecian world: while the interior was adorned with numerous paintings, among which a series representing one of the battles of Agathocles was especially celebrated. All these works of art, which had been spared by the generosity of Marcellus, were carried off by the insatiable Verres. (Cic. *Verr.* iv. 55, 56.) On the summit of the temple was a shield, which served as a landmark to sailors quitting or approaching the port. (Polemon, *ap. Athen.* xi. p. 462.) There can be no doubt that this temple, which must have stood on the highest point of the island, is the same which has been converted into the modern cathedral or church of *Sta Maria delle Colonne*. The columns of the sides, fourteen in number, are still perfect, though built into the walls of the church; but the portico and *façade* were destroyed by an earthquake. It was of the Doric order, and its dimensions (185 feet in length by 75 in breadth), which nearly approach those of the great temple of Neptune at Paestum, show that it must have belonged to the first class of ancient edifices of this description. The style of the architectural details and proportions of the columns would render it probable that this temple may be referred to the sixth century B. C., thus confirming an incidental notice of Diodorus (viii. Fr. 9), from which it would ap-

pear that it was built under the government of the Geomori, and therefore certainly prior to the despotism of Gelon. No other ancient remains are now extant in the island of Ortygia; but the celebrated fountain of Arethusa is still visible, as described by Cicero, near the southern extremity of the island, on its western shore. It is still a very copious source, but scarcely answering to the accounts of its magnitude in ancient times; and it is probable that it has been disturbed and its supply diminished by earthquakes, which have repeatedly afflicted the modern town of Syracuse.

At the extreme point of the island, and outside the ancient walls, probably on the spot where the castle built by John Maniaces now stands, was situated a temple of the Olympian Juno, with an altar from which it was the custom for departing sailors to take a cup with certain offerings, which they flung into the sea when they lost sight of the shield on the temple of Minerva (Polemon, *ap. Athen. l. c.*). Of the other edifices in the island the most remarkable were the Hexecontaclinus (οἶκος ὁ Ἑξηκοντάκλινος καλούμενος, Diod. xvi. 86), built, or at least finished, by Agathocles, but the purpose and nature of which are uncertain ; the public granaries, a building of so massive and lofty a construction as to serve the purposes of a fortress (Liv. xxiv. 21); and the palace of king Hieron, which was afterwards made the residence of the Roman praetors (Cic. *Verr.* iv. 52). The site of this is uncertain : the palace of Dionysius, which had been situated in the citadel constructed by him, was destroyed together with that fortress by Timoleon, and a building for the courts of justice erected on the site. Hence it is probable that Hieron, who was always desirous to court popularity, would avoid establishing himself anew upon the same site. No trace now remains of the ancient walls or works on this side of the island, which have been wholly covered and concealed by the modern fortifications. The remains of a tower are, however, visible on a shoal or rock near the N. angle of the modern city, which are probably those of one of the towers built by Agathocles to guard the entrance of the Lesser Harbour, or Portus Lacceius (Diod. xvi. 83): but no traces have been discovered of the corresponding tower on the other side.

2. ACHRADINA (Ἀχραδίνη, Diod., and this seems to be the more correct form of the name, though it is frequently written Acradina ; both Livy and Cicero, however, give Achradina), or "the outer city," as it is termed by Thucydides, was the most important and extensive of the quarters of Syracuse. It consisted of two portions, comprising the eastern part of the great triangular plateau already described, which extended from the angle of Epipolae to the sea, as well as the lower and more level space which extends from the foot of this table-land to the Great Harbour, and borders on the marshes of Lysimeleia. This latter plain, which is immediately opposite to the island of Ortygia, is not, like the tract beyond it extending to the Anapus, low and marshy ground, but has a rocky soil, of the same limestone with the table-land above, of which it is as it were a lower step. Hence the city, as soon as it extended itself beyond the limits of the island, spread at once over this area ; but not content with this, the inhabitants occupied the part of the table-land above it nearest the sea, which, as already mentioned in the general description, is partly separated by a cross valley or depression from the upper part of the plateau, or the heights of Epipolae. Hence this part of the city

was of considerable natural strength, and seems to have been early fortified by a wall. It is not improbable that, in the first instance, the name of Achradina was given exclusively to the heights *, and that these, as well as the island, had originally their own separate defences ; but as the city spread itself out in the plain below, this must also have been protected by an outer wall on the side towards the marshes. It has indeed been supposed (Grote's *Greece*, vol. vii. p. 556) that no defence existed on this side till the time of the Athenian expedition, when the Syracusans, for the first time, surrounded the suburb of Temenitis with a wall ; but no mention is found in Thucydides of so important a fact as the construction of this new line of defence down to the Great Harbour, and it seems impossible to believe that this part of the city should so long have remained unprotected.† It is probable indeed (though not certain) that the Agora was already in this part of the city, as we know it to have been in later times ; and it is highly improbable that so important a part of the city would have been placed in an unfortified suburb. But still more necessary would be some such defence for the protection of the naval arsenals or dockyards in the inner bight of the Great Harbour, which certainly existed before the Athenian invasion. It seems, therefore, far more natural to suppose that, though the separate defences of Ortygia and the heights of Achradina (Diod. xi. 67, 73) were not destroyed, the two were from an early period, probably from the reign of Gelon, united by a common line of defence, which ran down from the heights to some point near that where the island of Ortygia most closely adjoined the mainland. The existence of such a boundary wall from the time of the Athenian War is certain ; and there seems little doubt that the name of Achradina, supposing it to have originally belonged to the heights or table-land, soon came to be extended to the lower area also. Thus Diodorus describes Dionysius on his return from Gela as arriving at the gate of Achradina, where the outer gate of the city is certainly meant. (Diod. xiii. 113.) It is probable that this gate, which was that leading to Gela, is the same as the one called by Cicero the Portae Agragianae, immediately outside of which he had discovered the tomb of Archimedes. (Cic. *Tusc. Quaest.* v. 23.) But its situation cannot be determined : no distinct traces of the ancient walls remain on this side of Syracuse, and we know not how they may have been modified when the suburb of Neapolis was included in the city. It is probable, however, that the wall (as suggested by Col. Leake) ran from the brow of the hill near the amphitheatre in a direct line to the Great Harbour.

* These still abound in the wild pear-trees (ἀχράδες), from which the name, as suggested by Leake, was probably derived.

† The argument against this, urged by Cavallari, and derived from the existence of numerous tombs, especially the great necropolis of the catacombs, in this part of the city, which, as he contends, must have been without the walls, would prove too much, as it is certain that these tombs were ultimately included in the city ; and if the ordinary custom of the Greeks was deviated from at all, it may have been so at an earlier period. In fact we know that in other cases also, as at Agrigentum and Tarentum, the custom was violated, and persons habitually buried within the walls.

Of the buildings noticed by Cicero as still adorning Achradina in his day there are scarcely any vestiges . but the greater part of them were certainly situated in the lower quarter, nearest to the island and the two ports. The Forum or Agora was apparently directly opposite to the Pentapyla or fortified entrance of the island ; it was surrounded with porticoes by the elder Dionysius (Diod. xiv. 7), which are obviously those alluded to by Cicero (" pulcherrimae porticus," *Verr.* iv. 53). The temple of Jupiter Olympius, noticed by the orator, also adjoined the Agora ; it was built by Hieron II. (Diod. xvi. 83), and must not be confounded with the more celebrated temple of the same divinity on a hill at some distance from the city. The prytaneum, which was most richly adorned, and among its chief ornaments possessed a celebrated statue of Sappho, which fell a prey to the cupidity of Verres (Cic. *Verr.* iv. 53, 57), was probably also situated in the neighbourhood of the Agora ; as was certainly the Timoleonteum, or monument erected to the memory of Timoleon. (Plut. *Timol.* 39.) The splendid sepulchral monument which had been erected by the younger Dionysius in memory of his father, but was destroyed after his own expulsion, seems to have stood in front of the Pentapyla, opposite the entrance of the citadel. (Diod. xv. 74.) A single column is still standing on this site, and the bases of a few others have been discovered, but it is uncertain to what edifice they belonged. The only other ruins now visible in this quarter of the city are some remains of Roman baths of little importance. But beneath the surface of the soil there exist extensive catacombs, constituting a complete necropolis : these tombs, as in most similar cases, are probably the work of successive ages, and can hardly be referred to any particular period. There exist, also, at two points on the slope of the hill of Achradina, extensive quarries hewn in the rock, similar to those found in Neapolis near the theatre, of which we shall presently speak.

Traces of the ancient walls of Achradina, crowning the low cliffs which bound it towards the sea, may be found from distance to distance along the whole line extending from the quarries of the *Cappuccini* round to the little bay or cove of *Sta Panagia* at the NW. angle of the plateau. Recent researches have also discovered the line of the western wall of Achradina, which appears to have run nearly in a straight line from the cove of *Sta Panagia*, to the steep and narrow pass or hollow way that leads up from the lower quarter to the heights above, thus taking advantage of the partial depression or valley already noticed. The cove of *Sta Panagia* may perhaps be the Portus Trogiliorum of Livy (xxv. 23), though the similar cove of the *Scala Greca*, about half a mile further W., would seem to have the better claim to that designation. The name is evidently the same with that of Trogilus, mentioned by Thucydides as the point on the N. side of the heights towards which the Athenians directed their lines of circumvallation, but without succeeding in reaching it. (Thuc. vi. 99, vii. 2.)

3. Tycha (Τύχη), so called, as we are told by Cicero, from its containing an ancient and celebrated temple of Fortune, was situated on the plateau or table-land W. of Achradina, and adjoining the northern face of the cliffs looking towards Megara. Though it became one of the most populous quarters of Syracuse, no trace of its existence is found at the period of the Athenian siege ; and it may fairly be assumed that there was as yet no considerable

suburb on the site, which must otherwise have materially interfered with the Athenian lines of circumvallation, while the Syracusans would naturally have attempted to protect it, as they did that of Temenitis, by a special outwork. Yet it is remarkable that Diodorus notices the name, and even speaks of it as a distinct quarter of the city, as early as B. C. 466, during the troubles which led to the expulsion of Thrasybulus (Diod. xi. 68). It is difficult to reconcile this with the entire silence of Thucydides. Tycha probably grew up after the great wall erected by Dionysius along the northern edge of the plateau had completely secured it from attack. Its position is clearly shown by the statement of Livy, that Marcellus, after he had forced the Hexapylum and scaled the heights, established his camp *between* Tycha and Neapolis, with the view of carrying on his assaults upon Achradina. (Liv. xxv. 25.) It is evident therefore that the two quarters were not contiguous, but that a considerable extent of the table-land W. of Achradina was still unoccupied.

4. NEAPOLIS (Νεάπολις), or the New City, was, as its name implied, the last quarter of Syracuse which was inhabited, though, as is often the case, the New Town seems to have eventually grown up into one of the most splendid portions of the city. It may, however, well be doubted whether it was in fact more recent than Tycha ; at least it appears that some portion of Neapolis was already inhabited at the time of the Athenian invasion, when, as already mentioned, we have no trace of the existence of a suburb at Tycha. But there was then already a suburb called Temenitis, which had grown up around the sanctuary of Apollo Temenites. The statue of Apollo, who was worshipped under this name, stood as we learn from Cicero, within the precincts of the quarter subsequently called Neapolis ; it was placed, as we may infer from Thucydides, on the height above the theatre (which he calls ἄκρα Τεμενῖτις), forming a part of the table-land, and probably not far from the southern escarpment of the plateau. A suburb had apparently grown up around it, which was surrounded by the Syracusans with a wall just before the commencement of the siege, and this outwork bears a conspicuous part in the operations that followed. (Thuc. vi. 75.) But this extension of the fortifications does not appear to have been permanent, for we find in B. C. 396 the temples of Ceres and the Cora, which also stood on the heights not far from the statue of Apollo, described as situated in a suburb of Achradina, which was taken and the temples plundered by the Carthaginian general Himilco. (Diod. xiv. 63.) The name of Neapolis (ἡ Νέα πόλις) is indeed already mentioned some years before (Id. xiv. 9), and it appears probable therefore that the city had already begun to extend itself over this quarter, though it as yet formed only an unfortified suburb. In the time of Cicero, as is evident from his description, as well as from existing remains, Neapolis had spread itself over the whole of the southern slope of the table-land, which here forms a kind of second step or underfall, rising considerably above the low grounds beneath, though still separated from the heights of Temenitis by a second line of cliff or abrupt declivity. The name of Temenitis for the district on the height seems to have been lost, or merged in that of Neapolis, which was gradually applied to the whole of this quarter of the city. But the name was retained by the adjoining gate, which was called the Temenitid Gate

(Plut. *Dion.* 29, where there seems no doubt that we should read Τεμενῖτιδας for Μενῖτιδας), and seems to have been one of the principal entrances to the city.

Of the buildings described by Cicero as existing in Neapolis, the only one still extant is the theatre, which he justly extols for its large size ("theatrum maximum," *Verr.* iv. 53). Diodorus also alludes to it as the largest in Sicily (xvi. 83), a remark which is fully borne out by the existing remains. It is not less than 440 feet in diameter, and appears to have had sixty rows of seats, so that it could have accommodated no less than 24,000 persons. The lower rows of seats were covered with slabs of white marble, and the several cunei are marked by inscriptions in large letters, bearing the name of king Hieron, of two queens, Philistis and Nereïs, both of them historically unknown, and of two deities, the Olympian Zeus and Hercules, with the epithet of Εὐφρών. These inscriptions evidently belong to the time of Hieron II., who probably decorated and adorned this theatre, but the edifice itself is certainly referable to a much earlier period, probably as early as the reign of the elder Hieron. It was used not merely for theatrical exhibitions, but for the assemblies of the people, which are repeatedly alluded to as being held in it (Diod. xiii. 94; Plut. *Dion.* 38, *Timol.* 34, 38, &c.), as was frequently the case in other cities of Greece. The theatre, as originally constructed, must have been outside the walls of the city, but this was not an unusual arrangement.

Near the theatre have been discovered the remains of another monument, expressly mentioned by Diodorus as constructed by king Hieron in that situation, an altar raised on steps and a platform not less than 640 feet in length by 60 in breadth (Diod. xiv. 83). A little lower down are the remains of an amphitheatre, a structure which undoubtedly belongs to the Roman colony, and was probably constructed soon after its establishment by Augustus, as we find incidental mention of gladiatorial exhibitions taking place there in the reigns of Tiberius and Nero (Tac. *Ann.* xiii. 49; Val. Max. i. 7. § 8). It was of considerable size, the arena, which is the only part of which the dimensions can be distinctly traced, being somewhat larger than that of Verona. No traces have been discovered of the temples of Ceres and Libera or Proserpine on the height above : the colossal statue of Apollo Temenites had apparently no temple in connection with it, though it had of course its altar, as well as its sacred enclosure or τέμενος. The statue itself, which Verres was unable to remove on account of its large size, was afterwards transported to Rome by Tiberius (Suet. *Tib.* 74).

Immediately adjoining the theatre are extensive quarries, similar in character to those already mentioned in the cliffs of Achradina. The quarries of Syracuse (Latomiae or Lautumiae) are indeed frequently mentioned by ancient authors, and especially noticed by Cicero among the most remarkable objects in the city. (Cic. *Verr.* v. 27; Aelian, *V. H.* xii. 44.) There can be no doubt that they were originally designed merely as quarries for the extraction of the soft limestone of which the whole table-land consists, and which makes an excellent building stone; but from the manner in which they were worked, being sunk to a considerable depth, without any outlet on a level, they were found places of such security, that from an early period they were employed as prisons. Thus, after the Athenian expedition, the whole number of the captives, more than 7000 in number, were confined in these quarries (Thuc. vii. 86, 87; Diod. xiii. 33); and they continued to be used for the same purpose under successive despots and tyrants. In the days of Cicero they were used as a general prison for criminals from all parts of Sicily. (Cic. *Verr.* v. 27.) The orator in one passage speaks of them as constructed expressly for a prison by the tyrant Dionysius (*Ib.* 55), which is a palpable mistake if it refers to the Lautumiae in general, though it is not unlikely that the despot may have made some special additions to them with that view. But there is certainly no authority for the popular tradition which has given the name of the Ear of Dionysius to a peculiar excavation of singular form in the part of the quarries nearest to the theatre. This notion, like many similar ones now become traditional, is derived only from the suggestion of a man of letters of the 16th century.

5. EPIPOLAE ('Επίπολαι), was the name originally given to the upper part of the table-land which, as already described, slopes gradually from its highest point towards the sea. Its form is that of a tolerably regular triangle, having its vertex at Euryalus, and its base formed by the western wall of Achradina. The name is always used by Thucydides in this sense, as including the whole upper part of the plateau, and was doubtless so employed as long as the space was uninhabited; but as the

suburbs of Tycha and Temenitis gradually spread themselves over a considerable part of the heights, the name of Epipolae came to be applied in a more restricted sense to that portion only which was nearest to the vertex of the triangle. It is generally assumed that there subsequently arose a considerable town near this angle of the walls, and that this is the fifth quarter of the city alluded to by Strabo and those who spoke of Syracuse as a Pentapolis or aggregate of *five* cities. But there is no allusion to it as such in the passage of Cicero already quoted, or in the description of the capture of Syracuse by Marcellus; and it seems very doubtful whether there was ever any considerable population at this remote point. No vestiges of any ancient buildings remain within the walls; but the line of these may be distinctly traced along the top of the cliffs which bound the table-land both towards the N. and the S.; in many places two or three courses of the masonry remain; but the most important ruins are those at the angle or vertex of the triangle, where a spot named *Mongibellisi* is still crowned by the ruins of the ancient castle or fort of EURYALUS (Εὐρύηλος, Thuc., but the Doric form was Εὐρύαλος, which was adopted by the Romans). The ruins in question afford one of the best examples extant of an ancient fortress or castle, designed at once to serve as a species of citadel and to secure the approach to Epipolae from this quarter. The annexed plan will give a good idea of its general

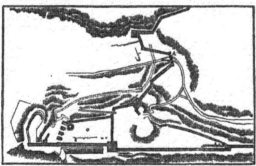

PLAN OF THE FORT EURYALUS.

form and arrangement. The main entrance to the city was by a double gate (A.), flanked on both sides by walls and towers, with a smaller postern or sally-port a little to the right of it. The fortress itself was an irregular quadrangle, projecting about 200 yards beyond the approach to the gate, and fortified by strong towers of solid masonry with a deep ditch cut in the rock in front of it, to which a number of subterraneous passages gave access from within. These passages communicating with the fort above by narrow openings and stairs, were evidently designed to facilitate the sallies of the besieged without exposing the fortress itself to peril. As the whole arrangement is an unique specimen of ancient fortification a view is added of the external, or N. front of the fort, with the subterranean openings.

There can be no doubt that the fortress at Mon-

gibellisi is the one anciently known as Euryalus. This clearly appears from the mention of that fort at the time of the siege of Syracuse by Marcellus, as one capable of being held by a separate garrison after the capture of the outer walls of Epipolae, and threatening the army of Marcellus in the rear, if he proceeded to attack Achradina. (Liv. xxv. 25, 26.) Euryalus is also mentioned by Thucydides at the time of the Athenian expedition, when it was still unfortified, as the point which afforded a ready ascent to the heights of Epipolae (Thuc. vi. 99, vii. 2); and it must indeed have always been, in a military point of view, the key of the whole position. Hence, the great care with which it was fortified after the occupation of Epipolae by the Athenians had shown the paramount importance of that position in case of a siege. The existing fortifications may, indeed, be in part the work of Hieron II. (as supposed by Col. Leake); but it is certain that a strong fort was erected there by Dionysius I.*, and

the importance of this was sufficiently shown in the reign of Agathocles, when the attack of Hamilcar

VIEW OF THE FORT EURYALUS.

was repulsed by means of a strong garrison posted at Euryalus, who attacked his army in flank, while advancing to the attack of Epipolae. (Diod. xx. 29.)

Some writers on the topography of Syracuse have supposed the fortress of *Mongibellisi* to be the ancient Hexapylum, and that Euryalus occupied the site of *Belvedere*, a knoll or hill on the ridge which is continued from *Mongibellisi* inland, and forms a communication with the table-land of the interior. But the hill of *Belvedere*, which is a mile distant from *Mongibellisi*, though somewhat more elevated than the latter point, is connected with it only by a narrow ridge, and is altogether too far from the table-land of Epipolae to have been of any importance in connection with it; while the heights of *Mongibellisi*, as already observed, form the true key of that position. Moreover, all the passages that relate to Hexapylum, when attentively considered, point to its position on the N. front of the heights, looking towards Megara and Thapsus: and Colonel Leake has satisfactorily shown that it was a fort constructed for the defence of the main approach to Syracuse on this side; a road which then, as now, ascended the heights at a point a short distance W. of the *Scala Greca*, where a depression or break in the line of cliffs affords a natural approach. (Leake, *Notes on Syracuse*, pp. 258, 342, &c.) The gate at Hexapylum thus led, in the first instance, into the suburb or quarter of Tycha, a circumstance completely in accordance with, if not necessarily required by, a passage in Livy (xxiv. 21), where the two are mentioned in close connection.

It is more difficult to determine the exact position of LABDALUM, where the Athenians erected a fort during the siege of Syracuse. The name is not subsequently mentioned in history, so that we have no knowledge of its relation to the fortifications as they existed in later times; and our only clue to its position is the description of Thucydides, that it stood "on the summit of the cliffs of Epipolae, looking towards Megara." It was probably situated (as placed by Göller and Mr. Grote) on the point of those heights which forms a slightly projecting

angle near the farmhouse now called *Targia*. Its purpose was, doubtless, to secure the communications of the Athenians with their fleet which lay at Thapsus, as well as with the landing-place at Leon.

It was not till the reign of the elder Dionysius (as we have already seen) that the heights of Epipolae were included within the walls or fortifications of Syracuse. Nor are we to suppose that even after that time they became peopled like the rest of the city. The object of the walls then erected was merely to secure the heights against military occupation by an enemy. For that purpose he in B. C. 402 constructed a line of wall 30 stadia in length, fortified with numerous towers, and extending along the whole N. front of the plateau, from the NW. angle of Achradina to the hill of Euryalus. (Diod. xiv. 18.) The latter point must at the same time have been occupied with a strong fort. The north side of Epipolae was thus securely guarded; but it is singular that we hear of no similar defence for the S. side. There is no doubt that this was ultimately protected by a wall of the same character, as the remains of it may be traced all around the edge of the plateau; but the period of its construction is uncertain. The portion of the cliffs extending from Euryalus to Neapolis may have been thought sufficiently strong by nature; but this was not the case with the slope towards Neapolis, which was easily accessible. Yet this appears to have continued the weakest side of the city, as in B. C. 396 Himilco was able to plunder the temples in the suburb of Temenitis with apparently little difficulty. At a later period, however, it is certain from existing remains, that not only was there a line of fortifications carried along the upper escarpment as far as Neapolis, but an outer line of walls was carried round that suburb, which was now included for all purposes as part of the city. Strabo reckons the whole circuit of the walls of Syracuse, including the fortifications of Epipolae, at 180 stadia (Strab. vi. p. 270); but this statement exceeds the truth, the actual circuit being about 14 English miles, or 122 stadia. (Leake, p. 279.)

It only remains to notice briefly the different localities in the immediate neighbourhood of Syracuse, which are noticed by ancient writers in connection with that city. Of these the most important

---

* This must have been the fort on Epipolae taken by Dion, which was then evidently held by a separate garrison. (Plut. *Dion.* 29.)

is the OLYMPIEUM, or Temple of Jupiter Olympius, which stood, as already mentioned, on a height, facing the southern front of Epipolae and Neapolis, from which it was about a mile and a half distant (Liv. xxiv. 33), the interval being occupied by the marshy plain on the banks of the Anapus. The sanctuary seems to have early attained great celebrity: even at the time of the Athenian expedition there had already grown up around it a small town, which was known as POLICHNE (ἡ Πολίχνη, Diod.), or the Little City. The military importance of the post, as commanding the bridge over the Anapus and the road to Helorus, as well as overlooking the marshes, the Great Harbour, and the lower part of the city, caused the Syracusans to fortify and secure it with a garrison before the arrival of the Athenians. (Thuc. vi. 75.) For the same reason it was occupied by all subsequent invaders who threatened Syracuse; by Himilco in B.C. 396, by Hamilcar in B.C. 309, and by Marcellus in B.C. 214. The remains of the temple are still visible: in the days of Cluverius, indeed, seven columns were still standing, with a considerable part of the substructure (Cluver. Sicil. p. 179), but now only two remain, and those have lost their capitals. They are of an ancient style, and belong probably to the original temple, which appears to have been built by the Geomori as early as the 6th century B.C.

The adjoining promontory of Plemmyrium does not appear to have been ever inhabited, though it presents a table-land of considerable height, nor was it ever permanently fortified. It is evident also, from the account of the operations of successive Carthaginian fleets, as well as that of the Athenians, that the Syracusans had not attempted to occupy, or even to guard with forts, the more distant parts of the Great Harbour, though the docks or arsenal, which were situated in the inner bight or recess of the bay, between Ortygia and the lower part of Achradina, were strongly fortified. The southern bight of the bay, which forms an inner bay or gulf, now known as the bay of Sta Maddalena, is evidently that noticed both during the Athenian siege and that by the Carthaginians as the gulf of DASCON. (Δάσκων, Thuc. vi. 66; Diod. xiii. 13, xiv. 72.) The fort erected by the Athenians for the protection of their fleet apparently stood on the adjacent height, which is connected with that of the Olympieum.

Almost immediately at the foot of the Olympieum was the ancient bridge across the Anapus, some remains of which may still be seen, as well as of the ancient road which led from it towards Helorus, memorable on account of the disastrous retreat of the Athenians. They did not, however, on that occasion cross the bridge, but after a fruitless attempt to penetrate into the interior by following the valley of the Anapus, struck across into the Helorine Way, which they rejoined some distance beyond the Olympieum. Not far from the bridge over the Anapus stood the monument of Gelon and his wife Demarete, a sumptuous structure, where the Syracusans were in the habit of paying heroic honours to their great ruler. It was adorned with nine towers of a very massive construction; but the monument itself was destroyed by Himilco, when he encamped at the adjacent Olympieum, and the towers were afterwards demolished by Agathocles. (Diod. xi. 38, xiv. 63.)

About a mile and a half SW. of the Olympieum is the fountain of CYANE, a copious and clear stream

rising in the midst of a marsh: the sanctuary of the nymph to whom it was consecrated (τὸ τῆς Κυάνης ἱερόν, Diod.), must have stood on the heights above, as we are told that Dionysius led his troops round to this spot with a view to attack the Carthaginian camp at the Olympieum (Diod. xiv. 72); and the marsh itself must always have been impassable for troops. Some ruins on the slope of the hill to the W. of the source are probably those of the temple in question. [CYANE.] The fountain of Cyane is now called La Pisma: near it is another smaller source called Pismotta, and a third, known as Il Cefalino, rises between the Cyane and the Anapus. The number of these fountains of clear water, proceeding no doubt from distant sources among the limestone hills, is characteristic of the neighbourhood of Syracuse, and is noticed by Pliny, who mentions the names of four other noted sources besides the Cyane and the more celebrated Arethusa. These he calls Temenitis, Archidemia, Magaea, and Milichia, but they cannot be now identified. (Plin. iii. 8. s. 14.) None of these springs, however, was well adapted to supply the city itself with water, and hence an aqueduct was in early times carried along the heights from the interior. The existence of this is already noticed at the time of the Athenian siege (Thuc. vi. 100); and the channel, which is in great part subterraneous, is still visible at the present day, and conveys a stream sufficient to turn a mill situated on the steps of the great theatre.

A few localities remain to be noticed to the N. of Syracuse, which, though not included in the city, are repeatedly alluded to in its history. LEON, the spot where the Athenians first landed at the commencement of the siege (Thuc. vi. 97), and where Marcellus established his winter quarters when he found himself unable to carry the city by assault (Liv. xxiv. 39), is probably the little cove or bay about 2 miles N. of the Scala Greca: this is not more than a mile from the nearest point of Epipolae, which would agree with the statement of Thucydides, who calls it 6 or 7 stadia from thence; Livy, on the contrary, says it was 5 miles from Hexapylum, but this must certainly be a mistake. About 3 miles further N. is the promontory of THAPSUS (ἡ Θάψος, now called Magnisi), a low but rocky peninsula, united to the mainland by a sandy isthmus, so that it formed a tolerably secure port on its S. side. On this account it was selected, in the first instance, by the Athenians for their naval camp and the station of their fleet, previous to their taking possession of the Great Harbour. (Thuc. vi. 97.) It had been one of the first points on the Sicilian coast occupied by Greek colonists, but these speedily removed to Megara (Thuc. vi. 4); and the site seems to have subsequently always remained uninhabited, at least there was never a town upon it. It was a low promontory, whence Virgil appropriately calls it 'Thapsus jacens." (Virg. Aen. iii. 689; Ovid, Fast. iv. 477.) About a mile inland, and directly opposite to the entrance of the isthmus, are the remains of an ancient monument of large size, built of massive blocks of stone, and of a quadrangular form. The portion now remaining is above 20 feet high, but it was formerly surmounted by a column, whence the name by which it is still known as L'Aguglia, or "the Needle." This monument is popularly believed to have been erected by Marcellus to commemorate the capture of Syracuse; but this is a mere conjecture, for which there is no foundation. It is probably in reality a sepulchral monument. (D'Orville, *Sicula*, p. 173; Swinburne, vol. ii. p. 318.)

The topography of Syracuse attracted attention from an early period after the revival of letters; and the leading features are so clearly marked by nature that they could not fail to be recognised. But the earlier descriptions by Fazello, Bonanni, and Mirabella, are of little value. Cluverius, as usual, investigated the subject with learning and diligence; and the ground has been carefully examined by several modern travellers. An excellent survey of it was also made by British engineers in 1808; and the researches and excavations carried on by the duke of Serra di Falco, and by a commission appointed by the Neapolitan government in 1839 have thrown considerable light upon the extant remains of antiquity, as well as upon some points of the topography. These have been discussed in a separate memoir by the architect employed, Saverio Cavallari, and the whole subject has been fully investigated, with constant reference to the ancient authors, in an elaborate and excellent memoir by Col. Leake. The above article is based mainly upon the researches of the last author, and the local details given in the

COINS OF SYRACUSAE.

great work of the duke of Serra di Falco, the fourth volume of which is devoted wholly to the antiquities of Syracuse. (Fazell. *de Reb. Sic.* iv. 1; Bonanni, *Le Antiche Siracuse*, 2 vols. fol. Palermo, 1717; Mirabella, *Dichiarazione della Pianta dell' antiche Siracuse*, reprinted with the preceding work; Cluver. *Sicil.* i. 12; D'Orville, *Sicula*, pp. 175—202; Smyth's *Sicily*, pp. 162—176; Swinburne, *Travels in the Two Sicilies*, vol. ii. pp. 318—346; Hoare, *Classical Tour*, vol. ii. pp. 140—176; Leake, *Notes on Syracuse*, in the *Transactions of the Royal Society of Literature*, 2nd series, vol. iii. pp. 239—354; Serra di Falco, *Antichità della Sicilia*, vol. iv; Cavallari, *Zur Topographie von Syrakus*, 8vo. Göttingen, 1845.)　　　　　[E. H. B.]

SYRASTRE'NE (Συραστρηνή, *Peripl. M. E.* c. 41; Ptol. vii. 1. § 2), a district of ancient India, near and about the mouths of the Indus. There can be no doubt that it is represented by the modern *Saurashtran*, for a long time the seat of a powerful nation. *Surashtra* means in Sanscrit "the beautiful kingdom." Ptolemy (*l. c.*) mentions a small village Syrastra, which may have once been its capital. It is probable that the Syrieni of Pliny (vi. 20. s. 23) were inhabitants of the same district.　　[V.]

SYRGIS (Σύργις, Herod. iv. 123), a considerable river of European Sarmatia, which flowed from the country of the Thyssagetae through the territory of the Maeotae, and discharged itself into the Palus Maeotis. Modern geographers, have variously attempted to identify it, Rennell (*Geogr. of Herod.* p. 90) considers it to be one of the tributaries of the *Wolga*. Gatterer (*Comment. Soc. Gott.* xiv. p. 36) takes it to be the *Donetz*, whilst Reichard identifies it with the *Irgitz*, and Linder (*Scythien*, p. 66) with the *Don* itself.　　　　[T. H. D.]

SY'RIA (Συρία : *Eth.* Σύριος), the classical name for the country whose ancient native appellation was Aram, its modern *Esh-Sham*.

I. *Name.*—The name Aram (אֲרָם), more comprehensive than the limits of Syria Proper, extends, with several qualifying adjuncts, over Mesopotamia and Chaldaea. Thus we read (1.) of Aram of the two rivers, or Aram Naharaim (אֲרָם נַהֲרַיִם, LXX. τὴν Μεσοποταμίαν, *Gen.* xxiv. 10), equivalent to Padan-Aram, or the Plain of Aram (פַדַּן אֲרָם, LXX. τῆς Μεσοποταμίας Συρίας, *Gen.* xxv. 20, xxviii. 2, 5, 6, 7, xxxi. 18), but comprehended also a mountain district called "the mountains of the east" (*Num.* xxii. 5, xxiii. 7; *Deut.* xxiii. 4). (2.) Aram Sobah (אֲרָם צוֹבָה, LXX. Σουβά, 1 *Sam.* xiv. 47; 2 *Sam.* viii. 3, x. 6, 8). (3.) Aram of Damascus (אֲרָם דַּמֶּשֶׂק, LXX. Συρία Δαμασκοῦ, 2 *Sam.* viii. 5). (4.) Aram Beth-Rehob (אֲרָם בֵּית־רְחוֹב, LXX. Ῥοώβ, 2 *Sam.* x. 6, 8). (5.) Aram Maacáh (מַעֲכָה, LXX. Μααχὰ, 1 *Chron.* xix. 6). Of these five districts thus distinguished, the first has no connection with this article. With regard to the second, fourth, and fifth, it is doubtful whether Sobah and Rehob were in Mesopotamia or in Syria Proper. Gesenius supposes the empire of Sobah to have been situated north-east of Damascus; but places the town, which he identifies with Nesebin, Nisibis, and Antiochia Mygdoniae, in Mesopotamia (*Lex. s. vv.* אֲרָם and צוֹבָה); but a comparison of 2 *Sam.* x. 6 with 1 *Chron.* xix. 6 seems rather to imply that Rehob was in Mesopotamia, Soba and Maacha in Syria Proper; for, in the former passage, we have the Aramites of Beth-Rehob, and the Aramites of Soba, and the king of Maacah,—in the latter, Aram Naharaim = Mesopotamia, and Aram Maacah and Zobah; from which we may infer the identity of Beth-Rehob and Mesopotamia, and the distinction between this latter and Maacah or Zobah : and again, the alliance between Hadadezer, king of Zobah, and the Aramites of Damascus (2 *Sam.* viii. 3—6; 1 *Chron.* xix. 3—6) would imply the contiguity of the two states ; while the expedition of the former " to recover his border," or " establish his dominion at the river Euphrates " (ver. 3), during which David attacked him, would suppose a march from west to east, through Syria, rather than in the opposite direction through Mesopotamia.

With regard to the origin of the name Aram, there are two Patriarchs in the early genealogies from whom it has been derived ; one the son of Shem, the progenitor of the Hebrew race, whose other children Uz, Asshur, Arphaxad, and Lud, represent ancient kingdoms or races contiguous to Syria; while Uz, the firstborn son of Aram, apparently gave his name to the native land of Job, at a very early period of the world's history. (*Gen.* x. 22, 23.) The other Aram was the grandson of Nahor, the brother of Abraham, by Kemuel, whose brother Huz is by some supposed to have given his name to the country of Job, as it can scarcely admit of a doubt that the third brother, Buz, was the patriarch from whom the neighbouring district took its name. (*Gen.* xxii. 20, 21; *Job*, i. 1, xxxii. 2.) But as we find the name Aram already applied to describe the country of Bethuel and Laban, the uncle and cousin of the later Aram, it is obvious that the country must have derived its name from the earlier, not from the later patriarch. (*Gen.* xxv. 20, xxviii. 5, &c.)

The classical name Syria is commonly supposed to be an abbreviation or modification of Assyria, and to date from the period of the Assyrian subjugation of the ancient Aram ; and this account of its origin is confirmed by the fact that the name Syria does not occur in Homer or Hesiod, who speak of the inhabitants of the country under the name of Arimi, (εἰν 'Αρίμοις, Hom. *Il. β.* 783. Hes. *Theog.* v. 304), in connection with the myth of Typhon, recorded by Strabo in describing the Orontes [ORONTES]; and this writer informs us that the Syrians were called Aramaei or Arimi (i. p. 42, xiii. p. 627, xvi. pp. 784, 785), which name was, however, extended too far to the west or north by other writers, so as to comprehend Cilicia, and the Sacae of Scythia. (See Bochart, *Geog. Sac.* lib. ii. cap. 6.) Herodotus, the earliest extant writer who distinctly names the Syrians, declares the people to be identical with the Assyrians, where he is obviously speaking of the latter, making the former to be the Greek, the latter the barbarian name (vii. 63); and this name he extends as far south as the confines of Egypt,—placing Sidon, Azotus, Cadytis, and, in short, the Phoenicians in general, in Syria (ii. 12, 158, 159), calling the Jews the Syrians in Palestine (ii. 104); and as far west as Asia Minor, for the Cappadocians, he says, are called Syrians by the Greeks (i. 72), and speaks of the Syrians about the Thermodon and Parthenius, rivers of Bithynia (ii. 104). Consistently with this early notice, Strabo, at a much later period, states that the name of Syri formerly extended from Babylonia as far as the gulf of Issus, and thence as far as the Euxine (xvi. p. 737); and in this wider sense

the name is used by other classical writers, and thus includes a tract of country on the west which was not comprehended within the widest range of the ancient Aram.

II. *Natural boundaries and divisions.* — The limits of Syria proper, which is now to be considered, are clearly defined by the Mediterranean on the west, the Euphrates on the east, the range of Amanus and Taurus on the north, and the great Desert of Arabia on the south. On the west, however, a long and narrow strip of coast, commencing at Marathus, and running south to Mount Carmel, was reckoned to Phoenice, and has been described under that name. In compensation for this deduction on the south-west, a much more ample space is gained towards the south-east, by the rapid trending away of the Euphrates eastward, between the 36th and 34th degree north lat., from near the 38th to the 41st degree of east longitude, thereby increasing its distance from the Mediterranean sea, from about 100 miles at Zeugma (*Bir*), to 250 miles at the boundary of Syria, south of Circesium (*Karkisia*). Commencing at the northern extremity of the Issicus Sinus (*Gulf of Iskanderún*), near Issus itself, the Amanus Mons (*Alma Dagh*), a branch of the Taurus, runs off first in a northern direction for 18 miles, then north-east for 30 more, until it joins the main chain (*Durdún Dagh*), a little westward of *Mar'ash*, from whence it runs due eastward to the Euphrates. The southern line cannot be accurately described, as being marked only by an imaginary line drawn through an interminable waste of sand. This irregular trapezium may now be subdivided.

For the purposes of a physical description, the ranges of Lebanon and Antilibanus may be assumed as landmarks towards the south, while the river Orontes affords a convenient division in the geography of the country towards the north ; for the valley of the Orontes may be regarded as a continuation northward of the great crevass of Coelesyria, the watershed being in the vicinity of Baalbek, so that " this depression extends along the whole western side of the country, having on each side, through nearly 6 degrees of latitude, an almost continuous chain of mountains, from which numerous offsets strike into the interior in different directions." (Col. Chesney, *Expedition for the Survey of the Euphrates and Tigris*, vol. i. p. 384.)

1. *The western range.*—Where the range of Amanus meets the coast at the *Gulf of Iskanderún*, near the river Issus, it leaves only a narrow pass between its base and the sea, formerly occupied by the Armenian, Syrian, or Amanidan gates of the various geographers, which will be again referred to below. This range then advances southwards under various names, approaching or receding from the coast, and occasionally throwing out bold headlands into the sea, as at *Ras Khanzeer, Ras Bosyt* (Posidium Prom.), *Ras-esh-Shaka*, &c. The part of the chain north of the Orontes is thus described by Col. Chesney (p. 384): " The base of the chain consists of masses of serpentines and diallage rocks, rising abruptly from plains on each side, and supporting a tertiary formation, terminating with bold rugged peaks and conical summits, having at the crest an elevation of 5387 feet. The sides of this mass are occasionally furrowed by rocky fissures, or broken into valleys, between which there is a succession of rounded shoulders, either protruding through forests of pines, oaks, and larches, or diversified by the arbutus, the myrtle, oleander, and other shrubs. Some basalt

appears near *Ayas*, and again in larger masses at some little distance from the NE. side of the chain. ...Southward of *Beilan* the chain becomes remarkable for its serrated sides and numerous summits, of which the *Akhma Tagh* shows about fifteen between that place and the valley of the Orontes." The sharp ridge of *Jebel Rhoms* terminates in the rugged and serrated peaks of *Cape Khanzir*, which overhangs the sea, and separates the *Gulf of Iskanderûn* from the *Bay of Antioch*. South of this is *Jebel Musa*, the Mons Pieria of classic writers, a limestone offset from *Mount Rhoms*, and itself imperfectly connected with the other classical mount, Casius, by the lower range of *Jebel Simân*. A little to the south of the *embouchure* of the Orontes, Mount Casius reaches an elevation of 5699 feet, composed of supra-cretaceous limestone, on the skirts of which, among the birch and larch woods, are still to be seen the ruins of the temple, said to have been consecrated by Cronus or Ham (Ammianus Marcell. xxii. 14), while the upper part of its cone is entirely a naked rock, justifying its native modern name *Jebel-el-Akra* (the bald mountain). From this point the mountain chain continues southward, at a much lower elevation, and receding further from the coast, throws out its roots both east and west, towards the Orontes on the one side and the Mediterranean on the other. This range has the general name of *Jebel Anzarieh* from the tribe that inhabits it, but is distinguished in its various parts and branches by local names, chiefly derived from the towns and villages on its sides or base. The southern termination of this range must be the intervening plains which Pliny places between Libanus and Bargylus ("interjacentes campi"), on the north of the former. (Plin. v. 20.) These plains Shaw finds in the *Jeune* (*fruitful*), as the Arabs call a comparatively level tract, which "commences a little south of *Maguzzel*, and ends at *Sumrah*, extending itself all the way from the sea to the eastward, sometimes five, sometimes six or seven leagues, till it is terminated by a long chain of mountains. These seem to be the Mons Bargylus of Pliny." *Sumrah* he identifies with Simyra,— which Pliny places in Coelesyria at the northern extremity of Mount Libanus,—but remarks that, as *Sumrah* lies in the Jeune, 2 leagues distant from that mountain, this circumstance will better fall in with Arca, where Mount Libanus is remarkably broken off and discontinued. (Shaw, *Travels in Syria*, pp. 268, 269, 4to ed.) We here reach the confines of Phoenice, to which a separate article has been devoted, as also to Mount Lebanon, which continues the coastline to the southern extremity of Syria.

2. *Coelesyria, and the valley of the Orontes.* — Although the name of Coelesyria (Hollow Syria) is sometimes extended so as to include even the coast of the Mediterranean — as in the passage above cited from Pliny — from Seleucis to Egypt and Arabia (Strabo, *ut infra*), and especially the prolongation of the southern valley along the crevass of the Jordan to the Dead Sea (see Reland, *Palaestina*, pp. 103, 458, 607, 774), yet, according to Strabo, the name properly describes the valley between Libanus and Antilibanus (xvi. 2. § 21), now known among the natives as *El-Bûkâ'a* (*the deep plain*). "Under this name is embraced the valley between Lebanon and Anti-Lebanon, from *Zahleh* southward ; including the villages on the declivities of both mountains, or rather at their foot : for the eastern declivity of Lebanon is so steep as to have very few

villages much above its base; and the western side of Anti-Lebanon is not more inhabited. Between *Zahleh* and its suburb, *Mu'allahah*, a stream called *El-Bûrdôny* descends from Lebanon and runs into the plain to join the *Lîtâny*. The latter river divides the *Bûkâ'a* from north to south ; and at its southern end passes out through a narrow gorge, between precipices in some places of great height, and finally enters the sea north of *Súr*, where it is called *Kâsimêyeh*" [LEONTES]. To the south of the *Bûkâ'a* is the *Merj 'Ayûn* (*meadow of the springs*), "between *Belâd Beshârah* and *Wâdy-et-Teim*, on the left of the *Lîtâny*. Here Lebanon and Anti-Lebanon come together, but in such a manner that this district may be said to separate rather than to unite them. It consists of a beautiful fertile plain, surrounded by hills, in some parts high, but almost every where arable, until you begin to descend towards the *Lîtâny*. The mountains farther south are much more properly a continuation of Lebanon than of Anti-Lebanon." (Dr. Eli Smith, in *Biblical Researches*, vol. iii. Appendix B. pp. 136, 140.) This then is the proper termination to the south of Coelesyria. The *Merj 'Ayûn* terminates in the *Erd-el-Huleh*, which is traversed by the several tributaries of the Jordan, and extends as far south as the *Bahr-el-Huleh*. [SAMACHONITIS LACUS; PALAESTINA, pp. 521, 522.]

To return now to the watershed. *Baalbek* gives its name to the remainder of the *Bûkâ'a*, from the village of *Zahleh* northward (Smith, *ut sup.* p. 143), in which direction, as has been stated, the remotest sources of the Orontes are found, not far from Baalbek, which lies in the plain nearer to the range of Antilibanus than to Lebanon. [ORONTES; HELIOPOLIS.] The copious fountain of *Labweh* is about 10 miles north-east of *Baalbek* ; and this village gives its name to the stream which runs for 12 miles through a rocky desert, until it falls into the basin of a much larger stream at the village of *Er-Ras* or *'Ain Zerka*, where is the proper source of the Orontes, now *El-'Asi*. The body of water now "becomes at least threefold greater than before, and continues in its rugged chasm generally in a north-easterly course for a considerable distance, until it passes near *Ribleh*," then runs north through the valley of *Homs*, having been fed on its way by numerous streams from the slopes of Lebanon and Antilibanus, draining the slopes of *Jebel Anzarieh*, and forming as it approaches *Homs* the *Bahr-el-Kades*, which is 6 miles long by about 2 wide. (*Chesney, ut sup.* p. 394; Robinson, *Journal of the R. G. S.* vol. xxiv. p. 32.) Emerging from the lake, it waters the gardens of *Homs* about a mile and a half to the west of the town, then running north to *Er-Rustan*, where is a bridge of ten arches, it is turned from its direct course by *Jebel Arbâyn* on its left bank, round the roots of which it sweeps almost in a semicircle, and enters *Hamah*, where it is crossed by a bridge of thirteen arches. It now continues its course north-west for about 15 miles to *Kalâat-es-Sejar* (Larissa), then due west for 8 miles, when it turns due north, and so continues to the *Jisr Hadid* mentioned below. About 20 miles below Larissa it passes *Kalâat-em-Medaik* (Apameia) on its right bank, distant about 2 miles; a little to the north of which it receives an affluent from the small lake *Et-Taka*, remarkable for its abundance of black-fish and carp (Burckhardt, *Syria*, p. 143; Chesney, p. 395), then, running through *Wady-el-Ghab*, enters the *Birket-el-Howash*, 8 miles north of Apameia, where its impetuosity is curbed and its waters dissipated in the morasses, so that it flows off in a diminished stream to *Jisr Shoyher*, to be again replenished in its course through the plain of *'Umk* by other affluents, until it reaches its northernmost point at *Jisr Hadid* (*the Iron Bridge*), a little below which it winds round to the west, and about 5 miles above Antioch receives from *Bahr-el-Abiad* (*the White Sea*) the *Nahr-el-Kowshit*, a navigable river, containing a greater volume of water than *El-Azy* itself. It now flows to the north of Antioch and the infamous groves of Daphne, through an exceedingly picturesque valley, in a south-west course to the sea, which it enters a little to the south of Seleucia, after a circuitous course of about 200 miles, between 34° and 36° 15' of north latitude, 36° and 37° of east longitude.

3. *Antilibanus and the eastern range.*—The mountain chain which confines Coelesyria on the east is properly designated Antilibanus, but it is further extended towards the north and south by offsets, which confine the valley of the Orontes and the Jordan valley respectively. Antilibanus itself, now called *Jebel-esh-Shurkeh* (*Eastern Mountain*), which is vastly inferior to Libanus both in majesty and fertility, has been already described, as has also its southern prolongation in Mount Hermon, now *Jebel-esh-Sheikh*, sometimes *Jebel-et-Telge* (*the Snow Mountain*). [ANTILIBANUS.] The northern chain, on the east of the Orontes valley, has not been sufficiently surveyed to admit of an accurate description, but there is nothing striking in the height or general aspect of the range, which throws out branches into the great desert, of which it forms the western boundary.

4. *The eastern desert.*—Although for the purposes of a geographical description the whole country east of the mountain chains above described may be regarded as one region, and the insufficient materials for a minute and accurate survey make it convenient so to regard it, yet it is far from being an uniform flat, presenting throughout the same features of desolation. On the contrary, so far as it has yet been explored, particularly to the south of the parallel of Damascus, the country is diversified by successions of hills and valleys, which often present large fertile tracts of arable land, cultivated in many parts by a hardy and industrious race of inhabitants. By far the richest of these is the plain of Damascus (*El-Ghútah*), at the foot of the eastern declivity of Antilibanus, the most excellent of the four earthly paradises of the Arabian geographers. (Dr. Eli Smith, in *Bib. Res.* vol. iii. Append. B. p. 147.) It owes its beauty, not less than its fertility, to the abundance of water conveyed to it in the united streams of the *Barada* and the *Phégeh*, which, issuing together from the eastern roots of Antilibanus, and distributed into numerous rivulets, permeate the city and its thousands of gardens, and finally lose themselves in the Sea of the Plain, *Bahr-el-Merj*, which the exploration of a recent traveller has found to consist of two lakes instead of one, as has been hitherto represented in all modern maps. (Porter, *Five Years in Damascus*, 1855, vol. i. pp. 377—382, and map.) Indeed, so much fresh light has been thrown on the south-west of Syria by Mr. Porter's careful surveys, that the geography of the whole country will have to be greatly modified in all future maps, as we are now, for the first time, in a position to define with some degree of accuracy the limits of several districts mentioned both by sacred and classical writers,

whose relative position even has hitherto been only matter of doubtful conjecture. The statements of Burckhardt, who has hitherto been the sole authority, require considerable correction.

The *Barada*, the ancient Abana, from its rise in Antilibanus, near the plain of *Zebdany* to its termination in the South and East Lakes, is computed to traverse a distance of 42 miles, and to water a tract equal to 311 square miles, inhabited by a population of 150,000 souls, or an average of 482 to every square mile, including Damascus and its suburbs. "The prevailing rock of the mountains through which it flows is limestone. In the higher regions it is hard and compact, but near Damascus soft and chalky, with large nodules of flint intermixed. Fossil shells and corals in great variety are found along the central chain of Antilibanus, through which the river first cuts. In the white hills near Damascus are large quantities of ammonites. At *Súk Wady Barada* (near its source) is a vast bed of organic remains, not less than a mile in length, and in some places exceeding 100 feet in thickness. Trunks of trees, branches of every size and form, and even the delicate tracery of the leaves may be seen scattered about in vast masses. There are in several places among the mountains traces of volcanic action. On a lofty summit, two hours' north-east of *Súk*, is what appears to be an extinct crater. The mountain has been rent, the limestone strata thrown back, and black porous trap-rock fills up the cavity. The plain of Damascus has a loamy soil intermixed with fine sand. The substratum is generally conglomerate, made up of rounded smooth pebbles, flint, and sand. The south-eastern portion of the plain is entirely volcanic." (Porter, *Journal of Sacred Literature*, vol. iv. p. 262.) The plain of Damascus is bounded towards the south by a low range of hills called *Jebel-el-Aswad* (*the Black Mountain*), the southern base of which is washed by a stream, which has lately been supposed by some travellers to represent the ancient Pharpar. It is now called *Nahr-el-Awaj*, which, rising in the roots of Hermon, runs in a course about north-east to a small lake named *Bahret-el-Heijány*, only about 4 miles south of the *Bahret-el-Kibliyah*, into which the Barada flows. It runs partly through a limestone and partly through a volcanic formation, which continues hence far to the south. (Porter, in *Journal of Sac. Lit.* vol. v. pp. 45—57, *Travels*, vol. i. pp. 297—322.) On the south side of the river, opposite to *Jebel-el-Aswad*, is another low mountain range called *Jebel Mánia*, and a higher elevation connected with this range commands a view of those ancient divisions of Southern Syria, which have hitherto been only conjecturally placed in modern maps. Their boundaries have notwithstanding been indelibly traced by the hand of nature, and the limits so clearly defined that they actually exist, mostly under their identical ancient names, as an evidence of the fidelity of classical and sacred geographers. But these will be more conveniently considered in connection with Trachonitis, round which they are grouped [TRACHONITIS], particularly as this part of the country may be regarded as debateable ground between Syria, Arabia, and Palestine.

Turning now to the north of Damascus and the east of the mountain range, the country between this city and Aleppo offers nothing worthy of particular notice; indeed its geography is still a blank in the map of Syria, except its western side, which is traversed by the *Haj* road, the most northern part of which has been described by Burckhardt, and its southern by the no less enterprising and more accurate Porter, in more recent times. (Burckhardt, *Syria*, p. 121, &c.; Porter, *Damascus*, vol. ii. p. 350, &c.)

The northern part of Syria is now comprehended in the pashalic of Aleppo. It is bounded on the east by the Euphrates, and on the north and west by the mountain chains of Taurus and Amanus, the former of which throws off other diverging branches to the south, until they ultimately flank the valley of the Orontes on the east, so continuing the connection between Antilibanus and its parent stock. Aleppo itself is situated in a rich and extensive plain, separated on the east by undulating hills from the almost unoccupied country, which consists of a level sheeptrack, extending from thence to the Euphrates. The sandy level of this Syrian desert is, however, diversified by occasional ranges of hills, and the plateaus are of various elevation, rising a little west of the meridian of Aleppo to a height of 1500 feet above the Mediterranean, and thence declining suddenly to the east and much more gradually to the west. It is on one of these ranges in the heart of the desert, northeast of Damascus, that Palmyra is situated, the only noticeable point in all the dreary waste, which has been described in an article of its own [PALMYRA]. The tract between Damascus and Palmyra has been frequently explored by modern travellers, as well as the ruins themselves; but there is no better account to be found of them than in Mr. Porter's book, already so frequently referred to (vol. i. pp. 149—254; compare Irby and Mangles, pp. 257—276).

III. *Ancient geographical divisions.*—The earliest classical notice of Syria, which could be expected to enter into any detail, is that of Xenophon in his *Anabasis*. Unhappily, however, this writer's account of the march of Cyrus through the north of Syria is very brief. The following notes are all that he offers for the illustration of its ancient geography. Issus he mentions as the last city of Cilicia, towards Syria. One day's march of 5 parasangs brought the army to the gates of Cilicia and Syria: two walls, 3 stadia apart,—the river Cersus (Κέρσος) flowing between,—drawn from the sea to the precipitous rocks, fitted with gates, allowing a very narrow approach along the coast, and so difficult to force, even against inferior numbers, that Cyrus had thought it necessary to send for the fleet in order to enable him to turn the flank of the enemy: but the position was abandoned by the general of Artaxerxes. One day's march of 5 parasangs brought them to Myriandrus (Μυρίανδρος), a mercantile city of the Phoenicians, on the sea. Four days' march, or 20 parasangs, to the river Chalus (Χάλος), abounding in a fish held sacred by the Syrians. Six days, or 30 parasangs, to the fountains of the Daradax (al. Dardes, Δάρδης), where were palaces and parks of Belesys, governor of Syria. Three days, 15 parasangs, to the city Thapsacus on the Euphrates (*Anab.* i. 4. §§ 4—18). It is to be remarked that the 9 days' march of 50 parasangs beyond this is said by Xenophon to have led through Syria, where he uses that term of the Aram Naharaim, of the Scriptures, equivalent to Mesopotamia. Of the places named by the historian in Syria Proper, Issus has been fully described [ISSUS]. The position of the Cilician and Syrian gates is marked by the narrow passage left between the base of the Amanus and the sea, where the ruins of two walls, separated by an interval of about 600 yards, still

preserve the tradition of the fortifications mentioned in the narrative. The Cersus, however, now called the *Merkez-su*, appears to have been diverted from its ancient channel, and runs to the sea in two small streams, one to the north of the northern wall, the other to the south of the southern. The site of Myriandrus has not yet been positively determined, but it must have been situated about half-way between *Iskanderún* (Alexandria) and *Arsús* (Rhosus), as Strabo also intimates (see below). From this point the army must have crossed the Amanus by the *Beilán* pass, and have marched through the plain of '*Umk*, north of the lake of Antioch, where three fordable rivers, the Labotas (*Kara-su*), the Oenoparas (*Aswad*), and the Arceuthus ('*Afrin*), must have been crossed on their march; which, however, are unnoticed by the historian. The river Chalus, with its sacred fish, is identified with the *Chalib* or *Koweik*, the river of Aleppo, the principal tributary to which in the mountains is still called *Balúkhlí-sú*, or *Fish-river*. The veneration of fish by the Syrians is mentioned also by Diodorus, Lucian, and other ancient writers. (Ainsworth, *Travels in the Track of the Ten Thousand*, pp. 57—65.) The source of the river Daradax, with the palaces and parks of Belesys, 30 parasangs, or 90 geographical miles, from Chalus, is marked by an ancient site called to the present day *Ba'lis*, "peculiarly positioned with regard to the Euphrates, and at a point where that river would be first approached on coming across Northern Syria in a direct line trending a little southward, and corresponding at the same time with the distances given by Xenophon." (Ainsworth, *l. c.* p. 66.) The ruins of a Roman castle, built upon a mound of ruins of greater antiquity, doubtless preserve the site of the satrap's palace; while the rich and productive alluvial soil of the plain around, covered with grasses, flowering plants, jungle, and shrubs, and abounding in game, such as wild boars, francolin, quails, landrails, &c., represents "the very large and beautiful paradise:" the river Daradax, however, is reduced to a canal cut from the Euphrates, about a mile distant, which separated the large park from the mainland; and Mr. Ainsworth thinks that the fact of the fountain being 100 feet wide at its source, "tends to show that the origin of a canal is meant, rather than the source of a river" (p. 67. n. 1). Thapsacus is described in a separate article. [THAPSACUS.]

Far more full, but still unsatisfactory, is the description of Syria given by Strabo, a comparison of which with the later notices of Pliny and Ptolemy, illustrated by earlier histories and subsequent Itineraries, will furnish as complete a view of the classical geography of the country as the existing materials allow. The notices of Phoenicia, necessarily intermingled with those of Syria, are here omitted as having been considered in a separate article [PHOENICIA]. On the north Syria was separated from Cilicia by Mons Amanus. From the sea at the gulf of Issus to the bridge of the Euphrates in Commagene was a distance of 1400 stadia. On the east of the Euphrates, it was bounded by the Scenite Arabs, on the south by Arabia Felix and Egypt, on the west by the Egyptian sea as far as Issus (xvi. p. 749). He divides it into the following districts, commencing on the north: Commagene, Seleucis of Syria; Coelesyria; Phoenice on the coast; Judaea inland. Commagene was a small territory, having Samosata for its capital, surrounded by a rich country. Seleucis, the fortress of Mesopotamia, was situated at the bridge of the Euphrates in this district, and was assigned to Commagene by Pompey. Seleucis, otherwise called Tetrapolis, the best of the before-named districts, was subdivided according to the number of its four principal cities, Seleucis of Pieria, Antioch, Apameia, and Laodiceia. The Orontes flowed from Coelesyria through this district, having to the east the cities of Bambyce, Beroea, and Heracleia, and the river Euphrates. Heracleia was 20 stadia distant from the temple of Athena at Cyrrhestia. This gave its name to Cyrrhestice which extended as far as Antiochis to the south, touched the Amanus on the north, and was conterminous with Commagene on the east. In Cyrrhestice were situated Gindarus, its capital, and near it Heracleum. Contiguous to Gindarus lay Pagrae of Antiochis, on the Amanus, above the plain of Antioch, which was watered by the Arceuthus, the Orontes, the Labotas, and the Oenoparas, in which was also the camp of Meleager; above these lay the table mount, Trapezae. On the coast were Seleuceia and Mount Pieria, attached to the Amanus, and Rhosus ('Ρωσός), between Issus and Seleuceia. South of Antiochis was Apameia, lying inland; south of Seleucis Mount Casius and Anticasius: but the former was divided from Seleuceia by the embouchure of the Orontes and the rock-hewn temple of Nymphaeum; then Posidium a small town, Heracleia, Laodiceia, &c. The mountains east of Laodiceia, sloping gradually on their west side, had a steeper inclination on the east towards Apameia (named by the Macedonians Pella) and the Chersonese, as the rich valley of the Orontes about that city was called. Conterminous with the district of Apamene, on the east, was the country of the phylarch of the Arabs, named Parapotamia, and Chalcidice, extending from the Massyas; while the Scenite Arabs also occupied the south, being less wild and less distinctively Arabs in proportion as they were brought nearer by position to the influences of Syrian civilisation. (*Ibid.* pp. 749—753.) Then follows the description of the coast, which belongs to Phoenicia (sup. p. 606), and his extraordinary mis-statement about Libanus and Antilibanus (p. 755) alluded to under those articles. According to this view, the western termination of Libanus was on the coast, a little to the south of Tripoli, at a place called Θεοῦ πρόσωπον, while Antilibanus commenced at Sidon. The two ranges then ran parallel towards the east, until they terminated in the mountains of the Arabians, above Damascus, and in the two Trachones [TRACHONITIS]. Between these two ranges lay the great plain of Coelesyria, divided into several districts, the width at the sea 200 stadia, the length inland about double the width; fertilised by rivers, the largest of which was the Jordan, and having a lake called Gennesaritis [TIBERIAS MARE]. The Chrysorrhoas, which rose near Damascus, was almost wholly absorbed in irrigation. The Lycus and Jordan were navigated by the Aradians. The westernmost of the plains, along the sea-border, was called Macra (Μάκρα πεδίον), next to which was Massyas, with a hilly district in which Chalcis was situated as a kind of acropolis of the district, which commenced at Laodiceia ad Libanum. This hilly district was held by the Ituraeans and Arabs [ITURAEA]. Above Massyas was the Royal Plain (Αὐλὼν Βασιλικὸς) and the country of Damascus, followed by the Trachones, &c. (pp. 755, 756). This very confused and inaccurate description has been sufficiently corrected in the account above given of the Physical Geography of Syria, and need not be further noticed than to observe that it is very strange that, after Syria had been occupied by the Macedonians and the Romans for so many years, and notwithstanding the frequent campaigns of the Roman legions in that country, even its main features were so little known.

Pliny confines Syria to the limits usually assigned it, that is he distinguishes between Syria and Palestine, which are confounded by Strabo. He describes Galilee as that part of Judaea which adjoins Syria (v. 14. s. 15), but coincides with Strabo in giving a description of the coast under the name of Phoenice (19. s. 17). His notion of the direction of the ranges of Libanus and Antilibanus is more correct than that of Strabo; but his description of the coast of Phoenice, like that of his predecessor, is far more correct than that of the interior of the country; while his grouping of the various districts is altogether arbitrary and incorrect. Thus, while he correctly describes Mount Lebanon as commencing behind Sidon, he makes it extend for 1500 stadia (a monstrous exaggeration, if the reading is correct) to Simyra, and this he calls Coelesyria. Then he loosely states the parallel range of Antilibanus to be equal to this, and adds a fact, unnoticed by other writers, that the two ranges were joined by a wall drawn across the intermediate valley. Within, i. e. east of, this last range ("post eum introrsus") he places the region of Decapolis and the tetrarchies which he had before enumerated (viz. Trachonitis, Paneas, Abila, Arca, Ampeloessa, Gabe), and the whole extent of Palestine ("Palaestinae tota laxitas"), —a confusion on the part of the author involving a double or triple error; for, 1st, unless Damascus be included in the Decapolis, the whole region lay south of Antilibanus; 2dly, the cities of the Decapolis lay in several tetrarchies, and therefore ought not to be distinguished from them as a separate district; 3dly, the tetrarchies themselves, which are wrongly enumerated, lay, for the most part, within Coelesyria proper, and only Abilene, in any proper sense, to the east of Antilibanus, although this description might loosely apply to Trachonitis also [TRACHONITIS]. But to descend to particulars.

Phoenice terminates to the north, according to Pliny, at the island Aradus, north of the river Eleutheros, near Simyra and Marathos. On the coast were situated Carne, Balanea, Paltos, Gabale, the promontory on which lay Laodiceia Libera, Diospolis, Heraclea, Charadrus, Posidium; then the promontory of Syria of Antioch, then that of Seleucia Libera, called also Pieria. Another egregious error follows this generally correct statement, and is accompanied with another example of exaggeration. Mons Casius he places above Seleucia ("super eam") —from which it is distant about 15 miles to the north, the Orontes intervening—and states its ascent to be xix. M.P., and its direct height iv. M.P., or nearly 20,000 feet!—its actual height being about 5,700 feet,—from the summit of which the sun might be seen above the horizon at the fourth watch, i. e. three hours before sunrise. North of this came the town Rhosos, behind which (" a tergo") Portae Syriae, between the Rhosii Montes and the Taurus; then Myriandros, on the coast, and Mount Amanus, on which was Bomitae, and which separated Syria from Cilicia (v. 20—22). In the interior the following districts belonged to Coelesyria: Apameia, divided by the river Marsyas from the tetrarchy of the Nazerini; Bambyce, otherwise called Hierapolis, but Mabog by the Syrians (famous for the worship of the monstrous Atargatis, the Derceto of the Greeks); Chalcis ad Belum, which gave its name to the region of Chalcidene, the most fertile in Syria; then Cyrrhestice, named from Cyrrhum; the Gazatae, Gindareni, Gabeni; two tetrarchies named Granucomatae; the Emeseni; Hylatae; the Ituraeans and their kindred Baetarveni; the Mariammitani, the tetrarchy of Mammisea, Paradisus, Pagrae, Pinaritae; two other Seleuciae, the one at the Euphrates, the other at Belus; the Cardytenses. All these he places in Coelesyria: the towns and peoples enumerated in the rest of Syria, omitting those on the Euphrates, which are separately described, are the Arethusii, Beroeenses, Epiphanoenses; on the east, the Laodiceans by Libanus, the Leucadii, Larisaei, besides seventeen tetrarchies with barbarous names not further specified. The towns named in connection with the Euphrates are, Samosata, the head of Commagene, xl. M. P. below the cataracts, where it receives the Marsyas; Cingilla the end, and Immea the commencement, of Commagene; Epiphania, Antiochia ad Euphraten; then Zeugma, lxxii. M. P. from Samosata, celebrated for the bridge over the Euphrates — whence its name — which connected it with Apameia on the left bank of the river; Europus; Thapsacus, then called Amphipolis. On reaching Ura, the river turned to the east, leaving the vast desert of Palmyra on the right. Palmyra was cccxxxvii. M. P. from the Parthian city of Seleuceia ad Tigrim, cciii. M. P. from the nearest part of the Syrian coast, and xxvii. M. P. from Damascus. Below ("infra") the deserts of Palmyra was the region Strelendena, and the above-named Hierapolis, Beroea, and Chalcis; and beyond ("ultra") Palmyra, Emesa and Elatius, half as near again ("dimidio propior") to Petra as was Damascus (Ib. cc. 23—26).

It is difficult to discover many of these names in their Latin disguise still further obscured by corrupt readings; but many of them will occur in the more accurate and methodical notices of Ptolemy, in connection with which a comparative Geography of Ancient and Modern Syria may be attempted. The boundaries of Syria are fixed by Ptolemy consistently with earlier writers. On the N., Cilicia, part of Cappadocia, and Mons Amanus; on the W. the Syrian sea; on the S. Judaea; on the E. the Arabian desert as far as the ford of the Euphrates, near Thapsacus; then the river itself as far as Cappadocia (Ptol. v. 15. §§ 1—8).

The districts and towns are enumerated under the following subdivisions:—

i. The Coast (§§ 2, 3) after Issus and the Cilician Gates. 1. Alexandreia by the Issus. 2. Myriandrus. 3. Rhossus. 4. The Rhossian Rock (σκόπελος). 5. Seleuceia of Pieria. 6. The mouth of the Orontes. 7. Poseidion. 8. Heracleia. 9. Laodiceia. 10. Gabala. 11. Paltos. 12. Balanaea. [Then follows Phoenice, from the Eleutherus to the Chorseus, S. of Dora. See Phoenice.] Of the above-named maritime towns of Syria, No. 2 alone has occurred in Xenophon, 5 parasangs S. of the Cilician Gates. Both this and most of the others occur in Strabo and Pliny, and the distances are furnished by the author of the Stadiasmus Maris Magni, and the Itinerarium Hierosolymitanum. Alexandreia (Iskanderín), not mentioned by Strabo or Pliny, was 45 stadia from the Cilician Pylae. Myriandrus was 80 stadia from Alexandreia. Its site has not been identified (Ainsworth, Travels in the Track of the Ten Thousand, p. 59), but is conjecturally, though probably, placed by Pococke on the river Dulgekan. (Observations

on Syria, p. 179.) Rhossus (now Arsús) is 90 stadia from Myriandrus; while the Rhossicus Scopulus, 80 stadia from Rhossus, is to be identified in the Ras Khanzeer, the southern promontory of the Gulf of Iskanderún, a well-known nautical feature on this coast. (Ib. p. 180; Chesney, Expedition, i. p. 410.) Between Seleuceia and the Rhossic rock the Stadiasmus inserts Georgia, 40 stadia from the former, 80 from the latter. Seleuceia is clearly marked by extensive and important ruins. [Seleuceia.] From Seleuceia to the Orontes, 40 stadia. Between the Orontes and Poseidion the Stadiasmus enumerates Nymphaeum, 15 stadia; Long Island (Μακρὰ νῆσος), one of the Pigeon Rocks, 50 stadia; Chaladrus, or Chaladropolis (obviously the Charadrus of Ptolemy), 10 stadia; Sidonia, 60 stadia, above which was a lofty mountain called the Throne (Θρόνος), distant 80 stadia from Poseidium. Heracleia (Ras-el-Basit), situated on a cape called Polia, was 100 stadia from Poseidium, and Laodiceia 120 stadia direct distance from Heracleia; between which the Stadiasmus inserts Pasieria and Albus Portus, the former 120 stadia from Polia, the latter 30 stadia from Laodiceia, with a like interval between the two. From Laodiceia the Stadiasmus reckons 200 stadia to Balaneae (Banias), in direct distance, subdivided as follows: from Laodiceia to a navigable river, probably Nahr-el-Kebir, 70 stadia; from that to Gabala (Jebili), 80; to Paltus (Boldo), 30; to Cape Balaneae, 70 stadia.

ii. By the Euphrates (§ 11). 1. Cholmadara. 2. Samosata.

iii. Pieria. (§ 12.) 1. Pinara. 2. Pagrae. 3. The Syrian Gates. This was the N.-western part of the country, where Bagras still marks about the centre of the district. [Pagrae.]

iv. Cyrrhestice (§ 13). 1. Ariseria. 2. Rhegias. 3. Buba. 4. Heracleia. 5. Niara. 6. Hierapolis. 7. Cyrrhus. 8. Berrhoea. 9. Baena. 10. Paphara. This district lay to the east of Pieria, and corresponded with the fertile plain watered by the three streams that flow into the lake of Antioch, the Labotas, the Arceuthus, and the Oenoparas of Strabo; on the last and easternmost of which, now called the Afrín, the modern village of Corus still represents the ancient Cyrrhus, the capital of the district to which it gave its name. This part of Syria is so little known that it is impossible to identify its other ancient towns, the names of which, however, might doubtless be recovered in existing villages or sites. The village of Corus, which has ruins in its vicinity, is situated on the slopes of the Taurus, about 40 miles N. by W. of Aleppo and 15 miles NW. of Kilis, the seat of the Turcoman government, whose limits nearly correspond with those of the ancient Cyrrhestice. (Chesney, Euphrates Expedition, vol. i. p. 422, and map i.)

v. By the Euphrates (§ 14). 1. Urima. 2. Arustis. 3. Zeugma. 4. Europus. 5. Caecilia. 6. Bethamania. 7. Gerrhe. 8. Arimara. 9. Eragiza or Errhasiga. These towns of the Euphrates were situated lower down the stream than those mentioned above (iii.), apparently between Samosat and the river Sajúr, a tributary of the Euphrates, which, rising near 'Ain Tab, enters that river a little below some ancient ruins, supposed to represent the Caecilia of Ptolemy (No. 5). The names of several of these towns are still preserved in the native villages situated between the Sajúr and the Euphrates; and it is clear that the geographer did not intend to say that all these towns were on the river. The castle of *Oroum*, not far above *Bireh-Jik* and *Port William*, is Urima (No. 1 in the list), to the west of which, not far from '*Ain Tab*, is the small village of *Arúl*, Aralis (No. 2). (Chesney, p. 419.)

vi. SELEUCIS (§ 15). 1. Gephyra. 2. Gindarus. 3. Imma. The Seleucis of Ptolemy comprehended a small part only of that district described under the same name by Strabo, probably that tract of coast to the north of the Orontes, in which Seleuceia Pieria was situated. [SELEUCIS; SELEUCEIA PIERIA.]

vii. CASSIOTIS (§ 16). 1. Antioch on the Orontes. 2. Daphne. 3. Bactialle. 4. Audeia (*al.* Lydia). 5. Seleuceia ad Belum. 6. Larissa. 7. Epiphaneia. 8. Rhaphaneae. 9. Antaradus. 10. Marathus. 11. Mariame. 12. Mamuga. This district comprehended the coast from the mouth of the Orontes to Aradus, so including part of Phoenice, while to the east it extended as far as the Orontes; thus corresponding nearly with the pashalic of Tripoli in the modern division of the country. This also was part of Strabo's Seleucis, in which he places Antioch. Of the towns recited, 7, 6, 5, 1, 2 were situated at or near the Orontes; 8, 9, and 10 on the coast (see under the names): 3, 4, 11, and 12 have not been identified.

viii. CHALYBONITIS (§ 17). 1. Thema. 2. Acoraca (*al.* Acoraba). 3. Derrhima. 4. Chalybon. 5. Spelunca; and, by the Euphrates, 6, Barbarissus. 7. Athis. Chalybonitis received its name from No. 4 in the list of cities, afterwards called Beroea by Seleucus Nicator, and so designated by Strabo, situated about half-way between Antioch and Hierapolis. [BEROEA, No. 3.] This fixes the district to the east of Cassiotis, in the pashalic of Aleppo, whose renowned capital called in Arabic *Chaleb*, is the modern representative of Chalybon, which had resumed its ancient name as early as the time of Ptolemy, unless it had rather retained it throughout among the natives. The district extended from the Orontes to the Euphrates. The sites have not been identified.

ix. CHALCIDICE (§ 18). 1. Chalcis. 2. Assapheidama. 3. Tolmidessa. 4. Maronias. 5. Coara. This district lay south of Aleppo, and therefore of Chalybonitis, according to Pococke (*Observations on Syria*, p. 149), which is confirmed by the existence of *Kennasserin*, which he takes to be identical in situation with Chalcis, and which, among Arab writers, gives its name to this part of Syria, and to the gate of Aleppo, which leads in this direction. [CHALCIS, No. 1.]

x. APAMENE (§ 19). 1. Nazaba (*al.* Nazama). And on the east of the Orontes, 2. Thelmenissus (*al.* Thelbenissus). 3. Apameia. 4. Emissa. This is comprehended in Strabo's Seleucis, and is easily identified with the district of *Homs*. [See EMESA, &c.]

xi. LAODICENE (§ 20). 1. Scabiosa Laodiceia, 2. Paradisus. 3. Jabruda. To the south of the former, higher up the Orontes, also comprehended in the Seleucis of Strabo. No. 1 is identical with Strabo and Pliny's Laodiceia ad Libanum, placed by Mr. Porter and Dr. Robinson at *Tell Neby Mîndan* on the left bank of the Orontes, near *Lake Homs*, Paradisus (2), still marked by a pyramid, on which are represented hunting scenes. (See above, p. 495, *s.v.* ORONTES.) Dr. Robinson so nearly agrees with this identification as to place Paradisus at *Júsieh-el-Kadim*, which is only a few miles distant from

the pyramid of *Hurmul* to the east. (Robinson, *Bib. Res.* 1852, p. 556; Porter, *Five Years in Damascus*, vol. ii. p. 339.) Jabruda (3) is distinctly marked by *Yabrúd* on the east of Antilibanus, a town mentioned by writers of sacred geography as an episcopal city in the fourth century, a distinction which it still retains.

xii. PHOENICE, inland cities (§ 21). 1. Arca. 2. Palaeobiblus. 3. Gabala. 4. Caesareia Panias. These have been noticed under the articles PHOENICE, &c.

xiii. COELESYRIA, cities of the Decapolis (§§ 22. 23). 1. Heliopolis. 2. Abila, named of Lysanias, 3. Saana. 4. Ina. 5. Damascus. 6. Samulis. 7. Abida. 8. *Hippus*. 9. Capitolias. 10. *Gadara*. 11. Adra. 12. *Scythopolis*. 13. *Gerasa*. 14. *Pella*. 15. *Dion*. 16. Gadôra. 17. *Philadelpheia*. 18. *Canatha*. The statement of the geographer that these are the cities of the Decapolis, preceding, as it does, the enumeration of eighteen cities, can only be taken to mean that the ten cities of the Decapolis were comprehended in the list, and that the remainder might be regarded as situated in that region. It is remarkable, too, that the name Coelesyria is here used in a more restricted and proper sense than at the heading of the chapter under consideration, where it is equivalent to Syria in its widest acceptation. According to Pliny the nine cities marked by italics in the above list, with the addition of Raphana, — apparently the Raphaneae of Ptolemy in Cassiotis, — properly constituted the cities of the Decapolis, according to most authorities. These and the remaining cities require a very large district to be assigned to this division of the country, comprehending the whole length of the *Búká'a*, i. e. Coelesyria Proper, from Heliopolis (1) (*Baalbek*) to Philadelpheia (17) (*Ammon*), and in width from Damascus almost to the Mediterranean. Abila of Lysanias (2), has only lately been identified, and attracted the notice which it deserves, as the capital of the tetrarchy of Abilene, mentioned by St. Luke, in connection perhaps with this same Lysanias, whose name is attached to it by the geographer. (*St. Luke*, iii. 1.) It is situated in the heart of Antilibanus, on the north side of the river *Barada*, where the numerous remains of antiquity and some inscriptions leave no doubt of the identity of the site. (De Saulcy, *Voyage autour de la Mer Morte*, vol. ii. pp. 593—604; Porter, *Damascus*, vol. i. pp. 15, 102, 261—273; Robinson, *Bib. Res.* 1852, pp. 479—484.)

xiv. PALMYRENE (§ 24). 1. Rhesapha. 2. Cholle. 3. Oriza. 4. Putea. 5. Adada. 6. Palmyra. 7. Adacha. 8. Danaba. 9. Goaria. 10. Aueria (*al.* Aueira). 11. Casama. 12. Odmana. 13. Atera; and, near the Euphrates, 14. Alalia. 15. Sura. 16. Alamatha. This district obviously lay to the east of the last-named, and south of Chalybonitis. It comprehended the vast desert region in which Palmyra is situated, but which is almost a blank on the map, so as to defy all attempts to identify the sites.

xv. BATANAEA (§ 26). 1. Gerra. 2. Elere. 3. Nelaxa. 4. Adrama. This district will best be considered in connection with Trachonitis. [G. W.]

IV. *History.*—The earliest accounts which we possess of Syria represent it as consisting of a number of independent kingdoms. Thus we hear of the kings of Maacha in the time of David (2 *Sam.* x. 6), of the kings of the neighbouring town of Geshur in the time of Solomon (*Ib.* iii. 3, xiii. 37), &c. But of all the Aramaean monarchies the most powerful in the time of Saul and David was Zobah, as appears from the number of men which that people brought into the field against David (*Ib.* viii. 4), and from the rich booty of which they were spoiled by the Israelites (*Ib.* v. 7). Even after sustaining a signal defeat, they were able in a little time to take the field again with a considerable force (*Ib.* x. 6). David nevertheless subdued all Syria, which, however, recovered its independence after the death of Solomon, B. C. 975. From this period Damascus, the history of which has been already given [DA-MASCUS, Vol. I. p. 748], became the most considerable of the Syrian kingdoms. Syria was conquered by Tiglath-Pileser, king of Assyria, about the year 747 B. C., and was annexed to that kingdom. Hence it successively formed part of the Babylonian and Persian empires; but its history presents nothing remarkable down to the time of its conquest by Alexander the Great. After the death of that conqueror in B. C. 323, Syria and Mesopotamia fell to the share of his general Seleucus Nicator. The sovereignty of Seleucus, however, was disputed by Antigonus, and was not established till after the battle of Ipsus, in 301 B. C., when he founded Antioch on the Orontes, as the new capital of his kingdom. [ANTIOCHEIA, Vol. I. p. 142.] From this period the descendants of Seleucus, known by the appellation of Seleucidae, occupied the throne of Syria down to the year 65 B. C., when Antiochus XIII Asiaticus was dethroned by Pompey, and Syria became a Roman province. (Plut. *Pomp.* 39; Appian, *Syr.* 46; Eutrop. vi. 14.) Into the history of Syria under the Seleucidae it is unnecessary to enter, since a table of that dynasty is given in the *Dictionary of Biography* [Vol. III. p. 769], and the public events will be found described in the lives of the respective monarchs.

The tract of which Pompey took possession under the name of Syria comprised the whole country from the gulf of Issus and the Euphrates to Egypt and the deserts of Arabia. (Appian, *Syr.* 50, *Mith.* 106.) The province, however, did not at first comprehend the whole of this tract, but consisted merely of a strip of land along the sea-coast, which, from the gulf of Issus to Damascus, was of slender breadth, but which to the S. of that city spread itself out as far as the town of Canatha. The rest was parcelled out in such a manner that part consisted of the territories of a great number of free cities, and part was assigned to various petty princes, whose absolute dependence upon Rome led to their dominions being gradually incorporated into the province. (Appian, *Syr.* 50.) The extent of the province was thus continually increased during the first century of the Empire; and in the time of Hadrian it had become so large, that a partition of it was deemed advisable. Commagene, the most northern of the ten districts into which, according to Ptolemy (v. 15), the upper or northern Syria was divided, had become an independent kingdom before the time of Pompey's conquest, and therefore did not form part of the province established by him. [COM-MAGENE, Vol. I. p. 651.] The extent of this province may be determined by the free cities into which it was divided by Pompey; the names of which are known partly from their being mentioned by Josephus (*Ant.* xiv. 4. § 4), and partly from the era which they used, namely that of B. C. 63, the year in which they received their freedom. In this way we are enabled to enumerate the following cities in the original province of Syria: Antiocheia, Se-

leuceia in Pieria, Epiphaneia, between Arethusa and Emesa, Apameia; nearly all the towns of the Decapolis, as Abila (near Gadara), Antiocheia ad Hippum or Hippos, Canatha, Dium, Gadara, Pella, and Philadelpheia; in Phoenicia, Tripolis, Sidon, Tyrus, Dora; in the north of Palestine, Scythopolis and Samaria; on the coast, Turris Stratonis (Caesareia), Joppe, Iamneia, Azotus, Gaza; and in the south, Marissa. The gift of freedom to so many cities is not to be attributed to the generosity of the Romans, but must be regarded as a necessary measure of policy. All these towns had their own jurisdiction, and administered their own revenues; but they were tributary to the Romans, and their taxes were levied according to the Roman system established on the organisation of the province. ("Syria tum primum facta est stipendiaria," Vell. Pat. ii. 37.) The first governors of Syria, and especially Gabinius, who was proconsul in the year 57 B. C., took much pains in restoring the cities which had been destroyed. (Joseph. *Ant.* xiv. 5, § 3.) The divisions established in Judaea by Gabinius have been noticed in another article. [PALAESTINA, Vol. II. p. 532.] Caesar, during his expedition against Pharnaces, B. C. 47, confirmed these cities in their rights, and likewise extended them to others, as Gabala, Laodiceia ad Mare, and Ptolemais. (Eckhel, vol. iii. p. 314, sq.; Norisius, *Ep. Syrom.* pp. 175—213, 450.) Of the regulations adopted in Syria during the reign of Augustus we have little information.

The same political reasons which dictated the establishment of these free cities, where it was possible to do so, rendered the continuance of dynastic governments necessary in the eastern and southern districts of the province, where either the nomadic character of the population, or its obstinate adherence to ancient institutions was adverse to the introduction of new and regular forms of government. These dynasties, however, like the free cities, were used as the responsible organs of the Roman administration, and were tributaries of Rome. Thus, in the histories of Commagene and Judaea, we find instances in which their sovereigns were cited to appear at Rome, were tried, condemned, and punished. The Roman idea of a province is essentially a financial one. A province was considered as a "praedium populi Romani" (Cic. *Verr.* ii. 3); and hence the dynasties of Syria may be considered as belonging to the province just as much as the free towns, since, like them, they were merely instruments for the collection of revenue. (Cf. Huschke, *Ueber den wur Zeit der Geburt Jesu Christi gehaltenen Census,* pp. 100—112.) Thus we find these petty sovereigns in other parts of the world regarding themselves merely as the agents, or procuratores, of the Roman people (Sall. *Jug.* 14; Maffei, *Mus. Ver.* p. 234); nor were they allowed to subsist longer than was necessary to prepare their subjects for incorporation with the province of which they were merely adjuncts.

The Syrian dynasties were as follows: 1. Chalcis ad Belum. 2. The dynasty of Arethusa and Emesa. 3. Abila. 4. Damascus. 5. Judaea. 6. Palmyra. These states have been treated of under their respective names, and we shall here only add a few particulars that may serve further to illustrate the history of some of them during the time that they were under the Roman sway. All that is essential to be known respecting the first three dynasties has already been recorded. With regard to Damascus, it may be added that M. Aemilius Scaurus, the first governor of Syria appointed by Pompey, after having punished its ruler, the Arabian prince Aretas, for the attacks which he had made upon the province before it had been reduced to order, concluded a treaty with him in B. C. 62. It is to this event that the coins of Scaurus refer, bearing the inscription REX ARETAS. (Eckhel, vol. v. p. 131; cf. Dion Cass. xxxvii. 15; Appian. *Syr.* 51; Joseph. *Ant.* xiv 4. § 5, 5. § 1.) Damascus was dependent on the Romans, and sometimes had a Roman garrison (Hieron. *in Isai.* c. 17; Joseph. *Ant.* xiv. 11. § 7), though it cannot be doubted that the Arabian kings were in possession of it, on the condition of paying a tribute. It has already been remarked that the city was in the possession of an ethnarch of Aretas in A. D. 39; and it was not till the year 105, when Arabia Petraea became a province, that Damascus was united with Syria, in the proconsulship of Cornelius Palma. (Eckhel, vol. iii. p. 330.)

On the other hand, Judaea appears to have been annexed to the province of Syria immediately after its conquest by Pompey in B. C. 63 (Dion Cass. xxxvii. 15, 16; Eutrop. vi. 14; Liv. *Ep.* 102; Strab. xvi. p. 762, sq.; Joseph. *B. J.* i. 7. § 7; Amm. Marc. xiv. 8. § 12); though it retained its own administration, with regard especially to the taxes which it paid to the Romans. (Joseph. *Ant.* xiv. 4. § 4, *B. J.* i. 7. § 6.) The race of the Jewish kings ended with Aristobulus, whom Pompey, after the capture of Jerusalem, carried to Rome to adorn his triumph (Appian, *Syr.* 50; Dion Cass. xxxvii. 16; Plut. *Pomp.* 45; Joseph. *Ant.* xiv. 4, &c.) Hyrcanus, the brother of Aristobulus, was left indeed in Judaea as chief priest and ethnarch, in which offices he was confirmed by Caesar; but his dignity was only that of a priest and judge. (Dion Cass. *l. c.*; and Joseph. *l. c.* and xiv. 7. § 2, 10. § 2.) The land, like the province of Syria, was divided for the convenience of administration into districts or circles of an aristocratic constitution (Joseph. *B. J.* i. 8. § 5); and during the constant state of war in which it was kept either by internal disorders, or by the incursions of the Arabians and Parthians, the presence of Roman troops, and of the governor of the province himself, was almost always necessary.

It has been already related [JERUSALEM, Vol. I. p. 26] that Antigonus, the son of Aristobulus, obtained possession of the throne with the assistance of the Parthians in B. C. 40. In the following year the Parthians were expelled from Syria by Ventidius (Dion Cass. xlviii. 39—41; Liv. *Epit.* 127); and in B. C. 38 Judaea was conquered by Sosius, Antony's legatus, Antigonus was captured and executed, and Herod, surnamed the Great, was placed upon the throne, which had been promised to him two years previously. (Dion Cass. xlix. 19—22; Plut. *Anton.* 34, sqq.; Tac. *Hist.* v. 9; Appian, *B. C.* v. 75; Strab. xvi. p. 765.) From this time, Judaea again became a kingdom. With regard to the relation of Herod to the Romans we may remark, that a Roman legion was stationed at Jerusalem to uphold his sovereignty, that the oath of fealty was taken to the king, and that the absolute dependence of the latter was recognised by the payment of a tribute and the providing of subsidiary troops. (Joseph. *Ant.* xv. 3. § 7, xvii. 2. § 4; Appian, *B. C.* v. 75.) Herod, therefore, is to be regarded only as a procurator of the emperor, with the title of king. Antony assigned part of the revenues of Judaea to Cleopatra. (Joseph. *Ant.* xv.

4. §§ 2, 4.) According to an ordinance of Caesar, the places in the jurisdiction of Jerusalem, with the exception of Joppa, had to pay a yearly tribute of a fourth of all agricultural produce, which was to be delivered the following year in Sidon, besides a tenth to be paid to Hyrcanus. (*Ibid.* xiv. 10. § 6.) In the seventh, or Sabbath year, however, the tribute was intermitted. Besides this tribute, there was a capitation tax; and it was for the organising of this tax that the census mentioned in the Gospel of St. Luke (ii. 1, 2) was taken in the year of our Saviour's birth, which appears to have been conducted by Herod's officers according to a Roman forma censualis. The division of Judaea among the sons of Herod, and its subsequent history till it was incorporated in the province of Syria by the emperor Claudius, A. D. 44 (Tac. *Ann.* xii. 23, *Hist.* v. 9), have been already narrated [Vol. II. p. 532], as well as the fate of Jerusalem under the emperors Titus and Hadrian. [Vol. II. p. 26, seq.]

With regard to Palmyra, the sixth of the dynasties before enumerated, we need here only add to what has been already said [Vol. II. p. 536] that it was united to the province of Syria by Hadrian, and bore from him the name of Ἀδριανὴ Πάλμυρα. (Steph. B. p. 498, ed Meineke; cf. Gruter, p. 86. 8.) But whether it became a colony with the Jus Italicum on that occasion or at a later period, cannot be determined.

Respecting the administration of the province of Syria, it may be mentioned that the series of Roman governors commences with M. Scaurus, who was left there by Pompey in the year 62 B. C. with the title of quaestor pro praetore. Scaurus was succeeded by two pro-praetores, L. Marcius Philippus, 61—60, and Lentulus Marcellinus, 59—58; when, on account of the war with the Arabs, Gabinius was sent there as proconsul, with an army (Appian, *Syr.* 51; cf. Joseph. xiv. 4, seq., *B. Jud.* i. 6—8; Eckhel, vol. v. p. 131). We then find the following names: Crassus, 55—53; Cassius, his quaestor, 53—51; M. Calpurnius Bibulus, proconsul. (Drumann, *Gesch. Roms,* vol. ii. pp. 101, 118—120). After the battle of Pharsalus, Caesar gave Syria to Sex. Julius Caesar, B. C. 47, who was put to death in the following year by Caecilius Bassus, an adherent of Pompey. (*Ib.* p. 125, iii. p. 768.) Bassus retained possession of the province till the end of 44, when Cassius seized it, and assumed the title of proconsul. (Cic. *ad Fam.* xii. 11.) After the battle of Philippi, Antony appointed to it his lieutenant, L. Decidius Saxa, B. C. 41, whose overthrow by the Parthians in the following year occasioned the loss of the whole province. (Dion Cass. xlviii. 24; Liv. *Epit.* 127.) The Parthians, however, were driven out by Ventidius, another of Antony's lieutenants, in the autumn of 39. (Dion Cass. *ib.* 39—43; Liv. *ib.*; Plut. *Ant.* 33.) Syria continued to be governed by Antony's officers till his defeat at Actium in 31, namely, C. Sosius, B. C. 38 (by whom, as we have said, the throne of Judaea was given to Herod), L. Munatius Plancus, B. C. 35, and L. Bibulus, B. C. 31. In B. C. 30, Octavian intrusted Syria to his legate, Q. Didius. After the division of the provinces between the emperor and senate in B. C. 27, Syria continued to have as governors legati Augusti pro praetore, who were always consulares. (Suet. *Tib.* 41; Appian, *Syr.* 51.) The most accurate account of the governors of Syria, from B. C. 47 to A. D. 69, will be found in Norisius, *Cenotaphia Pisana.* (Opp. vol. iii. pp. 424—531.) Their residence was Antioch, which, as the metropolis of the province, reached its highest pitch of prosperity. It was principally this circumstance that induced the emperor Hadrian to divide Syria into three parts (Spart. *Hadr.* 14), namely: I. SYRIA, which by way of distinction from the other two provinces was called Syria Coele, Magna Syria, Syria Major, and sometimes simply Syria. (Gruter, *Inscr.* 346. 1, 1091. 5; Orelli, *Inscr.* no. 3186, 4997; Galen, *de Antidot.* i. 2.) Antioch remained the capital till the time of Septimius Severus, who deprived it of that privilege on account of its having sided with Pescennius Niger, and substituted Laodiceia, which he made a colony in its stead (Capitol. *M. Anton.* 25; *Avid Cass.* 9; Ulp. *Dig.* 50. tit. 15. s. 1. § 3); and although Caracalla procured that its rights should be restored to Antioch, yet Laodiceia retained its title of metropolis, together with a small territory comprising four dependent cities, whilst Antioch, which had also been made a colony by Caracalla, was likewise called *Metrocolonia* (*Corp. Inscr. Gr.* no. 4472; Paul. *Dig.* 50. tit. 15. s. 8. § 5; Eckhel, iii. p. 302, sq., 319, sq.). II. SYRIA PHOENICE, or SYROPHOENICE, under a legatus Augusti pro praetore (Murat. 2009. 1, 2; Marini, *Atti, &c.* p. 744), consisted of three parts, with three metropolitan cities, namely: 1. Tyre, which first obtained the title of metropolis, with relation to the Roman province, under Hadrian (Suidas, ii. p. 147, Bernh.), though it had that appellation previously with relation to its own colonies (Strab. xvi. p. 756; Eckhel, vol. iii. p. 386). 2. Damascus, which from the time of Hadrian became a metropolis, with a small territory comprising five towns. (Just. Mart. *Dial. c. Tryphone,* c. 78; Tertull. *adv. Marcian,* iii. 13; Eckhel, vol. iii. pp. 331—333.) 3. Palmyra, which appears to have been the residence of a procurator Caesaris; whence we may infer that it was the centre of a fiscal circle (*Notit. Dign.* i. p. 85; Ulpian, *Dig.* 50. tit. 15. s. 1. § 5; Procop. *de Aed.* ii. 11; *Corp. Inscr. Gr.* no. 4485. 4496—4499.) A fourth metropolis, Emesa, was added under Heliogabalus (Eckhel, iii. p. 311; Ulpian, *Dig.* 50. tit. 15. s. 1. § 4). Trachonitis also formed a separate circle at this time, with the village of Phaina as its μετροκωμία (*Corp. Inscr. Gr.* 4551; Orell. *Inscr.* vol. ii. p. 437, no. 5040). III. SYRIA PALAESTINA, from the time of Hadrian administered by a legatus Augusti pro praet. The name of Syria Palaestina does not appear on coins till the time of the Antonines (Eckhel, iii. p. 435; cf. Aristid. ii. p. 470, Dind.; Galen. *de Simpl. Medic.* iv. 19; Just. Mart. *Apol.* i. 1; *Corp. Inscr. Gr.* no. 4029, 4151, &c.). Its metropolis was Caesareia, anciently Turris Stratonis (Eckhel, iii. p. 432).

This division of the province of Syria was connected with an alteration in the quarters of the three legions usually stationed in Syria. In the time of Dion Cassius (lv. 23) the Legio VI. Scythica was cantoned in Syria, the Legio III. Gallica in Phoenicia, and the Legio VI. Ferrata in Syria Palaestina. The system of colonisation which was begun by Augustus, and continued into the third century of our era, was also adapted to insure the security of the province. The first of these colonies was Berytus, where Augustus settled the veterans of the Legio V. Macedonica and VIII. Augusta. It was a Colonia juris Italici. (Eckhel, iii. p. 356; Orelli, *Inscr.* no. 514; Ulpian, *Dig.* 50. tit. 15. s. 1. § 1; Euseb. *Chron.* p. 155, Scal.) Augustus also founded Heliopolis (*Baalbek*), which received the jus Italicum under Septimius Severus (Ulpian, *l. c.*; Eckhel, iii.

p. 334). Under Claudius was founded Ptolemais (Ace), which did not possess the jus Italicum (Ulpian, *ib.* § 3; Plin. v. 1; Eckhel, iii. p. 424). Vespasian planted two colonies, Caesareia (Turris Stratonis) and Nicopolis (Emmaus) Paul. *Dig.* 50. tit. 15. s. 8. § 7; Eckhel, iii. p. 430); which latter, however, though originally a military colony, appears to have possessed neither the right, nor the name of a colonia (Eckhel, iii. p. 454; Joseph. *Bell. Jud.* vii. 6; Sozomen, *Hist. Eccles.* v. 21.) The chief colony founded by Hadrian was Aelia Capitolina (Jerusalem), whose colonists, however, were Greeks, and therefore it did not possess the jus Italicum. (Dion Cass. lxix. 12; Euseb. *Hist. Eccles.* iv. 6; Malalas, xi. p. 279, ed. Bonn; Ulpian, *l. c.* § 6.) Hadrian also probably founded Palmyra. Under Septimius Severus we have Laodiceia, Tyrus, and Sebaste (Samaria), of which the first two possessed the jus Italicum. (Ulpian, *ib.* § 3. and 7; Eckhel, iii. p. 319, 387, seq., 440, seq.) Caracalla founded Antioch and Emesa (Ulpian, *ib.* § 4; Paul. *ib.* § 5; Eckhel, iii. p. 302, 311), Elagabalus Sidon (Eckhel, iii. p. 371), and Philippus, apparently, Damascus (*ib.* p. 331). To these must be added two colonies whose foundation is unknown, Capitolias, of whose former name we are ignorant (Paul. *Dig.* 50. tit. 15. s. 8. § 7; Eckhel, iii. p. 328, seq.), and Caesareia ad Libanum (Arca). (Eckhel, *ib.* p. 361.)

At the end of the fourth century of our era, Syria was divided into still smaller portions, namely: 1. Syria prima, governed by a consularis, with the metropolis of Antioch and the following cities: Seleuceia, Laodiceia, Gabala, Paltos, Beroea, Chalcis. 2. Syria Secunda, under a praeses, with Apameia for its chief city, and the dependent towns of Epiphaneia, Arethusa, Larissa, Mariamne, Balaneia, Raphaneae, and Seleuceia ad Belum. Malalas (xiv. p. 265, ed. Bonn.) ascribes its separation from Syria Prima to the reign of Theodosius II., which, however, may be doubted. Böcking attributes the division to Theodosius the Great (*ad Not. Dignit.* i. p. 129). 3. Phoenicia Prima, under a consularis, with the metropolis of Tyrus and the cities Ptolemais, Sidon, Berytus, Byblos, Botryo, Tripolis, Arcae, Orthosias, Aradus, Antaradus, Caesarea Paneas. 4. Phoenicia Secunda, or Phoenicia ad Libanum, under a praeses, having Damascus for its capital, and embracing the cities of Emesa, Laodiceia ad Libanum, Heliopolis, Abila, Palmyra. It was first separated by Theodosius the Great. 5. Palaestina Prima, administered by a consularis, and in the years 383—385 by a proconsul. Its chief city was Caesareia, and it comprehended the towns of Dora, Antipatris, Diospolis, Azotus ad Mare, Azotus Mediterranea, Eleutheropolis, Aelia Capitolina (Jerusalem), Neapolis, Livias, Sebaste, Anthedon, Diocletianopolis, Joppa, Gaza, Raphia, Ascalon, &c. 6. Palaestina Secunda, under a praeses, with the capital of Scythopolis, and the towns of Gadara, Abila, Capitolias, Hippos, Tiberias, Dio Caesareia, and Gabae. 7. Palaestina Tertia. This was formed out of the former province of Arabia. (Procop. *de Aed.* v. 8.) It was governed by a praeses, and its chief city was Petra. (Cf. PALAESTINA, Vol. II. p. 533.)

With respect to these later subdivisions of Syria, the reader may consult Hierocles, p. 397, ed. Bonn, with the notes of Wesseling, p. 518, sqq.; the *Notitia Dignit.* i. p. 5, seq., and the commentary of Böcking, pp. 128—140, 511; Bingham, *Orig. Eccl.* vol. iii. p. 434, seq.; Norisius, *de Epoch. Syromaced.* in Opp. vol. ii. p. 374, sqq., p. 419, seq.

In the year 632, Syria was invaded by the Saracens, nominally under the command of Abu Obeidah, one of the " companions " of Mahomet, but really led by Chaled, " the sword of God." The easy conquest of Bosra inspirited the Moslems to attack Damascus; but here the resistance was more determined, and, though invested in 633, the city was not captured till the following year. Heraclius had been able to collect a large force, which, however, under the command of his general Werdan, was completely defeated at the battle of Aisnadin; and Damascus, after that decisive engagement, though it still held out for seventy days, was compelled to yield. Heliopolis and Emesa speedily shared the fate of Bosra and Damascus. The last efforts of Heraclius in defence of Syria, though of extraordinary magnitude, were frustrated by the battle of the Yermuk. Jerusalem, Aleppo, and Damascus successively yielded to the Saracen arms, and Heraclius abandoned a province which he could no longer hope to retain. Thus in six campaigns (633—639) Syria was entirely wrested from the Roman empire. (Gibbon, *Decline and Fall*, ch. 51; Marquardt, *Röm. Alterth.* vol. iii.) [T. H. D.]

SYRIAE PORTAE (Συρίαι πύλαι), a pass between Mount Amanus and the coast of the bay of Issus, which formed a passage from Cilicia into Syria. It was 3 stadia in length, and only broad enough to allow an army to pass in columns. (Xenoph. *Anab.* i. 4. § 4; Arrian, *Anab.* ii. 8; Plin. v. 18; Ptol. v. 15. § 12; Strab. xiv. p. 676.) This mountain pass had formerly been closed up at both ends by walls leading from the rocks into the sea; but in the time of Alexander they seem to have existed no longer, as they are not mentioned by any of his historians. Through the midst of this pass, which is now called the pass of *Beilan*, there flowed a small stream, which is still known under the name of *Merkez-su*, its ancient name being Cersus. [L. S.]

SYRIAS (Συριάς), a headland in the Euxine, on the coast of Paphlagonia, which, to distinguish it from the larger promontory of Carambis in its vicinity, was also called ἄκρα λεπτή. (Marcian, p. 72; Arrian, *Peripl. P. E.* p. 15; Anonym. *Peripl. P. E.* p. 7.) Its modern name is *Cape Indje*. [L.S.]

SYRIE'NI. [SYRASTRENE.]

SYRNOLA (*Itin. Hier.* p. 568), a town in the north-western part of Thrace, between Philippopolis and Parembole. [J. R.]

SYRO-PHOENICE. [SYRIA, p. 1079.]

SYROS or SYRUS (Σῦρος, also Συρίη, Hom. *Od.* xv. 403, and Σύρα, Diog. Laert. i. 115; Hesych.; Suid.: *Eth.* Σύριος: *Syra* (Σύρα), and the present inhabitants call themselves Συριῶται or Συριανοί, not Σύριοι), an island in the Aegaean sea, one of the Cyclades, lying between Rheneia and Cythnus, and 20 miles in circumference, according to some ancient authorities. (Plin. iv. 12. s. 22.) Syros produces good wine, but is upon the whole not fertile, and does not deserve the praises bestowed upon it by Homer (*l. c.*), who describes it as rich in pastures, cattle, wine, and wheat. It is usually stated upon the authority of Pliny (xxxiii. 12. s. 56) that Syros produced Sil or yellow ochre; but in Sillig's edition of Pliny, Scyros is substituted for Syros.

Syros had two cities even in the time of Homer (*Od.* xv. 412), one on the eastern, and the other on the western side of the island. The one on the eastern side, which was called Syros (Ptol. iii. 15. § 30), stood on the same site as the modern capital

of the island, which is now one of the most flourishing cities in Greece, containing 11,000 inhabitants, and the centre of a flourishing trade. In consequence of the numerous new buildings almost all traces of the ancient city have disappeared; but there were considerable remains of it when Tournefort visited the island. At that time the ancient city was abandoned, and the inhabitants had built a town upon a lofty and steep hill about a mile from the shore: this town is now called *Old Syra*, to distinguish it from the modern town, which has arisen upon the site of the ancient city. The inhabitants of *Old Syra*, who are about 6000 in number, are chiefly Catholics, and, being under the protection of France and the Pope, they took no part in the Greek revolution during its earlier years. Their neutrality was the chief cause of the modern prosperity of the island, since numerous merchants settled there in consequence of the disturbed condition of the other parts of Greece.

There are ruins of the second ancient city on the western coast, at the harbour of *Maria della Grazia*. Ross conjectures that its name may have been Grynche or Gryncheia, since we find the Γρυγχῆς, who are otherwise unknown, mentioned three times in the inscriptions containing lists of the tributary allies of Athens. There was another ancient town in the island, named Eschatia. (Böckh, *Inscr.* no. 2347, c.) Pherecydes, one of the early Greek philosophers, was a native of Syros. (Comp. Strab. x. pp. 485, 487; Scylax, p. 22; Steph. B. *s. v.*; Tournefort, *Voyage*, vol. i. p. 245, seq. Engl. tr.; Prokesch, *Erinnerungen*, vol. i. p. 55, seq.; Ross, *Reisen auf den Griech. Inseln*, vol. i. p. 5, seq., vol. ii. p. 24, seq.; Fiedler, *Reise*, vol. ii. p. 164, seq.)

SYRTICA REGIO (ἡ Συρτική, Ptol. iv. 3), a tract on the coast of N. Africa, between the Syrtis Major and Minor, about 100 miles in length. (Strab. xvii. p. 834, sq.; Mela, i. 7; Plin. v. 4. s. 4.) After the third century it obtained the name of the Regio Tripolitana, from the three principal cities, which were allied together, whence the modern name of *Tripoli* (*Not. Imp. Occid.* c. 45; Procop. *de Aed.* vi. 3; cf. Solinus, c. 27). Mannert conjectures (x. pt. ii. p. 133) that the emperor Septimius Severus, who was a native of Leptis, was the founder of this Provincia Tripolitana, which, according to the Not. Imp. (*l. c.*), was governed by its own duke (Dux) (Comp. Amm. Marc. xxviii. 6). The district was attributed by Ptolemy, Mela, and Pliny to Africa Propria; but in reality it formed a separate district, which at first belonged to the Cyrenaeans, but was subsequently wrested from them and annexed to Carthage, and, when the whole kingdom of the latter was subjected to the Romans, formed a part of the Roman province of Africa. For the most part the soil was sandy and little capable of cultivation, as it still remains to the present day (Della Cella, *Viaggio*, p. 50); yet on the borders of the river Cinyps and in the neighbourhood of the town of Leptis, there was some rich and productive land. (Herod. iv. 198; Scylax, p. 47; Strab. xvii. p. 835; Ovid, *ex Pont.* ii. 7. 25.) Ptolemy mentions several mountains in the district, as Mount Giglius or Gigius (τὸ Γίγιον ὄρος, iv. 3. § 20), Mount Thizibi (τὸ Θίζιβι ὄρος, *ib.*) Mount Zuchabbari or Chuzabarri (τὸ Ζουχάββαρι ἢ Χουζάβαρρι, *ib.*) and Mount Vasaluetum or Vasaleton (τὸ Οὐασάλουετον ἢ Οὐασάλετον ὄρος, *ib.* § 18). The more important promontories were Cephalae (Κεφαλαὶ ἄκρον, Ptol. iv. 3. § 13), near which also, on the W., the same author mentions another promontory, Trieron (Τριήρων or Τρίηρον ἄκρον, *ib.*) and Zeitha (τὰ Ζείθα, *ib.* § 12). The principal rivers were the Cinyps or Cinyphus (Ptol. *ib.* § 20), in the eastern part of the district, and the Triton, which formed its western boundary, and by which the three lakes called Tritonitis, Pallas, and Libya were supplied (*ib.* § 19). Besides these waters there were extensive salt lakes and marshes along the coast (Strab. *l. c.*; *Tab. Peut.* tab. vii.) The lotus is mentioned among the scanty products of this unfertile land (Plin. xxiv. 1. s. 1), and a peculiar kind of precious stones, called after the country Syrtides gemmae, was found on the coast (Id. xxxvii. 10. § 67). The tribes that inhabited the country beside the Nasamones, Psytti, and Macae, who in the earlier times at least spread themselves over this district, were the Lotophagi [Vol. II. p. 205], who dwelt about Syrtis Minor, and the Gindanes [Vol. I. p. 1002], who were situated to the W. of the former. Ptolemy, however, in place of these more ancient tribes, mentions others that are heard of nowhere else, as the Nigitimi, Samamycii, Nycpii, Nygbeni, Elaeones, Damnesii, &c. (iv. 3. §§ 23— 27). But Egyptian and Phoenician colonists had been mixed at a very early period with these aboriginal Libyan tribes, whom the Greeks found there when they settled upon the coast, and with whom, probably, they had for some time previously had connections. The most important towns of the Regio Syrtica were the three from which it subsequently derived its name of Tripolitana, that is, Leptis Magna, Oea, and Sabrata; besides which we find Tacape and other places mentioned by Ptolemy. Opposite to the coast lay the islands of Meninx and Cercina.　　　　　　　　[T. H. D.]

SYRTIS MAJOR and MINOR (Σύρτις μεγάλη καὶ μικρά, Ptol. iv. 3), two broad and deep gulfs in the Libyan sea on the N. coast of Africa, and in the district called after them Regio Syrtica. The name is derived from the Arabic, *Sert*, a desert from the desolate and sandy shore by which the neighbourhood of the Syrtes is still characterised. The navigation of them was very dangerous because of their shallow and sunken rocks, so that the smaller Syrtis was considered in ancient times as altogether unnavigable, and even into the larger one only small ships ventured. (Strab. xvii. p. 835; Scylax, p. 48; Polyb. i. 39; Mela, i. 7; Plin. v. 4. s. 4; Procop. *de Aed.* vi. 3.) The reports of modern travellers, however, do not tend to establish these dangers. (Lauthier, *Relazione* in Della Cella's *Viaggio*, p. 214, sqq.) The Greater Syrtis, which was the eastern one, now the *Gulf of Sidra*, extended from the promontory of Boreum on the E. side to that of Cephalae on the W. (Scyl. 46, sq.; Polyb. iii. 29; Strab. *l. c.* and ii. p. 123; Mela and Plin. *ll. cc.*) According to Strabo it was from 4000 to 5000 stadia in circumference (*l. c.*); but in another place (xvii. p. 835) he puts down the measure more accurately at 3930 stadia. Its depth, or landward recess, was from 1500 to 1800 stadia, and its diameter 1500 stadia. (Comp. Agathem. i. 3, and ii. 14). The smaller, or more western Syrtis (now *Gulf of Cabes*), was formed on the E. by the promontory of Zeitha and on the W. by that of Brachodes. (Scyl. p. 48; Polyb. i. 39, ii. 23, xii. 1; Strab. ii. p. 123, iii. p. 157, xvii. p. 834, &c.) According to Strabo it had a circumference of 1600 stadia and a diameter of 600 (comp. Agathem. *l. c.*). Particulars respecting the size of both will likewise be found in Mela i. 7; and *Itin. Ant.* p. 64. sqq. The shores of both were inhospitable, and sandy to such a degree that men and even ships were often overwhelmed by the huge cloud-like masses lifted by the wind (Diod. xx. 41; Sall. *Jug.* 79; Herod. iii. 25, 26, iv. 173; Lucan, ix. 294, sqq.); and it is affirmed by modern travellers that these descriptions of the ancients are not exaggerated. (See Browne's *Travels*, p. 282; Bruce, *Travels*, iv. p. 458; Beechey, *Expedition, &c.* ch. 10; Ritter, *Erdkunde*, i. p. 1030.) [T.H.D.]

SYSPIRI'TIS (Συσπιρῖτις, Strab. xi. p. 503), a district in Armenia Major.　　　　　　[T. H. D.]

SYTHAS. [ACHAIA, p. 13, b.]

T.

TAANACH (Θαανάκ and Θαανάχ), a town in Palestine, not far from Megiddo, with which it is generally mentioned, was originally one of the royal cities of the Canaanites. (*Josh.* xii. 21; *Judges*, v. 19; 1 *Kings*, iv. 12.) It was assigned to Manasseh (*Josh.* xvii. 11), but was afterwards one of the cities given to the Levites. (*Josh.* xxi. 25.) "Taanach by the waters of Megiddo" was the scene of the great battle of Deborah and Barak. (*Judges*, v. 19.) In the time of the Judges the Canaanitish inhabitants still remained in Taanach (*Judges*, i. 27), but in the reign of Solomon it appears an Israelitish town. (1 *Kings*, iv. 12.) Eusebius describes it as 3 Roman miles, and Jerome as 4 Roman miles from Legio, which is undoubtedly the Megiddo of Scripture. [LEGIO.] Taanach is still called *Ta'annuk*, a village standing on the slope of the hills which skirt the plain of Esdraelon towards the south. (Robinson, *Bibl. Res.* vol. ii. p. 316, vol. iii. p. 117, 2nd ed.; Stanley, *Sinai and Palestine*, p. 331.)

TABAE (Τάβαι; *Eth.* Ταβηνός), a town which, according to Strabo (xii. p. 570), was situated on the confines between Phrygia and Caria, and which, in another passage (p. 576), he evidently includes in Phrygia. The country was situated in a plain which derived from the town the name of Πεδίον Ταβηνόν. (Strab. xii. p. 576.) Stephanus Byz. (*s. v.*) on the other hand calls Tabae a Lydian town, though he at the same time mentions another in Caria; but it is highly probable that not only both are one and the same town, but also the same as the one assigned by Strabo to Phrygia, and that in point of fact the town was in Caria near the confines of Phrygia. Mythically the name of the place was derived from a hero Tabus, while others connected it with an Asiatic term τάβα, which signified a rock. (Steph. B. *l. c.*) The latter etymology is not inconsistent with Strabo's account, for though the town is described as being in a plain, it, or at least a part of it, may have been built on a rock. The plain contained several other little towns besides Tabae. Livy (xxxviii. 13), in his account of the expedition of Manlius, states that he marched in three days from Gordiutichos to Tabae. It must then have been a considerable place, for, having provoked the hostility of the Romans, it was ordered to pay 20 talents of silver and furnish 10,000 medimni of wheat. Livy remarks that it stood on the borders of Pisidia towards the shore of the Pamphylian sea. There can be no doubt that D'Anville is correct in identifying the modern *Thaous* or *Davas*, a place of some note north-east of *Moglah*, with the ancient Tabae. Col. Leake (*Asia Minor*, p. 153), relying too implicitly on Strabo, looks too far east for its site; for Hierocles

(p. 689) distinctly enumerates it among the Carian towns. *Davas* is a large and well-built town, and the capital of a considerable district; the governor's residence stands on a height overlooking the town, and commanding a most magnificent view. (Richter, *Wallfahrten*, p. 543; Franz, *Fünf Inschriften*, p. 30.)

It should be observed that Pliny (v. 27) mentions another town in Cilicia of the name of Tabae, of which, however, nothing is known. [L. S.]

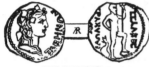

COIN OF TABAE.

TABALA (Τάβαλα), a town of Lydia near the river Hermus, is known only from coins found in the country; but it is no doubt the same as the one mentioned by Hierocles (p. 670) under the name of Gabala, which is perhaps only miswritten for Tabala. It is even possible that it may be the town of Tabae which Stephanus Byz. assigns to Lydia. Some trace of the ancient place seems to be preserved in the name of the village *Tonbaili* on the left bank of the Hermus, between *Adala* and *Kula*. [L. S.]

TABANA (Τάβανα, Ptol. iii. 6. § 6), a place in the interior of the Chersonesus Taurica. [T.H.D.]

TABASSI (Τάβασσοι, Ptol. vii. 1. § 65), a tribe of Indians who occupied the interior of the southern part of *Hindostán*, in the neighbourhood of the present province of *Mysore*. Their exact position cannot be determined, but they were not far distant from *M. Bettigo*, the most S. of the *W. Gháts*. They derived their name from the Sanscrit *Tapasja*, "woods." (Lassen, *Ind. Alterth.* vol. i. p. 243.) [V.]

TABERNAE, in Gallia, is placed by the Itineraries between Noviomagus (*Speier*) and Saletio(*Seltz*). The position of Tabernae is supposed to correspond to that of *Rheinzabern*. Tabernae is mentioned by Ammianus Marcellinus (xvi. 2), unless in this passage he means another place (No. 2) which has the same name.

2. Between Argentoratum (*Strassburg*) and Divodurum (*Metz*) is *Elsatz-Zabern*, or *Saverne* as the French call it, which is about 21 miles from *Strassburg*. This seems to be the place which Ammianus (xvi. 11) calls Tres Tabernae. When Julian was marching against the Alemanni, who were encamped near Argentoratum, he repaired Tres Tabernae, for the purpose of preventing the Germans from entering Gallia by this pass in the *Vosges*. Ammianus (xvi. 12) also gives the distance from Tres Tabernae to the German camp at Argentoratum at 14 "leugae," which is 21 Roman miles, and agrees very well with the distance between *Saverne* and *Strassburg* (D'Anville, *Notice, &c.*).

3. Tabernae is mentioned by Ausonius (*Mosella*, v. 8) on the road between Bingium (*Bingen*) and Noviomagus (*Neumagen*); but the geographers are not agreed about the position, whether it is *Bergzabern*, a place which is out of the way, *Baldenau*, or *Berncastel* on the *Mosel*. Ausonius says there is a spring thus:—

"Praeterea arentem sitientibus undique terris
Dumnissum riguasque perenni fonte Tabernas."
[G. L.]

TABIE'NI (Ταβιηνοί, Ptol. vi. 14. § 11), a people in the N. part of Scythia, on this side of the Imaus. [T. H. D.]

TABIE'NI. (Ταβιηνοί), an Aethiopian tribe, situated NW of the Regio Troglodytica, near the headland of Bazium (*Ras-el-Naschef*), mentioned by Ptolemy alone (iv. 27. § 28). [W. B. D.]

TABLAE, in Gallia, is marked in the Table between Lugdunum Batavorum (*Leiden*) and Noviomagus (*Nymegen*). D'Anville and others suppose it to be *Alblas*, a little above the junction of the *Leck* and the *Maas*, and opposite to *Dort*. [G. L.]

TABOR, a celebrated mountain in Galilee, called by the Greek writers Atabyrion, under which name it is described. [ATABYRIUM.]

TABRACA. [THABRACA.]

TABUDA, or TABULLAS in some editions of Ptolemy (ii. 9. § 3), a river of North Gallia. The mouth of this river is placed by Ptolemy between Gesoriacum (*Boulogne*) and the mouth of the Mosa (*Maas*). In another passage (ii. 9. § 9), after fixing the position of the Morini, whose towns were Gesoriacum and Taruanna, he adds, "Then after the Tabullas are the Tungri." All these indications seem to show that the Tabuda or Tabullas is the *Schelde*, which would be correctly placed between the Morini and the Tungri. Ortelius, cited by D'Anville and others, is said to have produced evidence from writings of the middle ages, that the *Schelde* was named Tabul and *Tabula*. [G. L.]

TABURNUS MONS (*Monte Taburno*), was the name given in ancient times to one of the most important mountain groups of the Apennines of Samnium. It is situated nearly due W. of Beneventum, between the valley of the Calor (*Calore*) and that of the smaller stream of the *Isclero*. Like the still more elevated mass of the *Monte Matese*, which fronts it on the N., it forms no part of the main chain of the Apennines (if that be reckoned, as usual, by the line of water-shed), but is considerably advanced towards the W., and its W. and NW. slopes consequently descend at once to the broad valley or plain of the Vulturnus, where that river receives its tributary the Calor. It is evidently these slopes and underfalls to which Virgil alludes as affording a favourable field for the cultivation of olives (Virg. *Georg.* ii. 38; Vib. Sequest. p. 33), with which they are covered at this day. But in another passage he alludes to the "lofty Taburnus" as covered with forests, which afforded pasture to extensive herds of cattle. (Id. *Aen.* xii. 715.) Gratius Faliscus also speaks of it as a rugged and rocky group of mountains (*Cyneget.* 509). We learn from that writer that it was included in the territory of the Candine Samnites [CAUDINI], and indeed the celebrated pass of the Caudine Forks was at a very short distance from the foot of Mount Taburnus. The name of *Monte Taburno* or *Taburo* is still commonly applied to the whole group, though the different summits, like those of the *Matese*, have each their peculiar name.

There is no ground for reading (as has been suggested) Τάβυρνον ὄρος for Αἴθυρνον ὄρος, in Polybius, iii. 100); the mountain of which that author is speaking must have been situated in quite a different part of Italy. [E. H. B.]

TACAPE (Τακάπη or Κάπη, Ptol. iv. 3. § 11), a town in the Roman province of Africa, in the Regio Syrtica and in the innermost part of the Syrtis Minor. The surrounding country is represented by Pliny (xvi. 27. s. 50, xviii. 22. s. 51) as exceedingly fruitful, but its harbour was bad. (Geogr. Nub. *Clim.* iii. pt. ii. p. 87.) In early times it was subject to Byzacium; but subsequently, as a Roman colony, belonged to the Regio Tripolitana, of which it was the most westerly town. In its neighbourhood were warm mineral springs called the Aquae Tacapitanae (*Itin. Ant.* p. 78), now *El-Hammah.* (Cf. Plin. v. 4. s. 3; *Itin. Ant.* pp. 48, 50, 59, &c., where it is called Tacapae). Now *Gabs, Cabes,* or *Quibes.*   [T. H. D.]

TACARAEI (Τακαραῖοι, Ptol. vii. 2. § 15), a mountain tribe of India extra Gangem, who lived in the extreme NW. near the junction of the Imaus and Emodus chains, adjoining the Mons Bepyrrhus. They must have occupied part of the district now called *Assam.*   [V.]

TACHOMPSO (Ταχομψώ, Herod. ii. 29; Tacompsos, Plin. vi. 29. s. 33; Mela, i. 9. § 2), a town in the Regio Dodecaschoenus, S. of Aegypt and the Cataracts. It stood upon an island of the Nile, and was inhabited by a mixed colony of Aegyptians and Aethiopians. The Coptic word Tachempsa signifies "the place of many crocodiles." Tachompso was seated on the E. bank of the river, lat. 23° 12′ N., nearly opposite the town of Pselcis. As Pselcis increased, Tachompso declined, so that it at last was regarded as merely a suburb of that town, and went by the name of Contra-Pselcis. Though supposed by some to have been near the modern village of *Conzo* in Lower Nubia, it is impossible to reconcile any known locality with the ancient descriptions of this place. Heeren (*African Nations,* vol. i. pp. 346, 383) supposes it to have been either at the island *Kalabshe* (Talmis) or 20 miles further S as *Ghyrshe.* Herodotus (*l. c.*) describes the island on which Tachompso stood as a plain contiguous to a vast lake. But neither such a lake nor island now appear in this part of the Nile's course. The lake may have been the result of a temporary inundation, and the island gradually undermined and carried away by the periodical floods.   [W. B. D.]

TACO'LA (Τάκωλα, Ptol. vii. 2. § 5), a place on the west coast of the Aurea Chersonesus, in India extra Gangem, which Ptolemy calls an emporium. There can be no doubt that it is represented now by either *Tavoy* or *Tenasserim.*   [V.]

TACU'BIS (Τακουβίς, Ptol. ii. 5. § 7), a place in Lusitania.   [T. H. D.]

TADER, a river on the S. coast of Hispania Tarraconensis. (Plin. iii. 3. s. 4.) It is probably indicated by Ptolemy (ii. 6. § 14) under Τέρεβος ποταμοῦ ἐκβολαί. Now the *Segura.*   [T. H. D.]

TADINUM (*Eth.* Tadinas: Ru. near *Gualdo*), a town of Umbria, mentioned by Pliny among the municipal towns of that region. (Plin. iii. 14. s. 19.) It is not noticed by any other ancient author previous to the fall of the Western Empire; but its name is repeatedly found in the epistles of Gregory the Great, and it is evidently the same place called by Procopius Taginae (Τάγιναι, Procop. *B. G.* iv. 29), near which the Gothic king Totila was defeated by Narses in a great battle, in which he was himself mortally wounded, A. D. 552. The site is clearly fixed by the discovery of some ruins and other ancient monuments in 1750 at a place about a mile and a half from *Gualdo,* where there is an old church consecrated in the middle ages to *Sta Maria di Tadino.* *Gualdo* is about 9 miles N. of Nocera (Nuceria), close to the line of the Flaminian Way: hence there is little doubt that we should substitute Tadinas for "Ptanias," a name obviously corrupt,

given in the Jerusalem Itinerary as a station on the Flaminian Way. (*Itin. Hier.* p. 614; Wesseling, *ad loc.*; Cramer, *Italy,* vol. i. p. 267.)   [E. H. B.]

TADMOR. [PALMYRA.]

TADU (Plin. vi. 29. s. 35; comp. Strab. xvii. p. 786), a small island of the Nile that formed the harbour of the city of Meroe. Bruce (*Travels,* vol. iv. p. 618) supposes Tadu to have been the modern *Curgo,* N. of *Schendy.* As, however, the site of Meroe is much disputed, that of Tadu is equally uncertain (Ritter, *Erdkund.* vol. i. p. 567). [W.B.D.]

TAE'NARUM (Ταίναρον, Herod. Strab. et alii; ἡ Ταιναρία ἄκρα, Ptol. iii. 16. § 9), a promontory at the extremity of Laconia, and the most southerly point of Europe, now called *C. Matapán.* The name of Taenarum, however, was not confined to the extreme point bearing the name of *Matapán.* It has been shown by Leake that it was the name given to the peninsula of circular form about seven miles in circumference, which is connected with the end of the great Taygetic promontory by an isthmus about half a mile wide in a direct distance. Hence Taenarum is correctly described by Strabo as an ἀκτὴ ἐκκειμένη (viii. p. 363). Leake conjectures with great probability that *Matapán* is merely another form of Μέτωπον, which may have been the name given by the ancients to the southern extremity of the peninsula. (*Morea,* vol. i. p. 301.) On either side of the isthmus, which connects the promontory of Taenarum with that of Taygetus, is a bay, of which the one on the east is called *Porto Quaglio,* corrupted into *Kaio,* and the one on the west *Marinári* or *Marmári.* The name of *Quaglio* was given to the eastern bay by the Venetians, because it was the last place in Europe at which the quails rested in the autumn before crossing over to Crete and Cyrene. *Porto Quaglio* is one of the best harbours in Laconia, being sheltered from the S. and SE.; it is nearly circular, with a narrow entrance, a fine sandy bottom, and depth of water for large ships. *Porto Marmári* is described as only a dangerous creek. In the Taenarian peninsula there are also two ports on its eastern side, of which the northern, called *Vathý,* is a long narrow inlet of the sea, while the southern, called *Asómato* or *Kistérnes,* is very small and ill sheltered. A quarter of a mile southward of the inner extremity of the last-mentioned port, a low point of rock projects into the sea from the foot of the mountain, which, according to the inhabitants of the peninsula, is the real *C. Matapán.* The western side of the peninsula is rocky and harbourless.

The whole of the Taenarian peninsula was sacred to Poseidon, who appears to have succeeded to the place of Helios, the more ancient god of the locality. (Hom. *Hymn. in Apoll.* 411.) At the extremity of this peninsula was the temple of Poseidon, with an asylum, which enjoyed great celebrity down to a late period. It seems to have been an ancient Achaean sanctuary before the Dorian conquest, and to have continued to be the chief sacred place of the Perioeci and Helots. The great earthquake, which reduced Sparta to a heap of ruins in B. C. 464, was supposed to have been owing to the Lacedaemonians having torn away some suppliant Helots from this sanctuary. (Thuc. i. 128, 133; Paus. iii. 25. § 4; Strab. viii. p. 363; Eurip. *Cycl.* 292.) Near the sanctuary was a cavern, through which Hercules is said to have dragged Cerberus to the upper regions. (Paus. Strab. *ll. cc.*; Pind. *Pyth.* iv. 77; *Taenariae fauces,* Virg. *Georg.* iv. 467;

Taenarus aperta umbris, Lucan, ix. 36.) There is a slight difference between Strabo and Pausanias in the position of the cave; the former placing it near the temple, which agrees with present appearances (see below); the latter describing the cave itself as the temple, before which stood a statue of Poseidon. Among the many dedicatory offerings to Poseidon the most celebrated was the brazen statue of Arion seated on a dolphin, which was still extant in the time of Pausanias. (Herod. i. 23, 24.) The temple was plundered for the first time by the Aetolians. (Polyb. ix. 34.)

Taenarum is said to have taken its name from Taenarus, a son either of Zeus or Icarius or Elatus. (Paus. iii. 14. § 2; Steph. B. *s. v.*; Schol. *ad Apoll. Rhod.* i. 102.) Bochart derives the word from the Phoenician *tinar* "rupes" (*Geograph. Sacra,* p. 459); and it is not improbable that the Phoenicians may have had a settlement on the promontory at an early period.

Pausanias (iii. 25. § 4) mentions two harbours in connection with the Taenarian promontory, called respectively PSAMATHUS (Ψαμαθοῦς), and the HARBOUR OF ACHILLES (ὁ λιμὴν Ἀχίλλειος). Scylax (p. 17) also mentions these two harbours, and describes them as situated back to back (ἀντίπνγος). Strabo (viii. p. 373) speaks of the former of these two harbours under the name of AMATHUS (Ἀμαθοῦς), but omits to mention the Harbour of Achilles. It would appear that these two harbours are the *Porto Quaglio* and the port of *Vathý* mentioned above, as these are the two most important in the peninsula. Leake identifies Psamathus with *Quaglio,* and the Harbour of Achilles with *Vathý,* but the French Commission reverse these positions. We have, however, no doubt that Leake is correct; for the ancient remains above the *Porto Quaglio,* the monastery on the heights, and the cultivated slopes and levels, show that the Taenarian population has in all ages been chiefly collected here. Moreover, no ancient writers speak of a town in connection with the Harbour of Achilles, while Strabo and others describe Amathus or Psamathus as a πόλις. (Steph. B. *s. v.* Ψαμαθοῦς; cf. Aeschin. *Ep.* 1; Plin. iv. 5. s. 8.) If we were to take the description of Scylax literally, Psamathus would be *Porto Quaglio,* and the Harbour of Achilles *Porto Marmóri;* and accordingly, they are so identified by Curtius; but it is impossible to believe that the dangerous creek of *Marmári* is one of the two harbours so specifically mentioned both by Scylax and Pausanias.

The remains of the celebrated temple of Poseidon still exist at *Asómato,* or *Kistérnes,* close to C. *Matapán* on the eastern side. They now form part of a ruined church; and the ancient Hellenic wall may be traced on one side of the church. Leake observes that the church, instead of facing to the east, as Greek churches usually do, faces southeastward, towards the head of the port, which is likely to have been the aspect of the temple. No remains of columns have been found. A few paces north-east of the church is a large grotto in the rock, which appears to be the cave through which Hercules was supposed to have dragged Cerberus; but there is no appearance of any subterranean descent, as had been already remarked by Pausanias. In the neighbourhood there are several ancient cisterns and other remains of antiquity.

There were celebrated marble quarries in the Taenarian peninsula. (Strab. viii. p. 367.) Pliny describes the Taenarian marble as black (xxxvi.

18. s. 29, 22. s. 43); but Sextus Empiricus (*Pyrrh. Hypot.* i. 130) speaks of a species that was white when broken to pieces, though it appeared yellow in the mass. Leake inquired in vain for these quarries.

At the distance of 40 stadia, or 5 English miles, north of the isthmus of the Taenarian peninsula, was the town TAENARUM or TAENARUS, subsequently called CAENEPOLIS. (Καινήπολις, Paus. iii. 25. § 9; Καινή, Ptol. iii. 16. § 9; Plin. iv. 15. s. 16; Steph. B. *s. v.* Ταίναρος; the same town is probably mentioned by Strab. viii. p. 360, under the corrupt form Κιναίδιον.) It contained a temple of Demeter and another of Aphrodite, the latter near the sea. The modern village of *Kypárisso* stands on the site of this town. Some ancient remains and inscriptions of the time of the Antonines and their successors have been found here. On the door-posts of a small ruined church are two inscribed quadrangular στῆλαι, decorated with mouldings above and below. One of the inscriptions is a decree of the Taenarii, and the other is by the community of the Eleuthero-Lacones (τὸ κοινὸν τῶν Ἐλευθερολακώνων). We have the testimony of Pausanias (iii. 21. § 7) that Caenepolis was one of the Eleuthero-Laconian cities; and it would appear from the above-mentioned inscription that the maritime Laconians, when they were delivered from the Spartan yoke, formed a confederation and founded as their capital a city in the neighbourhood of the revered sanctuary of Poseidon. The place was called the New Town (Caenepolis); but, as we learn from the inscriptions, it continued to be also called by its ancient name. For the inscriptions relating to Taenarum, see Böckh, *Inscr.* no. 1315—1317, 1321, 1322, 1389, 1393, 1483. (On the topography of the Taenarian peninsula, see Leake, *Morea,* vol. i. p 290, seq., *Peloponnesiaca,* p. 175, seq.; Boblaye, *Recherches, &c.,* p. 89, seq.; Curtius, *Peloponnesos,* vol. ii. p. 277, seq.)

TAEZALI (Ταίζαλοι or Ταίξαλοι, Ptol. ii. 3: § 15), a people on the eastern coast of Britannia Barbara. In their territory was the promontory called Ταίξαλον ἄκρον (*Ib.* § 5), now *Kinneird's Head.*   [T. H. D.]

TAGAE (Τάγαι, Polyb. x. 29. § 3), a town in the northern part of Parthia, situated in the defiles of the chain of Labutas, visited by Antiochus in his war against Arsaces. It has been conjectured by Forbiger that it is the same place as Tape, mentioned by Strabo (xi. p. 508) as a royal palace in the adjacent province of Hyrcania; but this conjecture seems unnecessary. Perhaps it may be represented by the present *Dameghan.*   [V.]

TAGARA (Τάγαρα, *Peripl. M. Erythr.* § 51, ed. Müller; Ptol. vii. 1. § 82), one of the two principal emporia of the interior of the *Deccan,* according to the author of the Periplus. It is not certain what modern town now represents this ancient site, but there is a fair presumption in favour of *Deoghir,* which was the seat of government down to A. D. 1293, and which is now in ruins, close to *Dowlatabad.* (Vincent, *Voyage of Nearchus,* ii. p. 413; Mannert, v. 1. p. 83; Ritter, *Erdk.* v. p. 513; Berghaus's Map.) Ptolemy, who places the town in Ariaca, probably copied from the author of the Periplus. It may be remarked that the distance given between Barygaza (*Beroach*), Paethana (*Pythan*), and Tagara (*Deoghir*), are not reconcileable with the actual position of these places.   [V.]

TAGASTE, or TAGESTENSE OPP. (Plin. v. 4. s. 4), a town of Numidia, whose spot is now marked by the ruins at *Tajilt* on the *Oued Hamise* or *Sugerast*, a tributary of the river *Mejerda*. (*Itin. Ant.* p. 44.) Tagaste is particularly distinguished by having been the birthplace of St. Augustine. (Aug. *Conf.* ii. 3.)   [T. H. D.]

TAGO'NIUS (Ταγώνιος, Plut. *Sert.* 17), a tributary of the Tagus in Hispania Tarraconensis, either the *Tajuna* or *Henares*. (Cf. Florez, *Esp. Sagr.* v. p. 40; Ukert, ii. pt. i. p. 389.) [T. H. D.]

TAGORI. [TAGRI.]

TAGRI (Τάγροι, Ptol. iii. 5. § 25), a people of European Sarmatia, on the borders of Dacia, and probably identical with the Tagori of Pliny (vi. 7. s. 7) and Jornandes (*Get.* 4).   [T. H. D.]

TAGUS (Τάγος, Ptol. ii. 5. § 4), one of the principal rivers of Spain, being considerably larger than the Anas and having its sources between Mounts Orospeda and Idubeda, in the country of the Celtiberi. (Strab. iii. pp. 139, 152, 162.) After a tolerably straight course of upwards of 300 miles in a westerly direction, it falls into the Atlantic ocean below Olisippo, where it is 20 stadia broad, and capable of bearing the largest ships. It was navigable as far up as Moron for smaller vessels. According to Strabo, at flood tides it overflowed the country at its mouth for a circumference of 150 stadia. It was celebrated for its fish and oysters (Strab. *ib.*; Mart. x. 78), and likewise for its gold sand (Plin. iv. 22. s. 35 ; Mela, iii. 1 ; Catull. xx. 30; Ov. *Met.* ii. 251, &c.); of which last, however, so little is now to be found that it hardly repays the amphibious paupers who earn a precarious living by seeking for it. (Ford's *Handbook of Spain*, p. 487; Dillon, i. p. 257.) The Tagonius alone, is named as a tributary. The Tagus is still called *Tajo* in Spain, *Tejo* in Portugal. (Cf. Liv. xxi. 5, xxvii. 19 ; Plin. iii. 3. s. 4, viii. 42. s. 67; Sen. *Thyest.* 352, &c.)   [T. H. D.]

TAHPA'NIS or TEHAPHE'NES (*Jerem.* xliii. 7, xliv. 1; *Ezek.* xxx. 18; *ἐν Τάφναις*, LXX.), is supposed to be the same place with the Daphne of Pelusium of the Greeks. It was the seat of a garrison under the native and the Persian kings of Aegypt (Herod. ii. 30), and was probably a place of considerable strength and importance, since it commanded the high road to Syria (Strab. xvii. p. 802). According to the Hebrew writers, Tahpanis was also occasionally a royal residence in Pharaonic times. In the reign of Psammitichus (B.C. 670, foll.) the troops quartered at Tahpanis, in common with the rest of the native Aegyptian army, offended by the king's favour to his Carian and Greek mercenaries, abandoned their country, and established themselves in the Regio Dodecaschoenus S. of Syene (Diodor. i. 67). From the Itineraries it appears that Daphne or Tahpanis was 16 Roman miles from Pelusium. *Tel-defenneh*, lying nearly in a direct line between the modern *Sala-kêëeh* and Pelusium, is supposed to be on the site of Tahpanis. [W.B.D.]

TALABRIGA (τὰ Ταλάβριγα, App. *Hisp.* 73), a town of Lusitania, between Eminium and Langobriga. (*Itin. Ant.* p. 421; Plin. ii. 5. s. 7, iv. 21. s. 35.) Variously identified with *Cacia, Aveiro, Talavera de la Reyna*, and *Villarinho*. [T. H. D.]

TALA'BROCA (Ταλαβρόκη, Strab. xi. p. 508), one of the four principal towns of Hyrcania noticed by Strabo. It is perhaps the same place that is called Tambrax by Polybius (x. 31). Its site cannot now be identified.   [V.]

TALACO'RY (Ταλάκωρυ, Ptol. vii. 4. § 7), a port on the north-western side of the island of Taprobane or *Ceylon*. It is described as an emporium, and has, probably, derived its name from the promontory of Cory, which was opposite to it, on the mainland. It appears to have been also called Aacote ('Αακότη).   [V.]

TALADUSII (Ταλαδούσιοι, Ptol. iv. 2. § 17), a people in the north part of Mauretania Caesariensis.   [T. H. D.]

TALAEUS MONS. [TALLAEUS.]

TALAMINA (Ταλαμίνη, Ptol. ii. 6. § 27), a town of the Seurri in Gallaecia.   [T. H. D.]

TALARES (Τάλαρες), a Molossian people of Epeirus, extinct in the time of Strabo (ix. p. 434).

TALAURA (Τάλαυρα), a mountain fortress in Pontus to which Mithridates withdrew with his most precious treasures, which were afterwards found there by Lucullus. (Dion Cass. xxxv. 14; Appian, *Mithr.* 115.) As the place is not mentioned by other writers, some suppose it to have been the same as Gaziura, the modern *Tourkhal* which is perched upon a lofty isolated rock. (Hamilton, *Researches*, vol. i. p. 360.)   [L. S.]

TALBENDA (Τάλβενδα or Τάλβανδα), a town in the interior of Pisidia, noticed only by Ptolemy (v. 5. § 8).   [L. S.]

TA'LETUM. [LACONIA, p. 108, b.]

TALIA (*Itin. Ant.* p.218), or TALIATA (*Not. Imp.*), erroneously called *Tavdris* by Ptolemy (iii. 9. § 4), Tabata by the Geogr. Rav. (iv. 7), and Faliata in the Tab. Peut. A place in Upper Moesia, between Novae and Egeta. Variously identified with *Tatalia, Gögerdsinlik*, and a place near *Ali Poreca*.   [T. H. D.]

TALICUS, a river of Scythia intra Imaum. (Amm. Marc. xxiii. 6. § 63.)   [T. H. D.]

TALLAEUS or TALAEUS MONS (Böckh, *Corp. Inscr. Graec.* vol. ii. p. 423; Hesych. *s. v.*), the station of Talus, the mythical man of bronze, and the guardian of the island of Crete. The well-known inscription which deplores the loss of Artemis, the chaste wife of Salvius Menas, is now buried by the mass of earth and stones heaped up at the entrance of the stalactitic cavern of *Melidhóni*. This grotto, memorable in modern times for the massacre of the Cretan Christians by the Mohammedans, is identified from the inscription with the spot where in ancient times human victims were presented before the statue of Talus. (Pashley, *Travels*, vol. i. pp. 126—139.)   [E. B. J.]

TALMEN (Ταλμήν, Arrian, *Indic.* c. 29), a port of Gedrosia at which the fleet of Nearchus found a secure harbour. It is not clear what place now may be identified with it, and different geographers have held different opinions. Vincent (*Voyage of Nearchus*, i. p. 271) thinks it is the bay formed by the mouth of a small river called by Ptolemy Candriaces or Hydriaces (vi. 8. § 8). It was probably close to the modern town, *Choubar Tiz* and *Purug*. (Cf. Gosselin, iii. p. 148.)   [V.]

TALMIS (*It. Anton.* p. 161; Olympiodor. *ap. Photium*, p. 62, ed. Bekker), a town in the Regio Dodecaschoenus, S. of Philae, from which it was five days' journey distant, situated in lat. 23° 30' N., and consequently immediately under the tropic of Cancer. Talmis stood on the western bank of the Nile, and is represented by the modern *Kalabsche*. The Libyan hills which rise immediately behind the town afforded an inexhaustible supply of materials for building, and the ancient quarries are still visible in their sides. The ruins of Talmis are of surpassing interest, and comparatively in good preservation, probably because, being excavated in the sandstone, they escaped mutilation or destruction by the Persians. The principal structure was a rock-temple at the foot of the hills, dedicated, as appears both from a hieroglyphical and a Greek inscription, to a deity named Mandulis or Malulis, a son of Isis. His mythical history is exhibited on bas-reliefs. But the sculptures at Talmis are of the highest interest, both as works of art and as historical monuments. Their execution is the work of various ages: some, as appears by their rude forms, ascending to a remote antiquity, others, as those in the temple of Mandulis, being of the best days of Aegyptian art. The temple was founded by Amunoph II., was rebuilt by one of the Ptolemies, and repaired in the reigns of the Caesars, Augustus, Caligula, and Trajan. The subjects of these sculptures represent partly the triumphs of the Pharaohs, and partly the tributes exacted by them from the conquered. On one wall is the warrior in his chariot putting to flight bearded men in short garments, armed with bows and arrows, and a sickle-shaped knife or sword. In another compartment the conqueror is in the act of putting his captives to death. Another represents the booty obtained after a victory, and, besides the captives, exhibits the spoils taken, e. g. lion-headed and lion-clawed chairs, knives, loaves, sandals, skins of animals, &c. These sculptures illustrate also the natural history of S. Aethiopia. They contain figures of lions, antelopes, and bulls, greyhounds, giraffes, ostriches and monkeys. The giraffes and ostriches point clearly to a country south of the utmost limit of Aegyptian dominion, and seem to indicate wars with the Garamantes and the kingdom of Bornoo. Herodotus (iii. 97) mentions ebony wood among the articles of tribute which every three years Aethiopia offered to the Persian king. Ebony as well as ivory, a product of the interior of Libya, appears on the walls of the temple of Mandulis. A coloured fac-simile of these sculptures is displayed in one of the rooms of the British Museum. At a short distance from Talmis stood another temple of scarcely inferior interest, and the space between is covered with heaps of earth and fragments of pottery, mixed with human bones and bandages that have been steeped in bitumen — the evident traces of a large necropolis. At Talmis has been also discovered an inscription in the Greek language, supposed to be of the age of Diocletian, in which Silco, king of Aethiopia and Nubia, commemorates his victories over the Blemmyes. The wealth of Talmis, apparent in its sculptures, was doubtless in great measure owing to its position as a commercial station between Aegypt and Aethiopia, but partly also to the emerald mines in its neighbourhood. In the fifth century A.D., the town and its neighbourhood were occupied by the Blemmyes, who had a regular government, since they had chiefs of tribes (φυλάρχοι) and were celebrated for their skill in divination. (Olympiodor. ap. Photium, p. 62.)   [W. B. D.]

TALUBATH (Ταλουβάθ, Ptol. iv. 6. § 25), a town of Gaetulia, in the NW. of Libya Interior, perhaps the modern Tafilet.   [T. H. D.]

TALUCTAE, a tribe of India extra Gangem, mentioned by Pliny (vi. 19. s. 22). They were probably seated beyond the Brahmaputra, in the mountains of Birmah. Sillig, in his recent edition of Pliny, has given the name as Thalutae. [V.]

TAMARA (Ταμαρή, Ptol. ii. 3. § 30), a town of

the Dumnonii, at the SW. extremity of Britannia Romana, at the mouth of the Tamarus. Now Tamerton near Plymouth. (Camden, p. 25.) [T.H.D.]

TAMARICI, a Gallaecian tribe on the river Tamaris in Hispania Tarraconensis. (Plin. iv. 20. s. 34; Mela, iii. 1.) According to Pliny (xxx. 2. s. 18) there were certain noted springs in their territory, which are undoubtedly the same described by Florez (Cantabria, p. 4) near the hermitage of S. Juan de fuentas divinas, 12 Spanish miles E. of Leon, and 5 N. of Saldanna. (Cf. Ukert, ii. pt. i. p. 302, note 80.)   [T. H. D.]

TAMARIS (called by Ptolemy, Ταμάρα, ii. 6. § 2), a small river of Gallaecia in Hispania Tarraconensis, which falls into the Atlantic ocean by the port of Ebora, between the Minius and the promontory Nerium. (Mela, iii. 1.) Now the Tambre. [T.H.D.]

TAMARUS (Tamaro), a river of Samnium, which falls into the Calor (Calore), about 5 miles above Beneventum. Its name is known only from the Itinerary of Antoninus, which places a station "super Tamarum fluvium" on the road from Bovianum to Equus Tuticus. (Itin. Ant. p. 103.) The line of this road is not very clear, but the modern name of the Tamaro leaves no doubt of the river meant. It rises in the mountains near Saepinum, only a few miles from Bovianum, and flows with a general direction from N. to S. till it joins the Calor as above indicated.   [E. H. B.]

TAMARUS (Τάμαρος, Ptol. ii. 3. § 4), a small river on the S. coast of Britannia Romana, now the Tamar.   [T. H. D.]

TAMASSUS (Ταμασσός, Ptol. v. 14. § 6 ; called also Tamasus by Pliny, v. 31. s. 35, Ταμάσος by Constantine Porphyr. de Them. i. p. 39, and Tamesa by Statius, Achill. i. 413; cf. coins in Eckhel, i. 3. p. 88), a town in the interior of the island of Cyprus, 29 miles SW. of Soloe, and on the road from that place to Tremithus. It lay in a fruitful neighbourhood (Ovid, M. x. 644), and in the vicinity of some extensive copper mines, which yielded a kind of rust used in medicine (Strab. xiv. p. 864). It is very probably the Τεμέση of Homer (Od. i. 184; Nitzch, ad loc ; cf. Mannert, vi. 1. p. 452), in which case it would appear to have been the principal market for the copper trade of the island in those early times. Hence some derive its name from the Phoenician word themaes, signifying smelting.   [T. H. D.]

TAMBRAX. [TALABROCA.]

TAMESA or TAMESIS (Τάμεσα, Dion Cass. xl. 3), a river on the E. coast of Britannia Romana, on which Londinium lay; the Thames. (Caes. B. G. v. 11; Tac. Ann. xiv. 32.)   [T. H. D.]

TAMESIS. [TAMESA.]

TAMIA (Ταμεία, Ptol. ii. 3. § 13), a town of the Vacomagi on the E. coast of Britannia Barbara, probably on Loch Tay.   [T. H. D.]

TAMIATHIS (Ταμίαθις, Steph. B. s. v.), was a considerable town in Lower Aegypt, situated at the mouth of the Phatnitic arm of the Nile. It is less celebrated in history than its representative, the modern Damiat or Damietta, which, since the era of the Crusades, has always been, until the rise of Alexandria in the present century, one of the most populous and commercial places in the Delta. Many antique columns and blocks from the ancient town are built into the walls of the mosques in the modern one. The present Damietta, indeed, does not occupy the site of Tamiathis, since, according to Abulfeda, the original town of that name was destroyed, on account of its exposed situation, and rebuilt higher up the Nile, about 5 miles further from the sea. The date of this change of position is fixed by Abulfeda in the year of the Hegira 648 (A.D. 1251). [W. B. D.]

TAMNA (Τάμνα, Strab. xvi. p. 768; Steph. B. s. v.; Tamna, Plin. vi. 28. s. 32: Θούμνα, Ptol. vi. 7. § 37; Thomna, Plin. xii. 14. s. 32: Eth. Ταμνίτης), a city of Arabia, and the chief town of the Cattabaneis (Catabani), according to Strabo, or of the Gebanitae, according to Pliny. It is described by Pliny as a large commercial town with 65 temples, to which caravans from Gaza in Palestine resorted. It is probably Sand, the present capital of Yemen.

TAMNUM, in Gallia, is placed by the Itineraries on a road from Burdigala (Bordeaux) to Mediolanum Santonum (Saintes); but in the Table the name is written Lamnum. The distance from Blavia or Blavium (Blaye) to Tamnum is xvi. in the Itins.; but the distance xxii. in the Table is nearer the truth, if Tallemont or Talmon is the site of Tamnum. Talmon is below Blaye on the right bank of the Gironde. [G. L.]

TAMUGADIS, a town in Numidia, on the E. side of Mount Aurasius, and 14 miles NE. of Lambese. (It. Ant. pp. 34, 40; Thamugadis, Tab. Peut.) It still retains the name of Temugadi. (Bruce.) Lapie identifies it with Ager Soudah. [T. H. D.]

TAMYNAE (Ταμύναι, Strab. et alii; Ταμύνα, Steph. B. s. v.: Eth. Ταμυναῖος, Ταμυνεύς), a town of Euboea in the territory of Eretria, at the foot of Mt. Cotylaeum, with a temple of Apollo, said to have been built by Admetus. (Strab. x. p. 447; Steph. B. s. vv. Τάμνυα, Κοτύλαιον.) It was taken by the Persians, when they attacked Eretria in B. C. 490 (Herod. vi. 101), but it is chiefly memorable for the victory which the Athenians, under Phocion, gained here over Callias of Chalcis, B. C. 350. (Aesch. c. Ctes. §§ 85—88, de Fals. Leg. 180; Dem. de Pac. 5; Plut. Phoc. 12.) Leake places Tamynae at the village of Ghymnó, at the foot of a high mountain, which he supposes to be the ancient Cotylaeum (Ancient Greece, vol. ii. p. 439); but Ulrichs regards Alivéri, where there are several ancient remains, as the site of Tamynae. (Rheinisches Museum, for 1847, p. 512.)

TAMY'RACA (Ταμυράκη, Ptol. iii. 5. § 8, viii. 10. § 3), a town and promontory of European Sarmatia in the neighbourhood of a lake (Arrian, Per. P. Eux. p. 20), and in the innermost part of the gulf of Carcinitis, now gulf of Achmeschid or Perekop. Hence, according to Strabo, the Sinus Carcinites was also called the gulf of Tamyracë (vii. p. 308). But the coast has undergone such extensive alterations at this part, that all attempts to determine the site of the town are unavailing. Some, indeed, have doubted its existence, as it is mentioned only by Ptolemy. (Cf. Neumann, Die Hellenen in Skythenlande, p. 375; Ukert, iii. 2. p. 457; Gail, Geogr. M. iii. p. 127.) [T. H. D.]

TAMYRACES SINUS. [CARCINA; TAMYRACA.]

TAMYRAS or DAMU'RAS (Ταμύρας, Strab. xvi. p. 756; Δαμοῦρας, Polyb. v. 68), a river of Phoenicia between Sidon and Berytus, the modern Nahred-Dâmúr. (Robinson, Bibl. Res. vol. ii. p. 488, 2nd ed.) [Comp. LEONTES.]

TANAGER or TANAGRUS (Tanagro), a river of Lucania, a tributary of the Silarus. It rises in the mountains near Lago Negro, flows for about

30 miles in a NNE. direction, through a broad and level upland valley called the Valle di Diano, till near La Polla it sinks into the earth, and emerges again through a cavern at a place thence called La Pertusa. This peculiarity is mentioned by Pliny, who calls it "fluvius in Atinate campo," without mentioning its name (Plin. ii. 103. s. 106, with Harduin's note): but this is known to us from Virgil, who notices it in connection with Mount Alburnus, which rises immediately to the W. of it, and the epithet "siccus" which he applies to it ("sicci ripa Tanagri") doubtless refers to this same peculiarity. (Virg. Georg. iii. 151; Serv. ad loc.; Vib. Seq. p. 19.) There is no doubt, also, that in the Itinerary we should read "Ad Tanagrum" for "Ad Tanarum," a station which it places on the road from Salernum to Nerulum. (Itin. Ant. p. 109.) The same Itinerary gives a station "Ad Calorem," as the next on this line of route, which seems to show that the river was then, as now, called in the upper part of its course Calor or Calore, while in the lower part it assumes the name of Tanagro or Negro. This part of the route, however, is very confused. [E. H. B.]

TANAGRA (Τάναγρα: Eth. Ταναγραῖος: the territory Ταναγραία, Paus. ix. 22. § 1, and Ταναγραϊκή or Ταναγρική, Strab. ix. p. 404: Adj. Ταναγρικός: Grimádha or Grimála), a town of Boeotia, situated upon the left bank of the Asopus, in a fertile plain, at the distance of 130 stadia from Oropus and 200 from Plataeae (Dicaearch. Stat. Gr. pp. 12, 14, ed. Hudson). Several ancient writers identified Tanagra with the Homeric Graea (Γραῖα, Hom. Il. ii. 498; Lycophr. 644); but others supposed them to be distinct places, and Aristotle regarded Oropus as the ancient Graea. (Steph. B. s. v. Τάναγρα; Strab. ix. p. 404; Paus. ix. 20. § 2.) It is possible, as Leake has remarked, that Tanagra, sometimes written Tanagraea, may be connected with the ancient name Graea, Tana, being an Aeolic suffix, and that the modern name Grimádha or Grimála may retain traces of the Homeric name. Tanagra was also called Poemandria, and its territory Poemandris, from the fertile meadows which surrounded the city. (Steph. B. s. v.; Strab. ix. p. 404.) The most ancient inhabitants of Tanagra are said to have been the Gephyraei, who came from Phoenicia with Cadmus, and from thence emigrated to Athens. (Herod. v. 57; Strab. ix. p. 404). From its vicinity to Attica the territory of Tanagra was the scene of more than one battle. In B. C. 457 the Lacedaemonians on their return from an expedition to Doris, took up a position at Tanagra, near the borders of Attica, with the view of assisting the oligarchical party at Athens to overthrow the democracy. The Athenians, with a thousand Argeians and some Thessalian horse, crossed Mount Parnes and advanced against the Lacedaemonians. Both sides fought with great bravery; but the Lacedaemonians gained the victory, chiefly through the treacherous desertion of the Thessalians in the very heat of the engagement. (Thuc. i. 107, 108; Diod. xi. 80.) At the beginning of the following year (B. C. 456), and only sixty-two days after their defeat at Tanagra, the Athenians under Myronides again invaded Boeotia, and gained at Oenophyta, in the territory of Tanagra, a brilliant and decisive victory over the Boeotians, which made them masters of the whole country. The walls of Tanagra were now razed to the ground. (Thuc. i. 108; Diod. xi. 81, 82.) In B. C. 426 the Athenians made an incursion into the territory of Tanagra, and

on their return defeated the Tanagraeans and Boeotians. (Thuc. iii. 91.) Dicaearchus, who visited
Tanagra in the time of Cassander, says that the city
stands on a rugged and lofty height, and has a white
chalky appearance. The houses are adorned with
handsome porticoes and encaustic paintings. The
surrounding country does not grow much corn, but
produces the best wine in Boeotia. Dicaearchus adds
that the inhabitants are wealthy but frugal, being for
the most part landholders, not manufacturers; and
he praises them for their justice, good faith, and hospitality. (*De Statu Graec.* p. 12.) In the time of
Augustus, Tanagra and Thespiae were the two most
prosperous cities in Boeotia. (Strab. ix. p. 403.)
Tanagra is called by Pliny (7. s. 12) a free
state; it is mentioned by Ptolemy (iii. 15. § 20);
and it continued to flourish in the sixth century.
(Hierocl. p. 645.) Its public buildings are described
at some length by Pausanias (ix. 20. § 3, seq.).
The principal temple was that of Dionysus, which
contained a celebrated statue of Parian marble, by
Calamis, and a remarkable Triton. Near it were
temples of Themis, Aphrodite and Apollo, and two of
Hermes, in one of which he was worshipped as
Criophorus, and in the other as Promachus. Near
the latter was the theatre, and probably at no great
distance the gymnasium, which contained a picture
of Corinna, who was a native of Tanagra. There
was also a monument of this poetess in a conspicuous
part of the city. Pausanias remarks as a peculiarity
in Tanagra, that all their sacred buildings were
placed by themselves, apart from the houses of the
town (ix. 22. § 2.) He likewise notices (ix. 22.
§ 4) that Tanagra was famous for its breed of fight-
ing-cocks, a circumstance which is mentioned by
other writers. (Varr. *de Re Rust.* iii. 9. § 6; Hesych.
s. v. Κολοίφρυξ; Suidas, *s. v.* Ταναγραῖοι ἀλεκτρο-
φίσκοι.) Tanagra possessed a considerable territory;
and Strabo (ix. p. 405) mentions four villages belonging to it, Eleon or Heleon, Harma, Mycalessus,
and Pharae. (Pherae, Plin iv. 7. s. 12).

The ruins of Tanagra are situated at an uninhabited spot, called *Grimádha* or *Grimóla*, situated
3 miles south of the village of *Skimdátari.* The
site is a large hill nearly circular, rising from the
north bank of the Asopus. The upper part of the
site is rocky and abrupt, looking down upon the town
beneath; and it was probably upon this upper height
that the sacred edifices stood apart from the other
buildings of the town. The walls of the city which
embraced a circuit of about two miles, may still be
traced, but they are a mere heap of ruins. About
100 yards below the height already described are the
remains of the theatre, hollowed out of the slope. On
the terrace below the theatre to the NE. are the
foundations of a public building, formed of marble of
a very dark colour with a green cast. The ground
is thickly strewn in every direction with remains of
earthenware, betokening the existence of a numerous
population in former times. (Leake. *Northern*

Greece, vol. ii. p. 454, seq.; Wordsworth, *Athens and
Attica,* p. 14, seq.; comp. K. O. Müller, *Orchomenos,*
p. 20.)

TA'NAIS (Τάναϊς, Ptol. iii. 5. § 14, v. 9. §§ 1, 2,
&c.), a famous river, which in the course of time
was universally assumed as the boundary between
Europe and Asia. (Strab. vii. 310, xi. 490; Mela,
i. 3; Scyl. p. 30, &c.) The older writers of antiquity thought that it rose from a large lake (Herod. iv. 57; Ephor. ap. Anon. *Per. P. Eux.* p. 4),
which is really the case, its source being in the lake
Ivan Osero, in the government of *Toula;* whilst later
writers held that it had its sources either in the
Caucasus (Strab. xi. 493; Ammian. xxii. 8), or in
the Rhipaean mountains. (Mela, i. 19; Lucan.
iii. 272; Procop. *B. G.* iv. 6, &c.) The last of
these hypotheses was most generally accepted; but
there was likewise a fourth which made it a branch
of the Ister (Strab. *l. c.*). Whilst Strabo, however,
adduces these different opinions, he himself holds
that its source was entirely unknown (ii. 107). It
is represented as flowing in so rapid a stream that
it never froze. (Mela, *l. c.*; cf. Nonnus, *Dionys.*
xxiii. 85.) It flows first in a SE. and then in a
SW. direction; and after receiving the Hyrgis (or
Syrgis) as a tributary, empties itself into the Palus
Maeotis (*Sea of Azof*) by two mouths. (Herod.
iv. 100.) These mouths, which are at the most
northern point of the Palus Maeotis, Strabo places
at the distance of 60 stadia from one another (vii.
310), whilst Artemidorus (ap. Eustath. *ad Dion.*
14) makes them only 7 stadia distant. At present,
however, the *Don* has 13 mouths. (Clarke, *Trav.*
i. p. 423.) The etymology of the name is discussed
by Plutarch (*de Flum.* 14) and Eustathius (*l. c.*);
but its true derivation is from the Scythian word
Don or *Dan,* signifying *water,* which occurs in the
names of other rivers, as Danubius, Eridanus, &c.
(Forbiger, *Handb. des Alt. Geogr.* p. 325, n. 16.)
The Tanais is frequently alluded to by the Latin
poets. (Hor. *Od.* iii. 10. 1; Virg. *G.* iv. 517; Ov.
Ex. Pont. iv. 10, 55, &c.) Clarke (*Travels,* i.
pp. 339, 448, note) would identify it with the
Danaets, from the similarity of the name, an hypothesis also accepted by Lindner (*Scythien,* p. 66);
but there can scarcely be a doubt that it should be
identified with the *Don.*   [T. H. D.]

TA'NAIS (Τάναϊς, Ptol. iii. 5. § 26, viii. 18. § 5),
a town of Asiatic Sarmatia, lying on the more southern mouth and between both mouths of the river of
the same name. It may also be described as situated
at the northernmost point of the Palus Maeotis, and
not far from the sea. It was a flourishing colony of
the Milesians, enjoying an extensive commerce, and
being the principal market of the surrounding tribes,
both of Europe and Asia, who here bartered slaves
and skins for the wine, apparel, and other articles of
more civilised nations. (Strab. xi. p. 493.) The inhabitants soon reduced a considerable part of the
neighbouring coasts to subjection, but were in turn
themselves subdued by the kings of the Bosporus
(Id. vii. p. 310, xi. p. 495). An attempt to regain
their independence only ended in the destruction of
their city by Polemon I. (Id. p. 493), a little before the
time when Strabo wrote. Pliny (vi. 7. s. 7) speaks
of Tanais as no longer existing in his time; but it
appears to have been subsequently restored (Ptol.
ll. cc.; Steph. B. p. 633), though it never recovered
its former prosperity. Clarke (i. p. 415) could discover no trace of it, nor even a probable site; but its
ruins are said to exist near the modern *Nedrigoska*

(cf. Gräfe, *Mém. de l'Ac. des Sc. à St. Petersb.* vi. Ser. vi. p. 24; Stempowsky, *Nouv. Jour. Asiat.* L p. 55; Böckh. *Inscr.* li. p. 1008).　[T. H. D.]

TANAITAE (*Ταναῖται*, Ptol. iii. 5. § 24), a people of European Sarmatia, dwelling NE. of the Roxolani, and between them and the Tanais.　[T. H. D.]

TANARUS (*Tanaro*), a river of Liguria, the most important of all the southern tributaries of the Padus. It rises in the Maritime Alps above *Ceva* (Ceba), flows at first due N., receives near *Cherasco* the waters of the *Stura*, a stream as considerable as itself, then turns to the NE., passes within a few miles of Pollentia (*Pollenza*), flows under the walls of Alba Pompeia and Asta (*Asti*), and discharges its waters into the Po about 15 miles below *Valenza* (Forum Fulvii). It receives many considerable tributaries besides the *Stura* already mentioned, of which the most important is the *Bormida*, the ancient name of which has not been preserved to us; but the *Orba*, a minor stream which falls into it a few miles above its junction with the *Tanaro*, is evidently the river Urbs, mentioned by Claudian (*B. Get.* 555), the name of which had given rise to an ambiguous prophecy, that had misled the Gothic king Alaric. The *Belbo*, which falls into the *Tanaro* a few miles above the *Bormida*, has been identified with the Fevus of the Tabula; but the names of rivers given in that document in this part of Italy are so corrupt, and their positions so strangely misplaced, that it is idle to attempt their determination. Though the Tanarus is one of the most important rivers of Northern Italy, its name is not mentioned by any of the geographers except Pliny; nor does it occur in history until long after the fall of the Western Empire. (Plin. iii. 16. s. 20; P. Diac. *Hist. Lang.* vi. 58.)　　　　　　　　　　　[E. H. B.]

TANATIS, according to Solinus (c. 12), an island in the neighbourhood of Britain. It is undoubtedly the same which Beda (*Hist. Eccl.* i. 25) calls Tanatos, and which still bears the name of *Thanet.*　　　　　　　　　　　[T. H. D.]

TANATIS. [TALIA.]

TANAUS. [ARGOS, Vol. I. p. 201, a.]

TANE'TUM or TANNE'TUM (*Τάνητον*, Ptol.: *Eth.* Tanetanus, Plin. : *S. Ilario*), a small town of Gallia Cispadana, on the Via Aemilia, between Regium Lepidum and Parma, and distant 10 miles from the former and 8 from the latter city. (*Itin. Ant.* p. 287; *Itin. Hier.* p. 616; *Tab. Peut.*) It is mentioned in history before the Roman conquest of this part of Italy, as a Gaulish village, to which the praetor L. Manlius retired after his defeat by the Boii in B. C. 218, and where he was surrounded and besieged by that people. (Pol. iii. 40; Liv. xxi. 25.) Its name is not again noticed in history, but it is mentioned both by Pliny and Ptolemy as a municipal town of Gallia Cispadana, though it appears to have never risen to be a place of importance. (Plin. iii. 15. s. 20; Ptol. iii. 1. § 46; Phlegon, *Macrob.* 1.) Livy calls the Gaulish town "vicus Pado propinquus," an expression which would lead to an erroneous idea of its position; for we learn from the Itineraries that it certainly stood on the Via Aemilia, at a distance of more than 10 miles from the Padus. The site is still occupied by a large village, which is now called, from the name of its principal church, Sant' *Ilario*; but a hamlet or village about half a mile to the N. still retains the name of *Taneto*. It is distant about 2 miles from the river *Enza*, the Nicia of Pliny (iii. 16. s. 20),

which flows into the *Po*, about 12 miles from the point where it crosses the Aemilian Way. [E. H. B.]

TANIS (*Τάνις*, Herod. ii. 166; Strab. xvii. p. 802; Ptol. iv. 5. § 52; the ZOAN of the Hebrews, *Numb.* xiii. 23; the Coptic TANI or ATHENNES, and the modern *San*). was a city of Lower Aegypt, situated, in lat. 30° 59', on the Tanitic arm of the Nile. [NILUS, Ostium Taniticum.] It was the capital of the Tanitic Nome. Although the name of Tanis does not appear in Aegyptian annals earlier than the xxi-st dynasty, which consisted of 21 Tanite kings, it had long previously been among the most important cities of the Delta. The branch of the Nile on which it stood was, with the exception of the Pelusiac, the most easterly, and the nearest to Palestine and Arabia. It is described in the Book of Numbers (*l. c.*) as founded only seven years later than Hebron; and Hebron, being extant in the time of Abraham, was one of the oldest towns in Palestine. Tanis owed its importance partly to its vicinity to the sea, and partly to its situation among the Deltaic marshes. It probably was never occupied by the Hyksos, but, during their usurpation, afforded refuge to the exiled kings and nobles of Memphis. It was a place of strength during the wars of the early kings of the New Monarchy—the xviiith dynasty—with the shepherds; and when the Aegyptians, in their turn, invaded Western Asia, the position of Tanis became of the more value to them. For after Aegypt became a maritime power, in its wars with Cyprus and Phoenicia, a city at no great distance from the coast would be indispensable for its naval armaments. To these purposes Tanis was better adapted than the more exposed and easterly Pelusium. The eastern arms of the Nile were the first that silted up, and the Pelusiac mouth of the river was at a very early period too shallow for ships of war. The greatness of Tanis is attested in many passages of the Hebrew writers. In the 78th Psalm the wonders that attended the departure of the Israelites from Aegypt are said to have been "wrought in the plain of Zoan." This Psalm, indeed, is somewhat later than David (B. C. 1055—1015); but it proves the tradition that Tanis was the capital of that Pharaoh who oppressed the Hebrew people. In the age of Isaiah (xix. 11, foll.), about 258 years later, Tanis was still reckoned the capital of the Delta, since the prophet speaks of the princes of Zoan and the princes of Noph (Memphis) as equivalent to the nobles of Aegypt. Again, Isaiah (xxx. 4) describes the ambassadors who were sent to Aegypt to form an alliance with its king as repairing to Zoan and Hanes, or Heracleopolis; and the desolation of Zoan is threatened by Ezekiel as the consequence of Nebuchadnezzar's invasion. Tanis probably declined as Sais and Memphis rose into importance; yet twenty years before the Christian era it was still a large town (Strab. xvii. p. 802); nor did it shrink into insignificance until nearly 80 A. D. (Joseph. *B. Jud.* iv. 11, § 4.) Its linen manufacture probably long sustained it. The marshy grounds in its environs was well suited to the cultivation of flax; and Pliny (ix. 1) speaks of the Tanitic linen as among the finest in Aegypt.

No city in the Delta presents so many monuments of interest as Tanis. The extensive plain of *San* is indeed thinly inhabited, and no village exists in the immediate vicinity of the buried city. A canal passes through, without being able to fertilise, the field of Zoan, and wild beasts and marsh fevei prevent all but a few fishermen from inhabiting it. The mounds which cover the site of Tanis are very high and of great extent, being upwards of a mile from north to south, and nearly three quarters of a mile from east to west. The arm in which the sacred enclosure of the temple of Pthah stood is about 1500 feet in length by 1250 broad. The enclosure, which is of crude brick, is 1000 feet long and about 700 wide. A gateway of granite or fine gritstone, bearing the name of Rameses the Great, stands on the northern side of this enclosure. The numerous obelisks and the greater part of the sculptures of the temple were contributed by Rameses. His name is also inscribed on two granite columns outside the enclosure, and apparently unconnected with the temple. Though in a very ruinous condition, the fragments of walls, columns, and obelisks sufficiently attest the former splendour of this building. The architecture is generally in the best style of Aegyptian art. and the beauty of the lotus-bud and palm capitals of the columns is much celebrated by travellers. Among the deities worshipped at Tanis were Pthah (Hephaestus), Maut, Ra, Horus, &c. The Pharaohs who raised these monuments were of various dynasties, ranging from the kings of the xviiith dynasty to the Aethiopian Tirhaka. The numerous remains of glass and pottery found here, and the huge mounds of brick, prove that the civil portions of Tanis were commensurate in extent and population with the religious. The modern village of San consists of mere huts. Early in the present century an attempt was made to establish nitre-works there; but they have been long abandoned; and the only occupation of the few inhabitants of this once flourishing city is fishing. North of the town, and between it and the coast of the Mediterranean, was the lake Tanis, the present *Menzaleh*. (Wilkinson, *Mod. Egypt and Thebes*, vol. i. pp. 407, 449, foll.; Kenrick, *Ancient Egypt*, vol. ii. p. 341.)   [W. B. D.]

TANUS (*Τάνος*, Artemidorus, *ap. Steph. B. s. v.*), a town in Crete of which there is a coin with the epigraph TANIΩN. (Eckhel, vol. ii. p. 321). [E.B.J.]

TANUS. [ARGOS, Vol. I. p. 201, a.]

TA'OCE (*Ταόκη*, Arrian, *Ind.* c. 39; Strab. xv. p. 728), a town or fortress of the district of Taocene, in Persis. It was, according to Strabo, the seat of one of the three treasuries of the kings of Persia. It is not certain from Arrian's statement whether he means the town or the district, but probably the former. The town appears to have been placed near the river Granis. Ptolemy speaks of a promontory and a town of this name (vi. 4. §§ 2 and 7). It is probable that it is the same place as that called by Al-Edrisi, *Toudj* or *Touj* (ii. p. 391, &c.). Where Dionysius (1069), enumerating the three palaces, speaks of the *Ταόκοι*, we ought most likely to read *Τωκοί* or *Τακοί*, with reference to the people of this district. The Granis is the river of *Abushir*. [GRANIS.] [V.]

TA'OCHI (*Τάοχοι*), a tribe in the interior of Pontus (Steph. B. *s. v.*), which is frequently noticed by Xenophon in the Anabasis (iv. 4. § 18). They lived in mountain fortresses in which they kept all their possessions (iv. 7. § 1, comp. 6. § 5, v. 15. § 17). They occupied the country near the frontiers of Armenia.   [L. S.]

TAPANI'TAE (*Ταπανῖται*, Ptol. iv. 5. § 21), a people in the interior of Marmarica. [T. H. D.]

TAPE. [TAGAE.]

TA'PHIAE, and more anciently TELEBO'IDES, a number of small islands off the western coast of Greece, between Leucas and Acarnania (Plin. iv. 12. a. 19), also called the islands of the Taphii or Teleboae (*Ταφίων, Τηλεβοῶν νῆσοι*, Strab. x. p. 459), who are frequently mentioned in the Homeric poems as pirates. (*Od.* xv. 427, xvi. 426.) When Athena visited Telemachus at Ithaca, she assumed the form of Mentes, the leader of the Taphians. (*Od.* i. 105.) The Taphians or Teleboans are celebrated in the legend of Amphitryon, and are said to have been subdued by this hero. (Herod. v. 59; Apollod. ii. 4. §§ 6, 7; Strab. *l. c.*; Plaut. *Amph.* i. 1; *Dict. of Biog.* art. AMPHITRYON.) The principal island is called Taphos (*Τάφος*) by Homer (*Od.* i. 417), and by later writers Taphiūs, Taphiussa, or Taphias (*Ταφιοῦς, Ταφιοῦσσα, Ταφιάς*, Strab. *l. c.*; Plin. *l. c.*; Steph. B. *s. v. Τάφος*), now *Meganisi*. The next largest island of the Taphii was Carnus, now *Kálamo*. (Scylax, p. 13; Steph. B. *s. v.*; Leake, *Northern Greece*, vol. iv. p. 16; Dodwell, vol. i. p. 60.) Stephanus B. mentions a town in Cephallenia, named Taphus, represented by the modern *Tafió*, where many ancient sepulchres are found. (Leake, *Northern Greece*, vol. iii. p. 67.)

TAPHIASSUS. [AETOLIA, p. 63.]

TAPHIS (*Itin. Anton.* p. 161; *Ταθίς*, Ptol. iv. 4. § 17; *Τάπις*, Olympiod. *ap. Phot.* p. 62, ed. Bekker), a town situated on the western bank of the Nile, in the Regio Dodecaschoenus, S. of Philae and the Lesser Cataract. The ruins of an ancient city have been discovered at *Teffah* in Lower Nubia, which are supposed to correspond with the ancient Taphis. It was in the neighbourhood of large stone-quarries. On the opposite side of the river was a suburb called Contra-Taphis. Both towns in the 5th century A. D. were occupied by the Blemmyes. [W. B. D.]

TAPHOS. [TAPHIAE.]

TAPHRAE or TAPHROS (*Τάφραι*, Steph. B. p. 642; cf. Mela. ii. 1; Plin. iv. 12. s. 26; *Τάφρος*, Ptol. iii. 6. § 5), that part of the neck of the Chersonesus Taurica which was cut through by a dyke and fortified (Herod. iv. 3). Pliny and Ptolemy (*ll. cc.*) mention a town called Taphrae; and Strabo (vii. 308) also notices at this spot a people called *Τάφριοι*. (Cf. D'Anville, *Mém de l'Ac. d. Inscr.* xxxvii. p. 581; Rennell, *Geogr. of Herod.* p. 96; Mannert, iv. p. 291.) *Perecop*, or *Prezecop*, the modern name of the isthmus, also signifies in Russian a ditch or entrenchment. (Clarke, *Trav.* ii. p. 316.)   [T. H. D.]

TAPHROS. [TAURUS.]

TAPORI, a people of Lusitania. (Plin. iv. 22. s. 25.)   [T. H. D.]

TAPOSI'RIS (*Ταπόσειρις*, Strab. xvii. p. 799; *Ταπόσιρις*, Ptol. iv. 5. § 34; Dioscorides, *Mater. Med.* iii. 24; *Ταφόσιρις*, Steph. B. *s. v.*; Tapostris, *Tab. Peut.*: the *Bosiri* of Leo Africanus), was a town in the Libyan Nome, west of the Delta, and about 25 miles distant from Alexandreia. There were probably several places of this name in Aegypt, since each Nome would be desirous to possess a " tomb of Osiris." Abulfeda mentions a *Basir* near Sebennytus, another in the Arsinoite Nome, the *Fyoum*; a third at *Gizeh*, close to the Pyramids. The town, however, in the Libyan Nome appears to have been the most considerable of all, inasmuch as it was the place where the prefect of Alexandreia held the periodical census of the Libyan Nome. Its market, indeed, was so much frequented that the emperor Justinian (A. D. 527, foll.) constructed at Taposiris a town-hall, and public baths. (Procop. *de Aedif.* vi. 1.) Nearer Alexandreia was a smaller town of this name. (Ταπόσειρις πλησίον 'Αλεξανδρείας, Steph. B. *s. v.*; ἡ μίκρα, Strab. xvii. p. 800.) [W. B. D.]

TAPPUAH or BETH-TAPPUAH, a city in Palestine, upon the mountains of Judah, not far from Hebron, which Robinson identifies with the ancient village of *Teffūh*, lying in the midst of olive-groves and vineyards. (*Josh.* xv. 53; Robinson, *Bibl. Res.* vol. ii. p. 71, 2nd ed.) There was another Tappuah in the plain of Judah (*Josh.* xv. 34); but which of these was the place conquered by Joshua, cannot be determined. (*Josh.* xii. 17.)

TAPRO'BANE (ἡ Ταπροβάνη, Strab. i. 63, xv. 690, &c.; Steph. B. *s. v.*; Ptol. vii. 4; Plin. vi. 22. s. 24; Mela, iii. 77; Ov. *ex Pont.* i. 5. 80), a very large island, now *Ceylon.* It is situated to the SE. of the peninsula of *Hindostán*, and is all but joined to the continent by a reef now called *Adam's Bridge*, and by an island called *Ramisir* or *Ramisceram Cor*, the Κῶρυ of Ptolemy (vii. 1. § 11) and the Insula Solis of Pliny (vi. 22. s. 24). (Comp. Duncan, *As. Res.* v. p. 39; Ritter, *Erdk.* vi. p. 63.)

Taprobane was not known to the writers of clas-sical antiquity before the time of Alexander the Great, and the various narratives which have reached the West subsequent to his invasion of the *Panjáb*, though often correct as to its natural productions, are singularly erroneous as to its position, its size, and its shape. Thus Onesicritus estimates it at 5000 stadia, though whether this number implies length, breadth, or circumference, is not stated by Strabo (xv. p. 690). If the last, he is nearly correct, Rennell considering this to be about 660 miles. (See *Map, and Memoir of India.*) He adds that it was twenty days' sail from the continent — the ships being badly con-structed and unfit for sailing; a view remarkably confirmed by Pliny, who notices the change in the length of the voyage owing to the improved kind of vessels, and the shallow character of the intervening strait (vi. 22. s. 24). Eratosthenes reduces the dis-tance to a navigation of seven days — the same time as Pliny states (*l. c.*); but this is far too great (Strab. xv. p. 691), as it is really little more than 50 miles from its nearest shores to the mainland of *Hindostán.* (Vincent, *Voy. of Nearchus*, i. p. 495; Boyd, in *Ind. Ann. Regist.* 1799.) Eratosthenes is still more erroneous in the position he assigns to the island, for he extends it 8000 stadia in the di-rection of Africa (Strab. *l. c.*), while the author of the *Periplus M. Erythr.* makes it reach almost to the coast of Azania (c. 61, ed. Müller) — an error which has probably led to that of Edrisi, who has confounded *C. Comorin* with *Madagascar*, and in his map has even placed this island to the E. of *Ceylon.* Strabo supposes that *Ceylon* is not less than Britain (ii. p. 130), and Ptolemy gives it a length of more than 1000 miles, and a breadth of more than 700 (i. 14. § 9, viii. 28. § 3). (Compare with this the statement of Marco Polo, which is, as to circum-ference, identical with Ptolemy, *l. c.*; and Caesar Frederick, *ap. Hackluyt's Voy.* ii. pp. 225—227.)

The history of ancient *Ceylon* falls naturally into three heads: 1. What may be gathered from the writers who followed the march of Alexander. 2. What we may learn from the Roman writers. 3. What may be obtained from the Byzantines.

Of the times preceding the invasion of India by Alexander we have no distinct notice in classical history; yet it may be inferred from Pliny that *some* report of its existence had reached the West,

where he states that it had long been the opinion that Taprobane was another world, and bore the name of Antichthonus, but that it was determined to be an island about the aera of Alexander (vi. 22. s. 24): while it is not impossible that Herodotus may have heard some tradition on the subject, since he states that cinnamon is produced in those countries in which Dionysus was brought up (iii. 111); from which passage, however, it cannot be determined whether the true cinnamon, that is the bark of the shrub, is intended, or some other kind of cassia.

To the first class of writers belong Onesicritus, the companion of Alexander, Megasthenes and Dai-machus, who were sent as ambassadors by Seleucus to Sandrocottus (*Chandragupta*) and his son Ami-trochates (*Amitraghâta*), from whose memorials almost all that is preserved in Strabo and in the earlier portion of the notice in Pliny has been taken. There is no reason to suppose that either Onesicritus or Megasthenes themselves visited this island; they probably collected, while in India, the narratives they subsequently compiled.

The second class of writers are of the period when the vast commerce of Alexandria had ex-tended to India subsequent to the death of Strabo, A. D. 24. (Groskurd, *Proleg. in Strab.* i. p. 16.) Previous to this period, some few ships may have reached India from Egypt: but, from Strabo's own statement, they appear to have been those only of private individuals (*l. c.*). Pliny, the writer of the Periplus of the Erythraean Sea, Marcian of Hera-clea, Mela, and Ptolemy, belong to this class, and, in the fulness of their narratives, show clearly how much additional knowledge had been acquired dur-ing the extension of the power of the early empe-rors of Rome.

Lastly, under the head of Byzantine writers, we have the remarkable account of the island in Cosmas Indicopleustes, the latest which belongs to the pe-riod of ancient or classical history.

The most important notice is that of Pliny (*l. c.*), who states that ambassadors from the island were received at Rome by the emperor Claudius, through the instrumentality of the freedman of a certain Annius Plocamus, who, after having been driven out of his course upon the island, remained there six months, and became intimate with the people and their rulers. He states that Plocamus landed at a port he calls Hippuros, which may be identified with the modern *Kudremalai*, which means the same in Sanscrit; and that the name of the king was Rachia, evidently the Indian *Rájah*: he adds that the island contained 500 towns, the chief of which was called Palaesimundum, and a vast lake Megisba, from which flowed two rivers, one called Cydara (*Kundara* or *Kadambo* in the *Annals*, now *Aripo*). It is not possible accurately to determine what modern place is to be identified with Megisba, but the *Mahawanso* speaks of enormous works of this nature attributed to Vasabha and other early kings. (*Mah.* pp. 65, 210, 221, 215.) Pliny adds some astronomical facts, which are not equally coincident with the truth; and remarks on the richness of the island in precious stones and metals, and on the fineness of the climate, which extended the life of man beyond its usual limits.

We may mention also, that Diodorus tells a remarkable story, which has been generally held to refer to *Ceylon*, though this is not capable of proof. According to him Iambulus, the son of a merchant, on his way to the spice countries, was taken prisoner by the Aethiopians, and, after a time, with one other companion, placed in a boat and left to his fate. After a long voyage, he came to an island, rich in all kinds of natural productions and 5000 stadia round (στρογγύλη μὲν ὑπαρχούσῃ τῷ σχήματι). Iambulus stayed there seven years, and thence went to Palibothra, where he was well received by the king, who is said to have been φιλέλλην (Diod. ii. 55, &c.). That the details of this voyage are fabulous no one can doubt, yet the narrative is probably founded on fact, and points to an early intercourse between the shores of Eastern Africa and India.

The fullest and by far the most interesting account of Ceylon, is that preserved by Cosmas Indicopleustes, which was published by Montfaucon (Coll. Nov. Patr. ii. p. 336). Cosmas, who flourished in the reign of Justinian, about A.D. 535, states that he obtained his information from a Greek named Sopatrus, whom he met at Adulis. According to this writer, the Taprobane of the Greeks is the Sielediba of the Hindus, an island lying beyond the Pepper Coast, or Malabar, and having near it a great number of small islands (i. e. the Maldives). He reckons it about 900 miles in length and breadth, a measure he deduces from a native measure called Gaudia (still said to be known in the island, and the same as the Tamil naliqual, Vincent, ii. p. 506). There were, at the time he received his information, two kings in the island, one the possessor of the Hyacinth (i. e. of the mountain districts which abound in precious stones), and the other of the plain country and coast, where in later times the Arabians, Portuguese, Dutch, and English, have in succession established factories. A Christian church, he adds, was established there ἐπιδημούντων Περσῶν Χριστιανῶν, with a priest and deacon ordained in Persia. There is no doubt that these were Nestorians, whose Catholicos resided at Ctesiphon, and who, on the Malabar coast, are often called Christians of St. Thomas. He determines the position of Sielediba, by stating that it is as far from it to China, as from the Persian Gulf to the island (p. 138). Again, he says, which is less correct, that Sielediba is five days' sail from the continent; and that on the continent is a place named Marallo (Maravoar?), which produces the pearl oysters; and adds, that the king of Ceylon sells elephants for their height; and that in India elephants are trained for war, while in Africa they are captured for their ivory. Horses imported from Persia pay no tax. It is remarkable that this notice of the elephants is in strict accordance with that of Aelian, who asserts that they were bred in Ceylon and transported in large native vessels to the opposite continent, and sold to the king of Calingae (Hist. An. xxvi. 18). Pliny (l. c.), on the authority of Onesicritus, affirms that larger and more warlike elephants are reared in this island than anywhere else in India, and that the hunting of them was a constant sport: and Ptolemy places under the Malea M. (Adam's Peak) his ἐλεφάντων νομαί, in the exact position in which they were, till lately, most abundant (vii. 4. § 8). The testimony of all modern travellers on the subject of the Ceylon elephant is, that those bearing great tusks, and therefore valuable for their ivory, are extremely rare in the island. (Compare also Dionys. Perieg. v. 593, who calls Ceylon μήτερα Ἀσιηγενέων ἐλεφάντων; Alex. Lychn. in Steph. B., who speaks of εὔρινοι ἐλέφαντες as the product of the island; Solin. c. 56; and Tzetzes Chil. viii. Hist. 215). Cosmas concludes his remarkable story with a notice

of a conference between the king of Ceylon and Sopatrus, in which the latter convinced the king that the Romans were a greater people than the Persians, by exhibiting some gold coins of Byzantium. It confirms the veracity of the narrator that we know from other sources that the Sassanian princes of the sixth century had only silver money, while at the capital of the Eastern Empire gold coin was not rare. There were many temples in the island, one of them famous for a hyacinth of extraordinary size.

Few islands have borne, at different times, so large a number of names: as many of these have considerable interest, we shall notice them in succession. The first, as we have stated, by which it was known to the Greeks was Ταπροβάνη. Several explanations have been given of this name; the best is probably Tamraparni (Sanscrit for red-leaved; cf. Burnouf, Journ. Asiat. viii. p. 147; Mahawanso, ed. Turnour, p. 50; Lassen, Inst. Ling. Pracrit. p. 246), a form slightly changed from the Pali Támbapanni, the spot where the first king Vigaya is said to have landed (Mahawanso, l. c.). This name is not unknown in other Indian writings: thus we find so named a place on the adjoining continent of Hindostán, and a river of the same district which flows from the Gháts into the sea near Tinnevelly (Wilson, Vishnu Purana, p. 176); and a pearl-fishery at the mouth of this stream is noticed in the Raghu-vansa (iv. p. 50; cf. also Vishnu Purana, p. 175, and Asiat. Research. viii. p. 330). Other interpretations of Taprobane may be found in Bochart (Geogr. Sacra, p. 692), who, after the fashion of the scholars of his day, derives it from two Hebrew words, and imagines it the Ophir of the Bible; Wahl (Erdbeschr. v. Ost-Indien, ii. 682, 683), Mannert (v. p. 285), Duncan (Asiat. Research. v. p. 39), Gladwin (Ayin Akberi, iii. 36), Bohler. (Altes Indien, i. 27), Vincent (Periplus, ii. p. 493), none of which are, however, free from objection. There can be no doubt that the early language of Ceylon approximated very closely to that of the adjoining continent, and was, in fact, a form of Tamil. (Cf. Rask, Cingal. Skrift. p. 1, Colombo, 1821; Buchanan Hamilton, ap. M. Martin's East India, ii. p. 795; cf. also Ptol. viii. 1. § 80). It may be observed that the name Támbapanni is found in the Girnar inscription of Asoka (B. c. 280), and would therefore naturally be known to the Seleucidan Greeks. (As. Journ. Beng. vii. p. 159.)

We may add that Pliny states that the ancient inhabitants were called by Megasthenes Palaeogoni (l. c.), doubtless the translation into Greek of some Indian name. It is not impossible that Megasthenes may have been acquainted with the Indian fable, which made the Rakshasas, or Giants, the children of the Earth, the earliest inhabitants of this island.

The next name we find applied to Ceylon was that of Simundu or Palaesimundu, which is found after the time of Strabo, but had, nevertheless, gone out of use before Ptolemy. (Ptol. l. c.; Steph. B. s. v. Taprobane; Peripl. M. E., ed. Hudson, p. 2; Marcian, ed. Hudson, p. 26, and pp. 2, 9.) There is a difficulty at first sight about these names, as to which form is the correct one: on the whole, we are inclined to acquiesce in that of Palaesimundu (Παλαισιμούνδου), on the authority of Marcian (l. c.) and of the Periplus (§ 61, ed. Müller). Pliny, too, in his account of the embassy to Rome, calls the city, where the royal palace was, Palaesimundu. There can be little doubt that this word is the Graecised form of the Sanscrit Páli-Simanta, the

Head of the Holy Law, which is confirmed by another name of analogous character, Andrasimundu (Ptol. vii. 4), a promontory now called Calpentyn (Mannert, l. c. p. 211). The ancient city noticed by Pliny, with the royal palace, must be that elsewhere called Anurogrammon, and by the natives Anurájápura, the royal seat of empire from B.C. 267 to A.D. 769 (Mahawanso, Intr. p. lxi.). (For other derivations of Palaesimundu, see Dodwell, Dissert. de Geogr. Min. p. 95; Wahl, Erdbeschr. ii. p. 684; Renaudot, Anc. Relat. des Indes, p. 133; Malte-Brun, Précis de Géogr. iv. 113; Mannert, i. p. 210; Paolino-a-St. Barth, Voyage aux Indes, ii. p. 482.) The conjecture of Wilford (As. Res. x. p. 148) that it may be Sumatra, and of Heeren (Soc. Reg. Götting. vol. vii. p. 32) that it is the town of " Pontgemolle," do not need refutation.

The other names which this island has borne appear to have been as follow: Salice, with its inhabitants, the Salae, Serendivus, Sielediba, Serendib, Zeilan, Ceylon. These are all closely connected and in reality euphonic modifications of one original form. The first, Salice, — perhaps more correctly Saline, — which seems to have been in use when Ptolemy wrote the common name of Taprobane (l. c.), is certainly derivable from Sinala, the Pali form of Sinhala (Mahaw. cap. vii. p. 50); from this would naturally come the Σιελε of Cosmas (Cosm. Indicopl. l. c.), the termination of this name, διϐα, being nothing more than the Sanscrit d'wipa, an island. (Cf. in the same neighbourhood the Lakkadive and Maldive islands.) The slight and common interchange of the L and R gives the Serendivus of Ammianus (xxii. 7). From this, again, we obtain the more modern forms of the Arabic, Dutch, and English. Sinhala would mean the abode of lions— which word is found with the same sense, and the form Sengkialo, in the narrative of the Chinese travellers who visited Ceylon in A.D. 412. (Foe-koue-ki, p. xli., cf. p. 328, Annot. p. 336). Besides these names there is one other whereby alone this island is known in the sacred Brahminical writings. This is Lanka (see Mahábh. ii. 30, v. 1177, iii. c. 278, &c.). It is most likely that this name had passed out of use before the time of Alexander, as it is not mentioned by any of the classical writers : it has been, however, preserved by the Buddhists, as may be seen from the notices in the Mahawanso (pp. 2, 3, 49, &c.). (Comp. also Colebrooke, Ess. ii. p. 427; Davis in As. Res. ii. p. 229.)

Ceylon is a very mountainous island, the greater masses being grouped towards the southern end, and forming thereby the watershed for most of its rivers. The ancients had a tolerably accurate knowledge of the position of these hills. To the N. were the Montes Galibi, terminating in a promontory called Boreum (now Cape Pedro), and overlooking the principal capital, Anurájápura. To the S. the great chain was known by the generic name of Malea, doubtless a form derived from the Sanscrit Mala, a mountain. The centre of this group is the well-known Adam's Peak—in the native Pali language, Samana Kúta (the Mountain of the Gods) (Upham, Sacred Books of Ceylon, iii. p. 202), and the high land now called Neura-Ellia.

The principal rivers of Ceylon, as known to the ancients, were the Phasis, which flowed from the Montes Galibi in a northern direction; the Ganges (now Mahávali - Ganga), the chief of all the streams whereby the island is watered, the principal source of which is in the S. range, of which

Adam's Peak is the pre-eminent mountain (Brooke on Mahavella-Ganga, Roy. Geograph. Journ. iii. p. 223), and whose course is nearly NE.; the Baraces, which rose in the M. Malea, and flowed SE. ; and the Soanas, which flows from the same source in a westerly direction. Besides these rivers was the celebrated lake called Megisba. the size of which has been extravagantly overstated by Pliny (vi. 22. s. 24). It is probable that this lake was formed by the connecting together of several great tanks, many remains of which still exist ; and thus Forbiger suggests that it may be near the mouths of the Mahávali-Ganga, in which neighbourhood there are still extraordinary remains of canals, earthworks, &c. (Brooke, l. c.). It was on the shores of this lake that Pliny placed the capital Palaesimundum, with a population of 200,000 souls. The island was rich in towns and peoples, which are not clearly distinguished by ancient writers ; of these the Anurogrammi with the town Anurogrammon (now Anurájápura) is the most important. The greatness of this place, which was the royal residence of the kings from B.C. 267 to A.D. 769 (Mahawanso, Introd. p. lxi.), is shown by the vast remains which still exist on the spot. (Chapman, Ancient Anurájápura, in Trans. Roy. As. Soc. ii. pl. ii. p. 463).

Other less known peoples and places were the Soani, Sandocandae, Rhogandani, Danae (now Tangalle), the Morduli with their seaport Mordulamne, the Nagadibi, Spartana (now Trincomali), Maagrammon (probably Tamankadawe), and the Modutti. For these and many more we are indebted to Ptolemy, who from his own account (i. 17. § 4), examined the journals and conversed with several persons who had visited the island. It is a strong confirmation of what he states, that a considerable number of the names preserved can be re-produced in the native Indian form.

The people who inhabited the island were for the most part of Indian descent, their language being very nearly connected with the Pali, one of the most widely spread Indian dialects. To this race belong all the monuments which remain of its former greatness, together with a very curious and authentic series of annals which have been of late brought to light by the exertions of Sir Alexander Johnston and the critical acumen of Mr. Turnour (Mahawanso) and Upham (Sacr. Hist. Books). There are, however, still existing in the island some few specimens of a wholly different race, locally known by the name of the Veddahs. These wild and uncivilised people are found in the valleys and woods to the E. and S. of the Mahávali-Ganga; and are, in all probability, the remains of the aboriginal race who dwelt in the land antecedent to the arrival of Vigaya and his Indian followers. In physiognomy and colour they bear a striking resemblance to the earliest inhabitants of the S. provinces of Hindostán and are, most likely, of similarly Scythic origin. (Knox, Account of Ceylon, Lond. 1657; Perceval, Account of Ceylon, Lond. 1803; Gardiner, Descr. of Ceylon, Lond. 1807; Davy, Ceylon and its Inhabitants, Lond. 1821; W. Hamilton, India, ii. 522; Ritter, iv. 2. p. 226; Lassen, Indische Alterth. i. p. 198 ; Dissert. de Taprobane, Bonn, 1832 ; Turnour, Mahawanso, Ceylon, 1836; Jour. Asiat. Beng. vi. 856; Chapman, Anc. City of Anurájápura, in Tr. R. As. Soc. iii. 463; Chitty, Ruins of Tammana Nuwera, in R. As. Soc. vi. 242; Brooke, Mahavella-Ganga, R. Geogr. Soc. iii. 223.)   [V.]

TAPSUS FLUVIUS. [Thapsus.]

TAPU'RA (Τάπουρα), a town of uncertain site in Armenia Minor, is mentioned only by Ptolemy (v. 7. § 3).   [L. S.]

TAPUREI (Ταπούρειοι, Ptol. vi. 14. §§ 12, 13), a tribe in Scythia intra Imaum.   [T. H. D.]

TAPU'RI (Τάπουροι or Τάπυροι, Strab. xi. p. 520; Plin. vi. 16. s. 18), a tribe whose name and probable habitations appear, at different periods of history, to have been extended along a wide space of country from Armenia to the eastern side of the Oxus. Strabo places them alongside the Caspian Gates and Rhagae, in Parthia, (xi. p. 514), or between the Derbices and Hyrcani (xi. p. 520), or in company with the Amardi and other people along the southern shores of the Caspian (xi. p. 523); in which last view Curtius (vi. 4. § 24, viii. 1. § 13), Dionysius (de Situ Orbis, 733), and Pliny (vi. 16. s. 18) may be considered to coincide. Ptolemy in one place reckons them among the tribes of Media (vi. 2. § 6), and in another ascribes them to Margiana (vi. 10. § 2). Their name is written with some differences in different authors; thus Τάπουροι and Τάπυροι occur in Strabo; Tapuri in Pliny and Curtius; Τάπυρροι in Steph. B. There can be no doubt that the present district of Taberistán derives its name from them. Aelian (V. H. iii. 13) gives a peculiar description of the Tapuri who dwelt in Media. (Wilson, Ariana, p. 157.)   [V.]

TAPU'RI MONTES, a chain of mountains, in Scythia, to the N. of the Jaxartes, apparently a portion of the Altai range, towards its western extremity (Ptol vi. 14. § 7). It may, however, be doubted whether this view of Ptolemy is really correct. It would seem more likely that they are connected with the Tapuri, a tribe who nearly adjoined the Hyrcani [TAPURI]; and this a notice in Polybius would appear clearly to imply (v. 44).   [V.]

TARACHI (Τάραχοι, Ptol. vii. 4. § 8), a tribe of Taprobane or Ceylon, who occupied the SE. corner of the island below the Malea mountains (Adam's Peak). They appear to have had a port called 'Ηλίου λιμήν, probably in the neighbourhood of the present Vintam. Near to them was a river called the Barace (Ptol. vii. 4. § 5). It is not unlikely that the river and the people had once the same name, which has since been modified by the change of the initial letters.   [V.]

TARANDRUS (Τάρανδρος: Eth. Ταράνδριος), a place in Phrygia of unknown site, is mentioned only by Stephanus Byz. (s. v.).   [L. S.]

TARANEI, a people in Arabia Deserta of unknown site. (Plin. vi. 28. s. 32.)

TARAS. [Tarentum.]

TARASCON (Ταρασκών: Tarascon), a town in the Provincia Narbonensis, on the east side of the Rhone, between Arles and Avignon. The railway from Avignon to Marseille passes through Tarascon, and there is a branch from Tarascon to Nîmes. Ptolemy (in whose text the name is written Ταρούσκων) enumerates Tarascon among the towns of the Salyes [SALYES]. Strabo (iv. p. 178) says that the road from Nemausus (Nîmes) to Aquae Sextiae passes through Ugernum (Beaucaire) and Tarascon, and that the distance from Nemausus to Aquae Sextiae is 53 Roman miles ; which, as D'Anville observes, is not correct. In another passage (iv. p. 187) Strabo makes the distance from Nîmes to the bank of the Rhone opposite to Tarascon about 100 stadia, which is exact enough. [TARUSCONIENSES.] [G. L.]

TARBA. [Tarrha.]

TARBELLI (Τάρβελλοι, Τάρβελοι) are mentioned by Caesar among the Aquitanian peoples (B. G. iii. 27). They lived on the shores of the Ocean, on the Gallic bay (Strab. iv. p. 190), of which they were masters. Gold was found abundantly in their country, and at little depth. Some pieces were a handful, and required little purification. The Tarbelli extended southwards to the Aturis (Adour) and the Pyrenees, as the passages cited from Tibullus (i. 7, 9) and Lucan (Pharsal. i. 421) show, so far as they are evidence :—

" Qui tenet et ripas Aturi, quo littore curvo
    Molliter admissum claudit Tarbellicus aequor."

Ausonius (Parent. iv. 11) gives the name " Tarbellus " to the Ocean in these parts. Ptolemy (ii. 7. § 9) places the Tarbelli south of the Bituriges Visci, and makes their limits extend to the Pyrenees. He names their city "Ὕδατα Αὐγούστα, or Aquae Tarbellicae. [AQUAE TARBELLICAE.] Pliny (iv. 19) gives to the Tarbelli the epithet of Quatuorsignani, a term which indicates the establishment of some Roman soldiers in this country, as in the case of the Cocossates, whom Pliny names Sexsignani. [COCOSSATES.] The country of the Tarbelli contained hot and cold springs, which were near one another.   [G. L.]

TARBESSUS (Ταρβησσός), a town of Pisidia, mentioned only by Strabo (xii. p. 570). [L. S.]

TARENTI'NUS SINUS (ὁ Ταραντῖνος κόλπος: Golfo di Taranto) was the name given in ancient as well as in modern times to the extensive gulf comprised between the two great promontories or peninsulas of Southern Italy. It was bounded by the Iapygian promontory (Capo della Leuca) on the N., and by the Lacinian promontory (Capo delle Colonne) on the S.; and these natural limits being clearly marked, appear to have been generally recognised by ancient geographers. (Strab. vi. pp. 261, 262 ; Mel. ii. 4. § 8 ; Plin. iii. 11. s. 16 ; Ptol. iii. 1. § 12.) Strabo tells us it was 240 miles in extent, following the circuit of the shores, and 700 stadia (87½ miles) across from headland to headland. Pliny reckons it 250 miles in circuit, and 100 miles across the opening. The latter statement considerably exceeds the truth, while Strabo's estimate is a very fair approximation. This extensive gulf derived its name from the celebrated city of Tarentum, situated at its N E. extremity, and which enjoyed the advantage of a good port, almost the only one throughout the whole extent of the gulf. (Strab. vi. p. 278.) But notwithstanding this disadvantage, its western shores were lined by a succession of Greek colonies, which rose into flourishing cities. Crotona, Sybaris, Metapontum, and, at a later period, Heraclea and Thurii, all adorned this line of coast ; the great fertility of the territory compensating for the want of natural harbours. On the northern or Iapygian shore, on the contrary, the only city was Callipolis, which never rose above a subordinate condition.   [E. H. B.]

TARENTUM (Τάρας, -αντος: Eth. Ταραντῖνος, Tarentinus : Taranto), one of the most powerful and celebrated cities of Southern Italy, situated on the N. shore of the extensive bay, which derived from it, both in ancient and modern times, the name of the gulf of Tarentum. (TARENTINUS SINUS: ὁ Ταραντῖνος κόλπος: Golfo di Taranto). It was included within the limits of the province of Calabria, as that term was used by the Romans; but the Greeks would generally have reckoned it a city of Magna Graecia, and not have regarded it as included in Iapygia. Its situation is peculiar, occupying a promontory or peninsula at the entrance of an extensive but shallow bay, now called the *Mare Piccolo*, but in ancient times known as the Port of Tarentum, an inlet of above 6 miles in length, and from 2 to 3 in breadth, but which was so nearly closed at its mouth by the peninsula occupied by the city, that the latter is now connected by a bridge with the opposite side of the harbour. There can be no doubt that the ancient city originally occupied only the same space to which the modern one is now confined, that of the low but rocky islet which lies directly across the mouth of the harbour, and is now separated from the mainland at its E. extremity by an artificial fosse or ditch, but was previously joined to it by a narrow neck of sand. This may probably have been itself a later accumulation; and it is not unlikely that the city was originally founded on an island, somewhat resembling that of Ortygia at Syracuse, which afterwards became joined to the mainland, and has again been artificially separated from it. As in the case of Syracuse, this island or peninsula afterwards became the Acropolis of the enlarged city, which extended itself widely over the adjoining plain.

Tarentum was a Greek city, a colony of Sparta, founded within a few years after the two Achaean colonies of Sybaris and Crotona. The circumstances that led to its foundation are related with some variation by Antiochus and Ephorus (both cited by Strabo), but both authors agree in the main fact that the colonists were a body of young men, born during the First Messenian War under circumstances which threw over their birth a taint of illegitimacy, on which account they were treated with contempt by the other citizens; and after an abortive attempt at creating a revolution at Sparta, they determined to emigrate in a body under a leader named Phalanthus. They were distinguished by the epithet of Partheniae, in allusion to their origin. Phalanthus, who was apparently himself one of the disparaged class, and had been the chief of the conspirators at Sparta, after consulting the oracle at Delphi, became the leader and founder of the new colony. (Antiochus, *ap.* Strab. vi. p. 278; Ephorus, *Ib.* p. 279; Serv. *ad Aen.* iii. 551; Diod. xv. 66; Justin, iii. 4; Scymn. Ch. 332.) Both Antiochus and Ephorus represent them as establishing themselves without difficulty on the spot, and received in a friendly manner by the natives; and this is far more probable than the statement of Pausanias, according to which they found themselves in constant warfare; and it was not till after a long struggle that they were able to make themselves masters of Tarentum. (Paus. x. 10. § 6.) The same author represents that city as previously occupied by the indigenous tribes, and already a great and powerful city, but this is highly improbable. The name, however, is probably of native origin, and seems to have been derived from that of the small river or stream which always continued to be known as the Taras; though, as usual, the Greeks derived it from an eponymous hero named Taras, who was represented as a son of Neptune and a nymph of the country. (Paus. *Ib.* § 8.) It is certain that the hero Taras continued to be an object of special worship at Tarentum, while Phalanthus, who was revered as their Oekist, was frequently associated with him, and gradually became the subject of many legends of a very mythical character,

in some of which he appears to have been confounded with Taras himself. (Paus. x. 10. §§ 6—8, 13. § 10; Serv. *ad Aen. l. c.*) Nevertheless, there is no reason to doubt the historical character of Phalanthus, or the Lacedaemonian origin of Tarentum, which was confirmed by numerous local names and religious observances still retained there down to a very late period. (Pol. viii. 30, 35.) The Roman poets also abound in allusions to this origin of the Tarentines. (Hor. *Carm.* iii. 5. 56, ii. 6. 11; Ovid. *Met.* xv. 50, &c.) The date of the foundation of Tarentum is given by Hieronymus as B. C. 708, and this, which is in accordance with the circumstances related in connection with it, is probably correct, though no other author has mentioned the precise date. (Hieron. *Chron.* ad Ol. xviii.)

The history of Tarentum, for the first two centuries of its existence, is, like that of most other cities of Magna Graecia, almost wholly unknown. But the main fact is well attested that it attained to great power and prosperity, though apparently at first overshadowed by the superior power of the Achaean cities, so that it was not till a later period that it assumed the predominant position among the cities of Magna Graecia, which it ultimately attained. There can be no doubt that it owed this prosperity mainly to the natural advantages of its situation. (Scymn. Ch. 332—336; Strab. vi. p. 278.) Though its territory was not so fertile, or so well adapted for the growth of grain as those of Metapontum and Siris, it was admirably suited for the growth of olives, and its pastures produced wool of the finest quality, while its port, or inner sea as it was called, abounded in shell-fish of all descriptions, among which the Murex, which produced the celebrated purple dye, was the most important and valuable. But it was especially the excellence of its port to which Tarentum owed its rapid rise to opulence and power. This was not only landlocked and secure, but was the only safe harbour of any extent on the whole shores of the Tarentine gulf; and as neither Brundusium nor Hydruntum, on the opposite side of the Messapian peninsula, had as yet attained to any eminence, or fallen into the hands of a seafaring people, the port of Tarentum became the chief emporium for the commerce of all this part of Italy. (Pol. x. 1; Flor. i. 18. § 3.) The story of Arion, as related by Herodotus (i. 24) indicates the existence of extensive commercial relations with Corinth and other cities of Greece as early as the reign of Periander, B. C. 625—585.

As the Tarentines gradually extended their power over the adjoining territories, they naturally came into frequent collision with the native tribes of the interior,—the Messapians and Peucetians; and the first events of their history recorded to us relate to their wars with these nations. Their offerings at Delphi noticed by Pausanias (x. 10. § 6, 13. § 10), recorded victories over both these nations, in one of which it appears that Opis, a king of the Iapygians, who had come to the assistance of the Peucetians, was slain; but we have no knowledge of the dates or circumstances of these battles. It would appear, however, that the Tarentines were continually gaining ground, and making themselves masters of the Messapian towns one after the other, until their progress was checked by a great disaster, their own forces, together with those of the Rhegians, who had been sent to their assistance, being totally defeated by the barbarians with great slaughter. (Herod. vii. 170; Diod. xi. 52.) So heavy was their loss that Herodotus, without stating the numbers, says it was the greatest slaughter of Greeks that had occurred up to his time. The loss seems to have fallen especially upon the nobles and wealthier citizens, so that it became the occasion of a political revolution, and the government, which had previously been an aristocracy, became thenceforth a pure democracy. (Arist. *Pol.* v. 3.) Of the internal condition and constitution of Tarentum previously to this time, we know scarcely anything, but it seems probable that its institutions were at first copied from those of the parent city of Sparta. Aristotle speaks of its government as a πολίτεια, in the sense of a mixed government or commonwealth; while Herodotus incidentally notices a king of Tarentum (iii. 156), not long before the Persian War, who was doubtless a king after the Spartan model. The institutions of a democratic tendency noticed with commendation by Aristotle (*Pol.* vi. 5) probably belong to the later and democratic period of the constitution. We hear but little also of Tarentum in connection with the revolutions arising out of the influence exercised by the Pythagoreans: that sect had apparently not established itself so strongly there as in the Achaean cities; though many Tarentines are enumerated among the disciples of Pythagoras, and it is clear that the city had not altogether escaped their influence. (Iambl. *Vit. Pyth.* 262, 266; Porphyr. *Vit. Pyth.* 56.)

The defeat of the Tarentines by the Messapians, which is referred by Diodorus to B. C. 473 (Diod. xi. 52), is the first event in the history of Tarentum to which we can assign a definite date. Great as that blow may have been, it did not produce any permanent effect in checking the progress of the city, which still appears as one of the most flourishing in Magna Graecia. We next hear of the Tarentines as interfering to prevent the Thurians, who had been recently established in Italy, from making themselves masters of the district of the Siritis. On what grounds the Tarentines could lay claim to this district, which was separated from them by the intervening territory of Metapontum, we are not informed; but they carried on war for some time against the Thurians, who were supported by the Spartan exile Cleandridas; until at length the dispute was terminated by a compromise, and a new colony named Heracleia was founded in the contested territory (B. C. 432), in which the citizens of both states participated, but it was agreed that it should be considered as a colony of Tarentum. (Antioch. *ap. Strab.* vi. p. 264; Diod. xii. 23, 36.) At the time of the Athenian expedition to Sicily, the Tarentines kept aloof from the contest, and contented themselves with refusing all supplies and assistance to the Athenian fleet (Thuc. vi. 44), while they afforded shelter to the Corinthian and Laconian ships under Gylippus (*Ib.* 104), but they did not even prevent the second fleet under Demosthenes and Eurymedon from touching at the islands of the Choerades, immediately opposite to the entrance of their harbour, and taking on board some auxiliaries furnished by the Messapians. (Id. vii. 33.)

Another long interval now elapses, during which the history of Tarentum is to us almost a blank; yet the few notices we hear of the city represent it as in a state of great prosperity. We are told that at one time (apparently about 380—360 B.C.) Archytas, the Pythagorean philosopher, exercised a paramount influence over the government, and filled

the office of Strategus or general no less than seven times, though it was prohibited by law to hold it more than once; and was successful in every campaign. (Diog. Laert. viii. 4. §§ 79—82.) It is evident, therefore, that the Tarentines were far from enjoying unbroken peace. The hostilities alluded to were probably but a renewal of their old warfare with the Messapians; but the security of the Greek cities in Italy was now menaced by two more formidable foes, Dionysius of Syracuse in the south, and the Lucanians on the north and west. The Tarentines, indeed, seem to have at first looked upon both dangers with comparative indifference: their remote position secured them from the immediate brunt of the attack, and it is even doubtful whether they at first joined in the general league of the Greek cities to resist the danger which threatened them. Meanwhile, the calamities which befel the more southern cities, the destruction of some by Dionysius, and the humiliation of others, tended only to raise Tarentum in comparison, while that city itself enjoyed an immunity from all hostile attacks; and it seems certain that it was at this period that Tarentum first rose to the preponderating position among the Greek cities in Italy, which it thenceforth enjoyed without a rival. It was apparently as an acknowledgment of that superiority, that when Tarentum had joined the confederacy of the Greek cities, the place of meeting of their congress was fixed at the Tarentine colony of Heracleia. (Strab. vi. p. 280.)

It was impossible for the Tarentines any longer to keep aloof from the contest with the Lucanians, whose formidable power was now beginning to threaten all the cities in Magna Graecia; and they now appear as taking a leading part in opposing the progress of those barbarians. But they were not content with their own resources, and called in successively to their assistance several foreign leaders and generals of renown. The first of these was the Spartan king Archidamus, who crossed over into Italy with a considerable force. Of his operations there we have no account, but he appears to have carried on the war for some years, as Diodorus places his first landing in Italy in B. C. 346, while the battle in which he was defeated and slain was not fought till the same time as that of Chaeroneia, B. C. 338. (Diod. xvi. 63. 88.) This action, in which Archidamus himself, and almost all the troops which he had brought with him from Greece perished, was fought (as we are told), not with the Lucanians, but with the Messapians, in the neighbourhood of Manduria, only 24 miles from Tarentum (Plut. *Agis.* 3; Paus. iii. 10. § 5; Diod. *l. c.*); but there can be no doubt, however, that both nations were united, and that the Lucanians lent their support to the Messapians, as the old enemies of Tarentum. Henceforth, indeed, we find both names continually united. A few years after the death of Archidamus, Alexander, king of Epirus, was invited by the Tarentines, and landed in Italy, B. C. 332. The operations of his successive campaigns, which were continued till B. C. 326, are very imperfectly known to us, but he appears to have first turned his arms against the Messapians, and compelled them to conclude a peace with the Tarentines, before he proceeded to make war upon the Lucanians and Bruttians. But his arms were attended with considerable success in this quarter also: he defeated the Samnites and Lucanians in a great battle near Paestum, and penetrated into the heart of the Brut-

tian territory. Meanwhile, however, he had quarrelled with his allies the Tarentines, so that he
turned against them, took their colony of Heracleia,
and endeavoured to transfer the congress of the
Greek cities from thence to a place on the river
Acalandrus, in the territory of Thurii. (Strab. vi.
p. 280; Liv. viii. 24; Justin. xii. 2.) Hence his
death, in B.C. 226, only liberated the Tarentines
from an enemy instead of depriving them of an ally.
They appear from this time to have either remained
tranquil or carried on the contest single-handed, till
B.C. 303, when we find them again invoking foreign
assistance, and, as on a former occasion, sending to
Sparta for aid. This was again furnished them,
and a large army of mercenaries landed at Tarentum
under Cleonymus, the uncle of the Spartan king.
But though he compelled the Messapians and Lucanians to sue for peace, Cleonymus soon alienated the
minds of his Greek allies by his arrogance and
luxurious habits, and became the object of general
hatred before he quitted Italy. (Diod. xx. 104.)
According to Strabo, the Tarentines subsequently
called in the assistance of Agathocles (Strab. vi. p.
280); but we find no mention of this elsewhere, and
Diodorus tells us that he concluded an alliance with
the Iapygians and Peucetians, which could hardly
have been done with favourable intentions towards
Tarentum. (Diod. xxi. p. 490.)

Not long after this the Tarentines first came into
collision with a more formidable foe than their neighbours, the Messapians and Lucanians. The wars of
the Romans with the Samnites, in which the descendants of the latter people, the Apulians and
Lucanians, were from time to time involved, had
rendered the name and power of Rome familiar to
the Greek cities on the Tarentine gulf and coast of
the Adriatic, though their arms were not carried
into that part of Italy till about B.C. 283, when
they rendered assistance to the Thurians against the
Lucanians [THURII]. But long before this, as
early as the commencement of the Second Samnite
War (B.C. 326), the Tarentines are mentioned in
Roman history as supporting the Neapolitans with
promises of succour, which, however, they never
sent; and afterwards exciting the Lucanians to war
against the Romans. (Liv. viii. 27.) Again, in
B.C. 321 we are told that they sent a haughty embassy to command the Samnites and Romans to
desist from hostilities, and threatened to declare war
on whichever party refused to obey. (Id. ix. 14.)
But on this occasion also they did not put their
threat in execution. At a subsequent period, probably about B.C. 303 (Arnold's *Rome*, vol. ii. p.
315), the Tarentines concluded a treaty with Rome,
by which it was stipulated that no Roman ships of
war should pass the Lacinian cape. (Appian, *Samnit.* 7.) It was therefore a direct breach of this
treaty when, in B.C. 302, a Roman squadron of ten
ships under L. Cornelius, which had been sent to
the assistance of the Thurians, entered the Tarentine gulf, and even approached within sight of the
city. The Tarentines, whose hostile disposition was
already only half concealed, and who are said to
have been the prime movers in organising the confederacy against Rome which led to the Fourth Samnite War (Zonar. viii. 2.), immediately attacked the
Roman ships, sunk four of them, and took one. After
this they proceeded to attack the Thurians on account of their having called in the Romans, expelled
the Roman garrison, and made themselves masters
of the city. (Appian, *Samn.* 7. § 1; Zonar. viii.

2.) The Romans sent an embassy to Tarentum to
complain of these outrages; but their demands being
refused, and their ambassador treated with con-
tumely, they had now no choice but to declare war
upon the Tarentines, B.C. 281. (Appian, *l. c.* § 2;
Zonar. *l. c.*; Dion Cass. *Fr.* 145.) Nevertheless,
the war was at first carried on with little energy;
but meanwhile the Tarentines, following their usual
policy, had invited Pyrrhus, king of Epirus, to their
assistance. That monarch readily accepted the over-
ture, and sent over his general Milo to occupy the
citadel of Tarentum with 3000 men, while he himself
followed in the winter. (Zonar. viii. 2; Plut. *Pyrrh.*
15, 16.)

It is usual to represent the Tarentines as at this
period sunk in luxury and effeminacy, so that they
were unable to defend themselves, and hence compelled to have recourse to the assistance of Pyrrhus.
But there is certainly much exaggeration in this
view. They were no doubt accustomed to rely much
upon the arms of mercenaries, but so were all the
more wealthy cities of Greece; and it is certain that
the Tarentines themselves (apart from their allies
and mercenaries), furnished not only a considerable
body of cavalry, but a large force or phalanx of
heavy-armed infantry, called the Leucaspids, from
their white shields, who are especially mentioned as
serving under Pyrrhus at the battle of Asculum.
(Dionys. xx. Fr. Didot. 1, 5.) It is unnecessary
here to repeat the history of the campaigns of that
monarch. His first successes for a time saved
Tarentum itself from the brunt of the war: but
when he at length, after his final defeat by Curius,
withdrew from Italy (B.C. 274), it was evident that
the full weight of the Roman arms would fall upon
Tarentum. Pyrrhus, indeed, left Milo with a garrison to defend the city, but the Tarentines themselves were divided into two parties, the one of which
was disposed to submit to Rome, while the other
applied for assistance to Carthage. A Carthaginian
fleet was actually sent to Tarentum, but it arrived
too late, for Milo had already capitulated and surrendered the citadel into the hands of the Roman
consul Papirius, B.C. 272. (Zonar. viii. 6; Oros.
iv. 3.)

From this time Tarentum continued subject to
Rome. The inhabitants were indeed left in possession of their own laws and nominal independence,
but the city was jealously watched; and a Roman
legion seems to have been commonly stationed there.
(Pol. ii. 24.) During the First Punic War the
Tarentines are mentioned as furnishing ships to the
Romans (Pol. i. 20): but with this exception we
hear no more of it till the Second Punic War, when
it became a military post of great importance.
Hannibal was from an early period desirous to make
himself master of the city, which, with its excellent
port, would at once have secured his communications
with Africa. It is evident also that there was a strong
Carthaginian party in the city, who shortly after
the battle of Cannae, opened negotiations with Hannibal, and renewed them upon a subsequent occasion
(Liv. xxii. 61, xxiv. 13); but they were kept down
by the presence of the Roman garrison, and it was
not till B.C. 212 that Nico and Philemenus, two of
the leaders of this party, found an opportunity to
betray the city into his hands. (Liv. xxv. 8—10;
Pol. viii. 26—33.) Even then the Roman garrison
still held the citadel; and Hannibal having failed in
his attempts to carry this fortress by assault, was
compelled to resort to a blockade. He cut it off on

the land side by drawing a double line of fortifications across the isthmus, and made himself master of the sea by dragging a part of the fleet which was shut up within the inner port (or *Mare Piccolo*), across the narrowest part of the isthmus, and launching it again in the outer bay. (Pol. viii. 34—36; Liv. xxv. 11.) This state of things continued for more than two years, during the whole of which time the Carthaginians continued masters of the city, while the Roman garrison still maintained possession of the citadel, and the besiegers were unable altogether to prevent them from receiving supplies from without, though on one occasion the Romans, having sent a considerable fleet under D. Quintius to attempt the relief of the place, this was met by the Tarentines, and after an obstinate conflict the Roman fleet was defeated and destroyed. (Liv. xxv. 15, xxvi. 39, xxvii. 3.) At length in B. c. 209 Fabius determined if possible to wrest from Hannibal the possession of this important post; and laid siege to Tarentum while the Carthaginian general was opposed to Marcellus. He himself encamped on the N. of the port, close to the entrance, so that he readily put himself in communication with M. Livius, the commander of the citadel. But while he was preparing his ships and engines for the assault, an accident threw in his way the opportunity of surprising the city, of which he made himself master with little difficulty. The Carthaginian garrison was put to the sword, as well as a large part of the inhabitants, and the whole city was given up to plunder. (Id. xxvii. 12, 15, 16; Plut. *Fab.* 21—23.) Livy praises the magnanimity of Fabius in not carrying off the statues and other works of art in which Tarentum abounded (Liv. xxvii. 16; Plut. *Fab.* 23); but it is certain that he transferred from thence to Rome a celebrated statue of Hercules by Lysippus, which long continued to adorn the Capitol. (Strab. vi. p. 278; Plin. xxxiv. 7. s. 18.) The vast quantity of gold and silver which fell into the hands of the victors sufficiently bears out the accounts of the great wealth of the Tarentines. (Liv. *l. c.*)

Tarentum had already suffered severely on its capture by Hannibal, and there can be no doubt that it sustained a still severer blow when it was retaken by Fabius. (Strab. vi. p. 278.) It was at first proposed to degrade it to a condition similar to that of Capua, but this was opposed by Fabius, and the decision was postponed till after the war. (Liv. xxvii. 25.) What the final resolution of the senate was, we know not; but Tarentum is alluded to at a subsequent period, as still retaining its position of an allied city, "urbs foederata." (Liv. xxxv. 16.) It is certain that it still remained the chief place in this part of Italy, and was the customary residence of the praetor or other magistrate who was sent to the S. of Italy. Thus we find in B. c. 185, L. Postumius sent thither to carry on investigations into the conspiracies that had arisen out of the Bacchanalian rites, as well as among the slave population. (Liv. xxxix. 29, 41.) But it is nevertheless clear that it was (in common with the other Greek cities of this part of Italy) fallen into a state of great decay; and hence, in B. c. 123, among the colonies sent out by C. Gracchus, was one to Tarentum, which appears to have assumed the title of Colonia Neptunia. (Vell. Pat. i. 15; Plin. iii. 11. s. 16; see Mommsen, in *Berichte der Sächsischen Gesellschaft* for 1849, pp. 49—51.) According to Strabo this colony became a flourishing one, and the

city enjoyed considerable prosperity in his day. But it was greatly fallen from its former splendour, and only occupied the site of the ancient citadel, with a small part of the adjoining isthmus. (Strab. vi. p. 278.) It was, however, one of the few cities which still retained the Greek language and manners, in common with Neapolis and Rhegium. (*Ib.* p. 253.) The salubrity of its climate, as well as the fertility of its territory, and, above all, the importance of its port, preserved it from the complete decay into which so many of the cities of Magna Graecia fell under the Roman government. It is repeatedly mentioned during the civil wars between Octavian, Antony, and Sex. Pompeius as a naval station of importance; and it was there that in B. c. 36 a fresh arrangement was come to between Octavian and Antony, which we find alluded to by Tacitus as the "Tarentinum foedus." (Appian, *B. C.* ii. 40, v. 50, 80, 84, 93 —99; Tac. *Ann.* i. 10.)

Even under the Empire Tarentum continued to be one of the chief seaports of Italy, though in some measure eclipsed by the growing importance of Brundusium. (Tac. *Ann.* xiv. 12, *Hist.* ii. 83.) An additional colony of veterans was sent there under Nero, but with little effect, most of them having soon again dispersed. (Tac. *Ann.* xiv. 27.) No subsequent mention of Tarentum is found in history until after the fall of the Western Empire, but it then appears as a considerable town, and bears an important part in the Gothic Wars on account of its strength as a fortress, and the excellence of its port. (Procop. *B. G.* iii. 23, 27, 37, iv. 26, 34.) It was taken by Belisarius, but retaken by Totila in A. D. 549, and continued in the hands of the Goths till it was finally wrested from them by Narses. From that time it continued subject to the Byzantine Empire till A. D. 661, when it was taken by the Lombard Romoaldus, duke of Beneventum (P. Diac. vi. 1); and afterwards fell successively into the hands of the Saracens and the Greek emperors. The latter did not finally lose their hold of it till it was taken by Robert Guiscard in 1063. It has ever since formed part of the kingdom of Naples. The modern city of Tarentum has a population of about 20,000 souls; it is the see of an archbishop, and still ranks as the most important city in this part of Italy. But it is confined to the space occupied by the ancient citadel, the extremity of the peninsula or promontory between the two ports: this is now an island, the low isthmus which connected it with the mainland having been cut through by king Ferdinand I., for the purpose of strengthening its fortifications.

Scarcely any remains are now extant of the celebrated and opulent city of Tarentum. "Never (says Swinburne) was a place more completely swept off the face of the earth." Some slight remains of an amphitheatre (of course of Roman date) are visible outside the walls of the modern city; while within it the convent of the Celestines is built on the foundations of an ancient temple. Even the extent of the ancient city can be very imperfectly determined. A few slight vestiges of the ancient walls are, however, visible near an old church which bears the name of *Sta Maria di Murveta*, about 2 miles from the gates of the modern city; and there is no doubt that the walls extended from thence, on the one side to the *Mare Piccolo*, on the other side to the outer sea. The general form of the city was thus triangular, having the citadel at the apex, which is now joined to the opposite shore by a bridge of seven arches. This was already the case in Strabo's time, though no mention of it is found at the time of the siege by Hannibal.

The general form and arrangement of the city cannot be better described than they are by Strabo. He says: "While the whole of the rest of the Tarentine gulf is destitute of ports, there is here a very large and fair port, closed at the entrance by a large bridge, and not less than 100 stadia in circumference. [This is beneath the truth: the *Mare Piccolo* is more than 16 miles (128 stadia) in circuit.] On the side towards the inner recess of the port it forms an isthmus with the exterior sea, so that the city lies upon a peninsula; and the neck of the isthmus is so low that ships can easily be drawn over the land from one side to the other. The whole city also lies low, but rises a little towards the citadel. The ancient wall comprises a circuit of great extent; but now the greater part of the space adjoining the isthmus is deserted, and only that part still subsists which adjoins the mouth of the port, where also the Acropolis is situated. The portion still remaining is such as to make up a considerable city. It has a splendid Gymnasium, and a good-sized Agora, in which stands the bronze colossal statue of Jupiter, the largest in existence next to that at Rhodes. In the interval between the Agora and the mouth of the port is the Acropolis, which retains only a few remnants of the splendid monuments with which it was adorned in ancient times. For the greater part were either destroyed by the Carthaginians when they took the city, or carried off as booty by the Romans, when they made themselves masters of it by assault. Among these is the colossal bronze statue of Hercules in the Capitol, a work of Lysippus, which was dedicated there as an offering by Fabius Maximus, who took the city." (Strab. vi. p. 278.)

In the absence of all extant remains there is very little to be added to the above description. But Polybius, in his detailed narrative of the capture of the city by Hannibal, supplies us with some local names and details. The principal gate on the E. side of the city, in the outer line of walls, seems to have been that called the Temenid Gate (αἱ πύλαι Τημένιδαι, Pol. viii. 30); outside of which was a mound or tumulus called the tomb of Hyacinthus, whose worship had obviously been brought from Sparta. A broad street called the Batheia, or Low Street, led apparently from this gate towards the interior of the city. This from its name may be conjectured to have lain close to the port and the water's edge, while another broad street led from thence to the Agora. (*Ib.* 31.) Another street called the Soteira (Σωτεῖρα) was apparently on the opposite side of the city from the Batheia, and must therefore have adjoined the outer sea. (*Ib.* 36.) Immediately adjoining the Agora was the Museum (Μουσεῖον), a public building which seems to have served for festivals and public banquets, rather than for any purposes connected with its name. (*Ib.* 27, 29.) There is nothing to indicate the site of the theatre, alluded to by Polybius on the same occasion, except that it was decidedly *within* the city, which was not always the case. Strabo does not notice it, but it must have been a building of large size, so as to be adapted for the general assemblies of the people, which were generally held in it, as was the case at Syracuse and in other Greek cities. This is particularly mentioned on several occasions; it was there that the Roman ambassadors

received the insult which finally led to the ruin of the city. (Flor. i. 18. § 3; Val. Max. ii. 2. § 5; Appian, *Samnit.* 7.)

Livy inaccurately describes the citadel as standing on lofty cliffs ("praealtis rupibus," xxv. 11): the peninsula on which it stood rises indeed (as observed by Strabo) a little above the rest of the city, and it is composed of a rocky soil; but the whole site is low, and no part of it rises to any considerable elevation. The hills also that surround the *Mare Piccolo* are of trifling height, and slope very gradually to its banks, as well as to the shore of the outer sea. There can be no doubt that the port of Tarentum, properly so called, was the inlet now called the *Mare Piccolo* or "Little Sea," but outside this the sea on the S. side of the city forms a bay or roadstead, which affords good shelter to shipping, being partially sheltered from the SW. by the two small islands of *S. Pietro* and *S. Paolo*, apparently the same which were known in ancient times as the CHOERADES. (Thuc. vii. 33.)

Tarentum was celebrated in ancient times for the salubrity of its climate and the fertility of its territory. Its advantages in both respects are extolled by Horace in a well-known ode (*Carm.* ii. 6), who says that its honey was equal to that of Hymettus, and its olives to those of Venafrum. Varro also praised its honey as the best in Italy (*ap. Macrob. Sat.* ii. 12). Its oil and wines enjoyed a nearly equal reputation; the choicest quality of the latter seems to have been that produced at Aulon (Hor. *l. c.*; Martial, xiii. 125; Plin. xiv. 6. s. 8), a valley in the neighbourhood, on the slope of a hill still called *Monte Melone* [AULON]. But the choicest production of the neighbourhood of Tarentum was its wool, which appears to have enjoyed an acknowledged supremacy over that of all parts of Italy. (Plin. xxix. 2. s. 9; Martial, *l. c.*; Varr. *R. R.* ii. 2. § 18; Strab. vi. p. 284; Colum. vii. 2. § 3.) Nor was this owing solely to natural advantages, as we learn that the Tarentines bestowed the greatest care upon the preservation and improvement of the breed of sheep. (Colum. vii. 4.) Tarentum was noted likewise for its breed of horses, which supplied the famous Tarentine cavalry, which was long noted among the Greeks. Their territory abounded also in various kinds of fruits of the choicest quality, especially pears, figs, and chestnuts, and though not as fertile in corn as the western shores of the Tarentine gulf, was nevertheless well adapted to its cultivation. At the same time its shores produced abundance of shell-fish of all descriptions, which formed in ancient times a favourite article of diet. Even at the present day the inhabitants of *Taranto* subsist to a great extent upon the shell-fish produced in the *Mare Piccolo* in a profusion almost incredible. Its Pectens or scallops enjoyed a special reputation with the Roman epicures. (Hor. *Sat.* ii. 4. 34.) But by far the most valuable production of this class was the Murex, which furnished the celebrated purple dye. The Tarentine purple was considered second only to the Tyrian, and for a long time was the most valuable known to the Romans. (Corn. Nep. *ap. Plin.* ix. 39. s. 63.) Even in the time of Augustus it continued to enjoy a high reputation. (Hor. *Ep.* ii. 1, 207.) So extensive were the manufactories of this dye at Tarentum that considerable mounds are still visible on the shore of the *Mare Piccolo*, composed wholly of broken shells of this species. (Swinburne's *Travels*, vol. i. p. 239.)

The climate of Tarentum, though justly praised by Horace for its mildness, was generally reckoned soft and enervating, and was considered as in some degree the cause of the luxurious and effeminate habits ascribed to the inhabitants ("molle Tarentum," Hor. *Sat.* ii. 4. 34, "imbelle Tarentum," Id. *Ep.* i. 7. 45.) It is probable that this charge, as in many other cases, was greatly exaggerated; but there is no reason to doubt that the Tarentines, like almost all the other Greeks who became a manufacturing and commercial people, indulged in a degree of luxury far exceeding that of the ruder nations of Central Italy. The wealth and opulence to which they attained in the 4th century B. C. naturally tended to aggravate these evils, and the Tarentines are represented as at the time of the arrival of Pyrrhus enfeebled and degraded by luxurious indulgences, and devoted almost exclusively to the pursuit of pleasure. To such an excess was this carried that we are told the number of their annual festivals exceeded that of the days of the year. (Theopomp. *ap. Athen.* iv. p. 166; Clearch. *ap. Athen.* xii. p. 522; Strab. vi. p. 280; Aelian, *V. H.* xii. 30.) Juvenal alludes to their love of feasting and pleasure when he calls it "coronatum ac petulans madidumque Tarentum" (vi. 297). It is certain, as already observed, that they were not incapable of war: they furnished a considerable body of troops to the army of Pyrrhus; and in the sea-fight with the Roman fleet off the entrance of the harbour, during the Second Punic War, they displayed both courage and skill in naval combat. (Liv. xxvi. 39.) In the time of their greatest power, according to Strabo, they could send into the field an army of 30,000 foot and 3000 horse, besides a body of 1000 select cavalry called Hipparchs. (Strab. vi. p. 280.) The Tarentine light cavalry was indeed celebrated throughout Greece, so that they gave name to a particular description of cavalry, which are mentioned under the name of Tarentines (Ταραντῖνοι), in the armies of Alexander the Great and his successors; and the appellation continued in use down to the period of the Roman Empire. (Arrian, *Anab.*; Id. *Tact.* 4; Pol. iv. 77, xi. 12; Liv. xxxv. 28; Aelian, *Tact.* 2. p. 14; Suidas, *s. v.* Ταραντῖνοι.) It is probable, however, that these may have been always recruited in great part among the neighbouring Messapians and Sallentines, who also excelled as light horsemen.

With their habits of luxury the Tarentines undoubtedly combined the refinements of the arts usually associated with it, and were diligent cultivators of the fine arts. The great variety and beauty of their coins is, even at the present day, a sufficient proof of this, while the extraordinary numbers of them which are still found in the S. of Italy attest the wealth of the city. Ancient writers also speak of the numbers of pictures, statues, and other works of art with which the city was adorned, and of which a considerable number were transported to Rome. (Flor. i. 18; Strab. vi. p. 278; Liv. xxvii. 16.) Among these the most remarkable were the colossal statue of Jupiter, mentioned by Strabo (*l. c.*), and which was apparently still standing in the Agora in his time; the bronze statue of Hercules by Lysippus already noticed; and a statue of Victory, which was also carried to Rome, where it became one of the chief ornaments of the Curia Julia. (Dion Cass. li. 22.) Nor were the Tarentines deficient in the cultivation of literature. In addition to Archytas, the Pythagorean philosopher, celebrated for his

mathematical attainments and discoveries, who long held at Tarentum a place somewhat similar to that of Pericles at Athens (Diog. Laert. viii. 4; Suid. *s. v.* Ἀρχύτας; Athen. xii. p. 545), Aristoxenus, the celebrated musician and disciple of Aristotle, was a native of Tarentum; as well as Rhinthon, the dramatic poet, who became the founder of a new species of burlesque drama which was subsequently cultivated by Sopater and other authors. (Suid. *s. v.* Ῥίνθων.) It was from Tarentum also that the Romans received the first rudiments of the regular drama, Livius Andronicus, their earliest dramatic poet, having been a Greek of Tarentum, who was taken prisoner when the city fell into their hands. (Cic. *Brut.* 18.)

Polybius tells us that Tarentum retained many traces of its Lacedaemonian origin in local names and customs, which still subsisted in his day. Such was the tomb of Hyacinthus already mentioned (Pol. viii. 30): the river Galaesus also was called by them the Eurotas (*Ib.* 35), though the native name ultimately prevailed. Another custom which he notices as peculiar was that of burying their dead within the walls of the city, so that a considerable space within the walls was occupied by a necropolis. (*Ib.* 30.) This custom he ascribes to an oracle, but it may have arisen (as was the case at Agrigentum and Syracuse) from the increase of the city having led to the original necropolis being inclosed within the walls.

The name of Tarentum (Taras) was supposed to be derived from a river of the name of TARAS (Τάρας), which is noticed by several ancient writers. (Steph. B. *s. v.* Τάρας; Paus. x. 10. § 8.) This is commonly identified with a deep, but sluggish, stream, which flows into the sea about 4 miles W. of the entrance of the harbour of Tarentum, and is still called *Tara*, though corrupted by the peasantry into *Fiume di Terra.* (Romanelli, vol. i. p. 281; Swinburne, vol. i. p. 271.) The more celebrated stream of the GALAESUS flowed into the *Mare Piccola* or harbour of Tarentum on its N. shore: it is commonly identified with the small stream called *Le Citrezze*, an old church near which still retains the name of *Sta Maria di Galeso.* [GALAESUS.] Another locality in the immediate neighbourhood of Tarentum, the name of which is associated with that of the city by Horace, is AULON, a hill or ridge celebrated for the excellence of its wines. This is identified by local topographers, though on very slight grounds, with a sloping ridge on the seashore about 8 miles SE. of Tarentum, a part of which bears the name of *Monte Melone*, supposed to be a corruption of *Aulone* [AULON]. A more obscure name, which is repeatedly mentioned in connection with Tarentum, is that of SATURIUM (Σατύριον). From the introduction of this name in the oracle alleged to have been given to Phalanthus (Strab. vi. p. 279), it seems probable that it was an old native name, but it is not clear that there ever was a town or even village of the name. It is more probable that it was that of a tract or district in the neighbourhood of Tarentum. Stephanus of Byzantium distinctly calls it χώρα πλησίον Τάραντος (*s. v.* Σατύριον); and the authority of Servius, who calls it a *city* (civitas) near Tarentum, is not worth much in comparison. There was certainly no *city* of the name in historical times. Virgil applies the epithet "Saturium" (as an adjective) to Tarentum itself (*Georg.* ii. 197; Serv. *ad loc.*: many commentators, however, consider "saturi" from "satur"

to be the true reading), and Horace speaks of " Sa-
tureianus cabellus" as equivalent to Tarentine.
(Sat. i. 6. 59.) The memory of the locality is preserved by a watch-tower on the coast, about seven
miles SE. of Tarentum, which is still called *Torre
di Saturo* (Romanelli, vol. i. p. 294; Zannoni *Carta
del Regno di Napoli*).

(Concerning the history and ancient institutions
of Tarentum, see Heyne, *Opuscula*, vol. ii. pp.
217—232; and Lorentz, *de Civitate Veterum Ta-
rentinorum*, 4to. Lips. 1833. The present state
and localities are described by Swinburne, vol. i. pp.
225—270; Keppel Craven, *Southern Tour*, pp.
174—190; and Romanelli, vol. i. pp. 282—289; but
from the absence of existing remains, the antiquities
of Tarentum have scarcely received as much attention as they deserve.)　　　　　　　　[E. H. B.]

COINS OF TARENTUM.

TARE'TICA (Ταρετική, or Τορετική ἄκρα, Ptol.
v. 9. § 9), a headland of Asiatic Sarmatia in the
Pontus Euxinus, and in the neighbourhood of the
modern town of *Sudaski*.　　　　　　　　[T. H. D.]

TARGINES (*Tacino*), a small river of Bruttium,
mentioned only by Pliny (iii. 10. s. 15) among the
rivers on the E. coast of that peninsula. It is probably the stream now called the *Tacino*, which rises
in the mountains of the *Sila*, and falls into the *Gulf
of Squillace* (Sinus Scylaceus).　　　　[E. H. B.]

TARI'CHEAE or TARICHAEAE (Ταριχέαι,
Strab. xvi. p. 764; Joseph. *Vita*, 32, 54, 73;
Ταριχαῖαι, Joseph. *B. J.* iii. 10. § 1, et alibi;
Ταριχέα, Steph. B. s. v.; Taricheae, Suet. *Tit.* 4;
Tarichea, Plin. v. 15: *Eth.* Ταριχεάτης), a city in
Lower Galilee situated below a mountain at the
southern end of the lake of Tiberias, and 30 stadia
from the city of Tiberias itself. (Joseph. *B. J.* iii.
10. § 1.) It derived its name from its extensive
manufactories for salting fish. (Strab. *l. c.*) It was
strongly fortified by Josephus, who made it his head-
quarters in the Jewish war; and it was taken by
Titus with great slaughter. (Joseph. *B. J.* iii. 10.
§§ 1—6.) Its ruins stand upon a rising ground,
called *Kerak*, where at present there is a Muslim
village, at the southern end of the lake. The river
Jordan, in issuing from the lake, runs at first south
for about a furlong, and then turns west for half a
mile. The rising ground *Kerak* stands in the
space between the river and lake, and was a place
easily defensible according to the ancient mode of
warfare. (Robinson, *Bibl. Res.* vol. ii. p. 387, 2nd
ed.)

TARNE (Τάρνη), is mentioned by Homer (*Il.* v.
44), and after him by Strabo (ix. p. 413), as a town
in Asia Minor: but Pliny (v. 30) knows Tarne only as
a fountain of Mount Tmolus in Lydia.　　[L. S.]

TARNIS (*Tarn*), a river in Gallia, a branch of
the *Garonne*. It rises near *Mount Losère*, in the
Cévennes, and flows in the upper part of its course
in a deep valley. After running near 200 miles it
joins the *Garonne* below *Moissac*. Sidonius Apollinaris (24, 44) calls it " citus Tarnis." [LESORA.]
Ausonius (*Mosella*, v. 465) speaks of the gold found
in the bed of the Tarn:—

" Et auriferum postponet Gallia Tarnem."
　　　　　　　　　　　　　　　　　　[G. L.]

TARODU'NUM (Ταρόδουνον), a town in the
south-west of Germany, between Mons Abnoba and
the Rhenus. (Ptol. ii. 11. § 30.) It is universally
identified with *Mark Zarten* near *Freiburg* in the
Breisgau, which, down to the 8th century, bore the
name of Zarduna, a name which is formed from
Tarodunum in the same way in which *Zabern* is
formed from Taberne.　　　　　　　　　[L. S.]

TARO'NA (Ταρῶνα, Ptol. iii. 6. § 5), a place in
the interior of the Chersonesus Taurica. [T. H. D.]

TARPHE (Τάρφη: *Eth.* Ταρφαῖος), a town of the
Locri Epicnemidii, mentioned by Homer (*Il.* ii. 533).
It was situated upon a height in a fertile and woody
country, and was said to have derived its name from
the thickets in which it stood. In the time of
Strabo it had changed its name into that of Pharygae
(Φαρύγαι), and was said to have received a colony
from Argos. It contained a temple of Hera Phary-
gaea. It is probably the modern *Pundonitza*. (Strab.
ix. p. 426; Groskurd and Kramer, *ad loc.*; Steph.
B. s. v.; Leake, *Northern Greece*, vol. iv. p. 179.)

TARPODIZUS (*It. Ant.* p. 230; *It. Hier.* p.
569; in Geog. Rav. iv. 6, Tarpodizon), a town in
the E. of Thrace, on the road from Byzantium to
Anchialus. According to Kiepert, its site answers
to that of the modern *Bujuk-Derbend*; according to
Reichard, to that of *Kodje-Tarla*; according to
Lapie, to that of *Develet-Agatch*. But in some
maps it is placed nearly due south of Sadame, and
on or near the river Artiscus: if this is correct,
Tarpodizus must have been in the neighbourhood of
Erekli.　　　　　　　　　　　　　　　　[J. R.]

TARQUI'NII (Ταρκυνία, Strab. Dionys.; Ταρ-
κουῖναι, Ptol: *Eth.* Tarquiniensis: *Corneto*), one of
the most ancient and important cities of Etruria,
situated about 4 miles from the Tyrrhenian sea,
and 14 miles from Centumcellae (*Civita Vecchia*),
near the left bank of the river Marta. All ancient
writers represent it as one of the most ancient of the
cities of Etruria; indeed according to a tradition
generally prevalent it was the parent or metropolis
of the twelve cities which composed the Etruscan
League, in the same manner as Alba was represented
as the metropolis of the Latin League. Its own
reputed founder was Tarchon, who according to some
accounts was the son, according to others the brother,
of the Lydian Tyrrhenus; while both versions represented him as subsequently founding all the other
cities of the league. (Strab. v. p. 219; Serv. *ad Aen.*
x. 179, 198.) The same superiority of Tarquinii
may be considered as implied in the legends that
represented the divine being Tages, from whom all
the sacred traditions and religious rites of the
Etruscans were considered to emanate, as springing
out of the soil at Tarquinii (Cic. *de Div.* ii. 23;
Censorin. *de Die Nat.* 4; Joan. Lyd. *de Ost.* 3.)
Indeed it seems certain that there was a close connec-

tion considered as subsisting between this Tages and Tarchon himself, the eponymous hero of Tarquinii. (Müller, *Etrusker*, vol. i. p. 73.) It is impossible here to discuss the historical bearings of these traditions, which seem to point to Tarquinii as the point from whence the power and civilisation of the Etruscans emanated as from a centre, while on the other hand there is another body of traditions which seems to represent that people as gradually extending themselves *from the north*, and Cortona as the first centre and stronghold of their power. [ETRURIA, Vol. I. p. 859.] A somewhat different version is given by Justin, who states that Tarquinii was founded by the Thessalians, probably meaning the Pelasgians from Thessaly, to whom Hellanicus ascribed the colonisation of Etruria in general. (Justin, xx. 1; Hellanic. *ap Dionys*. i. 28.)

But whatever value may be attached to these traditions, they may at least be admitted as proving the reputed high antiquity and early power of Tarquinii as compared with the other cities of Southern Etruria: and this is confirmed by the important position it appears to have held, when its name first appears in connection with the Roman history. Cicero calls it "urbem Etruriae florentissimam" at the time when Demaratus, the father of Tarquinius Priscus, was said to have established himself there. (Cic. *de Rep*. ii. 19.) It is remarkable indeed that the story which derived the origin of the Roman king Tarquinius from Corinth represented his father Demaratus as bringing with him Greek artists, and thus appears to ascribe the first origin or introduction of the arts into Etruria, as well as its religious institutions, to Tarquinii. (Plin. xxxv. 12. s. 43; Strab. v. p. 220.) It is unnecessary to repeat here the well-known story of the emigration of an Etruscan Lucumo from Tarquinii to Rome, where he became king under the name of Lucius Tarquinius. (Liv. i. 34; Dionys. iii. 46—48; Cic. *de Rep*. ii. 19, 20; Strab. v. p. 219.) The connection with Tarquinii is rejected by Niebuhr, as a mere etymological fable, but it is not easy to say on what grounds. The name of Tarquinius, as that of a gens or family, as well as that of the city, is undoubtedly Etruscan; the native form being "Tarcnas:" and the strong infusion of Etruscan-influence into the Roman state before the close of the regal period is a fact which cannot reasonably be questioned. It is remarkable also that the Roman traditions represented the Tarquinians as joining with the Veientes in the first attempt to restore the exiled Tarquin, B.C. 509, though from this time forth we do not again hear of their name for more than a century. (Liv. ii. 6, 7; Dionys. v. 14.) The story of the emigration of the elder Tarquin to Rome, as well as that of his father Demaratus from Corinth, may fairly be deemed unworthy of belief *in its present form;* but it is probable that in both cases there was a historical foundation for the fiction.

After the war already mentioned, in the first year of the Republic, no subsequent mention of Tarquinii occurs in Roman history till B.C. 398, when the Tarquinians took up arms, and ravaged the Roman territories, while their army was engaged in the siege of Veii. They were, however, intercepted on their march home, and all their booty taken from them. (Liv. v. 16.) Livy distinctly calls them on this occasion "novi hostes:" but from this time they took an active part in the wars of the Etruscans with Rome. The conquest of Veii in

B.C. 396, had indeed the effect of bringing the Romans into immediate collision with the cities which lay next beyond it, and among these Tarquinii and Volsinii seem to have taken the lead. Already in B.C. 389, we find the Tarquinians joining with the other cities of Southern Etruria in an attempt to recover Sutrium: the next year their territory was in its turn invaded by the Romans, who took the towns of Cortuosa and Contenebra, both places otherwise unknown, but which appear to have been dependencies of Tarquinii. (Liv. vi. 3, 4.) From this time we hear no more of them till B.C. 358, when the Tarquinians, having ravaged the Roman territories, the consul C. Fabius marched against them, but was defeated in a pitched battle, and 307 of the prisoners taken on the occasion were put to death in the Forum of Tarquinii, as a sacrifice to the Etruscan deities. (Liv. vii. 12, 15.) Shortly after, we find the Tarquinians and Faliscans again in arms, and in the first battle which occurred between them and the Romans they are said to have obtained the victory by putting forward their priests with flaming torches and serpents in their hands, to strike terror into their assailants. (Liv. vii. 16, 17). But the Etruscans were defeated in their turn by C. Marcius Rutilus, who was named dictator to oppose them: and two years later (B.C. 354) the Romans took a sanguinary revenge for the massacre of their prisoners, by putting to death, in the Forum at Rome, 358 of the captives taken from the Tarquinians, chiefly of noble birth. (*Ib.* 19.) But the spirit of the Tarquinians was not yet subdued, and with the support of the Faliscans and Caerites, who now for a short time took part against Rome, they continued the war till B.C. 351, when they sued for peace, and obtained a truce for forty years. (*Ib.* 19—22.)

This truce appears to have been faithfully observed, for we hear nothing more of hostilities with Tarquinii till B.C. 311, when the Tarquinians appear to have united with the other confederate cities of Etruria in attacking the Roman colony of Sutrium. They were, however, defeated by the Roman consul Aemilius Barbula, and again the next year by Q. Fabius, who followed up his victory by passing the Ciminian forest, and carrying his arms for the first time into Northern Etruria. There is no doubt that the Tarquinians, though not mentioned by name, bore a part in this contest as well as in the great battle at the Vadimonian lake in the following year (B.C. 309), as we find them soon after making their submission to Rome, and purchasing the favour of the consul Decius by sending him supplies of corn. (Liv. ix, 32, 35—39, 41.) They now obtained a fresh truce for forty years (*Ib.* 41); and from this time we hear no more of them as an independent nation. Whether this long truce, like the last, was faithfully observed, or the Tarquinians once more joined in the final struggles of the Etruscans for independence, we know not; but it is certain that they passed, in common with the other chief cities of Etruria, gradually into the condition of dependent allies of Rome, which they retained till the Social War (B.C. 90), when they as well as all the other Etruscans obtained the full Roman franchise. (Appian, *B. C.* i. 49.) The only mention of Tarquinii that occurs in this interval is during the Second Punic War, when the citizens came forward to furnish the expedition of Scipio with sail-cloth for his fleet. (Liv. xxviii. 45.) According to the Liber Coloniarum a body of colonists was sent thither by

Gracchus; but though it is there termed "Colonia Tarquinii," it is certain that it did not retain the title of a colony; Cicero distinctly speaks of it as a "municipium," and the Tarquinienses are ranked by Pliny among the ordinary municipal towns of Etruria. Its municipal rank is further confirmed by inscriptions recently discovered on the site. (*Lib. Col.* p. 219; Cic. *pro Caec.* 4; Plin. iii. 5. s. 8; Ptol. iii. 1. § 50; *Inscr. in Bullett. d. Inst. Arch.* 1830, pp. 198, 199.) From these last records we learn that it was apparently still a flourishing town in the time of the Antonines, and its name is still found in the Tabula near three centuries later (*Tab. Peut.*) It is probable, therefore, that it survived the fall of the Western Empire, and owed its final desolation to the Saracens.

At the present day the site of the ancient city is wholly desolate and uninhabited; but on a hill about a mile and a half distant stands the modern city of *Corneto*, the origin of which does not date further back than the eighth or ninth century. It was probably peopled with the surviving inhabitants of Tarquinii. The site of the latter is clearly marked: it occupied, like most Etruscan cities, the level summit of a hill, bounded on all sides by steep, though not precipitous escarpments, and occupying a space of about a mile and a half in length, by half a mile in its greatest breadth. It is still known as *Turchina*, though called also the *Piano di Civita.* Hardly any ruins are now visible, but the outline of the walls may be traced around the brow of the hill, partly by foundations still *in situ*, partly by fallen blocks. The highest point of the hill (furthest to the W. and nearest to the *Marta*) seems to have served as the Arx or citadel, and here the foundations of some buildings, supposed to be temples, may be traced. Numerous fragments of buildings of Roman date are also visible, and though insignificant in themselves, prove, in conjunction with the inscriptions already mentioned, that the site was well inhabited in Roman times. (Dennis's *Etruria*, vol. i. pp. 371—385.)

But by far the most interesting remains now visible at Tarquinii are those of the Necropolis, which occupied almost the whole of the hill opposite to the city, at the W. extremity of which stands the modern town of *Corneto.* The whole surface of the hill (says Dennis) "is rugged with tumuli, or what have once been such," whence the appellation by which it is now known of *Montarozzi.* Vast numbers of these tombs have been opened, and have yielded a rich harvest of vases, ornaments, and other objects of antiquity. But the most important are those of which the walls are adorned with paintings, which possess a double interest, both as works of art and from the light they throw upon Etruscan manners. It may indeed be asserted in general of the paintings in these tombs that while the influence of Greek *art* is unquestionably to be traced in their design and execution, the subjects represented and the manners they exhibit are purely Etruscan. The number of these painted tombs found at Tarquinii greatly exceeds those which have been discovered on the site of any other city of Etruria; but they still bear only a very small proportion to the whole number of tombs opened, so that it is evident this mode of decoration was far from general. The paintings in many of those first opened, which are figured in the works of Micali and Inghirami, have since been allowed to fall into decay, and have in great measure disappeared. Detailed descriptions of all the most interesting of them, as well as those more recently discovered, will be found in Dennis's Etruria (vol. i. pp. 281—364.)   [E. H. B.]

TARRACI'NA (Ταρράκινα, Strab.; Ταρράκηνα, Steph. B.: Eth. Ταρρακινῖτης, Tarracinensis: *Terracina*), a city of Latium in the more extended sense of that name, but originally a Volscian city, situated on the Tyrrhenian sea, about 10 miles from Circeii, and at the extremity of the Pomptine Marshes. It was also known by the name of ANXUR, and we learn from Pliny and Livy that this was its Volscian name, while Tarracina was that by which it was known to the Latins and Romans. (Plin. iii. 5. s. 9; Ennius ap. Fest. *s. v. Anxur*; Liv. iv. 59.) The name of Anxur is frequently used at a much later period by the Roman poets (Hor. *Sat.* i. 5. 26; Lucan. iii. 84; Martial, v. 1. 6, &c.), obviously because Tarracina could not be introduced in verse; but Cicero, Livy, and all other prose writers, where they are speaking of the Roman town, universally call it Tarracina. The Greek derivation of the latter name suggested by Strabo (v. p. 233), who says it was originally called Τραχινή, from its rugged situation, is probably a mere etymological fancy. The first mention of it in history occurs in the treaty between Rome and Carthage concluded in B. C. 509, in which the people of Tarracina are mentioned in common with those of Circeii, Antium, &c., among the subjects or dependencies of Rome. (Pol. iii. 22.) It seems certain therefore that Tarracina, as well as Circeii, was included in the Roman dominions before the fall of the monarchy. But it is clear that it must have again fallen under the dominion of the Volscians, probably not long after this period. It was certainly in the possession of that people, when its name next appears in history, in B. C. 406. On that occasion it was attacked by N. Fabius Ambustus, and taken by a sudden assault, while the attention of the Volscian armies was drawn off in another direction. (Liv. iv. 57; Diod. xiv. 16.) Livy speaks of it as having at this time enjoyed a long period of power and prosperity, and still possessing great wealth, which was plundered by the Roman armies. A few years afterwards (B. C. 402) it again fell into the hands of the Volscians, through the negligence of the Roman garrison (Liv. v. 8). In B. C. 400, it was again besieged by the Roman arms under Valerius Potitus, and though his first assaults were repulsed, and he was compelled to have recourse to a blockade, it soon after fell into his hands. (*Ib.* 12, 13.) An attempt of the Volscians to recover it in 397 proved unsuccessful (*Ib.* 16), and from this time the city continued subject to Rome. Nearly 70 years later, after the conquest of Privernum, it was thought advisable to secure Tarracina with a Roman colony, which was established there in B. C. 329. (Liv. viii. 21; Vell. Pat. i. 14.)

The condition of Tarracina as a Roman colony is not quite clear, for Velleius notices it as if it had been one of the "Coloniae Latinae," while Livy certainly does not consider it as such, for he omits its name among the thirty Latin colonies in the time of the Second Punic War, while he on two occasions mentions it in connection with the other maritime colonies, Antium, Minturnae, &c. In common with these, the citizens of Tarracina in vain contended for exemption from military service during the Second Punic War, and at a later period claimed exemption from naval service also. (Liv. xxvii. 38, xxxvi. 3.) There can, therefore, be no doubt that Tarracina was a "colonia maritima civium," and it seems to have early become one of the most important of the maritime towns subject to Rome. Its position on the Appian Way, which here first touched on the sea (Strab. v. p. 233; Hor. *Sat.* i. 5. 26), doubtless contributed to its prosperity; and an artificial port seems to have in some degree supplied the want of a natural harbour. (Liv. xxvii. 4.) In a military point of view also its position was important, as commanding the passage of the Appian Way, and the narrow defile of Lautulae, which was situated a short distance from the city on the side of Fundi. (Liv. xxii. 15.) [LAU-TULAE.]

Under the Roman Republic Tarracina seems to have continued to be a considerable and flourishing town. Cicero repeatedly notices it as one of the customary halting-places on the Appian Way, and for the same reason it is mentioned by Horace on his journey to Brundusium. (Cic. *de Orat.* ii. 59, *ad Fam.* vii. 23, *ad Att.* vii. 5; Hor. *Sat.* i. 5. 26; Appian, *B. C.* iii. 12; Val. Max. viii. 1. § 13.) At the outbreak of the civil war between Caesar and Pompey, Tarracina was occupied by the latter with three cohorts under the praetor Rutilius Lupus, but they abandoned their post, when Pompey withdrew to Brundusium. (Caes. *B. C.* i. 24; Cic. *ad Att.* viii. 11, B.) Again, during the civil war between Vespasian and Vitellius, Tarracina was evidently regarded as a place of importance in a military point of view, and was occupied by the partisans of Vespasian, but was wrested from them by L. Vitellius just before the death of his brother. (Tac. *Hist.* iii. 57, 76. 77.) It was at Tarracina also that the funeral convoy of Germanicus was met by his cousin Drusus and the chief personages of Rome. (Id. *Ann.* iii. 2.) The neighbourhood seems to have been a favourite site for villas under the Roman Empire: among others the Emperor Domitian had a villa there (Martial. v. 1. 6); and it was at another villa near the town, on the road to Fundi, that the emperor Galba was born. (Suet. *Galb.* 4.) In addition to the other natural advantages of the situation, there existed mineral springs in the neighbourhood, which seem to have been much frequented. (Martial, v. 1. 6, x. 51. 8.) The important position of Tarracina doubtless prevented its falling into decay as long as the Western Empire subsisted. Its name is found in the Itineraries as a " civitas " (*Itin. Ant.* p. 187; *Itin. Hier.* p. 611), and even after the fall of the Roman dominion it appears as a fortress of importance during the Gothic wars. (Procop. *B. G.* ii. 2, 4, &c.)

The position of Tarracina at the extremity of the Pomptine Marshes, just where a projecting ridge of the Volscian mountains runs down to the sea, and separates the marshy tract on the W. from a similar but much smaller tract on the E., which extends from thence towards Fundi, must in all ages have rendered it a place of importance. The ancient city stood on the hill above the marshes. Horace distinctly describes it as standing on lofty rocks, which were conspicuous afar, from their white colour:—

" Impositum saxis late candentibus Anxur "

(Hor. *Sat.* i. 5. 26); and the same circumstance is alluded to by other Latin poets. (Lucan, iii. 84; Sil. Ital. viii. 392.) Livy also describes the original Volscian town as " loco alto situm " (v. 12), though it extended also down the slope of the hill towards the marshes (" urbs prona in paludes," iv. 59.) At a later period it not only spread itself down the hill, but occupied a considerable level at the foot of it

(as the modern city still does), in the neighbourhood of the port. This last must always have been in great part artificial. but the existence of a regular port at Tarracina is noticed by Livy as early as B. C. 210. (Liv. xxvii. 4.) It was subsequently enlarged and reconstructed under the Roman Empire, probably by Trajan, and again restored by Antoninus Pius. (Capit. *Ant. P.* 8.) Its remains are still distinctly visible, and the whole circuit of the ancient basin, surrounded by a massive mole, may be clearly traced, though the greater part of it is now filled with sand. Considerable portions of the ancient walls also still remain, constructed partly in the polygonal style, partly in the more recent style known to the Romans as " opus incertum." Several ancient tombs and ruins of various buildings of Roman date are still extant in the modern city and along the line of the Via Appia. The modern cathedral stands on the site of an ancient temple, of which only the substructions and two columns remain. This is generally called, though on very uncertain authority, a temple of Apollo. The most celebrated of the temples at Tarracina was, however, that of Jupiter, which is noticed by Livy (xxviii. 11, xl. 45), and the especial worship of this deity in the Volscian city under the title of Jupiter Anxurus is alluded to by Virgil (*Aen.* vii. 799). He was represented (as we are told by Servius) as a beautiful youth, and the figure of the deity corresponding to this description is found on a Roman coin of the Vibian family. (Eckhel, vol. v. p. 340.) It is probable that this temple was situated in the highest part of the city, very probably in the ancient citadel, which occupied the summit of a hill above the town, where remains of its walls and substructions are still extant.

Tarracina was distant by the Via Appia 62 miles from Rome, and 18 from the Forum Appii. (*Itin. Ant.* p. 107; *Itin. Hier.* p. 611; Westphal, *Röm. Kamp.* p. 68.) Three miles from the city, at the side of the Via Appia, as well as of the canal which was frequently used by travellers, was the fountain of Feronia, celebrated by Horace, together with the sacred grove attached to it. [FERONIA.] [E.H.B.]

TA'RRACO (Ταρράκων, Ptol. ii. 6. § 17), an ancient city of Spain, probably founded by the Phoenicians, who called it *Tarchon*, which, according to Bochart, means " a citadel." This name was probably derived from its situation on a high rock, between 700 and 800 feet above the sea; whence we find it characterised as " arce potens Tarraco." (Auson. *Clar. Urb.* 9; cf. Mart. x. 104.) It was seated on the river Sulcis, on a bay of the Mare Internum, between the Pyrenees and the river Iberus. (Mela, ii. 6; Plin. iii. 3. s. 4.) Livy xxii. 22) mentions a " portus Tarraconis;" and according to Eratosthenes (ap. Strab. iii. p. 159) it had a naval station or roads (ναύσταθμον); but Artemidorus (ap. Strab. l. c.; Polyb. iii. 76) says with more probability that it had none, and scarcely even an anchoring place; and Strabo himself calls it ἀλίμενος. This answers better to its present condition; for though a mole was constructed in the 15th century with the materials of the ancient amphitheatre, and another subsequently by an Englishman named John Smith, it still affords but little protection for shipping. (Ford's *Handbook of Spain*, p. 222.) Tarraco lay on the main road along the S. coast of Spain. (*Itin. Ant.* pp. 391, 396, 399, 448, 452.) It was fortified and much enlarged by the brothers Publius and Cneius Scipio, who converted it into a fortress and arsenal against the Carthaginians. Subsequently it became the capital of the province named after it, a Roman colony, and "conventus juridicus." (Plin. *l. c.*; Tac. *Ann.* i. 78; Solin. 23, 26; Polyb. x. 34; Liv. xxi. 61; Steph. B. p. 637.) Augustus wintered at Tarraco after his Cantabrian campaign, and bestowed many marks of honour on the city, among which were its honorary titles of "Colonia Victrix Togata" and "Colonia Julia Victrix Tarraconensis." (Grut. *Inscr.* p. 382; Orelli, no. 3127; coins in Eckhel, i. p. 27; Florez, *Med.* ii. p. 579; Mionnet, i. p. 51, *Suppl.* i. p. 104; Sestini, p. 202.) According to Mela (*l. c.*) it was the richest town on that coast, and Strabo (*l. c.*) represents its population as equal to that of Carthago Nova. Its fertile plain and sunny shores are celebrated by Martial and other poets; and its neighbourhood is described as producing good wine and flax. (Mart. x. 104, xiii. 118; Sil. Ital. iii. 369, xv. 177; Plin. xiv. 6. s. 8, xix. 1. s. 2.) There are still many important ancient remains at *Tarragona*, the present name of the city. Part of the bases of large Cyclopean walls near the *Quartel de Pilatos* are thought to be anterior to the Romans. The building just mentioned, now a prison, is said to have been the palace of Augustus. But Tarraco, like most other ancient towns which have continued to be inhabited, has been pulled to pieces by its own citizens for the purpose of obtaining building materials. The amphitheatre near the sea-shore has been used as a quarry, and but few vestiges of it now remain. A circus, 1500 feet long, is now built over it, though portions of it are still to be traced. Throughout the town Latin, and even apparently Phoenician, inscriptions on the stones of the houses proclaim the desecration that has been perpetrated. Two ancient monuments, at some little distance from the town, have, however, fared rather better. The first of these is a magnificent aqueduct, which spans a valley about a mile from the gates. It is 700 feet in length, and the loftiest arches, of which there are two tiers, are 96 feet high. The monument on the NW. of the city, and also about a mile distant, is a Roman sepulchre, vulgarly called the "Tower of the Scipios;" but there is no authority for assuming that they were buried here. (Cf. Ford, *Handbook*, p. 219, seq.; Florez, *Esp. Sagr.* xxix. p. 68, seq.; Miñano, *Diccion.* viii. p. 398.)　　　[T. H. D.]

TARRACONENSIS PROVINCIA (called by the Greeks Ταρρακωνησία, Ptol. ii. 6, viii. 4. § 5, &c.; and Ἰβηρία ἡ περὶ Ταρράκωνα, Dion Cass. liii. 3), at first constituted, as already remarked [Vol. I. p. 1081], the province of Hispania Citerior. It obtained its new appellation in the time of Augustus from its chief city Tarraco, where the Romans had established themselves, and erected the tribunal of a praetor. The Tarraconensis was larger than the other two provinces put together. Its boundaries were, on the E. the Mare Internum; on the N. the Pyrenees, which separated it from Gallia, and further westward the Mare Cantabricum; on the W., as far southward as the Durius, the Atlantic ocean, and below that point the province of Lusitania; and on the S. the province of Lusitania and the province of Baetica, the boundaries of which have been already laid down. (Mela, ii. 6; comp. Strab. iii. p. 166; Plin. iv. 21. s. 35; Marcian, p. 34.) Thus it embraced the modern provinces of *Murcia, Valencia, Catalonia, Arragon, Navarre, Biscay, Asturias, Galli-*

cia, the N. part of *Portugal* as far down as the *Douro*, the N. part of *Leon*, nearly all the *Castiles*, and part of *Andalusia*. The nature of its climate and productions may be gathered from what has been already said [HISPANIA, Vol. I. p. 1086.] A summary of the different tribes. according to the various authorities that have treated upon the subject, has also been given in the same article [p. 1083], as well as the particulars respecting its government and administration [p. 1081.]　　　[T. H. D.]

TARRAGA (Τάρραγα, Ptol. ii. 6. § 67), called by the Geogr. Rav. (iv. 43) TERRACHA, a town of the Vascones in Hispania Tarraconensis (Plin. iii. 3. s. 4). Now *Larraga*. (Cf. Cellarius, *Orb. Ant.* i. p. 91.)　　　[T. H. D.]

TARRHA (Τάρρα, Pausan. ix. 16. § 13; Theophrast. *H. P.* ii. 2; Steph. B. *s. v.*; Orac. *ap. Euseb. P. E.* p. 133, ed. Stephan.; Τάρρος, *Stadiasm.* §§ 329, 330), a town on the SW. coast of Crete between Phoenice and Poecilassus, one of the earliest sites of the Apollo-worship, and the native country of the writer Lucillus. For Tarba (Τάρβα, Ptol. iii. 17. § 3) Meursius proposes to read Tarrha. There can be little or no doubt that its position should be fixed on the SW. coast of the island, at the very entrance of the glen of *Hághia Ruméli*, where the bold hanging mountains hem in the rocky bed of the river. (Pashley, *Travels*, vol. ii. p. 270). The Florentine traveller Buondelmonti, who visited Crete A. D. 1415, describes considerable remains of a temple and other buildings as existing on the site of the ancient city (*ap. Cornelius, Creta Sacra*, vol. i. p. 85).　　　[E. B. J.]

TARSATICA (Ταρσάτικα, Ptol. ii. 17. § 2), called in the *Itin. Ant.* p. 273, Tharsaticum, a place in Illyricum, on the road from Aquileia to Siscia through Liburnia, now *Tersat*, to the E. of *Fiume*. (Cf. Pliny, iii. 21. s. 25; *Tab. Peut.*)　　　[T. H. D.]

TARSHISH. [TARTESSUS.]

TA'RSIA (Ταρσία, Arrian, *Ind.* c. 37), a promontory on the coast of Carmania, visited by the fleet of Nearchus. The conjecture of Vincent (*Voyage of Nearchus*, i. p. 362) that it is represented by the present *Rás-al-Djerd* appears well founded. It is perhaps the same as the Themisteas Promontorium of Pliny (vi. 25) as suggested by Müller. (*Geog. Graec.* i. p. 360.)　　　[V.]

TA'RSIUM (Τάρσιον, Ptol. ii. 16. § 8), a place in Pannonia Inferior, now *Tersacz*.　　　[T. H. D.]

TA'RSIUS (Τάρσιος), a river of Mysia in the neighbourhood of the town of Zeleia, which had its source in Mount Temnus, and flowed in a north-eastern direction through the lake of Miletopolis, and, issuing from it, continued its north-eastern course till it joined the Macestus. (Strab. xiii. p. 587.) Strabo indeed states that the river flowed in numerous windings not far from Zeleia; but he can scarcely mean any other river than the one now bearing the name *Balikesri*, and which the Turks still call *Tarza*. Hamilton (*Researches*, vol. ii. p. 106) identifies it with the *Kara Su* or *Kara Dere Su*, which flows into *Lake Maniyas*.　　　[L. S.]

TARSU'RAS (Ταρσούρας, Arrian, *Per. P. Eux.* p. 10), a river of Colchis falling into the sea between the Singames and the Hippus. (Cf. Plin. vi. 4. s. 4.) It is probably the same river called Tassiaros in the *Tab. Peut.*　　　[T. H. D.]

TARSUS (Ταρσός: *Eth.* Ταρσηνός or Ταρσεύς), sometimes also called Tarsi (Ταρσοί), Tersus Τερσός), Tharsus (Θαρσός), or Ταρσὸς πρὸς τῷ Κύδνῳ, to distinguish it from other places of the same name was the chief city of Cilicia, and one of the most important places in all Asia Minor. It was situated in a most fertile and productive plain, on both sides of the river Cydnus, which, at a distance of 70 stadia from the city, flowed into a lagoon called Rhegma or Rhegmi. This lagoon formed the port of Tarsus, and was connected with the sea. The situation of the city was most favourable, for the river was navigable up to Tarsus, and several of the most important roads of Cilicia met there. Its foundation is ascribed to Sardanapalus, the Assyrian king, and the very name of the city seems to indicate its Semitic origin. But the Greeks claimed the honour of having colonised the place at a very early period; and, among the many stories related by them about the colonisation of Tarsus, the one adopted by Strabo (xiv. p. 673; comp. Steph. B. s. v.) ascribes the foundation to Argives who with Triptolemus arrived there in search of Io. The first really historical mention of Tarsus occurs in the Anabasis of Xenophon, who describes it as a great and wealthy city, situated in an extensive and fertile plain at the foot of the passes of Mount Taurus leading into Cappadocia and Lycaonia. (Anab. i. 2. § 23, &c.) The city then contained the palace of Syennesis, king of Cilicia, but virtually a satrap of Persia, and an equivocal ally of Cyrus when he marched against his brother Artaxerxes. When Cyrus arrived at Tarsus, the city was for a time given up to plunder, the troops of Cyrus being exasperated at the loss sustained by a detachment of Cilicians in crossing the mountains. Cyrus then concluded a treaty with Syennesis, and remained at Tarsus for 20 days. In the time of Alexander we no longer hear of kings; but a Persian satrap resided at Tarsus, who fled before the young conqueror and left the city, which surrendered to the Macedonians without resistance. Alexander himself was detained there in consequence of a dangerous fever brought on by bathing in the Cydnus. (Arrian, Anab. ii. 4; Curt. iii. 5.) After the time of Alexander, Tarsus with the rest of Cilicia belonged to the empire of the Seleucidae, except during the short period when it was connected with Egypt under the second and third Ptolemy. Pompey delivered Tarsus and Cilicia from the dominion of the eastern despots, by making the country a Roman province. Notwithstanding this, Tarsus in the war between Caesar and Pompey sided with the former, who on this account honoured it with a personal visit, in consequence of which the Tarsians changed the name of their city into Juliopolis. (Cass. B. Alex. 66; Dion Cass. xlvii. 24; Flor. iv. 2.) Cassius afterwards punished the city for this attachment to Caesar by ordering it to be plundered, but M. Antony rewarded it with municipal freedom and exemption from taxes. It is well known how Antony received Cleopatra at Tarsus when that queen sailed up the Cydnus in a magnificent vessel in the disguise of Aphrodite. Augustus subsequently increased the favours previously bestowed upon Tarsus, which on coins is called a "libera civitas." During the first centuries of the empire Tarsus was a place of great importance to the Romans in their campaigns against the Parthians and Persians. The emperor Tacitus, his brother Florian, and Maximinus and Julian died at Tarsus, and Julian was buried in one of its suburbs. It continued to be an opulent town until it fell into the hands of the Saracens. It was, however, taken from them in the second half of the 10th century by the emperor Nicephorus, but was soon after again restored to them, and has remained in

their hands ever since. The town still exists under the name of Tersoos, and though greatly reduced, it is still the chief town of that part of Karamania. Few important remains of antiquity are now to be seen there, but the country around it is as delightful and as productive as ever.

Tarsus was not only a great commercial city, but at the same time a great seat of learning and philosophy, and Strabo (xiv. p. 673, &c.) gives a long list of eminent men in philosophy and literature who added to its lustre; but none of them is more illustrious than the Apostle Paul, who belonged to one of the many Jewish families settled at Tarsus. (Acts, x. 30, xi. 30, xv. 22, 41, xxi. 39; comp. Ptol. v. 8. § 7; Diod. xiv. 20; Hierocl. p. 704; Stadiasm. Mar. M. § 156; Leake, Asia Minor, p. 214; Russegger, Reisen in Asien, i. 1. p. 395, foll., 2. p. 639, foll.)

Another town of the name of Tarsus is said to have existed in Bithynia (Steph. B. s. v.), but nothing is known about it.   [L. S.]

COIN OF TARSUS.

TA'RTARUS (Tartaro), a river of Venetia, near the borders of Gallia Transpadana. It is intermediate between the Athesis (Adige) and the Padus (Po); and its waters are now led aside by artificial canals partly into the one river and partly into the other, so that it may be called indifferently a tributary of either. In ancient times it seems to have had a recognised mouth of its own, though this was even then wholly artificial, so that Pliny calls it the "fossiones Philistinae, quod alii Tartarum vocant." (Plin. iii. 16. s. 20.) In the upper part of its course it formed, as it still does, extensive marshes, of which Caecina, the general of Vitellius, skilfully availed himself to cover his position near Hostilia. (Tac. Hist. iii. 9.) The river is here still called the Tartaro: lower down it assumes the name of Canal Bianco, and after passing the town of Adria, and sending off part of its waters right and left into the Po and Adige, discharges the rest by the channel now known as the Po di Levante. The river Atrianus (Ἀτριανὸς ποταμός), mentioned by Ptolemy (iii. 16. § 20), could be no other than the mouth of the Tartarus, so called from its flowing by the city of Adria; but the channels of these waters have in all ages been changing.   [E. H. B.]

TARTESSUS (Ταρτησσός, Herod. i. 163; Ταρτησσός and Ταρτεσσός, Diodor. Siculus, Frag. lib. xxv.), a district in the south of Spain, lying to the west of the Columns of Hercules. It is now the prevailing opinion among biblical critics that the Tarshish of Scripture indicates certain localities in the south of Spain, and that its name is equivalent to the Tartessus of the Greek and Roman writers. The connection in which the name of Tarshish occurs in the Old Testament with those of other places, points to the most western limits of the world, as known to the Hebrews (Genes. x. 4; 1 Chron. i. 7; Psalms, lxxii. 10; Isaiah, lxvi. 19);

and in like manner the word Tartessus, and its derivative adjectives, are employed by Latin writers as synonymous with the West (Ovid, *Met.* xiv. 416; Sil. Ital. iii. 399; Claud. *Epist.* iii. v. 14). Tarshish appears in Scripture as a celebrated emporium, rich in iron, tin, lead, silver, and other commodities; and the Phoenicians are represented as sailing thither in large ships (*Ezek.* xxvii. 12, xxviii 13; *Jerem.* x. 9). Isaiah speaks of it as one of the finest colonies of Tyre, and describes the Tyrians as bringing its products to their market (xxiii. 1, 6, 10). Among profane writers the antiquity of Tartessus is indicated by the myths connected with it (Strab. iii. p. 149; Justin, xliv. 4). But the name is used by them in a very loose and indefinite way. Sometimes it stands for the whole of Spain, and the Tagus is represented as belonging to it (Rutilius, *Itin.* i. 356; Claud. *in Rufin.* i. 101; Sil. Ital. xiii. 674, &c.). But in general it appears, either as the name of the river Baetis, or of a town situated near its mouth, or thirdly of the country south of the middle and lower course of the Baetis, which, in the time of Strabo, was inhabited by the Turduli. The Baetis is called Tartessus by Stesichorus, quoted by Strabo (iii. p. 148) and by Avienus (*Ora Marit.* i. 224), as well as the town situated between two of its mouths; and Miot (*ad Herod.* iv. 152) is of opinion that the modern town of *S. Lucar de Barameda* stands on its site. The country near the lower course of the Baetis was called Tartessis or Tartesia, either from the river or from the town; and this district, as well as others in Spain, was occupied by Phoenician settlements, which in Strabo's time, and even later, preserved their national customs. (Strab iii. p. 149, xvii. p. 832; Arr. *Exp. Alex.* ii. 16; App. *Hisp.* 2; Const. Porphyrog. *de Them.* i. p. 107, ed. Bonn.) There was a temple of Hercules, the Phoenician Melcarth, at Tartessus, whose worship was also spread amongst the neighbouring Iberians. (Arr. *l.c.*) About the middle of the seventh century B. C. some Samiot sailors were driven thither by stress of weather; and this is the first account we have of the intercourse of the Greeks with this distant Phoenician colony (Herod. iv. 152). About a century later, some Greeks from Phocaea likewise visited it, and formed an alliance with Arganthonius, king of the Tartessians, renowned in antiquity for the great age which he attained. (Herod. i. 163; Strab. iii. p. 151.) These connections and the vast commerce of Tartessus, raised it to a great pitch of prosperity. It traded not only with the mother country, but also with Africa and the distant Cassiterides, and bartered the manufactures of Phoenicia for the productions of these countries (Strab. i. p. 33; Herod. iv. 196; cf. Heeren, *Ideen,* i. 2. §§ 2, 3). Its riches and prosperity had become proverbial, and we find them alluded to in the verses of Anacreon (*ap. Strab.* iii. p. 151). The neighbouring sea (*Fretum Tartessium,* Avien. *Or. Mar.* 64) yielded the lamprey, one of the delicacies of the Roman table (Gell. vii. 16); and on a coin of Tartessus are represented a fish and an ear of grain (Mionnet, *Méd. Ant.* i. p. 26). We are unacquainted with the circumstances which led to the fall of Tartessus; but it may probably have been by the hand of Hamilcar, the Carthaginian general. It must at all events have disappeared at an early period, since Strabo (iii. pp. 148, 151), Pliny (iii. 1, iv. 22, vii. 48), Mela (ii. 6), Sallust (*Hist. Fr.* ii.), and others, confounded it with more recent Phoenician colonies, or took its name to be an ancient appellation of them.			[T. H. D.]

TARUALTAE (Ταρούαλται, Ptol. iv. 6. § 19), a people of Libya Interior.			[T. H. D.]

TARVEDUM. [ORCAS.]

TARUENNA or TARUANNA (Ταρούαννα, Ptol. ii. 9. § 8), a town in North Gallia, and according to Ptolemy an inland town of the Morini. [MORINI.] It is written Teruanna in the Table, where it is marked a capital town, and the modern name is *Térouenne.* It is mentioned in several Roman routes. The distance between Gesoriacum (*Boulogne*) in the Antonine Itin. and Taruenna does not agree with the true distance; nor does the distance in the same Itin. between Taruenna and Castellum (*Cassel*) agree with the actual measurement. In both instances we must assume that there is an error in the numerals of the Itin. D'Anville says that the Roman road appears to exist between *Térouenne* and the commencement of the *Boulonois,* or district of *Boulogne,* near *Devre,* where it passes by a place called *La Chaussée.* There are also said to be traces of a Roman road from Itius Portus (*Wissant*) to *Térouenne.*			[G. L.]

TARVESEDE (*It. Ant.* p. 279) or TARVESSEDO, according to the Peuting. Table, was a place in Rhaetia on the road from Mediolanum leading by Comum to Augusta Vindelicorum. Its exact site is now unknown, though it seems to have been situated near *Torre di Vercella.*			[L. S.]

TARVI'SIUM (Ταρβίσιον: Eth. Tarvisianus: *Treviso*), a town of Northern Italy, in the province of Venetia, situated on the left bank of the river Silis (*Sele*), about 15 miles from its mouth. The name is not mentioned by any of the geographers, though Pliny speaks of the Silis as flowing "ex montibus Tarvisanis," in a manner that would lead us to suppose it to have been a municipal town (Plin. iii. 18. s. 22), and this is confirmed by an inscription given by Muratori (*Inscr.* p. 328). After the fall of the Western Empire it appears as a considerable city, and is repeatedly noticed by Procopius during the Gothic Wars, as well as by Cassiodorus and Paulus Diaconus. (Cassiod. *Var.* x. 27; Procop. *B. G.* ii. 29, iii. 1, 2; P. Diac. *Hist. Lang.* ii. 12, iv. 3, v. 28, &c.) It retained this consideration throughout the middle ages, and is still a flourishing city under the name of *Treviso.* [E. H. B.]

TARUS (*Taro*), a river of Gallia Cispadana, one of the southern tributaries of the Padus, which crosses the Aemilian Way between 5 and 6 miles west of Parma. (Plin. iii. 16. s. 20; Geogr. Rav. iv. 36.)			[E. H. B.]

TARUSATES are mentioned by Caesar (*B. G.* iii. 27) among the Aquitanian peoples who submitted to P. Crassus: "Vocates, Tarusates, Elusates." After Crassus had defeated the Sotiates [SOTIATES] he entered the territory of the Vocates, and Tarusates, a statement which gives some indication of their position. Pliny (iv. 19) places the Tarusates between the Succasses and Basaboeates; but the MSS. reading in Pliny seems to be Latusates, which probably should be Tarusates. There appears to be no variation in the name in the MSS. of Caesar. D'Anville conjectures that the name Tarusates is preserved in *Tursan,* or *Teursan,* a part of the diocese of *Aire.* The town of *Aire* is on the Aturis (*Adour*).			[G. L.]

TARUSCONIENSES, as the name stands in Harduin's edition of Pliny (iv. 4), but the reading is doubtful. Harduin found Taruscunonienses in five MSS., and there are other variations. Besides *Tarascon* on the *Rhone,* there is *Tarascon* on the

Arriège, a branch of the *Garonne*. This Tarascon is in the *Pays de Foix*, and in a valley at the foot of the Pyrenees, which circumstance seems to indicate more probably the position of a small tribe or people than that of *Tarascon* on the *Rhône*. This *Tarascon* on the *Arriège* is mentioned in middle age documents under the name of Castrum Tarasco. Pliny's Tarasconienses, or whatever may be the true name, are enumerated among the Oppida Latina of Narbonensis. [G. L.]

TASCIACA, a town in Gallia, placed by the Table between Avaricum (*Bourges*) and Caesarodunum (*Tours*). The first station from Avaricum is Gabris, supposed to be *Chabris* on the *Cher*, and the next is Tasciaca, supposed to be *Tezée*, also on the *Cher*. But the number xxiiii. placed in the Table at the name of Tasciaca, which number should represent the distance from *Chabris* to *Tezée*, is nearly the distance between *Tezée* and *Tours*, and accordingly there is some error here. The Table gives no distance between Tasciaca and Caesarodunum. (D'Anville, *Notice;* Ukert, *Gallien.*) [G. L.]

TASCONI is the name of a Gallic people in the Narbonensis, mentioned by Pliny (iii. 4), as the name is read in five MSS. There is a small river *Tescon* or *Tescou*, which flows into the *Tarn*, near *Montauban*. D'Anville quotes a life of S. Théodard, archbishop of *Narbonne*, which speaks of this river as called Tasco by the people of that part. and as the limit between the territories of the Tolosani, or people of *Toulouse*, and the Caturcenses, or people of *Cahors*. This is a valuable passage, for it shows how far north the Narbonensis, to which the territory of *Toulouse* belonged, extended in this part of its frontier; and it also confirms the conjecture about the northern limits of the Ruteni Provinciales [RUTENI], who were also included in the Narbonensis. [G. L.]

TASTA. [DATIL.]

TATTA LACUS (ἡ Τάττα), a large salt lake on the frontiers between Lycaonia and Galatia; it had originally belonged to Phrygia, but was afterwards annexed to Lycaonia. Its waters were so impregnated with brine, that any substance dipped into it, was immediately incrusted with a thick coat of salt; even birds flying near the surface had their wings moistened with the saline particles, so as to become incapable of rising into the air, and to be easily caught. (Strab. xii. p. 568; Plin. xxxi. 41, 45; Dioscorid. v. 126.) Stephanus Byz. (*s. v.* Βοτίειον) speaks of a salt lake in Phrygia, which he calls Attaea (Ἄτταια), near which there was a town called Botieum, and which is probably the same as Lake Tatta. The Turks now call the lake *Tusla*, and it still provides all the surrounding country with salt. (Leake, *Asia Minor*, p. 70.) [L. S.]

TAUA. [TAUM.]

TAUA (Ταύα, Steph. B. *s. v.*; Ταούα, Ptol. iv. 5. § 50; Taba, *Itin. Ant.* p. 153), a town in Lower Aegypt, situated on the left bank of the Canopic arm of the Nile, S. of the city of Naucratis. It was the capital of the small Phthemphuthic Nome (Plin. v. 9. s. 9), and is supposed to be represented by the present *Thaouah*. (D'Anville, *Mémoire sur l'Egypte*, vol. i. p. 82.) [W. B. D.]

TAUCHI'RA or TEUCHI'RA (Ταύχειρα, Herod. iv. 171, et alii; Τεύχειρα, Hierocl. p. 732; Plin. v. 5. s. 5, &c.), a town on the coast of Cyrenaica, founded by Cyrene. It lay 200 stadia W. of Ptolemais. Under the Ptolemies it obtained the name

of Arsinoë. (Strab. xvii. p. 836; Mela, i. 8; Plin. *l. c.*) At a later period it became a Roman colony (*Tab. Peut.*), and was fortified by Justinian. (Procop. *de Aed.* vi. 3.) Tauchira was particularly noted for the worship of Cybele, in honour of whom an annual festival was celebrated. (Synes. *Ep.* 3.) It is the same town erroneously written Τάριχα by Diodorus (xviii. 20). It is still called *Tochira*. (Cf. Della Cella, *Viagg.* p. 198; Pacho, *Voyage*, p. 184.) [T. H. D.]

TA'VIUM (Ταούιον, Ταύιον) or TAVIA, a town in the central part of eastern Galatia, at some distance from the eastern bank of the river Halys, was the chief town of the Galatian tribe of the Trocmi, and a place of considerable commercial importance, being the point at which five or six of the great roads met. (Plin. v. 42; Strab. xii. p. 567; Ptol. v. 4. § 9; Steph. B. *s. v.* Ἄγκυρα; Hierocl. p. 696; *It. Ant.* pp. 201, 203.) It contained a temple with a colossal bronze statue of Zeus. Leake (*Asia Minor*, p. 311) is strongly inclined to believe that *Tshorum* occupies the site of ancient Tavium; but Hamilton (*Researches*, i. p. 379, &c.) and most other geographers, with much more probability, regard the ruins of *Boghas Kieui*, 6 leagues to the north-west of *Jazgat* or *Juzghat*, as the remains of Tavium. They are situated on the slope of lofty and steep rocks of limestone, some of which are adorned with sculptures in relief. There are also the foundations of an immense building, which are believed to be remains of the temple of Zeus. (Comp. Hamilton in the *Journal of the Roy. Geogr. Soc.* vol. vii. p. 74, foll.; Cramer, *Asia Minor*, ii. p. 98.) [L. S.]

TAULA'NTII (Ταυλάντιοι, Ptol. iii. 13. § 3), a people of Roman Illyria, in the neighbourhood of Epidamnus and Dyrrachium. In ancient times they were a powerful tribe, possessing several cities, and governed by their own kings, but subsequently they were reduced to subjection by the kings of Illyria, and at the time when the Romans waged war with Teuta they had sunk into insignificance. (Cf. Thucyd. i. 24; Arrian, *Anab.* i. 5; Mela, ii. 3; Liv. xlv. 26; Plin. iii. 22. s. 26.) Aristotle relates that they had a method of preparing mead from honey. (*Mir. Ausc.* t. ii. p. 716.) [T. H. D.]

TAUM, TAUS, or TAVA (Ταούα είσχυσις, Ptol. ii. 3. § 5), a bay on the E. coast of Britannia Barbara. (Tac. *Agr.* 22.) Now *Frith of Tay*. [T. H. D.]

TAUM (AD), a place in the SE. of Britannia Romana, in the territory of the Iceni (*Tab. Peut.*). Probably *Yarmouth*. [T. H. D.]

TAUNUS MONS, a range of hills in western Germany, beginning near the river Nicer (*Neckar*), and running northward till they reach the point where the Moenus (*Main*) joins the Rhenus. (Pomp. Mela, iii. 3; Tac. *Ann.* i. 56, xii. 28.) This range of hills still bears its ancient name, though it is sometimes simply called the *Höhe*, that is, the Height, Taunus being probably the Celtic word Dun or Daun, which signifies a height. In various places along this range of hills Roman inscriptions have been found, in which Cives Taunenses are mentioned, from which it may be inferred that there once existed a town of the name of Taunus. (Orelli, *Inscript.* nos. 181, 4981, 4982; Wilhelm, *Germanien*, p. 44.) [L. S.]

TAURA'NIA, a town of Campania, mentioned only by Pliny (iii. 5. s. 9) as having in his time entirely disappeared, like Stabiae. He affords no clue to its position. The name of Taurania (Ταυρανία) is found also in the older editions of Stephanus of

Byzantium; but it appears that the true reading is Taurasia. (Steph. B. *s. v.* ed. Mein.)　[E. H. B.]

TAURANI'TIUM, a district of Armenia Major lying N. of Tigranocerta, in the direction of Artaxata. (Tac. *Ann.* xiv. 24; Cf. Moses Chor. i. 5; Ritter, *Erdkunde,* x. p. 650, sq.)　[T. H. D.]

TAURA'SIA (*Taurasi*), an ancient city of Samnium, in the country of the Hirpini situated on the right bank of the river Calor, about 16 miles above its junction with the Tamarus. The name of the city is known only from the inscription on the tomb of L. Scipio Barbatus, which records it among the cities of Samnium taken by him during the Third Samnite War. (Orell. *Inscr.* 550.) It was probably taken by assault, and suffered severely, for no subsequent mention of the town occurs in history: but its territory ("ager, qui Taurasinorum fuerat"), which was doubtless confiscated at the same time, is mentioned long afterwards, as a part of the "ager publicus populi Romani," on which the Apuan Ligurians who had been removed from their own abodes were established by order of the senate. (Liv. xl. 38.) These Ligurians appear to have been settled in the plain on the banks of the Tamarus near its junction with the Calor; but there can be little doubt that the modern village of *Taurasi,* though 16 miles further S., retains the name, and marks (approximately at least) the site of the ancient Taurasia.

Several modern writers identify these Taurasini Campi with the Arusini Campi near Beneventum, which were the scene of the defeat of Pyrrhus by M'. Curius Dentatus (Flor. i. 18; Oros. iv. 2), and the suggestion is probable enough, though unsupported by any authority. [BENEVENTUM.]　[E. H. B.]

TAURAUNITES. [BAGRAUDANENE.]

TAURE'SIUM (Ταυρήσιον, Procop. *de Aed.* iv. 1. p. 266), a place in Moesia Superior, near Scupi or Justiniana Prima. It was situated in the Haemus, not far from the borders, and was the birthplace of the emperor Justinian. (Cf. Gibbon, vol. v. p. 79, ed. Smith.)　[T. H. D.]

TAURI (Ταῦροι, Strab. vii. p. 308), the inhabitants of the Chersonesus Taurica, or modern *Crimea.* They were probably the remains of the Cimmerians, who were driven out of the Chersonese by the Scythians. (Herod. iv. 11, 12; Heeren, *Ideen,* i. 2. p. 271; Mannert, iv. p. 278.) They seem to have been divided into several tribes: but the two main divisions of them were the nomad Tauri and the agricultural. (Strab. vii. p. 311.) The former possessed the northern part of the country, and lived on meat, mare's milk, and cheese prepared from it. The agricultural Tauri were somewhat more civilised; yet altogether they were a rude and savage people, delighting in war and plunder, and particularly addicted to piracy. (Herod. iv. 103; Strab. vii. p. 308; Mela, ii. 1; Tac. *Ann.* xii. 17.) Nevertheless, in early times at least, they appear to have been united under a monarchical government (Herod. iv. 119). Their religion was particularly gloomy and horrible, consisting of human sacrifices to a virgin goddess, who, according to Ammianus Marcellinus (xxii. 8. s. 34), was named Oreiloche, though the Greeks regarded her as identical with their Artemis, and called her Tauropolos. (Soph. *Aj.* 172; Eur. *Iph. Taur.* 1457; Diod. iv. 44; Ach. Tat. viii. 2; Strab. xiii. 535; Böckh, *Inscr.* ii. p. 89.) These victims consisted of shipwrecked persons, or Greeks that fell into their hands. After killing them, they stuck their heads upon poles, or,

according to Ammianus (*l. c.*), affixed them to the wall of the temple, whilst they cast down the bodies from the rock on which the temple stood. (Herod. iv. 103; Ov. *ex Pont.* iii. 2. 45, seq., *Trist.* iv. 4. 63.) According to a tradition among the Tauri themselves, this goddess was Iphigenia, the daughter of Agamemnon (Herod. *l. c.*) They had also a custom of cutting off the heads of prisoners of war, and setting them on poles above the chimneys of their houses, which usage they regarded as a protection of their dwellings (*Ib*). If the king died, all his dearest friends were buried with him. On the decease of a friend of the king's, he either cut off the whole or part of the deceased person's ear, according to his dignity. (Nic. Damasc. p. 160, Orell.)　　　　　　　　　　[T. H. D.]

TAURIA'NUM (*Traviano*), a town on the W. coast of Bruttium, near the mouth of the river Metaurus (*Marro*). Its name is mentioned by Mela, who places it between Scylla and Metaurum. It was probably, therefore, situated to the S. of the river, while the town of Metaurum was on its N. bank. Subsequently all trace of the latter disappears; but the name of Tauriana is still found in the Tabula, which places it 23 miles S. of Vibo Valentia. (Mel. ii. 4. § 8; *Tab. Peut.*) It became the see of a bishop in the later ages of the Roman empire, and retained that dignity down to the time of Gregory VII., when the town had fallen into complete decay. Its ruins, however, still exist, and the site is said to retain the name of *Traviano.* (Holsten. *Not. ad Cluver.* p. 299; Romanelli, vol. i. p. 70.)

There can be no doubt that the "Tauroentum oppidum" of Pliny (iii. 5. s. 10), which he mentions immediately after the "Metaurus amnis," is the same place that is called by Mela Taurianum. [E. H. B.]

TAU'RICA CHERSONE'SUS (ἡ Ταυρικὴ Χερσόνησος, Ptol. iii. Arg. 2, &c.), a peninsula stretching into the Pontus Euxinus from Sarmatia, or the country of the nomad Scythians, with which it is connected by a narrow isthmus, anciently called Taphrus, or Taphrae, now the isthmus of *Perecop.* The peninsula also bore the name of Chersonesus Scythica, and was sometimes styled simply Taurica. (Plin. iv. 12. s. 26; Scylax, i. p. 29, Huds.) It is now called the *Crimea,* from the once famous city of *Eski-Krim;* but since its incorporation with the Russian empire, the name of *Taurica* has also been again applied to it.

The isthmus which connects the peninsula with Sarmatia is so slender, being in some parts scarcely 40 stadia or 5 miles across (Strab. vii. p. 308; Clarke, *Trav.* ii. p. 314, 4th ed. 1816), as to make it probable that in a very remote period Taurica was an island. (Plin. *l. c.*; cf. Pallas, *Voyages,* &c., ii. p. 2, Fr. Transl. 4to.) The ancients compared it with the Peloponnesus, both as to size and shape (Strab. vii. p. 310; cf. Herod. iv. 99; and this comparison is sufficiently happy, except that Taurica throws out another smaller peninsula on its E. side, the Bosporan peninsula, or peninsula of *Kertsch,* which helps to form the S. boundary, or coast, of the Palus Maeotis. The Chersonese is about 200 miles across in a direct line from *Cape Tarchan,* its extreme W. point, to the *Straits of Kertsch,* and 125 miles from N. to S., from *Perecop* to *Cape Kikineis.* It contains an area of about 10,050 square miles. Nearly three-fourths of Taurica consist of flat plains little elevated above the sea; the remainder towards the S. is moun-

4 B 3

tainous. The NW. portion of the low country, or that which would lie to the W. of a line drawn from the isthmus to the mouth of the river *Alma*, consists of a sandy soil interspersed with salt lakes, an evidence that it was at one time covered by the sea (Pallas, *Ib.* p. 605, &c.); but the E. and S. part has a fertile mould. The mountain chain (Taurici Montes) begins to rise towards the centre of the peninsula, gently at first on the N., but increasing in height as the chain approaches the sea, into which it sinks steeply and abruptly. Hence the coast at this part presents huge cliffs and precipices, and the sea is so deep that the lead often finds no bottom at the distance of a mile or two from the shore. From these mountains, which extend from Symbolon, or *Balaclava*, on the W., to Theodosia, or *Caffa*, on the E., many bold promontories are projected into the sea, enclosing between them deep and warm valleys open to the S., and sheltered from the N. wind, where the olive and vine flourish, the apricot and almond ripen, and the laurel creeps among the dark and frowning cliffs. The most remarkable mountains of this chain are that anciently called the Cimmerium at the N. extremity, and the Trapezus at the S. (Strab. vii. p. 309.) The former, which is said to have derived its name from the Cimmerians, once dominant in the Bosporus, is now called *Aghirmisch-Daghi*. It lies nearly in the centre of the peninsula, to the NW. of the ancient Theodosia, and near the town of *Eski-Krim*, or *Old Crim*. Some writers, however, identify Cimmerium with *Mount Opouk*, on the S. coast of the peninsula of *Kertsch*. (Köhler, *Mém. de l'Acad. de St. Petersb.* 1824, p. 649, seq. ; Dubois de Montperreux, *Voyages, &c.* v. p. 253, seq.) But Trapezus is by far the highest mountain of Taurica. *Kohl* estimates its height at 5000 German feet (*Reisen in Südrussland*, i. p. 204); other authorities make it rather less, or 4740 feet. (Neumann, *Die Hellenen im Scythenlande*, p. 448.) According to Mr. Seymour, it is 5125 English feet high. (*Russia on the Black Sea*, p. 146.) Its form justifies its ancient name, and is said to resemble that of the *Table Mountain* at the *Cape of Good Hope* (Kohl, *Ib.*). A good idea of it may be obtained from the vignette in Pallas (ii. p. 196). As it stands somewhat isolated from the rest of the chain, it presents a very striking and remarkable object, especially from the sea. At present it is called *Tchatyr-Dagh*, or the *Tent Mountain*. The other mountains seldom exceed 1200 feet. Their geological structure presents many striking deviations from the usual arrangement, especially in the absence of granite. These anomalies are fully described by Pallas in his second volume of travels. That part of Taurica which lay to the E. of them was called the Rugged, or Rocky, Chersonesus (τρηκέη, Herod. *l. c.*) It is in these mountains that the rivers which water the peninsula have their sources, none of which, however, are considerable. They flow principally from the northern side, from which they descend in picturesque cascades. Only two are mentioned by the ancients, the Thapsis and the Istrianus. At present the most fertile districts of Taurica are the calcareous valleys among the mountains, which, though often covered with only a thin layer of mould, produce excellent wheat. The nature of the country, however, does not now correspond with the descriptions of the ancients. Strabo (*l. c.*) praises its fertility in producing corn, especially in that part which lies between Panticapaeum (*Kertsch*) and Theodosia (*Caffa*), which at present is a desolate and monotonous steppe. But this may probably be accounted for by the physical and political revolutions which the country has undergone. Taurica yielded a large tribute of wheat to Mithridates Eupator, King of Bosporus. That sovereign took much interest in promoting the cultivation of the country, especially by the planting of trees; but all his care to rear the laurel and the myrtle in the neighbourhood of Panticapaeum is said to have been vain, though other trees grew there which required a mild temperature. (Plin. xvi. s. 59.) Wine was produced in abundance, as at the present day, and the custom mentioned by Strabo (p. 307), of covering the vines with earth during the winter, is still observed, though Pallas considers it unnecessary (*Voyages, &c.* ii. p. 444.)

The interest connected with the ancient history of the Tauric Chersonese is chiefly derived from the maritime settlements of the Greeks, and our attention is thus principally directed to the coasts. An account of the barbarous people who inhabited the peninsula at the time when these settlements were made is given in a separate article [TAURI]. Its coasts, like those of the Euxine in general, were early visited by the Milesians, who planted some flourishing colonies upon it. Besides these we find a Dorian colony established near the site of the present *Sebastopol*; and, if we may believe Aeschines (*contra Ctesiph.* p. 141, sq.), the Athenians once possessed the town of Nymphaeon on the Cimmerian Bosporus, which, according to him, was betrayed to the Bosporan kings by Gylon, the maternal grandfather of Demosthenes (Cf. Crateros in Harpocration, *s. v.* Νύμφαιον.) The interior of the peninsula was but little known to the ancients, and we shall therefore best explain their connection with it by taking a survey of the coasts.

We shall begin on the NW. side, after the bay of Carcina or Tamyraca, which has been already described [CARCINA; TAMYRACA]. Fram this bay the peninsula stretches to its most westerly point, *Cape Tarchan*, which presents some high land ; but to the S. of *Tarchan* the coast sinks to a dead level as far as the river *Alma*, to the S. of which it again begins to rise in high cliffs. All the W. coast, however, presents no place of note in ancient history till we come to its extreme southern point, where a bald plateau of hills runs in a westerly direction into the sea. On the E. this tract is divided from the rest of the peninsula by a deep and broad valley, into which it falls by steep declivities. The harbour of *Sebastopol* (or *Roads of Aktiar*) on the N., which bites into the land for about 4 miles in a SE. direction, and that of *Balaclava* on the S. coast of the peninsula, which runs up towards the N., form an isthmus having a breadth, according to Strabo (p. 308), of 40 stadia, or 5 miles. This measurement is confirmed by Clarke (*Trav.* ii. p. 219), who, however, seems only to have been guided by his eye ; for in reality it is rather more, or about 6 miles. The S. coast of the little peninsula formed by this isthmus presents several promontories and small bays, with cliffs of from 500 to 700 feet in height.

So barren a spot presented no attractions to the Milesians, the chief colonisers of the Euxine ; but a more hardy race of emigrants, from the Dorian city of Heracleia in Pontus, found a new home upon it, and founded there the town of Chersonesus (Strab. *l. c.*). We learn from Pliny (iv. 12. s. 26) that it was at first called Megarice, apparently from the circumstance that Megara was the mother city of the Pontic Heracleots. From these settlers the little peninsula we have just described obtained the name of the CHERSONESUS HERACLEOTICA, or Heracleotic Chersonese, sometimes also called "the small Chersonesus" (ἡ μικρά, Strab. l. c.), by way of distinction from the great, or Tauric, peninsula.

The original city of Chersonesus seems to have been founded at the westernmost point of the peninsula, close to the present *Cape Fanary*. The date and occasion of its foundation are not ascertained; but Neumann conjectures that it may have been built about the middle of the fifth century B. C. (*Die Hellenen, &c.* p. 383). Considerable remains of the ancient city were visible so late as the end of the last century (Clarke, *Trav.* ii. pp. 292, seq.; Pallas, ii. pp. 70, seq); but every trace of them had vanished when Murawiew Apostol visited the spot (*Reise durch Taurien*, p. 62). They were destroyed by a certain Lieut. Kruse, who used the stones for building and converted the ground into a vineyard (Dubois de Montperreux, *Voyages, &c.* vi. p. 133). The ancient Chersonesus, however, had fallen into decay before the time of Strabo; but the new town was flourishing and appears from the ruins to have been seated on the W. side of what is now the Quarantine Harbour of *Sebastopol* (Neumann, p. 392). The place was much damaged towards the end of the fourteenth century by Olgierd, sovereign of Lithuania, since which time it has been gradually falling into ruins (Karamsin, *Russ. Gesch.* v. 13. Germ. tr.). The Turks carried away many of its sculptures and columns to adorn Constantinople. Nevertheless, the town, although almost entirely deserted, remained for three centuries in so perfect a state that a plan might have been drawn of it at the time when it came into the possession of the Russians; but its ruin was soon completed by its new masters, who blew up the walls and destroyed the graves and temples. (Clarke, ii. p. 207.) Pliny (iv. 12. s. 26) gives the circumference of its walls at 5 miles; but their outline could still be traced in 1820, and according to Dubois de Montperreux (vi. 138), was only about a quarter of that size. It is probable that Pliny may have confounded the town walls with the wall or rampart which extended across the isthmus, which, as we have already seen, Strabo describes as being 40 stadia, or 5 miles, broad. The same writer speaks of it in another place (p. 312) as being fortified with a wall. This wall ran from Ctenus, at the E. extremity of the harbour of *Sebastopol* to Symbolon (*Balaclava*) on the S. coast, and appears to have been made by the Bosporan kings as a defence against the Scythians. An account of its remaining vestiges is given by Clarke (ii. p. 285, seq.; cf. Seymour, p. 149.). The whole enclosure was anciently covered with gardens and villas, and the foundations of houses and of the boundary walls of fields and gardens may still be traced, as well as many remains of the town on the promontory between *Quarantine Bay* and *Streletska Bay*. Vestiges of the principal street show it to have been 20 feet broad. The town wall on the land side was near 2 miles long, built of limestone, and 5 or 6 feet thick, with 3 towers (Seymour, p. 150). Many antiquities and coins have been found in the ruins of Chersonesus. In the neighbourhood are graves of the most simple kind, hewn in the rock. They are easy of access, and present in this respect a remarkable contrast to those at Panticapaeum; but, from this cause, nothing but bones have been

found in them, whilst those at Panticapaeum have yielded valuable antiquities. According to Clarke (ii. 201, 210), the town of Eupatorium stood close to Chersonesus, though others have identified it with *Inkerman*. About the latter place, the ancient Ctenus, the rock is pierced all over with the subterranean dwellings of the ancient Tauri. On the top are the ruins of the castle built by Diophantes, general of Mithridates, to defend the Chersonese against the Tauro-Scythians. These caverns or crypts are now rapidly falling in. (Seymour, p. 140.) Similar caves are found in other parts of the peninsula.

The Heracleotic Chersonese was noted as the seat of the savage worship of Diana Tauropolis. The natives, or Tauri, themselves had a worship of a similar kind [TAURI]; but whether it was indigenous among them, or whether they borrowed it from the Dorian Heracleots who settled here, cannot be ascertained. The account of the Tauri themselves, that their virgin goddess was Iphigenia, the daughter of Agamemnon, would seem to lead to the latter conclusion; though it is well known that the nations of pagan antiquity readily adopted one another's deities when any similarity was observable in their rights and attributes; and from the account of Herodotus (iv. 103) it might perhaps be inferred that this horrible worship existed among the Tauri before the arrival of the Greeks. Artemis was a peculiarly Dorian deity, and was worshipped in several parts of Greece with human sacrifices. There was a tradition that the town of Chersonesus was founded by Artemis herself. The Heracleot Chersonites erected a famous temple on a headland which took the name of Parthenium from it. Strabo however merely calls the Parthenium "the temple of the virgin, a certain daemon" (p. 308), and does not mention Artemis. Opinions vary as to which is the real promontory of Parthenium. Many seek it at cape *Fanary* or *Chersonese*, which seems too near the town of Chersonesus, as Strabo places the temple at the distance of 100 stadia from the town, though *Fanary* answers to his description in other respects. Clarke and Pallas identify it with the *Aia Barun* or "Sacred Promontory" (Clarke, ii. p. 286, and note), between *Cape Fiolente* and *Balaclava*, which, besides its name, has also a ruin to recommend it; though the latter claim to notice is shared by *C. Fiolente*. Dubois de Montperreux (vi. p. 194, sq.) thinks that the temple may have stood on the spot now occupied by the monastery of St. George; whilst Neumann, again places it on the headland a little to the NW. of *C. Fiolente*. It will be seen that these opinions rest on little more than conjecture. On the coins of the Heracleotic Chersonese the image of Artemis occurs by far the most frequently. She sometimes appears with Apollo, sometimes with Hercules, the patron hero of the mother city, but more generally alone, and always as the goddess of the chase, never as Selene (Von Köhne, in the *Memoirs of the Archaeolog. and Numism. Society of St. Petersburg*, vol. ii. ap. Neumann, p. 420). On other coins a fish is frequently seen; and one has a plough on the obverse, and an ear of corn between two fishes on the reverse (*Ib.*). The bays of the Heracleotic peninsula abound with fish, which formed a great part of the riches of the country.

Of the history of the Heracleotic Chersonesus we know but little, but it may perhaps be inferred from the Inscription of Agasicles that its constitution was republican. It was important enough to take a part in political affairs as an independent city, at least as late as about the middle of the 2nd century B. C., when, like its mother city, Heracleia, it was a party to the alliance against Pharnaces I., king of Pontus, and Mithridates, satrap of Armenia. (Polyb. Frg. lib. xxvi. c. 6, vol. iv. p. 345, sqq., ed. Sweigh.) Soon afterwards, however, we find it struggling with the Taurians and their allies the Sarmatians for existence (Polyaen. *Strat.* viii. c. 56), and it was ultimately compelled to place itself under the protection of Mithridates the Great. Subsequently, however, it regained its independence, through the Romans, and under the name of Cherson or Chorson flourished till a late period of the middle ages, and even overturned the Bosporan kingdom. (Const. Porphyr. *de Adm. Imp.* c. 53.)

Leaving the Heracleotic Chersonese, we will now proceed to describe the remainder of the coast of the Tauric peninsula, which may be soon despatched, as an account of its different cities is given in separate articles. From the haven of Symbolon (*Balaclava*) to Theodosia (*Caffa*) the coast is correctly described by Strabo as craggy, mountainous, and stormy, and marked with many headlands (p. 309). The distance, however, which he assigns to this tract of 1000 stadia, or 125 miles, is rather too small. In both the Periplus of the Euxine the distance given is 1320 stadia, but this must include all the indentures of the coast. The most remarkable promontory in this part was the Criu-metopon, or Ram's Head, which has been variously identified. Some writers have taken it for the promontory of *Laspi*, which is in reality the most southern point of the peninsula. Some again have identified it with *Ai Petri*, and a still greater number with the *Aju-dagh*. But the account given by Arrian and the Anonymous agrees better with *Cape Aithodor*. These writers say that the Criu-metopon lay 220 stadia to the W. of Lampas. (Arrian, *Peripl.* p. 20; Anon. *Peripl.* p. 6.) Now Lampas is undoubtedly the present *Bijuk Lampat*, the distance between which and *Cape Aithodor* agrees very accurately with the preceding measurement. Scymnus indeed (ii. 320, Gail) states the distance at only 120 stadia; but this is evidently an error, as it is too short by half even for *Aju-dagh*. Cape Aithodor is not much N. of *Lapsi*, and from its position might easily have been taken by the Greeks for the southernmost point of the peninsula. (See Neumann, 451, sq.)

From the traces of Greek names, ruins, remains of marble columns, &c., it may be inferred that the whole of this tract was once in the hands of the Greeks. But these relics probably belong to the Byzantine times, since the older geographers mention only four places on this part of the coast, namely, Charax, Lagyra, Lampas, and Athenaeon.

To the E. of Theodosia the coast of the Euxine trends into a large bay, which, approaching the Palus Maeotis on the N., forms an isthmus about 12 miles broad, to the E. of which, as far as the Cimmerian Bosporus, extends the Bosporan peninsula, or that of *Kertsch*, which swells out to double the breadth of the isthmus. The western half of this peninsula is flat; but the eastern portion rises into hills, which surround the bay in which Panticapaeum was situated. It possessed several flourishing maritime towns, as Cazeka and Cimmericum on the S. coast; Nymphaeon Panticapaeum, the Bosporan capital, on the Cimmerian Bosporus; with some others of less note, as Myrmecium, Porthmion, and Hermisium. There

were also probably towns in the interior; but we know the name of only one, namely, Iluratum. (Ptol. iii. 6. § 6.) Beyond the Bosporan straits we have little to guide us but the accounts of Ptolemy. From those straits, the N. coast of the peninsula, which is high and chalky, proceeded in a westerly direction to the modern *Arabat*. Somewhere on this tract lay the Greek colony of Heracleion.

On the E. side of the Tauric peninsula, the *Tongue of Arabat*, a narrow slip of land scarcely raised above the level of the sea, 52 miles long and about half a mile broad, runs along the whole coast, dividing the Maeotis from the Σαπρὰ λίμνη, or *Putrid Sea*. But though Strabo knew that the latter formed the western portion of the Maeotis (p. 208), he is nowhere mentions the *Tongue of Arabat*. The *Putrid Sea* seems to be the Lacus Buges of Pliny (iv. 12. s. 26); but his description is not very intelligible. According to the accounts of recent travellers the *Putrid Sea*, now called the *Shivdshe*, does not appear to deserve its name, as it has neither an unpleasant smell nor are its shores unhealthy (Seymour, p. 33); yet in the times of Clarke and Pallas it seems to have possessed both these offensive qualities. (Clarke, *Trav.* vol. ii. p. 314, note.)

The chief feature in the history of the Chersonesus Taurica, is that of the kingdom of the Bosporus, a sketch of which has been already given. [BOSPORUS CIMMERIUS, Vol. I. p. 421, seq.] After the extinction of that dynasty, towards the end of the 4th century of our era, the peninsula fell into the hands of the Huns, of which race remnants still existed between Panticapaeum and Cherson in the 6th century. (Procop. *Goth.* iv. 5.) It was subsequently overrun by the Goths and other nations who followed the great stream of emigration. Justinian reunited the kingdom of the Bosporus to the Greek Empire; and the Byzantine emperors, till the fall of Constantinople, always regarded the Tauric peninsula as part of their dominions. But the Tatars had made themselves the actual masters of it before the middle of the 13th century. Under these possessors, the Genoese, who settled on the coasts towards the end of the same century, played the same part as the Greeks did when the country was possessed by the Tauri, and planted several flourishing colonies. (Neumann, *Die Hellenen im Skythenlande;* Georgii, *Alte Geographie,* vol. ii ; Clarke's *Travels,* vol. ii. ; Danby Seymour, *Russia on the Black Sea;* Forbiger, *Handb. der alt. Geogr.* vol. iii.) [T. H. D.]

TAURICI MONTES. [TAURICA CHERSONESUS.]

TAURINI (Ταυρῖνοι), a Ligurian tribe, who occupied the country on the E. slope of the Alps, down to the left bank of the Padus, in the upper part of its course. They were the most northerly of the Ligurian tribes, and from their geographical position would more naturally have been regarded as belonging to Cisalpine Gaul than to Liguria; but both Strabo and Pliny distinctly say they were a Ligurian tribe, and the same thing may be inferred from the omission of their name by Polybius where he is relating the successive settlements of the *Gaulish* tribes in the N. of Italy (Pol. ii. 17; Strab. iv. p. 204 ; Plin. iii. 17. s. 21). Their territory adjoined that of the Vagienni on the S., and that of the Insubres on the NE.; though the Laevi and Lebecii, tribes of which we know very little, must also have bordered on their NE. frontier (Pol. *l. c.*). The first mention of the Taurini in history is at the time of Hannibal's passage of the Alps (B. C. 218), when that general, on descending into the plains of Italy, found the Taurini on hostile terms with the Insubres, and, in consequence, turned his arms against them, took their principal city, and put the inhabitants to the sword. (Pol. iii. 60; Liv. xxi. 38, 39.) Neither Polybius nor Livy mention the name of this city, but Appian calls it Taurasia (*Annib.* 5): it was probably situated on the same site which was afterwards occupied by the Roman colony. The name of the Taurini is not once mentioned during the long wars of the Romans with the Cisalpine Gauls and Ligurians, and we are ignorant of the time when they finally passed under the Roman yoke. Nor have we any precise account of the foundation of the Roman colony in their territory which assumed the name of Augusta Taurinorum, though it is certain that this took place under Augustus, and it was doubtless connected with his final subjugation of the Alpine tribes in B. C. 8. From this time the name of the Taurini never again appears in history as that of a people; but during the latter ages of the Roman Empire the *city* of Augusta Taurinorum seems to have been commonly known (as was the case in many instances in Transalpine Gaul) by the name of the tribe to which it belonged, and is called simply Taurini in the Itineraries, as well as by other writers. (*Itin. Ant.* p. 341; *Itin. Hier.* p. 556; *Tab. Peut.*; Ammian. xv. 8. § 18.) Hence its modern name of *Torino* or *Turin.* This is the only city that we can assign with any certainty to the Taurini. On the W. their territory was bounded (at least in the days of Augustus) by the Segusiani and the other tribes subject to Cottius; and their limit in this direction is doubtless marked by the station Ad Fines, situated 18 miles from Augusta, on the road to Segusio (*Itin. Ant. l. c.*). But it appears probable that at an earlier period the nation of the Taurini was more widely spread, or their name used in a more comprehensive sense, so as to comprise the adjoining passes of the Alps; for Livy speaks of the Insubrian Gauls who crossed into Italy, " per Taurinos saltusque invios Alpes transcenderunt" (Liv. v. 34), and Strabo, in enumerating, after Polybius, the passes across the Alps, designates one of them as τὴν διὰ Ταυρινῶν (Strab. iv. p. 209.). Whether the pass here meant is the *Mont Genèvre* or the *Mont Cenis* (a much disputed point), it would not be included within the territory of the Taurini in the more restricted sense.   [E. H. B.]

TAURIS, an island of the Ionian sea, between Pharus and Corcyra, opposite to the NW. point of the peninsula of Hyllis and the mouth of the Naron. (Auct. *B. A.* 47.) Now *Torcola.*   [T. H. D.]

TAURISCI   [NORICUM, Vol. II. p. 447.]

TAUROEIS, TAUROE'NTIUM (Ταυρόεις, Ταυροέντιον: *Eth.* Ταυροέντιος). Steph. B. (*s. v.* Ταυρόεις), who calls it a Celtic town and a colony of the Massaliots, quotes the first book of Artemidorus' geography for a foolish explanation of the origin of the name. The place is mentioned by Caesar (*B. C.* ii. 4), who says " Tauroenta quod est castellum Massiliensium perveniunt;" by Strabo (iv. pp. 180, 184), by Scymnus Chius, and by Ptolemy (ii. 10. § 8), who places it between Massilia and Citharistes Promontorium. D'Anville erroneously supposes that Caesar uses Tauroenta for the plural number; but it is the accusative of Tauroeis. Strabo (iv. p. 184) enumerates the Massaliot settlements between Massilia and the Varus in this order: Tauroentium, Olbia, Antipolis, Nicaea. Mela (ii. 5) enumerates the places on this coast in a different order

from east to west: Athenopolis, Olbia, Tauroïs, Citharistes, and " Lacydon Massiliensium portus." Ptolemy, as we have seen, places Tauroeis between Massilia and Citharistes. In the Maritime Itin. the positions between Telo Martius (*Toulon*) and Immadrus seem to be out of order [IMMADRUS]; and they are to be placed thus — Aemines (*Embiez*), Tauroeis (*Taurenti*), Citharista [CITHARISTA], Carsici (*Cassis*), Immadrus, Massilia. Geographers have been much divided in opinion on the site of Tauroeis, but the modern name seems to determine the place to be at the right of the entry of the bay of *Ciotat.*   [G. L.]

TAUROME'NIUM (Ταυρομένιον; *Eth.* Ταυρομενίτης, Tauromenitanus: *Taormina*), a Greek city of Sicily, situated on the E. coast of Sicily, about midway between Messana and Catana. It was only about 3 miles from the site of the ancient Naxos, and there is no doubt that Tauromenium did not exist as a city till after the destruction of Naxos by Dionysius of Syracuse, B. C. 403; but the circumstances connected with its foundation are somewhat confused and uncertain. [NAXOS.] It appears, however, from Diodorus that after the destruction of Naxos, the remaining inhabitants of that city were driven into exile, and its territory was assigned by Dionysius to the neighbouring Siculi. These, however, did not re-occupy the site of the ancient city, but established themselves on a hill to the N. of it, which was called the hill of Taurus (ὁ λόφος ὁ καλούμενος Ταῦρος). Here they at first constructed only a temporary camp (in B. C. 396), but afterwards erected walls and converted it into a regular fortress or town, to which they gave the name of Tauromenium. (Diod. xiv. 58, 59.) The place was still in the hands of the Siculi in B. C. 394, and they held it against the efforts of Dionysius, who besieged the city in vain for great part of the winter, and though he on one occasion forced his way within the walls by a nocturnal surprise, was again driven out and repulsed with heavy loss. (*Ib.* 87, 88.) But by the peace concluded in B. C. 392, it was expressly stipulated that Tauromenium should be subject to Dionysius, who expelled the greater part of the Siculi that had settled there, and supplied their place with his own mercenaries. (*Ib.* 96.) From this time we hear no more of Tauromenium till B. C. 358, when we are told that Andromachus, the father of the historian Timaeus, brought together all the remains of the exiled Naxians, who were still scattered about in different parts of Sicily, and established them all at Tauromenium. (Id. xvi. 7.) This is related by Diodorus as if it were a new foundation, and even as if the *name* had then first been applied to the city, which is in direct contradiction with his former statements. What had become of the former inhabitants we know not, but there is little doubt that the account of this resettlement of the city is substantially correct, and that Tauromenium now for the first time became a Greek city, which was considered as taking the place of Naxos, though it did not occupy the same site. (Wesseling, *ad Diod.* xiv. 59.) Hence Pliny's expression, that Tauromenium had formerly been called Naxos (Plin. iii. 8. s. 14) is nearly, though not strictly, correct.

The new settlement seems to have risen rapidly to prosperity, and was apparently already a considerable town at the time of the expedition of Timoleon in B.C. 345. It was the first place in Sicily where that leader landed, having eluded the vigilance of the Carthaginians, who were guarding the straits of Messana, and crossed direct from Rhegium to Tauromenium. (Diod. xvi. 68; Plut. *Timol.* 10.) The city was at that time still under the government of Andromachus, whose mild and equitable administration is said to have presented a strong contrast with that of the despots and tyrants of the other Sicilian cities. He welcomed Timoleon with open arms, and afforded him a secure resting place until he was enabled to carry out his plans in other parts of Sicily. (Diod. *l. c.*; Plut. *l. c.*) It is certain that Andromachus was not deprived of the chief power, when all the other tyrants were expelled by Timoleon, but was permitted to retain it undisturbed till his death. (Marcellin. *Vit. Thucyd.* § 27.) We hear, however, very little of Tauromenium for some time after this. It is probable that it passed under the authority of Agathocles, who drove the historian Timaeus into exile; and some time after this it was subject to a domestic despot of the name of Tyndarion, who was contemporary with Hicetas of Syracuse and Phintias of Agrigentum. (Diod. xxii. *Exc. H.* p. 495.) Tyndarion was one of those who concurred in inviting Pyrrhus into Sicily (B.C. 278), and when that monarch landed with his army at Tauromenium, joined him with all his forces, and supported him in his march upon Syracuse. (Diod. *l. c.* pp. 495, 496.) A few years later we find that Tauromenium had fallen into the power of Hieron of Syracuse, and was employed by him as a stronghold in the war against the Mamertines. (*Ib.* p. 497.) It was also one of the cities which was left under his dominion by the treaty concluded with him by the Romans in B.C. 263. (Diod. xxiii. p. 502.) This is doubtless the reason that its name is not again mentioned during the First Punic War.

There is no doubt that Tauromenium continued to form a part of the kingdom of Syracuse till the death of Hieron, and that it only passed under the government of Rome when the whole island of Sicily was reduced to a Roman province; but we have scarcely any account of the part it took during the Second Punic War, though it would appear, from a hint in Appian (*Sic.* 5), that it submitted to Marcellus on favourable terms; and it is probable that it was on that occasion it obtained the peculiarly favoured position it enjoyed under the Roman dominion. For we learn from Cicero that Tauromenium was one of the three cities in Sicily which enjoyed the privileges of a "civitas foederata" or allied city, thus retaining a nominal independence, and was not even subject, like Messana, to the obligation of furnishing ships of war when called upon. (Cic. *Verr.* ii. 66, iii. 6, v. 19.) But the city suffered severe calamities during the Servile War in Sicily, B.C. 134—132, having fallen into the hands of the insurgent slaves, who, on account of the great strength of its position, made it one of their chief posts, and were able for a long time to defy the arms of the consul Rupilius. They held out until they were reduced to the most fearful extremities by famine, when the citadel was at length betrayed into the hands of the consul by one of their leaders named Sarapion, and the whole of the survivors put to the sword. (Diod. xxxiv. *Exc. Phot.* p. 528; Oros. v. 9.) Tauromenium again bore a conspicuous part during the wars of Sextus Pompeius in Sicily, and, from its strength as a fortress, was one of the principal points of the position which he took up in B.C. 36, for defence against Octavian. It became the scene also of a sea-fight between a part of the fleet of Octavian,

commanded by the triumvir in person, and that of Pompeius, which terminated in the defeat and almost total destruction of the former. (Appian, *B.C.* v. 103, 105, 106—111, 116; Dion Cass. xlix. 5.) In the settlement of Sicily after the defeat of Pompey, Tauromenium was one of the places selected by Augustus to receive a Roman colony, probably as a measure of precaution, on account of the strength of its situation, as we are told that he expelled the former inhabitants to make room for his new colonists. (Diod. xvi. 7.) Strabo speaks of it as one of the cities on the E. coast of Sicily that was still subsisting in his time, though inferior in population both to Messana and Catana. (Strab. vi. pp. 267, 268.) Both Pliny and Ptolemy assign it the rank of a "colonia" (Plin. iii. 8. s. 14; Ptol. iii. 4. § 9), and it seems to have been one of the few cities of Sicily that continued under the Roman Empire to be a place of some consideration. Its territory was noted for the excellence of its wine (Plin. xiv. 6. s. 8), and produced also a kind of marble which seems to have been highly valued. (Athen. v. p. 207.) Juvenal also speaks of the sea off its rocky coast as producing the choicest mullets. (Juv. v. 93.)

The Itineraries place Tauromenium 32 miles from Messana, and the same distance from Catana. (*Itin. Ant.* p. 90; *Tab. Peut.*) It continued after the fall of the Roman Empire to be one of the more considerable towns of Sicily, and, from the strength of its position was one of the last places that was retained by the Greek emperors; but it was taken by the Saracens in A.D. 906 after a siege of two years, and totally destroyed, a calamity from which it has never more than partially recovered. The present town of *Taormina* is a very poor place, with about 3500 inhabitants; but it still occupies the ancient site, on a lofty hill which forms the last projecting point of the mountain ridge that extends along the coast from Cape Pelorus to this point. The site of the town is about 900 feet above the sea, while a very steep and almost isolated rock, crowned by a Saracen castle, rises about 500 feet higher: this is undoubtedly the site of the ancient Arx or citadel, the inaccessible position of which is repeatedly alluded to by ancient writers. Portions of the ancient walls may be traced at intervals all round the brow of the hill, the whole of the summit of which was evidently occupied by the ancient city. Numerous fragments of ancient buildings are scattered over its whole surface, including extensive reservoirs of water, sepulchres, tesselated pavements, &c., and the remains of a spacious edifice, commonly called a Naumachia, but the real destination of which is difficult to determine. But by far the most remarkable monument remaining at *Taormina* is the ancient theatre, which is one of the most celebrated ruins in Sicily, on account both of its remarkable preservation and of the surpassing beauty of its situation. It is built for the most part of brick, and is therefore probably of Roman date, though the plan and arrangement are in accordance with those of Greek, rather than Roman, theatres; whence it is supposed that the present structure was rebuilt upon the foundations of an older theatre of the Greek period. The greater part of the seats have disappeared, but the wall which surrounded the whole cavea is preserved, and the *proscenium* with the back wall of the *scena* and its appendages, of which only traces remain in most ancient theatres, are here preserved in singular integrity, and contribute much to the picturesque effect, as well as to the interest, of the ruin. From the fragments of architectural decorations still extant we learn that it was of the Corinthian order, and richly ornamented. In size it ranks next to the theatre of Syracuse, among those of Sicily. Some portions of a temple are also visible, converted into the church of *S. Pancrazio*, but the edifice is of small size and of little interest. The ruins at *Taormina* are described in detail by the Duke of Serra di Falco (*Antichità della Sicilia*, vol. v. part iv.), as well as by most travellers in Sicily. (Swinburne's *Travels*, vol. ii. p. 380; Smyth's *Sicily*, p. 129, &c.)　　　　　　　　　[E. H. B.]

COIN OF TAUROMENIUM.

TAUROSCYTHAE (Ταυροσκύθαι, Ptol. iii. 5. § 25), called by Pliny Tauri Scythae (iv. 12. s. 26), a people of European Sarmatia, composed of a mixture of Taurians and Scythians. They were seated to the W. of the Jazyges, and the district which they inhabited appears to have been called Tauroscythia. (Cf. Strab. ap. Hudson, p. 87; Capit. *M. Ant.* 9; Procop. *de Aed.* iii. fin.)　　[T. H. D.]

TAURU'NUM (Ταύρουνον), a strong fortress in Lower Pannonia, at the point where the Savus joins the Danubius, on the road from Sirmium to Singidunum. It was the station of a small fleet of the Danubius. (Plin. iii. 28; Ptol. ii. 16. § 4; *It. Ant.* pp. 131, 241; *Tab. Peut.*; Geogr. Rav. iv. 19, where it is called Taurynum.) Its site is now occupied by the fortress of *Semlin*, opposite to *Belgrade*.　　　　　　　　　　[L. S.]

TAURUS MONS (ὁ Ταῦρος), one of the great mountain ranges of Asia, the name of which is believed to be derived from the Aramaic Tur or Tura, i. e., a high mountain or Alp; and accordingly is in reality a common noun applied to all the high mountains of Asia. The name has even been transferred to Europe, for the Taurian Chersonesus in Sarmatia and the Taurisci in the Norican Alps appear to owe their name to the same origin. We cannot wonder therefore when we find that Eratosthenes (*ap. Strab.* xv. 689) and Strabo (ii. pp. 68, 129, x. p. 490) apply the name to the whole range of mountains extending from the Mediterranean to the eastern ocean, although their connection is often broken. This extent of mountains is, according to Strabo's calculation (xi. p. 490), 45,000 stadia in length, and 3000 in breadth. But in the narrower and common acceptation Mount Taurus is the range of mountains in Asia Minor which begins at Cape Sacrum or Chelidonium on the coast of Lycia, which for this reason is called by Mela (i. 15) and Pliny (v. 28) Promontorium Tauri. It was, however, well known to the ancients that this promontory was not the real commencement, but that in fact the range extended to the south-western extremity of Asia Minor. (Strab. ii. p. 129, xi. p. 520, xiv. pp. 651, 666.) This range rises in the W. as a lofty and precipitous mountain, and runs without any interruptions, first in a northern direction between Lycia and Pamphylia, then in an eastern direction through Pisidia and Isauria as far as the frontiers of Cilicia and Lycaonia. There it separates into two main

branches. The one proceeds north-eastward under the name of Antitaurus (Ἀντίταυρος), and surpasses the other in height. It runs through Cappadocia, where it forms Mount Argaeus (Ἀργαῖος), and Armenia, where it is called Mons Capotes, and through the Montes Moschici it is connected with the Caucasus, while a more southerly branch, under the names of Abus and Macis or Massis, runs through Armenia towards the Caspian sea. The second branch, which separates itself on the frontiers of Cilicia and Lycaonia, retains the name of Taurus, and proceeds from Cilicia, where it forms the Portae Ciliciae, and sends forth Mons Amanus in a southern direction, while the main branch proceeds through Cappadocia. After being broken through by the Euphrates, it again sends forth a southern branch under the name of Mons Masius. The name Taurus ceases in the neighbourhood of Lake Arsissa, the mountains further east having other names, such as Niphates, Zagrus, &c. Most parts of Mount Taurus, which still bears its ancient name, were well wooded, and furnished abundance of timber to the maritime cities on the south coast of Asia Minor. [L. S.]

TAURUS PALUS, an *étang* on the coast of Narbonensis, west of the delta of the Rhone. It is named in the verses of Avienus, quoted in the article FECYI JUGUM; and to the verses there cited may be added the following verse:—

　"Taurum paludem namque gentici (gentili) vocant."

But I. Vossius in his edition of Mela (ii. 5, note) writes the verses of Avienus thus:—

　"In usque Taphrum pertinet,
　Taphron paludem namque gentili vocant;"

an alteration or corruption which D'Anville justly condemns, for the *étang* is still named *Taur*, or vulgarly *Tau*.　　　　　　　　　[G. L.]

TAXGAE'TIUM (Ταξγαίτιον), a place assigned by Ptolemy (ii. 12. § 5) to Rhaetia, but which more properly belonged to Vindelicia, was situated on the northern shore of the Lacus Brigantinus, and probably on the site of the modern *Lindau*. [L. S.]

TAXILA (Τάξιλα, Arrian, *Anab.* v. 8; Ταξίαλα, Ptol. vii. 1. § 45), a place of great importance in the Upper *Panjáb*, between the Indus and Hydaspes, which was visited by Alexander the Great. It is said to have been ruled at that time by a chief named Taxiles, who behaved in a friendly manner to the Grecian king. The country around was said to be very fertile, and more abundant than even Egypt (Strab. xv. pp. 698—714). There can be little doubt that it is represented by the vast ruins of *Manikyala*, which has in modern times been the scene of some very remarkable researches (Elphinstone, *Cabul*, p. 79; Burnes, *Travels*, i. p. 65, ii. p. 470.) The famous Topes of *Manikyala*, which were examined by General Ventura and others (*Asiatic Res.* xvii. p. 563), lie to the eastward of *Rawil-pindi*. Wilson considers Taxila to be the same as the *Takhsasila* of the Hindus (*Ariana*, p. 196).　　　　　　　　　[V.]

TAY'GETUS. [LACONIA, pp. 108, 109.]

TAZUS (Ταζός, Ptol. iii. 6. § 6). 1. A town in the SE. part of the Chersonesus Taurica.

2. A town of Asiatic Sarmatia, on the N. coast of the Pontus Euxinus. (Ptol. v. 9. § 9.)　[T. H. D.]

TEA'NUM (Τέανον: *Eth.* Teanensis: *Civitate*), sometimes also called TEANUM APULUM (Cic. *pro Cluent.* 9; Τέανον Ἄπουλον, Strab.; *Eth.* Teanenses Apuli), to distinguish it from the Campanian city of the same name, was a city of Apulia, situated on the right bank of the river Frento (*Fortore*), about 12 miles from its mouth. It appears to have been one of the most considerable cities of Apulia before its conquest by the Romans; but its name is first mentioned in B. C. 318, when, in conjunction with Canusium, it submitted to the Roman consuls M. Foslius Flaccinator and L. Plautius Venno. (Liv. ix. 20.) It is again noticed during the Second Punic War, when it was selected by the dictator M. Junius Pera as the place of his winter-quarters in Apulia. (Id. xxiii. 24.) Cicero incidentally notices it as a municipal town, at the distance of 18 miles from Larinum (Cic. *pro Cluent.* 9), and its name is found in all the geographers among the municipal towns of Apulia. (Strab. vi. p. 285; Mel. ii. 4. § 6; Plin. iii. 11. s. 16; Ptol. iii. 1. § 72.) Its municipal rank is confirmed also by an inscription, as well as by the Liber Coloniarum, and it is clear that it never attained the rank of a colony. (Orell. *Inscr.* 140; *Lib. Col.* p. 210.) Its ruins still exist at a place called *Civitate*, near the remains of a Roman bridge (now called the *Ponte di Civitate*), over the *Fortore*, by which the ancient road from Larinum to Luceria crossed that river. The distance from the site of Larinum agrees with that stated by Cicero of 18 miles (the Tabula erroneously gives only 12), and the discovery of inscriptions on the spot leaves no doubt of the identification. Considerable remains of the walls are still extant, as well as fragments of other buildings. From these, as well as from an inscription in which we find mention of the "Ordo splendidissimus Civitatis Theanensium," it seems probable that it continued to be a flourishing town under the Roman Empire. The period of its final decay is uncertain, but it retained its episcopal see down to modern times. (Holsten. *Not. ad Cluver.* p. 279; Romanelli, vol. ii. p. 291; Mommsen, *Inscr. R. N.* p. 271.)

Strabo speaks of Teanum as situated at some distance inland from a lake, the name of which he does not mention, but which is clearly the Lacus Pantanus of Pliny, now called the *Lago di Lesina*. From an inscription found on its banks it appears that this was comprised within the territory of Teanum, which thus extended down to the sea (Romanelli, *l. c.*), though about 12 miles distant from the coast.

Several Italian topographers have assumed the existence of a city in Apulia of the name of Teate, distinct from Teanum (Giovenazzi, *Sito di Ateja*, p. 13; Romanelli, vol. ii. p. 286); but there seems no doubt that the two names are only different forms of the same, and that the Teates Apuli of Livy (ix. 20) are in reality the people of Teanum. It is true that that writer mentions them as if they were distinct from the Teaneneses whom he had mentioned just before; but it is probable that this arises merely from his having followed different annalists, and that both statements refer in fact to the same people, and are a repetition of the same occurrence. (Mommsen, *Unter-Ital. Dialekt.* p. 301.) In like manner the Teate mentioned in the Liber Coloniarum (p. 261) is evidently the same place called in an earlier part of the same document (p. 210) Teanum. [E. H. B.]

TEA'NUM (Τέανον: *Eth.* Teanensis: *Teano*), sometimes called for distinction's sake TEANUM SIDICINUM (Liv. xxii. 57; Cic. *ad Att.* viii. 11; Plin. iii. 5. s. 9; Τέανον Σιδικῖνον, Strab. v. p. 237), an important city of Campania, situated in the interior of that province, on the Via Latina,

between Cales and Casinum. (Strab. v. p. 237.) It was therefore the frontier city of Campania, as that term was understood under the Roman Empire; but originally Teanum was not reckoned a Campanian city at all, but was the capital of the small independent tribe of the Sidicini. [SIDICINI.] It was indeed the only place of importance that they possessed, so that Livy in more than one instance alludes to it, where he is speaking of that people, merely as "their city," without mentioning its name (Liv. viii. 2, 17). Hence its history before the Roman conquest is identical with that of the people, which will be found in the article SIDICINI. The first mention of Teanum after the Roman conquest, is in B.C. 216, immediately after the battle of Cannae, when Marcellus sent forward a legion from Rome thither, evidently with the view of securing the line of the Via Latina. (Liv. xxii. 57.) A few years later, B. C. 211, it was selected as a place of confinement for a part of the senators of Capua, while they were awaiting their sentence from Rome; but the consul Fulvius, contrary to the opinion of his colleague App. Claudius, caused them all to be put to death without waiting for the decree of the senate. (Liv. xxvi. 15.) From this time Teanum became an ordinary municipal town : it is incidentally mentioned as such on several occasions, and its position on the Via Latina doubtless contributed to its prosperity. A gross outrage offered to one of its municipal magistrates by the Roman consul, was noticed in one of the orations of C. Gracchus (*ap.* A. Gell. x. 3), and we learn from Cicero that it was in his time a flourishing and populous town. (Cic. *de Leg. Agr.* ii. 31, 35, *ad Att.* viii. 11, d.) Its name repeatedly occurs in the Social War and the contest between Sulla and Marius (Appian, *B. C.* i. 45, 85); and at a later period it was the place where the commanders of the legions in Italy held a kind of congress, with a view to bring about a reconciliation between Octavian and L. Antonius (*Ib.* v. 20). It was one of the cities whose territory the tribune Rullus proposed by his law to divide among the Roman people (Cic. *l. c.*); but this misfortune was averted. It subsequently, however, received a colony under Augustus (*Lib. Col.* p. 238; Plin. iii. 5. s. 9), and seems to have retained its colonial rank under the Empire. (Mommsen, *Inscr. R. N.* 3989, 3999.) Strabo tells us that it was the largest and most populous town on the Via Latina, and the most considerable of the inland cities of Campania after Capua. (Strab. v. pp. 237, 248.) Inscriptions and existing remains confirm this account of its importance, but we hear little more of it under the Roman Empire. The Itineraries place it 16 miles from Casinum, and 18 from Venafrum: a cross road also struck off from Teanum to Allifae, Telesia, and Beneventum. (*Itin. Ant.* pp. 121, 304; *Tab. Peut.*) Another branch also communicated with Suessa and Minturnae.

Teanum was not more than 5 miles from Cales : the point where the territories of the two cities joined was marked by two shrines or aediculae of Fortune, mentioned by Strabo, under the name of *al δύο Τύχαι* (v. p. 249).

Teanum appears to have declined during the middle ages, and the modern city of *Teano* is a poor place, with only about 4000 inhabitants, though retaining its episcopal see. Many ruins of the ancient city are visible, though none of them of any great interest. They are situated below the modern city, which stands on a hill, and considerably nearer to

Calvi (Cales). The most important are those of an amphitheatre and a theatre, situated near the Via Latina; but numerous remains of other buildings are found scattered over a considerable space, though for the most part in imperfect preservation. They are all constructed of brick, and in the reticulated style, and may therefore probably be all referred to the period of the Roman Empire. Numerous inscriptions have also been found, as well as coins, vases, intaglios, &c., all tending to confirm the account given by Strabo of its ancient prosperity. (Romanelli, vol. iii. p. 456; Hoare's *Class. Tour,* vol. i. pp. 249—264; Mommsen, *Inscr. R. N.* pp. 208, 209).

At a short distance from *Teano* are some mineral springs, now called *Le Caldarelle,* which are evidently the same with the "aquae acidulae," mentioned both by Pliny and Vitruvius as existing near Teanum. (Plin. xxxi. 2. s. 5; Vitruv. viii. 3. § 17.) The remains of some ancient buildings, called *Il Bagno Nuovo,* are still visible on the spot. [E. H. B.]

COIN OF TEANUM SIDICINUM.

TEARI JULIENSES, the inhabitants of a town of the Ilercaones in Hispania Tarraconensis (Plin. iii. 3. § 4). It is called by Ptolemy Τιαριουλία, and is probably the modern *Trayguera.*   [T. H. D.]

TEARUS (Plin. iv. 11. s. 18; Τέαρος, Herod. iv. 90), now *Teare, Deara,* or *Dere,* a river in the SE. of Thrace, flowing in a SW. direction, until it joins the Contadesdos, their united waters falling into the Agrianes, one of the principal eastern tributaries of the Hebrus. Herodotus (*l. c.*) states that the sources of the Tearus are equidistant from Heraeum on the Propontis and Apollonia on the Euxine; that they are thirty-eight in number; and that, though they all issue from the same rock, some of them are cold, others warm. Their waters had the reputation, among the neighbouring people, of being pre-eminently medicinal, especially in cases of itch or mange (ψώρη). On his march towards the Danube, Darius halted his army for three days at the sources of the Tearus, and erected a pillar there, with an inscription commemorative of their virtues, and of his own.   [J. R.]

TEATE (Τεατέα, Strab. Ptol.: *Eth.* Teatinus: *Chieti*), the chief city of the Marrucini, was situated on a hill about 3 miles from the river Aternus, and 8 from the Adriatic. All the ancient geographers concur in representing it as the metropolis or capital city of the tribe (Strab. v. p. 241; Plin. iii. 12. s. 17: Ptol. iii. 1. § 60); and Silius Italicus repeatedly notices it with the epithets "great" and "illustrious" ("magnum Teate," Sil. Ital. viii. 520; Clarum Teate, Id. xvii. 453); but, notwithstanding this, we find no mention of it in history. Inscriptions, however, as well as existing remains, concur in proving it to have been a flourishing and important town under the Roman dominion. It was apparently the only municipal town in the land of the Marrucini, and hence the limits of its municipal district seem to have coincided with those of that people. We learn from the Liber Coloniarum that it received a body of colonists under Augustus, but it did not bear the title of a colony, and is uniformly styled in inscriptions a municipium. (*Lib. Colon.* p. 258; Orell. *Inscr.* 2175, 3853; Mommsen, *Inscr. R. N.* pp. 278, 279.) It derived additional splendour in the early days of the Empire from being the native place of Asinius Pollio, the celebrated statesman and orator; indeed the whole family of the Asinii seem to have derived their origin from Teate. Herius Asinius was the leader of the Marrucini in the Social War, and a brother of the orator is called by Catullus "Marrucine Asini." (Liv. *Epit.* lxxiii.; Catull. 12. 1.) The family of the Vettii also, to which belonged the Vettius Marcellus mentioned by Pliny (ii. 83. s. 85), appears to have belonged to Teate. (Mommsen, *l. c.* 5311.)

The Itineraries place Teate on the Via Valeria, though from the position of the town, on a hill to the right of the valley of the Aternus, the road must have made a considerable *détour* in order to reach it. (*Itin. Ant.* p. 310; *Tab. Peut.*) Its name is also noticed by P. Diaconus (ii. 20), and there seems no doubt that it continued throughout the middle ages to be a place of importance, and the capital of the surrounding district. *Chieti* is still one of the most considerable cities in this part of Italy, with above 14,000 inhabitants, and is the see of an archbishop. Still existing remains prove that the ancient city occupied the same site as the modern *Chieti*, on a long ridge of hill stretching from N. to S., though it must have been considerably more extensive. Of these the most important are the ruins of a theatre, which must have been of large size; those of a large edifice supposed to have been a reservoir for water, and two temples, now converted into churches. One of these, now the church of *S. Paolo*, and considered, but without any authority, as a temple of Hercules, was erected by the Vettius Marcellus above noticed; the other, from the name of *Sta Maria del Tricaglio* which it bears, has been conjectured to have been dedicated to Diana Trivia. All these edifices, from the style of their construction, belong to the early period of the Roman Empire. Besides these, numerous mosaics and other works of art have been discovered on the site, which attest the flourishing condition of Teate during the first two centuries of the Christian era. (Romanelli, vol. iii. pp. 104—109; Craven, *Abruzzi*, vol. ii. pp. 8, 9.) [E. H. B.]

COIN OF TEATE.

TEBENDA (Τέβενδα), a town in the interior of Pontus Galaticus (Ptol. v. 6. § 9), is no doubt the same as the Tebenna mentioned by Anna Comnena (p. 364, B.) as situated in the vicinity of Trapesus.   [L. S.]

TECELIA (Τεκελία), a town placed by Ptolemy

(ii. 11. § 27) in the north of Germany, perhaps in the country of the Chauci, on the left bank of the Visurgis (*Weser*). Its site must probably be looked for near or at the village of *Zetel*, about 3 miles from the western bank of the *Weser*. (Reichard, *Germanien*, p. 245.)   [L. S.]

TECMON (Τέκμων: *Eth.* Τεκμάνιος), a city of Molossis in Epeirus, incorrectly called by Stephanus B. a city of Thesprotia, taken by L. Anicius, the Roman commander, in B. C. 167. Leake supposes that *Gurimista*, near *Kúrendo*, about 20 miles to the W. of *Joánnina*, may have been the site of Tecmon or Horreum, which Livy mentions in connection with Tecmon. (Liv. xlv. 26; Steph. B. *s. v.*; Leake, *Northern Greece*, vol. iv. p. 83.)

TECTOSACES (Τεκτόσακες, Ptol. vi. 14. § 9), a people of Scythia within Imana.   [T. H. D.]

TECTOSAGES. [VOLCAE.]

TECTOSAGES, TECTOSAGAE, or TECTO-SAGI (Τεκτόσαγες, Τεκτοσάγαι), one of the three great tribes of the Celts or Gallograeci in Asia Minor, of which they occupied the central parts. For particulars about their history, see GALATIA. These Tectosages were probably the same tribe as the one mentioned by Polybius under the names of Aegosages or Rigosages. (Polyb. v. 33, 77, 78, 111.)   [L. S.]

TECUM. [TICHIS.]

TEDA'NIUS (Τηδάνιος), a small river of Illyricum (Ptol. ii. 16. § 3), on the frontier of the district called Iapydia (Plin. iii. 25), is in all probability the modern *Zermanja*.   [L. S.]

TE'GEA (Τεγέα, Steph. B. *s. v.*), a town of Crete, which according to legend, was founded by Agamemnon. (Vell. Pat. i. 1.) The coins which Sestini and Pellerin attributed to the Cretan Tegea have been restored by Eckhel (vol. ii. p. 321) to the Arcadian city of that name.   [E. B. J.]

TE'GEA (Τεγέα, Ion. Τεγέη: *Eth.* Τεγεάτης, Τεγεᾶτα), one of the most ancient and powerful towns of Arcadia, situated in the SE. of the country. Its territory, called TEGEATIS (Τεγεᾶτις), was bounded by Cynuria and Argolis on the E., from which it was separated by Mt. Parthenium, by Laconia on the S., by the Arcadian district of Maenalia on the W., and by the territory of Mantineia on the N. The Tegeatae are said to have derived their name from Tegeates, a son of Lycaon, and to have dwelt originally in eight, afterwards nine, demi or townships, the inhabitants of which were incorporated by Aleus in the city of Tegea, of which this hero was the reputed founder. The names of these nine townships, which are preserved by Pausanias, are: *Gareatae* (Γαρεᾶται), *Phylaceis* (Φυλακεῖς), *Cary-dtae* (Καρυᾶται), *Corytheis* (Κορυθεῖς), *Potachidae* (Ποταχίδαι), *Oeatae* (Οἰᾶται), *Manthyreis* (Μανθυρεῖς). *Echeuetheis* (Ἐχευήθεις), to which *Apheidantes* (Ἀφείδαντες) was added as the ninth in the reign of king Apheidas. (Paus. viii. 3. § 4, viii. 45. § 1; Strab. viii. p. 337.) The Tegeatae were early divided into 4 tribes (φυλαί), called respectively *Clareōtis* (Κλαρεῶτις, in inscriptions Κραριῶτις), *Hippothoïtis* (Ἱπποθοῖτις), *Apol'oneātis* (Ἀπολλωνεᾶτις), and *Athaneātis* (Ἀθανεᾶτις), to each of which belonged a certain number of metoeci (μέτοικοι) or resident aliens. (Paus. viii. 53. § 6; Böckh, *Corp. Inscr.* no. 1513.)

Tegea is mentioned in the Iliad (ii. 607), and was probably the most celebrated of all the Arcadian towns in the earliest times. This appears from its heroic renown, since its king Echemus is said

to have slain Hyllus, the son of Hercules, in single combat. (Herod. ix. 26; Paus. viii. 45. § 3.) The Tegeatae offered a long-continued and successful resistance to the Spartans, when the latter attempted to extend their dominion over Arcadia. In one of the wars between the two people, Charilaus or Charillus, king of Sparta, deceived by an oracle which appeared to promise victory to the Spartans, invaded Tegeatis, and was not only defeated, but was taken prisoner with all his men who had survived the battle. (Herod. i. 66; Paus. iii. 7. § 3, viii. 5. § 9, viii. 45. § 3, 47. § 2, 48. § 4.) More than two centuries afterwards, in the reign of Leon and Agesicles, the Spartans again fought unsuccessfully against the Tegeatae; but in the following generation, in the time of their king Anaxandrides, the Spartans, having obtained possession of the bones of Orestes in accordance with an oracle, defeated the Tegeatae and compelled them to acknowledge the supremacy of Sparta, about B. C. 560. (Herod. i. 65, 67, seq.; Paus. iii. 3. § 5, seq.) Tegea, however, still retained its independence, though its military force was at the disposal of Sparta; and in the Persian War it appears as the second military power in the Peloponnesus, having the place of honour on the left wing of the allied army. Five hundred of the Tegeatae fought at Thermopylae, and 3000 at the battle of Plataea, half of their force consisting of hoplites and half of light-armed troops. (Herod. vii. 202, ix. 26, seq., 61.) As it was not usual to send the whole force of a state upon a distant march, we may probably estimate, with Clinton, the force of the Tegeatae on this occasion as not more than three-fourths of their whole number. This would give 4000 for the military population of Tegea, and about 17,400 for the whole free population. (Clinton, *F. H.* vol. ii. p. 417.)

Soon after the battle of Plataea, the Tegeatae were again at war with the Spartans, of the causes of which, however, we have no information. We only know that the Tegeatae fought twice against the Spartans between B. C. 479 and 464, and were each time defeated; first in conjunction with the Argives, and a second time together with the other Arcadians, except the Mantineians at Dipaea, in the Maenalian district. (Herod. ix. 37; Paus. iii. 11. § 7.) About this time, and also at a subsequent period, Tegea, and especially the temple of Athena Alea in the city, was a frequent place of refuge for persons who had rendered themselves obnoxious to the Spartan government. Hither fled the seer Hegesistratus (Herod. ix. 37) and the kings Leotychides, and Pausanias, son of Pleistoanax. (Herod. vi. 72; Xen. *Hell.* iii. 5. § 25; Paus. iii. 5. § 6.)

In the Peloponnesian War the Tegeatae were the firm allies of the Spartans, to whom they remained faithful both on account of their possessing an aristocratical constitution, and from their jealousy of the neighbouring democratical city of Mantineia, with which they were frequently at war. [For details see MANTINEIA.] Thus the Tegeatae not only refused to join the Argives in the alliance formed against Sparta in B. C. 421, but they accompanied the Lacedaemonians in their expedition against Argos in 418. (Thuc. v. 32, 57.) They also fought on the side of the Spartans in the Corinthian War, 394. (Xen. *Hell.* iv. 2. § 13.) After the battle of Leuctra, however (371), the Spartan party in Tegea was expelled, and the city joined the other Arcadian towns in the foundation of Megalopolis and in the formation of the Arcadian confederacy. (Xen. *Hell.* vi. 5. § 6, seq.) When Mantineia a few years afterwards quarrelled with the supreme Arcadian government, and formed an alliance with its old enemy Sparta, Tegea remained faithful to the new confederacy, and fought under Epaminondas against the Spartans at the great battle of Mantineia, 362. (Xen. *Hell.* vii. 4. § 36, seq., vii. 5. § 5, seq.)

Tegea at a later period joined the Aetolian League, but soon after the accession of Cleomenes III. to the Spartan throne it formed an alliance with Sparta, together with Mantineia and Orchomenus. It thus became involved in hostilities with the Achaeans, and in the war which followed, called the Cleomenic War, it was taken by Antigonus Doson, the ally of the Achaeans, and annexed to the Achaean League, B. C. 222. (Pol. ii. 46, 54, seq.) In 218 Tegea was attacked by Lycurgus, the tyrant of Sparta, who obtained possession of the whole city with the exception of the acropolis. It subsequently fell into the hands of Machanidas, but was recovered by the Achaeans after the defeat of the latter tyrant, who was slain in battle by Philopoemen. (Pol. v. 17, xi. 18.) In the time of Strabo Tegea was the only one of the Arcadian towns which continued to be inhabited (Strab. viii. p. 388), and it was still a place of importance in the time of Pausanias, who has given us a minute account of its public buildings. (Paus. viii. 45—48, 53.) Tegea was entirely destroyed by Alaric towards the end of the 4th century after Christ. (Claud. *B. Get.* 576; comp. Zosim. v. 6.)

The territory of Tegea formed the southern part of the plain of *Tripolitzá*, of which a description and a map are given under MANTINEIA. Tegea was about 10 miles S. of the latter city, in a direct line, and about 3 miles SE. of the modern town of *Tripolitzá*. Being situated in the lowest part of the plain, it was exposed to inundations caused by the waters flowing down from the surrounding mountains; and in the course of ages the soil has been considerably raised by the depositions brought down by the waters. Hence there are scarcely any remains of the city visible, and its size can only be conjectured from the broken pieces of stone and other fragments scattered on the plain, and from the foundations of walls and buildings discovered by the peasants in working in the fields. It appears, however, that the ancient city extended from the hill of *Aio Sostis* (*St. Saviour*) on the N., over the hamlets *Ibrahim-Effendi* and *Paleó-Episkopí*, at least as far as *Akhúria* and *Piali*. This would make the city at least 4 miles in circumference. The principal remains are at *Piali*. Near the principal church of this village Leake found the foundations of an ancient building, of fine squared stones, among which were two pieces of some large columns of marble; and there can be little doubt that these are the remains of the ancient temple of Athena Alea. This temple was said to have been originally built by Aleus, the founder of Tegea; it was burnt down in B. C. 394, and the new building, which was erected by Scopas, is said by Pausanias to have been the largest and most magnificent temple in the Peloponnesus (Paus. viii. 45. § 4, seq.; for details see *Dict. of Biogr.* art. SCOPAS.) Pausanias entered the city through the gate leading to Pallantium, consequently the south-western gate, which must have been near *Piali*. He begins his description with the temple of Athena Alea, and then goes across the great agora to the theatre, the remains of which Ross

traces in the ancient foundations of the ruined church of *Paleó-Episkopí*. Perhaps this theatre was the splendid marble one built by Antiochus IV. Epiphanes in B. C. 175. (Liv. xli. 20.) Pausanias ends his description with the mention of a height (χωρίον ὑψηλόν, viii. 53. § 9), probably the hill *Aio Sostis* in the N. of the town, and apparently the same as that which Pausanias elsewhere calls the Watch-Hill (λόφος Φυλακτρίς, viii. 48. § 4), and Polybius the acropolis (ἄκρα, v. 17). None of the other public buildings of Tegea mentioned by Pausanias can be identified with certainty; but there can be no doubt if excavations were made on its site many interesting remains would be discovered, since the deep alluvial soil is favourable to their preservation.

The territory of Tegea N. of the city, towards Mantineia, is a plain of considerable size, and is usually called the Tegeatic plain (Τεγεατικὸν πεδίον). There was a smaller plain, separated from the former by a low range of mountains S. of *Tripolitzá*, and lying between Tegea and Pallantium: it was called the Manthyric plain (Μανθυρικὸν πεδίον), from Manthyrea, one of the ancient demi of Tegea, the ruins of which are situated SW. of Tegea, on a slope of Mt. Boreium. (Paus. viii. 44. § 7, comp. viii. 45. § 1, 47. § 1; Steph. B. s. v. Μανθυρέα.) The remainder of the Tegeatis on the E. and S. is occupied by the mountains separating it from Argolis and Sparta respectively, with the exception of a small plain running eastward from the Tegeatic plain to the foot of Mt. Parthenium, and probably called the Corythic plain, from Corytheis, one of the ancient demi of Tegea, which was situated in this plain. (Paus. viii. 45. § 1, 54. § 4.)

The plain of Tegea having no natural outlet for its waters is drained by natural chasms through the limestone mountains, called katavóthra. Of these the two most important are at the modern village of *Persová* and at the marsh of *Taki*. The former is situated in the Corythic plain above mentioned, at the foot of Mt. Parthenium, and the latter is the marsh in the Manthyric plain, SW. of Tegea. The chief river in the district is now called the *Sarantapótamos*, which is undoubtedly the Alpheius of Pausanias (viii. 54. § 1, seq.). The Alpheius rose on the frontiers of Tegea and Sparta, at a place called PHYLACE (Φυλάκη, near *Krya Vrysis*), one of the ancient demi of Tegea, and, as we may infer from its name, a fortified watch-tower for the protection of the pass. A little beyond Phylace the Alpheius receives a stream composed of several mountain torrents at a place named SYMBOLA (Σύμβολα); but upon entering the plain of Tegea its course was different in ancient times. It now flows in a north-easterly direction through the plain, receives the river of *Dhulianá* (the ancient Garates, Γαράτης, Paus. viii. 54. § 4), flows through the Corythic plain, and enters the katavóthra at *Persová*. Pausanias, on the other hand, says (viii. 54. § 2) that the Alpheius descends into the earth in the Tegeatic plain, reappears near Asea (SW. of Tegea), where, after joining the Eurotas, it sinks a second time into the earth, and again appears at Asea. Hence it would seem that the Alpheius anciently flowed in a north-westerly direction, and entered the katavóthra at the marsh of *Taki*, in the Manthyric plain. There is a tradition among the peasants that the course of the river was changed by a Turk, who acquired property in the neighbourhood, because the katavóthra at the *Taki* did not absorb quickly enough the waters of the marsh. The Garates therefore anciently flowed into the katavóthra at *Persová* without having any connection with the Alpheius. It probably derived its name from Garea or Garese, one of the ancient deini of Tegea, which may have been situated at the village of *Dhuliand.* (Ross, *Peloponnes*, p. 70, seq.; Leake, *Peloponnesiaca*, p. 112, seq.)

There were five roads leading from Tegea. One led due N. across the Tegeatic plain to Mantineia. [MANTINEIA.] A second led due S. by the valley of the Alpheius to Sparta, following the same route as the present road from *Tripolitsá* to *Mistrá.* A third led west to Pallantium. It first passed by the small mountain Cresium (Κρήσιον), and then ran across the Manthyric plain along the side of the *Taki.* Mount Cresium is probably the small isolated hill on which the modern village of *Vunó* stands, and not the high mountain at the end of the plain, according to the French map. Upon reaching the *Choma* (χῶμα), the road divided into two, one road leading direct to Pallantium, and the other SW. to Megalopolis through Asea. (Paus. viii. 44. § 1, seq.; Xen. *Hell.* vi. 5. § 9, αἱ ἐπὶ τὸ Παλλάντιον φέρουσαι πύλαι.) This choma separated the territories of Pallantium and Tegea, and extended as far south as Mount Boreium (*Krávori*), where it touched the territory of Megalopolis. There are still remains of this choma running NE. to SW. by the side of the marsh of *Taki.* These remains consist of large blocks of stone, and must be regarded as the foundations of the *choma*, which cannot have been a *chaussée* or causeway, as the French geographers call it, since χῶμα always signifies in Greek writers an artificial heap of earth, a tumulus, mound, or dyke. (Ross, p. 59.) A fourth road led SE. from Tegea, by the sources of the Garates to Thyreatis. (Paus. viii. 54. § 4.) A fifth road led NE. to Hysiae and Argos, across the Corythic plain, and then across Mt. Parthenium, where was a temple of Pan, erected on the spot at which the god appeared to the courier Pheidippides. This road was practicable for carriages, and was much frequented. (Paus. viii. 54. § 5, seq.; Herod. vi. 105, 106; *Dict. of Biogr.* art. PHEIDIPPIDES.) (Leake, *Morea*, vol. i. p. 88, seq., vol. ii. p. 333, *Peloponnesiaca*, pp. 112, seq., 369; Ross, *Peloponnes*, p. 66, seq.; Curtius, *Peloponnesos*, vol. i. p. 247, seq.; Koner, *Com. de Rebus Tegeatarum*, Berol. 1843.)

The Roman poets use the adjective Tegēēus or Tegaeaeus as equivalent to Arcadian: thus it is given as an epithet to Pan (Virg. *Georg.* i. 18), Callisto, daughter of Lycaon (Ov. *Ar. Am.* ii. 55, *Fast.* ii. 167), Atalanta (Ov. *Met.* viii. 317, 380), Carmenta (Ov. *Fast.* i. 627), and Mercury (Stat. *Silv.* i. 54)

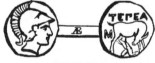

COIN OF TEGEA.

TEGIA'NUM (*Eth.* Tegianensis: *Diano*), a municipal town of Lucania, situated in the interior of that country, on the left bank of the river Tanager. Its name is found only in a corrupt form in Pliny,

who enumerates the Tergilani among the "populi" in the interior of Lucania (Plin. iii. 11. s. 15); but the Liber Coloniarum mentions the "Praefectura Tegenensis" among the Praefecturae of Lucania (*Lib. Col.* p. 209), and the correct form of the name is preserved by inscriptions. From the same source we learn that it was a town of municipal rank, while the discovery of them in the neighbourhood of *Diano* leaves no doubt that that place represents the ancient Tegianum. (Romanelli, vol. i. p. 415; Mommsen, *Inscr. R. N.* pp. 18, 19.) The modern city of *Diano* is a considerable place situated on a hill about 4 miles west of *La Sala*, and gives the name of *Valle di Diano* to the whole of the extensive upland valley which is traversed by the river *Tanagro* in the upper part of its course. Some remains of the ancient city are still visible in the plain at the foot of the hill (Romanelli, *l. c.*). [E. H. B.]

TEGLI'CIUM (*Itin. Ant.* p. 223), TEGULICIUM (*Tab. Peut.*), and TEGULITIA (Geogr. Rav. iv. 7), a place in Moesia Inferior, on the road between Candidiana and Dorostolum. It contained, according to the *Not. Imp.*, a garrison of light troops. Variously placed near *Veternicza* and *Tataritza.* Some modern writers identify it with the fortress in Moesia called Saltopyrgus by Procopius (*de Aedif.* iv. 7.) [T. H. D.]

TEGNA, in Gallia Narbonensis, was on the Roman road on the east bank of the Rhone between Vienna (*Vienne*) and Valentia (*Valence*). The name occurs in the Table, in which the place is fixed at xiii. from Valentia. Tegna is *Tein*, the name of which in the writings of a later date is Tinctum. A milestone at *Tein* marks the distance to Vienna xxxviii. *Tein* is right opposite to *Tournon*, which is on the west side of the river. *Tournon* is well situated, and the mountains there approach close to the *Rhone.* (D'Anville, *Notice, &c.*; Ukert, *Gallien.*) [G. L.]

TEGRA. [TIGRA.]

TEGULATA, in Gallia Narbonensis, is placed in the Itins. east of Aquae Sextiae (*Aix*) on the road to Ad Turrim (*Tourves*). The distance from Aquae Sextiae to Tegulata is xv. or xvi., and from Tegulata to Ad Turrim xvi. The distance measured along the road between Aquae Sextiae and Ad Turrim is said to exceed the direct distance between these two places, which is not more than 28 Roman miles. Tegulata is supposed to be *La Grande Peigière*, near the bourg of *Porrières* or *Pourrières*, perhaps somewhere about the place where C. Marius defeated the Teutones B. C. 102, and where a pyramid was erected to commemorate the great victory. This monument is said to have existed to the fifteenth century (A. Thierry, *Hist. des Gaulois, Deux. Partie*, c. 3); and the tradition of this great battle is not yet effaced. *Pourrières* is said to be a corruption of Putridi Campi. (D'Anville, *Notice, &c.*) [G. L.]

TEGULICIUM [TEGLICIUM].

TEGYRA (Τεγύρα: *Eth.* Τεγυρεύς), a village of Boeotia, near Orchomenus, and situated above the marshes of the river Melas. It was celebrated for its oracle and Temple of Apollo, who was even said to have been born there. In its neighbourhood was a mountain named Delos. Leake places Tegyra at *Xerópyrgo*, situated 3 miles ENE. of *Skripú* (Orchomenus), on the heights which bound the marshes. (Plut. *Pelop.* 16, *de Def. Or.* 5 and 8; Lycophr. 646; Steph. B. *s. v.*; Leake, *Northern Greece*, vol. ii. pp. 155, 159; comp. Ulrichs, *Reisen*, vol. i. p. 196.)

TEHAPHENES. [TAHPANIS.]

TEICHIUM (Τείχιον), a town of Aetolia Epictetus, on the borders of Locris, and one day's march from Crocyleium. (Thuc. iii. 96.)

TEKOAH (Θεκωέ, 1 Maccab. ix. 33; Θεκώα or Θεκουέ, Joseph. Vit. 75), a town of Palestine in Judah, to the south of Bethlehem. It was the residence of the wise woman who pleaded in behalf of Absalom; was fortified by Rehoboam; was the birthplace of the prophet Amos, and gave its name to the adjacent desert on the east. (2 Sam. xiv. 2; 2 Chron. xi. 6; Amos, i. 1; 2 Chron. xx. 20; 1 Macc. ix. 33.) Jerome describes Tekoah as situated upon a hill, 6 miles south of Bethlehem, from which city it was visible. (Hieron. Procem. in Amos. and Comm. in Jerem. vi. 1.) Its site still bears the name of Teku'a, and is described by Robinson as an elevated hill, not steep, but broad on the top, and covered with ruins to the extent of four or five acres. These consist chiefly of the foundations of houses built of squared stones; and near the middle of the site are the remains of a Greek church. (Robinson, Bibl. Res. vol. i. p. 486, 2nd ed.)

TELA, a place of the Vaccaei in Hispania Tarraconensis (Itin. Ant. p. 440). Variously identified with Fordesillas and Medina de Rio Seco. [T.H.D.]

TE'LAMON (Τελαμών: Telamone), a city on the coast of Etruria, situated on a promontory between the Mons Argentarius and the mouth of the Umbro (Ombrone), with a tolerable port adjoining it. The story told by Diodorus of its having derived its name from the hero Telamon, who accompanied the Argonauts on their voyage, may be safely dismissed as an etymological fable (Diod. iv. 56). There seems no reason to doubt that it was originally an Etruscan town, but no mention of its name occurs in history during the period of Etruscan independence. It is first noticed in B. C. 225, when a great battle was fought by the Romans in its immediate neighbourhood with an army of Cisalpine Gauls, who had made an irruption into Etruria, but were intercepted by the consuls C. Atilius and L. Aemilius in the neighbourhood of Telamon, and totally defeated. They are said to have lost 40,000 men slain, and 10,000 prisoners, among whom was one of their chiefs or kings (Pol. i. 27—31). The battle, which is described by Polybius in considerable detail, is expressly stated by him to have occurred "near Telamon in Etruria:" Frontinus, in speaking of the same battle, places the scene of it near Populonia (Strat. i. 2. § 7), but the authority of Polybius is certainly preferable. The only other mention of Telamon that occurs in history is in B. C. 87, when Marius landed there on his return from exile, and commenced gathering an army around him. (Plut. Mar. 41.) But there is no doubt that it continued to exist as a town, deriving some importance from its port, throughout the period of the Roman dominion. Its name is found both in Mela and Pliny, who calls it "portus Telamon," while Ptolemy notices only the promontory of the name (Τελαμών ἄκρον, Ptol. iii. 1. § 4; Plin. iii. 5. s. 8; Mel. ii. 4. § 9). The Itineraries prove that it was still in existence as late as the 4th century (Tab. Peut.; Itin. Marit. p. 500, where it is called "Portus Talamonis"); but from this time all trace of it disappears till the 14th century, when a castle was erected on the site. This, with the miserable village which adjoins it, still bears the name of Telamone; and the shores of the bay are lined with remains of Roman buildings, but of no great interest;

and there are no relics of Etruscan antiquity. (Dennis's Etruria, vol. ii. p. 258.) [E. H. B.]

TELCHI'NES. [RHODUS, p. 713.]

TELEBOAE. [TAPHIAE.]

TELE'BOAS (ὁ Τηλεβόας ποταμός, Xen. Anab. iv. 4. § 3), a river of Armenia Major, a tributary of the Euphrates. Probably identical with the ARSANIAS. [T. H. D.]

TELE'PHRIUS MONS. [EUBOEA.]

TELEPTE. [THALA.]

TELE'SIA (Τελεσία: Eth. Telesinus: Telese), a considerable city of Samnium, situated in the valley of the Calor, a short distance from its right bank, and about 3 miles above its confluence with the Vulturnus. It is remarkable that its name is never mentioned during the long wars of the Romans with the Samnites, though the valley in which it was situated was often the theatre of hostilities. Its name first occurs in the Second Punic War, when it was taken by Hannibal on his first irruption into Samnium, B. C. 217 (Liv. xxii. 13); but was recovered by Fabius in B. C. 214. (Id. xxiv. 20.) From this time we hear no more of it till it became an ordinary Roman municipal town. Strabo speaks of it as having in his time fallen into almost complete decay, in common with most of the cities of Samnium. (Strab. v. p. 250.) But we learn that it received a colony in the time of the Triumvirate (Lib. Colon. p. 238); and, though not mentioned by Pliny as a colony (the name is altogether omitted by him), it is certain, from inscriptions, that it retained its colonial rank, and appears to have continued under the Roman Empire to have been a flourishing and considerable town. (Orell. Inscr. 2626; Romanelli, vol. ii. p. 423; Mommsen, Inscr. R. N. 4840—4915.) It was situated on the line of the Via Latina, or rather of a branch of that road which was carried from Teanum in Campania through Allifae and Telesia to Beneventum (Itin. Ant. pp. 122, 304; Tab. Peut.), and this probably contributed to preserve it from decay.

The ruins of the ancient city are still visible about a mile to the NW. of the village still called Telese : the circuit of the walls is complete, inclosing a space of octagonal shape, not exceeding 1½ mile in circumference, with several gates, flanked by massive towers. The masonry is of reticulated work, and therefore probably not earlier than the time of the Roman Empire. The only ruins within the circuit of the walls are mere shapeless mounds of brick; but outside the walls may be traced the vestiges of a circus, and some remains of an amphitheatre. All these remains undoubtedly belong to the Roman colony, and there are no vestiges of the ancient Samnite city. The present village of Telese is a very small and poor place, rendered desolate by malaria; but in the middle ages it was an episcopal see, and its principal church is still dignified by the name of a cathedral. Its walls contain many Latin inscriptions, brought from the ancient city, the inhabitants of which migrated to the later site in the ninth century. (Craven, Abruzzi, vol. ii. pp. 173—175; Giustiniani, Dizion. Topogr. vol. ix. pp. 149, 150.)

Telesia was remarkable as being the birthplace of the celebrated Samnite leader, during the Social War, Pontius Telesinus; and it is probable (though there is no distinct authority for the fact) that it was also that of the still more celebrated C. Pontius, who defeated the Romans at the Caudine Forks. [E. H. B.]

TELIS. [RUSCINO.]

4 c

TELLE'NAE (Τελλήνη; Dion. Hal.; Τελλῆναι, Strab.: *Eth.* Τελληνεύς, Tellenensis), an ancient city of Latium, which figures in the early Roman history. According to Dionysius it was one of the cities founded by the Aborigines soon after their settlement in Latium (Dionys. i. 16), a proof at least that it was regarded as a place of great antiquity. Livy also reckons it as one of the cities of the Prisci Latini (i. 33), which may perhaps point to the same result, while Diodorus includes it in his list of the colonies of Alba. (Diod. vii. *ap. Euseb. Arm.* p. 185.) It was attacked by the Roman king Ancus Marcius, who took the city, and transported the inhabitants to Rome, where he settled them on the Aventine, together with those of Politorium and Ficana. (Liv. i. 33; Dionys. iii. 38, 43.) Tellenae, however, does not seem, like the other two places just mentioned, to have been hereby reduced to insignificance; for its name appears again in B. C. 493 among the confederate cities of the Latin League (Dionys. v. 61); and though this is the last mention that we find of it in history, it is noticed both by Strabo and Dionysius as a place still in existence in their time. (Dionys. i. 16; Strab. v. p. 231.) It is probable, however, that it had at that time fallen into complete decay, like Antemnae and Collatia; as it is only mentioned by Pliny among the once celebrated cities of Latium, which had left no traces of their existence in his day (Plin. iii. 5. s. 9), and from this time its name wholly disappears. The notices of Tellenae afford scarcely any clue to its position; though the circumstance that it continued to be inhabited, however slightly, down to the days of Augustus, would afford us more hope of being able to identify its site than is the case with Politorium, Apiolae, and other places, which ceased to exist at a very early period. It is this reason that has led Nibby to identify the ruins of an ancient city at *La Giostra*, as those of Tellenae, rather than Politorium, as supposed by Gell. [POLITORIUM.] The site in question is a narrow ridge, bounded by two ravines of no great depth, but with abrupt and precipitous banks, in places artificially scarped, and still presenting extensive remains of the ancient walls, constructed in an irregular style of massive quadrangular blocks of tufo. No doubt can exist that these indicate the site of an ancient city, but whether of Politorium or Tellenae, it is impossible to determine; though the remains of a Roman villa, which indicate that the spot must have been inhabited in the early ages of the Empire, give some additional probability to the latter attribution. *La Giostra* is situated on the right of the Via Appia, about 2 miles from a farm-house called *Fiorano*, immediately adjoining the line of the ancient highroad. It is distant 10 miles from Rome, and 3 from *Le Frattocchie*, on the Via Appia, adjoining the ruins of Bovillae. (Gell, *Top. of Rome*, pp. 280 —283; Nibby, *Dintorni*, vol. iii. pp. 146—153.)

Whether the proverbial expression of "tricae Tellenae" has any reference to the ancient city of Latium or not, can hardly be determined, the origin and meaning of the phrase being involved in complete obscurity. (Varro, *ap. Non.* i. p. 8; Arnob. *adv. Gentes*, v. p. 28, with Oehler's note.) [E. H. B.]

TELMESSUS, or TELMISSUS (Τελμησσός, Τελμισσός, or Τελμισός: *Eth.* Τελμισσεύς). 1. A flourishing and prosperous city in the west of Lycia, was situated near Cape Telmissis (Strab. xiv. p. 665), or Telmissus (Steph. B. *s. v.* Τελμισσός), on a bay which derived from it the name of

Sinus Telmisaicus. (Liv. xxxvii. 16; Lucan. viii. 248.) On the south-west of it was Cape Pedalium, at a distance of 200 stadia. Its inhabitants were celebrated in ancient times for their skill as diviners, and were often consulted by the Lydian kings. (Herod. i. 78; comp. Arrian, *Anab.* ii. 3. § 4.) In the time of Strabo, however, who calls it a small town (πολίχνη), it seems to have fallen into decay; though at a later period it appears to have been an episcopal see. (Hierocl. p. 684; comp. Pomp. Mela, i. 15; Plin. v. 28 ; Ptol. v. 3. § 2 ; Polyb. xxii. 27; *Stadiasm. Mar. M.* §§ 255, 256; Scylax, p. 39, where it is miswritten Θεανισσός.) Considerable remains of Telmessus still exist at *Myes* or *Meis;* and those of a theatre, porticoes, and sepulchral chambers in the living rock, are among the most remarkable in all Asia Minor. (Leake, *Asia Minor*, p. 128; Fellows, *Asia Minor*, p. 243, where some representations of the remains of Telmessus are figured; *Lycia*, p. 106, foll.)

2. A small town of Caria, at a distance of 60 stadia from Halicarnassus, is likewise sometimes called Telmessus, and sometimes Telmisus. (Suid. *s. v.* ; *Etym. Mag. s. v.*; Arrian, *Anab.* i. 25. § 8; Cic. *de Div.* i. 41; Plin. v. 29, xxx. 2.) The Carian Telmessus has often been confounded with the Lycian, and it is even somewhat doubtful whether the famous Telmessian soothsayers belonged to the Carian or the Lycian town. But the former must at all events have been an obscure place; and that it cannot have been the same as the latter is clear from the statement of Polemo in Suidas, that it was only 60 stadia from Halicarnassus. [L. S.]

TELMESSUS, according to Pliny (v. 29), a tributary of the river Glaucus in Caria, but it flowed in all probability near the town of Telmessus, which derived its name from it. [L. S.]

TELMI'SSICUS SINUS, a bay between Lycia and Caria, which derived its name from the Lycian town of Telmessus (Liv. xxxvii. 16; Lucan. viii. 248); but it is more commonly known by the name Glaucus Sinus, and is at present called the *Bay of Macri.* [L. S.]

TELMISSIS PROMONTORIUM. [TELMESSUS.]

TE'LOBIS (Τηλοβίς, Ptol. ii. 6. § 72), a town of the Jaccetani in Hispania Tarraconensis, now *Martorell.* (Cf. Laborde, *Itin.* i. § 73; Swinburne, Lett. 8.) [T. H. D.]

TELO MARTIUS (*Toulon*), in Gallia Narbonensis. This name is not mentioned by the geographers. It occurs in the Maritime Itin. and in the Notit. Imp. Occid., where a " procurator Baphii Telonensis Galliarum " is mentioned, which indicates the existence of a dyeing establishment there. In Lucan (iii. 592) Telo is the name of a pilot or helmsman, and Oudendorp supposes that the poet gave the man this name because he was of the town Telo; which seems a strange conjecture. And again Silius (xiv. 443) is supposed to allude to the same town, when he says—

" Et Neptunicolae transverberat ora Telonis."

The old Roman town is said to have been at or near *Toulouzan*, where the Lazaretto now is. (*Statist. du Dép. des Bouches du Rhône*, referred to by Ukert, *Gallien*, p. 428.) [G. L.]

TELONNUM, in Gallia. The Table has a name on the route between Aquae Bormonis (*Bourbon l'Archambault*) and Augustodunum (*Autun*), which name begins with *T* and ends with *onnum.* D'Anville gives good reasons for supposing that the place may be *Toulon-sur-Arroux;* and thus the modern name may enable us to correct the reading of the Table.　　　　　　　　　　　　　　　　[G. L.]

TELOS (Τῆλος: *Eth.* Τήλιος: *Dilos* or *Piscopia*), a small rocky island in the Carpathian sea, between Rhodus and Nisyrus, from the latter of which its distance is only 60 stadia. Strabo (x. p. 488) describes it as long and high, and abounding in stones fit for millstones. Its circumference was 80 stadia, and it contained a town of the same name, a harbour, hot springs, and a temple of Poseidon. The attribute long given to it by Strabo is scarcely correct, since the island is rather of a circular form. The family of the Sicilian tyrant Gelon originally came from Telos. (Herod. vii. 153.) According to Pliny (iv. 69) the island was celebrated for a species of ointment, and was in ancient times called Agathussa. (Steph. B. *s. v.* Τῆλος; Scylax, p. 38; *Stadiasm. Mar. Magni,* § 272.) The town of Telos was situated on the north coast, and remains of it are still seen above the modern village of *Episcopi.* The houses, it appears, were all built in terraces rising above one another, and supported by strong walls of unhewn stone. The acropolis, of which likewise a few remains exist, was at the top, which is now occupied by a mediaeval castle. Inscriptions have been found in Telos in great numbers, but, owing to the nature of the stone, many of them are now illegible. (Comp. Ross, *Hellenica,* i. p. 59, foll., *Reisen auf den Griech. Inseln,* iv. p. 42, foll.)　　　　　　　　　　　　　　　　[L. S.]

TELPHU'SA. [THELPUSA.]

TEMA, a tribe and district in Arabia, which took their name from Tema, one of the twelve sons of Ishmael. (*Gen.* xxv. 15; *Is.* xxi. 14; *Jer.* xxv. 23; *Job,* vi. 19.) Ptolemy mentions in Arabia Deserta a town Themma (Θέμμη, v. 19. § 6). Tema is distinguished in the Old Testament from Teman, a tribe and district in the land of the Edomites (Idumaea), which derived their name from Teman, a grandson of Esau. (*Gen.* xxxvi. 11, 15, 42; *Jer.* xlix. 7, 20; *Ezek.* xxv. 13; *Amos,* i. 12; *Hab.* iii. 3; *Obad.* 9.) The Temanites, like the other Edomites, are celebrated in the Old Testament for their wisdom (*Jerem.* xlix. 7; *Obad.* 8; *Baruch,* iii. 22, seq.); and hence we find that Eliphaz, in the book of Job, is a Temanite. (*Job,* ii. 11, iv. 1.) Jerome (*Onomast. s. v.*) represents Tema as distant 5 miles (Eusebius says 15 miles) from Petra, and possessing a Roman garrison.

TE'MALA (Τημάλα, Ptol. vii. 2. § 3), a river in the Aurea Regio, in the district of India extra Gangem, probably now represented by the great river of *Pegu,* the *Irawaddy.* Near it was a town which bore the same name.　　　　　　　　　　　　[V.]

TEMA'THIA. [MESSENIA, p. 341, b.]

TEME'NIUM (Τημένιον), a town in the Argeia, at the upper end of the Argolic gulf, built by Temenus, the son of Aristomachus. It was distant 50 stadia from Nauplia (Paus. ii. 38. § 2), and 26 from Argos. (Strab. viii. p. 368.) The river Phrixus flowed into the sea between Temenium and Lerna. (Paus. ii. 36. § 6, ii. 38. § 1.) Pausanias saw at Temenium two temples of Poseidon and Aphrodite and the tomb of Temenus (ii. 38. § 1). Owing to the marshy nature of the plain, Leake was unable to explore the site of Temenium; but Ross identifies it with a mound of earth, at the foot of which, in the sea, are remains of a dam forming a harbour, and upon the shore foundations of buildings, fragments of pottery, &c. (Leake,

Morea, vol. ii. p. 476; Ross, *Reisen im Peloponnes,* p. 149; Curtius, *Peloponnesos,* vol. ii. p. 383.)

TEMENOTHYRA (Τημένου θύραι, Paus. i. 35. § 7: *Eth.* Τημενοθυρεύς, Coins), a small city of Lydia, according to Pausanias (*l. c.*), or of Phrygia, according to Hierocles (p. 668, ed. Wess.). It would seem to have been situated upon the borders of Mysia, since the Trimenothuritae (Τριμενοθουρῖται) —which name is probably only another form of the Temenothyritae—are placed by Ptolemy (v. 2. § 15) in Mysia. (Eckhel, vol. iii. p. 119.)

TE'MESA or TEMPSA (Τεμέση and Τέμψα, Strab.; Τεμέση, Steph. B.; Τέμψα, Ptol.: *Eth.* Τεμεσαῖος, Tempsanus), an ancient city on the W. coast of Bruttium, a little to the N. of the Gulf of Hipponium, or *Golfo di Sta Eufemia.* Strabo tells us that it was originally an Ausonian city, but subsequently occupied by a colony of Aetolians who had accompanied Thoas to the Trojan War. (Strab. vi. p. 255.) Many writers appear to have supposed this to be the Temesa mentioned by Homer in the Odyssey on account of its mines of copper (*Odyss.* i. 184); and this view is adopted by Strabo; though it is much more probable that the place alluded to by the poet was Temesa in Cyprus, otherwise called Tamasus. (Strab. *l. c.*; Steph. B. *s. v.*; Schol. *ad Hom. Odyss. l. c.*) We have no account of Temesa having received a Greek colony in historical times though it seems to have become to a great extent Hellenised, like so many other cities in this part of Italy. At one period, indeed, we learn that it was conquered by the Locrians (about 480—460 B. C.); but we know not how long it continued subject to their rule. (Strab. *l. c.*) Neither Scylax nor Scymnus Chius mention it among the Greek cities in this part of Italy; but Livy says expressly that it was a Greek city before it fell into the hands of the Bruttians (Liv. xxxiv. 45). That people apparently made themselves masters of it at an early period of their career, and it remained in their hands till the whole country became subject to the dominion of Rome. (Strab. *l. c.*) During the Second Punic War it suffered severely at the hands, first of Hannibal, and then of the Romans; but some years after the close of the war it was one of the places selected by the Romans for the establishment of a colony, which was sent thither at the same time with that to Crotona, B. C. 194. (Liv. xxxiv. 45.) But this colony, the members of which had the privileges of Roman citizens, does not appear to have been numerous, and the town never rose to be a place of importance. Its copper mines, which are alluded to by several writers (Ovid, *Met.* xv. 706; Stat. *Silv.* i. 1. 42), had ceased to be productive in the days of Strabo (Strab. vi. p. 256). The only mention of Tempsa which occurs in Roman history is in connection with the great servile insurrection under Spartacus, when a remnant of the servile force seem to have established themselves at Tempsa, and for a time maintained possession of the town. (Cic. *Verr.*

v. 15, 16.) Its name is afterwards found in all the geographers, as well as in the Tabula, so that it must have subsisted as a town throughout the Roman Empire. (Strab. *l. c.*; Plin. iii. 5. s. 10; Ptol. iii. 1. § 9; *Tab. Peut.*) Pausanias expressly tells us it was still inhabited in his day; and Pliny also notices it for the excellence of its wine. (Paus. vi. 6. § 10; Plin. xiv. 6. s. 8.) The period of its destruction is unknown; but after the fall of the Roman Empire the name wholly disappears, and its exact site has never been determined. The best clue is that afforded by the Tabula (which accords well with the statements of Pliny and Strabo), that it was situated 10 miles S. of Clampetia. If this last town be correctly placed at *Amantea* [CLAMPETIA], the site of Tempsa must be looked for on the coast near the *Torre del Piano del Casale*, about 2 miles S. of the river *Savuto*, and 3 from *Nocera*. Unfortunately none of the towns along this line of coast can be fixed with anything like certainty. (Cluver. *Ital.* p. 1286; Romanelli, vol. i. p. 35.)

Near Temesa was a sacred grove, with a shrine or sanctuary of the hero Polites, one of the companions of Ulysses, who was said to have been slain on the spot, and whose spectre continued to trouble the inhabitants, until at length Euthymus, the celebrated Locrian athlete, ventured to wrestle with the spirit, and having vanquished it, freed the city from all further molestation. (Strab. vi. p. 255; Paus. vi. 6. §§ 7—11; Suid. *v.* Εὐθυμος.)   [E. H. B.]

TEMI'SDIA (ἡ Τεμισδία, Ptol. vi. 4. § 3), one of the districts into which ancient Persia was divided. It cannot now be determined exactly what its position was; but, as it adjoined the Mesabatae, it probably was part of a long narrow plain which extends through that province in a direction north-west and south-east. (Lassen, in Ersch und Gruber's *Encycl.* vol. xvii. p. 438.)   [V.]

TEMMICES. [BOEOTIA, p. 414.]

TEMNUS (Τῆμνον ὄρος), a mountain range of Mysia, extending from Mount Ida eastward into Phrygia, and dividing Mysia into two halves, a northern and a southern one. It contained the sources of the Macestus, Mysius, Caicus, and Evenus. (Strab. xiii. p. 616; Ptol. v. 2. § 13.) Hamilton (*Researches*, ii. p. 125) is inclined to believe that Mons Temnus is the same as the *Ak Dagh*, or, as it is commonly called in maps, *Morad Dagh.*   [L. S.]

TEMNUS (Τῆμνος: Eth. Τημνίτης), a town of Aeolis in Asia Minor, not far from the river Hermus, situated on a height, from which a commanding view was obtained over the territories of Cyme, Phocaea, and Smyrna. (Strab. xiii. p. 621.) From a passage in Pausanias (v. 13. § 4), it might be inferred that the town was situated on the northern bank of the Hermus. But this is irreconcilable with the statement that Temnus was 30 miles south of Cyme, and with the remarks of all other writers alluding to the place. Pliny (v. 29) also seems to be mistaken in placing Temnus at the mouth of the Hermus, for although the deposits of the river have formed an extensive alluvial tract of land, it is evident that the sea never extended as far as the site of Temnus. The town had already much decayed in the time of Strabo, though it never appears to have been very large. (Xenoph. *Hell.* iv. 8. § 5; Herod. i. 149; Polyb. v. 77, xx. 25; Cic. *pro Flacc.* 18.) In the reign of Tiberius it was much injured by an earthquake (Tac. *Ann.* ii. 47), and in the time of Pliny it had ceased

to be inhabited altogether. Its site is commonly identified with the modern *Menimen*, though Texier, in his *Description de l'Asie Mineure*, looks for it at the site of the village of *Guzal-Hissar*. [L. S.]

COIN OF TEMNUS.

TEMPE (τὰ Τέμπη, contr. of Τέμπεα), a celebrated valley in the NE. of Thessaly, is a gorge between Mounts Olympus and Ossa, through which the waters of the Peneius force their way into the sea. The beauties of Tempe were a favourite subject with the ancient poets, and have been described at great length in a well-known passage of Aelian; and more briefly by Pliny: but none of these writers appear to have drawn their pictures from actual observation; and the scenery is distinguished rather by savage grandeur than by the sylvan beauty which Aelian and others attribute to it. (Catull. lxiv. 285; Ov. *Met.* i. 568; Virg. *Georg.* ii. 469; Aelian, *V. H.* iii. 1; Plin. iv. 8. s. 15.) The account of Livy, who copies from Polybius, an eye-witness, is more in accordance with reality. This writer says, "Tempe is a defile, difficult of access, even though not guarded by an enemy; for besides the narrowness of the pass for 5 miles, where there is scarcely room for a beast of burden, the rocks on both sides are so perpendicular as to cause giddiness both in the mind and eyes of those who look down from the precipice. Their terror is also increased by the depth and roar of the Peneus rushing through the midst of the valley." (Liv. xliv. 6.) He adds that this pass, so inaccessible by nature, was defended by four fortresses, one at the western entrance at Gonnus, a second at Condylon, a third at Charax, and a fourth in the road itself, in the middle and narrowest part of the valley, which could be easily defended by ten men. The pass is now called *Lykóstomo*, or the *Wolf's Mouth.* Col. Leake gives about four miles and a half as the distance of the road through the valley. In this space the width of the gorge is in some parts less than 100 yards, comprehending in fact no more than the breadth of the road in addition to that of the river. The modern road follows in the track of the ancient military road made by the Romans, which ran along the right bank of the river. Leake remarks that even Livy in his description of Tempe seems to have added embellishments to the authority from which he borrowed; for, instead of the Peneius flowing rapidly and with a loud noise, nothing can be more tranquil and steady than its ordinary course. The remains of the fourth castle mentioned by Livy are noticed by Leake as standing on one side of an immense fissure in the precipices of Ossa, which afford an extremely rocky, though not impracticable descent from the heights into the vale; while between the castle and the river space only was left for the road. About half a mile beyond this fort there still remains an inscription engraved upon the rock, on the right-hand side of the road, where it ascends the hill: "L. Cassius Longinus Pro Cos. Tempe munivit." It is probable from the position of this inscription that it relates to the making of the road, though some refer it to defensive works erected by Longinus in Tempe. This Longinus appears to have been the L. Cassius Longinus who was sent by Caesar from Illyria into Thessaly. (Caes. *B. C.* lii. 34.) When Xerxes invaded Greece, B. c. 480, the Greeks sent a force of 10,000 men to Tempe, with the intention of defending the pass against the Persians; but having learnt from Alexander, the king of Macedonia, that there was another pass across Mt. Olympus, which entered Thessaly near Gonnus, where the gorge of Tempe commenced, the Greeks withdrew to Thermopylae. (Herod. vii. 173.)

It was believed by the ancient historians and geographers that the gorge of Tempe had been produced by an earthquake, which rent asunder the mountains, and afforded the waters of the Peneius an egress to the sea. (Herod. vii. 129; Strab. ix. p. 430.) But the Thessalians maintained that it was the god Poseidon who had split the mountains (Herod. *l. c.*); while others supposed that this had been the work of Hercules. (Diod. iv. 58; Lucan, vi. 345.)

The pass of Tempe was connected with the worship of Apollo. This god was believed to have gone thither to receive expiation after the slaughter of the serpent Pytho, and afterwards to have returned to Delphi, bearing in his hand a branch of laurel plucked in the valley. Every ninth year the Delphians sent a procession to Tempe consisting of wellborn youths, of which the chief youth plucked a branch of laurel and brought it back to Delphi. On this occasion a solemn festival, in which the inhabitants of the neighbouring regions took part, was celebrated at Tempe in honour of Apollo Tempeites. The procession was accompanied by a flute-player. (Aelian, *V. H.* iii. 1; Plut. *Quaest. Graec.* c. 11. p. 292, *de Musica*, c. 14. p. 1136; Böckh, *Inscr.* No. 1767, quoted by Grote, *Hist. of Greece*, vol. ii. p. 365.)

The name of Tempe was applied to other beautiful valleys. Thus the valley, through which the Helorus flows in Sicily, is called "Heloria Tempe" (Ov. *Fast.* iv. 477); and Cicero gives the name of Tempe to the valley of the Velinus, near Reate (*ad Att.* iv. 15). In the same way Ovid speaks of the "Heliconia Tempe" (*Am.* i. 1. 15).

(Leake, *Northern Greece*, vol. iii. p. 390, seq.; Dodwell, vol. ii. p. 109, seq.; Hawkins, in Walpole's *Collection*, vol. i. p. 517, seq.; Kriegk, *Das Thessalische Tempe*, Leipzig, 1835.)

TEMPSA. [TEMESA.]

TEMPY'RA (Ov. *Trist.* i. 10. 21; in Geogr. Rav. iv. 6, Tympira; in *It. Ant.* p. 322, Timpirum; and in *It. Hier.* p. 602, Ad Unimpara), a town in the S. of Thrace, on the Egnatian Way, between Trajanopolis and Maximianopolis. It was situated in a defile, which rendered it a convenient spot for the operations of the predatory tribes in its neighbourhood. Here the Thrausi attacked the Roman army under Cn. Manlius, on its return, loaded with booty, through Thrace from Asia Minor (B. c. 188); but the want of shelter exposed their movements to the Romans, who were thus enabled to defeat them. (Liv. xxxviii. 41.) The defile in question is probably the same as the Κορπίλων στενά mentioned by Appian (*B. C.* iv. 102), and through which, he states, Brutus and Cassius marched on their way to Philippi (Tafel, *de Viae Egnatiae Parte orient.* p. 34). Paul Lucas (*Trois Voy.* pp. 25, 27) regards it as corresponding to the modern *Gürschine*.   [J. R.]

TE'NCTERI or TE'NCHTERI (Τέγκτεροι, Τέγκτηροι, Τέγκεροι, and Ταγχρίαι or Ταγχαρέαι), an important German tribe, which is first mentioned by Caesar (*B. G.* iv. 1, 4). They appear, together with the Usipetes, originally to have occupied a district in the interior of Germany; but on being driven from their original homes by the Suevi, and having wandered about for a period of three years, they arrived on the banks of the Lower Rhine, and compelled the Menapii who inhabited both sides of the river to retreat to the western bank. Some time after this, the Germans even crossed the Rhine, established themselves on the western bank, in the country of the Menapii, and spread in all directions as far as the districts of the Eburones and Condrusi, who seem to have invited their assistance against the Romans. This happened in B.C. 56. The Germans demanded to be allowed to settle in Gaul; but Caesar, declaring that there was no room for them, promised to procure habitations for them in the country of the Ubii, who happened to have sent ambassadors to him at that time. The Germans asked for three days to consider the matter, requesting Caesar not to advance farther into their country. But, suspecting some treacherous design, he proceeded on his march, and an engagement ensued, in which the Romans were defeated and sustained serious losses. On the following day the chiefs of the Germans appeared before Caesar, declaring that their people had attacked the Romans without their orders, and again begged Caesar to stop his march. Caesar, however, not only kept the chiefs as his prisoners, but immediately ordered an attack to be made on their camp. The people, who during the absence of their chiefs had abandoned themselves to the feeling of security, were thrown into the greatest confusion by the unsuspected attack. The men, however, fought on and among their waggons, while the women and children took to flight. The Roman cavalry pursued the fugitives; and when the Germans heard the screams of their wives and children, and saw them cut to pieces, they threw away their arms and fled towards the Rhine; but as the river stopped their flight, a great number of them perished by the sword of the Romans, and others were drowned in the Rhine. Those who escaped across the river were hospitably received by the Sigambri, who assigned to the Tencteri the district between the *Ruhr* and the *Sieg.* (Caes. *B. G.* iv. 4—16; Livy, *Epit.* lib. cxxxviii.; Tac. *Germ.* 32, 33, *Ann.* xiii. 56, *Hist.* iv. 21, 64, 77; Plut. *Caes.* 21; Dion Cass. xxxix. 47, liv. 20, 21; Flor. iii. 10, iv. 12; Oros. iv. 20; Appian, *de Reb. Gall.* 4, 18; Ptol. ii. 11. § 8.) The Tencteri were particularly celebrated for their excellent cavalry; and in their new country, on the eastern bank of the Rhine, they possessed the town of Budaris (either *Monheim* or *Düsseldorf*), and the fort of Divitia (*Deutz*). In the reign of Augustus, the Tencteri joined the confederacy of the Cherusci (Liv. *l. c.*), and afterwards repeatedly appear joining other tribes in their wars against Rome, until in the end they appear as a part of the great confederacy of the Franks. (Greg. Tur. ii. 9; comp. Wilhelm, *Germanien*, p. 141; Reichard, *Germanien*, p. 31; Latham, *Tacit. Germ.* p. 110.)   [L. S.]

TE'NEA (Τενέα: Eth. Τενεάτης), the most important place in the Corinthia after the city of Corinth and her port towns, was situated south of the capital, and at the distance of 60 stadia from the latter, according to Pausanias. The southern gate of Corinth was called the Teneatic, from its leading to

Tenea. Stephanus describes Tenea as lying between Corinth and Mycenae. (*s. v. Tενία.*) The Teneatae claimed descent from the inhabitants of Tenedos, who were brought over from Troy as prisoners, and settled by Agamemnon in this part of the Corinthia; and they said that it was in consequence of their Trojan origin that they worshipped Apollo above all the other gods. (Paus. ii. 5. § 4.) Strabo also mentions here the temple of Apollo Teneates, and says that Tenea and Tenedos had a common origin in Tennus, the son of Cycnus. (Strab. viii. p. 380.) According to Dionysius, however, Tenea was of late foundation. (Cic. *ad Att.* vi. 2. § 3.) It was at Tenea that Oedipus was said to have passed his childhood. It was also from this place that Archias took the greater number of the colonists with whom he founded Syracuse. After the destruction of Corinth by Mummius, Tenea had the good fortune to continue undisturbed, because it is said to have assisted the Romans against Corinth. (Strab. *l. c.*) We cannot, however, suppose that an insignificant place like Tenea could have acted in opposition to Corinth and the Achaean League; and it is more probable that the Teneatae were spared by Mummius in consequence of their pretended Trojan descent and consequent affinity with the Romans themselves. However this may be, their good fortune gave rise to the line:

εὐδαίμων ὁ Κόρινθος, ἐγὼ δ᾽ εἴην Τενεάτης.

Tenea lay in the mountain valley through which flows the river that falls into the Corinthian gulf to the east of Corinth. In this valley are three places at which vases and other antiquities have been discovered, namely, at the two villages of *Chilimódi* and *Klénia*, both on the road to Nauplia, and the latter at the very foot of the ancient road Contoporia [see Vol. I. p. 201, b.], and at the village of *Athíki*, an hour east of *Chilimódi*, on the road to *Sophikó*. In the fields of *Athíki* there was found an ancient statue of Apollo, a striking confirmation of the prevalence of the worship of this god in the district. The Teneatae would therefore appear to have dwelt in scattered abodes at these three spots and in the intervening country; but the village of Tenea, properly so called, was probably at *Chilimódi*, since the distance from this place to Corinth corresponds to the 60 stadia of Pausanias.

Since one of the passes from the Argeia into the Corinthia runs by *Klénia* and *Chilimódi*, there can be little doubt that it was by this road that Agesilaus marched from the Argeia to Corinth in B.C. 391. (Xen. *Hell.* iv. 5. § 19.) In the text of Xenophon the words are ἐκεῖθεν ὑπερβαλὼν κατὰ Τεγέαν ἐς Κόρινθον, but Τενέαν ought to be substituted for Τεγέαν, since it is impossible to believe that Agesilaus could have marched from the Argeia to Corinth by way of Tegea. Moreover, we learn from Strabo (viii. p. 380) that the well-known name of Tegea was in other cases substituted for that of Tenea. In the parallel passage of the *Agesilaus* of Xenophon (ii. 17), the pass by Tenea is called κατὰ τὰ στενά. (Leake, *Morea*, vol. iii. p. 320, *Peloponnesiaca*, p. 400; Curtius, *Peloponnesos*, vol. ii. 549, foll.)

TENE'BRIUM (Τενέβριον ἄκρον, Ptol. ii. 6.§ 16), a promontory on the E. coast of Spain, near the mouth of the Iberus. Stephanus B. (*s. v.*) also mentions a district called Tenebria, and Ptolemy a harbour called Tenebrius, which Marca (*Hisp.* ii. 8) takes to be *Alfachs* near *Tarragona*, but which must be looked for to the SW. [T. H. D.]

TENEDOS (Τένεδος: *Eth. Τενέδιος: Tenedo,* Turk. *Bogsha-Adasai*), an island off the coast of Troas, from which its distance is only 40 stadia, while from Cape Sigeum it is 12 miles distant. (Strab. xiii. p. 604; Plin. ii. 106, v. 39.) It was originally called Leucophrys, from its white cliffs, Calydna, Phoenice, or Lyrnessus (Strab. *l.c.*: Paus. x. 14. § 3; Steph. B. *s.v.* Τένεδος; Eustath. *ad Hom. Il.* p. 33; Plin. *l. c.*), and was believed to have received the name of Tenedos from Tennes, a son of Cycnus (Strab. viii. p. 380; Diod. v. 83; Conon, *Narrat.* 28; Cic. *in Verr.* i. 19). The island is described as being 80 stadia in circumference, and containing a town of the same name, which was an Aeolian settlement, and situated on the eastern coast. (Herod. i. 149; Thucyd. vii. 57.) The town possessed two harbours, one of which was called Βόρειον (Arrian, *Anab.* ii. 2. § 2; Scylax, p. 35, who, however, notices only one), and a temple of the Smynthian Apollo. (Strab. *l. c.*; Hom. *Il.* i. 38, 452.) In the Trojan legend, the island plays a prominent part, and at an early period seems to have been a place of considerable importance, as may be inferred from certain ancient proverbial expressions which owe their origin to it, such as Τενέδιος πέλεκυς (Steph. B. *s. v.*; Apostol. xviii. 28; Diogenian. viii. 58; comp. Cic. *ad Quint. Frat.* ii. 11), Τενέδιος ἄνθρωπος (Zenob. vi. 9; Eustath. *ad Dionys.* 536), Τενέδιος αὐλητής (Steph. B. *s. v.*; Plut. *Quaest. Gr.* 28), Τενέδιος κακόν (Apostol. x. 80), and Τενέδιος ξυνήγορος (Steph. B. *s. v.*). The laws and civil institutions of Tenedos seem to have been celebrated for their wisdom, if we may credit Pindar, whose eleventh Nemean ode is inscribed to Aristagoras, a prytanis or chief magistrate of the island. We further know from Stephanus B. that Aristotle wrote on the polity of Tenedos. During the Persian wars the island was taken possession of by the Persians (Herod. vi. 31), and during the Peloponnesian War it sided with Athens and paid tribute to her (Thuc. *l. c.* ii. 2), which seems to have amounted to 3426 drachmae every year. (Franz, *Elem. Epigraph.* n. 52.) Afterwards, in B.C. 389, Tenedos was ravaged by the Lacedaemonians for its fidelity to Athens (Xen. *Hist. Gr.* v. 1. § 6); but though the peace of Antalcidas gave up the island to Persia, it yet maintained its connection with Athens. (Demosth. *c. Polycl.* p. 1223, *c. Theocr.* p. 1333.) In the time of Alexander the Great, the Tenedians threw off the Persian yoke, and, though reconquered by Pharnabazus, they soon again revolted from Persia. (Arrian, *Anab.* ii. 2, iii. 2.) During the wars of Macedonia with the Romans, Tenedos, owing to its situation near the entrance of the Hellespont, was an important naval station. (Polyb. xvi. 34, xxvii. 6; Liv. xxxi. 16, xliv. 28.) In the war against Mithridates, Lucullus fought a great naval battle near Tenedos. (Plut. *Luc.* 3; Cic. *p. Arch.* 9, *p. Mur.* 15.) In the time of Virgil, Tenedos seems to have entirely lost its ancient importance, and, being conscious of their weakness, its inhabitants had placed themselves under the protection of Alexandria Troas (Paus. x. 14. § 4). The favourable situation of the island, however, prevented its utter decay, and the emperor Justinian caused granaries to be erected in it, to receive the supplies of corn conveyed from Egypt to Constantinople. (Procop. *de Aed.* v. 1.) The women of Tenedos are reported to have been of surpassing beauty. (Athen. xiii. p. 609.) There are but few ancient remains in the island worthy of notice. (Chandler, *Travels in Asia Minor*, p. 22; Prokesch,

Denkwürdigkeiten, i. p. 111, foll.; Hemmer, *Respublica Tenediorum,* Hafniae, 1735.)　　[L. S.]

COIN OF TENEDOS.

TENEDOS (Τένεδος: *Eth.* Τενεδεύς), a fortified coast-town in the west of Pamphylia, 20 stadia to the west of Attalia. (Steph. B. *s. v.*; *Stadiasm. Mar. M.* §§ 224, 225.) It has been conjectured that this town is the same as Olbia, the remains of which are exactly 20 stadia from Attalia, and that one of the two names was Lycian and the other Greek. (Müller, *ad Stadiasm.* p. 490.)　[L. S.]

TENE'RICUS CAMPUS.　[BOEOTIA, p. 413, b.]

TE'NESIS REGIO (Τηνεσίς, Strab. xvi. p. 770), was, according to Strabo, who alone mentions it, an inland province of Aethiopia, lying due E. of the Sabae, and not far distant from the kingdom or city of Meroe. Tenesis was governed, at least when Strabo wrote, by a queen, who was also the sovereign of Meroe. This was one of the many districts of Aethiopia assigned by rumour to the Automoli, Sembritae, or Aegyptian war-caste, who abandoned their native country in the reign of Psammetichus [SEMBRITAE]. The lake Coloe and the sources of the Astapus are by some geographers placed in Tenesis. It was an alluvial plain bounded on the E. by the Abyssinian Highlands, and frequented by elephants, rhinoceroses, &c.　　　　　[W. B. D.]

TENOS (Τῆνος: *Eth.* Τήνιος; *Tino*), an island in the Aegaean sea, and one of the Cyclades, lying between Andros and Delos, distant from the former 1 mile and from the latter 15 miles. (Plin. iv. 12. s. 22.) It stretches from NW. to SE., and is 15 miles long according to Pliny (*l. c.*), or 150 stadia according to Scylax (p. 55). It was also called Hydrussa (Ὑδροῦσσα, Ὑδρόεσσα) from the number of its springs, and Ophiussa because it abounded in snakes. (Plin. *l. c.*; Mela, ii. 7. § 11; Steph. B. *s. v.*) The sons of Boreas are said to have been slain in this island by Hercules. (Apoll. Rhod. i. 1304, with Schol.) In the invasion of Greece by Xerxes, the Tenians were compelled to serve in the Persian fleet; but a Tenian trireme deserted to the Greeks immediately before the battle of Salamis (B. C. 480), and accordingly the name of the Tenians was inscribed upon the tripod at Delphi in the list of Grecian states which had overthrown the Persians. (Herod. viii. 82.) Pausanias relates that the name of the Tenians was also inscribed on the statue of Zeus at Olympia among the Greeks who had fought at the battle of Plataea (v. 23. § 2). The Tenians afterwards formed part of the Athenian maritime empire, and are mentioned among the subject allies of Athens at the time of the Sicilian expedition (Thuc. vii. 57). They paid a yearly tribute of 3600 drachmas, from which it may be inferred that they enjoyed a considerable share of prosperity. (Franz, *Elem. Epigr. Gr.* No. 49.) Alexander of Pherae took possession of Tenos for a

time (Dem. *c. Polycl.* p. 1207); and the island was afterwards granted by M. Antonius to the Rhodians (Appian, *B. C.* v. 7.) After the conquest of Constantinople by the Latins, Tenos fell to the share of the Venetians, and remained in their hands long after their other possessions in the Aegaean had been taken by the Turks. It was ceded by Venice to the Sultan by the peace of Passarovitz, 1718. It is still one of the most prosperous islands in the Aegaean, and the inhabitants are remarkable for their industry and good conduct. The present population is about 15,000 souls, of whom more than half are Catholics,—a circumstance which, by bringing them into closer connection with western Europe, has contributed to their prosperity.

The ancient city of Tenos, of the same name as the island, stood at the south-western end upon the same site as St. Nicolaos, the present capital. Scylax says that it possessed a harbour, and Strabo describes it as a small town. (Scyl. p. 22; Strab. x. p. 487; Ptol. iii. 14. § 30.) In the neighbourhood of the city there was a celebrated temple of Poseidon situated in a grove, where festivals were celebrated, which were much frequented by all the neighbouring people. (Strab. *l. c.*; Tac. *Ann.* iii. 63; Clem. *Protr.* p. 18; Böckh, *Inscr.* No. 2329, 2331.) The attributes of Poseidon appear on the coins of Tenos. There was another town in the island named Eriston (Ἠρίστον; Böckh, *Inscr.* 2336, 2337), which was situated in the interior at the village of *Komi.* Among the curiosities of Tenos was mentioned a fountain, the water of which would not mix with wine. (Athen. ii. p. 43, c.) The island was celebrated in antiquity for its fine garlic. (Aristoph. *Plut.* 18.) The chief modern production of the island is wine, of which the best kind is the celebrated Malvasia, which now grows only at Tenos and no longer at *Monembasia* in Peloponnesus, from which place it derived its name. (Tournefort, *Voyage, &c.* vol. i. p. 271, transl.; *Exped. Scientif.* vol. iii. p. 2; Fiedler, *Reise,* vol. ii. p. 241, seq.; Finlay, *Hist. of Greece under Othoman and Venetian Domination,* pp. 276, 287; and especially Ross, *Reise auf den Griech. Inseln,* vol. i. p. 11, seq., who cites a monograph, Marcaky Zallony, *Voyage à Tine, l'une des îles de l'Archipel de la Grèce,* Paris, 1809.)

COIN OF TENOS.

TE'NTYRA or TE'NTYRIS (τὰ Τέντυρα, Strab. xvii. p. 814; Ptol. iv. 5. §§ 6, 8; Steph. B. *s. v.*: *Eth.* Τεντυρίτης), the Coptic *Tentoré* and the modern *Denderah,* was the capital of the Tentyrite Nome in Upper Aegypt (Agatharch. *ap. Phot.* p. 447, ed. Bekker). It was situated in lat. 26° 9' N., on the western bank of the Nile, about 38 miles N. of Thebes. The name of the city was probably derived from the principal object of worship there—the goddess Athor (Aphrodite), being a contracted form of Thy-ê-Athor or abode of Athor. The hieroglyphic legend of the genius of the place contains the name of the town, and is generally attached to the head-dress of Athor, accompanied by the sign Kali or "the land." The Tentyrite Athor has a human face with the ears of a cow (Rosellini, *Monum. del Culto*, pl. 29. 3), and her attributes so closely resemble those of Isis, that it was long doubtful to which of the two goddesses the great temple at Tentyra was dedicated. Like Isis, Athor is delineated nursing a young child named *Ehôou*, said, in hieroglyphics, to be her son. He is the third member of the Tentyrite triad of deities.

The principal fabrics and produce of Tentyra were flax and linen. (Plin. xix. 1.) Its inhabitants held the crocodile in abhorrence, and engaged in sanguinary conflicts with its worshippers, especially with those of the Ombite Nome [OMBOS]. Juvenal appears to have witnessed one of these combats, in which the Ombites had the worst of it, and one of them, falling in his flight, was torn to pieces and devoured by the Tentyrites. Juvenal, indeed, describes this fight as between the inhabitants of contiguous nomes ("inter finitimos"); but this is incorrect, since Ombos and Tentyra are more than 50 miles apart. As, however, Coptos and Tentyra were nearly opposite to each other, and the crocodile was worshipped by the Coptites also, we should probably read Coptos for Ombos in Juvenal. (*Sat.* xv.) The latter were so expert in the chase of this animal in its native element, that they were wont to follow it into the Nile, and drag it to shore. (Aelian, *Hist. Anim.* x. 24; Plin. viii. 25. s. 38.) Seneca (*Nat. Quaest.* ii. 2) says that it was their presence of mind that gave the Tentyrites the advantage over the crocodile, for the men themselves were small sinewy fellows. Strabo (xvii. pp. 814, 815) saw at Rome the exhibition of a combat between the crocodile and men purposely imported from Tentyra. They plunged boldly into the tanks, and, entangling the crocodiles in nets, haled them backwards and forwards in and out of the water, to the great amazement of the beholders.

So long as Aegypt was comparatively unexplored, no ruins attracted more admiration from travellers than those of Tentyra. They are the first in tolerable preservation and of conspicuous magnitude that meet the eyes of those who ascend the Nile. They are remote from the highways and habitations of men, standing at the foot of the Libyan hills, amid the sands of the western desert. But though long regarded as works of a remote era, Aegyptian art was already on the decline when the temples of Tentyra were erected. The architecture, indeed, reflects the grandeur of earlier periods; but the sculptures are ungraceful, and the hieroglyphics unskilfully crowded upon its monuments. The most ancient of the inscriptions do not go farther back than the reigns of the later Ptolemies; but the names of the Caesars, from Tiberius to Antoninus Pius (A. D. 14—161), are of frequent occurrence. Tentyra, in common with Upper Aegypt generally, appears to have profited by the peace and security it enjoyed under the imperial government to enlarge or restore its monuments, which, since the Persian occupation of the country, had mostly fallen into decay. The principal structures at Tentyra are the great temple dedicated to Athor; a temple of Isis; a Typhonium; and an isolated building without a roof, of which the object has not been discovered. With the exception of the latter, these structures are inclosed by a crude brick wall, forming a square, each side of which occupies 1000 feet, and which is

in some parts 35 feet high and 15 feet thick. Full descriptions of the remains of Tentyra may be found in the following works: Belzoni's *Travels in Nubia*; Hamilton's *Aegyptiaca*; and Richardson's *Travels along the Mediterranean and Parts adjacent, in* 1816—1817. Here it must suffice to notice briefly the three principal edifices:—

1. *The Temple of Athor.*— The approach to this temple is through a dromos, commencing at a solitary stone pylon, inscribed with the names of Domitian and Trajan, and extending to the portico, a distance of about 110 paces. The portico is open at the top, and supported by twenty-four columns, ranged in four rows with quadrangular capitals, having on each side a colossal head of Athor, surmounted by a quadrangular block, on each side of which is carved a temple doorway with two winged globes above it. These heads of the goddess, looking down upon the dromos, were doubtless the most imposing decorations of the temple. To the portico succeeds a hall supported by six columns, and flanked by three chambers on either side of it. Next comes a central chamber, opening on one side upon a staircase, on the other into two small chambers. This is followed by a similar chamber, also with lateral rooms; and, lastly, comes the *naos* or sanctuary, which is small, surrounded by a corridor, and flanked on either side by three chambers. The hieroglyphics and picturesque decorations are so numerous, that nowhere on the walls, columns, architraves, or ceiling of the temple, is there a space of two feet unoccupied by them. They represent men and women engaged in various religious or secular employments; animals, plants, public ceremonies and processions, and the emblems of agriculture or manufactures. Occasionally, also, occur historical portraits of great interest, such as those of Cleopatra and her son Caesarion. The effect of this wilderness of highly-coloured basso-relievos was greatly enhanced by the mode by which the temple itself was lighted. The sanctuary itself is quite dark: the light is admitted into the chambers through small perforations in their walls. Yet the entire structure displays wealth and labour rather than skill or good taste, and, although so elaborately ornamented, was never completed. The emperor Tiberius finished the *naos*, erected the portico, and added much to the decoration of the exterior walls; but some of the cartouches designed for royal or imperial names have never been filled up.

On the ceiling of the portico is the famous zodiac of Tentyra, long imagined to be a work of the Pharaonic times, but now ascertained to have been executed within the Christian era. Though denominated a zodiac, however by the French savans, it is doubtful whether this drawing be not merely mythological, or at most astrological, in its object. In the first place the number of the supposed signs is incomplete. The crab is wanting, and the order of the other zodiacal signs is not strictly observed. Indeed if any astral signification at all be intended in the picture, it refers to astrology, the zodiac, as we know it, being unknown to the Aegyptians. Archaeologists are now pretty well agreed that a panegyris or procession of the Tentyrite triad with their cognate deities is here represented. The Greek inscription, which, long overlooked, determines the recent date of this portion of the temple, runs along the projecting summit of the cornice of the portico. It was engraved in the twenty-first year of Tiberius, A. D. 35 (Letronne, *Inscript.* p. 97). Upon the ceiling of one of the lateral chambers, behind the portico, and on the right side of the temple, was a smaller group of mythological figures, which has also been styled a planisphere or zodiac. This being sculptured on a kind of sandstone, was removeable, and by the permission of Mehemet Ali, in 1821, was cut out of the ceiling by M. Lelorrain, and brought to Paris. It was purchased by the French government, and is now in the Imperial Museum. It is probably a few years older than the larger zodiac.

2. *The Iseium.* — " The chapel of Isis is behind the temple of Athor." (Strab. xvii. p. 814.) It stands, indeed, immediately behind its SW. angle. It consists of one central and two lateral chambers, with a corridor in front. Among its hieroglyphics appear the names of Augustus, Claudius, and Nero. About 170 paces E. of this chapel stands a pylon, with a Greek inscription, importing that in the thirty-first year of Caesar (Augustus) it was dedicated to Isis. (Letronne, *Ib.* pp. 82, 84.)

3. *The Typhonium*, as it is denominated from the emblems of Typhon on its walls, stands about 90 paces N. of the great temple. It comprises two outer passage-chambers and a central and lateral adytum. A peristyle of twenty-two columns surrounds the sides and the rear of the building. On its walls are inscribed the names of Trajan, Hadrian, and Antoninus Pius. But although the symbols of the principle of destruction are found on its walls, Typhon can hardly have been the presiding deity of this temple. From the circumstance that all the other sculptures refer to the birth of Ehôou, Champollion (*Lettres sur l'Egypte*, vol. ii. p. 67) suggests that this was one of the chapels styled " Mammeisi," or " lying-in places," and that it commemorated the accouchment of Athor, mother of *Ehôou.* Typhon is here accordingly in a subordinate character, and symbolises not destruction, but darkness, chaos, or the " night primeval," which precedes creation and birth.

For the monuments of Tentyra, besides the works already enumerated, Wilkinson's *Ancient Egyptians* and *Modern Egypt and Thebes*, and the volumes in the *Library of Entertaining Knowledge*, entitled *British Museum, Egyptian Antiquities*, may be consulted; and for the zodiacs, Visconti, *Oeuvres* tom. iv.; Letronne, *Observations sur l'Objet des Représentations Zodiacales de l'Antiquité*, 8vo. Paris, 1824; or Halma, *Examen et Explications des Zodiaques Egyptiennes*, 8vo. 1822.　　[W. B. D.]

TENURCIO. [TINURTIUM.]

TEOS (Τέως: *Eth.* Τήιος), an Ionian city on the coast of Asia Minor, on the south side of the isthmus connecting the Ionian peninsula of Mount Mimas with the mainland. It was originally a colony of the Minyae of Orchomenos led out by Athamas, but during the Ionian migration the inhabitants were joined by numerous colonists from Athens under Nauclus, a son of Codrus, Apoecus, and Damasus; and afterwards their number was further increased by Boeotians under Geres. (Strab. xiv. p. 633; Paus. vii. 3. § 3; Herod. i. 142; Scylax, p. 37; Steph. B. *s. v.*) The city had two good harbours, one of which is mentioned even by Scylax, and the second, 30 stadia distant from the former, is called by Strabo Γερραίδαι (xiv. p. 644), and by Livy (xxxvii. 27) Geraesticus. Teos became a flourishing commercial town, and enjoyed its prosperity until the time of the Persian dominion, when its inhabitants, unable to bear the insolence of the barbarians, abandoned

their city and removed to Abdera in Thrace. (Herod. i. 168; Strab. *l. c.*) But though deserted by the greater part of its inhabitants, Teos still continued to be one of the Ionian cities, and in alliance with Athens. (Thucyd. iii. 32.) After the Sicilian disaster, Teos revolted from Athens, but was speedily reduced (Thucyd. viii. 16, 19, 20). In the war against Antiochus, the fleet of the Romans and Rhodians gained a victory over that of the Syrian king in the neighbourhood of this city. (Liv. *l. c.*; comp. Polyb. v. 77.) The vicinity of Teos produced excellent wine, whence Bacchus was one of the chief divinities of the place. Pliny (v. 38) erroneously calls Teos an island, for at most it could only be termed a peninsula. (Comp. Pomp. Mela, i. 17; Ptol. v. 2. § 6.) There still exist considerable remains of Teos at a place called *Sighajik*, which seems to have been one of the ports of the ancient city, and the walls of which are constructed of the ruins of Teos, so that they are covered with a number of Greek inscriptions of considerable interest, referring, as they do, to treaties made between the Teians and other states, such as the Romans, Aetolians, and several cities of Crete, by all of whom the inviolability of the Teian territory, the worship of Bacchus, and the right of asylum are confirmed. The most interesting among the ruins of Teos are those of the theatre and of the great and splendid temple of Bacchus; the massive walls of the city also may still be traced along their whole extent. The theatre commands a magnificent view, overlooking the site of the ancient city and the bay as far as the bold promontory of Myonnesus and the distant island of Samos. For a detailed description of these remains, see Hamilton, *Researches*, ii. p. 11, foll.; comp. Leake, *Asia Minor*, p. 350.　　　　　　　　　[L. S.]

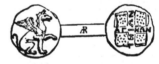

COIN OF TEOS.

TERACA'TRIAE (Τερακατρίαι), a German tribe in Noricum, on the banks of the Danube, probably on the south of the territory occupied by the Baemi (Ptol. ii. 11. § 26.)　　[L. S.]

TEREDON. [EUPHRATES].

TEREN (Τήρην, Diod. v. 72), a river in Crete, perhaps a tributary of the Amnisus, or the modern *Aposelemi.*　　　　　　　　　　[T. H. D.]

TERENUTHIS (Τερενοῦθις, *Not. Imp.*), the modern *Teranieh*, a town in Lower Aegypt, was situated on the left bank of the Canopic arm of the Nile. At this point a pass through the hills conducted to the Natron Lakes, about 30 miles to the W. of the town. The people of Terenuthis farmed of the government a monopoly for collecting and exporting natron. [NITRIAE.] Ruins at the modern hamlet of *Abou-Belleu* represent the ancient Terenuthis. (Sonnini, *Voyages*, vol. i. p. 228.)　　[W. B. D.]

TEREPS FLUVIUS. [TADER.]

TERESES FORTUNALES, a place in the W. of Hispania Baetica (Plin. iii. 1. s. 3).　　[T. H.'D.]

TERGESTE (Τέργεστε, Strab. Τέργεστον, Ptol.: *Eth.* Tergestinus: *Trieste*), a city of Venetia or Istria, situated on a bay to which it gave the name of TERGESTINUS SINUS, which forms the inner bight or extremity of the Adriatic sea towards the N. It was very near the confines of Istria and Venetia, so that there is considerable discrepancy between ancient authors as to which of these provinces it belonged, both Strabo and Ptolemy reckoning it a city of Istria, while Pliny includes it in the region of the Carni, which was comprised in Venetia. (Strab. v. p. 215, vii. p. 314; Plin. iii. 18. s. 22; Ptol. iii. 1. § 27.) Mela on the contrary calls it the boundary of Illyricum (ii. 4. § 3). From the time that the Formio, a river which falls into the sea 6 miles S. of *Trieste*, became fixed as the boundary of the provinces [FORMIO], there can be no doubt that Pliny's attribution is correct. It is probable that Tergeste was originally a native town either of the Carni or Istrians, but no mention is found of its name till after the Roman conquest, nor does it appear to have risen into a place of importance until a later period. The first historical mention of it is in B. C. 51, when we learn that it was taken and plundered by a sudden incursion of the neighbouring barbarians (Caes. *B. G.* viii. 24; Appian, *Illyr.* 18); but from the terms in which it is there noticed it is evident that it was already a Roman town, and apparently had already received a Roman colony. It was afterwards restored, and, to protect it for the future against similar disasters, was fortified with a wall and towers by Octavian in B. C. 32. (Gruter, *Inscr.* p. 266. 6.) It is certain that it enjoyed the rank of a Colonia from the time of Augustus, and is styled such both by Pliny and Ptolemy. (Plin. iii. 18. s. 22; Ptol. iii. 1. § 27.) That emperor also placed under the protection and authority of the city the neighbouring barbarian tribes of the Carni and Catali, and, by reducing to subjection their more formidable neighbours, the Iapodes, laid the foundations of the prosperity of Tergeste. The growth of this was mainly promoted by the advantages of its port, which is the only good harbour in this part of the Adriatic; but it was apparently overshadowed by the greatness of the neighbouring Aquileia, and Tergeste, though a considerable municipal town, never rose in ancient times to a commanding position. We even learn that in the reign of Antoninus Pius the citizens obtained the admission of the Carni and Catali—who had previously been mere subjects or dependents—to the Roman " civitas," in order that they might share the burthensome honours of the local magistracy. (Orell. *Inscr.* 4040.) The inscription from which we learn this fact is one of the most interesting municipal records preserved to us from ancient times, and has been repeatedly published, especially with notes and illustrations by C. T. Zumpt (*Decretum Municipale Tergestinum*, 4to. Berol. 1837) and by Göttling (*Fünfzehn Römische Urkunden*, p. 75). No subsequent mention of Tergeste is found in history under the Roman Empire; but it is certain that it continued to exist; and retained its position as a considerable town throughout the middle ages. But it is only within the last century that it has risen to the position that it now occupies of one of the most populous and flourishing cities on the Adriatic. The only remains of antiquity extant at *Trieste* are some portions of a Roman temple, built into the modern cathedral, together with several inscriptions (including the celebrated one already noticed) and some fragments of friezes, bas-reliefs, &c.

Tergeste is placed by the Itineraries at a distance of 24 miles from Aquileia, on the line of road which followed the coast from that city into Istria. (*Itin. Ant.* p. 270; *Tab. Peut.*) Pliny, less correctly,

calls it 33 miles from that city (Plin. *l. c.*). The spacious gulf on which it was situated, called by Pliny the TERGESTINUS SINUS, is still known as the *Gulf of Trieste*.   [E. H. B.]

TERGOLAPE, a town in Noricum, on the road from Ovilaba to Juvavum; was situated in all probability near *Lambach*. (*Tab. Peut.*; Muchar, *Norikum*, vol. i. p. 266.)   [L. S.]

TERIA (Τηρία), is mentioned in Homer (*Il.* ii. 829) in connection with a lofty mountain, or as a mountain itself (Τηρείης ὄρος αἰπύ), and, according to Strab (xii. p. 565, comp. xiii. p. 589), ought to be regarded as a height in the neighbourhood of Cyzicus; although others pointed out, at a distance of 40 stadia from Lampsacus, a hill with a temple of the Mother of the Gods, surnamed Tereia.   [L. S.]

TE'RIAS (Τηρίας: *Fiume di S. Leonardo*), a river of Sicily, on the E. coast of the island, flowing into the sea between Catana and Syracuse. It is mentioned by Pliny (iii. 8. s. 14) immediately after the Symaethus; and Scylax tells us it was navigable for the distance of 20 stadia up to Leontini. (Scyl. p. 4. § 13.) Though this last statement is not quite accurate, inasmuch as Leontini is at least 60 stadia from the sea, it leaves little doubt that the river meant is that now called the *Fiume di S. Leonardo*, which flows from the *Lake of Lentini* (which is not mentioned by any ancient author) to the sea. It has its outlet in a small bay or cove, which affords a tolerable shelter for shipping. Hence we find the mouth of the Terias twice selected by the Athenians as a halting-place, while proceeding with their fleet along the E. coast of Sicily. (Thuc. vi. 50, 96.) The connection of the Terias with Leontini is confirmed by Diodorus, who tells us that Dionysius encamped on the banks of that river near the city of Leontini. (Diod. xiv. 14.)   [E. H. B.]

TERICIAE. [TUICIAE.]

TERINA (Τερίνα, but Τέρεινα Lycophr.: *Eth.* Τερειναῖος, Terinaeus), a city on the W. coast of the Bruttian peninsula, near the *Gulf of St. Eufemia*, to which it gave the name of TERINAEUS SINUS. All writers agree in representing it as a Greek city and a colony of Crotona (Scymn. Ch. 307; Steph. B. *s. v.*; Scyl. p. 4. § 12; Strab. vi. p. 256; Plin. iii. 5. s. 10; Solin. 2. § 10), but we have no account of the time or circumstances of its foundation. It was regarded as the burial-place of the Siren Ligeia, a tradition which evidently pointed to the existence of a more ancient town on the spot than the Greek colony. (Lycophr. *Alex.* 726; Steph. B. *s. v.*) The name of Terina is scarcely mentioned in history during the flourishing period of Magna Graecia; but we learn from an incidental notice that it was engaged in war with the Thurians under Cleandridas (Polyaen. *Strat.* ii. 10. § 1)—a proof that it was at this time no inconsiderable city; and the number, beauty, and variety of its coins sufficiently attest the fact that it must have been a place of wealth and importance. (Millingen, *Numism. de l'Italie*, p. 53.) Almost the first notice of Terina is that of its conquest by the Bruttians, an event which appears to have taken place soon after the rise of that people in B. C. 356, as, according to Diodorus, it was the first Greek city which fell into their hands. (Diod. xvi. 15.) It was recovered from them by Alexander, king of Epirus, about 327 B. C. (Liv. viii. 24), but probably fell again under their yoke after the death of that monarch. It was one of the cities which declared in favour of Hannibal during the Second Punic

War; but before the close of the war that general found himself compelled to abandon this part of Bruttium, and destroyed Terina, when he could no longer hold it. (Strab. vi. p. 256.) The city never recovered this blow; and though there seems to have been still a town of the name in existence in the days of Strabo and Pliny, it never again rose to be a place of any importance. (Strab. l. c.; Plin. iii. 5. s. 10.) An inscription in which its name appears in the reign of Trajan (Orell. *Inscr.* 150) is in all probability spurious.

The site of Terina cannot be determined with any certainty; but the circumstance that the extensive bay now known as the *Gulf of Sta Eufemia* was frequently called the SINUS TERINAEUS (Plin. iii. 5. s. 10; ὁ Τεριναῖος κόλπος, Thuc. vi. 104), sufficiently proves that Terina must have been situated in its immediate proximity. The most probable conjecture is, that it occupied nearly, if not exactly, the same site as the *old* town of *Sta Eufemia* (which was destroyed by a great earthquake in 1638), about a mile below the modern village of the name, and near the N. extremity of the gulf to which it gives its name. Cluverius and other antiquarians have placed it considerably further to the N., near the modern *Nocera*, where there are said to be the ruins of an ancient city (Cluver. *Ital.* p. 1287; *Barrius, de Sit. Calabr.* ii. 10. p. 124); but this site is above 7 miles distant from the gulf, to which it could hardly therefore have given name. There is also reason to suppose that the ruins in question are those of a town which bore in ancient times the name of Nuceria, which it still retains with little alteration. [NUCERIA, No. 4.]

Lycophron seems to place Terina on the banks of a river, which he names OCINARUS (Ὠκίναρος, Lycophr. *Alex.* 729, 1009); and this name, which is not found elsewhere, has been generally identified with the river now called the *Savuto* (the Sabatus of the Itineraries), which flows by *Nocera*. But this identification rests on the position *assumed* for Terina: and the name of the Ocinarus may be equally well applied to any of the streams falling into the *Gulf of Sta Eufemia*.

The variety and beauty of the silver coins of Terina (which belong for the most part to the best period of Greek art), has been already alluded to. The winged female figure on the reverse, though commonly called a Victory, is more probably intended for the Siren Ligeia.　　　[E. H. B.]

COIN OF TERINA.

TERINAEUS SINUS. [HIPPONIATES SINUS.]

TERI'OLA CASTRA or TERI'OLIS, a fortress in Rhaetia, mentioned only in the *Notitia Imperii*, but generally identified with the castle near *Meran*, near which many Roman remains are found. (Comp. Pallhausen, *Beschreib. der Röm. Heerstrasse von Verona nach Augsburg*, p. 86.)　　　[L. S.]

TERMANTIA. [TERMES.]

TERMERA (τὰ Τέρμερα or Τέρμερον: Eth. Τερμερεύς), a maritime town of Caria, on the south coast

of the peninsula of Halicarnassus, near Cape Termerium. (Herod. v. 37; Strab. xiv. p. 657; Plin. v. 29; Steph. B. *s. v.*, who erroneously assigns the town to Lycia.) Under the Romans this Dorian town was a free city. According to Suidas (*s. v.*) the place gave rise to the proverbial expression Τερμέρια κακά, it being used as a prison by the rulers of Caria; but his remark that it was situated between Melos and Halicarnassus is unintelligible. Cramer supposes its site to be marked by the modern *Carbaglar* or *Gumishlu.*　　　[L. S.]

TERMERE (Τερμέρη), a place of uncertain site, mentioned only by Ptolemy (v. 2. § 16) as situated in the extreme north of Lydia, in the district Catacecaumene, near the two sources of the river Hermus.　　　[L. S.]

TERMERIUM. [TERMERA.]

TERMES (Τέρμες, Ptol. ii. 6. § 56), a town of the Arevaci in Hispania Tarraconensis. It is probably the same town called Τερμησός and Ταρμαντία by Appian (vi. 76 and 99). The inhabitants are called Termestini in Livy (*Epit.* liv.) and Tacitus (*Ann.* iv. 45; cf. coins in Sertini, p. 208). Termes was seated on a steep hill, and was often besieged without success by the Romans, till at last the inhabitants, on account of their hostile disposition towards Rome, were compelled in B. C. 97 to build a new city on the plain and without walls (App. vi. 99). It lay undoubtedly on the site of the present *Ermita de nuestra Señora de Termes*, 9 leagues W. of Numantia.　　　[T. H. D.]

TERMESSUS (Τερμησσός, Τερμησός, Τερμισσός, Τερμισσός, Τελμισσός: Eth. Τερμησσεύς), a town of Pisidia, celebrated for its natural strength no less than for its artificial fortifications, was situated on a height of Mount Taurus, at the entrance of the defiles which are traversed by the river Catarrhactes, and formed the means of communication between Pisidia, Pamphylia, and Lycia. (Strab. xiii. p. 630, xiv. p. 666; Ptol. v. 5. § 6, viii. 17. § 34; Polyb. xxii. 18; Steph. B. *s. v.*; Dion. Per. 859.) A peak of the mountain rising above the acropolis bore the name of Solymus; and the inhabitants of the town itself were, as Strabo says, called Solymi. They were certainly not Greeks, for Arrian (i. 27) distinctly calls them Pisidians and barbarians. Their town stood on a lofty height, precipitous on all sides; and the road running close by the place was very difficult, passing through a narrow gorge, which could be defended by a small force. Alexander the Great succeeded indeed in forcing his way through it, but despairing of the possibility of taking Termessus, he continued his march. Strabo (xiv. p. 666) therefore seems to be mistaken in stating that Alexander conquered the place. The consul Manlius, after relieving Isionda, passed along the same road. (Liv. xxxviii. 15.) The town of Termessus continued to exist down to a late period, when it was the see of a Christian bishop, who also had the administration of two neighbouring places, Jovia and Eudocia. (Hierocl. p. 680.) The site of ancient Termessus has not been difficult to discover by modern travellers, and considerable remains still exist at *Karabunar Kiui*, at the foot of the height on which the ancient fortress was situated. (Leake, *Asia Minor*, pp. 133 —135.) As to the coins of Termessus, which come down as far as the reign of the emperor Severus, see Sestini, p. 96. On some of these coins we read μειζόνων in addition to the name of the Termessians, a circumstance which confirms the statement of Stephanus B. that there was another town of the same name in Pisidia, which was called Lesser Termessus (Τερμησσὸς ἡ μικρά.)   [L. S.]

COIN OF TERMESSOS.

TERMETIS, a mountain of Lydia between Mounts Olympus and Tmolus, is mentioned only by Pliny (v. 31).   [L. S.]

TERMILAE (Τερμίλαι) is said to have been the ancient name of the inhabitants of Lydia, before the name Lydi came into use. These Termilae were believed to have come from Crete; and even in the time of Herodotus the Lydians were often called Termilae by the neighbouring nations. (Herod. i. 173, vii. 92; Paus. i. 19. § 4.)   [L. S.]

TERPO'NUS (Τέρπωνος), a town of the Iapodes in Illyria, of uncertain site. (Appian, B. Illyr. 18.)

TESA (Τησά, Marcian, Peripl. p. 23; Τεισά, Ptol. vi. 8. § 8), a small town on the coast of Gedrosia, visited by the fleet of Nearchus. It is probably the same as the Τάοι or Τρολοι of Arrian (Ind. c. 29), and may be represented by the present Tis. [V.]

TESEBA'RICE (Τισηβαρική, sc. χώρα, Peripl. Mar. Erythr. p. 1, ap. Hudson, Geogr. Min.), is supposed to have been a portion of the district inhabited by the Troglodytes. The modern Persian name Tres-u-Baresk closely resembles the ancient one, and is said to mean, when applied to a country. "low and flat," which designation would accord with the S. portion of the Regio Troglodytica in the level region of Aethiopia near the mouth of the Red Sea. (Vincent, Commerce and Navigation of the Ancients, vol. ii. p. 89. [TROGLODYTAE.] [W.B.D.]

TESTRINA. [ABORIGINES.]

TE'TIUS (Τέτιος, Ptol. v. 14. § 2), a river on the S. coast of Cyprus, probably the Tesis. [T. H. D.]

TETRADIUM. [TYRIAEUM.]

TETRANAULOCHUS. [NAULOCHUS, No. 3.]

TETRAPHYLIA, a town of Athamania in Epeirus, where the royal treasures were kept. (Liv. xxxviii. 1.)

TETRA'POLIS. 1. Of Attica. [MARATHON.]
2. Of Doris. [DORIS.]

TETRAPYRGIA (Τετραπυργία). 1. A town in the Cyrenaica, of uncertain site, situated above the harbour Plynus. (Strab. xvii. p. 838; Polyb. xxxi. 26.)

2. A town of Cappadocia in the district Garsauria. (Ptol. v. 6. § 14.)

TETRICA MONS, a mountain in the central range of the Apennines, adjoining the territory of the Sabines. Virgil enumerates the "Tetricae horrentes rupes" among the localities of that people, and Silius Italicus in like manner closely associates the "Tetrica rupes" with Nursia. Varro also speaks of the Montes Fiscellus and Tetrica as abounding in wild goats. (Virg. Aen. vii. 713 ; Sil. Ital. viii. 417; Varr. R. R. ii. 1. § 5.) From all these passages it is evident that it was one of the

lofty and rugged chain of the Central Apennines, which extend from the Monti della Sibilla, southwards as far as the Gran Sasso, separating Picenum from the country of the Sabines: and this position is confirmed by Servius and Vibius Sequester, of whom the former calls it "Mons in Piceno asperrimus," while the latter terms it "Mons Sabinorum." (Serv. ad Aen. l. c.; Vib. Seq. p. 33.) It cannot be identified with more accuracy. The two grammarians just quoted write the name "Tetricus Mons ;" but Varro, as well as Virgil and Silius, adopts the feminine form, which is not therefore one merely poetical.   [E. H. B.]

TETRISIUS [TIRIZIS].

TETUS (Τῆτος), a river on the Atlantic coast of Gallia, which Ptolemy (ii. 8. § 2) places between the Staliocanus Portus and Argenus, or the outlet of the river Argenus, if that is the true reading. It is impossible to determine what river is the Tetus. D'Anville assumes the place to be the bay of Seu, which receives the rivers Sée and Sélune. Others take the Tetus to be the Treguier or Trieu. (Ukert, Gallien, p. 144.)   [G. L.]

TEUCERA, in North Gallia, is placed by the Table about halfway between Nemetacum (Arras) and Samarobriva (Amiens). Tivre, on the road from Amiens to Arras, represents Teucera. (D'Anville, Notice, &c.)   [G. L.]

TEUCRI. [TROAS.]

TEUDE'RIUM (Τευδέριον), a place in the country of the Chauci Minores, on the river Amasia, in Germany (Ptol. ii. 11. § 28). Its site is commonly identified with that of the village of Dörgen, near Meppen.   [L. S.]

TEUDURUM, in North Gallia, is placed in the Antonine Itinerary on a route from Colonia Trajana [COLONIA TRAJANA] through Juliacum (Juliers) to Colonia Agrippina (Cologne). The place is Tuddern. The distance from Tuddern to the supposed site of Coriovallum is marked viii. [CORIOVALLUM.]   [G. L.]

TEUGLUSSA (Τεύγλουσσα), an island mentioned by Thucydides (viii. 42, where some read Τεύτλουσσα), which, from the manner he speaks of it, must have been situated between Syme and Halicarnassus. Stephanus B. also mentions the island on the authority of Thucydides, but calls it Teutlussa and an island of Ionia. There can be no doubt that the Scutlusa mentioned by Pliny (v. 36) is the same as the Teuglussa or Teutlussa of Thucydides.   [L. S.]

TEUMESSUS (Τευμησσός: Eth. Τευμήσσιος), a village in Boeotia, situated in the plain of Thebes, upon a low rocky hill of the same name. The name of this hill appears to have been also given to the range of mountains separating the plain of Thebes from the valley of the Asopus. [BOEOTIA, pp. 413, 414.] Teumessus was upon the road from Thebes to Chalcis (Paus. ix. 19. § 1), at the distance of 100 stadia from the former. (Schol. ad Eurip. Phoen. 1105.) It is mentioned in one of the Homeric hymns (Hymn. in Apoll. 228) with the epithet λεχεποίη or grassy, an epithet justified by the rich plain which surrounds the town. Teumessus is celebrated in the epic legends, especially on account of the Teumessian fox, which ravaged the territory of Thebes. (Paus. l. c.; Anton. Lib. 41; Palaeph. de Incredib. 8; see Dict. of Biogr. Vol. I. p. 667.) The only building at Teumessus mentioned by Pausanias was a temple of Athena Telchinia, without any statue. (Besides the authorities already quoted, see Strab.

ix. p. 409; Aristot. *Rhet.* iii. 6; Plin. iv. 7. s. 12: Steph. B. *s. v.*; Phot. *Lex.* p. 428; Leake, *Northern Greece*, vol. ii. p. 245, seq.)

TEURIOCHAEMAE (Τευριοχαῖμαι), a German tribe, occupying the country south of the Cherusci, on the north of Mons Sudeta, in the modern *Erzgebirge* and *Voigtland*. (Ptol. ii. 11. § 23.) [L. S.]

TEURISCI (Τευρίσκοι, Ptol. iii. 8. § 5), a Dacian tribe near the sources of the Tyras. [T. H. D.]

TEU'RNIA (Τεουρνία), a Celtic town in Noricum, on the left bank of the upper part of the river Dravus (Plin. iii. 27; Ptol. ii. 14. § 3). Its site is still marked by considerable ruins not far from the little town of *Spital*. (Comp. Orelli, *Inscript.* Nos. 498 and 5071; Eugippus, *Vit. S. Severi*, 17, 21, where it is called Tiburnia.) [L. S.]

TEUTHEA. [DYME.]

TEUTHEAS. [ACHAIA, p. 14, a.]

TEUTHIS (Τεῦθις: *Eth.* Τευθίδης), a town in the centre of Arcadia, which together with Theisoa and Methydrium belonged to the confederation (σύντέλεια) of Orchomenus. Its inhabitants were removed to Megalopolis upon the foundation of the latter. The *Paleócastron* of *Galatás* probably represents Teuthis. (Paus. viii. 27. §§ 4, 7, 28. § 4; Steph. B. *s. v.*; Ross, *Reisen im Peloponnes*, vol. i. p. 114.)

TEUTHRANIA (Τευθρανία), the name of the western part of Mysia about the river Caicus, which was believed to be derived from an ancient Mysian king Teuthras. This king is said to have adopted, as his son and successor, Telephus, a son of Heracles; and Eurypylus, the son of Telephus, appears in the Odyssey as the ruler of the Ceteii. (Strab. iii. p. 615; Hom. *Od.* x. 520; comp. MYSIA.)

In the district Teuthrania a town of the same name is mentioned as situated between Elaea, Pitane, and Atarneus (Strab. *l. c.*; Steph. B. *s. v.*; Xenoph. *Hist. Gr.* iii. 1. § 6), but no other particulars are known about it. [L. S.]

TEUTHRAS (Τεύθρας), the south-western part of Mt. Temnus in Teuthrania (Ctesias, *ap. Stob. Serm.* p. 213, ed. Bähr), is perhaps the mountain now called *Domacli*, which the caravans proceeding from *Smyrna* to *Brusa* have to traverse. (Lucas, *Trois-Voyage*, i. p. 133.) [L. S.]

TEUTHRO'NE (Τευθρώνη), a town of Laconia, situated upon the western side of the Laconian gulf, 150 stadia from Cape Taenarum. It was said to have been founded by the Athenian Teuthras. The chief deity worshipped here was Artemis Issoria. It had a fountain called Naia. Its ruins exist at the village of *Kotrónes*, and its citadel occupied a small peninsula, called *Skopos, Skopia* or *Skopópolis*. The distance assigned by Pausanias of 150 stadia from Teuthrone to Cape Taenarum is, according to the French Commission, only from 8 to 10 stadia in excess. Augustus made Teuthrone one of the Eleuthero-Laconian towns. (Paus. iii. 21. § 7, iii. 25. § 4; Ptol. iii. 16. § 9; Boblaye, *Recherches, &c.* p. 89; Curtius, *Peloponnesos*, vol. ii. p. 276.)

TEUTIBU'RGIUM or TEUTOBURGIUM (Τευτοβούργιον), a town in Lower Pannonia, near the confluence of the Dravus and Danubius, on the road from Mursa to Cornacum, was the station of the praefect of the sixth legion and a corps of Dalmatian horsemen. (*It. Ant.* p. 243; Ptol. ii. 16. § 5; *Notit. Imp.*; *Tab. Peut.*, where it is miswritten Tittoburgium.) The name seems to indicate that it was originally a settlement of the Teutones, which may have been founded at the time when they roamed over those countries, about B. C. 113. No remains are now extant, and its exact site is only matter of conjecture. (Muchar, *Norikum*, vol. i. p. 265.) [L. S.]

TEUTOBERGIENSIS SALTUS, a mountain forest in Western Germany, where in A.D. 9 the Roman legions under Varus suffered the memorable defeat, and where, six years later, their unburied remains were found by Drusus. (Tac. *Ann.* i. 60.) A general description of the locality without the mention of the name is found in Dion Cassius (lvi. 20, 21; comp. Vell. Pat. ii. 105, 118, foll.). This locality has in modern times been the subject of much discussion among German antiquaries; but the words of Tacitus seem to imply clearly that he was thinking of the range of hills between the sources of the Lupia and Amasis; that is, the range between *Lippspringe* and *Haustenbeck*. (Giefers, *De Alisone Castello deque Varianae Cladis Loco Commentatio*, p. 47, foll.) [L. S.]

TEUTONES or TEUTONI (Τεύτονες), the name of a powerful German tribe, which about B. C. 113 appeared on the frontiers of Gaul at the same time when the Cimbri, probably a Celtic people, after defeating the Romans in several battles, traversed Gaul and invaded Spain. The Teutones, however, remained behind ravaging Gaul, and were joined by the Ombrones. At length, in B. C. 102, they were defeated by C. Marius in a great battle near Aquae Sextiae, where, according to the most moderate accounts, 100,000 of them were slain, while 80,000 or 90,000 are said to have been taken prisoners. A body of 6000 men, who survived that terrible day, are said to have established themselves in Gaul between the *Maas* and *Schelde*, where they became the ancestors of the Aduatici. (Liv. *Epit.* lib. lxvii.; Vell. Pat. ii. 12; Flor. iii. 3; Plut. *Mar.* 36, foll.; Oros. v. 16; Caes. *B. G.* ii. 4, 29.) After this great defeat, the Teutones are for a long time not heard of in history, while during the preceding ten years they are described as wandering about the Upper Rhine, and eastward even as far as Pannonia. In later times a tribe bearing the name of Teutones is mentioned by Pomp. Mela (iii. 3), Pliny (xxxvii. 11), and Ptolemy (ii. 11. § 17) as inhabiting a district in the north-west of Germany, on the north of the river Albis, where according to Pliny, they dwelt even as early as the time of Pytheas of Massilia. The question here naturally presents itself whether these Teutones in the north of Germany were the same as those who in the time of Marius invaded Gaul in conjunction with the Cimbri, who in fact came from the same quarters. This question must be answered in the affirmative; or in other words, the Teutones who appeared in the south were a branch of those in the north-west of Germany, having been induced to migrate southward either by inundations or other calamities. The numerous body of emigrants so much reduced the number of those remaining behind, that thereafter they were a tribe of no great importance. That the name of Teutones was never employed, either by the Germans themselves or by the Romans, as a general name for the whole German nation, has already been explained in the article GERMANIA. Some writers even regard the Teutones as not Germans at all, but either as Slavonians or Celts. (Latham, *Epileg. ad Tac. Germ.* p. cx.) The fact that the country between the lower Elbe and the Baltic was once inhabited by the

Teutones seems to be attested by the names of Teutenwinkel, a village near Rostock, and Teutendorf, between Travemünde and Schwartau. [L. S.]

TEUTONO'ARI (Τευτονόαροι), a German tribe mentioned by Ptolemy (ii. 11. § 17) in close proximity to the Teutones, whence it may be inferred that they were only a branch of the Teutones. (Latham, Epileg. ad Tac. Germ. p. cxi.)　[L. S.]

THABOR.　[ATYBARIUM.]

THA'BRACA (Θάβρακα κολωνία, Ptol. vi. 3. §§ 5, 21, 28, viii. 14. § 3; Mela, i. 7), also called Tabraca (Plin. v. 3. s. 2, 6), a maritime city of Numidia, seated at the mouth of the Tusca. It was the border city towards Zeugitana, and a Roman colony. (Ptol., Plin., ll. cc.) The surrounding country was covered with thick woods. (Juv. S. x. 194.) Thabraca was the scene of the death of Gildo. (Claud. Laud. Stil. i. 359.) It still retains the name of Tabarka. (Cf. Itin. Ant. pp. 21, 495, 514; Aug. adv. Donat. vi. 32.)　　　[T. H. D.]

THABRASTA, a place in the Libyan Nomos (Itin. Ant. p. 72), identified by Lapie with Kasr Bowm Adjoubah.　　　　　　　　[T. H. D.]

THABU'SIUM, a fortress on the river Indus in Caria, not far from Cibyra. (Liv. xxxviii. 14.)

THAGULIS (Θαγουλίς, Ptol. iv. 3. § 43), or TAGULUS (Itin. Ant. p. 65), a town in Africa Propria, on the Syrtis Major, according to Lapie near Ali. Called Tagulis in Tab. Peut.　[T. H. D.]

THAGURA (called Thacora in Tab. Peut.), a place in Numidia, variously identified with El-Guettar and El-Matnainia. (Itin. Ant. p. 41.)　[T. H. D.]

THAGURUM (Θάγουρον ὄρος, Ptol. vi. 16. § 2), a mountain in Serica, stretching from the Ottorocorras in a northerly direction towards the Asmiraean mountains. It is in the S. part of the Mongol territory, and N. of the Hoang-ho.　　　　[T. H. D.]

THALA (Θάλα, Strab. xvii. p. 831), an important town of Numidia, with a treasury and arsenal. (Sall. J. 75, 77, 80, 89; Tac. Ann. iii. 21; Flor. iii. 1.) It is probably identical with Telepte (Τελεπτή, Procop. de Aed. vi. 6), a fortified town of Numidia, lying to the NW. of Capsa, and from which there was a road to Tacape on the Syrtis Minor (Itin. Ant. p. 77). Shaw (Trav. vol. i. p. 288, seq.) takes Ferreanah, both from its ruins and its situation, to have been the ancient Thala or Telepte (cf. Mannert, x. 2. p. 321), but Lapie seeks it at Haouch-el-Khima.　　　　　　[T. H. D.]

THALA (τὸ Θάλα ὄρος, Ptol. iv. 6. §§ 12, 14, 16), a mountain in the interior of Libya, near which dwelt a tribe of the same name (Θάλαι, Ptol. iv. 6. § 21).　　　　　　　　　[T. H. D.]

THA'LAMAE (Θαλάμαι). 1. A town of Elis, situated above Pylos on the frontiers of Achaia, and in the rocky recesses of Mount Scollis, probably near the modern village of Sandaméri, at the head of a narrow valley. It was here that the Eleians took refuge with their property and flocks, when their country was invaded by Philip in B. C. 219. (Xen. Hell. viii. 4. § 26; Polyb. iv. 75; Leake, Morea, vol. ii. p. 204, Peloponnesiaca, p. 220; Curtius, Peloponnesos, vol. ii. p. 38.)

2. (Also Θαλάμη, Ptol. iii. 16. § 22: Eth. Θαλαμάτης), a town of Laconia, distant 80 stadia north of Oetylus, and 20 stadia from Pephnus. (Paus. iii. 26. §§ 1, 2.) Pephnus was on the coast, on the eastern side of the Messenian gulf, and Thalamae was situated inland, probably at or near Platza, upon the river Miléa, the minor Pamisus of Strabo (viii. p. 361). Ptolemy (l. c.) also calls it

one of the inland towns of Laconia. Theopompus called Thalamae a Messenian town (Steph. B. s. v. Θαλάμαι), and we know that the Messenians said that their territory originally extended as far as the minor Pamisus. [LACONIA, p. 114, b.] Thalamae was said to have been founded by Pelops, and was called in the time of Strabo the Boeotian Thalamae, as if it had received a Boeotian colony. (Strab. viii. p. 360.) Thalamae is mentioned by Polybius (xvi. 16). It was subsequently one of the Eleuthero-Laconian towns. (Paus. iii. 21. § 7.) In the territory of Thalamae, on the road to Oetylus was a temple and oracle of Ino or Pasiphaë, in which the future was revealed to those that slept in the temple. Even the Spartan kings sometimes slept in the temple for this purpose. The temple probably stood upon the promontory Trachéla, where there are some ancient remains. (Paus. iii. 26. § 1; Plut. Agis, 9; Cic. de Divin. i. 43; Hermann, Gottesd. Alterth. § 41. 7.) (Leake, Peloponnesiaca, p. 178; Boblaye, Recherches, &c. p. 92; Curtius, Peloponnesos, vol. ii. p. 284.)

THALIADES. [ARCADIA, p. 193, No. 15.]

THALLI, a people of Asiatic Sarmatia, E. of the mouth of the Rha. (Plin. vi. 5. s. 5.)　[T. H. D.]

THAMANAEI, a people in central Asia, belonging to the fifteenth satrapy of Dareius Hystaspis. Their exact position is uncertain. (Herod. iii. 93, 117; Steph. B. s. v.)

THAMARA (Θαμαρά, Euseb. and Onom. s. v. Hazazon-Thamar; Θαμαρώ, Ptol. v. 16. § 8; Tab. Peut.; Tamar, Ezek. xlvii. 19, xlviii. 28), a town in Palestine, and one of the most southerly points in the country according to Ezekiel. According to Eusebius and Jerome it was a town and fortress one day's journey from Malatha on the way from Hebron to Ailah, and in their time was held by a Roman garrison. Robinson fixes it at Kurnub, the site with ruins 6 miles S. of Milh towards the pass es-Súfāh. (Bibl. Res. vol. ii. p. 202, 2nd ed.)

THAMBES (Θάμβης, Θάμμης, or Θάμης, Ptol. iv. 3. §§ 16, 25), a mountain in the eastern part of Numidia, in which the river Rubricatus has its sources.　　　　　　　　　　　[T. H. D.]

THAMNA (Θάμνα: Eth. Θαμνίτης), a large village of Palestine near Lydda, on the way to Jerusalem, which gave its name to the Toparchia Thamnitica. (Ptol. v. 16. § 8; Joseph. B. J. iii. 3, v. 4; Plin. v. 14. s. 15; Euseb. Onom. s. v.; Steph. B. s. v.; Robinson, Bibl. Res. vol. ii. p. 239, seq., 2nd ed.)

THAMONDACANA. [NIGRIR, p. 418, b.]

THAMUDE'NI (Θαμουδηνοί), a people of Arabia, dwelling upon the coast of the Arabian gulf, for more than 1000 stadia from about Moilah to Widjeh. (Diod. iii. 44; Agatharch. p. 59, Hudson, § 92, with Müller's note.) Ptolemy mentions the Thamydeni (Θαμυδηνοί) among the inland tribes of Arabia (vi. 7. § 21), but in another passage he places them upon the coast, under the slightly altered name of Thamyditae (Θαμυδῖται, vi. 7. § 4). In Pliny they are called Thamudeni (vi. 28. s. 32). Stephanus B. makes Thamuda (Θαμουδά) a neighbour of the Nabataeans. The name is evidently the same as Thamud, a celebrated tribe in early Arabian history.

THANA or THOANA (Θάνα, Θόανα, Ptol. v. 17. § 5; Thorma, Tab. Peut.), a town of Arabia Petraea, probably corresponds to Dhāna, a village visited by Burckhardt, on the declivity of a mountain N. of

Wady-el-Ghuweir. (Robinson, *Bibl. Res.* vol. ii. p. 168, 2nd ed.)

THAPSA. [RUBICADE.]

THA'PSACUS (Θάψακος), a town of considerable importance on the right bank of the Euphrates, in lat. 35° 15′ N. It is mentioned very early in ancient history, and is almost certainly the same as the Tiphsah, of the Old Testament (1 *Kings,* iv. 24; in the LXX. written Θάψα), which is mentioned as the eastern boundary of the kingdom of Solomon. There is some difference among ancient writers as to the province in which it should be included. Thus, Pliny (v. 24. s. 21) and Stephanus B. (*s. v.*) place it in Syria; Ptolemy (v. 19. § 3) in Arabia Deserta. The reason of this is, that it was a frontier town, and might therefore be claimed as belonging to one or more provinces. At Thapsacus was the most important passage of the Euphrates in the northern portion of that river's course. As such, we read it was used by Cyrus the younger, whose army forded it, the water reaching up to their breasts, there being probably at that time no bridge. (Xen. *Anab.* i. 4. § 11.) Some years later Dareius crossed it to meet Alexander in Cilicia, and recrossed it in haste after his defeat at Issus. (Arrian, ii. 13.) Alexander, pursuing Dareius, crossed the river also at the same spot, as the historian especially notices, on two bridges (probably of boats), which were joined together (iii. 7). Strabo, who makes frequent mention of Thapsacus, considers it, on the authority of Eratosthenes, as distant from Babylon about 4800 stadia, and from Commagene 2000 (ii. pp. 77, 78, 81, xvi. p. 746); and states that it was situated just at that spot where Mesopotamia is the widest (*l. c.*). There is no doubt that it derived its name from a Semitic verb, meaning to pass over (Winer, *Bibl. Wörterb. s. v.*) : hence another passage-place of the same name, which is mentioned in 2 *Kings,* xv. 16, but which is really in Palestine, has been often confounded with Tiphsah on the Euphrates. Pliny states that the name was changed by the Macedonian Greeks to Amphipolis (v. 24. s. 21), and Stephanus calls the Amphipolis of Seleucus Tourmeda. No trace of any of these names is now found in the country (Ritter, x. p. 1114), nor any ruins that can certainly be identified with its site. It was, however, probably near the present *Deir.* [V.]

THAPSIS (Θάψις, Diodor. xx. 23), a deep river of the Chersonesus Taurica, on which lay a royal castle. Ukert (iii. 2. p. 193) identifies it with the *Salgir.* But Köhler seeks the castle on *Mount Opuk,* 45 wersts south of Kertsch. (*Mém. de l'Ac. de St. Petersb.* ix. p. 649, seq.) [T. H. D.]

THAPSUS (Θάψος, Ptol. iv. 3. § 10), a maritime city of Byzacium, in Africa Propria. It lay on a salt lake, which, according to Shaw (*Trav.* p. 99), still exists, and on a point of land 80 stadia distant from the opposite island of Lopadussa. Thapsus was strongly fortified and celebrated for Caesar's victory over the Pompeians, B. C. 46. (Hirt. *B. Af.* 28, seq.) Shaw (*l. c.*) identifies it with the present *Demass,* where its ruins are still visible. (Cf. Strabo, xvii. pp. 831, 834 ; Liv. xxxiii. 48 ; Plin. v. 4. s. 3, &c.) [T. H. D.]

THAPSUS, a river of Numidia, falling into the sea near the town of Rusicade, probably the present *Oued Resas* (Vib. Sequest.) [T. H. D.]

THAPSUS. [SYRACUSAE.]

THARRANA, a place on the great line of road which led across the desert from the Euphrates to Hatrae (*Al-Hathr*). It is marked on the Tabula Peutingeriana. It has been conjectured by Mannert (v. 2. p. 233) that the name is a mistake for Charrana, another form of Charrae; but this hypothesis seems hardly tenable. Reichard believes it is represented by the present *Araban.* [V.]

THARRAS (Θάῤῥας, Ptol.: Ru. at *Capo del Sevo*), a city of Sardinia, mentioned only by Ptolemy (where the name is written in many MSS. and editions Tarrae or Tarras) and in the Itineraries, but which seems to have been one of the most considerable places in the island. It was situated on the W. coast, on a projecting point of land at the N. extremity of the *Gulf of Oristano,* where its ruins are still visible, though half buried in sand, and numerous minor antiquities have been discovered. From its position there can be little doubt that it was a Phoenician or Carthaginian settlement; but continued to be a considerable town under the Romans, and an inscription records the repair of the road from Tharras to Cornus as late as the reign of the emperor Philip. (De la Marmora, *Voy. en Sardaigne,* vol. ii. pp. 359, 477.) The Antonine Itinerary correctly places it 18 miles from Cornus and 12 from Othoca (*Oristano*). (*Itin. Ant.* p. 84; Ptol. iii. 3. § 2.) [E. H. B.]

THARSANDALA (Θαρσάνδαλα), a town in Thrace, between Byzantium and the wall of Anastasius, which was one of the numerous places fortified by Justinian. (Procop. *de Aed.* iv. 11. p. 305, Bonn.) According to Reichard, *Esatalcsa* now occupies its site. [J. R.]

THASOS (Θάσος, sometimes Θάσσος : *Eth.* Θάσιος: *Thaso* or *Tasso*), an island in the N. of the Aegaean sea, off the coast of Thrace, and distant only 3½ miles from the plain of the river Nestus or *Kara-Su.* It was distant half a day's sail from Amphipolis (Thuc. iv. 104), and 32 miles from Abdera. (Plin. iv. 12. s. 23.) It was also called Aeria or Aethra (Plin. *l. c.;* Steph. B. *s. v.*) and Chryse, from its gold mines (Eustath. *ad Dionys. Per.* 517), which were the chief source of the prosperity of the island. The earliest known inhabitants of Thasos were the Phoenicians, who were doubtless attracted to the island by its valuable mines, but who are said to have come thither in search of Europa, five generations before the birth of the Grecian Hercules. They were led by Thasos, the son of Agenor, from whom the island derived its name. (Herod. ii. 44, vi. 47; Paus. v. 25. § 12; Scymn. 660; Conon, c. 37; Steph. B. *s. v.*) Thasos was afterwards colonised in Ol. 15 or 18 (B. C. 720 or 708) by settlers from Paros, led by Telesicles, the father of the poet Archilochus. (Thuc. iv. 104; Strab. ix. p. 487; Clem. Alex. *Strom.* i. p. 144; Euseb. *Praep. Ev.* vi. 7.) There also existed at that time in the island a Thracian tribe called Saians, with whom the Parian settlers carried on war, but not always successfully; and on one occasion Archilochus was obliged to throw away his shield. (Archiloch. *Fragm.* 5, ed. Schneidewin; Aristoph. *Pac.* 1298, with the Schol.) The Greek colony rapidly rose in power, and obtained valuable possessions on the adjoining mainland, which contained even richer mines than those in the island. Shortly before the Persian invasion, the clear surplus revenue of the Thasians was 200, and sometimes even 300 talents yearly (46,000*l.,* 66,000*l.*), of which Scaptê Hylê produced 80 talents, and the mines in the island rather less. (Herod. vi. 46.) Besides Scaptê Hylê the Thasians also possessed upon the mainland Galepsus and Oesyma (Thuc. iv.

107; Diod. xii. 68), Stryme (Herod. vii. 118; Suid. s. v. Στρύμη), Datum, and at a later period Crenides. (Böckh, Publ. Econ. of Athens, p. 312, Engl. tr.) Herodotus, who visited Thasos, says that the most remarkable mines were those worked by the Phoenicians on the eastern side of the island between Aenyra and Coenyra opposite Samothrace, where a large mountain had been overturned in search of the gold. (Herod. vi. 47.) The Thasians appear to have been the only Greeks who worked the valuable mines in Thrace, till Histiaeus, the Milesian, settled upon the Strymon and built the town of Myrcinus, about B. C. 511. (Herod. v. 11, 23.) After the capture of Miletus (B. C. 494), Histiaeus made an unsuccessful attempt to subdue Thasos (Herod. vi. 28), but the growing power of the Thasians excited the suspicions of Dareius, who commanded them in B. C. 492 to pull down their fortifications and remove their ships of war to Abdera, — an order which they did not venture to disobey. (Herod. vi. 46.) When Xerxes marched through Thrace on his way to Greece, the Thasians, on account of their possessions on the mainland, had to provide for the Persian army as it marched through their territories, the cost of which amounted to 400 talents (92,800l.). (Herod. vii. 118.) After the defeat of the Persians, Thasos became a member of the confederacy of Delos; but disputes having arisen between the Thasians and Athenians respecting the mines upon the mainland, a war ensued, and the Athenians sent a powerful force against the island under the command of Cimon, B. C. 465. After defeating the Thasians at sea, the Athenians disembarked, and laid siege to the city both by land and sea. The Thasians held out more than two years, and only surrendered in the third year. They were compelled to raze their fortifications; to surrender their ships of war; to give up their continental possessions; and to pay an immediate contribution in money, in addition to their annual tribute. (Thuc. i. 100, 101; Diod. xi. 70; Plut. Cim. 14.) In B. C. 411 the democracy in Thasos was overthrown, and an oligarchical government established by Peisander and the Four Hundred at Athens; but as soon as the oligarchy had got possession of the power they revolted from Athens, and received a Lacedaemonian garrison and harmost. (Thuc. viii. 64.) Much internal dissension followed, till at length in B. C. 408 a party of the citizens, headed by Ecphantus, expelled the Lacedaemonian harmost Eteonicus with his garrison and admitted Thrasybulus, the Athenian commander. (Xen. Hell. i. 1. §§ 12, 32, i. 4. § 9; Dem. c. Lept. p. 474.) After the battle of Aegospotamos, Thasos passed into the hands of the Lacedaemonians; but it was subsequently again dependent upon Athens, as we see from the disputes between Philip and the Athenians. (Dem. de Halon. p. 80; Philipp. Epist. p. 159.) In the Roman wars in Greece Thasos submitted to Philip V. (Polyb. xv. 24), but it received its freedom from the Romans after the battle of Cynoscephalae, B. C. 197 (Polyb. xviii. 27, 31; Liv. xxxiii. 30, 35), and continued to be a free (libera) town in the time of Pliny (iv. 12. s. 23).

The city of Thasos was situated in the northern part of the island, and possessed two ports, of which one was closed. (Scylax, p. 27; Ptol. iii. 11. § 14.) It stood on three eminences; and several remains of the ancient walls exist, intermixed with towers built by the Venetians, who obtained possession of the island after the capture of Constantinople by the Turks. In the neighbourhood is a large statue of Pan cut in the rocks. No remains have been discovered of Aenyra and Coenyra; and the mines have long ceased to be worked.

Archilochus describes Thasos as an "ass's backbone overspread with wild wood" (. . . ἥδε δ᾽ ὥστ᾽ ὄνου ῥάχις ἕστηκεν, ὕλης ἀγρίης ἐπιστεφής, Fragm. 17, 18, ed. Schneidewin), a description which is still strikingly applicable to the island after the lapse of 2500 years, as it is composed entirely of naked or woody mountains, with only scanty patches of cultivable soil, nearly all of which are close to the sea-shore. (Grote, Hist. of Greece, vol. iv. p. 34.) The highest mountain, called Mount Ipsarió, is 3428 feet above the sea, and is thickly covered with fir-trees. There is not enough corn grown in the island for its present population, which consists only of 6000 Greek inhabitants, dispersed in twelve small villages. Hence we are surprised to find it called by Dionysius (Perieg. 532) Δημήτερος ἀκτή; but the praises of its fertility cannot have been written from personal observation, and must have arisen simply from the abundance possessed by its inhabitants in consequence of their wealth. Thasos produced marble and wine, both of which enjoyed considerable reputation in antiquity. (Athen. i. pp. 28, 32, iv. p. 129; Xen. Symp. 4. § 41; Virg. Georg. ii. 91.) The chief produce of the island at present is oil, maize, honey, and timber; the latter, which is mostly fir, is the principal article of export.

The coins of Thasos are numerous. The one figured below represents on the obverse the head of Dionysus, and on the reverse a figure of Hercules kneeling.

(Prokesch von Osten, Denkwürdigkeiten, vol. iii. p. 611, seq.; Cousinery, Voyage dans la Macédoine, vol. ii. p. 85, seq.; Griesbach, Reise, vol. i. p. 210, seq.; Journal of Geogr. Society, vol. vii. p. 64.)

COIN OF THASOS.

THAUBA'SIUM (Itin. Ant. p. 171; Thaubastenm, Not. Imp.), was a frontier town of Lower Aegypt, situated on the Canopic arm of the Nile, about 8 miles N. of Serapeium and the Natron Lakes. In Roman times Thaubasium was the head-quarters of a company of light auxiliary troops "II Ala Ulpia Afrorum." (Orelli, Inscript. no. 2552.) It is supposed to be at the modern Cheych-el-Nedy. (Champollion, l'Egypte, vol. ii. p. 71.)   [W. B. D.]

THAU'MACI (Θαυμακοί: Eth. Θαυμακός), a town of Phthiotis in Thessaly, was situated on the pass called Coela, on the road from Thermopylae and the Maliac gulf passing through Lamia. At this place, says Livy, the traveller, after traversing rugged mountains and intricate valleys, comes suddenly in sight of an immense plain like a vast sea, the extremity of which is scarcely visible. From the astonishment which it excited in the traveller, the city was supposed to have derived its name. It stood upon a lofty and precipitous rock. It was besieged by Philip in B. C. 199; but a reinforcement of Aetolians having made their way into the town, the king was obliged to abandon the siege. (Liv. xxxii. 4.) Thaumaci was taken by the consul Acilius in the war with Antiochus, B. C. 191. (Liv. xxxvi. 14; comp. Strab. ix. p. 434; Steph. B. *s. v.* Θαυμακία.) *Dhomokó* occupies the site of Thaumaci, and at this place inscriptions are found containing the ancient name. Its situation and prospect are in exact accordance with the description of Livy, who copied from Polybius, an eye-witness. Dodwell says that " the view from this place is the most wonderful and extensive he ever beheld," and Leake observes that " at the southern end of the town a rocky point, overtopping the other heights, commands a magnificent prospect of the immense plain watered by the Peneius and its branches." (Dodwell, vol. ii. p. 122; Leake, *Northern Greece,* vol. i. p. 458.)

THAUMA'CIA (Θαυμακία: *Eth.* Θαυμακιεύς), a town of Magnesia in Thessaly, one of the four cities whose ships in the Trojan War were commanded by Philoctetes. It was said to have been founded by Thaumacus, the son of Poeas. Leake supposes it to be represented by the paleókastro of *Askiti,* one of the villages on the Magnesian coast. This Thaumacia must not be confounded with Thaumaci in Phthiotis mentioned above. (Hom. *Il.* ii. 716; Strab. ix. p. 436; Steph. B. *s. v.*; Eustath. *ad Hom.* p. 329. 6; Plin. iv. 9. s. 16; Leake, *Northern Greece,* vol. iv. p. 416.)

THEA'NGELA (Θεάγγελα: *Eth.* Θεαγγελεύς), a town of Caria, which Alexander placed under the jurisdiction of Halicarnassus, is known as the birthplace of Philip, the historian of Caria. (Plin. v. 29; Athen. vi. p. 271; Steph. B. *s. v.*)

THEBAE (Θῆβαι, Herod. i. 182, ii. 42; Strab. xvii. pp. 805,815, foll.; Thebe, Plin. v. 9. s. 11), the No (*Ezekiel,* xxx. 14) or No-AMMON (*Nahum,* vv. 3, 8) of the Hebrew Scriptures; at a later period DIOS-POLIS the Great of the Greeks and Romans (Διόσ-πολις μεγάλη, Ptol. iv. 5. § 73; Steph. B. *s. v.*), was one of the most ancient cities of Aegypt, and even, according to Diodorus (i. 50, comp. xv. 45), of the world. Its foundation, like that of Memphis, was attributed to Menes, the first mortal king of Aegypt, i. e. it went back to the mythical period of Aegyptian history. By some writers, however, Memphis was reported to have been a colony of Thebes. It was the capital of the nome formed by the city itself and its environs, though Ptolemy (*l. c.*) describes it as pertaining to the Nome of Coptos. In all Upper Aegypt no spot is so adapted for the site of a great capital as the plain occupied by ancient Thebes. The mountain chains, the Libyan on the western, and the Arabian on the eastern, side of the Nile, sweep boldly from the river, and leave on both banks a spacious area, whose breadth, including the river, amounts to nearly 4 leagues, and the length from N. to S. is nearly as much. Towards the N. the plain is again closed in by the return of the hills to the Nile; but on the S., where the western chain continues distant, it remains open. The ground, therefore, on which Thebes stood was large enough to contain a city of at least equal extent with ancient Rome or modern Paris; and, according to Strabo, ancient Thebes covered the entire plain. Only a portion of it, however, was available for population. An immense area was covered with the temples and their avenues of sphinxes; and on the western side, as far as the Libyan hills, lay the monuments of the dead. On the eastern bank, therefore, the population

was generally collected; and there it was probably densely crowded, since ancient writers assign to Thebes an almost incredible number of inhabitants, and Diodorus (i. 45) describes the houses as consisting of many stories. The extent of the city is very differently stated by ancient authors. Rumours of its greatness had reached the Greeks of Homer's age, who (*Il.* ix. 381) speaks of its " hundred gates " and its 20,000 war-chariots, just as the Arabian story-tellers speak of the glories of Bagdad or Damascus under the Caliphs. Before the Persian invasion (B. C. 525) no Greek writer had visited Thebes; and after that catastrophe its dimensions had considerably shrunk, since Cambyses is said to have burnt all such portions of Thebes as fire would destroy, i. e. all the private buildings; and under the Persian viceroys no Aegyptian city was likely to regain its original proportions. It does not appear that Herodotus ever visited Upper Egypt, and his account of Thebes is extremely vague and meagre. Diodorus, on the contrary, who saw it after its capture by Ptolemy Lathyrus, about B. C. 87, beheld Thebes in the second period of its decay, and after Alexandreia had diverted much of its commerce to Berenice and the Arsinoite bay. He estimates its circuit at 140 stadia or about 17 miles. Strabo, again, who went thither with the expedition of Aelius Gallus in B. C. 24, beheld Thebes at a still lower stage of decadence, and assigns it a compass of about 10 miles. But at that time the continuity of its parts was broken up, and it was divided into certain large hamlets (κωμηδόν) detached from one another. Neither of these writers, accordingly, was in a position to state accurately the real dimensions of the city in its flourishing estate, i. e. between 1600 and 800 B.C. Modern travellers, again, have still further reduced its extent; for example, Sir Gardner Wilkinson supposes the area of Thebes not to have exceeded 5½ English miles. As, however, during the space of 2600 years (800 B.C.—1800 A.D.) there have been very material changes in the soil from the contraction of the habitable ground, partly by the depositions of the Nile, and partly by the drifting of the sands, it is scarcely possible for modern travellers to determine how far Aegyptian labour and art may once have extended their capital. An author quoted by Stephanus of Byzantium, probably Hecataeus, runs into the opposite extreme, and ascribes to Thebes a population (7,000,000) hardly possible for the entire Nile-valley, and an extent (400 stadia, or 50 miles) larger than the Theban plain itself. (Steph. B. *s. v.* Διόσπολις.) The name of Thebes is formed from the Tápé of the ancient Aegyptian language, pronounced Thaba in the Memphitic dialect of Coptic, and thence easily converted into Θῆβαι, Thebè, or Thebes. In hieroglyphics it is written AP or APE, with the feminine article, T-APE, the meaning of which is said to be " head," Thebes being the " head " or capital of the Upper Kingdom. Its later appellation of Diospolis Magna (Διόσπολις ἡ μεγάλη) answers also to the Aegyptian title Amunei or " abode of Amun,"—Ammon or Zeus, the ram-headed god, being the principal object of worship at Thebes. The name Tapè or Thebes applied to the entire city on either bank of the Nile; but the western quarter had the distinctive name of Pathyris, or, according to Ptolemy (iv. 5. § 69), Tathyris, as being under the special protection of Athor, who is sometimes called the President of the West. The necropolis, indeed, on the Libyan side was appropriately placed under the guardianship of this deity, since she was believed to receive the sun in her arms as he sank behind the *western* hills. This quarter, again, in the age of the Ptolemies, was termed " the Libyan suburb," which was subdivided also into particular districts, such as the Memnoneia (τὰ Μεμνόνεια, Young, *Hieroglyph. Literature*, pp. 69, 73) and Thynabunum, where the priests of Osiris were interred. (Wilkinson, *Anc. Egyptians*, vol. v. p. 387.)

The power and prosperity of Thebes arose from three sources — trade, manufactures, and religion. Its position on the Nile, near the great avenues through the Arabian hills to the Red Sea, and to the interior of Libya through the western desert, rendering it a common entrepôt for the Indian trade on the one side, and the caravan trade with the gold, ivory, and aromatic districts on the other, and its comparative vicinity to the mines which intersect the limestone borders of the Red Sea, combined to make Thebes the greatest emporium in Eastern Africa, until Alexandreia turned the stream of commerce into another channel. It was also celebrated for its linen manufacture — an important fabric in a country where a numerous priesthood was interdicted from the use of woollen garments (Plin. ix. 1. s. 4). The glass, pottery, and intaglios of Thebes were also in high repute, and generally the number and magnitude of its edifices, sacred and secular, must have attracted to the city a multitude of artisans, who were employed in constructing, decorating, or repairing them. The priests alone and their attendants doubtless constituted an enormous population, for, as regarded Aegypt, and for centuries Aethiopia also, Thebes stood in the relation occupied by Rome in medieval Christendom, — it was the sacerdotal capital of all who worshipped Ammon from Pelusium to Axume, and from the Oases of Libya to the Red Sea.

The history of Thebes is not entirely the same with that of Aegypt itself, since the predominance of the Upper Kingdom implies a very different era in Aegyptian annals from that of the lower, or the Delta. It may perhaps be divided into three epochs: 1. The period which preceded the occupation of Lower Aegypt by the Assyrian nomades, when it is doubtful whether Memphis or Thebes were the capital of the entire country, or whether indeed both the Thebaid and the Delta were not divided into several smaller states, such as that of Heliopolis in the N., and Abydus in the S., the rivals respectively of Memphis and Thebes. 2. The interval between the expulsion of the Assyrians by Thoutmosis, and the 21st dynasty of Tanite kings. During all this period, Thebes was unquestionably the capital of all the Nile-valley, from the Mediterranean to the island of Argo in lat. 19° 31' N. 3. The period of decadence, when the government of Aegypt was centered in the Delta, and Thebes was probably little more than the head-quarters of the sacerdotal caste and the principal refuge of old Aegyptian life and manners. And this threefold division is rendered the more probable by the consideration that, until the Assyrian empire became formidable, and Phoenicia important from its maritime power, Aethiopia, rather than Arabia or Syria, was the formidable neighbour of Aegypt.

Under the Old Monarchy there is no trace of Aegyptian dominion extending beyond the peninsula of Sinai, the northern shores of the Red Sea, or the Libyan tribes adjoining the Delta. During this period invasion was apprehended almost exclusively from the S. The Aethiopians were no less warlike, and perhaps as civilised, as the Aegyptians: the Nile afforded them direct ingress to the regions north of the Cataracts, and they were then, as the Syrians and north-eastern states became afterwards, the immediate objects of war, treaties, or intermarriages with the Pharaohs of Thebes. When the Theban state was powerful enough to expel the Assyrian nomades, it must have already secured the alliance or the subjection of Aethiopia; and the attention of its rulers was thenceforward directed to the eastern frontier of the Lower Kingdom. Accordingly we find that while only one nome in the Thebaid and one in Middle Aegypt were assigned to the native militia, the bulk of the Calasirians and Hermobytians was permanently quartered in the Delta.

The greatness of Thebes commences with the 18th dynasty of the Pharaohs, and the immediate cause of it appears to have been the collective efforts of the Upper Country to expel the Assyrian shepherds from the Delta. The Thebaid and its capital were, probably, at no period occupied by these invaders; since, according to Manetho's account of the 17th dynasty, there were then two contemporaneous kingdoms in Aegypt — the Delta governed by the Hyksos, and the Thebaid by native monarchs. Thoutmosis, king of Thebes, was the principal agent in the expulsion of the intruders, and his exploits against them are commemorated on the temples at *Karnak*. Memphis and the Delta, together with the lesser states, such as Xois, delivered from the invaders, thenceforward were under the dominion of the kings of Thebes. Its flourishing era lasted nearly eight centuries, i. e. from about 1600 to 800 B. C.

During this period the most conspicuous monarchs were Amenophis I., who appears, from the monuments, to have received divine honours after his decease, and to have been regarded as the second founder of the monarchy. He probably carried his arms beyond the north-eastern frontier of the Delta into Syria, and his presence in Aethiopia is recorded in a grotto at *Ibrim* near *Aboosimbel.* The victories or conquests of Amenophis in the N. and S. are inferred from the circumstance that in the sculptures he is represented as destroying or leading captive Asiatic and Aethiopian tribes. Next in succession is Thothmes I., with whose reign appears to have begun the series of Theban edifices which excited the wonder of the Greeks, who beheld them almost in their original magnificence, and of all subsequent travellers. The foundations, at least, of the palace of the kings were laid by this monarch. Thothmes also, like his predecessors, appears, from the monuments, to have made war with Assyria, and to have extended his dominion as high up the Nile as the island of Argo in upper Nubia. Thothmes II. maintained or even enlarged the realm which he inherited, since his name has been found at *Gebel-el-Birkel*, the Napata of the Romans, lat. 18° 30' N. At this period Aethiopia was apparently an appanage of the Theban kingdom, and its rulers or viceroys seem to have been of the blood royal of Aegypt, since now for the first time, and until the reign of Setei Menephthah (Rosellini, *Mon. Reg.* tab. xxxi.—iv.), we meet with the title of the royal son or prince of Aethiopia. The records of this reign have nearly perished; the great obelisks of *Karnak*, however, attest the flourishing condition of contemporary art. They were erected by Nemt Amen, the sister of Thothmes II., who appears, like the Nitocris of the

Old Monarchy, to have exercised the functions of royalty. The reign of Thothmes III. is one of the most splendid in the annals of the 18th dynasty. The frontiers of Aegypt extended S. a little beyond the second cataract, and E. nearly to Mount Sinai. Thothmes III. completed in Thebes itself many of the structures begun by his predecessors, e. g. the palace of the kings, — and generally enriched the cities of the Thebaid with sumptuous buildings. He commenced the temple at Amada, which was completed by Amunoph II. and Thothmes IV; and his name was inscribed on the monuments of Ombi, Apollinopolis Magna, and Eilithya. Thebes, however, was the centre of his architectural labours, and even the ruins of his great works there have served to adorn other capital cities. In the Hippodrome of Constantinople is a mutilated obelisk of the reign of Thothmes III., which was brought from Aegypt by one of the Byzantine emperors, and which originally adorned the central court of *Karnak*. Again the obelisk which Pope Sixtus V. set up in front of the church of St. John Lateran at Rome, the loftiest and most perfect structure of its kind, was first raised in this reign, and beare its founder's titles on the central column of its hieroglyphics. The records of this reign are inscribed on two interesting monuments, — a painting in a tomb at *Gournch* (Hoskins, *Travels in Aethiopia*, p. 437, foll.; Wilkinson, *Mod. Egypt and Thebes*, vol. ii. p. 234), and the great Tablet of *Karnak*; which is strictly an historical and statistical document, and which, there can be little doubt, is the very Tablet which the priests of Thebes exhibited and expounded to Caesar Germanicus in A. D. 16 (Tac. *Ann.* ii. 60). From the paintings and the hieroglyphics, so far as the latter have been read, on these monuments, it appears that in this reign tribute was paid into the Theban treasury by nations dwelling on the borders of the Caspian sea, on the banks of the Tigris, in the kingdom of Meroe or Aethiopia, and by the more savage tribes who wandered over the eastern flank of the great *Sahara*. Thirteen expeditions, indeed, of Thothmes III., are distinctly registered, and the 35th year of his reign, according to Lepsius, is recorded. At this period the kingdom of Thebes must have been the most powerful and opulent in the world. Of the son of Thothmes, Amunophis II., little is known; but he also added to the erections at Thebes, and reared other monuments in Nubia. Inscriptions found at *Surabit-el-Kaalim*, in the peninsula of Sinai, record his name, and at Primis (*Ibrim*) he appears in a *speos*, or excavated chapel, seated with two principal officers, and receiving the account of a great chase of wild beasts.

Next in importance, though not in succession, of the Theban kings of the 18th dynasty, is Amunoph, or Amenophis III. His name is found at *Toumbos*, near the third Cataract, and he permanently extended the frontiers of the Theban kingdom to Soleb, a degree further to S. than it had hitherto reached. These extensions are not only geographically, but commercially, important, inasmuch as the farther southward the boundaries extended, the nearer did the Aegyptians approach to the regions which produced gold, ivory, gems, and aromatics, and the more considerable, therefore, was the trade of Thebes itself. Only on the supposition that it was for many generations one of the greatest emporiums in the world can we understand the lavish expenditure of its monarchs, and its fame among northern nations as the greatest and richest of cities.

And this consideration is the more important towards a correct estimate of the resources of the Theban kingdom, since its proper territory barely sufficed for the support of its dense population, and there is no evidence of its having any remarkable traffic by sea. It is probable, indeed, that the dominions of Amenophis III. stretched to within five days' journey of Axume on the Red Sea; for a scarabaeus inscribed with his name and that of his wife Taia mentions the land of *Karoei* or *Kaloei*, supposed to be Coloe (Rosellini, *Mon. Stor.* iii. 1, 261; Birch, *Gall. Brit. Mus.* p. 83), as their southern limit. Thebes was enriched by this monarch with two vast palaces, one on the eastern, the other on the western bank of the Nile. He also commenced and erected the greater portion of the buildings at *Luxor*. On the walls of their chambers Amenophis was designated " The vanquisher of the Mennahoun," an unknown people, and the " Pacificator of Aegypt." From the fragment of a monolithal granite statue now in the Louvre, it may be inferred that his victories were obtained over negro races, and consequently were the results of campaigns in the interior of Libya and the S. of Aethiopia. Amenophis has a further claim to notice, since he was probably the Memnon, son of Aurora, whom Achilles slew at the siege of Troy. Of all the Aethiopian works the Memnonian statues, from their real magnitude and from the fabulous stories related of them, have attracted the largest share of attention. By the word Memnon the Greeks understood an Aethiopian or man of dark complexion (Steph. B. *s. v.*; Agathem. ap. Gr. *Geograph. Min.*), or rather, perhaps, a dark-complexioned warrior (comp. Eustath. *ad Il.* v. 639); and the term may very properly have been applied to the conqueror of the southern land, who was also hereditary prince of Aethiopia. The statues of Memnon, which now stand alone on the plain of Thebes, originally may have been the figures at the entrance of the long dromos of crio-sphinxes which led up to the Amenopheion or palace of Amenophis. Of the eastern and northern limits of the Theban kingdom under the third Amenophis, we have no evidence similar to that afforded by the tablet of *Karnak*; yet from the monuments of his battles we may infer that he levied tribute from the Arabians on the Red Sea and in the peninsula of Sinai, and at one time pushed his conquests as far as Mesopotamia. According to Manetho he reigned 31 years: his tomb is the most ancient of the sepulchres in the *Bab-el-Melook*; and even so late as the Ptolemaic age he had divine honours paid him by a special priest-college called " The pastophori of Amenophis in the Memnoneia." (Kenrick, *Ancient Aegypt*, vol. ii. p. 246.)

Setei Menephthah is the next monarch of the 18th dynasty who, in connection with Thebes, deserves mention. Besides the temples which he constructed at Amada in Nubia and at Silsilis (*Silseleh*), he began the great palace called Menephtheion in that city, although he left it to be completed by his successors Rameses II. and III. From the paintings and inscriptions on the ruins at *Karnak* and *Luxor* it appears that this monarch triumphed over five Asiatic nations as well as over races whose position cannot be ascertained, but whose features and dress point to the interior of Libya. The tomb and sarcophagus of Setei Menephthah were discovered by Belzoni in the *Bab-el-Melook*. (*Travels*, vol. i. p. 167.) If he be the same with the Sethos of the lists, he reigned 50 or 51 years. We now come to the name of Rameses II. and III., the latter of whom is the Sesostris of Herodotus, and who may therefore be regarded as a clearly historical personage. There can be no doubt of the greatness of Thebes under his sceptre. In this, as in many other instances where Aegypt is concerned, the monuments of the country enable us to approach the truth, while the credulity of the Greek travellers and historians in accepting the narrations of the Aegyptian priests — naturally eager, after their subjection by the Persians, to exalt their earlier condition — only tends to bewilder and mislead. Thus, for example, Diodorus (i. 54) was informed that Sesostris led into the field 600,000 infantry, 24,000 cavalry, and 27,000 chariots; and he appeals to the passage already cited from Homer to show that Thebes sent so many chariots out of its hundred gates. There is no evidence that the Aegyptians then possessed a fleet in the Mediterranean; yet Diodorus numbers among his conquests the Cyclades, and Dicaearchus (*Schol. in Apoll. Rhod.* iv. 272) assigns to him " the greater part of Europe." The monuments, on the contrary, record nothing so incredible of this monarch; although if we may infer the extent of his conquests and the number of his victories from the space occupied on the monuments by their pictorial records, he carried the arms of Aegypt beyond any previous boundaries, and counted among his subjects races as various as those which, nearly 17 centuries later, were ruled by Trajan and the Antonines. The reign of Rameses was of 60 years' duration, that is nearly of equal length with his life, for the first of his victories — that recorded on the propylaea of the temple of *Luxor*, and much more fully on those of *Aboosimbel* — was gained in his fifth year. We must refer to works professedly dealing with Aegyptian annals for his hisotry: here it will be sufficient to observe of Rameses or Sesostris that he added to Thebes the Rameseion, now generally admitted to be the " monument of Osymandyas," upon the western bank of the Nile; that he was distinguished from all his predecessors by the extent of his conquests and the wisdom of his laws; and among his subjects for his strength, comeliness, and valour. The very pre-eminence of Rameses III. has, indeed, obscured his authentic history. To him were ascribed many works of earlier and of later monarchs, — such as the canal of the Pharaohs, between the Nile and the Red Sea; the dykes and embankments which rendered the Delta habitable; the great wall, 1500 stadia in length, between Pelusium and Heliopolis, raised as a barrier against the Syrians and Arabians; a re-partition of the land of Aegypt; the law of hereditary occupation (Aristot. *Pol.* vii. 10); and foreign conquests, or at least expeditions into Western Asia, which rendered tributary to him even the Colchians and the Bactrians. (Tacit. *Ann.* ii. 60.)

With the 21st dynasty appear the traces of a revolution affecting the Upper Kingdom. Tanite and Bubastite Pharaohs are now lords of the Nile-valley: and these are succeeded by an Aethiopian dynasty, marking invasion and occupation of the Thebaid by a foreigner. Perhaps, as Aegypt became more involved with the affairs of Asia—a result of the conquests of the house of Rameses—it may have proved expedient to remove the seat of government nearer to the Syrian frontier. The dynasty of Sethos, the Aethiopian, however, indicates a revolt of the provinces S. of the cataracts; and even after the Aethiopians had withdrawn, the Lower Kingdom re-

tained its pre-eminence. The Saïte Pharaohs feared or despised the native militia, and surrounded themselves with foreign mercenaries. Greek colonies were established in the Delta; and Aegypt maintained a fleet — an innovation extremely prejudicial to Thebes, since it implied that the old isolation of the land was at an end, and that the seat of power was on the Syrian, and not on the Aethiopian frontier. The stages of its decline cannot be traced; but Thebes seems to have offered no opposition, after the fall of Memphis, to the Persians, and certainly, after its occupation by Cambyses, never resumed its place as a metropolitan city. That Thebes was partially restored after the destruction of at least its secular buildings by the Persians, admits of no doubt, since it was strong enough in B. C. 86 to hold out against the forces of Ptolemy Lathyrus. But although the circuit of its walls may have been undiminished, it seems never again to have been filled as before with a dense population. The foundation of Alexandreia was more fatal to Thebes than even the violence of Cambyses; and its rebellion against the Macedonians was perhaps prompted by jealousy of Greek commerce and religion. The hand of Lathyrus lay heavy on Thebes; and from this epoch probably dates the second stage of its decline. From the glimpses we gain of it through the writings of the Greeks and Romans, it appears to have remained the head-quarters of the sacerdotal order and of old Aegyptian life and manners. As a Macedonian or Roman prefecture, it took little or no part in the affairs of Aegypt; yet it profited by the general peace of the world under the Caesars, and employed its wealth or labour in the repair or decoration of its monuments. The names of Alexander and some of the Ptolemies, of the Caesars from Tiberius to the Antonines, are inscribed on its monuments; and even in the fourth century A. D. it was of sufficient importance to attract the notice of historians and travellers. Perhaps its final ruin was owing as much to the fanaticism of the Christians of the Thebaid, who saw in its sculptures only the abominations of idol-worship, as to its occupation by the Blemmyes and other barbarians from Nubia and Arabia. When the Saracens, who also were iconoclasts, broke forth from Arabia, Thebes endured its final desolation, and for many centuries its name almost disappears: nor can its monuments be said to have generally attracted the notice of Europeans, until the French expedition to Aegypt once again disclosed its monuments. From that period, and especially since the labours of Belzoni, no ancient city has been more frequently visited or described.

The growth of Thebes and the additions made to it by successive monarchs or dynasties have been partly traced in the foregoing sketch of its political history. A few only of its principal remains can here be noticed, since the ruins of this city form the subject of many works, and even the most condensed account of them would almost demand a volume for itself. Ancient Thebes, as has already been observed, occupied both the eastern and western banks of the Nile; and four villages, two, on each side of the river, now occupy a portion of its original area. Of these villages two, *Luxor* and *Karnak*, are on the eastern bank, and two, *Gourneh* and *Medinet-Aboo*, on the western. There is some difference in the character and purpose of the structures in the opposite quarters of the city. Those on the western bank formed part of its vast necropolis; and here are found the rock-hewn painted tombs,—" the tombs of the kings,"—whose sculptures so copiously illustrate the history, the arts, and the social life of Aegypt. On this side there are also the remains of temples, palaces, and halls of assembly or judicature, with their vast enclosure of walls and their long avenues of sphinxes. But the western quarter of Thebes was reserved principally for the dead, and for the service of religion and the state, while the mass of the population was contained in the eastern. Yet the numbers who inhabited the western side of the city must have been considerable, since each temple had its own establishment of priests, and each palace or public edifice its proper officers and servants. Still we shall probably be correct in describing the eastern quarter as the civil, and the western as the royal and ecclesiastical, portion of Thebes. At present no obelisks have been discovered in the western quarter, but, with this exception, the monuments of *Gourneh* and *Medinet-Aboo* yield little in grandeur, beauty, or interest to those of *Luxor* and *Karnak*, and in one respect indeed are the more important of the two, since they afford the best existing specimens of Aegyptian colossal or portrait statues.

Beginning then with the western quarter,—the Memnoneia of the Ptolemaic times,—we find at the northern limit of the plain, about three quarters of a mile from the river, the remains of a building to which Champollion has given the name of *Menephtheion*, because the name of Setei-Menephthah is inscribed upon its walls. It appears to have been both a temple and a palace, and was approached by a dromos of 128 feet in length. Its pillars belong to the oldest style of Aegyptian architecture, and its bas-reliefs are singularly fine.

The next remarkable ruin is the Memnoneium of Strabo (xvii. p. 728), the tomb of Osymandyas of Diodorus, now commonly called the *Rameseion* on the authority of its sculptures. The situation, the extent, and the beauty of this relic of Thebes are all equally striking. It occupies the first base of the hills, as they rise from the plain; and before the alluvial soil had encroached on the lower ground, it must have been even a more conspicuous object from the city than it now appears. The inequalities of the ground on which it was erected were overcome by flights of steps from one court to another, and the *Rameseion* actually stood on a succession of natural terraces improved by art. The main entrance from the city is flanked by two pyramidal towers: the first court is open to the sky, surrounded by a double colonnade, and 140 feet in length and 18 in breadth. On the left of the staircase that ascends to the second court still stands the pedestal of the statue of Rameses, the largest, according to Diodorus (i. 49), of the colossi of Aegypt. From the dimensions of its foot, parts of which still remain, it is calculated that this statue was 54 feet in height and 22 feet 4 inches in breadth across the shoulders. The court is strewn with its fragments. How it was erected, or how overthrown in a land not liable to earthquakes, are alike subjects of wonder; since, without mechanical aids wholly beyond the reach of barbarians, it must have been almost as difficult to cast it down from its pedestal as to transport it originally from the quarries. The walls of the second court are covered with sculptures representing the wars of Rameses III., a continuation and complement of the historical groups upon the interior walls of the pylon. Diodorus (i. 47) speaks of "monolithal figures, 16 cubits

high, supplying the place of columns," and these are probably the pillars of this second court. He also mentions the attack of a city surrounded by a river; and this group of sculpture, still extant, identifies the Memnoneium with the monument of Osymandyas. A third flight of stairs conducts from the court to a hall, which, according to Champollion was used for public assemblies. A sitting statue of Rameses flanked each side of the steps, and the head of one of them, now called the *young* Memnon adorns the British Museum. The columns and walls of the court are covered with sculptures partly of a religious, partly of a civil character, representing the homage of the 23 sons of Rameses to their parent and his offerings to the gods. Nine smaller apartments succeed to the hall. One of these was doubtless the library or "Dispensary of the Mind" ($\psi\upsilon\chi\tilde{\eta}\varsigma$ $\iota\alpha\tau\rho\epsilon\tilde{\iota}o\nu$) of which Diodorus (i. 49) speaks, since in it are found sculptures of Thoth, the inventor of letters, and his companion Saf, the "lady of letters" and "President of the Hall of Books." This chamber had also at one time an astronomical ceiling adorned with the figures or symbols of the Aegyptian months; but it was carried off by the Persians, and the Greek travellers, Diodorus, Hecataeus &c., knew of it only from hearsay. Of the nine original chambers, two only remain, the one just described, and a second, in which Rameses is depicted sacrificing to various divinities of the Theban Pantheon. Beneath the upper portion of the Memnoneium rock-sepulchres and brick graves have been discovered, both coeval with the Rameseian dynasty (Lepsius, *Rev. Arch.* Jan. 1845). The entire area of the Memnoneium was enclosed by a brick wall, in the double arches of which are occasionally imbedded fragments of still more ancient structures, the remains probably of the Thebes which the 18th dynasty of the Pharaohs enlarged and adorned. A dromos NW. of the Memnoneium, formed of not less than 200 sphinxes, and at least 1600 feet in length, led to a very ancient temple in a recess of the Libyan hills. This was probably a place of strength before the lowlands on each side of the Nile were artificially converted by drainage and masonry into the solid area upon which Thebes was built.

The next object which meets the traveller's eye is a mound of rubbish, the fragments of a building once occupying the ground. It is called by the Arabs *Koum-el-Hattam*, or mountain of sandstone, and is composed of the ruins of the Amenopheion, the palace or temple of Amunoph III.—the Memnon of the Greeks. About a quarter of a mile distant from the Amenopheion, and nearer to the Nile, are the two colossal statues called *Tama* and *Chama* by the natives, standing isolated on the plain and eminent above it. The most northerly of these statues is the celebrated vocal Memnon. Their present isolation, however, is probably accidental, and arises from the subsidence or destruction of an intermediate dromos, of which they formed the portals, and which led to the Amenopheion. These statues have already been described in the *Dictionary of Biography, s. v.* MEMNON [Vol. II. p. 1028.] It may be added here that the present height of these colossal figures, inclusive of the pedestal, is 60 feet. The alluvial soil, however, rises to nearly one half of the pedestal, and as there is an inscription of the age of Antoninus Pius, A. D. 139, foll., i. e. about 1720 years old, we obtain some measure of the amount of deposition in so many centuries. The blocks from which the statues are formed are composed of a coarse, hard breccia, intermixed with agatised pebbles. (Russegger, *Reisen*, vol. ii. pt. 1. p. 410.) The village of *Medinet-Aboo* stands about one third of a mile SW. of *Koum-el-Hattam*, upon a lofty mound formed by the ruins of the most splendid structure in western Thebes. It consisted of two portions, a temple and a palace, connected with each other by a pylop and a dromos. The temple was the work of successive monarchs of the name of Thothmes, and hence has received the name of the Thothmeseion. Apparently this site found favour with the sovereigns of Aegypt in all ages, since, either on the main building or on its numerous outworks, which extend towards the river, are inscribed the names of Tirhakah the Aethiopian, of Nectanebus, the last independent king of Aegypt, of Ptolemy Soter II., and of Antoninus Pius. The original Thothmeseion comprises merely a sanctuary surrounded by galleries and eight chambers ; the additions to it represent the different periods of its patrons and architects. The palace of Rameses—the southern Rameseion of Champollion—far exceeds in dimensions and the splendour of its decorations the Thothmeseion. It stands a little S. of the temple, nearer the foot of the hills. The dromos which connects them is 265 feet in length. The sculptures on the pylon relate to the coronation of Rameses IV. and his victories over the Aethiopians. A portion of the southern Rameseion seems to have been appropriated to the private uses of the king. The mural decorations of this portion are of singular interest, inasmuch as they represent Rameses in his hours of privacy and recreation.

The walls of the southern Rameseion generally are covered both on the inside and the out with representations of battles, sacrifices, religious processions and ceremonies, relating to the 18th dynasty. A plain succeeds, bounded by sand-hills and heaps of Nile-mud. It is variously described by modern travellers as the site of a race-course, of a camp or barrack, or an artificial lake, over which, according to Sir Gardner Wilkinson, the dead were ferried to the neighbouring necropolis. Whatever may have been its purpose, this plain is of considerable extent, being somewhat less than a mile and half in length, and more than half a mile in breadth.

The contrast between the portion of Thebes once crowded with the living, and that which was equally thronged with the dead, is less striking now, when the whole city is a desert or occupied only by a few straggling villages. But under the Pharaohs the vicinity of life and death must have been most solemn and expressive. From *Gourneh* to *Medinet-Aboo* the Libyan hills, along a curve of nearly 5 miles, are honey-combed with sepulchres, and conspicuous among them are the Tombs of the Kings, situated in the valley of *Bab-el-Melook*. The Theban necropolis is excavated in the native calcareous rock. The meaner dead were interred in the lower ground, where the limestone is of a softer grain, and more exposed to decomposition by wind and water. This portion of the cemetery has, accordingly, fallen into decay. But the upper and harder strata of the hills are of finer and more durable texture, and here the priest-caste and nobles were interred. The tombs of the lower orders are generally without sculpture, but filled with mummies of animals accounted sacred by the Aegyptians. A favourite companion in death appears to have been

the ape; and such numbers of this animal have been found in one portion of the necropolis that the valley containing their mummies bears the name of the "Apes' Burial Place." Upon the graves of the upper classes painting and sculpture were lavished in a measure hardly inferior to that which marks the sepulchres of the kings. The entire rock is tunnelled by them, and by the galleries and staircases which led to the various chambers. The entrances to these tombs are rectangular, and open into passages which either pierce the rock in straight lines, or wind through it by ascending and descending shafts. Where the limestone is of a crumbling nature, it was supported by brick arches, and drains were provided for carrying off standing or casual water. The walls of these passages and chambers were carefully prepared for the artist. Rough or carious portions were cut out, and their place filled up with bricks and plaster. Their entire surface was then covered with stucco, on which the paintings were designed and highly coloured. The decorations are rarely in relief, but either drawn on the flat surface, or cut into the stucco. They are mostly framed in squares of chequer and arabesque work. The subjects portrayed within these frames or niches are very various,—ranging through religious ceremonies and the incidents of public or private life. The ornaments of these tombs may indeed be termed the miniature painting of the Aegyptians. Within a space of between 40 and 50 feet no less than 1200 hieroglyphics are often traced, and finished with a minute delicacy unsurpassed even in buildings above ground, which were meant for the eyes of the living.

The Royal Sepulchres, however, form the most striking feature of the Theban necropolis. They stand in a lonely and barren valley, seemingly a natural chasm in the limestone, and resembling in its perpendicular sides and oblong shape a sarcophagus. At the lower end of this basin an entrance has been cut—there seems to be no natural mode of ingress—in the rock. Forty-seven tombs were, at one time, known to the ancients. (Diodor. i. 46.) Of these twenty or twenty-one have been counted by modern explorers. Here reposed the Theban Pharaohs from the 18th to the 21st dynasty. The only tombs, hitherto discovered, complete are those of Amunoph III., Rameses Meiamun, and Rameses III. To prepare a grave seems to have been one of the duties or pleasures of Aegyptian royalty ; and since the longest survivor of these monarchs rests in the most sumptuous tomb, it may be inferred that the majority of them died before they had completed their last habitation.

The queens of Aegypt were buried apart from the kings, in a spot about three-fourths of a mile NW. of the temple of *Medinet-Aboo*. Each of them bears the title of "Wife of Amun," indicating either that their consorts combined with their proper names that also of the great Theban deity, or that, after death, they were dignified by apotheosis. Twenty-four tombs have at present been discovered in this cemetery, twelve of which are ascertained to be those of the queens. The least injured of them by time or violence bears the name of Taia, wife of Amunoph III.

On the eastern bank of the Nile, the monuments are even more magnificent. The villages of *Luxor* and *Karnak* occupy a small portion only of the true Diospolis. The ruins at *Luxor* stand close to the river. The ancient landing place was a jetty of stone, which also served to break the current of the stream. The most remarkable monuments are two obelisks of Rameses III., respectively 70 and 60 feet high, one of which still remains there, while the other has been removed to the *Place de la Concorde* at Paris. Their unequal height was partially concealed from the spectator by the lower obelisk being placed upon the higher pedestal. Behind them were two monolithal statues of that monarch, in red Syenite granite. These are now covered from the breast downwards with rubbish and fluvial deposit, but were, originally, including their chairs or bases, 39 feet high. Next succeeds a court, surrounded by a corridor of double columns, 190 feet long and 170 broad. It is entered through a portal 51 feet in height, whose pyramidal wings are inscribed with the battles of Rameses. On the opposite side of the court a second portal, erected by Amunoph III., opens upon a colonnade which leads to a smaller court, and this again terminates with a portico composed of four rows of columns, eight in each row. Beyond the third portico follows a considerable number of apartments, flanking a sanctuary on the walls of which are represented the birth of Amunoph, and his presentation to Amun.

A dromos of *andro-sphinxes*, and various buildings now covered with sand and dried mud, formerly connected the quarter of eastern Thebes, represented by *Luxor*, with that represented by *Karnak*. Near to the latter place a portion of the dromos still exists, and a little to the right of it a second dromos of *crio-sphinxes* branches off, which must have been one of the most rémarkable structures in the city. It led up to the palace of the kings, and consisted of a double row of statues, sixty or seventy in number, each 11 feet distant from the next, and each having a lion's body and a ram's head. The SW. entrance of the palace is a lofty portal, followed by four spacious courts with intervening gateways.

The grandeur of the palace is, in some degree, lessened by later additions to its plan, for on the right side of the great court was a cluster of small chambers, while on its left were only two apartments. Their object is unknown, but they probably served as lodgings or offices for the royal attendants. In the first of the two main courts stand two obelisks of Thothmes I., one in fragments, the other still erect and uninjured. In a second court to the right of the first, there were two obelisks also : the one which remains is 92 feet high. The oldest portion of the palace of *Karnak* appears to be a few chambers, and some polygonal columns bearing the shield of Sesortasen I. To these—the nucleus of the later structures—Thothmes III. made considerable additions ; among them a chamber whose sculptures compose the great *Karnak* Tablet, so important a document for Aegyptian chronology.

But the Great Court is surpassed in magnificence by the Great Hall. This is 80 feet in height, and 329 feet long by 179 broad. The roof is supported by 134 columns, 12 in the centre and 122 in the aisles. The central columns are each 66 feet high, clear of their pedestals, and each 11 feet in diameter. The pedestals were 10 feet high, and the abacus over their capitals, on which rested the architraves of the ceiling, was 4 feet in depth. The columns were each about 27 feet apart from one another. The aisle-columns stood in 7 rows, were each 41 feet high, and 9 feet in girth. Light and air were admitted into the building through apertures in the side walls. The founder of the palace was Setei-Menephthah, of the 18th dynasty ; but one reign

cannot have sufficed for building so gigantic a court, and we know indeed not only that many of the historical bas-reliefs which cover the walls were contributed by his son Rameses II., but also that the latter added to the Great Hall, on its NW. side, a vast hypethral court, 275 feet in breadth, by 329 in length. This, like the hall, had a double row of columns down its centre, and a covered corridor round its sides. Four gateways opening to the four quarters gave admission into this court: and to the principal one which fronted the Nile an avenue of crio-sphinxes led up, headed by two granite statues of Rameses II.

The purpose for which these spacious courts and their annexed halls and esplanades were erected was perhaps partly religious, and partly secular. Though the kings of the 18th and succeeding dynasties had ceased to be chief-priests, they still retained many ceremonial functions, and the sacred calendar of Aegypt abounded in days of periodical meetings for religious objects. At such *panegyries* the priests alone were a host, and the people were not excluded. From the sculptures also it appears that the Court of Royal Palaces was the place where troops were reviewed, embassies received, captives executed or distributed, and the spoils or honours of victory apportioned. Both temples and palaces also served occasionally for the encampment of soldiers and the administration of justice. The temperature of the Thebaid rendered vast spaces indispensable for the congregation of numbers, and utility as well as pomp may have combined in giving their colossal scale to the structures of the Pharaohs.

In the Great Hall a great number of the columns are still erect. The many which have fallen have been undermined by water loosening the soil below: and they fall the more easily, because the architraves of the roof no longer hold them upright. The most costly materials were employed in some parts of the palace. Cornices of the finest marble were inlaid with ivory mouldings or sheathed with beaten gold.

These were the principal structures of the eastern moiety of Thebes: but other dromoi and gateways stand within the circuit of its walls, and by their sculptures or inscriptions attest that the Macedonian as well as the native rulers extended, renovated, or adorned the capital of the Upper Country. The eastern branch of the dromos which connects *Luxor* with *Karnak* appears from its remains to have been originally 500 feet in length, and composed of a double row of ram-headed lions 58 in number. The loftiest of Aegyptian portals stands at its SW. extremity. It is 64 feet high, but without the usual pyramidal propyla. It is indeed a work of the Greek era, and was raised by Ptolemy Euergetes I. Rameses IV. and Rameses VIII. added temples and a dromos to the city. Nor was Thebes without its benefactors even so late as the era of the Roman Caesars. The name of Tiberius was inscribed on one of its temples; and Hadrian, while engaged in his general survey of the Empire, directed some repairs or additions to be made to the temple of Zeus-Ammon. That Thebes, as Herodotus and Diodorus saw it, stood upon the site and incorporated the remains of a yet more ancient city, is rendered probable by its sudden expansion under the 18th dynasty of the Pharaohs, as well as by extant specimens of its architecture, more in affinity with the monuments S. of the cataracts than with the proper Aegyptian style. It seems hardly questionable that

Thebes was indebted for its greatness originally to its being the principal centre of Ammon-worship,—a worship which, on the one hand, connected it with Meroe, and, on the other, with the islands of the Libyan desert. The strength which the Thebaid and its capital thus acquired not only enabled it to rise superior to Abydus in the earlier period, but also to expel the Assyrian invaders from the Delta. It becomes then an interesting question which quarter of Thebes was its cradle? Did it spread itself from the eastern or the western shore of the Nile? Both Diodorus and Strabo are agreed in placing the "old town," with its Ammonian temple, on the eastern bank of the river; and this site too was the more accessible of the two, whether its population came from the left or, as it is more likely they did, from the right shore. Between *Luxor* and *Karnak* lies the claim to be considered as the site of the earliest Diospolis. Now in the former place there is no conspicuous trace of Ammon-worship, whereas the latter, in its ram-headed dromoi, abounds with symbols of it. At *Karnak*, every monument attests the presence of Ammon. Osiris indeed appears as his son or companion on the sculptures, and in some of the temple-legends they were represented as joint founders of the shrine. But Ammon was without doubt the elder of the two. We may accordingly infer that the first Thebes stood nearly on the site of the present *Karnak*, at a period anterior to all record: that it expanded towards the river, and was separated by the whole breadth of the stream and of the plain to the foot of the Libyan hills from the necropolis. Finally, that as its population became too large for the precincts of the eastern plain, a suburb, which grew into a second city, arose on the opposite bank of the Nile; and thus the original distinction between eastern and western Thebes partially disappeared, and the river, having thenceforward habitations on both its banks, no longer parted by a broad barrier the city of the living from the city of the dead.

(Kenrick, *Ancient Aegypt under the Pharaohs*, vol. i. pp. 149—178; Heeren, *Historical Researches, Thebes and its Monuments*, vol. ii. pp. 201—342; Champollion, *Lettres sur l'Egypte;* Hamilton, *Aegyptiaca;* Belzoni, *Travels, &c.*)

The territory of Thebes was named THEBAIS (ἡ Θηβαΐς, sc. χώρα, or οἱ ἄνω τόποι, the Upper Country, Ptol. iv. 5. § 62), the modern *Sais* or *Pathros*, and was one of the three principal divisions of Aegypt. Its frontiers to the S. varied accordingly as Aegypt or Aethiopia preponderated, the Theban Pharaohs at times ruling over the region above the Cataracts as far S. as Hiera Sycamina lat. 23° 6′ N.; while, at others, the kings of Meroe planted their garrisons N. of Syene, and, at one period, occupied the Thebais itself. But the ordinary limits of Upper Aegypt were Syene to S., lat. 24° 5′ N., and Hermopolis Magna to N., lat. 27° 45′ N. On the E. it was bounded by the Arabian, on the W. by the Libyan hills and desert. As rain seldom falls in the Thebais (Herod. iii. 10), and as its general surface is rocky or sandy, the breadth of cultivable land depends on the alluvial deposit of the Nile, and this again is regulated by the conformation of the banks on either side. For a similar cause the population of the Thebais was mostly gathered into towns and large villages, both of which are often dignified by ancient writers with the appellation of cities. But numerous cities were incompatible with the physical character of this region,

and its population must have been considerably below the estimate of it by the Greeks and Romans. The Thebais was divided into ten nomes (Strab. xvii. p. 787), and consequently ten halls in the Labyrinth were appropriated to its Nomarchs. But this number apparently varied with the boundaries of Upper Aegypt, since Pliny (v. 9) enumerates eleven, and other writers mention fourteen Nomes. The physical aspect of the Thebais requires especial notice, since it differed, both geologically and in its Fauna and Flora, from that of Lower Aegypt.

For the most part it is a narrow valley, intersected by the river and bounded by a double line of hills, lofty and abrupt on the eastern or Arabian side, lower and interrupted by sandy plains and valleys on the Libyan or western. The desert on either side produces a stunted vegetation of shrubs and herbs, which emit a slight aromatic odour. The cultivable soil is a narrow strip on each side of the Nile, forming, with its bright verdure, a strong contrast to the brown and arid hue of the surrounding district. The entire breadth of this valley, including the river, does not exceed 11 miles, and sometimes is contracted by the rocky banks of the Nile even to two.

Upper Aegypt belongs to Nubia rather than to the Heptanomis or the Delta. Herodotus (iii. 10) was mistaken in his statement that rain never falls in the Thebais. It is, however, of rare occurrence. Showers fall annually during four or five days in each year, and about once in eight or ten years heavy rains fill the torrent-beds of the mountains, and convert the valleys on either side of the Nile into temporary pools. That this was so even in the age of Hecataeus and Herodotus is proved by the circumstance that the lions on the cornices of the Theban temples have tubes in their mouths to let the water off.

But the fertility of the Thebais depends on the overflow of the Nile. From Syene nearly to Latopolis, lat. 25° 17′ N., the cultivable soil is a narrow rim of alluvial deposit, bounded by steep walls of sandstone. On the Arabian shore were the quarries from which the great temples of Upper Aegypt were constructed. At Apollinopolis Magna (*Edfu*) the sandstone disappears from the W. bank of the river, and on the E. it extends but a little below that city. Four miles below Eilithya, the limestone region begins, and stretches down nearly to the apex of the Delta, descending on the Libyan side in terraces to the Mediterranean. At this point a greater breadth of land is cultivable, and in the Arabian hills deep gorges open towards the Red Sea, the most considerable of which are the valleys that run from Eilithya in a SE. direction to Berenice, and from Coptos, past the porphyry quarries, to Cosseir on the Red Sea. The tanks and stations for the caravans which the Theban Pharaohs or the Ptolemies constructed in these valleys are still occasionally found buried in the sand. At Latopolis the Nile-valley is nearly 5 miles wide, but it is again contracted by the rocks at *Gebelein*, where, owing to the precipitous character of the banks, the road quits the river and crosses the eastern desert to Hermonthis.

The next material expansion of the Nile-valley is at the plain of Thebes. At this point both chains of hills curve boldly away from the river, and leave an area of more than 5 miles in length and 3 in breadth. At the northern extremity of this plain the banks again contract, and at *Gourneh* are almost close to the Nile. Re-opening again, the borders of the stream as far as Hermopolis Magna, the northern boundary of the Thebaid, generally extend inland on the E. side about one mile and a half, on the W. about two miles. They do not indeed observe an unbroken line, but the alluvial soil, where the mouths of the collateral valleys permit, occasionally stretches much farther into the country. Canals and dykes in the Pharaonic period admitted and retained the Nile's deposit to an extent unknown either in Grecian, Roman, or modern eras.

Seen from the river the Thebaid in the flourishing periods of Aegypt, presented a wide and animated spectacle of cultivation and industry, wherever the banks admitted of room for cities or villages. Of the scenery of the Nile, its teeming population and multitudinous river-craft, mention has already been made in the article NILUS. Among many others, the following objects were beheld by those who travelled from Syene to Hermopolis. At first the general appearance of the shores is barren and dreary. *Koum-Ombos*, the ancient Ombi, would first arrest attention by the brilliant colours of its temples, and, at certain seasons of the year, by the festivals held in honour of the crocodile-headed deity Sevak. At times also, if we may credit the Roman satirist (Juvenal, *Sat.* xv.), the shore at Ombi was the scene of bloody frays with the crocodile exterminators from Tentyra. Sixteen miles below Ombi was the seat of the special worship of the Nile, which at this point, owing to the escarped form of its sandstone banks, admits of a narrow road only on either side, and seems to occupy the whole breadth of Aegypt. Here too, and on the eastern bank especially are the vast quarries of stone which supplied the Theban architects with their durable and beautiful materials. Various landing-places from the river gave access to those quarries: the names of successive sovereigns and princes of the xviiith dynasty, their wars and triumphs, are recorded on the rocks; and blocks of stone and monolithal shrines are still visible in their galleries. The temples of Apollinopolis Magna (*Edfu*), the hypogaea of Eilithya, Thebes occupying either bank, Coptos, long the seat of Aegyptian commerce with India, the temples of Athor and Isis at Tentyra, the mouth of the ancient branch of the Nile, the canal of *Jusuf* at Diospolis Parva, the necropolis of Abydos, near which runs the highroad to the greater Oasis, the linen-works and stone-masons' yards of Chemmis or Panopolis (*Ekhmin*), the sepulchral chambers at Lycopolis, and, finally, the superb portico of Hermopolis Magna, all evince, within a compass of about 380 miles, the wealth, enterprise, and teeming population of Upper Aegypt.

The vegetation of this region announces the approach to the tropics. The productions of the desert, stunted shrubs and trees, resemble those of the Arabian and Libyan wastes. But wherever the Nile fertilises, the trees and plants belong rather to Aethiopia than to the lower country. The sycamore nearly disappears: the Theban palm and the date-palm take its place. The lotus (*Nymphaea Lotus* and *Nymphaea caerulea*) is as abundant in the Thebais as the papyrus in the Delta. It is the symbol of the Upper Land: its blue and white cups enliven the pools and canals, and representations of them furnished a frequent and graceful ornament to architecture. Its bulb afforded a plentiful and nutritious diet to the poorer classes. The deserts of the Thebais, which in Christian times swarmed with monasteries and hermitages, contained the wolf, hyaena, and

jackal: but the larger carnivorous animals of Libya were rarely seen in Aegypt. (Herod. ii. 65.) In the Pharaonic times the hippopotamus was found in the Nile below the Cataracts: more recently it has seldom been found N. of them. The crocodile, being an object of worship in several of the Theban nomes, was doubtless more abundant than it is now. From both papyri and sculptures we know that the Theban landowners possessed horned cattle and sheep in abundance, although they kept the latter for their wool and milk principally; and the chariots of Thebes attest the breeding and training of horses. From extant drawings on the monuments we know also that horticulture was a favourite occupation in Upper Aegypt.

The population of the Thebais was probably of a purer Aegyptian stamp than that of the Delta; at least its admixtures were derived from Arabia or Meroe rather than from Phoenicia or Greece. Its revolutions, too, proceeded from the south, and it was comparatively unaffected by those of the Lower Country. Even as late as the age of Tiberius, A.D. 14—37, the land was prosperous, as is proved by the extension and restoration of so many of its public monuments; and it was not until the reign of Diocletian that its ruin was consummated by the inroad of the Blemmyes, and other barbarous tribes from Nubia and the Arabian desert. [W. B. D.]

THEBAE (Θῆβαι, orig. Θήβη, Dor. Θήβα: *Eth.* Θηβαῖος, fem. Θηβαῖς, Thebanus, fem. Thebais), the chief city in Boeotia, was situated in the southern plain of the country, which is divided from the northern by the ridge of Onchestus. Both these plains are surrounded by mountains, and contained for a long time two separate confederacies, of which Orchomenus in the north and Thebes in the south were the two leading cities.

I. HISTORY.

No city in Greece possessed such long continued celebrity as Thebes. Athens and Sparta, which were the centres of Grecian political life in the historical period, were poor in mythical renown; while Argos and Mycenae, whose mythical annals are full of glorious recollections, sank into comparative insignificance in historical times, and Mycenae indeed was blotted out of the map of Greece soon after the Persian wars. But in the mythical ages Thebes shone pre-eminent, while in later times she always maintained her place as the third city of Greece; and after the battle of Leuctra was for a short period the ruling city. The most celebrated Grecian legends cluster round Thebes as their centre; and her two sieges, and the fortunes of her royal houses, were the favourite subjects of the tragic muse. It was the native city of the great seer Teiresias and of the great musician Amphion. It was the reputed birthplace of the two deities Dionysus and Hercules, whence Thebes is said by Sophocles to be "the only city where mortal women are the mothers of gods (οὖ δὴ μόναι τίκτουσιν αἱ θνηταὶ θεούς, Fragm. *ap.* Dicaearch, § 17, ed. Müller; Mure, *Tour in Greece,* vol. i. p. 253.)

According to the generally received tradition, Thebes was founded by Cadmus, the leader of a Phoenician colony, who called the city CADMEIA (Καδμεία), a name which was afterwards confined to the citadel. In the Odyssey, Amphion and Zethus, the two sons of Antiope by Zeus, are represented as the first founders of Thebes and the first builders of its walls. (*Od.* xi. 262.) But the logo-graphers placed Amphion and Zethus lower down in the series, as we shall presently see. The legends connected with the foundation of the city by Cadmus are related elsewhere. [*Dict. of Biogr. and Myth.* art. CADMUS.] The five Sparti, who were the only survivors of the warriors sprung from the dragon's teeth, were the reputed ancestors of the noblest families in Thebes, which bore the name of Sparti down to the latest times. It is probable that the name of their families gave origin to the fable of the sowing of the dragon's teeth. It appears certain that the original inhabitants of Thebes were called Cadmeii (Καδμεῖοι, *Il.* iv. 388, 391, v. 807, x. 288, *Od.* xi. 276) or Cadmeiones (Καδμείωνες, *Il.* iv. 385, v. 804, xxiii. 680), and that the southern plain of Boeotia was originally called the Cadmeian land (Καδμηῖς γῆ, Thuc. i. 12). The origin of these Cadmeians has given rise to much dispute among modern scholars. K. O. Müller considers Cadmus a god of the Tyrrhenian Pelasgians, and maintains that the Cadmeians are the same as the Tyrrhenian Pelasgians ; Welcker endeavours to prove that the Cadmeians were a Cretan colony; while other writers adhere to the old traditions that the Cadmeians were Phoenicians who introduced the use of letters into Greece. (Müller, *Orchomenos*, p. 111, seq., 2nd ed.; Thirlwall, *Hist. of Greece*, vol. i. p. 111.) It is useless, however, to enter into the discussion of a subject respecting which we possess no materials for arriving at a satisfactory conclusion. It is certain that the Greeks were indebted to the Phoenicians for their alphabet; but whether the Cadmeians were a Phoenician colony or some other race must be left uncertain.

But we must return to the legendary history of Thebes. Cadmus had one son, Polydorus, and four daughters, Ino, Semele, Autonoë, and Agave, all of whom are celebrated in the mythical annals. The tales respecting them are given in the *Dict. of Biogr. and Myth.*, and it is only necessary to mention here that Ino became the wife of Athamas and the mother of Melicertes ; Semele was beloved by Zeus and became the mother of the god Dionysus; Autonoë was the mother of the celebrated hunter Actaeon, who was torn to pieces by the dogs of Artemis; and Agave was the mother of Pentheus, who, when Cadmus became old, succeeded him as king of Thebes, and whose miserable end in attempting to resist the worship of Dionysus forms the subject of the *Bacchae* of Euripides. After the death of Pentheus, Cadmus retired to the Illyrians, and his son Polydorus became king of Thebes. Polydorus is succeeded by his son Labdacus, who leaves at his death an infant son Laius. The throne is usurped by Lycus, whose brother Nycteus is the father of Antiope, who becomes by Zeus the mother of the twin sons, Amphion and Zethus. Nycteus having died, Antiope is exposed to the persecutions of her uncle Lycus and his cruel wife Dirce, till at length her two sons, Amphion and Zethus, revenge her wrongs and become kings of Thebes. They fortify the city ; and Amphion, who had been taught by Hermes, possessed such exquisite skill on the lyre, that the stones, obedient to his strains, moved of their own accord, and formed the wall ("movit Amphion lapides canendo," Hor. *Carm.* iii. 11). The remainder of the legend of Amphion and Zethus need not be related; and there can be no doubt, as Mr. Grote has remarked, that the whole story was originally unconnected with the

Cadmeian family, as it still stands in the Odyssey, and has been interwoven by the logographers into the series of the Cadmeian myths. In order to reconcile the Homeric account of the building of the city by Amphion and Zethus with the usually received legend of its foundation by Cadmus, it was represented by later writers that, while Cadmus founded the Cadmeia, Amphion and Zethus built the *lower* city (τὴν πόλιν τὴν κάτω), and gave to the united city the name of Thebae. (Paus. ix. 5. §§ 2, 6.)

After Amphion and Zethus, Laius became king of Thebes; and with him commences the memorable story of Oedipus and his family, which is too well known to need repetition here. When Oedipus was expelled from Thebes, after discovering that he had murdered his father Laius and married his mother Jocasta, his two sons Eteocles and Polynices quarrelled for their father's throne. Their disputes led to the two sieges of Thebes by the Argive Adrastus, two of the most memorable events in the legendary history of Greece. They formed the subject of the two epic poems, called the Thebais and the Epigoni, which were considered only inferior to the Iliad and the Odyssey. Polynices, having been driven out of Thebes by Eteocles, retires to Argos and obtains the aid of Adrastus, the king of the city, to reinstate him in his rights. Polynices and Adrastus are joined by five other heroes, making the confederacy known under the name of the "Seven against Thebes." The names of these seven chiefs were Adrastus, Amphiaraüs, Capaneus, Hippomedon, Parthenopaeus, Tydeus, and Polynices; but there are discrepancies in the lists, as we shall notice more fully below: and Aeschylus (*Sept. c. Theb.* 461) in particular omits Adrastus, and inserts Eteocles in his place. The Seven Chiefs advanced against Thebes, and each attacked one of the celebrated gates of the city. Polynices and Eteocles fell by each other's hands; and in the general engagement which followed the combat of the two brothers, the Argives were defeated, and all their chiefs slain, with the exception of Adrastus, who was saved by the swiftness of his horse Areion, the offspring of Poseidon. A few years afterwards the sons of the Seven Chiefs undertook an expedition against Thebes, to avenge their fathers' fate, hence called the war of the Epigoni or Descendants. This expedition was also led by Adrastus, and consisted of Aegialeus, son of Adrastus, Thersander, son of Polynices, Alcmaeon and Amphilochus, sons of Amphiaraüs, Diomedes, son of Tydeus, Sthenelens, son of Capaneus, and Promachus, son of Parthenopaeus. The Epigoni gained a victory over the Cadmeians at the river Glisas, and drove them within their walls. Upon the advice of the seer Teiresias, the Cadmeians abandoned the city, and retired to the Illyrians under the guidance of Laodamas, son of Adrastus. (Apollod. iii. 7. § 4; Herod. v. 57—61 ; Paus. ix. 5. § 13 ; Diod. iv. 65, 66.) The Epigoni thus became masters of Thebes, and placed Thersander, son of Polynices, on the Throne. (For a full account of the legends of Thebes, see Grote, *Hist. of Greece*, vol. i. c. xiv.) According to the mythical chronology, the war of the Seven against Thebes took place 20 years before the Trojan expedition and 30 years before the capture of Troy; and the war of the Epigoni was placed 14 years after the first expedition against Thebes, and consequently only 4 years before the departure of the Greeks against Troy. (Clinton, *F. H.* vol. i. p. 140.)

There is another important event in the mythical times of Thebes, which was not interwoven with the series of the legends already related. This is the birth of Hercules at Thebes, and the important services which he rendered to his native city by his war against Orchomenus. It was stated that the Thebans were compelled to pay tribute to Erginus, king of Orchomenus; but that they were delivered from the tribute by Hercules, who marched against Orchomenus, and greatly reduced its power (Paus. ix. 37. § 2; Strab. ix. p. 414; Diod. iv. 18). This legend has probably arisen from the historical fact, that Orchomenus was at one time the most powerful city in Boeotia, and held even Thebes in subjection.

Thebes is frequently mentioned in Homer, who speaks of its celebrated seven gates (*Il.* iv. 406, *Od.* xi. 263); but its name does not occur in the catalogue of the Greek cities which fought against Troy, as it was probably supposed not to have recovered from its recent devastation by the Epigoni. Later writers, however, related that Thersander, the son of Polynices, accompanied Agamemnon to Troy, and was slain in Mysia by Telephus, before the commencement of the siege; and that upon his death the Thebans chose Peneleos as their leader, in consequence of the tender age of Tisamenus, the son of Thersander. (Paus. ix. 5. §§ 14, 15.) In the Iliad (ii. 494) Peneleos is mentioned as one of the leaders of the Boeotians, but is not otherwise connected with Thebes.

According to the chronology of Thucydides, the Cadmeians continued in possession of Thebes till 60 years after the Trojan War, when they were driven out of their city and country by the Boeotians, an Aeolian tribe, who migrated from Thessaly. (Thuc. i. 12; Strab. ix. p. 401.) This seems to have been the genuine tradition; but as Homer gives the name of Boeotians to the inhabitants of the country called Boeotia in later times, Thucydides endeavours to reconcile the authority of the poet with the other tradition, by the supposition that a portion of the Aeolic Boeotians had settled in Boeotia previously, and that these were the Boeotians who sailed against Troy. According to other accounts, Thebes was taken by the Thracians and Pelasgians during the Trojan War, and its inhabitants driven into exile in Thessaly, whence they returned at a later period. (Strab. ix. p. 401; Diod. xix. 53.)

Pausanias gives us a list of the kings of Thebes, the successors of Tisamenus, till the kingly dignity was abolished and a republic established in its place (ix. 5. § 16). But, with the exception of one event, we know absolutely nothing of Theban history, till the dispute between Thebes and Plataea in the latter end of the sixth century B. C.

The event to which we allude is the legislation of Philolaus, the Corinthian, who was enamoured of Diocles, also a Corinthian, and the victor in the Olympian games, B. C. 728. Both Philolaus and Diocles left their native city and settled at Thebes, where the former drew up a code of laws for the Thebans, of which one or two particulars are mentioned by Aristotle. (*Pol.* ii. 9. §§ 6, 7.) At the time when Thebes first appears in history, we find it under an oligarchical form of government, and the head of a political confederation of some twelve or fourteen Boeotian cities. The greater cities of Boeotia were members of this confederation, and the smaller towns were attached to one or other of these cities in a state of dependence. [BOEOTIA, p. 415.]

The affairs of the confederation were managed by certain magistrates or generals, called Boeotarchs, of whom there were eleven at the time of the battle of Delium (B. C. 424), two being elected by Thebes, and one apparently by each of the other members of the confederation (Thuc. iv. 91). But the real authority was vested in the hands of the Thebans, who used the power of the confederation with an almost exclusive view to Theban interests, and kept the other states in virtual subjection.

The first well-known event in Grecian history is the dispute, already mentioned, between Thebes and Plataea. The Plataeans, discontented with the supremacy of Thebes, withdrew from the Boeotian confederation, and surrendered their city to the Athenians. This led to a war between the Thebans and Athenians, in which the Thebans were defeated and compelled to cede to the Plataeans the territory S. of the Asopus, which was made the boundary between the two states. (Herod. vi. 108; Thuc. iii. 68.) The interference of Athens upon this occasion was bitterly resented by Thebes, and was the commencement of the long enmity between the two states, which exercised an important influence upon the course of Grecian history. This event is usually placed in B.C. 519, upon the authority of Thucydides (*l. c.*); but Mr. Grote brings forward strong reasons for believing that it must have taken place after the expulsion of Hippias from Athens in B. C. 510. (*Hist. of Greece*, vol. iv. p. 222.) The hatred which the Thebans felt against the Athenians was probably one of the reasons which induced them to desert the cause of Grecian liberty in the great struggle against the Persian power. But in the Peloponnesian War (B. C. 427) the Theban orator pleaded that their alliance with Persia was not the fault of the nation, but of a few individuals who then exercised despotic power. (Thuc. iii. 62.) At the battle of Plataea, however, the Thebans showed no such reluctance, but fought resolutely against the Athenians, who were posted opposite to them. (Herod. ix. 67.) Eleven days after the battle the victorious Greeks appeared before Thebes, and compelled the inhabitants to surrender their *medising* leaders, who were immediately put to death, without any trial or other investigation. (Herod. ix. 87, 88.) Thebes had lost so much credit by the part she had taken in the Persian invasion, that she was unable to assert her former supremacy over the other Boeotian towns, which were ready to enter into alliance with Athens, and would doubtless have established their complete independence, had not Sparta supported the Thebans in maintaining their ascendency in the Boeotian confederation, as the only means of securing the Boeotian cities as the allies of Sparta against Athens. With this view the Spartans assisted the Thebans in strengthening the fortifications of their city, and compelled the Boeotian cities by force of arms to acknowledge the supremacy of Thebes. (Diod. xi. 81; Justin, iii. 6.) In B.C. 457 the Athenians sent an army into Boeotia to oppose the Lacedaemonian forces in that country, but they were defeated by the latter near Tanagra. Sixty-two days after this battle (B. C. 456), when the Lacedaemonians had returned home, the Athenians, under the command of Myronides, invaded Boeotia a second time. This time they met with the most signal success. At the battle of Oenophyta they defeated the combined forces of the Thebans and Boeotians, and obtained in consequence possession of Thebes and of the other Boeotian towns. A democratical form of government was established in the different cities, and the oligarchical leaders were driven into exile. (Thuc. i. 108; Diod. xi. 81.) This state of things lasted barely ten years; the democracy established at Thebes was ill-conducted (Arist. *Pol.* v. 2. § 6); and in B.C. 447 the various Boeotian exiles, combining their forces, made themselves masters of Orchomenus, Chaeroneia, and some other places. The Athenians sent an army into Boeotia under the command of Tolmides; but this general was slain in battle, together with many of his men, while a still larger number were taken prisoners. To recover these prisoners, the Athenians agreed to relinquish their power over Thebes and the other Boeotian cities. The democratical governments were overthrown; the exiles were restored; and Thebes again became the bitter enemy of Athens. (Thuc. i. 113, iii. 62. Diod. xii. 6.) The Thebans were indeed more anti-Athenian than were the Spartans themselves, and were the first to commence the Peloponnesian War by their attempt to surprise Plataea in the night, B.C. 431. The history of this attempt, and of the subsequent siege and capture of the city, belongs to the history of Plataea. [PLATAEA.] Throughout the Peloponnesian War the Thebans continued the active and bitter enemies of the Athenians; and upon its close after the battle of Aegospotami they joined the Corinthians in urging the Lacedaemonians to destroy Athens, and sell its population into slavery. (Xen. *Hell.* ii. 2. § 19.) But soon after this event the feelings of the Thebans towards Athens became materially changed in consequence of their jealousy of Sparta, who had refused the allies all participation in the spoils of the war, and who now openly aspired to the supremacy of Greece. (Plut. *Lys.* 27; Justin, vi. 10.) They consequently viewed with hostility the Thirty Tyrants at Athens as the supporters of the Spartan power, and gave a friendly welcome to the Athenian exiles. It was from Thebes that Thrasybulus and the other exiles started upon their enterprise of seizing the Peiraeeus; and they were supported upon this occasion by Ismenias and other Theban citizens. (Xen. *Hell.* ii. 4. § 2.) So important was the assistance rendered by the Thebans on this occasion that Thrasybulus, after his success, showed his gratitude by dedicating in the temple of Hercules colossal statues of this god and Athena. (Paus. ix. 11. § 6.)

The hostile feelings of Thebes towards Sparta continued to increase, and soon produced the most important results. When Agesilaus was crossing over into Asia in B.C. 397, in order to carry on war against the Persians, the Thebans refused to take any part in the expedition, and they rudely interrupted Agesilaus when he was in the act of offering sacrifices at Aulis, in imitation of Agamemnon;—an insult which the Spartan king never forgave. (Xen. *Hell.* iii. 5. § 5; Plut. *Ages.* 6; Paus. iii. 9. §§ 3—5.) During the absence of Agesilaus in Asia, Tithraustes, the satrap of Asia Minor, sent an envoy to Greece to distribute large sums of money among the leading men in the Grecian cities, in order to persuade them to make war against Sparta. But before a coalition could be formed for this purpose, a separate war broke out between Thebes and Sparta, called by Diodorus (xiv. 81) the Boeotian war. A quarrel having arisen between the Opuntian Locrians and the Phocians respecting a strip of border land, the Thebans espoused the cause of the former and

invaded Phocis. Thereupon the Phocians invoked the aid of the Lacedaemonians, who were delighted to have an opportunity of avenging the affronts they had received from the Thebans. (Xen. *Hell.* iii. 5. §§ 3—5; Paus. iii. 9. § 9.) The Lacedaemonians made active preparations to invade Boeotia. Lysander, who had been foremost in promoting the war, was to lay siege to Haliartus, under the walls of which town Pausanias was to join him on a given day with the united Lacedaemonian and Peloponnesian forces. Thus menaced, the Thebans applied for assistance to their ancient enemies, the Athenians, who readily responded to their appeal, though their city was still undefended by walls, and they had no ships to resist the maritime power of Sparta. (Xen. *Hell.* iii. 5. § 16; Dem. *de Cor.* p. 258.) Orchomenus, however, seized the opportunity to revolt from Thebes, and joined Lysander in his attack upon Haliartus. (Xen. *Hell.* iii. 5. § 17; Plut. *Lys.* 28.) The death of Lysander under the walls of Haliartus, which was followed by the retreat of Pausanias from Boeotia, emboldened the enemies of Sparta; and not only Athens, but Corinth, Argos, and some of the other Grecian states joined Thebes in a league against Sparta. In the following year (B.C. 394) the war was transferred to the territory of Corinth; and so powerful were the confederates that the Lacedaemonians recalled Agesilaus from Asia. In the month of August Agesilaus reached Boeotia on his homeward march, and found the confederate army drawn up in the plain of Coroneia to oppose him. The right wing and centre of his army were victorious, but the Thebans completely defeated the Orchomenians, who formed the left wing. The victorious Thebans now faced about, in order to regain the rest of their army, which had retreated to Mount Helicon. Agesilaus advanced to meet them; and the conflict which ensued was one of the most terrible that had yet taken place in Grecian warfare. The Thebans at length succeeded in forcing their way through, but not without great loss. This was the first time that the Thebans had fought a pitched battle with the Spartans; and the valour which they showed on this occasion was a prelude to the victories which were soon to overthrow the Spartan supremacy in Greece. (Xen. *Hell.* iv. 3. §§ 15—21.)

We have dwelt upon these events somewhat at length in order to explain the rise of the Theban power; but the subsequent history must be related more briefly. After the battle of Coroneia the course of events appeared at first to deprive Thebes of the ascendency she had lately acquired. The peace of Antalcidas (B.C. 387), which was concluded under the influence of Sparta, guaranteed the independence of all the Grecian cities; and though the Thebans at first claimed to take the oath, not in their own behalf alone, but for the Boeotian confederacy in general, they were compelled by their enemy Agesilaus to swear to the treaty for their own city alone, since otherwise they would have had to contend single-handed with the whole power of Sparta and her allies. (Xen. *Hell.* v. 1. §§ 32, 33.) By this oath the Thebans virtually renounced their supremacy over the Boeotian cities; and Agesilaus hastened to exert all the Spartan power for the purpose of weakening Thebes. Not only was the independence of the Boeotian cities proclaimed, and a legal oligarchy organised in each city hostile to Thebes and favourable to Sparta, but Lacedaemonian garrisons were stationed in Orchomenus and Thespiae for the purpose of overawing Boeotia, and the city of Plataea was rebuilt to serve as an outpost of the Spartan power. (Paus. ix. 1. § 4). A more direct blow was aimed at the independence of Thebes in B. C. 382 by the seizure of the Cadmeia, the citadel of the city, by the Spartan commander, Phoebidas, assisted by Leontiades and a party in Thebes favourable to Sparta. Though Phoebidas appears to have acted under secret orders from the Ephors (Diod. xv. 20; Plut. *Agesil.* 24), such was the indignation excited throughout Greece by this treacherous act in time of peace, that the Ephors found it necessary to disavow Phoebidas and to remove him from his command; but they took care to reap the fruits of his crime by retaining their garrison in the Cadmeia. (Xen. *Hell.* v. 2. § 25.) Many of the leading citizens at Thebes took refuge at Athens, and were received with the same kindness which the Athenian exiles experienced at Thebes after the close of the Peloponnesian War. Thebes remained in the hands of the Spartan party for three years; but in B. C. 379 the Spartan garrison was expelled from the Cadmeia, and the party of Leontiades overthrown by Pelopidas and the other exiles. The history of these events is too well known to be repeated here. In the following year (B. C. 378) Thebes formed an alliance with Athens, and with the assistance of this state resisted with success the attempts of the Lacedaemonians to reduce them to subjection; but the continued increase of the power of the Thebans, and their destruction of the city of Plataea [PLATAEA] provoked the jealousy of the Athenians, and finally induced them to conclude a treaty of peace with Sparta, B. C. 371. This treaty, usually called the peace of Callias from the name of the leading Athenian negotiator, included all the parties in the late war with the exception of the Thebans, who were thus left to contend single-handed with the might of Sparta. It was universally believed that Thebes was doomed to destruction; but only twenty days after the signing of the treaty all Greece was astounded at the news that a Lacedaemonian army had been utterly defeated, and their king Cleombrotus slain, by the Thebans, under the command of Epaminondas, upon the fatal field of Leuctra (B. C. 371). This battle not only destroyed the prestige of Sparta and gave Thebes the ascendency of Greece, but it stript Sparta of her Peloponnesian allies, over whom she had exercised dominion for centuries, and led to the establishment of two new political powers in the Peloponnesus, which threatened her own independence. These were the Arcadian confederation and the restoration of the state of Messenia, both the work of Epaminondas, who conducted four expeditions into Peloponnesus, and directed the councils of Thebes for the next 10 years. It was to the abilities and genius of this extraordinary man that Thebes owed her position at the head of the Grecian states; and upon his death, at the battle of Mantineia (B. C. 362), she lost the pre-eminence she had enjoyed since the battle of Leuctra. During their supremacy in Greece, the Thebans were of course undisputed masters of Boeotia, and they availed themselves of their power to wreak their vengeance upon Orchomenus and Thespiae, the two towns which had been the most inimical to their authority, the one in the north and the other in the south of Boeotia. The Orchomenians had in B. C. 395 openly joined the Spartans and fought on their side; and the Thespians had withdrawn from the

Theban army just before the battle of Leuctra, when Epaminondas gave permission to any Boeotians to retire who were averse to the Theban cause. (Paus. ix. 13. § 8.) The Thespians were expelled from their city and Boeotia soon after the battle of Leuctra [THESPIAE]; and Orchomenus in B. C. 368 was burnt to the ground by the Thebans; the male inhabitants were put to the sword, and all the women and children sold into slavery. [ORCHOMENUS.]

The jealousy which Athens had felt towards Thebes before the peace of Callias had been greatly increased by her subsequent victories; and the two states appear henceforward in their old condition of hostility till they were persuaded by Demosthenes to unite their arms for the purpose of resisting Philip of Macedon. After the battle of Mantineia their first open war was for the possession of Euboea. After the battle of Leuctra this island had passed under the supremacy of Thebes; but, in B.C. 358, discontent having arisen against Thebes in several of the cities of Euboea, the Thebans sent a powerful force into the island. The discontented cities applied for aid to Athens, which was readily granted, and the Thebans were expelled from Euboea. (Diod. xvi. 7; Dem. *de Cherson.* p. 108, *de Cor.* p. 259, *c. Ctesiph.* p. 397.) Shortly afterwards the Thebans commenced the war against the Phocians, usually known as the Sacred War, and in which almost all the leading states of Greece were eventually involved. Both Athens and Sparta supported the Phocians, as a counterpoise to Thebes, though they did not render them much effectual assistance. This war terminated, as is well known, by the intervention of Philip, who destroyed the Phocian towns, and restored to Boeotia Orchomenus and the other towns which the Phocians had taken away from them, B.C. 346. The Thebans were still the allies of Philip, when the latter seized Elateia in Phocis towards the close of B.C. 339, as preparatory to a march through Boeotia against Athens. The old feeling of ill-will between Thebes and Athens still continued: Philip calculated upon the good wishes, if not the active co-operation, of the Thebans against their old enemies; and probably never dreamt of a confederation between the two states as within the range of probability. This union, however, was brought about by the eloquence of Demosthenes, who was sent as ambassador to Thebes, and who persuaded the Thebans to form an alliance with the Athenians for the purpose of resisting the ambitious schemes of Philip. In the following year (B. C. 338) Philip defeated the combined forces of Thebes and Athens at the battle of Chaeroneia, which crushed the liberties of Greece, and made it in reality a province of the Macedonian monarchy. On this fatal field the Thebans maintained the reputation they had won in their battles with the Spartans; and their Sacred Band was cut to pieces in their ranks. The battle was followed by the surrender of Thebes, which Philip treated with great severity. Many of the leading citizens were either banished or put to death; a Macedonian garrison was stationed in the Cadmeia; and the government of the city was placed in the hands of 300 citizens, the partisans of Philip. The Thebans were also deprived of their sovereignty over the Boeotian towns, and Orchomenus and Plataea were restored, and again filled with a population hostile to Thebes. (Diodor. xvi. 87; Justin, ix. 4; Paus. iv. 27. § 10, ix. 1. § 8.) In the year after Philip's death (B.C. 335) the Theban exiles got possession of the city, besieged the Macedonian garrison in the Cadmeia, and invited the other Grecian states to declare their independence. But the rapidity of Alexander's movements disconcerted all their plans. He appeared at Onchestus in Boeotia, before any intelligence had arrived of his quitting the north. ·He was willing to allow the Thebans an opportunity for repentance; but as his proposals of peace were rejected, he directed a general assault upon the city. The Theban troops outside the gates were driven back, and the Macedonians entered the town along with them. A dreadful carnage ensued; 6000 Thebans are said to have been slain, and 30,000 to have been taken prisoners. The doom of the conquered city was referred to the Grecian allies in his army, Orchomenians, Plataeans, Phocians, and other inveterate enemies of Thebes. Their decision must have been known beforehand. They decreed that Thebes should be razed to the ground, with the exception of the Cadmeia, which was to be held by a Macedonian garrison; that the territory of the city should be divided among the allies; and that all the inhabitants, men, women, and children should be sold as slaves. This sentence was carried into execution by Alexander, who levelled the city to the ground, with the exception of the house of Pindar (Arrian, *Anab.* i. 8, 9; Diodor. xvii. 12—14; Justin, xi. 4.) Thebes was thus blotted out of the map of Greece, and remained without inhabitants for the next 20 years. In B.C. 315, Cassander undertook the restoration of the city. He united the Theban exiles and their descendants from all parts of Greece, and was zealously assisted by the Athenians and other Grecian states in the work of restoration. The new city occupied the same area as the one destroyed by Alexander; and the Cadmeia was held by a garrison of Cassander. (Diodor. xix. 52—54, 78; Paus. ix. 7. § 4.) Thebes was twice taken by Demetrius, first in B. C. 293, and a second time in 290, but on each occasion he used his victory with moderation. (Plut. *Demetr.* 39, 40; Diod. xxi. p. 491. ed. Wess.)

Dicaearchus, who visited Thebes not long after its restoration by Cassander, has given a very interesting account of the city. "Thebes," he says (§ 12, seq. ed. Müller), "is situated in the centre of Boeotia, and is about 70 stadia in circumference; its site is level, its shape circular, and its appearance gloomy. The city is ancient, but it has been lately rebuilt, having been three times destroyed, as history relates*, on account of the insolence and haughtiness of its inhabitants. It is well adapted for rearing horses since it is plentifully provided with water, and abounds in green pastures and hills: it contains also better gardens than any other city in Greece. Two rivers flow through the town, and irrigate all the subjacent plain. There is also a subterraneous stream issuing from the Cadmeia, through pipes, said to be the work of Cadmus. Thebes is a most agreeable residence in the summer, in consequence of the abundance and coolness of the water, its large gardens, its agreeable breezes, its verdant appearance, and the quantity of summer and autumnal fruits. In the winter, however, it is a most disagreeable residence, from being destitute of fuel, and constantly exposed to floods and winds. It is often covered with snow and very muddy." Although Dicaearchus

* Dicaearchus probably means the capture of the city by the Epigoni; secondly by the Pelasgi, during the Trojan war; and lastly by Alexander.

in this passage gives to Thebes a circumference of 70 stadia, he assigns in his verses (*Stat. Graec.* 93) a much smaller extent to it, namely 43 stadia. The latter number is the more probable, and, being in metre was less likely to be altered; but if the number in prose is correct, it probably includes the suburbs and gardens outside the city walls. Dicaearchus also gives an account of the character of the inhabitants, which is too long to be extracted. He represents them as noble-minded and sanguine, but insolent and proud, and always ready to settle their disputes by fighting rather than by the ordinary course of justice.

Thebes had its full share in the later calamities of Greece. After the fall of Corinth, B.C. 146, Mummius is said to have destroyed Thebes (Liv. *Epit.* 52), by which we are probably to understand the walls of the city. In consequence of its having sided with Mithridates in the war against the Romans, Sulla deprived it of half its territory, which he dedicated to the gods, in order to make compensation for his having plundered the temples at Olympia, Epidaurus, and Delphi. Although the Romans afterwards restored the land to the Thebans, they never recovered from this blow (Paus. ix. 7. §§ 5, 6); and so low was it reduced in the time of Augustus and Tiberius that Strabo says that it was little more than a village (ix. p. 403). In the time of the Antonines, Pausanias found the Cadmeia alone inhabited, and the lower part of the town destroyed, with the exception of the temples (ix. 7. § 6). In the decline of the Roman Empire, Thebes became the seat of a considerable population, probably in consequence of its inland situation, which afforded its inhabitants greater security than the maritime towns from hostile attacks. In the eleventh and twelfth centuries Thebes was one of the most flourishing cities in Greece, and was celebrated for its manufactures of silk. In A.D. 1040 the Thebans took the field to oppose the Bulgarian invaders of Greece, but were defeated with great loss. (Cedren. p. 747, ed. Paris., p. 529, ed. Bonn.) In A.D. 1146 the city was plundered by the Normans of Sicily, who carried off a large amount of plunder (Nicetas, p. 50, ed. Paris., p. 98, ed. Bonn.) Benjamin of Tudela, who visited Thebes about 20 years later, speaks of it as still a large city, possessing 2000 Jewish inhabitants, who were very skilful manufacturers of silk and purple cloth (i. 47, ed. Asher; Finlay, *Byzantine Empire*, vol. i. p. 493, vol. ii. p. 199). The silks of Thebes continued to be esteemed even at a later period, and were worn by the emperors of Constantinople. (Nicetas, p. 297, ed. Paris., p. 609, ed. Bonn.) They were, however, gradually supplanted by those of Sicily and Italy; and the loss of the silk trade was followed by the rapid decline of Thebes. Under the Turks the city was again reduced, as in the time of Pausanias, to the site of the Cadmeia.

II. TOPOGRAPHY.

Thebes stood on one of the hills of Mount Teumessus, which divides southern Boeotia into two distinct parts, the northern being the plain of Thebes and the southern the valley of the Asopus. The Greeks, in founding a city, took care to select a spot where there was an abundant supply of water, and a hill naturally defensible, which might be easily converted into an acropolis. They generally preferred a position which would command the adjacent plain, and which was neither immediately upon the coast nor yet at a great distance from it. But as Boeotia lies between two seas, the founders of Thebes chose a spot in the centre of the country, where water was very plentiful, and where the nature of the ground was admirably adapted for defence. The hill, upon which the town stands, rises about 150 feet above the plain, and lies about 2 miles northward of the highest part of the ridge. It is bounded on the east and west by two small rivers, distant from each other about 6 or 7 stadia, and which run in such deep ravines as to form a natural defence on either side of the city. These rivers, which rise a little south of the city, and flow northward into the plain of Thebes, are the celebrated streams of Ismenus and Dirce. Between them flows a smaller stream, which divided the city into two parts, the western division containing the Cadmeia *, and the southern the hill Ismenius and the Ampheion. This middle torrent is called Cnopus by Leake, but more correctly Strophia (Callim. Hymn. in Del. 76) by Forchhammer. The Cnopus is a torrent flowing from the town Cnopia, and contributing to form the Ismenus, whence it is correctly described by the Scholiast on Nicander as the same as the Ismenus. (Strab. ix. p. 404; Nicand. Theriac. 889, with Schol.) The three streams of Ismenus, Dirce, and Strophia unite in the plain below the city, to which Callimachus (l. c.) appears to allude:—

Δίρκη τε Στροφίη τε μελαμψηφῖδος ἔχουσαι
Ἰσμηνοῦ χέρα πατρός.

The middle torrent is rarely mentioned by the ancient writers; and the Ismenus and Dirce are the streams alluded to when Thebes is called διπόταμος πόλις. (Eurip. Suppl. 622; comp. Phoen. 825. Bacch. 5, Herc. Fur. 572.) Both the Ismenus and Dirce, though so celebrated in antiquity, are nothing but torrents, which are only full of water in the winter after heavy rains. The Ismenus is the eastern stream, now called Ai Iánni, which rises from a clear and copious fountain, where the small church of St. John stands, from which the river derives its name. This fountain was called in antiquity Melia, who was represented as the mother of Ismenus and Tenerus, the hero of the plain which the Ismenus inundates. It was sacred to Ares, who was said to have stationed a dragon to guard it. (Callimach. Hymn. in Del. 80; Spanheim, ad loc.; Pind. Pyth. xi. 6; Paus. ix. 10. § 5; Forchhammer, Hellenica, p. 113.) The Dirce is the western stream, now called Platziótissa, which rises from several fountains, and not from a single one, like the Ismenus. A considerable quantity of the water of the Platziótissa is now diverted to supply the fountains of the town, and it is represented as the purest of the Theban streams; and it appears to have been so regarded in antiquity likewise, judging from the epithets bestowed upon it by the poets. (Ἀγνὸν ὕδωρ, Pind. Isthm. vi. 109, καλλίρροος, Isthm. viii. 43; ὕδωρ Διρκαῖον εὐτραφέστατον πωμάτων, Aesch. Sept. c. Theb. 307; καλλιπόταμος, Eurip. Phoen. 647; Δίρκης νᾶμα λευκόν, Herc. Fur. 578.) Though the position of Thebes and of its celebrated streams is certain, almost every point connected with its topography is more or less doubtful. In the other cities of Greece, which have been inhabited continuously, most of the ancient buildings

* The western division contains two eminences, and the question as to which of them was the Cadmeia will be discussed below.

have disappeared; but nowhere has this taken place more completely than at Thebes. Not a single trace of an ancient building remains; and with the exception of a few scattered remains of architecture and sculpture, and some fragments of the ancient walls, there is nothing but the site to indicate where the ancient city stood. In the absence of all ancient monuments, there must necessarily be great uncertainty; and the three writers who have investigated the subject upon the spot, differ so widely, that Leake places the ancient city to the south of the Cadmeia, and Ulrichs to the north of it, while Forchhammer supposes both the western heights between the Strophia and the Dirce to have been in a certain sense the Cadmeia, and the lower city to have stood eastward, between the Strophia and the Ismenus. In the great difficulty of arriving at any independent judgment upon the subject without a personal inspection of the site, we have adopted the hypothesis of Forchhammer, which seems consistent with the statements of the ancient writers.

The most interesting point in Theban topography is the position of the seven celebrated Theban gates. They are alluded to by Homer (Θήβης ἕδος ἑπταπύλοιο, Od. xi. 263) and Hesiod (ἑπτάπυλος Θήβη, Op. 161); and their names are given by seven different authors, whose statements will be more easily compared by consulting the following table. The numeral represents the order in which the gates are mentioned by each writer. The first line gives the names of the gates, the second the names of the Argive chiefs, the third the emblems upon their shields, and the fourth the names of the Theban chiefs.

Nonnus designates five of the gates by the names of the gods and the planets, and to the other two, to which he gives the names of Electrae and Oncaea, he also adds their position. Hyginus calls the gates by the names of the daughters of Amphion; and that of Ogygia alone agrees with those in the other writers. But, dismissing the statements of Nonnus and Hyginus, whose authority is of no value upon such a question, we find that the remaining five writers agree as to the names of all the seven gates, with two or three exceptions, which will be pointed out presently. The position of three of the gates is quite clear from the description of Pausanias alone. These are the ELECTRAE, PROETIDES, and NEITAE. Pausanias says that Electrae is the gate by which a traveller from Plataea enters Thebes (ix. 8. § 6); that there is a hill, on the right hand of the gate, sacred to Apollo, called the Ismenian, since the river Ismenus runs in this direction (ix. 10. § 2); and that on the left hand of the gate are the ruins of a house, where it was said that Amphitryon lived, which is followed by an account of other ancient monuments on the Cadmeia (ix. 11. § 1). Hence it is evident that the gate Electrae was in the south of the city, between the hills Ismenius and Cadmeia. The gate Proetides was on the north-eastern side of the city, since it led to Chalcis (ix. 18. § 1). The gate Neitae was on the north-western side of the city, since it led to Onchestus and Delphi; and the river which Pausanias crossed, could have been no other than the Dirce (ix. 25. §§ 1, 3, ix. 26. § 5). The names of these three gates are the same in all the five writers: the manuscripts of Apollodorus have the corrupt word Ὀχνηΐδας, which has been altered by the editors into Ὀγχαΐδας, instead of Νήϊται, which was the reading suggested by Porson (ad. Eurip. Phoen. 1150), and adopted by Valckenaer. (See Unger, Thebana Paradoxa, vol. i. p. 313.)

TABLE OF THE SEVEN GATES OF THEBES ACCORDING TO SEVEN WRITERS.

AESCHYLUS. Sept. c. Th. 360.	EURIPIDES. Phoeniss. 1130.	PAUSANIAS. IX. 8. § 4.	APOLLODORUS. III. 6. § 6.	STATIUS. Theb. VIII. 353, sqq.	NONNUS. Dionys. v. 69, sqq.	HYGINUS. 69. cf. 11.
1. Προιτίδες. Τυδεύς. πανσέληνος. Μελάνιππος.	2. Προιτίδες. 'Αμφιάραος. ἄσημα ὅπλα.	2. Προιτίδες. Τυδεύς. Μελάνιππος.	3. Προιτίδες. 'Αμφιάραος. cf. III. 6, 8, 6.	4. Proetides. Hypseus.	6. Ζηνός (?). cf. Schol. Lycoph. 1204.	Astycratia.
2. 'Ηλέκτραι. Καπανεύς. ἀνδρα πυρφόρον. Πολυφόντης.	6. 'Ηλέκτραι. Καπανεύς. γίγας γηγενής.	1. 'Ηλέκτραι. Καπανεύς.	6. 'Ηλέκτραι. Παρθενοπαῖος.	5. Electrae. Dryas.	4. 'Ηλέκτραι.	Cleodoxa.
3. Νήϊται. Ἐτέοκλος. ἀνὴρ ὑπλίτης κλίμακ. Μεγαρεύς.	1. Νήϊται. Παρθενοπαῖος. 'Αταλάντη.	3. Νήϊται. Πολυνείκης. ('Ετεοκλῆς.)	4. Νήϊται. 'Ιππομέδων.	2. Neitae. Eteocles.	2. 'Ερμάωνος (?).	Astynome.
4. Ὄγκας. 'Ιππομέδων. Τυφῶν πυρπνόον. Ὑπέρβιος.	5. Κρηναῖαι. Πολυνείκης. Ποτνιάδες πῶλοι. 'Ετεοκλῆς.	4. Κρηναῖαι. ('Ιππομέδων.)	7. Κρηνίδες. Τυδεύς (?).	7. Culmina Dircaea. Menoeceus. Haemon. X. 651.	1. 'Ογκαίη (ἐς ἑσπέριον κλίμα πήξας).	Chias.
5. Βορραῖαι. Παρθενοπαῖος. Σφίγξ. 'Ακτωρ.	3. Ὠγύγιαι. 'Ιππομέδων. ταυρότης.	7. Ὠγύγιαι. (Παρθενοπαῖος.)	2. Ὠγύγιαι. Καπανεύς.	1. Ogygiae. Creon. Echion. X. 494.	7. Κρόνου.	Ogygia.
6. 'Ομολωίδες. 'Αμφιάραος. σῆμα δ' οὐκ ἐπῆν. Λασθένης.	4. 'Ομολωίδες. Τυδεύς. λέοντος δέρος. Τι τὸν Προμηθεύς.	6. 'Ομολωίδες. 'Αμφιάραος (?). cf. Paus. ix. 8. § 3.	1. 'Ομολωίδες. 'Αδραστος.	3. Homoloides. Haemon.	3. 'Αφροδίτης.	Chloris.
7. Ἑβδομαι. Πολυνείκης. Δίκη. 'Ετεοκλῆς.	7. Ἑβδομαι. 'Αδραστος. ἑκατὸν ἐχίδναι ὕδρα.	5. Ὕψισται. ('Αδραστος.) (Διὸς ὑψίστου ἱερόν.)	5. Ὕψισται. Πολυνείκης.	6. Hypsistae. Eurymedon.	5. 'Αρεως.	Thera. (Νέαιρα.)

Of the other four gates, the Homoloides is also the same in all the five writers. Of the remaining three Aeschylus does not mention their proper names, but specifies two by their locality, one as near the temple of Athena Onca, and the other as the Northern gate (Βορραῖαι πύλαι), and describes the last simply as the Seventh gate. The names of these three gates are nearly the same in the other four writers, the one near the temple of Athena Onca being called Crenaeae, and in Statius Culmina Dircaea, the Northern gate Ogygiae, and the Seventh gate Hypsistae,—Euripides, however, also giving the name of Seventh to the last-mentioned gate.

Having described the position of the Electrae, Proetides, and Neitae, it remains to speak of the position of the other four, which we shall take in the order of Aeschylus. The fourth gate was probably situated on the western side of the city, and was called Crenaeae, because it was near one of the fountains of Dirce, now called Παραπόρτι, situated upon the right bank of the river. Near that fountain was a hill, called by the Greeks ὄγκος, whence Athena derived the name of Onca. Accordingly Statius, in calling the fourth gate Culmina Dircaea, connects both the fountain and the hill. Nonnus, who calls this gate Oncaea, describes it at the same time as situated towards the west. It is usually stated, on the authority of Hesychius, that the Oncaean gate is the same as the Ogygian; but this identification throws everything into confusion, while the change of three letters, proposed by Forch-

hammer, brings the statement of Hesychius into accordance with the other writers. (Ὄγκας 'Αθηνᾶς τὰς 'Ογκαίας [instead of 'Ωγυγίας] πύλας λέγει, i. e. Aesch. Sept. c. Theb. 486.)

The fifth gate was called Ogygian from Ogygus, the most ancient king of Thebes, in whose time the deluge is said to have taken place. Now there is no part of Thebes more exposed to inundation than the north of the city between the gates Neitae and Proetides, where the torrent Strophia descends into the plain. Here we may probably place the Ogygian gate, which Aeschylus calls the Northern, from its position.

The exact position of the sixth gate, called Homoloides, and of the seventh, designated by its number in Aeschylus and Euripides, but by the name of Hypsistae in the other writers, is doubtful. Forchhammer maintains that these gates were in the southern part of the city, one on either side of the gate Electrae; but none of his arguments are conclusive; and the position of these gates must be left uncertain. Pausanias relates that, after the victory of the Epigoni at Glisas, some of the Thebans fled to Homole in Thessaly; and that the gate, through which the exiles re-entered the city, when they were recalled by Thersander, was named the Homoloides, from Homole in Thessaly (ix. 8. §§ 6, 7). Forchhammer thinks that it would have been supposed that the exiles entered the city by the same gate by which they quitted it; and as the gate leading to Glisas must have been either in the southern or

eastern side of the city, the gate Homoloides must
have been on the southern side, as the Prœtides lay
towards the east. But this is mere conjecture; and
Leake supposes, with quite as much probability, that
the Homoloides was on the north-western side of the
city, since the Thebans would re-enter the city in
that direction on their return from Homole.

The divisions of the city, and its monuments, of
which Pausanias has given a full description, must
be treated more briefly. The city, as already remarked, was divided into two parts by the torrent
Strophia, of which the western half between the
Strophia and the Dirce was the Cadmeia, while the
eastern half between the Strophia and the Ismenus

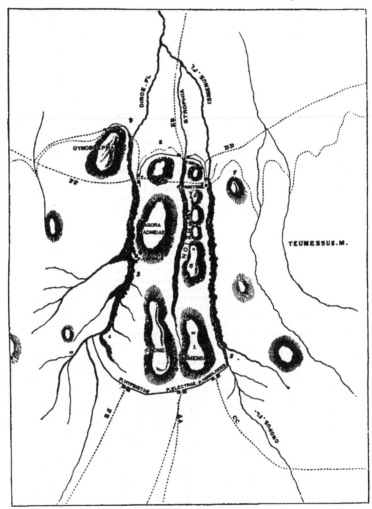

PLAN OF THEBES FROM FORCHHAMMER.

1. Temple of the Ismenian Apollo.
2. Melia, the fountain of the Ismenus.
3. Athena Onca.
4. Fountain of Dirce. *Paraporti.*
5. Theatre and Temple of Dionysus.
6. Monument of Amphion and Zethus.
7. Fountain of St. Theodore.
8. Syrma Antigonae.

9. House of Pindar.
A A. Road to Plataea.
B B. Road to Leuctra.
C C. Road to Tanagra.
D D. Road to Chalcis.
E E. Road to Acraephnium.
F F. Road to Thespiae.

was the lower city (ἡ κάτω πόλις), said to have been added by Amphion and Zethus. (Paus. ix. 5. §§ 2, 6.) The Cadmeia is again divided by a slight depression near the fountain of Dirce and the Crenaean gate into two hills, of which the larger and the higher one to the south was the acropolis proper, and was called the Cadmeia κατ' ἐξοχήν, while the northern hill formed the agora of the acropolis (τῆς ἀκροπόλεως ἀγορά, Paus. ix. 12. § 3). The eastern half of the city was also divided between the Strophia and the Ismenus into two parts, of which the southern consisted of the hill Ismenius, and the northern of several minor eminences, known under the general name of Ampheion. ('Αμφεῖον, Arrian, Anab. i. 8.) Aeschylus describes the tomb of Amphion as standing near the northern gate. (Βοῤῥαίαις πύλαις τύμβον κατ' αὐτὸν Διογενοῦς 'Αμφίονος, Sept. c. Theb. 528.) Hence Thebes consisted of four parts, two belonging to the acropolis, and two to the lower city, the former being the acropolis proper and the agora of the acropolis, and the latter being the hill Ismenius and the Ampheion.

Pausanias, leaving Potniae, entered Thebes on the south by the gate Electrae, before which he noticed the Polyandrium, or tomb of the Thebans who fell fighting against Alexander. (Paus. ix. 8. §§ 3, 4, 7, ix. 10. § 1.) The explanation of Forchhammer that Alexander laid siege to the city on the south, and that he did not return from the gate Electrae to the Proetides, as Leake supposes, seems the most probable. Accordingly the double lines of circumvallation, which the Thebans erected against the Macedonian garrison in the Cadmeia, must have been to the south of the city around the chief gates of the Cadmeia. (See Arrian, i. 7, 8.) Upon entering the city through the gate Electrae, Pausanias notices the hill Ismenius sacred to Apollo, named from the river Ismenus flowing by it (ix. 10. § 2). Upon the hill was a temple of Apollo, containing several monuments enumerated by Pausanias. This temple is likewise mentioned by Pindar and Herodotus, both of whom speak of the tripods situated in its treasury. (Pind. Pyth. xi. 7, seq.; Herod. v. 59.) Above the Ismenium, Pausanias noticed the fountain of the Ismenus, sacred to Ares, and guarded by a dragon, the name of which fountain was Melia, as we have already seen (ix. 10. § 5).

Next Pausanias, beginning again from the gate Electrae, turns to the left and enters the Cadmeia (ix. 11. § 1, seq.). He does not mention the acropolis by name, but it is evident from the list of the monuments which he gives that he was in the Cadmeia. He enumerates the house of Amphitryon, containing the bedchamber of Alcmena, said to have been the work of Trophonius and Agamedes; a monument of the children of Hercules by Megara; the stone called Sophronister; the temple of Hercules ('Ηράκλειον, Arrian, Anab. i. 8); and, near it, a gymnasium and stadium, both bearing the name of this God; and above the Sophronister an altar of Apollo Spodius.

Pausanias next came to the depression between the acropolis and the agora of the Cadmeia, where he noticed an altar and statue of Athena, bearing the Phoenician surname of Onga ("Ογγα), or Onca ("Ογκα) according to other authorities, and said to have been dedicated by Cadmus (ix. 12. § 2). We know from Aeschylus that there was originally a temple of Athena Onca in this locality, which stood outside the city near one of the gates, whence the goddess was called ἀγχίπτολις. Some derived the

name from a village named Onca or Oncae. (Aesch. Sept. c. Theb. 163, 487, 501, with Schol.; Schol. in Euripid. Phoen. 1069; Steph. B. s. v. 'Ογκαίαι; Hesych. s. v. "Ογκας; Schol. ad Pind. Ol. ii. 39, 48; Tzetzes, ad Lycophron. 1225; Phavorinus, s. v. "Ογκαι.) Sophocles also speaks of two temples of Athena at Thebes (πρὸς Παλλάδος διπλοῖς ναοῖς, Oed. Tyr. 20), in one of which, according to the Scholiast, she was surnamed Oncaea, and in the other Ismenia. In the valley between the two hills, there are still the remains of an aqueduct, partly under and partly above ground, to which Dicaearchus refers (φέρεται δὲ καὶ ἀπὸ τῆς Καδμείας ὕδωρ ἀφανὲς διὰ σωλήνων ἀγόμενον, l. c.)

In the agora of the Cadmeia the house of Cadmus is said to have stood; and in this place were shown ruins of the bedchamber of Harmonia and Semele; statues of Dionysus, of Pronomus, the celebrated musician, and of Epaminondas; a temple of Ammon; the place where Teiresias observed the flight of birds; a temple of Fortune; three wooden statues of Aphrodite, with the surnames of Urania, Pandemus, and Apostrophia; and a temple of Demeter Thesmophorus. (Paus. ix. 12. §§ 3—5, ix. 16. §§ 1—5.)

Crossing the torrent Strophia, Pausanias saw near the gate Proetides the theatre with the temple of Dionysus (ix. 16. § 6). In this part of the city, to which Forchhammer gives the name of Ampheion, the following monuments are mentioned by Pausanias (ix. 16. § 7, ix. 17. §§ 1—4): ruins of the house of Lycus and a monument of Semele; monuments of the children of Amphion; a temple of Artemis Euclea, and, near it, statues of Apollo Boedromius and of Hermes Agoraeus; the funeral pile (πυρά) of the children of Amphion, distant half a stadium from their tombs; two statues of Athena Zosteria; and the monument of Zethus and Amphion, being a mound of earth. As the lower city was deserted in the time of Pausanias, he does not mention the agora; but there is no doubt that it contained one, if not more, since Sophocles speaks of several agorae (Oed. Tyr. 20).

Outside the gate Proetides, on the road to Chalcis, Pausanias names the monuments of Melanippus, Tydeus, and the sons of Oedipus, and 15 stadia beyond the latter the monument of Teiresias. Pausanias also mentions a tomb of Hector and one of Asphodicus, at the fountain Oedipodeia, which is perhaps the modern fountain of St. Theodore. On the same road was the village Teumessus. (Paus. ix. 18, ix. 19. § 1.) After describing the road to Chalcis, Pausanias returns to the gate Proetides, outside which, towards the N., was the gymnasium of Iolaus, a stadium, the heroum of Iolaus, and, beyond the stadium, the hippodrome, containing the monument of Pindar (ix. 23. §§ 1, 2). Pausanias then comes to the road leading from the Ogygian or Northern gate, to Acraephnium, after following which he returns to the city, and enumerates the objects outside the gate Neitae. Here, between the gate and the river Dirce, were the tomb of Menoeceus, the son of Creon, and a monument marking the spot where the two sons of Oedipus slew each other. The whole of this locality was called the Syrma (Σύρμα) of Antigone, because, being unable to carry the dead body of her brother Polynices, she dragged it to the funeral pile of Eteocles. On the opposite side of the Dirce were the ruins of the house of Pindar, and a temple of Dindymene (ix. 25. §§ 1—3). Pausanias then appears to have returned to the gate Neitae and followed the road which ran from this gate to On-chestus. He first mentions a temple of Themis, then temples of the Fates and of Zeus Agoraeus, and, a little further, a statue of Hercules, surnamed Rhino-colustes, because he here cut off the noses of the heralds of Orchomenus. Twenty-five stadia beyond was the grove of Demeter Cabeiria and Persephone, and 7 stadia further a temple of the Cabeiri, to the

COIN OF THEBES.

right of which was the Teneric plain, and to the left a road which at the end of 50 stadia conducted to Thespiae (ix. 25. § 5, ix. 26. §§ 1, 6).

(Leake, *Northern Greece*, vol. ii. p. 218, seq., vol. iv. p. 573, seq.; Ulrichs, *Topographie von Theben*, in *Abhandl. der Bayer. Akad.* p. 413, seq. 1841; Unger, *Thebana Paradoxa*, 1839; Forchhammer, *Topographia Thebarum Heptapylarum*, Kiliae, 1854.)

THEBAE CORSICAE. [CORSEIA, No. 2.]

THEBAE PHTHIO'TIDES or PHTHIAE (Θῆ-βαι αἱ Φθιώτιδες, Polyb. v. 99; Strab. ix. p. 433; Thebae Phthiae, Liv. xxxii. 33), an important town of Phthiotis in Thessaly, was situated in the north-eastern corner of this district, near the sea, and at the distance of 300 stadia from Larissa. (Polyb. *l. c.*) It is not mentioned in the Iliad, but it was at a later time the most important maritime city in Thessaly, till the foundation of Demetrias, by Deme-trius Poliorcetes, about B. C. 290. ("Thebas Phthias unum maritimum emporium fuisse quondam Thes-salis quaestuosum et fugiferum," Liv. xxxix. 25.) It is first mentioned in B. C. 282, as the only Thessa-lian city, except Pelinnaeum, that did not take part in the Lamiac war. (Diod. xviii. 11.) In the war between Demetrius Poliorcetes and Cassander, in B. O 302, Thebes was one of the strongholds of Cassander. (Diod. xx. 110.) It became at a later time the chief possession of the Aetolians in northern Greece; but it was wrested from them, after an obstinate siege, by Philip, the son of Demetrius, who changed its name into Philippopolis. (Polyb. v. 99, 100; Diod. xxvi. p. 513, ed. Wesseling.) It was attacked by the consul Flamininus, previous to the battle of Cynoscephalae, B. C. 197, but without success. (Liv. xxxiii. 5; Polyb. xviii. 2.) After the defeat of Phi-lip, the name of Philippopolis was gradually dropped, though both names are used by Livy in narrating the transactions of the year B. C. 185. (Liv. xxxix. 25.) It continued to exist under the name of Thebes in the time of the Roman Empire, and is mentioned by Hierocles in the sixth century. ("Thebae Thessalae," Plin. v. 8. s. 15; Θῆβαι Φθιώ-τιδες, Ptol. iii. 13. § 17; Steph. B. *s. v.*; Hierocl. p. 642, ed. Wess.) The ruins of Thebes are situated upon a height half a mile to the north-east of *Ak-Ketjel*. The entire circuit of the walls and towers, both of the town and citadel, still exist; and the circumference is between 2 and 3 miles. The theatre, of which only a small part of the exterior circular wall of the cavea remains, stood about the

centre of the city, looking towards the sea. (Leake, *Northern Greece*, vol. iv. p. 358.)

THEBAIS. [THEBAE AEGYPTI.]

THEBE (Θήβη), a famous ancient town in Mysia, at the southern foot of Mount Placius, which is often mentioned by Homer as governed by Eetion, the father of Andromache (*Il.* i. 366, vi. 397, xxii. 479). The town is said to have been destroyed during the Trojan War by Achilles (*Il.* ii. 691; Strab. xiii. pp. 584, 585, 612, foll.) It must have been restored after its first destruction, but it was decayed in the time of Strabo, and when Pliny (v. 32) wrote it had entirely disappeared. The belief of some of the ancient grammarians (Etym. M. *s. v.*; Didym. *ad Hom. Il.* i. 336; Disc. *ad Hesiod. Scut.* 49; and Eustath. *ad Hom. Il.* ii. 691) that Thebe was only another name for Adramyttium, is contradicted by the most express testimony of the best writers. Xenophon (*Anab.* vii. 8. § 7) places it between Antandrus and Adramyttium, and Strabo, perhaps more correctly, between Adramyttium and Carina, about 80 stadia to the north-east of the former. (Comp. Pomp. Mela, i. 18; Steph. B. *s. v.*) Al-though this town perished at an early period, its name remained celebrated throughout antiquity, being at-tached to the neighbouring plain (Θήβης πεδίον, Campus Thebanus), which was famed for its fer-tility, and was often ravaged and plundered by the different armies, whom the events of war brought into this part of Asia. (Herod. vii. 42; Xenoph. *l. c.*; Strab. xiii. p. 588; Liv. xxxvii. 19.) Ste-phanus B. (*s. v.*) mentions another town of this name as belonging to the territory of Miletus in Asia Minor. 　　　　　　　　　　　　[L. S.]

THECHES (Θήχης), one of the highest points of Mount Paryadres in Pontus, south-east of Trapezus, on the borders of the country inhabited by the Ma-crones. From it the Ten Thousand Greeks under Xenophon for the first time descried the distant Euxine. (Xenoph. *Anab.* iv. 7. § 21.) Diodorus Siculus (xiv. 29) calls the mountain Χήνιον ὄρος; but it still bears its ancient name *Tekieh*. (Ritter, *Erdkunde*, ii. p. 768.) 　　　　　　　　　[L. S.]

THECOA. [TEKOAH.]

THEGANUSSA. [MESSENIA, p. 342, b.]

THEI'SOA (Θεισόα: Eth. Θεισοάτης). 1. A town of Arcadia, in the district Cynuria or Parrhasia, on the northern slope of Mt. Lycaeus, called after the nymph Theisoa, one of the nurses of Zeus. Its in-habitants were removed to Megalopolis upon the foundation of the latter city. Leake places it at the castle of *St. Helen* above *Lavdha*. Ross discovered some ancient remains N. of *Andritzéna*, which he conjectures may be those of Theisoa. (Paus. viii. 38. §§ 3, 9, viii. 27. § 4; Steph. B. *s. v.*; Leake, *Morea*, vol. ii. p. 315, *Peloponnesiaca*, p. 154; Ross, *Reisen im Peloponnes*, vol. i. p. 101; Boblaye, *Recherches*, p. 151.)

2. A town of Arcadia, in the territory of Orcho-menus, the inhabitants of which also removed to Megalopolis. It is mentioned along with Methy-drium and Teuthis as belonging to the confederation (συντέλεια) of Orchomenos. It is probably repre-sented by the ruins near *Dimitzana*. (Paus. viii. 27. §§ 4, 7, viii. 28. § 3; Ross, p. 115.)

THEIUM, a town of Athamania in Epeirus, of uncertain site. (Liv. xxxviii. 2.)

THELINE. [ARELATE.]

THELPU'SA (Θέλπουσα, Paus. and Coins; Τίλ-φουσα, Polyb., Diod., and Steph. B. *s. v.*: Eth. Θελ-πούσιος, Τελφούσιος), a town in the west of Arcadia, situated upon the left or eastern bank of the river Ladon. Its territory was bounded on the north by that of Psophis, on the south by that of Heraea, on the west by the Eleia and Tisatis, and on the east by that of Cleitor, Tripolis, and Theisoa. The town is said to have derived its name from a nymph, the daughter of the river Ladon, which nymph was probably the stream flowing through the lower part of the town into the Ladon. It is first mentioned in history in b. c. 352, when the Lacedaemonians were defeated in its neighbourhood by the Spartans. (Diod. xvi. 39.) In b. c. 222 it was taken by Antigonus Doson, in the war against Cleomenes, and it is also mentioned in the campaigns of Philip. (Polyb. ii. 54, iv. 60, 73, 77, Steph. B. *s. v.* Τέλφουσα; Plin. iv. 6. s. 20.) Its coins show that it belonged to the Achaean League. (Leake, *Peloponnesiaca,* p. 206.) When Pausanias visited Thelpusa, the city was nearly deserted, so that the agora, which was formerly in the centre of the city, then stood at its extremity. He saw a temple of Asclepius, and another of the twelve gods, of which the latter was nearly levelled with the ground. (Paus. viii. 25 § 3.) Pausanias also mentions two temples of some celebrity in the neighbourhood of Thelpusa, one above and the other below the city. The one above was the temple of Demeter Eleusinia, containing statues of Demeter, Persephone and Dionysus, made of stone, and which probably stood at the castle opposite to *Spáthari* (viii. 25. §§ 2, 3). The temple below the city was also sacred to Demeter, whom the Thelpusians called Erinnys. This temple is alluded to by Lycophron (1038) and Callimachus (*Fr.* 107). It was situated at a place called Onceium, where Oncus, the son of Apollo, is said once to have reigned (viii. 25. § 4, seq.; Steph. B. *s. v.* Ὄγκειον). Below this temple stood the temple of Apollo Oncaeates, on the left bank of the Ladon, and on the right bank that of the boy Asclepius, with the sepulchre of Trygon, said to have been the nurse of Asclepius (viii. 25. § 11). The ruins of Thelpusa stand upon the slope of a considerable hill near the village of *Vánena* (Βάνερα). There are only few traces of the walls of the city. At the ruined church of St. John, near the rivulet, are some Hellenic foundations and fragments of columns. The saint is probably the successor of Asclepius, whose temple, as we learn from Pausanias, stood longest in the city. There are likewise the remains of a Roman building, about 12 yards long and 6 wide, with the ruins of an arched roof. There are also near the Ladon some Hellenic foundations, and the lower parts of six columns. Below *Vánena* there stands upon the right bank of the Ladon the ruined church of St. Athanasius the Miraculous, where Leake found the remains of several columns. Half a mile below this church is the village of *Tumbíki*, where a promontory projects into the river, upon which there is a mound apparently artificial. This mound is probably the tomb of Trygon, and *Tumbíki* is the site of that the temple of Asclepius.

Pausanias, in describing the route from Psophis

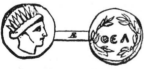

COIN OF THELPUSA.

to Thelpusa, after mentioning the boundaries between the territories of the two states [PSOPHIS], first crosses the river Arsen, and then, at the distance of 25 stadia, arrives at the ruins of a village Caus and a temple of Asclepius Causius, erected upon the roadside. From this place the distance to Thelpusa was 40 stadia. (Leake, *Morea,* vol. ii. pp. 97, seq., 250, seq., *Peloponnesiaca,* pp. 205, 222, 228; Boblaye, *Recherches, &c.* p. 152; Ross, *Reisen im Peloponnes.* p. 111; Curtius, *Peloponnesos,* vol. i. p. 370, seq.)

THELUTHA, a fortress situated on an island in the Euphrates. It is mentioned by Ammianus (xxiv. 2), who states that it was used as a treasury by the Persians. It is unquestionably the same as the Thilabus of Isidorus (*Stathm. Parth.* 1), who gives a similar description of it, and places it at no great distance from another island in the same river, Anatho. Zosimus, speaking of the same region, notices a fortified island, which he calls φρούριον ὀχυρότατον (iii. 15); probably the same place. It is doubtless represented now by an island which Colonel Chesney calls *Telbes, Tilbus,* or *Anatelbes* (i. p. 53 and Map.).   [V.]

THEMEOTAE (Θεμεῶται, Ptol. v. 9. § 17), a people of Asiatic Sarmatia.   [T. H. D.]

THEMMA. [TAMA].

THEMISCY'RA (Θεμίσκυρα), a plain in the north of Pontus, about the mouths of the rivers Iris and Thermodon, was a rich and beautiful district, ever verdant, and supplying food for numberless herds of oxen and horses. It also produced great abundance of grain, especially pannick and millet; and the southern parts near the mountains furnished a variety of fruits, such as grapes, apples, pears, and nuts in such quantities that they were suffered to waste on the trees. (Strab. ii. p. 126, xii. p. 547, foll.; Aeschyl. *Prom.* 722; comp. Apollod. ii. 5; Apollon. Rhod. ii. 370; Plin. vi. 3, xxiv. 102.) Mythology describes this plain as the native country of the Amazons.

A Greek town of the name of Themiscyra, at a little distance from the coast and near the mouth of the Thermodon, is mentioned as early as the time of Herodotus (iv. 86; comp. Scylax, p. 33; Paus. i. 2. § 1). Ptolemy (v. 6. § 3) is undoubtedly mistaken in placing it further west, midway between the Iris and Cape Heraclium. Scylax calls it a Greek town; but Diodorus (ii. 44) states that it was built by the founder of the kingdom of the Amazons. After the retreat of Mithridates from Cyzicus, Themiscyra was besieged by Lucullus. The inhabitants on that occasion defended themselves with great valour; and when their walls were undermined, they sent bears and other wild beasts, and even swarms of bees, against the workmen of Lucullus (Appian, *Mithrid.* 78). But notwithstanding their gallant defence, the town seems to have perished on that occasion, for Mela speaks of it as no longer existing (i. 19), and Strabo does not mention it at all. (Comp. Anon. *Peripl. P. E.* p. 11; Steph. B. *s. v.* Χαδισία.) Some suppose that the town of *Thermeh,* at the mouth of the Thermodon, marks the site of ancient Themiscyra; but Hamilton (*Researches,* i. p. 283) justly observes that it must have been situated a little further inland. Ruins of the place do not appear to exist, for those which Texier regards as indicating the site of Themiscyra, at a distance of two days' journey from the Halys, on the borders of Galatia, cannot possibly have belonged to it, but are in all probability the remains of Tavium.   [L. S.]

THEMISO'NIUM (Θεμισώνιον: Eth. Θεμισώνιος), a town of Phrygia, near the borders of Pisidia, whence in later times it was regarded as a town of Pisidia. (Strab. xii. p. 576; Paus. x. 32; Ptol. v. 2. § 26 ; Steph. B. s. v. ; Plin. v. 29 ; Hierocl. p. 674 ; Geogr. Rav i. 18.) Pausanias relates that the Themisonians showed a cave, about 30 stadia from their town, in which, on the advice of Heracles, Apollo, and Hermes, they had concealed their wives and children during an invasion of the Celts, and in which afterwards they set up statues of these divinities. According to the Peuting. Table, Themisonium was 34 miles from Laodiceia. Arundell (Discoveries, ii. p. 136), guided by a coin of the place, fixes its site on the river Azanes, and believes the ruins at Kai Hissar to be those of Themisonium; but Kiepert (in Franz's Fünf Inschriften, p. 29) thinks that the ruins of Kisel Hissar, which Arundell takes to mark the site of Cibyra, are those of Themisonium.   [L. S.]

THENAE (Θεναί, Callim. in Jov. 42; Steph. B. s. v. 'Ομφάλιον), a town of Crete close on the Omphalian plain, and near Cnossus. If not on the very site it must have been close to the Castello Temenos of the Venetians, which was built A. D. 961, when the Cretans, under their Saracenic leaders, were vanquished by Nicephorus Phocas and the forces of the Byzantine emperor. (Pashley, Travels, vol. i. p. 224: comp. Finlay, Byzantine Empire, vol. i. p. 377; Gibbon. c. lii.)   [E. B. J.]

THENAE (Θεναί), a maritime city of Byzacium in Africa Proper, at the mouth of a small river which fell into the Syrtis Minor, and 216 miles SE. of Carthage. (Plin. v. 4. s. 3.) By Strabo it is called ἡ Θένα (xvii. p. 831), and by Ptolemy Θαίνα, or Θέαιναι (i. 15. § 2, iv. 3. § 11). At a later period it became a Roman colony with the name of Aelia Augusta Mercurialis (Gruter, Inscr. p. 363; cf. Itin. Ant. p. 59, also pp. 46, 47, 48, 57). Now Thaini, or Tény.   [T. H. D.]

THEODORIAS. [VACCA.]

THEODORO'POLIS (Θεοδωρόπολις, Procop. de Aed. iv. 6, 7), a town of Moesia Inferior, founded by the emperor Justinian.   [T. H. D.]

THEODO'SIA (Θεοδοσία, Ptol. iii. 6. § 3), a flourishing colony of the Milesians, on the coast of the Chersonesus Taurica, in European Sarmatia, with a harbour capable of containing 100 ships. (Strab. vii. 309; Arrian, Per. P. Eux. p. 20.) In the dialect of the natives, it was called Ardabda ('Αρδάβδα, Anon. Per. P. Eux. p. 5), which is said to have signified, in the dialect of the Taurians, "seven gods" (Pallas, i. p. 416), and at a later period Kapha (Κάφα, Const. Porphyr. de Adm. Imp. c. 53); whilst by the Geogr. Rav. (iv. 3, v. 11) we find it named Theodosiopolis. It enjoyed an extensive commerce, particularly in corn (Dem. adv. Lept. p. 255), but appears to have been ruined before the age of Arrian, in the beginning of the second century. (Arrian, l. c.) Yet it continues to be mentioned by later writers (Polyaen. v. 23; Amm. Marc. xxii. 8. § 36; Oros. i. 2; Steph. B. s. v. &c.) Yet we should not, perhaps, allow these writers much authority; at all events the very name of the Milesian colony appears to have vanished in the time of the emperor Constantine Porphyrogenitus, under whom the site on which it stood was already called Kaffon (de Adm. Imp. c. 43; cf. Neumann, Die Hellenen im Skythenlande, p. 469.) Clarke imagined that he had discovered its ruins at Stara Crim, where there are still some magnificent remains of a

Greek city (Trav. ii. p. 154, sq.; cf. p. 150 and note); but the more general, and perhaps better founded opinion is, that it stood, near its namesake, the modern Caffa or Theodosia. (Cf. Raoul-Rochette, Ant. du Bosp. Cimm. p. 30; Dubois, v. p. 280.) For coins and inscriptions, see Köhler, Nov. Act. Acad. Petrop. xiv. p. 122, and Mém. de St. Petersb. ix. p. 649, sq.; Clarke, Trav. ii. 148, sq. [T. H. D.]

THEODOSIO'POLIS (also called APRI), a town in the SE. of Thrace, on the road from Cypsela to Byzantium, a short distance to the E. of the source of the river Melas. Ammianus (xxvii. 4. § 12) mentions it by the latter name as one of the two chief towns of Europa, the designation in his time of the SE. division of Thrace.   [J. R.]

THEODOSIO'POLIS (Θεοδοσιόπολις, Procop de Aed. iii. 5), a city in Armenia Major, founded by Theodosius II. to keep the Armenians in subjection. It was enlarged by the emperor Anastasius, and its fortifications were much strengthened by Justinian. (Procop. B. P. i. 10.) It lay S. of the Araxes and 42 stadia S. of the mountain in which the Euphrates rises, the present Bingöl. (Id. Ib. 17; cf. Ritter, Erdk. x. p. 79, seq.) Theodosiopolis enjoyed an extensive commerce. (Const. Porphyr. de Adm. Imp. 45.) Some writers identify it with Arzeroum (Ritter, Ib. pp. 80, 271, seq.; Zeune. p. 431); but according to D'Anville (Geogr. Anc. ii. p. 99, sq.) it lay 35 miles E. of that place. (Cf. Chardin, ii. p. 173, sq.; Hamilton, Asia Minor, &c. i. p. 178; Gibbon, Decline and Fall, iv. p. 168, ed. Smith.)   [T. H. D.]

THEODOSIO'POLIS, in Mysia. [PERPERENA.]

THEON OCHEMA. [LIBYA, p. 179, b.]

THEOPHA'NIUS (Θεοφάνιος, Ptol. v. 9. § 3), a river of Asiatic Sarmatia, which fell into the Palus Maeotis, between the greater and less Rhombites. (Cf. Amm. Marc. xxii. 8. § 29.)   [T. H. D.]

THEO'POLIS. This place in Gallia, with a pure Greek name, was near Sisteron, in the department of Basses-Alpes, on the left bank of the Druentia (Durance). An inscription cut on the slope of a rock in honour of Dardanus, praefect of the Praetorium of Gallia in the time of Honorius, and in honour of his mother, informs us that they made a road for this town by cutting both sides of the mountains, and they gave it walls and gates. The place is still called Théoux, and there are said to be remains there. (D'Anville, Notice, &c.) [G. L.]

THERA (Θήρα, Ion. Θήρη: Eth. Θηραίος: Santorin), an island in the Aegaean sea, and the chief of the Sporades, is described by Strabo as 200 stadia in circumference, opposite the Cretan island of Dia, and 700 stadia from Crete itself. (Strab. x. p. 484.) Pliny places Thera 25 Roman miles S. of Ios (iv. 12. s. 23). Thera is said to have been formed by a clod of earth thrown from the ship Argo, to have received the name of Calliste, when it first emerged from the sea, and to have been first inhabited by the Phoenicians, who were left there by Cadmus. Eight generations afterwards it was colonised by Lacedaemonians and Minyae under the guidance of the Spartan Theras, the son of Autesion, who gave his name to the island. (Herod. iv. 147, seq.; Pind. Pyth. iv. 457; Callin. ap. Strab. viii. p. 347, x. p. 484; Apoll. Rhod. iv. 1762; Paus. iii. 1. § 7, iii. 15. § 6, vii. 2. § 2.) Its only importance in history is owing to its being the mother-city of Cyrene in Africa, which was founded by Battus of Thera in B. C. 631. (Herod. iv. 150, seq.) At this time Thera contained seven districts (χῶροι, Herod. iv. 153.) Ptolemy (iii. 15. § 26) has preserved the names of two places, Eleusin or Eleusia, and Oea; and a third, called Melaenae, occurs in an inscription. (Böckh, *Inscr.* no. 2448.) Like Melos, Thera sided with the Lacedaemonians at the commencement of the Peloponnesian War (Thuc. ii. 9), but of its subsequent history we have no information.

Thera and the surrounding islands are remarkable as having been the scene of active volcanic operations in ancient as well as in modern times. In consequence of the survey made by command of the English Admiralty, we now possess precise information respecting these islands, the result of which, with additional particulars, is given by Lieutenant Leycester in a paper published in the Journal of the Royal Geographical Society, from which the following account is chiefly taken. Thera, now called *Santorin,* the largest of the group, has been likened in form to a horse-shoe; but a crescent with its two points elongated towards the west would be a more exact description. The distance round the inner curve is 12 miles, and round the outer 18, making the coast-line of the whole island 30 miles: its breadth is in no part more than 3 miles. Opposite to Thera westward is Therasia, which still bears the same name. (Strab. i. p. 57, v. p. 484; Steph. B. *s. v.* Θηρασία; Ptol. iii. 15. § 28; Plin. ii. 87. s. 89, iv. 12. s. 70.) Its circuit is 7½ miles, its length from N. to S. about 2½ miles, and its breadth a mile. About 1½ mile S. of Therasia, lies *Aspronisi,* or White Island, only a mile in circuit, and so called from being capped with a deep layer of pozzolana: the name of this island is not mentioned by the ancient writers. These three islands, Thera, Therasia, and *Aspronisi,* enclose an expanse of water nearly 18 miles in circumference, which is in reality the crater of a great volcano. The islands were originally united, and were subsequently separated by the eruption of the crater. In the centre of this basin three volcanic mountains rise, known by the name of *Kamméni* or the *Burnt,* (καμμένη, i. e. καυμένη instead of κεκαυμένη), and distinguished as the *Palaea* or Old, the *Nea* or New, and the *Mikra* or Little. It was formerly asserted that the basin was unfathomable, but its depth and shape have been clearly ascertained by the soundings of the English Survey. Supposing the basin could be drained, a gigantic bowl-shaped cavity would appear, with walls 2449 feet high in some places, and nowhere less than 1200 feet high, while the *Kamméni* would be seen to form in the centre a huge mountain 5½ miles in circumference with three summits, the *Palaea Kamméni,* the *Nea Kamméni,* and the *Mikra Kamméni,* rising severally from the bottom of the abyss to the height of 1606, 1629, and 1550 feet. The rim of the great crater thus exposed would appear in all parts unbroken, except at the northern point between Thera and Therasia, where there is a chasm or door into the crater about a mile in width, and 1170 feet in depth midway between the two islands. (See Map, B.) If we now suppose the waters of the Aegaean let in, the edges of the crater, forming the inner curve of Thera and Therasia, rise above the sea from the height of 500 to 1200 feet, and present frightful precipices, of the colour of iron dross, except where their summits are capped with a deep layer of pozzolana. The *Palaea Kamméni* is 328 feet above the water; the *Nea Kamméni* 351 feet; and the *Mikra Kamméni* 222 feet.

Thera, Therasia, and *Aspronisi* are all composed of volcanic matter, except the southern part of Thera, which contains *Mount Elias,* of limestone formation, the peak of which rises 1887 feet above the level of the sea, and is the highest land in the island. This mountain must have been originally a submarine eminence in the bed of the Mediterranean before the volcanic cone was formed (Lyell, *Principles of Geology,* p. 445, 9th ed).

The first appearance of the three *Kamménis* belongs to historical times, and has been narrated by several writers. The *Nea Kamméni,* which is the largest of the group, did not emerge till the year 1707; but the other two were thrown up in ancient times. The exact time of their appearance, however, is differently related, and it is difficult, and in some cases impossible, to reconcile the conflicting statements of ancient writers upon the subject. It appears certain that the oldest of these islands is the most southerly one, still called the *Palaea* or *Old Kamméni.* It burst out of the sea in B. C. 197, and received the name of Hiera, a name frequently given in antiquity to volcanic mountains. This fact is stated by Eusebius, Justin, Strabo, and Plutarch. It is related by Strabo that flames burst out of the sea for four days, and that an island was formed 12 stadia or 1½ English mile in circumference. (Euseb. *Chron.* p. 144, *Olymp.* 145. 4; Justin, xxx. 4; Strab. i. p. 57; Plut. *de Pyth. Or.* 11. p. 399.) The unanimous statement of these four writers is, however, at variance with that of Pliny (ii. 87. s. 89), who says "that in the 4th year of the 135th Olympiad [B. C. 237] there arose Thera and Therasia: between these islands, 130 years later [B. C. 107], Hiera, also called Automate; and 2 stadia from the latter, 110 years [A. D. 3] afterwards, in the consulship of M. Junius Silanus and L. Balbus, on the 8th of July, Thia." In another passage he says (iv. 12. s. 23): "Thera, when it first emerged from the sea, was called Calliste. Therasia was afterwards torn away from it; between the two there presently arose Automate, also called Hiera; and in our age Thia near Hiera." Seneca refers apparently to the events mentioned by Pliny, when he states (*Qu. Nat.* ii. 26), upon the authority of Posidonius, that an island arose in the Aegaean sea "in the memory of our ancestors" (majorum nostrorum memoria), and that the same thing happened a second time "in our memory " (nostra memoria) in the consulship of Valerius Asiaticus [A. D. 46]. (Comp. *Qu. Nat.* vi.21.)

According to the preceding statements there would have been five different eruptions of islands in the space of little more than 200 years. First Thera and Therasia themselves appeared in B. C. 237, according to Pliny; secondly Hiera, according to Eusebius, Justin, Strabo, and Plutarch, in B. C. 197; thirdly Hiera or Automate, according to Pliny, 130 years later than the first occurrence, consequently in B. C. 107; fourthly, according to Pliny, 110 years afterwards, Thia, that is in A. D. 3; fifthly, according to Seneca and other writers, who will be mentioned presently, an island in the reign of the emperor Claudius, A. D. 46.

Now it is evident that there is some gross error in the text of Pliny, or that he has made use of his authorities with a carelessness which is not unusual with him. The most surprising thing is, that he has omitted the eruptions of the islands in B. C. 197 and A. D. 46, which are guaranteed by several authorities. His statement that Thera and Therasia first appeared in the 4th year of the 135th Olympiad,

i. e. B. C. 237, is absurd, as they are mentioned by Callinus and Herodotus, and must have existed even long before the time of those writers; but if we suppose a slight error in the numerals in the text of Pliny (reading " Olympiadis cxxxxv anno quarto" instead of " Olympiadis cxxxv anno quarto "), we have the very year (B. C. 197) in which Eusebius and Justin place the appearance of Hiera. There can be little doubt, therefore, that Pliny's authorities referred to this event, and that it was only through carelessness that he spoke of the appearance of Thera and Therasia in that year. Thus the first statement of Pliny may be reconciled with the accounts of Eusebius, Justin, and the other writers. The appearance of the second island, to which he falsely transfers the name of Hiera from the earlier occurrence, must be placed in B. C. 67, according to the corrected chronology. This island no longer exists; and it must therefore either have been thrown up and disappeared again immediately, as was the case

in the eruption of 1650, or it was simply an addition to the ancient Hiera, of which there are some instances at a later period. It is apparently to this eruption that the statement of Posidonius, quoted by Seneca, refers. The last statement of Pliny that a new island, named Thia, was thrown up 2 stadia from Thia in the consulship of M. Junius Silanus and L. Balbus, on the 8th of July, is so exact that it seems hardly possible to reject it; but here again is an error in the data. If we take the numbers as they stand, this event would have happened in A.D. 3, or, according to the corrected numbers, in A. D. 43, whereas we know that M. Junius Silanus and L. Balbus were consuls in A.D. 19. No other writer, however, speaks of an eruption of an island in this year, which, if it actually happened, must again have disappeared. Moreover, it is strange that Pliny should have passed over the eruption of the real Thia, or *Mikra Kamméni*, which occurred in his lifetime, in the consulship of Valerius Asiaticus, and in

MAP OF THERA AND THE SURROUNDING ISLANDS.

A. Shoal formed by the submarine volcanic eruption in 1650.
B. Entrance to the crater.
C. *Mount Elias.*
D. *Messa-Vouno* and ruined city, probably Thera.
E. Submarine ruins at *Kamari*, probably Oea.
F. Ruins at *Perissa.*

G. *C. Erousiti.*
H. Ruins, probably of Eleusis.
I. Modern capital *Thera* or *Phira.*
K. Promontory of *Skaro.*
L. *Merovouli.*
M. *Eponomeria.*
N. *C. Kolumbo.*

the reign of Claudius, A. D. 46. This event, with the difference of only a single year, is mentioned by several writers. (Senec. *Qu. Nat.* ii. 26, vi. 21; Dion Cass. lx. 29; Aurel. Vict. *Caes.* 4, *Epit.* 4; Oros. vii. 6; Amm. Marc. xvii. 7; Georg. Cedren. i. p. 197, ed. Par.) Moreover Pliny himself, in another passage (iv. 12. s. 23), says that This appeared in our age (" in nostro aevo "), which can hardly apply to the consulship of Silanus and Balbus, since he was not born till A. D. 23.

In A. D. 726, during the reign of Leo the Isaurian, Hiera, or the *Palaea Kamméni*, received an augmentation on the NE. side. (Theoph. *Chronogr.* p. 338, ed. Paris.; Cedren. i. p. 454, ed. Paris.; Nicephor. p. 37, ed. Par.) There have been several eruptions in modern times, of which a full account is given by Lieut. Leycester and Ross. Of these one of the most important was in 1573, when the *Mikra Kamméni* is said to have been formed. But as we have already seen from several authorities that an island was formed in the reign of Claudius, A. D. 46. we must suppose either that the last-mentioned island sunk into the sea at some unknown period, and made its appearance a second time as the *Mikra Kamméni* in 1573, or that there was only an augmentation of the *Mikra Kamméni* in this year. The latter supposition is the more probable, especially since Father Richard, who records it, was not an eye-witness, but derived his information from old people in the island. There was another terrible eruption in 1650, which Father Richard himself saw. It broke out at an entirely different spot from all preceding eruptions, outside the gulf, off the NE. coast of Thera, about 3½ miles from *C. Kolumbo*, in the direction of Ios and Anydros. This submarine outbreak lasted about three months, covering the sea with pumice, and giving rise to a shoal, which was found by the English Survey to have 10 fathoms water over it. (See map, A.) At the same time the island of Thera was violently shaken by earthquakes, in which many houses were overthrown, and a great number of persons and animals were killed by the pestilential vapours emitted from the volcano. The sea inundated the flat eastern coast of the island to the extent of two Italian miles inland. The ruins of two ancient towns at *Perissa* and *Kamari* were disinterred, the existence of which was previously unknown, and which must have been overwhelmed by some previous eruption of volcanic matter. The road also, which then existed round *Cape Messa-Vouno*, was sunk beneath the waters.

For the next 50 years, or a little longer, the volcanic fires slept, but in 1707 they burst forth with redoubled fury, and produced the largest of the three burnt islands, the *Nea Kamméni*. It originally consisted of two islands. The first which rose was called the White Island, composed of a mass of pumice extremely porous. A few days afterwards there appeared a large chain of dark rocks, composed of brown trachyte, to which the name of the Black Island was given. These two islands were gradually united; and in the course of the eruptions, the black rocks became the centre of the actual island, the *Nea Kamméni*. The White Island was first seen on the 23rd of May, 1707, and for a year the discharges of the volcano were incessant. After this time the eruptions were less frequent; but they continued to occur at intervals in 1710 and 1711; and it was not till 1712 that the fires of the volcano became extinct. The island is now about 2½ miles in circuit, and has a perfect cone at its SE. side,

which is 351 feet high. From 1712 down to the present day there has been no further eruption.

There are several thermal and mineral springs at Thera and the surrounding islands, of which Lieut. Leycester gives an account, and which are more fully described by Landerer in the treatise entitled Περὶ τῶν ἐν Θήρᾳ (Σαντορίνῃ) Θερμῶν ὑδάτων, Athens, 1835. The most important are the iron springs in a bay on the SE. side of *Nea Kamméni*. There are springs on the NE. side of *Palaea Kamméni*, likewise near *Cape Exomiti* in the south of Thera, and at other places. Fresh water springs are very rare at Thera, and are only found round *Mount Elias* springing from the limestone. The inhabitants depend for their supply of water upon the rain which they catch in the tanks during the winter.

The principal modern town of the island is now called *Thera*, or *Phira*, and is situated in the centre of the curve of the gulf. When Tournefort visited Thera, the capital stood upon the promontory *Skaro*, a little to the N. of the present capital, and immediately under the town of *Merovouli*. The promontory *Skaro* projects about one third of a mile into the sea; and upon it are the remains of a castle built by the dukes of Naxos. The chief town in the island, after the capital, is *Epanomeria*, on the NW. promontory, and directly opposite to Therasia. As space is of the utmost value in this small island, all the principal towns are built upon the very edge of the cliffs, and present a very singular appearance, perched in some cases more than 900 feet above the sea. Wood being very scarce, the houses are excavated in the face of the vast beds of pozzolana. In order to make approaches to the towns upon the cliffs, the inhabitants have cut zig-zag stairs or roads in the sides of the precipices. The road upon the summit runs along the edge of the precipices, and, in many cases, over the habitations, which are built in the face of them. The population of the island in 1848 was about 14,000, and, including Therasia, about 14,380. In the time of Tournefort there were 10,000 inhabitants, so that the increase has been nearly a third in about 150 years. The island is carefully cultivated ; and the chief production is wine, which is mostly exported to the Russian ports in the Black Sea.

The antiquities of the island have been explained at length by Ross and Lieut. Leycester. There are remains of an ancient city situated on the SE. point of the island, upon the summit of *Messa-Vouno*, a mountain about 1100 feet above the level of the sea, connected with *Mount Elias* by the ridge of the *Sellada*. The mountain of *Messa-Vouno* slopes suddenly off to the precipices on the NE. side, which rise perpendicularly 600 feet above the water and form the cape of the same name. The walls exhibit masonry of all ages, from the most ancient Cyclopean to the regular masonry of later times. The walls may still be traced, and enclose a circuit of only seven-tenths of a mile : but the houses appear to have been built terrace-fashion upon the side of the hill. Several inscriptions, fragments of sculpture, and other antiquities, have been discovered here. The name of this city has been a subject of some dispute. In an inscription found below *Messa-Vouno*, at *Kamari*, in the church of *St. Nicholas*, the name Oea occurs, which, as we have already seen, is one of the two towns mentioned by Ptolemy. But in an inscription upon some steps cut out of the rock of *Messa-Vouno* we find Θήρα πόλις. Ross, however, does not consider this to be a proof that

Thera was the name of the city, supposing that ᵛᵈᴸⁱˢ here signifies only the political community of the Theraeans. On the other hand, it was so usual for the islands of the Aegaean to possess a capital of the same name, that, taken in connection with the inscription last mentioned, it is probable, either that Ptolemy has accidentally omitted the name of the capital, or that in his time the Theraeans had removed from the lofty site at *Messa-Vouno* to Oea upon the sea-coast at *Kamari*, where submarine ruins still exist. Upon the other or S. side of the *Cape Messa-Vouno*, at *Perissa*, there are also so many ancient remains as to lead us to suppose that this was the site of an ancient city, but no inscription has been discovered to give a clue to its name. Upon either side of the mountain of *Messa-Vouno* there are numerous tombs.

South of *Perissa* is *C. Exomiti*, and a little to the N. of this cape there are the remains of an ancient city, which is probably the Eleusis of Ptolemy. Here are the ruins of a mole under water, and upon the side of the mountain many curious tombs. There are likewise some ruins and tombs at *C. Kolumbo*, in the NE. of the island, which Ross conjectures may be the site of Melaenae. The island of Therasia possessed a town of the same name (Ptol. iii. 15. § 28), the ruins of which were discovered by Ross opposite *Epunomeria* in Thera. (Besides the earlier writers, such as Tournefort and others, the reader is particularly referred to Ross, *Reisen auf den Griechischen Inseln*, vol. i. pp. 53, seq., 86, seq., 180, seq.; and Lieut. Leycester, *Some Account of the Volcanic Group of Santorin or Thera*, in the *Journal of the Royal Geographical Society*, vol. xx. p. 1, seq.)

THERAMBOS or THRAMBUS (Θεράμβος, Herod. vii. 123; Θράμβος, Steph. B. *s. v.*; Θραμβηΐs, Scylax, p. 26; Θραμβουσία δειράς, Lycophr. 1404), a town of the peninsula Pallene, in Chalcidice in Macedonia, is called a promontory by Stephanus B., and is hence supposed by Leake (*Northern Greece*, vol. iii. p. 156) to have occupied a position very near the promontory Canastraeum, the most southerly point of Pallene; but from the order of the names in Scylax we would rather place it at the promontory upon the western side of the peninsula, called Posidium by Thucydides (iv. 129).

THERANDA, a town of Moesia, now *Trenonitza* (Geogr. Rav. iv. 15; *Tab. Peut.*). 　[T. H. D.]

THERAPNAE (Θεράπναι: *Eth.* Θεραπναῖος), a place in the territory of Thebes, between this city and the Asopus. (Eurip. *Bacch.* 1029; Strab. ix. p. 409; Leake, *Northern Greece*, vol. ii. p. 369.)

THERAPNE. [SPARTA, p. 1029, b.]

THERA'SIA. [THERA.]

THERIO'DES SINUS (Θηριώδης κόλπος, Ptol. vii. 3. § 2), a gulf on the coast of the Sinae, between the promontories Notium (Νότιον), and Satyron (Σατύρων). Perhaps the gulf of *Tonkin*, or that between the *Cape St. James* and the river of *Campodja*. 　[T. H. D.]

THERMA. [THESSALONICA.]

THERMAE (Θέρμαι, *Eth.* Thermitanus) was the name of two cities in Sicily, both of which derived their name from their position near hot springs.

1. The *northern* Thermae, sometimes called for distinction's sake THERMAE HIMERENSES (now *Termini*), was situated on the N. coast of the island, in the immediate neighbourhood of the more ancient city of Himera, to the place of which it may be considered as succeeding. Hence its history is given in the article HIMERA.

2. The *southern* Thermae, or THERMAE SELINUNTIAE (*Sciacca*), was situated on the SW. coast of the island, and, as its name imports, within the territory of Selinus, though at a distance of 20 miles from that city in the direction of Agrigentum. There can be no doubt that it occupied the same site as the modern town of *Sciacca*, about midway between the site of Selinus and the mouth of the river Halycus (*Platani*), where there still exist sulphureous waters, which are in constant use. (Smyth's *Sicily*, p. 217; Cluver, *Sicil.* p. 223.) We have no account of the existence of a town on the site during the period of the independence of Selinus, though there is little doubt that the thermal waters would always have attracted some population to the spot. Nor even under the Romans did the place attain to anything like the same importance with the northern Thermae; and there is little doubt that Pliny is mistaken in assigning the rank of a colonia to the southern instead of the northern town of the name. [HIMERA.] Strabo mentions the waters (τὰ ὕδατα τὰ Σελινούντια, Strab. vi. p. 275); and they are again noticed in the Itineraries under the name of Aquae Labodes or Labrodes (*Itin. Ant.* p. 89; *Tab. Peut.*)　　　　　　　[E. H. B.]

THERMAICUS SINUS. [THESSALONICA.]

THERMO'DON (Θερμώδων: *Thermeh*), a river of Pontus, celebrated in the story about the Amazons, is described by Pliny (vi. 3) as having its sources in the Amazonian mountains, which are not mentioned by any other ancient writer, but are believed still to retain their ancient name in the form of *Mason Dagh*. (Hamilton, *Researches*, i. p. 283.) Strabo (xii. p. 547) places its many sources near Phanaroea, and says that many streams combine to form the Thermodon. Its course is not very long, but its breadth was nevertheless three plethra, and it was a navigable river (Xen. *Anab.* v. 6. § 9, vi. 2. § 1; Arrian, *Peripl. P.E.* p. 16.) It discharged itself into the Euxine near the town of Themiscyra, at a distance of 400 stadia to the north-east of the mouth of the Iris. This river is very often noticed by ancient writers. See Aeschyl. *Prom.* 274, *Suppl.* 290; Herod. ix. 27; Scylax, p. 33; Strab. i. p. 52, vii. p. 298; Anon. *Peripl. P. E.* p. 10; Ptol. v. 6. § 4; Pomp. Mela. i. 19; Plin. xi. 19, xxxvii. 37; Virg. *Aen.* xi. 659; Ov. *ex Pont.* iv. 19. 51; Propert. iv. 4. 71. and many other passages. [L. S.]

THERMO'PYLAE (Θερμοπύλαι), or simply PYLAE (Πύλαι), that is, the *Hot Gates* or the *Gates*, a celebrated narrow pass, leading from Thessaly into Locris, and the only road by which an enemy can penetrate from northern into southern Greece. It lay between Mount Oeta and an inaccessible morass, forming the edge of the Maliac gulf. In consequence of the change in the course of the rivers, and in the configuration of the coast, this pass is now very different from its condition in ancient times; and it is therefore necessary first to give the statement of Herodotus and other ancient writers respecting the locality, and then to compare it with its present state. In the time of Herodotus the river Spercheius flowed into the sea in an easterly direction at the town of Anticyra, considerably W. of the pass. Twenty stadia E. of the Spercheius was another river, called Dyras, and again, 20 stadia further, a third river, named Melas, 5 stadia from which was the city Trachis. Between the mountains where Trachis stands and the sea the plain is widest. Still further E. was the Asopus, issuing from a rocky gorge (διασφάξ), and E. again is a small stream, named Phoenix, flowing into the Asopus. From the Phoenix to Thermopylae the distance, Herodotus says, is 15 stadia. (Herod. vii. 198—200.) Near the united streams of the Phoenix and the Asopus, Mt. Oeta approached so close to the morass of the gulf as to leave space for only a single carriage. In the immediate vicinity of the pass is the town of Anthela, celebrated for the temples of Amphictyon and of the Amphictyonic Demeter, containing seats for the members of the Amphictyonic council, who held here their autumnal meetings. At Anthela Mount Oeta recedes a little from the sea, leaving a plain a little more than half a mile in breadth, but again contracts near Alpeni, the first town of the Locrians, where the space is again only sufficient for a single carriage. At this pass were some hot springs, which were consecrated to Hercules (Strab. ix. p. 428), and were called by the natives Chytri or the Pans, on account of the cells here prepared for the bathers. Across this pass the Phocians had in ancient times built a wall to defend their country against the attacks of the Thessalians, and had let loose the hot water, so as to render the pass impracticable. (Herod. vii. 200, 176.) It appears from this description that the proper Thermopylae was the narrow pass near the Locrian town of Alpeni; but the name was also applied in general to the whole passage from the mouth of the Asopus to Alpeni. Taking the term in this acceptation, Thermopylae consisted of the two narrow openings, with a plain between them rather more than a mile in length and about half a mile in breadth. That portion of Mt. Oeta, which rises immediately above Thermopylae is called Callidromon by Livy and Strabo, but both writers are mistaken in describing it as the highest part of the range. Livy says that the pass is 60 stadia in breadth. (Liv. xxxvi. 15 ; Strab. ix. p. 428.)

In consequence of the accumulation of soil brought down by the Spercheius and the other rivers, three or four miles of new land have been formed, and the mountain forming the gates of Thermopylae is no longer close to the sea. Moreover, the Spercheius, instead of flowing into the sea in an easterly direction, considerably W. of Thermopylae, now continues its course parallel to the pass and at the distance of a mile from it, falling into the sea lower down, to the E. of the pass. The rivers Dyras, Melas, and Asopus, which formerly reached the sea by different mouths, now discharge their waters into the Spercheius. In addition to this there has been a copious deposit from the warm springs, and a consequent formation of new soil in the pass itself. The present condition of the pass has been described by Colonel Leake with his usual clearness and accuracy. Upon entering the western opening, Leake crossed a stream of warm mineral water, running with great rapidity towards the Spercheius, and leaving a great quantity of red deposit. This is undoubtedly the Phoenix, which probably derived its name from the colour of the sediment. After crossing a second salt-spring, which is the source of the Phoenix, and a stream of cold salt water, Leake entered upon that which Herodotus calls the plain of Anthela, which is a long triangular slope, formed of a hard gravelly soil, and covered with shrubs. There is an easy descent into this plain over the mountains, so that the western opening was of no importance in a military point of view. Upon reaching the eastern pass, situated at the end of the plain

of Anthela, the traveller reaches a white elevated soil formed by the deposit of the salt-springs of the proper Thermopylae. There are two principal sources of these springs, the upper or western being immediately at the foot of the highest part of the cliffs, and the lower or eastern being 200 yards distant. From the lower source the water is conducted in an artificial canal for a distance of 400 yards to a mill. This water emits a strong sulphureous vapour, and, as it issues from the mill, it pours out a great volume of smoke. Beyond the hill are conical heights, and in their neighbourhood are two salt ponds, containing cold water; but as this water is of the same composition as the hot springs, it is probably also hot at its issue. Leake observes that the water of these pools, like that of the principal hot source, is of a dark blue colour, thus illustrating the remark of Pausanias, that the bluest water he ever saw was in one of the baths at Thermopylae. (Paus. iv. 35. § 9.) The springs at this pass are much hotter, and have left a far greater deposit than those at the other end of the plain, at the opening which may be called the false Thermopylae. Issuing from the pass are foundations of a Hellenic wall, doubtless the remains of works by which the pass was at one time fortified; and to the left is a tumulus and the foundations of a circular monument. Upwards of a mile further is a deep ravine, in which the torrents descending from Mt. Callidromon, are collected into one bed, and which afford the easiest and most direct passage to the summit of the mountain. This is probably the mountain path by which the Persians, under Hydarnes, descended in the rear of Leonidas and his companions. This path, as well as the mountain over which it leads, is called Anopaea (ἡ Ἀνόπαια) by Herodotus, who does not use the name of Callidromon. He describes the path as beginning at the gorge of the Asopus, passing over the crest of the mountain, and terminating near Alpeni and the rock called Melampygus, and the seats of the Cercopes, where the road is narrowest. (Herod. vii. 216.) The history of the defence of Thermopylae by Leonidas is too well known to require to be related here. The wall of the Phocians, which Leonidas repaired, was probably built a little eastward of the western salt-spring. When the Spartan king learnt that Hydarnes was descending in his rear, he advanced beyond the wall into the widest part of the pass, resolved to sell his life as dearly as possible. Upon the arrival of Hydarnes, the Greeks retired behind the wall, and took up their position upon a hill in the pass (κολωνὸς ἐν τῇ εἰσόδῳ), where a stone lion was afterwards erected in honour of Leonidas. This hill Leake identifies with the western of the two small heights already described, as nearest to the position of the Phocian wall, and the narrowest part of the pass. The other height is probably the rock Melampygus.

Thermopylae is immortalised by the heroic defence of Leonidas ; but it was also the scene of some important struggles in later times. In B. C. 279 an allied army of the Greeks assembled in the pass to oppose the Gauls under Brennus, who were marching into southern Greece with the view of pillaging the temple of Delphi. The Greeks held their ground for several days against the attacks of the Gauls, till at length the Heracleotae and Aenianes conducted the invaders across Mount Callidromon by the same path which Hydarnes had followed two centuries before. The Greeks, finding their position no longer tenable, embarked on board their ships and retired without further loss. (Paus. x. 19—22.) In B.C. 207, when the Romans were carrying on war in Greece against Philip, king of Macedonia, the Aetolians, who were then in alliance with the Romans, fortified Thermopylae with a ditch and a rampart, but Philip shortly afterwards forced his way through the pass. (Liv. xxviii. 5, 7 ; Polyb. x. 41.) In B.C. 181, Antiochus, who was then at war with the Romans, took up his position at Thermopylae, which he fortified with a double rampart, a ditch, and a wall ; and, in order to prevent the Romans from crossing the mountains and descending upon his rear, he garrisoned with 2000 Aetolians the three summits, named Callidromum, Teichius, and Rhoduntia. The consul Acilius sent some troops against these fortresses and at the same time attacked the army of Antiochus in the pass. While the battle was going on in the pass, the Roman detachment, which had succeeded in taking Callidromum, appeared upon the heights, threatening the king's rear, in consequence of which Antiochus immediately took to flight. (Liv. xxxvi. 15—19.) There are still remains of three Hellenic fortresses upon the heights above Thermopylae, which probably represent the three places mentioned by Livy. Appian (Syr. 17) speaks only of Callidromum and Teichius, but Strabo (ix. p. 428) mentions Rhoduntia also. Procopius relates that the fortifications of Thermopylae were restored by Justinian (de Aed. iv. 2).

(On the topography of Thermopylae, see the excellent account of Leake, Northern Greece, vol. ii. pp. 5, seq., 40, seq. ; there is also a treatise by Gordon, Account of two Visits to the Anopaea or the Highlands above Thermopylae, Athens, 1838, which the writer of this article has not seen.)

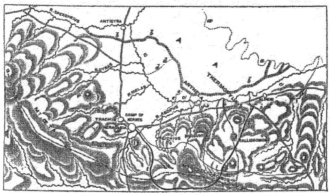

MAP OF THERMOPYLAE AND THE SURROUNDING COUNTRY.

AA. Alluvial deposits.
aa. Present line of coast.
bb. Present course of the Spercheius.
cc. Ancient line of coast.
dd. Present course of the Dyras.
ee. Present course of the Asopus.

ff. Track of the Persians under Hydarnes.
g. Hot springs at the western entrance, or the false Thermopylae.
h. Hot springs at the eastern entrance, or the real Thermopylae.
i. Phocian wall.

THERMUM, THERMUS or THERMA (τὸ Θέρμον, Pol. v. 8; τὰ Θέρμα, Strab. x. p. 463; Pol. v. 7; Θέρμος, Steph. B. s. v.: Eth. Θέρμιος: Vlokho), the chief city of Aetolia during the flourishing period of the Aetolian League, and the place where the meetings of the league were usually held and an annual festival celebrated. It possessed a celebrated temple of Apollo, in connection with which the festival was probably celebrated. It was situated in the very heart of Aetolia, N. of the lake Trichonis, and on a height of Mt. Panaetolium (Viena). It was considered inaccessible to an army, and from the strength of its situation was regarded as a place of refuge, and, as it were, the Acropolis of all Aetolia. The road to it ran from Metapa, on the lake Trichonis, through the village of Pamphia. The city was distant 60 stadia from Metapa, and 30 from Pamphia ; and from the latter place the road was very steep and dangerous, running along a narrow crest with precipices on each side. It was, however, surprised by Philip V., king of Macedonia, in his invasion of Aetolia in B.C. 218. The Aetolians, who had never imagined that Philip would have penetrated so far into their country, had deposited here all their treasures, the whole of which now fell into the hands of the king, together with a vast quantity of arms and armour. He carried off the most valuable part of the spoil, and burnt all the rest, among which were more than 15,000 suits of armour. Not content with this, he set fire to the sacred buildings, to retaliate for the destruction of Dium and Dodona. He also defaced all the works of art, and threw down all the statues, which were not less than 2000 in number, only sparing those of the Gods. (Pol. v. 6—9, 13.) A few years afterwards, when the Aetolians had sided with the Romans, Philip again surprised Thermus (about B. C. 206), when he destroyed everything which had escaped his ravages in his first attack. (Pol. xi. 4.) We have no further details of the history of Thermum. Polybius alludes, in one or two other passages (xviii. 31, xxviii. 4), to the meetings of the league held there. In the former of these passages Livy (xxxiii. 35) has misunderstood the words τὴν τῶν Θερμικῶν σύνυδον to mean the assembly held at Thermopylae.

Polybius's account of Philip's first invasion of Aetolia, which resulted in the capture of Thermum, supplies us with the chief information respecting the towns in the central plain of Aetolia. Philip set out from Limnaea, on the south-eastern corner of the Ambraciot gulf, crossed the Achelous between Stratus and Conope, and marched with all speed towards Thermum, leaving on his left Stratus, Agrinium, and Thestienses (Θεστιεῖς), and on his right Conope, Lysimachia, Trichonium, and Phoeteum. He thus arrived at Metapa, on the lake Trichonis, and from thence marched to Thermus, by that road already mentioned, passing by Pamphia in his way. He returned by the same road as far as Metapa, but from the latter place he marched in one day to a place called Acrae, where he encamped, and on the next day to Conope. After remaining a day at Conope, he marched up the Achelous, and crossed it near Stratus.

The remains of the walls of Thermum show that the city was about 2½ miles in circumference. It was in the form of a triangle on the slope of a pyramidal hill, bordered on either side by a torrent flowing in a deep ravine. The only remains of a public edifice within the walls consist of a square, pyramidal, shapeless mass of stones. (Leake, *Northern Greece*, vol. i. p. 126, &c.)

THERVINGI. [GOTHI, p. 1009.]

THE'SPIAE (Θεσπιαί, also Θέσπεια or Θέσπια, Hom. *Il.* ii. 498; Herod. viii. 50; Paus. ix. 26. § 6: *Eth.* Θεσπιεύς, Thespiensis, fem. Θεσπιάς, Θεσπίς: *Adj.* Θεσπιακός, Thespius, Thespiacus), an ancient city of Boeotia, situated at the foot of Mt. Helicon, looking towards the south and the Crissaean gulf, where stood its port-town Creusa or Creusis. (Strab. ix. p. 409; Paus. ix. 26. § 6; Steph. B. *s. v.*) Thespiae was said to have derived its name from Thespia, a daughter of Asopus, or from Thespius, a son of Erechtheus, who migrated from Athens. (Paus. *l. c.*; Diod. iv. 29.) The city is mentioned in the catalogue of Homer. (*Il.* ii. 498.) Thespiae, like Plataea, was one of the Boeotian cities inimical to Thebes, which circumstance affected its whole history. Thus Thespiae and Plataea were the only two Boeotian cities that refused to give earth and water to the heralds of Xerxes. (Herod. vii. 132.) Seven hundred Thespians joined Leonidas at Thermopylae; and they remained to perish with the 300 Spartans, when the other Greeks retired. (Herod. vii. 202, 222.) Their city was burnt by Xerxes, when he overran Boeotia, and the inhabitants withdrew to Peloponnesus (Herod. viii. 50.) The survivors, to the number of 1800, fought at the battle of Plataea in the following year, but they were reduced to such distress that they had no heavy armour. (Herod. ix. 30.) After the expulsion of the Persians from Greece, Thespiae was rebuilt, and the inhabitants recruited their numbers by the admission of strangers as citizens. (Herod. viii. 75.) At the battle of Delium (B. C. 424) the Thespians fought on the left wing against the Athenians, and were almost all slain at their post. (Thuc. iv. 93, seq.) In the following year (B. C. 423), the Thebans destroyed the walls of Thespiae, on the charge of *Atticism*, the Thespians being unable to offer any resistance in consequence of the heavy loss they had sustained while fighting upon the side of the Thebans. (Thuc. iv. 133.) In B. C. 414 the democratical party at Thespiae attempted

to overthrow the existing government; but the latter receiving assistance from Thebes, many of the conspirators withdrew to Athens. (Thuc. vi. 95.) In B. C. 372 the walls of Thespiae were again destroyed by the Thebans. According to Diodorus (xv. 46) and Xenophon (*Hell.* vi. 3. § 1) Thespiae was at this time destroyed by the Thebans, and the inhabitants driven out of Boeotia; but this happened after the battle of Leuctra, and Mr. Grote (*Hist. of Greece*, vol. x. p. 219) justly infers from a passage in Isocrates that the fortifications of the city were alone demolished at this period. Pausanias expressly states that a contingent of Thespians was present in the Theban army at the time of the battle of Leuctra, and availed themselves of the permission of Epaminondas to retire before the battle. (Paus. ix. 13. § 8, ix. 14. § 1.) Shortly afterwards the Thespians were expelled from Boeotia by the Thebans. (Paus. ix. 14. § 2.) Thespiae was afterwards rebuilt, and is mentioned in the Roman wars in Greece. (Polyb. xxvii. 1; Liv. xlii. 43.) In the time of Strabo, Thespiae and Tanagra were the only places in Boeotia that deserved the name of cities. (Strab. ix. p. 410.) Pliny calls Thespiae a free town (" liberum oppidum," iv. 7. s. 12). It is also mentioned by Ptolemy (iii. 15. § 20) and in the Antonine Itinerary (p. 326. ed. Wess.), and it was still in existence in the sixth century (Hierocl. p. 645, ed. Wess.).

Eros or Love was the deity chiefly worshipped at Thespiae; and the earliest representation of the god in the form of a rude stone still existed in the city in the time of Pausanias (ix. 27. § 1). The courtesan Phryne, who was born at Thespiae, presented to her native city the celebrated statue of Love by Praxiteles, which added greatly to the prosperity of the place in consequence of the great numbers of strangers who visited the city for the purpose of seeing it. (Dicaearch. § 25, ed. Müller; Cic. *Verr.* iv. 2; Strab. ix. p. 410, who erroneously calls the courtesan Glycera; Paus. ix. 27. § 3.) The story of the manner in which Phryne became possessed of this statue, and its subsequent history, are related in the life of PRAXITELES. [*Dict. of Biogr.* Vol. III. pp. 520, 521.] In the time of Pausanias there was only an imitation of it at Thespiae by Menodorus. Among the other works of art in this city Pausanias noticed a statue of Eros by Lysippus, statues of Aphrodite and Phryne by Praxiteles; the agora, containing a statue of Hesiod; the theatre, a temple of Aphrodite Melaena, a temple of the Muses, containing their figures in stone of small size, and an ancient temple of Hercules. (Paus. ix. 27.) Next to Eros, the Muses were specially honoured at Thespiae; and the festivals of the Ἐρωτίδια and Μούσεια celebrated by the Thespians on Mt. Helicon, at the end of every four years, are mentioned by several ancient writers. (Paus. ix. 31. § 3; Plut. *Amat.* 1; Athen. xiii. p. 561; K. F. Hermann, *Lehrbuch der gottesd. Alterth.* § 63, n. 4.) Hence the Muses are frequently called Thespiades by the Latin writers. (Varr. *L. L.* vii. 2; Cic. *Verr.* ii. 4, Ov. *Met.* v. 310; Plin. xxxvi. 5. s. 4, § 39, ed. Sillig.)

The remains of Thespiae are situated at a place called *Lefka* from a deserted village of that name near the village of *Erimókastro* or *Rimókastro*. Unlike most other Greek cities, it stands in a plain surrounded by hills on either side, and its founders appear to have chosen the site in consequence of its abundant supply of water, the sources of the river *Kanavdri* rising here. Leake noticed the foundations of an oblong or oval enclosure, built of very solid masonry of a regular kind, about half a mile in circumference; but he observes that all the adjacent ground to the SE. is covered, like the interior of the fortress, with ancient foundations, squared stones, and other remains, proving that if the enclosure was the only fortified part of the city, many of the public and private edifices stood without the walls. The site of some of the ancient temples is probably marked by the churches, which contain fragments of architraves, columns, and other ancient remains (Leake, *Northern Greece*, vol. ii. p. 479, seq.; Dodwell, vol. i. p. 253.)

COIN OF THESPIAE.

THESPRO'TI, THESPRO'TIA. [EPEIRUS.]
THESSA'LIA (Θεσσαλία or Θετταλία : *Eth.* Θεσσαλός or Θετταλός, Thessalus, *fem.* Θεσσαλίς, Θετταλίς, Thessalis : *Adj.* Θεσσαλικός, Θετταλικός, Thessalicus, Thessalius), the largest political division of Greece, was in its widest extent the whole country lying N. of Thermopylae as far as the Cambunian mountains, and bounded upon the W. by the range of Pindus. But the name of Thessaly was more specifically applied to the great plain, by far the widest and largest in all Greece, enclosed by the four great mountain barriers of Pindus, Othrys, Ossa and Pelion. and the Cambunian mountains. From Mount Pindus,—the Apennines or back-bone of Greece, — which separates Thessaly from Epeirus, two large arms branch off towards the eastern sea, running parallel to one another at the distance of 60 miles. The northern, called the Cambunian mountains, forms the boundary between Thessaly and Macedonia, and terminates in the summit of Olympus, which is the highest mountain in all Greece [OLYMPUS]. The southern arm, named Othrys, separates the plain of Thessaly from Malis, and reaches the sea between the Malian and Pagasaean gulfs [OTHRYS]. The fourth barrier is the range of mountains, first called Ossa and afterwards Pelion, which run along the coast of Thessaly upon the E., nearly parallel to the range of Pindus [OSSA; PELION]. The plain of Thessaly, which is thus enclosed by natural ramparts, is broken only at the NE. corner by the celebrated vale of Tempe, which separates Ossa from Olympus, and is the only way of entering Greece from the N., except by a pass across the Cambunian mountains. This plain, which is drained by the river Peneius and its affluents, is said to have been originally a vast lake, the waters of which were afterwards carried off through the vale of Tempe by some sudden convulsion, which rent the rocks of the valley asunder. (Herod. vii. 129.) [TEMPE.] The lakes of Nessonis and Boebeis, which are connected by a channel, were supposed by Strabo (ix. p. 430) to have been the remains of this vast lake. In addition to this plain there are two other districts included under the general name of Thessaly, of which one is the long and

narrow slip of rocky coast, called Magnesia, extending from the vale of Tempe to the gulf of Pagasae, and lying between Mounts Ossa and Pelion and the sea; while the other, known under the name of Malis, is quite distinct in its physical features from the rest of Thessaly, being a long narrow valley between Mounts Othrys and Oeta, through which the river Spercheius flows into the Maliac gulf.

The plain of Thessaly properly consists of two plains, which received in antiquity the name of Upper and Lower Thessaly; the Upper, as in similar cases, meaning the country near Mount Pindus most distant from the sea, and the Lower the country near the Thermaic gulf. (Strab. ix. pp. 430, 437.) These two plains are separated by a range of hills between the lakes Nessonis and Boebeis on the one hand, and the river Enipeus on the other. Lower Thessaly, which constituted the ancient division Pelasgiotis, extends from Mounts Titarus and Ossa on the N. to Mount Othrys and the shores of the Pagasaean gulf on the S. Its chief town was Larissa. Upper Thessaly, which corresponded to the ancient divisions Thessaliotis and Histiaeotis, of which the chief city was Pharsalus, stretches from Aeginium in the N. to Thaumaci in the S., a distance of at least 50 miles in a straight line. The road from Thermopylae into Upper Thessaly entered the plain at Thaumaci, which was situated at the pass called Coela, where the traveller came in sight of a plain resembling a vast sea. (Liv. xxxii. 4.) [THAUMACI.]

The river Peneius, now called the *Salambria* or *Salambria* (Σαλαμβρίας, Σαλαμπρίας), rises at the NW. extremity of Thessaly, and is composed of streams collected in the valleys of Mount Pindus and the offshoots of the Cambunian mountains. At first it flows through a contracted valley till it reaches the perpendicular rocks, named the *Meteóra*, upon the summits of which several monasteries are perched. Below this spot, and near the town of Aeginium or *Stagús*, the valley opens out into the vast plain of Upper Thessaly, and the river flows in a general southerly direction. At Tricca, or *Trikkala*, the Peneius makes a bend to the E., and shortly afterwards reaches the lowest point in the plain of Upper Thessaly, where it receives within a very short space many of its tributaries. Next it passes through a valley formed by a range of hills, of which those upon the right divide the plains of Upper and Lower Thessaly. It then emerges into the plain a few miles westward of Larissa; after passing which city it makes a sudden bend to the N., and flows through the vale of Tempe to the sea. Although the Peneius drains the greater part of Thessaly, and receives many tributaries, it is in the greater part of its course a shallow and sluggish river, except after the melting of the snows, when it sometimes floods the surrounding plain. Hence on either side of the river there is frequently a wide gravelly uncultivable space, described by Strabo as ποταμόκλυστος (ix. p. 430; Leake, *Northern Greece*, vol. i. p. 420). When the river is swollen in the spring, a channel near Larissa conducts the superfluous waters into the *Karaǧaï'r* or *Mavpoλίμνη*, the ancient Nessonis; and when this basin is filled, another channel conveys the waters into the lake of *Karla*, the ancient Boebeis. (Leake, iv. p. 403.) In the lower part of its course, after leaving Larissa, the Peneius flows with more rapidity, and is full of small vortices, which may have suggested to Homer the epithet ἀργυροδίνης (*Il.* ii. 753); though, as Leake has remarked, the poet carries his flattery to an extreme in comparing to silver the white hue of its turbid waters, derived entirely from the earth suspended in them. (*Northern Greece*, vol. iv. p. 291.)

The principal rivers of Thessaly, according to Herodotus (vii. 129), are the Peneius, Apidanus, Onochonus, Enipeus and Pamisus. The four latter rivers all flow from the S. Of these the most important is the Enipeus, now called the *Fersaliti*, which flows through the plain of Pharsalus, and falls into the Peneius near Piresiae in the lowest part of the plain. The Apidanus, now called *Vrysiá*, into which the Cuarius (*Sofadhítiko*) falls, is a tributary of the Enipeus. [ENIPEUS.] The Pamisus, now called the *Blúiri* or *Piliúri*, also joins the Peneius a little to the W. of the Enipeus. The Onochonus, which is probably the same as the Onchestus, flows into the lake Boebeis and not into the Peneius. [For details, see Vol. II. p. 483, a.] The chief tributary of the Peneius on the N. is the Titaresius, now called *Elassonítiko* or *Xeróghi*, which rises in Mt. Titarus, a part of the Cambunian range, and joins the main stream between Larissa and the vale of Tempe. Homer relates (*Il.* ii. 753, seq.) that the waters of the Titaresius did not mingle with those of the Peneius, but floated upon the surface of the latter like oil upon water, whence it was regarded as a branch of the infernal river Styx. (Comp. Lucan, vi. 375.) Leake calls attention to the fact that Strabo (ix. p. 441), probably misled by the epithet (ἀργυροδίνης) applied by the poet to the Peneius, has reversed the true interpretation of the poet's comparison of the Peneius and the Titaresius, supposing that the Peneius was the pellucid river, whereas the apparent reluctance of the Titaresius to mingle with the Peneius arises from the former being clear and the latter muddy. (*Northern Greece*, iii. p. 396, iv. p. 296.) The Titaresius was also called Eurotas (Strab. vii. p. 329) and Horcus or Orcus (Plin. iv. 8. s. 15).

The plain of Thessaly is the most fertile in all Greece. It produced in antiquity a large quantity of corn and cattle, which supported a numerous population in the towns, and especially a rich and proud aristocracy, who were at frequent feuds with one another and much given to luxury and the pleasures of the table (ἐκεῖ γὰρ δὴ πλείστη ἀταξία καὶ ἀκολασία, Plat. *Crit.* 15; Athen. xii. p. 564; Theopomp. *ap. Athen.* vi. p. 260; Dem. *Olynth.* p. 16). The Thessalian horses were the finest in Greece, and their cavalry was at all times efficient; but we rarely read of their infantry. The nobles, such as the Aleuadae of Larissa and the Scopadae of Crannon, supplied the poorer citizens with horses; but there was no class of free equal citizens, from which the hoplites were drawn in other Grecian states. (See Grote, *Hist. of Greece*, vol. ii. p. 367.) Hence the political power was generally either in the hands of these nobles or of a single man who established himself as despot. The numerous flocks and herds of the Scopadae at Crannon are alluded to by Theocritus (*Id.* xvi. 36), and the wealth of the Thessalian nobles is frequently mentioned by the ancient writers.

Thessaly is said to have been originally known by the names of Pyrrha, Aemonia, and Aeolis. (Rhian. *ap. Schol. Rhod.* iii. 1089; Steph. B. *s. v.* Αἰμονία; Herod. vii. 176.) The two former appellations belong to mythology, but the latter refers to the time when the country was inhabited by the Aeolian

Pelasgi, who were afterwards expelled from the country by the Thessalians. This people are said to have been immigrants, who came from Thesprotia in Epeirus, and conquered the plain of the Peneius. (Herod. vii. 176, comp. i. 57; Strab. ix. p. 444.) The Boeotians are said to have originally dwelt at Arne, in the country afterwards called Thessaly, and to have been expelled by the Thessalian invaders 60 years after the Trojan War. (Thuc. i. 12.) The expulsion of the Boeotians by the Thessalians seems to have been conceived as an immediate consequence of the immigration of the Thessalian invaders; but, however this may be, the name of Thessaly is unknown in Homer, who only speaks of the several principalities of which the country was composed. In the Homeric catalogue Pheidippus and Antiphus, who led the Greeks from Carpathus, Cos, and the neighbouring islands, are called the sons of Thessalus, the son of Hercules (Hom. *Il.* ii. 676); and, in order to connect this name with the Thessalians of Thesprotia, it was reported that these two chiefs had, upon their return from Troy, been driven by a storm upon the coast of Epeirus, and that Thessalus, the grandson of Pheidippus, led the Thessalians across Mount Pindus and imposed his name upon the country. (Vell. Pat. i. 2, 3; Steph. B. *s. v.* Δώρων; Polyaen. viii. 44.) There are many circumstances in the historical period which make it probable that the Thessalians were a body of immigrant conquerors; though, if they came from Thesprotia, they must have gradually dropt their original language, and learnt that of the conquered people, as the Thessalian was a variety of the Aeolic dialect. There was in Thessaly a triple division of the population analogous to that in Laconia. First, there were the Thessalians proper, the rich landed proprietors of the plain. Secondly, there were the descendants of the original inhabitants of the country, who were not expelled by the Thessalian conquerors, and who were more or less dependent upon them, corresponding to the Lacedaemonian Perioeci, but, unlike the latter, retaining their original names and their seats in the Amphictyonic council. These were the PERRHAEBI, who occupied the mountainous district between Mount Olympus and the lower course of the Peneius; the MAGNETES, who dwelt along the eastern coast between Mounts Pelion and Ossa and the sea; the ACHAEANS, who inhabited the district called Phthiotis, which extended S. of the Upper Thessalian plain, from Mount Pindus on the W. to the gulf of Pagasae on the S.; the DOLOPES, who occupied the mountainous regions of Pindus, S. of Phthiotis; and the MALIANS, who dwelt between Phthiotis and Thermopylae. The third class of the Thessalian population were the Penestae, serfs or dependent cultivators, corresponding to the Helots of Laconia, although their condition seems upon the whole to have been superior. They tilled the estates of the great nobles, paying them a certain proportion of the produce, and followed their masters to war upon horseback. They could not, however, be sold out of the country, and they possessed the means of acquiring property, as many of them were said to have been richer than their masters. (Archemach. *ap. Athen.* vi. p. 264; Plat. *Leg.* vi. p. 777; Aristot. *Pol.* ii. 6. § 3, vii. 9. § 9; Dionys. ii. 84.) They were probably the descendants of the original inhabitants of the country, reduced to slavery by the conquering Thesprotians; but when Theopompus states that they were the descendants of the conquered Perrhaebians and Magnetes (ap. *Athen.* vi. p. 265), this can only be true of a part of these tribes, as we know that the Penestae were entirely distinct from the subject Perrhaebians, Magnetes, and Achaeans. (Aristot. *Polit.* ii. 6. § 3.) The Penestae, like the Laconian Helots, frequently rose in revolt against their masters.

In the Homeric poems the names of Perrhaebi, Magnetes, Achaeans, and Dolopes occur; and Achaea Phthiotis was the residence of the great hero Achilles. This district was the seat of Hellen, the founder of the Hellenic race, and contained the original Hellas, from which the Hellenes gradually spread over the rest of Greece. ' (Hom. *Il.* ii. 683; Thuc. i. 3; Strab. ix. p. 431; Dicaearch. p. 21, ed. Hudson; Steph. B. *s. v.* 'Ελλάs). The Achaeans of Phthiotis may fairly be regarded as the same race as the Achaeans of Peloponnesus.

Thessaly Proper was divided at an early period into four districts or tetrarchies, named Thessaliotis, Pelasgiotis, Histiaeotis and Phthiotis. When this division was introduced is unknown. It was older than Hecataeus (Steph. B. *s. v.* Κράννων), and was ascribed to Aleuas, the founder of the family of the Aleuadae. (Hellenic. *Fragm.* 28, ed. Didot; Harpocrat. *s. v.* Τετραρχία; Strab. ix. p. 430.) This quadruple division continued to the latest times, and seems to have been instituted for political purposes; but respecting the internal government of each we have no precise information. The four districts were nominally united under a chief magistrate, called Tagus; but he seems to have been only appointed in war, and his commands were frequently disobeyed by the Thessalian cities. "When Thessaly is under a Tagus," said Jason, despot of Pherae, "she can send into the field an army of 6000 cavalry and 10,000 hoplites." (Xen. *Hell.* vi. 1. § 8.) But Thessaly was rarely united. The different cities, upon which the smaller towns were dependent, not only administered their own affairs independent of one another, but the three most important, Larissa, Pharsalus and Pherae, were frequently at feud with one another, and at the same time torn with intestine faction. Hence they were able to offer little resistance to invaders, and never occupied that position in Grecian history to which their population and wealth would seem to have entitled them. (Respecting the Thessalians in general, see Mr. Grote's excellent remarks, *Hist. of Greece,* vol. ii. p. 363, seq.)

The history of Thessaly may be briefly dismissed, as the most important events are related under the separate cities. Before the Persian invasion, the Thessalians had extended their power as far as Thermopylae, and threatened to overrun Phocis and the country of the Locrians. The Phocians built a wall across the pass of Thermopylae to keep off the Thessalians; and though active hostilities seem to have ceased before the Persian invasion, as the wall was at that time in ruins, the two nations continued to cherish bitter animosity towards one another. (Herod. vii. 176.) When Xerxes invaded Greece, the Thessalians were at first opposed to the Persians. It is true that the powerful family of the Aleuadae, whom Herodotus calls (vii. 6) kings of Thessaly, had urged Xerxes to invade Greece, and had promised the early submission of their countrymen; but it is evident that their party was in the minority, and it is probable that they were themselves in exile, like the Athenian Peisistratidae. The majority of the Thessalians sent envoys to the confederate Greeks at the Isthmus, urging them to send a force to the pass of Tempe, and promising them active co-operation in the defence. Their request was complied with, and a body of 10,000 heavy-armed infantry was despatched to Thessaly; but the Grecian commanders, upon arriving at Tempe, found that there was another pass across Mount Olympus, and believing it impossible to make any effectual resistance north of Thermopylae, retreated to their ships and abandoned Thessaly. (Herod. vii. 172, seq.) The Thessalians, thus deserted, hastened to make their submission to Xerxes; and under the influence of the Aleuadae, who now regained the ascendency in Thessaly, they rendered zealous and effectual assistance to the Persians. After the death of Leonidas and his heroic companions at Thermopylae, the Thessalians gratified their enmity against the Phocians by directing the march of the Persians against the Phocian towns and laying their country waste with fire and sword.

From the Persian to the Peloponnesian wars the Thessalians are rarely mentioned. After the battle of Oenophyta (B. C. 456) had given the Athenians the ascendency in Boeotia, Locris, and Phocis, they endeavoured to extend their power over Thessaly. With this view they marched into Thessaly under the command of Myronides in B. C. 454, for the purpose of restoring Orestes, one of the exiled nobles or princes of Pharsalus, whom Thucydides calls son of the king of the Thessalians. The progress of Myronides was checked by the powerful Thessalian cavalry; and though he advanced as far as Pharsalus, he was unable to accomplish anything against the city, and was compelled to retreat. (Thuc. i. 111; Diodor. xi. 85.) In the Peloponnesian War the Thessalians took no part; but the mass of the population was friendly to the Athenians, though the oligarchical governments favoured the Spartans. With the assistance of the latter, combined with his own rapidity and address, Brasidas contrived to march through Thessaly in B. C. 424, on his way to attack the Athenian dependencies in Macedonia (Thuc. iv. 78); but when the Lacedaemonians wished to send reinforcements to Brasidas in the following year, the Thessalians positively refused them a passage through their country. (Thuc. iv. 132.) In B. C. 395 the Thessalians joined the Boeotians and their allies in the league against Sparta; and when Agesilaus marched through their country in the following year, having been recalled by the Spartan government from Asia, they endeavoured to intercept him on his return; but their cavalry was defeated by the skilful manoeuvres of Agesilaus. (Xen. *Hell.* vi. 3. § 3, seq.)

About this time or a little earlier an important change took place in the political condition and relative importance of the Thessalian cities. Almost down to the end of the Peloponnesian War the powerful families of the Aleuadae at Larissa, of the Scopadae at Crannon, and of the Creondae at Pharsalus, possessed the chief power in Thessaly. But shortly before the close of this war Pherae rose into importance under the administration of Lycophron, and aspired to the supremacy of Thessaly. Lycophron overthrew the government of the nobles at Pherae, and made himself tyrant of the city. In prosecution of his ambitious schemes he attacked Larissa; and in B. C. 404 he gained a great victory over the Larissaeans and the other Thessalians who were opposed to him. (Xen. *Hell.* ii. 3. § 4.) In B. C. 395 Lycophron was still engaged in a contest with Larissa, which was then under the government of Medius, probably the head of the Aleuadae. Lycophron was supported by Sparta; and Medius accordingly applied for succour to the confederacy of Greek states which had been lately formed to resist the Lacedaemonian power. With their assistance Medius took Pharsalus, which was then occupied by a Lacedaemonian garrison, and is said to have sold all its inhabitants as slaves. (Diod. xiv. 82.) The return of Agesilaus, and his victory over the Thessalians, probably deprived Medius and his party of their power, and Larissa no longer appears as the rival of Pherae for the supremacy of Thessaly. Pharsalus soon recovered from the blow which it had received from Medius, and became, next to Pherae, the most important city in Thessaly. The inhabitants of Pharsalus agreed to entrust the supreme power to Polydamas, one of their own citizens, in whose integrity and abilities all parties placed the greatest confidence. The acropolis and the whole management of the finances were placed in his hands, and he discharged his trust to the satisfaction of all parties. (Xen. Hell. vi. 1. §§ 2, 3.)

Meantime the supreme power at Pherae had passed into the hands of Jason, a man of great energy and ability, and probably the son of Lycophron, though this is not expressly stated. He inherited the ambitious views of Lycophron, and meditated nothing less than extending his dominion over the whole of Greece, for which his central situation seemed to offer many facilities. He cherished even still more extensive projects of aggrandisement, and, once master of Greece, he looked forward to conquer the Persian empire, which the retreat of the Ten Thousand Greeks and the campaigns of Agesilaus in Asia seemed to point out as an easy enterprise. But the first step was his election as Tagus of Thessaly, and the submission of all the Thessalian cities to his authority. For this purpose it was necessary to obtain the acquiescence of Pharsalus, and although he might have gained his object by force, he preferred to effect it by negotiation, and accordingly frankly disclosed his schemes to Polydamas, and offered him the second place in Thessaly, if he would support his views. Polydamas asked the advice of the Spartans, and finding that he could receive from them no help, he acceded to the proposals of Jason, and induced the Pharsalians to espouse his cause. Soon after this, probably in B. C. 374, Jason was elected Tagus of Thessaly, and proceeded to settle the contingent of cavalry and heavy-armed troops which the Pharsalian cities were to furnish. He now possessed a force of 8000 cavalry and more than 20,000 infantry; and Alcetas I., king of Epeirus, and Amyntas II., king of Macedonia were his allies. (Xen. Hell. vi. 1. §§ 2—19; Diod. xv. 60.) He could in effect command a greater force than any other state in Greece; and from the disunion and exhaustion of the other Grecian states, it seemed not improbable that he might be able to carry his ambitious projects into effect. He had already formed an alliance with Thebes, and after the battle of Leuctra (B. C. 371) he was invited by the Thebans to join them in attacking the Lacedaemonian camp. But Jason's policy was to prevent any other power from obtaining the preponderance in Greece, and accordingly upon his arrival at Leuctra he advised the Thebans not to drive the Lacedaemonians to despair, and obtained a truce for the latter, which enabled them to secure their safety by a retreat. (Xen. Hell. vi. 4. § 20,

seq.) In the following year he announced his intention of marching to Delphi at the head of a body of Thessalian troops and presiding at the Pythian festival. Great alarm was felt throughout Greece; but before the time came, he was assassinated by seven youths as he sat in public to give audience to all comers. His death was felt as a relief by Greece; and the honours paid in many of the Grecian cities to his assassins prove the general fear which his ambitious schemes had excited. (Xen. Hell. vi. 4. §§ 28—32.)

Jason had so firmly established his power that he was succeeded in the post of Tagus of Thessaly by his two brothers Polyphron and Polydorus; but they did not possess his abilities or energy, and Thessaly again sank into political insignificance. Polyphron was assassinated by his brother Polydorus, who became sole Tagus. Polydorus exercised his authority with great cruelty; he put to death Polydamas of Pharsalus, and killed or drove into exile many other distinguished persons of this city and of Larissa. (Xen. Hell. vi. 4. §§ 33, 34.) At the end of a year he was also assassinated by Alexander, who was either his brother (Diod. xv. 61) or his nephew (Plut. Pelopid. 29.) Alexander surpassed even Polyphron in cruelty, and was guilty of gross enormities. The Aleuadae and other noble families, who were chiefly exposed to his vengeance, applied in their distress to Alexander, the youthful king of Macedonia, who had recently succeeded his father Amyntas. Alexander invaded Thessaly, defeated the tyrant, and took possession of Larissa and Crannon, which he garrisoned with his troops. (Diodor. xv. 61.) It would seem, however, that the necessities of his own kingdom compelled him shortly afterwards to withdraw his troops from Thessaly; since we find the Thessalian cities opposed to the tyrant inviting the aid of the Thebans. Accordingly, about B. C. 369, Pelopidas invaded Thessaly, and took Larissa and several other cities under his protection, apparently with the sanction of Alexander of Macedonia, with whom he formed an alliance. (Diodor. xv. 67.) In the following year (B.C. 368) Pelopidas again marched into Thessaly at the head of a Theban force, to protect Larissa and the other cities against the projects of Alexander of Pherae, who had solicited aid from Athens. Alexander was compelled to sue for peace; and Pelopidas, after arranging the affairs of Thessaly, marched into Macedonia, where the young king had been lately assassinated. Ptolemy, the regent of the kingdom, was also compelled to enter into alliance with Pelopidas, and to give him several hostages, among whom was the youthful Philip, afterwards king of Macedonia. (Diod. xv. 71; Plut. Pelop, c. 26.) By these means the influence of Thebes was extended over the greater part of Thessaly. Two years afterwards (B.C. 366) the Thebans obtained from the Persian court a rescript acknowledging their claims to the headship of Greece; and in the same year Pelopidas, accompanied by Ismenias, visited Thessaly with the view of obtaining the recognition of their claim from Alexander of Pherae and the other Thessalian cities. Alexander met them at Pharsalus, but when he found that they were not supported by any armed force, he seized them as prisoners and carried them off to Pherae. The first attempt of the Thebans to rescue their countryman proved unsuccessful; and the army which they sent into Thessaly was only saved from destruction by the genius of Epaminondas, who was then serving as a private, and was compelled by the soldiers to take the command. So greatly was Alexander strengthened in his power by this failure that all the Thessalian cities submitted to him, and the influence of Thebes in Thessaly was for a time destroyed. Subsequently a second expedition was sent into Thessaly under the command of Epaminondas, who compelled the tyrant to release Pelopidas and Ismenias, but without restoring Thebes to the commanding position which she had formerly held in Thessaly. (Diod. xv. 71—75; Plut. Pelop. 27—29; Cornel. Nep. Pelop. 5; Paus. ix. 15. § 1.) The continued oppressions of Alexander of Pherae became so intolerable that the Thessalian cities once more applied to Thebes for assistance. Accordingly in B. C. 364 Pelopidas was again sent into Thessaly at the head of a Theban army. In the first engagement Pelopidas was slain, but Alexander was defeated. (Diod. xv. 80, 81; Plut. Pelop. 31, 32; Cornel. Nep. Pelop. 5; respecting the different expeditions of Pelopidas into Thessaly, as to which there are discrepancies in the accounts, see Grote, Hist. of Greece, vol. x. p. 361, note, p. 391, note.) The death of Pelopidas, however, proved almost fatal to Alexander. Burning to revenge his loss, the Thebans sent a powerful army into Thessaly, which compelled him to renounce his supremacy in Thessaly, to confine himself to Pherae, and to submit to all the demands of Thebes. (Plut. Pelop. 35.)

After the death of Epaminondas at the battle of Mantineia (B. C. 362) the supremacy of Thebes in Thessaly was weakened, and Alexander of Pherae recovered much of his power, which he continued to exercise with his accustomed cruelty and ferocity till his assassination in B. C. 359 by his wife Thebe and her brothers. One of these brothers, Tisiphonus, succeeded to the supreme power, under the direction of Thebe; but his reign lasted only a short time, and he was followed in the government by Lycophron, another brother. (Xen. Hell. vi. 4. § 37; Diod. xvi. 14; Plut. Pelop. 35.) Meanwhile Philip, who had ascended the throne of Macedon in B. C. 369, had been steadily extending his dominions and his influence; and the Aleuadae of Larissa now had recourse to him in preference to Thebes. Accordingly Philip marched into Thessaly in B. C. 353. Lycophron, unable to resist him, invoked the aid of Onomarchus and the Phocians; and Philip, after a severe struggle was driven out of Thessaly. (Diodor. xvi. 35.) In the following year Philip returned to Thessaly, and gained a signal victory over Onomarchus and Lycophron. Onomarchus was slain in the battle; and when Philip followed up his victory by laying siege to Pherae, Lycophron surrendered the city to him, upon being allowed to retire to Phocis with his mercenaries. (Diodor. xvi. 37.) Thus ended the powerful dynasty of the tyrants of Pherae. Philip established a popular government at Pherae (Diod. xvi. 38), and gave nominal independence to the Thessalian cities. But at the same time he garrisoned Magnesia and the port of Pagasae with his troops, and kept steadily in view the subjugation of the whole country. An attempt made in B. C. 344 to restore the dynasty of the tyrants at Pherae gave him an opportunity of carrying his designs into effect. Not only did he garrison Pherae with his own troops, but he revived the ancient division of the country into four tetrarchies or tetradarchies, and placed at the head of each some of the chiefs of the Aleuadae, who were entirely devoted to his interests. The result of this arrangement was the entire subjection of Thessaly to Philip,

who drew from the country a considerable addition to his revenues and to his military resources. (Harpocrat. s. v. Τετραρχία; Dem. Olynth. i. § 23; Strab. ix. p. 440; Thirlwall, Hist. of Greece, vol. vi. pp. 12—14.) Upon the death of Philip the Thessalians were the first Grecian people who promised to support Alexander in obtaining the supremacy of Greece. (Diod. xvii. 4.) After the death of Alexander the Thessalians took an active part with the other Grecian states in attempting to throw off the Macedonian yoke, but by the victory of Antipater they were again united to the Macedonian monarchy, to which they remained subject till the defeat of Philip by the Romans at the battle of Cynoscephalae, B. C. 197. The Roman senate then declared Thessaly free (Liv. xxxiii. 32); but from this time it was virtually under the sovereignty of Rome. The government was vested in the hands of the more wealthy persons, who formed a kind of senate, which was accustomed to meet at Larissa. (Liv. xxxiv. 52, xxxvi. 8, xlii. 38.)

When Macedonia was reduced to the form of a Roman province, Thessaly was incorporated with it. (Strab. xvii. p. 840.) Under Alexander Severus it formed a separate province governed by a procurator (Gruter, Inscr p. 474. 4); and in the later constitution of the Empire after the time of Constantine, it also appears as a separate province under the administration of a praeses. (Not. Dig. i. p. 7; Böcking, i. p. 151; Marquardt, in Becker's Röm. Alterth. vol. iii. pt. i. p. 117.)

In giving an enumeration of the Thessalian tribes and cities, we will first describe the four tetrarchies already mentioned, and then take the other divisions of the country.

1. HESTIAEOTIS or HISTIAEOTIS (Ἑστιαιῶτις, Ἱστιαιῶτις), inhabited by the Hestiaeotae (Ἑστιαιῶται), was the northern part of Thessaly, of which the Peneius may be described in general as its southern boundary. It occupied the passes of Olympus, and extended westward as far as Pindus. (Plin. iv. 1; Strab. ix. pp. 430, 437, 438.) It was the seat of the Perrhaebi (Περραιβοί), a warlike and powerful tribe, who possessed in historical times several towns strongly situated upon the mountains. They are mentioned by Homer (Il. ii. 749) as taking part in the Trojan War, and were regarded as genuine Hellenes, being one of the Amphictyonic states (Aeschin. de Fals. Leg. p. 122). The part of Hestiaeotis inhabited by them was frequently called Perrhaebia, but it never formed a separate Thessalian province. The Perrhaebi are said at one time to have extended south of the Peneius as far as the lake Boebeis, but to have been driven out of this district by the mythical race of the Lapithae. (Strab. ix. pp. 439, 440.) It is probable that at an early period the Perrhaebi occupied the whole of Hestiaeotis, but were subsequently driven out of the plain and confined to the mountains by the Thessalian conquerors from Thesprotia. Strabo states that Hestiaeotis, was formerly, according to some authorities, called Doris (ix. p. 437), and Herodotus relates that the Dorians once dwelt in this district at the foot of Mts. Ossa and Olympus (i. 56). It is said to have derived the name of Hestiaeotis from the district of this name in Euboea, the inhabitants of which were transplanted to Thessaly by the Perrhaebi (Strab. ix. p. 437); but this is an uncertified statement, probably founded alone upon similarity of name. Homer mentions another ancient tribe in this part of Thessaly called the Aethices, who are placed by Strabo upon

the Thessalian side of Pindus near the sources of the Peneius. They are described as a barbarous tribe, living by plunder and robbery. (Hom. *Il.* ii. 744; Strab. vii. p. 327, ix. p. 434; Steph. B. *s. v.* Αἰθικία.) The towns of Hestiaeotis were: OXYNEIA, PIALIA, AEGINIUM, MELIBOEA, PHALORIA, ERICINIUM, PELINNAEUM, TRICCA, OECHALIA, SILANA, GOMPHI, PHECA or PHECADUM, ITHOME, LIMNAEA, PHACIUM, PHAESTUS, PHARCADON, MYLAE, MALLOEA, CYRETIAE, ERITIUM, OLOOSSON, AZORUS, DOLICHE, PYTHIUM, ELONE subsequently LEIMONE, EUDIERU, LAPATHUS, GONNUS or GONNI, CHARAX, CONDYLON, PHALANNA, ORTHE, ATRAX.

2. PELASGIOTIS (Πελασγιῶτις), inhabited by the Pelasgiotae (Πελασγιῶται), extended S. of the Peneius, and along the western side of Pelion and Ossa, including the district called the Pelasgic plain. (Strab. ix. p. 443.) The name shows that this district was originally inhabited by Pelasgians; and its chief town was Larissa, a well known name of Pelasgic cities. The towns of Pelasgiotis were: ELATEA, MOPSIUM, METROPOLIS, GYRTON or GYRTONA, ARGURA, LARISSA, SYCURIUM, CRANNON, AMYRUS, ARMENIUM, PHERAE, CYNOSCEPHALAE, SCOTUSSA, PALAEPHARUS.

3. THESSALIOTIS (Θεσσαλιῶτις), the central plain of Thessaly and the upper course of the river Peneius, so called from its having been first occupied by the Thessalian conquerors from Epeirus. Its towns were: PEIRESIAE, PHYLLUS, METROPOLIS, CIERIUM, EUHYDRIUM, PHARSALUS, the most important in the district, THETIDIUM.

4. PHTHIOTIS (Φθιῶτις), inhabited by the Achaean Phthiotae (Ἀχαιοὶ Φθιῶται), under which name they are usually mentioned as members of the Amphictyonic league. This district, according to Strabo, included the southern part of Thessaly, extending from the Maliac gulf on the E. to Dolopia and Mount Pindus on the W., and stretching as far N. as Pharsalus and the Thessalian plains. (Strab. ix. p. 430.) Phthiotis derived its name from the Homeric Phthia (Φθίη, *Il.* i. 155, ii. 683), which appears to have included in the heroic times not only Hellas and Dolopia, which is expressly called the furthest part of Phthia (*Il.* ix. 484), but also the southern portion of the Thessalian plain, since it is probable that Phthia was also the ancient name of Pharsalus. (Leake, *Northern Greece*, vol. iv. p. 484, seq.) The cities of Phthiotis were: Amphanaeum (Scylax, p. 25), or Amphanae (Ἀμφαναί, Steph. B. *s. v.*), on the promontory Pyrrha and on the Pagasaean gulf; THEBAE, ERETRIA, PHYLACE, ITON, HALUS, PTELEUM, ANTRON, LARISSA, CREMASTE, PROERNA, PRAS, NARTHACIUM, THAUMACI, MELITAEA, CORONEIA, XYNIAE, LAMIA, PHALARA, ECHINUS.

5. MAGNESIA (Μαγνησία), inhabited by the Magnetes (Μάγνητες), was the long and narrow slip of country between Mts. Ossa and Pelion on the W. and the sea on the E., and extending from the mouth of the Peneius on the N. to the Pagasaean gulf on the S. The Magnetes were members of the Amphictyonic league, and were settled in this district in the Homeric times. (*Il.* ii. 756.) The Thessalian Magnetes are said to have founded the Asiatic cities of Magnesia on Mt. Sipylus and of Magnesia on the river Maeander. (Aristot. *ap. Athen.* iv. p. 173; Conon, 29; Strab. xiv. p. 647). The towns of Magnesia were: CERCINIUM, BOEBE, GLAPHYRAE, AESONIS, PA-

GASAE, IOLCUS, DEMETRIAS, NELIA, APHETAE, HOMOLE or HOMOLIUM, EURYMENAE, MELIBOEA, THAUMACIA, CASTHANAEA, RHIZUS, MAGNESIA, OLIZON, MYLAE, SPALAETHRA, CORACAE, METHONE.

6. DOLOPIA (Δολοπία), inhabited by the Dolopes (Δόλοπες), a mountainous district in the SW. corner of Thessaly, lying between Mt. Tymphrestus, a branch of Pindus, on the one side, and Mt. Othrys on the other. The Dolopes were, like the Magnetes, an ancient Hellenic people, and members of the Amphictyonic league. They are mentioned by Homer (*Il.* ix. 484) as included in Phthia, but were governed by a subordinate chieftain of their own. Though nominally belonging to Thessaly, they seem practically to have been independent: and their country was at a later period a constant subject of contention between the Aetolians and the kings of Macedonia. The only place in Dolopia of the slightest importance was CTIMENE.

7. OETAEA (Οἰταία), inhabited by the Oetaei (Οἰταῖοι), was the mountainous district around Mt. Oeta in the upper valley of the Spercheius, and to the E. of Dolopia. The Oetaeans appear to have been the collective name of the various predatory tribes, dwelling upon the northern declivities of Mt. Oeta, who are mentioned as plundering both the Malians on the east, and the Dorians on the south (Thuc. iii. 92—97, viii. 3.) The most important of these tribes were the Aenianes (Αἰνιᾶνες), called Enianes (Ἐνιῆνες) by Homer (*Il.* ii. 749) and Herodotus (vii. 132), an ancient Hellenic Amphictyonic race. (Paus. x. 8. § 2; Harpocrat. *s. v.* Ἀμφικτύονες.) They are said to have first occupied the Dotian plain in Pelasgiotis; afterwards to have wandered to the borders of Epeirus, and finally to have settled in the upper valley of the Spercheius, where Hypata was their chief town. (Plut. *Quaest. Gr.* 13. p. 294; Strab. i. p. 61, ix. p. 442.) Besides HYPATA, which was the only place of importance in Oetaea, we find mention of SPERCHIAE and MACRA COME by Livy (xxxii. 13), and of Sosthenis (Σωσθενίς), Homilae (Ὁμίλαι), Cypaera (Κύπαιρα) and Phalachthia (Φαλαχθία) by Ptolemy (iii. 13. § 45.)

8. MALIS, the lower valley of the Spercheius, described in a separate article. [MALIS.]

COIN OF THESSALIA.

THESSALIOTIS. [THESSALIA.]

THESSALONI'CA (Θεσσαλονίκη; Θετταλονίκη, Polyb. xxiii. 4; Scymn. Ch. 625; Θεσσαλονικεία, Strab. vii. *Epit.* 3; *Eth.* Θεσσαλονικεύς), a large and important city, the capital of Roman Macedonia, situated at the head of the Thermaic gulf, in the district anciently called Mygdonia.

1. SITUATION.—This is well described by Pliny (iv. 10) as "medio flexu litoris [sinus Thermaici]." The gulf extends about 30 leagues in a NW. direction from the group of the Thessalian islands, and then turns to the NE., forming a noble basin be-

tween *Capes Vardir* and *Karaburnu*. On the edge of this basin is the city, partly on the level shore and partly on the slope of a hill, in 40° 38' 47" N. lat., and 22° 57' 22" E. long. The present appearance of the city, as seen from the sea, is described by Leake, Holland, and other travellers as very imposing. It rises in the form of a crescent up the declivity, and is surrounded by lofty whitened walls with towers at intervals. On the E. and W. sides of the city ravines ascend from the shore and converge towards the highest point, on which is the citadel called 'Επταπύργιον, like that of Constantinople. (A view of Thessalonica from the sea is given by Cousinéry). The port is still convenient for large ships, and the anchorage in front of the town is good. These circumstances in the situation of Thessalonica were evidently favourable for commanding the trade of the Macedonian sea. Its relations to the inland districts were equally advantageous. With one of the two great levels of Macedonia, viz. the plain of the " wide-flowing Axius " (Hom. *Il.* ii. 849), to the N. of the range of Olympus, it was immediately connected. With the other, viz. the plain of the Strymon and Lake Cercinitis, it communicated by a pass across the neck of the Chalcidic peninsula. Thus Thessalonica became the chief station on the Roman Via Egnatia, between the Hadriatic and the Hellespont. Its distance from Pella, as given by the Itineraries, is 27 miles, and from Amphipolis (with intermediate stations; see *Act. Apost.* xvii. 1) 67 miles. It is still the chief centre of the trade of the district. It contains a population of 60,000, or 70,000, and (though Adrianople may possibly be larger) it is the most important town of European Turkey, next after Constantinople.

2. Name.—Two legendary names, which Thessalonica is said to have borne in early times, are Emathia (Zonar. *Hist.* xii. 26) and Halia (Steph. B. *s. v.*), the latter probably having reference to the maritime position of the town. During the first period of its authentic history, it was known under the name of Therma (Θέρμα, Aesch.; Θέρμη, Herod., Thucyd.; Θέρμαι, Mal. *Chronog.* p. 190, ed. Bonn), derived, in common with the designation of the gulf (Thermaicus Sinus), from the hot salt-springs, which are found on various parts of this coast, and one of which especially is described by Pococke as being at a distance of 4 English miles from the modern city. (See Scylax, p. 278, ed. Gail.) Three stories are told of the origin of the name Thessalonica. The first (and by far the most probable) is given by Strabo (vii. *Epit.* 10), who says that Therma was rebuilt by Cassander, and called after his wife Thessalonica, the daughter of Philip: the second is found in Steph. B. (*s. v.*), who says that its new name was a memorial of a victory obtained by Philip over the Thessalians (see Const. Porphyrog. *De Them.* ii. p. 51, ed Bonn): the third is in the *Etym. Magn.* (*s. v.*), where it is stated that Philip himself gave the name in honour of his daughter. Whichever of these stories is true, the new name of Thessalonica, and the new eminence connected with the name, are distinctly associated with the Macedonian period, and not at all with the earlier passages of true Greek history. The name, thus given, became permanent. Through the Roman and Byzantine periods it remained unaltered. In the Middle Ages the Italians gave it the form of *Salonichi* or *Saloniki*, which is still frequent. In Latin chronicles we find *Salonicia*. In German poems of the thirteenth century the name appears, with a Teutonic termination,

as *Salnek*. The uneducated Greeks of the present day call the place Σαλονίκη, the Turks *Selanik*.

3. Political and Military History. — Thessalonica was a place of some importance, even while it bore its earlier name of Therma. Three passages of chief interest may be mentioned in this period of its history. Xerxes rested here on his march, his land-forces being encamped on the plain between Therma and the Axius, and his ships cruising about the Thermaic gulf; and it was the view from hence of Olympus and Ossa which tempted him to explore the course of the Peneius. (Herod. vii. 128, seqq.) A short time (B. C. 421) before the breaking out of the Peloponnesian War, Therma was occupied by the Athenians (Thucyd. i. 61); but two years later it was given up to Perdiccas (Id. ii. 29). The third mention of Therma is in Aeschines (*de Fals. Leg.* p. 31, ed. Bekk.), where it is spoken of as one of the places taken by Pausanias.

The true history of Thessalonica begins, as we have implied above, with the decay of Greek nationality. The earliest author who mentions it under its new name is Polybius. It seems probable that it was rebuilt in the same year (B. C. 315) with Cassandreia, immediately after the fall of Pydna and the death of Olympias. [Cassandreia.] We are told by Strabo (*l. c.*) that Cassander incorporated in his new city the population, not only of Therma, but likewise of three smaller towns, viz. Aeneia and Cissus (which are supposed to have been on the eastern side of the gulf), and Chalastra (which is said by Strabo (vii. *Epit.* 9) to have been on the further side of the Axius, whence Tafel (p. xxii.) by some mistake infers that it lay between the Axius and Therma). It does not appear that these earlier cities were absolutely destroyed; nor indeed is it certain that Therma lost its separate existence. Pliny (*l. c.*) seems to imply that a place bearing this name was near Thessalonica; but the text is probably corrupt.

As we approach the Roman period, Thessalonica begins to be more and more mentioned. From Livy (xliv. 10) this city would appear to have been the great Macedonian naval station. It surrendered to the Romans after the battle of Pydna (Ib. xliv. 45), and was made the capital of the second of the four divisions of Macedonia (Ib. xlv. 29). Afterwards, when the whole of Macedonia was reduced to one province (Flor. ii. 14), Thessalonica was its most important city, and virtually its metropolis, though not so called till a later period. [Macedonia.] Cicero, during his exile, found a refuge here in the quaestor's house (*pro Planc.* 41); and on his journeys to and from his province of Cilicia he passed this way, and wrote here several of his extant letters. During the first Civil War Thessalonica was the head-quarters of the Pompeian party and the senate. (Dion Cass. xli. 20.) During the second it took the side of Octavius and Antonius (Plut. *Brut.* 46; Appian, *B. C.* iv. 118), and reaped the advantage of this course by being made a free city. (See Plin. *l. c.*) It is possible that the word ἐλευθερίας, with the head of Octavia, on some of the coins of Thessalonica, has reference to this circumstance (see Eckhel, ii. p. 79); and some writers see in the *Vardár* gate, mentioned below, a monument of the victory over Brutus and Cassius.

Even before the close of the Republic Thessalonica was a city of great importance, in consequence of its position on the line of communication between Rome and the East. Cicero speaks of it as *posita in gremio imperii nostri.* It increased in size and rose in importance with the consolidation of the Empire. Strabo in the first century, and Lucian in the second, speak in strong language of the amount of its population. The supreme magistrates (apparently six in number) who ruled in Thessalonica as a free city of the Empire were entitled πολίταρχαι, as we learn from the remarkable coincidence of St. Luke's language (*Act. Ap.* xvii. 6) with an inscription on the *Vardár* gate. (Böckh, 1967. Belley mentions another inscription containing the same term.) In *Act. Ap.* xvii. 5, the δῆμος is mentioned which formed part of the constitution of the city. Tafel thinks that it had a βουλή also.

During the first three centuries of the Christian era, Thessalonica was the capital of the whole country between the Adriatic and the Black Sea ; and even after the founding of Constantinople it remained practically the metropolis of Greece, Macedonia, and Illyricum. In the middle of the third century, as we learn from coins, it was made a Roman *colonia ;* perhaps with the view of strengthening this position against the barbarian invasions, which now became threatening. Thessalonica was the great safeguard of the Empire during the first shock of the Gothic inroads. Constantine passed some time here after his victory over the Sarmatians; and perhaps the second arch, which is mentioned below, was a commemoration of this victory : he is said also by Zosimus (ii. p. 86, ed. Bonn) to have constructed the port, by which we are, no doubt, to understand that he repaired and improved it after a time of comparative neglect. Passing by the dreadful massacre by Theodosius (Gibbon's *Rome,* ch. xxvii.), we come to the Sclavonic wars, of which the Gothic wars were only the prelude, and the brunt of which was successfully borne by Thessalonica from the middle of the sixth century to the latter part of the eighth. The history of these six Sclavonic wars, and their relation to Thessalonica, has been elaborated with great care by Tafel.

In the course of the Middle Ages Thessalonica was three times taken ; and its history during this period is thus conveniently divided into three stages. On Sunday, July 29th, 904, the Saracen fleet appeared before the city, which was stormed after a few days' fighting. The slaughter of the citizens was dreadful, and vast numbers were sold in the various slave-markets of the Levant. The story of these events is told by Jo. Cameniata, who was crozier-bearer to the archbishop of Thessalonica. From his narrative it has been inferred that the population of the city at this time must have been 220,000. (*De Excidio Thessalonicensi,* in the volume entitled *Theophanes Continuatus* of the Bonn ed. of the Byz. writers, 1838.) The next great catastrophe of Thessalonica was caused by a different enemy, the Normans of Sicily. The fleet of Tancred sailed round the Morea to the Thermaic gulf, while an army marched by the Via Egnatia from Dyrrhachium. Thessalonica was taken on Aug. 15th, 1185, and the Greeks were barbarously treated by the Latins. Their cruelties are described by Nicetas Choniates (*de Andron. Comneno,* p. 388, ed. Bonn, 1835). The celebrated Eustathius was archbishop of Thessalonica at this time; and he wrote an account of this capture of the city, which was first published by Tafel (Tübingen, 1832), and is now printed in the Bonn ed.

of the Byz. writers. (*De Thessalonica a Latinis capta,* in the same vol. with Leo Grammaticus, 1842.) Soon after this period follows the curious history of western feudalism in Thessalonica under Boniface, marquis of Montferrat, and his successors, during the first half of the 13th century. The city was again under Latin dominion (having been sold by the Greek emperor to the Venetians) when it was finally taken by the Turks under Amurath II., in 1430. This event also is described by a writer in the Bonn Byzantine series (Joannes Anagnostes, *de Thessalonicensi Excidio Narratio,* in the same volume with Phranzes and Cananus, 1838).

For the medieval history of Thessalonica see Mr. Finlay's works, *Medieval Greece* (1851), pp. 70, 71, 135—147; *Byzantine and Greek Empires,* vol. i. (1853), pp. 315—332, vol. ii. (1854), pp. 182, 264 —266, 607. For its modern condition we must refer to the travellers, especially Beaujour, Cousinéry, Holland, and Leake.

4. ECCLESIASTICAL HISTORY. — The annals of Thessalonica are so closely connected with religion, that it is desirable to review them in this aspect. After Alexander's death the Jews spread rapidly in all the large cities of the provinces which had formed his empire. Hence there is no doubt that in the first century of the Christian era they were settled in considerable numbers at Thessalonica: indeed this circumstance contributed to the first establishment of Christianity there by St. Paul (*Act. Ap.* xvii. 1). It seems probable that a large community of Jews has been found in this city ever since. They are mentioned in the seventh century during the Sclavonic wars; and again in the twelfth by Eustathius and Benjamin of Tudela. The events of the fifteenth century had the effect of bringing a large number of Spanish Jews to Thessalonica. Paul Lucas says that in his day there were 30,000 of this nation here, with 22 synagogues. More recent authorities vary between 10,000 and 20,000. The present Jewish quarter is in the south-east part of the town.

Christianity, once established in Thessalonica, spread from it in various directions, in consequence of the mercantile relations of the city. (1 *Thess.* i. 8.) During the succeeding centuries this city was the bulwark, not simply of the Byzantine Empire, but of Oriental Christendom,—and was largely instrumental in the conversion of the Sclavonians and Bulgarians. Thus it received the designation of " The Orthodox City." It is true that the legends of Demetrius, its patron saint (a martyr of the early part of the fourth century), disfigure the Christian history of Thessalonica; in every siege success or failure seems to have been attributed to the granting or withholding of his favour: but still this see has a distinguished place in the annals of the Church. Theodosius was baptized by its bishop; even his massacre, in consequence of the stern severity of Ambrose, is chiefly connected in our minds with ecclesiastical associations. The see of Thessalonica became almost a patriarchate after this time; and the withdrawal of the provinces subject to its jurisdiction from connection with the see of Rome, in the reign of Leo Isauricus, became one of the principal causes of the separation of East and West. Cameniata, the native historian of the calamity of 904, was, as we have seen, an ecclesiastic. Eustathius, who was archbishop in 1185, was, beyond dispute, the most learned man of his age, and the author of an invaluable commentary on the Iliad and Odyssey, and of theological works, which have been recently published by Tafel. A list of the Latin archbishops of Thessalonica from 1205 to 1418, when a Roman hierarchy was established along with Western feudalism, is given by Le Quien (*Oriens Christianus*, iii. 1089). Even to the last we find this city connected with questions of religious interest. Symeon of Thessalonica, who is a chief authority in the modern Greek Church on ritual subjects, died a few months before the fatal siege of 1430; and Theodore Gaza, who went to Italy soon after this siege, and, as a Latin ecclesiastic, became the translator of Aristotle, Theophrastus, and Hippocrates, was a native of the city of Demetrius and Eustathius.

5. REMAINS OF ANTIQUITY. — The two monuments of greatest interest at Thessalonica are two arches connected with the line of the Via Egnatia. The course of this Roman road is undoubtedly preserved in the long street which intersects the city from east to west. At its western extremity is the *Vardár* gate, which is nearly in the line of the modern wall, and which has received its present name from the circumstance of its leading to the river *Vardár* or *Axius*. This is the Roman arch believed by Beaujour, Holland, and others to have been erected by the people of Thessalonica in honour of Octavius and Antonius, and in memory of the battle of Philippi. The arch is constructed of large blocks of marble, and is about 12 feet wide and 18 feet high; but a considerable portion of it is buried deep below the surface of the ground. On the outside face are two bas-reliefs of a Roman wearing the toga and standing before a horse. On this arch is the above-mentioned inscription containing the names of the *politarchs* of the city. Leake thinks from the style of the sculpture, and Tafel from the occurrence of the name Flavius in the inscription, that a later date ought to be assigned to the arch. (A drawing of it is given by Cousinéry). The other arch is near the eastern (said in Clarke's *Travels*, iv. p. 359, by mistake, to be near the western) extremity of the main street. (A drawing of this arch also is given by Cousinéry and an imaginary restoration by Pococke.) It is built of brick and faced with marble, and formerly consisted of three archways. The sculptured camels give an oriental aspect to the monument; and it is generally supposed to commemorate the victory of Constantine over Licinius or over the Sarmatians.

Near the line of the main street, between the two above-mentioned arches are four Corinthian columns supporting an architrave, above which are Caryatides. This monument is now part of the house of a Jew; and, from a notion that the figures were petrified by magic, it is called by the Spanish Jews *Las Incantadas*. The Turks call it *Sureth-Maleh*. (A view will be found in Cousinéry, and a more correct one, with architectural details, in Stuart and Revett's *Athen. Antiq.* vol. iii. ch. 9. p. 53). This colonnade is supposed by some to have been part of the Propylaea of the Hippodrome, the position of which is believed by Beaujour and Clarke to have been in the south-eastern part of the town, between the sea and a building called the *Rotunda*, now a mosque, previously the church *Eski-Metropoli*, but formerly a temple, and in construction similar to the Pantheon at Rome. (Pococke has a ground-plan of this building.) Another mosque in Thessalonica, called *Eski-Djumà*, is said by Beaujour to have been a temple consecrated to Venus Thermaea.

The city walls are of brick, and of Greek construction, resting on a much older foundation, which consists of hewn stones of immense thickness. Everywhere are broken columns and fragments of sculpture. Many remains were taken in 1430 to Constantinople. One of the towers in the city wall is called the Tower of the Statue, because it contains a colossal figure of Thessalonica, with the representation of a ship at its feet. The castle is partly Greek and partly Venetian. Some columns of verd antique, supposed to be relics of a temple of Hercules, are to be noticed there, and also a shattered triumphal arch, erected (as an inscription proves) in the reign of Marcus Aurelius, in honour of Antoninus Pius and his daughter Faustina.

In harmony with what has been noticed of its history, Thessalonica has many remains of ecclesiastical antiquity. Leake says that in this respect it surpasses any other city in Greece. The church of greatest interest (now a mosque) is that of St. Sophia, built, according to tradition, like the church of the same name at Constantinople, in the reign of Justinian, and after the designs of the architect Anthemius. This church is often mentioned in the records of the Middle Ages, as in the letters of Pope Innocent III. and in the account of the Norman siege. It remains very entire, and is fully described by Beaujour and Leake. The church of St. Demetrius (apparently the third on the same site, and now also a mosque) is a structure of still greater size and beauty. Tafel believes that it was erected about the end of the seventh century; but Leake conjectures, from its architectural features, that it was built by the Latins in the thirteenth. Tafel has collected with much diligence the notices of a great number of churches which have existed in Thessalonica. Dapper says, that in his day the Greeks had the use of thirty churches. Walpole (in Clarke's *Travels*, iv. p. 349) gives the number as sixteen. All travellers have noticed two ancient pulpits, consisting of "single blocks of variegated marble, with small steps cut in them," which are among the most interesting ecclesiastical remains of Thessalonica.

6. AUTHORITIES. — The travellers who have described Thessalonica are numerous. The most important are Paul Lucas, *Second Voyage*, 1705 ; Pococke, *Description of the East*, 1743—1745 ; Beaujour, *Tableau du Commerce de la Grèce*, translated into English, 1800 ; Clarke, *Travels in Europe, &c.* 1810—1823 ; Holland, *Travels in the Ionian Isles &c.*, 1815 ; Cousinéry, *Voyage dans la Macédoine*, 1831 ; Leake, *Northern Greece*, 1835 ; Zachariä, *Reise in den Orient*, 1840; Grisebach, *Reise durch Rumelien*, 1841; Bowen, *Mount Athos, Thessaly, and Epirus*, 1852.

In the *Mémoires de l'Académie des Inscriptions*, tom. xxxviii. Sect. hist. pp. 121—146, is an essay on the subject of Thessalonica by the Abbé Belley ; but the most elaborate work on the subject is that by Tafel, the first part of which was published at Tübingen in 1835. This was

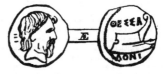

COIN OF THESSALONICA.

4 F 3

afterwards reprinted as "Prolegomena" to the *Dissertatio de Thessalonica ejusque Agro Geographica*, Berlin, 1839. With this should be compared his work on the *Via Egnatia*. To these authorities we ought to add the introduction to some of the commentaries on St. Paul's *Epistles to the Thessalonians*, —especially those of Koch (Berlin 1849) and Lünemann (Göttingen, 1850).   [J. S. H.]

THE'STIA. [THESTIENSES.]

THESTIENSES (Θεστιεῖς, Pol. v. 7), are usually called the inhabitants of a town Thestia in Aetolia. But no town of this name is mentioned by the ancient writers, and it is not improbable that the town itself was called Θεστιεῖς. The name occurs only in Polybius, and the exact site of the place is unknown. We only learn, from the narrative of Polybius, that it was situated in the Northern part of the upper plain of Aetolia. The name is perhaps connected with Thestius, one of the old Aetolian heroes.

THETI'DIUM (Θετίδιον, Strab. ix. p. 431; Polyb. xviii. 3, 4; Θετίδειον, Eurip. *Androm.* 20; Θεστίδειον, Steph. B. *s. v.*: *Eth.* Θετιδεύς), a place in Thessaly, close to Pharsalus, where Flamininus encamped at the end of the second march from Pherae towards Scotussa, before the battle of Cynoscephalae. It derived its name from Thetis, the mother of Achilles, the national hero of the Achaean Phthiotae. Leake places it at or near *Magula*, on the opposite bank of the Enipeus. (*Northern Greece*, vol. iv. pp. 472, 473.)

THEUDO'RIA, one of the chief towns of the Athamanes in Epeirus, is identified by Leake with the modern *Thodhóriana*, a village situated near *Mount Tzumérka* in a pass which leads from the Achelous to the Arachthus. (Liv. xxxviii. 1; Leake, *Northern Greece*, vol. iv. p. 212.)

THEUMA, a town of Thessaly, near the frontiers of Dolopia. (Liv. xxxii. 13.)

THEUPROSOPON. [PHOENICIA, p. 606, a.]

THEVESTE (Θεουέστη, Ptol. iv. 3. § 30), an important town of Numidia, but which is only mentioned in the later writers. It was a Roman colony (Gruter, *Inscr.* p. 600; *Itin. Ant.* p. 27), and the place where many roads running in a SE. direction into the Roman province of Africa, had their commencement. (Cf. *Itin. Ant.* pp. 33, 46, 47, 53, 54.) It is the town of *Tebessa*, recently discovered by General Negrier, considerable ruins of which still exist, especially the ancient walls, the circumference of which indicates a town capable of containing 40,000 inhabitants. (See Letronne, in *Rev. Archéol.* iv. p. 360, sqq.; *Sur l'Arc de Triomphe de Teveste, &c.*, Paris, 1847; Jahn's *Jahrbücher*, lii. p. 409.)   [T. H. D.]

THIA. [THERA.]

THIANNICE (Θιαννική, Arrian, *Per. P. Eux.* p. 7), or THIANITICE (Θιανιτική, Anon. *Per. P. Eux.* p. 14), a district of Asia in the Pontus Euxinus, which was separated from Colchis by the river Ophis. Its name probably should be Sannice, as the Sanni, or Tzani, were a well-known people in this region. (Cf. Mannert, iv. p. 378, vi. pt. 2. p. 421; Gail, *ad Arrian.* p. 95.)   [T. H. D.]

THIAR, a town of the Contestani in Hispania Tarraconensis, between Carthago Nova, and Ilici (*Itin. Ant.* p. 401). Variously identified with *San Gines* and *Orihuela*, near which latter place are many ruins. (Florez, *Esp. Sagr.* v. p. 30, vii. p. 124.) [T. H. D.]

THIBA (Θίβα: *Eth.* Θίβιος), a district in Pontus, so called from an Amazon slain there by Hercules. The inhabitants were said to be socerers, whose

breath was poisonous, and who would not perish if thrown into the water, but would float on the surface. (Eustath. *ad Dionys. Per.* 828; Steph. B. *s. v.* Θιβαΐς; Plut. *Symp.* v. 7. § 1; Phylarch. *ap. Plin.* vii. 2. s. 2.)

THILSAPHATA (Amm. Marc. xxv. 8), a fortified town in the south of Mesopotamia, probably the present *Tel el Hava*, between *Mosul* and the *Sinjar*, in the neighbourhood of the *Tigris*.   [V.]

THILUTHA, an impregnable fortress on an island in the Euphrates, near Anatho, which defied the arms of Julian (Amm. Marc. xxiv. 2). Zosimus (iii. 15) speaks of this island, and of the impregnable fortress (φρούριον ὀχυρότατον) situated upon it, but without mentioning its name. It is described by Isidorus Charax (*Mans. Parth.* § 1, ed. C. Müller) as an island in the Euphrates, containing a treasury of the Parthians, and distant two schoeni from Anatho. The old editions read Ὀλαβούς; but the MSS. have Ὀλαβούς, which Müller has changed into Θιλαβούς, and there can be little doubt of the propriety of this correction. It corresponds to the island called *Tilbus* by Chesney (vol. i. p. 57), and in his map *Telbes* or *Anatelbes*, containing ruins of very ancient buildings. (See Müller, *ad Isid. Char. l. c.*)

THINAE (Θῖναι, or Σῖναι, Ptol. vii. 3. § 6, viii. 27. § 12), or THINA (Θῖνα, Arrian, *Per. M. Erythr.* p. 36), a capital city of the Sinae, who carried on here a large commerce in silk and woollen stuffs. It appears to have been an ancient tradition that the city was surrounded with brazen walls; but Ptolemy remarks that these did not exist there, nor anything else worthy of remark. The ancient writers differ very considerably as to its situation. According to the most probable accounts it was either *Nankin*, or rather perhaps *Thsin*, *Tin*, or *Tein*, in the province *Schensi*, where, according to the accounts of the Chinese themselves, the first kingdom of *Sin*, or *China*, was founded. (Cf. Ritter, *Erdkunde*, ii. p. 199.)   [T. H. D.]

THINO'DES (τὸ Θινῶδες ὄρος, i. e. *the Sand Hill*, Ptol. iv. 5. § 18), a mountain of Egypt, belonging to the Libyan chain, on the S. borders of Marmarica.   [T. H. D.]

THIRMIDA, a place in Numidia, the situation of which is totally unknown. (Sall. *Jug.* 12.) [T. H. D.]

THIS. [ABYDUS.]

THISBE (Θίσβη, Hom., Paus., Steph. B. *s. v.*; Θίσβαι, Strab., Xen.: *Eth.* Θισβαῖος), a town of Boeotia, described by Strabo as situated at a short distance from the sea, under the southern side of Helicon, bordering upon the confines of Thespiae and Coroneia. (Strab. ix. p. 411.) Thisbe is mentioned by Homer, who says that it abounds in wild pigeons (πολυτρήρωνά τε Θίσβην, *Il.* ii. 502); and both Strabo and Stephanus B. remark that this epithet was given to the city from the abundance of wild pigeons at the harbour of Thisbe. Xenophon remarks that Cleombrotus marched through the territory of Thisbe on his way to Creusis before the battle of Leuctra. (*Hell.* vi. 4. § 3.) The only public building at Thisbe mentioned by Pausanias (ix. 32. § 3) was a temple of Hercules, to whom a festival was celebrated. The same writer adds that between the mountain on the sea-side and the mountain at the foot of which the town stood, there is a plain which would be inundated by the water flowing into it, were it not for a mole or causeway constructed through the middle, by means of which the water is diverted every year into the part of the plain lying on one side of the causeway, while that on the other is cultivated. The ruins of Thisbe are found at *Kakósia.* " The position is between two great summits of the mountain, now called *Karamingki* and *Paleovund,* which rise majestically above the vale, clothed with trees, in the upper part, and covered with snow at the top. The modern village lies in a little hollow surrounded on all sides by low cliffs connected with the last falls of the mountain. The walls of Thisbe were about a mile in circuit, following the crest of the cliffs which surround the village; they are chiefly preserved on the side towards *Dobrená* and the south-east. The masonry is for the most part of the fourth order, or faced with equal layers of large, oblong, quadrangular stones on the outside, the interior as usual being filled with loose rubble. On the principal height which lies towards the mountain, and which is an entire mass of rock, appear some reparations of a later date than the rest of the walls, and there are many Hellenic foundations on the face of this rock towards the village. In the cliffs outside the walls, to the north-west and south, there are many sepulchral excavations." (Leake, *Northern Greece,* vol. ii. p. 506.) Leake observed the mole or causeway which Pausanias describes, and which serves for a road across the marsh to the port. The same writer remarks that, as the plain of Thisbe is completely surrounded by heights, there is no issue for the river which rises in the Ascraea and here terminates. " The river crosses the causeway into the marsh by two openings, the closing of which in the winter or spring would at any time cause the upper part of the plain to be inundated, and leave the lower part for cultivation in the summer; but as the river is now allowed to flow constantly through them, the western side is always in a state of marsh, and the ground has become much higher on the eastern side."

The port of Thisbe is now called *Vathý.* The shore is very rocky, and abounds in wild pigeons, as Strabo and Stephanus have observed; but there is also a considerable number at *Kakósia* it-elf. The Roman poets also allude to the pigeons of Thisbe. Hence Ovid (*Met.* xi. 300) speaks of the " Thisbaeae columbae," and Statius (*Theb.* vii. 261) describes Thisbe as " Dionaeis avibus circumsona." Thisbe is mentioned both by Pliny (iv. 7. s. 12) and Ptolemy (iii. 15. § 20).

THISOA. [THEISOA.]

. THIUS. [MEGALOPOLIS.]

THMUIS (Θμουίς, Herod. ii. 168; Aristides, *Aegypt.* vol. iii. p. 610; Ptol. iv. 5. § 51), the modern *Tmai,* was a town in Lower Aegypt, situated upon a canal E. of the Nile, between its Tanite and Mendesian branches. It was the capital of the Thmuite Nome, in which the Calasirian division of the Aegyptian army possessed lands. At the time of Herodotus's visit to the Delta the Thmuite Nome had been incorporated with the Mendesian. Their incorporation was doubtless owing, partly to the superior size of the latter, and partly to their having a common object of worship in the goat Mendes (*Pan*), of whom *Thmu* was in the old Aegyptian language (Hieronym. *in Isaiam,* xlvi. 1) the appellation. In the reigns of Valentinian and Theodosius the Great (A. D. 375, foll.) Thmuis was a town of some consequence, governed by its own magistrates, and exempt from the jurisdiction of the Alexandrian prefect (Amm. Marc. xxii. 16. § 6). It was also an episcopal see, and one of its bishops, Serapion, is mentioned by Heracleanus. (*ap. Photium,* p. 65, ed.

Bekker.) Remains of the ancient city are supposed to exist at *Tel-etmai* or *'Tmai,* SW. of *Mansoorah.* A monolithal shrine and many sarcophagi of granite have been found there, and a factitious mound at the village of *Ternay,* raised above the level of the inundation, is probably an Aegyptian work. (Champollion, *Egypte sous les Pharaons,* vol. ii. p. 114.) That dykes were essential to the preservation of the city appears from the description of it by Aristides (*l. c.*), who represents Thmuis as standing upon and surrounded by flat and marshy grounds. [W.B.D.]

THOAE. [ECHINADES.]

THOANA. [THANA.]

THO'ARIS or THOA'RIUS (Θόαρις or Θοάριος), a small coast river in Pontus Polemoniacus (Arrian, *Peripl. P. E.* p. 16; Anon. *Peripl. P. E.* p. 11), is now called *Gheurek, Irmak,* or perhaps more correctly *Thurek Irmak.* (Hamilton, *Researches,* i. p. 279.) [L. S.]

THO'CNIA (Θώκνία, Θόκνεια: *Eth.* Θωκνεύς), a town of Arcadia in the district Parrhasia, situated upon a height on the river Aminius, which flows into the Helisson, a tributary of the Alpheius. The town was said to have been founded by Thocnus, the son of Lycaon, and was deserted in the time of Pausanias, as its inhabitants had been removed to Megalopolis. It is placed by Leake in the position of *Vromoséla.* (Paus. viii. 3. § 2, 27. § 4, 29. § 5; Steph. B. *s. v.*; Leake, *Morea,* vol. ii. p. 293.)

THOMNA. [TAMNA.]

THONITIS LACUS. [THOSPITIS.]

THORAE. [ATTICA, p. 331, a.]

THO'RICUS (Θορικός: *Eth.* Θορίκιος: *Therikó*), a town of Attica on the SE. coast, and about 7 or 8 miles N. of the promontory of Sunium, was originally one of the twelve cities into which Attica is said to have been divided before the time of Theseus, and was afterwards a demus belonging to the tribe Acamantis. (Strab. ix. p. 397.) It continued to be a place of importance during the flourishing period of Athenian history, as its existing remains prove, and was hence fortified by the Athenians in the 24th year of the Peloponnesian War. (Xen. *Hell.* i. 2. § 1.) It was distant 60 stadia from Anaphlystus upon the western coast. (Xen. *de Vect.* 4. § 43.) Thoricus is celebrated in mythology as the residence of Cephalus, whom Eos or Aurora carried off to dwell with the gods. (Apollod. ii. 4. § 7; Eurip. *Hippol.* 455.) It has been conjectured by Wordsworth, with much probability, that the idea of Thoricus was associated in the Athenian mind with such a translation to the gods, and that the " Thorician stone " (Θορίκιος πέτρος) mentioned by Sophocles (*Oed. Col.* 1595), respecting which there has been so much doubt, probably has reference to such a migration, as the poet is describing a similar translation of Oedipus.

The fortifications of Thoricus surrounded a small plain, which terminates in the harbour of the city, now called *Porto Mandri.* The ruins of the walls may be traced following the crest of the hills on the northern and southern sides of the plain, and crossing it on the west. The acropolis seems to have stood upon a height rising above the sheltered creek of *Frangó Limióna,* which is separated only by a cape from *Porto Mandri.* Below this height, on the northern side, are the ruins of a theatre, of a singular form, being an irregular curve, with one of the sides longer than the other. In the plain, to the westward, are the remains of a quadrangular colonnade, with Doric columns. (Leake, *Demi of Attica,*

p. 68, seq. 2nd ed.; Wordsworth, *Athens and Attica*, p. 208, seq.)

THORNAX (Θόρναξ). 1. A mountain near the city of Hermione in Argolis, between which and Mt. Pron the road ran from Hermione to Halice. It was subsequently called Coccygium, because Zeus was said to have been here transformed into a cuckoo; and on its summit was a temple of Zeus Coccygius. (Paus. ii. 36. §§ 1, 2; Leake, *Peloponnesiaca*, p. 288; Curtius, *Peloponnesos*, vol. ii. p. 463.)

2. A mountain in Laconia, on the road from Sparta to Sellasia, upon which stood a colossal statue of Apollo Pythaeus. (Herod. i. 69; Paus. iii. 10. § 8; Steph. B. *s. v.*; Leake, *Morea*, vol. ii. p. 534, *Peloponnesiaca*, pp. 348, 352; Boblaye, *Rech.* p. 75; Ross, *Peloponnes*, p. 190; Curtius, *Peloponnesos*, vol. ii. pp. 237, 259.)

THO'SPIA (Θωσπία, Ptol. v. 13. § 19, viii. 19. § 12), the capital of the district Thospitis. [T. H. D.]

THOSPI'TIS (Θωσπῖτις, Ptol. v. 13. § 18), a district of Armenia Major. It lay at the northern side of the LACUS THOSPITES (ἡ Θωσπῖτις λίμνη, Ptol. *ib.* § 7), through which the Tigris flowed (Plin. vi. 27. s. 31). It is perhaps the same lake called Thonitis or Thopitis by Strabo (Θωνῖτις or Θωπῖτις, xi. p. 529), and Priscian (Lacus Thonitidis, *Perieg.* 913), the water of which is described by Strabo as nitrous and undrinkable. It is probably the modern *Wan*, in the district of *Tosp*, and hence called by the Armenians *Dzow Tospai*. [T. H. D.]

THRA'CIA (Θρῄκη, Hom.; Θρηΐκίη, Herod. i. 168, or Θρηΐκη, iv. 99; Attic, Θρᾴκη: Eth. Θρᾷιξ, Hom.; Θρῇϊξ, Herod. viii. 116; Attic, Θρᾷξ; Trag. Θρῇξ: Thrax, Threx, the latter form being chiefly, if not exclusively, employed of gladiators), a country at the south-eastern extremity of Europe, and separated from Asia only by the Propontis and its two narrow channels, the Bosporus and the Hellespont.

I. NAME. — Besides its ordinary name, the country had, according to Steph. B. (*s. v.*). two older appellations, Πέρκη and 'Αρία; and Gellius (xiv. 6) mentions Sithon as another. Respecting the origin of these names, various conjectures have been made both in ancient and in modern times; but as none of them, with the exception to be presently mentioned, are of much value, it is not worth while to devote any space to their consideration. * The exception alluded to is the etymology adopted by Col. Mure (*Hist. of Lang. and Lit. of Anc. Greece*, i. p. 153, note), which is far more probable and satisfactory than any other that the present writer has seen, and which derives the name Thrace from the adjective τραχεῖα, "rugged," by the common transfer of the aspirate. Thus the name would indicate the geographical character of the various districts to which it is given; for, as we shall see, it was by no means confined to the country which is the special subject of the present notice.

II. EXTENT. — In the earliest times, the region called Thrace had no definite boundaries, but was often regarded as comprising all that part of Europe which lies to the north of Greece. Macedonia, in the south, is spoken of by Hecataeus as belonging to it (cf. Mel. ii. 2, sub fin., where the Chalcidic peninsula is described under the title of Thrace); and

Scythia, in the north, is included in it by Steph. B. (*s. v.* Σκύθαι: cf. Amm. xxvii. 4. § 3). This explains the fable reported by Andron (Tzetz. *ad Lycophr.* 894), to the effect that Oceanus had four daughters, Asia, Libya, Europa, and Thracia; thus elevating the last-named country to the rank of one of the four quarters of the known—or rather unknown—world. But as the Greeks extended their geographical knowledge, the designation Thrace became more restricted in its application, and at length was generally given to that part of Europe which is included within the following boundaries: the Ister on the N. (Strab. ii. p. 129; Plin. iv. 18; Mel. ii. 2); the Euxine and the Bosporus on the E.; the Propontis, the Hellespont, the Aegean, and the northern part of Macedonia, on the S.; the Strymon, or subsequently, i. e. in the time of Philip II. and his son Alexander the Great, the Nestus (Strab. vii. pp. 323, 330; Ptol. iii. 11), and the countries occupied by the Illyrians, on the W., where, however, the boundary was never very settled or accurately known. (Plin. and Mel. *ll. cc.*) These were the limits of Thrace until the Romans subdued the country, when, in the reign of Augustus, it was divided into two parts, separated by the Haemus; the portion to the south of that mountain chain retaining the name of Thrace, while the part between the Ister and the Haemus received the appellation of Moesia, and was constituted a Roman province. [MOESIA, Vol. II. p. 367.] But even after this period both countries were sometimes included under the old name, which the Latin poets frequently used in its earliest and widest extent of meaning. (Cf. Heyne, *ad Virg. Aen.* xi. 659; Burman, *ad Val. Flacc.* iv. 280; Muncker, *ad Hygin. Fab.* 138; Tzschucke, *ad Mel.* ii. 2. p. 63.) As the little that is known about Moesia is stated in the article above referred to, the present will, as far as possible, be confined to Thrace proper, or south of the Haemus, corresponding pretty nearly to the modern *Roumelia*, which, however, extends somewhat more to the west than ancient Thrace.

III. PHYSICAL GEOGRAPHY, CLIMATE, PRODUCTIONS, &c. — Many circumstances might have led us to expect that the ancients would have transmitted to us full information respecting Thrace: its proximity to Greece; the numerous Greek colonies established in it; the fact that it was traversed by the highroad between Europe and Asia; and that the capital of the Eastern Empire was situated in it,—all these things seem calculated to attract attention to the country in an unusual degree, and to induce authors of various kinds to employ their pens in recording its natural and political history. Yet the latest and most profound historian of Greece is compelled to admit that, apart from two main roads, "scarcely anything whatever is known of [the interior of] the country." (Grote, vol. xii. p. 34, note. For this various reasons may be assigned; but the principal one is the barbarous character, in all ages, of the occupants of the land, which has, at least until very recently, precluded the possibility of its exploration by peaceful travellers. * Those who have

---

* Those who are curious about such matters may consult Steph. B. *s. v.*; Eustath. *ad Dion. Per.* 322, 323; Sickler, *Handb.* i. p. 480; Berkel *ad Steph. B.* p. 400; Tzschucke. *ad Mel.* ii. 2. p. 62; Kenrick, *Philol. Mus.* i. p. 618.

* Even one of the latest travellers there, M. Viquesnel, commissioned by the French government, and countenanced by the Turkish authorities, found it impossible to induce his guides to conduct him to a certain district which he wished to visit, although he offered to take as numerous an escort as they pleased. (See *Archives des Missions scient. et litt.* vol. i. p. 210.)

traversed it have been almost invariably engaged in military enterprises, and too much occupied with their immediate objects to have either opportunity or inclination, even had they possessed the necessary qualifications, to observe and describe the natural features of the country. What adds to the difficulty of the writer on the classical geography of Thrace is the unfortunate loss of the whole of that portion of the seventh book of Strabo which was devoted to the subject. Strabo, in several parts of his work, treats incidentally of Thrace: but this is a poor substitute for the more systematic account of it which has perished, and of which little more than a table of contents has been preserved in the meagre epitome which alone remains of it.

In modern times, several travellers have endeavoured, with various degrees of success, to explore the country; and some of them have published the results of their investigations; but it is evident from their very frequent disagreement as to the sites of the places which they attempt to identify with those mentioned in ancient writers, that as yet the necessary data have not been obtained; and the Itineraries, instead of assisting, not seldom add to the difficulty of the task, and render its accomplishment almost hopeless. Moreover, the extent of country examined by these travellers was very limited. "The mountainous region of Rhodope, bounded on the west by the Strymon, on the north and east by the Hebrus, and on the south by the Aegean, is a *terra incognita*, except the few Grecian colonies on the coast. Very few travellers have passed along or described the southern or king's road; while the region in the interior, apart from the highroad, was absolutely unexplored until the visit of M. Viquesnel in 1847. (Grote, *l. c.*)

The results of this traveller's researches have not yet, we believe, appeared in a complete and connected form. His reports to the French minister by whom he was commissioned are published in the work already referred to; but most of them are mere outlines, written on the spot from brief notes. They contain much that is valuable and interesting; but no one except their author could make full use of them; and it is to be hoped that he may be able to employ the materials so ably collected in the composition of a work that would dispel much of the obscurity that at present rests upon the country. M. Viquesnel was engaged little more than a year in Thrace, a period evidently insufficient for its complete exploration; accordingly he seems to have devoted his principal attention to its geology, especially of the the mountain systems, above all in the district of Rhodope.

According to Ami Boué's chart of the geological structure of the globe, copied in Johnston's *Physical Atlas*, the three principal geological formations in Thrace are: (1) the crystalline schistous, comprehending all the granitoid rocks; this occupies the W. portion of the country, and a small district on the Euxine, immediately S. of the Haemus: (2) the tertiary, extending over the basin of the Hebrus: (3) the primary stratifications, or the transition series, including the carboniferous formations; this occupies the SE. part of the country, and a region S. of the Haemus, and W. of the tertiary formation above mentioned. Near the sources of the *Bourghas*, Viquesnel found volcanic rocks (p. 213).

The surface of Thrace is, on the whole, decidedly mountainous, the vast plains spoken of by Virgil (*Aen.* iii. 13) belonging to Moesia. From the great range of Haemus, three chains of mountains branch off towards the SE., and with their various ramifications occupy nearly the entire country. The most westerly of these begins at the NW. extremity of the boundary line, and soon separates into two almost parallel ranges, the Pangaeus and Rhodope, which are separated from each other by the river Nestus: the former filling up the whole space between that river and the Strymon, the latter the district E. of the Nestus and SW. of the Hebrus. Both Pangaeus and Rhodope extend down to the coast of the Aegean, and the latter is continued parallel to it as far E. as the Hebrus. The central offshoot of the Haemus branches off between the sources of the Hebrus and the Tonzus, and extends to their junction near Hadrianopolis. The most easterly chain diverges from the Haemus about 100 miles W. of the Euxine, to the W. shore of which it is nearly parallel, though it gradually approaches nearer to it from N. to S.: it extends as far as the Bosporus, and with its lateral offshoots occupies nearly the whole country between the E. tributaries of the Hebrus and the Euxine. The central and E. ranges appear to have had no general distinctive names; at least we are not aware that any occur in ancient writers: the modern name of the most easterly is the *Strandja-Dagh*. A continuation of this range extends along the shore of the Propontis, and is now called the *Tekir-Dagh*.

The loftiest peaks, among these mountains, belong to Rhodope, and attain an elevation of about 8500 feet (Viquesnel, p. 325); the summits of the *Strandja-Dagh*, are 2600 feet high (Id. p. 314); those of the *Tekir-Dagh*, 2300 (Id. p. 315); the other mountains are from 2000 to 600 feet in height (Id. pp. 314, 315). The Haemus is not more than 4000 feet high, in that portion of it which belongs to Thrace. It is obvious from these measurements that the statements of some of the ancients that the summits of the Thracian mountains were covered with eternal snow (Θρηκῶν ὄρεα νιφόεντα, Hom. *Il.* xiv. 227), and that from the highest peak of the Haemus the Adriatic and the Euxine could be seen, are mere fancies. Strabo (vii. pp. 313, 317) points out the inaccuracy of this notion. An interesting account is given by Livy (xl. 21, 22) of the ascent of Haemus by Philip V., who shared in the popular belief in question. Livy states plainly enough his conviction that Philip's labour, which was far from slight, was thrown away; but he and his attendants were prudently silent upon the subject, not wishing, says Livy, to be laughed at for their pains. Yet Florus, who alludes to the same circumstance (ii. 12), but makes Perseus the mountain-climber, assumes that the king's object was accomplished, and that the bird's-eye view of his dominions, obtained from the mountain top, assisted him in forming a plan for the defence of his kingdom; with reference to his meditated war with Rome. Mela too repeats the erroneous statement (ii. 2).

The main direction of the rivers of Thrace is from N. to S., as might be inferred from the foregoing description of its mountain system. The Strymon forms its W. boundary. In the lower part of its course, it expands into a considerable width, and was called Lake Cercinitis, into which flowed a smaller river, the Angites (Herod. vii. 113); next, towards the E., comes the Nestus; then, in succession, the Travus, which falls into Lake Bistonis, the Schoenus, the Hebrus, the principal river of Thrace, and lastly the Melas. All these rivers fall into the Aegean. Several small streams flow into the Hellespont and the Propontis, of which we may mention Aegospotami, renowned, notwithstanding its insignificant size, the Arzus, and the Erginus. The rivers which fall into the Euxine are all small, and few of them are distinguished by name in the geographers, though doubtless not so unhonoured by the dwellers upon their banks: among them Pliny (iv. 18) mentions the Pira and the Orosines. The Hebrus drains at least one-half, probably nearer two-thirds, of the entire surface of Thrace; and on its banks, or on those of its tributaries, most of the level portions of the country are situated, as well as nearly all the inland towns. Its principal affluents are the Arda (in some maps called the Harpessus), and the Suemus on the W., the Tonzus, Artiscus. and Agrianes on the E.

The Thracian coast of the Aegean is extremely irregular in its outline, being broken up by bays which enter far into the land, yet appear to be of comparatively little depth. Most of them, indeed, are at the mouths of rivers, and have probably been filled up by alluvial deposits. It was perhaps for this reason that several of them were called *lakes*, as if they had been regarded as belonging to the land rather than to the sea; e. g. Lake Cercinitis, already mentioned, which seems, indeed, to have been little more than a marsh, and in Kiepert's map its site is so represented; Lake Bistonis, east of Abdera; and Stentoris Lacus, at the mouth of the Hebrus. The gulf of Melas, formed by the northern shore of the Chersonesus and the opposite coast of what may be called the mainland, is an exception to this description of the Thracian bays. The coasts on the Propontis and the Euxine are comparatively unbroken, the only gulf of any extent being Portus Hellodos, near Anchialus, which is known in modern times, by the name of the bay of *Bourghas*, as one of the best harbours in the Euxine, the Thracian shore of which was regarded by the ancients as extremely dangerous. [SALMYDESSUS.]

The principal promontories were, Ismarum, Serrheum, Sarpedonium, and Mastusium, on the southern coast; Thynias and Haemi Extrema, on the eastern.

For an account of one of the most remarkable parts of Thrace, see CHERSONESUS, Vol. I. p. 608.

Off the southern coast are situated the islands of Thasos, Samothrace, and Imbros; the first is separated from the mainland by a channel about 5 miles wide; the other two are considerably more distant from the shore.

The climate of Thrace is always spoken of by the ancients as being extremely cold and rigorous: thus Athenaeus (viii. p. 351) describes the year at Aenus as consisting of eight months of cold and four months of winter; but such statements are not to be taken literally, since many of them are mere poetical exaggerations, and are applied to Thrace as the representative of the north in general The Haemus was regarded as the abode of the north wind, and the countries beyond it were believed to enjoy a beautifully mild climate. (See Niebuhr, *Ethnog. and Geog.* i. p. 16, Eng. trans.; Soph. *Antig.* 985; Eurip. *Rhes.* 440; Theophr. *de Caus.* v. 17; Virg. *Georg.* iii. 350 seq.; Ov. *Pont.* iv. 10. 41, *ib.* 7. 8; *Trist.* iii. 10: &c.). Even after making full allowance for the undoubted effect of vast forests, undrained marshes, and very partial cultivation, in lowering the average temperature of a country, it is difficult to believe that a land, the northern boundary of which (i. e. of Thrace Proper) is in the same parallel of latitude as Tuscany and the Pyrenees, and the highest mountains of which are less than 9000 feet above the

level of the sea, can have had a very severe climate. That the winter was often extremely cold, there can be no doubt. The Hebrus was sometimes frozen over: not to dwell upon the "Hebrus nivali compede vinctus" of Horace (*Ep.* i. 3. 3; cf. Virg. *Aen.* xii. 331, and the epigram, attributed by some to Caesar, beginning, "Thrax puer adstricto glacie dum ludit in Hebro"), Florus (iii. 4) relates that, in the campaign of Minucius in southern Thrace, a number of horsemen in his army were drowned while trying to cross that river on the ice. Xenophon states that the winter which he passed in Thrace, in the mountainous district of the Thyni, was so cold that even wine was frozen in the vessels, and that many Greek soldiers had their noses and ears frostbitten; the snow also lay deep upon the ground. And that this was not an exceptional season may be inferred from Xenophon's remarks on the dress of the Thracians, which seemed to him to have been devised with special reference to the climate, and to prevent such mishaps as those which befel the Greeks (*Anab.* vii. 4. §§ 3, 4). Tacitus (*Ann.* iv. 51) assigns the early and severe winter of Mount Haemus among the causes which prevented Poppaeus Sabinus (A. D. 26) from following up his first success over the rebellious Thracians.[*] Pliny (xvii. 3) says that the vines about Aenus were often injured by frosts, after the Hebrus was brought nearer to that city; the allusion probably being to the formation of the western mouth of the river, nearly opposite to Aenus, the floating ice and the cold water brought down by which would have some effect in lowering the temperature of the neighbourhood. Mela (ii. 2, init.) describes Thrace generally as agreeable neither in climate nor in soil, being, except in the parts near the sea, barren, cold, and very ill adapted for agriculture and fruit-trees of all kinds, except the vine, while the fruit even of that required to be protected from the cold by a covering of the leaves, in order to ripen. This last remark throws some doubt upon the accuracy of the writer; for the shading of the grapes from the direct rays of the sun is obviously more likely to prevent than to promote their arrival at maturity; and hence, as is well known, it is the practice in many parts of Europe to *remove* the leaves with a view to this object.

However this may be, it is certain that Thrace did produce wine, some kinds of which were famous from very early times. Homer, who bestows upon Thrace the epithet ἐριβῶλαξ (*Il.* xi. 485), represents Nestor reminding Agamemnon that the Grecian ships bring to him cargoes of wine from that country every day (*Ib.* ix. 76); and the poet celebrates the excellence of the produce of the Maroneian vineyards. (*Od.* ix. 197, seq.) Pliny (xiv. 6) states that this wine still maintained its reputation, and describes it as black, perfumed, and growing rich with age; a description which agrees with Homer's (*l. c.*). Paul Lucas says that he found the Thracian wine excellent. (*Voy. dans la Turquie,* i. p. 25; see also, Athen. i. p. 31.) Thrace was fertile in corn (Plin. xvii. 3), and its wheat is placed by Pliny high in the scale of excellence as estimated by weight. It has, he says (xviii. 12), a stalk consisting of several coats (*tunicae*),

---

[*] M. Viquesnel states, on two occasions, that he was compelled to change his route in consequence of heavy and continuous snow-storms, in the month of November (pp. 213, 312). The wind also was extremely violent.

to protect it, as he supposes, from the severity of the climate; by which also he accounts for the cultivation, in some parts of the country, of the *triticum trimestre* and *bimestre*, so called because those varieties were reaped in the third and second month respectively after they were sown. Corn was exported from Thrace, and especially from the Chersonesus to Athens (Theoph. *de Plantis*, viii. 4; Lys. *in Diogit.* p. 902), and to Rome (Plin. *l. c.*). Millet was cultivated in some parts of Thrace; for Xenophon (*Anab.* vii. 5. § 12) states that on the march to Salmydessus, Seuthes and his allies traversed the country of the "millet-eating Thracians" (cf. Strab. vii. p. 315.) The less important vegetable productions of Thrace may be briefly mentioned: a species of water-chestnut (*tribulus*) grew in the Strymon, the leaves of which were used by the people who lived on its banks to fatten their horses, while of its nuts they made a very sweet kind of bread. (Plin. xxi. 58, xxii. 12.) Roses (*Rosa centifolia*) grew wild on the Pangaeus, and were successfully transplanted by the natives (Id. xxi. 10). The mountains, in general, abounded in wild-thyme and a species of mint (Id. xix. 55). A sort of morel or truffle (*iton*) was found in Thrace (Id. xix. 12; Athen. ii. p. 62), and a styptic plant (*ischaemon*), which was said to stop bleeding from even divided blood-vessels, (Theoph. *de Plant.* ix. 15; Plin. xxv. 45.) Several varieties of ivy grew in the country, and were sacred to Dionysus. (Theoph. *de Plant.* iii. 16; Plin. xvi. 62.) Herodotus (iv. 74) states that the Scythians had hemp both wild and cultivated; and as he proceeds to say that the Thracians made clothing of it, we may fairly infer that it grew in Thrace also. "The Athenians imported their timber chiefly from the country about the Strymon, for the Thracian hills abounded in oak and fir-trees." (Niebuhr, *Lect. Anc. Hist.* i. p. 292, Eng. trans.). M. Viquesnel states that the *Strandja-dagh* is covered with forests of oak (p. 314), and that in some parts of the district of Rhodope tobacco is now cultivated (p. 320).

Among the animals of Thrace, white horses are repeatedly mentioned. The famous steeds of Rhesus were "whiter than snow." (Hom. *Il.* x. 437; Eurip. *Rhes.* 304.) When Xerxes reached the banks of the Strymon in his onward march, the magi sacrificed white horses (Herod. vii. 113), which were probably Thracian, for the same reason, whatever that was, that the human victims spoken of in the next chapter were the children of natives. Xenophon states that, during a banquet given by Seuthes, a Thracian entered, leading a white horse, which he presented to his prince, with an encomium on its fleetness (*Anab.* vii. 3. § 26). Virgil speaks of Thracian horses with white spots (*Aen.* v. 565, ix. 49). Horses were no doubt plentiful in Thrace: Homer (*Il.* xiv. 227) calls the Thracians ἱπποπόλοι; and cavalry always formed a large part of their armies. Thus Thucydides (ii. 98) estimates the number of horsemen in the army with which Sitalces invaded Macedonia at about 50,000. One of the twelve labours of Hercules was to bring to Mycenae the savage mares of Diomedes, king of the Bistones in Thrace, who fed them with human flesh. (Ov. *Met.* ix. 194.) Herodotus (vii. 126) states that lions were found throughout the country bounded on the W. by the Achelous and on the E. by the Nestus; a statement which is repeated by Aristotle (*H. A.* vi. 31, viii. 28); so that the part of Thrace between the Strymon and the Nestus must have been in-

fested, at least in early times, by those formidable animals. Herodotus says that they attacked the baggage-camels of Xerxes during the march of his army from Acanthus to Therme (vii. 125). Cattle, both great and small, were abundant, and seem to have constituted the chief wealth of a people who, like most barbarians, considered agriculture a base occupation. (Herod. v. 6.) The fertile valleys were well adapted for oxen, and the thyme-covered hills for sheep; and it is clear, from several passages in Xenophon, that even the wildest Thracian tribes were rich in this kind of wealth. (*Anab.* vii. § 48, 7. § 53.) Aristotle informs us that the Thracians had a peculiar method of fattening swine (*H. A.* viii. 6). He attributes the smallness of their asses to the coldness of the climate (*Ib.* 28). Cranes are often mentioned as belonging to Thrace. (Virg. *Georg.* i. 120; Ov. *A. A.* iii. 182; Juv. xiii. 167.) Aristotle says that an aquatic bird of the pelican kind (πελεκᾶνες) migrates from the Strymon to the Ister (*H. A.* viii. 11); and that the people in some marshy districts of Thrace were assisted in catching water-fowl by hawks; which do not seem to have been trained for the purpose, but, though wild, to have been induced by a share of the game, to second the proceedings of their human associates (*Ib.* ix. 36). Eels were caught at certain seasons in the Strymon (*Ib.* viii. 2, ad fin.). The tunny fishery was a source of great wealth to Byzantium. (Strab. vii. p. 320.)

The principal mineral productions of Thrace were gold and silver, most of which came from the mountainous district between the Strymon and the Nestus. There, at the southern extremity of the Pangaeus, was situated Crenides, founded by the Thasians, and afterwards called Philippi, in a hill near which, named the hill of Dionysus (Appian, *B. C.* iv. 106), were the most productive gold mines of Thrace, to get possession of which was Philip's principal object in annexing the district in question to his dominions. He is said to have derived from the mines an annual income of 1000 talents. (Diod. xvi. 8; cf. Strab. vii. p. 323.) * Strabo (xiv. p. 680) says that the wealth of Cadmus came from the mines of the Pangaeus; and Pliny refers to the same tradition when he states (vii. 57) that according to some authorities, the Pangaeus was the place where Cadmus first discovered gold-mines, and the art of melting their produce (*conflatura*). Herodotus (vii. 112) mentions silver, as well as gold, mines in the Pangaeus, which in his time were in the possession of the native tribes called Pieres, Odomanti, and Satrae. He states also (vi. 46) that the Thasians had gold mines at Scapte Hyle, near Abdera, from which they derived an (annual) revenue of about 80 talents; and that a part of the revenues of Peisistratus came from the Strymon, by which the mines on its banks are probably meant (i. 64). (See also, ix. 75; Eurip. *Rhes.* 921; Strabo (or rather his epitomiser), vii. p. 331.) According to Pliny (xxxiii. 21) gold was found in the sands of the Hebrus; and this is confirmed by Paul Lucas (*l. c.*), and by Viquesnel, who states (p. 204) that in rainy years the affluents of that river are frequented by gold-finders, who wash the sands which contain gold in grains (*en paillettes*). Thucydides was interested in gold mines and works near Amphipolis, as he himself informs us (iv. 105). Of the other minerals of Thrace we may mention the

* On these mines, see Niebuhr, *Lect. Ethnog. and Geog.* i. pp. 285, 295, Eng. trans.

opal (*paederos*, Plin. xxxvii. 46); the *Thracia gemma*, one variety of which seems to resemble the bloodstone (*ib.* 68); a stone which burnt in water (Id. xxxiii. 30); and nitre, which was found near Philippi (Id. xxxi. 46). In addition to these, M. Viquesnel mentions fine marble, which is quarried from the mountains of *Lidja* (p. 200); excellent iron, manufactured at *Samakov* (p. 209); alum, produced at *Chaphané* (p. 213); and potter's clay, in the district of Rhodope, used by the Turks in the fabrication of earthenware (p. 319). He states also that Rhodope abounds in mineral waters (*ib.*), and that there are warm springs at *Lidja* (p. 212).

A few miscellaneous notes will conclude this part of our subject.

The narrow portion of Thrace between the Euxine, Bosporus and Propontis, is sometimes called the Delta (τὸ Δέλτα, Xen. *Anab.* vii. 1. § 33, 5. § 1).

Reference is several times made to violent natural convulsions, which destroyed various Thracian cities. Thus Strabo (i. 59) says that it appeared that some cities were swallowed up by a flood in Lake Bistonis; and he (vii. p. 319), Pliny (iv. 18), and Mela (ii. 2) speak of the destruction of Bizone, on the Euxine, by earthquakes.

Livy (xl. 22) describes the region between Maedica and the Haemus as without inhabitants (*solitudines*).

Herodotus (vii. 109) speaks of a lake near Pistyrus (on the coast N. of Abdera), about 30 stadia in circumference, abounding in fish, and extremely salt.

Thrace possessed two highroads, "both starting from Byzantium; the one (called the King's road, from having been in part the march of Xerxes in his invasion of Greece, Liv. xxxix. 27; Herod. vii. 115), crossing the Hebrus and the Nestus, touching the northern coast of the Aegean sea at Neapolis, a little south of Philippi, then crossing the Strymon at Amphipolis, and stretching through Pella across Inner Macedonia and Illyria to Dyrrhachium. The other road took a more northerly course, passing along the upper valley of the Hebrus from Adrianople to Philippopolis, then through Sardica (*Sophia*) and Naissus (*Nisch*), to the Danube near Belgrade, being the highroad now followed from Constantinople to Belgrade." (Grote, vol. xii. p. 34, note.) Herodotus (*l. c.*) remarks, with evident surprise, that the King's road had not, up to his time, been destroyed by the Thracians, a circumstance which he seems to attribute to the almost religious respect with which they regarded the "great king." It may be safely inferred that people who were considered to have done something wonderful in abstaining from breaking up a road, were not great makers or maintainers of highways; and it is clear from Livy's account of the march of Manlius (xxxviii. 40, 41) along this very road (afterwards called by the Romans, Via Egnatia, *q. v.*), that, although it was the principal line of communication between Europe and Asia, it was at that time (B. C. 188) in a very bad condition. From this some conception may be formed of the deplorable state in which the roads of the interior and mountainous districts must have been, and in which, indeed, they still remain. (Viquesnel, p. 312.) The Thracians no doubt were well aware that their independence would soon be lost, if there were an easy access for disciplined armies to every part of their country. Such paths as they possessed were sufficient for their own purposes of depredation, of ambush, and, when overpowered, of flight.

IV. ETHNOLOGY, MANNERS, RELIGION, ETC.—

The first point to be determined here is, whether the Thracians mentioned in the ancient writers as extending over many parts of Greece, as far south as Attica, were ethnologically identical with those who in historical times occupied the country which is the subject of the present article. And before discussing the topic, it will be convenient to lay before the reader some of the principal passages in the classics which bear upon it.

It is Strabo who makes the most distinct statements on the point. He says (vii. p. 321), "Hecataeus the Milesian states that, before the Hellenes, barbarians inhabited Peloponnesus. But in fact nearly all Greece was originally the abode of barbarians, as may be inferred from the traditions. Pelops brought a people with him into the country, to which he gave his name, and Danaus came to the same region with followers from Egypt, at a time when the Dryopes, Caucones, Pelasgi, Leleges, and other similar races had settlements within the Isthmus; and indeed without it too, for the Thracians who accompanied Eumolpus had Attica and Tereus possessed Daulis in Phocis; the Phoenician companions of Cadmus occupied Cadmeia, the Aones, Temmices, and Hyantes Boeotia." Strabo subsequently (ix. 401) repeats this statement respecting Boeotia, and adds that the descendants of Cadmus and his followers, being driven out of Thebes by the Thracians and Pelasgians, retired into Thessaly. They afterwards returned, and, having joined the Minyans of Orchomenos, expelled in their turn the Pelasgians and Thracians. The former went to Athens, where they settled at the foot of Hymettus, and gave the name of Pelasgicum to a part of the city (cf. Herod. vi. 137): the Thracians, on the other hand, were driven to Parnassus. Again (ix. p. 410) he says, speaking of Helicon: "The temple of the Muses, and Hippocrene, and the cave of the Leibethridan nymphs are there; from which one would conjecture that those who consecrated Helicon to the Muses were Thracians; for they dedicated Pieria, and Leibethrum, and Pimpleia to the same goddesses. These Thracians were called Pierians (Πίερες); but their power having declined, the Macedonians now occupy these (last named) places." This account is afterwards (x. p. 471) repeated, with the addition that " the cultivators of ancient music, Orpheus, Musaeus, Thamyris, and Eumolpus, were Thracians."

The difficulty that presents itself in these passages,—and they are in general agreement with the whole body of Greek literature,—arising from the confounding under a common name of the precursors of Grecian poetry and art with a race of men designated as barbarous, is well stated by K. O. Müller (*Hist. of Greek Liter.* p. 26, seq.): " It is utterly inconceivable that, in the later historic times, when the Thracians were contemned as a barbarian race, a notion should have sprung up that the first civilisation of Greece was due to them; consequently we cannot doubt that this was a tradition handed down from a very early period. Now, if we are to understand it to mean that Eumolpus, Orpheus, Musaeus, and Thamyris were the fellow-countrymen of those Edonians, Odrysians, and Odomantians, who in the historical age occupied the Thracian territory, and who spoke a barbarian language, that is, one unintelligible to the Greeks, we must despair of being able to comprehend these accounts of the ancient Thracian minstrels, and of assigning them a place in the history of Grecian civilisation; since it is manifest that at this early period, when there was scarcely any intercourse between different nations, or knowledge of foreign tongues, poets who sang in an unintelligible language could not have had more influence on the mental development of the people than the twittering of birds."

Müller therefore concludes that the Thracians of the ante-historical era, and those of subsequent times, belonged to distinct races. "When we come to trace more precisely the country of these Thracian bards, we find that the traditions refer to Pieria, the district to the east of the Olympus range, to the north of Thessaly, and the south of Emathia or Macedonia: in Pieria likewise was Leibethra, where the Muses are said to have sung the lament over the tomb of Orpheus : the ancient poets, moreover, always make Pieria, not Thrace, the native place of the Muses, which last Homer clearly distinguishes from Pieria. (*Il.* xiv. 226.) It was not until the Pierians were pressed in their own territory by the early Macedonian princes that some of them crossed the Strymon into Thrace Proper, where Herodotus (vii. 112) mentions the castles of the Pierians at the time of the expedition of Xerxes. It is, however, quite conceivable that in early times, either on account of their close vicinity, or because all the north was comprehended under one name, the Pierians might, in Southern Greece, have been called Thracians. These Pierians, from the intellectual relations which they maintained with the Greeks, appear to be a Grecian race; which supposition is also confirmed by the Greek names of their places, rivers, fountains, &c., although it is probable that, situated on the limits of the Greek nation, they may have borrowed largely from neighbouring tribes. (See Müller's *Dorians*, vol. i. pp. 472, 488, 501.)" After referring to the accounts of the Thracians in Southern Greece, Müller adds: "From what has been said, it appears sufficiently clear that these Pierians or Thracians, dwelling about Helicon and Parnassus in the vicinity of Attica, are chiefly signified when a Thracian origin is ascribed to the mythical bards of Attica."

Colonel Mure, after referring to the foregoing view, which be designates as " plausible," goes on as follows: " But the case admits of another, and perhaps more satisfactory explanation. It is certain that, in the mythical geography, a tract of country on the frontiers of Boeotia and Phocis, comprehending Mount Parnassus and Helicon, bore the name of Thrace. [See the etymology, *ante.*] In this region the popular mythology also lays the scene of several of the most celebrated adventures, the heroes of which are called Thracians." The author then applies this explanation to the stories of Tereus and Procne, and of Lycurgus, " king of Thrace; " and proceeds thus: " Pausanias makes the ' Thracian ' bard Thamyris virtually a Phocian. He assigns him for mother a nymph of Parnassus called Argiope. His father, Philammon, is described as a native of the same region, son of Apollo, by the nymph Chione, and brother of Autolycus, its celebrated robber chieftain. The divine grandsire is obviously here but a figure of his own sacred region; the grandmother Chione, as her name bears, of its snow. Others call the latter heroine Leuconoë. The names of these heroines are all so many varied modes of typifying the same ' snow-white' Parnassus. This view of the ' Thracian ' character of these sages becomes the more plausible, if it be remembered that the region of Central Greece, in which

the Hellenic Thrace was situated, is that from which first or chiefly, the seeds of elementary culture were propagated throughout the nation. Here tradition places the first introduction of the alphabet. Here were also the principal seats of Apollo and the Muses. In the heart of the same region was situated the Minyean Orchomenos, the temple of the Graces, rivalling Thebes herself in the splendour of her princes and zeal for the promotion of art. Among the early masters of poetry or music, not vulgarly styled Thracians, the most illustrious, Amphion and Linus, are Boeotians. Nor was this region of Central Greece less favoured in respect of its religious institutions. It was not only the favourite seat of Apollo, the Muses, and the Graces, but the native country of the Dionysiac rites, zeal for the propagation of which is a characteristic of the Thracian sages." (*Hist. of Lang. and Lit. of Ant. Greece*, i. pp. 150—153; cf. Niebuhr, *Lect. on Ethnog. and Geog.* i. p. 287.)

In thus entirely disconnecting these early " Thracians," from those of later times, we have the authority of Thucydides (ii. 29), who, in speaking of Teres, the father of Sitalces, remarks : " This Teres had no connection whatever with Tereus, who married Procne, daughter of Pandion of Athens ; they did not even belong to the same Thrace. Tereus dwelt at Daulia, a city of the country now called Phocis, and which was then occupied by the Thracians." And he proceeds to show that it was not likely that Pandion would form an alliance with any one who lived so far from Athens as the country of the Odrysae.[*]

The consideration of the ethnological relations of the early Thracians hardly falls within the scope of this article ; but since identity of name has often caused them to be confounded with the historical inhabitants of Thrace, it may be desirable briefly to discuss the subject in this place.

The view which seems to the present writer to be best supported by the evidence, and to explain most satisfactorily the ancient authors, is that which regards the mythical Thracians as members of the widely extended race to which the name of Pelasgians is usually given. It is clear from Homer that a close connection existed between the people of Southern Thrace and the Trojans, who were probably Pelasgians, and who are at the same time represented by him as agreeing, in language, religion, and other important respects, with the Greeks. Again, Homer mentions among the auxiliaries of Priam, the Caucones, who are named along with the Pelasgians (*Il.* x. 429), and the Cicones (*Il.* ii. 846). These two names bear so close a resemblance to each other as to suggest the probability of the cognate origin of the tribes so designated. Now the Cicones were undoubtedly Thracians (*Odys.* ix. 39, seqq.) ; while as to the Caucones, Strabo (xii. p. 542) informs us that they occupied part of the coast of Bithynia, and were regarded by some as Scythians, by others as Macedonians, by others again as Pelasgians. It will be remembered that Caucones are mentioned by him (vii. p. 321) among the earliest inhabitants of Peloponnesus. Another noticeable fact is, that in the passage of Strabo already quoted (ix. p. 401), he represents the Thracians and Pelasgians as acting in

---

[*] Yet subsequent prose writers, to say nothing of poets, fall into the error of making Tereus an inhabitant of Thrace Proper ; and Pliny (iv. 18) even mentions the castle there in which the crime of Tereus was perpetrated !

concert. The same author (xiii. p. 590) points out the similarity of many Thracian names of places to those existing in the Trojan territory. Finally, the names of the places mentioned by Strabo (vii. p. 321) as common to Pieria and the southern Thracians, are evidently Greek (see Müiler's *Dorians*, i. p. 501); and, as we have seen, the name Thrace itself is in all probability a significant Greek word.

These considerations appear to us to lead to the conclusion already stated, namely, that the mythical Thracians, as well as those spoken of by Homer, were Pelasgians; and hence that that race once occupied the northern as well as the other shores of the Aegean, until, at a comparatively late period, its continuity was broken by the irruption of the historical Thracians from the north into the country between the Strymon and the Euxine. The circumstance that the Greeks designated these barbarians by the name which had been borne by those whom they supplanted, admits of easy explanation, and history abounds in instances of a similar kind. But it may be doubted whether the Thracians had any general designation in their own language: they probably called themselves Edones, Denseletae, Thyni, Satrae, and so on; but we have no evidence that they really were all branches of a common stock. Under these circumstances, it was inevitable that the Greeks should bestow upon them the name of the earlier possessors of the country; and those Thracians who were brought in contact with the more civilised race would probably adopt it. (On the foregoing question, see Niebuhr, *Lect. on Anc. Hist.* i. pp. 142, 212; *Lect. on Ethnog. and Geog.* i. p. 287; Wachsmuth, *Hist. Ant.* i. p. 44, seqq.)

Respecting the historical Thracians we have tolerably full information, but not of that kind which will enable us to arrive at any very definite conclusions as to their ethnological relations. That they belonged to an extensively diffused race, whose early abodes were in the far northern regions, may be regarded as sufficiently proved by the concurrent testimony of the ancient writers. Herodotus, in a well-known passage (v. 3), says that the Thracian nation is the greatest in the world, after the Indians, and that its subdivisions, of which the Getae are one, have many names, according to the countries which they severally occupy. Strabo too (vii. p. 295) states that the Getae and the Mysi were Thracians (as to the Mysi, see also i. p. 6), who extended north of the Danube (vii. p. 296). In confirmation of his assertion that the Getae were ethnologically akin to the Thracians, he adduces the identity of their language (vii. p. 303). He adds (vii. p. 305) that the Daci also spoke this language. From his remark (vii. p. 315) about the Iapodes, it would seem that he regarded the Illyrians also as nearly allied to, if not actually a branch of, the Thracians. In another passage (x. p. 471) he says that the Phrygians were colonists of the Thracians; to which race also the Saraparae, a nation still farther towards the east, north of Armenia, were reported to belong (xi. p. 531). "The Bithyni, previously called Mysi, were so named, as is admitted by most authorities, from the Thracian Bithyni and Thyni, who emigrated to that country (i. e. Asia Minor; cf. Herod. vii. 75). And I conjecture that the Bebryces, who settled in Mysia before the Bithyni and Mysi, were also Thracians. The Mysians themselves are said to be colonists of those Thracians who are now called Mysi. As the Mariandyni are in all respects like the Bithyni, they too are probably Thracians." (Strab. xii. pp. 541, 542.) Justin

couples the Thracians with the Illyrians and Dardani (xi. 1). In the west and south-west it is impossible to define the Thracian boundary: we have seen that Mela describes the whole of the Chalcidic peninsula as part of Thrace (cf. Thucyd. ii. 79); and there is no doubt that they extended as far south as Olympus, though mixed up with Macedonians, who were the preponderating race in that quarter. In later times the intrusive and undoubtedly distinct races which were mingled with the Thracians near the Danube, were sometimes confounded with them. Thus Florus (iii. 4) calls the Scordisci the most savage of all the Thracians.

Of the language of the Thracians scarcely a trace exists. They were too barbarous to have any literary or artistic memorials, so that the principal guides of the ethnologist are wanting. Strabo (vii. p. 319) states that *bria*, which occurs as the termination of several names of Thracian towns, signified "city" or "town." This and a few proper names constitute all that remains of their language.

The following is the account which Herodotus gives of the customs of the Thracians. They sell their children into foreign slavery. The women while unmarried enjoy perfect freedom in their intercourse with men; but after marriage they are strictly guarded. The men pay large sums of money for their wives to the parents of the latter. 'To be tattooed is considered an indispensable mark of noble birth. (Cf. Strab. vii. p. 315.) Idleness is most honourable; the cultivator of the soil is regarded as the meanest of men; to live by war and plundering is most noble. The only gods they worship are Ares, Dionysus, and Artemis. But their kings differ in this respect from their subjects; for they worship Hermes especially, and swear by him alone, from whom they say that they are descended. When a wealthy man dies, his corpse lies in state for three days: his friends then make a great feast, at which, after bewailing the departed, they slaughter victims of every kind: the body is then buried, having sometimes been previously burnt. A mound is raised above the grave, upon which athletic games are celebrated (v. 6—8; cf. Xen. *Hell.* iii. 2. § 5). Besides these customs, which were common to all the Thracians, Herodotus mentions some which were peculiar to certain tribes; as, for instance, that which prevailed among the people to the north of the Crestonians. "Among them, each man has many wives. When any man dies, a great contest arises among his widows on the question as to which of them was most beloved by their husband; and in this their relations take a very active part. She in whose favour the point is decided, receives the congratulations of both men and women, and is then slain upon her husband's grave by her nearest male relation. The other widows regard themselves as extremely unfortunate, for they are considered to be disgraced." (*Ib.* 5.) Herodotus here seems to speak of polygamy as confined to a certain tribe of Thracians; but Strabo (vii. p. 297) represents this custom as general among them. In a note upon this passage, Casaubon quotes from Heracleides Ponticus to the effect that Thracians often had as many as thirty wives, whom they employed as servants, a practice still common in many eastern countries. Xenophon furnishes us with an illustration of the Thracian custom of purchasing wives. He states that at his first interview with Seuthes, the Thracian prince proposed to give his daughter in marriage to Xenophon; and if the Greek himself had a daughter, offered to buy her as a wife. (*Anab.* vii. 2. § 38; cf. Mela, ii. 2.)

The want of union among the Thracians is mentioned by Herodotus (v. 3) as the only cause of their weakness. Their tribes, like the Highland clans, seem to have been constantly engaged in petty warfare with one another, and to have been incapable of co-operating even against foreign foes, except for very brief periods, and rarely with any higher object than plunder. Until a late period (Flor. iv. 12. §17) they appear to have been destitute of discipline, and this, of course, rendered their bravery of comparatively little avail. Thus we learn from Thucydides (ii. 96, 98) that, although Sitalces was the most powerful Thracian king that had ever reigned—(he seems indeed to have been subsequently regarded as a kind of national hero; Xen. *Anab.* vi. 1. § 6),—yet a large part of the army with which he invaded Macedonia consisted of mere volunteers, formidable chiefly for their numbers, and attracted to his standard by his offers of pay, or by their hope of plunder. Any one, in fact, who held out these inducements, could easily raise an army in Thrace. Thus Clearchus no sooner received supplies of money from Cyrus the Younger, than he collected a force in the Chersonesus, which, although in great part undoubtedly Thracian, was employed by him in making war upon other Thracians, until he was required to join Cyrus in Asia Minor (*Ib.* i. 1. § 9, 2. § 9, &c.). So when Seuthes undertook the expedition against his so-called revolted subjects, his army was soon tripled by volunteers, who hastened from other parts of Thrace to serve him, as soon as they heard of his enterprise (*Ib.* vii. 4. § 21). Such soldiers could not, of course, be depended upon for one moment after a reverse. A considerable number of Thracian mercenaries in the army of Cyrus took the earliest opportunity to desert to Artaxerxes after the battle of Cunaxa (*Ib.* ii. 2. § 7).

Tacitus (*Ann.* iv. 46) informs us that the principal cause of the insurrection (A. D. 26) of the Thracians who dwelt in the elevated mountain districts (probably of Rhodope), was their dislike of the conscription, which, it would appear, the Romans had introduced into Thrace. This was a yoke to which they could not submit; they were not accustomed to obey even their own rulers, except when it pleased them; and when they sent troops to the assistance of their princes, they used to appoint their own commanders, and to war against the neighbouring tribes only. (Cf. Liv. xlii. 51; Xen. *Anab.* vii. 4. § 24, 7. § 29, seq.)

Thracian troops were chiefly light-armed infantry and irregular horse. (Xen. *Anab.* i. 2. § 9, vii. 6. § 27, *Memor.* iii. 9. § 2; Curt. iii. 9.) The bravest of the foot-soldiers in the army of Sitalces were the free mountaineers of Rhodope, who were armed with short swords (μαχαιροφόροι; Thucyd. ii. 98). The equipment of the Asiatic Thracians is described by Herodotus (vii. 75), and as this description agrees with what Xenophon states respecting Seuthes' forces (*Anab.* vii. 4. § 4), it is no doubt substantially true of the Thracians generally. They wore caps covering their ears, made of fox-skins, cloaks, and party-coloured mantles ((ειραl, ? = plaids) ; their boots, which came high up the leg, were made of deer-skin; their arms were shields, javelins, and daggers (cf. Thucyd. vii. 27). The Thracians in the army of Philip V. were armed with very long *rhomphaeae*, a word which some translate *javelins*, others *swords*. (Liv. xxxi. 39;

Plut. *Paul. Aemil.* 17.) Thracian soldiers fought with impetuosity and with no lack of bravery; but they, like all barbarian and undisciplined troops were incapable of sustained efforts. Livy (xlii. 59) describes them as rushing to the attack like wild beasts long confined in cages: they hamstrung the horses of their adversaries, or stabbed them in the belly. When the victory was gained on this occasion (the first encounter in the war between the Romans and Perseus), they returned to their camp, singing loud songs of triumph, and carrying the heads of the slain on the tops of their weapons (*Ib.* 60). When defeated, they fied with rapidity, throwing their shields upon their backs, to protect them from the missiles of the pursuers. (Xen. *Anab.* vii. 4. § 17.)

About the time of the Peloponnesian War, Thrace began to be to the countries around the Aegean what Switzerland has long, to its disgrace, been to the despotic powers of modern Europe, a land where men might be procured to fight for any one who could hold out sufficient inducements in the shape of pay or plunder. (Thucyd. vii. 27, et alibi; Xen. *Anab.* i. pass.; Just. xi. 1 & 9.) The chief causes of this, apart from the character of its people, appear to have been the want of any central government, and the difficult nature of the country, which rendered its savage independence tolerably secure; so that there was nothing to restrain those who might wish to seek their fortune in foreign warfare. During the period of Macedonian supremacy, and after its close, under the Roman power, Thracians are often mentioned as auxiliaries in Macedonian and Roman armies; but few of these, it is probable, were volunteers. (Liv. xxxi. 39, xlii. 29, 51, et al.; Caes. *B. C.* iii. 4; Vell. Pat. ii. 112; Tac. *Hist.* i. 68, &c.) Cicero (*de Prov. Cons.* 4) seems to imply that Thracians were sometimes hired to assassinate like the modern Italian bravos; these were perhaps gladiators, of whom great numbers were Thracians. Caligula gave the command of his German bodyguard to Thracians. (Suet. *Calig.* 55.)

Another point in which the Thracians remind us of the natives of India, is mentioned by Thucydides (ii. 97) in these words: "The tribute of the barbarians and of the Greek cities received by Seuthes, the successor of Sitalces, might be reckoned at 400 talents of silver, reckoning gold and silver together. The presents in gold and silver amounted to as much more. And these presents were made not only to the king, but also to the most influential and distinguished of the Odrysae. For these people, like those of Thrace generally, differ in this respect from the Persians, that they would rather receive than give; and among them it is more shameful not to give when you are asked, than to be refused when you ask. It is true that abuses arise from this custom ; for nothing can be done without presents." (Cf. Liv. xlii. 19, xlv. 42; Tac. *Germ.* 15.) Xenophon (*Anab.* vii. 3) gives some amusing illustrations of this practice among the Thracians.

Mention is often made of the singing and dancing of the Thracians, especially of a martial kind. Xenophon (*Anab.* vi. 1. § 5, seq.) gives an account of a dance and combat performed by some Thracians, to celebrate the conclusion of a peace between the remnant of the 10,000 Greeks and the Paphlagonians: they danced fully armed to the music of the flute, jumping up nimbly to a considerable height, and fencing with their swords: at last, one man struck another, to all appearance mortally and he fell as if dead, though in reality not in the least injured. His antagonist then stripped off his armour, and went out singing the praises of Sitalces, while the other man was carried out like a corpse by his comrades (cf. *Ib.* vii. 3. § 32, seq.; Tac. *Ann.* iv. 47).

Their music was rude and noisy. Strabo (x. p. 471) compares it to that of the Phrygians, whom, indeed, he regards as descended from the Thracians. Xenophon, in the passage last referred to, says that they played on horns and on trumpets made of raw ox-hide. Their worship of Dionysus and Cotytto was celebrated on mountain tops with loud instruments of music, shouting, and noises like the bellowing of cattle. (Strab. x. p. 470.)

Their barbarity and ferocity became proverbial. Herodotus (viii. 116) tells a story of a king of the Bisaltae, who punished his six sons for disobeying him by putting out their eyes. Seuthes, with his own hand, transfixed some of the Thyni who had been taken prisoners (Xen. *Anab.* vii. 4. § 6). Rhascuporis invited his nephew to a banquet, plied him with wine, then loaded him with fetters, and afterwards put him to death. (Tac. *Ann.* ii. 64, seqq.) Thucydides (vii. 27, seq.) gives an instance of the ferocity of the Thracians in their massacre of the inhabitants of Mycalessus.

A truly barbarian trait in the character of the Thracians was their faithlessness, even to one another. This is especially shown in their disregard of their obligations towards the hostages whom they gave as securities for their observance of their engagements with others. Seuthes had received from the Thyni a number of old men as hostages; yet the Thyni, seeing a favourable opportunity, as they supposed, for renewing hostilities, at once seized it, apparently without a thought of the but too probable consequences of such conduct to their helpless countrymen. (Xen. *Anab.* vii. 4. § 21; cf. Liv. xl. 22). Some of the tribes inhabiting the Thracian coast of the Euxine were systematic wreckers [SALMYDESSUS]. Robbery, as we have seen, was considered honourable by them; and plunder was their chief inducement to engage in war. (Strab. vii. p. 318; Cic. *Pis.* 34; Liv. xxvi. 25, xxxviii. 40, seq.) Strabo (iii. pp. 164, 165), Mela (ii. 2), and Tacitus (*Ann.* iv. 51) bear witness to the bravery of the Thracian women.

The deity most worshipped by the Thracians was Dionysus, whom they, as well as the Phrygians, called Sabazius. (Schol. *Aristoph. Vesp.* 9.) The mythical stories respecting Orpheus and Lycurgus are closely connected with the worship of this god, who had an oracle on Rhodope, in the country of the Satrae, but under the direction of the Bessi [SATRAE]. Herodotus (vii. 111) states that the mode of delivering the answers of this oracle resembled that which prevailed at Delphi. He compares also the worship of Artemis (whose Thracian name was Bendis or Cotytto), as he had seen it celebrated by Thracian and Paeonian women, with some of the ceremonies at Delos (iv. 33). These resemblances may be accounted for on the supposition that the Thracian rites were derived from the original Pelasgian population, remnants of which may have maintained themselves amid the mountain fastnesses; as Niebuhr holds (*Ethnog. and Geog.* i. p. 287) was the case with the Paeonians, who are mentioned by Herodotus in the passage last referred to. (On the Thracian divinities, see Strabo, x. pp. 470, 471; Soph. *Antig.* 955, seq.; Plin. xvi. 62; and the articles BENDIS, COTYS, and RHEA, in the *Dict. Biog. and Myth.*)

It has sometimes been asserted that the Thracians were accustomed to sacrifice human victims to their divinities; but this appears to be either an incorrect generalisation, or a confounding of them with other races; for we find no reference to such a custom in any of the ancient accounts of their manners. Herodotus, it is true, states (ix. 119) that when the Persian Oeobazus fell into the hands of the Apsinthii, after the taking of Sestus by the Athenians, they sacrificed him to their local god, Pleistorus; but from the next words (τρόπῳ τῷ σφετέρῳ) it is clear that he regarded the practice as characteristic of the Apsinthii, and not as one common to all Thracians: nor is it conceivable that he would have omitted to mention so striking a circumstance, in his general description of Thracian manners, which has been already quoted (v. 3. seqq); for the practice of slaying the favourite wife on the tomb of her deceased husband cannot with any propriety be called a sacrifice.

Whether indulgence in wine was regarded as a part of the homage due to Dionysus, or simply as a means of sensual gratification, certain it is that it was prevalent in Thrace, and frequently attended with violent and sanguinary quarrels: "Natis in usum laetitiae scyphis pugnare Thracum est," says Horace, and evidence is not wanting in support of the accusation. Ammianus (xxvii. 4. § 9) describes the Odrysae as so fond of bloodshed that in their banquets, after eating and drinking to satiety, they used to fall to blows with one another. Tacitus (*Ann.* iv. 48) relates that the Thracians serving with Poppaeus Sabinus against their fellow-countrymen, indulged to such a degree in feasting and drinking that they kept no guard at night, so that their camp was stormed by their exasperated brethren, who slew great numbers of them. Xenophon tells us that at his first interview with Seuthes, they drank horns of wine to each other's health, according to the Thracian custom (*Anab.* vii. 2. § 23). At the banquet which Seuthes afterwards gave to Xenophon and some other important persons the drinking seems to have been deep. Xenophon admits that he had indulged freely; and he was evidently astonished that when Seuthes rose from the table, he manifested no signs of intoxication. (*Ib.* 3. § 26, seqq.) The Thracians are said to have had a custom, which prevailed in England as late as the last century, of compelling all the guests to drink the same quantity. (Callim. *ap. Athen.* x. p. 442.) The Odrysian auxiliaries of Dercyllidas poured great quantities of wine upon the graves of their slain comrades. (Xen. *Hell.* iii. 2. § 5.) It would appear from Mela (ii. 2), that some of the Thracians were unacquainted with wine, but practised another mode of producing intoxication: while feasting, they threw into the fires around which they were seated certain seeds, the fumes of which caused a cheerful kind of drunkenness. It is possible that these may have been the seeds of hemp, which, as we have seen, probably grew in Thrace, and contains, as is well known, a narcotic principle.

The Thracians against whom Seuthes led his forces lived in villages (*Ib.* § 43), the houses being fenced round with large stakes, within the inclosure formed by which their sheep were secured (*Ib.* 4. § 14; cf. Tac. *Ann.* iv. 49).

Pliny (vii. 41) states that the Thracians had a custom of marking their happy or unhappy days, by placing a white or a black stone in a vessel at the close of each day. On any one's death, the vessel belonging to him was emptied, the stones were separately counted, and his life pronounced to have been happy or the reverse, as the white or the black were more numerous.

V. HISTORY.—Thrace is one of those countries whose people, not being sufficiently civilised to establish a national government or to possess a national literature, cannot have histories of their own. We become acquainted with the Thracians at second hand, as it were, through the narrations of foreigners, who necessarily make them subordinate to their own countrymen; and therefore it is only in connection with foreign states that their history has been recorded. Hence it is fragmentary, and, consequently, often obscure; nor would its importance, indeed, repay the labour that might be employed in elucidating it, even if we possessed the requisite materials. Destitute of union, the Thracians, notwithstanding their numbers, their wide diffusion, their powers of endurance, and their contempt of death, exerted no perceptible influence upon the general course of history; but were reduced, in spite of their wild love of independence, to assist, as humble allies or subjects, in the aggrandisement of the more civilised or politic races with which they came in contact. These were the Greeks, the Persians, the Macedonians, and the Romans, with the successors of the last in the Eastern Empire. We shall now briefly state the leading points of their history, as connected with that of the nations just mentioned ; referring the reader for details, especially as to the little that is known of their purely internal affairs, to the articles in this work which relate to the BESSI, ODRYSAE, and other prominent Thracian tribes.

We pass over the alleged conquest of Thrace by Sesostris (Herod. ii. 103; Diod. i. 53), and that said to have been effected by the Teucri and Mysi before the Trojan War (Herod. vii. 20 ; cf. Eurip. *Rhes.* 406, seq.), and come at once to the strictly historical periods.

The first connection of the Greeks with Thrace was through colonies planted upon its various coasts, the original object of which seems generally to have been of a commercial kind. Only an approximation to the date of most of these can be made, since the majority were established long before the commencement of authentic history. Byzantium and Selymbria, colonies of Megara, belong to the seventh century B. C., the year 675 B. C. being assigned for the foundation of the former. In 651 B. C. an unsuccessful attempt is said to have been made by settlers from Clazomenae to establish themselves at Abdera (Solin. x. 10); but that city was not actually founded till 560 B. C., and then by emigrants from Teos. (Herod. i. 168.) Mesembria, on the Euxine, was a colony of the Byzantians and Chalcedonians, who abandoned their cities on the approach of the Phoenician fleet, B. C. 493. (Id. vi. 33). When Dicaea, Maronea, and Aenus, all on the south coast, were established, is not known; which is the case also with Cardia and Sestus in the Chersonesus. That these settlements were generally exposed to the hostility of their Thracian neighbours, there can be no doubt, though we rarely have their infant struggles so fully recorded as in the instance of Amphipolis. The Athenians sent no less than 10,000 men (B. C. 465) to found a colony there; and they succeeded in driving off the Edonians who occupied the country; but having advanced into the interior, they

were defeated at Drabescus by the natives, and compelled to abandon the country. About thirty years afterwards, however, the Athenians returned, and this time overcame all resistance. Sometimes the relation between the Greeks and the Thracians was of a more friendly description. Thus, in the time of Peisistratus, the Dolonci, who dwelt in the Chersonesus, invited Miltiades (the elder) to rule over them, as they were unable to cope with their neighbours the Apsinthii; and this led to the Athenians obtaining a firm footing in that most important and valuable district. (Herod. vi. 34, seq.) By these various means, the Greeks had obtained possession of nearly the whole coast of Thrace, a considerable period before the commencement of the great contest between themselves and the Persian empire. Of the interior they appear to have known scarcely anything whatever; and although in some cases the surrounding barbarians may have been brought into subjection (Byzantium is said to have reduced the Bithynian Thracians to the condition of tributary perioeci), yet this was rarely the case. On the contrary, it is clear from Thucydides (ii. 97), that the Greeks sometimes paid tribute to the native kings. The Greeks, even when dwelling among hostile strangers, showed their tendency to separation rather than to union; and hence their settlements on the Thracian coast never gained the strength which union would have conferred upon them. Each city had a government and to a great extent a history of its own; and we must therefore refer the reader for information respecting those states to the separate articles in this work devoted to them.

The first Persian expedition to Thrace was that of Darius, who crossed the Bosporus with his army about B. C. 513 (or 508, as some authorities hold). As the principal object of Darius was to chastise the Scythians for their invasion of Asia in the reign of Cyaxares, he took the shortest route through Thrace, where he met with no opposition. The Greeks whom he found there were required to follow in his train to the Danube: among them was the younger Miltiades, the destined hero of Marathon, who then ruled over the Chersonesus, as his uncle had formerly done, and who had married the daughter of a Thracian king. (Herod. vi. 39.)[*] On returning from the north, Darius directed his march to the Hellespont, and before crossing from Sestus into Asia, erected a fort at Doriscus, near the mouth of the Hebrus. (Herod. iv. 89—93, 143, 144, vii. 59.) Megabazus was left with 80,000 men to subdue the whole of Thrace, a task which he began by besieging Perinthus, which, though previously weakened by the attacks of the Paeonians, made a brave but fruitless resistance. After this, Megabazus reduced the country into subjection, though perhaps only the districts near the sea. (Herod. v. 1, 2, 10.) That his conquests extended as far as the Strymon appears from Darius's grant of a district upon that river to Histiaeus, who founded there the town of Myrcinus. (Herod. v. 11.) Megabazus soon returned to Asia ; and it seems probable that he took with him the greater part of his army; for if the Persians had maintained

---

[*] Instances occur in later times of the intermarriage of Greeks with Thracians: thus the wife of Sitalces was a daughter of Pythes, a citizen of Abdera (Thucyd. ii. 29); and Iphicrates married a daughter of the Thracian king Cotys. (Nep. *Iph.* 3.)

a powerful force in Thrace, the Paeonians could hardly have succeeded in making their escape from Phrygia back to the Strymon (Id. v. 98), nor could the revolted Ionians (B. C. 498) have taken Byzantium and all the other cities in that country. (Id. v. 103.) It is to this period that we must refer the invasion of the Scythians, who are said to have advanced as far as the Chersonesus, thus occasioning the temporary flight of Miltiades, who, they were aware, had assisted Darius in his attack upon their country. (Id. vi. 40.)

After the suppression of the Ionian revolt (B. C. 493), the Phoenician fleet sailed to the Hellespont, and again brought the country under the Persian dominion, Cardia being the only city which they were unable to take. (Id. vi. 33.) Miltiades made his escape from the Chersonesus to Athens, on hearing of the approach of the hostile fleet. (Ib. 41.)

Next year Mardonius led an army across the Hellespont, and advanced as far as Macedonia; but his fleet having been wrecked off Mount Athos, and his land forces having suffered considerably in a war with the Thracians, who then occupied the country W. of the Strymon, he retraced his steps, and transported his shattered army into Asia (Id. vi. 43, seqq.).

It was not till B. C. 480 that the vast army under the command of Xerxes crossed the Hellespont by the famous bridges which spanned the strait from Abydos to Sestus. Of his march through Thrace, Herodotus gives an interesting account (vii. 108—115); but, as he met with no opposition, we need not dwell upon these circumstances.

After the disastrous battle of Salamis, Xerxes, with an escort of 60,000 men, hastened back by the same road which he had so recently trod in all the overweening confidence of despotic power: in Thrace, his miserable troops suffered greatly from hunger and consequent disease, but do not appear to have been openly attacked. (Herod. viii. 115, seqq.)

Next year (B. C. 479) was fought the battle of Plataeae in which Thracians formed part of the motley host arrayed against Greek freedom (Id. ix. 32). Artabazus led the 40,000 men, who alone remained of the Persian army, by forced marches through Thessaly, Macedonia, and Thrace. He struck through the interior of the latter country, probably for fear of the Greek cities on the coast; but he encountered enemies as much to be dreaded, and lost a great part of his army by hunger, fatigue, and the attacks of the Thracians, before he reached Byzantium.

It was now the turn of the victorious Greeks to assail their foes in their own territories. Thrace, with the exception of Doriscus, was soon cleared of the Persians. After the battle of Mycale, their fleet sailed to the Hellespont, where the Athenians laid siege to Sestus, which was taken early in the following year (B. C. 478) [SESTUS]. Eion, at the mouth of the Strymon, made a desperate resistance; but at length (B. C. 476) fell into the hands of Cimon and the Athenians, after its Persian governor had put to death all his family, and finally himself. (Herod. vii. 107; cf. Thucyd. i. 98). Byzantium had been taken by Pausanias the year before. Thus the Persians were driven out of Europe, and the Greek settlements in Thrace resumed their internal freedom of action, though most of them, it is probable, were under the supremacy of Athens, as the chosen head of the great Greek confederacy.

During the administration of Pericles, 1000 Athenian citizens were settled in the Thracian Chersonesus, which was always the chief stronghold of Athens in that quarter. Under the auspices of the same statesman, in B. C. 437, the Athenians succeeded in founding Amphipolis, the contests for the possession of which occupy a very prominent place in the subsequent history of Greece. [AMPHIPOLIS, Vol. I. p. 126.]

About this time flourished the most powerful Thracian kingdom that ever existed, that of the Odrysae, for the history of which see ODRYSAE, Vol. II. pp. 463—465. At the commencement of the Peloponnesian War (B.C. 431), the Athenians entered into an alliance with Sitalces, the king of the Odrysae (Thucyd. ii. 29), who, they hoped, would enable them to subdue all opposition to their supremacy in the Chalcidic peninsula. In consequence of this alliance, Sitalces led (B. C. 429) a vast host into Macedonia, the ruler of which supported the enemies of Athens: he encountered no opposition, yet was compelled by want of supplies to return to Thrace, about a month after he had left it (Ib. 95—101). But although Sitalces was an ally of Athens, this did not prevent Brasidas from having great numbers of light-armed Thracians in his armies, while commanding the Spartan forces in the neighbourhood of Amphipolis (B. C. 422).

It would occupy too much space to relate minutely the various turns of fortune which occurred in Thrace during the Peloponnesian War. The principal struggle in this quarter was for the command of the Bosporus and Hellespont, so important, especially to the Athenians, on account of the corn trade with the Euxine, from which Athens drew a large part of her supplies. Hence many of the most important naval battles were fought in the Hellespont; and the possession of Byzantium and Sestus was the prize of many a victory. The battle of Aegospotami, which terminated the long contest for supremacy, took place to the S. of Sestus, B. C. 405. By the peace concluded next year, Athens gave up all her foreign possessions; and those in the east of Thrace fell into the hands of the Spartans and Persians. [See BYZANTIUM, SESTUS, &c.]

When the remnant of the 10,000 Greeks returned (B. C. 400) to Europe, they were engaged by Seuthes, an Odrysian prince, to assist him in recovering the dominions which had belonged to his father, in the south eastern part of Thrace. (Xen. Anab. vii. pass.) Having thus been reinstated in his principality, he showed his gratitude to the Greeks, by sending auxiliaries to Dercyllidas, who commanded the Spartan forces against the Persians, with whom they were now (B. C. 399) at war (Xen. Hell. iii. 2). Next year Dercyllidas crossed over into the Chersonesus, and erected a wall across its northern extremity, as a protection to the Greek inhabitants, who were exposed to constant attacks from their barbarous neighbours (Ib. 2. §§ 8—10). The same general successfully defended Sestus from the combined forces of Conon and Pharnabazus (B.C. 394: Ib. iv. 8. § 5, seqq.) But in B. C. 390 Thrasybulus restored Athenian influence in Thrace, by forming an alliance with two native princes, and by establishing democracy at Byzantium (Ib. § 25, seqq.); and his success was confirmed by the victory of Iphicrates over Anaxibius the next year (ib. § 34). The peace of Antalcidas, however, released all the Greek states from their connection with Athens, and virtually gave the supremacy to Sparta (B. C. 387).

Nothing of any importance happened in Thrace after this event till the accession of Philip II. to the throne of Macedonia (B. C. 359). This able but unscrupulous monarch at once began his career of aggrandisement towards the east. He contrived to get possession of Amphipolis (B. C. 358), and thus obtained a secure footing from which he might extend his dominions in Thrace as opportunity offered. At this time there were three native Thracian princes, probably brothers, who seem to have ruled over most of the country. According to Justin (viii. 3), Berisades and Amadocus, two of them, chose Philip as judge of their disputes; of which position he treacherously availed himself to seize upon their dominions. Though this statement is not supported, we believe, by any other ancient author, yet it is probably true; for such conduct is highly characteristic of the Macedonian monarch; and the almost entire disappearance from history of these Thracian princes soon after Philip's accession, would thus be accounted for. Cersobleptes, the third brother, who seems to have had the E. portion of Thrace, maintained a long struggle against his ambitious neighbour. In B. C. 357 he ceded the Chersonesus to the Athenians, who sent a colony to occupy it four years afterwards. [See CERSO-BLEPTES, Dict. Biog. Vol. I. p. 674 : SESTUS.] Philip at various times marched into Thrace, and repeatedly defeated Cersobleptes, whom he at length (B. C. 343) completely subdued and rendered tributary. Next year he established colonies in the eastern part of Thrace, and acts of hostility occurred between him and Diopeithes, the Athenian commander in that quarter. Philip was occupied the next three years in Thrace, and laid siege to Perinthus and Byzantium, which were in alliance with Athens, whose forces, commanded by Phocion, compelled Philip to abandon the sieges; and he soon afterwards left Thrace, to advance towards the south against the confederate Greeks. On his departure Phocion recovered several of the cities in which Macedonian garrisons had been placed.

Notwithstanding these checks, Philip had brought under his command a great part of Thrace, especially on the south coast: he had, above all, completely incorporated with his kingdom the district between the Strymon and the Nestus, and from the mines of the Pangaeus, which he seized in B. C. 356, he obtained abundant supplies of the precious metals.

Philip was assassinated B. C. 336: next year his successor, Alexander the Great, marched across the Haemus to attack the Triballi; but his chief attention was bestowed upon the preparations for the Asiatic expedition, which he entered upon next year, crossing the Hellespont from Sestus.

On the death of Alexander (B. C. 323), Thrace was allotted to Lysimachus, who was soon involved in hostilities with Seuthes, a king of the Odrysae. The reader is referred to the account of Lysimachus [Dict. Biog. Vol. II. pp. 867—870] for details respecting his government of Thrace: the result of his various wars was that his sway was firmly established over all the countries south of the Danube, as far as the confines of Macedonia; the Greek cities on the Euxine were garrisoned by his troops; and though many of the native tribes, in the more inaccessible districts, no doubt retained their freedom, yet he had completely defeated all their attacks upon his power. In B. C. 309 he founded Lysimachia, near the northern extremity of the Chersonesus and made it his capital. Having engaged in a war with Seleucus, the ruler of Syria, he advanced to meet his antagonist in Asia, and was defeated and slain at Corupedion (B. C. 281), upon which Seleucus passed

over into Europe and took possession of Thrace. Next year, however, he was assassinated by Ptolemy Ceraunus, who was thereupon acknowledged king; but shortly afterwards a vast horde of Celts invaded the country, and Ptolemy was slain in a battle with them. Anarchy now prevailed for some years in the country: the Celts again advanced to the south in B. C. 279, and under Brennus penetrated as far as Delphi, on their repulse from which they retreated northwards, and some of them settled on the coast of Thrace.

For nearly fifty years after this time little mention is made of Thrace in history; it appears to have been annexed to Macedonia; but the rulers of that kingdom were too insecure, even in their central dominions, to be able to exercise much control over such a country as Thrace, inhabited now by races differing so widely as the Thracians, the Greeks, and the Celts, and offering so many temptations to the assertion of independence. [See ANTIGONUS GONATAS, DEMETRIUS II., and PYRRHUS, in Dict. Biog.].

About B. C. 247, the fleet of Ptolemy Euergetes captured Lysimachia and other important cities on the coast; and they remained for nearly half a century under the kings of Egypt. (Polyb. v. 34, 58.)

In B. C. 220, Philip V. ascended the throne of Macedonia. Under him the Macedonian power regained something of its old prestige; and had it not been brought into collision with Rome, it might have become as extensive as in former times. But Philip unfortunately directed his ambitious views in the first instance towards the West, and thus soon encountered the jealous Republic. It was not till B. C. 211 that Philip commenced his enterprises against Thrace: he then led an army into the country of the Maedi, who were in the habit of making incursions into Macedonia. Their lands were laid waste, and their capital, Iamphorina, compelled to surrender. Having made peace with the Romans (B. C. 205), he invaded Thrace, and took Lysimachia. In B. C. 200, he again attacked that country, both by sea and land; and it is evident that he did not anticipate much resistance, since he took with him only 2000 infantry and 200 cavalry. Yet with this insignificant force, aided by the fleet, he made himself master of the whole of the south coast, and of the Chersonesus. He then laid siege to Abydos, and after a desperate resistance took it (Liv. xxxi. 16). This seems to have hastened the declaration of war on the part of the Romans; a war which lasted till B. C. 196, when Philip was reduced to procure peace by surrendering all his conquests, and withdrawing his garrisons from the Greek cities (Liv. xxxiii. 30). L. Stertinius was sent to see that these terms were complied with (ib. 35). But scarcely had the cities been evacuated by the Macedonian garrisons, when Antiochus the Great crossed the Hellespont, and took possession of the Chersonesus, which he claimed as a conquest of Seleucus (ib. 38). He refused to comply with the demand of the Romans, that he should withdraw his army from Europe; but left his son Seleucus to complete the restoration of Lysimachia, and to extend his influence, which seems to have been done by placing garrisons in Maroneia and Aenus.

In the war which ensued between the Romans and Antiochus (B. C. 190), Philip rendered the former good service, by providing everything necessary for their march through Thrace, and securing them from molestation by the native tribes (Liv. xxxvii. 7). Antiochus was defeated by Scipio at Magnesia, and sued for peace, which was at length granted to him (B. C. 188) on condition of his abandoning all his dominions west of the Taurus (Liv. xxxviii. 38). The Romans gave the Chersonesus and its dependencies to their ally Eumenes (ib. 39). As indicative of the internal condition of Thrace, even along the great southern road, the account which Livy (ib. 40, seq.) gives of the march of the consul Manlius' army through the country on its return from Asia Minor, is highly interesting. The army was loaded with booty, conveyed in a long train of baggage-waggons, which presented an irresistible temptation to the predatory tribes through whose territories its route lay. They accordingly attacked the army in a defile, and were not beaten off until they had succeeded in their object of sharing in the plunder of Asia.

The possession of the Chersonesus by Eumenes soon led to disagreements with Philip, who was charged by Eumenes (B.C. 185) with having seized upon Maroneia and Aenus, places which he coveted for himself. (Liv. xxxix. 24, 27). The Romans insisted upon the withdrawal of the Macedonian garrisons (B.C. 184), and Philip, sorely against his will, was obliged to obey. He wreaked his anger upon the defenceless citizens of Maroneia, by conniving at, if not actually commanding, the massacre of a great number of them (ib. 33, 34). In the course of the disputes about these cities, it was stated that at the end of the war with Philip, the Roman commissioner, Q. Fabius Labeo, had fixed upon the king's road, which is described as nowhere approaching the sea, as the S. boundary of Philip's possessions in Thrace; but that Philip had afterwards formed a new road, considerably to the S., and had thus included the cities and lands of the Maronitae in his territories (ib. 27).

In the same year, Philip undertook an expedition into the interior of Thrace, where he was fettered by no engagements with the Romans. He defeated the Thracians in a battle, and took their leader Amadocus prisoner. Before returning to Macedonia he sent envoys to the barbarians on the Danube to invite them to make an incursion into Italy (ib. 35). Again in B.C. 183, Philip marched against the Odrysae, Dentheletae and Bessi, took Philippopolis, which its inhabitants had abandoned at his approach, and placed a garrison in it, which the Odrysae, however, soon afterwards drove out (ib. 53). In B.C. 182, Philip removed nearly all the inhabitants of the coast of Macedonia into the interior, and supplied their places by Thracians and other barbarians, on whom he thought he could more safely depend in the war with the Romans, which he now saw was inevitable (Liv. xl. 3). He had done something of the same kind a few years before (Id. xxxix. 24).

Philip's ascent of the Haemus, already referred to, took place in B.C. 181: on the summit he erected altars to Jupiter and the Sun. On his way back his army plundered the Dentheletae; and in Maedica he took a town called Petra. (Liv. xl. 21, seq.)

Philip died in B.C. 179, and his successor Perseus continued the preparations which his father had made for renewing the war with Rome, which did not begin, however, till B. C. 171. The Romans had formed an alliance the year before with a number of independent Thracian tribes, who had sent ambassadors to Rome for the purpose, and who were likely to be formidable foes to Perseus. The Romans took care to send valuable presents to the principal Thracians, their ambassadors having no

doubt impressed upon the senate the necessity for compliance with this national custom. (Liv. xlii. 19.)

The advantage of this alliance was soon seen. Cotys, king of the Odrysae, was an ally of Perseus, and marched with him to meet the Romans in Thessaly, but with only 1000 horse and 1000 foot, a force which shows how greatly the power of the Odrysian monarchy had declined since the reign of Sitalces (ib. 51). Cotys commanded all the Thracians in Perseus's army in the first engagement with the Roman cavalry, which was defeated (ib. 57, seq.). When Perseus retreated into Macedonia a report was brought that the Thracian allies of Rome had invaded the dominions of Cotys, whom Perseus was therefore obliged to dismiss for their protection (ib. 67), and he does not seem to have personally taken any further part in the war, though he probably sent part of his forces to assist Perseus (xliv. 42). His son Bitis fell into the hands of the Romans, after the battle of Pydna (B.C. 168), which put an end to the Macedonian kingdom. Cotys sent ambassadors to Rome to endeavour to ransom his son, and to excuse himself for having sided with Perseus. The senate rejected his offers of money, but liberated his son, and gave a considerable sum to each of the Thracian ambassadors. The reason it assigned for this generosity was the old friendship which had existed between Rome and Cotys and his ancestors. The Romans were evidently unwilling to engage in a war with the Thracian people at this time; and were anxious to secure friends among them for the sake of the peace of Macedonia, which, though not yet nominally made a province, was completely in their power. They sent (B. c. 167) three commissioners to conduct Bitis and the other Thracians home; and at the same time, no doubt, to make observations on the state of that country. (Liv. xlv. 42).

After the fall of Perseus, the senate divided his dominions into four districts (regiones), the first of which included the territory between the Strymon and the Nestus, and all the Macedonian possessions east of the latter, except Aenus, Maroneia, and Abdera: Bisaltica and Sintice, west of the Strymon, also belonged to this district, the capital of which was Amphipolis. (Ib. 29.) It is important to recollect that the Thrace spoken of by the Latin historians subsequently to this time does not include the territories here specified, which thenceforth constituted an integral part of Macedonia.

From the year B. c. 148, when the Romans undertook the direct government of that country, they were brought into contact with the various barbarous nations on its frontiers, and were continually at war with one or another of them. For some years, however, their chief occupation was with the Scordisci, a people of Celtic origin which had settled south of the Danube, and often made devastating incursions into the more civilised regions of the south. They are sometimes called Thracians (e. g. by Florus, iii. 4; cf. Amm. xxvii. 4. § 4), which is the less surprising when we remember that great numbers of Celts had settled in Southern Thrace, and would soon be confounded under a common name with the other occupants of the country. The history of all this period, up to the time of Augustus, is very obscure, owing to the loss of so great a part of Livy's work; enough, however, appears in other writers to show that Thrace was left almost entirely to its native rulers, the Romans rarely interfering with it except when provoked by the predatory incursions of its people into Macedonia: they then sometimes made retaliatory expeditions into Thrace ; but seem generally to have made their way back as soon as the immediate object was accomplished. The relation existing between the Romans and the Thracians, for more than a century after the conquest of Macedonia, thus bears a close resemblance to that which has long existed between our own countrymen and the Caffres.

During the years B. C. 110, 109, the Consul M. Minucius Rufus was engaged in hostilities with the Scordisci and Triballi; and, according to Florus (l.c.), laid waste the whole valley of the Hebrus (cf. Eutr. iv. 27). In B. C. 104, Calpurnius Piso penetrated into the district of Rhodope (Flor. l. c.). In B. C. 92, the Maedi defeated the praetor, C. Sentius, and then ravaged Macedonia (Cic. Pis. 34 ; Liv. Epit. 70). After the breaking out of the Mithridatic War (B.C. 88), mention is made in several successive years of the incursions of the Thracians into the Roman provinces, and it is probable that they were acting in concert with Mithridates, whose general Taxiles, in B. C. 86, led a vast army through Thrace, and Macedonia to the assistance of Archelaus. (Liv. Epit. 74, 76, 81, 82). On the final defeat of Archelaus, Sulla directed his march towards Asia through, Thrace B. C. 84, and, either to punish the people for their connection with Mithridates, or because they opposed his passage, made war upon them with complete success (Id. 83). C. Scribonius Curio defeated the Dardani, and penetrated to the Danube, being the first Roman who had ventured into that part of Europe (B. C. 75 ; Liv. Epit. 92 ; Eutr. vi. 2). Curio was succeeded as governor of Macedonia by M. Lucullus (B. C. 73), who defeated the Bessi in a pitched battle on Mount Haemus, took their capital, and ravaged the whole country between the Haemus and the Danube (Liv. Epit. 97 ; Eutr. vi. 10). The Bessi were again conquered in B. C. 60 by Octavius, the father of Augustus (Suet. Aug. 3 ; cf. Ib. 94 ; Freinsh. Suppl. cxxxv. 2). In the years B. C. 58, 57, Piso, so well known to us from Cicero's celebrated speech against him, was governor of Macedonia ; and, if we may believe Cicero, acted in the most cruel and faithless manner towards the Bessi and other peaceable Thracian tribes. (Pis. 34, de Prov. Cons. 2, seq.). From the latter passage it appears that although Thrace was not under the government of Rome, yet the Romans claimed the right of way through it to the Hellespont; for Cicero calls the Egnatian Way " via illa nostra militaris."

In the civil war between Caesar and Pompey, several Thracian princes furnished the latter with auxiliary forces. Why they interfered in the contest, and why they preferred Pompey to Caesar, are matters of conjecture only. Pompey had been chiefly engaged all his life in the East, Caesar in the West ; and that is probably sufficient to account for the greater influence of Pompey in Thrace. (Caes. B. C. iii. 4 ; Flor. iv. 2 ; Dion Cass. xli. 51, 63, xlvii. 25).

At the time of Caesar's death two brothers, Rhascuporis and Rascus [Dict. Biog. Vol. III. p. 647] ruled over the greater part of Thrace ; and when the war broke out between the triumvirs and the republican party, Rhascuporis sided with the latter, while Rascus aided the former. By this plan they hoped to be safe, whichever party might be victorious; and it is said that their expectations were realised.

When the power of Rome was at length wielded by Augustus without a rival, the relation of Thrace to the Roman state seems to have become in many respects like that which the native princes of India long bore to the British. The Thracian kings were generally allowed to exercise, without restraint, their authority over their own subjects, and when needful it was supported by the arms of Rome. But all disputes among the native rulers were referred to the decision of the emperors, who disposed of the country as its acknowledged lords. These subject princes were expected to defend Thrace from external and internal foes ; to assist the Romans in the field ; to allow them to enlist troops, and in other ways to exercise the rights of sovereignty. For illustrations of these statements we must refer the reader to Tacitus, especially to the following passages : Ann. ii. 64— 67, iii. 38, 39, iv. 5, 46—51. The few Thracian coins which are extant afford a proof of the dependent character of the Thracian kings ; they bear on the obverse the effigy of the reigning emperor, on the reverse that of the native prince. [See Dict. Biog. Vol. III. p. 653.]

The interference of the Romans in the government of Thrace was not submitted to by the nation at large without several severe struggles. The most formidable of these occurred about B. c. 14, the fullest account of which is given by Dion Cassius (lib. liv.). The leader in this insurrection was Vologaesus, a Bessian priest of Bacchus, who availed himself of his sacerdotal character to inflame the religious feelings of his countrymen. Having thus assembled a large army, he attacked, defeated, and slew Rhascuporis, a king under Roman protection ; his uncle, Rhoemetalces, was next assailed and compelled to flee : the insurgents pursued him as far as the Chersonesus, where they devastated the country and captured the fortified places. On receiving information of these proceedings, Augustus ordered L. Piso, the governor of Pamphylia, to transport his army into Thrace, where, after a three years' war and several reverses, he at length succeeded in subduing the Bessi, who had adopted Roman arms and discipline. They soon afterwards made a second attempt to regain their independence ; but were now easily crushed. (Vell. Pat. ii. 98 ; Tac. Ann. vi. 10; Sen. Ep. 83; Flor. iv. 12 ; Liv. Epit. 137.)

After this war, the Romans gradually absorbed all the powers of government in the country. Germanicus visited it in A. D. 18, and introduced reforms in its administration (Tac. Ann. ii. 54). A system of conscription seems to have been imposed upon the Thracians about A. D. 26 (Ib. iv. 46). The last native prince of whom we find any mention is Rhoemetalces II., who, in A. D. 38, was made by Caligula ruler over the whole country; and at length, in the reign of Vespasian (A. D. 69—79), Thrace was reduced into the form of a province. (Suet. Vesp. 8; Eutr. vii. 19; cf. Tac. Hist. i. 11.) The date of this event has been disputed on the authority of the Eusebian Chronicle, which states that it took place in A. D. 47, in the reign of Claudius; but the statement of Suetonius is express on the point. It is possible that Rhoemetalces II. may have died about the year last mentioned ; and if Claudius refused to appoint a successor to him, this would be regarded as equivalent to incorporating the country in the Roman empire, although its formal constitution as a province was delayed ; as we know was commonly the case. It is remarkable that Moesia was made a province upwards of 50 years before Thrace Proper, its first propraetor being mentioned in A. D. 15. (Tac. Ann. i. 79; cf. Ib. ii. 66; Plin. iii. 26. s. 29.)

Thrace now shared in the general fortunes of the Roman world, on the division of which into the Eastern and Western Empires, it was attached to the former, being governed by the *Vicarius Thraciarum*, who was subordinate to the *Praefectus Praetorio Orientis*. Its situation rendered it extremely liable to the inroads of barbarians, and its history, so far as it is known, is little else than a record of war and devastation. The Goths made their first appearance there in A. D. 255; the emperor Probus, about A. D. 280, established in it 100,000 Bastarnae. In A. D. 314, and again in 323, the emperor Licinius was defeated at Hadrianople by Constantine, who, in A. D. 334, settled a multitude of Sarmatians in Thrace, which, in 376, received another accession to its heterogeneous population, Valens having given permission to the Goths to reside in it. This gave rise to innumerable wars, the details of which are recorded by Ammianus (lib. xxxi.). In 395 the devoted country was overrun by Alaric, and in 447 by the more dreadful Attila. Through all these misfortunes, however, Thrace remained in connection with the Eastern Empire, the capital of which was within its boundaries, until the year 1353, when the Turks, who had crossed over into Europe in 1341, obtained possession of the Thracian fortresses. Their leader Amurath conquered the whole country, except Constantinople, and made Hadrianople his capital. At length, in 1453, Constantinople itself was taken, and the Turks have ever since been the undisputed lords of Thrace.

VI. TOPOGRAPHY.— Under this head we shall merely collect such names as will serve to direct the reader to articles in this work, where fuller information is given.

Pliny (iv. 18; cf. Mela, ii. 2; Amm. xxvii. 4) enumerates the following as the principal Thracian tribes: Denseletae, Maedi, Bisaltae, Digeri, Bessi, Elethi, Diobessi, Carbilesi, Brysae, Sapaei, Odomanti, Odrysae, Cabyleti, Pyrogeri, Drugeri, Caenici, Hypsalti, Beni, Corpilli, Bottiaei, Edoni, Selletae, Priantae, Dolonci, Thyni, Coeletae. To these we may add, the Apsinthii, Bistones, Cicones, Satrae, Dii, and Trausi.

Of the towns mentioned by Pliny (*l. c.*), these belonged to Thrace Proper: 1. On the coast (i.) of the Aegean: Oesyma, Neapolis, Datum, Abdera, Tirida, Dicaea, Maronea, Zone, and Aenus; to these must be added Amphipolis, Pistyrus, Cosinthus, and Mesembria; (ii.) of the Chersonesus: Cardia, Lysimachia, Pachyta, Callipolis, Sestus, Elaeus, Coelos, Tiristasis, and Panormus; besides these there were Alopeconnesus and Agora; (iii.) of the Propontis: Bisanthe, Perinthus, and Selymbria; (iv.) of the Bosporus: Byzantium; (v.) of the Euxine: Mesembria, Anchialus, Apollonia, Thynias, Salmydessus, and Phinopolis. 2. In the interior: Philippopolis, Philippi, Scotusa, Topiris, Doriscus, Cypsela, Apros, and Develton. This is a very scanty list; but many of the principal inland towns were founded after Pliny's time: their names also were often changed. The following are some of the chief towns in the interior: Hadrianopolis, Plotinopolis, Trajanopolis, Tempyra, Nicopolis, Beroea, Iamporina, and Petra.

Besides the rivers mentioned in the course of this article, the following occur: the Bathynias, Pydaras or Atyras, Bargus, Cossinites, Compsatus, and Xerogypsus.

As to the political divisions of Thrace, Pliny (*l. c.*) states that it was divided into fifty *strategiae*; but he describes Moesia as part of Thrace. According to Ptolemy (iii. 11. § 8. seq.), its districts were Maedica, Denthaletica, Sardica, Bessica, Drosica, Bennica, Usdicesica, Selletica, Samaica, Coeletica, Sapaica, Corpilica, Caenica, and Astica.

Ammianus (*l. c.*) states that in the 4th century Thrace was divided into six provinces, but of these only four belonged to Thrace south of the Haemus: (i.) Thrace Proper (speciali nomine), including the W. part of the country; principal cities, Philippopolis and Beroea: (ii.) Haemimontus, i. e. the NE. district; chief towns, Hadrianopolis and Anchialus: (iii.) Europa, comprehending the SE. district; cities, Apri and Perinthus (Constantinople, being the capital of the whole Eastern Empire, was not regarded as belonging to any province): (iv.) Rhodopa, comprising the SW. region; principal cities, Maximianopolis, Maronea, and Aenus.

The principal modern writers in whose works information will be found respecting Thrace, have been mentioned in the course of this article. Among the other authors whom the reader may consult, we may name the following: Dapper, *Beschryving der Eilanden in de Archipel*, Amst. 1688, of which Latin and French translations were published at Amsterdam in 1703. Paul Lucas, *Voyages dans la Turquie, l'Asie, &c.* 2 vols. Amst. 1720. Choiseul, *Voyage Pittoresque dans l'Empire Ottoman :* of this work the first volume was published at Paris in 1782, the first part of the second not till 1809; the author died in 1817. A new edition, with many corrections and additions, was published in 4 vols. 8vo. at Paris in 1842. This work is devoted chiefly to the antiquities of the country; of which the plates contained in the illustrative Atlas which accompanies the book give many representations. Ami Boué's, *La Turquie d'Europe*, 4 vols. 8vo. Paris, 1840, is the most complete work yet written on the subject; its author, a man of great scientific acquirements, made two journeys in Turkey, in 1836, when he was accompanied by M. Viquesnel, and in 1838. The first volume contains an elaborate account of the physical geography, geology, vegetation, fauna, and meteorology of the country; but takes little or no notice of its classical geography. A map is prefixed to it, which was a vast improvement on all that had preceded it; but it is now in its turn superseded by that of Kiepert, who has employed in its construction the materials afforded by M. Viquesnel's reports already referred to. (Comp. Gatterer, *De Herodoti ac Thucydidis Thracia*, contained in the *Commentationes Soc. Reg. Gottin.* vol. iv. pp. 87—112, vol. v. pp. 57—88. [J. R.]

THRACIA, in Asia. A district in Asia Minor on the coast of the Euxine, is sometimes called Thrace, and its inhabitants Thracians. (Herod. i. 28; Xen. *Anab.* vi. 2. § 14, et al.) This country is more commonly called Bithynia. [See BITHYNIA, Vol. I. p. 404.] [J. R.]

THRA'CIUS BO'SPORUS. [BOSPORUS.]

THRASYME'NUS LACUS [TRASIMENUS.]

THRAUSTUS (Θραῦστος, Xen) or THRAESTUS (Θραιστός), a town in the mountainous district of Acroreia in Elis, of unknown site. (Xen. *Hell.* vii. 14. § 14; Diod. xiv. 17.)

THRIA. [ATTICA, p. 328, b.]

THROASCA (Θρόασκα), a place in Carmania, mentioned by Ptolemy (vi. 8. § 14). Perhaps the modern *Girost*. [V.]

THRONI (Θρόνοι), a town and promontory on the SE. coast of Cyprus, distant 700 stadia from the promontory Curias. On the promontory of Throni

·Pococke observed an ancient tower. (Strab. xiv. p. 682; Ptol. v. 14. §§ 2, 3; Engel. *Kypros*, vol. i. p. 99.)

THRO'NIUM (Θρόνιον: *Eth.* Θρόνιος, Θρονίτης, Θρονιεύς). 1. The chief town of the Locri Epicnemidii, situated 20 stadia from the coast and 30 stadia from Scarpheia, upon the river Boagrius, which is described by Strabo as sometimes dry, and sometimes flowing with a stream two plethra in breadth. (Strab. ix. p 436.) It is mentioned by Homer, who speaks of it as near the river Boagrius. (*Il.* ii. 533.) It was at one time partly destroyed by an earthquake. (Strab. i. p. 60.) At the beginning of the Peloponnesian War (B.C. 431) Thronium was taken by the Athenians. (Thuc. ii. 26; Diod. xii. 44.) In the Sacred War it was taken by Onomarchus, the Phocian general, who sold its inhabitants into slavery, and hence it is called by Scylax a Phocian city. (Diod. xvi. 33; Aesch. *de Fals. Leg.* p. 45, 33; Scylax. p. 23.) (Thronium is also mentioned by Polyb. ix. 41, xvii. 9; Eurip. *Iph. Aul.* 264; Liv. xxxii. 5, 6, xxxiii. 3, xxxv. 37, xxxvi. 20; Paus. v. 22. § 4; Lycophr. 1148; Ptol. iii. 15. § 7; Plin. iv. 7. s. 12; Steph. B. *s. v.*) The site of Thronium was ascertained by Meletius who found above the village *Románi*, at a place named *Paleókastro*, where some remains of the city still exist, a dedicatory inscription of the council and demus of the Thronienses. (Leake, *Northern Greece*, vol. ii. pp. 177, 178.)

2. A town in Greek Illyria in the neighbourhood of Amantia [AMANTIA], said to have been founded after the Trojan War by the Abantes of Euboea and the inhabitants of the Locrian Thronium. It was taken at an early period by the inhabitants of the neighbouring town of Apollonia, and annexed to their territory, as appears from an epigram inscribed on a dedicatory offering of the Apolloniatae at Olympia. (Paus. v. 22. §§ 3, 4.)

THRYON, THRYOESSA. [EPITALIUM.]

THULE (Θούλη, Ptol. ii. 6. § 32), a celebrated island in the Northern Ocean, discovered by the navigator Pytheas. Pytheas arrived at it after a voyage of six days from the Orcades, in which it may be computed that he had accomplished about 3000 stadia. (Plin. ii. 77.) According to the account of Pytheas, he reached the polar circle, so that on this island the longest day was twenty-four hours, and there was constant day during the six summer months and constant night during the six winter ones. It was deficient in animals, and even the most necessary fruits, but produced a little corn. From the time of its discovery it was regarded as the most northerly point of the known world, although no further knowledge was obtained respecting it; and this view seems to be confirmed by its name, since in Gothic *Tiel* or *Tiule* (τέλος. goal) denoted the remotest land. (Strab. i. p. 63, ii. pp. 104, 114, iv. p. 201; Agath. i. 8; Prisc. *Perieg.* 587, sqq.; Mela, iii. 6; Plin. iv. 16. s. 30; Tac. *Agr.* 10; Virg. *G.* i. 30; Solin. c. 22, &c.; cf. Praetorius, *de Orbe Goth.* iii. 4. 3. p. 33; D'Anville, *Sur la Navig. de Pytheas*, p. 439; Rudbeck, *Atlant.* i. p. 514.) Ptolemy is the only writer who places Thule a great deal further S., though he undoubtedly had in view the island discovered by Pytheas; and according to him it would seem to have been the largest of the Shetland islands, or the modern *Mainland* (see ii. 3. § 32, i. 24. §§ 4, 6, 17, 20, vi. 16. § 21, vii. 5. § 12, viii. 3. § 3). Most modern geographers incline to the opinion that Pytheas meant *Iceland*; though according to others his

Thule is to be variously sought in *Norway*; in that part called *Thile* or *Thilemark* ; in *Jutland*, the extreme point of which is called *Thy* or *Thyland*; or in the *whole Scandinavian peninsula* (Malte-Brun, *Geogr. Univ.* i. p. 120; Ortelius, *Theatr. Orb.* p. 103.) [T. H. D.]

THUMATA (Θουμάτα, Ptol. vi. 7. § 33; Plin. vi. 28. s. 32; Thamatha, *Not. Imp. Rom.* § 22, p. 37), a town of Arabia Felix, according to Ptolemy, and described by Pliny as distant 10 days' sail from Petra, and subject to the king of the Characeni.

THUMNA. [TAMNA.]

THUNU'DROMON (Θουνούδρομον, Ptol. iv. 3. § 29), a Roman colony in Numidia. It seems to be the same place as the Tynidrumense oppidum of Pliny (v. 4. s. 4). [T. H. D.]

THU'RIA (Θουρία: *Eth.* Θουριάτης), a town of Messenia, situated in the eastern part of the southern Messenian plain, upon the river Aris (*Pidhima*), and at the distance of 80 stadia from Pharae, which was about a mile from the coast (Paus. iv. 31. § 1). It was generally identified with the Homeric Antheia, though others supposed it to be Aepeia. (Paus. *l. c.*; Strab. viii. p. 360.) It must have been a place of considerable importance, since the distant Messenian gulf was even named after it (ὁ Θουριάτης κόλπος, Strab. *l. c.*). It was also one of the chief towns of the Lacedaemonian Perioeci after the subjugation of Messenia ; and it was here that the Third Messenian War took its rise, B.C. 464 (Thuc. i. 101). On the restoration of the Messenians by Epaminondas, Thuria, like the other towns in the country, was dependent upon the newly-founded capital Messene ; but after the capture of this city by the Achaeans in B.C. 182, Thuria, Pharae, and Abia joined the Achaean League as independent members. (Polyb. xxv. 1.) Thuria was annexed to Laconia by Augustus (Paus. *l. c.*); but it was restored to Messenia by Tiberius. [MESSENIA, p. 345. a.] Pausanias found two cities of this name. The Thuriatae had descended from the summit of the lofty hill of the upper city to dwell upon the plain ; but without abandoning altogether the upper city, where a temple of the Syrian goddess still stood within the town walls (Paus. iv. 31. § 2). There are considerable remains of both places. Those of Upper Thuria are on the hill of the village called *Paleókastro*, divided from the range of mountains named *Makryplái* by a deep ravine and torrent, and which commands a fine view of the plain and gulf. The remains of the walls extend half a mile along the summit of the hill. Nearly in the centre of the ruins is a quadrangular cistern, 10 or 12 feet deep, cut out of the rock at one end, and on the other side constructed of masonry. The cistern was divided into three parts by two cross walls. Its whole length is 29 paces ; the breadth half as much. On the highest part of the ridge there are numerous ruins, among which are those of a small Doric temple, of a hard brown calcareous stone, in which are cockle and muscle shells, extremely perfect. In the plain at *Palea Lutra* are the ruins of a large Roman building, standing in the middle of fig and mulberry grounds. Leake observes that " it is in an uncommon state of preservation, part even of the roof still remaining. The walls are 17 feet high, formed of equal courses of Roman tiles and mortar. The roof is of rubble mixed with cement. The plan does not seem to be that of a bath only, as the name would imply, though there are many appearances of the building having contained baths : it seems rather to have been the palace of some Roman governor. As there are no sources of water here, it is to be supposed that the building was supplied by an aqueduct from the neighbouring river of *Pidhíma.*" (Leake, *Morea,* vol. i. pp. 354, seq. 360; Boblaye, *Recherches, &c.* p. 105; Ross, *Reisen im Peloponnes,* p. 2; Curtius, *Peloponnesos,* vol. ii. p. 161.)

THU'RII (Θούριοι : *Eth.* Θουρῖνος, Thurinus), called also by some Latin writers and by Ptolemy THURIUM (Θούριον, Ptol.), a city of Magna Graecia, situated on the Tarentine gulf, within a short distance of the site of Sybaris, of which it may be considered as having taken the place. It was one of the latest of all the Greek colonies in this part of Italy, not having been founded till nearly 70 years after the fall of Sybaris. The site of that city had remained desolate for a period of 58 years after its destruction by the Crotoniats [SYBARIS]; when at length, in B.C. 452, a number of the Sybarite exiles and their descendants made an attempt to establish themselves again on the spot, under the guidance of some leaders of Thessalian origin; and the new colony rose so rapidly to prosperity that it excited the jealousy of the Crotoniats, who, in consequence, expelled the new settlers a little more than 5 years after the establishment of the colony. (Diod. xi. 90, xii. 10.) The fugitive Sybarites first appealed for support to Sparta, but without success: their application to the Athenians was more successful, and that people determined to send out a fresh colony, at the same time that they reinstated the settlers who had been lately expelled from thence. A body of Athenian colonists was accordingly sent out by Pericles, under the command of Lampon and Xenocritus; but the number of Athenian citizens was small, the greater part of those who took part in the colony being collected from various parts of Greece. Among them were two celebrated names,—Herodotus the historian, and the orator Lysias, both of whom appear to have formed part of the original colony. (Diod. xii. 10; Strab. vi. p. 263; Dionys. *Lys.* p. 453; *Vit. X. Orat.* p. 835; Plut. *Peric.* 11, *Nic.* 5.) The new colonists at first established themselves on the site of the deserted Sybaris, but shortly afterwards removed (apparently in obedience to an oracle) to a spot at a short distance from thence, where there was a fountain named Thuria, from whence the new city derived its name of Thurii. (Diod. *l. c.*; Strab *l. c.*) The foundation of Thurii is assigned by Diodorus to the year 446 B. C.; but other authorities place it three years later, B. C. 443, and this seems to be the best authenticated date. (Clinton, *F. H.* vol. ii. p. 54.) The protection of the Athenian name probably secured the rising colony from the assaults of the Crotoniats, at least we hear nothing of any obstacles to its progress from that quarter; but it was early disturbed by dissensions between the descendants of the original Sybarite settlers and the new colonists, the former laying claim not only to honorary distinctions, but to the exclusive possession of important political privileges. These disputes at length ended in a revolution, and the Sybarites were finally expelled from the city. They established themselves for a short time upon the river Traens, but did not maintain their footing long, being dislodged and finally dispersed by the neighbouring barbarians. (Diod. xii. 11, 22; Arist. *Pol.* v. 3.) The Thurians meanwhile concluded a treaty of peace with Crotona, and the new city rose rapidly to prosperity. Fresh colonists poured in from all quarters, especially the Peloponnese; and though it continued to be generally regarded as an Athenian colony, the Athenians in fact

formed but a small element of the population. The citizens were divided, as we learn from Diodorus, into ten tribes, the names of which sufficiently indicate their origin. They were,—the Arcadian, Achaean, Elean, Boeotian, Amphictyonic, Dorian, Ionian, Athenian, Euboean, and Nesiotic, or that of the islanders. (Diod. xii. 11.) The form of government was democratic, and the city is said to have enjoyed the advantage of a well-ordered system of laws; but the statement of Diodorus, who represents this as owing to the legislation of Charondas, and that lawgiver himself as a citizen of Thurii, is certainly erroneous. [*Dict. of Biogr.* art. CHARONDAS.] The city itself was laid out with great regularity, being divided by four broad streets or " plateae," each of which was crossed in like manner by three others. (Diod. xii. 10.)

Very shortly after its foundation, Thurii became involved in a war with Tarentum. The subject of this was the possession of the fertile district of the Siritis, about 30 miles N. of Thurii, to which the Athenians had a claim of long standing [SIRIS], which was naturally taken up by their colonists. The Spartan general, Cleandridas, who had been banished from Greece some years before, and taken up his abode at Thurii, became the general of the Thurians in this war, which, after various successes, was at length terminated by a compromise, both parties agreeing to the foundation of the new colony of Heracleia in the disputed territory. (Diod. xii. 23, 36, xiii. 106; Strab. vi. p. 264; Polyaen. *Strat.* ii. 10.) [HERACLEIA.] Our knowledge of the history of Thurii is unfortunately very scanty and fragmentary. Fresh disputes arising between the Athenian citizens and the other colonists were at length allayed by the oracle of Delphi, which decided that the city had no other founder than Apollo. (Diod. xii. 35.) But the same difference appears again on occasion of the great Athenian expedition to Sicily, when the city was divided into two parties, the one desirous of favouring and supporting the Athenians, the other opposed to them. The latter faction at first prevailed, so far that the Thurians observed the same neutrality towards the Athenian fleet under Nicias and Alcibiades as the other cities of Italy (Thuc. vi. 44); but two years afterwards (B. C. 213) the Athenian party had regained the ascendency; and when Demosthenes and Eurymedon touched at Thurii, the citizens afforded them every assistance, and even furnished an auxiliary force of 700 hoplites and 300 dartmen. (Id. vii. 33, 35.) From this time we hear nothing of Thurii for a period of more than 20 years, though there is reason to believe that this was just the time of its greatest prosperity. In B. C. 390 we find that its territory was already beginning to suffer from the incursions of the Lucanians, a new and formidable enemy, for protection against whom all the cities of Magna Graecia had entered into a defensive league. But the Thurians were too impatient to wait for the support of their allies, and issued forth with an army of 14,000 foot and 1000 horse, with which they repulsed the attacks of the Lucanians; but having rashly followed them into their own territory, they were totally defeated, near Lalis, and above 10,000 of them cut to pieces (Diod. xiv. 101).

This defeat must have inflicted a severe blow on the prosperity of Thurii, while the continually increasing power of the Lucanians and Bruttians, in their immediate neighbourhood would prevent them from quickly recovering from its effects. The city continued also to be on hostile, or at least unfriendly, terms with Dionysius of Syracuse, and was in consequence chosen as a place of retirement or exile by his brother Leptines and his friend Philistus (Diod. xv. 7). The rise of the Bruttian people about B. C. 356 probably became the cause of the complete decline of Thurii, but the statement of Diodorus that the city was *conquered* by that people (xvi. 15) must be received with considerable doubt. It is certain at least that it reappears in history at a later period as an independent Greek city, though much fallen from its former greatness. No mention of it is found during the wars of Alexander of Epirus in this part of Italy; but at a later period it was so hard pressed by the Lucanians that it had recourse to the alliance of Rome; and a Roman army was sent to its relief under C. Fabricius. That general defeated the Lucanians, who had actually laid siege to the city, in a pitched battle, and by several other successes to a great extent broke their power, and thus relieved the Thurians from all immediate danger from that quarter. (Liv. *Epit.* xi.; Plin. xxxiv. 6. s. 15; Val. Max. i. 8. § 6.) But shortly after they were attacked on the other side by the Tarentines, who are said to have taken and plundered their city (Appian, *Samn.* 7. § 1); and this aggression was one of the immediate causes of the war declared by the Romans against Tarentum in B. C. 282.

Thurii now sunk completely into the condition of a dependent ally of Rome, and was protected by a Roman garrison. No mention is found of its name during the wars with Pyrrhus or the First Punic War, but it plays a considerable part in that with Hannibal. It was apparently one of the cities which revolted to the Carthaginians immediately after the battle of Cannae, though, in another passage, Livy seems to place its defection somewhat later. (Liv. xxii. 61, xxv. 1.) But in B. C. 213, the Thurians returned to their alliance with Rome, and received a Roman garrison into their city. (Id. xxv. 1.) The very next year, however, after the fall of Tarentum, they changed sides again, and betrayed the Roman troops into the hands of the Carthaginian general Hanno. (Id. xxv. 15; Appian, *Hann.* 34.) A few years later (B. C. 210), Hannibal, finding himself unable to protect his allies in Campania, removed the inhabitants of Atella who had survived the fall of their city to Thurii (Appian, *Hann.* 49); but it was not long before he was compelled to abandon the latter city also to its fate; and when he himself in B. C. 204 withdrew his forces into Bruttium, he removed to Crotona 3500 of the principal citizens of Thurii, while he gave up the city itself to the plunder of his troops. (Appian, *l. c.* 57.) It is evident that Thurii was now sunk to the lowest state of decay; but the great fertility of its territory rendered it desirable to preserve it from utter desolation: hence in B. C. 194, it was one of the places selected for the establishment of a Roman colony with Latin rights. (Liv. xxxiv. 53; Strab. vi. p. 263.) The number of colonists was small in proportion to the extent of land to be divided among them, but they amounted to 3000 foot and 300 knights. (Liv. xxxv. 9.) Livy says merely that the colony was sent "in Thurinum agrum," and does not mention anything of a change of name; but Strabo tells us that they gave to the new colony the name of COPIAE, and this statement is confirmed both by Stephanus of Byzantium, and by the evidence of coins, on which, however, the name is written COPIA. (Strab. *l. c.*; Steph. Byz. *s. v.* Θούριοι;

Eckhel, vol. i. p. 164.) But this new name did not continue long in use, and Thurii still continued to be known by its ancient appellation. It is mentioned as a municipal town on several occasions during the latter ages of the Republic. In B. C. 72 it was taken by Spartacus, and subjected to heavy contributions, but not otherwise injured. (Appian, *B. C.* i. 117.) At the outbreak of the Civil Wars it was deemed by Caesar of sufficient importance to be secured with a garrison of Gaulish and Spanish horse; and it was there that M. Coelius was put to death, after a vain attempt to excite an insurrection in this part of Italy. (Caes. *B. C.* iii. 21, 22.) In B. C. 40 also it was attacked by Sextus Pompeius, who laid waste its territory, but was repulsed from the walls of the city. (Appian, *B. C.* v. 56, 58.)

It is certain therefore that Thurii was at this time still a place of some importance, and it is mentioned as a still existing town by Pliny and Ptolemy, as well as Strabo. (Strab. vi. p. 263; Plin. iii. 11. s. 15; Ptol. iii. 1. § 12.) It was probably, indeed, the only place of any consideration remaining on the coast of the Tarentine gulf, between Crotona and Tarentum; both Metapontum and Heraclea having already fallen into almost complete decay. Its name is still found in the Itineraries (*Itin. Ant.* p. 114, where it is written "Turios;" *Tab. Peut.*); and it is noticed by Procopius as still existing in the 6th century. (Procop. *B. G.* i. 15.) The period of its final decay is uncertain; but it seems to have been abandoned during the middle ages, when the inhabitants took refuge at a place called *Terranova*, about 12 miles inland, on a hill on the left bank of the Crathis.

The exact site of Thurii has not yet been identified, but the neighbourhood has never been examined with proper care. It is clear, from the statements both of Diodorus and Strabo, that it occupied a site *near to, but distinct from,* that of Sybaris (Diod. xii. 10; Strab. *l. c.*): hence the position suggested by some local topographers at the foot of the hill of *Terranova*, is probably too far inland. It is more likely that the true site is to be sought to the N. of the *Coscile* (the ancient Sybaris), a few miles from the sea, where, according to Zannoni's map, ruins still exist, attributed by that geographer to Sybaris, but which are probably in reality those of Thurii. Swinburne, however, mentions Roman ruins as existing in the peninsula formed by the rivers Crathis and Sybaris near their junction, which may perhaps be those of Thurii. (Swinburne, *Travels,* vol. i. pp. 291, 292; Romanelli, vol. i. p. 236.) The whole subject is very obscure, and a careful examination of the localities is still much needed.

The coins of Thurii are of great beauty; their number and variety indeed gives us a higher idea of the opulence and prosperity of the city than

COIN OF THURII.

we should gather from the statements of ancient writers.   [E. H. B.]

THU'RIUM. [BOEOTIA, p. 412, b.]

THYA'MIA. [PHLIUS, p. 602, b.]

THY'AMIS (Θύαμις), a river of Epeirus, flowing into the sea near a promontory of the same name. (Ptol. iii. 14. §§ 4, 5.) It formed the northern boundary of Thesprotia, which it separated from Cestrine, a district of Chaonia (Thuc. i. 46; Strab. vii. p. 324; Paus. i. 11. § 2; Cic. ad Att. vii. 2, de Leg. ii. 3; Plin. iv. 1.) It is now called Kalamá, apparently from the large reeds and aquatic plants which grow upon one of its principal tributaries. Its ancient name seems to have been derived from the Θύα or juniper, which, Leake informs us, though not abundant near the sources of the river, is common in the woody hills which border the middle of its course. The historian Phylarchus related (ap. Athen. iii. p. 73) that the Egyptian bean, which grew only in marshy places and nowhere but in Egypt, once grew for a short time upon the banks of the Thyamis. (Leake, Northern Greece, vol. i. p. 103, vol. iv. p. 97.)

THY'AMUS (Θύαμος), a mountain lying to the S. of Argos Amphilochicum, identified by Leake with Spartovúni. (Thuc. iii. 106; Leake, Northern Greece, vol. iv. p. 251.)

THYATEIRA (τὰ Θυάτειρα: Eth. Θυατειρηνός), a considerable city in the north of Lydia, on the river Lycus, and on the road leading from Sardes in the south to Germa in the north. It was anciently called Pelopeia, Euhippa, and Semiramis. (Plin. v. 31, Steph. B. s. v. Θυάτειρα.) Strabo (xiii. p. 625) calls it a Macedonian colony, which probably means only that during the Macedonian period it was increased and embellished, for Stephanus B., admitting that it previously existed under other names, relates that Seleucus Nicator gave it the name of Thygateira or Thyateira on being informed that a daughter (Θυγάτηρ) was born to him. But whatever we may think of this etymology, it seems clear that the place was not originally a Macedonian colony, but had existed long before under other names, and at one period belonged to Mysia. After the time of Antiochus Nicator, however, it became an important place, and is often noticed in history. When the two Scipios arrived in Asia on their expedition against Antiochus the Great, the latter was encamped near Thyateira, but retreated to Magnesia. (Liv. xxxvii. 8, 21, 37.) After the defeat of the Syrian king, the town surrendered to the Romans. (Liv. xxxvii. 44; Polyb. xvi. 1, xxxii. 25; comp. Appian, Syr. 30; Strab. xiii. p. 646; Plut. Sulla, 15; Ptol. v. 2. § 16; It. Ant. p. 336.) In Christian times Thyateira appears as one of the seven Churches in the Apocalypse (ii. 18); in the Acts of the Apostles (xvi. 14) mention is made of one Lydia, a purple-seller of Thyateira, and at a still later period we hear of several bishops whose see it was. In the middle ages the Turks changed the name of the town into Akhissar, which it still bears. (Mich. Duc. p. 114.) Sir C. Fellows (Asia

COIN OF THYATEIRA.

Min. p. 22), who calls the modern place Aksa, states that it teems with relics of an ancient splendid city, although he could not discover a trace of the site of any ruin or early building. These relics consist chiefly of fragments of pillars, many of which have been changed into well-tops or troughs. (Comp. Arundell, Seven Churches, p. 188, foll.; Wheeler and Spon, vol. i. p. 253; Lucas, Troisième Voy. p. 192, &c.; Prokesch, Denkwürdigkeiten, iii. p. 60, foll.)   [L. S.]

THYIA (Θυιά), a place in Phocis, where the Delphians erected an altar to the winds, derived its name from Thyia, a daughter of Cephissus or Castalius, and the mother of Delphus by Apollo. (Herod. vii. 178; Dict. of Biogr. art. THYIA.)

THYMBRA (Θύμβρη or Θύμβρα), a town of Troas, in the vicinity of Ilium. (Hom. Il. x. 430; Steph. B. s. v.; Plin. v. 33.) Strabo (xiii. p. 598) speaks of it only as a plain traversed by the river Thymbrius. The valley of Thymbra and the hill in it, called Callicolone (Hom. Il. xx. 53, 151; Strab. l. c.), are said still to retain their ancient names. (Prokesch. Denkwürdigkeiten, i. p. 145, foll.) The town of Thymbra must have perished at an early period; but its name remained celebrated in religion, for Apollo, who had had a temple at Thymbra, is frequently called Thymbraeus (Θυμβραῖος; Virg. Aen. iii. 85; Eurip. Rhesus, 224; Steph. B. s. v. Θύμβρα).   [L. S.]

THYMBRARA (Θύμβραρα), a place near Sardes, not far from the small river Pactolus, at which the contingents of the Persian army furnished by the inhabitants of Asia Minor used to assemble. (Xen. Cyrop. vi. 2. § 11, vii. 1. § 45; Steph. B. s. v.) Some are inclined to identify this place with Thybarna, mentioned by Diodorus Siculus (xiv. 80); but this latter place could hardly be said to be situated on, or even near the Pactolus.   [L. S.]

THYMBRES, a tributary of the Sangarius in Phrygia (Liv. xxxviii. 18), is no doubt the same as the Tembrogius of Pliny (vi. 1) and the Timbrius in the Argonautica bearing the name of Orpheus (713), where the river is described as abounding in fish.   [L. S.]

THY'MBRIA (Θυμβρία), a small town of Caria, only 4 stadia east of Myus on the banks of the Maeander; in its neighbourhood there was a so-called Charonium, or cave from which poisonous vapours issued. (Strab. xiv. p. 636.)   [L. S.]

THY'MBRIUM (Θύμβριον: Eth. Thymbrianus), a town of Phrygia, at a distance of 10 parasangs to the west of Tyriaeum (Xenoph. Anab. i. 2. § 13; Hierocl. p. 673; Conc. Constant. iii. p. 505.) Vibius Sequester (p. 25. ed. Oberlin) mentions a forest Thymbra in Phrygia, which seems to have been near the town of Thymbrium.   [L. S.]

THY'MBRIUS (Θύμβριος), a small river of Troas in the neighbourhood of Ilium; it was a tributary of the Scamander, and on its banks stood the town of Thymbra (Strab. xiii. p. 598; Eustath. ad Hom. Il. x. 430.) There still exists in that district a small river called Timbrek, which, however, does not flow into the Scamander, but into a bay of the sea; if this be the ancient Thymbrius, the plain of Thymbra must have been at a considerable distance from Ilium. For this reason, Col. Leake is inclined to identify the Thymbrius rather with the Kamara Su, which still is a tributary of the Scamander or Mendere Su (Asia Minor, p. 289.)   [L. S.]

THYME'NA (Θύμηνα), a place on the coast of Paphlagonia, at a distance of 90 stadia from Aegialus. (Arrian, *Peripl. P. E.* p. 15; Anonym. *Peripl. P. E.* p. 6.) Ptolemy (v. 4. § 2) mentions it under the name of Thymaena, and states that it was also called Teuthrania. [L. S.]

THYMIATE′RION (Θυμιατήριον, Hanno, *Peripl.* p. 2), called by Scylax (p. 23) Θυμιατηρίας, the first Carthaginian colony planted by Hanno on the west coast of Mauretania, 26 miles south-west of Lixus, on the Sinus Emporicus. There is no further mention of it. It has been variously identified with *Marmora*, *Larache*, and *Tangier*, but perhaps most correctly with the first. [T. H. D.]

THY′MNIAS, a bay on the south-west coast of Caria, on the south-west of the bay of Schoenus, and between Capes Aphrodisium and Posidium. (Pomp. Mela. i. 16; Plin. v. 29.) [L. S.]

THYMOETADAE. [ATTICA, p. 325, b.]

THYNI (Plin. iv. 11. s. 18, v. 32. s. 43; Θυνοί, Herod. i. 28), a people in the SE. part of Thrace, between the Agrianes and the mountains which separate its head-waters from the Euxine. At a very early period, a portion of the tribe, along with the related race of the Bithyni, emigrated to Asia Minor, where they occupied the district afterwards called Bithynia; but part of which seems originally to have been named more directly from the Thyni, since we find the names Θυνιακὴ Θρῴκη (Memnon. c. 18), Θυνίς (Scymn. 727, and 236), Θυνία (Steph. B. p. 315), and Thynia (Amm. xxii. 8. § 14). Respecting the Asiatic Thyni, see also Strabo, vii. p. 295, xii. p. 541; and the article BITHYNIA.

Of the Thyni who remained in Europe scarcely any notice is taken by the ancient historians. When Xenophon and the remnant of the 10,000 Greeks entered the service of Seuthes, one expedition in which they were employed had for its object the subjugation of the Thyni, who were said to have defeated Teres, an ancestor of Seuthes (*Anab.* vii. 2. § 22). Xenophon gives them the somewhat equivocal character of being the most warlike of all people, especially by night: and he had personal experience of their fondness for nocturnal fighting; for, having encamped in their villages at the foot of the mountains, to which the Thyni had retired on the approach of Seuthes and his forces, he was attacked by them on the next night, and narrowly escaped being burnt to death in the house in which he had taken up his quarters (*Ib.* 4. § 14, seq.). But this attack having failed, the Thyni again fled to the mountains, and soon afterwards submitted to Seuthes. Xenophon visited the country of the Thyni in the winter (*Ib.* 6. § 31), which he describes as being extremely severe, there being deep snow on the ground, and so low a temperature, that not only water, but even wine in the vessels was frozen; and many of the Greeks lost noses and ears through frostbite. (*Ib.* 4. § 3.) [J. R.]

THY′NIAS (Θυνίας), a small island in the Euxine at a distance of one mile from the coast of Thynia or Bithynia; its distance from the port of Rhoë was 20 stadia, and from Calpe 40. (Plin. vi. 13; Arrian, *Peripl. P. E.* p. 13.) The island had only 7 stadia in circumference, and had at first been called Apollonia from a temple of Apollo which existed in it. (Plin., Arrian, *ll. cc.*; Apollon. Rhod. ii. 177, 675; Anon. *Peripl. P. E.* p. 3.) According to Ptolemy (v. 1. § 15) it was also called Daphnusia, and obtained its name of Thynias from the Thyni, who inhabited the opposite coast. The island had a port and a naval station belonging to Heracleia (Scylax, p. 34; Arrian, *l. c.*); and Mela (ii. 7)

is probably mistaken in believing that the island contained a town of the same name. (Comp. Strab. xii. p. 543, where it is called Thynia; Marcian, p. 69; Steph. B. *s. v.*; Orph. *Argon.* 717, where it bears the name Thyneis.) The modern name of the island is *Kirpeh.* [L. S.]

THY′NIAS (Mela ii. 2. § 5; Plin. iv. 11. s. 18; Θυνίας, Strabo vii. p. 319, xii. p. 541: Scymn. 727; Arrian. *Per. P. Eux.* p. 24; Anon. *Per. P. Eux.* p. 15; Ptol. iii. 11. § 4; Steph. B. *s. v.*), a promontory on the Thracian coast of the Euxine, N. of Salmydessus, which was probably at one time in the territories of the Thyni, although Strabo (vii. p. 319) speaks of the district as belonging to the people of Apollonia. Pliny (*l. c.*) mentions a town of the same name, which in some maps is placed a little to the south of the promontory, on the site of the modern *Inada* or *Iniada*; but which, according to Dapper (*de l'Archip.* p. 515), is still called *Thinno.* [J. R.]

THYNOS or TYNOS, a town mentioned only by Pliny (v. 22) as situated between Mopsus and Zephyrium in Cilicia. [L. S.]

THYRAEUM (Θυραῖον: *Eth.* Θυραῖος), a town of Arcadia in the district Cynuria, said to have been founded by Thyraeus, a son of Lycaon. It is placed by Leake at *Palamári.* (Paus. viii. 3. § 3, 35. § 7; Steph. B. *s. v.*; Leake, *Peloponnesiaca,* p. 240.)

THYRAEUM. [MEGALOPOLIS, p. 310, a.]

THY′REA, THYREA′TIS. [CYNURIA.]

THYREA′TES SINUS. [CYNURIA, p. 727, a.]

THYREUM. [THYRIUM.]

THYRGO′NIDAE. [ATTICA, p. 330, a.]

THYRIDES (Θυρίδες), a promontory of Laconia, on the western coast of the Taygetic peninsula, now called *Cape Grosso.* It is of a semicircular form, nearly 7 miles in circumference, and rises from the sea to the height of 700 feet. There are many apertures and clefts in the rocks, the abodes of innumerable pigeons, and from the window-like form of these holes the whole promontory has received the name of Thyrides. Strabo describes it as a ῥοώδης κρημνός, "a precipitous cape beaten by the winds," distant 130 stadia from Taenarum (reckoning from the northern point of Thyrides); Pausanias, as a promontory (ἄκρα), situated 70 stadia from Taenarum (reckoning from the southern point of the promontory). Pausanias likewise calls it a promontory of Taenarum, using the latter word in its widest sense, to signify the whole peninsula of *Mani.* According to Strabo, the Messenian gulf terminated at this promontory. Pliny (iv. 12. s. 56) mentions three islands of the name of Thyrides in the Asinaean gulf. (Paus. iii. 25. § 9; Strab. viii. pp. 360, 362; Leake, *Morea,* vol. i. p. 302, seq.; Boblaye, *Recherches,* &c. p. 91; Curtius, *Peloponnesos,* vol. ii. p. 281.)

THY′RIUM, or THY′REUM (Θύριον, Pol. iv. 25; Θύρεον, Pol. iv. 6; Θούριον, Pol. xxviii. 5; Θύρρειον, Anth. Graec. ix. 553: *Eth.* Θυριεύς, Thyriensis), a city in Acarnania, the exact site of which is unknown. It placed by Pouqueville in the interior near the sources of the Anapus; and his authority is followed by K. O. Müller and others. This, however, is evidently a mistake. Cicero tells us (*ad Fam.* xvi. 5) that in sailing from Alyzia to Leucas, he touched at Thyrium, where he remained two hours; and from this statement, as well as from the history of the events in which Thyrium is mentioned, we may infer that it was situated on or near the Ionian sea, and that it was the first town on the coast S. of the canal which separated Leucas from the mainland. It is placed by Leake in the plain of Zavérdha, but no ruins of it have been discovered. Its name does not occur in Strabo. Thyrium is first mentioned in B. C. 373, when its territory was invaded by Iphicrates. (Xen. Hell. vi. 2. § 37.) Xenophon describes it as a place of importance; and it appears as one of the chief cities of Acarnania at the time of the Roman wars in Greece, when its name frequently occurs. At this period Thyrium was one of the places at which the meetings of the Acarnanian League were usually held. [ACARNANIA.] It was one of the many towns whose ruin was occasioned by the foundation of NICOPOLIS, to which its inhabitants were removed by order of Augustus. (Pol. iv. 6, 25, xvii. 10, xxii. 12, xxviii. 5; Liv. xxxvi. 11, 12, xxxviii. 9, xliii. 17; Anth. Graec. l. c.; Leake, Northern Greece, vol. iv. p. 16.)

COIN OF THYRIUM.

THYRSUS or TYRSUS (Θύρσος ποταμός, Ptol.; Θόρσος, Paus.; Tirso), the most considerable river of Sardinia, which still retains its ancient name almost unaltered. It has its sources in the mountains in the NE. corner of the island, and flows into the Gulf of Oristano on the W. coast, after a course of above 75 miles. About 20 miles from its mouth it flowed past Forum Trajani, the ruins of which are still visible at Fordungianus; and about 36 miles higher up are the Bagni di Benetutti, supposed to be the Aquae Lesitanae of Ptolemy. The Itineraries give a station "ad Caput Tyrsi" (Itin. Ant. p. 81), which was 40 M.P. from Olbia by a rugged mountain road: it must have been near the village of Buduso. (De la Marmora, Voy. en Sardaigne, vol. ii. p. 445.) Pausanias tells us that in early times the Thyrsus was the boundary between the part of the island occupied by the Greeks and Trojans and that which still remained in the hands of the native barbarians. (Paus. x. 17. § 6.) [E. H. B.]

THYSDRUS (Θύσδρος, Ptol. iv. 3. § 39), the oppidum Tusdritanum or Thysdritanum of Pliny (v. 4. s. 4), a city of Byzacium, in the Roman province of Africa, lying midway between Thenae and Thapsus, and west of the promontory Brachodes. It was here that the emperor Gordianus first set up the standard of rebellion against Maximin (Herodian. vii. 4, seq.; Capitol. Gord. c. 7, seq.), and it was from him, probably, that it derived its title of a Roman colony. We find the name variously written, as Tusdra, by Hirtius or whoever was the author of the history of the African War (B. Afr. 26, 27, &c.), and Tusdrus, in the Itin. Ant. (p. 59). Now El Jemme or Legem, with extensive ruins, especially of a fine amphitheatre in a tolerably perfect state. (Shaw, Travels, vol. i. p. 220, sqq.) [T. H. D.]

THYSSA'GETAE (Θυσσαγέται, Herod. iv. 22), a numerous people of Asiatic Sarmatia, living principally by the chase. They dwelt to the north-east of a great desert of 7 days' journey, which lay between them and the Budini. Stephanus B. (s. v.) erroneously places them on the Maeotis, apparently from misunderstanding Herodotus. They are called

Thussagetae by Mela (i. 19) and Pliny (iv. 12 s. 26), and Thyssagetae by Valerius Flaccus (vi. 140). [T. H. D.]

THYSSUS (Θύσσος), a town of Chalcidice in Macedonia, situated on the W. or S. side of the peninsula of Acte or Mt. Athos. Its exact position is uncertain, but it appears that Thyssus and Cleonae occupied the central part of the W. or S. coast of the peninsula, and that one of them may be placed at Zográfu or Dhokhiári, and the other at Xeropotámi. (Herod. vii. 22; Thuc. iv. 109, v. 35; Scylax. p. 26; Strab. vii. p. 331; Plin. iv. 10. s. 17; Leake, Northern Greece, vol. iv. pp. 149—152.)

TIARANTUS (Τιαραντός, Herod. iv. 48), a river in Scythia, flowing into the Ister from the N. Mannert identifies it with the Syl (iv. p. 105; cf. Ukert, iii. 2. p. 184). [T. H. D.]

TIARIULIA. [TEARI JULIENSES.]

TIASA. [LACONIA, p. 110, a.]

TIASUM (Τίασον or Τίασσον, Ptol. iii. 8. § 9), a town in Dacia, in the neighbourhood of the modern Fokschani. [T. H. D.]

TIBARANI, a tribe of Cilicia, about Mount Amanus and in the vicinity of Pindenissus, which was subdued by Cicero during his proconsular administration of that country, but is otherwise unknown. (Cic. ad Fam. xv. 4.) [L. S.]

TIBARE'NI (Τιβαρηνοί), a tribe on the coast of Pontus, occupying the country between the Chalybes and the Mosynoeci, on the east of the river Iris. They are mentioned as early as the time of Herodotus (iii. 94), and were believed to be of Scythian origin. (Schol. ad Apoll. Rhod. ii. 378, 1010; Xen. Anab. v. 5. § 2; Scylax, p. 33; Steph. B. s. v. Τιβαρηνία.) Strabo (xi. p. 527) describes them as inhabiting the mountains branching off from the Montes Moschici and Colchici, and mentions Cotyura as their principal town. (Comp. Xen. l. c.; Plin. vi. 4.) They appear to have been a harmless and happy people, who performed all their duties in a joyous manner. (Schol. ad Apoll. Rhod. l. c.; Steph. B. l. c.; Anon. Peripl. P. E. p. 12; Pomp. Mela, i. 19.) Their arms consisted of wooden helmets, small shields, and short spears with long points. (Herod. vii. 78.) Xenophon and his Greeks spent three days in travelling through their country. (Xen. l. c., vii. 8. § 25; Diod. Sic. xiv. 30; Dionys. Per. 767; Pomp. Mela, i. 2; Val. Flacc. v. 149; Strab. ii. p. 129, vii. p. 309, xi. p. 549, xii. p. 555.) [L. S.]

TIBERIACUM, in North Gallia, is placed in the Antonine Itin. between Juliacum (Juliers) and Colonia Agrippina (Cologne), viii. from Juliacum and x. from Colonia. D'Anville and others fix Tiberiacum at Berghem, at the passage of the river Erft, which flows between Juliers and Cologne. Others place Tiberiacum at Tarren, south of Berghem, where the bridge is. D'Anville adds "that a place situated in the direction between Juliers and Berghem is called Stein-Stras, that is to say, Lapidea Strata (Stone Street), just as in our provinces they say Chemin Perré." (D'Anville, Notice, &c.; Ukert, Gallien, p. 544.) [G. L.]

TIBE'RIAS (Τιβεριάς, Joseph. Ant. xviii. 3, B. J. ii. 8, iii. 16; Steph. B. s. v.; Ptol. viii. 20. § 16), the principal town of Galilaea, on the SW. bank of the sea of Tiberias or Gennesareth. It was situated in the most beautiful and fruitful part of that state (Joseph. Ant. xviii. 2. § 3), and was adorned with a royal palace and stadium. (Joseph. Vit. 12, 13, 64.) It was built by the

tetrarch Herodes Antipas, in honour of the Roman
emperor Tiberius, from whom it derived its name.
(Joseph. *l. c.*) It is stated to have been 30 stadia
from Hippo, 60 from Gadara, and 120 from Scythopolis (Joseph. *Vit.* 65); distances which are not
much at variance with that of Joliffe, who states
that it is 20 miles English from Nazareth and 90
from Jerusalem. (*Travels,* p. 40.)

From the time of Herodes Antipas to that of the
reign of Agrippa II., Tiberias was probably the
capital of the province (Joseph. *Vit.* 9), and it was
one of the four cities which Nero added to the
kingdom of Agrippa. (Joseph. *Ant.* xx. 8. § 4.)
In the last Jewish War, Tiberias, from its great
strength, played an important part (Joseph. *B. J.* ii.
20); as, after Sepphoris, it was held to be the
largest place in Galilaea (Joseph, *Vit.* 65), and was
very strongly fortified. (*B. J.* iii. 10. § 1.) The
inhabitants derived their sustenance in great measure from their fisheries in the adjoining sea.
(Joseph. *Vit.* 12.) On the destruction of Jerusalem, and for several centuries subsequently,
Tiberias was famous for its academy of learned
Jews. (Lightfoot, *Hor. Hebr.* p. 140.)

In the immediate neighbourhood of Tiberias were
the celebrated hot springs of Emmaus (Joseph.
B. J. ii. 21, *Ant.* xviii. 2.) [EMMAUS.] It is not
certain whether Tiberias occupied the site of Chinnereth, though Hieronymus thinks so (*Onom. s. v.
Chinnereth*); it seems more likely that this place
belonged to the tribe of Naphthali. (Josh. xix.
35; Reland, *Palaest.* p. 161.) Nor is there any better
reason for identifying it, as some have done, with
Chammath (Joseph. xix. 35) or Rakkah, which was
the Rabbinical notion. (Cf. Hieron. *Megil.* fol. 701;
Lightfoot, *Chorograph. Cent.* cap. 72—74.) The
modern name of Tiberias is *Tabariek*; it is not,
however, built actually on the site of the old town,
though close to its ruins. When Joliffe was there, it
had a population of 11,000 (*Travels,* pp. 48—58.)
It was nearly destroyed by an earthquake on New
Year's Day, 1837, since which time it has never
been completely rebuilt. (Russegger, iii. p. 132;
Strauss. p. 356; Robinson, iii. p. 500.)   [V.]

TIBE'RIAS MARE (λίμνη Τιβερίας, Pausan. v.
7. § 4; Ptol. v. 16. § 4; λίμνη ἡ Τιβερίων, Joseph.
B. J. iv. 26), the principal lake or sea of Palestine in
the province of Galilaea. It was bordered on the
W. side by the tribes of Issachar and Zabulon, and
on the E. by the half-tribe of Manasseh. The
waters were fresh (Joseph. *B. J.* iii. 35) and
full of fish (Joseph. *B. J.* iv. 26; *Matth.* iv.
18; *Luke.* v. 1, &c.), and its size is variously
stated, by Josephus (*l. c.*), to have been 140 stadia
long by 40 broad, and by Pliny, to have been 16 M. P.
long and 6 M. P. broad (v. 15). It was traversed
in a direction NW. and SE. by the river Jordan.
[JORDANES; PALAESTINA.] This sea is known
by many different names in the Bible and profane
history. Its earliest title would seem to have been
Chinnereth (*Numb.* xxxiv. 11; *Josh.* xiii. 27; LXX.
Χεννερέθ.) From this form has probably arisen
its second appellation of Gennesareth (ἡ λίμνη Γεν-
νεσαρὴτ, *Matth.* xiv. 34, &c.; ὕδωρ Γεννησὰρ, 1
Maccab. ii. 67; ἡ λίμνη Γεννησὰρ, Joseph. *B. J.*
ἡ λίμνη Γεννεσαρῖτις, Joseph. *Ant.* xviii. 3; Strab.
xvi. p. 755; Genasara, Plin. v. 15.) A third
appellation it has derived from the province with
which it was most nearly connected, viz. the sea of
Galilee (Θάλασσα τῆς Γαλιλαίας, *Matth.* iv. 18;
Mark, vii. 31, &c.; and with a double title, Θάλασσα

τῆς Γαλιλαίας, τῆς Τιβεριάδος, *John* vi. 1). Pliny,
in describing the same localities, speaks of a town
called Tarichaea, from whence also he says the
adjoining lake was sometimes named (*l. c.*; cf.
also Strab. xvi. p. 764). The present name is
Bahr-al-Tabarieh. (Pococke, ii. p. 103; Thevenot
p. 387; Haselquist, i. p. 181; Robinson, iii. pp. 499
—509, &c.)   [V.]

TIBERIO'POLIS (Τιβεριούπολις), a town in
Phrygia Major, in the neighbourhood of Eumenia.
(Ptol. v. 2. § 25; Socrat. *Hist. Eccles.* vii. 46.).
Its site is yet uncertain, but Kiepert (in Franz,
Fünf Inschriften, p. 33) is disposed to regard the
extensive ruins near *Suleiman* as the remnants of
Tiberiopolis. Hamilton (*Researches,* i. p. 127, foll.),
probably more correctly, regards them as the ruins
of Blaundos. (Comp. Arundell, *Discoveries,* i. p.
81, foll.)   [L. S.]

TI'BERIS (ὁ Τίβερις: *Tevere, Tiber*: the forms
Tibris, Tybris, and Thybris are chiefly poetical, as
is Θύμβρις also in Greek: the Latin poets use also
Tiberinus as an adjective form, as Tiberinus pater,
Tiberinum flumen, &c., and thence sometimes Tiberinus by itself as the name of the river), one of
the most important rivers of Central Italy. It has
its sources in the Apennines above Tifernum, but in
the territory of Arretium (Plin. iii. 5. s. 9), on the
confines of Etruria and Umbria, and flows at first in
a southerly direction, passing by the walls of Tifernum, which derived from it the name of Tiberinum
(*Città di Castello*), and afterwards within a few miles
of Perusia on the E., and within a still shorter distance
to the W. of Tuder (*Todi*). From thence it still preserves a general S. direction, notwithstanding considerable windings, till it receives the waters of the
Anio (*Teverone*), a few miles from the walls of
Rome, from which point it has a general SW. course
to the sea at Ostia. Pliny estimates the upper part
of its course at 150 miles, to which must be added
about 35 more for the lower part, giving as a total
185 miles (Plin. *l. c.*; Strab. v. p. 218); but this estimate is below the truth, the whole course of the
river being about 180 geogr. or 225 Roman miles.
During the whole of its course from Tifernum to the
sea the Tiber formed in ancient times the eastern
boundary of Etruria, separating that country from
Umbria in the upper part of its course, afterwards
from the territory of the Sabines, and, in the lower
part, from the mouth of the Anio downwards, dividing it from Latium. (Strab. v. p. 219; Plin. *l. c.*)
It receives numerous confluents or tributaries, of
which the most important are, the TINIA, an inconsiderable stream which joins it from the E. a little
below Perusia, bringing with it the waters of the
more celebrated Clitumnus; the CLANIS, which
falls into it from the right bank, descending from the
marshy tract near Clusium; the NAR, a much
more considerable stream, which is joined by the
VELINUS a few miles above Interamna, and discharges their combined waters into the Tiber, a few
miles above Ocriculum; and the ANIO, which falls
into the Tiber at Antemnae, 3 miles above Rome.
These are the only affluents of the Tiber of any geographical importance, but among its minor tributaries, the ALLIA on its left bank, a few miles above
the Anio, and the CREMERA on the right, are names
of historical celebrity, though very trifling streams,
the identification of which is by no means certain.
[See the respective articles.] Two other streams of
less note, which descend from the land of the Sabines
and fall into the Tiber between Ocriculum and Ere-

tum, are, the HIMELLA (*Asia*) and the FARFARUS or FABARIS (*Farfa*).

The Tiber is unquestionably, in a merely geographical point of view, the most important river of Central Italy, but its great celebrity is derived from its flowing under the walls of Rome, or rather through the heart of the city, after this had attained to its full extension. The detailed account of the river in this part of its course must be sought in the article ROMA: we need here only mention that after flowing under the Milvian Bridge [PONS MILVIUS or MULVIUS] the river makes a considerable bend to the W. so as to approach the foot of the Vatican hills, and leave, on the other side, between its left bank and the nearest ridge of hills, a broad tract of plain, early known as the Campus Martius, the whole of which was eventually included within the imperial city. A short distance lower down, but still within the walls of the city, its stream was divided into two by an island known as the INSULA TIBERINA, and reported by tradition to have been formed by alluvial accumulations within the period of Roman history. It is remarkable that this is the only island of any consideration in the whole course of the river, with the exception of that called the INSULA SACRA, at its mouth, formed by the two arms of the river, and which is undoubtedly of late growth, and in great part of artificial formation.

The Tiber was at all times, like most rivers which are supplied, principally by mountain streams, a turbid, rapid, and irregular river, that must always have presented considerable difficulties to navigation. The yellow and muddy hue of its turbid waters is repeatedly alluded to by the Roman poets ("flavum Tiberim," Hor. *Carm.* i. 2. 13; "suo cum gurgite flavo," Virg. *Aen.* ix. 816; &c.), and the truth of Virgil's description, "Vorticibus rapidis et multa flavus arena," (*Aen.* vii. 31), must be familiar to every one who has visited Rome. In the upper part of its course, as we learn from Pliny, the river was with difficulty navigable, even for small boats; nor did its first tributaries, the Tinia and Clanis contribute much to its facilities in this respect, though their waters were artificially dammed up, and let off from time to time in order to augment the main stream. (Plin. iii. 5. s. 9.) But from the point of its junction with the Nar, the Tiber became navigable for larger vessels, and even from an early period extensive supplies of various kinds were brought down the river to Rome. (Liv. ii. 34, v. 54; Cic. *de Rep.* ii. 5; &c.) In the more flourishing period of the city the navigation of the Tiber was of course enormously increased; and vast supplies of timber, stone, and other materials for building, as well as corn and provisions, were continually introduced by means of the river and its tributaries. (Strab. v. p. 235.) Corn was brought down the Tiber even from the neighbourhood of Tifernum, when the upper part of the stream was navigable. (Plin. *Ep.* v. 6.) It seems also to have been used as an ordinary mode of travelling, as we are told that in A. D. 20, Piso, the murderer of Germanicus, proceeded from Narnia to Rome by descending the Nar and the Tiber. (Tac. *Ann.* iii. 9.) At the present day the river is navigated by boats of large size as far as the confluence of the *Nera*, and small steamers ascend as far as *Borghetto*, a few miles from *Otricoli*.

But it was from Rome itself to the sea, a distance of 27 miles by the river (Strab. v. p. 232), that the navigation of the Tiber was the most important. Pliny speaks of it as in this part of its course na-

vigable for the largest vessels (" quamlibet magnarum navium ex Italo mari capax "), and as becoming the receptacle of merchandise from every part of the world. The latter statement may be readily admitted; but the former is calculated to astonish any one acquainted with the river in its present condition yet it is partly confirmed by the distinct statement of Strabo (v. p. 232), that the larger class of merchant vessels used to ride at anchor in the open sea off the mouth of the river, until they had been lightened of a part of their cargoes, which they discharged into barges, and afterwards proceeded up the river to Rome. Dionysius gives the same account, with the exception that vessels which exceeded 3000 amphorae in burden were unable to enter the river at all, and forced to send their cargoes up by barges. (Dionys. iii. 44.) But all kinds of rowing vessels, not excepting the largest ships of war, were able to ascend the river (*Ib.*); and thus we find the younger Cato on his return from Cyprus proceeding at once in his galley to the Navalia within the walls of Rome. (Plut. *Cat. Min.* 39.) We learn also from Livy that the ships of war which had been taken from Perseus king of Macedonia, though of unusual size (" inusitatae ante magnitudinis "), were carried up the river as far as the Campus Martius (Liv. xlv. 42); and even the gigantic vessel constructed for the purpose of bringing the obelisk that was set up in the Circus Maximus, was able to ascend as far as the Vicus Alexandri, within three miles of Rome (Ammian. xvii. 4. § 14). The chief difficulties that impeded the navigation of the river in the time of Strabo were caused by its own accumulations at its mouth, which had destroyed the port of Ostia. These were afterwards in great measure removed by the construction of an artificial port, called the PORTUS AUGUSTI, commenced by Claudius, and enlarged by Trajan, which communicated by an artificial canal or arm with the main stream of the river. (The history of these works, and the changes which the mouths of the Tiber underwent in consequence, are fully given in the article OSTIA.) The importance of the navigation of the Tiber led to the formation of distinct bodies or corporations in connection with it, called Navicularii and Lenuncularii, both of which are frequently mentioned in inscriptions of imperial times (Preller, p. 147).

Another disadvantage under which the Tiber laboured, in common with most rivers of mountain origin, arose from the frequent inundations to which it was subject. These appear to have occurred in all ages of the Roman history; but the earliest recorded is in B. C. 241, immediately after the close of the first Punic War (Oros. iv. 11), which is said to have swept away all the houses and buildings at Rome in the lower part of the city. Similar inundations, which did more or less damage to the city are recorded by Livy in B. C. 215, 202, 193, and again in 192 and 189 (Liv. xxiv. 9, xxx. 38, xxxv. 9, 21, xxxviii. 28) and there is little doubt that it is only from the loss of the detailed annals that we do not hear again of the occurrence of similar catastrophes till near the close of the Republic. Thus we find a great inundation of the Tiber noticed as taking place in B. C. 54 (Dion Cass. xxxix. 61), which is alluded to by Cicero (*ad Q. Fr.* iii. 7); and several similar inundations are known to have occurred in the time of Augustus, in B. C. 27, 23 and 22, of which the first is probably that alluded to by Horace in a well-known ode. (Hor. *Carm.* i. 2. 13; Orell. *Excurs. ad l. c.*; Dion Cass. liii. 20,

33, liv. 1.) Great attention was bestowed by Augustus upon the subject, and he first instituted magistrates with the title of Curatores Tiberis, whose special duty was to endeavour to restrain the river within due bounds, to preserve the embankments, &c. (Suet. *Oct.* 37.) These officers received increased powers under Tiberius, and continued down to the close of the Empire. We frequently meet with mention in inscriptions of the " Curatores alvei Tiberis et riparum," and the office seems to have been regarded as one of the most honourable in the state. (Dion Cass. lvii. 14; Orell. *Inscr.* 1172, 2284, &c.; Gruter, *Inscr.* pp. 197, 198.) But it is evident that all their efforts were ineffectual. In the reign of Tiberius so serious was the mischief caused by an inundation in A. D. 15 that it was proposed in the senate to diminish the bulk of the waters by diverting some of the chief tributaries of the stream, such as the Nar, Velinus and Clanis. (Tac. *Ann.* i. 76; Dion Cass. lvii. 14.) This plan was, however, abandoned as impracticable; and in A. D. 69 another inundation took place, which appears to have caused still more damage than any that had preceded it (Tac. *Hist.* i. 86). It is strange that in face of these facts Pliny should assert that the Tiber was so confined within artificial banks as to have very little power of outbreak, and that its inundations were rather subjects of superstitious alarm than formidable in themselves. (Plin. iii. 5. s. 9.) During the later ages of the Empire indeed we hear but little of such outbreaks of the Tiber, but this is very probably owing only to the scanty nature of our records. One great inundation is, however, recorded as doing great mischief in the reign of Trajan, another in that of Macrinus, and a third in that of Valerian. (Dion Cass. lxxviii. 25; Vict. *Caes.* 34, *Epit.* 13.) One of the most destructive of all is said to have been that of A. D. 590, which added to the various calamities that at that time almost overwhelmed the city. (*Hist. Miscell.* xviii. p. 583; Greg. Turon. x. 1.) At the present day the lower parts of Rome are still frequently flooded by the river, for though the soil of these parts of the city has unquestionably been raised, in some places many feet, the bed of the Tiber has undoubtedly been also elevated, though probably in a less degree. The whole subject of the inundations and navigation of the Tiber, and the measures taken in ancient times in connection with them, is fully illustrated by Preller in an article entitled *Rom und der Tiber* in the *Berichte der Sächsischen Gesellschaft* for 1848 and 1849.

The Tiber appears to have been in ancient times occasionally frozen, at least partially; a circumstance to which the Latin poets repeatedly allude. But we must not construe their rhetorical expressions too strictly; and it is clear from the terms in which Livy notices its being frozen over in the extraordinary winter of B. C. 398, that such an occurrence was of extreme rarity. ("Insignis annus hieme gelida ac nivosa fuit, adeo ut viae clausae, Tiberis innavigabilis fuerit, Liv. v. 13.) St. Augustin also alludes to such a winter (apparently the same noticed by Livy), "ut Tiberis quoque glacie duraretur," as a thing unheard of in his times. (Augustin, *Civ. Dei,* iii. 17.)

It was a tradition generally received among the Romans that the Tiber had been originally called Albula; and that it changed its name in consequence of Tiberinus, one of the fabulous kings of Alba, having been drowned in its waters. (Liv. i. 3; Dionys.

i. 71; Vict. *Orig. G. Rom.* 18.) Virgil, however, who calls the king Thybris, assigns him to an earlier period, prior to the landing of Aeneas (*Aen.* viii. 330). Hence the river is not unfrequently called by the Roman poets Albula. (Sil. Ital. vi. 391, viii. 455, &c.) It had naturally its tutelary divinity or river-god, who, as we learn from Cicero, was regularly invoked in their prayers by the augurs under the name of Tiberinus (Cic. *de N. D.* iii. 20). He is frequently introduced by the Roman poets as " pater Tiberinus" (Enn. *Ann.* i. p. 43; Virg. *Aen.* viii. 31, 72; &c.)   [E. H. B.]

TIBIGENSE OPPIDUM, a town in Africa Propria, apparently the Thigiba (Θιγίβα) of Ptolemy (iv. 3. § 29; Plin. v. 4. s. 4).   [T. H. D.]

TIBILIS, a town in the interior of Numidia, 54 miles from Cirta, having hot mineral springs (Aquae Tibilitanae) (August. *Ep.* 128; *Itin. Ant.* p. 42), commonly identified with *Hammam Meskutin* in the mountains near the river *Seibonse;* but, according to D'Avezac and the map of the province of Constantine (Par. 1837), it is *Hammam-el-Berda,* somewhat more to the N.   [T. H. D.]

TIBISCUM (Τίβισκον, Ptol. iii. 8. § 10), a town of Dacia, on the river Tibiscus. By the Geogr. Rav. it is called Tibis (iv. 14), and in the Tab. Peut. Tiviscum. Its ruins exist at *Kavaran,* at the junction of the *Temess* (Tihincna) and *Bistra* (cf. Ukert, iii. 2. p. 616).   [T. H. D.]

TIBISCUS (Τίβισκος, Ptol. iii. 8. § 1), a tributary river of the Danube in Dacia. We also find it called Tibissus (*Inscr.* Grut. p. 448. 3) and Tibisia (Geogr. Rav. iv. 14). Several authors identify it with the Tisianus or Tysia (the modern *Theiss*), with which, indeed, Ptolemy seems to have confounded it, as he does not mention the latter (Mannert, iv. p. 203; Sickler, i. p. 196; cf. Ukert, iii. 2. p. 603). But Forbiger, after Reichard, identifies it with the *Temess;* his grounds for that opinion being that Jornandes (*Get.* c. 34) and the Geographer of Ravenna (*l. c.*) mention the Tysia and Tibisia as two distinct rivers, and that the site of the ancient town of Tibiscum appears to point to the *Donesz* (*Handb. d. alt. Geogr.* iii. p. 1103, note). It is probable that the Pathissus of Pliny (iv. 12. s. 25) and Parthiscus of Ammianus Marcellinus (xvii. 13. § 4) are the same river, though some identify them with the Tisianus.   [T. H. D.]

TIBISIS (Τίβισις), a large river of Scythia, which Herodotus describes as rising in Mt. Haemus, and flowing into the Maris (iv. 49). It is identified by some with the *Kara Low.*

TIBULA (Τίβουλα, Ptol.), a town of Sardinia, near the N. extremity of the island, which appears to have been the customary landing-place for travellers coming from Corsica; for which reason the Itineraries give no less than four lines of route, taking their departure from Tibula as a starting-point. (*Itin. Ant.* pp. 78—83.) It is very unfortunate therefore that its position is a matter of great uncertainty. That assigned to it by Ptolemy would place it on the site of *Castel Sardo* on the N. coast of the island, and only about 18 miles from *Porto Torres,* but this is wholly incompatible with the statements of the Itineraries, and must certainly be erroneous. Indeed Ptolemy himself places the Tibulates, or Tibulatii (Τιβουλάτιοι), who must have been closely connected with the town of that name, in the extreme N. of the island (Ptol. iii. 3. § 6), and all the data derived from the Itineraries concur in the same result. The most probable position is, therefore, that assigned it by De la Marmora, who fixes it on the port or small bay called *Porto di Lungo Sardo*, almost close to the northernmost point of the island, the Errebantium Prom. of Ptolemy. (De la Marmora, *Voy. en Sardaigne*, vol. ii. pp. 421—432, where the whole question is fully examined and discussed.)   [E. H. B.]

TIBUR (ἡ Τιβουρίνων or Τιβουρήνων πόλις, Polyb. vi. 14; τὰ Τίβουρα, Strab. v. p. 238; τὸ Τίβουρ, Ptol. iii. 1. § 58; ἡ Τίβυρις, Steph. B. p. 564: *Eth.* Tibura, Liv. vii. 9; Virg. *Aen.* xi. 757; Hor. *S.* i. 6. 108; Tac. *Ann.* xiv. 22, &c.; Tiburtinus, Cic. *Phil.* v. 7; Prop. iv. 7. 85; Plin. *Ep.* vii. 29, &c.; Tiburnus, Stat. *Silv.* i. 3. 74; Prop. iii. 22, 23: now *Tivoli*), an ancient and celebrated town of Latium, seated on the Anio, to the NE. of Rome, from which it was distant 20 Roman miles (*Itin. Ant.* p. 309; cf. Mart. iv. 57; Procop. *B. G.* ii. 4). Tibur lies on an offshoot or spur thrown out from the northern side of what is now called *Monte Ripoli*, at a level of between 800 and 900 feet above the sea. This ledge extends across the bed of the Anio to *Monte Catillo* on its north bank, thus forming a natural barrier over which the river leaps into the valley below, from a height of about 80 feet, and forms the celebrated waterfall so frequently mentioned by the ancient writers (Strab. *l. c.*; Dionys. H. v. 37; Hor. *Od.* i. 7. 13, &c.). The town lay principally on the cliff on the left or southern bank, where it is half encircled by the Anio. It is probable that at a remote period the waterfall was lower down the river than it is at present, since there are tokens that the stream once washed the substructions of the terrace on which the round temple is built; especially a broken wheel embedded in the cliff at a height of 150 feet above the abyss called the *Grotto of Neptune.* The awful catastrophe in A. D. 105 recorded by the younger Pliny (*Ep.* viii. 17), when the Anio burst its banks and carried away whole masses of rock — *montes* he calls them — with the groves and buildings upon them, must have produced a remarkable change in the character of the fall. We may gather, from some descriptions in Propertius (iii. 16. 4) and Statius (*Silv.* i. 3. 73), that previously to that event the Anio leaped from a high rock, but that its fall was broken towards its lower part by projecting ledges, which caused it to form small lakes or pools. From the time of Pliny the cataract probably remained much in the same state down to the year 1826, when the river again swept away a number of houses on the left bank, and threatened so much danger to the rest that it was found necessary to divert its course by forming a tunnel for its waters through *Monte Catillo* on the right bank. This alteration spoiled the romantic points of view on the side of the grottoes of Neptune and the Sirens; but the fall is still a very fine one. Scarcely inferior to it in picturesque beauty are the numerous small cascades, called *Cascatelle*, on the western side of the town. These are formed by water diverted from the Anio for the supply of various manufactories, which, after passing through the town, seeks its former channel by precipitating itself over the rock in several small streams near what is commonly called the villa of Maecenas. Nothing can be finer than the view of these cascades from the declivities of *Monte Peschiavatore*, whence the eye ranges over the whole of the *Campagna*, with Rome in the distant background.

The country around Tibur was not very fertile in grain; but it was celebrated for its fruit-trees and orchards ("pomosi Tiburis arva," Col. *R. R.* x. p. 347, ed. Lugd 1548; cf. Propert. iv. 7. 81: "Pomosis Anio qua spumifer incubat arvis"), and especially for its grapes and figs (Plin. xiv. 4. s. 7, xv. 19). Its stone, now called *travertino*, was much used at Rome for building, whither it was easily conveyed by means of the Anio, which became navigable at Tibur (Strab. *l. c.*). Vast remains of ancient quarries may still be seen on the banks of that river (Nibby, *Viaggio Ant.* i. 112). Of this material were constructed two of the largest edifices in the world, the Colosseum and the Basilica of St. Peter. The air of Tibur was healthy and bracing, and this was one of the recommendations, together with its beautiful scenery, which made it a favourite retirement of the wealthy Romans. Besides its salubrity, the air was said to possess the peculiar property of bleaching ivory (Sil. It. xii. 229; Mart. viii. 28. 12). Tibur was also famed for its pottery (Sen. *Ep.* 119).

The foundation of Tibur was long anterior to that of Rome (Plin. xvi. 87). According to Dionysius of Halicarnassus (i. 16), it was one of the cities founded by the Siculi when they had possession of Italy; in proof of which statement he adduces the fact that in his own time part of the town was still called Sicelion; a name which would also indicate its having been one of the chief cities of that people. Another legend affirmed that the Siculi were expelled by Tiburtus, Coras and Catillus II., sons of Catillus I. The last was the son of Amphiaraus, the celebrated Theban king and prophet, who flourished about a century before the Trojan War. Catillus migrated to Italy in consequence of a ver sacrum. Tiburtus, or Tiburnus, the eldest of his three sons, became the eponymous hero of the newly founded city; for such it may be called, since the Siculi dwelt only in unwalled towns, which were subsequently fortified by the Greek colonists of Italy. According to Cato's version of the legend, Tibur was founded by Catillus, an officer of Evander (Solin. i. 2). From these accounts we may at all events infer the high antiquity of Tibur. The story of its Greek origin was very generally adopted by the Roman poets, whence we find it designated as the "moenia Catili" by Horace (*Od.* i. 18. 2; cf. *Ib.* ii. 6. 5; Virg. *Aen.* vii. 670; Ov. *Fast.* iv. 71, *Amor.* iii. 6. 45; Stat. *Silv.* i. 3. 74: Sil. It. iv. 225, viii. 364). Tibur possessed a small surrounding territory, the limits of which, however, we are unable to fix, all that we know respecting it being that the towns of Empulum and Sassula, besides one or two others, at one time belonged to it. Both these places lay in what is called the *Valle di Siciliano*, to the NE. of the town, the name of which is probably connected with the Sicelion of Dionysius. Empulum is identified with the present *Ampiglione*, a place about 4 miles distant from Tibur. Sassula probably lay 2 or 3 miles beyond Empulum, in the same direction. The boundary between the Tiburtine territory and that of the Sabines was very uncertain. Augustus adopted the Anio as the limit; yet considerable uncertainty seems to have prevailed even subsequently to the assumption of that boundary. Thus according to Tacitus (*Ann.* xiv. 22), the territory of Tibur extended beyond the Anio, and included Sublaqueum, the modern *Subiaco*, which is commonly assigned to the Aequi. Originally Tibur with its territory seems to have belonged to the Sabines. Pliny enumerates Tibur among the Sabine towns (iii. 12. s. 17).

We know nothing of the history of Tibur except in connection with that of Rome. The first occasion on which we find it mentioned is in the time of the decemvirate, B. C. 446, when M. Claudius, the infamous tool of the decemvir Appius, went into exile there (Liv. iii. 58). It does not appear, however, as taking any active part in affairs till B. C. 357; in which year the Tiburtines shut their gates against the Roman consuls C. Sulpicius and C. Licinius Calvus, who were returning from a successful expedition against the Hernici. There appear to have been previous disputes and complaints between the Tiburtines and Romans, and the latter seized the opportunity to declare war (Liv. vii. 9). But hostilities were suspended for a time by an incursion of the Gauls, who crossed the Anio and advanced to within 3 miles of Rome. This invasion of the Gauls was assisted by the Tiburtines ; and therefore, after the barbarians had been repulsed by the prodigious valour of Manlius Torquatus, the consul C. Poetelius was sent against them with an army in the following year. But the Gauls returned to the assistance of the Tiburtines; and, to meet this emergency, Q. Servilius Ahala was named dictator. The Gauls again advanced close to the walls of Rome, and a great battle was fought just outside the Porta Collina, in the sight of all the citizens. After a desperate conflict, the barbarians were defeated and fled to Tibur for refuge. Here they were intercepted by the consul Poetelius, who drove them into the city, as well as the Tiburtines who had come to their aid. For this achievement a triumph was awarded to Poetelius, which we find recorded in the *Fasti Capitolini* as well as by Livy. This triumph, however, excited the ridicule of the Tiburtines, who denied that the Romans had ever met them in a fair and open field : and in order to wipe out this affront, they made, in the following year, a nocturnal attempt upon Rome itself. But when day dawned and two armies, led by the two consuls, marched out against them from different gates, they were scarcely able to sustain the first charge of the Romans (Liv. vii. 11, 12). Yet the war continued for several years. In B. C. 350, the consul M. Popilius Laenas devastated their territory (*ib.* 17), and in the following year Valerius Poplicola took Empulum, one of their dependent cities (*ib.* 18; cf. EMPULUM). Sassula also yielded in 348 to the arms of M. Fabius Ambustus; and the Tiburtines would have lost all the rest of their territory had they not laid down their arms and submitted to the Roman consul. The triumph of Fabius is recorded in the *Fasti* and by Livy (*ib.* 19). Yet a few years later we find the Tiburtines joining the Latin league against the Romans ; and even after the overthrow of the Latins they allied themselves with the Praenestini and Veliterni to defend Pedum (Id. viii. 12). In B. C. 335, the consul L. Furius Camillus, attacked and completely defeated them under the walls of that place, in spite of a sortie of the inhabitants, and then took the town by escalade. All Latium was now subdued, and we do not again hear of the Tiburtines taking up arms against Rome (*ib.* 13). For this exploit Camillus not only obtained a triumph, but also an equestrian statue in the forum, a rare honour in that age. In the Senatusconsultum subsequently drawn up for the settlement of Latium, Tibur and Praeneste were treated with more severity than the other cities, except Velitrae. They were deprived of part of their territory, and were not admitted to the

Roman franchise like the rest. The cause of this severity was not their recent insurrection, the guilt of which they shared with the rest of the Latin cities, but their having formerly joined their arms with those of the Gauls (*ib.* 14). Thus Tibur remained nominally free and independent, so that Roman exiles might resort to it (Polyb. vi. 14). Hence we find the tibicines taking refuge there when they fled from the rigour of the censors (B. C. 310), who had deprived them of the good dinners which they were accustomed to enjoy in the temple of Jupiter; an event more important than at first sight it might seem to be, since, without the tibicines, neither sacrifices, nor several other important ceremonies, could be performed at Rome. On this occasion the rights of the Tiburtines were respected. The senators sent ambassadors to them as to an independent city, to request their assistance in procuring the return of the fugitives. The Tiburtines, like able diplomatists, took the pipers by their weak side. They invited them to dinner and made them drunk, and during the night carted them in waggons to Rome, so that when they awoke in the morning sober, they found themselves in the Forum (Liv. ix. 30). The story is also told by Ovid with his usual felicity (*Fast.* vi. 665, sqq.). Other instances might be adduced in which Tibur enjoyed the privilege of affording an asylum. That of M. Claudius, before alluded to, was of course previous to the conquest of Latium by the Romans; but we find Cinna taking refuge at Tibur after the murder of Caesar (App. *B. C.* i. 65) : and Ovid (*ex Ponto*, i. 3, 81, sq.) notes it as the most distant land of exile among the ancient Romans.

It was at Tibur that Syphax, king of Numidia, expired, in B. C. 201, two years after being captured in Africa. He had been brought thither from Alba, and was destined to adorn the triumph of Scipio; a humiliation which he escaped by his death (Liv. xxx. 45). Some centuries later Tibur received a more interesting captive, the beautiful and accomplished Zenobia. The former queen of the East resided near the villa of Hadrian, in the unostentatious manner of a Roman matron; and at the time when Trebellius Pollio wrote her history, the estate still bore her name. (Poll. *XXX. Tyr.* 26.)

In the Barberini palace at Rome is preserved a bronze tablet on which is engraved the following fragment of a Senatusconsultum: *Propterea . quod . scibamus . ea . vos . merito . nostro . facere . non . potuisse . neque . vos . dignos . esse . quei . faceretis . neque . id . vobeis . neque . rei . poplicae . vostras . oitile . esse . facere*. This monument, first acquired by Fulvio Orsini, and left by him to Cardinal Farnese, is published by Gruter (*Inscr.* ccccxcix. 12). The tenour seems to show that the Tiburtines had been accused of some grave offence from which they succeeded in exculpating themselves; but, as there is nothing to fix the date of the inscription, various opinions have been entertained respecting the occasion of it. As the style seems to belong to about the middle of the 7th century of Rome, Nibby (*Dintorni,* iii. p. 172) is of opinion that the document refers to the social war; that the Tiburtines had cleared themselves from the charge of taking part in that league, and were in consequence admitted to the Roman franchise, at the same time with many other Latin and Etruscan cities. This conjecture is by no means improbable. If, however, Tibur received the franchise before the civil wars of Marius and Sulla, the latter must have taken it away when he deprived the rest of the municipal cities of it, with the exception of Anagnia (Cic. *pro Dom.* 30), but it was probably regained on the abdication of the dictator. The treasure deposited at Tibur in the temple of Hercules was appropriated by Octavian during his war against Lucius Antonius, when so many other temples were plundered at Rome and in its neighbourhood. (App. *B. C.* v. 24.) From this period we have no notices of Tibur till the time of the Gothic war in the 6th century of our era. During the siege of Rome by Vitiges, Belisarius placed 500 men in it, and afterwards garrisoned it with Isaurians. (Procop. *B. G.* ii. 4.) But under his successor Totila a party of the Tiburtines having introduced the Goths by night into the city, the Isaurians fled, and the Goths murdered many of the inhabitants with circumstances of great cruelty (*Ib.* iii. 10.) Great part of the city must have been destroyed on this occasion, since it appears further on (c. 24) that Totila having retired to Tivoli, after a vain attempt upon Rome, rebuilt the fortress.

At present there are but few traces of the boundaries of the ancient city; yet there are certain points which, according to Nibby (*Dintorni,* iii. p. 186, seq.), enable us to determine the course of the walls with some degree of accuracy, and thus to estimate its circumference, at all events during the time of its subjection to the Romans. These points are determined partly by the nature of the ground, partly by existing remains, and partly by positive testimony. The nature of the ledge upon which the town is built shows that the walls must have traversed the edge of it towards the N. and E.; and this assumption is confirmed by some remains. The two temples commonly known as those of the Sibyl and of Drusilla in the quarter called *Castro Vetere,* and the evident pains taken to isolate this part, indicate it to have been the ancient acropolis or arx, and probably the Sicelion of Dionysius. On the W. the boundary is marked by some remains of the walls and of the gate opening on the road to Rome. On investigating this track, we find that it inclined inwards towards the church of the *Annunziata,* leaving out all that part now occupied by the *Villa d'Este* and its appurtenances. From that church it proceeded towards the modern gate of *Santa Croce* and the citadel built by Pope Pius II. on the site of the ancient amphitheatre. Thence to the Anio two points serve to fix the direction of the walls: first, the church of *S. Clemente,* which was certainly outside of them, since, according to the testimony of Marzi, some sepulchral stones were discovered there; second, the church of *S. Vincenzo,* which was certainly within them, as vestiges of ancient baths may still be seen at that spot. From the fortress of Pius II. the wall seems to have proceeded in an almost direct line to the Anio between the church of *S. Bartolommeo* and the modern gate of *S. Giovanni.* It did not extend to the opposite bank, as a small sepulchre of the imperial times has recently been discovered there, at the spot where the tunnel for diverting the Anio was opened; where also were found remains of an ancient bridge. Thus the plan of the city, with the abatement of some irregularities, formed two trapeziums joined together at their smallest sides. The arx also formed a trapezium completely isolated, and was connected with the town by a bridge on the same site as the present one of *S. Martino.* The circumference of the city, including the arx, was about

8000 Roman feet, or 1½ miles. The remains of the wall which still exist are of three different epochs. The rarest and most ancient consist of trapezoidal masses. Others, near the *Porta Romana* or *del Colle,* are of opus incertum, and belong to the time of Sulla. The gate itself, though composed of quadrilateral masses, is of the style of the gates of Rome of the age of Justinian. From the nature of the place and the direction of the ancient roads, Tibur must have had five gates; namely, three towards the W., one towards the S., and one towards the E., without counting that which communicated with the citadel; but with the exception of the Reatina, where the aqueduct called Anio Vetus began, their names are unknown, and even with regard to that the reading is doubtful. (Front. *Aq.* p. 30.)

The ancient remains existing at *Tivoli,* to call them by the names under which they commonly pass, are, the temple and portico of Hercules, the temples of Vesta and Sibylla, the thermae or baths, the two bridges and the little tomb recently discovered, the temple of Tussis, the villas of Maecenas, of Varus, &c.

Tibur was famed for the worship of Hercules, and hence the epithet of Herculean, so frequently applied to it by the Roman poets (Prop. ii. 32. 5; Sil. It. iv. 224; Mart. i. 13. 1, &c.; cf. Stat. *Silv.* iii. 1. 183.) The temple of that demigod at Tibur was, with the exception of the vast temple of Fortune at Praeneste, the most remarkable presented by any city in the neigbourhood of Rome. Thus Strabo (*l. c.*) mentions the Heracleum and the waterfall as the distinguishing features of Tibur, just as he alludes to the temple of Fortune as the principal object at Praeneste. And Juvenal (xiv. 86, seq.) censures the extravagance of Cetronius in building by saying that his villas at Tibur and Praeneste outdid the fanes of Hercules and Fortune at those places. The name of Heracleum used by Strabo of the former, as well as the term τέμενος applied to it by Stephanus Byzantinus, show that it embraced a large tract of ground, and as Augustus is said to have frequently administered justice in its porticoes (Suet. *Oct.* 72), they must have been of considerable size. It possessed a library, which, however, in the time of the Antonines appears to have fallen into decay. (A. Gell. *N. A.* xix. 5.) We have already seen that it had a treasury. There was also an oracle, which, like that at Praeneste, gave responses by means of sortes. (Stat. *Silv.* i. 3. 79.) Some antiquaries seek this vast temple behind the tribune of the present cathedral, where there are some remains of a circular cella composed of materials of a rhomboidal shape, thus marking the transition in the mode of building which took place about the age of Augustus from the opus incertum to the opus reticulatum. But it would be difficult to regard these vestiges as forming part of a temple 150 feet in circumference; nor was it usual to erect the principal Christian church on the foundations of a heathen temple. Nibby therefore (*Dintorni,* iii. p. 193), after a careful investigation, and a comparison of the remains at *Palestrina* with those of the so-called villa of Maecenas at *Tivoli,* is inclined to regard the latter, which will be described further on, as belonging to the celebrated temple of Hercules. It is probable, however, that there were several temples to that deity at Tibur, just as there were at Rome. The principal one was doubtless that dedicated to Hercules Victor Tiburs; but there was also one of Hercules Saxanus, which will be described by and by; and the remains at the cathedral may have belonged to a third. It is pretty certain, however, that the Forum of Tibur was near the cathedral, and occupied the site of the present *Piazza dell' Ormo* and its environs, as appears from a Bull of Pope Benedict VII. in the year 978, referred to by Ughelli in his *Italia Sacra* (t. i. p. 1306), and copied by Marini (*Papiri Diplomatici*, p. 316). In this Bull, the object of which was to determine the rights and jurisdiction of the bishop of *Tivoli*, many places in the town are mentioned by their ancient names; as the Forum, the Vicus Patricius, the Euripus, the Porta Major, the Porta Obscura, the walls, the postern of Vesta, the district of Castrum Vetus, &c. The round temple at the cathedral belonged therefore to the Forum, as well as the crypto-porticus, now called *Porto di Ercole* in the street *del Poggio*. The exterior of this presents ten closed arches about 200 feet in length, which still retain traces of the red plaster with which they were covered. Each arch has three loopholes to serve as windows. The interior is divided into two apartments or halls, by a row of twenty-eight slender pillars. Traces of arabesque painting on a black ground may still be seen. The mode of building shows it to be of the same period as the circular remains.

In that part of the city called *Castro Vetere*, which Nibby identifies with the arx, are two temples, one round, the other oblong, both of which have been variously identified. The round one, a charming relic of antiquity, is commonly regarded as the temple of the Sibyl. We know that the tenth and last of the Sibyls, whose name was Albunea, was worshipped at Tibur (Varro, ap. Lactant. *de Falsa Rel.* i. 6; cf. δεκάτη ἡ Τιβουρτία ὀνόματι Ἀλβουναία, Suid. p. 3302 Gaisf.); and Horace evidently alludes to her when he speaks of the "domus Albuneae resonantis" at that place. (*Od.* i. 7. 12.) It can scarcely be doubted therefore that she had a fane at Tibur. But Nibby is of opinion that the epithet of "resonantis," which alludes to the noise of the waterfall, is inapplicable to the situation of the round temple on the cliff; for though it immediately overhung the fall, before the recent diversion of the stream, the cataract, as before shown, must in the time of Horace have been lower down the river. This objection however, may perhaps be considered as pressing a poetical epithet rather too closely; nor is there anything to show how far the fall may have been removed by the catastrophe described by the younger Pliny. Some writers have ascribed the temple to Vesta, an opinion which has two circumstances in its favour: first, we know that Vesta was worshipped at Tibur, from inscriptions recording the Vestal virgins of the Tiburtini; secondly, the temples of Vesta were round, like the celebrated one near the Roman forum. Unfortunately, however, for this hypothesis, the Bull of Pope Benedict before referred to shows that the district of Vesta was on the opposite side of the river. Hence Nibby (*Dintorni*, iii. p. 205) regards the building in question as the temple of Hercules Saxanus. We know that round temples were sometimes erected to that deity, as in the Forum Boarium at Rome; and the epithet of Saxanus is applicable to the one in question, from its being seated on a rock. It may be observed, however, that Saxanus is not a usual derivative form from Saxum; and on the whole it may perhaps be as satisfactory to follow the ancient tradition which ascribes the temple to the Sibyl. It is of the style called peripteral, or having columns all round. These were originally eighteen in number, but only ten now remain, of which seven are isolated and three are built into the wall of a modern structure; but in such a manner that the sides towards the cell are visible. The columns are of *travertino*, of the Corinthian order, and channelled: hence the temple bears considerable resemblance to that in the Forum Boarium at Rome. According to the Bull before quoted, it was, in the 10th century, a church dedicated to the Virgin Mary.

The same was the case with the adjoining temple, which was dedicated to S. George. This building is also principally of *travertino*. It has four columns in front, now hidden by modern houses, and six at each side, five of which are built into the walls of the cella to the extent of two-thirds of their circumference. Hence it was of the style called prostylos tetrastylos pseudo-peripteros. The columns are of the Ionic order. From an inscription found near it, some writers have inferred that the temple was dedicated to the worship of Drusilla, the sister of Caligula: but the style of building is considerably earlier, and belongs to the age of Sulla. Others have called it the temple of the Sibyl. Professor Nibby (*Dintorni*, iii. p. 210) started a novel hypothesis, and regarded it as the temple of Tiburtus, or Tiburnus. It is certain that the eponymous founder of the city enjoyed divine honours in it, as we see from Horace ("Tiburni lucus," *Od.* i. 7. 13) and Statius ("illa recubat Tiburnus in umbra," *Silv.* i. 3. 74). But these expressions refer to a sacred grove or τέμενος, probably with a shrine, or perhaps merely an altar, and therefore situated, in all likelihood, in the outskirts of the town, and not in a narrow crowded place like the arx. And we must here point out a little inconsistency into which the learned professor has fallen: for whilst he objects to the round temple being called that of Vesta, on the ground that it was not within hearing of the waterfall, when that was in its ancient state, yet he regards the square one, which immediately adjoins it, as the temple of Tiburnus, because it was close to the cataract. On the whole, therefore, we must for the present content ourselves with one of the ancient names for this building, or else, which may perhaps be the safer course, leave it altogether unidentified.

The catastrophe of 1826 brought to light the remains of a bridge; and another still more perfect one was discovered in 1832, in the progress of the works for diverting the course of the river. At the same time the workmen came upon a small tomb, between the Via Valeria and the banks of the river, containing several skeletons and monumental stones. Among these was a cenotaph to Senecio, who was consul for the fourth time A. D. 107, and several inscriptions. Under this tomb was an ancient aqueduct, intended to distribute the waters of the Anio among the adjacent villas.

There are no other remains in the town except some fine opus reticulatum et lateritium, near the church of S. Andrea. At this spot were discovered, in 1778, some large and handsome columns with Corinthian capitals, and also the pedestal of a statue to Fur. Maecius Graecus, with an inscription connecting it with some embellishment of the baths. Hence we may conclude that the thermae were situated here.

Outside the city, on the Via Constantiana, is the building known as the temple of Tussia, for which appellation, however, no authority exists. Externally it is of an octagon form, but round inside.

Nibby holds that it is not anterior to the 4th century of our era, its construction resembling that of the villa of Maxentius on the Via Appia. There are traces of painting of the 13th century, showing that then, if not previously, it was a Christian church. A little further on we come to an inscription which records the levelling of the Clivus Tiburtinus in the time of Constantius and Constans. The name of the latter is purposely effaced, no doubt by the order of Magnentius. This monument was discovered in 1736, and re-erected by order of the magistrates of Tibur at the same spot where it was found.

The delightful country in the vicinity of Tibur caused many villas to be erected there during the latter period of the Republic and under the first Caesars, as we see from the writings of Catullus, Horace, Propertius, Statius, and other poets. Of these villas, however, of which we shall mention only the more interesting, there are but few remains, and scarcely any that can be identified with certainty. The most striking are those commonly called the villa of Maecenas on the SW. side of the town, near the *Cascatelle.* Ligorio was the first who called this building the villa of Maecenas; but there is no authority for the assumption. It was probably founded on a wrong conception of a passage in Horace (*Od.* iii. 29. 6, seq.), which is also quoted by Mr. Cramer (*Italy*, vol. ii. p. 60) under a misapprehension that it contains an allusion to a residence possessed by Maecenas at Tibur, instead of to his town-house on the Esquiline. The plan of this building published by Marquez and Uggeri is correct. It was founded on gigantic substructions, the magnitude of which may be best observed on the N. side, or that towards the valley of the Anio. It is an immense quadrilateral edifice, 637½ feet long, and 450 broad, surrounded on three sides by sumptuous porticoes. The fourth side, or that which looks towards Rome, which is one of the long sides, had a theatre in the middle of it, with a hall or saloon on each side. The porticoes are arched, and adorned on the side towards the area with half columns of the Doric order. Behind is a series of chambers. An oblong tumulus now marks the site of the house, or, according to Nibby, who regards it as the temple of Hercules, of the Cella. The pillars were of travertine, and of a beautiful Ionic order. One of them still existed on the ruins as late as 1812. This immense building intercepted the ancient road, for which, as appears from an inscription preserved in the Vatican, a vault or tunnel was constructed, part of which is still extant. Hence it gave name to the *Porta Scura*, or *Obscura*, mentioned in the Bull of Benedict, which it continued to bear at least as late as the 15th century.

To our apprehension, the plan here laid down is rather that of a palace or villa, than of a temple, nor do we perceive the resemblance, insisted on by Nibby, to the temple of Fortune at Praeneste. It is not probable that the chief fane of Hercules, the patron deity of Tibur, should have been erected outside the town, nor would it have been a convenient spot for Augustus to administer justice, as we have mentioned that he did in his frequent retirements to Tibur, in the porticoes of the temple of Hercules. The precincts of the Forum would have been more adapted to such a purpose. But if that emperor so much frequented Tibur, evidently the favourite among all his country retreats (Suet. *l. c.*), he must have had a suitable residence for his reception. Might

not this villa have been his palace? Nibby himself observes that the style of building is of the Augustan, or transition, period; and a subject would scarcely have ventured to occupy the highroad with his substructions. But we offer this notion as a mere conjecture in favour of which we can adduce nothing but its probability.

Catullus had a paternal estate in the neighbourhood of Tibur; and the pretended site of his house is still pointed out in the valley by *Monte Catillo.* It is evident, however, from his address to his farm (*Carm.* 42), that it was more distant from the town, and lay at a point where the boundary between the Sabine and the Tiburtine territory was uncertain. He himself wished to be considered as in the latter, probably as the more fashionable and aristocratic situation; but his ill-wishers persisted in asserting that it was Sabine. Horace had also a residence at Tibur, besides his Sabine farm; and, according to his biographer, it was situated near the grove of Tiburnus (Suet. *Vit. Hor.*); but whether it was at the spot now pointed out, near the hermitage of *S. Antonio*, on the road from *Tivoli* to the *Cascatelle*, is very problematical, the remains there being, according to Nibby (*Dintorni*, iii. p. 221), of a period anterior to that of Horace. Nibby would identify them as belonging to the villa of Sallust, who, if we may trust the *Declamatio in Sallustium* (c. 7) falsely ascribed to Cicero, had a residence at Tibur. But this is mere conjecture. Equally uncertain is the site of the villa of Vopiscus, a poet of the age of Domitian; of which Statius has left us a pretty description (*Silv.* i. 3). The grounds seem to have extended on both sides of the river, and from certain particulars in the description, Nibby (*Dintorni*, iii. p. 216) imagines that he has discovered the spot near the place commonly assigned to the villa of Catullus and the grove of Tiburnus, in the valley between *M. Catillo* and *M. Peschiavatore.* The Cynthia of Propertius, whose real name was Hostia (Appul. *Apol.* ii. p. 405, ed. Bosscha), lived and died at Tibur (Prop. iii. 30, iv. 7. 85, &c.); so that scarcely any place was more associated with the domestic life of the Roman poets. The situation of the villa of Quintilius Varus, a little further on the same road, is rather better supported than most of the others. Horace alludes to the estate of Varus at Tibur, which appears to have lain close to the town (*Od.* i. 18. 2). A tract on the declivity of *Monte Peschiavatore*, opposite to the *Cascatelle*, bore the name of *Quintiliolo* as far back as the 10th century, and the little church at this spot is called *La Madonna di Quintiliolo*, an appellation which may possibly have been derived from the family name of Varus. Here are the remains of a magnificent villa, in which marble pavements, columns, capitals, statues, consular coins, &c., have been discovered, and especially, in 1820, two beautiful marble Fauns, now in the Vatican. Just below this villa is the *Ponte Acquoria*, as well as the surrounding district, takes its name, literally "the golden water," from a beautifully clear spring which rises near it. This bridge was traversed by the primitive Via Tiburtina. One arch of it still remains, constructed of large blocks of travertine. Near it is another bridge of bricks of the imperial times, as well as a modern one of the 15th century, but none of these are at present in use. On the other side of the river, which is crossed by a rude wooden bridge, the road ascends the Clivus Tiburtinus in returning towards the town. Portions of the pavement are in complete preservation. Under a rock on the right is an ancient artificial cave, called by the local antiquaries *Il Tempio del Mondo*, but which was probably either a sepulchre, or one of those caves consecrated by the ancients to the rustic tutelary deities. This road joins the Via Constantia before mentioned, leading up to the ruins of the so-called villa of Maecenas.

Outside the *Porta S. Croce* is a district called *Carciano*, a corruption of the name of Cassianum which it bore in the 10th century, derived from a magnificent villa of the gens Cassia which was situated in it. In the time of Zappi, in the 16th century, a great part of this building was extant. The splendour of this residence is attested by the numerous beautiful statues found there, many of which were acquired by Pope Pius VI. and now adorn the Vatican. In the neighbourhood of Tibur are also the remains of several aqueducts, as the Anio Vetus, the Aqua Marcia, and the Aqua Claudia. The ruins of the sumptuous villa of Hadrian lie about 2 miles S. of the town. A description of it would be too long for this place, and it will suffice to say that, in a circuit of about 8 miles, it embraced, besides the imperial palace and a barracks for the guard, a Lyceum, an Academy, a fac-simile of the Poecile at Athens and of the Serapeum at Alexandria, a vale of Tempe, a Tartarus, a tract called the Elysian Fields, a stream called the Euripus, numerous temples, &c. (Cf. Nibby, *Viaggio Antiquario*, vol. i.; *Analisi della Carta de' Dintorni di Roma*, v. viii.; Gell, *Topography of Rome and its vicinity*, ed. Bunbury; Ant. del Ré, *Antichità Tiburtine*; Cabrale and F. del Ré, *Della Villa e de' Monumenti antichi della Città e del Territorio di Tivoli*; Santo Viola, *Storia di Tivoli*; Keller, *De vetere cum novo Tibure comparato* : concerning the villa of Hadrian, Piero Ligorio, *Pianta della Villa Tiburtina*; Fea, *ap. Winckelmann*, ii. p. 379.)　　　[T. H. D.]

TIBURES or TIBURI (Τεισούρων in gen., Ptol. ii. 6. § 37), a branch of the Astures in Hispania Tarraconensis, whose principal town was Nemetobriga.　　　[T. H. D.]

TICHIS (*Tech*), a river of Gallia Narbonensis, placed by Mela (ii. 5) in the "Ora Sardonum" [SARDONES]. The Tichis is the Tecum of Pliny (iii. 4). The *Tet* and the *Tech*, two small rivers, cross the territory of *Rousillon* from west to east. The Tichis is named Illiberis or Illeris by other writers. [ILLIBERIS.]　　　[G. L.]

TI'CHIUM. [TEICHIUM.]

TICHIUSSA (Τειχιοῦσσα), is mentioned twice by Thucydides (viii. 26, 28) as a fortified place in Caria in the territory of Miletus. Stephanus B. speaks of it under the name of Τειχιόεσσα, and Athenaeus knew it under the name of Τειχιοῦς (viii. p. 351.) It seems to have been situated on the north coast of the bay of Iassus.　　　[L. S.]

TICHOS or TEICHOS. [DYME.]

TICINUM (Τίκινον: *Eth*. Ticinensis: *Pavia*), a city of Gallia Transpadana, situated on the river Ticinus, from which it derived its name, about 5 miles above the junction of that stream with the Padus. According to Pliny it was founded by the two tribes of the Laevi and Marici, at the period of the first Gaulish immigrations into this part of Italy. (Plin. iii. 17. s. 21.) But it is remarkable that no mention is found of any town on the site during the operations of P. Scipio against Hannibal in B.C. 218, though he must have crossed the Ticinus in the immediate neighbourhood of the spot where the

city afterwards stood. It is probable, indeed, that in this, as in many other cases, the rise of a town upon the spot was mainly owing to the existence of a convenient passage across the river. There seems no reason to doubt that under the Roman government Ticinum had grown up into a considerable municipal town before the close of the Republic, though its name is not noticed in history. But it is mentioned by all the geographers, and repeatedly figures in history during the Roman Empire. It is included by Ptolemy among the cities of the Insubres, and would naturally be so reckoned, though not of Insubrian origin, as soon as the river Ticinus came to be considered as the boundary of that people. (Strab. v. p. 217, Plin. iii. 17. s. 21; Ptol. iii. 1. § 36.)

The earliest mention of Ticinum in history is on occasion of the death of Drusus, the father of Germanicus, when we are told that Augustus advanced as far as Ticinum to meet his funeral procession. (Tac. *Ann.* iii. 5.) Its name is also repeatedly mentioned during the civil wars of A.D. 69, when its position on the great highroad that led from the foot of the Alps to join the Aemilian Way at Placentia, rendered it an important post. It was the scene of a serious sedition among the troops of Vitellius, while that emperor halted there. (Id. *Hist.* ii. 17, 27, 30, 68, 88.) At a later period it was at Ticinum that the emperor Claudius (the second of the name) was saluted with the imperial title, while he was commanding the garrison of the city. (Vict. *Caes.* 33, *Epit.* 34.) It was there also that Constantius took leave of his nephew Julian, whom he had just raised to the rank of Caesar. (Ammian. xv. 8. § 18.) From these frequent notices of Ticinum it seems probable that it had already risen under the Roman Empire into a flourishing municipal town, and derived importance from its position, the great highroad which formed the continuation of the Aemilian Way from Placentia to the foot of the Alps passing through Ticinum, until the increasing importance of Mediolanum, which became the second capital of Italy, made it customary to proceed through that city instead of following the direct route. (*Itin. Ant.* pp. 283, 340, 347.)

But though Ticinum was undoubtedly a considerable town under the Roman Empire, it was not till after the fall of that empire that it rose to the position it subsequently occupied. In A.D. 452, indeed, it had sustained a great calamity, having been taken and devastated by Attila (Jornand. *Get.* 42); but the Gothic king Theodoric, being struck with the importance of its position, not only raised it from its ruins, but erected a royal palace there, and strengthened the city with fresh fortifications, until it became one of the strongest fortresses in this part of Italy. It consequently bears an important part in the Gothic wars, that people having made it their chief stronghold in the north of Italy (Procop. *B. G.* ii. 12, 25, iii. 1, iv. 32, &c.), in which the royal treasures and other valuables were deposited. At the time of the Lombard invasion, it offered a prolonged resistance to the arms of Alboin, and was not taken by that monarch till after a siege of more than three years, A.D. 570 (P. Diac. *Hist. Lang.* ii. 26, 27). It thenceforth became the residence of the Lombard kings, and the capital of the kingdom of Italy, and continued to hold this position till A.D. 774, when Desiderius, the last of the Lombard kings, was compelled to surrender the city to Charlemagne, after a blockade of more than 15 months.

4 H 3

From this time Ticinum sank again into the condition of an ordinary provincial town, which it has retained ever since. Before the close of the Lombard period we find that it was already designated by the name of Papia, from which its modern appellation of *Pavia* is derived. Paulus Diaconus calls it "Ticinus quae alio nomine Papia appellatur" (P. Diac. ii. 15); and the anonymous Geographer of Ravenna gives the same double appellation (Geogr. Ravenn. iv. 30). The most probable explanation of this change of name is that when Ticinum became admitted to the rights of a Roman municipium its inhabitants were enrolled in the Papian tribe, a fact which we learn from inscriptions (Gruter, *Inscr.* p. 1093. 7; Murat. *Inscr.* p. 1087. 1, p. 1119. 4), and that in consequence of this the city came to be known as "Civitas Papia," in contradistinction to Mediolanum, which belonged to the Ufentine tribe. (Aldini, *Antiche Lapidi Ticinesi*, pp. 43—60.)

The modern city of *Pavia* contains no remains of antiquity except a few sarcophagi and inscriptions. These confirm the municipal condition of the city under the Roman Empire, but are not in themselves of much interest.　　　　　　　　　[E. H. B.]

TICINUS (Τίκινος: *Ticino*), a considerable river of Northern Italy, and one of the most important of the northern tributaries of the Padus. It has its sources among the high Alps, in the Mons Adula or *Mont St. Gothard*, and, where it first emerges from the Alpine valleys forms an extensive lake, called the LACUS VERBANUS or *Lago Maggiore.* Where it issues from this again it is a deep, clear, and rapid stream, and flows through the level plains of *Lombardy*, with a course of above 60 miles, passing under the walls of Ticinum (*Pavia*), and discharging its waters into the Padus or *Po*, about 3 miles below that city. (Strab. iv. p. 209, v. p. 217; Plin. ii. 103. s. 106, iii. 19. s. 23.) Throughout this lower part of its course (from the *Lago Maggiore* to the *Po*) it is navigable for vessels of considerable burden; but the extreme rapidity of the current renders the navigation inconvenient if not dangerous. Its banks are low and marshy, the river being bordered on each side by a belt of thickets and marshy woods. This character of its banks is noticed by Claudian (*de VI. Cons. Hon.* 194), while Silius Italicus alludes to the beautiful clearness of its waters. (Sil. Ital. iv. 82.)

The Ticinus appears to have been recognised at an early period as the boundary between the Insubrians and their neighbours the Libicii and Laevi (Liv. v. 34, 35). From its geographical position it must always have presented a formidable barrier to any invader advancing into Italy after having crossed the Cottian, Graian or Pennine Alps, and for this reason its banks have been the scene of many successive battles. Even in the first descent of the Gauls into the plains of Northern Italy, we are told that they defeated the Etruscans in a battle near the river Ticinus (Liv. v. 34). But much the most celebrated of the contests which were fought on its banks was that between Hannibal and P. Scipio in B.C. 218, shortly after the descent of the Carthaginian general into Italy. The precise scene of this action cannot, however, be determined; but it appears to have been fought on the W. or right bank of the Ticinus, at a short distance from the Padus, and probably not far from the site of Ticinum or *Pavia.* Livy marks it more distinctly as being within 5 miles of a place called Victumvii (?); but as no other mention of this obscure name occurs, this lends us no assistance.

(Liv. xxi. 45.) The narrative of Polybius is far from clear and has given rise to considerable discussion. Scipio, who had hastened from Pisae into Cisalpine Gaul, on hearing that Hannibal had actually crossed the Alps and descended into the plains of Italy, advanced to meet him, crossed the Padus by a bridge constructed for the occasion, and afterwards crossed the Ticinus in like manner. After this, Polybius tells us, "both generals advanced along the river, on the side facing the Alps, the Romans having the stream on their left hand, the Carthaginians on their right" (iii. 65). It is clear that this is not consistent with the statement that the Romans had crossed the Ticinus[*], as in ascending that river they would have had the stream on their right, unless we suppose "the river" to mean not the Ticinus but the Padus, which is at least equally consistent with the general plan of operations. Hannibal was in fact advancing from the country of the Taurini, and no reason can be assigned why he should have turned so far to the N. as to be descending the Ticinus, in the manner supposed by those who would place the battle near *Vigevano* or *Borgo S. Siro.* If we are to understand the river in question to be the Ticinus, the words of Polybius above quoted would necessarily require that the battle should have been fought on the *left* bank of the Ticinus, which is at variance with all the other particulars of the operations, as well as with the probabilities of the case. The battle itself was a mere combat of cavalry, in which the Roman horse was supported by a portion of their light-armed troops. They were, however, defeated, and Scipio at once retreated to the bridge over the Padus, leaving a small body of troops to break up that over the Ticinus. These troops, 600 in number, were cut off and made prisoners by Hannibal, who, however, gave up the attempt to pursue Scipio, and turned up the stream of the Padus, till he could find a point where he was able to construct a bridge of boats across it. (Pol. iii. 65, 66.) The account of Livy (which is based mainly upon that of Polybius, though he must have taken some points, such as the name of Victumvii, from other sources) agrees with the above explanation, though he certainly seems to have transferred what Polybius relates as occurring at the bridge over the Ticinus to that over the Padus. It appears also by his own account that there was considerable discrepancy among his authorities as to the point at which Hannibal eventually crossed the Padus. (Liv. xxi. 45—47.) It may therefore on the whole be assumed as probable that the battle was fought at a short distance W. of the Ticinus, and not close to the banks of that river: the circumstance that Scipio had encamped on the banks of the Ticinus just before, and advanced from thence to meet Hannibal will explain why the battle was always called the "pugna ad Ticinum" or "apud Ticinum."

Two other battles were fought in the same neighbourhood before the close of the Roman empire: one

---

[*] Polybius, indeed, does not distinctly say that the Romans crossed the Ticinus, but it is implied in his whole narrative, as he tells us that the consul ordered a bridge to be built over the Ticinus with the purpose of crossing that river, and afterwards relates their advance without further allusion to it (iii. 64. 65). But after narrating the defeat and retreat of Scipio, he says that Hannibal followed him as far as the bridge on *the first river*, which can be no other than the Ticinus. (*Ib.* 66.)

in A.D. 270, in which the Alemanni, who had invaded Italy, were finally defeated by the Emperor Aurelian (Vict. *Epit.* 35): the other in A.D. 352, between the rival emperors Magnentius and Constantius. (*Ib.* 42.)   [E. H. B.]

TIERNA (called by Ptol. Δίερνα, iii. 8. § 10), a town of Dacia on the Danube, opposite to the castle of Zernes (*Old Orsova*) in Moesia. In inscriptions we find it called Statio Tsiernensis (Murat. p. 332. 3; Griselini, i. p. 265); in the Digest (*de Cens.* i. 8), Colonia Zernensium; and in the *Not. Imp.* (c. 3), Trans Diernis.   [T. H. D.]

TIFATA (τὰ Τιφατηνὰ ὄρη, Dion Cass.: *Monte di Maddaloni*), a mountain ridge on the borders of Campania and Samnium, only about a mile from the city of Capua. It is one of the last outlying masses of the Apennines, and is a long, narrow ridge of no great elevation, but above 12 miles in length from E. to W., and presenting a bold and steep mountain front towards the Campanian plain, upon which it looks directly down. The name was derived according to Festus from the woods of evergreen oak with which it was covered, "Tifata" being equivalent to "ilicета," though whether it was an Oscan or old Latin word, we are not told. (Fest. *s. v. Tifata.*) It is first mentioned during the war between the Samnites and Campanians which immediately preceded the First Samnite War. On that occasion the Samnites in the first instance occupied the ridge itself with a strong force, and afterwards drew out their main army into the plain below, where they soon defeated the Campanians in a pitched battle. (Liv. vii. 29.) Livy calls it on this occasion " Tifata, imminentes Capuae colles," and elsewhere "montem imminentem Capuae" (xxvi. 5), which well describes its character and situation. It was this opportune position with regard to Capua and the surrounding plain, that caused it to be selected by Hannibal as a post where he established his camp in B. C. 215, and from whence he long carried on his operations against the various cities of Campania. (Id. xxiii. 36, 37, 39, 43, xxvi. 5; Sil. Ital. xii. 487.) At a later period it was in the plain at the foot of Tifata that Sulla defeated the Marian general Norbanus, B. C. 83; and in gratitude for this victory, he consecrated a considerable tract of territory to Diana, the tutelary goddess of the mountain. (Vell. Pat. ii. 25.) We hence learn that that divinity had a celebrated temple on Tifata, and the "Dianae Tifatinae fanum" is noticed also in inscriptions found at Capua. From one of these we learn that the consecrated territory was again assigned to the goddess by Vespasian. (Orell. *Inscr.* 1460, 3055.) As the Tabula marks a station "Ad Dianae" near the W. extremity of the ridge, it is probable that the temple was situated in that neighbourhood. (*Tab. Peut.*) From the same authority we learn that Jupiter, who was worshipped on so many of the highest points of the Apennines, had a temple also on Tifata, to which it gives the name of Jovis Tifatinus. It is placed in the Tabula at the E. extremity of the ridge. (*Tab. Peut.*) Again in B. C. 48 the fastnesses of this mountain ridge afforded a shelter to Milo when driven from Capua. (Dion Cass. xlii. 25.) This is the last time its name is mentioned in history, and it is not noticed by any of the geographers : in the middle ages the name seems to have been wholly forgotten; and the mountain is now called from a neighbouring village the *Monte di Maddaloni.* But the descriptions of Livy and Silius Italicus leave no doubt of

the identification. It is indeed, from its proximity to Capua and the abruptness with which it rises from the plain, one of the most striking natural features of this part of Campania.   [E. H. B.]

TIFERNUM (Τίφερνον) was the name of two cities or towns of Umbria, which were distinguished by the epithets Tiberinum and Metaurense (Plin. iii. 14. s. 19).

1. TIFERNUM TIBERINUM, which appears to have been the most considerable place of the name, was situated on or near the site of the modern *Città di Castello*, in the upper valley of the Tiber, about 20 miles E. of *Arezzo*. The Tifernates Tiberini are enumerated among the municipal communities of Umbria by Pliny (*l. c.*); but our principal knowledge of the town is derived from the epistles of the younger Pliny, whose Tuscan villa was situated in its neighbourhood. For this reason the citizens had chosen him at a very early age to be their patron; and in return for this honour he had built a temple there at his own expense. (Plin. *Ep.* iv. 1.) He afterwards adorned this with statues of the various Roman emperors, to which he in one of his letters begs leave to add that of Trajan (*Ib.* x. 24). From the circumstance that Pliny's villa itself was in Etruria (whence he always calls it his *Tuscan* villa), while Tifernum was certainly in Umbria, it is evident that the frontier of the two countries ran very near the latter place, very probably as that of the Tuscan and Roman States does at the present day, between *Città di Castello* and *Borgo S. Sepolcro.* The position of Tifernum on nearly the same site with the former of these cities seems to be well established by the inscriptions found there and reported by Cluverius (Cluver. *Ital.* p. 624; Gruter, *Inscr.* p. 494. 5). But it was probably situated rather further from the Tiber, as Pliny describes it as being, like Perugia and Ocriculum, " not far" from that river (Plin. iii. 5. s. 9), while the modern *Città di Castello* almost adjoins its banks.

The precise site of Pliny's Tuscan villa cannot be ascertained, as the terms in which he describes its position (*Ep.* v. 6) will apply to many localities on the underfalls of the Apennines in the upper valley of the Tiber. It is, however, most probable that it was situated (as suggested by Cluverius) in the neighbourhood of *Borgo S. Sepolcro*, about 10 miles N. of *Città di Castello*, rather than in the immediate vicinity of Tifernum. (Cluver. *Ital.* p. 590.)

2. TIFERNUM METAURENSE was evidently, as its name implies, situated on the other side of the Apennines, in the valley of the Metaurus. Its name is mentioned only by Pliny among ancient writers ; but it is found in several inscriptions (in which the citizens are termed, as by Pliny, Tifernates Metaurenses), and the discovery of these at *S. Angelo in Vado* leaves no doubt that Tifernum occupied the same site as that town, near the sources of the Metaurus, about 20 miles above *Fossombrone.* (Forum Sempronii). (Cluver. *Ital.* p. 621; Orell. *Inscr.* 3049, 3305, 3902.)

It is uncertain which of the towns above mentioned is the Tifernum of Ptolemy (iii. 1. § 53); perhaps the first has the better claim.   [E. H. B.]

TIFERNUS (Τίφερνος, Ptol.: *Biferno*), one of the most considerable rivers of Samnium, which has its sources in the heart of that country, near Bovianum (*Bojano*), in a lofty group of mountains, now known by the same name as the river (*Monte Biferno*). This is evidently the same which is called by Livy the TIFERNUS MONS, which the Samnite army had occupied as a stronghold in B. c. 295: but notwithstanding the strength of the position, they were attacked and defeated there by the Roman consul L. Volumnius Flamma (Liv. x. 30, 31). Upon two other occasions during the Samnite wars Livy speaks of Tifernus or Tifernum in a manner that would leave it uncertain whether this mountain fastness is meant, or a town of the same name (Liv. ix. 44, x. 14); but as we have no other mention of a town of Tifernum in Samnium, it is perhaps more probable that in all these cases the mountain of that name is meant. The group thus named is a part of that known collectively as the *Monte Matese*,—one of the most conspicuous mountain masses in Samnium. [SAMNIUM.] The river Tifernus has a course of above 60 miles from its source to the Adriatic, in a general direction from SW. to NE. In the lower part of its course, after leaving the confines of Samnium, it constituted in ancient times the boundary between Apulia and the Frentani. (Mel. ii. 4. § 6; Plin. iii. 11, s. 16, 12. s. 17; Ptol. iii. 1. § 18, where the MSS. have Φέτερνος; but this is probably a mistake for Τίφερνος.)   [E. H. B.]

TIGAVA CASTRA (*It. Ant.* p. 38; Tigavae, Plin. v. 2. s. 1; Τιγαῦα, Ptol. iv. 2. § 26), a fortress in Mauretania Caesariensis, between Oppidum Novum and Malliana, variously identified with *El-Herba, Cantara, Abd-el-Kader*.

TIGRA (called Τίγα by Procopius, *de Aed.* iv. 7), a fortress in Moesia Inferior, near the Danube, and between Sexantaprista and Appiaria (*Itin. Ant.* p. 222). In the *Not. Imp.* it is called Tegra. Variously identified with *Marotin* and a place near *Olughissar*.   [T. H. D.]

TIGRANOCERTA (τὰ Τιγρανόκερτα, Strab. xi. pp. 522, 532; Ptol. v. 13. § 22; ἡ Τιγρανοκέρτα, Plut. *Lucull.* 25, &c.), literally, the city of Tigranes, since κέρτα (*kert, gerd*, or *karta*) meant, in the Armenian dialect, *city* (Hesych. iii. p. 237). The later capital of Armenia, built by Tigranes on an eminence by the river Nicephorius, a city of considerable size and strongly fortified. It was in a great measure populated with Greeks and Macedonians, taken thither by force from Cappadocia and Cilicia. After Lucullus gained his victory over Tigranes before its walls, he caused a great part of the still unfinished town to be pulled down, and permitted its kidnapped inhabitants to return to their homes. Nevertheless, the town continued to exist, though we hear but little of it subsequently to this event. (Cf. Strab. *ll. cc.* and xii. p. 539, xvi. p. 747; App. *Mithr.* 67; Plut. *Lucull.* 25, sqq.; Tac. *Ann.* xii. 50, xiv. 24, xv. 4; Plin. vi. 9. s. 10.) It has been variously identified with the ruins of *Sert* on the *Chabur*, with *Mejafarkin*, and with *Amid* or *Amadiah*. (See Ainsworth, ii. p. 361; St. Martin, i. p. 173; Ritter, *Erdk.* x. p. 87, xi. p. 106, sqq.)   [T. H. D.]

TIGRIS, a celebrated river of Asia. We find various forms of its name, both in Greek and Latin writers. The earlier and more classical Greek form is ὁ Τίγρης, *gen.* Τίγρητος (Herod. vi. 20; Xen. *Anab.* iv. 1. § 3; Arr. *Anab.* vii. 7, &c.), whilst the form ὁ Τίγρις, *gen.* Τίγριδος, and sometimes Τίγριος, is more usual among the later writers. (Strab. ii. p. 79, xv. p. 728; Ptol. v. 13. § 7; Plut. *Lucull.* 22, &c.) Amongst the Romans the *nom.* is constantly Tigris, with the *gen.* Tigris and *acc.* Tigrin and Tigrim among the better writers (Virg. *Ecl.* i. 63; Lucan, iii. 261; Plin. vi. s. 9; Curt. iv. 5, &c.); but sometimes Tigridis, Tigridem (Lucan, iii. 256;

Eutrop. ix. 18; Amm. Marc. xxiii. 6. § 20, &c.) According to Pliny, the river in the upper part of its course, where it flowed gently, was called Diglito; but lower down, where it moved with more rapidity, it bore the name of Tigris, which, in the Median language, signified an arrow (cf. Strab. xi. p. 529; Curt. iv. 9; Isid. *Or.* xii. c. 2, &c.) Josephus (*Ant.* i. 1, 2, sq.) and Zonaras (*Ann.* i. 2) mention that it bore the name of Diglad; and in its earliest course it is still called *Daghele, Didschle* or *Dadschla*.

According to the general testimony of the ancients the Tigris rose in Armenia (Xen. *Anab.* iv. 1. § 3; Eratosth. *ap. Strab.* ii. p. 80; Plin. vi. 27. s. 31; Ptol. *l. c.*, &c.). Diodorus, indeed, places its sources in the territory of the Uxii in Persia (xvii. 67); but he has here confounded the Tigris with the Pasitigris. Herodotus (v. 52) observes that there were three rivers bearing the name of Tigris, but that they did not spring from the same source; one of them rising in Armenia, another in the country of the Matieni, whilst he does not mention the origin of the third. These two branches, which are not mentioned by any other ancient writer, are the more western and proper sources of the Tigris in Sophene, to the NE. of the cataracts of the Euphrates. The more eastern of them forms the little river Nymphius or Nymphaeus (now the *Batman Su* or river of *Miafarakin*.) The union of these two sources forms the main western arm of the Tigris, which flows for between 100 and 200 miles, first in a NE., then in a S., and lastly in an E. direction, before it joins the main eastern branch of the river, about 62 miles SE. of Tigranocerta. The authors subsequent to Herodotus do not notice his correct account of these sources, but confine themselves entirely to the eastern branch. According to Strabo (xi. pp. 521, 529) this rose in Mount Niphates, at a distance of 2500 stadia from the sources of the Euphrates. But Pliny, who has written in most detail concerning this eastern branch, describes it as rising in a plain of Armenia Major, at a place called Elegosine (vi. 27. s. 31). It then flowed through the nitrous lake of Arethusa, without, however, mingling its waters with those of the lake, and after losing itself at a place called Zoroanda (near the present *Hasur*), under a chain of the Taurus (the *Nimrud Dagh*), burst again from the earth, and flowed through a second lake, the Thospites. After emerging from this, it again sank into the earth with much noise and foam (cf. Strab. xvi. p. 746; Prisc. *Perieg.* 913; Amm. Marc. xxiii. 6. § 15, &c.), and, after a subterranean passage of 25 miles, reappeared at a place called Nymphaeum (cf. Justin, xlii. 3). The account of Strabo, however, varies very considerably from the preceding one of Pliny. The former writer mentions only one lake (xi. p. 529), the description of which entirely resembles Pliny's Arethusa, but which Strabo calls Arsene or Thopitis, meaning evidently the Thospites of Pliny, the present *Wan* in *Tosp*, on which is situated the town of *Ardschisch*, with which the Tigris is in reality quite unconnected. Subsequently the river approaches the Euphrates in the neighbourhood of Seleucia, forming in this part of its course the boundary between Assyria and Mesopotamia. Diodorus Siculus (ii. 11) and Curtius (v. 1) erroneously represent it as flowing through Media, which it does not even touch. Near Seleucia, it was connected with the Euphrates by means of canals (Arrian, *Anab.* vii. 7). After this, it again retires from the Euphrates, till at last, bending its course to the SW., it completely unites with that river, at a place called by Pliny (*l. c.*) Digba, 1000 stadia above their common embouchure in the Persian gulf. Many of the ancients were aware that the two rivers joined one another, and had a common mouth (Plin. *ib.*; Strab. ii. p. 79; Procop. *B. P.* i. 17, &c.), whilst others were of opinion that the Euphrates had a separate embouchure (Onesicritus, ap. *Strab.* xv. p. 729; Arrian, *Anab. l. c.*; and *Ind.* 41; Nearch. p. 37, Huds.). But even those who recognised their junction were not agreed as to which stream it was that received the other, and whether their united course, now the *Shat-el-Arab*, should be called Tigris or Euphrates. Most writers adopted the former name, but Nearchus and Onesicritus preferred that of the Euphrates (cf. Arrian, *Indic.* 41). It is not impossible, however, that the Euphrates may at one time have had a separate mouth (cf. Plin. *l. c.*; Ritter, *Erdk.* x. p. 27). There was also a difference of opinion as to the number of mouths by which the united stream emptied itself into the Persian gulf. Its western mouths were entirely unknown to the ancient Greeks, as Antiochus Epiphanes was the first who caused the coast to the W. of the Tigris to be accurately surveyed; and amongst later conquerors, Trajan alone penetrated as far as this neighbourhood. Hence the ancient Greeks, as well as Pliny (*l. c.*), speak of only one mouth, the breadth of which is given by the latter at 10 miles. Ptolemy, however, mentions two mouths (vi. 3. § 2) at a distance of 1½ degrees apart, which is confirmed by Onesicritus (ap. Philostorg. *Hist. Eccl.* iii. 7, 8), according to whom the island between these mouths was inhabited by the Meseni. But probably by the eastern mouth was meant that of the river Eulaeus, the present *Karún*, one arm of which unites with the Tigris, whilst the other falls into the sea by an independent mouth. This river was also called Pasitigris by the ancients (Παστίγρις, Strab. xv. p. 729), that is, "the little Tigris," from the old Persian word *pas*, signifying "small;" whence also among the modern Persians it bears the name of *Didjlahi-Kudak*, which means the same thing. Hence we may explain how the united stream of the Tigris and Euphrates itself was throughout its course called Pasitigris by some writers (Strab. *l. c.*; Plin. *l. c.*); whilst others regarded the Pasitigris as quite a separate stream, rising in the territory of the Uxii, and disemboguing into the Persian gulf (Nearch. ap. *Strab. l. c.*; Arrian, *Ind.* 42; Diodor. xvii. 67; Curt v. 3, init). This last view would make it identical with the present *Karún* (cf Kinneir, *Mem.* p. 59; Gosselin, *Recherches, &c.* ii. p. 86, sqq; Vincent, *Peripl.* iii. p. 67, not. &c.). The other affluents of the Tigris were the Nicephorius or Centritis, the Zabatus or Lycus, the Bumadus, the Caprus, the Tornadotus or Torna, apparently the same as the Physcus of Xenophon (*Anab.* ii. 4. § 25), the Gyndes or Delas, the Choaspes, and the Coprates, which fell into the main stream after joining the Eulaeus. All these rivers were on the left or eastern bank of the Tigris. The stream of the Tigris was very rapid, and according to Strabo (p. 529) from its very source; whilst Pliny (*l. c.*) more correctly ascribes this quality only to its lower course. It was, in fact, owing to the large quantity of water which the Tigris received by means of the canals which connected it with the Euphrates, none of which was returned through the same channels, owing to the

bed of the Tigris being at a lower level. (Arrian, *l. c.*; Dion Cass. lxviii. 28; Strab. *l. c.*; Hor. *Od.* iv. 14, 46; Lucan, iii. 256, &c.) In ancient times many dams had been constructed in its course from Opis to its mouth, designed to retain its waters for the purpose of irrigating the adjoining districts (cf. Heeren, *Ideen,* i. 2. p. 171; Tavernier, *Voyages,* i. p. 185; Niebuhr, *Reise,* ii. p. 243). These, however, were all cut through by Alexander, in order to improve the navigation, which began as high up as Opis (Arrian, *l. c.*; Strab. 739, sq.). Between *Mosul* and the confluence of the greater *Zab,* and 3 hours' journey above the latter, there still remains an ancient dam of masonry thrown across the stream (Ritter, *Erdkunde,* x. p. 5, sqq.). [T. H. D.]

TIGUADRA, a small island off the coast of Spain, opposite the town of Palma, in the island of Balearis Major. (Plin. iii. 5. s. 11.) [T. H. D.]

TIGURINUS PAGUS. [HELVETII.]

TILADAE (Τιλάδαι, Ptol. vii. 2. § 15), a race who lived under the Mons Maeandrus in Western India. They are probably the same as the Taluctae of Pliny (vi. 19. s. 22). [TALUCTAE.] [V.]

TILAVEMPTUS (Τιλαούεμπτος : *Tagliamento*), a river of Venetia, which has its sources in the Alps, above 80 miles from the sea, and after traversing the broad plain of the *Frioul,* falls into the Adriatic sea between Aquileia and Concordia. (Plin. iii. 18. s. 22; Ptol. iii. 1. § 26.) It is the most considerable river in this part of Italy, and, like all the neighbouring rivers, is subject to be swollen by floods and winter rains, so that it leaves a broad bed of shingle, great part of which is dry at ordinary seasons. The name is found in Pliny and Ptolemy; and it is doubtless the same river which is described by Strabo, though without mentioning its name, as separating the territory of Aquileia from the province of Venetia, and which he says was navigable for 1200 stadia from its mouth. (Strab. v. p. 214.) This last statement is indeed a great exaggeration; but the valley of the *Tagliamento* is one of the natural openings of this part of the Alps, and was followed by the line of a Roman road, which proceeded from Aquileia by Julium Carnicum (*Zuglio*) over the pass of the *Monte di Sta Croce* into the valley of the *Gail.* [ALPES, p. 110.]

Pliny speaks (*l. c.*) of a "Tilaventum majus minusque," but it is impossible to say what river he meant to designate under the latter appellation. The name is written in the Tabula "Tiliabinte," while it assumes very nearly its modern form in the Geographer of Ravenna. (Taliamentum, Geogr. Rav. iv. 36.) [E. H. B.]

TILENE, in Gallia. The name is File in the Table, or Filena as some say. D'Anville altered it to Tilene, and he finds the place on a road in the Table from Andomatunum (*Langres*) to Cabillonum (*Challon-sur-Saône*). The place is *Til-le-Château,* the Tile Castrum of the eleventh century. Some documents of that time have Tiricastrum and Tricastel, and accordingly the place is vulgarly called *Tré-château* or *Tri-château.* [G. L.]

TILPHOSSA FONS. [BOEOTIA, p. 412, a.]
TILPHO'SSIUM or TILPHOSSAEUM. [BOEOTIA, p. 412, a.]

TILURIUM (Geogr. Rav. iv. 31), or TILURI PONS (*Itin. Ant.* p. 337), a place in Dalmatia, on the river Tilurus. It appears to be the same place as the Tribulium of Pliny (iii. 22. s. 26). Now *Trigl.* [T. H. D.]

TILURUS, a river of Dalmatia falling into the sea near Dalminium. (*Itin. Ant.* p. 337; *Tab. Peut.*) Now the *Czettina*.　　　[T. H. D.]

TIMACHUS, a river in Upper Moesia, a tributary of the Danube, which it joined between Dorticum and Florentiana. (Plin. iii. 26. s. 29: *Tab. Peut.*) Now the *Timok*.　　　[T. H. D.]

TIMACUM MAJUS and MINUS (Τίμακον, Ptol. iii. 9. § 5), two towns of Moesia Superior situated on the Timachus. (Geogr. Rav. iv. 7; *Tab. Peut.*) One still exists by the name of *Timok;* but Mannert seeks the larger town near *Iperik*, and the smaller one near *Geurgowatz*.　　　[T. H. D.]

TIMALINUM, a place in Gallaecia in Hispania Tarraconensis (*Itin. Ant.* pp. 425, 430). Variously identified with *Villartelin* and *Fontaneira*. [T.H.D.]

TIMA'VUS (Τίμαυος: *Timao*), a river of Venetia, flowing into the Adriatic sea between Aquileia and Tergeste, about 12 miles E. of the former city. Notwithstanding its classical celebrity, it is one of the shortest of rivers, being formed by copious sources which burst out from the rock at the foot of a lofty cliff, and immediately constitute a broad and deep river, which has a course of little more than a mile before it discharges itself into the sea. There can be no doubt that these sources are the outlets of some subterranean stream, and that the account of Posidonius (*ap. Strab.* v. p. 215), who says that the river after a course of some length falls into a chasm, and is carried under .ground about 130 stadia before it issues out again and falls into the sea, is substantially correct. Such subterranean passages are indeed not uncommon in *Carniola*, and it is impossible to determine from what particular river or lake the waters of the Timavus derive their origin; but the popular notion still regards them as the outflow of a stream which sinks into the earth near *S. Canzian*, about 13 miles from the place of their reappearance. (Cluver. *Ital.* p. 193.) The number of the sources is variously stated : Virgil, in the well-known passage in which he describes them (*Aen.* i. 245), reckons them nine in number, and this agrees with the statement of Mela; while Strabo speaks of seven; and this would appear from Servius to have been the common belief (Serv. *ad Aen. l. c.*; Mel. ii. 4. § 3), which is supported also by Martial, while Claudian follows Virgil (Mart. iv. 25. 6; Claudian, *de VI. Cons. Hon.* 198). Cluverius, on the other hand, could find but six, and some modern travellers make them only four. Strabo adds that, according to Polybius, all but one of them were *salt*, a circumstance which would imply some connection with the sea, and, according to Cluverius, who described them from personal observation, this was distinctly the case in his time; for though at low water the stream issued tranquilly from its rocky sources, and flowed with a still and placid current to the sea, yet at high tides the waters were swollen, so as to rush forth with much greater force and volume, and inundate the neighbouring meadows: and at such times, he adds, the waters of all the sources but one become perceptibly brackish, doubtless from some subterranean communication with the sea. (Cluver. *Ital.* p. 194.) It appears from this account that Virgil's remarkable expressions—

" Unde per ora novem, vasto cum murmure montis
It *mare* proruptum, et *pelago* premit arva sonanti "

—are not mere rhetorical exaggerations, but have a foundation in fact. It was doubtless from a reference to the same circumstance that, according to

Polybius (*ap. Strab. l. c.*), the stream was called by the natives " the source and mother of the sea " (μητέρα τῆς θαλάττης.) It is probable that the communication with the sea has been choked up, as no modern traveller alludes to the phenomenon described by Cluverius. The *Timao* is at present a very still and tranquil stream, but not less than 50 yards broad close to its source, and deep enough to be navigable for vessels of considerable size. Hence it is justly called by Virgil "magnus Timavus" (*Ecl.* viii. 6); and Ausonius speaks of the " aequoreus amnis Timavi " (*Clar. Urb.* xiv. 34).

Livy speaks of the " lacum Timavi," by which he evidently means nothing more than the basin formed by the waters near their source (Liv. xli. 1): it was close to this that the Roman consul A. Manlius established his camp, while C. Furius with 10 ships appears to have ascended the river to the same point, where their combined camp was attacked and plundered by the Istrians. According to Strabo there was a temple in honour of Diomed erected near the sources of the Timavus, with a sacred grove attached to it. (Strab. v. p. 214). There were also warm springs in the same neighbourhood, which are now known as the *Bagni di S. Giovanni.*　　　[E. H. B.]

TIMOLAEUM (Τιμολάιον), a fort or castle on the coast of Paphlagonia, 40 or 60 stadia to the north of Climax, and 100 or 150 stadia from Cape Carambis. (Marcian, p. 71; Anon. *Peripl. P. E.* p. 6.)　　　[L. S.]

TIMONI'TIS (Τιμωνῖτις), a district in the interior of Paphlagonia, near the borders of Bithynia. (Strab. xii. p. 562; Ptol. v. 1. § 12.) Pliny (v. 42) mentions its inhabitants under the name of Timoniacenses, and Stephanus B. knows Timonium (Τιμώνιον) as a fort in Paphlagonia, from which the district no doubt derived its name.　　　[L. S.]

TINA (Τίνα or Τίννα, Ptol. ii. 3. § 5), a river on the E. coast of Britannia Romana, forming the boundary between it and Britannia Barbara, and still called the *Tyne*.　　　[T. H. D.]

TINCONCIUM, in Gallia, is placed in the Itins. on a road between Avaricum (*Bourges*) and Decetia (*Décise*). In the Table the name is Tincollo. The distance in the Itins. is the same (xx.) from Avaricum to Tinconcium (*Sancoins*), which is named Tincentium in some middle-age documents. The Itins. do not agree in the distance between Tinconcium and Decetia.　　　[G. L.]

TINFADI, a place in Numidia, 22 miles W. of Thevesta (*Itin. Ant.* p. 33). According to Lapie, the ruins on the *Oued Hrhia.*　　　[T. H. D.]

TINGENTERA. [TRANSDUCTA.]

TINGIS (Τίγγις, Strab. iii. p. 140, and Τίγα, xvii. p. 827; in Ptol. iv. 1. § 5, Τίγγις Καισάρεια), a very ancient city on the N. coast of Mauretania. Mela (i. 5) calls it Tinge, Pliny (v. 1. s. 1) Tingi. It lay 60 miles W. of the promontory of Abyla (*Itin. Ant.* p. 9, &c) and 30 miles from Belo on the opposite coast of Spain (Plin. *l. c.*). Mela and Pliny record the tradition of its foundation by Antaeus, whilst according to Plutarch it was founded by Sophax, a son of Hercules and the widow of Antaeus (*Sert.* 9). In that neighbourhood was the fabled grave of Antaeus, and his skeleton 60 cubits long (Strab. xvii. 829, cf. iii. p. 422). These mythic legends serve at least to indicate the great antiquity of the place. (Cf. Strab. *l. c.*; Solin. c. 45.) It was raised by Augustus to the rank of a free city

(Dion Cass. xlviii. 45), and in the time of Claudius became a Roman colony (Plin. *l. c.*; *Itin. Ant.* 8, 12) and the capital of the province of Tingitana. It was also a place of considerable trade. Now *Tangier*. [T. H. D.]

TI'NIA (Τενέας: *Tinia*), a small river of Umbria, falling into the Tiber, a few miles below Perusia. The name is given by the ancient geographers to the affluent of the Tiber (one of the first tributaries which that river receives), but at the present day the stream called the *Tinia* loses its name after its junction with the *Topino*, a more considerable stream. Four small rivers indeed bring down their united waters to the Tiber at this point: 1, the *Maroggia*, which rises between *Todi* and *Spoleto*, and brings with it the waters of the *Clitumno*, the ancient CLITUMNUS; 2, the *Timia*, which joins the Clitumnus near Mevania (*Bevagna*); 3, the *Topino*, which descends from the Apennines near *Nocera*, and turns abruptly to the NW., after receiving the waters of the *Timia*; and 4, the *Chiascio*, which joins the *Topino* from the N. only 3 miles from the point where it falls into the Tiber. Though thus augmented from various quarters the Tinia was always an inconsiderable stream. Pliny speaks of it as navigable with difficulty even for boats, and Silius Italicus calls it "Tiniae inglorius humor." (Sil. Ital. viii. 452; Plin. iii. 5. s. 9; Strab. v. p. 227.) [E. H. B.]

TINNE'TIO, a place in Rhaetia, mentioned only in the Antonine Itinerary (p. 257), but still retaining its ancient name in the form of *Tinzen.* [L. S.]

TINU'RTIUM, in Gallia, is placed in the Itins. near the *Saône*, between Cabillonum (*Challon*) and Matisco (*Mâcon*). The Antonine Itin. marks M.P. xxi., leugas xiiii. between Cabillonum and Tinurtium, which is *Tournus.* The Table gives only xii., which appears to be nearer the truth. The two Itins. do not agree in the distance between Tinurtium and Matisco. Spartianus (*Vita Septim. Severi*, c. 11) says that Severus defeated Clodius Albinus at Tinurtium, or Trinurtium, for the reading is perhaps doubtful. (Is. Casaubon, in Aelium Spartianum notae). Dion (lxxv. c. 6), Herodian (iii. 7), and Eutropius (viii. 18) speak of Clodius Albinus being defeated by Severus at or near Lugdunum (*Lyon*). The name Tinurtium appears to be sometimes miswritten Tiburtium. [G. L.]

TIORA MATIENA. [ABORIGINES.]

TIPARENUS, an island off the coast of Hermionis in Argolis, mentioned only by Pliny (iv. 12. s. 19.) It is frequently identified with *Spétzia ;* but Leake remarks that Tiparenus has no appearance of a Greek name, and conjectures that it is an error for Tricarenus, the same as the Tricrana of Pausanias (ii. 34. § 8) and the modern *Trikhiri.* (Leake, *Morea*, vol. ii. p. 465; Ross, *Wanderungen in Griechenland*, vol. ii. p. 21).

TIPASA (Τίπασα, Ptol. iv. 2. § 5). 1. A town in Mauretania Caesariensis, endowed with the jus Latii by the emperor Claudius (Plin. v s. 1) and subsequently a Roman colony (*Itin. Ant.* p. 15). It lay between Icosium and Caesarea (*Ib.*). Procopius (*B. V.* ii. 10) mentions two columns near Tipasa in the SE. of Mauretania, which had on them the following inscription in the Phoenician language: "We are fugitives from the face of Joshua, the robber, and his son Nave." Now *Tefessad* or *Tefesah.*

2. A town in Numidia, on the road from Sicca to Cirta (*Itin. Ant.* p. 41). Now *Tebessa* or *Tifech.* [T. H. D.]

TIPHAE. . [SIPHAE.]

TIPHSAH. [THAPSACUS.]

TIPSUM or TIPSUS (*It. Hier.* p. 569), a place in Thrace, now *Sundukli* or *Karassivi*, according to Lapie. [J. R.]

TIRIDA. [STABULUM DIOMEDIS.]

TIRISSA (Geogr. Rav. iv. 6), called by Arrian Τερψισίας (*Per. P. Eux.* p. 24), and in the Tab. Peut. Trissa; a fortified place on the promontory of Tirizis. From its situation on this bold headland it was sometimes called simply Ἄκρα (Steph. B. p. 53; Hierocl. p. 637), and hence at present *Ekerne* or *Kavarna.* [T. H. D.]

TIRISTASIS (Plin. iv. 11. s. 18; Τειρίστασις, Scyl. p. 28; Τιρίστασις, Epist. Phil. ad Ath. sp. Dem. p. 159, R.), a town of the Thracian Chersonesus, on the coast of the Propontis. It was included in the dominions of Philip, who in the letter above referred to complains that the Athenian general Diopeithes had taken it and sold its inhabitants for slaves (B. C. 340) [DIOPEITHES, *Dict. Biog.*] According to Choiseul, its site is still occupied by a village bearing the same name. [J. R.]

TIRIZIS (Τίριζις, Strab. vii. p 319), a very projecting headland of Moesia in the Pontus Euxinus. The name varies, being written Τίριζα in Anon. (*Perip. P. Eux.* p. 13), Τιριστρίς or Τιριστρία ἄκρα by Ptolemy (iii. 10. § 8), and Tiristis by Mela (ii. 2). Now *Cupe Gülgrad.* [T. H. D.]

TIRYNS (Τίρυνς: *Eth.* Τιρύνθιος: the name is perhaps connected with τύῤῥις, Lepsius, *Tyrrh. Pelasger*, p. 13), one of the most ancient cities of Greece, lay a short distance SE. of Argos, on the right of the road leading to Epidaurus (Paus. ii. 25. § 8), and at the distance of 12 stadia from Nauplia. (Strab. viii. p. 373.) Its massive walls, which have been regarded with wonder in all ages, are said to have been the work of the Cyclopes, and belong to the same age as those of Mycenae. (Paus. ii. 16. § 5, ii. 25. § 8, vii. 25. § 6, ix. 36. § 5; Strab. *l. c.*; Plin. vii. 56. s. 57.) Hence Homer calls the city Τίρυνς τειχιόεσσα. (*Il.* ii. 559.) Pindar speaks of the Κυκλώπια πρόθυρα of Tiryns (*Fragm.* 642, ed. Böckh), and Pausanias says that the walls are not less worthy of admiration than the pyramids of Egypt (ix. 36. § 5.) In another passage he describes the walls as consisting of wide masses of stone (ἀργοὶ λίθοι), of such a size, that a yoke of oxen could not stir the least of them, the interstices being filled in with smaller stones to make the whole more compact and solid. (Paus. ii. 25. § 8.) The foundation of Tiryns ascends to the earliest mythical legends of the Argeia. It was said to have derived its name from Tiryns, the son of Argus (Paus. ii. 25. § 8), and to have been founded by Proetus. (Strab. viii. p. 372; Paus. ii. 16. § 2) According to the common tradition, Megapenthes, the son of Proetus, ceded Tiryns to Perseus, who transmitted it to his descendant Electryon. Alcmena, the daughter of Electryon, married Amphitryon, who would have succeeded to the crown, had he not been expelled by Sthenelus, king of Argos. Their son Hercules afterwards regained possession of Tiryns, where he lived for many years, and hence is frequently called Tirynthius by the poets. (Hes. *Scut.* 81; Pind. *Ol.* x. 37, *Isthm.* vi. 39; Virg. *Aen.* vii. 662; Ov. *Met.* vii. 410.) Although Tiryns was thus closely connected with the Heraclidae, yet the city remained in the hands of the old Achaean population after the return of the Heraclidae and the conquest of Peloponnesus by the

Dorians. The strong fortress of Tiryns was dangerous to the neighbouring Dorian colony of Argos. After the dreadful defeat of the Argives by Cleomenes, their slaves took possession of Tiryns and held it for many years, (Herod. vi. 83.) In the Persian War the Tirynthians sent some men to the battle of Plataea. (Herod. ix. 28.) Subsequently their city was taken by the Argives, probably about the same time as Mycenae, B. C. 468. The lower city was entirely destroyed; the citadel was dismantled; and the inhabitants fled to Epidaurus and Halieis, a town on the coast of Hermionis. (Strab. viii. p. 373; Ephorus, *ap. Steph. B. s. v.* 'Αλιεῖς; Eustath. *ad Hom. Il.* ii. 559, p. 286,) It was probably owing to this circumstance that Stephanus B. (*s. v.* Τίρυνς) was led into the mistake of saying that Tiryns was formerly called Halieis. The Tirynthians, who did not succeed in effecting their escape, were removed to Argos. (Paus. ii. 25. § 8.) From this time Tiryns remained uninhabited; and when Pausanias visited the city in the second century of our era, he saw nothing but the remains of the walls of the citadel. and beneath them towards the sea the so-called chambers of the daughters of Proetus. No trace of the lower city appears to have been left. The citadel was named Licymna, after Licymnius, son of Electryon, who was slain at Tiryns by Tleptolemus, son of Hercules. (Strab. vii. p. 373; Pind. *Ol.* vii. 47.) Hence Statius calls the marshes in the neighbourhood of Tiryns "stagna Licymnia." (*Theb.* iv. 734.) Theophrastus represents the Tirynthians as celebrated for their laughing propensities, which rendered them incapable of attention to serious business (*ap. Athen.* vi. p. 261, d.).

The ruins of the citadel of Tiryns are now called *Paleó Anápli.* They occupy the lowest and flattest of several rocky hills, which rise like islands out of the plain. The impression which they produce upon the beholder is well described by Col. Mure: "This colossal fortress is certainly the greatest curiosity of the kind in existence. It occupies the table summit of an oblong hill, or rather knoll, of small extent or elevation, completely encased in masses of enormous stones, rudely piled in tiers one above another, into the form alternately of towers, curtain walls, abutments, gates, and covered ways. There is not a fragment in the neighbourhood indicating the existence of suburb or outer town at any period; and the whole, rising abruptly from the dead level of the surrounding plain, produces at a distance an effect very similar to that of the hulk of a man-of-war floating in a harbour." The length of the summit of the rock, according to Col. Leake's measurement, is about 250 yards, the breadth from 40 to 80, the height above the plain from 20 to 50 feet, the direction nearly N. and S. The entire circuit of the walls still remains more or less preserved. They consist of huge masses of stone piled upon one another, as Pausanias describes. The wall is from about 20 to 25 feet in thickness, and it had two entrances, one on the eastern, and the other on the southern side. "In its general design the fortress appears to have consisted of an upper and lower enclosure of nearly equal dimensions, with an intermediate platform, which may have served for the defence of the upper castle against an enemy in possession of the lower. The southern entrance led by an ascent to the left into the upper inclosure, and by a direct passage between the upper inclosure and the eastern wall of the fortress into the lower inclosure, having also a branch

to the left into the middle platform, the entrance into which last was nearly opposite to the eastern gate. Besides the two principal gates, there was a postern in the western side. On either side of the great southern entrance, that is to say, in the eastern as well as in the southern wall, there were galleries in the body of the wall of singular construction. In the eastern wall, where they are better preserved, there are two parallel passages, of which the outer has six recesses or niches in the exterior wall. These niches were probably intended to serve for the protracted defence of the gallery itself, and the galleries for covered communications leading to towers or places of arms at the extremity of them. The passage which led directly from the southern entrance, between the upper inclosure and the eastern wall into the lower division of the fortress, was about 12 feet broad. About midway, there still exists an immense door-post, with a hole in it for a bolt, showing that the passage might be closed upon occasion. The lower inclosure of the fortress was of an oval shape, about 100 yards long and 40 broad; its walls formed an acute angle to the north, and several obtuse angles on the east and west. Of the upper inclosure of the fortress very little remains. There is some appearance of a wall of separation, dividing the highest part of all from that next to the southern entrance; thus forming four interior divisions besides the passages." (Leake.) The general appearance of these covered galleries is shown in the accompanying drawing from Gell's *Itinerary.* (Leake, *Morea,* vol. ii. p. 350, seq.; Mure, *Tour in Greece,* vol. ii. p. 173, seq.; Curtius, *Peloponnesos,* vol. ii. p. 388, seq.)

GALLERY AT TIRYNS.

TISAEUM (Τισαῖον: *Bardjóia*), a lofty mountain on the promontory of Aeantium in Magnesia in Thessaly, at the entrance of the Pagasaean gulf, on which stood a temple of Artemis, and where in B. C. 207 Philip V., son of Demetrius, caused watch-fires to be lighted, in order to obtain immediate knowledge of the movements of the Roman fleet. (Apoll. Rhod. i. 568; Val. Flacc. ii. 6; Polyb. x. 42; Liv. xxviii. 5; Leake, *Northern Greece,* vol. iv. p. 397.)

TISCANUS (Jornand. *Get.* 5), or Tysca (*Ib.* 34; Geogr. Rav. iv. 14); a river in Thrace, a tributary of the Danube, the modern *Theiss.* [T.H.D.]

TISEBARICE. [Tesebarica.]

TI'SIA (Τισία: *Eth.* Τισιδρης), a town of the Bruttii, mentioned by Appian in his account of the operations of Hannibal in that country. It had been occupied by that general with a Carthaginian garrison, but was betrayed by one of the citizens into the hands of the Romans, who held it for a short time, but it was soon recovered by Hannibal. (Appian, *Hann.* 44.) It is probably the same place which is called Isia by Diodorus, from whom we learn that it was besieged without success by the leaders of the Italian forces during the Social War. (Diod. xxxvii. *Exc. Phot.* p. 240.) On both occasions it appears as a strong fortress, situated apparently in the neighbourhood of Rhegium; but no other mention is found of the city, which is not noticed by any of the geographers, and must probably have ceased to exist, like so many of the smaller towns of Bruttium. The name is, however, found in Stephanus of Byzantium, who confirms the correctness of the form Tisia, found in Appian. (Steph. B. *s. v.*) Its site is wholly uncertain.　[E. H. B.]

TISSA (Τίσσα, Ptol.; Τίσσαι, Steph. B.: Eth. Τισσαῖος, Tisaiensis, Cic., Tissinensis, Plin.), a town in the interior of Sicily, repeatedly mentioned by ancient authors, but without any clue to its position. As its name is cited from Philistus by Stephanus of Byzantium (*s. v.*), it must have existed as a Siculian town from an early period, but its name is not found in history. Under the Romans it continued to subsist as a municipal town, though a very small place. Cicero calls it "perparva et tenuis civitas," and Silius Italicus also ter.ns it "parvo nomine Tisse." (Cic. *Verr.* iii. 38; Sil. Ital. xiv. 267.) It is again noticed by Pliny and Ptolemy among the towns of the interior of Sicily, but all trace of it is subsequently lost. The only clue to its site is derived from Ptolemy, who places it in the neighbourhood of Aetna. It has been fixed by Cluverius and others on the site of the modern town of *Randazzo*, at the northern foot of Aetna, but this is a mere conjecture. (Plin. iii. 8. s. 14; Ptol. iii. 4. § 12; Cluver. *Sicil.* p. 308.)　　　[E. H. B.]

TITACIDAE. [Attica, p. 330, a.]

TITANE (Τιτάνη, Paus.; Τίτανα, Steph. B. *s. v.*: Eth. Τιτάνιος), a place in the Sicyonia, upon the left bank of the Asopus, distant 60 stadia from Sicyon, and 40 from Phlius. It was situated upon the summit of a hill, where Titan, the brother of the Sun, is said to have dwelt, and to have given his name to the spot. It was celebrated for a temple of Asclepius, reported to have been built by Alexander, the son of Machaon, the son of Asclepius. This temple still existed in the time of Pausanias, in the middle of a grove of cypress trees, in which the servants of the god attended to the patients who came thither for the recovery of their health. Within the temple stood statues of Asclepius and Hygieia, and of the heroes Alexanor and Euamerion. There was also a temple of Athena at Titane, situated upon a hill, and containing an ancient wooden statue of the goddess. In descending from the hill there was an altar of the Winds. (Paus. ii. 11. §§ 5—8, ii. 12. § 1, ii. 27. § 1.) Stephanus B. (*s. v.*) refers the Τιτάνοιό τε λευκὰ κάρηνα of Homer (*Il.* ii. 735) to Titane, but those words indicate a mountain in Thessaly. [Vol. I. p. 248, b.] The ruins of Titane were first discovered by Ross. Leake heard that there were some ancient foundations on the summit of the hill above *Liópesi*, which he supposed to be the remains of the temple of Asclepius at Titane; but although Hellenic remains exist in this site, there can be no doubt that Titane is represented by the more important *Paleókastron* situated further S., and a few minutes N. of the village of *Voivónda*. This *Paleókastron* stands upon a projecting spur of the mountains which run eastward towards the Asopus, and terminate just above the river in a small hill, which is surrounded by beautiful Hellenic walls, rising to the height of 20 or 30 ft. on the S. and SW. side,

and flanked by three or four quadrangular towers. On this hill there stands a chapel of St. Tryphon, containing fragments of Doric columns. This was evidently the acropolis of the ancient city, and here stood the temple of Athena mentioned by Pausanias. The other parts of this projecting ridge are covered with ancient foundations; and upon this part of the mountain the temple of Asclepius must have stood. (Leake, *Morea*, vol. iii. p. 354, seq.; Ross, *Reisen im Peloponnes*, p. 49, seq.; Curtius, *Peloponnesos*, vol. ii. p. 500, seq.)

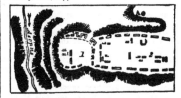

TITANUS. [Asterium.]

TITARE'SIUS. [Thessalia, p. 1166, a.]

TITARUS. [Thessalia, p. 1166, a.]

TITHOREA. [Neon.]

TITHRO'NIUM (Τιθρώνιον: Eth. Τιθρωνιεύς), a frontier town of Phocis, on the side of Doris. Livy, who calls it Tritonon, describes it as a town of Doris (xxviii. 7), but all other writers place it in Phocis. It was destroyed by the army of Xerxes together with the other Phocian towns. It is placed by Pausanias in the plain at the distance of 15 stadia from Amphiclea. The site of Tithronium is probably indicated by some ruins at *Mulki* below *Versand*, where a torrent unites with the Cephissus. (Herod. viii. 33; Paus. x. 3. § 2, x. 33. § 11; Steph. B. *s. v.*; Leake, *Northern Greece*, vol. ii. p. 87.)

TITTHIUM. [Epidaurus, p. 841, a.]

TITULCIA, a town of the Carpetani in Hispania Tarraconensis, on the road from Emerita to Caesaraugusta (*Itin. Ant.* pp. 436, 438, &c.) It seems to be the same town called Τιτουακία by Ptolemy (ii. 6. § 57). Variously placed near *Torrejon*, at *Getafe*, and at *Bayona*.　[T. H. D.]

TITYRUS (Τίτυρος, Strab. x. p. 479), a mountain in the NW. part of Crete, not far from Cydonia. Upon it was the sanctuary or temple called Dictynnaeum. (Strab. *ib.*) One of its spurs formed the headland also called Tityrus (*Stadiasm.* p. 302) or Psacum. (*Cape Spada.*)　[T. H. D.]

TIUS or TIUM (Τῖος or Τῖον: Eth. Τιανός), a town on the coast of Bithynia, or, according to others, belonging to Paphlagonia. It was a Greek town situated at the mouth of the river Billaeus, and seems to have belonged to Paphlagonia until Prusias annexed it to Bithynia. (Memnon, 17—19; Pomp. Mela, i. 19; Marcian, p. 70; Arrian, *Peripl. P. E.* p. 14; Anon. *Peripl. P. E.* p. 2.) In Strabo's (xii. pp. 542, 543, 565) time, Tius was only a small place but remarkable as the birthplace of Philetaerus, the founder of the royal dynasty of Pergamum. (Comp. Plin. vi. 1.) There are coins of Tius as late as the reign of Gallienus, on which the ethnic name appears as Τιανοί, Τεῖοι, and Τειανοί. (Sestini, p. 71; Eckhel, ii. p. 438.)　[L. S.]

TLOS (Τλώς or Τλῶς), an ancient and important

city of Lycia. It is not often mentioned by ancient writers, but we know from Artemidorus (*ap. Strab.* xiv. p. 665) that it was one of the six cities forming the Lycian confederacy. Strabo only remarks further that it was situated on the road to Cibyra. (Comp. Plin. v. 28; Ptol. v. 3. § 5; Steph. B. *s. v.*; Hierocl. p. 659.) Until recently the site of this town was unknown, though D'Anville had correctly conjectured that it ought to be looked for in the valley of the Xanthus. Sir C. Fellows was the first modern traveller who saw and described its beautiful remains, the identity of which is established beyond a doubt by inscriptions. These ruins exist in the upper valley of the Xanthus, at a little distance from its eastern bank, almost due north of the city of Xanthus, and about 5 miles from the village of *Doover*. They are, says Sir Charles, very extensive, consisting of extremely massive buildings, suited only for palaces; the design appears to be Roman, but not the mode of building nor the inscriptions. The original city must have been demolished in very early times, and the finely wrought fragments are now seen built into the strong walls, which have fortified the town raised upon its ruins. The theatre was large, and the most highly and expensively finished that he had seen; the seats not only are of marble, but the marble is highly wrought and has been polished, and each seat has an overhanging cornice often supported by lions' paws. There are also ruins of several other extensive buildings with columns; but the most striking feature in the place is the perfect honeycomb formed in the sides of the acropolis by excavated tombs, which are cut out of the rock with architectural ornaments, in the form of triangles, &c., some showing considerable taste. (Fellows, *Asia Minor*, p. 237, foll., *Lycia*, p. 132, foll., where some of the remains are figured and a number of inscriptions given.)   [L. S.]

TMARUS. [Dodona, p. 783, b.]

TMOLUS (Τμῶλος), a mountain range on the south of Sardes, forming the watershed between the basins of the Hermus in the north and the Cayster in the south, and being connected in the east with Mount Messogis. It was said to have received its name from a Lydian king Timolus, whence Ovid (*Met.* vi. 16) gives this name to the mountain itself. Mount Tmolus was celebrated for the excellent wine growing on its slopes (Virg. *Georg.* ii. 97; Senec. *Phoen.* 602; Eurip. *Bacch.* 55, 64; Strab. xiv. p. 637; Plin. v. 30). It was equally rich in metals; and the river Pactolus, which had its source in Mount Tmolus, at one time carried from its interior a rich supply of gold. (Strab. xiii. pp. 591, 610, 625; Plin. xxxiii. 43; comp. Hom. *Il.* ii. 373; Aesch. *Pers.* 50; Herod. i. 84, 93, v. 101; Ptol. v. 2. § 13; Dion. Per. 831.) On the highest summit of Mount Tmolus, the Persians erected a marble watch-tower commanding a view of the whole of the surrounding country (Strab. xiii. p. 625). The Turks now call the mountain *Bous Dagh*. (Richter, *Wallfahrten*, pp. 512, 519.)   [L. S.]

TMOLUS, a town of Lydia, situated on Mount Tmolus, which was destroyed during the great earthquake in A. D. 19. (Tac. *Ann.* ii. 47; Plin. v. 30; Euseb. *Chron. ad Ann. V. Tib.*; Niceph. Call. i. 17.) Some coins are extant with the inscription Τμωλείτων. (Sestini, p. 114.)   [L. S.]

TO'BIUS (Τόβιος or Τούβιος, Ptol. ii. 3. § 5), a river on the western coast of Britannia Romana, now the *Towy*.   [T. H. D.]

TOCAE (Τῶκαι), a very large city of Numidia,

mentioned only by Diodorus (xx. 57), is perhaps the same as TUCCA.

TOCHARI (Τόχαροι, Ptol. vi. 11. § 6), a powerful Scythian people in Bactriana, which also spread itself to the E. of the Jaxartes over a portion of Sogdiana, and even as far as the borders of Serica. (Plin. vi. 17. s. 20; Amm. Marc. xxiii. 6. § 57.)   [T. H. D.]

TOCOLOSIDA (Τοκολόσιδα, Ptol. iv. 1. § 14), the most southern place in the Roman possession in Mauretania Tingitana. (*Itin. Ant.* p. 23.) Variously identified with *Magilla*, *Fortin* near *Sidi Casseni*, and *Mergo* or *Amergo*.   [T. H. D.]

TOCOSANNA (Τοκοσάννα, Ptol. vii. 2. § 2), a river which falls into the *Bay of Bengal* at its NE. end. It is probably that now called the river of *Arracan*, which is formed by the junction near its mouth of three other rivers. (Lassen, *Map of Anc. India.*)   [V].

TODUCAE (Τοδούκαι, also Δούκαι or Τοδούκεσσες, Ptol. iv. 2. § 21), a people in Mauretania Caesariensis, on the left bank of the Ampsaga.   [T. H. D.]

TOE'SOBIS (Τοίσοβις, Ptol. ii. 3. § 2), a river on the western coast of Britannia Romana, now the *Conway*.   [T. H. D.]

TOGARMAH. [ARMENIA.]

TOGISONUS (*Bacchiglione*), a river of Venetia, mentioned only by Pliny, who describes it as flowing through the territory of Patavium, and contributing a part of its waters to the artificial canals called the Fossiones Philistinae, as well as to form the port of Brundulus (Plin. iii. 16. s. 20.) The rivers in this part of Italy have changed their course so frequently that it is very difficult to identify them: but the most probable conjecture is that the Togisonus of Pliny is the modern *Bacchiglione*, one arm of which still flows into the sea near the *Porto di Brondolo*, while the other joins the *Brenta* (Medoacus) under the walls of *Padova* (Patavium).   [E. H. B.]

TOLBIACUM, in North Gallia, on the road from Augusta Trevirorum (*Trier*) to Colonia Agrippina (*Cologne*). The distance of Tolbiacum from Colonia is xvi. in the Antonine Itin. Tolbiacum is *Zülpich*, south-west of *Bonn*, on the direct road from *Trier* to *Cologne*. The words " vicus supernorum " or " vicus supenorum," which occur in the MSS. of the Itin. after the name " Tolbiaco," have not been explained. Several writers have proposed to alter them. Tacitus (*Hist.* iv. 79) places Tolbiacum within the limits of the territory of the Agrippinenses or the Colonia Agrippina.   [G. L.]

TOLENTI'NUM or TOLLENTI'NUM (*Eth.* Tolentinas, ātis: *Tolentino*), a town of Picenum, in the valley of the Flusor or *Chienti*, about 12 miles below Camerinum (*Camerino*). It is mentioned by Pliny among the municipal towns of Picenum, and its municipal rank is attested by the Liber Coloniarum, which mentions the "ager Tolentinus," and by inscriptions. (Plin. iii. 13. s. 18; *Lib. Col.* pp. 226, 259; Orell. *Inscr.* 2474; Gruter, *Inscr.* pp. 194. 2, 410. 2.) The modern city of *Tolentino*, which retains the ancient site as well as name, is situated on the present highroad from Rome to Ancona; but as no ancient road descended the valley of the Flusor, the name is not found in the Itineraries.   [E. H. B.]

TOLE'NUS (*Turano*), a river of Central Italy, which rises in the mountains between Carseoli and the lake Fucinus, flows within a short distance of the walls of the former city, and falls into the Velinus a few miles below Reate. Its name is mention^d only by Ovid and Orosius, in reference to a great battle fought on its banks during the Social War, between the Roman consul Rutilius and the Marsi, in which the Romans were defeated with great slaughter and Rutilius himself slain. (Ovid, *Fast.* vi. 565; Oros. v. 18.)　　　[E. H. B.]

TOLE'RIUM (Τολέριον, Steph. B.: *Eth.*Τολερῖνος, Toleriensis: *Valmontone ?*), an ancient town of Latium, the name of which occurs in the early Roman history, but which appears to have ceased to exist at an early period. Its name is found in the list given by Dionysius of the thirty Latin cities which formed the league in B. C. 493 (Dionys. v. 61, according to the Vatican MS.; Niebuhr, vol. ii. note 21): and it is again mentioned among the places taken by Coriolanus at the head of the Volscian army in B.C. 486 (Dionys. viii. 17; Plut. *Coriol.* 28). According to the narrative given by Dionysius, and by Plutarch who copies him, it was the first place attacked by Coriolanus in that campaign, and its reduction was followed in succession by that of Bola, Labicum, Pedum and Corbio. It is singular that no mention of Tolerium occurs in the narrative of the same operations by Livy (ii. 39), and it seems probable that the name of Trebiam, which is found in that author (for which the best MSS. give Trebium), is a corruption for Tolerium, a name otherwise little known and therefore liable to alteration by copyists. (Cluver. *Ital.* p. 969; Bormann, *Alt-Latinische Chorographie*, p. 203.) The only other notice of Tolerium is found in Pliny, who enumerates the "Tolerienses" among the "populi" of Latium who had formerly shared in the sacrifices on the Alban Mount, but were in his time utterly extinct (iii. 5. s. 9). We have no account of the period of its destruction or final decay. The only clue to its position is that derived from the narratives above referred to, and it seems very doubtful how far we are justified in drawing strict topographical inferences from such relations. It may, however, be admitted as probable that Tolerium was situated in the same neighbourhood with Bola, Labicum, and Pedum; and the conjecture of Nibby, who would place it at *Valmontone*, derives at least some support from the circumstance that the latter town stands just at the source of the river *Sacco*, called in ancient times the Trerus or Tolerus [TRERUS]. The name of *Valmontone*, is of modern origin, but it in all probability occupies an ancient site: some vestiges of its ancient walls are still visible, as well as some remains of Roman date, while the scarped sides of the rocks which surround it, and render the position one of great natural strength, abound in ancient sepulchres. Gell, however, regards it as the site of Vitellia rather than Tolerium, a conjecture which has also much to recommend it. [VITELLIA.] *Valmontone* is 5 miles S. of *Palestrina* and about 3 miles beyond *Lugnano*, on the line of the modern Via Latina, and 26 from Rome. (Nibby, *Dintorni*, vol. iii. pp. 370, 377; Gell, *Top. of Rome*, p. 436; Abeken, *Mittel-Italien*, p. 76.) [E. H. B.]

TOLE'TUM (Τόληγτον, Ptol. ii. 6. § 57: *Eth.* Toletani, Plin. iii. 3. s. 4; Orelli, *Inscr.* no. 980), the capital of the Carpetani, in Hispania Tarraconensis, situated on the Tagus, and on the road from Emerita to Caesaraugusta, and connected also by another road with Laminium. (*Itin. Ant.* pp. 438, 446.) It was a very strong town, though only of moderate size, and famed for its manufacture of arms and steel-ware. (Liv. xxxv. 7, 22, xxxix, 30; Grat. *Cyneg.* 341; cf. Miñano, *Diccion.* viii. p.

453.) According to an old Spanish tradition, Toledo was founded in the year 540 B. C. by Jewish colonists, who named it *Toledoch*, that is, "mother of people," whence we might perhaps infer a Phoenician settlement. (Cf. Miñano, *l. c.*; Puente, *Travels*, i. p. 27.) It is still called *Toledo*, and contains several remains of Roman antiquities, and especially the ruins of a circus. (Cf. Florez, *Esp. Sagr.* v. p. 22; Puente, i. p. 165, seq.) [T. H. D.]

TOLIAPIS (Τολίαπις, Ptol. ii. 3. § 33), a small island on the E. coast of Albion, opposite to the country of the Trinobantes. *Sheppy* seems the only island with which it is at all possible to identify it; yet it lies farther S. than the account of Ptolemy appears to indicate.　　　[T. H. D.]

TOLISTOBOGII, TOLISTOBOGI, or TOLISTOBOII. [GALATIA.]

TOLLENTI'NUM. [TOLENTINUM.]

TOLOBIS, a coast town of the Ilercaones, in Hispania Tarraconensis. (Mela, ii. 6.) [T. H. D.]

TO'LOPHON (Τολοφών: *Eth.* Τολοφώνιος), a town of the Locri Ozolae, possessing a large harbour according to Dicaearchus (66; comp. Thuc. iii. 101; Steph. B. *s. v.*). According to Leake it occupied the valley of *Kiseli.* (*Northern Greece*, vol. ii. p. 620.)

TOLO'SA or THOLO'SA (Τολώσσα, Τολῶσα, Τόλοσα, Dion Cass. xxxviii. c. 32: *Eth.* Tolosates, Tolosenses, Tolosani), in Gallia, is *Toulouse*, in the department of *Haute-Garonne*, on the right bank of the *Garonne*.

The identity of Tolosa and *Toulouse* is easily proved from the Itineraries and other evidence. In Caesar's time Tolosa was within the Roman Provincia. (*B. G.* i. 10.) When Caesar is speaking of the intention of the Helvetii to migrate into the country of the Santones, he remarks that the Santones are not far from the territory of the Tolosates, who are in the Provincia. He considered that it would be dangerous to the Provincia if the warlike Helvetii, the enemies of Rome, should be so near to an open country, which produced a great deal of grain. The commentators have found some difficulty in Caesar's expression about the proximity of the Santones and the Tolosates, for the Nitiobriges and Petrocorii were between the Santones and the Tolosates; but Caesar only means to say that the Helvetii in the country of the Santones would be dangerous neighbours to the Provincia. In Caesar's time Tolosa and Carcaso, both in the basin of the *Garonne*, were fully organised as a part of the Provincia; for when P. Crassus invaded Aquitania, he summoned soldiers from the muster-rolls of these towns to join him in his army. (*B. G.* iii. 20.) Tolosa being situated on the neck of land where Gallia is narrowest [GALLIA TRANSALPINA, Vol. I. p. 949] and in a position easy of access from the west, north, and east, was one of the places threatened by the Galli in the great rising of B. c. 52; but Caesar with his usual vigilance protected the province on this side by placing a force at Tolosa. (*B. G.* vii. 7.)

Tolosa was an old town of the Volcae Tectosages which existed probably many centuries before it was conquered by the Romans. A great quantity of gold and silver was collected there, the gold the produce of the auriferous region near the Pyrenees, and both the precious metals the offerings of Gallic superstition. The treasure was kept in chambers in the temples, and also in sacred tanks. This is the story of Posidonius (Strab. iv. p. 188), who had travelled in Gallia; and it is more probable than the tradition that the gold of Tolosa was the produce of the plunder of Delphi by Brennus and his men, among whom it is said there were some Tectosages (Justin, xxxii. c. 3); for it is very doubtful if any of Brennus' soldiers got back to Gallia, if we admit that they came from Gallia. Tolosa was in some kind of alliance with Rome (Dion Cass. xxxiv. 97) about B. C. 106; but the Teutones and Cimbri at this time had broken into Gallia, and fear or policy induced the Tolosates to side with them. Q. Servilius Caepio (consul B. C. 106) made this a pretext for attacking Tolosa, which he took and plundered of its treasures, either in B. C. 106 or in the following year. This act of sacrilege was supposed to have been punished by the gods, for Caepio was defeated by the Cimbri B. C. 105, and his army was destroyed. (Liv. Epit. 67; Orosius, v. 15; Gell. iii. 9.) The treasure of Tolosa never reached Rome, and perhaps Caepio himself laid hold of some of it. However this may be, the "Aurum Tolosanum" became a proverb. All who had touched the consecrated treasure came to a miserable end. It seems that there was inquiry made into the matter at Rome, for Cicero (De Nat. Deorum, iii. 30) speaks of a "quaestio auri Tolosani."

The Tolosani or Tolosates were that division of the Tectosages which was nearest to the Aquitani. A place called Fines, between Tolosa and Carcaso, denotes the boundary of the territory of Tolosa in that direction, as this term often indicates a territorial limit in the Roman geography of Gallia [FINES]; and another place named Fines marks the boundary on the north between the Tolosates and the Cadurci.

Pliny (iii. 4) mentions Tolosa among the Oppida Latina of Narbonensis, or those towns which had the Latinitas, and, as Ptolemy (ii. 10. § 9) names it a Colonia, we must suppose that it was made a Colonia Latina. Tolosa maintained its importance under the Empire. Ausonius (Ordo Nob. Urb. xii.) describes Tolosa as surrounded by a brick wall of great circuit, and as a populous city, which had sent out inhabitants enough to found four other cities. The name Palladia, which Martial (Ep. ix. 101), Sidonius Apollinaris, and Ausonius give to Tolosa appears to refer to the cultivation of the liberal arts in this Gallic city —

" Te sibi Palladiae antetulit toga docta Tolosae."

(Auson. Parent. iii. 6; and Commem. Profess. Burdig. xvii. 7.)   [G. L.]

TOLOUS, a place of the Ilergetes in Hispania Tarraconensis. (Itin. Ant. p. 391.) Probably Mon-zon.   [T. H. D.]

TO'MARUS. [DODONA, p. 783, b.]

TOME'RUS (Τόμηρος, Arrian, Ind. 24), a river, or rather torrent of Gedrosia, called Tonberos or Tomberos by Pliny (vi. 23. s. 25. § 93, ed. Sillig.), and Tubero by Mela (iii. 7). According to the distances in Arrian, this river is the Muklow or Hingul.

TOMEUS. [MESSENIA, p. 341, b.]

TOMIS or TOMI (Τόμις, Strab. vii. p. 319; Ov. Tr. iii. 9. 33; Geogr. Rav. iv. 6, &c.: Τόμοι, Ptol. iii. 10. § 8; Tomi, Plin. iv. 11. s. 18; Stat. S. i. 2, 255; Itin. Ant. p. 227, &c.; in Mela, ii. 2, Tomoe: we also find the Greek form Τομεύς, Steph. B. s. v.; Arrian, Per. P. Eux. p. 24), a town of Lower Moesia, on the Euxine, and the

capital of the district of Scythia Minor (Sozom. H. Eccl. vii. 25; Hierocl. p. 637). It was situated at a distance of about 300 stadia or 36 miles from Istros or Istropolis (Anon. Per. P. Eux. p. 12; Itin. Ant. p. 227), but according to the Tab. Peut. 40 miles. It was a Milesian colony, and according to the legend the place where Medea cut up her brother's body, or where their father Aeëtes got together and buried the pieces (Ov. l. c.; Apollod. i. 9, 25; Hygin. Fab. 13.) The legend is no doubt connected with the name of the town, which, however, is still better known as the place of banishment of Ovid. Now Tomisvar or Jeni Pangola.   [T. H. D.]

COIN OF TOMIS OR TOMI.

TO'MISA (Τόμισα: Eth. Τομισηνός, Τομισεύς, a town of Sophene, in Armenia, was ceded by Lucullus to the Cappadocians. (Polyb. xxxiv. 13; Strab. xii. p. 535, xiv. pp. 663, 664; Steph. B. s. v.)

TONBEROS. [TOMERUS.]

TONICE. [NICONIS DROMUS.]

TONOSA, a town of Cappadocia, 50 miles from Sebastia, still called Tonus. (It. Ant. pp. 181, 182, 212.)

TONSUS, or TONZUS (Τόνσος, Zos. ii. 22. § 8 ; cf. Lampr. Elag. 7), the principal tributary of the Hebrus in Thrace. It rises in the Haemus: its general course for about 70 miles is almost due E.; it then makes a sudden bend to the S., and, after a farther southerly course of nearly the same length, falls into the Hebrus, a short distance from Hadrianopolis. Now Tunsca or Toondja.   [J. R.]

TOPI'RIS (Plin. iv. 11. s. 18; Τόνιρίς or Τουηρίς, Ptol. iii. 11. § 13), or TOPIRUS (It. Ant. p. 321; in p. 331, it is corrupted into Otopisus; and in It. Hier. p. 603, into Epyrus; Tab. Peut.; Τόπιρος, Hierocl. p. 634), a town in the SW. of Thrace, a little NE. from the mouth of the Nestus, and a short distance W. of Abdera. In the time of Procopius (B. G. iii. 38) it was the first of the maritime cities of Thrace, and is described as distant 12 days' journey from Byzantium. Very little is known about this place. In later times it was called Rhusion (Ρούσιον, Hierocl. l. c.; cf. Aposposm. Geo. in Hudson. iv. p. 42 ; and Anna Comn. p. 212), and was the seat of a bishopric. (Conc. Chalced.) Justinian rebuilt its walls, which had been demolished, and made them stronger than before. (Procop. de Aed. iv. 11.) According to Paul Lucas and Boudoue, the modern Tosbur occupies its site; but Lapie identifies it with Kara-Giuensi.   [J. R.]

TOREA'TAE. [TORETAE.]

TORECCADAE. [TORETAE.]

TO'RETAE (Τορεταί, Steph. B. s. v.; Dionys. Per. 682; Plin. vi. 5; Mela, i. 2; Avien. Orb. Terr. 867) or TOREA'TAE (Τορεᾶται, Strab. xi. p. 495), a tribe of the Maeotae in Asiatic Sarmatia. Ptolemy (v. 9. § 9) mentions a Τορετική ἄκρα in Asiatic Sarmatia; and in another passage (iii. 5. § 25) he speaks of the Τορεκκάδαι as a people in European Sarmatia, who are perhaps the same as the Toretae or Toreatae.

TORNADOTUS, a small river of Assyria, mentioned by Pliny (vi. 27. s. 31), and a tributary of the Tigris. It is probably the same stream as that noticed by Xenophon under the name of the Physcus. (*Anab.* ii. 4. § 25.) It may be the modern *Torna* or *Odorneh*. Mannert (vi. 2. p. 317) takes it to be the same as the Adiabas of Ammianus (xxiii. 6); but the Adiabas is more likely to be that elsewhere called the Zabatus (now *Záb*). [V.]

TORNATES, an Aquitanian people, whose name is preserved in Pliny (iv. 19). There is no indication of their position, unless it be the name *Tour-nai*, a small town on the *Arros*, a branch of the *Adour*, and in the diocese of *Tarbes*, which, under the name of Turba, was the chief place of the Bigerriones. [BIGERRIONES.] [G. L.]

TORONAICUS SINUS. [TORONE.]

TORO'NE (Τορώνη: Eth. Τορωναῖος), a town of Chalcidice in Macedonia, situated upon the SW. coast of the peninsula of Sithonia. It was said to have derived its name from Torone, a daughter of Proeteus or Poseidon and Phoenice. (Steph. B. s. v. Τορώνη.) It was a Greek colony, founded by the Chalcidians of Euboea, and appears to have been originally the chief settlement of the Chalcidians in these parts. Hence the gulf lying between the peninsulas of Sithonia and Torone was generally called the Toronaean, now the *Gulf of Kassándhra*. (Τορωναϊκὸς κόλπος, Steph. B. s. v. Τορώνη; Ptol. iii. 13. § 13; Τορωνικὸς κόλπος, Strab. vii. p. 330; Scymn. Ch. 640; Toronaicum mare, Liv. xliv. 11; Toronaeus sinus, Tac. *Ann.* v. 10.) Like the other Greek cities in these parts, Torone furnished ships and men to the army of Xerxes in his invasion of Greece. (Herod. vii. 122.) After the Persian War Torone came under the dominion of Athens. In B.C. 424 a party in the town opened the gates to Brasidas, but it was retaken by Cleon two years afterwards. (Thuc. iv. 110, seq., v. 2.) At a later time it seems to have been subject to Olynthus, since it was recovered by the Athenian general Timotheus. (Diodor. xv. 81.) It was annexed by Philip, along with the other Chalcidian cities, to the Macedonian empire. (Diodor. xvi. 53.) In the war against Perseus, B. C. 169, it was attacked by a Roman fleet, but without success. (Liv. xliv. 12.) Theophrastus related that the Egyptian bean grew in a marsh near Torone (ap. *Athen.* iii. p. 72, d.); and Archestratus mentions a particular kind of fish, for which Torone was celebrated (ap. *Athen.* vii. p. 310, c.). The harbour of Torone was called Cophos (Κωφός), or "deaf," because being separated from the sea by two narrow passages, the noise of the waves was never heard there: hence the proverb κωφότερος τοῦ Τορωναίου λιμένος. (Strab. vii. p. 330; Mela, ii. 3; Zenob. *Prov. Graec.* cent. iv. pr. 68.) This port is apparently the same as the one called by Thucydides (v. 2) the harbour of the Colophonians, which he describes as only a little way from the city of the Toronaeans. Leake conjectures that we ought perhaps to read Κωφῶν instead of Κολοφωνίων. It is still called Κωφό, and Torone likewise retains its ancient name. (Leake, *Northern Greece*, vol. iii. pp. 119, 155, 455.)

TORYNE (Τορύνη, Plut. *Ant.* 62; Τορώνη, Ptol. iii. 14. § 5), a town of Thesprotia in Epeirus, off which the fleet of Augustus was moored a short time before the battle of Actium, seems from the

order of the names in Ptolemy to have stood in one of the bays between the mouth of the river Thyamis and Sybota, probably at *Parga*. (Leake, *Northern Greece*, vol. i. p. 103, vol. iii. p. 8.)

TOTTAEUM, a place in Bithynia of uncertain site (*It. Ant.* p. 141; *It. Hieros.* p. 573, where it is called Tutaium; *Concil. Chalced.* p. 98); but some look for its site near *Geiveh*, and others near *Kara-kaia*. [L. S.]

TOXANDRI. These inhabitants of North Gallia are first mentioned by Pliny (iv. 17) in a passage which has been interpreted several ways. Pliny's Belgica is limited on the north by the Scaldis (*Schelde*). [GALLIA TRANS., Vol. I. p. 960.] Pliny says: "A Scaldi incolunt extera Toxandri pluribus nominibus. Deinde Menapii, Morini." D'Anville and others explain "extera" to signify beyond the limits of the *Schelde*, that is, north and east of this boundary; and Cluver places the Toxandri in the islands of *Zeeland*. D'Anville supposes that they took a part of their territory from the Menapii, and that this newly acquired country was the *Campen* north of *Brabant* and the bishopric of *Liége*. This conjecture is supposed to be confirmed by the passage of Ammianus Marcellinus (xvii. 8), in which he says that Julian marched against the Franci named Salii, who had dared to fix themselves on Roman ground "apud Toxiandriam locum." The geographers who are best acquainted with the Netherlands fix Toxiandri locus at *Tessender Lo*, a small place in the *Campen* to the north of *Brabant*. Ukert (*Gallien*, p. 372) gives a different meaning to the word "extera." He remarks that Pliny, describing the north coast of Europe (iv. 14), says: "Toto autem hoc mari ad Scaldim usque fluvium Germanicae accolunt gentes," and he then enumerates the peoples as far as the Scaldis. Afterwards (c. 17) he adds "a Scaldi incolunt," &c.; and a few lines further, a word "introrsus" is opposed to this "extera"; from which Ukert concludes that "extera" here means the coast country, a meaning which it has in two other passages of Pliny (ii. 67, iv. 13). After describing the nations which occupy the "extera," or coast, Pliny mentions the peoples in the interior, and in the third place the Germanic peoples on the Rhine. Accordingly Ukert concludes that we must look for the Toxandri in the neighbourhood of *Ghent* and *Bruges*. [G. L.]

TRACANA (Τράκανα, Ptol. iii. 5. § 27), an inland city of European Sarmatia. [T. H. D.]

TRACHIS or TRACHIN (Τραχίς, Herod., Thuc., et alii; Τραχίν, Strab.: Eth. Τραχίνιος). 1. A city of Malis, in the district called after it Trachinia. It stood in a plain at the foot of Mt. Oeta, a little to the N. or rather W. of Thermopylae, and derived its name from the rocks which surrounded the plain. It commanded the approach to Thermopylae from Thessaly, and was, from its position, of great military importance. (Herod. vii. 176; Strab. ix. p. 428; Steph. B. s. v.) The entrance to the Trachinian plain was only half a plethrum in breadth, but the surface of the plain was 22,000 plethra, according to Herodotus. The same writer states that the city Trachis was 5 stadia from the river Melas, and that the river Asopus issued from a gorge in the mountains, to the S. of Trachis. (Herod. vii. 198.) According to Thucydides, Trachis was 40 stadia from Thermopylae and 20 from the sea (Thuc. iii. 92.) Trachin is mentioned in Homer as one of the cities subject to Achilles (*Il.* ii. 682), and is celebrated in the legends of Hercules as the scene of this hero's death. (Soph. *Trach.* passim.) It became a place of historical importance in consequence of the colony founded here by the Lacedaemonians in the sixth year of the Peloponnesian War, B. C. 426. The Trachinians and the neighbouring Dorians, who suffered much from the predatory incursions of the Oetaean mountaineers, solicited aid from the Spartans, who eagerly availed themselves of this opportunity to plant a strong colony in this commanding situation. They issued an invitation to the other states of Greece to join in the colony; and as many as 10,000 colonists, under three Spartan oecists, built and fortified a new town, to which the name of HERACLEIA was given, from the great hero, whose name was so closely associated with the surrounding district. (Thuc. iii. 92; Diod. xii. 59.) It was usually called the Trachinian Heracleia, to distinguish it from other places of the same name, and by later writers Heracleia in Phthiotis, as this district was subsequently included in the Thessalian Phthiotis. ('Ηράκλεια ἡ ἐν Τραχινίᾳ, Xen. *Hell.* i. 2. § 18; Diod. xii. 77, xv. 57; 'Ηρακλεῶται οἱ ἐν Τραχῖνι, Thuc. v. 51; 'Η. ἡ Τραχὶν καλουμένη πρότερον, Strab. ix. p. 428; Heraclea Trachin dicta, Plin. iv. 7. s. 14; 'Η. Φθιώτιδος, Ptol. iii. 13. § 46.) The new colonists also built a port with docks near Thermopylae. It was generally expected that this city, under the protection of Sparta, would become a formidable power in Northern Greece, but it was attacked from the beginning by the Thessalians, who regarded its establishment as an invasion of their territory; and the Spartans, who rarely succeeded in the government of dependencies, displayed haughtiness and corruption in its administration. Hence the city rapidly dwindled down; and in B. C. 420 the Heracleots were defeated with great loss by the neighbouring Thessalian tribes, and Xenares, the Lacedaemonian governor, was slain in the battle. Sparta was unable at the time to send assistance to their colony; and in the following year the Boeotians, fearing lest the place should fall into the hands of the Athenians, took possession of it, and dismissed the Lacedaemonian governor, on the ground of misconduct. (Thuc. v. 51, 52.) The Lacedaemonians, however, regained possession of the place; and in the winter of B. C. 409—408, they experienced here another disaster, 700 of the Heracleots being slain in battle, together with the Lacedaemonian harmost. (Xen. *Hell.* i. 3. § 18.) But, after the Peloponnesian War, Heracleia again rose into importance, and became the head-quarters of the Spartan power in Northern Greece. In B. C. 399 Herippidas, the Lacedaemonian, was sent thither to repress some factious movements in Heracleia; and he not only put to death all the opponents of the Lacedaemonians in the town, but expelled the neighbouring Oetaeans and Trachinians from their abodes. (Diod. xiv. 38; Polyaen. ii. 21.) In B. C. 395 the Thebans, under the command of Ismenias, wrested this important place from the Spartans, killed the Lacedaemonian garrison, and gave the city to the old Trachinian and Oetaean inhabitants. (Diod. xiv. 82.) The walls of Heracleia were destroyed by Jason, lest any state should seize this place and prevent him from marching into Greece. (Xen. *Hell.* vi. 4. § 27.) At a later time Heracleia came into the hands of the Aetolians, and was one of the main sources of their power in Northern Greece. After the defeat of Antiochus at Thermopylae, B. C. 191, Heracleia was besieged by the Roman consul Acilius Glabrio, who divided his army into four bodies, and directed his attacks upon four points at once; one body being stationed on the river Asopus, where was the gymnasium; the second near the citadel outside of the walls (extra muros), which was almost more thickly inhabited than the city itself; the third towards the Maliac gulf; and the fourth on the river Melas, opposite the temple of Diana. The country around was marshy, and abounded in lofty trees. After a siege of twenty-four days the Romans succeeded in taking the town, and the Aetolians retired to the citadel. On the following day the consul seized a rocky summit, equal to the citadel in height, and separated from it only by a chasm so narrow that the two summits were within reach of a missile. Thereupon the Aetolians surrendered the citadel. (Liv. xxxvi. 24.) Leake remarks that it seems quite clear from this account of Livy that the city occupied the low ground between the rivers *Karvunariá* (Asopus) and *Mavra-Néria* (Melas), extending from the one to the other, as well as a considerable distance into the plain in a south-eastern direction. There are still some vestiges of the citadel upon a lofty rock above; and upon its perpendicular sides there are many catacombs excavated. "The distance of the citadel above the town justifies the words *extra muros*, which Livy applies to it, and may explain also the assertion of Strabo (*l. c.*), that Heracleia was six stadia distant from the ancient Trachis; for, although the town of Heracleia seems to have occupied the same position as the Trachis of Herodotus, the citadel, which, according to Livy, was better inhabited in the Aetolian War than the city, may very possibly have been the only inhabited part of Heracleia two centuries later." (Leake, *Northern Greece*, vol. ii. pp. 26—29.)

2. Surnamed PHOCICA (ἡ Φωκική), a small city of Phocis, situated upon the confines of Boeotia, and on the road to Lebadeia. (Strab. ix. p. 423; Paus. x. 3. § 2.)

TRACHONI'TIS (Τραχωνῖτις, *Luke*, iii. 1; Joseph. *Ant.* xvi. 9, *B. J.* iii. 3; Plin. v. 18. s. 16; Τράχων, Joseph. *Ant.* xiii. 16), according to Josephus, a portion of Palestine which extended in a NE. direction from the neighbourhood of the sea of Galilee in the direction of Damascus, having the Syrian desert and Auranitis on its eastern frontier, Ituraea on the S., and Gaulanitis on the W. It was considered as the northern portion of Peraea (Περαία, i. e. Πέραν τοῦ Ἰορδανου, *Judith*, i. 9; *Matth.* iv. 25.) According to Strabo, it lay between Damascus and the Arabian mountains (xvi. p. 755); and from other authorities we may gather that it adjoined the province of Batanaea (Joseph. *B. J.* i. 20. § 4), and extended between the Regio Decapolitana (Plin. v. 15) as far S. as Bostra (Euseb. *Onomast. s. v. Ituraea.*) It derived its name from the rough nature of the country (τραχών, i. e. τραχὺς καὶ πετρώδης τόπος); and Strabo mentions two τραχῶνες (xvi. p. 755, 756), which Burckhardt considers to be the summits of two mountain ranges on the road from *Mekka* to *Damascus*, near the village of *Al-Kesswe.* (*Travels*, p. 115.) The inhabitants of Trachonitis are called by Ptolemy, οἱ Τραχωνῖται Ἄραβες (v. 15. § 26), and they seemed to have maintained their character for remarkable skill in shooting with the bow and plundering (Joseph. *B. J.* ii. 4. § 2), for which the rocky nature of the country they inhabited, full as it was of clefts, and holes and secret fastnesses, was peculiarly well suited (Joseph. *Ant.* xv. 10. § 1.) Trachonitis belonged originally to the tetrarchy of Philippus, the son of Herod the

Great (Joseph. *Ant.* xvii. 8. § 1, *B. J.* ii. 6. § 3); but it subsequently formed part of the dominion of Herodes Agrippa. (Joseph. *Ant.* xviii. 6. § 10, *B. J.* iii. 3. § 5; Philo, *Opp.* ii. p. 593.)

The whole district has been recently explored and examined with much care and judgment by the Rev. J. L. Porter of Damascus, who has shown that the ancient accounts of this province, properly weighed, coincide with remarkable accuracy with what we know of it now. According to him, it must have been to the NW. of Batanaea, and have extended along the stony tract at the base of the *Jebel Haurán*, as Kenath (now *Kunawát*) was a city of Trachon (Euseb. *Onomast. s. v. Canath*), while the Targums extend it, though improbably, as far S. as Bostra. Mr. Porter observes that the name is sometimes applied in a more general sense by ancient writers, so as to include the neighbouring provinces (as in *Luke*, iii. 1, where the "Region of Trachonitis" must be understood as embracing Batanaea and Auranitis; Joseph. *Ant.* xvii. 14. § 4.) He thinks, too, that the plain on the western side as far as the *Háj* road was embraced in Trachonitis, and likewise that on the north to the *Jebel Khiyárah*, with a considerable section of the plain on the east, N. of *Ard-al-Bathanyeh.* The Argob of *Numb.* xxxiv. 15, 1 *Kings*, iv. 13, &c., Mr. Porter considers to be the same district as Trachonitis, the latter being the Greek rendering of the Hebrew form. (Porter, *Five Years in Damascus*, ii. pp. 259—262, 268—272; Robinson, iii. p. 907; Russegger, iii. p. 279; Winer, *Bibl. Realwörterbuch.*)   [V.]

TRACHY. [ORCHOMENUS, p. 490, a.]

TRACTARI, a tribe in the Chersonesus Taurica (Plin. iv. 12. s. 26).   [T. H. D.]

TRAELIUS. [TRAGILUS.]

TRAENS or TRAÏS (*Τράεις* or *Τράεντ, -εντος: Trionto*), a river of Bruttium celebrated for the sanguinary defeat of the Sybarites on its banks by their rivals the Crotoniats, which led to the destruction of the city of Sybaris, B. C. 510. (Iambl. *Vit. Pyth.* § 260.) It is singular that the banks of a stream which had been the scene of such a catastrophe should be again selected by the remnant of the Sybarites who were expelled from the new colony of Thurii shortly after its foundation [THURII] for the site of their settlement. They, however, did not remain long, being expelled and put to the sword by the neighbouring barbarians, whom Diodorus by a remarkable anachronism calls Bruttians, apparently within a few years of their establishment. (Diod. xii. 22.) The name of the river is not found in any of the geographers, but there can be little doubt of its being the one still called the *Trionto*, which falls into the gulf of Tarentum a few miles E. of *Rossano*, and gives name also to an adjoining headland, the *Capo di Trionto*.   [E. H. B.]

TRA'GIA (*Τραγία*), also called Tragiae (*Τραγίαι*), Tragia, Tragaeae (*Τραγαίαι*), or Tragaea (*Τραγαία*), a small island off the south coast of Samos, near which Pericles, in B. C. 440, defeated the Samians in a naval engagement. (Thucyd. i. 116; Plin. iv. 71, v. 135; Plut. *Per.* 25; Strab. xiii. p. 635; Steph. B. *s. v.* Τραγαία.) Respecting the Tragasaeae Salinae, see HALESION.   [L. S.]

TRA'GIA or TRAGAEA. [NAXOS, p. 406, a.]

TRA'GILUS (*Τράγιλος*: *Eth.* Τραγιλεύς, Steph. B. *s. v.*), a town of Macedonia, and doubtless the same as the Βράγιλος or Δράγιλος found in Hierocles (p. 639) among the towns of the first or consular Macedonia. In the Table there is a place "Triulo"

marked as 10 miles from Philippi. This is apparently a corruption of "Traelio," since numerous coins (one of which is figured below) have been found near Amphipolis with the inscription TRAIAIΩN. Leake conjectures with much probability that the real name was Tragilus, and that in the local form of the name the Γ may have been omitted, so that the TPAIAIΩN of the coin may represent the Hellenic Τραγιλίων. (Eckhel, vol. ii. p. 81; Leake, *Northern Greece*, vol. iii. p. 228.)

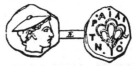

COIN OF TRAGILUS OR TRAELIUS.

TRAGU'RIUM (*Τραγούριον*, Strab., Ptol.; *Τραγύριον*, Polyb.), an important town of Dalmatia, situated upon an island, which was separated from the mainland by an artificial canal. According to the Antonine Itinerary, it was distant 16 miles from Praetorium and 13 from Salonae. Pliny calls it "Tragurium civium Romanorum," and says that it was celebrated for its marble. Its name is preserved in the modern *Trau*. (Polyb. xxxii. 18; Strab. ii. p. 124, vii. p. 315; Ptol. ii. 17. § 14; Plin. iii. 22. s. 26; Mela, ii. 3; *It. Ant.* p. 272; *Tab. Peut.*; Geogr. Rav. iv. 16.)

TRAGUS. [CAPHYAE.]

TRAIA CAPITA (*Itin. Ant.* p. 399), more correctly TRIA CAPITA (Geog. Rav. v. 3), since it lay near the three mouths of the Iberus, a town of the Cosetani, in Hispania Tarraconensis, between Dertosa and Tarraco. Variously identified with *Tivisa* and *Torre del Aliga*.   [T. H. D.]

TRAJA'NI MUNIMENTUM, a fort or castle built by Trajan on the southern bank of the river Moenus, not far from its junction with the Rhenus. (Amm. Marc. xvii. 1.) The site is uncertain, nor is it known what the Munimentum really was.   [L. S.]

TRAJA'NI PORTUS. [OSTIA.]

TRAJANO'POLIS (*Τραιανόπολις*), a town in Mysia, in the district occupied by the tribe of the Thraemenothyritae, on the frontiers of Phrygia. (Ptol. v. 2. §§ 14, 15.) The Cilician city of Selinus also for a time bore the name of Trajanopolis. [SELINUS.]   [L. S.]

TRAJANO'POLIS (*Τραιανόπολις*), an important town in the S. of Thrace, which was probably founded by or in honour of the emperor Trajan, about the time when Plotinopolis was founded, to perpetuate the name of his wife Plotina. Its exact site appears to be somewhat doubtful. Some authorities describe it as situated on the right bank of the Hebrus, near the pass in the range of Mount Rhodope, through which that river flows, and about 40 miles from its mouth. Now this is the site of the modern *Orikhova*, with which accordingly it is by some identified. It would be difficult, however, to reconcile this with the various distances given in the Itineraries: e. g. Trajanopolis is stated to be 9000 paces from Tempyra, and 29,000 from Cypsela; whereas the site above mentioned is nearly equidistant from those assigned to Tempyra and Cypsela, being, however, more distant from the former. But this is only one example out of many showing how extremely imperfect is our knowledge of the geography of Thrace, both ancient and modern. In the map of the Society for the Diffusion of Useful Knowledge Trajanopolis is placed on the Egnatian Way at a considerable distance W. of the Hebrus, and at a point which fulfils tolerably well the conditions of distance from the two places above mentioned.

Trajanopolis became the capital of the province of Rhodope, and continued to be a place of importance until the fourth century. It is remarkable, however, that it is not mentioned by Ammianus in his general description of Thrace (xxvii. 4); according to him, the chief cities of Rhodope were Maximianopolis, Maronea, and Aenus. (Ptol. iii. 11. § 13; Hierocl. p. 631; Procop. de Aed. iv. 11; Const. Porph. de Caerim. ii. 54; Cantacuz. i. 38, iii. 67. et alibi; It. Ant. pp. 175, 322, 332, 333; It. Hier. p. 602; Geog. Rav. iv. 6; cf. Mannert, vii. p. 224.)   [J. R.]

TRAJECTUM, in North Gallia, is not mentioned in any Roman writing before the Itin. of Antoninus. It was on the Roman road which ran along the Rhine from Lugdunum Batavorum, and the site is Utrecht in the kingdom of the Netherlands, at the bifurcation of the old Rhine and the Vecht. The modern name contains the Roman name abbreviated, and the part U seems to be a corruption of the word Oude (Vetus); but D'Anville observes that the name is written Utrecht as early as 870.   [G. L.]

TRAJECTUS in Gallia, placed by the Antonine, Itin. on a road which runs from Aginnum (Agen) through Excisum and Trajectus to Vesunna (Périgueux). Trajectus is xxi. from Excisum (Ville Neuve), and xviii. from Vesunna, and it marks the passage of the Duranius (Dordogne) between these two positions at a place called Pontons on the Dordogne, opposite to which on the other bank of the river is La Linde, mentioned in the Table under the name of Diolindum. [DIOLINDUM.]   [G. L.]

TRAIS. [TRAENS.]

TRALLES or TRALLIS (Τράλλεις, Τράλλις: Eth. Τραλλιανός), a large and flourishing city of Caria, on the southern slope of mount Messogis, a little to the north of the Scamander, a small tributary of which, the Eudon, flowed close by the city, while another passed right through it. Its acropolis was situated on a lofty eminence in the north of the city. Tralles was said to have been founded by Argives in conjunction with a body of Thracians, whence its name Tralles was believed to be derived (Strab. xiv. pp. 648, 649; Hesych, s. v.; Diod. Sic. xvii. 65; Plut. Ages. 16), for it is said to have previously been called Anthea, Evanthea, Erymna, Charax, Seleucia, and Antiochia (Steph. B. s. vv. Τράλλις, Χάραξ; Etym. M. p. 389; Plin. v. 29). Others, however, state that it was a Pelasgian colony, and originally bore the name of Larissa (Agath. ii. 17; Schol. ad Hom. Il. x. 429). It was situated in a most fertile district, at a point where highroads met from the south, east, and west; so that it must have been a place of considerable commerce. (Cic. ad Att. v. 14, ad Fam. iii. 5, ad Quint. Frat. i. 1; Strab. xiv. p. 663.) The inhabitants of Tralles were celebrated for their great wealth, and were generally appointed asiarchs, that is, presidents of the games celebrated in the district. But the country in which Tralles was situated was much subject to earthquakes; in the reign of Augustus many of its public buildings were greatly damaged by a violent shock; and the emperor gave the inhabitants a handsome sum of money to repair the losses they had sustained. (Strab. xii. p. 579.) Out of gratitude, the Trallians petitioned to be permitted to erect a temple in honour

of Tiberius, but without effect. (Tac. Ann. iv. 55.) According to Pliny (xxxv. 49), king Attalus had a palace at Tralles. A statue of Caesar was set up in the temple of Victoria at Tralles; and during the presence of Caesar in Asia a miracle is said to have happened in the temple, respecting which see Caes. Bell. Civ. iii. 105; Plut. Caes. 47; and Val. Max. i. 6. The city is very often mentioned by ancient writers (Xen. Anab. i. 4. § 8, Hist. Gr. iii. 2. § 19; Polyb. xxii. 27; Liv. xxxvii. 45, xxxviii. 39; Diod. xiv. 36, xix. 75; Juven. iii. 70; Ptol. v. 2. § 19; Hierocl. p. 659). During the middle ages the city fell into decay, but was repaired by Andronicus Palaeologus (G. Pachymer, p. 320). Extensive ruins of the place still exist above the modern Ghiusel Hissar, in a position perfectly agreeing with the description of Strabo. (See Arundell, Seven Churches, pp. 58, 65, 293; Leake, Asia Minor, pp. 243, 246; Fellows, Asia Minor, p. 276, Lycia, p. 16; Hamilton, Researches, i. p. 533.) As to the coins of Tralles, which are very numerous, see Sestini, p. 89. [L. S.]

COIN OF TRALLES.

TRALLES or TRALLIS (Τράλλης), a town in Phrygia, on the west of Apamea, and 15 miles east of Hierapolis, not far from the banks of the Maeander (Hierocl. p. 667; Conc. Const. ii. p. 243; Conc. Nicaen. ii. p. 51; Tab. Peut.). The ruins seen by Arundell (Seven Churches, p. 231) near the village of Kuslar are probably those of Tralles. [L. S.]

TRA'LLIA (Τραλλία: Eth. Τραλλός, Τραλλεύς, Steph. B. s. v.), a district of Illyria, whose inhabitants, the Tralli, are mentioned several times by Livy (xxvii. 32, xxxi. 35, xxxiii. 4).

TRALLICON, a town of Caria, mentioned only by Pliny (v. 29), situated on the river Harpasus; but in his time it had already ceased to exist. [L. S.]

TRAMPYA. [TYMPHAEA.]

TRANSCELLENSIS MONS, a mountain in Mauretania, between Caesarea and the river Chinalaph. (Amm. Marc. xxix. 5. § 20.) [T. H. D.]

TRANSDUCTA (Τρανσδούκτα, Ptol. ii. 4. § 6), and in a fuller form, JULIA TRANSDUCTA or TRADUCTA, a town of the Bastuli, in Hispania Baetica, to the E. of Mellaria. It is doubtless the same place which Strabo (ii. p. 140) calls Ιουλία Ιόζα, and sets down between Belon and Gades, whither the Romans transplanted the inhabitants of Zelis, in Mauretania Tingitana. According to Ukert (ii. pt. i. p. 345) it is also the Tingentera of Mela (ii. 6), who informs us that he was born there; though it is not easy to see how it could have had so many names. But the ground for the conjecture is that Tingentera, according to Mela, was inhabited by Phoenicians, who had been transported thither, which in some respects resembles Strabo's account of Julia Ioza. It is sought at the modern Tarifa, or in its neighbourhood. For coins see Flores, Med. ii. p. 596; Eckhel, Doctr. Num. i. 1. p. 30; Mionnet, I.

p. 26, and Suppt. i. pp. 19, 45; Sestini, p. 90; Flores, *Esp. Sagr.* x. p. 50; *Mém. de l'Acad. des Inscr.* xxx. p. 103.)   [T. H. D.]

TRANSMARISCA (Τρομάρισκα, Ptol. iii. 10. § 11; Τραμαρίσκας and Τρασμάρικα, Procop. *de Aed.* iv. 7. p. 292; Stamarisca, Geogr. Rav. iv. 7), a strong fortress of Lower Moesia, opposite to the spot where the Mariscus flows into the Danube. It was the head-quarters of two cohorts of the Legio XI. Claudia, and also of some light-armed troops. (*Itin. Ant.* p. 223; *Not. Imp.*; *Tab. Peut*). Now *Turtukai, Tuturkai*, or *Toterkan.*   [T. H. D.]

TRANSMONTA'NI (Τρανσμοντανοί, Ptol. iii. 5. § 21), the name of a tribe in European Sarmatia dwelling between the sources of the Borysthenes and the Peucinian mountains.   [T. H. D.]

TRAPEZO'POLIS (Τραπεζόπολις or Τραπεζούπολις: *Eth.* Trapezopolitae), a town situated, according to Ptolemy (ii. 2. § 18), in Caria, but according to Socrates (*Hist. Eccles.* vii. 36) and Hierocles (p. 665), in Phrygia. The former is the more correct statement, for the town stood on the southern slope of Mount Cadmus, to the south-east of Antiochia, and, according to the Notitia Imperii, afterwards belonged to the province of Pacatiana. It is possible that the ruins which Arundell (*Discoveries,* ii. p. 147) found at *Kesiljah-bouluk* may be those of Trapezopolis.   [L. S.]

TRA'PEZUS (Τραπεζοῦς: *Eth.* Τραπεζούντιος: now *Tarabosan* or *Trebizond*), an important city on the coast of Pontus, on the slope of a hill, 60 stadia to the east of Hermonassa, in the territory of the Macrones (Anon. *Peripl. P. E.* p. 13), was a colony founded by the Sinopians, who formed many establishments on this coast. (Xenoph. *Anab.* iv. 8. § 22; Arrian, *Peripl. P. E.* pp. 1, 3, 6; Scylax, p. 33.) It derived its name probably from its form, being situated on an elevated platform, as it were a table above the sea; though the town of Trapezus in Arcadia pretended to be the mother-city of Trapezus in Pontus (Paus. viii. 27. § 4). Trapezus was already a flourishing town when Xenophon arrived there on his memorable retreat; and he and his men were most hospitably treated by the Trapezuntians. (Xen. *Anab.* v. 5. § 10.) At that time the Colchians were still in possession of the territory, but it afterwards was occupied by the Macrones. The real greatness of Trapezus, however, seems to have commenced under the dominion of the Romans. Pliny (vi. 4) calls it a free city, a distinction which it had probably obtained from Pompey during his war against Mithridates. In the reign of Hadrian, when Arrian visited it, it was the most important city on the south coast of the Euxine, and Trajan had before made it the capital of Pontus Cappadocicus, and provided it with a larger and better harbour. (Arrian, *Peripl. P. E.* p. 17; comp. Tac. *Ann.* xiii. 39, *Hist.* iii. 47; Pomp. Mela, i. 19: Strab. vii. pp. 309, 320, xi. p. 499, xii. p. 548; Steph. B. *s. v.*) Henceforth it was a strongly fortified commercial town; and although in the reign of Gallienus it was sacked and burnt by the Goths (Zosim. i. 33; Eustath. *ad Dion. Per.* 687), it continued to be in such excellent condition, that in the reign of Justinian it required but few repairs. (Procop. *de Aed.* iii. 7.) From the Notitia Imperii (c. 27) we learn that Trapezus was the station of the first Pontian legion and its staff. Some centuries later a branch of the imperial house of the Comneni declared themselves independent of the Greek Empire, and made Trapezus the seat of their principality. This small principality maintained its independence even for some time after the fall of Constantinople; but being too weak to resist the overwhelming power of the Turks, it was obliged, in A. D. 1460, to submit to Mohammed II., and has ever since that time been a Turkish town. (Chalcond. ix. p. 263, foll.; Duc. 45; comp. Gibbon, *Decline,* c. xlviii. foll.) The port of Trapezus, called Daphnus, was formed by the acropolis, which was built on a rock running out into the sea. (Anon. *Peripl. P. E.* p. 13.) The city of Trebizond is still one of the most flourishing commercial cities of Asia Minor, but it contains no ancient remains of any interest, as most of them belong to the period of the Lower Empire. (Tournefort, *Voyage au Levant,* iii., lettre 17, p. 79, foll.; Fontanier, *Voyages dans l'Orient,* p. 17—23; Hamilton's *Researches,* i. p. 240.) The coins of Trapezus all belong to the imperial period, and extend from the reign of Trajan to that of Philip. (Eckhel, i. 2. p. 358; Sestini, p. 60.)   [L. S.]

TRA'PEZU'S (Τραπεζοῦς, -οῦντος: *Eth.* Τραπεζούντιος), a town of Arcadia, in the district Parrhasia, a little to the left of the river Alpheius, is said to have derived its name from its founder Trapezeus, the son of Lycaon, or from *trapeza* (τράπεζα), "a table," because Zeus here overturned the table on which Lycaon offered him human food. (Paus. viii. 3. §§ 2, 3; Apollod. iii. 8. § 1.) It was the royal residence of Hippothous, who transferred the seat of government from Tegea to Trapezus. On the foundation of Megalopolis, in B. C. 371, the inhabitants of Trapezus refused to remove to the new city; and having thus incurred the anger of the other Arcadians, they quitted Peloponnesus, and took refuge in Trapezus on the Pontus Euxeinus, where they were received as a kindred people. The statues of some of their gods were removed to Megalopolis, where they were seen by Pausanias. Trapezus stood above the modern *Mavridi.* (Paus. viii. 5. § 4, 27. §§ 4—6, viii. 29. § 1, 31. § 5; Herod. vi. 127; Steph. B. *s. v.*; Leake, *Morea,* vol. ii. p. 292; Ross, *Reisen im Peloponnes,* vol. i. p. 90.)

TRAPEZUS MONS. [TAURICA CHERSONESUS.]

TRA'RIUM (Τράριον), a town of Mysia, mentioned by Strabo in conjunction with Perperena (xiii. p. 607.) Tzetzes (*ad Lycophr.* 1141, 1159) mentions a mountain named Traron(Τράρων) in the Troad.

TRASIMENUS LACUS* (ἡ Τρασουμένη or Τρασυμένα λίμνη, Strab.; ἡ Ταρσιμένη λίμνη, Pol.: *Lago di Perugia*), one of the most extensive and important of the lakes of Etruria, situated between Cortona and Perusia. It is the largest of all the lakes of Etruria, being above 10 miles in length by 8 in breadth: and differs from all the other considerable lakes of that country in not being of volcanic origin. It is merely formed in a depressed basin, surrounded on all sides by hills of moderate elevation, and having no natural outlet. The hills on the N. side of the lake, which extend from Crotona to Perusia, are considerably more elevated than those that form the other sides of the basin, but even these scarcely rise to the dignity of mountains. The lake itself is of small depth, nowhere exceeding 30 feet, and its banks are almost everywhere low, flat, and covered with reeds. No con-

---

* This is the form universally found in the best MSS. of Latin writers: there is no good ancient authority for the orthography of THRASIMENUS or THRASYMENUS, so generally adopted by modern writers.

siderable town was situated on its shores: Perusia, from which it derives its modern name of the *Lago di Perugia*, stands on a lofty hill about 10 miles to the E. of it; Clusium is situated about 9 miles to the SW. and Cortona between 6 and 7 to the NW. The highroad from Arretium to Perusia followed the northern shore of the lake for a considerable distance.

The lake Trasimenus derives its chief celebrity from the great victory obtained upon its shores by Hannibal over the Roman consul, C. Flaminius, B. C. 217, one of the greatest defeats sustained by the Roman arms during the whole course of their history. The circumstances of this battle are more clearly related and more readily understood with reference to the actual localities than those of any of the other great battles of Hannibal. The Carthaginian general, after crossing the Apennines, and effecting his toilsome march through the marshes of Etruria, had encamped in the neighbourhood of Faesulae (Pol. iii. 80, 82). Flaminius was at this time posted with his army at Arretium, and Hannibal, whose object was to draw him into a general battle, moved along the upper valley of the Arnus, and passing within a short distance of the consul's camp, advanced along the road towards Rome (i. e. by Perusia), laying waste the country as he advanced. Flaminius on this hastily broke up his camp, and followed the Carthaginian army. Hannibal had already passed the city of Cortona on his left, and was advancing along the N. shore of the lake, which lay on his right hand, when, learning that Flaminius was following him, he determined to halt and await his attack, taking advantage of the strong position which offered itself to him. (Pol. iii. 82; Liv. xxii. 4.) The hills which extend from Cortona to the lake, called by Livy the "montes Cortonenses," and now known as the *Monte Gualandro*, descend completely to the bank of the lake, or at least to the marshes that border it, at a point near the NW. angle of the lake, now marked by a village and a round tower called *Borghetto*. This spur of the hills completely separates the basin of the lake from the plains below Cortona, and it is not until after surmounting it that the traveller by the modern road comes in sight of the lake, as well as of the small plain or valley, shut in between its N. shore and the *Gualandro*, which was the actual scene of the catastrophe. "Arrived at the highest point of the road, the traveller has a partial view of the fatal plain, which opens fully upon him as he descends the *Gualandro*. He soon finds himself in a vale, enclosed to the left, and in front, and behind him by the *Gualandro* hills, bending round in a segment larger than a semicircle, and running down at each end to the lake, which obliques to the right and forms the chord of this mountain arc. The position cannot be guessed at from the plains of Cortona, nor appears to be so completely enclosed, unless to one who is fairly within the hills. It then indeed appears a place made as it were on purpose for a snare, 'locus insidiis natus.' (Liv. xxii. 4.) *Borghetto* is then found to stand in a narrow marshy pass close to the hill and to the lake, whilst there is no other outlet at the opposite turn of the mountains than through the little town of *Passignano*, which is pushed into the water by the foot of a high rocky acclivity. There is a woody eminence branching down from the mountains into the upper end of the plain nearer to the site of *Passignano*, and on this stands a village called

Torre" (more properly *Tuoro*). (Hobhouse, *Notes and Illustrations to Childe Harold*, canto iv. st. 63.)

From this description of the localities by an eyewitness, which agrees almost exactly with that given by Livy (xxii. 4), the details of the battle are rendered perfectly clear. Hannibal occupied the hill last-mentioned with the main body of his troops, his heavy-armed African and Spanish infantry, while he sent round his light-armed troops to occupy the slopes of *Monte Gualandro* on his right, so as to threaten the left flank of the advancing Roman army, while he posted his cavalry and the Gaulish troops on the hills on the left between *Borghetto* and the present road. Flaminius advanced the next morning almost before daylight, while a thick fog rising from the lake still further concealed the position of the enemy. He therefore advanced through the pass, in ignorance of the bodies of troops that hung upon both his flanks, and, seeing only the array in front on the hill of *Tuoro*, began to draw up his forces for battle in the plain in front of them. But before he was able to commence the engagement, he found himself suddenly attacked on all sides at once: the surprise was complete, and the battle quickly became a mere promiscuous massacre. Flaminius himself fell early in the day, and numbers of the Roman troops were driven into the lake, and either perished in its waters or were put to the sword by the enemy's cavalry. A body of about 6000 men having forced their way through the enemy, occupied a hill on which there stood an Etruscan village, but finding themselves wholly isolated, surrendered the next day to Maharbal. Sixteen thousand Roman troops perished in this disastrous battle: the site of the chief slaughter is still marked by a little rivulet which traverses the plain, and is known at the present day by the name of the *Sanguineto*.* (Hobhouse, *l. c.*) The details of the battle are given by Polybius (iii. 83, 84) and Livy (xxii. 4—6). It is remarkable that in this instance the localities are much more clearly and accurately described by Livy than by Polybius: the account given by the latter author is not incompatible with the existing local details, but would not be easily understood, unless we were able to correct it by the certainty that the battle took place on this particular spot. The narratives of Appian and Zonaras add nothing to our knowledge of the battle. (Appian, *Annib.* 9, 10; Zonar. viii. 25.) Numerous allusions to and notices of the memorable slaughter at the lake of Trasimene are found in the later Roman writers, but they have preserved no additional circumstances of interest. The well-known story related by Livy, as well as by Pliny and later writers, that the fury of the combatants rendered them unconscious of the shock of an earthquake, which occurred during the battle, is easily understood without any prodigy, such shocks being frequently very local and irregular phenomena. (Plin. ii. 84. s. 86, xv. 18. s. 20; Cic. *de N. D.* ii. 3,

---

* The name of *Ossaja*, a village on the road from Cortona to the lake, has been thought to be also connected with the slaughter of the battle, but this is very improbable. *Ossaja* is several miles distant from the lake, and on the other side of the hills. (Hobhouse, *l. c.*) It is probable moreover that the modern name is only a corruption of *Orsaja* or *Orsaria*. (Niebuhr, *Lectures*, vol. ii. p. 102.)

de Div. ii. 8; Eutrop. iii. 9; Flor. ii. 6. § 13; Oros. iv. 15; Val. Max. i. 6. § 6; Sil. Ital. i. 49, v. 1, &c.; Ovid, *Fast.* vi. 770; Strab. v. p. 226.)

The lake is now commonly known as the *Lago di Perugia*, though frequently called on maps and in guide-books the *Lago Trasimeno*.   [E. H. B.]

TRAUSI (Τραυσοί, Herod. v. 3, 4; Thrausi, Liv. xxxviii. 41), a Thracian people, who appear, in later times at least, to have occupied the SE. offshoots of Mount Rhodope, to the W. of the Hebrus, and about Tempyra. Herodotus tells us that the Trausi entertained peculiar notions respecting human life, which were manifested in appropriate customs. When a child was born, his kinsfolk, sitting around him, bewailed his lot in having to encounter the miseries of mortal existence; whereas when any one died, they buried him with mirth and rejoicing, declaring him to have been freed from great evils, and to be now in perfect bliss.*

As to the Thrausi spoken of by Livy, see TEM-PYRA.

Suidas and Hesychius (*s. v.*) mention a Scythian tribe called the Trausi, who, according to Steph. B. (*s. v.*), were the same people as the Agathyrsi. The last-named author speaks of a Celtic race also, bearing this appellation. On this slight foundation the strange theory has been built that the Thracian Trausi were the original stock of the Celts; and by way of supporting this notion, its propounders arbitrarily read Τραυσοί instead of Πραῦσοι in Strabo, iv. p. 187, where Strabo expressly says that he was unable to state what was the original abode of the Prausi: had he been writing about the Thracian Trausi we may safely assume that no such ignorance would have been acknowledged. Cf. Ukert, ii. pt. 2, p. 230.   [J. R.]

TRAVUS (Τραῦος, Herod. vii. 109), a small river in the S. of Thrace, which falls into the λίμνη Βιστονίς, a shallow aestuary penetrating far into the land, NE. of Abdera. The Travus is the principal outlet for the drainage of that part of southern Thrace which is included between the Nestus and the Hebrus.   [J. R.]

TREBA or TRE'BIA. 1. (*Eth.* Trebias, Ἄτις: *Trevi*), a municipal town of Umbria, situated at the western foot of the Apennines, between Fulginium and the sources of the Clitumnus, about 4 miles from the latter. It is mentioned by Pliny among the municipal cities of Umbria, and its name is found in an inscription among the "xv Populi Umbriae:" in both these authorities the name of the people is written Trebiates. The Jerusalem Itinerary, which places it on the Via Flaminia, 4 miles from Sacraria (at the sources of the Clitumnus) and 5 from Fulginium, writes the name Trevis, thus approximating closely to the modern name of *Trevi*. The modern town is still a considerable place standing on a hill which rises abruptly from the valley of the Clitumnus. (Plin. iii. 14. s. 19; *Itin. Hier.* p. 613; Orell. *Inscr.* 98).

2. (Τρήβα, Ptol.: *Eth.* Trebanus: *Trevi*), a city of Latium. in the upper valley of the Anio, about 5 miles from the sources of that river and 10 above *Subiaco*. It is mentioned both by Pliny and Ptolemy, as well as by Frontinus, who calls it Treba Augusta (Plin. iii. 5. s. 9; Ptol. iii. 1. § 62; Fron-

tin. *de Aquaed.* 93); and in an inscription, which proves it to have been a town of municipal rank under the Roman Empire. (Orell. *Inscr.* 4101.) But its name is not mentioned in history, and it was apparently never a place of importance, for which its secluded position is alone sufficient to account. The ancient name and site are retained by the modern village of *Trevi*, a poor place, surrounded on all sides by lofty mountains.   [E. H. B.]

TRE'BIA (ὁ Τρεβίας: *Trebbia*), a considerable river of Gallia Cispadana, falling into the Padus about 2 miles W. of Placentia. From its proximity to the latter city Pliny designates it as "Trebias Placentinus." (Plin. iii. 16. s. 20; Strab. v. p. 217.) It has its sources in the Ligurian Apennines near *Montebruno*, and has a course of above 50 miles from thence to the Po. Throughout the greater part of this course it flows through a mountain valley, passing under the walls of *Bobbio* (celebrated in the middle ages for its convent, from which some of the most valuable MSS. of ancient authors have been derived), and does not emerge from the hills which form the underfalls of the Apennines till within about 12 miles of its mouth. For the remainder of its course it flows through the fertile plain of the Padus, and crosses the Via Aemilia about 3 miles W. of Placentia. It appears probable that the Trebia was fixed by Augustus as the western limit of the Eighth Region, and continued from that period to be regarded as the limit of Gallia Cispadana towards Liguria. This is not distinctly stated, but may probably be inferred from the circumstance that Placentia was situated in the Eighth Region, while Iria (*Voghera*), the next town to the W., was certainly in Liguria. (Plin. iii. 5. s. 7, 15. s. 20.) Like most of the rivers which flow from the Apennines, the Trebia varies very much according to the season: in summer it is but a scanty stream, winding through a broad bed of stones, but in winter and after heavy rains it becomes a formidable torrent.

The chief celebrity of the Trebia is derived from the battle which was fought on its banks in B.C. 218 between Hannibal and the Roman consul Sempronius, and which was the first of the decisive victories obtained by the Carthaginian general. Unfortunately the movements which preceded and led to this battle, and the exact site on which it occurred, are very difficult to determine. Scipio after his defeat on the Ticinus had recrossed the Padus and withdrawn to Placentia, where the presence of a Roman colony afforded him a secure stronghold. Hannibal on the other hand effected his passage of the Padus higher up, above its junction with the Ticinus, and then advanced along the right bank of the river, till he approached Placentia, and established his camp within 5 miles of that of Scipio. (Pol. iii. 66.) The defection of the Boian Gauls having soon after given the alarm to Scipio, he broke up his camp and withdrew "to the hills that bordered the river Trebia." (*Ib.* 67.) In this movement, it is clear, from what we are told immediately afterwards that, he *crossed* the river Trebia (*Ib.* 68): his former camp therefore, though in the neighbourhood of Placentia, must have been on the W. side of the Trebia. In this new position, which was one of considerable natural strength (*Ib.* 67), Scipio awaited the arrival of Sempronius with his army, who was advancing from Ariminum, and succeeded in effecting a junction with his colleague, without opposition from Hannibal. (*Ib.* 68.) The attention of the Carthaginian general had been apparently drawn off

* Mela has followed Herodotus very closely in the following passage (ii. 2): "Lugentur apud quosdam puerperia, natique deflentur: funera contra festa sunt, et veluti sacra, cantu lusuque celebrantur."

to the W. ; where the town of Clastidium was betrayed into his hands. Meanwhile Sempronius, who was newly arrived, after a short interval of repose, was eager for a general engagement, and his confidence was increased by a partial success in a combat of cavalry, in the plain between the Trebia and the Padus (*Ib.* 69.) Hannibal, who on his side was equally desirous of a battle, took advantage of this disposition of Sempronius, and succeeded in drawing him out of his camp, where he could not venture to attack him, into the plain below, which was favourable to the operations of the Carthaginian cavalry and elephants. For this purpose he sent forward a body of Numidian horse, who crossed the Trebia and approached the Roman camp, but, as soon as a body of Roman cavalry and light-armed troops were sent out against them, retreated skirmishing until they had recrossed the river. Sempronius followed with his whole army, and crossed the Trebia, not without difficulty, for the river was swollen with late rains, and was only just fordable for the infantry. His troops suffered severely from cold and wet, and when the two armies met in order of battle, early began to feel themselves inferior to the enemy : but the victory was decided by a body of 1000 foot and 1000 horse, under the command of Mago, the brother of Hannibal, which had been placed by that general in ambuscade, in the hollow bed of a stream which crossed the field of battle, and by a sudden onset on the rear of the Roman army, threw it into complete confusion. A body of about 10,000 Roman infantry succeeded in forcing their way through the centre of the enemy's line, but finding themselves isolated, and their retreat to their camp quite cut off, they directed their march at once towards Placentia, and succeeded in reaching that city in safety. The other troops were thrown back in confusion upon the Trebia, and suffered very heavy loss in passing that river ; but those who succeeded in crossing it, fell back upon the body already mentioned and made good their retreat with them to Placentia. Thither also Scipio on the following day repaired with that part of the Roman forces which had not been engaged in the battle. (Pol. iii. 70—74.)

From the view above given of the battle and the operations that preceded it, which coincides with that of General Vaudoncourt (*Campagnes d'Annibal en Italie,* vol. i. pp. 93—130), it seems certain that the battle itself was fought on the *left* bank of the Trebia, in the plain, but a short distance from the foot of the hills ; while the Roman camp was *on* the hills, and on the right bank of the Trebia. It is certain that this view affords much the most intelligible explanation of the operations of the armies, and there is nothing in the narrative of Polybius (which has been exclusively followed in the above account) *inconsistent* with it, though it must be admitted that some difficulties remain unexplained. Livy's narrative on the contrary is confused, and though based for the most part on that of Polybius, seems to be mixed up with that of other writers. (Liv. xxi. 52—56.) From his account of the retreat of the Roman army and of Scipio to Placentia after the battle, it seems certain that he considered the Roman camp to be situated on the left bank of the river, so that Scipio must necessarily cross it in order to arrive at Placentia, and therefore he must have conceived the battle as fought on the right bank : and this view has been adopted by many modern writers, including Niebuhr and Arnold ; but the difficulties in its way greatly exceed those which arise on the con-

trary hypothesis. Niebuhr indeed summarily disposes of some of these, by maintaining, in opposition to the distinct statements of Polybius, that Hannibal had crossed the Padus below Placentia, and that Sempronius joined Scipio from Genua and not from Ariminum. Such arbitary assumptions as these are worthless in discussing a question, the decision of which must rest mainly, if not entirely, on the authority of Polybius. (Niebuhr's *Lectures on Roman History* vol. ii. pp. 94—96 ; Arnold, *Hist. of Rome,* vol. iii. pp. 94—101.) Cramer adopts the views of General Vaudoncourt. (*Anct. Italy,* vol. i. p. 82.)

The battle on the Trebia is alluded to by Lucan, and described by Silius Italicus : it is noticed also by all the epitomisers of Roman history ; but none of these writers add anything to our knowledge of the details. (Lucan, ii. 46 ; Sil. Ital. iv. 484—666 ; Corn. Nep. *Hann.* 4 ; Eutrop. iii. 9 ; Oros. iv. 14 ; Flor. ii. 6. § 12.)   [E. H. B.]

TREBULA (Τρήβουλα: *Eth.* Trebulanus: *Treglia*), a city of Campania, situated in the district N. of the Vulturnus, in the mountain tract which extends from near *Cajazzo* (Calatia) to the Via Latina. Pliny terms the citizens "Trebulani cognomine Balinienses," probably to distinguish them from those of the two cities of the same name among the Sabines (Plin. iii. 5. s. 9) ; but the Campanian town seems to have been the most considerable of the three, and is termed simply Trebula by Ptolemy, as well as by Livy. The first mention of the name occurs in B. C. 303, when we are told that the Trebulani received the Roman franchise at the same time with the Arpinates. (Liv. x. 1.) There seems no doubt that the Campanian city is here meant : and this is quite certain in regard to the next notice in Livy, where he tells us that the three cities of Compulteria, Trebula, and Saticula, which had revolted to Hannibal, were recovered by Fabius in B. C. 215. (Id. xxiii. 39.) The "Trebulanus ager" is mentioned also by Cicero among the fertile districts of Campania, which Rullus proposed to distribute among the poorer Roman citizens (Cic. *de Leg. Agr.* ii. 25) ; and we learn from Pliny that it was noted for its wines, which had rapidly risen in estimation in his day. (Plin. xiv. 6. s. 8.) The Liber Coloniarum also mentions Trebula among the municipal towns of Campania. It appears to have received a fresh body of settlers under Augustus, but without attaining the rank of a colony. (*Lib. Col.* p. 238 ; Plin. iii. 5. s. 9 ; Ptol. iii. 1. § 68.) The site of Trebula, which was erroneously fixed by Cluverius and some local writers to the S. of the Vulturnus, appears to be correctly identified by local antiquarians with a place called *Treglia* or *Tregghia,* at the foot of the *Pizzo S. Salvatore,* about 6 miles N. of the Vulturnus and 8 NE. of *Capua.* There are said to be considerable ancient remains upon the spot, which together with the resemblance of name would seem clearly to establish the position of the ancient city. (Romanelli, vol. iii. pp. 575, 576 ; Trutta, *Antichità Allifane. Diss.* xxiii ; Abeken, *Mittel-Italien,* p. 99.)   [E. H. B.]

TREBULA (Τρήβουλα: *Eth.* Trebulanus), was the name of two cities or towns of the Sabines, apparently at no great distance from one another, which were called for the sake of distinction Trebula Mutusca and Trebula Suffenas.

1. TREBULA MUTUSCA, called by Virgil simply MUTUSCAE, while the full name is preserved to us by Pliny, the only author who mentions both places ("Trebulani qui cognominantur Mutuscaei, et qui

Suffenates," Plin. vi. 12. s. 17). Its site is clearly fixed at *Monte Leone*, sometimes called *Monte Leone della Sabina*, a village about 2 miles on the right of the Via Salaria, between *Osteria Nuova* and *Poggio S. Lorenzo*. Here there are considerable ruins, including those of a theatre, of thermae or baths, and portions of the ancient pavement. Several inscriptions have also been found here, some of which have the name of the people, "Plebs Trebulana," "Trebulani Mutuscani," and "Trebulani Mut.," so that no doubt can remain of their attribution. (Chaupy, *Maison d'Horace*, vol. iii. pp. 93—96; Orell. *Inscr.* 923, 3442, 3963.) As this seems to have been much the most considerable place of the two, it is probably that meant by Strabo, who mentions Trebula without any distinctive adjunct but in conjunction with Eretum (Strab. v. p. 228). The Liber Coloniarum also mentions a "Tribule, municipium" (p. 258) which is probably the same place. Martial also alludes to Trebula as situated among cold and damp mountain valleys (v. 72), but it is not certain which of the two places he here refers to. Virgil speaks of Mutusca as abounding in olives ("oliviferaeque Mutuscae," *Aen.* vii. 711), which is still the case with the neighbourhood of *Monte Leone*, and a village near it bears in consequence the name of *Oliveto*.

2. TREBULA SUFFENAS, the name of which is known only from Pliny, is of very uncertain site. Chaupy would place it at *Rocca Sinibaldi*, in the valley of the *Turano*, but this is mere conjecture. Guattani on the other hand fixes it on a hill near *Stroncone*, between *Rieti* and *Terni*, where there are said to be distinct traces of an ancient town. (Chaupy, *l.c.*; Guattani *Mon. della Sabina*, vol. i. p. 190.) It is probable that the Tribula (Τρίβολα) of Dionysius, mentioned by him among the towns assigned by Varro to the Aborigines (Dionys. i. 14) may be the same with the Trebula Suffenas of Pliny. In this case we know that it could not be far from Reate.   [E. H. B.]

TREIA (*Eth.* Treiensis: Ru. near *Treja*), a municipal town of Picenum, situated on the left bank of the river Potentia, about 9 miles below Septempeda (*S. Severino*) and 5 above Ricina. Pliny is the only geographer that mentions it; but it is probable that the Τραίανα of Ptolemy is only a corruption of its name. (Plin. iii. 13. s. 18; Ptol. iii. 1. § 52.) The Treienses are enumerated by Pliny among the municipal communities of Picenum, and the municipal rank of the town is further attested by several inscriptions. (Orell. *Inscr.* 516, 3899.) It seems indeed to have been a considerable place. The Itinerary of Antoninus places it on the branch of the Via Flaminia which led direct to Ancona: it was 9 miles from Septempeda and 18 from Auximum. (*Itin. Ant.* p. 312.) Cluverius says that he could find no trace either of the place or the name; but the ruins were pointed out by Holstenius as still existing on the left bank of the *Potenza*, at the foot of the hill occupied by the village of *Montecchio*. The latter place has since adopted the ancient name of *Treja*, and having been augmented by the population of several neighbouring villages, is now become a considerable town. (Cluver. *Ital.* p. 738; Holsten. *Not. ad Cluv.* p. 136.)   [E. H. B.]

TREMERUS INS. [DIOMEDEAE INSULAE.]

TRE'MITHUS (Τρεμιθοῦς, Steph. B. *s. v.*; Τρεμιθοῦς, Ptol. v. 14. § 6; Τρίμυθος, Constant. *de Them.* i. 15, p. 39, ed. Bonn; Τρεμιθούντων, Hierocl. p. 707: *Eth.* Τοεμιθούσιος, Τοεμιθοπολίτης), a town in the interior of Cyprus, was the seat of a bishopric and a place of some importance in the Byzantine times. According to the Peutinger Table it was 18 miles from Salamis, 24 from Citium, and 24 from Tamassus. Stephanus B. calls it a village of Cyprus, and derives its name from the turpentine trees (τερέβινθοι) which grew in its neighbourhood. (Engel, *Kypros*, vol. i. p. 148.)

TRE'MULA, a town in Mauretania Tingitana. (*Itin. Ant.* p. 24.) Variously identified with *Exadschen* and *Soe el Campa*.   [T. H. D.]

TREPONTIUM or TRIPUNTIUM, a place on the Appian Way near the entrance of the Pontine Marshes, 4 miles nearer Rome than Forum Appii. It is not mentioned as a station in the Itineraries, but we learn from an inscription of the time of Trajan that it was from thence the part of the road which was restored by that emperor began. This important work, as we are informed by another inscription, was continued for *nineteen miles*, a circumstance that explains the origin of the name of DECENNOVIUM, which occurs at a later period in connection with the Pontine Marshes. Procopius calls the Decennovium a *river;* but it is evident that it was in reality an artificial cut or canal, such as must always have accompanied the highroad through these marshes, and as we know already existed in the days of Horace from Forum Appii. The importance of this work will account for the circumstance that we find the Pontine Marshes themselves called by Cassiodorus "Decennovii Paludes." (Cassiod. *Var.* ii. 32, 33; Procop. *B. G.* i. 11.) The site of Trepontium is clearly marked at the distance of 39 miles from Rome, by the name of *Torre di Treponti*, together with the remains on the 3 ancient bridges, from which it derives its name (Chaupy, *Maison d'Horace*, vol. iii. pp. 387—392; D'Anville, *Analyse de l'Italia*, pp. 184—187.)

The inscriptions above cited are given by Sir R. Hoare, *Class. Tour*, vol. i. pp. 97, 98; and by the Aboé Chaupy (*l. c.*). The name of Τρανένtιον, found in Strabo (v. p. 237) among the cities on the left of the Appian Way, can hardly be other than a corruption of Trepontium, but it is wholly out of place in that passage, and is supposed by Kramer to be an interpolation.   [E. H. B.]

TRERES (Τρῆρες), a people repeatedly mentioned by Strabo, generally as a tribe of, or at least, as closely connected with, the Cimmerii, but in a few passages as Thracians. They are not named by Homer or Herodotus. Strabo was evidently undecided whether to regard them as a distinct race, or as identical with the Cimmerii, in whose company they several times made destructive inroads into Asia Minor. "The Cimmerii, whom they name Treres also, or some tribe of them, often overran the southern shores of the Euxine and the adjoining countries, sometimes throwing themselves upon the Paphlagonians, at other times upon the Phrygians, at the time when they say Midas died from drinking bull's blood. And Lygdamis led his army as far as Lydia and Ionia, and took Sardes, but perished in Cilicia. And the Cimmerii and Treres often made such expeditions. But they say that the Treres and Cobus [their leader] were at last driven out [of Asia] by Madys, the king of the Scythians."[*] (Strab. i. p. 61). "Callisthenes states

---

[*] The reading in the text is ὑπὸ Μάδυος τοῦ τῶν Κιμμερίων βασιλέως; but as just before we find Μάδυος τοῦ Σκυθικοῦ, we can have no hesita-

that Sardes was taken several times; first by the
Cimmerians; then by the Treres and Lycians, as
Callinus also shows; lastly in the time of Cyrus and
Croesus." (Id. xiii. p. 627). "In olden times, it
befel the Magnetes [the people of Magnesia on the
Maeander] to be utterly destroyed by the Treres,
a Cimmerian tribe." (Id. xiv. p. 647; see also xi.
p. 511, xii. p. 573; CIMMERII, Vol. I. p. 623, seq.;
Müller, *Hist. Lit. Anc. Greece*, pp. 108, 109; and
cf. Herod. i. 6, 15, 16, 103.)

Various attempts have been made to fix the dates
of these events; but the means of doing so appear
to be wanting, and hence scholars have arrived at
very different conclusions on the subject. Strabo
infers from some expressions of Callinus that the
destruction of Sardes preceded that of Magnesia,
which latter occurred, he considers, after the time
of that poet, and during the age of Archilochus,
who alludes to it.

Thucydides (ii. 96) states that the kingdom of
Sitalces was bounded on the side next to the Triballi
by the Treres and Tilataei, who dwelt on the northern
slope of Mount Scombrus (Scomius), and extended
towards the W. as far as the river Oscius (Oescus).
Whether this relative clause applies to the Treres
as well as to the Tilataei is doubtful; but the col-
location of the words seems to confine it to the
latter.

Strabo (i. p. 59) speaks of the Treres as dwelling
with the Thracians; and says that the Treres, who
were Thracians, possessed a part of the Troad after
the time of Priam (xiii. p. 586).

Pliny does not mention the Treres as a Thracian
people; but in the description of Macedonia (iv. 10.
s. 17), says that they, with the Dardani and Pieres,
dwelt on its borders; it is not clear, however, which
borders are meant. (Cf. Theopom. *Frag.* 313,
where they are called Τρᾶρες; and Steph. B. p. 664,
where also a district of Thrace inhabited by them is
named Τρῆρος.)

It is possible that these Thracian Treres were the
descendants of a body of the Cimmerian Treres, left
N. of the Haemus when the main body advanced to
Asia Minor; for there can be little doubt that Niebuhr's view respecting the course of their inroads is
correct. "The general opinion, which is presupposed
in Herodotus also, is that the Cimmerians invaded
Asia Minor from the E., along the coasts of the
Euxine. But it would seem that, on the contrary,
they came through Thrace, for they make their first
appearance in Ionia and Lydia. The former road is
almost entirely impassable for a nomadic people, as
the Caucasus extends to the very shores of the
Euxine." (*Lect. Anc. Hist.* i. p. 32, note.)

In confirmation of the conjecture above made, we
may refer to the parallel case mentioned by Caesar
(*B. G.* ii. 29), that the Aduatuci, a Belgian tribe,
were the descendants of the 6000 men whom the
Cimbri and Teutoni, on their march towards Italy,
left behind them W. of the Rhine, to guard that part
of their property which they were unable to take with
them any farther.   [J. R.]

TRERUS (Τρῆρος, Strab.: *Sacco*), a river of Latium, and one of the principal tributaries of the Liris
(*Garigliano*), into which it discharges its waters
close to the ruins of Fabrateria. (Strab. v. p. 237.)
Its name is mentioned only by Strabo, but there is
no doubt of its identification: it is still called the

Tolero in the lower part of its course, near its junction with the *Garigliano*, but more commonly known
as the *Sacco*. It has its sources in the elevated
plain which separates the mountains about Praeneste from the Volscian group; and the broad valley
through which it flows for above 40 miles before it
joins the *Garigliano* must always have formed a
remarkable feature in this part of Italy. Throughout its extent it separates the main or central
ranges of the Apennines from the outlying mass of
the *Monti Lepini* or Volscian mountains, and hence
it must, from an early period, have constituted one
of the natural lines of communication between the
plains of Latium proper (the modern *Campagna di
Roma*) and those of Campania. After the whole
district had fallen under the power of Rome it was
the line followed by the great highroad called the
Via Latina. [VIA LATINA.]   [E. H. B.]

TRES ARBORES, the Three Trees, was a Mutatio or relay for horses mentioned in the Jerusalem
Itin. between Vasatae and Elusa (*Eause*). The
site is unknown.   [G. L.]

TRES TABERNAE, was the name of a station
on the Via Appia, between Aricia and Forum Appii,
which is noticed not only in the Itineraries (*Itin.
Ant.* p. 107; *Tab. Peut.*), but by Cicero and in
the Acts of the Apostles. From the former we
learn that a branch road from Antium joined the
Appian Way at this point (Cic. *ad Att.* ii. 12);
while in the latter it is mentioned as the place
where many of the disciples met St. Paul on his
journey to Rome. (*Acts*, xxviii. 15.) It was
probably therefore a village or place of some importance from the traffic on the Appian Way. Its
position would appear to be clearly determined by
the Antonine Itinerary, which gives 17 miles from
Aricia to Tres Tabernae, and 10 from thence to
Forum Appii: and it is a strong confirmation of
the accuracy of these data that the distance thus
obtained from Forum Appii to Rome corresponds
exactly with the true distance of that place, as
marked by ruins and ancient milestones. It is
therefore wholly unnecessary to change the distances
in the Itinerary, as proposed by D'Anville and
Chaupy, and we may safely fix Tres Tabernae at
a spot about 3 miles from the modern *Cisterna*, on
the road to *Terracina*, and very near the commencement of the Pontine Marshes. The Abbé
Chaupy himself points out the existence of ancient
remains on this spot, which he supposes to be those
of the station Ad Sponsas mentioned only in the
Jerusalem Itinerary. It is far more likely that
they are those of Tres Tabernae; if indeed the two
stations be not identical, which is very probable.
This situation would also certainly accord better
than that proposed by Chaupy with the mention of
Tres Tabernae in Cicero, who there joined the
Appian Way on his road from Antium to his
Formian villa, not to Rome. (Cic. *ad Att.* ii. 12,
13, 14; Chaupy, *Maison d'Horace*, vol. iii. p. 383;
D'Anville, *Analyse de l'Italie*, p. 195; Westphal,
Röm. Kampagne, p. 69.)   [E. H. B.]

TRES TABERNAE, in Gaul. [TABERNAE.]

TRETA (Τρῆτα, Strab. xiv. p. 683), in Cyprus,
called Τρῆτοι in the *Stadiasmus Maris Magni* (p.
285, ed. Hoffmann), where it is placed 50 stadia
from Palaepaphus or Old Paphus, was apparently a
promontory in the SW. of the island, and probably
the same as the one called Φρούριον by Ptolemy (v.
14. § 2).

TRETUM (Τρῆτον ἄκρον, Ptol. iv. 3. § 3), a

promontory of Numidia at the W. point of the Sinus Oleachites. (Strab. xvii. p. 829, 832.) It probably derived its name from the numerous caves in the cliffs, which are still the lurking places of the piratical tribes of this coast. Now *Sebba Rus.*   [T. H. D.]

TRETUM PROM. (Τρητόν, *Stadiasm.* §327), the NW. promontory of Crete now called *Grabiusa*, the CORYCUS of Ptolemy.   [E. B. J.]

TRETUS. [ARGOS, p. 201, b.]

TREVA (Τρηοϐα), a town of the Saxones in north-western Germany (Ptol. ii. 11. § 27), which must have been situated somewhere in the *Trave*, but as no further details are known, it is impossible to fix its site with any degree of certainty.   [L. S.]

TREVENTUM or TEREVENTUM (Eth. Treventinus, Plin.; but inscriptions have Terventinas and Tereventinas: *Trivento*), a town of Samnium, in the country of the Pentri, situated on the right bank of the Trinius (*Trigno*), not far from the frontiers of the Frentani. Its name is not noticed in history, but Pliny mentions it among the municipal towns of Samnium in his time: and we learn from the Liber Coloniarum that it received a Roman colony, apparently under the Triumvirate (Plin. iii. 14. s. 17; *Lib. Colon.* p. 238). It is there spoken of as having been thrice besieged ("ager ejus ... post tertiam obsidionem adsignatus est"), probably during the Social War and the civil wars that followed; but we have no other account of these sieges; and the name is not elsewhere mentioned. But from existing remains, as well as inscriptions, it appears to have been a place of considerable importance, as well as of municipal rank. The modern *Trivento*, which is still the see of a bishop and the capital of the surrounding district, stands on a hill above the river *Trigno*, but the ruins of ancient buildings and fragments of masonry are scattered to a considerable extent through the valley below it. (Romanelli, vol. ii. p. 473.) The inscriptions which have been discovered there are given by Mommsen (*Inscr. R. N.* pp. 269, 270).   [E. H. B.]

TREVERI or TREVIRI (Τρηούϊροι, Τριϐηροι, Ptol.). There is authority for both forms of the name. The position of the Treviri is determined by several passages of Caesar. The Treviri bordered on the Rhine (*B. G.* iii. 11, iv. 10), and south of them along the Rhine were the Triboci or Tribocci. The Arduenna Silva extended through the middle of the territory of the Treviri from the Rhine to the commencement of the territory of the Remi (*B. G.* v. 3). The Treviri were separated from the Germans by the Rhine (*B. G.* vii. 63, viii. 25); the Ubii were their neighbours on the opposite side of the Rhine (*B. G.* vi. 29, 35). In Caesar's time the Treviri differed little from the Germans in their way of living and their savage temper. Tacitus remarks (*de Mor. Germ.* c. 28) that the Treviri and Nervii affected a Germanic origin, and it is probable that the Treviri were mixed with Germans, but Caesar supposed them to be a Gallic people. Mela (iii. 2) calls them the most renowned of the Belgae. When Hieronymus speaks of the resemblance between the language of the Galatae of Asia and of the Treviri, he means to say that the Treviri are Galli [GALATIA, Vol. I. p. 931]. Strabo (iv. p. 194) speaks of the Nervii as being German. He says: " The Nervii are neighbours of the Treviri, and they (the Nervii) are also a German people;" which remark about the Nervii being also German does not refer to the Treviri, but to the Triboci, whom he had just spoken of as a German nation which had settled on the Gallic side of the Rhine.

It seems impossible to determine whether Caesar includes the Treviri among the Belgae or the Celtae. Some geographers include them in the Gallia of Caesar in the limited sense, that is, in the country of the Celtae, which lay between the *Garonne* and the *Seine*, and between the Ocean and the Rhine. If this determination is correct, the Mediomatrici also of course belong to Caesar's Gallia in the limited sense. [MEDIOMATRICI.]

The Treviri are often mentioned by Caesar, for they had a strong body of cavalry and infantry, and often gave him trouble. From one passage (*B. G.* vi. 32) it appears that the Segni and Condrusi, German settlers in Gallia, were between the Treviri and the Eburones; and the Condrusi and Eburones were dependents of the Treviri (*B. G.* iv. 6). Caesar constructed his bridges over the Rhine in the territory of the Treviri (*B. G.* vi. 9); and Strabo speaks of a bridge over the Rhine in the territory of the Treviri. It appears then that the Treviri occupied a large tract of country between the Mosa (*Maas*) and the Rhine, which country was intersected by the lower course of the Mosella (*Mosel*), for Augusta Trevirorum (*Trier*), on the Mosella, was the chief town of the Treviri in the Roman imperial period and probably a town of the Treviri in Caesar's time. It is not possible to fix the exact limits of the Treviri on the Rhine, either to the north or the south. When the Germans were settled on the west side of the Rhine by Agrippa and after his time, the Treviri lost part of their territory; and some modern writers maintain that they lost all their country on the Rhine, a conclusion derived from a passage of Pliny (iv. c. 17), but a conclusion by no means certain. Another passage of Pliny, cited by Suetonius (*Calig.* c. 8), says that Caligula was born " in Treveris, vico Ambiatino, supra Confluentes," and this passage places the Treviri on the Rhine. Ptolemy in his geography gives the Treviri no place on the Rhine: he assigns the land on the west bank of the river to the Germania Inferior and Germania Superior. The bishopric of *Trier* used to extend from the *Maas* to the *Rhine*, and along the Rhine from the *Ahr* below *Andernach* as far south as *Bingen*. The limits of the old country of the Treviri and of the diocese may have been the same, for we find many examples of this coincidence in the geography of Gallia. The rugged valley of the *Ahr* would be a natural boundary of the Treviri on the north.

Tacitus gives the Treviri the name of Socii (*Ann.* i. 63); and in his time, and probably before, they had what the Romans called a Curia or senate. The name of the Treviri often appears in the history of the war with Civilis (Tacit. *Hist.* iv.). The Treviri under the Empire were in that part of Gallia which was named Belgica, and their city Augusta Trevirorum was the chief place, and under the later emperors frequently an imperial residence. [AUGUSTA TREVIRORUM.]   [G. L.]

TREVIDON, a place in Gallia, mentioned by Sidonius Apollinaris (*Propempt.*), the position of which is partly determined by the fact of the poet fixing Trevidon in the mountainous region of Central France, and partly by the existence of a place named *Trève* on the boundary of the old province of *Rouergue*, and on a little river named *Trevesel.* The mountain in which the *Trevesel* rises (*Lesperou*) is the

" Vicinum nimis heu ! jugum Rutenis "

of Sidonius. [RUTENI.]   [G. L.]

TREVIRI. [TREVERI.]

TRIACONTASCHOENUS (Τριακοντάσχοινος, Ptol. iv. 7. § 32), a district so named by Ptolemy after the analogy of the Dodecaschoenus of Egypt, and forming the most northern part of Aethiopia on the W. side of the Nile, between the cataracts of that river and the Aethiopian mountains. [T.H.D.]

TRIADITZA (Τριάδιτζα; Nicet. Chon. iii. p. 214; Apost. Geog. Huds. iv. p. 43), a town in Upper Moesia, at the confluence of the sources of the Oescus, and the capital of the district called in late times Dacia Interior. It was situated in a fertile plain, and its site is identified with that of some extensive ruins S. of Sophia.   [J. R.]

TRIBALLI (Τριβαλλοί), a Thracian people which appears to have been in early times a very widely diffused and powerful race, about the Danube; but which, being pressed upon from the N. and W. by various nations, became gradually more and more confined, and at length entirely disappeared from history. Herodotus speaks of the Triballic plain, through which flowed the river Angrus, which fell into the Brongus, a tributary of the Ister (iv. 49). This is probably the plain of Kossovo in the modern Servia.

Thucydides states (ii. 96) that on the side of the Triballi, who were independent at the beginning of the Peloponnesian War, the territories of Sitalces were bounded by the Treres and Tilataei, whose W. limit was the river Oscius (Oescus), which must therefore, at that time, have been the E. frontier of the Triballi. (Cf. Plin. iii. 29, iv. 17; Strab. vii. pp. 317, 318.) Strabo (vii. p. 305) informs us that the Triballi were much exposed to the inroads of migrating hordes driven out of their own countries by more powerful neighbours, some expelled by the Scythians, Bastarnae, and Sauromatae, from the N. side of the Danube, who either settled in the islands of that river, or crossed over into Thrace; others from the W., set in motion by the Illyrians.

The earliest event recorded of them is the defeat which they gave to Sitalces, king of the Odrysae, who made an expedition against them, B. C. 424, in which he lost his life (Thuc. iv. 101). In B.C. 376 the Triballi crossed the Haemus, and with 30.000 men advanced as far S. as the territory of Abdera, which they ravaged without opposition. On their return, however, loaded with booty, the people of Abdera took advantage of their careless and disorderly march, to attack them, killing upwards of 2000 men. The Triballi thereupon marched back to take revenge for this loss; and the Abderites, having been joined by some of the neighbouring Thracians, gave them battle; in the midst of which they were deserted by their treacherous allies and, being surrounded, were slain almost to a man. The Triballi then prepared to lay siege to Abdera which would now have been quite unable to resist them for more than a very short time; but at this critical moment, Chabrias appeared before the town with the Athenian fleet, which had recently defeated the Lacedaemonian fleet at Naxos. Chabrias compelled the Triballi to retire from Abdera, and garrisoned the city when he departed. (Diod. xv. 36). In B.C. 339, Philip II., after raising the siege of Byzantium, marched to the Danube, where he defeated the Getae, and took much booty. On his return through the country of the Triballi, the latter posted themselves in a defile, and refused to allow the Macedonian army to pass, unless Philip gave to them a part of the plunder. A fierce battle ensued, in which Philip

was severely wounded, and would have been slain, but for his son Alexander, who threw himself before his father, and thus saved his life. The Triballi were at length defeated, and probably professed submission to Philip, so long, at least, as he was in their country.

On Alexander's accession to the throne, he thought it necessary to make his power felt by the barbarians on the frontiers of his kingdom, before he quitted Europe for his great enterprise against the Persian empire. Accordingly, in the spring of B. C. 335, he marched from Amphipolis in a north-easterly direction, at the head of a large force. In ten days he reached the pass by which he intended to cross the Haemus, where a body of Thracians had assembled to oppose his progress. They were defeated, and Alexander advanced against the Triballi, whose prince, Syrmus, having had timely information of Alexander's movements, had already withdrawn, with the old men, women, and children into an island of the Danube, called Peuce, where many other Thracians also had sought refuge. The main force of the Triballi posted themselves in woody ground on the banks of the river Lyginus, about 3 days' march from the Danube. Having ventured out into the open plain, however, they were completely defeated by the Macedonians, with a loss of 3000 men. (Arrian, Anab. i. 2.)

Alexander then marched to the Danube, opposite to Peuce; but he was unable to make himself master of that island, because he had few boats, and the enemy were strongly posted at the top of the steep sides of the island. Alexander therefore abandoned the attempt to take it, and crossed the Danube to make war on the Getae. It would appear, however, that he had made sufficient impression on the Triballi to induce them to apply to him for peace, which he granted before his return to Macedonia. It was probably some time after these events that the Triballi were attacked by the Autariatae, a powerful Illyrian tribe, who seem to have completely subdued them, great numbers being killed, and the survivors driven farther towards the east. (Strab. vii. pp. 317, 318.) Hence, in B. c. 295, the Gauls, with only 15,000 foot and 3000 horse, defeated the combined forces of the Triballi and Getae (Just. xxv. 1.) When the Romans began to extend their dominion in the direction of the Danube, the Triballi were a small and weak people, dwelling about the confluence of the Oescus with the Danube, near the town Oescus (cf. Ptol. iii. 10. § 10, viii. 11. § 6).

Pliny (vii. 2) states that, according to Isigonus, there were people among the Triballi who fascinated by their look, and destroyed those whom they gazed upon too long, especially with angry eyes : adults were more liable to be injured by them than children. This is probably the same superstition as the modern one respecting the "evil eye," which is peculiarly prevalent among the Slavonian races. (Arrian, Anab. i. 1. § 4, 2. § 4, seqq., 3. § 3, seq., 4. § 6, v. 26. § 6, vii. 9. § 2 ; Steph. B. s. v.; Mannert, vii. p. 25, seqq.]   [J. R.]

TRIBOCI or TRIBOCCI, a German people in Gallia. Schneider (Caesar, B. G. i. 51) has the form " Triboces " in the accusative plural. Pliny has Tribochi, and Strabo Tribocchi (Τριβόκχοι). In the passage of Caesar (B. G. iv. 10) it is said that all the MSS. have " Tribucorum " (Schneider, note).

The Triboci were in the army of the German king Ariovistus in the great battle in which Caesar defeated him; and though Caesar does not say that they were Germans, his narrative shows that he considered them to be Germans. In another passage (*B. G.* iv. 10) Caesar places the Triboci on the Rhine between the Mediomatrici and the Treviri, and he means to place them on the left or Gallic side of the Rhine. Strabo (iv. p. 193), after mentioning the Sequani and Mediomatrici as extending to the Rhine, says, " Among them a German people has settled, the Tribocchi, who have passed over from their native land." Pliny also (iv. 17) and Tacitus (*German.* c. 28) say that the Tribocci are Germans. The true conclusion from Caesar is that he supposed the Tribocci to be settled in Gallia before B. C. 58.

Ptolemy (ii. 9. § 17) places the Tribocci in Upper Germania, but he incorrectly places the Vangiones between the Nemetes and the Tribocci, for the Nemetes bordered on the Tribocci. However he places the Tribocci next to the Rauraci, and he names Breucomagus (Brocomagus) and Elcebus (Helcebus) as the two towns of the Tribocci. D'Anville supposes that the territory of the Tribocci corresponded to the diocese of *Strassburg.* Saletio (*Seltz* or *Sets*), we may suppose, belonged to the Nemetes, as in modern times it belonged to the diocese of *Speier;* and it is near the northern limits of the diocese of *Strassburg.* On the south towards the Rauraci, a place named *Markelsheim*, on the southern limit of the diocese of *Strassburg* and bordering on that of *Basle*, indicates a boundary by a Teutonic name (*mark*), as Fines does in those parts of Gallia where the Roman tongue prevailed. The name of the Tribocci does not appear in the Notit. Provinc., though the names of the Nemetes and Vangiones are there; but instead of the Tribocci we have Civitas Argentoratum (*Strassburg*), the chief place of the Tribocci. Ptolemy makes Argentoratum a city of the Vangiones. [G.L.]

TRI'BOLA (Τριβόλα, App. *Hisp.* 62, 63), a town of Lusitania, in the mountainous regions S. of the Tagus, probably the modern *Trevoens.* [T.H.D.]

TRIBULIUM. [TRILURIUM.]

TRIBUNCI, a place in Gallia, which we may assume to have been near Concordia, for Ammianus (xvi. 12), after speaking of the battle near *Strassburg*, in which Chnodomarius, king of the Alemanni, was defeated by Julian, says that the king hurried to his camp, which was near Concordia and Tribunci. But neither the site of Concordia nor of Tribunci is certain. [CONCORDIA.] [G. L.]

TRICARA'NUM. [PHLIUS, p. 602, a.]

TRICASSES, a people of Gallia Lugdunensis. (Plin. iv. 18.) In Ptolemy (ii. 8. § 13) the name is Tricasii (Τρικάσιοι), and their city is Augustobona (Αὐγουστόβονα). They border on the Parisii. The name appears in the form Tricassini in Ammianus (xvi. 1) and in an inscription. In the Notit. Provinc. the name Civitas Tricassium occurs; and the name of the people has been transferred to the town, which is now *Troyes* on the *Seine*, the chief town of the French department of *Aube.* Caesar does not mention the Tricasses, and his silence has led to the conjecture that in his time they were comprised within the powerful state of the Senones. [G. L.]

TRICASTI'NI (Τρικαστινοί), a Gallic people between the Rhone and the Alps. Livy (v. 34) describing the march of Bellovesus and his Galli into Italy, says they came to the Tricastini: " The Alps next were opposed to them;" from which it is inferred that the Tricastini were near the Alps. But nothing exact can be inferred from the narrative, nor from the rest of this confused chapter. In the

description of Hannibal's march (Liv. xxi. 34) it is said that Hannibal, after settling the disputes of the Allobroges, being now on his road to the Alps, did not make his march straight forward, but turned to the left into the territory of the Tricastini; and from the country of the Tricastini he went through the uttermost part of the territory of the Vocontii into the country of the Tricorii, and finally reached the Druentia (*Durance.*) It would be out of place to examine this question fully, for it would require some pages to discuss the passages in Livy. He means, however, to place the Tricastini somewhere between the Allobroges and part of the border of the Vocontian territory. The capital of the Vocontii is Dea Vocontiorum, or *Die* in the department of *Drome ;* and the conclusion is that the Tricastini were somewhere between the Isara (*Isère*) and the Druna (*Drome*). This agrees with the position of Augusta Tricastinorum [AUGUSTA TRICASTINORUM] as determined by the Itins.

Ptolemy (ii. 10. § 13) places the Tricastini east of the Segallauni, whose capital is Valentia, and he names as the capital of the Tricastini a town Noeomagus, which appears to be a different place from Augusta Tricastinorum. D'Anville places the Tricastini along the east bank of the Rhone, north of Arausio (*Orange*), a position which he fixes by his determination of Augusta Tricastinorum; and he adds, " that the name of the Tricastini has been preserved pure in that of *Tricastin.*" But the Tricastini of Livy and Ptolemy are certainly not where D'Anville places them. [G. L.]

TRICCA (Τρίκκη : *Eth.* Τρικκαῖος : *Trikkala*), an ancient city of Thessaly in the district Histiaeotis, stood upon the left bank of the Peneius, and near a small stream named Lethaeus. (Strab. ix. p. 438, xiv. p. 647.) This city is said to have derived its name from Tricca, a daughter of Peneius. (Steph. B. s. v.) It is mentioned in Homer as subject to Podaleirius and Machaon, the two sons of Asclepius or Aesculapius, who led the Triccaeans to the Trojan War (Hom. *Il.* ii. 729, iv. 202); and it possessed a temple of Asclepius, which was regarded as the most ancient and illustrious of all the temples of this god. (Strab. ix. p. 437.) This temple was visited by the sick, whose cures were recorded there, as in the temples of Asclepius at Epidaurus and Cos. (Strab. viii. p. 374.) There were probably physicians attached to the temple; and Leake gives an inscription in four elegiac verses, to the memory of a "god-like physician named Cimber, by his wife Andromache," which he found upon a marble in a bridge over the ancient Lethaeus. (*Northern Greece*, vol. iv. p. 285.) In the edict published by Polysperchon and the other generals of Alexander, after the death of the latter, allowing the exiles from the different Greek cities to return to their homes, those of Tricca and of the neighbouring town of Pharcadon were excepted for some reason, which is not recorded. (Diod. xviii. 56.) Tricca was the first town in Thessaly at which Philip V. arrived after his defeat on the Aous. (Liv. xxxii. 13.) Tricca is also mentioned by Liv. xxxvi. 13 ; Plin. iv. 8. s. 15 ; Ptol. iii. 13. § 44 ; Them. *Orat.* xxvii. p. 333. Procopius, who calls the town Tricattūs (Τρικάττους), says that it was restored by Justinian (*de Aedif.* iv. 3); but it is still called Tricca by Hierocles (p. 642) in the sixth century, and the form in Justinian may be a corruption. In the twelfth century it already bears its modern name (Τρίκκαλα, Anna Comn. v. p. 137, ed. Paris.; Eustath. *ad Il.* ii. p.

330.) *Trikkala* is now one of the largest towns in this part of Greece. The castle occupies a hill projecting from the last falls of the mountain of *Khassiá*; but the only traces of the ancient city which Leake could discover were some small remains of Hellenic masonry, forming part of the wall of the castle, and some squared blocks of stone of the same ages dispersed in different parts of the town. (Leake, *Northern Greece*, vol. i. p. 425, seq., vol. iv. p. 287.)

TRICCIA'NA, a place in Pannonia, in the valley called Cariniana (*It. Ant.* p. 267). It is probably the same as the Gurtiana noticed in the Peut. Table, as the difference in the statements about the distances amounts only to 2 miles.   [L. S.]

TRICESIMAE, in Gallia, one of the places mentioned by Ammianus Marcellinus (xviii. 2) in the list of those places along the Rhenish frontier which Julian repaired. Ammianus mentions Tricesimae between Quadriburgium and Novesium. [QUADRIBURGIUM.]   [G. L.]

TRICESIMUM, AD, in Gallia. D'Anville observes that the ancient Itins. contain many positions with similar names, which names of places are derived from the distances which they indicate from the principal towns; for the distances within the dependent territory were measured from the principal towns. This Tricesimum is measured from Narbo (*Narbonne*), as the Jerusalem Itin. shows, on the road to *Toulouse*, through *Carcassonne*. *Trebes* on the canal of Languedoc may represent the name; and Tricesimum may be near that place. [G. L.]

TRICHO'NIS LACUS. [AETOLIA, p. 64, a.]

TRICHO'NIUM (Τριχώνιον: *Eth.* Τριχωνιεύς), a town of Aetolia, from which the lake Trichonis derived its name. [Respecting the lake, see Vol. I. p. 64, a.] Its position is uncertain. Leake places it S. of the lake at a place called *Gavala*, and Kiepert, in his map E. of the lake. But since Strabo mentions it along with Stratus as situated in a fertile plain, it ought probably to be placed N. of the lake (Strab. x. p. 450; Pol. v. 7; Steph. B. *s. v.*). It was evidently a place of importance, and several natives of this town are mentioned in history. (Pol. iv. 3, v. 13, xvii. 10; Paus. ii. 37. § 3; Leake, *Northern Greece*, vol. i. p. 155.)

TRICOLO'NI. [MEGALOPOLIS, p. 309.]

TRICO'MIA (Τρικωμία), a place in the eastern part of Phrygia, on the road from Dorylaeum to Apamea Cibotus (Ptol. v. 2. § 22; *Tab. Peut.*), is placed by the Table at a distance of 28 miles from Midaeum and 21 from Pessinus.   [L. S.]

TRICORII (Τρικόριοι), a people between the Rhone and the Alps. Hannibal in his march from the Rhone to the Alps passed into the country of the Tricorii, as Livy says [TRICASTINI]. Strabo (iv. pp. 185, 203) says in one passage that above the Cavares are "the Vocontii and Tricorii and Iconii and Meduli," from which we learn that he considered the Tricorii as neighbours of the Vocontii; and in another passage he says, "after the Vocontii are the Iconii and Tricorii, and next to them the Meduli, who occupy the highest summits of the Alps." Some geographers conclude that the Tricorii must be on the *Drac*, a branch of the *Isère*, in the southern part of the diocese of *Grénoble*, But if the Tricorii were in the valley of the *Drac*, we do not therefore admit that Hannibal's march to the Alps was through that valley.   [G. L.]

TRICORNE'NSII. [TRICORNIUM.]

TRICO'RNIUM (Τρικόρνιον, Ptol. iii. 9. § 3), or TRICORNIA CASTRA (*Itin. Hieros.* p. 564), a town in the territory of the Tricornensii, a people of Upper Moesia, on the borders of Illyria.. Variously identified with *Ritopk* and *Tricorni* or *Kolumbacs*.   [T. H. D.]

TRICORYTHUS [MARATHON.]

TRICRANA (Τρίκρανα), an island off the coast of Hermionis in Argolis (Paus. ii. 34. § 8), perhaps the same as the Tiparenus of Pliny. [TIPARENUS.]

TRICRE'NA. [PHENEUS, p. 595, a.]

TRIDENTI'NI (Τριδεντίνοι), an Alpine tribe occupying the southern part of Rhaetia, in the north of Lacus Benacus, about the river Athesis. (Strab. iv. p. 204; Plin. iii. 23.) They, with many other Alpine tribes, were subdued in the reign of Augustus.   [L. S.]

TRIDENTUM or TRIDENTE (Τριδέντε: *Trento* or *Trent*), the capital of the Tridentini in the south of Rhaetia, on the eastern bank of the Athesis, and on the highroad from Verona to Veldidena. (Plin. iii. 23; Justin, xx. 5; *It. Ant.* pp. 275, 281; Paul. Diac. i. 2, iii. 9, iv. 42, v. 36; Flor. iii. 3; Ptol. iii. 1. § 31; *Tab. Peut.*) The town is said to have derived its name from the trident of Neptune, which is still shown fixed in the wall of the ancient church of S. Vigil. The place seems to have been made a Roman colony (Orelli, *Inscript.* Nos. 2183, 3744, 3905, 4823). Theodoric the Great surrounded Tridentum with a wall, of which a considerable portion still exists. (Comp. Pallhausen, *Beschreib. der Röm. Heerstrasse von Verona nach Augsburg*, p. 28, foll.; Benedetto Giovanelli, *Discorso sopra un' Iscrizione Trentina*, Trento, 1824, and by the same author, *Trento, Citta de' Resj e Colonia Romana*, Trento, 1825.)   [L. S.]

TRIE'RES (Τριήρης, Polyb. v. 68; Strab. xvi. p. 754), a small fortified place in Phoenicia, on the northern declivity of Lebanon, and about 12 miles distant from Tripolis. It is in all probability the same place as the Tridis of the *Itin. Hierosol.* (p. 583). Lapie identifies it with *Enty*, others with *Belmont*.   [T. H. D.]

TRIE'RUM (Τριήρων or Τρίηρον ἄκρον, Ptol. iv. 3. § 13), a headland of the Regio Syrtica in Africa, Propria. Ritter (*Erdk.* i. p. 928) identifies it with the promontory of Cephalae mentioned by Strabo (xvii. p. 836), the present *Cape Cefalo* or *Mesurata*. Ptolemy indeed mentions this as a separate and adjoining promontory; but as *Cefalo* still exhibits three points, it is possible that the ancient names may be connected, and refer only to this one cape. (See Blaquiere, *Letters from the Mediterranean*, i. p. 18; Della Cella, *Viaggio*, p. 61.) [T. H. D.]

TRIFANUM. [VESCIA.]

TRIGABOLI. [PADUS.]

TRIGISAMUM, a town of Noricum, mentioned only in the Peuting. Table, as situated not far from the mouth of the river Trigisamus (*Trasen*), which flows into the Danubius. It still bears the name of *Traismaur*. (See Muchar, *Noricum*, vol. i. p. 269.)   [L. S.]

TRIGLYPHON (Τρίγλυφον τὸ καὶ Τρίλιγγον, Ptol. vii. 2. § 23), the metropolis and royal residence (βασίλειον) of Cirrhadia, a district at the NE. corner of the *Bay of Bengal*. It is doubtless the present *Tipperah* (*Tripúra*), which is situated on the *Gumpty* (*Gomáti*), a small river which flows into the *Brachmaputra* near its mouth.   [V.]

TRIGUNDUM, a place in the territory of the Callaici Lucenses, in Gallaecia. (Hispania Tarraconensis). (*Itin. Ant.* p. 424.) Variously identified with *Berreo* and *Arandon*.   [T. H. D.]

TRILEUCUM (Τρίλευκον ἄκρον, Ptol. ii. 6. § 4), a promontory in the territory of the Callaici Lucenses, on the N. coast of Hispania Tarraconensis, known also by the name of Κάρου ἄκρον. (Marcian, p. 44.) Now Cape Ortegal.   [T. H. D.]

TRIMA'MMIUM (Τριμμάριον or Τριμάμμιον, Ptol. iii. 10. § 10), a castle on the Danube, in Lower Moesia. (Itin. Ant. p. 222; called Trimamium in the Tab. Peut. and by the Geogr. Rav. iv. 7.) Variously identified with Murotín, Dikalika, and the ruins near Pirgo or Birgos. [T. H. D.]

TRIMENOTHYRA. [TEMENOTHYRA.]

COIN OF TRIMENOTHYRA.

TRIMONTIUM (Τριμόντιον, Ptol. ii. 3. § 8), a town of the Selgovae, in Britannia Barbara, probably near Longholm, in the neighbourhood of the Solway Frith.   [T. H. D.]

TRI'MYTHUS. [TREMITHUS.]

TRINA'CIA. [TYRACIA.]

TRINA'CRIA. [SICILIA.]

TRINA'SUS (Τρίνασος, Paus. iii. 22. § 3 : Τρίνασσος, Ptol. iii. 16. § 9), a town or rather fortress of Laconia, situated upon a promontory near the head of the Laconian gulf, and 30 stadia above Gythium. It is opposite to three small rocks, which gave their name to the place. The modern village is for the same reason still called Trínisa (τὰ Τρίνησα). There are considerable remains of the ancient walls. The place was built in a semi-circular form, and was not more than 400 or 500 yards in circuit. (Leake, Morea, vol. i. p. 232 ; Boblaye, Recherches, &c. p. 94 ; Ross, Wanderungen in Griechenland, vol. ii. p. 239; Curtius, Peloponnesos, vol. ii. p. 287.)

TRINEMEIA. [ATTICA, p. 330, b.]

TRI'NIUS (Trigno), a considerable river of Samnium, which has its sources in the rugged mountain district between Agnone and Castel di Sangro, and has a course of about 60 miles from thence to the Adriatic. During the lower part of its course it traverses the territory of the Frentani, and falls into the sea about 5 miles SE. of Histonium (Il Vasto). The only ancient writer who mentions it is Pliny (iii. 12. s. 17), who calls it " flumen portuosum:" it is, indeed, the only river along this line of coast the mouth of which affords shelter even for small vessels.   [E. H. B.]

TRINOBANTES (called by Ptolemy Τρινόαντες, ii. 3. § 22), a people on the E. coast of Britannia Romana, situated N. of London and the Thames, in Essex and the southern parts of Suffolk, whose capital was Camalodunum (Colchester). They submitted to Caesar when he landed in Britain, but revolted against the Romans in the reign of Nero. (Caes. B. G. v. 20; Tac. Ann. xiv. 31.) [T.H.D.]

TRINURTIUM. [TINURTIUM.]

TRIOBRIS, a river of Gallia named by Sidonius Apollinaris (Propempt.). It is a branch of the Oltis (Lot), and is now named Truyère. [G. L.]

TRIO'CALA (Τριόκαλα: Eth. Triocalinus : Rn. near Calatabellotta), a city of Sicily, situated in the interior of the island, about 12 miles from Thermae Selinuntiae (Sciacca). As the name is cited by Stephanus of Byzantium (who writes the name Τρίκαλα) from Philistus, it is probable that it was a Siculian town or fortress as early at least as the time of the elder Dionysius; but no notice of it is now found in history until the second Servile War in Sicily in B. C. 103—100. On that occasion Triocala was selected, on account of its great natural strength and other advantages, by Tryphon, the leader of the insurgents, as his chief stronghold: he fortified the rocky summit on which it was situated, and was able to hold out there, as in an impregnable fortress, after his defeat in the field by L. Lucullus. (Diod. xxxvi. 7, 8.) The circumstances of its fall are not related to us, but Silius Italicus alludes to it as having suffered severely from the effects of the war. (" Servili vastata Triocala bello," xiv. 270). Cicero nowhere notices the name among the municipal towns of Sicily, but in one passage mentions the " Triocalinus ager" (Verr. v. 4); and the Triocalini again appear in Pliny's list of the municipal towns of Sicily. The name is also found in Ptolemy, but in a manner that gives little information as to its position. (Plin. iii. 8. s. 14; Ptol. iii. 4. § 14.) It was an episcopal see during the early part of the middle ages, and the site is identified by Fazello, who tells us that the ruins of the city were still visible in his time a short distance from Calatabellotta, a town of Saracen origin, situated on a lofty hill about 12 miles inland from Sciacca; and an old church on the site still preserved the ancient appellation. (Fazell. de Reb. Sic. x. 472; Cluver. Sicil. p. 374).   [E. H. B.]

TRIO'PIUM (Τριόπιον ἄκρον: C. Crio), the promontory at the eastern extremity of the peninsula of Cnidus, forming at the same time the southwestern extremity of Asia Minor. (Thucyd. viii. 35, 60; Scylax, p. 38; Pomp. Mela, i. 16.) On the summit of this promontory a temple of Apollo, hence called the Triopian, seems to have stood, near which games were celebrated, whence Scylax calls the promontory the ἀκρωτήριον ἱερόν. According to some authorities the town of Cnidus itself also bore the name of Triopium, having, it is said, been founded by Triopas. (Steph. B. s. v. Τριόπιον; Plin. v. 29, who calls it Triopia; Eustath. ad Hom. Il. iv. 341; CNIDUS.)   [L. S.]

TRIPHYLIA. [ELIS.]

TRIPODISCUS (Τριποδίσκος, Thuc. iv. 70 ; Τριποδίσκοι, Paus. i. 43. § 8 ; Τρίποδοι, Τριποδίσκιον, Strab. ix. p. 394 ; Τριποδίσκη, Herod. ap. Steph. B. s. v. Τριποδίσκοι : Eth. Τριποδίσκιος, Steph. B. ; Τριποδισκαῖος), an ancient town of Megaris, said to have been one of the five hamlets into which the Megarid was originally divided. (Plut. Quaest. Graec. c. 17.) Strabo relates that, according to some critics, Tripodi was mentioned by Homer, along with Aegirusa and Nisaea, as part of the dominions of Ajax of Salamis, and that the verse containing these names was omitted by the Athenians, who substituted for it another to prove that Salamis in the time of the Trojan War, belonged to Athens. (Strab. l. c.) Tripodiscus is celebrated in the history of literature as the birthplace of Susarion, who is said to have introduced comedy into Attica, and to have removed from this place to the Attic Icaria. (Aspas. ad Aristot. Eth. Nic. iv. 2; Dict. of Biogr. Vol. III. p. 948.) We learn from Thucydides (l. c.) that Tripodiscus was situated at the foot of Mount Geraneia, at a spot convenient for the junction of troops marching from Plataea in the one direction, and from the Isthmus in the other. Pausanias (*l. c.*) also describes it as lying at the foot of Geraneia on the road from Delphi to Argos. This author relates that it derived its name from a tripod, which Coroebus the Argive brought from Delphi, with the injunction that wherever the tripod fell to the ground he was to reside there and build a temple to Apollo. (Comp. Conon, *Narrat.* 19.) Leake noticed the vestiges of an ancient town at the foot of Mt. Geraneia, on the road from Plataea to the Isthmus, four or five miles to the NW. of Megara. (Leake, *Northern Greece*, vol. ii. p. 410.)

TRIPOLIS (Τρίπολις, Ptol. v. 15. § 4 : *Eth.* Τριπολίτης : *Adj.* Tripoliticus, Plin. xiv. 7. s. 9), an important maritime town of Phoenicia, situated on the N. side of the promontory of Theuprosopon. (Strab. xvi. p. 754.) The site of Tripolis has been already described, and it has been mentioned that it derived its name, which literally signifies *the three cities*, from its being the metropolis of the three confederate towns, Tyre, Sidon, and Aradus [PHOENICIA, Vol. II. p. 606]. Each of those cities had here its peculiar quarter, separated from the rest by a wall. Tripolis possessed a good harbour, and, like the rest of the Phoenician towns, had a large maritime commerce. (Cf. Joannes Phocas, c. 4; Wesseling, *ad Itin. Ant.* p. 149.) Respecting the modern *Tripoli* (*Tarablus* or *Tripoli di Soria*); see Pococke, vol. ii. p. 146, seq.; Maundrell, p. 26; Burckhardt, p. 163, seq., &c.; cf. Scylax, p. 42; Mela, i. 12; Plin. v. 20. s. 17 ; Diod. xvi. 41 ; Steph. B. *s. v.*; Eckhel, vol. iii. p. 372.)　　[T. H. D.]

COINS OF TRIPOLIS IN PHOENICIA.

TRIPOLIS (Τρίπολις : *Eth.* Τριπολίτης). 1. A town of Phrygia, on the northern bank of the upper course of the Maeander, and on the road leading from Sardes by Philadelphia to Laodiceia. (*It. Ant.* p. 336; *Tab. Peut.*) It was situated 12 miles to the north-west of Hierapolis, and is not mentioned by any writer before the time of Pliny (v. 30), who treats it as a Lydian town, and says that it was washed by the Maeander. Ptolemy (v. 2. § 18) and Stephanus B. describe it as a Carian town, and the latter (*s.v.*) adds that in his time it was called Neapolis. Hierocles (p. 669) likewise calls it a Lydian town. Ruins of it still exist near Yeniji or

Kash Yeniji. (Arundell, *Seven Churches*, p. 245; Hamilton, *Researches*, i. p. 525; Fellows, *Asia Minor*, p. 287.)

2. A fortress in Pontus Polemoniacus, on a river of the same name, and with a tolerably good harbour. It was situated at a distance of 90 stadia from Cape Zephyrium. (Arrian, *Peripl. P. E.* p. 17; Anon. *Peripl. P.E.* p. 13; Plin. vi. 4.) The place still exists under the name of *Tireboli*, and is situated on a rocky headland. (Hamilton, *Researches*, i. p. 257.)　　　　　[L. S.]

TRIPOLIS (Τρίπολις). 1. A district in Arcadia. [Vol. I. p. 193, No. 12.]

2. A district in Laconia. [Vol. II. p. 113, b.]

3. A district of Perrhaebia in Thessaly, containing the towns Azorus, Pythium, and Doliche. (Liv. xlii. 53.) [AZORUS.]

TRIPOLITANA REGIO. [SYRTICA.]

TRIPONTIUM, a town of Britannia Romana, apparently in the territory of the Coritani. (*Itin. Ant.* p. 477.) Variously identified with *Lilbourn*, *Calthorpe*, and *Rugby.*　　　　　[T. H. D.]

TRIPYEGIA. [AEGINA, p. 34, b., p. 35, a.]

TRISANTON (Τρισάντων, Ptol. ii. 3. § 4), a river on the S. coast of Britannia Romana; according to Camden (p. 137) the river *Test*, which runs into *Southampton Water*; according to others the river *Arun.*　　　　　[T. H. D.]

TRISCIANA (Τρισκίανα, Procop. *de Aed.* iv. 4, p. 282), a place in Moesia Superior, perhaps the present *Feristina* or *Pristina.*　　　[T. H. D.]

TRISSUM (Τρισσόν, Ptol. iii. 7. § 2), a place in the country of the Jazyges Metanastae. [Cf. JAZYGES, Vol. II. p. 7.]　　　　　[T. H. D.]

TRITAEA. 1. (Τρίταια : *Eth.* Τριταιεύς ; in Herod. i. 145, Τριταιέεις is the name of the people), a town in Achaia, and the most inland of the 12 Achaean cities, was distant 120 stadia from Pharae. It was one of the four cities, which took the lead in reviving the Achaean League in B. C. 280. In the Social War (B. C. 220, seq.) it suffered from the attacks of the Aetolians and Eleians. Its territory was annexed to Patrae by Augustus, when he made the latter city a colony after the battle of Actium. Its site is probably represented by the remains at *Kastritza*, on the Selinus, near the frontiers of Arcadia. (Herod. i. 145 ; Pol. ii. 41, iv. 6, 59, 60; Strab. viii. p. 386; Paus. vii. 22. § 6. seq.; Steph. B. *s. v.*; Leake, *Morea*, vol. ii. p. 117.)

2. (Tritea, Plin. iv. 3. s. 4 : *Eth.* Τριτέες, Herod. viii. 33), one of the towns of Phocis, burnt by Xerxes, of which the position is uncertain. (Leake, *Northern Greece*, vol. ii. p. 89.)

3. (Τρίτεια, Steph. B. *s. v.* : *Eth.* Τριταιέες, Thuc. iii. 101), a town of the Locri Ozolae, described by Stephanus B. as lying between Phocis and the Locri Ozolae. Hence it is placed by Leake not far from Delphi and Amphissa, on the edge, perhaps, of the plain of *Sálona.* (Leake, *Northern Greece*, vol. ii. p. 621.)

TRITIUM, a town of the Autrigones, in Hispania Tarraconensis, in the jurisdiction of Clunia. (Plin. iii. 3. s. 4; *Itin. Ant.* pp. 450, 454.) Variously identified with *Carceda*, *Rodilla*, and a place near *Monasterio.*　　　　　[T. H. D.]

TRITIUM METALLUM (Τρίτιον Μέταλλον, Ptol. ii. 6. § 55), a town of the Berones, in Hispania Tarraconensis, now called *Tricio*, near *Nájera.* (Florez, *Cantabr.* p. 182.)　　　[T. H. D.]

TRITIUM TUBORICUM (Τρίτιον Τουβόρικον, Ptol. ii. 6. § 66), a town of the Barduli, in Hispania Tarraconensis, on the river Deva or Devales. (Mela, iii. 1.) It is commonly identified with *Motrico*, which, however, does not lie on the Deva; and Mannert (i. p. 365) seeks it near *Mondragon*, in *Guipuscoa*.   [T. H. D.]

TRITON (ὁ Τρίτων ποταμός, Ptol. iv. 3. § 19, &c.), a river of Libya, forming, according to Ptolemy, the boundary of the Regio Syrtica towards the W. It rose in Mount Vasalaetus, and, flowing in a northerly direction, passed through three lakes, the Libya Palus, the lake Pallas, and the lake Tritonitis (ἡ Τριτωνῖτις λίμνη, *Ib.*); after which it fell into the sea in the innermost part of the Syrtis Minor between Macomada and Tacape, but nearer to the latter.

The lake Tritonitis of Ptolemy is called, however, by other writers Tritonis (ἡ Τριτωνὶς λίμνη, Herod. iv. 179). Herodotus seems to confound it with the Lesser Syrtis itself; but Scylax (p. 49), who gives it a circumference of 1000 stadia, describes it as connected with the Syrtis by a narrow opening, and as surrounding a small island,—that called by Herodotus (*ib.* 178) Phla (Φλά), which is also mentioned by Strabo (xvii. p. 836), as containing a temple of Aphrodite, and by Dionysius. (*Perieg.* 267.) This lake Tritonis is undoubtedly the present *Schibkah-el-Loudjah*, of which, according to Shaw (*Travels*, i. p. 237), the other two lakes are merely parts; whilst the river Triton is the present *El-Hammah*. This river, indeed, is no longer connected with the lake (Shaw, *Ib.*); a circumstance, however, which affords no essential ground for doubting the identity of the two streams; since in those regions even larger rivers are sometimes compelled by the quicksands to alter their course. (Cf. Ritter, *Erdkunde*, i. p. 1017). Scylax (*l. c.*) mentions also another island called Tritonos (Τρίτωνος) in the Syrtis Minor, which last itself is, according to him, only part of a large Sinus Tritonites (Τριτωνίτης κόλπος).

Some writers confound the lake Tritonis with the lake of the Hesperides, and seek it in other districts of Libya ; sometimes in Mauretania, in the neighbourhood of Mount Atlas and the Atlantic Ocean, sometimes in Cyrenaica near Berenice and the river Lathon or Lethon. The latter hypothesis is adopted by Lucan (ix. 346, seq.), the former by Diodorus Siculus (iii. 53), who also attributes to it an island inhabited by the Amazons. But Strabo (*l. c.*) especially distinguishes the lake of the Hesperides from the lake Tritonis.

With this lake is connected the question of the epithet *Tritogeneia*, applied to Pallas as early as the days of Homer and Hesiod. But though the Libyan river and lake were much renowned in ancient times (cf. Aeschyl. *Eum.* 293; Eurip. *Ion*, 872, seq.; Pind. *Pyth.* iv. 36, &c.), and the application of the name of Pallas to the lake connected with the Tritonis seems to point to these African waters as having given origin to the epithet, it is nevertheless most probable that the brook Triton near Alalcomenae in Boeotia has the best pretensions to that distinction. (Cf. Pausan. ix. 33. § 5; Schol. *ad Apollon. Rhod.* i. 109, iv. 1315; Müller, *Orchomenos*, p. 355; Leake, *Northern Greece*, vol. ii. p. 136, seq.; Kruse, *Hellas*, vol. ii. pt. 1 p. 475.   [T. H. D.]

TRITON (Τρίτων, Diod. v. 72), a river of Crete at the source of which Athene was said to have been born. From its connection with the Omphalian plain, it is identified with the river discharging

itself into the sea on the N. coast of the island which is called *Platyperama*, but changes its name to *Ghiofiro* as it approaches the shore. (Pashley, *Travels*, vol. i. p. 225.)   [E. B. J.]

TRITON (Τρίτων), a river of Boeotia. [Vol. I. p. 413. a.]

TRITURRITA. [PISAE.]

TRIVICUM (*Trevico*), a town of Samnium, in the country of the Hirpini, not far from the frontiers of Apulia. Its name is known to us only from Horace, who slept there (or at least at a villa in its immediate neighbourhood) on his well-known journey to Brundusium. (Hor. *Sat.* i. 5. 79.) It appears therefore that it was situated on the Via Appia, or the line of road then frequented from Rome to Brundusium. But this was not the same which was followed in later times, and is given in the Itineraries under that name, a circumstance which has given rise to much confusion in the topography of this part of Italy. (VIA APPIA.) There can be no doubt that Trivicum occupied nearly, if not exactly, the same site with the modern *Trevico:* the ancient road appears to have passed along the valley at the foot of the hill on which it was situated. It was here that stood the villa to which Horace alludes, and some remains of Roman buildings, as well as of the pavement of the ancient road, still visible in the time of Pratilli, served to mark the site more accurately. (Pratilli, *Via Appia*, iv. 10. p. 507; Romanelli, vol. ii. p. 350.) It probably never was a municipal town, as its name is not mentioned by any of the geographers.   [E. H. B.]

TRIUMPILI'NI, an Alpine people of Northern Italy, who are mentioned by Augustus in the inscription in which he recorded the final subjugation of the Alpine tribes (ap. Plin. iii. 20. s. 24). It appears from Pliny that the whole people was reduced to slavery and sold together with their lands. According to Cato they were of Euganean race, as well as their neighbours the Camuni, with whom they are repeatedly mentioned in common. (Plin. *l. c.*) Hence there is little doubt that they were the inhabitants of the district still called *Val Trompia*, the upper valley of the *Mella*, and separated only by an intervening ridge of mountains from the *Val Cumonica*, the land of the Camuni.   ·   [E. H. B.]

TROAS (Τρωάς, Τροίη, Τροία, or Ἰλιὰς γῆ), the territory ruled over by the ancient kings of Troy or Ilium, which retained its ancient and venerable name even at a time when the kingdom to which it had originally belonged had long ceased to exist. Homer himself nowhere describes the extent of Troas or its frontiers, and even leaves us in the dark as to how far the neighbouring allies of the Trojans, such as the Dardanians, who were governed by princes of their own, of the family of Priam, were true allies or subjects of the king of Ilium. In later times, Troas was a part of Mysia, comprising the coast district on the Aegean from Cape Lectum to the neighbourhood of Dardanus and Abydus on the Hellespont; while inland it extended about 8 geographical miles, that is, as far as Mount Ida, so as to embrace the south coast of Mysia opposite the island of Lesbos, together with the towns of Assus and Antandrus. (Hom. *Il.* xxiv. 544: Herod. vii. 42.) Strabo, from his well-known inclination to magnify the empire of Troy, describes it as extending from the Aesepus to the Caicus, and his view is adopted by the Scholiast on Apollonius Rhodius (i. 1115). In its proper and more limited sense, however, Troas was an undulating plain, traversed by the terminal branches of Ida running out in a north-western direction, and by the small rivers SATNIOIS, SCAMANDER, SIMOIS, and THYMBRIUS. This plain gradually rises towards Mount Ida, and contained, at least in later times, several flourishing towns. In the Iliad we hear indeed of several towns, and Achilles boasts (*Il.* ix. 328) of having destroyed eleven in the territory of Troy; but they can at best only have been very small places, perhaps only open villages. That Ilium itself must have been far superior in strength and population is evident from the whole course of events; it was protected by strong walls, and had its acropolis. [ILIUM.]

The inhabitants of Troas, called Troes (Τρῶες), and by Roman prose-writers Trojani or Teucri, were in all probability a Pelasgian race, and seem to have consisted of two branches, one of which, the Teucri, had emigrated from Thrace, and become amalgamated with the Phrygian or native population of the country. Hence the Trojans are sometimes called Teucri and sometimes Phryges. (Herod. v. 122, vii. 43; Strab. i. p. 62, xiii. p. 604; Virg. *Aen.* i. 38, 248, ii. 252, 571, &c.) The poet of the Iliad in several points treats the Trojans as inferior in civilisation to his own countrymen; but it is impossible to say whether in such cases he describes the real state of things, or whether he does so only from a natural partiality for his own countrymen.

According to the common legend, the kingdom of Troy was overturned at the capture and burning of Ilium in B. C. 1184; but it is attested on pretty good authority that a Trojan state survived the catastrophe of its chief city, and that the kingdom was finally destroyed by an invasion of Phrygians who crossed over from Europe into Asia. (Xanthus, *ap.* Strab. xiv. p. 680, xii. p. 572.) This fact is indirectly confirmed by the testimony of Homer himself, who makes Poseidon predict that the posterity of Aeneas should long continue to reign over the Trojans, after the race of Priam should be extinct. [L. S.]

TROCHOEIDES LACUS. [DELOS, p. 759, b.]

TROCHUS. [CENCHREAE, p. 584, a.]

TROCMADA (Τρόκμαδα), a place of uncertain site in Galatia, which probably derived its name from the tribe of the Trocmi, is mentioned only by late Christian writers (*Conc. Chalced.* pp. 125, 309, 663; *Conc. Constant.* iii. p. 672: *Conc. Nicaen.* ii. p. 355, where its name is Τρόκναδα; Hierocl. p. 698, where it is miswritten Ῥεγετνακδὅη.) [L. S.]

TROCMI [GALATIA].

TROES. [TROAS.]

TROESA. [TESA.]

TROEZEN (Τρωζήν), a city in "Massilia of Italy," as Stephanus (*s. v.*) says, if his text is right; but perhaps he means to say "a city of Massilia in Italy." Eustathius (*ad Il.* p. 287) says that it is in "Massaliotic Italy." Charax is Stephanus' authority. This brief notice adds one more to the list of Massaliotic settlements on the coast of the Mediterranean; but we know nothing of Troezen. [G. L.]

TROEZEN (Τροιζήν; also Τροιζήνη, Ptol. iii. 16. § 12 : *Eth.* Τροιζήνιος: the territory γῆ Τροιζηνία, Eurip. *Med.* 683; ἡ Τροιζηνὶς γῆ, Thuc. ii. 56), a city of Peloponnesus, whose territory formed the south-eastern corner of the district to which the name of Argolis was given at a later time. It stood at the distance of 15 stadia from the coast, in a fer-

tile plain, which is described below. (Strab. viii. p. 373.) Few cities of Peloponnesus boasted of so remote an antiquity; and many of its legends are closely connected with those of Athens, and prove that its original population was of the Ionic race. According to the Troezenians themselves, their country was first called Oraea from the Egyptian Orus, and was next named Althepia from Althepus, the son of Poseidon and Leis, who was the daughter of Orus. In the reign of this king, Poseidon and Athena contended, as at Athens, for the land of the Troezenians, but, through the mediation of Zeus, they became the joint guardians of the country. Hence, says Pausanias, a trident and the head of Athena are represented on the ancient coins of Troezen. (Comp. Mionnet, *Suppl.* iv. p. 267. § 189.) Althepus was succeeded by Saron, who built a temple of the Saronian Artemis in a marshy place near the sea, which was hence called the Phoebaean marsh (Φοιβαία λίμνη), but was afterwards named Saronis, because Saron was buried in the ground belonging to the temple. The next kings mentioned are Hyperes and Anthas, who founded two cities, named Hypereia and Antheia. Aëtius, the son of Hyperes, inherited the kingdom of his father and uncle, and called one of the cities Poseidonias. In his reign, Troezen and Pittheus, who are called the sons of Pelops, and may be regarded as Achaean princes, settled in the country, and divided the power with Aëtius. But the Pelopidae soon supplanted the earlier dynasty; and on the death of Troezen, Pittheus united the two Ionic settlements into one city, which he called Troezen after his brother. Pittheus was the grandfather of Theseus by his daughter Aethra; and the great national hero of the Athenians was born and educated at Troezen. The close connection between the two states is also intimated by the legend that two important demi of Attica, Anaphlystus and Sphettus, derived their names from two sons of Troezen. (Paus. ii. 30. §§ 5—9.) Besides the ancient names of Troezen already specified, Stephanus B. (*s. v.* Τροιζήν) mentions Aphrodisias, Saronia, Poseidonias, Apollonias and Anthanis. Strabo likewise says (ix. p. 373) that Troezen was called Poseidonia from its being sacred to Poseidon.

At the time of the Trojan War Troezen was subject to Argos (Hom. *Il.* ii. 561); and upon the conquest of the Peloponnesus by the Dorians, it received a Dorian colony from Argos. (Paus. ii. 30. § 10.) The Dorian settlers appear to have been received on friendly terms by the ancient inhabitants, who continued to form the majority of the population; and although Troezen became a Doric city, it still retained its Ionic sympathies and traditions. At an early period Troezen was a powerful maritime state, as is shown by its founding the cities of Halicarnassus and Myndus in Caria. (Paus. ii. 30. § 8; Herod. vii. 99; Strab. viii. p. 374.) The Troezenians also took part with the Achaeans in the foundation of Sybaris, but they were eventually driven out by the Achaeans. (Aristot. *Pol.* v. 3.) It has been conjectured with much probability that the expelled Troezenians may have been the chief founders of Poseidonia (Paestum), which Solinus calls a Doric colony, and to which they gave the ancient name of their own city in Peloponnesus. [PAESTUM.]

In the Persian War the Troezenians took an active part. After the battle of Thermopylae, the harbour of Troezen was appointed as the place of rendezvous for the Grecian fleet (Herod. viii. 42); and when the Athenians were obliged to quit Attica upon the approach of Xerxes, the majority of them took refuge at Troezen, where they were received with the greatest kindness by the semi-Ionic population. (Herod. viii. 41; Plut. *Them.* 10.) The Troezenians sent 5 ships to Artemisium and Salamis, and 1000 men to Plataeae, and they also fought at the battle of Mycale. (Herod. viii. 1, ix. 28, 102.) After the Persian war the friendly connection between Athens and Troezen appears to have continued ; and during the greatness of the Athenian empire before the thirty years' peace (B. C. 455) Troezen was an ally of Athens, and was apparently garrisoned by Athenian troops ; but by this peace the Athenians were compelled to relinquish Troezen. (Thuc. i. 115, iv. 45.) Before the Peloponnesian War the two states became estranged from one another ; and the Troezenians, probably from hostility to Argos, entered into close alliance with the Lacedaemonians. In the Peloponnesian War the Troezenians remained the firm allies of Sparta, although their country, from its maritime situation and its proximity to Attica, was especially exposed to the ravages of the Athenian fleet. (Thuc. ii. 56, iv. 45.) In the Corinthian War, B. C. 394, the Troezenians fought upon the side of the Lacedaemonians (Xen. *Hell.* iv. 2. § 16) ; and again in B. C. 373 they are numbered among the allies of Sparta against Athens. (Xen. *Hell.* vi. 2. § 3.) In the Macedonian period Troezen passed alternately into the hands of the contending powers. In B. C. 303 it was delivered, along with Argos, from the Macedonian yoke, by Demetrius Poliorcetes ; but it soon became subject to Macedonia, and remained so till it was taken by the Spartan Cleonymus in B. C. 278. (Polyaen. *Strat.* ii. 29. § 1 ; Frontin. *Strat.* iii. 6. § 7.) Shortly afterwards it again became a Macedonian dependency ; but it was united to the Achaean League by Aratus after he had liberated Corinth. (Paus. ii. 8. § 5.) In the war between the Achaean League and the Spartans, it was taken by Cleomenes, in B. C. 223 (Polyb. ii. 52 ; Plut. *Cleom.* 19) ; but after the defeat of this monarch at Sellasia in B. C. 221, it was doubtless restored to the Achaeans. Of its subsequent history we have no information. It was a place of importance in the time of Strabo (viii. p. 373), and in the second century of the Christian era it continued to possess a large number of public buildings, of which Pausanias has given a detailed account. (Paus. ii. 31, 32.)

According to the description of Pausanias, the monuments of Troezen may be divided into three classes, those in the Agora and its neighbourhood, those in the sacred inclosure of Hippolytus, and those upon the Acropolis. The Agora seems to have been surrounded with stoas or colonnades, in which stood marble statues of the women and children who fled for refuge to Troezen at the time of the Persian invasion. In the centre of the Agora was a temple of Artemis Soteira, said to have been dedicated by Theseus, which contained altars of the infernal gods. Behind the temple stood the monument of Pittheus, the founder of the city, surmounted by three chairs of white marble, upon which he and two assessors are said to have administered justice. Not far from thence was the temple of the Muses, founded by Ardalus, a son of Hephaestus, where Pittheus himself was said to have learnt the art of discourse; and before the temple was an altar where sacrifices were offered to the Muses and to Sleep, the deity whom the Troezenians considered the most friendly to these goddesses.

Near the theatre was the temple of Artemis Lyceia, founded by Hippolytus. Before the temple there was the very stone upon which Orestes was purified by nine Troezenians. The so-called tent of Orestes, in which he took refuge before his expiation, stood in front of the temple of Apollo Thearius, which was the most ancient temple that Pausanias knew. The water used in the purification of Orestes was drawn from the sacred fountain Hippocrene, struck by the hoof of Pegasus. In the neighbourhood was a statue of Hermes Polygius, with a wild olive tree, and a temple of Zeus Soter, said to have been erected by Aëtius, one of the mythical kings of Troezen.

The sacred enclosure of Hippolytus occupied a large space, and was a most conspicuous object in the city. The Troezenians denied the truth of the ordinary story of his being dragged to death by his horses, but worshipped him as the constellation Auriga, and dedicated to him a spacious sanctuary, the foundation of which was ascribed to Diomede. He was worshipped with the greatest honours; and each virgin, before her marriage, dedicated a lock of her hair to him. (Eurip. *Hippol.* 1424; Paus. ii. 32. § 1.) The sacred enclosure contained, besides the temple of Hippolytus, one of Apollo Epibaterius, also dedicated by Diomede. On one side of the enclosure was the stadium of Hippolytus, and above it the temple of Aphrodite Calascopia, so called because Phaedra beheld from this spot Hippolytus as he exercised in the stadium. In the neighbourhood was shown the tomb of Phaedra, the monument of Hippolytus, and the house of the hero, with the fountain called the Herculean in front of it.

The Acropolis was crowned with the temple of Athena Polias or Sthenias; and upon the slope of the mountain was a sanctuary of Pan Lyterius, so called because he put a stop to the plague. Lower down was the temple of Isis, built by the Halicarnassians, and also one of Aphrodite Ascraea.

The ruins of Troezen lie west of the village of *Dhamalá.* They consist only of pieces of wall of Hellenic masonry or of Roman brickwork, dispersed over the lower slopes of the height, upon which stood the Acropolis, and over the plain at its foot. The Acropolis occupied a rugged and lofty hill, commanding the plain below, and presenting one of the most extensive and striking prospects in Greece. There are in the plain several ruined churches, which probably mark the site of ancient temples; and several travellers have noticed the remains of the temple of Aphrodite Calascopia, overlooking the cavity formerly occupied by the stadium. The chief river of the plain flows by the ruins of Troezen, and is now called *Potámi.* It is the ancient Taurius, afterwards called Hyllicus (Paus. ii. 32. § 7), fed by several streams, of which the most important was the Chrysorrhoas, flowing through the city, and which still preserved its water, when all the other streams had been dried up by a nine years' drought. (Paus. ii. 31. § 10.)

The territory of Troezen was bounded on the W. by that of Epidaurus, on the SW. by that of Hermione, and was surrounded on every other side by the sea. The most important part of the territory was the fertile maritime plain, in which Troezen stood, and which was bounded on the south by a range of mountains, terminating in the promontories Scyllaeum and Bucephala, the most easterly points of the Peloponnesus. [SCYLLAEUM.] Above the promontory Scyllaeum, and nearly due E. of Troezen, was a large bay, protected by the island of

Calaureia, named Pogon, where the Grecian fleet was ordered to assemble before the battle of Salamis (Herod. viii. 42; Strab. viii. p. 873.) The port-town, which was named Celenderis (Paus. ii. 32. § 9), appears to have stood at the western extremity of the bay of Pogon, where some ancient remains are found. The high rocky peninsula of Methana, which belonged to the territory of Troezen and is united to the mainland by a narrow isthmus, is described in a separate article. [METHANA.] There were formerly two islands off the coast of Troezen, named Calaureia and Sphaeria (afterwards Hiera), which are now united by a narrow sandbank. (Leake, *Morea*, vol. ii. p. 442, seq.; Boblaye, *Recherches, &c.* p. 56; Curtius, *Peloponnesos*, vol. ii. p. 431, seq.)

TROGI'LIUM (Τρωγίλιον), a promontory formed by the western termination of Mount Mycale, opposite the island of Samos. Close to this promontory there was an island bearing the same name. (Strab. xiv. p. 636; Steph. B. *s. v.* Τρώγιλος, according to whom it was also called Trogilia; *Act. Apost.* xx. 15, where its name is Trogyllion.) Pliny (v. 31. s. 37) speaks of three islands being called Trogiliae, their separate names being Philion, Argennon, and Sandalion.   [L. S.]

TROGI'LIUM, a town of Lusitania, according to Luitprand (*Adversaria*, § 30, ap. Wessel. *ad Itin.* p. 438), the same place which Pliny (iv. 35) calls Castra Julia. It is incontestably the Turcalion of the Geogr. Rav. (iv. 35) and the modern *Truxillo.* (Cf. Florez, *Esp. Sagr.* xiii. p. 114, and Ukert, ii. pt. i. p. 395.)   [T. H. D.]

TROGI'TIS (Τρωγῖτις), a small lake in Lycaonia, mentioned only by Strabo (xii. p. 568), and probably the same as the one now called *Ilghun.*   [L. S.]

TROGLO'DYTAE (Τρωγλοδύται, Ptol. iii. 10. § 9; Diodor. iii. 14; Strab. xvii. pp. 786, 819; Agatharchid. *ap. Phot.* p. 454, ed. Bekker; Plin. ii. 70. s. 71 vi. 29. s. 34; ἡ Τρωγλοδύτις or Τρωγλοδυτική, κε. χώρα, Diodor. i. 30; Ptol. iv. 7, 27.) Under the term Troglodytae the ancients appear to have included various races of men. For we meet with them in Mauretania (Strab. xvii. p. 828); in the interior of Libya east of the Garamantes, along the Arabian shore of the Red Sea, as well as on the opposite coast of Aethiopia and Aegypt, and on both in such numbers that the districts were each of them named "Regio Troglodytica;" and even on the northern side of the Caucasus (Strab. xi. p. 506). The Caucasian Troglodytae were in a higher state of civilisation than their eastern namesakes, since they cultivated corn.

But the race most commonly known as Troglodytae inhabited either shore of the Red Sea, and were probably a mixture of Arabian and Aethiopian blood. Their name, as its composition imports (τρώγλη, δύω), was assigned to them because they either dug for themselves cabins in the lime and sandstone hills of that region, or availed themselves of its natural caverns. Even in the latter case, the villages of the Troglodytae were partly formed by art, since long tunnels, for the passage or stabling of their herds, were cut between village and village, and the rocks were honeycombed by their dwellings. Bruce saw at *Gojam* in Nubia a series of such caverns, inhabited by herdsmen, and witnessed the periodical passage of the cattle in *Sennaar* from the lowlands to the hills. The same cause led to similar migrations in ancient times, viz., the appearance of the gadfly in the marshes, immediately after the cessation of the periodical rains.

The accounts of the Regio Troglodytica that extended from the Sinus Arsinoites to Berenice may be assumed as applicable to the Troglodytae generally. The catacombs of Naples will perhaps give the most accurate image of their dwellings. The *Ababdeh*, who now inhabit this region, exhibit many of their peculiar manners and customs. Their language was described by the Greeks as a shriek or whistle, rather than as articulate speech; a portion at least of them were serpent-eaters. (Herod. iv. 183.) But their general occupation was that of herdsmen.

Agatharchides of Cnidos is the earliest writer who mentions the Troglodytae (*ap. Photium*, p. 454, ed. Bekker). According to him and Strabo (xvii. p. 786) animal food was their staple diet; and they eat not only the flesh but also the bones and hides of their cattle. Their drink was a mixture of milk and blood. Since, however, only the older and sicklier beasts were slaughtered for food, it may be presumed that the better animals were reserved for the Aegyptian and Aethiopian markets. The hides supplied their only article of raiment; but many of them went naked, and the women tattooed their bodies, and wore necklaces of shells. The pastoral habits of the Troglodytae rendered them so swift of foot as to be able to run down the wild beasts which they hunted; and they must have been acquainted with the use of weapons, since they were not only hunters, but robbers, against whom the caravans passing from the interior of Libya to Berenice on the Red Sea were obliged to employ a guard of soldiers, stationed at Phulacôn (Φυλάκων κώμη: *Tab. Peut.*), about 25 miles from Berenice. Troglodytae also served among the light troops in the army of Xerxes, B. C. 480, and acted as guides to the caravans, since the Ichthyophagi whom Cambyses employed as explorers of Meroe were a tribe of Troglodytae. (Herod. iii. 19.) Among the common people a community of women existed: the chiefs alone, who may have been of a superior race, having wives appropriated. For the abstraction or seduction of a chieftain's wife an ox was the penalty. During their retirement in caverns they seem to have lived peaceably together, but as soon as they sallied forth with their herds into the pastures they were incessantly at war with one another, on which occasions the women were wont to act as mediators. They practised the rite of circumcision, like the Arabians and Aethiopians generally. According to Agatharchides the Troglodytae differed as much from the rest of mankind in their sepulchral customs as in their habitations. They bound the corpse neck and heels together, affixed it to a stake, pelted it with stones amid shouts of laughter, and when it was quite covered with stones, placed a horn upon the mound, and went their ways. But they did not always wait for natural death to perform this ceremony, since, accounting inability to procure a livelihood among intolerable evils, they strangled the aged and infirm with an ox-tail. Their civilisation appeared so low to Aristotle (*Hist. Anim.* viii. 12) that he describes the Troglodytae as pigmies who, mounted on tiny horses, waged incessant wars with the cranes in the Aethiopian marshes. A tribe on the frontiers of *Abyssinia*, called *Barnagas* by the natives, corresponds, according to modern accounts, with the ancient Troglodytae. (Vincent, *Commerce and Navigation of the Ancients*, vol. ii. p. 89.) [W. B. D.]

TROICUS MONS (Τρωικὸν ὄρος, Strab. xvii. p. 809; Steph. B. *s. v.*; Τρωικοῦ λίθου ὄρος, Ptol. iv. 5. § 27), was a long range of hills east of the Nile, which threw out several abrupt spurs into the Heptanomis of Aegypt. It stood in the parallel of Heracleopolis, i. e. in Lat. 31° N. From this calcareous range was quarried, according to Strabo, the stone used in the construction of the Pyramids. [W. B. D.]

TROJA. [ILIUM; TROAS.]

TRONIS. [DAULIS, p. 756, b.]

TROPAEA AUGUSTI. [MONOECI PORTUS.]

TROPAEA DRUSI (Τρόπαια Δρούσου), a trophy erected on a hill on the banks of the *Elbe* by Drusus, to mark the point to which he had advanced in the north of Germany. (Dion Cass. lv.1; Flor. iv. 12; Ptol. ii. 11. § 28, who speaks of it as if it were a town.) [L. S.]

TROPAEA POMPEII (τὰ Πομπηίου τρόπαια, or ἀναθήματα, Strab. iii. p. 160, iv. p. 178), a trophy or monument erected by Pompey on the summit of the Pyrenees, recording the subjugation of 876 Spanish cities. (Plin. iii. 3. s. 4, iv. 7. s. 27, xxxvii. 2. s. 6.) It stood at the spot named Summum Pyrenaeum in the *Itin. Ant.* (p. 397), and according to some on the boundary between Gaul and Spain. [T. H. D.]

TROSMIS (Τρόσμις, Hierocl. p. 637; Τρισμίς or Τροισμίς, Ptol. iii. 10. § 11), a town of some importance in Lower Moesia, on the Danube, where, according to the *Itin. Ant.* (p. 225), the Legio I. Jovia had its head quarters, though the *Not. Imp.* (c. 28) more correctly mentions the Legio II. Herculea. Lapie identifies it with *Matchin.* (Cf. Ovid, *ex Pont.* iv. 9, v. 79.) [T. H. D.]

TROSSULUM, a town of Etruria, which, according to a story current among the Romans, was taken by a body of cavalry alone, unsupported by infantry; an exploit thought to be so singular, that the Roman knights were for some time called Trossuli on account of it. (Plin. xxxiii. 2. s. 9; Festus, *s. v.* Trossuli, p. 367.) No other mention is found of it; and it was probably a small place which had disappeared in the time of the geographers, but Pliny tells us (*l. c.*) that it was situated 9 miles from Volsinii, on the side towards Rome. It is said that the name was still retained by a place called *Trosso* or *Vado di Trosso*, about 2 miles from *Monte Fiascone*, as late as the 17th century, but all trace of it is now lost. (Holsten. *Not. ad Cluver.* p. 67; Dennis's *Etruria*, vol. i. p. 517.) [E. H. B.]

TRUENTUM. [CASTRUM TRUENTINUM.]

TRUENTUS or TRUENTI'NUS (Τρουεντῖνος: *Tronto*), a considerable river of Picenum, which rises in the Apennines above *Amatrice*, flows under the walls of *Ascoli* (Asculum), and falls into the Adriatic about 5 miles S. of *S. Benedetto*. It gave name to a town which was situated at its mouth, and is called by Pliny Truentum, but more commonly CASTRUM TRUENTINUM. Though one of the most considerable of the rivers of Picenum, the Truentus has very much the character of a mountain torrent, and is only navigable for about 5 miles near its mouth. (Strab. v. p. 241; Plin. iii. 13. s. 18; Mel. ii 4. § 6; Ptol. iii. 1. § 21.) [E. H. B.]

TRUTULENSIS PORTUS. [RUTUPIAE.]

TRYBACTRA (Τρυβάκτρα, Ptol. vi. 12. § 6), a place to the NW. of Alexandreia Oxiana, probably represented by the present *Bokhára.* [V.]

TUAESIS (Τούαισις, Ptol. ii. 3 § 13), a town

on the E. coast of Britannia Barbara, which stood on an estuary of the same name (Ptol. *ib.* § 5), now the *Murray Frith.* [T. H. D.]

TUATI VETUS, a town in Hispania Baetica, belonging to the jurisdiction of Corduba. (Plin. iii. 3. s. 3.) Ukert (ii. pt. i. p. 370) is of opinion that it should be call Tucci Vetus. [T. H. D.]

TUBANTES or TUBANTII (Τούβαντοι or Τούβάντιοι), a German tribe which was allied with the Cherusci, and seems originally to have dwelt between the *Rhine* and *Yssel*; but in the time of Germanicus they appear in the country south of the *Lippe*, that is, the district previously occupied by the Sigambri (Tac. *Ann.* i. 51, xiii. 55, foll.) They seem to have followed the Cherusci still farther to the south-east, as Ptolemy (ii. 11. § 23) places them on the south of the Chatti, near the *Thüringer Wald*, between the rivers *Fulda* and *Werra* (Comp. Tac. *Germ.* 36). In the end we find them again as a member of the confederacy of the Franks. (Nazarius, *Paneg. Const.* 18.) The name Subattii in Strabo (vii. p. 292) is probably only an error of the transcriber, whence Kramer has changed it into Τούβάντιοι. (Wilhelm. *Germanien*, p. 130.) [L.S.]

TUBUCCI, a place in Lusitania between Scalabris and Mundobriga. (*Itin. Ant.* p. 420.) Probably *Abrantes.* [T. H. D.]

TUBURBO MAJUS and MINUS (Θουβουρβώ, Ptol. iv. 3. § 35), two neighbouring towns in the interior of Byzacium. The latter is still called *Tebourba*; the former is variously identified with *Tubersole* and *Zaghouan.* Pliny (v. 4. s. 4) writes the name Tuburbis. (*Itin. Ant.* pp. 44, 48; *Tab. Peut.*) [T.H.D.]

TUBUSUPTUS (Τουβούσουπτος, Τουβούσουπτος, or Τουβούσιππος, Ptol. iv. 2. § 31, viii. 13. § 12), a town of Mauretania Caesariensis, 18 miles SE. of Saldae. (*Itin. Ant.* p. 32.) According to Ammianus Marcellinus it was situated close to Mons Ferratus (xxix. 5. § 11). From Pliny (v. 2. s. 1) we learn that it was a Roman colony since the time of Augustus. It was once a place of some importance, but afterwards declined, though even at a late period it seems to have had a Roman garrison (*Not. Imp.*, where it is called Tubusubdus). Variously identified with *Burg, Bordj, Ticla*, and a place on the *Djebel Afroun.* [T. H. D.]

TUCABA (Τούκαβα, Ptol. iv. 6. § 25), a place in the interior of Libya. [T. H. D.]

TUCCA (Τούκκα, Ptol. iv. 2. § 28). 1. A town of Mauretania Caesariensis. Ptolemy places it in the interior; but according to Pliny (v. 2. s. 1) it was on the sea, at the mouth of the river Ampsaga. (Cf. *Tab. Peut.*)

2. A town in the district of Byzacium in Africa Proper. (Ptol. iv. 3. § 32.) From inscriptions found in a village still called *Dugga* it may be inferred that the place should be more correctly called Tugga. According to the *Itin. Ant.* (pp. 47, 49, 51) it lay 50 miles N. of Sufetula, the modern *Sbaitha* or *Sfaitla*, and also bore the name of Terebentina or Terebinthina, probably from its being situated in a neighbourhood abounding with the Terebinth tree. Tucca was a fortified town. (Procop. *de Aed.* vi. 5.) It is probably the same place called Tuccabori by St. Augustin (*adv. Donat.* vi. 24.) (Cf. Wessel. *ad Itin.* p. 48.)

3. A town of Numidia. (Ptol. iv. 3. § 29.) [T. H. D.]

TUCCI (Τούκκι, Ptol. ii. 4. § 11), a town of Hispania Baetica, between Ilipla and Italica (*Itin. Ant.* p. 432.) According to Pliny (iii. 3. s. 3) it

4 K 3

had the surname of Augusta Gemella. Commonly identified with *Tejada*. (Cf. Florez, *Esp. Sagr.* xii. p. 355.)   [T. H. D.]

TUCRIS (Τούκρις, Ptol. ii. 6. § 56), a town of the Arevaci in Hispania Tarraconensis [T. H. D.]

TUDE (Τοῦδαι and Τοῦνδαι, Ptol ii. 6. § 45), a fort or castle of the Gruii or Gravii, in Hispania Tarraconensis, E. of Limia, and on the road from Bracara to Asturica. (*Itin. Ant.* p. 429.) It is called Tyde by Pliny (iv. 20. s. 34), and according to an ancient tradition it was the seat of an Aetolian colony under Diomed; a tale probably occasioned by the similarity of its name to that of Tydeus. (Sil. Ital. iii. 367, xvi. 369; Plin. *l. c.*; Avien. *Descr. Orb.* 650.) It is the modern *Tuy.* [T. H. D.]

TUDER (Τοῦδερ: *Eth.* Tudertinus: *Todi*), one of the most considerable cities of Umbria, situated on a lofty hill, rising above the left bank of the Tiber, about 26 miles S. of Perusia and 18 W. of Spoletium. There is no doubt that it was an ancient Umbrian city, but no mention of the name occurs in history previous to the Roman conquest. Silius Italicus tells us that it was celebrated for the worship of Mars (Sil. Ital. iv. 222, viii. 462), and notices its position on a lofty hill. (Id. vi. 645.) The first notice of it in history is on occasion of a prodigy which occurred there at the time of the invasion of the Cimbri and Teutones (Plut. *Mar.* 17; Plin. ii. 57. s. 58); and shortly after we learn that it was taken by Crassus, as the lieutenant of Sulla, during the wars of the latter with the partisans of Marius. (Plut. *Crass.* 6.) It received a colony under Augustus, and assumed the title of "Colonia Fida Tuder," probably in consequence of some services rendered during the Perusian War, though its name is not mentioned by Appian. (Plin. iii. 14. s. 19; *Lib. Colon.* p. 214; Murat. *Inscr.* pp. 1111. 4, 1120. 3; Orell. *Inscr.* 3726.) It appears from inscriptions to have been a flourishing and important town under the Roman Empire, and is mentioned by all the geographers among the chief towns of Umbria. (Strab. v. p. 227; Plin. *l. c.*; Ptol. iii. 1. § 54.) It was not situated on the Flaminian Way, but the Tabula gives a line of road, which led from Ameria to Tuder, and thence to Perusia. (*Tab. Peut.*) Its great strength as a fortress, arising from its elevated position, is already alluded to by Strabo (*l. c.*), and rendered it a place of importance during the Gothic Wars, after the fall of the Western Empire. (Procop. *B. G.* ii. 10, 13.) It is again mentioned as a city under the Lombards (P. Diac. iv. 8); and there can be no doubt that it continued throughout the middle ages to be a considerable city. It is now much decayed, and has only about 2500 inhabitants, but still retains the title of a city.

Considerable ancient remains still attest its former consideration. Among these the most remarkable are the walls of the city, some portions of which are apparently of great antiquity, resembling those of Perusia, Volaterrae, and other Etruscan cities, but they are in general more regular and less rude. Other parts of the walls, of which three distinct circuits may be traced, are of regular masonry and built of travertine. These are certainly of Roman date. There are also the remains of an ancient building, called by local antiquarians the temple of Mars, but more probably a basilica of Roman date. Numerous coins and other small objects have been found at *Todi:* among the latter the most interesting is a bronze statue of Mars, now in the *Museo Gregoriano* at Rome. The coins of Tuder, which are

numerous, belong to the class called Aes Grave, being of brass and of large size, resembling the earliest coinage of Volaterrae, Iguvium, &c. They all have the name written in Etruscan characters TVTERE, which we thus learn to have been the native form of the name. [E. H. B.]

TUE'ROBIS (Τουέροβις, Ptol ii. 3. § 11), a river on the W. coast of Britannia Romana, now the *Tivy.* [T. H. D.]

TUFICUM (Τούφικον: *Eth.* Tuficanus), a municipal town of Umbria, mentioned both by Pliny and Ptolemy, as well as in an inscription, which confirms its municipal rank; but its site is wholly uncertain. (Plin. iii. 14. s. 19; Ptol. iii. 1. § 53; Orell. *Inscr.* 87.)   [E. H. B.]

TU'GENI (Τωΰγενοί). [HELVETII, Vol. I. p. 1041.]

TUGIA, a town of the Oretani, in Hispania Tarraconensis. (Plin. iii. 3. s. 4; *Itin. Ant.* p. 404.) Its site is marked by some ruins at *Toya*, near *Quesada*, at the sources of the *Guadalquivir*. (Cf. Florez, *Esp. Sagr.* v. pp. 24, 34; D'Anville, *Geogr. Anc.* i. p. 34.)   [T. H. D.]

TUGIENSIS SALTUS, a part of the chain of Mount Orospeda, which derived its name from the town of Tugia, and in which, according to Pliny (iii. 1. s. 3), the Baetis had its source, whence it would appear to be the same branch called by others Mons Argentarius. [Cf. OROSPEDA.] [T. H. D.]

TUICIAE or TERICIAE, as some read it, in Gallia Narbonensis, between Glanum [GLANUM] and Aquae Sextiae (*Aix*). It is placed in the Table between Glanum and Pisavae, xl. from Glanum and xv. from Pisavae. D'Anville fixes Tuiciae or Tericiae, as he reads the name, about *Aiquières* or *Aureille*. This second name, as he observes, seems to have some relationship to that of the Roman road described in the Antonine Itin. under the name of Via Aurelia as far as Arelate (*Arles*). It is said that there are many remains at a place named *Jean-Jean* about a mile from *Aiquières*. [G. L.]

TULCIS, a small river on the E. coast of Hispania, near Tarraco. (Mela, ii. 6.) It is probably the modern *Gaya.* [T. H. D.]

TULINGI. [HELVETII, Vol. I. p. 1042.]

TULIPHURDUM (Τουλίφουρδον), a place in Germany, probably in the country of the Chauci Minores, on the right bank of the Visurgis. (Ptol. ii. 11. § 28.) Wilhelm (*Germanien*, p. 161) identifies it with the modern *Verden*; but this is a mere conjecture.   [L. S.]

TULISU'RGIUM (Τουλισούργιον), a town in Germany, probably belonging to the country of the Dulgibini. (Ptol. ii. 11. § 28.) Not to mention other conjectures as to its modern representative, Zeuss (*Die Deutschen*, p. 7) and Wilhelm (*Germanien*, p. 46) are of opinion that the reading in Ptolemy is wrong, and that we should read Τευτιβούργιον, which they regard as the place from which the Teutoburgiensis Saltus derived its name; and it is accordingly believed that the remains of an ancient wall, now called the *Hünenring*, on Mount Grotenburg, near *Detmold*, marks the site of the ancient Teutoburgium. But all this is no more than a plausible conjecture.   [L. S.]

TULLICA (Τούλλικα, Ptol. ii. 6. § 64), a town of the Carieti in Hispania Tarraconensis. [T. H. D.]

TULLO'NIUM (Τουλόνιον, Ptol. ii. 6. § 66), a town of the Barduli in Hispania Tarraconensis, on the road from Pompelo to Asturica. (*Itin. Ant.* p. 455.) Probably the modern *Alegria.* [T. H. D.]

TULLUM (Τούλλον), in Gallia Belgica, is one of the cities of the Leuci, who bordered on the Mediomatrici. (Ptol. ii. 9. § 13.) Nasium is the other city [Nasium]. The Notitia of the Provinces of Gallia mentions Tullum thus : " Civitas Leucorum Tullo." *Toul*, which is Tullum, has preserved its name instead of taking the name of the people, like most other capital towns. *Toul* is in the department of the *Meurthe*. 　　[G. L.]

TUNES (Τύνης, Polyb. i. 30; Τόβνις, or Τύνις, Strab. xvii. p. 834, &c.), a strongly fortified town, once of some importance, in the Roman province of Africa. According to Polybius (xiv. 20), who is followed by Livy (xxx. 9), it was 120 stadia or 15 miles from Carthage, from which it lay in a SW. direction; but the Tab. Peut., in which it is written Thunis, places it more correctly at a distance of only 10 miles from that city. It is said to have been situated at the mouth of a little river called Catada, in the bay of Carthage, but there are now no traces of any such river. On the present state of *Tunis*, see Blaquière, *Lett.* i. p. 161, seq.; Ritter *Erdkunde*, i. p. 914, seq. 　　　　　　[T. H. D.]

TUNGRI (Τούγγροι), are placed by Ptolemy (ii. 9. § 9) east of the Tabullas river, and their chief place is Atuacutum, which is Aduatuca or *Tongern* [Aduatica]. Tacitus (*German.* c. 2) says. " Those who first crossed the Rhine and expelled the Galli, are now called Tungri, but were then named Germani." Tacitus speaks of the Tungri in two other passages (*Hist.* iv. 55. 79); and in one of them he appears to place the Tungri next to the Nervii. The name of the Eburones, whom Caesar attempted to annihilate [Eburones], disappears in the later geography, and the Tungri take their place. (Plin. iv. 31.) D'Anville observes (*Notice, &c.*) that the name of the Tungri extended over a large tract of country, and comprehended several peoples; for in the Notit. of the Provinces of Gallia, the Tungri divide with the Agrippinenses all Germania Secunda; and there is some evidence that the bishops of *Tongern* had once a territory which bordered on that of *Reims*.

Ammianus (xv. 11) gives the name of the people, Tungri, to one of the chief cities of Germania Secunda; the other is Agrippina (*Cologne*). This shows that *Tongern* under the later Empire was a large place. Many Roman remains have been dug up there; and it is said that the old Roman road may still be traced through the town. 　　[G. L.]

TUNNOCELUM, according to the Notitia Imp. a place on the coast of Britannia Romana, at the end of the wall of Hadrian. the station of the Cohors I. Aelia Classica. Horsley (p. 91) and others place it at *Bowness*, on *Solway Frith;* Camden, with less probability, seeks it at *Tynemouth*, on the E. coast. 　　　　　　[T. H. D.]

TUNTOBRIGA (Τουττόβριγα, Ptol. ii. 6. § 39), a town of the Callaici in Hispania Tarraconensis. 　　　　　　[T. H. D.]

TURANIANA, a place in Hispania Baetica, not far from the coast, between Murgis and Urci. (*Itin. Ant.* p. 405.) Variously identified with *Torque, Torbiscon*, and *Tabernas*. 　　[T. H. D.]

TURBA, a town of the Edetani in Hispania Tarraconensis. (Liv. xxxiii. 44.) Perhaps the modern *Tuejar* on the *Guadalaviar*. 　　[T. H. D.]

TURBA. [Bigerriones.]

TURBULA (Τούρβουλα, Ptol. ii. 6. § 61), a town of the Bastetani in Hispania Tarraconensis. D'Anville (*Geogr. An.* i. p. 28) and Mentelle (*Esp.*

Anc. p. 177) identify it with *Teruel;* but Ukert (ii. pt. i. p. 407) more correctly declares it to be *Tovorra* in *Murcia*. The inhabitants are called Τορβολῆται by App. *Hisp.* 10. 　　　　　　[T. H. D.]

TURCAE (Τοῦρκοι, Suid. *s. v.*), a Scythian people of Asiatic Sarmatia, dwelling on the Palus Maeotis, which appears to be identical with the Ἰύρκαι of Herodotus (iv. 22, &c.). The various hypotheses that have been started respecting the Turcae only show that nothing certain is known respecting them. (Cf. Mannert, iv. p. 130; Heeren, *Ideen*, i. 2, pp. 189, 281, 307; Schaffarik, *Slav. Alterth.* i. p. 318, &c.) Humboldt (*Central-Asien*, i. p. 245, ed. Mahlmann) opposes the notion that these Turcae or Jyrcae were the ancestors of the present Turks. 　　　　　　[T. H. D.]

TURCILINGI, a tribe in northern Germany which is not noticed before the fifth century of our era, and then is occasionally mentioned along with the Rugii. (Jornand. *Get.* 15; Paul. Diac. i. 1.) 　　　　　　[L. S.]

TURDETA'NI (Τουρδητανοί, Ptol. ii. 4. § 5, &c.), the principal people of Hispania Baetica; whence we find the name of Turdetania (Τουρδητανία or Τουρτυταρία) used by Strabo (iii. p. 136) and Stephanus Byz. (p. 661) as identical with Baetica. Their territory lay to the W. of the river Singulis (now *Xenil*), on both sides of the Baetis as far as Lusitania on the W. The Turdetani were the most civilised and polished of all the Spanish tribes. They cultivated the sciences; they had their poets and historians, and a code of written laws, drawn up in a metrical form (Strab. iii. pp. 139, 151, 167; Polyb. xxxiv. 9). Hence they were readily disposed to adopt the manners and customs of their conquerors, and became at length almost entirely Romans; but with these characteristics we are not surprised to find that they are at the same time represented by Livy (xxxiv. 17) as the most unwarlike of all the Spanish races. They possessed the Jus Latii. Some traits in their manners are noted by Diodorus Sic. (v. 33), Silius Italicus (iii. 340, seq.), and Strabo (iii. 164). Their superior civilisation was no doubt derived from their intercourse with the Phoenicians whose colony of Tartessus lay in their neighbourhood. 　　[T. H. D.]

TURDULI (Τουρδοῦλοι, Ptol. ii. 4. § 10), a people in Hispania Baetica, very nearly connected with the Turdetani, and ultimately not to be distinguished from them. (Strab. iii. p. 139; Polyb. xxxiv. 9). They dwelt to the E. and S. of the Turdetani, down to the shores of the Fretum Herculeum. A branch of them called the Turduli Veteres appears to have migrated into Lusitania, and to have settled to the S. of the Durius; where it is probable that in process of time they became amalgamated with the Lusitanians (Strab. iii. p. 151; Mela, iii. 1. § 7; Plin. iii. 1. s. 3, iv. 21. s. 35; cf. Florez, *Esp. Sagr.* ix. p. 7). 　　[T. H. D.]

TURECIONICUM or TURECIONNUM, in Gallia Narbonensis, is placed in the Table on a road between Vienna (*Vienne*) and Cularo (*Grenoble*). Turecionicum is between Vienna and Morginnum (*Moirans*). The site is unknown. 　　[G. L.]

TURIA or TURIUM, a river in the territory of the Edetani in Hispania Tarraconensis, which enters the sea in the neighbourhood of Valentia (Mela, ii. 6; Plin. iii. 3. s. 4; Vib. Seq. p. 227, ed. Bip.) It was famed for the proelium Turiense between Pompey and Sertorius (Plut. *Pomp.* 18, *Sert.* 19; Cic. *p. Balb.* 2). Now the *Guadalaviar*. 　　[T. H. D.]

TURIASO (Τουριασώ and Τουριασσώ, Ptol. ii. 6. § 58; Turiasson, Geogr. Rav. iv. 43: Eth. Turiasonensis, Plin. iii. 3. s. 4), a town of the Celtiberi in Hispania Tarraconensis, on the road from Caesaraugusta to Numantia (Itin. Ant. pp. 442, 443). According to Pliny (l. c.) it was a civitas Romana in the jurisdiction of Caesaraugusta. A fountain in its neighbourhood was said to have the quality of hardening iron (Id. xxxiv. 14. s. 41). The town is now called Tarrasona. For coins see Florez, Med. ii. p. 600, iii. p. 124; Mionnet, i. p. 53, and Suppl. i. p. 167; Sestini p. 207.   [T. H. D.]

TURICUM. [HELVETII, Vol. I. p. 1041.]

TURIGA. [CURGIA.]

TURISSA (called by Ptolemy Τρούρισα, ii. 6. § 67), a town of the Vascones in Hispania Tarraconensis, on the road from Pompelo to Burdigala (Itin. Ant. p. 455.) Variously identified with Ituren and Osteriz.   [T. H. D.]

TURMO'DIGL [MURBOGI.]

TU'RMOGUM (Τούρμογον, Ptol. ii. 5. § 8), a town in the interior of Lusitania.   [T. H. D.]

TURMULI, a town of Lusitania on the Tagus, and on the road from Emerita to Caesaraugusta. (Itin. Ant. p. 433.) Variously identified with Alconetar and Puente de Alcuñete.   [T. H. D.]

TURNACUM or TORNACUM, a city of North Gallia, is first mentioned in the Roman Itins. In the Notit. Imp. mention is made of a military force under the name of Numerus Turnacensium; and of a "Procurator Gynaecii Tornacensis Belgicae Secundae." This procurator is explained to be a superintendent of some number of women who were employed in making clothing for the soldiers. Hieronymus about A. D. 407 speaks of Turnacum as one of the chief towns of Gallia; and Audoenus, in his life of S. Eligius (St. Eloi) in the seventh century, says of it, "quae quondam regalis extitit civitas." Turnacum was within the limits of the ancient territory of the Nervii. The Flemish name is Doórnick, which the French have corrupted into Tournai. Tournai is on the Schelde, in the province of Hainault, in the kingdom of Belgium.

There are silver corns of Turnacum, with the legend DVRNACOS and DVRNACVS. On one side there is the head of an armed man, and on the other a horseman armed. On some there is said to be the legend DVBNO REX. Numerous Roman medals have been found at Tournai, some of the time of Augustus and others as late as Claudius Gothicus and Tetricus, and even of a later date. The tomb of Childeric I., who died A. D. 481, was discovered at Tournai in the seventeenth century, and a vast quantity of gold and silver medals, and other curious things; among which was the golden ring of Childeric, with his name on it, CHILDIRICI REGIS. Such discoveries as these, which have been made in various places in Belgium, show how little we know of the Roman history of this country. (D'Anville, Notice, &c.; Ukert, Gallien; Recueil d'Antiquités Romaines et Gauloises trouvées dans la Flandre proprement dite, par M. J. de Bast.) [G.L.]

TUROBRICA, a town of Hispania Baetica in the jurisdiction of Hispalis (Plin. iii. 1. s. 3). [T.H.D.]

TU'RODI (Τουροδοί, Ptol.ii. 6. § 40), a people in Hispania Tarraconensis, probably a subdivision of the Callaici Bracarii, in whose territory were the baths called Ὕδατα λαιδ.   [T. H. D.]

TU'RONES, TU'RONI, TURO'NII. Some of Caesar's troops wintered in the country of the Turones after the campaign of B. C. 57 (B. G. ii. 35). The Turones are mentioned again (B. G. viii. 46), where we learn that they bordered on the Carnutes; and in another place (vii. 4) they are mentioned with the Pictones, Cadurci, Aulerci, and other states of Western Gallia. When Vercingetorix (B. C. 52) was rousing all Gallia against Caesar, he ordered the Turones to join him. The contingent which they were called on to furnish against Caesar, during the siege of Alesia was 8000 men (vii. 75). But the Turones never gave Caesar much trouble, though Lucan calls them "instabiles" (i. 437), if the verse is genuine.

In Ptolemy (ii. 8. § 14), the name is Τουρογυεῖς, and the capital is Caesarodunum or Tours on the Loire. In the insurrection of Sacrovir in the time of Tiberius, the Turonii, as Tacitus calls them (Ann. iii. 41, 46), rose against the Romans, but they were soon put down. They are in the Lugdunensis of Ptolemy. The chief part of the territory of the Turones was south of the Loire, and their name is the origin of the provincial name Touraine. Ukert (Gallien, p. 329) mentions a silver coin of the Turoni. On one side there is a female head with the legend "Turonos," and on the other "Cantorix" with the figure of a galloping horse.   [G. L.]

TURO'NI (Τούρωνοι), a German tribe, described as occupying a district on the south of the country once inhabited by the Chatti, perhaps on the northern bank of the Moenus. (Ptol. ii. 11. § 22.) [L. S.]

TUROQUA (in the Geogr. Rav. iv. 43, TURAQUA), a town of the Callaici in Hispania Tarraconensis on the road from Bracara to Lucus Augusti (Itin. Ant. p. 430.) Variously identified with Touren (or Turon) and Ribavadia.   [T. H. D.]

TURRES, a place in the interior of Moesia Superior. (Itin. Ant. p. 135; Itin. Hieros. p. 566; Geogr. Rav. iv. 7.) Procopius (de Aed. iv. 4. p. 285) calls it Τουρρίθας, which is intended for Turribus. Variously identified with Ssarköi and Tchardah.   [T. H. D.]

TURRES (AD). 1. A town of the Oretani in Hispania Tarraconensis (Itin. Ant. p. 445). Variously identified with Calatrava and Oreto.

2. A town in the territory of the Contestani in the same province (Itin. Ant. p. 400). Identified either with Castralla or Olleria.   [T.H.D.]

TURRES ALBAE (Πύργοι Λευκοί, Ptol. ii. 5. § 6), a place of the Celtici in Lusitania. [T. H. D.]

TURRIGA (Τούρριγα or Τούργυνα, Ptol. ii. 6. § 23), a town of the Callaici Lucenses in Hispania Tarraconensis.   [T. H. D.]

TURRIM, AD, in Gallia Narbonensis, east of Aquae Sextiae (Aix), is placed in the Antonine Itin. between Matavonium and Tegulata (TEGULATA). The name Turris is preserved in that of Tourves, which is written Torreves and Torvis in some middle age documents. (D'Anville, Notice, &c.)   [G. L.]

TURRIS. 1. TURRIS CAESARIS, a place in Numidia, whence there was a road through Sigus to Cirta. (Itin. Ant. p. 34.) Usually identified with Twill, but by Lapie with Djebel Guerionu.

2. [EUPHRANTA TURRIS.]

3. TURRIS HANNIBALIS, a strong fortress in the territory of Carthage, where Hannibal took ship when flying to king Antiochus. (Liv. xxxiii. 48.) Justin calls it the Rus urbanum Hannibalis (xxxi. 2). It seems to have been situated between Acholla and Thapsus, at the spot where the Tab. Peut. places Sullectis.

4. TURRIS TAMALLENI, in Africa Proper, on the road from Tacape to Leptis Magna. (Itin. Ant. pp 73, 74.) Now Telemin.   [T. H. D.]

TURRIS LIBYSSONIS (Πύργος Λιβύσσωνος, Ptol.: *Porto Torres*), a town of Sardinia, and apparently one of the most considerable in the island. It is situated on the N. coast about 15 miles E. of the Gorditanian promontory (the *Capo del Falcone*), and on the spacious bay now called *Golfo dell' Asinara*. Pliny tells us it was a Roman colony, and we may probably infer from its name that there was previously no town on the spot, but merely a fort or castellum. (Plin. iii. 12. s. 17.) It is noticed also by Ptolemy and in the Itineraries, but without any indication that it was a place of any importance. (Ptol. iii. 3. § 5; *Itin. Ant.* p. 83.) But the ancient remains still existing prove that it must have been a considerable town under the Roman Empire; and we learn from the inscriptions on ancient milestones that the principal road through the island ran directly from Caralis to Turris, a sufficient proof that the latter was a place much frequented. It was also an episcopal see during the early part of the middle ages. The existing port at *Porto Torres*, which is almost wholly artificial, is based in great part on Roman foundations; and there exist also the remains of a temple (which, as we learn from an inscription, was dedicated to Fortune, and restored in the reign of Philip), of thermae, of a basilica and an aqueduct, as well as a bridge over the adjoining small river, still called the *Fiume Turritano*. The ancient city continued to be inhabited till the 11th century, when the greater part of the population migrated to *Sassari*, about 10 miles inland, and situated on a hill. This is still the second city of the island. (De la Marmora, *Voy. en Sardaigne*, vol. ii. pp. 363, 465—472; Smyth's *Sardinia*, pp. 263—266.) [E. H. B.]

TURRIS STRATO'NIS. [CAESAREIA, p. 470, a.]

TURRUS FLUVIUS. [AQUILEIA.]

TURU'LIS (Τούρουλις, Ptol. ii. 6. § 15), a river in the territory of the Edetani in Hispania Tarraconensis, between the Iberus and the Fretum Herculis. Ukert (ii. pt. i. p. 293) thinks that it is probably identical with the Saetabis of Mela (ii. 6) and the Uduba of Pliny (iii. 3. s. 4), the present *Mijares* or *Myares*. [T. H. D.]

TURUM (*Eth.* Turinus: *Turi*), a town of Apulia, mentioned only by Pliny, who enumerates the Turini among the towns of that province. (Plin. iii. 11. s. 16.) The name is written Tutini in our present text of Pliny; but it is probable that we should read Turini, and that the site is marked by the present village of *Turi*, near *Conversano*, about 6 miles W. of *Polignano*. (Romanelli, vol. ii. p. 180.) [E. H. B.]

TURUNTUS (Τουροῦντος, Ptol. iii. 5. § 2), a river of European Sarmatia which fell into the Northern Ocean, and which, according to Marcian (p. 55), had its source in the Rhipaean mountains, but Ptolemy seems to place it in Mount Alaunus or Alanus. Mannert (iv. p. 258) takes it to be the *Windaw*. [T. H. D.]

TURUPTIA'NA (Τουρουπτίανα, Ptol. ii. 6. § 23), a town of the Callaici Lucenses in Hispania Tarraconensis. [T. H. D.]

TUSCA, a river forming the W. boundary of the Roman province of Africa, which, after a short course to the N., fell into the sea near Tabraca. (Plin. v. ss. 2, 3.) [T. H. D.]

TUSCA'NIA (*Eth.* Tuscaniensis: *Toscanella*), a city of Southern Etruria, situated about 12 miles NE. of Tarquinii. It is mentioned only by Pliny, who enumerates the Tuscanienses among the municipal communities of Etruria, and in the Tabula,

which places it on the Via Clodia, between Blera and Saturnia, but in a manner that would afford little clue to its true position were it not identified by the resemblance of name with the modern *Toscanella*. (Plin. iii. 5. s. 8; *Tab. Peut.*) The name is found in an inscription, which confirms its municipal rank. (Murat. *Inscr.* p. 328.) But it appears to have been in Roman times an obscure town, and we find no allusion to it as of ancient Etruscan origin. Yet that it was so is rendered probable by the tombs that have been discovered on the site, and some of which contain sarcophagi and other relics of considerable interest; though none of these appear to be of very early date. The tombs have been carefully examined, and the antiquities preserved by a resident antiquary, Sig. Campanari, a circumstance which has given some celebrity to the name of *Toscanella*, and led to a very exaggerated estimate of the importance of Tuscania, which was apparently in ancient times never a place of any consideration. It was probably during the period of Etruscan independence a dependency of Tarquinii. The only remains of ancient buildings are some fragments of reticulated masonry, undoubtedly of the Roman period. (Dennis's *Etruria*, vol. i. pp. 440—460.) [E. H. B.]

TUSCI (Τοῦσκοι, Ptol. v. 9. § 22), a people of Asiatic Sarmatia between the Caucasus and the Montes Ceraunii. [T. H. D.]

TU'SCIA. [ETRURIA.]

TUSCULA'NUM. [TUSCULUM, p. 1243, b.]

TU'SCULUM (Τούσκουλον, Ptol. iii. l. § 61; Τούσκλον, Strab. v. p. 237; Τούσκλος, Steph. B. p. 673: *Eth.* Tusculanus, Cic. *Balb.* 20; Liv. iii. 7, &c.: *Adj.* Tusculus, Tib. i. 7. 57; Stat. *Silv.* iv. 4. 16; Tusculanensis, Cic. *Fam.* ix. 6: *Frascati* and *Il Tuscolo*), a strong and ancient city of Latium, lying on the hills which form a continuation of Mount Albanus on the W. When Dionysius of Halicarnassus (x. 20) places it at a distance of 100 stadia, or 12½ miles, from Rome, he does not speak with his accustomed accuracy, since it was 120 stadia, or 15 miles, from that city by the Via Latina. Josephus (*Ant.* xviii. 7. § 6) places the imperial villa of Tiberius at Tusculum at 100 stadia from Rome, which, however, lay at some distance to the W. of the town. Festus (*s. v. Tuscos*) makes Tusculum a diminutive of Tuscus, but there is but slight authority to connect the town with the Etruscans. According to common tradition, it was founded by Telegonus, the son of Ulysses and Circe; and hence we find its name paraphrased in the Latin poets as "Telegoni moenia" (Ov. *Fast.* iii. 91, iv. 71; Prop. iii. 30. 4; Sil. It. xii. 535) and "Circaea moenia" (Hor. *Epod.* i. 30); and the hill on which it stood called "Telegoni juga parricidae" (Id. *Od.* iii. 29. 8), "Circaeum dorsum" (Sil. It. vii. 691), and "Telegoni jugera" (Stat. *Silv.* i. 3. 83). Thus Tusculum did not claim so remote an origin as many other Latin cities; and, as being founded a generation after the Trojan War, Virgil, a learned antiquary, consistently omits all notice of it in his *Aeneid.* The author of the treatise entitled *Origo Gentis Romanae* mentions that it was made a dependency or colony of Alba by Latinus Silvius (c. 17. § 6). After the destruction of Alba by Tullus Hostilius it appears to have recovered its independence, and to have become a republic under the government of a dictator.

But to descend from these remote periods to the more historical times. In the reign of Tarquinius

Superbus, who courted the friendship of the Latin cities, Octavius Mamilius of Tusculum was the foremost man of all the race, tracing his descent from Ulysses and Circe. Him Tarquin conciliated by the gift of his daughter in marriage, and thus obtained the powerful alliance of his family and connections. (Liv. i. 49; Dionys. iv. 45.) The genealogical pretensions of the gens Mamilia are still to be seen on their coins, which bear on the obverse the head of Mercury, and on the reverse Ulysses in his travelling dress and with his dog. The alliance of Mamilius with Tarquin, however, was the main cause of the Latin War. After his expulsion from Rome, and unsuccessful attempt to regain his crown by means of the Etruscans, Tarquin took refuge with his son-in-law at Tusculum (Liv. ii. 15), and by his assistance formed an alliance with the confederacy of the thirty Latin cities. (*Ib.* 18). The confederate army took up a position near Lake Regillus, a small sheet of water, now dry, which lay at the foot of the hill on which Tusculum is seated. This was the scene of the famous battle so fatal to the Latins, in B. C. 497. Mamilius, who commanded the Latin army, was killed by the hand of Titus Herminius; Tarquinius Superbus himself, who, though now advanced in years, took a part in the combat, was wounded; and the whole Latin army sustained an irretrievable defeat (*ib.* 19, 20; Dionys. vi. 4, seq.).

After the peace which ensued, the Tusculans remained for a long while the faithful allies of Rome; an attachment which drew down on their territory the incursions of the Volsci and Aequi, B. C. 461, 460. (Liv. iii. 7, 8.) In B. C. 458, when the Roman capitol was seized by the Sabine Appius Herdonius, the Tusculans gave a signal proof of their love and fidelity towards Rome. On the next morning after the arrival of the news, a large body of them marched to that city and assisted the Romans in recovering the capitol; an act for which they received the public thanks of that people (*ib.* 18; Dionys. x. 16); and soon afterwards, Lucius Mamilius, the Tusculan dictator was rewarded with the gift of Roman citizenship. (Liv. *ib.* 29.) In the following year the Romans had an opportunity of repaying the obligation. The Aequi had seized the citadel of Tusculum by a nocturnal assault. At that time, Fabius with a Roman army was encamped before Antium; but, on hearing of the misfortune of the Tusculans, he immediately broke up his camp and flew to their assistance. The enterprise, however, was not of such easy execution as the expulsion of Herdonius, and several months were spent in combats in the neighbourhood of Tusculum. At length the Tusculans succeeded in recapturing their citadel by reducing the Aequi to a state of famine, whom they dismissed after compelling them to pass unarmed under the yoke. But as they were flying homewards the Roman consul overtook them on Mount Algidus, and slew them to a man. (*Ib.* 23; Dionys. x. 20.)

In the following year, the Aequi, under the conduct of Gracchus, ravaged the Labican and Tusculan territories, and encamped on the Algidus with their booty. The Roman ambassadors sent to expostulate with them were treated with insolence and contempt. Then Tit. Quinctius Cincinnatus was chosen dictator, who defeated the Aequi, and caused them, with their commander Gracchus, to pass ignominiously under the yoke. (Liv. *ib.* 25—28.) Algidus became the scene of a struggle between the Romans and Aequi on two or three subsequent occa-

sions, as in B. C. 452 and 447. (*Ib.* 31, 42.) In the latter battle the Romans sustained a severe defeat, being obliged to abandon their camp and take refuge in Tusculum. After this, we do not again hear of the Tusculans till B. C. 416. At that period, the Romans, suspecting the Labicans of having entered into a league with the Aequi, charged the Tusculans to keep a watch upon them. These suspicions were justified in the following year, when the Labicans, in conjunction with the Aequi, ravaged the territory of Tusculum and encamped upon the Algidus. The Roman army despatched against them was defeated and dispersed, owing to the dissensions among its chiefs. Many of these, however, together with the *élite* of the army, took refuge at Tusculum; and Q. Servilius Priscus, being chosen dictator, changed the face of affairs in eight days, by routing the enemy and capturing Labicum. (Id. iv. 45—47.)

This steady friendship between Tusculum and Rome, marked for so many years by the strongest tokens of mutual goodwill, was at length interrupted by an occurrence which took place in B. C. 379. In that year the Tusculans, in conjunction with the Gabinians and Labicans, accused the Praenestines before the Roman senate of making inroads on their lands; but the senate gave no heed to their complaints. Next year Camillus, after defeating the Volscians, was surprised to find a number of Tusculans among the prisoners whom he had made, and, still more so when, on questioning them, he found that they had taken up arms by public consent. These prisoners he introduced before the Roman senate, in order to prove how the Tusculans had abandoned the ancient alliance. So war was declared against Tusculum, and the conduct of it entrusted to Camillus. But the Tusculans would not accept this declaration of hostilities, and opposed the Roman arms in a manner that has scarcely been paralleled before or since. When Camillus entered their territory he found the peasants engaged in their usual avocations; provisions of all sorts were offered to his army; the gates of the town were standing open; and as the legions defiled through the streets in all the panoply of war, the citizens within, like the countrymen without, were seen intent upon their daily business, the schools resounded with the hum of pupils, and not the slightest token of hostile preparation could be discerned. Then Camillus invited the Tusculan dictator to Rome. When he appeared before the senate in 'the Curia Hostilia, not only were the existing treaties with Tusculum confirmed, but the Roman franchise also was shortly afterwards bestowed upon it, a privilege at that time but rarely conferred.

It was this last circumstance, however, together with their unshaken fidelity towards Rome, that drew down upon the Tusculans the hatred and vengeance of the Latins; who, in the year B. C. 374, having burnt Satricum, with the exception of the temple of Matuta, directed their arms against Tusculum. By an unexpected attack, they obtained possession of the city; but the inhabitants retired to the citadel with their wives and children, and despatched messengers to Rome with news of the invasion. An army was sent to their relief, and the Latins in turn became the besieged instead of the besiegers; for whilst the Romans encompassed the walls of the city, the Tusculans made sorties upon the enemy from the arx. In a short time the Romans took the town by assault and slew all the

Latins. (*Ib.* 33.) Servius Sulpicius and L. Quinctius, both military tribunes, were the Roman commanders on this occasion; and on some rare gold coins, still extant, of the former family, are seen on the obverse the heads of Castor and Pollux, deities peculiarly worshipped at Tusculum (Cic. *Div.* i. 43; cf. Festus, *s. v. Stroppus*), and on the reverse the image of a city with the letters TVSCVL on the gate.

From this period till the time of the great Latin war we have little to record of Tusculum except the frustrated attempt of the Veliterni on its territory (Liv. iv. 36) and the horrible devastations committed on it by the Gauls, when in alliance with the Tiburtines, in B. C. 357. (Id. vii. 11.) After their long attachment to Rome we are totally at a loss to conjecture the motives of the Tusculans in joining the Latin cities against her. The 'war which ensued is marked by the well-known anecdote of Titus Manlius, who, being challenged by Geminus Mettius, the commander of the Tusculan cavalry, attacked and killed him, against strict orders to the contrary; for which breach of military discipline he was put to death by his father. (Id. viii. 7.) The war ended with the complete subjugation of the Latins; and by the famous senatus-consultum regulating the settlement of Latium, the Tusculans were treated with great indulgence. Their defection was ascribed to the intrigues of a few, and their right of citizenship was preserved to them. (*Ib.* 14.) This settlement took place in B. C. 335. In 321 the Tusculans were accused by the tribune, M. Flavius, of having supplied the Veliterni and Privernates with the means of carrying on war against Rome. There does not appear to have been any foundation for this charge; it seems to have been a mere calumny; nevertheless the Tusculans, with their wives and children, having put on mourning habits, went in a body to Rome, and implored the tribes to acquit them of so odious an imputation. This spectacle moved the compassion of the Romans, who, without further inquiry, acquitted them unanimously; with the exception of the tribe Pollia, which voted that the men of Tusculum should be scourged and put to death, and the women and children sold, agreeably to the laws of war. This vote remained indelibly imprinted on the memory of the Tusculans to the very latest period of the Roman Republic; and it was found that scarce one of the tribe Papiria, to which the Tusculans belonged, ever voted in favour of a candidate of the tribe Pollia. (*Ib.* 37.)

Tusculum always remained a municipium, and some of its families were distinguished at Rome. (Id. vi. 21—26; Orell. *Inscr.* 775, 1368, 3042.) Among them may be mentioned the gens Mamilia, the Porcia, which produced the two Catos, the Fulvia, Coruncania, Juventia, Fonteia, &c. (Cic. p. *Planc.* 8, p. *Font.* 14; Corn. Nep. *Cat.* 1; Val. Max. iii. 4. § 6.)

Hannibal appears to have made an unsuccessful attempt upon, or perhaps rather a mere demonstration against, Tusculum in B. C. 212. (Liv. xxvi. 9; cf. Sil. It. xii. 534.) In the civil wars of Marius and Sulla, its territory seems to have been distributed by the latter. (Auct. *de Coloniis*.) Its walls were also restored, as well as during the wars of Pompey. We have no notices of Tusculum under the Empire. After the war of Justinian and the inroads of the Lombards, Tusculum regained even more than its ancient splendour. For several cen-

turies during the middle ages the counts of Tusculum were supreme in Rome, and could almost dispose of the papal chair. The ancient city remained entire till near the end of the 12th century. At that period there were constant wars between the Tusculans and Romans, the former of whom were supported by the German emperors and protected by the popes. According to Romualdus, archbishop of Salerno (*apud Baronium*, vol. xix. p. 340), the walls of Tusculum were razed in the pontificate of Alexander III. in the year 1168; but perhaps a more probable account by Richard de S. Germano (*ap. Muratori, Script.* t. vii. p. 972) ascribes the destruction of the city to the permission of the German emperor in the year 1191.

Towards the end of the Republic and beginning of the Empire, Tusculum was one of the favourite resorts of the wealthy Romans. Strabo (v. p. 239) describes the hill on which it was built as adorned with many villas and plantations, especially on the side that looked towards Rome. But though the air was salubrious and the country fine, it does not appear, like Tibur, to have been a favourite resort of the Roman poets, nor do they speak of it much in their verses. The Anio, with its fall, besides other natural beauties, lent a charm to Tibur which would ·have been sought in vain at Tusculum. Lucullus seems to have been one of the first who built a villa there, which seems to have been on a magnificent scale, but with little arable land attached to it. (Plin. xviii. 7. s. 1.) His parks and gardens, however, which were adorned with aviaries and fishponds, extended to the Anio, a distance of several miles; whence he was noted in the report of the censors as making more use of the broom than the plough. (*Ib.* and Varr. *R. R.* i. 13, iii. 3, seq.; Columella, i. 4.) On the road towards Rome, in the *Vigna Angelotti*, is the ruin of a large circular mausoleum, 90 feet in diameter inside, and very much resembling the tomb of Caecilia Metella on the Via Appia. It evidently belongs to the last period of the Republic; and Nibby (*Dintorni*, p. 344) is inclined to regard it as the sepulchre of Lucullus, mentioned by Plutarch (*Vit. Luc.* 43), though that is commonly identified with a smaller mausoleum between *Frascati* and the *Villa Rufinella*. Besides the villa of Lucullus, we hear of those of Cato, of Cicero and his brother Quintus, of Marcus Brutus, of Q. Hortensius, of T. Anicius, of Balbus, of Caesar, of L. Crassus, of Q. Metellus, &c. It would now be vain to seek for the sites of most of these; though it may perhaps be conjectured that Cato's stood on the hill to the NE. of the town, which seems to have been called Mons Porcius from it, and still bears the name of *Monte Porzio*. So much interest, however, is attached to the villa of Cicero (Tusculanum), as the favourite retirement in which he probably composed a great portion of his philosophical works, and especially the *Disputations* which take their name from it, that we shall here present the reader with the chief particulars that can be collected on the subject. Respecting the site of the villa there have been great disputes, one school of topographers seeking it at *Grotta Ferrata*, another at the *Villa Rufinella*. Both these places lie to the W. of Tusculum, but the latter nearer to it, and on an eminence, whilst *Grotta Ferrata* is in the plain. We have seen from Strabo that the Roman villas lay chiefly on the W. side of the town; and it will be found further on that Cicero's adjoined those of Lucullus and Gabinius, which were the most splendid and remarkable, and must therefore have belonged to those noticed by Strabo. The scholiast on Horace (*Epod.* i. 30) describes Cicero's as being "ad latera superiora" of the Tusculan hill; and if this authority may be relied on, it disposes of the claims of *Grotta Ferrata.* The plural "latera" also determines us in favour of the W. side of the town, or *Villa Rufinella,* where the hill has two ridges. At this spot some valuable remains were discovered in 1741, especially a beautiful mosaic, now in the *Museo Pio Clementino.* The villa belonged originally to Sulla (Plin. xxii. 6. s. 6). It was, as we have said, close to that of Lucullus, from which, in neighbourly fashion, Cicero was accustomed to fetch books with his own hand. (*De Fin.* iii. 2.) It was likewise near that of the consul Gabinius (*pro Dom.* 24, *post Red.* 7), which also stood on the Tusculan hill (*in Pis.* 21), probably on the site of the *Villa Falconieri.* In his oration *pro Sestio* (43), Cicero says that his own villa was a mere cottage in comparison with that of Gabinius, though the latter, when tribune, had described it as "pictam," in order to excite envy against its owner. Yet from the particulars which we learn from Cicero himself, his retirement must have been far from deficient in splendour. The money which he lavished on it and on his villa at Pompeii brought him deeply into debt. (*Ep. ad Att.* ii. 1.) And in another letter (*Ib.* iv. 2) he complains that the consuls valued that at Tusculum at only *quingentis millibus,* or between 4000*l.* and 5000*l.* This would be indeed a very small sum, to judge by the description of it which we may collect from his own writings. Thus we learn that it contained two *gymnasia* (*Div.* i. 5), an upper one called Lyceum, in which, like Aristotle, he was accustomed to walk and dispute in the morning (*Tusc. Disp.* ii. 3), and to which a library was attached (*Div.* ii. 3), and a lower one, with shady walks like Plato's garden, to which he gave the name of the Academy. (*Tusc. Disp.* ii. 3.) The latter was perhaps on the spot now occupied by the *Casino* of the *Villa Rufinella.* Both were adorned with beautiful statues in marble and bronze. (*Ep. ad Att.* i. 1. 8, 9, 10.) The villa likewise contained a little atrium (atriolum, *Ib.* i. 10, *ad Quint. Fr.* iii. 1), a small portico with exedria (*ad Fam.* vii. 23), a bath (*Ib.* xiv. 20), a covered promenade ("tecta ambulatiuncula," *ad Att.* xiii. 29), and an horologium (*ad Fam.* xvi. 18). In the excavations made in the time of Zuzzeri, a sun-dial was discovered here, and placed in the *Collegio Romano.* The villa, like the town and neighbourhood, was supplied with water by the Aqua Crabra. (*De Leg. Agr.* iii. 31.) But of all this magnificence scarce a vestige remains, unless we may regard as such the ruins now called *Scuola di Cicerone,* close to the ancient walls. These consist of a long corridor with eight chambers, forming apparently the ground floor of an upper building, and if they belonged to the villa they were probably granaries, as there is not the least trace of decoration.

We will now proceed to consider the remains at *Frascati.* Strabo (v. p. 239) indicates where we must look for Tusculum, when he describes it as situated on the high ridge connected with Mount Albanus, and serving to form with it the deep valley which stretches out towards Mount Algidus. This ridge was known by the name of the Tusculani Colles. We have already seen that Tusculum was composed of two distinct parts, the town itself and the arx or citadel, which was isolated from it, and

seated on a higher point; so elevated, indeed, that when the Aequi had possession of it, as before narrated, they could descry the Roman army defiling out of the gates of Rome. (Dionys. x. 20.) It was indeed on the very nut, or pinnacle, of the ridge, a point isolated by cliffs of great elevation, and approachable only by a very steep ascent. According to Sir W. Gell (*Topogr. &c.* p. 429) it is 2079 French feet above the level of the sea. Here a few traces of the walls of the citadel remain, from which, and from the shape of the rock on which the town stood, we may see that it formed an irregular oblong, about 2700 feet in circumference. There must have been a gate towards the town, where the ascent is less steep; and there are also vestiges of another gate on the E. side, towards *La Molara,* and of a road which ran into the Via Latina. Under the rock are caves, which probably served for sepulchres. The city lay immediately under the arx, on the W. side. Its form was a narrow oblong approaching to a triangle, about 3000 feet in length, and varying in breadth from about 1000 to 500 feet. Thus it is represented of a triangular shape on the coins of the gens Sulpicia. Some vestiges of the walls remain, especially on the N. and S. sides. Of these the ancient parts consist of large quadrilateral pieces of local tufo, some of them being 4 to 5 feet long. They are repaired in places with opus incertum, of the age of Sulla, and with opus reticulatum. Including the arx, Tusculum was about 1½ mile in circumference. Between the town and the citadel is a large quadrilateral piscina, 86 feet long by 67½ broad, divided into three compartments, probably intended to collect the rain water, and to serve as a public washing-place. One of the theatres lies immediately under this cistern, and is more perfect than any in the vicinity of Rome. The scena, indeed is partly destroyed and covered with earth; but the benches or rows of seats in the cavea, of which there are nine, are still nearly entire, as well as the steps cut in them for the purpose of commodious descent. There are three flights of these steps, which consequently divide the cavea into four compartments, or cunei. The spectators faced the W., and thus enjoyed the magnificent prospect over the Alban valley and the plains of Latium, with Rome and the sea in the distance. Abeken (*Mittel-Italien,* p. 200), considers this theatre to belong to the early times of the Empire. Sir W. Gell, on the other hand, pronounces it to be earlier. (*Topogr. of Rome,* p. 429.) Near this edifice were discovered in 1818, by Lucien Buonaparte, the beautiful bronze statue of Apollo and those of the two Rutiliae. The last are now in the Vatican, in the corridor of the *Museo Chiaramonti.* At the back of this structure are vestiges of another theatre, or odeum; and at its side two parallel walls, which bounded the street leading to the citadel. On the W. of the theatre is an ancient road in good preservation, leading to one of the gates of the city, where it is joined by another road. Close to the walls near the piscina is an ancient cistern, and at its side a small fountain with an inscription; a little further is a Roman milestone, recording the distance of 15 miles. Besides these objects, there are also remains of a columbarium and of an amphitheatre, but the latter is small and not of high antiquity. Many fragments of architecture of an extremely ancient style are strewed around. Within the walls of the town, in what appears to have been the principal street, several inscriptions still remain, the chief of which is one on a kind of pedestal, recording that the object to which it belonged was sacred to Jupiter and Liberty. Other inscriptions found at Tusculum are preserved in the *Villa Rufinella*. One of them relates to M. Fulvius Nobilior, the conqueror of Aetolia; another to the poet Diphilos, mentioned by Cicero in his letters to Atticus (ii. 19).

Near the hermitage at *Camaldoli* was discovered in 1667 a very ancient tomb of the Furii, as recorded by Falconieri, in his *Inscrr. Athleticae.* p. 143, seq. It was cut in the rock, and in the middle of it was a sarcophagus, about 5 feet long, with a pediment-shaped cover. Round it were twelve urns placed in *loculi*, or coffins. The inscriptions on these urns were in so ancient a character that it bore a great resemblance to the Etruscan and Pelasgic. The form of the P resembled that in the sepulchral inscriptions of the Scipios, as well as that of the *l*. The diphthong OV was used for V, and P for F. The inscriptions on the urns related to the Furii, that on the sarcophagus to Luc. Turpilius. There were also fragments of fictile vases, commonly called Etruscan, and of an elegant cornice of terra cotta, painted with various colours. (Nibby, *Dintorni*, iii. p. 360.)

We shall only add that the ager Tusculanus, though now but scantily supplied with water, formerly contributed to furnish Rome with that element by means of the Aqua Tepula and Aqua Virgo. (Front. *Aq.* 8, seq.)

Respecting Tusculum the reader may consult Canina, *Descrizione dell' antico Tusculo*; Nibby, *Dintorni di Roma*, vol. iii.; Gell, *Topography of Rome and its Vicinity*, ed. Bunbury; Abeken, *Mittel-Italien*; Compagnoni, *Mem. istoriche dell' antico Tusculo*. On Cicero's villa, Cardoni, *De Tuscul. M. T. Ciceronis*; Zuzzeri, *Sopra d' una antica Villa scopertasul Dorso del Tusculo.*   [T. H. D.]

TUSCUM MARE. [TYRRHENUM MARE.]

TUTA'TIO, a place in Noricum of uncertain site (*It. Ant.* p. 277; *Tab. Peut.*, where it is called Tutastio.)   [L. S.]

TU'THOA (Τουθόα), a river of western Arcadia, flowing into the Ladon, on the confines of Thelpusa and Hernea. It is now called *Langádhia*, and joins the Ladon opposite to the small village of *Renéri.* (Paus. viii. 25. § 12 ; Leake, *Morea*, vol. ii. p. 95, *Peloponnesiaca*, p. 223.)

TU'TIA, a small stream in the neighbourhood of Rome, mentioned only by Livy and Silius Italicus, who inform us that Hannibal encamped on its banks, when he was commencing his retreat from before the walls of Rome. (Liv. xxvi. 11; Sil. Ital. xiii. 5.) Livy places it 6 miles from the city, and it is probable that it was on the Salarian Way, by which Hannibal subsequently commenced his retreat: in this case it may probably be the stream now called the *Fiume di Conca*, which crosses that road between 6 and 7 miles from Rome, and has been supposed by Gell and Nibby to be the Allia. [ALLIA.] Silius Italicus expressly tells us that it was a very small stream, and little known to fame. The name is written Turia in many editions of that poet, but it appears that the best MSS. both of Silius and of Livy have the form Tutia. [E. H. B.]

TU'TIA (Τουττία, Plut. *Sert.* 19), a place in the territory of the Edetani in Hispania Tarraconensis not far from Sucro, the scene of a battle between Pompey and Sertorius (Plut. *l. c.*; Florus, iii. 22.) It is thought to be the modern *Tous.* But perhaps

the conjecture of Ukert (ii. pt. i. p. 413) is correct that in both these passages we should read Turia.   [T. H. D.]

TUTICUM. [EQUUS TUTICUS.]

TUTZIS (*It. Anton.* p. 162), a small fortified town in Aethiopia, situated 12 miles N. of Tachompso, upon the western side of the Nile. The ruins of Tutzis are supposed to be near, and NW. of the present village of *Gyrseh.* (Belzoni, *Travels*, vol. i. p. 112.)   [W. B. D.]

TY'ANA (τὰ Τύανα; Eth. Τυανεύς or Τυανίτης), also called Thyana or Thiana, and originally Thoana, from Thoas, a Thracian king, who was believed to have pursued Orestes and Pylades thus far, and to have founded the town (Arrian, *Peripl. P. E.* p. 6; Steph. B. *s. v.*). Report said that it was built, like Zela in Pontus, on a causeway of Semiramis; but it is certain that it was situated in Cappadocia at the foot of Mount Taurus, near the Cilician gates, and on a small tributary of the Lamus (Strab. xii. p. 537, xiii. p. 587.) It stood on the highroad to Cilicia and Syria at a distance of 300 stadia from Cybistra, and 400 stadia (according to the Peut. Table 73 miles) from Mazaca (Strab. *l. c.* ; Ptol. v. 6. § 18 ; comp. Plin. vi. 3 ; *It. Ant.* p. 145). Its situation on that road and close to so important a pass must have rendered Tyana a place of great consequence, both in a commercial and a military point of view. The plain around it, moreover, was extensive and fertile, and the whole district received from the town of Tyana the name of Tyanitis (Τυανῖτις, Strab. *l. c.*). From its coins we learn that in the reign of Caracalla the city became a Roman colony; afterwards, having for a time belonged to the empire of Palmyra, it was conquered by Aurelian, in A. D. 272 (Vopisc. *Aurel.* 22, foll.), and Valens raised it to the rank of the capital of Cappadocia Secunda (Basil. Magn. *Epist.* 74, 75 ; Hierocl. p. 700; Malala, *Chron.*; *Not. Imp.*) Its capture by the Turks is related by Cedrenus (p. 477). Tyana is celebrated in history as the native place of the famous impostor Apollonius, of whom we have a detailed biography by Philostratus. In the vicinity of the town there was a temple of Zeus on the borders of a lake in a marshy plain. The water of the lake itself was cold, but a hot well, sacred to Zeus, issued from it (Philostr. *Vit. Apoll.* i. 4; Amm. Marc. xxiii. 6; Aristot. *Mir. Ausc.* 163.) This well was called Asmabaeon, and from it Zeus himself was surnamed Asmabaeus. These details about the locality of Tyana have led in modern times to the discovery of the true site of the ancient city. It was formerly believed that *Kara Hissar* marked the site of Tyana; for in that district many ruins exist, and its inhabitants still maintain that their town once was the capital of Cappadocia. But this place is too far north to be identified with Tyana; and Hamilton (*Researches*, ii. p. 302, foll.) has shown most satisfactorily, what others had conjectured before him, that the true site of Tyana is at a place now called *Kiz Hissar*, south-west of *Nigdeh*, and between this place and *Erekli.* The ruins of Tyana are considerable, but the most conspicuous is an aqueduct of granite, extending seven or eight miles to the foot of the mountains. There are also massy foundations of several large buildings, shafts, pillars, and one handsome column still standing. Two miles south of these ruins, the hot spring also still bubbles forth in a cold swamp or lake. (Leake, *Asia Minor*, 61; Eckhel, iii. p. 195; Sestini, p. 60.)   [L. S.]

TYBIACAE (Τυβίακαι, Ptol. vi. 14. § 11), a

people of Scythia intra Imaum, on the banks of the Rha.   [T. H. D.]

TYDE. [TUDE.]

TYLE (Τύλη, Polyb. iv. 46), a town of Thrace, on the coast of the Euxine, where the Gauls established a seat of government (βασίλειον), and which Reichard identifies with *Kilios*. Steph. B. (p. 670) calls it Τύλις, and places it on the Haemus. [J. R.]

TYLISSUS, a town of Crete (Plin. iv. 20), the position of which can only be conjectured. On its ancient coins are found on the reverse a young man holding in his right hand the head of an ibex or wild goat, and in his left a bow. These types on the coins of Tylissus led the most distinguished numismatist of the last century (Eckhel, vol. ii. p. 321) to fix its situation somewhere between Cydonia and Elyrus, the bow being common on the coins of the one, and the ibex's head on those of the other, of these two cities. Höck (*Kreta*, vol. i. p. 433) and Torres Y. Ribera (*Periplus Cretae*, p. 324) adopt this suggestion of Eckhel, and place Tylissus on the S. coast at the W. extremity of the island near the modern *Sélino-Kastéli*. (Pashley, *Travels*, vol. i. p. 162.)   [E. B. J.]

TYLUS or TYRUS (Τύλος, Ptol. vi. 7. § 47; Τύρος, Strab. xvi. p. 766; Steph. B. s. v.), an island in the Persian gulf, off the coast of Arabia. It has been already mentioned that according to some traditions, this island was the original seat of the Phoenicians, who named the city of Tyre after it when they had settled on the coasts of the Mediterranean. [PHOENICIA, p. 607.] Pliny describes the island as abounding in pearls. (Plin. vi. 28. s. 32, xii. 10. s. 21, xvi. 41. s. 80; Arrian, *Anab.* vii. 20; Theophr. *Hist. Plant.* iv. 9, v. 6)   [T. H. D.]

TYMANDUS (Τύμανδος: Eth. Τυμανδηνός), a place in Phrygia, between Philomelium and Sozopolis. (*Conc. Chalced.* pp. 244, and 247: in this passage the reading Μανδηνῶν πόλις is corrupt; Hierocl. p. 673, where the name is miswritten Τύμανδρος.) It is possible that Tymandus may be the same as the Dymas mentioned by Livy (xxxviii. 15), for which some MSS. have Dimas or Dinias.   [L. S.]

TYMBRES, a tributary of the Sangarius, in the north of Phrygia (Liv. xxxviii. 18), is in all probability the same river as the one called by Pliny (vi. 1) Tembrogius, which joined the Sangarius, as Livy says, on the borders of Phrygia and Galatia, and, flowing in the plain of Dorylaeum, separated Phrygia Epictetus from Phrygia Salutaris. It seems also to be the same river as the Thyaris and Bathys mentioned in Byzantine writers. (Cinnamus, v. 1. p. 111; Richter, *Wallfahrten*, p. 522, foll.) [L. S.]

TYMPHAEA, TYMPHAEI. [TYMPHE.]

TYMPHE (Τυμφή), a mountain on the confines of Macedonia, Epeirus, and Thessaly, a part of the range of Pindus, which gave its name to the district TYMPHAEA (Τυμφαία), and to the people, the TYMPHAEI (Τυμφαῖοι, Steph. B. s. v.). As it is stated that the river Arachthus rose in Mt. Tymphe, and that Aeginium was a town of the Tymphaei (Strab. vii. pp. 325, 327), Mt. Tymphe may be identified with the summits near *Métzovo*, and the Tymphaei may be regarded as the inhabitants of the whole of the upper valley of the Peneius from *Métzovo* or *Kalabáka*. The name is written in some editions of Strabo, Stymphe and Stymphaei, and the form Stymphaea also occurs in Arrian (i. 7); but the orthography without the s is perhaps to be preferred. The

question whether Stymphalis or Stymphalia is the same district as Tymphaea has been discussed elsewhere. [STYMPHALIS.] Pliny in one passage calls the Tymphaei an Aetolian people (iv. 2. s. 3), and in another a Macedonian (iv. 10. s. 17), while Stephanus B. describes the mountain as Thesprotian, and Strabo (*l. c.*) the people as an Epirotic race.

Stephanus B. mentions a town Tymphaea, which is probably the same place called Trampya (Τραμπύα) by others, where Polysperchon, who was a native of this district, murdered Hercules, the son of Alexander the Great. (Lycophr. 795; Diodor. xx. 28, with Wesseling's note; Steph. B. s. v. Τραμπύα.) (Leake, *Northern Greece*, vol. i. p. 422, vol. ii. pp. 275, 276.)

TYMPHRESTUS. [PINDUS.]

TYNDARIS (Τυνδαρίς, Strab.; Τυνδάριον, Ptol.: Eth. Τυνδαρίτης, Tyndaritanus: Tindaro), a city on the N. coast of Sicily, between Mylae (*Milazzo*) and Agathyrna. It was situated on a bold and lofty hill standing out as a promontory into the spacious bay bounded by the *Punta di Milazzo* on the E., and the *Capo Calavà* on the W., and was distant according to the Itineraries 36 miles from Messana. (*It. Ant.* p. 90; *Tab. Peut.*) It was a Greek city, and one of the latest of all the cities in Sicily that could claim a purely Greek origin, having been founded by the elder Dionysius in B. C. 395. The original settlers were the remains of the Messenian exiles, who had been driven from Naupactus, Zacynthus, and the Peloponnese by the Spartans after the close of the Peloponnesian War. These had at first been established by Dionysius at Messana, when he repeopled that city [MESSANA]; but the Spartans having taken umbrage at this, he transferred them to the site of Tyndaris, which had previously been included in the territory of Abacaenum. The colonists themselves gave to their new city the name of Tyndaris, from their native divinities, the Tyndaridae or Dioscuri, and readily admitting fresh citizens from other quarters, soon raised their whole population to the number of 5000 citizens. (Diod. xiv. 78.) The new city thus rose at once to be a place of considerable importance. It is next mentioned in B. C. 344, when it was one of the first cities that declared in favour of Timoleon after his landing in Sicily. (Id. xvi. 69.) At a later period we find it mentioned as espousing the cause of Hieron, and supporting him during his war against the Mamertines, B. C. 269. On that occasion he rested his position upon Tyndaris on the left, and on Tauromenium on the right. (Diod. xxii. *Exc. H.* p. 499.) Indeed the strong position of Tyndaris rendered it in a strategic point of view as important a post upon the Tyrrhenian, as Tauromenium was upon the Sicilian sea, and hence we find it frequently mentioned in subsequent wars. In the First Punic War it was at first dependent upon Carthage; and though the citizens, alarmed at the progress of the Roman arms, were at one time on the point of revolting to Rome, they were restrained by the Carthaginians, who carried off all the chief citizens as hostages. (Diod. xxiii. p. 502.) In B. C. 257, a sea-fight took place off Tyndaris, between that city and the Liparaean islands, in which a Roman fleet under C. Atilius obtained some advantage over the Carthaginian fleet, but without any decisive result. (Poly. i. 25; Zonar. viii. 12.) The Roman fleet is described on that occasion as touching at the promontory of Tyndaris, but the city had not yet fallen into their hands, and it was not till after the fall of Panormus, in B. C. 254, that

Tyndaris expelled the Carthaginian garrison, and joined the Roman alliance. (Diod. xxiii. p. 505.) We hear but little of Tyndaris under the Roman government, but it appears to have been a flourishing and considerable city. Cicero calls it "nobilissima civitas" (*Verr.* iii. 43), and we learn from him that the inhabitants had displayed their zeal and fidelity towards the Romans upon many occasions. Among others they supplied naval forces to the armament of Scipio Africanus the Younger, a service for which he requited them by restoring them a statue of Mercury which had been carried off by the Carthaginians, and which continued an object of great veneration in the city, till it was again carried off by the rapacious Verres. (Cic. *Verr.* iv. 39—42, v. 47.) Tyndaris was also one of seventeen cities which had been selected by the Roman senate, apparently as an honorary distinction, to contribute to certain offerings to the temple of Venus at Eryx. (*Ib.* v. 47; Zumpt, *ad loc.*; Diod. iv. 83.) In other respects it had no peculiar privileges, and was in the condition of an ordinary municipal town, with its own magistrates, local senate, &c., but was certainly in the time of Cicero one of the most considerable places in the island. It, however, suffered severely from the exactions of Verres (Cic. *Verr. ll. cc.*), and the inhabitants, to revenge themselves on their oppressor, publicly demolished his statue as soon as he had quitted the island. (*Ib.* ii. 66.)

Tyndaris again bore a considerable part in the war between Sextus Pompeius and Octavian (B. C. 36). It was one of the points occupied and fortified by the former, when preparing for the defence of the Sicilian straits, but was taken by Agrippa after his naval victory at Mylae, and became one of his chief posts, from which he carried on offensive warfare against Pompey. (Appian, *B. C.* v. 105, 109, 116.) Subsequently to this we hear nothing more of Tyndaris in history; but there is no doubt of its having continued to subsist throughout the period of the Roman Empire. Strabo speaks of it as one of the places on the N. coast of Sicily which, in his time, still deserved the name of *cities*; and Pliny gives it the title of a Colonia. It is probable that it received a colony under Augustus, as we find it bearing in an inscription the titles of "Colonia Augusta Tyndaritanorum." (Strab. vi. p. 272; Plin. iii. 8. s. 14; Ptol. iii. 4. § 2; Orell. *Inscr.* 955.) Pliny indeed mentions a great calamity which the city had sustained, when (he tells us) half of it was swallowed up by the sea, probably from an earthquake having caused the fall of part of the hill on which it stands, but we have no clue to the date of this event; (Plin. ii. 92. s. 94.) The Itineraries attest the existence of Tyndaris, apparently still as a considerable place, in the fourth century. (*Itin. Ant.* pp. 90, 93; *Tab. Peut.*)

The site of Tyndaris is now wholly deserted, but the name is retained by a church, which crowns the most elevated point of the hill on which the city formerly stood, and is still called the *Madonna di Tindaro*. It is 650 feet above the sea-level, and forms a conspicuous landmark to sailors. Considerable ruins of the ancient city are also visible. It occupied the whole plateau or summit of the hill, and the remains of the ancient walls may be traced, at intervals, all round the brow of the cliffs, except in one part, facing the sea, where the cliff is now quite precipitous. It is not improbable that it is here that a part of the cliff fell in, in the manner recorded by Pliny (ii. 92. s. 94). Two gates of the city are also

still distinctly to be traced. The chief monuments, of which the ruins are still extant within the circuit of the walls, are: the theatre, of which the remains are in imperfect condition, but sufficient to show that it was not of large size, and apparently of Roman construction, or at least, like that of Tauromenium, rebuilt in Roman times upon the Greek foundations; a large edifice with two handsome stone arches, commonly called a Gymnasium, but the real purpose of which is very difficult to determine; several other edifices of Roman times, but of wholly uncertain character, a mosaic pavement, and some Roman tombs. (Serra di Falco, *Antichità della Sicilia*, vol. v. part vi.; Smyth's *Sicily*, p. 101; Hoare's *Classical Tour*, vol. ii. p. 217, &c.) Numerous inscriptions, fragments of sculpture, and architectural decorations, as well as coins, vases, &c. have also been discovered on the site. 　　　　　　　　　　　[E. H. B.]

TYNDIS (Τύνδις, Ptol. vii. 1. § 16), a river of India intra Gangem, which flowed into the *Bay of Bengal*. There is great doubt which of two rivers, the Manades (*Mahanadda*) or the Maesolus (*Godávery*), represents this stream. According to Mannert it was the southern branch of the former river (v. 1. p. 173). But, on the whole, it is more likely that it is another name for the *Godávery*. 　　　[V.]

TYNIDRUMENSE OPP. [THUNUDROMON.]

TYNNA (Τύννα), a place in Cataonia or the southern part of Cappadocia, in the neighbourhood of Faustinopolis, is mentioned only by Ptolemy (v. 7. § 7). 　　　　　　　　　　　[L. S.]

TYPAEUS. [OLYMPIA.]

TYPA'NEAE (Τυπανέαι, Polyb. Steph. B.; Τυμπανέαι, Strab.; Τυμπάνεια, Ptol.: *Eth.* Τυπανεάτης), a town of Triphylia in Elis, mentioned by Strabo along with Hypana. It was taken by Philip in the Social War. It was situated in the mountains in the interior of the country, but its exact site is uncertain. Leake supposes it to be represented by the ruins near *Platianá*; but Boblaye supposes these to be the remains of Aepy or Aepium [AKPY], and that Typaneae stood on the hill of *Makrysia*. (Strab. viii. p. 343; Polyb. iv. 77—79; Steph. B. s. v; Ptol. iii. 16. § 18; Leake, *Morea*, vol. ii. p. 82; Boblaye, *Recherches, &c.* p. 133; Ross, *Reisen in Peloponnes*, p. 105; Curtius, *Peloponnesos*, vol. ii. p. 89.)

TYRA'CIA or TYRACI'NA (Τυρακίναι, Steph. B: *Eth.* Tyraciensis, Plin.), a city of Sicily, of which very little is known. It is noticed by Stephanus as "a small but flourishing city;" and the Tyracienses are mentioned by Pliny among the municipal communities of the interior of Sicily. (Steph. B. *s. v.*; Plin. iii. 8. s. 14.) It is doubtful whether the "Tyracinus, princeps civitatis," mentioned by Cicero (*Verr.* iii. 56) is a citizen of Tyracia or one of Helorus who bore the proper name of Tyracinus. In either case the name was probably derived from the city: but though the existence of this is clearly established, we are wholly without any clue to its position.

Several writers would identify the TRINACIA (Τρινακία) of Diodorus (xii. 29), which that writer describes as having been one of the chief towns of the Siculi, until it was taken and destroyed by the Syracusans in B. C. 439, with the Tyracinae of Stephanus and Tyracia of Pliny. Both names being otherwise unknown, the readings are in both cases uncertain: but Diodorus seems to represent Trinacia as having been totally destroyed, which would sufficiently account for its not being again mentioned in history.: and there is no other reason for assuming the two places to be identical. (Cluver. *Sicil.* p. 388; Holsten. *Not. ad Steph. B. s. v.*; Wesseling, *ad Diod. l. c.*)   [E. H. B.]

TYRALLIS (Τύραλλίς), a place in Cappadocia, on the south-west of Cabassus, on the river Cydnus. (Ptol. v. 7. § 7.)   [L. S.]

TYRAMBAE (Τυράμβαι, Ptol. v. 9. § 17), a people of Asiatic Sarmatia, whose chief city was Tyrambe (Τυράμβη, *ib.* § 4, &c.: Strab. xi. p. 494), in the neighbourhood of the river Rhombites Minor.   [T. H. D.]

TYRANGI'TAE (Τυραγγεῖται, Τυραγγέται, or Τυρεγέται, Strab. vii. p. 289, &c.; Ptol. iii. 5. § 25), literally, the Getae of the Tyras, an immigrant tribe of European Sarmatia dwelling E. of the river Tyras, near the Harpii and Tagri, and, according to Ptolemy, the northern neighbours of Lower Moesia. Pliny (v. 12. s. 26) calls them, with more correct orthography, Tyragetae, and represents them as dwelling on a large island in the Tyras.   [T. H. D.]

TYRANNOBOAS (Τυραννοβόας), an emporium on the western coast of Bengal between Mandagara and Byzantium, noticed by the author of the Periplus (p. 30.) It cannot now be identified with any place.   [V.]

TYRAS (ὁ Τύρας, Strab. ii. p. 107), one of the principal rivers of European Sarmatia. According to Herodotus (iv. 51) it rose in a large lake, whilst Ptolemy (iii. 5. § 17, 8. § 1, &c.) places its sources in Mount Carpates, and Strabo (*l. c.*) says that they are unknown. The account of Herodotus, however, is correct, as it rises in a lake in Gallicia. (Georgii, *Alte-Geogr.* p. 269.) It ran in an easterly direction parallel with the Ister, and formed part of the boundary between Dacia and Sarmatia. It fell into the Pontus Euxinus to the NE. of the mouth of the Ister; the distance between them being, according to Strabo, 900 stadia (Strab. vii. p. 305, seq.), and, according to Pliny (iv. 12. s. 26), 130 miles (from the Pseudostoma). Scymnus (*Fr.* 51) describes it as of easy navigation, and abounding in fish. Ovid (*ex Pont.* iv. 10. 50) speaks of its rapid course. At a later period it obtained the name of Danastris or Danastus (Amm. Marc. xxxi. 3. § 3; Jornand. *Get.* 5; Const. Porphyr. *de Adm. Imp.* 8), whence its modern name of *Dniester* (*Neister*), though the Turks still call it *Tural.* (Cf. Herod. iv. 11, 47, 82; Scylax, p. 29; Strab. i. p. 14; Mela, ii. 1, &c.; also Schaffarik, *Slav. Alterth.* i. p. 505.) The form Τύρις is sometimes found. (Steph. B. p. 671; Suid. *s. v.* Σκύθαι and Ποσειδώνιος.)   [T. H. D.]

TYRAS (Τύρας, Ptol. iii. 10. § 16), a town of European Sarmatia, situated at the mouth of the river just described. (Herod. iv. 51; Mela, ii. 1.) It was originally a Milesian colony (Scymn. *Fr.* 55; Anon. *Peripl. P. Eux.* p. 9); although Ammianus Marcellinus (xxii. 8. § 41), apparently from the similarity of the name, which he writes "Tyros," ascribes its foundation to the Phoenicians from Tyre. Pliny (iv. 12. s. 26; cf. Steph. B. p. 671) identifies it with an older town named Ophiusa ("gelidis pollens Ophiusa venenis," Val. Flacc. vi. 84). Ptolemy, however (*l. c.*), makes them two different towns; and places Ophiusa somewhat more N., and towards the interior. Scylax knows only Ophiusa, whilst the later writers, on the other hand, knew only Tyras. (Cf. Neumann, *Die Hellenen im Skythenlande*, p. 357, seq.) It probably lay on the site of the present *Ackermann.* (Clarke, *Travels*, ii. p. 124; Kohl, *Reisen in Südrussland*, i. 167.)   [T. H. D.]

TYRIAEUM (Τυριαῖον: *Eth.* Tyrienses), a town of Lycaonia, which according to Xenophon (*Anab.* i. 2. § 24) was 20 parasangs west of Iconium, and according to Strabo (xiv. p. 663) on the eastern frontier of Phrygia, and probably on the road from Synnada to Laodiceia, and between the latter and Philomelium. Near this town Cyrus the Younger reviewed his forces when he marched against his brother. (Comp. Plin. v. 25; Hierocl. p. 672 ; and *Conc. Chalced.* p. 401, where the name is written Τυρδίον.) It is possible that Tyriaeum may be the same town as the Totarion or Tetradion of Ptolemy (v. 4. § 10), the Tyrasion in the *Conc. Chalced.* (p. 669), and the Tyganion of Anna Comnena (xv. 7, 13). Its site seems to be marked by the modern *Ilgun* or *Ilghun.* (Hamilton, *Researches*, ii. p. 200 ; Kiepert in Franz, *Fünf Inschriften*, p. 36.) [L. S.]

TYRICTACA (Τυρικτάκη or Τωριτάκη, Ptol. iii. 6. § 4), a town in the Chersonesus Taurica. (Cf. Anon. *Peripl. P. Eux.* p. 4., where it is written Τυριστάκη.) Dubois de Montperreux identifies it with some ruins found on lake *Thurbach.* (*Voy. autour du Caucase*, v. p. 247.)   [T. H. D.]

TYRISSA (Τόρισσα, Ptol. iii. 13. § 39 : *Eth.* Tyrissaeus, Plin. iv. 10. s. 17), a town of Emathia in Macedonia, placed by Ptolemy next to Europus.

TYRI'TAE (Τυρῖται, Herod. iv. 51), certain Greeks settled at the mouth of the Tyras, probably Milesians who built the town of that name. [T. H. D.]

TYRRHE'NIA, TYRRHE'NI. [ETRURIA.]

TYRRHE'NUM MARE (τὸ Τυρρηνικὸν πέλαγος), was the name given in ancient times to the part of the Mediterranean sea which adjoins the W. coast of Italy. It is evident from the name itself that it was originally employed by the Greeks, who universally called the people of Etruria Tyrrhenians, and was merely adopted from them by the Romans. The latter people indeed frequently used the term TUSCUM MARE (Liv. v. 33; Mel. ii. 4. § 9), but still more often designated the sea on the W. of Italy simply as "the lower sea," MARE INFERUM, just as they termed the Adriatic ' the upper sea " or MARE SUPERUM. (Mel. ii. 4. § 1; Plin. iii. 5. s. 10; Liv. *l. c.*) The name of Tyrrhenum Mare was indeed in all probability never in use among the Romans, otherwise than as a mere geographical term; but with the Greeks it was certainly the habitual designation of that portion of the Mediterranean which extended from the coast of Liguria to the N. coast of Sicily, and from the mainland of Italy to the islands of Sardinia and Corsica en the W. (Polyb. i. 10, 14, &c.; Strab. ii. p. 122, v. p. 211, &c. ; Dionys *Per.* 83; Scyl. §§ 15, 17; Agathem. ii. 14.) The period at which it came into use is uncertain; it is not found in Herodotus or Thucydides, and Scylax is the earliest author now extant by whom the name is mentioned. [E. H. B.]

TYRRHINE. [OGYRIS.]

TYRSUS. [THYRSUS.]

TYRUS (Τύρος, Herod. ii. 44, &c.: *Eth.* Τύριος, Tyrius), the most celebrated and important city of Phoenicia. By the Israelites it was called Tsor (*Josh.* xix. 29, &c.), which means a rock but by the Tyrians themselves Sor or Sur (Theodoret. *in Ezek.* xxvi.), which appellation it still retains. For the initial letter *t* was substituted by the Greeks, and from them adopted by the Romans ; but the latter also used the form Sara or Sarra, said to be derived from the Phoenician name of the purple fish ; whence also the adjective Sarra-nus. (Plaut. *Truc.* 2, 6, 58 : Virg. *Georg.* ii. 506; Juv. x. 38; Gell. xiv. 6, &c.) The former of these etymologies is the preferable one. (Shaw, *Travels*, ii. p. 31.) The question of the origin of Tyre has been already discussed, its commerce, manufactures and colonies described, and the principal events of its history narrated at some length [PHOENICIA, p. 608, seq.], and this article will therefore be more particularly devoted to the topography, and to what may be called the material history, of the city.

Strabo (xvi. p. 756) places Tyre at a distance of 200 stadia from Sidon, which pretty nearly agrees with the distance of 24 miles assigned by the *Itin. Ant.* (p. 149) and the *Tab. Peuting.* It was built partly on an island and partly on the mainland. According to Pliny (v. 19. s. 17) the island was 22 stadia, or 2¾ miles, in circumference, and was originally separated from the continent by a deep channel 7/10ths of a mile in breadth. In his time, however, as well as long previously (cf. Strab. *l. c.*), it was connected with the mainland by an isthmus formed by the mole or causeway constructed by Alexander when he was besieging Tyre, and by subsequent accumulations of sand. Some authorities state the channel to have been only 3 stadia (Scylax, p. 42) or 4 stadia broad (Diodor. Sic. xvii. 60; Curt. iv. 2); and Arrian (*Anab.* ii. 18) describes it as shallow near the continent and only 6 fathoms in depth at its deepest part near the island. The accretion of the isthmus must have been considerable in the course of ages. William of Tyre describes it in the time of the Crusades as a bow-shot across (xiii. 4); the Père Roger makes it only 50 paces (*Terre Sainte*, p. 41); but at present it is about ⅓ of a mile broad at its narrowest part, near the island.

That part of the city which lay on the mainland was called Palae-Tyrus, or Old Tyre; an appellation from which we necessarily infer that it existed previously to the city on the island; and this inference is confirmed by Ezekiel's prophetical description of the siege of Tyre by Nebuchadnezzar, king of Babylon, the particulars of which are not suitable to an island city. Palae-Tyrus extended along the shore from the river Leontes on the N., to the fountain of *Ras-el-Ain* on the S., a space of 7 miles; which, however, must have included the suburbs. When Strabo says (xvi. p. 758) that Palae-Tyrus was 30 stadia, or 3¾ miles, distant from Tyre, he is probably considering the southern extremity of the former. Pliny (*l. c.*) assigns a circumference of 19 miles to the two cities. The plain in which Palae-Tyrus was situated was one of the broadest and most fertile in Phoenicia. The fountain above mentioned afforded a constant supply of pure spring water, which was received into an octagon reservoir, 60 feet in diameter and 18 feet deep. Into this reservoir the water gushes to within 3 feet of the top. (Maundrell, *Journey*, p. 67.) Hence it was distributed through the town by means of an aqueduct, all trace of which has now disappeared (Robinson, *Palest.* iii. p. 684.) The unusual contrast between the bustle of a great seaport and the more tranquil operations of rural life in the fertile fields which surrounded the town, presented a striking scene which is described with much felicity in the *Dionysiaca* of Nonnus (40, 327, sqq.).

The island on which the new city was built is the largest rock of a belt that runs along this part of the coast. We have no means of determining the origin of the island city; but it must of course have

arisen in the period between Nebuchadnezzar and Alexander the Great. The alterations which the coast has undergone at this part render it difficult to determine the original size of the island. Maundrell (p. 66) estimated it at only 40 acres; but he was guided solely by his eye. The city was surrounded with a wall, the height of which. where it faced the mainland, was 150 feet. (Arrian, *Anab.* ii. 18.) The foundations of this wall, which must have marked the limits of the island as well as of the city, may still be discerned, but have not been accurately traced. The measurement of Pliny before cited must doubtless include the subsequent accretions, both natural and artificial. The smallness of the area was, however, compensated by the great height of the houses of Tyre, which were not built after the eastern fashion, but story upon story, like those of Aradus, another Phoenician island city (Mela, ii. 7), or like the insulae of Rome. (Strab. *l. c.*) Thus a much larger population might be accommodated than the area seems to promise. Bertou, calculating from the latter alone, estimates the inhabitants of insular Tyre at between 22,000 and 23,000. (*Topogr. de Tyr*, p. 17.) But the accounts of the capture of Tyre by Alexander, as will appear in the sequel, show a population of at least double that number; and it should be recollected that, from the maritime pursuits of the Tyrians, a large portion of them must have been constantly at sea. Moreover, part of the western side of the island is now submerged, to the extent of more than a mile; and that this was once occupied by the city is shown by the bases of columns which may still be discerned. These remains were much more considerable in the time of Benjamin of Tudela, in the latter part of the 12th century, who mentions that towers, markets, streets, and halls might be observed at the bottom of the sea (p. 62, ed. Asher).

Insular Tyre was much improved by king Hiram, who in this respect was the Augustus of the city. He added to it one of the islands lying to the N., by filling up the intervening space. This island, the outline of which can no longer be traced, previously contained a temple of Baal, or, according to the Greek way of speaking, of the Olympian Jupiter. (Joseph. *c. Apion*, i. 17.) It was by the space thus gained, as well as by substructions on the eastern side of the island, that Hiram was enabled to enlarge and beautify Tyre, and to form an extensive public place, which the Greeks called Eurychorus. The artificial ground which Hiram formed for this purpose may still be traced by the loose rubbish of which it consists. The frequent earthquakes with which Tyre has been visited (Sen. *Q. N.* ii. 26) have rendered it difficult to trace its ancient configuration; and alterations have been observed even since the recent one of 1837 (Kenrick, *Phoenicia*, p. 353, &c.).

The powerful navies of Tyre were received and sheltered in two roadsteads and two harbours, one on the N., the other on the S. side of the island. The northern, or Sidonian roadstead, so called because it looked towards Sidon (Arrian, ii. 20), was protected by the chain of small islands already mentioned. The harbour which adjoined it was formed by a natural inlet on the NE. side of the island. On the N., from which quarter alone it was exposed to the wind, it was rendered secure by two sea-walls running parallel to each other, at a distance of 100 feet apart, as shown in the annexed plan. Portions of these walls may still be traced. The eastern side of the harbour was enclosed by two ledges of rock, with the assistance of walls, having a passage between them about 140 feet wide, which formed the mouth of the harbour. In case of need this entrance could be closed with a boom or chain. At present this harbour is almost choked with sand, and only a small basin, of about 40 yards in diameter, can be traced (Shaw, *Travels*, vol. ii. p. 30); but in its original state it was about 300 yards long, and from 230 to 240 yards wide. Part of the modern town of *Sur*, or *Sour*, is built over its southern portion, and only vessels of very shallow draught can enter.

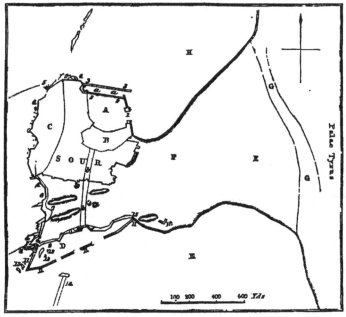

PLAN OF TYRE.
(From Kenrick's "*Phoenicia*.")

A. Northern harbour.
B. Supposed limit of ancient harbour
C. Tract of loose sand.
D. Southern, or Egyptian, harbour.
E. Southern, or Egyptian, roadstead.
FF. Isthmus formed by Alexander's mole.
GG. Depression in the sand.
H. Northern, or Sidonian, roadstead.
aa. Portions of inner sea-wall, visible above water.
bb. Ancient canal.
1. Entrance of northern harbour.
2, 2. Original line of sea-wall.
3, 3. Outer wall, now below water.
4, 4, 4, 4. Line of rocks, bordered on the E. by a wall, not of ancient construction.
5. Ledge of rocks projecting 90 feet into the sea.

6. Columns united to the rock.
7. Rock, below 5 feet of rubbish.
8. Ledge of rocks extending 200 feet into the sea.
9. Remains of a wall, with irons for mooring.
10. Masonry, showing the entrance of the canal.
11,11,11,11. Walls of the Cothon or harbour, about 28 feet broad.
12, 12. Portions of wall overturned in the harbour.
13. Rocky islets.
14. Supposed submarine dyke or breakwater.
15. Commencement of the isthmus, covering several yards of the harbour wall.
16. Angle of the ancient wall of circumvallation, and probable limit of the island on the E.

The southern roadstead was called the Egyptian, from its lying towards that country, and is described by Strabo (*l. c.*) as unenclosed. If, however, the researches of Bertou may be relied upon (*Topogr. de Tyr*, p. 14), a stupendous sea-wall, or breakwater, 35 feet thick, and running straight in a SW. direction, for a distance of 2 miles, may still be traced. The wall is said to be covered with 2 or 3 fathoms of water, whilst within it the depth is from 6 to 8 fathoms. Bertou admits, however, that this wall has never been carefully examined; and if it had existed in ancient times, it is impossible to conceive how so stupendous a work should have escaped the notice of all the writers of antiquity. According to the same authority, the whole southern part of the island was occupied by a *cothon*, or dock, separated from the roadstead by a wall, the remains of which are still visible. This harbour, like the northern one, could be closed with a boom; whence Chariton (vii. 2. p. 126, Reiske) takes occasion to compare the security of Tyre to that of a house with bolted doors. At present, however, there is nothing to serve for a harbour, and even the roadstead is not secure in all winds. (Shaw, ii. p. 30.) The northern and southern harbours were connected together by means of a canal, so that ships could pass from one to the other. This canal may still be traced by the loose sand with which it is filled.

We have already adverted to the sieges sustained by Tyre at the hands of Shalmaneser, Nebuchadneszar, Alexander, and Antigonus. [PHOENICIA, pp. 610—613]. That by Alexander was so remarkable, and had so much influence on the topography of Tyre, that we reserved the details of it for this place, as they may be collected from the narratives of Arrian (*Anab.* ii. 17—26), Diodorus Siculus (xvii. 40—45), and Q. Curtius (iv. 4—27). The insular situation of Tyre, the height and strength of its walls, and the command which it possessed of the sea, seemed to render it impregnable; and hence the Tyrians, when summoned by Alexander to surrender, prepared for an obstinate resistance. The only method which occurred to the mind of that conqueror of overcoming the difficulties presented to his arms by the site of Tyre, was to connect it with the mainland by means of a mole. The materials for such a structure were at hand in abundance. The deserted buildings of Palae-Tyrus afforded plenty of stone, the mountains of Lebanon an inexhaustible supply of timber. For a certain distance, the mole, which was 200 feet in breadth, proceeded rapidly and successfully, though Alexander's workmen were often harassed by parties of Tyrian troops, who landed in boats, as well as by the Arabs of the Syrian desert. But as the work approached the island, the difficulties increased in a progressive ratio. Not only was it threatened with destruction from the depth and force of the current, often increased to violence by a southerly wind, but the workmen were also exposed to the missiles of the Tyrian slingers and bowmen, aimed both from vessels and from the battlements of the city. To guard themselves from these attacks, the Macedonians erected two lofty wooden towers at the extremity of the mole, and covered them with hides as a protection against fire. The soldiers placed on these towers occasioned the Tyrians considerable annoyance. At length, however, the latter succeeded in setting fire to the towers by means of a fire-ship filled with combustibles; and afterwards, making a sortie in their boats, pulled up the stakes which protected the mole, and destroyed the machines which the fire had not reached. To complete the discomfiture of the Macedonians, a great storm arose and carried away the whole of the work which had been thus loosened.

This misfortune, which would have damped the ardour of an ordinary man, only incited Alexander to renew his efforts with greater vigour and on a surer plan. He ordered a new mole to be constructed, broader than the former one; and in order to obviate the danger of destruction by the waves, he caused it to incline towards the SW., and thus to cross the channel diagonally, instead of in a straight line. At the same time he collected a large fleet from Sidon, whither he went in person, from Soli, Mallus, and other places; for, with the exception of Tyre, all Phoenicia was already in the hands of Alexander. He then made an incursion into Coelesyria, and chased away the Arabs who annoyed his workmen employed in cutting timber in Antilibanus. When he again returned to Tyre with his fleet, which he had joined at Sidon, the new mole had already made great progress. It was formed of whole trees with their branches, covered with layers of stone, on which other trees were heaped. The Tyrian divers, indeed, sometimes succeeded in loosening the structure by pulling out the trees; but, in spite of these efforts, the work proceeded steadily towards completion.

The large fleet which Alexander had assembled struck terror into the Tyrians, who now confined themselves to defensive measures. They sent away the old men, women, and children to Carthage, and closed the mouths of their harbours with a line of triremes. It is unnecessary to recount all the incidents which followed, and we shall therefore confine ourselves to the most important. Alexander had caused a number of new machines to be prepared, under the direction of the ablest engineers of Phoenicia and Cyprus. Some of these were planted on the mole, which now very nearly approached the city; others were placed on board large vessels, in order to batter the walls on other sides. Various were the devices resorted to by the Tyrians to frustrate these attempts. They cut the cables of the vessels bearing the battering rams, and thus sent them adrift; but this mode of defence was met by the use of iron mooring chains. To deaden the blows of the battering engines, leathern bags filled with sea-weed were suspended from the walls, whilst on their summit were erected large wheel-like machines filled with soft materials, which being set in rapid motion, either averted or intercepted the missiles hurled by the Macedonians. A second wall also was commenced within the first. On the other hand, the Macedonians, having now carried the mole as far as the island, erected towers upon it equal in height to the walls of the town, from which bridges were projected towards the battlements, in order to take the city by escalade. Yet, after all the labour bestowed upon the mole, Tyre was not captured by means of it. The Tyrians annoyed the soldiers who manned the towers by throwing out grappling hooks attached to lines, and thus dragging them down. Nets were employed to entangle the hands of the assailants; masses of red-hot metal were hurled amongst them, and quantities of heated sand, which, getting between the interstices of the armour, caused intolerable pain. An attempted assault from the bridges of the towers was repulsed, and does not appear to have been renewed. But a breach was made in the walls by battering rams fixed on vessels; and whilst this was assaulted by means of ships provided with bridges, simultaneous attacks were directed against both the harbours. The Phoenician fleet burst the boom of the Egyptian harbour, and took or destroyed the ships within it. The northern harbour, the entrance of which was undefended, was easily taken by the Cyprian fleet. Meanwhile Alexander had entered with his troops through the breach. Provoked by the long resistance of the Tyrians and the obstinate defence still maintained from the roofs of the houses, the Macedonian soldiery set fire to the city, and massacred 8000 of the inhabitants. The remainder, except those who found shelter on board the Sidonian fleet, were sold into slavery, to the number of 30,000; and 2000 were crucified in expiation of the murders of certain Macedonians during the course of the siege. The lives of the king and chief magistrates were spared.

Thus was Tyre captured, after a siege of seven months, in July of the year B. C. 332. Alexander then ordered sacrifices and games in honour of the Tyrian Hercules, and consecrated to him the battering ram which had made the first breach in the walls. The population, which had been almost destroyed, was replaced by new colonists, of whom a considerable portion seem to have been Carians. The subsequent fortunes of Tyre have already been recorded. [PHOENICIA, p. 613.]

For the coins of Tyre see Eckhel, *Doctr. Num.*

P. i. vol. iii. pp. 379—393, and 408, seq. Respecting its history and the present state of its remains, the following works may be advantageously consulted: Hengstenberg, *De Rebus Tyriorum;* Kenrick, *Phoenicia;* Pococke, *Description of the East;* Volney, *Voyage en Syrie;* Richter, *Wallfahrt;* Bertou, *Topographie de Tyr;* Maundrell, *Journey from Aleppo to Damascus;* Shaw's *Travels;* Robinson, *Biblical Researches,* &c.　　　　　　　　[T. H. D.]

COIN OF TYRUS.

TYSANUSA, a port on the coast of Caria. on the bay of Schoenus, and a little to the east of Cape Posidium (Pomp. Mela. i. 16). Pliny (v. 29) mentions Tisanusa as a town in the same neighbourhood. 　　　　　　　　[L. S.]

TYSIA. [TISIANUS.]

TZURU'LUM (Τζουρουλὸν, Procop. *B. Goth.* iii. 38; Anna Comn. vii. p. 215, x. p. 279; Theophyl. vi. 5; in Geog. Rav. iv. 6, and *Tab. Peut.,* Surallum and Syrallum; in *It. Ant.* pp. 138, 230, Izirallum, but in p. 323, Tirallum; and in *It. Hier.* p. 569, Tunorullum), a strong town on a hill in the SE. of Thrace, not far from Perinthus, on the road from that city to Hadrianopolis. It has retained its name with little change to the present day, being the modern *Tchorlu* or *Tchurlu.*　　　　　　　　[J. R.]

U, V.

VABAR, a river of Mauretania Caesariensis, which fell into the sea a little to the W. of Saldae. Ptolemy (iv. 2. § 9) mentions it under the name of Οὐαβαρ as if it had been a town; and Maffei (*Mus. Ver.* p. 463) thought that he had discovered such a place in the name of Bavares, in an African inscription (cf. Orelli, *Inscr.* no. 529). In Pliny (v. 2. s. 1) and Mela (i. 6) the name is erroneously written Nabar. It is probably the present *Buberak.*　　　　　　　　[T. H. D.]

VACALUS. [BATAVI.]

VACCA. 1. (Sall. *J.* 29, &c.) or VAGA (Sil. It. iii. 259; Οὐάγα, Ptol. iv. 3. § 28; Βάγα, Procop. *de Aed.* vi. 5), an important town and place of considerable commerce in the interior of Numidia, lying a long day's journey SW. of Utica. Pliny (v. 4) calls it Vagense Oppidum. It was destroyed by Metellus (Sall. *J.* 69; but afterwards restored and inhabited by the Romans. Justinian surrounded it with a wall, and named it Theodoria, in honour of his consort. (Procop. *l. c.;* cf. Strab. xvii. p. 831; Sall. *J.* 47, 68; Plut. *Mar.* 8. p. 409.) Now *Bayjah* (Begia, *Beggia, Bedeja*) in *Tunis,* on the borders of *Algiers.* (Cf. Shaw, *Travels,* i. p. 183.) Vaga is mentioned by the Geogr. Nub. (*Clim.* iii. 1. p. 88) under the name of Bagia, and by Leo Afric. (p. 406, Lorsbach) under that of Beggia, as a place of considerable commerce.

2. A town in Byzacium in Africa Proper, lying to the S. of Ruspinum (Hirt. *B. Afr.* 74). This is

probably the "aliud Vagense oppidum" of Pliny (*l. c.*).　　　　　　　　[T. H. D.]

VACCAEI (Οὐακκαῖοι, Ptol. ii. 6. § 50), an important people in the interior of Hispania Tarraconensis, bounded on the W. by the Astures, on the N. by the Cantabri, on the E. by the Celtiberi (to whom Appian, *Hisp.* 51, attributes them), and on the S. by the Vettones and the river Durius. Hence their district may be considered as marked by the modern towns of *Zamora, Toro, Palencia, Burgos,* and *Valladolid.* Their chief cities were Pallantia (*Palencia*) and Intercatia. According to Diodorus (v. 34) they yearly divided their land for tillage among themselves, and regarded the produce as common property, so that whoever kept back any part for himself was capitally punished. (Cf. Liv. xxx. 7, xl. 47; Polyb. iii. 14; Strab. iii. pp. 152, 162; Plin. iii. 3. s. 4; Plut. *Sert.* 21.) [T. H. D.]

VACOMAGI (Οὐακομάγοι, Ptol. ii. 3. § 13), a people in Britannia Barbara, near the Taezali, never subdued by the Romans. Camden (p. 1217) seeks them on the borders of *Loch Lomond.* Ptolemy (*l. c.*) ascribes four towns to them.　　　　　　　　[T. H. D.]

VACUA (Οὐακούα, Strab. iii. p. 153; Οὐακος, Ptol. ii. 5. § 4), a river in Lusitania, which entered the Atlantic ocean between the Durius and Munda, in the neighbourhood of Talabrica. Pliny (iv. 21. s. 35) calls it Vacca. The present *Vouga.* [T. H. D.]

VACUATAE (Οὐακούατα: or Βακούατα, Ptol. iv. 6. § 10), a people in the S. of Mauretania Tingitana, extending as far as the Little Atlas. [T.H.D.]

VADA, a place on or near the Rhine, in North Gallia. Tacitus (*Hist.* v. 21) in his history of the war of Civilis speaks of Civilis attacking on one day with his troops in four divisions, Arenacum, Batavodurum, Grinnes, and Vada. The history shows that Grinnes and Vada were south or on the south side of the stream which Tacitus calls the Rhenus. [GRINNES.]　　　　　　　　[G. L.]

VADA SABBATA (Σαβάτων Οὐάδα, Strab.; Σάββατα, Ptol.: *Vado*), a town and port on the sea-coast of Liguria, about 30 miles W. of Genua. It was situated on a bay which affords one of the best roadsteads along this line of coast, and seems to have been in consequence much frequented by the Roman fleets. In B. c. 43 it was the first point at which M. Antonius halted after his defeat at Mutina, and where he effected his junction with Ventidius, who had a considerable force under his command. (Cic. *ad Fam.* xi. 10, 13.) D. Brutus, in his letter to Cicero, speaks of it as "inter Apenninum et Alpes," a phrase which obviously refers to the notion commonly entertained that this was the point of demarcation between the two chains of mountains, a view adopted also by Strabo (iv. p. 202). A pass led into the interior across the Apennines from Vada to Aquae Statiellae which was probably that followed by Antony. Brutus speaks in strong terms of the rugged and difficult nature of the roads in all directions from this point, (*Ib.*): but at a later period · a regular road was constructed across the mountains from Vada to Aquae Statiellae, as well as in both directions along the coast. (*Itin. Ant.* p. 295; *Tab. Peut.*) Under the Roman Empire we learn that Vada continued to be a place of considerable trade (Jul. Capit. *Pert.* 9, 13); and it is still mentioned as a port in the Maritime Itinerary (p. 502). Some doubt has arisen with regard to its precise position, though the name of *Vado* would seem to be obviously derived from it; but that of Sabbata or Sabatia, on the other hand, is apparently connected with that of *Savona,* a town with a small but secure port about 4 miles N. of *Vado*. Livy indeed mentions Savo (undoubtedly the same with *Savona*) as a sea-port town of the Ligurians, where Mago established himself during the Second Punic War (Liv. xxviii. 46) ; but the name does not occur again in any writer, and hence Cluverius supposed that this was the place afterwards called Sabbata. There seems, however, no doubt that Sabbata or Sabatia, Vada Sabbata, or Vada Sabatia, and Vada simply (as the name is written by Cicero), are all only different forms of the same name, and that the Roman town of Vada was situated on, or very near, the same site as the present *Vado*, a long straggling fishing village, the bay of which still affords an excellent roadstead. The distinctive epithet of Sabbata or Sabatia was evidently derived from its proximity to the original Ligurian town of Savo.   [E. H. B.]

VADA'VERO, a mountain near Bilbilis in the territory of the Celtiberi, in Hispania Tarraconensis. It appears to be mentioned only by Martial (i. 50. 6), who characterises it by the epithet of "sacred," and adverts to its rugged character.   [T. H. D.]

VADA VOLATERRANA. [VOLATERRAE].

VADICASSII (Οὐαδικάσσιοι), a people of Gallia Lugdunensis, whom Ptolemy (ii. 8. § 16) places on the borders of Belgica, and next to the Meldae. He assigns to the Vadicassii a city Noeomagus. D'Anville concludes that following Ptolemy's data we may place his Vadicassii in *Valois*, which is between *Meaux* and *Soissons*. He remarks that *Valois* is Vadisus in the capitularies of Charles the Bald, and Vadensis in the later acts. Other geographers have different opinions. In many of the editions of Pliny (iv. 18) we find enumerated "Andegavi, Viducasses, Vadiocasses, Unelli;" but only one MS. has "Vadiocasses," and the rest have Bodiocasses or Bodicasses, which we must take to be the true reading, and they seem to be the same as the BAIOCASSES. (D'Anville, *Notice*, &c.; Ukert, *Gallien*.)   [G. L.]

VADIMO'NIS LACUS (ἡ Οὐάδμων λίμνη, Polyb.: *Laghetto di Bassano*), a small lake of Etruria, between the Ciminian hills and the Tiber, celebrated in history as the scene of two successive defeats of the combined Etruscan forces by the Romans. In the first of these battles, which was fought in B. C. 309, the Etruscans had raised a chosen army, enrolled with peculiar solemnity (lege sacrata) ; but though they fought with the utmost valour and obstinacy, they sustained so severe a defeat at the hands of the Roman Consul Q. Fabius Maximus, that, as Livy remarks, this disastrous day first broke the power of Etruria (Liv. ix. 39). The second battle was fought near 30 years later (B. c. 283), in which the allied forces of the Etruscans and Gauls were totally defeated by the consul P. Cornelius Dolabella. (Polyb. ii. 20 ; Eutrop. ii. 10 ; Flor. i. 13.) But though thus celebrated in history, the Vadimonian lake is a very trifling sheet of water, in fact, a mere pool or stagnant pond, now almost overgrown with reeds and bulrushes. It was doubtless more extensive in ancient times, though it could never have been of any importance, and scarcely deserves the name of a lake. But it is remarkable that the younger Pliny in one of his epistles describes it as a circular basin abounding in floating islands, which have now all disappeared, and probably have contributed to fill up the ancient basin. Its waters are whitish and highly sulphureous, resembling, in this respect, the Aquae Albulae near Tibur, where the phenomenon of floating islands still occasionally occurs. (Plin. *Ep.* viii.

20.) It enjoyed the reputation, probably on account of this peculiar character, of being a sacred lake. But the apparent singularity of its having been twice the scene of decisive conflicts is sufficiently explained by its situation just in a natural pass between the Tiber and the wooded heights of the Ciminian forest, which (as observed by Mr. Dennis) must always have constituted a natural pass into the plains of Central Etruria. The lake itself, which is now called the *Laghetto di Bassano* from a neighbouring village of that name, is only a very short distance from the Tiber, and about 4 miles above *Orte*, the ancient Horta. (Dennis's *Etruria*, vol. i. pp. 167—170.)   [E. H. B.]

VAGA, a town of the Cantii in Britannia Romana (*Not. Imp.*)   [T. H. D.]

VAGA. [VACCA.]

VAGEDRUSA, the name of a river in Sicily, mentioned by Silius Italicus (xiv. 229), according to the old editions of that author; but there can be no doubt that the true reading is that restored by Ruperti, "vage Chrysa," and that the river Chrysas is the one meant. (Ruperti, *ad l. c.*)   [E. H. B.]

VAGIENNI (Βαγιεννοί), a Ligurian tribe, who inhabited the region N. of the Maritime Alps, and S. of the territory of the Taurini. According to Pliny they extended as far to the W. as the Mons Vesulus or *Monte Viso*, in the main chain of the Alps (Plin. iii. 16. s. 20), while their chief town or capital under the Roman rule, called Augusta Vagiennorum, was situated at *Bene*, between the rivers *Stura* and *Tanaro*, so that they must have occupied an extensive territory. But it seems impossible to receive as correct the statement of Velleius (i. 15) that the Roman colony of Eporedia (*Ivrea*) was included within their limits. [EPOREDIA.] It is singular that Pliny more than once speaks of them as being descended from the Caturiges, while at the same time he distinctly calls them a Ligurian tribe, and the Caturiges are commonly reckoned a Gaulish one. It seems probable, however, that many of the races which inhabited the mountain valleys of the Alps were of Ligurian origin; and thus the Caturiges and Segusiani may very possibly have been of a Ligurian stock like their neighbours the Taurini, though subsequently confounded with the Gauls. We have no account of the period at which the Vagienni were reduced under the Roman yoke, and their name is not found in history as an independent tribe. But Pliny notices them as one of the Ligurian tribes still existing in his time, and their chief town, Augusta, seems to have been a flourishing place under the Roman Empire. Their name is sometimes written Bagienni (Orell. *Inscr.* 76), and is found in the Tabula under the corrupt form Bagitenni. (*Tab. Peut.*)   [E. H. B.]

VAGNIACAE, a town of the Cantii in Britannia Romana, between Noviomagus and Durobrivae. Camden (p. 226) identifies it with *Maidstone*, Horsley (p. 424), with more probability, with *Northfleet*. Others have sought it near *Longfield*, and at *Wrotham*.   [T. H. D.]

VAGORITUM (Οὐαγόριτον). [ARVII.]

VAHALIS. [BATAVI; RHENUS.]

VALCUM, a place near the confines of Upper and Lower Pannonia, not far from Lake Peiso (*Itin. Ant.* p. 233), but its exact site is uncertain.   [L. S.]

VALDASUS, a southern tributary of the Savus, flowing from the mountains of Illyricum, and joining the Savus not far from the town of Basante (Plin. iii. 28, where some read Valdanus or Vadasus) ; its modern name is *Bosna*.   [L. S.]

VALE'NTIA (*Eth.* Valentinus: *Nuragus*), a town in the interior of Sardinia, SE. of Usellis. It seems to have been a considerable place, as the Valentini are one of the few names which Pliny thought it worth while to mention among the Sardinian towns. Ptolemy also notices the Valentini among the tribes or " populi " of the island, and there can be little doubt that the Valeria of the same author is only a false reading for Valentia. (Plin. iii. 12. s. 17; Ptol. iii. 3. §§ 6, 7.) Its remains are still visible at a village called *Nuragus*, near the town of *Isili*, about 12 miles from the ruins of Usellis. The adjoining district is still called *Parte Valenza*. (De la Marmora, *Voy. en Sardaigne*, vol. ii. p. 407.)   [E.H.B.]

VALE'NTIA, the later name of a Roman province in the S. part of Britannia Barbara, or of the country lying N. of the Picts' wall, as far as *Graham's Dike*, including *Northumberland, Dumfries*, &c. This district was wrested from the Picts and Scots in the time of Valentinian, and formed by Theodosius into a Roman province, but it remained only a short time in the possession of the Romans. (Ammian. Marc. xxviii. 3; *Not. Imp.*)   [T. H. D.]

VALE'NTIA (Οὐαλεντία, Ptol. ii. 6. § 62), a considerable town of the Edetani in Hispania Tarraconensis, situated on the river Turium, at a distance of 3 miles from its mouth, and on the road from Carthago Nova to Castulo. (Plin. iii. 3. s. 4; Vib. Seq. p. 18; *Itin. Ant.* p. 400.) Ptolemy (*l. c.*) erroneously attributes it to the Contestani. It became at a later period a Roman colony (Plin. *l. c.*), in which apparently the consul Junius Brutus settled the soldiers of Viriathus. (Liv. *Epit.* lv.) Pompey destroyed it. (*Epist. Pomp. ap. Sallust*, ed. Corte, p. 965; cf. Plut. *Pomp.* 18.) It must, however, have been restored soon afterwards, since Mela mentions it as being still an important place (ii. 6), and coins of it of a late period are preserved. (Cf. Florez, *Med.* ii. p. 610, iii. p. 125; Mionnet, i. p. 55, *Suppl.* i. p. 110; Sestini, p. 209; Eckhel, i p. 60.) The town still bears the same name, but has few antiquities to show.   [T. H. D.]

COIN OF VALENTIA IN SPAIN.

VALE'NTIA (Οὐαλεντία), in Gallia Narbonensis, a colonia in the territory of the Cavari, as Pliny says (iii. 4); but D'Anville proposes to alter the meaning of this passage of Pliny by placing a full stop between " Cavarum " and " Valentia." However, Valentia (*Valence*) was not in the country of the Cavari, but in the territory of the Segallauni, as Ptolemy (ii. 10. § 12) says, who calls it " colonia." *Valence* is a town on the east bank of the Rhone, a few miles below the junction of the *Isère*. In the middle ages it was the capital of the Valentinois, and in the fifteenth century it became the seat of a university.   [G. L.]

VALENTIA, in Bruttium. [HIPPONIUM.]

VALEPONGA or VALEBONGA, a town of the Celtiberi in Hispania Tarraconensis, on the road from Luminium to Caesaraugusta. (*Itin. Ant.* p. 477.) Variously identified with *Val de Meca* and *Valsalobre*.   [T. H. D.]

VALE'RIA, the name of the NE. part of Lower Pannonia, which was constituted as a separate province by the emperor Galerius, and named Valeria in honour of his wife. (Aurel. Vict. *de Caes.* 40; Amm. xvi. 10, xxviii. 3.) This province was bounded on the E. and N. by the Danubius, on the S. by the Savus, and on the W. by Lake Peiso. (Comp. PANNONIA, p. 531, and Muchar, *Norikum*, vol. i. p. 3.)   [L. S.]

VALE'RIA (Οὐαλερία, Ptol. ii. 6. § 58), a town of the Celtiberi in Hispania Tarraconensis, on the Sucro. At a later period it became a Roman colony in the jurisdiction of Carthago Nova. (Plin. iii. 3. s. 4.) Now *Valera la Vieja*, with ruins. (Of. Florez, *Esp. Sagr.* viii. p. 198, with v. p. 19, and vii. p. 59.)   [T. H. D.]

VALERIANA (Βαλεριάνα, Procop. *de Aed.* iv. 6), a place in Moesia Inferior. (*Itin. Ant.* p. 220.) Probably near *Ostova*.   [T. H. D.]

VALI (Οὐάλοι, Ptol. v. 9. § 21), a people of Asiatic Sarmatia, between Mount Ceraunus and the river Rha. (Plin. vi. 7. s. 7.)   [T. H. D.]

VALINA (Οὐάλεινα or Βαλίνα), a place in Upper Pannonia, commonly identified with the modern *Valbach*. (Ptol. ii. 15. § 6.)   [L. S.]

VALLA. [BALLA.]

VALLATA, a town of the Astures in Hispania Tarraconensis, between Asturica and Interamnium. (*Itin. Ant.* pp. 448, 453.) Variously identified with *Bañeza, Puente de Orvijo, S. Martin de Camino*, and *Villar de Majardin*.   [T. H. D.]

VALLATUM, a town in Vindelicia, not far from the S. bank of the Danubius, on the road from Reginum to Augusta Vindelicorum; it was the station of the staff of the third legion and the second Valerian squadron of cavalry. (*It. Ant.* p. 250; *Not. Imp.*) It occupied, in all probability, the same site as the modern *Wahl*, on the little river *Ilm*.   [L. S.]

VALLIS PENNINA, or POENINA, as the name is written in some inscriptions, is the long valley down which the Rhone flows into the *Lake of Geneva*. In the Notitia of the Gallic Provinces all the inhabitants of this valley are included in the name Vallenses, for we read " Civitas Vallensium, hoc est, Octodurum." [OCTODURUS.] But there were four peoples in the *Vallais*, as it seems, NANTUATES, VERAGRI, SEDUNI, and VIBERI. The name Vallis Pennina went out of use, and it was called Pagus Vallensis. The name Vallis is preserved in that of the canton *Wallis* or *Vallais*, which is the largest valley in Switzerland. [GALLIA TRANSALPINA, Vol. I. p. 950; RHODANUS.] [G.L.]

VALLUM ROMANUM. Under this title we propose to give a short account of the remarkable work constructed by the Romans across our island, from near the mouth of the *Tyne* on the E. to the *Solway Frith* on the W., and of which considerable remains still exist. The history of the formation of this line of fortification is involved in a good deal of obscurity, and very different opinions have been entertained respecting its authors; and neither the Latin writers nor the inscriptions hitherto found among the ruins of the wall and its subsidiary works are sufficient to settle the disputed points, though they suggest conjectures more or less probable.

The origin of the barrier may have been the forts and stationary camps which Agricola (A. D. 79) caused to be erected in Britain (Tac. *Agr.* 20); but the account which. Tacitus gives of this measure is so vague that it is quite impossible to found any certain conclusion on his words. In A. D. 120, Hadrian. visited Britain, where he determined on fixing the boundary of the Roman Empire considerably to the S. of the most N. conquests of Agricola. He chose this boundary well, as it coincides with a natural one. The *Tyne* flows almost due E., just S., and nearly parallel to the 55° N. lat., for more than two thirds of the breadth of the island. The valley of the *Tyne* is separated from that of the *Irthing*, a branch of the *Eden*, by the N. extremity of the great chain of hills sometimes called the Backbone of England; and the *Irthing*, with the *Eden*, completes the boundary to the *Solway Frith.* In order to strengthen this natural frontier, Hadrian, as we are informed by Spartianus, "drew a wall (*murus*) 80,000 paces in length, to divide the barbarians from the Romans;" which wall followed the same general direction as the line above indicated.

Eutropius (viii. 19) states that the Emperor Septimius Severus, who was in Britain during A. D. 208—211, constructed a rampart (*vallum*) from sea to sea, for the protection of the Roman provinces in the S. of the island.

Now, as will be seen from the following description, the lines of works designated by the general name, Roman Wall, consist of two main parts, a stone wall and an earthen rampart; and most writers on the subject have regarded these as two distinct, though connected, works, and belonging to two different periods; the earthwork has generally been ascribed to Hadrian, the stone wall to Severus. Such is the opinion of Horsley, whose judgment, as Mr. Bruce emphatically admits, is always deserving of the highest consideration. Mr. Bruce himself expresses an opinion, founded on repeated and careful examination of all the remains of the wall, " that the lines of the barrier are the scheme of one great military engineer. . . . . The wall of Hadrian was not a fence such as that by which we prevent the straying of cattle; it was a line of military operation, similar in its nature to the works which Wellington raised at *Torres Vedras.* A broad belt of country was firmly secured. Walls of stone and earth crossed it. Camps to the north and south of them broke the force of an enemy in both directions; or, in the event of their passing the outer line, enabled the Romans to close upon them both in front and rear. Look-out stations revealed to them the movements of their foes; beacons enabled them to communicate with neighbouring garrisons; and the roads, which they always maintained, assisted them in concentrating their forces upon the points where it might be done with the best effect. Such, I am persuaded, was the intention of the Roman wall, though some still maintain that the murus and vallum are independent structures, the productions of different periods" (pp. ix. x. *Pref.* 2nd ed.)

We confess that the reasoning here does not seem to us to be very conclusive. Grant that the system of defence has consistency and unity, yet it by no means follows that the whole was executed at one time. The earliest works were probably detached stationary camps; the next step would naturally be to connect them together by a wall, whether of earth or stone; and if experience should afterwards prove that this barrier was insufficient, it would be an obvious proceeding to strengthen it by a parallel fortification. The common opinion, therefore, that Agricola commenced the defensive line, Hadrian strengthened it, and Severus completed it, appears to be probable in itself, and is supported by the little that we find upon the subject in the classical writers. If we may assume that the words *murus* and *vallum* were used by Spartianus and Eutropius in their strict significations, it would seem that the stone wall was the work of Hadrian, the earthen rampart of Severus. That some portion of the barrier was executed under the direction of the latter, is rendered still more probable by the fact that the Britons called the wall *gual Sever, gal Sever,* or *mur Sever,* as Camden states. It has been designated by various names in later times; as the *Picts' Wall,* the *Thirl Wall,* the *Kepe Wall;* but is now generally called the *Roman Wall.*

The following description is taken almost entirely from Mr. Bruce's excellent work, mentioned at the end of this article.

The barrier consists of three parts: (i.) a stone wall or *murus,* strengthened by a ditch on its northern side; (ii.) an earthen wall or *vallum,* south of the stone wall; (iii.) stations, castles, watchtowers, and roads: these lie for the most part between the stone wall and the earthen rampart.

The whole of the works extend from one side of the island to the other, in a nearly straight line, and comparatively close to one another. The wall and rampart are generally within 60 or 70 yards of each other, though the distance of course varies according to the nature of the country. Sometimes they are so close as barely to admit of the passage of the military way between them; while in one or two instances they are upwards of half a mile apart. It is in the high grounds of the central region that they are most widely separated. Here the wall is carried over the highest ridges, while the rampart runs along the adjacent valley. Both works, however, are so arranged as to afford each other the greatest amount of support which the nature of the country allows.

The stone wall extends from *Wallsend* on the *Tyne* to *Bowness* on the *Solway,* a distance which Horsley estimates at 68 miles 3 furlongs, a measurement which almost exactly coincides with that of General Roy, who gives the length of the wall at 68½ miles. The vallum falls short of this length by about 3 miles at each end, terminating at *Newcastle* on the E. side, and at *Drumburgh* on the W.

For 19 miles out of Newcastle, the present highroad to *Carlisle* runs upon the foundations of the wall, which pursues a straight course wherever it is at all possible, and is never curved, but always bends at an angle.

In no part is the wall perfect, so that it is difficult to ascertain what its original height may have been. Bede, whose monastery of Jarrow was near its eastern extremity, and who is the earliest authority respecting its dimensions, states that in his time it was 8 feet thick and 12 high. Sir Christ. Ridley, writing in 1572, describes it as 3 yards broad, and in some places 7 yards high. Samson Erdeswick, a well-known antiquary, visited the wall in 1574, when he ascertained its height at the W. end to be 16 feet. Camden, who saw the wall in 1599, found a part of it on a hill, near *Carvoran,* to be 15 feet high and 9 broad. Allowing for a battlement, which would probably soon be destroyed, we may conclude that the average height was from 18 to 19 feet. The thickness varies from 6 to 9¼ feet.

The wall was everywhere accompanied on its northern side by a broad and deep fosse, which may still be traced, with trifling interruptions, from sea to sea, even where the wall has quite disappeared. It traverses indifferently alluvial soil and rocks of sandstone, limestone, and basalt. Thus, on *Tapper Moor*, enormous blocks of whinstone lie just as they were lifted out of the fosse. East of *Heddon on the Wall*, the fosse is 34 feet wide at the top, 14 at the bottom, and about 9 deep. In some places it is 40 feet wide at the top, and in others 20 feet deep.

Hodgson, in his *History of Northumberland* (iii. p. 276), states a fact curious if true: "A little W. of *Portgate*, the earth taken out of the fosse lies spread abroad to the N. in lines, just as the workmen wheeled it out and left it. The tracks of their barrows, with a slight mound on each side, remain unaltered in form." It is scarcely credible, however, that slight elevations of earth, and superficial traces in it, should, for more than a thousand years, have successfully resisted the constant operation of the natural agencies which are sufficient to disintegrate the hardest rocks.

The VALLUM, or earth wall, is uniformly S. of the stone wall. It consists of three ramparts and a fosse. One rampart is close to the S. edge of the ditch. Of the other two, which are considerably larger, one is situated N., the other S. of the ditch, at the distance of about 24 feet from it. These larger ramparts are even now, in some places, 6 or 7 feet high. They are composed of earth, in which masses of stone are often imbedded, for the sake of which they are sometimes quarried. The fosse of the vallum was probably smaller than that of the murus.

No outlets through the S. lines of fortification have been discovered; so that the gateways of the stations appear to have originally been the only means of communication with the country.

At distances averaging nearly 4 miles, stationary camps were erected along the line. Some of these, though connected with the wall, were evidently built before it.

The stations are four-sided and nearly square, but somewhat rounded at the corners, and contain an area averaging from 3 to 6 acres, though some of them are considerably larger. A stone wall, about 5 feet thick, encloses them, and was probably in every instance strengthened by a fosse and one or more earthen ramparts. The stations usually stand upon ground with a southern inclination.

The great wall either falls in with the N. wall of the stations, or else usually comes up to the N. cheek of their E. and W. gateways. The vallum in like manner generally approaches close to the S. wall of the stations, or comes up to the S. side of the E. and W. portals. At least three of the stations, however, are quite detached from both lines of fortification, being to the S. of them. These may have been erected by Agricola.

Narrow streets intersecting one another at right angles traverse the interior of the stations; and abundant ruins outside the walls indicate that extensive suburbs were required for the accommodation of those connected with the soldiers stationed in the camps. The stations were evidently constructed with exclusive reference to defence; and hence no traces of tessellated pavements or other indications of luxury and refinement have been discovered in the mural region.

According to Horsley, there were 18 stations on the line of the wall, besides some in its immediate vicinity;

but Hodgson reduces the number to 17, believing that in one instance Horsley mistook a mere temporary encampment for a station.

In ascertaining the number and names of the stations, our principal literary authority is the *Notitia Imperii*, supposed to have been compiled about the end of the reign of the emperor Theodosius the younger. The 69th section of this document contains a list of the prefects and tribunes under the Duke of Britain: the portion relating to our subject is headed, "*Item per lineam Valli*," and contains the names of 23 stations, evidently arranged in their order from E. to W. The heading, however, manifestly implies, not, as it seems sometimes to have been interpreted, that all the stations were actually *on* the line of the wall, but that they were *along* it, that is, parallel to, or at no great distance from it. It is clear, therefore, that as remains of stations exist both to the N. and to the S. of the wall, as well as actually on its line, nothing but the remains themselves can enable us to name the stations with certainty.

Now the first 12 stations mentioned in the Notitia have been accurately identified by means of inscriptions found in the ruins of the stations. Of these we subjoin a list, with the ancient and modern names, taken chiefly from the plan prefixed to Mr. Bruce's work:—

Segedunum	- -	*Wallsend.*
Pons Aelii	- -	*Newcastle.*
Condercum	- -	*Benwell.*
Vindobala	- -	*Rutchester.*
Hunnum -	- -	*Halton Chesters.*
Cilurnum -	- -	*Walwick Chesters.*
Procolitia -	- -	*Carrawburgh.*
Borcovicus	- -	*Housesteads.*
Vindolana	- -	*Little Chesters, or Chesterholm.*
Aesica	- -	*Great Chesters.*
Magna (Magnæ)	- -	*Carvoran.*
Amboglanna	- -	*Birdoswald.*

All these are on the actual line of the wall, except Vindolana and Magna, which are a little to the S. of it.

West of Amboglanna no evidence has yet been discovered to identify any of the stations; and it is to be feared that many antiquities which might have enabled us to do so have been destroyed; for it appears that the country people, even quite recently, regarded stones bearing inscriptions as "unlucky," calling them "witch-stones," the evil influence of which was to be extirpated by pounding them to powder. Besides this, stone is scarce in that part of the country; and hence the materials of the wall and stations have been extensively employed in the construction of dikes and other erections in the neighbourhood.

It appears from the plan already referred to that there were stations at the places now called *Cambeck Fort, Stanwix, Burgh, Drumburgh*, and *Bowness;* the first a little to the S., all the rest on the line of the wall.

Of the remaining eleven stations mentioned in the Notitia, the plan identifies Alionis with *Whitley Castle*, some miles S. of the wall. Mr. Bruce places Bremetenracum a little W. of the village of *Brampton;* Petriana, he thinks, is probably the same as *Cambeck Fort.*

It is possible that something may yet be done to elucidate what is still obscure in connection with these most interesting monuments of Roman Britain; and the Duke of Northumberland had, in 1853, given directions to competent persons to make an accurate and complete survey of the whole line of the barrier, from sea to sea. Whether any results of this investigation have yet been published, we are not aware.

Of the identified stations the most extensive and important are Vindobala, Cilurnum, Procolitia, and Borcovicus. At the first, great numbers of coins and other antiquities have been found. The second has an area of 8 acres, and is crowded with ruins of stone buildings. A great part of the rampart of Procolitia is entire, and its northern face, which is formed of the main line of wall, is in excellent preservation. Borcovicus, however, surpasses all the other stations in magnitude and in the interest which attaches to its remains. It is 15 acres in extent, besides a large suburb on the S. Within it no less than 20 streets may be traced ; and it seems to have contained a Doric temple, part of a Doric capital and fragments of the shafts of columns having been discovered in it, besides a great number of altars, inscriptions, and other antiquities.

The remaining portions of this great fortification may be briefly described.

The CASTELLA, or mile-castles as they are called, on account of being usually a Roman mile from one another, are buildings about 60 or 70 feet square. With two exceptions, they are placed against the S. face of the wall ; the exceptions, at Portgate and near Aesica, seem to have projected equally N. and S. of the wall. The castella have usually only one entrance, of very substantial masonry, in the centre of the S. wall ; but the most perfect specimen of them now existing has a N. as well as a S. gate.

Between each two castella there were four smaller buildings, called turrets or watch-towers, which were little more than stone sentry-boxes, about 3 feet thick, and from 8 to 10 feet square in the inside.

The line of the wall was completed by military roads, keeping up the communications with all its parts and with the southern districts of the island. As these were similar in their construction to other Roman roads, it is not necessary to say more respecting them in this place.

The following works contain detailed information of every kind connected with the Roman Wall :— Horsley's *Britannia Romana ;* Warburton's *Vallum Romanum*, 4to. Lond. 1753 ; W. Hutton's *History of the Roman Wall*, 1801 ; Roy's *Military Antiquities of the Romans in Britain ;* the 3rd vol. of Hodgson's *History of Northumberland;* and lastly, *The Roman Wall; an Historical and Topographical Description of the Barrier of the lower Isthmus, &c. Deduced from numerous personal Surveys.* By the Rev. J. C. Bruce, M. A., 2nd edit. Lond. 1853, 4to. This work contains full descriptions of all the antiquities hitherto discovered along the line of the wall, and great numbers of well executed engravings of the most interesting objects, besides maps and plans of the works. [J. R.]

VALVA (Οὔαλουα, Ptol. iv. 2. § 16), a mountain in Mauretania Caesariensis. [T. H. D.]

VAMA (Οὔαμα, Ptol. ii. 4. § 15), a town of the Celtici in Hispania Baetica. [T. H. D.]

VANCIANIS. [BATIANA.]

VANDABANDA (Οὐανδαβάνδα, Ptol. vi. 12. § 4), a district of Sogdiana, between the Mons Caucasus (*Hindú-Kúsh*) and the Imaus (*Himáleh*). It is probably nearly the same as the present *Badakhshán* (Wilson, *Ariana*, p. 164). [V.]

VANDALI, VANDALII, VINDILI, or VANDULI (Οὐανδαλοί, Βανδῆλοι, Βανδίλοι), a powerful branch of the German nation, which, according to Procopius (*Bell. Goth.* i. 3), originally occupied the country about the Palus Maeotis, but afterwards inhabited an extensive tract of country on the south coast of the Baltic, between the rivers Vistula and Viadrus, where Pliny (iv. 28) mentions the Burgundiones as a tribe of the Vindili. At a somewhat later period we find them in the country north of Bohemia, about the *Riesengebirge*, which derived from them the name of Vandalici Montes (Οὐανδαλικὰ ὄρη ; Dion Cass. lv. 1.) In the great Marcomannian war, they were allied with the Marcomanni, their southern neighbours, and in conjunction with them and the Quadi attacked Pannonia. (Jul. Capitol. *M. Aurel.* 17 ; Eutrop. viii. 13 ; Vopisc. *Prob.* 18 ; Dexippus, *Exc. de Leg.* p. 12.) In the reign of Constantine they again appear in a different country, having established themselves in Moravia, whence the emperor transplanted them into Pannonia (Jornand. *Get.* 22), and in the reign of Probus they also appear in Dacia. (Vopisc. *Prob.* 38.) In A. D. 406, when most of the Roman troops had been withdrawn from Gaul, the Vandals, in conjunction with other German tribes, crossed the Rhine and ravaged Gaul in all directions ; and their devastations in that country and afterwards in Spain have made their name synonymous with that of savage destroyers of what is beautiful and venerable. Three years later they established themselves in Spain under their chief Godigisclus. Here again they plundered and ravaged, among many other places, Nova Carthago and Hispalis, together with the Balearian islands. At last, in A. D. 429, the whole nation, under king Genseric, crossed over into Africa, whither they had been invited by Bonifacius, who hoped to avail himself of their assistance against his calumniators. But when they were once in Africa, they refused to quit it. They not only defeated Bonifacius, but made themselves masters of the whole province of Africa. This involved them in war with the Empire, during which Sicily and the coasts of Italy were at times fearfully ravaged. On one occasion, A. D. 455, Genseric and his hordes took possession of Rome, which they plundered and sacked for fourteen days. And not only Rome, but other cities also, such as Capua and Nola, were visited in a similar way by these barbarians. Afterwards various attempts were made to subdue or expel them, but without success, and the kingdom of the Vandals maintained itself in Africa for a period of 105 years, that is, down to A. D. 534, when Belisarius, the general of the Eastern Empire, succeeded in destroying their power, and recovered Africa for the Empire. As to the nationality of the Vandals, most German writers claim them for their nation (Zeuss, *Die Deutschen*, p. 57 ; Wilhelm, *Germanien*, p. 87) ; but Dr. Latham (on *Tac. Epileg.* p. lxxxviii. foll.) and others prefer regarding them as a Slavonic people, though their arguments are chiefly of an etymological nature, which is not always a safe guide in historical inquiries. (Papencordt, *Gesch. der Vandal. Herrschaft in Africa*, Berlin, 1837 ; Hansen, *Wer veranlasste die Berufung der Vandalen nach Africa?* Dorpat, 1843 ; Friedländer, *Die Münzen der Vandalen*, Leipzig, 1849.) [L. S.]

VANDALICI MONTES. [VANDALI.]

VANDUARA, or VANDOGARA (Οὐανδόυαρα, Ptol. ii. 3. § 9), a town of the Damnonii in Britannia Barbara. Now *Paisley*. (Cf. Camden, p. 1214.) [T. H. D.]

VANESIA, a place in Gallia Aquitanica, fixed by the Jerusalem Itin. between Elusa (*Eause*) and Auscius, the capital of the Ausci, xii. from Elusa and viii. from Auscius. The place is supposed by D'Anville to be the passage of the *Baise*, a branch of the *Garonne* which comes from the Pyrenees. [G. L.]

VANGIONES (Οὐαγγίονες). There were Vangiones in the army of Ariovistus when Caesar defeated him. (*B. G.* i. 51.) Caesar means to say that they were Germans, but he does not say whether they were settled in Gallia. Pliny and Tacitus (*Ann.* xii. 27, *Germ.* c. 28) also describe the Vangiones as Germans and settled on the left bank of the Rhine, where they are placed by Ptolemy (ii. 9. § 17); but Ptolemy makes a mistake in placing the Nemetes north of the Vangiones, and making the Vangiones the neighbours of the Tribocci, from whom in fact the Vangiones were separated by the Nemetes. In the war of Civilis (Tacit. *Hist.* iv. 70), Tutor strengthened the force of the Treviri by levies raised among the Vangiones, Caracates [CARACATES], and Tribocci. The territory of the Vangiones seems to have been taken from that of the Mediomatrici. Their chief town was Borbetomagus (*Worms*). [BORBETOMAGUS.] [G. L.]

VA'NNIA (Οὐαννία, Ptol. iii. 1. § 32), according to Ptolemy a town of the Bechuni in Carnia or *Carniola* (cf. Plin. iii. 19. s. 23). Variously identified with *Venzone* and *Cividato*. [T. H. D.]

VAPINCUM, in Gallia Narbonensis, is not mentioned by any authority earlier than the Antonine and Jerusalem Itins. In the Notitia of the Gallic Provinces it is styled " Civitas Vapincensium." The initial letter of the name has been changed to G, as in many other instances in the French language, and the modern name is *Gap*, which is the capital of the department of *Hautes-Alpes*, and on a small stream which flows into the *Durance*. [G. L.]

VARA, or VARAE, a town in Britannia Romana, between Conovium and Deva. (*Itin. Ant.* p. 482.) Variously identified with *St. Asaph*, *Rudland*, and *Bodvary*. [T. H. D.]

VARADA (Οὐάραδα, Ptol. ii. 6. § 57), a town of the Carpetani in Hispania Tarraconensis. [T.H.D.]

VARADETUM, in Gallia, is placed by the Table on a road from Divona (*Cahors*) to Segodunum (*Rodez*); and the distance from Divona is xv. D'Anville places Varadetum at *Varaie*, which is on the road between *Cahors* and *Rodez*; but the distances do not agree. Others fix the site at *Puijourdes*. [G. L.]

VARAE. [VARA.]

VARAGRI. [VERAGRI.]

VARAR (Οὐάραρ, Ptol. ii. 6. § 5), an estuary on the E. coast of Britannia Barbara, very probably the present *Frith of Cromarty*. [T. H. D.]

VARCIANI (Οὐαρκιανοί), a tribe in Upper Pannonia, which is mentioned by both Pliny (iii. 28) and Ptolemy (ii. 15. § 2), but of which nothing is known, except that it probably occupied the western portion of Slavonia. [L. S.]

VARCILENSES, the inhabitants of a town of the Carpetani in Hispania Tarraconensis. (*Inscr.* in Morales, *Ant.* pp. 17, 26, 28.) The modern *Varciles* still contains some ruins of the old town. [T. H. D.]

VARDAEI (Οὐαρδαῖοι, Ptol. ii. 17. § 8), an Illyrian tribe dwelling opposite to the island of Pharos (cf. Plin. iii. 23. s. 26). By Strabo they are called Ardiaei (Ἀρδιαῖοι, vii. p. 315). In the Epitome of Livy (lvi.) they are said to have been subdued by the consul Fulvius Flaccus. [T. H. D.]

VARDANES (Οὐαρδάνης, Ptol. v. 9 §§ 5 and 28), a river of Asiatic Sarmatia, represented as falling into the Euxine to the SW. of the Atticitus. Probably, however, it was only the southern arm of the latter, the present *Kuban*. (Cf. Ukert, iii. pt. ii. p. 202.) [ATTICITUS.] [T. H. D.]

VARDO, a tributary of the Rhone, which rises in the *Cévennes*, and is formed by two branches named respectively *Gardon d'Alais* and *Gardon d'Anduse*, from the names of these two towns. The Vardo flows in a deep valley, and passes under the great Roman aqueduct now named *Pont du Gard*, below which it enters the *Rhône* on the west bank, near a place named *Cons*. The name Vardo occurs in Sidonius Apollinaris; and in a Latin poem of three or four centuries' later date the name is Wardo, from which the modern name *Gardon* is formed, according to a common change of V into G. [VAPINCUM.] [G. L.]

VARDULI (Οὐαρδοῦλοι, Ptol. ii. 6. §§ 9, 66; Βάρδουλοι, Strab. iii. p. 162; where we also learn that at an earlier period they were called Βαρδυῆται), a people in Hispania Tarraconensis, who dwelt westward of the Vascones, as far as the N. coast (in the present *Guipuscoa* and *Alava*). (Mela, iii. 1; Plin. iii. 3. s. 4, iv. 20. s. 34.) [T. H. D.]

VARGIO'NES (Οὐαργίωνες), a German tribe, between the eastern bank of the Rhenus and Mons Abnoba, that is, perhaps between the *Ruhr* and the *Rauhe Alp*. (Ptol. ii. 11. § 9.) [L. S.]

VARIA. 1. (Οὐαρία: *Vicovaro*), a town of the Sabines, situated in the valley of the Anio, on the right bank of the river, about 8 miles above Tibur. The name is corruptly written in most editions of Strabo Valeria (Οὐαλερία), for which there is no doubt that we should read Varia (Οὐαρία, Strab. v. p. 237; Kramer, *ad loc.*). Strabo there calls it a Latin city, as well as Carseoli and Alba, both of which were certainly Aequian towns, and subsequently included in Latium. But Horace speaks of it as the town to which the peasantry from his Sabine farm and the neighbouring villages used to resort (Hor. *Ep.* i. 14. 3), in a manner that certainly seems to imply that it was the municipal centre of that district, and if so, it must have then been reckoned a Sabine town. It is not mentioned by Pliny, but according to his limitation was certainly included among the Sabines, and not in Latium. It was probably never a large place, though the remains of the ancient walls still extant prove that it must at one time have been a fortified town. But it early sank into a mere village; the old commentator on Horace calls it " Oppidum in Sabinis olim, nunc vicus " (Schol. Cruq. *ad l. c.*): and hence in the middle ages it came to be called Vicus Varia, whence its modern appellation of *Vicovaro*. It is still a considerable village of above 1000 inhabitants, standing on a hill to the left of the Via Valeria, and a short distance above the Anio, which flows in a deep valley beneath. The Tabula and the old commentary on Horace both place it 8 miles above Tibur, which is very nearly exact. (*Tab. Peut.* Comm. Cruq. *l. c.*)

2. Pliny mentions among the cities of Calabria a place called Varia, " cui cognomen Apulae " (iii. 11. s. 16); but the name is otherwise unknown, and it is probable that we should read " Uria ;" the place meant being apparently the same that is called by other writers Hyria or Uria [HYRIA]. [E. H. B.]

VA'RIA (Οὐαρία, Strab. iii. p. 162 ; Οὐάρεια, Ptol. ii. 6. § 55), a town of the Berones in Hispania Tarraconensis, situated on the Iberus, which here began to be navigable (Plin. ii. 3. s. 4), and where also the main road through Spain crossed the river, between Calagurra and Tritium. (*Itin. Ant.* p. 393, where, under the name of Verela, the same town is undoubtedly meant.) Usually identified with *Varea* (cf. Florez, *Cantabr.* p. 198), though some have sought it at *Logroño*, and others at *Murillo de Rio Leza.* 　　　　　　[T. H. D.]

VARIA'NA (Βαριάνα), a town in Lower Moesia on the Danube, was the garrison of a portion of the fifth legion and of a squadron of horse. (*It. Ant.* p. 220; Procop. *de Aed.* iv. 6; *Notit. Imp.*, where it is called Variniana and Varina.) Its site is marked by the town of *Orcaja* or *Orcava.* 　[L. S.]

VARIANAE, a place in Pannonia, on the road running along the left bank of the Savus from Siscia to Sirmium. (*It. Ant.* pp. 260, 265.) Its exact site is only matter of conjecture. 　　　[L. S.]

VARI'NI, a German tribe mentioned by Pliny (iv. 28) as a branch of the Vindili or Vandali, while Tacitus (*Germ.* 40) speaks of them as belonging to the Suevi. But they must have occupied a district in the north of Germany, not far from the coast of the Baltic, and are probably the same as the Pharodini (Φαροδεινοί) of Ptolemy (ii. 11. § 13), in the country between the Chalusus and Suebus; it is highly probable, also, that the Varni (Οὐάρνοι) of Procopius (*B. Goth.* ii. 15, iii. 35, iv. 20, &c.) are the same people as the Varini. The Viruni (Οὐίρουνοι) of Ptolemy (ii. 11. § 17), who dwelt north of the Albis, seem to have been a branch of the Varini. (Comp. Cassiod. *Var.* iii. 3, where they are called Guarni; Wersebe, *Beschreib. der Gau zwischen Elbe, Saale, &c.* p. 70.) 　[L. S.]

VARISTI. [NARISCI.]

VARUS (Οὔαρος), a river which the ancient geographers make the boundary of Gallia and Italia, as it is now the boundary of France and Italy. (Mela, ii. 4; Ptol. ii. 10. § 1.) It is only the lower part of the *Var* which forms the boundary between Italy and France. The river gives its name to the French department of *Var*, the eastern limit of which is the lower course of the river *Var*. The larger part of the *Var* is in the Sardinian territory. It is only the mouth of the *Var* which Ptolemy names when he fixes the limit between Italy and Gallia Narbonensis. D'Anville remarks on the line of Lucan (i. 404) —

" Finis et Hesperiae promoto limite Varus "—

that he alludes to the extension of the boundary of Italy westward from the summit of the Alpia Maritima, which is Italy's natural boundary. He adds that the dependencies of the province of the Alpes Maritimae comprehended Cemenelium (*Cimiez*) and its district, which are on the Italian side of the *Var* and east of Nicaea (*Nizza*). [CEMENELIUM.] But D'Anville may have mistaken Lucan's meaning, who seems to allude to the extension of the boundary of Italy from the Rubicon to the Varus, as Vibius Sequester says : " Varus nunc Galliam dividit, ante Rubicon " (ed. Oberl.). However, the critics are not agreed about this passage. (D'Anville, *Notice, &c.*; Ukert, *Gallien*, p. 81.) 　　　　[G. L.]

VASADA (Οὐάσαδα), a town of Lycaonia, a little to the south-west of Laodiceia (Ptol. v. 4. § 10; Hierocl. p. 675; *Conc. Chalced.* p. 674, where it is miswritten Οὔσαδα; *Conc. Const.* iii. p. 675, where it bears the name of 'Αδσαδα). Its site is probably marked by the ruins near *Chamur Chanak*, between *Ilgun* and *Ladik.* (Hamilton,

Researches, ii. p. 190, in the *Journ. of the Roy. Geogr. Soc.* viii. p. 144; Kiepert, in Franz, *Fünf Inschriften*, p. 36.) 　　　　　　[L. S.]

VASALAETUS (Οὐασάλαιτον or Οὐασάλετον ὄρος, Ptol. iv. 3. §§ 18, 26), a mountain at the S. boundary of the Regio Syrtica. 　　[T. H. D.]

VASATAE. [COSSIO or COSSIUM.]

VASATES. It is probable that the name Vasarii in Ptolemy (ii. 7. § 15) should be Vasatii, as D'Anville says, and so it is printed in some Greek texts. But Ptolemy makes them border on the Gabali and places them farther north than *Bordeaux*, though he names their chief town Cossium. The Vocates are enumerated by Caesar (*B. G.* iii. 23, 27) among the Aquitanian peoples who submitted to P. Crassus in B. C. 56. [COSSIO or COSSIUM.] [G.L.]

VA'SCONES (Οὐάσκωνες, Strab. iii. pp. 155, 116; Οὐάσκωνες, Ptol. ii. 8. §§ 10, 67), a people in the NE. part of Hispania Tarraconensis, between the Iberus and the Pyrenees, and stretching as far as the N. coast, in the present *Navarre* and *Guipuscoa*. Their name is preserved in the modern one of the *Basques*; although that people do not call themselves by that appellation, but *Euscaldunac*, their country *Euscaleria*, and their language *Euscara*. (Ford's *Handbook of Spain*, p. 557; cf. W. v. Humboldt, *Untersuch.* &c. p. 54.) They went into battle bareheaded. (Sil. Ital. iii. 358.) They passed among the Romans for skilful soothsayers. (Lamp. *Alex. Sev.* 27.) Their principal town was Pompelo (*Pamplona*). (Cf. Malte-brun, *Moeurs et Usages des anciens Habitans d'Espagne*, p. 309.) [T.H.D.]

VA'SCONUM SALTUS, the W. offshoot of the Pyrenees, running along the Mare Cantabricum, and named after the Vascones, in whose territory it was. (Plin. iv. 20. s. 34; Auson. *Ep.* 15.) It may be more precisely defined as that portion of the chain now called *Sierra de Orcamo, S. de Augana*, and *S. Sejos*, forming the E. part of the Cantabrian chain. 　　　　　　　　　　[T.H.D.]

VASIO (Οὐασιών: *Eth.* Vasiensis), a town of the Vocontii in Gallia Narbonensis, and the only town which Ptolemy (ii. 10. § 17) assigns to them. Vasio is mentioned by Mela (ii. 5) as one of the richest towns of the Narbonensis; and Pliny (iii. 4) names Vasio and Lucus Augusti as the two chief towns of the Vocontii. The ethnic name Vasiensis appears in the Notitia of the Gallic Provinces (Civitas Vasiensium), and in inscriptions. The place is *Vaison* in the department of *Vaucluse*, on the *Ouvèze*, a branch of the Rhone. It is now a small, decayed place; but there are remains which show that it may have been what Mela describes it to have been. The ancient remains are spread over a considerable surface. There is a Roman bridge of a single arch over the *Ouvèze*, which still forms the only communication between the town and the faubourg. The bridge is built on two rocks at that part of the river where the mountains which shut in the bed of the river approach nearest. There are also the remains of a theatre ; the semicircle of the cavea is clearly traced, and the line of the proscenium is indicated by some stones which rise above the earth. There are also the remains of a quay on the banks of the river which was destroyed by an inundation in 1616. The quay was pierced at considerable intervals by sewers which carried to the river the water and filth of the town : these sewers are large enough for a man to stand in upright. There are also traces of the aqueducts which brought to the town the waters of the great spring of *Groseau*.

(Breton, *Mém. de la Société Royale des Antiquaires de France*, tom. xvi., quoted by Richard et Hocquart, *Guide du Voyageur*.)   [G. L.]

VATEDO, in Gallia, mentioned in the Table, is a place east of *Bordeaux*, supposed to be *Vaires* on the left bank of the *Dordogne*, a branch of the *Garonne*.   [G. L.]

VATRENUS (*Santerno*), a river of Gallia Cispadana, one of the southern tributaries of the Padus. It had its sources in the Apennines, flowed under the walls of Forum Cornelii (*Imola*), and joined the southern branch of the Padus (the Spineticum Ostium) not far from its mouth, for which reason the port at the entrance of that arm of the river was called the Portus Vatreni. (Plin. iii. 16. s. 20.) The *Santerno* now flows into the *Po di Primaro* (the modern representative of the Spinetic branch), above 16 miles from its mouth: but the channels of both are in this part artificial. In this lower part it must always have been more of a canal than a river, whence Martial uses its name as typical of a sluggish stream. (Martial, iii. 67. 2.)   [E. H. B.]

UBERAE, a nation in India extra Gangem, mentioned by Pliny (vi. 19. s. 22). It possessed a large town of the same name. It is not possible to determine its exact position; but, from the names of other nations mentioned by Pliny in connection with the Uberae, it is probable that this people lived near the mouths of the *Brahmaputra*.   [V.]

U'BII (Οὔβιοι), a German people who in Caesar's time lived on the east bank of the Rhine and opposite to the Treviri, for Caesar having made his bridge in the country of the Treviri passed over into the country of the Ubii. Owing to their proximity to the Rhine they were somewhat more civilised than the other Germans, being much visited by merchants and accustomed to Gallic manners (*B. G.* iv. 3, 18, vi. 29, 35). The Sigambri were the neighbours of the Ubii on the north. The Suevi were pressing the Ubii hard, when the Ubii applied to Caesar for help: they gave him hostages, and offered to supply him with a large number of boats to cross the river, from which we may infer that they were accustomed to navigate the Rhine. (*B. G.* iv. 16.) In the time of Augustus (Strab. iv. p. 194), the nation crossed the Rhine, and Agrippa assigned them lands on the west bank of the river, the policy of the Romans being to strengthen the Rhenish frontier against the rest of the Germans. (Tacit. *Germ.* c. 28, *Annal.* xii. 27; Sueton. *Aug.* c. 21.) In the new territory of the Ubii was Colonia Agrippina (*Cöln*), and hence the people had the name of Agrippinenses, which was one of the causes why the Germans east of the Rhine hated them. They were considered as traitors to their country, who had assumed a new name. (Tacit. *Hist.* iv. 28.) North of the Ubii on the west side of the Rhine were the Gugerni [GUGERNI]; and south of them were the Treviri. [COLONIA AGRIPPINA; ARA UBIORUM.]   [G. L.]

UBIO'RUM ARA. [ARA UBIORUM.]

UBISCI. [BITURIGES VIVISCI.]

U'CENA (Οὔκενα), a town of the tribe of the Trocmi in Galatia. (Ptol. v. 4. § 9.)   [L. S.]

UCENI, a people of Gallia Narbonensis, who are mentioned in the trophy of the Alps quoted by Pliny (iii. 20), and placed between the Meduli and Caturiges. The site of these people is uncertain. D'Anville supposes that they were in that part of the mountain region of the Alps which con-

tains the bourg d'*Oisans*. But other geographers place them in the district of *Oze*, or near *Hues*, both of which places are on the right bank of the river *Romanche*, which flows into the *Drac*, a branch of the *Isère*. (Ukert, *Gallien*, p. 317.)   [G. L.]

UCETIA, in Gallia Narbonensis, north of *Nîmes*. This place is known only from the Roman remains which have been discovered there, and from the inscription VCETIAE on a stone found at *Nîmes*. The place is *Uzes*, north of the river *Gardon*, from which place the water was brought to *Nîmes* by the aqueduct over the *Gardon*. [NEMAUSUS.] Ucetia appears in the Notitia of the Provinces of Gallia under the name of Castrum Uceciense. Ucetia was a bishopric as early as the middle of the fifth century.   [G. L.]

UCHALICCENSES (Οὐχαλικκεῖς, Ptol. iv. 6. § 20), an Aethiopian tribe in the interior of Libya.   [T. H. D.]

UCHEIMERIUM (Οὐχειμέριον, Procop. *B. Goth.* iv. 14), a mountain fortress in the Regio Lazica, in Colchis.   [T. H. D.]

UCIA (Οὔκια, Ptol. ii. 4. § 13), a town of the Turdetani in Lusitania.   [T. H. D.]

UCIENSE, a town in Hispania Baetica, on the road from Corduba to Castulo. (*Itin. Ant.* p. 403.) Variously identified with *Marmolejo, Andujar*, and *S. Julian*.   [T. H. D.]

UCUBIS, a place in Hispania Baetica, in the neighbourhood of Corduba and the Flumen Salsum. (Hirt. *B. H.* 7.) According to Ukert (ii. pt. i. p. 361) between *Osuna* and *Antequera*.   [T. H. D.]

UCULTUNIACUM. [CURGOLA.]

UDAE (Οὔδαι, Ptol. v. 9. § 23), a people of Asiatic Sarmatia on the Caspian sea. They are probably the people mentioned under the name of Udini by Pliny (vi. 12. s. 15). They appear to have derived their name from the river Udon. [T. H. D.]

UDON (Οὔδων, Ptol. v. 9. § 12), a river of Asiatic Sarmatia, which rises in the Caucasus and falls into the Caspian sea between the Rha and the Alonta. Most probably the modern *Kuma*. [J. R.]

UDUBA. [TURULIS.]

UDURA (Οὔδουρα, Ptol. ii 6. § 72), a town of the Jaccetani in Hispania Tarraconensis, probably the modern *Cardona*.   [T. H. D.]

VECTA or VECTIS (Οὐηκτίς, Ptol. ii. 3. § 33), an island on the S. coast of Britannia Romana, lying opposite to the Portus Magnus (*Portsmouth*). It was known to the Romans before their conquest of Britain, through the Massiliots, who had here a station for their tin trade. (Diod. v. 22, 38.) At that time the channel between the island and the mainland become almost dry at ebb tide, so that the Britons carried their tin in carts to the island. It was first conquered by Vespasian, in the reign of Claudius. (Suet. *Vesp.* 4.) Now the *Isle of Wight*. (Cf. *Itin. Ant.* p. 509; Eum. *Pan. Const.* 15; Mela, iii. 6; Plin. iv. 16. s. 30.)   [T. H. D.]

VECTURIONES, a subdivision of the Picts in Britannia Barbara, according to Ammianus (xxvii. 8).   [T. H. D.]

VEDIANTII (Οὐεδιάντιοι, Ptol. iii. 1. § 41), a Ligurian tribe, who inhabited the foot of the Maritime Alps near the mouth of the *Var*. Both Pliny (iii. 5. s. 7) and Ptolemy assign to them the town of Cemenelium or *Cimiez* near *Nice*: the latter also includes in their territory Sanitium; but this must certainly be a mistake, that town, which answers to the modern *Senes*, being far off to the NW. (D'Anville, *Géogr. des Gaules*, p. 682.)   [E. H. B.]

VEDINUM (*Udine*), a city of Venetia, mentioned only by Pliny (iii. 19. s. 23) among the municipalities of that country. It was situated in the plain of the Carni, 11 miles W. of *Cividale* (Forum Julii), and 22 NNW. of Aquileia. In Pliny's time it was apparently an inconsiderable place, but rose into importance in the middle ages, and is now a flourishing and populous city, and the capital of the whole province of the *Friuli*. Many MSS. of Pliny write the name Nedinates, which has been adopted both by Harduin and Sillig, but it is probable that the old reading Vedinates is correct. [E. H. B.]

VEDRA (Οὐέδρα, Ptol. ii. 3. § 6), a river in the N. part of the E. coast of Britannia. The name would lead us to the conclusion that it is the *Wear* (Camden, p. 944), yet Horsley (p. 103) and others have taken it to be the *Tyne*. [T. H. D.]

VEGIA (Οὐεγία or Οὐερία), or VEGIUM (Plin. iii. 21. s. 25), a town of Liburnia, the present *Vezzo*. [T. H. D.]

VEGISTUM (Οὐέγιστον), or, as some read, Vetestum (Οὐέτεστον), a town of Galatia, in the territory of the Tolistobogi, between Mounts Didymus and Celaenus (Ptol. v. 4. § 7), is perhaps the same place as the Vetissum of the Peutinger Table. [L. S.]

VEII (Οὐήιοι, Strab. v. p. 226; Οὐιοί, Dionys. H. ii. 54: *Eth.* Veientes, Cic. *Div.* i. 44; Liv. i. 15, &c.: *Adj.* Veius (trisyl.), Propert. iv. 10. 31), an ancient and purely Tuscan city of Etruria. According to Festus (*ap. P. Diac. s. v.*) Veia was an Oscan word, and signified a waggon (plaustrum); but there is nothing to show that this was the etymology of the name of the town.

Among the earlier Italian topographers, a great diversity of opinion prevailed respecting the site of Veii. Nardini was the first writer who placed it at the present *Isola Farnese*, the correctness of which view is now universally admitted. The distance of that spot northwards from Rome agrees with the distance assigned by Dionysius of Halicarnassus (*l. c.*) to Veii, namely, "about 100 stadia," which is confirmed by the Tabula Peut., where it is set down at 12 miles. In Livy, indeed (v. 4), it is mentioned as being "within the 20th milestone;" but this is in a speech of App. Claudius, when the orator is using round numbers, and not solicitous about strict accuracy; whilst the two writers before cited are professedly giving the exact distance. Nor can the authority of Eutropius (i. 4), who places Veii at 18 miles from Rome, be admitted to invalidate the testimony of these authors, since Eutropius is notoriously incorrect in particulars of this description. There are other circumstances which tend to show that *Isola Farnese* is the site of ancient Veii. Thus the Tab. Peuting. further indicates that the city lay on the Via Cassia. Now following that road for a distance of about 12 miles from Rome, the locality not only exactly corresponds with the description of Dionysius, but also the remains of city walls and sepulchres, and traces of roads in various directions, have been found there. Moreover at the same spot were discovered, in the year 1810, stones bearing inscriptions which related exclusively to Veii and the Veientines.

We know little of the history of Veii but what concerns the wars it waged with the Romans. It is called by Eutropius (i. 20), "civitas antiquissima Italiae atque ditissima," and there can be no doubt that it was in a flourishing state at the time of the foundation of Rome. At that period the Etruscan, or Veientine, territory was separated from the Latin by the river Albula, afterwards called Tiberis ; and

consequently neither the Mons Vaticanus nor Janiculensis then belonged to the Romans. (Liv. i. 3.) To the SW. of Rome it extended along the right bank of the Tiber down to the sea, where it contained some Salinae, or salt-works, at the mouth of the river. (Dionys. ii. 55.) The district immediately opposite to Rome seems to have been called Septem Pagi (*Ib.*). On the N. of Rome the territory of Veii must at one time have extended as far as Mount Soracte, since the ager Capenatis belonged to it, Capena being a colony of Veii (Cato, *ap. Serv. Aen.* vii. 697); though in the history of the wars between Rome and Veii, Capena appears as an independent city. [CAPENA, Vol. I. p. 504.] On the NW. it may probably have stretched as far as the Mons Ciminus ; but here, as well as more to the S., its limits are uncertain, and all we know is that in the latter direction it must have been bounded by the territory of Caere. (Cf. Müller, *Etrusker*, ii. 2. p. 1, &c.) The ager Veiens is stigmatised by Horace and others as producing an execrable sort of red wine (*Sat.* ii. 3. 143; cf. Pers. v. 147 ; Mart. i. 103. 9, ii. 53. 4, &c.). We learn from Dionysius (ii. 54) that the city was of about the same size as Athens, and therefore nearly as large as Rome within the walls of Servius. [ROMA, Vol. II. p. 756.]

The political constitution of Veii, like that of the other Etruscan cities, seems originally to have been republican, though probably aristocratically republican, with magistrates annually elected. It was perhaps their vicinity to ambitious and aspiring Rome, and the constant wars which they had to wage with that city, that induced the Veientines to adopt the form of an elective monarchy, in order to avoid the dissensions occasioned by the election of annual magistrates under their original constitution, and thus to be enabled, under a single leader, to act with more vigour abroad ; but this step procured them the ill-will of the rest of the Etruscan confederacy (Liv. v. 1, cf. iv. 17). Monarchy, however, does not appear to have been permanent among them ; and we only know the names of two or three of their kings, as Tolumnius (*ib.*), Propertius (Serv. *Aen.* vii. 697), and Morrius (*Ib.* viii. 285).

The first time that the Veientes appear in history is in the war which they waged with Romulus in order to avenge the capture of their colony, Fidenae. According to the narrative of Livy, this war was terminated by one decisive battle in which Romulus was victorious (i. 15); but Dionysius (ii. 54, seq.) speaks of two engagements, and represents the Romans as gaining the second by a stratagem. Both these writers, however, agree with regard to the results of the campaign. The loss of the Veientines was so terrible, both in the battle and in the subsequent flight, in which numbers of them were drowned in attempting to swim the Tiber, that they were constrained to sue for peace. The terms imposed upon them by Romulus show the decisive nature of his victory. They were compelled to surrender that part of their territory in the neighbourhood of Rome called Septem Pagi, probably from its containing seven villages ; to give up the salt-works which they possessed at the mouth of the Tiber ; and to provide 50 hostages as security for the due execution of the treaty. On these conditions they obtained a peace for 100 years, with the restoration of their prisoners ; though such of the latter as preferred to remain at Rome were presented with the freedom of the city and lands on the left bank of the Tiber. The district of Septem Pagi thus acquired probably comprehended the Vatican and Janiculan hills, and became the seat of the 5th Roman tribe, the Romilia or Romulia. (Varr. *L. L.* v. 9. § 65, Müll.; Paul. *ap. Fest. s. v. Romulia Trib.*)

This peace seems to have lasted about 60 or 70 years, when war again broke out between the Veientines and Romans in the reign of Tullus Hostilius, and this time also on account of Fidenae, which appears to have become a Roman colony after its capture by Romulus. The cause of the war was the treacherous conduct of the Fidenates during the Roman struggle with Alba. When called to account, they refused to give any explanation of their conduct, and procured the assistance of the Veientines. Tullus crossed the Anio (*Teverone*) with a large army, and the battle which took place at a spot between that river and the town of Fidenae was the most obstinate and bloody which had yet been recorded in the Roman annals. Tullus, however, gained a signal victory over the Fidenates and their allies the Veientines. The battle is remarkable for the vows made by Tullus, of twelve Salian priests, and of temples to Pavor and Pallor. These were the second set of Salians, or those attached to the worship of Quirinus [cf. ROMA, p. 829]; and the appropriateness of the vow will be perceived when we consider that the Fidenates, in their answer to the Romans, had asserted that all their engagements towards Rome had expired on the death of that deified hero. (Liv. i. 27; Dionys. iii. 23, sqq.)

The war was renewed under Ancus Marcius by forays on both sides, which, however, seem to have been begun by the Veientines. Ancus 'overthrew them in two pitched battles, the last of which was decisive. The Veientines were obliged to surrender all the tract on the right bank of the Tiber called the Silva Maesia. The Roman dominion was now extended as far as the sea; and in order to secure these conquests, Ancus founded the colony of Ostia at the mouth of the Tiber. (Liv. i. 33; Dionys. iii. 41.)

The next time that we find the Veientines in collision with Rome, they had to contend with a leader of their own nation. L. Tarquinius, an emigrant from Tarquinii to Rome, had distinguished himself in the wars of Ancus Marcius against Veii, and was now in possession of the Roman sovereignty. The Veientines, however, on this occasion did not stand alone, but were assisted by the other Etruscan cities, who complained of insults and injuries received from Tarquin. The Veientines, as usual, were discomfited, and so thoroughly, that they did not dare to leave their city, but were the helpless spectators of the devastation committed on their lands by the Romans. The war was terminated by Tarquin's brilliant victory at Eretus, which enabled him to claim the sovereignty of all Etruria, leaving, however, the different cities in the enjoyment of their own rights and privileges. It was on this occasion that Tarquin is said to have introduced at Rome the institution of the twelve lictors and their fasces, emblems of the servitude of the twelve Etruscan cities, as well as the other Etruscan insignia of royalty. (Dionys. iii. 57: Flor. i. 5.) It should be observed that on this subject the accounts are very various; and some have even doubted the whole story of this Etruscan conquest, because Livy does not mention it. That historian, however, when he speaks of the resumption of the war under Servius Tullius, includes the other Etruscans with the Veientines, as parties to the truce which had expired (" bellum cum Veientibus (jam

enim indutiae exierant) *aliisque Etruscis* sumptum," i. 42), although the Etruscans had not been concerned in the last Veientine war he had recorded. (Cf. Dionys. iv. 27.) This war under Servius Tullius was the last waged with the Veientines during the regal period of Rome.

When the second Tarquin was expelled from Rome, the Etruscans endeavoured to restore him. Veii and Tarquinii were the two most forward cities in the league formed for this purpose. The first battle, which took place near the Silvia Arsia, was bloody but indecisive, though the Romans claimed a dubious victory. But the Etruscans having obtained the assistance of Porsena, Lars of Clusium, the Romans were completely worsted, and, at the peace which ensued, were compelled to restore to the Veientines all the territory which had been wrested from them by Romulus and Ancus Marcius. This, however, Porsena shortly afterwards restored to the Romans, out of gratitude for the hospitality which they had displayed towards the remnant of the Etruscan army after the defeat of his son Aruns at Aricia. (Liv. ii. 6—15; Dionys. v. 14, sqq.; Plut. *Publ.* 19.)

The Veientines could ill brook being deprived of this territory; but, whilst the influence of Porsena and his family prevailed in the Etruscan League, they remained quiet. After his death the war again broke out, B. C. 483. For a year or two it was a kind of border warfare characterised by mutual depredations. But in B.C. 481, after a general congress of the Etruscans, a great number of volunteers joined the Veientines, and matters began to assume a more serious aspect. In the first encounters the Romans were unsuccessful, chiefly through a mutiny of the soldiers. They seem to have been disheartened by their ill success; their army was inferior in number to that of the Veientines, and they endeavoured to decline an engagement. But the insults of the enemy incensed the Roman soldiery to such a degree that they insisted on being led to battle. The contest was long and bloody. The Etruscans at one time were in possession of the Roman camp; but it was recovered by the valour of Titus Siccius. The Romans lost a vast number of officers, amongst whom were the consul Manlius, Q. Fabius, who had been twice consul, together with many tribunes and centurions. It was a drawn battle; yet the Romans claimed the victory, because during the night the Etruscans abandoned their camp, which was sacked by the Romans on the following day. But the surviving consul, M. Fabius Vibulanus, on his return to Rome, refused a triumph, and abdicated his office, the duties of which he was prevented from discharging by the severity of his wounds. (Dionys. ix. 5, sqq.; Liv. ii. 42—47.)

Shortly after this, the Veientines, finding that they were unable to cope with the Romans in the open field, adopted a most annoying system of warfare. When the Roman army appeared, they shut themselves up within their walls; but no sooner had the legions retired, than they came forth and scoured the country up to the very gates of Rome. The Fabian family, which had given so many consuls to Rome, and which had taken so prominent a part in the late war, now came forward and offered to relieve the commonwealth from this harassing annoyance. The whole family appeared before the senate, and by the mouth of their chief, Caeso Fabius, then consul for the third time, declared, that, as a continual rather than a large guard was required for the Veientine war, they were willing to undertake the duty and to maintain the majesty of the Roman name, without calling upon the state for either soldiers or money. The senate thankfully accepted the offer. On the following morning 306 Fabii met in the vestibule of the consul's house. As they passed through the city to the place of their destination, they stopped at the capitol and offered up vows to the gods for the success of their enterprise. Then they passed out of Rome by the right arch of the Porta Carmentalis, and proceeded straight to the river Cremera, where there was a spot that seemed adapted by nature as a fortress for their little garrison. It appears, however, that the Fabii were accompanied by their clients and adherents, and the whole band probably amounted to 3000 or 4000. (Dionys. ix. 15; P. Diac. *s. v. Scelerata Porta.*) The place which they chose as the station of their garrison was a precipitous hill which seemed to have been cut and isolated by art; and they further strengthened it with entrenchments and towers. The spot has been identified with great probability by Nardini, and subsequently by other topographers, with a precipitous hill about 6 miles from Rome, on the left of the Via Flaminia, where it is traversed by the Cremera (now the *Valcha*). and on the right bank of that stream. It is the height which commands the present *Osteria della Valchetta.* (Nibby, *Dintorni di Roma,* vol. iii. p. 399; Dennis, *Etruria,* vol. i. p. 43.)

The position here taken up by the Fabii not only enabled them to put a complete stop to the marauding expeditions of the Veientines, but even to commit depredations themselves on the territory of Veii. The Veientines having made many vain attempts to dislodge them, at length implored the succour of the Etruscans; but the Fabii on their side were supported by a consular army under Aemilius, and the Veientines and their allies were defeated. This success rendered the Fabii still more enterprising. After occupying their fortress two years with impunity they began to extend their excursions; and the Veientines on their side sought to draw them onwards, in which they at length succeeded. By a feigned flight, they enticed the Fabii into an ambuscade and slew them, 13th Feb. B. C. 476. (Ov. *Fast.* ii. 195, sqq.; Liv. ii. 48—50; Dionys. ix. 16—19; Florus, i. 12, &c.)

Elated with this success, the Veientines, united with the Etruscans, now marched towards Rome and pitched their camp on the Janiculan hill, at a distance of only 6 stadia from the city. Thence passing the Tiber, they penetrated as far as the ancient temple of Hope, which stood near the modern *Porta Maggiore.* Here an indecisive action took place, which was renewed at the Porta Collina with the same result; but two engagements of a more decisive character on the Janiculan hill obliged the allied army to retreat. In the following year the Veientines allied themselves with the Sabines, but were completely defeated under the walls of their own city by the consul Pub. Valerius. The war was brought to a termination in the following year. in the consulship of C. Manlius, who concluded with them a truce of 40 years, the Veientines engaging to pay a tribute in corn and money. (Liv. ii. 51—54; Dionys. ix. 23, sqq.)

But such terms were merely nominal, and in a few years hostilities were renewed. We hear of some forays made by the Veientines in B. C. 442 (Liv. iv. 1); but there was no regular war till seven years later, when the Veientines, who were at that time governed by Lars, or King, Tolumnius,

excited the Roman colony Fidenae to rebel; and in order completely to compromise the Fidenates, Tolumnius ordered them to slay the Roman ambassadors who had been despatched to demand an explanation. Both sides flew to arms; one or two obstinate engagements ensued; but the allies who had been joined by the Falisci also, were overthrown in a decisive battle under the walls of Fidenae, in which Tolumnius was killed by the Roman military tribune, A. Cornelius Cossus. (Liv. iv. 17—19; cf. Propert. iv. 10. 22, sqq.)

Three years afterwards, Rome being afflicted with a severe pestilence, the Veientines and Fidenates were emboldened to march upon it, and encamped before the Porta Collina; but on the appearance of a Roman army under the dictator Aulus Servilius, they retreated. Servilius having pursued and routed them near Nomentum, marched to Fidenae, which he at length succeeded in taking by means of a cuniculus or mine. (Liv. iv. 22.)

Although the Veientines obtained a truce after this event, yet they soon violated it, and began to commit depredations in the Roman territory, B. C. 427; and even defeated a Roman army whose operations had been paralysed through the dissensions of the three military tribunes who commanded it. The Fidenates now rose and massacred all the Roman colonists, and again allied themselves with the Veientines, who had also enlisted a great number of Etruscan volunteers in their service. These events occasioned great alarm at Rome. Mamercus Aemilius was created dictator, and, marching against the enemy, encamped in the peninsula formed by the confluence of the Anio and the Tiber. Between this spot and Fidenae a desperate battle was fought: stratagems were employed on both sides; but at length the allies were completely defeated, and the Romans entered the gates of Fidenae along with the flying enemy. The city was sacked and destroyed and the inhabitants sold as slaves; but on the other hand the Romans granted the Veientines a truce of 20 years. (Liv. iv. 31—35.)

At the expiration of this truce, the Romans resolved to subdue Veii, as they had done Fidenae, and it was besieged by an army commanded by six military tribunes. At this news the national assembly of the Etruscans met at the fane of Voltumna, to consider what course they should pursue. The Veientines had again resorted to the regal form of government; but unfortunately the person whom they elected for their king, though rich and powerful, had incurred the hatred of the whole Etruscan nation by his oppressions and imperious manners, but especially by his having hindered the performance of certain sacred games. The Etruscans consequently declared that, unless he was deposed, they should afford the Veientines no assistance. But the latter were afraid to adopt this resolution, and thus they were abandoned to their fate. Nevertheless, they contrived to prolong the siege for a period of ten years, during which the Romans were several times discomfited. It is worthy of remark that it was during this siege that the Roman soldiers, being obliged to pass the winter out of Rome, first received a fixed regular stipend. The Capenates, the Falisci, and the Tarquinienses in vain endeavoured to relieve the beleaguered city.

The length of the siege had begun to weary the Romans, when, according to the legend, the means of its capture was suggested by an extraordinary portent. The waters of Lake Albanus swelled to such an extent that they threatened to inundate the surrounding country. The oracle of Delphi was consulted on the occasion, and the response involved not only the immediate subject of the application, but also the remoter one of the capture of Veii. According to the voice from the sacred tripod, that city would be taken when the waters of the lake were made to flow off without running directly into the sea; and the prophecy was confirmed by the revelation of a Veientine haruspex made during the interval of the embassy to Delphi. All that we can infer from this narrative is that the formation of the emissary for draining the Alban lake was contemporary with the siege of Veii [cf. ALBANUS LACUS, Vol. I. p. 29]: the rest must be referred to the propensity of the ancients to ascribe every great event to the intervention of the gods; for we have already seen that Fidenae was captured by means of a cuniculus, a fact which there does not appear to be any valid reason to doubt, and therefore the emissary of the lake cannot be regarded as having first suggested to the Romans the method of taking a city by mine.

The honour of executing this project was reserved for the dictator M. Furius Camillus. Fortune seemed to have entirely deserted the Veientines: for though the pleading of the Capenates and Falisci on their behalf had made some impression on the national assembly of the Etruscans, their attention was diverted in another direction by a sudden irruption of the Cisalpine Gauls. Meanwhile Camillus, having defeated some bodies of troops who endeavoured to relieve Veii, erected a line of forts around it, to cut off all communication with the surrounding country, and appointed some corps of miners to work continually at the cuniculus. When the mine was completed, he ordered a picked body of his most valiant soldiers to penetrate through it, whilst he himself diverted the attention of the inhabitants by feigned attacks in different quarters. So skilfully had the mine been directed that the troops who entered it emerged in the temple of Juno itself, in the highest part of the citadel. The soldiers who guarded the walls were thus taken in the rear; the gates were thrown open, and the city soon filled with Romans. A dreadful massacre ensued; the town was sacked, and those citizens who had escaped the sword were sold into slavery. The image of Juno, the tutelary deity of Veii, was carried to Rome and pompously installed on Mount Aventine, where a magnificent temple was erected to her, which lasted till the abolition of paganism. (Liv. v. 8, 12, 13, 15—22; Cic. Div. i. 44, ii. 32; Plut. Cam. 5, sq.; Flor. i. 12.)

Veii was captured in the year 396 B. C. Its territory was divided among the citizens of Rome at the rate of seven jugera per head. A great debate arose between the senate and the people whether Veii should be repopulated by Roman citizens, and thus made as it were a second capital; but at the persuasion of Camillus the project was abandoned. But though the city was deserted, its buildings were not destroyed, as is shown by several facts. Thus, after the battle of the Allia and the taking of Rome by the Gauls, the greater part of the Romans retired to Veii and fortified themselves there; and when the Gauls were expelled, the question was mooted whether Rome, which had been reduced to ashes, should be abandoned, and Veii converted into a new capital. But the eloquence of Camillus again decided the Romans for the negative, and the question

was set at rest for ever. This took place in B. C. 389. Some refractory citizens, however, who disliked the trouble of rebuilding their own houses at Rome, took refuge in the empty ones of Veii, and set at nought a senatusconsultum ordering them to return; but they were at length compelled to come back by a decree of capital punishment against those who remained at Veii beyond a day prescribed. (Liv. v. 49, sqq., vi. 4.)

From this time Veii was completely deserted and went gradually to decay. Cicero (ad Fam. xvi. 9) speaks of the measuring of the Veientine territory for distribution; and it was probably divided by Caesar among his soldiers in B. C. 45. (Plut. Caes. 57.) Propertius also describes its walls as existing in his time; but the space within consisted of fields where the shepherd fed his flock, and which were then under the operation of the decempeda (iv. 10. 29). It is, however, rather difficult to reconcile this chronology, unless there were two distributions. Caesar also appears to have planted a colony at the ancient city, and thus arose the second, or Roman, Veii, which seems to have been considerable enough to sustain an assault during the wars of the triumvirs. The inhabitants were again dispersed, and the colony was not re-erected till towards the end of the reign of Augustus, when it assumed the name of municipium Augustum Veiens, as appears from inscriptions. (Cf. Auct. de Coloniis.) When Florus, who flourished in the reign of Hadrian, asserts (i. 12) that scarcely a vestige remained to mark the spot where Veii once stood, he either writes with great carelessness or is alluding to the ancient and Etruscan Veii. The existence of the municipium in the reigns of Augustus and Tiberius is attested by several monuments discovered in its ruins; and some inscriptions also found there show that it was in existence at least as late as the reign of Constantius Chlorus. The monuments alluded to consist partly of sculptures relating to those emperors and their families, and partly of inscriptions. Amongst the latter the most important is now preserved in the Capitoline Museum at Rome, recording the admission of Caius Julius Gelotes, a freedman of Augustus, to the office of an Augustalis, by the centumviri of Veii. It is dated in the consulship of Gaetulicus and Calvisius Sabinus, A. U. C. 779==B. C. 26, or the 13th year of the reign of Tiberius. It is published by Fabretti (Inscr. p. 170), but more correctly from the original by Nibby in his Dintorni di Roma (vol. iii. p. 409). The accents are worthy of note. Among the centumvirs whose names are subscribed to this decree are those of two of the Tarquitian family, namely, M. Tarquitius Saturninus and T. Tarquitius Rufus. This family, which produced a celebrated writer on Etruscan divination (Macrob. Sat. iii. 7), seems to have belonged to Veii and to have enjoyed considerable importance there, as two other inscriptions relating to it have been discovered. One of these records the restoration of a statue erected in honour of M. Tarquitius Saturninus by the 22nd Legion; the other is a tablet of Tarquitia Prisca dedicated to her husband M. Saenius Marcellus. (Nibby, Ib. p. 410, sq.) The family of Priscus is the most celebrated of the Gens Tarquitia. One of these was the accuser of Statilius Taurus in the reign of Claudius, and was himself condemned under the law of repetundae in the reign of Nero. (Tac. Ann. xii. 59, xiv. 44.) There are various coins of the Tarquitii. (Eckhel, D. N. V. p. 322.) After the era of Constantine we have no notices of Veii except in the Tab. Peutingeriana and the Geographer of Ravenna. It was probably destroyed by the Lombards. At the beginning of the 11th century a castle was erected on the precipitous and isolated hill on the S. side of Veii, which was called *la Isola*, and is now known by the name of the *Isola Farnese*.

Sir William Gell was the first who gave an exact plan of Veii in the *Memorie dell'Istituto* (Fasc. l.), and afterwards in his *Topography of Rome and its Vicinity*. He traced the vestiges of the ancient walls, which were composed of irregular quadrilateral masses of the local *tufa*, some of which were from 9 to 11 feet in length. Mr. Dennis, however, failed to discover any traces of them (*Etruria*, vol. i. p. 15), and describes the stone used in the fortifications of Veii, as being cut into smaller pieces than usual in other Etruscan cities. These remains, which are principally to be traced in the N. and E., as well as the streams and the outline of the cliffs, determine the extent of the city in a manner that cannot be mistaken. They give a circumference of about 7 miles, which agrees with the account of Dionysius, before referred to, when he compares the size of Veii with that of Athens. It has been debated whether the isolated rock, called the *Isola Farnese*, formed part of the city. Nibby (*Dintorni*, vol. iii. p. 424) and others are of opinion that it was the arx or citadel. On the other hand Sir William Gell and Mr. Dennis hold that this could not have been the case ; and it must be confessed that the reasons advanced by the latter (vol. i. p. 42, note 5) appear decisive ; namely, 1, the *Isola* is separated from the city by a deep glen, so that, had it been the citadel, Camillus by its capture would not have obtained immediate possession of the town, as we learn from Livy's narrative, before referred to, that he did : 2, the remains of Etruscan tombs on the *Isola* show that it must have been a cemetery, and consequently without the walls. The two authorities last cited identify the citadel with the hill now called the *Piazza d' Armi* at the SE. extremity of the town, in the angle formed by the junction of the stream called *Fosso de' due Fossi* with that called *Fosso di Formello*. These two streams traverse the southern and eastern boundaries of ancient Veii. The latter of these streams, or *Fosso di Formello*, is thought to be the ancient Cremera. The other rivulet rises at *La Torretta*, about 12 miles from Rome. Near Veii it forms a fine cataract, precipitating itself over a rock about 80 feet high. From this spot it runs in a deep channel among precipices, and separates the *Isola* from the rest of Veii. It then receives the *Rivo del Pino* or *della Storta*, whence its name of *Fosso de' due Fossi*. After joining the *Fosso di Formello*, or Cremera, the united stream is now called *La Valca*, and falls into the Tiber about 6 miles from Rome, near the Via Flaminia.

Topographers have discovered 9 gates, to which they have assigned imaginary names from local circumstances. It would be impossible to explain the exact sites of these gates without the assistance of a plan, and we shall therefore content ourselves with enumerating them in the order in which they occur, premising only that all writers do not call them alike. The westernmost gate, called the *Porto de' Sette Pagi*, from its being supposed to have led to the district called the Septem Pagi, is situated near the *Ponte dell' Isola*. Then proceeding round the S. side of the city, the next gate occurs near the *Fosso dell' Isola*; and, from its leading to the rock of *Isola*, which,

as we have seen, was thought by some topographers to be the ancient citadel, has been called the *Porta dell' Arce*. The next gate on the E. is the *Porta Campana*; and after that, by the *Piazza d' Armi*, is the *Porta Fidenate*. Near this spot was discovered, in 1840, the curious staircase called *La Scaletta*. Only eight steps of uncemented masonry, seated high in the cliff, remain, the lower part having fallen with the cliff. After passing the *Piazza d' Armi*, in traversing the northern side of the city by the valley of the Cremera, the gates occur in the following order : the *Porta di Pietra Pertusa*; the *Porta delle Are Muzie*; the *Porta Capenate*; the *Porta del Colombario*, so named from the columbarium near it ; and lastly the *Porta Sutrina*, not far from the *Ponte di Formello*.

The Municipium Veiens, which succeeded the ancient town, was undoubtedly smaller ; for Roman sepulchres and columbaria, which must have been outside the Municipium, have been discovered within the walls of Etruscan Veii. It was perhaps not more than 2 miles in circumference. On the spot probably occupied by the Forum, were discovered the colossal heads of Augustus and Tiberius, and the colossal statue of the latter, crowned with oak and in a sitting posture, which are now in the Vatican, in the corridor of the *Museo Chiaramonte*. Several other fragments of statues have been found, as well as 24 marble columns, 12 of which now adorn the *Piazza Colonna* at Rome, and the rest are employed in the Chapel of the Sacrament in the new Basilica of St. Paul.

The remains of Etruscan Veii are portions of the walls, the bridge near the *Porta di Pietra Pertusa*, the bridge, or tunnel, called *Ponte Sodo*, and the tombs and sepulchral grottoes. Of the walls we have already spoken. The remains of the bridge consist of a piece of wall about 20 feet wide on the bank of the stream, which seems to have formed the pier from which the arch sprung, and some large blocks of hewn tufo which lie in the water. The piers of the bridge called *Ponte Formello* are also possibly Etruscan, but the arch is of Roman brickwork. The *Ponte Sodo* is a tunnel in the rock through which the stream flows. Nibby (*Dintorni*, vol. iii. p. 433), describes it as 70 feet long, 20 wide, and 15 high : but Mr. Dennis, who waded through it, says that it is 240 feet long, 12 to 15 wide and nearly 20 high (*Etruria*, vol. i. p. 14). It is in all probability an Etruscan excavation, or has at all events been enlarged by art. An ancient road ran over it ; and from above it is scarcely visible. No trace remains of the cuniculus of Camillus. The vicinity of Veii abounds with tombs excavated in the rock, and sepulchral tumuli, some of which are Roman. Among the tombs is a very remarkable one, discovered in the winter of 1842, and still open to inspection. It consists of a long passage in the tumulus, or mound, called *Poggio Michele*, leading to a door in the middle of the mound, and guarded at each end by sculptured lions. This is the entrance to a low dark chamber, hewn out of the rock, the walls of which are covered with paintings of the most grotesque character, consisting of horses, men, sphinxes, dogs, leopards, &c. On either side a bench of rock, about 2½ feet high, projects from the wall, on each of which, when the tomb was first opened, a skeleton reposed ; but these soon crumbled into dust. One of them, from the arms lying near, was the remains of a warrior ; the other skeleton was probably that of his wife. On the floor were large jars containing human ashes, and also several small vases of the most archaic Etruscan pottery. Within was another smaller chamber also containing cinerary urns. A complete description of this remarkable sepulchre will be found in Mr. Dennis's *Etruria* (vol. i. ch. 2).

For the history and antiquities of Veii the following works may be consulted ; Nibby, *Dintorni di Roma*, vol. iii., and *Viaggio Antiquario*, vol. i. ; Canina, *L'antica Città di Veji descritta ;* Abeken, *Mittelitalien ;* Müller, *Etrusker ;* Sir W. Gell, *Topography of Rome and its Vicinity;* Dennis, *Cities and Cemeteries of Etruria.* [T. H. D.]

VELATODURUM, in Gallia, is placed by the Antonine Itin. on the road from Vesontio (*Besançon*) to Epamanduodurum (*Mandeure*) xxii. from Besançon and xii. from *Mandeure*. But these two numbers exceed the distance between *Besançon* and *Mandeure*. The termination *durum* seems to show that Velatodurum was on a stream ; and D'Anville conjectures that it is near *Clereval* on the *Doubs*, where there is a place named *Pont-pierre*. But this is merely a guess. [EPAMANDUODU-RUM.] [G. L.]

VELAUNI, a people mentioned in the Trophy of the Alps (Plin. iii. 20), between tne Neruaii and Suetri. If the geographical position of these people corresponds to their position in Pliny's list of tribes, we know in a general way where to place them. [NERUSII; SUETRI.] [G. L.]

VELDIDENA, one of the most important towns of Rhaetia, on the southern bank of the river Oenus, and on the road leading from Tridentum to Augusta Vindelicorum. (*It. Ant.* pp. 258, 259, 275, 280.) According to coins which have been found on its site, it was made a Roman colony with the surname Augusta. Its site is now occupied by the convent of *Wilden* in the neighbourhood of *Inspruck*, on the little river *Sihl*. (See Roschmann, *Veldidena Urbs antiquissima Augusti Colonia*, Ulm, 1744, 4to.) [L. S.]

VELEIA (*Eth.* Veleias, ātis: Ru. near *Montepolo*), a town of Liguria, situated on the frontiers of Gallia Cisalpina, about 20 miles S. of Placentia (*Piacenza*), in the hills which form the lower slopes of the Apennines. The Veleiates are mentioned by Pliny among the Ligurian tribes; and in another passage he speaks of "oppidum Veleiatium," which was remarkable for the longevity of some of its inhabitants (vii. 49. s. 50). He there describes it as situated " circa Placentiam in collibus," but its precise site was unknown until its remains were discovered in 1760. From the mode in which these are buried, it seems certain that the town was overwhelmed by a vast landslip from the neighbouring mountain. Systematic excavations on the spot, which have been carried on since 1760, have brought to light several buildings of the ancient city, including the amphitheatre, a basilica, the forum, and several temples: and the great number of bronze ornaments and implements of a domestic kind, as well as statues, busts, &c., which have been discovered on the spot, have given celebrity to Veleia as the Pompeii of Northern Italy. Unfortunately the great weight of the superincumbent mass has crushed in the buildings, so that all the upper part of them is destroyed, and the larger statues have suffered severely from the same cause. The inscriptions found there attest that Veleia was a flourishing municipal town in the first centuries of the Roman Empire. One of these is of peculiar interest as containing a detailed account of the investment of a large sum of money by the em-

peror Trajan in the purchase of lands for the maintenance of a number of poor children of both sexes. This remarkable document contains the names of numerous farms and villages in the neighbourhood of Veleia, and shows that that town was the capital of an extensive territory (probably the same once held by the Ligurian tribe of the Veleiates) which was divided into a number of Pagi, or rural districts. The names both of these and of the various "fundi" or farms noticed are almost uniformly of Roman origin, — thus affording a remarkable proof how completely this district had been Romanised before the period in question. The Tabula Alimentaria Trajana, as it is commonly called, has been repeatedly published, and illustrated with a profusion of learning, especially by De Lama. (*Tavola Alimentaria Veleiate detta Trajana*, 4to. Parma. 1819.) A description of the ruins and antiquities has been published by Antolini (*Le Rovine di Velja*, Milano, 1819). The coins found at Veleia are very numerous, but none of them later than the time of Probus : whence it is reasonably inferred that the catastrophe which buried the city occurred in the reign of that emperor. [E. H. B.]

VELIA (Οὐέλια, or Οὐίλεια, Ptol. ii. 6. § 65), a town of the Caristi in Hispania Tarraconensis, on the road from Pompelo to Asturica (*Itin. Ant.* p. 454, where it is called Beleia). (Cf. Plin. iii. 3. s. 4; Geogr. Rav. iv. 45.) Variously identified with *Viana, Bernedo*, and *Yrузsa*. [T. H. D.]

VELIA (Ύέλη or Ἐλέα : *Eth.* Ύελήτης or Ἐλεάτης, Veliensis: *Castell' a Mare della Brucca*), one of the principal of the Greek colonies in Southern Italy, situated on the shores of the Tyrrhenian sea, about midway between Posidonia and Pyxus. There is some uncertainty respecting the correct form of the name. Strabo tells us that it was originally called Hyele (Ύέλη), but was in his day called Elea (Ἐλέα), and Diogenes Laertius also says that it was at first called Hyele and afterwards Elea. (Strab. vi. p. 252; Diog. Laert. ix. 5. § 28; Steph. B. s. v.) But it is certain from the evidence of its coins, which uniformly bear the legends ΎΕΛΗ and ΎΕΛΗΤΩΝ, that the name of Hyele continued in use among the people themselves as long as the city continued; while,on the other hand, the name of Ἐλέα is already found in Scylax (p. 4. § 12), and seems to have been certainly that in use among Attic writers from an early period, where the Eleatic school of philosophy rendered the name familiar. Strabo also tells us that some authors wrote the name Ele (Ἐλη), from a fountain of that name; and this form, compared with Ύέλη and the Latin form Velia, seems to show clearly that the diversity of names arose from the Aeolic Digamma, which was probably originally prefixed to the name, and was retained in the native usage and in that of the Romans, while it was altogether dropped by the Attics. (Münter, *Velia*, p. 21.) It is not improbable that the name was derived from that of the neighbouring river, the Hales of Cicero (*Alento*), of which the name is written Ἐλέης by Strabo and Βελέα by Stephanus of Byzantium. (Cic. *ad Fam.* vii. 20; Strab. vi. p. 254.) Others, however, derived it from the marshes (ἔλη) at the mouth of the same river.

There is no trace of the existence of any town on the site of Velia before the establishment of the Greek colony there, and it is probable that this, like most of the Greek colonies in Southern Italy, was founded on a wholly new site. It was a colony from Phocaea in Ionia, and derived its origin from the voluntary expatriation of the inhabitants of that city in order to avoid falling under the Persian yoke, at the time of the conquest of Ionia by Harpagus, B. C. 544. The Phocaean emigrants proceeded in a body to Corsica, where they had already founded the colony of Alalia about 20 years before; and in the first instance established themselves in that island, but, having provoked the enmity of the Tyrrhenians and Carthaginians by their piracies, they sustained such severe loss in a naval action with the combined fleets of these two powers, that they found themselves compelled to abandon the colony. A part of the emigrants then repaired to Massilia (which was also a Phocaean colony), while the remainder, after a temporary halt at Rhegium, proceeded to found the new colony of Hyele or Velia on the coast of Lucania. This is the account given by Herodotus (i. 164—167), with which that cited by Strabo from Antiochus of Syracuse substantially agrees. (Strab. vi. p. 254.) Later writers have somewhat confused the narrative, and have represented the foundation of Massilia and Velia as contemporaneous (Hygin. ap. A. Gell. x. 16; Ammian. Marc. xv. 9. § 7); but there is no doubt that the account above given is the correct one. Scylax alone represents Velia as a colony of Thurii. (Scyl. p. 4. § 12.) If this be not altogether a mistake it must refer to the admission at a later period of a body of fresh colonists from that city; but of this we find no trace in any other author. The exact date of the foundation of Velia cannot be determined, as we do not know how long the Phocaeans remained in Corsica, but it may be placed approximately at about 540 B. C.

There is no doubt that the settlers at Velia, like those of the sister colony of Massilia, followed the example of their parent city, and devoted themselves assiduously to the cultivation of commerce; nor that the city itself quickly became a prosperous and flourishing place. The great abundance of the silver coins of Velia still in existence, and which are found throughout the S. of Italy, is in itself sufficient evidence of this fact; while the circumstance that it became the seat of a celebrated school of philosophy, the leaders of which continued through successive generations to reside at Velia, proves that it must have been a place of much intellectual refinement and cultivation. But of its history we may be said to know absolutely nothing. Strabo tells us that it was remarkable for its good government, an advantage for which it was partly indebted to Parmenides, who gave his fellow-citizens a code of laws which the magistrates from year to year took an oath to obey. (Strab. vi. p. 254; Diog. Laert. ix. 3. § 23.) But the obscure story concerning the death of Zeno, the disciple of Parmenides, who was put to death by a tyrant named Nearchus or Diomedon, would seem to show that it was not free from the same kind of violent interruptions by the rise of despotisms as were common to most of the Greek cities. (Diog. Laert. ix. 5; Cic. Tusc. ii. 22.) Strabo also tells us that the Eleans came off victorious in a contest with the Posidonians, but of the time and circumstances of this we are wholly ignorant; and he adds that they maintained their ground against the Lucanians also. (Strab. l. c.) If this is correct they would have been one of the few Greek cities which preserved their national existence against those barbarians, but their name is not found in the scanty historical notices that we possess of the wars between the Lucanians and the cities of Magna Graecia. But the statement of Strabo is in some

degree confirmed by the fact that Velia was certainly admitted at an early period (though on what occasion we know not) to the alliance of Rome, and appears to have maintained very friendly relations with that city. It was from thence, in common with Neapolis, that the Romans habitually derived the priestesses of Ceres, whose worship was of Greek origin. (Cic. pro Balb. 24; Val. Max. i. 1. § 1.) Cicero speaks of Velia as a well-known instance of a "foederata civitas," and we find it mentioned in the Second Punic War as one of those which were bound by treaty to contribute their quota of ships to the Roman fleet. (Cic. l. c.; Liv. xxvi. 39.) It eventually received the Roman franchise, apparently in virtue of the Lex Julia, B. C. 90. (Cic. l. c.) Under the Roman government Velia continued to be a tolerably flourishing town, and seems to have been from an early period noted for its mild and salubrious climate. Thus we are told that P. Aemilius was ordered to go there by his physicians for the benefit of his health, and we find Horace making inquiries about it as a substitute for Baiae. (Plut. Aemil. 39; Hor. Ep. i. 15. 1.) Cicero's friend Trebatius had a villa there, and the great orator himself repeatedly touched there on his voyages along the coast of Italy. (Cic. Verr. ii. 40, v. 17, ad Fam. vii. 19, 20, ad Att. xvi. 6, 7.) It appears to have been at this period still a place of some trade, and Strabo tells us that the poverty of the soil compelled the inhabitants to turn their attention to maritime affairs and fisheries. (Strab. vi. p. 254.) It is probable that the same cause had in early times co-operated with the national disposition of the Phocaean settlers to direct their attention especially to maritime commerce. We hear nothing more of Velia under the Roman Empire. Its name is found in Pliny and Ptolemy, but not in the Itineraries, which may, however, probably proceed from its secluded position. It is mentioned in the Liber Coloniarum (p. 209) among the Praefecturae of Lucania; and its continued existence as a municipal town is proved by inscriptions. (Mommsen, Inscrip. R. N. 190, App. p. 2.) It became an episcopal see in the early ages of Christianity, and still retained that dignity as late as the time of Gregory the Great (A. D. 599). It is probable that the final decay of Velia, like that of Paestum, was owing to the ravages of the Saracens in the 8th and 9th centuries. The bishopric was united with that of Capaccio, which had succeeded to that of Paestum. (Münter, Velia, pp. 69—73.) During the middle ages there grew up on the spot a fortress which was called Castell' a Mare della Brucca, and which still serves to mark the site of the ancient city.

The ruins of Velia are situated on a low ridge of hill, which rises about a mile and a half from the mouth of the river Alento (the ancient Hales), and half a mile from the coast, which here forms a shallow but spacious bay, between the headland formed by the Monte della Stella and the rocky point of Porticello near Ascea. The mediaeval castle and village of Castell' a Mare della Brucca occupy the point of this hill nearest the sea. The outline of the ancient walls may be traced at intervals round the hill for their whole extent. Their circuit is not above two miles, and it is most likely that this was the old city or acropolis, and that in the days of its prosperity it had considerable suburbs, especially in the direction of its port. It is probable that this was an artificial basin, like that of Metapontum, and its site is in all probability marked by a marshy pool which still exists between the ruins of the ancient city and the mouth of the *Alento*. This river itself, however, was sufficient to afford a shelter and place of anchorage for shipping in ancient times (Cic. *ad Att.* xvi. 7), and is still resorted to for the same purpose by the light vessels of the country. No other ruins exist on the site of the ancient city except some masses of buildings, which, being in the reticulated style, are unquestionably of Roman date: portions of aqueducts, reservoirs for water, &c. are also visible. (The site and existing remains of Velia are described by Münter, *Velia in Lucanien*, 8vo. Altona, 1818, pp. 15—20, and by the Duc de Luynes, in the *Annali dell' Instituto*, 1829, pp. 381—386.)

It is certain that as a Greek colony Velia never rose to a par with the more opulent and flourishing cities of Magna Graecia. Its chief celebrity in ancient times was derived from its celebrated school of philosophy, which was universally known as the Eleatic school. Its founder Xenophanes was indeed a native of Colophon, but had established himself at Velia, and wrote a long poem, in which he celebrated the foundation of that city. (Diog. Laert. ix. 2. § 20.) His distinguished successors Parmenides and Zeno were both of them born at Velia, and the same thing is asserted by some writers of Leucippus, the founder of the atomic theory, though others represent him as a native of Abdera or Melos. Hence Diogenes Laertius terms Velia "an inconsiderable city, but capable of producing great men" (ix. 5. § 28).   [E. H. B.]

COIN OF VELIA.

VELINUS (*Velino*), a considerable river of Central Italy, which has its sources in the lofty group of the Apennines between Nursia (*Norcia*) and Interocrea (*Antrodoco*). Its actual source is in the immediate neighbourhood of the ancient Falacrinum, the birthplace of Vespasian, where an old church still bears the name of *Sta Maria di Fonte Velino*. The upper part of its course is from N. to S.; but near *Antrodoco* it turns abruptly to the W., pursues that direction as far as *Rieti*, and thence flows about NNW. till it discharges its waters into the Nar (*Nera*) about 3 miles above *Terni* (Interamna). Just before reaching that river it forms the celebrated cascade now known as the *Falls of Terni* or *Cascata delle Marmore*. This waterfall is in its present form wholly artificial. It was first formed by M'. Curius Dentatus, who opened an artificial channel for the waters of the Velinus, and thus carried off a considerable part of the Lacus Velinus, which previously occupied a great part of the valley below Reate. There still remained, however, as there does to this day, a considerable lake, called the Lacus Velinus, and now known as the *Lago di Piè di Lugo*. It was on the banks of this lake that the villa of Axius, the friend of Cicero and Varro, was situated. (Cic. *ad Att.* iv. 15; Varro, *R.R.* ii. 1, 8.) Several smaller lakes still exist a little higher up the valley: hence we find Pliny speaking in the plural

of the VELINI LACUS (Plin. iii. 12. s. 17; Tac. *Ann.* i. 79; Vib. Seq. p. 24.) The character and confirmation of the lower valley of the Velinus are fully described in the article REATE. Pliny has made a complete confusion in his description of the Nar and Velinus. [NAR.] The latter river receives near *Rieti* two considerable streams, the *Salto* and the *Turano*: the ancient name of the first is unknown to us, but the second is probably the Tolenus of Ovid. (*Fast.* vi. 565.) It flows from the mountain district once occupied by the Aequiculi, and which still retains the name of *Cicolano*. [TOLENUS.]   [E. H. B.]

VELITRAE (Οὐέλιτραι : *Eth.* Οὐελιτρανός, Veliternus : *Velletri*), a city of Latium situated on the southern slope of the Alban hills, looking over the Pomptine Marshes, and on the left of the Via Appia. There can be no doubt that it was included within the limits of Latium, as that name was usually understood, at least in later times : but there is great uncertainty as to whether it was originally a Latin or a Volscian city. On the one hand Dionysius includes the Veliterni in his list of the thirty cities of the Latin League, a document probably derived from good authority (Dionys. v. 61). On the other hand both Dionysius himself and Livy represent Velitrae as a Volscian city at the earliest period when it came into collision with Rome. Thus Dionysius, in relating the wars of Ancus Marcius with the Volscians, speaks of Velitrae as a city of that people which was besieged by the Roman king, but submitted, and was received to an alliance on favourable terms. (Id. iii. 41.) Again in B. C. 494, just about the period when its name figures in Dionysius as one of the Latin cities, it is mentioned both by that author and by Livy as a Volscian city; which was wrested from that people by the consul P. Virginius (Id. vi. 42 ; Liv. ii. 30). According to Livy a Roman colony was sent there the same year, which was again recruited with fresh colonists two years afterwards. (Liv. ii. 31, 34.) Dionysius, on the contrary, makes no mention of the first colony, and represents that sent in B. C. 492 as designed to supply the exhausted population of Velitrae, which had been reduced to a low state by a pestilence. (Dionys. vii. 13, 14.) It appears certain at all events that Velitrae received a Roman colony at this period ; but it had apparently again fallen into decay, as it received a second body of colonists in B. C. 404. (Diod. xiv. 34.) Even this did not suffice to secure its allegiance to Rome : shortly after the Gaulish war, the Roman colonists of Velitrae joined with the Volscians in their hostilities, and after a short time broke out into open revolt. (Liv. vi. 13, 21.) They were indeed defeated in B. C. 381, together with the Praenestines and Volscians, who supported them, and their city was taken the next year (*ib.* 22, 29); but their history from this time is a continued succession of outbreaks and hostile enterprises against Rome, alternating with intervals of dubious peace. It seems clear that they had really assumed the position of an independent city, like those of the neighbouring Volscians, and though the Romans are said to have more than once taken this city, they did not again restore it to the position of a Roman colony. Thus notwithstanding its capture in B. C. 380, the citizens were again in arms in 370, and not only ravaged the territories of the Latins in alliance with Rome, but even laid siege to Tusculum. They were quickly defeated in the field, and Velitrae itself in its turn was besieged by a Roman army ; but the siege was protracted for more than two years, and it is not quite clear whether the city was taken in the end. (Liv. vi. 36, 37, 38, 42.) In B. C. 358 they again broke out, and ravaged the Roman territories, but we hear nothing of their punishment (Liv. vii. 15): and in B. C. 340, on the outbreak of the great Latin War, they are represented as among the first to join in the defection. It is evident indeed that they were at this time still a powerful people : their troops bore an important part in two successive campaigns, but shared in the general defeat of the Latins on the banks of the Astura, B. C. 338. (Liv. viii. 3, 12, 13 ; *Fast. Capit.*) After the close of the war they were selected for the severest punishment, on the especial ground of their having been originally Roman citizens. Their walls were destroyed, and their local senators transported beyond the Tiber, under a severe penalty in case of their return. Their place was, however, supplied by a body of fresh colonists, so that the city continued to be not less populous than before. (Liv. viii. 14.)

From this time Velitrae sank into the condition of an ordinary municipal town, and we hear little of it in history. It is mentioned incidentally on occasion of some prodigies that occurred there (Liv. xxx. 38, xxxii. 1, 9), but with this exception its name is not again mentioned till the close of the Republic. We hear, however, that it was a flourishing municipal town, and it derived some celebrity at the commencement of the Empire from the circumstance of its having been the native place of the Octavian family, from which the emperor Augustus was descended. The Octavii indeed claimed to be descended from the ancient Roman family of the same name ; but it is certain that both the grandfather and great-grandfather of Augustus were merely men of equestrian rank, who held municipal magistracies in their native town. (Snet. *Aug.* 1, 2 ; Dion Cass. xlv. 1.) According to the Liber Coloniarum, Velitrae had received a fresh body of colonists in the time of the Gracchi ; but it continued to retain its municipal rank until the reign of Claudius, when it received a military colony, and from this time assumed the title of a Colonia, which we find it bearing in inscriptions (*Lib. Colon.* p. 238 ; Zumpt, *de Col.* p. 383 ; Orell. *Inscr.* 1740, 3652). No mention of the city occurs in history under the Roman Empire, but its name is found in the geographers, and inscriptions testify that it continued to exist as a flourishing town down to near the close of the Empire. (Strab. v. p. 237 ; Plin. iii. 5. s. 9 ; Sil. Ital. viii. 376 ; Nibby, *Dintorni,* vol. iii. p. 450.) It appears to have subsequently suffered severely from the ravages of the barbarians, but continued to subsist throughout the middle ages: and the modern city of *Velletri* still occupies the site of the ancient one, though it has no remains of antiquity. Its position is very similar to that of Lanuvium (*Civita Lavinia*), on a projecting rock or spur of hill, standing out from the more elevated group of the Alban hills, and rising like a headland above the plain of the Pomptine Marshes, which lie stretched out beneath it. The inscriptions which have been discovered there have been published by Cardinali (*Inscrizioni Antiche Veliterne,* 4to. Roma, 1823). From one of these we learn that the ancient city possessed an amphitheatre, which was repaired as late as the reign of Valentinian, but no traces of it are now visible. It had also temples of Apollo, Hercules and Mars, as well as of the Sabine divinity Sancus. (Liv. xxxii. 1.)

Pliny notices the territory of Velitrae as producing a wine of great excellence, inferior only to the Falernian (Plin. xiv. 6. s. 8).   [E. H. B.]

VELLAVI or VELAUNI, a people of Gallia. In the passage of Caesar (*B. G.* vii. 75) some editions have Velauni, but it is certain that whatever is the true form of the name, these Velauni are the Vellaioi (Οὐελλαῖοι) of Strabo (p. 190). The Gabali and Velauni in Caesar's time were subject to the Arverni. In Ptolemy (ii. 7. § 20) the name is Velauni (Οὐέλαυνοι), but he puts them next to the Auscii, which is a great mistake. D'Anville says that the diocese of *Pui* represents their territory ; but that this cannot be said of the small province of *Vellay,* which was annexed to *Languedoc* in the ante-revolutionary division of France. In the Notit. of the Provinces of Gallia, the capital of the Vellavi is Civitas Vellavorum [REVESSIO]. [G L.]

VELLAUNI. [VELAUNI.]

VELLAUNODUNUM, in Gallia. In B. C. 52 Caesar, leaving two legions and all the baggage at Agedincum (*Sens*), marches on Genabum (*Orléans*). On the second day he reaches Vellaunodunum. (*B. G.* vii. 11.) In two days Caesar made a vallum round Vellaunodunum, and on the third day the place surrendered, and the people gave up their arms. There is no evidence about the site of Vellaunodunum, except that it was on the road from *Sens* to *Orléans,* and was reached in the second day's march from *Sens,* and that Caesar reached *Orléans* in two days from Vellaunodunum. Caesar was marching quick. D'Anville conjectures that Vellaunodunum may be *Beaune,* in the old province of *Gâtinois ;* for *Beaune* is about 40 Roman miles from *Sens,* and the Roman army would march that distance in two days. *Beaune* is named Belna in the Pagus Vastinensis (*Gâtinois, Gastinois, Vastinois ;* VAPINCUM), in the acts of a council held at *Soissons* in 862, and D'Anville thinks that Belna may be a corruption of Vellauna, which is the name of Vellaunodunum, if we cut off the termination *dunum.* (D'Anville, *Notice, &c.*)   [G. L.]

VELLEIA [VELEIA].

VE'LLICA (Οὐέλλικα, Ptol. ii. 6. § 51), a town of the Cantabri in Hispania Tarraconensis. Ukert (ii. pt. i. p. 144) places it in the neighbourhood of *Villelba,* to the N. of *Aquilar de Campo.* [T.H.D.]

VELLOCASSES. [VELOCASSES.]

VELOCASSES, as Caesar (*B. G.* ii. 4) writes the name, Vellocasses in Pliny (iv. 18), and in Ptolemy Οὐενελιοκάσιοι (ii. 8. § 8). Caesar places them in the country of the Belgae, and consequently north of the *Seine.* The number of fighting men that they could muster in B. C. 57 was estimated at 10,000, unless Caesar means that they and the Veromandui together had this number. In the division of Gallia by Augustus, the Velocasses were included in Lugdunensis. Their chief town was Rotomagus (*Rouen*) on the north bank of the *Seine.* West of the Velocasses were the Caleti, whose country extended along the coast north of the *Seine.* That part of the country of the Velocasses which is between the rivers *Andelle* and *Oise,* became in modern times *Vexin Normand* and *Vexin Français,* the little river *Epte* forming the boundary between the two *Vexins.*   [G. L.]

VELPI MONTES (τὰ Οὐέλπα ὄρη, Ptol. iv. 4. § 8), a range of mountains on the W. borders of Cyrenaica, in which were the sources of the river Lathon.   [T. H. D.]

VELTAE (Οὐέλται, Ptol. iii. 5. § 22), a people of European Sarmatia, dwelling on both banks of the river Rhubon, identical, according to Ukert (iii. pt. ii. p. 435), with the Slavonian Veleti, or Lutizi, who dwelt on the *Oder*.   [T. H. D.]

VEMA'NIA, a town of Vindelicia, on the road between Augusta Vindelicorum and Brigantium (*It. Ant.* pp. 237, 251, 259; *Tab. Peut.*), seems to have been a place of some importance, as it was the station of the prefect of the third legion, who had to guard the frontier from this town to Campodunum. (*Not. Imp.*) The place now occupying the site is called *Wangen*. [L. S.]

VENAFRUM (Οὐέναφρον: *Eth.* Venafranus: *Venafro*), an inland city of Campania, situated in the upper valley of the Vulturnus, and on the Via Latina, 16 miles from Casinum and 18 from Teanum. (*Itin. Ant.* p. 303.) It was the last city of Campania towards the N., its territory adjoining on the W., that of Casinum (*S. Germano*), which was included in Latium, in the more extended sense of that name, and that of Aesernia on the NE., which formed part of Samnium. It stood on a hill rising above the valley of the Vulturnus, at a short distance from the right bank of that river. (Strab. v. p. 238.) No mention is found in history of Venafrum before the Roman conquest of this part of Italy, and it is uncertain to what people it originally belonged; but it is probable that it had fallen into the hands of the Samnites before that people came into collision with Rome. Under the Roman government it appears as a flourishing municipal town: Cato, the most ancient author by whom it is mentioned, notices it as having manufactures of spades, tiles, and ropes (Cato, *R. R.* 135): at a later period it was more noted for its oil, which was celebrated as the best in Italy, and supplied the choicest tables of the great at Rome under the Empire. (Hor. *Carm.* ii. 6. 16, *Sat.* ii. 4. 69; Juv. v. 86; Martial, xiii. 98; Strab. v. pp. 238, 242; Varr. *R. R.* i. 2. § 6; Plin. xv. 2. s. 3.) The only occasion on which Venafrum figures in history is during the Social War, B. C. 88, when it was betrayed into the hands of the Samnite leader Marius Egnatius, and two Roman cohorts that formed the garrison were put to the sword. (Appian, *B. C.* i. 41.) Cicero more than once alludes to the great fertility of its territory (Cic. *de Leg. Agr.* ii. 25, *pro Planc.* 9), which was one of those that the tribune Rullus proposed by his agrarian law to divide among the Roman citizens. This project proved abortive, but a colony was planted at Venafrum under Augustus, and the city continued henceforth to bear the title of a Colonia, which is found both in Pliny and in inscriptions. (Plin. iii. 5. s. 9; *Lib. Col.* p. 239; Zumpt, *de Colon.* p. 347; Mommsen, *Inscr. R. N.* 4643, 4703.) These last, which are very numerous, sufficiently attest the flourishing condition of Venafrum under the Roman Empire: it continued to subsist throughout the middle ages, and is still a town of about 4000 inhabitants. It retains the ancient site as well as name, but has few vestiges of antiquity, except the inscriptions above mentioned and some shapeless fragments of an edifice supposed to have been an amphitheatre. The inscriptions are published by Mommsen. (*Inscr. R. N.* pp. 243—249.)   [E. H. B.]

VENANTODUNUM, apparently a town of the Catyeuchlani in Britannia Romana, perhaps *Huntingdon*. The name appears in the Not. Imp.; though Camden (p. 502) notes it as coined by Leland.   [T. H. D.]

VENASA (Οὐήνασα), a rather important town in the district of Morimene in Cappadocia, possessing a celebrated temple of Zeus, to which no less than

3000 slaves belonged. The high priest enjoyed an annual income of fifteen talents, arising from the produce of the lands belonging to the temple. This sacerdotal dignity was held for life, and the priest was next in rank to the high priest of Comana. (Strab. xii. p. 537.)   [L. S.]

VENDUM (Οὐένδον, Strab. iii. p. 207, vii. p. 314), a town of the Iapodes in Illyria, and on the borders of Pannonia. It is probably the modern *Windisch-Grätz*; but some have identified it with *Brindjel*.   [T. H. D.]

VE'NEDAE (Οὐενέδαι, Ptol. iii. 5. § 19), or VENEDI (Tac. *Germ.* 46; Plin. iv. 13. s. 27), a considerable people of European Sarmatia, situated on the N. declivity of the mountains named after them, and along the Sinus Venedicus about the river Chronos, and as far as the E. bank of the Vistula. They were the northern neighbours of the Galindae and Gythones; but Tacitus was doubtful whether he should call them Germans or Sarmatians, though they more resembled the former than the latter in some of their customs, as the building of houses, the carrying of shields, and the habit of going on foot, whilst the Sarmatians travelled on horseback or in waggons. They sought a precarious livelihood by scouring the woods and mountains which lay between the Peucini and the Fenni. Whether they were the forefathers of the Wends is very problematical. (Cf. Schafarik, *Slav. Alterth.* i. p. 75, seq., p. 151, seq. &c., *Ueber die Abkunft der Slaven*, p. 24.)   [T. H. D.]

VENEDICI MONTES (τὰ Οὐενεδικὰ ὄρη, Ptol. iii. 5. § 15), certain mountains of European Sarmatia, bounding the territory of the Venedae on the S. They were probably the low chain of hills which separates *East Prussia* from *Poland*. [T. H. D.]

VENEDICUS SINUS (Οὐενεδικὸς κόλπος, Ptol. iii. 5. § 1), a bay of the Sarmatian ocean, or *Baltic*, named after the Venedae who dwelt upon it. It lay to the E. of the Vistula, and was in all probability the *Gulf of Riga*; a view which is strengthened by the name of *Vindau* belonging to a river and town in *Courland*.   [T. H. D.]

VE'NELL [UNELLI.]
VENELIOCASIL [VELOCASSES.]
VE'NERIS MONS. [APHRODISIUS MONS.]
VE'NERIS PORTUS. [PORTUS VENERIS.]
VE'NERIS PROM. [HISPANIA, Vol. I. p. 1084.]
VE'NETI (Οὐένετοι), a Celtic people, whose country Caesar names Venetia (*B. G.* iii. 9). The Veneti lived on the coast of the Atlantic (*B. G.* ii. 34), and were one of the Armoric or Maritime states of Celtica. On the south they bordered on the Nannetes or Nannetes, on the east they had the Redones, and on the north the Osismii, who occupied the most western part of *Bretagne*. Strabo (iv. p. 195) made a great mistake in supposing the Veneti to be Belgae. He also supposes them to be the progenitors of the Veneti on the coast of the Hadriatic, whom others supposed to be Paphlagonians; however, he gives all this only as conjecture. The chief town of the Veneti was Dariorigum, afterwards Veneti, now *Vannes* [DARIORIGUM.] The river *Vilaine* may have been the southern boundary of the Veneti.

Caesar (*B. G.* iii. 9) describes the coast of Venetia as cut up by aestuaries, which interrupted the communication by land along the shore. Most of the towns (*Ib.* 12) were situated at the extremity of tongues of land or peninsulas, so that when the tide was up the towns could not be reached on foot, nor could ships reach them during the ebb, for the water was then too shallow. This is the character of the coast of the French department of *Morbihan*, which corresponds pretty nearly to Caesar's Venetia. On this coast there are many bays and many "lingulae" as Caesar calls them (*Pointes*). The most remarkable peninsula is *Quiberon*, which runs out into the sea near 10 miles, and is insulated at high water. The Veneti commanded the sea in these parts, and as the necessities of navigation often drove vessels to their ports, they made them pay for the shelter. The Veneti had trade with Britain, with *Devonshire* and *Cornwall*, the parts of the island which were nearest to them. They were the most powerful maritime state on the Atlantic.

Their vessels were made nearly flat-bottomed, in order that they might the better take the ground when they were left dry by the ebb. The heads were very high, and the sterns strong built, to stand the violence of their seas. The material was oak. Instead of ropes they had chain cables, the use of which has been revived in the present century. Strabo (iv. p. 195) writes as if the ropes of the rigging were chains, which is very absurd, and is contradicted by Caesar, who says that the yards were fastened to the masts by ropes, which the Romans cut asunder in the sea-fight with the Veneti (iii. 14). Instead of sails they used skins and leather worked thin, either because they had no flax and did not know its use, or, as Caesar supposes it to be more likely, because flaxen sails were not suited for the tempests of that coast.

The Veneti rose against the Romans in the winter of B. C. 57, and induced many other neighbouring states to join them, even the Morini and Menapii. They also sent to Britain for help. Caesar, who was absent in Italy during the winter (B.C. 57—56), sent orders to build ships on the *Loire*, probably in the territory of the Andes, Turones and Carnutes, where his legions were quartered, and the ships were floated down to the Ocean. He got his rowers from the Provincia. In the meantime he came himself into Gallia. He protected his rear against attack by sending Labienus to the country of the Treviri, to keep the Belgae quiet and to stop the Germans from crossing the Rhine. He sent P. Crassus with twelve cohorts and a large body of cavalry into Aquitania to prevent the Celtae from receiving any aid from these parts; and he kept the Unelli [UNELLI], Curiosolites and Lexovii in check by sending Q. Titurius Sabinus into those parts with three legions. D. Brutus commanded Caesar's fleet and the Gallic ships furnished by the Pictones and Santones, and other states that had been reduced to obedience.

Caesar began the campaign by besieging the Venetian towns that were situated on the extremities of the tongues of land; but as the Veneti had abundance of ships, they removed themselves by water from one town to another, when they could no longer resist the besieger. They did this during a great part of the summer, and Caesar could not prevent it, for he had not yet got together all his ships. After taking several of their towns he waited for the remainder of his fleet. The Veneti with about 220 of their best equipped ships came out of port to meet the Romans. The Roman ships could not do the Gallic ships any damage by driving the heads of their vessels against them, for the Gallic ships were too high at the prow and too strong; nor could the Romans have attacked them by raising wooden frameworks on their decks, for the Gallic ships were too high. The only advantage

that the Roman ships had was in the oars, which the Gallic ships had not. They could only trust to their sails. The Romans at last fixed sharp hooks at the end of long poles, and laying hold of the enemy's rigging with them, and then putting their own vessels in motion by the oars, they cut the ropes asunder, and the yards and sails falling down, the Venetian ships were useless. Everything now depended on courage, in which the Romans had the advantage; and the men were encouraged by the presence of Caesar and the army, which occupied all the hills and higher ground which commanded a view of the sea. The Roman ships got round the Venetian, two or three about each, for they had the advantage in number of vessels, and the men began to board the enemy. Some ships were taken and the rest tried to sail away, but a dead calm came on and they could not stir. A very few ships escaped to the land at nightfall. The battle lasted from the fourth hour in the morning to sunset. Thus was destroyed the first naval power that was formed on the coast of the Atlantic. The Veneti lost their ships, all their young men of fighting age, and most of their men of mature age and of rank. They surrendered unconditionally. Caesar put to death all the members of the Venetian state assembly, on the ground that they had violated the law of nations by imprisoning Q. Velanius and T. Silius, who had been sent into their country in the previous winter to get supplies for the Roman troops who were quartered along the *Loire* (*B. G.* iii. 7, 8). The rest of the people were sold by auction; all, we must suppose, that Caesar could lay hold of. Thus the territory of the Veneti was nearly depopulated, and an active commercial people was swept from the earth. The Veneti never appear again as a powerful state. When Vercingetorix was rousing all Gallia to come against Caesar at Alesia (B.C. 52), the contingent of all the Armoric states, seven or eight in number, was only 6000 men (*B. G.* vii. 75).

Dion Cassius (xxxix. 40—43) has four chapters on the history of this Venetian war, which, as usual with him, he puts in confusion, by misunderstanding Caesar and making his own silly additions. [G. L.]

VENETIA (Οὐενετία; Eth. Οὐένετος or Ἕνετος, Venetus), a province or region of Northern Italy, at the head of the Adriatic sea, extending from the foot of the Alps, where those mountains descend to the Adriatic, to the mouths of the Padus, and westward as far as the river Athesis (*Adige*), or the lake Benacus. But the boundaries of the district seem to have varied at different times, and there is some difficulty in determining them with accuracy. In early times, indeed, before the Roman conquest, we have no account of the exact line of demarcation between the Veneti and the Cenomani, who adjoined them on the W., though according to Livy, Verona was a city of the latter people (v. 35). After the Roman conquest, the whole of Venetia was at first included as a part of Cisalpine Gaul, and was not separated from it till the time of Augustus, who constituted his Tenth Region of Venetia and Istria, but including within its limits not only Verona, but Brixia and Cremona also (Plin. iii. 18. s. 22, 19. s 23), both of which were certainly cities of the Cenomani, and seem to have continued to be commonly considered as belonging to Cisalpine Gaul. (Ptol. iii. 1. § 31.) Some authors, however, extended the appellation of Venetia still further to the W., so as to include not only Brixia and Cremona, but Bergomum also, and regarded the Addua as the boundary

(P. Diac. *Hist. Lang.* ii. 14). But in the later period of the Roman Empire the Athesis seems to have been generally recognised as the W. boundary of Venetia, though not so strictly as to exclude Verona, the greater part of which was situated on the right bank of the river. Towards the N. the boundary was equally indefinite : the valleys and southern slopes of the Alps were occupied by Rhaetian and Euganean tribes; and it is probable that the limit between these and the Veneti, on their S. frontier, was always vague and arbitrary, or at least determined merely by nationality, not by any geographical boundary, as is the case at the present day with the German and Italian races in the same region. Thus Tridentum, Feltria, and Belunum, were all of them properly Rhaetian towns (Plin. iii. 19. s. 23), though included in the Tenth Region of Augustus, and for that reason often considered as belonging to Venetia.

On the E. the limits of Venetia were more definite. The land of the Carni, who occupied the greater part of the modern *Frioul*, was generally considered as comprised within it, while the little river Formio (*Risano*), a few miles S. of Tergeste, separated it from Istria. (Plin. iii. 18. s. 22.) Several authors, however, regard Tergeste as an Istrian city [TER-GESTE], and must therefore have placed the boundary either at the Timavus, or where the Alps come down so close to the sea, between that river and Tergeste, as to prevent the road being continued along the coast. There can be no doubt that this point forms the natural boundary of Venetia on the E., although the Formio continued under the Roman Empire to constitute its political limit.

The physical peculiarities of the region thus limited are very remarkable. The greater part of Venetia is, like the neighbouring tract of Cisalpine Gaul, a broad and level plain, extending, without interruption, to the very foot of the Alps, and furrowed by numerous streams, which descend from those mountains with great rapidity and violence. These streams, swollen by the melting of the Alpine snows, or by the torrents of rain which descend upon the mountains, as soon as they reach the plain spread themselves over the country, forming broad beds of sand and pebbles, or inundating the fertile tract on each side of their banks. Continually stagnating more and more, as they flow through an almost perfectly level tract, they form, before reaching the sea, considerable sheets of water; and the action of the tides (which is much more perceptible at the head of the Adriatic than in any other part of that sea or of the Mediterranean) combining to check the outflow of their waters, causes the formation of extensive salt-water lagunes, communicating with the sea only through narrow gaps or openings in the long line of sandy barriers that bounds them. Such lagunes, which occupy a great extent of ground S. of the present mouth of the *Po* [PADUS], are continued on from its N. bank to the neighbourhood of Altinum; and from thence, with some interruptions, to the mouth of the *Isonzo*, at the head or inmost bight of the Adriatic. So extensive were they in ancient times that there was an uninterrupted line of inland navigation by these lagunes, which were known as the Septem Maria, from Ravenna to Altinum, a distance of above 80 miles. (*Itin. Ant.* p. 126.) Great physical changes have naturally taken place in the course of ages in a country so constituted. On the one hand there is a constant tendency to the filling up of the lagunes with the silt and mud brought

down by the rivers, which converts them first into marshes, and eventually into firm land. On the other hand the rivers, which have for ages been confined within artificial banks, keep pushing on their mouths into the sea, and thus creating backwaters which give rise to fresh lagunes. At the same time, the rivers thus confined, from time to time break through their artificial barriers and force new channels for themselves; or it is found necessary to carry them off by new and artificial outlets. Thus all the principal streams of Venetia, from the *Adige* to the *Piave*, are at the present day carried to the sea by artificial canals; and it is doubtful whether any of them have now the same outlet as in ancient times.

In the eastern portion of Venetia, from the *Piave* to the foot of the Alps near Aquileia, these physical characters are less marked. The coast is indeed bordered by a belt of marshes and lagunes, but of no great extent: and within this, the rivers that descend from the Alps have been for the most part left to wander unrestrained through the plain, and have in consequence formed for themselves broad beds of stone and shingle, sometimes of surprising extent, through which the streams in their ordinary condition roll their diminished waters the trifling volume of which contrasts strangely with the breadth and extent of their deposits. Such is the character especially of the *Tagliamento*, the largest river of this part of Italy, as well as of the *Torre*, the *Natisone*, and other minor streams. The irregularity of their channels, resulting from this state of things, is sufficiently shown by the fact that the rivers Turrus and Natiso, which formerly flowed under the walls of Aquileia, have now changed their course, and join the *Isonzo* at a distance of more than 4 miles from that city. [AQUILEIA.]

Of the history of Venetia previous to the Roman conquest we know almost nothing. It was occupied at that time by two principal nations, the VENETI from whom it derived its name, in the W., and the CARNI in the E.; the former extending from the Athesis to the Plavis, or perhaps to the Tilaventus, the latter from thence to the borders of Istria. But the origin and affinities of the Veneti themselves are extremely obscure. Ancient writers represent them as a very ancient people (Polyb. ii. 17), but at the same time are generally agreed that they were not the original inhabitants of the tract which they occupied. This was reported by tradition to have been held in the earliest ages by the Euganeans (Liv i. 1), a people whom we still find lingering in the valleys and underfalls of the Alps within the historical period, but of whose origin and affinities we know absolutely nothing. [EUGANEI.] In regard to the Veneti themselves it cannot fail to be remarked that we meet with three tribes or nations of this name in other parts of the world, besides those of Italy, viz. the Gaulish tribe of the Veneti on the coast of Armorica; the Venedi or Veneti of Tacitus, a Sarmatian or Slavonian tribe on the shores of the Baltic; and the Heneti or Eneti, who are mentioned as existing in Paphlagonia in the time of Homer. (*Iliad,* ii. 85.) The name of this last people does not subsequently appear in history, and we are therefore wholly at a loss as to their ethnical affinities, but it is not improbable that it was the resemblance or rather identity of their name with that of the Italian Veneti (according to the Greek form of the latter) that gave rise to the strange story of Antenor having migrated to Venetia after the siege of Troy, and there founded the city of Patavium. (Liv. i. 1; Virg. *Aen.* i. 242 ; Serv. *ad loc.*) This legend, so generally adopted by the Romans and later Greeks, seems to have been current as early as the time of Sophocles. (Strab. xiii. p. 608.) Some writers, however, omitted all mention of Antenor. and merely represented the tribe of the Heneti, after having lost their leader Pylaemenes in the Trojan War, as wandering through Thrace to the head of the Adriatic, where they ultimately established themselves. (Id. xii. p. 543; Scymn. Ch. 389.) Whether there be any foundation for this story or not, it is evident that it throws no light upon the national affinities of the Italian Veneti. The other two tribes of the same name would seem to lead our conjectures in two different directions. From the occurrence of a tribe of Veneti among the Transalpine Gauls, just as we find among that people a tribe of Cenomani and of Senones, corresponding to the two tribes of that name on the Italian side of the Alps. it would seem a very natural inference that the Veneti also were a Gaulish race, who had migrated from beyond the Alps. To this must be opposed the fact that, while a distinct historical tradition of the successive migrations of the Gaulish tribes in the N. of Italy has been preserved and transmitted to us (Liv. v. 34, 35). no trace is recorded of a similar migration of the Veneti; but, on the contrary, that people is uniformly distinguished from the Gauls: Livy expressly speaks of them as occupying the same tract which they did in his time not only before the first Gaulish migration, but before the plains of Northern Italy were occupied by the Etruscans (*Ib.* 33); and Polybius emphatically, though briefly, describes them as a different people from the Gauls their neighbours, and using a different language, though resembling them much in their manners and habits (ii. 17). Strabo also speaks of them as a distinct people from the Gauls, though he tells us that one account of their origin derived them from the Gaulish people of the same name that dwelt on the shores of the ocean. (Strab. iv. p. 195, v. p. 212.) But there is certainly no ground for rejecting the distinct statement of Polybius, and we may safely acquiesce in the conclusion that they were *not* of Celtic or Gaulish origin.

On the other hand the existence of a tribe or people on the southern shores of the Baltic, who were known to the Romans (through their German neighbours) as Venedi or Veneti, a name evidently identical with that of the *Wenden* or *Wends*, by which the Slavonian race in general is still known to the Germans, would lead us to regard the Italian Veneti also as probably a Slavonian tribe : and this seems on the whole the most plausible hypothesis. There is nothing improbable in the circumstance that the Slavonians may at an early period have extended their migrations as far as the head of the Adriatic, and left there a detached branch or offshoot of their main stock. The commercial intercourse of the Veneti with the shores of the Baltic, a traffic which we find already established at a very early period, may be the more readily explained if we suppose it to have been carried on by tribes of the same origin. Herodotus indeed represents the Veneti as an Illyrian tribe (i. 196, v. 9) ; but it seems probable that the name of Illyrians was applied in a vague sense to all the mountaineers that occupied the eastern coasts of the Adriatic, and some of these may in ancient times have been of Slavonian origin, though the true

Illyrians (the ancestors of the present Albanians) were undoubtedly a distinct people.

Of the history of the Veneti as an independent people we know almost nothing ; but what little we do learn indicates a marked difference between them and their neighbours the Gauls on one side, and the Liburnians and Illyrians on the other. They appear to have been a commercial, rather than a warlike, people : and from the very earliest dawn of history carried on a trade in amber, which was brought overland from the shores of the Baltic, and exchanged by them with Phoenician and Greek merchants. Hence arose the fables which ascribed the production of that substance to the land of the Veneti, and ultimately led to the identification of the Eridanus of Northern Europe with the Padus of Northern Italy. [ERIDANUS.] Herodotus mentions a peculiar custom as existing among the Veneti in his day, that they sold their daughters by auction to the highest bidder, as a mode of disposing of them in marriage (i. 196). We learn also that they habitually wore black garments, a taste which may be said to be retained by the Venetians down to the present day, but was connected by the poets and mythographers with the fables concerning the fall of Phaëton. (Scymn. Ch. 396.) Another circumstance for which they were distinguished was the excellence of their horses, and the care they bestowed on breeding and training them, a fact which was appealed to by many as a proof of their descent from Antenor and "the horsetraining Trojans." (Strab. v. pp. 212,215.) It is clear that they were a people considerably more advanced in civilisation than either the Gauls or the Ligurians, and the account given by Livy (x. 2) of the landing of Cleonymus in the territory of Patavium (B.C. 302) proves that at that period Patavium at least was a powerful and well organised city. Livy indeed expressly contrasts the Veneti with the Illyrians, Liburnians, and Istrians, "gentes ferae et magna ex parte latrociniis maritimis iufames." (*Ib.*) On this occasion we are told that the citizens of Patavium were kept in continual alarm on account of their Gaulish neighbours, with whom they seem to have been generally on unfriendly terms. Thus at a still earlier period we are informed by Polybius that the retreat of the Senonian Gauls, who had taken the city of Rome, was caused by an irruption of the Venetians into the Gaulish territory (ii. 18). It was doubtless this state of hostility that induced them, as soon as the Roman arms began to make themselves felt in Northern Italy, to conclude an alliance with Rome against the Gauls (B.C. 215), to which they appear to have subsequently adhered with unshaken fidelity. (Polyb. ii. 23, 24.) Hence while we afterwards find the Romans gradually carrying their arms beyond the Veneti, and engaged in frequent hostilities with the Carni and Istrians on the extreme verge of Italy, no trace is found of any collision with the Venetians. Nor have we any account of the steps by which the latter passed from the condition of independent allies to that of subjects of the Roman Republic. But it is probable that the process was a gradual one, and grew out of the mere necessity of the case, when the Romans had conquered Istria and the land of the Carni, in which last they had established, in B.C. 181, the powerful colony of Aquileia. It is certain that before the close of the Republic the Veneti had ceased to have any independent existence, and were comprised, like the Gaulish tribes, in the province of Gallia Cisalpina, which was placed under the authority of Caesar, B.C.

59. The period at which the Veneti acquired the Roman franchise is uncertain : we are only left to infer that they obtained it at the same time as the Transpadane Gauls, in B. C. 49.	(Dion Cass. xli. 56.)

Under the Roman Empire, Venetia (as already mentioned) was included, together with Istria, in the Tenth Region of Augustus. The land of the Carni (Carnorum regio, Plin. iii. 18. s. 22) was at this time considered, for administrative purposes, as a part of Venetia; though it is still described as distinct by Ptolemy (iii. 1. §§ 25, 26); and there is no doubt that the two nations were originally separate. But as the population of both districts became thoroughly Romanised, all traces of this distinction were lost, and the names of Venetia and Istria alone remained in use. These two continued to form one province, and we meet with mention, both in inscriptions and in the Notitia, of a "Corrector Venetiae et Histriae," down to the close of the Roman Empire. (Notit. Dign. ii. p. 65; Böcking, ad loc. p. 441; Orell. Inscr. 1050, 3191.) The capital of the united provinces was Aquileia, which rose under the Roman Empire to be one of the most flourishing cities of Italy. Its importance was derived, not from its wealth and commercial prosperity only, but from its situation at the very entrance of Italy, on the highroad which became the great means of communication between the Eastern and Western Empires. The same circumstance led to this part of Venetia becoming the scene of repeated contests for power between rival emperors. Thus it was before Aquileia that the Emperor Maximin perished in A.D. 238; it was on the banks of the river Alsa (Ausa) that the younger Constantine was defeated and slain, in A.D. 340; again, in 388, the contest between Maximus and Theodosius the Great was decided in the same neighbourhood; and in 425, that between the usurper Joannes and the generals of Theodosius II. [AQUILEIA.] Finally, in A. D. 489, it was on the river Sontius (Isonzo) that Odoacer was defeated by the Gothic king Theodoric. (Hist. Miscell. xvi. p. 561.)

It seems certain that Venetia had become under the Roman Empire a very opulent and flourishing province: besides Aquileia, Patavium and Verona were provincial cities of the first class; and many other towns such as Concordia, Altinum, Forum Julii, &c., whose names are little known in history, were nevertheless opulent and considerable municipal towns. But it suffered with peculiar severity from the inroads of the barbarians before the close of the Empire. The passage across the Julian Alps from the valley of the Save to the plains of Aquileia, which presents few natural difficulties, became the highway by which all the barbarian nations in succession descended into the plains of Italy; and hence it was Venetia that felt the first brunt of their fury. This was especially the case with the invasion of Attila in A. D. 452, who, having at length reduced Aquileia after a long siege, razed it to the ground; and then, advancing with fearful rapidity, devastated in like manner the cities of Concordia, Altinum, Patavium, Vicentia, Verona, Brixia, and Bergomum, not one of which was able to oppose any effectual resistance. (Hist. Miscell. xv. p. 549.) The expression of the chronicler that he levelled these cities with the ground is probably exaggerated; but there can be no doubt that they suffered a blow from which three of them at least, Concordia, Altinum, and Aquileia, never recovered. In the midst of this devastation many fugitives from the ruined cities took refuge in the extensive lagunes that bordered the coasts of Venetia, and established themselves on some small islands in the midst of the waters, which had previously been inhabited only by fishermen. It was thus that the refugees from Aquileia gave origin to the episcopal city of Grado, while those from Patavium settled on a spot then known as Rivus Altus, in the midst of the lagunes formed by the Meduacus, where the new colony gradually grew up into a wealthy city and a powerful republic, which retained the ancient name of the province in that of Venezia or Venice. "This emigration (observes Gibbon) is not attested by any contemporary evidence ; but the fact is proved by the event, and the circumstances might be preserved by tradition." (Decl. and Fall, ch. 35, note 55.) A curious letter of Cassiodorus (Var. xii. 24), written in A. D. 523, describes the islands of Venetia as inhabited by a population whose sole occupation and resource was derived from their fisheries : and it is remarkable, that he already appears to confine the appellation of Venetia to these islands, an usage which had certainly become prevalent in the time of Paulus Diaconus, who says, in speaking of the ancient province, "Venetis enim non solum in paucis insulis, quas nunc Venetias dicimus, constat" (ii. 14). It is clear, therefore, that the transfer the name of the province to the island city, which has continued ever since, was established as early as the eighth century.

The original land of the Veneti, as already observed, was almost entirely a plain. The underfalls of the Alps, and the hills that skirt the foot of that range, were for the most part inhabited by tribes of mountaineers, who were of the same race with the Rhaetians and Euganeans, with whom, so far as we can discover, the Veneti themselves had nothing in common. But a portion of this district was comprised within the limits of the province of Venetia, as this came to be marked out under Augustus; so that the boundary line between Venetia and Rhaetia was carried apparently from the head of the Lake Benacus (Lago di Garda) across the valley of the Athesis (Adige) to the ridge which separates the valley of the Plavis from that of the Meduacus, so as to exclude the Val Sugana, while it included the whole valley of the Piave (Plavis), with the towns of Feltria and Belunum, both of which are expressly ascribed by Pliny to the Tenth Region. Thence the boundary seems to have followed the ridge which divides the waters that fall into the Adriatic from the valleys of the Drave and Gail, both of which streams flow eastward towards the Danube, and afterwards swept round in a semicircle, till it nearly touched the Adriatic near Trieste (Tergeste).

Within these limits, besides the underfalls of the Alps that are thrust forward towards the plain, there were comprised two distinct groups of hills, now known as the Colli Euganei and Monti Berici, both of them wholly isolated from the neighbouring ranges of the Alps, and, in a geological sense, unconnected with them, being both clearly of volcanic origin. The name of the Euganean hills, applied to the more southerly of the two groups, which approaches within a few miles of Patavium (Padova), is evidently a relic of the period when that people possessed the greater part of this country, and is doubtless derived from a very early time. The appellation is not noticed by any ancient geographer, but the name of Euganeus Collis is given by Lucan to the hill above the baths of Aponus, one of the group in question; and Martial gives the name of "Euganeae Oras" to the hills near the town of Ateste (*Este*), at the southern extremity of the same range. (Lucan. vii. 192; Martial. x. 93). There can, therefore, be no doubt that this beautiful range of hills was known in ancient times as the Euganei Colles.

The rivers of Venetia are numerous, but, for the reasons already mentioned, not always easy to identify. Much the largest and most important is the ATHESIS (*Adige*), which at one period formed the boundary of the province, and which, emerging from the Alps, near Verona, sweeps round in a great curve till it pours its waters into the Adriatic only a few miles N. of the mouths of the Padus. The next river of any magnitude is the MEDUACUS or *Brenta*, which flows under the walls of Patavium, and receives as a tributary the *Bacchiglione*, apparently the Meduacus Minor of Pliny. After this (proceeding eastwards) comes the SILIS (*Sele*), a small stream flowing by the town of Altinum: next, the PLAVIS (*Piave*), a much more important river, which rises in the Alps above Belunum (*Belluno*), flows past that city and Feltria (*Feltre*), and enters the sea a few miles E. of Altinum: then the LIQUENTIA (*Livenza*), and the ROMATINUS (*Lemene*), a small river flowing under the walls of Concordia. Next to this comes the TILAVEMPTUS (*Tagliamento*), the most important of the rivers of the E. portion of Venetia, having its sources in the high ranges of the Alps above Julium Carnicum, whence it traverses the whole plain of the Carni, nearly in a direct line from N. to S. Beyond this come several minor streams, which it is not easy to identify with certainty: such are the Varanus and Anassus of Pliny, probably the *Stella* and the torrent of *Cormor*; and the ALSA, which still bears the name of *Ausa*. E. of these, again, come three considerable streams, the TURRUS, NATISO, and SONTIUS, which still preserve their ancient names, as the *Torre*, *Natisone*, and *Isonzo*, but have undergone considerable changes in the lower part of their course, the Natiso having formerly flowed under the walls of Aquileia, about 4 miles W. of its present channel, while the *Isonzo*, which now unites with it, originally followed an independent channel to the sea, near *Monfalcone*. The *Isonzo* receives a considerable tributary from the E., the *Wippach* or *Vipao*, which descends from the elevated table-land of the *Karst*, and was known in ancient times as the FLUVIUS FRIGIDUS. It was by the valley of this river that the great highroad from the banks of the Danube, after crossing the dreary highlands of *Carniola*, descended to Aquileia and the plains of Venetia. On the extreme confines of the province the little river TIMAVUS must be mentioned, on account of its classical celebrity, though of no geographical importance; and the FORMIO (*Risano*), a few miles S. of Tergeste, which, from the time of Pliny, constituted the limit between Venetia and Istria. (Plin. iii. 18. s. 22.)

The cities and towns of Venetia may now be enumerated in geographical order. Farthest to the W., and situated on the Athesis, was the important city of VERONA. Considerably to the E. of this was VICENTIA, and beyond that again, PATAVIUM. S. of Vicentia, at the southern extremity of the Euganean hills, was ATESTE (*Este*). On the border of the lagunes, at their N. extremity, was ALTINUM, and 30 miles farther to the E., CONCORDIA. Inland from these lay OPITERGIUM and TARVISIUM,

both of them considerable towns; and on the slopes of the hills forming the lowest underfalls of the Alps, the smaller towns of ACELUM (*Asolo*) and Ceneta (*Ceneda*), the name of which is found in Agathias and Paulus Diaconus (Agath. *Hist. Goth.* ii. 8; P. Diac. ii. 13), and was in all probability a Roman town, though not mentioned by any earlier writer. Still farther inland, in the valley of the Plavis, were FELTRIA and BELUNUM. E. of the Tilavemptus, and therefore included in the territory of the Carni, were AQUILEIA, near the sea-coast; FORUM JULII, N. of the preceding; VEDINUM (*Udine*), farther to the W.; and JULIUM CARNICUM. in the upper valley of the Tilavemptus, and in the midst of the Alps. TERGESTE, on the E. side of the bay to which it gave its name, was the last city of Venetia, and was indeed by many writers considered as belonging to Istria. [TERGESTE].

Besides these, there were in the land of the Carni several smaller towns, the names of which are mentioned by Pliny (iii. 19. s. 23.), or are found for the first time in Paulus Diaconus and the Geographer of Ravenna, but were in all probability Roman towns, which had grown up under the Empire. Of these, Flamonia (Plin.) is probably *Flagogna*, in the valley of the *Tagliamento*; Osopum (P. Diac. iv. 38) is still called *Osopo*, and Glemona, *Gemona*, higher up in the same valley; and Artemia, *Artegna*, a few miles SE. of the preceding. Cormones (*ib.*) is still called *Cormons*, a small town between *Cividale* and *Gradisca*; and PUCINUM (Plin., Ptol.) is *Duino*, near the sources of the Timavus.

The other obscure names mentioned by Pliny (*l. c.*), and of which he himself says, "quos scrupulose dicere non attineat," were apparently for the most part mountain tribes or communities, and cannot be determined with any approach to certainty.

Venetia was traversed by a great line of highroad, which proceeded from Aquileia to Verona, and thence to Mediolanum, and formed the great highway of communication from the latter city to the Danube and the provinces of the Eastern Empire. It passed through Concordia, Altinum, Patavium, Vicentia, and Verona. From Patavium a branch struck off through Ateste and Anneianum (probably *Legnago* on the *Adige*) to join the Aemilian Way at Mutina. A still more direct line of communication was established from Altinum to Ravenna by water, through the lagunes and artificial canals which communicated from one to another of these sheets of water. This line of route (if such it can be called) is briefly indicated by the Antonine Itinerary ("inde [a Ravenna] navigantur Septem Maria Altinum usque," p. 126); while the stations are given in detail by the Tabula; but from the fluctuations that the lagunes have undergone, few of them can be identified with any certainty.   [E. H. B.]

VENETIA, in Gaul. [VENETI.]

VENETICAE INSULAE, in Gallia, mentioned by Pliny (iv. 19), are the numerous small islands along the coast of Venetia, or the modern department of *Morbihan*. The largest is *Belle-île*. The others are *Houat*, *Hedic*, *Groain*, and some others. Perhaps the peninsula of *Quiberon* may be included [VENETI; VINDILIS].   [G.L.]

VENETUS LACUS. [BRIGANTINUS LACUS.]

VENIA'TIA, a place in Gallaecia in Hispania Tarraconensis, on the road from Bracara to Asturica. (*Itin. Ant.* p. 423.) Variously identified with *Vinhaes*, *Varzona*, and *Requejo*. [T. H. D.]

VENICO'NES (Οὐενίκωνες, Ptol. ii. 3. § 14), a

people on the E. coast of Britannia Barbara, S. of the estuary of the Tuaesis (*Murray Frith*), in *Forfarshire* and *Aberdeenshire*. [T. H. D.]

VENNENSES, a tribe of the Cantabri in Hispania Tarraconensis. (Plin. iii. 3. s. 4.) [T.H.D.]

VENNI'CNII (Οὐεννίκνιοι, Ptol. ii. 2. § 3), a people in the NW. part of Hibernia, between the promontories Boreum and Vennicnium. [T. H. D.]

VENNI'CNIUM PROM. (Οὐεννίκνιον ἄκρον, Ptol. ii. 2. § 2), the most northerly headland of Hibernia, usually identified with *Malin Head*; but Camden (p. 1411) takes it to have been *Rame's Head*. [T. H. D.]

VE'NNONES (Οὐέννονες or Οὐίννονες), a tribe of Rhaetia (Ptol. ii. 12. § 3), or according to Strabo (iv. pp. 204, 206), of Vindelicia. They are described as the wildest among the Rhaetian tribes, and are no doubt the same as the Vennonetes who, according to Pliny (iii. 24), were mentioned among the nations of the Alpine Trophy. They seem to have inhabited the district about the sources of the Athesis, which bore the name of Venonesgowe or Finesgowe as late as the eleventh century. (Von Hormayr, *Gesch. Tirols*. i. 1. p. 35.) [L. S.]

VENONAE, a town in Britannia Romana apparently belonging to the Coritavi, at which the road from London to the NW. part of Britain separated, one branch proceeding towards Deva, the other taking a NE. direction towards Lindum and Eboracum. There was also another branch to the SW. towards Venta Silurum, so that the two main roads which traversed the whole island must have crossed here. (*Itin. Ant.* pp. 470, 477, 479.) Variously identified with *Highcross*, *Claybrook*, and *Wigston Parva*. [T. H. D.]

VENOSTES, probably a branch of the Vennones, a Rhaetian tribe, were mentioned in the Alpine Trophy, of which the inscription is quoted by Pliny (iii. 24). In the middle ages their district bore the name of Venusta Vallis. (Zeuss, *Die Deutschen*, p. 237.) [L. S.]

VENTA, the name of several towns in Britannia Romana. 1. Venta Belgarum (Οὐέντα, Ptol. ii. 3. § 28), in the SW. of Britain, on the road from Londinium to Calleva and Isca Dumnoniorum. (*Itin. Ant.* p. 478, &c.; Geogr. Rav. v. 31.) Now *Winchester*, where there are some Roman remains. (Camden, p. 138.)

2. Venta Silurum on the W. coast of Britannia Romana, on the road from Londinium to Isca Silurum, and near the estuary of the Sabrina. (*Itin. Ant.* p. 485.) Now *Caer Went* in *Monmouthshire*, where there are traces of the ancient walls, and where Roman antiquities are (or were) occasionally found. (Camden, p. 713.)

3. Venta Icenorum, a town of the Iceni, on the E. coast of Britannia Romana (Ptol. ii. 3. § 21), to which there was a road from London. (*Itin. Ant.* p. 479.) Most probably *Caistor*, on the river *Wensum*, a little S. of *Norwich*, which probably rose from the ruins of *Caistor*. Here are traces of Roman remains. (Camden, p. 460.) [T. H. D.]

VE'NTIA (Οὐεντία), in Gallia Narbonensis, a town of the Allobroges, mentioned only by Dion Cassius (xxxvii. 47) in his history of the war between the Allobroges and C. Pomptinus the governor of Gallia Provincia (B. C. 62). Manlius Lentinus, a legatus of Pomptinus, came upon this town, but was driven from it. The place appears to be near the Isara (*Isère*) from Dion's narrative, and D'Anville following De Valois supposes it to be

Vinai, between *Moirenc* and *S. Marcellin*, at some distance from the bank of the *Isère*. As Ventia is unknown otherwise, it may be a blunder of Dion, and the place may be Vienna. [G. L.]

VENTISPONTE, a town in Hispania Baetica (Hirt. *B. Hisp.* 27), which appears from still extant inscriptions to have been not far from *Puente de Don Gonzalo*. (Ukert, ii. pt. i. p. 368.) It appears on coins under the name of Ventipo. (Florez, *Med.* ii. p. 617; Eckhel, i. p. 31; Mionnet, i. p. 27; Sestini, p. 92.) [T. H. D.]

COIN OF VENTISPONTE OR VENTIPO.

VENUSIA (Οὐενουσία: *Eth.* Venusinus: *Venosa*), a city of Apulia, situated on the Appian Way, about 10 miles S. of the river Aufidus. It nearly adjoined the frontiers of Lucania, so that, according to Horace, himself a native of the place, it was doubtful whether it belonged properly to Lucania or to Apulia, and the territory of the city, as assigned to the Roman colony, included a portion of that of both nations. (Hor. *Sat.* ii. 1. 34, 35.) This statement of Horace leaves it doubtful to what people Venusia originally belonged, though it is more probable that it was an Apulian city, and that it received only an accession of territory from Lucania. Later writers, indeed, distinctly assigned it to Apulia. (Plin. iii. 11. s. 16; Ptol. iii. 1. § 73; *Lib. Colon.* p. 210.) But no mention of it is found in history till the occasion of its capture by the Roman consul L. Postumius, in B. C. 262 (Dionys. *Exc. Vales.* p. 2335), when we are told that it was a populous and important town. A large part of the inhabitants was put to the sword, and, shortly afterwards, a Roman colony was established there by order of the senate. (Dionys. *l. c.*; Vell. i. 14; Hor. *l. c.*) The colonists are said to have been 20,000 in number, which must be either a mistake or an exaggeration; but there seems no doubt that the new colony became a populous and flourishing place, and was able to render important services to the Roman state during the Second Punic War. It was at Venusia that the consul Terentius Varro took refuge with 700 horse after the great defeat at Cannae (B. C. 216), and where he was gradually able to gather around him a force of about 4000 horse and foot. The Venusians vied with one another in showing them the utmost attention, and furnished them with clothing, arms, and other necessaries. (Liv xxii. 49, 54; Polyb. iii. 116, 117.) Again, at a later period of the war, when so many of the Roman colonies proved unable to satisfy the repeated demands of the senate, the Venusians were among those who continued steadfast, and declared themselves ready to furnish the troops and supplies required of them. (Liv. xxvii. 10.) It was after this, through several successive campaigns, the head-quarters of the Roman commanders in Apulia. (*Ib.* 20, 41; Appian, *Annib.* 50.) But the colony suffered severely from all these exertions, and, in B. C. 200, after the close of the war, it was found necessary to recruit its exhausted strength with a fresh body of colonists. (Liv. xxxi. 49.) From this time Venusia seems to have always continued to be a flourishing town and one of the most considerable places in this part of Italy. It bore an important part in the Social War, having early joined in the outbreak, and became one of the principal strongholds of the allies in the south of Italy. (Appian, B. C. i. 39, 42.) In the second year of the war its territory was ravaged by the Roman praetor Cosconius, but we do not learn that the city itself fell into his hands. (Ib. 52.) At all events it did not suffer severely, as it is afterwards mentioned by Appian as one of the most flourishing cities of Italy (Ib. iv. 3) ; and Strabo also notices it as one of the few cities in this region which retained their consideration in his time (v. p. 250). It received a colony of veterans under the Triumvirate (Appian, B. C. iv. 3 ; Zumpt, de Colon. p. 332). and seems to have retained the rank of a Colonia under the Empire, as we find it bearing that designation both in Pliny and in inscriptions. (Plin. iii. 11. s. 16 ; Orell. Inscr. 867 ; Mommsen, Inscr. R. N. 735, 745.) Its position on the Appian Way doubtless contributed to its prosperity, and it is mentioned more than once by Cicero as a customary halting-place in proceeding from Rome to Brundusium. (Cic. ad Att. v. 5, xvi. 5.) It appears indeed that the great orator had himself a villa there, as one of his letters is dated " de Venusino" (ad Fam. xiv. 20). But the chief interest of Venusia is undoubtedly derived from its having been the birthplace of Horace, who was born there in the consulship of L. Manlius Torquatus and L. Aurelius Cotta, B. c. 65. (Hor. Carm. iii. 21. 1.) The works of the poet abound in allusions to the neighbourhood of his native city, the fountain of Bandusia, the forests of Mount Vultur, &c. But it does not appear that he ever resided there in the latter years of his life, having lost his paternal estate, which was confiscated in the civil wars. (Id. Ep. ii. 2.)

We hear nothing of Venusia under the Roman Empire, but it is certain from the Liber Coloniarum, which mentions it among the Civitates Apuliae, and from the Itineraries, that it continued to exist as a city, and apparently one of the most considerable in this part of Italy. (Ptol. iii. 1. § 73 ; Lib. Colon. pp. 210, 261; Itin. Ant. pp. 104, 113, 121 ; Tab. Peut.) This is further confirmed by inscriptions, in one of which it is called "splendida civitas Venusinorum." (Mommsen, I. R. N. 706.) It retained the same consideration throughout the middle ages, and is still an episcopal city with about 6000 inhabitants. Its antiquities have been illustrated with a profusion of erudition by Italian writers, but it has few ancient remains of much interest ; though fragments of ancient edifices, mosaic pavements, &c. have been found on the site, as well as numerous inscriptions. These last have been collected and published by Mons. Lupoli, in his Marmora Venusina

COIN OF VENUSIA.

(added as an appendix to the Iter Venusinum, 4to. Neapoli, 1797), and more recently by Mommsen, in his Inscriptiones Regni Neapolitani (pp. 39—48). Concerning the antiquities of Venusia in general, see the work of Lupoli above quoted, and that of Cimaglia (Antiquitates Venusinae, 4to. Neapol. 1757.) [E. H. B.]

VEPITENUM or VIPITENUM, a place in the district occupied by the Venostes in Rhaetia, between Veldidena and Tridentum. (It. Ant. pp. 275, 280 ; Tab. Peut.) Its modern representative is, in all probability, the town of Sterzing on the Eisach, at the foot of the Brenner. [L. S.]

VERAGRI (Οὐάραγροι). The Veragri are placed by Caesar (B. G. iii. 1, 6) in the Valais of Switzerland between the Nantuates and the Seduni, [NANTUATES; SEDUNI]. Their town was Octodurus (Martigny), whence the Veragri are called Octodurenses by Pliny [OCTODURUS]. Dion Cassius (xxxix. 5), using Caesar as he generally used him, says that the Veragri extended from the territory of the Allobroges and the Leman lake to the Alps; which is not true. Strabo (iv. p. 204) mentions the Varagri, as he calls them, between the Caturiges and the Nantuatae ; and Pliny (iii. 20) between the Seduni and the Salassi: the Salassi are on the Italian side of the Alps in the Val d'Aosta. Livy (xxi. 38) places the Veragri among the Alps and on the road to the pass of the Pennine Alps, or the Great St. Bernard, which is correct. He says that the pass was occupied by half German tribes. [G. L.]

VERBANUS LACUS (ὁ Οὐερβανὸς λίμνη! Lago Maggiore), one of the principal lakes of Northern Italy, formed by the river Ticinus, where it first issues from the valleys of the Alps. (Plin. iii. 19. s. 24.) It is the largest of the three great lakes of Northern Italy, whence its modern name of Lago Maggiore; though Virgil appears to have considered the Larius as the largest, as he calls it, " Te, Lari maxime," and singularly enough does not mention the Verbanus at all. (Georg. ii. 159.) Strabo, by a strange mistake, describes the river Addua as flowing from the Lake Verbanus, and the Ticinus from the Larius (iv. p. 209): this may, perhaps, be an error of the copyists, but is more probably an accidental blunder of the author. He gives the length of the lake at 400 stadia, or 40 geog. miles, which is somewhat below the truth, the actual length being 46 geog. miles: its breadth does not exceed 4 or 5 miles, except in one part, where it expands to a width of from 8 to 10 miles. [E. H. B.]

VERBICAE or VERBICES (Οὐέρβικαι or Οὐερβίκες, Ptol. iv. 1. § 10), a people of Mauretania Tingitana. [T. H. D.]

VERBIGENUS PAGUS. [HELVETII, Vol. I. p. 1041.]

VERBINUM, in Gallia, is placed by the Itins. on a road from Bagacum (Bavai) to Durocortorum (Reims). Duronum is between Bagacum and Verbinum [DURONUM]. All the several distances between Bagacum and Durocortorum do not agree in the Antonine Itin. and the Table. The sum total of these distances in the Table is 53 M. P., and the Itin., though it makes the several distances amount to 63 M. P., still gives the sum total at 53 M. P. But these must be Gallic leagues, as D'Anville shows. He supposes Verbinum to be Vervins, which in fact is the same name as Verbinum. The table writes it Vironum. Vervins is in the department of Aisne, about 20 miles NE. of Laon. [G. L.]

VERCELLAE (Οὐερκέλλαι, Ptol. iii. 1. § 36;

Οὐερκέλλοι, Strab. v. p. 218; Βερκέλλαι, Plut. *Mar.* 25: *Vercelli*), the chief city of the Libici, in Gallia Cisalpina. It lay on the W. bank of the Sessites (*Sesia*); but perhaps the ancient town should be sought at *Borgo Vercelli*, about 2 miles from the modern city. In the time of Strabo it was an unfortified village (*l. c.*), but subsequently became a strong and not unimportant Roman municipium. (Tac. *Hist.* i. 70; cf. *De clar. Orator.* 8; also Orell. *Inscr.* 3044, 3945.) Here the highroad from Ticinum to Augusta Praetoria was crossed by a road running westwards from Mediolanum. (*Itin. Ant.* pp. 282. 344, 347, 350.) At the beginning of the 5th century it was rapidly falling to decay. (Hieron. *Epist.* 17.) There were some gold mines at a place called Ictimuli, or Vicus Ictimulorum, in the district of Vercellae (Strab. *l. c.*; Plin. xxxiii. 4. s. 21), which must have been of considerable importance, as the last cited authority mentions a law forbidding that more than 5000 men should be employed in them. The true position of these mines has, however, been the subject of some dispute. The question is fully discussed by Durandi in his treatise *Dell' antica Condizione del Vercellese.* The city was distinguished for its worship of Apollo, whence it is called Apollineae Vercellae by Martial (x. 12. 1); and there was in its vicinity a grove, and perhaps a temple sacred to that deity (Stat. *Silv.* i. 4. 59), which is probably to be sought at a small place called *Pollone*, at the foot of the Alps. (Cf. Cic. *Fam.* xi. 19; Plin. iii. 17. s. 21; Bellini, *Antichità di Vercelli*.)   [T. H. D.]

VEREASUECA, a harbour belonging to the town of Argenomescum. in the territory of the Cantabri, in Hispania Tarraconensis. (Plin. iv. 20. s. 34.) Probably *Puerto de S. Martin.* (Cf. Florez, *Esp. Sagr.* xxiv. p. 44.)   [T. H. D.]

VERELA. [VARIA.]

VERETUM (Οὐερητόν, Strab., Ptol.: *Eth.* Veretinus: *Sta Maria di Vereto*), a town of Calabria, in the district or territory of the Sallentines, and within a few miles of the Iapygian promontory. Strabo tells us that it was formerly called Baris, and describes it as if it were a seaport town; but both Pliny and Ptolemy rank it among the inland towns of the Sallentines; and there seems no doubt that its site is marked by the old church of *Sta Maria di Vereto*, the name of which is found on old maps, between the villages of *Salve* and *Roggiano*, about 6 miles from the *Capo di Leuca*, and 10 from *Ugento*, the correct distance given in the Tabula from Uxentum to Veretum. (Strab. vi. p. 281; Plin. iii. 11. s. 16; Ptol. iii. 1. § 76; *Tab. Peut.*; Galateo, *de Sit. Iapyg.* p. 99; Holsten. *ad Cluver.* p. 283; Romanelli. vol. ii. p. 35.) The "ager Veretinus" is mentioned also in the Liber Coloniarum (p. 262) among the "civitates Calabriae," and doubtless comprised the whole district as far as the Iapygian promontory.   [E. H. B.]

VERGAE. [BRUTTII.]

VERGELLUS, a rivulet or torrent, which crossed the field of battle of Cannae. It is not indeed mentioned by either Livy or Polybius in their circumstantial accounts of the battle, but it is noticed by both Florus and Valerius Maximus in connection with a story that seems to have been current among the Romans, that its course was choked up by the dead bodies of the slain, to such an extent that the Carthaginian troops crossed over them as a bridge. (Flor. ii. 6. § 18; Val. Max. ix. 2, Ext. § 2.) The same incident is alluded to by other writers, but

without mentioning the name of the stream. (Sil. Ital. viii. 668; Lucian, *Dial. Mort.* 12. § 2.) The stream meant is probably a rivulet which falls into the Aufidus on its right bank between Cannae and Canusium, and is wholly dry in summer.   [E. H. B.]

VERGENTUM, a place in Hispania Baetica, with the surname of Julii Genius. (Plin. iii. 1. s. 3.) Now *Gelves* or *Gines*.   [T. H. D.]

VERGI'LIA (Οὐεργγιλία, Ptol. ii. 6. § 61: *Eth.* Vergilienses, Plin. iii. 3. s. 4), a town of the Bastetani, in Hispania Tarraconensis. It has been identified by some writers with *Murcia.* (D'Anville, *Geogr. Anc.* i. p. 31; Mentelle, *Esp. Anc.* p. 186.)   [T. H. D.]

VERGIUM, a fortress in Hispania Tarraconensis (Liv. xxxiv. 21). Reichard, but perhaps without adequate grounds, identifies it with the present *Berga.*   [T. H. D.]

VERGOANUM. [LERINA.]

VERGUNNI, the name of an Alpine people mentioned in the Trophy of the Alps (Plin. iii. 20). They are supposed to be represented by the name *Vergons* or *Vergon*, between *Senez* [SANITIUM] and *Glandèves*, and about half-way between these two places.   [G. L.]

VERISA (Βήρισα), a town in the interior of Pontus, on the road from Sebastopolis to Sebastia. (*It. Ant.* pp. 205, 214; Basil. Magn. *Epist. ult.*) Its site is yet uncertain, some identifying it with *Cora*, others with *Baulus.*   [L. S.]

VERLU'CIO, a place in Britannia Romana, on the road from Isca Silurum to Calleva (*Itin. Ant.* p. 486), and apparently in the territory of the Dobuni. It has been variously identified with the village of *Leckham* on the *Avon*, with *Westbury, Spy Park*, and *Whetham.*   [T. H. D.]

VERNEA, a fort in Rhaetia, on a steep height above the banks of the river Athesis, not far from Tridentum, where its site is still marked by the *Dos di Trent.* (Cassiod. *Var.* iii. 48; Paul. Diac. iii. 31, where it is called Ferruge; Pallhausen, *Beschreib. der Röm. Heerstrasse von Verona nach Augsburg*, p. 28.)   [L. S.]

VERNODUBRUM, a river of Gallia Narbonensis mentioned by Pliny (iii. 4) after the Tecum, which is the Tichis [TICHIS] of Mela. Pliny does not mention the Telis or Tetis (*Tet*), and it has been conjectured that he gives the name of Vernodubrum to the Telis. But there is a river *Gly* or *Agly*, north of the *Tet* and not far from it, which flows into the Mediterranean past *Rivesaltes*, and a branch of the *Gly* is still named *Verdouble* or *Verdoubra*, which is certainly the Vernodubrum. (D'Anville, *Notice, &c.*)   [G. L.]

VERNOSOL, in Aquitania, is placed in the Antonine Itin. on a road from Beneharnum [BENEHARNUM] to Tolosa (*Toulouse*). This circuitous road ran through Lugdunum Convenarum and Calagorris. Vernosol is between Calagorris (*Cazères*) and *Toulouse*. Vernosol is *Vernose*.   [G. L.]

VERODUNENSES. This name does not occur in any document earlier than the Notitia of the Gallic Provinces, which was probably drawn up at the commencement of the fifth century of our era. Civitas Verodunensium in the Notitia is the capital of a people, and is named last in the first of the two Belgicae. The name Virodunum occurs in the Antonine Itin. and so the name is written on some medals. It is placed on a route from Durocortorum (*Reims*) to Divodurum (*Metz*). In the middle age writings it is Viredunum, Viridunum, and Virdu- num, which last abbreviated form comes nearest to *Verdun*, which is the capital of the Verodunenses. *Verdun* is west of *Metz*, in the department of *Meuse*, and on the *Meuse* or *Maas*. There was a place named Fines [FINES, No. 13] between Virodu- num and Divodurum, which probably marked the limit between the Verodunenses and the Medioma- trici.　　　　　　　　　　　　　[G. L.]

VERODUNUM. [VERODUNENSES.]

VEROLA'MIUM and VERULA'MIUM (Οὐρολά- νιον, Ptol. ii. 3. § 21), the capital of the Catyeuch- lani in Britannia Romana, on the road from Lon- dinium to Lindum and Eboracum. (*Itin. Ant.* pp. 471, 476, 479.) It was probably the residence of Cassi- vellaunus, which was taken by Caesar (*B. Gall.* v. 21), and subsequently became a considerable Roman municipium, (Tac. *Ann.* xiv. 33.) It is *Old Ve- rulam*, near *St. Alban's*, in *Hertfordshire*, which latter town rose from its ruins; and its celebrated abbey church is said to be built in great part of Roman bricks. (Camden, p. 350, seq.)　　[T. H. D.]

VEROMANDUI (Οὐερομάνδυες, Ptol. iii. 9. § 11), a Belgic people, who in B.C. 57 were supposed to be able to raise 10,000 fighting men (Caesar, *B. G.* ii. 4); unless Caesar's text means that they and the Velocasses together mustered this number [VE- LOCASSES]. They joined the Nervii and the Atre- bates in the attack on Caesar's army on the Sabis (*Sambre*). The Veromandui attacked the eleventh and eighth legions, which were in Caesar's centre, and they were driven back to the river. They are not mentioned again in the Commentaries.

The Veromandui had the Ambiani and the Atrebates on the west, and the Suessiones on the south. On the north they were neighbours of the Nervii. Their chief town was afterwards Augusta Veromanduorum, *St. Quentin*, on the *Somme*, in the department of *Aisne*, and in the old division of France named *Vermandois*. The name Civitas Ve- romanduorum occurs in the Notitia of the Gallic Provinces. [AUGUSTA VEROMANDUORUM.] [G.L.]

VEROMETUM, a town of the Coritani in Bri- tannia Romana, between Ratae and Margidunum. (*Itin. Ant.* pp. 477, 479, where it is also called Vernometum.) Camden (p. 575) places it at *Bur- rough Hill*, near *Willoughby on the Wold*, in the S. part of *Nottinghamshire*.　　　　　　　[T. H. D.]

VERONA (Οὐήρωνα, Ptol. iii. 1. § 31 ; Θυήρων, Strab. iv. p. 206, v. p. 213; Βερῶνη, Procop. *B.G.* ii. 29, iii. 3, &c.; and Βερῶνα, *Ib.* iv. 33 : *Eth.* Vero- nensis : *Verona*), an important town in Gallia Transpadana, seated on the river Athesis (" Verona Athesi circumflua," Sil. It. viii. 595), and chiefly on its W. bank. There is some difficulty in deter- mining whether Verona was a city of the Euganei or of the Cenomani, from the little knowledge which we possess of the respective boundaries of those peoples, and from the confusion which prevails upon the subject in ancient authors. By Ptolemy (*l. c.*), who does not mention the Euganei, it is ascribed to the Cenomani; and Catullus (lxvii. 34), in a passage, however, which has been banished by some editors as not genuine, Brixia, which undoubtedly belonged to the Cenomani, is styled the mother city of Verona. Pliny, on the other hand (iii. 19. s. 23), gives Verona partly to the Rhaeti and partly to the Euganei, and Strabo (*l. c.*) attributes it to the former. Some have sought a solution of this difficulty by assuming that the city belonged originally to the Euganei, but was subsequently occupied by the Cenomani, referring to

Livy, v. 35. (Cf. Justin, xx. 5.) We know little or nothing of the early history of Verona. Under the Roman dominion it became a colony with the surname of Augusta, and one of the finest and most flourishing cities in that part of Italy (Tac. *H.* iii. 8; *Itin. Ant.* p. 128 ; Strab. v. p. 213; Grut. *Inscr.* p. 166. 2.) The surrounding country was exceed- ingly fruitful, producing good wine, excellent apples, and abundance of spelt (alica, Plin. xviii. 11. s. 29, xiv. 1. s. 3, xv. 14. s. 14; Cassiod. *Var.* xii. 4). The Rhaetian wine also is praised by Virgil. (*G.* ii. 94; cf. Strab. iv. 206; Suet. *Oct.* 77.) The situation of Verona rendered it a great thoroughfare and the centre of several highroads (*Itin. Ant.* pp. 128, 174, 275, 282; *Itin. Hier.* p. 558.)

Verona was celebrated in history for the battle fought by Marius in the Campi Raudii, in its neighbourhood, against the Cimbri. (Vell. Pat. ii. 12; Florus, iii. 3.) From an inscription still extant on one of its gates, now called the *Porta de' Borsari*, the walls of Verona appear to have been newly erected in the reign of the emperor Gallienus, A. D. 265. It was besieged by Constantine on his march from Gaul to Rome, and, though obstinately defended by Ruricius Pompeianus, obliged to surrender at dis- cretion. (*Paneg. Vet.* ix. 9. sqq.) It was likewise the scene of the victory of Theodoric over Odoacer. (Jornand. *Get.* 57.) Theodoric made it one of his residences, and often held his court there: a repre- sentation of his palace is still extant upon a seal. (Gibbon, *Decl. and Fall,* vol. v. p. 22, ed. Smith.) It was at Verona that the splendid wedding took place between king Autharis and Theudelinda. (Procop. *B. G.* iii. 5; Paul. Diac. iii. 29.) But, more than by all these events, Verona is illustrious as having been the birthplace of Catullus (Ovid. *Amor.* iii. 15. 7; Mart. x. 103; Plin. xxxvi. 6. s. 7); though it is exceedingly doubtful whether the re- mains of a villa on the *Lago di Garda*, commonly called the villa of Catullus, could really have be- longed to him. The honour sometimes claimed for Verona of having given birth to the architect Vi- truvius Pollio arises from a mistaken interpretation of the inscription on the arch of the Gavii, formerly existing at Verona, but pulled down in the year 1805. The inscription related to the great architect's less celebrated namesake, Vitruvius Cerdo. (*Descriz. di Verona,* pt. i. p. 86.) Some are of opinion that the elder Pliny also was born at Verona, but it is more probable that he was a native of Comum. In the life of him ascribed to the pen of Suetonius, he is styled Novocomensis ; and when he calls himself in his Preface the *conterraneus* of Catullus, that epi- thet by no means necessarily implies that he was the fellow-citizen of the poet, but rather that he was merely his fellow-countryman, or from the same province.

The amphitheatre at Verona is a very striking monument of antiquity. Although not nearly so large as the Colosseum, it is in a much better state of preservation, owing to the pains which have al- ways been taken to keep it in repair. It is also of a more costly material than the Roman amphitheatre; for whilst the latter is built of *travertino*, that at Verona is of marble, from some quarries in the neigh- bourhood. The substructions are of Roman brick- work. The date of its erection cannot be ascer- tained, but it must undoubtedly have been posterior to the time of Augustus. A great part of the ex- ternal arcade was thrown down by an earthquake in the year 1184. Its form is elliptical, the larger diameter being 513 feet externally and 248 internally; the smaller one, 410 feet externally and 147 feet internally. The banks or rows of seats are at present 45 in number, but, from the repairs and alterations which the building has undergone, it is not certain whether this was the original number. It is estimated that it would afford seats for about 22,000 persons.

There are also a few remains of a Roman theatre, on the left bank of the *Adige*, at the foot of the hill immediately under the castle of *S. Pietro.* It appears from two decrees of king Berengarius, dated in 895 and 913, that the theatre was then regarded as of the highest antiquity, and had in great part gone to ruin; on which account its destruction was allowed. (*Descriz. di Verona,* pt. ii. p. 108, sqq.)

We have already alluded to the ancient gate called the *Porta de' Borsari.* It is evidently older than the walls of Gallienus, the elevation of which in the space of 8 months is recorded upon it; since a previous inscription has been erased in order to make room for the new one. It is a double gate, of a very florid style of architecture, concerning the merits of which architects have held widely different opinions. The walls of Gallienus, to judge of them from the vestiges which still remain, were of a construction sufficiently solid, notwithstanding the shortness of the time in which they were erected. The other remains of antiquity at Verona, as the *Porta de' Leoni,* the baths, &c., do not require any particular description in this place.

The chief works on Verona and its antiquities are the splendid ones of Count Scip. *Maffei,* entitled *Verona Illustrata,* and *Museum Veronense.* Onuphrius Panvinius also described its remains (*Antiq. Veron.* lib. viii. Pat. 1668). Some account of them will likewise be found in the *Descrizione di Verona e della sua Provincia,* by Giovambatista da Pertico. 8vo. Verona, 1820.   [T. H. D.]

VERONES. [BERONES.]

VERRUCINI, a Gallic people near the Alps in the Provincia. Pliny (iii. 4) says: "Regio Camatullicorum, dein Suelteri, supraque Verrucini." [CAMATULLICI; SUELTERI.] There is nothing to guide us in fixing the position of the Verrucini, except their position with respect to these two other tribes, and the fact that there is a place named *Vérignon,* between *Draguignan* and *Ries. Draguignan* is in the department of *Var,* and *Ries* is on the site of Reii [REII APOLLINARES].   [G. L.]

VERRUGO or VERRUCA (Ἐρρουκα, Diod.: *Colle Ferro?*), a town or fortress in the territory of the Volsci, which is repeatedly mentioned during the wars of the Romans with that people. The name first occurs in B. C. 445, when we are told that the place had been recently occupied and fortified by the Romans, evidently as a post of offence against the Volscians; a proceeding which that people resented so much that it became the occasion of a fresh war. (Liv. iv. 1.) We do not know at what period it fell again into the hands of the Volscians, but in B. C. 409 it was recovered and again garrisoned by the Romans. (*Ib.* 55, 56; Diod. xiv. 11.) It, however, fell once more into the hands of the Volscians in B. C. 407 (Liv. iv. 58), and apparently continued in their possession till B. C. 394, when it was again occupied with a garrison by the military tribune C. Aemilius, but lost soon after in consequence of the defeat of his colleague Sp. Postumius. (Liv. v. 28; Diod. xiv. 98.) From this time it wholly disappears from history. It is very doubtful whether it ever was a

town, the manner in which it is mentioned by Livy, in connection with the Arx Carventana, seeming to prove that it was a mere fort or stronghold, garrisoned and fortified, on account of its natural strength and advantageous position. Its site cannot be determined with any certainty, but from the name itself there can be no doubt that it was situated on a projecting knoll or peak; hence its site has been sought by Nibby (followed by Abeken) at *Colle Ferro,* near *Segni; Colle Sacco,* in the same neighbourhood, has as plausible a claim. (Nibby, *Dintorni,* vol. iii. p. 473; Gell, *Top. of Rome,* p. 458; Abeken, *Mittel-Italien,* p. 75.)   [E. H. B.]

VERTACOMICORI, a pagus of the Vocontii in Gallia Provincia, to whom Pliny (iii. 17) attributes the foundation of Novaria in Gallia Cisalpina [NOVARIA]. The name seems to be preserved in *Vercors,* a district in the old country of the Vocontii, in the northern part of the diocese of *Die* [DEA VOCONTIORUM]. In some middle age documents the name appears in the abbreviated form Vercorium, which is the next step to *Vercors* (D'Anville. *Notice, &c.*).   [G. L.]

VERTERAE, a town of the Brigantes in Britannia Romana. (*Itin. Ant.* pp. 467, 476.) Variously identified with *Brough* in *Westmoreland* and *Bowes.*   [T. H. D.]

VERTINAE (Οὐερτίναι: *Verzino*), a small town of Bruttium, mentioned only by Strabo (vi. p. 254), who places it in the interior of that country. Its name is still retained by the village of *Verzino,* about 7 miles NW. of *Strongoli,* the ancient Petelia.   [E. H. B.]

VERUBIUM (Οὐερούβιον, Ptol. ii. 3. § 5), a promontory on the N. coast of Britannia Barbara, most probably *Noss Head.*   [T. H. D.]

VERVES (Οὐερουείς, Ptol. iv. 1. § 10), a people of Mauretania Tingitana.   [T. H. D.]

VERULAE (*Eth.* Verulanus: *Veroli*), a city of the Hernici, but included in Latium in the more extensive sense of that name, situated in the Apennines N. of the valley of the *Sacco,* between Alatrium and the valley of the Liris. It was apparently one of the chief cities of the Hernici, and was certainly a member of the Hernican League: but its name is not mentioned separately in history till the final war of that people with Rome, in B. C. 306. On that occasion the citizens of Verulae, together with those of Alatrium and Ferentinum, took part against the Anagnians, and refused to join in the hostilities against Rome. For this reason they were rewarded after the termination of the war by being left in possession of their own laws and magistrates, which they preferred to receiving the Roman "civitas." (Liv. ix. 42, 43.) The period at which they ultimately became Roman citizens is uncertain. Florus vaguely asserts that a triumph had been celebrated over the people of Verulae (Flor. i. 11. § 6) but this is probably a mere rhetorical flourish: there is no occasion known in history to which it can be referred. Under the Roman dominion Verulae became a quiet and somewhat obscure country town. According to the Liber Coloniarum it received a body of colonists in the time of the Gracchi, and again under the reign of Nerva. But it is probable that it always retained its municipal rank. It is mentioned by Pliny among the municipal towns of the Fifth Region (Plin. iii. 5. s. 9), but is not again noticed in history. Its secluded position probably rendered it a place of small importance. The ancient site is still occupied by the modern town of *Veroli*, which retains also some portions of the ancient walls in the polygonal or Cyclopean style. (Westphal, *Röm. Kamp.* p. 87; Abeken, *Mittel-Italien*, p. 147.)　　　　　　　　　　[E. H. B.]

VERULAMIUM. [VERULAMIUM.]

VERURIUM (*Ὀυερούριον*, Ptol. ii. 5. § 7), a town in the N. part of Lusitania, perhaps *S. Vincent de Beira*.　　　　　　　　　　　　[T. H. D.]

VESASPE (*Ὀυέσασπη*, Ptol. vi. 2. § 12), a town in Media Atropatene, perhaps the same as the present *Casbin*.　　　　　　　　　　　　[V.]

VESCELIA, a town of the Oretani in Hispania Tarraconensis (Liv. xxxv. 22), perhaps· *Vilches*. (Ukert, ii. pt. i. p. 413.)　　　　　　[T. H. D.]

VESCELLIUM or VERCELLIUM, a town of the Hirpini, of uncertain site. Its name is mentioned by Livy (xxiii. 37) as having been recovered by the praetor M. Valerius, after it had revolted to the Carthaginians. The reading in Livy is very uncertain, but Pliny also mentions the Vescellani among the municipal communities of the Hirpini. (Plin. iii. 11. s. 16.)　　　　　　　　　　　[E. H. B.]

VESCI FAVENTIA (*Ὀυέσκις*, Ptol. ii. 4. § 11), a town in Hispania Baetica, between Singili and Astigi. (Plin. iii. 1. s. 3.)　　　　　[T. H. D.]

VESCIA (*Eth.* Vescinus), a city of Latium, in the most extended sense of that name, but originally a city of the Ausones, situated in a plain to the S. of the Liris (*Garigliano*). Livy in one passage tells us distinctly that the Ausones had three cities, Ausona, Minturnae, and Vescia, all of which were betrayed into the hands of the Romans by a party within their walls, and the inhabitants put to the sword in B. C. 314. (Liv. ix. 25.) The name of Vescia is mentioned also about 25 years before as affording shelter to the remains of the Latin army defeated by the consuls Manlius and Decius in B. C. 340. (Id. viii. 11.) But after the capture of the city in 314, no mention of it again occurs, and it is probable that it never recovered from that calamity. Minturnae indeed is the only one of these three cities which again appears in history; but the "ager Vescinus" is repeatedly mentioned (Liv. x. 20, 21, 31), and would seem to have extended from the banks of the Liris as far as the extreme point of the ridge of Mount Massicus. The Roman colony of Sinuessa, which was situated just where that ridge abuts upon the sea, is expressly said to have been planted "in saltu Vescino." (Liv. x. 21.) But all trace of the city seems to have been lost. Pliny does not even notice the name among the *extinct* cities of Latium and Campania, and we are wholly without a clue to its precise situation.　　　　　　　[E. H. B.]

VESCITANIA, a district in Spain mentioned only by Pliny (iii. 3. s. 4). [OSCA.] [T. H. D.]

VESDIANTII. [VEDIANTII.]

VESERIS, a river of Campania, the name of which is known only in connection with the great battle fought with the Latins by T. Manlius Torquatus and P. Decius Mus, B. C. 340. That battle is described by Livy as having been fought "haud procul radicibus Vesuvii montis, qua via ad Veserim ferebat" (viii. 8), an expression which would leave us in doubt whether Veseris was the name of a town or of a river. In another passage he refers to the same battle as having been fought "ad Veserim" (x. 28); and Cicero also twice notices it as "pugna ad Veserim" or "apud Veserim." (Cic. *de Fin.* i. 7, *de Off.* iii. 31.) Valerius Maximus uses the latter

phrase (vi. 4. § 1). The only author whose expressions are free from ambiguity is Aurelius Victor, who distinctly speaks of that celebrated battle as having been fought "apud Veserim fluvium" (*de Vir. Ill.* 28), and adds that the Romans had pitched their camp on its banks (" positis apud Veserim fluvium castris," *Ib.* 26). The authority of Victor is not indeed worth much on points of detail, but there is no reason to reject it in this instance, as it is certainly not at variance with the phrases of Livy and Cicero. The Veseris was probably a small stream, and is not mentioned on any other occasion, or by any geographer, so that it is wholly impossible now to identify it.　　　　　　　　[E. H. B.]

VESIO'NICA, a town of Umbria mentioned only by Pliny, who names the Vesionicates among the municipal communities of that country. (Plin. iii. 14. s. 19.) It is supposed to be represented by *Civitella di Benezzone*, in the upper valley of the Tiber, 7 miles SE. of *Perugia*. (Cluver. *Ital.* p. 627.)　　　　　　　　　　　　[E. H. B.]

VESO'NTIO (*Ὀυισόντιον*, Ptol. ii. 9. § 21: *Besançon*), in Gallia, the chief city of the Sequani. The name occurs in Dion Cassius (xxxviii. 34, lxiii. 24), where Reimarus has written Βεσοντίωνα for the MSS. reading Ὀυεσοντίωνα, without any reason. In Ausonius (*Gratiarum Act.*) the form Visontio occurs, and he speaks of a "municipalis schola" in the place. The orthography of the word varied, as we might expect; and other forms occur in Ammianus. D'Anville says that the name is Vesant on a milestone which bears the name of Trajan, and was found at *Mandeure* [EPAMANDUODURUM, in which article the name is incorrectly printed Vesont].

When Caesar (B. C. 58) was marching through the country of the Sequani towards the German king Ariovistus, he heard that the German was intending to occupy Vesontio, but Caesar got there before him (*B. G.* i. 38.) He describes the town as nearly surrounded by the *Doubs* [DUBIS], and he says that the part which was not surrounded by the river was only 600 Roman feet wide. This neck of land was filled by an eminence, the base of which on each side was washed by the river. There was a wall along this neck of land, which made it a strong fortress, and the wall connected the heights with the town. Caesar's description is exact except as to the width of the neck of land, which D'Anville says is about 1500 Roman feet; and accordingly either Caesar was mistaken, or there is an error in his text in the numerals, which is always a possible thing. Vesontio when Caesar took it was well supplied with everything for war, and its position made it a strong place. Caesar set out from Vesontio to fight the German king, whom he defeated in the plain between the *Vosges* and the Rhine. The battle-field was only 5 miles from the Rhine (*B. G.* i. 53, in which passage the true reading is "milia passuum...circiter quinque," not "quinquaginta.") In the winter of B. C. 58—57 Caesar quartered his men among the Sequani, and we may assume that Vesontio was one of the places where he fixed his troops.

Vesontio has been several times sacked and destroyed by Alemanni, by Huns, and others. It is a town built on the ruins of former towns. The ground has been raised above 20 feet, and where it has been dug into, Roman remains, medals, and other antiquities have been discovered.

The modern town of *Besançon* consists of two parts. The upper town, once called *La Ville*, is built on the peninsula, and the citadel stands on the steep rock which Caesar describes as occupying the neck of land, where the river does not flow. The lower town is on the other side of the river opposite to the peninsula, with which it is connected by a stone bridge, the foundations of which are Roman.

There is a Roman triumphal arch with a single passage. The date of its construction does not appear. This arch which was nearly hidden by rubbish and buildings has been partially uncovered and restored within the present century. It is decorated with sculptures. There are some remains of the aqueduct which supplied Vesontio with water from a distant source. It was constructed of a soft stone. It terminated in the town in a vast reservoir of an oval form, which was covered by a roof supported by columns. The water was distributed from the reservoir all through the town: and in many parts of *Besançon* there have been found traces of the conduits which conveyed the water to the private houses. (*Penny Cyclopaedia,* art. *Besançon;* Richard et Hocquart, *Guide du Voyageur.*) [G. L.]

VESPA'SIAE. [NURSIA.]

VESPERIES, a town of the Varduli in Hispania Tarraconensis. (Plin. iii. 20. s. 34.) It is identified with the present *Bermeo.* (Cf. Mentelle, *Esp. Mod.* p. 37.)   [T. H. D.]

VESTINI (Ὀυηστῖνοι), a people of Central Italy, who occupied a mountainous tract extending from the coast of the Adriatic to the lofty mountains near the sources of the Aternus. Here they met the Sabines, whose territory bounded them on the W.; thence they were bounded by the high mountain range which forms the southern barrier of the valley of the Aternus, and separated them from the Aequi and Marsi; while towards the S. and E. the river Aternus itself, from the point where it takes the sudden bend towards the NE., became the limit of their territory, and their frontier towards the Peligni and Marrucini. Along the coast of the Adriatic they held only the narrow space between the mouth of the Aternus and that of the Matrinus, a distance of about 6 miles; the latter river apparently formed the northern limit of their territory from its mouth to its source, and thence to the high ridge of the Central Apennines their exact frontier cannot be traced. But it is almost immediately after passing the point where the Vestini adjoined the Praetutii on the one hand and the Sabines on the other, that the chain of the Apennines rises abruptly into the lofty group or mass, of which the *Monte Corno* (commonly called the *Gran Sasso d' Italia*) is the highest summit. This mountain is the most elevated in the whole range of the Apennines, attaining to a height of 9500 feet; and those immediately adjoining it are but little inferior, forming a rugged and irregular mass of mountains, which is continued without interruption by a range of inferior but still very considerable elevation, in a SE. direction. This range is almost continuous with the equally lofty ridge of the *Monte Morrone,* the two being separated only by the deep and narrow gorge below *Popoli,* through which the Aternus finds its way to the sea. Hence the territory of the Vestini is naturally divided into two distinct regions, the one consisting of the upper valley of the Aternus, W. of the lofty mountain range above described, the other of the tract on the E. of the same mountains, sloping gradually thence to the sea. This last district is very hilly and rugged, but has the advantage of a far milder climate than that of the basin of the Aternus, which is a bleak and cold upland region, having much analogy

with the valley of the Peligni (of which it may be considered in some degree as a continuation), but from its considerable elevation above the sea (2380 feet in its upper part) suffering still more severely from cold in winter. The Vestini, however, did not occupy the whole of the valley of the Aternus; Amiternum, near the sources of that river, which was one of the oldest abodes of the Sabines, having continued, even in the days of Pliny, to belong to that people, and though Ptolemy assigns it to the Vestini, it is probable that in this, as in many similar cases, he was guided by geographical views rather than the real ethnical distribution of the tribes. (Strab. v. p. 228; Plin. iii. 12. s. 17; Ptol. iii. 1. § 59.) But the precise line of demarcation between the Vestini and the Sabines, cannot now be determined.

No author has left to us any distinct statement concerning the origin and affinities of the Vestini, but there seems to be no reason to doubt that they were, in common with the other tribes by which they were surrounded, a Sabine race. It would indeed have been almost impossible for that people to have extended themselves to the S., and sent forth their numerous colonies, the Peligni, the Samnites, &c., had not the valley of the Aternus been already occupied by a kindred and friendly race. The close connection which we find subsisting between the four tribes of the Vestini, Marrucini, Peligni, and Marsi, may be also taken as a strong presumption of their common origin, and there seem good reasons for supposing them all to have been derived from a Sabine stock. The first mention of the Vestini in history occurs in B. C. 324, when they concluded an alliance with the Samnites against Rome. It was feared that their example would be speedily followed by the Marrucini, Peligni, and Marsi, but this was not the case, and the Vestini, unsupported by their allies, were unable to resist the Roman arms: they were defeated and dispersed by the consul D. Junius Brutus, and took refuge in their fortified towns, of which Cutina and Cingilia were successively taken by assault. (Liv. viii. 29.) From this time we hear nothing more of the Vestini till B. C. 301, when they concluded a treaty with the Romans, which appears to have been an alliance on favourable terms (Id. x. 3); and from this time the Vestini became the faithful allies of the rising republic. In the enumeration of the forces of the Italian allies in B. C. 225, Polybius mentions the Vestini, together with the Marsi, Marrucini, and Frentani (the Peligni being omitted), and estimates their joint contingent at 20,000 foot and 4000 horse soldiers (ii. 24); but we have no means of judging of the proportion furnished by each nation.

No other mention is found in history of the Vestini, with the exception of casual notices of their troops serving as auxiliaries in the Roman armies (Ennius, *Ann. Fr.* viii. 6; Liv. xliv. 40), until the outbreak of the Social War, in B. C. 90. On this occasion they followed the example of the Marsi and Peligni, as well as of their more immediate neighbours the Picentines, and were among the first to declare themselves in insurrection against Rome. Liv. Epit. lxxii.; Oros. v. 18; Appian, *B. C.* i. 39.) There can be no doubt that throughout that contest they furnished their contingent to the armies of the Marsi; but their name is not specially mentioned till towards the close of the war, when we learn that they were defeated and reduced to submission, apparently somewhat sooner than the other confederates. (Liv. Epit. lxxv., lxxvi.; Appian, B. C. i. 52; Oros. v. 18.) There is no doubt that they at this time received the Roman franchise, and henceforth became merged in the ordinary condition of Roman citizens. Hence we hear nothing more of them in history, though it is evident that they retained their existence as a separate tribe, which is recognised by all the geographers, as well as by inscriptions. (Strab. v. p. 241; Plin. iii. 12. s. 17; Ptol. iii. 1. § 59; Orell. Inscr. 4036.) From the last source we learn that they were enrolled in the Quirinian tribe. Their territory was included in the Fourth Region of Augustus (Plin. l. c.), but in the later division of Italy it was separated into two, the maritime district being united with Picenum, while the inland portion or valley of the Aternus was included (together with the Sabines and Peligni) in the province of Valeria. (Lib. Colon. pp. 227, 228; Bingham's Eccles. Antiq. ix. ch. 5, sect. 3.) We learn from Juvenal that they continued to retain their primitive simplicity and rustic habits of life even under the Roman Empire. (Juv. xiv. 181.) Silius Italicus speaks of them as a race, hardy and warlike, and habituated to the chase: their rugged mountains were doubtless still the refuge of many wild animals. (Sil. Ital. viii. 513.) The more inland parts of their territory abounded in excellent upland pastures, which produced a kind of cheese that was highly esteemed at Rome. (Plin. xi. 42. s. 97; Martial, xiii. 31.)

The most important physical feature of the territory of the Vestini is the Monte Corno or Gran Sasso d' Italia, which, as already observed, is the highest summit of the Apennines. This was identified by Cluver, who has been followed by most later writers, with the Cunarus Mons of Servius (ad Aen. x. 185). But Silius Italicus (viii. 517) places the Mons Fiscellus, a name much better known, among the Vestini; and though this is opposed to the statement of Pliny that that mountain contains the sources of the Nar, there seems much reason to believe that Pliny has here confounded the Nar with its tributary the Velinus [NAR], which really rises in a group closely connected with the Gran Sasso, and that it was therefore that remarkable mountain range which was known to the ancients as the Mons Fiscellus.

The following towns are noticed by ancient writers as belonging to the Vestini. PINNA, now called Civita di Penne, appears to have been the chief of those which were situated on the eastern slope of the mountains. Lower down, and only a few miles from the sea, was ANGULUS, now Civita S. Angelo. ATERNUM, at the mouth of the river of the same name, now Pescara, was the seaport of the Vestini, and, being the only one along this line of coast for some distance, served also as that of the Marrucini. In the valley of the Aternus were: PELTUINUM (Ansedonia), about 14 miles S. of Aquila; AVEIA, the remains of which are still visible at Fossa, about 6 miles S. of Aquila; and PITINUM, still called Torre di Pitino, about 2 miles E. of the same city, which must have immediately adjoined the territory of Amiternum. FURCONIUM, the ruins of which are still visible at Civita di Bagno, a little to the S. of Aquila, though an important place in the early part of the middle ages, is not mentioned by any writer before Paulus Diaconus (Hist. Lang. ii. 20), and was certainly not a municipal town in the time of the Romans. PRIFERNUM (mentioned only in the Tab. Peut.) is of very uncertain site, but is supposed to have been near As-

sergio. Aquila, the present capital of this district, is a wholly modern city, having been founded by the emperor Frederic II. in the 13th century, when its population was gathered together from the surrounding towns of Amiternum, Aveia, Furconium, &c., the complete desolation of which apparently dates from this period. AUFINA, which according to Pliny (iii. 12. s. 17) was in his time united for municipal purposes with Peltuinum, still retains the name of Ofena. CUTINA and CINGILIA, two towns of the Vestini mentioned by Livy (viii. 29), are wholly unknown, and the sites assigned to them by Romanelli, at Civita Aquana and Civita Retenga respectively, are merely conjectural.

The topography of the Vestini is specially illustrated in the work of Giovenazzi (Della Città d' Aveja nei Vestini, 4to. Roma, 1773), as well as by Romanelli (vol. iii. pp. 241—284). [E. H. B.]

VESUBIA'NI, a people mentioned in the inscription of the arch of Susa. The resemblance of name has led geographers to place the Vesubiani in a valley through which runs a torrent called Vesubia, which falls into the Var. The Esubiani, who are mentioned in the inscription of the Trophy of the Alps (Pliny, iii. 20) seem to be the same as the Vesubiani, for the only difference is a V. But D'Anville places the Esubiani on the Ubaye and the Ubayette, which two streams unite above Barcelonette in the department of Basses-Alpes. [G. L.]

VESULUS MONS (Monte Viso), one of the most lofty summits of the Alps, which, from its prominent position near the plains of Italy, and its great superiority in height over any of the neighbouring peaks, is one of the most conspicuous mountains of the whole Alpine range as viewed from the Italian side. Hence it is one of the very few individual summits of the Alps of which the ancient name can be identified with certainty. It is mentioned by both Pliny and Mela as containing the sources of the Padus; and the former adds that it was the highest summit of the Alps, which is a mistake, but not an unnatural one, considering its really great elevation (12,580 feet) and its comparatively isolated position. (Plin. iii. 16. s. 20; Mela, ii. 4. § 4.) Virgil also mentions the forests of "the pine-clad Vesulus" as affording shelter to numerous wild boars of the largest size. (Virg. Aen. x. 708; Serv. ad loc.) [E. H. B.]

VESUNNA (Οὐέσοννα), according to Ptolemy (ii. 7. § 12) the capital of the Petrocorii, a people of Aquitania. In inscriptions the name is written Vesunna. The place occurs in the Itins., and its position is Périgueux, in the old province of Périgord, which name as well as Périgueux is a memorial of the name of the people, Petrocorii. But it is said that the remains of the old town are still called La Vésone. Périgueux is on the Ille, a branch of the Dordogne, and it is the capital of the department of Dordogne.

There is no Roman city in France of which we know so little that contains so many remains as Périgueux. Foundations of ancient buildings, mosaics, statues, and ruins of edifices show its former magnitude. The tour de Vésone, a round building constructed of small stones and of rough materials, is supposed to have been the cella of a temple, or a tomb, as some conjecture. It is about 200 feet in circumference. There were seven bridges at Vesunna, four of which have been repaired or rebuilt. There are some remains of an amphitheatre of large dimensions. Several aqueducts supplied the

town with water. There are also remains of a Roman citadel. On a hill which commands Vesunna,
and is separated from it by the river *Ille*, there are
the remains of a Roman camp, which is called *Camp
de César*, though Caesar never was there; but
some of his successors may have been. There are
several other Roman camps about *Périgueux*. Several Roman roads have been traced leading to *Périgueux*. Vesunna seems to have been an important
position in Aquitania during the imperial government of Rome. There is a French work on the
antiquities of *Vésone* by M. Wlgrin de Tailleffer,
2 vols. 4to. 1821, Périgueux.   [G. L.]

VESUVIUS MONS (Οὐεσούϊος, or Οὐεσούϊος:
Monte Vesuvio), sometimes also called by Latin
writers VESEVUS, and VESVIUS or VESBIUS (Βέσ-
βιος, Dion Cass.), a celebrated volcanic mountain of
Campania, situated on the shore of the gulf called
the Crater or *Bay of Naples*, from which it rises
directly in an isolated conical mass, separated on all
sides from the ranges of the Apennines by a broad
tract of intervening plain. It rises to the height of
4020 feet, and its base is nearly 30 miles in circumference.

Though now celebrated for the frequency as well
as violence of its eruptions, Vesuvius had in ancient
times been so long in a quiescent state that all tradition of its having ever been an active volcano was
lost, and until after the Christian era it was noted
chiefly for the great fertility of the tract that extended around its base and up its sloping sides
(Virg. *Georg.* ii. 227; Strab. v. p. 247), a fertility
which was in great measure owing to the deposits of
fine volcanic sand and ashes that had been thrown
out from the mountain. There were not indeed
wanting appearances that proved to the accurate
observer the volcanic origin and nature of Vesuvius:
hence Diodorus speaks of it as "bearing many signs
of its having been a burning mountain in times long
past" (Diod. iv. 21); but though he considers it as
having on this account given name to the Phlegraean
plains, he does not allude to any historical or traditional evidence of its former activity. Strabo
in like manner describes it as "surrounded by
fields of the greatest fertility, with the exception
of the summit, which was for the most part
level, and wholly barren, covered with ashes, and
containing clefts and hollows, formed among rocks
of a burnt aspect, as if they had been eaten away by
fire; so that a person would be led to the conclusion
that the spot had formerly been in a state of conflagration, and had craters from which fire had burst
forth, but that these had been extinguished for want
of fuel" (v. p. 247). He adds that the great fertility of the neighbourhood was very probably owing
to this cause, as that of Catana was produced by
Mount Aetna. In consequence of this fertility, as
well as of the beauty of the adjoining bay, the line of
coast at the foot of Vesuvius was occupied by several
flourishing towns, and by numbers of villas belonging to wealthy Roman nobles.

The name of Vesuvius is twice mentioned in history before the Christian era. In B. C. 340 it was
at the foot of this mountain that was fought the
great battle between the Romans and the Latins, in
which P. Decius devoted himself to death for his
country. (Liv. viii. 8.) The precise scene of the
action is indeed uncertain, though it was probably
in the plain on the N. side. Livy describes it as
"haud procul radicibus Vesuvii montis, qua via ad
Veserim ferebat;" but the situation of the Veseris is

wholly uncertain. [VESERIS.] Again, at a later
period (B. C. 73) we are told that Spartacus, with
the fugitive slaves and gladiators under his command, took refuge on Mount Vesuvius as a stronghold, and by a sudden sally from it defeated the
Roman general Claudius Pulcher, who had been sent
against him. (Flor. iii. 20. § 4; Plut. *Crass.* 9;
Appian, *B. C.* i. 116; Vell. Pat. ii. 30; Oros. v. 24;
Frontin. *Strat.* i. 5. § 21.)

But it was the fearful eruption of the 24th of
August, A. D. 79, that first gave to Vesuvius the
celebrity that it has ever since enjoyed. That great
catastrophe is described in detail in a well-known letter of the younger Pliny to the historian Tacitus; and
more briefly, but with the addition of some fabulous
circumstances, by Dion Cassius. (Plin. *Ep.* vi. 16,
20; Dion Cass. lxvi. 21—23; Vict. *Epit.* 10.) It
is remarkable that in recording this, the earliest
eruption of the mountain, Pliny particularly notices
the form assumed by the cloud of ashes that, rising
from the crater in a regular column to a considerable
height, afterwards spread out laterally so as to form
a head like that of a stone-pine: an appearance
which has been observed in many subsequent eruptions. The other phenomena described are very
much the same as are common to all similar eruptions: but the mass of ashes, sand, and pumice
thrown out was so vast as not only to bury the cities
of Herculaneum and Pompeii at the foot of the volcano under an accumulation many feet in depth,
but to overwhelm the more distant town of Stabiae,
where the elder Pliny perished by suffocation, and
to overspread the whole bay with a cloud of ashes
such as to cause a darkness more profound than that
of night even at Misenum, 15 miles distant from
the foot of the mountain. (Plin. *l. c.*) On the other
hand the outflow of lava was inconsiderable, and if
any streams of that kind broke out at this time they
probably did not descend to the inhabited regions:
at least we hear nothing of them, and the popular
notion that Herculaneum was overwhelmed by a
current of *lava* is certainly a mistake. [HERCU-
LANEUM.] So great and unexpected a calamity
naturally excited the greatest sensation, and both the
poets and the prose writers of Rome for more than a
century after the event abound with allusions to it.
Tacitus speaks of the *Bay of Naples* as "pulcer-
rimus sinus, ante quam Vesuvius mons ardescens faciem loci verteret." (*Ann.* iv. 67.) Martial, after
descanting on the beauty of the scene when the
mountain and its neighbourhood were covered with
the green shade of vines, adds:—

"Cuncta jacent flammis et tristi mersa favilla"
                                (iv. 44);

and Statius describes Vesuvius as

"Aemula Trinacriis volvens incendia flammis."
                                (*Silv.* iv. 4. 80.)

(See also Val. Flacc. iii. 208, iv. 507; Sil. Ital.
xvii. 594; Flor. i. 16. § 5.)

A long interval again elapsed before any similar
outbreak. It is probable indeed that the mountain
continued for some time at least after this first eruption to give signs of activity by sending forth smoke
and sulphurous vapours from its crater, to which
Statius probably alludes when he speaks of its summit still threatening destruction ("necdum lethale
minari cessat apex," *Silv.* iv. 4. 85). But the
next recorded eruption, and probably the next of
any magnitude, occurred in A. D. 203, and is
noticed by Dion Cassius (lxxvi. 2). This is pro-

bably the one alluded to by Galen (*de Meth.* v. 12), and it seems certain from the description given by Dion Cassius of the state of the mountain when he wrote (under Alexander Severus) that it was then in a state of occasional, but irregular, activity, much resembling that which exists at the present day. (Dion Cass. lxvi. 21.) The only other eruption that we find mentioned under the Roman Empire occurred in A. D. 472 under the reign of Anthemius. (Marcellin. *Chron.* ad ann.) A fourth, which took place in the reign of Theodoric king of the Goths (A. D. 512), is noticed by both Cassiodorus and Procopius, who describe in considerable detail the phenomena of the mountain. It appears certain that these later eruptions were accompanied by the discharge of streams of lava, which caused great mischief to the surrounding country. (Cassiod. *Ep.* iv. 50; Procop. *B. G.* ii. 4, iv. 35.)

It would be foreign to our subject to trace the history of the mountain through the middle ages, but it may be mentioned that its eruptions seem to have been far more rare and separated by longer intervals than they have been for more than two centuries past; and in some instances at least these intervals were periods of perfect quiescence, during which the mountain was rapidly losing its peculiar aspect. Even as late as 1611, after an interval of little more than a century, the sides of the mountain were covered with forests, and the crater itself was overgrown with shrubs and rich herbage. (Daubeny *on Volcanoes*, p. 225.)

At the present day Vesuvius consists of two distinct portions: the central cone, which is now the most elevated part of the mountain; and a ridge which encircles this on three sides at some distance, and is separated from it by a level valley or hollow called the *Atrio del Cavallo*. This outer ridge, of which the highest point, near its N. extremity, is called *Monte Somma*, was probably at one time continuous on all sides of the circle, but is now broken down on the S. and W. faces: hence the appearance of Vesuvius as viewed from Naples or from the W. is that of a mountain having two peaks separated by a deep depression. This character is wholly at variance with the description given by Strabo, who tells us that the summit was *nearly level*, but with clefts and fissures in it, from which fire appeared to have formerly issued (v. p. 247.) Hence it is probable that the mountain was then a single truncated cone, and that the vast crater-like hollow of which the *Atrio del Cavallo* forms part, was first created by the great eruption of A. D. 79, which blew into the air the whole mass of the then existing summit of the mountain, leaving the present ridge of *Monte Somma* standing, enclosing a vast crater, within which the present cone has gradually formed. (Daubeny *on Volcanoes*, p. 215; Lyell's *Principles of Geology*, p. 365, 8th edit.) It has indeed been frequently assumed from the accounts of the operations of Spartacus already mentioned (Flor. iii. 20; Plut. *Crass.* 9) that the mountain had even then a crater, within which that leader and his band were enclosed by the Roman general: but it is very doubtful whether the passages in question bear out this interpretation, which seems at variance with the account given by Strabo, whose description has every appearance of being derived from personal observation.

(Concerning the history of the different eruptions of Vesuvius see Della Torre, *Storia del Vesuvio*, 4to., Napoli, 1755; and the geological work of Dr. Daubeny. ch. xii.)   [E. H. B.]

VETERA. [CASTRA VETERA.]

VETTONA (*Eth.* Vettonensis: *Bettona*), a municipal town of Umbria, situated about 5 miles E. of the Tiber, between Perusia and Mevania. It is mentioned by Pliny among the municipalities of Umbria, and its name is found also in an inscription among the "xv Populi Umbriae;" while another mentions it in connection with Perusia, from which it was only about 10 miles distant, as measured on the map, though the Tabula calls it 14 miles from that city and 20 from Tuder. (Plin. iii. 14. s. 19; Orell. *Inscr.* 95, 98: *Tab. Peut.*) Vettona continued in the middle ages to be a city of considerable importance, but it was destroyed by the Perugians in 1352. The ancient site is, however, still marked by the village of *Bettona*, about a mile from the left bank of the Tinia. [E. H. B.]

VETTONES (Οὐέττωνες, Strab. iii. p. 152; Οὐέττονες, Ptol. ii. 5. § 9), one of the principal peoples of Lusitania. (Caes. *B. C.* i. 38; Plin. iv. 21. s. 38; Grut. *Inscr.* p. 383. 7.) Strabo alone (*l. c.*) assigns them to Hither Iberia, or the Provincia Tarraconensis. We find their country called Vettonia by Prudentius (*Hymn. in Eulal.* v. 186) and in an inscription. (Orelli, no. 3664.) It was watered by the Tagus, and separated by the Durius from Asturia on the N. On the W., where their boundary corresponded very nearly with that of modern *Portugal*, they adjoined the proper Lusitani. On the E. they neighboured on the Carpetani in Hispania Tarraconensis, and their boundary would be described by a line drawn from the modern *Simancas* in a SW. direction over *Puente del Arzobispo* to *Truxillo*. On the S. they were bounded by the province of Baetica, so that their country comprehended a part of *Estremadura* and *Leon*. Their principal towns were Salmantica (*Salamanca*), Cecilionicum (*Baños?*), Capara (*las Ventas de Capara*), Sentice (in the neighbourhood of *Los Santos*), Cottaeobriga (*Almeida*), Augustobriga (*Ciudad Rodrigo?*), &c. In their country grew the herba Vettonica (Plin. xxv. 7. s. 46), still known under the name of *betony;* an account of which is given in the treatise *De Herba Betonica*, ascribed to Antonius Musa.   [T. H. D.]

VETULO'NIA or VETULO'NIUM (Οὐετουλώνιον, Ptol. iii. 1. § 49: *Eth.* Vetuloniensis), one of the twelve principal cities of the Etruscan confederation (Dionys. iii. 51; Plin. iii. 5. s. 8). Yet we hear nothing of its political history; and all we know respecting it is, that it was reputed to be the town in which the Etruscan insignia of magistracy, afterwards adopted by the Romans, such as the lictors, fasces, sella curulis, toga praetexta, &c., as well as the trumpet, were first used. (Sil. It. viii. 483, sqq.; cf. Dionys. iii. 61; Strab. v. p. 220; Macr. *S.* i. 6; Flor. i. 5; &c.)

The destruction of Vetulonia, and the silence of history respecting it, have caused even its site to be a matter of doubt. Thus it has been sought at or near *Viterbo* (Annio, *Antiqq. Var. Volum.*), at *Massa Marittima*, the ancient Massa Veternensis (Amm. Marc. xiv. 11. § 25), or in a dense wood 5 miles to the W. of that town (Ximenes, *ap. Inghirami, Ricerche di Vetulonia*, p. 62; cf. Targioni-Tozzetti, *Viaggi in Toscana*, iv. p. 116); on the site of *Vulci* (Luc. Buonaparte, *Ann. Inst.* 1829, p. 188, sqq.; and Valeriani, *Mus. Chius.* i. p. 68); on the hill of *Castiglione Bernardi*, near *Monte Rotondo* (Inghirami, *Ricerche di Vetulonia*, Ambrosch), and at *Orbetello* (Ennolao Barbaro, *ap. Dempster, Etrur.*

Reg. ii. 56). But till very recently the opinion most commonly adopted was that of Leandro Alberti, an antiquary of the 16th century, who placed it on *Monte Calvi* (*Descris. d' Italia*, p. 27), in a wood called *Selva di Vetleta;* and who has been followed by Cluverius (*Ital. Ant.* ii. 2. p. 472), by Müller (*Etrusker,* i. p. 211), &c. It is now, however, generally admitted that Vetulonia is to be identified with the remains of a city, discovered in 1842 by Sig. Pasquinelli, an Italian engineer, at *Magliano*, a village between the *Osa* and the *Albegna*, and 8 or 10 miles to the N. of *Orbetello.* To Mr. Dennis (*Cities and Sepulchres of Etruria*, vol. ii. ch. 48), however, is to be assigned the credit of first identifying these remains as those of the lost Etruscan city. Their site agrees with what we learn respecting that of Vetulonia. Pliny and Ptolemy (*ll. cc.*) agree in placing the latter among the inland colonies of Etruria; yet Pliny (ii. 103. s. 106) also describes it as being not far from the sea, and as having hot springs, the Aquae Vetuloniae, in its neighbourhood. Now, all the necessary conditions are fulfilled by the remains alluded to. The circuit of the walls, about 4½ miles, shows it to have been an important city; its situation with regard to the sea agrees with the account of Pliny; and near *Telamonaccio*, at a distance of only 200 or 300 yards from the coast, and in the vicinity of the newly found city, warm springs still exist. For other reasons which led Mr. Dennis to the opinion which he formed, the reader is referred to his work before cited, and to his paper in the *Classical Museum*, vol. ii. p. 229, seq. For coins of Vetulonia, see Eckhel, vol. i. pt. i. p. 94. [T. H. D.]

VETU′RII. [GENUA.]

VEXALLA AEST. (Οὐεξάλλα ἀσχνσις, Ptol. ii. 3. § 3), a bay on the W. coast of Britannia Romana, near the mouth of the river Sabrina, now *Bridgewater Bay.*   [T. H. D.]

UFENS (*Ufente*), a river of Latium, rising at the foot of the Volscian mountains, and flowing through the Pontine Marshes, whence its course is slow and stagnant, and it is described by both Virgil and Silius Italicus, as a sluggish and muddy stream. (Virg. *Aen.* vii. 801; Sil. Ital. viii. 382.) Claudian also calls it "tardatus suis erroribus Ufens." (*Prob. et Ol. Cons.* 257.) It joins the Amasenus (still called *Amaseno*) during its course through the marshes to the sea at *Terracina*, but the present channels of both rivers are artificial, and it is uncertain whether they united their streams in ancient times or not. The name is corrupted by Strabo into Aufidus (Αὔφιδος, v. p. 233), but he correctly describes it as one of the chief agents in the formation of the Pontine Marshes. The ancient form of the name was Oufens, whence the Roman tribe Oufentina derived its name, being composed originally of citizens settled in the territory and neighbourhood of Privernum (Fest. *s. v. Oufentina*, p. 194).   [E. H. B.]

UFFUGUM [BRUTTII].

UGERNUM (Οὔγερνον), a town of Gallia Narbonensis, on the road from Nemausus through Ugernum and Tarascon to Aquae Sextiae (*Aix*). Strabo (iv. p. 178) has described this road. The genitive VOERNI occurs in an inscription found at *Nîmes.* Ugernum is represented by *Beaucaire.* The Table marks the distance from Nemausus (*Nîmes*) to Ugernum xv., which is near the truth. In the last century the Roman road between Nemausus and Ugernum was discovered with several milestones on it in their original position, and numbered, as it

seems, from Nemausus the ancient capital of the district. These milestones gave the opportunity of ascertaining the length of the Roman mile. The name of *Beaucaire* is a corruption of the middle-age name of Bellum-quadrum. If any trace of the name Ugernum exists, it is in the name of *Gernegue*, the lower part of *Tarascon*, which is on the opposite side of the river, for *Beaucaire* and *Tarascon* stand face to face. But in order to admit this, we must suppose that *Gernegue* represents an island Gernica, which, according to a middle-age document, was between *Beaucaire* and *Tarascon*, and that by some change in the river the island has become part of the mainland on the east side of the river; and it is said that this fact about the island is certain. (D'Anville, *Notice, &c.*; *Penny Cyclopaedia*, art. *Beaucaire.*)   [G. L.]

UGIA (Οὔγια, Ptol. ii. 4. § 12), a town of the Turdetani in Hispania Baetica, on the road from Cades to Corduba. (*Itin. Ant.* p. 410.) It is probably the town called Urgia by Pliny (iii. 1. s. 3), with the surnames of Castrum Julium or Caesaris Salutariensis, and possessing the Jus Latii. Now *Las Cabezas*, where there are some antiquities. (Cf. Ukert, ii. pt. i. p. 356.)   [T. H. D.]

VIA AEMILIA (ἡ Αἰμιλία ὁδός), one of the most celebrated and important of the Roman highways, and the first that was constructed by them in Northern Italy. The period of its first construction is clearly marked by Livy, who tells us that M. Aemilius Lepidus, the consul of B. C. 187, after having effectually subdued the Ligurians, carried a highroad from Placentia to Ariminum, that it might there join the Flaminian Way ("Viam ab Placentia, ut Flaminiae committeret, Ariminum perduxit," Liv. xxxix. 2). Strabo indeed gives a different view of the case, and speaks of the Aemilian Way as constructed in the first instance only from Ariminum to Bononia, and thence sweeping round the marshes, and skirting the roots of the Alps to Aquileia (v. p. 217). But there is every reason to suppose that this last branch of the road was not constructed till long afterwards; and there is no doubt of the correctness of Livy's statement that the original Via Aemilia, and the only one that was generally recognised as such, was the line of road from Ariminum to Placentia. It was this celebrated highway—which is still in use at the present day, and, being carried the whole way through a level plain, preserves almost a straight line during a course of 180 miles—that became the means of carrying Roman civilisation into the heart of Cisalpine Gaul; and so great was its influence upon the population that it traversed, that the whole district between the Apennines and the Padus, constituting the Eighth Region of Augustus, and commonly called by geographers Gallia Cispadana, came to be known as Aemilia, and was eventually constituted into a province under that name. The period at which this took place is uncertain, but the appellation was doubtless in popular use long before it became an official designation; and as early as the first century we find Martial employing the expressions, "Aemiliae de regione viae," and even "tota in Aemilia" (Martial. iii. 4. 2, vi. 85. 6). As indeed all the principal towns of the district (with the single exception of Ravenna) were situated on the Via Aemilia, the use of this designation seems extremely natural.

We have no account of the period at which the Via Aemilia was continued from Placentia to Mediolanum, though there is little doubt that it would take place soon after the complete subjugation of the Transpadane Gauls. Nor do we know with any certainty whether the name of Via Aemilia was ever applied in common usage to this portion of the road, or to the branches that led from Mediolanum to the foot of the Alps, as well as from that city by Verona to Patavium. But as Strabo distinctly applies the name to the branch that led by Patavium to Aquileia, we may here most conveniently include all the principal highroads of the N. of Italy under one view in the present article.

1. The main or trunk line of the Via Aemilia from Ariminum to Placentia. The stations on this road are thus given in the Antonine Itinerary, where they are repeated more than once (pp. 99, 126, 287); and, from the direct line of the road, the distances are subject to no doubt :—

From Ariminum (*Rimini*) to

Caesena (*Cesena*)	- - - xx.	M.P.
Faventia (*Faenza*)	- - - xxiv.	
Forum Cornelii (*Imola*)	- - x.	
Bononia (*Bologna*)	- - - xxiv.	
Mutina (*Modena*)	- - - xxv.	
Regium (*Reggio*)	- - - - xvii.	
Parma (*Parma*)	- - - xviii.	
Fidentiola (*Borgo S. Donino*)	xv.	
Placentia (*Piacenza*)	- - - xxiv.	

The same line is given more in detail in the Jerusalem Itinerary (p. 615, &c.), with which the Tabula substantially agrees; but the distances are more correctly given in the latter.

The stations enumerated are:—

Competu (*I. H.*) Ad Confluentes (*Tab.*)	- - - xii.	M.P.
Caesena (*Cesena*)	- - - viii.	
Forum Populii (*Forlimpopoli*)	vii.	
Forum Livii (*Forli*)	- - - vii.	
Faventia (*Faenza*)	- - - x.	
Forum Cornelii (*Imola*)	- - x.	
Claterna (*Quaderna*)	- - xiv.	
Bononia (*Bologna*)	- - - x.	
Forum Gallorum	- - - xvii.	
Mutina (*Modena*)	- - - viii.	
Regium (*Reggio*)	- - - xvii.	
Tannetum (*Taneto*)	- - - xi.	
Parma (*Parma*)	- - - vii.	
Fidentia (*Borgo S. Donino*)	xv.	
Florentia (*Firenzuola*)	- - x.	
Placentia (*Piacenza*)	- - - xv.	

The general agreement in the distances above given (which are those of the Tabula) with those of the Antonine Itinerary, though the division is different, sufficiently shows the accuracy of the two. The distances in the Jerusalem Itinerary are, for this line of route, generally less accurate. Some obscure Mutationes mentioned in the one document, and not in the other, have been omitted in the above list.

2. Continuation of the Via Aemilia from Placentia to Mediolanum. This line is summarily given in the Antonine Itinerary thus:—

From Placentia to Laus

Pompeia (*Lodi Vecchio*) -	xxiv.	M.P.
Thence to Mediolanum (*Milan*)	xvi.	

The same distances are thus divided in the Jerusalem Itinerary:—

Ad Rotas	- - - - - -	xi. M.P.
Tres Tabernae	- - - -	v.
Laus	- - - - - -	viii.
Ad Nonum	- - - - -	vii.
Mediolanum	- - - - -	vii. (ix. ?)

The intermediate stations are unknown, and are

expressly called mere Mutationes, or places for changing horses.

3. From Mediolanum to Augusta Praetoria, at the foot of the Alps, the distances, as given in the Antonine Itinerary, are :—

From Mediolanum to

Novaria (*Novara*)	- - - xxxiii.	M.P.
Vercellae (*Vercelli*)	- - - xvi.	
Eporedia (*Ivrea*)	- - - xxxiii.	
Vitricium (*Verres*)	- - - xxi.	
Augusta Praetoria (*Aosta*)	- xxv.	

The same authority gives a circuitous line of route from Mediolanum to Vercellae (where it rejoins the preceding) by

Ticinum (*Pavia*)	- - - xxii.	M.P.
Laumellum (*Lomello*)	- - xxii.	
Vercellae (*Vercelli*)	- - xxvi.	

4. From Mediolanum to Aquileia. The stations given in the Itineraries are as follows:—

Med. to Argentia - - - - x. M.P.

Pons Aureoli (*Pontirolo*)	x.
Bergamum (*Bergamo*)	- xiii.
Brixia (*Brescia*)	- xxxviii.(xxxii.)
Sirmio (*Sermione*)	- xxii.
Verona (*Verona*)	- xxii.
Vicentia (*Vicenza*)	- xxxiii.
Patavium (*Padova*)	- xxvii. (xxii.)
Altinum (*Altino*)	- xxxiii.
Concordia (*Concordia*)	- xxxi.
Aquileia (*Aquileia*)	- xxxi.

(In the above line of route the minor stations (Mutationes) given in the Jerusalem Itinerary are omitted. For an examination of them, and a careful comparison of all the Roman roads through Cisalpine Gaul, see Walckenaer, *Géographie des Gaules*, vol. iii. pp. 2—13.)

5. From Bononia to Aquileia. This is the road of which Strabo expressly speaks as a continuation of the Via Aemilia (v. p. 217), but it is probable that he did not mean to say that it branched off directly from Bononia ; at least the only line given in the Itineraries turns off from the main line of the Via Aemilia at Mutina, and thence proceeds to

Vicus Serninus (?)	- - - xxiii.	M.P.
Vicus Varianus (*Bariano*, on the N. bank of the *Po*)	- xx.	
Anneianum (*Legnago?*)	- - xvii.	
Ateste (*Este*)	- - - xx.	
Patavium (*Padova*)	- - - xxv.	

whence it followed the same line to Aquileia as that given above. Another line of road, which though more circuitous was probably more frequented, led from Mutina by Colicaria (an uncertain station) to Hostilia (*Ostiglia*), where it crossed the Padus, and thence direct to Verona (xxx. M. P.). (*Itin. Ant.* p. 282.)

6. From Placentia to Dertona, where it communicated with the road constructed by Aemilius Scaurus across the Apennines to Vada Sabata. (Strab. v. p. 217.) The stations on this short line were:—

From Placentia to

Comillomagus	- - - - -	xxv. M.P.
Iria (*Voghera*)	- - - -	xvi.
Dertona (*Tortona*)	- - -	x.

The first station, Comillomagus, or Camillomagus, as the name is written in the Tabula, is unknown, but must have been situated a short distance to the W. of Broni.

7. Lastly, a branch of the Via Aemilia led from Placentia to Ticinum (*Pavia*), whence it was carried westwards to Augusta Taurinorum (*Turin*) and

the foot of the Cottian Alps. This was therefore one of the great highroads leading to Gaul.
But the stations on it, as given in the Tabula, are
very confused, and can only partially be restored by
the assistance of the Antonine Itinerary, which nowhere gives this road in its entirety. At Ticinum it
was joined by another road leading from Mediolanum
to that city. The stations, as given in the Jerusalem
Itinerary (p. 556), are as follows :—

Ticinum
Durii (*Dorno*) - - - - xii. M. P.
Laumellum (*Lomello*) - - - ix.
Ad Cottias (*Cozzo*) - - - xii.
Ad Medias - - - - - - xiii.
Rigomagus (*Trino Vecchio*) - x.
Cesta (?) - - - - - - viii.
Quadratae (near *Londaglio*) - xi.
Ad Decimum - - - - - - xii.
Taurini (*Turin*) - - - - x.
Ad Fines (*Avigliano*) - - xvi.
Ad Duodecimum - - - - xii.
Segusio (*Susa*) - - - - xii.

The rest of the route over the Cottian Alps is given
in the article ALPES.   [E. H. B.]

VIA AEMILIA SCAURI, is the name given, for
the sake of distinction, to a road which was constructed by Aemilius Scaurus long after the more
celebrated Via Aemilia above described. Strabo,
the only author who distinctly mentions the two,
says that Aemilius Scaurus, after having drained the
marshes on the S. side of the Padus, constructed the
Aemilian Way through Pisae and Luna as far as Sabata, and thence through Dertona. (Strab. v. p. 217.)
Whether " the other Aemilian Way," as Strabo calls
it, had been already continued from Placentia to
Dertona, or this also was first effected by Scaurus,
we know not ; but it is clear that the two were
thus brought into connection. The construction of
this great work must be assigned to the censorship
of M. Aemilius Scaurus, in B. C. 109, as we learn from
Aurelius Victor (*Vir. Ill.* 72), who, however, probably
confounds it with the more celebrated Via Aemilia
from Placentia to Ariminum. But a comparison of
the two authors leaves no doubt as to the road really
meant. The name seems to have gradually fallen
into disuse, probably on account of the ambiguity
arising between the two Viae of the same name ; and
we find both the coast-road from Pisae to Vada
Sabata, and that across the mountains from the
latter place by Aquae Statiellae to Dertona, included
by the Itineraries as a part of the Via Aurelia, of
which the former at least was in fact a mere continuation. Hence it will be convenient to discuss the
stations and distances along these lines, under the
general head of VIA AURELIA.   [E. H. B.]

VIA AMERINA, is the name given in an inscription of the time of Hadrian (Orell. *Inscr.* 3306)
to a line of road, which must obviously be that leading direct from Rome to Ameria. This, as we learn
from the Tabula, branched off from the Via Cassia
at Baccanae (*Baccano*), and proceeded through Nepete and Falerii to Ameria. The stations and distances as there given are:—

Rome to Baccanae - - - - xxi. M. P.
Nepete (*Nepi*) - - - - ix.
Falerii (*Sta Maria di*
Falleri) - - - - v.
Castellum Amerinum - xii.
Ameria (*Amelia*) - - ix.

The sum of these distances (56 miles) agrees
precisely with the statement of Cicero, who, in the

oration *Pro Sexto Roscio Amerino* (c. 7. § 18), observes that it was 56 miles from Ameria to Rome.
According to the Tabula a prolongation of the
same road led from Ameria to Tuder, and thence
by a circuitous route through Vettona and Perusia
to Clusium, where it rejoined the Via Cassia. The
first station to Ameria is omitted : thence to

Tuder (*Todi*), was - - - vi. M. P.
Vettona (*Bettona*) - - - - xx.
Perusia (*Perugia*) - - - xiv.

The distance from that city to Clusium is again
omitted.   [E. H. B.]

VIA APPIA (ἡ ᾿Αππία ὁδός), the greatest and
most celebrated of all the Roman highways in Italy,
which led from Rome direct to Brundusium, and thus
became the principal line of communication with
Greece, Macedonia and the East. Hence it became, in
the flourishing times of the Roman Empire, the most
frequented and important of the Roman roads, and is
called by Statius " regina viarum." (*Silv.* ii. 2. 12.)
Martial also calls it " Appia . . . Ausoniae maxima
fama viae" (ix. 102). The former author terms it
" annosa Appia," in reference to its great antiquity
(*Ib.* iv. 3. 163.) It was indeed the earliest of all
the Roman highways, of the construction of which
we have any definite account, and very probably the
first of all that was regularly made as a great public
work; the Via Salaria, Tiburtina, &c., having doubtless long been in use as mere natural roads, before
they were converted into solidly constructed Viae.
There must in like manner have always been some
kind of road communicating from Rome with Alba
and Aricia; but it is evident, from the perfectly
straight line followed by the Via Appia from a
point very little without the gates of Rome to Aricia,
that this must have been a new work, laid out and
executed at once. The original construction of the
Via Appia was undoubtedly due to the censor
Appius Claudius Caecus, who commenced it in B. C.
312, and completed it as far as Capua before the
close of his censorship. (Liv. ix. 29 ; Diod. xx. 36;
Frontin. *de Aquaed.* 5; Orell. *Inscr.* 539.) From
Capua it was undoubtedly carried on to Beneventum,
and again at a subsequent period to Brundusium;
but the date of these continuations is unknown. It
is evident that the last at least could not have taken
place till after the complete subjugation of the south
of Italy in B. C. 266, and probably not till after the
establishment of the Roman colony at Brundusium,
B. C. 244. Hence it is certainly a mistake when
Aurelius Victor speaks of Appius Claudius Caecus
as having carried the Appian Way to Brundusium.
(Vict. *Vir. Ill.* 34.) The continuation and completion of this great work has been assigned to
various members of the Claudian family; but this is
entirely without authority.

Strabo distinctly speaks of the Appian Way as extending, in his time, from Rome to Brundusium; and
his description of its course and condition is important.
After stating that almost all travellers from Greece and
the East used to land at Brundusium, he adds: " From
thence there are two ways to Rome, the one adapted
only for mules, through the country of the Peucetians,
Daunians, and Samnites, to Beneventum, on which
are the cities of Egnatia, Caelia, Canusium, and Herdonia; the other through Tarentum, deviating a little
to the left, and going round about a day's journey,
which is called the Appian, and is better adapted for
carriages. On this are situated Uria (between Brundusium and Tarentum) and Venusia, on the confines
of the Samnites and Lucanians. Both these roads,

starting from Brundusium, meet at Beneventum. Thence to Rome the road is called the Appian, passing through Caudium, Calatia, Capua, and Casilinum, to Sinuessa. The whole distance from Rome to Brundusium is 360 miles. There is yet a third road, from Rhegium, through the Bruttians and Lucanians, and the lands of the Samnites to Campania, where it joins the Appian; this passes through the Apennine mountains, and is three or four days' journey longer than that from Brundusium." (Strab. v. p. 283.) It is not improbable that the first of these branches, which Strabo distinctly distinguishes from the true Appian Way, is the Via Numicia or Minucia (the reading is uncertain), mentioned by Horace as the *alternative* way by which it was customary to proceed to Brundusium. (Hor. *Ep.* i. 18. 20.) But Strabo gives us no information as to how it proceeded from Herdonia, in the plains of Apulia, through the mountains to Beneventum. It is, however, probable that it followed nearly the same line as the high road afterwards constructed by *Trajan, through Aecae and Equus Tuticus. This is indeed one of the principal natural passes through this part of the Apennines, and is still followed, with little deviation, by the modern highroad from Naples to *Brindisi* and *Taranto.* But it is worthy of remark, that Horace and his companions in their journey to Brundusium, of which he has left us the poetical Itinerary (*Sat.* l. 5), appear not to have followed this course, but to have taken a somewhat more direct route through Trivicum, and a small town not named (" oppidulum quod versu dicere non est"), to Canusium. This route, which does not agree with either of those mentioned by Strabo, or with those given in the Itineraries, was probably disused after that constructed by Trajan, through Equus Tuticus and Aecae, had become the frequented line. It was to that emperor that the Appian Way was indebted for many improvements. He restored, if he was not the first to construct, the highroad through the Pontine Marshes from Forum Appii to Tarracina (Dion Cass. lxviii. 15; Hoare, *Class. Tour,* vol. i. p. 28) ; and he at the same time constructed, at his own expense, a new line of highroad from Beneventum to Brundusium (Gruter, *Inscr.* p. 151. 2), which is undoubtedly the Via Trajana celebrated by coins. (Eckhel, vol. iv. p. 421.) It is probable (as already pointed out) that he did no more than render practicable for carriages a line of route previously existing, but accessible only to mules; and that the Via Trajana coincided nearly with the road described by Strabo. But from the time that this road was laid open to general traffic, the proper Via Appia through Venusia to Tarentum, which traversed a wild and thinly-peopled country, seems to have fallen much into disuse. It is, however, still given in the Antonine Itinerary (p. 120) though not as the main line of the Appian Way. The latter appellation seems indeed to have been somewhat vaguely used under the Empire, and the same Itinerary bestows the name on the line, already indicated by Strabo (*l. c.*), that proceeded S. through Lucania and Bruttium to Rhegium, on the Sicilian Strait, a route which never went near Beneventum or Brundusium at all.

The Appian Way long survived the fall of the Western Empire. That portion of it which passed through the Pontine Marshes, which was always the most liable to suffer from neglect, was restored by Theodoric (Gruter, *Inscr.* p. 152. 8); and Procopius, who travelled over it 40 years later,

speaks with admiration of the solidity and perfection of its construction. " The Appian Way (says he) extends from Rome to Capua, a journey of five days for an active traveller. Its width is such as to admit of the passage of two waggons in contrary directions. The road itself is worthy of the highest admiration, for the stone of which it is composed, a kind of mill-stone, and by nature very hard, was brought by Appius from some distant region, since none such is found in this part of the country. He then, after having smoothed and levelled the stones, and cut them into angular forms, fitted them closely together, without inserting either bronze or any other substance. But they are so accurately fitted and joined together, as to present the appearance of one compact mass naturally united, and not composed of many parts. And notwithstanding the long period of time that has elapsed, during which they have been worn by the continual passage of so many carriages and beasts of burden, they have neither been at all displaced from their original position, nor have any of them been worn down, or even lost their polish." (Procop. *B. G.* i. 14.) The above description conveys an accurate impression of the appearance which the Appian Way must have presented in its most perfect state. The extraordinary care and accuracy with which the blocks that composed the pavement of the Roman roads were fitted together, when first laid down, is well seen in the so-called Via Triumphalis, which led to the Temple of Jupiter, on Mons Albanus. [AL-BANUS MONS.] But it is evident from many other examples, that they became much worn down with time; and the pavement seen by Procopius had doubtless been frequently restored. He is also mistaken in supposing that the hard basaltic lava (silex) with which it was paved, had to be brought from a distance: it is found in the immediate neighbourhood, and, in fact, the Appian Way itself, from the *Capo di Bove* to the foot of the Alban Hills, runs along a bank or ridge composed of this lava. Procopius also falls into the common mistake of supposing that the road was originally constructed by Appius Claudius such as he beheld it. But during the long interval it had been the object of perpetual care and restoration; and it is very doubtful how far any of the great works along its line, which excited the admiration of the Romans in later ages, were due to its original author. Caius Gracchus in particular had bestowed great pains upon the improvement of the Roman roads; and there is much reason to believe that it was in his time that they first assumed the finished appearance which they ever afterwards bore. (Plut. *C. Gracch.* 7.) Caesar also, when a young man, was appointed " Curator Viae Appiae," which had become a regular office, and laid out large sums of money upon its improvement. (Plut. *Caes.* 5.) The care bestowed on it by successive emperors, and especially by Trajan, is attested by numerous inscriptions.

It is very doubtful, indeed, whether the original Via Appia, as constructed by the censor Appius, was carried through the Pontine Marshes at all. No mention is found of his draining those marshes, without which such a work would have been impossible; and it is much more probable that the road was originally carried along the hills by Cora, Norba, and Setia, by the same line which was again in use in the last century, before the Pontine Marshes had been drained for the last time by Pius VI. This conjecture is confirmed by the circumstance that Lucilius, in describing his journey from Rome to Capua, complains of the extremely hilly character of the road in approaching Setia. (Lucil. *Fragm.* iii. 6, ed. Gerlach.) Even in the time of Horace, as we learn from his well-known description of the journey to Brundusium, it was customary for travellers to continue their route from Forum Appii by water, embarking at that point on the canal through the Pontine Marshes (Hor. *Sat.* i. 5. 11, &c.). But the very existence of this canal renders it probable that there was at that time a road by the side of it, as we know was the case in Strabo's time, notwithstanding which he tells us that the canal was much used by travellers, who made the voyage in the night, and thus gained time. (Strab. v. p. 233.)

It will be convenient to divide the description of the Appian Way, as it existed under the Roman Empire, and is given in the Itineraries, into several portions. The first of these from Rome to Capua was the main trunk line, upon which all its branches and extensions depended. This will require to be described in more detail, as the most celebrated and frequented of all the Roman highways.

1. From Rome to Capua.

The stations given in the Antonine Itinerary are:—

From Rome to Aricia (*Laricia*)	-	-	-	xvi. M.P.
Tres Tabernae	-	-	-	xvii.
Appii Forum	-	-	-	x.
Tarracina (*Terracina*)	-	-	xviii.
Fundi (*Fondi*)	-	-	-	xvi. (xiii.)
Formiae (*Mola di Gaëta*)				xiii.
Minturnae (near *Tragletto*)				ix.
Sinuessa (*Mondragone*)	-			ix.
Capua (*Sta Maria*)	-	-	xvi.(xxvi.)

The above stations are for the most part well known, and admit of no doubt. Those in the neighbourhood of the Pontine Marshes have indeed given rise to much confusion, but are in fact to be easily determined. Indeed, the line of the road being almost perfectly straight from Rome to Tarracina renders the investigation of the distances a matter of little difficulty.

The Jerusalem Itinerary (p. 611) subdivides the same distance as follows:

Rome to Ad Nonum (mutatio)	-	-	ix. M.P.
Aricia (civitas)	-	-	-	vii.
Sponsae or Ad Sponsas (mutatio)	xix.
Appii Forum (do.)	-	-	-	vii. (xii.?)
Ad Medias (do.)	-	-	-	ix.
Tarracina (civitas)	-	-	-	x.
Fundi (do.)	-	-	-	-	xiii.
Formiae (do.)	-	-	-	-	xii.
Minturnae (do.)	-	-	-	ix.
Sinuessa (do.)	-	-	-	ix.
Pons Campanus (mutatio)	-	ix.
Ad Octavum (do.)	-	-	-	ix.
Capua (civitas)	-	-	-	viii.

The intermediate stations were (as they are expressly called in the Itinerary itself) mere Mutationes, or posthouses, where relays of horses were kept. The determination of their position is therefore of no interest, except in connection with the distances given, which vary materially from those of the other Itinerary, though the total distance from Rome to Capua (125 miles) is the same in both.

The Appian Way issued from the Porta Capena, in the Servian walls of Rome, about half a mile outside of which it separated from the Via Latina, so that the two roads passed through different gates in the walls of Aurelian. That by which the Via Appia finally quitted Rome was known as the Porta Appia;

it is now called the *Porta S. Sebastiano.* The first milestone on the road stood about 120 yards outside this gate; the distances always continuing to be measured from the old Porta Capena. The buildings and tombs which bordered the Via Appia in that portion of it which lay between the two gates, are described in the article ROMA, p. 821. It was apparently in this part of its course, just outside the original city, that it was spanned by three triumphal arches, erected in honour of Drusus (the father of the emperor Claudius), Trajan, and L. Verus. One only of these still remains, just within the *Porta S. Sebastiano*, which, from its plain and unadorned style of architecture, is probably that of Drusus. Outside the Porta Appia the road descends to a small stream or brook, now called *Acquataccia*, which it crosses by a bridge less than half a mile from the gate: this trifling stream is identified, on good grounds, with the river Almo, celebrated for the peculiar sacred rites with which it was connected [ALMO]. A short distance beyond this the road makes a considerable bend, and ascends a bank or ridge before it reaches the second milestone. From that point it is carried in a straight line direct to the remains of Bovillae at the foot of the Alban Hills, running the whole way along a slightly elevated bank or ridge, formed in all probability by a very ancient current of lava from the Alban Mount. This long, straight line of road, stretching across the *Campagna*, and bordered throughout by the remains of tombs and ruins of other buildings, is, even at the present day, one of the most striking features in the neighbourhood of Rome, and, when the edifices which bordered it were still perfect, must have constituted a magnificent approach to the Imperial City. The whole line has been recently cleared and carefully examined. It is described in detail by the Car. Canina (in the *Annali dell' Instituto di Corrispondenza Archeologica* for 1852 and 1853; and more briefly by Desjardins, *Essai sur la Topographie du Latium*, 4to. Paris, 1854, pp. 92—130. We can here mention only some of the most interesting of the numerous monuments that have been thus brought to light, as well as those previously known and celebrated.

On the right of the road, shortly after crossing the *Almo*, are the remains of a vast sepulchre, which now serve to support the tavern or *Osteria dell'Acquataccio*; this is clearly identified by the inscriptions discovered there in 1773, as the monument of Abascantius, a freedman of Domitian, and of his wife Priscilla, of which Statius has left us in one of his poems a detailed description (Stat. *Silv.* v. 1). On the left of the road, almost exactly 3 miles from Rome, is the most celebrated of all the monuments of this kind, the massive sepulchre of Caecilia Metella, the daughter of Q Metellus Creticus, and wife of Crassus the triumvir. Converted into a fortress in the middle ages, this tower-like monument is still in remarkable preservation, and, from its commanding position, is a conspicuous object from all points of the surrounding country. It is popularly known as the *Capo di Bove*, from the bucranium which appears as an ornament in the frieze. (A view of this remarkable monument is given in the article ROMA, p. 822.) Before reaching the *Capo di Bove*, the road passes some extensive remains of buildings on the left, which appear to have formed part of an imperial villa constructed by the emperor Maxentius, attached to which are the remains of a circus, also the work of the same emperor, and which, from their remarkably perfect condition, have thrown much light on the general plan of these edifices. [ROMA, p. 844.]

Proceeding onwards from the tomb of Caecilia Metella, the road is bordered throughout by numerous sepulchres, the most remarkable of which is the tomb of Servilius Quartus, on the left, about 3¾ miles from Rome. The remarkable preservation of the ancient road in this part of its course, shows the accuracy of the description above cited from Procopius ; but it is remarkable that this, the greatest and most frequented highway of the Roman empire, was only just wide enough to admit of the passage of two carriages abreast, being only 15 feet broad between the raised *crepidines* which bordered it. After passing a number of obscure tombs on both sides of the way, there occurs, just beyond the fifth mile from Rome, a remarkable enclosure, of quadrangular form, surrounded by a low wall of Alban stone. This has frequently been supposed to be the Campus Sacer Horatiorum, alluded to by Martial (iii. 47) as existing on the Appian Way, and which preserved the memory of the celebrated combat between the Horatii and Curiatii. This was believed to have been fought just about 5 miles from Rome (Liv. i. 23), which would accord well with the position of the enclosure in question ; but it is maintained by modern antiquaries that this, which was certainly of a sacred character, more probably served the purposes of an Ustrinum, or place where the bodies of the dead were burned, previously to their being deposited in the numerous sepulchres that lined both sides of the Appian Way. These still form a continuous cemetery for above two miles farther. The most massive of them all, which must, when entire, have greatly exceeded even that of Caecilia Metella in magnitude, and from its circular form is known as the *Casal Rotondo*, occurs near the 6th mile from Rome, on the left of the Via Appia. From a fragment of an inscription found here, it is probable that this is the tomb of Messala Corvinus, the friend of Augustus and patron of Tibullus, and is the very monument, the massive solidity of which is more than once referred to by Martial ("Messalae saxa," viii. 3. 5; "marmora Messalae," x. 2. 9). Somewhat nearer Rome, on the same side of the road, are extensive ruins of a different description, which are ascertained to be those of a villa of the Quintilii, two brothers celebrated for their wealth, who were put to death by Commodus (Dion Cass. lxxii. 5), after which the villa in question probably became an imperial residence.

Some remains of a small temple, just 8 miles from Rome, have been supposed to be those of a temple of Hercules, consecrated or restored by Domitian at that distance from the city (Martial, iii. 47. 4, ix. 65. 4, 102. 12); but though the site of the temple in question is clearly indicated, it appears that the existing remains belong to an edifice of earlier date. Exactly 9 miles from Rome are the ruins of a villa of imperial date, within which is a large circular monument of brick, supposed with good reason to be the tomb of Gallienus, in which the emperor Flavius Severus also was buried. (Vict. *Epit.* lx.) Close to this spot must have been the station Ad Nonum mentioned in the Jerusalem Itinerary (*l. c.*). The road is still bordered on both sides by tombs; but none of these are of any special interest. At the *Osteria delle Fratocchie* (between 11 and 12 miles from Rome) the ancient Via is joined by the modern road to *Albano*: it here commences the ascent of the Alban Hills, which continues (though at first very gradually) for above 3

miles. A little farther on are the remains of Bovillae; the principal ruins of which lie a short distance to the right of the road. [BOVILLAE.] The Tabula marks that place as a station on the Via Appia, but erroneously places it 10 miles from Rome, while the real distance is 12 miles. Thence the road (still retaining its straight line) ascended the hill to *Albano, nearly on the site of the ALBANUM of Domitian, which, as we learn from Martial, was just 14 miles from Rome. (Martial, ix. 65. 4, 102. 12.) The remains of the imperial villa border the road on the left for some distance before reaching the modern town. Two miles farther was Aricia, which is correctly placed by both the Itineraries 16 miles from Rome. The station was probably below the town, outside of the walls, as the Via Appia here deviates from the straight line which it has pursued so long, and descends into the hollow below the city by a steep slope known as the Clivus Aricinus. A little farther on it is carried over the lowest part of the valley by a causeway or substruction of massive masonry, one of the most remarkable works of the kind now extant. [ARICIA.]

The remainder of the road will not require to be described in such detail. From Aricia it was continued, with a slight deviation from the direct line, avoiding the hills of *Genzano* and those which bound the *Lake of Nemi*, on the left, and leaving Lanuvium at some distance on the right, till it descended again into the plain beyond the Alban Hills and reached the station of Tres Tabernae. An intermediate station, Sub Lanuvio, indicated only in the Tabula, must have been situated where a branch road struck off to the city of Lanuvium. The position of Tres Tabernae has been much disputed, but without any good reason. That of Forum Appii, the next stage, is clearly established [FORUM APPII], and the 43rd milestone of the ancient road still exists on the spot; thus showing that the distances given in the Antonine Itinerary are perfectly correct. This being established, it is clear that Tres Tabernae is to be placed at a spot 10 miles nearer Rome, and about 3 miles beyond the modern *Cisterna*, where there are still ruins of ancient buildings, near a mediaeval tower called the *Torre d'Annibale*. The ancient pavement is still visible in many places between Aricia and Tres Tabernae, and no doubt can exist as to the course of the road. This was indeed carried in a perfectly straight line from the point where it descended into the plain, through the Pontine Marshes to within a few miles of *Terracina*. The position of the station Ad Sponsas, mentioned in the Jerusalem Itinerary, cannot be determined, as the distances there given are incorrect. We should perhaps read xii. for vii. as the distance from Forum Appii, in which case it must be placed 2 miles nearer Rome than Tres Tabernae. Between the latter station and Forum Appii was TRIPONTIUM, at which commenced the canal navigation called Decennovium from its being 19 miles in length. The site of this is clearly marked by a tower still called *Torre di Tre Ponti*, and the 19 miles measured thence along the canal would terminate at a point 3 miles from *Terracina*, where travellers quitted the canal for that city. An inscription records the paving of this part of the road by Trajan. The solitary posthouse of *Mesa*

* It was probably this long ascent that was known as the CLIVUS VIRBII, mentioned by Persius (vi. 55).

is evidently the station Ad Medias of the Jerusalem Itinerary. A short distance from *Terracina* the Via Appia at length deviated from the direction it had so long pursued, and turning to the left ascended the steep hill on which the ancient city stood [TARRACINA], while the modern road is carried round the foot of this hill, close to the sea. The distance of Tarracina from Rome is correctly given at 61 miles in the Antonine Itinerary.

From *Terracina* the line of the ancient road may still be traced distinctly all the way to *Fondi*, and is flanked by ruins of villas, dilapidated tombs, &c., through a great part of its course. It first ascended the hill above the city as far as the convent of *San Francesco*, and afterwards descended into the valley beneath, joining the modern highroad from Rome to Naples about 3 miles from *Terracina*, just before crossing the frontier of the Papal States. The narrow pass at the foot of the mountains, which the road here follows, between the rocks and the marshy lake of *Fondi*, is the celebrated defile of LAUTULAE, or Ad Lautulas, which more than once bears a conspicuous part in Roman history. [LAUTULAE.] The distance from Tarracina to Fundi is overstated in the Antonine Itinerary: the true distance does not exceed 13 miles, as correctly given in the Jerusalem Itinerary. From Fundi to Formiae (*Mola di Gaëta*), a distance of 13 miles, the road passed through a rugged and mountainous country, crossing a complete mountain pass: the substructions of the ancient way are in many places still visible, as well as portions of the pavement, and numerous ruins of buildings, for the most part of little interest. The bridges also are in several instances the ancient ones, or at least rest upon ancient substructions. The ruins of Formiae and of the numerous villas with which it was adorned line the shores at *Mola di Gaëta*, and bound the road for a space of more than 2 miles: other ruins, principally sepulchral, are scattered along its line almost all the way thence to MINTURNAE. The ruins of this latter city stand on the right bank of the Liris (*Garigliano*), a short distance from its mouth, and about a mile and a half below the village of *Traghetto*. The line of the ancient road from *Mola* thither is clearly traced and susceptible of no doubt: the distance is correctly given as 9 miles. Here the Via Appia crossed the Liris, and was continued nearly in a straight line through a level and marshy district along the sea-coast to Sinuessa, the ruins of which are found near the village of *Mondragone*. The distance of 9 miles between the two (given in both Itineraries) is somewhat less than the truth. It was at Sinuessa that the Appian Way finally quitted the coast of the Tyrrhenian sea (Strab. v. p. 233), and struck inland towards Capua, passing by the stations of Pons Campanus and Ad Octavum But this part of its course has not been very distinctly traced, and there is some difficulty as to the distances given. The three subdivisions of the Jerusalem Itinerary would give 26 miles for the total distance from Sinuessa to Capua; and the coincidence of this sum with the statement of the Antonine Itinerary, as given by Wesseling, is a strong argument in favour of the reading xxvi. M. P. instead of xvi. adopted by Pinder. The latter number is certainly too small, for the *direct* distance between the two points is not less than 21 miles, and the road must have deviated from the straight line on account of the occurrence of the marshes of the Savo, as well as of the river Vulturnus. It is

probable, therefore, that it made a considerable bend, and that the distance was thus prolonged: but the question cannot be settled until this part of the road has been more accurately traced than has hitherto been done. The distances given in the Tabula are too inaccurate to be of any use; but it appears probable from that document that the Pons Campanus was a bridge over the little river Savo, and not, as might have been suspected, over the Vulturnus, which the Appian Way did not cross till it arrived at Casilinum, 3 miles from Capua. It was here that it united with the Via Latina. (Strab. v. p. 237; *Tab. Peut.*)

The total distance from Rome to Capua (if we adopt 26 miles as that from Sinuessa) was therefore 131 miles. This portion of the Via Appia as far as Minturnae has been traced with much care by Westphal (*Römische Kampagne*, pp. 22—70), as well as by Chaupy (*Maison d'Horace*, vol. iii. pp. 365—461) and Sir R. Hoare (*Classical Tour*, vol. i. pp. 81—148); but all these accounts are deficient in regard to the portion between Minturnae and Capua.

Several minor branches or cross lines parted from the Via Appia during this first portion of its course. Of these it may suffice to mention : 1. The VIA ARDEATINA, which quitted the Via Appia at a short distance beyond the Almo, just after passing the *Osteria dell' Acquataccio*: it proceeded in a nearly straight line to Ardea, 23 miles from Rome. [ARDEA.] 2. The VIA ANTIATINA, which branched off from the Appian Way just before reaching Bovillae, and proceeded direct to Antium, 38 miles from Rome. It probably followed nearly the same line as the modern road, but its precise course has not been traced. 3. The VIA SETINA quitted the Appian Way, shortly after passing Trepontium, and proceeded in a direct line to Setia (*Sezze*) : considerable portions of the ancient pavement still remain. 4. A branch road, the name of which is unknown, diverged from the Via Appia at Minturnae, and proceeded to Teanum (18 miles distant) on the Via Latina, whence it was continued through Allifae and Telesia to Beneventum. [VIA LATINA.] 5. The VIA DOMITIANA, constructed by the emperor of that name, of which Statius has left us a pompous description. (*Silv.* iv. 3.) It was a continuation of the coast-road from Sinuessa, being carried across the Vulturnus close to its mouth by a bridge which must really have been a work of great difficulty ; thence it followed closely the line of coast as far as Cumae, whence it struck across to Puteoli. The road communicating between that city and Neapolis was previously in existence. The distances on this road, as given in the Antonine Itinerary (p. 122), are:—

From Sinuessa to Liternum   xxiv. M. P. (this must be a mistake for xiv.)

thence to Cumae - vi.
Puteoli - iii.
Neapolis - x.

There was also a direct road from Capua to Neapolis (*Tab. Peut.*), passing through Atella, which was midway between the two cities.

2. From Capua to Beneventum.

This portion of the road may be very briefly disposed of. From Capua it was continued along in the plain as far as Calatia, the site of which is fixed at *Le Galazze*, near *Maddaloni* ; it then entered the Apennines, and, passing through the valley of *Arienzo*, commonly supposed to be the celebrated valley of the Candine Forks, reached Candium, which must have been situated about 4 miles beyond Arpaja, on the road to Beneventum. The distances given along this line are :—

From Capua to Calatia - - - vi. M. P.
  Ad Novas - - - vi.
  Caudium - - - ix.
  Beneventum - - xi.

(*Itin. Ant.* p. 111; *Itin. Hier.* p. 610; *Tab. Peut.*) It was at Beneventum, as above shown, that the two main branches of the Appian Way separated : the one proceeding by Venusia and Tarentum to Brundusium; the other by Equus Tuticus and Canusium to Barium, and thence along the coast of the Adriatic. We proceed to give these two branches separately.

3. From Beneventum to Brundusium, through Venusia and Tarentum.

The line of this road is given in the Antonine Itinerary (p. 120) as well as in the Tabula; but in this last it appears in so broken and confused a form that it would be unintelligible without the aid of the other authority. But that this line was the original Via Appia is proved not only by the distinct testimony of Strabo, and by incidental notices which show that it was the frequented and customary route in the time of Cicero (Cic. *ad Att.* v. 5, 7), but still more clearly by an inscription of the time of Hadrian, in which the road from Beneventum to Aeculanum is distinctly called the Via Appia. The greater part of the line from Beneventum to Venusia, and thence to Tarentum, was carried through a wild and mountainous country; and it is highly probable that it was in great measure abandoned after the more convenient line of the Via Trajana was opened. It appears that Hadrian restored the portion from Beneventum to Aeculanum, but it is doubtful whether he did so farther on. Nevertheless the general course of the road can be traced, though many of the stations cannot be fixed with certainty. The latter are thus given in the Antonine Itinerary :—

From Beneventum to
 Aeculanum - - - - - xv. M. P.
 Sub Romulea - - - - xxi.
 Pons Aufidi - - - - - xxii.
 Venusia (*Venosa*) - - - xviii.
 Silvium (*Garagnone*) - - xx.
 Blera (*Gravina*) - - - xiii.
 Sub Lupatia - - - - xiv.
 Canales - - - - - - xiii.
 Tarentum (*Taranto*) - - xx.

Aeculanum, or Eclanum as the name is written in the Itineraries, is fixed beyond a doubt at *Le Grotte*, near *Mirabella*, just 15 miles from Beneventum, where a town grew up on its ruins in the middle ages with the name of Quintodecimum. [AECULANUM.] The site of Romulea is much less certain, but may perhaps be placed at *Bisaccia*, and the station Sub Romulea in the valley below it. The Pons Aufidi is the *Ponte Sta Venere*, on the road from *Lacedogna* to *Venosa*, which is unquestionably an ancient bridge, and the distance from Venusia agrees with that in the Itinerary, which is confirmed also in this instance by the Tabula. The latter authority gives as an intermediate station between Sub Romulea and the Pons Aufidi, Aquilonia, which is probably *Lacedogna;* but the distances given are certainly incorrect. In this wild and mountainous country it is obviously impossible at present to determine these with any accuracy. From Venusia again the Via Appia appears to have passed, in as direct

a line as the nature of the country will allow, to Tarentum; the first station, Silvium, may probably be placed at *Garagnone*, and the second, Plera, or Blera, at or near *Gravina;* but both determinations are very uncertain. Those of Sub Lupatia and Canales are still more vague, and, until the course of the ancient road shall have been traced upon the spot by some traveller, it is idle to multiply conjectures.

From Tarentum to Brundusium the Antonine Itinerary gives 44 M. P., which is nearly correct; but the intermediate stations mentioned in the Tabula, Mesochoron, Urbius, and Scamnum, cannot be identified. Urbius may perhaps be a corruption of Urium or Hyrium, the modern *Oria*, which is nearly midway between the two cities.

Besides the main line of the Via Appia, as above described, the Itineraries mention several branches, one of which appears to have struck off from Venusia to Potentia, and thence to have joined the highroad to Rhegium, while another descended from Venusia to Heraclea on the gulf of Tarentum, and thence followed the E. coast of the Bruttian peninsula. These lines are briefly noticed in the articles LUCANIA and BRUTTII, but they are very confused and uncertain.

4. From Beneventum by Canusium and Barium to Brundusium.

It was this line of road, first constructed by Trajan, and which was originally distinguished as the VIA TRAJANA, that became after the time of that emperor the frequented and ordinary route to Brundusium, and thus came to be commonly considered as the Via Appia, of which it had in fact taken the place. Its line is in consequence given in all the Itineraries, and can be traced with little difficulty. It passed at first through a rugged and mountainous country, as far as Aecae in Apulia, from which place it was carried through the plains of Apulia to Barium, and afterwards along the sea-coast to Brundusium: a line offering no natural difficulties, and which had the advantage of passing through a number of considerable towns. Even before the construction of the Via Trajana it was not uncommon (as we learn from the journey of Horace) for travellers to deviate from the Appian Way, and gain the plains of Apulia as speedily as possible.

The first part of this road from Beneventum to Aecae may be traced by the assistance of ancient milestones, bridges, &c. (Mommsen, *Topogr. degli Irpini*, in the *Bullet. dell' Inst. Arch.* for 1848, pp. 6, 7.) It proceeded by the villages of *Paduli, Buonalbergo,* and *Casalbore,* to a place called *S. Eleuterio*, about 2 miles S. of *Castelfranco*, which was undoubtedly the site of Equus Tuticus, a much disputed point with Italian topographers. [EQUUS TUTICUS.] This is correctly placed by the Antonine Itinerary 21 miles from Beneventum ; the Jerusalem Itinerary, which makes it 22 miles, divides the distance at a station called Forum Novum, which must have been situated at or very near *Buonalbergo*. From Equus Tuticus, the road followed a NE. direction to Aecae (the site of which is clearly known as that of the modern *Troja*), and thence turned in a direction nearly due E. to Herdonia (*Ordona*). The object of this great bend was probably to open a communication with Luceria and the other towns of Northern Apulia, as well as perhaps to avoid the defile of the *Cervaro*, above *Bovino*, through which the modern road passes. At Aecae the Via Trajana descended into the great plain of Apulia, across which it was carried in a nearly straight line to Barium (*Bari*). The remainder of its course presents no difficulties, and the stations are, for the most part, well-known towns. The whole line is thus given in the Antonine Itinerary (pp. 112, 116):—

From Beneventum to

		M. P.
Equus Tuticus (*S. Eleuterio*)	-	xxi.
Aecae (*Troja*) - - - - - -		xviii.*
Herdonia (*Ordona*) - - - -		xviii.
Canusium (*Canosa*) - - - -		xxvi.
Rubi (*Ruvo*) - - - - - -		xxiii.
Butuntum (*Bitonto*) - - - -		xi.
Barium (*Bari*) - - - - - -		xi.
Turres (?) - - - - - - -		xxi.
Egnatia (*Torre di Gnazia*) - - -		xvi.
Speluncae (?) - - - - - -		xx.
Brundusium (*Brindisi*) - - - -		xviii.

The two stations of Turres between Barium and Egnatia, and Speluncae between Egnatia and Brundusium, cannot be identified; it is evident from the names themselves that they were not towns, but merely small places on the coast so called. The Jerusalem Itinerary has two stations, Turres Aurelianae, and Turres Juliae, between Egnatia and Barium, but, from the distances given, neither of these can be identified with the Turres of the Antonine Itinerary. The other intermediate stations mentioned by the same authority are unimportant Mutationes, which can be identified only by a careful survey on the spot.

The Tabula gives (though in a very confused manner) an intermediate line of route, which appears to have been the same as that indicated by Strabo (v. p. 283), which quitted the coast at Egnatia, and proceeded through Caelia to Brundusium. The stations given are:—

		M. P.
Canusium to Rudiae	- - -	xii.
Rubi	- - - -	xiv.
Butuntum	- -	ix.
Caelia (*Ceglie*)	-	ix.
Ehetium (*Azetium?*)	—	
Norve (?) - - -		ix.
Ad Veneris (?) - -		viii.
Egnatia - - -		viii.

It is certain that the Via Trajana was continued, probably by Trajan himself, from Brundusium to Hydruntum (*Otranto*), and was thence carried all round the Calabrian peninsula to Tarentum. The road from Brundusium to Hydruntum passed through Lupiae (*Lecce*), in the interior of the peninsula, which is correctly placed 25 miles from each of the above cities. (*Itin. Ant.* p. 118.) The stations on the other line, which is given only in the Tabula, are as follow:—

	M. P.
Hydruntum to Castrum Minervae (*Castro*)	viii.
Veretum (*Sta Maria di Vereto*) - - - - -	xii.
Uxentum (*Ugento*) - -	x.
Baletium (*Aletium*) - -	x.
Neretum (*Nardò*) - -	x.
Manduria (*Manduria*) -	xxix.
Tarentum (*Taranto*) -	xx.

The above distances appear to be correct.

Lastly, a branch struck off from the Via Trajana at Barium which proceeded direct to Tarentum. It is probable that this came to be adopted as the most convenient mode of reaching the latter city when

the original Via Appia had fallen into disuse. The distance is correctly given as 60 miles. (*Itin. Ant.* p. 119.)

Besides the above, which may be considered as all in some degree branches of the Via Trajana, there was another line, probably constructed at a late period, which struck across from Equus Tuticus to Venusia, so as to form a cross communication between the Via Trajana and the old Via Appia. This is set down in the Antonine Itinerary (p. 103) as part of a long line proceeding from the N. of Italy to the S.; but the intermediate stations between Equus Tuticus and Venusia cannot be determined.

5. From Capua by Nuceria to Rhegium.

This line of road is indicated by Strabo in the passage above cited (v. p. 283) as existing in his time, but he certainly did not include it under the name of the Via Appia. It seems, however, to have subsequently come to be regarded as such, as the Antonine Itinerary puts it under the heading, "Ab Urbe Appia via recto itinere ad Columnam" (*Itin. Ant.* p. 106.)*, and inasmuch as it was a continuation of the original Appian Way, it was, strictly speaking, as much entitled to bear the name as the Via Trajana. Strabo does not tell us whether it was passable in his day for carriages or not, and we have no account in any ancient author of its construction. But we learn the period at which it was first opened from a remarkable inscription discovered at *La Polla*, in the valley of *Diano*, which commemorates the construction of the road from Rhegium to Capua, and adds the distances of the principal towns along its course: unfortunately the first line, containing the name of the magistrate by whom it was opened, is wanting; and the name of M. Aquilius Gallus, inserted by Gruter and others, is a mere conjecture. There is little doubt that the true restoration is the name of P. Popilius Laenas, who was praetor in B.C. 134, and who, after clearing the mountains of Lucania and Bruttium of the fugitive slaves who had taken refuge in them, appears to have first constructed this highroad through that rugged and mountainous country. (Mommsen, *Inscr. R. N.* 6276; Ritschl. *Mon. Epigr.* pp. 11, 12.) There is, therefore, no foundation whatever for the name of VIA AQUILIA, which has been given by some modern writers (Romanelli, Cramer, &c.) to this line of road: it was probably at first called VIA POPILIA, after its author, who, as was usual in similar cases, founded at the same time a town which bore the name of Forum Popilii, and occupied the site of *La Polla* [FORUM POPILII]; but no mention of this name is found in any ancient author, and it seems to have been unknown to Strabo. The distances given in the inscription above mentioned (which are of the greatest value, from their undoubted authenticity), are:—

		M. P.
From Capua to Nuceria	- - -	xxxiii.
[Forum Popilii] -	- -	li.
Muranum	- - -	lxxiv.
Consentia	- - -	xlix.
Valentia	- - -	lvii.
Ad Statuam	- -	li.
Rhegium	- - -	vi.

The point designated as "Ad Fretum ad Statuam" is evidently the same as the Columna of the Itineraries, which marked the spot from which it was

---

* This distance must be above the truth: the direct distance is not more than 8 miles.

* The words "Appia via" may, however, refer only to the first part of this route, which certainly followed the true Appian Way as far as Capua.

usual to cross the Sicilian straits. The total distance from Capua to Rhegium, according to the above description, is 321 miles. The Antonine Itinerary makes it 337 miles. It is difficult to judge how far this discrepancy is owing to errors in the distances as given in our MSS., or to alterations in the line of road; for though it is evident that the road given in the Itinerary followed *generally* the same line as that originally constructed by Popilius, it is probable that many alterations had taken place in particular parts; and in the wild and mountainous tracts through which the greater part of it was carried, such alterations must frequently have been rendered necessary. The determination of the particular distances is, for the same reason, almost impossible, without being able to trace the precise course of the ancient road, which has not yet been accomplished. The stations and distances, as given in the Antonine Itinerary, are as follow:—

		M. P.
From Capua to Nola	- - - -	xxi. (xix.)*
Nuceria (*Nocera*)	-	xvi.* (xiv.)
Ad Tanarum	- -	xxv.
Ad Calorem	- -	xxiv.
In Marcelliana	- -	xxv.
Caesariana	- - -	xxi.
Nerulum (*LaRotonda*)		xxiii.
Sub Murano (near *Murano*)	- - -	xiv.
Caprasiae (*Tarsia*)	-	xxi.
Consentia (*Cosenza*)		xxviii.
Ad Sabatum fluvium		xviii.
Ad Turres	- - -	xviii.
Vibona (*Monte Leone*)		xxi.
Nicotera (*Nicotera*)	-	xviii.
Ad Mallias	- - -	xxiv.
Ad Columnam	- -	xiv.

The stations between Nuceria and Nerulum cannot be determined. Indeed the only points that can be looked upon as certain, in the whole line from Nuceria to Rhegium, are Sub Murano, at the foot of the hill on which stands the town of *Murano*, Consentia (*Cosenza*), Vibo Valentia (*Monte Leone*), and Nicotera, which retains its ancient name. Nerulum and Caprasiae may be fixed with tolerable certainty by reference to these known stations, and the distances in this part of the route appear to be correct. The others must remain uncertain, until the course of the road has been accurately traced.

At Nerulum the above line of road was joined by one which struck across from Venusia through Potentia (*Potenza*) to that place. It was a continuation of the cross-road already noticed from Equus Tuticus to Venusia; this line, which is given in the Antonine Itinerary (p. 104), was called, as we learn from the inscriptions on milestones still extant, the VIA HERCULIA, and was therefore in all probability the work of the Emperor Maximianus. (Mommsen, *I. R. N.* p. 348.) The stations mentioned in the Itinerary (*l. c.*) are:—

		M. P.
From Venusia to Opinum	- - -	xv.
Ad fluv. Bradanum		xxix.

* Both these distances are overstated, and should probably be corrected as suggested by the numbers in parentheses. The same distances are given in the Tab. Peut. thus:—

		M. P.
Capua to Suessula	- - -	ix.
Nola	- - - - - -	ix.
Ad Teglanum	-- - - - -	v.
Nuceria	- - - - -	ix.

From Venusia to Potentia (*Potenza*)	xxiv.
Acidii (?) - - -	xxiv.
Grumentum (*Saponara*) - - -	xxviii.
Semuncla (?) - -	xxvii.
Nerulum - - -	xvi.

None of the above stations can be identified, except Potentia and Grumentum, and the distances are in some cases certainly erroneous. The same line of route is given in the Tabula, but in a very confused and corrupt manner. The stations there set down are wholly different from those in the Itinerary, but equally uncertain. Anxia (*Anzi*), between Potentia and Grumentum is the only one that can be identified.

The principal work on the Via Appia is that of Pratilli (*Della Via Appia*, fol. Napoli, 1745); but, unfortunately, little dependence can be placed upon it. Parts of the route have been carefully and accurately examined by Westphal, Chaupy, and other writers already cited, but many portions still remain to be explored; and accurate measurements are generally wanting. Nor does there exist any map of the kingdom of Naples on which dependence can be placed in this respect.   [E. H. B.]

VIA AQUILIA. [VIA APPIA, No. 5.]

VIA ARDEATINA. [ARDEA.]

VIA AURELIA, one of the principal highways of Italy, which led from Rome to Pisae in Etruria, and thence along the coast of Liguria to the Maritime Alps. It was throughout almost its whole extent a maritime road, proceeding, in the first instance, from Rome to Alsium on the Tyrrhenian sea, whence it followed the coast-line of Etruria, with only a few trifling deviations, the whole way to Pisae. The period of its construction is quite uncertain. Its name sufficiently indicates that it was the work of some magistrate of the name of Aurelius; but which of the many illustrious men who bore this name in the latter ages of the Republic was the author of it, we are entirely uninformed. We know with certainty that it was in use as a well-known and frequented highway in the time of Cicero, who mentions it as one of the three roads by which he might proceed to Cisalpine Gaul ("ab infero mari Aurelia," *Phil.* xii. 9). It may also be probably inferred that it was in existence as far as Pisae, when the road was carried from that city to Vada Sabata and Dertona, the construction of which is ascribed by Strabo to Aemilius Scaurus, in B.C. 109 (Strab. v. p. 217). [VIA AEMILIA SCAURI.] This continuation of the Aurelian Way seems to have been commonly included under the same general name as the original road; though, according to Strabo, it was properly called the Aemilian Way, like its more celebrated namesake in Cisalpine Gaul. It was apparently not till the reign of Augustus that the line of road was carried along the foot of the Maritime Alps, from Vada Sabata to Cemenelium, and thence into Gaul. It is certain, at least, that the ancient road, of which the traces are still visible, was the work of that emperor; and we know also that the Ligurian tribes who inhabited the Maritime Alps were not completely reduced to subjection till that period. [LIGURIA.] The Itineraries, however, give the name of Via Aurelia to the whole line of road from Rome to Arelate in Gaul; and though little value can be attached to their authority on this point, it is not improbable that the name was frequently used in this more extended sense; just as that of the Via Appia was applied to the whole line from Rome to Brundusium, though originally carried only as far as Capua.

The stations from Rome, as far as Luna in Etruria, are thus given in the Antonine Itinerary (p. 290, &c.):

		M.P.
Lorium (near *Castel Guido*)	-	xii. M.P.
Ad Turres (*Monteroni*))	-	x.
Pyrgi (*Sta Severa*)	- -	xii.
Castrum Novum (*T. di Chiaruccia*)	viii.
Centum Cellae (*Civita Vecchia*)	v.
Martha (Ad Martam fl.)	- -	x.
Forum Aurelii (*Montalto?*)	-	xxiv.
Cosa (*Ansedonia*)	- -	xxv.
Ad lacum Aprilem (Prilem)	-	xxii.
Salebro (?)	- -	xii.
Manliana (?)	- -	ix.
Populonium (Ru. of *Populonia*)	xii.
Vada Volaterrana (*Vada*)	-	xxv.
Ad Herculem (near *Livorno*)	-	xviii.
Pisae (*Pisa*)	- -	xii.
Papiriana (*Viareggio ?*)	- -	xi.
Luna (*Luni*)	- -	xxiv.

The stations thence along the coast of Liguria as far as the river Varus have been mentioned in the article LIGURIA; and the distances along this part of the line, in both the Antonine Itinerary and the Tabula, are so confused and corrupt that it is useless to attempt their correction. Even of that part of the Via Aurelia above given, along the coast of Etruria, several of the stations are very uncertain, and some of the distances are probably corrupt. From Rome to Centum Cellae, indeed, the road has been carefully examined and the distances verified (Westphal, *Röm. Kamp.* pp. 162—169); but this has not been done farther on: and as the road traversed the *Maremma*, which was certainly in the latter ages of the Roman Empire, as at the present day, a thinly-peopled and unhealthy district, several of the stations were probably even then obscure and unimportant places. The Tabula, as usual, gives a greater number of such stations, several of which may be identified as the points where the road crossed rivers and streams whose names are known. But the route is given very confusedly, and the distances are often incorrect, while in some cases they are omitted altogether.

From Rome to			M.P.
Lorium (*Castel Guido*)	-	-	xii.
Baebiana (?)	-	-	—
Alsium (*Palo*)	-	-	vi.
Pyrgi (*Sta Severa*)	-	-	x
Punicum (*Sta Marinella*)	-	—
Castrum Novum (*Torre di Chiaruccia*)	ix.
Centum Cellas (*Civita Vecchia*)	iv.
(Ad) Minionem fl. (*River Mignone*)	—
Graviscae	-	-	-	—
Tabellaria (?)	-	-	v.
Ad Martam fl.	-	-	ii.
Forum Aurelii (*Montalto?*)	-	iii.
(Ad) Arminiam fl. (*River Fiora*)	iv.
Ad Novas, or Ad Nonas	-	iii.
Sub Cosam	-	-	ii.
Cosa (*Ansedonia*)	-	-	ii.
(Ad) Albiniam fl. (*R. Albegna*)	ix.
Telamonem (*Porto Talamone*)	-	iv.
Hastam	-	-	viii.
(Ad) Umbronem fl. (*R. Ombrone*)	viiii.(?)
Salebro (?)	-	-	xii.
Manliana (?)	-	-	ix.
Populonium (Ru. of *Populonia*)	xii.
Vada Volaterrana (*Vada*)	-	xx.(?)
Ad Fines	-	-	viii.(?)
(Ad) Piscinas	-	-	xiii.(?)
Turrita (*Triturrita*)	-	xvi.(?)
Pisae (*Pisa*)	-	-	ix.(?)

The distances between Populonium and Pisae, as well as those between Centum Cellas and Cosa, are in many cases unintelligible; and it is often impossible to say to which of the stages they are meant to refer.

The Via Aurelia (in the more extended sense of the term, as used in the Itineraries) communicated with Cisalpine Gaul and the Via Aemilia by two different routes; the one, which according to Strabo was constructed by Aemilius Scaurus at the same time that he continued the Via Aurelia to Vada Sabata, led from that place across the Apennines to Aquae Statiellae, and thence to Dertona, to which place the Via Aemilia had probably already been prolonged. (Strab. v. p. 217.) The other, which was known as the Via Postumia, and was therefore probably constructed at a different period, led from Dertona across the mountains direct to Genua. Both these lines are given in the Antonine Itinerary and in the Tabula; though in the former they are confused and mixed up with the direct line of the coast-road. [LIGURIA.]

1. From Genua to Dertona the stations were:—
Libarnum (Ru. between *Arquata*
    and *Serravalle*) - - xxxvi. M.P.
Dertona (*Tortona*) - - xxxv.
The continuation of this route thence to Placentia will be found under VIA AEMILIA.

2. From Dertona to Vada Sabata:—
D. to Aquae Statiellas (*Acqui*) xxvii. M.P.
    Crixia (?) - - xx. (xxii. *Tab.*)
    Canalicum (?) - x. (xx. *Tab.*)
    Vada Sabata (*Vado*) xii.
(For the correction of these distances and more detailed examination of the routes in question, see Walckenaer, *Géographie des Gaules*, vol. iii. p. 22.)   [E. H. B.]

VIA CANDA'VIA. [VIA EGNATIA.]

VIA CASSIA, was the name given to one of the principal highroads of Italy which led from Rome through the heart of Etruria to Arretium, and thence by Florentia to Luca. The period of its construction, as well as the origin of its name, is unknown. We learn only from a passage of Cicero that it was a well-known and frequented highway in his time, as that orator mentions it as one of the three roads by which he could proceed to Cisalpine Gaul. (Cic. *Phil.* xii. 9.) In the same passage, after speaking of the Flaminian Way as passing along the Upper Sea, and the Aurelian along the Lower, he adds : "Etruriam discriminat Cassia." Hence it is clear that it was the principal road through the centre of that province, and is evidently the same given in the Antonine Itinerary (p. 285), though it is there erroneously called the Via Clodia. But indeed the occurrence of the Forum Cassii upon this line is in itself a sufficient proof that it was the Cassian and not the Clodian Way. The stations there set down, with their distances, are as follow:—

From Rome to Baccanae (*Baccano*)	- -	M.P. xxi.
Sutrium (*Sutri*)	- - -	xii.
Forum Cassii (near *Vetralla*)	- - - -	xi.
Volsinii (*Bolsena*)	- -	xxviii.
Clusium (*Chiusi*)	- -	xxx.
Ad Statuas	- -	xii.
Arretium (*Arezzo*)	- -	xxv.
Ad Fines	- -	xxv.
Florentia (*Firenze*)	- -	xxv.
Pistoria (*Pistoja*)	- -	xxv.
Luca (*Lucca*)	- - -	xxv.

The Via Cassia branched off from the Via Flaminia just after crossing the Tiber by the Milvian Bridge, 3 miles from Rome. It then ascended the table-land, and proceeded over a dreary and monotonous plain to Baccanae (*Baccano*), situated in the basin or crater of an extinct volcano. Two intermediate small stations are given in the Tabula: Ad Sextum, which, as its name imports, was situated 6 miles from Rome, and therefore 3 from the Pons Milvius; and Veii, 6 miles farther: but it is probable that the ancient Via Cassia, like the modern highroad, passed *by*, but not *through*, the ancient city; so that the station indicated was probably that where the road turned off to Veii, near the *Isola Farnese*. The Via Clodia separated from the Cassia about 3 miles beyond the station Ad Sextum, and struck off through Careiae (*Galera*) and Sabate (*Bracciano*) to Forum Clodii. The Tabula again gives an intermediate station, between Sutrium and Forum Cassii, called Vicus Matrini, the ruins of which are still visible 7 miles beyond *Sutri;* and that of the Aquae Passeris, now called the *Bagni di Serpa*, 12 miles beyond Forum Cassii. The stations given in that document can thus be identified as far as Clusium. They are :—

Ad Sextum	-	vi. M.P.
Veii (near *Isola Farnese*)	-	vi.
Baccanae (*Baccano*)	-	ix.
Sutrium (*Sutri*)	-	xii.
Vicus Matrini	-	(omitted, but should be vii.)
Forum Cassii (*Vetralla*)	-	iv.
Aquae Passeris (*Bagni di Serpa*)		xi.
Volsinii (*Bolsena*)	-	ix.
Ad Palliam Fluvium (*R. Paglia*)	—	
Clusium (*Chiusi*)	-	ix.

But from Clusium to Florentia the names of the stations are wholly unknown, and cannot be identified, with the exception of Arretium; and the entire route is given in so confused a manner that it is impossible to make anything of it.

Livy tells us that C. Flaminius, the colleague of M. Aemilius Lepidus in B.C. 187, after having effectually reduced the Ligurian tribes that had infested the territory of Bononia, constructed a road from Bononia to Arretium (Liv. xxxix. 2). But it is remarkable that we never hear anything more of this line of road, which would seem to have fallen into disuse; though this pass across the Apennines, which is still traversed by the modern highroad from *Florence* to *Bologna*, is one of the easiest of all. Cicero indeed might be thought to allude to this route when he speaks of proceeding into Cisalpine Gaul by the Via Cassia (*l. c.*); but the absence of any allusion to its existence during the military operations at that period, or on any other occasion, seems to prove conclusively that it had not continued in use as a military highway.

(For a careful examination and description of the portion of the Via Cassia near Rome, see Westphal, *Röm. Kamp.* pp. 147—153; Nibby, *Vie degli Antichi*, pp. 75—82.) [E. H. B.]

VIA CIMINIA, a name known only from an inscription of the time of Hadrian (Orell. *Inscr.* 3306), was probably a short cut constructed across the range of the Ciminian hills, leaving the Via Cassia to the left, and following nearly the same line as the modern road over the same hills. (Holsten. *Not. ad Cluv.* p. 67.) [CIMINUS MONS.] [E. H. B.]

VIA CLODIA, was the name of a highroad that branched off from the Via Cassia, to the left, about

10 miles from Rome, near the inn of *La Storta*, where remains of the ancient pavement, indicating its direction, may still be seen. The name of the Via Clodia is known to us only from the Itineraries, and from inscriptions of imperial date (Orell. *Inscr.* 822, 3143); but from the form of the name there can be no doubt that it dates from the republican period, though we have no account when or by whom this line of road was constructed. The Itineraries indeed seem to have regarded the Via Clodia as the main line, of which the Via Cassia was only a branch, or rather altogether confounded the two; but it is evident from the passage of Cicero above quoted, that the Via Cassia was, properly speaking, the main line, and the Clodia merely a branch of it. At the same time, the occurrence of a Forum Clodii on the one branch, as well as a Forum Cassii on the other, leave no doubt which were the true lines designated by these names. The course of the Via Clodia as far as Sabate (*Bracciano*) admits of no doubt, though the distances given in the Tabula are corrupt and uncertain; but the position of Forum Clodii is uncertain, and the continuation of the line is very obscure. It appears indeed to have held a course nearly parallel with that of the Via Cassia, through Blera, Tuscania, and Saturnia; but from the latter place the Tabula represents it as proceeding to Succosa (Sub Cosa), which would be an abrupt turn at right angles, and could never have been the direction of the principal line of road. It is probable that this was either carried up the valley of the Ombrone to Siena (Sena Julia), or proceeded across the marshy plains of that river to join the Via Aurelia. But this is mere conjecture. The stations, as given in the Tabula (the only one of the Itineraries in which the true Via Clodia is found), are as follow :—

From Rome to Ad Sextum	-	vi. M.P.
Careiae (*Galera*)	-	ix.
Ad Novas	-	viii.
Sabate (*Bracciano*)		—
Forum Clodii		—
Blera (*Bieda*)	-	xvi. (?)
Marta (Ad Martam fl.)		ix.
Tuscania (*Toscanella*)		—
Maternum (*Farnese*?)		xii.
Saturnia (*Saturnia*)		xviii.

The Antonine Itinerary, without giving the route in detail, says simply—

A Roma Foro Clodii, M.P. xxxii.

If this distance be correct, Forum Clodii must be placed either at or a little beyond *Oriuolo*, which is 6 miles beyond Sabate (*Bracciano*). The distance of *Oriuolo* from Rome by the line of the Via Clodia (as measured on Gell's map), somewhat exceeds 31 miles. But the distance from Blera must, in that case, be greatly overstated; the actual distance from Oriuolo to Bieda being scarcely more than 10 miles. (Westphal, *Röm. Kampagne*, pp. 154—158; Dennis's *Etruria*, vol. i. p. 273: but the distances there cited, in the note from the Tabula, are incorrect.) [E. H. B.]

VIA DOMITIANA. [VIA APPIA, No. 1.]

VIA EGNATIA (ἡ Ἐγνατία ὁδός, Strab. vii. p. 322, seq.), a Roman military road, which connected Illyria, Macedonia, and Thrace. We are almost totally in the dark with regard to the origin of this road. The assumption that it was constructed by a certain person named Egnatius, who was likewise the founder of the town Egnatia, or Gnatia, between Barium and Brundusium, on the coast of Apulia, is a mere conjecture, which cannot be supported by any authority. We may, however, make some approximation towards ascertaining the date of its construction, or, at all events, that of a portion of it. Strabo, in the passage cited at the head of this article, says that Polybius estimated the length of the via, between the coast of the Adriatic and the city of Thessalonica, at 267 Roman miles; whence it appears that this portion of it at least was extant in the time of Polybius. Consequently, as that historian flourished in the first half of the 2nd century B. C., we may infer with tolerable certainty that the road must have been commenced shortly after the reduction of Macedonia by the Romans in B. C. 168. Whether the eastern portion of the road, namely, that between Thessalonica and Cypsela, a town 10 miles beyond the left, or E., bank of the Hebrus, was also completed in the time of Polybius, is a point which cannot be so satisfactorily ascertained. For although Strabo, in the same passage, after mentioning the length of the road, from its commencement to its termination at Cypsela, proceeds to say that, if we follow Polybius, we must add 178 stadia to make up the number of Roman miles, because that writer computed 8 stadia and 2 plethra, or 8¼ stadia, to the Roman mile, instead of the usual computation of exactly 8; yet Strabo may then be speaking only of the historian's general practice, without any reference to this particular road. And, on the whole, it may perhaps be the more probable conclusion that the eastern portion of the road was not constructed till some time after the Romans had been in possession of Macedonia.

According to the same geographer, who is the chief authority with regard to this via, its whole length was 535 Roman miles, or 4280 stadia; and although the first portion of it had two branches, namely, one from Epidamnus or Dyrrachium and another from Apollonia, yet, from whichever of those towns the traveller might start, the length of the road was the same. Into the accuracy of this statement we shall inquire further on. Strabo also mentions that the first part of the road was called in Candavium (ἐπὶ Κανδαουίας), and this name frequently occurs in the Roman writers. Thus Cicero (ad Att. iii. 7) speaks of travelling "per Candaviam," and Caesar (B. C. iii. 79) mentions it as the direct route into Macedonia. It does not, however, very clearly appear to how much of the road this name was applicable. Tafel, who has written a work on the Via Egnatia, is of opinion that the appellation of Candavia may be considered to extend from the commencement of the via, including the two branches from Dyrrachium and Apollonia, to the town of Lychnidus. (De Via mil. Rom. Egnatia, Proleg. p. xcix. Tubing. 1842.) But this limitation is entirely arbitrary; and unsupported by any authority; and it would perhaps be a juster inference from the words of Strabo to assume that the name "Candavia" was applicable to the road as far as Thessalonica, as Col. Leake appears to have done. (Northern Greece, vol. iii. p. 311.) The point to be determined is, what does Strabo mean by "the first part?" The road in its whole extent he says is called "Via Egnatia," and the first part "in Candaviam" ('Η μὲν οὖν πᾶσα 'Εγνατία καλεῖται. Η δὲ πρώτη ἐπὶ Κανδαουίας λέγεται, κ. τ. λ.); and from what follows it is evident that he contemplated the division of the parts at Thessalonica, since he gives the separate measurement as far as that town, which is just half the whole length of the road.

We will consider the road as far as Thessalonica, or the Via Candavia, first. and then proceed to the remainder of the Egnatian Way. Strabo (l. c. and p. 326) lays down the general direction of the road as follows: After passing Mount Candavia, it ran to the towns of Lychnidus and Pylon; which last, as its name implies, was the border town between Illyria and Macedonia. Hence it proceeded by Barnus to Heracleia. and on through the territory of the Lyncestae and Eordaei through Edessa and Pella to Thessalonica. The whole extent of this line, as we have already seen, was 267 Roman miles; and this computation will be found to agree pretty accurately with the distance between Dyrrachium and Thessalonica as laid down in the Antonine Itinerary. According to that work, as edited by Parthey and Pinder (Berlin, 1848), who have paid great attention to the numbers, the stations and distances between those two places, starting from Dyrrachium, were as follow (p. 151):—

Clodiana				33 miles.
Scampa	-	-	-	20 "
Tres Tabernae	-	-	28 "
Lignidus (Lychnidus)	-	-	27 "
Nicias	-	-	-	32 "
Heracleia	-	-	-	11 "
Cellae	-	-	-	34 "
Edessa	-	-	-	28 "
Pella	-	-	-	28 "
Thessalonica	-	-	-	28 "
				269 "

The difference of 2 miles probably arises from some variation in the MSS. of the Itinerary. It should be observed, however, that, according to Wesseling's edition (p. 318, seq.), the distance is 11 miles more, or 280 miles, owing to variations in the text. According to the Tab. Peut. the whole distance was 279 miles, or 10 more than that given in the Itinerary; but there are great discrepancies in the distances between the places.

The last-named work gives 307 miles as the sum of the distances between Apollonia and Thessalonica; or 38 miles more than the route between Dyrrachium and the latter town. Both these routes united, according to the Itinerary, at Clodiana; and the distance from Apollonia to Clodiana was 49 miles, while that from Dyrrachium to the same place was only 33. This accounts for 16 miles of the difference, and the remainder, therefore, must be sought in that part of the road which lay between Clodiana and Thessalonica. Here the stations are the same as those given in the route from Dyrrachium, with the exception of the portion between Lychnidus and Heracleia; where, instead of the single station of Nicias, we have two, viz., Scirtiana, 27 miles from Lychnidus, and Castra, 15 miles from Scirtiana. And as the distance between Castra and Heracleia is stated at 12 miles, it follows that it was 11 miles farther from Lychnidus to Heracleia by this route than by that through Nicias. This, added to the 16 miles extra length to Clodiana, accounts for 27 miles of the difference; but there still remain 11 miles to make up the discrepancy of 38; and, as the stations are the same, this difference arises in all-probability from variations in the MSS.

According to the Itin. Hierosol. (p. 285, seq., Berlin ed.), which names all the places where the horses were changed, as well as the chief towns, the total distance between Apollonia and Thessalonica was 300 miles; which differs very slightly from that of the Itinerary, though there are several variations in the route.

Now, if we apply what has been said to the remark of Strabo, that the distance from Thessalonica was the same whether the traveller started from Epidamnus (Dyrrachium) or from Apollonia, it is difficult to perceive how such could have been the case if the junction of the two branches existed in his time also at Clodiana; since, as we have already seen, it was 16 miles farther to that place from Apollonia than from Dyrrachium according to the Itin. Ant.; and the Itin. Hierosol. makes it 24 miles farther. Indeed the maps would seem to show that if the two branches were of equal length, their junction must have taken place to the E. of Lake Lychnitis; the branch from Dyrrachium passing to the N. of that lake, and that from Apollonia to the S. But, although Burmeister, in his review of Tafel's work (in Zimmerman's *Zeitschrift für die Alterthumswissenschaft*, 1840, p. 1148), adopted such an hypothesis, and placed the junction at Heracleia, it does not appear that the assumption can be supported by any authority.

Clodiana, where the two branches of the Via Egnatia, or Candavia, united, was seated on the river Genusus (the *Tjerma* or *Skumbi*). From this point the valley of the river naturally indicated the course of the road to the E. (Leake, *Northern Greece*, vol. iii. p. 312.)

We will now proceed to consider the second, or eastern, portion of the Egnatian Way, viz., that between Thessalonica and Cypsela.

The whole length of this route, according to Strabo, was 268 Roman miles; and the distances set down in the Itin. Ant. amount very nearly to that sum, or to 265, as follows. (Pind. and Parth. p. 157; Wess. p. 330, seq.)

Apollonia	-	-	-	36 miles.
Amphipolis	-	-	-	32 „
Philippi	-	-	-	32 „
Acontisma	-	-	-	21 „
Otopisus (Topirus)	-	-	18 „
Stabulum Diomedis	-	-	22 „
Maximianopolis	-	-	18 „
Brizice or Brendice	-	-	20 „
Trajanopolis	-	-	-	37 „
Cypsela	-	-	-	29 „
				265 „

Another route given in the same Itinerary (Wess. p. 320, seq.) does not greatly vary from the above, but is not carried on to Cypsela. This adds the following stations:—Melissurgis, between Thessalonica and Apollonia, Neapolis, between Philippi and Acontisma, Cosintas, which according to Tafel (pars ii. p. 21) is meant for the river Cossinites, between Topirus and Maximianopolis, and Milolitum and Tempyra, between Brendice and Trajanopolis. The Itin. Hierosol. makes the distance only 250 miles.

Many remains of the Egnatian Way are said to be still traceable, especially in the neighbourhood of Thessalonica. (Beaujour, *Voy. militaire dans l'Empire Othoman*, vol. i. p. 205.)   [T. H. D.]

VIA FLAMINIA (ἡ Φλαμινία ὁδός), one of the most ancient and important of the highroads of Italy, which led from Rome direct to Ariminum, and may be considered as the *Great North Road* of the Romans, being the principal and most frequented line of communication with the whole of the north of Italy. It was also one of the first of the great

highways of which we know with certainty the period of construction, having been made by C. Flaminius during his censorship (B. C. 220), with the express purpose of opening a free communication with the Gaulish territory, which he had himself reduced to subjection a few years before. (Liv. *Epit.* xx.) It is therefore certainly a mistake, when Strabo ascribes it to C. Flaminius (the son of the preceding), who was consul together with M. Aemilius Lepidus, the author of the Aemilian Way, in B. C. 187, and himself constructed a road from Bononia to Arretium. (Liv. xxxix. 2 ; Strab. v. p. 217.) It is certain that the Flaminian Way was in existence long before, and its military importance was already felt and known in the Second Punic War, when the consul Sempronius proceeded by it to Ariminum, to watch the movements and oppose the advance of Hannibal. (Liv. xxii. 11.) Throughout the period of the Republic, as well as under the Empire, it was one of the best known and most frequented of the highways of Italy. Cicero, in one of the Philippics, says there were three ways which led from Rome to Cisalpine Gaul : the Flaminian by the Upper Sea (the Adriatic), the Aurelian by the Lower, and the Cassian through the midst of Etruria (*Phil.* xii. 9). During the contest between the generals of Vespasian and Vitellius (A. D. 69) the military importance of the Flaminian Way was fully brought out, and it was felt that its possession would be almost decisive of the victory. (Tac. *Hist.* i. 86, iii. 52, &c.) Tacitus alludes to the extent to which this great highway was at this period frequented, and the consequent bustle and crowding of the towns on its course (*Ib.* i. 64). Most of these, indeed, seem to have grown up into flourishing and populous places, mainly in consequence of the traffic along the line of road.

So important a highway was naturally the object of much attention, and great pains were taken not only to maintain, but to restore and improve it. Thus, in B. C. 27, when Augustus assigned the care of the other highways to different persons of consular dignity, he reserved for himself that of the Via Flaminia, and completely restored it throughout its whole length from Rome to Ariminum, a service which was acknowledged by the erection of two triumphal arches in his honour, one at Rome, the other at Ariminum, the latter of which is still standing. [ARIMINUM.] Again, at a later period, Vespasian added materially to the convenience of the road by constructing a tunnel through the rock at a place called Intercisa, now known as *Il Furlo*, a work which still subsists in its integrity. [INTERCISA.] This remarkable passage is particularly noticed by the poet Claudian, who has left us a general description of the Flaminian Way, by which the emperor Honorius proceeded, in A. D. 404, from Ravenna to Rome. (Claudian, *de VI. Cons. Hon.* 494—522.) Indeed, it is evident that in the latter ages of the Empire, when the emperors for the most part took up their residence at Mediolanum or Ravenna, the Flaminian Way, which constituted the direct line of communication between those cities and Rome, must have become of still greater importance than before.

One proof of the important influence exercised by this great line of highway, is afforded by the circumstance that, like the Aemilian Way, it gave name to one of the provinces of Italy in the later division of that country under the Empire; though, by a strange confusion or perverseness, the name of Flaminia was given, not to the part of Umbria which was actually traversed by the Via Flaminia, but to the eastern portion of Gallia Cispadana, which should naturally have been included in Aemilia. [ITALIA, p. 93.]

There is no doubt, from the description of Claudian above cited, compared with the narrative in Tacitus of the movements of the Vitellian and Vespasian armies in A. D. 69, that the main line of the Via Flaminia continued the same throughout the Roman Empire, but we find it given in the Itineraries with some deviations. The principal of these was between Narnia and Forum Flaminii, where the original road ran direct from Narnia to Mevania, while a branch or loop made a circuit by Interamna and Spoletium, which appears to have come to be as much frequented as the main line, so that in both the Antonine and Jerusalem Itineraries this branch is given, instead of the direct line. Another route given in the Antonine Itinerary (p. 811) follows the line of the old Flaminian Way as far as Nuceria, but thence turns abruptly to the right across the main ridge of the Apennines, and descends the valley of the Potentia to Ancona. Though given in the Itinerary under the name of the Via Flaminia, it may well be doubted whether this route was ever properly so called. Before enumerating the stations and distances along this celebrated line of road, as recorded in the different Itineraries, it will be well to give a brief general description of its course, especially of that part of it nearest to Rome.

The Via Flaminia issued from the gate of the same name, the Porta Flaminia, which was situated nearly on the same site as the modern *Porta del Popolo*, but a little farther from the Tiber, and was carried thence in a direct line to the Pons Milvius (*Ponte Molle*), where it crossed the Tiber. This celebrated bridge, which so often figures in Roman history, was reckoned to be 3 miles from Rome, though only 2 from the Porta Flaminia, the distances being as usual computed from the ancient gate, the Porta Ratumena. After crossing the Tiber, the Flaminian Way turned to the right, keeping pretty close to the river, while the Via Cassia, which diverged from it at this point, ascended the table-land and proceeded nearly due N. The line of the Via Flaminia is here distinctly marked by the remains of several ancient sepulchres, with which its course was studded on both sides, like the Via Appia and Latina, for some miles from the gates of Rome. The number of such sepulchres on the line of the Via Flaminia is particularly noticed by Juvenal (i. 171). One of these, which was discovered in the 17th century at a place called *Grotta Rossa*, obtained much celebrity from being supposed to be that of the family of Ovid, though in reality it belonged to a family of the name of Nasonius, which could have no connection with the poet, whose cognomen only was Naso.

Six miles from the Milvian Bridge (at a place now called *Prima Porta*) was the station of Saxa Rubra, or Ad Rubras as it is called in the Itineraries, which, from its proximity to Rome, and its position on the great northern highway, is repeatedly mentioned in history. [SAXA RUBRA.] It was here that the VIA TIBERINA parted from the Flaminia, and, turning off to the right, followed closely the valley of the river, while the main line of the more important highway ascended the table-land, and held nearly a straight course to the station of Rostrata Villa, which is placed by the Antonine Itinerary 24 miles from Rome. The exact site of this cannot be identified, but it must have been a little short of *Rignano*. It is not mentioned in the Tabula or Je-

rusalem Itinerary, both of which, on the contrary, give another station, Ad Vicesimum, which, as its name imports, was situated 20 miles from Rome, and, therefore, 11 from Ad Rubras. It must therefore have been situated a little beyond the *Monte di Guardia*, but was evidently a mere Mutatio, or station for changing horses, and no ruins mark the site. But the course of the Via Flaminia can be traced with certainty across this table-land to the foot of Soracte, by portions of the ancient pavement still existing, and ruined tombs by the roadside. The next station set down in the Jerusalem Itinerary and the Tabula is Aqua Viva, 12 miles beyond Ad Vicesimum, and this is identified beyond a doubt with the *Osteria dell' Acqua Viva*, which is just at the required distance (32 miles) from Rome. Thence the ancient road proceeded direct to the Tiber, leaving *Civita Castellana* (the ancient Fescennium) on the left, and crossed the Tiber a little above *Borghetto*, where the remains of the ancient bridge are still visible, and still known as the *Pile di Augusto*. Thence it proceeded in a straight line to Ocriculum, the ruins of which are situated below the modern town of *Otricoli*. Ocriculum was 12 M. P. from Aqua Viva, or 44 from Rome, according to the detailed distances of the Jerusalem Itinerary, which are exactly correct. The Antonine Itinerary makes the distance in one place 45, in another 47 miles. (*Itin. Ant.* pp. 125, 311; *Itin. Hier.* p. 613. For a detailed examination of this first portion of the Via Flaminia, see Westphal, *Römische Kampagne*, pp. 133—145; Nibby, *Vie degli Antichi*, pp. 57—74.)

The remainder of the route must be more briefly described. From Ocriculum it led direct to Narnia (12 miles), where it crossed the Nar by the famous bridge, the ruins of which are still the admiration of travellers, and, quitting altogether the valley of the Nar, crossed the hills nearly in a straight line due N. to Mevania (*Bevagna*), passing by a station Ad Martis (16 M. P.), and thence to Mevania (16 M. P.): whence it proceeded to Forum Flaminii, at the foot of the Apennines. But the distances here have not been examined in detail, and most of the Itineraries (as already mentioned) give the circuitous or loop line (nearly coinciding with the modern road) by Interamna and Spoletium to Forum Flaminii. The stations on this road were according to the Itin. Ant. :—

Interamna (*Terni*) - - -	viii.	M. P.
Spoletium (*Spoleto*) - - -	xviii.	
Forum Flaminii - - - -	xviii.	

but the Jerusalem Itinerary, which gives them in greater detail, makes the total distance somewhat greater. The stations as there set down are :—

Interamna (*Terni*) - - - -	viii.	M.P.
Tres Tabernae - - - - -	iii.	
Fanum Fugitivi - - - -	x.	
Spoletium (*Spoleto*) - - -	vii.	
Sacraria (*Le Vene*, at the sources		
of the Clitumnus) - - -	viii.	
Treba (*Trevi*) - - - -	iiii.	
Fulginium (*Foligno*) - - -	v.	
Forum Flaminii - - - -	iii.	

The position of Forum Flaminii is well ascertained at a place called *S. Giovanni in Forifiamma*, where its ruins are still visible. This is, however, little more than 2 miles from *Foligno*, but is correctly placed by the Itineraries 12 miles from Nuceria (*Nocera*). There can be no doubt that the foundation of the town of Forum Flaminii was contemporary with the construction of the highroad itself: it was judiciously placed just at the entrance of the Apennines, where the passage of those mountains may be considered to have commenced. Thence the highway followed nearly the same line as the modern road from *Foligno* to *Fano*, skirting the main ridge of the Apennines, and the principal stations can be identified without difficulty. It passed by Helvillum (*Sigillo*), crossed the central ridge of the Apennines at *La Schieggia* (probably Ad Ensem of the Tabula), and descended into the valley of the *Cantiano*, a tributary of the Metaurus, passing by Cales or Calles (*Cagli*), Intercisa (the *Passo del Furlo*), and emerging into the valley of the Metaurus at Forum Sempronii (*Fossombrone*), whence it descended the course of that river to Fanum Fortunae (*Fano*) on the Adriatic, and thence along the coast to Ariminum (*Rimini*), where it joined the Via Aemilia.

We may now recapitulate the distances as given, first, in the Antonine Itinerary (p. 125):—

From Rome to
Rostrata Villa -	- xxiv. M. P.
Ocriculum (*Otricoli*)	- - xxi.
Narnia (*Narni*) -	- - xii.
Ad Martis (near *Massa*)	- xvi.
Mevania (*Bevagna*) -	- xvi.
Nuceria (*Nocera*) -	- xviii.
Helvillum (*Sigillo*) -	- xiv.
Calles (*Cagli*)	- - xxiii.
Forum Sempronii (*Fossombrone*)	xviii.
Fanum Fortunae (*Fano*)	- xvi.
Pisaurum (*Pesaro*) -	- viii.
Ariminum (*Rimini*) -	- xxiv.

These distances are all approximately correct. The stations are given more in detail in the Jerusalem Itinerary (p. 613), as follow:—

From Rome to
Ad Rubras (*Prima Porta*)	- ix. M. P.
Ad Vicesimum -	- - xi.
Aqua Viva(*Osteria dell' Acqua Viva*)	xii.
Ocriculum (*Otricoli*) -	- xii.
Narnia (*Narni*) -	- xii.
Interamna (*Terni*) -	- viii.
Tres Tabernae -	- - iii.
Fanum Fugitivi (*Monte Somma*)	- x.
Spoletium (*Spoleto*) -	- vii.
Sacraria (*Le Vene*) -	- viii.
Trebia (*Trevi*) -	- iv.
Fulginium (*Foligno*) -	- v.
Forum Flaminii (*S. Gio. in Foriamma*)	- - iii.
Nuceria (*Nocera*) -	- xii.
Ptaniae, probably Tadinum (*Gualdo*)	viii.
Herbellonium (?) -	- vii.
Ad Ensem (*La Schieggia*)	- x.
Ad Calem (*Cagli*) -	- xiv.
Intercisa (*Il Furlo*) -	- ix.
Forum Sempronii (*Fossombrone*)	- ix.
Ad Octavum -	- ix.
Fanum Fortunae (*Fano*)	- viii.
Pisaurum (*Pesaro*) -	- viii.
Ariminum (*Rimini*) -	- xxiv.

The whole distance from Rome to Ariminum according to this Itinerary is therefore 222 miles, while the Antonine (following the more direct line) makes it 210 miles. The Tabula adds nothing to our knowledge of this route; and the distances are much less correct than in the other two Itineraries.

The branch of the Flaminian Way which struck off from the main line at Nuceria and crossed the Apennines direct to Ancona, is thus given in the Antonine Itinerary (p. 311):—

From Nuceria to
Dubii (?) -	- - viii. M. P.
Prolaqueum (*Pioraco*)	- - viii.
Septempeda (*S. Severino*)	- - xv.
Treia (Ru. near *Treia*)	- ix.
Auximum (*Osimo*)	- - xviii.
Ancona - -	- - xii.

Thence a road was carried along the coast by Sena Gallica to Fanum Fortunae, where it rejoined the main line of the Via Flaminia. The stations were:—
Ad Aesim fl. (*R. Esino*)	- viii. M. P.
Sena Gallica (*Sinigaglia*)	- xii.
Ad Pirum (?) -	- - viii.
Fanum Fortunae (*Fano*)	- viii.

All the above distances appear to be at least approximately correct. (For a full and careful examination of the line of the Via Flaminia, and the distances of the stations upon it, see D'Anville, *Analyse Géographique de l'Italie*, pp. 147—162.)   [E. H. B.]

VIA LABICANA (ἡ Λαβικανὴ ὁδὸς) was one of the highroads that issued from the Porta Esquilina at Rome. It was evidently originally nothing more than a road that led to the ancient city of Labicum (16 miles from Rome), but was subsequently continued in the same direction, and, after sweeping round the E. foot of the Alban hills, it joined the Via Latina at the station Ad Pictas, in the plain between them and the Volscian mountains. (Strab. v. p. 237.) This route was in many respects more convenient than the proper Via Latina, as it avoided the ascent and descent of the Alban hills: and hence it appears to have become, in the later ages of the Empire, the more frequented road of the two; so that the Antonine Itinerary gives the Via Labicana as the regular highroad from Rome to Beneventum, and afterwards gives the Via Latina as falling into it. (*Itin. Ant.* pp. 304, 306.) But this is decidedly opposed to the testimony of Strabo (*l. c.*), and the usage of the Augustan age, which is generally followed by modern writers. Hence the Via Labicana will be here given only as far as the point where it joins the Latina.

The stations set down in the Antonine Itinerary are merely—
From Rome to Ad Quintanas - -	xv. M. P.
Ad Pictas - - -	x.

The Tabula subdivides the latter stage into two; viz., Ad Statuas, iii. M. P., and thence to Ad Pictas, vii. ; thus confirming the distance in the Itinerary. The station Ad Quintanas was undoubtedly situated at the foot of the hill on which stands the village of *La Colonna*, occupying the site of the ancient LABICUM. The line of the ancient road from Rome thither followed nearly the same course, though with fewer windings, as the modern road to *Palestrina* and *Valmontone*. It is described in the article LABICUM.   [E. H. B.]

VIA LATINA (ἡ Λατινὴ ὁδὸς) was one of the principal of the numerous highroads that issued from the gates of Rome, and probably one of the most ancient of them. Hence we have no account of the time of its construction, and it was doubtless long in use as a means of communication before it was paved and converted into a regular highroad. Some road or other must always have existed between Rome and Tusculum; while again beyond the Alban hills the valley of the *Sacco* (*Trerus*) is one of the

natural lines of communication that must have been
in use from the earliest times. But it is not probable that the line of the Via Latina was completed
as a regular road till after the complete reduction
of both the Latins and Volscians under the Roman
authority. It is true that Livy speaks of the Via
Latina as if it already existed in the time of Coriolanus (ii. 39), but he in fact uses the name only as
a geographical description, both in this passage and
again in the history B. C. 296, when he speaks of
Interamna as a colony " quae via Latina est" (x. 36).
Neither passage affords any proof that the *road* was
then in existence; though there is no doubt that there
was already a way or line of communication. The
course of the Via Latina is, indeed, more natural for
such a line of way than that of the more celebrated
Via Appia, and must have offered less difficulties
before the construction of an artificial road. Nor
did it present any such formidable passes in a military point of view as that of Lautulae on the Appian Way, for which reason it was the route chosen
both by Pyrrhus when he advanced towards Rome
in B. C. 280, and by Hannibal in B. C. 211.
(Liv. xxvi. 8, 9.) On the latter occasion the Carthaginian general seems certainly to have followed
the true Via Latina across Mount Algidus and by
Tusculum (Liv. l. c.) ; Pyrrhus, on the contrary,
turned aside from it as he approached Praeneste,
which was the farthest point that he reached in his
advance towards Rome.

Whatever may have been the date of the construction of the Via Latina, it is certain that long before
the close of the Republic it was one of the best
known and most frequented highways in Italy.
Strabo speaks of it as one of the most important of
the many roads that issued from the gates of Rome
(v. p. 237), and takes it as one of the leading and
most familiar lines of demarcation in describing the
cities of Latium. (*Ib.*) It was, however, in one
respect very inferior to its neighbour the Via Appia,
that it was not capable of any considerable extension,
but terminated at Casilinum, where it joined the
Via Appia. (Strab. l. c.) There was, indeed, a
branch road that was continued from Teanum by
Allifae and Telesia to Beneventum; but though this
is given in the Itineraries in connection with the Via
Latina (*Itin. Ant.* pp. 122, 304), it certainly was
not generally considered as forming a part of that
road, and was merely a cross line from it to the
Appian. On the other hand, the main line of the
Via Latina, which descended the valley of the *Sacco*,
received on its way the two subordinate lines of road
called the VIA LABICANA and VIA PRAENESTINA,
which issued from Rome by a different gate, but
both ultimately joined the Via Latina, and became
merged in it. (Strab. l. c.) Such at least is Strabo's
statement, and doubtless was the ordinary view of
the case in his time. But it would seem as if at a
later period the Via Labicana came to be the more
frequented road of the two, so that the Antonine
Itinerary represents the Via Latina as joining the
Labicana, instead of the converse. (*Itin. Ant.* p.
306.)

The stations, as given in the Itinerary just cited,
are as follow:—

Ad Decimum	-	-	-	x. M. P.
Roboraria	-	-	-	iii. (vi.)
Ad Pictas	-	-	-	xvii.
Compitum Anagninum		-		xv.
Ferentinum (*Ferentino*)		-		viii.
Frusino (*Frosinone*)		-	-	vii.

Fregellanum (*Ceprano*)		-	xiv.	M.P.
Fabrateria (*S. Giovanni in Carico*)		-	-	iii.
Aquinum (*Aquino*)		-	-	viii.
Casinum (*S. Germano*)		-	-	vii.
Teanum (*Teano*)		-	-	xxvii.
Cales (*Calvi*)		-	-	vi.
Casilinum (*Capova*)		-	-	vii.
Capua (*Sta Maria*)		-	-	iii.

(The four last stages are supplied from the
Tabula. The Antonine Itinerary gives only the
branch of the road that led, as above noticed, to
Beneventum.)

It will be observed that, in its course,
as above set down, from Rome to Ferentinum,
the Via Latina did not pass through any town of
importance, the stations given being mere Mutationes, or places for changing horses. But, on
account of the importance of this line of road, it
will be necessary to describe it somewhat more in
detail.

The Via Latina issued from the Porta Capena together with the Via Appia. It was not till about
half-way between that gate and the later Porta
Appia (*Porta di S. Sebastiano*), that the two separated, and the Via Latina pursued its own course
through the gate in the walls of Aurelian that derived from it the name of Porta Latina. From this
gate (now long closed) to a point 2 miles from the
Porta Latina, where it crosses the modern road from
Rome to *Albano*, the line of the ancient road may be
readily traced by portions of the pavement, and ruins
of sepulchres, with which the Latin Way. as well as the
Flaminian and Appian (Juv. *Sat.* i. 171), was bordered.
From that point the road may be seen proceeding in a
perfectly straight line, which is marked from distance
to distance by tombs and other ruins, to the foot of
the Tusculan hills. The only one of these ruins
which deserves any notice is that commonly called
the temple of Fortuna Muliebris, which is in reality
a sepulchre of imperial times. About 9 miles from
the Porta Capena is a farm or hamlet called *Mor-
rena*, near which are the extensive remains of a
Roman villa, supposed to be that of Lucullus; and
about a mile farther must be placed the station Ad
Decimum, the 10 miles being undoubtedly reckoned
from the Porta Capena. Almost immediately from
this point began the ascent of the Tusculan hills: the
road still preserved nearly its former direction, leaving *Grotta Ferrata* on the right, and the citadel of
Tusculum on the left; it then passed, as it is described by Strabo (v. p. 237), between Tusculum
and the Alban Mount, following the line of a deep
valley or depression between them, till it reached the
foot of Mount Algidus, and, passing through a kind
of notch in the ridge of that mountain, at a place now
called La Cava, descended to the station Ad Pictas
in the plain below. The course of the ancient road
may be distinctly traced by remains of the pavement still visible at intervals ; the second station,
Roboraria (if the distance of six miles given in
some MSS. be correct), must have stood near
the ruins of a mediaeval castle called *Molara*.
Thence to Ad Pictas the distance is stated at
17 miles, which is certainly greatly above the truth.
It was at this station that the Via Labicana joined
the Latina; and from this circumstance, compared
with the distances given thence to Ferentinum,
we may place the site of Ad Pictas somewhere near
the *Osteria di Mezza Selva*, about 10 miles beyond
Roboraria. Strabo calls it 210 stadia 26¼ miles)

from Rome, but it is not clear whether he measured the distance by the Via Latina or the Labicana (v. p. 237). The actual distance of Ferentinum (concerning which there is no doubt) from Rome is 49 miles; and the Compitum Anagninum is correctly placed 8 miles nearer the city, which would exactly agree with the point on the present highroad where the branch to Anagnia still turns off. Both the Itinerary and the Tabula place Ad Pictas 15 miles from the Compitum Anagninum, and this distance would fix it 10 miles from Roboraria, or 26 from Rome, thus agreeing closely with the statement of Strabo. We may, therefore, feel sure that the position above assigned to Ad Pictas, a point of importance, as that where the two roads joined, is at least approximately correct.

The next stations admit of no doubt, and the distances are correct. It was at the Compitum Anagninum, 15 miles beyond Ad Pictas, that the Via Praenestina joined the Latina, which was carried thence down the valley of the Sacco, nearly in the line of the present highroad, by Ferentinum and Frusino, both of which still retain their ancient names, to Fregellanum (Ceprano) on the Liris, whence it turned S. to Fabrateria Nova (the ruins of which are still visible at S. Giovanni in Carico), on the right bank of the Liris. Here it crossed that river by a bridge, of which the ruins are still extant, whence the course of the ancient road may be traced without difficulty through Aquinum, Casinum, Teanum, and Cales to Casilinum on the Vulturnus, where it fell into the Via Appia. Portions of the ancient pavement, sepulchres, and other ruins mark the line of the ancient way throughout the latter part of its course. At a station given in the Tabula under the name of Ad Flexum (9 miles from Casinum) a branch road turned off to Venafrum, whence it ascended the valley of the Vulturnus to Aesernia, and thence into the heart of Samnium. The Antonine Itinerary represents the Via Latina as following this cross-road, and making a bend round by Venafrum, but there can be no doubt that the regular highroad proceeded direct to Teanum. The remains of the ancient road may be distinctly traced, proceeding from Teanum nearly due N. through Cajanello and Tora to S. Pietro in Fine, which was probably the site of the station Ad Flexum. This would be 18 miles from Teanum. The Tabula gives the distance as viii., for which there is no doubt we should read xviii.

The branch part of the Via Latina, already alluded to, which was carried to Beneventum, quitted the main road at Teanum, crossed the Vulturnus to Allifae, and thence was carried up the valley of the Calor by Telesia to Beneventum. The distances are thus given in the Antonine Itinerary (p. 304):—

Teanum to Allifae (Alife)	-	-	xvii. M.P.
Telesia (Telese)	-	-	xxv.
Beneventum	-	-	xvii.

(The first part of the Via Latina from Rome to the valley of the Liris is examined and discussed in detail by Westphal, Röm. Kamp. pp. 78—97; and Nibby, Vie degli Antichi, pp. 110—119.) [E.H.B.]

VIA LAURENTINA. [LAURENTUM.]
VIA NOMENTANA. [NOMENTUM.]
VIA OSTIENSIS, was, as its name imports, the road leading from Rome to Ostia, which must naturally have been an extremely frequented route when the city was at the height of its prosperity. It followed in its general direction the left bank of the Tiber, but cutting off the more considerable bends

and windings of the river. It issued from the Porta Ostiensis, now called the Porta S. Paolo, from the celebrated basilica of St. Paul, about 1½ mile outside the gate, and situated on the line of the ancient road. Three miles from Rome it passed through a village, or suburb, known as the Vicus Alexandri (Ammian. xvii. 4. § 14): it was at this point that the Via Laurentina struck off direct to Laurentum, 16 miles distant from Rome [LAURENTUM]; while the Via Ostiensis, turning a little to the right, pursued thenceforth nearly a straight course all the way to Ostia. On this line, 11 miles from Rome, is the Osteria di Mala Fede, where a road branches off to Porcigliano, which undoubtedly follows the same line as that mentioned by the younger Pliny, by which his Laurentine villa could be approached as conveniently as by the Via Laurentina. (Plin. Ep. ii. 17.) Five miles farther the highroad reached Ostia, which was 16 miles from Rome. (Itin. Ant. p. 301.) [OSTIA].   [E. H. B.]

VIA POPILIA. [VIA APPIA, No. 5.]
VIA PORTUENSIS, was the road that led from Rome to the Portus Trajani, or the new port of the city constructed under the Empire on the right bank of the Tiber. [OSTIA.] The name could not, of course, have come into use until after the construction of this great artificial port to replace the natural harbour of Ostia, and is only found in the enumeration of the Vine in the Curiosum Urbis and Notitia (pp. 28, 29, ed. Preller). But the line of the road itself may still be traced without difficulty. It issued from the Porta Portuensis, in the walls of Aurelian, and followed, with little deviation, the right bank of the Tiber, only cutting off the minor windings of that river. The Antonine Itinerary places the city of Portus 19 miles from Rome (p. 300); but this is certainly a mistake, the real distance being just about the same as that of Ostia, or 16 miles. (Nibby, Dintorni, vol. iii. p. 624.) From Portus a road was carried along the coast by Fregenae (9 miles) to Alsium (9 miles), where it joined the VIA AURELIA. (Itin. Ant. p. 300.)   [E. H. B.]

VIA POSTUMIA, was, as we learn from an inscription (Orell. Inscr. 3121), the proper name of the road that crossed the Apennines direct from Dertona to Genua. But it appears to have fallen into disuse; at least we do not find it mentioned by any ancient writer, and the road itself is included by the Itineraries under the general name of the Via Aurelia. It has therefore been considered more convenient to describe it in that article.   [E. H. B.]

VIA PRAENESTINA (ἡ Πραινεστινὴ ὁδός, Strab.), was the name of one of the highroads that issued from the Porta Esquilina at Rome, and led (as its name implies) direct to Praeneste. The period of its construction is unknown; but it is evident that there must have been from a very early period a highway, or line of communication from Rome to Praeneste, long before there was a regular paved road, such as the Via Praenestina ultimately became. The first part of it indeed, as far as the city of Gabii, 13 miles from Rome, was originally known as the VIA GABINA, a name which is used by Livy in the history of the early ages of the Republic (Liv. ii. 11), but would seem to have afterwards fallen into disuse, so that both Strabo and the Itineraries give the name of Via Praenestina to the whole line. (Strab. v. p. 238; Itin. Ant. p. 302.) In the latter period of the Republic, indeed, Gabii had fallen very much into decay, while Praeneste was still an important and flourishing town, which will sufficiently account for the one appellation having become merged in the other. A continuation of the same road, which was also included under the name of the Via Praenestina, was carried from the foot of the hill at Praeneste, through the subjacent plain, till it fell into the Via Latina, just below Anagnia.

The stations on it mentioned in the Antonine Itinerary (p. 302) are:—

From Rome to Gabii   -   -   -   xii. M. P.
        Praeneste   -   -   -   xi.
        Sub Anagnia   -   -   xxiv.

The Tabula gives the same distances as far as Praeneste, which are very nearly correct. Strabo reckons it 100 stadia (12½ miles) from Rome to Gabii, and the same distance thence to Praeneste. The continuation from Praeneste to Sub Anagnia is given only in the Antonine Itinerary, but the distance is overstated; it does not really exceed 18 miles.

The Via Praenestina issued from the Porta Esquilina at Rome, together with the Via Labicana (Strab. v. p. 237): it passed through the Porta Praenestina in the later circuit of the walls, now called Porta Maggiore; and separated from the Via Labicana immediately afterwards, striking off in a nearly direct line towards Gabii. About 3 miles from Rome it passed the imperial villa of the Gordians, the magnificence of which is extolled by Julius Capitolinus (Gordian. 32), and is still in some degree attested by the imposing and picturesque ruins at a spot called Torre dei Schiavi. (Nibby, Dintorni, vol. iii. pp. 707—710.) Nine miles from Rome the road is carried over the valley of a small stream by a viaduct of the most massive construction, still known as the Ponte di Nona: and 3 miles farther it passes the still existing ruins of the city of Gabii. Thence to Praeneste the line of the road was not so direct: this part of the Campagna being intersected by deep gullies and ravines, which necessitated some deviations from the straight line. The road is however clearly marked, and in many places retains its ancient pavement of basaltic lava. It is carried nearly straight as far as a point about 5 miles beyond Gabii, where it passes through a deep cutting in the tufo rock, which has given to the spot the name of Cavamonte: shortly afterwards it turns abruptly to the right, leaving the village of Gallicano (the probable site of PEDUM) on the left, and thence follows the line of a long narrow ridge between two ravines, till it approaches the city of Praeneste. The highroad doubtless passed only through the lower part of that city. Portions of the ancient pavement may be seen shortly after quitting the southern gate (Porta del Sole), and show that the old road followed the same direction as the modern one, which leads through Cavi and Paliano, to an inn on the highroad below Anagni, apparently on the very same site as the station Sub Anagnia (or Compitum Anagninum, as it is called in another route) of the Itinerary.

(Westphal, Röm. Kamp. pp. 97—107; Nibby, Dintorni di Roma, pp. 625—630.)   [E. H. B.]

VIA SALARIA (ἡ Σαλαρία ὁδός, Strab.), one of the most ancient and well-known of the highroads of Italy, which led from Rome up the valley of the Tiber, and through the land of the Sabines to Reate, and thence across the Apennines into Picenum, and to the shores of the Adriatic. We have no account of the period of its construction as a regular road, but there can be little doubt that it was a fre-

quented route of communication long before it was laid down as a regular highway: and the tradition that its name was derived from its being used by the Sabines to carry into their own country the salt that they obtained from the Roman salt-works at the mouth of the Tiber, in itself seems to point to an early age. (Fest. s. v. Salaria.) It was indeed, with the exception of the Via Latina, the only one of the great Roman highways, the name of which was not derived from that of its first constructor. But it cannot be inferred from the expressions of Livy that the battle of the Allia was fought "ad undecimum lapidem," and that the Gauls on a subsequent occasion encamped "ad tertium lapidem via Salaria trans pontem Anienis" (Liv. v. 37, vii. 9), that the regular road was then in existence, though there is no doubt that there was a much frequented line of communication with the land of the Sabines. We learn from the latter passage that a bridge had been already constructed over the Anio; and it is probable that the Via Salaria was constructed in the first instance only as far as Reate, and was not carried across the mountains till long afterwards. Even in the time of Strabo there is no evidence that it reached to the Adriatic: that author speaks of it merely as extending through the land of the Sabines, but as not of great extent (οὐ πολλὴ οὖσα, Strab. v. p. 228), which renders it improbable that it had then been carried to the Upper Sea. But the Itineraries give the name of Salaria to the whole line of road from Rome to Castrum Truentinum on the Adriatic, and thence to Adria.

The Salarian Way issued from the Porta Collina of the ancient city together with the Via Nomentana (Strab. l. c.; Fest. s. v. Salaria); but they diverged immediately afterwards, so that the one quitted the outer circuit of the city (as bounded by the walls of Aurelian) through the Porta Salaria, the other through the Porta Nomentana. Between 2 and 3 miles from Rome the Via Salaria crossed the Anio by a bridge, called the Pons Salarius, which was the scene of the memorable combat of Manlius Torquatus with the Gaul. (Liv. vii. 9.) The present bridge is ancient, though not strictly of Roman date, having been constructed by Narses, to replace the more ancient one which was destroyed by Totila. On a hill to the left of the road, just before it descends to the river, is the site of the ancient city of ANTEMNAE, and a hill to the right of the road immediately after crossing the river is worthy of notice, as the spot where the Gauls encamped in B. C. 361 (Liv. l. c.), and where Hannibal pitched his camp when he rode up to reconnoitre the walls of Rome. (Id. xxvi. 10.) Between 5 and 6 miles from Rome, after passing the Villa Spada, the road passes close to Castel Giubileo, a fortress of the middle ages, which serves to mark the site of the ancient FIDENAE. From this point the road is carried through the low grounds near the Tiber, skirting the foot of the Crustumian hills, which border it on the right. Several small streams descend from these hills, and, after crossing the road, discharge themselves into the Tiber; and there can be no doubt that one of these is the far-famed Allia, though which of them is entitled to claim that celebrated appellation is still a very disputed point. [ALLIA.] The road continued to follow the valley of the Tiber till, after passing Monte Rotondo, it turned inland to Eretum, the site of which is probably to be fixed at Grotta Marozza and is marked in the Itineraries as 18 miles from Rome. Here the Via Nomentana again fell into the Salaria. (Strab. v. p. 228.) Hence to Reate the latter road traversed a hilly country, but of no great interest, following nearly the same line as the modern road from Rome to *Rieti.* The intermediate station of Ad Novas or Vicus Novus, as it is called in the Antonine Itinerary is still marked by ruins near the *Osteria Nuova,* 32 miles from Rome, and 16 from *Rieti.* Here an old church still bore at a late period the name of *Vico Nuovo.*

The stations on the original Via Salaria, from Rome to Reate, are correctly given, and can clearly be identified.

From Rome to

Eretum (*Grotta Marozza*)	-	xviii. M. P.
Vicus Novus (*Ost. Nuova*)	-	xiv.
Reate (*Rieti*) -	- - -	xvi.

From Reate the Via Salaria (or the continuation of it as given in the Itineraries) proceeded nearly due E. by Cutiliae, which is identified by its celebrated lake, or rather mineral springs, to Interocrea (*Antrodoco*), situated at the junction of two natural passes or lines of communication through the central Apennines. The one of these leads from Interocrea to Amiternum, in the upper valley of the Aternus, and was followed by a cross-road given in the Tabula, but of which both the stations and the distances are extremely confused : the other, which is the main valley of the Velinus, and bears nearly due N., was ascended by the Via Salaria as far as Falacrinum, 16 miles from Interocrea, and near the sources of the Velinus. Thence that road crossed the ridge of the Apennines and descended into the valley of the *Tronto* (Truentus), which river it followed to its mouth at Castrum Truentinum, passing on the way by the strongly situated city of Asculum (*Ascoli*). The distances on this line of route are thus correctly given in the Antonine Itinerary (p. 307):

From Reate to

Cutiliae (near *Paterno*)	- -	viii. M. P.
Interocrea (*Antrodoco*)	- -	vi.
Falacrinum (near *Civita Reale*)	-	xvi.
Vicus Badies -	- - -	ix.
Ad Centesimum*	- -	x.
Asculum (*Ascoli*)	- -	xii.
Castrum Truentinum	- -	xx.

From this last point two roads branched off, the one turning N., and proceeding along the coast of the Adriatic to Ancona ; the other proceeding S. along the same coast to Castrum Novum (near *Giulia Nuova*), and thence to Adria (*Atri*). The latter branch is given in the Itinerary as a part of the Via Salaria ; but it is clear that neither of them properly belonged to that highway, both being in fact only portions of the long line of road which followed the coast of the Adriatic continuously from Ancona to Brundusium, and which is given in the Antonine Itinerary in connection with the Via Flaminia. (*Itin. Ant.* pp. 313—316). (The course of the Via

---

* It is clear from the name that this station was distant 100 miles from Rome, while the distances above given would make up only 97 miles : but it is uncertain at what precise point the deficiency occurs. The Tabula gives 9 miles from Reate to Cutiliae, and 7 thence to Interocrea : if these distances be adopted the result is 99 miles, leaving a discrepancy of only one mile. In either case the approximation is sufficient to show the general correctness of the Itineraries.

Salaria is examined, and the distances discussed in detail by D'Anville, *Analyse Géographique de l'Italie* pp. 163—169.)   [E. H. B.]

VIA SUBLACENSIS.   [VIA VALERIA.]

VIA TIBERINA, a name found in inscriptions, and noticed by the Notitia and Curiosum among the roads that issued from the gates of Rome, was in all probability the road that quitted the Via Flaminia at Saxa Rubra, and followed the right bank of the Tiber until it rejoined the Via Flaminia, between *Acqua Viva* and *Borghetto.* The existence of such a road is known from remains of it still visible ; and it is the only one to which the name of Via Tiberina can well be applied. (Westphal, *Röm. Kamp.* pp. 134, 138.)   [E. H. B.]

VIA TIBURTINA.   [VIA VALERIA.]

VIA TRAJANA.   [VIA APPIA, No. 4.]

VIA VALERIA (ἡ Οὐαλερία ὁδός, Strab.), one of the most celebrated and important of the Roman highways, which led from Rome, or, more strictly speaking, from Tibur, to the lake Fucinus and the land of the Marsi, and thence was subsequently continued to the Adriatic, at the mouth of the Aternus. The period of its construction is uncertain. It has indeed been frequently supposed to have derived its name from, and to have been the work of, M. Valerius Maximus, who was censor with C. Junius Bubulcus in B. C. 307 ; but the expression of Livy, that the two constructed roads "per agros," would certainly seem to refer to cross-roads in the neighbourhood of Rome ; and it is very improbable that the construction of so celebrated a highway as the Via Valeria should not have been more distinctly stated. (Liv. ix. 43.) The Via Valeria, indeed, was properly only a continuation of the Via Tiburtina, which led from Rome to Tibur ; and though the Itineraries include the whole line of route under the name of the Via Valeria, it appears that the distinction was still kept up in the time of Strabo, who distinctly speaks of the Valerian Way as *beginning from* Tibur, and leading to the Marsi, and to Corfinium, the metropolis of the Peligni (Strab. v. p. 238). The expressions of the geographer would naturally lead us to conclude that the Via Valeria was in his time carried as a regular highway as far as Corfinium ; but we learn from an inscription, that this was not the case, and that the regularly constructed road stopped short at Cerfennia, at the foot of the Mons Imeus or *Forca di Caruso,* a steep and difficult pass, over which the highway was not carried till the reign of Claudius, who at the same time continued it to the mouth of the Aternus. (Orell. *Inscr.* 711.) It appears that the portion thus added at first bore the name of the Via Claudia Valeria (*Inscr. l. c.*); but the distinction was soon lost sight of, and the whole line of route from Rome to the Adriatic was commonly known as the Via Valeria. (*Itin. Ant.* p. 308.) It will be convenient here to adopt the same usage, and consider the whole course of the road under one head.

The Via Tiburtina, as the road from Rome to Tibur was properly called, must undoubtedly have been of very ancient origin. There must indeed have existed from the earliest ages of Rome a frequented highway or communication between the two cities ; but we are wholly ignorant as to the time when a regularly made road, with its solid pavement and all the other accessories of a Roman via, was constructed from the one city to the other. The road as it existed in the time of the Roman Empire may be distinctly traced by portions still remaining of the pavement, or by sepulchres and fragments of ancient buildings, so that no doubt can exist as to its precise course. It quitted the original city by the Porta Esquilina, passed through the Porta Tiburtina (now *Porta S. Lorenzo*) in the walls of Aurelian, and then proceeded nearly in a straight line to the Anio, which it crossed by a bridge about 4 miles from Rome. This bridge, now called the *Ponte Mammolo*, is in its present state the work of Narses, having been restored at the same time as those on the Via Salaria and Nomentana, after their destruction by Totila, A. D. 549. From this bridge the ancient road followed very nearly the same line as the modern one as far as the *Lago di Tartaro*, a small lake or pool of sulphureous waters, similar in character to the more considerable pool called the *Solfatara* or *Aquae Albulae*, about 2 miles farther on, and a mile to the left of the highroad. Leaving this on the left, the Via Tiburtina proceeded almost perfectly straight to the *Ponte Lucano*, at the foot of the hill of *Tivoli*, where it recrossed the Anio. There can be no doubt that this bridge retains its ancient name of Pons Lucanus, though this is not mentioned by any ancient author; but the origin of the name is evident from the massive sepulchre of the Plautian family (a structure not unlike the celebrated tomb of Caecilia Metella on the Appian Way), which stands close to the bridge, and which was constructed by M. Plautius Lucanus, who was censor together with Tiberius in the reign of Augustus. From the inscription on an ancient milestone it appears that this part of the road was constructed by him at the same time; and it is probable that the original Via Tiburtina was carried from the *Lago di Tartaro* in a different direction, bearing away more to the left, so as to leave the Aquae Albulae on the right; while the road constructed by Plautius, like the modern highroad, passed between that lake and Tibur. The 14th milestone was found near the spot where the road crosses the artificial channel that carries off the waters of the lake. From the *Ponte Lucano* the ancient road ascended the hill of Tibur by a very steep and straight ascent, passing through or under a portion of the vaulted substructions of the so-called villa of Maecenas. [TIBUR.]

The Itineraries all agree in stating the distance of Tibur from Rome at 20 miles ; but it in reality little exceeds 18 by the direct road, which crossed the *Ponte Lucano*, as above described. The Tabula gives the Aquae Albulae as an intermediate station, but places it 16 M. P. from Rome, though the true distance is only 14.

From Tibur the Via Valeria ascended the valley of the Anio, passing by the town of Varia (*Vicovaro*), 8 miles from Tibur, to a point marked by an inn, now called *Osteria Ferrata*, 5 miles beyond *Vicovaro* and 13 from *Tivoli*. This point, where the Anio makes a sudden bend, is evidently the site of the station Ad Lamnas of the Tabula, whence a side road struck off to the right, ascending the upper valley of the Anio to Sublaqueum (*Subiaco*), whence the road derived the name of VIA SUBLACENSIS, by which it is mentioned by Frontinus (*de Aquaeduct.* 15). The road is given in the Tabula, but in so confused a manner that it is impossible to make it out. Sublaqueum was in reality 48 miles from Rome by this route, or 28 from Tibur.

The Via Valeria, on the other hand, turned to the left at the *Osteria Ferrata*, and crossed the hills to Carseoli, the ruins of which are still visible at some distance nearer Rome than the modern village of

Carsoli. Thence it ascended a steep mountain-pass, where portions of the ancient road, with its pavement and substructions, are still visible, and descended again into the basin of the Lake Fucinus. After passing by, rather than through, Alba Fucensis, it was carried along the N. shore of the lake to Cerfennia, the site of which is clearly identified at a spot just below the village of *Coll' Armeno*. [CERFENNIA.] Here, as already mentioned, the original Via Valeria terminated ; but the continuation of it, as constructed by Claudius, and given in the Itineraries, ascended the steep mountain-pass of the MONS IMEUS, and thence descended into the valley of the Aternus, on the banks of which, near its confluence with the *Gizio*, stood the city of Corfinium. Three miles from that city was a bridge over the Aternus (near the site of the present town of *Popoli*), which constituted an important military position. [ATERNUS.] Below this point the river flows through a narrow pass or defile, through which the Via Valeria also was carried. The station Interpromium, marked in the Itineraries as 12 miles from Corfinium, must be placed at the *Osteria di S. Valentino*, below the village of the same name. Thence the road descended the valley of the Aternus to its mouth, which is correctly placed by the Itineraries 21 miles from Interpromium, and 9 beyond Teate (*Chieti*).

The distances given in the Antonine Itinerary from Rome to this point are as follow :—

Rome to Tibur (*Tivoli*) - -	XX. M.P.	
Carseoli (Ru. near *Carsoli*)	xxii.	
Alba Fucentia (*Alba*) -	xxv.	(xxii.)
Cerfennia (*Sta Felicita*)	xxxii.	(xiii.)
Corfinium (*S. Pelino*) -	xvi.	(xvii.)
Interpromium (*Ost. di S.*		
Valentino) -	xi.	(xii.)
Teate (*Chieti*) - -	xvii.	(xii.)

The distances stated in parentheses are the corrections suggested by D'Anville, who examined the whole of this line of route with much care, and are confirmed by the discovery of ancient milestones, which leave no doubt as to the actual distances. The general correctness of the result thus obtained is confirmed by a statement of Pliny (iii. 5. s. 6), in which he estimates the breadth of Italy in its central part, as measured from the mouths of the Tiber to that of the Aternus at 136 miles. Here the mention of the Aternus leaves little doubt that the measurement was taken along the Via Valeria. Now the corrected distances above given amount to 118 miles from Rome to Teate, or 125 miles to the mouth of the Aternus; and if to this be added 16 miles from Rome to Ostia, the result is 141 miles, agreeing, within 5 miles, with the statement of Pliny.

(For a full examination of this whole line of route, see D'Anville, *Analyse Géogr. de l'Italie*, pp. 170—182, and Kramer, *Der Fuciner See*, pp. 59 —62. The Via Tiburtina and the first part of the Valeria are also described and examined by Westphal, *Röm. Kamp.* pp. 108—121, and Nibby, *Vie degli Antichi*, pp. 96—104)

The proper termination of the Via Valeria, as continued by Claudius, was undoubtedly at the mouth of the Aternus. But the Antonine Itinerary continues it on to Hadria, which it places at 14 M.P. from Teate ; but this distance is much below the truth : we should perhaps read 24 M.P. The probability is, that at the mouth of the Aternus it fell into the line of road previously existing along the coast of the Adriatic, and which, without belonging properly to any of the three highways that proceeded from Rome to that sea, served to connect the Valerian. Salarian, and Flaminian Ways. For this reason it may be useful to set down here the stations and distances along this line of coast, from the mouth of the Aternus to Ancona. They are thus given in the Antonine Itinerary (p. 313):—

From the Ostia Aterni (*Pescara*) to

Hadria (*Atri*) - - -	xvi.	M. P.
Castrum Novum (near *Giulia Nuova*) - - -	xv.	
Castrum Truentium (at the mouth of the *Tronto*) - -	xii.	
Castellum Firmanum (*Porto di Fermo*) - - -	xxiv.	
Potentia (*Potenza*) - -	xxii.	
Numana (*Humana*) - -	x.	
Ancona - - - -	viii.	

Here the coast-road joined one branch of the Via Flaminia; and the distances from Ancona to Ariminum will be found in the article on that road. [VIA FLAMINIA.]

The Via Valeria, like the Aemilia and Flaminia, gave name to one of the later divisions or provinces of Italy under the Roman Empire, which was called Valeria. It comprised the land of the Marsi, Peligni, and Vestini, through which the road really passed, as well as the land of the Sabines, which was traversed by the Via Salaria. [ITALIA, p. 93.] [E. H. B.]

VIADUS (Oὐίαδος), a river of Germany, west of the Vistula, mentioned by both Ptolemy (ii. 11. § 2) and Marcianus (p. 53) as flowing into the Mare Suevicum or Baltic. Neither of these authors mentions either its source or its course, but it is generally assumed to be the *Oder*. Ptolemy in another passage (ii. 11. § 15) mentions, according to the common reading, a river ʼIαδούα, which some regard as a tributary of the Viadus, and others as a name of the upper Viadus; but Wilberg, the latest editor of Ptolemy, treating ʼIαδούα as a corrupt reading, has altered it to Oὐίαδος. [L. S.]

VIANA (Oὐίανα), a place in Rhaetia, on the road from Vemania to Augusta Vindelicorum (Ptol. ii. 12. § 4); it is marked in the Peutinger Table as Viaca, and its site is now occupied by a place called *Wageck*. [L. S.]

VIATIA. [BEATIA.]

VIBI FORUM. [FORUM VIBII.]

VIBINUM, or VIBONIUM (ʼIβώνιον: *Bovino*), a town of Apulia, in the interior of that country, 7 miles S. of Aecae (*Troja*) and 15 from Luceria. Its correct name is given by Pliny, who enumerates the Vibinates among the municipal communities of Apulia, and by inscriptions which are still extant at *Bovino*, an episcopal town situated on one of the lower slopes of the Apennines, on the right of the river Cervaro (Cerbalus). (Plin. iii. 11. s. 16; Holsten, *Not. ad Cluver*. p. 272.) There is no doubt that it is the place of which the name is corruptly written in Ptolemy, Vibarnum (Oὐίβαρνον, iii. 1. § 72), and which is called by Polybius Vibonium (ʼIβώνιον, for which we should probably read Oὐιβώνιον, Schweigh. *ad loc*.). The latter author distinctly places it among the Daunian Apulians, and mentions that Hannibal established his camp there, and thence laid waste the territory of Arpi and other neighbouring cities. (Polyb. iii. 88.) [E. H. B.]

VIBIONES (Oὐιβίωνες or ʼIβίωνες, Ptol. iii. 5. § 23), a people of European Sarmatia, on the N. side of Mount Bodinus, probably on the river *Ivo* or *Jevisa* in *Volhynia*. [T. H. D.]

VIBO, VIBO VALENTIA. [HIPPONIUM.]

VIBONENSIS SINUS, another name of the Hipponiates Sinus. [HIPPONIUM.]

VICENTIA or VICETIA (Oὐικετία: *Eth.* Vicentinus: *Vicenza*), a city of Venetia in the N. of Italy, situated between Patavium and Verona, and distant 22 miles from the former and 33 from the latter city (*Itin. Ant.* p. 128; *Itin. Hier.* p. 559). No mention is found of Vicentia before the Roman conquest of this part of Italy, and the earliest record of its existence is an inscription of the republican period which informs us that the limits between its territory and that of the Atestini were fixed and determined by the proconsul Sex. Atilius Saranus in B. C. 136. (Orell. *Inscr.* 3110.) It is also incidentally mentioned as one of the municipal towns in the N. of Italy, in B. C. 43. (Cic. *ad Fam.* xi. 19.) Strabo notices it as one of the minor towns of Venetia, and Tacitus tells us that it was taken by Antonius, the general of Vespasian, on his advance from Patavium to Verona, in a manner that sufficiently proves it not to have been a town of any great importance. (Tac. *Hist.* iii. 8; Strab. v. p. 214.) But it always continued to be a municipal town, and the younger Pliny mentions a cause in which the Vicentini were engaged before the Roman Senate in defence of their municipal rights. (Plin. *Ep.* v. 4, 14.) We learn also from Suetonius that it was the birthplace of the grammarian Remmius Palaemon. (Suet. *Gramm.* 23.) It is noticed also by both Pliny and Ptolemy, as well as in the Itineraries, and evidently continued till near the close of the Roman Empire, to be a municipal town of some consideration, though very inferior to its opulent neighbours, Verona and Patavium. (Plin. iii. 19. s. 23; Ptol. iii. 1. § 30; Orell. *Inscr.* 3219.) It suffered severely in common with most of the cities of Venetia from the invasion of Attila (A. D. 452), by whom it was laid waste with fire and sword (*Hist. Miscell.* xv. p. 549), but it recovered from this catastrophe, and appears again under the Lombards as a considerable city of Venetia (P. Diac. ii. 14. v. 39). During the middle ages it became for some time an independent republic, and is still a populous city with about 30,000 inhabitants, but has no remains of antiquity.

The name is written in inscriptions Vicetia, which has been restored by recent editors as the true reading both in Pliny and in Tacitus, but it is certain that before the close of the Roman Empire the name Vicentia (which has been retained in the modern *Vicenza*) was already in use. [E. H. B.]

VICIANUM, a place in Moesia (*Tab. Peut.*), probably the Βίρζανα of Procopius (*de Aed.* iv. 4. p. 281), and the present *Nova Berda*. [T. H. D.]

VICTO'RIA (Oὐικτωρία, Ptol. ii. 3. § 9), the most eastern place belonging to the Damnonii in Britannia Barbara. Camden (p. 1190) thinks that it is Bede's *Caer Guidi*, and that it stood on *Inchkeith Island*, in the *Frith of Forth*; but Horsley is of opinion that it is *Abernethy*, near *Perth*. [T. H. D.]

VICTO'RIAE MONS, a mountain in Hispania Citerior, near the Iberus. (Liv. xxiv. 41.) [T. H. D.]

VICTO'RIAE PORTUS, a haven belonging to Juliobriga, a town of the Cantabri in Hispania Tarraconensis. (Plin. iv. 20. s. 34.) Now *Santonna*. (Cf. Florez, *Esp. Sagr.* xxiv. p. 9.) [T. H. D.]

VICTUMVIAE. [TICINUS.]

VICUS ALEXANDRI. [VIA OSTIENSIS.]

VICUS AMBIATINUS. [AMBIATINUS.]

VICUS AQUA'RIUS, a place in the territory of the Vaccaei in Hispania Tarraconensis. (*Itin. Ant.*

p. 439.) Variously identified with *Villafafla* and *Villasecco*.   [T. H. D.]

VICUS AQUENSIS. [AQUAE CONVENARUM.]

VICUS CAECI'LIUS, a place in Lusitania belonging to the Vettones, on the road from Augusta Emerita to Caesaraugusta. (*Itin. Ant.* p. 434.) Variously identified with *Naralconcejo* and *S. Esteran.*   [T. H. D.]

VICUS CUMINA'RIUS, a place of the Carpetani in Hispania Tarraconensis, somewhat S. of the Tagus, and E. of Toletum. Probably the modern *St. Cruz de la Zarza*, which is still renowned for its cumin. (Morales, *Antig.* p. 77; Florez, *Esp. Sagr.* v. p. 22.) Others have identified it with *Ocaña* and *Bayona.*   [T. H. D.]

VICUS DOLUCENSIS, in Gallia. The name occurs only on an inscription found at *Halinghen*, near *Boulogne*, the ancient Gesoriacum [GESORIACUM]. Vicus Dolucensis may be the old name of *Halinghen.* (Ukert, *Gallien.*)   [G. L.]

VICUS HE'LENAE, in Gallia, mentioned by Sidonius Apollinaris (*Major. Carm.* 5. 216), in the country of the Atrebates; but geographers disagree about the site. Some place it at *Hedin* or *Hesdin*, on the *Canche*, but that river is in the country of the Morini. Others fix it at a place called *Lens*, and others in other places. (Ukert, *Gallien.*) [G. L.]

VICUS ICTIMULORUM. [ICTIMULI.]

VICUS JULII or ATURES, in Aquitania. The name Civitas Aturensium occurs in the Notitia of the Gallic Provinces. The name Atures also occurs in Sidonius Apollinaris (ii. ep. 1). In the passage of Tibullus, cited under ATURUS [Vol. I. p. 336] "Atur" is said to be a correction of Scaliger, the MSS. having Atax : —

" Quem tremeret forti milite victus Atur ;"

but the great critic is probably right.

At the council of *Agde* (Agatha), A. D. 506, there is a subscription by a bishop " de civitate Vico Juli," and the same name occurs in Gregory of Tours. D'Anville affirms that Atures and Vicus Julii are the same place, relying on a Notice, where we read " Civitas Adtorensium Vico Juli." The name of the river Atur was also given to a people Atures, who have given their name to the town of *Aire*, which is on the *Adour*. (D'Anville, *Notice, &c.*)   [G. L.]

VICUS JULIUS, in Gallia, is mentioned only in the Notitia of the Empire as a post under the orders of the general residing at Mogontiacum (*Mains*). It is placed between Tabernae (*Rhein-Zabern*) and Nemetes (*Speier*). D'Anville supposes Vicus Julius to be *Germersheim*, at the place where the *Queich* enters the Rhine.   [G. L.]

VICUS MATRINI. [VIA CASSIA.]

VICUS NOVUS. [VIA SALARIA.]

VICUS SPACORUM. [SPACORUM VICUS.]

VICUS VARIANUS. [VIA AEMILIA, No. 5.]

VIDRUS (Οὔιδρος), a small coast river in the west of Germany, between the Rhenus and the Amisia (Ptol. ii. 11. § 1; Marcian. p. 51), is probably the same as the *Wecht.*   [L. S.]

VIDUA (Οὐιδούα, Ptol. ii. 2. § 2), a river on the N. coast of Hibernia; according to Camden (p. 1411), the *Crodagh*. Others identify it with the *Culmore.*   [T. H. D.]

VIDUBIA or VIDUBIO, in Gallia, appears in the Table on a road from Andematunnum (*Langres*) to Cabillio, which is Cabillonum (*Châlon sur-Saône*). The road passes through File or Tile [TILE] to Vi-

dubia. The distance in the Table between Tile and *Châlon*, 39 leagues, is correct : and it is 19 from Tile to Vidubia. D'Anville fixes Vidubia at *St. Bernard*, on the little river *Vouge*, a branch of the *Saône.* (D'Anville, *Notice, &c.*)   [G. L.]

VIDUCASSES, a Celtic people in Gallia Lugdunensis. Pliny (iv. 18) mentions them before the Bodiocasses, who are supposed to be the Baiocasses [BAIOCASSES]. Ptolemy (ii. 8. § 5) writes the name Οὐιδουκαίσιοι or Οὐιδουκάσσιοι, for we must assume them to be the Viducasses, though he places the Viducassii next to the Osismii, and the Veneti between the Viducassii and the Lexovii. But the Viducasses are between the Baiocasses and the Lexovii. The boundary between the Viducasses and the Baiocasses is indicated by a name *Fins* (Fines), which often occurs in French geography.

There is a place named *Vieux* SW. of *Caen*, in the department of *Calvados*, some distance from the left bank of the river *Orne*. This place is mentioned in the titles or muniments of the neighbouring abbey of *Fontenai*, on the other side of the *Orne*, under the name of Videocae or Veocae, of which *Vieux* is a manifest corruption, as D'Anville shows, like Tricasses, Trecae, *Troies*, and Durocasses, Drocae, *Dreux*. There is or was a stone preserved in the *château of Torigni*, in the arrondissement of *Saint Lô*, in the department of *Manche*, which contains the inscription ORDO CIVITATIS VIDVCAS. This marble, which was found at *Vieux* in 1580, is said to be the pedestal of a statue placed in the third century of our aera in honour of T. Sennius Solemnis. In the excavations made at *Vieux* in 1705 were found remains of public baths, of an aqueduct, a gymnasium, fragments of columns, of statues, and a great number of medals of the imperial period, besides other remains. Inscriptions, of the date A. D. 238, found on the spot show that this city had temples and altars erected to Diana, to Mars, and to Mercury. (*Nouveaux Essais sur la Ville de Caen*, par M. L'Abbé Delarue, 2 vols. Caen, 1842, cited by Richard et Hocquart, *Guide du Voyageur.*)

The name of this old town is unknown, but the remains show that it was a Roman city, probably built on a Celtic site; and several Roman roads branch off from it. Some geographers suppose it to be the Araegenus or Araegenue of the Table, which D'Anville would fix at *Bayeux*. But the site of Araegenus is doubtful. [AUGUSTODURUS.] [G. L.]

VIENNA (Οὐίενα, Οὐίεννα : *Eth.* Viennensis : *Vienne*), a city of the Allobroges (Ptol. ii. 10. § 11) in Gallia Narbonensis, on the east bank of the *Rhône*; and the only town which Ptolemy assigns to the Allobroges. Stephanus (*s. v.* Βίεννος) gives this form of the word and an Ethnic name Βιέννιος, and he suggests also Βιεννήσιος and Βιενναῖος from a form Βιέννη. He has preserved a tradition about Vienna being a Cretan colony from Biennus in Crete; and accordingly, if this were true, its origin is Hellenic. Dion Cassius (xlvi. 50) has a story about some people being expelled from Vienna by the Allobroges, but he does not say who they were. [LUGDUNUM.]

The position of Vienna is easily fixed by the name and by its being on the Roman road along the east side of the *Rhône*. There is a difficulty, however, as D'Anville observes, in the Antonine Itinerary, which makes Vienna xxiii. from Lugdunum, and adds the remark that by the shorter cut it is xvi. The number xvi. occurs also in the

Table. It is remarked, too, that Seneca (*De Morte Claudii*, c. 6) says that Claudius was born at Lugdunum (*Lyon*), "ad sextum decimum lapidem a Vienna." The real distance from Vienna to the *Rhône* at *Lyon* is about 17 M. P.; but D'Anville suggests that the territory of Lugdunum may have had a narrow strip on the south side of the *Rhône*. There can be no road of 23 M. P. from Lugdunum to Vienna, unless it be one on the west bank of the *Rhône*. Strabo (iv. pp. 184, 186) makes the distance between Lugdunum and Vienna 200 stadia or 20 M. P., which is too much.

Vienna is first mentioned by Caesar (*B. G.* vii. 9), and only once mentioned. He had crossed the *Cévennes* into the *Auvergne* in the depth of winter, and he went again over the mountains to Vienna to meet a newly-levied cavalry force, which some time before he had sent on thither. Under the Empire Vienna was a great city, and there was rivalry and enmity between it and Lugdunum. (Tacit. *Hist.* i. 65.) Mela speaks of it as a flourishing place; and under the Empire it was a Colonia (Plin. iii. 4; Tacit. *Hist.* i. 66), before the time of Claudius, who speaks of it in his Oratio (*super Civitate Gallis danda*); "Ornatissima ecce Colonia valentissimaque .Viennensium, quam longo jam tempore senatores huic curiae confert." (J. Lipsius, *Excurs. ad Tacit. Ann.* lib. xi.) This passage shows that Vienna had already supplied members to the Roman senate, and it must have been a Romana Colonia. Martial (vii. 88) calls it "pulcra":—

"Fertur habere meos, si vera est fama, libellos,
Inter delicias pulcra Vienna suas."

So Pliny says that his works were in the booksellers' shops at Lugdunum. [LUGDUNUM.] These facts present a curious contrast between the book trade in a French provincial town under the Empire and at the present day, when a man would not find much. Vienna was also noted for the wine (Martial, xiii. 107) that grew in the neighbourhood; and some of the best wines of the *Rhône* are still made about *Vienne*. This town afterwards gave name to the subdivision of Narbonensis named Viennensis.

The modern town of *Vienne* is in the department of *Isère*, on the little river *Gère*, which flows through *Vienne* to the *Rhône*. The modern town is in the narrow valley of the *Gère*, and extends to the banks of the *Rhône*. The Roman town was placed on two terraces in the form of amphitheatres. There still exist the foundations of the massive Roman walls above 19,000 feet in circuit which enclosed Vienna. These walls, even in the weakest parts, were about 20 feet thick; and it appears that there were round towers at intervals. There are at *Vienne* the remains of some arcades. which are supposed to have formed the entrance to the Thermae. They are commonly called triumphal arches, but there is no reason for this appellation. One of the arcades bears the name of the emperor Gratian. There is a temple which M. Schneider has conjectured to have been dedicated to Augustus and Livia, if his deciphering of the inscription may be trusted. This is one of the best preserved Roman monuments of its kind in France after the *Maison Carrée* of *Nîmes* [NEMAUSUS]. It is now a Museum, and contains some valuable ancient remains and inscriptions. This building is of the Corinthian order, with six columns in front and eight on each side; the columns are above 3 feet in diameter, and 35 feet high, including the base of the capitals.

There is a singular monument near *Vienne*, sometimes called Pontius Pilate's tomb, there being a tradition that Pilate was banished to Vienna. But even if Pilate was sent to Vienna, that fact will not prove that this is his monument. It is a pyramid supported on a quadrangular construction, on the sides of which there are four arcades with semicircular arches at the top; and there are columns at each of the angles of the construction. Each side of the square of this basement is about 21 feet long, and the height to the top of the entablature of the basement is nearly 22 feet. The pyramid with its smaller base rests on the central part of the quadrangular construction; it is about 30 feet high, and the whole is consequently about 52 feet high. The edifice is not finished. It has on the whole a very fine appearance. There is a drawing of it in the *Penny Cyclopaedia* (art. *Vienne*), made on the spot in 1838 by W. B. Clarke, architect.

The remains of the amphitheatre have been found only by excavation. It was a building of great magnitude, the long diameter being above 500 feet and the smaller above 400 feet, which dimensions are about the same as those of the amphitheatre of Verona. It has been used as a quarry to build the modern town out of. Three aqueducts supplied Vienna with water during the Roman period. These aqueducts run one above another on the side of the hill which borders the left bank of the *Gère*, and they are nearly parallel to one another, but at different elevations. The highest was intended to supply the amphitheatre when a naumachia was exhibited. There are also remains of a fourth aqueduct large enough for four persons to walk in upright and abreast. These aqueducts were almost entirely constructed under ground, with a fall of about one in a thousand, and for the most part lined inside with a red cement as high up as the spring of the arches.

The Roman road, sometimes called the Via Domitia, ran from Arelate (*Arles*) along the E. side of the river to Lugdunum (*Lyon*). Where it enters *Vienne*, it is now more than 3 feet below the surface of the ground, and its depth increases as it goes farther into the town. It is constructed of large blocks of stone. Another road went from Vienna to the Alpis Graia (*Little St. Bernard*) through BERGINTRUM; and it is an interesting fact to find that several villages on this road retain names given to them in respect of the distance from *Vienne*: thus *Septème* is 7 miles, *Oytier* 8 miles, and *Diémos* 10 Roman miles from *Vienne*. Another road led from *Vienne* through CULARO (*Grenoble*) to the Alpis Cottia (*Mont St. Genèvre*). (See Richard et Hocquart, *Guide du Voyageur*, for references to modern works on the antiquities of *Vienne*, and particularly M. Mermet's work, 8vo. Vienne, 1829, which contains the answers to a series of questions proposed by the Académie des Inscriptions et Belles Lettres; also the references in Ukert, *Gallien*, p. 453.)   [G. L.]

VIGESIMUM, AD. 1. A station in Gallia Narbonensis, the distance of which from a given point determined its name, as we see in the case of other names of places derived from numerals. [DUODECIMUM, AD; VIENNA.] The place is xx. M. P. from Narbo (*Narbonne*) on the road to Spain, and may be at or near a place called *La Palme*.

2. There is another Ad Vigesimum which occurs in the Itin. of *Bordeaux* to Jerusalem, on the road from *Toulouse*. These numerals show that such cities

had the privilege of reckoning their roads from the capital to the limit of their territories, where a Fines often occurs. [FINES.] (D'Anville, *Notice, &c.*) [G. L.]

VILLA FAUSTINI, a place of the Iceni in Britannia Romana, on the road from Londinium to the northern boundary wall. (*Itin. Ant.* p. 474.) Camden (p. 438) identifies it with *St. Edmund's Bury;* but others have placed it near *Thetford*, at *Wulpit*, and at *Tornham Parva.* [T. H. D.]

VIMINA'CIUM (Ούιμινάκιον, Ptol. iii. 9. § 3), an important town of Moesia Superior, lying somewhat E. of the mouth of the Margus, and connected with Constantinople by a highroad which passed through Naissus. (*Itin. Ant.* p. 133; *Itin. Hierosol.* p. 564.) It was the head-quarters of the Legio VII. Claudia. (*Ib.*; cf. Eutrop. ix. 13 ; Procop. *de Aed.* iv. 6. p. 287 ; Theophyl. i. 5, viii. 12, &c.) By the later Greeks the name is written Βιμινάκιον. Variously identified with *Ram* or *Rama*, and *Kostolacs.* (Cf. Maraili, *Danub.* ii. p. 10 ; Mannert, vii. p. 78.) [T. H. D.]

VIMINA'CIUM (Ούιμινάκιον, Ptol. ii. 6. § 50), a town of the Vaccaei in Hispania Tarraconensis, to the E. of Pallancia. (*Itin. Ant.* pp. 449, 453.) Identified with *Valderaduci* or *Beceril.* [T. H. D.]

VINCEIA, a town of Moesia Superior, between Mons Aureus and Margum, and 6 miles from the former. (*Itin. Ant.* p. 132) In the *Itin. Hierosol.* (p. 564) it is called Vingeius or Vingeium. Lapie identifies it with *Semendria.* [T. H. D.]

VINCUM. [BINGIUM.]

VINDA (Ούίνδία, Ptol. v. 4. § 7), a place in Galatia, between Pessinus and Ancyra, near the modern *Ilidja.* (*It. Ant.* pp. 201, 202.) [L. S.]

VINDALUM, or VINDALIUM (Ούίνδαλον), in Gallia Narbonensis, a place where Domitius Ahenobarbus defeated the Allobroges, B. C. 121. [GALLIA TRANSALPINA, Vol. I. p. 954.] Strabo (iv. p. 185) says that Vindalum is at the confluence of the Sulgas [SULGAS] and the *Rhône.* Florus (iii. 2) names this river Vindalicus or Vindelicus. The Sulgas is the *Sorgue.* D'Anville, relying, as he often does, on a mere resemblance of name, would place Vindalium at *Vedene*, which is about a mile from the junction of the *Sorgue* and the *Rhône.* Others would place Vindalium at *Port de la Traille*, the place where the *Sorgue* joins the *Rhône.* [G. L.]

VINDANA PORTUS (Ούίνδανα λιμήν), a bay on the north-west coast of Gallia (Ptol. ii. 8. § 1), and placed by Ptolemy between the mouth of the Herius [HERIUS] and the Promontorium Gobaeum. D'Anville supposes the Vindana to be the bay of *Morbihan*, at the bottom of which was the capital of the Veneti, now *Vannes.* Other geographers have made other guesses : the bay of *Douarnez*, the mouth of the *Blavet*, and others still. [G. L.]

VINDELEIA (Ούινδέλεια, Ptol. ii. 6. § 53), a town of the Autrigones in Hispania Tarraconensis, between Virovesca and Deobriga. (*Itin. Ant.* p. 454.) Probably *Pancorbo.* [T. H. D.]

VINDELI'CIA (Ούινδελικία or Βινδελικία), the most western of the four Danubian provinces of the Roman empire. , In the time of Augustus, it formed a distinct province by itself, but towards the end of the first century after Christ it was united with Rhaetia. At a still later period the two countries were again separated, and Rhaetia Proper appears under the name Rhaetia Prima, and Vindelicia under that of Rhaetia Secunda. We have here to speak only of the latter or Vindelicia, as it appears

in the time of Augustus, when it was bounded on the north by Germania Magna, that is, by the Danube and the Vallum Hadriani or Limes, on the west by the territory of the Helvetii, on the south by Rhaetia, and on the east by Noricum, from which it was separated by the river Oenus (*Inn*). The line of demarcation between Vindelicia and Rhaetia is not mentioned anywhere, but was in all probability formed by the ridge of the Rhaetian Alps. Vindelicia accordingly embraced the north-eastern parts of *Switzerland*, the south-eastern part of *Baden*, the southern part of *Würtemberg* and *Bavaria*, and the northern part of *Tirol* (Ptol. ii. 12. § 1, 13. § 1, viii. 7. § 1 ; Sext. Ruf. 8 ; Agathem. ii. 4.) The country is for the most part flat, and only its southern parts are traversed by off-shoots of the Rhaetian Alps. As to the products of Vindelicia in ancient times, we have scarcely any information, though we are told by Dion Cassius (liv. 22) that its inhabitants carried on agriculture, and by other authors that the country was very fertile. (Solin. 21 ; Isid. *Orig.* i. 4.) The chief rivers of Vindelicia are : the Danube, the upper part of which flowed through the country, and farther down formed its boundary. All the others are Alpine rivers and tributaries of the Danube, such as the ILARGUS, GUNTIA, LICUS, VIRDO, ISARUS, and the OENUS, which separated Vindelicia from Noricum. The Lacus Brigantinus in the south-west also belonged to Vindelicia.

The inhabitants of Vindelicia, the Vindelici, were a kindred race of the Rhaeti, and in the time of Augustus certainly Celts, not Germans, as some have supposed. Their name contains the Celtic root *Vind*, which also occurs in several other Celtic names, such as Vindobona, Vindomagus, Vindonissa, and others. (Zeuss, *Die Deutschen*, p. 228, foll.; Diefenbach, *Celtica*, ii. 1. p. 134, foll.) Others, without assuming that the Vindelicians were Germans, believe that their name is connected with the German *Wenden*, and that it was used as a general designation for nations or tribes that were not Germans, whence the modern *Wend* and also the name of the Vandali or Vindili. (Comp. Horat. *Carm.* iv. 4. 18 ; Strab. iv. pp. 193, 207, vii. pp. 293, 313 ; Tac. *Ann.* ii. 17, *Hist.* iii. 5 ; Suet. *Aug.* 21; Vell. Pat. ii. 39; Plin. iii. 24.) After their subjugation by Tiberius, many of them were transplanted into other countries. (Strab. vii. p. 207 ; Dion Cass. liv. 22.) The principal tribes into which, according to Strabo, Pliny, and Ptolemy, the Vindelici were divided, were : the BRIGANTII, RUNICATAE, LEUNI, CONSUANTAE, BENLAUNI, BREUNI, and LICATII. Their more important towns were : Augusta Vindelicorum, their capital, Reginum, Arbor Felix, Brigantium, Vemania, Campodunum, Abodiacum, Abusina, Quintiana Castra, Batava Castra, Vallatum, Isinisca, Pons Oeni, and a few others, which are treated of in separate articles. (Comp. Rayser, *Der Oberdonaukreis Bayerns unter den Römern*, Augsburg, 1830 ; J. Becker, *Drusus und die Vindelicier*, in Schneidewin's *Philologus*, v. p. 119, foll.) [L. S.]

VINDENAE, a place in Upper Moesia, on the road from Naissus to Scodra. (*Tab. Peut.*) [T. H. D.]

VI'NDERIS (Ούινδέριος ποταμοῦ ἐκβολαί, Ptol. ii. 2. § 8), a little river on the E. coast of Hibernia, perhaps that which falls into *Strangford Bay ;* but Camden (p. 1403) places it more to the N. near *Carrickfergus.* [T. H. D.]

VINDILI. [VANDALI.]

VINDILIS INSULA, on the Atlantic coast of

Gallia, is mentioned in the Maritime Itin. after Uxantis and Sina or Sena. Middle age documents prove that the island of *Belle-tle* was once named *Guedel*, and this is the name Vindilis, the interchange of Gu or G and W or V being common. [VAPINCUM.] Though this is the only evidence, it is sufficient, for the names agree, and *Belle-tle* is not likely to have been omitted in the Itin., when smaller islands along the coast are mentioned.   [G. L.]

VINDINUM. [SUINDINUM.]

VINDIUS MONS (Οὐίνδιον ὄρος, Ptol. vii. 1. § 28), a chain of mountains in *Hindostán*, extending NE. and SW. nearly, along the N. bank of the Namadus (now *Nerbudda*), in lat. 21°, long. 117° 30′. They are now known by the name of the *Vindhya Ms.*, and form the principal watershed of the *Nerbudda* and *Tapti*, which flow into the Indian Ocean, a little to the N. of *Bombay*, and of the *Soane* and *Andomati*, which are great tributaries of the Ganges. [V.]

VI′NDIUS or VINNIUS (Οὐί. διον ὄρος, Ptol. ii. 6. § 21), a mountain in Hispania Tarraconensis, which ran in a W. direction from the Saltus Vasconum and formed the boundary between the Cantabri and the Astures. It formed, therefore, the W. portion of the Cantabrian chain. The Iberus had its source in it.   [T. H. D.]

VINDOBALA, a station on the wall of Hadrian in Britain, which was garrisoned by the Cohors I. Frixagorum. Camden (p. 1090) identifies it with *Walls-End*; whilst Horsley (p. 105) and others take it to be *Rutchester*. (*Not. Imp.*; Geo. Rav. v. 31.) [VALLUM ROMANUM.]   [T. H. D.]

VINDOBO′NA or VENDOBONA (Οὐινδόβουνα: *Vienna*), a town on the Danube in Upper Pannonia, was originally a Celtic place, but afterwards became a Roman municipium, as we learn from inscriptions. (Gruter, *Inscript.* p. 4.) This town, which according to Ptolemy (ii. 15. § 3) for some time bore the name of Juliobona (Ἰουλιόβονα), was situated at the foot of Mons Cetius, on the road running along the right bank of the river, and in the course of time became one of the most important military stations on the Danube; for after the decay of Carnuntum it was not only the station of the principal part of the Danubian fleet, but also of the Legio x. Gemina. (*It. Ant.* pp. 233, 248, 261, 266; *Tab. Peut.*; Aurel. Vict. *de Caes.* 16; Agathem. ii. 4; Jornand. *Get.* 50, where it is called Vindomina.) Vindobona suffered severely during the invasion of the Huns under Attila, yet continued to be a flourishing place, especially under the dominion of the Longobards. (Jornand. *l. c.*) It is well known that the emperor M. Aurelius died at Vindobona. (Aurel. Vict. *de Caes.* 16, *Epit.* 18; comp. Fischer, *Brevis Notitia Urbis Vindobonae*, Vindobonae, 1767; Von Hormayr, *Geschichte Wiens*, i. p. 43, foll.; Muchar, *Norikum*, vol. i. p. 166, foll.)   [L. S.]

VINDOGLA′DIA, a place in Britannia Romana, probably in the territory of the Belgae on the road from Venta Belgarum to Isca Dumnoniorum. (*Itin. Ant.* pp. 483, 486.) The Geogr. Rav. (v. 31) calls it Bindogladia. Some place it at *Pentridge*, near *Old Sarum*, where are remains of Roman fortifications. Camden, however (p. 61), identifies it with *Winburn*, and Horsley (p. 472) with *Cranburn*.   [T. H. D.]

VINDOLANA, a station on Hadrian's boundary wall in Britain, where the Cohors IV. Gallorum lay in garrison. (*Not. Imp.*) By the Geo. Rav. (v. 31) it is called Vindolanda. Camden (p. 1087) identifies it with *Old Winchester*, Horsley (p. 89, &c.) with *Little Chesters*. [VALLUM ROMANUM.] [T.H.D.]

VINDOMAGUS (Οὐινδόμαγος), in Gallia Narbonensis, one of the two cities which Ptolemy (ii. 10. § 10) assigns to the Volcae Arecomici. There is nothing to determine the position of Vindomagus, except the fact that there is a town *Vigan*, where some remains have been found. *Le Vigan* is NW. of *Nismes*, and on the southern border of the *Cévennes*.   [G. L.]

VINDOMIS or VINDOMUM, a place belonging probably to the Belgae in Britannia Romana on the road from Venta Belgarum to Calleva. (*Itin. Ant.* pp. 483, 486.) Horsley (p. 459) identifies it with *Farnham*; others have sought it at *E. Sherborne*, and at *Whitchurch*.   [T. H. D.]

VINDOMORA, a town of the Brigantes in the N. part of Britannia Romana. (*Itin. Ant.* p. 464.) It is commonly identified with *Ebchester* at the NW. boundary of Durham (Horsley, p. 398), where there are remains of a fort, and where Roman antiquities have been discovered. (Cf. Camden, p. 1086; *Philos. Trans.* No. 278.)   [T. H. D.]

VINDONISSA, in Gallia, is mentioned by Tacitus (*Hist.* iv. 61, 70). It was the station of the twenty-first legion, A. D. 71, which entered Rhaetia from Vindonissa. The place is *Windisch*, in the Swiss canton of *Aargau*, near the junction of the *Aar*, *Reuss*, and *Limmath*. Vindonissa was once a large place, and many Roman remains and coins have been found there. In the *Bärlisgrube* there are traces of an amphitheatre, and on the road from *Braunneckberg* to *Königsfelden* the remains of an aqueduct. The name of the XXL Legion has been discovered in inscriptions found at *Windisch*. Near *Windisch* is the former convent and monastery of *Königsfelden*, where some of the members of the Habsburg family are buried. Several Roman roads help to fix the position of Vindonissa. The Table places it at the distance of xxii. from Augusta Rauracorum (*Augst*) [AUGUSTA RAURACORUM]; and another road went from Vindonissa past Vitodurum [VITODURUM] to Arbor Felix in Rhaetia. Vindonissa is named Vindo in a Panegyric of Constantine by Eumenius, and Castrum Vindonissense in Maxima Sequanorum in the Notitia of the Gallic Provinces. When Christianity was established in these parts, Vindonissa was the see of the first bishopric, which was afterwards removed to *Constanz*. In the third and fourth centuries Vandals and Alemanni damaged the town. The Huns afterwards ravaged Vindonissa, and Childebert king of the Franks destroyed it in the sixth century. (D'Anville, *Notice*, &c.; Ernesti, *Note on Tacit. Hist.* iv. 70; Neigebaur, *Neuestes Gemälde der Schweiz.*)   [G. L.]

VINIOLAE, a place of the Oretani in Hispania Tarraconensis, between Acatucci and Mentesa Bastia. (*Itin. Ant.* p. 402.) Variously identified with *Hinojares* and as a place on the river *Borosa*. [T.H.D.]

VINNIUS. [VINDIUS.]

VINO′VIA (in Ptol. Οὐιννούϊον, ii. 3. § 16), a town of the Brigantes in the N. of Britannia Romana. (*Itin. Ant.* p. 465.) Now *Binchester* near *Bishop Auckland*, with remains of Roman walls and other antiquities. (Camden, p. 945.) In the *Not. Imp.* and by the Geogr. Rav. (v. 31) it is called Vinonia.   [T. H. D.]

VI′NTIUM (Οὐίντιον: *Vence*), in Gallia Narbonensis, the chief town of the Nerusii. [NERUSII.] Inscriptions have been found at *Vence* with the words CIVIT. VINT.; and in the Notitia of the Gallic Provinces it is placed in the Alpes Maritimae under the name of Civitas Vintiensium or

Venciensium. *Vence* is in the department of *Var*, near the river *Var*. (D'Anville, *Notice, &c.*) [G. L.]

VI'NZELA (Οὐίνζελα), a town of Galatia, in the territory of the Tectosages. (Ptol. v. 4. § 8.) A second town of the same name is mentioned by Ptolemy (v. 5. § 8) in the south-east of Pisidia.   [L. S.]

VIOLVASCENSIS PAGUS. [MARTIALIS.]

VIPITENUM, a town in Rhaetia belonging to the Venostes, situated between Veldidena and Tridentum. (*Itin. Ant.* pp. 275, 280.) Some place it in the *Ober-Wipthal;* others identify it with *Sterzing* on the *Eisach*, at the foot of the *Brenner*.   [T. H. D.]

VIPOSCIANA, a place in Mauretania Tingitana, on the road from Tocolosida to Tingis. (*Itin. Ant.* p. 23.) Mannert (x. pt. ii. p. 487) supposes that it is the place called Prisciana by Mela (iii. 10. sub fin.), and Πτισκίανα or Πισκιάνα by Ptolemy (iv. 1. § 14). The same author identifies it with *Mergo*, whilst Lapie takes it to be *Soc-el-Arba*, and Graberg di Hemsö, *Dar-el-Hhamara*. [T. H. D.]

VIRACELLUM (Βιράκελλον, Ptol.), a town of Etruria, mentioned only by Ptolemy (iii. 1. § 47), who places it among the inland towns in the NW. corner of that country. It is supposed by Cluverius to be represented by *Verrucola* or *Verrucchia* in the mountains between the *Serchio* and the *Magra* (Cluver. *Ital.* p. 75), but the identification is very doubtful.   [E. H. B.]

VIRDO (the *Wertach*), a small river in the territory of the Licatii in Vindelicia, a tributary of the Licus, which it joins a little below Augusta Vindelicorum. (Paul. Diac. *Langob.* ii. 13; Venant. Fort. *Vita S. Mart.* iv. 646, where it is less correctly called Vindo or Vinda).   [L. S.]

VIRGULAE. [BERGULE, Vol. I. p. 393, a.]

VIRIBALLUM. [CORSICA, Vol. I. p. 691, a.]

VIRITIUM (Οὐιρίτιον), a place in northern Germany, mentioned only by Ptolemy (ii. 11. § 27), was probably in the territory of the Sidini, on the site of the modern town of *Wrietzen* on the *Oder*. (Wilhelm. *Germanien*, p. 275.)   [L. S.]

VIROCO'NIUM (Οὐιροκόνιον, Ptol. ii. 3. § 19), a town of the Cornavii in Britannia Romana, on the road from Deva to Londinium, with a by-road from Maridunum. (*Itin. Ant.* pp. 482, 484.) It is the town called Urioconium in another route of the Itinerary (p. 469). Now *Wroxeter*, with ruins and antiquities. (Camden, p. 652.)   [T. H. D.]

VIRODUNUM. [VERODUNENSES.]

VIROMAGUS. [BROMAGUS.]

VIROSIDUM (*Not. Imp.*), a fort or castle at the N. boundary of Britannia Romana and in the territory of the Brigantes, the station of the Cohors VI. Nerviorum. Camden (p. 1022) places it near *Warwik Cumberland;* whilst others seek it on the S. coast of *Solway Frith*, and at *Preston*.   [T. H. D.]

VIROVESCA (Οὐιροούεσκα, Ptol. ii. 6. § 53), a town of the Autrigones in Hispania Tarraconensis, on the road from Pompelo to Asturica (*Itin. Ant.* pp. 394, 450, 454; Plin. ii. 3. s. 4). It is the modern *Briviesca*. (Cf. Florez, *Esp. Sagr.* xxiv. p. 10, xxvii. p. 13.) Coins in Sestini (p. 211).   [T.H.D.]

VIROVIACUM, in Gallia, in the Table, Virovinum, is placed on a route from Castellum (*Cassel*) to Turnacum (*Tournay*). The Antonine Itinerary fixes it xvi. from each place. The distances in the Table do not agree; but the site is certain. It is *Wervic* or *Verwick*, a large village on the *Lys*, 3 leagues from *Lille* in the French department of *Nord*. In 1514 a medal of C. Julius Caesar was dug up at *Werwic*,

and some time afterwards other medals of the time of the Antonini. There is a tradition also of the remains of an ancient edifice having been seen here, and a fragment of a statue (Bast, *Recueil d'Antiquités Romaines et Gauloises trouvées dans la Flandre proprement dite*, Gand, 1804.)   [G. L.]

VIRUEDRUM (Οὐιρουεδροὺμ ἄκρον, Ptol. ii. 3. § 5), a promontory on the N. coast of Britannia Barbara, and the most N. point of the island. It is apparently the present *Dungsby Head*. (Camden, p. 1280.)   [T. H. D.]

VIRUNI. [VARINI.]

VIRU'NUM (Οὐίρουνον). 1. One of the most important towns in the interior of Noricum, south of Noreia, and on the road from Aquileia to Lauriacum. (Plin. iii. 27; Ptol. ii. 14. § 3; Steph. Byz. s. v. Βέρουνος; Suid. s. v. Βηρούνιον; *It. Ant.* p. 276; *Tab. Peut.*, where it is called Varunum.) But notwithstanding its importance, which is attested by its widely scattered remains about the village of *Mariasaal* near *Klagenfurt*, no details about it are known, except, from inscriptions, the fact that it was a Roman colony, with the surname of Claudia. (Gruter, *Inscript.* p. 569; Orelli, *Inscript.* no. 1317, 5074; comp. Muchar, *Noricum*, vol. i. p. 271.)

2. A town in the country of the Sidini in Germania, of unknown site, and mentioned only by Ptolemy (ii. 11. § 27).   [L. S.]

VIRUS (Οὐίρου ἐκβολαί, Ptol. ii. 6. § 3), a river in the N. part of the W. coast of Hispania Tarraconensis. Variously identified with the *Landrove* and the *Allones*.   [T. H. D.]

VISBU'RGII (Οὐισβούργιοι), a tribe in the south-east of Germany, about the sources of the Vistula, and placed by Ptolemy (ii. 11. § 21) near the Quadi, in the district to which Tacitus (*Germ.* 43) assigns the Gothini.   [L. S.]

VISO'NTIUM (Οὐισόντιον, Ptol. ii. 6. § 54), a town of the Pelendones in Hispania Tarraconensis, perhaps *Vinnesa* or *Binoesca*.   [T. H. D.]

VISPI (Οὐίσποι), a tribe in the south-west of Germany, is mentioned only by Ptolemy (ii. 11. § 10); nothing certain can be said as to the precise district they inhabited.   [L. S.]

VI'STULA, VISTILLUS (Οὐιστούλα, Οὐιστούλας: *Vistula* or *Weichsel*), one of the great rivers of Germany, separating, according to Ptolemy (viii. 10. § 2; comp. ii. 11. § 4, iii. 5. § 5), Germany from Sarmatia, while Pomp. Mela (iii. 4), who calls the river Visula, describes it as forming the boundary between Scythia and Sarmatia. It cannot be expected that either Greeks or Romans should have possessed much information about this distant river. Ptolemy says that it had its origin in the Hercynia Silva, and discharged itself into the Sarmatian ocean (the *Baltic*), and Marcianus (p. 53) ascribes to it a course of from 1850 to 2000 stadia in length. This is all the information to be gathered from the ancient authors. (Comp. Plin. iv. 27. s. 28; Solin. 20; Geogr. Rav. iv. 4; Amm. Marc. xxii. 8, where it is called Bisula; Jornand. *Get.* 3.) Jornandes in two passages (*Get.* 5 and 17) speaks of a river Viscla, which some geographers regard as identical with the modern *Wisloka*, a tributary of the Vistula, but it is probably no other than the Vistula itself, whose modern German name *Weichsel* seems to be formed from Viscla.   [L. S.]

VISURGIS (Οὐίσουργις, Βίσουργις, Οὐίσουργος, or Οὐισσούργιος: *Weser*), one of the principal rivers in north-western Germany, which was tolerably well known to the Romans, since during their wars in Germany they often advanced as far as its banks, and at one time even crossed it; but they seem to have been unacquainted with its southern course, and with its real origin; for it is formed by the confluence of the *Werra* and the *Fulda*, while Ptolemy (ii. 11. § 1) imagined that it had its sources in Mons Melibocus. Marcianus (p. 51) states that its length amounted to from 1600 to 1780 stadia. The Visurgis flowed into the German Ocean in the country of the Chauci. (Comp. Pomp. Mela, iii. 4; Plin. iv. 27; Tac. *Ann.* i. 70, ii. 9; Vell. Pat. ii. 105; Sidon. Apoll. *Carm.* xxiii. 243; Strab. vii. p. 291; Dion Cass. xliv. 33, lv. 1, 2, 8, lvi. 18.)   [L. S.]

VITE'LLIA (Βιτελλία, Steph. B.: *Eth.* Βιτελλῖνος, Vitelliensis), an ancient town of Latium, which was, however, apparently situated in the territory of the Aequi, or at least on their immediate frontiers, so that it is hard to determine whether it was properly a Latin or an Aequian town. But the circumstance that its name is not found in the list of the cities of the Latin League given by Dionysius (v. 61) is strongly in favour of the latter supposition. Its name is first mentioned by Livy (ii. 39) in the account of the celebrated campaign of Coriolanus, whom he represents as taking Vitellia at the same time as Corbio, Labicum, and Pedum: but in the more detailed narratives of the same campaign by Dionysius and Plutarch, no notice is found of Vitellia. The name is again mentioned by Livy in B.C. 393, when the city fell into the hands of the Aequi, who surprised it by a night attack (Liv. v. 29.) He there calls it "Coloniam Romanam," and says it had been settled by them in the territory of the Aequi; but we have no previous account of this circumstance; nor is there any statement of its recovery by the Romans. A tradition preserved to us by Suetonius recorded that the Roman colony was at one time entrusted to the sole charge of the family of the Vitellii for its defence (Suet. *Vitell.* 1); but there can be little doubt that this is a mere family legend. All trace of Vitellia, as well as Tolerium and other towns in the same neighbourhood, disappears after the Gaulish invasion, and the only subsequent mention of the name occurs in the list given by Pliny (iii. 5. s. 9) of the cities of Latium which were in his time utterly extinct. The site is wholly uncertain, though it seems probable that it may be placed in the same part of Latium as Tolerium, Bola, Labicum, and other towns on the frontiers of the Aequian territory. It has been placed by Gell at *Valmontone*, a place which in all probability occupies an ancient site, and this would do very well for Vitellia, but that it is equally suitable for Tolerium, which must be placed somewhere in the same neighbourhood, and is accordingly fixed by Nibby at *Valmontone* [TOLERIUM.] The latter writer would transfer Vitellia to *Civitella* (called also *Civitella d' Olevano*), situated in the mountains between *Olevano* and *Subiaco*; but this seems decidedly too far distant from the other cities with which Vitellia is connected. It would be much more plausible to place Vitellia at *Valmontone* and Tolerium at *Lugnano*, about 3 miles NW. of it, but that *Lugnano* again would suit very well for the site of Bola, which we are at a loss to fix elsewhere [BOLA]. The fact is that the determination of the position of these cities, which disappeared in such early times, and of which no record is preserved by inscriptions or other ancient monuments, must remain in great measure conjectural. (Gell. *Top. of Rome*, p. 436; Nibby, *Dintorni*, vol. i. p. 467, vol. iii. p. 370.)   [E. H. B.]

VITIA (Οὐιτία, Strab. xi. pp. 508, 514, 531: *Eth.* Οὐίτιοι), a small district in Media Atropatene, noticed by Strabo in his account of that province. It appears to have been in the northern part near the tribes of the Dribyces and Amardi.   [V.]

VITIS [UTIS].

VITODURUM or VITUDURUM, in Gallia, is mentioned in an inscription, in which it is said that the emperors Diocletian and Maximianus "murum Vitodurensem a solo instauraverunt." The Antonine Itin. places it between Vindonissa (*Windisch*) and Fines (*Pfin*) [FINES, No. 15.] At *Winterthur* in the Swiss canton of *Zürich* there is in the town library a collection of Roman coins and cut stones, most of which have been found in the neighbourhood of the town and in the adjacent village of *Oberwinterthur*, which is the site of Vitodurum. (D'Anville, *Notice, &c.*)   [G. L.]

VITRICIUM (*Verres*), a town or village of the Salassi, on the high road leading from Eporedia (*Ivrea*), to Augusta Praetoria (*Aosta*). It is known only from the Itineraries, which place it 25 miles from Augusta, and 21 from Eporedia (*Itin. Ant.* pp. 345, 347, 351), but is undoubtedly identical with *Verres*, a large village in the *Val d' Aosta*, at the entrance of the *Val Challant*.   [E. H. B.]

VIVANTAVARIUM (Οὐιβανταουάριον, Ptol. iii. 5. § 30), a place in European Sarmatia, between the rivers Axiaces and Tyras.   [T. H. D.]

VIVISCI, VIBISCI. [BITURIGES VIVISCI.]

VIVISCUS, in Gallia. In the Antonine Itin. the name is Bibiscus. The place is *Vevay*, or near it, in the Swiss canton of *Waadt* or *Vaud*. See the article PENNELOCUS.   [G.L.]

ULCAEI LACUS (Οὐλκαῖα ἕλη), a succession of lakes and swamps in Pannonia, between the mouths of the Dravus and Savus. (Dion Cass. lv. 32.) They seem to be the same as the Palus Hiulca mentioned by Aurelius Victor (*Epit.* 41) as being near Cibalae in Pannonia. (Comp. Zosim. ii. 18.) These lakes now bear the name of *Laxincze*.   [L. S.]

ULCI'SIA CASTRA, a fort in Pannonia, on the road running along the right bank of the Danubius from Aquincum to Bregetio (*It. Ant.* p. 269), is now called *Ssent Endre*.   [L. S.]

ULIA (Οὐλία, Strab. iii. p. 141), a town in Hispania Baetica, on a hill, on the road from Gades to Corduba. (*Itin. Ant.* p. 412.) It was a Roman municipium, with the surname of Fidentia, and belonged to the jurisdiction of Corduba (Plin. iii. 3. s. 4; Hirt. *B. H.* 3, 4, *B. Alex.* 61; Dion Cass. xliii. 31.) From inscriptions it appears to be the present *Monte Mayor*, where there are ruins. (Cf. Morales, *Ant.* p. 5; Florez, *Esp. Sagr.* x. p. 150, xii. p. 5; coins in Florez, *Med.* ii. p. 620, iii. p. 130; Mionnet, i. p. 27, *Suppl.* i. p. 47.)   [T. H. D.]

COIN OF ULIA.

ULIARUS INSULA (*Eth.* Olarionensis, Sidonius Apollinaris), is placed by Pliny in the Aquitanicus Sinus (iv. 19). It is the *Ile d'Oléron*, which belongs to the department of *Charente Inférieure*, and is separated from the mainland by a narrow strait.   [G. L.]

ULIZIBERA (Οὐλιζίβηρα, or Οὐλιζίβιρρα, Ptol. iv. 3. § 37), the Ulnsubritanum of Pliny (v. 4. s. 4), a town of Byzacium in Africa Proper, S. of Hadrumetum.   [T. H. D.]

ULLA (called by Ptolemy Οὐία, ii. 6. § 2), a river on the W. coast of Hispania Tarraconensis, which enters the sea between the Minius and the promontory of Nerium. (Mela, iii. 1.) It is still called *Ulla*.   [T. H. D.]

ULMANETES. [SILVANECTES.]

ULMI or ULMUS, a place frequently mentioned in the Itineraries as situated in the interior of Lower Pannonia on the road leading from Siccia to Cibalae and Sirmium (*It. Ant.* pp. 131, 232, 261, 267 ; *It. Hieros.* p. 563 ; *Tab. Peut.*) ; but its exact site is uncertain.   [L. S.]

ULMUS, a place in Upper Moesia, between Naissus and Remesiana. (*Itin. Hieros.* p. 566.) According to Lapie near *Pauclita.*   [T. H. D.]

ULPIA'NUM. 1. (Οὐλπιανόν, Ptol. iii. 9. § 6), called also ULPIANA (Οὐλπιανά, Hierocl. p. 656), a town of Upper Moesia on the southern declivity of Mt. Scomius. It was enlarged and adorned by Justinian, whence it obtained the name of Justiniana Secunda. (Procop. *de Aed.* iv. 1, *Goth.* iv. 25.) It is commonly identified with the present *Giustendil*; but Leake (*Northern Greece*, iii. p. 475) takes that town to represent the ancient Pantalia or Pantalia in Thrace.

2. A place in Dacia, apparently in the neighbourhood of *Klausenburg.* (Ptol. iii. 8. § 7.) [T. H. D.]

ULTERIOR PORTUS. [ITIUS PORTUS.]

ULUBRAE (*Eth.* Ulubrensis), a small town of Latium on the borders of the Pontine Marshes. It is not mentioned in history previous to the establishment of the Roman dominion, but is noticed repeatedly by Latin writers of the best period, though always as a poor and decayed town, a condition which appears to have resulted from its marshy and unhealthy position. Hence Cicero jestingly terms its citizens little frogs (*ranunculi*, *Ep. ad Fam.* vii. 18), and both Horace and Juvenal select it as an almost proverbial example of a deserted and melancholy place. (Hor. *Ep.* i. 11. 30 ; Juv. x. 101.) Still it appears from the expressions of the latter, that it still retained the rank of a municipal town, and had its own local magistrates ; and in accordance with this, we find the Ulubrenses enumerated by Pliny among the municipal towns of the First Region. (Plin. iii. 5. s. 9.) The same thing is attested by inscriptions (Orell. *Inscr.* 121—123), and the discovery of these at the place now called *Cisterna*, about eight miles from *Velletri*, and 35 from Rome, immediately at the entrance of the Pontine Marshes, leaves no doubt that Ulubrae was situated somewhere in that neighbourhood. But the village of Cisterna (called in the middle ages Cisterna Neronis), does not appear to occupy an ancient site, and the exact position of Ulubrae is still undetermined. (Nibby, *Dintorni di Roma*, vol. i. p. 463.) [E.H.B.]

UMBENNUM, in Gallia Narbonensis, is placed in the Jerusalem Itin. between Batiana [BATIANA] and Valentia (*Valence*).   [G. L.]

UMBRAE, one of many tribes placed by Pliny near the mouth of the Indus, adjoining, perhaps

within, the larger district of Pattalene (vi. 20. s. 23).   [V.]

UMBRANICI, a people of Gallia Narbonensis, who had the Jus Latii. (Plin. iii. 4.) There is no further notice of these people who had this political privilege, except the occurrence of the name Umbranica or Umbranicia in the Table.   [G. L.]

UMBRIA (ἡ Ὀμβρική: *Eth.* Umber, Umbri, Ὄμβρικός), was one of the principal divisions of Central Italy, situated to the E. of Etruria, and extending from the valley of the Tiber to the shores of the Adriatic. The name was, however, at different periods applied within very different limits. Umbria, properly so called, may be considered as extending only from the Tiber, which formed its W. limit through the greater part of its course, and separated Umbria from Etruria, to the great central range of the Apennines from the sources of the Tiber in the N. to the *Monti della Sibilla* in the S. But on the other side of this range, sloping down to the Adriatic, was an extensive and fertile district extending from the frontiers of Picenum to the neighbourhood of Ariminum, which had probably been at one time also occupied by the Umbrians, but, before it appears in Roman history, had been conquered by the Gaulish tribe of the Senones. Hence, after the expulsion of these invaders, it became known to the Romans as "Gallicus ager," and is always so termed by historians in reference to the earlier period of Roman history. (Liv. xxiii. 14, xxxix. 44 ; Cic. *Brut.* 14, &c.) On the division of Italy into regions by Augustus, this district was again united with Umbria, both being included in the Sixth Region. (Plin. iii. 14. s. 19.) But even Pliny, in describing this union, distinguishes the "ager Gallicus" from Umbria Proper (" Jungitur his sexta regio *Umbriam complexa agrumque Gallicum* circa Ariminum," *Ib.*): it is evident therefore that the name of Umbria did not at that time in common usage include the territory on the shores of the Adriatic. In like manner Ptolemy designates the coast from Ancona to Ariminum (termed by Pliny the "Gallica ora") as "the land of the Senones" (Ptol. iii. 1. § 22), a term which had certainly become inappropriate long before his time. It was according to Pliny (*l. c.*) this portion of the Gaulish territory which was properly designated as Gallia Togata, a name afterwards extended and applied to the whole of Cisalpine Gaul. (Hirt. *B. G.* viii. 24; Cic. *Phil.* viii. 9, &c.) It was not, therefore, till a late period that the name of Umbria came into general use as including the whole of the Sixth Region of Augustus, or the land from the Tiber to the Adriatic.

Umbria, in this more extended sense of the name, was bounded on the W. by the Tiber, from a point near its source to a little below Ocriculum, which was the most southern city included within the province. Thence the E. frontier ascended the valley of the Nar, which separated Umbria from the land of the Sabines, almost to the sources of that river in the great central chain of the Apennines. Thence it followed a line nearly parallel with the main ridge of those mountains, but somewhat farther to the E. (as Camerinum, Matilica, and other towns situated on the E. slopes of the Apennines were included in Umbria), as far as the sources of the Aesis (*Esino*), and then descended that river to its mouth. We know that on the coast the Aesis was the recognised boundary between Umbria and Picenum on the S., as the little river Rubicon was between Umbria and Gallia Cisalpina on the N.

From the mouth of the latter stream the frontier must have followed an irregular line extending to the central range of the Apennines, so as to include the upper valleys of the Sapis and Bedesis; thence it rejoined the line already traced from the sources of the Tiber.

All ancient authors agree in representing the Umbrians as the most ancient people of Italy (Plin. iii. 14. s. 19; Flor. i. 17; Dionys. i. 19), and the traditions generally received described them as originally spread over a much more extensive region than that which ultimately retained their name, and occupying the whole tract from sea to sea, including the territories subsequently wrested from them by the Etruscans. That people, indeed, was represented as gaining possession of its new settlements step by step, and as having taken not less than 300 towns from the Umbrians. (Plin. l. c.) This number is doubtless fabulous, but there seems to be good reason for regarding the fact of the conquest as historical. Herodotus, in relating the Lydian tradition concerning the emigration of the Tyrrhenians, represents the land as occupied, at the time of their arrival, by the Umbrians. (Herod. i. 94.) The traditions reported by Dionysius concerning the settlements of the Pelasgians in Italy, all point to the same result, and represent the Umbrians as extending at one period to the neighbourhood of Spina on the Adriatic, and to the mouths of the Padus. (Dionys. i. 18—20.) In accordance with this we learn incidentally from Pliny that Butrium, a town not far from Ravenna, was of Umbrian origin. (Plin. iii. 15. s. 20.) The name of the river Umbro (Ombrone), on the coast of Etruria, was also in all probability a relic of their dominion in that part of Italy. On the whole we may fairly assume as a historical fact, the existence of the Umbrians at a very early period as a great and powerful nation in the northern half of Central Italy, whose dominion extended from sea to sea, and comprised the fertile districts on both sides of the Apennines, as well as the mountains themselves. According to Zenodotus of Troezen (ap. Dionys. ii. 49), the powerful race of the Sabines itself was only a branch or offshoot of the Umbrians; and this statement is to a great extent confirmed by the result of recent philological researches. [SABINI.]

If the Umbrians are thus to be regarded as one of the most ancient of the races established in Italy, the question as to their ethnological affinities becomes of peculiar interest and importance. Unfortunately it is one which we can answer but very imperfectly. The ancient authorities upon this point are of little value. Most writers, indeed, content themselves with stating that they were the most ancient people of Italy, and apparently consider them as Aborigines. This was distinctly stated by Zenodotus of Troezen, who had written a special history of the Umbrian people (Dionys. ii. 49); and the same idea was probably conveyed by the fanciful Greek etymology that they were called Ombricans or Ombrians, because they had survived the deluge caused by floods of rain (ὄμβροι; Plin. iii. 14. s. 19). Some writers, however, of whom the earliest seems to have been one Bocchus, frequently quoted by Solinus, represented the Umbrians as of Gaulish origin (Solin. 2. § 11; Serv. ad Aen. xii. 753; Isidor. Orig. ix. 2); and the same view has been maintained by several modern writers, as the result of philological inquiries. Researches of this latter kind have indeed of late years thrown much light upon the affinities of the Umbrian language, of which we

possess an important monument in the celebrated tables of Iguvium. [IGUVIUM.] They have clearly established, on the one hand its distinctness from the language of the neighbouring Etruscans, on the other its close affinity with the Oscan, as spoken by the Sabellian tribes, and with the old Latin, so that the three may fairly be considered as only dialects of one and the same family of languages. [ITALIA, p. 86.] The same researches tend to prove that the Umbrian is the most ancient of these cognate dialects, thus confirming the assertions of ancient writers concerning the great antiquity of the nation. But, while they prove beyond a doubt that the Umbrian, as well as the nearly related Oscan and Latin, was a branch of the great Indo-Teutonic family, they show also that the three formed to a great extent a distinct branch of that family or an independent group of languages, which cannot with propriety be assigned to the Celtic group, any more than to the Teutonic or Slavonic.

The history of the Umbrians is very imperfectly known to us. The traditions of their power and greatness all point to a very early period; and it is certain that after the occupation of Etruria as well as of the plains of the Padus by the Etruscans, the Umbrians shrunk up into a comparatively obscure mountain people. Their own descendants the Sabines also occupied the fertile districts about Reate and the valley of the Velinus, which, according to the traditions reported by Dionysius, had originally been held by the Umbrians, but had been wrested from them by the Pelasgians (Dionys. ii. 49.) At a much later period, but still before the name of the Umbrians appears in Roman history, they had been expelled by the Senonian Gauls from the region on the shores of the Adriatic. Livy indeed represents them as having previously held also a part of the territory which was subsequently occupied by the Boians, and from which they were driven by the invasion of that people (Liv. v. 35).

It was not till the Romans had carried their arms beyond the immediate neighbourhood of the city, and penetrated beyond the barrier of the Ciminian forest, that they came into contact with the Umbrians. Their first relations were of a friendly nature. The consul Fabius having sent secret envoys through the land of the neighbouring Etruscans into Umbria, received from the tribe of the Camertes promises of support and assistance if he should reach their country. (Liv. ix. 36.) But the Umbrian people seem to have been divided into different tribes, which owned no common government and took different lines of policy. Some of these tribes made common cause with the Etruscans and shared in their defeat by Fabius. (Ib. 37.) This disaster was followed by two other defeats, which were sustained by the Umbrians alone, and the second of these, in which their combined forces were overthrown by the consul Fabius near Mevania (B. C. 308), appears to have been a decisive blow. It was followed, we are told, by the submission of all the Umbrian tribes, of whom the people of Ocriculum were received into the Roman alliance on peculiarly favourable terms. (Liv. ix. 39, 41.)

From this time we hear no more of hostilities with the Umbrians, with the exception of an expedition against a mere marauding tribe of mountaineers (Liv. x. 1), till B. C. 296, when the Samnite leader Gellius Egnatius succeeded in organising a general confederacy against Rome, in which the Umbrians and Senonian Gauls took part, as well as the Etruscans and Samnites. (Liv. x. 21.) Their combined forces were, however, overthrown in the great battle of Sentinum (*Ib.* 26, 27; Polyb. ii. 19); and this is the last time that the Umbrians, as a people, appear in arms against the Roman power. We are indeed told in the epitome of Livy that the Umbrians were again defeated, and reduced to submission at the same time as the Sallentines, in B. C. 266 (Liv. *Epit.* xv.); but there seems no doubt that this refers only to the outlying tribe or people of the Sarsinates (on the N. of the Apennines, and adjoining the Boian Gauls), as the Fasti, in recording the events of the year, mention both consuls as triumphing only "de Sarsinatibus" (*Fast. Capit.*) We have no account of the terms on which the Umbrians were received into submission, or of the manner in which they passed, like their neighbours the Etruscans, into the condition of dependent allies of Rome : it is certain only that the different tribes and cities were, according to the usual Roman policy, admitted on very different terms. Ocriculum, as already mentioned, enjoyed special privileges ; and the same was the case with the Camertes, who, even in the days of Cicero, retained a peculiarly favoured position, and had a treaty which secured them a nominal independence and equality. (Liv. xxviii. 45 ; Cic. *pro Balb.* 20.) The fertile district of the "Gallicus ager" was in great part occupied by Roman colonies. of which Sena Gallica was founded as early as B. C. 289, Ariminum in B. C. 268, and Pisaurum in B. C. 183. But besides these, a considerable part of that territory was divided among Roman citizens, by a law of the tribune, C. Flaminius, in B. C. 232. (Cic. *Brut.* 14.) The other Umbrians continued in the position of dependent allies of Rome, and appear to have remained uniformly faithful to the powerful republic. Thus, in B. C. 282, we are told that they were solicited by the envoys of the Tarentines (Dion Cass. *Fr.* 144), but apparently without effect : nor does it appear that their constancy was for a moment shaken by the successes of Hannibal: and before the close of the Second Punic War we find them coming forward with the offer of volunteers for the army of Scipio. (Liv. xxviii. 45.) In the Social War they are said to have for a time broken out into revolt, and were defeated in a battle by the legate C. Plotius ; but it is probable that the defection was a very partial one, and the Romans wisely secured the fidelity of the Umbrians as well as of the Etruscans by bestowing on them the Roman franchise, B. C. 90. (Liv. *Epit.* lxxiv.; Oros. v. 18; Appian, *B. C.* i. 49.)

From this time the name of the Umbrians as a nation disappears from history, though it continued, as already mentioned, to be well known as one of the territorial divisions of Italy. (Tac. *Hist.* iii. 41, 42; Jul. Capit. *Gordiani,* 4; &c.) In the early ages of the empire it was still one of the districts which supplied the most numerous recruits to the praetorian cohorts. (Tac. *Ann.* iv. 5.) As long as the division of Italy into regions subsisted, the name of Umbria continued to be applied to the sixth region; but from an early period, certainly long before the time of Constantine, it was united for administrative purposes with Etruria, and its name seems to have become gradually merged in that of the more important province. Thus Servius tells us that Umbria was a part of Tuscia (Serv. *ad Aen.* xii. 753), and the Liber Coloniarum includes the ancient Umbrian cities of Hispellum, Tuder, Ameria, &c., among the "Civitates Tusciae." (*Lib. Colon.* p. 224.) On the other hand, the district E. of the Apennines, the ancient Ager Gallicus, was now again separated from Umbria, and became known by the name of Picenum Annonarium. (Mommsen, *de Lib. Col.* p. 211.)

Of the Umbrians as a nation during their period of independence we know almost nothing. We learn only that they enjoyed the reputation of brave and hardy warriors; and the slight resistance that they opposed to the Roman arms was probably owing to their want of political organisation. So far as we learn, they appear to have been divided into several tribes or "populi," such as the Camertes, Sarsinates, &c., each of which followed its own line of policy without any reference to a common authority. No trace is found in history of the existence among them of any national league or council such as existed among the Etruscans and Latins; and even where the Umbrians are spoken of in general terms, it is often doubtful whether the whole nation is really meant.

The physical characters of Umbria are almost wholly determined by the chain of the Apennines, which, as already described, enters the province near the sources of the Tiber, and extends thence without interruption to the lofty group of the *Monti della Sibilla* (the ancient Mons Fiscellus) at the sources of the Nar, and on the confines of Picenum and the land of the Sabines. The Apennines do not rise in this part of the chain to so great an elevation as they attain farther south, but their principal summits within the Umbrian territory range from 4000 to 5500 feet in height; while their numerous ramifications fill up a space varying from 30 to 50 miles in breadth. A very large portion of Umbria is therefore a mountain country (whence it is termed "montana Umbria" by Martial. iv. 10), though less rugged and difficult of access than the central regions of Italy farther to the S. On the W. the mountain district terminates abruptly on the edge of a broad valley or plain which extends from near *Spoleto* to the neighbourhood of *Perugia*, and is thence continued up the valley of the Tiber as far as *Città di Castello*. But beyond this plain rises another group of hills, connected with the main chain of the Apennines by a ridge which separates *Spoleto* from *Terni*, and which spreads out through almost the whole extent of country from the valley of the Nar to that of the Tiber. It is on the outlying hills or underfalls of this range that the ancient Umbrian cities of Tuder and Ameria were placed. The broad valley between this group and the main mass of the central Apennines is a fertile and delightful district, and was renowned in ancient times for the richness and luxuriance of its pastures, which were watered by the streams of the Tinia and Clitumnus. Here we find within a short distance of one another the towns of Treba, Hispellum, Mevania, and Assisium. This district may accordingly be looked on as the heart of Umbria properly so called.

On the E. of the central chain the Apennines descend more gradually to the sea by successive stages, throwing off like arms long ranges of mountains, sinking into hills as they approach the Adriatic. The valleys between them are furrowed by numerous streams, which pursue nearly parallel courses from SW. to NE. The most considerable of these are the AESIS (*Esino*), which formed the established limit between Umbria and Picenum; the SENA, which flowed under the walls of Sena Gallica (*Sinigaglia*); the far more celebrated METAURUS, which entered the sea at Fanum Fortunae (*Fano*); the PISAURUS, which gave name to the city of Pisaurum (*Pesaro*); the CRUSTUMIUS, now called the *Conca;* and the ARIMINUS (*Marecchia*), which gave its name to the celebrated city of Ariminum, and seems to have been regarded by Pliny as the northern boundary of Umbria, though that limit was certainly marked at an earlier period by the far-famed though trifling stream of the RUBICON. The river SAPIS also flowed through the Umbrian territory in the upper part of its course, and gave name to the Sapinia Tribus, mentioned by Livy as one of the divisions of the Umbrian nation.

All the waters which descend on the W. of the Umbrian Apennines discharge themselves into the Tiber. None of them are considerable streams, and the TINIA and CLITUMNUS are the only two the ancient names of which have been preserved to us. The NAR, a much more important river, the sources of which are in the Sabine territory, seems to have formed the boundary between Umbria and the land of the Sabines, through a considerable part of its course; but it entered the Umbrian territory near Interamna (*Terni*). and traversed it thence to its junction with the Tiber.

Two principal passes crossed the main chain of the Apennines within the limits of Umbria, and served to maintain the communication between the two portions of that country. The one of these was followed by the main line of the Flaminian Way, which proceeded almost due N. from Forum Flaminii, where it quitted the valley of the Clitumnus, and passed by Nuceria, Tadinum, and Helvillum, to the crest of the mountain chain, which it crossed between the last place and Cales (*Cagli*), and descended by the narrow ravine of the *Furlo* (Intercisa) into the valley of the Metaurus, which it then followed to the Adriatic at *Fano* (Fanum Fortunae). This celebrated road continued throughout the period of the Roman Empire to be the main line of communication, not only from the plains of Umbria to the Adriatic, but from Rome itself to Ariminum and Cisalpine Gaul. Its military importance is sufficiently apparent in the civil war between Vitellius and Vespasian. (Tac. *Hist.* i. 86, iii. 50, 52, &c.) Another line of road given in the Antonine Itinerary, quitted this main line at Nuceria, and, turning abruptly to the E., crossed a mountain pass to Proliaqueum (*Pioraco*), in the valley of the *Potenza*, and descended that valley to Septempeda in Picenum (*S. Severino*), and thence to Ancona. This pass has been in modern times wholly abandoned. The present road from Rome to Ancona turns to the E. from *Foligno* (Fulginium) and crosses the mountain ridge between that place and *Camerino*. descending to *Tolentino* in the valley of the *Chienti* (Flusor).

The towns of Umbria were numerous, though few of them were of any great importance. 1. On the W. of the Apennines, and beginning with those nearest to Rome, were: OCRICULUM, near the left bank of the Tiber; NARNIA and INTERAMNA, on the banks of the Nar; AMERIA and CARSULAE, a few miles to the N. of Narnia; TUDER, on a hill on the left bank of the Tiber; SPOLETIUM, in the hills which separate the valley of the *Maroggia* from that of the Nar; TREBA, MEVANIA, HISPELLUM, FULGINIUM, and ASSISIUM, all situated in or bordering on the broad valley above mentioned; ARNA and TIFERNUM TIBERINUM in the upper valley of the Tiber, and IGUVIUM in the mountains at a short distance from it. VESIONICA was probably situated at *Civitella di Benezzone*, also in the valley of the Tiber. On the Flaminian Way, exactly at the entrance of the

mountains, stood FORUM FLAMINII, and higher up, on the same line of road, NUCERIA, TADINUM, and HELVILLUM.

2. On the E. of the central ridge of the Apennines, but still high up among the mountains, were situated CAMERINUM, near the sources of the Flusor; PROLAQUEUM (*Pioraco*), near those of the Potentia; PITULUM (*Piolo*), in the same valley; MATILICA and ATTIDIUM, both in the upper valley of the Aesis; SENTINUM, in a lateral branch of the same valley; TUFICUM and SUASA, both of them in the valley of the *Cesano*; CALLES (*Cagli*), on the Flaminian Way; TIFERNUM METAURENSE and URBINUM METAURENSE, both of them in the upper valley of the Metaurus; FORUM SEMPRONII (*Fossombrone*), lower down in the same valley; URBINUM HORTENSE (*Urbino*), between the valleys of the Metaurus and the Pisaurus; SESTINUM (*Sestino*), near the sources of the latter river; PITINUM PISAURENSE, probably at *Piagnino* in the same valley; SARSINA, in the upper valley of the Sapis; and MEVANIOLA, which is fixed by Cluverius, on the faith of inscriptions discovered there, at *Galeata*, in the upper valley of the Bedesis or *Ronco* (Cluver. *Ital.* p. 623), and is therefore the most northerly town that was included in Umbria.

3. Along the coast of the Adriatic were the important towns of SENA GALLICA; FANUM FORTUNAE, PISAURUM, and ARIMINUM. To the above must be added AESIS or AESIUM (*Jesi*), on the left bank of the river of the same name, and OSTRA, the ruins of which are said to exist between the rivers *Cesano* and *Nigolo*. (Abeken, *Mittel-Italien.* p. 41.)

In addition to the above long list of towns, the position of which can be assigned with tolerable certainty, the following obscure names are enumerated by Pliny among the towns or communities of Umbria still existing in his time: the Casuentillani, Dolates surnamed Salentini, Forojulienses surnamed Concubienses, Forobrentani, Pelestini, Vindinates, and Viventani. The above towns being totally unknown, the correct form and orthography of the names is for the most part uncertain. The same is the case with several others which the same writer enumerates as having in his day ceased to exist. (Plin. iii. 14. s. 19.) Strabo also mentions a place called Larolum as being situated on the Flaminian Way, in the neighbourhood of Narnia and Ocriculum (v. p. 227), which is otherwise wholly unknown, and the name is probably corrupt.

Of the natural productions of Umbria the most celebrated were its cattle, especially those of the valley of the Clitumnus [CLITUMNUS]; but its mountain tracts afforded also pasturage to flocks of sheep, which were driven southwards as far as Metapontum and Heraclea. (Varr. *R. R.* ii. 9. § 6.) The lower portions of the country abounded in fruit-trees, vines, and olives; but when Propertius terms his native Umbria "terris fertilis uberibus," this can be understood only of the tracts on the W. of the Apennines, of which he is there speaking (Propert. i. 22. 9), not of the more extensive mountain regions.

The name of Umbria is still given to one of the provinces of the Papal States, of which *Spoleto* is the capital; but this is merely an official designation, the name having been wholly lost in the middle ages, and being no longer in use as a popular appellation.　　　　　　　　　　[E. H. B.]

UMBRO (*Ombrone*), a river of Etruria, and next to the Arnus the most considerable in that country. It rises in the hills between *Siena* and *Arezzo*, and has a course of above 50 miles in a SSW. direction till it flows into the Tyrrhenian sea, about 16 miles N. of the promontory of *Monte Argentaro*. Pliny terms it a navigable river (" navigiorum capax "), and Rutilius describes it as forming at its mouth a tranquil and secure port. (Plin. iii. 5. s. 8 ; Rutil. *Itin.* i. 337—340.) It flows near the modern city of *Grosseto*, and within a few miles of the ruins of Rusellae. The name of Umbro is considered to be connected with the Umbrians, who held this part of Italy previous to its conquest by the Etruscans : and according to Pliny, the coast district extending from its mouth to Telamon, was still known as the " tractus Umbriae." (Plin. *l. c.*) [E. H. B.]

UNELLI or VENELI (Οὐένελοι), one of the Armoric or maritime states of Gallia. (*B. G.* ii. 34, iii. 11.) Caesar mentions them with the Veneti, Osismi, Curiosolitae, and other maritime states. The Unelli and the rest submitted to P. Crassus in B.C. 57; but in B.C. 56 it was necessary to send a force again into the country of the Unelli, Curiosolitae, and Lexovii. Q. Titurius Sabinus had the command of the three legions who were to keep the Unelli and their neighbours quiet. The commander of the Unelli was Viridovix, and he was also at the head of all the forces of the states which had joined the Unelli, among whom were the Aulerci Eburovices and the Lexovii. The force of Viridovix was very large, and he was joined by desperate men from all parts of Gallia, robbers and those who were too idle to till the ground. The Roman general entrenched himself in his camp, and made the Galli believe that he was afraid and was intending to slip away by night. The trick deceived the Galli, and they attacked the Roman camp, which was well placed on an eminence with a sloping ascent to it about a mile in length. On the Galli reaching the Roman camp exhausted by a rapid march up the hill and encumbered with the fascines which they carried for filling up the ditch, the Romans sallied out by two gates and punished the enemy well for their temerity. They slaughtered an immense number of the Galli, and the cavalry pursuing the remainder let few escape. This clever feat of arms is told clearly in the Commentaries.

The Unelli sent a contingent of 6000 men to attack Caesar at the siege of Alesia. (*B. G.* vii. 75.)

Ptolemy (ii. 8. § 2) names Crociatonum the capital of the Veneli. [CROCIATONUM.] The people occupied the peninsula of *Cotantin* or *Cotentin*, which is now comprehended in the department of *La Manche*, except a small part which is included in the department of *Calvados*. [G. L.]

UNSINGIS, according to a reading in Tacitus (*Ann.* i. 70), a river in the north-west of Germany; but the correct reading in that passage is *ad Amisiam*, as Ritter has shown in his note upon it, Unsingin being only a conjecture of Alting manufactured out of the modern name of a river called *Unse* or *Hunse*. [L. S.]

VOBARNA [BRIXIA].

VOCANUS AGER, a district in Africa Propria, between Carthage and Thapsus. (Liv. xxxiii. 48.) [J. R.]

VOCARIUM or VACORIUM (Οὐακόριον), a place in Noricum, on the great road leading from Augusta Vindelicorum to Aemona. (Ptol. ii. 14. § 3 ; *Tab. Peut.*) Its exact site is matter of conjecture only. [L. S.]

VOCATES. [VASATES.]

VOCE'TIUS MONS. This name occurs in Tacitus (*Hist.* i. 68), and nowhere else. The history shows that Tacitus is speaking of the country of the Helvetii. The Vocetius is conjectured to be that part of the Jura which is named *Boetsberg*. The road from *Bâle* runs through the *Frickthal* over the *Bötzberg* to Baden and the *Zürich*. The Helvetii fled from Caecina (A. D. 70) into the Vocetius, where many were caught and massacred. Aventicum, the chief city (caput gentis), surrendered to Caecina. [AVENTICUM.] It has been proposed to write Vogesus for Vocetius in the passage of Tacitus; but there is no reason for the alteration. [G. L.]

VOCONII FORUM. [FORUM VOCONII.]

VOCO'NTII (Οὐοκόντιοι), a people of Gallia Narbonensis, between the *Rhône* and the Alps. The only city which Ptolemy (ii. 10. § 17) assigns to them is Vasio [VASIO]. On the north they bordered on the Allobroges, as we learn from Caesar's march (*B. G.* i. 10). Strabo places the Cavares west of the Vocontii, but he has not fixed the position of the Cavares well [CAVARES]. The position of the Vocontii, and the extent of their country, are best shown by looking at the position of Vasio, which was in the south part of their territory, and of Dea [DEA], which is in the north part, and Lucus Augusti, which lies between them [LUCUS AUGUSTI].

In the Notitia of the Gallic Provinces we find both Civitas Deentium and Civitas Vasiensium or Vasionensium.

The Vocontii were between the *Isère* and the *Durance*, their southern limit being probably a little south of *Vaison*. D'Anville supposes that the Vocontii occupied the dioceses of *Vaison* and *Die*, and also a part of the country comprised in the diocese of *Gap* [VAPINCUM], and a part of the diocese of Sisteron, which borders on *Vaison*. Pliny (iii. 4) calls the Vocontii a " Civitas foederata," a people who had a " foedus " with Rome; and besides the chief places, Vasio and Lucus Augusti, he says they have nineteen small towns. Pliny (ii. 58) mentions that he had been in the country of the Vocontii, where he saw an aerolite which had lately fallen (" delatum " should perhaps be " delapsum "). The Vocontii occupied the eastern part of the department of *Drôme*, which is a mountainous country, being filled with the lower offsets of the Alps, and containing numerous valleys drained by mountain streams. Part of the country is fitted for pasture. Silius Ital. (iii. 466) has :—

" Tum faciles campos, jam rura Vocontia carpit;"

for he makes Hannibal pass through the Vocontii to the Alps, as Livy (xxi. 31) does. [G. L.]

VODGORIACUM, in Gallia, is the first place in the Itins. on the road from Bagacum (*Bavai*) to Aduatuca (*Tongern*). This remarkable Roman road is called the *Chaussée de Brunehaut*, or the *Haut Chemin*. The distance of Vodgoriacum from Bagacum is xii., and the place is supposed to be *Voudrei* or *Vaudre*. (D'Anville, *Notice, &c.*) [G.L.]

VOGESUS. [VOSEGUS.]

VOLANA. [SAMNIUM.]

VOLANDUM, a castle in Armenia Major, lying a day's journey W. of Artaxata. (Tac. *Ann.* xiii. 39.) [T. H. D.]

VOLATERRAE (Οὐολατέρραι: *Eth.* Volaterranus: *Volterra*), one of the most important and powerful of all the Etruscan cities. It was situated on a lofty hill, rising above the valley of the Cecina, about 5 miles N. of that river and 15 from the sea. Strabo has well described its remarkable situation on the summit of a hill, which required a steep ascent of 15 stadia from whatever side the approached, while the summit itself presented a level surface of considerable extent, bounded on all sides by precipices, and crowned by the walls of the ancient city. (Strab. v. p. 223.) The hill on which it stands is, according to modern measurements, more than 1700 English feet in height above the sea, and completely overlooks all the surrounding heights, so that the position of the city is extremely commanding. It is indeed the most striking instance of the kind of position which the Etruscans seem to have generally preferred for their cities.

There can be no doubt of the great antiquity of Volaterrae, nor that it was, from the earliest period of Etruscan history with which we have any acquaintance, one of the twelve principal cities of the Etruscan confederation: this conclusion, to which we should be irresistibly led by the still existing proofs of its ancient greatness, is confirmed by the earliest notice of it that we find in history, where it appears as one of the five Etruscan cities which furnished support to the Latins in their war with Tarquinius Priscus. (Dionys. iii. 51.) But from this time we find no subsequent mention of Volaterrae in history till a much later period. Its remoteness from Rome will indeed sufficiently account for the fact that its name never figures in the long protracted wars of the Romans with the southern Etruscans ; but even after the Roman arms had been carried into the heart of Etruria, and the cities of Perusia and Arretium took active part in the wars, we find no mention of Volaterrae. In B. c. 298, however, we are told that the Roman consul L. Scipio was encountered near Volaterrae by the combined forces of the Etruscans (Liv. x. 12), among which there is little doubt that those of the Volaterrans themselves were included, though this is not expressly stated. But we do not again find their name noticed in the extant accounts of these wars, and the terms on which they were finally reduced to submission by the Romans are unknown to us. We learn only that in common with most of the Etruscans they were received on the footing of dependent allies, and they appear among the "socii" who in the Second Punic War came forward to furnish supplies for the fleet of Scipio, B. c. 205. On that occasion the Volaterrans provided materials for ship-building as well as corn. (Liv. xxviii. 45.) From this time we hear no more of Volaterrae till the civil wars between Marius and Sulla, when the city espoused the cause of the former, and from its great natural strength became the last stronghold of the Marian party in Etruria, and indeed in Italy. It was besieged by Sulla himself long after every other city in Italy had submitted, and did not surrender till after a siege or rather blockade of two years' duration. (Strab. v. p. 223; Liv. Epit. lxxxix.; Cic. pro Rosc. Amer. 7, pro Caec. 7.) As a punishment for its obstinacy, its territory was confiscated by the conqueror; but it appears that it was never actually divided, and the citizens who had survived the calamities of the war remained in possession of their lands, as well as of the rights of Roman citizens, which had been doubtless conferred upon them in common with the other Etruscans by the Lex Julia in B. c. 89. (Cic. pro Dom. 30, ad Fam. xiii. 4, 5, ad Att. i. 19.) It appears that another attempt was made to dispossess them by an agrarian law in the consulship of Cicero, but this calamity was averted from them by the efforts of the great

orator, to whom the citizens in consequence became warmly attached (Id. ad Fam. xiii. 4), and it appears probable that Caesar subsequently confirmed them in the possession both of their lands and municipal privileges. (Ib.)

Volaterrae, however, certainly received a colony under the Triumvirate (Lib. Col. p. 214), but does not appear to have retained the title of a Colonia: it is expressly included by Pliny among the municipal towns of Etruria. (Plin. iii. 5. s. 8; Ptol. iii. 1. § 48.) We find no mention of the name in history under the Roman Empire; but it is certain that the city continued to exist; and it appears again, after the fall of the Western Empire, as a place of importance during the wars of the Goths with Narses (Agath. B. G. i. 11). It continued to subsist throughout the middle ages, and still retains the title of a city and its episcopal see; though it has little more than 4000 inhabitants, and occupies only a small portion of the area of the ancient city. The latter is clearly marked out, having comprised the whole level surface of the hill, a very irregular space, above a mile and a half in length and more than 1000 yards in its greatest breadth: the whole circuit of the ancient walls is above three miles and a quarter. Very large portions of these walls are still visible, and these massive fortifications are incontestably the finest specimens of the kind now existing in Etruria: they resemble in their general style of construction those of Faesulae and Cortona, but are composed of a different material, a soft, arenaceous limestone, which composes the whole summit of the hill on which Volterra stands. This stone, however, like the macigno of Fiesole and Cortona, lends itself readily to the horizontal structure, and is wholly distinct from the hard Apennine limestone of which the polygonal walls of Cosa and other cities are composed. These walls may be traced, at intervals, all round the brow of the hill, following the broken and irregular outlines of its summit, and frequently taking advantage of projecting points to form bold salient angles and outworks. Two of the ancient gates are still preserved ; of which the one called the Porta all' Arco still serves as the principal entrance to the city. It is of very massive construction, but regularly built, and surmounted by an arch of perfectly regular form and structure, adorned with three sculptured heads, projecting in relief from the keystone and two of the principal voussoirs. The antiquity of this arch has been a subject of much dispute among antiquarians; some maintaining it to be a specimen of genuine Etruscan architecture, others ascribing it to the Roman period. The arguments in favour of the latter view seem on the whole to preponderate; though there is no reason to doubt that the Etruscans were acquainted with the true principles of the construction of the arch. (Dennis's Etruria, vol. ii. pp. 146—150; Micali, Antichi Popoli Italiani, vol. iii. pp. 4, 5.*) The other gate, on the N. side of the Etruscan walls, now known as the Porta di Diana or Portone, is of similar plan and construction to the Porta all' Arco; but the arch is wanting.

No other remains of ancient edifices are now extant on the site of Volaterrae, except some portions of Thermae, of Roman date and little interest ; but the sepulchres which have been excavated on all sides of the city, but particularly on the N. slope of the hill, have yielded a rich harvest of Etruscan antiqui-

---

* The gate itself is figured by Micali, pl. 7, 8 ; and by Abeken, Mittel-Italien, pl. 2, fig. 4.

4 P 4

ties. Among these the most conspicuous are the sepulchral urns, or rather chests, for ashes, resembling small sarcophagi, and generally formed of alabaster, a material which is quarried in the immediate neighbourhood. Many of them are adorned with sculptures and bas-reliefs, some of them purely Etruscan in character, others taken from the Greek mythology, and there is no doubt that many of them belong to a period long after the fall of Etruscan independence. The inscriptions are for the most part merely sepulchral, and of little interest; but those of one family are remarkable as preserving to us the original Etruscan form (Ceicna) of the well-known family of the Caecinae, who figure frequently in Roman history [CAE-CINA, *Biogr. Dict.*]. Indeed, the first of this family of whom we have any knowledge—the Aulus Caecina defended by Cicero in B. C. 69—was himself a native of Volaterrae (Cic. *pro Caec.* 7). His son was the author of a work on the "Etruscan discipline," which is frequently referred to as a valuable source of information in regard to that department of antiquities (Cic. *ad Fam.* vi. 6; Plin. i. *Arg. Lib.* ii; Senec. *Nat. Quaest.* ii. 39).

There is no doubt that Volaterrae in the days of its independence possessed an extensive territory. Strabo distinctly tells us (v. p. 223) that its territory extended down to the sea-coast, where the town of VADA, or as it was called for distinction's sake, VADA VOLATERRANA, constituted its sea-port. It was not indeed a harbour or port in the strict sense of the word; but a mere roadstead, where the shoals, from which it derived its name, afforded a good anchorage and some shelter to shipping. Hence it was, in the Roman times, a frequented station for vessels proceeding along the coast of Etruria (Cic. *pro Quinct.* 6: Plin. iii. 5. s 8; *Itin. Marit.* p. 501); and Rutilius, in particular, has left us an exact description of the locality (Rutil. *Itin.* i. 453—462). The site is still marked by a mediaeval tower on the coast, called *Torre di Vada*.

The coins of Volaterrae are numerous, and belong to the class called Aes Grave, from their large size and weight; but they are distinguished from all other Etruscan coins of this class by their having the name of the city in full; whence we learn that the Etruscan form of the name was FELATHRI, or VELATHRI, as on the one of which a figure is annexed.   [E. H. B.]

COIN OF VOLATERRAE.

VOLCAE, a people of South Gallia, divided into Volcae Arecomici and Volcae Tectosages (Οὐόλκαι Ἀρικόμιοι, Οὐόλκαι Τεκτοσάγες, Ptol. ii. 10. §§ 9, 10; Οὐόλκαι Ἀρικόμισκοι, Strabo).

Ptolemy says that the Tectosages occupied the most western parts of the Narbonensis, and that these are their cities: Illiberia, Ruscino, Tolosa Colonia, Cessero, Carcaso, Baeterrae, and Narbo Colonia. Next to them and extending to the *Rhône* he places the Arecomici, or Aricomii, as the name is in Ptolemy's text; and he assigns to the Arecomii

only Vindomagus [VINDOMAGUS] and Nemausus Colonia (*Nismes*). These two nations occupied all the Provincia from the *Rhône* to its western limits; and if Livy is not mistaken (xxi. 26), at the time of Hannibal's invasion of Italy, the Volcae had also possessions east of the *Rhône*.

The Cebenna (*Cévennes*) formed a natural boundary between the Volcae Arecomici and the Gabali and Ruteni. As to the limits between the Tectosages and the Arecomici there is great difficulty; for while Ptolemy assigns Narbo to the Tectosages, Strabo (iv. p. 203) says that Narbo is the port of the Arecomici; and it is clear that he supposed the Arecomici to have possessed the greater part of the Provincia, which is west of the *Rhône*, and that he limited the country of the Tectosages to the part which is in the basin of the *Garonne*. He makes the Tectosages extend also northwards to the *Cévennes*, in the western prolongation of this range. The chief city of the Arecomici was Nemausus [NEMAUSUS]; and the chief city of the Tectosages was Tolosa; and if Narbo belonged to the Arecomici, we must limit the Tolosates, as already observed, to the basin of the *Garonne*. [NARBO; TOLOSA.]

There is some resemblance between the names Volcae and Belgae, and there is some little evidence that the Volcae were once named Belcae or Belgae. But it would be a hasty conclusion from this resemblance to assume a relationship or identity between these Volcae and the Belgae of the north of Gallia. There was a tradition that some of the Volcae Tectosages had once settled in Germany about the Hercynia Silva; and Caesar (*B. G.* vi. 24) affirms, but only from hearsay, that these Volcae in his time still maintained themselves in those parts of Germany, and that they had an honourable character and great military reputation. He adds that they lived like the other Germans. The Tectosages also were a part of the Gallic invaders who entered Macedonia and Greece, and finally fixed themselves in Asia Minor in Galatia [GALATIA]. With the Roman conquest of Tolosa ended the fame of the Volcae Tectosages in Europe.   [G. L.]

VOLCARUM STAGNA. [STAGNA VOLCARUM.]

VOLCEIUM or VOLCENTUM (*Eth.* Volcentanus, Plin.; Volceianus, *Inscr.*: *Buccino*), a municipal town of Lucania, situated in the mountains W. of Potentia, a few miles from the valley of the Tanager. The name is variously written by ancient authors. Livy mentions the Volcentes as a people who in the Second Punic War revolted to Hannibal and received a Carthaginian garrison into their town, but, in B. C. 209, returned to the Roman alliance. (Liv. xxvii. 15.) There can be no doubt that these are the same people as the Volcentani of Pliny, who are enumerated by that author among the municipal communities of the interior of Lucania (Plin. iii. 10. s. 15), and it is certain that the Ulci or Volci of Ptolemy (Οὔλκοι, Ptol. iii. 1. § 70) refers to the same place, the correct name of which, as we learn from inscriptions, was Volceii or Vulceii, and the people Volceiani. (Mommsen, *Inscr. R. N.* pp. 15, 16.) The discovery of these inscriptions at *Buccino* leaves no doubt that this town occupies the site of the Lucanian city of Vulceii. (Romanelli, vol. i. p. 422; Holsten. *Not. ad Cluver.* p. 290.) It appears to have been a considerable municipal town under the Roman Empire, and is one of the "Praefecturae Lucaniae" mentioned in the Liber Coloniarum (p. 209).   [E. H. B.]

VOLCI (Ουόλκοι, Ptol.: *Eth.* Volciens: Ru. near *Ponte della Badia*), a city of Etruria, situated in the plain on the right bank of the river Armina (*Fiora*), about 8 miles from its mouth. Very little mention is found of it in history. The name of the city is known from Ptolemy as well as from Pliny, who enumerates, among the municipal towns of Etruria, the "Volcentini cognomine Etrusci," an appellation evidently used to distinguish them from the people of Volcentum in Lucania. (Plin. iii. 5. s. 8; Ptol. iii. 1. § 49.) The name is quoted also by Stephanus of Byzantium, who writes it Ὄλκιον, from Polybius. (Steph. B. *s. v.*) But the only indication that they had once been a powerful people, and their city a place of importance, is found in the Fasti Capitolini, which record a triumph in the year B. C. 280 over the Volsinienses and Volcientes (*Fast. Capit.* ad ann. 473). This was one of the last struggles of the Etruscans for independence, and it was doubtless in consequence of the spirit shown on this occasion by the Volcientes that the Romans shortly afterwards (in B. C. 273) established a colony at Cosa, in their territory. (Vell. Pat. i. 14; Plin. iii. 5. s. 8.) It is expressly stated on this occasion by Pliny, that Cosa was a dependency of Volci (Cosa Volcientium), a statement which has been ignored by those modern writers who have represented Cosa as an independent and important Etruscan city. But while this is very doubtful in the case of Cosa, the evidence, though scanty, is conclusive that Volci was such; and there is even reason to suppose, from a monument discovered at *Cervetri*, that it was at one time reckoned one of the twelve chief cities of the Etruscan League. (*Ann. d. Inst. Arch.* 1842, pp. 37—40.) But notwithstanding these obscure hints of its greatness, the name of Volci was almost forgotten, and its site unknown, or at least regarded as uncertain, when the first discovery of its necropolis in 1828 led to subsequent researches on the spot, which have brought to light a number of painted vases greatly exceeding that which has been discovered on any other Etruscan site. The unprecedented number, beauty, and variety of these works of art have given a celebrity in modern times to the name of Volci which is probably as much in excess of its real importance in ancient times as in the somewhat parallel case of Pompeii. It is impossible here to enter into any detailed account of the result of these excavations. It is calculated that above 6000 tombs in all have been opened, and the contents have been of the most varied kind, belonging to different periods and ages, and varying from the coarsest and rudest pottery to the finest painted vases. The same tombs have also yielded very numerous objects and works of art in bronze, as well as delicate works in gold and jewellery; and after making every allowance for the circumstance that the cemetery at Volci appears to have enjoyed the rare advantage of remaining undisturbed through ages, it affords incontestable proof that it must have belonged to a wealthy and populous city. The necropolis and its contents are fully described by Mr. Dennis (*Etruria*, vol. i. pp. 397—427). The results of the excavations, in regard to the painted vases discovered, are given by Gerbard in his *Rapporto su i Vasi Volcenti*, published in the *Annali dell' Instituto* for 1831. It is remarkable that only one of the thousands of tombs opened was adorned with paintings similar to those found at Tarquinii, and, in this instance, they are obviously of late date. The site of the city itself has been carefully ex-

plored since these discoveries have attracted so much interest to the spot. It stood on the right bank of the river Armina, just below the point where that stream is spanned by a noble bridge, now called the *Ponte della Badia*, undoubtedly a work of Roman times, though the foundations *may be* Etruscan. The few remaining relics of antiquity still visible on the site of the city, which occupied a plateau of about 2 miles in circumference, are also of Roman date, and mostly belong to a late period. Inscriptions also have been discovered, which prove it to have continued to exist under the Roman Empire; and the series of coins found there shows that it was still in existence, at least as late as the fourth century of the Christian era. In the middle ages it seems to have totally disappeared, though the plain in which it stood continued to be known as the *Pian di Voci*, whence Holstenius correctly inferred that this must have been the site of Volci. (Holsten. *Not. ad Cluver.* p. 40.) The necropolis was, for the most part, on the other side of the river; and it is here that the excavations have been carried on most diligently. The site of Volci (which is now wholly uninhabited) is about 8 miles from *Montalto*, a small town at the mouth of the *Fiora*, where that river was crossed by the Via Aurelia. (Dennis, *l. c.*)   [E. H. B.]

VOLCIANI, a people in Hispania Tarraconensis. (Liv. xxi. 19.)   [T. H. D.]

VOLENOS, a fort in Rhaetia, in the territory of Tridentum, which was destroyed by the Franks (Paul. Diac. *Longob.* iii. 31), and is generally identified with the modern village of *Volano* on the *Adige*, south of *Caliano*.   [L. S.]

VOLIBA (Ουόλιβα, Ptol. ii. 3. § 30), a town of the Dumnonii in Britannia Romana, near the W. extremity of the island. Most probably *Falmouth*. (Camden, p. 16.)   [T. H. D.]

VOLOBRIGA (Ουολόβριγα, Ptol. ii. 6. § 41), a town in Gallaecia in Hispania Tarraconensis belonging to the Nemetatae.   [T. H. D.]

VOLOGATIS, in Gallia Narbonensis, is placed by the Jerusalem Itin. after Lucus (*Luc*), on the road to Vapincum (*Gap*) past Mons Saleucus. The distance from Lucus is ix.; and D'Anville supposes that Vologatis may be a place named *Lèches*, but the distance ix. is too much. Others fix the place at *Beaurière*; and others propose *Lethes* or *Beaumont.* All this is uncertain.   [V.]

VOLOGE'SIA (Ουολγεσία, Ptol. v. 20. § 6), a city built by and named after Vologeses, one of the Arsacidan kings of Parthia, in the immediate neighbourhood of Seleuceia upon the Tigris. It is called by Pliny, Vologesocerta (vi. 26. s. 30), the latter portion of the name implying the "city of." The extensive ruins, still existing, on both sides of the Tigris, are probably those of the two great cities of Seleuceia and Vologesia.   [G. L.]

VOLSAS (Ουόλσας κόλπος, Ptol. ii. 3. § 1), a bay on the W. coast of Britain, probably *Loch Brey*. (Horsley, p. 378.)   [T. H. D.]

VOLSCI (Ουόλσκοι, Strab.; Ουολουσκοι, Dionys.), an ancient people of Central Italy, who bear a prominent part in early Roman history. Their territory was comprised within the limits of Latium as that name was employed at a late period, and under the Roman Empire; but there is no doubt that the Volscians were originally a distinct people from the Latins, with whom, indeed, they were almost always on terms of hostility. On the other hand they appear as constantly in alliance with the Aequi; and there is little doubt that these two nations were kindred races, though always distinguished from each another as two separate peoples. We have no statement in any ancient writer as to the ethnic origin or affinities of the Volscians, and are left almost wholly to conjecture on the subject. But the remains of the language, few and scanty as they are, afford nevertheless the safest foundation on which to rest our theories; and these lead us to regard the Volscians as a branch of the same family with the Umbrians and Oscans, who formed the aboriginal population of the mountain tracts of Central Italy. It would appear, indeed, as if they were more closely connected with the Umbrians than either the Sabines and their Sabellian offshoots, or the Oscans properly so called ; it is probable, therefore, that the Volscians had separated at a still earlier period from the main stock of the Umbrian race. (Mommsen, *Unter-Ital. Dialekt.* pp. 319—326 ; Schwegler, *Röm. Gesch.* vol. i. p. 178.) The only notice of their language that occurs in Roman authors, also points to it distinctly as different from Oscan (Titinius, *ap. Fest.* v. *Obscum*, p. 189), though the difference was undoubtedly that of two cognate dialects, not of two radically distinct languages.

When the Volscians first appear in Roman history, it is as a powerful and warlike nation, who were already established in the possession of the greater part at least of the territory which they subsequently occupied. Their exact limits are not, indeed, to be determined with accuracy; and it is probable that they underwent considerable fluctuations during their long wars with the Latins and Romans. But there seems no doubt that from a very early period they held the whole of the detached mountain group S. of the Tolerus (*Sacco*), termed by modern geographers the *Monti Lepini*, together with the valley of the Liris, and the mountain district of Arpinum, Sora, and Atina. Besides this they were certainly masters at one time of the plains extending from the Volscian Apennines to the sea, including the Pomptine Marshes and the fertile tract that borders on them. This tract they had, according to Cato, wrested from the Aborigines, who were its earliest possessors (Cato *ap. Priscian.* v. p. 668).

The first mention of the Volscians in Roman history is in the reign of the second Tarquin, when they appear as a numerous and warlike people. It is clear that it was the great extension of the Roman power under its last king (which must undoubtedly be admitted as a historical fact), and the supremacy which he had assumed over the Latin League, that first brought him into collision with the Volscians. According to the received history he marched into their country and took their capital city, Suessa Pometia, by assault. (Liv. i. 53 ; Dionys. iv. 50 ; Cic. *de Rep.* ii. 24.) The tradition that it was the spoils there obtained which enabled him to build the Capitol at Rome, sufficiently proves the belief in the great power and wealth of the Volscians at this early period ; and the foundation of the two colonies of Circeii and Signia, both of which are expressly ascribed to Tarquin, was doubtless intended to secure his recent conquests, and to impose a permanent check on the extension of the Volscian power. It is evident, moreover, from the first treaty with Carthage, preserved to us by Polybius (iii. 22), that the important cities of Antium and Tarracina, as well as Circeii, were at this time subject to Tarquin, and could not, therefore, have been in the hands of the Volscians.

But the dissolution of the power of Tarquin, and the loss of the supremacy of Rome over the Latins, seem to have allowed the Volscians to regain their former superiority ; and though the chronology of the earliest years of the Republic is hopelessly confused, we seem to discern clearly that it was the increasing pressure of the Volscians and their allies the Aequians upon the Latins that caused the latter people to conclude the celebrated treaty with Rome under Sp. Cassius, B. C. 493, which became the foundation of the permanent relation between the two states. (Liv. ii. 33 ; Dionys. vi. 95.) According to the received annals, the wars with the Volscians had already recommenced prior to this period; but almost immediately afterwards occurs the great and sudden development of their power which is represented in a legendary form in the history of Coriolanus. Whatever may have been the origin of that legend, and however impossible it is to receive it as historically true, there is no doubt that it has a historical foundation in the fact that many of the Latin cities at this period fell successively into the power of the Volscians and their allies the Aequians ; and the two lines of advance, so singularly mixed up in the received narrative of the war, which represents all these conquests as made in a single campaign, appear to represent distinctly the two separate series of conquests by which the two nations would respectively press on towards Rome. (Niebuhr, vol. ii. pp. 95, 259; Schwegler, *Röm. Gesch.* vol. ii. pp. 274, 275.)*

It is impossible here to give more than a very brief outline of the long series of wars with the Volscians which occupy so prominent a place in the early history of Rome for a period of nearly two centuries. Little historical value can be attached to the details of those wars as they were preserved by the annalists who were copied by Livy and Dionysius ; and it belongs to the historian of Rome to endeavour to dispel their confusion and reconcile their discrepancies. But in a general point of view they may be divided (as remarked by Niebuhr), into four periods. The first of these would comprise the wars down to B. C. 459, a few years preceding the Decemvirate, including the conquests ascribed to Coriolanus, and would seem to have been the period when the Volscians were at the height of their power. The second extends from B. C. 459 to 431, when the dictator A. Postumius Tubertus is represented as gaining a victory over the allied forces of the Volscians and Aequians (Liv. iv. 26—29), which appears to have been really an important success, and proved in a manner the turning point in the long struggle between the two nations. From this time till the capture of Rome by the Gauls (B. C. 390) the wars with the Volscians and Aequians assume a new character ; the tide had turned, and we find the Romans and their allies recovering one after another the towns which had fallen into the hands of their enemies. Thus Labicum and Bola were regained in B. C. 418 and 414, and Ferentinum, a Hernican city, but which had been taken by the Volscians, was again wrested from them in B. C. 413. (Liv. iv. 47, 49, 51.) The frontier fortresses of Verrugo and Carventum were indeed taken and retaken; but the capture of Anxur or Tarracina in B. C. 399, which from that period

---

* It is worthy of notice that Antium, which at the commencement of the Republic appears as a Latin city, or at least as subject to the supremacy of Rome, is found at the very outbreak of these wars already in the hands of the Volscians.

continued constantly in the hands of the Romans must have been a severe blow to the power of the Volscians, and may be considered as marking an era in their decline. Throughout this period it is remarkable that Antium, one of the most powerful cities of the Volscians, continued to be on peaceful terms with Rome ; the war was carried on almost exclusively upon the NE. frontier of the Volscians, where they were supported by the Aequians, and Ecetra was the city which appears to have taken the lead in it.

The capture of Rome by the Gauls marks the commencement of the fourth period of the Volscian Wars. It is probable that their Aequian allies suffered severely from the same invasion of the barbarians that had so nearly proved the destruction of Rome [AEQUI], and the Volscians who adjoined their frontier, may have shared in the same disaster. But on the other hand, Antium, which was evidently at this period a powerful city, suddenly broke off its friendly relations with Rome ; and during a period of nearly 13 years (B. C. 386—374), we find the Volscians engaged in almost perpetual hostilities with Rome, in which the Antiates uniformly took the lead. The seat of war was now transferred from the Aequian frontier to the southern foot of the Alban hills : and the towns of Velitrae and Satricum were taken and retaken by the Volscians and Romans. Soon after the conclusion of peace with the Antiates we hear for the first time of Privernum, as engaging in hostilities with Rome, B. C. 358, and it is remarkable that it comes forward single-handed. Indeed, if there had ever been any political league or bond of union among the Volscian cities, it would seem to have been by this time completely broken up. The Antiates again appear repeatedly in arms ; and when at length the general defection of the Latins and Campanians broke out in B. C. 340, they were among the first to join the enemies of Rome, and laid waste the whole sea-coast of Latium, almost to the walls of Ostia. But they shared in the defeat of the Latin armies, both at Pedum and on the Astura : Antium itself was taken, and received a colony of Romans within its walls, but at the same time the citizens themselves were admitted to the Roman franchise. (Liv. viii. 14.) The people of Fundi and Formiae, both of them probably Volscian cities, received the Roman franchise at the same time, and Tarracina was soon after occupied with a Roman colony. The Privernates alone ventured once more to provoke the hostility of the Romans in B. C. 327, but were severely punished, and their city was taken by the consul C. Plautius. Nevertheless, the inhabitants were admitted to the Roman Civitas ; at first, indeed, without the right of suffrage, but they soon afterwards obtained the full franchise, and were enrolled in the Ufentine tribe. The greater part of the Volscians, however, was included in the Pomptine tribe.

Of the fate of the cities that were situated on the borders of the valley of the Trerus, or in that of the Liris, we have scarcely any information ; but there is reason to suppose that while the Antiates and their neighbours were engaged in hostilities with Rome, the Volscians of the interior were on their side fully occupied with opposing the advance of the Samnites. Nor were their efforts in all cases successful. We know that both Arpinum and Fregellae had been wrested from the Volscians by the Samnites, before the Romans made their appearance in the contest (Liv. viii. 23, ix. 44), and it is probable that the other cities of the Volscians readily took shelter

under the protection of Rome, for security against their common enemy. It seems certain, at all events, that before the close of the Second Samnite War (B. C. 304), the whole of the Volscian people had submitted to the authority of Rome, and been admitted to the privileges of Roman citizens.

From this time their name disappears from history. Their territory was comprised under the general appellation of Latium, and the Volscian people were merged in the great mass of the Roman citizens. (Strab. v. pp. 228, 231 ; Plin. iii. 5. s. 9 ; Cic. pro Balb. 13.) But a rude and simple mountain-people would be naturally tenacious of their customs and traditions ; and it is clear, from the manner in which Juvenal incidentally alludes to it, that even under the Roman Empire, the name of the Volscians was by no means extinct or forgotten in the portion of Central Italy which was still occupied by their descendants. (Juv. Sat. viii. 245.)

The physical geography of the land of the Volscians will be found described in the article LATIUM. Of the peculiar characters of the people themselves, or of any national customs or institutions that distinguished them from their Latin neighbours, we know absolutely nothing. Their history is a record only of the long struggle which they maintained against the Roman power, and of the steps which led to their ultimate subjugation. This is the only memory that has been transmitted to us, of a people that was for so long a period the most formidable rival of the Roman Republic.   [E. H. B.]

VOLSINIENSIS LACUS (ἡ περὶ Οὐολσινίους λίμνη, Strab. v. p. 226: Lago di Bolsena), a considerable lake of Etruria, scarcely inferior in size to that of Trasimene. It took its name from the town of Volsinii, which stood on its NE. shore ; but it was also sometimes called Lacus Tarquiniensis, as its western side adjoined the territory of Tarquinii. (Plin. ii. 96.) Notwithstanding its great size, it is probable, from the nature of the surrounding hills and rocks, that it is the crater of an extinct volcano (Dennis, Etruria, vol. i. p. 514). In this lake the river Marta has its source. It abounded in fish, and its sedgy shores harboured large quantities of water-fowl, with which articles it supplied the Roman markets. (Strab. l. c.; Colum. viii. 16.) It contained two islands, of which, as well as of the lake itself, wonderful stories were related by the ancients. They were remarked to be ever changing their forms (Plin. l. c.), and on one occasion during the Second Punic War its waters are said to have flowed with blood. (Liv. xxvii. 23.) The shores of the lake were noted for their quarries. (Plin. xxxvi. 22. s. 49.) In a castle on one of the islands queen Amalasontha was murdered by order of her husband Theodatus. (Procop. B. Goth. i. c. 4, p. 23, ed. Bonn.)   [T. H. D.]

VOLSINII or VULSINII (Οὐολσίνιον, Strab. v. p. 226; Οὐολσίνιον, Ptol. iii. 1. § 50: Bolsena), an ancient city of Etruria, situated on the shore of a lake of the same name (Lacus Volsiniensis), and on the Via Clodia, between Clusium and Forum Cassii. (Itin. Ant. p. 286; Tab. Peut.) But in treating of Volsinii we must distinguish between the Etruscan and the Roman city. We know that the ancient town lay on a steep height (Zonaras, Ann. viii.7 ; cf. Aristot. Mir. Ausc. 96); while Bolsena, the representative of the Roman Volsini, is situated in the plain. There is considerable difference of opinion as to where this height should be sought. Abeken (Mittelitalien, p. 34, seq.) looks for it at Monte Fiascone, at the southern extremity of the lake; whilst Müller (*Etrusker*, i. p. 451) seeks it at *Orvieto*, and adduces the name of that place==Urbs Vetus, "the old city," as an argument in favour of his view; but Mr. Dennis (*Etruria*, vol. i. p. 508) is of opinion that there is no reason to believe that it was so far from the Roman town, and that it lay on the summit of the hill, above the amphitheatre at *Bolsena*, at a spot called *Il Piazzano*. He adduces in support of this hypothesis the existence of a good deal of broken pottery there, and of a few caves in the cliffs below.

Volsinii appears to have been one of the most powerful cities of Etruria, and was doubtless one of the 12 which formed the Etruscan confederation, as Volsinii is d signated by Livy (x. 37) and Valerius Maximus (ix. 1. extern. 2) as one of the "capita Etruriae." It is described by Juvenal (iii. 191) as seated among well-wooded hills.

We do not hear of Volsinii in history till after the fall of Veii. It is possible that the success of the Roman arms may have excited the alarm and jealousy of the Volsinienses, as their situation might render them the next victims of Roman ambition. At all events, the Volsinienses, in conjunction with the Salpinates, taking advantage of a famine and pestilence which had desolated Rome, made incursions into the Roman territory in B. C. 391. But they were easily beaten; 8000 of them were made prisoners; and they were glad to purchase a twenty years' truce on condition of restoring the booty they had taken, and furnishing the pay of the Roman army for a twelvemonth. (Liv. v. 31, 32.)

We do not again hear of Volsinii till the year B. C. 310, when, in common with the rest of the Etruscan cities, except Arretium, they took part in the siege of Sutrium, a city in alliance with Rome. (Liv. ix. 32.) This war was terminated by the defeat of the Etruscans at lake Vadimo, the first fatal shock to their power. (*Ib.* 39.) Three years afterwards we find the consul P. Decius Mus capturing several of the Volsinian fortresses. (*Ib.* 41.) In 295, L. Postumius Megellus ravaged their territory and defeated them under the walls of their own city, slaying 2800 of them; in consequence of which they, together with Perusia and Arretium, were glad to purchase a forty years' peace by the payment of a heavy fine. (Id. x. 37.) Not more than fourteen years, however, had elapsed, when, with their allies the Vulcientes, they again took up arms against Rome. But this attempt ended apparently in their final subjugation in B. C. 280. (Liv. *Ep.* xi.; *Fast. Cons.*) Pliny (xxxiv. 7. s. 16) retails an absurd story, taken from a Greek writer called Metrodorus Scepsius, that the object of the Romans in capturing Volsinii was to make themselves masters of 2000 statues which it contained. The story, however, suffices to show that the Volsinians had attained to a great pitch of wealth, luxury, and art. This is confirmed by Valerius Maximus (*l. c.*), who also adds that this luxury was the cause of their ruin, by making them so indolent and effeminate that they at length suffered the management of their commonwealth to be usurped by slaves. From this degrading tyranny they were rescued by the Romans. (Flor. i. 21; Zonaras, *l. c.*; A. Victor, *Vir. Illustr.* 36; Oros. iv. 5.)

The Romans, when they took Volsinii, razed the town, and compelled the inhabitants, as we have already intimated, to migrate to another spot. (Zonaras, *l. c.*) This second, or Roman, Volsinii con-

tinued to exist under the Empire. It was the birthplace of Sejanus, the minister and favourite of Tiberius. (Tac. *Ann.* iv. 1, vi. 8.) Juvenal (x. 74) alludes to this circumstance when he considers the fortunes of Sejanus as dependent on the favour of Nursia, or Norsia, an Etruscan goddess much worshipped at Volsinii, into whose temple there, as in that of Jupiter Capitolinus at Rome, a nail was annually driven to mark the years. (Liv. vii. 3; Tertull. *Apol.* 24.) According to Pliny, Volsinii was the scene of some supernatural occurrences. He records (ii. 54) that lightning was drawn down from heaven by king Porsenna to destroy a monster called Volta that was ravaging its territory. Even the commonplace invention of hand-mills, ascribed to this city, is embellished with the traditional prodigy that some of them turned of themselves! (Id. xxxvi. 18. s. 29.) Indeed, in the whole intercourse of the Romans with the Etruscans, we see the ignorant wonder excited by a cultivated people in their semi-barbarous conquerors.

From what has been already said it may be inferred that we should look in vain for any traces of the Etruscan Volsinii. Of the Roman city, however, some remains are still extant at *Bolsena*. The most remarkable are those of a temple near the Florence gate, vulgarly called *Tempio di Norzia*. But the remains are of Roman work; and the real temple of that goddess most probably stood in the Etruscan city. The amphitheatre is small and a complete ruin. Besides these there are the remains of some baths, cippi, sepulchral tablets, a sarcophagus with reliefs representing the triumph of Bacchus, &c.

For the coins of Volsinii, see Müller, *Etrusker*, vol. i. pp. 324, 333; for its history, &c., Adami, *Storia di Volseno*; Dennis, *Etruria*, vol. i.; Abeken, *Mittelitalien*. [T. H. D.]

VOLTUMNAE FANUM [FANUM VOLTUMNAE].

VOLUBILIANI. [VOLUBILIS.]

VOLUBILIS (Οὐολούβιλις, Ptol. iv. 1. § 14), a town of Mauretania Tingitana, seated on the river Subur, and on the road from Tocolosida to Tingis, from the former of which places it was only 4 miles distant. (*Itin. Ant.* p. 23.) It lay 35 miles SE. from Banasa, and the same distance from the coast. (Plin. v. 1. s. 1; Mela, iii. 10.) It was a Roman colony (*Itin. Ant. l. c.*) and a place of some importance. Ptolemy calls the inhabitants of the surrounding district, Volubiliani (Οὐολουβίλιανοι, iv. 1. § 10). In the time of Leo Africanus (p. 279, ed. Lorsbach) it was a deserted town between *Fes* and *Mequinez*, bearing the name of *Valili* or *Gualili*, the walls of which were 6 Italian miles in circumference. That position is now occupied by the town of *Zanitat-Mula-Driss*, on mount *Zarhon*. At some distance to the NW. are the splendid ruins of *Kassr Faraun* (Pharaoh's castle), with Roman inscriptions; but to what ancient city they belong is unknown. (Cf. Mannert, x. pt. ii. p. 486; Graberg di Hemsö, p. 28; Wimmer, *Gemälde von Afrika*, i. p. 439.) [T. H. D.]

VOLUCE (probably the Οὐέλουκα of Ptol. ii. 6. § 56), a town of the Pelendones in Hispania Tarraconensis, on the road from Asturica to Caesaraugusta, and 25 miles W. of Numantia. (*Itin. Ant.* p. 442.) Variously identified with *Velucha* (*Velache*), *Valecha*, and *Calatañazor*. [T. H. D.]

VOLUNTII (Οὐολούντιοι, Ptol. ii. 2. § 9), a people on the E. coast of Hibernia. [T. H. D.]

VOLUSTA'NA. [CAMBUNII MONTES.]

VOMANUS (*Vomano*), a river of Picenum, which rises in the lofty group of the Apennines now known as the *Gran Sasso d'Italia*, and flows into the Adriatic, after passing within a few miles to the N. of the city of Adria (*Atri*). Its name is mentioned by Pliny only (iii. 13. § 18).   [E. H. B.]

VORDENSES, in Gallia Narbonensis, an ethnic name which occurs in an inscription found at *Apt*, the site of Apta Julia [APTA JULIA]. The inscription states that the "Vordenses pagani" dedicate this monument to their patronus, who is designated " IIII vir " of the Colonia Apta. The place is supposed to be *Gordes*, which is contiguous to the diocese of *Apt*, and in that of *Cavaillon*. The change of *Vord* into *Gord* is easily explained. [VARINCUM.] (D'Anville *Notice, &c*) [G. L.]

VOREDA, a town of the Brigantes in Britannia Romana, on the road from Cataracton to Luguvallium. (*Itin. Ant.* p. 467.) It is variously identified with *Old Penrith*, *Whelp Castle*, and *Coal Hills*. By the Geogr. Rav. (v. 31) it is called Bereda.   [T. H. D.]

VORGA'NIUM (Οὐοργάνιον), in Gallia Lugdunensis, the capital of the Osismii [OSISMII], a Celtic people in the north-west part of *Bretagne* (Ptol. ii. 8. § 5). This seems to be the same place as the Vorginum of the Table; and it appears on a route which leads from the capital of the Namnetes through the capital of the Veneti, and ends on the coast at Gesocribate, or Gesobrivate, as some would write it. Between the capital of the Veneti and Vorginum is Sulis, supposed to be at the junction of the *Suel* and the *Blavet* [SULIS]. From Sulis to Vorginum the distance is marked xxiiii., and this brings us to a place named *Karhes* (D'Anville). But all this is very uncertain. Others fix Vorginum at a place named *Guemené*   [G. L.]

VORO'GIUM, in Gallia, is placed in the table on a road from Augustonemetum (*Clermont Ferrand*) through Aquae Calidae (*Vichy*) to Ariolica (*Avrilli*). The distance is marked viii. from Aquae Calidae, and xiiii. from Vorogium to Ariolica. There is a place named *Vouroux*, which is the same name as Vorogium. *Vouroux* is near the small town of *Varennes*, and somewhat nearer to the banks of the Allier. The direct distance from the springs of *Vichy* to *Varennes* is somewhat less than the Itin. distance of viii. Gallic leagues, but the 8 leagues are not more than we may assign to the distance from *Vichy* to *Varennes* along the river. But the Itin. distance from Vorogium to Ariolica is somewhat too large compared with the real distance. (D'Anville, *Notice, &c.*)   [G. L.]

VOSALIA. [VOSAVA.]

VOSAVA or VOSAVIA, in North Gallia, is placed by the Table on the Roman road along the west bank of the Rhine, and between Bontobrice or Baudobrica (*Boppart*) [BAUDOBRICA] and Bingium (*Bingen*). It stands half-way between these places and at the distance of viiii. Vosava is *Oberwesel* on the Rhine, north of *Bingen;* and it is almost certain, as D'Anville suggests, that the name is erroneously written in the Table, and that it should be Vosalia.   [G. L.]

VO'SEGUS (*Vogesen, Vasgau, Vosges*). The form Vosegus has better authority than Vosegus (Schneider's *Caesar, B. G.* iv. 10) ; and the modern name also is in favour of the form Vosegus. Lucan is sometimes quoted as authority for the form Vogesus:

"Castraque quae Vogesi curvam super ardua rupem
Pugnaces pictis cohibebant Lingonas armis."
    (*Pharsal.* i. 397.)
The name is Βοσῆκον in the Greek version of the Commentaries.

Caesar says that the Mosa (*Maas*) rises in the Vosegus, by which he means that the hills in which the *Maas* rises belong to the *Vosges*. But he says no more of this range. The battle with Ariovistus, B. C. 58. was fought between the southern extremity of the *Vosges* and the *Rhine*, but Caesar (*B. G.* i. 43, 48) gives no name to the range under which Ariovistus encamped in the great plain between the *Vosges* and the *Rhine*. D'Anville observes that an inscription in honour of the god Vosegus was found at *Berg-Zabern* on the confines of *Alsace* and the *Palatinate*, which proves that the name Vosegus extended as far as that place. It seems likely that the name was given to the whole range now called *Vosges*, which may be considered as extending from the depression in which is formed the canal of the *Rhône* and *Rhine*, between *Béfort* and *Altkirch*, to the bend of the *Rhine* between *Mains* and *Bingen*, a distance of above 170 miles. The range of the *Vosges* is parallel to the Rhine. The hilly country of the *Faucilles* in which the *Maas* rises is west of the range to which the name of *Vosges* is now given. The *Vosges* are partly in France and partly in Rhenish *Bavaria* and *Hesse Darmstadt.*

The territory of the Sequani originally extended to the Rhine, and the southern part of the *Vosges* was therefore included in their limits. North of the Sequani and west of the *Vosges* were the Leuci and Mediomatrici; and east of the *Vosges* and between the *Vosges* and the *Rhine* were the Rauraci, Triboci, Nemetes, Vangiones, and Caracates.

In the Table the Silva Vosagus is marked as a long forest on the west side of the Rhine. Pliny (xvi. 39) also speaks of the range of the Vosegus as containing timber.   [G. L.]

UR, a castle of the Persians mentioned by Ammianus Marcellinus (xxv. 8), in his account of the war between Julian and the Persians. It must have been situated in Mesopotamia, at no great distance from Hatra (*Al-Hathr*). It has been generally supposed that Ur is the same place as that mentioned in Genesis (xi. 28); but the recent researches of Colonel Rawlinson have demonstrated that the Ur whence Abraham started was situated in the S. part of Babylonia, at a place now called *Mugeher*. (*Journ. Roy. As. Soc.* 1855.)   [V.]

URANO'POLIS (Οὐρανόπολις), a town in the peninsula Acte of Chalcidice in Macedonia, of which we know nothing, except that it was founded by Alexarchus, the brother of Cassander, king of Macedonia (Athen. iii. p. 98; Plin. iv. 10. s. 17). As Pliny does not mention Sane in his list of the towns of Acte, it has been conjectured by Leake that Uranopolis occupied the site of Sane. (*Northern Greece*, vol. iii. p. 149.)

URANO'POLIS (Οὐρανόπολις), a town of Pisidia, in the district of Cabalia, to the north-west of Termessus, and south-east of Isionda. (Ptol. v. 5. § 6.)   [L. S.]

URBA, a town of Gallia, in the territory of the Helvetii. It is placed in the Antonine Itin. between Lacus Lausonius and Ariolica [ARIOLICA], xviii. from Lacus Lausonius and xxiiii. from Ariolica. Urba is *Orbe* in the Swiss Canton *Waadt* or *Pays de Vaud*, on the road from the Lake of *Neuf-*

châtel to the *Lake of Geneva*, and on a hill nearly surrounded by the river *Orbe*.   [G. L.]

URBANA COLONIA, mentioned by Pliny only (xiv. 6. s. 8), was a colony founded by Sulla in a part of the territory of Capua, adjoining the Falernus ager. From its name it would appear probable that it was a colony of citizens from Rome itself, who were settled by the dictator in this fertile district. It is doubtful whether there ever was a town of the name, as no allusion is found to it as such, and the district itself was reunited to that of Capua before the time of Pliny. (Plin. *l. c.*; Zumpt, *de Col.* p. 252.)   [E. H. B.]

URBATE, a place in Lower Pannonia, on the road from Siscia to Sirmium (*It. Ant.* p. 268 ; *Tab. Peut.*); its exact site is unknown.   [L. S.]

URBIACA, a town of the Celtiberi, in Hispania Tarraconensis. (*Itin. Ant.* p. 447.) Probably the Urbicua of Livy (xl. 16). Variously identified with *Albaroches*, *Checa*, and *Molina.*   [T. H. D.]

URBIGENUS PAGUS. [HELVETII, Vol. I. p. 1041.]

URBINUM (Οὐρβῖνον), was the name of two cities or municipal towns of Umbria, situated within a short distance of each other, which were distinguished by the epithets Hortense and Metaurense. (Plin. iii. 14. s. 19.)

1. URBINUM HORTENSE (*Urbino*), apparently the more considerable of the two, and for that reason frequently called simply Urbinum, was situated on a hill between the valleys of the Metaurus and the Pisaurus (*Foglia*), rather more than 20 miles from the Adriatic. It is mentioned by Pliny among the municipal towns of Umbria, and is incidentally noticed by Tacitus as the place where Fabius Valens, the general of Vitellius, was put to death, in A.D. 69, after he had fallen into the hands of the generals of Vespasian. (Tac. *Hist.* iii. 62.) Its municipal rank is confirmed by numerous inscriptions, which prove it to have been a town of some importance. (Orell. *Inscr.* 3714; Gruter, *Inscr.* p. 387. 8, p. 392. 1, &c.) Procopius also notices it during the Gothic Wars, and correctly describes it as situated on a steep and lofty hill; it was at that time a strong fortress, but was besieged and taken by Belisarius in A.D. 538. (Procop. *B. G.* ii. 19.) From this time it seems to have continued to be a place of consideration, and in the middle ages became the seat of government of a race of independent dukes. It is still a considerable city, and one of the capitals of the delegation of *Urbino* and *Pesaro*, but has no remains of antiquity, except the inscriptions above noticed.

2. URBINUM METAURENSE (*Urbania*), was situated, as its name imports, in the valley of the Metaurus, on the right bank of the river, about 6 miles below *S. Angelo in Vado* (Tifernum Metaurense), and 9 from *Urbino*. Its municipal rank is attested by an inscription, in which the inhabitants are termed Urvinates Mataurenses, as well as by Pliny (Gruter, *Inscr.* p. 463. 4; Plin. iii. 14. s. 19); but it seems never to have been a place of much importance. In the middle ages it fell into complete decay, and was replaced by a village called *Castel Durante*, which, in 1625, was enlarged and raised to the dignity of a city by Urban VIII., from whom it derives its present name of *Urbania*. (Cluver. *Ital.* p. 620; Rampoldi, *Diz. Top.* vol. iii. p. 1278.) [E. H. B.]

URBS SALVIA (Οὐρβσα Σαλουΐα, Ptol. iii. 1. § 52: *Eth.* Urbis Salviensis or Urbisalviensis: *Urbisaglia*), a town of Picenum, mentioned by Pliny among the municipal towns of that district. (Plin. iii. 13.

s. 18.) It was situated on a hill above the valley of the Flusor (*Chienti*), about 2 miles from the right bank of that river, and 7 miles E. of Tolentinum. The testimony of Pliny to its municipal rank is confirmed by the Liber Coloniarum, which mentions the "ager Urbis Salviensis," as well as by an inscription (*Lib. Col.* p. 226 ; Orell. *Inscr.* 1870); and it seems to have been a flourishing town until it was taken and destroyed by Alaric, a calamity from which it never recovered, so that it still lay in ruins in the time of Procopius. (Procop. *B. G.* ii. 16.) Dante also notices it in the 13th century as in complete ruins (*Par.* xvi. 73); but the name has always survived, and is still attached to the modern *Urbisaglia*, which is, however, a mere village, dependent on *Macerata*. The Itineraries give two lines of crossroads which passed through Urbs Salvia, the one from Septempeda (*S. Severino*) to Firmum (*Fermo*), the other from Auximum through Ricina and Urbs Salvia to Asculum. (*Itin. Ant.* p. 316; *Tab. Peut.*)   [E. H. B.]

URBS VETUS (*Orvieto*), a city of Etruria mentioned by Paulus Diaconus (*Hist. Lang.* iv. 33) together with Balneum Regis (*Bagnaréa*) in the same neighbourhood. No mention of either name occurs in any writer before the fall of the Roman Empire, but it is probable that the Urbiventum (Οὐρβίεντον) of Procopius, which figures in the Gothic Wars as a fortress of some importance, is the same place as the Urbs Vetus of P. Diaconus. (Procop.*B. G.* ii. 20.) There is no doubt that the modern name of *Orvieto* is derived from Urbs Vetus; but the latter is evidently an appellation given in late times, and it is doubtful what was the original name of the city thus designated. Niebuhr supposes it to be Salpinum, noticed by Livy in B. C. 389 (Liv. v. 31 ; Niebuhr, vol. ii. p. 493) [SALPINUM], while Italian antiquaries in general identify it with Herbanum. [HERBANUM.] But both suggestions are mere conjectures. [E. H. B.]

URCESA (Οὐρκεσα or Οὐρκαισα, Ptol. ii. 6 § 58), a town of the Celtiberi in Hispania Tarraconensis. According to some, the modern *Requena*, whilst others identify it with *Veles* or *Orgas*. (Coins in Sestini p. 212.)   [T. H. D.]

URCI (Plin. iii. 3. s. 4; Οὐρκη, Ptol. ii. 6. § 14), a town of the Bastetani in Hispania Tarraconensis, on the borders of Baetica, or according to another boundary line, which makes the latter reach as far as Barca, in Baetica itself, on a bay named after it, and on the road from Castulo to Malaca. (Mela, ii. 6, where the editions incorrectly have Urgi and Virgi; *Itin. Ant.* p. 404.) Variously identified with *Abruceña*, *Puerto de Aguilas*, and *Aleodus.* Ukert, however (ii. pt. i. p. 352), would seek it in the neighbourhood of *Almeria*.   [T. H. D.]

URCITANUS SINUS, a small bay either on the S. coast of Hispania Tarraconensis or in Baetica, named after the town of Urci. It was separated by the Promontorium Charidemi from the Sinus Massienus on the E. (Mela, ii. 6.) Now the bay of *Almeria*.   [T. H. D]

URGAO, a town in Hispania Baetica, on the road from Corduba to Castulo (*Itin. Ant.* p. 403), with the surname of Alba. (Plin. iii. 1. s. 3.) In the editions of the Itinerary it is called Urcao and Vircao; and according to inscriptions in Gruter (ccxlix. 3, ccxliii. 6), it was a municipium, with the name of Albense Urgavonense. Most probably *Arjona*. (Cf. Morales, *Ant.* p. 74; Florez, *Esp. Sagr.* xii. p. 379.)   [T. H. D.]

URGO. [GORGONA.]

URIA. [HYRIUM.]

U'RIA LACUS. [AETOLIA, p. 64, a.]

URIAS SINUS. [APULIA.]

URISIUM (*It. Hier.* p. 569), a town in Thrace, on the road between Tarpodizus and Bergule: according to Reichard it corresponds to the modern *Alpiuli* or *Alpuli*; but according to Lapie, to *Kirk-Kilissia.*   [J. R.]

URIUM (Οὔριον, Ptol. ii. 4. § 12). 1. A town in Hispania Baetica, on the borders of Lusitania; according to Reichard, now *Torre del Oro.*

2. A river in Hispania Baetica, between the Baetis and the Anas, which entered the sea near the town just named. (Plin. iii. 1. a. 3.) Now the *Tinto.*   [T. H. D.]

URPANUS, a small river of Pannonia, a tributary of the Savus, is now called the *Verbass.* (Plin. iii. 28; *Tab. Peut.*, where it is called Urbas.) [L. S.]

URSI PROMONTORIUM. [SARDINIA.]

URSO (Οὔρσων, Strab. iii. p. 141), a strong mountain town in Hispania Baetica, the last refuge of the Pompeians. It was a Roman colony, with the surname of Genua Urbanorum, and was under the jurisdiction of Astigi. (Plin. iii. 1. s 3; Hirt. *B. H.* 26. 41, 65; Appian, *B. H.* 16.) It is the modern *Osuña*, where some inscriptions and ruins have been found. (Cf. Muratori, p. 1095; Florez, *Esp. Sagr.* x. p. 77.) For coins of Urso, see Florez, *Med.* ii. p. 624, iii. p. 130; Mionnet, i. p. 28, *Suppl.* i. p. 47; Sestini, p. 94.   [T. H. D.]

COIN OF URSO.

URSOLAE or URSOLI, a place in Gallia Narbonensis, fixed by the Antonine Itin. on the road between Valentia (*Valence*) and Vienna (*Vienne*), xxii. from Valentia, and xxvi. from Vienna. This agrees pretty well with the whole distance between *Valence* and *Vienne.* There are no means of determining the site of Ursoli except the distances; and D'Anville fixes on *S. Valier*, a place on the right bank of the *Galaure* near the place where it enters the Rhone.   [G. L.]

URUNCI, a place in Gallia between the *Vosges* and the Rhine. It occurs twice in the Antonine Itin., and in both cases the road from Urunci runs to Mons Brisiacus. [MONS BRISIACUS.] In one route it is placed between Larga (*Largitzen*) and Mons Brisiacus, xviii. from Larga, and xxiiii. from Brisiacus. This route is from south to north-east. The other route is from Arialbinnum, supposed to be *Binning* near *Basle*, to Mons Brisiacus, from south to north, and Urunci is xxiii. M. P. or 15 leugae from Mons Brisiacus. D'Anville supposes that Urunci may be a place named *Rucsen* or *Ricsen*, on the line of the road from Larga to Mons Brisiacus or *Breisach.*   [G. L.]

USAR, the most easterly river of Mauretania. (Plin. v. 2. s. 1.) It seems to be the river called Ἄσαρ by Ptolemy (iv. 2. § 10), and is probably the *Ajebby*, which falls into the gulf of *Bugie.*   [T. H. D.]

USARGALA (Οὐσάργαλα, Ptol. iv. 6. § 7, &c.), a very extensive mountain chain in the country of the Garamantae on the N. border of Libya Interior, and S. of Numidia and Mauretania, stretching in a NW. direction as far as Atlas. It is in this mountain that the river Bagradas has its source.   [T. H. D.]

U'SBIUM (Οὔσβιον), a town mentioned by Ptolemy (ii. 11. § 30) in the south-east of Germania, probably in the territory of the Marcomanni, seems to be identical with the modern *Ispern*, on a rivulet of the same name.   [L. S.]

US'CANA, the chief town of the Penestae, a people of Illyricum, which contained 10,000 inhabitants at the time of the Roman war with Perseus. At the commencement of this war it appears to have been in the hands of Perseus, and the first attempt of the Roman commander, App. Claudius, to obtain possession of the place proved unsuccessful, B. C. 170. (Liv. xliii. 10.) It would seem, however, to have been afterwards taken by the Romans, since we read that Perseus in the following year surprised Uscana, marching thither in three days from Stubera. (Liv. xliii. 17, 18.) Shortly afterwards L. Coelius, the Roman commander in Illyricum, made an unsuccessful attack upon Uscana. (*Ib.* 21.) The site of this town is uncertain.

U'SCENUM (Οὔσκενον, or Οὔσκαινον, Ptol. iii. 7. § 2), a town of the Jazyges Metanastae. [T.H.D.]

USCUDAMA, a town belonging to the Bessi, near Mount Haemus, which M. Lucullus took by assault. (Eutr. vi. 10.)   [J. R.]

USELLIS (Οὐσέλλις, Ptol.: *Usellus*), a city of Sardinia, situated in the interior of the island, about 16 miles from the *Gulf of Oristano* on the W. coast, and the same distance S. of Forum Trajani. Its name is not found in the Itineraries, and the only author who mentions it is Ptolemy (iii. 3. § 2), who erroneously places it on the W. coast of the island: but the existing ruins, together with the name of *Usellus*, still borne by a village on the site, leave no doubt of its true situation. It is about 3 miles NE. of the modern town of *Ales.* Ptolemy styles it a colonia, and this is confirmed by an inscription in which it bears the title of "Colonia Julia Augusta." It would hence appear probable that the colony must have been founded under Augustus, though Pliny tells us distinctly that Turris Libyssonis was the only colony existing in Sardinia in his time. (De la Marmora, *Voy. en Sardaigne*, vol. ii. pp. 367, 466.)   [E. H. B.]

USILLA (Οὐσίλλα, Ptol. iv. 3. § 10), a place in Byzacium in Africa Proper. It is the Usula of the *Itin. Ant.* (p. 59), lying between Thyadrus and Thenae. Variously identified with *Inchilla* or *Sidi Makelouf*, and *Inshillah.*   [T. H. D.]

USI'PETES or USI'PI (Οὐσίπεται, Οὔσιποι), a German tribe, mostly mentioned in conjunction with the Tencteri, with whom they for a long time shared the same fate, until in the end, having crossed the lower Rhine, they were treacherously attacked and defeated by Julius Caesar. (Caes. *B. G.* iv. 4, &c.; Appian, *de Reb. Gall.* 18; comp. TENCTERI.) After this calamity, the Usipetes returned across the Rhine, and were received by the Sigambri, who assigned to them the district on the northern bank of the Luppia, which had previously been inhabited by the Chamavi and Tubantes, and in which we henceforth find the Usipetes as late as the time of Tacitus. (*Ann.* xiii. 55, *Hist.* iv. 37, *Germ.* 32; Dion Cass. liv. 32, foll.) Afterwards the Usipetes are met with farther south, opposing Germanicus on his return from the country of the Marsi. (Tac. *Ann.* i. 50, 51; comp. Dion Cass. xxxix. 47; Plut. *Caes.* 22.) In Strabo (vii. p. 292) they appear under the name of Οὐίσποι, and Ptolemy (ii. 11. § 10) mentions a tribe of the name of Οὐίσποι, whom some believe to be the same as the Usipetes; but if this be correct, it would follow that the Usipetes migrated still farther south, as Ptolemy places these Vispi on the upper Rhine; but as no other authority places them so far south, the question is altogether-uncertain. About the year A. D. 70, the Usipetes took part in the siege of Moguntiacum (Tac. *Ann.* xiii. 54), and in A. D. 83 a detachment of them is mentioned as serving in the Roman army in Britain. (Id. *Agric.* 27.) Afterwards they disappear from history. (Comp. Zeuss, *Die Deutschen*, p. 88; Wilhelm, *Germanien*, p. 139.)   [L. S.]

USPE, a town of the Siraci in Sarmatia, lying E. of the Tanais. It lay on a height, and was fortified with a ditch and walls; but the latter were composed only of mud confined in hurdles. (Tac. *Ann.* xii. 16.)   [T. H. D.]

USSADIUM (Οὐσσάδιον, or Οὐσάδιον ἄκρον, Ptol. iv. 1. §§ 4 and 12). a promontory of Mauretania Tingitana, lying SW. of the promontory of Hercules. Now *Cape Osem*.   [T. H. D.]

USTICA. [OSTEODES.]

USUERNA or USUERVA. [HOSUERBAS.]

UTHINA (Οὔθινα, Ptol. iv. 3. § 34), a town of Zeugitana, in Africa Propria, between Tabraca and the river Bagradas. (Cf. Id. viii. 14. § 11; Plin. v. 4. s. 4.) Erroneously written Uthica in Tab Peut. Now *Udine*.   [T. H. D.]

UTICA (ἡ Ἰτύκη, Polyb. l. 75; Ptol. iv. 3. § 6; Οὐτίκη, Dion Cass. xli. 41; *Eth.* Uticensis; Liv. xxix. 35; Caes. *B. C.* ii. 36), a colony founded by the Tyrians on the N. coast of Zeugitana in Africa. (Vell. Pat. i. 2; Mela, i. 7; Justin. xviii. 4, &c.) The date of its foundation is said to have been a few years after that of Gades, and 287 years before that of Carthage. (Vell. Pat. *l. c.*; Aristot. *Mirab. Ausc.* 146; Gesenius, *Monum. Script. Linguaeque Phoenic.* p. 291; Sil. Ital. *Pun.* iii. 241, sqq. &c.) Its name signified in Phoenician, "ancient," or "noble" (עתיקה, Gesen. *ib.* p. 420, and *Thes. Ling. Heb.* p. 1085). Utica was situated near the mouth of the river Bagradas, or rather that of its western arm, in the Bay of Carthage, and not far from the promontory of Apollo, which forms the western boundary of the bay. (Strab. xvii. p. 832; Liv. *l. c.*; Ptol. *l. c.*; Appian, *B. C.* ii. 44, seq.; Procop. *B. V.* ii. 15, &c.) It lay 27 miles NW. of Carthage. (*Itin. Ant.* p. 22.) The distance is given as 60 stadia in Appian (*Pun.* 75), which is probably an error for 160; and as a day's sail by sea. (Scylax, *Geogr. Min.* i. p. 50, ed. Huds.) Both Utica and Tunes might be descried from Carthage. (Strab. *l. c.*; Polyb. i. 73; Liv. xxx. 9.) Utica possessed a good harbour, or rather harbours, made by art, with excellent anchorage and numerous landing places. (Appian, *l. c.*; cf. Barth, *Wanderungen durch die Küstenländer des Mittelmeers*, pp. 111, 125.) On the land side it was protected by steep hills, which, together with the sea and its artificial defences, which were carefully kept up, rendered it a very strong place. (Liv. xxix. 35; App. *Pun.* 16, 30, 75; Diod. xx. 54; Plut. *Cat. Min.* 58.) The surrounding country was exceedingly fertile and well cultivated, and produced abundance of corn, of which there was a great export trade to Rome. (Liv. xxv. 31.)

The hills behind the town, as well as the district near the present *Porto Farina*, contained rich veins of various metals; and the coast was celebrated for producing vast quantities of salt of a very peculiar quality. (Plin. xxxi. 7. s. 39; Caes. *B. C.* ii. 37; Polyb. xii. 3, seq.; Diod. xx. 8, &c.) Among the buildings of the town, we hear of a temple of Jupiter (Plut. *Cat. Min.* 5) and of one of Apollo, with its planks of Numidian cedar near twelve centuries old (Plin. xvi. 40. s. 79); of a forum of Trajan, and a theatre outside the city. (Tiro Prosper, *ap. Morcelli, Afr. Christ.* iii. p. 40; Caes. *B. C.* ii. 25.) The tomb and statue of Cato on the sea-shore were extant in the time of Plutarch (*Ib.* 79). Shaw (*Travels*, vol. i. p. 160, seq.) has the merit of having first pointed out the true situation of this celebrated city, the most important in N. Africa after Carthage. Before the time of Shaw, it was sought sometimes at *Biserta*, sometimes at *Porto Farina*; but that learned traveller fixed it near the little miserable *Duar*, which has a holy tomb called *Boo-shatter*; and with this view many writers have agreed (Falbe, *Recherches sur l'Emplacement de Carthage*, p. 66; Barth, *Wanderungen, &c.* p. 109; Semilasso, pp. 39, 46; Ritter, *Afrika*, p. 913, &c.) Since the Roman times the muddy stream of the Bagradas has deposited at its mouth a delta of from 3 to 4 miles in extent, so that the innermost recess of the Bay of Carthage, on which ancient Utica was situated, as well as the eastern arm of the river itself, have been converted into a broad morass, in which traces are still visible of the quays which formerly lined the shore, and of the northern mole which enclosed the harbour. More towards the E., at the margin of the chain of hills which at an earlier period descended to the sea, may be discerned blocks of masonry belonging to the ancient town wall. On the declivity of the hills towards the SE. are the remains of six cisterns, or reservoirs, 136 feet long, 15 to 19 feet broad, and 20 to 30 feet deep, covered with a remarkably thin arched roof. These are connected with an aqueduct, which may be traced several miles from *Boo-shatter*, in the direction of the hills: but its most remarkable remains are a treble row of arches by which it was carried over a ravine. These reservoirs may probably have served to furnish water for a naumachia in the neighbouring amphitheatre, which is hollowed out of the hills, and is capable of containing about 20,000 persons. The ancient site of the city is covered with ruins. Near its centre rises the highest summit of the chain of hills on which stood the citadel and, probably, also the ancient temple of Apollo. The ruins of other temples and castles have been discovered, as well as the site of the senate house (Plut. *Cat. Min.* 67), which has been thought to be determined by the excavation of a number of statues. These are now preserved in the museum at *Leyden*.

In the course of time, as is usual with such connections, Utica became severed from the mother-city, and first appears in history as independent of it. In the first commercial treaty between Rome and Carthage, in the year 509 B. C., Utica was probably included in it among the allies of the Carthaginians (Polyb. iii. 22); in the second, in B. C. 348, it is expressly named (*ib.* 24; Diodor. xvi. 69, who however confounds the two treaties), as well as in the alliance concluded by Hannibal with Philip of Macedon in the Second Punic War, B. C. 215 (Polyb. viii. 9). Subsequently, however, Utica appears to have thrown off her dependence upon, or perhaps we should rather call it her alliance with Carthage, and, with other cities of N. Africa, to have joined the Sicilian Agathocles, the opponent of Carthage; to have afterwards revolted from that conqueror, but to have been again reduced to obedience (Diod. xx. 17, 54: cf. Polyb. i. 82). In the First Punic War, Utica remained faithful to Carthage; afterwards it joined the Libyans, but was compelled to submit by the victorious Carthaginians (Polyb. ib. 88: Diod. Fr. xxv.). In the Second Punic War also we find it in firm alliance with Carthage, to whose fleets the excellent harbour of Utica was very serviceable. But this exposed it to many attacks from the Romans, whose freebooting excursions were frequently directed against it from Lilybaeum, as well as to a more regular, but fruitless siege by Scipio himself (Liv. xxv. 31, xxvii. 5, xviii. 4, xxix. 35, xxx. 3, &c.; Polyb. xiv. 2; Appian, Punic. 16, 25, 30). In the third war, however, the situation of Carthage being now hopeless, the Uticenses indulged their ancient grudge against that city, and made their submission to Rome by a separate embassy (Polyb. xxxvi. 1; Appian, Pun. 75, 110, 113). This step greatly increased the material prosperity of Utica. After the destruction of Carthage, the Romans presented Utica with the fertile district lying between that city and Hippo Diarrhytus. It became the chief town of the province, the residence of the Roman governor, the principal emporium for the Roman commerce, and the port of debarcation for the Roman armaments destined to act in the interior of Africa. Owing to this intimate connection with Rome, the name of Utica appears very frequently in the later history of the republic, as in the accounts of the Jugurthine War, of the war carried on by Pompey at the head of Sulla's faction, against the Marian party under Domitius and his ally the Numidian king Iarbas, and in the struggle between Caesar and the Pompeians, with their ally Juba. It is unnecessary to quote the numerous passages in which the name of Utica occurs in relation to these events. In the last of these wars, Utica was the scene of the celebrated death of the younger Cato, so often related or adverted to by the ancients (Plut. Cat. Min. 58, seq.; Dion Cass. xliii. 10, sqq.; Val. Max. iii. 2. § 14; Cic. pro Ligar. 1, &c.; cf. Dict. of Biogr. Vol. I. p. 649). Augustus presented the Uticenses with the Roman civitas, partly as a reward for the inclination which they had manifested for the party of his uncle, and partly also to indemnify them for the rebuilding of Carthage (Dion Cass. xlix. 16; cf. Sext. Rufus, Brev. 4). We know nothing more of Utica till the time of Hadrian, who visited N. Africa in his extensive travels, and at whose desire the city changed its ancient constitution for that of a Roman colony (Spartian. Hadr. 13; Gell. N. Att. xvi. 13). Thus it appears in the Tab. Peut. with the appellation of Colonia, as well as in an inscription preserved in the museum of Leyden (Col. Jul. Ael. Hadr. Utic., ap. Janssen, Mus. Lugd. Batav. Inscr. Gr. et Lat.). Septimius Severus, an African by birth, endowed it, as well as Carthage and his birthplace Leptis Magna, with the Jus Italicum. We find the bishops of Utica frequently mentioned in the Christian period from the time of the great Synod under Cyprian of Carthage in 256, down to 684, when a bishop of Utica appeared in the Council of Toledo. The city is said to have witnessed the martyrdom of 300 persons at one time (cf. Morcelli, Afr. Christ. i. p. 362, ii. p. 150; Munter, Primod. Eccl. Afr. p. 32; Augustin, c. Donat. vii. 8). Utica probably fell with Carthage, into the hands of the Vandals under

Genseric in 439. Subsequently it was recovered by the Byzantine emperors, but in the reign of the Chalif Abdelmalek was conquered by the Arabians under Hassan; and though it appears to have been again recovered by John the prefect or patrician, it finally sank under the power of the Saracens during the reign of the same Chalif, and on its second capture was destroyed (cf. Papencordt, die Vandal Herrschaft in Afr. p. 72, sq., 151, sq.; Weil, Gesch. der Chalifer, i. p. 473, sqq.; Gibbon, Decl. and Fall, vi. 350, sqq. ed. Smith). The remains of its marbles and columns were carried away in the preceding century, to serve as materials for the great mosque of Tunis (Semilasso, p. 43.)

Several coins of Utica are extant bearing the heads of Tiberius or Livia; a testimony perhaps of the gratitude of the city for the rights bestowed upon it by Augustus (cf. Mionnet, Med. Ant. vi. p. 589; Supp. viii. p. 208).   [T. H. D.]

UTIDAVA (Οὐτίδαυα, Ptol. viii. 8. § 7), a town in Dacia, E. of the Aluta. Identified with the ruins at Kosmin, near the confluence of the Kutschur and the Pruth (cf. Ukert, iii. pt. ii. p. 620.) [T. H. D.]

UTII (Οὔτιοι), one of the nations belonging to the fourteenth satrapy of the Persian empire (Herod. iii. 93), which was armed in the same manner as the Pactyes (Id. vii. 68), and, according to Bobrik's conjecture, perhaps dwelt in Pactyica. (Geog. des Herod. p. 181.)   [J. R.]

UTIS or VITIS (Montone), a river of Gallia Cisalpina, which rises in the Apennines, flows under the walls of Forlì (Forum Livii), and subsequently by the city of Ravenna, and enters the Adriatic about 5 miles from that city. At the present day it joins the Ronco (the Bedesis of Pliny), before reaching the latter city, but in ancient times it probably discharged its waters by a separate channel into the lagunes which at that time surrounded Ravenna. The name is written Vitis by Pliny (iii. 14. s. 19), but it is probable that Utis or Utens is the more correct form, which is found in Livy. According to that author it at one time formed the boundary between the Boian and Senonian Gauls. (Liv. v 35.)   [E. H. B.]

UTTARIS, a town of the Callaici in the NW. of Hispania Tarraconensis, on the road from Lucus Augusti to Asturica, between Pons Neviae and Bergidum. (Itin. Ant. pp. 425, 430.) Variously identified with Cerredo, Doncos, and Castro de la Ventosa.   [T. H. D.]

UTUS, an affluent of the Danube in Moesia. The Utus had its sources in Mount Haemus, and formed the E. boundary of Dacia Ripensis (Plin. iii. 26. s. 29). Now the Vid.   [T. H. D.]

UTUS (Οὔτος, Procop. de Aed. iv. 1), a town of Moesia Inferior, a little to the S. of the confluence of the like-named river with the Danube, and between Oescus and Securisca (Itin. Ant. p. 221). Variously identified with Staroselitsi, Hutalidsch, and a place near Brestovats.   [T. H. D.]

VULCANI FORUM. [PUTEOLI.]

VULCANIAE INSULAE. [AEOLIAE INSULAE.]

VULCHALO is mentioned by Cicero (pro Fonteio, 9) as a place in the west part of Gallia Narbonensis, but nothing more is known of it. [G. L.]

VULGIENTES. [APTA JULIA.]

VULSINII. [VOLSINII.]

VULTUR MONS (Monte Voltore), one of the most celebrated mountains of Southern Italy, situated on the confines of Apulia, Lucania, and the country of the Hirpini. It commences about 5 miles to the S. of the modern city of *Melfi*, and nearly due W. of *Venosa* (Venusia), and attains an elevation of 4433 feet above the level of the sea. Its regular conical form and isolated position, as well as the crater-like basin near its summit, at once mark it as of volcanic origin; and this is confirmed by the nature of the rocks of which it is composed. Hence it cannot be considered as properly belonging to the range of the Apennines, from which it is separated by a tract of hilly country, forming as it were the base from which the detached cone of *Monte Voltore* rises. No ancient author alludes to the volcanic character of Mount Vultur; but the mountain itself is noticed, in a well known passage, by Horace, who must have been very familiar with its aspect, as it is a prominent object in the view from his native city of Venusia. (*Carm.* iii. 4. 9—16.) He there terms it "Vultur Apulus," though he adds, singularly enough, that he was without the limits of Apulia (" altricis extra limen Apuliae ") when he was wandering in its woods. This can only be explained by the circumstance that the mountain stood (as above stated) on the confines of three provinces. Lucan also incidentally notices Mt. Vultur as one of the mountains that directly fronted the plains of Apulia. (Lucan, ix. 185.)

The physical and geological characters of Mount Vultur are noticed by Romanelli (vol. ii. p. 233), and more fully by Daubeny (*Description of Volcanoes*, chap. 11). [E. H. B.]

VULTURNUM (Οὐουλτούρνον: *Castel Volturno*), a town of Campania, situated on the sea-coast at the mouth of the river of the same name, and on its S. bank. There is no trace of the existence of any town on the site previous to the Second Punic War, when the Romans constructed a fortress (castellum) at the mouth of the river with the object of securing their possession of it, and of establishing a magazine of corn for the use of the army that was besieging Capua. (Liv. xxv. 20, 22.) It is probable that this continued to exist and gradually grew into a town; but it was in B. C. 194, a colony of Roman citizens was established there, at the same time with Liternum and Puteoli. (Id. xxxiv. 45; Varr. *L. L.* v. 5.) The number of colonists was in each case but small, and Vulturnum does not appear to have ever risen into a place of much importance. But it is noticed by Livy as existing as a town in his time (" ad Vulturni ostium, ubi nunc urbs est," xxv. 20), and is mentioned by all the geographers. (Strab. v. p. 238; Plin. iii. 5. a. 9; Mel. ii. 4. § 9; Ptol. iii. 1. § 6.) We learn also that it received a fresh colony under Augustus (*Lib. Colon.* p. 239), and retained its colonial rank down to a late period. It became an episcopal see before the close of the Roman Empire, and appears to have continued to subsist down to the 9th century, when it was destroyed by the Saracens. In the 17th century a new fortress was built nearly on the ancient site, which is called *Castel Volturno* or *Castell' a Mare di Volturno.* But from the remains of the ancient city still visible it appears that this occupied a site somewhat nearer the sea than the modern fortress. Several inscriptions have been found on the spot, which attest the colonial rank of Vulturnum as late as the age of the Antonines. (Mommsen, *I. R. N.* 3535—3539.) [E. H. B.]

VULTURNUS (Οὐουλτούρνος: *Volturno*), the most considerable river of Campania, which has its sources in the Apennines of Samnium, about 5 miles S. of Aufidena, flows within a few miles of

Aesernia on its left bank, and of Venafrum on its right, thence pursues a SE. course for about 35 miles, till it receives the waters of the Calor (*Calore*), after which it turns abruptly to the WSW., passes under the walls of Casilinum (*Capoua*), and finally discharges itself into the Tyrrhenian sea about 20 miles below that city. Its mouth was marked in ancient times by the town of the same name (Vulturnum), the site of which is still occupied by the modern fortress of *Castel Volturno* [VULTURNUM]. (Strab. v. pp. 238, 249; Plin. iii. 5. a. 9; Mel. ii. 4. § 9.) The Vulturnus is a deep and rapid, but turbid stream, to which character we find many allusions in the Roman poets. (Virg. *Aen.* vii. 729; Ovid. *Met.* xv. 714; Lucan. ii. 423; Claudian. *Paneg. Prob. et Ol.* 256; Sil. Ital. viii. 530.) A bridge was thrown over it close to its mouth by Domitian, when he constructed the Via Domitia that led from Sinuessa direct to Cumae. (Stat. *Silv.* iv. 3. 67, &c.) From the important position that the Vulturnus occupies in Campania, the fertile plains of which it traverses in their whole extent from the foot of the Apennines to the sea, its name is frequently mentioned in history, especially during the wars of the Romans with the Campanians and Samnites, and again during the Second Punic War. (Liv. viii. 11, x. 20, 31, xxii. 14, &c.; Polyb. iii. 92.) Previous to the construction of the bridge above mentioned (the remains of which are still visible near the modern *Castel Volturno*), there was no bridge over it below Casilinum, where it was crossed by the Via Appia. It appears to have been in ancient times navigable for small vessels at least as far as that city. (Liv. xxvi. 9; Stat. *Silv.* iv. 3. 77.)

Its only considerable tributary is the CALOR, which brings with it the waters of several other streams, of which the most important are the TAMARUS and SABATUS. These combined streams bring down to the Vulturnus almost the whole waters of the land of the Hirpini; and hence the Calor is at the point of junction nearly equal in magnitude to the Vulturnus itself. [E. H. B.]

VUNGUS, VICUS, in North Gallia, is placed by the Antonine Itin. on the road from Durocortorum (*Reims*) to Augusta Trevirorum (*Trier*). Vungus is between Durocortorum and Epoissum (*Iptsch, Ivois*), or Epusum [EPOISSUM], and marked xxii. leugae from each place. The direction of this road from *Reims* is to the passage of the *Maas* or *Meuse* at *Mouzon;* and before it reaches *Ivois* it brings us to a place named *Vonc,* near the river *Aisne*, a little above *Attigni.* This is a good example, and there are many in France, of the old Gallic names continuing unchanged. Flodoard, in his history of *Reims*, speaks of " Municipium Vongum," and the " Pagus Vongensis circa Axonnae ripas." The Axonna is the *Aisne.* The Roman road may be traced in several places between *Reims* and *Vonc;* and there is an indication of this road in the place named *Vau d'Etré* (de strata), at the passage of the river *Suippe.* [G. L.]

UXACONA, a town belonging apparently to the Cornavii in Britannia Romana, on the road from Deva to Londinium, and between Urioconium and Pennocrucium. Camden (p. 653) and others identify it with *Okenyate,* a village in *Shropshire ;* Horsley (p. 419) and others with *Sheriff Hales.* [T. H. D.]

UXAMA (Οὔξαμα 'Αργέλλαι, Ptol. ii. 6. § 56), a town of the Arevaci in Hispania Tarraconensis, on the road from Asturica to Caesaraugusta, 50 miles W. of Numantia, and in the neighbourhood of Clunia (*Itin. Ant.* p. 441), where, however, the more recent editions read Vasama. (Plin. iii. 3. s. 4; Flor. iii. 22; Sil. Ital. iii. 384.) It is called Uxuma in the Geogr. Rav. (iv. 43); and according to Ukert (ii. pt. i. p. 455), is probably the Ἀξεἰνιον of Appian (vi. 47). Now *Osma*.   [T. H. D.]

UXAMABARCA (Οὐξαμαβάρκα, Ptol. ii. 6. § 53), a town of the Autrigones in Hispania Tarraconensis. (Murat. *Inscr.* p. 1095. 8.) Ukert (ii. pt. i. p. 446) identifies it with *Osma* in *Biscaya*. [T. H. D.]

UXANTIS INSULA, for so the name should be read in the Maritime Itin., is Pliny's Axantos (iv. 30), an island off the Atlantic coast of Gallia. Uxantis is *Ouessant*, or *Ushant*, as the English often write it, a small island belonging to the department of *Finistère*, and nearly in the latitude of *Brest*.   [G. L.]

UXELLA (Οὔξελλα, Ptol. ii. 3. § 10), called by the Geogr. Rav. (v. 30) Uxeli, a city of the Dumnonii in Britannia Romana. Camden (p. 18) identifies it with the little town of *Lostwithiel* in *Cornwall*; whilst Horsley (p. 378) and others take it to be *Exeter*.   [T. H. D.]

UXELLODU'NUM, in Gallia. In B. C. 51 Drappes a Senon and Lucterius a Cadurcan, who had given the Romans much trouble, being pursued by C. Caninius Rebilus, one of Caesar's legates, took refuge in Uxellodunum, a town of the Cadurci (*B. G.* viii. 32—44): Uxellodunum was in a position naturally strong, protected by rocks so steep that an armed man could hardly climb up, even if no resistance were made. A deep valley surrounded nearly the whole elevation on which the town stood, and a river flowed at the bottom of the valley. The interval where the river did not flow round the steep sides of this natural fortress was only 300 feet wide, and along this part ran the town wall. Close to the wall was a large spring, which supplied the town during the siege, for the inhabitants could not get down the rocks to the river for water without risk of their lives from the Roman missiles. Caninius began his blockade of Uxellodunum by making three camps on very high ground, with the intention of gradually drawing a vallum from each camp, and surrounding the place. On the river side his camps were of course separated from the town by the deep valley in which the river flowed; he may have planted two camps here and one on the land side of Uxellodunum.

The townsmen remembering what had happened at Alesia the year before, sent out Lucterius and Drappes to bring supplies into the place. Lucterius and Drappes took all the fighting men for this purpose except 2000, and they collected a large quantity of corn; but as Lucterius was attempting to carry it into the town by night, the Romans surprised him, and cut his men to pieces. The other part of the force which had gone out was with Drappes about 12 miles off. Caninius sent his cavalry and light German troops against Drappes to surprise him, and he followed with a legion. His success was most complete. Drappes was taken prisoner and his force destroyed or captured. Caninius was now enabled to go on with his circumvallation without fear of interruption from without, and C. Fabius arriving the next day with his troops undertook the blockade of part of the town.

Caesar hearing the news about Uxellodunum and resolving to check all further risings in Gallia by one signal example more, hurried to the place with all his cavalry, ordering C. Calenus and two legions to follow him by regular marches. He found the place shut in, but it was well supplied with provisions, as the deserters told him; and there remained nothing to do but to cut off the townsmen from the water. By his archers and slingers, and by his engines for discharging missiles (tormenta) placed opposite those parts of the town where the descent to the river was easiest, he attempted to prevent the enemy from coming down to the river to get water. His next operation was to cut them off from the spring, and this was the great operation of the siege on which depended the capture of the town. Caesar dealt with his enemies as a doctor with a disease — he cut off the supplies. (Frontinus, *Strat.* iv. 7. 1.) He moved his vineae towards that part of the town where the spring lay under the wall, and this was the isthmus which connected the hill fort with the open country. He also began to construct mounds of earth, while the townsmen from the higher ground annoyed the Romans with missiles. Still the Romans pushed on their vineae and their earthworks, and at the same time began to form mines (cuniculi) to reach the source of water and draw it off. A mound of earth 9 feet high was constructed, and a tower of ten stories was placed upon it, not high enough to be on a level with the top of the wall, but high enough to command the summit level of the spring. Thus they prevented the enemy from reaching the spring, and a great number of cattle, horses, and men died of thirst. The townsmen now tumbled down blazing barrels filled with fat, pitch, and chips of wood, and began a vigorous onset to prevent the Romans from quenching the flames; for the burning materials being stopped in their descent by the vineae and mounds, set the Roman works on fire. On this Caesar ordered his men to scale the heights on all sides and to divert the defendants from the land side by a feint of attacking the walls. This drew the enemy from the fire; and all their force was employed in manning the walls. In the meantime the Romans put out the fire or cut it off. The obstinate resistance of the enemy was terminated by the spring being completely dried up by the diversion of the water through the subterraneous passages which the Romans had constructed; and they surrendered after many of them had died of thirst. To terrify the Galli by a signal example, Caesar cut off the hands of all the fighting men who remained alive.

The attack and defence of Uxellodunum contain a full description of the site. This hill-fort was surrounded by a river on all sides except one, and on this side also the approach to it was steep. It is agreed that Uxellodunum was somewhere either on the Oltis (*Lot*) or on the Duranius (*Dordogne*). D'Anville places it at *Puech d'Issolu*, on a small stream named the *Tourmente*, which flows into the *Dordogne* after passing *Puech d'Issolu*. He was informed by some person acquainted with the locality that the spring still exists, and we may assume that to be true, for Caesar could not destroy the source: he only drew off the water, so that the besieged could not get at it. D'Anville adds that what appeared to be the entrance of the place is called in the country *le portail de Rome*, and that a hill which is close to the *Puech*, is named *Bel-Castel*. But this distinguished geographer had no exact plan of the place, and had not seen it. Walckenaer (*Géog. des Gaules*, i. p. 353) affirms that the plan of *Puech* d'Issoln made by M. Cornnan, at the request of Turgot does not correspond to the description in the Gallic War, for the river *Tourmente* washes only one of the four sides of this hill; he also says, that nothing appears easier than to turn the river towards the west on the north side of the town, and to prevent its course being continued to the south. But the author of the eighth book of the Gallic War says that Caesar could not deprive the defenders of Uxellodunum of the water of the river by diverting its course, "for the river flowed at the very foot of the heights of Uxellodunum, and could not be drawn off in any direction by sinking ditches." There is a plan of *Capdenac* in Caylus' *Antiquités* (tom. v. pl. 100, p. 280), and Walckenaer observes that this also corresponds very imperfectly with the description. The researches of Champollion (*Nouvelles Recherches sur Uxellodunum*), which are cited by Walckenaer, appeared in 1820. Walckenaer makes some objection to *Capdenac*, on grounds which are not very strong. He says that the *Lot* is above 300 feet wide where it surrounds *Capdenac*, and one cannot conceive how archers placed on one bank could have prevented the besieged from getting water on the other side. If the archers and slingers were on the river in boats or rafts, which is likely enough, this objection is answered, even if it be true that an archer or slinger could not kill a man at the distance of 300 feet. Walckenaer makes some other objections to *Capdenac*, but they are mainly founded on a misunderstanding or a perversion of the Latin text.

It is possible that we have not yet found Uxellodunum, but a journey along the banks of the Lot, for that is more probably the river, might lead to the discovery of this interesting site of Caesar's last great military operation in Gallia. The position of the place, the attack, and the defence, are well described; and it cannot be difficult to recognise the site, if a man should see it before his eyes. Nothing could be easier to recognise than Alesia. It is impossible for any man to doubt about the site of Alesia who has seen *Alise* [MANDUBII]. In the case of Uxellodunum, we have not the help of a corresponding modern name, unless it be a place not yet discovered. [G. L.]

UXELLODUNUM, a station on the wall of Hadrian in Britannia Romana, where the Cohors I. Romanorum was in garrison (*Not. Imp.*). Probably *Brough*. [T. H. D.]

UXELLUM (Οὔξελλον, Ptol. ii. 3. § 8), a town of the Selgovae in Britannia Barbara. Camden (p. 1193) takes it to have been on the river *Esse* in *Eusedale*; whilst Horsley (p. 366) identifies it with *Caerlaverock* near *Dumfries*. [T. H. D.]

UXENTUM (Οὔξεντον, Ptol.: *Eth.* Uxentinus: *Ugento*), a town of Calabria, in the territory of the Sallentines, situated about 5 miles from the sea-coast, and 16 from the Iapygian Promontory (*Capo di Leuca*). It is mentioned by both Pliny and Ptolemy among the inland towns which they assign to the Sallentines, and is placed by the Tabula on the road from Tarentum to the extremity of the peninsula. (Plin. iii. 11. s. 16; Ptol. iii. 1. § 76; *Tab. Peut.*) The name is corruptly written in the Tabula Uhintum, and in Pliny the MSS. give Ulentini, for which the older editors had substituted Valentini. Hence Ptolemy is the only authority for the form of the name (though there is no doubt that the place meant is in all cases the same); and as coins have the Greek legend OZAN, it is doubtful

whether Uxentum or Uzentum is the more correct form. The site is clearly marked by the modern town of *Ugento*, and the ruins of the ancient city were still visible in the days of Galateo at the foot of the hill on which it stands. (Galateo, *de Sit. Iapyg.* p. 100; Romanelli, vol. ii. p. 43.) Many tombs also have been found there, in which coins, vases, and inscriptions in the Messapian dialect have been discovered. [E. H. B.]

COIN OF UXENTUM.

UXENTUS (τὸ Οὔξεντον, Ptol. vii. 1. §§ 24, 76), a chain of mountains in the *Deccan* of India, between lat. 22° and 24° and long. 136° and 143°, probably those called *Gondwana*. They formed the watershed of several rivers which flowed into the *Bay of Bengal*, as the Adamas, Dosaron and Tyndis. [V.]

U'XII (Οὔξιοι, Arrian, *Anab.* iii. 17; Strab. xi. p. 524, xv. pp. 729, 744), a tribe of ancient Persia, who lived on the northern borders of that province between Persis and Susiana, to the E. of the Pasitigris and to the W. of the Oroatis. They were visited by Alexander the Great on his way from Susa; and their capital town, Uxia (Strab. xv. p. 744), was the scene of a celebrated siege, the details of which are given by Arrian and Curtius. It has been a matter of considerable discussion where this city was situated. The whole question has been carefully examined by the Baron de Bode, who has personally visited the localities he describes. (*Geogr. Journ.* xiii. pp. 108—110.) He thinks Uxia is at present represented by the ruins near *Shikaftohi-Suleimán* in the *Bakhtyari* Mountains, to the E. of *Shuster*. [V.]

UZ, a district of Western Asia, to which the prophet Job belonged. (*Job*, i. 1.) It cannot be certainly determined where it was; hence, learned men have placed it in very different localities. Winer, who has examined the question, inclines to place it in the neighbourhood of Edom, adjoining Arabia and Chaldaea. (*Biblisch. Realwörterb. s. v. Uz.*) The people are perhaps represented in classical geography by the Αὐσῖται or Αἰσῖται of Ptolemy (v. 19. § 2), a tribe who lived on the borders of Babylonia. In *Genesis* x. 23, Uz is called the son of Aram: hence Josephus says, Οὖσος κτίζει τὴν Τραχωνῖτιν καὶ Δαμασκόν (*Antiq.* i. 6. § 4); but there is no sufficient evidence to show that the "land of Uz" of Job is connected with Northern Mesopotamia. [V.]

UZITA (Οὔζιτα, or Οὔζικα, Ptol. iv. 3. § 37), a town of Byzacium·in Africa Propria, lying S. of Hadrumetum and Ruspina, and W. of Thysdrus. (Cf. Hirt. *B. Afr.* 41, 51.) [T. H. D.]

X.

XANTHUS (Ξάνθος: *Eth.* Ξάνθιος), the greatest and most celebrated city of Lycia, was situated according to Strabo (xiv. p. 666) at a distance of 70 stadia from the mouth of the river Xanthus, and according to the Stadiasmus (§ 247) only 60 stadia. Pliny (v. 28) states the distance at 15 Roman miles, which is much too great. (Comp. Steph. B. *s. r.*; Ptol. v. 3. § 5 ; Mela, i. 15 ; Polyb. xxvi. 7.) This famous city was twice destroyed, on each of which occasions its inhabitants defended themselves with undaunted valour. The first catastrophe befell the city in the reign of Cyrus, when Harpagus besieged it with a Persian army. On that occasion the Xanthians buried themselves, with all they possessed, under the ruins of their city. (Herod. i. 176.) After this event the city must have been rebuilt ; for during the Roman civil wars consequent upon the murder of Caesar, Xanthus was invested by the army of Brutus, as its inhabitants refused to open their gates to him. Brutus, after a desperate struggle, took the city by assault. The Xanthians continued the fight in the streets, and perished with their wives and children in the flames, rather than submit to the Romans. (Dion Cass. xlvii. 34 ; Appian, *B. C.* iv. 18, foll.) After this catastrophe, the city never recovered. The chief buildings at Xanthus were temples of Sarpedon (Appian, *l. c.*), and of the Lycian Apollo. (Diod. v. 77.) At a distance of 60 stadia down the river and 10 stadia from its mouth, there was a sanctuary of Leto on the bank of the Xanthus. (Strab. *l. c.*) The site of Xanthus and its magnificent ruins were first discovered and described by Sir C. Fellows in his *Excursion in Asia Minor*, p. 225, foll. (comp. his *Lycia*, p. 164, foll.) These ruins stand near the village of *Koonik*, and consist of temples, tombs, triumphal arches, walls, and a theatre. The site, says Sir Charles, is extremely romantic, upon beautiful hills, some crowned with rocks, others rising perpendicularly from the river. The city does not appear to have been very large, but its remains show that it was highly ornamented, particularly the tombs. The architecture and sculptures of the place, of which many specimens are in an excellent state of preservation, and the inscriptions in a peculiar alphabet, have opened up a page in the history of Asia Minor previously quite unknown. The engravings in Fellows' works furnish a clear idea of the high perfection which the arts must have attained at Xanthus. (See also Spratt and Forbes, *Travels in Lycia*, i. p. 5, and ii., which contains an excellent plan of the site and remains of Xanthus ; E. Braun, *Die Marmorwerke von Xanthos in Lykia*, Rhein. Mus. Neue Folge, vol. iii. p. 481, foll.)

A large collection of marbles, chiefly sepulchral, discovered at Xanthus by Sir C. Fellows, and brought to England in 1842 and 1843, has been arranged in the British Museum. Of these a full account is given in the Supplement to the *Penny Cyclopaedia*, vol. ii. p. 713, foll.   [L. S.]

XANTHUS (Ξάνθος), an important river in the W. of Lycia, which is mentioned even in Homer (*Il.* ii. 877, v. 479), and which, according to Strabo (xiv. p. 665), was anciently called Sirbes, that is in Phoenician and Arabic "reddish yellow," so that the Greek name Xanthus is only a translation of the Semitic Sirbes or Zirba. The Xanthus has its sources in Mount Taurus, on the frontiers between Lycia and Pisidia, and flows as a navigable river in a SW. direction through an extensive plain (Ξάνθου πεδίον, Herod. i. 176), having Mount Bragus on the W. and Massicytes on the E., towards the sea, into which it discharges itself about 70 stadia S. of the city of Xanthus, and a little to the NW. of Pinara. (Herod. *l. c.* ; Ptol. v. 3. § 2 ; Dion. *Per.* 848 ; Ov. *Met.* ix. 645 ; Mela, i. 15 ; Plin. v. 28.) Now the *Eshen* or *Essenide*. (Fellows, *Lycia*, pp. 123, 278.)

Respecting Xanthus as a name of the Trojan river Scamander, see SCAMANDER.   [L. S.]

XANTHUS. [BUTHROTUM.]

XATHRI (Ξάθροι, Arrian, *Anab.* vi. 15), a tribe of free Indians mentioned by Arrian as dwelling along the banks of the Hydraotes (*Iravâti*) in the *Panjáb*. There can be little doubt that they derive their name from the Indian caste of the *Kshatriyas*.   [V.]

XENAGORAE INSULAE (Ξεναγόρου νῆσοι), according to Pliny (v. 35), a group of eight small islands off the coast of Lycia, which the Stadiasmus (§ 218) states were situated 60 stadia to the east of Patara. They are commonly identified with a group of islands in the bay of *Kalamaki*.   [L. S.]

XENIPPA, a small place in the NE. part of Sogdiana, noticed by Curtius (viii. 2. § 14) ; perhaps the present *Urtippa*.   [V.]

XEROGYPSUS (Ξηρόγυψος, Anna Comn. vii. 11, p. 378, Bonn), a small river in the SE. of Thrace, which falls into the Propontis, not far from Perinthus. In some maps it is called the Erginus, upon the authority of Mela (ii. 2).   [J. R.]

XERXE'NE (Ξερξηνή, Strab. xi. p. 528), a district on the Euphrates, in the NW. part of Armenia, more properly, however, belonging to Cappadocia. It is called Derxene by Pliny (v. 24. s. 20), and this perhaps is the more correct name. (Cf. Ritter, *Erdk.* x. p. 769.)   [T. H. D.]

XIME'NE (Ξιμήνη), a district in the most southern part of Pontus, on the Halys, and near the frontiers of Cappadocia, was celebrated for its salt-works. (Strab. xii. p. 561.)   [L. S.]

XION (Ξιών, Scylax, p. 53), a river on the W. coast of Libya Interior.   [T. H. D.]

XIPHONIUS PORTUS (Ξιφώνειος Λιμήν, Scyl. p. 4 : *Bay of Augusta*), a spacious harbour on the E. coast of Sicily, between Catana and Syracuse. It is remarkable that this, though one of the largest and most important natural harbours on the coasts of Sicily, is rarely mentioned by ancient authors. Scylax, indeed, is the only writer who has preserved to us its name as that of a port. Strabo speaks of the Xiphonian Promontory (τὸ τῆς Ξιφωνίας ἀκρωτήριον, vi. p. 267), by which he evidently means the projecting headland near its entrance, now called the *Capo di Santa Croce*. Diodorus also mentions that the Carthaginian fleet, in B. C. 263 touched at *Xiphonia* on its way to Syracuse (εἰς τὴν Ξιφωνίαν, xxiii. 4. p. 502). None of these authors allude to the existence of a town of this name, and it is probably a mistake of Stephanus of Byzantium, who speaks of Xiphonia as *a city* (*s. v.*). The harbour or bay of *Augusta* is a spacious gulf, considerably larger than the Great Harbour of Syracuse, and extending from the *Capo di Santa Croce* to the low peninsula or promontory of *Magnisi* (the ancient Thapsus). But it is probable that the port designated by Scylax was a much smaller one, close to the modern city of *Augusta*, which occupies a low peninsular point or tongue of land that projects from near the N. extremity of the bay, and strongly resembles the position of the island of Ortygia, at Syracuse, except that it is not quite separated from the mainland. It is very singular that so remarkable and advantageous a situation should not have been taken advantage of by the Greek colonists in Sicily ; but we have no trace of any ancient town on the spot, unless it were the site of the ancient Megara. [MEGARA.] The modern town of *Augusta*, or *Agosta*, was founded in the 13th century by Frederic II.   [E. H. B.]

XOIS (Ξόις, Strab. xvii. p. 802; Ptol. iv. 5. § 50; Ξόης, Steph. B. s. v.), a town of great antiquity and considerable size, was situated nearly in the centre of the Delta, upon an island formed by the Sebennytic and Phatnitic branches of the Nile. It belonged to the Sebennytic Nome. The 14th dynasty, according to Manetho, consisted of 76 Xoite kings. This dynasty immediately preceded that of the shepherd kings of Aegypt. It seems probable, therefore, that Xois, from its strong position among the marshes formed by the intersecting branches of the river, held out during the occupation of the Delta by the Hyksos, or at least compromised with the invaders by paying them tribute. By some geographers it is supposed to be the Papremis of Herodotus (ii. 59, iii. 12). Champollion (l'Egypte sous les Pharaons, vol. ii. p. 214) believes its site to have been at Sakkra, which is the Arabian synonyme of the Coptic Xeos and of the old Aegyptian Skhoo (Niebuhr, Travels, vol. i. p. 75.) The road from Tamiathis to Memphis passed through Xois. [W.B.D.]

XYLENO'POLIS, a town said by Pliny, on the authority it would seem of Onesicritus or Nearchus, to have been founded by Alexander the Great (vi. 23. s. 26). It must have been in the southern part of Sinde; but its position cannot be recognised, as Pliny himself states that the authors to whom he refers did not say on what river it was situated. [V.]

XYLICCENSES (οἱ Ξυλικκεῖς Αἰθίοπες, Ptol. iv. 6. § 23), an Aethiopian people in Libya Interior, between the mountains Arangas and Arualtes. [T.H.D.]

XYLINE COME, a village in Pisidia, between Corbasa and Termessus, is mentioned only by Livy (xxxviii. 15). A place called Xyline, in the country of the Cissians in Pontus, is noticed by Ptolemy (v. 6. § 6). [L. S.]

XYLO'POLIS (Ξυλόπολις), a town of Mygdonia in Macedonia (Ptol. iii. 13. § 36), whose inhabitants, the Xylopolitae, are mentioned by Pliny also (iv. 10. s. 17).

XY'NIA or XY'NIAE (Ξυνία: Eth. Ξυνιεύς), a town near the southern confines of Thessaly, and the district of the Aenianes (Liv. xxxiii. 3), which gave its name to the lake Xynias (Ξυνίας), which Stephanus confounds with the Boebeis (Apollon. Rhod. i. 67; Catull. lxiii. 287; Steph. B. s. v. Ξυνία). Xynia, having been deserted by its inhabitants, was plundered by the Aetolians in B.C. 198 (Liv. xxxii. 13). In the following year Flamininus arrived at this place in three days' march from Heraclea (Liv. xxxiii. 3; comp. Liv. xxxix. 26). The lake of Xynias is now called Taukli, and is described as 6 miles in circumference. The site of the ancient city is marked by some remains of ruined edifices upon a promontory or peninsula in the lake. (Leake, Northern Greece, vol. i. p. 460, vol. iv. p. 517.)

XY'PETE. [ATTICA, p. 325, a.]

Z.

ZABA (Ζάβα), a small place on the northern coast of Taprobane or Ceylon, noticed by Ptolemy (vii. 4. § 13). It has not been identified with any modern site. [V.]

ZABAE (Ζάβαι, Ptol. i. 14. §§ 1, 4, 6, 7, vii. 2. § 6, viii. 27. § 4), a town of some importance in India intra Gangem, on the sinus Gangeticus, perhaps the modern Ligor. [J. R.]

ZA'BATUS (Ζάβατος), a river of Assyria, first noticed by Xenophon (Anab. ii. 5. § 1, iii. 3. § 6), and the same as the Lycus of Polybius (v. 51),

Arrian (Anab. iii. 15), and Strabo (ii. p. 79, xvi. p. 737). It is called Zabas by Ammianus (xviii. 14) and Zerbis by Pliny (vi. 26. s. 30). There can be no doubt that it is now represented by the Greater Záb, a river of considerable size, which, rising in the mountains on the confines of Armenia and Kurdistán, flows into the Tigris a little to the S. of the great mound of Nimrud (Tavernier, ii. c. 7; Layard, Nineveh and its Remains, i. p. 192.) [V.]

ZABE. [BERZABDA.]

ZABE (Ζάβη, Procop. B. Vand. ii. 20, p. 501, ed. Bonn), a district in Mauretania Sitifensis. According to the Not. Imp. it contained a town of the same name, which must be that called Zabi in the Itin. Ant. (p. 30). Lapie identifies it with the present Msilah. [T. H. D.]

ZACATAE (Ζακάται, Ptol. v. 9. § 16), a people of Asiatic Sarmatia. [T. H. D.]

ZACYNTHUS (Ζάκυνθος: Eth. Ζακύνθιος: Zante), an island in the Sicilian sea, lying off the western coast of Peloponnesus, opposite the promontory Chelonatas in Elis, and to the S. of the island of Cephallenia, from which it was distant 25 miles, according to Pliny, (iv. 12. s. 19) but according to Strabo, only 60 stadia (x. p. 458). The latter is very nearly correct, the real distance being 8 English miles. Its circumference is stated by Pliny at 36 M. P., by Strabo at 160 stadia; but the island is at least 50 miles round, its greatest length being 23 English miles. The island is said to have been originally called Hyrie (Plin. l. c.), and to have been colonized by Zacynthus, the son of Dardanus, from Psophis in Arcadia, whence the acropolis of the city of Zacynthus was named Psophis. (Paus. viii. 24. § 3; Steph. B. s. v.) We have the express statement of Thucydides that the Zacynthians were a colony of Achaeans from Peloponnesus (ii. 66). In Homer, who gives the island the epithet of "woody" (ὑλήεις and ὑλήεσσα), Zacynthus forms part of the dominions of Ulysses. (Il. ii. 634, Od. i. 246, ix. 24, xvi. 123, 250; Strab. x. p. 457.) It appears to have attained considerable importance at an early period; for according to a very ancient tradition Saguntum in Spain was founded by the Zacynthians, in conjunction with the Rutuli of Ardea. (Liv. xxi. 7; Plin. xvi. 40. s. 79; Strab. iii. p. 159.) Bocchus stated that Saguntum was founded by the Zacynthians 200 years before the Trojan War (ap. Plin. l. c.) In consequence probably of their Achaean origin, the Zacynthians were hostile to the Lacedaemonians, and hence we find that fugitives from Sparta fled for refuge to this island. (Herod. vi. 70, ix. 37.) In the Peloponnesian War the Zacynthians sided with Athens (Thuc. ii. 7, 9); and in B.C. 430 the Lacedaemonians made an unsuccessful attack upon their city. (Ib. 66.) The Athenians in their expedition against Pylus found Zacynthus a convenient station for their fleet. (Id. iv. 8, 13.) The Zacynthians are enumerated among the autonomous allies of Athens in the Sicilian expedition. (Id. vii. 57.) After the Peloponnesian War, Zacynthus seems to have passed under the supremacy of Sparta; for in B.C. 374, Timotheus, the Athenian commander, on his return from Corcyra, landed some Zacynthian exiles on the island, and assisted them in establishing a fortified post. These must have belonged to the anti-Spartan party; for the Zacynthian government applied for help to the Spartans, who sent a fleet of 25 sail to Zacynthus. (Xen. Hell. vi. 2. § 3; Diodor. xv. 45, seq.; as to the statements of Diodorus, see Grote, Hist. of Greece, vol. x. p. 192.) The Zacynthians assisted Dion in his expedition to Syracuse with the view of expelling the tyrant Dionysius, B. C. 357. (Diod. xvi. 6, seq.; Plut. *Dion*, 22, seq.) At the time of the Roman wars in Greece we find Zacynthus in the possession of Philip of Macedon. (Polyb. v. 102.) In B. C. 211 the Roman praetor M. Valerius Laevinus, took the city of Zacynthus, with the exception of the citadel. (Liv. xxvi. 24.) It was afterwards restored to Philip, by whom it was finally surrendered to the Romans in B. C. 191. (Id. xxxvi. 32.) In the Mithridatic War it was attacked by Archelaus, the general of Mithridates, but he was repulsed. (Appian, *Mithr.* 45.) Zacynthus subsequently shared the fate of the other Ionian islands, and is now subject to Great Britain.

The chief town of the island, also named Zacynthus (Liv. xxvi. 14; Strab. x. p. 458; Ptol. iii. 14. § 13), was situated upon the eastern shore. Its site is occupied by the modern capital, *Zante*, but nothing remains of the ancient city, except a few columns and inscriptions. The situation of the town upon the margin of a semi-circular bay is very picturesque. The citadel probably occupied the site of the modern castle. The beautiful situation of the city and the fertility of the island have been celebrated in all ages (καλὰ πόλις ἀ Ζάκυνθος, Theocr. *Id.* iv. 32; Strab., Plin., *ll. cc.*). It no longer deserves the epithet of " woody," given to it by Homer (*l. c.*) and Virgil ("nemorosa Zacynthos," *Aen.* iii. 270); but its beautiful olive-gardens, vineyards, and gardens, justify the Italian proverb, which calls *Zante* the " flower of the Levant."

The most remarkable natural phenomenon in *Zante* is the celebrated pitch-wells, which are accurately described by Herodotus (iv. 195), and are mentioned by Pliny (xxxv. 15. s. 51). They are situated about 12 miles from the c j, in a small marshy valley near the shore of the *Bay of Chieri*, on the SW. coast. A recent observer has given the following account of them: " There are two springs, the principal surrounded by a low wall ; here the pitch is seen bubbling up under the clear water, which is about a foot deep over the pitch itself, with which it comes out of the earth. The pitch-bubbles rise with the appearance of an India-rubber bottle until the air within bursts, and the pitch falls back and runs off. It produces about three barrels a day, and can be used when mixed with pine-pitch, though in a pure state it is comparatively of no value. The other spring is in an adjoining vineyard ; but the pitch does not bubble up, and is in fact only discernible by the ground having a burnt appearance, and by the feet adhering to the surface as one walks over it. The demand for the pitch of *Zante* is now very small, vegetable pitch being preferable." (Bowen, in Murray's *Handbook for Greece*, p. 93.)

The existence of these pitch-wells, as well as of numerous hot springs, is a proof of the volcanic

COIN OF ZACYNTHUS.

agency at work in the island ; to which it may be added that earthquakes are frequent.

Pliny mentions Mt. Elatus in Zacynthus (" Mons Elatus ibi nobilis," Plin. *l. c.*), probably Mt. *Skopo*, which raises its curiously jagged summit to the height of 1300 feet above the eastern extremity of the bay of *Zante*. (Dodwell, *Tour through Greece*, vol. i. p. 83, seq.)

ZADRACARTA. [TAGAE.]

ZAGATIS (Ζάγατις), a coast river in the E. part of Pontus, discharging itself into the Euxine about 7 stadia to the east of Athenae; probably the same river as the modern *Sucha Dere*. (Arrian, *Peripl. P. E.* p. 17; Anon. *Peripl. P. E.* p. 15.) [L. S.]

ZAGO'RUS, or ZAGO'RUM (Ζάγωρος, or Ζάγωρον, Marcian. p. 73 ; Ζάγειρα, Ptol. v. 4. § 5; Ζάγωρα, Arrian, *Peripl. P. E.* p. 15; Zacoria, *Tab. Peut.*), a town of Paphlagonia, on the coast of the Euxine, between Sinope and the mouth of the Halys, from the latter of which it was distant about 400 stadia. [L. S.]

ZAGRUS MONS (ὁ Ζάγρος, τὸ Ζάγρον ὄρος, Polyb. v. 44 ; Ptol. vi. 2. § 4 ; Strab. xi. p. 522), the central portion of the great chain of mountains which, extending in a direction nearly N. and S. with an inclination to the W. at the upper end, connects the mountains of Armenia and the Caucasus with those of Susiana and Persis. It separates Assyria from Media, and is now represented by the middle and southern portion of the mountains of *Kurdistán*, the highest of which is the well known *Rowandiz*. Near this latter mountain was the great highroad which led from Assyria and its capital Nineveh into Media, and, at its base, was in all probability the site of the pass through the mountains, called by Ptolemy αἱ τοῦ Ζάγρου πύλαι (vi. 2. § 7), and by Strabo, ἡ Μηδικὴ πύλη (xi. p. 525). Polybius notices the difficulty and danger of this pass (v. 44), which, from Colonel Rawlinson's narrative, would seem to have lost none of its dangers (Rawlinson, in *Trans. Geogr. Soc.* vol. x., *Pass and Pillar of Keli-Shin*). [V.]

ZAITHA or ZAUTHA (Ζαυθά, Zosim. iii. 14), a small town or fortified place in Mesopotamia, on the Euphrates, to the SE. of Circesium. It is said by Ammianus to have been called Zaitha (or more properly Zaita) from the olive trees (xxiii. 5. § 7), which we must suppose grew there, though the climate is very hot for that tree. He adds that it was celebrated for the monument erected by the soldiers to the emperor Gordianus. Zosimus, on the other hand, places this monument at Dara (*l. c.*), in which Eutropius agrees with him (ix. 2). Ptolemy calls it Zeitha (Ζεῖθα, v. 18. § 2). [DURA.] [V.]

ZALACUS (τὸ Ζάλακον ὄρος, Ptol. iv. 2. §§ 14, 19), a mountain chain of Mauretania near the river Chinalaph, the highest and most rugged branch of the Atlas in this neighbourhood. Now the *Wannash-reese* or *Guenesseris*. (Cf. Shaw, *Travels*, i. p. 74.) [T. H. D.]

ZALDAPA (Ζάλδαπα, Procop. *de Aed.* iv. 11. p. 308), a town in the interior of Lower Moesia. It is called Saldapa by Theophylact (Σάλδαπα, i. 8), and Zeldepa by Hierocles. (Ζέλδεπα, p. 637). [T. H. D.]

ZALE'CUS (Ζάληκος, or Ζάλισκος, in Ptol. v. 4. § 3), a small river on the coast of Paphlagonia, discharging itself into the Euxine at a distance of 210 stadia west of the Halys. (Marcian. p. 73.) At its mouth there was a small town of the same name, about 90 stadia from Zagorus, or Zagorum (Anon.

Peripl. P. E. p. 9) ; and this place seems to be the same as the one mentioned in the Peut. Table under the corrupt name of Halega, at a distance of 25 Roman miles from Zacoria. Hamilton (*Researches,* i. p. 298) identifies the site of Zalecus with the modern *Alatcham,* where some ruins and massive walls are still seen.   [L. S.]

ZALICHES (Ζαλίχης), a town in the interior of Paphlagonia, or what, at a late period, was called Hellenopontus, probably near some mountain forest, as Hierocles (p. 701) calls it Σάλτος Ζαλίχης (*Novell.* 28 ; Conc. Nicaen. ii. p. 355, where a bishop of Zaliches is mentioned, and p. 163, from which it would seem that at one time the place bore the name of Leontopolis.)   [L. S.]

ZAMA (Ζάμα μείζων, Ptol. iv. 3. § 33), a town of Numidia, situated five days' journey to the SW. of Carthage. (Polyb. xv. 5; Liv. xxx. 29.) It lay between Sicca Veneria and Suffetula, and bore the name of "Regia;" .whence we find it erroneously written Zamareigia in the *Tab. Peut.* Zama is particularly renowned as the scene of Scipio's victory over Hannibal in 201 B.C. It was a very strong place, and hence adopted as a residence by Juba, who brought his harem and his treasure hither, as to a place of safety. (Hirt. *B. Afr.* 91; Vitruv. viii. 3. (or 4.) § 24.) Strabo represents it as destroyed by the Romans, and as being in a ruinous state in his time (xvii. pp. 829, 831). But it must have been subsequently restored, since Pliny (v. 4. s. 4) mentions the Zamense oppidum as a free city. It also appears in the *Tab. Peut.,* and a bishop of Zama is mentioned by St. Augustine. (*De Civ. Dei,* vii. 16.) In an inscription in Gruter (364. 1) Zama Regia appears with the title of a colony (Col. Aelia Hadriana); though it is not mentioned as a colony in any of the ancient writers. It is the present *Jama,* SE. of *Kess.* (Cf. Dion Cass. xlviii. 23; Sall. *J.* 60, 61.)   [T. H. D.]

ZAMA (Ζάμα), a town of the district of Chammanene, in Cappadocia, on the borders of Galatia. (Ptol. v. 18. § 12 ; *Tab. Peut.*)   [L. S.]

ZAMAE FONS, a spring in Africa, probably near the town of Zama, which had the property of rendering the voice clear and strong. (Plin. xxxi. 2. s. 12.)   [T. H. D.]

ZAMAZII (Ζαμάζιοι, Ptol. iv. 6. § 18), a people of Libya Interior.   [T. H. D.]

ZAMENSE OPPIDUM. [ZAMA.]

ZAMES (Ζάμης, Ptol. vi. 7. §§ 20, 21), a mountain chain in the interior of Arabia Felix, which stretched as far as the borders of Arabia Deserta. It is probably the present *Jabel Aared,* or *Imaryeh.*   [T. H. D.]

ZANCLE. [MESSANA.]

ZAO PROMONTORIUM, a headland on the coast of Gallia Narbonensis, and east of Massilia (*Marseille*). Pliny (iii. 4), after mentioning Massilia says, "Promontorium Zao, Citharista Portus. Regio Camatullicorum. Dein Suelteri." It is not easy to identify Zao. Ukert conjectures that it may be *Bec de Sormion.* In the *Statistique du Dép. des Bouches du Rhône,* it is supposed to be *Cap de la Croisette.* This is a rocky coast, which has undergone little change for many centuries. (Ukert, *Gallien,* p. 120.)   [G. L.]

ZAPAORTENI. [APAVARCTICENE.]

ZARA (Ζάρα), a town in the northern part of Armenia Minor, or perhaps more correctly in Pontus, on the road from Caesarea to Satala, and at the same time on that from Arabissus to Nicopolis. It

still bears the name of *Zara* or *Sara.* (*It. Ant.* pp. 182, 207, 213.)   [L. S.]

ZARADRUS (Ζαράδρος, Ptol. vii. 1. § 27), the upper portion of the Hyphasis, the most eastern of the five rivers of the *Panjâb,* now the *Sutledge.* There is some doubt about the orthography of this name, which in some editions is written Zadrades. There can be no doubt that in either case it is derived from the Sanscrit name *Satadru,* and that it is the same as the Hesydrus of Pliny (vi. 17. s. 21).   [V.]

ZARAI, a town in the interior of Numidia, on the road from Lamasba to Sitifis. (*Itin. Ant.* p. 35.) In the *Tab. Peut.* it is called Zaras. Variously identified with *Jigbah, Ngaous,* and *Zéryah.*   [T. H. D.]

ZARANGI. [DRANGAE.]

ZARATAE, or ZARETAE (Ζαράται, Ptol. vi. 14. § 11), a people of Scythia on the Imaus.   [T.H.D.]

ZARAX (Ζάραξ, Paus., Polyb.; Ζάρηξ, Ptol.: Eth. Ζαρήκιος, Steph. B.), a town on the eastern coast of Laconia, with a good harbour, situated upon a promontory, which is a projection of Mt. Zarax. [Vol. II. p. 109, b.] Like Prasiae and some other places on this part of the Laconian coast, it passed into the hands of the Argives in the time of the Macedonian supremacy; and this was apparently the reason why it was destroyed by Cleonymus, the son of Cleomenes. From this disaster it never recovered. Augustus made it one of the Eleuthero-Laconian towns; but Pausanias found in it nothing to mention but a temple of Apollo at the end of the harbour. It is now called *Hiéraka,* which is evidently a corruption of Zarax, and there are still ruins of the ancient town. The promontory bears the same name, and the port, which is on its northern side, is described as small but well sheltered. Pausanias says that Zarax was 100 stadia from Epidaurus Limera, but this distance is too great. (Paus. iii. 24. § 1 ; comp. i. 38. § 4, iii. 21. § 7 ; Polyb. iv. 36 ; Ptol. iii. 15. § 10 ; Plin. iv. 5. s. 17 ; Steph. B. s. v.; Leake, *Morea,* vol. i. p. 219 ; Boblaye, *Recherches, &c.* p. 101; Curtius, *Peloponnesos,* vol. ii. p. 291.)

ZARAX MONS. [LACONIA, p. 109, b.]

ZARGIDAVA (Ζαργίδαυα, Ptol. iii. 10. § 15), a town of Moesia Inferior, on the Danube. [T. H. D.]

ZARIASPA. [BACTRA.]

ZARIASPAE. [BACTRA.]

ZARIASPIS. [BACTRUS.]

ZARMIZEGETHUSA. [SARMIZEGETHUSA.]

ZAUE'CES (Ζαυῆκες, Herod. iv. 193), a people of Libya, dwelling in a woody and mountainous country abounding in wild beasts, to the S. of the subsequent Roman province of Africa, and near the tribe of the Maxyes. A custom prevailed among them for the women to drive the chariots in war; which Heeren conjectures may have occasioned the placing of the Amazons in this neighbourhood. (*Ideen,* ii. 1. p. 41.)   [T. H. D.]

ZAUTHA. [ZAITHA.]

ZEA PORTUS. [ATHENAE, p. 304, seq.]

ZEBULON. [PALAESTINA.]

ZEGRENSII (Ζεγρήνσιοι, Ptol. iv. 1. § 10), a people of Mauretania Tingitana.   [T. H. D.]

ZEITHA (Ζείθα, Ptol. iv. 3. § 12), a promontory of the Regio Syrtica forming the E. point of the Syrtis Minor.   [T. H. D.]

ZELA (τὰ Ζῆλα), a town in the interior of Pontus, on the left bank of the Iris, towards the Galatian frontier, was believed to have been erected on a mound constructed by Semiramis. (Strab. xii. p. 561, comp. pp. 512, 559.) It seems to have originally been a place consecrated to the worship of the goddess Anaitis, to whom a temple was built there by the Persians in commemoration of a victory over the Sacae. The chief priest of this temple was regarded as the sovereign of Zela and its territory (Ζηλῆτις). Notwithstanding this, however, it remained a small place until Pompey, after his victory over Mithridates, raised it to the rank of a city by increasing its population and extending its walls. Zela is celebrated in history for a victory obtained in its vicinity by Mithridates over the Romans under Triarius, and still more for the defeat of Pharnaces, about which Caesar sent to Rome the famous report " Veni, Vidi, Vici." (Plin. vi. 3; Appian, *Mithrid.* 89 ; Plut. *Caes.* 50; Dion Cass. xlii. 47, where the place is erroneously called *Ζέλεια*; Hirt. *Bell. Alex.* 73, where it is called Ziela; Ptol. v. 6. § 10 Hierocl. p. 701; Steph. B. *s. v.*) Zela was situated at a distance of four days' journey (according to the Peut. Table 80 miles) from Tavium, and south-east of Amasia. The elevated ground on which the town was situated, and which Strabo calls the mound of Semiramis, was, according to Hirtius, a natural hill, but so shaped that it might seem to be the work of human hands. According to Hamilton (*Researches*, i. p. 306), is a black-coloured isolated hill rising out of the plain, and is now crowned with a Turkish fortress, which still bears the name of *Zilleh*.   [L. S.]

ZELA'SIUM. [POSIDIUM, p. 662, No. 4.]

ZELDEPA. [ZALDAPA.]

ZELEIA (Ζέλεια), a town of Troas, at the foot of Mount Ida and on the banks of the river Aesepus, at a distance of 80 stadia from its mouth. It is mentioned by Homer (*Il.* ii. 824, iii. 103), who calls it a holy town. (Comp. Strab. xii. p. 565, xiii. pp. 585, 587, 603 ; Steph. B. *s. v.*) Arrian (*Anab.* i. 13) mentions it as the head-quarters of the Persian army before the battle of the Granicus: it existed in the time of Strabo ; but afterwards it disappears. Some travellers have identified it with the modern *Biga*, between *Bozaegee* and *Sorricui.*   [L. S.]

ZELETIS. [ZELA.]

ZENOBII INSULAE (Ζηνοβίου νησία, Ptol. vi. 7. § 47), seven small islands lying in the Sinus Sachalites, at the entrance of the Arabian Gulf. (Cf. Arrian. *Per. M. Eryth.* p. 19.)   [V.]

ZENODO'TIUM (Ζηνοδότιον, Dion Cass. xl. 12; Steph. B. *s. v.*), a strong castle in the upper part of Mesopotamia, which was held by the Parthians during the war between them and the Romans under Crassus. It is called by Plutarch, Zenodotia (*Crass.* c. 17). It cannot be identified with any modern site, but it was, probably, not far distant from Edessa.   [V.]

ZENO'NIS CHERSONESUS (Ζήνωνος Χερσόνησος, Ptol. iii. 6. § 4), a point of land on the N. coast of the Chersonesus Taurica in European Sarmatia, probably the narrow tongue of *Arabat*, between the *Sea of Azof* and the *Putrid Sea.* [T.H.D.]

ZE'PHYRE, a small island off the promontory Sammonium in Crete. (Plin. iv. 12. s. 20.)

ZEPHY'RIA. [HALICARNASSUS.]

ZEPHY'RIUM (Ζεφύριον), the name of a great number of promontories, as 1. At the western extremity of the peninsula of Myndus in Caria, now called *Gumichle* or *Angeli.* (Strab. xiv. p. 658.)

2. On the coast of Cilicia, between Cilicia Tracheia and Pedias, a little to the west of the town of Anchiale. (Strab. xiv. p. 671.) It contained a fort of the same name, and was 120 stadia from Tarsus,

and 13 miles east of Soli. (*Stadiasm.* § 157 ; *Tab. Peut.*; comp. Scyl. p. 40; Ptol. v. 8. § 4; Liv. xxxiii. 20; Plin. v. 22; Hierocl. p. 704.) When Pliny (xxxiv. 50) states that the best molybdaena was prepared at Zephyrium, he no doubt alludes to this place, since we know from Dioscorides (v. 100) that this mineral was obtained in the neighbouring hill of Corycus, and that there it was of excellent quality. Leake (*Asia Minor*, p. 214) looks for it near the mouth of the river *Mertis.*

3. On the coast of Cilicia, near the mouth of the river Calycadnus. (Strab. xiv. p. 670; Ptol. v. 8. § 3.)

4. A town on the coast of Paphlagonia, 60 stadia to the west of Cape Carambis. (Arrian, *Peripl. P. E.* p. 15; Anon. *Peripl. P. E.* p. 6 ; Ptol. v. 4. § 2.)

5. A town and promontory on the coast of Pontus, in the country of the Mosynoeci, 90 stadia to the west of Tripolis. (Ptol. v. 6. § 11; Arrian, *Peripl. P. E.* p. 17 ; Scylax, p. 33 ; Anon. *Peripl. P. E.* p. 13 ; *Tab. Peut.*) The cape still bears the name of *Zafra* or *Zefreh*, and Hamilton (*Researches*, i. p. 261) regards the modern *Kaik Liman* as occupying the site of the ancient Zephyrium.   [L. S.]

ZEPHYRIUM PROMONTORIUM (τὸ Ζεφύριον: *Capo di Bruzzano*), a promontory on the E. coast of the Bruttian peninsula, between Locri and the SE. corner of Bruttium. It is mentioned principally in connection with the settlement of the Locrian colonists in this part of Italy, whose city thence derived the name of LOCRI EPIZEPHYRII. According to Strabo, indeed, these colonists settled in the first instance on the headland itself, which had a small port contiguous to it, but after a short time removed to the site of their permanent city, about 15 miles farther N. (Strab. vi. pp. 259, 270.) The Zephyrian Promontory is mentioned by all the geographers in describing the coast of Bruttium, and is undoubtedly the same now called the *Capo di Bruzzano*, a low but marked headland, about 10 miles N. of *Cape Spartivento*, which forms the SE. extremity of the Bruttian peninsula. (Strab. l. c.; Plin. iii. 5. s. 10 ; Mel. ii. 4. § 8 ; Ptol. iii. 1. § 10 ; Steph. Byz. *s. v.*)   [E. H. B.]

ZEPHY'RIUM (Ζεφύριον ἄκρον, Ptol. iii. 17. § 5). 1. A promontory on the E. part of the N. coast of Crete, near the town of Apollonia. Now *Ponta di Tigani.*

2. A promontory on the W. coast of Cyprus, near Paphos, probably the cape which closes the bay of *Baffo* to the W. (Ptol. v. 14. § 1 ; Strab. xiv. p. 683.)

3. A promontory in the E. part of Cyrenaica, 150 stadia to the W. of Darnis. (Strab. xvii. p. 799, who attributes it to Marmarica; Ptol. iv. 4. § 5; *Stadias. M. Magni*, §§ 47, 48.) Now *Cape Derne.*

4. Another promontory of Cyrenaica, with a harbour. (Strab. xvii. p. 838.)

5. A promontory near Little Taposiris in Lower Aegypt, having a temple of Arsinoë-Aphrodite. (Strab. xvii. p. 800.) Hence that goddess derived the epithet of Zephuritis (Ζεφυρῖτις, Athen. vii. p. 318, D.; Callim. *Ep.* 31; Steph. B. *s. v.*).

6. A town of the Chersonesus Taurica, mentioned only by Pliny (iv. 12. s. 26).   [T. H. D.]

ZERNES (Ζέρνης, Procop. *de Aed.* iv. 6. p. 288), a fortress in Upper Moesia, apparently the present *Old Orsowa*, at the mouth of the *Tzerna*. [T.H.D.]

ZERYNTHUS (Ζήρυνθος, Lycophr. 77 ; Steph. B. *s. v.*), a town of Thrace not far from the borders of the Aenianes. It contained a cave of Hecate, a temple of Apollo, and another of Aphrodite, which two deities hence derived the epithet of Zerynthian. (Cf. Liv. xxxviii. 41; Ov. *Trist.* i. 10. 19; Tzetz. *ad Lycophr.* 449, 958.) [T. H. D.]

ZESUTERA (*It. Hier.* p. 602), a town in the SE. of Thrace, on the Egnatian Way, between Apri and Siracellae, which Lapie identifies with *Kahraman*. [J. R.]

ZEUGITANA REGIO, the more northern part of the Roman province of Africa. Pliny seems to be the earliest writer who mentions the name of Zeugitana (v. 4. s. 3). A town of Zeugis is mentioned by Aethicus (*Cosmogr.* p. 63), and a Zeugitanus, apparently a mountain, by Solinus (" a pede Zeugitano," c. 27), which is perhaps the same as the Mons Zignensis of Victor (*de Persec. Vandal.* iii.), the present *Zow-wan;* and according to Shaw (*Travels,* i. p. 191, sq.), if the existence of a town or mountain so named is not altogether problematical, the province probably derived its name from either one or the other. The district was bounded on the S. by Byzacium, on the W. by Numidia, from which it was divided by the river Tusca (now *Zaine*), and on the N. and E. by the Mare Internum. After the time of Caesar it appears to have been called Provincia Vetus, or Africa Propria, as opposed to the later acquired Numidia. (Dion Cass. xliii. 10; Plin. *l. c.;* Mela, i. 7.) Strabo mentions it only as ἡ Καρχηδονία, or the province of Carthage (vi. p. 267, &c.). It embraced the modern *Frigeah* (which is doubtless a corruption of the ancient name of Africa) or northern part of the kingdom of *Tunis*. Zeugitana was watered by the Bagradas, and was a very fertile country. There were no towns of importance in the interior, but on the coast we find Siagul, Neapolis, Curubis, Aspis or Clupea, Carpis, Tunes, Carthago, Castra Cornelia, Utica, and Hippo Diarrhytus. For further particulars concerning this province see AFRICA. [T. H. D.]

ZEUGMA. 1. (Ζεῦγμα, Ptol. v. 15. § 14), a town founded by Seleucus Nicator, in the province of Cyrrhestica, in Syria. It derived its name from a bridge of boats which was here laid across the Euphrates, and which in the course of time became the sole passage over the river, when the older one at Thapsacus, 2000 stadia to the S., had become impracticable, or at all events very dangerous, owing to the spreading of the Arabian hordes. (Plin. v. 24. s. 21; Strab. xvi. p. 746; Steph. B. s. v.) Zeugma lay on the right bank of the Euphrates, opposite to Apamea, 72 miles SW. of Samosata, 175 miles NE. of the maritime Seleucia, and 36 miles N. of Hierapolis. (Plin. *l. c.,* and v. 12. s. 13; Strab. xvi. p. 749; *Tab. Peut.*) It was therefore opposite to the modern *Bir* or *Biredjik*, which occupies the site of the ancient Apamea. (Cf. Ritter, *Erdkunde*, x. p. 944, seq.) In the time of Justinian, Zeugma had fallen into decay, but was restored by that emperor. Procop. *de Aed.* ii. 9, p. 237, ed. Bonn.) (Cf.

COIN OF ZEUGMA.

Polyb. v. 43; Dion Cass. xl. 17, xlix. 19; Lucan, viii. 236; *Itin. Ant.* pp. 184, 185, &c.)

2. A place in Dacia. (Ptol. iii. 8. § 10). Mannert (iv. p. 210) identifies it with the Pons Augusti of the Geogr. Rav. (iv. 14) and Tab. Peut.; concerning which see above, p. 656.) [T. H. D.]

ZICCHI (Ζικχοί, Arrian, *Perip. P. Eux.* p. 19), ZINCHI (Ζιγχοί, Ptol. v. 9. § 18), or ZINGI (Plin. vi. 7. s. 7), a savage piratical tribe of Asiatic Sarmatia, on the coast of the Pontus Euxinus, between Sanigae and Achaei. They are called by Procopius Ζῆχοι and Ζῆαχοι (*B. Goth.* iv. 4, *B. Pers.* ii. 29), and by Strabo, Ζυγοί (i. p. 129, xi. pp. 492, 495), if, indeed, he means the same people, as he places them in the interior on the Caucasus. [T. H. D.]

ZIGAE, a people of Sarmatia, on the Tanais (Plin. vi. 7. s. 7). [T. H. D.]

ZIGERE, a place in Lower Moesia, in the neighbourhood of Axiopolis (Plin. iv. 11. s. 18). [T.H.D.]

ZIGUENSIS MONS. [ZEUGITANA.]

ZIKLAG, a town in the tribe of Simeon (*Jos.* xix. 5), which at first belonged to the Philistine city of Gath (1 *Sam.* xxvii. 5), but was annexed to the kingdom of Israel by David. (1 *Chron.* xii. 1.) It appears to be the same as that called Σέκελλα by Josephus (*Ant.* vi. 14) and Σίκελα by Stephanus B. It is now entirely destroyed. (Robinson, *Travels,* ii. p. 424.) [V.]

ZILIA (Mel. iii. 10; Ζιλεία or Λιξεία, Ptol. iv. 1. § 2), a town on the W. coast of Mauretania Tingitana, which fell into the sea near the town of the same name, N. of the Lixius. It is still called *Ar-Zila*. [T. H. D.]

ZILIA (Mel. iii. 10; Ζιλία, Ζιλεῖαι, and Ζειλία, Ptol. iv. 1. § 13, viii. 13. § 4; Ζῆλις and Ζέλης, Strab. xvii. p. 827, iii. p. 140), a town of some importance on the W. coast of Mauretania Tingitana, at the mouth of the like-named river, and on the road from Lix to Tingis, from which latter place it was 24 miles distant (*Itin. Ant.* p. 8, where, and in Plin. v. 1. s. 1, it is called Zilis). It was founded by the Carthaginians, and made a colony by the Romans, with the surname of Julia Constantia. (Plin. *l. c.*) According to Strabo (iii. p. 140), the Romans transplanted the inhabitants, as well as some of the citizens of Tingis, to Julia Joza in Spain. The place is still called *Azila, Azila, Ar-Zila.* [T. H. D.]

ZIMARA (Ζίμαρα), a town in Armenia Minor, on the road from Satala to Melitena, between Analiba and Teucira (*It. Ant.* p. 208; Ptol. v. 7. § 2; *Tab. Peut.*) The exact site is still matter of uncertainty, some finding traces of it near *Pashash*, others near *Divriki*, and others near *Kemakh*. (Ritter, *Erdkunde,* x. p. 800.) [L. S.]

ZINGIS PROMONTORIUM (Ζίγγις Ptol. i. 17. § 9, iv. 7. § 11), probably the Modern *Maroe*, was a headland on the eastern coast of Africa about lat. 10° N. It was conspicuous from its forked head and its elevation above a level shore of nearly 400 miles in extent. [W. B. D.]

ZIOBERIS, a small river of Parthia mentioned by Curtius (vi. 4. § 4). It is probably the same as the Stiboites (Στιβοίτης) of Diodorus (xvii. 75), which flowed under the earth in some places, and at length fell into the Rhidagus (Curt. vi. 4. § 6). [V.]

ZION. [SION.]

ZIPH. [SIPH.]

ZIPHA (Ζίφα, Ζόφα, or Ζίφαρ, Ptol. iv. 8. § 6), a mountain in the interior of Libya. [T. H. D.]

ZIPHE'NE (Ζιφήνη, Joseph. *Antiq.* vi. 13), a district of Palaestina, in the neighbourhood of Mt.

Carmel, which probably took its name from Ziph. (*Josh.* xv. 14.) Steph. Byz. notices it, quoting from Josephus. [SIPH.]　　　　　　　　[V.]

ZIRIDAVA (Ζιρίδαυα, Ptol. iii. 8. § 8), a town in Dacia, most probably *Szereka* on the *Broosch* (cf. Katancsich. *Istri Accolae*, ii. p. 296). [T.H.D.]

ZIRINAE (*Tab. Peut.*; Ζειρινία, Steph. B. p. 287; Zernae, with various readings, in *It. Ant.* p. 322), a town in Thrace, on the Hebrus, between Trajanopolis and Plotinopolis. Reichard places it on the site of *Zernits*; but Lapie identifies it with *Termalitza.*　　　　　　　　　　　　　[J. R.]

ZITHA, or ZEITHA (Ζείθα, Ptol. v. 18. § 6), a small place in Mesopotamia near the Euphrates, noticed by Ptolemy. It is in all probability the same as the Sitha of Zosimus (iii. 15).　　　[V.]

ZITHA (Ζείθα, Ptol. iv. 3. § 12), a promontory in Africa Propria between the two Syrtes and W. of Sabathra. On it lay the place called Pons Zitha.　　　　　　　　　　　　　[T. H. D.]

ZOARA (Ζοάρα, Steph. B. *s. v.*), a small town at the southern end of the Lacus Asphaltites in Judaea, to which Lot escaped from the burning of Sodom. (*Gen.* xiv. 2, 8, xix. 22.) Josephus, in describing the same lake, states that it extends μέχρι Ζοάρων 'Αραβίας (iv. c. 27). During the latter times of the Roman Empire, there was a guard maintained in that part of the country, a corps of native mounted bowmen (" Equites sagittarii Indigenae Zoarae"), who were under the command of the Dux Palaestinae. (*Notit. Imper.*)　　　　　　　　[V.]

ZOELAE, a town of the Astures in Hispania Tarraconensis, not far from the sea, and noted for the cultivation of flax. (Plin. iii. 3. s. 4, xix. 1. s. 2: comp. Florez, *Esp. Sagr.* xvi. p. 17; *Inscr. in Spon. Misc.* p. 278. 3; Orelli, no. 156.) [T.H.D.]

ZOE'TIA. [MEGALOPOLIS, p. 309, b.]

ZOMBIS (Ζομβίς, Steph. B. *s. v.*), a small place in Upper Media, noticed by Ammianus (xxiii. 6). [V.]

ZONE (Plin. iv. 11. s. 18; Mela, ii. 2. § 8; Ζώνη, Herodot. vii. 59; Scyl. p. 27; Steph. B. p. 291; Schol. *Nicand. Ther.* 462; Schol. *Apoll. Rhod.* i. 29), a town on the S. coast of Thrace, on a promontory of the same name, a short distance to the W. of the entrance of the Lacus Stentoris. According to Apollonius and Mela (*ll. cc.*) it was to this place that the woods followed Orpheus, when set in motion by his wondrous music.　　[J. R.]

ZORAMBUS (Ζωράμβος), a small stream on the coast of Gedrosia, mentioned by Marcian (*Peripl.* c. 29, ed. Müller), called Zorambes by Ptolemy (vi. 8. § 9).　　　　　　　　　　　　[V.]

ZORLANAE (*Tab. Peut.*; in Geog. Rav. v. 12, Strolanae), a place in Thrace, on the road from Siracellae to Aenus.　　　　　　　　　[J. R.]

ZOROANDA (Plin. vi. 27. s. 31), a place on the range of Mount Taurus, where the Tigris fell into a cavern, and reappeared on the other side of the mountain; perhaps the spot discovered by Rich, 11 leagues from *Julamerik*, where an eastern tributary of the Tigris suddenly falls into a chasm in the mountain. (Rich, *Koordistan*, i. p. 378; cf. Ritter, *Erdk.* x. p. 86, seq.; D'Anville, *l'Euphr. et le Tigre*, p. 74.)　　　　　　　　　　　　[J. R.]

ZOSTER. [ATTICA, p. 330, b.]

ZUCHABBARI (Ζουχάββαρι, Ptol. iv. 3. § 20), a mountain at the S. borders of the Regio Syrtica.　　　　　　　　　　　　[T. H. D.]

ZUCHABBARI. [SUCCABAR.]

ZUCHIS (Ζοῦχις, Strab. xvii. p. 835), a lake 400 stadia long, with a town of the same name upon it, in Libya, not far from the Lesser Syrtis. Stephanus B. (p. 290) mentions only the town, which, according to Strabo, was noted for its purple dyes and salt fish. It seems to be the place called Χουζίς by Ptolemy (iv. 3. § 41.)　　　　　　[T. H. D.]

ZUGAR (Ζούγαρ, Ptol. iv. 3. § 40), a town of Africa Propria, between the rivers Bagradas and Triton.　　　　　　　　　　　　　[T. H. D.]

ZUMI (Ζοῦμοι), a German tribe occupying a district in the neighbourhood of the Lugii, are mentioned by Strabo (vii. p. 209), the only author that notices them, as having been subdued by Maroboduus.　　　　　　　　　　　　　[L. S.]

ZUPHONES(Ζούφωνες,Diod. xx. 38), a Numidian tribe in the vicinity of Carthage.　　　[T. H. D.]

ZURMENTUM (Ζούρμεντον, Ptol. iv. 3. § 37), a town of Byzacium, in Africa Propria, lying to the S. of Hadrumetum.　　　　　　　[T. H. D.]

ZUROBARA (Ζουρόβαρα, Ptol. iii. 8. § 9), a town of Dacia, situated where the *Marosch* falls into the *Theiss.*　　　　　　　　　　　[T. H. D.]

ZUSIDAVA (Ζουσίδαυα, Ptol. iii. 8. § 8), a town of Dacia, probably on the site of the ruins called *Tschetatie de Pómunt*, below *Burlau* (cf. Ukert, iii. pt. ii. p. 691).　　　　　　　　　[T. H. D.]

ZYDRE'TAE (Ζυδρῆται or Ζυδρεῖται, Arrian, *Peripl. Pont. Eux.* p. 11), a people of Colchis, on the coast of the Pontus Euxinus, on the S. side of the Phasis, and between the Machelones and the Lazi.　　　　　　　　　　　[T. H. D.]

ZYGANTIS (Ζυγαντίς, Hecat. *Fr. ap. Steph. B.* p. 290), a town of Libya, whose inhabitants were noted for their preparation of honey. Hence Klausen (*ad Hecat.* p. 134) identifies them with the Gyzantes of Herodotus (iv. 194), on the W. side of the lake Tritonis, of whom that historian relates the same thing.　　　　　　　　　　　[T. H. D.]

ZYGENSES (Ζυγεῖς, Ptol. iv. 5. § 22), a people on the coast of the Libyan Nomos in Marmarica.　　　　　　　　　　　　　[T. H. D.]

ZYGI (Ζυγοί, Strab. xi. p. 496), a wild and savage people on the Pontus Euxinus in Asiatic Sarmatia, and on the heights stretching from the Caucasus to the Cimmerian Bosporus. They were partly nomad shepherds, partly brigands and pirates, for which latter vocation they had ships specially adapted (cf. Id. ii. 129, xi. 492, xvii. 839). Stephanus B. (p. 290) says that they also bore the name of Ζυγριανοί; and we find the form Zygii (Ζύγιοι) in Dionysius (*Perieg.* 687) and Avienus (*Descrip. Orb.* 871.)　　　　　[T. H. D.]

ZYGOPOLIS (Ζυγόπολις, Strab. xii. p. 548), a town in Pontus, in the neighbourhood of Colchis. Stephanus B. (p. 290) conjectures that it was in the territory of the Zygi, which, however, does not agree with Strabo's description.　　　　　[T. H. D.]

ZYGRIS (Ζυγρίς, Ptol. iv. 5. § 4), a village on the coast of the Libyan Nomos in Marmarica, which seems to have given name to the people called Zygritae dwelling there (Ζυγρῖται, Ptol. *ib.* § 22.)　　　　　　　　　　　　[T. H. D.]

ZYGRITAE. [ZYGRIS.]

ZYMETHUS (Ζύμηθος, Ptol. iv. 4. § 11), a town in the interior of Cyrenaica.　　　　[T. H. D.]

INDEX.

In this Index, modern names are distinguished from ancient by being printed in italics. The references are to the first volume, unless they have ii. prefixed. The letter *a* refers to the first column of the page, *b* to the second.

Names which occur in the alphabetical arrangement of the Work itself appear in the Index only when additional information respecting them is given incidentally in other articles.

INDEX.

In this Index, modern names are distinguished from ancient by being printed in italics. The references are to the first volume, unless they have ii. prefixed. The letter *a* refers to the first column of the page, *b* to the second.

Names which occur in the alphabetical arrangement of the Work itself appear in the Index only when additional information respecting them is given incidentally in other articles.

Aa, ii. 917, a.
Ababdeh, ii. 1236. b.
Abacaenum, ii. 987, a.
Abalus, 380. b.
Abana, ii. 1072, b.
Abaris, 43, b.
Abasci, 643, a.
Abbassia, 602, b.
Abbasia. ii. 904, a.
Abbatone, Monte, 46ª, b.
Abd-el-Kader, ii. 1208, a.
'Abd er-Rabbi, ii. 377, b.
Abdelacru, El Valle de, ii. 421, b.
Abdera, ii. 1190, a-
Abelterium, ii. 220, a.
Abensberg, 7, b.
Aberdeenshire, 772, a ; ii. 1276, a.
Abergavenny, 1004, a.
Abernethy. ii. 1307, b.
Abia, ii. 345, b.
Abida, ii. 1076, b.
Abieta, ii. 7, b.
Abii Scythae, ii. 943, b.
Abil or *Ibel-el-Hawa*, ii. 232, b.
Abil or *Ibel-el-Kamkh*, ii. 232, b.
Abila, ii. 1076, b.
Abinta, ii. 7, b.
Abissa, 380, a.
Abisso, 1039. b ; ii. 986, a.
Abi hasia, 643, a.
Ablois. 400, b.
Abn-Goosh, 824, b.
Abobrica, 934, b.
Aboccis or Abuncis, 60, b.
Abonitichos, ii. 547, b.
Aboosimbel, 4, b ; 60, b.
Aborangi, 80, a.
Abou-Beilew, ii. 1129, b.
Aboukir, 501, b.
Aboisir, ii. 642, a.
Abrantes, 187, a ; ii. 219, b ; ii. 1237, b.
Abrincatui, 218. b.
Abrostola, 931, a.
Abruccha. ii. 1326, b.
Abruzzo, ii. 667, b.
Abruzzo Citeriore, 915, b.
Absyrtides, ii. 74, a.
Abu Dis, 371, b.
Abullionte, 161, b ; 406, b.
Abus, Mt., 188, a.
Abuschaar, ii. 387, b.
Abushir, 1065, b ; ii. 332, a ; ii. 509, a.
Abydus, 40, a.
Abyla, ii. 298, a.
Abyssinia, 57, a ; 976, a.
Acacesium, 192, b.
Academy (Athens). 303, a.
Acalandrus, ii. 209, b.
Acamantis, 729, a.
Acamas, Cape, 729, b.
Acampsis, ii. 658, a.
Acampsis. 216, b.
Acarra, 17, a.

Accous, 241, b.
Accua, 167, a.
Acelum, ii. 1275, b.
Acerenza, 19, b.
Acerra, 11, b.
Acesines, 61, a ; 802, a ; ii. 985, b.
Acestaei, ii. 987, a.
Achaea, 705, b.
Achaei, 572, b ; ii. 917, b.
Acharnae, 18, a ; 326, a.
Acharnian Gate (Athens), 263, b.
Achates, ii. 985, b.
Acherini, ii. 987, a.
Acherontia, 167, a.
Achillis Insula, 20, b.
Achiado Kampos, 1108, a.
Achman-Tanah, ii. 328, b.
Achneschid, Gulf of, ii. 1087, a.
Achne, 566, a.
Achradina (Syracuse), ii. 1063, b.
Achzib. 802, b ; ii. 607, a.
Acidava, 744, b.
Aridll, ii. 1295, b.
Acimincum, ii. 542, a.
Acinasis, ii. 658, b.
Acinipo, 583, a.
Acinippo, 583, a.
Aciris, ii. 209, b.
Acis, ii. 986, a.
Acithius, ii. 985, b.
Ackermann, ii. 1248, a.
Acmonia, 744, b.
Acontisma, 807, b ; ii. 1299, a.
Acontium, 192, b.
Acontium, Mt., 412, a.
Acoraca. ii. 1076, a.
Acqua Sparta, 527, a.
Acquanile, 1103, a.
Acqualaccia, 106, a.
Acque Dolci. 72, b.
Acque Grandi, 21, a.
Acqui, 169, b ; ii. 188, a, b ; ii. 1296, b.
Acqui di Benetutti, ii. 912, a.
Acra, 422, a ; ii. 297, b.
Acrabatta, ii. 532, b.
Acrabatta, ii. 532, a.
Acrabbim, ii. 529, b.
Acrae, 67, a ; ii. 987, a, b.
Acraephium, 219, b.
Acragas. ii. 985, b.
Acre, 11, a.
Acremonte, 21, b.
Acri or *Agri*, 21, a.
Acriae, ii. 112, b.
Acridophagi, 58, a.
Acrilla, ii. 341, b.
Acro-Lochias, 96, a.
Acropolis (Athens), 255, a.
Actium, 10, b.
Acvnka, 1006. b.
Acunum, ii. 449, a.
Acusiorum Colonia, 577, a.
Ad, 178, a.

Ad Aquas, 744, b ; 934, a.
Ad Duos Pontes, 934, b.
Ad Martis, 110, a.
Ad Mediam, 744, b.
Ad Monilia, ii. 188, b.
Ad Navalia, ii. 188, b.
Ad Putea, 582, a.
Ad Solaria, ii. 188, b.
Ad Taum, 442, b.
Ad Tricesimum, 111, a.
Ad Turrem, ii. 600, a.
Ad Turres, ii. 219, b.
Adacha, ii. 1076, b.
Adada, ii. 1076, b.
Adala, 321, a.
Adalia, 320, b ; ii. 536, b.
Adalia, Bay of. 634, b.
Adam's Peak, ii. 1093, a.
Adamas, ii. 46, b.
Adar, ii. 529, b.
Adda, 24, b.
Addanus, 521, a.
Adeba, ii. 31, a.
Adelsathri, ii. 48, a.
Adelsberg, ii. 643, a.
Aden, 24, b ; 181, b.
Aderno, 25, b ; ii. 987, a.
Adertisus Pagus, 319, b.
Adhem, ii. 485, a.
Adiabarae, 60, a.
Adienus, ii. 658, b.
Adige, 309, a ; ii. 1275, a.
Adisathrus, M., ii. 46, b.
Adjisu, ii. 709, b.
'Adlan, ii. 494, a.
Adnon, or *Adlown*, ii. 606. b.
Adonaea (Rome), ii. 806, a.
Adonis, ii. 606, a.
Adour, 110, a ; 336, a.
Adour, 337, a ; 348, b.
Adra, 2, b ; ii. 1076, b.
Adrama, ii. 1076, b.
Adramitae, 181, b.
Adramiti, 25, a.
Adranum. ii. 987, a.
Adranus, ii. 985, a.
Adrapsa, 365, a.
Adratum. 25, a.
Adria, ii. 628, b.
Adria, 26, a.
Adriana, Privata (Rome), ii. 827, a.
Adrianople, 1023, b.
Adriatic, 27, a.
Adrum, flumen, Ad, ii. 220, a.
Adsaneta, ii. 1035, b.
Adula, Mons, 107, a.
Adule, 347, b.
Adummim, ii. 529, b.
Adyrmachidae, ii. 277, a.
Aebura, 525, b.
Aecae, 167, a ; ii. 1294, a.
Aeculanum, ii. 896, b.
Adepsus, 827, b.
Aedonia, ii. 277, b ; 641, a.
Aedonia, Ps. ii. 277, b.
Aega, 498, a.

Aegae, 14, b ; 624, a; 872, b
Aegaeae, 83, a.
Aegaleum, ii. 341, b.
Aegeira, 14, b.
Aegeus, Gate of (Athens), 263, b.
Aegialus, ii. 547, b.
Aegida, ii. 73, b.
Aegila, 32, b.
Aegileia, 32, b.
Aegilia, 331, a.
Aegilips, ii. 97, b.
Aegilium, 509, a.
Aegilus, 32, b.
Aeginium, ii. 1170, a.
Agiroessa, 53, a.
Aegirus, ii. 160, b.
Aegitium, 67, a ; ii. 203, a.
Aegys, 192, b.
Aegytae, 192, b.
Aegium, 14, a, b.
Aelanticus, Sinus, 174, b.
Aelea, ii. 237, a.
Aelia, ii. 1157, a.
Aelius, Pons (Rome), ii. 850, a.
Aemilia, Basilica (Rome), ii. 787, b.
Aemilia, Porticus (Rome), ii. 812, a.
Aemilius, Pons (Rome), ii. 848, a.
Aemines, ii. 1113, b.
Aemona, ii. 542, a; ii. 461, b.
Aenus, 587, b ; ii. 1190, a, b.
Aenyra, ii. 1136, a.
Aeolis, ii. 889, a.
Aepeia, 730, a; ii. 1191, b.
Aepy, 821, b.
Aequa, 496, a.
Aequum, 748, a.
Aesarus, 450 b.
Aesculapius, Temple of (Rome), ii. 840, b.
Aeseitae, 181, a.
Aesernia, ii. 896, a.
Aesica, ii. 1296, b.
Aesim, Ad, ii. 1301, b.
Aesinus, 56, a.
Aesis, or Aesium, ii. 1317, b.
Aesones, ii. 32, a.
Aesonis, ii. 1170, a.
Aestraei, ii. 512, a.
Aethiopia, 976, a.
Aex, ii. 282, a.
Aexone, 327, b.
Aezani, ii. 278, a.
Affghans, 243, a.
Afile, 67, a.
Afliano, Monte, 67, a.
Afghanistan, 209, b ; ii. 552, a.
Afium Karahissar, ii. 1035, b.
Afiom Cara-hissar, ii. 675, a.
Afiom Kara-Hissar, 776, a.
Afka, 157, a.

Africae, Caput (Rome), ii. 818, b.
Afrikeah, 68, b. .
Afrm, ii. 1075, b.
Afren, ii. 445, b.
Afxia, ii. 484, b.
Agader, ii. 718, a.
Agadir, 893, a.
Agamede, ii. 165, b.
Agata dei Goti, Sia, ii. 896, b.
Agatha, ii. 1308, a.
Agathyrna, ii. 986, b.
Agathyrsi, ii. 916, b.
Agavi, 4, a.
Agdami, ii. 284, b.
Agde, 187, b; ii. 1308, a.
Agdinitia, 521, a.
Ages, 73, b; 457,b; ii. 441, b.
Ager Soudah, ii. 1087, a.
Aghaliman, 1090, a.
Aghra, 327, b; ii. 320, a; ii. 892, a.
Aghia Kyriaki, 128, a.
Aghia Thymia, ii. 386, b.
Aghion Oros, Gulf of, ii. 1006, b.
Aghirmisch Daghi, 623, b; ii. 1110, a.
Aghous, ii. 390, a.
Aghri Tagh, 7, a; 215, b.
Aginnum, 457, b; ii. 441, b.
Agiria, 582, a.
Aglasoum, ii. 873, a.
Aglaurium (Athens), 296, b.
Agualvar, ii. 230, a.
Agnavae, 744, b.
Agneum, 705, b.
Agnone, 172, a.
Agnus, 327, b.
Agognas, 497, a.
Agonensis, Porta (Rome), ii. 757, a.
Agora, ii. 1190, a.
Agora (Athens), 293, b.
Agoritae, ii. 917, b.
Agosta, ii. 311, a.
Agrae, 327, b.
Agrae (Athens), 302, b.
Agraei, 181, a.
Agramaut, 254, b.
Agrapidho-Khori, ii. 682, a.
Agri, ii. 209, b.
Agrianes, ii. 512, a; ii. 1178, a.
Agri-Dagh, 7, a; 215, b.
Agrinium, 67, a.
Agrippa, Pedestal of, (Athens,) 770, b.
Agrippae, Campus (Rome), ii. 839, b.
Agrippae, Thermae (Rome), ii. 847, a.
Agroeira, 321, a.
Agryle, 327, b.
Agubeni, 181, a.
Agueda, ii. 230, a.
Aguilar, ii. 64, a.
Aguias, Puerto de, ii. 1326, b.
Agulenitza, 843, b.
Agulon, 346, b.
Aguntum, ii. 448, a.
Agylla, 466, b.
Agyrium, ii. 986, b.
Ahatkoi, 21, a.
Ahmed-nagar, ii. 47, a; ii. 482, b.
Ai Andhrea, ii. 160, a.
Ai Janni, ii. 1151, a.
Ai Petri, ii. 1112, a.
Ai Vasili, 10, b; 804, b.
Aia or L'aia, 1065, b.
Aia Barun, ii. 1111, b.
Aia-burum, 708, a.
Aia Kyriake, ii. 341, b.
Ajan, 354, a.
Aiamsi, 1051, a.
Aianteion, 423, b.
Ajasmat-koi, 53, a.
Aidin, ii. 243, b.
Aidinjik, 740, a.
Aidos or Avido, 7, b.
Ajeby, 337, a.
Ajeboy, ii. 1327, a.
Aigues Mortes, ii. 656, b.
Aiguillon, L., ii. 629, b.

Ajmir, ii. 692, b.
Ain-dur, ii. 395, b.
Ain-el-Ghazal, ii. 277, b.
Ain-el-Hiyeh, ii. 270, b.
Ain-el-Weiabeh, ii. 103, b.
Ain-er-Ressul, ii. 529, b.
Ain Ersen, 45, a.
Ain-es-Sultan, ii. 16, b.
Ain-el-Tyn, 504, b.
Ain Etan, 855, a.
Ain Hajla, 396, a.
Ain-Hazel, ii. 117, a.
'Ain-Jidi, 124, b.
'Ain-Jidiy, 826, b.
'Ain Kades or Kudes, ii. 103, b.
Ain or Kusr Hajlah, ii. 529, b.
Ain Semit, ii. 1001, b,
'Ain Shems, 399, b.
Ain Tab, 147, b; ii. 439, b.
Ainadzjik, ii. 419, a.
Aintab, 147, b; ii. 439, b.
Aio Mamas, ii. 481, a.
Aio Merkurio, 230, a.
Aio Vlasi, ii. 542, b.
Aiquières, ii. 1238, b.
Aire, ii. 1308, a.
Airuruk, ii. 11, b.
Aisme, 352, a.
Aisne, 352, b.
Aissumm, 169, b.
Aiteachtuath, 320, b.
Aithodor, Cape, ii. 1112, a.
Aix, 169, b.
Aju-dagh, ii. 1112, a.
Ak-Dagh, ii. 1124, a.
Ak-Ketjel, ii. 1155, a.
Ak-serai, 193, b.
Ak-su, 248, b; 471, a; 594, a.
Akaba, 49, a.
Akabah, Gulf of, 174, b.
Akabet et Kebira, 732, a.
Akburun, ii. 558, b. -
Akhaltskaï, 1004, a.
Akhmo, 804, b.
Akhissar, ii. 1194, a.
Akhmim, ii. 543, b.
Akjah Kalek, 672, b.
Akjah Tash, 651. a.
Akialt, 132, b.
Akibi, ii. 916, b.
Akir, 805, a.
Akka, 11, a.
Akkerkuf, 363, a.
Akkerman, ii. 419, a.
Akra, 74, a.
Akrata, 13, b; 30, b.
Akridha, ii. 36, b; ii. 223, b.
Akroteri, 524, a; 789, a.
Akshehr, 147, a; ii. 600, b.
Aktash, ii. 505, a.
Akte, 477, b.
Aktiar, Roads of, ii. 1110, b.
Al Hathr, 219, a.
Al Hermar, 359, b; 363, a.
Al Hiera, 158, a.
Al Madam, 715, a.
Al Natroun, 733, b.
Alaba, 582, a.
Alabanda, 239, a, b; 520, a.
Alabus, ii. 986, a.
Alaçer do Sal, ii. 876, b.
Alacks, 86, a.
Alatcham, ii. 1336, a.
Ala-dagh, ii. 1336, a.
Aladan, ii. 933, a.
Aladja, 926, a.
Alaesa, ii. 986, b.
Alagon, 581, b.
Alagonia, ii. 112, b.
Alajor, ii. 903, a.
Alakananda, 973, a.
Alakhai, ii. 236, b.
Alalis, ii. 1076, b.
Alamassus, 2, a.
Alamatha, ii. 1076, b.
Alambater, ii. 549, b.
Alameda, 249, a.
Alange, ii. 219, b.
Alani Scythae, ii. 943, b.
Alanorsi, ii. 943, b.
Alanquer, 183, b; ii. 220, a.
Alara, ii. 678, a.
Alaro, ii. 873, b.
Alasan, 86, a.

Alatri, 85, b.
Alava, 346, b; ii. 1256, b.
Alauni, ii. 916, b.
Alaya, 617, b; 667, b; ii. 1084, a.
Alba, 87, a; 89, a; ii. 188, a; ii. 1316, b.
Alba Docilia, ii. 188, b.
Alba Fucensis, 55, a.
Alba Fucentia, ii. 1306, b.
Alba Pompeia, ii. 188, a.
Albana, 89, b.
Albania, ii. 36, a.
Albano, 90, a; ii. 1291, b.
Albanopolis, ii. 37, b.
Albanum, ii. 1291, b.
Albanus, 69, b.
Albanus, Mons, 83, b.
Albaragena, 28, b.
Albarracin, 666, a; ii. 198, b.
Albaroches, ii. 1326, a.
Albegna, 93, a; 857, a; ii. 1296, a.
Al-Beisha, ii. 284, b.
Albenga, 93, a; 110 a; ii. 53, b; ii. 188, a.
Albingaunum, ii. 188, b.
Albinia, 857, a.
Albiniam Fl., Ad, ii. 1296, a.
Albintemellium, ii. 188, b.
Albintimilio, 110, a.
Albion, 432, a.
Albiosc, 92, b.
Albissola, 86, a; ii. 188, b.
Albium, ii. 53, b.
Albium, Ingaunum, ii. 188, a.
Albium Intemelium, ii. 188.
Albona, ii. 74, a.
Albonica, 582, a.
Albor, ii. 661, a.
Al Bostan, 650, b.
Albrus, 748, a.
Ablias, ii. 1082, b.
Albula, ii. 1199, a.
Albulates, 93, b.
Altum, Prom., ii. 606, a.
Alburnus, Mons, 156, a.
Albus Portus, ii. 1075, b.
Alcançer do Sal, ii. 220, a.
Alcala, 525, b.
Alcala de Guadaira, ii. 493, a.
Alcala de Henares, 632, a.
Alcanadre, ii. 579, b.
Alcaniz, 807, b.
Alcantara, 61, a; ii. 445, b.
Alcaroches, 582, a.
Alcaudete, ii. 376, b
Alce, 525, a.
Alces, 480, a.
Alchatria, ii. 1042, b.
Al-Chasrin, ii. 283, b.
Alcolea, 228, a.
Alcomenus, 83, a.
Alconetar, ii. 1240, a.
Alcorrucen, ii. 871, b.
Alcoy, ii. 872, b.
Alcudia, 374, b.
Alcunnete, Puente de, ii. 1240, a.
Aldborough, ii. 74, b.
Aldea el Muro, 34), a.
Alderney, 949, b; ii. 717, b.
Aldrington, 442, a.
Alea, 192, b.
Alenume, 86, a.
Alecippe, ii. 108, a.
Alegrana, ii. 149, a.
Alegranza, 906, b; ii. 678, b.
Alegria, ii. 1238, b.
Aleksam, ii. 491, a.
Alento, ii. 210, a.
Aleria, 691, b.
Alesiaeum, 821, a.
Alessa, 812, b.
Alessandreia, Capo de, 481, b.
Aleta, ii. 987, a.
Aletium, 474, b.
Aletrium, 1073, b.
Alexandreia, 365, a; 521, a; ii. 552, a; ii. 1075, a.
Alexandreia Ultima, 102, b.
Alexandreum, 102, a.
Alexandri, Nymphaeum Divi (Rome), ii. 827, a.

Alexandrina, Aqua (Rome), ii. 851, a.
Alexandrinae, Thermae (Rome), ii. 847, a; ii. 838, a; ii. 839, b.
Alexandropolis, 102, a.
Alexandroschene, 94, a.
Alexsnitza, ii. 592, b.
Alfacks, ii. 1126, a.
Alfaques, Puerto de los, ii. 8, b.
Alfarache, S. Juan de, ii. 500, b.
Alfaterni, 55, a.
Alfeo, 130, a.
Alfidena, 337, a.
Alford, 427, a.
Algarte, ii. 220, a.
Algeria, ii. 296, b; ii. 453, b.
Algier, 68, b; ii. 12, b.
Alhama, 168 b; 228, a.
Alhama Sierra de, ii. 33, a.
Al Haratch, ii. 296, a.
Al-Hathr, ii. 486, b.
Alhowareah, 170, b.
Ali, ii. 1184, a.
Ali Tagh, ii. 440, a.
Alia, 525, b.
Alia, 529, b.
Alicata, 79, b; 805, a; ii. 601, a.
Alicante, 21, b; ii. 211, b.
Alice, 450, a; 1025, b.
Alice, Capo dell', 857, a; 706, a.
Alichurg, 212, b.
Alicudi, 51, b.
Aliedha, ii. 474, b.
Alifaka, ii. 888, b.
Alife, 105, a.
Aliga, Torre del, ii. 1219, b.
Aligora, ii. 1020, a.
Aliki, 886, a.
Aliphera, 192, a.
Alisc, 95, a.
Alizeda, ii. 1022, b.
Alishona, 871, a.
Alishtar, ii. 440, a.
Alista, 691, b.
Allium, 821, a.
Aliveri, 871, b; ii. 1087, a.
Al-Kairwan, 72, a.
Al-Karn, ii. 350, b.
Alksay, 89, b.
Allahabad, ii. 60, b; ii. 351, a.
Allahsher, ii. 597, b.
Allante, 193, a.
Allaria, 705, b.
Allier, 341, a.
Allifae, ii. 896, b.
Allobon, 581, b.
Alloeira, 321, a.
Allones, 933, b; ii. 1312, b.
Allotriges, 502, a.
Alma, 857, a.
Alme, 857, a; ii. 1110, a.
Almadagh, ii. 468, a.
Almaden, ii. 319, b; ii. 1014,b.
Almakarana, ii. 857, b.
Alme, 821, b.
Almeida, ii. 56, b; ii. 1285, b.
Almeria, 22, b; ii. 1326, b.
Almissa, ii. 483, a.
Almopia, 624, a.
Almunia, 581, b; ii. 420, a.
Alon, 810, b.
Alonae, 655, b.
Aloni, 1028, b.
Alonistena, 1088, b.
Alontas, 571, b.
Alope, ii. 202, b.
Alopece, 327, b.
Alopeconnesus, ii. 1190, a.
Alpruli, or Alpuli, ii. 1327, a.
Alora, ii. 39, b.
Alos, 17, a.
Aloeygna, ii. 47, a.
Alpe Pennino, in, ii. 188, b.
Alpe Summa, 110, a; ii. 188, b.
Alpenus, ii. 202, b.
Alpes Carnicae, 108, a.
Alpes Cottiae, 107, a.
Alpes Dalmaticae, 108, a.
Alpes Graiae, 107, b.
Alpes Juliae, 108, b.
Alpes Maritimi, 107, a.

Alpes Noricae, 108, a.
Alpes Pannonicae, 108. b.
Alpes Penninae or Poeninae, 108, a.
Alpes Rhaeticae, 108, a.
Alpes Venetae, 108, b.
Alps or Aps, 87, b.
Alpujarras, ii. 33, a.
Alsa, ii. 1275, a.
Alberto Lago d', 877, a.
Al-Sibkah, 68. a.
Alsietinus, Lacus, 866, b; 887, a.
Alsium, 670, b; ii. 1296, a.
Alsodux, ii. 1326, b.
Alt, 744, b.
Alta Semita (Rome), ii. 831, b.
Altai, 347, a; 826, b; ii. 69, b.
Altai range. ii. 1094, a.
Altamura, 167, b.
Altano, Capo, ii. 911, a.
Altbreusach, ii. 369, b.
Alt Buda, 20, b.
Alter da Chao, ii. 290, a.
Altilia, ii. 672, a.
Altino, 112, b; ii. 1297, b. 1287, b.
Altinum, ii. 1275, a; ii. 1287, b.
Alt-Salankemen, 20, b.
Alt-Stadt, 683, b.
Altum Tash, 655, b.
Altus, ii, 384, a.
Aluntium, ii. 966, b.
Alutas, 744, b.
Aluena, 817, b; 1103, b.
Almgmamo, 652, b.
Alvona, ii. 74, a.
Aluta, 744, b.
Aluta, 187, b.
Alvum, ii. 74, a.
Alyzia, 10, b.
Alura, ii. 872, b.
Amaci, 249, b.
Amadassa, 2, a.
Amadoci, ii. 917, a.
Amage, ii. 946, a.
Amalek, 178, a.
Amantini, ii. 542, a.
Amanus Mons, ii. 468, a.
Amaraea, ii. 468, b.
Amardocaea, 361, a.
Amardus, 320, a; 489, a.
Amaseno, 117, a.
Amasia, 444, b.
Amasra, 117, a.
Amasra or Amasserah, 118, a.
Amastris, ii. 547, a.
Amata, 119, a; 296, a.
Amathus, 729, b; 730, a.
Amathusia, 729, a.
Amazergh, 975. b.
Amazones, ii. 917, a.
Amazygh or Amazergi, 926, a.
Amba, ii. 593, a.
Ambar, 824, a.
Ambastae, ii. 48, a.
Ambastus, ii. 1002, b.
Ambriakia, ii. 878, a.
Ambelokipo, 327, b.
Ambibari, 218, b.
Ambitui, 931, a.
Ambleside, 773, b.
Amboglanna, ii. 1256, b.
Ambracus, 120, b.
Ambrose, St., 850, b.
Ambrysus, ii. 605, a.
Ambucote, ii. 922, a.
Ameland, 346, a.
Amelia, 121, b; ii. 1288, a.
Amenanus, ii. 986, a.
Amergo, ii. 1214, b.
Ameria, 462, b; ii. 1288, a; ii. 1317, a.
Amerinum, Castellum, ii. 1288, a.
Amestratus, ii. 987, a.
Amid or Amadiah, ii. 1206, a.
Ameira, ii. 219, b.
Amicus, 119, a; ii. 868, b.
Amilias, 193, a.
Aminachae, ii. 47, a.
Amisus, 476, a, b.
Amiternum, ii. 1283, b.

Ammas, ii. 597, b.
Ammaus, ii. 682, a.
Ammedera, ii. 455, a.
Ammon, ii. 1076, b.
Ammone, Il Vasto d', 915, b; 1089, b.
Ammons, 427, b.
Ammonium, 40, a; ii. 457, b.
Ammous, 248, a; 824, b.
Amnias, ii. 547, a.
Amnisus, 705, b; ii. 1129, b.
Amorgo, 124, a.
Amorium, 981, a.
Ampelos, 705, b.
Ampelusia, ii, 296, a.
Amphe, 866, a.
Ampheia, ii. 345, b.
Amphicaea, ii. 604, b.
Amphidoli, 821, a.
Amphimalla, 705, b.
Amphimatrium, 705, b.
Amphipagus, 669, b.
Amphipolis, 807, b; ii. 236, b; ii. 1190, a; ii. 1299, a.
Amphitheatre (Rome), ii. 836, a.
Amphitheatrum Castrense (Rome), ii. 837, b.
Amphitrope, 331, b.
Amphitus, ii. 342, a.
Ampighione, 826, a; ii. 1300, b.
Amposta, ii. 31, a.
Ampsaga, 68, a; ii. 297, b; ii. 454, a, b.
Ampurias, 825, b.
Ampurias, Gulf of, ii. 52, a.
Amram Ibn Ali, 359, b.
Amu Darja, 364, b.
Amutria, 744, b.
Amsous, 385, a; 824, b.
Amymone, 201, a.
Amvrus, ii. 1170, a.
Anabus, ii. 1, b.
Anace, 17, a.
Anactarium (Athens), 299, b.
Anactorium, 10, b.
Anadoli Dagh, ii. 480, a.
Anadoli Kawak, 424, b.
Anagni, 129, a.
Anagninum, Compitum, ii. 1302, b.
Anagombri, ii. 278, a.
Anagrana, ii. 283, a, b.
Anagyrus, 331, a.
Anah, 131, a.
Anamba, ii. 924, b.
Anamis, 521, a.
Anamo, ii. 237, a.
Anamour, ii. 395, b.
Anamour, Cape, 617, a.
Anamur, 136, b; ii. 640, b.
Anao Portus, ii. 424, a.
Anaphe, 130, a.
Anaphlystus, 331, a.
Anepli, Paleo, ii. 1212, a.
Anaplus, 424, a.
Anapo, 130, a; ii. 985, b.
Anapus, 9, a; 19, b; ii. 985, b.
Anarel, Scythae, ii. 943, b.
Anarto-phracti, ii. 916, a.
Anaselitza, 209, a, ii. 286, b; ii. 491, b.
Anasseh, 1050, b.
Anassus, ii. 1275, a.
Anatelbes, 1174, b; ii. 1156, b.
Anatolia Sta, ii. 197, a.
Anatoliko, 64, a; ii. 671, b.
Anawyso, 130, a; 331, a.
Anaway or Amnasy, 132, a.
Anaxium, 1030, a.
Ancaster, 488, b; 876, b.
Anchesmus, 285, a.
Anchialus, ii. 1190, a.
Anchitae, 363, b.
Ancinale, 450, b.
Ancona, ii. 1301, b.
Ancona, 133, a.
Ancome, ii. 449, a.
Ancrina, ii. 987, a.
Ancyra, 929, a.
Ancyraeum Prom., 424, b.
Andalusia, ii. 1105, b.
Andania, ii. 345, b.
Andania, 129, b; 321, a.
Andelle, ii. 718, b.

Andera, ii. 929, a.
Anderab, 368. a.
Andernach, 150, a; ii. 470, a.
Andethanna, ii. 494, b.
Andetrium, 748, a.
Andhamati, 973, b.
Andiantes, ii. 542, a.
Andilalo, ii. 475, a.
Andomatis, 973, b.
Andover, 135, a.
Andraki, 735, b.
Andraristus, ii. 561, b.
Andredeseage, 135, a.
Andredesweald, 135, a.
Andreotissa, ii. 630, a.
Andres de Zarracones, 168, b.
Andrew, St., 624, b; 727, a, b; ii. 668, a.
Andritsana, ii. 1155, b.
Andro, 136, a.
Andronicus Cyrrhestes, Horologium of (Athens), 290, a.
Andropolis, 39, b.
Andropolite Nome, 39, b.
Androssano, ii. 282, a.
Andujar, ii. 1260, b.
Andujar la Vieja, ii. 74, b.
Anduse, 136, a.
Anemoreia, ii. 605, a.
Anemosa, 192, b.
Anemurium, 617, a.
Aneritae, ii. 278, a.
Angeli, ii. 1337, a.
Angelo, Civita S., ii. 1283, a.
Angelo in Vado, S., ii. 1207, b.
Angelo, Monte S., 67, a; ii. 115, a.
Angelum, 137, a; 916, a.
Anger, 136, b.
Angers. 443, a; ii. 102, a.
Anghelokastro, 655, b; ii. 671, b.
Anghista, 136, b; 372, b.
Anghustri, ii. 571, a.
Angites. 372, b; ii. 1177, b.
Angitola, 450, a.
Angitula, 450, a.
Angkistri, Cape, ii. 515, a; ii. 688, b.
Anglesey, Isle of, ii. 308, b.
Angiona, Sta Maria d', ii. 539, b.
Angora, 133, b.
Angoulême, ii. 13, a.
Angulus, ii. 1263, a.
Angustia, 744, b.
Anhydrus, 322, b.
Ani, 486, a.
Anio Novus (Rome), ii. 840, b.
Anio Vetus (Rome), ii. 840, b.
Ankustri, C., ii. 515, a; ii. 688, b.
Annelanum, ii. 1287, b.
Annius Verus, House of (Rome), ii. 818, a.
Annum, 916, a.
Anoge, ii. 97, b.
Anonax, 123, b.
Anopolis, 185, a; 705, b.
Anse, 229, b.
Ansedonia, 695, b; ii. 572, b; ii. 1283, a; ii. 1296, a.
Antaeopolis, 40, a.
Antaeopolite Nome, 40, a.
Antakieh, 142, a.
Antandro, 138, b.
Antaradus, 560, b; ii. 606, a; ii. 1076, a.
Antas, ii. 912, a.
Antephelo, or Andifilo, 147, b.
Antequera, 148, a; ii. 1022, b.
Antequa, 347, a.
Anternacha, 150, a.
Anthana, 193, a.
Anthedon, 410, b.
Antheia, ii. 1191, b.
Anthena, 726, a.
Antibes, 110, a; 148, a; 787, b; ii. 507, b.
Antiboul, 148, a.
Anticirrha, ii. 203, a.
Anticites, 667, b; ii. 587, a.

Antigoneia, ii. 237, a; ii. 384, a.
Antino, Civita d', ii. 282, a.
Anti-Gozzo, ii. 484, b.
Antilibanus, ii. 1072, b.
Antimelos, ii. 648, b.
Antinopolis, 47, b.
Antinum, ii. 282, a.
Antiocheia, 560, b.
Antiochiana, 508, b; ii. 222, b.
Antioco, Isola di S., ii. 911, b.
Antioco, S., ii. 1045, b.
Antiparo, ii. 473, b.
Antipatria, 766, a.
Antipaxo, ii. 559, b.
Antipolis, 110, a; 787, b; ii. 507, b.
Antipyrgos, ii. 277, b.
Antirrhium, 13, a; 600, b.
Antissa, ii. 165, a.
Antonine Column (Rome), ii. 838, b.
Antonini, Columna (Rome), ii. 839, a.
Antonini, Templum (Rome), ii. 839, a.
Antoniniana, Aqua (Rome), ii. 841, a.
Antoninianae, Thermae (Rome), ii. 847, b.
Antoninopolis, 557, a.
Antoninus and Faustina, Temple of (Rome), ii. 795, b.
Antoninus, Pons (Rome), ii. 850, a.
Antonio river, St., ii. 1034, b.
Antonius, House of (Rome), ii. 804, b.
Antrain, 901, a.
Antrim, 754, b.
Antrodoco, 6, b; ii. 59, a; ii. 1306, a.
Antron, ii. 1170, a.
Antunnacum, ii. 460, a.
Anurafepura, ii. 1099, b.
Anurogrammon, ii. 1083, b.
Anuren, ii. 494, b.
Anxano, 916, a.
Anxantia, ii. 282, a.
Anxanum, 167, a; 916, a.
Anxia, ii. 1295, b.
Anxi. ii. 1296, b.
Aornus, 243, a; 365, a.
Aorsi, 572, b; ii. 916, b; ii. 943, b.
Aosta, 110, a; 339, a.
Aosta, Val d', ii. 880, a.
Aous, ii. 530, a.
Aoust-en-Dios, 340, b.
Aouste, 340, b.
Apamea, 239, a.
Apameia, ii. 1076, a.
Apameia Cibotus, 342, a.
Apameia Rhagiana, 611, b.
Apamene, ii. 1076, a.
Apamo Porta, 308, b.
Apano-Khrepa, ii. 243, b.
Apano-Khrepa, M., ii. 244, a.
Apanomi, 1002, a.
Ape Mountains, ii. 965, a.
Apennines, 188, b.
Aperantia, 67, a.
Apesas, ii. 416, b.
Aphaca, ii. 606, a.
Aphek, 157, a.
Aphetae, ii. 1170, b.
Aphrstis, 824, a.
Aphrces, ii. 468, a.
Aphrodisias, 239, b; 521, a.
Aphrodisium, 192, b; 797, a; ii. 455, a.
Aphrodite Pandemus, Temple of (Athens), 297, a; 301, a.
Aphrodite Urania, Sanctuary of (Athens), 298, b.
Aphroditopolis, 39, b.
Aphroditopolite Nome, 39, b; 40, a.
Apis, ii. 277, b.
Apiaus, ii. 511, b.
Apiotheca, Port, ii. 205, b.
Apiothica, 703, a.
Apocopa, M., ii. 46, b.
Apodoti, 63, a.
Apokorona, 1070, a.

Apoturo, Lake of, 64, a.
Apollinare (Rome), ii. 833, a.
Apollinares, Aquae, 870, b.
Apollinis, Area (Rome), ii. 805, a.
Apollinis, Templum (Rome), ii. 842, a.
Apollinopolis, 40, a.
Apollo and Pan, Cave of (Athens), 286, a.
Apollo Coelispex (Rome), 815, b.
Apollo Sandaliarius, Statue of (Rome), ii. 827. b.
Apollo, Statue of (Rome), ii. 770, a.
Apollo, Temple of (Rome), ii. 804, b; ii. 833, a.
Apollonia, 705, b; 733, b; ii. 236, b; ii. 987, a; ii. 1011, a; ii. 1190. a; ii. 1209, a.
Apollonias, 705, b.
Apolloniatis, 406, b; 822, b.
Apollonis, 239, b.
Apollonite Nome, 40, a.
Aposelemi, 124, a; ii. 1129, b.
Apostolia, 739, a; 785, a.
Appii Forum, ii. 1290, a.
Appia, Porta (Rome), ii. 760, b.
Appleby, 1, b.
Apri, ii. 1190, b.
Aprilem, Ad Lacum, ii. 1296, a.
Aprilis Lacus, 857, b.
Apros, ii. 1190, a.
Aprustum, 451, a.
Apsarus, ii. 658, b.
Apsidae, 643, a.
Apsinthii, ii. 1190, a.
Apsinthus, 50, b.
Apsorrus, 7, a.
Apt, 163, b.
Aptera, 705, b.
Apuani, ii. 187, a.
Apula, 744, b.
Aqua Alsietina (Rome), ii. 850, b.
Aqua Appia (Rome), ii. 850, a.
Aqua Marcia (Rome), ii. 850, b.
Aqua Tepula (Rome), ii. 850, b.
Aqua Virgo (Rome), ii. 850, b.
Aqua Viva, ii. 1301, a.
Aquae, ii. 188, b.
Aquae Bilbitanorum, 581, b.
Aquae Caeretanae, 168, a.
Aquae Calidae, 344, b; ii. 115, b.
Aquae Laevae, 934, a.
Aquae Lesitanae, ii. 912, a.
Aquae Nismeii, 427, a.
Aquae Originis, 934, a.
Aquae Passeris, ii. 1297, a.
Aquae Querquennae, 934, a.
Aquae Quintinae, 934, b.
Aquae Sextiae Colonia, ii. 887, a.
Aquae Solis, 442, a.
Aquae Statiellae, ii. 148, a.
Aquae Sulis, 387, b.
Aquae Tarbellicae, 389, b.
Aquae Voconiae, ii. 115, b.
Aquana, Civita, ii. 1283, b.
Aquensil, ii. 299, a.
Aquila, 350, b; ii. 1283, b.
Aquileia, ii. 1275, b.
Aquileia, 171, b.
Aquillius, Palace of C. (Rome), ii. 828, b.
Aquilon, 346, b.
Aquilonia, ii. 896, b; ii. 1293, a.
Aquincum, ii. 542, a.
Aquino, 172, a; ii. 1302, b.
Aquinum, ii. 1302, b.
Ar, 197, a.
Araayr, 220, b.
Arab Hissa, 81, b; 520, a.
Araba, ii. 952, b.
Arabah, ii. 555, a.
Araban, ii. 1135, b.
Arabat, ii. 692, b; ii. 1337, a.

Arabat-el-Matfoon, 8, a.
Arabat, Tongue of, ii. 1112, b.
Arabi Hissar, ii. 559, b.
Arabia, 174, a.
Arabian Sea, 175, b.
Arabicus Sinus, 174, b.
Arabisci, ii. 542, a.
Arabistan, 174, a.
Arabitae, 983, b.
Arachoeii, 211, a.
Arachoti, 210, b.
Arachona, ii. 236, b.
Aracnea, ii. 116, a.
Aracynthus, 63, a, b.
Aradillos, 185, a.
Araducta. 934, a.
Aradus, ii. 606, a.
Araegenus, 341, a.
Araf, 161, b.
Aragon, 581, a; 807, a.
Aragus or Arak, 187, a.
Arakhova, 555, a.
Arakli. 326, b.
Aral, Sea of, ii. 505, a.
Aram Naharaim, ii. 333, a.
Arandos, ii. 1230, b.
Arantos, 934, b.
Araphen, 332, a.
Ararat, 215, a.
Ararat, 7, a.
Ararene, ii. 283, b.
Araros. ii. 938, b.
Aras, 188, a.
Aratias. 25, a.
Aravelli, ii. 46, b.
Araviana, 347, a.
Arauni, or Arandis, ii. 220, a.
Arauris, ii. 178, a.
Arausio, 577, a.
Araxa, 517, b.
Araxes, 175, a.
Araxus, 13, b.
Arbace, 197, b.
Arbe, 188, b; ii. 339, b
Arbil, 189, a.
Arbon, 1041, b.
Arbor Felix, 1041, b.
Arbor Sancta (Rome), ii. 818, b.
Arbora, C. del, ii. 662, a.
Arbucias, ii. 947, a.
Arca, ii. 1076, b.
Arcachon, Pointe d', 720, a.
Arcadia, 705, b.
Arce, 222, a.
Arcesine, 524, a.
Arceuthus, ii. 1075, a.
Archabis, ii. 658, b.
Archaeopolis, 643, a; ii. 376, a.
Archias, 424, a.
Archipelago, 31, a.
Arci, 720. a.
Arcidava, 744, b.
Arcinna, 744, b.
Arcis-sur-Aube, 210, a.
Arcobadara, 744, b.
Arcobriga, 581, b.
Arconii, 19, b.
Arcos, 193, b, 194, a.
Arcti Prom., ii. 911, b.
Arcus Argentarius (Rome), ii. 813, a.
Ard-al-Bathanych, ii.1219,a.
Arda, ii. 1178, a.
Ardanis Prom., ii. 277, b.
Ardea, 194, a.
Ard-el-Hulch. 750, a.
Arden, 196, a.
Arden, 705, b.
Ardennes, 196, a.
Ardham, ii. 587, a; ii. 696, a.
Ardhenitza, ii. 553, b.
Ardius, 748, a.
Ardon, 196, a.
Ardscherud, 225, a.
Ardschich, ii. 396, b.
Area Capitolina (Rome), ii. 768, a.
Arebrigium, 110, b.
Arechthea, 120, b.
Areiopagus (Athens), 281, b.
Arek, 186, a; ii. 471, a.
Arelate, ii. 448, a.
Arelatum Colonia, ii. 887, a.
Arena, 772, b.
Arenas Gordas, 197, a.

Arenio, 916, a.
Areschkui, ii. 997, b.
Arevacae, 581, b.
Arezzo, 222, b; ii. 1296, b.
Argaliki, M., 338, b; ii. 269, a.
Arganthonius, 406, a.
Argara, ii. 47, a.
Argaricus, S. ii. 46, b.
Argennum, ii. 387, a.
Argenomescus, 502, b.
Argenomescum, 502, b.
Argentanum, 451, a.
Argentarius, 367, b.
Argentaro Monte, 198, a.
Argenteus (river), ii. 507, b.
Argentia, ii. 1287, b.
Argentiera, 625, a.
Argentiere, 198, b.
Argentina, 451, a.
Argentiolum, 250, a.
Argentos, 198, b.
Argentoratum Civitas, ii. 1219, a.
Argenis, 198, b; ii. 507, b.
Arghasm, 184, b; 220, b.
Arghyrokastro, 209, b; 810, a.
Argiro, S. Filippo d', 80, b.
Argish, or Erjish Dagh, 198, a.
Argithea, 254, b.
Argob, 380, b
Argonautarum, Porticùs (Rome), ii. 837, a.
Argos, 566, a.
Argos, The Mills of, 201, a.
Argostoli, 699, b.
Argous, Portus, ii. 40, a.
Argum, 593, a.
Argura, ii. 1170, a.
Argusto, 162, b.
Argyle, 750, a.
Argyleshire, 593, a; 842, b.
Argyra, 17, a.
Argyronium Prom., 424, b.
Ariaca, ii. 47, a, 49, b.
Ariacae, ii. 943, b.
Arichi, ii. 917, b.
Aricia, ii. 1290, a.
Arienzo, ii. 1292, b.
Arigaeum, 241, b.
Arii, 210, b.
Arimara, ii. 1075, b.
Ariminum, ii. 1317, b.
Arjish, 224, b.
Arjona, ii. 1326, b.
Ariklar, 392, b.
Aripo, ii. 1091, b.
Aris, ii. 1191, b.
Ariseria, ii. 1075 b.
Aritium Praetorium, ii. 220, a.
Arivates, ii. 542, a.
Ariusia, 609, b.
Arizanti, ii. 301, b.
Arixxo, 210, a.
Arkadia, 728, b.
Arkand, Ab, 184, b.
Arkassa, 524, a.
Arkava, 193, b.
Arkecko, 29, a; 347, b.
Arkhadhia, ii. 342, b.
Arlape, ii. 448, a.
Arles, 187, b; 196, b.
Armadoci, ii. 917, a.
Armene, ii. 547, b.
Armenium, ii. 1170, a.
Armenta, 857, a.
Armentarium (Rome), ii. 819, a.
Armi, Capo dell', ii. 171, a.
Armilustrum (Rome), ii. 810, a.
Armirum Fl., Ad, ii. 1296,a.
Armiro, 125, b.
Armyro, Polis S., ii. 644, b.
Arna, ii. 1317. a.
Arnaudkoi, 424, a.
Arne, 22, a.
Arnestum, 167, a.
Arnheim, 197, a.
Arnissa, 380, a.
Arno, 219, b.
Arnoba, or Arbona, 4, b.
Aroanius, 633, a; ii. 676, a.

Arochas, 450, b.
Aroche, 228. a.
Aromata, 57, b.
Aron, 772, b.
Aronches, ii. 968, a.
Arpa, 290, b.
Arpaja, 573, b; ii. 1293, a.
Arpa-Chai. 1031, a.
Arpa Su, 519, a.
Arpas, Kalessi, 1081, a.
Arpi, 167, a.
Arquata, ii. 174, a; ii. 1296, b.
Arrabo, ii. 541, b; ii. 542, a.
Arrabo, 222, b.
Arracas, ii. 1214, b.
Arragon, ii. 1, b.
Arragon, ii. 1105, a.
Arrabas, ii. 46, b.
Arras, 319, b; ii. 417, a.
Arretium, ii. 1296, b.
Arrhene, 229, b.
Arriaca, 593, a.
Arrotrehae, 296, a.
Arrouches, ii. 219, b.
Arsa, 224, b.
Arsacia, 247, b.
Arsama, ii 474, b.
Arschelia, 225, b.
Arsenaria, ii. 297, b.
Arsene, 216, b; 229, b.
Arsingam, or Arzendjan, 354, b.
Arsinoe, 67, a; 730, a.
Arsinoite Nome, 39, b.
Arsissa, 216, b; 224, b.
Arsuf, 162, a.
Arsus, ii. 1075, b.
Arta, 119, b; 184, b.
Arta, Gulf of, 121, a.
Artabri, 932, b.
Artabrorum, Portus, 430, a.
Artabrorum, Sinus, 933, b.
Artacana, 226, b.
Artager, 227, a.
Artaki, 226, b.
Artamis, 364, b.
Artegna, ii. 1275, b.
Artemia, ii. 1275, b.
Artemis Brauronia, Temple of (Athens), 281, a.
Artemis Munychia, Temple of (Athens), 307, b.
Artemisium, Mt., 201, b.
Artemus, 773, a.
Artiscus, ii. 1178, a.
Artois, 319, b.
Artzenheim, 198, a.
Arvarni, ii. 47, a.
Aruci, 583, a.
Arve, 229. a.
Arverni, 173, a; 341, a.
Arul, ii. 1076, a.
Arulis, ii. 1076, a.
Arulos, ii. 237, a.
Arun, ii. 1222, b.
Arunda, 582, a.
Arupium, ii. 2, b.
Arusini Campi, 291, a.
Arustis, ii. 1075, b.
Arutela, 744, b.
Arzan, ii. 297, b.
Arzar-Palanca, ii. 692, b.
Arucroum, ii. 1157, b.
Arxew, 224, a.
Arzila, ii. 298, a.
Ar-Zila, ii. 1238, b.
Asaac, 247, b.
Asabi, Cape of, 383, b.
Asaei, ii. 917, b.
Asaph, St., ii. 1258, a.
Asapheidama, ii. 1076, a.
Asaro, 243, b.
Asburg, 231, a.
Asca, ii. 284, b.
Ascatancae, ii. 943, b.
Ascerris, ii. 1, b.
Aschelon, 17, a.
Asclepieium, or Temple of Asclepius (Athens), 301, a.
Ascoli, 231, b; ii. 628, b; ii. 1305, a.
Ascordus, ii. 237, a.
Ascra, 1035, a.
Ascrivium, 748, a.
Asculum, 167, a; ii. 628, b; ii. 1305, a.

Ascurus, ii. 656, b.
Asea, 192, b.
Asfersà, ii. 506, a.
Ashdod, 355, a.
Asher, Tribe of, ii. 530, a.
Ashira, 212, b.
Au Kur, ii. 439, b.
Asinara, Golfo dell', ii. 911, a.
Asinara, Isola dell', ii. 911, a.
Asinaria, Porta (Rome), ii. 760, b.
Asinarus, ii. 966, a.
Asine, 647, a; ii. 345, b.
Asmea, ii. 965, b.
Asloiae, ii. 943, b.
Asnar, ii. 412, b.
Askem, or Asyn Kalessi, ii. 5, a.
Askiti, ii. 1137, a.
Askuian, 230, a.
Asmani, ii. 943, b.
Asuniraea, ii. 968, b.
Avolo, 11, a; ii. 1273, b.
Asomato, ii. 1084, a.
Asopus, ii. 112, b; ii. 1218, b.
Aspa Luca, 389, b.
Aspacara, ii. 968, b.
Aspadana, 578, b.
Aspd Rud, 488, a.
Aspelia, 729, a.
Aspern, 559, a.
Asphaltites, Lake, ii. 522, a.
Aspiona, 364, b.
Aspis, ii. 1338, a.
Asplsii Scythae, ii. 943, b.
Aspithra, ii. 1002, b.
Aspro, 559, b.
Aspra Spitia, 140, a.
Aspromonte, 155, b.
Aspronisi, ii. 1158, a.
Aspropotamo, 18, b.
Assacen, or Aspasii, 1006, b.
Assam, ii. 1043, a.
Asseconia, 934, b.
Assenik, ii. 1642, b.
Assergio, ii. 669, a; ii. 1283, a.
Assisi, 240, b.
Assisium, ii. 1317, a.
Asso, 244, a; 588, b.
Assorcy, 934, b.
Assorus, ii. 364, a; ii. 966, b.
Assouan, ii. 1054, a.
Assus, 588, b.
Asta, ii. 188, a.
Astaboras, 57, b; ii. 711, a.
Astacus, 9, b; 10, b.
Astale, 705, b.
Astapus, ii. 295, a; ii. 429, b.
Astelephus, 643, a.
Astcrabad, 680, a.
Asterion 201, a.
Asterusia, 705, b.
Asti, 247, b; ii. 188, a.
Astibon, ii. 237, a.
Astica, ii. 1190, b.
Astingi, ii. 917, a.
Astorga, 170, a; 250, b.
Astrabe, 566, a.
Astrakhan, ii. 917, b.
Astro, 249, a.
Astropalaea, 250, b.
Astros, 727, a.
Asturias, 250, a; ii. 1105, a.
Asturica, 170, a.
Asturicani, ii. 917, b.
Asty (Athens), 259, b.
Astypalaea, 250, a; 695, a.
Asylum (Rome), ii. 770, b.
Asyn Kalesi, 379, b.
Atagis, 110, b.
Atalanta, 624, a.
Ataroth-Addar, ii. 530, a.
Atbara, ii. 711, a.
Atcca, 330, b.
Ateila, Sta Maria di, 253, b.
Atena, 311, a.
Atenak, 255, a.
Atera, ii. 1076, b.
Aterno, 254, a.
Aternum, ii. 1283, a.
Ateste, ii. 1275, a; ii. 1297, b.
Atfyeh, 156, a.
Athamanes, 65, a.
Athanagia, ii. 32, a.

Athena, 726, a.
Athenae Diades, 872, b.
Athenaeum, 192, b.
Athens, 255, a.
Athesis, ii. 1275, a.
Athkar, ii. 1126, a.
Athis, ii. 1076, a.
Athmonum, 326, b.
Athribis, 39, b.
Athribite Nome, 39, b.
Athrulla, ii. 283, b.
Athyrnia, ii. 386, b.
Athyto, 158, b.
Atiliana, 347, a.
Atilius, ii. 210, a.
Atina, 311, a; ii. 210, a.
Atlas, High, 317, b.
Atlas, Island of, 314, a.
Atlas, Lesser, 318, a.
Atlas, Major, 319, a.
Atlas, Middle, 316, a.
Atlas, Minor, 319, a.
Atlit, ii. 1053, b.
Atrax, ii. 1170, a.
Atrecht, 319, b.
Atrek, 1106, a; ii. 299, a; ii. 920, b.
Atrs, 26, b.; ii. 626, b; ii. 1307, a.
Atrcb, 310, a.
Atripaldi, 3, b.
Atta Vicus, 221, b.
Attacum, 582, a.
Attalia, 321, b.
Attanae, 181, b.
Attea, 52, a.
Attene Regio, 321, b.
Atteva, or Attoba, 60, b.
Attidium, ii. 1317, b.
Attigno, 536, a.
Attok, ii. 641, a.
Atur, ii. 1306, a.
Atures, 173, a.
Aturus, 170, a.
Atyras, ii. 1190, a.
Atzikolo, 1006, b.
Avampon, 349, a.
Avareni, ii. 915, b; ii. 916, a.
Avarmo, ii. 685, a.
Avart, 181, b.
Avaur, 352, b.
Aubarr, ii. 577, b.
Auch, 338, a; 344, a; 389, a.
Auchanitis, 361, a.
Aucus, ii. 2, b.
Aude, 253, a.
Audela, ii. 1076, a.
Audierne, 1004, a.
Audum, 336, b.
Audus, ii. 454, a.
Aveia, ii. 1283, a; ii. 1283, b.
Avetro, ii. 220, b.
Avella, 3, a.
Avella Vecchia, 3, a.
Avellino, 3, a.
Avenches, 850, b.
Avendone, ii. 3, b.
Avenio, 577, a.
Aventia, 857, a.
Aventine (Rome), ii. 810, a.
Auerua, ii. 1076, b.
Auerxperg, 276, a.
Avezron, ii. 860, a.
Auddena, 513, b; ii. 896, a.
Aufidi, Pons, ii. 1293, a.
Aufina, ii. 1283, b.
Augana, S. de, ii. 1299, b.
Augeiae, 32, b; ii. 202, b.
Augilae, ii. 278, a.
Augsburg, 340, b.
Augst, 339, b; 380, b.
Augusta, ii. 311, a; ii. 945, a.
Augusta, Bay of, ii. 1333, b.
Augusta Praetoria, 110. a.
Augusta Rauracorum, 380, b.
Augusta Taurinorum, ii. 188, a.
Augusta Vagiennorum, ii. 188, a; ii. 1253, b.
Augusti Fornix (Rome), ii. 794, b.
Augusti Portus, 870, b.
Augusti Solarium (Rome), ii. 817, b.
Augusti Templum (Rome), ii. 805, b.
Augustobriga, ii. 1285, b.

Augusto-phratensis, 652, a.
Augustus, Palace of (Rome), ii. 806, a.
Auguturi, 210, b.
Aujcink, 337, b.
Avigliano, ii. 1288, a.
Avignon, 350, b; 577, a.
Avila, ii. 459, b.
Avjliak. 338, a.
Aulad Naim, ii. 676, b.
Aulad Sliman, ii. 676, b.
Aulan Tagh, 383, a.
Auidby, ii. 560, b; ii. 667, a.
Aulon, 193, a; 331, b; 705, b; ii. 521, b.
Aulon, 342, b.
Aunis, ii. 903, b.
Avoca, ii. 16, a.
Avola, b, a.
Avola, Fiume di, ii. 966, a.
Avon, 337, b.
Aups, 57, b.
Avranches, 7, a.
Avranchin, 7, a.
Auray, 1057, a.
Aurea Domus (Rome), ii. 806, a.
Aureae Chersonesi, Prom., ii. 46, b.
Aurelle, ii. 1238, b.
Aurelia, Porta (Rome), ii. 758, b; ii. 761, a.
Aurelii, Forum, ii. 1296, a.
Aurelium, Tribunal (Rome), ii. 788, a.
Aurelius, Pons (Rome), ii. 850, a.
Aurelius, Arch of M., (Rome), ii. 840, a.
Aureoli, Pons, ii. 1287, b.
Aureus, Mons, 691, a.
Auribeau, 1091, a.
Aurigny, ii. 717, b.
Avro-Kastro, 242, b.
Ausa, 344, b.
Ausa, 111, b; ii. 1275, a.
Ausancalio, ii. 3, b.
Auschisae, ii. 278, a.
Ausci, 173, a.
Auser, 857, a.
Ausera, ii. 373, a.
Ausirus, ii. 447, a; ii. 541, a.
Ausurii, 344, b.
Autern, ii. 16, a.
Autolula, 346, b.
Automala, ii. 277, a.
Autrito, 34', b.
Autun, 400, b.
Auvergne, 226, b.
Avus, 933, a.
Auwaich, ii. 606, b.
Auxacia, ii 943, b.
Auxacitis, ii. 943, b.
Auxrrre, 346, b; 416, a.
Auximum, ii. 698, b; ii. 1301, b.
Awerie, ii. 593, a.
Axenus, 18, b.
Axius, ii. 213, a; ii. 1173, a.
Axum, 347, b.
Axus, 705, b.
Arus, 353, b.
Axylis, 783, b.
Ayamonte, 854, b.
Ayan, ii. 474, b; ii. 681, b.
Ayas Kala, 31, a.
Ayasaluk, 837, b.
Ayash, ii. 946, a.
Argaulic, 839, a.
Aygux-Sec, 169, b.
Ayodhiya, ii. 50, a.
Azab, ii. 863, b.
Azak-deniz-i, ii. 244, b.
Azali, ii. 542, a.
Azani, 463, b.
Axelburg, ii. 969, b.
Azenia, 331, a.
Azerbaijan, 320, a.
Asetium, 167, a.
Azila, ii. 1338, b.
Azilaref, 354, a.
Aziz, 23, b.
Azizis, 744, b.
Azmon, ii. 529, b
Azorus, ii. 1170, a
Azotus, 17, a.
Azov, Sea of, ii. 244, b.

Azwaga, 224, a.
Azurnis, 987, a.
Azzah, 961, b.
Azzila, ii. 1338, b.

Baalbec, 896, b; 1034, b; ii. 1076, b.
Baara, 355, a.
Baba, ii. 153, a.
Baba, Cape, 1030, a; ii. 662, a.
Baba Dagh, 463, b.
Baba Kelam, 355, b.
Babel, 355, b.
Babel, 460, b.
Bab-el-Mandeb, C., 175, b.
Bab-el-Mandeb, G. of, 175, b.
Bab-el-Mandeb, Straits of, ii. 534, b.
Bab-el-Melook, ii. 1142, a.
Baboul, 360, a.
Babras, 355, b.
Babul, ii. 299, a.
Babyla, 752, a.
Bacasia, ii. 1, b.
Babytace, 366, b.
Bacatae, ii. 278, a.
Baccanae, ii. 1286, a; ii. 1296, b.
Baccanas, 172, a.
Baccano, 122, a; 363, b; 856, b; ii. 1296, b.
Bacchyliones, ii. 1214, b; ii. 1275, a.
Bacolo, 364, a.
Bactaialle, ii. 1076, a.
Busuatas, ii. 840, a.
Bacuoro, 169, a.
Bada, ii. 237, a.
Badaca, 343, b.
Badajoz, 367, a.
Badakkshen, 364, a; ii. 1257, a.
Badara, 330, a.
Badavero, 542, a.
Badclona, 368, b. ii. 115, b.
Baden-Baden, 168, a.
Badesas, S. Juan de las, 561, a.
Badiza, 451, a.
Baebiana, ii. 1296, a.
Baecolicus, M., 734, a.
Baecula, 344, b.
Baedyes, 933, a.
Baena, ii. 1075, b.
Baena, ii. 376, b.
Baetana, 210, a; ii. 47, a.
Baeterrae, ii. 1290, a.
Baetis, 368, a.
Baetulo, ii. 115, b.
Baeturia, 563, a.
Baena, 384, b.
Baffa, ii. 548, a.
Baffi, Lake of, 1049, b; ii. 144, a.
Baffo, Bay of, ii. 1337, b.
Bafio, ii. 564, b.
Bagacum, ii. 420, a.
Bagaria, Fiume di, ii. 966, a.
Bages, ii. 1, bx
Baghdad, ii. 302, b.
Baghras, ii. 515, a.
Bagienna, 340, b.
Bagienni, ii. 1253, b.
Bagitenni, ii. 1253, b.
Bagna, ii. 1021, b.
Bagnara, 451, b.
Bagneau, ii. 1037, a.
Bagnères-de-Bigorre, 168, b.
Bagni d'Abano, 162, b.
Bagni di Ferrata, 170, a.
Bagni di Grotta, 169, a.
Bagni del Sasso, 169, a.
Bagni di Serpa, ii. 1297, a.
Bagni di Stigliano, 168, a.
Bagno, Civita di, ii. 1283, a.
Bagrada, 591, a; ii. 578, b.
Bagradas, 58, a; 316, a; 570, b.
Bagras, ii. 106, b; ii. 1075, b.
Bahbeyt, 459, a; ii. 67, b.
Bahiouda, ii. 330, a.
Bahr-el-Abiad, ii. 429, b.
Bahr-el-Azrek, 644, b; ii. 295, a; ii. 429, b.

Bahr-el-Huleh, ii. 519, b; ii. 887, b.
Bahr-el-Tabarich, ii.1197, b.
Bahram, 321, b.
Bakrein, 1032, b.
Bakrein, Gulf of, 321, b; 919, a.
Baya, 371, b.
Baiocasses, 218, b.
Bajore, 384, a.
Baue, ii. 1258, a.
Baitna, ii. 117, a.
Balisida, 189, b.
Baux, 383, a.
Bakhir or Bakri, ii. 395, a.
Bakhtegan, 737, b.
Bakhtiars, 097, a.
Bakhtyars, M., ii. 549, a.
Bakir, 471, a.
Bakou, 90, a.
Bakoua, ii. 550, b.
Balaguer, ii. 32, a; ii. 473, a.
Balaklava, ii. 515, b; ii. 1055, a; ii. 1110, a.
Balamont. 162, a.
Balamut, 655, a.
Balaneae, ii. 1075, a, b.
Balarus, Portus, 401, b.
Balatonli, 691, b.
Balbi, Crypta (Rome), ii. 834, b.
Balbi, Theatrum (Rome), ii. 834, a.
Balbura, 462, a.
Balbus, Theatre of (Rome), ii. 845, a.
Baldenau, ii. 1082, a.
Bâle, ii. 695, a.
Baleao, 375, a.
Baletium, 474, b; ii. 1294, a.
Balikesri, 469, b; ii. 356, a; ii. 1105, b.
Balkan, 1025, a.
Balkh, 264, a.
Balkri, 740, a.
Ballashan Pomt, ii. 65, a.
Balluercanes, ii. 947, b.
Balomum, 983, b.
Balaa, ii. 220, a.
Balsio, 681, b.
Baltaliman, 424, a.
Baltia, i, b; 380, b.
Baltic, 375, b; 641, b; ii. 920, a.
Baltic Sea, ii. 1045, b.
Baltistan, ii. 41, b.
Baluchistan, 184, a.
Balyra, ii. 341, b; ii. 342, a.
Bamberg, ii. 287, a.
Bambola, 402, b.
Bamburg, 384, b.
Bamian, ii. 552, a.
Ban, 199, b.
Banados, ii. 541, a.
Bancs, 383, a.
Bandel d' Agoa, 159, a.
Bañeza, ii. 1254, b.
Bangalore, 210, a; 1070, a.
Bangor, 427, a.
Bangpa-Kung, ii. 1002, b.
Bani Teude, 355, b.
Bantas, 372, b; ii. 519, b; ii. 540, a; ii. 1075, b.
Banitza, 200, b.
Bantubae, ii. 299, a.
Banuri, ii. 298, b.
Bannos, 579, b.
Bannos de Bande, 934, a.
Bannos de Bande or Orense, 168, b.
Bañolas, 344, b.
Baños de Molgas, 934, a.
Baños, ii. 1285, b.
Banostor, 419, b.
Banoub, ii. 483, b.
Bantia, 167, a; ii. 210, a.
Bantry Bay River, ii. 16, b.
Banturarii, ii. 299, a.
Banxi, ii. 210, a.
Banxi, Sta Maria di, 376, b.
Baptans, 369, b; 488, a.
Baptana or Batana, 369, b.
Baraces, ii. 1093, b
Barada, ii. 1072, b; ii. 1076, b.
Barameda, St. Lucar de, ii. 1107, a.

Barbara, Cape of St.. ii. 878, a.
Barbargis, ii, 91?, b.
Barbariana, 347, a.
Barbaricini, ii. 912, b.
Barbarissus, ii. 1076, a.
Borbaro, Monte, 980, a.
Barbate, 388, b.
Barbentane, 388, b.
Barbesula, 377, a.
Rarbitza, 88?, a.
Barca, 378, a.
Barcelona, 378, b.
Barcino, ii. 115, b.
Bardarium, 3?2, b.
Bardengau, ii. 119, b.
Barderate, ii. 188, a.
Bardewik, ii. 119, b.
Bardiah, Port, ii. 384, b.
Bardilui, 368, b.
Bardjoua, ii. 1212, b.
Bardscy, 808, a.
Bardulum, 167, a.
Hardyali, 502, a.
Bardyetae, 502, a.
Barege, ii. 687, b.
Bareka, ii. 634, a.
Bargeny, ii. 699, a.
Bargus, ii. 1190, a.
Bargyleticus, Sinus, 519, b.
Bari, 379, b; ii. 1294, a.
Bariano, ii. 1287, b.
Barin, ii. 550, b.
Barium, 167, a; ii. 1294, a.
Barkah, Desert of, ii. 277, a.
Barkal, 58, b.
Barletta, 167, a.
Barna, 366, b.
Baroach, 366, a.
Barpana, 857, b.
Barrameda, S. Lucar de, ii. 473, a.
Barre, 799, a.
Barrow, ii. 16, a.
Barsita, 420, b.
Bartan-Su, or Barthne, ii. 553, b.
Bartolomeo, Plume di S., 706, b; ii 986, a.
Barygaza, 366, a; ii. 47, a; ii. 49, b; ii. 255, a; ii. 1048, a.
Barygazenua, S., ii. 46, b; ii. 484, a.
Bas-Assiz, ii. 678, a.
Basanarne, ii. 47, a.
Basel or Bâle, 380, b.
Baselice, ii. 376, b.
Bashan-havoth-Jair, 380, b.
Bashkele, 248, a.
Bassege, 366, b.
Basiento, 565, b; ii. 209, b.
Basilia, i, b.
Basilica (Rome), ii. 787, b.
Basilicata, ii. 206, b.
Basilis, 192, b.
Basiluzzo, 51, b.
Basir, ii. 1090, b.
Bassum, 57, b.
Basle, ii. 718, b.
Raslyan, ii. 920, b.
Basques, ii. 1259, b.
Basrah, 904, b.
Bassachitae, ii. 278, a.
Bassae, ii. 596, b.
Bassano, Laghetto, or Lago di, 857, b; ii. 1253, a.
Rassen, ii. 47, a; ii. 1002, a.
Bassin d' Arcachon, 416, b.
Basta, 474, b.
Basternae, ii. 917, a.
Bastide, Vieille, La, ii. 13, a.
Batae, 427, b.
Batanea, ii. 532, a; ii. 1076, b.
Batanael, 181, a.
Batenburg, 382, b.
Bath, 169, b; 887, b; 442, a.
Bathos, 192, b.
Bathy, ii. 98, a.
Bathynias, ii. 1190, a.
Bathyrsus, 382, b.
Bathys, ii. 658, b; ii. 1246, a.
Batl, ii. 47, a.
Batia or Vatia, 6, b.
Batiae, 833, a.

Batmow-Su, ii. 1208, b.
Batnae, 737, a.
Batnek, 399, b.
Batn-el-Baharah, 591, b.
Batnis, 383, a.
Baio, 450, a.
Batrus, 425, b.
Batta, ii. 215, a.
Batulum, ii. 897, a.
Batum Flumen, 450, a.
Bavai, ii. 420, a.
Bavaria, ii. 447, a.
Bavay, 852, b; 368, b.
Bavlus, ii. 1278, b.
Baumes-les-Nones, ii. 205, a.
Bauota, 474, b.
Bauron, 773, b.
Bautzheim, ii. 1084, a.
Bayax, 372, b.
Bayeus, 341, a; 372, b; ii. 173, a.
Bayjah, ii. 1252, a.
Baylen, 367, a.
Bayona, 525, a; 934, b; ii. 1213, b; ii. 1308, a.
Bayonne, 949, a; ii. 125, a.
Bazas, 697, a.
Bazilbak, ii. 988, a.
Bram-Castle, 376, a.
Béarn, 390, a.
Beaucaire, ii. 1296, a.
Beaune, ii. 1269, b.
Bcauvais, 341, a; 470, b.
Bebek, 424, a.
Beblius, 748, a.
Bec de Sormion, ii. 1336, a.
Beceril, 250, a; ii. 1310, a.
Becerra, 402, a.
Bechires, ii. 658, b.
Bectileth, 863, b.
Bedaium, ii. 448, a.
Beder, 210, a.
Bedesia, ii. 1317, b.
Bedoun, Cape, 159, a.
Bedoya, S. Maria de, ii. 280, a.
Beds, 571, a.
Bedschajah, ii. 484, a.
Bedunia, 250, b.
Bedunenses, 249, b.
Bretz. 395, b.
Beg Basar, ii. 116, b.
Begacum, 852, b.
Beger de la Miel, ii. 330, a.
Beghe, ii. 598, b.
Beglos, 424, b.
Behistun, 369, b.
Behut, 1100, b.
Bei Skeher, ii. 65, b.
Beila, ii. 220, a; ii. 559, b.
Beiud, 400, a.
Beyer de la Frontera, 395, b.
Reilan, 113, b; ii. 1080, a.
Beilo, ii. 32, a.
Beira, S. Vincent de, ii. 1291, a.
Beiram-Dere, ii. 514, b.
Beirut, 894, b.
Beishe, ii. 284, b.
Beit-el-Maa, 752, a.
Beit-el-Moie, 752, a.
Beit-Jebrin, 397, b; 978, b; ii. 273, b.
Beit-Ilfah, 399, b.
Beitin, 396, b.
Beitir, 396, a.
Beitlahem, 397, a.
Beit-Nettif, ii. 422, a.
Beit-Safa, ii. 363, b.
Beit-'ur-et-Tahta, and el-Fokn, 398, a.
Beknesch, ii. 508, a.
Belad-el-Arab, 174, a.
Belbey, ii. 559a, .
Helbina, 331, a.
Belchite, 807, b.
Beled-el-Jerid, 316, b.
Belerion, 963, b.
Belgeda, 582, a.
Belgites, ii. 542, a.
Belgrade, ii. 1006, b.
Beli Kessr, ii. 355, a.
Belia, 807, b.
Belias, 375, a.

Belici, 706, b; 1106, b; ii. 89, b; ii. 988, b.
Belisdak, 401, b.
Belikas, 326, a.
Belikke, 375, a.
Bétin, 386, a.
Bellegarde, ii. 656, b.
Belle-Ile, ii. 1275, b; ii. 1311, a.
Bellentre, 392, b.
Belli, 581, b.
Bellona, Aedes (Rome), ii. 823, a.
Belluono, 389, a.
Belmont, ii. 1230, b.
Belonia, 388, b.
Belsinum, 582, a.
Belsinum, ii. 1275, b.
Belus, ii. 607, a.
Bembe, ii. 573, b.
Bembibre, 250, a.
Bembina, ii. 417, a.
Ben Ghasi, 1063, a.
Benarnum, 390, a.
Benavente, 250, b; ii. 220, a.
Benbodagh, ii. 1012, b.
Benda, 210, a.
Bender-begh, 371, b.
Bender-rik, ii. 716, a.
Bene, 705, b.
Bene, ii. 1258, b.
Bene, 340, b; ii. 188, a.
Benearnum, ii. 32, a; ii. 687, b.
Benedetto, S. ii. 279, b.
Beneficence, Temple of (Rome), ii. 770, a.
Benefutti Bagni di, ii.1196, a.
Benevente, 214, b.
Benevento, 390, a.
Benezzone, Civitella di, ii. 1781, b; ii. 1317, a.
Bengal, Bay of, ii. 46, b; ii. 52, a.
Rengasi, ii. 131, a.
Bengerwad, ii. 600, a.
Benghazi, 733, b.
Beni, ii. 1190, a.
Beni-hassam, ii. 1031, b.
Beni-Kahtam, 363, b; 566, a; 698, a.
Beni Khaled, 601, b.
Beni-Omran, 376, b.
Beni-Shammar, 363, b.
Benizert, 1070, a; ii. 1014, b.
Henjamin, tribe of, ii. 530, a.
Benlauni, ii. 1310, b.
Bennica, ii. 1190, b.
Benwell Hill, 654, b.
Benwell, ii. 1256, b.
Bepyrrhus Mons, ii. 10, a; ii. 46, b; ii. 243, a.
Berbera, ii. 254, a.
Berbers, 925, a.
Berchem or Berghen, ii. 102, a.
Bercouats, 391, b.
Berda, Nova, ii. 1307, b.
Beregra, ii. 626, b.
Berek Marsah, ii. 549, b.
Bereki, 1103, a.
Berenice, 346, a.
Berga, 392, b; ii. 1278, b.
Bergamah, ii. 576, a.
Bergamo, 393, a; ii. 1287, b.
Bergamum, ii. 1287, b.
Bergau, ii. 575, a.
Bergax, ii. 575, a.
Berghem, ii. 1196, b.
Bergidum, 250, a; ii. 32, a.
Bergion, ii. 420, a.
Bergium, ii. 287, a.
Bergma, 471, a; ii. 390, a.
Bergusia, ii. 32, a.
Bergzabern, ii. 1082, a.
Beriam Kalesi, 244, a.
Beris, ii. 658, b.
Berlinguas, ii. 204, a.
Bermerara, 1058, b.
Bermeo, ii. 1292, a.
Bernard, Little St., 107, b.
Bernard, St., ii. 1308, b.
Bernardino, S., 28, b.
Berncastel, ii. 1062, a.
Bernedo, ii. 1266, b.
Bernet, 389, a.

Beroach, 742, b; ll. 47, a; ll. 49, b; ll. 1048, a.
Beroea, 634, a; 737, a; ll. 237, a; ll. 1190, a.
Berreo, 934, b; ll. 1230, b.
Berrhoea, ll. 1075, b.
Berrus, ll. 31, b.
Bersical, ll. 32, a.
Bersovia, 744, b.
Bertinoro, 911, b.
Bertrand de Cominge, or Comminges, S., 389, a; 666, a.
Bertzentze, ll. 157, b.
Berua, 394, b.
Berwick, ll. 504, b.
Berwickshire, 750, a; 923, a.
Berytus, ll. 606, a.
Besa, 331, b.
Besançon, ll. 1281, b.
Besares or Bezares, 367, b.
Beschiktasche or Cradle Stone, 423, b.
Beseda, 561, a.
Besh-Shekr, ll. 575, a.
Besidiae, 451, a.
Besikia, 418, a; ll. 384, a.
Besos, 368, b; ll. 113, b.
Bessapara, 395, b.
Bessi, ll. 1190, a.
Bessica, ll. 1190, b.
Besynga, ll. 46, b.
Betamxos, 430, a.
Beth-Amar, 355, a.
Besh-Arbel, 189, a.
Beth-hogia, ll. 529, b.
Beth-horon, ll. 530, a.
Beth-Leboath, 397, a.
Beth Takkara, 363, a.
Bethamania, ll. 1075, b.
Bethleptaphene, ll. 532, b.
Beth-sa-lisa, 355, a.
Bethshean, ll. 530, b.
Bethshemesh. ll. 529, b.
Bettigi, ll. 48, a.
Bettigo, 427, b; ll. 675, b.
Bettigo, M. ll. 1082, a.
Bettona, ll. 1285, b; ll. 1288, b.
Betuwe, 382, a.
Bevagna, ll. 352, b; ll. 1301, a.
Beverley, ll. 550, b; ll. 667, a.
Beyadhye. 367, a.
Beylik, 1023, b.
Bezers, 367, a.
Bezira, 243, a.
Bhagirathi, 973, a.
Bhotan, 825, b.
Bhourda, ll. 641, a.
Bhulgar Dagh, 618, b.
Bianco, Cape, 669, b; 1049, a.
Bias, ll. 342, b.
Biball, 933, a.
Bibalorum Forum, 934, a.
Bibmo, 401, b.
Bibium, ll. 3, b.
Bibliotheca Graeca and La-tina (Rome), ll. 801, b.
Bibliothecae Graeca et La-tina (Rome), ll. 804, b.
Bibulus, Tomb of Caius (Rome), ll. 750, a.
Bidborg, 384, b.
Bidino, S. Gio. di, ll. 987, a.
Bidis, ll. 987, a.
Bidué, 401, b.
Bidué, St. 720, b.
Biecz, 402, a.
Bieda, 409, a; ll. 1297, b.
Biel, ll. 582, b.
Bienne, ll. 582, b.
Biennus, 705, b.
Bièvre, 401, b.
Biferno, 166, b; ll. 1207, b.
Biga, ll. 1337, a.
Bigerriones, 173, a.
Bigorre, 402, a.
Bilbilis, 581, b.
Bibitanorum, Aq., 168, b.
Bilecha, 375, a.
Billaeus, 406, a.
Bimbelli, ll. 187, b.
Binchester, ll. 1311, b.
Bin Gol, 183, a.
Bingen, 402, b.
Bingol, ll. 1157, b.

Binoesca, ll. 1312, b.
Biouk-Lambat, ll. 118, b.
Bir, 876, b.
Bir Bin Kilisseh, 770, b.
Bir or Birehjik, 408, a; ll. 1338, b.
Birdoswald, ll. 1256, b.
Birgos, ll. 1231, a.
Birgus, ll. 16, a.
Birkel Mount, ll. 397, a.
Birket el-Duarah, ll. 441, b.
Birket-el-Kerun, ll. 365, b.
Birket-el-Maroud, ll. 278, a.
Birmah, ll. 1086, a.
Birs-s-Nimrud, 359, b.
Birtha, 737, a; 877, a.
Birziminium. 748, a.
Bisaccia, ll. 855, a; ll. 1293, a.
Bisagno, 968, a; ll. 187, b.
Bisaltae, ll. 1190, a.
Bisan, 787, a.
Bisanthe, ll. 1190, a.
Biscarga, ll. 31, b.
Biscay, ll. 1105, a.
Biscay, Bay of, 314, a; 501, b.
Biscaya, 346, b.
Bisceglia, 167, a.
Biserta, ll. 1228, b.
Bisharyes, ll. 241, a.
Bishop's Waltham, 631, b.
Bishore, 384, a.
Bisignano, 451, a.
Bisitun, 369, b.
Bissikeni, ll. 600, b.
Bistones, ll. 1190, a.
Bistonis, Lake, ll. 1176, a.
Bisur, 420, a; 730, a.
Bithyas, 802, b.
Bitia, ll. 912, a.
Bitiae Portus, ll. 911, b.
Bitlis-chäi, ll. 424, b.
Bitolia, ll. 561, a.
Bitonto, 167, b; ll. 1294, a.
Bitti, ll. 48, a.
Bittigo, M., ll. 46, b.
Bituriges Cubi, 173, a.
Bituriges Vivisci, 173, a.
Bivados, 642, a.
Bivona, 1070, b; ll. 99, a.
Blum, ll. 237, a.
Bixeria, 1070, a; ll. 1014, b.
Bixone. ll, 1180, a.
Black Forest, 4, b; ll. 270, b.
Black Mountains, 383, b.
Black Sea, 886, a; ll. 920, a.
Black Sod Bay, ll. 175, a.
Blackwater, 645, b; 742, b; 808, b.
Blanc, Cape, 94, a.
Blanc, Cape, 499, a; 730, a; ll. 357, a.
Blanda, ll. 115, b; ll. 210, a.
Blandiana, 744, b.
Blanes, ll. 115, b; ll. 420, a.
Blanil, ll. 16, a.
Blannot, 428, b.
Blariacum, 570, a.
Blaundos, ll. 1197, b.
Blavet, 408, b; ll. 1310, a.
Bloye, 408. b.
Blemmyes, 58, a.
Blendium, 502, b.
Blera, 870, b; ll. 1298, a; ll. 1297, b.
Blerick, 407, b; 570, a.
Blessed, Islands of the, 906, a.
Blitira, 241, a.
Bliuri, ll. 537, b.
Blois, 523, a.
Bludin, ll. 642, b.
Boactes, ll. 188, a.
Boarium, Forum (Rome), ll. 813, a.
Bobardia, 383, b.
Bobia, 410, a.
Bochstein, 1019, a.
Bodenset, 429, b.
Bodetia, ll. 188, b.
Bodiocasses, 372, b.
Bodoa, ll. 220, a.
Bodrum or Boudroum,1026,b.
Boduni, 571, a.
Bodvary, ll. 1258, a.
Boeae, ll. 112, b.
Boebe, 705, b; ll. 1170, a.
Boerus, ll. 384, a.

Boctuborg, ll. 1318, b.
Bog, 1103, b.
Bogatz, ll. 556, a.
Bogdsha-Adassi, ll. 1126, b.
Boghas, 423, a.
Boghaz, ll. 1036, a.
Boghaz Hissan Kalch, ll. 253, a.
Boghaz Kieui, ll. 1108, b.
Bogopol, 889, a.
Boheim, 417, b.
Bohemia, 417, b.
Böhmerwald, 922, a.
Bohrus, 456, b.
Boienkerm, 417, b.
Boii, 756, a; ll. 542, a.
Booodurum, ll. 448, a.
Boisvinet, Ponote de, ll.629,b.
Bojuk-Ada, ll. 635, b.
Bojuk-Derbend, ll. 1101, b.
Bokhara, ll. 1237, a.
Bokhori, 64, a.
Bokhusia,13, b; 457, a; 693, b.
Boklu, 55, b.
Bokomadhi, ll. 559, b.
Bokomadhi, Cape, 638, a.
Bolat, 406, a.
Bolbitic arm of the Nile, ll. 433, b.
Bolax, 821, b.
Bolcascove, ll. 560, a; ll. 1054, b.
Boldo, ll. 537, b; ll. 1075, b.
Bolimnos, ll. 192, b.
Bolina, 13, b.
Bolinaeus, 13, b.
Bolite, 17, a.
Bolingae, ll. 48, a.
Bolitae, ll. 552, a.
Bologna, 419, a; ll. 1287, a.
Bolomia, 383, b.
Bolonidia, 841, a.
Bolor, ll. 41, a.
Bolsena, Lago di, 837, a; 856, b; ll. 1324, b.
Bolsena, ll. 1296, b; ll. 1297, a; ll. 1323, b.
Bomba, 733, b; ll. 277, b; ll. 641, a.
Bomilia, G. of, 733, b.
Bombareek, C., 520, b; 1031, a; ll. 549, b.
Bomarzo, ll. 644, b.
Bomi, 63, b.
Bon, Cape, 317, b; ll. 330, a.
Bona, Cape, ll. 5, a.
Bona Dea, Temple of the (Rome), ll. 811, a.
Bonah, 68, a; 69, a.
Bonah, Gulf of, 1070, a.
Bondino, ll. 509, a.
Boni Eventus, Porticus (Rome), ll. 839, b.
Bonifacio, 691, a.
Bonifacio. Straits of, 718, b.
Bonnar, ll. 686, b.
Bonn, 173, b; 418, b; ll. 192, a.
Bononia, ll. 1297, a.
Bontobrice. 383, b.
Bonus, 419, b.
Boobian, 877, a.
Boolok, ll. 955, b.
Boo-Shatter, ll. 1328, b.
Boosura, 631, b; 730, a.
Boppart, 383, b.
Borcani, 167, b.
Borcovicus, ll. 1256, b.
Borcum, 457, b.
Bordeaus, 170, a; 407, b; 457, b.
Bordj, ll. 1237, b.
Boreigonol, 5, b.
Boreum, 732, a; 733, b; ll. 1093, a.
Borgas, ll. 663, a.
Borghetto, 897, b.
Boria, 581, b.
Borjeiyah, ll. 401, a.
Borinanum, ll. 7, b.
Bormida, ll. 1035, a.
Borneo, 570, a; ll. 47, a.
Boron, ll. 188, b.
Boroan, ll. 1311, b.
Borrello, 934, b.
Borsippus, 360, a.

Bortinae, ll. 32, a.
Boruech, ll. 916, b.
Bosa, ll. 911, b.
Bosa, ll. 911, b.
Boschavir, 1018, a.
Bosco dell' Abadia, 376, b.
Boscovitza, ll. 1036, a.
Bosna, ll. 1254, a.
Bosnia, 747, a; ll. 36, a; ll. 541, a.
Bossuth, 366, b.
Bost, 403, a.
Bostam, 369, b.
Boston, 576, b.
Boatreus, ll. 606, b.
Boterdum, 582, a.
Botom, Botm, or Botam, ll. 506, a.
Botrys, ll. 606, a.
Bottiaei, ll. 1190, a.
Botzen, 384, a.
Boudroum, 589, b.
Bougie, ll. 454, a.
Bovianum, ll. 896, b.
Boujayah, G. of 326, b.
Bovino, 167, a; ll. 1307, a.
Boul, 456, b.
Bouleuterium, (Athens), 296, b.
Boulness, ll. 1239, a.
Boulogne, 442, b; 1000, a.
Boulovan, ll. 654, a.
Boun Ajonbah, ll. 277, b.
Bourbon l' Anci,169, a; 427, a.
Bourbon l'Archambault, 168, a.
Bourdeaux, 170, a; 407, b; 457, b.
Bourg d'Oysans, ll. 832, b.
Bourges, 350, a; 407, a.
Bourghaz, ll. 1176, a.
Bourgom, 393, a.
Bouriques, ll. 646, a.
Bournoubut, ll. 319, b.
Bous Dagh, ll. 1214, a.
Bowes, ll. 144, b; ll. 1290, b.
Bowness, 922, b; ll. 1256, b.
Boyne, the, 427, a; ll. 459, b.
Boyuk Mender, ll. 243, a.
Bazaar Su, ll. 589, a.
Bozburun, 198, a.
Bozburun, Cape, ll. 662, a.
Bra, 379, a.
Bracara, ll. 220, b.
Bracara Augusta, 250, a.
Bracarii, Callaeci, 932, b.
Bracciano, ll. 1297, b.
Bracciano, Lago di, 856, b; 857, a; ll. 864, a.
Brachma, 427, b.
Brachmani Magi, ll. 48, a.
Brachyle, 593, b.
Bradano, 165, b; 427, b; ll. 209, b.
Bradanus, 166, b; ll. 209, b.
Braga, 250, a; 427, a; ll. 220, b.
Bragança, 934, a.
Brahmaputra, 795, a; ll. 10, a; ll. 1260, a.
Brahmini, ll. 46, b.
Brahmins, the, 427, a.
Braga, ll. 277, a.
Bram, 1033, a.
Brampton, 429, a; ll.1256, b.
Brancaster, 428, b; 442, b.
Brandone, Monte, 564, b.
Brannodunum, 442, b.
Brasiae, ll. 112, b.
Brattia, ll. 37, a.
Bratuspante, 428, b.
Brauron, 232, a.
Brazza, 428, b; ll. 37, a.
Brecz, 391, b.
Brega, ll. 634, a.
Bréganson, ll. 472, b; ll. 576, b.
Bregentz, 429, b.
Bregenz, 110, b.
Bregetio, ll. 542, a.
Bremen, ll. 585, b.
Bremenium, 750. a.
Brementacae, 429, a.
Bremervörde, ll. 565, b.
Brenta, ll. 305, b; ll. 1275, a.
Brenthe, 111, b; 193, a.
Brescello, 443, a.

Brescia, 443, b; ii. 1287, b.
Brescon, 408, a.
Breslaw, ii. 215, a.
Bressure, ii. 951, a.
Brest, 443, a; 1000, a.
Brettoratz, ii. 1329, b.
Bretagne, 708, b; ii. 499, b; ii. 504, a.
Breuci, ii. 542, a.
Breuni, ii. 1310, b.
Brevia, 934, b.
Brey, Loch, ii. 1321, b.
Briançon, 110, a; 429, b.
Briare, 385, b; 443. a.
Bridgeford. East, ii. 274, a.
Bridgewater Bay, ii. 1286, a.
Brieuc, St. 401, b; 720, b.
Brigaecini, 249, b.
Brigaecium, 250. b.
Brigantes, ii. 16, a.
Brigantia, 110. b.
Brigantii, ii. 1310, b.
Brigantio, 110, a.
Brihuega, 582, a.
Brilessus, 322, a.
Brindjel, ii. 1270, b.
Brindisi, 444, b.
Briniates, ii. 187, a.
Brmnos, 347, a; 770, a.
Bruonnois, 424, b.
Brion, 430, a.
Brioude, 442, b.
Britannicum, Mare, ii. 460. b.
Brivain, 443, a.
Brviesca, ii. 1312, a.
Brivodurum, 385, b.
Brixen, 940, b.
Brixentes. 940, a.
Brixia, ii. 1287, b.
Bruxia, 429, b.
Brizice, or Brendice, ii. 1219, a.
Brockley Hill, ii. 1046, a.
Brodon, 444, a.
Bromi, ii. 1287, b.
Brough, 708, b; ii. 1280, b; ii. 1332, a.
Broughtern, ii. 211, b.
Broughton, 430. a.
Broussa, ii. 674, b.
Brucca, Castell' e Mare della, ii. 1266, b.
Brucheium, 97, a.
Brucida, ii. 36, b.
Brucla, 744, b.
Bruges, ii. 1217, b.
Brugh, 427, a.
Brugnato, 430, a.
Bruma, 1046, a.
Brusmath, 444, a.
Brunecken, 429, a.
Brutti Praesentis, Domus (Rome), ii. 828, a.
Bruttianus, Campus (Rome), ii. 844, b.
Bruxxano, Capo di, 641, b; ii. 1337, b.
Brychon, ii. 569, a.
Bryelice, 338, a.
Brysae, ii. 1190, a.
Brystacia, 451, a.
Bua, 384, a.
Buba, ii. 1075, b.
Bubastite Nome, 39, b.
Bubastus, 39, b; ii. 434, a.
Bubban, 400, b.
Buberak, ii. 1252, a.
Bubon, 462, a.
Bubula, ad Capita (Rome). ii. 801, b.
Buca, 915, b.
Buccia, or Buccina, 363, b.
Buccino. ii. 210, a; ii.1320, b.
Bucephala, ii. 47, b.
Buchaetium, 833, a.
Buchovisna, 1001, a.
Bucra, ii. 985, a.
Budaris, ii. 1125, a.
Budelli Isola dei, 719, a.
Budelli, Isole dei, ii. 911, b.
Budini, ii. 917, a.
Budissin or Budia, 383, a.
Budja, ii. 236, b.
Budii, ii. 301, b.
Budorum, ii. 878, b.
Badrio, 459, b.

Budua, ii. 220, a.
Buduzo, ii. 1196, a.
Budwus, ii. 278, a.
Buges, Lacus, ii. 1112, b.
Buhtan Chai, 585, a.
Buktanchoï, 216, b.
Bujeiyak, ii. 297, b; ii. 881, a.
Bules, 416, b.
Bujuk-dereh, 424, a.
Buka'a, ii. 1076, b.
Bukowina. 743, b.
Bulanes, ii. 918, b.
Buldur, or Burdur, Lake of, 230, b.
Bulis, ii. 603, a.
Bulla Regia, ii. 455, a.
Bullene, 162, a.
Bulum, 934, b.
Bulwudun, 781, a; ii. 645, b.
Bumadus, ii. 1209, a.
Bunarbaschi, ii. 926, b.
Bunbury. 427, a.
Bunderuk, 430, a.
Bunich, 419, b.
Bun-pur, 983, b.
Buon Riposo, ii. 204, b.
Buonalbergo, 910, b; 1073, b; ii. 1293, b.
Buphagium, 193, a.
Buphras, ii. 341, b.
Bura, 14, b.
Buraicus, 13, b; 457, a.
Burbida, 934, b.
Burdigala, 170, a.
Burdur or Buldur, 131, b.
Bureïka Kalyvia, ii. 586, b.
Büren, ii. 582, b.
Burg, ii. 1237, b.
Burgh, 442, b; ii. 550, b; ii. 1256, b.
Burgh Castle, 442, b; 977, b.
Burgh on the Sands. 351, b.
Burgh St. Peter, 442. b.
Burghausen, 384, b.
Burgos, 581, a; 770, a; ii. 1252, b.
Burlia, M., ii. 870, b.
Burlos, 459, b.
Burmasaka, 701, b.
Burres, 934, b.
Burrinna, 807, a; ii. 964, a.
Burridava, 744, b.
Burrindus, ii. 677, a.
Burrium, 409, b.
Burrough Hill, ii. 1279, a.
Bursada, 582, a.
Busento, ii. 209, b.
Busae, ii. 301, b.
Bushashim, 607, a.
Busir, 458, b.
Busiris, 39, b.
Busirite Nome, 39. b.
Buskard, Mts., ii. 583, a.
Bassière, 427, a.
Busta Gallica, Ad (Rome), ii. 815, b.
Butera, ii. 242, a.
Buthrotum, 832, b.
Buthrotus, 450, a.
Buto, 39, b.
Butua, 748, a.
Butuntum, 167, a.
Butunium, ii. 1294, a.
Buxentum, ii. 209, b.
Buyati, 331, b.
Buzenses, ii. 278, a.
Buzi, ii. 414, a.
Buzrak, 424, b.
Byblus, ii. 606, a.
Byltae, ii. 41, b; ii. 943, b.
Byzantium, 657, a; ii. 1190, a.
Byzeres, ii. 658, b.

Cabandene, ii. 1050 b.
Cabanes, Villa de, 807, a.
Cabarnis, ii. 552, b.
Cabeiri, ii. 901, b.
Cabendena, 821, a.
Cabez, ii. 1083, a.
Cabes, Gulf of, ii. 1081, a.
Cabezas, Las, ii. 1286, b.
Cabezas Rubias, ii. 857, a.
Cabo de Palos, ii. 924, a.
Cabo Quilates, ii. 969, b.
Cabo Villano. ii. 969, b.
Cabra, 367, a.

Cabra, Col de, 980, a.
Cabrera, 374, b; ii. 342, b.
Cabul, 558, a; ii. 552, a.
Cabul River, ii. 552, a; ii. 585, b.
Cabulistan, ii. 552, a.
Cabyleti, ii. 1190, a.
Caceres, 562, a.
Cachagae Scythae, ii. 943, b.
Cachales, ii. 418, b.
Cacia, ii. 1085, a.
Cacobae. ii. 47. a.
Cacus, Cave of (Rome), ii. 810, a; ii. 817, a.
Cacyparis, ii. 986, b.
Cacyrum, ii. 987, a.
Cadière, 477, b.
Cadix or Cadiz, 923, a.
Cadmus, 463, b; 519, a.
Caduret, 173, a.
Cadusii, ii. 302, a.
Cadytis, ii. 17, b.
Caecilia, ii. 1073, b.
Caecilia Metella, Mausoleum of (Rome), ii. 821, b.
Caeciliana, ii. 220, a.
Caecina, 857, a.
Caecinus, 450, a.
Caedici, 55, a.
Caedrius, ii. 911, a.
Caelia, 167, a; 474, b; ii. 1294, a.
Caelian Hill (Rome), ii. 817, a.
Caelimontana, Porta (Rome), ii. 755, b.
Caelimontani, Arcus (Rome), ii. 851, a.
Caena, ii. 986, b.
Caendar, 921, b.
Caenon, 463, a.
Caenepolis, ii. 112, b.
Caenica, ii. 1190, b.
Caenci. ii. 1190, a.
Caenus, 705, b.
Caenyr, ii. 706, a.
Caeretanus, Amnis, 466, b.
Caeritis Amnis, 468, b.
Caerlaverock, ii. 1332, a.
Caerleon, 418, b.
Caericon-on-Usk. ii. 66, b.
Caernarvon, ii. 951, a; ii. 971, a.
Caernarvonshire, ii. 491, a.
Caer Went, ii. 1276, a.
Caesada, 525, a; 582, a.
Caesar, Statue of (Rome), 793, a.
Caesaraugusta, 250, a.
Caesarea, 949, b.
Caesarela Panias, ii. 1076, b.
Caesarea Philippi, ii. 540, a.
Caesariana, ii. 210, b; ii. 1295, a.
Caesaris, Horti (Rome), ii. 841, b.
Caesaromagus, 341, a.
Caesarum, Nemus (Rome), ii. 841, b.
Caesena, ii. 1287, a.
Caesius, 89, b.
Caffa, ii. 1110, a; ii. 1157, b.
Cafsa, 510, a.
Cagli, ii. 1301, a; ii. 1317, b.
Cagliari, 513, b.
Cahors, 464, a; 517, a; 780, a.
Caianum (Rome), ii. 844, b.
Caiazzo, 476, b.
Cajazzo, ii. 896, b.
Caistor, 442, b; 488, b; ii. 1276, a.
Caithness, 687, a.
Calabreña, ii. 952, b.
Calabria, ii. 206, b.
Calabria Citra, 447, a.
Calabria Ultra, 447, a.
Calachene, 606, b.
Calacta, ii. 986, b.
Caladunum, 934, a.
Calae Caras, ii. 46, b.
Calagum, 400, b.
Calagurris, 394, a; 469, a.
Calahorra, 394, a; 469, a; 475, b.
Calais, Pas de, 916, b.
Calamae, ii. 345, b.

Calamos, ii. 606, a.
Calamotia, 810, a.
Calamyda, 706, b.
Calandro, 8, b; ii. 209, b.
Calanta Manor, ii. 1324, b.
Calas Lumneonas, 148, a.
Calasarna, ii. 210, a.
Calatabellotta, ii. 986, b; ii. 1231, a.
Calatafimi, ii. 948, a.
Calatia, ii. 896, b; ii. 1292, b.
Calatrava, ii. 219, b; ii. 1240, b.
Calbis, 519, a; ii. 53, a.
Calcus, ii. 455, a.
Calcutta, 972, b; ii. 47. a.
Caldas del Rey, 168, b; 934, b.
Caldelas, 934, a; ii. 883, a.
Caldelas, Castro de. 934, a.
Caldes de Malavella, 168, b.
Caldnoven, 485, a.
Caldo, Rio, 934, a.
Caleia, 167, a.
Calem, ii. 220, b.
Calem, Ad, ii. 1301, a.
Calentum, 583, a.
Cales, ii. 1302, b.
Caletes, 218, b.
Calianria, ii. 461, b.
Calicat, 698, a.
Caligula, Bridge of (Rome), ii. 806, b.
Calinapatnam, 480, b; 972, b.
Calinapattana, ii. 47, a.
Calindaea, ii. 384, a.
Calingae, 972, b; ii. 47, a.
Calingapatam, 750, b.
Calitri, 1073, b.
Callenses Emanici, 583, a.
Calles, ii. 1301, a; ii. 1317, b.
Calleva, 387, b.
Calleva Attrebatum, 320, a; 442, a.
Callia, 193, a.
Callian, ii. 182, b.
Calliarus, ii. 1072, b.
Callicolone, ii. 1194, b.
Callicula, Mons, 166, a.
Callene, ii. 49, b.
Callifae, ii. 896, b.
Calliga, 480, b.
Calligicum, ii. 46, b.
Callinusa, 730, a.
Callipari, 450, b.
Callipeuce. ii. 174, a.
Callipolis, 474, b; ii. 1190, a.
Callipus, ii. 220, a.
Callirrhoë, Fountain of, (Athens), 292, a.
Calnen, 67, a.
Calmex, Cape, 67, b.
Calonato, 1103. a.
Caloni, ii. 688, b.
Calor, 1072, a; ii. 209, b. 209, b.
Calorem, Ad, ii. 210, b; ii. 1295, a.
Calthorpe, ii. 1232, b.
Calvados. ii. 173, a.
Calne, 479, b; ii. 1302, b.
Calvi, Monte, ii. 1286, a.
Calvisii, 481, b.
Calvus, 582, a.
Calydon, 67, a.
Calzadilla de Mendigos, ii. 964, a.
Camala, 250, b.
Camara, 705, b.
Camaran, 651, a.
Camarana, 486, a.
Camarana, Fiume di, 1069, b; ii. 985, b.
Camarica, 502, b.
Camarina Palus, ii. 986, a.
Cambadene, 369, a.
Cambaetum, 934, a.
Cambalidus, Mons, 369, b.
Cambay, ii. 255 a.
Cambay, Gulf of, ii. 46, b; ii. 47, a; ii. 484, a.
Cambeck Fort, ii. 585, a; ii. 1256, b.
Cambo, 488, a.
Camboya, ii. 1002, b.
Camboricum, 488, b.
Cambrai, ii. 421, a.

Cambray, 486, a.
Cambridge, 488, b.
Cambyses, 320, a.
Cambysis, 60, b.
Camelobosci, 521, a.
Camelodunum, 442, a.
Camenarum Lucus and Aedes of (Rome), ii. 820, a.
Cameno, ii. 947, b.
Camerino, 489, a.
Camerinum, ii. 1317, b.
Camicus, 79, b; ii. 985, b; ii. 986, b.
Cammino, S. Martin de, ii. 1254, b.
Camirus, ii. 713, b.
Cammanene, 807, b.
Campan, 497, b.
Companella, Punta della, ii. 359, b; ii. 514, b.
Campanus, Pons, ii. 1290, a.
Campo di Annibale, 92, a.
Campo di Giove, ii. 568, b.
Campo Mayor, ii. 220, a.
Campo, S. Maria del, ii. 886, a.
Campodia, ii. 1161, a.
Campus de Marianicis, 169, b.
Campus Major (Rome), ii. 835, a.
Campus Martialis (Rome), ii. 818, a.
Campus Martius (Rome), ii. 832, a; ii. 834, b.
Campus Minor (Rome), ii. 835, a.
Campylus, 19, b; 61, a.
Camudolanum, 571, a.
Camulodunum, 645, b.
Canaan, ii. 516, a.
Canach, 515, a.
Canal Bianco, 26, b.
Canale del Cefalo, 474, a.
Canales, ii. 1293, a.
Canalicum, ii. 188, b; ii. 1296, b.
Canaria, 906, b.
Canaries, 314, a.
Canasis, 983, b.
Canatha, ii. 1076, b.
Canca, 499, b.
Canche, 442, b.
Candanum, ii. 7, b.
Candavia, ii. 36, b.
Candia, 703, a.
Cane, 472, a.
Canelate, 691, b.
Canentelus, ii. 903, b.
Canet, 725, b.
Cani, 465, a.
Cannae, 167, a.
Canne, 499, b.
Canne, Fiume delle, ii. 965, b.
Cannes, 1091, a.
Cannete, ii. 870, a.
Canneto, 385, a.
Canobus, 39, a.
Canopic arm of the Nile, ii. 433, b.
Canopic Canal (Nile), ii. 434, a.
Conosa, 503, a; ii. 1294, a.
Cantaber, Oceanus, 314, a.
Cantabria, 894, b.
Cantae, 502, b.
Cantalice, 6, a.
Cantanus, 705, b.
Cantara, 12, a; ii. 1208, a.
Cantara, F. ii. 985, b.
Cantaro, 1100, a; ii. 986, a.
Canterbury, 442, a.
Canthi, ii. 255, a.
Canthi, S., ii. 46, b.
Cantium Promontorium, 502, b.
Caniyre, Mull of, 750, a; 842, b.
Canusium, 167, a; ii. 1294, a.
Capara, ii. 1285, b.
Capara, Las Ventas de, ii. 1285, b.
Cap Blanc, 198, a.
Capdenac, ii. 1332, a.
Cape Guardafui, 57, b.

Capena, Porta (Rome), ii. 755, a.
Capenus, Sinus, 604, a.
Caphareus, 871, b.
Caphardagon, 396, b.
Caphusa, 505, b.
Caphyae, 193, a.
Caphyatis, 193, a.
Capilla, ii. 219, b; ii. 361, b.
Capissene, 505, b.
Capitanata, 164, b.
Capitium, ii. 987, a.
Capitol (Rome), ii. 761, a.
Capitolias, ii. 1076, b.
Capitolium, Vetus (Rome), ii. 829, b.
Capixa, 505, b.
Capo dell' Alice, 450, b.
Capo dell' Armi, 447, a.
Capo d' Istria, ii. 73, b.
Capo S. Teodoro, 85, b.
Capoccia S. Angelo di, ii. 306, b.
Capori, 933, a.
Capova, 556, b; ii. 1302, b.
Capoua, Sia Maria di, 510, a.
Cappadocicus, Pontus, 508, a.
Cappadoxa, 508, a.
Capiadosso, 635, b.
Capraia, 509, a.
Capraja, 857, b.
Capraria, 374, b; 857, b; 906, b.
Capraria, Ardicula (Rome), ii. 835, a.
Caprasia, 451, a, b.
Caprasiae, ii. 1008, a.
Capreae or Caprae, Palus (Rome), ii. 835, a.
Caprera, Isola di, 719, a; ii. 911, b.
Capri, 509, a.
Capri-Su, 886, a.
Capris, 241, b.
Caprus, 189, a; ii. 1034, b; ii. 1209, a.
Capua, ii. 1290, a.
Caput Bubali, 744, b.
Caput Vada, 67, b; 427, b.
Caput Vadorum, ii. 859, b.
Carabash, 194, a.
Carabia, ii. 384, a.
Caracallae, Thermae (Rome), ii. 847, b.
Caracca, 525, a.
Caracena, 525, b.
Curacodes Portus, ii. 911, a.
Caracuel, ii. 219, b.
Carae, 582, a.
Caralis, ii. 911, b.
Caralis, Prom., ii. 911, b.
Caralitanum Prom., ii. 911, b.
Carambis, 406, a; ii. 547, a.
Caranusca, 515, a.
Caratae, ii. 943, a.
Caravis, 591, b.
Carbaglar, ii. 1131, b.
Carbulesi, ii. 1190, a.
Carbuna, 474, b.
Carbo, C., 336, b; ii. 454, a.
Carbones, ii. 916, b.
Carcaso, ii. 1370, a.
Carcassone, 515, b.
Carceda, ii. 1232, b.
Carcer Mamertinus (Rome), ii. 781, a.
Carchemish, 627, a.
Carci, ii. 47, a.
Carcines, 450, b.
Carcorus, ii. 541, b.
Carcurium, ii. 219, b.
Cardia, ii. 1190, a.
Cardona, ii. 1, b; ii. 1260, b.
Cardua, 582, a.
Careiae, ii. 1297, b.
Carentan, 708, b.
Cariatain, ii. 283, b.
Carico, S. Giovanni in, 889, a; ii. 1302, b.
Caridia, 516, a.
Carife, 481, b.
Carinae (Rome), ii. 822, b.
Carini, Muro di, ii. 987, b.

Cariniola, 893, a.
Carinthia, 541, a.
Carmethia, ii. 541, a; ii.447,a.
Caripeta, ii. 283, b; ii. 284, b.
Carius, 521, a.
Cariza, 520, a.
Carlburg, 999, b.
Carlisle, ii. 215, a.
Carlopago, or Cerlobago, ii. 497, b.
Carlsburg, 167, b.
Carlstadi, ii. 855, a.
Carmana, 521, a.
Carmanaça, 973, b.
Carmania Deserta, ii. 365, b; ii. 349, a.
Carmarthen, 775, a; ii. 276,b.
Carmel, M., ii. 606, a.
Carmentalis, Porta (Rome), ii. 751, a.
Carmono, 521, b.
Carn-al-Manazil, or Carn-al-Manzil, ii. 357, b; ii. 358, b.
Carna, Carana, or Carnon, ii. 358, b.
Carneates, ii. 601, b.
Carniola, ii. 447, a; ii. 541, a.
Carnion, 49, a; ii. 309, b.
Carnsore Point, 1065, b; ii. 872, a.
Carnuntum, ii. 542, a.
Carnus, 113, b.
Caronia, 475, a.
Caronia, Bosco di, 1051, b.
Carovigno, 474, b; 515, b.
Carpas, 923, b.
Carpas, 730, a.
Carpathian Mountains, 523, b; ii. 482, a; ii. 917. a; ii. 920, a.
Carpella, 520, b.
Carpelia, Prom., ii. 549, b.
Carpentras, 524, b.
Carpi, ii. 917, a.
Carpiani, ii. 917, a.
Carpis, ii. 1338, a.
Carrea Potentia, ii. 188, a.
Carrawburgh, ii. 1256, b.
Carrickfergus, ii. 1310, b.
Carro, 775, a.
Carru, 526, a.
Carry, ii. 43, a.
Carseoli, 55, a; ii. 1306, b.
Carsici, ii. 1113, b.
Carcisia Portus, 515, b.
Carsidava, 744, b.
Carsoli, 526, b; 527, a; ii. 1306, b.
Carsulae, ii. 1317, a.
Carta, 1105, a.
Carta la Vieja, or Carta Vieja, 554, a; ii. 31, b.
Cartagena, 552, b; ii. 290, a.
Cartalias, 807, a.
Cartenna, ii. 297, b.
Carthaea, 587, a.
Carthagena, ii. 636, a.
Carthago Spartaria, ii. 636, a.
Carthago Vetus, ii. 31, b.
Carvathos, ii. 220, a.
Carulnae, ii. 946, b; ii. 1256, b.
Carura, ii. 47, a.
Carusa, ii. 547, b.
Caryae, 193, a.
Carystum, ii. 188, a.
Carystus, 872, b.
Casa Mara, or Casamari, 592, a.
Casale di Conca, ii. 973, a.
Casale, Torre del Piano del, ii. 1124, a.
Casaluce, ii. 362, b.
Casama, ii. 1076, b.
Casbona, ii. 1281, a.
Cashmir, ii. 47, b; ii. 50, b.
Casil Montes, ii. 508, a.
Casilinum, ii. 1302, b.
Casinum, ii. 1302, b.
Casiotis, 37, a.
Casius, 37, a; 89, b.
Casmenae, ii. 987, a.
Casmonates, ii. 187, b.
Caspatyrus, 972, a; ii. 50, b.
Caspeira, 558, b.
Caspeirai, ii. 48, a.

Caspiae Pylae, 90, a.
Caspian Sea, 559, b.
Caspii, ii. 302, a.
Caspiria, ii. 47, b.
Caspius, 572, a.
Cassaei, 822, b.
Cassaro, 463, a; ii. 987, a.
Cassel, 561, b; ii. 327, b.
Cassibili, 463, a; ii. 986, a.
Casali Forum, 870, b; ii. 1296, b; ii. 1297, a.
Cassobury, 560, b.
Cassiope, 669, b; 671, b; 832, b.
Cassiotis, ii. 1076, a.
Cassope, 833, a.
Castabala, 507, b.
Castamouni, 561, a.
Casteggio, 630, b; ii. 40, b; ii. 188, a.
Castel d' Asso, 894, a.
Castel d' Asso, or Castellaccio, 351, b.
Castel dell' Osa, 644, a.
Castel dell' Uovo, 495, b.
Castel Franco, 908, b.
Castel Guido, ii. 1296, a.
Castel Nuovo, 224, b.
Castel-Pinon, Sommet de, ii. 1047, a.
Castel Rodrigo, ii. 86, b.
Castel Sardo, ii. 912, a.
Castel Vecchio Subequo, ii. 1048, a.
Castel Vetere, 575, b.
Castell' a Mare, ii. 1033, b.
Castellana, Civita, 891, b; 807, b.
Castello, Città di, ii. 1207, b.
Castello Termenos, ii. 1157, a.
Castellon de la Plana, ii. 964, a.
Castellum Menapiorum, ii. 337, b.
Castelnaudari, ii. 1023, b.
Castelnon, 349, b.
Casthanaea, ii. 1170, b.
Castiglione, 920, a.
Castiglione Bernardi, ii. 1285, b.
Castiglione, Lago di, ii. 668, b.
Castile, Old and New, 525, a.
Castiles, the, ii. 1105, b.
Castle Acre, 442, b.
Castle of the Morea, 13, a.
Castle Over, 672, a.
Castle Rising, 442, b.
Castle-steeds, ii. 585, a.
Castleford, ii. 153, b.
Castor, 793, a.
Castor and Pollux, Temple of (Rome), ii. 784, a; ii. 834, b.
Castore, 6, b.
Castra, ii. 36, b.
Castra (Rome), ii. 839, b.
Castra Cornelia, ii. 1338, a.
Castra Hannibalis, 451, a.
Castra Nova, 744, b.
Castra Peregrina (Rome), ii. 818, a.
Castra Trajana, 744, b.
Castralla, ii. 1240, b.
Castrense, Amphitheatrum (Rome), ii. 847, a.
Castro, 61, a; 564, a; ii. 390, b; ii. 912, a; ii. 1035, b; ii. 1294, a.
Castro de la Ventosa, 250, a.
Castro del Rio, ii. 718, a.
Castro Giovanni, 828, a.
Castro Reale, Fiume di, ii. 204, a.
Castro, Rio de, 904, a; 933, b.
Castro Zarvi, ii. 1042, a.
Castrum Minervae, 474, b.
Castrum Novum, 870, b; ii. 628, b; ii. 491, b, ii. 1307, a.
Castuera, 228, a.
Castulo, 561, a; ii. 491, b.
Casuentiliani, ii. 1317, b.
Casuentus, ii. 209, b.
Catabathmus Major, 732, a.
Catabeda, ii. 46, b.

Catnea, 521, a.
Catalonia, ii. 1105, a.
Catania, 567, a.
Catania, 507, b.
Catanri, ii. 542, a.
Catarrhactes, 320, b; ii. 538, a.
Catherine, C. St., 669, b.
Catiline's House (Rome), ii. 804, b.
Catobriga, ii. 290, a.
Cattaro, 570, a.
Cattarus, 748, a.
Cattigara, ii. 47, a.
Cattrick Bridge, 569, b.
Catularia, Porta (Rome), ii. 757, b.
Catull, Porticus (Rome), ii. 804, b.
Cava Canim, 499, a.
Cavado, 427, a.
Cavado, R., 933, a.
Cavaillon, 462, a; 577, a.
Cavalaire, Pointe, 1049, a.
Cavaliere, ii. 386, b.
Cavallo, C., 336, b.
Caucana, ii. 985, a.
Caucasus, 571, a; 591, a; ii. 917, b.
Cauchabeni, 181, a.
Cauci, ii. 16, a.
Caudebec, ii. 206, a.
Caudine Forks, ii. 1223, a.
Caveri, ii. 46, b; ii. 48, a.
Caviones, 351, b.
Canlares, 575, a.
Cauni, ii. 299, a.
Caunil, 518, a.
Caunus, 239, b; 514, a.
Cavoli, Isola dei, ii. 911, b.
Caus, ii. 32, a.
Causennae, 488, b.
Caussèque, 641, b.
Cautes Bacchiae, 424, a.
Caus, Pays de, ii. 102, a.
Canolla, 479, b.
Cazeca, 472, a.
Canères, 476, a.
Canlona, 565, a; ii. 491, b.
Cea, 250, b.
Ceba, ii. 188, a.
Cecilionicum, ii. 1285, b.
Cecina, 464, a; 857, a.
Cecropium (Athens), 278, a.
Cedonie, 744, b.
Cefalo, Cape, ii. 1230, b.
Cefalu, 588, b.
Ceglie, 464, b; 465, a; ii. 1294, a.
Ceice, ii. 961, a.
Ceirtadae (Athens), 302, b.
Cela Nova, ii. 879, a.
Celadus, 933, a.
Celano, Lago di, 917, b.
Celegeri, ii. 367, b.
Celeia, ii. 448, a.
Celenae, Aquae, 934, b.
Celenae, or Cilenae, Aquae, 168, b.
Celenderis, ii. 1236, a.
Celenna, ii. 897, a.
Celidoni, 606, b.
Cella, ii. 461, a.
Cellae, ii. 236, b; ii. 1298, b.
Celsa, ii. 32, a.
Cema, Mons, 107, b.
Cembaro, or Cembalo, ii. 515, b.
Cemenelion, 110, a.
Cemenelium, ii. 188, a.
Cemenelo, 110, a.
Cenaeum, 871, a.
Cenchreae, 682, b.
Ceneda, ii. 1275, a.
Ceneta, ii. 1275, b.
Cenis, Mont, 107, b.
Centesimum, Ad, ii. 1335, a.
Centobriga, 582, a.
Centorbi, 585, b; ii. 987, a.
Centrites, or Centritis, 216, b; ii. 1209, a.
Centron, 585, a; 907, b.
Centum Cellae, 870, b; ii. 1296, a.
Centum Puteae, 744, b.
Centumcellae, 870, b; ii. 1296, a.

Centuria, 691, b.
Centuripa, ii. 987, a.
Centuripi, 61, a.
Cepet, Cape, 526, b.
Cephalae, ii. 1230, b.
Cephalae, Prom., ii. 1080, b.
Cephale, 332, b.
Cephalo, 587, b.
Cephaloedium, ii. 966, b.
Cephalonia, 587, b.
Cephisia, 326, b.
Cephisia, 411, b.
Cephisus, 200, b; 323, a.
Cepi Milesiorum, 422, a.
Ceprano, 914, a; ii. 1302, b.
Ceralto, S. Columba de, ii. 1, b.
Ceramaicus, 325, a.
Ceramaicus (Athens), 298, b; 301, b.
Ceramaicus, Outer (Athens), 303, a. [b.
Ceramic Gate (Athens), 262
Ceramic, ii. 237, a.
Cerastis, 729, a.
Cerata, 322, a.
Ceraunilia, 167, a.
Cerax, 756, a.
Cerbalus, 166, b.
Cerbani, 515, a.
Cerberion, 422, a.
Cerbia, 730, a.
Cercernae, Aquae, 168. b.
Cercetium, M., ii. 630, b.
Cercina, 461, a; ii. 1081, a.
Cercinitis, Lake, ii. 1177, b.
Cereinium, ii. 1170, a.
Cerdagne, 593, a.
Ceres, 705, b.
Ceres, Temple of (Rome), ii. 816, b.
Cereste, 628, b.
Ceresus, ii. 1, b.
Cerfenna, in, 592, b.
Cerfennia, ii. 282, a; ii. 1306, b.
Cerisdae, 325, a.
Cerignola, 167, a; 590, b.
Cerigo, 738, a.
Cerigotto, 32, b.
Cerilli, 451, a.
Cerinthus, 872, b.
Cermalus (Rome), ii. 802, b.
Cerredo, 934, b; ii. 1329, b.
Cerreto, 651, b.
Cersie, 744, b.
Cersus, ii. 1080, a.
Certima, 582, a.
Certis, 367, b.
Cerraro, 166, b; 591, a; 926, a.
Cervera, 593, b.
Cervetri, 466, b.
Cervia, ii. 52, a.
Cervini, 691, b.
Cerycetum, 414, a.
Ceryneia, 14, b.
Cerynia, 730, a.
Cerynites, 13, b; 457, a.
Cexada, 197, b.
Cesano, 1000, a; ii. 1317, b.
Cesarieux, 565, b.
Cesarini, 898, a.
Cesena, 470, b; ii. 1287, a.
Cessero, ii. 1320, a.
Ceste, ii. 1288, a.
Cestius, Pons (Rome), ii. 849, b.
Cestria, 594, a; 832, b.
Cestrus, ii. 538, a.
Cetaria, ii. 986, b.
Cetium, ii. 448, a.
Cette, 408, a; ii. 404, a.
Cettina, ii. 657, b.
Cesa, 578, b; ii. 188, a.
Cèvennes, 578, b; ii. 54, b; ii. 494, b.
Ceuta, b.
Ceylon, 59, b; ii. 49, b; ii. 715, b; ii. 1091, a.
Chaalla, ii. 283, a.
Chaberis, ii. 46, b.
Chaberus, ii. 48, a.
Chabcuil, 592, a.
Chabiones, 351, b.
Chablais, ii. 396, a.

Chaboras, ii. 338, b.
Chabur, 135, b.
Chadisius, ii. 658, b.
Chacham, ii. 1012, a.
Chaedini, ii. 927, b.
Chaenides, ii. 917, b.
Chaeonoetae, 572, a.
Chaeroneia, 219, b.
Chaetae, ii. 344, a.
Chai Kieu, 578, a.
Chailli, 400, b.
Chailly, 475, b.
Chalach, 478, a.
Chaladrus, ii. 1075, b.
Chalaeum, ii. 203, a.
Chalastra, ii. 384, a.
Chalcidice, ii. 1076, a.
Chalcidicum (Rome), ii. 791, b.
Chalcis, 63, b; 67, a; 600, b; 633, a; ii. 1076, a.
Chalcitis, 770, a; ii. 47, a.
Chalybonitis, ii. 1076, a.
Cham, ii. 551, b.
Chamanene, 508, a.
Chamari, 363, b.
Chandrabagha, 502, a.
Chandrabhaga, 12, a.
Changeri, 974, a.
Chancel, English, 814, a.
Chammer Chmah, ii. 1259, a.
Chantelle-le-Chtel, 502, b.
Chantelle-la-Vieille, 502, b.
Chaours, 570, b.
Chapsylar, 731, b.
Characene, ii. 1050, b.
Characitani, 525, b.
Charadra, ii. 604, b.
Charadrus, 13, b; 200, b.
Charaunael Scythae, ii. 943, b.
Charax, ii. 1170, a.
Chardak, 131, a.
Charente, 515, a; ii. 903, b.
Charente Inférieure, ii. 503, a.
Chariels, 643, a.
Charindas, 320, a; 1106, a.
Chariot of the Gods, ii. 448, a.
Charisia, 193, a.
Charlieu, 520, a.
Charma Su, 590, b.
Charmans, ii. 920, a.
Charpagne, ii. 929, a.
Charran, 526, a.
Chartrain, 823, a.
Chartres, 346, b; 823, a.
Charvati, 327, a.
Chassenon, 557, a.
Chastiels, 329, b.
Chat Bay, 604, a.
Chatae Scythae, ii. 943, b.
Château du Loir, 901, a.
Chatramotitae, 181, b.
Chattani, ii. 278, a.
Chaves, 168, b; 934, a.
Chauke, ii. 3, b.
Chaule-burnau, 809, b.
Chaulu-bernau, 730, a.
Chaurana, ii. 943, b.
Chaussée de Brunehaut, ii. 1318, b.
Checa, 582, a; ii. 1326, a.
Cheimarrhus, 201, a.
Cheimerium, 833, a.
Chel Minar, ii. 578, a.
Chelae, 474, a.
Chelendrch, 580, a.
Chelenophagi, 58, a.
Cheli, 1028, b.
Chemmis, 40, a.
Chemmite Nome, 39, b; 40, a.

Chenab, 12, a.
Chene, 465, b.
Chenei, ii. 1008, a.
Cheppe, 893, b.
Cherbourg, 673, b.
Cherkas, 591, b.
Cherkaskaia, 991, b.
Cherronesus, 807, a.
Chersinos, ii. 917, a.
Cherso, 7, a.
Cherson, ii. 917, a.
Chersonesus, 705, b; ii. 277, b; ii. 911, a.
Chersonesus Magna, 732, a.
Chester, 427, a; 687, a.
Chester, Little, ii. 1311, a.
Chesterford, 488, b; ii. 12, a.
Chesterholm, ii. 1256, b.
Chesterton, 793, a.
Cheyich-el-Nedy, ii. 1136, b.
Chiana, 630, a.
Chiaruccia, T. di, ii. 1296, a.
Chiavenna, 110, b; 631, b.
Chichester, 135, a; 442, a; ii. 697, b.
Chicnti, ii. 629, a.
Chieri, 826, a.
Chiers, 469, a.
Chiese, 584, b; 637, b.
Chieti, ii. 279, b; 1117, a; ii. 1306, b.
Chilimodi, ii. 1125, a.
Chilney Isle, 400, b.
Chimaera, 832, b.
China, ii. 967, b.
Chinalaph, ii. 297, b.
Chinchilla, 582, a.
Chinese, the, ii. 1002, a.
Chinnereth, ii. 1197, a.
Chionitae, 1097, b.
Chios, 239, b.
Chirin-Koi, 53, a.
Chituae, ii. 290, b.
Chivasso, ii. 589, b.
Chiusi, 636, b.
Chiusi, Lago di, 857, b.
Chlomo, M., 412, a.
Choaspes, ii. 641, a; ii. 1050, b; ii. 1209, a.
Chobanlar, 732, a.
Chobus, 643, a.
Choerius, 3, b.
Choes, ii. 118, b.
Cholle, ii. 1076, b.
Cholleidae, 331, a.
Choimadara, ii. 1075, b.
Chonae, 648, b.
Chone, 451, a.
Chorasmi, ii. 1019, a.
Choros Rixamarum, 582, a.
Choubar Tiz, ii. 1085, b.
Christopolis, 21, b.
Chronos, ii. 460, b.
Chronus, ii. 917, a.
Chrysas, ii. 985, a.
Chryse, ii. 49, b.
Chryso, 706, b.
Chrysoana, ii. 46, b.
Chrysondyon, 641, a.
Chrysorrhoas, 643, a.
Chunt, ii. 917, a.
Chur, 730, a.
Churmut, 476, a.
Churn, 794, a.
Chuzabarri, M., ii. 1080, b.
Chydas, ii. 986, a.
Chytra, 614, b.
Chytrus, 730, a.
Ciadia, 934, a.
Cibalae, ii. 542, a.
Cibotus, 239, a.
Cibyra, 575, a; ii. 1157, a.
Cibyratica, 239, a.
Cicero, House of (Rome), ii. 804, b.
Cichyrus, 833, a.
Cicolano, 6, a; 58, b.
Cicones, ii. 1190, a.
Cidaritae, 1097, b.
Cierium, ii. 1170, a.
Cigarrosa, 250, a.
Cigno, 691, a.
Cilebenali, 691, b.
Cilicia, 507, b.
Cilini, 933, a.
Cilla, 53, a.
Cilly, 580, a.

Cilonis, Domus (Rome), ii. 822, a.
Cilurnum, ii. 1256, b.
Cimbricum, Mare, ii. 460, b.
Cimetra, ii. 896, b.
Cimex, 110, a; 583, b; ii. 188, a.
Cimmo, Monte, 623, a.
Ciminus, Lacus, 656, b; 857, a.
Cimmericum, 422, a.
Cimoli, 625, a.
Cimolis, ii. 547, b.
Cinca, 625, a.
Cingilia, ii. 1283, b.
Cingoli, 625, a; ii. 628, b.
Cingulum, ii. 628, b.
Cnifo, 625, b.
Cinium, 374, b.
Cinna, ii. 1, b.
Cinnaba, M., ii. 299, a.
Cinnamomifera, 752, a.
Cinniana, ii. 52, a.
Cinyps, ii. 1081, a.
Ciotat, 628, b; ii. 1113, b.
Cipiona, 466, a.
Circars, 480. b; 972, b; ii. 47, a; ii. 245, a.
Circassia, 591, b; ii. 917, b.
Circeo, or *Circello, Monte*, 626, a.
Circidius, 691, a.
Circus Agonalis (Rome), ii. 814, a.
Circus Maximus (Rome), ii. 812, b; ii. 842, a.
Cirella Vecchia, 592, b.
Cirencester, 387, b.; 442, a; 673, b.
Cirenchester, 793, b.
Ciro, 706, a.
Cirphis, ii. 605. a.
Cirrodes, ii. 1019, a.
Cirta, 69, a.
Cisamus, 705, b.
Cispius (Rome), ii. 822, a.
Cissa, ii. 74, a.
Cissus, ii. 384, a.
Cisterna, ii. 1226, b.
Cisterna, ii. 1314, a.
Cisthene, 53, a.
Cité, 779, a.
Cithaeron, 322, a.
Citium, 624, a; 730, a.
Città Nuova. ii. 74, a.
Cittadella, Monte della, 626, a.
Ciudad Rodrigo, 341, a; ii. 461, b.
Ciudadela, 374, b.
Cividale, 385, a; 522, b.
Cividato, ii. 1258, a.
Civita, 5:6, b.
Cività d'Antino, 141, b.
Cirita di Bagno, 350, b.
Cirita Ducale, 6, b.
Cirità Lavinia, ii. 120, b.
Civita Retenga, 625, a.
Civita Vecchia, 195, a; 585, a, 794, b; ii. 896, b; ii. 1296, a.
Civitas Cadurcorum, 464, a.
Civitas Romana, ii. 115, b.
Civitate. ii. 1115, b.
Civitella, 55, a; 625, a; ii. 1313, a.
Civitella di Tronto, 391, b.
Cius, 452, a.
Clampetia, 451, a.
Clanis, 857, a.
Clanius, 495, a.
Clare, 972, b.
Clastidium, ii. 40, b; ii. 188, a.
Claterna, ii. 1287, b.
Claudia, Aqua (Rome), ii. 850, b.
Claudia, Porticus (Rome), ii. 828, a.
Claudionerium, 226, a.
Claudiopolis, 4, a; 569, a; 406, b.
Claudius, Arch of (Rome), ii. 840, a.
Claudius Centumalus (Rome), ii. 818, a.
Clavenna, 110, b.

Claves Ponti, 424, a.
Clausa, Porta (Rome), ii. 756, a; ii. 759, a.
Clausen, ii. 1041, b.
Claybrook, ii. 1276, a.
Cleitor, 193, a.
Cleitoria, 193, a.
Clemente, ii. 560, b.
Clemente, S., 582, a.
Clementino, S., 1018, b.
Clepsydra, Fountain of (Athens), 286, a.
Clermont, 341, a.
Clewsburg, 694, b.
Clew Bay, ii. 175, a.
Climberris, 389, a.
Climax, 201, b; ii. 606, a.
Climberrum, 338, b.
Clisobra, ii. 48, a.
Cliternia, 55, a; 167, a.
Clitunno, 635, b.
Clivus Urbius (Rome), ii. 824, a.
Cloaca Maxima (Rome), ii. 815, a.
Clodiana, ii. 36, b.; ii. 1298, b.
Clodianus, ii. 52, a.
Clodii, Forum, 870, b.; ii. 1297, b.
Clogher Head, ii. 65, a.
Cluacina, Shrine of (Rome), ii. 783, a.
Cluana, ii. 628, b.
Cluna, 197, b.
Clunium, 691, b.
Clupea, ii. 1338, a.
Clupium, Lake of, 857, b.
Clusius, 684, b.
Cluson, 977, a.
Cluvia, ii. 896, b.
Clyde, 636, a.
Clypea, 67, b.
Cnacalus, 505, a.
Cnausum, 193, a.
Cnemis, ii. 202, b.
Cnidos, 239, b.
Cnopus, 413, b.
Cnossus, 705, b.
Coal Hills, ii. 1325, a.
Coara, ii. 1076, a.
Coblentz, 119, a; 655, a.
Cobus, 643, a.
Coca, 571, a.
Cocconagae, ii. 48, a.
Coccygium, ii. 1176, a.
Cochin, 698, a; ii. 47, a.
Cockermouth, 630, a.
Cocoates, 173, a.
Cucsou, 715, b.
Codanus Sinus, ii. 460, b.
Codesera, ii. 219, b; ii. 965, a.
Codeta (Rome), ii. 841, a.
Codozoso, Castro de, 934. a.
Codos de Ladoco, ii. 115, a.
Codrion, 756, a.
Coedamusii, ii. 298, b.
Coele, 325, a.
Coele (Athens), 302, b.
Coelerini, 933, a.
Coelesyria, ii. 1071, a; ii. 1076, b.
Coelesyria Proper, ii. 1076, b.
Coeletae, ii. 1190, a.
Coeletica, 642, a; ii. 1190, b.
Coeliobriga, 934, a.
Coelos, ii. 1190, a.
Coenyra, ii. 1136, a.
Coeron, 669, a.
Corsfeld, 471, a.
Cosnou or *Couznou*, 697, a.
Coeus, ii. 342, a.
Cognac, 654, a.
Cogni, ii. 12, a.
Combatore, ii. 47, a; ii. 675, b.
Combra, ii. 220, a.
Corr, 110, b.
Counlou, ii. 1042, a.
Colapiani, ii. 542, a.
Colapis, ii. 3, b; ii. 541, b.
Colchester, 442, a; 645, a.
Colchi, ii. 47, a; ii. 658, b.
Colchicus, S., ii. 46, b.
Colenda, 197, b.

Coletiani, ii. 542, a.
Coli, 643, a.
Colias, Cape, 805, b.
Colinca, 729, a.
Coll' Armeno, 592, b.
Coliat or *Collati*, 481, a.
Collatia, 167, a.
Collatina, 167, a.
Collatina, Porta (Rome), ii. 757, b.
Colle Faustiniano, 56, b.
Colle Piccolo, 6, b.
Colle Sacco, ii. 1280, b.
Collina, Porta (Rome), ii. 755, b.
Collioure, 725, b; ii. 35, a.
Collops Magnus, ii. 484, a.
Collytus, 325, a.
Collytus (Athens), 302, a.
Cöln, 646, a.
Colney, 442, b.
Colobi, 58, a, 59, b.
Coloe, 59, b; 1021, a.
Colone, Cape, 498, a.
Colonides, ii. 345, b.
Colonna, La, ii. 690, b.
Colonne, Capo delle, ii. 107, b.
Colonus, 326, a.
Colonus (Athens), 303, a.
Colosseum (Rome), ii. 827, b; ii. 846, b.
Colubraria, 373, a.
Columba, 374, a.
Columbaria, 857, b.
Columbaria (Rome), ii. 821, b.
Columbarium, ii. 911, b.
Columna Bellica (Rome), ii. 833, a.
Columna Cochlis (Rome), ii. 839, a.
Columna Lactaria (Rome), ii. 833, a.
Columnam, Ad, ii. 1295, a.
Comacchio, 459, b.
Comaceni, 691, b.
Comari, ii. 943, a.
Comaria, ii. 46, b; ii. 47, a.
Combré, 651, a.
Comedae, ii. 943, a.
Comedorum Montes, ii. 41, b.
Comidava, 744, b.
Comillomagus, ii. 1287, b.
Comini, 55, a.
Comnium, ii. 896, b.
Como, 1045, b.
Comitium (Rome), ii. 775, b.
Commagene, 977, a; ii. 439, b.
Commenaces, 973, b.
Commodianae, Thermae (Rome), ii. 839, b; ii. 847, b.
Commores, 116, a.
Como, 653, a.
Como, Lago di, ii. 128, a.
Comorin, ii. 47, a.
Comorin, Cape, 643, b; 650, b; ii. 46, b.
Competu, ii. 1267, a.
Complega, 582, a.
Compleutica, 934, a.
Compludo, 934, a.
Compsatus, ii. 1190, a.
Cona, 973, b.
Conaponti, ii. 917, b.
Conca, 714, a.
Conca, Fiume di, ii. 1245, a.
Concam, ii. 49, b; ii. 256, b.
Concangii, 499, b.
Concanii, 502, a.
Concejo de Pilonna, ii. 511, b.
Concord, Temple of (Rome), ii. 781, b; ii. 783, a; ii. 827, b.
Concordia, 653, b; ii. 1287, b.
Concordia, ii. 1275, a; ii. 1287, b.
Concubienses, ii. 1317, b.
Condabora, 582, a.
Condat, Condé, or *Conc*, 654, a.
Condate, 443, a.
Condercum, ii. 1256, b.
Condochates, 973, b.
Cundom, ii. 441, b.

Condraa, 675, b.
Condreu, 654, b.
Condros, 469, a.
Condros or *Condrost*, 655, a.
Conembrica, ii. 220, a.
Conflans, 110, b.
Conflans, L'Hôpital de, ii. 678, a.
Confluenta, 197, b.
Confluentes, 119, a.
Confluentes, Ad, ii. 1287, a.
Congleton, 654, b.
Congosta, 250, a.
Conguaso, 655, b.
Coniaci, 502, a.
Conisci, 502, a.
Conistorgis, 583, a.
Connaught, 346, a; ii. 16, a.
Conope, 64, a; 67, a.
Consabrum, 525, a.
Consentia, 451, a, b; ii. 1294, b; ii. 1295, a.
Conserans, 656, b.
Consilinum or Cosilinum, ii. 210, a.
Constantine, Arch of (Rome), ii. 809, a.
Constantineh, 627, a.
Constantini, Basilica (Rome), ii. 808, b.
Constantinianae, Thermae (Rome), ii. 848, a.
Constantinople, 659, b.
Constantinople, Channel of, 423, a.
Constanz, Lake of, 429, b.
Consuantae, ii. 1310, b.
Consuegra, 525, a.
Contacassyla, ii. 47, a; ii. 245, a.
Contessa, 809, a.
Contoporia, 201, b.
Contosolia, ii. 219, b.
Contra-Taphis, 60, a.
Contrebia, 582, a.
Contrebria, 394, b.
Convenae, 173, a.
Conway, ii. 1214, b.
Cooa, 682, a.
Conxo, ii. 1083, a.
Coolioo, 480, b.
Copais, 411, b.
Cophanta, 521, a.
Cophen, ii. 5 2, a.
Cophos, ii. 1217, a.
Coprates, 874, a; ii. 1050, b; ii. 1209. a.
Coptite Nome, 40, a.
Cora, ii. 127*n*, b.
Coracae, ii. 1170, b.
Corace, 450, b; 563, a.
Coracesium, 617, b.
Coracium Prom., 494, b.
Coradsche, 613, a.
Corallius, 412, b.
Corancali, ii. 47, a.
Corax, 63, b.
Coraxi, 643, a; ii. 943, b.
Corbega, 668, b.
Corbeil, 687, b.
Corbiana, 842, b; ii. 1050, b.
Corbridge, 429, a; 692, a.
Corchuela, ii. 860, a.
Corcollo, ii. 690, a.
Corcyra Nigra, ii. 37, a.
Corda, 515, a.
Cordoba or *Cordova*, 672, a.
Cordova, 368, a.
Corduba, 368, a.
Coressia, 587, a.
Corfinium, ii. 1306, b.
Corfu, 669, b.
Cori, 667, a.
Corifanio, 694, b.
Cornenses, 167, b.
Corineum, 387, b.
Cornium, 442, a.
Corinthia, Porticus (Rome) ii. 834, b.
Coriondi, ii. 16, a.
Corisopiti, 218, b.
Corium, 705, b.
Cormachite, 709, a.
Cormeilles, 720, b.
Cormones, ii. 1275, b.
Cormons, ii. 1275, h.

4 B 4

Cormor, ii. 1275, a.
Cornelii, Forum, ii. 1287, a.
Corneto, ii. 1101, b.
Cornificies, Domus (Rome), ii. 822, a.
Corniscarum Divarum, Lucus (Rome), ii. 841, a.
Corno Monte, ii. 1283, a.
Cornucates, ii. 542, a.
Cornuselle, Lago di, ii. 696, b.
Cornus, ii. 911, b.
Cornwall, 560, b.
Corodamum, 175, b.
Coromandel Coast, ii. 245, a.
Corone, 53, b; ii. 345, b.
Coroneia, 332, a, ii. 1170, a.
Coronta, 10, b.
Coronus, M., ii. 440, a.
Coropassus, ii. 222, b.
Corpiliaca, ii. 1190, b.
Corpilli, ii. 1190, b.
Corragum, 756, a.
Correse, 719, a.
Corseia, ii. 202, b
Corscp, 669, a.
Corsuelt, 720, b.
Corsica, 689, b.
Corsil Point. ii. 448, b.
Corso, Capo, 691, a.
Corstorpitum, 429, a.
Corsula, 6, b.
Corte, 60, a.
Cortex, 686, b.
Cortes, ii. 872, b.
Cortona, 692, a.
Cortyk, 693, b.
Corudeia, 606, b.
Coruña, 195, b.
Coruña, Bay of, 196, a.
Coruña del Conde, 636, b.
Corus, 737, a; ii. 1075, b.
Cory, ii. 46, b.
Cory Island, 532, b.
Coryceum, ii. 357, a.
Corycus, 705, b; ii. 1227, a.
Corydallus, 325, a.
Coryphantis, 53, a.
Coryphasium, ii. 341, b; ii. 682, b.
Corytheis, 192, b.
Cos, 229, b.
Cos or Cox, 696, b.
Cosa, ii. 1296, a.
Cosam, Sub, ii. 1296, a.
Cosanus, 870, b.
Cosavaha, 573, b.
Coscile, ii. 309, b; ii. 1052,a; ii. 1193, a.
Cosenus, ii. 452, b.
Cosenza, 656, a; ii. 1295, a.
Coscyr, ii. 284, a.
Cosi, 697, b.
Cosinthus, ii. 1190, a.
Cosmano, Monte di S., ii. 2, b.
Cosne, 443, a; 654, a.
Cossinites, ii. 1190, a.
Cossoanus, 973, b.
Cossopo, 671, b.
Costa Balaenae, ii. 188, b.
Costa Balenae, 110, a.
Costambol Chai, 124, a.
Costantineh, 69, a.
Costoboci, ii. 916, a; ii. 917, a.
Cotace, 498, b.
Cotacene, 569, b.
Cotantin, or Cotentin, ii. 1318, a.
Côte d'Or, ii. 257, b.
Cotoxtin, ii. 696, b.
Cotrone, 709, b.
Cotschiolan-Kami, 641, b.
Cotta, 696, b.
Cottaeobriga, ii. 1285, b.
Cottiara, ii. 47, a.
Cottiaris, ii. 1002, b.
Cottias, Ad, ii. 1288, a.
Cottopatam, ii. 424, b.
Coturga or Cortuga, ii. 987, a.
Cotylia or Cutilia, 6, b.
Cotyora, 602, a.
Cotyura, ii. 1196, b.
Courland, 56, b.
Courtrai, 693, a.

Couserans, 656, b.
Coutances, 687, a.
Coyns, 844, a; ii. 290, a.
Cozo, ii. 1288, a.
Cramont, 107, b.
Cranburn, ii. 1311, a.
Craneia, 130, b.
Cranii, 588, a.
Crannon, ii. 1170, a.
Crapis, ii. 299, b.
Crassum, Prom., ii. 911, a.
Crataeis, 450, a.
Crathis, 13, b; 450, b.
Crau, 912, b.
Crausundon, ii. 569, a.
Crawfurd, 642, a; 673, b.
Creil, ii. 198, a.
Cremaste, ii. 1170, a.
Cremides, ii. 1136, a.
Cremona, 701, b.
Cremonis Jugum, 107, b.
Crenides, ii. 599, a.
Creonium, 766, a.
Creophagi, ii. 1.
Creopolum, 201, b.
Crepsa, 7, a.
Crescentino, ii. 690, a.
Creus, C., ii. 52, a.
Crimca, ii. 1109, a.
Crimessus, ii. 986, a.
Crimisa, 451, a.
Crimisa, Cape, 447, b.
Crio, C., ii. 1231, b.
Criscia, ii. 1296, b.
Crisophos, 225, b.
Crissa, ii. 605, a.
Crisset, 713, a.
Cristo, Monte, 557, b.
Crithote, 9, b.
Crius, 13, b.
Crixia, ii. 188, b.
Croatia, ii. 36, a; ii. 541, a.
Crocchio, 450, b.
Croce, Capo di Sta, ii. 985, a.
Croce, Monte Sta, 730, a.
Croce Sta, ii. 480, b.
Crocodilopolis, 39, b.
Crocyleia, ii. 98, a.
Crocyleum, 67, a; ii. 203, a.
Crodagh, ii. 1308, a.
Croisette, Cap de la, ii. 1336, a.
Cromarty, Firth, ii. 203, a; ii. 206, a; ii. 1258, a.
Cromer, 442, b.
Cromi, or Cromnus, 192, b.
Cromitis, 192, b.
Crommion, Cape, 730, a.
Cromna, ii. 547, a.
Cropia, 326, a.
Crotalus, 450, b.
Cruz de la Zarza, St., ii. 1308, a.
Cryptos, 729, a.
Ctenus, ii. 515, b.
Ctimene, ii. 1170, b.
Ctista, 973, b
Cuarius, 412, b; ii. 101, a.
Cuba, 58, a.
Cubu, ii. 1041, b.
Cucullo, 715, a.
Cucusis, 369, a.
Cuenca, 525, b; 581, a; 582, a.
Cuellar, 643, b.
Cuerva, 29, b.
Cuesta, Castello de la, ii. 500, b.
Cuglieri, 1020, b.
Cullera, 607, a; ii. 1042, b.
Culmore, ii. 696, b; ii. 1308,a.
Cuma, 716, a.
Cume, 53, a.
Cuminarius, Vicus, 525, a.
Cumnock, 672, a.
Cunarus, Mons, 156, a.
Cuneus, M., ii. 220, a.
Cunici, 374, b.
Cuniculariae, Insulae, ii. 911, b.
Cunicularium Prom., ii.911, b.
Cupra Maritima, ii. 628, b.
Cupra Montana, ii. 628, b.
Cure, 613, a.
Curetes, 9, b.

Curgia, 583, a.
Curge, ii. 1083, b.
Curia, 110, b.
Curiae Veteres (Rome), ii. 804, a.
Curiae, 730, a.
Curiga, 583, a.
Curion, 729, b.
Curiosolites, 218, b.
Curium, 63, b; 730, a.
Curmsul, ii. 46, b.
Curaus, 773, b.
Curris-on-Gore, 720, a.
Curtius, Lacus (Rome), ii. 783, a.
Curubis, ii. 1338, a.
Curzola, 672. a; ii. 37, a.
Cutatisium, 634, a.
Cutch, 184, a; ii. 52, a; ii. 255, a; ii. 559, a.
Cutch, Gulf of, 502, b; ii. 46, b.
Cutilia, ii. 1305, a.
Cutilian Lake, 721, a.
Cutina, 625, a; ii. 1283, b.
Cyamosorus, ii. 985, b.
Cyane, ii. 985, b.
Cyaneae, Insulae, 434, a.
Cyathus, 18, b; 64, n.
Cyblstra, 507, b; 569, a.
Cycloborus, 323, a.
Cyclopis, Atrium or Antrum (Rome), ii. 818, b.
Cydara, ii. 1091, b.
Cydathenaeum (Athens), 302, b; 325, a.
Cydnus, 618, b.
Cydonia, 705, b.
Cyiza, 983, b.
Cylindrina, ii. 47, b.
Cynaetha, 193, a.
Cynia, 64, a.
Cynopolis, 40, a.
Cynopolite Nome, 40, a.
Cynos, Sema, 158, a.
Cynosarges (Athens), 308, b.
Cynoscephalae, ii. 1170, a.
Cynuria, 193, a.
Cynus, ii. 202. b.
Cypaera, ii. 1170, b.
Cyparus, 729, a.
Cyparissus, ii. 342, b.
Cyprus, Vicus (Rome), ii. 824, a.
Cyprus, Keys of, 730, a.
Cypsela, 192, b; 380, b; ii. 1190, a; ii. 1299, a.
Cyretiae, ii. 1170, a.
Cyrrhestice, ii. 1075, b.
Cyrrhus, 634, a; 727, a; ii. 1075, b.
Cyrus, 89, a; 330, a; 559, a; 571, b.
Cyta, 643, a.
Cytaes, 422, a.
Cytaeum, 705, b.
Cytherrus, 342, b.
Cytherus, 1046, a.
Cytni, ii. 542, a.
Cytorus, ii. 547, a, b.
Cyzicus, 239, b.
Cxettina, ii. 1210, a.
Czibru, 614, b.
Czur, ii. 710. a.

Dabistan, 1106, a.
Dachinabades, ii. 47, a.
Dactonium, 934, b.
Dades, 730, a.
Dadichia, ii. 1208, b.
Daedala, 517, b.
Daesitiatae, ii. 541, b.
Daetichae, ii. 47, b.
Dagasira, 983, b.
Daghele, ii. 1208, b.
Daghcstan, 89, b.
Dahistan, 1106, a.
Dahr-el-Maghair, ii. 283, b.
Daisan, ii. 932, b.
Dakash, 227, a; 364, b; 366, b.
Dakhinabhada, ii. 47, a.
Dukkeh, 781, b; ii. 675, a.
Dalamon Tchy, 606, a; 745, b.
Dalin, ii. 13, b.

Dalhay, ii. 192, b.
Dalluntum, 748, a.
Dalmatia, ii. 36, a.
Dalminium, 748, a.
Damanhur, 1059, a.
Damania, 807, b.
Damasi, Montes, ii. 10, a; ii. 46, b.
Dameghan, ii. 1084, b.
Damghan, 1083, b.
Dhanghan, 689, a.
Damiat, or Damietta, ii. 1066, b.
Damour, ii. 606, b.
Dan, tribe of, ii. 529, b.
Danaba, ii. 1076, b.
Danala, 931, a.
Danastia, or Danastus, ii. 1248, a.
Danae, ii. 1093, b.
Dandagula, 480, b; ii. 47, a.
Danube, 750, b.
Danusg, Gulf of, ii. 460, b.
Daphne, 560, b; ii. 1076, a.
Daphnidis, Balneum (Rome), ii. 828, a.
Daphnusia, ii. 1195, a.
Dar-Charamatah, 605, b.
Dara-ben, or Derra-bin, 752, b.
Darachcni, 181, b.
Daradrae, ii. 41, b.
Daram, 770, a.
Darantasia, 110, b; 384, a.
Darapaa, 365, a.
Dardanelles, 754, a; 1038, b.
Dardanelles, Peninsula of the, 608, a.
Dardani, ii. 367, b.
Dardania, ii. 901, b.
Dardare, ii. 41, b.
Dardas, 788, a.
Darfour, 782, b.
Dargamanis, 364, b.
Dargamenes, ii. 552, a.
Dariel, Pass of, 187, a.
Daritis, 210, b.
Dorkiah Tagh, ii. 440, a.
Darnii, ii. 16, a.
Dartsch, ii. 533, a.
Dascyleium, 452, a.
Daseae, 192, b.
Darnis, 733, b.
Dar-el-Hhamara, ii. 1312, a.
Daroca, 582, a.
Darrha, 784, b.
Dashour, 9, a.
Daskalio, 634, b.
Datii, 173, a.
Datiule, 51, b.
Datum, ii. 1136, a; ii. 1190, a.
Davas, ii. 1081, b.
Daventry, ii. 68, a.
Davis, 779, b; ii. 944, a.
Dava, River of, 111, b.
Daulia, 830, a.
Daulis, ii. 543, a; ii. 605, a.
Davno, 748, b.
Davron, 777, a.
Dax or Dacqs, 170, a.
Daz, 389, b; 416, b.
Daxe, 756, a.
Dchas, 784, a.
Dea Carna (Rome), ii. 817, a.
Dea Vocontiorum, 340, b.
Deara, or Dere, ii. 1117, a.
Ueb, 368, b.
Debae, 625, a.
Deboma, 830, a.
Debot or Debou, ii. 550, a.
Debrende, ii. 666, a.
Debreux, 781, a.
Deburiah, 742, a.
Deccan, ii. 47, a; ii. 48, a.
Decelea, 330, a.
Decianae, Thermae (Rome), ii. 848, a.
Decimium, Ad, ii. 1288, a; ii. 1302, a.
Decius, 757, b.
Decumana, Porta (Rome), ii. 789, a.
Decx, 786, b.
Dedebey, ii. 309, b.

Dederiani, ii. 318, a; ii. 483, a.
Dee, 881, a; 779, b; ii. 971, a.
Dee (Aberdeenshire), 772, a.
Dee (in Cheshire), 771, b.
Dee (in Galloway), 772, a.
Derr, 188, b; ii. 1125, a.
Derr Diwan, ii. 355, a.
Dekhuni, 193, a.
Delftland, 501, a.
Delas, ii. 1209, a.
Deli Chai, 116, a.
Deli Hassami, 755, b.
Deliktash, ii. 480, a.
Dellys, ii. 860, a.
Delphi, Mt., 871, a.
Delphinium, ii. 496, a.
Delta, ii. 1180, a.
Demass, ii. 1135, a.
Demawend, 559, a; ii. 440, a.
Dembra, 644, b.
Dembre, ii. 387, b.
Demeter Chloe, Temple of (Athens), 301, a.
Demetrias, ii. 552, b; ii. 1170, b.
Demir Kapi, 1042, a; ii. 14, a; ii. 237, a; ii. 1036, a; ii. 1037, a.
Demir Kapu, 561, a.
Demirissar, ii. 463, b.
Demmcerger-derasy, 103, b.
Demonia, 1103, a.
Demotica, 774, a; ii. 642, b.
Denair, 183, a; 342, a.
Denbighshire, ii. 491, a.
Denderah, ii. 1127, b.
Dendra, 737, a; ii. 353, b.
Denderobosa, 983, b.
Denia, 773, a.
Denizli, 554, a.
Denmark, 1094, a.
Denseletae, ii. 1190, a.
Dentheletica, ii. 1190, b.
Dentheliates, Ager, ii. 345, b.
Densem, 791, a.
Deobriga, 347, a.
Deoghir, ii. 47, a; ii. 49, b; ii. 1084, b.
Dervan, 60, a.
Derbend, ii. 506, a.
Derbend Bournou, 132, b.
Derbent, 89, b.
Derders, ii. 41, b.
Derea, 193, a.
Deren, 318, b.
Derendah, 746, b.
Deris, ii. 277, b.
Derkus, ii. 601, a.
Derna, 733, b; 754, b.
Derne Jailasi, ii. 493, b.
Derrhima, ii. 1076, a.
Dertona, ii. 188, a, b; ii. 1287, b.
Dertum, 167, a.
Dervenaki, 201, b.
Derwent, 771, a.
Derxene, ii. 1333, b.
Despoto Dagh, ii. 713, a.
Deste, 933, a.
Desudaba, ii. 243, b.
Deva, 427, a.
Deva, 771, a.
Devanagari, ii. 49, b.
Develton, ii. 1190, a.
Dèves et le bois de Dève, 756, b.
Devol, 755, b; 830, a.
Devriki, ii. 426, a.
Deuriopus, ii. 512, a.
Deux, 779, b; ii. 1125, b.
Dewlet-Agatch, ii. 1101, b.
Dhadki, 125, b.
Dhafar, ii. 904, b.
Dhafni, 322, a; 326, a.
Dhamala, ii. 1235, b.
Dhamasi, ii. 349, b.
Dhana, ii. 1134, b.
Dhaskalio, 331, b.
Dhavlia, 756, a; ii. 543, a.
Dhefteropoli, 932, b.
Dhemniko, 736, b.
Dhesfina, ii. 300, b.
Dhiles, 760, b.
Dhilissi, 758, a.
Dhionysiodhes, 777, a.

Dhistomo, 121, a.
Dhokhlari, ii. 1196, b.
Dhoko, 166, b.
Dhomoko, ii. 1137, a.
Dragonera, 804, b.
Dhrogonares, 804, b.
Dhrakmerra, M., ii. 268, b.
Dhrama, 787, b.
Dhramia, 1101, a.
Dhramissus, ii. 555, b.
Dhrepano, 771, a; 789, a.
Dhrepano, C., ii. 13, a.
Dhysta, 797, a.
Dia, 422, a.
Diacria, 322, b.
Diades, 254, b.
Diala, 1021, b.
Diana, Temple of (Rome), ii. 810, a; ii. 826, b; ii. 834, b.
Dianae, Sacellum (Rome), ii. 817. a.
Dianum, Ad, ii. 36, b.
Dianium, 857, b.
Diawa, ii. 210, a; ii. 1120, a.
Diaskilli, 755, a.
Djayrah, 1105, a.
Dibbeh, ii. 429, b.
Dicaea, 403, b; ii. 1190, a.
Dictynna, 705, b.
Didier, S., 110, b.
Didjlahi-Kudak, ii. 1209, a.
Didschle, ii. 1208, b.
Diduri, ii. 917, b.
Didyma, 774, a.
Didyme, 51, b.
Die, 340, b; 488, b; 737, a; ii. 213, a; ii. 1318, b.
Djebel Afroun, ii. 1237, b.
Djebel Feeh, 57, b.
Djebel Feel, 976, a.
Djebel Guerioum, ii. 1240, b.
Djebel Zabareh, ii. 1016, a, b.
Djeheyne, ii. 995, a.
Djerrahi, 1034, a.
Djezzret el Sag, 812, a.
Diessen, ii. 657, b.
Dieuze, 757, b.
Djezret Tyran, ii. 63, b.
Digeri, ii. 1190, a.
Diglad, ii. 1208, b.
Diglito, ii. 1208, b.
Digne, 349, a; 409, b; 776, a.
Dii, ii. 1190, a.
Djihoun, ii. 506, b.
Dijon, 773, a.
Dikalika, ii. 1231, a.
Dikeli-Koi, 252, b.
Dikelrick, ii. 881, a.
Dil, 787, b.
Dilos, ii. 1123, a.
Dimastus, ii. 383, b.
Dimitzana, ii. 1155, b.
Dimotico, 1018, a.
Dinan, 893, b.
Dinaretum, 632, b; 730, a.
Dindymene, Mons, 463, b.
Dine, 202, b.
Dingle Bay, 787, b.
Dinia, 349, a; 409, b.
Dio d'Ouro, 752, b.
Dio Rud, 686, b.
Diobessi, 295, b; ii. 1190, a.
Diochares, Gate of (Athens), 263, b.
Dioclea, 748, a.
Diocletianae, Thermae (Rome), ii. 847, b.
Diaforti, ii. 222, a.
Djoliba, ii. 428, a.
Dioneia (Athens), 302, b; 825, a.
Diomean Gate (Athens), 263, b.
Dion, ii. 1076, b.
Dionysiac Theatre (Athens), 284, b.
Dionysopolis, ii. 47, b.
Dionysus, Theatre of (Athens), 283, b.
Diope, 193, a.
Diopolis, 462, b.
Dioscuri, Temple of the (Athens), 299, b.
Dioscurias, 572, a; 643, a.
Diospolis, 396, b.
Diospolis Magna, ii. 1137, b

Djovata, 379, a.
Diour, 229, b.
Dipaea, 192, b.
Dipo, ii. 220, a.
Dipoena, 193, a.
Dipylum (Athens), 262, b.
Dirce, 413, b.
Diribitorium (Rome), ii. 837, a.
Dirillo, 18, a; ii. 985, b.
Dirini, 167, b.
Dirphys, 871, b.
Discus, Protos and Deuteros, 424, b.
Ditis Patris, Aedes (Rome), ii. 816, b.
Ditis Patris et Proserpinae, Ara (Rome), ii. 835, a.
Ditis, Sacellum (Rome), ii. 782, b.
Dittaino, 614, a; ii. 371, b; ii. 985, a.
Dittam, 581, b.
Dio Rud, 521, a.
Diveriigi, ii. 942, b.
Divet, 775, a.
Divitia, ii. 1125, b.
Divle, 770, b.
Dium, 705, b; 872, b.
Divona, 464, a; 517, a.
Divriki, ii. 1338, b.
Dius Fidius, Sacrarium of (Rome), ii. 830, a.
Djustencil, ii. 569, a.
Divus Claudius, Temple of (Rome), ii. 817, b.
Diwaniyah, 363, a.
Diyaleh, ii. 1001, b.
Diyar Bekr, 122, b.
Diz, ii. 1050, b.
Dixful, 666, b; 874, a.
Dnieper, 420, b.
Dniester, 84, a; ii. 1248, b.
Doanas, 825, b; ii. 46, b.
Dobo, 456, a.
Dobrmcne, 380, a.
Dobuni, 571, a.
Docidava, 744, b.
Dodona, 833, a.
Doganlu, ii. 331, b.
Doghiran, 780, b.
Doiram, ii. 237, a.
Dolabella, Arch of (Rome), ii 817, b.
Dolates, ii. 1317, b.
Dole, 77, a.
Doliche, ii. 1170, a.
Dolomene, 606, b.
Dolonci, ii. 1190, a.
Dolopes, 65, a.
Dolopia, ii. 1170, b.
Dolus, ii. 967, a.
Domacki, ii. 1133, a.
Dombai, 342, a.
Domerus, 807, b.
Domitiae, Horti (Rome), ii. 842, b.
Domitian, Statue of (Rome), ii. 795, a.
Domoun Dagh, ii. 480, a.
Domus Transitoria (Rome), ii. 805, b.
Don, ii. 1088, b.
Don Cossacks, 456, a.
Don Kosaks, ii. 917, b.
Donauweschingen, ii. 144, a.
Doncaster, 751, a.
Doncos, 934, b; ii. 1329, b.
Donerx, ii. 1199, b.
Dunetz, ii. 1069, b.
Dongola, 60, a.
Donino, or Domnino Borgo, S., 900, a.
Dnoat-ei-Kuuma, 877, a.
Doodenweerd, 791, a.
Dooree, 184, b.
Doornick, ii. 1240, a.
Doover, ii. 1214, a.
Dor, ii. 530, b.
Dora, 470, b; ii. 607, a.
Dora, 791, b; ii. 1006, b.
Dora Baltea, 107, b; 791, b.
Dora Riparia, 107, b; 792, a.
Doraclum, 788, a.
Dorchester, 442, a.

Dorchester (in Dorsetshire), 792, a.
Dorchester (in Oxfordshire), 792, a.
Dordogne, 791, b.
Doreiade, 382, b.
Dörgen, ii. 1132, b.
Dorias, ii. 46, b.
Doris, 519, b.
Dorisci, 210, b.
Doriscus, ii. 1190, a.
Dorium, ii. 345, b.
Dorno, ii. 1288, a.
Dornoch Firth, ii. 203, a
Dorsetshire, 847, b.
Dosaron, ii. 46, b.
Dos di Trent, ii. 1278, b.
Dotan, 787, a.
Douarnez, ii. 1310, a.
Dovaslam, ii. 331, b.
Doubs, 790, b.
Dover, 442, a; 790, b.
Dover, Straits of, 814, a; 916, b; ii. 460, b.
Douro, 477, b.
Dowlatabad, ii. 1084, b.
Down, 784, b; ii. 101, b.
Draa, 24, b.
Drabescus, 807, b.
Drac, ii. 1230, a.
Drago, 1105, b; ii. 985, b.
Dragoncello, 898, a.
Drako, 307, a.
Drangae, 210, b.
Drapsaca, 365, a.
Drasti, C. 669, b.
Drau, 788, a.
Draudacum, ii. 754. a.
Dravus, ii. 541, b.
Drecanon, 694, b.
Drepane, 669, b.
Drepanon, 729, b.
Drepanum, 13, a.
Drepas, 365, a.
Dreux, 793, b.
Drilae, ii. 658, b.
Drillophyllitae, ii. 48, a.
Drim, 789, a.
Drin at Struga, the, ii. 36, b.
Drima, 789, a.
Drinus, ii. 541, b.
Drivicnza, 789, b.
Drius, ii. 406, b.
Drôme, 789, b; ii. 1318, b.
Drone, 787, b.
Drosica, ii. 1190, b.
Drubetis, 744, b.
Druentia, 107, b.
Drugeri, ii. 1190, a.
Drummburgh, 922, b; ii. 1256, b.
Drusus, Arch of (Rome), ii. 820, b.
Drybactae, ii. 1019, a.
Drylitae, ii. 299, a.
Drymaea, ii. 604, b.
Drymus, 329, b.
Dschidscheli, ii. 454, a.
Dschirdscheh, 60, a.
Dshens-sheer, ii. 497, a.
Dshib, 94, a.
Djatal-Borgas, 393, a.
Djedile, ii. 930, a.
Djibel-Fil, 812, b.
Djibra Palanca, 614, b.
Djiir-Erkene, ii. 642, b.
Duar, ii. 1328, b.
Dubil, ii. 1301, b.
Dublin, 797, a; ii. 16, a; ii. 256, b.
Ducato, Cape, ii. 168, b.
Duden Su, 320, b; 569, b; 641, a.
Due Torri, Colle di, ii. 271, a.
Duero, 792, a.
Dugga, ii. 1237, b.
Dujik Tagh, 505, b.
Duilia, Columna (Rome), ii. 785, b.
Duno, ii. 74, a; ii. 678, a; ii. 1275, b.
Duklista, 784, a.
Dulcigno, ii. 473, a.
Dulgehan, ii. 1075, a.
Dulopolis, 705, b.
Dumbarton, 593, a.
Dumbrek Chai, ii. 1002, a.

Dumfries, 750, a; ii. 1254, a.
Dumfries-shire, ii. 956, a.
Dumna, 49, a; ii. 420, a.
Dumno, 748, b.
Dûna, ii. 716. a.
Duna, ii. 917. a.
Dunany Point, ii. 65, a.
Dungsby Head, ii. 1312, b.
Dunkeron, ii. 101, b.
Dummow, 488, b.
Dunnet Head, ii. 487, a.
Dunoen, ii. 420, a.
Dunsley Bay, 791, a; 922, a.
Dunstable, 793, b.
Dunum, ii. 101, b; ii. 16. a.
Duodecimum, Ad, ii. 1283. a.
Dur, ii. 696, b.
Dur, or Dura, 791, a.
Durance, 107, b; 570, b; 771. b; 789, b; ii. 689, b.
Durazzo, 796, b.
Durdus, M., ii. 299, a.
Duren, ii. 271, a.
Duria, 107, b.
Durli, ii. 1288, a.
Durius, 477, b.
Durnoravia, 442, a.
Durobrivis, 488, b.
Durocortorum, 380, b.
Durolipons, 488, b.
Duronia, ii. 896, b.
Durotriges, 387, b.
Durovernum, 442. a.
Dusseldorf, ii. 1125, b.
Dury Dhaker, 742, b.
Dyar Bekir, 229, b.
Dycallio, 248, b.
Dyme, 14, b.
Dyrin, 791, b.
Dyrta, 243, a.
Dyscelados, 579, b.
Dyspontium, 821, a.
Dystus, 872, b.

E' Syrout, ii. 226, b.
East Riding of Yorkshire, ii. 550, b.
Eastbourne, 135, a.
Eastern Counties, 902, b.
Eause, 822, a.
Eba, 870, a.
Ebajik, 454, a.
Ebchester, 831, a; ii. 1311, b.
Ebellinum, ii. 32, a.
Eblana. ii. 16, a.
Eboli, 799, a; ii. 210. a.
Ebora, ii. 210, a.
Ebora de Alcobaza, 799, a.
Ebot, 8, a.
Ebro, ii. 10, a.
Ebrodunum, 107, b.
Ebrudunum, ii. 904, a.
Eburi, ii. 210, a.
Eburodono, 110, a.
Ebusus, 373, a.
Ecbatana, ii. 301, b.
Ecclesia, ii. 152, b.
Ecclippa, 94, a.
Ecdipna, ii. 606, a.
Echaea, 424, b.
Echedameia, ii. 605, a.
Echelidae, 325, b.
Echetla. ii. 947, a.
Echinus, 10, b; ii. 1170, a.
Echternach, ii. 494, b.
Ecija, 249, a; ii. 504, b.
Ecnomus, 79, b.
Ecsemil, ii. 232, a.
Ed-Doad, 807, b.
Eden, ii. 174, a.
Eder, 25, a.
Edessa, 31, a; 624, a; ii. 236, b; ii. 1298, b.
Edeta, 807, a.
Edfou, 159, b.
Edhra, 807, b.
Edjmal, 396, b.
Edinburgh, 562, a; 750, a.
Edoni, ii. 1190, a.
Edrei, 380, b.
Edremit, 25, a.
Edrene, 10.3, b.
Edrum, 940, a.
Edschmiadzin, 569, b.
Eetionia. 308, a.
Egara, ii. 115, b.

Egelasta, 582, a.
Egerdir, ii. 494, a.
Egeria, Valley of (Rome), ii. 820, a.
Eghina, 82, b.
Egina, Gulf of, ii. 920, a.
Egnatia, 167, a; ii. 1294, a.
Egri-Limen, ii. 619, b.
Egripo, 599, a; 871, a.
Egurri, 249, b.
Ehden, ii. 174, a.
Ehetium, ii. 1294, a.
Eidumannia, 645, b.
Ejerdir, ii. 954, a.
Ein-el-Hye, ii. 270, a.
Einieh, 825, b.
Eion, 807, b.
Eira, ii. 345, b.
Eira, Mountains of, ii. 341, b.
Eiresidae, 327, a.
Eisach, 110, b; ii. 31, a.
Eisadicae, 572, a.
Ekatermoslav, ii. 916, b.
Ekerne, ii. 1211, b.
Ekron, ii. 529, b. a.
El-Ahsa, 181, b.
El-Al, 811, b.
El-Alcater, 380, a.
El-Aliah, 20, a.
El-Araish, 826, a; ii. 501, b.
El-Arish, ii. 709, b.
El-'Asi, ii. 494, a.
El-Azyr, 821, b.
El-'Aujeh, ii. 592, a.
El-Azariyeh, 396, a.
El-Bacharieh, ii. 458, b.
El-Berrocal, ii. 116, a.
El-Birch, 885, a.
El-Budsche, ii. 570, a.
El-Chairy, ii. 277, b.
El-Chaulan, ii. 283, a.
El-Commandante, ii. 219, b.
El-Dakkel, ii. 458, b.
El-Djedur, ii. 101, a.
El-Farafreh, ii. 458, b.
El-Ferrol, 430, a.
El-Fyoom, 225, a.
El-Garib, 789, a.
El-Ghor, 342, b; ii. 521, b.
El-Guettar, ii. 1134, a.
El-Hadramaut, 181. b.
El-Hammah, ii. 1233, a.
El-Hammat-ei-Khabs, 170, a.
El-Haura, ii. 284, a.
El-Herba, ii. 1208, a.
El-Hessue, ii. 699, a.
El-Hesuf, 771, a; ii. 277, b.
El-Hilal, ii. 404, a.
El-Hodna, 317, b.
El-Hosin, 971, b.
El-Jib, 1001. b.
El-Kas, or El-Katish, 37, a.
El-Katich, or El-Kas, 558, a.
El-Katif, 999, a.
El-Khadarah, ii. 486, a.
El-Khaii, ii. 425, b.
El-Khargeh, ii. 459, a.
El-Khubeibeh, 824, b.
El-Khuds, ii. 17, b.
El Khulil, 1033, a.
El-Kods, ii. 27, b.
El-Kulah, 992, a.
El-Kureyetem, ii. 104, a.
El-Lahum, ii. 677, b.
El-Litani, ii. 606, b.
El-Marabba, ii. 275, b.
El-Matnainia, ii. 1134, a.
El-Medinah, 378, a; ii. 131, a.
El-Mejdel, ii. 354, b.
El-Mengaleh, ii. 160, a.
El-Merjeh, 378, a.
El-Mesaourat, ii. 330, b.
El-Mahhad, 978. b.
El-Mrzairib, 232, b.
El-Mith, ii. 368, a.
El-Natroun, 852, b.
El-Padron, 934, b; ii. 117, b.
El-Rif, 37, a.
El-Rocadillo, 527, b.
El-Siwah, ii. 457, b.
El-Skandersuh. 93, a.
El-Tayibeh, 839, a.
El-Term, ii. 104, b.
El-Zemmineh, ii. 277, b.

El-Zerka, ii. 1, a.
Elaea, 705, b; 730, a; 833, a.
Elaeatis, 19, b.
Elaeum, ii. 341, b.
Elaeus, 67, a; 202, b; 330, b; ii. 1190, a.
Elafonisi, ii. 483, b.
Elagabalus, Gardens and Circus of (Rome), ii. 827, b.
Elaphonezia, ii. 377, a.
Elaphus, ii. 310, a.
Elasona, ii. 583, a.
Elassona, ii. 474, b.
Elassonitiko, ii. 463, a.
Elaté, 372, a.
Elatea, ii. 1170, a.
Elatreia, or Elatea, 523, a.
Elaver, 341, a.
Elba, ii. 39, b.
Elbassan, 496, b; ii. 36, b.
Elbe, 93, a.
Elbourz, ii. 962, a.
Elburz, M., 671, b; ii. 554, a.
Elcethium, ii. 987, a.
Elche, ii. 32, a.
Electra, ii. 342, a.
Electris, ii. 901, b.
Elefthero-Khori, ii. 474. b.
Eleni, 481, b.
Elephantophagi, 58, a.
Elephas, 57, b.
Elephas Herbarius (Rome), ii. 832, b.
Elere, ii. 1076. b.
Elethesna, 815, a.
Eletht, ii. 1190, a.
Eleusin, ii. 1158, a.
Eleusinium (Athens), 301, a.
Eleusis, ii. 1161, a.
Eleussa, 331, a.
Eleutrio, S., 844, a; 1073, b; ii. 1294, a.
Eleutherae, 329, a.
Eleutherion, 201, a.
Eleutherna, 705, b.
Eleutheropolis, 354, a.
Eleutherus, ii. 606, a; ii. 986, a.
Elia, Capo di S., ii. 911, b.
Elias, Mt., 609, b; 871, b; ii. 1160, b.
Eliberre, 838, b.
Elineia, ii. 236, b.
Elimiotis, ii. 550, a.
Elis, 193, a.
Elisari, 821, b.
Ell, 1034, a.
Elindka, ii. 1032, a.
Elland, 488, a.
Ellebri, ii. 14, a.
Ellinikokastro, 134, b.
Ellopium, 67, a.
Elmah Dagh, 24, b.
Elne, ii. 34, b.
Elone, ii. 1170, a.
Elpidio a Marc, S., 636, a; ii. 628, b.
Elsatz-Zabern, ii. 1082, a.
Elten, 103, b.
Elulli, ii. 299. a.
Eluro, ii. 115, b.
Elusates, 173, a.
Elwend, ii. 495, a; ii. 534, a.
Elwend, M., ii. 4, b.
Elymbo, ii. 479, b.
Elymbo, Mt., 331, a.
Elymia, 192, b.
Elyrus, 705, b.
Emathia, ii. 1171, a.
Emba, ii. 11, b.
Embeshanda, 708, b.
Embics, ii. 661, a.
Embiex, ii. 1113, b.
Embolima, 243, a.
Embro, ii. 42, a.
Embrum, 107, b; 798, b.
Emineh Burnu, ii. 463, a.
Eminium, ii. 210, a.
Emissa, ii. 1076, a.
Emmaus, 385, a; ii. 532, b.
Emodus, ii. 46, a.
Empulum, ii. 1200, b.
Emporiae, Gulf of, ii. 52, a.
Emporium (Rome), ii. 812, a.
Ems, 122, b; 444, b.

Emsfukrew, 128, a.
En-Nasirah, ii. 407, a.
Ena, ii. 987, a.
Enabasi, ii. 299, a.
Enba, 490, b.
Enchelariae, 786, a.
Endor, ii. 530, b.
Ene, 826, b.
Engarek, 133, b.
Engedi, 124, b.
Engern, 137, a.
English Channel, ii. 460, b.
Engyum, ii. 986, b.
Enneacrunus (Athens), 292, a.
Enneakhoria, ii. 42, b.
Ennsdorf, ii. 636, a.
Enos, 50, a.
Enosis, ii. 911, b.
Ensem, Ad, ii. 1301, a.
Enernch, 141, b.
Enshemesh, ii. 529, b.
Entella, ii. 187, b; ii. 986, b.
Enty, ii. 1230, b.
Enyora, ii. 270, a.
Eordaea, ii. 236, b; ii. 568, b.
Eoritae, 184, a.
Epacra, 330, b.
Epakto, ii. 402, b.
Epanomeria, ii. 1160, b; ii. 1161, a.
Epanterii, ii. 187, b.
Epaphroditiani, Horti (Rome), ii. 826, a.
Epe, 53, b.
Epetium, 748, a.
Ephesia, 5, a.
Ephesus, 239, a.
Ephialtium, 534, a.
Ephron, M., ii. 529, b.
Ephthalitae, 1097, b.
Ephyra, 67, a; 193, a; 821, a.
Epidaurus, 748, a.
Epidaurus Limera, ii. 112, b.
Epideires, 392, a.
Epidian Promontory, 750, a.
Epidii, 750, a.
Epidium, Prom. 593, a.
Epidotium, ii. 3, b.
Epila, 581, b.
Epiodorus, 642, b.
Epiphaneia, 560, b; ii. 1076, a.
Epipolae (Syracuse), ii. 1066, a.
Episcopiano, 607, b.
Episkopi, 1004, b.
Episkopiano, ii. 356, b.
Epitalium, 821, a.
Epoissum, ii. 494, b.
Epomeus, Mt., 49, b.
Eporedia, ii. 1287, b.
Epiermach, ii. 494, b.
Equa, 496, a.
Equabona, ii. 220, a.
Equestrian Gate (Athens), 263, b.
Equus Tuticus, 1073, b; ii. 1294, a.
Er-Ram, ii. 691, a.
Eragiza, or Errhasiga, ii. 1075, b.
Erana, 116, a; ii. 346, a.
Erannoboas, ii. 534, a.
Erannoboas, 973, b; ii. 48, a.
Erasinus, 13, b; 201, a; 323, b.
Eraskh, 188 a.
Erbad, 189, b.
Erbessus, 79, b.
Ercolano, 1052, b.
Ercte, ii. 985, a.
Erd-Mukhna, ii. 412, b.
Erdek, 226, b.
Erdini, ii. 16, a.
Erechtheum (Athens), 275, a.
Erekli, 1050, a; ii. 1101, b.
Erekli, or Eregli, 849, a.
Erenopoli, 1018, a.
Erenuesis, 478, b.
Eresso, 846, a.
Eressus, ii. 168, a.
Bretria, ii. 1170, a.
Eretum, ii. 1305, a.
Erga, ii. 32, a.
Ergavica, 582, a.

Ergetium, il. 987, a.
Ergina, 74, b.
Ergitium, 167, a.
Ergonisi, ii. 469, a.
Ericinium, il. 1170. a.
Ericusa, 51, b.
Erikho, li. 493, a.
Erimon, 451, a.
Erineum, 17, a.
Erineus, il. 986, a.
Eriss, il. 165, a.
Erisso, 9, a.
Eriston, it. 1127, b.
Eritium, il. 1170, a.
Erkene, 848, b.
Erkle, 353, a.
Ermeni, 1058, b.
Ermitade Muestra; Señora
   de Termes, ii. 1131, b.
Ernatia, il. 231, b.
Erne, Loch, 346, a.
Erness, 219, b.
Erochus, ii. 604, b.
Erpeditani, ii. 16, a.
Erquica, ii. 697, a.
Errebantium, Prom., ii.
   911, a.
Ersad, ii. 916, b.
Erse, 229, a.
Erwend, il. 495, a.
Erycinum, ii. 912, a.
Erymanthus, 184, b; il.
   676, a.
Erymini, ii. 943, b.
Erythini, ii. 547, b.
Erythrae, il. 203, a; 705, b.
Erythraeum Mare, 174, b.
Erzeroom, 7, a.
Evagebirge, ii. 1185, a.
Erzi, 692, a.
Erzugan, 613, b.
Erzrum, 614, b.
Es-Serr, il. 952, b.
Es-Sham, 749, a.
Es-Shirrah, il. 521, b.
Esaro, 450, b.
Escaut, il. 926, b.
Escaut-pont, il. 637, b.
Esch, 854, b.
Eschatiotis, 685, b.
Escoussé, or Escoursé, il.
   951, a.
Esdom, il. 1018, a.
Esdraelon, il. 530, b.
Esdud, 355, a.
Esh-Sham, ii. 1069, b.
Esh-Sherah, ii. 583, b.
Eshinoon, 1058, b.
Esino, 56, a; ii. 1301, b.
Esker, il. 469, b.
Eski-Eregli, il. 577, a.
Eski-Hissar, il. 122, a; il.
   642, b; ii. 712, b; ii. 1037, b
Eski-Kalen, il. 577, a.
Eski-Kara Hissar, 400, a;
   il. 1055, b.
Eski-Krim, ii. 1109, b.
Eski-Samsun, 122, b.
Eski-Sbchr, 786, b.
Eski-Stambul, 102, b.
Eskihissar, il. 122, a; il. 642,
   b; ii. 712, b; il. 1037, b.
Eskupshi, il. 930, a.
Esky Adalia, 616, a; il.
   993, a.
Esne, 46, a.
Esneh, il. 144, a.
Espartel, C., 125, a.
Espejo, 336, a; ii. 101, a; il.
   376, b.
Espichel, C., il. 253, a.
Esquers, il. 499, b.
Esquilina, Porta (Rome),
   il. 755, b.
Esquiline (Rome), il. 872, a.
Esquilinus, Campus (Rome),
   il. 825, a.
Esquilinus, Lucus (Rome),
   ii. 826, b.
Esquillade, P, il. 1037, a.
Essex, il. 1231, a.
Essenide, il. 1333, a.
Essina, il. 425, b.
Este, 254, a; il. 1275, a; il.
   1287, b.
Estevan de Val de Orres, S.,
   250, a.

Estevan, S., ii. 1306, a.
Esthen, 56, b.
Esthonia, 1073, b; 1091, b.
Estiae, 494, b.
Estiffen, ii. 1036, a.
Estola, 249, b.
Estoy, ii. 220, a; il. 501, a.
Estrella, Sierra de la, 1057, a.
Estremadura, 525, a.
Estreung in Chaussée, or
   Estrun Cauchie, 794, b.
Et-Taiyibch, ii. 484, b.
Et-Tell, 398. b.
Etang de l'Estouma, 912, b.
Etea, 705, b.
Etini, il. 987, a.
Etovissa, 807, a.
Etymander, 183, b.
Eua, 193, a.
Eva, 726, a.
Evan, il. 341, b.
Evander, Altar of (Rome),
   il. 810, a.
Evandriana, il. 220, a.
Evarchus, ii. 547, a.
Euburiates, ii. 187, a.
Eucleia, Temple of (Athens),
   296, a; 297, b.
Eucratidia, 364, b.
Eudieru, il. 1170, a.
Evenus, 600, b.
Evergetae, 210, b.
Eufemia, Sta, ii. 117, b; ii.
   1131, a.
Eufemia, Golfo di Sta,
   1070, b.
Eufemia, Gulf of St., ii. 397,
   b; il. 1130. b.
Euganei, Colli, 873, b.
Eugeia, 193, a.
Euhydrium, il. 1170, a.
Eulaeus, 366, b; il. 1209, a;
   il. 1050, b.
Euonymus, 51, b.
Evora, 797, a; il. 220, a.
Eupagium, 821, a.
Eupalium, ii. 203, a.
Eupatorium, ii. 1111, b.
Euphrantas, il. 600, a.
Euphratensis, 652, a.
Euploea, 495, b.
Euryidae, 326, a.
Euran Sheher, il. 407, a.
Evreokastro, 331, b.
Evreux, 799, b; il. 303, a.
Evreux, Vieil, il. 303, a.
Euristus, ii. 561, b.
Euroea, 833, a.
Europae, Porticus (Rome),
   il. 839, b.
Europe, 877, b.
Europus, 624, a; 737, a; il.
   1075, b.
Eurymedon, il. 538, a.
Eurynenae, 833, a; il. 1170, b.
Eurysaces, Monument of
   (Rome), il. 827, a.
Eurysaces, Porta (Rome),
   ii. 760, a.
Eurytanes, 65, a.
Euryteiae, 17, a.
Eutaea, 192, b.
Rutre, 193, a.
Eutresia, 193, a.
Eutresil, 193, a.
Ewenny, 418, b.
Exarkho, 1, b.
Exeter, il. 66, b; il. 1331, a.
Exmouth, il. 65, a.
Exobugitae, il. 917, a.
Exomti, C., ii. 1161, a.
Eygur, il. 289, b.
Exadschen, ii. 1225, b.
Exatalexa, il. 1135, b.
Exeuga, il. 903, a.
Exevo, 232, a.
Ezion-Geber, 392, b.
Ezla, 249, b.

Fabius, or Fabianus, Fornix
   (Rome), il. 758, b.
Fabrateria, il. 1302, b.
Fabricius, Pons (Rome), ii.
   849, b.
Fachs, il. 593, a.

Facialcaxar, ii. 885, b.
Faenza, 894, a; il. 1287, a.
Faga, 412, a; il. 300, b.
Faga, M., il. 483, a.
Farr Head, 754, b; il. 718, b.
Falais, 28, b.
Falconara, 239, b; il. 986, a.
Falacrinum, il. 1306, a.
Faleria, ii. 628, b.
Faleria, Portus, 870, a.
Falerii, il. 1288, a.
Falese, Porto, 890, b.
Falleri, Sta Maria di, 890, b;
   il. 1288, a.
Fallerona, 890, b.
Fallerone, ii. 628, b.
Falmouth, ii. 1321, b.
Fama Julia, 883, a.
Famagosta, 730, a.
Famich, 152, a.
Fammars, 893, b.
Famnenne, Pays de, ii.
   511, b.
Fanari, 19, b; 304, a; ii.
   99, a.
Fanary, Cape, ii. 1111, a; ii.
   1111, b.
Fano, 150, a; 893, a; il.
   1301, a.
Fanum Fortunae, il. 1301, a;
   il. 1317, b.
Fanum Fugitivo, il. 1300, b.
Faouet, le, 893, b.
Farfa, 889, a.
Farfarus, 889, a.
Farina, C., 159, a.
Farina, Porto, il. 1328, b.
Farmaco, il. 589, a.
Farnay, 911, a.
Farndon, ii. 657, b.
Farnese, il. 295, b; il. 1042, b.
   il. 1297, b.
Farnese, Isola, il. 1261, a; il.
   1297, a.
Farnham, il. 1311, b.
Faro, Capo di, il. 571, b.
Farras, 60, b.
Farsan, il. 1017, b.
Fasana, 808, b.
Faventia, il. 1287, a.
Faveria, ii. 73, b.
Favignana, 32, a.
Faunus, Temple of (Rome)
   il. 840, b.
Favonii, Portus, 691, b.
Fayen, il. 182, b.
Fazukla, 58, a.
Febris, Altar of (Rome),
   il. 826, b.
Fecrussa, il. 585, b.
Fenss, 901, b.
Ferra, ii. 220, b.
Feiran, Wady, il. 588, a.
Felibedjik, il. 600, a.
Felice, S., 626, a.
Felicita, Sta, il. 1306, b.
Felicudi, 51, b.
Felines, 900, b.
Felipe, S., il. 1035, b.
Felix, Cape, 57, b; 812, b;
   976, a.
Fellerdagh, 148, a.
Felonica, 896, b.
Feltre, 894, b.
Feltria, il. 1275, b.
Felujah, 362, a.
Fenestella, Porta (Rome),
   il. 757, a.
Penny Stratford, il. 246, a.
Ferath Maian, 904, b.
Ferentina, Porta (Rome),
   il. 757, b.
Ferentino, 895, a; il. 1302, a.
Ferentium, 1073, b.
Ferentinum, il. 1302, a.
Ferento, 894, b.
Ferentum, 167, a.
Feretrius, Temple of Ju-
   piter (Rome), il. 769, a.
Feritor, il. 187, b.
Fermanagh, 846, a.
Fermo, 901, b; il. 628, b.
Fermo, Porto di, il. 628, b.
   il. 1307, a.
Fermosel, il. 461, a.
Fermoselle, il. 461, b.

Peronia, il. 912, a.
Perrah, il. 620, a.
Perrera, 907, a.
Perrecanah, il. 1134, a.
Ferreira, il. 692, b.
Ferrières, 169, a.
Ferro, 906, b.
Ferro, Capo di, il. 911, b.
Ferro, Cap, il. 1037, a.
Ferro, Colle, il. 1280, a.
Ferrol, Bay of, 196, a.
Ferrol and Coruña, Bay of,
   430, a.
Ferrol, G. of, 933, b.
Fersala, il. 501, a.
Fersaliti, 827, b.
Ferse, 912, a.
Fessah, 344, b.
Feurs, 910, b.
Fex, il. 296, b.
Fezzan, 732, a; 974, b; li.
   457, a.
Fiano, 902, b.
Fiascone, Monte, 894, a.
Fibreno, 897, b.
Ficaria, 691, b; il. 911, b.
Fichtel-, Erz-, and Riesen-
   gebirge, 1056, b.
Ficus Ruminalis (Rome),
   il. 802, b.
Fidentia, il. 1287, a.
Fidentiola, il. 1287, a.
Fidhari, 600, b.
Fidhart, or Fidharo, 888, b.
Fidil, Vicus (Rome), il.
   811, b.
Fiesole, 889, b.
Figlinas, Ad, il. 188, b,
   il. 53, a.
Fil-burun, 424, b.
Filadelfo, S., 113, a.
File, il. 1209, b.
Filena, il. 1209, b.
Filey Bay, 922, a.
Fill, 329, b.
Fillea, or Filma, il. 599, a.
Filurrna, 1046, b; il. 231, a;
   il. 236, b; il. 322, a.
Filyas, 402, b.
Fineka, Cape, il. 193, a.
Fines, il. 115, b.
Fines, Ad, il. 1288, a; il.
   1296, a.
Finiki, il. 605, a.
Finistère, 1004, a.
Finisterre, C., 934, b.
Finni, il. 913, b.
Fins, 573, a.
Fiora, 857, a; il. 1296, a.
Fiorenzuola, 904, a; il. 1287,
   a.
Fir-Bolgs, 320, b.
Firstina, il. 1232, b.
Firmanum, Castellum, il.
   1307, a.
Firmanum, Castrum, il.
   628, b.
Firmum, il. 628, b.
Firth of Forth, 409, b.
Fiscellus, Mons, 156, a.
Fischament, 55, a.
Fismes, 901, a.
Fittre, 607, a.
Fiume della Maddalena,
   495, a.
Fiume delle Canne, 490, a.
Fiume di Jaco, 21, a.
Fiume di Noto, 239, b.
Fiume di Pescara, 254, a.
Fiume Freddo, 12, a; 81, a.
Fiume Salso, il. 585, b.
Fiumenica, 450, b; 706, a;
   1103, a.
Fiumicino, il. 857, a.
Flacciana Area (Rome), il.
   804, b.
Flagogna, il. 1275, b.
Flamborough, 923, a; il. 667,
   a.
Flaminia, Porta (Rome),
   il. 758, b.
Flaminia Prata, or Campus
   Flaminius (Rome), il.
   832, b.
Flaminii, Forum, il. 1300, b;
   il. 1301, a.
Flaminius, Circus (Rome),

ii. 832, a; ii. 833, b; ii.
844, a.
Flamonia, ii. 1275, b.
Flavia Solva, 902, b.
Flaviae, Aquae, 168, b;
934, a.
Flaviae, Templum Gentis
(Rome), ii. 831, b.
Flaviano, S., 864, b.
Flavionavia, 250, b.
Flavium, Amphitheatrum,
(Rome), ii. 846, b.
Flenium, 912, a.
Fleva, or Flega, 331, a.
Flevum Castellum, 903, b.
Flintshire, ii. 491, a.
Florae, Circus (Rome), ii.
831, a; ii. 844, b.
Flora, Temple of (Rome),
ii. 829, b.
Florence, 903, b.
Florentia, ii. 1287, a.
Florius, 933, b.
Flumendosa, ii. 911, a.
Flumentana, Porta (Rome),
ii. 781, a.
Flumeniorgia, ii. 912, a.
Flusor, ii. 629, a.
Fluvia, ii. 52, a.
Fogria Nova, ii. 603, b.
Fokia, Cape, 1101, a.
Fokschani, ii. 1196, b.
Foligno, 919, a; ii. 1300, b;
ii. 1301, a.
Fondi, 919, a; ii. 1290, a.
Fonsatiko, ii. 594, a.
Fontainebleau, 169, a.
Fontana Grande, 376, a.
Fontaneira, 934, b; ii.
1210, a.
Fonte Bello, 376, a; 774, b.
Fontinalis, Porta (Rome),
ii. 750, b.
Forca Carruso, ii. 42, a.
Forca Carusa, 186, b.
Forca di Caruso, ii. 282, b.
Forcassi, Sta Marie ia,
907, b.
Forchia, 874, a.
Fordcsillas, ii. 1121, a.
Fordongianus, 911, b.
Fordungianus, ii. 911, b;
ii. 912, a; ii. 1196, a.
Forenza, 896, a.
Forex, or Foreste, 911, a.
Forfarshire, ii. 1276, a.
Foriflamma, S. Gio. m, ii.
1301, a.
Forli, 910, a; ii. 1287, a.
Forlimpopoli, 910, b; ii.
1287, a.
Formeniera, 873, a.
Formiae, ii. 1290, a.
Formiche di Grosseto,
857, b.
Formio, ii. 1275, a.
Fornovo, 910, a.
Forobrentani, ii. 1317, b.
Forojulienses, ii. 1317, b.
Fors Fortuna, Temple of
(Rome), ii. 841, a, b.
Fortin, ii. 1214, b.
Fortore, 166, b; 916, b.
Fortuna, Altar of (Rome),
ii. 830, b.
Fortuna Mammosa (Rome),
ii. 821, b.
Fortuna Primigenia, Temple
of (Rome), ii. 830, b.
Fortuna Publica, Temple of
(Rome), ii. 830, b.
Fortuna Respiciens, Sacel-
lum of (Rome), ii. 804, a.
Fortuna Respiciens, Temple
of (Rome), ii. 826, b.
Fortuna Seia (Rome), ii.
826, b.
Fortuna, Temple of (Rome),
ii. 814, a.
Fortuna Temples of (Rome),
ii. 830, b.
Fortuna Virilis, Temple of
(Rome), ii. 814, a.
Fortunae, Ara (Rome), ii.
838, a.
Fortunae Dubiae, Vicus
(Rome), ii. 811, b.

Fortunae Equestris, Aedes,
(Rome), ii. 834, b.
Fortune, Temple of (Rome),
ii. 769, b.
Forty Saints, ii. 482, b.
Forum (Rome), ii. 778, b.
Forum Augusti (Rome),
ii. 799, a.
Forum Boarium (Rome),
ii. 812, b.
Forum Cigurrorum, 250, a.
Forum during the Republic
(Rome), ii. 783, b.
Forum Esquilinum (Rome),
ii. 827, a.
Forum Flaminii, ii. 1317, b.
Forum Fulvii, ii. 188, a.
Forum Gallorum, ii. 32, a;
ii. 1287, a.
Forum Julii, 108, b; 522, b;
ii. 1275, b.
Forum Julium (Rome), ii.
797, a.
Forum Livii, ii. 1287, a.
Forum Novum, 1073, b; ii.
1293, b.
Forum Olitorium (Rome),
ii. 832, b.
Forum Piscarium (Rome),
ii. 833, a.
Forum Piscatorium (Rome),
ii. 786, b.
Forum Pistorium (Rome),
ii. 812, b.
Forum Popilii, ii. 706, b;
ii. 1294, b.
Forum Popillii, ii. 210, a.
Forum Populii, ii. 1287, a.
Forum Segustavarum, 911,
a.
Forum Trajani, ii. 1196, a.
Forum Transitorium
(Rome), ii. 799, b.
Forum Vibii, ii. 188, a.
Forum under the Empire
(Rome), ii. 789, a.
Forum under the Kings
(Rome), ii. 778, b.
Forum Vulcani, 497, a.
Posenbrock, 912, a.
Fos-les-Martigues, 913, a.
Fossa, ii. 911, b.
Fossa, ii. 1283, a.
Fossae, 719, a.
Fosso dell' Incastro, 195, b;
563, b.
Fosso delle Fratocchie, 156,
b.
Fosso di Valca or Varca,
701, a.
Fossombrone, 911, a; ii.
1301, a; ii. 1317, b.
Foug. 901, b.
Foul Bay, 57, b; ii. 42, b.
Fox, 912, b.
Fraga, ii. 32, a.
Francoli, ii. 1041, b.
Frango Limiona, 685, a.
Francovryn, 232, b.
Frank Mountain, 1061, b.
Frangu Cap de la, ii. 170,
b.
Frascati, ii. 1241, b.
Frascolari, ii. 985, b.
Fratuertium, 474, b.
Fratulum, 1073, b.
Fraxinus, ii. 219, b.
Freddo, Fiume, 706. b.
Fregellanum, ii. 1302, b.
Fregenae, 870, b.
Frejus, 908, b; ii. 1045, a.
Fren-Kevi, ii. 484, b.
Frento, 166, b.
Friesland, 917, a.
Frigidus, Fluvius, ii.
1275, a.
Frikea, 68, b.
Friniates, ii. 187, a.
Frioul, 108, b.
Fritzlar, ii. 450, b.
Friuli, Cividale di, 909, a.
Frontignan, Etang de, ii.
1035, a.
Frosinone, 917, a; ii. 1302,
a.
Frusino, ii. 1302, a.

Frebio, ii. 677, a.
Fucino, Lago, 917, b.
Fucugirola, ii. 1043, a.
Fuenllana, ii. 118, a.
Fuente de la Onejuna, ii. 322,
a.
Fuente de Saburra, ii. 974, a.
Fuente Ventura, ii. 678, b.
Fuerteventura, 906, b.
Fugitivi, Fanum, ii. 1301, a.
Fuka, 157, a; ii. 416, b.
Fulfulae, ii. 896, b.
Fulginium, ii. 1300, b; ii.
1301, a; ii. 1317, a.
Fulvia, Basilica (Rome), ii.
787, a.
Fundi, ii. 1290, a.
Funduklu, 423, b.
Fünfkirchen, ii. 1022, a.
Furconium, 350, b; ii. 1283,
a, b.
Furculae, 574, b.
Furinae Lucus (Rome), ii.
841, a.
Furlo, IL, ii. 1301, a.
Furna, 759, b.
Furrah, ii. 620, a.
Fyne, Loch, ii. 154, b.

Gabae, ii. 578, b.
Gabala, ii. 1075, a, b; ii. 1076,
a.
Gabalf, 173, a.
Gabiana, 822, b.
Gabiene, ii. 1050, b.
Gabii, 4, a.
Gabriel, St., 850, b.
Gabs, ii. 1063, a.
Gad, tribe of, ii. 531, a.
Gadara, ii. 521, b; 1076, b.
Gadeni, 750, a.
Gadora, ii. 1076, b.
Gaeta, 471. b.
Gaeta, Mola di, 904, b; ii.
1290, a.
Gaganaea, 744, b.
Gaggera, Fiume, ii. 986, a.
Gagliano, 926, b.
Gaknavi, 973, a.
Gaidharonisi, 331, a; ii. 558,
b.
Galactophagi, 4, a.
Galactophagi Scythae, ii.
943, b.
Galactopotae, 4, a.
Galadrae, 830, a.
Galanda, 932, b.
Galandos, ii. 191, a.
Galaria, ii. 987, a.
Galatae, 477, a.
Galatas, Palaeocastron of, ii.
1133, a.
Galaticus, Pontus, 508, a.
Galarathi, ii. 468, b.
Galaxie, 477, a.
Galbiana et Aniciana, Horrea
(Rome), ii. 812, a.
Galeata, ii. 1317, b.
Galefon, 1010, a.
Galepsus, ii. 1133, b.
Galera, 516, b; ii. 1297, b.
Galibi, M., ii. 1093, a.
Galicia, 743, b; 932, b.
Galilee, ii. 531, b.
Galilee, Sea of, ii. 1197, a.
Galindae, ii. 916, a.
Galisteo, ii. 860, a.
Galizia, ii. 870, a.
Gallaeci, 933, a.
Gallaeci Lucenses, 226, a.
Gallego, ii. 32, a.
Galicae, 897, b.
Gallican, ii. 49, b.
Gallica Flavia, ii. 32, a.
Gallicano, ii. 560, a.
Gallica, ii. 1109, a.
Gallicum, 703, a; ii. 32, a;
ii. 237, a.
Gallicum, Fretum, ii. 460,
b.
Gallicus, ii. 32, a.
Gallieni, Arcus (Rome), ii.
827, a.
Galliko, 803, b; ii. 237, a.
Gallinaro, 93, b.
Gallinaria Insula, 93, b.

Gallipoli, 481, b; 482, a;
606, a.
Galloway, ii. 986, a.
Gallo, C., ii. 341, b.
Galaforo, 604, b.
Galway, 346, a.
Gowalik, 486, a.
Gamalitica, ii. 532, a.
Gambia, 752, b; ii. 295, a.
Gandaki, 973, b.
Gandar, 922, b.
Gandarae, ii. 47, b.
Gandari, ii. 1019, a.
Gandaritis, ii. 565, b.
Gandava, 184, a.
Gandharas, ii. 47, b; ii. 1019,
a.
Gangani, ii. 16, a; ii. 47. b.
Ganganorum, Prom., 499, b.
Gangara or Gaetara, 90, a.
Gangarides, Calingae, 480, b.
Gange, ii. 47. a; ii. 49, b.
Gangeticus, Sinus, ii. 46, b;
ii. 52, a.
Gangi, ii. 986, b.
Gangi Vetere, 927, a.
Ganuari, 466, a.
Gap, 488, b; ii. 1258, a; ii.
1318, b.
Garagnone, ii. 1001, b; ii.
1293, a, b.
Garaphi M., ii. 299, a.
Garbos, ii. 399, b.
Gorde, C. de, ii. 454, a.
Gardhiki, ii. 127, b; ii. 868,
b; ii. 586, b; ii. 587, b.
Gardo, Cape del, 57, a.
Gardon d'Alais, ii. 1258. b.
Gardon d'Anduze, ii.
1258, b.
Gardum, ii. 657, b.
Garea, 192, b.
Garen, 514, b.
Gargano, Monte, 976, a.
Gargettus, 327, a, b.
Gargyttes, 977, a.
Gariannonum, 442, b.
Gariennus, 645, b.
Gargitiano, ii. 196, a.
Garites, 173, a.
Garito, 327, a.
Garsai, Mont, 214, a.
Garonne, 977, a.
Garsaouria, 508, b.
Garsauritis, 507, b.
Garulli, ii. 187, b.
Garumni, 173, a.
Gasorus, 807, b.
Gastritzi, ii. 226, b.
Gasuan, 817, a.
Gata, C. de, 604, a.
Gatheae, 192, b.
Gathestas, ii. 309, b.
Gatte, Capo delle, 730, a; ii.
228, a.
Gavala, ii. 626, a; ii. 1230, a.
Gavata or delle Gatte, Capo,
720, a.
Gavdapoulo, ii. 484, b.
Gave d'Aspe, ii. 1047, a.
Gaulanitis, ii. 532, a.
Gaulos, ii. 470. b.
Gaureleon, 136, a.
Gauri, 1006, b.
Gaurion, 136, a.
Gaurion, 136, a.
Gaya, ii. 1238, b.
Gaza, 320, b.
Gazuan, Mount, 978, a
Ge Curotrophus, Temple of
(Athens), 301, a.
Gebal Shamil, 520, b.
Gebel-el-Sammn, ii. 606, b.
Gebel-esh-Sheikh, 380. b.
Gebel Shammar, 363, b.
Gebae, 745, b.
Gedrosem, 210, b.
Gedrosii, 210, b.
Gedrusii, 210, b.
Geroch, ii. 1217, b.
Gelae, 90, a; ii. 302, a.
Geles, ii. 983, b.
Gelbus, 1002, a.
Geldern, 604, a.
Geldub, Geib, or Gellep,
482, b.
Gelduba, 482, b.

Gellep or *Gelb*, 986, a.
Geloni, 643, a.
Gelves, ii. 1278, b.
Gemblou, 986, b.
Gemella, 11, a.
Gemeri, 1021, a.
Gemina, 250, b.
Geminae, 934, a.
Geminae, S., 527, a.
Gemona, ii. 1275, b.
Gemoniae, Scalae (Rome), ii. 783, b.
Gendevar, 499, a.
Genethes, ii. 658, b.
Geneva, Lake of, ii. 155, b.
Genèvre, Mont, 107, b; ii. 296, a.
Gennaro, Monte, ii. 211, b.
Gennesareth, ii. 1197, a.
Genoa, ii. 188, b.
Genoa, Gulf of, ii. 189, a.
Genua, ii. 188, a, b.
Genuates, ii. 187, a.
Genusium, 167, b.
Genusus, ii. 533, a.
George, St., ii. 107, a.
Georgen, St., ii. 107, a.
Georgia, ii. 9, a; ii. 922, a.
Gephyra, ii.1076, a.
Gephyra, Mutatio, ii. 236, b.
Gerace, ii. 109, a.
Geraestus, 871, b.
Gerasa, ii 1076, b.
Gerash, 988, b.
Gerasi, 613, a.
Gerasus, 714, b.
Gerenia, ii. 112, b.
Gergen Kal'-ah-si, 218, b.
Gergitha, 471, a.
Gergove, 991, a.
Gerione, 999, b.
Germalus (Rome), ii. 802, b.
German Ocean, 998, a; ii. 400, b.
Germaniciana, Victoria (Rome), ii. 806, b.
Germanicum, Mare, ii. 460, b.
Germano, S., ii. 1302, b.
Germany, 992, b.
Germasioo, 992, a.
Gerine, 931, a.
Germe, 701, b.
Germersheim, ii. 1308, a.
Germizera, 744, b.
Gerona, 344, b.
Geronthrae, ii. 112, b.
Gerra, ii. 1076, b.
Gerraei, 181, b.
Gerraicus Sinus, 321, b.
Gerrhe, ii. 1075, b.
Gerrhi, ii. 917, b.
Gerrhus, 89, b.
Gers, 977, a.
Gertus, 999, b.
Gerun, ii. 471, a.
Gerunda, 844, b.
Gerunium, 167, a; 756, a.
Gerus, 756, a.
Gesocribate, 443, a.
Gesoriacum, 442, b.
Getae, 746, b.
Getae, Horti (Rome), ii. 842, a.
Getafe, 525, a; ii. 1213, b.
Gevaudan, 920, a.
Gevini, ii. 917, a.
Grurgowatz, ii. 1210, a.
Ghafsah, 510, a.
Ghamari, C., 552, a.
Ghara, ii. 658, a.
Ghats, ii. 46, b.
Ghaur or *Ghor*, 612, a.
Ghaur or *Ghorian*, 364, b.
Ghax, 982, a.
Ghazni, 980, b.
Ghebae, ii. 182, b.
Ghela, 20, b.
Ghella, ii. 461, a.
Ghellak, 562, b.
Ghent, ii. 1217, b.
Ghera, 157, b.
Gheraki, 999, b.
Gherba, 591, b.
Ghermano, 36, b.
Ghermotzuma, ii. 676, a.
Gherra or *Gera*, 11, b.

Gharsek, 554, b.
Gheurek, ii. 1175, b.
Ghialbra, 873, a.
Ghidek, ii. 625, b.
Ghiedia, 463, b.
Ghiedia Chai, 463, b.
Ghieukler, 463, b.
Ghio, 629, a.
Ghioftro, ii. 1223, b.
Ghiouriston, 722, a.
Ghir, C. 317, b.
Ghirne, 593, b.
Ghiuk-Su, 484, a.
Ghrustendil, ii. 237, a; ii. 559, a; 933, a.
Ghuzel Hissar, ii. 1220, b.
Ghore, 977, a.
Ghori, 364, b.
Ghremnah, 734, a.
Ghuriano, M., 1018, b.
Ghysto-Kastro, 329, a; ii. 642, a.
Ghymno, ii. 1087, a.
Ghynekokastro, ii. 671, a.
Ghyrahe, ii. 1063, a.
Giannuti, 773, a; 857, b.
Giaour Irmak, 124, a.
Giarretta, 61, a; ii. 985, a.
Gibraltar, 483, a.
Gibraltar, Straits of, 225, a.
Giens, ii. 661, b.
Gieritza, ii. 1023, b.
Gieuk Bonar, 463, b.
Gifil, 744, b.
Giglio, 857, b; ii. 29, b.
Giglius, M., ii. 1080, b.
Gigonza, ii. 874, a.
Gigurri, 249, b.
Gihon, 364, b.
Gijon, ii. 442, a.
Gilan, 464, a; 986, a.
Giligammae, ii. 277, b.
Gillette, 971, a.
Ginaea, ii. 887, b.
Gindarus, ii. 1076, a.
Gines, ii. 1278, b.
Gines, San, ii. 1174, a.
Ginosa, 167, b; 988, a.
Giostra, La, ii. 644, b; ii. 1122, a.
Giovanni di Bidino, S. 401, b.
Giovanni pro Fiamma, or *m. Foriflamma*, 908, a.
Giove, Monte, 686, b.
Giovenazzo, 167, a.
Gircaro, 1091, b.
Girgenti, 74, b.
Giromagny, 1018, a.
Gironde, 407, b.
Girone, 999, b.
Girost, ii. 1190, b.
Gitanae, 833, a.
Giva, 379, a.
Giubileo, Castel, 809, a.
Giudicello, 121, b; ii. 986, a.
Giulia Nuova, 564, b; ii. 6з8, b; ii. 1307, a.
Giuliano, S., 852, b.
Giupan, 810. a.
Giustendil, ii. 1314, a.
Givyza, 745, b.
Giza, ii. 690, b.
Gizzo, ii. 567, b.
Glagovacz, ii. 64, a.
Glandimarium, 934, a.
Gianum, ii. 887, a.
Glaphyrae, ii. 1170, a.
Glarentza, 724, b.
Glarentza, C., 606, b.
Glastonbury, ii. 168, a.
Glava, ii. 469, b.
Glaucanitae, ii. 47, b.
Glaucus, 13, b; 517, b.
Glaucus, Sinus, 1003, b.
Glemona, ii. 1275, b.
Glen Luce, 750, a.
Glevum, 442, a.
Glinditiones, 748, a.
Gloucester, 442, a.
Gloucestershire, 571, a; 781, a.
Glunista, 790, a.
Gmund, ii. 288, b.
Gnaxia, Torre di, ii. 1294, a.
Goa, ii. 47, a.
Goaria, ii. 1076, a.
Goaris, 210, a.

Godaikh, 569, b.
Godavari, ii. 46, b; ii. 47, a. ii. 245, a.
Godavery, ii. 1247, b.
Godeim, 498, b.
Godesberg, 173, b.
Godmanchester, 488, b.
Godo, 420, a.
Goffras, 571, a.
Gogerddinlik, ii. 1085, b.
Gogvyn, 569, a; 715, b.
Gókdje Deniz, Lake, ii. 223, b.
Golden Horn, 614, a.
Goleutz, 932, b.
Golewitza, 463, a.
Golfo di Squillace, 447, b.
Golfo di Sta Eufemia, 447, b.
Golo, 691, a.
Goloe, 463, a.
Gomera, 906, b.
Gomeroon, ii. 873, a.
Gomphi, ii. 1170, a.
Gondali, ii. 48, a.
Gondwana, ii. 1332, b.
Goniek, 163, a; 722, b.
Gonnus, or *Gonni*, ii. 1170, a.
Gonzalo, Puente de Don, ii. 1006, b.
Gophna, ii. 532, b.
Gordes, ii. 1325, a.
Gorditanum Prom., ii. 911, a.
Gordyaean Mts., 216, a.
Gorgon, 857, b.
Gorgona, 857, b; 1005, a.
Gorgoro, ii. 227, b.
Gorr, ii. 552, a; 488, b; 754, a.
Goritza, 769, b.
Gorkum, 559, a.
Gormak, 463, b.
Gormanum, ii. 7, b.
Gortho, 674, a.
Gortyna, 705, b.
Gortynia, 624, a.
Gortys, or Gortyna, 193, a.
Gorya, ii. 47, b.
Gorydala, 241, b.
Gothard, Mont St. ii. 161, a.
Gothard, St. 107, a.
Gou-el-Kebber, 138, b.
Govind, ii. 702, b.
Gourabeli, ii. 448, b.
Gouril, 673, b.
Goutchka, Lake of, 217, a.
Gozo, 979, b; ii. 470, b.
Graan, 1018, a.
Graan Harb. 688, a.
Grabaea, 748, a.
Grabusa, 694, a; ii. 1227, a.
Grachatz, ii. 4, b.
Graciosa, 906; ii. 678, b.
Gracsanwicza, 1018, b.
Gradischie, ii. 920, b.
Gradstza, 456, b.
Grado, 171, b.
Graecostasis Imperial (Rome), ii. 791, b.
Graen, or *Grane*, 601, b.
Grahovo, 1009, b.
Grambousa, 699, a.
Gramsta, ii. 236, b; ii. 491, b.
Grammiccia, 504, b.
Grammium, 705, b.
Grampian Hills, 1018, a.
Gran, 999, a.
Gran Canaria, 906, b.
Gran Michele, 803, b; ii. 987, a.
Gran Sasso, ii. 1132, b.
Gran Sasso d'Italia, 123, b; ii. 1283, a; ii. 1325, a.
Granada, ii. 34, b; 491, b.
Granatula, ii 491, b.
Grande, Fiume, 1069, a. ii. 986, a.
Grandes, ii. 170, b.
Grandimirum, 934, a.
Granja, La, ii. 32, a.
Granis, 371, b.
Granitza, 412, b; 1035, b.
Granvillars, 1018, a.
Granville, 1018, a.
Grasse, 1091, a.

Gratian, Arch of (Rome), ii. 839, b.
Gratianus, Pons (Rome), i. 850, a.
Graubündten, 499, b.
Grave, Pointe de, 720, a.
Gravia, 739, a.
Gravil, 983, a.
Gravina, 167, b; ii. 641, a; ii. 1293, a.
Graviscae, ii. 1296, a.
Great Britain, 432, a.
Great Chesters, ii. 1256, b.
Greatchester, 56, a.
Grebius, 810, a.
Greco Capo, ii. 295, a.
Greece, 1010, a.
Grega, Capo della, 730, a.
Grenoble, 570, a; 715, b.
Greoulz, 1019, a.
Gresst, ii. 260, b.
Grevena, 815, b; ii. 236, b; ii. 550, a.
Grevene, 815, b.
Gridinum, 364, b.
Grimadka, or *Grimala*, ii. 1087, b.
Grimaud, Gulf of, ii. 888, b.
Grion, 519, a.
Grisnex, Cap., ii. 90, a.
Grisons, 108, a; ii. 700, a.
Grissia, 744, b.
Gritziano, ii. 588, b.
Groain, ii. 1275, b.
Grodno, ii. 30, a; ii. 916, a.
Groede, or *Gronde*, 1019, a.
Groningen, 619, a.
Gros Kemba, 488, a.
Grossa, ii. 37, a.
Grosso, Cape, ii. 1196, a.
Grotta Maronsa, 847, b; ii. 1305, a.
Grotiaglie, 474, b.
Grovii, 933, a.
Gruii, 933, a.
Grumentum, ii. 210, a; ii. 1205, b.
Grumo, 167, b; 1019, b.
Grumum, 167, b.
Grusia, ii. 9, a.
Grynaei, ii. 943, b.
Grynexa, 53, a.
Guadajoz,ii.886, a; ii. 1000,b.
Guadalajara, 224, a.
Guadalaviar, ii. 1239, b.
Guadalimar, 368, a.
Guadalquivir, 367, b.
Gnaulel, C., 606, a.
Guadiamar, 368, a; ii. 329, a.
Guadiana, 130, b.
Guadiana, S. Lucar de, ii. 666, b.
Guadiaro, 377, a.
Guadix el viejo, 11 a.
Gualdo, ii. 1083, a; ii. 1301,a.
Gualili, ii. 1334, b.
Guaon, Rio de, ii. 1034, b.
Guardafui, Cap, 2з0, b; 752, a.; ii. 340, b.
Gubbio, ii. 30, a.
Guebara, ii. 694, b.
Guedel, ii. 1311. a.
Guenet, 754, b.
Guemené, ii. 1325, a.
Guenesera, ii. 1335, b.
Guernsey, 949, b; ii. 920, b.
Guevra, or *Guerm*, ii. 63, b.
Guglionisi, 916, a.
Guido, Castel di, ii. 205, a.
Guienne, 173, a.
Guigurra, 250, a.
Guipuscoa, ii. 1258, b.
Guipuzcoa, 346, b.
Guirvan, 89, b.
Guisona, 627, b; ii. 1, b.
Guitinez, 934, b.
Gulgrad, 523, b.
Gulgrad, Cape, ii. 1211, b.
Gunecheh, 649, a.
Gunichie, ii. 1337. a.
Gumishkie, ii. 1131, b.
Gunduk, 655, a.
Gunyunta, 374, b.
Guntia, ii. 1310, a.
Gunty, 652, a.
Güniz, 1090, b.

Gura, ii. 505, a.
Gurgam, ii. 299, a; ii. 920, b; ii. 1017, b.
Gwrgo, 795, b.
Gurgures, Montes, 156, a.
Gurk, 516, a.
Gurkan, 1106, a.
Gurla, 19, b.
Gurna Longa, ii. 371, b.
Gurrea, ii. 32, a.
Gurschine, ii. 1125, a.
Gurtlana, ii. 1230, a.
Gurulis Vetus and Nova, ii. 912, a.
Gustendil, ii. 1038, b.
Gutae, ii. 927, b.
Guzal-Hissar, ii. 1194, b.
Guzel-hissar, ii. 252, a.
Guzerat, ii. 52, a; ii. 125, b.
Gymnosophistae, ii. 48, a.
Gyndes, ii. 1209, a.
Györgg, 391, b.
Gypopolis, 424, a.
Gyrach, ii. 1245, b.
Gyrton, or Gyrtona, ii. 1170, a.
Gythium, ii. 112, b.
Gythones, ii. 915, b.
Gyxantes, 461, a; ii. 1339, b.
Gyxis, ii. 277, b.

Hadadrimmon, ii. 299, a.
Haddington, 923, a; ii. 504, b.
Hadgrnella, 694, b.
Hadjar-selseleh, ii. 482. a.
Haciba, 607, a.
Hadji Tous Ghkieul, 131, a.
Hadramaut, 25, a; 605, b; ii. 359, a.
Hadria, ii. 1307, a.
Hadrian, Aqueduct of (Athens), 293, b.
Hadrian, Arch of (Athens), 293, a.
Hadriani, Circus (Rome), ii. 844, b.
Hadriani, Mausoleum or Moles (Rome), ii. 842, b.
Hadrianopolis, ii. 1190, a.
Hadrianum (Rome), ii. 839, a.
Hadrumetum, 68, a.
Haemi Extrema, ii. 1178, a.
Haemimontus, ii. 1190, b.
Haemoniae, 192, b.
Haemus, ii. 463, a; ii. 1177, b.
Haffur, 874, a.
Hafoom, ii. 485, b.
Hagar, 1032, b.
Haghia Rumeli, ii. 1105, b.
Hagho Galene, ii. 1046, a.
Haghio Kyrko, ii. 197, a.
Haghio Myro, ii. 703, a.
Haghios Epiphanios, 729, b.
Haghios Georghios, ii. 351, b.
Haghios Nikolaos, 466, a.
Haghios Stavros, ii. 480, b.
Haghios Theodhoros, 456, a.
Haghius Dheka, 1006, a.
Hagisik, ii. 496, b.
Hagnus, 327, b.
Haj, ii. 1219, a.
Haifa, ii. 1053, b.
Haimava, ii. 46, a.
Hamburg, 522, b.
Harx, 1031, b.
Halae, ii. 202, b.
Halae Aexonides, 327, b.
Halae Araphenides, 332, a.
Haleb, 394, a.
Halesus, ii. 986, a.
Halex, 450, a.
Halia, ii. 1171, a.
Halicarnassus, 239, b
Halice, 1058, a.
Halicyae, ii. 986, b.
Halicyrna, 67, a.
Halimus, 327, b.
Halinghen, ii. 1308, a.
Halton, 1098, b.
Halton Chesters, ii. 1256, b.
Halus, 193, a; ii. 1170, a.
Halycus, ii. 985, b; ii. 1161, b.

Halys, 490, b; ii. 658, b
Hamadan, 320, b; 799, b; ii. 301, b.
Hamah, 843, a.
Hamamat, ii. 681, a.
Hamawli Ghieul, ii. 404, a.
Hamath Zobah, 598, b.
Hamaxobii, ii. 916, b.
Hamburg, ii 276, b.
Hami, 240, b.
Hamiz, 370, b.
Hammam, 876, b.
Hammam-el-Berda, 170, a; ii. 1199, b.
Hammam-el-Enf, ii. 299, b.
Hammam Gurbos, 168, b.
Hammam l'Enf, 168, b.
Hammam Meriga, 168, b.
Hammam Meskutin, ii. 1199, b.
Hammam Mezkoutin, 170, a.
Hammam Truxxa, 169, a.
Hampshire, ii. 951, a.
Handakur, ii. 506, a.
Hannibalis, Parva, 374, b.
Hanover, 606, a.
Hanxzabek, ii. 883, b.
Haouch Alowna, ii. 988, a.
Haouch-el-Khrma, ii. 1134, a.
Harau, 526, a.
Harb nation, 579, b.
Harb tribe, 815, a.
Harfleur, 523, b.
Harma, 329, b; 413, b.
Harmatelia, 437, b.
Harmosica, 127, a.
Harmozon, 520, b.
Harmuza, 521, a.
Harpa, 1031, a.
Harpasus, 519, a.
Harpessus, ii. 1178, a.
Harpinna, 821, a.
Hartz Mountain, 1056, b.
Harx, M., ii.319, b; ii. 961, b.
Hasbeia river, ii. 619, b.
Hascooe, 926, a.
Hassis, 353, a.
Hasta, ii. 188, b.
Hastam, ii. 1296, a.
Hatera, ii. 237, a.
Havagichay, 1025, b.
Havilah, 606. a.
Haura, ii. 284, a.
Hauran, the, 1031, b.
Housberge, ii. 14, a.
Haustenbeck, ii. 1133, b.
Haut Chemm, ii. 1318, b.
Hawks, Island of, ii. 911, b.
Hawr or El-Hawra, ii. 283, a.
Hay, 49, a.
Hazaras, 972, b; ii. 914, b.
Hazezon-Tamar, 124, b.
Hazur, ii. 1208, b.
Hebberstow, ii. 667, a.
Hebrides, 1033, b; ii. 717, b.
Helorus, ii. 986, a.
Hecale, 330, b.
Hecate, 760, b.
Hecatombaeon, 17, a.
Hecutounesi, 53, a.
Hecatostylon (Rome), ii. 834, a.
Hedic, ii. 1275, b.
Hedin or Hesdin, ii. 1308, a.
Hedjaz, 181, b; 579, b.
Hedylium, 412, a.
Hedython, ii. 1050, b.
Hejax, 181, b; 579, b.
Heins, 901, a.
Helchou, ii. 600, b.
Helen, St., ii. 1155, b.
Helene, Cape, ii. 662, a.
Heles, ii. 210, a.
Helfendorf, ii. 67, b.
Helice, 14, b.
Helicon, 376, b; ii. 986, a.
Hellcranon, 833, a.
Heliogabali, Circus (Rome), ii. 844, b.
Heliogabalus, Temple of (Rome), ii. 806, b.
Heliopolis, 39, b; ii. 1076, b.
Heliopolite Nome, 39, a.
Helisson, 111, b; 192, b.
Hellenica, 625, a.
Hellenico, 727, b.
Hellenista, 53, b.

Helleporus, 450, b.
Hellodos, Portus, ii. 1178, a.
Helmend, 163, b.
Helorus, 450, b.
Helvillum, ii. 1301, a; ii. 1317, b.
Hem Ryck, 713, a.
Hembury, ii. 372, a.
Hems, 824, b.
Henares, ii. 1088, a.
Heniochi, 572, a; 643, a; ii. 917, b.
Henly, 182, a.
Hephaestus, Temple of (Athens), 298, b.
Hephaestiadae, 336, b.
Hephaestias, ii. 186, b.
Heptacometae, 461, b; ii. 658, b.
Hequaesi, 933, a.
Heraclea, 21, a, ii. 1296, b.
Heraclela, 10, b; 53, a; 254, b; 588, b; 821, a; ii. 36, b; ii. 237, a; ii. 1075, b.
Heraclean Promontory, 1049, a.
Heracleopolis, 39, b.
Heracleote Nome, 39, b.
Heracles, Couch of, 424, b.
Heracleum, 705, b.
Heracleustes, ii. 384, a.
Heraea, 193, a.
Heraeatis, 193, a.
Heraeum, 685, a; ii. 912, a.
Herakie, 1050, a.
Herat, 102, a; 210, a.
Heratemis, ii. 578, b.
Herault, 187, b; ii. 175, a.
Herbanum, 870, b.
Herbellonium, ii. 1301, a.
Herbessus, ii. 986, b; ii. 987, a.
Herbita, ii. 987, a.
Herbulenses, ii. 987, a.
Hercates, ii. 187, b.
Herculem, Ad, ii. 1296, a.
Hercules Custos (Rome), ii. 833, a.
Hercules Musarum (Rome), ii. 833, b.
Hercules Olivarius (Rome), ii. 815, b.
Hercules, Pillars of, 1054, a.
Hercules, Round Temple of (Rome), ii. 813, b.
Hercules Sullanus (Rome), ii. 826, b.
Hercules, Temple of (Rome), ii. 813, b.
Hercules Victor (Rome), ii. 826, b.
Hercules Arenae, 733, b.
Herculis Insula, ii. 911, a.
Herculis Labronis, or Liburni, Portus, 870, a.
Herculis, Magna Ara (Rome), ii. 813, b.
Herculis Portus, ii. 911, b.
Hercuniatae, ii. 542, a.
Hercyna, 412, b.
Herdonia, 167, a. ii. 1294, a.
Heri Rud, 214, b.
Herran Gate (Athens), 263, b.
Herius, 443, a; 791, b.
Hermaeum, ii. 277, b.
Hermaeum, Promontorium, 424, a; ii. 911, a.
Hermandus, 184, b.
Hermes, ii. 333, b; ii. 384, b.
Hermon, Mount, 380, b.
Hermonthis, 40, a.
Hermonthite Nome, 40, a.
Hermopolis, 39, b.
Hermopolite Nome, 39, b.
Hermus, 325, b.
Herodeum, ii. 532, a.
Herodium, ii. 532, a.
Heroopolis, 39, b; 174, b.
Heroopolite Nome, 39, a.
Herpeditani, ii. 299, a.
Hergam Kalch, 124, b.
Hervelt, 563, a.
Herzegovina, ii. 36, a.
Hesban, 1062, b.
Hesperides, 733, b.
Hesperidum, Lacus, 733, b.

Hessen, 605, b.
Hessus, ii. 303, a.
Hestiae, 424, a.
Hestiaeotis, ii. 1169, b.
Hetriculum, 451, a.
Hezham, 351, b; 830, b.
Hex, 1031, b.
Hesron, ii. 529, b.
Hicesia, 51, b.
Hiera, 51, a; 477, a; ii. 165, b.
Hiera Sycaminus, 60, a.
Hieraka, 327, a; ii. 1336, b.
Hierapetra, Kastele af, 1065, a.
Hierapolis, 737, a; ii. 1075, b.
Hierapytna, 705, b.
Hierasus, 744, b.
Hières, Isles d', ii. 597, a; ii. 684, b; ii. 1087, a.
Hierocepia, 730, a.
Hieromax, 922, b.
Hieron, 424, b.
Hieron, 841, a.
Hierus Fluvius, 691, a.
Highcross, ii. 1276, a.
Higuera, C., ii. 466, a.
Higuera, S. Iago della, ii. 948, a.
Hiisban, 1062, b.
Hillah, 363, a.
Hilmend, 850, b.
Himalaya, ii. 41, a; ii. 46, a.
Himalayan Range, 825, b.
Himavat, 825, a.
Himera, ii. 985, b; ii. 986, a.
Himyari, 1090, a.
Hindostan, ii. 667, b.
Hindu Kush, 364, b; 505, b; ii. 41, a; ii. 46, a; ii. 552, a.
Hingul, ii. 1216, a.
Hinojares, ii. 1311, b.
Hipparis, ii. 985, b.
Hippasil, 241, b.
Hippemolgi, 4, a.
Hippi Prom., 1070, a; ii. 454, a.
Hippo, 69, a; 525, b.
Hippo Diarrhytus, ii. 1338, a.
Hippo Regius, 68, a; ii. 455, a.
Hippo Zarytus, 68, a.
Hippocrene, 1035, b.
Hippocronium, 705, b.
Hippocura, 210, a; ii. 47, a.
Hippodameian Agora (Athens), 308, a.
Hippolytus, Tomb of (Athens), 301, a.
Hipponensis Sinus, 1070, a.
Hipponian Gulf, 447, b.
Hipponium, 448, a.
Hippophagi Sarmatae, ii. 917, b.
Hippophagi Scythae, ii. 543, b.
Hippuros, ii. 1091, b.
Hippus, 643, a; ii. 1076, b.
Hiranyavaka, ii. 48, a; ii. 534, a; 973, b.
Hirmeniy, ii. 1042, a.
Hirminius, ii. 985, b.
Hispalis, 368, a.
Hispellum, ii. 1317, a.
Hissan Ghorab, 499, a.
Histiaea, 871, a.
Histiaeotis, ii. 1167, a; ii. 1169, b.
Histoë, 705, b.
Histonios, 916, a.
Histonium, 915, b.
Hit, ii. 65, a; ii. 508, a.
Hoang-ho, 881, a.
Höchst, ii. 376, b.
Höhe, ii. 1108, b.
Hohenembs, 749, b.
Hollow Elis, 817, a.
Holme, 442, b.
Holipade, 367, a.
Holy Land, the, ii. 516, a.
Holwan, 596, a.
Holwood Hill, ii. 450, a.
Homeritae, 181, b.
Homilae, ii. 1170, b.
Homole or Homolium, ii. 1170, b.

Homs, ii. 1076, a.
Honam, ii. 966, b.
Honaver, ii. 441, b.
Honos and Virtus, Temple of (Rome), ii. 769, b; ii. 819, a.
Honosca, 807, a.
Hoozoomlce, 485, b.
Hoplias, 413, a.
Hoplites, 413, a.
Horatiana, Pila (Rome), ii. 780, a.
Horbeyt, ii. 588, b.
Horibel, 1091, a.
Horitae, 983, b.
Hormarah, ii. 555, a.
Hormuz, ii. 471, a.
Hornsea, ii. 607, a.
Horreum, 813, a.
Horta, 870, b.
Hortensius, House of (Rome), ii. 804, b.
Hortorum, Collis (Rome), ii. 831, b.
Horum Ziche, 187, a.
Horusen, ii. 696, a.
Horzoom, 575, a; 615, a.
Hosaca, ii. 912, a.
Hostolrick, ii. 115, b.
Hostilia, ii. 1287, b.
Hostilia, Curia (Rome), ii. 779, a.
Houat, ii. 1275, b.
Houat, Isle de, ii. 973, b.
Houlz, ii. 286, b.
House-Steeds, 420, a.
Housesteads, ii. 1256, b.
How, 778, a.
Hu, 778, a.
Huarte Araquil, 183, b.
Huesca, ii. 32, a; ii. 498, a.
Huelva, ii. 483, a.
Huex, ii. 1260, b.
Huines, 901, a.
Humago, ii. 74, a.
Humana, ii. 1307, a.
Humber, 7, a; 429, b.
Hundu de devant et Men-foulet, 1091, a.
Hünenring, ii. 1238, b.
Hungory, 743, b; ii. 541, a.
Hilningen, 210, b.
Hunnum, ii. 1256, b.
Hunse, ii. 1318, a.
Huntingdon, ii. 1270, a.
Hunts, 571, a.
Hutalidsch, ii. 1329, b.
Hüsban, 1063, a.
Huy, 655, a.
Hyampolis, ii. 604, b.
Hybla, ii. 987, a.
Hybla Major, ii. 987, a.
Hyccara, ii. 986, b; ii. 987, b.
Hydata, 744, b.
Hydra, 64, a; ii. 987, a.
Hydra, 1101, a.
Hydrabad, 210, a; 1070, a; ii. 47, a; ii. 49, b.
Hydramum, 705, b.
Hydraotes, 25, a; 501, b.
Hydruntum, 474, b.
Hydrus, 1102, a.
Hydrussa, 586, b.
Hylaethus, ii. 202, b.
Hyle, ii. 203, a.
Hylea, 3, b.
Hyleësa, ii. 552, b.
Hylias, 450, b.
Hylica, 413, b.
Hypachaei, 620, b.
Hypacyris, 999, a.
Hypana, 821, b.
Hypanis, 571, b.
Hypata, ii. 1170, b.
Hypatus, 414, a; 1003, b.
Hyperacrii, 322, b.
Hyphantelum, 412, a.
Hypsas, 706, b; ii. 59, b; ii. 985, b.
Hypseremos, 485, a.
Hypsilibounos, ii. 387, a.
Hypsitanae, Aquae, ii. 912 a.
Hypsus, 193, a.
Hyrcana, 1106, a.
Hyria, 64, a; 474, b.
Hyrie, 64, a.

Hyrium, 167, a.
Hyrium or Hyrina, 496, a.
Hyrmine, 821, a.
Hyrtacina, 705, b.
Hysalti, ii. 1190, a.
Hysia, 193, a.
Hyssus, ii. 658, b.

Ja'ferët, ii. 297, b.
Jabbok, 390, b.
Jaders, ii. 33, a.
Jabel Aared, ii. 1336, a.
Jablanatz, ii. 648, b; ii. 678, b.
Jabneel, ii. 529, b.
Jabruda, ii. 1076, b.
Jabul, 598, b.
Jaca, ii. 1, b.
Jacca, ii. 1, b.
Jact, Furme di, ii. 966, a.
Jadera, ii. 33, a.
Jaen, 343, a.
Jaeta, ii. 986, b.
Jaffa, 470, b ; ii. 62, b.
Jaffuleen, ii. 387, a.
Jah Jirm, 1033, b.
Jaik, 746, b.
Jakli, ii. 106, b.
Jalbus, 571, a.
Jaliso, ii. 3, a.
Jalloo, 338, a.
Jalousa, 730, a.
Jaiowa, ii. 970, b.
Iysus, ii. 713, b.
Jama, ii. 1336, a.
Jamanitae, ii. 284, a.
Jamboli. 750, a.
James, Cape, St., ii. 1161, a.
Jamnia, 396, b; ii. 532, a.
Jamno or Jamna, 374, b.
Jamporina, ii. 1190, a.
Jamuna, 973, b; ii. 60, b.
Janar Dagh, ii. 480, a.
Jangaucari, ii. 299, a.
Jani (Rome), ii. 788, b.
Janiculum (Rome), ii. 840, b.
Janohah, ii. 530, a.
Janot, 199, a.
Jantra, ii. 5, b.
Janula, 323, a.
Janus Curiatius (Rome), ii. 824, b.
Janus Quadrifrons (Rome). ii. 813, a.
Janus, Temple of (Rome), ii. 778, b ; ii. 832, b.
Japati, or Japti, ii. 396, a.
Japhia, ii. 530, b.
Iapis, 323, a.
Iapodes, ii. 542, a.
Iapydes, ii. 542, a.
Jarrow, ii. 243, a.
Iasili, ii. 542, a.
Jask, C., 520, b ; 746, a.
Jasoon, ii. 5, a.
Iasus, 519, a.
Jathrippa, ii. 283, b.
Jatinum, 475, b.
Jatioa, ii. 872, b.
Jato, ii. 2, b.
Java, 209, a ; ii. 1, a.
Javols, 135, a.
Javeur Dagh, 114, b.
Jaxamatae, ii. 47, a.
Jaxartae, ii. 943, b.
Jaxartes, 188, b.
Ibera, 807, a.
Iberingae, ii. 47, a.
Ibi, ii. 10, b.
Ibrahim Rud, 129, b ; 521, a ; 1030, b.
Ibrim, 60, a ; ii. 396, b ; ii. a.
Icaria, 328, b.
Icarus, 364, b.
Iceland, ii. 1191, a.
Ichana, ii. 987, a.
Ichthyophagi, 58, a ; 210, b ; 983, b ; ii. 241, a.
Iciani, 488, b.
Ickburg, ii. 12, a.
Icklingham, 488, b.
Ichthys, 817, b ; ii. 593, b.
Ictis, 963, b.

Ida, ii. 13, a.
Idanusa la Vieja, 808, a.
Idomenia, ii. 237, a.
Idomene, 624, a.
Idrae, ii. 916, b.
Idrar-n-Deren, 318, b.
Idria, ii. 129, a.
Idro, 808, a ; 940, a ; 1102, a.
Idubeda, Mt., 502, b.
Jean-Jean, ii. 1234, b.
Jebel-'Ajlun, ii. 253, b.
Jebel Akdar, 732, b.
Jebel Allaki or Ollaki, 392, a.
Jebel Amour, 318, a.
Jebel Athal, ii. 276, b.
Jebel Attarus, ii. 413, b.
Jebel Aurus, 342, b.
Jebel Barkah, 1054, a.
Jebel Deira, 348, b.
Jebel-el-Akra, 557, b.
Jebel-el-Mina, 8, a; ii. 298, a.
Jebel-es-Sur, ii. 973, b.
Jebel-ash-Shurki, 140, b.
Jebel-et-Tur, 251, b.
Jebel Furcidis, 397, a.
Jebel Hadrar, 317, b.
Jebel Hauran, ii. 1219, a.
Jebel Khtyarah, ii. 1219, a.
Jebel Kurrux, 463, a.
Jebel Miltun, 317, b.
Jebel Mokattem, 181, b
Jebel Nad'ur, ii. 255, a.
Jebel Ouanseris, 133 b.
Jebel-Sanam, 362, b.
Jebel-Soudan, 253, b.
Jebel-Tedla, 318, b.
Jebel Truzza, ii. 256, b.
Jebel Zaiout, 8, a.
Jebili, ii. 1075, b.
Jedur, 982, b.
Jehan, 114, a.
Jehudia, ii. 666, b.
Jekaterinoslav, 113, b.
Jellom, 1002, a.
Jellapoor, 454, b.
Jelum, 454, b ; 1100, b.
Jemme, El, ii. 1196, a.
Jens Pangula, ii. 1216, b.
Jemibola, ii. 413, a.
Jenikale, ii. 388, b.
Jenikor, 424, a.
Jenin, ii. 887, b.
Jenne, 855, a.
Jerabriga, ii. 220, a.
Jeracovouni, ii. 505, a.
Jerbah, 67, b ; ii. 329, a.
Jericho, ii. 530, a ; 532, b.
Jerichus, ii. 532, a.
Ierne, 432, a.
Jerraki, ii. 1050, b.
Jersey, 949, b.
Jerun, ii. 471, a.
Jess, 56, a ; ii. 1317, b.
Jespus, ii. 1, b.
Jexiral-el-Arab, 174, a.
Jexireh-Ibn-Omar, 400, a.
Jezreel, 854, a ; ii. 530, b.
Igilgili, ii. 454, a.
Igilgilis, 336, b ; ii. 297, b.
Igilium, 857, b.
Igualeda, ii. 1, b.
Iguvium, ii. 1317, a.
Igylliones, ii. 916, a.
Jihua, 619, b.
Jijeli, 336, b ; ii. 29, b ; ii. 297, b.
Jilgitia, 1002, a.
Jigbah, ii. 1336, b.
Ijon, ii. 232, b.
Ikirman, 1035, a.
Iksal, 608, b.
Il Castellare, 150, a.
Il Gran Sasso d'Italia, 156, a.
Il Lagno, 630, a.
Il Lago, 504, a.
Il Pigio, 505, b.
Il Vasto, 1089, b.
Ilargus, ii. 1310, b.
Ilario, S, ii. 1089, a.
Ilchester, ii. 67, b.
Ildum, 807, a.
Ilghun, ii. 1236, a.
Iigun, ii. 600, b.
Iigun or Ilghun, ii. 1248, a.
Ilidja, ii. 1310, a.

Illci, 655, b.
Iljeh, 811, b.
Ilipa, 368, a.
Ilipula, 367, b.
Ilissus, Ionic Temple on the (Athens), 298, a.
Ilistra, ii. 222, b.
Ilium, 239, b ; 756, a.
Ilkley, ii. 473, b.
Iller, ii. 31, a.
Illiberris, 585, b ; 635, a.
Illiberis, ii. 1390, a.
Ilisera, ii. 33, a.
Ilmend, 850, b.
Ilori, 1072, a.
Ilva, 719, a ; ii. 911, b.
Iluro, 389, b ; ii. 115, b.
Imachara, ii. 987, a.
Imaus, ii. 46, a.
Imaryeh, ii. 1336, a.
Imelie, 1065, b.
Imeus, Mons, 136, b.
Imma, ii. 1076, a.
Imola, 907, b ; ii. 1287, a.
Imru, ii. 42, a.
Imus Pyrenaeus, ii. 42, b.
In Alpe Maritima, ii. 188, b.
Indus, 519, a.
Industria, ii. 188, a.
Ineboli, 5, a.
Inek-bazar, ii. 252, a.
Incusa, 60, b ; ii. 987, a.
Infreschi, Capo degli, ii. 209, b.
Ingauni, ii. 187, a.
Ingena, 7, a.
Ingersheim, ii. 43, a.
Inia, ii. 468, b.
Iniada, ii. 1195, b.
Inje-Kara, 1025, b
Inigt-Chat, 745, b.
Inimakaic, ii. 601, a.
Inkerman, ii. 111), b.
Inn, 80, b.
Innerlochy, ii. 205, a.
Innstadt, 417, b.
Inoi, ii. 268, a.
Inopus, 759, b.
Insani Montes, ii. 911, a.
Inskillah, ii. 1377, b.
Inspruck, ii. 1266, a.
Insula Tiberina (Rome), ii. 849, b.
Insulae Diomedeae, 167, a.
Isi-Sandt, ii. 870, a.
Intemelii, ii. 187, a.
Intepeh, ii. 715, b.
Intercatia, 250, b.
Inter duos Pontes (Rome), ii. 840, b; ii. 841, a.
Interamna, ii. 628, b; ii. 667, b ; ii. 1317, a.
Interamnium, 250, a.
Interamnium Flavium, 250, a.
Intercatia, ii. 1282, b.
Intercisa, ii. 1301, a.
Interocrea, ii. 1305, a.
Interpromium, ii. 279, b; ii. 1306, b.
Intibili, 807, a.
Inycum, ii. 986, b.
Joannina, 783, a ; 831, a.
Iobacchi, ii. 278, a.
Jobares or Jomanes, 973, b.
Iol, ii. 297, b.
Iolcus, 1170, b.
Jomanes, 480, b.
Iomnium, ii. 297, b.
Ionopolis, 5, a.
Joppa, 470, b ; ii. 532, b.
Jorak, 216, b.
Jordan, the, ii. 519, a.

Jorham, 178, a.
Jorjen, 1106, a.
Jorquera, 582, a; ii. 886, a.
Joruk, 163, a.
Jouanon, 391, b.
Jouare, 777, a.
Jouncuc. ii. 63, b.
Joviacum, ii. 448, a.
Jovis Arboratoris, Temple of (Rome), ii. 816, b.
Jovis Larene, ii. 868, b.
Jovis Pistoris, Ara (Rome), ii. 770, a.
Jourre or Jourve, 1091, b.
Iperix, ii. 1210, a.
Iphistiadae, 326, b.
Ipnua, ii. 203, a.
Ipsambul, 4, b; 60, b; ii. 896, b.
Ipsara. ii. 677, a.
Ipsili Hissar, ii. 64, a.
Iptsch, 843, b; ii. 494, b.
Itacus, ii. 449, b.
Ishnik, ii. 422, b.
Isser. ii. 966, b.
Ira, 3, b; ii. 345 b.
Iran, 211, a.
Iranonia, 748, a.
Irasa, 45, a.
Iravati, ii. 422, a.
Irawaddy, ii. 46, b; 780, b; 825, b; ii. 1123, a.
Irbid, 189, a.
Ireby, 189, a.
Ireland, 432, a; ii. 16, a; ii. 420, a.
Irenopolis, 393, b.
Irgits, ii. 1069, b.
Iri, 240, a.
Iria, ii. 188, a; ii. 1287, b.
Iria Flavia, 934, b.
Iris, 117, a; ii. 658, b.
Irmak, ii. 1175, b.
Irom, ii. 10, b.
Irrawaddy, 780, b; 825, b; ii. 46, b; ii. 1123, a.
Irrish, ii. 711, a.
Irsak, 692, a.
Is, 361, a.
Isar, ii. 65, b.
Isarus, ii. 1310, b.
Isaza, 442, b.
Isauritis, 507, b.
Isborus, ii. 1034, b.
Isburus, ii. 985, b.
Isca Legionum, 418, b.
Ischia, 49, a.
Iscia, ii. 469, a.
Isclero, 573, b.
Isem, ii. 67, b.
Iseo, Lagos', ii. 947, a.
Isernia, 55, b.
Isfahan, 801, a.
Ishekle, 874, b.
Ishekli, ii. 572, b.
Ishyun, ii. 297, b.
Isia, ii. 1212, b.
Isidoro di Teulada, ii. 912, a.
Isla, ii. 658, b.
Isis and Serapis, Temple of (Rome), ii. 828, a.
Isis Patricia, Temple of (Rome), ii. 826, b.
Isis, Temple of (Rome), ii. 838, a.
Isium, (Rome), ii. 818, a.
Isium, Mt., 57, b.
Iskanderiah, 365, a.
Iskanderun, ii. 1075, a.
Iskenderun, 102, b; 618, a; ii 69, b.
Isker, ii. 469, b; ii. 1024, b.
Iskuria, 778, a.
Iskuryah, 363, a.
Islama, 701, b.
Islands of the Blessed, 906, a.
Isle de Maire, ii. 42, a.
Islute, ii. 933, a.
Ismaron, 403, b.
Ismarum, ii. 1178, a.
Ismenus, 413, b.
Iznik, 422, b.
Isnikmid or Ismid, ii. 425, a.
Isola Plana, ii. 637. b.
Isole di S. Pietro et S. Paolo, 612. b.
Isole di Tremiti. 167, a.

Isomantus, 418, a.
Isondaa, ii. 917, b.
Isonzo, ii. 1022, a; ii. 1275, a.
Ispala, 731, b.
Ispern, ii. 1327, b.
Issa, 6, b; 579, b; ii. 37, a.
Issachar, Tribe of, ii. 530, a.
Issedon, ii. 943, b; ii. 968, b.
Issenovrs, ii. 282, b.
Issoria, 833, a.
Issus, 618, a.
Istere, ii. 74, a.
Istib, ii. 237, a.
Istone, Mt., 669, b.
Istonium, 582, a; 916, a.
Istria, ii. 72, b.
Istron, 705, b.
Itagnua, ii. 97, a.
Italy, ii. 74, b.
Itanus, 705, b.
Itchiman, 1035, a.
Ithaceslae, 451, a.
Ithome, ii. 341, b; ii. 1170, a.
Ithoria, 67, a.
Iton, ii. 1170, a.
Itonian Gate (Athens), 263, b.
Itshil, ii. 538, a.
Itskale, ii. 403, b.
Ituren, ii. 1240, a.
Iva-Ivitsa-Ivmka, ii. 10, b.
Juan de Fuentas divrnas S. ii. 1086, b.
Juan de la Badesas, S., 395, a.
Jubeil, 460, a.
Jubi, C., 317, b.
Jubleins, 772, b; ii. 442, b.
Jucar, 582, a.
Judaea, ii. 516, a; ii. 532, a.
Judah, Tribe of, ii. 529, b.
Judenburg, ii. 15, a.
Ivernus, ii. 101, b.
Jufna, 1005, a.
Jugarius, Vicus (Rome), ii. 775, a.
Ivia, 333, b.
Ivixa, 973, a.
Juiasmerik, ii. 1339, a.
Julia, Aqua (Rome), ii. 850, b.
Julia, Basilica (Rome), ii. 793, a.
Julia, Curia (Rome), ii. 789, b.
Julia Libyca, 593, b.
Julia Martia, Col.. 748, a.
Julia, Porticus (Rome), ii. 827, b.
Julia, Septa (Rome), ii. 836, b.
Julian S., ii. 1260, b.
Juliers or Jillich, ii. 102, a.
Juliobona, 429, a; 480, b.
Juliobrica, 502, b.
Juliobriga, 502, b.
Juliomagus, 443, a.
Jullium, 587, a.
Jullium Carnicum, 108, b; 522, a; ii. 1275, b.
Jum-burun, 424, b.
Jumna, 480, b; 973, b; ii. 60, b.
Juncaria, ii. 52, a; ii. 687, b.
Juncarius Campus, ii. 52, a.
Juno Lucina, Lucus of (Rome), ii. 826, b.
Juno Moneta, Temple of (Rome), ii. 770, a.
Juno Regina (Rome), ii. 810, a.
Juno Regina, Temple of (Rome), ii. 834, b.
Juno Sororia (Rome), ii. 824, b.
Juno, Temple of (Rome), ii. 832, b; ii. 833, b.
Junonia, 906, b.
Junonia Minor, 906, b.
Junquera, ii. 52, a; ii. 687, b.
Ivorina, ii. 3, b; ii. 243, h.
Jupiter Capitolinus, Temple of (Rome), ii. 768, a.
Jupiter Conservator, Sacellum of (Rome), ii. 770, a.

Jupiter Custos, Temple of (Rome), ii. 770, a.
Jupiter Dolichenus (Rome), ii. 812, a.
Jupiter Elicius (Rome), ii. 810, a.
Jupiter Fagutalis (Rome), ii. 826, b.
Jupiter Inventor (Rome), ii. 810, a.
Jupiter Propugnator, Temple of (Rome), ii. 804, a.
Jupiter Stator, Temple of (Rome), ii. 804, a; ii. 823, b.
Jupiter, Statue of (Rome), ii. 770, a.
Jupiter, Temple of (Rome), ii. 811, a, ii. 840, b.
Jupiter Tonans, Temple of (Rome), ii. 770, a.
Jupiter Victor, Temple of (Rome), ii. 804, a.
Jupiter Viminalis, Altar of (Rome), ii. 828, b.
Jura, 1021, a.
Ivrea, 845, b; ii. 1287, b.
Jurkup, ii. 499, b.
Jusagora, ii. 385, b.
Juscha Tagh, 424, b.
Jusrich-el-Kadim, ii. 1076, a.
Justinopolis, 22, b; ii. 73, b.
Jutland, 607, b; 622, b; ii. 1191, b.
Juturnae, Aedes (Rome), ii. 835, b.
Juvavum, ii. 448, a.
Juventas, Temple of (Rome), ii. 804, a; ii. 816, b.
Jwna, 933, b.
Ixburg, 442, b.
Ixias, 451, a.
Ixumati, 973, b.
Jyrcae, ii. 1239, b.
In Ogklu, 811, b.
Inama, 772, b.
Ismid, 406, b.
Insur, ii. 1016, a.

Kabudiah, C., ii. 859, b.
Kabul, 505, b; 666, a; ii. 118, b; ii. 497, b.
Kabulistan, 184, a.
Kadesh-Barnea, ii. 529, b.
Kadeshah, ii. 27, b.
Kadi-Kioi, 596, b.
Kaemuria, ii. 223, a.
Kaf. 370, b.
Kaffa, ii. 99, b.
Kahienberg, 594, b.
Kahramun, ii. 1338, a.
Kahtanys, 569, a.
Kai Hissar, ii. 1157, a.
Kaiguez, 576, a.
Katpha, ii. 1053, b.
Kaisar Koi, 776, b.
Kaisariyeh, 469, b.
Kaiserstuhl, 911, b.
Kakaletri, ii. 64, a.
Kakava, 784, a.
Kaki-skala, 63, b; 600, b.
Kakoreos, ii. 317, b.
Kakoreuma, ii. 418, b.
Kakosia, ii. 1175, a.
Kokou-oros, 1050, b.
Kal-at-en-cjm, 1064, b.
Kalaat Shyzar, ii. 128, a.
Kalabshe, ii. 1083, a; ii. 1085, a.
Kalama, ii. 1194, a.
Kalamaki, 683, a; ii. 619, b.
Kalamata, ii. 342, b; ii. 345, b; ii. 588, a.
Kalami, 476, a; ii. 345, b.
Kalamo, ii. 113, b; 523, a; ii. 1090, b.
Kalanca, 483, b.
Kalantchak, 999, a.
Kalapodhi, ii. 400, b.
Kalassy, 31, a.
Kalavryta, 13, b; 457, a; 725, b.
Kalcfoni, 850, b.
Kaliari, 385, b.
Kalibiah, 242, a.

Kalichi-Su, 608, a.
Kalhuno, 48, a.
Kalinkoi, ii. 575, a.
Kalliannec, 481, b.
Kallimakhi, C., 327, b.
Kallogria, 795, b.
Kalogria, 13, b.
Kalolimno, 795, a.
Kalos, Port, 872, a.
Kalotikos, ii. 388. b.
Kalpaki, ii. 490, b.
Kalyvia, 556, a.
Kama, 871, a.
Kamara, 49, a.
Kamara-Su, ii. 1194. b.
Kamares, 790, a; ii. 551, a.
Kamari, ii. 1160, b.
Kamarina, 860, b.
Kamcsik, ii. 718, a.
Kamek, ii. 118, b.
Kamenitza, 13, b; ii. 588, a.
Kamili, Cape, 842. b.
Kammeil, 1020, a.
Kammeni Mikra, ii. 1158, a.
Kammeni Nea, ii. 1158, a.
Kammeni Palaea, ii. 1158, a.
Kamulor, ii. 288, b.
Kan or Kum, 611, b.
Kana, 498, a; ii. 103, b.
Kanareh, ii. 872, a.
Kanavari, 413, b.
Kamdahar, 184, a; 972, a; ii. 498, a.
Kandia, 240, a; 809, a.
Kandili, 118, a; 524, a; 871, a.
Kangawar, 658, b.
Kangreh, 974, a.
Kanu, 603, b; 727, a.
Kanouge, 480, b.
Kantawos, 476, b.
Kantsilieres, 778, b.
Kapoudia, 427, b.
Kapoudiah, 67, b.
Kaprena, 1003, b.
Kapurna, 595, a; ii. 842, b.
Kara-bagh, ii. 504, b.
Kara-Bel, ii. 555. a.
Kara Bouroun, ii. 600, b.
Kara Burnu, 50, a; ii. 171, a; ii. 599. a.
Kara Burun, ii. 317, b.
Kara Devlit, 566, b.
Kara Haghio Ghiorghi, ii. 456, a.
Kara Kapu, 114, a.
Kara Kaya, 561, a.
Kara Su, 124, a; 519, a; 577, a; 876, a; 1106, a; ii. 319, a; ii. 1038, b.
Kara Su, or Kara Dere Su, ii. 1105, b.
Karaboa, ii. 668, b.
Karaburnu, 50, a; ii. 171, a; ii. 599, a.
Karabunar Kiwi, ii. 1131, b.
Karadagh, 891, b.
Karedash, 617, b; ii. 3, b; ii. 245, b.
Karadja, ii. 213, a.
Karadjelek, ii. 914, b.
Karadjoli, ii. 586, b.
Karadran, 603, b.
Karagask, ii. 715, b.
Kara Gruenzi, ii. 1216, b.
Karahissar, 727, b.
Karakala, ii. 1217, b.
Karakoul, ii. 509, a.
Kara Low, ii. 1199, b.
Karaman, 617, b; ii. 125, a.
Karamusal, 849, a.
Karansebes, ii. 288, b.
Karasa, ii. 422, a.
Karassiui, ii. 1211, b.
Karasu, 124, a; 519, a; 577, a; 876, a; 1106, a; ii. 319, a; ii. 1038, b.
Karatour, ii. 370, a; ii. 421, b.
Karatula, ii. 309. b.
Karavaren, ii. 231, b.
Karauli, 1032, a.
Karavostasi, 795, a.
Karback, 513, b.
Kardhenitsa, ii. 486, b.
Kardhiki, Old, ii. 568, b.
Kardkitsa, 22, a; 412 a.

Kardiotissa, ii. 116, b.
Karek, 186, a; 720, a.
Kareotae, ii. 916, b.
Karkez, ii. 1325, a.
Karja Baghlar, ii. 289, a; ii. 333. b.
Karibdtsche, 424, a.
Karitena, 111, b; 459, a.
Karitena, River of. 111, a.
Karitza, 886, a; 1090, b.
Karkaa, ii. 529, b.
Karkar, 672, a.
Karkenah. 461, a; 591, b.
Karki, 600, b.
Karkisia, 627, a.
Karla, 410, a.
Karlich, 513, b.
Karlonisi, 804, b.
Karmelis. 979, a.
Karn-al-Manzil, 520, b.
Karnak, ii. 1140, b.
Karnaka, ii. 484, a.
Kärnchen, 522, b.
Karpusli, ii. 497, a.
Kars, 613, b; ii. 946, a.
Kartali, ii. 920, b.
Kartero, 466 b.
Karieroli, ii. 226, b.
Karthäuser, 513, b.
Karun, 366, b; 612, a; ii. 1209, a; ii. 1050, b.
Karutes, ii. 644, b.
Karvunaria, ii. 1218, b.
Karweiler, 513, b.
Karyones, ii. 916, b.
Karysto, 555, b.
Kasalmak, ii. 64, b.
Kaschgar, ii. 466, b; ii. 505, a.
Kaschmir. 558, a; 972, a; ii. 41, b; ii. 509, a.
Kaschnia, ii. 654, a.
Kashmir, 558, a; 972, a; ii. 41, b; ii. 509, a.
Kash Yeniji, ii. 1282, b.
Kasimich, ii. 606, b.
Kasimiyeh, 818, a.
Kasr, 359, b.
Kasr Bourn Adjoubah, ii. 1134, a.
Kasr-Safran, 875, a.
Kasr-Serjan, 604, a.
Kasvandhra, 560, a; 597, b; ii. 535, b.
Kasnr-Assciie, ii. 973, b.
Kass'r Jebir, ii. 398, a.
Kass'r Ounga, ii. 413, a.
Kasr Faraun, ii. 1324, b.
Kastania, 805, a.
Kastanitza, 728, a.
Kastelia, 647, a.
Kasteliana, ii. 42, b.
Kasteloryzo, ii. 317, a.
Kastoria, 580, b; ii. 236, b; ii. 491, b.
Kastri, 19, b; 128, b; 760, b; 847, b; ii. 129, a; ii. 352, b; ii. 539, b; ii. 676, b.
Kastritza, 783, a; ii. 1232, b.
Kastro, ii. 156, b.
Katakolo, 817, b.
Katakolo, C. of, ii. 893, b.
Katara, 321, b.
Katara, 373, a.
Katara Soo, 373, a.
Katavothra, ii. 469, a.
Katerina, 1031, b; ii. 237, a; ii. 363, a.
Katiff Bay, 604, a.
Katirli, 198, a.
Kuto, or Palea-Akhaia, ii. 473, b.
Katranitza, 830, a.
Kattegattet, ii. 460, b.
Kattregam, ii. 370, b; ii. 395, b.
Kattuariorum, Pagus, 604, a.
Katuna, ii. 300, b.
Katura, 321, b.
Katzana, 220, a; 633, a.
Katzanes, 633, a.
Katzingri, ii. 353, b.
Katzula, 851, a.
Kavala, 21, b.
Kavallers, 612, b.
Kavallo, ii. 411, a.
Kavalo, ii. 688, b.
Kavaran, ii. 1199, b.

Kavarna, ii. 1211, b.
Kavo Doro, 504, b; 871, b.
Kavo Grosso, 1070, b.
Kavo Krio, 708, a.
Kavo-Posidhi, ii. 328, a.
Kavo Siravro, 779, b.
Kavkas, 571, a; 591, a.
Kazan, ii. 917, b.
Kazam, Eastern, ii. 917, b.
Kazdag, 976, b.
Kchitais, 643, a; 721, a.
Kebban Ma'dem, 754, b.
Kedes, ii. 104, a.
Kedesh, ii. 530, b.
Kedus, 463, b.
Kefalari, 413, a.
Kefulosi, 1029, a.
Kejelikut, 424, a.
Keff, ii. 975, a.
Kefken, 606, b.
Keft, 666, b.
Keish, or Kens, 567, a.
Keishm, 646, b.
Kekhries, 682, b.
Kelat-al-Gherrah, 362, b.
Kelberina, 121, a.
Kelefina, ii. 469, a.
Kelenderi, 392, b.
Keleukol, 248, b.
Kelisman, 631, b.
Kellen, 646, a.
Kellen, or Kelln, 647, a.
Kellnet, Kennell, or Kendel, 482, b.
Kelvedon, 801, b.
Kem Kasir, 459, b.
Kemakh, 486, a; ii. 1338, b.
Kemer, ii. 551, a.
Kemer Dagh, ii. 198, b, ii. 484, b.
Kempten, 497, b.
Kenath, ii. 1219, a.
Kenchester, ii. 246, a.
Kendal, 653, b.
Kenmare River, ii. 16, b.
Kennasserin, ii. 1076, a.
Kennelbach, 482, b.
Kennet, 718, b.
Kent, 388, a; 502, b.
Kentros, 579, b.
Kephalari, 201, a.
Kephiz Burns, 753, b.
Kephr, 497, b.
Kepse, ii. 953, b.
Kerak, 603, a; ii. 105, a; ii. 1101, a.
Kerasonde, ii. 589, b.
Kerasonde Ada, ii. 600. b.
Kerasunt, 197, b; ii. 589, b.
Kerasunt Ada. 197, b.
Keratia, 332, b.
Kereli, 514, a, 668, a.
Kerempe, 406, a; 514, b.
Keresoun, 590, a.
Kerrwen, 607, a.
Kerka, ii. 421, b.
Kerketi, ii. 917, b.
Kerkhah, 612, a, 1021, b; ii. 1050, b.
Kerman, 102, a.
Kermentchik, ii. 411, b.
Keronus, 607, b.
Keraus, 116, a.
Kertch, ii. 545, b; ii. 1109, b.
Kertesick, 592, b.
Kertsch, ii. 542, b; ii. 1109, b.
Kervaiara, ii. 192, b.
Kesem, ii. 373, a.
Keshish Dagh, ii. 480, a.
Kesi Gah-bouluk, ii. 1221, a.
Kesker, 603, b.
Kesrawan, ii. 172, b.
Kesrt, 469, b.
Kesri-Shirin, ii. 5, b.
Kessel, 561, b.
Kestaneh Dagh, ii. 332, b.
Keswick, Great, 932, a.
Keupris, ii. 1001, b.
Keuslar, ii. 321, b.
Khabas, 462, a.
Khabour, 175, a; 188, a; 594, b; ii. 333, b.
Khabs, Gulf of, 67, b.
Khabur, 175, a, 188, a; 594, b; ii. 233, b.
Khadros, 502, b.
Khaiaffa, ii. 259, a; ii. 889, b.

Khaifa, 521, b.
Khaliki, 18, b; 600, b.
Khali, 321, b.
Khamil, 240, b.
Khan Minich, 504, b.
Khan of Krevata, 877, a; 535, a.
Khania, 723, a.
Khara, M., 556, b.
Kharezm, 498, b.
Kharput, 520, b.
Kharput Dawassi, 360, b; ii. 439, b.
Khartoum, ii. 330, a.
Kharnati, ii. 380, b.
Khash Rud, ii. 484, b.
Khasia, 329, b; ii. 640, b.
Khatoun, Serai, ii. 232, a.
Khaulam, Bay of, ii. 151, a.
Khawak, ii. 440, a.
Khawarezm, 613, a.
Khazir, 456, b.
Khedhcyre, 784, b.
Kheli, ii. 289, a.
Kheli, Port, 1058, a.
Khelidonia, 606, b.
Khcimos, 385, b.
Kherson, 113, b.
Khersonesos, 607, b.
Khilidhromia, ii. 574, b.
Khmiara, 591, a; 609, a.
Khio, 609, a.
Khirlet-el-Gerar, 988, b.
Khicmutsi, 606, b.
Khodjend, 102, b.
Kholo, ii. 101, a.
Khomari, 364, b.
Khonar, 871, a.
Khonos, 649, b.
Khoorukan, 781, a.
Khoos, 614, b.
Khorasan, 209, b; ii. 274, a; ii. 421, a.
Khorassan, 1106, a.
Khore-essern, 1052, a.
Khorkkhorhoundkh, Canton of, 613, a.
Khorsabad, ii. 438, a.
Khoriiatzi, 628, a.
Khortus, ii. 593, b.
Khosis, 689, a.
Khotussa, 505, a.
Khowaybah, ii. 283, b.
Khispa, 414, a.
Khudar, 723, b.
Khulm, 364, a; 865, a.
Khurbet-es-Sumrah, 1072, a.
Khuzistan, 628, a; 697, a.
Khwaremsans, ii. 1019, a.
Kiapiche, 505, b.
Kedeyre, 579, b.
Kidras, or Kidros, 739, b.
Kiengarch, 974, a.
Kier, ii. 916, a.
Kiladhia, ii. 289, a.
Kiladhia, Port, 1058, a.
Kilian, ii. 1017, a.
Kilisbahr, 642, a.
Kilimra, 499, a.
Kilios, ii. 1246, a.
Kilis, ii. 1075, b.
Kilkenny, 429, b.
Kilkiij, 703, a.
Kill, 986, a.
Killiar, ii. 101, b.
Killiala Bay, ii. 175, a.
Kinburun, ii. 213, a.
Kinchan, 825, b.
Kinderton, 654, b.
Kineta, 244, a; 686, a; 709, a.
Kingston, ii. 667, a.
Kinla, or Kinogbu, 625, b.
Kinncird's Head, ii. 1084, b.
Kinnisrm, 598, b.
Kio, 629, a.
Kjölen, Mt., ii. 972, a.
Ktopikens, ii. 1017, b.
Kipula, 1070, b.
Kir-Shekr, 508, a.
Kiroly, St. ii. 556, a.
Kiraias, 627, a; ii. 1019, a.
Kirchenhacher, 808, b.
Kircudbright, 750, a.
Kirghis, ii. 69, a.
Kirghiz-Kazaks, 746, b.
Kirghiz Tartars, 85, a.

Kirjath-Jearim, ii. 539, b.
Kirk Hiss, 125, b.
Kirk-Kilissia, ii. 1327, a.
Kirkintilloch, ii. 1084, b.
Kirman, 520, b; 521, a; 998, a; ii. 365, b; ii. 549, a.
Kirmanshah, 369, b.
Kirpek, ii. 1195, b.
Kirpe Liman, 483, b.
Kisamo Kasteli, 627, b.
Kiseli, ii. 1218, b.
Kishon, ii. 607, a.
Kisil, Irmak, 1029, b.
Kissarlik, ii. 34, a.
Kissavo, ii. 500, b.
Kissavo, Mt., 1090, b.
Kisternes, ii. 1084, a.
Kistna, ii. 46, b; ii. 245, b; ii. 254, a.
Kiti, 730, a; 745, b.
Kürini, 585, b.
Kitro, 629, a; ii. 681, b.
Kitvina, 323, a; 326, b.
Kitz Hissar, ii. 1245, b.
Kizil-Deria, ii. 5, b.
Kizil Ermak, 490, b.
Kizil Koum, ii. 5, b.
Kizil Osien, 117, a.
Kizil-Uzen, 4x8, a.
Kizliman, ii. 318, a; ii. 1084, a.
Kizlinan, C., ii. 662, a.
Klausemburg, ii. 1314, a.
Klenes, 634, a.
Klenra, ii. 1126, a.
Klephho-limani, 325, b.
Klimino, 821, b.
Klisali, ii. 384, a.
Klisali, 800, a.
Klisura, 839, b; ii. 197, b; ii. 470, a; ii. 568, b.
Knisoro, 199, b.
Kodad, 641, b.
Kodor, 248, b.
Kodje-Taria, ii. 1101, b.
Koghthen, 649, a.
Koh-i-Baba, ii. 862, a.
Kohik, ii. 5, b.
Kohistug, 520, b.
Kohitem, ii. 584, b.
Koisou, 89, b.
Kokala, 125, b.
Kokhla, ii. 640, a.
Koknaio, 22, b.
Kokkina, ii. 687, a.
Kukkinoplo, ii. 689, a.
Koklobaski, 850, a.
Kokora, ii. 317, b.
Köln, 646, a.
Kolonnes, Cape, 331, a; ii. 1047, b.
Kolugha, ii. 506, a.
Kolumbacz, ii. 1230, b.
Kolumbatz, ii. 449, a.
Kolumbo, C, ii. 1161, a.
Komis, 651, b.
Komcit, 601, b; 999, a.
Konfoda, ii. 256, a.
Komia, 353, a.
Konispoli, 873, a.
Komitza, ii. 550, a.
Koniyeh, ii. 12, a.
Kong Mountains, ii. 392, a.
Kunkum, 1004, a.
Kontokyneghi, 476, b.
Konuklia, 730, a; ii. 548, a.
Koonik, ii. 1333, a.
Kop Tagh, ii. 373, b.
Koraka, 694, a; ii. 357, a.
Koraki, M.. ii. 269, a.
Koraku, 199, b.
Korana, ii. 3, b.
Kordufan, 57, a; ii. 241, b; ii. 451, a.
Korghos, 693, b.
Koritza, 755, b.
Korn-el-Maghsal, ii. 284, b.
Kurna, 362, b.
Koroni, 240, a; 647, a; 841, a.
Koros, 989, b.
Korti, 60, a; ii. 922, a.
Kosa Arabatskaia, 454, b.
Kosa Djarilgatch, 20, a.
Kosa Tendra, 90, a.
Kosur, 81, b.
Kosmas, ii. 956, a.
Kosmas, St., 306, b.

Kosmin, ii. 1329, b.
Kossev, 37, b.
Köstendil, ii. 223, b.
Kostenduje, 687, a.
Kostolacz, ii. 1310, a.
Kostroma, ii. 917, b.
Kotrones, ii. 1133, a.
Kotroni, 157, a.
Kotroni, M., ii. 269, b.
Kotumbul, ii. 1017, b.
Kousi, 666, b.
Koukuoba, ii. 924, b.
Koula, 566, b.
Koum-el-Akmar, 81, b.
Koum-el-Hattam, ii. 1141, b.
Koum-Ombos, ii. 482, a.
Koumpans, 656, a.
Koundoux, ii. 41, b.
Kour, 89, b.
Kouskawooda, 999, a.
Koutchouk-Lambat, ii. 118, b.
Koutschuk-Tzschekmetsche, ii. 697, a.
Kouwik, 602, a.
Kopunjik, ii. 334, a; ii. 438, a.
Krainburg, ii. 129, a.
Krato, 700, a.
Kranova, ii. 60, b.
Kremidhi, 842, a.
Krevata, ii. 9?9, a.
Krio, Cape, 452, b; 638, a.
Kriti, 703, a.
Kriu-metopon, Prom., ii. 1112, a.
Kronia, ii. 1040, a.
Krusi, 668, b.
Kskatryas, 870, a; ii. 1333, b.
Kuban, 336, a; 687, b; 1058, b; ii. 567, a; ii. 1258, b.
Kudremalai, ii. 1091, b.
Kufah, 362, b.
Kufo, 666, b; ii. 1217, a.
Kugal'nik, 1031, b.
Kuh-i-Nuh, 7, a.
Kuik, 594, b.
Kukla, 730, a; ii. 548, a.
Kula, ii. 626, b.
Kulaat-ed-Dammim, ii. 629, b.
Kulakia, 596, a.
Kulat-el-Mudik, 132, a.
Kulai Ibn Ma'an, 1?9, a.
Kufat, Ibn Ma'an, ii. 63, b.
Kulei Hissar, ii. 227, b.
Kulle-bagdschessi, 424, b.
Kulogli, ii. 682, a.
Kulpa, 642, a; ii. 3, b.
Kuluri, ii. 877, a.
Kum-Firwz, 188, b.
Kuma, ii. 68, a; ii. 1260, b.
Kumani, Palcokastro of, ii. 130, a.
Kumanovo, 771, b; ii. 243, b.
Kumaras, 364, b.
Kumaro, 1092, b.
Kumawat, ii. 1219, a.
Kundara, 329, b.
Kundura, 850, a.
Kundux, 364, a; 364, b; 764, a.
Kunjah, ii. 12, a.
Kunupeli, 816, b; 1107, b.
Künzen, ii. 690, b.
Kur, 589, a; 5?1, b; 737, b.
Kur-ab, 737, b.
Kurachi, ii. 47, b; ii. 569, a.
Kurbak, 720, b.
Kurdistan, 244, b; 320, a; 612, a; 672, b.
Kurds, 516, b.
Kurgh Dagh, ii. 245, b.
Kürghan-Tippa, ii. 506, a.
Kurisches Haff, ii. 460, b.
Kuriyat-el-anub, 824, b.
Kurko, 694, a; ii. 357, a.
Kurmel, 521, a;
Kurna, 686, b.
Kurnub, ii. 1134, b.
Kurt-aga, 484, a; 1028, a.
Kurte Ardschisch, 1101, a.
Kurtzolari, 804, b.
Kurudere, 341, b.
Kurutchesme, 424, a.
Kuryet-el-'Enab, ii. 104, b.
Kuryet-el-Gat, 978, b.
Kushuntu Tepe, 579, a.

Kusiek, 721, a.
Kuslar, ii. 1220, b.
Kuer Hajla, 396, a.
Kuss, 160, a.
Kutahiyah, 697, b; 776, b.
Kutms, 721, a.
Kutchulan, 641, b.
Kutfuk Kara-Su, 849, b.
Kutschuk Kasnardtjik, ii. 536, a.
Knttug, ii. 555, a.
Kutufarma, ii. 309, b.
Kutzopodki, ii. 889, b.
Kurela, ii. 341, b.
Klülk Tep, ii. 74, a.
Kyparissos, 380, b.
Kyparisso, ii. 1084, b.
Kyra, 579, b.
Kyradhes, 978, b.
Kyveri, 987, a.

La Baleza, 250, b.
La Beaumette, 756, b.
La Brosse, ii. 642, b.
La Caffarella, 105, b.
La Caillole, 107, b.
La Calera, 720, a.
La Cava dell' Aglio, 103, b.
La Chaise, 565, b.
La Clitadella, 848, b.
La Civita, 803, a.
La Colonna, ii. 105, a.
La Combe, 488, b.
La Cortinella, 343, a.
La Corutta, 430, a.
La Cousinière, 696, b.
La Crau, ii. 124, a.
La Foresta, 6, a.
La Gajola, 495, b.
La Linde, 777, a.
La Manche, 708, b.
La Medulas, 250, a.
La Polla, ii. 210, a; ii. 706, b.
La Punta, 23, b.
La Rotonda, ii. 210, a.
La Riccia, 211, b.
La Roca, ii. 115, b; ii. 667, a.
La Serra, 343, a.
La Tor etta, ii. 644, b.
La Tuille, 214, b.
La Ville Auxerre, 613, a.
Laara, 321, a; ii. 253, b.
L'Arek, ii. 471, a.
Labecia, ii. 284, b.
Laberus, ii. 101, a.
Labicum, ii. 690, b.
Laborini, Campi, 497, a.
Labotas, ii. 1075, b.
Labus, or Labutas, ii. 554, a.
Lacedaemon, ii. 1024, b.
Lacedogna, 172, a; ii. 896, b; ii. 1293, a.
Lacladae, 326, a.
Laconimurgis, Constantia Julia, 583, a.
Lacter, 694, b.
Lacus Pastorum, or Pastoris (Rome), ii. 828, a.
Ladakh, ii. 50, a.
Ladenburg, ii. 217, a.
Laaik, ii. 122, a.
Ladikiyeh, ii. 123, b.
Ladoceia, 192, b.
Laea, 733, b.
Laeron, 933, b.
Laestrygones, ii. 515, b.
Laevae, Aquae, 168, b.
Lagan, ii. 203, a.
Lagni, 197, b.
Lagno, 495, a.
Lagnus Sinus, ii. 460, b.
Lago d'Averno, 350, b.
Lago d'Iseo, 497, b.
Lago di Albano, 91, a.
Lago di Castiglione, 162, b.
Lago di Fusaro, 20, a; 495, b.
Lago di Garda, 389, a.
Lago di Patria, 496, a, b.
Lago di Vico, 662, b.
Lagonzn, or Lagussa, 331, a.
Lagos Bura, 403, b.

Lagous, ii. 228, a.
Lahn, ii. 144, b.
Lahore, ii. 902, b.
Laii, 609, b.
Laisse, ii. 146, b.
Lakena, ii. 116, b.
Lamas, 617, b.
Lamas, or Lamuno, ii. 119, a.
Lamato, 450, a; 1070, b; ii. 117, b.
Lambach, ii. 1110, b.
Lambaesa, ii. 455, a.
Lambardo, ii. 63, b.
Lambay Island, ii. 192, b.
Lambiri, ii. 717, a.
Lambro, 804, b.
Lambro, ii. 117, a.
Lametium, 451, a.
Lametus, 450, a; 1070, b; ii. 117, b.
Lamia, ii. 1170, a.
Lamiani, Horti (Rome), ii. 826, a.
Laminium, 528, a.
Lanium, 362, b.
Lamorika, 331, a.
Lampedusa, ii. 205, a.
Lamptra, 331, a.
Lamsaki, ii. 119, a.
Lamus, 617, b.
Lanark, 750, a; 1090, b.
Lancaster, ii. 204, b.
Lance, 250, b.
Lanchester, 630, b; 830, b.
Lanciano, 150, a; 916, a.
Lanciati, 249, b.
Landrone, ii. 1312, b.
Land's End, 386, a; 963, b.
Landizi, 738, b.
Langadhia, ii. 1245, a.
Langeia, 634, a.
Langiana, 744, b.
Langobriga, ii. 220, b.
Langon, 17, a.
Langres, 134, b.
Lanzarate Sin Clara, ii. 678, b.
Lanzarote, 906, b.
Lanzerote, ii. 678, b.
Lao, ii. 209, b.
Lao, or Laino, ii. 149, b.
Laodicea, 239, a.
Laodicea, Scabiosa, ii. 1076, a.
Laoussa, 812, b.
Lapathus, ii. 1170, a.
Lapethus, 730, a.
Laphystium, 1035, b.
Lapicini, ii. 187, b.
Lapis Manalis (Rome), ii. 820, b.
Lapithas, 817, b.
Lapitho, or Lapta, 730, a; ii. 123.
Lappa, or Lampa, 705, b.
Lar, 169, b; ii. 716, a.
Larache, ii. 1195, a.
Laraiche, ii. 298, a.
Laranda, 508, b; 617, b; ii. 222, b.
Larbuss, ii. 125, b.
Larenda, ii. 125, a.
Lares Permarini, Temple of the (Rome), ii. 835, b.
Largitxen, ii. 125, a.
Loriccia, ii. 1290, a.
Larice, ii. 47, a.
Larino Vecchio, ii. 125, b.
Larinum, 167, a; 916, a.
Larissa, ii. 1076, a; ii. 1170, a; ii. 1220, a.
Laristan, 520, a.
Larius, ii. 542, b.
Larnaki, 596, a.
Larnika, 628, b.
Larnum, ii. 115, b.
Larolum, ii. 1317, b.
Larraga, ii. 1105, b.
Larum Ruralium, Vicus (Rome), ii. 841, a.
Larymna, ii. 202, b.
Larysium, 1022, b.
Las, ii. 112, b.
Las Ventas de Caparra, 503, b.
Lasion, 821, a.
Laspi, ii. 1112, a.

Lasthenes, or Leosthenes, Sinus, 424, a.
Lastigi, 583, a.
Laterani, Palace of the (Rome), ii. 818, b.
Lathon, 733, b.
Latiano, 474, b.
Latiaris, Hill (Rome), ii. 830, a.
Latina, Porta (Rome), ii. 760, b.
Lato, 486, a.
Latobici, ii. 542, a.
Latopolis, 46, a.
Latria, 886, a.
Latuata, 566, a.
Lavagna, ii. 188, a.
Lauenburg, ii. 107, a.
Lavenza, 557, a.
Lavernalis, Porta (Rome), ii. 755, a.
Laverus, ii. 16, a.
Lavinasene, 507, b.
Lavisse, 628, a.
Laumellum, ii. 1287, b; ii. 1288, a.
Lavra, 23, a.
Laureacum, ii. 448, a.
Laureata, 748, a.
Lauretum (Rome), ii. 810, a.
Laury, ii. 149, b.
Laus, ii. 209, b; ii. 1287, a.
Laus Pompeia, ii. 1287, a.
Lausanne, ii. 150, b.
Lauterburg, 653, b.
Lautolae (Rome), ii. 813, a.
Lautumiae (Rome), ii. 787, b.
Lavsac, 388, b.
Laznsæe, ii. 1313, b.
Laybach, 49, a; ii. 403, b; ii. 461, a.
Luzi, 643, a.
Lazians, ii. 151, a.
Le Boulu, ii. 1034, a.
Le Canet, 911, b.
Le Castelle, 563, a.
Le L'Uttreuse, 926, a.
Le Colonne, 391, a.
Le Fau, 900, b.
Le Ga, 980, a.
Le Galauxe, ii. 1292, b.
Le Grotte, 30, a.
Le Grotte a Mare, 719, a; ii. 628, b.
Le Mofete, 127, b.
Le Murelle, ii. 647, a.
Leban, ii. 182, b.
Lebanon, M., ii. 173, a.
Lebda, ii. 162, a.
Leben, 705, b.
Lebrija, ii. 394, b.
Lebuini, 933, a.
Lecce, 95, a; ii. 216, b.
Lech, 340, b; ii. 182, b.
Leche, ii. 205, b.
Leches, ii. 1321, b.
Leckenheim, 561, b.
Leckham, ii. 1278, b.
Lecticariorum, Castra (Rome), ii. 842, a.
Lectoure, ii. 115, a.
Leda, ii. 152, b.
Ledon, ii. 604, b.
Ledus, ii. 973, a.
Leersum, ii. 167, b.
Lefka, ii. 172, a.
Lefka, or Lafka, 13, b.
Lefke, 406, b; 971, a; ii. 168, a.
Lefkimo, 669, b.
Lefkosia, ii. 171, b.
Lefta, 811, a.
Leftheridha, ii. 1034, b.
Lefthero-Khori, 849, a.
Leftro, ii. 172, b.
Legae, 90, a.
Legem, ii. 1196, a.
Leghistan, 89, b.
Legnano, 907, a; ii. 1287, b.
Legrana, ii. 149, a.
Leguin, or Letum, ii. 987, a.
Leguse, or el-Lejjun, ii. 153, b.
Leibethrium, 412, b; 1035, b.
Leicester, 871, a; ii. 692, b.
Leiden, 912, a; ii. 214, b.
Leimone, ii. 1170, a.

Leinster, ii. 16, a.
Leintwardine, 428, b.
Leipsydrium, 226, b.
Leipzig, ii. 217, b.
Lekhonia, ii. 414, a.
Lelantum, 671, b.
Leleges, 9, b.
Leman Lake, ii. 155, b.
Lemavi, 933, a.
Lemba, ii. 117, b.
Lemene, ii. 1275, a.
Lemenc, Mont, ii. 155, b.
Lemovices, 173, a; 218, b.
Lemta, ii. 161, b.
Lenaeum (Athens), 300, b.
Lenidhi, 729, a.
Leontia, ii. 448, a.
Lens, ii. 1308, a.
Lenthni, ii. 158, a; ii. 987, a.
Leodhoro, ii. 266, b.
Leon, 280, b; ii. 153, b; ii. 1105, b.
Leonardo, Fiume di S., ii. 986, a; ii. 1130, b.
Leondari, ii. 172, b; ii. 284, b.
Leone, Castel, ii. 1041, a.
Leone, Monte, ii. 1225, a; ii. 1296, a.
Leonessa, 6, a.
Leonica, 807, b.
Leontes, ii. 606, b.
Leontini, ii. 987, a.
Leontium, 14, b.
Leontopolis, 47, b.
Leontopolite Nome, 39, b.
Leopus, 413, b.
Lepanto, ii. 402, b.
Lepanto, Gulf of, 673, b.
Lepe, ii. 116, a.
Lepe di Ronda, ii. 33, a.
Lepreum, 821, b.
Lepsina, 812, b.
Leptis, 68, a.
Leptis Magna, ii. 1081, a.
Ler, 923, b.
Lerici, ii. 188, a.
Lerida, ii. 31, b.
Lérins, ii. 163, a.
Lerissae, 53, a.
Leros, 483, a.
Leros, ii. 164, a.
Les Chaberies Montvoison, 592, a.
Less, ii. 1, b; ii. 912, a.
Lesch, ii. 197, a.
Leser, ii. 167, a.
Lesghi, ii. 153, b.
Leshkerrek, 338, a.
Lesna, ii. 37, a; ii. 589, b.
Lesina, Lago di, 167, a; 454, a.
Lesser Zab, 509, b.
Lesitanae, Aquae, ii. 1196, a.
Lesta, Monte di, ii. 197, b.
Lete, ii. 384, a.
Letopolite Nome, 39, b.
Letrini, 821, a.
Letitchang, ii. 187, b.
Levant, or Titan, l'Isle, du ii. 1087, a.
Levantina Val, ii. 161, a.
Levanzo, 21, a; 455, a.
Leuca, 474, b.
Leuca, ii. 167, b.
Leuca, Capo di, 474, b.
Leuca, Capo Sta Maria di, ii. 4, b.
Leucae, 405, b.
Leucas, 4, a; 10, a.
Leucasia, ii. 342, a.
Leucaxium, 193, a.
Leucate, Étang de, ii. 1023, a.
Leucates, ii. 168, b.
Leuce, 20, b; 456, a.
Leuce Come, ii. 243, a.
Leucimme, 669, b.
Leucogaeus, Collis, 496, b.
Leucolla, 730, a.
Leuconia, ii. 171, a.
Leucopetra, 447, a.
Leucosia, 730, a; ii. 210, a; ii. 901, b.
Leucosyri, ii. 656, b.
Leuctra, 193, b; ii. 112, b.
Leuctrum, 17, a.

Levituosa, 708, b.
Levidhi, 823, a.
Lewke, ii. 166, a.
Leuni, ii. 1310, a.
Levool, ii. 927, a.
Leyden, 646, a.
Leynas, 655, a.
Lrytonstone, 794, b.
Leyva, 347, a.
Lex, ii. 153, a; ii. 972, a.
Lezuna, 582, a; ii. 174, b.
Li Brioni, ii. 74, a.
Li Galli, 495, b.
Liamone, 691, a.
Libana, 582, a.
Libarium, ii. 188, b.
Libarna, ii. 188, a.
Libarnum, ii. 1296, b.
Liber and Libera, Temple of (Rome), ii. 816, b.
Libertas, Temple of (Rome), ii. 811, a.
Libisosia, 582, a.
Libitinensis, Porta (Rome), ii. 757, a.
Libous, ii. 16, a.
Libokhovo, 1024, a.
Libunca, 934, b.
Libya, Lake, ii. 1081, a.
Libyarchae, ii. 278, a.
Licata, 805, a.
Licaili, ii. 1310, b.
Liochiano, 635, b.
Licenza, 774, a.
Licinini, 691, b.
Licodia, Sta Maria di, 61, a.
Licogas, Bois de, ii. 205, b.
Licosa, Punta della, ii. 171, b; ii. 662, a.
Licosa, Punta di, ii. 210, a; ii. 514, b.
Licus, 340, b; ii. 1310, b.
Lide, 519, a.
Liegnitz, ii. 215, a.
Liens, ii. 203, a.
Liesma, ii. 589, b.
Lietzen, 923, b.
Liffy, ii. 16, a.
Ligagnan, 465, b.
Ligea, 691, a.
Ligoidus, ii. 1296, b.
Ligor, ii. 1334, a.
Lilaea, ii. 604, b.
Lilbours, ii. 1232, b.
Lille Belt, ii. 460, b.
Lillebonne, 429, a; 480, b.
Lima, 583, a; 933, a.
Lima, Ponte de, 934, a.
Limaea, 691, a.
Liman Naim, ii. 471, a.
Limasol, Old, 118, b; 730, a.
Limburg, 799, a.
Limene, 474, b.
Lamenia, 730, a.
Limenia, ii. 671, a.
Limna, 934, a.
Limnae, 533, a.
Limlei, 933, a.
Limnae, ii. 191, a.
Limnae, ii. 345, b.
Limnae (Athens), 302, a.
Limnaea, 10, b; ii. 1170, a.
Limni, 31, a; 32, b.
Limoges, 341, b; ii. 157, a.
Limon, 493, b.
Limosa, 711, a.
Limousin, ii. 157, a.
Limyrica, ii. 47, a.
Linares, ii. 1001, a.
Lincoln, 442, a; ii. 193, b.
Lincolnshire, 902, b.
Lindau, ii. 1115, b.
Lindos, ii. 193, b.
Landum, 442, a.
Linlithgow, 713, b.
Linstock Castle, ii. 473, a.
Lint, ii. 157, b.
Liogest, 332, b.
Lion, Golfe du, 971, a.
Lionardo, Fiume, S. 1069, a.
Lionda, Punta di, ii. 187, b.
Lionti, ii. 494, a.
Liopesi, ii. 1213, a.
Liossa, 330, b.
Lipara, 51, a.

Lipari, 51, a; ii. 194, b.
Lipari Islands, 51, a.
Lappe, 444, b; 471, a; ii. 217, b.
Lippspringe, ii. 1133, b.
Lipso, 30, a; ii. 161, b.
Lipsokutali, ii. 878, a.
Liquentia, ii. 1275, a.
Lisboa, ii. 474, a.
Lisbon, ii. 474, a.
Lisseur, 429, a; ii. 172, a; ii. 449, b.
Lissa, ii. 1, b; ii. 37, a.
Lessa, ii. 68, a; ii. 37, a.
Lissan-el-Kahpe, ii. 931, a.
Lisse, ii. 167, a.
Lissus, 706, b; 748, a.
Lista, 6, b.
Litana Silva, 417, a.
Litany, ii. 158, a.
Literna Palus, 495, a, b.
Liternus, 495, a.
Lithodha, 871, a; 883, b.
Lithuania, ii. 30, a.
Litokhoro, 827, b; ii. 174, b; ii. 479, b; ii. 630, a.
Littamo, 111, a.
Little Altai, 126, a.
Littleborough, ii. 948, a.
Little Chesters, ii. 1256, b.
Litubium, ii. 188, a.
Livadhi, 413, b; ii. 516, a; ii. 689, a.
Livadhia, ii. 151, a.
Livadhostra, 706, a.
Livanates, 723, a.
Livanitis, ii. 470, a.
Ljubenye, 1002, b.
Liven-dael, ii. 167, b.
Livenza, ii. 196, a; ii. 1275, a.
Liviae, Porticus (Rome), ii. 827, b.
Livorno, ii. 175, b; ii. 1296, a.
Livvon, ii. 175, a.
Lixuri, ii. 533, b.
Lixus, 826, a; ii. 299, a; ii. 297, b; ii. 452, b; ii. 501, b.
Lnzard, 750, a.
Lixier, St., 656, b.
Lizizis, 744, b.
Llan-dewybrevy, ii. 213, b.
Llobregat, 378, b; ii. 857, a.
Llobregat Menor, 636, a.
Lo Cantaro, 82, a.
Lobera, ii. 964, b.
Lobetum, ii. 196, b.
Locano, 450, b.
Loch Corrib, 345, a.
Locobriga, 250, a.
Locras, 691, a.
Lodève, 654, b; ii. 221, b.
Lodi Vecchio, ii. 150, a; ii. 1287, a.
Logatecs, ii. 204, b.
Logrono, 394, a; ii. 1259, a.
Lohr, ii. 199, a.
Loire, ii. 182, b.
Lombardy, ii. 700, a.
Lomello, ii. 146, b; ii. 1287, b; ii. 1288, a.
Lomond, Loch, ii. 1252, b.
Long Island, ii. 1075, b.
Loncio, 711, a.
Loncium, ii. 448, a.
Londaglio, ii. 1288, a.
London, ii. 203, b.
Longfield, ii. 1253, b.
Longholm, ii. 1231, a.
Longo, 534, a.
Longos, 597, b; ii. 1018, a.
Longovardho, ii. 342, b.
Longus, ii. 718, b.
Lopbis, 413, a.
Lorbeus, ii. 125, b.
Lorca, 816, a.
Lorch, ii. 148, b; ii. 192, a.
Lorenzo Guaxxome, S. 383, a.
Lorenzo, Sierra de, ii. 14, a.
Lorium, ii. 1296, a.
Los Santos, ii. 964, a.
Lossae, ii. 206, a.
Lostwithiel, ii. 1231, a.
Lot, 464, a.
Lot, the, ii. 474, b.

Loth, ii. 206, a.
Lotophagi, ii. 1081, a.
Loucopibra, 750, a.
Loussiaikkevi, ii. 205, b.
Lora, ii. 33, a.
Lozère, 920, a.
Lozère, Mont, ii. 166, b.
Luanci, 933, a.
Lubaeni, 933, a.
Lübeck, ii. 276, b.
Luc, 488, b.
Luca, ii. 1296, b.
Lucanua, 450, b.
Lucar de Barrameda, 796, b.
Lucar la Mayor, S., 186, a.
Lucca, ii. 206, a; ii. 1296 b.
Lucenses, Callaici, 933, b.
Lucentum, 655, b.
Lucera, ii. 210, b.
Luceria, 167, a.
Lucia, Fiume di Santa, ii 204, a.
Luciol or Luriol, ii. 205, a.
Luco, ii. 212, b.
Luco Bormani, 110, a.
Lucretilis, Mons, 186, a.
Lucrino, Lago, ii. 212, a.
Lucullus, Gardens of (Rome), ii 832, a.
Lucus, 934, b.
Lucus Angitiae, ii. 282, a.
Lucus Asturum, 250, b.
Lucus Augusti, 226, a; 934, b.
Lucus Bormani, ii. 188, b.
Ludiovo, 428, b.
Lodus Magnus (Rome), ii. 896, a.
Ludus Matutinus et Galli-cus (Rome), ii. 819, a.
Lufer Su, 755, b.
Lugdunum, 646, a.
Lugdunum Convenarum, 389, a.
Lugnano, 417, b.
Lugo, 934, b; ii. 213, a; ii. 282, a.
Lugudonec, ii. 912, a.
Luki, 737, a.
Lukin, 139, b.
Luku, 201. a; 726, b.
Lumone, 110, a.
Lumonem, ii. 188, b.
Luna, ii. 188, b; ii. 1296, a.
Luna, Temple of (Rome), ii. 811, a; ii. 816, a; ii. 1296, a.
Lunarium, ii. 115, b.
Lüneburg, ii. 173, a.
Lungo Sardo, ii. 911, a, b.
Lungo Sardo, Porto di, ii. 1200, a.
Lungones, 249, b; 250, b.
Luni, ii. 188, b; ii. 215, a; ii. 1296, a.
Lupod, ii. 717, a.
Lupatia, 167, b.
Lupatia, Sub, ii. 1293, a.
Lupercal (Rome), ii. 802, b.
Lupia, 444, b.
Lupiae, 474, b.
Lupta, ii. 217, b.
Lusatia, ii. 962, a.
Lusi, 193, a.
Lugna, ii. 287, a.
Luso, ii. 356, b.
Lusones, 581, b.
Lutraki, 685, b.
Lütur, ii. 876, a.
Luxeuil, ii. 222, a.
Luxor, ii. 1140, b.
Lus, 396, b.
Luxara, ii. 442, b.
L'urghor, ii. 168, a.
Lybixadha, 509, b; ii. 1034, b.
Lycabettus, 285, a.
Lycabettus (Athens), 303, b.
Lycaea, 193, a.
Lycastus, ii. 558, b.
Lyceum (Athens), 303, b.
Lychnidus, 756, a; ii. 36, b.
Lycoa, 192, b.
Lycopolis, 40, a.
Lycopolite Nome, 40,
Lycorea, ii. 608, a.

Lycormas, 888, b.
Lycosura, 192, b.
Lyctus, 705, b.
Lycuria, 191, a; ii. 227, a.
Lycus, 189, a; 485, a; ii. 606, a; ii. 658, b; ii. 1209, a.
Lydd, 778, b.
Lydda, ii. 532, a, b.
Lydda, 396, b; 778, a.
Lydia, 560, b; ii. 987, a.
Lygovitz, ii. 332, b.
Lykotimo, ii. 341, b.
Lykostomo, 1005, a; ii. 237, a; ii. 1124, b.
Lykurio, ii. 167, a.
Lymen, ii. 192, b.
Lynne, ii. 155, a.
Lympne, 442, a.
Lympiada, 1004, a.
Lyncestis, ii. 236, b; ii. 512, a.
Lynncloch, ii. 205, a.
Lyon, ii. 213, b.
Lyons, Gulf of, ii. 189, a.
Lyria, 807, a.
Lysicrates, Choragic Monument of (Athens), 291, a.
Lysimachia, 64, a; 67, a; ii. 1190, a.
Lysimelia Palus, ii. 986, a.
Lystra, 770, b.
Lytarmis Prom., ii. 232, b.
Lytto, ii. 227, a.

Magrammon, ii. 1093, b.
Maarat, 222, b.
Maaren, ii. 260, b.
Maarra, 222, b.
Maarsares, 362, a.
Maas, ii. 372, b.
Maastricht, ii. 657, a.
Mabny, or Mably, ii. 413, a.
Maca or Masis, ii. 380, b.
Macae, ii. 1081, a.
Maçaka, ii. 289, b.
Macalla, 451, a,
Macanitae, ii. 299, a.
Macarese, 192, b.
Macaris, 729, a; 730, a.
Macauley, ii. 448, a.
Maccarese, Torre di, 914, b.
Macchurebi, ii. 298, b.
Maccocalingae, 480. b.
Maccurae, ii. 299, a.
Macela, 175, b.
Macella, ii. 986, b.
Macellaro, ii. 247, b.
Macellum Livianum (Rome), ii. 827, a.
Macellum Magnum (Rome), 817, b.
Macerata, ii. 629, a; ii. 717, b.
Machaetegi, ii. 943, b.
Machecoul, ii. 693, a.
Macheiresta, 643, a.
Machelones, 643, a.
Mackcaco, Cape, 950, a.
Machures, ii. 298, b.
Machuali, ii. 298, b.
Macistus, 821, b.
Macolicum, ii. 16, a; ii. 101, b.
Macomades, ii. 413, a.
Mâcon, 428, b; ii. 296, a.
Macopsisa, ii. 912, a.
Macoraba, 181, b.
Macra, ii. 187, b.
Macra Come, ii. 1170, b.
Macri, 519, b; 628, a.
Macri, Bay of, ii. 1122, b.
Macrini, 691, b.
Macrobii, 58, a.
Macrones. ii. 658, b.
Macynia, 67, a.
Macynium, 63, b.
Madagascar, ii. 329, b.
Maddalena, Fiume della, ii. 946, b.
Maddalena, Isola della, 719, a; ii. 601, a; ii. 911, b.
Maddaloni, Monte di, ii. 1207, a.
Madeba, ii. 242, b.

Madeira, 314, a; 346, b; 906, b; ii. 678, b.
Madrinu, ii. 985, b.
Madonia, Monte, 79, b; 1051, b; ii. 985, b.
Madonna, Monti di, ii. 413, b.
Madonna, C.. 128, b.
Madras, 228, b; ii. 47, a. ii. 254, a; ii. 1017, b; ii. 1019, a; ii. 1023, b.
Madrid, 525, a.
Madura, ii. 365, b.
Maeandrus, M.. ii. 46, b.
Maecenas, House of (Rome), ii. 825, a.
Maecenatis, Horti (Rome), ii. 825, a.
Maedi, ii. 1190, a.
Maedica, ii. 1180, a; ii. 1190, b.
Maenalia, 192, b; ii. 244, a
Maenalus, 192, b.
Maenaria, 207, a.
Maenia, Columna (Rome). ii. 785, a.
Maera, 192, b.
Maesoli, ii. 47, a.
Maesolia, 480, b; ii. 47, a.
Maesolus, ii. 46, b; ii. 47, a; ii. 245, a; ii. 1247, b.
Mafrag, 218, b.
Magarsus, 617, b.
Magas, ii. 253, b.
Magelli, ii. 187, b.
Maggiore, Lago, ii. 1277, b.
Mugharab-el-Heabes, ii. 584, b.
Magharat-el-Heabes, ii. 277, b.
Magi, ii. 301, b.
Magilla, ii. 1214, b.
Magliano, ii. 1286, a.
Magnae, ii. 1256, b.
Magnesia, ii. 1170, a, b.
Magnesia ad Sipylum, 239, b.
Magni, ii. 585, a.
Magnin, ii. 985, a.
Magnus, Portus, ii. 297, b.
Mago, 374, a.
Magoras, ii. 606, b.
Magra, ii. 240, a.
Magrali, ii. 241, a.
Magreda, 496, b.
Magulone, Etang de, ii. 1035, a.
Magugliano, 466, a.
Magula, 218, b; 328, b; ii. 1024, b; ii. 1174, a.
Maguas, ii. 283, b; ii. 284, b.
Mah-Sabadan, 369, b; ii. 1050, b.
Maha-Nadi, 787, a
Mahadah, ii. 277, b.
Mahalu, 607, a.
Mahanada, ii. 1247, b.
Mahanadi, ii. 46, b.
Makarrakah, Wady, 1063, b.
Makavali-Ganga, ii. 1093, a.
Mahavelle-Ganga, 974, a.
Mahé, 1004, a.
Maher Mountains, ii. 332, a.
Mahi, ii. 243, b.
Masdn, ii. 413, a.
Maydel Jar, 899, a.
Maidstone, ii. 1253, b.
Majella, ii. 278, b.
Majerdah, ii. 47, a.
Mam, ii. 266, a.
Main, the, ii. 365, b.
Mamland, ii. 1191, a.
Mainroth, ii. 329, a.
Mamz, ii. 368, a.
Majorca, 373, a.
Maito, ii. 242, b.
Makares, ii. 406, a.
Makariotissa, 1035, b.
Makri, 804, b; 1003, b.
Makri, Cape, ii. 969, a.
Makrikhori, 811, a.
Makro-Teikho, 640, a.
Makronisi, 1034, a.
Makryplai, ii. 341, b; ii. 1191, b.
Makrysia, ii. 1247, b.

Mala Fortuna, Altar of (Rome), ii. 826, b.
Malacca, 342, b; ii. 47, a; ii. 49, b; ii. 577, a.
Malacca, Straits of, ii. 52, a; ii. 254, a.
Malaei Colon, ii. 46, b.
Malaga, ii. 254, a.
Malakasa, 330, a.
Malan, C., ii. 254, a.
Malanga, 228, b; ii. 47, a.
Malathria, 779, a; ii. 237, a.
Malntia, ii. 322, a.
Malavella, Caldas de, ii. 115, b.
Malaza, 163, b.
Malchubii, ii. 298, b.
Maldon, 645, b.
Maldysem, ii. 182, b.
Malea, 192, b.
Malea Mountains, ii. 1093, a; ii. 1094, a.
Maleatis, 192, b.
Malecca, ii. 220, a.
Malesina, 1025, a.
Malestraou, ii. 296, a.
Maleum, ii. 46, b.
Malevos, 201, b.
Malfatano, Porto di, 1056, b.
Malfatiano, Porto, ii. 911, b.
Malgara, ii. 1012, a.
Malia, 197, b.
Malia, ii. 254, b.
Maliapur, ii. 265, a.
Malin Head, 430, a; ii. 1276, a.
Malleos, 515, a.
Mallias, Ad, ii. 1295, a.
Mallorati, 373, a.
Malloes, ii. 1170, a.
Mallow, ii. 101, b.
Malo, ii. 256, a.
Malo, St., 720, b.
Malogniti, 811, b; ii. 167, a.
Malta, ii. 302, a.
Malva, 67, b; 317, b; ii. 376, a.
Malum Punicum, ad (Rome), ii. 831, b.
Malus, ii. 309, b.
Mameda, Sierra de, ii. 307, a.
Mamertium, 451, a.
Mamilla, Turris (Rome), ii. 825, a.
Mamora, 376, a.
Mamuga, ii. 1076, a.
Mamurti, Clivus (Rome), ii. 829, b.
Mamurius, Statue of (Rome), ii. 829, a.
Mamurra, House of (Rome), ii. 818, a.
Man, Isle of, ii. 368, b.
Mana, 14, a.
Manaar, 642, b.
Manaar, Bay of, ii. 46, b.
Manades, ii. 1247, b.
Manaskhert, ii. 265, b.
Manasseh, Half-tribe of, ii. 531, a.
Manasseh, Tribe of, ii. 530, a.
Manavgat, 617, a.
Mancester, ii. 259, b.
Mancha, ii. 491, b.
Manchester, ii. 256, b.
Mancipium, 424, b.
Mandagara, ii. 47, a.
Mandalae, ii. 47, b.
Mandeure, 831, b.
Mandili, 871, b; 988, b.
Mandria, Casal della, ii. 645, b.
Mandrum, 364, b.
Manduria, 474, b; ii. 1294, a.
Manduria, ii. 259, b; ii. 1294, a.
Manfredonia, Gulf of, 166, b.
Mangalor, ii. 675, b.
Mangalore, ii. 47, a; ii. 49, b; ii. 380, a.
Manhem, 561, b.
Mani, 1022, b.
Manikyala, ii. 47, b; ii. 1115, b.

Manissa, ii. 252, b.
Manisyas, 755, a; ii. 255, b.
ii. 643, a.
Manliana, ii. 1296, a.
Mannu, Capo, 687, b; ii. 911, a.
Manouffelsciffy, ii. 368, b.
Manresa, ii. 1, b.
Mans, 584, a; 772, b.
Mansilla, 150, b.
Mansio Luco, 488, b.
Mansio Vabincum, 489, b.
Manchyrea, 192, b.
Mantinae, 216, b.
Mantineia, 192, b.
Mantinice, 192, b; ii. 264, b.
Mantinum, 691, b.
Mantotte, ii. 365, b.
Mantova, ii. 265, a.
Mantua, 525, a.
Manyez, ii. 266, b.
Mar-Ujvar, ii. 556, a.
Marais de Fox, le, 913, a.
Marakiah, ii. 270, b.
Maratea, 407, b; ii. 210, d.
Marateca, ii. 220, a.
Maratha, 193, a.
Marathesium, ii. 413, a.
Marathia, 875, a.
Marathon, 330, b.
Marathona, ii. 267, b.
Marathonisi, 699, a.
Marathus, 560, b; ii. 605, a; ii. 606, a; ii. 1076, a.
Marathusa, 705, b.
Marbella, ii. 881, b.
Marbury, ii. 296, b.
Marcelli, Theatrum (Rome), ii. 845, a.
Marcelliana, In, ii. 1295, a.
Marcellina, ii. 306, b.
Marcellus, Theatre of (Rome), ii. 832, b.
March, 381, a; ii. 287, a.
Marcheville, 901, a.
Marciae, 934, b.
Marcianes, Basilica (Rome), ii. 839, a.
Marcugliana Vecchia, 714, b.
Marciliana, ii. 210, b.
Marciliana, 656, b; ii. 271, a.
Marco, San, 112, b.
Marcodava, 744, b.
Mardastan, ii. 272, a.
Mardin, ii. 276, a.
Mardus, 320, a.
Mardyeni, ii. 1019, a.
Mare Creticum, 31, b.
Mare Icarium, 31, b.
Mare Myrtoum, 31, b.
Mare Thracium, 31, b.
Mareb, ii. 275, a; ii. 264, a; ii. 863, b.
Mares, ii. 658, b.
Maretimo, 32, a.
Margana, 821, a.
Margg, ii. 656, b.
Margiana, 146, b.
Marglian, 772, b.
Marguerite, Sainte, ii. 597, a.
Margus, ii. 4, b; ii. 243, b.
Mari, ii. 277, a.
Maria de Riberedonda, S., 347, a.
Maria del Campo, 582, a.
Maria, Isola di Sta, 719, a.
Maria, S., ii. 380, a.
Maria, Sta., ii. 1290, a.
Mariaba, ii. 283, b; ii. 284, a.
Mariame, 560, b; ii. 1076, a.
Mariana, 691, b.
Marianum, 691, a, b.
Marianus, 367, b.
Mariasnal, ii. 1812, b.
Maribba, ii. 275, b.
Marmella, Sta, ii. 678, b; ii. 1296, a.
Marines, ii. 369, b.
Marino, 563, b; 896, a.
Mariolates, 417, b; 603, a.
Marios, ii. 112, b.
Marrouth, ii. 273, b.
Maris, 73, a; ii. 938, b.
Marius, 744, b.
Maritza, 1033, a.
Marium, 730, a.

Marius, Trophies of (Rome), ii. 827, a.
Mark, ii. 270, b ; ii. 494, b.
Mark Zarten, ii. 1101, b.
Markah, ii. 425, b.
Market Weighton, 758, a.
Markhoula, 248, b.
Markopulo, 327, b.
Marmagen, ii. 271, b.
Marmara, 111, b.
Marmara or Marmaria, ii. 491, b.
Marmariae, 374, b.
Marmarians, ii. 1054, a.
Marmolejo, ii. 1260, b.
Marmora, ii. 670, b ; ii. 1195, a.
Marmora, Sea of, ii. 671, a.
Marmorce, ii. 626, a.
Marna, ii. 256, b.
Marne, ii. 276, b.
Marocco, 409, b ; 925, a.
Marocco, Empire of, ii. 296, b.
Maroc, ii. 1338, b.
Marogna, ii. 278, b.
Maronea, 403, b ; ii. 896, b ; ii. 1190, a.
Maroneia, 331, b ; ii. 1190, b.
Maronias, ii. 1076, a.
Maros, ii. 938, b.
Marosch, 73, a ; ii. 276, b ; ii. 287, a ; ii. 55., b.
Marotin, ii. 1208, a.
Marpessa, Mt., ii. 533, a.
Marqurz, ii. 501, a.
Marragiu, Capo di, ii. 911, a.
Marrok, 222, b.
Marrama del Pantano, 896, a.
Marrs, 159, a ; ii. 849, a.
Marruvium, 6, b.
Mars-el-Kibir, ii. 253, a.
Mars, Temple of (Rome), ii. 819, b ; ii. 834, b
Mars Ultor, Temple of (Rome), ii. 770, a ; ii. 799, b.
Marsa-al-Halal, 733, b.
Marsa Kibir, ii. 297, b.
Marsa Sollom, 732, a.
Marsa Sousa, 733, b.
Marsa Zaffran, 242, b.
Marsa Zeitoun, 127, b.
Marsah Saloum, ii. 277, b.
Marsala, ii. 189, b.
Marsala, Fiume di, ii. 985, b.
Marseille, 92, b ; ii. 290, a.
Marses, 362, a.
Marsico Vetere, 3, b.
Marsyabae, ii. 283, b.
Marsyas, Statue of (Rome), ii. 785, b.
Marta, 857, a.
Marta, 857, a ; ii. 286, a ; ii. 1297, b.
Martaban, ii. 533, a.
Martaban, Gulf of, ii. 52, a.
Martam Fl., Ad, ii. 1296, a.
Marteni, 181, a.
Martha, ii. 1296, a.
Martignano, Lago di, 112, a ; 856, b ; 857, a.
Martigny, 110, b ; ii. 462, b.
Martigues, ii. 276, b.
Martin, C. St., ii. 642, b.
Martin, Puerto de S., ii. 1278, a.
Martinach, ii. 462, b.
Martis, Ad, ii. 1301, a.
Martis, Aedes (Rome), ii. 835, b.
Martis, Ara (Rome), ii. 835, b.
Martorell, ii. 1, b ; ii. 115, b ; ii. 1122, b.
Martorris, S., 476, a.
Martos, ii. 101, a ; ii. 376, b.
Marvao, ii. 306, a.
Marvoa, ii. 219, b.
Marussi, 326, b.
Marzo, Colle, ii. 271, a.
Masalia, ii. 49, b.
Masani, 181, a.
Mascilanae, 744, b.
Mases, 1058, a.
Masices, ii. 299, a.

Maslus, Mons, ii. 333, b.
Masora, 421, b.
Massa, ii. 1301, a.
Massa Marittima, ii. 289, a ; ii. 1185, b.
Massa Veternensis, ii. 1285, 334, a.
Massabatica, 822, b.
Massaca, or Mazaga, 243, a.
Massacara, ii. 912, a.
Massaei, ii. 943, b.
Massaesylli, 68, b.
Massafran, ii. 956, b.
Massagetae, ii. 943, a.
Masseure, 389, a.
Massylli, 68, b.
Mastaura, ii. 295, a.
Mastico, Cape, 609, b.
Mastusium, ii. 1178, a.
Masulipatam, 663, b ; ii. 49, b.
Masulipattana, ii. 47, a ; ii. 245, a.
Mataju, Cape, ii. 859, b.
Matala, ii. 295, b.
Matalia, 705, b.
Matapan, C., ii. 1083, b.
Matauranga, 219, b ; 616, b.
Matarieh, 1034, b.
Mataro, ii. 115, b.
Matchin, ii. 1237, a.
Mateo, S., 807, a.
Mateola, 167, b.
Mater Matuta, Temple of (Rome), ii. 814, a.
Matera, 167, b ; ii. 295, b.
Materi, ii. 917, b.
Maternum, ii. 1297, b.
Mathia, ii. 341, b.
Mathias, Ponte St., 1001, a.
Mathura, ii. 47, a.
Matiani, ii. 302, a.
Matidies, Basilica (Rome), ii. 839, a.
Matiene, 6, b.
Matilica, ii. 296, a.
Matilica, ii. 1317, b.
Matium, 705, b.
Matricem, Ad, 748, a.
Matrini, Vicus, ii. 1297, a.
Matrinum, ii. 628, b.
Matris Deum, Aedes (Rome), ii. 803, b ; ii. 816, b.
Matter, ii. 295, b.
Matuta (Rome), ii. 832, b.
Mavalipuram, ii. 255, a.
Mavra Litharia, 32, b.
Mavra-Neria, ii. 318, b ; ii. 1218, b.
Maurensii, ii. 299, a.
Mavria, ii. 1221, b.
Maurice Bourg S., 110, b.
Maurice, St., 392, b.
Mauntenne, 977, a ; ii. 306, a.
Mausoleum (Rome), ii. 837, b
Mausta, 629, a.
Mavro-potamo, 137, a.
Mavro-Vuni, 322, b.
Mavromati, ii. 338, b ; ii. 340, a.
Mauromolo, ii. 601, a.
Mavropotami, 413, a.
Mavrozumeno, ii. 342, a.
Maxentius, Circus of (Rome), ii. 844, b.
Maxera, 1106, a.
Maximianopolis, 657, a ; ii. 1190, b ; ii. 1299, a.
Mayfa, Wady, ii. 216, a.
Mayfah, Wady, ii. 245, a.
Mayktang, ii. 1002, b.
Mayn, 355, a.
Mayo, 346, a.
Mazagan, ii. 680, b.
Mazandcran, 1106, a.
Mazani, ii. 541, b.
Mazari, Punta di, ii. 473, a
Mazarus, ii. 985, b.
Mazcyne, ii. 260, a.
Mazi, 1026, b.
Mazices, ii. 299, a.
Mazifun, or Marsifun, ii. 593, b.
Mazuma, ii. 1042, a.
Mazxara, ii. 299, b.
Mazzara, Fiume di, ii. 300, a ; ii. 985, b.
Mearus, 933, b.

Menus, 475, b ; ii. 5, b ; ii. 319, a.
Meca, Val de, ii. 1234, b.
Mecca, 181, b ; ii. 243, b.
Mecklenburg, 873, b ; ii. 324, a.
Medania, 152, b.
Medaura, ii. 455, a.
Medcenet Ashoyeh, 310, b.
Medellin, ii. 349, a.
Medeon, 10, b ; ii. 605, a.
Medghova, 18, b.
Medias, Ad, ii. 1288, a ; ii. 1290, a.
Medilli or Medellu-Adassi, ii. 164, b.
Medina de Rio Seco, ii. 1121, a.
Medina Sidonia, 239, b.
Mrdinek, ii. 283, b.
Medinet-Aboo, ii. 1140, b.
Medinet-el-Fyoom, 225, b.
Medinet-Nimrour, 363, b.
Medingen, ii. 302, b.
Mediolanum, 457, b.
Mediolium, 582, a.
Medion, 748, a.
Mediterranean Sea, ii. 57, a.
Medma, 448, a.
Médoc, ii. 306, a.
Medocae, ii. 917, b.
M. dolino, Golfo di, ii. 74, a.
Meduacus, ii. 1275, a.
Meduacus Minor, ii. 1275, a.
Meduli, 173, a.
Meditis, Lucus (Rome), ii. 826, b.
Megabari, 58, a.
Megalo-Kastron, 160, b ; ii. 296, a.
Megalo Potamo, 323, a ; ii. 289, b ; ii. 500, a.
Megalonesi, ii. 385, b.
Meganis, ii. 1090, b.
Meganitas, 13, b.
Megalia, ii. 317, a.
Megaris or Megalia, 495, b.
Megarishuzzer, ii. 283, b.
Megiddo, ii. 530, b.
Megisba, L., ii. 1093, b.
Megistus, ii. 717, a.
Megue, 566, b ; ii. 244, a.
Mehadia, 744, b.
Mehatet-el-Haj, 197, a.
Mehediah, 376, a.
Mejafuskin, ii. 1208, a.
Mejdel, ii. 245, b.
Meyerdah, 318, a ; 370, b ; 371, b.
Melichus, 13, b.
Meillan, Chateau, ii. 302, b.
Meinaer, ii. 243, a.
Memet Borja, 1050, a.
Meionis, 729, a.
Meiraques, 169, b.
Meis, ii. 1122, b.
Meissen, ii. 217, b.
Mekaberab, ii. 307, a.
Mekka, 757, a.
Mekka or Mecca, ii. 239, a.
Mekran, 982, b.
Melada, ii. 37, a.
Melae, ii. 895, b.
Melaena, 609, b.
Melanae, Kara Burnu, ii. 357, a.
Melanae, 329, b ; ii. 1158, a ; ii. 1161, a.
Melanenae, 193, a.
Melanchlaeni, 643, a ; ii. 917, b.
Melangels, 192, b.
Melanippera, 606, b.
Melankavi, 685, a.
Melanthius, ii. 658, b.
Melas, 413, a ; 617, a ; ii. 538, a ; ii. 986, a ; ii. 1177, b ; ii. 1218, b.
Melasgerd, ii. 265, b.
Melasso, ii. 386, a ; ii. 559, b.
Meleagri, Porticus (Rome), ii. 837, b.
Meleda, 778, b ; ii. 321, b.
Melemko, ii. 463, b.
Melet Irmak, ii. 318, b.
Melfa, ii. 324, a.
Melfort, Loch, ii. 205, a.

Meliboea, ii. 1170, a, b.
Melidhoni, ii. 1085, b.
Melilah, ii. 298, a.
Melilla, ii. 858, b.
Melissurgis, ii. 236, b.
Melissurgus, ii. 236, b ; ii. 322, b.
Melita, ii. 37, a.
Melitaea, ii. 1170, a.
Melite, 9, b ; 325, a ; ii. 901, b.
Melite (Athens), 301, b.
Melitelum, 669, b.
Melitene, 507, b.
Melitian Gate (Athens), 363, b.
Melitisch Chai, 393, a.
Mella, ii. 317, b.
Mellay, 570, b.
Melleck, ii. 537, b.
Mellisurgis, ii. 364, a.
Melone, Monte, ii. 629, a ; ii. 645, b ; ii. 1110, b.
Meloria, 857, b.
Melphes, ii. 209, b.
Melun, ii. 322, b.
Memel, ii. 917, a.
Memnones, 60, a.
Memphite Nome, 38, b.
Menaenum, ii. 987, a.
Menapia, 363, a ; ii. 16, a.
Menapii, ii. 16, a.
Menavgat-Su, ii. 319, a.
Mende, 138, a.
Mendeli, 324, a ; 1021, b ; ii. 149, a.
Mendere-Su, ii. 926, b.
Meudes, 38, b.
Mendesian arm of the Nile, ii. 433, a.
Mendesian Nome, 39, b.
Mendiculeia, ii. 32, a.
Mendoya, 250, a ; ii. 417, b.
Menduria, 471, a.
Menduria or Mendveghora, ii. 267, a.
Menelaite Nome, 39, a.
Menidhi, 326, b.
Menmmen, ii. 1124, b.
Meninx, 67, b ; 891, b ; ii. 1081, a.
Menlaria, 658, b.
Mennodunum, 444, a.
Menoba, 368, a.
Menorca, 373, a.
Mensich, ii. 678, a.
Mentana, ii. 444, b.
Mentelite Nome, 39, b.
Mentone, ii. 188, b.
Menuthias, ii. 668, a.
Menzaleh, 1051, a ; ii. 540, b.
Mephyla, 6, a.
Mequinenza, ii. 463, a.
Mera, 412, b.
Meran, ii. 1131, a.
Merave, ii. 396, b.
Mercury, Temple of (Rome), ii. 816, b.
Merghem or Merville, ii. 359, a.
Mergo, ii. 1214, b ; ii. 1312, a.
Merj' Ayun, ii. 222, b.
Merida, 338, b.
Merij Ibn 'Amr, 854, b.
Merinum, 167, a.
Merionethshire, ii. 491, a.
Merk, ii. 494, b.
Merkez-su, ii. 1080, a.
Mermere, ii. 670, b.
Mero, 933, b ; ii. 300, a.
Meroe, ii. 429, b.
Merom, Waters of, ii. 520, a.
Meronda, 332, b.
Merorouli, ii. 1160, b.
Mers Irmak, 595, a.
Mersey, 388, b.
Mertesi, 685, a.
Mertin, ii. 1337, b.
Mertola, ii. 220, a ; ii. 388, b.
Merv, 147, a.
Merw Rud, ii. 274, b.
Merva, 934, a.
Merula, ii. 187, b.
Merula, ii. 331, b.

4 s 3

Merum-Ruremonde, ii. 300, b.
Merut, ii. 425, b.
Mesa, ii. 1291, b.
Mesa de Asia, 247, b.
Mesagne, 474, b; ii. 338, a.
Mesaibronus, 424, a.
Mese, ii. 385, b; ii. 684, b.
Mese or Mese, ii. 346, a.
Mesembria, ii. 1190, a.
Meshech, ii. 373, a.
Meshed Ali, 362, b.
Mesheddizar, ii. 256, b.
Mesima, 450, a; ii. 105, b.
Meskianah, 370, b.
Mesma, 450, a.
Mesobatene, 369, b.
Mesoboa, 193, a.
Mesochoron, 474, b.
Mesogaea, 312, b.
Mesoghia, 322, b.
Mesolonghi, 64, a; 810, a;
  ii. 641, b.
Mesorughi, ii. 445, b.
Mesr-Wostani, 104b, b.
Messa-Vouno, ii. 1160, b.
Messabatae, ii. 1050, b.
Messapia, 474, b; ii. 203, a.
Messapium, 414, a.
Messelerius, Castel, ii. 473, b.
Messina, ii. 334, a.
Messis or Mensis, ii. 370, b.
Mesta, Port, 609, b.
Mesve or Mèves, ii. 289, b.
Mesurata, 587, b; ii. 1230, b.
Meta Sudans (Rome), ii.
  809, b.
Metagonitae, ii. 298, a; ii.
  299, a.
MetagoniumProm., ii. 297, b.
Metalla, ii. 912, a.
Metapa, 67, a.
Metauro or Metro, ii. 348, b.
Metaurum, 451, a.
Metaurus, 450, a.
Metelin, ii. 917, b.
Metelino, ii. 164, b.
Metella, Tomb of Caecilia
  (Rome), ii. 822, a.
Metelli, Porticus (Rome), ii.
  833, b.
Metein, ii. 308, a.
Meterees, ii. 349, a.
Methana, ii. 349, b.
Methone, ii. 346, a; ii. 1170,
  b.
Methora, ii. 48, a.
Methoricl, 210, b.
Methydrium, 193, a.
Methymna, 705, b; ii. 165, a.
Metia, Porta (Rome), ii.
  737, b.
Metlika, ii. 3, b.
Metronis, Porta (Rome),
  ii. 760, b.
Metroon (Athens), 296, b.
Metropisti, 331, b.
Metropolis, 10, b; 521, a; ii.
  1170, a.
Metropolitanus, 776, a.
Metulum, ii. 3, b.
Metz, 779, b; ii. 305, a.
Metzovo, ii. 108, a; ii. 1246, a.
Mevania, ii. 1301, a; ii.
  1317, a.
Mevaniola, ii. 1317, b.
Mezalocha, ii. 969, a.
Mezapho, ii. 334, a.
Mezeiu, ii. 1019, b.
Mezioumta, ii. 421, b.
Mezzo, 810, a.
Miacum, 197, b; 523, a.
Miafarakin, ii. 1208, b.
Miafare Kyn, ii. 287, a.
Mica Aurea (Rome), ii. 819,
  a.
Micalitza, ii. 717, a.
Micaza, ii. 551, b.
Michael, Mount St., 963, b.
Michmash, ii. 355, a.
Michmethah, ii. 530, a.
Midsleby, 408, a.
Middlesex, 645, a.
Midea, 202, b.
Midhurst, ii. 353, a.
Midjek, ii. 884, a.
Midland Counties, 902, b.

Midyan, ii. 354, b.
Miera, ii. 907, a.
Migalgara, ii. 1012, a.
Migdol, ii. 246, a.
Mignone, 857, a; ii. 359, b.
Mignone, River, ii. 1296, a.
Migonium, 1022, b.
Mijares, ii. 1241, a.
Mikanafxi, 614, b.
Milan, ii. 303, a.
Milazzo, ii. 384, b.
Milden, ii. 360, a.
Milea, ii. 574, b.
Miletus, 705, b.
Mileum, ii. 455, a.
Miliana, ii. 260, a.
Miliiarium Aureum(Rome),
  ii. 794, b.
Milo, ii. 322, b.
Miltopae, Statio, 474, b.
Mimisan, ii. 998, a.
Minara, ii. 639, b.
Mincio, ii. 359, a.
Mineo, ii. 326, b; ii. 987, a.
Minerva Capta (Rome), ii.
  817, a.
Minerva Chalcidica (Rome),
  ii. 838, a.
Minerva Medica, Temple of
  (Rome), ii. 826, b.
Minerva, Promontory of, ii
  514, b.
Minerva, Temple of (Rome),
  ii. 791, b; ii. 811, a; ii.
  820, b.
Minervae, Aedes (Rome),
  ii. 799, b.
Minervae, Castrum, ii. 1294,
  a.
Mingrelia, 602, b; ii. 260, b.
Minho, 502, b; ii. 359, b.
Minio, 857, a.
Minionem Fl., ii. 1296, a.
Minius, 502, b.
Minnagara, ii. 47, a.
Minni, 215, a.
Minoa, 705, b; ii. 552, b;
  ii. 1011, a.
Minorca, 373, a.
Minsk, ii. 916, a.
Minthe, 817, b.
Mintro, ii. 220, a.
Minturnae, ii. 1290, a.
Minucia, or Minutia, Porta
  (Rome), ii. 755, a.
Minuciae, Porticus Frumen-
  taria (Rome), ii. 834, b.
Minutiae, Porticus Vetus
  (Rome), ii. 834, b.
Minyas, 181, b.
Miolans, ii. 414, b.
Mirabella, ii. 896, b.
Mirabello, Castel, ii. 360, b.
Miraka, 1031, b; ii. 632, a.
Miramar, ii. 473, a.
Miranda, 850, a.
Miranda de Ebro, 347, a;
  770, a.
Mirandella, ii. 631, a.
Mirandola, 643, b.
Miritza, ii. 507, b.
Mirobriga, ii. 219, b.
Mirza-Mombarrik, ii. 678, a.
Miseno, Capo di, ii. 361, b.
Misenatium, Castra (Rome),
  ii. 828, a.
Misis, 618, b.
Missen Head, ii. 448, b.
Mistra, ii. 1024, b.
Mistretta, 122, a; ii. 987, a.
Mithridatium, 531, a.
Mitranich, ii. 325, a.
Mitylen, ii. 164, b; ii. 390, b.
M'lit, 778, b.
Mnemium, 57, b.
Mocha, ii. 49, b.
Mochha, ii. 675, b.
Mocassus, 508, a.
Modena, ii. 377, b; ii. 1287, a.
Modguli, ii. 365, b.
Modhia, 804, b.
Modica, ii. 375, b; ii. 987.
  a.
Modogalingae, 480, b.
Modomastite, 521, a.
Modom, ii. 350, a.
Modura, ii. 47, a; ii. 48, a.

Modutti, ii. 1093, b.
Moesi, ii. 367, b.
Mogador, C. 1056, a.
Moghostan, 520, b.
Moghostan, 520, b.
Mogh'rib-al-aksa, ii. 296, b.
Moglena, 106, a.
Moglenitiko, ii. 213, a.
Mogou, ii. 906, a.
Mogrus, ii. 658, b.
Moguer, ii. 474, a.
Mohalidik, ii. 717, a.
Mojabra, 338, a.
Mougte de Brone, ii. 246, a.
Moilah, ii. 283, b; ii. 1134, b.
Moirans, ii. 371, b.
Mojur, 508, a.
Mokri, 348, b.
Moldavia, 628, a; 743, b.
Molfetta, 167, a.
Molibae, 59, b.
Molines, 581, a; ii. 1326, a.
Motivo, ii. 165, a.
Molivopyrgo, ii. 500, a.
Molo, ii. 929, a.
Molochath, 67, b; 317, b.
Mologeni, ii. 943, b.
Mologhusta, ii. 256, b.
Moloschuijawoda, 999, b.
Molpa, ii. 209, b; ii. 334, a.
Molycreia, ii. 203, a.
Molycreium, 67, a.
Monbag, Caldas de, ii. 115,
  b.
Monaco, 98, b; 154, a; ii.
  188, a; ii. 369, a.
Monalus, ii. 986, a.
Monasterace, ii. 390, a.
Monasteri, ii. 561, a.
Monasterio, ii. 1233, b.
Monclova, 348, a; ii. 460, a.
Monda, ii. 376, b.
Mondego, ii. 376, b.
Mondejar, 535, a.
Mondragon, ii. 1223, a.
Mondragone, ii. 290, a; ii.
  1008, b; ii. 1290, a.
Moneglia, ii. 188, b.
Monems, ii. 369, a.
Monemvasia, Old, 842, a.
Monestier or Monetier, ii.
  1033, b.
Moneta (Rome), ii. 828, a.
Monghir, ii. 257, a.
Mongibello, 61, a.
Mongoi territory, ii. 1134, a.
Mongri, ii. 64, a.
Monheim, ii. 1125, b.
Monmouth, 409, b.
Monopoli, 167, a.
Mons Panachaicus, 13, a.
Mons Silicis, 254, b.
Monselice, 254, b.
Mont-martin, 993, b.
Montalto, 907, a; ii. 1296, a.
Montanchers, ii. 1023, b.
Montaroza, ii. 1103, a.
Montbruson, 169, b.
Monte Affliano, 56, b.
Monte Alburno, 94, a.
Monte Cavo, 88, b; 91, b.
Monte Comero, 718, b. 470.
Monte Cristo, 857, b; ii.
Monte d' Oro, 799, a.
Monte del Hacho, 8, a.
Monte di Postiglione, 94, a.
Monte di San Nicola, 49, b.
Monte di Sta Croce, 343, a.
Monte Fortino, 803, a.
Monte Mayor, ii. 1313, b.
Monte Melone, 342, b.
Monte-Negro, ii. 36, a.
Monte Santo, 309, a.
Monte Somma, ii. 1301, a.
Montélimart, 577, a.
Montepolo, ii. 1266, a.
Montercau, 654, a.
Monteroni, ii. 1296, a.
Monteu, ii. 188, a.
Montedi di Po, ii. 53, a.
Montgomeryshire, ii. 491, a.
Monti Albani, 91, b.
Monti della Sibilla, 156, a;
  902, a.
Monti di Leoncessa, 6, a.

Monti Lepini, 91, b.
Manticelli, 867, a.
Montobriga, ii. 219, b.
Montone, ii. 1329, b.
Montoro, 843, b.
Monza, ii. 364, b.
Monxon, ii. 32, a; ii. 328,
  b; ii. 1216, a.
Mopsium, ii. 1170, a.
Mopsuestia, 618, b.
Muraça, 776, b.
Morad Dagh, 463, b; 775, b;
  ii. 1194, a.
Moram, Cape, ii. 473, a.
Morano, ii. 210, a; ii. 376, b.
Morava, ii. 243, b; ii. 274, a.
Moravia, ii. 230, a.
Morawa, ii. 14, a.
Morawa Hissar, 1091, a.
Morbihan, Bay of, ii. 1310,
  a.
Mordulus, ii. 102, b.
Mordulmne, ii. 1093, b.
Morduli, ii. 1093, b.
Morecambe Bay, ii. 371, b.
Morena, Sierra, ii. 276, a;
  ii. 299, a.
Moresby, 189, a; ii. 370, b.
Morgantia, ii. 987, a.
Morgnou, Cape, ii. 42, b.
Morikl, ii. 930, a.
Morillus, ii. 384, a.
Morimene, 507, b.
Moritsi, 413, b; ii. 1030, b.
Morius, 412, b.
Mormas, 524, b.
Morno, 1102, b; ii. 202, b.
Murosca, 502, b.
Morontobaça, 983, a.
Morotales, 525, b.
Morrone, ii. 278, b.
Moschice, ii. 373, b.
Moschiel, 572, a.
Mosel or Moselle, ii. 373, b.
Mosel, Upper, ii. 170, b.
Mossinus or Mosynus, 519, a.
Mostaghamom, ii. 297, b.
Mostar, ii. 296, a.
Morul, ii. 334, a; ii. 438, a.
Mosyll, 59, b.
Mosynoeci, ii. 638, b.
Moulavrna, ii. 967, a.
Mothoni, ii. 350, a.
Mothri, ii. 1233, a.
Motril, ii. 926, a.
Möttling, ii. 3, b.
Motyca, ii. 987, a.
Motychanus, ii. 985, b.
Motyum, 79, b.
Moudon, 444, a; ii. 360, a.
Moukhtar, 186, b.
Moura, 228, a.
Mouro, Porto, ii. 450, b.
Mornouk, 975, b.
Moussa, 214, b.
Moussoldja, ii. 515, b.
Moustiers, 110, b.
Mout or Mood, ii. 897, b.
Moutiersen Tarentaise, 384,
  a; 752, b.
Mouxon, ii. 373, b.
Moyments, ii. 879, a.
Mozetra, ii. 905, a.
Mrisa, ii. 299, b.
Msarata, 587, b.
Msilah, ii. 1334, b.
Mucia Prata (Rome), ii.
  841, a.
Mucialis, Collis (Rome), ii.
  830, a.
Mucuni, ii. 296, b.
Mucrae, ii. 897, a.
Muel, 562, a; ii. 969, a.
Muenna, 352, b.
Muga, 636, a.
Mugello, Val di, ii. 246, a
Mugcyer, 363, a.
Mugula, ii. 466, b.
Muhr, ii. 377, a.
Mujelebe, 359, b.
Muin-Mura, ii. 46, b; ii.
  243, a.
Mukhmas, ii. 353, a.
Muklow, ii. 1216, a.
Mulcy Bu Selham, ii. 376, a.
Mulki, ii. 1213, b.
Mull of Cantyre, 593, a.

Multan, 1030, b.
Mulucha, 67, b; ii. 297, b.
Muluwi, ii. 376, a.
Mulwia, 317, b.
Munda, 582, a.
Mundo, Sierra del, ii.496, b.
Mundritza, 1103, b.
Mungava, 228, a.
Munscheeker, 515, a.
Munster, ii. 16, a.
Muntesha, ii. 386, b.
Munvicia, ii. 14, a.
Munychia, 259, b.
Munychia (Athens), 306, a.
Muqueyer, ii. 438, b; ii. 487, a.
Murad, 7, a.
Murad-chai, 875, a; ii.1008, a.
Murano, Sub, ii. 210, b; ii. 1295, a.
Murano, 451, b; ii. 1295. a.
Muranum, 451, b; ii 210, a, ii. 1294, b.
Murcia, 665, b; ii.491, b; ii. 1105, a; ii. 1278, b.
Murcia, Sacellum of (Rome), ii. 816, a.
Murgantia, ii. 896, b.
Murghab, ii. 4, b; ii. 274, b; ii. 555, a.
Murillo de Rio Leza, ii. 1259, a.
Murius, ii. 541, b.
Muro, 913, b.
Muro di Carmi, 1100, b.
Muros, 934, b.
Murotin, ii. 1231, a.
Murray Firth, ii. 203, a; ii. 1037, a.
Mursia, ii. 542, a.
Murviedro, ii. 874, a.
Murus, 110, b; 525, b.
Murustaga, ii. 297, b.
Musa, Wady, ii. 583, a.
Musakt, Cape, 457, a.
Muscat, 714, b.
Musconisi, 1034, a.
Museium (Athens), 233, b.
Muskakos-Su, ii. 663, a.
Musopale, ii. 47, a.
Musscidom, Cape, ii. 233, a; ii. 238, a.
Mustapha Palanca, ii. 698, a.
Mutania, 152, b.
Mutatio Vologatis, 488, b.
Mut Khan, ii. 440, a.
Mutatorium Caesaris (Rome), ii. 820, b.
Mutila, ii. 73. b.
Mutina, ii. 1287, a.
Mutistratum, ii. 987, a.
Mutuscae, ii. 1224, b.
Muxa, ii. 49, b.
Muziris, ii. 49, b.
Muxon, ii. 377, b.
Mydonius, ii. 333, b.
Myares, ii. 1241, a.
Mycenae, 705, b.
Myceni, ii. 299, a.
Mychus, ii. 605, a.
Myconus, ii. 383, b.
Myenus, 63, b.
Myes, ii. 1122, b.
Mygdonii Cadi, 463, b.
Mykono, ii. 383, b.
Mylae, ii. 966, b; ii. 1170, a, b.
Mylasa, 239, b.
Myonia, ii. 203, a.
Myous, 355, a.
Myra, ii. 387, b.
Myrad-chai, 224, a.
Myrcinus, 807, b.
Myrlandrus, ii. 1075, a.
Myrina, 53, a; ii. 156, b.
Myrlea, 152, b.
Myrmecium, 422, a.
Myrrhinus, 332, b.
Myrtilis, ii. 220, a.
Myrtuntium, 9, b.
Mysia Major, ii. 389, a.
Mysia Minor, ii. 389, a.
Mysore, ii. 1089, a.
Mytila, 451, a.
Mytika, ii. 427, a.
Mytilene, 339, b.

Mytistratum, ii. 987, a.
Myupoli, 329, a.
Naab, ii. 394, b.
Naaman, ii. 607, a.
Naarath, ii. 530, a.
Nabat, ii. 394, a.
Nabathaei, 181, b.
Nabel, ii. 413, b.
Nabend, 371, b; 521, a.
Nabui, ii. 410, b.
Nablus, 385, a; ii. 412, b.
Nachdgevan, ii. 406, b.
Nacmusii, ii. 299, a.
Nacona, ii. 987, a.
Nadin, ii. 414, a.
Naebis, 427, a.
Naenia, Sacellum of (Rome), ii. 828, b.
Naevia, Porta (Rome), ii. 755, a.
Naftia, Lago di, ii. 533, b.
Naga-gebel-ardam, ii. 330, b.
Nagadibt, ii. 1093, b.
Nagar, ii. 47, b; ii. 395, a.
Nagara, ii. 47, b.
Nagnatae, 346, a; ii. 16, a.
Nagy-Banja, ii. 552, a.
Nahar-Malcha, ii. 954, b.
Nahe, ii. 401, b.
Nahr Abu-Zubara, ii. 103, b.
Nahr-al-Hualt, ii. 384, b.
Nahr-awan, ii. 485, a.
Nahr-Beirut, ii. 253, b.
Nahr-ed-Damur, ii. 253, b; ii 1087, a.
Nahr-el-Auly, 428, b; ii. 158, a.
Nahr-el-Ibrahim, 24, b; ii. 606, a.
Nahr el-Kebir, 815, a; ii. 606, a.
Nahr-el-Kelb, ii. 328, a; ii. 606, a.
Nahr-el-Mukutta, 627, b.
Nahr-le-Dan, 750, b.
Nahr-Malcha, 362, a.
Nahr-Malka, ii. 237, b.
Nahr Na' Man, 389, a.
Nahr Zerka, 708, b.
Naissus, ii. 1180, a.
Nais or Nais, ii. 401, b.
Nakah-el-Hajar, ii. 266, a.
Nakhilu, ii. 461, b; ii. 578, b.
Nakil-Samara, 635, a.
Naksheb, ii. 404, a.
Nalata, 748, a.
Nalon, ii. 395, a.
Namadus, ii. 46, b; ii. 47, a; ii 549, b.
Namare, ii. 448, a.
Namastae, ii. 943, b.
Namfi, 130, a.
Nanaguna, ii. 46, b.
Nandira, ii. 47, a.
Nanichae, ii. 47, b.
Nanm Noss, ii. 232, b.
Nankin, ii. 1003, a; ii. 1174, b.
Nannetes, 218, b.
Nantrs, 654, b; ii. 396, a.
Naparis, ii. 938, b.
Napata, 58, b.
Nape, ii. 165, b.
Napetium, 451, a.
Napht-ii, Tribe of, ii. 530, a.
Naples, ii. 407, b.
Naples, Bay of, 700, a.
Napoca, 744, b.
Napoul, 1091, a.
Navuka, Mts. ii. 10, a; ii. 46, b.
Naralconcrjo, ii. 1308, a.
Naranja, 355, b.
Narbaci, 933, a.
Narbasorum, Forum, 934, a.
Narbo Colonia, ii. 1320, a.
Narbonne, ii. 398, a.
Narborough, 442, b.
Narcra, ii. 324, a.
Nardinium, 250, b.
Nardo, 93, a; ii. 419, b; ii. 1294, a.
Narenta, ii. 399, b.
Naris, ii. 202, b.

Naria, 984, b.
Narmada, ii. 46, b; ii. 47, a.
Narni, ii. 399, a; ii. 1301, a.
Narnia, ii. 1301, a; ii. 1317, a.
Narona, 748, a; ii. 38, a.
Narraga, 362, a.
Narthacium, ii. 1170, a.
Naryn Chara, ii. 716, b.
Nasamones, ii. 278, a; ii. 1081, a.
Nasi, 193, a.
Naski, ii. 916, b.
Nassau, ii. 396, b.
Natiolum, 167, a.
Natiso, ii. 1275, a.
Natisone, ii. 401, b; ii. 1275, a.
Natron Lakes, ii. 441, b.
Navalia (Rome). ii. 835, b.
Navalis, Porta (Rome), ii. 754, b.
Navari, ii. 917, a.
Navarino, ii. 682. b.
Navarre, ii. 1105, a.
Navarreins, 380, b.
Navern, ii. 392, b.
Naveras, 132, a.
Navia, 933, b; ii. 402, b.
Navia de Suarna, 934, b.
Naviae, Pons, 934, b.
Navilubio, 933, b.
Naumachiae (Rome), ii. 842, a.
Naupactus, ii. 903, a.
Nauportus, ii. 541, b; ii. 542, a.
Naustathmus, 733, b.
Naulu, ii. 406, b.
Naxus, 705, b.
Naye, 389, b; ii. 486, a.
Nazaba, ii. 1076, a.
Nazarre E'tang de St., ii. 1023, a.
Nazuk, 197, a.
Neaethus, 450, b.
Neapolis, 167, a; 385, a; 465, b; 807, b; ii. 74, a; ii. 1180, a; ii. 1190, a; ii. 1338, a.
Neapolis (Syracuse), ii. 1065, a.
Neapolitanae Aquae, ii. 912, a.
Neath, 418, b; ii. 427, b.
Neba, ii. 413, b.
Nebt Abri, 4, a.
Nebis, 933, a.
Nebousan, ii. 483, b.
Nebrodes, Mons, 79. b.
Neby Samoil, ii. 363, a; ii. 691, b.
Neckar, ii. 217, a; ii. 424, b.
Nectiberes, ii. 299, a.
Nede, 193, a.
Neder Rhyn, 555, a.
Nedjran, ii. 283, a, b.
Nedon, ii. 342, b.
Nedrigoska, ii. 1.88, b.
Nedum, 418, b.
Neetum, ii. 987, a.
Nefter, 932, a; ii. 469, b.
Nefteropoli, 931, b.
Negombo, ii. 668, b.
Negra, ii. 283, b.
Negram, ii. 284, a.
Negranes, ii. 284, a.
Negretto, Capo, ii. 912, a.
Negropont, 699, a; 871, a.
Neh, ii. 428, a.
Neister, ii. 1248, a.
Nekhori, ii. 711, a.
Nelaxa, ii. 1076, b.
Nelia, ii. 1170, b.
Neliceram, ii. 49, b.
Neliseram, ii. 414, a.
Nelkynda, ii. 49, b.
Nemetacum, 319, b.
Nella-Mella, ii. 498, a.
Nellore, ii. 284, a.
Nelus, 933, b.
Nemertzika, 55, a.
Nemetatae, 933, a.
Nemetobriga, 250, a.
Nemetocenna, 319, b.
Nemossus, 341, a.
Neutidava, 744, b.

Neocaesarea, 402, b.
Neokhoirio, ii. 236, b.
Neokhori, 207, a; ii. 309, b; ii. 569, b.
Neokhorio, 126, b; 403, b; 709, a.
Neon Teichos, 52, a.
Neopatra, 1103, b.
Nepaul, 825, b.
Nepete, 870, b; ii. 1288, a.
Nephtoah, ii. 529, b.
Nepi, ii. 419, a; ii. 1288, a.
Nepthalitae, 1097, b.
Neptune, Temple of (Rome), ii. 834, b; ii. 837, a.
Nera, ii. 284, a.
Nera, ii. 397, b.
Nerbudda, ii. 46, b; ii. 47, a; ii. 48, a; ii. 396, a; ii. 594, b.
Neretum, 96, a; 474, b; ii. 1294, a.
Neris, 169, a; 726, a.
Nerium, Promontory of, 934, b.
Nero, Statue of (Rome), ii. 806, a.
Neroassus, ii. 446, a.
Neronianae Thermae (Rome), ii. 838, a; ii. 847, a.
Neroniani Arcus (Rome), ii. 851, a.
Neronianus, Pons (Rome), ii. 850, a.
Neronis, Circus (Rome), ii. 844, b.
Neronis, Horti (Rome), ii. 842, a.
Nervii, ii. 103, b.
Nersae, 53, b; 55, a.
Nertobriga, 581, b.
Nertobriga Concordia Julia, 583, a.
Nerva, 346, b.
Nervae, Forum (Rome), ii. 799, b.
Nervion, 346, b; ii. 420, a.
Nerulum, ii. 210, a, b; ii. 1295, a.
Nessactium, ii. 73, b.
Nesca, ii. 284, b.
Nestane, 192, b.
Nestania, 193, a.
Nestus, ii. 1177, b.
Nesto, ii. 422, a.
Netherby, 56, a; 562, b.
Netium, 167, a.
Neto, 450, b; ii. 407, b.
Nettuno, 149, b.
Neva, ii. 917, a.
Nevada, Sierra, ii. 33, a; ii. 1021, a.
Nevers, 443, a; ii. 449, a.
Neufchâteau, ii. 449, a.
Nevirnum, 443, a.
Neunagen, ii. 450, a.
Neumark, ii. 447, a.
Neura-Ellia, ii. 284, b; ii. 1093, a.
Neury-sur-Berenjon, ii. 449, a.
Neuss, 458, b; 646, a; ii. 449, a.
Neusiädie, ii. 667, b.
Neuville, ii. 442, b; ii. 450, a.
Newcastle, 429, a; ii. 1256, b.
Newenden, 135, a.
Nevera Ellia, ii. 284, b; ii. 1053, a.
Newton Kyme, 477, b.
Neytra, ii. 414, a.
Ngaous, ii. 1336, b.
Niamtz, 651, a.
Niara, ii. 1075, b.
Niausta, 823, b.
Nicaea, 691, b; ii. 36, b; ii. 47, b; ii. 188, a; ii. 202, b.
Nice, ii. 188, a; ii. 423, b.
Nicephorius, ii. 1209, a.
Nicer, ii. 217, a.
Nicholas, St., 1035, b.
Nicl, ii. 425, b.
Nicias, ii. 1298, b.
Nicolo, S., 609, b.
Nicolo, Cape S., ii. 317, b.
Nicolo dell Arena, S., 61, a.
Nicomedeia, 406, b.

Nicopolis, 494, b; 833, a; ii. 1190, a.
Nicosia, 1052, b; ii. 877, a.
Nicotera, 451, a; ii. 1295, a.
Nicotera, ii. 427, b; ii. 1295, a.
Nicsar, ii. 418, a.
Niebla, ii. 33, a.
Niedda, Capo, 687, b.
Niederwallsee, ii. 115, a.
Niemen, ii. 460, b.
Nienhus, ii. 450, b.
Nieto, ii. 407, b.
Nifer, 755, b.
Niffer, 363, a.
Nigde, 463, a; 561, a.
Nigeira, ii. 429, b.
Nigolo, ii. 1317, b.
Nigritia, ii. 551, b.
Nigritis, Lacus, ii. 429, b.
Nijni Novgorod, 456, a; ii. 17, b.
Nikaria, ii. 10, b.
Nike Apteros, Temple of (Athens), 269, a.
Nikolao, C. 841, n.
Nikolaos, C. St., 685, a.
Nikoraki, 638, a.
Nizosta, ii. 171, b.
Niksar, 463, b.
Nile, the, ii. 430, a.
Nimrs, ii. 414, b.
Nimrud, 475, a; ii. 128, a; ii. 438, b.
Nimrud Tagh, ii. 440, a.
Nims, ii. 417, a.
Ninaea, 451, a.
Ninfa, ii. 456, a.
Ningum, ii. 74, a.
Nimittaci, ii. 350, a.
Nineveh, ii. 487, a.
Ninus, 745, b.
Nio, ii. 63, a.
Nipal, 746, a; 749, b.
Nipal Himalayas, 742, a.
Niphates, ii. 439, b.
Nirae or Nissa, ii. 456, b.
Nisch, ii. 1180, a.
Nishadha, ii. 552, a.
Nisibin, ii. 440, b.
Nisida, ii. 421, b.
Nissa, ii. 396, a; ii. 421, a.
Nisyrus, 524, a.
Nith, ii. 450, b.
Nitiobriges, 173, a.
Nitrae, ii. 47, a.
Nitrariae, 39, b.
Nitriote Nome, 39, b.
Nivaria, 906, b.
Nivitza, 114, b.
Nizhni Novogorod, 456, a; ii. 917, b.
Nixoro, ii. 1034, b.
Nixworo, 597, b.
Nizza, ii. 423, b.
Nizzy le Comte, ii. 359, a.
No, ii. 1137, a.
No-ammon, ii. 1137, a.
Noae, ii. 987, a.
Noara, ii. 442, n; ii. 987, a.
Nocara, ii. 116, b.
Nocera, 829, b; ii. 452, a, b; ii. 1295, a; ii. 1301, a.
Nocera dei Pagani, ii. 451, b.
Noega, 250, b.
Noegaucesia, 502, b.
Nogat, 999, a.
Nokra or Maaden-en-Nokra, ii. 283, b.
Nola, ii. 1295, a.
Nola, ii. 442, b.
Nomentana, Porta (Rome), ii. 759, a.
Nomia, Mt. ii. 341, b.
Nom, Valle di, 987, a.
Nonacris, 193, a.
Nonum, Ad, ii. 1287, a; ii. 1290, a.
Nora, ii. 911, b.
Norba, 167, a.
Norcia, ii. 455, b.
Norma, ii. 446, a.
Norosbes, ii. 943, b.
Norossi, ii. 943, b.
North Elmham, 442, b.
North Fambridge, 501, b.

Northfleet, ii. 1283, b.
North Foreland, 502, b.
Northampton, 571, a.
Northumberland, 750, a; ii. 504, b; ii. 1254, a.
Northwich, 654, b.
Norve, ii. 1294, a.
Norway, ii. 419, b.
Norwich, 442, a.
Noss Head, 394, b; ii. 1280, b.
Nostia, 193, b.
Noti Cornu, 57, b; ii. 425, b.
Notium, 53, a; 609, b.
Noto, Val di, 1052, a.
Noto Vecchio, ii. 422, a; ii. 987, a.
Nottingham, 576, b.
Nova Augusta, 197, b.
Nova Via (Rome), ii. 806, b; ii. 821, b.
Nova Zembla, ii. 232, a.
Nouam, ii. 449, a.
Novana, ii. 628, b.
Novantae, 750, a.
Novara, ii. 448, b; ii. 1287, b.
Novaria, ii. 1287, b
Novas, Ad, ii. 1497, b.
Novas or Nonas, Ad, ii. 1296, a.
Nove, Monte di, ii. 448, b; ii. 628, b.
Novesium, 458, b; 646, a.
Novgorod, 456, a.
Novigrad, ii. 449, b.
Noviomagus, 382, b; 429, a; 646, a.
Novito, F., 450, a.
Novium, 226, a.
Novograd, ii. 448, b.
Nouph, ii. 483, b.
Noya, ii. 442, b.
Noyon, ii. 450, a.
Noxia, 322, a.
Nuba, 58, a.
Nubia, 57, a.
Nuceria, 451, a; ii. 1294, b; ii. 1295, a; ii. 1301, a; ii. 1317, b.
Nucerium, ii. 1301, a.
Numana, ii. 628, b; ii. 1307, a.
Numidia, New, 71, a.
Numidicus, Sinus, ii. 297, b.
Numistro, ii. 210, a.
Num, C., 317, b.
Nura, 374, a.
Nuragus, ii. 1254, a.
Nymegen, 382, b; 646, a; ii. 450, a.
Nymphaeum, 310, a; 748, a; 421, a; ii. 1075, b.
Nymphaeus Portus, ii. 911, a.
Nymphlus or Nymphaeus, ii. 1208, b.
Nyon, 646, b.

Oaeneum, ii. 574, a.
Oanus, ii. 985, b.
Oarus, 455, a.
Oasis Magna, ii. 459, a.
Oasis Minor, ii. 458, b.
Oasis Trinytheos, ii. 458, b.
Ober-Glinzburg, 1020, b.
Ober-Laybach, ii. 404, a.
Obernburg, ii. 192, a.
Ober-W'pthal, ii. 1312, a.
Oberwesel, ii. 1325, n.
Oberwinterthur, 1041, b; ii. 1313, b.
Obi, ii. 232, b.
Obilae, ii. 278, a.
Obilinum, 110, b.
Oboca, ii. 16, a.
Oca, Sierra de, ii. 14, a.
Ocalen, 413, a.
Ocana, 525, a.
Ocana, ii. 461, b; ii. 1308, a.
Occhiala or Occhula, 803, b.
Ocelis, 20, b.
Ocelum, 934, b; ii. 188, a.
Oche, 871, b.
Ochosbanes, ii. 347, a.
Ochus, 364, b; ii. 421, a, ii. 578, b.
Ocilis, 582, a.

Ocinarus, 450, a; ii. 1131, a.
Ocitis, 49, a.
Ocra, 522, b.
Ocra, Mons, 108, b.
Ocriculum, ii. 1301, a; ii. 1817, a.
Octavia, Porticus (Rome), ii. 834, b.
Octaviae, Porticus (Rome), ii. 833, b.
Octavian, Statue of (Rome), ii. 793, a.
Octavum, Ad, ii. 1290, a; ii. 1301, a.
Octodurus, 110, b.
Octogesa, ii. 32, a.
Odeium (Athens), 297, a.
Odeium of Herodes or Regilla (Athens), 286, a.
Odeium of Pericles (Athens), 300, b.
Odemira, ii. 361, b.
Odenvald. 1056, b.
Oder, ii. 1042, b; ii. 1307, a.
Oderzo, ii. 485, a.
Odessa, ii. 67, b.
Odeum (Rome), ii. 838, b; ii. 845, b.
Odiel, ii. 223, a.
Odmana, ii. 1076, b.
Odomanti, ii. 512, a; ii. 1190, a.
Odorneh, ii. 1217, a.
Odrysae, ii. 1190, a.
Odysseae, Portus, ii. 983, a.
Oea, 325, b; ii. 1081, a; ii. 1158, a; ii. 1160, b.
Oeanthe, ii. 203, a.
Oeaso, 949, a; 950, a.
Oechalia, 65, a; 193, b; ii. 345, b; ii. 1170, a.
Oecharites, 347, a.
Oedenburg, ii. 928, b.
Oeneon, ii. 203, a.
Oeneus, ii. 541, b.
Oenia, 10, b.
Oeniadae, 10, b.
Oenius, ii. 658, b.
Oenoanda, 462, a.
Oenoe, 329, a; 330, b; 602, b; 685, b; 821, a; ii. 268, a.
Oenone, or Oenopia, 33, a.
Oenoparas, ii. 1075, b.
Oenus, ii. 1310, b.
Ornussae, ii. 342, b.
Oeroe, 413, b.
Oesel, 380, b; 1091, b.
Oesyma, 807, b; ii. 1135, b; ii. 1190, a.
Oetaea, ii. 1170, b.
Oetylus, ii. 112, b.
Oeum Cerameicum, 326, a.
Oeum Deceleicum, 330, a.
Of, ii. 484, b.
Ofanto, 166, b; 337, a.
Ofena, 337, b; ii. 1283, b.
Ogdaemi, ii. 287, a.
Oglasa, 857, b.
Oglio, 497, b; 940, a; ii. 474, a.
Ogyris, ii. 471, a.
Oisans, d', ii. 1260, b.
Oise, 442, b; ii. 65, n.
Okenyate, ii. 1330, b.
Okridha, ii. 243, b.
Oktap Dagh, ii. 198, b.
Oktax Dagh, ii. 484, b.
Olarso, 949, a.
Olbasa, 508, b.
Olbia, 225, b; 321, a; ii. 54, a; ii. 60, a; ii. 911, b; ii. 912, a; ii. 1196, a.
Olbianus, Portus, ii. 911, b.
Olbiopolis, 213, a.
Oleachites, 644, b.
Olcinium, 748, a.
Old Carlisle, ii. 473, a.
Old Penrith, 554, b.
Old Town, 409, b; 932, a.
Oldenburg, 606, a.
Oleastrum, 698, a; 807, a; ii. 31, b.
Olenus, 14, b; 17, a; 67, a.
Oléron, 389, b; ii. 39, b.
Oléron, Ile d', ii. 1314, a.

Olerus, 705, b.
Olesa, ii. 857, a.
Olevano, 55, a.
Olevano, Civitella d', ii. 1318, a.
Olgassys, 406, a; ii. 547, a.
Oliba, 394, b.
Oligyrtum, 192, b.
Olina, 934, b.
Olivula, Portus, ii. 424, a.
Olizon, ii. 1170, b.
Ollerra, ii. 1240, b.
Ollius, 497, b; 940, a.
Olmeius, 413, a.
Olmo, Monte dell', ii. 559, a; ii. 629, a.
Olmones, 1102, b.
Olondae, ii. 917, b.
Olonos, 850, b.
Oloosson, ii. 1170, a.
Olos Borion, 161, b.
Olou Bouxar, ii. 65, b.
Olpae, 10, a; ii. 203, a.
Oltis, 464, a.
Olwera, ii. 33, a.
Olughissar, ii. 1208, a.
Olus, 705, b.
Olympieium (Athens), 289, a.
Olympus, 730, a.
Olympum, ii. 237, a.
Olynta, ii. 37, a.
Om Keiss, 922, b.
Omalis, 973, b.
Oman, 181, b; 383, b; 605, b; 698, a; ii. 481, b.
Oman, Gulf of, 174, b; 175, b.
Omana, 983, b.
Omani, 383, b.
Omanitae, 181, b; 608, a.
Ombite, Nome, 40, a.
Omboa, 40, a.
Umbrios, 906, b.
Ombrone, 857, a; ii. 1296, a; ii. 1317, b.
Ombrones, ii. 916, a.
Omphalium, 705, b.
Onchesmus, 832, b.
Omenagara, ii. 47, a.
Oncium, or Oncae, 193, a.
Onda, ii. 964, a.
Oneum, 748, a.
Onobalas, ii. 986, a.
Onuphis, 39, b.
Onuphite Nome, 39, b.
Ooracta, 521, a; 686, b.
Opheltius, Mount, ii. 198, b.
Ophionenses, 65, a.
Ophir, 59, b.
Ophis, ii. 658, b.
Ophiusa, 873, a; 729, b.
Ophlimus, ii. 688. b.
Opblones, ii. 916, b.
Opis, or Opio, 914, a.
Opimia, Basilica (Rome), ii. 784, a.
Opini, 691, b.
Opitergium, ii. 1275, a.
Oporto, 477, b; ii. 220, b.
Opouk, 623, b.
Opouk, Mount, ii. 1110, a.
Oppenheim, 418, b.
Oppidum Novum, 389, b.
Oppius (Rome), ii. 822, a.
Ops, Aedes of (Rome), ii. 782, b.
Ops, Temple of (Rome), ii. 769, b.
Optatiana, 744, b.
Opuk, Mount, ii. 1035, n.
Opus, 821, a; ii. 202, b.
Ora, 243, a; 521, a.
Orae, or Ori, 983, b.
Orak, Ada, 194, a.
Oran, ii. 297, b.
Orange, 187, b; 577, a.
Orbe, 367, a; ii. 1325, b.
Orbetello, ii. 1285, b.
Orbis, ii. 718, a, b.
Orbis, 367, a.
Orbitanium, ii. 896, b.
Orbo, Fiume, 691, a.
Orcajo or Orcaeva, ii. 1259, n.
Orcaino, Sierra de, ii. 1259, b.
Orchamps, 713, a.

Orcheni, 181. a.
Orchies, ii. 493, a.
Orchoe, 601, a.
Orchomenia, 193, a.
Orchomenus, 193, a.
Ordessus, ii. 938, b.
Ordona, 1086, b; ii. 1294, a.
Ordou, 602, a; 698, a.
Ordunna, 255, a.
Ordunna, ii. 420, a.
Ore Sund, ii. 460, b.
Oreine, ii. 532, b.
Oreitae, 983, b.
Orense, 934, a; ii. 883, a.
Oreos, ii. 492, b.
Oreste, Monte S., ii. 1023, a.
Oresthasium, 192, b.
Orestis, ii. 236, b.
Orestis, Portus, 451, b.
Oreszovits, ii. 469, b.
Orethus, ii. 986, a.
Oreto, ii. 986, a; ii. 1240, b.
Orfa4, 806, b.
Orfana, ii. 586, a.
Orgagna, ii. 32, a.
Orgamenes, 364, b.
Organa, 521, a; ii. 471, a.
Orgas. ii. 1326, b.
Orgusi, ii. 943, b.
Orgessus, 756, a.
Orgia, ii. 32, a.
Oria, 336, a; 1106, b; ii. 1293, b.
Oribucia, ii. 487, a.
Origenomesci, 502, b.
Originis, Aquae, 168, b.
Orihuela, ii. 1174, a.
Orikhova, ii. 1219, b.
Orinael, ii. 917, b.
Oristano, 687, b; ii. 912, a.
Oristano, Gulf of, ii. 911, b.
Oriuolo, 907, b.
Orixa, ii. 1076, b.
Orkney Islands, ii. 487, a.
Orléans, 523, a; 986, b.
Orléans, Forest of, 901, a.
Ormenium, 406, a.
Ormuz, 1030, b; ii. 471, a.
Ormylia, ii. 969, a.
Orne, ii. 474, a.
Orniaci, 249, b; 250, b.
Ornithonopolis, ii. 605, b.
Oro, Torre del, ii. 1327, a.
Oroascus, 521, a.
Oroatis, ii. 578, b; ii. 1050, b.
Orobatis, 243, a.
Orobiae, 872, b.
Oropesa, 807, a.
Oropo, ii. 496, a.
Orosei, Fiume di, ii. 911, a.
Orosines, ii. 1178, a.
Oroxvar, 999, b; ii. 689, b.
Oroum, ii. 1076, a.
Orphei, Lacus (Rome), ii. 828, a.
Orrock, ii. 496, b.
Orsaria, ii. 74, a.
Orso, Capo dell', ii. 911, b.
Orsova, Old, ii. 1207, a.
Orsova, Old, ii. 1338, a.
Ortakoi, 424, a.
Orte, 1091, a.
Ortegal, Cape, ii. 1231, a.
Orthe, ii. 1170, a.
Orthes, ii. 32, a.
Orthez, 389, b.
Orthopagum, 412, b.
Orthosia, ii. 606, a.
Ortona a Mare, ii. 497, b.
Ortona, 915, b; 916, a.
Ortosa, ii. 497, a.
Ortospanum, 505, b; ii. 552, a.
Ortygia (Syracuse), ii. 1062, b.
Orudil, M., ii. 46, b.
Orvieto, 1052, a; ii. 886, a; ii. 1326, b.
Orvinium, 6, a.
Orwell, 808, b.
Oryx, 193, a.
Osa, 837, a.
Osaca, ii. 912, a.
Osburg, 442, b.
Osca, ii. 32, a.
Oscm, Cape, ii. 1328, a.
Osenik, ii. 1042, b.

Oseriates, ii. 542, a.
Osero, 7, a; ii. 329, b.
Osli, ii. 916, b.
Osmo, 347, a; ii. 628, b; ii. 1301, b.
Osmigiri, ii. 1006, a.
Osismii, 218, b.
Osma, 347, a; ii. 1231, a.
Osma in Biscoya, ii. 1331, a.
Osmida, 705, b.
Osopa, ii. 1275, b.
Osopum, ii. 1275, b.
Osprizo,Capo di S., ii. 424, a.
Osquidates Campestres, 173, a.
Osroene, ii. 439, b.
Ossa, 817, b; 857, a.
Ossau, ii. 500, a.
Ossera, 807, b; ii. 501, a.
Osvetes, 85, a.
Ossigerda, 807, b.
Ossonoba, ii. 220, a.
Ostanitza, 663, a; ii. 323, b.
Osteria, 129, b.
Osteria dell' Acqua Viva, ii. 1301, a.
Osteria del Cavaliere, 526, b.
Osteria della Molara, ii. 718, b.
Osteria delle Fratocchie, 426, a.
Osteria di S. Valentino, ii. 59, a.
Osteria, Nuova, ii. 1305, a.
Osteriz, ii. 1240, a.
Ostia, ii. 501, b.
Ostia Aterni, 916, a; ii. 1307, a.
Ostiensis, Porta (Rome), ii. 758, a; ii. 760, b.
Ostiglia, 1091, b; ii. 1287, b.
Ostoea, ii. 1254, b.
Ostra, ii. 1317, b.
Ostrovo, 219, b; 581, a; 830, a; ii. 236, b.
Ostur, ii. 504, b.
Osuli, ii. 917, a.
Osuña, ii. 1023, b.
Osuna, ii. 1327, a.
Oswald, St., 25, a.
Othoca, ii. 912, a.
Otmarsheim, ii. 1034, a.
Otopisus, ii. 1299, a.
Otranto, 1101, b.
Otriculi, ii. 462, a; ii. 1301, a.
Ottochatz, ii. 3, b.
Ottadini, 750, a.
Ottaviolca, 507, b.
Ottorocorra, ii. 968, b.
Ovar, ii. 689, b.
Ovaschik, 248, a.
Oude, ii. 50, a.
Oudi, ii. 504, b.
Oudjenar, ii. 584, b.
Oued Hrhia, ii. 1210, b.
Oued Resas, ii. 1135, a.
Overborough, 427, a; 429, a.
Ovetsant, 949, a; ii. 1331, a.
Ovetum, 250, b.
Ovidiopol, ii. 429, b.
Oviedo, 250, b.
Owcin, ii. 47, a; ii. 49, b; ii. 508, a.
Ovilaba, ii. 448, a.
Ovile (Rome), ii. 836, a.
Oulan Adassi, 20, b.
Oulx, ii. 286, b.
Ovo, Castell dell', ii. 317, a.
Oural, 455, a.
Ovrio-Kastro, 600, b; ii. 701, a.
Ovrio-Nisi, or Ovrio-Kastro, 685, a.
Ovrogue, 187, a; ii. 220, a.
Oursuf, 1020, b.
Outlouk, 999, a.
Outzen, 455, a.
Oxi Rupes, ii. 506, a.
Oxia, 80, a.
Oxiana, 102, b.
Oxici, 804, b.
Oxicad, 442, b.
Oxumagis, 973, b.
Oxus, 364, b.
Oxydrancae, ii.1019, a.
Oxyneia, ii. 1170, a.

Ovarco, 949, a; ii. 466, a.
Oyarzun, ii. 466, a.
Ozal, 353, a.
Oxe, ii. 1260, b.
Ozene, ii. 47, a; ii. 49, b.

Pabillonis, R. di, ii. 911, a.
Pachnamunis, 39, b.
Pachyta, ii. 1190, a.
Pacis, Ara (Rome), ii. 838, a.
Pactia, ii. 552, b.
Pactius, 474, a.
Padargus, ii. 578, b.
Padova, ii 556, a; ii. 1287, b.
Padria, 1020, b.
Paduli di Castiglione, 857, b.
Padan Aram, ii. 333, a.
Paderborn, ii. 595, b.
Padula, ii. 210, a.
Paeania, 332, b.
Paeanium, 67, a.
Paronidae, 326, a.
Puesici, 249, b.
Paetovis, ii. 542, a.
Pagasae, ii. 1170, a.
Pagidas, 371, b.
Paglia, 857, a; ii. 1297, a.
Paglione, ii. 187, b; ii. 559, a.
Pago, ii. 379, b.
Pagrae, ii. 106, b; ii. 1075, b.
Pagras, ii. 515, a.
Pagus Forensis, 911, a.
Pagyritae, ii. 916, b.
Pahang, 375, a.
Pakholi, ii. 585, b.
PAKI, ii. 220, b.
Pausley, ii. 1257, b.
Palachthia, ii. 1170, b.
Palaea, 730, a.
Palaeo Foggia, ii. 6-2, b.
Palaeobiblus, ii. 1076, b.
Palaeogula, ii. 960, b.
Palaeokastro, ii. 646, a.
Palaeokastron, 823, b.
Palaepaphos, 163, b; 730, a.
Palaepharus, ii. 1170, a.
Palaerus, 10, b.
Palaesimundum, ii. 1093, b.
Palaeste, 832, b; ii. 492, b.
Palaibyblus, ii. 606, a.
Palamarı, ii. 310, a; ii. 1195, b.
Palamidhi, ii. 403, b.
Palancia, ii. 535, a.
Palantia, 250, a.
Palasa, ii. 492, b; ii. 516, a.
Palace, Sta Maria le, 82, b.
Palatia, 524, a; ii. 351, b.
Palatine (Rome), ii. 802, a.
Palatium, 6, a.
Palazzo, ii. 535, b.
Palazzolo, 91, b; 89, a; 92, b; ii. 987, a; ii. 987, b.
Pale, 588, a.
Palea, 411, a.
Pal a, M., 1162, b.
Palea Piva, ii. 153, a; ii. 418, b; ii. 560, a.
Palea-Khora, 34, b; 106, b; ii. 1036, b.
Palea Larissa, 699, b.
Palea Lutra, ii. 1191, b.
Palea Venetia, 594, a.
Palencia, ii. 535, a; ii. 1252,b.
Paleofanaro, ii. 620, b.
Paleokastro, 243, a; 331, b; 700, a; 737, a; 850, a; 1102, b; ii. 189, a; ii. 352, a; ii. 715, b; ii. 1191, a, b.
Paleokastron, 1038, b.
Paleomiri, ii. 310, a.
Polcopanaghia, 592, b.
Paleopoli, 932, b; 102, b; ii. 260, b.
Paleoprevesa, ii. 427, a.
Paleopyrgo, 728, a.
Paleo Vraona, 334, a.
Paleoeuni, 1035, a.
Palermo, ii. 545, a.
Palermo, ii. 543, b.
Palestrina, ii. 663, b.
Palibothra, ii. 47, b.
Paliki, ii. 533, b.

Palicorum, Lacus, ii. 986, a.
Palindromus, 175, b.
Palinuro, Capo di, ii. 209, b.
Palinurus, ii. 209, b.
Palio, ii. 533, b.
Paliuri, Capr, 498, b.
Paliuro, Capo, ii. 534, b.
Pallurus, ii. 277, b.
Pals's Bay, 198, a; ii. 46, b.
Paliacottas, 362, b.
Pallae, 691, b.
Pallaeopas, 362, b.
Pallano, Monte di, 916, a.
Pallano, Monte, ii. 535, b.
Pallanti, 6, a.
Pallantia, 197. b; ii. 1252, b.
Pallantiani, Horti (Rome), ii. 826, a.
Pallantium, 192, b.
Pallanum, 916, a.
Pallas, ii. 1081, a.
Pallene, 327, a; 560, a.
Pallene, Peninsula of, 597, b.
Pallis, 857, a.
Pallam Fluvium, Ad, ii. 1297, a.
Palma, 374, b.
Palma, 906, b.
Palmajola, 857, b.
Palmaria, ii. 658, a.
Palmaruola, ii. 536, a; ii. 658, a.
Palmas, Golfo di, ii. 911, b.
Palme, La, ii. 1309, b.
Palmyrene, ii. 1076, b.
Palo, 112, a; 167, b; ii. 535, a; ii. 1296, a.
Paloda, 744, b.
Palombara, 489, a.
Palombara, 489, a.
Palos, ii. 474, a.
Paltos, ii. 1075, b.
Paltus, ii. 1075, b.
Palu, 628, b.
Paludi Pontine, ii. 654, b.
Palumbinum, ii. 896, b.
Palus Tritonis, 68, a.
Pambuk-Kalessi, 1064, a.
Pamisus, ii. 341, b; ii. 574, b.
Pamphia, 67, a.
Pamplona, ii. 654, b.
Panactum, 329, a, b.
Panaetolium, 63, b.
Panagia di Cordialissa, ii. 117, a.
Panaria, 51, b.
Panaro, ii. 934, a.
Panathenaic Stadium (Athens), 292, b.
Panban, 644, a.
Panchrysos, 392, a.
Pancorbo, ii. 1310, a.
Pandavas, ii. 588, b; ii. 540, a.
Pandja, ii. 47, a.
Pandicora, ii. 254, a.
Pandikki, ii. 546, b.
Pandion, ii. 47, a.
Pandosia, 833, a; 451, a; ii. 210, a.
Pandous, ii. 47, a.
Paneium, 331, a.
Pangaeus, ii. 1177, b.
Pani, 331, a.
Panjab, 224, a; 509, b; ii. 255, b; ii. 422, a; ii. 507, b; ii. 666, b.
Panjab, Upper, ii. 1115, b.
Paniardi, ii. 943, b.
Pankala, ii. 507, b.
Pannona, 705, b.
Pannonios, Ad, 744, b.
Panon, ii. 541, a.
Panopeus, ii. 605, a.
Panopolis, 40, a; 465, b.
Panopolite Nome, 40, a.
Panormo, 331, b.
Panormus, 17, a; 331, b; 588, b; 705, b; ii. 277, b; ii. 1190, a.
Pantagias, ii. 986, a.
Pantaleo, S., ii. 374, b.
Pantalia, ii. 1038, b.
Pantalia or Pautalia, ii. 1314, a.
Pantalica, 848, b.
Pantanus, Lacus, 167, a.
Panteichion, 434, b.

Panticlaria, 607, b.
Pantheon of Agrippa (Rome), ii. 836, b.
Panticapes, 999, a.
Pantomatrium, 706, b.
Panyasus, ii. 533, a.
Paola, Potro di, 626, a.
Papa, Rocca di, 889, a.
Papadha, 457, a.
Papadhates, ii. 221, a.
Papadoula, 699, a.
Papaduia, 700, b.
Paphara, ii. 1075, b.
Papiriana, ii. 1296, a.
Papremis, ii. 1334, a.
Para, ii. 550, b.
Parabita, 474, b.
Paracheloitis, 9, a.
Parachoathras, ii. 554, a.
Parachoatras, M., ii. 4, b.
Paradisus, ii. 1076, a.
Paraepaphitis, 591, a.
Paraetacae, 822, b.
Paraetaceni, ii. 301, b.
Paraetonium, ii. 277, b.
Paragon Sinus, 175, b.
Paralia, 322, b; 596, a.
Paralimni, 413, b; 812, a; 1080, b; ii. 582, b.
Parapotamii, ii. 604, b.
Parca, ii. 7, b.
Parco di Colonna, 806, a.
Parembole, 60, a.
Parembolis, ii. 549, b.
Parentium, ii. 73, b.
Parenzo, ii. 73, b; ii. 550, a.
Parietinis, 582, a.
Parga, ii. 1217, b.
Paris, ii. 270, b.
Parma, ii. 1287, a.
Parma, ii. 851, a; ii. 1287, a.
Paroes, 322, a.
Paro, ii. 552, b.
Parolissum, 744, b.
Paropamisadae, 210, b.
Paropamisus, 364, b; ii. 46, a; ii. 552, a.
Paropus, ii. 986, b.
Paroreia, 193, a; ii. 310, a; ii. 512, a.
Parrhasia, 192, b.
Parrhasii, 192, b.
Parstrymonia, ii. 512, a.
Parialegre, ii. 219, b.
Parthalis, 480, b; ii. 47, a.
Parthenius, Portus, 451, b.
Parthenon (Athens), 270, a.
Parthiscus, ii. 1199, b.
Parthnico, ii. 987, b.
Partenkirchen, ii. 853, b.
Parthens, ii. 553, b.
Parthenium, 403, b.
Parthenium, 422, a; ii. 967, b; ii. 1111, b.
Parthorum, Septem Domus (Rome), ii. 821, b.
Parthus, ii. 853, b.
Partiscum, ii. 7, b.
Parupium, ii. 3, b.
Paryadres, 572, a; ii. 658, b.
Paryeti, 184, a.
Pas de Calais, ii. 460, b.
Pasagarda, ii. 578, b.
Paschalimani, 306, b.
Pasha Limane, 379, b.
Pasha Limani, 555, b.
Pashash, ii. 1338, b.
Pasicae, ii. 1019, a.
Pasieria, ii. 1075, b.
Pasires, 210, b.
Pasitigris, ii. 1209, a.
Pasmaktchi, 722, b.
Paso, Cape, ii. 1337, b.
Passaiae, ii. 47, a.
Passaron, 833, a.
Pass of Derbend, 90, a.
Passau, 381, b.
Passava, 32, b; ii. 130, a.
Passaro, Capo, ii. 508, a.
Passenex, or Palmee, ii. 377, b.
Passerano, ii. 928, a.
Passeria, Aquae, 870, a.
Passo del Furlo, ii. 56, b.
Passo di Portella, ii. 150, b.
Pataliputra, ii. 47, b.

Patavissa, 744, b.
Patavium, ii. 1275, a; ii. 1287, b.
Patera, ii. 555, b.
Paterno, 721, a; 1099, b; ii. 1306, a.
Paternum, 451, a.
Pathiasus, ii. 1199, b.
Pathmetic arm of the Nile, ii. 433, a.
Pathros, ii. 1144, b.
Patmo, ii. 557, b.
Patna, ii. 47, b; ii. 534, a.
Patrae, 14, a; 17, a; ii. 36, b.
Patraeus, 422, a.
Patrasso, Patras or Patra, ii. 557, b.
Patreis, 14, b.
Patridava, 744, b.
Patrington, ii. 667, a.
Patroclus, Island of, 331, a.
Pattala, ii. 47, b; ii. 49, b.
Pattalene, ii. 47, b.
Patteres, 128, b.
Patyorus, ii. 887, a.
Patuca, 691, b.
Pavia, ii. 1205, a; ii. 1287, b.
Paula, 737, a.
Paulian, St., ii. 12, a.
Paulien or Paulhan, S., ii. 699, b.
Pavilitza, ii. 596, a.
Paulli, Basilica (Rome), ii. 787, a.
Paulo, ii. 187, b.
Pauna or Panna, ii. 897, a.
Paunton, ii. 657, b.
Paus, 193, a.
Pauslippus, Mons, 495, b.
Pausulae, ii. 629, a.
Pautalia, ii. 237, a.
Pautilza, ii. 1314, a.
Pax Augusta, 542, a.
Pax Julia, ii. 220, a.
Pasi, Cape, ii. 930, a.
Paxo, ii. 559, b.
Pays de Caux, 480, b.
Peace, Temple of (Rome), ii. 808, a.
Peccana, ii. 1032, a.
Pedalium, 227, b; 730, a.
Pedalium, Prom. 638, a.
Pedasus, ii. 346, a.
Pediaeus, 729, b.
Pedro, Cape, ii. 1098, a.
Peebles, 750, a.
Pegae, 111, b.
Pegae, ii. 1042, b.
Peguere, La Grande, ii. 1190, b.
Peirae, 17, a.
Peiraeus, 259, b.
Peiraeeus (Athens), 306, a.
Piraeum, 685, b.
Peiraeus, 665, a.
Peiraic Gate (Athens), 263, a.
Peiresiae, ii. 1170, a.
Peirus, 13, b; 19, a.
Peusenberg, 5, a.
Peitho, Temple of (Athens), 301, a.
Pekhely, ii. 585, b.
Pel, ii. 570, a.
Pelagonia, ii. 512, a.
Pelasgiotis, ii. 1167, a; ii. 1170, a.
Peleces, 326, a.
Pelendones, 581, b.
Pelendova, 744, b.
Pelestini, ii. 1317, b.
Pelinaeus, 609, b.
Pelinnaeum, ii. 1170, a.
Pelino, S., 673, a; ii. 1306, b.
Pelisame, ii. 633, b.
Pella, 17, a; ii. 236, b; ii. 532, a; ii. 1076, b; ii. 1298, b.
Pellegrino, Monte, 845, b.
Pellene, 14, b.
Pelodes, 459, a.
Pelontium, 280, b.
Pelso or Peiso, ii. 541, b.
Peltuinum, ii. 1283, a.

Pelusian arm of the Nile, ii. 433, a.
Pelva, 748, a.
Pembrokeshire, 775, a.
Penaflor, ii. 32, b.
Penarium, Aedes (Rome), ii. 808, a.
Penausende, ii. 974, a.
Penkridge, ii. 574, a.
Pennaecrite, ii. 950, b.
Pennaus, ii. 496, a.
Pennalda de Castro, 636, b.
Penne, ii. 874, a.
Penne, Civita di, ii. 631, a; ii. 1283, a.
Pennelocus, ii. 574, a.
Penrith, Old, 429, a; ii. 555, a; ii. 1235, a.
Pentapylium (Rome), ii. 804, a.
Pentele, 327, a.
Pentelensia, Mons, 332, a.
Penteleum, 193, a.
Penteli, 332, a.
Pentelicus, 332, a.
Pentridge, ii. 1311, a.
Penza, ii. 917, b.
Pera, ii. 165, b.
Perabod, ii. 951, a.
Perachora, 688, b.
Peraea, 517, b; ii. 522, a.
Perasthes, 192, b.
Percea, 367, b.
Perdikobrysus, 22, b.
Pers de Sorceda, S., ii. 947, a.
Percop, ii. 1090, b.
Perekop, Gulf of, 516, a; ii. 1087, a.
Perengadi Tagh, ii. 373, b.
Pergaeus, ii. 1283, b.
Pergamum, 471, a; 705, b.
Pergamus, 807, b.
Pergusa, ii. 986, a.
Perierbidi, ii. 917, b.
Pergeus, 457, b.
Pergord, ii. 585, a.
Perigueus, 457, b; 654, a; 692, a; ii. 585, a.
Perim, 776, b.
Perimula, ii. 46, b.
Perimulicus, Sinus, ii. 46, b; ii. 52, a.
Perin Dagh, ii. 487, a.
Perinthus, ii. 1190, a, b.
Perissa, ii. 1161, a.
Permoessus, 413, a.
Perrhidae, 330, a.
Perrigus, ii. 1015, a.
Perschmbah, 698, a.
Pershendi, ii. 643, a.
Persian Gulf, 174, b; ii. 578, b; ii. 557, a.
Persicus Sinus, 174, b.
Pertuis, ii. 585, a.
Pertus, Col de, ii. 1047, a.
Pertusa, ii. 32, a.
Perugia, ii. 579, b; ii. 1288, b.
Perugia, Lago di, ii. 1221, b.
Perusia, ii. 1288, b.
Pesaro, ii. 633, b; ii. 1301, a.
Pescara, 252, b; ii. 1283, a; ii. 1307, a.
Peschiera, 195, b.
Peshawur, 505, b.
Pessinus, 929, a.
Pessium, ii. 7, b.
Pesth, ii. 7, b.
Pesto, ii. 512, b.
Petala, 804, a.
Petalidha, ii. 385, b; 688, a.
Petalius, ii. 541, b.
Petavonium, 240, a.
Petella, 451, a; ii. 210, a.
Peteon, 562, a.
Peterwarden, ii. 254, b.
Petit Col d'Ornon et Querele, 570, a.
Petitarus, 18, b.
Petra, ii. 966, b; ii. 1190, a.
Petra, 412, a; 787, a.
Petra Thermastis, 423, b.
Petralis, ii. 363, a.
Petras Parvus, ii. 277, b.
Petrocorii, 173, a.
Petri, Porta Sti (Rome), ii. 758, b.

Petrodava, 744, b.
Petrosaca, 192, b.
Petrowics, ii. 377, a.
Pettau, ii. 562, b.
Pettineo, 82, b; ii. 986, a.
Pettini, 810, a.
Petuaria, ii. 550, b; ii. 667, a.
Petusias, 562, a.
Peucela, 243, a.
Peucelaotis, ii. 47, b.
Peucini, 281, a; ii. 367, b.
Pevensey, 135, a.
Pfahlgraben, ii. 192, a.
Pfahlheim, ii. 191, b.
Pfahlrain, ii. 191, b.
Pfünzen, ii. 686, a.
Phacelinus, ii. 996, a.
Phacium, ii. 1170, a.
Phaedrias, 192, b.
Phaestus, 17, a; 705, b; ii. 1170, a.
Phagres, 807, b.
Phalacrian Prom., ii. 984, a.
Phalacrum, 669, b.
Phalaesae, 192, b.
Phalanna, ii. 1170, a.
Phalanthum, 193, a.
Phalara, ii. 1170, a.
Phalarus, 412, b.
Phalasarna, 705, b.
Phaleric Wall (Athens), 260, a.
Phalerum, 259, b; 336, a.
Phalerum (Athens), 304, b.
Phalesina, 403, b.
Phaloria, ii. 1170, a.
Phana, 67, a.
Phanae, 609, b.
Phanagoria, 422, a.
Phanari, 306, b.
Phanote, 833, a.
Pharbaethite Nome, 39, b.
Pharcedon, ii. 1170, a.
Pharae, 17, a.
Phareis, 14, b.
Pharillon, 96, a.
Pharmacia, 424, a.
Pharnazia, 197, b.
Pharmatheous, ii. 656, b.
Pharos, ii. 37, a.
Pharsalus, ii. 1170, a.
Pharygae, ii. 202, b.
Phasiani, ii. 658, b.
Phasis, 571, b; ii. 658, b; ii. 1093, a.
Phatnitic arm of the Nile, ii. 433, a.
Phavonae, ii. 927, b.
Phaura, 231, a.
Phazania, 732, a; 974, b; ii. 457, a.
Pheca, or Phecadum, ii. 1170, a.
Phegeae, 230, b.
Pheia, 521, a.
Phelleus, 322, b.
Pbellon, 817, b.
Pheneatis, 192, a.
Pheneus, 193, a.
Pherae, 67, a; ii. 345, b; ii. 1170, a.
Phi-Beseth, 453, a.
Phicium, 412, a.
Phigalia, 193, a.
Phigalice, 193, a.
Phigamus, ii. 656, b.
Phiklia, ii. 890, a.
Philadelpheia, ii. 1076, b.
Philadelphia, 123, b; 239, a.
Philaidae, 332, b.
Philak, ii. 598, a.
Philara, ii. 364, a.
Phdilippeville, ii. 656, b.
Philippi, 807, b; ii. 1190, a; ii. 1299, a.
Philippi, Domus (Rome), ii. 818, b.
Philippi, Porticus (Rome), ii. 823, b.
Phdilippo, ii. 1033, b.
Phdilipppopoli, ii. 600, a.
Philippopolis, ii. 1190, a; ii. 1190, a.

Philoteras, 37, b; 81, b.
Phtniki, ii. 168, a.
Phinopolis, ii. 1190, a.
Phintias, 79, b; 805, a.
Phinton, 719, a.
Phintonis, ii. 911, b.
Pkira, ii. 1160, b.
Phiraesi, ii. 927, b.
Phlegra, ii. 535, b.
Phlya, 332, b.
Phlygonium, ii. 605, a.
Phocas, Column of (Rome), ii. 797, a.
Phocaea, 239, b.
Phoebatae, 755, b.
Phoebia, 457, a.
Phoenice, 832, b; ii. 1076, b.
Phoenicium, 412, a.
Phoenicusa, 51, b.
Phoenix, 13, b; 705, b.
Phoezon, 192, b.
Phorbantia, 454, b.
Phorbia, ii. 383, b.
Phoriela, 193, b.
Phoron Limen, 325, b.
Photice, 833, a.
Pkrat Misan, ii. 332, a.
Phrateria, 744, b.
Phreattys (Athens), 308, a.
Phriconis, 53, a.
Phrixa, 821, b.
Phrugundiones, ii. 915, b.
Phrurium, 730, a.
Phtheirophagi, 572, a; ii. 917, b.
Phthemphuthite Nome, 29, b.
Phthiotis, ii. 1167, a; ii. 1170, a.
Phturis, 60, b.
Phurui, 418, a; 668, b.
Phuth, ii. 297, b.
Phycus, 733, b.
Phylace, 192, b; 833, a; ii. 1170, a.
Phyle, 329, b.
Phyllitae, ii. 48, a.
Phyllus, ii. 1170, a.
Physca, 830, a; ii. 384, a.
Physco, ii. 626, a.
Physcus, 519, b; ii. 1209, a.
Phyteum, 67, a.
Phytia, or Phoetelae, 10, b.
Piacenza, ii. 636, a.
Piacularis, Porta (Rome), ii. 757, b.
Piagnino, ii. 1317, b.
Piali, ii. 1119, a.
Pialia, ii. 1170, a.
Piana, 1038, b.
Piano dell' Ausente, 345, a.
Piano di Civita, ii. 1103, a.
Pianosa, 857, b; ii. 637, b.
Piave, ii. 641, a; ii. 1275, a.
Picaria, 748, a.
Pictas, Ad, ii. 1301, b; ii. 1302, a.
Pictones, 173, a.
Picuina, ii. 585, a.
Pidhavro, 841, a.
Pidhima, 214, b; ii. 1191, b.
Piè di Lugo, Lago del, 6, b.
Piè Feguiè, lou, 894, b.
Piena, ii. 629, b.
Pieria, ii 629, b: ii. 1075, b.
Pierre Pertuse, 795, a.
Pierus, ii. 629, b.
Pietas, Temple of (Rome), ii. 832, b.
Pictola, 135, b.
Pictra della Nave, 451, a.
Pietro, Isola di S., ii. 911, b.
Pietro Vernotico, 375, a.
Pifano, St., 729, b.
Pigeon Rocks, ii. 1075, b.
Piguntia, 748, a.
Pikermi, 330, b.
Pikerni, ii. 264, b.
Pila, 730, a.
Pilisch, ii. 969, a.
Piliuri, ii. 537, b.
Pimprama, 25, a.
Pinaka, 559, b.
Pinal, ii. 64, b.
Pinara, ii. 1075, b.
Pinarus, 116, a.

Pincensil, ii. 367, b.
Pincian Hill (Rome), ii. 828, b; ii. 831, b.
Pinciana, Domus (Rome), ii. 831, b.
Pinciana, Porta (Rome), ii. 759, a.
Pindus, 785, a.
Pineta di Castel Volurno, 971, a.
Pinetum, 934, a.
Pinguente, ii. 74, a.
Pinhel, 934, a; ii. 631, a.
Pinhetra, ii. 631, a; ii. 220, a.
Pinna, ii. 1283, a.
Pinos, ii. 35, a.
Pintia, 934, b.
Pinum, 744, b.
Piolo, ii. 635, b; ii. 1317, b.
Piomba, La, ii. 296, a.
Piaroco, ii. 671, a; ii. 1301, b; ii. 1317, b.
Piperno Vecchia, ii. 669, b.
Piquentum, ii. 74, a.
Pira, ii. 1178, a.
Pirano, ii. 74, a.
Piranon, ii. 74, a.
Pirgo, ii. 1231, a.
Pirnari, ii. 540, b.
Pirum, Ad, 744, b; ii. 1301, b.
Pisa, 821, a.
Pisa, ii. 632, a; ii. 1296, a.
Pisae, ii. 1296, a.
Pisanus, Portus, 870, a.
Pisatello, ii. 857, a.
Pisatis, 817, a.
Pisaurum, ii. 1301, a; ii. 1317, b.
Piscina Publica (Rome), ii. 820, b.
Piscinas, Ad, ii. 1296, a.
Piscopia, 720, b; ii. 1123, a.
Piscopia, F., 464, b.
Piscopo, F., 450, a.
Pisma, La, 741, b.
Pismesh Kalasi, ii. 352, a.
Pismesh Kalesi, ii. 395, a.
Pissaeum, ii. 561, b.
Pissantini, 755, b.
Pistoja, ii. 634, b; ii. 1296, b.
Pistoria, ii. 1296, b.
Pisyrus, ii. 1180, a; ii. 1190, a.
Pitaue, 53, a.
Pitanus, 691, a.
Pithecusa, 49, a.
Pitino, Torre ni, ii. 1283, a.
Pitinum, ii. 1283, a.
Pitinum Pisaurense, ii. 1317, b.
Pitsunda, ii. 635, b.
Pitulum, ii. 1317, b.
Pitynda, ii. 47, a.
Pityodes, 770, a.
Pityonnesus, ii. 571, a.
Pityusa, 769, b.
Pityusae, 373, a.
Pizzighettone, 11, b.
Piagiaria, ii. 219, b.
Planasia, 857, b.
Planaticus, Portus, ii. 74, a.
Platamodes, ii. 341, b.
Platamona, 158, b; ii. 174, a.
Platanaki, 1003, b.
Plotani, 1029. a; ii. 965, b; ii. 1161, b.
Platania, ii. 4, b; ii. 576, b.
Plataniston, ii. 226, b.
Platanius, ii. 202, a.
Platanodes, ii. 341, b.
Platanus, ii. 606, b.
Plate, 485, a.
Platea, 582, a; 733, b; ii. 277, b.
Platiana, ii. 1247, b.
Plattensee, ii. 572, a.
Platyperama, ii. 1233, b.
Plaxa, ii. 1134, a.
Plaxiotissa, ii. 1181, a.
Plavis, ii. 1275, a.
Plera, ii. 167, b.
Plessidhi, ii. 569, a.
Pleuron, 67, a.
Pleutauri, 502, a.
Plexoa, ii. 572, b.
Pliassa, ii. 568, b.
Plistia, ii. 896, b.

Plora, ii. 682, a.
Plotheia, 330, b.
Plotinopolis, ii. 1190, a.
Plubium, ii. 912, a.
Plumbaria Insula, ii. 911, b.
Plyni, Ps., ii. 277, b.
Pnigeus, ii. 619, b.
Pnyx (Athens), 382, a.
Po di Primaro, ii. 1032, b.
Po, the, 849, a; ii. 509, a.
Podend, ii. 511, b; ii. 642, b.
Podlachia, ii. 8, a.
Podolia, ii. 30, a; ii. 916, a.
Poecilasium, 705, b.
Poeeessa, 587, a.
Poetelius, Lucus (Rome), ii. 826, b.
Point du Galle, ii. 64, a.
Point Zingis, 57, b.
Poitiers, ii. 192, b.
Pola, ii. 643, a.
Pola de Lena, ii. 511, b.
Polaticum, Promontorium, ii. 74, a.
Polcevera, ii. 187, b; ii. 660, b.
Polemoiiacus, Pontus, 508, a.
Polenza, ii. 188, a; ii. 646, a.
Poli, 417, b.
Poliana, ii. 1000, a.
Policastro, 460, a; ii. 210, a.
Polichna, 705, b.
Polichne, ii. 34b, b.
Policoro, 21, a; 1046, b.
Polignano, 167, a; ii. 411, a.
Polighero, 161, a.
Polinartlum, 870, b.
Polin, 566, a.
Polikrusoko, 225, b.
Polis, ii. 125, a.
Polis (Athens), 259, a.
Politeia, 17, a.
Polluna, ii. 165, b.
Polla, 910, b.
Pollentia, 374, b; 375, a; ii. 188, a; ii. 629, a.
Pollenza, 374, b.
Pollina, 160, a.
Pollina, ii. 236, b; ii. 986, a; ii. 987, a.
Pollina, or Pollona, 160, b.
Poltyobria, 50, b.
Polybos, ii. 645, b.
Polyfengo, ii. 601, b.
Polyfengo, Mt., 187, a.
Polykhrono, ii. 411, a.
Polyphagi, 572, a.
Polyportu, 1063, b.
Polyrrhenia, 705, b.
Polystylus, 3, b.
Polytimetus, ii. 5, b.
Pombeiro, ii. 876, b.
Pomegue, ii. 1037, a.
Pompeii, ii. 646, a.
Pompeii, Curia (Rome), ii. 834, a.
Pompeii, Porticus (Rome), ii. 834, a.
Pompeii, Theatrum (Rome), ii 834, a; ii. 844, b.
Pompey, Statue of (Rome), ii. 793, a.
Ponches, ii. 657, b.
Pondicherry, ii. 643, a; ii. 1017, b.
Pondikonisi, 804, b.
Ponferrada, 250, a.
Pons Aelii, ii. 1256, b.
Pons Aluti, 744. b.
Pons Augusti, 744, b.
Pons Nartiae, 934, b.
Pons Neviae, 934, b.
Pons Servilii et Claudanum, ii. 36, b.
Pons Vetus Stenarum, 744, b.
Pont-Audemer, 429, a.
Pont-Authon, 429, a.
Pont du Gard, ii. 415, b.
Pont l'Esquit, 389, b.
Pont-pierre, ii. 1260, a.
Pont St. Esprit, ii. 963, b.
Ponta di Tigani, ii. 1337, b.
Ponta Tyrsidi, 1057, a.
Pontarlier, 214, b.
Ponte della Badia, ii. 1321, a.

Ponte Molle, ii. 646, b.
Ponte Salara, ii. 657, a.
Pontevedra, 934, b.
Pontia, ii. 469, a.
Pontikokastro, ii. 563, b.
Pontinus, 201, a.
Pontirolo, ii. 656, b; ii. 1287, b.
Pontoise, 442, b.
Pontons, ii. 1220, a.
Pontour, ii. 656, b.
Pontremoli, 163, b.
Ponza, ii. 658, a.
Populonia, ii. 659, b; ii. 1296, a.
Populonium, 870, a; ii. 1296, a.
Porata, ii. 938, b.
Porcari, ii. 545, a; ii. 986, a.
Porcia, Basilica (Rome), 786, a.
Porcifera, ii. 187, b.
Porjani, ii. 568, b.
Poro, 477, b.
Porpax, ii. 986, a.
Porphyrium, 531, b; ii. 606, b.
Porquerolez, ii. 654, b; ii. 1037. a.
Port Mahon, 874, b.
Port-sur-Saône, ii. 661, a.
Porta, ii. 626, a.
Porta Armidio e Lucola, ii. 171, a.
Porta Arnio dia e Lucolas, 730, a.
Porta Collina (Rome), ii. 749, b.
Porta Panaghia, 308, b.
Porta Sanqualis (Rome), ii. 749, b.
Portae, Duodecim (Rome), ii. 757, b.
Porteros, ii. 1037, a.
Portela de Abade, ii. 879, a.
Portigate, ii. 1287, a.
Porticus - and Nationes (Rome), ii. 837, b.
Porticus Polae (Rome), ii. 839, b.
Porticus Eumenia (Athens), 301, a.
Porto, 477, b; ii. 503, b.
Porto Badisco, 564, a.
Porto Barbato, 395, b.
Porto Bufalo, ii. 661, a.
Porto Cavaliere, 703, a.
Porto Cetareo, 474, b.
Porto Cunte, ii. 911, a.
Porto d'Anxo, 148, b.
Porto d'Ercole, 198, b.
Porto Fanari, 839, b.
Porto Favone, 691, b.
Porto Ferrato, ii. 40, a.
Porto Fino, ii. 188, a; ii. 661, a.
Porto Fresnco, 685, a.
Porto Leone, 307, a.
Porto Rafti, 331, b.
Porto Santo, ii. 678, b.
Porto Vecchio, 691, a.
Porto Venere, ii. 188, a.
Portsmouth, ii. 253, a; ii. 1260, b.
Portuensis, Porta (Rome), ii. 761, a.
Portugal, 932, b; ii.1105,b.
Portugalete, 902, b.
Portuosus, Sinus, ii. 515, b.
Portus, ii. 503, b.
Portus Adurni, 442, a.
Portus Agasus, 167, a.
Portus Azarius, 354, b.
Portus Delphini, ii. 188, a.
Portus Dubris, 442, a.
Portus Garnae, 167, a.
Portus Herculis, 196, b; 451, b.
Portus Herculis Monoeci, ii. 188, a.
Portus Lemanis, 442, a.
Portus Lugudonis, ii. 912, a.
Portus Magnus, ii. 1260, b.
Portus Monoeci, 93, b.
Portus Mullerum, 424, a.
Portus Veneris, ii. 188, a.

Posada, ii. 912, a.
Poseidion, ii. 1075, a.
Poseidium, 524, a.
Poseidonium, 175, b.
Posidei, ii. 662, a.
Posidium. 609, b; ii. 514, b.
Posidonia, ii. 210, a; ii. 514, b.
Posseda, ii. 662, b.
Potala, ii. 47, b.
Potami, ii. 547, b.
Potamus, 331, b.
Potentia, ii. 210, a; ii. 628, b; ii. 1295, b; ii. 1307, a.
Potenza, ii. 210, a; ii. 663, a; ii. 1295. b; ii. 1307, a.
Potenza, Sta Maria, a, ii. 628, b; ii. 662, b.
Potidania, 67, a; ii. 203, a.
Potisje, ii. 7, b.
Potsdam, ii. 962, a.
Poulemon, ii. 644, a.
Pouleman Chai, ii. 995, b.
Pourbal, ii. 220, a.
Poybueno, 250, a.
Pozzo di Ratignano, or La- tignano, 721, a.
Pozzuoli, ii. 678, b.
Praenestina, Porta (Rome), ii. 759, a.
Praesidium, 691, b; 934, a.
Praesus, 705, b; ii. 667, a.
Praetoria Augusta, 744, b.
Praetorian Camp (Rome), ii. 831, b.
Praetorium, 744, b; 748, a; ii. 115, b.
Pragelas, 977, a.
Prague, ii. 696, a.
Pras, ii. 1170, a.
Prasa, 625, a.
Prasiaca, ii. 47, b.
Prasiae, 331, b.
Prasias, 592, a.
Prasoncis, ii. 385, b.
Prasomei, 1102, a.
Prasum, 57, a.
Prat de Trajan, 743, b.
Prati di Ro, 497, a.
Pratica, ii. 145, a.
Pratishthana, ii. 60, b.
Pravadi, ii. 271, a; ii. 1017, b.
Pravista, ii. 576, b.
Prò St. Didier, 196, a.
Precinus, 173, a
Pregel, 1020, b; ii. 917, a.
Prelius Lucus, 587, b.
Premedi, ii. 482, b.
Premnis, 60, a.
Prespa, ii. 36, b.
Prestia, ii. 642, a.
Preston, ii. 1312, a.
Prevcniza, 156, b.
Prevcra, ii. 426, a.
Perecop, ii. 1090, b.
Pria, 934, b.
Priansus, 705, b.
Priantae, ii. 1190, a.
Prifernum, ii. 1263, a.
Prima Porta, ii. 925, b; ii. 1301, a.
Primis, ii. 396, b.
Primis Magna, 60, a.
Principato Citeriore, ii. 206, b.
Prinko, 1040, a.
Prinkipo, 770, a.
Prinus, 201, b.
Pristina, ii. 1232, b.
Probalinthus, ii. 268, a; 330, b.
Probatia, 412, b.
Probi, Pons (Rome), ii. 850, a.
Prochyta, 49, b.
Procida, 49, b; ii. 670, a.
Procolitia, ii. 1256, b.
Prodhromo, 689, a.
Proerna, ii. 1170, a.
Progeri, ii. 1190, a.
Prolaqueum, ii. 1301, b; ii. 1317, b.
Prolog, 748, a.
Promarens, 444, a.
Promethei, Lacus (Rome), ii. 820, b.

Promina, ii. 671, a.
Promona, 748, a.
Promontorium Magnum, ii. 46, b.
Proni, 588, a.
Propylaea (Athens), 268, a.
Proschium, 67, a.
Proseis, 192, b.
Prosigna, 689, a; 1025 b; ii. 202, a.
Prosopite Nome, 39, b.
Prospalta, 332, a.
Prote, ii. 634, b.
Prote, ii. 671, b.
Provati, 804, b.
Provins, 73, b.
Prussia, 56, b.
Pruth, ii. 687, b.
Prytaneium (Athens), 296, a.
Prytanis, ii. 658, b.
Psaphara, 140, b.
Psaphis, 330, a.
Psara, 609, b.
Pscelcis, 60, a; 781, b.
Psessii, ii. 917, b.
Pseudavari, 349, b.
Psilorití, ii. 13, b.
Psophidia, 193, a.
Psophis, 17, a; 193, a.
Psychium, 705, b.
Psyra, 609, b.
Psyttaleia, ii. 878, a.
Psytti, ii. 1081, a.
Ptaniae, ii. 1301, a.
Ptelco, ii. 677, a.
Pteleum, ii. 1170, a
Ptolederma, 193, a.
Ptolemais, 733, b.
Ptovis, ii. 586, a.
Ptoum, 412, a.
Ptychia, 671, b.
Publica, Villa (Rome), ii. 836, b.
Publicius, Clivus (Rome), ii. 811, a.
Pucinum, ii. 74, a; ii. 1275, b.
Pudicitia Patricia (Rome), ii. 815, a.
Pudicitiae Plebeiae, Sacel- lum (Rome), ii. 830 b.
Puebla de la Reyna, ii. 696, b.
Puech d' Issolu, ii. 1331, b.
Puenta de la Guardia vieja, ii. 377, a.
Puente de Arçobispo, 341, a.
Puente de Don Gonzalo, ii. 1276, b.
Puente de Don Guarray, ii. 453, a.
Puente de Orvijo, ii. 1254, b.
Puente de Orvigo, 250, a.
Puente do Sora, ii. 220, a.
Puente, Rio de la, 923, b.
Puerta de Daroca, 582, a.
Puerto de S. Maria, ii. 329, a.
Puglia petrosa, 164, b.
Puglia piana, 164, b.
Puhra, 983, b.
Puigcerdà, 593, b.
Puijourdes, ii. 1258, a.
Pula, Capo di, ii. 445, b; ii. 911, b.
Pulcrum Littus (Rome), ii. 803, a.
Pullaria, ii. 74, a
Pullopice, 110, a.
Pullopicem, ii. 188, b.
Pulska, ii. 678, b.
Pulianah, ii. 642, a.
Pulvinar Solis (Rome), ii. 831, a.
Pulvran, 737, b; ii. 307, a.
Pundonitza, 638, a; ii. 424, b; ii. 486, a; ii. 1101, b.
Punhete, ii. 219, b.
Punicum, ii. 1296, a.
Punjab, ii. 709, a.
Punon, ii. 586, a.
Punta de Falcone, ii. 911, a.
Punta dei Barbieri, 753, b.
Punta del Pezzo, 466, a; ii. 706, a.
Punta dell' Alice, 417, b.

Punta della Penna, 454, a.
Punta di Promontore, ii. 74, a.
Punta di Stilo, 641, a.
Pupulum, ii. 912, a.
Pura, 983, b.
Purali, 183, b.
Purpurariae. 906, b.
Purug, ii. 1085, b.
Puskkalavati, ii. 47, b.
Pussiano, Lago di, 877, a.
Putea, ii. 1076, b.
Puteal Libonis (Rome), ii. 788, a.
Puteal Scribonianum, (Rome), ii. 788, a.
Putrid Lake, 454, b.
Putrid Sea, ii. 1112, b.
Puy de Jussat, 990, b.
Pydarus, ii. 1190, a.
Pylae, 193, b.
Pylene, 67, a.
Pylorus, 705, b.
Pyramus, 114, a; 619, b.
Pyranthus, 705, b.
Pyrathi, ii. 686, b.
Pyrenaei, Portus, ii. 52, a.
Pyrenaeus, Imus, 515, a.
Pyrenaeus, Summus, 515, a.
Pyrenees, the, ii. 687. a.
Pyrgaki, 231, a; 1035, a.
Pyrgi, 821, a; ii. 1296, a.
Pyrgo, or Pyrgako, ii. 351, b.
Pyrgos, 625, a.
Pyrrha, ii. 165, a.
Pyrrhicus, ii. 112, b.
Pyrucheium, 97, a.
Pyrustae, ii. 541, b.
Pythan, ii. 642, a.
Pythium, ii. 1170, a.
Pyxites, ii. 658, b.
Pyxus, ii. 209, b.

Quabes, ii. 1083, a.
Quaceran, 933, a.
Quad-Dra (Wady-Dra), ii. 452, b.
Quaderna, 631, a; ii. 1287, a.
Quadratae, ii. 1288, a.
Quaeri, ii. 74, a.
Quaglio, Porto, ii. 1084, a.
Qualburg, ii. 690, a.
Quarantine Bay, ii. 1111, a.
Quarnéro, Canal del, 902, a.
Quarnero, Golfo di, 224, b; ii. 74, a.
Quarte, ii. 690, a.
Quentin, St., 340, b.
Querci, 464, a.
Quernquernae, Aquae, 168, b.
Querquerni, 933, a.
Querquetulana, Porta (Rome), ii. 755, b.
Quiberon, ii. 1275, b.
Quilates, C., 501, a.
Quimper, 686, b.
Quinctia, Prata (Rome), ii. 842, b.
Quing, ii. 53. a.
Quinta, 934, b.
Quintanas, Ad. ii. 1301, b.
Quirinal Hill (Rome), ii. 828. b.
Quirinalis, Porta (Rome), ii. 757, a.
Quirinalis, Sacellum (Rome), ii. 829. a.
Quirini, Vallis (Rome), ii. 828. b.
Quirinus, Temple of (Rome), ii. 829, a.
Quiset-Hissar, ii. 419, a.
Quiza, ii. 297, b.
Quorra, ii. 428, a.

Raab, 222, b.
Rabat, ii. 876, a.
Rabba, ii. 690, b.
Rabbath, 123, b.
Radepont, ii. 718, b.
R'adea, ii. 299, b.
Rafina, 332, a.
Ragusa, Fiume di, ii. 985, b.
Ragusa-Vecchia, 640, a.
Rajib, 199, b.
Rayyuts, 570, a.

Rakhamytes, ii. 310, a.
Rakhsi, 188, a.
Rakka, ii. 699, a.
Rakli, 588, b.
Ram-gur, ii. 692, a.
Ram-nagar, ii. 692, a.
Ram-Ullah, ii. 691, b.
Rama, ii. 115, b; ii. 153, a.
Ramaam Kor, 693, b.
Rama, or Ram, ii. 1310, a.
Ramae, 110, a.
Ramatheum Sophim, ii. 691, b.
Ramatuelle 487, b.
Hame, ii. 692, a.
Ram's Head, ii. 1276, a.
Ramguna, ii. 253, a.
Ramiseram, 693, b.
Ramiseram Cor, ii. 1020, a.
Ramlah, 591, b.
Ramleh, 213, a; ii. 691, a.
Ramsey, ii. 192, b.
Randazzo, ii. 1213, a.
Raphanea, 560, b.
Rapolla, 167, b.
Raposera, ii. 219, b.
Kapsani, 232, a; 655, a; ii. 124, a.
Ras, 188, a.
Ras Addar, 317, b; ii. 330, a.
Ras Aferwi, 317, b.
Ras-al-Aïn, ii. 709, a.
Ras-al-Djerd, ii. 1105, b.
Ras-al-Hamrak, ii. 468, b.
Ras-al-Harsbah, ii. 297, b.
Ras-al-Kanais, 170, b; ii. 620, a.
Ras-al-Kanatir, ii. 297, b.
Ras-al-Milhr, ii. 328, b.
Ras-al-Naxat, 733, b.
Ras-al-Sarr, 344, a.
Ras-Bad, 367, a.
Ras Bergawaad, ii. 600, a.
Ras Broom, ii. 669, b.
Ras-el-Abiad, 499, a; ii. 606, b.
Ras-el-Auf, ii. 161, b.
Ras-el-Basit, ii. 1075, b.
Ras-el-Char, 608, a.
Ras-el-Dwaer, ii. 68, a.
Ras-el-Had, 175, b; 687, b.
Ras-el-Hadd, 499, b.
Ras-el-Hamrah, 1070, a; ii. 454, a.
Ras-el-Harsbah, ii. 346, a.
Ras-el-Harzeit, ii. 277, b.
Ras-el-Jerd, 520, b.
Ras-el-Kaanis, ii. 277, b.
Ras-el-Mellah, ii. 277, b.
Ras-el-Naschef, 384, a.
Ras-el-Ouad, ii. 575, a.
Ras-el-Raxat, ii. 625, b.
Ras-el-Shukkur, ii. 29c, a.
Ras-es-Shekah, ii. 606, a.
Ras-es-Tin, 608, a; 732, a; ii. 277, b.
Ras Fartak, ii. 871, a.
Ras Fartask, ii. 1052, a.
Ras Ghamart, 531, a.
Ras Guadel, ii. 549, b.
Ras Hadid, ii. 454, a; ii. 1037, a.
Ras Kelb, 499, b.
Ras Khanzeer, ii. 1075, b.
Ras Lmouf, ii. 599, a.
Ras Halem, ii. 277, b.
Ras Metznkoub, 336, b.
Ras Mohammed, 175, b; ii. 662, a.
Ras Musendom, 175, b.
Ras-, or Tarf-, esh-Shakhar, 125, a.
Ras Seryada, 398, b.
Ras Sem, 733, b; ii. 625, b.
Ras Sidi Ali-al-Mekh, 159, a.
Ras Sidi Bou Said, 531, a.
Ras Tanhub, ii. 620, a.
Ras Teyonas, 732, a; 733, b.
Rag-ud-Dehar, ii. 297, b.
Ras-ud-Dehir, ii. 346, a.
Raswalta Sillan, ii. 606, a.
Rasa, ii. 919, a.
Rasboistje, ii. 171, a.
Raschid, 418, a.
Rashat, 321, b.
Rasocolmo, Capo di, ii. 985, a.
Rasocolmo, Cape, ii. 402, b.

Rassova, 852, a.
Rastan, 197, a.
Ratanea, 748, a.
Ratlaria, 745, a.
Ratisbon, ii. 697, a.
Ratonrau, ii. 1037, a.
Ratonou, ii. 926, b.
Ratumena, Porta (Rome), ii. 750. a.
Ratzeburg, ii. 107, a.
Rauduscula, Porta (Rome) ii. 755, a.
Ravee, 25, a.
Ravrguano, 26, a.
Ravrnna, ii. 693, a.
Rauke Alp, 1054, b; ii. 1258, b.
Ravi, ii. 422, a; 1101, a.
Raum, ii. 695, a.
Raxatin, 678, a.
Razzoli, Isola der, 719, a.
Reate, Civita, 890, b; ii. 1305, a.
Recco, ii. 717, b.
Reculver, ii. 697, b.
Red Sea, 174, b; 182, a; ii. 857, a.
Refah, ii. 692, b.
Rega, ii. 858, b.
Regen, ii. 696, b.
Regensburg, ii. 697, a.
Regenwalde, ii. 858, b.
Reggio, ii. 697, a; ii. 703, a; ii. 1287, a.
Regia (Rome), ii. 779, a.
Regio Judaeorum, 97, a.
Regio Transtiberina (Rome), ii. 841, a.
Regium, ii. 1287, a.
Regnum, 442, a.
Reims, 794, a.
Remagen, ii. 718, a.
Rematiasri, 760, b.
Remi, St., 1002, a.
Remich, ii. 717, b.
Rendina, ii. 1038, b.
Renfrew, 750, a.
Reno, ii. 709, a.
Rennes, 654, a; ii. 696, a.
Reol, ii. 717, b.
Rronda, ii. 644, a.
Repton, ii. 698, b.
Requejo, ii. 1275, b.
Requena, ii. 198, b; ii. 1326, b.
Rergintrum, 110, b.
Resina, 496, a; 1054, a.
Respa, 167, a.
Retenga, Civita, ii. 1283, b.
Retigonium, or Rerigouium, 750, a.
Retimo, ii. 710, b.
Retina, 496, a.
Retino, C., ii. 546, b.
Retortillo, ii. 102, a.
Reix, Pays de, ii. 692, b.
Reuben, Tribe of, ii. 531, a.
Rhaabeni, 181, a.
Rhacalani, ii. 855, b.
Rhacotis, 98, b.
Rhades, 24, b.
Rhaeba, ii. 16, a.
Rhaeteae, 193, a.
Rhage, 571, a.
Rhakalani, ii. 917, a.
Rhambacia, 983, b.
Rhamidava, 744, b.
Rhamnus, 705, b.
Rhaphaneae, ii. 1076, a.
Rhaptum, 57, b.
Rhaptus, ii. 702, b.
Rhaucus, 705, b.
Rhausium, 748, a.
Rheban, ii. 700, a.
Rhedones, 218. b.
Rhegias, ii. 1075, b.
Rhegium, ii. 1294, b.
Rkeinns, 380, b.
Rheinbreitbach, ii. 192. a.
Rheinzabern, ii. 1082, a.
Rheitl, 328, a.
Rhrneia, 760, b.
Rheon, ii. 376, a.
Rhesapha, ii. 1076, b.
Rhey, ii. 701, a.
Rhibii, ii. 943, b.
Rhigia, ii. 16, a.

Rhine, the, ii. 706, b.
Rhithymna, 705, b.
Rhithymnos, ii. 710, b.
Rhium, 13, a.
Rhizophagi, 58, a.
Rhizo-Kastron, ii. 710, b.
Rhizus, 748, a; ii. 1170, b.
Rho, 497, a.
Rhobogdii, ii. 16, a.
Rhobusci, ii. 943, b.
Rhoda, Gulf of, ii. 52, a.
Rhodes, ii. 713, a.
Rhodes, 617, a.
Rhodope, ii. 1177, b.
Rhodupa, ii. 1190, b.
Rhogandani, ii. 1093, b.
Rhoganis, 371, b.
Rhogonis, ii. 678, b.
Rhoxkia, ii. 711, a.
Rhon, 1056, b.
Rhone, the, ii. 711, b.
Rhoplutae, 184, a.
Rhossian Rock, the, ii. 1075, a.
Rhossus, ii. 1075, a, b.
Rhotanus, 94, b; 691. a.
Rhossicus Scopulus, ii. 1075. b.
Rhubon, ii. 917, a.
Rhusibis, Portus, 229, b.
Rhymmus, ii. 716, b.
Rhyncus, 10, b.
Rhynenburg, ii. 296, a.
Rhynland, 501, a.
Rhypes, 14, b.
Rhytium, 705, b.
Riazan, ii. 917, b.
Ribadavia, ii. 1240, b.
Ribavedonda, S. Maria de, ii. 947, b.
Ribble, 388, b; ii. 971, a.
Ribble-chester, ii. 718, a.
Ribchester, 641, a.
Riceiacum, 515, a.
Richborough, 442, a; 855, a; ii. 860, b.
Richmond, ii. 718, a.
Ricina, ii. 188, b; ii. 629, a.
Ricsen, ii. 1327, a.
Riduna, 949, b.
Riechester, 429, a.
Ries, ii. 718, b.
Riesengebirge, ii. 1287, b.
Riesgau, ii. 718, b.
Rieti, 6, a; ii. 695, a.
Riez, ii. 698, a.
Riga, Gulf of, 723, b; ii. 1270, b.
Rigae, 542, a.
Rigul, ii. 717, b.
Rigomagus, ii. 1288, a.
Riha, ii. 15, b.
Rima-el-Luhf, ii. 706, b.
Rimini, 213, b.
Rimokastro, ii. 172, a.
Ringwood, ii. 697, b.
Rinteln, ii. 14, a.
Rio Caldo, 168, b.
Rio d'Ave, 933, a.
Rio d'Aye, 351, b.
Rio de la Kalameta, 476, a.
Rio de la Puente, ii. 414, a.
Rio Grande, ii. 422, b.
Rio Torto, ii. 453, a.
Rio Verde, ii. 881, b.
Rion, 571, b.
Rioni, or Rion. ii. 593, a.
Ripatransone, 719, a; ii. 624, b.
Risano, 905, b; ii. 710, b; ii. 1275, a.
Risingham, 1023, a.
Ritopk, ii. 1230, b.
Ritri, 852, a.
Riva, ii. 703, a.
Rivière, 978, a.
Ritrière d'Aurai, 442, a.
Rixton, ii. 718, a.
Rizah, 483, a.
Rzch, ii. 710, b; ii. 711, a.
Roa, ii. 693, a.
Roannec, ii. 718, b.
Robbio, or Robio, 497, a.
Roberti, ii. 636, b.
Robledo, 934, a.
Robogk, ii. 718, b.
Roboraria, ii. 1302, a.

Roboretum, 934, a.
Roca, C. da, ii. 216, b.
Rocca, 705, b.
Rocca d'Entella, 829, a.
Rocca di Papa, 89, a.
Rocca Giovane, 774, b.
Rocca Massima, 854, b.
Rocca Monfina, 343, b.
Rocca Priore, 669, a.
Roche Bernard, 791, b.
Rochelle, ii. 903, b.
Rochester, 792, a.
Rochester, High, 750, a.
Rodasto, or Rodostshig, 403, b.
Rodez, 654, b; ii. 951, a.
Rodi, 1106, b.
Rodicio, 934, a.
Rodilla, ii. 1232, b.
Rodrigo, Ciudad, ii. 1285, b.
Rogrus, 497, a.
Rogus, 603, a.
Rohcbeh, ii. 698, a.
Roja, 93, b; ii. 55, a; ii. 187, b; ii. 860, a.
Rore, ii. 718, b.
Rorno, ii. 553, b.
Rom, ii. 695, a.
Roma and Venus, Temple (of Rome), ii. 809, a.
Roman Kings, statues of (Rome), ii. 770, a.
Roman People, Statue of the Genius of (Rome), ii. 796, b.
Romanca, C., ii. 253, a.
Romani, ii. 1191, a.
Romatinus, ii. 1275, a.
Rome, ii. 719, a.
Rome and Augustus, Temple of (Athens), 281, a.
Romechi, ii. 855, a.
Romigik, 786, b.
Romula, 744, b.
Romulea, ii. 896, b.
Romulea, Sub, ii. 1293, a.
Romuli Aedes (Rome), ii. 803, a.
Romuli, Casa (Rome), ii. 802, b.
Ronaldsa, ii. 461, b.
Ronaldsha, St., 49, a.
Ronco, ii. 1317, b.
Ronda, 228, a.
Ronda la Vieja, 20, b; 228, a.
Ronda, Sierra de, ii. 130, b.
Roomburg, ii. 667, a.
Rosalia, Monte Sta, ii. 985, a.
Rosas, ii. 52, a; ii. 711, b.
Roscianum, 481, a, b.
Roselle, ii. 859, a.
Rosetta, 418, a.
Rossa di Teulada, Isola, ii. 911, b.
Rossano, 451, a; ii. 855, a.
Rosso, Castel, ii. 317, a.
Rostra (Rome), ii. 785, a.
Rostrata, Columna (Rome), ii. 785, b.
Rostrata Villa, ii. 1301, a.
Rotas, Ad, ii. 1287, a.
Rotomagus, 429, a.
Rotonda, La, ii. 421, a; ii. 1295, a.
Rotondo, Monte, 691, a.
Rouen, 429, a; 480, b.
Rouergue, ii. 860, a.
Rovies, ii. 494, b.
Rovigno, ii. 74, a.
Roumelia, ii. 1176. b.
Roussillon, ii. 859, a; ii. 1023, b.
Rowandi, ii. 495, a.
Rowandiz, 390, a; ii. 495, a; ii. 1335, b.
Rowton, ii. 860, b.
Roxburgh, 923, a; ii. 504, b.
Roxolani, ii. 917, a.
Royan, ii. 450, a.
Ruad, 185, a.
Ruaditae, ii. 278, a.
Rubi, 167, a; ii. 1294, a.
Rubra, 691, b.
Rubras, Ad, ii. 1301, a.
Rubricata, ii. 115, b.
Rubricatus, 68, a; 378, b; ii. 454, b.

Rucconium, 744, b.
Rucsen, ii. 1377, a.
Ruda, 810, a.
Rudge, ii. 253, b.
Rudiae, 474, b; ii. 1294, a.
Rudiana, 521, a.
Rudland, ii. 1258, a.
Rueda, ii. 951, a.
Rufea or Rofta, 111, a.
Ruffach, ii. 858, a.
Rufrae, ii. 897, a.
Rufrium, ii. 896, b.
Rugby, ii. 1232, b.
Rügenwalde, ii. 858, b.
Rugge, ii. 716, a.
Ruhr, ii. 858, b; ii. 1258, b.
Rum Kala, 152, b.
Rum Kala'h, 876, b.
Rumili, 600, b.
Rumili, Castle of, 13, a.
Rumili-Hisar, 424, a.
Rumili-Kavak, 424, a.
Runicatae, ii. 1310, b.
Runn of Cutch, ii. 255, a.
Runovich, ii. 449, a.
Rupes Tarpeia (Rome), ii. 771, b.
Rus, ii. 858, b.
Rusadir, ii. 297, b.
Rusadir Prom., ii. 297, b.
Ruscino, ii. 1320, a.
Rusellae, 870, a.
Rusicada, ii. 454, a.
Rusicade, ii. 455, a.
Rusidava, 744, b.
Rusloi, ii. 716, b.
Rustschuk, ii. 609, b; ii. 926, b; ii. 972, a.
Rusqueur, ii. 1012, a.
Rusucurrium, ii. 297, b.
Rutchester, ii. 1256, b; ii. 1811, a.
Ruteni, 173, a.
Rutigliano, 354, b.
Rutschuck, ii. 669, b; ii. 926, b; ii. 972, a.
Rutuba, 93, b; ii. 55, a; ii. 187, b.
Rutupae, 442, a.
Ruver, 550, b.
Ruvigno, ii. 74, a.
Ruvo, ii. 856, a; ii. 1294, n. a.
Ryan, Loch, 7, a; ii. 639, a.

Sa-el-Hadjar, ii. 874, b.
Sa-Minagur, ii. 360, a.
Saaba, ii. 863, b.
Saale, ii. 876, a.
Saale (in Franconia), ii. 876, a.
Saana, ii. 1076, b.
Saarburg, ii. 657, b.
Saaret, 147, b.
Sabaei, 161, b.
Sabakhah, 598, b.
Sabalet-es-Sahib, ii. 369, b.
Sabanja, 406, b.
Sabaracus, Sinus, ii. 52, a.
Sabarae, ii. 48, a.
Sabaria, ii. 542, a.
Sabaricus, S., ii. 46, b.
Sabate, 870, b; ii. 1297, b.
Sabatinus, Lacus, 856, b; 857, a.
Sabatium, ii. 237, a.
Sabatum Fluvium, Ad, ii. 1295, a.
Sabatus, 450, a; ii. 461, b.
Sabbatha, 25, a.
Sabbato, 3, b; ii. 864, b.
Sabbia, ii. 284, a.
Sabee, 383, b.
Sabina, Monte Leone della, ii. 1225, a.
Sabiote, ii. 880, a.
Sabis, 521, a.
Sables d'Olonne, ii. 947, b.
Sabrata, ii. 1081, a.
Sabyholm, ii. 864, a.
Sacala, 983, a.
Sacani, ii. 917, b.
Sacastene, 366, a.
Sacco, 1059, b; ii. 1226, a.
Sacer Fluvius, 691, a; ii. 911, a.
Sachbs, ii. 946, b.

Saclas, ii. 882, b.
Sacra Via (Rome), ii. 773, a.
Sacrani, 5, a.
Sacraria, ii. 1300, b.
Sacred Gate (Athens), 263,a.
Sacred Promontory, 691, a.
Sadji, ii. 902, a.
Sado, ii. 220, a.
Saelini, 249, b; 250, b.
Saepinum, ii. 896, b.
Saepone, 583, a.
Saeprus, ii. 911, a.
Saetabicula, 655, b.
Saetabis, 655, b; ii. 1241, a.
Saetlani, ii. 943, b.
Saftt, 229, b.
Sagaraucae, ii. 943, b.
Sagarra, 379, a; ii. 1, b.
Sagarre, ii. 1034, b.
Sagartii, ii. 302, a.
Sagida, ii. 48, a.
Sagres, ii. 448, a.
Sagrus, 513, b.
Sahara, 175, b; 252, b; 925, a.

Saja, ii. 924, b.
Saians, ii. 1135, b.
Said, 37, a.
Saigon, or *Saung*, ii. 964, a.
Saillans, 754, a.
St. David's Head, ii. 462, b.
St. Edmund's Bury, ii. 1310, a.

St. Etienne, Val, 805, b.
St. Florentin, 799, a.
St. George, 385, b; 588, b; ii. 509, a; ii. 585, a.
St. George, Cape, 310, a; ii. 964, b.
St. George, Hill of (Athens), 295, a.
St. George, Monastery of, ii. 995, a.
St. George, River of, 341, a.
St. James, Cape, ii. 924, b; ii. 1002, b.
St. Jean d'Acre, 11, a.
St. Jean, Pied-de-Port, 515, a; ii. 42, b.
St. John, ii. 167, b.
St. John, C., ii. 46, b.
St. John, River, 613, b; ii. 1034, b.
St. John's Foreland, ii. 65, a.
St. Martin sous le Boulou, 385, b.
St. Mary, Cape, ii. 254, b.
St. Michael's, Mount, ii.12,b.
St. Paul trois Châteaux, 840, b.
St. Pierre d'Eixonne, 822, a.
St. Remi, ii. 887, a.
Saint-Vallier, ii. 182, b.
Saintes, 457, b; ii. 303, a; ii. 903, b.
Ste Reine d'Alise, 95, a.
Saintonge, ii. 903, b.
Sais, 39, b.
Sais, ii. 1144, a.
Sakarya, or *Sakari*, ii. 902, b.
Sakasthan, 366, a.
Sak Adassi, or *Sakßadassi*, 609, a.
Sakkra, ii. 1334, a.
Sala, 229, b; ii. 297, b.
Salaceni, ii. 48, a.
Salacia, 934, a; ii. 220, a.
Salado, ii. 662, b; ii. 886, a.
Salamanca, ii. 219, b; ii. 883, b; ii. 1285, b.
Salamonde, 934, a; ii. 876, b.
Salandrella, 8, b.
Salaniana, 934, a.
Salapia, 167, a.
Salapina Palus, 167, a.
Salaria, Porta (Rome), ii. 759, a.
Salassi, 109, a.
Salassii, ii. 298, b.
Salban, 452, a.
Salburg, 227, a.
Saldae, 68, a; ii. 454, a.
Saldae, Pa., ii. 297, b.
Saldatti, ii. 318, b.
Saldapa, ii. 1335, b.
Salebro, ii. 1296, a.

Salemi, 1027, b.
Salentini, ii. 1317, b.
Salßon, 488, b; ii. 370, a.
Salerno, ii. 882, b.
Salerno, Gulf of, ii. 514, b.
Sales, ii. 884, b.
Salgir, ii. 1135, a.
Salha, 938, a.
Salhadschar, ii. 402, b.
Sali, ii. 916, b.
Sallentes, 934, a.
Salina, 51, b.
Salinae, 167, a; 744, b.
Saline, 167, a.
Saline, Le, 1018, b.
Salinello, ii. 667, b.
Salines, 628, b.
Salinsae, ii. 299, a.
Saliorum, Curia (Rome), ii. 804, a.
Salis, ii. 882, a.
Saliunca, 347, a.
Sallee, 229, b; ii. 876, a.
Sallentia, 474, b.
Sallmax, ii. 1020, b.
Salluntum, 746, a.
Sallustianae, Thermae (Rome), ii. 831, a.
Sallustiani, Horti (Rome), ii. 831, a.
Salluatii, Circus (Rome), ii. 831, a; ii. 844, b.
Salmantica, ii. 1285, b.
Salmantice, ii. 219, b.
Salme, ii. 883, b.
Salmone, 821, a.
Salmydessus, ii. 599, a; ii. 1190, a.
Salnay, or *Sandye*, ii. 883, b.
Salnek, ii. 1171, b.
Salo, 402, b; ii. 210, a.
Salodurum, ii. 581, b.
Salomon, C., ii. 897, a.
Salom, C., ii. 961, a.
Salona, 748, a; ii. 38, a.
Salona, 127, a; ii. 1232, b.
Salonace, ii. 1171, b.
Salonicki, or *Saloniki*, or *Salonicia*, ii. 1171, a.
Saloniki, ii. 236, b.
Salpesa, 583, a.
Salpi, ii. 879, a.
Salpi, Lago di, 167, a.
Salses, or *Salçes*, ii. 886, a.
Salso, Fiume, 1068, b; ii. 985, a.
Salsum Flumen, 877, a.
Salt Sea, the, ii. 527, a.
Salteras, ii. 514, b.
Saltici, 582, a.
Salto, 6, a.
Salvatierra, 214, b; ii. 220, a.
Salwen, ii. 46, b.
Salurn, ii. 886, a.
Salus, Sacellum of (Rome), ii. 830, a.
Salus, Temple of (Rome), ii. 830, a.
Salutaris, Collis (Rome), ii. 830, a.
Saluzzo, 911, b.
Salzburg, ii. 103, a; ii. 172, b; ii. 447, a.
Samaica, ii. 1190, b.
Samallus, 726, a.
Samana Kuta, ii. 1093, a.
Samandrakt, ii. 901, a.
Samara, 709, a; ii. 545, b.
Samarcand, ii. 266, b.
Samargah, 362, b.
Samaria, ii. 532, a.
Samariana, 1106, a.
Samata, 414, a.
Sambea, 369, b.
Sambre, ii. 870, a.
Same, 588, a.
Samhar, ii. 947, a.
Samicum, 821, a.
Samidah, 362, b.
Samigae, 643, a.
Somisat, ii. 901, a.
Samnitae, ii. 943, b.
Samo, ii. 889, a; ii. 897, b.
Samos, 239, b.
Samosata, 877, a.
Samothraki, ii. 901, a.
Samour, 89, b.

Samsoon, ii. 669, a.
Samsun, 406, a.
Samulis, ii. 1076, b.
Sax, ii. 870, a; ii. 1089, b.
San Germano, 557, a.
San Selomi, ii. 947, a.
Sana, ii. 1087, a.
Saoarae, ii. 917, b.
Sancas, ii. 284, b.
Sandakli, ii. 572, b.
Sandameri, ii. 1134, a.
Sandamerrotiko, ii. 932, b.
Sandarlik, ii. 388, b.
Sandava, 744, b.
Sanderli, ii. 635, a.
Sanderli, or *Sandarlio*,724,b.
Sandocandae, ii. 1093, b.
Sandoway, ii. 872, a.
Sandrabatis, ii. 48, a.
Sandras, 934, a.
Sandrixetes, ii. 542, a.
Sandrovecs, 526, b.
Sandukli, 878, a; ii. 1000, b.
Sandukli Chai, ii. 459, b.
Sane, ii. 1325, b.
Sanga, ii. 264, b.
Sangro, 513, b; ii. 873, b.
Sanuarium (Rome), ii. 819,a.
Sanisera, 374, b.
Sanitium, ii. 1260, b.
Sannio, 915, b.
Sant' Andrea, 682, b.
Santa Cruz, 593, a; 798, b.
Santa Cruz de la Zarza, 525, a.
Santa Felice, 6, a.
Santa Maria, ii. 153, a.
Santa Maria della Luna, 95, a.
Santander, 502, b.
Santarem, ii. 220, a; ii.926,b.
Santaver, 582, a.
Santerno, ii. 1260, a.
Santiago de Villela, 934, a.
Santiago o' Compostella, 934, b.
Santis, ii. 974, a.
Santones, 173, a.
Santonna, ii. 102, a; ii. 1307, a.
Santorin, ii. 1157, b.
Santos, Los, ii. 1285, b.
Sanza, ii. 210, a; ii. 1021, b.
Saône, 187, b; ii. 950, b.
Sapaci, ii. 1190, a.
Sapalca, ii. 1190, b.
Sapan Tagh, ii. 440, a.
Sapienza, ii. 342, b.
Sapis, ii. 1317, b.
Saponara, 1019, a; ii. 210, a; ii. 1295, b.
Sapor, ii. 577, b.
Sapothraeni, ii. 917, b.
Sapri, ii. 210, a; ii. 990, b.
Sar, 933, b; ii. 920, a.
Sara, ii. 1336, b.
Sarabat, ii. 508, b.
Suracatin, ii. 973, b.
Saraceni, 181, a; 363, b.
Saragossa, 469, a.
Sarahkafik, 161, b.
Sarakino, ii. 12, a.
Saralapia, ii. 912, a.
Saram, ii. 172, a.
Saranda, 111, a.
Sarandaforo, 323, a.
Sarandi, ii. 1010, b.
Saranga, 983, a.
Saranga, ii. 905, b.
Sarapana, 643, a.
Sarapionis, ii. 425, b.
Sarasvati or *Sarsooti*, ii. 1020, b.
Saratov, ii. 917, b.
Saravati, 973, b.
Saravene, 507, b.
Sardara, Bagni di, ii. 912, a.
Sardica, ii. 1180, a; ii. 1190, b.
Sardinia, ii. 907, a.
Sardo, Castel, ii. 1199, b.
Sardonix, M., ii. 46, b.
Sarepta, ii. 606, b.
Sargens, ii. 920, b.
Sargantha, 197, b.
Sargati, ii. 916, b.
Sargarausene, 507, b; 508, a.

Saria, 524, a.
Sarigueu, 424, a.
Sarighioli, ii. 568, b.
Sorighrul, ii. 236, b.
Sarlat, ii. 835, a.
Sarmadium, 474, b.
Sarmatians, Hyperborean, ii. 917, b.
Sarmatians, Royal, ii. 917, b.
Sarmaticum, Mare, ii. 460, b.
Sarmizegethusa, 745, b; 744, b.
Sarnelus, 1106, a.
Sarnia, 949, b.
Sarno, 495, a; ii. 920, b.
Sarnus, 495, a.
Saros, ii. 318, b.
Sarpedonium, ii. 1178, a.
Sarre, ii. 906, a.
Sars, 933, b.
Sarsina, ii. 1317, b.
Sarsma, ii. 921, a.
Sart, ii. 907, a.
Sarug, 383, a.
Sarum, Old, ii. 1073, a.
Sarus, 24, a; 619, a.
Sasano, ii. 948, a.
Sasemo, Sassono, or *Sassa*, ii. 922, a.
Sasima, 474, b.
Sasones, ii. 943, b.
Sassula, ii. 1200, b.
Sation, 786, a.
Satomou, ii. 1042, b.
Satrae, ii. 1190, a.
Saturn, Temple of (Rome), ii. 781, b; ii. 782, a.
Saturnia, 870, a; ii. 1297, b.
Saturnia, ii. 934, a; ii. 1297, b.
Satyrs, Cape of the, ii. 1002, a.
Sav-Su, 886, a.
Savari, ii. 916, b.
Saubusse, ii. 974, a.
Save, 747, b; ii. 925, b.
Saverne, ii. 1082, a.
Save, ii. 474, a.
Savmes, ii. 924, b.
Savio, ii. 904, a.
Saulieu, ii. 996, a.
Savo, 495, a.
Savone, 495, a; ii. 924, b.
Savorra, Punta della, ii. 911, b.
Savoy, 752, b; ii. 904, a.
Saurashtran, ii. 47, a; ii. 52, a; ii. 419, b; ii. 1069, b.
Sauromatae, 572, b.
Sautpura, ii. 46, b.
Savus, ii. 841, b.
Savuto, 450. a; ii. 461, b; ii. 864, b; ii. 1131, a.
Saw, ii. 1019, a.
Sarmundham, ii. 1015, b.
Saxons, ii. 926, a.
Saxum Sacrum (Rome), ii. 811, a.
Sbaitha, ii. 1237, b.
Sebba or *Sbibah*, ii. 1045, b.
Scala, C., 588, b.
Scala Ghadova, 744, a.
Scala Nova, ii. 413, a; ii. 681, b.
Scalabis, ii. 219, b.
Scalea, ii. 149, b.
Scamander, ii. 996, a.
Scambonidae (Athens), 302, a.
Scambonidae, 325, a.
Scamnum, 474, b.
Scampa, 830, a; ii. 1298, b.
Scampae, ii. 36, b.
Scampis, 988,a.
Scandalium, 94, a.
Scandarium, 694, b.
Scanderoon, ii. 69, b.
Scania, ii. 928, a.
Scapte Hyle, ii. 1135, b.
Scarbantia, ii. 542, a.
Scardona, ii. 38, a.
Scardona, ii. 928, b.
Scarphae, ii. 202, b.
Scauri, Clivus (Rome), ii. 817, b.
Scaurus, House of (Rome), ii. 804, b.

Scelerata, Porta (Rome), ii. 751, a.
Sceleratus, Campus (Rome), ii. 831, a.
Sceleratus, Vicus (Rome), ii. 834, a.
Scenitae, 181, a.
Schar-Dagh, ii. 928, b.
Scharapani, 643, a; ii. 905, b.
Scharnitz, ii. 928, b.
Schebba, ii. 859, b.
Scheker-Su, ii. 318, b.
Scheib, 117, a, 904, b.
Scheide, ii. 926, b; ii. 1082, b.
Schemnitza, ii. 500, a.
Schenkenschanz, 458, a.
Schera, ii. 986, b.
Scheria, 670, a.
Schibkah-el-Loudjah, ii. 1233, a.
Schieggia, La, ii. 1301, a.
Schieland, 501, a.
Schirvan, 89, b.
Schiso, Capo di, ii. 404, a.
Schleswig, ii. 864, a.
Schockl, 554, b.
Schoenus, 413, b; 683, a; ii. 1177, b.
Schola Quaestorum et Capulatorum (Rome), ii. 828, b.
Schola Xantha (Rome), ii. 788, b.
Schonen, ii. 928, a.
Schwan, ii. 888, b.
Schwangau, 665, b.
Schwarzwald, 1056, b.
Schwerne, ii. 1042, b.
Schwemegraben, ii. 192, a.
Scinecca, ii. 1161, b.
Scicli, 558, a.
Scicli, Fiume di, ii. 965, b.
Scidrus, ii. 210, a.
Sciaz, 193, a.
Scilla, ii. 935, a.
Scillus, 821, b.
Scilly Isles, 560, b; ii. 1001, b.
Scinde, ii. 10, a.
Scinde, Lower, ii. 47, b.
Scio, 609, a.
Scioëssa, 13, a.
Scipios, Tomb of the (Rome), ii. 621, a.
Sciradium, ii. 878, a.
Scirtiana, ii. 36, b.
Scirtonium, 192, b.
Scirum, 326, a; 328, a.
Scissum, ii. 1, a.
Scletrinas, 424, a.
Scodra, 748, a; ii. 36, a.
Scoedises, ii. 658, b.
Scuglio, 495, b.
Scolia, 17, a.
Scone, ii. 928, a.
Scopelus, 1029, a.
Scopuli Tyndarei, ii. 277, b.
Scordisci, ii. 367, b; ii. 542, a.
Score, ii. 149, a.
Scorobax, ii. 547, a.
Scoti, ii. 16, b.
Scotussa, ii. 1190, a.
Scotussa, ii. 1170, a.
Scrofes, 804, b.
Scurgola, ii. 282, a.
Scutari, 614, a; ii. 36, a; ii. 105, a; ii. 932, b.
Scydises, 572, a.
Scylax. ii. 658, b.
Scyllacium, 447, b.
Scyllaeum, 451, a.
Scylleticus Sinus, ii. 935, a.
Scymmitae, ii. 917, b.
Scyrus, ii. 309, b.
Scythae, ii. 367, b.
Scythica, ii. 943, b.
Scythopolis, ii. 1076, b.
Seal, ii. 641, a.
Seaton, ii. 372, a.
Seba' Burdj, ii. 536, a.
Seba Rus, ii. 454, a.
Sebaket-Bardoil, ii. 1012, b.
Sebaste, 462, b.
Sebastia, 647, a.

Sebastian, St., ii. 372, b.
Sebastopol, 714, b; ii. 515, b; ii. 1110, b.
Sebastopolis, 643, a; 647, a; 778, a.
Sebba Rus, ii. 1237, a.
Sebato, 111, a.
Sebboh, ii. 288, a.
Sebcha-es-Sukara, 531, a.
Seben, ii. 1041, b.
Sebennytic arm of the Nile, ii. 433, a.
Sebennytic Nome, 39, b.
Sebethus, 495, a.
Sebinus, Lacus, 497, b.
Sebta, 8, b.
Secchia, ii. 947, a.
Seche, ii. 1011, a.
Seckingen, ii. 902, a.
Secx, 854, b.
Sedeh-Aram, ii. 333, a.
See, ii. 1132, b.
Seewalchen, ii. 107, a.
Sefert, ii. 269, a.
Sefid-Rud, 117, a; 489, a.
Segarra, ii. 31, b.
Segasamunclum, 347, a.
Segedunum, ii. 1256, b.
Segesta, ii. 188, a; ii. 986, b.
Segestan, or Seistan, ii. 870, b.
Segeste, 522, b.
Segiclar, 873, a.
Segida, 197, b.
Segida Restituta Julia, 583, a.
Segigeck, 844, b.
Segikler, ii. 946, a.
Segisamunculum, 347, a.
Segni, ii. 998, a.
Segodunum, 317, a.
Segontia, 197, b; 581, b.
Segorbe, ii. 950, b.
Segovia, 197, b.
Segre, 593, a.
Segura, 368, a; ii. 1083, a.
Seguino, 107, b; ii. 1288, a.
Sehegm, ii. 950, b.
Seibouse, ii. 716, a.
Seiches, 169, b.
Srid-el-Ghazu, ii. 675, a.
Seidi Sheher, ii. 65, b.
Seif Tawil, ii. 425, b.
Sejestan, or Seistan, 366, a; 787, b.
Seihan, ii. 922, a.
Seijo, ii. 961, a.
Scitlans, ii. 883, b.
Scille, ii. 883, a.
Sein, ii. 963, a.
Seme, 305, b; ii. 965, b.
Sejont, ii. 951, a.
Sejo, S. ii. 1229, b.
Seir, ii. 583, a.
Seiras, 193, a.
Seiscola, ii. 220, a.
Seissel, 654, b.
Sela, ii. 209, b.
Selandib, ii. 49, b.
Selanik, ii. 1171, b.
Selas, ii. 342, b.
Selbit, ii. 972, a.
Sele, 483, a; ii. 1000, a, b; ii. 1275, a.
Seierstreh, ii. 954, a.
Selemnus, i3, b.
Selenga, 347, a.
Selenit, ii. 959, a.
Seleuceia, 560, b; ii. 1075, a.
Seleuceia ad Belum, ii. 1076, a.
Seleucis, ii. 1076, a.
Seleucus, Mons, 48°, b.
Selgovae, 642, a; 780, a.
Selino-Kastell, ii. 1246 a.
Selinus, 13, b; ii. 985, b.
Selkirk, 750, a.
Sella, ii. 983, a.
Sellada, ii. 1160, b.
Seletae, ii. 1190, a.
Selletica, ii. 1190, b.
Sellium, ii. 220, a.
Selmen, ii. 876, b.
Seloni, San, ii. 115, b.
Selos, 821, b; ii. 154, b.
Selovia, 748, a.
Sélzune, ii. 1132, b.

Selymbria, ii. 1190, a.
Semachidae, 330, b.
Semanthini, Mts. ii. 46, b.
Sembritae, 69, b.
Semellitani, ii. 987, a.
Semendria, ii. 1310, a.
Semenhoud, ii. 946, b.
Semiramidis, Mt., 520, b.
Semirus, 450, b.
Semlin, ii. 1115. a.
Semo Sancus, Sacellum of (Rome), ii. 840, b.
Semo Sancus, Sacrarium of (Rome), ii. 830, a.
Sempronia, ii. 787, b.
Sempronii, Forum, ii. 1301, a; ii. 1317, b.
Sempnat, ii. 901, a.
Semuncia, ii. 1295, b.
Sena, 870, a.
Sena Gallica, ii. 1301, b; ii. 1317, b.
Senacula (Rome), ii. 620, b; ii. 833, a.
Senaculum (Rome), ii. 780, a.
Senez, ii. 903, a; ii. 1260, b.
Senga, ii. 963, a.
Seni Beti, ii. 1008, a.
Senia, ii. 3, b.
Senkera, 363, a.
Senlis, 341, a; ii. 1001, b.
Senmut, ii. 898, b.
Senn, 465, b.
Sennaar, 57, a; ii. 429, b.
Sens, 73, b.
Senyfa, ii. 1006, a.
Sentice, ii. 1285, b.
Sentino, ii. 964, a.
Sentinum, ii. 1317, b.
Sentites, ii. 278, a.
Senum, 474, b.
Senus, ii. 16, a.
Senzina, Lake of, 413, b.
Sepelaci, 807, a.
Srpino, ii. 896, b.
Sepomana, ii. 74, a.
Septem Aquae, 6, b.
Septem Fratres, 8, a.
Septempeda, ii. 629, a; ii. 1301, b.
Septimiana, Porta (Rome), ii. 842, b.
Septimius Severus, Mausoleum of (Rome), ii. 821, b.
Septizonium (Rome), ii. 806, a.
Sepyra, 116, a.
Sera, ii. 968, b.
Serakhs, ii. 1014, b.
Serapeion, 424, a.
Serapis, Temple of (Rome), ii. 830, b; ii. 838, a.
Serbal, ii. 1003, b.
Serbera, 593, b.
Sercada, S. Pere de, ii. 115, b.
Serchio, 344, b; 857, a.
Serdica, 745, a; ii. 237, a.
Seret, 1065, a.
Sereth, ii. 491, a.
Seretium, 748, a.
Serguntia, 197, b.
Seria, 583, a.
Serippo, 583, a.
Serki Serai, ii. 65, b.
Sermione, ii. 1014, a; ii. 1287, b.
Sermo, 582, a.
Sermoneta, ii. 1046, a.
Sernnius, Vicus, ii. 1287, b.
Serpent's Island, 20, b.
Serpho, ii. 968, b.
Serrapilli, ii. 542, a.
Serravalle, ii. 174, a; ii. 1296, b.
Serres, ii. 1013, b.
Serretes, ii. 542, a.
Serrheum, ii. 1178, a.
Se'rt, 219, a.
Sert, ii. 1208. a.
Sertes, C., 520, b.
Servi, ii. 917, b.
Servia, ii. 583, a.
Sesamus, ii. 547, a.
Sesta, 497, a; ii. 969, b.
Sessa, ii. 1043, a.

Sessola, ii. 1044, b.
Sestini, 250, b.
Sestino, ii. 969, b; ii. 1317, b.
Sestinum, ii. 1317, b.
Sestium, 451, a.
Sestri, ii. 188, a; ii. 950, a.
Sestus, ii. 1190, a.
Setelcis, ii. 1, b.
Seterrae or Becerrae, ii. 115, b.
Sethraite Nome, 29, b.
Setif, ii. 1015, b.
Setortialacta, 197, b.
Setx, ii. 883, a.
Sevanga, Lake, ii. 223, b.
Sevangha, Lake of, 217, a.
Sevastopol, 714, b; ii. 515, b; ii. 1110, b.
Seudre, ii. 903, b.
Sewra, Sania, ii. 687, b; ii. 1296, a.
Severi, Arcus (Rome), ii. 796, a.
Severiana, Aqua (Rome), ii. 851, a.
Severianae, Thermae (Rome), ii. 847, b.
Severm, 513, b.
Severina, Sta, ii. 974, a.
Severine, Sta, 451, a.
Severino, S. ii. 629, a; ii. 1301, b.
Severino, San, ii. 965, a.
Severn, the, ii. 870, b.
Severo, S., 167, a.
Severus, Mons, 186, a.
Sevilla, 568, a; 1074, a.
Seu, ii. 1139, b.
Sevilla la Vieja, ii. 97, a.
Seumara, 181, a.
Sevo, Capo del, ii. 1135, b.
Sevri, Hissar, ii. 581, b.
Sextum, Ad, ii. 1297, a.
Seurri, 933, a.
Sewad, ii. 47, b.
Sewel, ii. 1046, a.
Sewestan, 184, a; ii. 868, b.
Sevano, 1000, a.
Sezze, ii. 971, a.
Sfaitla, ii. 1045, b; ii. 1287, b.
Shabanja, ii. 1048, a.
Shahpur, 366, b; ii. 577, b.
Shamelik, ii. 635, b.
Shangallas, 58, a.
Shannon, the, ii. 964, a.
Shannon, ii. 16, a.
Shat-al-Arab, ii. 332, b; 875, b; ii. 1209, a.
Shechem, 991, b; ii. 411, b.
Sheduan, ii. 904, a.
Shelidam, 606, b.
Shelif, 317, b.
Shellif, 133, b.; 609, a.
Sheppy, ii. 1215, b.
Sherban, 227, b.
Sherborne, E., ii. 1311, b.
Sherboro, ii. 448, a.
Sheriff Hales, ii. 1330, b.
Shetland Islands, 49, a; ii. 487, a.
Skrweitch, 354, a.
Shuckron, ii. 529, b.
Shihos, ii. 711, a.
Shijam, 248, b.
Shikaftoht-Suleiman, ii.1332, b.
Shinar, 360, b.
Shivashe, ii. 1112, b.
Shiur, 570, a.
Shaffri, ii. 904, a.
Shogh, ii. 952, b.
Shropshire, 687, a.
Shunem, ii. 530, b.
Shur, 521, a; 686, b; ii. 886, a.
Shuster, ii. 1050, a.
Shutta, 397, b.
Si Kiang, 698, a.
Si Kiang, the, ii. 1002, b.
Siagui, ii. 1338, a.
Siam, Gulf of, ii. 46, b; ii. 253, a.
Siamata, 414, a; 1003, b.
Siapul or Siapuch, ii. 974, a.
Sibae, ii. 47, b.
Silverena, 451, a.
Sibilla, Monti della, ii. 1132, b.

Sibuzates, 173, a.
Sibyls, Statues of the three (Rome), ii. 786, a.; ii. 796, b.
Sicca Veneres, 370, b.
Sicca, ii. 455, a.
Sichem, ii. 411, b.
Siciliano, ii. 923, a.
Sicilinum, 1073, b.
Sicily, ii. 975, a.
Sicoris, 593, a.
Siculiana, 490, a.
Sicum, 748, a.
Sidas Kaleh, ii. 971, a.
Siddim, Vale of, ii. 522, a.
Side, ii. 995, a.
Sidenus, ii. 658, b.
Sidero, C. S., ii. 897, a.
Sidhiro-kafinio, ii. 270, b.
Sidhiro-peliko, 319, b.
Sidi Makelouf, ii. 1327, b.
Sidodone, 521, a.
Sidonia, ii. 10:5, b.
Sidra, Gulf of, 67, b; ii. 1061, a.
Sidri, 184, a.
Siebengebirge, ii. 709, b.
Sieg, ii. 974, b.
Sicna, ii. 963, a.
Sienna, 589, b.
Sierra Cazorla, 367, b.
Sierra Morena, 367, b.
Sierra Nevada, 367, b.
Severa, ii. 916, b.
Sicverovcsi, ii. 909, b.
Sigarra, ii. 31, b.
Sighajik, ii. 1129, b.
Sigillo, 1045, a; ii. 1301, a.
Sign, ii. 971, b.
Siguenza, 581, b; ii. 874, a.
Sihun, 619, a; ii. 922, a.
Sjeoer, ii. 994, b.
Siktno, ii. 988, a.
Sila, 156, a; ii. 999, b; ii. 1000, a.
Silana, ii. 1170, a.
Silarus, 483, a; ii. 209, b.
Silchester, 320, a; 387, b; 442, a; 481, a.
Sileniae, ii. 878, a.
Silesia, ii. 1000, b.
Silis, ii. 1275, a.
Silili, ii. 1001, a.
Silivri, ii. 961, a.
Silva Marciana, 4, b.
Silvestro, S., 897, b.
Silvium, 167, b; ii. 1293, a.
Silun, ii. 1001, a.
Silvum, ii. 74, a.
Simancas, ii. 963, b.
Simas, 424, a.
Simaul-Su, ii. 238, a.
Simbirsk, ii. 917, b.
Simbri, 691, b.
Simeon, Tribe of, ii. 529, b.
Simeto, 61, a; ii. 985, a; ii. 1054, b.
Similttu, ii. 485, a.
Simissa, ii. 338, b.
Simmari, 450, b.
Simois, ii. 986, a.
Simylla, 210, a; ii. 46, b; ii. 47, a.
Simyra, ii. 606, a.
Sinaab, ii. 486, a.
Sinab, ii. 1009, a.
Sinae, Bay of the, ii. 1002, b.
Sinaja-woda. 889, a.
Sinanbey, 452, a.
Sinanu, ii. 307, a.
Sind, ii. 1016, a.
Sind or Sindhu, ii. 53, a.
Sinde, ii. 1334, a.
Sindus, ii. 384, a.
Sinei or Signer, ii. 950, b.
Sines, ii. 361, b.
Sincu, 374, b.
Singames, 643, a.
Singan. ii. 966, b.
Singar, ii. 1006, b; ii. 1007, a.
Singara, 360, b.
Singarus, M., ii. 333, b.
Singitic Gulf, 597, b.
Singiticus, Sinus, ii. 1006, b.
Singulis, 368, a; ii. 1239, b.
Singar, 360, b; 811, b; ii. 333, b; ii. 384, a.
Sinibaldi, Rocca, ii. 1225, a.

Sinigaglia, ii. 962, b; ii. 1301, b.
Sinna, 748, a.
Sinno, ii. 209, b; ii. 1012, b.
Sinonia, ii. 658, a.
Sinope, 406, a; ii. 547, b.
Sinotium, 748, a.
Sinub, 406, a.
Sinuessa, ii. 1290, a.
Sinus Amycus, 424, b.
Sinus Immundus, 57, b.
Sinus Magnus, ii. 46, b.
Sinus Paragon, 174, b.
Sinus Profundus, 424, a.
Sinus Urius, 166, b.
Sion, ii. 947, b.
Siounik' h, ii. 870, b.
Sipontum, 167, a.
Sephno, or Siphanto, ii. 1010, b.
Siponto, Sta Maria di, ii. 1011, a.
Sir Scruh, ii. 440, a.
Siracui, ii. 917, b.
Siraci, 572, b.
Sirenusae Insulae, 495, b.
Sirghie, 369, a; 590, a.
Sirhind, ii. 48, a.
Siris, ii. 209, b; ii. 210, a.
Sirmio, ii. 1287, b.
Sirmium, ii. 542, a.
Sirom. Pont de, ii. 1012, b.
Sisapo, ii. 219, b.
Sisar, 336, b; ii. 454, a.
Siscia, ii. 3, b; ii. 542, a.
Sissek, ii. 3, b.
Sisteron, ii. 962, a; ii. 1318, b.
Sistov, ii. 947, b.
Sita-Rhegian, ii. 1015, a.
Sitges, ii. 1041, b.
Sitha, ii. 1339, a.
Sithonian Peninsula, 597, b.
Sitifensis, 336, b.
Sittacene, 822, b.
Sitten, ii. 947, b.
Sittocatis, 973, b.
Sitzhanli, 776, a.
Siwas, ii. 946, a.
Sixeboli, 160, b.
Skaftscha, ii. 551, b.
Skala, ii. 496, a.
Skalanova, ii. 266, b.
Skandole, ii. 928, a.
Skaphidaki, 584, a.
Skaphidi, 796, b; ii. 593, b.
Skardhamula, 516, a.
Skarmanga, 31, b.
Skaro, ii. 1160, b.
Skarpanto, 524, a.
Skiada, ii. 486, b.
Skiatho, ii. 930, b.
Skino, 685, b.
Skipeu, Mt. ii. 473, b.
Sklatima, ii. 587, a; ii. 626, a.
Sklavokhori, 128, a.
Skopelo, 1029, a.
Skopos, or Skopopolis, ii.1133, a.
Skotini, 94, b.
Skripu, ii. 488, b.
Skroponeri, 410, b; 412, a.
Skumbi, 988, a; ii. 36, b; ii. 533, a.
Skumbi River, ii. 36, b.
Skurta, 329, b.
Skutari, 32, b.
Skyro, ii. 935, b.
Slack, 488, a.
Slavonia, ii. 541, a.
Sleat, Sound of, ii. 101, b.
Sligo Bay, ii. 173, a.
Smerna, 817, b.
Smyrna, 53, a.
Smyrna, ii. 1016, a.
Sneim, ii. 594, b.
Soana, 89, b.
Soanes, ii. 1039, b.
Soane, 814, b.
Soanes, 572, a.
Soani, ii. 1093, b.
Soara-esch-Schurkia, ii. 870, b.
Soatra, ii. 222, b.
Soba, ii. 691, b.
Sobad-Koh, ii. 106, b.
Soboridae, 59, b.

Sobusse, ii. 974, a.
Socanaa, 1106, a.
Socossli, ii. 299, a.
Socotorra, 777, b.
Soe-el-Arba, ii. 1312, a.
Soe el Campa, ii. 1225, b.
Soeta, ii. 943, b.
Sofala, ii. 484, a.
Sofia, 804, b; ii. 237, a; ii. 943, a.
Sohagpur, ii. 44, a.
Sohajpur, ii. 873, b.
Sohar, 714, b; ii. 677, b.
Sohegurli, ii. 947, b.
Soier-el-Rexiam, 349, a.
Soissons, 339, b; ii. 1044, a.
Sokar, ii. 235, a.
Sokho, 796, b; ii. 500, b.
Sokhta Kalesi, 226, a.
Sol, Temple of (Rome), ii. 830, b.
Solam, ii. 973, b.
Solano, Fiume di, 450, a; 700, a.
Solanio, ii. 1021, a.
Solaro, ii. 188, b.
Sole, Città del, ii. 1020, b.
Soleto, ii. 1019, a.
Soletum, 474, b.
Soleure, or Solothurn, ii.884, b.
Solfatara, 94, a; 497, a.
Solfeld, 902, b.
Soli, 53, b; 729, b.
Soliman Koh, ii. 550, b.
Solivela, ii. 1034, b.
Sollanco, 250, b.
Sollanco, or Sollancia, ii. 119, b.
Sollium, 10, b.
Solomatis, 973, b.
Solothurn, ii. 562, b.
Solsona, ii. 1, b; ii. 971, a.
Solta, ii. 27, a; ii. 480, b.
Soluatum, ii. 986, b.
Soluny, 642, a; 750, a.
Solway Firth, ii. 101, a.
Solvay Frith, ii. 1312, a.
Solygeia, 685, a.
Somerset, 388, a.
Somma, ii. 893, b.
Sömmering, 534, b.
Sommet de Castel-Pinon, ii. 42, b.
Sontia, ii. 210, a.
Sontius, ii. 1275, a.
Sonus, 844, b; 973, b.
Suo Ood Guse, 575, a.
Soorcah, ii. 1048, b.
Sopheue, ii. 439, b.
Sophia, ii. 1180, a; ii. 1226, a.
Sophon. 406, a.
Sopoto, ii. 576, a.
Sor, ii. 1248, b.
Sora, ii. 1092, a.
Sorae, ii. 48, a; ii. 299, a.
Sorano, ii. 1042, b.
Sorbitan, ii. 952, b.
Sors, Monte, 1051, b.
Soria, 581, a.
Soringi, ii. 47, a.
Sornum, 744, b.
Sorrento, ii. 1049, a.
Sas, ii. 1024, a.
Sosias, or Sossius, ii. 985, b.
Sospita (Rome), ii. 832, b.
Sosthenis, ii. 1170, b.
Soteriopolis, 778, a.
Sotiates, 173, a.
Sovana, ii. 1041, a.
Souches, ii. 1019, a.
Souic, ii. 974, b.
Soulosse, ii. 1020, a.
Sour, ii. 1048, b.
Sour Guzlon, 349, a.
Sourman, 1108, b.
South Brabant, 28, b.
South Creake, 442, b.
Southampton, 631, b.
Southwold, ii. 101A, b.
Sontius, ii. 1275, a.
Souzou, ii. 1024, b.
Spa, 904, b.
Spada, C, ii. 675, a.
Spadha, Cape, 463, b.
Spain, 1074, a.
Spalaethra, ii. 1170, b.
Spalmadoret, ii. 469, a.

Sparagi, I. del, 719, a.
Spartana, ii. 1093, b.
Spartel, Cape, 125, a; ii. 296, a.
Spartivento, Cape, 1056, a.
Spartovuni, 74, a.
Spata, 832, b.
Spauta, 320, b.
Spauta, Lake of, 216, b.
Specea, 718, b.
Speier, ii. 450, a.
Spello, 1089, a.
Spelunca, ii. 1076, a.
Speluncae, 464, b; ii. 1294, a.
Spene, ii. 1032, b.
Sperchiae, ii. 1170, b.
Sperlinga, 1052, b.
Sperlonga, 464, b; ii. 1031, b.
Spes, Temple of (Rome), ii. 831, b.
Spes Vetus, Temple of (Rome), ii. 826, b.
Spessart, 1056, b.
Sphaeria, 477, a.
Sphecela, 729, b.
Spetzsa, 647, a; 840, a; ii. 1211, a.
Sphendale, 330, a.
Sphentanium, 748, a.
Sphettus, 332, b.
Sphingium, 412, a.
Spina Longa, ii. 406, b.
Spineticum Ostium, ii. 1032, b.
Spria, ii. 602, b.
Spirnatsa, ii. 533, a.
Spitul, ii. 1133, a.
Splügen, 28, b; 107, a.
Spoletium, ii. 1300, b; ii. 1301, a; ii. 1317, a.
Spoleto, ii. 1300, b; ii. 1301, a; ii. 1032, b.
Spoliarium (Rome), ii. 819, a.
Sponsae, or Ad Sponsas, ii. 1290, a.
Spurn Head, 7, b; ii. 461, b.
Spyck, 550, a.
Spy Park, ii. 1278, b.
Squillace, ii. 934, b.
Squillace, Gulf of, ii. 935, a.
Srbec, ii. 906, a.
Srmager, 558, b.
Stoghanli Dere, ii. 1017, b.
Ssulu Derbend, ii. 104:, a.
Stabula IV., Factionum (Rome), ii. 834, b.
Stabulum Diomedis, ii. 1299, a.
Stadium (Rome), ii. 838, b.
Stafford, 687, a.
Stagus, 35, a.
Stala, ii. 226, b.
Stalimene, ii. 157, a.
Stampalia, 250, b.
Standia, 772, a.
Staneclum, 748, a.
Stanko, or Stanchio, 604, b.
Stanuex, 655, b; ii. 1256, b.
Stara Orun, ii. 1157, a.
Stari-Krim, 701, b.
Staroselitsu, ii. 1329, b.
Statiellae Aquae, 1296, b.
Statielli, ii. 187, a.
Statilius Taurus, Amphitheatre of, ii. 845, b.
Statonia, 870, a.
Statuam, Ad, ii. 1294, b.
Stavani, ii. 916, a.
Stavoren, 903, b.
Stavros, ii. 1034, b.
Stavros, C., ii. 602, a.
Steckborn, 911, b.
Steigerwald, 1056, b.
Stein, 974, b.
Stein Am Anger. ii. 864, a.
Stein-Strass, ii. 1196, b.
Steiria, 332, a.
Stelac, 705, b.
Stella, ii. 1275, a.
Stennitsa, 1105, b.
Stena, ii. 14, a.
Stenas, ii. 202, a.
Stenia, 424, a.
Stentoris, Lacus, ii. 1178, a.
Stenyclarus, ii. 345, b.
Stephane, ii. 547, b.
Stephanio, ii. 1036, a.

Stercoraria, Porta (Rome), ii. 757, a ; ii. 782, b.
Sterna, ii. 231, a.
Sternaccio, ii. 1039, a.
Sternes, ii. 360. a.
Sterzing, ii. 1277, b ; ii. 1312, a.
Stilo, Capo di, 641, b.
Stiris, ii. 605, a.
Stirling, 750, a ; 1090, b.
Stoa Basileius (Athens), 296, a.
Stoa Poecile (Athens), 296, b.
Stobi, ii. 237, a ; ii. 551, b.
Stoborrum, ii. 454, a.
Stobretz, 833, a.
Stoeni, or Stoni, 872, b.
Stomogil, ii. 471, b.
Stonas, ii. 237, a.
Storah, Bay of, 644, b.
Store Belt, ii. 460, b.
Stour, 808, b.
Stowmarket, ii. 1015, b.
Stranitja-Dagh, ii. 1177, b.
Strangford Bay, ii. 1310, b.
Strasvaraer, 750, a.
Strapellum, 167, b.
Strassburg, 198, b; ii. 1229, a.
Stratford, 651, a.
Stratia, ii. 407, a.
Stratiotiki, 304, a ; 306, b.
Stratoni, ii. 1037, b.
Stratonicea, 239, b.
Stratus, 10, b.
Straubing, ii. 969, b.
Strcfi, 738, b.
Strehlen, ii. 1037, b.
Strel, or Strey, ii. 914, b.
Streletska Bay, ii. 1111, a.
Streniae, Sacellum (Rome), ii. 826, b.
Strepsa, ii. 384, a.
Streton, 437, a ; ii. 574, a.
Strgas, ii. 1037, b.
Strivali, ii. 1038, a.
Strofadia, ii. 1038, b.
Stromboli, 51, b.
Stroncone, ii. 1225, a.
Strongoli, ii. 582, a.
Strongyle, 51, b.
Strongylus, 520, b.
Strovitzi, ii. 161, b.
Struchates, ii. 301, b
Struma, ii. 1038, a.
Strumitza, 249, a.
Struthophagi, 88, a.
Struttina, 412, a.
Strawiki, 1102, b.
Stryme, ii. 1186, a.
Strymon, ii. 1177, b.
Studenita, Mount, ii. 691, a.
Stühlingen, ii. 144, a.
Stura, ii. 188, a.
Stura, ii. 1039, a ; ii. 1040, a.
Sturni, ii. 916, b.
Sturnium, 474, b.
Styllagium, 821, b.
Stymbara, ii. 861, a.
Stymphalia, 192, b.
Stymphalus, 192, b.
Styra, 872, b.
Styria, ii. 447, a.
Su Vermexs, ii. 1017, a.
Suabeni, ii. 943, b.
Suachen, ii. 1042, a.
Suana, 870, a.
Suani, 643, a.
Suanocolchi, ii. 917, b.
Suardeni, ii. 917, b.
Suarium Forum (Rome), ii. 840, a.
Suasa, ii. 1317, b.
Suastene. ii. 47, b.
Suastus, 1006, b ; ii. 1041, b.
Subasani, 691, b.
Sublaco, ii. 1041, b.
Sublicius, Pons (Rome), ii. 848, a.
Subur, ii. 1041, b.
Subur, 696, b ; ii. 297, b.
Subura (Rome), ii. 824, b.
Sucasses, 173, a.
Succat, ii. 1042, a.
Succosa, ii. 34, a.

Sucha Dere, ii. 1335, b.
Sucro, 807, a.
Suda, 125, b.
Sudak, 306, b.
Sudaski, ii. 1101, a.
Sudeni, ii. 916, a.
Sudertum, 870, a.
Sudeten, ii. 1042, b.
Sudha, ii. 170, b.
Sudhena, ii. 217, b.
Sudras, ii. 1018, b.
Sudusra, 569, b.
Suecca, ii. 1043, b.
Suemus, ii. 1178, a.
Suesbula, or Vesbula, 6, a.
Suessona, 341, a.
Suevicum, Mare, ii. 460, b.
Suex, 638, a.
Suez, G. of, 174, b.
Suffenas, Trebula, ii. 1225, a.
Suffolk, ii. 1231, a.
Suffimar, 127, b.
Sugdaja, 306, b.
Sukha, 1033, b.
Sukum, 668, b.
Sulak, 89, b.
Sülchen, ii. 902, a.
Sulci, ii. 911, b.
Sulcitanus Portus, ii. 911, b.
Suleiman, ii. 1197, b.
Sulemanii, 408, a.
Suli, 839, b ; ii. 268, a.
Sulia, 705, b.
Sulima, 786, b.
Sulinari, 83, a.
Sulla, Statue of (Rome), ii. 793, a.
Sulmona, ii. 1046, b.
Sulones, ii. 915, b.
Sulpicius Portus, ii. 911, b.
Sultan-hissar, ii. 456, b.
Sultania, 753, b.
Sumaro, 635, a.
Sumatia, 192, b.
Sumatra, 209, a ; ii. 1, a.
Sumaya, ii. 329, a.
Sumerm, 336, b.
Sumusat, 876, b.
Summum Choragium (Rome), ii. 828. a.
Summus Pyrenaeus, ii. 42, b.
Sumrah, ii. 1002, a.
Sun, Temple of the (Rome), ii. 816, a.
Suna, 6, a.
Sunani, ii. 917, b.
Sundukli, ii. 1311, b.
Sungaria, ii. 289, b.
Sunjuk-kala, 1074, a.
Sunium, 331, a.
Suntelgebirge, 1066, a.
Superatti, 249, b ; 250, b.
Supil, ii. 934, a.
Sur, ii. 1248, b.
Sora, ii. 1076, b.
Suram, ii. 1048, b.
Suranae, Thermae (Rome), ii. 848, a.
Surapend, ii. 914, a.
Surasene, ii. 48, a.
Sure, ii. 1048, b.
Surianae et Declanae, Thermae (Rome), ii. 811, b.
Surium, 643, a.
Surovigli, ii. 1038, a.
Surrey, ii. 697, b.
Sus, ii. 1050, a.
Susa, 107, b ; 1024, a ; ii. 188, a ; ii. 931, b ; ii. 931, b ; ii. 1288, a.
Susaki, ii. 997, a.
Susam Adassi, ii. 397. b.
Sussex, 388, a ; ii. 697. b.
Susu, or Surugheril, 238, a.
Surugheril, ii. 717, a.
Sutherland, 517, a ; 522, b.
Sutlxi, ii. 1270, a.
Sutledge, 1106, a ; ii. 48, a ; ii. 1336, b.
Sutri, ii. 1051, a; ii. 1296, b ; ii. 1297, a.

Sutrium, ii. 1296, b; ii. 1297, a.
Suvala, 603, a.
Suvasta, or Suwad, 1006, b.
Suwasti, or Suwad, ii. 1041, b.
Suxannecourt, ii. 948, a.
Sweden, ii. 928, a ; ii. 1045, b.
Swine, ii. 1042, b.
Syagrus, 175, b ; ii. 871, a.
Sybaris, ii. 209, b ; ii. 1193, b.
Sybota, 833, a.
Sybritia, 705, b.
Sycurium, ii. 1170, a.
Syderis, 1106, a.
Syebi, ii. 943, b.
Sykoon, or Sykan, 24, a.
Syia, 705, b.
Sykena, 13, b.
Sykta, ii. 1006, b.
Syl, ii. 1196, b.
Sylimma, ii. 1047, a.
Syllacium, 451, b.
Symaethus, 61, a ; ii. 985, a.
Symbolon, ii. 1110, a.
Symbolon, Portus, ii. 515, b.
Symi, ii. 1055, a.
Symmachus, House of (Rome), ii. 818, b.
Synnada, 239, a ; 776, a.
Syphaeum, 451, a.
Syr-Daria, ii. 6, a.
Syra, ii. 1060, a.
Syracuse, ii. 1055, b.
Syracusanus, Portus, 691, a.
Syrastrene, ii. 47, a ; ii. 255, a.
Syrgis, 455, a.
Syrian Gates, the, ii. 1075, b.
Syriam, 313, a.
Syrnus, ii. 547, a.
Syrtis, Greater, 67, b.
Syrtis, Lesser, 67, b.
Syspiratis, 488, a.
Sythas, or Syx, 13, b.
Szala Egerszek, ii. 876, a.
Szarkol, ii. 1240, b.
Szasvaros, 996, b.
Szekszard, ii. 1035, b.
Saent Endre, ii. 1313, b.
Szereka, ii. 1339, a.
Szlatina, ii. 881, a.
Szombathely, ii. 864, a.
Szőny, 429, a.
Szgr, ii. 2, b.

Taanach, ii. 530, b.
Taanath-shiloh, ii. 530, a.
Ta'annuk, ii. 1081, b.
Tab, 220, b ; ii. 1050, b.
Tabarich, ii. 1197, a.
Tabarka, ii. 1134, a.
Tabassi, ii. 48, a.
Taberistan, ii. 1094, a.
Tabernae Novae (Rome), ii. 782, b.
Tabernae, Tres, 1290, a.
Tabernae Veteres (Rome), ii. 782, b.
Tabernas, ii. 1239, a.
Tabieni, ii. 943, b.
Tabilba, ii. 277, a.
Tabor, 251, b ; ii. 530, b.
Tabraca, ii. 455, a.
Tabris, 801, a.
Tabularium (Rome), ii. 770, b.
Taburno, Monte, 156, a; ii. 1082, b.
Taburnus, Mons, 156, a.
Tacape, ii. 1081, a.
Tacarael, ii. 47, a.
Tacazae, 57, b; ii. 711, a.
Tachompso, 60, a.
Tachta, 158, b.
Tacna, 450, b.
Tacmo, ii. 1101, a.
Tadcaster, 477, b.
Tader, 358, a.
Tadiates, 55, a.
Tadinum, ii. 1317, b.
Taesburg, 442, b.
Taf, ii. 703, a.
Tafilet, ii. 1086, a.
Tafio, 588, b ; ii. 1090, b.
Tafna, ii. 997, b.

Taganrog, 701, b.
Tagara, ii. 47, a ; ii. 49, b.
Taggia, ii. 187, b.
Taghtaku, ii. 1021, b.
Tagliamento, 529, a; ii. 1209, b ; ii. 1275, a, b.
Tagonius, 525, b.
Tagri, ii. 917, a.
Taguria, 364, b.
Tajilt, ii. 1085, a.
Tajo, ii. 1085, a.
Taguha, 535, b ; ii. 1085, a.
Tak Kesra, 715, a.
Taka, ii. 711, a.
Takht-i-Solciman, 231, a ; 801, a.
Takhyno, 392, b ; 591, b.
Takt, 111, b ; ii. 663, a.
Takmak, 999, a.
Takt Tiridate, 227, a.
Takurs, ii. 1019, a.
Talabriga, ii. 220, b.
Talabroca, 1106, a.
Taladusii, ii. 299, a.
Talamas-Su, 486, a.
Talamina, 934, b.
Talamone, Porto, ii. 1296, a.
Talanda, ii. 202, a ; ii. 400, b; ii. 486, a.
Talamdonisi, 262, a.
Talarenses, ii. 987, a.
Talavera de la Reyna, ii. 1085, a.
Talca, los Campos de, ii. 97, a.
Talmon, ii. 1087, a.
Talos, or Calos, Tomb of (Athens), 301, a.
Taluctae, ii. 1209, b.
Taman, 422, a ; ii. 587, a ; ii. 1006, a.
Tamankadawe, ii. 232, a ; ii. 1093, b.
Tamar, ii. 1066, b.
Tamaris, 933, b.
Tamaro, ii. 1086, b.
Tamasa, 972, b.
Tamassus, 729, b ; 730, a.
Tambov, ii. 917, b.
Tambre, 933, b ; ii. 1086, b.
Tamerion, ii. 1086, b.
Tammacum, ii. 283, b.
Tammacus, ii. 284, b.
Tamraparni, ii. 1019, a.
Tamukhari, 561, b.
Tamusch, 248, b.
Tamyras, ii. 606, b.
Tanager, ii. 209, b.
Tanagro, ii. 209, b ; ii. 1087, a.
Tanagrum, Ad, ii. 210, b.
Tanaltae, ii. 916, b.
Tanaro, ii. 188, a ; ii. 1089, a
Tanarum, Ad, ii. 1295, a.
Tanarus, ii. 188, a.
Taneto, ii. 1287, a.
Tangala, or Tangalle, 750, b.
Tangalle, ii. 1093, b.
Tangier, ii. 296, a ; ii. 1195, a ; ii. 1211, a.
Tanis, 39, b.
Tanite Nome, 39, b.
Tanitic arm of the Nile, ii. 433, a.
Tanka, Cape, ii. 481, b.
Tannetum, ii. 1287, a.
Tantura, 470, b ; 784, b.
Tanus, 201, a
Tanus, or Tanaus, 726, b.
Taoce, ii. 578, b.
Taochan Adassi, ii. 117, a.
Taochi, ii. 658, b.
Taormina, ii. 1113, b.
Tapanitae, ii. 278, a.
Tape, 1106, a.
Taphiassus, 63, b ; 600, b.
Taphii, 9, b.
Taphus, 60, a.
Taphus, 588, b.
Taposiris, ii. 277, b ; ii. 642, a.
Taprobane, 59, b.
Tapures, ii. 943, b.
Tapyri, 364, b ; ii. 302, a.
Tara, 505, a ; ii. 1100, b.
Taraba, ii. 275, a.

Tarabosam, ii. 1221, a.
Tarabuxum, ii. 242, a.
Taranto, ii. 1094, b; ii. 1293, a; ii. 1294, a.
Taranto, Golfo di, ii. 1094, b.
Tarascon, ii. 887, a.
Tarascon, ii. 1094, a; ii. 1108, a.
Tarazona, 581, b.
Tarbelli, 173, a; 949, a.
Tarbellicae, 416, b.
Tarbcs, 402, a.
Tarbet Ness, 502, b.
Tardajoz, 770, b.
Tarentinus, Portus, 474, b.
Tarentum, ii. 1293, a; ii. 1294, a.
Tarentum (Rome), ii. 835, a.
Targines, 450, b.
Tarifa, ii. 101, b; ii. 1220, b.
Tarn, ii. 1101, b.
Tarne, 17, a.
Taro, ii. 1107, b.
Tarpeian Rock (Rome), ii. 771, b.
Tarphe, ii. 202, b.
Tarrabenii, 691, b.
Tarracina, ii. 1290, a.
Tarraco, 696, b; ii. 31, b.
Tarragona, ii. 1106, a.
Tarrazona, ii. 1240, a.
Tarrega, ii. 1, b.
Tarrcn, ii. 1196, b.
Tarrha, 705, b.
Tarsia, 520, b.
Tarsia, 451, a, b; ii. 1295, a.
Tarsiana, 521, a.
Tarsuras, 643, a.
Tarsus, 618, a.
Tartals, 1025, b.
Tartaro, 26, b; ii. 1106, b.
Tartessus, 528, b.
Tartus, 138, b.
Tarty, ii. 46, b.
Tarvisium, ii. 1275, a.
Tarusates, 173, a.
Tarza, ii. 1106, b.
Tasch-Katschik, 578, b.
Tash Kupri, ii. 654, b.
Taskora, 354, b.
Tasm, 178, a.
Tasso, ii. 1135, b.
Tatalia, ii. 1085, b.
Tatari, 1021, b.
Tataritza, ii. 1120, b.
Tateza, 784, b.
Tatoy, 310, a.
Tatta, ii. 360, a; ii. 556, b.
Tatta, L., 508, b.
Tattaea, 425. b.
Tau, E'tang de, ii. 1035, a.
Tava, 39, b.
Taval, ii. 47, a.
Tavas, ii. 53, a.
Tavia, 929, a; ii. 187, b.
Tavignano, 94, b; 691, a.
Tavira, 375, a; ii. 220, a.
Tavium, ii. 1156, b.
Taukli, ii. 1334, a.
Taukra, 733, b.
Tavola, 691, a.
Tavoy, ii. 47, a; ii. 1063, a.
Taur, or Tau, ii. 1115, b.
Taurania, 496, a.
Taurasi, ii. 1109, a.
Taurasia, 1073, a.
Taurenti, ii. 1113, b.
Tauri, Aquae, 870, b.
Tauriana, ii. 237, a.
Taurini, ii. 187, a; ii. 1288, a.
Tauroscythae, ii. 917, a.
Taurubulae, 509, b.
Taurunum, ii. 542, a.
Taurus, 618, b; ii. 1035, a.
Taxila, ii. 47, b.
Tay, Frith of, ii. 1106, b.
Tay, Loch, ii. 1086, b.
Tayf, ii. 284, b.
Tayne, 562, a.
Tchandeli, ii. 635, a.
Tchardah, ii. 1240, b.
Tchatyr-Dagh, ii. 1110, a.
Tchavdour-Hissar, 353, b; 463, b.
Tcherezelan, ii. 947, b.
Tchiraly, 693, b.
Tchoukoorbye, 148, a.

Tchorocsou, 1003, b.
Tchoruk-Su, ii. 227, b.
Tchoterlek Irmak, ii. 935, a.
Tchourbache, Lake of, ii. 456, a.
Teano, ii. 1302, b.
Teano Marrucino, 916, a.
Teanum, 167, a; ii. 1302, b.
Teare, ii. 1117, a.
Teate, ii. 279, b; ii. 1306, b.
Teba, 321, b.
Tebessa, ii. 1174, a; ii. 1211, a.
Tebourba, ii. 1237, b.
Tech, 588, b; 736, b; ii. 1205, a.
Tecmon, 823, a.
Tectosaces, ii. 943, b.
Tectosages, 928, a; ii. 1320, a.
Tedanius, ii. 208, a.
Tedjen, ii. 431, a; ii. 461, b.
Tedjin, 1106, a; ii. 299, a.
Tedlez, ii. 297, b.
Tedmor, ii. 536, a.
Tefessad, or Tefecah, ii. 1211, a.
Teffuk, 60, a; ii. 1090, b.
Teffuk, ii. 1091, a.
Tegea, 192, b.
Tegeatis, 192, b.
Teglanum, ii. 210, a.
Tegula, ii. 912, a.
Tegulata, ii. 188, b.
Tejada, ii. 1238, a.
Teichium, 67, a; ii. 202, a.
Teichos, 17, a; 798, b.
Teima, ii. 283, b.
Tein, ii. 1120, b; ii. 1174, b.
Tejo, ii. 1085, a.
Tekieh, ii. 545, a; ii. 1155, b.
Tekir-Dagh, ii. 1177, b.
Tekke, ii. 538, a.
Tekrit, 402, b.
Tekrova, ii. 592, b.
Teku'a, ii. 1121, a.
Tel-Arka, 189, b.
Tel-Basta, ii. 434, a.
Tel-Bustak, 453, a.
Tel-defenneh, ii. 1085, a.
Tel Eide, 363, a.
Tel el Hava, ii. 1174, b.
Tel-Essabe, ii. 160, a.
Tel Siphr, 363, a.
Telamonaccio, ii. 1286, a.
Telamone, ii. 1121, a.
Telamonem, ii. 1296, a.
Telamonis, Portus, 870, b.
Telawe, 227, a.
Telbes, ii. 1156, b; ii. 1174, b.
Teleboae, 9, b.
Telemra, ii. 1240, b.
Teiendos, 485, a.
Telese, ii. 1191, b.
Telesia, ii. 896, b.
Telethrius, M., 871, a.
Teligul, 352, a.
Telis, ii. 1278, b.
Tell, 316, b.
Tell 'Arad, 185, a.
Tell-el-Ful, ii. 363, a.
Tell-ei-Kadi, ii. 519, b.
Tell-el-Kady, 750, a.
Tell-es-Safieh, ii. 363, b.
Tell Hum, 504, b.
Tell Neby Mindan, ii. 1076, a.
Tell-Zakariya, 398, a.
Tellaro, or Telloro, 1039, b.
Tellus, Temple of (Rome), ii. 823, a.
Telo-Vumi, 322, b.
Telobis, ii. 1, b.
Temathia, ii. 341, b.
Tembrogius, ii. 1194, b.
Temendjex, Cape, ii. 859, b.
Temenia, 1107, b.
Temenion, 202, b.
Temes, 926, a.
Temesvar, Banat of, 743, b.
Temesx, ii. 1199, b.
Temminch, Wady, ii. 533, a; ii. 586, b.
Temminch, 354, b.
Temnus, 53, a.
Temo, ii. 911, a.

Tempestas, Temple of (Rome), ii. , b.
Tempe, 48, a.
Tempyra, ii. 1190, a.
Temruk, 422, a.
Temugadi, ii. 1087, a.
Temua, or Termus, ii. 911, a.
Tenasserim, ii. 1082, a.
Tenedo, ii. 1136, b.
Tenelum, 17, a.
Teneric Plain, 413, b.
Tenerife, 906, b.
Tenesis, 59, b.
Tenex, 529, a; ii. 297, b.
Tensift, Wady, ii. 625, a.
Tentyra, 40, a.
Tentyrite Nome, 40, a.
Teos, 239, b.
Tepelené, 151, b.
Tera, 730, a.
Terame, ii. 55, b.
Terame, ii. 55, a; ii. 636, b; ii. 667, b.
Teranich, ii. 1129, b.
Terebintina, ii. 1237, b.
Teredon, 362, b.
Terek, 105, a; 571, b; ii. 68, b.
Terentum (Rome), ii. 835, a.
Tereses, Fortunatae, 583, a.
Tereventum, ii. 896, b.
Tergedum, 60, a.
Tergiiani, ii. 210, a.
Terias, ii. 986, a.
Terina, 448, a.
Terinaean Gulf, 447, b.
Terinaeus Sinus, ii. 1130, a.
Termalitza, ii. 1339, a.
Termera, 239, b.
Termes, 197, b.
Termini, 1065, b; ii. 1161, a.
Termini, Fiume di, 1069, a.
Termuser, 523, a.
Termoli, 454, a; 916, a.
Termi, 6, b; ii. 55, b.
Tirouenne, ii. 1107, b.
Terra, di Bari, 164, b.
Terra, Fiume di, ii. 1100, b.
Terra Nova, ii. 54, a.
Terracina, ii. 1103, b; ii. 1290, a.
Terranova, 983, b; ii. 472, a; 912, a; ii. 1003, b.
Terranova, Fiume di, ii. 985, b.
Terranova, Gulf of, ii. 911, a.
Tersaca, ii. 1105, b.
Tersat, ii. 1105, b.
Tersoos, 618, a; ii. 1106, a.
Tersoos Tchy, 618, b.
Teruel, ii. 1239, b.
Tervitziana, 886, a.
Tescom, or Tescou, ii. 1108, a.
Testi, 730, a; ii. 1133, a.
Tessender Lo, ii. 1217, b.
Test, ii. 1232, b.
Testet, 756, a.
Tet, 725, b.
Tête de Buch, 416, b.
Tetius, 730, a.
Tetraphylia, 254, b.
Tetraxi, ii. 64, a; ii. 341, b.
Tetrica Mons, 156, a.
Teucheira, 226, a; 733, b.
Tevere, ii. 1197, b.
Teverone, 137, a.
Teufelshecke, ii. 192, a.
Teulada, Capo di, ii. 911, a; ii. 912, a.
Teurnia, ii. 448, a.
Teursan, ii. 1107, b.
Trutendorf, ii. 1134, a.
Teutenwinkel, ii. 1134, a.
Teuthis, 193, a.
Teuthrania, ii. 389, a; ii. 1195, a.
Teuthrone, ii. 112, b.
Teyonas, 420, a.
Texle, ii. 1106, a.
Texxoul, ii. 117, b.
Thacori, ii. 1019, a.
Thaema, ii. 283, b.
Thalamae, 821, a; ii. 112, b.
Thaliades, 193, a.

Thames, ii. 1086, b.
Thamna, ii. 532, a, b.
Thamucadis, ii. 456, a.
Thamud, 176, a.
Thamydeni, 181, b.
Thana, ii. 535, b.
Thanatu, 886, a.
Thanet, ii. 1089, a.
Thaouah, ii. 1108, a.
Thaous, ii. 1081, b.
Thapsacus, 877, a.
Thapsus, ii. 985, a.
Tharros, ii. 911, b.
Thaso, ii. 1135, b.
Thaumaci, ii. 1170, a.
Thaumacia, ii. 1170, b.
Theava, ii. 31, b.
Thebae, ii. 1170, a.
Thebais, ii. 1144, a.
Thebanua, Campus, ii. 1155, b.
Theganussa, ii. 342, b.
Thelsoa, 193, a.
Thens, 581, a; ii. 1199, b; ii. 1212, b.
Thetus, ii. 309, b.
Thelepte Lares, ii. 455, a.
Thetford, ii. 1310, a.
Thelmenissus, ii. 1076, a.
Thelpusa, 193, a.
Thelpusia, 193, a.
Thema, ii. 1076, a.
Themis, Temple of (Athens), 301, a.
Themistocles, Tomb of (Athens), 308, a.
Thenae, 193, b; 705, b.
Theodonia, Villa, 515, a.
Theodore, Mons S., ii. 160, b.
Theodosia, ii. 1110, a; ii. 1157, b.
Theodosiopolis, 514, b.
Theodosius, Arch of (Rome), ii. 879, b.
Theoux, ii. 1157, b.
Thera, 341, b.
Therapeia, 494, a.
Therasia, 51, a; ii. 1156, a.
Theriso, ii. 1175, b.
Theriodes Sinus, ii. 1002, b.
Therma, 685, b; ii. 1171, a.
Thermae, ii. 966, b.
Thermae (Rome), ii. 827, a.
Thermek, 1050, a; ii. 1156, b; ii. 1161, b.
Thermessa, 51, a.
Thermia, 738, b.
Thermodon, 413, b; ii. 656, b.
Thermum, 67, a.
Theseïum (Athens), 287, b.
Thespiae, ii. 172, a.
Thessaliotis, ii. 1167, a; ii. 1170, a.
Thessalonica, ii. 226, b.
Thestienses, 67, a.
Thestius, 18, b.
Thetford, ii. 12, a; ii. 1015, b.
Thetidium, ii. 1170, a.
Theu-prosopon, ii. 606, a.
Theudoria, 364, b.
Theveste, ii. 455, a.
Thiaki, ii. 97, b.
Thibuga, ii. 1199, b.
Thiengea, ii. 144, a.
Thile, or Thdemark, ii. 1191, b.
Thinae, ii. 1003, a.
Thmah, ii. 50, a.
Thinite Nome, 40, a.
Thionville, 485, a; ii. 515, a.
This, 8, a; 40, a.
Thiviers, 900, b.
Thmuis, 39, b.
Thmuite Nome, 39, b.
Thoanteium, 524, a.
Thoaria, ii. 568, b.
Thoas, 18, b.
Thochares, 192, b.
Thochoriana, ii. 1174, a.
Tholo, ii. 717, a.
Tholus (Athens), 296, b.
Tholus Cybeles (Rome), ii. 803, b.
Thonitis, ii. 1176, a.
Thopitis, ii. 1175, a.
Thora, 6, b.

Thorae, 331, a.
Thorax, 67, a.
Thorda, 748, a; ii. 271, a; ii. 883, b.
Thorotzsko, 781, a.
Thospites, 216, b.
Thospitis, 224, b; ii. 229, b.
Thosibi, M., ii. 1080, b.
Thraces, ii. 367, b.
Thrasyllus, Monument of (Athens), 285, a.
Thraustus, 821, a.
Thria, 328, b.
Thriasian Gate (Athens), 262, b.
Thrius, 17, a.
Throana, ii. 968, b.
Throasca, 521, a.
Throne, ii. 1075, b.
Throni, 730, a.
Thronium, ii. 202, b.
Thryon, 821, a.
Thssn, ii. 1003, a; ii. 1174, b.
Thulla, 29, a.
Thurbach, ii. 1248, b.
Thurch Irmak, ii. 1175, b.
Thuria, 53, b; ii. 345, b.
Thurii, ii. 210. a.
Thüringer Wald, 922, a; 1035, b; ii. 319, b; ii. 961, b; ii. 1237, b.
Thurium, 412, b.
Thusaazetae, ii. 1196, b.
Thy, or *Thyland*, ii. 1191, b.
Thyamia, ii. 602, b.
Thyamus, 74, a.
Thyaris, ii. 1246, a.
Thybarna, ii. 1194, b.
Thymaeus, ii. 917, b.
Thymoetadae. 325, b.
Thyni, ii. 1190, a.
Thynias, 161, a; ii. 1178, a; ii. 1190, a.
Thyraeum, 193, a, b; ii. 310, a.
Thyrea, 726, a.
Thyreatis, 726, b.
Thyrgonidae, 330, a.
Thyrium, 10, b.
Thyraus, ii. 911, a, b.
Dangli, 847, b.
Tiarantus, ii. 938, b.
Tiariulia, ii. 31, a.
Tiasum, 744, b.
Djaterli, ii. 400, b.
Tibareni, 507, b; ii. 656, b.
Tiber, ii. 1179, b.
Tiber, *St.*, 594, a.
Tiberiacum, ii. 102, a.
Tiberiana, Domus (Rome), ii. 805, a.
Tiberii, Arcus (Rome), ii. 795, a.
Tiberina, Insula (Rome), ii. 840, b.
Tiberinus, Sacellum of (Rome), ii. 840, b.
Tiberius, Arch of (Rome), ii. 834, b.
Tibiga, ii. 455, a.
Tibiscus, 744, b.
Tibula, ii. 911, b; ii. 912, a.
Tibures, 249, b.
Tiburtina, Porta (Rome), ii. 759, a; ii. 760, a.
Ticarius, 691, a.
Tichis, ii. 52, a.
Ticino, ii. 1206, a.
Ticinum, ii. 1287, b; ii. 1288, a.
Ticla, ii. 1237, b.
Tieium, 572, b.
Tjerma, 968, a; ii. 533, a.
Tierna, 744, b.
Tjersemba, 815, b; ii. 226, b; ii. 550, a.
Tiévre, ii. 1132, b.
Tjeutroa, 689, a.
Tifata, Mons, 156, a; 481, b.
Tifcch, ii. 1211, a.
Tifernum Metaurense, ii. 1207, b; ii. 1317, a.
Tifernum Tiberinum, ii. 1907, b; 1317, a.
Tifernus, 166, b.
Tiffech, 370, b.
Tigani, *C.*, ii. 1337, b.

Tigilium Sororium (Rome), ii. 834, b.
Tigullia, ii. 188, a.
Til-le-Château, ii. 1209, b.
Tiladae, ii. 47, a.
Tilavemptus, 522, a; ii. 1275, a.
Tilbus, ii. 1156, b; ii. 1174, b.
Tilium, ii. 912, a.
Tilphossium, 412, a.
Tilurium, 748, a.
Tilurus, ii. 557, b.
Tima, ii. 283, b.
Timachi, ii. 367, b.
Timalibum, 934, b.
Tmao, ii. 1210, a.
Timavus, ii. 1275, a.
Timbrek, ii. 1194, b.
Timbrius, ii. 1194, b.
Timethus, ii. 986, a.
Tinia, ii. 1211, a.
Timnah, ii. 529, b.
Timok, ii. 1210, a.
Tin, ii. 1174, b.
Tindaro, ii. 1246, b.
Tinek, ii. 573, b.
Tingentera, ii. 1230, b.
Tingis, ii. 296, a.
Tinnetio, 110, b.
Tino, ii. 1127, a.
Tinto, ii. 1327, a.
Tinzen, 110, b; ii. 1211, a.
Tiora, 6, b.
Tiorbadji, ii. 682, b.
Tipasa, 270, b.
Tiperak, ii. 47, a.
Tiphsah, ii. 1135, a.
Tipperah, ii. 1230, b.
Tiquadra, 374, b.
Tiran, ii. 63, b.
Tireboli, ii. 1232, b.
Tirida, 403, b; ii. 1190, a.
Tirich, ii. 127, b.
Tiriscum, 744, b.
Tiristasis, ii. 1190, a.
Tirso, ii. 911, a.
Tisia, 481, a.
Tisianus, 744, b.
Tisinanus, ii. 1199, b.
Tissa, ii. 907, a.
Titacidae, 330, a.
Titaresius, ii. 463, a.
Titel, ii. 718, a.
Tithorea, ii. 418, b; ii. 604, b.
Tithronium, ii. 604, b.
Titi, Thermae (Rome), ii. 847, a.
Titiani, 691, b.
Titti, 581, b.
Tituacia, 525, a.
Titulcia, 525, a.
Titus, Arch of (Rome), ii. 809, b.
Tityrus, ii. 675, a.
Tivisa, ii. 1219, b.
Tiviscum, 744, b.
Tivoli, ii. 1200, a.
Tivy, ii. 1238, b.
Tix, 498, b.
Tmai, ii. 1175, a.
Tmutarakan, 422, a; ii. 587, a.
Tobruk, ii. 277, b.
Tochira, ii. 1108, b.
Tucola, ii. 47, a.
Tocosanna, ii. 46, b.
Todi, ii. 1238, a; ii. 1288, b.
Toducae, ii. 298, b.
Togarmah, 215, a.
Tokhari, 364, b.
Toledo, ii. 1215, b.
Tolentino, ii. 629, a; ii. 1214, b.
Tolentinum, ii. 628, b.
Tolistobogii, 928, a.
Tolmeita, 733, b.
Tolmidessa, ii. 1076, a.
Tulon, 240, a.
Tolophon, ii. 203, a.
Tolosa Colonia, ii. 1320, a.
Tolosochorion, 931, a.
Tolous, ii. 32, a.
Tomeus, ii. 341, b.
Tomiswar, ii. 1216, b.
Tommasa, *Città*, 906, b.
Tonnor, 756, a.

Tombaibl, ii. 1082, a.
Tongern, 26, b; 904, b; ii. 1239, a.
Tongquén, *Gulf of*, ii. 1002, b.
Tonice, ii. 425, b.
Tonitn, ii. 1161, a.
Tonus, ii. 1216, b.
Tonsus, ii. 1178, a.
Toondja, ii. 1216, b.
Toornae, ii. 943, b.
Topiris, ii. 1190, a.
Toplika, ii. 63, b.
Topoita, 666, a.
Tor di Patria, ii. 196, a.
Torcola, ii. 1112, a.
Torbiscom, ii. 1239, a.
Tordera, ii. 115, b; ii. 129, a.
Tordera, *C.*, ii. 216, b.
Tordino, 383, a.
Torienzo, 198, b.
Torienzo, or *Torneras*, 250, b.
Torino, 339, b; ii. 1112, a.
Torinos, ii. 32, a.
Torna, ii. 1217, a.
Tornadotus, or Torna, ii. 1209, a.
Torneras, 198, b.
Tornese, *C.*, 608, b.
Tornese, *Kastro*, 1107, b.
Tornham Parva, ii. 1310, a.
Toro, ii. 461, a; ii. 1252, b.
Toro Grande, 509, b.
Toro Piccolo, 509, b.
Torquati, Balneum (Rome), ii. 820, b.
Torquatiani, Horti (Rome), ii. 896, a.
Torque, ii. 1239, a.
Torquemada, ii. 661, a.
Torre, 170, b; ii. 425, b; ii. 1275, a.
Torre d'Agnazzo, 808, b.
Torre de los Herberos, ii. 493, a.
Torre de Mongat, ii. 115, b.
Torre del Pulci, ii. 956, a.
Torre del Filosopho, 62, b.
Torre di Astura, 249, b.
Torre di Chiaruccia, 564, b.
Torre di Mare, ii. 346, b.
Torre di Martin Sicuro, 564, b.
Torre di Patermò, ii. 146, b.
Torre di Patria, 971, a.
Torre di Pitino, ii. 635, b.
Torre di Rivoli, 167, a.
Torre di S. Cataldo, 474, b.
Torre di Scupello, 594, a.
Torre di Terracima, 897, a.
Torre Vignola, ii. 912, a.
Torrecilla de aldea Tejada, 583, b.
Torrejon, ii. 1213, b.
Torres, *Porto*, ii. 911, b; ii. 1241, a.
Tortona, 771, a; ii. 188, a, b; ii. 1287, b.
Tortoorcar, ii. 997, b.
Tortosa, 771, a; ii. 270, a.
Toryne, 833, a.
Tosbur, ii. 1216, b.
Toscanella, ii. 1341, a; ii. 1297, b.
Towdj, or *Towj*, ii. 1090, a.
Tovis, ii. 556, a.
Towl, 134, b; ii. 1289, a.
Toulon, ii. 1122, b.
Toulon-sur-Arrous, ii. 1122, a.
Toulouse, ii. 1215, b.
Toulouzan, ii. 1122, b.
Tovorra, ii. 1239, b.
Tourbali, ii. 352, a.
Touren, 934, b.
Touren, or *Turon*, ii. 1240, b.
Tourkhal, 786, b; ii. 1085, b.
Tournai, ii. 328, a; ii. 1217, a; ii. 1240, a.
Tours, 470, b; ii. 1240, b.
Touwerx, ii. 1240, b.
Tous, ii. 1245, a.
Tousa, 772, a.
Towareij, 359, b.

Tovey, ii. 1214, a.
Toya, ii. 1238, b.
Trachis, ii. 606, a.
Trachonitis, ii. 532, a.
Traena, or Trais, 460, b.
Tragia, ii. 406, a.
Tragilus, 807, b.
Traglecito, ii. 1290, a.
Tragurium, 748, a.
Tragus, 505, a.
Traja Capita, ii. 31, b.
Trajan, Arch of (Rome), ii. 820, b.
Trajan, Column of (Rome), ii. 801, a.
Trajan, House of (Rome), ii. 812, a.
Trajan, Temple of (Rome), ii. 802, a.
Trajana, 646, a.
Trajana, Aqua (Rome), ii. 851, a.
Trajaner-dorf, 26, a.
Trajani, Forum (Rome), ii. 800, a; ii. 811, b.
Trajani, Thermae (Rome), ii. 847, a.
Trajanopolis, ii. 1190, a; ii. 1299, a.
Trajanus, Portus, 870, a.
Trajectus Genusi, ii. 36, b.
Trajetto, ii. 361, a.
Traille, Port de la, ii. 1310, a.
Traina, ii. 40, b.
Traismour, ii. 1230, b.
Tralles, 239, a.
Trans, 167, a.
Transmontani, ii. 916, a.
Transtiberine Wall (Rome), ii. 757, b.
Transylvania, 743, b.
Tranupara, ii. 237, a.
Trapezus, 192, b.
Trau, ii. 1219, b.
Travancore, 698, a.
Trave, ii. 1227, a.
Traviano, ii. 1109, b.
Traun, 7k7, b.
Trausi, ii. 1190, a.
Travus, ii. 1177, b.
Trayguera, ii. 31, a; ii. 1117, a.
Tré-château, or *Tri-château*, ii. 1209, b.
Tre Ponti, Torre di, ii. 1291, b.
Treba, ii. 1300, b; ii. 1317, a.
Trebbia, ii. 1223, b.
Trebes, ii. 1230, a.
Trebia, ii. 188, a; ii. 1301, a.
Trebizond, ii. 1221, a.
Treglia, ii. 1224, b.
Tregoso, ii. 188. a.
Treguier, or *Tricu*, ii. 1132, b.
Treia, ii. 629, a; ii. 1301, b.
Treja, ii. 629, a; ii. 1225, a.
Trelo-Yani, 1102, b; ii. 474, a.
Tremithus, 730, a.
Tremiti, Isole di, 777, a.
Trenonitza, ii. 1161, a.
Trento, or *Trent*, ii. 1230, b.
Trepano, 730, a.
Trepillus, ii. 384, a.
Treponti, 907, a.
Treponti, Torre di, ii. 1225, a.
Trerus, 1059, b.
Tres Forcas, Cap, ii. 297, b; ii. 346, a.
Tres Insulae, ii. 297, b.
Tres Prom., ii. 454, a.
Tres Tabernae, ii. 36, b; ii. 1287, a; ii. 1298, b.
Treta, 730, a.
Treton, 201, b.
Tretus, 201, b; 729, b.
Trèves, 340, a; ii. 1227, b.
Treventum, ii. 896, b.
Trèves, 340, a; ii. 1227, b.
Trevi, ii. 1293, a; ii. 1300, b; ii. 1301, a.

Trevico, ii. 896, b; ii. 1233, b.
Treviso, ii. 1107, b.
Trevocus, ii. 1229, a.
Trez-u-Bareek, ii. 1182, a.
Triballi, ii. 367, b.
Tribula, 6. a.
Tribulium, ii. 1209, b.
Tribunal Praetoris (Rome), ii. 788, a.
Tricastini, ii. 1229, b.
Tricca, ii. 1170, a.
Trichonium, 67, a.
Tricio, 394, a; ii. 1222, b.
Tricoloni, 193, a; ii. 309, b.
Tricomia, 931, a.
Tricornesii, ii. 367, b.
Tricorni, ii. 1230, b.
Tricorythus, 330, b.
Tricrana, ii. 1211, a.
Tridis, ii. 1230, b.
Trieb, 810, a.
Trier, 340, a; ii. 1227, b.
Trieris, ii. 606, a.
Trieron, ii. 1061, a.
Trieste, ii. 1129, b.
Trigaecini, 429, b.
Trigemina, Porta (Rome), ii. 754, b.
Trigeminam, Extra Portam (Rome), 812, a.
Trigi, ii. 657, b; ii. 1209, b.
Triglyphon, ii. 47, a.
Trigno, ii. 1231, a.
Trilgundum, 934, b.
Trikala, 1094, a.
Trikardho, 9, b; ii. 466, b.
Trikeri, 29, b; 187, a.
Trikeri, 616, a.
Trikhiri, ii. 474, a; ii. 1211, a.
Trikkala, ii. 1229, b.
Trimontium, 515, a.
Trimcomalee, ii. 516, a; ii. 548, b.
Trincomali, ii. 1093, b.
Trinemeia, 330, b.
Trinisa, ii. 1231, a.
Trino Vecchio, ii. 718, a; ii. 1288, a.
Trinobantes, 645, a.
Trinquetaille, 196, b.
Triocala, ii. 986, b.
Trionto, 450, b; ii. 1319, a.
Triphulum, 744, b.
Triphylia, 817, b.
Tripi, 1, a.
Tripoli, ii. 465, b; ii. 1080, b; ii. 1232, a.
Tripolis, ii. 606, a.
Tripolitana, Regio, ii. 1080, b.
Tripolitza, ii. 535, b.
Tripontium, 907, a; ii. 1201, b.
Tripotamo, ii. 676, a.
Tripura, ii. 47, a; ii. 1230, b.
Trisum, ii. 7, b.
Tristolus, ii. 551, b.
Tritaea, 17, a; ii. 203, a; ii. 604, b.
Tritaeis, 14, b.
Tritium, 347, a.
Tritium Metallum, 394, a.
Triton, 413, a; 733, b.
Tritonis, 312, b.
Tritonis, Lake, ii. 1233, a.
Tritonitis, ii. 1061, a.
Tritonos, ii. 1233, a.
Triturrita, ii. 1296, a.
Triudad, 934, a.
Trivento, ii. 896, b; ii. 1227, b.
Trivicum, ii. 896, b.
Triumphalis, Porta (Rome), ii. 751, b.
Troas, 102, b; ii. 389, a.
Trobis, ii. 694, b.
Trocmi, 928, a.
Troesa, 983, b.
Troglodytae, 58, a.
Troglodytes, ii. 367, b.
Trogyllum, ii. 380, a.
Troja, 29, b; ii. 1294, a.
Tromileia, 17, a.
Trompia, Val, ii. 1233, b.
Tronto, 231, b; 383, a; ii. 1237, a; ii. 1307, a.

Tronto, Civitella di, ii. 629.
Tropaea, 192, a.
Tropea, 451, b; 1056, a.
Tropez, St., 309, a.
Trosso, ii. 1237, a.
Troye, 471, a.
Truentinum, Castrum, ii. 628, b; ii. 1306, a; ii. 1307, a.
Truentus, 231, b; 383, a.
Truxillo, ii. 1236, a.
Truyère, ii. 1231, a.
Trychonis, 64, a.
Tsana, ii. 675, a.
Tscherimiss, ii. 102, b.
Tschernawode, 505, a.
Tschernigow, 697, b.
Tschetatie de Pomanni, ii. 1339, b.
Tsettina, ii. 657, b.
Tshambil Bel, ii. 934, b.
Tshangit, ii. 413, a; ii. 540, b.
Tsharuk, ii. 606, b.
Tsheremiss, 213, a.
Tshesme, ii. 619, b.
Tshigri, 583, b.
Tshili, ii. 317, b.
Tshina, ii. 286, a; 696, b.
Tshina Chi, 519, a.
Tshorok, ii. 68, a.
Tshorum, ii. 1108, b.
Tshusashes, ii. 102, b.
Trumar, 187, a.
Tuaricks, 926, a.
Tuaryks, ii. 299, b.
Tubersole, ii. 1237, b.
Tubucci, ii. 219, b.
Tuburnica, ii. 455, a.
Tucca, ii. 1214, b.
Tucris, 197, b.
Tucumbrit, ii. 997, b.
Tuddern, ii. 1123, b.
Tude, 934, a.
Tuder, ii. 1288, b; ii. 1317, a.
Tuficum, ii. 1317, b.
Tucfar, 807, a; ii. 1239, a.
Tugen, 1041, b.
Tugeni, 1041, b.
Tulsi, 502, b.
Tuleil-el-Pull, 1001, b.
Tulensli, ii. 298, b.
Tullianum (Rome), ii. 783, b.
Tullum, 134, b.
Tumbiki, ii. 482, b; ii. 1156, a.
Tuncza, ii. 1216, b.
Tunes, 68, a; ii. 1338, a.
Tunis, ii. 1239, a.
Tuntobriga, 934, a.
Tuola, 691, a.
Turambae, ii. 917, b.
Turano, 6, a; ii. 1215, a.
Turba, 402, a; 807, a.
Turbia, 110, a; ii. 188, b.
Turcalion, ii. 1236, a.
Turchal, or *Turkhal*, ii. 946, b.
Turchina, ii. 1103, a.
Turduli, 583, a.
Turenum, 167, a.
Turi, 167, b; ii. 1241, a.
Turiaso, 581, b.
Turin, 339, b; ii. 1113, a; ii. 1288, a.
Turiva, 364, b.
Turks, ii. 1239, b.
Turiure, 456, a.
Turmentini, 167, b.
Turnacum, ii. 326, a.
Turniki, 227, b.
Turnis, ii. 16, a.
Turnuk, 184, b.
Turobriga, 583, a.
Turodi, 933, a.
Turoqua, 934, a.
Turqueville, 708, b.
Turres, ii. 1294, a.
Turres, Ad, ii. 1295, a; ii. 1296, a.
Turris Libysonis, ii. 911, b.
Turrita, ii. 1296, a.
Turrus, 170, b; ii. 1275, a.
Tursan, ii. 1107, b.
Turum, 167, b.
Turuntus, ii. 917, a.
Turuptiana, 934, b.
Tusca, 68, a; ii. 454, b.

Tuscania, 870, a; ii. 1297, b.
Tuscamp, 855, a.
Tusci, ii. 917, b.
Tuscolo, Il, ii. 1241, b.
Tuscus, Vicus (Rome), ii. 775, a.
Tusdra, ii. 1196, a.
Tutaium, ii. 1317, b.
Tutela, 582, a.
Tutinek, ii. 413, a.
Tutini, 167, b.
Tutzis, 60, a.
Tuy, 934, a; ii. 1288, a.
Tux Koi, 506, b.
Tuzla, 1025, b; ii. 1108, a.
Tuzla, or *Tusla*, ii. 923, a.
Twill, ii. 1340, b.
Tyanitis, 507, b.
Tybiacae, ii. 943, b.
Tycha (Syracuse), ii. 1064, b.
Tyde, ii. 1236, a.
Tylissus, 706, b.
Tymphaei, 6b, a.
Tymphrestus, 68, b; ii. 680, a.
Tyndaris, ii. 966, b.
Tyndis, ii. 46, b; ii. 47, a; ii. 254, a.
Tyne, 429, b; ii. 1210, b; ii. 1261, a.
Tynemouth, ii. 1239, a.
Tynna, ii. 498, a.
Typanese, 821, b.
Tyracini, ii. 987, a.
Tyrangetae, ii. 917, a.
Tyras, 84, a.
Tyriaeum, ii. 222, b.
Tyridromum, ii. 455, a.
Tyro, ii. 668, a.
Tyrol, 108, a; ii. 447, a; ii. 700, a.
Tysia, 744, b; ii. 1199, b.
Tzakonia, 736, a.
Tzamali, 243, b.
Tzana, 644, b.
Tzangon, ii. 566, b.
Tzerigo, 738, b.
Tzerkovi, ii. 570, b.
Tzimbaru, 308, b; 385, b.
Tzurela, 32, b.

Vacca, ii. 1252, b.
Vacca, Val de, ii. 332, a.
Vacci Prata, (Rome), ii. 804, b.
Vaccina, 466, b.
Vacuatae, ii. 299, a.
Vada, ii. 1296, a.
Vada Sabbata, or Sabata, 110, a; ii. 188, a; ii. 1296, a.
Vada Volaterrana, 670, a; ii. 1296, a.
Vadimonian Lake, 857, b.
Vadinia, 502, b.
Fado, 110, a; ii. 188, a; ii. 1252, b; ii. 1296, b.
Fado di Trosso, ii. 1237, a.
Vagense Oppidum, ii. 1252, b.
Vagienni, ii. 187, a.
Vagoritum, 229, a.
Vahalis, or Vacalus, 381, b.
Varparu, ii. 1019, a.
Vaires, ii. 1260, a.
Vaison, ii. 1259, b; ii. 1318, b.
Val Camonica, 497, b.
Val d'Aosta, 109, a.
Val de Meca, 582, a.
Val di Viu, 977, a.
Valais, ii. 574, a; ii. 947, b; ii. 1254, b; ii. 1277, b.
Valbach, ii. 1254, b.
Valdasus, ii. 541, b.
Valderaduci, ii. 1310, a.
Valderaduci, 250, a.
Vaiebonga, 582, a.
Valecha, ii. 1324, b.
Valence, 340, b; ii. 1254, a.
Valencia, 665, b; 807, a; ii. 1105, a.
Valencia, Gulf of, ii. 1042, b.
Valentia, 340, b; 577, a; 655, b; ii. 912, a; ii. 1294, b.
Valencia de S. Juan, 250, a.

Valentinian, Arch of (Rome), ii. 839, b.
Valentino, Ost. di S., ii. 1305, b.
Valentinum, ii. 188, a.
Valenza, 906, a; ii. 188, a.
Valera la Vieja, 562, a; ii. 1254, b.
Valeria, 582, a.
Valerius, 691, a.
Valesio, 375, a.
Vali, ii. 917, b.
Falier, S., ii. 1327, a.
Valiti, ii. 1324, b.
Valladolid, ii. 631, a; ii. 1252, b.
Vallata, 250, a.
Vallis Murcia (Rome), ii. 816, a.
Valmontone, ii. 1215, a; ii. 1313, a.
Valois, ii. 1252, a.
Valona, 342, a.
Valpo, ii. 63, b.
Valsalobre, ii. 1254, b.
Valsolebre, 582, a.
Valtetui, ii. 310, a.
Vama, 583, a.
Van, 216, b; 294, a; 227, b; 673, b; ii. 8, b; ii. 296, b.
Vanacem, 691, b.
Vandotena, ii. 533, b.
Vanena, ii. 1156, a.
Vannes, 784, a.
Var, ii. 188, b; ii. 1269, a.
Var-chonites, 349, b.
Vara, 409, b; 430, a; ii. 188, a.
Varagri, ii. 1277, b.
Varese, ii. 1256, a.
Varanus, ii. 1278, a.
Varassova, 63, b; 600, b.
Varaz, Mt., 379, b.
Varciani, ii. 542, a.
Varcilenses, 525, b.
Varcolen, 525, b; ii. 1256, a.
Vardanes, 571, b.
Vardar, ii. 1173, a.
Vardari, 352, b; ii. 213, a.
Vardhari, Bridge of the, ii. 236, b.
Vardkust, 63, b.
Varduli, 502, a.
Varea, 394, b; ii. 1269, a.
Varentri, ii. 287, a.
Varkeiy, ii. 920, b.
Vari, 129, b; 331, a.
Varia, 55, a; 774, b.
Variadhes, 896, a.
Varianus Vicus, ii. 1287, b.
Varin, ii. 550, b.
Varlam, C., 606, b.
Varna, 364, b; ii. 463, b; ii. 546, b.
Varnakova, 35, b.
Varoi, 364, b.
Varo, 748, a.
Varsa, ii. 47, b.
Varum Flumen, 110, a; ii. 188, b.
Varus, ii. 187, b.
Varzana, ii. 1275, b.
Vasaeluetum, M., ii. 1080, b.
Vasnta, ii. 223, b.
Vasates, 173, a.
Vasgau, ii. 1325, a.
Vasilika, ii. 989, b.
Vasiliko, ii. 342, a.
Vaste, 380, b.
Vathy, 341, b; 847, b; 1105, b; ii. 1175, a.
Vathy, Port of, ii. 1084, a.
Vaticanus, Mons, or Collis (Rome), ii. 842, b.
Vaticanus, Pons (Rome), ii. 850, a.
Vatika, 409, b.
Vatopedhi, 603, a.
Vatriae, 11, b.
Vaudre, ii. 1318, b.
Vaugelas, 488, b; 980, a.
Ubaye, ii. 1283, b.
Ubayette, ii. 1283, b.
Ubus, ii. 454, b.

Uoero, 197, b.
Ucutrinacum, 562, a.
Udine, ii. 1261, a; ii. 1275, b; ii. 1329 a.
Ududa, ii. 1941, a.
Udura, ii. 1, b.
Vedene, ii. 1310, a.
Vedianti, ii. 187, a.
Vedinum, ii. 1275, b.
Vexesack, ii. 14, a.
Veglia, 720, a.
Veine, 756, b.
Vejovis, Temple of (Rome), ii. 770, a.
Vela, ii. 620, a.
Velabrum (Rome), ii. 812, b.
Veldidana, 110, b.
Velebich, ii. 3, b.
Veleiates, ii. 187, b.
Veles, 1326, b.
Velexa, or *Velesxo*, 460, b.
Velestino, ii. 595, b.
Veleti, ii. 1270, a.
Velex Malaga, ii. 244, a.
Veliborae, ii. 16, a.
Vellavi, 173, a.
Vellica. 502, b.
Velpi, M., 733, b.
Vehuca, 197, b.
Velia (Rome), ii. 802, a; ii. 807, a.
Velilla, 581, a; ii. 32, a.
Velino, ii. 1268, a.
Velino, Mount, 5, b.
Velitxa, ii. 418, b.
Vellay, ii. 1269, b.
Velletri, ii. 1268, b.
Veltae, ii. 916, a.
Velucha, ii. 1324, b.
Velvendo, 375, a.
Velvitxi, 13, b.
Velukhi, ii. 630, b.
Veluwe, 367, a.
Venafro, ii. 1270, a.
Venaria, 857, a.
Vénasque, 524, b.
Vencx, ii. 491, a; ii. 1311, b.
Vendeleia, 347, a.
Vendelxabai, ii. 1020, a.
Vendre Port, ii. 661, b.
Vendrell, ii. 533, b.
Vendres Porte, ii. 52, a.
Vene, Le, ii. 1300, b.
Venedi. ii. 916, a.
Venedicus, Sinus, ii. 460, b.
Veneni, ii. 187, b.
Venere, Ponte Sta, ii. 1293, a.
Veneris Calvae, Aedes (Rome), ii. 770, a.
Veneris Libitinae, Lucus (Rome), ii. 826, b.
Veneris, Ad, ii. 1294, a.
Veneti, 754, b.
Venetiko, ii. 342, b.
Venxa, 818, b.
Venuatia, 934, a.
Vennicnii, ii. 16, a.
Venosa, ii. 1276, b; ii. 1293, a.
Venta, 387, b.
Venta Belgarum, 442, a.
Venta Icenorum, 442, a.
Ventoux, Castro de la, ii. 1329, b.
Venus Capitolina, Temple of (Rome), ii. 769, b.
Venus Cluacina, Shrine of (Rome), ii. 783, a.
Venus Erycina, Temple of (Rome), ii. 830, b.
Venus Genitrix, Temple of (Rome). ii. 797, a.
Venus, Temple of (Rome), ii. 804, b; ii. 817, a.
Venus Victrix, Temple of (Rome), ii. 769, b.
Venusia, 167, a; ii. 1293, a.
Venusta Vallis, ii. 1276, a.
Venxone, ii. 1258, a.
Vera, 320, b.
Vera, 379, a.
Veramin, 885, b.
Verbaxx, ii. 1327, a.
Verbicae, ii. 299, a.
Vercella, Torre di, ii. 1107, b.
Vercellae, ii. 1287, b.

Vercelli, ii. 1278, a; ii. 1287, b.
Vercellium, 1073, b.
Vercors, ii. 1280, b.
Verde, C., 225, a.
Verden, ii. 1238, b.
Verdouble, or *Verdoubre*, ii. 1278, b.
Verdun, ii. 1279, a.
Vereja, ii. 236, b.
Verela, 394, a.
Vercto, Sta Maria di, ii. 1278, a; ii. 1294, a.
Veretum, 474, b; ii. 1294, b.
Vergae, 451, a.
Vergons, ii. 1278, b.
Vérignon, ii. 1280, a.
Vernose, ii. 1278, b.
Verôcxe, or *Verovitx*, ii. 969, a.
Veroli, ii. 1280, b.
Verona, ii. 1276, a; ii. 1287, b.
Verona, ii. 1279, a; ii. 1287, b.
Verovesca, 347, a.
Verrex, 110, a; ii. 1287, b; ii. 1313, b.
Verria, 353, a; 823, b; ii. 237, a.
Verrucola, or *Verrucchia*, ii. 1312, a.
Versuglia, 857, a.
Vertinae, ii. 210, a.
Verves, ii. 299, a.
Verveins, ii. 1277, b.
Verulam, Old, ii. 1279 a.
Verus, Arch of (Rome), ii. 820, b.
Verwick, ii. 1312, a.
Verxino, ii. 1280, b.
Vescellium, 1073, b.
Vescovio, 910, a.
Vesidia, 857, a.
Vestorica, ii. 1317, a.
Vespasian, Temple of (Rome), ii. 781, b.
Vespasian and Titus, Temple of (Rome), ii. 795, a.
Vestae, Aedes (Rome), ii. 778, b.
Vesulus, Mons, 107, b.
Vesunna, 457, b.
Vesuvio, Monte, ii. 1284, a.
Vetera, 173, b; 482, b.
Veternicxa, ii. 1120, b.
Vetlclta, Selva di, ii. 1286, a.
Vetojo, Laghetto di, ii. 448, b.
Vetralla, 907, b; ii. 1296, b; ii. 1297, a.
Vettona, ii. 1288, b.
Vetturi, Castel, ii. 989, b.
Veturii, ii. 187, a.
Vevai, 444, a.
Vevay, 110, b; ii. 1313, b.
Vexin Français, ii. 1269 b.
Vexin Normand, ii. 1269, b.
Vex, ii. 442, b.
Vexxo, ii. 1261, a.
Ufente, ii. 1286, a.
Uffugum, 451, a.
Ugento, 95, a; ii. 1294, a; ii. 1332, a.
Uglian, ii. 196, b.
Via Lata (Rome), ii. 832, a; ii. 839, b.
Via Tecta (Rome), ii. 837, b.
Viana, ii. 1266, b.
Viana de Bollo, 934, a.
Vianos, 401, b.
Viareggio, ii. 1296, a.
Viatka, ii. 917, b.
Vibinum, 167, a.
Vibiones, ii. 916, b.
Vibona, ii. 1295, a.
Vic de Osane, 343, b.
Vicentia, ii. 1275, a; ii. 1287, b.
Vicenxa, ii. 1287, b; 1307, b.
Vichy, 168, a.
Vico, 340, b.
Vico, Lago di, 856, b; 857, a.
Vicovaro, 774, b; ii. 1258, b.
Victilianae, Aedes (Rome), ii. 818, b.

Victoria, Sanctuary of (Rome), ii. 803, b.
Victoriae, Clivus (Rome), ii. 803, b.
Victoriae Jullobrigensium, Portus, ii. 109, a.
Victory, Statue of (Rome), ii. 795, a.
Vicus Badies, ii. 1305, a.
Vicus Cumurius, 525, a.
Vicus Longus (Rome), ii. 829, a.
Vicus Novus, ii. 1305, a.
Vicus Patricius (Rome), ii. 822, b.
Vicus Spacorum, 934, b.
Vicus Virginis, ii. 188, b.
Vid, ii. 1329, b.
Vidi, ii. 150, b.
Vido, 671, b; ii. 400, a.
Viducasses, 218, b.
Vicille Tour, 389, b.
Viena, 63, b.
Vienna, ii. 1311, a.
Vienne, 187, b; ii. 1308, b.
Vietri, 497, b; ii. 271, a.
Viexx, ii. 1308, b.
Vieux-Brisach, ii. 269, b.
Vieux-Châtel, ii. 442, b.
Vieux Seurre, 779, a.
Vigan, ii. 1311, b.
Vigo, 934, b.
Ujjayini, ii. 47, a.
Vilaine, 443, a; 791, b; 1057, a.
Vilches, ii. 1281, a.
Villa de dos Hermaños, ii. 493, a.
Villa Fasila, 93, b.
Villa Faustini, 488, b.
Villa Velha, ii. 219, b.
Villnfafila, ii. 1308, a.
Villafranca, Gulf, ii. 424, a.
Villalpando, ii. 399, a.
Villano, C., 186, b.
Villanueva, ii. 1034, b; ii. 1041, b.
Villanueva de Sitges, ii. 1034, b.
Villar de Mafardin, ii. 1254, b.
Villar Pedroso, 341, a.
Villarinho, ii. 1065, a.
Villaroane, 250, a.
Villartelin, ii. 1210, a.
Villaxecco, ii. 1308, a.
Ville Neuve, 889, a.
Villebaudon, ii. 153, b.
Villciba, ii. 1269, b.
Villeneuve, ii. 574, a.
Vilna, ii. 916, a.
Vimala, 973, b.
Viminacium, 250, a.
Viminal Hill (Rome), ii. 828, b.
Viminalis, Collis (Rome), ii. 828, b.
Viminalis, Porta (Rome), ii. 756, a.
Viminalis sub aggere, Campus (Rome), ii. 826, a.
Vinai, ii. 1276, b.
Vincent, Cape St., 377, a; ii. 872, a.
Vindeleia, 347, a.
Vindhya, 746, a; ii. 46, b; ii. 48, a; ii. 1311, a.
Vindhya Mountains, ii. 692, b; ii. 914, a; ii. 1022, a.
Vindia, 931, a.
Vindicari, ii. 11, b.
Vindicari Porto, ii. 40, b.
Vindinates, ii. 1317, b.
Vindios, M., 746, a.
Vindius, M., ii. 46, b; ii. 549, b.
Vindo, 340, b.
Vindobala, ii. 1251, b.
Vindobona, ii. 542, a.
Vindolana, ii. 1256, b.
Vindonissa, 1041, b.
Vinitya, Ms., ii. 692, b.
Vinexxa, ii. 1312, b.
Vinhaes, 934, a; ii. 1275, b.
Viniola, ii. 912, a.
Vinkoucxe, 614, b.

Vins, ii. 296, b
Vinxam, ii. 1094, a.
Vintimiglia, 110, a.
Vintimiglia, 93, b; ii. 188, a.
Vintium, ii. 421, a.
Viosa, Vuissa, or *Voruxxe*, 151, b.
Viosa, ii. 550, a.
Vipao, 916, b; ii. 1275, a.
Vipeteno, 111, a.
Vipsania, Porticus (Rome), ii. 839, b.
Vique, or *Vich*, 344, a.
Viraplaca, Sacellum of, Dea (Rome), ii. 804, a.
Virdo. ii. 1310, b.
Viro Valentia, 451, b.
Virovesca, 347, a.
Viruni, ii. 1259, a.
Virunum, ii. 448, a.
Virus, 933, b.
Viskardho, 588, b.
Viso, Monte, 107, b; ii. 1263, b.
Vissuch, ii. 4, a.
Vistritxa, 1025, b.
Vistula, ii. 1312, b.
Viterbo, 894, a; ii. 1285, b.
Vithari, 1063, b; ii. 586, a
Vito, S., 153, b.
Vitodurum, 1041, b.
Vitricium, 110, a; ii. 1287, b.
Vitruvius Vaccus, house of (Rome), ii. 804, b.
Vittoria, ii. 1045, b.
Vittorino, Sam, 122, b.
Vitylo, ii. 470, a.
Vitxch, ii. 689, a.
Vivaraxx, 1048, a.
Vivel, 389, a.
Viventani, ii. 1317, b.
Viviscum, 110, b.
Viviscus, 444, a.
Vlaardingen, 902, b; 912, a.
Vladimir, ii. 917, b.
Ulai, 874, b.
Vlakho-makkala, ii. 60, b.
Vlakholivadho, ii. 629, b.
Ulan Robat, 184, a.
Vleuten, 903, a.'
Ulgxx, ii. 473, b.
Vlic-Stroom, 908, b.
Vlieland, 903, b.
Vlikha, 208, b.
Ulken, ii. 473, a.
Ulla, 933, b.
Ulla, 933, b; ii. 1314, a.
Vlokho, 248, b; ii. 1163, a.
Ulpia, Basilica (Rome), ii. 800, b.
Ulpianum, 744, b.
Ulster, ii. 16, a.
Ulubad, 161, b.
Ulurtini, 167, b.
Um-el-Jemal, 896, b.
Um Lakis, ii. 107, a.
Umago, ii. 74, a.
Umana, ii. 483, a; ii. 698, b.
Umbilicus Romae (Rome), ii. 794, b.
Umbro, 857, a.
Umbronem, Fl. Ad, ii. 1296, a.
Umgheier, 863, a.
Unelli, 218, b.
Unich, 602, b; ii. 468, a.
Unknown Land, ii. 917, b.
Unna, ii. 466, b.
Unxe, ii. 1318, a.
Vocanae, Aquae, 168, b.
Vocates, 173, a.
Vodae. ii. 917, b.
Vodhena, 806, a; 822, b; ii. 236, b.
Vodiae. ii. 16, a.
Vogdhani, 1099, a.
Vogescn, ii. 1325, a.
Voghera, ii. 64, b; ii. 188, a; ii. 1287, b.
Voidhxa, 13, a.
Voigtland, ii. 1133, a.
Voirodu, ii. 320. a.
Voivonda, ii. 1213, a.
Volana, ii. 896, b.
Volano, ii. 1321, b.
Volanxa, 418, a.

Volcentum, or Volcelum, ii. 210, a.
Volga, 455, a; ii. 298, a; ii. 699, b.
Volkynis, ii. 30, a; ii. 916, a.
Volo, ii. 60, b; ii. 515, a.
Volobriga, 934, a.
Vologatis, Mutatio, 980. a.
Volpo, Cape, 158, a; 726, a.
Volsiniensis, Lacus, 857, a.
Volsinii, ii. 1296, b; 1297, a.
Volterra, ii. 1318. b.
Voltore, Monte, ii. 1329, b.
Volturno, ii. 1330, a.
Volturno, Castel, ii. 1330, a.
Volubiliani, ii. 299, a.
Volvic, ii. 286, b.
Voluntii, ii. 16, a.
Voluptas, Sacellum (Rome), ii. 812, b.
Vomano, 383. a.
Vomanus, 383, a.
Vona, 419, b.
Vona, Cape, ii. 5, a.
Vonitza, 10, b; 129, a.
Voorbourg, 908, b.
Voroncsh, ii. 917, b.
Vortumnus, Ara of (Rome), ii. 811, a.
Vosges, ii. 1325, a.
Vostitza, 13, b; 35, b.
Voturi, 931, a.
Voudrei, ii. 1318, a.
Vouga, ii. 1253, b.
Vouria, 668, a.
Vouroux, ii. 1326, a.
Uphrenus, ii. 468, a.
Ur, 601, a.
Ur of the Chaldees, ii. 438, b; ii. 487, a.
Vrashori, ii. 346, a.
Ural, 746, b.
Ural Chain, ii. 289, a.
Uralian Range, ii. 102, b.
Urania, 780, a.
Vrania, ii. 243, b; ii. 267, b.
Uranopolis. 23, a.
Vraona, 332, a; 312, b.
Vravnitza, 250, b.
Urbania, ii. 1326, a.
Urbi, 210, b.
Urbiaca, 582, a.
Urbiei, 770, a.
Urbino, ii. 1317, b; ii.1326, a.
Urbinum Hortense, ii. 1317. b.
Urbinum Metaurense, ii. 1317, b.
Urbisaglia, ii. 628, b; ii. 645, b; ii. 1326, a.
Urbius, ii. 1293, b.
Urbo, 934, b.
Urbs Salvia, ii. 628, b; ii. 645, b.
Urcinium, 691, b.
Uresmea, ii. 253, b.
Urfah, 806, b; ii. 439, b.
Urgo, 857, b.
Urgub, ii. 499, b.
Urgub or Urkup, ii. 871, a.
Uria, 64, a; 474, b.
Uriconium, 442, a.
Urima, ii. 1075, b; ii. 1076, a.
Urium, 167, a.
Urmiah, 320, b.
Uroconium, 427, a.
Vroil, 214, a.
Vromona, 804, b.
Vromoseia, ii. 1175, b.
Uroxcicr, 427, a.
Urpanus, ii. 541, b.
Ursentini, ii. 210, a.
Urtas, Wady, 1061, b.
Urtippa, ii. 1333, b.
Urumiah, Sea of, ii. 1031, a.
Urumyyah, 216, b; ii. 286, b.
Usar, 337, a; ii. 297, b.
Uscana, ii. 574, a.
Uscenum, ii. 7, b.
Uschkub, ii. 934, a.
Uscosium, 916, a.
Usdicesica, ii. 1190, b.
Ucossio, 916, a.
Uscudama, 395, b.
Usdom, ii. 1018, a.
Uscit, 815, b.

Uselle, ii. 3, b.
Usellis, ii. 912, a.
Uselius, 1327, b.
Uses, ii. 1260, b.
Ushak, 113, a; 890, a; 902, b.
Ushant, ii. 1331, a.
Usk, 409, b.
Usseglio, 977, b.
Ustica, ii. 501, a.
Ulatur or Utacoow, ii. 427, a.
Uterni, ii. 16, a.
Utica, 68, a.
Utidava, 714, b.
Utrecht, ii. 1290, a.
Uttarakurw, ii. 505, a.
Uttaru, 934, b.
Vulaubus, 912, a.
Vulcan, Temple of (Rome), ii. 834, b.
Vulcaniello, 52, b.
Vulcani Insula, 51, b.
Vulcano, 51, b.
Vulci, ii. 1285, b.
Vuliasmeui, 331, a; 685, b.
Vulsiniensis, Lacus, 856, b.
Vuriemi, 241, a.
Vuriendi, 241, a.
Vurkano, ii. 336, b.
Vurvuri, ii. 630, a.
Vutundro, 459, a.
Vuvo, 19, b.
Uxama, 197, b.
Uxama Barca, 347, a.
Uxantis Insula, 949, a.
Uxeau, ii. 188, a; 461, a.
Uxelum, 515, a.
Uxeutum, 95, a; 474, b; ii. 1294, a.
Uxentus, M., ii. 46, b.
Uxii, 822, b.
Usum Kiupri, ii. 642, b.
Uxumi, 755, b; 756, a.

Waal, 381, b.
Wad-al-Gored, 229, b.
Wad Daab, 1090, a.
Wad-el-Boul, 456, b.
Wad-el-Gored, 779, b.
Wad-el-Jenan, 336, b.
Wad-el-Kebir, 127, b; ii. 297, b.
Wad Mrssa, ii. 322, a.
Wadi Quasam, 625, b.
Wadi Roumel, 127, b.
Wady-er-Rcma, ii. 300, a.
Wady-el-Arabah, 174, b.
Wady-el-Kebir, 68, a.
Wady-el-Khos, ii. 452, b.
Wady-el-Majib, 219, b.
Wady-ez-Suni, 810, a.
Wady-esh-Sheikh, ii. 699, a.
Wady-es-Zarm, 68, a.
Wady Etam, 855, a.
Wady-Ghurandel, 815, b.
Wady Kelt, 607, b; ii. 329, b.
Wady Maharrakah, 60, a.
Wady Malekh, 113, b.
Wady Maid, ii. 468, a.
Wady Mulwia, or Mohalow, 67. b.
Wady Seibous, 68, a.
Wady-Tensift, 229, b.
Wady Waseit, 815, b.
Wageck, ii. 1307, a.
Wageningen, 555, a.
Wahl, ii. 1254, b.
Wahran ii. 297, b.
Wallachia, 743, b.
Wallis, ii. 1254, b.
Wallscnd, ii. 1256, b.
Walls-end, ii. 1311, a.
Walwick Chesters, 563, b; ii. 1256, b.
Wan, ii. 1176, a.
Wangen, ii. 1270, a.
Wannash-reese, ii. 1235, b.
Warka, 363, a.
Warick, 1019, a.
Warka, 363, a; 601, a; ii. 487, a.
Warne, ii. 1042, b.
Warwick, ii. 666, b.
Warwick, ii. 1312, b.
Wash, the, ii. 348, b.
Washoti Mountains, 367, b; 982, b.

Watchcross, 1, b.
Water-Newton, 446, b.
Wear, ii. 1261, a.
Wechi, ii. 1306, a.
Wechsel, ii. 1312, b.
Weissenburg, 167, b.
Weis, ii. 505, a.
Wernet, 754, b.
Wends, ii. 1270, b.
Weriech, 340, b; ii. 1312, a.
Werwic, ii. 1312, a.
Weser, ii. 1312, b.
Westbury, ii. 1278, b.
Weston, 212. b.
Wexford, 672, b.
Weymouth, ii. 63, a.
Whelp Castle, ii. 1255, a.
Whetacre, 442, b.
Whetham, ii. 1278, b.
Whitchurch, ii. 1311, b.
White Sea, 31, b.
Whiterne, ii. 211, b.
Whitley Castle, ii. 1256, b.
Widjeh, ii. 1134, b.
Wicabaden, 169, a.
Wight, Isle of, ii. 1260, b.
Wigston Parva, ii. 1276, a.
Wigton Bay, ii. 15, a.
Wigtonshire, 780, a; ii. 448, b.
Wilden, 110, b; 1266, a.
Wilts, 388, a.
Wimburn, ii. 1311, a.
Winchester, 387, b; 442, a; ii. 1276, a.
Winchester, Old, ii. 1311, a.
Windaw, ii. 1241, a.
Windisch, 1041, b; ii. 1311, b.
Windisk-Garstein, 923, b.
Windisch-Grätz, ii. 1270, b.
Windsor, Old, ii. 687, b.
Wines, 901, a.
Wippack, 916, b; ii. 1275, a.
Wismar, ii. 107, a; ii. 276, b.
Wissant or Wilsand, ii. 99, b.
Wittenberg, ii. 217, b.
Woad Nafn, ii. 330, b.
Woodcote, ii. 450. a.
Worcester, 478, b.
Woringen, 456, b.
Worms, 420, a.
Wrietzen, ii. 1312, a.
Writtle, 470, b.
Wrotham, ii. 1253, b.
Wroxeter, 442, a; ii. 1312, a.
Wulpit, ii. 1310, a.
Würtzburg, ii. 951, a.
Wustani, 37, a.
Wyck-te-Durstede, 382, b.

Xalon, ii. 884, b.
Xanten, 173, b; 482, b; 562, b.
Xativa, ii. 1036, b.
Xelsa, 581, a.
Xenil, 368, a; ii. 1229, b.
Xeres, 247, b.
Xeres de la Frontera, 239, b.
Xeria, 200, b.
Xerilo, 49, a.
Xerogypsus, ii. 1190, a.
Xerokambi, 1031, b.
Xerokampo, ii. 110, a.
Xeropegado, 707, a.
Xeropigadho, 700, b.
Xeropotami, ii. 1196, b.
Xeropyrgu, ii. 1120, b.
Xigonza, ii. 874, a.
Ximeira, 8, a.
Ximena de la Frontera, 343, a; 377, a.
Xingi, ii. 152, b.
Xiphonian Port, ii. 985, a.
Xiphonian Prom., ii. 984, b.
Xucar, ii. 1043, b.
Xuria, 125, a.
Xylofago, 504, b; 871, b.
Xylopolis, ii. 384, a.
Xyniae, ii. 1170, a.
Xypete, 235, a.

Yabes, Wady, ii. 1, b.
Yabrud, ii. 1076, b.

Yafa, ii. 62, b; ii. 359, a.
Yalobutch, 147, a.
Yambo, 746, a.
Yanar, 608, b.
Yapha, ii. 530, b.
Yars, 645, b; 977, b.
Yarmak, 923, b.
Yarmouth, ii. 1108, b.
Yarmuk, ii. 286, a; ii. 521, b.
Yaroo, 722, a.
Yathrib, ii. 131, a.
Yebna, 396, b; ii. 3, b.
Yechil or Yekil Irmak, ii. 63, a.
Yellow River, 384, a.
Yenema, ii. 401, a.
Yemen, 181, b; ii. 284, a; ii. 337, a.
Yeni Kalc, Strait of, 421, b.
Yenifi, ii. 1127, a.
Yenikale, ii. 388, b.
Yenikiug, ii. 569, b.
Yenisheher, ii. 127, a.
Yenisheri, ii. 997, b.
Yenne, 855, a.
Yents, 485, a.
Yerma, 992, b.
Yeshil Ermak, 117, a.
Yonne, ii. 11, a.
Yori, 488, b.
York, 797, b.
Ypek, ii. 631, a.
Ypsili, ii. 64, b.
Ypsili Hissar, 336, a.
Yruna, ii. 1266, b.
Ysarche, ii. 31, a.
Yssel, 471, a; ii. 392, b.
Ystvytk, ii. 1038, b.
Yueti, 746, b.
Yutta, ii. 103, a.
Yverdum, 798, b; ii. 904, a.

Zab, 189, a; ii. 1234, b.
Zabi, ii. 1334, b.
Zabatus, ii. 1209, a.
Zacatae, ii. 917, b.
Zacynthus, ii. 582, b.
Zadracarta, 1106, a.
Zafra, ii. 1337, b.
Zagora, 413, a; 1035, b.
Zagatis, ii. 658, b.
Zaghouam, ii. 1237, b.
Zagora, 412, a, b; 772, a; 982, a; ii. 569, a; ii. 917, a.
Zagori, ii. 550, a.
Zahle, 598, b.
Zalecus, ii 547, a.
Zalongo, 560, b.
Zama, 490, b.
Zamareni, 363, b.
Zamargai, ii. 484, a.
Zamocma, ii. 974, a.
Zamora, ii. 461, a; ii. 964, a; ii. 1252, b.
Zanah, 772, b.
Zandvoort, 501, a.
Zanfour, 243, b.
Zanziat-Mula-Driza, ii. 1324, b.
Zannone, ii.658, a; ii.1007, a.
Zante, ii. 1334, b.
Zanxibar, ii. 329, b; ii. 668, a.
Zaphran, ii. 297, b.
Zaptal, 840, a.
Zara, ii. 2, a; ii. 64, b; ii. 1336, b.
Zaragoza, 250, a; 469, a.
Zarah, or Zerrah, 210, a.
Zaraka, ii. 1040, a.
Zarangae, 210, b.
Zaratae, ii. 943, b.
Zarax, ii. 1312, a.
Zarepthah, ii. 606, b.
Zarfa, 344, a.
Zarlaspa, 364, b.
Zariaaspes, 364, b.
Zarnata, 3, b; 989, b.
Zarmource, 696, b.
Zarvi, ii. 1042, a.
Zarsosa, ii. 964, a.
Zavitsa, 726, b.
Zea, 586, b.
Zeb, ii. 607, a.
Zebeye, 797, a.

Zabra, 614, b.
Zebulun, Tribe of, ii. 530, a.
Zee Hill, 20, b.
Zefreh, ii. 1337, b.
Zefreh, Cape, ii. 600, b.
Zegrensii, ii. 299, a.
Zeitha, ii. 1061, a.
Zeitoun Bouroun, ii. 254, b.
Zeldepa, ii. 1335, b.
Zellete, 622, b.
Zembra, 32, b.
Zemenic, ii. 970, b.
Zeng, ii. 963, a.
Zephyrian Promontory, 641, a.
Zephyrium Promontorium, 730, a.
Zephyrium, 733, b.
Zerin, 854, a.
Zermagna, ii. 205, a.
Zerna, ii. 1012, a.
Zernes, ii. 1207, a.
Zernitz, ii. 1339, a.

Zershell, ii. 60, a; ii. 297, b.
Zervokhia, ii. 569, a.
Zervokhori, 1046, b.
Zeryah, ii. 1336, b.
Zetei, ii. 1118, a.
Zetta, 776, b.
Zeugg, ii. 3, b.
Zeugma, 737, a; 744, b; ii. 1075, b.
Zcyla, 336, b.
Zia, ii. 406, b.
Zib, 94, a; 802, b.
Ziberuch, Su, ii. 456, a.
Ziboviti, 136, b.
Zibru, 614, b.
Zicchi, ii. 917, b.
Zikeli, 622, b.
Zikhna, ii. 463, b; ii. 922, a.
Zillis, ii. 298, a.
Zille, 630, b.
Zilleh, ii. 1337, a.
Zimeno Derveni, ii. 980, a.
Zin, ii. 529, b.

Zinari, 625, a.
Zingane, ii. 908, a.
Zingebar, ii. 668, a.
Ziridava, 744, b.
Zirknitz, Lake, ii. 215, a.
Zituni, ii. 117, b.
Zituni, Gulf of, ii. 255, a.
Zmievoi, 20, b.
Znaim, ii. 625, b.
Zochasa, 641, a.
Zoelae, 249, b.
Zoetelum, 198, a.
Zof, ii. 1037, a.
Zografu, ii. 1196, b.
Zone, ii. 1190, a.
Zoroanda, ii. 1208, b.
Zorzo di Magnes, St., 773, b.
Zoster, 531, a.
Zowamour, 32, b.
Zowan, ii. 64, a.
Zowan, Mount, ii. 549, a.
Zrna Rjeka, 849, b.
Zuchabbari, M., ii. 1080, b.

Zuglio, 110, b; 522, a; ii. 102, b.
Zugra, ii. 570, b.
Zuider Zee, 903, a.
Zuia-Sarakini, 457, a.
Zulla, 29, a.
Zunra, ii. 32, a.
Zurka, 380, b.
Zurobara, 744, b.
Zurzach, 911, b.
Zusidava, 744, b.
Zworte Kuikenbuurt, ii. 429, b.
Zydowo, ii. 971, a.
Zydretae, 643, a.
Zygenses, ii. 278, a.
Zygi, 872, b.
Zygus, ii. 277, b.
Zygos, 63, b; 185, a; ii. 503, a.
Zygos, Lake of, 64, a.
Zygritae, ii. 278, a.
Zyria, 724, a.

THE END.

LONDON: PRINTED BY
SPOTTISWOODE AND CO., NEW-STREET SQUARE
AND PARLIAMENT STREET

ND - #0034 - 130924 - C0 - 229/152/40 - PB - 9781390992854 - Gloss Lamination